INSIGHT INTO ETHICS

Focus on Ethics

BUSINESS LAW

TEXT AND CASES

THIRTEENTH EDITION

Kenneth W. Clarkson
University of Miami

Roger LeRoy Miller
Institute for University Studies
Arlington, Texas

Frank B. Cross
Herbert D. Kelleher
Centennial Professor in Business Law
University of Texas at Austin

CENGAGE
Learning™

Australia • Brazil • Japan • Mexico • Singapore • United Kingdom • United States

CENGAGE
Learning™

Business Law
TEXT AND CASES

THIRTEENTH EDITION

Kenneth W. Clarkson
Roger LeRoy Miller
Frank B. Cross

Senior Vice President,
Global Product Management
Higher Education:
Jack W. Calhoun

Vice President and
General Manager,
Social Sciences
& Qualitative Business:
Erin Joyner

Product Director:
Michael Worls

Senior Product Manager:
Vicky True-Baker

Senior Content Developer:
Jan Lamar

Product Assistant:
Tristann Jones

Marketing Director:
Kristen Hurd

Senior Marketing Manager:
Robin LeFevre

Marketing Coordinator:
Chris Walz

Senior Art Director:
Michelle Kunkler

Senior Content Project Manager:
Ann Borman

Senior Media Developer:
Kristen Meere

Manufacturing Planner:
Kevin Kluck

Compositor:
Parkwood Composition Service

Cover and Internal Designer:
Red Hangar Design

Design Elements:
linen texture: Lisa-Blue/iStockphoto; justice scales:
imagedb.com/Shutterstock; gavel: koosen/Shutterstock;
media network: solarseven/Shutterstock; building
windows: Nneirda/Shutterstock; puzzle icon: Shebeko/
Shutterstock; spotlight: Ivan Lord/Shutterstock; ethics
scale: Lightspring/Shutterstock; magnifying glass icon:
sergign/Shutterstock; globe: mj007/Shutterstock;
compass: TADDEUS/Shutterstock; Insight Global globe:
evantravels/Shutterstock

© 2015, 2012 Cengage Learning

ALL RIGHTS RESERVED. No part of this work covered by the copyright herein may be reproduced, transmitted, stored or used in any form or by any means graphic, electronic, or mechanical, including but not limited to photocopying, recording, scanning, digitizing, taping, Web distribution, information networks, or information storage and retrieval systems, except as permitted under Section 107 or 108 of the 1976 United States Copyright Act, without the prior written permission of the publisher.

For product information and technology assistance, contact us at
Cengage Learning Customer & Sales Support
1-800-354-9706
For permission to use material from this text or product,
submit all requests online at
www.cengage.com/permissions.
Further permissions questions can be e-mailed to
permissionrequest@cengage.com.

Library of Congress Control Number: 2013946695

ISBN-13: 978-1-285-18524-8

Cengage Learning
200 First Stamford Place, 4th Floor
Stamford, CT 06902
USA

Cengage Learning is a leading provider of customized learning solutions with office locations around the globe, including Singapore, the United Kingdom, Australia, Mexico, Brazil, and Japan. Locate your local office at: **www.cengage.com/global.**

Cengage Learning products are represented in Canada by Nelson Education, Ltd.

To learn more about Cengage Learning, visit **www.cengage.com.**

Purchase any of our products at your local college store or at our preferred online store **www.cengagebrain.com.**

Printed in Canada
1 2 3 4 5 6 7 17 16 15 14 13

BRIEF CONTENTS

CONTENTS

CONCEPT SUMMARIES

EXHIBITS

The study of business law and, more generally, the legal environment of business has universal applicability. A student entering any field of business must have at least a passing understanding of business law in order to function in the real world.

Additionally, students preparing for a career in accounting, government and political science, economics, and even medicine can use much of the information they learn in a business law and legal environment course. In fact, every individual throughout his or her lifetime can benefit from a knowledge of contracts, real property law, landlord-tenant relationships, and other topics. Consequently, we have fashioned this text as a useful "tool for living" for all of your students (including those taking the CPA exam).

For the Thirteenth Edition, we have spent a great deal of effort making this book more contemporary, exciting, and visually appealing than ever before. We have also added many new features and special pedagogical devices that focus on the legal, ethical, global, and e-commerce environments, while addressing core curriculum requirements.

UNIQUE NEW DIGITAL LEARNING SYSTEMS

Before we discuss the many new aspects of this text, however, we wish to point out the exciting new digital products offered in conjunction with the text.

MindTap

New for *Business Law,* Thirteenth Edition, MindTap is a fully online, highly personalized learning experience built on Cengage Learning content. MindTap combines student learning tools—such as readings, multimedia, activities and assessments from CengageNOW™—into a singular Learning Path that guides students through their course.

Instructors can personalize the experience by customizing authoritative Cengage Learning content and learning tools. MindTap offers instructors the ability to add their own content in the Learning Path with apps that integrate into the MindTap framework seamlessly with Learning Management Systems (LMS).

CengageNOW for *Business Law*: Interactive Assignment System

CengageNOW™ is a powerful course management tool that provides control and customization to optimize the student learning experience and produce desired outcomes. The application features a variety of question types to test simple reading comprehension, complex critical thinking, legal reasoning, and case analysis skills. CengageNOW includes:

- An Interactive book.
- Auto-graded homework with the following consistent question types:
  - Worksheets—Interactive worksheets prepare students for class by ensuring reading and comprehension.
  - Video Activities—Real-world video exercises make business law engaging and relevant.
  - Brief Hypotheticals—These applications provide students practice in spotting the issue and applying the law in the context of a short, factual scenario.
  - Case Problem Blueprints—Promote deeper critical thinking and legal reasoning by guiding students step-by-step through a case problem, building on acquired knowledge to truly assess their understanding of legal principles.
- Personalized Student Plan with multimedia study tools and videos.
- Test Bank.
- Reporting and Assessment options.

By using the optional CengageNOW system, students can complete the assignments online and can receive instant feedback on their answers. Instructors can utilize CengageNOW to upload their course syllabi, create and customize homework assignments, and keep track of their students' progress. Instructors can also communicate with their students about assignments and due dates, and create reports summarizing the data for an individual student or for the whole class.

CourseMate

CourseMate for *Business Law* brings business law concepts to life with interactive learning, study, and exam preparation tools that support the printed textbook. Built-in engagement tracking tools allow you to assess the study activities of your students.

Additionally, *Business Law* CourseMate includes an interactive online textbook, which contains the complete content of the print textbook enhanced by the many advantages of a digital environment.

Cengage Learning Testing Powered by Cognero

Cengage Learning Testing Powered by Cognero is a flexible, online system that allows you to do the following:

- Author, edit, and manage *Test Bank* content from multiple Cengage Learning solutions.
- Create multiple test versions in an instant.
- Deliver tests from your LMS, your classroom, or wherever you want.

START RIGHT AWAY! *Cengage Learning Testing Powered by Cognero* works on any operating system or browser.

- No special installs or downloads are needed.
- Create tests from school, home, the coffee shop—anywhere with Internet access.

WHAT WILL YOU FIND

- *Simplicity at every step.* A desktop-inspired interface features drop-down menus and familiar intuitive tools that take you through content creation and management with ease.
- *Full-featured test generator.* Create ideal assessments with your choice of fifteen question types—including true/false, multiple choice, opinion scale/Likert, and essay). Multi-language support, an equation editor and unlimited metadata help ensure your tests are complete and compliant.
- *Cross-compatible capability.* Import and export content into other systems.

COMPLETE SERIES OF *BUSINESS LAW* TEXTS

We also want instructors to know that there is now an entire family of derivative texts based on these materials for instructors wishing to customize the text for their purposes. (See **www.cengagebrain.com** or your local sales representative for more information on the entire series of *Business Law* texts.) The series includes:

- ***Business Law: Text and Cases, The First Course*** includes the first twenty-four chapters of *Business Law,* plus four chapters on Agency and Employment, and four chapters on Business Organizations.
- ***Business Law: Text and Cases, An Accelerated Course*** includes a total of nineteen chapters, all but eight of which combine materials from chapters of *Business Law.* This text provides a brief version of the core content suitable for a one-semester course.
- ***Business Law: Text and Cases, Commercial Law for Accountants*** is designed for those entering the field of accounting and includes topics from *Business Law* that accountants need to know. It covers business organizations, agency, employment, negotiable instrument law, sales and lease contracts, creditors' rights and bankruptcy, government regulation, property, and professional liability.

WHAT IS NEW IN THE THIRTEENTH EDITION

Instructors have come to rely on the coverage, accuracy, and applicability of *Business Law.* To make sure that our text engages your students, solidifies their understanding of legal concepts, and provides the best teaching tools available, we now offer the following items either in the text or in conjunction with the text.

New Chapter on Internet Law, Social Media, and Privacy

For the Thirteenth Edition, we have included an entirely new chapter (Chapter 9) entitled **Internet Law, Social Media, and Privacy.** Social media have entered the mainstream and become a part of everyday life for many businesspersons. Throughout the text, we recognize this trend by incorporating the Internet and social media as they relate to the topics under discussion.

We also give the legal issues surrounding the Internet, social media, and privacy special emphasis in this new chapter. This chapter examines some of the laws pertaining to the Internet, intellectual property, and privacy. It also discusses recent legal developments concerning the protection of social media passwords and the use of social media by employers and law enforcement.

New *Managerial Strategy* Features

For the Thirteenth Edition, we have created a new feature entitled **Managerial Strategy** that focuses on the management aspects of business law. Special emphasis is given to sustainability, ethical trends, and changing managerial responsibilities.

Each feature includes a short section entitled **Managerial Implications** that provides concrete information for managers and connects the topic under discussion to operating a business. Each feature also concludes with two **Business Questions** that prompt students to further examine the issues discussed. **Suggested answers to all the *Business Questions* are included in both the *Instructor's Manual* and the *Answers Manual* for this text.**

Topics examined in these features include:

- Budget Cuts for State Courts Can Affect Businesses (Chapter 2).
- Facing Breach of Contract Issues (Chapter 22).
- Changing Social Media Policies (Chapter 34).
- Small Business Owners Now Have Recourse When Cyber Thieves Empty Their Bank Accounts (Chapter 38).

New Appendix to Chapter 19 Focuses on Reading and Analyzing Contracts

Because reading and analyzing contracts is such a crucial skill for businesspersons, a special **new Appendix to Chapter 19** has been added. This appendix follows the last contracts chapter and explains how to read and analyze a contract. Then, it presents an example of an employee noncompetition and nondisclosure agreement. The sample contract is annotated so that students can quickly see what each contract provision means.

New Highlighted and Numbered *Examples* and *Case in Point* Illustrations

Many instructors use cases and examples to illustrate how the law applies to business. For this edition, we have expanded both our in-text examples and our discussion of case law by adding highlighted numbered **Examples** and **Cases in Point** in every chapter.

These two features are uniquely designed and consecutively numbered throughout each chapter for easy reference. *Examples* illustrate how the law applies in a specific situation. *Cases in Point* present the facts and issues of an actual case and then describe the court's decision and rationale. The numbered *Examples* and *Cases in Point* features are integrated throughout the text to help students better understand how courts apply the principles in the real world.

New *Spotlight Cases* and *Spotlight Case Problems*

For the Thirteenth Edition of *Business Law*, certain cases and case problems have been carefully chosen as exceptionally good teaching cases. **Spotlight Cases** and **Spotlight Case Problems** are labeled either by the name of one of the parties or by the subject involved. Some examples include *Spotlight on Amazon, Spotlight on Apple, Spotlight on the Seattle Mariners, Spotlight on Commercial Speech, and Spotlight on Internet Porn.*

Instructors will find these *Spotlight Cases* useful to illustrate the legal concepts under discussion. Students will enjoy studying these cases because the parties are often familiar and the cases involve interesting and memorable facts. **Suggested answers to all case-ending questions and case problems are included in both the *Instructor's Manual* and the *Answers Manual* for this text.**

New *ExamPrep* Section with Two *Issue Spotters*

For this edition, we have added a new section called *ExamPrep* at the conclusion of each chapter. The section includes **two new *Issue Spotters* related** to the chapter's topics that facilitate student learning and review of the materials. Suggested answers to the *Issue Spotters* in every chapter are provided in Appendix E at the end of the text.

New *Legal Reasoning Group Activities*

For instructors who want their students to engage in group projects, each chapter of the Thirteenth Edition includes a **special new *Legal Reasoning Group Activity*.** Each activity begins by describing a business scenario and then requires each group of students to answer a specific question pertaining to the scenario based on the information that they learned in the chapter. These projects may be used in class to spur discussion or as homework assignments. **Suggested answers to the *Legal Reasoning Group Activities* are included in both the *Instructor's Manual* and the *Answers Manual* for this text.**

New *Insight* Features

For the Thirteenth Edition, we have created **new *Insight into [E-Commerce, Ethics, the Global Environment, or Social Media]* features** that appear in selected chapters. These features provide valuable insights into how the courts and the law are dealing with specific issues. Each of these features ends with a **Legal Critical Thinking** question that explores some cultural, environmental, or technological aspect of the issue. The following are some of the topics explored in these features:

- *Insight into E-Commerce*—Do Computers Have Free Speech Rights? (Chapter 4).
- *Insight into Ethics*—Warning Labels for Video Games (Chapter 7).
- *Insight into the Global Environment*— Is It Legal to Resell Textbooks Purchased Abroad? (Chapter 8).
- *Insight into Social Media*—"Catfishing": Is That Online "Friend" Who You Think It Is? (Chapter 15).
- *Insight into E-Commerce*—Smartphone-Based Payment Systems (Chapter 25).
- *Insight into Social Media*—Social Media Estate Planning (Chapter 51).

Suggested answers to the *Legal Reasoning Group Activities* are included in both the *Instructor's Manual* and the *Answers Manual* for this text.

New *Case Analysis Cases* with Four *Legal Reasoning Questions*

In every chapter of the Thirteenth Edition of *Business Law*, we have included one longer case excerpt— labeled **Case Analysis Case**— followed by **four *Legal Reasoning Questions.*** The questions are designed to guide students' analysis of the case and build their legal reasoning skills. These *Case Analysis Cases* may be used for case-briefing assignments and are also tied to the *Special Case Analysis* questions found in every unit of the text (one per unit). **Suggested answers to the *Legal Reasoning Questions* are included in both the *Instructor's Manual* and the *Answers Manual* for this text.**

Improved Ethics Coverage

For the Thirteenth Edition of *Business Law*, we have significantly revised and updated the chapter on ethics and business decision making (Chapter 5). The chapter now presents a more practical, realistic, case-study approach to business ethics and the dilemmas facing businesspersons today. It also provides step-by-step guidance for making ethical business decisions.

The emphasis on ethics is reiterated in materials throughout the text, particularly the *Insight into Ethics* features, the *Focus on Ethics* features that conclude every unit, and the pedagogy that accompanies selected cases and features. We also discuss **corporate governance issues** as appropriate in the corporate law chapters and in the *Focus on Ethics* feature concluding Unit Eight on business organizations. Finally, each chapter in the text includes *A Question of Ethics* case problem that provides a modern-day example of the kinds of ethical issues faced by businesspersons and explores the ways that courts can resolve them.

ADDITIONAL FEATURES OF THIS TEXT

Business Law, Thirteenth Edition, includes a number of pedagogical devices and special features, including those discussed here.

Emphasis on Business and on Critical Thinking

For the Thirteenth Edition, we have focused on making the text more business related. To that end, we have carefully chosen cases, features, and problems that are relevant to operating a business. In addition, we recognize that today's business leaders must often think "outside the box" when making business decisions. For this reason, we have included numerous critical thinking and legal reasoning elements in this text. Almost all of the features and cases presented in the text conclude with some type of critical thinking question.

Cases may include one or more of the following critical thinking questions:

- *What If the Facts Were Different?*
- *The Ethical Dimension*
- *The E-Commerce Dimension*
- *The Global Dimension*
- *The Legal Environment Dimension*

Suggested answers to all questions following cases can be found in both the *Instructor's Manual* and the *Answers Manual* that accompany this text.

Managerial Implications in Selected Cases

In addition to the critical thinking questions, we have included special case pedagogy at the end of selected cases that have particular importance for business managers. This section, called *Managerial Implications*, points out the significance of the court's ruling in the case for business owners and managers.

Special Case Analysis Questions

For nearly every unit in the text, we also provide a *Special Case Analysis* question that is based on the *Case Analysis Case* excerpt in that chapter. The *Special Case Analysis* questions are designed to build students' analytical skills and appear in the *Business Case Problems* at the end of selected chapters.

The *Special Case Analysis* questions test students' ability to perform IRAC (Issue, Rule, Application, and Conclusion) case analysis. Students must identify the legal issue presented in the chapter's *Case Analysis Case*, understand the rule of law, determine how the rule applies to the facts of the case, and describe the court's conclusion. Instructors can assign these questions as homework or use them in class to elicit student participation and teach case analysis. **Suggested answers to the *Special Case Analysis* questions can be found in both the *Instructor's Manual* and the *Answers Manual* that accompany this text.**

Reviewing Features in Every Chapter

In the Thirteenth Edition of *Business Law,* we continue to offer a *Reviewing* feature at the end of every chapter to help solidify students' understanding of the chapter materials. Each *Reviewing* feature presents a hypothetical scenario and then asks a series of questions that require students to identify the issues and apply the legal concepts discussed in the chapter.

These features are designed to help students review the chapter topics in a simple and interesting way and see how the legal principles discussed in the chapter affect the world in which they live. An instructor can use these features as the basis for in-class discussion or encourage students to use them for self-study prior to completing homework assignments. **Suggested answers to the questions posed in the *Reviewing* features can be found in both the *Instructor's Manual* and the *Answers Manual* that accompany this text.**

Concept Summaries

When key areas of the law need additional emphasis, we provide a *Concept Summary.* These summaries have always been a popular pedagogical tool in this text. It now includes more than fifty of these summaries, many of which have been expanded or revised.

Exhibits

When appropriate, we also illustrate important aspects of the law in graphic form in exhibits. In all, more than one hundred exhibits are featured in *Business Law,* Thirteenth Edition. Several of these exhibits are new, and we have modified existing exhibits to achieve better clarity.

Case Problems

Every chapter includes a 2012 or 2013 case problem in the *Business Case Problems* that appear at the end of the chapter. These problems are designed to clarify how modern courts deal with the business issues discussed in the chapter.

At the request of instructors, we have given every business scenario and case problem a label that identifies the chapter topic to which the question relates. These labels make it easier for instructors who wish to assign only certain questions to their students. In addition, for this edition, we have added page references to the text where the problem's answer can be found.

We have also included two special problems—the *Spotlight Case Problems* (mentioned earlier), which are based on good teaching cases with interesting facts, and the *Business Case Problem with Sample Answer* (discussed next).

Suggested answers to all chapter-ending business scenarios and case problems are included in both the *Instructor's Manual* and the *Answers Manual* that accompany this text.

Business Case Problem with Sample Answer in Each Chapter

In response to those instructors who would like students to have sample answers available for some of the questions and case problems, we include a *Business Case Problem with Sample Answer* in each chapter.

The *Business Case Problem with Sample Answer* is based on an actual case, and students can access a sample answer in Appendix F at the end of the text.

BUSINESS LAW ON THE WEB

The Web site for the Thirteenth Edition of *Business Law* can be found by going to **www.cengagebrain.com** and entering ISBN 9781285185248. The Web site offers a broad array of teaching/learning resources, including the following:

- **Practice quizzes** for every chapter in this text.
- **Interactive flashcards** and a **Glossary** for every chapter in this text.

- **Appendix A: How to Brief Cases and Analyze Case Problems** that appears in the book is also posted on the Web site.
- **Legal reference materials** including a "Statutes" page that offers links to the full text of selected statutes referenced in the text, a Spanish glossary, and other important legal resources.
- **CourseMate,** which students can purchase access to, provides additional study tools, including an e-book, additional quizzes, flashcards, key terms, and PowerPoint slides.

THE MOST COMPLETE SUPPLEMENTS PACKAGE AVAILABLE TODAY

This edition of *Business Law* is accompanied by a vast number of teaching and learning supplements, which is available on the password-protected portion of the Instructor's Companion Web Site.

In addition, the complete teaching/learning package for the Thirteenth Edition includes numerous other supplements, including those listed below. For further information on the *Business Law* teaching/learning package, contact your local sales representative or visit the *Business Law* Web site.

Instructor's Companion Web Site

The Instructor's Companion Web Site includes the following supplements:

- **Instructor's Manual.** Includes sections entitled "Additional Cases Addressing This Issue" at the end of selected case synopses.
- **Answers Manual.** Provides answers to all questions presented in the text, including the questions in each case, feature, and unit-ending feature.
- **Test Bank.** A comprehensive test bank that contains multiple choice, true/false, and short essay questions.
- **Case-Problem Cases.**
- **Case Printouts.**
- **PowerPoint slides.**
- *Instructor's Manual* for the *Drama of the Law* video series.

Software, Video, and Multimedia Supplements

- ***Business Law* Digital Video Library**— Provides access to ninety videos, including the *Drama of the Law* videos and video clips from actual Hollywood movies. Access to our Digital Library is available in an optional package with each new text at no additional cost. You can access the *Business Law* Digital Video Library, along with corresponding *Video Questions* that are related to specific chapters in the text, at **www.cengagebrain.com**.
- **CengageNow** (described on the first page of this preface).
- **MindTap** (described on the first page of this preface).
- **CourseMate** (described on the first page of this preface).
- **Westlaw®**—(Ten free hours for qualified adopters).

FOR USERS OF THE TWELFTH EDITION

First of all, we want to thank you for helping make *Business Law* the best-selling business law text in America today. Second, we want to make you aware of the numerous additions and changes that we have made in this edition—many in response to comments from reviewers.

New Chapter and Special Pedagogy

For this edition, we have added more material on Internet law and social media throughout the text. We have also created an entire chapter (Chapter 9) on Internet law, social media, and privacy. We have combined coverage of intentional torts and negligence in one chapter (Chapter 6), and now cover strict liability and product liability in the same chapter (Chapter 7).

We have also added the following entirely new elements for the Thirteenth Edition:

- New highlighted and numbered *Examples* and *Cases in Point.*
- New *Managerial Strategy* features.

- New *Insight into Social Media* features.
- New *Spotlight Cases and Spotlight Case Problems.*
- *Classic Cases.*
- Four *Legal Reasoning Questions* at the conclusion of *Case Analysis Cases.*
- *Appendix to Chapter 19: Reading and Analyzing Contracts.*
- *Issue Spotters* in every chapter.
- *Legal Reasoning Group Activities* in every chapter.
- *Appendix E* (Answers to the *Issue Spotters*), *Appendix F* (Sample Answers for *Business Case Problems with Sample Answer*).

Significantly Revised Chapters

Every chapter of the Thirteenth Edition has been revised as necessary to incorporate new developments in the law or to streamline the presentations. Other major changes and additions for this edition include the following:

- Chapter 4 (Business and the Constitution)— The chapter has been revised and updated to be more business oriented. It has numerous new *Examples* and *Cases in Point,* many of which are based on United States Supreme Court decisions.
- Chapter 5 (Business Ethics)—This chapter has been thoroughly revised with all new cases, business scenarios, and many new case problems. It includes a new section on business ethics and social media, as well as an in depth discussion of stakeholders and corporate social responsibility. The chapter also provides step-by-step guidance on making ethical business decisions and includes materials on global business ethics. An *Insight into the Global Environment* feature examines bribery and the Foreign Corrupt Practices Act.
- Chapter 6 (Torts) and Chapter 7 (Strict Liability and Product Liability)—Our torts coverage has been substantially revised, reorganized, and streamlined. The materials are up to date and business oriented. Intentional torts and negligence are covered in one chapter, and strict liability and product liability are covered in the next. Each chapter includes a *Spotlight Case* and Chapter 7 presents an *Insight into Ethics* feature discussing warning labels for video games.

- Chapter 8 (Intellectual Property Rights)—The materials on intellectual property rights have been thoroughly revised and updated to reflect the most current laws and trends. There is a discussion of the dispute between Apple, Inc. and Samsung Electronics Company over smartphones. A feature discusses a 2013 United States Supreme Court decision on the resale on eBay of textbooks purchased abroad.

- Chapter 9 (Internet Law, Social Media, and Privacy)—This chapter is all new and was created for the Thirteenth Edition to explore timely topics. It discusses legal issues that are unique to the Internet, such as spam, domain name disputes, cybersquatting, digital copyright laws, and file-sharing. It also discusses social media, company-wide social media networks, state legislation on social media, the Electronic Communications Privacy Act, and password protection. The chapter also covers online defamation, data collection and cookies, and online privacy.

- Chapters 11 through 19 (the Contracts and E-Contracts unit)—Throughout this unit, we have added many highlighted and numbered *Examples, Cases in Point,* and updates to clarify and enhance our already superb contract law coverage. The discussion of online contracting and electronic signatures has been merged with the coverage of tradition contracts. Numerous *Spotlight Cases* have been added to this unit, including *Spotlight on Amazon, Spotlight on Columbia Pictures, Spotlight on the Improv,* and *Spotlight on PC Magazine.*

- Chapters 20 through 24 (the unit on Domestic and International Sales and Lease Contracts)—We have streamlined and simplified our coverage of the Uniform Commercial Code. We have added numerous new *Examples* and *Cases in Point* throughout the unit to increase student comprehension. New pedagogy, business scenarios, and case problems have been added to Chapter 23 (Warranties), and the materials on product liability have been moved out of this chapter. The chapter now includes a *Spotlight on DaimlerChrysler* case and a *Spotlight on Apple* case problem. It also contains a classic case and a 2013 *Case Analysis Case.* We have also expanded our discussion of international sales and lease contracts in Chapter 24 (International Law in a Global Economy). Chapter 24 now also discusses international dispute resolution and includes a feature on border searches of electronic devices. All three cases presented in Chapter 24 are new, and an important 2013 United States Supreme Court decision has been selected as a *Spotlight on International Torts.*

- Chapters 25 through 28 (the unit on Negotiable Instruments)—We have updated this entire unit and revised the materials to make difficult concepts more comprehensible for students. Chapter 25 contains an *Insight into E-Commerce* feature on smartphone-based payment systems as well as a *Spotlight Case* on casino markers.

- Chapters 29 through 31 (the unit on Creditors' Rights and Bankruptcy)—This unit has been revised to be more up to date and comprehensible. We have also streamlined the materials to focus on those concepts that students need to know. Chapter 30 (Secured Transactions) was substantially reworked to clarify the general principles and exceptions. Chapter 31 (Bankruptcy Law) includes updated dollar amounts of various provisions of the Bankruptcy Code.

- Chapter 34 (Employment, Immigration, and Labor Law) and Chapter 35 (Employment Discrimination and Diversity)—These two chapters covering employment law have been thoroughly updated to include discussions of legal issues facing employers today. In Chapter 34, we have updated minimum wage figures and Social Security and Medicare percentages, and have included a discussion of the Affordable Care Act (Obamacare). The materials on immigration law have been streamlined and updated and include a discussion of state immigration legislation and its constitutionality. A *Managerial Strategy* feature in Chapter 34 covers changing social media policies, and there is a new *Cases Analysis Case* on labor law. Chapter 35 includes new numbered lists of elements, two new cases, and an *Insight into Ethics* feature on appearance-based discrimination. We discuss relevant United States Supreme Court decisions affecting employment issues throughout both chapters.

- Chapters 36 through 42 (the Business Organizations unit)—This unit has been revised and updated to improve the flow and clarity. We provide more practical information and recent examples. Limited liability companies and other small-business organizational forms—as well as issues affecting owners of small businesses—are covered in Chapter 38. The chapter discusses financing considerations, such as crowdfunding, and includes a *Managerial Strategy* feature discussing what small-business owners can do if they become victims of cyber thieves. New cases and many new Case Analysis Cases have been added in the corporate law chapters. An *Insight into Ethics* feature in Chapter 40 addresses the issue of when lying is a federal crime. The chapter on securities law (Chapter 42) has been substantially revised, updated, and simplified.
- Chapter 43 through 47 (the Government Regulation unit)—This unit has been streamlined and updated. The Dodd-Frank Wall Street Reform and Consumer Protection Act is covered in Chapter 44 (Consumer Law). Chapter 44 also includes a *Spotlight on Honda* case and a *Spotlight on McDonald's* case problem. The materials on air pollution and water pollution in Chapter 45 (Environmental Law) have been updated, and a recent decision from the United States Supreme Court decision is presented. Chapter 46 (Antitrust Law) has several new examples and expanded coverage of leading cases, including a discussion of price fixing and e-books. Updated thresholds for interlocking directorates have been incorporated. Chapter 47 (Professional Liability

and Accountability) includes a new discussion of the use of global accounting rules by the United States. A *Managerial Strategy* feature in Chapter 47 discusses professionals' responsibilities for protecting data in the cloud.
- Chapter 48 (Personal Property and Bailments)—Many new *Examples, Cases in Point,* and numbered lists have been added to help clarify the materials. There is a *Classic Case* on gifts, and a new case on whether a bailee is negligent for losing computer data while replacing a hard drive.
- Chapter 49 (Real Property and Landlord-Tenant Law)—Parts of this chapter have been significantly revised. Several new terms were added. The discussion of eminent domain for economic development was updated. A *Spotlight Case* covers whether the buyer of an allegedly haunted house can seek rescission of the sale. The *Case Analysis Case* is on whether a town can use a condemnation action to acquire rights of way for a natural gas pipeline that is not being built to furnish natural gas to the residents of that town. The discussion of zoning laws has been reworked and several numbered lists explain permissible uses of land and requirements for variances.
- Chapter 51 (Wills and Trusts)—This chapter has been revised for more streamlined presentation, especially in the discussion of capacity and intent. The cases illustrate undue influence, disinheritance, and revocation of wills. Numbered lists have been added to improve comprehension, and an *Insight into Social Media* feature addresses social media estate planning.

ACKNOWLEDGMENTS
FOR PREVIOUS EDITIONS

Since we began this project many years ago, a sizable number of business law professors and others have helped us in various phases of the undertaking. The following reviewers offered numerous constructive criticisms, comments, and suggestions during the preparation of all previous editions.

Jeffrey E. Allen
University of Miami

Judith Anshin
Sacramento City College

Thomas M. Apke
California State University, Fullerton

Raymond August
Washington State University

William Auslen
San Francisco City College

Mary B. Bader
Moorhead State University

Frank Bagan
County College of Morris

John J. Balek
Morton College, Illinois

Michael G. Barth
University of Phoenix

David L. Baumer
North Carolina State University

Barbara E. Behr
Bloomsburg University of Pennsylvania

Robert B. Bennett, Jr.
Butler University

Robert C. Bird
University of Connecticut

Heidi Boerstler
University of Colorado at Denver

Maria Kathleen Boss
California State University, Los Angeles

Lawrence J. Bradley
University of Notre Dame

Dean Bredeson
University of Texas at Austin

Doug Brown
Montana State University

Kristi K. Brown
University of Texas at Austin

William J. Burke
University of Massachusetts, Lowell

Kenneth Burns
University of Miami

Daniel R. Cahoy
Pennsylvania State University

Rita Cain
University of Missouri—Kansas City

Jeanne A. Calderon
New York University

Joseph E. Cantrell
DeAnza College, California

Donald Cantwell
University of Texas at Arlington

Thomas D. Cavenagh
North Central College—Naperville, Illinois

Robert Chatov
State University of New York, Buffalo

Corey Ciocchetti
University of Denver

Nanette C. Clinch
San Jose State University, California

Robert J. Cox
Salt Lake Community College

Thomas Crane
University of Miami

Angela Crossin
Purdue University, Calumet

Kenneth S. Culott
University of Texas at Austin

Larry R. Curtis
Iowa State University

Richard Dalebout
Brigham Young University

William H. Daughtrey, Jr.
Virginia Commonwealth University

Michael DeAngelis
University of Rhode Island

James Doering
University of Wisconsin, Green Bay

John V. Dowdy
University of Texas at Arlington

Michele A. Dunkerley
University of Texas at Austin

Paul Dusseault
Herkimer County Community College

Nena Ellison
Florida Atlantic University

O. E. Elmore
Texas A&M University

Robert J. Enders
California State Polytechnic University, Pomona

Michael Engber
Ball State University

David A. Escamilla
University of Texas at Austin

James S. Fargason
Louisiana State University

Frank S. Forbes
University of Nebraska at Omaha

Joe W. Fowler
Oklahoma State University

Stanley G. Freeman
University of South Carolina

Joan Gabel
Florida State University

Christ Gaetanos
State University of New York, Fredonia

Chester S. Galloway
Auburn University

Bob Garrett
American River College, California

Gary L. Giese
University of Colorado at Denver

Thomas Gossman
Western Michigan University

Dr. J. Keaton Grubbs
Stephen F. Austin State University

Patrick O. Gudridge
University of Miami School of Law

Jacqueline Hagerott
Franklin University

James M. Haine
University of Wisconsin, Stevens Point

Gerard Halpern
University of Arkansas

Christopher L. Hamilton
Golden West College, California

JoAnn W. Hammer
University of Texas at Austin

Charles Hartman
Wright State University, Ohio

Richard A. Hausler
University of Miami School of Law

Harry E. Hicks
Butler University, Indianapolis

Janine S. Hiller
Virginia Polytechnic Institute and State University

Rebecca L. Hillyer
Chemeketa Community College

E. Clayton Hipp, Jr.
Clemson University

Anthony H. Holliday, Jr.
Howard University

Telford Hollman
University of Northern Iowa

June A. Horrigan
California State University, Sacramento

John P. Huggard
North Carolina State University

Terry Hutchins
Pembroke State University,
North Carolina

Robert Jesperson
University of Houston

Debra Johnson
University of Montana at Billings

Bryce J. Jones
Northeast Missouri State University

Margaret Jones
Southwest Missouri State College

Peter A. Karl III
SUNY Institute of Technology at Utica

Jack E. Karns
East Carolina University

Tamra Kempf
University of Miami

Judith Kenney
University of Miami

Barbara Kincaid
Southern Methodist University

Carey Kirk
University of Northern Iowa

Nancy P. Klintworth
University of Central Florida

Kurtis P. Klumb
University of Wisconsin
at Milwaukee

Kathleen M. Knutson
College of St. Catherine,
St. Paul, Minnesota

Vonda M. Laughlin
Carson-Newman College

M. Alan Lawson
Mt. San Antonio College

Leslie E. Lenn
St. Edwards University

Susan Liebeler
Loyola University

Stuart MacDonald
University of Central Oklahoma

Thomas E. Maher
California State University, Fullerton

Sal Marchionna
Triton College, Illinois

Gene A. Marsh
University of Alabama

Karen Kay Matson
University of Texas at Austin

Woodrow J. Maxwell
Hudson Valley Community College,
New York

Bruce E. May
University of South Dakota

Gail McCracken
University of Michigan, Dearborn

John W. McGee
Southwest Texas State University

Cotton Meagher
University of Nevada at Las Vegas

Christopher Meakin
University of Texas at Austin

Roger E. Meiners
University of Texas at Arlington

Gerald S. Meisel
Bergen Community College, New Jersey

Richard Mills
Cypress College

David Minars
City University of New York, Brooklyn

Leo Moersen
The George Washington University

Alan Moggio
Illinois Central College

Violet E. Molnar
Riverside City College

James E. Moon
Meyer, Johnson & Moon, Minneapolis

Melinda Ann Mora
University of Texas at Austin

Bob Morgan
Eastern Michigan University

Barry S. Morinaka
Baker College—Michigan

Melanie Morris
Raritan Valley Community College

Joan Ann Mrava
Los Angeles Southwest College

Dwight D. Murphey
Wichita State University

Daniel E. Murray
University of Miami School of Law

Paula C. Murray
University of Texas

Gregory J. Naples
Marquette University

George A. Nation III
Lehigh University

Caleb L. Nichols
Western Connecticut State University

John M. Norwood
University of Arkansas

Jamie O'Brien
University of Notre Dame

Michael J. O'Hara
University of Nebraska at Omaha

Rick F. Orsinger
College of DuPage, Illinois

Daniel J. O'Shea
Hillsborough Community College

Thomas L. Palmer
Northern Arizona University

Charles M. Patten
University of Wisconsin, Oshkosh

Patricia Pattison
Texas State University, San Marcos

Peyton J. Paxson
University of Texas at Austin

Ralph L. Quinones
University of Wisconsin, Oshkosh

Carol D. Rasnic
Virginia Commonwealth University

Marvin H. Robertson
Harding University

Bert K. Robinson
Kennesaw State University

Gary K. Sambol
Rutgers State University

Rudy Sandoval
University of Texas, San Antonio

Sidney S. Sappington
York College of Pennsylvania

Martha Sartoris
North Hennepin Community College

Barbara P. Scheller
Temple University

S. Alan Schlact
Kennesaw State University, Georgia

Lorne H. Seidman
University of Nevada at Las Vegas

Ira Selkowitz
University of Colorado at Denver

Roscoe B. Shain
Austin Peay University

Bennett D. Shulman
Lansing Community College, Michigan

S. Jay Sklar
Temple University

Dana Blair Smith
University of Texas at Austin

Michael Smydra
*Oakland Community College—
Royal Oak*

Arthur Southwick
University of Michigan

Sylvia A. Spade
University of Texas at Austin

John A. Sparks
Grove City College, Pennsylvania

Robert D. Sprague
University of Wyoming

Elisabeth Sperow
*California Polytechnic University,
San Luis Obispo*

Brenda Steuer
North Harris College, Houston

Craig Stilwell
Michigan State University

Irwin Stotsky
University of Miami School of Law

Larry Strate
University of Nevada at Las Vegas

Charles R. B. Stowe
Sam Houston State University

Raymond Mason Taylor
North Carolina State University

Ray Teske
University of Texas at San Antonio

H. Allan Tolbert
Central Texas College

Jesse C. Trentadue
University of North Dakota

Edwin Tucker
University of Connecticut

Gary Victor
Eastern Michigan University

William H. Volz
Wayne State University

David Vyncke
Scott Community College, Iowa

William H. Walker,
*Indiana University–Purdue University,
Fort Wayne*

Diana Walsh
County College of Morris

Robert J. Walter
University of Texas at El Paso

Gary Watson
*California State University,
Los Angeles*

John L. Weimer
Nicholls State University, Louisiana

Marshall Wilkerson
University of Texas at Austin

Melanie Stallings Williams
California State University—Northridge

Arthur D. Wolfe
Michigan State University

Elizabeth A. Wolfe
University of Texas at Austin

Daniel R. Wrentmore
Santa Barbara City College

Eric D. Yordy
Northern Arizona University

Norman Gregory Young
*California State Polytechnic University,
Pomona*

Ronald C. Young
*Kalamazoo Valley Community College,
Michigan*

ACKNOWLEDGMENTS FOR THE THIRTEENTH EDITION

In preparing the Thirteenth Edition of *Business Law*, we received valuable suggestions for how to improve the text from the following individuals:

Kylar William Broadus, Esq.
Lincoln University in Missouri

Elizabeth K. Brunn, Esq.
*University of Baltimore; University
of Maryland University College*

Arthur J. Casey
*San Jose State University, College of
Business, Organization and Management*

Julia M. Dunlap, Esq.
University of California, San Diego

Paul Dusseault
Herkimer Community College (SUNY)

Maria Elena Ellison
Florida Atlantic University

Denise M. Farag
Linfield College

John D. Grigsby
Pennsylvania College of Technology

Paul Guymon
William Rainey Harper College

Debra M. Johnson
Montana State University—Billings

Anne E. Kastle
Edmonds Community College

Lisa Quinn Knych
Syracuse University,
Whitman School of Management

Peter Kwiatkowski, Esq.
Baldwin Wallace University

Meg Costello Lambert
Oakland Community College—
Auburn Hills Campus

Robert B. Long
Oakland Community College

Michael Martin, J.D., M.B.A., LL.M.
University of Northern Colorado,
Monfort College of Business

Jennifer Merton, J.D.
University of Massachusetts
at Amherst

Dr. Kelly E. O'Donnell, J.C.D
California Lutheran University,
Thousand Oaks, California

Carlton Perkins
Texas Southern University

Darren A. Prum
The Florida State University

Norberto Ruiz
Chabot College

Thomas F. Taylor
Campbell University

Katherine Hannan Wears, J.D.
Clarkson University School of Business

Bob Zaffram
Erie Community College,
Buffalo, New York

We also wish to extend special thanks to Diane May, Winona State University, for her contributions to the Thirteenth Edition, specifically for preparing the Blueprint Cases that are included in both CengageNOW and MindTap for this edition.

As in all past editions, we owe a debt of extreme gratitude to the numerous individuals who worked directly with us or at Cengage Learning. In particular, we wish to thank Vicky True-Baker and Rob Dewey for their helpful advice and guidance during all of the stages of this new edition. We extend our thanks to Jan Lamar, our longtime developmental editor, for her many useful suggestions and for her efforts in coordinating reviews and ensuring the timely and accurate publication of all supplemental materials. We are also indebted to Kristen Hurd for her excellent marketing advice and Mike Worls for his support.

Our production manager and designer, Ann Borman, made sure that we came out with an error-free, visually attractive Thirteenth Edition. We appreciate her efforts. We are also indebted to the staff at Parkwood Composition, our compositor. Their ability to generate the pages for this text quickly and accurately made it possible for us to meet our ambitious printing schedule.

We especially wish to thank Katherine Marie Silsbee for her management of the entire project, as well as for the application of her superb research and editorial skills. We also wish to thank William Eric Hollowell, who co-authored the *Instructor's Manual* and the *Test Bank* for his excellent research efforts. We were fortunate enough to have the copyediting of Pat Lewis and the proof-reading services of Beverly Peavler. We are grateful for the efforts of Vickie Reierson and Roxanna Lee for their proofreading and other assistance, which helped to ensure an error-free text. Finally, we thank Suzanne Jasin of K & M Consulting for her many special efforts on this project.

In addition, we would like to give special thanks to all of the individuals who were instrumental in developing and implementing the new CengageNOW for *Business Law:* Interactive Assignment System. These include Rob Dewey, Vicky True, Jan Lamar, Lisa Lysne, and Kristen Meere at Cengage, and Katherine Marie Silsbee, Roger Meiners, Lavina Leed Miller, William Eric Hollowell, Kimberly Wallan, Kristi Wiswell, and Joseph Zavaleta who helped develop the content for this unique Web-based product.

Through the years, we have enjoyed an ongoing correspondence with many of you who have found points on which you wish to comment. We continue to welcome all comments and promise to respond promptly. By incorporating your ideas, we can continue to write a business law text that is best for you and best for your students.

K.S.C.
R.L.M.
F.B.C.

Dedication

To Ed Dumke,

Whose penetrating insights
continue to sharpen
my intellectual analyses.
What a delight knowing you!

R. L. M.

To my parents and sisters.

F. B. C.

BUSINESS LAW

CLARKSON · MILLER · CROSS

UNIT ONE

THE LEGAL ENVIRONMENT OF BUSINESS

CONTENTS

CHAPTER 1

LAW AND LEGAL REASONING

One of the important functions of law in any society is to provide stability, predictability, and continuity so that people can know how to order their affairs. If any society is to survive, its citizens must be able to determine what is legally right and legally wrong. They must know what sanctions will be imposed on them if they commit wrongful acts. If they suffer harm as a result of others' wrongful acts, they must know how they can seek compensation. By setting forth the rights, obligations, and privileges of citizens, the law enables individuals to go about their business with confidence and a certain degree of predictability.

Although law has various definitions, they are all based on the general observation that **law** consists of *enforceable rules governing relationships among individuals and between individuals and their society*. These "enforceable rules" may consist of unwritten principles of behavior established by a nomadic tribe. They may be set forth in a law code, such as the Code of Hammurabi in ancient Babylon (c. 1780 B.C.E.) or the law code of one of today's European nations. They may consist of written laws and court decisions created by modern legislative and judicial bodies, as in the United States. Regardless of how such rules are created, they all have one thing in common: they establish rights, duties, and

privileges that are consistent with the values and beliefs of their society or its ruling group.

In this introductory chapter, we first look at an important question for any student reading this text: How does the legal environment affect business decision making? We next describe the major sources of American law, the common law tradition, and some basic schools of legal thought. We conclude the chapter with sections offering practical guidance on several topics, including how to find the sources of law discussed in this chapter (and referred to throughout the text) and how to read and understand court opinions.

BUSINESS ACTIVITIES AND THE LEGAL ENVIRONMENT

Laws and government regulations affect almost all business activities—from hiring and firing decisions to workplace safety, the manufacturing and marketing of products, business financing, and more. To make good business decisions, a basic knowledge of the laws and regulations governing these activities is beneficial—if not essential.

Realize also that in today's business world, a knowledge of "black-letter" law is not enough. Businesspersons are also pressured to make ethical decisions. Thus, the study of business law necessarily involves an ethical dimension.

Many Different Laws May Affect a Single Business Decision

As you will note, each chapter in this text covers specific areas of the law and shows how the legal rules in each area affect business activities. Though compartmentalizing the law in this fashion promotes conceptual clarity, it does not indicate the extent to which a number of different laws may apply to just one decision.

LESSONS FROM FACEBOOK When Mark Zuckerberg started Facebook as a Harvard student, he probably did not imagine all the legal challenges his company would face as a result of his business decisions.

• As you may know from the movie, *The Social Network,* shortly after Facebook was launched, others claimed that Zuckerberg had stolen their ideas for a social networking site. Their claims involved alleged theft of intellectual property (see Chapter 8), fraudulent misrepresentation (see Chapter 15), partnership law and securities law. Facebook ultimately paid a significant amount ($65 million) to settle those claims out of court (see Chapter 2).

- Facebook has also been sued repeatedly for violating users' privacy (such as by disseminating private information to third parties for commercial purposes—see Chapters 4 and 9).
- In 2012, a *class-action* lawsuit was filed against Facebook that seeks damages of $15 billion for violating users' privacy (and federal wiretapping law) by tracking their Web site usage.
- Facebook's business decisions have also come under scrutiny by federal regulators, such as the Federal Trade Commission (FTC) and the Securities and Exchange Commission (SEC).
- In 2011, the company settled a complaint filed by the FTC alleging that Facebook failed to keep "friends" lists and other user information private.
- In 2012, Facebook conducted a much-anticipated initial public offering (IPO) of its stock. The IPO did not go well, however, and many investors suffered losses. Facebook is facing dozens of lawsuits (including class actions) related to business decisions made with regard to the IPO and alleged violations of securities laws.
- The SEC is also investigating whether Facebook engaged in any wrongdoing with regard to its IPO and trading of stock.

POINTS TO CONSIDER A key to avoiding business disputes is to think ahead when starting or running a business or entering a contract. Learn what you can about the laws pertaining to that specific enterprise or transaction. Have some idea of the legal ramifications of your business decisions and seek the advice of counsel when in doubt. Exhibit 1–1 on the following page illustrates the various areas of law that may influence business decision making.

Ethics and Business Decision Making

Merely knowing the areas of law that may affect a business decision is not sufficient in today's business world. Businesspersons must also take ethics into account. As you will learn in Chapter 5, *ethics* generally is defined as the principles governing what constitutes right or wrong behavior.

Today, business decision makers need to consider not just whether a decision is legal, but also whether it is ethical. Often, as in several of the claims against Facebook discussed above, disputes arise in business because one party feels that he or she has been treated unfairly. Thus, the underlying reason for bringing some lawsuits is a breach of ethical duties (such as when a partner or employee attempts to secretly take advantage of a business opportunity).

Throughout this text, you will learn about the relationship between the law and ethics, as well as about some of the types of ethical questions that often arise in business. For example, the unit-ending *Focus on Ethics* features are devoted solely to the exploration of ethical questions pertaining to topics treated within the unit. We have also included *Ethical Dimension* questions for selected cases that focus on ethical considerations in today's business climate and *Insight into Ethics* features that appear in selected chapters. A *Question of Ethics* case problem is included at the conclusion of every chapter to introduce you to the ethical aspects of specific cases involving real-life situations. Additionally, Chapter 5 offers a detailed look at the importance of business ethics.

SECTION 2
SOURCES OF AMERICAN LAW

There are numerous sources of American law. *Primary sources of law,* or sources that establish the law, include the following:

1. The U.S. Constitution and the constitutions of the various states.
2. Statutory law—including laws passed by Congress, state legislatures, or local governing bodies.
3. Regulations created by administrative agencies, such as the Food and Drug Administration.
4. Case law and common law doctrines.

We describe each of these important sources of law in the following pages.

Secondary sources of law are books and articles that summarize and clarify the primary sources of law. Examples include legal encyclopedias, treatises, articles in law reviews, and compilations of law, such as the *Restatements of the Law* (which will be discussed shortly). Courts often refer to secondary sources of law for guidance in interpreting and applying the primary sources of law discussed here.

EXHIBIT 1-1 **Areas of the Law That May Affect Business Decision Making**

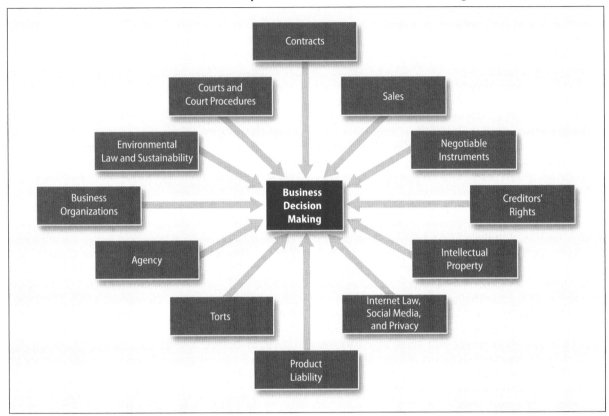

Constitutional Law

The federal government and the states have separate written constitutions that set forth the general organization, powers, and limits of their respective governments. **Constitutional law** is the law as expressed in these constitutions.

According to Article VI of the U.S. Constitution, the Constitution is the supreme law of the land. As such, it is the basis of all law in the United States. A law in violation of the Constitution, if challenged, will be declared unconstitutional and will not be enforced, no matter what its source. Because of its importance in the American legal system, we present the complete text of the U.S. Constitution in Appendix B and discuss it in depth in Chapter 4.

The Tenth Amendment to the U.S. Constitution reserves to the states all powers not granted to the federal government. Each state in the union has its own constitution. Unless it conflicts with the U.S. Constitution or a federal law, a state constitution is supreme within the state's borders.

Statutory Law

Laws enacted by legislative bodies at any level of government, such as statutes passed by Congress or by state legislatures, make up the body of law known as **statutory law.** When a legislature passes a statute, that statute ultimately is included in the federal code of laws or the relevant state code of laws (discussed later in this chapter).

Statutory law also includes local **ordinances**— statutes (laws, rules, or orders) passed by municipal or county governing units to govern matters not covered by federal or state law. Ordinances commonly have to do with city or county land use (zoning ordinances), building and safety codes, and other matters affecting the local community.

A federal statute, of course, applies to all states. A state statute, in contrast, applies only within the state's borders. State laws thus may vary from state to state. No federal statute may violate the U.S. Constitution, and no state statute or local ordinance may violate the U.S. Constitution or the relevant state constitution.

UNIFORM LAWS During the 1800s, the differences among state laws frequently created difficulties for businesspersons conducting trade and commerce among the states. To counter these problems, a group of legal scholars and lawyers formed the National Conference of Commissioners on Uniform State Laws (NCCUSL, **www.uniformlaws.org**) in 1892 to draft **uniform laws** (model statutes) for the states to consider adopting. The NCCUSL still exists today and continues to issue uniform laws.

Each state has the option of adopting or rejecting a uniform law. *Only if a state legislature adopts a uniform law does that law become part of the statutory law of that state.* Note that a state legislature may adopt all or part of a uniform law as it is written, or the legislature may rewrite the law however the legislature wishes. Hence, even though many states may have adopted a uniform law, those states' laws may not be entirely "uniform."

The earliest uniform law, the Uniform Negotiable Instruments Law, was completed by 1896 and adopted in every state by the 1920s (although not all states used exactly the same wording). Over the following decades, other acts were drawn up in a similar manner. In all, more than two hundred uniform acts have been issued by the NCCUSL since its inception. The most ambitious uniform act of all, however, was the Uniform Commercial Code.

THE UNIFORM COMMERCIAL CODE One of the most important uniform acts is the Uniform Commercial Code (UCC), which was created through the joint efforts of the NCCUSL and the American Law Institute.[1] The UCC was first issued in 1952 and has been adopted in all fifty states,[2] the District of Columbia, and the Virgin Islands.

The UCC facilitates commerce among the states by providing a uniform, yet flexible, set of rules governing commercial transactions. Because of its importance in the area of commercial law, we cite the UCC frequently in this text. We also present the full UCC in Appendix C. From time to time, the NCCUSL revises the articles contained in the UCC and submits the revised versions to the states for adoption.

Administrative Law

Another important source of American law is **administrative law,** which consists of the rules,

orders, and decisions of administrative agencies. An **administrative agency** is a federal, state, or local government agency established to perform a specific function. Administrative law and procedures constitute a dominant element in the regulatory environment of business.

Rules issued by various administrative agencies now affect almost every aspect of a business's operations. Regulations govern a business's capital structure and financing, its hiring and firing procedures, its relations with employees and unions, and the way it manufactures and markets its products. Regulations enacted to protect the environment also often play a significant role in business operations.

FEDERAL AGENCIES At the national level, the cabinet departments of the executive branch include numerous **executive agencies.** The U.S. Food and Drug Administration, for example, is an agency within the U.S. Department of Health and Human Services. Executive agencies are subject to the authority of the president, who has the power to appoint and remove their officers.

There are also major **independent regulatory agencies** at the federal level, such as the Federal Trade Commission, the Securities and Exchange Commission, and the Federal Communications Commission. The president's power is less pronounced in regard to independent agencies, whose officers serve for fixed terms and cannot be removed without just cause.

STATE AND LOCAL AGENCIES There are administrative agencies at the state and local levels as well. Commonly, a state agency (such as a state pollution-control agency) is created as a parallel to a federal agency (such as the Environmental Protection Agency). Just as federal statutes take precedence over conflicting state statutes, federal agency regulations take precedence over conflicting state regulations.

Case Law and Common Law Doctrines

The rules of law announced in court decisions constitute another basic source of American law. These rules include interpretations of constitutional provisions, of statutes enacted by legislatures, and of regulations created by administrative agencies.

Today, this body of judge-made law is referred to as **case law.** Case law—the doctrines and principles announced in cases—governs all areas not covered by

---

1. This institute was formed in the 1920s and consists of practicing attorneys, legal scholars, and judges.
2. Louisiana has not adopted Articles 2 and 2A (covering contracts for the sale and lease of goods), however.

statutory law or administrative law and is part of our common law tradition. We look at the origins and characteristics of the common law tradition in some detail in the pages that follow.

See *Concept Summary 1.1* below for a review of the sources of American law.

SECTION 3
THE COMMON LAW TRADITION

Because of our colonial heritage, much of American law is based on the English legal system, which originated in medieval England and continued to evolve in the following centuries. Knowledge of this system is necessary to understanding the American legal system today.

Early English Courts

The origins of the English legal system—and thus the U.S. legal system as well—date back to 1066, when the Normans conquered England. William the Conqueror and his successors began the process of unifying the country under their rule. One of the means they used to do this was the establishment of the king's courts, or *curiae regis*.

Before the Norman Conquest, disputes had been settled according to the local legal customs and traditions in various regions of the country. The king's courts sought to establish a uniform set of customs for the country as a whole. What evolved in these courts was the beginning of the **common law**—a body of general rules that applied throughout the entire English realm. Eventually, the common law tradition became part of the heritage of all nations that were once British colonies, including the United States.

COURTS OF LAW AND REMEDIES AT LAW The early English king's courts could grant only very limited kinds of **remedies** (the legal means to enforce a right or redress a wrong). If one person wronged another in some way, the king's courts could award as compensation one or more of the following: (1) land, (2) items of value, or (3) money.

The courts that awarded this compensation became known as **courts of law,** and the three remedies were called **remedies at law.** (Today, the remedy at law normally takes the form of monetary **damages**—an amount given to a party whose legal interests have been injured.) This system made the procedure for settling disputes more uniform. When a complaining party wanted a remedy other than economic compensation, however, the courts of law could do nothing, so "no remedy, no right."

COURTS OF EQUITY *Equity* is a branch of law—founded on notions of justice and fair dealing—that seeks to supply a remedy when no adequate remedy at law is available. When individuals could not obtain an adequate remedy in a court of law, they petitioned the king for relief. Most of these petitions were decided by an adviser to the king, called a **chancellor,** who had the power to grant new and unique remedies. Eventually, formal chancery courts, or **courts of equity,** were established.

CONCEPT SUMMARY 1.1
Sources of American Law

SOURCE	DESCRIPTION
Constitutional Law	The law as expressed in the U.S. Constitution and the state constitutions. The U.S. Constitution is the supreme law of the land. State constitutions are supreme within state borders to the extent that they do not violate a clause of the U.S. Constitution or a federal law.
Statutory Law	Laws (statutes and ordinances) enacted by federal, state, and local legislatures and governing bodies. None of these laws can violate the U.S. Constitution or the relevant state constitution. Uniform laws, when adopted by a state, become statutory law in that state.
Administrative Law	The rules, orders, and decisions of federal, state, and local government administrative agencies.
Case Law and Common Law Doctrines	Judge-made law, including interpretations of constitutional provisions, of statutes enacted by legislatures, and of regulations created by administrative agencies.

REMEDIES IN EQUITY The remedies granted by the equity courts became known as **remedies in equity,** or equitable remedies. These remedies include specific performance, an injunction, and rescission. *Specific performance* involves ordering a party to perform an agreement as promised. An *injunction* is an order to a party to cease engaging in a specific activity or to undo some wrong or injury. *Rescission* is the cancellation of a contractual obligation. We will discuss these and other equitable remedies in more detail at appropriate points in the chapters that follow, particularly in Chapter 19.

As a general rule, today's courts, like the early English courts, will not grant equitable remedies unless the remedy at law—monetary damages—is inadequate. ▶ **Example 1.1** Ted forms a contract (a legally binding agreement—see Chapter 11) to purchase a parcel of land that he thinks will be perfect for his future home. The seller **breaches,** or fails to fulfill, this agreement. Ted could sue the seller for the return of any deposits or down payment he might have made on the land, but this is not the remedy he really seeks. What Ted wants is to have the court order the seller to perform the contract. In other words, Ted wants the court to grant the equitable remedy of specific performance because monetary damages are inadequate in this situation. ◀

EQUITABLE MAXIMS In fashioning appropriate remedies, judges often were (and continue to be) guided by so-called **equitable maxims**—propositions or general statements of equitable rules. Exhibit 1–2 below lists some important equitable maxims.

The last maxim listed in that exhibit—"Equity aids the vigilant, not those who rest on their rights"—merits special attention. It has become known as the

equitable doctrine of **laches** (a term derived from the Latin *laxus,* meaning "lax" or "negligent"), and it can be used as a defense. A **defense** is an argument raised by the **defendant** (the party being sued) indicating why the **plaintiff** (the suing party) should not obtain the remedy sought. (Note that in equity proceedings, the party bringing a lawsuit is called the **petitioner,** and the party being sued is referred to as the **respondent.**)

The doctrine of laches arose to encourage people to bring lawsuits while the evidence was fresh. What constitutes a reasonable time, of course, varies according to the circumstances of the case. Time periods for different types of cases are now usually fixed by **statutes of limitations.** After the time allowed under a statute of limitations has expired, no action (lawsuit) can be brought, no matter how strong the case was originally.

Legal and Equitable Remedies Today

The establishment of courts of equity in medieval England resulted in two distinct court systems: courts of law and courts of equity. The courts had different sets of judges and granted different types of remedies. During the nineteenth century, however, most states in the United States adopted rules of procedure that resulted in the combining of courts of law and equity. A party now may request both legal and equitable remedies in the same action, and the trial court judge may grant either or both forms of relief.

The distinction between legal and equitable remedies remains relevant to students of business law, however, because these remedies differ. To seek the proper remedy for a wrong, one must know what

EXHIBIT 1–2 Equitable Maxims

1. *Whoever seeks equity must do equity.* (Anyone who wishes to be treated fairly must treat others fairly.)
2. *Where there is equal equity, the law must prevail.* (The law will determine the outcome of a controversy in which the merits of both sides are equal.)
3. *One seeking the aid of an equity court must come to the court with clean hands.* (The plaintiff must have acted fairly and honestly.)
4. *Equity will not suffer a wrong to be without a remedy.* (Equitable relief will be awarded when there is a right to relief and there is no adequate remedy at law.)
5. *Equity regards substance rather than form.* (Equity is more concerned with fairness and justice than with legal technicalities.)
6. *Equity aids the vigilant, not those who rest on their rights.* (Equity will not help those who neglect their rights for an unreasonable period of time.)

remedies are available. Additionally, certain vestiges of the procedures used when there were separate courts of law and equity still exist. For example, a party has the right to demand a jury trial in an action at law, but not in an action in equity. Exhibit 1–3 below summarizes the procedural differences (applicable in most states) between an action at law and an action in equity.

The Doctrine of *Stare Decisis*

One of the unique features of the common law is that it is *judge-made* law. The body of principles and doctrines that form the common law emerged over time as judges decided legal controversies.

CASE PRECEDENTS AND CASE REPORTERS When possible, judges attempted to be consistent and to base their decisions on the principles suggested by earlier cases. They sought to decide similar cases in a similar way and considered new cases with care because they knew that their decisions would make new law. Each interpretation became part of the law on the subject and thus served as a legal **precedent.** A precedent is a decision that furnishes an example or authority for deciding subsequent cases involving identical or similar legal principles or facts.

In the early years of the common law, there was no single place or publication where court opinions, or written decisions, could be found. By the fourteenth century, portions of the most important decisions from each year were being gathered together and recorded in *Year Books,* which became useful references for lawyers and judges. In the sixteenth century, the *Year Books* were discontinued, and other forms of case publication became available. Today, cases are published, or "reported," in volumes called **reporters,** or *reports*. We describe today's case reporting system in detail later in this chapter.

STARE DECISIS AND THE COMMON LAW TRADITION
The practice of deciding new cases with reference to former decisions, or precedents, became a cornerstone of the English and American judicial systems. The practice formed a doctrine known as **stare decisis**[3] (a Latin phrase meaning "to stand on decided cases"). Under this doctrine, judges are obligated to follow the precedents established within their jurisdictions. The term *jurisdiction* refers to a geographic area in which a court or courts have the power to apply the law—see Chapter 2.

Once a court has set forth a principle of law as being applicable to a certain set of facts, that court must apply the principle in future cases involving similar facts. Courts of lower rank (within the same jurisdiction) must do likewise. Thus, *stare decisis* has two aspects:

1. A court should not overturn its own precedents unless there is a compelling reason to do so.
2. Decisions made by a higher court are binding on lower courts.

CONTROLLING PRECEDENTS Controlling precedents in a jurisdiction are referred to as binding authorities. A **binding authority** is any source of law that a court must follow when deciding a case. Binding authorities include constitutions, statutes, and regulations that govern the issue being decided, as well as court decisions that are controlling precedents within the jurisdiction. United States Supreme Court case decisions, no matter how old, remain controlling until they are overruled by a subsequent decision of the Supreme Court or changed by further legislation or a constitutional amendment.

STARE DECISIS AND LEGAL STABILITY The doctrine of *stare decisis* helps the courts to be more efficient because, if other courts have analyzed a similar case,

3. Pronounced *ster*-ay dih-*si*-ses.

EXHIBIT 1–3 Procedural Differences between an Action at Law and an Action in Equity

Procedure	Action at Law	Action in Equity
Initiation of lawsuit	By filing a complaint	By filing a petition
Parties	Plaintiff and defendant	Petitioner and respondent
Decision	By jury or judge	By judge (no jury)
Result	Judgment	Decree
Remedy	Monetary damages	Injunction, specific performance, or rescission

their legal reasoning and opinions can serve as guides. *Stare decisis* also makes the law more stable and predictable. If the law on a subject is well settled, someone bringing a case can usually rely on the court to rule based on what the law has been in the past.

DEPARTURES FROM PRECEDENT Although courts are obligated to follow precedents, sometimes a court will depart from the rule of precedent if it decides that the precedent should no longer be followed. If a court decides that a ruling precedent is simply incorrect or that technological or social changes have rendered the precedent inapplicable, the court might rule contrary to the precedent. Cases that overturn precedent often receive a great deal of publicity.

▶ **Case in Point 1.2** The United States Supreme Court expressly overturned precedent in the case of *Brown v. Board of Education of Topeka.*[4] The Court concluded that separate educational facilities for whites and blacks, which it had previously upheld as constitutional,[5] were inherently unequal. The Court's departure from precedent in this case received a tremendous amount of publicity as people began to realize the ramifications of this change in the law. ◀

Note that judges do have some flexibility in applying precedents. For instance, a lower court may avoid applying a precedent set by a higher court in its jurisdiction by distinguishing the two cases based on their facts. When this happens, the lower court's ruling stands unless it is appealed to a higher court and that court overturns the decision.

WHEN THERE IS NO PRECEDENT Occasionally, courts must decide cases for which no precedents exist, called cases of *first impression.* For instance, as you will read throughout this text, the extensive use of the Internet has presented many new and challenging issues for the courts to decide.

In deciding cases of first impression, courts often look at **persuasive authorities** (precedents from other jurisdictions) for guidance. A court may also consider legal principles and policies underlying previous court decisions or existing statutes. Other factors that courts look at include fairness, social values and customs, and **public policy** (governmental policy based on widely held societal values).

Stare Decisis and Legal Reasoning

In deciding what law applies to a given dispute and then applying that law to the facts or circumstances of the case, judges rely on the process of **legal reasoning.** Through the use of legal reasoning, judges harmonize their decisions with those that have been made before, as the doctrine of *stare decisis* requires.

Students of business law and the legal environment also engage in legal reasoning. For example, you may be asked to provide answers for some of the case problems that appear at the end of every chapter in this text. Each problem describes the facts of a particular dispute and the legal question at issue. If you are assigned a case problem, you will be asked to determine how a court would answer that question, and why. In other words, you will need to give legal reasons for whatever conclusion you reach.[6] We look here at the basic steps involved in legal reasoning and then describe some forms of reasoning commonly used by the courts in making their decisions.

BASIC STEPS IN LEGAL REASONING At times, the legal arguments set forth in court opinions are relatively simple and brief. At other times, the arguments are complex and lengthy. Regardless of the length of a legal argument, however, the basic steps of the legal reasoning process remain the same. These steps, which you can also follow when analyzing cases and case problems, form what is commonly referred to as the *IRAC method* of legal reasoning. IRAC is an acronym formed from the first letters of the following words: *Issue, Rule, Application,* and *Conclusion.* To apply the IRAC method, you would ask the following questions:

1. **Issue**—*What are the key facts and issues?* Suppose that a plaintiff comes before the court claiming *assault* (words or acts that wrongfully and intentionally make another person fearful of immediate physical harm—see Chapter 6). The plaintiff claims that the defendant threatened her while she was sleeping. Although the plaintiff was unaware that she was being threatened, her roommate heard the defendant make the threat. The legal issue is whether the defendant's action constitutes the tort (civil wrong) of assault, given that the plaintiff was unaware of that action at the time it occurred.

4. 347 U.S. 483, 74 S.Ct. 686, 98 L.Ed. 873 (1954). A later section in this chapter explains how to read legal citations.
5. See *Plessy v. Ferguson,* 163 U.S. 537, 16 S.Ct. 1138, 41 L.Ed. 256 (1896).
6. See Appendix A for further instructions on how to analyze case problems.

2. **Rule**—*What rules of law apply to the case?* A rule of law may be a rule stated by the courts in previous decisions, a state or federal statute, or a state or federal administrative agency regulation. In our hypothetical case, the plaintiff **alleges** (claims) that the defendant committed a tort. Therefore, the applicable law is the common law of torts—specifically, tort law governing assault (see Chapter 6). Case precedents involving similar facts and issues thus would be relevant. Often, more than one rule of law will be applicable to a case.

3. **Application**—*How do the rules of law apply to the particular facts and circumstances of this case?* This step is often the most difficult because each case presents a unique set of facts, circumstances, and parties. Although cases may be similar, no two cases are ever identical in all respects. Normally, judges (and lawyers and law students) try to find **cases on point**—previously decided cases that are as similar as possible to the one under consideration. (Because of the difficulty—and importance—of this step in the legal reasoning process, we discuss it in more detail in the next subsection.)

4. **Conclusion**—*What conclusion should be drawn?* This step normally presents few problems. Usually, the conclusion is evident if the previous three steps have been followed carefully.

There Is No One "Right" Answer

Many people believe that there is one "right" answer to every legal question. In most legal controversies, however, there is no single correct result. Good arguments can usually be made to support either side of a legal controversy. Quite often, a case does not involve a "good" person suing a "bad" person. In many cases, both parties have acted in good faith in some measure or in bad faith to some degree.

Additionally, each judge has her or his own personal beliefs and philosophy (see the discussion in the next section), which shape the legal reasoning process, at least to some extent. This means that the outcome of a particular lawsuit before a court cannot be predicted with absolute certainty. Sometimes, even though the law would seem to favor one party's position, judges, through creative legal reasoning, have found ways to rule for the other party to prevent injustice.

Legal reasoning and other aspects of the common law tradition are reviewed in *Concept Summary 1.2* below.

The Common Law Today

Today, the common law derived from judicial decisions continues to be applied throughout the United States. Common law doctrines and principles, how-

---

CONCEPT SUMMARY 1.2
The Common Law Tradition

ASPECT	DESCRIPTION
Origins of the Common Law	The American legal system is based on the common law tradition, which originated in medieval England. Following the conquest of England in 1066 by William the Conqueror, king's courts were established throughout England, and the common law was developed in these courts.
Legal and Equitable Remedies	Remedies at law (money or items of value, such as land) and remedies in equity (including specific performance, injunction, and rescission of a contractual obligation) originated in the early English courts of law and courts of equity, respectively.
Case Precedents and the Doctrine of *Stare Decisis*	In the king's courts, judges attempted to make their decisions consistent with previous decisions, called precedents. This practice gave rise to the doctrine of *stare decisis*. This doctrine, which became a cornerstone of the common law tradition, obligates judges to abide by precedents established in their jurisdictions.
***Stare Decisis* and Legal Reasoning**	Legal reasoning is the reasoning process used by judges in applying the law to the facts and issues of specific cases. Legal reasoning involves becoming familiar with the key facts of a case, identifying the relevant legal rules, applying those rules to the facts, and drawing a conclusion.

ever, govern only areas *not* covered by statutory or administrative law. In a dispute concerning a particular employment practice, for instance, if a statute regulates that practice, the statute will apply rather than the common law doctrine that applied before the statute was enacted.

COURTS INTERPRET STATUTES Even in areas governed by statutory law, though, judge-made law continues to be important because there is a significant interplay between statutory law and the common law. For instance, many statutes essentially codify existing common law rules, and regulations issued by various administrative agencies usually are based, at least in part, on common law principles. Additionally, the courts, in interpreting statutory law, often rely on the common law as a guide to what the legislators intended.

Furthermore, how the courts interpret a particular statute determines how that statute will be applied. If you wanted to learn about the coverage and applicability of a particular statute, for example, you would necessarily have to locate the statute and study it. You would also need to see how the courts in your jurisdiction have interpreted and applied the statute. In other words, you would have to learn what precedents have been established in your jurisdiction with respect to that statute. Often, the applicability of a newly enacted statute does not become clear until a body of case law develops to clarify how, when, and to whom the statute applies.

RESTATEMENTS OF THE LAW CLARIFY AND ILLUSTRATE THE COMMON LAW The American Law Institute (ALI) has published compilations of the common law called *Restatements of the Law*, which generally summarize the common law rules followed by most states. There are *Restatements of the Law* in the areas of contracts, torts, agency, trusts, property, restitution, security, judgments, and conflict of laws. The *Restatements*, like other secondary sources of law, do not in themselves have the force of law, but they are an important source of legal analysis and opinion. Hence, judges often rely on them in making decisions.

Many of the *Restatements* are now in their second, third, or fourth editions. We refer to the *Restatements* frequently in subsequent chapters of this text, indicating in parentheses the edition to which we are referring. For example, we refer to the third edition of the *Restatement of the Law of Contracts* as simply the *Restatement (Third) of Contracts*.

SCHOOLS OF LEGAL THOUGHT

How judges apply the law to specific cases, including disputes relating to the business world, depends in part on their philosophical approaches to law. Thus, the study of law, or **jurisprudence,** involves learning about different schools of legal thought and how the approaches to law characteristic of each school can affect judicial decision making.

Clearly, a judge's function is not to *make* the laws—that is the function of the legislative branch of government—but to interpret and apply them. From a practical point of view, however, the courts play a significant role in defining the laws enacted by legislative bodies, which tend to be expressed in general terms. Judges thus have some flexibility in interpreting and applying the law. It is because of this flexibility that different courts can, and often do, arrive at different conclusions in cases that involve nearly identical issues, facts, and applicable laws.

The Natural Law School

An age-old question about the nature of law has to do with the finality of a nation's laws at a given point in time. What if a particular law is deemed to be a "bad" law by a substantial number of that nation's citizens? According to the **natural law** theory, a higher or universal law exists that applies to all human beings, and written laws should imitate these inherent principles. If a written law is unjust, then it is not a true (natural) law and need not be obeyed.

The natural law tradition is one of the oldest and most significant schools of jurisprudence. It dates back to the days of the Greek philosopher Aristotle (384–322 B.C.E.), who distinguished between natural law and the laws governing a particular nation. According to Aristotle, natural law applies universally to all humankind.

The notion that people have "natural rights" stems from the natural law tradition. Those who claim that a specific foreign government is depriving certain citizens of their human rights are implicitly appealing to a higher law that has universal applicability. The question of the universality of basic human rights also comes into play in the context of international business operations. ▶ **Example 1.3** U.S. companies that have operations abroad often hire foreign workers as employees. Should the same laws that protect

U.S. employees apply to these foreign employees? This question is rooted implicitly in a concept of universal rights that has its origins in the natural law tradition. ◄

The Positivist School

In contrast to natural law, *positive,* or national, law (the written law of a given society at a particular time) applies only to the citizens of that nation or society. Those who adhere to **legal positivism** believe that there can be no higher law than a nation's positive law.

According to the positivist school, there are no "natural rights." Rather, human rights exist solely because of laws. If the laws are not enforced, anarchy will result. Thus, whether a law is "bad" or "good" is irrelevant. The law is the law and must be obeyed until it is changed—in an orderly manner through a legitimate lawmaking process.

A judge with positivist leanings probably would be more inclined to defer to an existing law than would a judge who adheres to the natural law tradition.

The Historical School

The **historical school** of legal thought emphasizes the evolutionary process of law by concentrating on the origin and history of the legal system. This school looks to the past to discover what the principles of contemporary law should be. The legal doctrines that have withstood the passage of time—those that have worked in the past—are deemed best suited for shaping present laws. Hence, law derives its legitimacy and authority from adhering to the standards that historical development has shown to be workable.

Adherents of the historical school are more likely than those of other schools to strictly follow decisions made in past cases.

Legal Realism

In the 1920s and 1930s, a number of jurists and scholars, known as *legal realists,* rebelled against the historical approach to law. **Legal realism** is based on the idea that law is just one of many institutions in society and that it is shaped by social forces and needs. The law is a human enterprise, and judges should take social and economic realities into account when deciding cases.

Legal realists also believe that the law can never be applied with total uniformity. Given that judges are human beings with unique personalities, value systems, and intellects, different judges will obviously bring different reasoning processes to the same case. Female judges, for instance, might be more inclined than male judges to consider whether a decision might have a negative impact on the employment of women or minorities.

Legal realism strongly influenced the growth of what is sometimes called the **sociological school**, which views law as a tool for promoting justice in society. In the 1960s, for example, the justices of the United States Supreme Court helped advance the civil rights movement by upholding long-neglected laws calling for equal treatment for all Americans, including African Americans and other minorities. Generally, jurists who adhere to this philosophy of law are more likely to depart from past decisions than are jurists who adhere to other schools of legal thought.

Concept Summary 1.3 on the following page reviews the schools of jurisprudential thought.

SECTION 5
CLASSIFICATIONS OF LAW

The law may be broken down according to several classification systems. For example, one classification system divides law into substantive law and procedural law. **Substantive law** consists of all laws that define, describe, regulate, and create legal rights and obligations. **Procedural law** consists of all laws that outline the methods of enforcing the rights established by substantive law.

Note that many statutes contain both substantive and procedural provisions. ▶ **Example 1.4**   A state law that provides employees with the right to *workers' compensation benefits* for on-the-job injuries is a substantive law because it creates legal rights. Procedural laws establish the method by which an employee must notify the employer about an on-the-job injury, prove the injury, and periodically submit additional proof to continue receiving workers' compensation benefits. ◄

Other classification systems divide law into federal law and state law, private law (dealing with relationships between private entities) and public law (addressing the relationship between persons and their governments), and national law and international law. Here we look at still another classification

---

CONCEPT SUMMARY 1.3
Schools of Jurisprudential Thought

SCHOOL OF THOUGHT	DESCRIPTION
Natural Law School	One of the oldest and most significant schools of legal thought. Those who believe in natural law hold that there is a universal law applicable to all human beings.
Positivist School	A school of legal thought centered on the assumption that there is no law higher than the laws created by the government.
Historical School	A school of legal thought that stresses the evolutionary nature of law and looks to doctrines that have withstood the passage of time for guidance in shaping present laws.
Legal Realism	A school of legal thought that advocates a less abstract and more realistic and pragmatic approach to the law and takes into account customary practices and the circumstances surrounding the particular transaction.

---

system, which divides law into civil law and criminal law, as well as at what is meant by the term *cyberlaw*.

Civil Law and Criminal Law

Civil law spells out the rights and duties that exist between persons and between persons and their governments, as well as the relief available when a person's rights are violated. Typically, in a civil case, a private party sues another private party who has failed to comply with a duty (note that the government can also sue a party for a civil law violation). Much of the law that we discuss in this text is civil law. Contract law, for example, covered in Chapters 11 through 19, is civil law. The whole body of tort law (see Chapters 6 and 7) is also civil law.

Criminal law, in contrast, is concerned with wrongs committed *against the public as a whole.* Criminal acts are defined and prohibited by local, state, or federal government statutes. Criminal defendants are thus prosecuted by public officials, such as a district attorney (D.A.), on behalf of the state, not by their victims or other private parties. (See Chapter 10 for a further discussion of the distinction between civil law and criminal law.)

Cyberlaw

As mentioned, the use of the Internet to conduct business transactions has led to new types of legal issues. In response, courts have had to adapt traditional laws to situations that are unique to our age.

Additionally, legislatures at both the federal and the state levels have created laws to deal specifically with such issues.

Frequently, people use the term **cyberlaw** to refer to the emerging body of law that governs transactions conducted via the Internet. Cyberlaw is not really a classification of law, nor is it a new *type* of law. Rather, it is an informal term used to refer to both new laws and modifications of traditional laws that relate to the online environment. Throughout this book, you will read how the law in a given area is evolving to govern specific legal issues that arise in the online context. We have also devoted Chapter 9 entirely to Internet law, social media, and privacy.

SECTION 6
HOW TO FIND PRIMARY SOURCES OF LAW

This text includes numerous references, or *citations,* to primary sources of law—federal and state statutes, the U.S. Constitution and state constitutions, regulations issued by administrative agencies, and court cases.

A **citation** identifies the publication in which a legal authority—such as a statute or a court decision or other source—can be found. In this section, we explain how you can use citations to find primary sources of law. Note that in addition to being published in sets of books, as described next, most federal and state laws and case decisions are available online.

Finding Statutory and Administrative Law

When Congress passes laws, they are collected in a publication titled *United States Statutes at Large.* When state legislatures pass laws, they are collected in similar state publications. Most frequently, however, laws are referred to in their codified form—that is, the form in which they appear in the federal and state codes. In these codes, laws are compiled by subject.

UNITED STATES CODE The *United States Code* (U.S.C.) arranges all existing federal laws by broad subject. Each of the fifty subjects is given a title and a title number. For instance, laws relating to commerce and trade are collected in Title 15, "Commerce and Trade." Titles are subdivided by sections.

A citation to the U.S.C. includes both title and section numbers. Thus, a reference to "15 U.S.C. Section 1" means that the statute can be found in Section 1 of Title 15. ("Section" may be designated by the symbol §, and "Sections," by §§.) In addition to the print publication, the federal government provides a searchable online database of the *United States Code* at **www.gpo.gov** (click on "Libraries" and then "Core Documents of Our Democracy" to find the U.S.C.).

Commercial publications of federal laws and regulations are also available. For instance, Legal Solutions from Thomson Reuters (formerly West Group) publishes the *United States Code Annotated* (U.S.C.A.). The U.S.C.A. contains the official text of the U.S.C., plus notes (annotations) on court decisions that interpret and apply specific sections of the statutes. The U.S.C.A. also includes additional research aids, such as cross-references to related statutes, historical notes, and library references. A citation to the U.S.C.A. is similar to a citation to the U.S.C.: "15 U.S.C.A. Section 1."

STATE CODES State codes follow the U.S.C. pattern of arranging law by subject. They may be called codes, revisions, compilations, consolidations, general statutes, or statutes, depending on the preferences of the states.

In some codes, subjects are designated by number. In others, they are designated by name. ▶ **Example 1.5** "13 Pennsylvania Consolidated Statutes Section 1101" means that the statute can be found in Title 13, Section 1101, of the Pennsylvania code. "California Commercial Code Section 1101" means that the statute can be found under the subject heading "Commercial Code" of the California code in Section 1101. Abbreviations are often used. For example, "13 Pennsylvania Consolidated Statutes Section 1101" is abbreviated "13 Pa. C.S. § 1101," and "California Commercial Code Section 1101" is abbreviated "Cal. Com. Code § 1101." ◀

ADMINISTRATIVE RULES Rules and regulations adopted by federal administrative agencies are initially published in the *Federal Register,* a daily publication of the U.S. government. Later, they are incorporated into the *Code of Federal Regulations* (C.F.R.).

Like the U.S.C., the C.F.R. is divided into fifty titles. Rules within each title are assigned section numbers. A full citation to the C.F.R. includes title and section numbers. ▶ **Example 1.6** A reference to "17 C.F.R. Section 230.504" means that the rule can be found in Section 230.504 of Title 17. ◀

Finding Case Law

Before discussing the case reporting system, we need to look briefly at the court system (which will be discussed in detail in Chapter 2). There are two types of courts in the United States, federal courts and state courts.

Both the federal and the state court systems consist of several levels, or tiers, of courts. *Trial courts,* in which evidence is presented and testimony given, are on the bottom tier (which also includes lower courts that handle specialized issues). Decisions from a trial court can be appealed to a higher court, which commonly is an intermediate *court of appeals,* or *appellate court.* Decisions from these intermediate courts of appeals may be appealed to an even higher court, such as a state supreme court or the United States Supreme Court.

STATE COURT DECISIONS Most state trial court decisions are not published in books (except in New York and a few other states, which publish selected trial court opinions). Decisions from state trial courts are typically filed in the office of the clerk of the court, where the decisions are available for public inspection. (Increasingly, they can be found online as well.)

Written decisions of the appellate, or reviewing, courts, however, are published and distributed (in print and online). As you will note, most of the state court cases presented in this textbook are from state appellate courts. The reported appellate decisions are published in volumes called *reports* or *reporters,* which are numbered consecutively. State appellate court decisions are found in the state reporters of that particular state. Official reports are published by the state, whereas unofficial reports are published by nongovernment entities.

Regional Reporters. State court opinions appear in regional units of the National Reporter System, published by West Group (now Thomson Reuters). Most lawyers and libraries have these reporters because they report cases more quickly and are distributed more widely than the state-published reporters. In fact, many states have eliminated their own reporters in favor of the National Reporter System.

The National Reporter System divides the states into the following geographic areas: *Atlantic* (A., A.2d, or A.3d), *North Eastern* (N.E. or N.E.2d), *North Western* (N.W. or N.W.2d), *Pacific* (P., P.2d, or P.3d), *South Eastern* (S.E. or S.E.2d), *South Western* (S.W., S.W.2d, or S.W.3d), and *Southern* (So., So.2d, or So.3d). (The *2d* and *3d* in the preceding abbreviations refer to *Second Series* and *Third Series,* respectively.) The states included in each of these regional divisions are indicated in Exhibit 1–4 on the following page, which illustrates the National Reporter System.

Case Citations. After appellate decisions have been published, they are normally referred to (cited) by the name of the case; the volume, name, and page number of the state's official reporter (if different from the National Reporter System); the volume, name, and page number of the National Reporter; and the volume, name, and page number of any other selected reporter. (Citing a reporter by volume number, name, and page number, in that order, is common to all citations. The year that the decision was issued is often included at the end in parentheses.) When more than one reporter is cited for the same case, each reference is called a *parallel citation.*

Note that some states have adopted a "public domain citation system" that uses a somewhat different format for the citation. For example, in Wisconsin, a Wisconsin Supreme Court decision might be designated "2013 WI 40," meaning that the case was decided in the year 2013 by the Wisconsin Supreme Court and was the fortieth decision issued by that court during that year. Parallel citations to the *Wisconsin Reports* and the *North Western Reporter* are still included after the public domain citation.

▶ **Example 1.7** Consider the following case citation: *Colbert v. Carr,* 140 Conn.App. 229, 57 A.3d. 878 (2013). We see that the opinion in this case can be found in Volume 140 of the official *Connecticut Appellate Court Reports,* on page 229. The parallel citation is to Volume 57 of the *Atlantic Reporter, Third Series,* page 878. ◀

When we present opinions in this text (starting in Chapter 2), in addition to the reporter, we give the name of the court hearing the case and the year of the court's decision. Sample citations to state court decisions are explained in Exhibit 1–5 on pages 17–19.

FEDERAL COURT DECISIONS Federal district (trial) court decisions are published unofficially in the *Federal Supplement* (F.Supp. or F.Supp.2d), and opinions from the circuit courts of appeals (reviewing courts) are reported unofficially in the *Federal Reporter* (F., F.2d, or F.3d). Cases concerning federal bankruptcy law are published unofficially in the *Bankruptcy Reporter* (Bankr. or B.R.).

The official edition of the United States Supreme Court decisions is the *United States Reports* (U.S.), which is published by the federal government. Unofficial editions of Supreme Court cases include the *Supreme Court Reporter* (S.Ct.) and the *Lawyers' Edition of the Supreme Court Reports* (L.Ed. or L.Ed.2d). Sample citations for federal court decisions are also listed and explained in Exhibit 1–5 on pages 17–19.

UNPUBLISHED OPINIONS Many court opinions that are not yet published or that are not intended for publication can be accessed through Westlaw® (abbreviated in citations as "WL"), an online legal database maintained by Thomson Reuters (formerly West Group). When no citation to a published reporter is available for cases cited in this text, we give the WL citation (see Exhibit 1–5 on pages 17–19 for an example).

OLD CASE LAW On a few occasions, this text cites opinions from old, classic cases dating to the nineteenth century or earlier. Some of these are from the English courts. The citations to these cases may not conform to the descriptions just presented because the reporters in which they were originally published were often known by the names of the persons who compiled the reporters.

SECTION 7
HOW TO READ AND UNDERSTAND CASE LAW

The decisions made by the courts establish the boundaries of the law as it applies to almost all business relationships. It thus is essential that businesspersons know how to read and understand case law.

EXHIBIT 1-4 National Reporter System—Regional/Federal

Regional Reporters	Coverage Beginning	Coverage
Atlantic Reporter (A., A.2d, or A.3d)	1885	Connecticut, Delaware, District of Columbia, Maine, Maryland, New Hampshire, New Jersey, Pennsylvania, Rhode Island, and Vermont.
North Eastern Reporter (N.E. or N.E.2d)	1885	Illinois, Indiana, Massachusetts, New York, and Ohio.
North Western Reporter (N.W. or N.W.2d)	1879	Iowa, Michigan, Minnesota, Nebraska, North Dakota, South Dakota, and Wisconsin.
Pacific Reporter (P., P.2d, or P.3d)	1883	Alaska, Arizona, California, Colorado, Hawaii, Idaho, Kansas, Montana, Nevada, New Mexico, Oklahoma, Oregon, Utah, Washington, and Wyoming.
South Eastern Reporter (S.E. or S.E.2d)	1887	Georgia, North Carolina, South Carolina, Virginia, and West Virginia.
South Western Reporter (S.W., S.W.2d, or S.W.3d)	1886	Arkansas, Kentucky, Missouri, Tennessee, and Texas.
Southern Reporter (So., So.2d, or So.3d)	1887	Alabama, Florida, Louisiana, and Mississippi.

Federal Reporters		
Federal Reporter (F., F.2d, or F.3d)	1880	U.S. Circuit Courts from 1880 to 1912; U.S. Commerce Court from 1911 to 1913; U.S. District Courts from 1880 to 1932; U.S. Court of Claims (now called U.S. Court of Federal Claims) from 1929 to 1932 and since 1960; U.S. Courts of Appeals since 1891; U.S. Court of Customs and Patent Appeals since 1929; U.S. Emergency Court of Appeals since 1943.
Federal Supplement (F.Supp. or F.Supp.2d)	1932	U.S. Court of Claims from 1932 to 1960; U.S. District Courts since 1932; U.S. Customs Court since 1956.
Federal Rules Decisions (F.R.D.)	1939	U.S. District Courts involving the Federal Rules of Civil Procedure since 1939 and Federal Rules of Criminal Procedure since 1946.
Supreme Court Reporter (S.Ct.)	1882	United States Supreme Court since the October term of 1882.
Bankruptcy Reporter (Bankr.)	1980	Bankruptcy decisions of U.S. Bankruptcy Courts, U.S. District Courts, U.S. Courts of Appeals, and the United States Supreme Court.
Military Justice Reporter (M.J.)	1978	U.S. Court of Military Appeals and Courts of Military Review for the Army, Navy, Air Force, and Coast Guard.

NATIONAL REPORTER SYSTEM MAP

Legend: Pacific, North Western, South Western, North Eastern, Atlantic, South Eastern, Southern

EXHIBIT 1–5 How to Read Citations

STATE COURTS

285 Neb. 88, 825 N.W.2d 429 (2013)[a]

> *N.W.* is the abbreviation for Thomson Reuters's publication of state court decisions rendered in the *North Western Reporter* of the National Reporter System. *2d* indicates that this case was included in the *Second Series* of that reporter. The number 825 refers to the volume number of the reporter; the number 429 refers to the page in that volume on which this case begins.

> *Neb.* is an abbreviation for *Nebraska Reports,* Nebraska's official reports of the decisions of its highest court, the Nebraska Supreme Court.

213 Cal.App.4th 1, 152 Cal.Rptr.3d 30 (2013)

> *Cal.Rptr.* is the abbreviation for the unofficial reports—titled *California Reporter*— of the decisions of California courts.

102 A.D.3d 774, 958 N.Y.S.2d 440 (2013)

> *N.Y.S.* is the abbreviation for the unofficial reports—titled *New York Supplement*—of the decisions of New York courts.

> *A.D.* is the abbreviation for *Appellate Division*, which hears appeals from the New York Supreme Court—the state's general trial court. The New York Court of Appeals is the state's highest court, analogous to other states' supreme courts.

319 Ga.App. 777, 736 S.E.2d 480 (2013)

> *Ga.App.* is the abbreviation for *Georgia Appeals Reports,* Georgia's official reports of the decisions of its court of appeals.

FEDERAL COURTS

___ U.S. ___, 133 S.Ct. 721, 184 L.Ed.2d 553 (2013)

> *L.Ed.* is an abbreviation for *Lawyers' Edition of the Supreme Court Reports*, an unofficial edition of decisions of the United States Supreme Court.

> *S.Ct.* is the abbreviation for Thomson Reuters's unofficial reports—titled *Supreme Court Reporter*—of decisions of the United States Supreme Court.

> *U.S.* is the abbreviation for *United States Reports*, the official edition of the decisions of the United States Supreme Court. The blank lines in this citation (or any other citation) indicate that the appropriate volume of the case reporter has not yet been published and no page number is available.

a. The case names have been deleted from these citations to emphasize the publications. It should be kept in mind, however, that the name of a case is as important as the specific page numbers in the volumes in which it is found. If a citation is incorrect, the correct citation may be found in a publication's index of case names. In addition to providing a check on errors in citations, the date of a case is important because the value of a recent case as an authority is likely to be greater than that of older cases from the same court.

Continued

EXHIBIT 1-5 How to Read Citations—Continued

FEDERAL COURTS (Continued)

705 F.3d 315 (8th Cir. 2013)

> *8th Cir.* is an abbreviation denoting that this case was decided in the U.S. Court of Appeals for the Eighth Circuit.

___ F.Supp.2d ___ (D.D.C. 2013)

> *D.D.C.* is an abbreviation indicating that the U.S. District Court for the District of Columbia decided this case.

ENGLISH COURTS

9 Exch. 341, 156 Eng.Rep. 145 (1854)

> *Eng.Rep.* is an abbreviation for *English Reports, Full Reprint,* a series of reports containing selected decisions made in English courts between 1378 and 1865.

> *Exch.* is an abbreviation for *English Exchequer Reports*, which includes the original reports of cases decided in England's Court of Exchequer.

STATUTORY AND OTHER CITATIONS

18 U.S.C. Section 1961(1)(A)

> *U.S.C.* denotes *United States Code*, the codification of *United States Statutes at Large*. The number 18 refers to the statute's U.S.C. title number and 1961 to its section number within that title. The number 1 in parentheses refers to a subsection within the section, and the letter A in parentheses to a subsection within the subsection.

UCC 2–206(1)(b)

> *UCC* is an abbreviation for *Uniform Commercial Code*. The first number 2 is a reference to an article of the UCC, and 206 to a section within that article. The number 1 in parentheses refers to a subsection within the section, and the letter b in parentheses to a subsection within the subsection.

Restatement (Third) of Torts, Section 6

> *Restatement (Third) of Torts* refers to the third edition of the American Law Institute's *Restatement of the Law of Torts*. The number 6 refers to a specific section.

17 C.F.R. Section 230.505

> *C.F.R.* is an abbreviation for *Code of Federal Regulations*, a compilation of federal administrative regulations. The number 17 designates the regulation's title number, and 230.505 designates a specific section within that title.

EXHIBIT 1–5 How to Read Citations—Continued

WESTLAW® CITATIONS[b]

2013 WL 285688

> *WL* is an abbreviation for Westlaw. The number 2013 is the year of the document that can be found with this citation in the Westlaw database. The number 285688 is a number assigned to a specific document. A higher number indicates that a document was added to the Westlaw database later in the year.

UNIFORM RESOURCE LOCATORS (URLs)

web2.westlaw.com[c]

> The suffix *com* is the top-level domain (TLD) for this Web site. The TLD *com* is an abbreviation for "commercial," which usually means that a for-profit entity hosts (maintains or supports) this Web site.

> *westlaw* is the host name—the part of the domain name selected by the organization that registered the name. In this case, West Group (now Thomson Reuters) registered the name. This Internet site is the Westlaw database on the Web.

> *web2* describes Web sites that use software allowing users to interact and collaborate with each other in a social media dialogue, rather than limiting users to the passive viewing of static content.

http://www.uscourts.gov

> This is "The Federal Judiciary Home Page." The host is the Administrative Office of the U.S. Courts. The TLD *gov* is an abbreviation for "government." This Web site includes information and links from, and about, the federal courts.

> *www* is an abbreviation for "World Wide Web." The Web is a system of Internet servers that support documents formatted in *HTML* (hypertext markup language) and other formats as well.

http://www.law.cornell.edu/index.html

> This part of a URL points to a Web page or file at a specific location within the host's domain. This page is a menu with links to documents within the domain and to other Internet resources.

> This is the host name for a Web site that contains the Internet publications of the Legal Information Institute (LII), which is a part of Cornell Law School. The LII site includes a variety of legal materials and links to other legal resources on the Internet. The TLD *edu* is an abbreviation for "educational institution" (a school or a university).

http://www.ipl.org/div/news

> This part of the Web site points to a static *news* page at this Web site, which provides links to online newspapers from around the world.

> *ipl* is an abbreviation for "Internet Public Library," which is an online service that provides reference resources and links to other information services on the Web. The IPL is supported chiefly by the School of Information at the University of Michigan. The TLD *org* is an abbreviation for "organization" (normally nonprofit).

> *div* is an abbreviation for "division," which is the way that the Internet Public Library tags the content on its Web site as relating to a specific topic.

b. Many court decisions that are not yet published or that are not intended for publication can be accessed through Westlaw, an online legal database.

c. The basic form for a URL is "service://hostname/path." The Internet service for all of the URLs in this text is *http* (hypertext transfer protocol). Because most Web browsers add this prefix automatically when a user enters a host name or a hostname/path, we have generally omitted the *http://* from the URLs listed in this text.

The cases that we present in this text have been condensed from the full text of the courts' opinions and are presented in a special format. In approximately two-thirds of the cases (including the cases designated as Classic and Spotlight), we have summarized the background and facts, as well as the court's decision and remedy, in our own words. In those cases, we have included only selected portions of the court's opinion ("in the language of the court"). In the remaining one-third of the cases (labeled "Case Analysis Cases"), we have provided a longer excerpt from the court's opinion without summarizing the background and facts or decision and remedy.

The following sections will provide useful insights into how to read and understand case law.

Case Titles and Terminology

The title of a case, such as *Adams v. Jones,* indicates the names of the parties to the lawsuit. The *v.* in the case title stands for *versus,* which means "against." In the trial court, Adams was the plaintiff—the person who filed the suit. Jones was the defendant. If the case is appealed, however, the appellate court will sometimes place the name of the party appealing the decision first, so the case may be called *Jones v. Adams* if Jones is appealing.

Because some appellate courts retain the trial court order of names, it is often impossible to distinguish the plaintiff from the defendant in the title of a reported appellate court decision. You must carefully read the facts of each case to identify the parties. Otherwise, the discussion by the appellate court may be difficult to understand.

The following terms, phrases, and abbreviations are frequently encountered in court opinions and legal publications.

PARTIES TO LAWSUITS As mentioned previously, the party initiating a lawsuit is referred to as the *plaintiff* or *petitioner,* depending on the nature of the action. The party against whom a lawsuit is brought is the *defendant* or *respondent.* Lawsuits frequently involve more than one plaintiff and/or defendant.

When a case is appealed from the original court or jurisdiction to another court or jurisdiction, the party appealing the case is called the **appellant.** The **appellee** is the party against whom the appeal is taken. (In some appellate courts, the party appealing a case is referred to as the petitioner, and the party against whom the suit is brought or appealed is called the respondent.)

JUDGES AND JUSTICES The terms *judge* and *justice* are usually synonymous and represent two designations given to judges in various courts. All members of the United States Supreme Court, for instance, are referred to as justices, and justice is the formal title often given to judges of appellate courts, although this is not always the case. In New York, a *justice* is a judge of the trial court (called the Supreme Court), and a member of the Court of Appeals (the state's highest court) is called a *judge.*

The term *justice* is commonly abbreviated to J., and *justices,* to JJ. A United States Supreme Court case might refer to Justice Sotomayor as Sotomayor, J., or to Chief Justice Roberts as Roberts, C.J.

DECISIONS AND OPINIONS Most decisions reached by reviewing, or appellate, courts are explained in written **opinions.** The opinion contains the court's reasons for its decision, the rules of law that apply, and the judgment. You may encounter several types of opinions as you read appellate cases, including the following:

- When all the judges (or justices) agree, a *unanimous opinion* is written for the entire court.
- When there is not unanimous agreement, a **majority opinion** is generally written. It outlines the views of the majority of the judges deciding the case.
- A judge who agrees (concurs) with the majority opinion as to the result but not as to the legal reasoning often writes a **concurring opinion.** In it, the judge sets out the reasoning that he or she considers correct.
- A **dissenting opinion** presents the views of one or more judges who disagree with the majority view.
- Sometimes, no single position is fully supported by a majority of the judges deciding a case. In this situation, we may have a **plurality opinion.** This is the opinion that has the support of the largest number of judges, but the group in agreement is less than a majority.
- Finally, a court occasionally issues a ***per curiam opinion*** (*per curiam* is Latin for "of the court"), which does not indicate which judge wrote the opinion.

A Sample Court Case

To illustrate the various elements contained in a court opinion, we present an annotated court opinion in Exhibit 1–6 on page 22. The opinion is from an actual case decided by a federal trial court located in California.

Background of the Case. In 2011, Amazon.com launched an Appstore for viewing and downloading applications to Android devices, such as the Kindle Fire. Apple products (iPads, iPhones, iPods) use the term APP STORE. In this case, Apple claims that Amazon's use of the name "Appstore" constitutes false advertising and trademark infringement (discussed in Chapter 8). The issue before the court here is whether Amazon's use of "Appstore" might mislead the public into thinking that Amazon's Appstore is affiliated with Apple and offers the same content.

Editorial Practice. You will note that triple asterisks (* * *) and quadruple asterisks (* * * *) frequently appear in the opinion. The triple asterisks indicate that we have deleted a few words or sentences from the opinion for the sake of readability or brevity. Quadruple asterisks mean that an entire paragraph (or more) has been omitted.

Additionally, when the opinion cites another case or legal source, the citation to the case or source has been omitted to save space and to improve the flow of the text. These editorial practices are continued in the other court opinions presented in this book. In addition, whenever we present a court opinion that includes a term or phrase that may not be readily understandable, a bracketed definition or paraphrase has been added.

Briefing Cases. Knowing how to read and understand court opinions and the legal reasoning used by the courts is an essential step in undertaking accurate legal research. A further step is "briefing," or summarizing, the case.

Legal researchers routinely brief cases by reducing the texts of the opinions to their essential elements. Generally, when you brief a case, you first summarize the background and facts of the case, as the authors have done for the cases presented in this text. You then indicate the issue (or issues) before the court. An important element in the case brief is, of course, the court's decision on the issue and the legal reasoning used by the court in reaching that decision.

Detailed instructions on how to brief a case are given in Appendix A, which also includes a briefed version of the sample court case presented in Exhibit 1–6 on the following page.

THE SAMPLE COURT CASE STARTS ON THE FOLLOWING PAGE.

EXHIBIT 1-6 A Sample Court Case

This section contains the citation—the name of the case, the name of the court that heard the case, the year of the decision, and reporters in which the court's opinion can be found.	**APPLE, INC. v. AMAZON.COM, INC.** United States District Court, Northern District of California, __ F.Supp.2d __ , 2013 WL 11896 (2013).
This line provides the name of the judge (or justice) who authored the court's opinion.	Phyllis J. *HAMILTON*, District Judge. * * * *
The court divides the opinion into three sections, each headed by an explanatory heading. The first section summarizes the factual background of the case.	**BACKGROUND** This is a * * * false advertising case. Plaintiff Apple Inc. ("Apple") **alleges** that defen-
To *allege* is to assert to be true as described.	dant Amazon.com Inc. ("Amazon") has been improperly using the term "APP STORE"
	in connection with sales of apps for Android devices and the Kindle Fire (Amazon's
	tablet computer). Since July 2008, Apple has sold applications ("apps") for its mobile devices
	through its APP STORE service. * * * On March 22, 2011, Amazon launched the Amazon Appstore for Android.
The Lanham Act is a federal statute enacted in 1946 that protects the owner of a trademark against the use of a similar mark if any consumer confusion might result.	Apple filed this action [in the same month, asserting] false advertising under Section 43(a) of the **Lanham Act.**
A *summary judgment* is a judgment that a court enters without beginning or continuing a trial. This judgment can be entered only if no facts are in dispute and the only question is how the law applies to the facts.	Amazon now seeks * * * **summary judgment,** as to the * * * cause of action for false advertising.
The second major section of the opinion responds to the defendant's motion.	**DISCUSSION** * * * * * * * A false advertising claim under Section 43(a) has five elements [including] a false statement of fact by the defendant in a commercial advertisement about its own or another's product.
To *grant* is to approve, warrant, or order a motion or some other request.	* * * Amazon argues that summary judgment should be **granted** as to this claim because Apple has not identified a single false statement that Amazon has made about the nature, characteristics, or quality of the Amazon Appstore for Android (or the Amazon Appstore, which allows viewing and downloading of apps for the Kindle Fire).

EXHIBIT 1-6 A Sample Court Case—Continued

Apple essentially alleges that by using the word "Appstore" in the name of Amazon's store, Amazon implies that its store is affiliated with or sponsored by Apple.

* * * *

Apple argues that * * * Amazon's service ("Appstore") does not possess the characteristics and qualities that the public has come to expect from the name APP STORE, based on their familiarity with Apple's service. For this reason, Apple argues, Amazon's use of "Appstore" misleads the public—in particular because (according to Apple) it "implies a false **equivalence** without cuing consumers to test this claim." Apple contends that because its APP STORE offers so many more apps than Amazon's Appstore, consumers will be misled into thinking that Amazon's Appstore will offer just as many.

> An *equivalence* is a characteristic or quality corresponding in effect or function, or nearly equal or virtually identical, to another.

* * * The court finds no support for the proposition that Amazon has expressly or impliedly communicated that its Appstore for Android possesses the characteristics and qualities that the public has come to expect from the Apple APP STORE and/or Apple products.

That is, Apple has failed to establish that Amazon made any false statement (express or implied) of fact that actually deceived or had the tendency to deceive a substantial segment of its audience. The mere use of "Appstore" by Amazon to designate a site for viewing and downloading/purchasing apps cannot be **construed** as a representation that the nature, characteristics, or quality of the Amazon Appstore is the same as that of the Apple APP STORE. Apple has pointed to no advertisement by Amazon that qualifies as a false statement under Section 43(a) of the Lanham Act. Nor is there **sufficient evidence** to raise a **triable** issue.

> To *construe* is to interpret or explain the sense of something according to judicial standards.

> *Sufficient evidence* is evidence that is sufficient to satisfy an unprejudiced mind seeking the truth.

> A *triable* issue is an issue that is subject to judicial examination and trial.

* * * If an advertisement is not false on its face (i.e., if there is no express or explicit false statement), the plaintiff must produce evidence, usually in the form of market research or consumer surveys, showing exactly what message was conveyed that was sufficient to constitute false advertising. Here, Apple has presented no evidence that

Continued

EXHIBIT 1-6 A Sample Court Case—Continued

In this context, *attribute* refers to the elements or properties of the App Store that are closely associated with Apple.

consumers or customers understand "app store" to include specific qualities or characteristics or **attributes** of the Apple APP STORE, or that any customers were misled by Amazon's use of the term.

Apple asserts that its APP STORE offers many more apps than Amazon's does, and that the apps are **"seamlessly integrated"** with all Apple devices. However, there is

Here, *seamlessly integrated* means coordinated to operate without any awkward transitions or interruptions.

no evidence that a consumer who accesses the Amazon Appstore would expect that it would be identical to the Apple APP STORE, particularly given that the Apple APP STORE sells apps solely for Apple devices, while the Amazon Appstore sells apps solely for Android and Kindle devices. Further, the integration of Apple devices has more to do with Apple's technology than it does with the nature, characteristics, or qualities of the APP STORE.

Apple fails to make clear how [Amazon's use of Appstore] constitutes a "statement" that implies something false about the nature, characteristics, or qualities of Apple's

Showing is the act of establishing through evidence and argument.

APP STORE, because it has made no **showing** that such (implied) statement deceived or had a tendency to deceive users of Amazon's Appstore.

In the third major section of the opinion, the court states its decision.

CONCLUSION

* * * Amazon's motion for summary judgment as to the * * * cause of action for false advertising is GRANTED.

Reviewing: Law and Legal Reasoning

Suppose that the California legislature passes a law that severely restricts carbon dioxide emissions from automobiles in that state. A group of automobile manufacturers files suit against the state of California to prevent the enforcement of the law. The automakers claim that a federal law already sets fuel economy standards nationwide and that fuel economy standards are essentially the same as carbon dioxide emission standards. According to the automobile manufacturers, it is unfair to allow California to impose more stringent regulations than those set by the federal law. Using the information presented in the chapter, answer the following questions.

1. Who are the parties (the plaintiffs and the defendant) in this lawsuit?
2. Are the plaintiffs seeking a legal remedy or an equitable remedy?
3. What is the primary source of the law that is at issue here?
4. Where would you look to find the relevant California and federal laws?

DEBATE THIS ... *Under the doctrine of* stare decisis, *courts are obligated to follow the precedents established in their jurisdiction unless there is a compelling reason not to. Should U.S. courts continue to adhere to this common law principle, given that our government now regulates so many areas by statute?*

Terms and Concepts

administrative agency 5	damages 6	*per curiam* opinion 20
administrative law 5	defendant 7	petitioner 7
allege 10	defense 7	plaintiff 7
appellant 20	dissenting opinion 20	plurality opinion 20
appellee 20	equitable maxims 7	precedent 8
binding authority 8	executive agency 5	procedural law 12
breach 7	historical school 12	public policy 9
case law 5	independent regulatory agency 5	remedy 6
case on point 10	jurisprudence 11	remedy at law 6
chancellor 6	laches 7	remedy in equity 6
citation 13	law 2	reporter 8
civil law 13	legal positivism 12	respondent 7
common law 6	legal realism 12	sociological school 12
concurring opinion 20	legal reasoning 9	*stare decisis* 8
constitutional law 4	majority opinion 20	statute of limitations 7
court of equity 6	natural law 11	statutory law 4
court of law 6	opinion 20	substantive law 12
criminal law 13	ordinance 4	uniform law 5
cyberlaw 13	persuasive authorities 9	

ExamPrep

Issue Spotters

1. Under what circumstances might a judge rely on case law to determine the intent and purpose of a statute? **(See page 5.)**

2. After World War II, several Nazis were convicted of "crimes against humanity" by an international court. Assuming that these convicted war criminals had not disobeyed any law of their country and had merely been following their government's orders, what law had they violated? Explain. **(See page 11.)**

- **Check your answers to the Issue Spotters against the answers provided in Appendix E at the end of this text.**

Before the Test

Go to **www.cengagebrain.com**, enter the ISBN 9781285185248, and click on "Find" to locate this textbook's Web site. Then, click on "Access Now" under "Study Tools," and select Chapter 1 at the top. There, you will find a Practice Quiz that you can take to assess your mastery of the concepts in this chapter, as well as Flashcards and a Glossary of important terms.

Business Scenarios

1–1. Binding versus Persuasive Authority. A county court in Illinois is deciding a case involving an issue that has never been addressed before in that state's courts. The Iowa Supreme Court, however, recently decided a case involving a very similar fact pattern. Is the Illinois court obligated to follow the Iowa Supreme Court's decision on the issue? If the United States Supreme Court had decided a similar case, would that decision be binding on the Illinois court? Explain. **(See page 8.)**

1–2. Sources of Law. This chapter discussed a number of sources of American law. Which source of law takes priority in the following situations, and why? **(See page 3.)**

(a) A federal statute conflicts with the U.S. Constitution.

(b) A federal statute conflicts with a state constitutional provision.

(c) A state statute conflicts with the common law of that state.

(d) A state constitutional amendment conflicts with the U.S. Constitution.

1–3. *Stare Decisis.* In the text of this chapter, we stated that the doctrine of *stare decisis* "became a cornerstone of the English and American judicial systems." What does *stare decisis* mean, and why has this doctrine been so funda-

mental to the development of our legal tradition? **(See page 8.)**

1–4. Remedies. Assume that Arthur Rabe is suing Xavier Sanchez for breaching a contract in which Sanchez promised to sell Rabe a painting by Vincent Van Gogh for $30 million. **(See page 6.)**

(a) In this lawsuit, who is the plaintiff and who is the defendant?

(b) Suppose that Rabe wants Sanchez to perform the contract as promised. What remedy would Rabe seek from the court?

(c) Now suppose that Rabe wants to cancel the contract because Sanchez fraudulently misrepresented the painting as an original Van Gogh when in fact it is a copy. What remedy would Rabe seek?

(d) Will the remedy Rabe seeks in either situation be a remedy at law or a remedy in equity? What is the difference between legal and equitable remedies?

(e) Suppose that the trial court finds in Rabe's favor and grants one of these remedies. Sanchez then appeals the decision to a higher court. On appeal, which party will be the appellant (or petitioner), and which party will be the appellee (or respondent)?

Business Case Problems

1–5. Spotlight on AOL—Common Law. AOL, LLC, mistak-

enly made public the personal information of 650,000 of its members. The members filed a suit, alleging violations of California law. AOL asked the court to dismiss the suit on the basis of a "forum-selection" clause in its member agreement that designates Virginia courts as the place where mem-

ber disputes will be tried. Under a decision of the United States Supreme Court, a forum-selection clause is unenforceable "if enforcement would contravene a strong public policy of the forum in which suit is brought." California courts have declared in other cases that the AOL clause contravenes a strong public policy. If the court applies the doctrine of *stare decisis,* will it dismiss the suit?

Explain. [*Doe 1 v. AOL LLC*, 552 F.3d 1077 (9th Cir. 2009)] **(See page 6.)**

1–6. BUSINESS CASE PROBLEM WITH SAMPLE ANSWER—Reading Citations.

 Assume that you want to read the entire court opinion in the case of United States v. Yi, *704 F.3d 800 (9th Cir. 2013). Refer to the subsection entitled "Finding Case Law" in this chapter, and then explain specifically where you would find the court's opinion.* **(See page 14.)**

- **For a sample answer to Problem 1–6, go to Appendix F at the end of this text.**

1–7. A QUESTION OF ETHICS—The Common Law Tradition.

 On July 5, 1884, Dudley, Stephens, and Brooks— "all able-bodied English seamen"—and a teenage English boy were cast adrift in a lifeboat following a storm at sea. They had no water with them in the boat, and all they had for sustenance were two one-pound tins of turnips. On July 24, Dudley proposed that one of the four in the lifeboat be sacrificed to save the others. Stephens agreed with Dudley, but Brooks refused to consent—and the boy was never asked for his opinion. On July 25, Dudley killed the boy, and the three men then fed on the boy's body and blood. Four days later, a passing vessel rescued the men. They were taken to England and tried for the murder of the boy. If the men had not fed on the boy's body, they would probably have died of starvation within the four-day period. The boy, who was in a much weaker condition, would likely have died before the rest. [Regina v. Dudley and Stephens, 14 Q.B.D. (Queen's Bench Division, England) 273 (1884)] **(See page 6.)**

(a) The basic question in this case is whether the survivors should be subject to penalties under English criminal law, given the men's unusual circumstances. Were the defendants' actions necessary but unethical? Explain your reasoning. What ethical issues might be involved here?

(b) Should judges ever have the power to look beyond the written "letter of the law" in making their decisions? Why or why not?

Legal Reasoning Group Activity

1–8. Court Opinions. Read through the subsection in this chapter entitled "Decisions and Opinions." **(See page 20.)**

(a) One group will explain the difference between a concurring opinion and a majority opinion.

(b) Another group will outline the difference between a concurring opinion and a dissenting opinion.

(c) A third group will explain why judges and justices write concurring and dissenting opinions, given that these opinions will not affect the outcome of the case at hand, which has already been decided by majority vote.

CHAPTER 2

COURTS AND ALTERNATIVE DISPUTE RESOLUTION

The United States has fifty-two court systems—one for each of the fifty states, one for the District of Columbia, and a federal system. Keep in mind that the federal courts are not superior to the state courts. They are simply an independent system of courts, which derives its authority from Article III, Section 2, of the U.S. Constitution. By the power given to it under the U.S. Constitution, Congress has extended the federal court system to U.S. territories such as Guam, Puerto Rico, and the Virgin Islands.[1]

As we shall see, the United States Supreme Court is the final controlling voice over all of these fifty-two systems, at least when questions of federal law are involved. The Supreme Court's decisions—whether on affirmative action, health-care reform, immigration, or same-sex marriage—represent the last word in the most controversial legal debates in our society. Nevertheless, many of the legal issues that arise in our daily lives, such as the use of social media by courts, employers, and law enforcement, have not yet come before the nation's highest court. The lower courts usually resolve such pressing matters, making these courts equally important in our legal system.

Although an understanding of our nation's court systems is beneficial for anyone, it is particularly crucial for businesspersons, who will likely face a lawsuit at some time during their careers. Anyone involved in business should be familiar with the basic requirements that must be met before a party can bring a lawsuit before a particular court. We discuss these requirements in this chapter. It is also increasingly important for businesspersons to understand the various methods of alternative dispute resolution, which are discussed at the end of this chapter.

---

1. In Guam and the Virgin Islands, territorial courts serve as both federal courts and state courts. In Puerto Rico, they serve only as federal courts.

SECTION 1

THE JUDICIARY'S ROLE IN AMERICAN GOVERNMENT

As you learned in Chapter 1, the body of American law includes the federal and state constitutions, statutes passed by legislative bodies, administrative law, and the case decisions and legal principles that form the common law. These laws would be meaningless, however, without the courts to interpret and apply them. The essential role of the judiciary—the courts—in the American governmental system is to interpret the laws and apply them to specific situations.

Judicial Review

As the branch of government entrusted with interpreting the laws, the judiciary can decide, among other things, whether the laws or actions of the other two branches are constitutional. The process for making such a determination is known as **judicial review.** The power of judicial review enables the judicial branch to act as a check on the other two branches of government, in line with the system of checks and balances established by the U.S. Constitution.[2]

The Origins of Judicial Review in the United States

The power of judicial review is not mentioned in the U.S. Constitution (although many constitutional scholars believe that the founders intended the judi-

---

2. In a broad sense, judicial review occurs whenever a court "reviews" a case or legal proceeding—as when an appellate court reviews a lower court's decision. When discussing the judiciary's role in American government, however, the term *judicial review* refers to the power of the judiciary to decide whether the actions of the other two branches of government violate the U.S. Constitution.

ciary to have this power). The United States Supreme Court explicitly established this power in 1803 in the case *Marbury v. Madison.*[3] In that decision, the Court stated, "It is emphatically the province [authority] and duty of the Judicial Department to say what the law is. . . . If two laws conflict with each other, the courts must decide on the operation of each. . . . [I]f both [a] law and the Constitution apply to a particular case, . . . the Court must determine which of these conflicting rules governs the case. This is of the very essence of judicial duty." Since the *Marbury v. Madison* decision, the power of judicial review has remained unchallenged. Today, this power is exercised by both federal and state courts.

SECTION 2
BASIC JUDICIAL REQUIREMENTS

Before a lawsuit can be brought before a court, certain requirements must be met. These requirements relate to jurisdiction, venue, and standing to sue. We examine each of these important concepts here.

Jurisdiction

In Latin, *juris* means "law," and *diction* means "to speak." Thus, "the power to speak the law" is the literal meaning of the term **jurisdiction.** Before any court can hear a case, it must have jurisdiction over the person (or company) against whom the suit is brought (the defendant) or over the property involved in the suit. The court must also have jurisdiction over the subject matter of the dispute.

JURISDICTION OVER PERSONS OR PROPERTY
Generally, a particular court can exercise *in personam* **jurisdiction** (personal jurisdiction) over any person or business that resides in a certain geographic area. A state trial court, for example, normally has jurisdictional authority over residents (including businesses) of a particular area of the state, such as a county or district. A state's highest court (often called the state supreme court[4]) has jurisdictional authority over all residents within the state.

A court can also exercise jurisdiction over property that is located within its boundaries. This kind of jurisdiction is known as *in rem* **jurisdiction,** or "jurisdiction over the thing." ▶ **Example 2.1**   A dispute arises over the ownership of a boat in dry dock in Fort Lauderdale, Florida. The boat is owned by an Ohio resident, over whom a Florida court normally cannot exercise personal jurisdiction. The other party to the dispute is a resident of Nebraska. In this situation, a lawsuit concerning the boat could be brought in a Florida state court on the basis of the court's *in rem* jurisdiction. ◀

Long Arm Statutes and Minimum Contacts. Under the authority of a state **long arm statute,** a court can exercise personal jurisdiction over certain out-of-state defendants based on activities that took place within the state. Before a court can exercise jurisdiction, though, it must be demonstrated that the defendant had sufficient contacts, or *minimum contacts*, with the state to justify the jurisdiction.[5]

Generally, the minimum-contacts requirement means that the defendant must have sufficient connection to the state for the judge to conclude that it is fair for the state to exercise power over the defendant. For instance, if an out-of-state defendant caused an automobile accident within the state or breached a contract formed there, a court will usually find that minimum contacts exist to exercise jurisdiction over that defendant. Similarly, a state may exercise personal jurisdiction over a nonresident defendant that is sued for selling defective goods within the state.

▶ **Case in Point 2.2**   An Xbox game system caught fire in Bonnie Broquet's home in Texas and caused substantial personal injuries. Broquet filed a lawsuit in a Texas court against Ji-Haw Industrial Company, a nonresident company that made the Xbox components. Broquet alleged that Ji-Haw's components were defective and had caused the fire. Ji-Haw argued that the Texas court lacked jurisdiction over it, but a state appellate court held that the Texas long arm statute authorized the exercise of jurisdiction over the out-of-state defendant.[6] ◀

Corporate Contacts. Because corporations are considered legal persons, courts use the same principles to determine whether it is fair to exercise jurisdiction

---

3. 5 U.S. (1 Cranch) 137, 2 L.Ed. 60 (1803).

4. As will be discussed shortly, a state's highest court is often referred to as the state supreme court, but there are exceptions. For instance, in New York the supreme court is a trial court.

5. The minimum-contacts standard was first established in *International Shoe Co. v. State of Washington,* 326 U.S. 310, 66 S.Ct. 154, 90 L.Ed. 95 (1945).

6. *Ji-Haw Industrial Co. v. Broquet,* 2008 WL 441822 (Tex.App.—San Antonio 2008).

over a corporation.[7] A corporation normally is subject to personal jurisdiction in the state in which it is incorporated, has its principal office, and/or is doing business. Courts apply the minimum-contacts test to determine if they can exercise jurisdiction over out-of-state corporations.

The minimum-contacts requirement is usually met if the corporation advertises or sells its products within the state, or places its goods into the "stream of commerce" with the intent that the goods be sold in the state. ▶ **Example 2.3** A business is incorporated under the laws of Maine but has a branch office and manufacturing plant in Georgia. The corporation also advertises and sells its products in Georgia. These activities would likely constitute sufficient contacts with the state of Georgia to allow a Georgia court to exercise jurisdiction over the corporation. ◀

Some corporations do not sell or advertise products or place any goods in the stream of commerce. Determining what constitutes minimum contacts in these situations can be more difficult. ▶ **Case in Point 2.4** Independence Plating Corporation is a New Jersey corporation that provides metal-coating services. Its only office and all of its personnel are located in New Jersey, and it does not advertise out of state. Independence had a long-standing business relationship with Southern Prestige Industries, Inc., a North Carolina company. Eventually, Southern Prestige filed suit in North Carolina against Independence for defective workmanship. Independence argued that North Carolina did not have jurisdiction over it, but the court held that Independence had sufficient minimum contacts with the state to justify jurisdiction. The two parties had exchanged thirty-two separate purchase orders in a period of less than twelve months.[8] ◀

JURISDICTION OVER SUBJECT MATTER Subject-matter jurisdiction refers to the limitations on the types of cases a court can hear. Certain courts are empowered to hear certain kinds of disputes.

General and Limited Jurisdiction. In both the federal and the state court systems, there are courts of *general* (unlimited) *jurisdiction* and courts of *limited jurisdiction*. A court of general jurisdiction can decide cases involving a broad array of issues. An example of a court of general jurisdiction is a state trial court or a federal district court.

An example of a state court of limited jurisdiction is a probate court. **Probate courts** are state courts that handle only the disposition of a person's assets and obligations after that person's death, including issues relating to the custody and guardianship of children. An example of a federal court of limited subject-matter jurisdiction is a bankruptcy court. **Bankruptcy courts** handle only bankruptcy proceedings, which are governed by federal bankruptcy law.

A court's jurisdiction over subject matter is usually defined in the statute or constitution that created the court. In both the federal and the state court systems, a court's subject-matter jurisdiction can be limited by any of the following:

1. The subject of the lawsuit.
2. The sum in controversy.
3. Whether the case involves a felony (a more serious type of crime) or a misdemeanor (a less serious type of crime).
4. Whether the proceeding is a trial or an appeal.

Original and Appellate Jurisdiction. The distinction between courts of original jurisdiction and courts of appellate jurisdiction normally lies in whether the case is being heard for the first time. Courts having original jurisdiction are courts of the first instance, or trial courts. These are courts in which lawsuits begin, trials take place, and evidence is presented. In the federal court system, the *district courts* are trial courts. In the various state court systems, the trial courts are known by different names, as will be discussed shortly.

The key point here is that any court having original jurisdiction normally serves as a trial court. Courts having appellate jurisdiction act as reviewing, or appellate, courts. In general, cases can be brought before appellate courts only on appeal from an order or a judgment of a trial court or other lower courts.

JURISDICTION OF THE FEDERAL COURTS Because the federal government is a government of limited powers, the jurisdiction of the federal courts is limited. Federal courts have subject-matter jurisdiction in two situations: when a federal question is involved and when there is diversity of citizenship.

Federal Questions. Article III of the U.S. Constitution establishes the boundaries of federal judicial power. Section 2 of Article III states that "the judicial Power shall extend to all Cases, in Law and Equity, arising under this Constitution, the Laws of the United

---

7. In the eyes of the law, corporations are "legal persons"—entities that can sue and be sued.
8. *Southern Prestige Industries, Inc. v. Independence Plating Corp.,* 690 S.E.2d 768 (N.C. 2010).

States, and Treaties made, or which shall be made, under their Authority."

In effect, this clause means that whenever a plaintiff's cause of action is based, at least in part, on the U.S. Constitution, a treaty, or a federal law, a **federal question** arises. If a case involves a federal question, the case comes under the judicial power of the federal courts. A person who claims that her constitutional rights have been violated, for instance, can file the lawsuit in a federal court. Note that in a case based on a federal question, a federal court will apply federal law.

Diversity of Citizenship. Federal district courts can also exercise original jurisdiction over cases involving **diversity of citizenship.** The most common type of diversity jurisdiction[9] requires *both* of the following:

1. The plaintiff and defendant must be residents of different states.
2. The dollar amount in controversy must exceed $75,000.

---

9. Diversity jurisdiction also exists in cases between (1) a foreign country and citizens of a state or of different states and (2) citizens of a state and citizens or subjects of a foreign country. Cases based on these types of diversity jurisdiction occur infrequently.

For purposes of diversity jurisdiction, a corporation is a citizen of both the state in which it is incorporated and the state in which its principal place of business is located. A case involving diversity of citizenship can be filed in the appropriate federal district court. If the case starts in a state court, it can sometimes be transferred, or "removed," to a federal court.

A large percentage of the cases filed in federal courts each year are based on diversity of citizenship. As noted before, a federal court will apply federal law in cases involving federal questions. In a case based on diversity of citizenship, in contrast, a federal court will apply the relevant state law (which is often the law of the state in which the court sits).

The following dispute focused on whether diversity jurisdiction existed. A boat owner was severely burned when his boat exploded after being filled with excessive fuel at a marina in the U.S. Virgin Islands. The owner filed a suit in a federal district court against the marina and sought a jury trial. The defendant argued that a plaintiff in an admiralty, or maritime (on the sea), case does not have a right to a jury trial unless the court has diversity jurisdiction. The defendant claimed that because it, like the plaintiff, was a citizen of the Virgin Islands, the court had no such jurisdiction.

CASE ANALYSIS

Case 2.1   Mala v. Crown Bay Marina, Inc.
United States Court of Appeals, Third Circuit, 704 F.3d 239 (2013).

**IN THE LANGUAGE
OF THE COURT**
SMITH, Circuit Judge.
* * * *

Kelley Mala is a citizen of the United States Virgin Islands. * * * He went for a cruise in his powerboat near St. Thomas, Virgin Islands. When his boat ran low on gas, he entered Crown Bay Marina to refuel. Mala tied the boat to one of Crown Bay's eight fueling stations and began filling his tank with an automatic gas pump. Before walking to the cash register to buy oil, Mala asked a Crown Bay attendant to watch his boat.

By the time Mala returned, the boat's tank was overflowing and fuel

was spilling into the boat and into the water. The attendant manually shut off the pump and acknowledged that the pump had been malfunctioning in recent days. Mala began cleaning up the fuel, and at some point, the attendant provided soap and water. Mala eventually departed the marina, but as he did so, the engine caught fire and exploded. Mala was thrown into the water and was severely burned. His boat was unsalvageable.

* * * Mala sued Crown Bay in the District Court of the Virgin Islands. Mala's * * * complaint asserted * * * that Crown Bay negligently maintained its gas pump. [Negligence is the failure to exercise the standard of

care that a reasonable person would exercise in similar circumstances. Negligence is a tort—a breach of a legal duty that proximately causes harm or injury to another—that forms the basis for a claim subject to applicable state law.] The complaint also alleged that the District Court had admiralty and diversity jurisdiction over the case, and it requested a jury trial.

* * * *

* * * Crown Bay filed a motion to strike Mala's jury demand. Crown Bay argued that plaintiffs generally do not have a jury-trial right in admiralty cases—only when the court also has

CASE 2.1 CONTINUES ➡

diversity jurisdiction. And Crown Bay asserted that the parties were not diverse in this case * * * . In response to this motion, the District Court ruled that both Mala and Crown Bay were citizens of the Virgin Islands. The court therefore struck Mala's jury demand, but nevertheless opted to empanel an advisory jury. [The court could accept or reject the advisory jury's verdict.]

* * * At the end of the trial, the advisory jury returned a verdict of $460,000 for Mala—$400,000 for pain and suffering and $60,000 in compensatory damages. It concluded that Mala was 25 percent at fault and that Crown Bay was 75 percent at fault. The District Court ultimately rejected the verdict and entered judgment for Crown Bay.

* * * *

This appeal followed.

* * * *

Mala * * * argues that the District Court improperly refused to conduct a jury trial. This claim ultimately depends on whether the District Court had diversity jurisdiction.

The Seventh Amendment [to the U.S. Constitution] creates a right to civil jury trials in federal court: "In Suits at common law * * * the right

of trial by jury shall be preserved." Admiralty suits are not "Suits at common law," which means that when a district court has only admiralty jurisdiction the plaintiff does not have a jury-trial right. But [a federal statute] allows plaintiffs to pursue state claims in admiralty cases as long as the district court also has diversity jurisdiction. In such cases [the statute] preserves whatever jury-trial right exists with respect to the underlying state claims.

Mala argues that the District Court had both admiralty and diversity jurisdiction. As a preliminary matter, the court certainly had admiralty jurisdiction. The alleged tort occurred on navigable water and bore a substantial connection to maritime activity.

The grounds for diversity jurisdiction are less certain. *District courts have jurisdiction only if the parties are completely diverse. This means that no plaintiff may have the same state or territorial citizenship as any defendant.* The parties agree that Mala was a citizen of the Virgin Islands. [Emphasis added.]

Unfortunately for Mala, the District Court concluded that Crown Bay also was a citizen of the Virgin Islands. Mala rejects this conclusion.

Mala bears the burden of proving that the District Court had diversity jurisdiction. Mala failed to meet that burden because he did not offer evidence that Crown Bay was anything other than a citizen of the Virgin Islands. Mala contends that Crown Bay admitted to being a citizen of Florida, but Crown Bay actually denied Mala's allegation.

Absent evidence that the parties were diverse, we are left with Mala's allegations. *Allegations are insufficient at trial. And they are especially insufficient on appeal,* where we review the District Court's underlying factual findings for clear error. Under this standard, we will not reverse unless we are left with the definite and firm conviction that Crown Bay was in fact a citizen of Florida. Mala has not presented any credible evidence that Crown Bay was a citizen of Florida— much less evidence that would leave us with the requisite firm conviction. [Emphasis added.]

* * * Accordingly, the parties were not diverse and Mala does not have a jury-trial right.

* * * *

* * * For these reasons we will affirm the District Court's judgment.

LEGAL REASONING QUESTIONS

1. What is "diversity of citizenship"?
2. How does the presence—or lack—of diversity of citizenship affect a lawsuit?
3. What did the court conclude with respect to the parties' "diversity of citizenship" in this case?
4. How did the court's conclusion affect the outcome?

EXCLUSIVE VERSUS CONCURRENT JURISDICTION When cases can be tried only in federal courts or only in state courts, exclusive jurisdiction exists. Federal courts have **exclusive jurisdiction** in the following types of cases:

1. Federal crimes.
2. Bankruptcy.
3. Most patent and copyright claims.
4. Any lawsuits against the United States.

5. Some areas of admiralty law (law governing seaborne transportation and ocean waters).

State courts also have exclusive jurisdiction over certain subjects—for example, divorce and adoption.

When both federal and state courts have the power to hear a case, as is true in suits involving diversity of citizenship, **concurrent jurisdiction** exists. When concurrent jurisdiction exists, a party may choose to bring a suit in either a federal court or a state court.

Many factors can affect a party's decision to litigate in a federal versus a state court. Examples include the availability of different remedies, the distance to the respective courthouses, or the experience or reputation of a particular judge. For instance, if the dispute involves a trade secret, a party might conclude that a federal court—which has exclusive jurisdiction over copyrights and patents—would have more expertise in the matter. A party might also choose a federal court over a state court if a state court has a reputation for bias against certain types of cases or plaintiffs.

In contrast, a plaintiff might choose to litigate in a state court if the court has a reputation for awarding substantial amounts of damages or if the judge is perceived as being pro-plaintiff. The concepts of exclusive and concurrent jurisdiction are illustrated in Exhibit 2–1 below.

Jurisdiction in Cyberspace

The Internet's capacity to bypass political and geographic boundaries undercuts the traditional basis on which courts assert personal jurisdiction. This basis includes a party's contacts with a court's geographic jurisdiction.

As already discussed, for a court to compel a defendant to come before it, there must be at least minimum contacts—the presence of a salesperson within the state, for instance. When a defendant's only contacts with the state are through a Web site, however, it is more difficult to determine whether these contacts are sufficient for a court to exercise jurisdiction.

THE "SLIDING-SCALE" STANDARD The courts have developed a "sliding-scale" standard to determine when they can exercise personal jurisdiction over an out-of-state defendant based on the defendant's Web activities. The sliding-scale standard identifies three types of Internet business contacts and outlines the following rules for jurisdiction:

1. When the defendant conducts substantial business over the Internet (such as contracts and sales), jurisdiction is proper.
2. When there is some interactivity through a Web site, jurisdiction may be proper, depending on the circumstances. Even a single contact can satisfy the minimum-contacts requirement in certain situations.
3. When a defendant merely engages in passive advertising on the Web, jurisdiction is never proper.[10] An Internet communication is typically considered passive if people have to voluntarily access it to read the message and active if it is sent to specific individuals.

▶ **Case in Point 2.5** A Louisiana resident, Daniel Crummey, purchased a used recreational vehicle (RV) from sellers in Texas after viewing photos of it on eBay. The sellers' statements on eBay claimed that "Everything works great on this RV and will provide comfort and dependability for years to come. This RV will go to Alaska and back without problems!"

---

10. For a leading case on this issue, see *Zippo Manufacturing Co. v. Zippo Dot Com, Inc.,* 952 F.Supp. 1119 (W.D.Pa. 1997).

EXHIBIT 2–1 Exclusive and Concurrent Jurisdiction

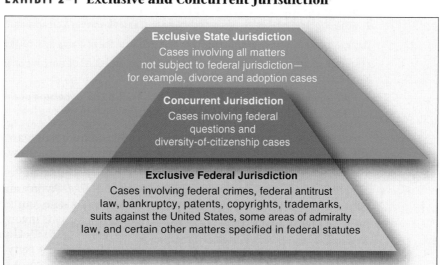

Exclusive State Jurisdiction
Cases involving all matters
not subject to federal jurisdiction—
for example, divorce and adoption cases

Concurrent Jurisdiction
Cases involving federal
questions and
diversity-of-citizenship cases

Exclusive Federal Jurisdiction
Cases involving federal crimes, federal antitrust
law, bankruptcy, patents, copyrights, trademarks,
suits against the United States, some areas of admiralty
law, and certain other matters specified in federal statutes

Crummey picked up the RV in Texas, but on the drive back to Louisiana, the RV quit working. He filed a suit in Louisiana against the sellers, alleging that the vehicle was defective. The sellers claimed that the Louisiana court lacked jurisdiction. The court found that Louisiana had jurisdiction because the sellers had used eBay to market and sell the RV to a Louisiana buyer—and had regularly used eBay to sell vehicles to remote parties in the past.[11] ◄

Concept Summary 2.1 reviews the various types of jurisdiction, including jurisdiction in cyberspace.

---

11. *Crummey v. Morgan,* 965 So.2d 497 (La.App. 1 Cir. 2007). But note that a single sale on eBay does not necessarily confer jurisdiction. Jurisdiction depends on whether the seller regularly uses eBay as a means for doing business with remote buyers. See *Boschetto v. Hansing,* 539 F.3d 1011 (9th Cir. 2008).

INTERNATIONAL JURISDICTIONAL ISSUES Because the Internet is international in scope, it obviously raises international jurisdictional issues. The world's courts seem to be developing a standard that echoes the requirement of minimum contacts applied by the U.S. courts.

Most courts are indicating that minimum contacts—doing business within the jurisdiction, for example—are enough to compel a defendant to appear and that a physical presence in the country is not necessary. The effect of this standard is that a business firm has to comply with the laws in any jurisdiction in which it targets customers for its products. This situation is complicated by the fact that many countries' laws on particular issues—free speech, for instance—are very different from U.S. laws.

CONCEPT SUMMARY 2.1
Jurisdiction

TYPE OF JURISDICTION	DESCRIPTION
Personal	Exists when a defendant is located in the territorial boundaries within which a court has the right and power to decide cases. Jurisdiction may be exercised over out-of-state defendants under state long arm statutes. Courts have jurisdiction over corporate defendants that do business within the state, as well as corporations that advertise, sell, or place goods into the stream of commerce in the state.
Property	Exists when the property that is subject to a lawsuit is located within the territorial boundaries within which a court has the right and power to decide cases.
Subject Matter	Limits the court's jurisdictional authority to particular types of cases. 1. *Limited jurisdiction*—Exists when a court is limited to a specific subject matter, such as probate or divorce. 2. *General jurisdiction*—Exists when a court can hear cases involving a broad array of issues.
Original	Exists with courts that have the authority to hear a case for the first time (trial courts).
Appellate	Exists with courts of appeal and review. Generally, appellate courts do not have original jurisdiction.
Federal	1. *Federal questions*—A federal court can exercise jurisdiction when the plaintiff's cause of action is based at least in part on the U.S. Constitution, a treaty, or a federal law. 2. *Diversity of citizenship*—A federal court can exercise jurisdiction in cases between citizens of different states when the amount in controversy exceeds $75,000 (or in cases between a foreign country and citizens of a state or of different states and in cases between citizens of a state and citizens or subjects of a foreign country).
Concurrent	Exists when both federal and state courts have authority to hear the same case.
Exclusive	Exists when only state courts or only federal courts have authority to hear a case.
Jurisdiction in Cyberspace	The courts have developed a sliding-scale standard to use in determining when jurisdiction over a Web site owner or operator in another state is proper.

The following case illustrates how federal courts apply a sliding-scale standard to determine if they can exercise jurisdiction over a foreign defendant whose only contact with the United States is through a Web site.

Case 2.2   Gucci America, Inc. v. Wang Huoqing

United States District Court, Northern District of California, ___ F.Supp.2d ___ (2011).

BACKGROUND AND FACTS Gucci America, Inc., is a New York corporation headquartered in New York City. Gucci manufactures and distributes high-quality luxury goods, including footwear, belts, sunglasses, handbags, and wallets, which are sold worldwide. In connection with its products, Gucci uses twenty-one federally registered trademarks (trademark law will be discussed in Chapter 8). Gucci also operates a number of boutiques, some of which are located in California.

Wang Huoqing, a resident of the People's Republic of China, operates numerous Web sites. When Gucci discovered that Wang Huoqing's Web sites offered for sale counterfeit goods—products bearing Gucci's trademarks but not genuine Gucci articles—it hired a private investigator in San Jose, California, to buy goods from the Web sites. The investigator purchased a wallet that was labeled Gucci but was counterfeit. Gucci filed a trademark infringement lawsuit against Wang Huoqing in a federal district court in California seeking damages and an injunction to prevent further infringement. Wang Huoqing was notified of the lawsuit via e-mail (see the discussion of *service of process* on page 52) but did not appear in court. Gucci asked the court to enter a default judgment—that is, a judgment entered when the defendant fails to appear. First, however, the court had to determine whether it had personal jurisdiction over Wang Huoqing based on the Internet sales.

IN THE LANGUAGE OF THE COURT
Joseph C. *SPERO*, United States Magistrate Judge.

* * * *

* * * Under California's long-arm statute, federal courts in California may exercise jurisdiction to the extent permitted by the Due Process Clause of the Constitution. The Due Process Clause allows federal courts to exercise jurisdiction where * * * the defendant has had sufficient minimum contacts with the forum to subject him or her to the specific jurisdiction of the court. The courts apply a three-part test to determine whether specific jurisdiction exists:

(1) The nonresident defendant must do some act or consummate some transaction with the forum or perform some act by which he purposefully avails himself of the privilege of conducting activities in the forum, thereby invoking the benefits and protections of its laws; (2) the claim must be one which arises out of or results from the defendant's forum-related activities; and (3) exercise of jurisdiction must be reasonable.

* * * *

In order to satisfy the first prong of the test for specific jurisdiction, a defendant must have either purposefully availed itself of [taken advantage of] the privilege of conducting business activities within the forum or purposefully directed activities toward the forum. *Purposeful availment typically consists of action taking place in the forum that invokes the benefits and protections of the laws of the forum, such as executing or performing a contract within the forum.* To show purposeful availment, a plaintiff must show that the defendant "engage[d] in some form of affirmative conduct allowing or promoting the transaction of business within the forum state." [Emphasis added.]

"In the Internet context, the Ninth Circuit utilizes a sliding scale analysis under which 'passive' websites do not create sufficient contacts to establish purposeful availment, whereas

CASE 2.2 CONTINUES ▶

CASE 2.2 CONTINUED interactive websites may create sufficient contacts, depending on how interactive the website is." * * * *Personal jurisdiction is appropriate where an entity is conducting business over the Internet and has offered for sale and sold its products to forum [California] residents.* [Emphasis added.]

Here, the allegations and evidence presented by Plaintiffs in support of the Motion are sufficient to show purposeful availment on the part of Defendant Wang Huoqing. Plaintiffs have alleged that Defendant operates "fully interactive Internet websites operating under the Subject Domain Names" and have presented evidence in the form of copies of web pages showing that the websites are, in fact, interactive. * * * Additionally, Plaintiffs allege Defendant is conducting counterfeiting and infringing activities within this Judicial District and has advertised and sold his counterfeit goods in the State of California. * * * Plaintiffs have also presented evidence of one actual sale within this district, made by investigator Robert Holmes from the website bag2do.cn. * * * Finally, Plaintiffs have presented evidence that Defendant Wang Huoqing owns or controls the twenty-eight websites listed in the Motion for Default Judgment. * * * Such commercial activity in the forum amounts to purposeful availment of the privilege of conducting activities within the forum, thus invoking the benefits and protections of its laws. Accordingly, the Court concludes that Defendant's contacts with California are sufficient to show purposeful availment.

DECISION AND REMEDY *The U.S. District Court for the Northern District of California held that it had personal jurisdiction over the foreign defendant, Wang Huoqing. The court entered a default judgment against Wang Huoqing and granted Gucci an injunction.*

WHAT IF THE FACTS WERE DIFFERENT? *Suppose that Gucci had not presented evidence that Wang Huoqing had made one actual sale through his Web site to a resident (the private investigator) of the court's district. Would the court still have found that it had personal jurisdiction over Wang Huoqing? Why or why not?*

THE LEGAL ENVIRONMENT DIMENSION *Is it relevant to the analysis of jurisdiction that Gucci America's principal place of business is in New York rather than California? Explain.*

Venue

Jurisdiction has to do with whether a court has authority to hear a case involving specific persons, property, or subject matter. **Venue**[12] is concerned with the most appropriate location for a trial. For instance, two state courts (or two federal courts) may have the authority to exercise jurisdiction over a case. Nonetheless, it may be more appropriate or convenient to hear the case in one court than in the other.

The concept of venue reflects the policy that a court trying a case should be in the geographic neighborhood (usually the county) where the incident occurred or where the parties reside. Venue in a civil case typically is where the defendant resides, whereas venue in a criminal case normally is where the crime occurred. Pretrial publicity or other factors, though, may require a change of venue to another community, especially in criminal cases in which the defendant's right to a fair and impartial jury has been impaired.

▶ **Example 2.6** Police raid a compound of religious polygamists in Texas and remove many children from the ranch. Authorities suspect that some of the girls were being sexually and physically abused. The raid receives a great deal of media attention, and people living in the nearby towns would likely be influenced by this publicity. If the government files criminal charges against a member of the religious sect, that individual may request a change of venue to another location. ◀

Note, though, that venue has lost some significance in today's world because of the Internet and 24/7 news reporting. Courts now rarely grant requests for a change of venue. Because everyone has instant access to all information about a purported crime, courts reason that no community is more or less informed or prejudiced for or against a defendant.

Standing to Sue

Before a party can bring a lawsuit to court, that party must have **standing to sue,** or a sufficient stake in

---

12. Pronounced *ven*-yoo.

a matter to justify seeking relief through the court system. Standing means that the party that filed the action in court has a legally protected interest at stake in the litigation. At times, a person can have standing to sue on behalf of another person, such as a minor (child) or a mentally incompetent person.

Standing can be broken down into three elements:

1. *Harm.* The party bringing the action must have suffered or will imminently suffer harm—an invasion of a legally protected interest. The controversy must be real and substantial rather than hypothetical.
2. *Causation.* There must be a causal connection between the conduct complained of and the injury.
3. *Remedy.* It must be likely, as opposed to merely speculative, that a favorable court decision will remedy, or make up for, the injury suffered.

▶ **Case in Point 2.7**   The federal government's Legal Services Corporation (LSC) subsidizes legal services for people who cannot afford them. LSC restricts the use of its funds to certain purposes. In an attempt to cut costs, the state of Oregon tried to consolidate some of its legal assistance programs with similar programs provided by other organizations, including LSC. LSC did not approve, however, because Oregon's plan would integrate programs receiving federal funds with programs that engaged in restricted activities.

Oregon filed a suit against LSC, alleging that the state's ability to provide legal services to its citizens was frustrated, but the court dismissed the suit. Oregon had not accepted any federal funds and was not injured by the federal government's decision to subsidize certain private activities. The state had no standing to sue the federal government over federal subsidies to private parties.[13] ◀

S E C T I O N   3
THE STATE AND FEDERAL COURT SYSTEMS

As mentioned earlier in this chapter, each state has its own court system. Additionally, there is a system of federal courts. Although no two state court systems are exactly the same, the right-hand side of Exhibit 2–2 below illustrates the basic organizational framework characteristic of the court systems in many states. The exhibit also shows how the federal court system is structured. We turn now to an examination of these court systems, beginning with the state courts.

The State Court Systems

Typically, a state court system includes several levels, or tiers, of courts, as shown in Exhibit 2–2. State courts may include (1) trial courts of limited jurisdiction, (2) trial courts of general jurisdiction, (3) appellate courts

---

13. *Oregon v. Legal Services Corp.,* 552 F.3d 965 (9th Cir. 2009).

EXHIBIT 2–2 The State and Federal Court Systems

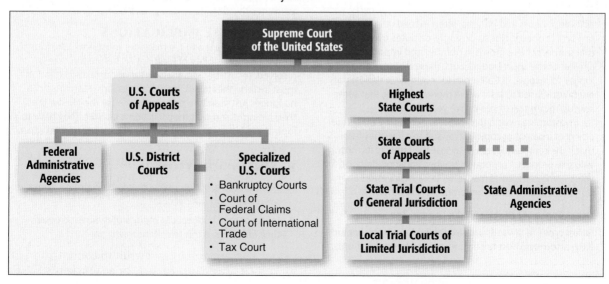

(intermediate appellate courts), and (4) the state's highest court (often called the state supreme court).

Generally, any person who is a party to a lawsuit has the opportunity to plead the case before a trial court and then, if he or she loses, before at least one level of appellate court. Finally, if the case involves a federal statute or federal constitutional issue, the decision of a state supreme court on that issue may be further appealed to the United States Supreme Court. (See this chapter's *Managerial Strategy* feature below for a discussion of how state budget cuts are making it more difficult to bring cases in some state courts.)

MANAGERIAL STRATEGY

Budget Cuts for State Courts Can Affect Businesses

In the United States, businesses use the courts far more than anyone else. Most civil court cases involve a business suing another business for breach of contract or fraud, for instance. Additionally, when one company fails to pay another company for products or services, the unpaid company will often turn to the court system. If that firm does not have ready access to the courts, its financial stability can be put at risk.

Court Budgets Have Been Reduced

According to the National Center for State Courts, since 2008 forty-two state legislatures have reduced funding for their state courts. California's courts have experienced the steepest cuts—$844 million from their annual budget since 2011. Recently, the Alabama legislature cut its court funding by almost 9 percent. As a result, the state's chief justice ordered courthouses to close on Fridays. The number of weeks that jury trials are available to civil litigants in Alabama has been reduced by 50 percent.

Intellectual Property Cases Take Longer to Resolve

Today, the value of a company's intellectual property, such as its copyrights and patents, often exceeds the value of its physical property. Not surprisingly, disputes over intellectual property have grown in number and importance. As a result of the court budget cuts, these disputes also take longer to resolve. In California, for example, a typical patent lawsuit used to last twelve months. Today, that same lawsuit might take three to five years.

Investors are reluctant to invest in a company that is the object of a patent or copyright lawsuit because they fear that if the company loses, it may lose the rights to its most valuable product. Consequently, when litigation drags on for years, some companies may suffer because investors abandon them even though the companies are otherwise healthy.

Other Types of Litigation Take Longer, Too

Other types of lawsuits are also taking longer to conclude. Now attorneys must tell businesses to consider not only the cost of bringing a lawsuit, but also the length of time involved. The longer the litigation lasts, the larger the legal bills and the greater the drain on company employees' time. Roy Weinstein, managing director of Micronomics in California, argues that the economic impact of court delays on businesses is substantial. During the years that a lawsuit can take, some businesses find that they cannot expand or hire new employees, and they are reluctant to spend on additional marketing and advertising.

In fact, it is not unusual for a company to win its case but end up going out of business. As a result of putting its business on hold for years, the company becomes insolvent.

Some Meritorious Cases Are Never Filed

Facing long delays in litigation with potential negative effects on their companies, business managers are becoming reluctant to bring lawsuits, even when their cases clearly have merit. In Alabama, for instance, the number of civil cases filed has dropped by more than a third in the last few years. Judge J. Scott Vowell of Jefferson County attributes this decline to delays and higher court costs.

MANAGERIAL IMPLICATIONS

Before bringing a lawsuit, a manager must now take into account the possibility of long delays before the case is resolved. A cost-benefit analysis for undertaking litigation must include the delays in the calculations. Managers can no longer just stand on principle because they know that they are right and that they will win a lawsuit. They have to look at the bigger picture, which includes substantial court delays.

BUSINESS QUESTIONS

1. *What are some of the costs of increased litigation delays caused by court budget cuts?*

2. *In response to budget cuts, many states have increased their filing fees. Is this fair? Why or why not?*

The states use various methods to select judges for their courts. Usually, voters elect judges, but in some states judges are appointed. For instance, in Iowa, the governor appoints judges, and then the general population decides whether to confirm their appointment in the next general election. The states usually specify the number of years that judges will serve. In contrast, as you will read shortly, judges in the federal court system are appointed by the president of the United States and, if they are confirmed by the Senate, hold office for life—unless they engage in blatantly illegal conduct.

TRIAL COURTS Trial courts are exactly what their name implies—courts in which trials are held and testimony is taken. State trial courts have either general or limited jurisdiction.

General Jurisdiction. Trial courts that have general jurisdiction as to subject matter may be called county, district, superior, or circuit courts.[14] State trial courts of general jurisdiction have jurisdiction over a wide variety of subjects, including both civil disputes and criminal prosecutions. In some states, trial courts of general jurisdiction may hear appeals from courts of limited jurisdiction.

Limited Jurisdiction. Courts of limited jurisdiction as to subject matter are generally inferior trial courts or minor judiciary courts. Limited jurisdiction courts might include local municipal courts (which could also have separate traffic courts and drug courts) and domestic relations courts (which handle divorce and child-custody disputes).

Small claims courts are inferior trial courts that hear only civil cases involving claims of less than a certain amount, such as $5,000 (the amount varies from state to state). Procedures in small claims courts are generally informal, and lawyers are not required (in a few states, lawyers are not even allowed). Decisions of small claims courts and municipal courts may sometimes be appealed to a state trial court of general jurisdiction.

A few states have also established Islamic law courts, which are courts of limited jurisdiction that serve the American Muslim community. These courts decide cases with reference to the *sharia*, a system of law used in most Islamic countries that is derived from the Qur'an and the sayings and doings of Muhammad and his followers.

Appellate, or Reviewing, Courts. Every state has at least one court of appeals (appellate court, or reviewing court), which may be an intermediate appellate court or the state's highest court. About three-fourths of the states have intermediate appellate courts.

Generally, courts of appeals do not conduct new trials, in which evidence is submitted to the court and witnesses are examined. Rather, an appellate court panel of three or more judges reviews the record of the case on appeal, which includes a transcript of the trial proceedings. The appellate court hears arguments from attorneys and determines whether the trial court committed an error.

Reviewing courts focus on questions of law, not questions of fact. A **question of fact** deals with what really happened in regard to the dispute being tried—such as whether a party actually burned a flag. A **question of law** concerns the application or interpretation of the law—such as whether flag-burning is a form of speech protected by the First Amendment to the U.S. Constitution. Only a judge, not a jury, can rule on questions of law.

Appellate courts normally defer (or give weight) to the trial court's findings on questions of fact because the trial court judge and jury were in a better position to evaluate testimony. The trial court judge and jury can directly observe witnesses' gestures, demeanor, and other nonverbal behavior during the trial. An appellate court cannot.

HIGHEST STATE COURTS The highest appellate court in a state is usually called the supreme court but may be designated by some other name. For instance, in both New York and Maryland, the highest state court is called the Court of Appeals. The highest state court in Maine and Massachusetts is the Supreme Judicial Court, and in West Virginia, it is the Supreme Court of Appeals.

The decisions of each state's highest court on all questions of state law are final. Only when issues of federal law are involved can the United States Supreme Court overrule a decision made by a state's highest court. ▶ **Example 2.8** A city enacts an ordinance that prohibits citizens from engaging in door-to-door advocacy without first registering with the mayor's office and receiving a permit. A religious group then sues the city, arguing that the law violates the freedoms of speech and religion guaranteed by the First Amendment. If the state supreme court upholds the law, the group could appeal the decision to the United States Supreme Court—because a constitutional (federal) issue is involved. ◀

---

14. The name in Ohio and Pennsylvania is Court of Common Pleas. The name in New York is Supreme Court, Trial Division.

The Federal Court System

The federal court system is basically a three-tiered model consisting of (1) U.S. district courts (trial courts of general jurisdiction) and various courts of limited jurisdiction, (2) U.S. courts of appeals (intermediate courts of appeals), and (3) the United States Supreme Court.

Unlike state court judges, who are usually elected, federal court judges—including the justices of the Supreme Court—are appointed by the president of the United States, subject to confirmation by the U.S. Senate. All federal judges receive lifetime appointments under Article III of the U.S. Constitution, which states that federal judges "hold their offices during good Behaviour." In the entire history of the United States, only seven federal judges have been removed from office through impeachment proceedings.

U.S. DISTRICT COURTS At the federal level, the equivalent of a state trial court of general jurisdiction is the district court. U.S. district courts have original jurisdiction in matters involving a federal question and concurrent jurisdiction with state courts when diversity jurisdiction exists. Federal cases typically originate in district courts. There are other federal courts with original, but special (or limited), jurisdiction, such as the federal bankruptcy courts and others shown in Exhibit 2–2 on page 37.

There is at least one federal district court in every state. The number of judicial districts can vary over time, primarily owing to population changes and corresponding changes in caseloads. Today there are ninety-four federal judicial districts. Exhibit 2–3 below shows the boundaries of both the U.S. district courts and the U.S. courts of appeals (discussed next).

U.S. COURTS OF APPEALS In the federal court system, there are thirteen U.S. courts of appeals—referred to as U.S. circuit courts of appeals. Twelve of the federal courts of appeals (including the Court of Appeals for the D.C. Circuit) hear appeals from the federal district courts located within their respective judicial circuits, or geographic boundaries (shown in Exhibit 2–3 on the

EXHIBIT 2–3 **Geographic Boundaries of the U.S. Courts of Appeals and U.S. District Courts**

Source: Administrative Office of the United States Courts.

previous page).[15] The Court of Appeals for the Thirteenth Circuit, called the Federal Circuit, has national appellate jurisdiction over certain types of cases, such as those involving patent law and those in which the U.S. government is a defendant.

The decisions of a circuit court of appeals are binding on all courts within the circuit court's jurisdiction and are final in most cases, but appeal to the United States Supreme Court is possible.

THE UNITED STATES SUPREME COURT The highest level of the three-tiered federal court system is the United States Supreme Court. According to the U.S. Constitution, there is only one national Supreme Court. All other courts in the federal system are considered "inferior." Congress is empowered to create other inferior courts as it deems necessary. The inferior courts that Congress has created include the second tier in our model—the U.S. circuit courts of appeals—as well as the district courts and the various federal courts of limited, or specialized, jurisdiction.

The United States Supreme Court consists of nine justices. Although the Supreme Court has original, or trial, jurisdiction in rare instances (set forth in Article III, Sections 1 and 2), most of its work is as an appeals court. The Supreme Court can review any case decided by any of the federal courts of appeals. It also has appellate authority over cases involving federal questions that have been decided in the state courts. The Supreme Court is the final authority on the Constitution and federal law.

Appeals to the Supreme Court. To bring a case before the Supreme Court, a party requests the Court to issue a writ of *certiorari.*[16] A **writ of *certiorari*** is an order issued by the Supreme Court to a lower court requiring the latter to send it the record of the case for review. The Court will not issue a writ unless at least four of the nine justices approve of it. This is called the **rule of four.**

Whether the Court will issue a writ of *certiorari* is entirely within its discretion, and most petitions for writs are denied. (Although thousands of cases are filed with the Supreme Court each year, it hears, on average, fewer than one hundred of these cases.)[17] A

---

15. Historically, judges were required to "ride the circuit" and hear appeals in different courts around the country, which is how the name "circuit court" came about.
16. Pronounced sur-shee-uh-*rah*-ree.
17. From the mid-1950s through the early 1990s, the Supreme Court reviewed more cases per year than it has since then. In the Court's 1982–1983 term, for example, the Court issued written opinions in 151 cases. In contrast, during the Court's 2012–2013 term, the Court issued written opinions in only 79 cases.

denial of the request to issue a writ of *certiorari* is not a decision on the merits of the case, nor does it indicate agreement with the lower court's opinion. Also, denial of the writ has no value as a precedent. Denial simply means that the lower court's decision remains the law in that jurisdiction.

Petitions Granted by the Court. Typically, the Court grants petitions in cases that raise important constitutional questions or when the lower courts have issued conflicting decisions on a significant issue. The justices, however, never explain their reasons for hearing certain cases and not others, so it is difficult to predict which type of case the Court might select.

See *Concept Summary 2.2* on the next page to review the courts in the federal and state court systems.

SECTION 4

ALTERNATIVE DISPUTE RESOLUTION

Litigation—the process of resolving a dispute through the court system—is expensive and time consuming. Litigating even the simplest complaint is costly, and because of the backlog of cases pending in many courts, several years may pass before a case is actually tried. For these and other reasons, more and more businesspersons are turning to **alternative dispute resolution (ADR)** as a means of settling their disputes.

The great advantage of ADR is its flexibility. Methods of ADR range from the parties sitting down together and attempting to work out their differences to multinational corporations agreeing to resolve a dispute through a formal hearing before a panel of experts. Normally, the parties themselves can control how they will attempt to settle their dispute. They can decide what procedures will be used, whether a neutral third party will be present or make a decision, and whether that decision will be legally binding or nonbinding. ADR also offers more privacy than court proceedings and allows disputes to be resolved relatively quickly.

Today, more than 90 percent of civil lawsuits are settled before trial using some form of ADR. Indeed, most states either require or encourage parties to undertake ADR prior to trial. Many federal courts have instituted ADR programs as well. In the following pages, we examine the basic forms of ADR.

CONCEPT SUMMARY 2.2
Types of Courts

TYPE OF COURT	DESCRIPTION
Trial Courts	Trial courts are courts of original jurisdiction in which actions are initiated. 1. *State courts*—Courts of general jurisdiction can hear any case that has not been specifically designated for another court. Courts of limited jurisdiction include, among others, domestic relations courts, probate courts, municipal courts, and small claims courts. 2. *Federal courts*—The federal district court is the equivalent of the state trial court. Federal courts of limited jurisdiction include the bankruptcy courts and others shown in Exhibit 2–2 on page 37.
Intermediate Appellate Courts	Courts of appeals are reviewing courts. Generally, appellate courts do not have original jurisdiction. About three-fourths of the states have intermediate appellate courts. In the federal court system, the U.S. circuit courts of appeals are the intermediate appellate courts.
Supreme Courts	The highest state court is that state's supreme court, although it may be called by some other name. Appeal from state supreme courts to the United States Supreme Court is possible only if a federal question is involved. The United States Supreme Court is the highest court in the federal court system and the final authority on the Constitution and federal law.

Negotiation

The simplest form of ADR is **negotiation,** a process in which the parties attempt to settle their dispute informally, with or without attorneys to represent them. Attorneys frequently advise their clients to negotiate a settlement voluntarily before they proceed to trial. Parties may even try to negotiate a settlement during a trial or after the trial but before an appeal.

Negotiation traditionally involves just the parties themselves and (typically) their attorneys. The attorneys, though, are advocates—they are obligated to put their clients' interests first.

Mediation

In **mediation,** a neutral third party acts as a mediator and works with both sides in the dispute to facilitate a resolution. The mediator normally talks with the parties separately as well as jointly, emphasizes points of agreement, and helps the parties to evaluate their options.

Although the mediator may propose a solution (called a mediator's proposal), he or she does not make a decision resolving the matter. The mediator, who need not be a lawyer, usually charges a fee for his or her services (which can be split between the parties). States that require parties to undergo ADR before trial often offer mediation as one of the ADR options or (as in Florida) the only option.

One of the biggest advantages of mediation is that it is less adversarial than litigation. In mediation, the mediator takes an active role and attempts to bring the parties together so that they can come to a mutually satisfactory resolution. The mediation process tends to reduce the antagonism between the disputants, allowing them to resume their former relationship while minimizing hostility. For this reason, mediation is often the preferred form of ADR for disputes between business partners, employers and employees, or other parties involved in long-term relationships.

Arbitration

A more formal method of ADR is **arbitration,** in which an arbitrator (a neutral third party or a panel of experts) hears a dispute and imposes a resolution on the parties. Arbitration differs from other forms of ADR in that the third party hearing the dispute makes a decision for the parties. Exhibit 2–4 on the following page outlines the basic differences among the three traditional forms of ADR.

Usually, the parties in arbitration agree that the third party's decision will be *legally binding,* although the parties can also agree to *nonbinding* arbitration. (Arbitration that is mandated by the courts often is not binding on the parties.) In nonbinding arbitration, the parties can go forward with a lawsuit if they do not agree with the arbitrator's decision.

EXHIBIT 2-4 Basic Differences in the Traditional Forms of ADR

Type of ADR	Description	Neutral Third Party Present	Who Decides the Resolution
Negotiation	Parties meet informally with or without their attorneys and attempt to agree on a resolution. This is the simplest and least expensive method of ADR.	No	The parties themselves reach a resolution.
Mediation	A neutral third party meets with the parties and emphasizes points of agreement to bring them toward resolution of their dispute. 1. This method of ADR reduces hostility between the parties. 2. Mediation is preferred for resolving disputes between business partners, employers and employees, or others involved in long-term relationships.	Yes	The parties, but the mediator may suggest or propose a resolution.
Arbitration	The parties present their arguments and evidence before an arbitrator at a hearing, and the arbitrator renders a decision resolving the parties' dispute. 1. This ADR method is the most formal and resembles a court proceeding because some rules of evidence apply. 2. The parties are free to frame the issues and set the powers of the arbitrator. 3. If the parties agree that the arbitration is binding, then the parties' right to appeal the decision is limited.	Yes	The arbitrator imposes a resolution on the parties that may be either binding or nonbinding.

In some respects, formal arbitration resembles a trial, although usually the procedural rules are much less restrictive than those governing litigation. In a typical arbitration, the parties present opening arguments and ask for specific remedies. Both sides present evidence and may call and examine witnesses. The arbitrator then renders a decision.

THE ARBITRATOR'S DECISION The arbitrator's decision is called an **award.** It is is usually the final word on the matter. Although the parties may appeal an arbitrator's decision, a court's review of the decision will be much more restricted in scope than an appellate court's review of a trial court's decision. The general view is that because the parties were free to frame the issues and set the powers of the arbitrator at the outset, they cannot complain about the results. A court will set aside an award only in the event of one of the following:

1. The arbitrator's conduct or "bad faith" substantially prejudiced the rights of one of the parties.
2. The award violates an established public policy.
3. The arbitrator exceeded her or his powers—that is, arbitrated issues that the parties did not agree to submit to arbitration.

ARBITRATION CLAUSES Almost any commercial matter can be submitted to arbitration. Frequently, parties include an **arbitration clause** in a contract (a written agreement—see Chapter 11) specifying that any dispute arising under the contract will be resolved through arbitration rather than through the court system. Parties can also agree to arbitrate a dispute *after* it arises.

ARBITRATION STATUTES Most states have statutes (often based, in part, on the Uniform Arbitration Act of 1955) under which arbitration clauses will be enforced. Some state statutes compel arbitration of certain types of disputes, such as those involving public employees.

At the federal level, the Federal Arbitration Act (FAA), enacted in 1925, enforces arbitration clauses in contracts involving maritime activity and interstate commerce. Because of the breadth of the commerce clause (see Chapter 4), arbitration agreements involving transactions only slightly connected to the flow of interstate commerce may fall under the FAA. The FAA established a national policy favoring arbitration.

In the following case, the parties had agreed to arbitrate disputes involving their contract, but a state law allowed one party to void a contractual provision that required arbitration outside the state. The court had to decide if the FAA *preempted* (took priority over, or blocked—see Chapter 4) the state law.

CASE 2.3

Cleveland Construction, Inc. v. Levco Construction, Inc.

Court of Appeals of Texas, First District, 359 S.W.3d 843 (2012).

BACKGROUND AND FACTS Cleveland Construction, Inc. (CCI), was the general contractor on a project to build a grocery store in Houston, Texas. CCI hired Levco Construction, Inc., as a subcontractor to perform excavation and grading. The contract included an arbitration provision stating that any disputes would be resolved by arbitration in Ohio. When a dispute arose between the parties, Levco filed a suit against CCI in a Texas state court. CCI sought to compel arbitration in Ohio under the Federal Arbitration Act (FAA), but a Texas statute allows a party to void a contractual provision that requires arbitration outside Texas. The Texas court granted an emergency motion preventing arbitration. CCI appealed.

 IN THE LANGUAGE OF THE COURT
Evelyn N. *KEYES*, Justice.

* * * *

[Texas] Business and Commerce Code section 272.001 provides:

If a contract contains a provision making * * * any conflict arising under the contract subject to * * * arbitration in another state, that provision is voidable by the party obligated by the contract to perform the construction * * * .

Levco argues * * * that it "exercised its option to void the requirement in the Contract to arbitrate in Lake County, Ohio."

*The FAA preempts all otherwise applicable inconsistent state laws * * * under the Supremacy Clause of the United States Constitution. The FAA declares written provisions for arbitration "valid, irrevocable, and enforceable, save upon such grounds as exist at law or in equity for the revocation of any contract."* [Emphasis added.]

* * * Applying section 272.001 as Levco asks us to do here would prevent us from enforcing a term of the parties' arbitration agreement—the venue—on a ground that is not recognized by the FAA or by general state-law contract principles. We hold that the FAA preempts application of this provision under the facts of this case. * * * By allowing a party to * * * declare void a previously bargained-for provision, application of section 272.001 would undermine the declared federal policy of rigorous enforcement of arbitration agreements.

DECISION AND REMEDY *The Texas appellate court reversed the trial court, holding that the FAA preempts the Texas statute. CCI could compel arbitration in Ohio.*

THE LEGAL ENVIRONMENT DIMENSION *How would business be affected if each state could pass a statute, like the one in Texas, allowing parties to void out-of-state arbitration?*

THE SOCIAL DIMENSION *Considering the relative bargaining power of the parties, was it fair to enforce the arbitration clause in this contract? Why or why not?*

THE ISSUE OF ARBITRABILITY The terms of an arbitration agreement can limit the types of disputes that the parties agree to arbitrate. Disputes can arise, however, when the parties do not specify limits or when the parties disagree on whether the particular matter is covered by their arbitration agreement.

When one party files a lawsuit to compel arbitration, it is up to the court to resolve the issue of *arbitrability.* That is, the court must decide whether the matter is one that must be resolved through arbitration.

If the court finds that the subject matter in controversy is covered by the agreement to arbitrate, then a party may be compelled to arbitrate the dispute. Usually, a court will allow the claim to be arbitrated if the court finds that the relevant statute (the state arbitration statute or the FAA) does not exclude such claims.

No party, however, will be ordered to submit a particular dispute to arbitration unless the court is convinced that the party has consented to do so. Additionally, the courts will not compel arbitration if it is clear that the arbitration rules and procedures are inherently unfair to one of the parties.

MANDATORY ARBITRATION IN THE EMPLOYMENT CONTEXT A significant question for businesspersons has concerned mandatory arbitration clauses in employment contracts. Many employees claim they are at a disadvantage when they are forced, as a condition of being hired, to agree to arbitrate all disputes and thus waive their rights under statutes designed to protect employees. The United States Supreme Court, however, has held that mandatory arbitration clauses in employment contracts are generally enforceable.

▶ **Case in Point 2.9** In a landmark decision, *Gilmer v. Interstate Johnson Lane Corp.*,[18] the Supreme Court held that a claim brought under a federal statute prohibiting age discrimination could be subject to arbitration. The Court concluded that the employee had waived his right to sue when he agreed, as part of a required application to be a securities representative, to arbitrate "any dispute, claim, or controversy" relating to his employment. ◀

Compulsory arbitration agreements often spell out the rules for a mandatory proceeding. For example, an agreement may address in detail the amount and payment of filing fees and other expenses. Employment-related agreements often require the parties to split the costs, but some courts have overturned those provisions when an individual worker lacked the ability to pay.[19]

Other Types of ADR

The three forms of ADR just discussed are the oldest and traditionally the most commonly used forms. In addition, a variety of new types of ADR have emerged in recent years, including those described here.

1. In **early neutral case evaluation,** the parties select a neutral third party (generally an expert in the subject matter of the dispute) and then explain their respective positions to that person. The case evaluator assesses the strengths and weaknesses of each party's claims.
2. In a **mini-trial,** each party's attorney briefly argues the party's case before the other party and a panel of representatives from each side who have the authority to settle the dispute. Typically, a neutral third party (usually an expert in the area being disputed) acts as an adviser. If the parties fail to reach an agreement, the adviser renders an opinion as to how a court would likely decide the issue.
3. Numerous federal courts now hold **summary jury trials,** in which the parties present their arguments and evidence and the jury renders a verdict. The jury's verdict is not binding, but it does act as a guide to both sides in reaching an agreement during the mandatory negotiations that immediately follow the trial.
4. Other alternatives being employed by the courts include summary procedures for commercial litigation and the appointment of special masters to assist judges in deciding complex issues.

Providers of ADR Services

Both government agencies and private organizations provide ADR services. A major provider of ADR services is the **American Arbitration Association (AAA).** The AAA was founded in 1926 and now handles more than 200,000 claims a year in its numerous offices worldwide.

Cases brought before the AAA are heard by an expert or a panel of experts in the area relating to the dispute and are usually settled quickly. Generally, about half of the panel members are lawyers. To cover its costs, the AAA charges a fee, paid by the party filing the claim. In addition, each party to the dispute pays a specified amount for each hearing day, as well as a special additional fee in cases involving personal injuries or property loss.

Hundreds of for-profit firms around the country also provide dispute-resolution services. Typically, these firms hire retired judges to conduct arbitration hearings or otherwise assist parties in settling their disputes. The judges follow procedures similar to those of the federal courts and use similar rules. Usually, each party to the dispute pays a filing fee and a designated fee for a hearing session or conference.

18. 500 U.S. 20, 111 S.Ct. 1647, 114 L.Ed.2d 26 (1991).
19. See, for example, *Davis v. O'Melveny & Myers, LLC,* 485 F.3d 1066 (9th Cir. 2007); and *Nagrampa v. MailCoups, Inc.,* 469 F.3d 1257 (9th Cir. 2006).

Online Dispute Resolution

An increasing number of companies and organizations are offering dispute-resolution services using the Internet. The settlement of disputes in these online forums is known as **online dispute resolution (ODR).** The disputes resolved in these forums have most commonly involved rights to domain names (Web site addresses—see Chapter 9) or the quality of goods sold via the Internet, including goods sold through Internet auction sites.

ODR may be best for resolving small- to medium-sized business liability claims, which may not be worth the expense of litigation or traditional ADR methods. Rules being developed in online forums may ultimately become a code of conduct for everyone who does business in cyberspace. Most online forums do not automatically apply the law of any specific jurisdiction. Instead, results are often based on general, more universal legal principles. As with offline methods of dispute resolution, any party may appeal to a court at any time if the ODR is nonbinding arbitration.

Some cities use ODR as a means of resolving claims against them. ▶ **Example 2.10** New York City uses Cybersettle.com to resolve auto accident, sidewalk, and other personal-injury claims made against the city. Parties with complaints submit their demands, and the city submits its offers confidentially online. If an offer exceeds a demand, the claimant keeps half the difference as a bonus, plus the original claim. ◀

SECTION 5
INTERNATIONAL DISPUTE RESOLUTION

Businesspersons who engage in international business transactions normally take special precautions to protect themselves in the event that a party with whom they are dealing in another country breaches an agreement. Often, parties to international contracts include special clauses in their contracts providing for how disputes arising under the contracts will be resolved.

Forum-Selection and Choice-of-Law Clauses

As you will read in Chapter 20, parties to international transactions often include forum-selection and choice-of-law clauses in their contracts. These clauses designate the jurisdiction (court or country) where any dispute arising under the contract will be litigated and which nation's law will be applied.

When an international contract does not include such clauses, any legal proceedings arising under the contract will be more complex and attended by much more uncertainty. For instance, litigation may take place in two or more countries, with each country applying its own national law to the particular transactions.

Furthermore, even if a plaintiff wins a favorable judgment in a lawsuit litigated in the plaintiff's country, the defendant's country could refuse to enforce the court's judgment. As will be discussed in Chapter 24, the judgment may be enforced in the defendant's country for reasons of courtesy. The United States, for example, will generally enforce a foreign court's decision if it is consistent with U.S. national law and policy. Other nations, however, may not be as accommodating as the United States, and the plaintiff may be left empty-handed.

Arbitration Clauses

International contracts also often include arbitration clauses that require a neutral third party to decide any contract disputes. In international arbitration proceedings, the third party may be a neutral entity (such as the International Chamber of Commerce), a panel of individuals representing both parties' interests, or some other group or organization.

The United Nations Convention on the Recognition and Enforcement of Foreign Arbitral Awards[20] has been implemented in more than 145 countries, including the United States. This convention assists in the enforcement of arbitration clauses, as do provisions in specific treaties among nations. The American Arbitration Association provides arbitration services for international as well as domestic disputes.

International Treaties and Arbitration

International treaties (formal agreements among several nations—see Chapter 24) sometimes also stipulate arbitration for resolving disputes. This is a tactic that has been used in the past to increase foreign investment. ▶ **Example 2.11** In the 1990s, Argentina encouraged foreign investment by forming bilateral investment treaties with other nations, including the United States and France. The treaties required Argentina to protect investors' property rights and provided that any grievances would be settled by arbi-

---

20. June 10, 1958, 21 U.S.T. 2517, T.I.A.S. No. 6997 (the "New York Convention").

tration at the International Centre for the Settlement of Investment Disputes (ICSID), which is part of the World Bank. Foreign investment in Argentina skyrocketed, in part, because companies had the security of knowing that disputes would be settled by the ICSID rather than by Argentina's courts.

After Argentina's economy collapsed in 2001, companies that had suffered significant losses filed claims against Argentina with the ICSID. The ICSID, however, resolved most claims in Argentina's favor. The few companies that won awards from the ICSID, such as Philip Morris International, then had to ask courts in Argentina to enforce the judgments. These problems have caused some nations to withdraw from the ICSID. Others, including Australia, have indicated that they will not enter any future trade agreements that require their domestic investors who invest in other countries to submit to arbitration. ◄

Reviewing: Courts and Alternative Dispute Resolution

Stan Garner resides in Illinois and promotes boxing matches for SuperSports, Inc., an Illinois corporation. Garner created the concept of "Ages" promotion—a three-fight series of boxing matches pitting an older fighter (George Foreman) against a younger fighter. The concept had titles for each of the three fights, including "Battle of the Ages." Garner contacted Foreman and his manager, who both reside in Texas, to sell the idea, and they arranged a meeting in Las Vegas, Nevada. During negotiations, Foreman's manager signed a nondisclosure agreement prohibiting him from disclosing Garner's promotional concepts unless the parties signed a contract. Nevertheless, after negotiations fell through, Foreman used Garner's "Battle of the Ages" concept to promote a subsequent fight. Garner filed a suit against Foreman and his manager in a federal district court located in Illinois, alleging breach of contract. Using the information presented in the chapter, answer the following questions.

1. On what basis might the federal district court in Illinois exercise jurisdiction in this case?
2. Does the federal district court have original or appellate jurisdiction?
3. Suppose that Garner had filed his action in an Illinois state court. Could an Illinois state court exercise personal jurisdiction over Foreman or his manager? Why or why not?
4. Assume that Garner had filed his action in a Nevada state court. Would that court have had personal jurisdiction over Foreman or his manager? Explain.

DEBATE THIS . . . *In this age of the Internet, when people communicate via e-mail, texts, tweets, Facebook, and Skype, is the concept of jurisdiction losing its meaning?*

Terms and Concepts

alternative dispute resolution (ADR) 41
American Arbitration Association (AAA) 45
arbitration 42
arbitration clause 43
award 43
bankruptcy court 30
concurrent jurisdiction 32
diversity of citizenship 31
early neutral case evaluation 45

exclusive jurisdiction 32
federal question 31
in personam jurisdiction 29
in rem jurisdiction 29
judicial review 28
jurisdiction 29
litigation 41
long arm statute 29
mediation 42
mini-trial 45
negotiation 42

online dispute resolution (ODR) 46
probate court 30
question of fact 39
question of law 39
rule of four 41
small claims court 39
standing to sue 36
summary jury trial 45
venue 36
writ of *certiorari* 41

ExamPrep

Issue Spotters

1. Sue uses her smartphone to purchase a video security system for her architectural firm from Tipton, Inc., a company that is located in a different state. The system arrives a month after the projected delivery date, is of poor quality, and does not function as advertised. Sue files a suit against Tipton in a state court. Does the court in Sue's state have jurisdiction over Tipton? What factors will the court consider? **(See page 29.)**

2. The state in which Sue resides requires that her dispute with Tipton be submitted to mediation or nonbinding arbitration. If the dispute is not resolved, or if either party disagrees with the decision of the media-

tor or arbitrator, will a court hear the case? Explain. **(See page 43.)**

• Check your answers to the Issue Spotters against the answers provided in Appendix E at the end of this text.

Before the Test

Go to **www.cengagebrain.com**, enter the ISBN 9781285185248, and click on "Find" to locate this textbook's Web site. Then, click on "Access Now" under "Study Tools," and select Chapter 2 at the top. There, you will find a Practice Quiz that you can take to assess your mastery of the concepts in this chapter, as well as Flashcards and a Glossary of important terms.

Business Scenarios

2–1. Standing. Jack and Maggie Turton bought a house in Jefferson County, Idaho, located directly across the street from a gravel pit. A few years later, the county converted the pit to a landfill. The landfill accepted many kinds of trash that cause harm to the environment, including major appliances, animal carcasses, containers with hazardous content warnings, leaking car batteries, and waste oil. The Turtons complained to the county, but the county did nothing. The Turtons then filed a lawsuit against the county alleging violations of federal environmental laws pertaining to groundwater contamination and other pollution. Do the Turtons have standing to sue? Why or why not? **(See page 36.)**

2–2. Jurisdiction. Marya Callais, a citizen of Florida, was walking along a busy street in Tallahassee, Florida, when a large crate flew off a passing truck and hit her, causing numerous injuries. She experienced a great deal of pain and suffering, incurred significant medical expenses, and could not work for six months. She wants to sue the trucking firm for $300,000 in damages. The firm's headquarters are in Georgia, although the company does business in Florida. In what court might Callais bring suit—a Florida state court, a Georgia state court, or a federal court? What factors might influence her decision? **(See page 29.)**

Business Case Problems

**2–3. BUSINESS CASE PROBLEM
WITH SAMPLE ANSWER: Arbitration Clause.**

 Kathleen Lowden sued cellular phone company T-Mobile USA, Inc., contending that its service agreements were not enforceable under Washington state law. Lowden requested that the court allow a class-action suit, in which her claims would extend to similarly affected customers. She contended that T-Mobile had improperly charged her fees beyond the advertised price of service and charged her for roaming calls that should not have been classified as roaming.

T-Mobile moved to force arbitration in accordance with the provisions that were clearly set forth in the service agreement. The agreement also specified that no class-action suit could be brought, so T-Mobile also asked the court to dismiss the request for a class-action suit. Was T-Mobile correct that Lowden's only course of action was to file for arbitration personally? Why or why not? [Lowden v. T-Mobile USA, Inc., 512 F.3d 1213 (9th Cir. 2008)] **(See page 43.)**

• For a sample answer to Problem 2–3, go to Appendix F at the end of this text.

2–4. Venue. Brandy Austin used powdered infant formula to feed her infant daughter shortly after her birth. Austin claimed that a can of Nestlé Good Start Supreme Powder Infant Formula was contaminated with *Enterobacter sakazakii* bacteria. The bacteria can cause infections of the bloodstream and central nervous system, in particular, meningitis (inflammation of the tissue surrounding the brain or spinal cord). Austin filed an action against Nestlé in Hennepin County District Court in Minnesota. Nestlé argued for a change of venue because the alleged tortious action on the part of Nestlé occurred in South Carolina. Austin is a South Carolina resident and gave birth to her daughter in that state. Should the case be transferred to a South Carolina venue? Why or why not? [*Austin v. Nestlé USA, Inc.,* 677 F.Supp.2d 1134 (D.Minn. 2009)] **(See page 36.)**

2–5. Arbitration. PRM Energy Systems owned patents licensed to Primenergy to use in the United States. Their contract stated that "all disputes" would be settled by arbitration. Kobe Steel of Japan was interested in using the technology represented by PRM's patents. Primenergy agreed to let Kobe use the technology in Japan without telling PRM. When PRM learned about the secret deal, the firm filed a suit against Primenergy for fraud and theft. Does this dispute go to arbitration or to trial? Why? [*PRM Energy Systems v. Primenergy,* 592 F.3d 830 (8th Cir. 2010)] **(See page 42.)**

2–6. Spotlight on the National Football League—Arbitration.

 Bruce Matthews played football for the Tennessee Titans. As part of his contract, he agreed to submit any dispute to arbitration. He also agreed that Tennessee law would determine all matters related to workers' compensation. After Matthews retired, he filed a workers' compensation claim in California. The arbitrator ruled that Matthews could pursue his claim in California but only under Tennessee law. Should this award be set aside? Explain. [*National Football League Players Association v. National Football League Management Council,* 2011 WL 1137334 (S.D.Cal. 2011)] **(See page 42.)**

2–7. Minimum Contacts. Seal Polymer Industries sold two freight containers of latex gloves to Med-Express, Inc., a company based in North Carolina. When Med-Express failed to pay the $104,000 owed for the gloves, Seal Polymer sued in an Illinois court and obtained a judgment against Med-Express. Med-Express argued that it did not have minimum contacts with Illinois and therefore the Illinois judgment based on personal jurisdiction was invalid. Med-Express stated that it was incorporated under North Carolina law, had its principal place of business in North Carolina, and therefore had no minimum contacts with Illinois. Was this statement alone sufficient to prevent the Illinois judgment from being collected against Med-Express in North Carolina? Why or why not? [*Seal Polymer Industries v. Med-Express, Inc.,* 725 S.E.2d 5 (N.C.App. 2012)] **(See page 29.)**

2–8. Arbitration. Horton Automatics and the Industrial Division of the Communications Workers of America,

the union that represented Horton's workers, negotiated a collective bargaining agreement. If an employee's discharge for a workplace-rule violation was submitted to arbitration, the agreement limited the arbitrator to determining whether the rule was reasonable and whether the employee violated it. When Horton discharged employee Ruben de la Garza, the union appealed to arbitration. The arbitrator found that de la Garza had violated a reasonable safety rule, but "was not totally convinced" that Horton should have treated the violation more seriously than other rule violations. The arbitrator ordered de la Garza reinstated. Can a court set aside this order? Explain. [*Horton Automatics v. The Industrial Division of the Communications Workers of America, AFL-CIO,* 2013 WL 59204 (5th Cir. 2013)] **(See page 42.)**

2–9. A QUESTION OF ETHICS: Agreement to Arbitrate.

 Nellie Lumpkin, who suffered from various illnesses, including dementia, was admitted to the Picayune Convalescent Center, a nursing home. Because of her mental condition, her daughter, Beverly McDaniel, filled out the admissions paperwork and signed the admissions agreement. It included a clause requiring parties to submit to arbitration any disputes that arose. After Lumpkin left the center two years later, she sued, through her husband, for negligent treatment and malpractice during her stay. The center moved to force the matter to arbitration. The trial court held that the arbitration agreement was not enforceable. The center appealed. [Covenant Health & Rehabilitation of Picayune, LP v. Lumpkin, 23 So.3d 1092 (Miss.App. 2009)] **(See page 42.)**

(a) Should a dispute involving medical malpractice be forced into arbitration? This is a claim of negligent care, not a breach of a commercial contract. Is it ethical for medical facilities to impose such a requirement? Is there really any bargaining over such terms? Discuss fully.

(b) Should a person with limited mental capacity be held to the arbitration clause agreed to by the next-of-kin who signed on behalf of that person? Why or why not?

Legal Reasoning Group Activity

2–10. Access to Courts. Assume that a statute in your state requires that all civil lawsuits involving damages of less than $50,000 be arbitrated. Such a case can be tried in court only if a party is dissatisfied with the arbitrator's decision. The statute also provides that if a trial does not result in an improvement of more than 10 percent in the position of the party who demanded the trial, that party must pay the entire costs of the arbitration proceeding. **(See page 42.)**

(a) One group will argue that the state statute violates litigants' rights of access to the courts and to trial by jury.

(b) Another group will argue that the statute does not violate litigants' rights of access to the courts.

(c) A third group will evaluate how the determination on rights of access would be changed if the statute was part of a pilot program and affected only a few judicial districts in the state.

CHAPTER 3
COURT PROCEDURES

American and English courts follow the *adversarial system of justice.* Although parties are allowed to represent themselves in court (called *pro se* representation),[1] most parties to lawsuits hire attorneys to repre-

sent them. Each lawyer acts as his or her client's advocate, presenting the client's version of the facts in such a way as to convince the judge (or the judge and jury, in a jury trial) that this version is correct.

Most of the judicial procedures that you will read about in the following pages are rooted in the adversarial framework of the American legal sys-

tem. In this chapter, after a brief overview of judicial procedures, we illustrate the steps involved in a lawsuit with a hypothetical civil case (criminal procedures will be discussed in Chapter 10). We also discuss how judges are coping with courtroom tweeting in this chapter's *Insight into Social Media* feature on page 64.

---

1. This right was definitively established in *Faretta v. California,* 422 U.S. 806, 95 S.Ct. 2525, 45 L.Ed.2d 562 (1975).

SECTION 1
PROCEDURAL RULES

The parties to a lawsuit must comply with the procedural rules of the court in which the lawsuit is filed. Although people often think that substantive law determines the outcome of a case, procedural law can have a significant impact on a person's ability to pursue a legal claim. Procedural rules provide a framework for every dispute and specify what must be done at each stage of the litigation process.

Procedural rules are complex, and they vary from court to court and from state to state. There is a set of federal rules of procedure as well as various sets of rules for state courts. Additionally, the applicable procedures will depend on whether the case is a civil or criminal proceeding. All civil trials held in federal district courts are governed by the **Federal Rules of Civil Procedure (FRCP).**[2]

Stages of Litigation

Broadly speaking, the litigation process has three phases: pretrial, trial, and posttrial. Each phase involves specific procedures, as discussed throughout this chapter. Although civil lawsuits may vary greatly in terms of complexity, cost, and detail, they typically progress through the specific stages charted in Exhibit 3–1.

To illustrate the procedures involved in a civil lawsuit, we will use a simple hypothetical case. The case arose from an automobile accident, which occurred when a car driven by Antonio Carvello, a resident of New Jersey, collided with a car driven by Jill Kirby, a resident of New York. The accident took place at an intersection in New York City. Kirby suffered personal injuries, which caused her to incur medical and hospital expenses as well as lost wages for four months. In all, she calculated that the cost to her of the accident was $100,000.[3] Carvello and Kirby have been unable to agree on a settlement, and Kirby now must decide whether to sue Carvello for the $100,000 compensation she feels she deserves.

Consulting with an Attorney

As mentioned, rules of procedure often affect the outcome of a dispute—a fact that highlights the impor-

---

2. The United States Supreme Court has authority to establish these rules, as spelled out in 28 U.S.C. Sections 2071–2077. Generally, though, the federal judiciary appoints committees that make recommendations to the Supreme Court. The Court then publishes any proposed changes in the rules and allows for public comment before finalizing the rules.

3. In this example, we are ignoring damages for pain and suffering and for permanent disabilities. Often, plaintiffs in personal-injury cases seek such damages.

EXHIBIT 3-1 Stages in a Typical Lawsuit

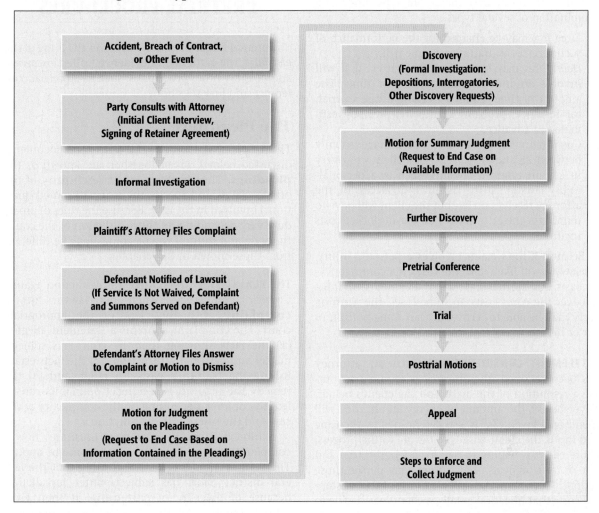

Accident, Breach of Contract, or Other Event

↓

Party Consults with Attorney (Initial Client Interview, Signing of Retainer Agreement)

↓

Informal Investigation

↓

Plaintiff's Attorney Files Complaint

↓

Defendant Notified of Lawsuit (If Service Is Not Waived, Complaint and Summons Served on Defendant)

↓

Defendant's Attorney Files Answer to Complaint or Motion to Dismiss

↓

Motion for Judgment on the Pleadings (Request to End Case Based on Information Contained in the Pleadings)

Discovery (Formal Investigation: Depositions, Interrogatories, Other Discovery Requests)

↓

Motion for Summary Judgment (Request to End Case on Available Information)

↓

Further Discovery

↓

Pretrial Conference

↓

Trial

↓

Posttrial Motions

↓

Appeal

↓

Steps to Enforce and Collect Judgment

tance of obtaining the advice of counsel. The first step taken by almost anyone contemplating a lawsuit is to seek the guidance of a qualified attorney.[4]

In the hypothetical Kirby-Carvello case, assume that Kirby consults with a lawyer. The attorney will advise her regarding what she can expect in a lawsuit, her probability of success at trial, and the procedures that will be involved. If more than one court would have jurisdiction over the matter, the attorney will also discuss the advantages and disadvantages of filing in a particular court. In addition, the attorney will indicate how long it will take to resolve the dispute through litigation in a particular court and provide an estimate of the costs involved.

The attorney will also inform Kirby of the legal fees that she will have to pay in an attempt to collect damages from the defendant, Carvello. Attorneys base their fees on such factors as the difficulty of a matter, the amount of time involved, the experience and skill of the attorney in the particular area of the law, and the cost of doing business. In the United States, legal fees range from $175 to $700 per hour or even higher (the average fee is between $200 and $425 per hour). In addition, the client must also pay various expenses related to the case (called "out-of-pocket" costs), such as court filing fees, travel expenses, and the cost of expert witnesses and investigators.

---

4. Normally, you will seek out an attorney who is licensed to practice in your state.

TYPES OF ATTORNEYS' FEES For a particular legal matter, an attorney may charge one type of fee or a combination of several types.

1. *Fixed fees* may be charged for the performance of such services as drafting a simple will.
2. *Hourly fees* may be charged for matters that will involve an indeterminate period of time. The amount of time required to bring a case to trial, for instance, probably cannot be precisely estimated in advance.
3. *Contingency fees* are fixed as a percentage (usually between 25 and 40 percent) of a client's recovery in certain types of lawsuits, such as a personal-injury lawsuit.[5] If the lawsuit is unsuccessful, the attorney receives no fee, but the client will have to reimburse the attorney for all out-of-pocket costs incurred.

Because Kirby's claim involves a personal injury, her lawyer will likely take the case on a contingency-fee basis, but she may have to pay an amount up front to cover the court costs. In some cases, the winning party may be able to recover at least some portion of her or his attorneys' fees from the losing party.

SETTLEMENT CONSIDERATIONS Once an attorney has been retained, the attorney is required to pursue a resolution of the matter on the client's behalf. Nevertheless, the amount of energy an attorney will spend on a given case is also determined by the time and funds the client wishes to devote to the process. If the client is willing to pay for a lengthy trial and one or more appeals, the attorney may pursue those actions. Often, however, after learning of the substantial costs that litigation entails, a client may decide to pursue a settlement of the claim. Attempts to settle the case may be ongoing throughout the litigation process.

Another important consideration in deciding whether to pursue litigation is the defendant's ability to pay the damages sought. Even if Kirby is awarded damages, it may be difficult to enforce the court's judgment if, for example, the amount exceeds the limits of Carvello's automobile insurance policy. (We will discuss the problems involved in enforcing a judgment later in this chapter.)

SECTION 2
PRETRIAL PROCEDURES

The pretrial litigation process involves the filing of the *pleadings,* the gathering of evidence (called *discovery*), and possibly other procedures, such as a pretrial conference and jury selection.

The Pleadings

The *complaint* and *answer* (and other legal documents discussed below), taken together, are known as the **pleadings.** The pleadings inform each party of the other's claims and specify the issues (disputed questions) involved in the case. Because the rules of procedure vary depending on the jurisdiction of the court, the style and form of the pleadings may be different from those shown in this chapter.

THE PLAINTIFF'S COMPLAINT Kirby's action against Carvello commences when her lawyer files a **complaint**[6] with the clerk of the appropriate court. The complaint contains a statement alleging (1) the facts showing that the court has subject-matter and personal jurisdiction, (2) the facts establishing the plaintiff's basis for relief, and (3) the remedy the plaintiff is seeking. Complaints can be lengthy or brief, depending on the complexity of the case and the rules of the jurisdiction.

Exhibit 3–2 on the next page illustrates how a complaint in the Kirby-Carvello case might appear. The complaint asserts facts indicating that the federal district court has subject-matter jurisdiction because of diversity of citizenship. It then gives a brief statement of the facts of the accident and alleges that Carvello negligently drove his vehicle through a red light, striking Kirby's car and causing serious personal injury and property damage. The complaint goes on to state that Kirby is seeking $100,000 in damages, although in some state civil actions the plaintiff need not specify the amount of damages sought.

Service of Process. Before the court can exercise personal jurisdiction over the defendant (Carvello)—in effect, before the lawsuit can begin—the court must

---

5. Note that attorneys may charge a contingency fee only in certain types of cases and are typically prohibited from entering into this type of fee arrangement in criminal cases, divorce cases, and cases involving the distribution of assets after death.

6. Sometimes, the document filed with the court is called a *petition* or a *declaration* instead of a complaint.

EXHIBIT 3-2 A Typical Complaint

IN THE UNITED STATES DISTRICT COURT
FOR THE SOUTHERN DISTRICT OF NEW YORK

CIVIL NO. 9-1047

JILL KIRBY

                              Plaintiff,

v.   COMPLAINT

ANTONIO CARVELLO

                              Defendant.

The plaintiff brings this cause of action against the defendant, alleging as follows:

1. This action is between the plaintiff, who is a resident of the State of New York, and the defendant, who is a resident of the State of New Jersey. There is diversity of citizenship between the parties.
2. The amount in controversy, exclusive of interest and costs, exceeds the sum of $75,000.
3. On September 10th, 2014, the plaintiff, Jill Kirby, was exercising good driving habits and reasonable care in driving her car through the intersection of Boardwalk and Pennsylvania Avenue, New York City, New York, when the defendant, Antonio Carvello, negligently drove his vehicle through a red light at the intersection and collided with the plaintiff's vehicle.
4. As a result of the collision, the plaintiff suffered severe physical injury, which prevented her from working, and property damage to her car.

WHEREFORE, the plaintiff demands judgment against the defendant for the sum of $100,000 plus interest at the maximum legal rate and the costs of this action.

By ___*Joseph Roe*___

Joseph Roe
Attorney for Plaintiff
100 Main Street
New York, New York

1/3/15

have proof that the defendant was notified of the lawsuit. Formally notifying the defendant of a lawsuit is called **service of process.**

The plaintiff must deliver, or serve, a copy of the complaint and a **summons** (a notice requiring the defendant to appear in court and answer the complaint) to the defendant. The summons notifies Carvello that he must file an answer to the complaint within a specified time period (twenty days in the federal courts) or suffer a default judgment against him. A **default judgment** in Kirby's favor would mean that she would be awarded the damages alleged in her complaint because Carvello failed to respond to the allegations. A typical summons is shown in Exhibit 3–3 on the following page.

Method of Service. How service of process occurs depends on the rules of the court or jurisdiction in

EXHIBIT 3–3 A Typical Summons

```
                    UNITED STATES DISTRICT COURT
              FOR THE SOUTHERN DISTRICT OF NEW YORK

                                      CIVIL ACTION, FILE NO. 9-1047

     JILL KIRBY

                          Plaintiff,

     v.                                        SUMMONS

     ANTONIO CARVELLO

                          Defendant.


     To the above-named Defendant:

     You are hereby summoned and required to serve upon Joseph Roe,
     plaintiff's attorney, whose address is 100 Main Street, New York, NY, an
     answer to the complaint which is herewith served upon you, within 20 days
     after service of this summons upon you, exclusive of the day of service.
     If you fail to do so, judgment by default will be taken against you for
     the relief demanded in the complaint.


     C. H. Hynek                        January 3, 2015
     ─────────────────                  ─────────────────
     CLERK                              DATE


     John Dolan
     ─────────────────
     BY DEPUTY CLERK
```

which the lawsuit is brought. Under the Federal Rules of Civil Procedure, anyone who is at least eighteen years of age and is not a party to the lawsuit can serve process in federal court cases. In state courts, the process server is often a county sheriff or an employee of an independent company that provides process service in the local area.

Usually, the server hands the summons and complaint to the defendant personally or leaves it at the defendant's residence or place of business. In some states, process can be served by mail if the defendant consents (accepts service). When the defendant cannot be reached, special rules provide for alternative means of service, such as publishing a notice in the local newspaper. In some situations, courts have allowed service of process via e-mail, as long as it is reasonably calculated to provide notice and an opportunity to respond.

In cases involving corporate defendants, the summons and complaint may be served on an officer or on a *registered agent* (representative) of the corporation. The name of a corporation's registered agent can usually be obtained from the secretary of state's office in the state where the company incorporated its business (and, frequently, from the secretary of state's office in any state where the corporation does business).

Waiver of Formal Service of Process. In many instances, the defendant is already aware that a lawsuit is being filed and is willing to waive (give up) her or his right to be served personally. The Federal Rules of Civil Procedure (FRCP) and many states' rules allow defendants to waive formal service of process, provided that certain procedures are followed. Kirby's attorney, for example, could mail to defendant Carvello a copy of the complaint, along with "Waiver of Service of Summons" forms for Carvello to sign. If Carvello signs and returns the forms within thirty days, formal service of process is waived.

Moreover, under the FRCP, defendants who agree to waive formal service of process receive additional time to respond to the complaint (sixty days, instead of twenty days). Some states provide similar incentives to encourage defendants to waive formal service of process and thereby reduce associated costs and foster cooperation between the parties.

THE DEFENDANT'S RESPONSE Typically, the defendant's response to the complaint takes the form of an **answer.** In an answer, the defendant either admits or denies each of the allegations in the plaintiff's complaint and may also set forth defenses to those allegations. Under the federal rules, any allegations that are not denied by the defendant will be deemed by the court to have been admitted. If Carvello admits to all of Kirby's allegations in his answer, a judgment will be entered for Kirby. If Carvello denies Kirby's allegations, the matter will proceed further.

Affirmative Defenses. Carvello can also admit the truth of Kirby's complaint but raise new facts to show that he should not be held liable for Kirby's damages. This is called raising an **affirmative defense.** As will be discussed in subsequent chapters, defendants in both civil and criminal cases can raise affirmative defenses. For example, Carvello could assert Kirby's own negligence as a defense by alleging that Kirby was driving negligently at the time of the accident. In some states, a plaintiff's contributory negligence operates as a complete defense. In most states, however, the plaintiff's own negligence constitutes only a partial defense (see Chapter 6).

Counterclaims. Carvello could also deny Kirby's allegations and set forth his own claim that the accident occurred as a result of Kirby's negligence and therefore she owes Carvello for damage to his car. This is appropriately called a counterclaim. If Carvello files a **counterclaim,** Kirby will have to submit an answer to the counterclaim.

Dismissals and Judgments before Trial

Many actions for which pleadings have been filed never come to trial. The parties may, for example, negotiate a settlement of the dispute at any stage of the litigation process. There are also numerous procedural avenues for disposing of a case without a trial. Many of them involve one or the other party's attempts to get the case dismissed through the use of various motions.

A **motion** is a procedural request submitted to the court by an attorney on behalf of her or his client. When a motion is filed with the court, the filing party must also send to, or personally serve, the opposing party a *notice of motion*. The notice of motion informs the opposing party that the motion has been filed. **Pretrial motions** include the motion to dismiss, the motion for judgment on the pleadings, and the motion for summary judgment, as well as the other motions listed in Exhibit 3–4 on the following page.

MOTION TO DISMISS Either party can file a **motion to dismiss** asking the court to dismiss the case for the reasons stated in the motion. Normally, though, it is the defendant who requests dismissal.

A defendant can file a motion to dismiss if the plaintiff's complaint fails to state a claim for which relief (a remedy) can be granted. Such a motion asserts that even if the facts alleged in the complaint are true, they do not give rise to any legal claim against the defendant. For example, if the allegations in Kirby's complaint do not constitute negligence on Carvello's part, Carvello can move to dismiss the case for failure to state a claim. Defendant Carvello could also file a motion to dismiss on the grounds that he was not properly served, that the court lacked jurisdiction, or that the venue was improper.

If the judge grants the motion to dismiss, the plaintiff generally is given time to file an amended complaint. If the judge denies the motion, the suit will go forward, and the defendant must then file an answer. Note that if Carvello wishes to discontinue the suit because, for example, an out-of-court settlement has been reached, he can likewise move for dismissal. The court can also dismiss a case on its own motion.

EXHIBIT 3-4 Pretrial Motions

MOTION TO DISMISS

A motion normally filed by the defendant in which the defendant asks the court to dismiss the case for a specified reason, such as improper service, lack of personal jurisdiction, or the plaintiff's failure to state a claim for which relief can be granted.

MOTION TO STRIKE

A motion filed by the defendant in which the defendant asks the court to strike (delete) certain paragraphs from the complaint. Motions to strike help to clarify the underlying issues that form the basis for the complaint by removing paragraphs that are redundant or irrelevant to the action.

MOTION TO MAKE MORE DEFINITE AND CERTAIN

A motion filed by the defendant to compel the plaintiff to clarify the basis of the plaintiff's cause of action. The motion is filed when the defendant believes that the complaint is too vague or ambiguous for the defendant to respond to it in a meaningful way.

MOTION FOR JUDGMENT ON THE PLEADINGS

A motion that may be filed by either party in which the party asks the court to enter a judgment in his or her favor based on information contained in the pleadings. A judgment on the pleadings will be made only if there are no facts in dispute and the only question is how the law applies to a set of undisputed facts.

MOTION TO COMPEL DISCOVERY

A motion that may be filed by either party in which the party asks the court to compel the other party to comply with a discovery request. If a party refuses to allow the opponent to inspect and copy certain documents, for example, the party requesting the documents may make a motion to compel production of those documents.

MOTION FOR SUMMARY JUDGMENT

A motion that may be filed by either party in which the party asks the court to enter judgment in his or her favor without a trial. Unlike a motion for judgment on the pleadings, a motion for summary judgment can be supported by evidence outside the pleadings, such as witnesses' affidavits, answers to interrogatories, and other evidence obtained prior to or during discovery.

In the following case, one party filed a complaint against two others, alleging a breach of contract. The defendants filed a motion to dismiss on the ground that the venue was improper. The court denied the motion, and the defendants appealed.

CASE ANALYSIS

Case 3.1   Espresso Disposition Corp. 1 v. Santana Sales & Marketing Group, Inc.
Florida Court of Appeal, Third District, 105 So.3d 592 (2013).

IN THE LANGUAGE OF THE COURT
CORTIÑAS, J. [Judge]

* * * *

Espresso Disposition Corporation 1 and Rowland Coffee Roasters, Inc. (collectively "Appellants") seek review of the trial court's order denying their motions to dismiss [Santana Sales & Marketing Group, Inc.'s

("Appellee's")] third amended complaint. Appellants claim that the trial court erred in denying their motions to dismiss because the plain and unambiguous language in the parties' * * * agreement contains a mandatory forum selection clause [a provision in a contract designating the court, jurisdiction, or tribunal that will decide any disputes arising under the contract] requiring that all lawsuits

brought under the agreement shall be in Illinois.

Espresso Disposition Corporation 1 and Santana and Associates entered into the * * * agreement in 2002. The agreement provides for a mandatory forum selection clause in paragraph 8. The provision states:

> The venue with respect to any action pertaining to this Agreement shall be the State of Illinois. The laws of

CASE 3.1 CONTINUED

the State of Illinois shall govern the application and interpretation of this Agreement.

However, Appellee filed a lawsuit against Appellants alleging a breach of the agreement in Miami–Dade County, Florida. In fact, Appellee filed four subsequent complaints—an initial complaint, amended complaint, second amended complaint, and third amended complaint—after each and every previous pleading's dismissal was based upon venue as provided for in the agreement's mandatory forum selection clause. Appellee's third amended complaint alleges the forum selection clause was a mistake that was made at the time the agreement was drafted. Additionally, Appellee attached an affidavit [a sworn statement] which states that, in drafting the agreement, Appellee * * * copied a form version of an agreement between different parties, and by mistake, forgot to change the venue provision from Illinois to Florida. In response, Appellants filed their motions to dismiss the third amended complaint, which the trial court denied.

Florida appellate courts interpret a contractual forum selection clause under a *de novo* standard of review. [The courts review the issue anew, as if the lower courts had not ruled on the issue.] Likewise, as the trial court's order denying appellant's motion to dismiss is based on the interpretation of the contractual forum selection clause, this court's standard of review is *de novo*. Therefore, the narrow issue before this court is whether the * * * agreement provides for a mandatory forum selection clause that is enforceable under Florida law.

Florida courts have long recognized that forum selection clauses such as the one at issue here are presumptively valid. *This is because forum selection clauses provide a degree of certainty to business contracts by obviating [preventing] jurisdictional struggles and by allowing parties to tailor the dispute resolution mechanism to their particular situation. Moreover, forum selection clauses reduce litigation over venue, thereby conserving judicial resources, reducing business expenses, and lowering consumer prices.* [Emphasis added.]

Because Florida law presumes that forum selection clauses are valid and enforceable, the party seeking to avoid enforcement of such a clause must establish that enforcement would be unjust or unreasonable. Under Florida law, the clause is only considered unjust or unreasonable if the party seeking avoidance establishes that enforcement would result in no forum at all. There is absolutely no set of facts that Appellee could plead and prove to demonstrate that Illinois state courts do not exist. Illinois became the twenty-first state in 1818, and has since established an extensive system of state trial and appellate courts. Clearly, Appellee failed to establish that enforcement would be unreasonable since the designated forum—Illinois—does not result in Appellee's having "no forum at all."

Further, as we have said on a number of occasions, if a forum selection clause unambiguously mandates that litigation be subject to an agreed upon forum, then it is [an] error for the trial court to ignore the clause. Generally, the clause is mandatory where the plain language used by

the parties indicates exclusivity. Importantly, if the forum selection clause states or clearly indicates that any litigation must or shall be initiated in a specified forum, then it is mandatory. Here, the agreement's plain language provides that the venue for any action relating to a controversy under the agreement any litigation "shall be the State of Illinois." The clear language unequivocally renders the forum selection clause mandatory.

Appellee would have us create an exception to our jurisprudence on mandatory forum selection clauses based on their error in cutting and pasting the clause from another agreement. Of course, the origin of "cutting and pasting" comes from the traditional practice of manuscript-editing whereby writers used to cut paragraphs from a page with editing scissors, that had blades long enough to cut an 8½ inch-wide page, and then physically pasted them onto another page. Today, the cut, copy, and paste functions contained in word processing software render unnecessary the use of scissors or glue. However, what has not been eliminated is the need to actually read and analyze the text being pasted, especially where it is to have legal significance. Thus, in reviewing the mandatory selection clause which Appellant seeks to enforce, we apply the legal maxim "be careful what you ask for" and enforce the pasted forum.

Accordingly, we reverse [the] trial court's denial of the motions to dismiss Appellee's third amended complaint on the basis of improper venue, and remand for entry of an order of dismissal.

LEGAL REASONING QUESTIONS

1. Compare and contrast a motion to dismiss with other pretrial motions. Identify their chief differences.

2. Why did the appellants in this case file a motion to dismiss?

3. What is the effect of granting a motion to dismiss?

4. Did the court grant or deny the appellants' motion? Why did the court take this action?

MOTION FOR JUDGMENT ON THE PLEADINGS At the close of the pleadings, either party may make a **motion for judgment on the pleadings.** This motion asks the court to decide the issue solely on the pleadings without proceeding to trial. The judge will grant the motion only when there is no dispute over the facts of the case and the sole issue to be resolved is a question of law. For example, in the Kirby-Carvello case, if Carvello had admitted to all of Kirby's allegations in his answer and had raised no affirmative defenses, Kirby could file a motion for judgment on the pleadings.

In deciding a motion for judgment on the pleadings, the judge may consider only the evidence contained in the pleadings. In contrast, in a motion for summary judgment, discussed next, the court may consider evidence outside the pleadings, such as sworn statements and other materials that would be admissible as evidence at trial.

MOTION FOR SUMMARY JUDGMENT Either party can file a **motion for summary judgment,** which asks the court to grant a judgment in that party's favor without a trial. The motion can be made before or during the trial. As with a motion for judgment on the pleadings, a court will grant a motion for summary judgment only if no facts are in dispute and the only question is how the law applies to the facts. In determining whether no facts are in contention, the court considers the evidence in the light most favorable to the other party.

To support a motion for summary judgment, a party can submit evidence obtained at any point before the trial that refutes the other party's factual claim. The evidence may consist of **affidavits** (sworn statements by parties or witnesses) or copies of documents, such as contracts, e-mails, and letters obtained through the course of discovery (discussed

next). Of course, the evidence must be *admissible* evidence—that is, evidence that the court would allow to be presented during the trial. As mentioned, the use of additional evidence is one feature that distinguishes the motion for summary judgment from the motion to dismiss and the motion for judgment on the pleadings.

Discovery

Before a trial begins, the parties can use a number of procedural devices to obtain information and gather evidence about the case. Kirby, for example, will want to know how fast Carvello was driving. She will also want to learn whether he had been drinking, was under the influence of medication, and was wearing corrective lenses if required by law to do so while driving.

The process of obtaining information from the opposing party or from witnesses prior to trial is known as **discovery.** Discovery includes gaining access to witnesses, documents, records, and other types of evidence. In federal courts, the parties are required to make initial disclosures of relevant evidence to the opposing party.

Discovery prevents surprises at trial by giving both parties access to evidence that might otherwise be hidden. This allows the litigants to learn as much as they can about what to expect at a trial before they reach the courtroom. Discovery also serves to narrow the issues so that trial time is spent on the main questions in the case. A court can impose sanctions on a party who fails to respond to discovery requests.

The question in the following case was what a court could do when a plaintiff failed to disclose the names of expert witnesses during discovery, even though the court deemed that such witnesses were necessary to establish the plaintiff's claim.

CASE 3.2

Blankenship v. Collier
Supreme Court of Kentucky, 302 S.W.3d 665 (2010).

BACKGROUND AND FACTS In February 2004, Horace Collier was admitted to Caritas Medical Center with abdominal pain. The following day, after undergoing tests and being diagnosed by Dr. Robert Blankenship as having appendicitis, Collier had an appendectomy. One year later, Collier sued Blankenship and Caritas Health Services in a Kentucky state court, contending that they had been negligent because they had failed to evaluate and treat him in a timely manner. Specifically, Collier claimed that he had been ignored for several hours while awaiting treatment and had suffered severe abdominal pain. He also

CASE 3.2 CONTINUED

claimed that the X-ray of his abdomen had not been stored properly, causing further delay in his diagnosis and treatment. Collier alleged that as a result of the defendants' medical negligence, he had sustained permanent physical and mental injuries, prolonged pain and mental anguish, impairment of his power to work and earn income, and significant medical expenses.

More than nine months later, Collier had not yet disclosed the identities of any expert witnesses who would testify on his behalf, and the court ordered him to do so by January 30, 2006. At Collier's request, this deadline was later extended—to February 28. Finally, on March 14, 2006, after Collier had still had not disclosed any names, the defendants filed motions for summary judgment, arguing that there could be no issue of material fact in this medical malpractice (negligence by professionals—see Chapter 6) case without expert testimony. The trial court granted the motions. Collier appealed, arguing that summary judgment was inappropriate because it was being used only as a sanctioning tool to punish him for failing to timely disclose his experts. He further asserted that there was a "serious question" as to whether he would even need experts to prove his medical malpractice claim. The intermediate appellate court agreed and reversed the trial court's decision. The defendants appealed the decision to the Supreme Court of Kentucky.

IN THE LANGUAGE OF THE COURT
Opinion of the court by Justice *ABRAMSON*.

* * * *

* * * Although a defendant is permitted to move for a summary judgment at any time, this Court has cautioned trial courts not to take up these motions prematurely and to consider summary judgment motions "only after the opposing party has been given ample opportunity to complete discovery." Thus, even though an appellate court always reviews the substance of a trial court's summary judgment ruling *de novo* [anew] * * * to determine whether the record reflects a genuine issue of material fact, *a reviewing court must also consider whether the trial court gave the party opposing the motion an ample opportunity to respond and complete discovery before the court entered its ruling.* In a medical malpractice action, where a sufficient amount of time has expired and the plaintiff has still "failed to introduce evidence sufficient to establish the respective applicable standard of care," then the defendants are entitled to summary judgment as a matter of law. The trial court's determination that a sufficient amount of time has passed and that it can properly take up the summary judgment motion for a ruling is reviewed for an abuse of discretion. [Emphasis added.]

In this case, the issue before this Court is not simply whether Collier had failed to establish a genuine issue of material fact at the time Dr. Blankenship and Caritas filed their summary judgment motions—without a doubt, there is no genuine issue of material fact in the record because Collier has no expert to support his claim of medical negligence. Rather, the more specific issue is whether the trial court was correct to take up the defendants' summary judgment motions and enter a ruling when it did and, secondarily, whether the court was required first either to enter a separate order requiring Collier to obtain expert testimony or to enter an order sanctioning Collier for failing to meet the court's expert disclosure deadline.

Having carefully reviewed the record, we conclude that the defendants' summary judgment motions were properly before the trial court and it did not abuse its discretion in taking them up and deciding to rule on the motions approximately four months after they were filed and seventeen months after the lawsuit was initiated. Collier had completely failed to identify any expert witnesses and could not sustain his burden of proof without expert testimony and, thus, no material issue of fact existed in the record and the defendants were entitled to summary judgment as a matter of law. Because Collier never disputed that a medical expert was necessary to prove his claim of medical negligence and continually represented to the trial court that he would obtain an expert witness, no separate ruling stating the obvious—the need for an expert witness—was required before the court ruled on the defendants' summary judgment motions. Further, * * * the trial court was not required to enter a sanctions order prior to granting the defendants' summary judgment motions.

CASE 3.2 CONTINUES ▶

DECISION AND REMEDY *The Supreme Court of Kentucky reversed the decision of the lower ap-pellate court and reinstated the trial court's decision. The trial court had not abused its discretion by granting summary judgment for the defendants.*

THE ETHICAL DIMENSION *Collier contended that there was a "serious question" as to whether he would even need experts to prove his medical malpractice claim. Is it fair to Collier to prevent the trial from proceeding, even though the lack of expert testimony might have made it difficult—if not impossible—for him to win the case? Explain.*

MANAGERIAL IMPLICATIONS *Business owners and managers should be aware that initiating discovery procedures and responding to discovery requests in a timely fashion are important in any litigation. Although the court in this case claimed that summary judgment was not a sanction imposed on the plaintiff for delays during discovery, one could argue (as a dissenting judge did) that it was indeed a sanction—and a very harsh one. Courts have also dismissed cases when the plaintiffs have caused undue delay by not meeting procedural deadlines.*

DISCOVERY RULES The FRCP and similar state rules set forth the guidelines for discovery activity. Generally, discovery is allowed regarding any matter that is relevant to the claim or defense of any party. Discovery rules also attempt to protect witnesses and parties from undue harassment, and to safeguard privileged or confidential material from being disclosed. Only information that is relevant to the case at hand—or likely to lead to the discovery of relevant information—is discoverable.

If a discovery request involves privileged or confidential business information, a court can deny the request and can limit the scope of discovery in a number of ways. For instance, a court can require the party to submit the materials to the judge in a sealed envelope so that the judge can decide if they should be disclosed to the opposing party.

DEPOSITIONS Discovery can involve the use of depositions. A **deposition** is sworn testimony by a party to the lawsuit or by any witness, recorded by an authorized court official. The person deposed gives testimony and answers questions asked by the attorneys from both sides. The questions and answers are recorded, sworn to, and signed. These answers, of course, will help the attorneys prepare their cases.

Depositions also give attorneys the opportunity to ask immediate follow-up questions and to evaluate how their witnesses will conduct themselves at trial. In addition, depositions can be employed in court to **impeach** (challenge the credibility of) a party or a witness who changes his or her testimony at the trial. A deposition can also be used as testimony if the witness is not available at trial.

INTERROGATORIES Discovery can also involve **interrogatories,** which are written questions for which written answers are prepared and then signed under oath. The main difference between interrogatories and written depositions is that interrogatories are directed to a party to the lawsuit (the plaintiff or the defendant), not to a witness. The party usually has thirty days to prepare answers.

The party's attorney often drafts the answers to interrogatories in a manner calculated to give away as little information as possible. Whereas depositions elicit candid answers not prepared in advance, interrogatories are designed to obtain accurate information about specific topics, such as how many contracts were signed and when. The scope of interrogatories is also broader because parties are obligated to answer questions, even if that means disclosing information from their records and files. Note that, as with discovery requests, a court can impose sanctions on a party who fails to answer interrogatories.

▶ **Case in Point 3.1** Computer Task Group, Inc. (CTG), hired William Brotby as an information technology consultant. As a condition of his employment, Brotby signed an agreement that restricted his ability to work for CTG's customers if he left CTG. Less than two years later, Brotby left CTG and began working for Alyeska Pipeline Service Company, a CTG client, in breach of the agreement. CTG sued Brotby. During discovery, Brotby refused to respond fully to CTG's interrogatories. He gave contradictory answers, made frivolous objections, filed baseless motions, and never disclosed all the information that CTG sought. The court ordered

Brotby to comply with discovery requests five times. Nevertheless, Brotby continued to make excuses and changed his story repeatedly, making it impossible for CTG to establish basic facts with any certainty. Eventually, CTG requested and the court granted a default judgment against Brotby based on his failure to cooperate.[7] ◄

REQUESTS FOR ADMISSIONS One party can serve the other party with a written request for an admission of the truth of matters relating to the trial. Any fact admitted under such a request is conclusively established as true for the trial. For example, Kirby can ask Carvello to admit that his driver's license was suspended at the time of the accident. A request for admission shortens the trial because the parties will not have to spend time proving facts on which they already agree.

REQUESTS FOR DOCUMENTS, OBJECTS, AND ENTRY UPON LAND A party can gain access to documents and other items not in her or his possession in order to inspect and examine them. Carvello, for example, can gain permission to inspect and copy Kirby's car repair bills. Likewise, a party can gain "entry upon land" to inspect the premises.

REQUESTS FOR EXAMINATIONS When the physical or mental condition of one party is in question, the opposing party can ask the court to order a physical or mental examination by an independent examiner. If the court agrees to make the order, the opposing party can obtain the results of the examination. Note that the court will make such an order only when the need for the information outweighs the right to privacy of the person to be examined.

ELECTRONIC DISCOVERY Any relevant material, including information stored electronically, can be the object of a discovery request. The federal rules and most state rules (as well as court decisions) specifically allow individuals to obtain discovery of electronic "data compilations." Electronic evidence, or **e-evidence,** consists of all computer-generated or electronically recorded information, such as e-mail, voice mail, tweets, blogs, social media posts, spreadsheets, documents, and other data stored electronically.

E-evidence can reveal significant facts that are not discoverable by other means. Computers, smartphones, cameras, and other devices automatically

record certain information about files—such as who created the file and when, and who accessed, modified, or transmitted it—on their hard drives. This information is called **metadata,** which can be thought of as "data about data." Metadata can be obtained only from the file in its electronic format—not from printed-out versions.

▶ **Example 3.2** In 2012, John McAfee, the programmer responsible for creating McAfee antivirus software, was wanted for questioning in the murder of his neighbor in Belize. McAfee left Belize and was on the run from police, but he allowed a journalist to come with him and photograph him. When the journalist posted photos of McAfee online, some metadata were attached to a photo. The police used the metadata to pinpoint the latitude and longitude of the image and subsequently arrested McAfee in Guatemala. ◄

E-Discovery Procedures. The Federal Rules of Civil Procedure deal specifically with the preservation, retrieval, and production of electronic data. Although traditional interrogatories and depositions are still used to find out whether e-evidence exists, a party usually must hire an expert to retrieve the evidence in its electronic format. The expert uses software to reconstruct e-mail, text, and other exchanges to establish who knew what and when they knew it. The expert can even recover computer files that the user thought had been deleted.

Advantages and Disadvantages. Electronic discovery has significant advantages over paper discovery. Electronic versions of documents, e-mail, and text messages can provide useful—and often quite damaging—information about how a particular matter progressed over several weeks or months. E-discovery can uncover the proverbial smoking gun that will win the lawsuit, but it is also time consuming and expensive, especially when lawsuits involve large firms with multiple offices. Also, many firms are finding it difficult to fulfill their duty to preserve electronic evidence from a vast number of sources.

A party that fails to preserve e-evidence may even find itself at such a disadvantage that it will settle a dispute rather than continue litigation. ▶ **Case in Point 3.3** Advanced Micro Devices, Inc. (AMD), sued Intel Corporation, one of the world's largest microprocessor suppliers, for violating antitrust laws. Immediately after the lawsuit was filed, Intel began collecting and preserving the electronic evidence

---

7. *Computer Task Group, Inc. v. Brotby,* 364 F.3d 1112 (9th Cir. 2004).

on its servers and instructed its employees to retain documents and e-mails related to competition with AMD. Nevertheless, many employees saved only copies of the e-mails that they had received and not e-mails that they had sent. In addition, Intel did not stop its automatic e-mail deletion system, causing other information to be lost. In the end, although Intel produced data equivalent to "somewhere in the neighborhood of a pile 137 miles high" in paper, its failure to preserve e-discovery led it to settle the dispute.[8] ◄

Pretrial Conference

After discovery has taken place and before the trial begins, the attorneys may meet with the trial judge in a **pretrial conference,** or hearing. Usually, the conference consists of an informal discussion between the judge and the opposing attorneys after discovery has taken place. The purpose is to explore the possibility of a settlement without trial and, if this is not possible, to identify the matters in dispute and to plan the course of the trial. In particular, the parties may attempt to establish ground rules to restrict the number of expert witnesses or discuss the admissibility or costs of certain types of evidence.

The Right to a Jury Trial

The Seventh Amendment to the U.S. Constitution guarantees the right to a jury trial for cases at law in *federal* courts when the amount in controversy exceeds $20. Most states have similar guarantees in their own constitutions (although the threshold dollar amount is higher than $20).

The right to a trial by jury need not be exercised, and many cases are tried without a jury. In most states and in federal courts, one of the parties must request a jury, or the judge presumes the parties waive this right. If there is no jury, the judge determines the truth of the facts alleged in the case.

Jury Selection

Before a jury trial commences, a panel of jurors must be selected. Although some types of trials require twelve-person juries, most civil matters can be heard by six-person juries. The jury selection process is known as **voir dire.**[9] In most jurisdictions, attorneys for the plaintiff and the defendant ask prospective jurors oral questions to determine whether they are biased or have any connection with a party to the action or with a prospective witness. In some jurisdictions, the judge may do all or part of the questioning based on written questions submitted by counsel for the parties.

During *voir dire,* a party may challenge a certain number of prospective jurors *peremptorily*—that is, ask that an individual not be sworn in as a juror without providing any reason. Alternatively, a party may challenge a prospective juror *for cause*—that is, provide a reason why an individual should not be sworn in as a juror. If the judge grants the challenge, the individual is asked to step down. A prospective juror, however, may not be excluded by the use of discriminatory challenges, such as those based on racial criteria or gender.

See *Concept Summary 3.1* on the facing page for a review of pretrial procedures.

SECTION 3
THE TRIAL

Various rules and procedures govern the trial phase of the litigation process. There are rules governing what kind of evidence will or will not be admitted during the trial, as well as specific procedures that the participants in the lawsuit must follow. Today, some judges also have rules prohibiting or limiting the use of social media by jurors and others during trials, as discussed in this chapter's *Insight into Social Media* feature on page 64.

Opening Statements

At the beginning of the trial, both attorneys are allowed to make **opening statements** setting forth the facts that they expect to prove during the trial. The opening statement provides an opportunity for each lawyer to give a brief version of the facts and the supporting evidence that will be used during the trial. Then the plaintiff's case is presented. In our hypothetical case, Kirby's lawyer would introduce evidence (relevant documents, exhibits, and the testimony of witnesses) to support Kirby's position.

---

8. *In re Intel Corp. Microprocessor Antitrust Litigation,* 2008 WL 2310288 (D.Del. 2008).

9. Pronounced *vwahr deehr.* These verbs based on Old French mean "to speak the truth." In legal language, the phrase refers to the process of questioning jurors to learn about their backgrounds, attitudes, and similar attributes.

CONCEPT SUMMARY 3.1
Pretrial Procedures

PROCEDURE	DESCRIPTION
The Pleadings	1. *The plaintiff's complaint*—The plaintiff's statement of the cause of action and the parties involved, filed with the court by the plaintiff's attorney. After the filing, the defendant is notified of the suit through service of process. 2. *The defendant's response*—The defendant's response to the plaintiff's complaint may take the form of an answer, in which the defendant admits or denies the plaintiff's allegations. The defendant may raise an affirmative defense and/or assert a counterclaim.
Pretrial Motions	1. *Motion to dismiss*—May be made by either party to request that the judge dismiss the case for reasons stated in the motion (such as failure to state a claim for which relief can be granted). 2. *Motion for judgment* on the pleadings—May be made by either party and will be granted only if no facts are in dispute and only questions of law are at issue. 3. *Motion for summary judgment*—May be made by either party and will be granted only if no facts are in dispute and only questions of law are at issue. Unlike the motion for judgment on the pleadings, the motion for summary judgment may be supported by evidence outside the pleadings, such as testimony and other evidence obtained during discovery.
Discovery	The process of gathering evidence concerning the case, which may involve the following: 1. *Depositions* (sworn testimony by either party or any witness). 2. *Interrogatories* (in which parties to the action write answers to questions with the aid of their attorneys). 3. Requests for admissions, documents, examinations, or other information relating to the case. 4. Requests for electronically recorded information, such as e-mail, text messages, voice mail, and other data.
Pretrial Conference	A pretrial hearing, at the request of either party or the court, to identify the matters in dispute after discovery has taken place and to explore the possibility of settling the dispute without a trial. If no settlement is possible, the parties plan the course of the trial.
Jury Selection	In a jury trial, the selection of members of the jury from a pool of prospective jurors. During a process known as *voir dire,* the attorneys for both sides may challenge prospective jurors either for cause or peremptorily (for no cause).

Rules of Evidence

Whether evidence will be admitted in court is determined by the **rules of evidence.** These are a series of rules that the courts have created to ensure that any evidence presented during a trial is fair and reliable. The Federal Rules of Evidence govern the admissibility of evidence in federal courts.

EVIDENCE MUST BE RELEVANT TO THE ISSUES Evidence will not be admitted in court unless it is relevant to the matter in question. **Relevant evidence** is evidence that tends to prove or disprove a fact in question or to establish the degree of probability of a fact or action. For example, evidence that the defendant was in another person's home when the victim was shot would be relevant—because it would tend to prove that the defendant was not the shooter.

HEARSAY EVIDENCE NOT ADMISSIBLE Generally, hearsay is not admissible as evidence. **Hearsay** is testimony someone gives in court about a statement made by someone else who was not under oath at the

INSIGHT INTO SOCIAL MEDIA
To Tweet or Not to Tweet Inside the Courtroom

About two-thirds of all adult Internet users access social networking sites such as Twitter and Facebook.[a] Ordinarily, this is not a problem, but what if the adult is a member of a jury hearing a case? Typically, a trial judge will instruct jurors not to communicate with anyone about the case they are hearing. Nevertheless, many jurors are apparently ignoring these instructions when it comes to social media. When former Baltimore mayor Sheila Dickson was being tried for corruption, for example, five members of the jury communicated with each other via Facebook. Their posts were detected by a newspaper reporter. (Before the judge could sanction the jurors, the case was settled.)

Many judges worry that what jury members say online could be construed as generating bias about the case. Furthermore, they might reveal information about a trial before the information was supposed to be released to the public. Another problem is that jurors may look for information about the case and learn details that are not admissible at trial. The use of social media by journalists in the courtroom raises similar concerns.

How Can a Judge Know Who Is Tweeting?

A major difficulty with policing social media use by jurors and journalists is that a judge rarely knows who is tweeting. When the Federal Judicial Center asked judges if they would know if a juror violated a social media ban, almost 80 percent said no. About the only way a judge can learn that a juror has ignored the ban is if someone has access to the juror's postings and then informs the court, as happened in the Dickson trial mentioned above.

Some defense attorneys are asking judges to require jurors to disclose their Twitter "handles." Supposedly, the defense can then make sure that the jurors are not researching or tweeting about the case.

What Should Be the Policy Concerning Reporters?

Despite judges' efforts to prohibit anyone in the courtroom from using social media during a trial, reporters argue that social media are useful for providing "play-by-play" commentary for the public as events unfold. Judges respond

that reporters "feverishly" tweeting on their smartphones distract jurors and witnesses.

The judge in the high-profile sexual abuse case of former Penn State assistant football coach Jerry Sandusky did allow reporters to tweet during pretrial hearings, but he prohibited photographs and verbatim transmittals via social media. During the trial itself, the judge banned live tweets. To ensure that reporters did not tweet, he required them to disclose their Twitter "handles" and asked a member of the sheriff's department to track their accounts.

Later, the same judge developed stricter guidelines. Now he places a digital clock in the front of the courtroom and requires reporters to synchronize their smartphones, tablet devices, and laptops with the clock. When court is adjourned, the time is noted. Any reporter who transmitted information earlier than that time may be fined or jailed.[b]

A Different Approach from the United Kingdom

The United Kingdom has taken a different approach to social media in the courtroom. For the past several years, journalists have been able to use their Twitter accounts without even asking the judge's permission. The Lord Chief Justice—the most senior judge—issued *Practice Guidance Notes* that allow for the "use of live text-based forms of communications (including Twitter)."[c] The chief justice said that live communications would enable the media to produce fair and accurate reports of court proceedings.

Only text-based communications are permitted, however. Reporters are still prohibited from making sound recordings or taking photographs in the courtrooms.

LEGAL CRITICAL THINKING
INSIGHT INTO THE TECHNOLOGICAL ENVIRONMENT

Why is it so difficult for judges to effectively prohibit social media communications from the courtroom?

---

a. Pew Research Center Survey, Summer 2012

b. *Decorum Order Governing the Sentencing Hearing,* in the Court of Common Pleas of Centre County, Pennsylvania, *Commonwealth of Pennsylvania v. Jerold A. Sandusky.* October 3, 2012. By the order of the court John M. Cleland, S.J.

c. Lord Chief Justice of England and Wales, December 14, 2011.

---

time of the statement. Literally, it is what someone heard someone else say. For example, if a witness in the Kirby-Carvello case testified in court concerning what he or she heard another observer say about the accident, that testimony would be hearsay, or secondhand knowledge. Admitting hearsay into evidence carries many risks because, even though it may be relevant, there is no way to test its reliability.

Examination of Witnesses and Potential Motions

Because Kirby is the plaintiff, she has the burden of proving that her allegations are true. Her attorney begins the presentation of Kirby's case by calling the first witness for the plaintiff and examining, or questioning, the witness. (For both attorneys, the types of questions and the manner of asking them are governed by the rules of evidence.) This questioning is called **direct examination.** After Kirby's attorney is finished, the witness is subject to **cross-examination** by Carvello's attorney. Then Kirby's attorney has another opportunity to question the witness in *redirect examination,* and Carvello's attorney may follow the redirect examination with a *recross-examination.* When both attorneys have finished with the first witness, Kirby's attorney calls the succeeding witnesses in the plaintiff's case, each of whom is subject to examination by the attorneys in the manner just described.

EXPERT WITNESSES As part of their cases, both the plaintiff and the defendant may present testimony from one or more expert witnesses, such as forensic scientists, physicians, and psychologists. An *expert witness* is a person who, by virtue of education, training, skill, or experience, has scientific, technical, or other specialized knowledge in a particular area

beyond that of an average person. In Kirby's case, her attorney might hire an accident reconstruction specialist to establish Carvello's negligence or a physician to testify to the extent of Kirby's injuries.

Normally, witnesses can testify only about the facts of a case—that is, what they personally observed. When witnesses are qualified as experts in a particular field, however, they can offer their opinions and conclusions about the evidence in that field. Expert testimony is an important component of litigation today. Because numerous experts are available for hire and expert testimony is powerful and effective with juries, there is tremendous potential for abuse. Therefore, in federal courts and most state courts, judges act as gatekeepers to ensure that the experts are qualified and that their opinions are based on scientific knowledge.[10]

If a party believes that the opponent's expert witness is not a qualified expert in the relevant field, that party can make a motion to prevent the witness from testifying. In the following case, a court had refused to allow an expert to testify as to his opinion because the plaintiffs had failed to file a discovery report outlining the expert's testimony and credentials. The appellate court had to decide whether to reverse the trial court's decision regarding the expert's testimony.

---

10. See Paul C. Giannelli and Edward J. Imwinkelried, *Scientific Evidence,* 4th ed. (Newark, N.J.: LexisNexis, 2007), Sections 1.06 and 1.16.

CASE 3.3

Downey v. Bob's Discount Furniture Holdings, Inc.
United States Court of Appeals, First Circuit, 633 F.3d 1 (2011).

BACKGROUND AND FACTS Yvette Downey bought a children's bedroom set from Bob's Discount Furniture Holdings, Inc., in 2004. Soon, Downey and her daughter, Ashley Celester, began to experience skin irritation. In July 2005, they discovered insects on Ashley's body and in their home. Downey immediately called Allegiance Pest Control and spoke to Edward Gordinier, a licensed and experienced exterminator. Gordinier inspected Downey's home that day. He found bedbugs throughout the house and identified Ashley's bedroom set as the main source of the infestation. Downey informed Bob's about the problem. Although Bob's retrieved the bedroom set and refunded the purchase price, it refused to pay for the costs of extermination or any other damages. Downey and her daughter filed a lawsuit in a federal district court seeking compensation for health problems, emotional distress, and economic loss.

Before the trial, the plaintiffs named Gordinier as a witness but did not submit a written report describing his anticipated testimony or specifying his qualifications. Rule 26 of the Federal Rules of Civil Procedure requires that a written report be filed for an expert witness who is retained or specially employed to provide expert testimony. The plaintiffs asserted that Gordinier had not been specially employed as an expert and, therefore, no such disclosures were required. The defendants argued that Gordinier could not testify as to his expert opinion because the plaintiffs had not filed a written report. The district court agreed with

CASE 3.3 CONTINUES ▶

CASE 3.3 CONTINUED

the defendants and allowed Gordinier to testify only about the facts, such as his inspection of the premises, not about his opinion of the source of the bedbug infestation. The court granted a judgment for the defendants based, in part, on their claim that the plaintiffs had not proved that the furniture was infested with bedbugs when it was delivered. The plaintiffs appealed.

IN THE LANGUAGE OF THE COURT
SELYA, Circuit Judge.

* * * *

* * * Rule 26 "is an integral part of the machinery devised to facilitate the management of pretrial discovery." Among other things, the rule provides for wide-ranging pretrial disclosures in connection with anticipated expert testimony. *At its most basic level, the rule obligates a party who wishes to offer expert testimony to disclose "the identity of any witness it may use at trial to present evidence under Federal Rule of Evidence 702, 703, or 705."* In the case at hand, the plaintiffs seasonably [within a reasonable time period] complied with this identification requirement, naming Gordinier as a potential expert witness regarding causation. [Emphasis added.]

Other, more stringent disclosure requirements pertain to a witness who is "retained or specially employed to provide expert testimony in the case or . . . whose duties as the party's employee regularly involve giving expert testimony." The proponent of a witness falling into this subset must submit to the opposing party "a written report containing, [among other things,] detailed information as to the qualifications and intended testimony of the witness."

* * * *

As the text of Rule 26(a)(2)(B) makes plain, the rule covers two types of experts: (i) "retained or specially employed" experts who meet certain criteria and (ii) employees of a party who meet certain criteria. Because there is no suggestion that Gordinier was regularly employed by the plaintiffs, the lens of our inquiry narrows to whether he was "retained or specially employed."

The circumstances suggest that he was not. For one thing, there is no evidence that Gordinier was a person who held himself out for hire as a purveyor of expert testimony. For another thing, there is no evidence that he was charging a fee for his testimony.

Interpreting the words "retained or specially employed" in a common-sense manner, consistent with their plain meaning, we conclude that as long as an expert was not retained or specially employed in connection with the litigation, and his opinion about causation is premised on personal knowledge and observations made in the course of treatment, no report is required under the terms of Rule 26(a)(2)(B).

DECISION AND REMEDY *The U.S. Court of Appeals for the First Circuit held that Gordinier was not the type of expert witness for whom a report was required. Therefore, the court reversed the district court's judgment and remanded the case for a new trial.*

THE LEGAL ENVIRONMENT DIMENSION *Why can only an expert testify about the source of a bedbug infestation?*

THE ETHICAL DIMENSION *Is it fair to require plaintiffs who hire expert witnesses to pay for and submit written reports that specify what the experts will say at trial? Why or why not?*

POTENTIAL MOTION AND JUDGMENT At the conclusion of the plaintiff's case, the defendant's attorney may ask the judge to direct a verdict for the defendant on the ground that the plaintiff has presented no evidence to support her or his claim. This is called a **motion for a judgment as a matter of law** (or a **motion for a directed verdict** in state courts). In considering the motion, the judge looks at the evidence in the light most favorable to the plaintiff and grants the motion only if there is insufficient evidence to raise an issue of fact. (Motions for directed verdicts at this stage of a trial are seldom granted.)

DEFENDANT'S EVIDENCE The defendant's attorney then presents the evidence and witnesses for the defendant's case. Witnesses are called and examined by the defendant's attorney. The plaintiff's attorney has the right to cross-examine them, and there may be a redirect examination and possibly a recross-examination.

At the end of the defendant's case, either attorney can move for a directed verdict. Again, the test is whether the jury can, through any reasonable interpretation of the evidence, find for the party against whom the motion has been made. After the defendant's attorney has finished introducing evidence, the plaintiff's attorney can present a **rebuttal** by offering additional evidence that refutes the defendant's case. The defendant's attorney can, in turn, refute that evidence in a **rejoinder.**

Closing Arguments, Jury Instructions, and Verdict

After both sides have rested their cases, each attorney presents a **closing argument.** In the closing argument, each attorney summarizes the facts and evidence presented during the trial and indicates why the facts and evidence support his or her client's claim. In addition to generally urging a verdict in favor of the client, the closing argument typically reveals the shortcomings of the points made by the opposing party during the trial.

JURY INSTRUCTIONS Attorneys usually present closing arguments whether or not the trial was heard by a jury. If it was a jury trial, the attorneys will have met with the judge before the closing arguments to determine how the jury will be instructed on the law. The attorneys can refer to these instructions in their closing arguments. After closing arguments are completed, the judge instructs the jury in the law that applies to the case (these instructions are often called *charges*). The jury then retires to the jury room to deliberate a verdict.

Juries are instructed on the standard of proof they must apply to the case. In most civil cases, the standard of proof is a *preponderance of the evidence.*[11] In other words, the plaintiff (Kirby in our hypothetical case) need only show that her factual claim is more likely to be true than the defendant's. (As you will read in Chapter 10, in a criminal trial the prosecution has a higher standard of proof to meet—it must prove its case *beyond a reasonable doubt.*)

---

11. Note that some civil claims must be proved by "clear and convincing evidence," meaning that the evidence must show that the truth of the party's claim is *highly* probable. This standard is often applied in situations that present a particular danger of deception, such as allegations of fraud.

VERDICT Once the jury has reached a decision, it issues a **verdict** in favor of one party. The verdict specifies the jury's factual findings. In some cases, the jury also decides on the amount of the *award* (the compensation to be paid to the prevailing party). After the announcement of the verdict, which marks the end of the trial itself, the jurors are dismissed.

See *Concept Summary 3.2* on the next page for a review of trial procedures.

SECTION 4
POSTTRIAL MOTIONS

After the jury has rendered its verdict, either party may make a posttrial motion. The prevailing party usually requests that the court enter a judgment in accordance with the verdict. The nonprevailing party frequently files one of the motions discussed next.

Motion for a New Trial

At the end of the trial, the losing party may make a motion to set aside the adverse verdict and any judgment and to hold a new trial. After looking at all the evidence, the judge will grant the **motion for a new trial** only if she or he believes that the jury was in error and that it is not appropriate to grant judgment for the other side.

Usually, a new trial is granted only when the jury verdict is obviously the result of a misapplication of the law or a misunderstanding of the evidence presented at trial. A new trial can also be granted on the grounds of newly discovered evidence, misconduct by the participants during the trial (such as when a juror has made prejudicial and inflammatory remarks), or an error by the judge.

Motion for Judgment N.O.V.

If Kirby wins and if Carvello's attorney has previously moved for a judgment as a matter of law, then Carvello's attorney can make a second *motion for a judgment as a matter of law* (the terminology used in federal courts). State courts may use different terms for these motions. In many state courts, if the defendant's attorney moved earlier for a directed verdict, he or she may now make a **motion for judgment n.o.v.**—from the Latin *non obstante veredicto,* meaning "notwithstanding the verdict." Such a motion will be

---

CONCEPT SUMMARY 3.2
Trial Procedures

PROCEDURE	DESCRIPTION
Opening Statements	Each party's attorney is allowed to present an opening statement indicating what the attorney will attempt to prove during the course of the trial.
Examination of Witnesses	1. Plaintiff's introduction and direct examination of witnesses, cross-examination by defendant's attorney, possible redirect examination by plaintiff's attorney, and possible recross-examination by defendant's attorney. 2. Both the plaintiff and the defendant may present testimony from one or more expert witnesses. 3. At the close of the plaintiff's case, the defendant may make a motion for a directed verdict (or for judgment as a matter of law), which, if granted by the court, will end the trial before the defendant presents witnesses. 4. Defendant's introduction and direct examination of witnesses, cross-examination by plaintiff's attorney, possible redirect examination by defendant's attorney, and possible recross-examination by plaintiff's attorney. 5. Possible rebuttal of defendant's argument by plaintiff's attorney, who presents more evidence. 6. Possible rejoinder by defendant's attorney to meet that evidence.
Closing Arguments, Jury Instructions, and Verdict	Each party's attorney argues in favor of a verdict for his or her client. The judge instructs (or charges) the jury as to how the law applies to the issue, and the jury retires to deliberate. When the jury renders its verdict, the trial comes to an end.

granted only if the jury's verdict was unreasonable and erroneous.

If the judge grants the motion, then the jury's verdict will be set aside, and a judgment will be entered in favor of the opposing party (Carvello). If the motion is denied, Carvello may then appeal the case. (Kirby may also appeal the case, even though she won at trial. She might appeal, for example, if she received a smaller monetary award than she had sought.)

SECTION 5
THE APPEAL

Either party may appeal not only the jury's verdict but also the judge's ruling on any pretrial or posttrial motion. Many of the appellate court cases that appear in this text involve appeals of motions for summary judgment or other motions that were denied by trial court judges.

Note that a party must have legitimate grounds to file an appeal (some legal error) and that few trial court decisions are reversed on appeal. Moreover, the expenses associated with an appeal can be considerable.[12]

Filing the Appeal

If Carvello decides to appeal the verdict in Kirby's favor, then his attorney must file a *notice of appeal* with the clerk of the trial court within a prescribed period of time. Carvello then becomes the *appellant* or *petitioner*. The clerk of the trial court sends to the reviewing court (usually an intermediate court of appeals) the *record on appeal*. The record contains all the pleadings, motions, and other documents filed with the court and a complete written transcript of the proceedings, including testimony, arguments, jury instructions, and judicial rulings.

Carvello's attorney will file an appellate *brief* with the reviewing court. The **brief** is a formal legal document outlining the facts and issues of the case, the judge's rulings or jury's findings that should be reversed or modified, the applicable law, and argu-

---

12. See, for example, *Phansalkar v. Andersen Weinroth & Co.*, 356 F.3d 188 (2d Cir. 2004).

ments on Carvello's behalf (citing applicable statutes and relevant cases as precedents). The attorney for the *appellee* (Kirby, in our hypothetical case) usually files an answering brief. Carvello's attorney can file a reply, although it is not required. The reviewing court then considers the case.

Appellate Review

As mentioned in Chapter 2, a court of appeals does not hear any evidence. Rather, it reviews the record for errors of law. Its decision concerning a case is based on the record on appeal and the briefs and arguments. The attorneys present oral arguments, after which the case is taken under advisement. The court then issues a written opinion. In general, appellate courts do not reverse findings of fact unless the findings are unsupported or contradicted by the evidence.

An appellate court has the following options after reviewing a case:

1. The court can *affirm* the trial court's decision. (Most decisions are affirmed.)
2. The court can *reverse* the trial court's judgment if it concludes that the trial court erred or that the jury did not receive proper instructions.
3. The appellate court can *remand* (send back) the case to the trial court for further proceedings consistent with its opinion on the matter.
4. The court might also affirm or reverse a decision *in part*. For example, the court might affirm the jury's finding that Carvello was negligent but remand the case for further proceedings on another issue (such as the extent of Kirby's damages).
5. An appellate court can also *modify* a lower court's decision. If the appellate court decides that the jury awarded an excessive amount in damages, for example, the court might reduce the award to a more appropriate, or fairer, amount.

Higher Appellate Courts

If the reviewing court is an intermediate appellate court, the losing party may decide to appeal the decision to the state's highest court, usually called its supreme court. Although the losing party has a right to ask (petition) a higher court to review the case, the party does not have a right to have the case heard by the higher appellate court. Appellate courts normally have discretionary power and can accept or reject an appeal. Like the United States Supreme Court, state supreme courts generally deny most petitions for appeal.

If the petition for review is granted, new briefs must be filed before the state supreme court, and the attorneys may be allowed or requested to present oral arguments. Like the intermediate appellate courts, the supreme court can reverse or affirm the lower appellate court's decision or remand the case. At this point, the case typically has reached its end (unless a federal question is at issue and one of the parties has legitimate grounds to seek review by a federal appellate court).

Concept Summary 3.3 on the next page reviews the options that the parties may pursue after the trial.

SECTION 6
ENFORCING THE JUDGMENT

The uncertainties of the litigation process are compounded by the lack of guarantees that any judgment will be enforceable. Even if the jury awards Kirby the full amount of damages requested ($100,000), for example, Carvello's auto insurance coverage might have lapsed. If so, the company would not pay any of the damages. Alternatively, Carvello's insurance policy might be limited to $50,000, meaning that Carvello personally would have to pay the remaining $50,000.

Requesting Court Assistance in Collecting the Judgment

If the defendant does not have the funds available to pay the judgment, the plaintiff can go back to the court and request that the court issue a *writ of execution*. A **writ of execution** is an order directing the sheriff to seize and sell the defendant's nonexempt assets, or property (certain assets are exempted by law from creditors' actions). The proceeds of the sale are then used to pay the damages owed, and any excess proceeds are returned to the defendant. Alternatively, the nonexempt property itself could be transferred to the plaintiff in lieu of an outright payment. (There are creditors' remedies available, and there are issues of exempt and nonexempt property.)

Availability of Assets

The problem of collecting a judgment is less pronounced, of course, when a party is seeking to satisfy a judgment against a defendant with substantial assets that can be easily located, such as a major corporation.

CONCEPT SUMMARY 3.3
Posttrial Options

PROCEDURE	DESCRIPTION
Posttrial Motions	1. *Motion for a new trial*—If the judge believes that the jury was in error but is not convinced that the losing party should have won, the motion normally is granted. It can also be granted on the basis of newly discovered evidence, misconduct by the participants during the trial, or error by the judge. 2. *Motion for judgment n.o.v.* (*"notwithstanding the verdict"*)—The party making the motion must have filed a motion for a directed verdict at the close of the presentation of evidence during the trial. The motion will be granted if the judge is convinced that the jury was in error.
Appeal	Either party can appeal the trial court's judgment to an appropriate court of appeals. 1. *Filing the appeal*—The appealing party must file a notice of appeal with the clerk of the trial court, who forwards the record on appeal to the appellate court. Attorneys file appellate briefs. 2. *Appellate review*—The appellate court does not hear evidence but bases its opinion, which it issues in writing, on the record on appeal and the attorneys' briefs and oral arguments. The court may affirm or reverse all (or part) of the trial court's judgment and/or remand the case for further proceedings consistent with its opinion. Most decisions are affirmed on appeal. 3. *Further review*—In some cases, further review may be sought from a higher appellate court, such as a state supreme court. If a federal question is involved, the case may ultimately be appealed to the United States Supreme Court.

Usually, one of the factors considered by the plaintiff and his or her attorney before a lawsuit is initiated is whether the defendant has sufficient assets to cover the amount of damages sought. In addition, during the discovery process, attorneys routinely seek information about the location of the defendant's assets that might potentially be used to satisfy a judgment.

Reviewing: Court Procedures

Ronald Metzgar placed his fifteen-month-old son, Matthew, awake and healthy, in his playpen. Ronald left the room for five minutes and on his return found Matthew lifeless. A toy block had lodged in the boy's throat, causing him to choke to death. Ronald called 911, but efforts to revive Matthew were to no avail. There was no warning of a choking hazard on the box containing the block. Matthew's parents hired an attorney and sued Playskool, Inc., the manufacturer of the block, alleging that the manufacturer had been negligent in failing to warn of the block's hazard. Playskool filed a motion for summary judgment, arguing that the danger of a young child choking on a small block was obvious. Using the information presented in the chapter, answer the following questions.

1. Suppose that the attorney the Metzgars hired agreed to represent them on a contingency-fee basis. What does that mean?
2. How would the Metzgars' attorney likely have served process (the summons and complaint) on Playskool, Inc.?

3. Should Playskool's request for summary judgment be granted? Why or why not?

4. Suppose that the judge denied Playskool's motion and the case proceeded to trial. After hearing all the evidence, the jury found in favor of the defendant. What options do the plaintiffs have at this point if they are not satisfied with the verdict?

DEBATE THIS . . . *Some consumer advocates argue that attorneys' high contingency fees—sometimes reaching 40 percent—unfairly deprive winning plaintiffs of too much of their awards. Should the government cap contingency fees at, say, 20 percent of the award? Why or why not?*

Terms and Concepts

affidavit 58
affirmative defense 55
answer 55
brief 68
closing argument 67
complaint 52
counterclaim 55
cross-examination 65
default judgment 53
deposition 60
direct examination 65
discovery 58
e-evidence 61
Federal Rules of Civil Procedure (FRCP) 50

hearsay 63
impeach 60
interrogatories 60
metadata 61
motion 55
motion for a directed verdict 66
motion for a judgment as a matter of law 66
motion for a new trial 67
motion for judgment *n.o.v.* 67
motion for judgment on the pleadings 58
motion for summary judgment 58
motion to dismiss 55

opening statement 62
pleadings 52
pretrial conference 62
pretrial motion 55
rebuttal 67
rejoinder 67
relevant evidence 63
rules of evidence 63
service of process 53
summons 53
verdict 67
voir dire 62
writ of execution 69

ExamPrep

Issue Spotters

1. At the trial, after Sue calls her witnesses, offers her evidence, and otherwise presents her side of the case, Tom has at least two choices between courses of actions. Tom can call his first witness. What else might he do? **(See page 65.)**

2. After the trial, the judge issues a judgment that includes a grant of relief for Sue, but the relief is less than Sue wanted. Neither Sue nor Tom is satisfied with this result. Who can appeal to a higher court? **(See page 68.)**

• **Check your answers to the Issue Spotters against the answers provided in Appendix E at the end of this text.**

Before the Test

Go to **www.cengagebrain.com**, enter the ISBN 9781285185248, and click on "Find" to locate this textbook's Web site. Then, click on "Access Now" under "Study Tools," and select Chapter 3 at the top. There, you will find a Practice Quiz that you can take to assess your mastery of the concepts in this chapter, as well as Flashcards and a Glossary of important terms.

Business Scenarios

3–1. Discovery Rules. In the past, the rules of discovery were very restrictive, and trials often turned on elements of surprise. For example, a plaintiff would not necessarily know until the trial what the defendant's defense was going to be. In the last several decades, however, new rules of discovery have substantially changed this situation. Now each attorney can access practically all of the evidence that the other side intends to present at trial, with the exception of certain information—namely, the opposing attorney's work product. Work product is not a precise concept. Basically, it includes all of the attorney's thoughts on the case. Can you see any reason why such information should not be made available to the opposing attorney? Discuss fully. **(See page 58.)**

3–2. Motions. When and for what purpose is each of the following motions made? Which of them would be appropriate if a defendant claimed that the only issue between the parties was a question of law and that the law was favorable to the defendant's position? **(See page 55.)**

(a) A motion for judgment on the pleadings.

(b) A motion for a directed verdict.

(c) A motion for summary judgment.

(d) A motion for judgment *n.o.v.*

3–3. Motion for a New Trial. Washoe Medical Center, Inc., admitted Shirley Swisher for the treatment of a fractured pelvis. During her stay, Swisher suffered a fatal fall from her hospital bed. Gerald Parodi, the administrator of her estate, and others filed an action against Washoe seeking damages for the alleged lack of care in treating Swisher. During *voir dire*, when the plaintiffs' attorney returned a few minutes late from a break, the trial judge led the prospective jurors in a standing ovation. The judge joked with one of the prospective jurors, whom he had known in college, about his fitness to serve as a judge and personally endorsed another prospective juror's business. After the trial, the jury returned a verdict in favor of Washoe. The plaintiffs moved for a new trial, but the judge denied the motion. The plaintiffs then appealed, arguing that the tone set by the judge during *voir dire* prejudiced their right to a fair trial. Should the appellate court agree? Why or why not? **(See page 67.)**

3–4. Discovery. Advance Technology Consultants, Inc. (ATC), contracted with RoadTrac, LLC., to provide software and client software systems for the products of global positioning satellite (GPS) technology being developed by RoadTrac. RoadTrac agreed to provide ATC with hardware with which ATC's software would interface. Problems soon arose, however. ATC claimed that RoadTrac's hardware was defective, making it difficult to develop the software. RoadTrac contended that its hardware was fully functional and that ATC had simply failed to provide supporting software. ATC told RoadTrac that it considered their contract terminated. RoadTrac filed a suit in a Georgia state court against ATC alleging breach of contract. During discovery, RoadTrac requested ATC's customer lists and marketing procedures. ATC objected to providing this information because RoadTrac and ATC had become competitors in the GPS industry. Should a party to a lawsuit have to hand over its confidential business secrets as part of a discovery request? Why or why not? What limitations might a court consider imposing before requiring ATC to produce this material? **(See page 58.)**

Business Case Problems

3–5. Discovery. Rita Peatie filed a suit in a Connecticut state court against Wal-Mart Stores, Inc., to recover for injuries to her head, neck, and shoulder. Peatie claimed that she had been struck two years earlier by a metal cylinder falling from a store ceiling. The parties agreed to nonbinding arbitration. Ten days before the hearing, the plaintiff asked for, and was granted, four more months to conduct discovery. On the morning of the rescheduled hearing, she asked for more time, but the court denied this request. The hearing was held, and the arbitrator ruled in Wal-Mart's favor. Peatie filed a motion for a new trial, which was granted. Five months later, she sought through discovery to acquire any photos, records, and reports held by Wal-Mart regarding her alleged injury. The court issued a "protective order" against the request, stating that the time for discovery had long been over. On the day of the trial—four years after the alleged injury—the plaintiff asked the court to lift the order. Should the court do so? Why or why not? [*Peatie v. Wal-Mart Stores, Inc.,* 112 Conn. App. 8, 961 A.2d 1016 (2009)] **(See page 58.)**

3–6. Jury Misconduct. Michelle Fleshner worked for Pepose Vision Institute (PVI), a surgical practice. She was fired after she provided information to the U.S. Department of Labor about PVI's overtime pay policy. She sued for wrongful termination, and the jury awarded her $125,000. After the trial, a juror told PVI's attorneys that another juror had made anti-Semitic statements during jury deliberations. The comments concerned a witness who testified on PVI's behalf. According to the juror, the other juror said, about the witness: "She is a Jewish witch." "She is a penny-pinching Jew." "She was such a cheap Jew that she did not want to pay Plaintiff unemployment compensation." Another juror confirmed the remarks. PVI filed a motion for a new trial on the basis of juror misconduct. The trial judge held that the comments did not prevent a fair trial from occurring. PVI appealed. Do you think such comments are sufficient to require a new trial, or must a juror's bias be discovered during *voir dire* for it to matter? Explain. [*Fleshner v. Pepose Vision Institute,* 304 S.W.3d 81 (Mo. 2010)] **(See page 62.)**

3–7. Service of Process. Dr. Kevin Bardwell owns Northfield Urgent Care, LLC, a Minnesota medical clinic. Northfield ordered flu vaccine from Clint Pharmaceuticals, a licensed distributer of flu vaccine located in Tennessee. The parties signed a credit agreement that specified that any disputes would be litigated in the Tennessee state courts. When Northfield failed to pay what it owed for the vaccine, Clint Pharmaceuticals filed a lawsuit in Tennessee and served process on the clinic via registered mail to Dr. Bardwell, the registered agent of Northfield. Bardwell's wife, who worked as a receptionist at the clinic and handled inquiries on the clinic's Facebook site, signed for the letter. Bardwell did not appear on the trial date, however, and the Tennessee court entered a default judgment against Northfield. When Clint Pharmaceuticals attempted to collect on the judgment in Minnesota, Bardwell claimed that the judgment was unenforceable. He asserted that he had not been properly served because his wife was not a registered agent. Should the Minnesota court invalidate the Tennessee judgment? Was service of process proper when it was mailed to the defendant medical clinic and the wife of the physician who owned the clinic opened the letter? Explain. [*Clint Pharmaceuticals v. Northfield Urgent Care, LLC,* 2012 WL 3792546 (Minn.App. 2012).] **(See page 52.)**

3–8. BUSINESS CASE PROBLEM
WITH SAMPLE ANSWER: Discovery.

Jessica Lester died from injuries suffered in an auto accident caused by the driver of a truck owned by Allied Concrete Co. Jessica's widower, Isaiah, filed a suit against Allied for damages. The defendant requested copies of all of Isaiah's Facebook photos and other postings. Before responding, Isaiah "cleaned up" his Facebook page. Allied suspected that some items had been deleted, including a photo of Isaiah holding a beer can while wearing a T-shirt that declared "I [heart] hotmoms." Can this material be

recovered? If so, how? What effect might Isaiah's "postings" have on the result in this case? Discuss. [Allied Concrete Co. v. Lester, *736 S.E.2d 699 (2013)]* **(See page 58.)**

• **For a sample answer to Problem 3–8, go to Appendix F at the end of this text.**

3–9. A QUESTION OF ETHICS: Service of Process.

*Narnia Investments, Ltd., filed a suit in a Texas state court against several defendants, including Harvestons Securities, Inc., a securities dealer. (Securities are documents evidencing the ownership of a corporation, in the form of stock, or debts owed by it, in the form of bonds.) Harvestons is registered with the state of Texas. Thus, a party may serve a summons and a copy of a complaint on Harvestons by serving the Texas Securities Commissioner. In this case, the return of service indicated that process was served on the commissioner "by delivering to JoAnn Kocerek defendant, in person, a true copy of this [summons] together with the accompanying copy(ies) of the [complaint]." Harvestons did not file an answer, and Narnia obtained a default judgment against the defendant for $365,000, plus attorneys' fees and interest. Five months after this judgment, Harvestons filed a motion for a new trial, which the court denied. Harvestons appealed to a state intermediate appellate court, claiming that it had not been served in strict compliance with the rules governing service of process. [*Harvestons Securities, Inc. v. Narnia Investments, Ltd., 218 S.W.3d 126 (Tex.App.—Houston 2007)]* **(See page 52.)**

(a) Harvestons asserted that Narnia's service was invalid, in part, because "the return of service states that process was delivered to 'JoAnn Kocerek'" and did not show that she "had the authority to accept process on behalf of Harvestons or the Texas Securities Commissioner." Should such a detail, if it is required, be strictly construed and applied? Should it apply in this case? Explain.

(b) Who is responsible for ensuring that service of process is accomplished properly? Was it accomplished properly in this case? Why or why not?

Legal Reasoning Group Activity

3–10. Court Procedures. Bento Cuisine is a lunch-cart business. It occupies a street corner in Texarkana, a city that straddles the border of Arkansas and Texas. Across the street—and across the state line, which runs down the middle of the street—is Rico's Tacos. The two businesses compete for customers. Recently, Bento has begun to suspect that Rico's is engaging in competitive behavior that is illegal. Bento's manager overheard several of Rico's employees discussing these competitive tactics while on a break at a nearby Starbucks. Bento files a lawsuit against Rico's in a federal court based on diversity jurisdiction. **(See page 55.)**

(a) The first group will discuss whether Rico's could file a motion claiming that the federal court lacks jurisdiction over this dispute.

(b) The second group will assume that the case goes to trial. Bento believes that it has both the law and the facts on its side. Nevertheless, at the end of the trial, the jury decides against Bento, and the judge issues a ruling in favor of Rico's. If Bento is unwilling to accept this result, what are its options?

(c) As discussed in this chapter, hearsay is literally what a witness says he or she heard another person say. A third group will decide whether Bento's manager can testify about what he heard some of Rico's employees say to one another while at a coffee shop. This group will also discuss what makes the admissibility of hearsay evidence potentially unethical.

CHAPTER 4

BUSINESS AND THE CONSTITUTION

L aws that govern business have their origin in the lawmaking authority granted by the U.S. Constitution, which is the supreme law in this country.[1] As mentioned in Chapter 1, neither Congress nor any state may pass a law that is in conflict with the Constitution.

Constitutional disputes frequently come before the courts. For instance, numerous states challenged the Obama administration's Affordable Care Act on constitutional grounds. The United States Supreme Court decided in 2012 that the provisions of this law, which require most Americans to have health insurance by 2014, did not exceed the constitutional authority of the federal government. The Court's decision in the

matter continues to have a significant impact on the business environment.

In this chapter, we examine some basic constitutional concepts and clauses and their significance for businesspersons. We then look at certain freedoms guaranteed by the first ten amendments to the Constitution—the Bill of Rights—and discuss how these freedoms affect business activities.

---

1. See Appendix B for the full text of the U.S. Constitution.

SECTION 1
THE CONSTITUTIONAL POWERS OF GOVERNMENT

Following the Revolutionary War, the states adopted the Articles of Confederation. The Articles created a *confederal form of government* in which the states had the authority to govern themselves and the national government could exercise only limited powers. When problems arose because the nation was facing an economic crisis and state laws interfered with the free flow of commerce, a national convention was called, and the delegates drafted the U.S. Constitution. This document, after its ratification by the states in 1789, became the basis for an entirely new form of government.

A Federal Form of Government

The new government created by the U.S. Constitution reflected a series of compromises made by the convention delegates on various issues. Some delegates wanted sovereign power to remain with the states. Others wanted the national government alone to exercise sovereign power. The end result was a compromise—a **federal form of government** in

which the national government and the states *share* sovereign power.

FEDERAL POWERS The Constitution sets forth specific powers that can be exercised by the national government. It further provides that the national government has the implied power to undertake actions necessary to carry out its expressly designated powers (or *enumerated powers*). All other powers are expressly "reserved" to the states under the Tenth Amendment to the U.S. Constitution.

REGULATORY POWERS OF THE STATES As part of their inherent **sovereignty** (independence), state governments have the authority to regulate affairs within their borders. As mentioned, this authority stems, in part, from the Tenth Amendment, which reserves all powers not delegated to the national government to the states or to the people.

State regulatory powers are often referred to as **police powers.** The term encompasses more than just the enforcement of criminal laws. Police powers also give state governments broad rights to regulate private activities to protect or promote the public order, health, safety, morals, and general welfare. Fire and building codes, antidiscrimination laws, parking regulations, zoning restrictions, licensing requirements, and thousands of other state statutes have been enacted pursuant to states' police powers.

Local governments, including cities, also exercise police powers.[2] Generally, state laws enacted pursuant to a state's police powers carry a strong presumption of validity.

Relations Among the States

The U.S. Constitution also includes provisions concerning relations among the states in our federal system. Particularly important are the *privileges and immunities clause* and the *full faith and credit clause.*

THE PRIVILEGES AND IMMUNITIES CLAUSE Article IV, Section 2, of the Constitution provides that the "Citizens of each State shall be entitled to all Privileges and Immunities of Citizens in the several States." This clause is often referred to as the interstate **privileges and immunities clause.**[3] It prevents a state from imposing unreasonable burdens on citizens of another state—particularly with regard to means of livelihood or doing business.

When a citizen of one state engages in basic and essential activities in another state (the "foreign state"), the foreign state must have a *substantial reason* for treating the nonresident differently from its own residents. Basic activities include transferring property, seeking employment, or accessing the court system. The foreign state must also establish that its reason for the discrimination is *substantially related* to the state's ultimate purpose in adopting the legislation or regulating the activity.[4]

THE FULL FAITH AND CREDIT CLAUSE Article IV, Section 1, of the U.S. Constitution provides that "Full Faith and Credit shall be given in each State to the public Acts, Records, and judicial Proceedings of every other State." This clause, which is referred to as the **full faith and credit clause,** applies only to civil matters. It ensures that rights established under deeds, wills, contracts, and similar instruments in one state will be honored by other states.

It also ensures that any judicial decision with respect to such property rights will be honored and enforced in all states.

▶ **Example 4.1** The legal issues raised by same-sex marriage involve, among other things, the full faith and credit clause because that clause requires each state to honor marriage decrees issued by another state. Therefore, if same-sex partners marry in Washington, which legalized same-sex marriage in 2012, and the couple later moves to another state, that state would be required to recognize the validity of their marriage. ◀

The full faith and credit clause has contributed to the unity of American citizens because it protects their legal rights as they move about from state to state. It also protects the rights of those to whom they owe obligations, such as a person who is awarded monetary damages by a court. The ability to enforce such rights is extremely important for the conduct of business in a country with a very mobile citizenry.

The Separation of Powers

To make it difficult for the national government to use its power arbitrarily, the Constitution provided for three branches of government. The legislative branch makes the laws, the executive branch enforces the laws, and the judicial branch interprets the laws. Each branch performs a separate function, and no branch may exercise the authority of another branch.

Additionally, a system of **checks and balances** allows each branch to limit the actions of the other two branches, thus preventing any one branch from exercising too much power. Some examples of these checks and balances include the following:

1. The legislative branch (Congress) can enact a law, but the executive branch (the president) has the constitutional authority to veto that law.
2. The executive branch is responsible for foreign affairs, but treaties with foreign governments require the advice and consent of the Senate.
3. Congress determines the jurisdiction of the federal courts, and the president appoints federal judges, with the advice and consent of the Senate. The judicial branch has the power to hold actions of the other two branches unconstitutional.[5]

---

2. Local governments derive their authority to regulate their communities from the state, because they are creatures of the state. In other words, they cannot come into existence unless authorized by the state to do so.
3. Interpretations of this clause commonly use the terms *privilege* and *immunity* synonymously. Generally, the terms refer to certain rights, benefits, or advantages enjoyed by individuals.
4. This test was first announced in *Supreme Court of New Hampshire v. Piper,* 470 U.S. 274, 105 S.Ct. 1272, 84 L.Ed.2d 205 (1985). For another example, see *Lee v. Miner,* 369 F.Supp.2d 527 (D.Del. 2005).

5. As discussed in Chapter 2, the power of judicial review was established by the United States Supreme Court in *Marbury v. Madison,* 5 U.S. (1 Cranch) 137, 2 L.Ed. 60 (1803).

The Commerce Clause

To prevent states from establishing laws and regulations that would interfere with trade and commerce among the states, the Constitution expressly delegated to the national government the power to regulate interstate commerce. Article I, Section 8, of the U.S. Constitution explicitly permits Congress "[t]o regulate Commerce with foreign Nations, and among the several States, and with the Indian Tribes." This clause, referred to as the **commerce clause,** has had a greater impact on business than any other provision in the Constitution. The commerce clause provides the basis for the national government's extensive regulation of state and even local affairs.

Initially, the courts interpreted the commerce clause to apply only to commerce between the states (*interstate* commerce) and not commerce within the states (*intrastate* commerce). In 1824, however, the United States Supreme Court decided the landmark case of *Gibbons v. Ogden*.[6] The Court held that commerce within the states could also be regulated by the national government as long as the commerce *substantially affected* commerce involving more than one state.

THE EXPANSION OF NATIONAL POWERS UNDER THE COMMERCE CLAUSE As the nation grew and faced new kinds of problems, the commerce clause became a vehicle for the additional expansion of the national government's regulatory powers. Even activities that seemed purely local in nature came under the regulatory reach of the national government if those activities were deemed to substantially affect interstate commerce. In 1942, the Supreme Court held that wheat production by an individual farmer intended wholly for consumption on his own farm was subject to federal regulation.[7]

▶ **Case in Point 4.2**   In *Heart of Atlanta Motel v. United States*,[8] a landmark case decided in 1964, the Supreme Court upheld the federal government's authority under the commerce clause to prohibit racial discrimination nationwide in public facilities. The case was brought by an Atlanta motel owner who refused to rent rooms to African Americans, in violation of the Civil Rights Act of 1964. The Court concluded that local motels and restaurants do affect interstate commerce. The Court stated that "if it is interstate commerce that feels the pinch, it does not matter how local the operation that applies the squeeze." ◀

THE COMMERCE CLAUSE TODAY Today, at least theoretically, the power over commerce authorizes the national government to regulate almost every commercial enterprise in the United States. The breadth of the commerce clause permits the national government to legislate in areas in which Congress has not explicitly been granted power.

In the last twenty years, the Supreme Court has on occasion curbed the national government's regulatory authority under the commerce clause. In 1995, the Court held—for the first time in sixty years—that Congress had exceeded its regulatory authority under the commerce clause. The Court struck down an act that banned the possession of guns within one thousand feet of any school because the act attempted to regulate an area that had "nothing to do with commerce."[9] Subsequently, the Court invalidated key portions of two other federal acts on the ground that they exceeded Congress's commerce clause authority.[10]

MEDICAL MARIJUANA AND THE COMMERCE CLAUSE
In one notable case, however, the Supreme Court did allow the federal government to regulate noncommercial activities taking place wholly within a state's borders. ▶ **Case in Point 4.3**   More than a dozen states, including California, have adopted laws that legalize marijuana for medical purposes. Marijuana possession, however, is illegal under the federal Controlled Substances Act (CSA).[11] After the federal government seized the marijuana that two seriously ill California women were using on the advice of their physicians, the women filed a lawsuit. They argued that it was unconstitutional for the federal statute to prohibit them from using marijuana for medical purposes that were legal within the state.

The Supreme Court, though, held that Congress has the authority to prohibit the *intrastate* possession and noncommercial cultivation of marijuana as part of a larger regulatory scheme (the CSA).[12] In other

---

6. 22 U.S. (9 Wheat.) 1, 6 L.Ed. 23 (1824).
7. *Wickard v. Filburn,* 317 U.S. 111, 63 S.Ct. 82, 87 L.Ed. 122 (1942).
8. 379 U.S. 241, 85 S.Ct. 348, 13 L.Ed.2d 258 (1964).

9. The Court held the Gun-Free School Zones Act of 1990 to be unconstitutional in *United States v. Lopez,* 514 U.S. 549, 115 S.Ct. 1624, 131 L.Ed.2d 626 (1995).
10. *Printz v. United States,* 521 U.S. 898, 117 S.Ct. 2365, 138 L.Ed.2d 914 (1997), involving the Brady Handgun Violence Prevention Act of 1993; and *United States v. Morrison,* 529 U.S. 598, 120 S.Ct. 1740, 146 L.Ed.2d 658 (2000), concerning the federal Violence Against Women Act of 1994.
11. 21 U.S.C. Sections 801 *et seq.*
12. *Gonzales v. Raich,* 545 U.S. 1, 125 S.Ct. 2195, 162 L.Ed.2d 1 (2005).

words, state medical marijuana laws do not insulate the users from federal prosecution. ◀

THE "DORMANT" COMMERCE CLAUSE The Supreme Court has interpreted the commerce clause to mean that the national government has the *exclusive* authority to regulate commerce that substantially affects trade and commerce among the states. This express grant of authority to the national government is often referred to as the "positive" aspect of the commerce clause. But this positive aspect also implies a negative aspect—that the states do *not* have the authority to regulate interstate commerce. This negative aspect of the commerce clause is often referred to as the "dormant" (implied) commerce clause.

The dormant commerce clause comes into play when state regulations affect interstate commerce. In this situation, the courts weigh the state's interest in regulating a certain matter against the burden that the state's regulation places on interstate commerce. Because courts balance the interests involved, it is difficult to predict the outcome in a particular case.

In the following case, the plaintiffs—a group of California wineries and others—contended that a Massachusetts statute discriminated against out-of-state wineries in violation of the dormant commerce clause. A federal district court agreed and enjoined (prevented) the enforcement of the statute. The commonwealth of Massachusetts appealed the trial court's decision.

CASE ANALYSIS

Case 4.1   Family Winemakers of California v. Jenkins[a]
United States Court of Appeals, First Circuit, 592 F.3d 1 (2010).

IN THE LANGUAGE OF THE COURT
LYNCH, Chief Judge.

* * * *

The ratification of the Twenty-first Amendment ended Prohibition[b] and gave states substantial control over the regulation of alcoholic beverages. Most states, including Massachusetts, then imposed a three-tier system to control the sale of alcoholic beverages within their territories. The hallmark of the three-tier system is a rigid, tightly regulated separation between producers, wholesalers, and retailers of alcoholic beverages. Producers can ordinarily sell alcoholic beverages only to licensed in-state wholesalers. Wholesalers then must obtain licenses to sell to retailers. Retailers, which

include stores, taverns, restaurants, and bars, must in turn obtain licenses to sell to consumers or to serve alcohol on their premises. Recently, as to wine, Massachusetts has adjusted the separation between these three tiers * * *.

* * * *

Wineries have heralded direct shipping as a supplemental avenue of distribution because of its economic advantages, especially for wineries that do not rank among the fifty to one hundred largest producers. Direct shipping lets consumers directly order wines from the winery, with access to their full range of wines, not just those a wholesaler is willing to distribute. Direct shipping also avoids added steps in the distribution chain, eliminating wholesaler and retailer price markups.

Before 2005, Massachusetts's * * * winery licensing law * * * allowed only in-state wineries to obtain licenses to combine distribution methods through wholesalers, retailers, and direct shipping to consumers. [After the United States Supreme Court] invalidated similar facially

discriminatory state laws, [the 2005 Massachusetts law] was held to be invalid under the Commerce Clause.

In 2006, the Massachusetts legislature enacted [a new law regulating wineries, which] does not distinguish on its face between in-state and out-of-state wineries' eligibility for direct shipping licenses, but instead distinguishes between "small" or "large" wineries through [a] 30,000 gallon cap.

* * * *

* * * All wineries producing over 30,000 gallons of wine—all of which are located outside Massachusetts—can apply for a "large winery shipment license[.]" * * * "Large" wineries can either choose to remain completely within the three-tier system and distribute their wines solely through wholesalers, or they can completely opt out of the three-tier system and sell their wines in Massachusetts exclusively through direct shipping [to consumers]. They cannot do both. * * * By contrast, "small" wineries can simultaneously use the traditional

---

a. The case was brought against Eddie J. Jenkins, the chair of the Massachusetts Alcoholic Beverages Control Commission, in his official capacity.

b. The Eighteenth Amendment to the U.S. Constitution, adopted in 1919, prohibited the sale of alcoholic beverages, giving rise to the so-called Prohibition Era. The Twenty-first Amendment, ratified in 1933, repealed the Eighteenth Amendment.

CASE 4.1 CONTINUES ◆

wholesaler distribution method, direct distribution to retailers, and direct shipping to reach consumers.

* * * *

* * * *Discrimination under the Commerce Clause "means differential treatment of in-state and out-of-state economic interests that benefits the former and burdens the latter," as opposed to state laws that "regulate * * * evenhandedly with only incidental effects on interstate commerce[.]"* [Emphasis added.]

* * * Plaintiffs argue that Massachusetts's choice of 30,000 gallons as the demarcation [separation] point between "small" and "large" wineries, along with [a] production exception for fruit wine, has both a discriminatory effect and [a] purpose. The discriminatory effect is because [the law's] definition of "large" wineries encompasses the wineries which produce 98 percent of all wine in the United States, all of which are located out-of-state and all of which are deprived of the benefits of combining distribution methods. All wines produced in Massachusetts, on the other hand, are from "small" wineries that can use multiple distribution methods. Plaintiffs also say that [the law]

is discriminatory in purpose because the gallonage cap's particular features, along with legislators' statements and [the law's] process of enactment, show that [the law's] true purpose was to ensure that Massachusetts's wineries obtained advantages over their out-of-state counterparts.

* * * *

* * * State laws that alter conditions of competition to favor in-state interests over out-of-state competitors in a market have long been subject to invalidation.

* * * Here, the totality of the evidence introduced by plaintiffs demonstrates that [the law's] preferential treatment of "small" wineries that produce 30,000 gallons or less of grape wine is discriminatory. Its effect is to significantly alter the terms of competition between in-state and out-of-state wineries to the detriment of the out-of-state wineries that produce 98 percent of the country's wine.

[The 2006 law] confers a clear competitive advantage to "small" wineries, which include all Massachusetts's wineries, and creates a comparative disadvantage for "large" wineries, none of which are

in Massachusetts. "Small" wineries that obtain a * * * license can use direct shipping to consumers, retailer distribution, and wholesaler distribution simultaneously. Combining these distribution methods allows "small" wineries to sell their full range of wines at maximum efficiency because they serve complementary markets. "Small" wineries that produce higher-volume wines can continue distributing those wines through wholesaler relationships. They can obtain new markets for all their wines by distributing their wines directly to retailers, including individual bars, restaurants, and stores. They can also use direct shipping to offer their full range of wines directly to Massachusetts consumers, resulting in greater overall sales.

* * * *

We conclude that [the 2006 law] altered the competitive balance to favor Massachusetts's wineries and disfavor out-of-state competition by design.

* * * *

We *affirm* the judgment of the district court.

LEGAL REASONING QUESTIONS

1. The court held that the Massachusetts statute discriminated against out-of-state wineries "by design" (intentionally). How can a court determine legislative intent?

2. Suppose that most "small" wineries, as defined by the 2006 Massachusetts law, were located out of state. How could the law be discriminatory in that situation?

3. Suppose that the state had only required the out-of-state wineries to obtain a special license that was readily available. Would this have affected the outcome of the case? Explain.

4. When it is difficult to predict how the law might be applied—as in cases arising under the dormant commerce clause—what is the best course of conduct for a business?

The Supremacy Clause and Federal Preemption

Article VI of the U.S. Constitution, commonly referred to as the **supremacy clause,** provides that the Constitution, laws, and treaties of the United States are "the supreme Law of the Land." When there is a

direct conflict between a federal law and a state law, the state law is rendered invalid. Because some powers are *concurrent* (shared by the federal government and the states), however, it is necessary to determine which law governs in a particular circumstance.

When Congress chooses to act (legislate) exclusively in an area in which the federal government and the states have concurrent powers, **preemption** occurs. A valid federal statute or regulation will take precedence over a conflicting state or local law or regulation on the same general subject.

FEDERAL STATUTES MAY SPECIFY PREEMPTION Sometimes, the federal statute will include a preemption provision to make it clear that Congress intends the legislation to preempt any state laws on the matter. ▶ **Case in Point 4.4** A man who alleged that he had been injured by a faulty medical device (a balloon catheter that was inserted into his artery following a heart attack) sued the manufacturer.

The case ultimately came before the United States Supreme Court, which noted that the Medical Device Amendments of 1976 had included a preemption provision. The medical device had passed the U.S. Food and Drug Administration's rigorous premarket approval process. Therefore, the Court concluded that the federal regulation of medical devices preempted the injured party's state common law claims for negligence, strict liability, and implied warranty (see Chapters 6 and 7).[13] ◀

WHEN THE STATUTE DOES NOT EXPRESSLY MENTION PREEMPTION Often, it is not clear whether Congress, in passing a law, intended to preempt an entire subject area against state regulation. In those situations, the courts determine whether Congress intended to exercise exclusive power over a given area.

No single factor is decisive as to whether a court will find preemption. Generally, congressional intent to preempt will be found if a federal law regulating an activity is so pervasive, comprehensive, or detailed that the states have no room to regulate in that area. Also, when a federal statute creates an agency—such as the National Labor Relations Board—to enforce the law, matters that come within the agency's jurisdiction will likely preempt state laws.

The Taxing and Spending Powers

Article I, Section 8, of the U.S. Constitution provides that Congress has the "Power to lay and collect Taxes, Duties, Imposts, and Excises." Section 8 further requires uniformity in taxation among the states, and thus Congress may not tax some states while exempting others.

In the distant past, if Congress attempted to regulate indirectly, by taxation, an area over which it had

no authority, the courts would invalidate the tax. Today, however, if a tax measure is reasonable, it generally is held to be within the national taxing power. Moreover, the expansive interpretation of the commerce clause almost always provides a basis for sustaining a federal tax.

Article I, Section 8, also gives Congress its spending power—the power "to pay the Debts and provide for the common Defence and general Welfare of the United States." Congress can spend revenues not only to carry out its expressed powers but also to promote any objective it deems worthwhile, so long as it does not violate the Bill of Rights. The spending power necessarily involves policy choices, with which taxpayers (and politicians) may disagree.

SECTION 2
BUSINESS AND THE BILL OF RIGHTS

The importance of a written declaration of the rights of individuals caused the first Congress of the United States to submit twelve amendments to the U.S. Constitution to the states for approval. Ten of these amendments, known as the **Bill of Rights,** were adopted in 1791 and embody a series of protections for the individual against various types of interference by the federal government.[14]

The protections guaranteed by these ten amendments are summarized in Exhibit 4–1 on the following page.[15] Some of these constitutional protections apply to business entities as well. For example, corporations exist as separate legal entities, or *legal persons,* and enjoy many of the same rights and privileges as *natural persons* do.

Limits on Federal and State Governmental Actions

As originally intended, the Bill of Rights limited only the powers of the national government. Over time, however, the United States Supreme Court "incorporated" most of these rights into the protections against state actions afforded by the Fourteenth Amendment to the Constitution.

---

13. *Riegel v. Medtronic, Inc.,* 552 U.S. 312, 128 S.Ct. 999, 169 L.Ed.2d 892 (2008).

14. Another of these proposed amendments was ratified more than two hundred years later (in 1992) and became the Twenty-seventh Amendment to the Constitution. See Appendix B.

15. See the Constitution in Appendix B for the complete text of each amendment.

EXHIBIT 4-1 Protections Guaranteed by the Bill of Rights

First Amendment: Guarantees the freedoms of religion, speech, and the press and the rights to assemble peaceably and to petition the government.

Second Amendment: States that the right of the people to keep and bear arms shall not be infringed.

Third Amendment: Prohibits, in peacetime, the lodging of soldiers in any house without the owner's consent.

Fourth Amendment: Prohibits unreasonable searches and seizures of persons or property.

Fifth Amendment: Guarantees the rights to indictment by grand jury, to due process of law, and to fair payment when private property is taken for public use; prohibits compulsory self-incrimination and double jeopardy (being tried again for an alleged crime for which one has already stood trial).

Sixth Amendment: Guarantees the accused in a criminal case the right to a speedy and public trial by an impartial jury and with counsel. The accused has the right to cross-examine witnesses against him or her and to solicit testimony from witnesses in his or her favor.

Seventh Amendment: Guarantees the right to a trial by jury in a civil case involving at least twenty dollars.[a]

Eighth Amendment: Prohibits excessive bail and fines, as well as cruel and unusual punishment.

Ninth Amendment: Establishes that the people have rights in addition to those specified in the Constitution.

Tenth Amendment: Establishes that those powers neither delegated to the federal government nor denied to the states are reserved to the states and to the people.

a. Twenty dollars was forty days' pay for the average person when the Bill of Rights was written.

THE FOURTEENTH AMENDMENT The Fourteenth Amendment, passed in 1868 after the Civil War, provides, in part, that "[n]o State shall . . . deprive any person of life, liberty, or property, without due process of law." Starting in 1925, the Supreme Court began to define various rights and liberties guaranteed in the U.S. Constitution as constituting "due process of law," which was required of state governments under that amendment.

Today, most of the rights and liberties set forth in the Bill of Rights apply to state governments as well as the national government. In other words, neither the federal government nor state governments can deprive persons of those rights and liberties.

JUDICIAL INTERPRETATION The rights secured by the Bill of Rights are not absolute. Many of the rights guaranteed by the first ten amendments are set forth in very general terms. The Second Amendment states that people have a right to keep and bear arms, but it does not explain the extent of this right. As the Supreme Court noted in 2008, this does not mean that people can "keep and carry any weapon whatsoever in any manner whatsoever and for whatever purpose."[16] Legislatures can prohibit the carrying of concealed weapons or certain types of weapons, such as machine guns.

Ultimately, it is the United States Supreme Court, as the final interpreter of the Constitution, that gives meaning to these rights and determines their boundaries. Changing public views on controversial topics, such as privacy in an era of terrorist threats or the rights of gay men and lesbians, may affect the way the Supreme Court decides a case. On several occasions, justices on the Supreme Court have even mentioned that they have considered foreign laws in reaching a decision.

Freedom of Speech

A democratic form of government cannot survive unless people can freely voice their political opinions and criticize government actions or policies. Freedom of speech, particularly political speech, is thus a prized right, and traditionally the courts have protected this right to the fullest extent possible.

Symbolic speech—gestures, movements, articles of clothing, and other forms of expressive conduct—is also given substantial protection by the courts. The Supreme Court has held that the burning of the American flag as part of a peaceful protest is a constitutionally protected form of expression.[17] Similarly, wearing a T-shirt with a photo of a presidential candidate is a constitutionally protected form of expression. ▶ **Example 4.5** As a form of expression, Nate

---

16. *District of Columbia v. Heller,* 554 U.S. 570, 128 S.Ct. 2783, 171 L.Ed.2d 637 (2008).

17. *Texas v. Johnson,* 491 U.S. 397, 109 S.Ct. 2533, 105 L.Ed.2d 342 (1989).

has gang signs tattooed on his torso, arms, neck, and legs. If a reasonable person would interpret this conduct as conveying a message, then it might be a protected form of symbolic speech. ◀

An interesting topic in today's legal environment is whether computers should have free speech rights.

For a discussion of this issue, see this chapter's *Insight into E-Commerce* feature below.

REASONABLE RESTRICTIONS Expression—oral, written, or symbolized by conduct—is subject to reasonable restrictions. A balance must be struck between

---

INSIGHT INTO E-COMMERCE
Do Computers Have Free Speech Rights?

When you do a Web search using Bing, Google, or any other search engine, the program inherent in the engine gives you a list of results. When you use a document-creation program, such as Microsoft Word, it often guesses what you intend and corrects your misspellings automatically. Do computers that make such choices engage in "speech," and if so, do they enjoy First Amendment protection? This question is not as absurd as it may seem at first.

Are Google's Search Results "Speech"?

More than a decade ago, a company dissatisfied with its rankings in Google's search results sued. Google argued that its search results were constitutionally protected speech. The plaintiff, Search King, Inc., sought an injunction against Google, but a federal district court decided in Google's favor. The court ruled that the ranking of results when a search is undertaken "constitutes opinions protected by the First Amendment. . . . *Page Ranks* are opinions—opinions are the significance of particular Web sites as they correspond to a search query." Therefore, the First Amendment applied to the search results.[a]

Google versus the Federal Trade Commission

For the last few years, Google has been the dominant search engine. Yet in the 1990s, the federal government was worried that Microsoft's search engine was too dominant and was crushing the search engines of Yahoo!, AltaVista, and Lycos. Today, of course, AltaVista and Lycos no longer exist, and Microsoft's new search engine, Bing, is a relatively minor player in the field.

Fast-forward to 2011. The Federal Trade Commission (FTC) contemplated bringing charges against Google for favoring its own offerings, such as restaurant reviews, in its search results. Now it was Microsoft that was encouraging the FTC to proceed. After a nineteen-month investiga-

tion, in early 2013 the FTC announced that it would *not* prosecute Google. The FTC's decision was a blow to search engines that compete with Google, including Microsoft's Bing.

The First Amendment Protection Argument

Google commissioned Eugene Volokh and Donald Falk, two legal experts in this field, to research the issue of whether search engine results are protected by the First Amendment.[b] The researchers concluded that search engine results are the same as the editorial judgments that a newspaper makes in deciding which wire service stories to run and which op-ed and business columnists to feature. The authors further claim that free speech applies to editorial choices no matter what their format. Search engines are protected even when they are "unfair" in ranking search results. Whether the search engine uses a computerized algorithm to compile its rankings is irrelevant.

Columbia Law professor Tim Wu disagrees. He argues that the First Amendment was intended to protect humans against the evils of state censorship and that protecting a computer's speech is not related to that purpose. At best, he says, search engine results are *commercial speech,* which has always received limited protection under the First Amendment. After all, computers make trillions of invisible decisions each day. Is each of those decisions protected speech?

LEGAL CRITICAL THINKING
INSIGHT INTO SOCIAL MEDIA

Facebook has numerous computers, all programmed by humans, of course. If Facebook's computers make decisions that allow your private information to be shared without your knowledge, should the First Amendment protect Facebook? Why or why not?

---

a. *Search King, Inc. v. Google Technology, Inc.,* 2003 WL 21464568 (W.D.Okla. 2003). See also *Langdon v. Google, Inc.,* 474 F.Supp.2d 622 (D.Del. 2007).

b. Eugene Volokh and Donald Falk, "First Amendment Protection for Search Engine Search Results: White Paper Commissioned by Google" (UCLA School of Law Research Paper No. 12-22, April 20, 2012).

a government's obligation to protect its citizens and those citizens' exercise of their rights. Reasonableness is analyzed on a case-by-case basis.

Content-Neutral Laws. Laws that regulate the time, manner, and place, but not the content, of speech receive less scrutiny by the courts than do laws that restrict the content of expression. If a restriction imposed by the government is content neutral, then a court may allow it. To be content neutral, the restriction must be aimed at combatting some societal problem, such as crime or drug abuse, and not be aimed at suppressing the expressive conduct or its message. Courts have often protected nude dancing as a form of symbolic expression but typically allow content-neutral laws that ban all public nudity.

▶ **Case in Point 4.6**   Ria Ora was charged with dancing nude at an annual "anti-Christmas" protest in Harvard Square in Cambridge, Massachusetts, under a statute banning public displays of open and gross lewdness. Ora argued that the statute was overbroad and unconstitutional, and a trial court agreed. On appeal, however, a state appellate court upheld the statute as constitutional in situations in which there was an unsuspecting or unwilling audience.[18] ◀

Laws That Restrict the Content of Speech. If a law regulates the content of the expression, it must serve a

compelling state interest and must be narrowly written to achieve that interest. Under the **compelling government interest** test, the government's interest is balanced against the individual's constitutional right to free expression. For the statute to be valid, there must be a compelling government interest that can be furthered only by the law in question.

The United States Supreme Court has held that schools may restrict students' speech at school events. ▶ **Case in Point 4.7**   Some high school students held up a banner saying "Bong Hits 4 Jesus" at an off-campus but school-sanctioned event. The Supreme Court ruled that the school did not violate the students' free speech rights when school officials confiscated the banner and suspended the students for ten days. Because the banner could reasonably be interpreted as promoting drugs, the Court concluded that the school's actions were justified. Several justices disagreed, however, noting that the majority's holding creates an exception that will allow schools to censor any student speech that mentions drugs.[19] ◀

At issue in the following case was an Indiana state law that barred most sex offenders from using social networking sites such as Facebook, instant messaging services such as Twitter, and chat programs that the offenders knew were accessible to minors. Was this law unconstitutional under the First Amendment?

---

18. *Commonwealth v. Ora,* 451 Mass. 125, 883 N.E.2d 1217 (2008).

19. *Morse v. Frederick,* 551 U.S. 393, 127 S.Ct. 2618, 168 L.Ed.2d 290 (2007).

CASE 4.2

Doe[a] v. Prosecutor, Marion County, Indiana
United States Court of Appeals, Seventh Circuit, 705 F.3d 694 (2013).

BACKGROUND AND FACTS   John Doe was convicted of child exploitation in Marion County, Indiana. After his release from prison, he was not subject to court supervision, but was required to register as a sex offender with the state. Under an Indiana statute that covered child exploitation and other sex offenses, Doe could not use certain Web sites and programs. Doe filed a suit in a federal district court against the Marion County prosecutor, alleging that the statute violated his right to freedom of speech under the First Amendment. Doe asked the court to issue an injunction to block enforcement of the law. The court held that "the regulation is narrowly tailored to serve a significant state interest" and entered a judgment for the defendant. Doe appealed to the U.S. Court of Appeals for the Seventh Circuit.

 IN THE LANGUAGE OF THE COURT
FLAUM, Circuit Judge.

* * * *

Indiana Code Section 35-42-4-12 prohibits certain sex offenders from "knowingly or intentionally using: a social networking Web site" or "an instant messaging or chat room program"

---

a.   The names *John Doe* and *Jane Doe* are used as placeholders in litigation to represent a party whose true identity is either unknown or being with held for some reason.

CASE 4.2 CONTINUED

that "the offender knows allows a person who is less than eighteen (18) years of age to access or use the Web site or program." The law applies broadly to all individuals required to register as sex offenders.

* * * *

This case presents a single legal question * * * . The statute clearly implicates Doe's First Amendment rights * * * . It not only precludes [prohibits] expression through the medium of social media, it also limits his right to receive information and ideas. The Indiana law, however, is content neutral because it restricts speech without reference to the expression's content. As such, it may impose reasonable time, place, or manner restrictions. To do so, the law * * * must be narrowly tailored to serve a significant governmental interest.

The state initially asserts an interest in "protecting public safety, and specifically in protecting minors from harmful online communications." Indiana is certainly justified in shielding its children from improper sexual communication.

* * * *

* * * The state agrees there is nothing dangerous about Doe's use of social media as long as he does not improperly communicate with minors. Further, there is no disagreement that illicit communication comprises a minuscule subset of the universe of social network activity. As such, *the Indiana law targets substantially more activity than the evil it seeks to redress.* * * * *Indiana has other methods to combat unwanted and inappropriate communication between minors and sex offenders.* For instance, [under Indiana Code Section 35-42-4-6] it is a felony in Indiana for persons over twenty-one to "solicit" children under sixteen "to engage in: (1) sexual intercourse; (2) deviate sexual conduct; or (3) any fondling intended to arouse or satisfy the sexual desires of either the child or the older person." A separate statute goes further. [Indiana Code Section 35-42-4-13] punishes mere "inappropriate communication with a child" and communication "with the intent to gratify the sexual desires of the person or the individual." Significantly, both statutes have enhanced penalties for using a computer network and better advance Indiana's interest in preventing harmful interaction with children (by going beyond social networks). They also accomplish that end more narrowly (by refusing to burden benign Internet activity). That is, they are neither over nor under-inclusive like the statute at issue here. [Emphasis added.]

* * * *

For the foregoing reasons, we REVERSE the district court's decision, and REMAND with instructions to enter judgment in favor of Doe and issue the injunction.

DECISION AND REMEDY *The U.S. Court of Appeals for the Seventh Circuit reversed the lower court's judgment in the defendant's favor and remanded the case for the entry of a judgment for Doe. A law that concerns rights under the First Amendment must be narrowly tailored to accomplish its objective. The blanket ban on social media in this case did not pass this test.*

THE LEGAL ENVIRONMENT DIMENSION *What is an injunction? What did the plaintiff in this case hope to gain by seeking an injunction?*

THE SOCIAL DIMENSION *Could a state effectively enforce a law that banned all communication between minors and sex offenders through social media sites? Why or why not?*

CORPORATE POLITICAL SPEECH Political speech by corporations also falls within the protection of the First Amendment. Many years ago, the United States Supreme Court struck down as unconstitutional a Massachusetts statute that prohibited corporations from making political contributions or expenditures that individuals were permitted to make.[20] The Court

has also held that a law forbidding a corporation from including inserts with its bills to express its views on controversial issues violates the First Amendment.[21]

Corporate political speech continues to be given significant protection under the First Amendment. ▶ **Case in Point 4.8** In *Citizens United v. Federal*

---

20. *First National Bank of Boston v. Bellotti,* 435 U.S. 765, 98 S.Ct. 1407, 55 L.Ed.2d 707 (1978).

21. *Consolidated Edison Co. v. Public Service Commission,* 447 U.S. 530, 100 S.Ct. 2326, 65 L.Ed.2d 319 (1980).

Election Commission,[22] the Supreme Court issued a landmark decision that overturned a twenty-year-old precedent on campaign financing. The case involved Citizens United, a nonprofit corporation that has a *political action committee* (an organization that registers with the government and campaigns for or against political candidates).

Citizens United had produced a film called *Hillary: The Movie* that was critical of Hillary Clinton, who was seeking the Democratic nomination for presidential candidate. Campaign-finance law restricted Citizens United from broadcasting the movie, however. The Court ruled that the restrictions were unconstitutional and that the First Amendment, prevents limits from being placed on independent political expenditures by corporations. ◄

COMMERCIAL SPEECH The courts also give substantial protection to *commercial speech,* which consists of communications—primarily advertising and marketing—made by business firms that involve only their commercial interests. The protection given to commercial speech under the First Amendment is less extensive than that afforded to noncommercial speech, however.

A state may restrict certain kinds of advertising, for instance, in the interest of preventing consumers from being misled. States also have a legitimate interest in roadside beautification and therefore may impose restraints on billboard advertising. ▶ **Case in Point 4.9** Café Erotica, a nude dancing establishment, sued the state after being denied a permit to erect a billboard along an interstate highway in Florida. The state appellate court decided that because the law directly advanced a substantial government interest in highway beautification and safety, it was not an unconstitutional restraint on commercial speech.[23] ◄

Generally, a restriction on commercial speech will be considered valid as long as it meets three criteria:

1. It must seek to implement a substantial government interest.
2. It must directly advance that interest.
3. It must go no further than necessary to accomplish its objective.

At issue in the following case was whether a government agency had unconstitutionally restricted commercial speech when it prohibited the inclusion of a certain illustration on beer labels.

---

22. 558 U.S. 310, 130 S.Ct. 876, 175 L.Ed.2d 753 (2010).

23. *Café Erotica v. Florida Department of Transportation,* 830 So.2d 181 (Fla.App. 1 Dist. 2002); review denied by *Café Erotica We Dare to Bare v. Florida Department of Transportation,* 845 So.2d 888 (Fla. 2003).

SP TLIGHT on Beer Labels

Case 4.3 Bad Frog Brewery, Inc. v. New York State Liquor Authority
United States Court of Appeals, Second Circuit, 134 F.3d 87 (1998).

BACKGROUND AND FACTS Bad Frog Brewery, Inc., makes and sells alcoholic beverages. Some of the beverages feature labels that display a drawing of a frog making the gesture generally known as "giving the finger." Bad Frog's authorized New York distributor, Renaissance Beer Company, applied to the New York State Liquor Authority (NYSLA) for brand label approval, as required by state law before the beer could be sold in New York.

The NYSLA denied the application, in part, because "the label could appear in grocery and convenience stores, with obvious exposure on the shelf to children of tender age." Bad Frog filed a suit in a federal district court against the NYSLA, asking for, among other things, an injunction against the denial of the application. The court granted summary judgment in favor of the NYSLA. Bad Frog appealed to the U.S. Court of Appeals for the Second Circuit.

IN THE LANGUAGE OF THE COURT
Jon O. *NEWMAN,* Circuit Judge:

★ ★ ★ ★

★ ★ ★ To support its asserted power to ban Bad Frog's labels [NYSLA advances] ★ ★ ★ the State's interest in "protecting children from vulgar and profane advertising" ★ ★ ★ .

CASE 4.3 CONTINUED

[This interest is] substantial * * * . *States have a compelling interest in protecting the physical and psychological wellbeing of minors * * * .* [Emphasis added.]

* * * *

* * * NYSLA endeavors to advance the state interest in preventing exposure of children to vulgar displays by taking only the limited step of barring such displays from the labels of alcoholic beverages. *In view of the wide currency of vulgar displays throughout contemporary society, including comic books targeted directly at children, barring such displays from labels for alcoholic beverages cannot realistically be expected to reduce children's exposure to such displays to any significant degree.* [Emphasis added.]

* * * If New York decides to make a substantial effort to insulate children from vulgar displays in some significant sphere of activity, at least with respect to materials likely to be seen by children, NYSLA's label prohibition might well be found to make a justifiable contribution to the material advancement of such an effort, but its currently isolated response to the perceived problem, applicable only to labels on a product that children cannot purchase, does not suffice. * * * A state must demonstrate that its commercial speech limitation is part of a substantial effort to advance a valid state interest, not merely the removal of a few grains of offensive sand from a beach of vulgarity.

* * * *

* * * Even if we were to assume that the state materially advances its asserted interest by shielding children from viewing the Bad Frog labels, it is plainly excessive to prohibit the labels from all use, including placement on bottles displayed in bars and taverns where parental supervision of children is to be expected. Moreover, to whatever extent NYSLA is concerned that children will be harmfully exposed to the Bad Frog labels when wandering without parental supervision around grocery and convenience stores where beer is sold, that concern could be less intrusively dealt with by placing restrictions on the permissible locations where the appellant's products may be displayed within such stores.

DECISION AND REMEDY *The U.S. Court of Appeals for the Second Circuit reversed the judgment of the district court and remanded the case for the entry of a judgment in favor of Bad Frog. The NYSLA's ban on the use of the labels lacked a "reasonable fit" with the state's interest in shielding minors from vulgarity. In addition, the NYSLA had not adequately considered alternatives to the ban.*

WHAT IF THE FACTS WERE DIFFERENT? *If Bad Frog had sought to use the offensive label to market toys instead of beer, would the court's ruling likely have been the same? Why or why not?*

THE LEGAL ENVIRONMENT DIMENSION *Whose interests are advanced by the banning of certain types of advertising?*

UNPROTECTED SPEECH The United States Supreme Court has made it clear that certain types of speech will not be protected under the First Amendment. Speech that violates criminal laws (threatening speech and pornography, for example) is not constitutionally protected. Other unprotected speech includes fighting words, or words that are likely to incite others to respond violently. Speech that harms the good reputation of another, or defamatory speech (see Chapter 6), also is not protected under the First Amendment.

Obscene Speech. The First Amendment, as interpreted by the Supreme Court, also does not protect obscene speech. Establishing an objective definition of obscene speech has proved difficult, however, and

the Court has grappled from time to time with this problem. In *Miller v. California,*[24] the Supreme Court created a test for legal obscenity, including a set of requirements that must be met for material to be legally obscene. Under this test, material is obscene if all of the following are true:

1. The average person finds that it violates contemporary community standards.
2. The work taken as a whole appeals to a prurient (arousing or obsessive) interest in sex.
3. The work shows patently offensive sexual conduct.
4. The work lacks serious redeeming literary, artistic, political, or scientific merit.

---

24. 413 U.S. 15, 93 S.Ct. 2607, 37 L.Ed.2d 419 (1973).

Because community standards vary widely, the *Miller* test has had inconsistent applications, and obscenity remains a constitutionally unsettled issue. Numerous state and federal statutes make it a crime to disseminate obscene materials, including child pornography.

Online Obscenity. Congress's first two attempts at protecting minors from pornographic materials on the Internet—the Communications Decency Act (CDA) of 1996[25] and the Child Online Protection Act (COPA) of 1998[26]—failed. Ultimately, the United States Supreme Court struck down both the CDA and COPA as unconstitutional restraints on speech, largely because the wording of these acts was overbroad and would restrict nonpornographic materials.

In 2000, Congress enacted the Children's Internet Protection Act (CIPA),[27] which requires public schools and libraries to install **filtering software** on computers to keep children from accessing adult content. Such software is designed to prevent persons from viewing certain Web sites based on a site's Internet address or its **meta tags,** or key words. The CIPA was challenged on constitutional grounds, but in 2003 the Supreme Court held that the act does not violate the First Amendment. The Court concluded that because libraries can disable the filters for any patrons who ask, the system is reasonably flexible and does not burden free speech to an unconstitutional extent.[28]

Virtual Pornography. In 2003, Congress enacted the Prosecutorial Remedies and Other Tools to end the Exploitation of Children Today Act (Protect Act).[29] The act makes it a crime to knowingly advertise, present, distribute, or solicit "any material or purported material in a manner that reflects the belief, or that is intended to cause another to believe, that the material or purported material" depicts actual child pornography.

Thus, it is a crime to intentionally distribute virtual child pornography—which uses computer-generated images, not actual people—without indicating that it is computer generated. In a case challenging the constitutionality of the Protect Act, the Supreme Court held that the statute was valid because it does not

prohibit a substantial amount of protected speech.[30] Rather, the act generally prohibits offers to provide, and requests to obtain, child pornography—both of which are unprotected speech. Nevertheless, because of the difficulties of policing the Internet, as well as the constitutional complexities of prohibiting online obscenity through legislation, it remains a problem worldwide.

Freedom of Religion

The First Amendment states that the government may neither establish any religion nor prohibit the free exercise of religious practices. The first part of this constitutional provision is referred to as the **establishment clause,** and the second part is known as the **free exercise clause.** Government action, both federal and state, must be consistent with this constitutional mandate.

THE ESTABLISHMENT CLAUSE The establishment clause prohibits the government from establishing a state-sponsored religion, as well as from passing laws that promote (aid or endorse) religion or show a preference for one religion over another. Although the establishment clause involves the separation of church and state, it does not require a complete separation.

Applicable Standard. Establishment clause cases often involve such issues as the legality of allowing or requiring school prayers, using state-issued vouchers to pay tuition at religious schools, and teaching creation theories versus evolution. Federal or state laws that do not promote or place a significant burden on religion are constitutional even if they have some impact on religion. For a government law or policy to be constitutional, it must not have the primary effect of promoting or inhibiting religion.

Religious Displays. Religious displays on public property have often been challenged as violating the establishment clause, and the United States Supreme Court has ruled on a number of such cases. Generally, the Court has focused on the proximity of the religious display to nonreligious symbols, such as reindeer and candy canes, or to symbols from different religions, such as a menorah (a nine-branched candelabrum used in celebrating Hanukkah). The Supreme Court

25. 47 U.S.C. Section 223(a)(1)(B)(ii).

26. 47 U.S.C. Section 231.

27. 17 U.S.C. Sections 1701–1741.

28. *United States v. American Library Association,* 539 U.S. 194, 123 S.Ct. 2297, 156 L.Ed.2d 221 (2003).

29. 18 U.S.C. Section 2252A(a)(5)(B).

30. *United States v. Williams,* 553 U.S. 285, 128 S.Ct. 1830, 170 L.Ed.2d 650 (2008).

took a slightly different approach when it held that public displays having historical, as well as religious, significance do not necessarily violate the establishment clause.[31]

▶ **Case in Point 4.10** Mount Soledad is a prominent hill near San Diego. There has been a forty-foot cross on top of Mount Soledad since 1913. In the 1990s, a war memorial with six walls listing the names of veterans was constructed next to the cross. The site was privately owned until 2006, when Congress authorized the property's transfer to the federal government "to preserve a historically significant war memorial."

Steve Trunk and the Jewish War Veterans filed lawsuits claiming that the cross violated the establishment clause because it endorsed the Christian religion. A federal appellate court agreed, finding that the primary effect of the memorial as a whole sent a strong message of endorsement of Christianity and exclusion (of non-Christian veterans). Although the inclusion of a cross in a war memorial does not always violate the establishment clause, the cross in this case physically dominated the site. Also, the cross was originally dedicated to religious purposes, had a long history of religious use, and was the only portion visible to drivers on the freeway below.[32] ◀

THE FREE EXERCISE CLAUSE The free exercise clause guarantees that a person can hold any religious belief that she or he wants, or a person can have no religious belief. The constitutional guarantee of personal freedom restricts only the actions of the government and not those of individuals or private businesses.

Restrictions Must Be Necessary. The government must have a compelling state interest for restricting the free exercise of religion, and the restriction must be the only way to further that interest. ▶ **Case in Point 4.11** Members of a particular Mennonite church must use horses and buggies for transportation, but they can use tractors to take their agricultural products to market. Their religion requires the tractors to have steel cleats on the tires, and they drove tractors with cleats on county roads for many years. Then the county passed an ordinance that prohibited the use of steel cleats because the cleats tend to damage newly surfaced roads.

When a member of the church received a citation for driving a tractor with cleats, he claimed that the ordinance violated the church's right to freely exercise its religion. Ultimately, the court ruled in his favor. The county had not met its burden of showing that the ordinance served a compelling state interest and was the least restrictive means of attaining that interest. There was no evidence of how much the cleats harmed the roads, other events also harmed the roads, and the county had allowed the cleats to be used for many years. Therefore, the ordinance was not carefully tailored to achieve the stated objective of road preservation.[33] ◀

Public Welfare Exception. When religious *practices* work against public policy and the public welfare, though, the government can act. For instance, the government can require that a child receive certain types of vaccinations or medical treatment if his or her life is in danger—regardless of the child's or parent's religious beliefs. When public safety is an issue, an individual's religious beliefs often have to give way to the government's interest in protecting the public.

▶ **Example 4.12** In the Muslim faith, it is a religious violation for a woman to appear in public without a scarf over her head. Due to public safety concerns, many courts today do not allow any headgear to be worn in courtrooms. A courthouse in Georgia prevented a Muslim woman from entering because she refused to remove her scarf. As she left, she uttered an expletive at the court official and was arrested and brought before the judge, who ordered her to serve ten days in jail. ◀

Searches and Seizures

The Fourth Amendment protects the "right of the people to be secure in their persons, houses, papers, and effects." Before searching or seizing private property, law enforcement officers must usually obtain a **search warrant**—an order from a judge or other public official authorizing the search or seizure.

SEARCH WARRANTS AND PROBABLE CAUSE To obtain a search warrant, law enforcement officers must convince a judge that they have reasonable grounds, or probable cause, to believe a search will reveal evidence of a specific illegality. To establish **probable cause,** the officers must have trustworthy evidence that would convince a reasonable person that the proposed search or seizure is more likely justified than not.

---

31. *Van Orden v. Perry,* 545 U.S. 677, 125 S.Ct. 2854, 162 L.Ed.2d 607 (2005).
32. *Trunk v. City of San Diego,* 629 F.3d 1099 (9th Cir. 2011).
33. *Mitchell County v. Zimmerman,* 810 N.W.2d 1 (Iowa Sup.Ct. 2012).

Furthermore, the Fourth Amendment prohibits *general* warrants. It requires warrants to include a particular description of whatever is to be searched or seized. General searches through a person's belongings are impermissible. The search cannot extend beyond what is described in the warrant. Although search warrants must be specific, if a warrant is issued for a person's residence, officers may search items found in that residence even though they belong to other individuals.

▶ **Case in Point 4.13** Paycom Billing Services, Inc., an online payment service, stores vast amounts of customer credit-card information. Christopher Adjani, a former Paycom employee, threatened to sell Paycom's confidential client information if the company did not pay him $3 million. Pursuant to an investigation, the Federal Bureau of Investigation (FBI) obtained a search warrant to search Adjani's person, automobile, and residence, including computer equipment. When the FBI agents served the warrant, they discovered evidence of the criminal scheme in the e-mail communications on a computer in Adjani's residence that belonged to Adjani's live-in girlfriend. The court held that the search of the computer was proper given the involvement of computers in the alleged crime.[34] ◀

SEARCHES AND SEIZURES IN THE BUSINESS CONTEXT

Because of the strong government interest in protecting the public, a warrant normally is not required for seizures of spoiled or contaminated food. Nor are warrants required for searches of businesses in such highly regulated industries as liquor, guns, and strip mining.

The standard used for highly regulated industries is sometimes applied in other contexts as well, such as screening for airline travel. ▶ **Case in Point 4.14** Christian Hartwell was attempting to board a flight from Philadelphia to Phoenix, Arizona. When he walked through the security checkpoint, he set off the alarm. Airport security took him aside and eventually discovered that he had two packages of crack cocaine in his pocket. When Hartwell was convicted of possession of drugs, he appealed, claiming that the airport search was suspicionless and violated his Fourth Amendment rights. A federal appellate court held that airports can be treated as highly regulated industries and that suspicionless checkpoint screening of airline passengers is constitutional.[35] ◀

---

34. *United States v. Adjani*, 452 F.3d 1140 (9th Cir. 2006); *cert.* denied, 549 U.S. 1025, 127 S.Ct. 568, 166 L.Ed.2d 420 (2006).
35. *United States v. Hartwell*, 436 F.3d 174 (3d Cir. 2006).

Generally, however, government inspectors do not have the right to enter business premises without a warrant, although the standard of probable cause is not the same as that required in nonbusiness contexts. The existence of a general and neutral enforcement plan will normally justify issuance of the warrant. Lawyers and accountants frequently possess the business records of their clients, and inspecting these documents while they are out of the hands of their true owners also requires a warrant.

Self-Incrimination

The Fifth Amendment guarantees that no person "shall be compelled in any criminal case to be a witness against himself." Thus, in any court proceeding, an accused person cannot be forced to give testimony that might subject him or her to any criminal prosecution. The guarantee applies to both federal and state proceedings because the due process clause of the Fourteenth Amendment extends the protection to state courts.

The Fifth Amendment's guarantee against self-incrimination extends only to natural persons. Therefore, neither corporations nor partnerships receive Fifth Amendment protection. When a partnership is required to produce business records, it must do so even if the information provided incriminates the individual partners of the firm. In contrast, sole proprietors and sole practitioners (those who fully own their businesses) cannot be compelled to produce their business records. These individuals have full protection against self-incrimination because they function in only one capacity, and there is no separate business entity.

SECTION 3

DUE PROCESS AND EQUAL PROTECTION

Other constitutional guarantees of great significance to Americans are mandated by the *due process clauses* of the Fifth and Fourteenth Amendments and the *equal protection clause* of the Fourteenth Amendment.

Due Process

Both the Fifth and Fourteenth Amendments provide that no person shall be deprived "of life, liberty, or property, without due process of law." The **due** process clause** of these constitutional amendments has two aspects—procedural and substantive. Note that the due process clause applies to "legal persons" (that is, corporations), as well as to individuals.

PROCEDURAL DUE PROCESS *Procedural* due process requires that any government decision to take life, liberty, or property must be made equitably. In other words, the government must give a person proper notice and an opportunity to be heard. Fair procedures must be used in determining whether a person will be subjected to punishment or have some burden imposed on her or him.

Fair procedure has been interpreted as requiring that the person have at least an opportunity to object to a proposed action before an impartial, neutral decision maker (which need not be a judge). ▶ **Example 4.15**   Doyle Burns, a nursing student in Kansas, poses for a photograph standing next to a placenta used as a lab specimen. Although she quickly deletes the photo from her library, it ends up on Facebook. When the director of nursing sees the photo, Burns is expelled. She sues for reinstatement and wins. The school violated Burns's due process rights by expelling her from the nursing program for taking a photo without giving her an opportunity to present her side to school authorities. ◀

SUBSTANTIVE DUE PROCESS *Substantive* due process focuses on the content of legislation rather than the fairness of procedures. Substantive due process limits what the government may do in its legislative and executive capacities. Legislation must be fair and reasonable in content and must further a legitimate governmental objective. A city cannot, for instance, pass an ordinance that allows police officers to break up any group of two or more persons who are standing together if one of those persons is believed to be a gang member.

If a law or other governmental action limits a fundamental right, the state must have a legitimate and compelling interest to justify its action. Fundamental rights include interstate travel, privacy, voting, marriage and family, and all First Amendment rights. Thus, a state must have a substantial reason for taking any action that infringes on a person's free speech rights.

In situations not involving fundamental rights, a law or action does not violate substantive due process if it rationally relates to any legitimate government purpose. In these circumstances, only state conduct that is arbitrary or shocks the conscience will violate

substantive due process. Under this test, almost any business regulation will be upheld as reasonable.

Equal Protection

Under the Fourteenth Amendment, a state may not "deny to any person within its jurisdiction the equal protection of the laws." The United States Supreme Court has interpreted the due process clause of the Fifth Amendment to make the **equal protection clause** applicable to the federal government as well. Equal protection means that the government cannot enact laws that treat similarly situated individuals differently.

Equal protection, like substantive due process, relates to the substance of a law or other governmental action. When a law or action limits the liberty of *all* persons, it may violate substantive due process. When a law or action limits the liberty of *some* persons but not others, it may violate the equal protection clause. ▶ **Example 4.16**   If a law prohibits all persons from buying contraceptive devices, it raises a substantive due process question. If it prohibits only unmarried persons from buying the same devices, it raises an equal protection issue. ◀

In an equal protection inquiry, when a law or action distinguishes between or among individuals, the basis for the distinction—that is, its classification—is examined. Depending on the classification, the courts apply different levels of scrutiny, or "tests," to determine whether the law or action violates the equal protection clause. The courts use one of three standards: strict scrutiny, intermediate scrutiny, or the "rational basis" test.

STRICT SCRUTINY If a law or action prohibits or inhibits some persons from exercising a fundamental right, the law or action will be subject to "strict scrutiny" by the courts. Under this standard, the classification must be necessary to promote a *compelling state interest.* Also, if the classification is based on a *suspect trait*—such as race, national origin, or citizenship status—it must be necessary to promote a compelling government interest.[36]

Compelling state interests include remedying past unconstitutional or illegal discrimination but do not include correcting the general effects of "society's discrimination." ▶ **Example 4.17**   For a city to give preference to minority applicants in awarding con-

---

36. See *Johnson v. California,* 543 U.S. 499, 125 S.Ct. 1141, 160 L.Ed.2d 949 (2005).

struction contracts, it normally must identify past unconstitutional or illegal discrimination against minority construction firms. Because the policy is based on suspect traits (race and national origin), it will violate the equal protection clause *unless* it is necessary to promote a compelling state interest. ◄ Generally, few laws or actions survive strict-scrutiny analysis by the courts.

INTERMEDIATE SCRUTINY A higher standard, that of *intermediate scrutiny,* is applied in cases involving discrimination based on gender or discrimination against illegitimate children (children born out of wedlock). Laws using these classifications must be *substantially related to important government objectives.* For instance, an important government objective is preventing illegitimate teenage pregnancies. Because males and females are not similarly situated in this regard, a law that punishes men but not women for statutory rape will be upheld, even though it treats men and women unequally.

The state also has an important objective in establishing time limits (called *statutes of limitation*) for how long after an event a particular type of action can be brought. Nevertheless, the limitation period must be substantially related to the important objective of preventing fraudulent or outdated claims. ► **Example 4.18** A state law requires illegitimate children to bring paternity suits within six years of their births in order to seek support from their fathers. A court will strike down this law if legitimate children are allowed to seek support from their parents at any time. Distinguishing between support claims on the basis of legitimacy is not related to the important government objective of preventing fraudulent or outdated claims. ◄

THE "RATIONAL BASIS" TEST In matters of economic or social welfare, a classification will be considered valid if there is any conceivable *rational basis* on which the classification might relate to a legitimate government interest. It is almost impossible for a law or action to fail the rational basis test. ► **Example 4.19** A city ordinance prohibits all pushcart vendors, except a specific few, from operating in a particular area of the city. It will be upheld under the equal protection clause if the city provides a rational basis—such as reducing the traffic in the particular area—for the ordinance. ◄ In contrast, a law that provides unemployment benefits only to people over six feet tall would clearly fail the rational

basis test because it could not further any legitimate government objective.

SECTION 4
PRIVACY RIGHTS

The U.S. Constitution does not explicitly mention a general right to privacy. In a 1928 Supreme Court case, *Olmstead v. United States,*[37] Justice Louis Brandeis stated in his dissent that the right to privacy is "the most comprehensive of rights and the right most valued by civilized men." The majority of the justices at that time, however, did not agree with Brandeis.

It was not until the 1960s that the Supreme Court endorsed the view that the Constitution protects individual privacy rights. In a landmark 1965 case, *Griswold v. Connecticut,*[38] the Supreme Court held that a constitutional right to privacy was implied by the First, Third, Fourth, Fifth, and Ninth Amendments.

Federal Statutes Affecting Privacy Rights

In the 1960s, Americans were sufficiently alarmed by the accumulation of personal information in government files that they pressured Congress to pass laws permitting individuals to access their files. Congress responded in 1966 with the Freedom of Information Act, which allows any person to request copies of any information on her or him contained in federal government files.

In 1974, Congress passed the Privacy Act, which also gives persons the right to access such information. Since then, Congress has passed numerous other laws protecting individuals' privacy rights with respect to financial transactions, electronic communications, and other activities in which personal information may be gathered and stored by organizations.

Since the 1990s, one of the major concerns of individuals has been how to protect privacy rights in cyberspace and to safeguard private information that may be revealed online. The increasing value of personal information for online marketers has exacerbated the situation. Chapter 9 discusses online privacy in more detail.

PRETEXTING A *pretext* is a false motive put forth to hide the real motive, and *pretexting* is the process of

---

37. 277 U.S. 438, 48 S.Ct. 564, 72 L.Ed. 944 (1928).
38. 381 U.S. 479, 85 S.Ct. 1678, 14 L.Ed.2d 510 (1965).

obtaining information by false means. Pretexters may try to obtain personal data by claiming that they are taking a survey for a research firm, a political party, or even a charity. The Gramm-Leach-Bliley Act[39] makes pretexting to obtain financial information illegal, but it does not mention lying to obtain *nonfinancial* information (for purposes other than identity theft).

▶ **Example 4.20** To find out who had leaked confidential company information to the press, Patricia C. Dunn, the chair of Hewlett-Packard, hired private investigators. They used false pretenses to access individuals' personal cell phone records. Dunn claimed that she had not been aware of the investigators' methods and had assumed that they had obtained the information from a public record. Criminal charges were filed but later dropped. Nevertheless, the scandal was highly publicized, and several civil lawsuits followed. Hewlett-Packard wound up paying millions to settle these lawsuits, including $14.5 million in fines to settle a claim filed by the California attorney general. ◀

To clarify the law on pretexting to gain access to phone records, Congress enacted the Telephone Records and Privacy Protection Act.[40] This act makes it a federal crime to pretend to be someone else or to make false representations for the purpose of obtaining another person's confidential phone records. The Federal Trade Commission investigates and prosecutes violators, who can be fined and sentenced to up to ten years in prison.

MEDICAL INFORMATION Responding to the growing need to protect the privacy of individuals' health records—particularly computerized records—Congress passed the Health Insurance Portability and Accountability Act (HIPAA).[41] This act defines and limits the circumstances in which an individual's "protected health information" may be used or disclosed.

HIPAA also requires health-care providers and health-care plans, including certain employers who sponsor health plans, to inform patients of their privacy rights and of how their personal medical information may be used. The act also states that a person's medical records generally may not be used for purposes unrelated to health care—such as marketing,

for example—or disclosed to others without the individual's permission. Congress later expanded HIPAA's provisions to apply to vendors (those who maintain personal health records for health-care providers) and to electronic records shared by multiple medical providers. Congress also authorized the Federal Trade Commission to enforce HIPAA and pursue violators.

THE USA PATRIOT ACT The USA Patriot Act was passed by Congress in the wake of the terrorist attacks of September 11, 2001, and then reauthorized in 2006.[42] The Patriot Act has given government officials increased authority to monitor Internet activities (such as e-mail and Web site visits) and to gain access to personal financial information and student information. Law enforcement officials can now track the telephone and e-mail communications of one party to find out the identity of the other party or parties. Privacy advocates argue that this law adversely affects the constitutional rights of all Americans, and it has been widely criticized in the media.

To gain access to these communications, the government must certify that the information likely to be obtained by such monitoring is relevant to an ongoing criminal investigation. The government need not provide proof of any wrongdoing.[43]

▶ **Example 4.21** In 2012, General David Petraeus, who ran the wars in Iraq and Afghanistan, resigned as director of the Central Intelligence Agency after his extramarital affair with Paula Broadwell, his biographer, became public. Apparently, after Petraeus broke off the affair with Broadwell, she sent harassing e-mails to another woman. When she reported the harassment, the FBI investigated, accessed Petraeus's e-mail accounts, and discovered that he had communicated with Broadwell via messages left in a draft folder on his e-mail account. Although there was no evidence that Petraeus did anything illegal, he was urged to resign and did so. ◀

Other Laws Affecting Privacy

State constitutions and statutes also protect individuals' privacy rights, often to a significant degree. Privacy rights are also protected to some extent under

39. Also known as the Financial Services Modernization Act, Pub. L. No. 106-102 (1999), 113 Stat. 1338, codified in numerous sections of 12 U.S.C.A.
40. 18 U.S.C. Section 1039.
41. HIPAA was enacted as Pub. L. No. 104-191 (1996) and is codified in 29 U.S.C.A. Sections 1181 *et seq.*

42. The Uniting and Strengthening America by Providing Appropriate Tools Required to Intercept and Obstruct Terrorism Act of 2001, also known as the USA Patriot Act, was enacted as Pub. L. No. 107-56 (2001) and reauthorized by Pub. L. No. 109-173 (2006).
43. See, for example, *American Civil Liberties Union v. National Security Agency*, 493 F.3d 644 (6th Cir. 2007), in which a federal appeals court upheld the government's warrantless monitoring of electronic communications.

tort law (see Chapter 6), Internet law (see Chapter 9), and employment law. Additionally, the Federal Trade Commission has played an active role in protecting the privacy rights of online consumers.

Reviewing: Business and the Constitution

A state legislature enacted a statute that required any motorcycle operator or passenger on the state's highways to wear a protective helmet. Jim Alderman, a licensed motorcycle operator, sued the state to block enforcement of the law. Alderman asserted that the statute violated the equal protection clause because it placed requirements on motorcyclists that were not imposed on other motorists. Using the information presented in the chapter, answer the following questions.

1. Why does this statute raise equal protection issues instead of substantive due process concerns?
2. What are the three levels of scrutiny that the courts use in determining whether a law violates the equal protection clause?
3. Which standard of scrutiny, or test, would apply to this situation? Why?
4. Applying this standard, or test, is the helmet statute constitutional? Why or why not?

DEBATE THIS ... *Legislation aimed at "protecting people from themselves" concerns the individual as well as the public in general. Protective helmet laws are just one example of such legislation. Should individuals be allowed to engage in unsafe activities if they choose to do so?*

Terms and Concepts

Bill of Rights 79
checks and balances 75
commerce clause 76
compelling government interest 82
due process clause 89
equal protection clause 89
establishment clause 86

federal form of government 74
filtering software 86
free exercise clause 86
full faith and credit clause 75
meta tags 86
police powers 74
preemption 79

privileges and immunities clause 75
probable cause 87
search warrant 87
sovereignty 77
supremacy clause 78
symbolic speech 80

ExamPrep

Issue Spotters

1. Can a state, in the interest of energy conservation, ban all advertising by power utilities if conservation could be accomplished by less restrictive means? Why or why not? **(See page 84.)**
2. Suppose that a state imposes a higher tax on out-of-state companies doing business in the state than it imposes on in-state companies. Is this a violation of equal protection if the only reason for the tax is to protect the local firms from out-of-state competition? Explain. **(See page 77.)**

• Check your answers to the Issue Spotters against the answers provided in Appendix E at the end of this text.

Before the Test

Go to **www.cengagebrain.com**, enter the ISBN 9781285185248, and click on "Find" to locate this textbook's Web site. Then, click on "Access Now" under "Study Tools," and select Chapter 4 at the top. There, you will find a Practice Quiz that you can take to assess your mastery of the concepts in this chapter, as well as Flashcards and a Glossary of important terms.

Business Scenarios

4–1. Commerce Clause. A Georgia state law requires the use of contoured rear-fender mudguards on trucks and trailers operating within Georgia state lines. The statute further makes it illegal for trucks and trailers to use straight mudguards. In approximately thirty-five other states, straight mudguards are legal. Moreover, in Florida, straight mudguards are explicitly required by law. There is some evidence suggesting that contoured mudguards might be a little safer than straight mudguards. Discuss whether this Georgia statute violates any constitutional provisions. **(See page 76.)**

4–2. Freedom of Religion. Thomas worked in the nonmilitary operations of a large firm that produced both military and nonmilitary goods. When the company discontinued the production of nonmilitary goods, Thomas was transferred to a plant producing military equipment. Thomas left his job, claiming that it violated his religious principles to participate in the manufacture of goods to be used in destroying life. In effect, he argued, the transfer to the military equipment plant forced him to quit his job. He was denied unemployment compensation by the state because he had not been effectively "discharged" by the employer but had voluntarily terminated his employment. Did the state's denial of unemployment benefits to Thomas violate the free exercise clause of the First Amendment? Explain. **(See page 86.)**

4–3. Equal Protection. With the objectives of preventing crime, maintaining property values, and preserving the quality of urban life, New York City enacted an ordinance to regulate the locations of commercial establishments that featured adult entertainment. The ordinance expressly applied to female, but not male, topless entertainment. Adele Buzzetti owned the Cozy Cabin, a New York City cabaret that featured female topless dancers. Buzzetti and an anonymous dancer filed a suit in a federal district court against the city, asking the court to block the enforcement of the ordinance. The plaintiffs argued, in part, that the ordinance violated the equal protection clause. Under the equal protection clause, what standard applies to the court's consideration of this ordinance? Under this test, how should the court rule? Why? **(See page 89.)**

Business Case Problems

4–4. Spotlight on Plagiarism—Due Process. The Russ College of

Engineering and Technology of Ohio University announced in a press conference that it had found "rampant and flagrant plagiarism" in the theses of mechanical engineering graduate students. Faculty singled out for "ignoring their ethical responsibilities" included Jay Gunasekera, chair of the department. Gunasekera was prohibited from advising students. He filed a suit against Dennis Irwin, the dean of Russ College, for violating his due process rights. What does due process require in these circumstances? Why? [*Gunasekera v. Irwin,* 551 F.3d 461 (6th Cir. 2009)] **(See page 88.)**

4–5. Commerce Clause. Under the federal Sex Offender Registration and Notification Act (SORNA), sex offenders must register and update their registration as sex offenders when they travel from one state to another. David Hall, a convicted sex offender in New York, moved to Virginia, where he did not update his registration. He was charged with violating SORNA. He claimed that the statute is unconstitutional, arguing that Congress cannot criminalize interstate travel if no commerce is involved. Is that reasonable? Why or why not? [*United States v. Guzman,* 591 F.3d 83 (2d Cir. 2010)] **(See page 76.)**

4–6. BUSINESS CASE PROBLEM WITH SAMPLE ANSWER: Establishment Clause.

Judge James DeWeese hung a poster in his courtroom showing the Ten Commandments. The American Civil Liberties Union (ACLU) filed a suit, alleging that the poster violated the estab-lishment clause. DeWeese responded that his purpose was not to promote religion but to express his view about "warring" legal philosophies—moral relativism and moral absolutism. "Our legal system is based on moral absolutes from divine law handed down by God through the Ten Commandments." Does this poster violate the establishment clause? Why or why not? [American Civil Liberties Union of Ohio Foundation, Inc. v. DeWeese, 633 F.3d 424 (6th Cir. 2011)] **(See page 86.)**

- **For a sample answer to Problem 4–6, go to Appendix F at the end of this text.**

4–7. The Dormant Commerce Clause. In 2001, Puerto Rico enacted a law that requires specific labels on cement sold in Puerto Rico and imposes fines for any violations of these requirements. The law prohibits the sale or distribution of cement manufactured outside Puerto Rico that does not carry a required label warning that the cement may not be used in government-financed construction projects. Antilles Cement Corp., a Puerto Rican firm that imports foreign cement, filed a complaint in federal court, claiming that this law violated the dormant commerce clause. (The dormant commerce clause doctrine applies not only to commerce among the states and U.S. territories, but also to international commerce.) Did the 2001 Puerto Rican law violate the dormant commerce clause? Why or why not? [*Antilles Cement Corp. v. Fortuno,* 670 F.3d 310 (1st Cir. 2012)] **(See page 77.)**

4–8. Freedom of Speech. Mark Wooden sent an e-mail to an alderwoman for the city of St. Louis. Attached was a nineteen-minute audio file that compared her to the biblical character Jezebel. The audio said she was a "bitch in the Sixth Ward," spending too much time with the rich and powerful and too little time with the poor. In a menacing, maniacal tone, Wooden said that he was "dusting off a sawed-off shotgun," called himself a "domestic terrorist," and referred to the assassination of President John Kennedy, the murder of federal judge John Roll, and the shooting of Representative Gabrielle Giffords. Feeling threatened, the alderwoman called the police. Wooden was convicted of harassment under a state criminal statute. Was this conviction unconstitutional under the First Amendment? Discuss. [*State v. Wooden*, 388 S.W.3d 522 (Mo. 2013)] **(See page 80.)**

4–9. A QUESTION OF ETHICS: Defamation.

 Aric Toll owns and manages the Balboa Island Village Inn, a restaurant and bar in Newport Beach, California. Anne Lemen lives across from the inn. Lemen complained to the authorities about the inn's customers, whom she called "drunks" and "whores." She referred to Aric's wife as "Madam Whore" and told neighbors that the owners were involved in illegal drugs and prostitution. Lemen told the inn's bartender Ewa Cook that Cook "worked for Satan." She repeated her statements to potential customers, and the inn's sales dropped more than 20 percent. The inn filed a suit against Lemen. [Balboa Island Village Inn, Inc. v. Lemen, 40 Cal.4th 1141, 156 P.3d 339 (2007)] **(See page 85.)**

(a) Are Lemen's statements about the inn's owners, customers, and activities protected by the U.S. Constitution? Should such statements be protected? In whose favor should the court rule? Why?

(b) Did Lemen behave unethically in the circumstances of this case? Explain.

Legal Reasoning Group Activity

4–10. Free Speech and Equal Protection. For many years, New York City has had to deal with the vandalism and defacement of public property caused by unauthorized graffiti. In an effort to stop the damage, the city banned the sale of aerosol spray-paint cans and broad-tipped indelible markers to persons under twenty-one years of age. The new rules also prohibited people from possessing these items on property other than their own. Within a year, five people under age twenty-one were cited for violations of these regulations, and 871 individuals were arrested for actually making graffiti.

Lindsey Vincenty and other artists wished to create graffiti on legal surfaces, such as canvas, wood, and clothing. Unable to buy her supplies in the city or to carry them in the city if she bought them elsewhere, Vincenty and others filed a lawsuit on behalf of themselves and other young artists against Michael Bloomberg, the city's mayor, and others. The plaintiffs claimed that, among other things, the new rules violated their right to freedom of speech.

(a) One group will argue in favor of the plaintiffs and provide several reasons why the court should hold that the city's new rules violate the plaintiffs' freedom of speech. **(See page 80.)**

(b) Another group will develop a counterargument that outlines the reasons why the new rules do not violate free speech rights. **(See page 80.)**

(c) A third group will argue that the city's ban violates the equal protection clause because it applies only to persons under age twenty-one. **(See page 89.)**

CHAPTER 5

BUSINESS ETHICS

One of the most complex issues businesspersons and corporations face is ethics. It is not as well defined as the law, and yet it can have tremendous impacts on a firm's finances and reputation. Consider, for instance, the experience of the Chick-fil-A restaurant chain in 2012 when its chief operating officer made several statements about the company's commitment to supporting traditional marriage.

After those comments were made, it became public knowledge that Chick-fil-A had made donations to Christian organizations perceived to be opposed to same-sex marriage. Opponents of same-sex marriage held support rallies and Chick-fil-A appreciation days. Supporters of same-sex marriage held "kiss-ins" at local Chick-fil-A restaurants. Some politicians denounced Chick-fil-A's position and said that they would block expansion of the company in their cities. Eventually, Chick-fil-A issued a statement saying that it had ceased donations to any organization that promotes discrimination in any way. Chick-fil-A no longer sponsors charities that discriminate against same-sex couples or those who identify as gay, lesbian, bisexual, or transgendered.

Chick-fil-A was not accused of violating any laws, but its actions raised questions about the role of corporations and the effect of corporate ethics on profit. This chapter addresses some of those same questions. First, we look at business ethics—its definitions, its importance, and its relationship to the law. Next, we examine the philosophical bases for making ethical decisions. Finally, we discuss the application of business ethics to global situations.

SECTION 1
BUSINESS ETHICS

At the most basic level, the study of **ethics** is the study of what constitutes right or wrong behavior. It is a branch of philosophy focusing on morality and the way moral principles are derived and implemented. Ethics has to do with the fairness, justness, rightness, or wrongness of an action.

The study of **business ethics** typically looks at the decisions businesses make or have to make and whether those decisions are right or wrong. It has to do with how businesspersons apply moral and ethical principles in making their decisions. Those who study business ethics also evaluate what duties and responsibilities exist or should exist for businesses.

At the end of every unit in this book, we present a series of ethical issues in features called *Focus on Ethics*. In each of these features, we expand on the concepts of business ethics discussed in this chapter.

Why Is Studying Business Ethics Important?

Over the last two hundred years, the public perception of the corporation has changed from an entity that primarily generates revenues for its owners to an entity that participates in society as a corporate citizen. Originally, the only goal or duty of a corporation was to maximize profits. Although many people today may view this idea as greedy or inhumane, the rationale for the profit-maximization theory is still valid.

PROFIT MAXIMIZATION In theory, if all firms strictly adhere to the goal of profit maximization, resources flow to where they are most highly valued by society. Corporations can focus on their strengths, and other entities that are better suited to deal with social problems and perform charitable acts can specialize in those activities. The government, through taxes and other financial allocations, can shift resources to those other entities to perform public services. Thus, in an ideal world, profit maximization leads to the most efficient allocation of scarce resources.

THE RISE OF CORPORATE CITIZENSHIP Over the years, as resources were not sufficiently reallocated to cover the costs of social needs, many people became dissatisfied with the profit-maximization theory. Investors and others began to look beyond profits and dividends and to consider the **triple bottom line**—a corporation's profits, its impact on people, and its impact on the planet. Magazines and Web sites began to rank companies based on their environmental impacts and their ethical decisions. The corporation came to be viewed as a "citizen" that was expected to participate in bettering communities and society.

Even so, many still believe that corporations are fundamentally money-making entities that should have no responsibility other than profit maximization.

The Importance of Ethics in Making Business Decisions

Whether one believes in the profit-maximization theory or corporate citizenship, ethics is important in making business decisions. Corporations should strive to be "good citizens." When making decisions, a business should evaluate:

1. The legal implications of each decision.
2. The public relations impact.
3. The safety risks for consumers and employees.
4. The financial implications.

This analysis will assist the firm in making decisions that not only maximize profits but also reflect good corporate citizenship.

LONG-RUN PROFIT MAXIMIZATION In attempting to maximize profits, however, corporate executives and employees have to distinguish between *short-run* and *long-run* profit maximization. In the short run, a company may increase its profits by continuing to sell a product, even though it knows that the product is defective. In the long run, though, because of lawsuits, large settlements, and bad publicity, such unethical conduct will cause profits to suffer. Thus, business ethics is consistent only with long-run profit maximization. An overemphasis on short-term profit maximization is the most common reason that ethical problems occur in business.

▶ **Case in Point 5.1** When the powerful narcotic painkiller OxyContin was first marketed, its manufacturer, Purdue Pharma, claimed that it was unlikely to lead to drug addiction or abuse. Internal company documents later showed that the company's executives knew that OxyContin could be addictive, but kept this risk a secret to boost sales and maximize short-term profits.

Subsequently, Purdue Pharma and three former executives pleaded guilty to criminal charges that they misled regulators, patients, and physicians about OxyContin's risks of addiction. Purdue Pharma agreed to pay $600 million in fines and other payments. The three former executives agreed to pay $34.5 million in fines and were barred from federal health programs for a period of fifteen years. Thus, the company's focus on maximizing profits in the short run led to unethical conduct that hurt profits in the long run.[1] ◀

THE INTERNET CAN RUIN REPUTATIONS In the past, negative information or opinions about a company might remain hidden. Now, however, cyberspace provides a forum where disgruntled employees, unhappy consumers, or special interest groups can post derogatory remarks. Thus, the Internet has increased the potential for a major corporation (or other business) to suffer damage to its reputation or loss of profits through negative publicity.

Wal-Mart and Nike in particular have been frequent targets for advocacy groups that believe that those corporations exploit their workers. Although some of these assertions may be unfounded or exaggerated, the courts generally have refused to consider them *defamatory* (the tort of defamation will be discussed in Chapter 6). Most courts regard online attacks as simply the expression of opinion and therefore a form of speech protected by the First Amendment. Even so, corporations often incur considerable expense in running marketing campaigns to thwart bad publicity and may even face legal costs (if the complaint leads to litigation).

IMAGE IS EVERYTHING The study of business ethics is concerned with the purposes of a business and how that business achieves those purposes. Thus, business ethics is concerned with the image of the business and the impacts that the business has on the environment, customers, suppliers, employees, and the global economy.

Unethical corporate decision making can negatively affect suppliers, consumers, the community, and society as a whole. It can also have a negative impact on the reputation of the company and the

---

1. *United States v. Purdue Frederick Co.,* 495 F.Supp.2d 569 (W.D.Va. 2007).

individuals who run that company. Hence, an in-depth understanding of business ethics is important to the long-run viability of any corporation today.

The Relationship of Law and Ethics

Because the law does not codify all ethical requirements of all persons, compliance with the law is not always sufficient to determine "right" behavior. Laws have to be general enough to apply in a variety of circumstances. Laws are broad in their purpose and their scope. They prohibit or require certain actions to avoid significant harm to society.

When two competing companies secretly agree to set prices on products, for instance, society suffers harm—typically, the companies will charge higher prices than they could if they continued to compete. This harm inflicted on consumers has negative consequences for the economy, and so colluding to set prices is an illegal activity. Similarly, when a company is preparing to issue stock, the law requires certain disclosures to potential investors. This requirement is meant to avoid harms that come with uninformed investing, such as occurred in the 1920s and contributed to the stock market crash and the Great Depression.

MORAL MINIMUM Compliance with the law is sometimes called the **moral minimum.** If people and entities merely comply with the law, they are acting at the lowest ethical level society will tolerate. The study of ethics goes beyond those legal requirements to evaluate what is right for society.

Businesspersons must remember that just because an action is legal does not mean it is ethical. For instance, no law specifies the salaries that publicly held corporations (companies that sell their shares to the public) can pay their officers (executive employees). Nevertheless, if a corporation pays its officers an excessive amount relative to other employees, or relative to what officers at other corporations are paid, the executives' compensation might be viewed as unethical.

In the following case, the court had to determine if a repair shop was entitled to receive full payment of an invoice or a lesser amount given its conduct in the matter.

CASE 5.1

Johnson Construction Co. v. Shaffer
Court of Appeal of Louisiana, Second Circuit, 87 So.3d 203 (2012).

BACKGROUND AND FACTS   A truck owned by Johnson Construction Company needed repairs. John Robert Johnson, Jr., the company's president, took the truck with its attached fifteen-ton trailer to Bubba Shaffer, doing business as Shaffer's Auto and Diesel Repair. The truck was supposedly fixed, and Johnson paid the bill. The truck continued to leak oil and water. Johnson returned the truck to Shaffer, who again claimed to have fixed the problem. Johnson paid the second bill. The problems with the truck continued, however, so Johnson returned the truck and trailer a third time. Shaffer gave a verbal estimate of $1,000 for the repairs, but he ultimately sent an invoice for $5,863.49. Johnson offered to settle for $2,480, the amount of the initial estimate ($1,000), plus the costs of parts and shipping. Shaffer refused the offer and would not return Johnson's truck or trailer until full payment was made. Shaffer also charged Johnson a storage fee of $50 a day and 18 percent interest on the $5,863.49.

Johnson Construction filed a suit against Shaffer alleging unfair trade practices. The trial court determined that Shaffer had acted deceptively and wrongfully in maintaining possession of the trailer, on which no work had been performed. The trial court awarded Johnson $3,500 in general damages, plus $750 in attorneys' fees. Shaffer was awarded the initial estimate of $1,000 and appealed.

 IN THE LANGUAGE OF THE COURT
LOLLEY, J. [Judge]

* * * *

* * * At the outset, we point out that Mr. Johnson maintained he had a verbal agreement with Bubba Shaffer, the owner of Shaffer's Auto Diesel and Repair, that the repairs to the truck would cost $1,000. Mr. Johnson also testified that he was not informed otherwise.

CASE 5.1 CONTINUES ▶

CASE 5.1 CONTINUED   The existence or nonexistence of a contract is a question of fact, and the finder of fact's determination may not be set aside unless it is clearly wrong.

* * * *

* * * At the trial of the matter, the trial court was presented with testimony from Mr. Johnson, Mr. Shaffer, and Michael Louton, a mechanic employed by Shaffer. * * * The trial court did not believe Mr. Johnson was informed of the cost for the additional work.

* * * We cannot say that the trial court was clearly wrong in its determination. * * * The trial court viewed Mr. Shaffer's testimony on the issue as "disingenuous" and we cannot see where that was an error.

As for the amount that Shaffer contends is due for storage, had it invoiced Mr. Johnson the amount of the original estimate in the first place, there would have been no need to store the truck or trailer. * * * We cannot see how Shaffer would be entitled to any payment for storage when it failed to return the truck and trailer where an offer of payment for the agreed upon price had been conveyed.

* * * *

* * * So considering, we see no error in the trial court's characterization of Shaffer's actions with the trailer as holding "hostage in an effort to force payment for unauthorized repairs." * * * Shaffer had no legal right to retain possession of the trailer * * * . *Thus, the trial court did not err in its determination that Shaffer's retention of Johnson Construction's trailer [for four years!] was a deceptive conversion of the trailer.* [Emphasis added.]

DECISION AND REMEDY   *The state appellate court affirmed the judgment of the trial court in favor of Johnson Construction Company. It affirmed the award of $3,500, plus $750 in attorneys' fees, as well as Shaffer's original award of $1,000.*

WHAT IF THE FACTS WERE DIFFERENT?   *Suppose that Shaffer had invoiced Johnson for only $1,500. Would the outcome have been different?*

THE ETHICAL DIMENSION   *Would it have been ethical for Shaffer's mechanic to lie to support his employer's case? Discuss.*

ETHICS AND PRIVATE LAW   Most companies attempt to link ethics and law through the creation of internal codes of ethics. Company codes are not law. Instead, they are rules that the company sets forth that it can also enforce (by terminating an employee who does not follow them, for instance). Codes of conduct typically outline the company's policies on particular issues and indicate how employees are expected to act.

▶ **Example 5.2**   Google's code of conduct starts with the motto "Don't be evil." The code then makes general statements about how Google promotes integrity, mutual respect, and the highest standard of ethical business conduct. Google's code also provides specific rules on a number of issues, such as privacy, drugs and alcohol, conflicts of interest, co-worker relationships, and confidentiality—it even has a dog policy. The company takes a stand against employment discrimination that goes further than the law requires. It prohibits discrimination based on sexual orientation, gender identity or expression, and veteran status. ◀

Numerous industries have also developed their own codes of ethics. The American Institute of Certified Public Accountants (AICPA) has a comprehensive Code of Professional Conduct for the ethical practicing of accounting. The American Bar Association has model rules of professional conduct for attorneys, and the American Nurses Association has a code of ethics that applies to nurses. These codes can give guidance to decision makers facing ethical questions. Violation of a code may result in discipline of an employee or sanctions against a company from the industry organization. Remember, though, that these internal codes are not laws, so their effectiveness is determined by the commitment of the industry or company leadership to enforcing the codes.

ETHICAL UNCERTAINTY   Ethics can be a difficult subject for corporate officers to fully understand. Because it is often highly subjective and subject to change over time without any sort of formal process, ethics is less certain than law.

The law can also be uncertain, however, and contains numerous "gray areas" that make it difficult to predict with certainty how a court will apply a given law to a particular action. Uncertainty can make decision making difficult, especially when a law requires a court to determine what is "foreseeable" or "reasonable" in a particular situation. Because a business has no way of predicting how a specific court will decide these issues, decision makers need to proceed with caution and evaluate an action and its consequences from an ethical perspective.

Ethics is based more on judgment than research. A company that can show it acted ethically, responsibly, and in good faith (honestly) has a better chance of succeeding in a dispute than one that cannot make such a showing.

In the following case, the court concluded that the employer's response to complaints about a hostile work environment was so inadequate that it not only violated the employee's rights but was unethical enough to warrant a large penalty against the corporation. Notice the court's language about the company's behavior.

CASE 5.2

May v. Chrysler Group, LLC
United States Court of Appeals, Seventh Circuit, 692 F.3d 734 (2012).

COMPANY PROFILE *Chrysler Group, LLC, is the parent company of Fiat, Chrysler, Dodge, Jeep, and several other automobile manufacturers. (An LLC is a limited liability company.) Chrysler Group was created in 2009 to manage the consolidation of the different automobile companies during the economic downturn of the late 2000s. The company employs more than 64,000 people at thirty-two manufacturing facilities. Its 2013 revenue was estimated to be $60 billion.*

BACKGROUND AND FACTS Between 2002 and 2005, Otto May, Jr., a pipefitter at Chrysler's Belvedere Assembly Plant, was the target of more than fifty racist, homophobic, and anti-Semitic messages and graffiti. He found six death-threat notes in his toolbox, his bike and car tires were punctured, and someone poured sugar into the gas tank of his car twice. At one point, a dead bird wrapped in toilet paper to look like a member of the Ku Klux Klan (including the white pointed hat) was left at his work station. May complained to Chrysler. The director of human resources met with May, documented the complaints, and initiated an internal investigation. As part of that investigation, records were checked to determine who was in the building when the incidents occurred, and the handwriting on the notes and graffiti was analyzed.

The director held two meetings with about sixty employees (out of more than a thousand plant employees). At the meetings, the director reminded the workers that harassment was not acceptable. The harassers were never caught, and the harassment continued after the meetings. Chrysler's headquarters became involved only after the Anti-Defamation League wrote a letter on May's behalf. May sued Chrysler for hostile work environment harassment and was awarded $709,000 in compensatory damages and $3.5 million in punitive damages (or punishment). The judge overturned the punitive damages award, and May appealed.

 IN THE LANGUAGE OF THE COURT
TINDER, Circuit Judge.

* * * *

May can recover punitive damages only if he presented sufficient evidence for the jury to conclude that Chrysler acted with "malice or with reckless indifference to [his] federally protected rights." * * * *No evidence of "egregious" or "outrageous" conduct by the employer is required, although, of course, such a showing could support a conclusion that the employer acted with the requisite mental state.* [Emphasis added.]

We have already explained why it was appropriate for Chrysler to be held responsible for the hostile work environment. Its response was shockingly thin as measured against the gravity of May's harassment.

CASE 5.2 CONTINUES ▶

* * * *

* * *[A]lthough the district court did not rule on whether the jury's $3.5 million award of punitive damages is "grossly excessive" and therefore violates due process, * * * we asked the parties for supplemental briefing so that we might consider that question now. After reviewing the parties' submissions, we are convinced that the punitive damage award does not violate the Constitution and should therefore be reinstated in full. The award is substantial—five times the original compensatory damages and eleven times the remitted amount—but Chrysler's long-term recklessness in the face of repeated threats of violence against May and his family is sufficiently reprehensible [shameful] to support it.

DECISION AND REMEDY   *The federal appellate court reinstated the punitive damages award based on the reprehensible and unethical nature of Chrysler's failure to sufficiently address the harassment.*

THE ETHICAL DIMENSION   *Does an organization have an ethical obligation to secure a safe and harassment-free workplace for its employees? Why or why not? Discuss.*

MANAGERIAL IMPLICATIONS   *It is clear from this opinion that employers have a significant duty to take complaints of harassment seriously. Even if Chrysler believed that May was harassing himself (perhaps in order to obtain compensation from the company), as the company implied at the trial, it had an obligation to do a serious investigation, to set up clear policies and procedures, and to follow those procedures when a complaint was made.*

SECTION 2
BUSINESS ETHICS AND SOCIAL MEDIA

Although most young people think of social media—Facebook, Twitter, Pinterest, Google+, MySpace, LinkedIn, and the like—as simply ways to communicate rapidly, businesses face ethical issues with respect to these same social media platforms.

Hiring Procedures

In the past, to learn about a prospective employee, the employer would ask the candidate's former employers for references. Today, employers are likely to also conduct Internet searches to discover what job candidates have posted on their Facebook pages, blogs, and tweets. Nevertheless, many people believe that judging a job candidate based on what she or he does outside the work environment is unethical.

Sometimes, too, the opposite situation occurs, and job candidates are rejected because they *do not* participate in any social media. Given that the vast majority of younger people do use social media, some employers have decided that the failure to do so raises a red flag. Some consider this employer behavior to be unethical as well.

The Use of Social Media to Discuss Work-Related Issues

Because so many Americans use social media many times a day, they often discuss work-related issues there. Numerous companies have provided strict guidelines about what is appropriate and inappropriate when making posts at one's own or others' social media accounts. A number of companies have fired employees for such activities as criticizing other employees or managers through social media outlets. Until recently, such disciplinary measures were considered ethical and legal.

Today, in contrast, a ruling by the National Labor Relations Board (NLRB—the federal agency that investigates unfair labor practices) has changed the legality of such actions. ▶ **Example 5.3**   Costco's social media policy specified that its employees should not make statements that would damage the company, harm another person's reputation, or violate the company's policies. Employees who violated these rules were subject to discipline and could be fired.

In 2012, the NLRB ruled that Costco's social media policy violated federal labor law, which protects employees' right to engage in "concerted activities." Employees can freely associate with each other and have conversations about common workplace issues without employer interference. This right extends to social media posts. Therefore, Costco cannot broadly prohibit its employees from criticizing the company or co-workers, supervisors, or managers via social media. ◄

Ethics in Reverse

While most of the discussion in this chapter involves business ethics, employee ethics is also an important issue. For instance, is it ethical for employees to make negative posts in social media about other employees or, more commonly, about managers? After all, negative comments about managers reflect badly on those managers, who often are reluctant to respond via social media to such criticism. Disgruntled employees may exaggerate the negative qualities of managers whom they do not like.

Some may consider the latest decision by the National Labor Relations Board outlined in *Example 5.3* above to be too lenient toward employees and too stringent toward management. There is likely to be an ongoing debate about how to balance employees' right to free expression against employers' right to prevent inaccurate negative statements being spread across the Internet.

SECTION 3
ETHICAL PRINCIPLES AND PHILOSOPHIES

As Dean Krehmeyer, executive director of the Business Roundtable's Institute for Corporate Ethics, once said, "Evidence strongly suggests being ethical—doing the right thing—pays." Instilling ethical business decision making into the fabric of a business organization is no small task, even if ethics "pays." How do business decision makers decide whether a given action is the "right" one for their firms? What ethical standards should be applied?

Broadly speaking, **ethical reasoning**—the application of morals and ethics to a situation—applies to businesses just as it does to individuals. As businesses make decisions, they must analyze the alternatives in a variety of ways, one of which is the ethical implications.

Generally, the study of ethics is divided into two major categories—duty-based ethics and outcome-based ethics. **Duty-based ethics** is rooted in the idea that every person has certain duties to others, including both humans and the planet. Those duties may be derived from religious principles or from other

philosophical reasoning. **Outcome-based ethics** focuses on the impacts of a decision on society or on key *stakeholders*.

Duty-Based Ethics

Duty-based ethics focuses on the obligations of the corporation. It deals with standards for behavior that traditionally were derived from revealed truths, religious authorities, or philosophical reasoning. These standards involve concepts of right and wrong, and duties owed and rights to be protected.

Corporations today often describe these values or duties in their mission statements or strategic plans. Some companies base their statements on a nonreligious rationale, but others still derive their values from religious doctrine (such as the statements of Chick-fil-A, discussed in the introduction to this chapter).

RELIGIOUS ETHICAL PRINCIPLES Nearly every religion has principles or beliefs about how one should treat others. In the Judeo-Christian tradition, which is the dominant religious tradition in the United States, the Ten Commandments of the Old Testament establish these fundamental rules for moral action. The principles of the Muslim faith are set out in the Qur'an, and Hindus find their principles in the four Vedas.

Religious rules generally are absolute with respect to the behavior of their adherents. ▶ **Example 5.4**   The commandment "Thou shalt not steal" is an absolute mandate for a person who believes that the Ten Commandments reflect revealed truth. Even a benevolent motive for stealing (such as Robin Hood's) cannot justify the act because the act itself is inherently immoral and thus wrong. ◄

For businesses, religious principles can be a unifying force for employees or a rallying point to increase employee motivation. They can also be problematic, however, because different owners, suppliers, employees, and customers may all have different religious backgrounds. As the introduction to this chapter illustrated, taking an action based on religious principles, especially when those principles address socially or politically controversial topics, can lead to negative publicity and even to protests or boycotts.

PRINCIPLES OF RIGHTS Another view of duty-based ethics focuses on basic rights. The principle that human beings have certain fundamental rights (to life, freedom, and the pursuit of happiness, for example) is deeply embedded in Western culture. As discussed in Chapter 1, the natural law tradition embraces the concept that certain actions (such as killing another person) are morally wrong because they are contrary to nature (the natural desire to continue living).

Those who adhere to this **principle of rights,** or "rights theory," believe that a key factor in determining whether a business decision is ethical is how that decision affects the rights of others. These others include the firm's owners, its employees, the consumers of its products or services, its suppliers, the community in which it does business, and society as a whole.

Conflicting Rights. A potential dilemma for those who support rights theory, however, is that they may disagree on which rights are most important. When considering all those affected by a business decision to downsize a firm, for example, how much weight should be given to employees relative to shareholders? Which employees should be laid off first—those with the highest salaries or those who have worked there for less time (and have less seniority)? How should the firm weigh the rights of customers relative to the community, or employees relative to society as a whole?

Resolving Conflicts. In general, rights theorists believe that whichever right is stronger in a particular circumstance takes precedence. ▶ **Example 5.5** Murray Chemical Corporation has to decide whether to keep a chemical plant in Utah open, thereby saving the jobs of a hundred and fifty workers, or shut it down. Closing the plant will avoid contaminating a river with pollutants that would endanger the health of tens of thousands of people. In this situation, a rights theorist can easily choose which group to favor because the value of the right to health and well-being is obviously stronger than the basic right to work. (Not all choices are so clear-cut, however.) ◀

KANTIAN ETHICAL PRINCIPLES Duty-based ethical standards may also be derived solely from philosophical reasoning. The German philosopher Immanuel Kant (1724–1804) identified some general guiding principles for moral behavior based on what he thought to be the fundamental nature of human beings. Kant believed that human beings are qualitatively different from other physical objects and are endowed with moral integrity and the capacity to reason and conduct their affairs rationally.

People Are Not a Means to an End. Based on this view of human beings, Kant said that when people are treated merely as a means to an end, they are being treated as the equivalent of objects and are being denied their basic humanity. For instance, a manager who treats subordinates as mere profit-making tools is less likely to retain motivated and loyal employees than a manager who respects his or her employees. Management research has shown that employees who feel empowered to share their thoughts, opinions, and solutions to problems are happier and more productive.

Categorical Imperative. When a business makes unethical decisions, it often rationalizes its action by saying that the company is "just one small part" of the problem or that its decision would have "only a small impact." A central theme in Kantian ethics is that individuals should evaluate their actions in light of the consequences that would follow if everyone in society acted in the same way. This **categorical imperative** can be applied to any action.

▶ **Example 5.6** CHS Fertilizer is deciding whether to invest in expensive equipment that will decrease profits but will also reduce pollution from its factories. If CHS has adopted Kant's categorical imperative, the decision makers will consider the consequences if every company invested in the equipment (or if no company did so). If the result would make the world a better place (less polluted), CHS's decision would be clear. ◀

Outcome-Based Ethics: Utilitarianism

In contrast to duty-based ethics, outcome-based ethics focuses on the consequences of an action, not on the nature of the action itself or on any set of preestablished moral values or religious beliefs. Outcome-based ethics looks at the impacts of a decision in an attempt to maximize benefits and minimize harms. The premier philosophical theory for outcome-based decision making is **utilitarianism,** a philosophical theory developed by Jeremy Bentham (1748–1832) and modified by John Stuart Mill (1806–1873)—both British philosophers.

"The greatest good for the greatest number" is a paraphrase of the major premise of the utilitarian approach to ethics.

COST-BENEFIT ANALYSIS Under a utilitarian model of ethics, an action is morally correct, or "right," when, among the people it affects, it produces the greatest amount of good for the greatest number or creates the least amount of harm for the fewest people. When an action affects the majority adversely, it is morally wrong. Applying the utilitarian theory thus requires the following steps:

1. A determination of which individuals will be affected by the action in question.
2. A **cost-benefit analysis,** which involves an assessment of the negative and positive effects of alternative actions on these individuals.
3. A choice among alternative actions that will produce maximum societal utility (the greatest positive net benefits for the greatest number of individuals).

Thus, if expanding a factory would provide hundreds of jobs but generate pollution that could endanger the lives of thousands of people, a utilitarian analysis would find that saving the lives of thousands creates greater good than providing jobs for hundreds.

PROBLEMS WITH THE UTILITARIAN APPROACH There are problems with a strict utilitarian analysis. In some situations, an action that products the greatest good for the most people may not seem to be the most ethical. ▶ **Example 5.7** Phazim Company is producing a drug that will cure a disease in 85 percent of patients, but the other 15 percent will experience agonizing side effects and a horrible, painful death. A quick utilitarian analysis would suggest that the drug should be produced and marketed because the majority of patients will benefit. Many people, however, have significant concerns about manufacturing a drug that will cause such harm to anyone. ◀

Corporate Social Responsibility

In pairing duty-based concepts with outcome-based concepts, strategists and theorists developed the idea of the corporate citizen. **Corporate social responsibility (CSR)** combines a commitment to good citizenship with a commitment to making ethical decisions, improving society, and minimizing environmental impact.

CSR is a relatively new concept in the history of business, but a concept that becomes more important every year. Although CSR is not imposed on corporations by law, it does involve a commitment to self-regulation in a way that attends to the text and intent of the law, ethical norms, and global standards. A survey of U.S. executives undertaken by the Boston College Center for Corporate Citizenship found that more than 70 percent of those polled agreed that cor-

porate citizenship must be treated as a priority. More than 60 percent said that good corporate citizenship added to their companies' profits.

CSR can be an incredibly successful strategy for companies, but corporate decision makers must not lose track of the two descriptors in the title: *corporate* and *social*. The company must link the responsibility of citizenship with the strategy and key principles of the business. Incorporating both the social and the corporate components of CSR and making ethical decisions can help companies grow and prosper.

THE SOCIAL ASPECTS OF CSR First, the social aspect requires that corporations demonstrate that they are promoting goals that society deems worthwhile and are moving toward solutions to social problems. Because business controls so much of the wealth and power of this country, business, in turn, has a responsibility to society to use that wealth and power in socially beneficial ways. Companies may be judged on how much they donate to social causes, as well as how they conduct their operations with respect to employment discrimination, human rights, environmental concerns, and similar issues.

Some corporations publish annual social responsibility reports, which may also be called corporate sustainability (referring to the capacity to endure) or citizenship reports. ▶ **Example 5.8** The Hitachi Group has Web pages dedicated to its CSR initiatives and includes reports outlining its environmental strategies, its human rights policies, and its commitment to diversity. The software company Symantec Corporation issues corporate responsibility reports to demonstrate its focus on critical environmental, social, and governance issues. In its 2012 report, Symantec pointed out that 88 percent of facilities it owns or leases on a long-term basis are certified as environmentally friendly by the LEED program. LEED stands for Leadership in Energy and Environmental Design. Certification requires the achievement of high standards for energy efficiency, material usage in construction, and other environmental qualities. ◀

THE CORPORATE ASPECTS OF CSR Arguably, any socially responsible activity will benefit a corporation. The corporation may see an increase in goodwill from the local community for creating a park. Corporations may see increases in sales if they are viewed as good citizens.

At times, the benefit may not be immediate. Constructing a new plant that meets the high LEED standards may cost more initially. Nevertheless, over the life of the building, the savings in maintenance and utilities may more than make up for the extra cost of construction.

Surveys of college students about to enter the job market confirm that young people are looking for socially responsible employers. Socially responsible activities may cost a corporation now, but may lead to more impressive, and more committed employees. Corporations that engage in meaningful social activities retain workers longer, particularly younger ones.

Corporate responsibility is most successful when a company undertakes activities that are significant and related to its business operations. ▶ **Example 5.9** In 2012, the Walt Disney Company announced that in an effort to curb childhood obesity, it was issuing strict nutritional standards for all products advertised through its media outlets. In addition to focusing on a major social issue, the initiative was intended to clarify Disney's mission and values, as well as enhance its reputation as a trustworthy, family-friendly company. The initiative has been praised by commentators and politicians and is expected to increase Disney's revenue in the long term. ◀

STAKEHOLDERS One view of CSR stresses that corporations have a duty not just to shareholders, but also to other groups affected by corporate decisions—called **stakeholders.** The rationale for this "stakeholder view" is that, in some circumstances, one or more of these other groups may have a greater stake in company decisions than the shareholders do.

Under this approach, a corporation considers the impact of its decisions on its employees, customers, creditors, suppliers, and the community in which it operates. Stakeholders could also include advocacy groups such as environmental groups and animal rights groups. To avoid making a decision that may be perceived as unethical and result in negative publicity or protests, a corporation should consider the impact of its decision on the stakeholders. The most difficult aspect of the stakeholder analysis is determining which group's interests should receive greater weight if the interests conflict.

For instance, during the last few years, layoffs numbered in the millions. Nonetheless, some corporations succeeded in reducing labor costs without layoffs. To avoid slashing their workforces, these employers turned to alternatives such as (1) four-day workweeks, (2) unpaid vacations and voluntary furloughs, (3) wage freezes, (4) pension cuts, and (5) flexible work schedules. Some companies asked their workers to accept wage cuts to prevent layoffs, and the workers agreed.

Companies finding alternatives to layoffs included Dell (extended unpaid holidays), Cisco Systems (four-day end-of-year shutdowns), Motorola (salary cuts), and Honda (voluntary unpaid vacation time).

SECTION 4
MAKING ETHICAL BUSINESS DECISIONS

Even if officers, directors, and others in a company want to make ethical decisions, it is not always clear what is ethical in a given situation. Thinking beyond things that are easily measured, such as profits, can be challenging. Although profit projections are not always accurate, they are more objective than considering the personal impacts of decisions on employees, shareholders, customers, and even the community. But this subjective component to decision making potentially has a great influence on a company's profits.

Companies once considered leaders in their industry, such as Enron and the worldwide accounting firm Arthur Andersen, were brought down by the unethical behavior of a few. A two-hundred-year-old British investment banking firm, Barings Bank, was destroyed by the actions of one employee and a few of his friends. Clearly, ensuring that all employees get on the ethical business decision-making "bandwagon" is crucial in today's fast-paced world.

Individuals entering the global corporate community, even in entry-level positions, must be prepared to make hard decisions. Sometimes, there is no "good" answer to the questions that arise. Therefore, it is important to have tools to help in the decision-making process and a framework for organizing those tools. Business decisions can be complex and may involve legal concerns, financial questions, possibly health and safety concerns, and ethical components.

A Systematic Approach

Organizing the ethical concerns and issues and approaching them systematically can help a businessperson eliminate various alternatives and identify the strengths and weaknesses of the remaining alternatives. Ethics consultant Leonard H. Bucklin of CorporateEthics.US™ has devised a procedure that he calls Business Process Pragmatism™. It involves five steps:

Step 1: Inquiry. First, the decision maker must understand the problem. To do this, one must identify the parties involved (the stakeholders) and collect the relevant facts. Once the ethical problem or problems are clarified, the decision maker lists any relevant legal and ethical principles that will guide the decision.

Step 2: Discussion. In this step, the decision maker lists possible actions. The ultimate goals for the decision are determined, and each option is evaluated using the laws and ethical principles listed in Step 1.

Step 3: Decision. In this step, those participating in the decision making work together to craft a consensus decision or consensus plan of action for the corporation.

Step 4: Justification. In this step, the decision maker articulates the reasons for the proposed action or series of actions. Generally these reasons should come from the analysis done in Step 3. This step essentially results in documentation to be shared with stakeholders explaining why the proposal is an ethical solution to the problem.

Step 5: Evaluation. This final step occurs once the decision has been made and implemented. The solution should be analyzed to determine if it was effective. The results of this evaluation may be used in making future decisions.

The Importance of Ethical Leadership

Talking about ethical business decision making is meaningless if management does not set standards. Furthermore, managers must apply the same standards to themselves as they do to the company's employees.

ATTITUDE OF TOP MANAGEMENT One of the most important ways to create and maintain an ethical workplace is for top management to demonstrate its commitment to ethical decision making. A manager who is not totally committed to an ethical workplace rarely succeeds in creating one. Management's behavior, more than anything else, sets the ethical tone of a firm. Employees take their cues from management.

▶ **Example 5.10** Devon, a BioTek employee, observes his manager cheating on her expense account. Later, when Devon is promoted to a managerial position, he "pads" his expense account as well, knowing that he is unlikely to face sanctions for doing so. ◀

Managers who set unrealistic production or sales goals increase the probability that employees will act unethically. If a sales quota can be met only through high-pressure, unethical sales tactics, employees will try to act "in the best interest of the company" and will continue to behave unethically.

A manager who looks the other way when she or he knows about an employee's unethical behavior also sets an example—one indicating that ethical transgressions will be accepted. Managers have found that discharging even one employee for ethical reasons has a tremendous impact as a deterrent to unethical behavior in the workplace. This is true even if the company has a written code of ethics. If management does not enforce the company code, the code is essentially nonexistent.

The following case demonstrates the types of situations that can occur when management demonstrates a lack of concern about ethics.

CASE ANALYSIS

Case 5.3   Moseley v. Pepco Energy Services, Inc.

United States District Court, District of New Jersey, 2011 WL 1584166 (2011).

IN THE LANGUAGE OF THE COURT
Joseph H. *RODRIGUEZ*, District Judge.

* * * Plaintiff Moseley is an employee of Defendant Pepco Energy Services, Inc. ("PES"). He has been employed

by PES or its corporate predecessors for over twenty-five years. PES, a subsidiary of Defendant Pepco Holdings, Inc. ("PHI"), provides deregulated energy and energy-related services for residential, small business, and large commercial customers.
* * * *

In 1998, Thomas Herzog held the position of Vice President of CTS. * * * In or around 2002, CTS merged with Potomic Electric Power Company, Inc., and each company became a subsidiary of PHI. Following the merger, according to Plaintiff, he continued to work for PHI, still as

CASE 5.3 CONTINUES ▶

Maintenance Manager at Midtown Thermal, until December 31, 2009.

* * * *

Following the 2002 merger with PHI, employees were required to complete an annual ethics survey. By March of 2007, Plaintiff and two co-workers had discussed their respective observations of Herzog's conduct, which they deemed questionable and possibly unethical. Specifically, they felt that Herzog improperly used company assets and improperly hired immediate family members and friends who did not appear on the payroll. The three decided to disclose this information on PHI's annual "Ethics Survey."

The three planned to reveal that Herzog employed his daughter, Laurie, as his secretary in the summer of 2005 and the beginning of 2006 without posting the position first and in violation of PHI's anti-nepotism policy.

* * * *

Next, Herzog hired his girlfriend's daughter as his secretary after his daughter had gone back to school. Plaintiff believed this was in violation of Company policy because the position again was not posted. Herzog also hired his son as a project manager, again through a third party independent contractor, Walter Ratai. Plaintiff thought this was wrong because (1) Herzog circumvented the Company's hiring process, (2) it violated Company policy, and (3) Herzog's son was being paid $75.00/hr, which was more than Plaintiff was making. * * * In addition, Plaintiff had learned that Herzog was improperly using the Company's Eagles' tickets for personal use. Finally, Herzog had leased a new SUV with Company funds, but which was not approved by the Company.

* * * *

[After the surveys were completed, an] investigation ensued. Following the investigation, effective on or about May 10, 2007, Herzog was escorted out of the building. * * * On March 8, 2008, Plaintiff received his annual performance evaluation * * * ; for the first time in twenty-three years, Plaintiff's performance review was negative. Plaintiff feels that this negative performance review was a further act of retaliation for his disclosure of Herzog's conduct.

* * * *

On or about June 11, 2008 the Plant/Operations Manager position was posted * * * . Plaintiff applied for the position, but it was offered to [another person]. Plaintiff alleges that he "was not promoted to the position of Plant/Operations Manager despite his experience performing the job for the previous two and a half years, qualifications for same and seniority, as a direct and proximate result of his prior complaints and/or disclosures regarding the Herzog illegal conduct and activities."

* * * *

The New Jersey Legislature enacted the Conscientious Employee Protection Act (CEPA) to "protect and encourage employees to report illegal or unethical workplace activities." * * * CEPA prohibits a New Jersey employer from taking "retaliatory action" against an employee who objects to "any activity, policy or practice which the employee reasonably believes" is in violation of applicable law. * * * "To prevail on a claim under this provision, a plaintiff must establish that: (1) he reasonably believed that [the complained-of] conduct was violating a law or rule or regulation promulgated pursuant to law; (2) he objected to the conduct; (3) an adverse employment action was taken against him; and (4) a causal connection exists between the whistleblowing activity and the adverse employment action.

* * * *

The first element of the prima facie case [a case sufficient to be sent to the jury] under CEPA is that the Plaintiff reasonably believed that the complained-of conduct (1) was violating a "law, rule, or regulation promulgated pursuant to law, including any violation involving deception of, or misrepresentation to, any shareholder, investor, client, patient, customer, employee, former employee, retiree or pensioner of the employer or any governmental entity"; or "(2) is fraudulent or criminal, including any activity, policy or practice of deception or misrepresentation which the employee reasonably believes may defraud any shareholder, investor, client, patient, customer, employee, former employee, retiree or pensioner of the employer or any governmental entity."

Although Defendants have argued that Plaintiff merely disclosed a violation of Company policy, Moseley has testified that in March 2007, he reported what he believed to be "unethical conduct, misappropriation of company funds, and theft" by his direct supervisor. * * * *Moreover, a plaintiff need not demonstrate that there was a violation of the law or fraud, but instead that he "reasonably believed" that to be the case.* The facts in this case support an objectively reasonable belief that a violation of law or fraudulent conduct was being committed by Plaintiff's supervisor. [Emphasis added.]

Regarding the causal connection between Plaintiff's whistleblowing activity and the negative adverse employment actions taken against him, Plaintiff stresses that he was employed by the Defendants for twenty-five years without a negative employment evaluation or any form of discipline until immediately after he disclosed the wrongful conduct of his supervisor. Not only did Plaintiff then receive a negative performance evaluation, but the posted position of Plant Manager was given to [another], despite [the other's] alleged past negative history and despite that Plaintiff asserts he had been acting in that job for over two years. Plaintiff contends that this is sufficient evidence of pretext.

The Court is unable to find as a matter of law that Defendants' infer-

CASE 5.3 CONTINUED

ences prevail or that a jury could not reasonably adopt a contrary inference of retaliation. There are questions of fact as to how much the individuals responsible for Plaintiff's negative performance evaluations knew about Plaintiff's complaints. "[A] finding of the required causal connection may be based solely on circumstantial evidence that the person ultimately responsible for an adverse employment action was aware of an employee's whistle-blowing activity." Because jurors may infer a causal connection from the surrounding circumstances, as well as temporal proximity, the Court will not grant summary judgment. [Emphasis added.]

* * * *

IT IS ORDERED on this 26th day of April, 2011 that Defendants' motion for summary judgment is hereby DENIED.

LEGAL REASONING QUESTIONS

1. Using duty-based ethical principles, what facts or circumstances in this case would lead Moseley to disclose Herzog's behavior?

2. Using outcome-based ethical principles, what issues would Moseley have to analyze in making the decision to report Herzog's behavior? What would be the risks to Moseley? The benefits?

3. Under the Business Process Pragmatism™ steps, what alternatives might Moseley have had in this situation?

4. Regardless of who wins this case at trial, in performing Step 5 (Evaluation) of the Business Process Pragmatism™ procedure, what changes should the company take with regard to the complaint process?

BEHAVIOR OF OWNERS AND MANAGERS Business owners and managers sometimes take more active roles in fostering unethical and illegal conduct. This may indicate to their co-owners, co-managers, employees, and others that unethical business behavior will be tolerated. Business owners' misbehavior can have negative consequences for themselves and their business. Not only can a court sanction the owners and managers, but it can also issue an injunction that prevents them from engaging in similar patterns of conduct in the future.

▶ **Example 5.11** Lawyer Samir Zia Chowhan posted a help-wanted ad on Craigslist seeking an "energetic woman" for the position of legal secretary. The ad stated that the position included secretarial and paralegal work, as well as "additional duties" for two lawyers in the firm. Applicants were asked to send pictures and describe their physical features.

When a woman applied for the job, Chowhan sent her an e-mail saying that "in addition to the legal work, you would be required to have sexual interaction with me and my partner, sometimes together sometimes separate." He also explained that she would need to perform sexual acts at the job interview so that he and his partner could determine whether she would be able to handle these duties. The woman filed a complaint with the Illinois Bar Association, which suspended Chowhan's law license for a year for making false statements about the ad. Because the bar association's ethics rules prohibited attorneys from having sex with their clients, but not with potential employees, Chowhan could only be disciplined for lying. ◀

THE SARBANES-OXLEY ACT The Sarbanes-Oxley Act of 2002[2] requires companies to set up confidential systems so that employees and others can "raise red flags" about suspected illegal or unethical auditing and accounting practices. (The Sarbanes-Oxley Act covers additional issues, and excerpts from and explanatory comments on this important law appear in Appendix D of this text.)

Some companies have implemented online reporting systems to accomplish this goal. In one such system, employees can click on an icon on their computers that anonymously links them with EthicsPoint, an organization based in Portland, Oregon. Through EthicsPoint, employees can report suspicious accounting practices, sexual harassment, and other possibly unethical behavior. EthicsPoint, in turn, alerts management personnel or the audit committee at the designated company to the possible problem. Those who have used the system say that it is less inhibiting than calling a company's toll-free number.

SECTION 5
GLOBAL BUSINESS ETHICS

Just as different religions have different moral codes, different countries, regions and even states have different ethical expectations and priorities. Some of

---

2. 15 U.S.C. Sections 7201 *et seq.*

these differences are based in religious values, whereas others are cultural in nature. As a result of the various cultures and religions throughout the world, making ethical business decisions can be even more difficult.

For instance, in certain countries the consumption of alcohol and specific foods is forbidden for religious reasons. It would be considered unethical for a U.S. business to build a factory to produce alcohol and employee local workers in a culture in which alcohol is forbidden.

International transactions often involve issues related to employment and financing. Congress has addressed some of these issues, not eliminating the ethical components but clarifying some of the conflicts between the ethics of the United States and the ethics of other nations. For example, the Civil Rights Act of 1964 and the Foreign Corrupt Practices Act (discussed in more detail below) have clarified the U.S. ethical position on employment issues and bribery in foreign nations. (Other nations, including Mexico, have also enacted laws that prohibit bribery, as discussed in this chapter's *Insight into the Global Environment* feature on the following page.)

The Monitoring of Employment Practices of Foreign Suppliers

Many businesses contract with companies in developing nations to produce goods, such as shoes and clothing, because the wage rates in those nations are significantly lower than those in the United States. Yet what if a foreign company hires women and children at below-minimum-wage rates, for example, or requires its employees to work long hours in a workplace full of health hazards? What if the company's supervisors routinely engage in workplace conduct that is offensive to women? What if plants located abroad routinely violate labor and environmental standards?

▶ **Example 5.12** Apple, Inc., owns Pegatron Corporation, a subsidiary company based in China, which supplies parts for iPads and other Apple products. In December 2011, there was an explosion at a Pegatron factory in Shanghai. Dozens of employees were injured when aluminum dust from polishing cases for iPads caught fire and caused the explosion. Allegations surfaced that the conditions at the factory violated labor and environmental standards. California-based Apple did not comment on the issue. ◀

Given today's global communications network, few companies can assume that their actions in other nations will go unnoticed by "corporate watch" groups that discover and publicize unethical corpo-

rate behavior. As a result, U.S. businesses today usually take steps to avoid such adverse publicity—either by refusing to deal with certain suppliers or by arranging to monitor their suppliers' workplaces to make sure that the employees are not being mistreated.

The Foreign Corrupt Practices Act

Another ethical problem in international business dealings has to do with the legitimacy of certain side payments to government officials. In the United States, the majority of contracts are formed within the private sector. In many foreign countries, however, government officials make the decisions on most major construction and manufacturing contracts because of extensive government regulation and control over trade and industry.

Side payments to government officials in exchange for favorable business contracts are not unusual in such countries, nor are they considered to be unethical. In the past, U.S. corporations doing business in these nations largely followed the dictum "When in Rome, do as the Romans do."

In the 1970s, however, the U.S. media uncovered a number of business scandals involving large side payments by U.S. corporations to foreign representatives for the purpose of securing advantageous international trade contracts. In response to this unethical behavior, in 1977 Congress passed the Foreign Corrupt Practices Act[3] (FCPA), which prohibits U.S. businesspersons from bribing foreign officials to secure beneficial contracts.

PROHIBITION AGAINST THE BRIBERY OF FOREIGN OFFICIALS The first part of the FCPA applies to all U.S. companies and their directors, officers, shareholders, employees, and agents. This part prohibits the bribery of most officials of foreign governments if the purpose of the payment is to motivate the official to act in his or her official capacity to provide business opportunities.

The FCPA does not prohibit payment of substantial sums to minor officials whose duties are ministerial. A ministerial action is a routine activity such as the processing of paperwork with little or no discretion involved in the action. These payments are often referred to as "grease," or facilitating payments. They are meant to accelerate the performance of administrative services that might otherwise be carried out at a slow pace. Thus, for instance, if a firm makes a payment to a minor official to speed up an import licensing process, the firm has not violated the FCPA.

---

3. 15 U.S.C. Sections 78dd-1 *et seq.*

INSIGHT INTO THE GLOBAL ENVIRONMENT
Bribery and the Foreign Corrupt Practices Act

Many countries have followed in the footsteps of the United States by passing their own anticorruption laws, some of which are similar to our Foreign Corrupt Practices Act. Nevertheless, some countries are still not diligent in weeding out corruption—of government officials, for instance.

Mexico Faces a Corruption Issue

Recently, Mexico passed an anticorruption law that prevents hospital administrators from approving contracts. Medical device supplier Orthofix International NV, based in Texas, faced a problem after passage of the new law. It wanted to continue providing bone-repair products to Mexico. It therefore bribed regional government officials instead of hospital administrators. Over several years, Orthofix paid more than $300,000 in bribes to Mexican officials to retain government health-care contracts. Employees at Orthofix called these bribes "chocolates." The contracts generated almost $8.7 million in revenues for the company.

The Bribing Process

Before the anticorruption law was enacted, Orthofix's Mexican subsidiary, Promeca, regularly offered cash and gifts, such as vacation packages, televisions, and laptops, to hospital employees in order to secure sales contracts. These employees then submitted falsified receipts for imaginary expenses such as meals and new car tires. When the bribes became too large to hide in this manner, Promeca's employees falsely attributed the payments to promotional and training expenses. After the new law was passed, Mexico formed a special national committee to approve medical contracts. Promeca employees then sim-

ply bribed committee members to ensure that the company was awarded the contracts.

No Compliance Policy or Training to Prevent Violations

As it turned out, Orthofix did not provide any training in how to prevent violations of the Foreign Corrupt Practices Act or have a compliance policy in place in Mexico. Orthofix did create a code of ethics and antibribery training materials, but they were only distributed in English. When Orthofix managers found out about Promeca's overbudget expenses, they questioned the amounts, but initially took no further steps.

The U.S. Government Investigates

Sometime after Orthofix learned of the payments, it self-reported them to the U.S. Securities and Exchange Commission (SEC). After negotiations with the SEC, Orthofix agreed to terminate the Promeca executives who had engaged in the bribery and to end Promeca's operations. Orthofix required mandatory training for all employees and strengthened its auditing of company payments. In addition, the company paid more than $7 million in penalties.

LEGAL CRITICAL THINKING
INSIGHT INTO THE LEGAL ENVIRONMENT

Because managers are potentially responsible for all actions of their foreign subsidiaries whether or not they knew of the illegal conduct, what actions should Orthofix's upper management have taken before this corruption scandal came to light?

Generally, the act, as amended, permits payments to foreign officials if such payments are lawful within the foreign country. Payments to private foreign companies or other third parties are permissible—unless the U.S. firm knows that the payments will be passed on to a foreign government in violation of the FCPA. The U.S. Department of Justice also uses the FCPA to prosecute foreign companies suspected of bribing officials outside the United States.

ACCOUNTING REQUIREMENTS To prevent bribes from being concealed in the corporate financial records, the second part of the FCPA is directed toward accountants. All companies must keep detailed records that

"accurately and fairly" reflect their financial activities. Their accounting systems must provide "reasonable assurance" that all transactions entered into by the companies are accounted for and legal. These requirements assist in detecting illegal bribes. The FCPA prohibits any person from making false statements to accountants or false entries in any record or account.

PENALTIES FOR VIOLATIONS The FCPA provides that business firms that violate the act may be fined up to $2 million. Individual officers or directors who violate the FCPA may be fined up to $100,000 (the fine cannot be paid by the company) and may be imprisoned for up to five years.

Reviewing: Business Ethics

James Stilton is the chief executive officer (CEO) of RightLiving, Inc., a company that buys life insurance policies at a discount from terminally ill persons and sells the policies to investors. RightLiving pays the terminally ill patients a percentage of the future death benefit (usually 65 percent) and then sells the policies to investors for 85 percent of the value of the future benefit. The patients receive the cash to use for medical and other expenses, the investors are "guaranteed" a positive return on their investment, and RightLiving profits on the difference between the purchase and sale prices. Stilton is aware that some sick patients might obtain insurance policies through fraud (by not revealing the illness on the insurance application). Insurance companies that discover this will cancel the policy and refuse to pay. Stilton believes that most of the policies he has purchased are legitimate, but he knows that some probably are not. Using the information presented in this chapter, answer the following questions.

1. Would a person who adheres to the principle of rights consider it ethical for Stilton not to disclose the potential risk of cancellation to investors? Why or why not?
2. Using Immanuel Kant's categorical imperative, are the actions of RightLiving, Inc. ethical? Why or why not?
3. Under utilitarianism, are Stilton's actions ethical? Why or why not? What difference does it make if most of the policies are legitimate and will be paid rather than being fraudulently procured and void?
4. Using the Business Process Pragmatism™ steps discussed in this chapter, discuss the decision process Stilton should use in deciding whether to disclose the risk of fraudulent policies to potential investors.

DEBATE THIS . . . *Executives in large corporations are ultimately rewarded if their companies do well, particularly as evidenced by rising stock prices. Consequently, should we let those who run corporations decide what level of negative side effects of their goods or services is "acceptable"?*

Terms and Concepts

business ethics 95	duty-based ethics 101	principle of rights 102
categorical imperative 102	ethical reasoning 101	stakeholders 104
corporate social responsibility (CSR) 103	ethics 95	triple bottom line 96
cost-benefit analysis 103	moral minimum 97	utilitarianism 102
	outcome-based ethics 101	

ExamPrep

Issue Spotters

1. News, Inc., is always looking for ways to increase the number of its viewers. Recently, it was the first network to interview surviving witnesses on location after a tragic school shooting. Are there ethical concerns about putting traumatized children on the news immediately after an event like this? Why or why not? **(See page 104.)**

2. Johnny Sport is a world-famous athlete. He is careful to avoid using any performance-enhancing drugs that are banned by his sport's oversight organization. Is it ethical for Johnny to take a performance-enhancing drug that has not been banned? Why or why not? **(See page 104.)**

• **Check your answers to the Issue Spotters against the answers provided in Appendix E at the end of this text.**

Before the Test

Go to **www.cengagebrain.com**, enter the ISBN 9781285185248, and click on "Find" to locate this textbook's Web site. Then, click on "Access Now" under "Study Tools," and select Chapter 5 at the top. There, you will find a Practice Quiz that you can take to assess your mastery of the concepts in this chapter, as well as Flash-cards and a Glossary of important terms.

Business Scenarios

5–1. Business Ethics. Jason Trevor owns a commercial bakery in Blakely, Georgia, that produces a variety of goods sold in grocery stores. Trevor is required by law to perform internal tests on food produced at his plant to check for contamination. On three occasions, the tests of food products containing peanut butter were positive for salmonella contamination. Trevor was not required to report the results to U.S. Food and Drug Administration officials, however, so he did not. Instead, Trevor instructed his employees to simply repeat the tests until the results were negative. Meanwhile, the products that had originally tested positive for salmonella were eventually shipped out to retailers.

Five people who ate Trevor's baked goods that year became seriously ill, and one person died from a salmonella infection. Even though Trevor's conduct was legal, was it unethical for him to sell goods that had once tested positive for salmonella? Why or why not? **(See page 95.)**

5–2. Ethical Conduct. Internet giant Zoidle, a U.S. company, generated sales of £2.5 billion in the United Kingdom in 2013 (approximately $4 billion in U.S. dollars). Its net profits before taxes on these sales were £200 million, and it paid £6 million in corporate tax, resulting in a tax rate of 3 percent. The corporate tax rate in the United Kingdom is between 20 percent and 24 percent.

The CEO of Zoidle held a press conference stating that he was proud of his company for taking advantage of tax loopholes and for sheltering profits in other nations to avoid paying taxes. He called this practice "capitalism at its finest." He further stated that it would be unethical for Zoidle not to take advantage of loopholes and that it would be borderline illegal to tell shareholders that the company paid more taxes than it had to pay because it felt it should. Zoidle receives significant benefits for doing business in the United Kingdom, including tremendous sales tax exemptions and some property tax breaks. The United Kingdom relies on the corporate income tax to provide services to the poor and to help run the agency that regulates corporations. Is it ethical for Zoidle to avoid paying taxes? Why or why not? **(See page 97.)**

Business Case Problems

5–3. Spotlight on Pfizer, Inc.—Corporate Social Responsibility. Methamphetamine (meth) is an addictive drug made chiefly in small toxic labs (STLs) in homes, tents, barns, or hotel rooms. The manufacturing process is dangerous and often results in explosions, burns, and toxic fumes. Government entities spend time and resources to find and destroy STLs, imprison meth dealers and users, treat addicts, and provide services for affected families. Meth cannot be made without ingredients that are also used in cold and allergy medications. Arkansas has one of the highest numbers of STLs in the United States. To recoup the costs of fighting the meth epidemic, twenty counties in Arkansas filed a suit against Pfizer, Inc., which makes cold and allergy medications. What is Pfizer's ethical responsibility here, and to whom is it owed? Why? [*Ashley County, Arkansas v. Pfizer, Inc.*, 552 F.3d. 659 (8th Cir. 2009)] **(See page 103.)**

5–4. Ethical Leadership. David Krasner, who worked for HSH Nordbank AG, complained that his supervisor, Roland Kiser, fostered an atmosphere of sexism that was demeaning to women. Among other things, Krasner claimed that career advancement was based on "sexual favoritism." He objected to Kiser's relationship with a female employee, Melissa Campfield, who was promoted before more qualified employees, including Krasner. How do a manager's attitudes and actions affect the workplace? [*Krasner v. HSH Nordbank AG*, 680 F.Supp.2d 502 (S.D.N.Y. 2010)] **(See page 105.)**

5–5. BUSINESS CASE PROBLEM WITH SAMPLE ANSWER: Online Privacy.

 *Facebook, Inc., launched a program called "Beacon" that automatically updated the profiles of users on Facebook's social networking site when those users had any activity on Beacon "partner" sites. For example, one partner site was Blockbuster.com. When a user rented or purchased a movie through Blockbuster.com, the user's Facebook profile would be updated to share the purchase. The Beacon program was set up as a default setting, so users never consented to the program, but they could opt out. What are the ethical implications of an opt-in program versus an opt-out program in social media? [Lane v. Facebook, Inc., 696 F.3d 811 (9th Cir. 2011)] **(See page 101.)**

• For a sample answer to Problem 5–5, go to Appendix F at the end of this text.

5–6. Business Ethics on a Global Scale. After the fall of the Soviet Union, the new government of Azerbaijan began converting certain state-controlled industries to private ownership. Ownership in these companies could be purchased through a voucher program. Frederic Bourke, Jr., and Viktor Kozeny wanted to purchase the Azerbaijani oil company, SOCAR, but it was unclear whether the Azerbaijani president would allow SOCAR to be put up for sale. Kozeny met with one of the vice presidents of SOCAR (who was also the son of the president of Azerbaijan) and other Azerbaijani leaders to discuss the sale of SOCAR. To obtain their cooperation, Kozeny set up a series of parent and subsidiary companies through which the Azerbaijani leaders would eventually receive two-thirds of the SOCAR profits without ever investing any of their own funds. In return, the Azerbaijani leaders would attempt to use their influence to convince the president to put SOCAR up for sale. Assume that Bourke and Kozeny are operating out of a U.S. company. Discuss the ethics of this scheme, both in terms of the Foreign Corrupt Practices Act (FCPA) and as a general ethical issue. What duties did Kozeny have under the FCPA? [*United States v. Kozeny,* 667 F.3d 122 (2d Cir. 2011)] **(See page 107.)**

5–7. Business Ethics. Mark Ramun worked as a manager for Allied Erecting and Dismantling Co., where he had a tense relationship with his father, who was Allied's president. After more than ten years, Mark left Allied, taking 15,000 pages of Allied's documents on DVDs and CDs, which constituted trade secrets. Later, he joined Allied's competitor, Genesis Equipment & Manufacturing, Inc. Genesis soon developed a piece of equipment that incorporated elements of Allied equipment. How might business ethics have been violated in these circumstances? Discuss. [*Allied Erecting and Dismantling Co. v. Genesis Equipment & Manufacturing, Inc.,* 2013 WL 85907 (6th Cir. 2013)] **(See page 95.)**

5–8. A QUESTION OF ETHICS: Consumer Rights.

 Best Buy, a national electronics retailer, offered a credit card that allowed users to earn "reward points" that could be redeemed for discounts on Best Buy goods. After reading a newspaper advertisement for the card, Gary Davis applied for, and was given, a credit card. As part of the application process, he visited a Web page containing Frequently Asked Questions as well as terms and conditions for the card. He clicked on a button affirming that he understood the terms and conditions. When Davis received his card, it came with seven brochures about the card and the reward point program. As he read the brochures, he discovered that a $59 annual fee would be charged for the card. Davis went back to the Web pages he had visited and found a statement that the card "may" have an annual fee. Davis sued, claiming that the company did not adequately disclose the fee. [Davis v. HSBC Bank Nevada, N.A., 691 F.3d 1152 (9th Cir. 2012)] **(See page 96.)**

(a) Online applications frequently have click-on buttons or check boxes for consumers to acknowledge that they have read and understand the terms and conditions of applications or purchases. Often, the terms and conditions are so long that they cannot all be seen on one screen and users must scroll to view the entire document. Is it unethical for companies to put terms and conditions, especially terms that may cost the consumer, in an electronic document that is too long to read on one screen? Why or why not? Does this differ from having a consumer sign a hard-copy document with terms and conditions printed on it? Why or why not?

(b) The Truth-in-Lending Act requires that credit terms be clearly and conspicuously disclosed in application materials. Assuming that the Best Buy credit-card materials had sufficient legal disclosures, discuss the ethical aspects of businesses strictly following the language of the law as compared to following the intent of the law.

Legal Reasoning Group Activity

5–9. Global Business Ethics. Pfizer, Inc., developed a new antibiotic called Trovan (trovafloxacinmesylate). Tests showed that in animals Trovan had life-threatening side effects, including joint disease, abnormal cartilage growth, liver damage, and a degenerative bone condition. Several years later, an epidemic of bacterial meningitis swept across Nigeria. Pfizer sent three U.S. physicians to test Trovan on children who were patients in Nigeria's Infectious Disease Hospital. Pfizer did not obtain the patients' consent, alert them to the risks, or tell them that Médecins Sans Frontières (Doctors without Borders) was providing an effective conventional treatment at the same site. Eleven children died in the experiment, and others were left blind, deaf, paralyzed, or brain damaged. Rabi Abdullahi and other Nigerian children filed a suit in a U.S. federal court against Pfizer, alleging a violation of a customary international law norm prohibiting involuntary medical experimentation on humans.

(a) One group should use the principles of ethical reasoning discussed in this chapter to develop three arguments that Pfizer's conduct was a violation of ethical standards.

(b) A second group should take a pro-Pfizer position and argue that the company did not violate any ethical standards (and counter the first group).

(c) A third group should come up with proposals for what Pfizer might have done differently to avert the consequences.

UNIT ONE Focus on Ethics

Ethics and the Legal Environment of Business

In Chapter 5, we examined the importance of ethical standards in the business context. We also offered suggestions on how business decision makers can create an ethical workplace. Certainly, it is not wrong for a businessperson to try to increase his or her firm's profits. But there are limits, both ethical and legal, to how far businesspersons can go. In preparing for a career in business, you will find that a background in business ethics and a commitment to ethical behavior are just as important as a knowledge of the specific laws that are covered in this text. Of course, no textbook can give an answer to each and every ethical question that arises in the business environment. Nor can it anticipate the types of ethical questions that will arise in the future, as technology and globalization continue to transform the workplace and business relationships.

The most we can do is examine the types of ethical issues that businesspersons have faced in the past and that they are facing today. In the *Focus on Ethics* sections in this book, we provide examples of specific ethical issues that have arisen in various areas of business activity.

In this initial *Focus on Ethics* feature, we look first at the relationship between business ethics and business law. We then examine various obstacles to ethical behavior in the business context. We conclude the feature by exploring the parameters of corporate social responsibility through a discussion of whether corporations have an ethical duty to the community or society at large.

Business Ethics and Business Law

Business ethics and business law are closely intertwined because ultimately the law rests on social beliefs about right and wrong behavior in the business world. Thus, businesspersons, by complying with the law, are acting ethically. Mere legal compliance (the "moral minimum" in terms of business ethics), however, is often not enough. This is because the law does not—and cannot—provide the answers for all ethical questions.

In the business world, numerous actions may be unethical but not necessarily illegal. Consider an example. Suppose that a pharmaceutical company is banned from marketing a particular drug in the United States because of the drug's possible adverse side effects. Yet no law prohibits the company from selling the drug in foreign markets—even though some consumers in those markets may suffer serious health problems as a result of using the drug. At issue here is not whether it would be legal to market the drug in other countries but whether it would be *ethical* to do so. In other words, the law has its limits—it cannot make all ethical decisions for us. Rather, the law assumes that those in business will behave ethically in their day-to-day dealings. If they do not, the courts will not come to their assistance.

LEGAL REASONING

1. *Can you think of a situation in which a business firm may be acting ethically but not in a socially responsible manner? Explain.*

Obstacles to Ethical Business Behavior

People sometimes behave unethically in the business context, just as they do in their private lives. Some businesspersons knowingly engage in unethical behavior because they think that they can "get away with it"—that is, no one will ever learn of their unethical actions.

Examples of this kind of unethical behavior include padding expense accounts, casting doubts on the integrity of a rival co-worker to gain a job promotion, and stealing company supplies or equipment. Obviously, these acts are unethical, and many of them are illegal as well. In some situations, however, businesspersons who would choose to act ethically may be deterred from doing so because of situational circumstances or external pressures.

Ethics and the Corporate Environment Individuals in their personal lives normally are free to decide ethical issues as they wish and to follow through on those decisions. In the business world, and particularly in the corporate environment, rarely is such a decision made by *one* person. If you are an officer or a manager of a large company, for example, you will find that the decision as to what is right or wrong for the company is not totally yours to make. Your input may weigh in the decision, but ultimately a corporate decision is a collective undertaking.

Additionally, collective decision making, because it places emphasis on consensus and unity of opinion, tends to hinder individual ethical assertiveness. For example, suppose that a director has ethical misgivings about a planned corporate venture that promises to be highly profitable. If the other directors have no such misgivings, the director who does may be swayed by the others' enthusiasm for the project and downplay her or his own criticisms.

Furthermore, just as no one person makes a collective decision, so no one person (normally) is held accountable for the decision. The corporate enterprise thus tends to shield corporate personnel from both individual exposure to the consequences of their decisions (such as direct contact with someone who suffers harm from a corporate product) and personal accountability for those decisions.

Ethics and Management Much unethical business behavior occurs simply because management does not always make clear what ethical standards and behaviors are expected of the firm's employees. Although most firms now issue ethical policies or codes of conduct, these policies and codes are not always effective in creating an ethical workplace. At times, this is because the firm's ethical policies are not communicated clearly to employees or do not bear on the real ethical issues confronting decision makers. Additionally, particularly in a large corporation, unethical behavior in one corporate

FOCUS ON ETHICS CONTINUES ▶

department may simply escape the attention of those in control of the corporation or the corporate officials responsible for implementing and monitoring the company's ethics program.

Unethical behavior may also occur when corporate management, by its own conduct, indicates that ethical considerations take a second seat. If management makes no attempt to deter unethical behavior—through reprimands or employment terminations, for example—it will be obvious to employees that management is not very serious about ethics. Likewise, if a company gives promotions or salary increases to those who clearly use unethical tactics to increase the firm's profits, then employees who do not resort to such tactics will be at a disadvantage. An employee in this situation may decide that because "everyone else does it," he or she might as well do it too.

Of course, an even stronger encouragement of unethical behavior occurs when employers engage in blatantly unethical or illegal conduct and expect their employees to do so as well. An employee in this situation faces two options, neither of which is satisfactory: participate in the conduct or "blow the whistle" on (inform authorities of) the employer's actions—and, of course, risk being fired. (Whistleblowing is a controversial issue because it is sometimes difficult to prove employers' motivations for dismissals.)

LEGAL REASONING

2. *What might be some other deterrents to ethical behavior in the business context, besides those discussed in this* Focus on Ethics *feature?*

Corporate Social Responsibility

As discussed in Chapter 5, just what constitutes corporate social responsibility has been debated for some time. In particular, questions arise concerning a corporation's ethical obligations to its community and to society as a whole.

A Corporation's Duty to the Community In some circumstances, the community in which a business enterprise is located is greatly affected by corporate decisions and therefore may be considered a stakeholder. Assume, for example, that a company employs two thousand workers at one of its plants. If the company decides that it would be profitable to close the plant, the employees—and the community—would suffer as a result. To be considered ethical in that situation (and, in some circumstances, to comply with laws governing plant shutdowns), a corporation must take both the employees' needs and the community's needs into consideration when making its decision.

Another ethical question sometimes arises when a firm moves into a community. Does the company have an obligation to evaluate first how its presence will affect that community (even though the community is not a stakeholder yet)? This question has surfaced in regard to the expansion of Wal-Mart Stores, Inc., into smaller communities. Generally, most people in such communities welcome the lower prices and wider array of goods that Wal-Mart offers relative to other, smaller stores in the area. A vocal minority of people in some communities, however, claim that smaller stores often find it impossible to compete with Wal-Mart's prices and thus are forced to go out of business. Many of these smaller stores have existed for years and, according to Wal-Mart's critics, enhance the quality of community life. These critics claim that it is unethical of Wal-Mart to disregard a town's interest in the quality and character of its community life.

In addition to expanding, Wal-Mart has been consolidating some of its smaller stores into large "superstores." As it consolidates, Wal-Mart is closing stores in some of the very towns in which it drove its smaller competitors out of business. This development raises yet another ethical question: Does a store such as Wal-Mart have an obligation to continue operations in a community once it has driven its competitors out of business?

LEGAL REASONING

3. *Why are consumers and the public generally more concerned with ethical and socially responsible business behavior today than they were, say, fifty years ago?*

A Corporation's Duty to Society Perhaps the most disputed area of corporate social responsibility is the nature of a corporation's duty to society at large. Those who contend that corporations should first and foremost attend to the goal of profit maximization would argue that it is by generating profits that a firm can best contribute to society. Society benefits from profit-making activities because profits can only be realized when a firm markets products or services that are desired by society. These products and services enhance the standard of living, and the profits accumulated by successful business firms generate national wealth. Our laws and court decisions promoting trade and commerce reflect the public policy that the fruits of commerce (wealth) are desirable and good. Because our society values wealth as an ethical goal, corporations, by contributing to that wealth, automatically are acting ethically.

Those arguing for profit maximization as a corporate goal also point out that it would be inappropriate to use the power of the corporate business world to further society's goals by promoting social causes. Determinations as to what exactly is in society's best interest involve questions that are essentially political. Therefore the public, through the political process, should have a say in making those determinations. Thus, the legislature—not the corporate boardroom—is the appropriate forum for making such decisions.

Critics of the profit-maximization view believe that corporations should become actively engaged in seeking and furthering solutions to social problems. Because business controls so much of the wealth and power of this country, business has a responsibility to use its resources in socially beneficial ways. Corporations should therefore promote human rights, strive for equal treatment of minorities and women in the workplace, take steps to preserve the environment, and generally not profit from activities that society has deemed unethical. The critics also point out that it is ethically irresponsible to leave decisions concerning social welfare up to the government, because many social needs are not being met sufficiently through the political process.

LEGAL REASONING

4. *Suppose that an automobile manufacturing company has to choose between two alternatives: contributing $1 million annually to the United Way or reinvesting the $1 million in the company. In terms of ethics and social responsibility, which is the better choice? Why?*

It Pays to Be Ethical

Most corporations today have learned that it pays to be ethically responsible—even if this means less profit in the short run (and it often does). Today's corporations are subject to more intensive scrutiny—by both government agencies and the public—than corporations of the past. "Corporate watch"

groups monitor the activities of U.S. corporations, including activities conducted in foreign countries. Through the Internet, complaints about a corporation's practices can easily be disseminated to a worldwide audience. Similarly, dissatisfied customers and employees can voice their complaints about corporate policies, products, or services in Internet chat rooms and other online forums. Thus, if a corporation fails to conduct its operations ethically or to respond quickly to an ethical crisis, its goodwill and reputation (and future profits) will likely suffer as a result.

There are other reasons as well for a corporation to behave ethically. For example, companies that demonstrate a commitment to ethical behavior—by implementing ethical programs, complying with environmental regulations, and promptly investigating product complaints, for example—often receive more lenient treatment from government agencies and the courts. Additionally, investors may shy away from a corporation's stock if the corporation is perceived to be socially irresponsible. Finally, unethical (and/or illegal) corporate behavior may result in government action, such as new laws imposing further requirements on corporate entities.

LEGAL REASONING

5. *Have Internet chat rooms and online forums affected corporate decision makers' willingness to consider the community and public interest when making choices? Are corporate decision makers more apt to make ethical choices in the cyber age?*

BUSINESS LAW

CLARKSON · MILLER · CROSS

UNIT TWO

TORTS AND CRIMES

CONTENTS

CHAPTER 6

TORTS

P art of doing business today—and, indeed, part of everyday life—is the risk of being involved in a lawsuit. The list of circumstances in which businesspersons can be sued is long and varied. A customer who is injured by a security guard at a business establishment, for instance, may sue the business owner, claiming that the security guard's conduct was intentionally wrongful. The parents of a young girl who is bitten while feeding a dolphin may file a suit against Sea World, alleging *negligence* (to be explained later in this chapter).

Any time that one party's allegedly wrongful conduct causes injury to another, an action may arise under the law of *torts* (the word *tort* is French for "wrong"). Through tort law, society compensates those who have suffered injuries as a result of the wrongful conduct of others.

Many of the lawsuits brought by or against business firms are based on the tort theories discussed in this chapter and the next chapter, which covers strict liability and product liability. In addition, Chapter 9 discusses how tort law applies to wrongful actions in the online environment.

SECTION 1
THE BASIS OF TORT LAW

Two notions serve as the basis of all **torts:** wrongs and compensation. Tort law is designed to compensate those who have suffered a loss or injury due to another person's wrongful act. In a tort action, one person or group brings a lawsuit against another person or group to obtain compensation (monetary damages) or other relief for the harm suffered.

The Purpose of Tort Law

Generally, the purpose of tort law is to provide remedies for the violation of various *protected interests*. Society recognizes an interest in personal physical safety. Thus, tort law provides remedies for acts that cause physical injury or that interfere with physical security and freedom of movement. Society recognizes an interest in protecting property, and tort law provides remedies for acts that cause destruction of or damage to property.

Damages Available in Tort Actions

Because the purpose of tort law is to compensate the injured party for the damage suffered, you need to have an understanding of the types of damages that plaintiffs seek in tort actions.

COMPENSATORY DAMAGES A plaintiff is awarded **compensatory damages** to compensate or reimburse the plaintiff for actual losses. Thus, the goal is to make the plaintiff whole and put her or him in the same position that she or he would have been in had the tort not occurred. Compensatory damages awards are often broken down into *special damages* and *general damages*.

Special damages compensate the plaintiff for quantifiable monetary losses. Such losses might include medical expenses, lost wages and benefits (now and in the future), extra costs, the loss of irreplaceable items, and the costs of repairing or replacing damaged property.

▶ **Case in Point 6.1** Seaway Marine Transport operates the *Enterprise*, a large cargo ship, which has twenty-two hatches for storing coal. When the *Enterprise* positioned itself to receive a load of coal on the shores of Lake Erie, in Ohio, it struck a land-based coal-loading machine operated by Bessemer & Lake Erie Railroad Company. A federal court found Seaway liable and awarded $522,000 in special damages to compensate Bessemer for the cost of repairing the damage to the loading boom.[1] ◄

General damages compensate individuals (not companies) for the nonmonetary aspects of the harm suffered, such as pain and suffering. A court might award general damages for physical or emotional pain and suffering, loss of companionship, loss of consortium (losing the emotional and physical benefits of a spousal relationship), disfigurement, loss of reputation, or loss or impairment of mental or physical capacity.

PUNITIVE DAMAGES Occasionally, the courts also award **punitive damages** in tort cases to punish the wrongdoer and deter others from similar wrongdoing. Punitive damages are appropriate only when the defendant's conduct was particularly egregious (reprehensible).

Usually, this means that punitive damages are available in *intentional* tort actions and only rarely in negligence lawsuits (negligence actions will be discussed later in this chapter). They may be awarded, however, in suits involving *gross negligence*. Gross negligence can be defined as an intentional failure to perform a manifest duty in reckless disregard of the consequences of such a failure for the life or property of another.

Courts exercise great restraint in granting punitive damages to plaintiffs in tort actions because punitive damages are subject to limitations under the due process clause of the U.S. Constitution (see Chapter 4). The United States Supreme Court has held that to the extent an award of punitive damages is grossly excessive, it furthers no legitimate purpose and violates due process requirements.[2] Consequently, an appellate court will sometimes reduce the amount of punitive damages awarded to a plaintiff on the ground that it is excessive and thereby violates the due process clause.[3]

Tort Reform

Tort law performs a valuable function by enabling injured parties to obtain compensation. Nevertheless, critics contend that certain aspects of today's tort law

encourage too many trivial and unfounded lawsuits, which clog the courts and add unnecessary costs. They say that damages awards are often excessive and bear little relationship to the actual damage suffered, which inspires more plaintiffs to file lawsuits. The result, in the critics' view, is a system that disproportionately rewards a few plaintiffs while imposing a "tort tax" on business and society as a whole. For instance, to avoid *medical malpractice* (see page 132) suits, physicians and hospitals often order more tests than necessary.

TYPES OF REFORMS The federal government and a number of states have begun to take some steps toward tort reform. Measures to reduce the number of tort cases can include any of the following:

1. Limiting the amount of both punitive damages and general damages that can be awarded.
2. Capping the amount that attorneys can collect in *contingency fees* (attorneys' fees that are based on a percentage of the damages awarded to the client—see Chapter 3).
3. Requiring the losing party to pay both the plaintiff's and the defendant's expenses.

FEDERAL REFORM At the federal level, the Class Action Fairness Act (CAFA) of 2005[4] shifted jurisdiction over large interstate tort and product liability class-action lawsuits from the state courts to the federal courts. (A *class action* is a lawsuit in which a large number of plaintiffs bring the suit as a group. *Product liability* suits involve the manufacture, sale, and distribution of dangerous and defective goods—see Chapter 7 for details.)

The CAFA prevents plaintiffs' attorneys from *forum shopping*—looking for a state court known to be sympathetic to their clients' cause. Previously, some state courts had been predisposed to award large damages in class-action suits, even when the case had only a weak connection to that jurisdiction. State courts no longer have jurisdiction over class actions under the CAFA.

STATE REFORMS At the state level, more than half of the states have placed caps ranging from $250,000 to $750,000 on noneconomic general damages (for example, pain and suffering), especially in medical malpractice suits. More than thirty states have limited punitive damages, with some imposing outright bans.

Note that the supreme courts in about half a dozen states have declared their state's damages caps to be unconstitutional. ► **Case in Point 6.2** Naython

1. *Bessemer & Lake Erie Railroad Co. v. Seaway Marine Transport,* 357 F.3d 596 (6th Cir. 2010).
2. *State Farm Mutual Automobile Insurance Co. v. Campbell,* 538 U.S. 408, 123 S.Ct. 1513, 155 L.Ed.2d 585 (2003).
3. See, for example, *Buell-Wilson v. Ford Motor Co.,* 160 Cal.App.4th 1107, 73 Cal.Rptr.3d 277 (2008).
4. 28 U.S.C. Sections 1711–1715, 1453.

Watts was born with disabling brain injuries because Cox Medical Centers, in Missouri, and its associated physicians were negligent in providing health-care services. At the age of six, Naython cannot walk, talk, or feed himself; has the mental capacity of a two-year-old; suffers from seizures; and needs around-the-clock care. His mother, Deborah Watts, sued the medical center on his behalf. Watts won a $1.45 million jury award for noneconomic damages plus $3.37 million for future medical damages.

The trial court reduced the noneconomic damages award to $350,000—the statutory cap under Missouri's law. State law also required the trial court to split the future damages award into two parts, with half the amount payable in yearly installments for fifty years (Naython's life expectancy). Watts appealed. Missouri's highest court struck down the state's damages cap, holding that it violated the state constitution's right to trial by jury. The court reasoned that the amount of damages is a fact for the jury to determine, and the legislature cannot place caps on jury awards independent of the facts of a case.[5] ◄

Classification of Torts

There are two broad classifications of torts: *intentional torts* and *unintentional torts* (torts involving negligence). The classification of a particular tort depends largely on how the tort occurs (intentionally or negligently) and the surrounding circumstances. Intentional torts result from the intentional violation of person or property (fault plus intent). Negligence results from the breach of a duty to act reasonably (fault without intent).

Defenses

Even if a plaintiff proves all the elements of a tort, the defendant can raise a number of legally recognized *defenses* (reasons why the plaintiff should not obtain damages). The defenses available may vary depending on the specific tort involved. A common defense to intentional torts against persons, for instance, is *consent*. When a person consents to the act that damages her or him, there is generally no liability. The most widely used defense in negligence actions is *comparative negligence* (see page 137). A successful defense releases the defendant from partial or full liability for the tortious act.

---

5. *Watts v. Lester E. Cox Medical Centers*, 376 S.W.3d 633 (Mo. 2012).

INTENTIONAL TORTS AGAINST PERSONS

An **intentional tort,** as the term implies, requires intent. The **tortfeasor** (the one committing the tort) must intend to commit an act, the consequences of which interfere with another's personal or business interests in a way not permitted by law. An evil or harmful motive is not required—in fact, the person committing the action may even have a beneficial motive for doing what turns out to be a tortious act.

In tort law, *intent* means only that the person intended the consequences of his or her act or knew with substantial certainty that specific consequences would result from the act. The law generally assumes that individuals intend the *normal* consequences of their actions. Thus, forcefully pushing another—even if done in jest—is an intentional tort (if injury results), because the object of a strong push can ordinarily be expected to fall down.

In addition, intent can be transferred when a defendant intends to harm one individual, but unintentionally harms a second person. This is called **transferred intent. ▶ Example 6.3**   Alex swings a bat intending to hit Blake but misses and hits Carson instead. Carson can sue Alex for the tort of battery (discussed shortly) because Alex's intent to harm Blake can be transferred to Carson. ◄

Assault

An **assault** is any intentional and unexcused threat of immediate harmful or offensive contact—words or acts that create a reasonably believable threat. An assault can occur even if there is no actual contact with the plaintiff, provided that the defendant's conduct creates a reasonable apprehension of imminent harm in the plaintiff. Tort law aims to protect individuals from having to expect harmful or offensive contact.

Battery

If the act that created the apprehension is *completed* and results in harm to the plaintiff, it is a **battery**— an unexcused and harmful or offensive physical contact *intentionally* performed. **▶ Example 6.4**   Ivan threatens Jean with a gun and then shoots her. The pointing of the gun at Jean is an assault. The firing of the gun (if the bullet hits Jean) is a battery. ◄

The contact can be harmful, or it can be merely offensive (such as an unwelcome kiss). Physical injury need not occur. The contact can involve any part of the body or anything attached to it—for instance, a hat, a purse, or a jacket. The contact can be made by the defendant or by some force set in motion by the defendant, such as by throwing a rock. Whether the contact is offensive is determined by the *reasonable person standard.*[6]

If the plaintiff shows that there was contact, and the jury (or judge, if there is no jury) agrees that the contact was offensive, then the plaintiff has a right to compensation. A plaintiff may be compensated for the emotional harm or loss of reputation resulting from a battery, as well as for physical harm. A defendant may assert self-defense or defense of others in an attempt to justify his or her conduct.

False Imprisonment

False imprisonment is the intentional confinement or restraint of another person's activities without justification. False imprisonment interferes with the freedom to move without restraint. The confinement can be accomplished through the use of physical barriers, physical restraint, or threats of physical force. Moral pressure does not constitute false imprisonment. It is essential that the person being restrained does not wish to be restrained. (The plaintiff's consent to the restraint bars any liability.)

Businesspersons often face suits for false imprisonment after they have attempted to confine a suspected shoplifter for questioning. Under the "privilege to detain" granted to merchants in most states, a merchant can use *reasonable force* to detain or delay persons suspected of shoplifting and hold them for the police. Although laws pertaining to this privilege vary from state to state, generally any detention must be conducted in a *reasonable* manner and for only a *reasonable* length of time. Undue force or unreasonable detention can lead to liability for the business.

Cities and counties may also face lawsuits for false imprisonment if they detain individuals without reason. ▶ **Case in Point 6.5** Police arrested Adetokunbo Shoyoye for an unpaid subway ticket and for a theft that had been committed by someone who had stolen his identity. A court ordered him to be released, but a county employee mistakenly confused Shoyoye's paperwork with that of another person—who was scheduled to be sent to state prison. As a result, instead of being released, Shoyoye was held in county jail for more than two weeks. Shoyoye later sued the county for false imprisonment and won.[7] ◀

Intentional Infliction of Emotional Distress

The tort of *intentional infliction of emotional distress* involves an intentional act that amounts to extreme and outrageous conduct resulting in severe emotional distress to another. To be **actionable** (capable of serving as the ground for a lawsuit), the act must be extreme and outrageous to the point that it exceeds the bounds of decency accepted by society.

OUTRAGEOUS CONDUCT Courts in most jurisdictions are wary of emotional distress claims and confine them to situations involving truly outrageous behavior. Generally, repeated annoyances (such as those experienced by a person who is being stalked), coupled with threats, are enough. Acts that cause indignity or annoyance alone usually are not sufficient.

▶ **Example 6.6** A father attacks a man who has had consensual sexual relations with the father's nineteen-year-old daughter. The father handcuffs the man to a steel pole and threatens to kill him unless he leaves town immediately. The father's conduct may be sufficiently extreme and outrageous to be actionable as an intentional infliction of emotional distress. ◀

LIMITED BY THE FIRST AMENDMENT When the outrageous conduct consists of speech about a public figure, the First Amendment's guarantee of freedom of speech also limits emotional distress claims.

▶ **Case in Point 6.7** *Hustler* magazine once printed a false advertisement that showed a picture of the late Reverend Jerry Falwell and described him as having lost his virginity to his mother in an outhouse while he was drunk. Falwell sued the magazine for intentional infliction of emotional distress and won, but the United States Supreme Court overturned the decision. The Court held that creators of parodies of public figures are protected under the First Amendment from intentional infliction of emotional distress claims. (The Court used the same standards that apply to public figures in defamation lawsuits, discussed next.)[8] ◀

---

6. The *reasonable person standard* is an "objective" test of how a reasonable person would have acted under the same circumstances. See "The Duty of Care and Its Breach" later in this chapter.

7. *Shoyoye v. County of Los Angeles,* 203 Cal.App.4th 947, 137 Cal.Rptr.3d 839 (2012).

8. *Hustler Magazine, Inc. v. Falwell,* 485 U.S. 46, 108 S.Ct. 876, 99 L.Ed.2d 41 (1988). For another example of how the courts protect parody, see *Busch v. Viacom International, Inc.,* 477 F.Supp.2d 764 (N.D.Tex. 2007), involving a false endorsement of televangelist Pat Robertson's diet shake.

Defamation

As discussed in Chapter 4, the freedom of speech guaranteed by the First Amendment is not absolute. The courts are required to balance the vital guarantee of free speech against other pervasive and strong social interests, including society's interest in preventing and redressing attacks on reputation.

Defamation of character involves wrongfully hurting a person's good reputation. The law imposes a general duty on all persons to refrain from making false, defamatory *statements of fact* about others. Breaching this duty in writing or other permanent form (such as a digital recording) involves the tort of **libel.** Breaching this duty orally involves the tort of **slander.** The tort of defamation also arises when a false statement of fact is made about a person's product, business, or legal ownership rights to property.

To establish defamation, a plaintiff normally must prove the following:

1. The defendant made a false statement of fact.
2. The statement was understood as being about the plaintiff and tended to harm the plaintiff's reputation.
3. The statement was published to at least one person other than the plaintiff.
4. If the plaintiff is a public figure, she or he must prove *actual malice* (discussed on page 125).

STATEMENT-OF-FACT REQUIREMENT Often at issue in defamation lawsuits (including online defamation, which will be discussed later in this chapter) is whether the defendant made a statement of fact or a *statement of opinion*. Statements of opinion normally are not actionable because they are protected under the First Amendment.

In other words, making a negative statement about another person is not defamation unless the statement is false and represents something as a fact rather than a personal opinion. ▶ **Example 6.8** The statement "Lane cheats on his taxes," if false, can lead to liability for defamation. The statement "Lane is a jerk," however, cannot constitute defamation because it is an opinion. ◀

THE PUBLICATION REQUIREMENT The basis of the tort of defamation is the publication of a statement or statements that hold an individual up to contempt, ridicule, or hatred. *Publication* here means that the defamatory statements are communicated (either intentionally or accidentally) to persons other than the defamed party. ▶ **Example 6.9** If Rodriques sends Andrews a private handwritten letter falsely accusing him of embezzling funds, the action does not constitute libel. If Peters falsely states that Gordon is dishonest and incompetent when no one else is around, the action does not constitute slander. In neither instance was the message communicated to a third party. ◀

The courts have generally held that even dictating a letter to a secretary constitutes publication, although the publication may be privileged (a concept that will be explained shortly). Moreover, if a third party merely overhears defamatory statements by chance, the courts usually hold that this also constitutes publication. Defamatory statements made via the Internet are actionable as well. Note also that any individual who repeats or republishes defamatory statements normally is liable even if that person reveals the source of the statements.

DAMAGES FOR LIBEL Once a defendant's liability for libel is established, general damages are presumed as a matter of law. General damages are designed to compensate the plaintiff for nonspecific harms such as disgrace or dishonor in the eyes of the community, humiliation, injured reputation, and emotional distress—harms that are difficult to measure. In other words, to recover damages, the plaintiff need not prove that he or she was actually harmed in any specific way as a result of the libelous statement.

DAMAGES FOR SLANDER In contrast to cases alleging libel, in a case alleging slander, the plaintiff must prove *special damages* to establish the defendant's liability. The plaintiff must show that the slanderous statement caused her or him to suffer actual economic or monetary losses.

Unless this initial hurdle of proving special damages is overcome, a plaintiff alleging slander normally cannot go forward with the suit and recover any damages. This requirement is imposed in slander cases because oral statements have a temporary quality. In contrast, a libelous (written) statement has the quality of permanence and can be circulated widely, especially through tweets and blogs. Also, libel usually results from some degree of deliberation by the author.

SLANDER *PER SE* Exceptions to the burden of proving special damages in cases alleging slander are made for certain types of slanderous statements. If a false statement constitutes "slander *per se*," it is actionable with no proof of special damages required. In most states, the following four types of declarations are considered to be slander *per se*:

1. A statement that another has a particular type of disease (such as a sexually transmitted disease or mental illness).
2. A statement that another has committed improprieties while engaging in a profession or trade.
3. A statement that another has committed or has been imprisoned for a serious crime.
4. A statement that a person (usually only unmarried persons and sometimes only women) is unchaste or has engaged in serious sexual misconduct.

DEFENSES TO DEFAMATION Truth is normally an absolute defense against a defamation charge. In other words, if a defendant in a defamation case can prove that the allegedly defamatory statements of fact were true, normally no tort has been committed.

Other defenses to defamation may exist if the speech is *privileged* or concerns a public figure. Note that the majority of defamation actions are filed in state courts, and state laws differ somewhat in the defenses they allow, such as privilege (discussed shortly).

At the heart of the following case were allegedly defamatory statements posted online that criticized a doctor for what the son of one of the doctor's patients perceived as rude and insensitive behavior.

CASE ANALYSIS

Case 6.1 McKee v. Laurion
Supreme Court of Minnesota, 825 N.W.2d 725 (2013).

IN THE LANGUAGE OF THE COURT
PAGE, Justice.

* * * *

On April 17, 2010, Kenneth Laurion, the father of Dennis Laurion (Laurion), was admitted to St. Luke's Hospital in Duluth [Minnesota] after suffering a hemorrhagic stroke. On April 19, Kenneth Laurion was transferred from the intensive care unit (ICU) of St. Luke's to a private room. The attending physician arranged for Dr. [David] McKee, a neurologist, to examine Kenneth Laurion. Dr. McKee had never met Kenneth Laurion before he examined him on April 19.

Three family members were present in Kenneth Laurion's hospital room when Dr. McKee's examination began: Laurion, his mother, and his wife. The examination lasted no longer than 20 minutes, during which time Dr. McKee made certain statements and acted in a manner that, as a whole, the Laurions perceived as rude and insensitive. After Kenneth

Laurion had been discharged from the hospital, Laurion posted the following statements regarding Dr. McKee on various "rate-your-doctor" websites:

> My father spent 2 days in ICU after a hemorrhagic stroke. He saw a speech therapist and a physical therapist for evaluation. About 10 minutes after my father transferred from ICU to a ward room, Dr. McKee walked into a family visit with my dad. He seemed upset that my father had been moved. Never having met my father or his family, Dr. McKee said, "When you weren't in ICU, I had to spend time finding out if you transferred or died." When we gaped at him, he said, "Well, 44 percent of hemorrhagic strokes die within 30 days. I guess this is the better option." * * * When my father said his gown was just hanging from his neck without a back, Dr. McKee said, "That doesn't matter." My wife said, "It matters to us; let us go into the hall."

* * * *

After learning of Laurion's online postings from another patient, Dr.

McKee commenced this action [in a Minnesota state court] against Laurion, asserting claims for defamation * * *. Laurion moved for summary judgment seeking dismissal of Dr. McKee's lawsuit. The * * * court granted Laurion's motion * * *, concluding that * * * the statements were * * * substantially true.

The court of appeals * * * reversed the [lower] court * * *. The [appellate] court concluded that * * * there were genuine issues of material fact as to the statements' falsity.

* * * *

*Truth is a complete defense to a defamation action and true statements, however disparaging, are not actionable. * * * If the statement is true in substance, minor inaccuracies of expression or detail are immaterial. Minor inaccuracies do not amount to falsity so long as the substance, the gist, the sting, of the libelous charge is justified. A statement is substantially true if it would have the same effect on the mind of the reader or listener as that which the pleaded truth would have produced.*

CASE 6.1 CONTINUES ➡

The plaintiff has the burden of proving falsity in order to establish a successful defamation claim. [Emphasis added.]

Viewing the evidence here in a light most favorable to Dr. McKee, we conclude that there is no genuine issue of material fact as to the falsity of [the] statements * * * . As to Statement 1 (Dr. McKee said he had to "spend time finding out if you transferred or died."), Dr. McKee described his account of the statement in his deposition testimony:

> I made a jocular [funny] comment * * * to the effect of I had looked for Kenneth Laurion up in the intensive care unit and was glad to find that, when he wasn't there, that he had been moved to a regular hospital bed, because you only go one of two ways when you leave the intensive care unit; you either have improved to the point where you're someplace like this or you leave because you've died.

In light of the substantial similarity between Statement 1 and Dr. McKee's account, we conclude that any differences between the two versions are nothing more than minor inaccuracies that cannot serve as a basis for satisfying the falsity element of a defamation claim. Here, the gist or sting of Laurion's and Dr. McKee's versions are the same. Both communicate the notion that patients in the intensive care unit who have suffered a hemorrhagic stroke leave the intensive care unit either because they have been transferred to a regular room or they have died. Therefore, the substance of Statement 1 is justified given the similarity of the two versions. In other words, Dr. McKee's account of what he said would produce the same effect on the mind of the reader as Statement 1. The minor inaccuracies of expression in Statement 1 as compared to Dr. McKee's version of what he said do not give rise to a genuine issue as to falsity. For these reasons, we conclude that there is no genuine issue of material fact as to the falsity of Statement 1.

As to Statement 2 (Dr. McKee said, "Well, 44 percent of hemorrhagic strokes die within 30 days. I guess this is the better option."), Dr. McKee acknowledged in his deposition that during the examination of Kenneth Laurion, he communicated to those present that some ICU patients die. However, he denies referencing a specific percentage. Thus, Dr. McKee posits that Statement 2 is false, or that, at the least, there is a genuine issue of material fact as to the falsity of Statement 2 because he never stated a specific percentage. The problem for Dr. McKee with respect to Statement 2 is that the gist or sting of Statement 2 is the mention of hemorrhagic stroke patients dying and not the percentage referenced. Statement 2 squarely satisfies the test for substantial truth because it would have the same effect on the reader regardless of whether a specific percentage is referenced (or whether the percentage is accurate). The presence or absence of a specific percentage within Statement 2, without more, has no bearing on how a reader would perceive the statement because the gist or sting of Dr. McKee's reference to death does not change based on the statistical reference. Nor does the presence, absence, or inaccuracy of the stated percentage, without more, cast Dr. McKee in a more negative light than does his discussion of patients dying. That is especially true when the reader is given no context for the statistics. Therefore, we conclude that there is no genuine issue of material fact as to the falsity of Statement 2.

As to Statement [3] (Dr. McKee said, "That doesn't matter" that the patient's gown did not cover his backside), Dr. McKee testified that he told the patient that the gown "looks like it's okay" because it did not appear that the gown was at risk of falling off. We are not persuaded that there is any meaningful difference between the two versions of the statements sufficient to create a genuine issue as to the falsity of Statement [3]. The substance or gist of the two versions is the same. Commenting that the gown "looks like it's okay" is another way of communicating that "it didn't matter" that the gown was not tied in the back. Thus, any inaccuracy of expression does not change the meaning of what Dr. McKee admits to having said. For these reasons, we conclude that Statement [3] is not actionable.

* * * *

Because the [three] statements at issue, viewed individually or in the context of the entire posting, are not actionable, we conclude that the [lower] court properly granted summary judgment in favor of Laurion.

Reversed.

LEGAL REASONING QUESTIONS

1. What are the required elements to establish a claim of defamation? Which party has to plead and prove these elements?

2. Which element of the claim is undercut by the "truth"?

3. How did the court's interpretation of the "truth" affect its decision in this case?

4. Suppose that Laurion had posted online, "When I mentioned Dr. McKee's name to a friend who is a nurse, she said, 'Dr. McKee is a real tool!' " Would this statement have been defamatory? Explain.

Privileged Communications. In some circumstances, a person will not be liable for defamatory statements because she or he enjoys a **privilege,** or immunity. Privileged communications are of two types: absolute and qualified.[9] Only in judicial proceedings and certain government proceedings is an *absolute privilege* granted. Thus, statements made by attorneys and judges in the courtroom during a trial are absolutely privileged, as are statements made by government officials during legislative debate.

In other situations, a person will not be liable for defamatory statements because he or she has a *qualified,* or *conditional, privilege.* An employer's statements in written evaluations of employees, for instance, are protected by a qualified privilege. Generally, if the statements are made in good faith and the publication is limited to those who have a legitimate interest in the communication, the statements fall within the area of qualified privilege.

▶ **Example 6.10** Jorge has worked at Sony Corporation for five years and is being considered for a management position. His supervisor, Lydia, writes a memo about Jorge's performance to those evaluating him for the position. The memo contains certain negative statements, which Lydia honestly believes are true. If Lydia limits the disclosure of the memo to company representatives, her statements will likely be protected by a qualified privilege. ◀

Public Figures. Politicians, entertainers, professional athletes, and others in the public eye are considered **public figures.** In general, public figures are considered "fair game," and false and defamatory statements about them that are published in the media will not constitute defamation unless the statements are made with **actual malice.**

To be made with actual malice, a statement must be made *with either knowledge of its falsity or a reckless disregard of the truth.*[10] Statements made about public figures, especially when they are communicated via a public medium, usually are related to matters of general public interest. Public figures generally have some access to a public medium for answering belittling falsehoods about themselves. For these reasons, public figures have a greater burden of proof in defa-

mation cases (to show actual malice) than do private individuals.

Invasion of Privacy

A person has a right to solitude and freedom from prying public eyes—in other words, to privacy. As mentioned in Chapter 4, the courts have held that certain amendments to the U.S. Constitution imply a right to privacy. Some state constitutions explicitly provide for privacy rights, as do a number of federal and state statutes. Tort law also safeguards these rights through the tort of *invasion of privacy.* Generally, to sue successfully for an invasion of privacy, a person must have a reasonable expectation of privacy, and the invasion must be highly offensive.

INVASION OF PRIVACY UNDER THE COMMON LAW
The following four acts qualify as an invasion of privacy under the common law:

1. *Intrusion into an individual's affairs or seclusion.* Invading someone's home or searching someone's briefcase or laptop without authorization is an invasion of privacy. This tort has been held to extend to eavesdropping by wiretap, unauthorized scanning of a bank account, compulsory blood testing, and window peeping. ▶ **Example 6.11** A female sports reporter for ESPN is digitally videoed while naked through the peephole in the door of her hotel room. She will probably win a lawsuit against the man who took the video and posted it on the Internet. ◀

2. *False light.* Publication of information that places a person in a false light is also an invasion of privacy. For instance, it is an invasions of privacy to write a story about a person that attributes ideas and opinions not held by that person. (Publishing such a story could involve the tort of defamation as well.) ▶ **Example 6.12** An Arkansas newspaper prints an article with the headline "Special Delivery: World's oldest newspaper carrier, 101, quits because she's pregnant!" Next to the article is a picture of a ninety-six-year-old woman who is not the subject of the article (and not pregnant). She sues the paper for placing her in a false light and probably will prevail. ◀

3. *Public disclosure of private facts.* This type of invasion of privacy occurs when a person publicly discloses private facts about an individual that an ordinary person would find objectionable or embarrassing. A newspaper account of a private

---

9. Note that the term *privileged communication* in this context is not the same as privileged communication between a professional, such as an attorney, and his or her client.
10. *New York Times Co. v. Sullivan,* 376 U.S. 254, 84 S.Ct. 710, 11 L.Ed.2d 686 (1964). As mentioned earlier, the First Amendment also protects the creator of a parody from liability for defamation of a public figure.

citizen's sex life or financial affairs could be an actionable invasion of privacy. This is so even if the information revealed is true, because it should not be a matter of public concern.

Note, however, that news reports about public figures' personal lives are often not actionable because a public figure's behavior *is* a legitimate public concern. For instance, when U.S. Congressman Anthony Weiner posted partially nude photos of himself on Twitter, his action was a matter of legitimate public concern. In contrast, the same online communications by a neighbor would likely not be a matter of public concern.

4. *Appropriation of identity.* Using a person's name, picture, likeness, or other identifiable characteristic for commercial purposes without permission is also an invasion of privacy. An individual's right to privacy normally includes the right to the exclusive use of her or his identity. ▶ **Example 6.13** An advertising agency asks a singer with a distinctive voice and stage presence to do a marketing campaign for a new automobile. The singer rejects the offer. If the agency then uses someone who imitates the singer's voice and dance moves in the ad, it would be actionable as an appropriation of identity. ◀

APPROPRIATION STATUTES Most states today have codified the common law tort of appropriation of identity in statutes that establish the distinct tort of appropriation or right of publicity. States differ as to the degree of likeness that is required to impose liability for appropriation, however.

Some courts have held that even when an animated character in a video or a video game is made to look like an actual person, there are not enough similarities to constitute appropriation. ▶ **Case in Point 6.14** The Naked Cowboy, Robert Burck, is a street entertainer in New York City who performs for tourists wearing only a white cowboy hat, white cowboy boots, and white underwear. He carries a guitar strategically placed to give the illusion of nudity and has become famous. Burck sued Mars, Inc., the maker of M&Ms candy, over a video it showed on billboards in Times Square that depicted a blue M&M dressed exactly like The Naked Cowboy. The court, however, held that the use of Burck's signature costume did not amount to appropriation.[11] ◀

---

11. *Burck v. Mars, Inc.,* 571 F.Supp.2d 446 (S.D.N.Y. 2008).

Fraudulent Misrepresentation

A misrepresentation leads another to believe in a condition that is different from the condition that actually exists. Although persons sometimes make misrepresentations accidentally because they are unaware of the existing facts, the tort of **fraudulent misrepresentation,** or *fraud,* involves *intentional* deceit for personal gain. The tort includes several elements:

1. A misrepresentation of material facts or conditions with knowledge that they are false or with reckless disregard for the truth.
2. An intent to induce another party to rely on the misrepresentation.
3. A justifiable reliance on the misrepresentation by the deceived party.
4. Damages suffered as a result of that reliance.
5. A causal connection between the misrepresentation and the injury suffered.

For fraud to occur, more than mere **puffery,** or *seller's talk,* must be involved. Fraud exists only when a person represents as a fact something he or she knows is untrue. For instance, it is fraud to claim that the roof of a building does not leak when one knows that it does. Facts are objectively ascertainable, whereas seller's talk (such as "I am the best accountant in town") is not.

Normally, the tort of fraudulent misrepresentation occurs only when there is reliance on a *statement of fact.* Sometimes, however, reliance on a *statement of opinion* may involve the tort of fraudulent misrepresentation if the individual making the statement of opinion has superior knowledge of the subject matter. For instance, when a lawyer makes a statement of opinion about the law in a state in which the lawyer is licensed to practice, a court might treat it as a statement of fact.

Abusive or Frivolous Litigation

Tort law recognizes that people have a right not to be sued without a legally just and proper reason. It therefore protects individuals from the misuse of litigation. If the party that initiated a lawsuit did so out of malice and without a legitimate legal reason, and ended up losing that suit, the party can be sued for *malicious prosecution.*

Abuse of process can apply to any person using a legal process against another in an improper manner or to accomplish a purpose for which the process was not designed. The key difference between the torts of abuse of process and malicious prosecution is the level of proof. Abuse of process is not limited to prior litigation and does not require the plaintiff to prove malice. It can be based on the wrongful use of subpoenas, court orders to attach or seize real property, or other types of formal legal process.

Concept Summary 6.1 below reviews intentional torts against persons.

SECTION 3
BUSINESS TORTS

The torts known as *business torts* generally involve wrongful interference with another's business rights. Business torts involving wrongful interference generally fall into two categories: interference with a contractual relationship and interference with a business relationship.

Wrongful Interference with a Contractual Relationship

Three elements are necessary for wrongful interference with a contractual relationship to occur:

1. A valid, enforceable contract must exist between two parties.

2. A third party must know that this contract exists.

3. This third party must *intentionally induce* a party to the contract to breach the contract.

▶ **Case in Point 6.15**   A landmark case in this area involved an opera singer, Joanna Wagner, who was under contract to sing for a man named Lumley for a specified period of years. A man named Gye, who knew of this contract, nonetheless "enticed" Wagner to refuse to carry out the agreement, and Wagner began to sing for Gye. Gye's action constituted a tort because it interfered with the contractual relationship between Wagner and Lumley. (Of course, Wagner's refusal to carry out the agreement also entitled Lumley to sue Wagner for breach of contract.)[12] ◀

The body of tort law relating to wrongful interference with a contractual relationship has increased greatly in recent years. In principle, any lawful contract can be the basis for an action of this type. The contract could be between a firm and its employees or a firm and its customers. Sometimes, a competitor of a firm draws away one of the firm's key employees. Only if the original employer can show that the competitor knew of the contract's existence, and intentionally

_____

12. *Lumley v. Gye,* 118 Eng.Rep. 749 (1853).

CONCEPT SUMMARY 6.1
Intentional Torts against Persons

NAME OF TORT	DESCRIPTION
Assault and Battery	Any unexcused and intentional act that causes another person to be apprehensive of immediate harm is an assault. An assault resulting in physical contact is a battery.
False Imprisonment	An intentional confinement or restraint of another person's movement without justification.
Intentional Infliction of Emotional Distress	An intentional act that amounts to extreme and outrageous conduct resulting in severe emotional distress to another.
Defamation (Libel or Slander)	A false statement of fact, not made under privilege, that is communicated to a third person and that causes damage to a person's reputation. For public figures, the plaintiff must also prove that the statement was made with actual malice.
Invasion of Privacy	Publishing or otherwise making known or using information relating to a person's private life and affairs, with which the public has no legitimate concern, without that person's permission or approval.
Fraudulent Misrepresentation (Fraud)	A false representation made by one party, through misstatement of facts or through conduct, with the intention of deceiving another and on which the other reasonably relies to his or her detriment.
Abusive or Frivolous Litigation	The filing of a lawsuit without legitimate grounds and with malice. Alternatively, the use of a legal process in an improper manner.

induced the breach, can damages be recovered from the competitor.

Wrongful Interference with a Business Relationship

Businesspersons devise countless schemes to attract customers. They are prohibited, however, from unreasonably interfering with another's business in their attempts to gain a greater share of the market.

There is a difference between *competitive practices* and *predatory behavior*—actions undertaken with the intention of unlawfully driving competitors completely out of the market. Attempting to attract customers in general is a legitimate business practice, whereas specifically targeting the customers of a competitor is more likely to be predatory.

▶ **Example 6.16** A shopping mall contains two athletic shoe stores: Joe's and Zappato's. Joe's cannot station an employee at the entrance of Zappato's to divert customers to Joe's by telling them that Joe's will beat Zappato's prices. Doing this would constitute the tort of wrongful interference with a business relationship because it would interfere with a prospective economic advantage. Such behavior is commonly considered to be an unfair trade practice. If this type of activity were permitted, Joe's would reap the benefits of Zappato's advertising. ◀

Generally, a plaintiff must prove that the defendant used predatory methods to intentionally harm an established business relationship or prospective economic advantage. The plaintiff must also prove that the defendant's interference caused the plaintiff to suffer economic harm.

Defenses to Wrongful Interference

A person will not be liable for the tort of wrongful interference with a contractual or business relationship if it can be shown that the interference was justified, or permissible. Bona fide competitive behavior—through aggressive marketing and advertising strategies, for instance—is a permissible interference even if it results in the breaking of a contract.

▶ **Example 6.17** Taylor Meats advertises so effectively that it induces Sam's Restaurant to break its contract with Burke's Meat Company. In that situation, Burke's Meat Company will be unable to recover against Taylor Meats on a wrongful interference theory. The public policy that favors free competition through advertising outweighs any possible instability that such competitive activity might cause in contractual relations. ◀

INTENTIONAL TORTS AGAINST PROPERTY

Intentional torts against property include trespass to land, trespass to personal property, conversion, and disparagement of property. These torts are wrongful actions that interfere with individuals' legally recognized rights with regard to their land or personal property.

The law distinguishes real property from personal property. *Real property* is land and things permanently attached to the land, such as a house. *Personal property* consists of all other items, including cash and securities (stocks, bonds, and other ownership interests in companies).

Trespass to Land

A **trespass to land** occurs when a person, without permission, does any of the following:

1. Enters onto, above, or below the surface of land that is owned by another.
2. Causes anything to enter onto land owned by another.
3. Remains on land owned by another or permits anything to remain on it.

Actual harm to the land is not an essential element of this tort because the tort is designed to protect the right of an owner to exclusive possession.

Common types of trespass to land include walking or driving on another's land, shooting a gun over another's land, and throwing rocks at a building that belongs to someone else. Another common form of trespass involves constructing a building so that part of it extends onto an adjoining landowner's property.

ESTABLISHING TRESPASS Before a person can be a trespasser, the real property owner (or another person in actual and exclusive possession of the property, such as a renter) must establish that person as a trespasser. For instance, "posted" trespass signs expressly establish as a trespasser a person who ignores these signs and enters onto the property. A guest in your home is not a trespasser—unless he or she has been asked to leave and refuses. Any person who enters onto another's property to commit an illegal act (such as a thief entering a lumberyard at night to steal lumber) is established impliedly as a trespasser, without posted signs.

DAMAGES At common law, a trespasser is liable for any damage caused to the property and generally cannot hold the owner liable for injuries that the trespasser sustains on the premises. This common law rule is being abandoned in many jurisdictions, however, in favor of a *reasonable duty of care* rule that varies depending on the status of the parties.

For instance, a landowner may have a duty to post a notice that guard dogs patrol the property. Also, if young children were attracted to the property by some object, such a swimming pool or a sand pile, and were injured, the landowner may be held liable for their injuries. This is the so-called *attractive nuisance doctrine.* An owner can normally use reasonable force, however, to remove a trespasser from the premises—or detain the trespasser for a reasonable time—without liability for damages.

DEFENSES AGAINST TRESPASS TO LAND One defense to a claim of trespass is to show that the trespass was warranted—such as when a trespasser enters a building to assist someone in danger. Another defense exists when the trespasser can show that she or he had a *license* to come onto the land.

A **licensee** is one who is invited (or allowed to enter) onto the property of another for the licensee's benefit. A person who enters another's property to read an electric meter, for example, is a licensee. When you purchase a ticket to attend a movie or sporting event, you are licensed to go onto the property of another to view that movie or event.

Note that licenses to enter onto another's property are *revocable* by the property owner. If a property owner asks an electric meter reader to leave and she or he refuses to do so, the meter reader at that point becomes a trespasser.

Trespass to Personal Property

Whenever any individual wrongfully takes or harms the personal property of another or otherwise interferes with the lawful owner's possession and enjoyment of personal property, **trespass to personal property** occurs. This tort may also be called *trespass to chattels* or *trespass to personalty.*[13] In this context,

harm means not only destruction of the property, but also anything that diminishes its value, condition, or quality.

Trespass to personal property involves intentional meddling with a possessory interest (one arising from possession), including barring an owner's access to personal property. ▶ **Example 6.18** Kelly takes Ryan's business law book as a practical joke and hides it so that Ryan is unable to find it for several days before the final examination. Here, Kelly has engaged in a trespass to personal property (and also *conversion,* the tort discussed next). ◀

If it can be shown that trespass to personal property was warranted, then a complete defense exists. Most states, for instance, allow automobile repair shops to hold a customer's car (under what is called an *artisan's lien*) when the customer refuses to pay for repairs already completed.

Conversion

Any act that deprives an owner of personal property or of the use of that property without the owner's permission and without just cause can constitute **conversion.** Even the taking of electronic records and data may form the basis of a conversion claim. Often, when conversion occurs, a trespass to personal property also occurs because the original taking of the personal property from the owner was a trespass. Wrongfully retaining the property is conversion.

Conversion is the civil side of crimes related to theft, but it is not limited to theft. Even when the rightful owner consented to the initial taking of the property, so no theft or trespass occurred, a failure to return the property may still be conversion. ▶ **Example 6.19** Chen borrows Mark's iPad mini to use while traveling home from school for the holidays. When Chen returns to school, Mark asks for his iPad back, but Chen says that he gave it to his little brother for Christmas. In this situation, Mark can sue Chen for conversion, and Chen will have to either return the iPad or pay damages equal to its replacement value. ◀

Conversion can occur even when a person mistakenly believed that she or he was entitled to the goods. In other words, good intentions are not a defense against conversion. Someone who buys stolen goods, for instance, may be sued for conversion even if he or she did not know the goods were stolen. If the true owner brings a tort action against the buyer, the buyer must either return the property to the owner or pay the owner the full value of the property (despite having already paid the purchase price to the thief).

---

13. Pronounced *per*-sun-ul-tee.

Disparagement of Property

Disparagement of property occurs when economically injurious falsehoods are made about another's product or property rather than about another's reputation (as in the tort of defamation). *Disparagement of property* is a general term for torts that can be more specifically referred to as *slander of quality* or *slander of title*.

SLANDER OF QUALITY The publication of false information about another's product, alleging that it is not what its seller claims, constitutes the tort of **slander of quality,** or **trade libel.** To establish trade libel, the plaintiff must prove that the improper publication caused a third person to refrain from dealing with the plaintiff and that the plaintiff sustained economic damages (such as lost profits) as a result.

An improper publication may be both a slander of quality and a defamation of character. For instance, a statement that disparages the quality of a product may also, by implication, disparage the character of a person who would sell such a product.

SLANDER OF TITLE When a publication falsely denies or casts doubt on another's legal ownership of property, resulting in financial loss to the property's owner, the tort of **slander of title** occurs. Usually, this is an intentional tort in which someone knowingly publishes an untrue statement about another's ownership of certain property with the intent of discouraging a third person from dealing with the person slandered. For instance, it would be difficult for a car dealer to attract customers after competitors published a notice that the dealer's stock consisted of stolen automobiles.

See *Concept Summary 6.2* below for a review of intentional torts against property.

SECTION 5
UNINTENTIONAL TORTS (NEGLIGENCE)

The tort of **negligence** occurs when someone suffers injury because of another's failure to live up to a required *duty of care*. In contrast to intentional torts, in torts involving negligence, the tortfeasor neither wishes to bring about the consequences of the act nor believes that they will occur. The person's conduct merely creates a risk of such consequences. If no risk is created, there is no negligence. Moreover, the risk must be foreseeable. In other words, it must be such that a reasonable person engaging in the same activity would anticipate the risk and guard against it. In determining what is reasonable conduct, courts consider the nature of the possible harm.

Many of the actions giving rise to the intentional torts discussed earlier in the chapter constitute negligence if the element of intent is missing (or cannot be proved). ▶ **Example 6.20** Juan walks up to Maya and intentionally shoves her. Maya falls and breaks her arm as a result. In this situation, Juan is liable for the intentional tort of battery. If Juan carelessly bumps into Maya, however, and she falls and breaks her arm as a result, Juan's action constitutes

---

CONCEPT SUMMARY 6.2
Intentional Torts against Property

NAME OF TORT	DESCRIPTION
Trespass to Land	The invasion of another's real property without consent or privilege. Once a person is expressly or impliedly established as a trespasser, the property owner has specific rights, which may include the right to detain or remove the trespasser.
Trespass to Personal Property	The intentional interference with an owner's right to use, possess, or enjoy his or her personal property without the owner's consent.
Conversion	The wrongful possession or use of another person's personal property without just cause.
Disparagement of Property	Any economically injurious falsehood that is made about another's product or property; an inclusive term for the torts of *slander of quality* and *slander of title*.

negligence. In either situation, Juan has committed a tort. ◄

To succeed in a negligence action, the plaintiff must prove each of the following:

1. *Duty.* The defendant owed a duty of care to the plaintiff.
2. *Breach.* The defendant breached that duty.
3. *Causation.* The defendant's breach caused the plaintiff's injury.
4. *Damages.* The plaintiff suffered a legally recognizable injury.

The Duty of Care and Its Breach

Central to the tort of negligence is the concept of a **duty of care.** The basic principle underlying the duty of care is that people are free to act as they please so long as their actions do not infringe on the interests of others. When someone fails to comply with the duty to exercise reasonable care, a potentially tortious act may have been committed.

Failure to live up to a standard of care may be an act (accidentally setting fire to a building) or an omission (neglecting to put out a campfire). It may be a careless act or a carefully performed but, nevertheless, dangerous act that results in injury. Courts consider the nature of the act (whether it is outrageous or commonplace) and the manner in which the act is performed (carelessly versus cautiously). In addition, courts look at the nature of the injury (whether it is serious or slight) in determining whether the duty of care has been breached. Creating a very slight risk of a dangerous explosion might be unreasonable, whereas creating a distinct possibility of someone's burning his or her fingers on a stove might be reasonable.

THE REASONABLE PERSON STANDARD Tort law measures duty by the **reasonable person standard.** In determining whether a duty of care has been breached, the courts ask how a reasonable person would have acted in the same circumstances. The reasonable person standard is said to be objective. It is not necessarily how a particular person *would* act. It is society's judgment of how an ordinarily prudent person *should* act. If the so-called reasonable person existed, he or she would be careful, conscientious, even tempered, and honest.

The courts frequently use the hypothetical reasonable person standard in other areas of law as well. That individuals are required to exercise a reasonable standard of care in their activities is a pervasive con-

cept in business law. Many of the issues discussed in subsequent chapters of this text have to do with the duty of reasonable care.

In negligence cases, the degree of care to be exercised varies, depending on the defendant's occupation or profession, her or his relationship with the plaintiff, and other factors. Generally, whether an action constitutes a breach of the duty of care is determined on a case-by-case basis. The outcome depends on how the judge (or jury, if it is a jury trial) decides a reasonable person in the position of the defendant would have acted in the particular circumstances of the case.

THE DUTY OF LANDOWNERS Landowners are expected to exercise reasonable care to protect individuals coming onto their property from harm. In some jurisdictions, as mentioned earlier, landowners may even have a duty to protect trespassers against certain risks. Landowners who rent or lease premises to tenants are expected to exercise reasonable care to ensure that the tenants and their guests are not harmed in common areas, such as stairways, entryways, and laundry rooms.

The Duty to Warn Business Invitees of Risks. Retailers and other companies that explicitly or implicitly invite persons to come onto their premises have a duty to exercise reasonable care to protect these **business invitees.** The duty normally requires storeowners to warn business invitees of foreseeable risks, such as construction zones or wet floors, about which the owners knew or *should have known.*

► **Example 6.21** Liz enters a supermarket, slips on a wet floor, and sustains injuries as a result. If there was no sign or other warning that the floor was wet at the time Liz slipped, the supermarket owner would be liable for damages. A court would hold that the owner was negligent by failing to exercise a reasonable degree of care to protect customers against the foreseeable risk of injury from slipping on the wet floor. The owner should have taken care to avoid this risk or warn the customer of it (by posting a sign or setting out orange cones, for example). ◄

The landowner also has a duty to discover and remove any hidden dangers that might injure a customer or other invitee. Hidden dangers might include uneven surfaces or defects in the pavement of a parking lot or a walkway. Store owners also have a duty to protect customers from slipping and injuring themselves on merchandise that has fallen off the shelves, for example. Thus, the owners of business premises should evaluate and frequently reassess potential hazards on the property to ensure the safety of business invitees.

Obvious Risks Provide an Exception. Some risks, of course, are so obvious that an owner need not warn of them. For example, a business owner does not need to warn customers to open a door before attempting to walk through it. Other risks, however, even though they may seem obvious to a business owner, may not be so in the eyes of another, such as a child. In addition, even if a risk is obvious, that does not necessarily excuse a business owner from the duty to protect its customers from foreseeable harm.

▶ **Case in Point 6.22** Giorgio's Grill is a restaurant in Florida that becomes a nightclub after hours. At those times, traditionally, as the manager of Giorgio's knew, the staff and customers throw paper napkins into the air as the music plays. The napkins land on the floor, but no one picks them up. One night, Jane Izquierdo went to Giorgio's. Although she had been to the club on prior occasions and knew about the napkin-throwing tradition, she slipped and fell, breaking her leg. She sued Giorgio's for negligence, but lost at trial because a jury found that the risk of slipping on the napkins was obvious. A state appellate court reversed, however, holding that the obviousness of a risk does not discharge a business owner's duty to its invitees to maintain the premises in a safe condition.[14] ◀

THE DUTY OF PROFESSIONALS If an individual has knowledge or skill superior to that of an ordinary person, the individual's conduct must be consistent with that status. Professionals—including physicians, dentists, architects, engineers, accountants, and lawyers, among others—are required to have a standard minimum level of special knowledge and ability. Therefore, in determining what constitutes reasonable care in the case of professionals, the law takes their training and expertise into account. Thus, an accountant's conduct is judged not by the reasonable person standard, but by the reasonable accountant standard.

If a professional violates his or her duty of care toward a client, the client may bring a suit against the professional, alleging **malpractice,** which is essentially professional negligence. For instance, a patient might sue a physician for *medical malpractice.* A client might sue an attorney for *legal malpractice.*

---

14. *Izquierdo v. Gyroscope, Inc.,* 946 So.2d 115 (Fla.App. 2007).

Causation

Another element necessary to a negligence action is *causation.* If a person breaches a duty of care and someone suffers injury, the person's act must have caused the harm for it to constitute the tort of negligence.

COURTS ASK TWO QUESTIONS In deciding whether the requirement of causation is met, the court must address two questions:

1. *Is there causation in fact?* Did the injury occur because of the defendant's act, or would it have occurred anyway? If the injury would not have occurred without the defendant's act, then there is causation in fact.

   Causation in fact usually can be determined by use of the *but for* test: "but for" the wrongful act, the injury would not have occurred. This test determines whether there was an actual cause-and-effect relationship between the act and the injury suffered. In theory, causation in fact is limitless. One could claim, for example, that "but for" the creation of the world, a particular injury would not have occurred. Thus, as a practical matter, the law has to establish limits, and it does so through the concept of proximate cause.

2. *Was the act the proximate, or legal, cause of the injury?* **Proximate cause,** or *legal cause,* exists when the connection between an act and an injury is strong enough to justify imposing liability. Proximate cause asks whether the injuries sustained were foreseeable or were too remotely connected to the incident to trigger liability. Judges use proximate cause to limit the scope of the defendant's liability to a subset of the total number of potential plaintiffs that might have been harmed by the defendant's actions.

   ▶ **Example 6.23** Ackerman carelessly leaves a campfire burning. The fire not only burns down the forest but also sets off an explosion in a nearby chemical plant that spills chemicals into a river, killing all the fish for a hundred miles downstream and ruining the economy of a tourist resort. Should Ackerman be liable to the resort owners? To the tourists whose vacations were ruined? These are questions of proximate cause that a court must decide. ◀

Both of these causation questions must be answered in the affirmative for liability in tort to arise. If there is causation in fact but a court decides that the defendant's action is not the proximate cause of the plaintiff's injury, the causation requirement has not been met. Therefore, the defendant normally will not be liable to the plaintiff.

FORESEEABILITY Questions of proximate cause are linked to the concept of foreseeability because it would be unfair to impose liability on a defendant unless the defendant's actions created a foreseeable risk of injury.

Probably the most cited case on the concept of foreseeability and proximate cause is the *Palsgraf* case, which is presented next. In determining the issue of proximate cause, the court addressed the following question: Does a defendant's duty of care extend only to those who may be injured as a result of a foreseeable risk, or does it also extend to a person whose injury could not reasonably be foreseen?

CLASSIC CASE 6.2

Palsgraf v. Long Island Railroad Co.

Court of Appeals of New York, 248 N.Y. 339, 162 N.E. 99 (1928).

BACKGROUND AND FACTS The plaintiff, Helen Palsgraf, was waiting for a train on a station platform. A man carrying a package was rushing to catch a train that was moving away from a platform across the tracks from Palsgraf. As the man attempted to jump aboard the moving train, he seemed unsteady and about to fall. A railroad guard on the car reached forward to grab him, and another guard on the platform pushed him from behind to help him board the train.

In the process, the man's package, which (unknown to the railroad guards) contained fireworks, fell on the railroad tracks and exploded. There was nothing about the package to indicate its contents. The repercussions of the explosion caused scales at the other end of the train platform to fall on Palsgraf, causing injuries for which she sued the railroad company. At the trial, the jury found that the railroad guards had been negligent in their conduct. The railroad company appealed. The appellate court affirmed the trial court's judgment, and the railroad company appealed to New York's highest state court.

IN THE LANGUAGE OF THE COURT
CARDOZO, C.J. [Chief Justice]

* * * *

The conduct of the defendant's guard, if a wrong in its relation to the holder of the package, was not a wrong in its relation to the plaintiff, standing far away. Relatively to her it was not negligence at all.
* * * *

* * * What the plaintiff must show is "a wrong" to herself; i.e., a violation of her own right, and not merely a wrong to someone else[.] * * * *The risk reasonably to be perceived defines the duty to be obeyed[.]* * * * Here, by concession, there was nothing in the situation to suggest to the most cautious mind that the parcel wrapped in newspaper would spread wreckage through the station. If the guard had thrown it down knowingly and willfully, he would not have threatened the plaintiff's safety, so far as appearances could warn him. His conduct would not have involved, even then, an unreasonable probability of invasion of her bodily security. Liability can be no greater where the act is inadvertent. [Emphasis added.]

* * * One who seeks redress at law does not make out a cause of action by showing without more that there has been damage to his person. If the harm was not willful, he must show that the act as to him had possibilities of danger so many and apparent as to entitle him to be protected against the doing of it though the harm was unintended. * * * The victim does not sue * * * to vindicate an interest invaded in the person of another. * * * He sues for breach of a duty owing to himself.

* * * [To rule otherwise] would entail liability for any and all consequences, however novel or extraordinary.

CASE 6.2 CONTINUES ➡

DECISION AND REMEDY *Palsgraf's complaint was dismissed. The railroad had not been negligent toward her because injury to her was not foreseeable. Had the owner of the fireworks been harmed, and had he filed suit, there could well have been a different result.*

IMPACT OF THIS CASE ON TODAY'S LAW *The Palsgraf case established foreseeability as the test for proximate cause. Today, the courts continue to apply this test in determining proximate cause—and thus tort liability for injuries. Generally, if the victim or the consequences of a harm done were unforeseeable, there is no proximate cause. Note, though, that in the online environment, distinctions based on physical proximity, such as that used by the court in this case, are largely inapplicable.*

THE GLOBAL DIMENSION *What would be the advantages and disadvantages of a universal principle of proximate cause applied everywhere by all courts in all relevant cases? Discuss.*

The Injury Requirement and Damages

For a tort to have been committed, the plaintiff must have suffered a *legally recognizable* injury. To recover damages (receive compensation), the plaintiff must have suffered some loss, harm, wrong, or invasion of a protected interest. Essentially, the purpose of tort law is to compensate for legally recognized harms and injuries resulting from wrongful acts. If no harm or injury results from a given negligent action, there is nothing to compensate—and no tort exists.

For instance, if you carelessly bump into a passerby, who stumbles and falls as a result, you may be liable in tort if the passerby is injured in the fall. If the person is unharmed, however, there normally can be no suit for damages because no injury was suffered.

As mentioned at the start of this chapter, compensatory damages are the norm in negligence cases. Occasionally, though, a court will award punitive damages if the defendant's conduct was *grossly negligent,* meaning that the defendant intentionally failed to perform a duty with reckless disregard of the consequences to others.

Negligence *Per Se*

Certain conduct, whether it consists of an action or a failure to act, may be treated as **negligence *per se*** ("in or of itself"). Negligence *per se* may occur if an individual violates a statute or an ordinance providing for a criminal penalty and that violation causes another to be injured. The statute must be designed to prevent the type of injury that the plaintiff suffered and must clearly set out what standard of conduct is expected. The statute must also indicate when, where, and of whom that conduct is expected. The standard of conduct required by the statute is the duty that the

defendant owes to the plaintiff, and a violation of the statute is the breach of that duty.

▶ **Case in Point 6.24** A Delaware statute states that anyone "who operates a motor vehicle and who fails to give full time and attention to the operation of the vehicle" is guilty of inattentive driving. Michael Moore was cited for inattentive driving after he collided with Debra Wright's car when he backed a truck out of a parking space. Moore paid the ticket, which meant that he pleaded guilty to violating the statute. The day after the accident, Wright began having back pain, which eventually required surgery. She sued Moore for damages, alleging negligence *per se.* The court ruled that the inattentive driving statute sets forth a sufficiently specific standard of conduct to warrant application of negligence *per se.*[15] ◀

Good Samaritan Statutes

Most states now have what are called **Good Samaritan statutes.**[16] Under these statutes, someone who is aided voluntarily by another cannot turn around and sue the "Good Samaritan" for negligence. These laws were passed largely to protect physicians and medical personnel who volunteer their services in emergency situations to those in need, such as individuals hurt in car accidents.[17] Indeed, the California Supreme Court has interpreted that state's Good Samaritan statute to mean that a person who renders

---

15. *Wright v. Moore,* 931 A.2d 405 (Del.Supr. 2007).
16. These laws derive their name from the Good Samaritan story in the Bible. In the story, a traveler who had been robbed and beaten lay along the roadside, ignored by those passing by. Eventually, a man from the region of Samaria (the "Good Samaritan") stopped to render assistance to the injured person.
17. See, for example, the discussions of various state statutes in *Chamley v. Khokha,* 730 N.W.2d 864 (N.D. 2007), and *Mueller v. McMillian Warner Insurance Co.,* 2006 WI 54, 290 Wis.2d 571, 714 N.W.2d 183 (2006).

nonmedical aid is not immune from liability.[18] Thus, only medical personnel and persons rendering medical aid in emergencies are protected in California.

Dram Shop Acts

Many states have also passed **dram shop acts**,[19] under which a bar's owner or bartender may be held liable for injuries caused by a person who became intoxicated while drinking at the bar. The owner or bartender may also be held responsible for continuing to serve a person who was already intoxicated.

Some states' statutes also impose liability on *social hosts* (persons hosting parties) for injuries caused by guests who became intoxicated at the hosts' homes. Under these statutes, it is unnecessary to prove that the bar owner, bartender, or social host was negligent.

▶ **Example 6.25** Jane hosts a Super Bowl party at which Brett, a minor, sneaks alcoholic drinks. Jane is potentially liable for damages resulting from Brett's drunk driving after the party. ◀

SECTION 6
DEFENSES TO NEGLIGENCE

Defendants often defend against negligence claims by asserting that the plaintiffs have failed to prove the existence of one or more of the required elements for negligence. Additionally, there are three basic *affirmative* defenses in negligence cases (defenses that a defendant can use to avoid liability even if the facts are as the plaintiff states): *assumption of risk, superseding cause,* and *contributory and comparative negligence.*

Assumption of Risk

A plaintiff who voluntarily enters into a risky situation, knowing the risk involved, will not be allowed to recover. This is the defense of **assumption of risk,** which requires:

1. Knowledge of the risk.
2. Voluntary assumption of the risk.

The defense of assumption of risk is frequently asserted when the plaintiff was injured during recreational activities that involve known risk, such as skiing and skydiving. Courts do not apply the assumption of risk doctrine in emergency situations. Note that assumption of risk can apply not only to participants in sporting events, but also to spectators and bystanders who are injured while attending those events.

In the following *Spotlight Case,* the issue was whether a spectator at a baseball game voluntarily assumed the risk of being hit by an errant ball thrown while the players were warming up before the game.

---

18. *Van Horn v. Watson,* 45 Cal.4th 322, 197 P.3d 164, 86 Cal.Rptr.3d 350 (2008).
19. Historically, a dram was a small unit of liquid, and distilled spirits (strong alcoholic liquor) were sold in drams. Thus, a dram shop was a place where liquor was sold in drams.

SP TLIGHT on the Seattle Mariners

Case 6.3 Taylor v. Baseball Club of Seattle, LP
Court of Appeals of Washington, 132 Wash.App. 32, 130 P.3d 835 (2006).

BACKGROUND AND FACTS Delinda Taylor went to a Seattle Mariners baseball game at Safeco Field with her boyfriend and two minor sons. Their seats were four rows up from the field along the right field foul line. They arrived more than an hour before the game so that they could see the players warm up and get their autographs. When she walked in, Taylor saw that Mariners pitcher, Freddy Garcia, was throwing a ball back and forth with José Mesa right in front of their seats.

As Taylor stood in front of her seat, she looked away from the field, and a ball thrown by Mesa got past Garcia and struck her in the face, causing serious injuries. Taylor sued the Mariners for the allegedly

CASE 6.3 CONTINUES ▶

CASE 6.3 CONTINUED

negligent warm-up throw. The Mariners filed a motion for summary judgment in which they argued that Taylor, a longtime Mariners fan, was familiar with baseball and the inherent risk of balls entering the stands. Thus, the motion asserted, Taylor had assumed the risk of her injury. The trial court granted the motion and dismissed Taylor's case. Taylor appealed.

 IN THE LANGUAGE OF THE COURT
DWYER, J. [Judge]

* * * *

* * * For many decades, courts have required baseball stadiums to screen some seats—generally those behind home plate—to provide protection to spectators who choose it.

A sport spectator's assumption of risk and a defendant sports team's duty of care are accordingly discerned under the doctrine of primary assumption of risk. * * * "Implied *primary* assumption of risk arises where a plaintiff has impliedly consented (often in advance of any negligence by defendant) to relieve defendant of a duty to plaintiff regarding specific *known* and appreciated risks." [Emphasis in original.]

* * * *

Under this implied primary assumption of risk, defendant must show that plaintiff had full subjective understanding of the specific risk, both its nature and presence, and that he or she voluntarily chose to encounter the risk.

* * * It is undisputed that the warm-up is part of the sport, that spectators such as Taylor purposely attend that portion of the event, and that the Mariners permit ticket-holders to view the warm-up.

* * * We find the fact that Taylor was injured during warm-up is not legally significant because that portion of the event is necessarily incident to the game.

* * * *

Here, there is no evidence that the circumstances leading to Taylor's injury constituted an unusual danger. It is undisputed that it is the normal, every-day practice at all levels of baseball for pitchers to warm up in the manner that led to this incident. *The risk of injuries such as Taylor's are within the normal comprehension of a spectator who is familiar with the game.* Indeed, the possibility of an errant ball entering the stands is part of the game's attraction for many spectators. [Emphasis added.]

* * * The record contains substantial evidence regarding Taylor's familiarity with the game. She attended many of her sons' baseball games, she witnessed balls entering the stands, she had watched Mariners' games both at the Kingdome and on television, and she knew that there was no screen protecting her seats, which were close to the field. In fact, as she walked to her seat she saw the players warming up and was excited about being in an unscreened area where her party might get autographs from the players and catch balls.

DECISION AND REMEDY *The state intermediate appellate court affirmed the lower court's judgment. As a spectator who chose to sit in an unprotected area of seats, Taylor voluntarily undertook the risk associated with being hit by an errant baseball thrown during the warm-up before the game.*

WHAT IF THE FACTS WERE DIFFERENT? *Would the result in this case have been different if it had been Taylor's minor son, rather than Taylor herself, who had been struck by the ball? Should courts apply the doctrine of assumption of risk to children? Discuss.*

THE LEGAL ENVIRONMENT DIMENSION *What is the basis underlying the defense of assumption of risk? How does that basis support the court's decision in this case?*

Superseding Cause

An unforeseeable intervening event may break the causal connection between a wrongful act and an injury to another. If so, the intervening event acts as a **superseding cause**—that is, it relieves the defendant of liability for injuries caused by the intervening event.

▶ **Example 6.26** While riding his bicycle, Derrick negligently hits Julie, who is walking on the sidewalk. As a result of the impact, Julie falls and fractures her hip. While she is waiting for help to arrive, a small aircraft crashes nearby and explodes, and some of the fiery debris hits her, causing her to sustain severe burns. Derrick will be liable for the damages related to Julie's fractured hip, because the risk of injuring her with his bicycle was foreseeable. Normally, Derrick will not be liable for the burns caused by the plane crash—because the risk of a plane crashing nearby and injuring Julie was not foreseeable. ◄

Contributory Negligence

All individuals are expected to exercise a reasonable degree of care in looking out for themselves. In the past, under the common law doctrine of **contributory negligence,** a plaintiff who was also negligent (failed to exercise a reasonable degree of care) could not recover anything from the defendant. Under this rule, no matter how insignificant the plaintiff's negligence was relative to the defendant's negligence, the plaintiff would be precluded from recovering any damages. Today, only a few jurisdictions still hold to this doctrine.

Comparative Negligence

In most states, the doctrine of contributory negligence has been replaced by a **comparative negligence** standard. Under this standard, both the plaintiff's and the defendant's negligence are computed, and the liability for damages is distributed accordingly. Some jurisdictions have adopted a "pure" form of comparative negligence that allows the plaintiff to recover, even if the extent of his or her fault is greater than that of the defendant. Under pure comparative negligence, if the plaintiff was 80 percent at fault and the defendant 20 percent at fault, the plaintiff may recover 20 percent of his or her damages.

Many states' comparative negligence statutes, however, contain a "50 percent" rule that prevents the plaintiff from recovering any damages if she or he was more than 50 percent at fault. Under this rule, a plaintiff who is 35 percent at fault could recover 65 percent of his or her damages, but a plaintiff who is 65 percent (more than 50 percent) at fault could recover nothing.

Reviewing: Torts

Elaine Sweeney went to Ragged Mountain Ski Resort in New Hampshire with a friend. Elaine went snow tubing down a snow-tube run designed exclusively for snow tubers. There were no Ragged Mountain employees present in the snow-tube area to instruct Elaine on the proper use of a snow tube. On her fourth run down the trail, Elaine crossed over the center line between snow-tube lanes, collided with another snow tuber, and was injured. Elaine filed a negligence action against Ragged Mountain seeking compensation for the injuries that she sustained. Two years earlier, the New Hampshire state legislature had enacted a statute that prohibited a person who participates in the sport of skiing from suing a ski-area operator for injuries caused by the risks inherent in skiing. Using the information presented in the chapter, answer the following questions.

1. What defense will Ragged Mountain probably assert?
2. The central question in this case is whether the state statute establishing that skiers assume the risks inherent in the sport bars Elaine's suit. What would your decision be on this issue? Why?
3. Suppose that the court concludes that the statute applies only to skiing and not to snow tubing. Will Elaine's lawsuit be successful? Explain.
4. Now suppose that the jury concludes that Elaine was partly at fault for the accident. Under what theory might her damages be reduced in proportion to the degree to which her actions contributed to the accident and her resulting injuries?

DEBATE THIS . . . *Each time a state legislature enacts a law that applies the assumption of risk doctrine to a particular sport, participants in that sport suffer.*

Terms and Concepts

actionable 121	dram shop act 135	puffery 126
actual malice 125	duty of care 131	punitive damages 119
assault 120	fraudulent misrepresentation 126	reasonable person standard 131
assumption of risk 135	Good Samaritan statute 134	slander 122
battery 120	intentional tort 120	slander of quality 130
business invitee 131	libel 122	slander of title 130
causation in fact 132	licensee 129	superseding cause 136
comparative negligence 137	malpractice 132	tort 118
compensatory damages 118	negligence 130	tortfeasor 120
contributory negligence 137	negligence *per se* 134	trade libel 130
conversion 129	privilege 125	transferred intent 120
defamation 122	proximate cause 132	trespass to land 128
disparagement of property 130	public figure 125	trespass to personal property 129

ExamPrep

Issue Spotters

1. Jana leaves her truck's motor running while she enters a Kwik-Pik Store. The truck's transmission engages, and the vehicle crashes into a gas pump, starting a fire that spreads to a warehouse on the next block. The warehouse collapses, causing its billboard to fall and injure Lou, a bystander. Can Lou recover from Jana? Why or why not? **(See page 132.)**

2. A water pipe bursts, flooding a Metal Fabrication Company utility room and tripping the circuit breakers on a panel in the room. Metal Fabrication contacts Nouri, a licensed electrician with five years' experience, to check the damage and turn the breakers back on. Without testing for short circuits, which Nouri knows that he should do, he tries to switch on a breaker. He is electrocuted, and his wife sues Metal Fabrication for damages, alleging negligence. What might the firm successfully claim in defense? **(See page 135.)**

- Check your answers to the Issue Spotters against the answers provided in Appendix E at the end of this text.

Before the Test

Go to **www.cengagebrain.com**, enter the ISBN 9781285185248, and click on "Find" to locate this textbook's Web site. Then, click on "Access Now" under "Study Tools," and select Chapter 6 at the top. There, you will find a Practice Quiz that you can take to assess your mastery of the concepts in this chapter, as well as Flashcards and a Glossary of important terms.

Business Scenarios

6–1. Defamation. Richard is an employee of the Dun Construction Corp. While delivering materials to a construction site, he carelessly backs Dun's truck into a passenger vehicle driven by Green. This is Richard's second accident in six months. When the company owner, Dun, learns of this latest accident, a heated discussion ensues, and Dun fires Richard. Dun is so angry that he immediately writes a letter to the union of which Richard is a member and to all other construction companies in the community, stating that Richard is the "worst driver in the city" and that "anyone who hires him is asking for legal liability." Richard files a suit against Dun, alleging libel on the basis of the statements made in the letters. Discuss the results. **(See page 122.)**

6–2. Wrongful Interference. Lothar owns a bakery. He has been trying to obtain a long-term contract with the owner of Martha's Tea Salons for some time. Lothar starts a local advertising campaign on radio and television and in the newspaper. This advertising campaign is so persuasive that Martha decides to break the contract she has had with Harley's Bakery so that she can patronize Lothar's bakery. Is Lothar liable to Harley's Bakery for the tort of wrongful interference with a contractual relationship? Is Martha liable for this tort? Why or why not? **(See page 127.)**

6–3. Liability to Business Invitees. Kim went to Ling's Market to pick up a few items for dinner. It was a stormy day, and the wind had blown water through the market's door each time it opened. As Kim entered through the door, she slipped and fell in the rainwater that had accumulated on the floor. The manager knew of the weather conditions but had not posted any sign to warn customers of the water hazard. Kim injured her back as a result of the fall and sued Ling's for damages. Can Ling's be held liable for negligence? Discuss. **(See page 131.)**

Business Case Problems

6–4. Spotlight on Intentional Torts—Defamation. Sharon Yeagle

was an assistant to the vice president of student affairs at Virginia Polytechnic Institute and State University (Virginia Tech). As part of her duties, Yeagle helped students participate in the Governor's Fellows Program. The *Collegiate Times,* Virginia Tech's student newspaper, published an article about the university's success in placing students in the program. The article's text surrounded a block quotation attributed to Yeagle with the phrase "Director of Butt Licking" under her name. Yeagle sued the *Collegiate Times* for defamation. She argued that the phrase implied the commission of sodomy and was therefore actionable. What is *Collegiate Times's* defense to this claim? [*Yeagle v. Collegiate Times,* 497 S.E.2d 136 (Va. 1998)] **(See page 123.)**

6–5. Proximate Cause. Galen Stoller was killed at a railroad crossing when an AMTRAK train hit his car. The crossing was marked with a stop sign and a railroad-crossing symbol, but there were no flashing lights. Galen's parents filed a suit against National Railroad Passenger Corp. (AMTRAK) and Burlington Northern & Santa Fe Railroad Corp., alleging negligence in the design and maintenance of the crossing. The defendants argued that Galen had not stopped at the stop sign. Was AMTRAK negligent? What was the proximate cause of the accident? Discuss. [*Henderson v. National Railroad Passenger Corp.,* __ F.3d __ (10th Cir. 2011)] **(See page 132.)**

6–6. Business Torts. Medtronic, Inc., is a medical technology company that competes for customers with St. Jude Medical S.C., Inc. James Hughes worked for Medtronic as a sales manager. His contract prohibited him from working for a competitor for one year after leaving Medtronic. Hughes sought a position as a sales director for St. Jude. St. Jude told Hughes that his contract with Medtronic was unenforceable and offered him a job. Hughes accepted. Medtronic filed a suit, alleging wrongful interference. Which type of interference was most likely the basis for this suit? Did it occur here? Explain. [*Medtronic, Inc. v. Hughes,* __ N.W.2d __ (Minn.App. 2011)] **(See page 127.)**

6–7. Intentional Infliction of Emotional Distress. While living in her home country of Tanzania, Sophia Kiwanuka signed an employment contract with Anne Margareth Bakilana, a Tanzanian living in Washington, D.C. Kiwanuka traveled to the United States to work as a babysitter and maid in Bakilana's house. When Kiwanuka arrived, Bakilana confiscated her passport, held her in isolation, and forced her to work long hours under threat of having her deported.

Kiwanuka worked seven days a week without breaks and was subjected to regular verbal and psychological abuse by Bakilana. Kiwanuka filed a complaint against Bakilana for intentional infliction of emotional distress, among other claims. Bakilana argued that Kiwanuka's complaint should be dismissed because the allegations were insufficient to show outrageous intentional conduct that resulted in severe emotional distress. If you were the judge, in whose favor would you rule? Why? [*Kiwanuka v. Bakilana,* 844 F.Supp.2d 107 (D.D.C. 2012)] **(See page 121.)**

6–8. BUSINESS CASE PROBLEM WITH SAMPLE ANSWER: Negligence.

At the Weatherford Hotel in Flagstaff, Arizona, in Room 59, a balcony extends across thirty inches of the room's only window, leaving a twelve-inch gap with a three-story drop to the concrete below. A sign prohibits smoking in the room but invites guests to "step out onto the balcony" to smoke. Toni Lucario was a guest in Room 59 when she climbed out of the window and fell to her death. Patrick McMurtry, her estate's personal representative, filed a suit against the Weatherford. Did the hotel breach a duty of care to Locario? What might the Weatherford assert in its defense? Explain. [McMurtry v. Weatherford Hotel, Inc., *293 P.3d 520 (Ariz.App. 2013)]* **(See page 130.)**

- **For a sample answer to Problem 6–8, go to Appendix F at the end of this text.**

6–9. A QUESTION OF ETHICS: Wrongful Interference with a Contractual Relationship.

White Plains Coat & Apron Co. is a New York– based linen rental business. Cintas Corp. is a competitor. White Plains had five-year exclusive contracts with some of its customers. As a result of Cintas's soliciting of business, dozens of White Plains' customers breached their contracts and entered into rental agreements with Cintas. White Plains filed a suit against Cintas, alleging wrongful interference. [White Plains Coat & Apron Co. v. Cintas Corp., 8 N.Y.3d 422, 867 N.E.2d 381 (2007)] **(See page 127.)**

(a) What are the two important policy interests at odds in wrongful interference cases? Which of these interests should be accorded priority?

(b) The U.S. Court of Appeals for the Second Circuit asked the New York Court of Appeals to answer a question: Is a general interest in soliciting business for profit a sufficient defense to a claim of wrongful interference with a contractual relationship? What do you think? Why?

Legal Reasoning Group Activity

6–10. Negligence. Donald and Gloria Bowden hosted a cookout at their home in South Carolina, inviting mostly business acquaintances. Justin Parks, who was nineteen years old, attended the party. Alcoholic beverages were available to all of the guests, even those like Parks, who were between the ages of eighteen and twenty-one. Parks consumed alcohol at the party and left with other guests. One of these guests detained Parks at the guest's home to give Parks time to "sober up." Parks then drove himself from this guest's home and was killed in a one-car accident. At the time of death, he had a blood alcohol content of 0.291 percent, which exceeded the state's limit for driving a motor vehicle. Linda Marcum, Parks's mother, filed a suit in a South Carolina state court against the Bowdens and others, alleging that they were negligent. **(See page 130.)**

(a) The first group will present arguments in favor of holding the social hosts liable in this situation.

(b) The second group will formulate arguments against holding the social hosts liable based on principles in this chapter.

(c) The states vary widely in assessing liability and imposing sanctions in the circumstances described in this problem. The third group will determine the reasons why courts do not treat social hosts the same as parents who serve alcoholic beverages to their underage children.

CHAPTER 7

STRICT LIABILITY AND PRODUCT LIABILITY

In this chapter, we look at a category of tort called **strict liability,** or *liability without fault.* Under the doctrine of strict liability, a person who engages in certain activities can be held responsible for any harm that results to others, even if the person used the utmost care.

We open this chapter with an examination of this doctrine and then look at an area of tort law of particular importance to businesspersons—product liability. The manufacturers and sellers of products may incur **product liability** when product defects cause injury or property damage to consumers, users, or bystanders (people in the vicinity of the product when it fails).

Although multimillion-dollar product liability claims often involve big automakers, pharmaceutical companies, or tobacco companies, many businesses face potential liability. For instance, in the last few years, there have been numerous reports of energy drinks, such as Monster, Red Bull, Rockstar, and 5-hour Energy, having serious adverse effects—especially on young people.

Several individuals have been hospitalized, and some have even died after consuming energy drinks. In 2012, the federal government issued a report concerning the adverse effects of these products and launched an investigation into their safety. Parents of a teenage girl who died after consuming two Monster energy drinks then filed a lawsuit against Monster Beverage Corporation in California—perhaps the first case in a wave of lawsuits against makers of energy drinks.

SECTION 1
STRICT LIABILITY

The modern concept of strict liability traces its origins, in part, to an English case decided in 1868. ▶ **Case in Point 7.1** In the coal-mining area of Lancashire, England, the Rylands, who were mill owners, had constructed a reservoir on their land. Water from the reservoir broke through a filled-in shaft of an abandoned coal mine nearby and flooded the connecting passageways in an active coal mine owned by Fletcher.

Fletcher sued the Rylands, and the court held that the defendants (the Rylands) were liable, even though the circumstances did not fit within existing tort liability theories. The court held that a "person who for his own purposes brings on his land and collects and keeps there anything likely to do mischief if it escapes . . . is *prima facie*[1] answerable for all the damage which is the natural consequence of its escape."[2] ◀ British courts liberally applied the doctrine that emerged from the case.

Initially, few U.S. courts accepted this doctrine, presumably because the courts were worried about its effect on the expansion of American business. Today, however, the doctrine of strict liability is the norm rather than the exception.

Abnormally Dangerous Activities

Strict liability for damages proximately caused by an abnormally dangerous, or ultrahazardous, activity is one application of strict liability. Courts apply the doctrine of strict liability in these situations because of the extreme risk of the activity. Abnormally dangerous activities are those that involve a high risk of serious harm to persons or property that cannot be completely guarded against by the exercise of reasonable care.

---

1. *Prima facie* is Latin for "at first sight." Legally, it refers to a fact that is presumed to be true unless contradicted by evidence.

2. *Rylands v. Fletcher,* 3 L.R.–E & I App. [Law Reports, English & Irish Appeal Cases] (H.L. [House of Lords] 1868).

Activities such as blasting or storing explosives qualify as abnormally dangerous. Even if blasting with dynamite is performed with all reasonable care, there is still a risk of injury. Considering the potential for harm, it seems reasonable to ask the person engaged in the activity to pay for injuries caused by that activity. Although there is no fault, there is still responsibility because of the dangerous nature of the undertaking.

Other Applications of Strict Liability

Persons who keep wild animals are strictly liable for any harm inflicted by the animals. The basis for applying strict liability is that wild animals, should they escape from confinement, pose a serious risk of harm to people in the vicinity. An owner of domestic animals (such as dogs, cats, cows, or sheep) may be strictly liable for harm caused by those animals if the owner knew, or should have known, that the animals were dangerous or had a propensity to harm others.

A significant application of strict liability is in the area of product liability—liability of manufacturers and sellers for harmful or defective products. Liability here is a matter of social policy and is based on two factors:

1. The manufacturer can better bear the cost of injury because it can spread the cost throughout society by increasing the prices of its goods.
2. The manufacturer is making a profit from its activities and therefore should bear the cost of injury as an operating expense.

We will discuss product liability in greater detail next. Strict liability is also applied in certain types of *bailments* (a bailment exists when goods are transferred temporarily into the care of another).

SECTION 2
PRODUCT LIABILITY

Those who make, sell, or lease goods can be held liable for physical harm or property damage caused by those goods to a consumer, user, or bystander. This is called *product liability*. Product liability may be based on the theories of negligence, misrepresentation, strict liability, and warranties (see Chapter 23). Multiple theories of liability can be, and often are, asserted in the same case. We look here at product liability based on negligence and on misrepresentation.

Based on Negligence

In Chapter 6, *negligence* was defined as the failure to exercise the degree of care that a reasonable, prudent person would have exercised under the circumstances. If a manufacturer fails to exercise "due care" to make a product safe, a person who is injured by the product may sue the manufacturer for negligence.

DUE CARE MUST BE EXERCISED Manufacturers must use due care in all of the following areas:

1. Designing the product.
2. Selecting the materials.
3. Using the appropriate production process.
4. Assembling and testing the product.
5. Placing adequate warnings on the label to inform the user of dangers of which an ordinary person might not be aware.
6. Inspecting and testing any purchased components used in the product.

PRIVITY OF CONTRACT NOT REQUIRED A product liability action based on negligence does not require *privity of contract* between the injured plaintiff and the defendant-manufacturer. As will be discussed in Chapter 17, *privity of contract* refers to the relationship that exists between the parties to a contract. Privity is the reason that normally only the parties to a contract can enforce that contract.

In the context of product liability law, privity is not required. A person who is injured by a defective product may bring a negligence suit even though he or she was not the one who actually purchased the product—and thus is not in privity. A manufacturer, seller, or lessor is liable for failure to exercise due care to *any person* who sustains an injury proximately caused by a negligently made (defective) product. Relative to the long history of the common law, this exception to the privity requirement is a fairly recent development—it dates to the early part of the twentieth century.[3]

Based on Misrepresentation

When a user or consumer is injured as a result of a manufacturer's or seller's fraudulent misrepresentation, the basis of liability may be the tort of fraud. In

---
3. A landmark case in this respect is *MacPherson v. Buick Motor Co.*, 217 N.Y. 382, 111 N.E. 1050 (1916).

this situation, the misrepresentation must have been made knowingly or with reckless disregard for the facts. The intentional mislabeling of packaged cosmetics, for instance, or the intentional concealment of a product's defects would constitute fraudulent misrepresentation.

The misrepresentation must be of a material fact, and the seller must have intended to induce the buyer's reliance on the misrepresentation. Misrepresentation on a label or advertisement is enough to show an intent to induce the reliance of anyone who may use the product. In addition, the buyer must have relied on the misrepresentation.

SECTION 3
STRICT PRODUCT LIABILITY

As discussed at the beginning of this chapter, under the doctrine of strict liability, people may be liable for the results of their acts regardless of their intentions or their exercise of reasonable care. In addition, liability does not depend on privity of contract. Thus, the injured party does not have to be the buyer, as required under contract warranty theory (see Chapter 23). In the 1960s, courts applied the doctrine of strict liability in several landmark cases involving manufactured goods, and it has since become a common method of holding manufacturers liable.

Strict Product Liability and Public Policy

The law imposes strict product liability as a matter of public policy. This public policy rests on the threefold assumption that:

1. Consumers should be protected against unsafe products.
2. Manufacturers and distributors should not escape liability for faulty products simply because they are not in privity of contract with the ultimate user of those products.
3. Manufacturers and distributors can better bear the costs associated with injuries caused by their products—because they can ultimately pass the costs on to all consumers in the form of higher prices.

DEVELOPMENT OF THE DOCTRINE California was the first state to impose strict product liability in tort on manufacturers. ▶ **Case in Point 7.2**   William Greenman was injured when his Shopsmith combination power tool threw off a piece of wood that struck him in the head. He sued the manufacturer, claiming that he had followed the product's instructions and the product must be defective. In a landmark decision, *Greenman v. Yuba Power Products, Inc.,*[4] the California Supreme Court set out the reason for applying tort law rather than contract law (including laws governing warranties) in cases involving consumers who were injured by defective products.

According to the *Greenman* court, the "purpose of such liability is to [e]nsure that the costs of injuries resulting from defective products are borne by the manufacturers . . . rather than by the injured persons who are powerless to protect themselves." ◀ Today, the majority of states recognize strict product liability, although some state courts limit its application to situations involving personal injuries (rather than property damage).

STATED PUBLIC POLICY Public policy may be expressed in a statute or in the common law. Sometimes, public policy may be revealed in a court's interpretation of a statute, as in the following case.

---

4. 59 Cal.2d 57, 377 P.2d 897, 27 Cal.Rptr. 697 (1962).

SP●TLIGHT on Injuries from Vaccines

Case 7.1   Bruesewitz v. Wyeth, LLC
Supreme Court of the United States, __ U.S. __, 131 S.Ct. 1068, 179 L.Ed.2d 1 (2011).

COMPANY PROFILE   *Wyeth, LLC—a subsidiary of Pfizer, Inc.—is an international pharmaceutical and health-care company with its corporate headquarters in Madison, New Jersey. Wyeth develops, makes, and markets medical therapies, clinical programs, nutritional supplements, prescription drugs, and other health-care products,*

CASE 7.1 CONTINUES ▶

CASE 7.1 CONTINUED *including over-the-counter medications. Wyeth was incorporated in 1926. In 1994, the company bought Lederle Laboratories. Since 1948, Lederle had been making the diphtheria, tetanus, and pertussis (DTP) vaccine for children.*

BACKGROUND AND FACTS When Hannah Bruesewitz was six months old, her pediatrician administered a dose of the DTP vaccine according to the Centers for Disease Control's recommended childhood immunization schedule. Within twenty-four hours, Hannah began to experience seizures. She suffered more than one hundred seizures during the next month. Her doctors diagnosed her with "residual seizure disorder" and "developmental delay." Hannah's parents, Russell and Robalee Bruesewitz, filed a claim for relief in the U.S. Court of Federal Claims under the National Childhood Vaccine Injury Act (NCVIA) of 1986, which set up a no-fault compensation program for persons injured by vaccines. The claim was denied. The Bruesewitzes then filed a suit in a state court against Wyeth, LLC, the maker of the vaccine, alleging strict product liability. The suit was moved to a federal district court, which held that the claim was preempted by the NCVIA, which includes provisions protecting manufacturers from liability for "a vaccine's unavoidable, adverse side effects." The U.S. Court of Appeals for the Third Circuit affirmed the district court's judgment. The Bruesewitzes appealed to the United States Supreme Court.

IN THE LANGUAGE OF THE COURT
Justice *SCALIA* delivered the opinion of the Court.

* * * *

In the 1970's and 1980's vaccines became, one might say, victims of their own success. They had been so effective in preventing infectious diseases that the public became much less alarmed at the threat of those diseases, and much more concerned with the risk of injury from the vaccines themselves.

Much of the concern centered around vaccines against * * * DTP, which were blamed for children's disabilities * * * . This led to a massive increase in vaccine-related tort litigation. * * * This destabilized the DTP vaccine market, causing two of the three domestic manufacturers to withdraw.

* * * *

To stabilize the vaccine market and facilitate compensation, Congress enacted the NCVIA in 1986. The Act establishes a no-fault compensation program designed to work faster and with greater ease than the civil tort system. A person injured by a vaccine, or his legal guardian, may file a petition for compensation in the United States Court of Federal Claims.

* * * *

Successful claimants receive compensation for medical, rehabilitation, counseling, special education, and vocational training expenses; diminished earning capacity; pain and suffering; and $250,000 for vaccine-related deaths. Attorney's fees are provided * * * . These awards are paid out of a fund created by a * * * tax on each vaccine dose.

The *quid pro quo* [something done in exchange] for this, designed to stabilize the vaccine market, was the provision of significant tort-liability protections for vaccine manufacturers. * * * *Manufacturers are generally immunized from liability * * * if they have complied with all regulatory requirements * * * . * * * And most relevant to the present case, the Act expressly eliminates liability for a vaccine's unavoidable, adverse side effects.* [Emphasis added.]

* * * *

The Act's structural *quid pro quo* leads to the * * * conclusion: The vaccine manufacturers fund from their sales an informal, efficient compensation program for vaccine injuries; in exchange they avoid costly tort litigation.

DECISION AND REMEDY *The United States Supreme Court affirmed the lower court's judgment. The NCVIA preempted the Bruesewitzes' claim against Wyeth for compensation for the injury to their daughter caused by the DTP vaccine's side effects. The Court found that the NCVIA's compensation program strikes a balance between paying victims harmed by vaccines and protecting the vaccine industry from collapsing under the costs of tort liability.*

THE ECONOMIC DIMENSION *What is the public policy expressed by the provisions of the NCVIA?*

THE POLITICAL DIMENSION *If the public wants to change the policy outlined in this case, which branch of the government—and at what level—should be lobbied to make the change? Explain.*

The Requirements for Strict Product Liability

After the *Restatement (Second) of Torts* was issued in 1964, Section 402A became a widely accepted statement of how the doctrine of strict liability should be applied to sellers of goods (including manufacturers, processors, assemblers, packagers, bottlers, wholesalers, distributors, retailers, and lessors).

The bases for an action in strict liability that are set forth in Section 402A of the *Restatement (Second) of Torts* can be summarized as a set of six requirements, which are listed here. Depending on the jurisdiction, if these requirements are met, a manufacturer's liability to an injured party can be almost unlimited.

1. The product must be in a *defective condition* when the defendant sells it.
2. The defendant must normally be engaged in the *business of selling* (or otherwise distributing) that product.
3. The product must be *unreasonably dangerous* to the user or consumer because of its defective condition (in most states).
4. The plaintiff must incur *physical harm* to self or property by use or consumption of the product.
5. The defective condition must be the *proximate cause* of the injury or damage.
6. The *goods must not have been substantially changed* from the time the product was sold to the time the injury was sustained.

PROVING A DEFECTIVE CONDITION Under these requirements, in any action against a manufacturer, seller, or lessor, the plaintiff need not show why or in what manner the product became defective. The plaintiff does, however, have to prove that the product was defective at the time it left the hands of the seller or lessor. The plaintiff must also show that this defective condition made the product "unreasonably dangerous" to the user or consumer.

Unless evidence can be presented to support the conclusion that the product was defective when it was sold or leased, the plaintiff will not succeed. If the product was delivered in a safe condition and subsequent mishandling made it harmful to the user, the seller or lessor normally is not strictly liable.

UNREASONABLY DANGEROUS PRODUCTS The *Restatement* recognizes that many products cannot be made entirely safe for all uses. Thus, sellers or lessors are liable only for products that are *unreasonably* dangerous. A court could consider a product so defective as to be an **unreasonably dangerous product** in either of the following situations:

1. The product was dangerous beyond the expectation of the ordinary consumer.
2. A less dangerous alternative was *economically* feasible for the manufacturer, but the manufacturer failed to produce it.

As will be discussed next, a product may be unreasonably dangerous due to a flaw in the manufacturing process, a design defect, or an inadequate warning.

Product Defects

The *Restatement (Third) of Torts: Products Liability* defines the three types of product defects that have traditionally been recognized in product liability law—manufacturing defects, design defects, and inadequate warnings.

MANUFACTURING DEFECTS According to Section 2(a) of the *Restatement (Third) of Torts,* a product "contains a manufacturing defect when the product departs from its intended design even though all possible care was exercised in the preparation and marketing of the product." Basically, a manufacturing defect is a departure from a product unit's design specifications that results in products that are physically flawed, damaged, or incorrectly assembled. A glass bottle that is made too thin and explodes in a consumer's face is an example of a product with a manufacturing defect.

Quality Control. Usually, such defects occur when a manufacturer fails to assemble, test, or adequately check the quality of a product. Liability is imposed on the manufacturer (and on the wholesaler and retailer) regardless of whether the manufacturer's quality control efforts were "reasonable." The idea behind holding defendants strictly liable for manufacturing defects is to encourage greater investment in product safety and stringent quality control standards.

Expert Testimony. Cases involving allegations of a manufacturing defect are often decided based on the opinions and testimony of experts. ▶ **Case in Point 7.3** Kevin Schmude purchased an eight-foot stepladder and used it to install radio-frequency shielding in a hospital room. While Schmude was standing on the ladder, it collapsed, and he was seriously injured. He filed a lawsuit against the ladder's maker, Tricam Industries, Inc., based on a manufacturing defect.

Experts testified that the preexisting holes in the ladder's top cap did not properly line up with the holes in the rear right rail and backing plate. As a result of the misalignment, the rivet at the rear legs of the ladder was more likely to fail. A jury concluded that this manufacturing defect made the ladder unreasonably dangerous and awarded Schmude more than $677,000 in damages.[5] ◄

DESIGN DEFECTS Unlike a product with a manufacturing defect, a product with a design defect is made in conformity with the manufacturer's design specifications. Nevertheless, the product results in injury to the user because the design itself was faulty. A product "is defective in design when the foreseeable risks of harm posed by the product could have been reduced or avoided by the adoption of a reasonable alternative design by the seller or other distributor, or a predecessor in the commercial chain of distribution, and the omission of the alternative design renders the product not reasonably safe."[6]

To successfully assert a design defect, a plaintiff has to show that:

1. A reasonable alternative design was available.
2. The defendant's failure to adopt the alternative design rendered the product not reasonably safe.

In other words, a manufacturer or other defendant is liable only when the harm was reasonably preventable.

According to the *Restatement*, a court can consider a broad range of factors. These include the magnitude and probability of the foreseeable risks as well as the relative advantages and disadvantages of the product as it was designed and as it could have been designed.

Risk-Utility Analysis. Most courts engage in a risk-utility analysis to determine whether the risk of harm from the product as designed outweighs its utility to the user and to the public. ▶ **Case in Point 7.4** Jodie Bullock smoked cigarettes manufactured by Philip Morris for forty-five years. When she was diagnosed with lung cancer, Bullock brought a product liability suit against Philip Morris. She presented evidence that by the late 1950s, scientists had proved that smoking caused lung cancer. Nonetheless, Philip Morris had issued full-page announcements stating that there was no proof that cigarette smoking caused cancer and that "numerous scientists" questioned "the validity of the statistics." At trial, the judge instructed the jury to consider the gravity of the danger posed by the design, as well as the likelihood that the danger would cause injury.

The jury found that there was a defect in the design of the cigarettes and that they had been negligently designed. It awarded Bullock $850,000 in compensatory damages and $28 million in punitive damages. Philip Morris appealed, claiming that no evidence had been offered to show that there was a safer design for cigarettes. Nonetheless, the reviewing court found that the jury had been properly instructed. The court affirmed the award but remanded the case for a reconsideration of the proper amount of punitive damages.[7] ◄

Consumer-Expectation Test. Other courts apply the consumer-expectation test to determine whether a product's design was defective. Under this test, a product is unreasonably dangerous when it fails to perform in the manner that would reasonably be expected by an ordinary consumer. The court applied this test in the following case.

---

5. *Schmude v. Tricam Industries, Inc.,* 550 F.Supp.2d 846 (E.D.Wis. 2008).
6. *Restatement (Third) of Torts: Products Liability,* Section 2(b).

7. *Bullock v. Philip Morris USA, Inc.,* 159 Cal.App.4th 655, 71 Cal.Rptr.3d 775 (2008).

CASE ANALYSIS

Case 7.2 Wilson Sporting Goods Co. v. Hickox
District of Columbia Court of Appeals, 59 A.3d 1267 (2013).

IN THE LANGUAGE OF THE COURT
McLEESE, Associate Judge.
* * * *

* * * At an annual retreat for Major League Baseball umpires, a Wilson [Sporting Goods Company] representa- tive gave [Edwin] Hickox an umpire's mask with what the representative claimed was a new, safer design. Several months later, Mr. Hickox wore the mask while working behind home plate as an umpire during a game in Washington, D.C. In the top of the ninth inning, a foul-tipped ball struck the mask. The impact of the ball gave Mr. Hickox a concussion and dam- aged a joint between the bones in Mr. Hickox's inner ear. As a result, Mr. Hickox suffered permanent hearing loss of mild to moderate severity.

CASE 7.2 CONTINUED

The mask was a traditional umpire's mask, but had a newly designed throat guard that angled forward instead of extending straight down. According to the Hickoxes, the throat guard should have had a center wire and should have extended straight down with no forward angle. Because the mask lacked these features, when the ball hit the throat guard, the mask did not deflect the ball but rather temporarily trapped the ball, concentrating the ball's energy at the point of impact. As a result, the mask was driven into Mr. Hickox's jaw with great force.

* * * *

In contrast to the Hickoxes' version of events, Wilson contended the following at trial. The ball hit the mask above the throat guard, not on it, and so the same injury would have occurred even if the mask had not had a throat guard at all. Wilson intended the mask to provide protection by deflecting balls away from the wearer's head, and the mask accomplished this objective during the incident.

* * * *

[Hickox and his wife filed a suit in a District of Columbia court against Wilson, claiming product liability based on a design defect.] The jury rendered verdict for the Hickoxes * * * , awarding $750,000 to Mr. Hickox and $25,000 to his wife. [Wilson appealed, arguing that the evidence was insufficient to support the verdict.]

* * * *

There are two tests commonly used to determine whether a product's design was defective: the consumer-expectation test and the risk-utility test.

Wilson explicitly assented at trial to jury instructions that required the jury to make findings under a consumer-expectation test. Specifically, the jury was told that "a design is defective if the product fails to perform as safely as an ordinary customer would expect when the product is used in an intended or reasonably foreseeable manner."

* * * Accordingly, we employ the consumer-expectation test to evaluate the sufficiency of the evidence in this case.

* * * The evidence indicated that the mask at issue was more dangerous than comparable masks sold at the time, such as hockey-style masks, because the mask could concentrate energy at the point of impact, rather than distribute energy evenly throughout the padded area of the mask. Because the energy possessed by a pitched baseball is adequate to cause severe injury, the jury could reasonably have concluded that a mask that concentrated energy would increase the risk of severe injury.

The jury could also have relied on the existence of safer, commercially available alternatives to draw inferences about the level of safety an ordinary user would expect. There was evidence that alternative masks with detachable throat guards and no forward angle work well and do not excessively restrict the umpire's movement. There also was evidence that Mr. Hickox would not have suffered injury to his ear had he been wearing a hockey-style mask or a mask with a center wire and no forward angle.

In addition, the jury could have concluded that the statements made by Wilson's representative to Mr. Hickox

about the mask reflected Wilson's standard marketing approach, and that an ordinary consumer therefore would have expected the mask to perform more safely than other models. There was evidence that Wilson's representative told Mr. Hickox that the mask would disperse energy and protect against concussion, and that the mask was the best and safest technology. Mr. Hickox also testified that he believed that companies like Wilson tested new products and did not sell them unless they were safe to use. Jurors could consider such testimony in combination with their own reasonable inferences to determine an ordinary consumer's expectations. [Emphasis added.]

Evidence of industry practice can also be relevant to reasonable consumer expectations. Wilson's objective in designing the mask was to disperse energy, not to concentrate it. At the time of the incident, Wilson tested its hockey-style masks to determine if they met impact-intensity standards, but did not perform such testing on its baseball masks. At a time when Wilson used energy dispersal as a design objective for its baseball masks and when impact-intensity standards existed for football helmets, *a reasonable juror could infer that an ordinary consumer would have expected baseball masks to disperse rather than concentrate energy.* In sum, considering all the evidence, a reasonable juror could conclude that an ordinary consumer would have expected the mask to perform more safely than it did. [Emphasis added.]

* * * *

The judgment of the trial court is therefore *Affirmed.*

LEGAL REASONING QUESTIONS

1. What is the "consumer-expectation test"?

2. What factors did the court consider in determining whether the evidence in this case was sufficient to establish reasonable consumer expectations?

3. Can a jury make "inferences" to arrive at a verdict? Explain.

4. How did the appellate court's conclusion in this case affect the parties?

INADEQUATE WARNINGS A product may also be deemed defective because of inadequate instructions or warnings. A product will be considered defective "when the foreseeable risks of harm posed by the product could have been reduced or avoided by the provision of reasonable instructions or warnings by the seller or other distributor . . . and the omission of the instructions or warnings renders the product not reasonably safe."[8]

Content of Warnings. Important factors for a court to consider include the risks of a product, the "content and comprehensibility" and "intensity of expression" of warnings and instructions, and the "characteristics of expected user groups."[9] Courts apply a "reasonableness" test to determine if the warnings adequately alert consumers to the product's risks. For instance, children will likely respond readily to bright, bold, simple warning labels, whereas educated adults might need more detailed information.

An action alleging that a product is defective due to an inadequate label can be based on state law. (For a discussion of a case involving a state law that required warning labels on violent video games, see this chapter's *Insight into Ethics* feature on page 150.)

In the following case, the court had to decide whether the plaintiff could pursue a theory of recovery alleging both a design defect and inadequate warnings.

---

8. *Restatement (Third) of Torts: Products Liability,* Section 2(c).

9. *Restatement (Third) of Torts: Products Liability,* Section 2, Comment h.

CASE 7.3

Johnson v. Medtronic, Inc.
Missouri Court of Appeals, 365 S.W.3d 226 (2012).

BACKGROUND AND FACTS In 2005, Jeffrey Johnson was taken to the emergency room for an episode of atrial fibrillation, a heart rhythm disorder. Dr. David Hahn used a defibrillator manufactured by Medtronic, Inc., to deliver electric shocks to Johnson's heart. The defibrillator had synchronous and asynchronous modes, and it reverted to the asynchronous mode after each use. Dr. Hahn intended to deliver synchronized shocks, which required him to select the synchronous mode for each shock.

Unfortunately, Dr. Hahn did not read the device's instructions, which Medtronic provided both in a manual and on the device itself. As a result, he delivered a synchronized shock, followed by twelve asynchronous shocks that endangered Johnson's life. Johnson and his wife filed a product liability suit against Medtronic, asserting both that Medtronic had provided inadequate warnings about the defibrillator and that the device had a design defect. The trial court found for Medtronic under both product liability theories. The Johnsons appealed.

 IN THE LANGUAGE OF THE COURT
James Edward *WELSH,* Judge.

* * * *

Jeffrey Johnson was not damaged as a result of the [defibrillator] being sold without an adequate warning, at least as described by the Johnsons. The undisputed facts established that Dr. Hahn failed to read or in any way follow the instructions * * * , and the Johnsons have not contended that the manner in which the instructions were provided failed to effectively communicate to users * * * .

* * * *

* * * We nevertheless conclude that [the Johnsons] have raised [enough evidence about] whether the [defibrillator] was * * * in a defective condition and unreasonably dangerous when put to a reasonably anticipated use and whether Dr. Hahn's actions constituted a "reasonably anticipated use" of the device.

* * * *

We recognize that Dr. Hahn's actions in this case were contrary to the instructions provided by Medtronic, both on a label on the defibrillator and in its instruction manual. However, *the fact that a particular use of a product is contrary to the manufacturer's instructions does not, per se, establish that the use could not be anticipated.* [Emphasis added.]

CASE 7.3 CONTINUED The fact that we have rejected the Johnsons' failure to warn claim does not mandate a similar result as to the product defect claim. As the Missouri Supreme Court emphasized recently, "Design defect and failure to warn theories constitute distinct theories aimed at protecting consumers from dangers that arise in different ways."

In other words, in certain instances, a manufacturer may be held liable where it chooses to warn of the danger (even admittedly adequately warn) rather than preclude the danger by design.

DECISION AND REMEDY *The Missouri appellate court held that the Johnsons could not pursue a claim based on the inadequacy of Medtronic's warnings, but that they could pursue a claim alleging a design defect. The court therefore affirmed the trial court's decision in part and reversed it in part.*

THE LEGAL ENVIRONMENT DIMENSION *What could Medtronic have done to avoid possible liability to plaintiffs like the Johnsons? Was there a reasonable alternative design for the defibrillator?*

THE ECONOMIC DIMENSION *Could Hahn or the hospital be held liable for Johnson's injury on a product liability theory? Explain.*

Obvious Risks. There is no duty to warn about risks that are obvious or commonly known. Warnings about such risks do not add to the safety of a product and could even detract from it by making other warnings seem less significant. As will be discussed later in the chapter, the obviousness of a risk and a user's decision to proceed in the face of that risk may be a defense in a product liability suit based on an inadequate warning.

▶ **Case in Point 7.5** Sixteen-year-old Gary Crosswhite failed in an attempt to do a back flip on a trampoline and was paralyzed as a result. There were nine warning labels affixed to the trampoline, an instruction manual with safety warnings, and a placard attached to the entrance that advised users not to do flips. Crosswhite sued the manufacturer for inadequate warnings. The court found that the warnings were sufficient to make the risks obvious and insulate the manufacturer from liability for Crosswhite's injuries.[10] ◀

Risks that may seem obvious to some users, though, will not be obvious to all users, especially when the users are likely to be children. A young child may not be able to read or understand warning labels or comprehend the risk of certain activities. To avoid liability, the manufacturer would have to prove that the warnings it provided were adequate to make the risk of injury obvious to a young child.[11]

Foreseeable Misuses. Generally, a seller must warn those who purchase its product of the harm that can result from the foreseeable misuse of the product as well. The key is the foreseeability of the misuse. Sellers are not required to take precautions against every conceivable misuse of a product, just those that are foreseeable.

Market-Share Liability

Ordinarily, in all product liability claims, a plaintiff must prove that the defective product that caused his or her injury was the product of a specific defendant. In a few situations, however, courts have dropped this requirement when plaintiffs could not prove which of many distributors of a harmful product supplied the particular product that caused the injuries. Under a theory of **market-share liability,** a court can hold each manufacturer responsible for a percentage of the plaintiff's damages that is equal to the percentage of its market share.

▶ **Case in Point 7.6** John Smith suffered from hemophilia (a blood-clotting disorder). Because of his condition, Smith received injections of a blood protein known as antihemophiliac factor (AHF) concentrate. Smith later tested positive for the acquired immune deficiency syndrome (AIDS) virus. Because there was no way to determine which manufacturer was responsible for the particular AHF received by Smith, the court held that all of the manufacturers of AHF could be held liable.[12] ◀

Many jurisdictions do not recognize this theory of liability because they believe that it deviates too significantly from traditional legal principles.

---

10. *Crosswhite v. Jumpking, Inc.,* 411 F.Supp.2d 1228 (D.Or. 2006).

11. See, for example, *Bunch v. Hoffinger Industries, Inc.,*123 Cal.App.4th 1278, 20 Cal.Rptr.3d 780 (2004).

12. *Smith v. Cutter Biological, Inc.,* 72 Haw. 416, 823 P.2d 717 (1991). See also *Sutowski v. Eli Lilly & Co.,* 82 Ohio St.3d 347, 696 N.E.2d 187 (1998); and *In re Methyl Tertiary Butyl Ether ("MTBE") Products Liability Litigation,* 447 F.Supp.2d 289 (S.D.N.Y. 2006).

INSIGHT INTO ETHICS
Warning Labels for Video Games

Almost every product that you purchase in the physical world has one or more warning labels. Indeed, some critics argue that these labels have become so long and ubiquitous that consumers ignore them. In other words, putting warnings on just about everything defeats their original purpose.

Until recently, video games have largely escaped mandated warning labels, although the video game industry has instituted a voluntary rating system to provide information about a video game's content. Each video game is assigned one of six age-specific ratings, ranging from "Early Childhood" to "Adults Only."

Should video games, whether downloaded or bought on a CD-ROM or DVD, have additional warnings to advise potential users (or their parents) that the games might be overly violent? When the California legislature enacted a law imposing restrictions and a labeling requirement on the sale or rental of "violent video games" to minors, this issue became paramount.[a]

Video Software Dealers Sue the State

The Video Software Dealers Association, along with the Entertainment Software Association, immediately brought a suit in federal district court seeking to invalidate the law. The court granted summary judgment in favor of the plaintiffs.

The act defined a violent video game as one in which "the range of options available to a player includes killing, maiming, dismembering, or sexually assaulting an image of a human being." While agreeing that some video games are unquestionably violent by everyday standards, the trial court pointed out that many video games are based on popular novels or motion pictures and have extensive plot lines.

Accordingly, the court found that the definition of a violent video game was unconstitutionally vague and thus violated the First Amendment's guarantee of freedom of speech. The court also noted the existence of the voluntary rating system. The U.S. Court of Appeals for the Ninth Circuit affirmed the district court's decision.[b]

The United States Supreme Court's Decision

The state of California appealed to the United States Supreme Court, but in 2011 the Court affirmed the decision in favor of the video game and software industries. The Court noted that video games are entitled to First Amendment protection. Because California had failed to show that the statute was justified by a compelling government interest and that the law was narrowly tailored to serve that interest, the Court ruled that the statute was unconstitutional.[c]

LEGAL CRITICAL THINKING
INSIGHT INTO THE SOCIAL ENVIRONMENT

Should victims of a mass shooting be able to sue the manufacturer of a violent video game for a design defect if the shooter had been a devoted player of that violent game?

***

a. California Civil Code Sections 1746–1746.5.

b. *Video Software Dealers Association v. Schwarzenegger,* 556 F.3d 950 (9th Cir. 2009).

c. *Brown v. Entertainment Merchants Association,* ___ U.S. ___, 131 S.Ct. 2729, 180 L.Ed.2d 708 (2011).

***

Jurisdictions that do recognize market-share liability apply it only when it is difficult to determine which company made a particular product. Cases usually involve drugs or chemicals.

Other Applications of Strict Product Liability

Almost all courts extend the strict liability of manufacturers and other sellers to injured bystanders. Thus, if a defective forklift that will not go into reverse injures a passerby, that individual can sue the manufacturer for product liability (and possibly bring a negligence action against the forklift operator as well).

Strict product liability also applies to suppliers of component parts. ▶ **Example 7.7** Toyota buys brake pads from a subcontractor and puts them in Corollas without changing their composition. If those pads are defective, both the supplier of the brake pads and Toyota will be held strictly liable for the injuries caused by the defects. ◀

DEFENSES TO PRODUCT LIABILITY

Defendants in product liability suits can raise a number of defenses. One defense, of course, is to show that there is no basis for the plaintiff's claim. If a defendant can show that the plaintiff has *not* met the requirements (such as causation) for an action in negligence, for instance, generally the defendant will not be liable.

Similarly, in a case involving strict product liability, a defendant can claim that the plaintiff failed to meet one of the requirements. For instance, if the defendant shows that the goods were altered after they were sold, normally the defendant will not be held liable. Defendants may also assert the defenses discussed next.

Preemption

A defense that has been successfully raised by defendants in recent years is preemption—that government regulations preempt claims for product liability (see *Spotlight Case* 7.1 on page 143, for example). An injured party may not be able to sue the manufacturer of defective products that are subject to comprehensive federal regulatory schemes. Medical devices, for instance, are subject to extensive government regulation and undergo a rigorous premarket approval process.

Assumption of Risk

Assumption of risk can sometimes be used as a defense in a product liability action. To establish assumption of risk, the defendant must show the following:

1. The plaintiff knew and appreciated the risk created by the product defect.
2. The plaintiff voluntarily assumed the risk—by express agreement or by words or conduct—even though it was unreasonable to do so.

For instance, if a buyer failed to heed a seller's product recall, the buyer may be deemed to have assumed the risk of the product defect that the seller had offered to repair. (See Chapter 6 for a more detailed discussion of assumption of risk.)

Some states do not allow the defense of assumption of risk in strict product liability claims, however.

▶ **Case in Point 7.8** When Savannah Boles became a customer of Executive Tans, she signed a contract that included a clause stating that she was using a tanning booth at her own risk. The clause also stated that she released the manufacturer and others from any liability for any injuries. Later, Boles's fingers were partially amputated when they came into contact with a tanning booth's fan. Boles sued the manufacturer for strict product liability. The Colorado Supreme Court held that assumption of risk was not applicable because strict product liability is driven by public-policy considerations. The theory focuses on the nature of the product rather than the conduct of either the manufacturer or the person injured.[13] ◀

Product Misuse

Similar to the defense of voluntary assumption of risk is that of **product misuse,** which occurs when a product is used for a purpose for which it was not intended. The courts have severely limited this defense, however, and it is now recognized as a defense *only when the particular use was not foreseeable.* If the misuse is reasonably foreseeable, the seller must take measures to guard against it.

Comparative Negligence (Fault)

Comparative negligence or fault (see Chapter 6) can also affect strict liability claims. Today, courts in many jurisdictions consider the negligent or intentional actions of both the plaintiff and the defendant when apportioning liability and damages. A defendant may be able to limit some of its liability if it can show that the plaintiff's misuse of the product contributed to his or her injuries.

When proved, comparative negligence differs from other defenses in that it does not completely absolve the defendant of liability, but it can reduce the total amount of damages that will be awarded to the plaintiff. Note that some jurisdictions allow only intentional conduct to affect a plaintiff's recovery, whereas other states allow ordinary negligence to be used as a defense to product liability.

▶ **Case in Point 7.9** Dan Smith, a mechanic, was not wearing a hard hat at work when he was asked to start the diesel engine of an air compressor. Because the compressor was an older model, he had to prop open a door to start it. When the engine started, the door fell from its position and hit Smith's head. The injury caused him to suffer from seizures. Smith sued the

---

13. *Boles v. Sun Ergoline, Inc.,* 223 P.3d 724 (Col.Sup.Ct. 2010).

manufacturer, claiming that the engine was defectively designed. The manufacturer contended that Smith had been negligent by failing to wear a hard hat and propping open the door in an unsafe manner. Smith argued that ordinary negligence could not be used as a defense in product liability cases. The court ruled that defendants can use the plaintiff's ordinary negligence to reduce their liability proportionately.[14] ◄

Commonly Known Dangers

The dangers associated with certain products (such as matches and sharp knives) are so commonly known that, as mentioned, manufacturers need not warn users of those dangers. If a defendant succeeds in convincing the court that a plaintiff's injury resulted from a *commonly known danger,* the defendant will not be liable.

► **Case in Point 7.10** In a classic example from 1957, Marguerite Jamieson was injured when an elastic exercise rope slipped off her foot and struck her in the eye, causing a detachment of the retina. Jamieson claimed that the manufacturer should be liable because it had failed to warn users that the exerciser might slip off a foot in such a manner. The court stated that to hold the manufacturer liable in these circumstances "would go beyond the reasonable dictates of justice in fixing the liabilities of manufacturers." After all, stated the court, "almost every physical object can be inherently dangerous or potentially dangerous in a sense. . . . A manufacturer cannot manufacture a knife that will not cut or a hammer that will not mash a thumb or a stove that will not burn a finger. The law does not require [manufacturers] to warn of such common dangers."[15] ◄

Knowledgeable User

A related defense is the *knowledgeable user* defense. If a particular danger (such as electrical shock) is or should be commonly known by particular users of a product (such as electricians), the manufacturer need not warn these users of the danger.

► **Case in Point 7.11** The parents of teenagers who had become overweight and developed health problems filed a product liability suit against McDonald's. The teenagers claimed that the fast-food chain had failed to warn customers of the adverse health effects of eating its food. The court rejected this claim, however, based on the knowledgeable user defense.

The court found that it is well known that the food at McDonald's contains high levels of cholesterol, fat, salt, and sugar and is therefore unhealthful. The court's opinion, which thwarted future lawsuits against fast-food restaurants, stated: "If consumers know (or reasonably should know) the potential ill health effects of eating at McDonald's, they cannot blame McDonald's if they, nonetheless, choose to satiate their appetite with a surfeit [excess] of supersized McDonald's products."[16] ◄

Statutes of Limitations and Repose

As noted in Chapter 1, statutes of limitations restrict the time within which an action may be brought. The statute of limitations for product liability cases varies according to state law. Usually, the injured party must bring a product liability claim within two to four years. Often, the running of the prescribed period is **tolled** (that is, suspended) until the party suffering an injury has discovered it or should have discovered it.

To ensure that sellers and manufacturers will not be left vulnerable to lawsuits indefinitely, many states have passed **statutes of repose,** which place *outer* time limits on product liability actions. For instance, a statute of repose may require that claims be brought within twelve years from the date of sale or manufacture of the defective product. If the plaintiff does not bring an action before the prescribed period expires, the seller cannot be held liable.

14. *Smith v. Ingersoll-Rand Co.,* 14 P.3d 990 (Alaska 2000).
15. *Jamieson v. Woodward & Lothrop,* 247 F.2d 23 (D.C.Cir. 1957).
16. *Pelman v. McDonald's Corp.,* 237 F.Supp.2d 512 (S.D.N.Y. 2003).

Reviewing: Strict Liability and Product Liability

Shalene Kolchek bought a Great Lakes Spa from Val Porter, a dealer who was selling spas at the state fair. Kolchek signed an installment contract. Porter then handed her the manufacturer's paperwork and arranged for the spa to be delivered and installed for her. Three months later, Kolchek left her six-year-old daughter, Litisha, alone in the spa. While exploring the spa's hydromassage jets, Litisha stuck her index finger into one of the jet holes and was unable to remove her finger from the jet.

Litisha yanked hard, injuring her finger, then panicked and screamed for help. Kolchek was unable to remove Litisha's finger, and the local police and rescue team were called to assist. After a three-hour operation that included draining the spa, sawing out a section of the spa's plastic molding, and slicing the jet casing, Litisha's finger was freed. Following this procedure, the spa was no longer functional. Litisha was taken to the local emergency room, where she was told that a bone in her finger was broken in two places. Using the information presented in the chapter, answer the following questions.

1. Under which theories of product liability can Kolchek sue Porter to recover for Litisha's injuries?
2. Would privity of contract be required for Kolchek to succeed in a product liability action against Great Lakes? Explain.
3. For an action in strict product liability against Great Lakes, what six requirements must Kolchek meet?
4. What defenses to product liability might Porter or Great Lakes be able to assert?

DEBATE THIS ... *All liability suits against tobacco companies for lung cancer should be thrown out of court now and forever.*

Terms and Concepts

market-share liability 149

product liability 141

product misuse 151

statute of repose 152

strict liability 141

tolling 152

unreasonably dangerous product 145

ExamPrep

Issue Spotters

1. Rim Corporation makes tire rims that it sells to Superior Vehicles, Inc., which installs them on cars. One set of rims is defective, which an inspection would reveal. Superior does not inspect the rims. The car with the defective rims is sold to Town Auto Sales, which sells the car to Uri. Soon, the car is in an accident caused by the defective rims, and Uri is injured. Is Superior Vehicles liable? Explain your answer. **(See page 142.)**

2. Real Chocolate Company makes a box of candy and sells it to Sweet Things, Inc., a distributor. Sweet sells the box to a Tasty Candy store, where Jill buys it. Jill gives it to Ken, who breaks a tooth on a stone the same size and color as a piece of the candy. If Real, Sweet, and Tasty were not negligent, can they be liable for the injury? Why or why not? **(See page 143.)**

- Check your answers to the Issue Spotters against the answers provided in Appendix E at the end of this text.

Before the Test

Go to **www.cengagebrain.com**, enter the ISBN 9781285185248, and click on "Find" to locate this textbook's Web site. Then, click on "Access Now" under "Study Tools," and select Chapter 7 at the top. There, you will find a Practice Quiz that you can take to assess your mastery of the concepts in this chapter, as well as Flashcards and a Glossary of important terms.

Business Scenarios

7–1. Strict Liability. Danny and Marion Klein were injured when part of a fireworks display went astray and exploded near them. They sued Pyrodyne Corp., the pyrotechnic company that was hired to set up and discharge the fireworks. The Kleins alleged, among other things, that the company should be strictly liable for damages caused by the fireworks display. Will the court agree with the Kleins? What factors will the court consider in making its decision? Discuss fully. **(See page 141.)**

7–2. Product Liability. Jason Clark, an experienced hunter, bought a paintball gun. Clark practiced with the gun and knew how to screw in the carbon dioxide cartridge, pump the gun, and use its safety and trigger. Although Clark was aware that he could purchase protective eyewear, he chose not to buy it. Clark had taken gun safety courses and understood that it was "common sense" not to shoot anyone in the face. Clark's friend, Chris Wright, also owned a paintball gun and was similarly familiar with the gun's use and its risks.

Clark, Wright, and their friends played a game that involved shooting paintballs at cars whose occupants also had the guns. One night, while Clark and Wright were cruising with their guns, Wright shot at Clark's car, but hit Clark in the eye. Clark filed a product liability lawsuit against the manufacturer of Wright's paintball gun to recover for the injury. Clark claimed that the gun was de-

fectively designed. During the trial, Wright testified that his gun "never malfunctioned." In whose favor should the court rule? Why? **(See page 142.)**

7–3. Defenses to Product Liability. Baxter manufactures electric hair dryers. Julie purchases a Baxter dryer from her local Ace Drugstore. Cox, a friend and guest in Julie's home, has taken a shower and wants to dry her hair. Julie tells Cox to use the new Baxter hair dryer that she has just purchased. As Cox plugs in the dryer, sparks fly out from the motor, and sparks continue to fly as she operates it. Despite this, Cox begins drying her hair. Suddenly, the entire dryer ignites into flames, severely burning Cox's scalp. Cox sues Baxter on the basis of negligence and strict liability in tort. Baxter admits that the dryer was defective but denies liability, particularly because Cox was not the person who purchased the dryer. In other words, Cox had no contractual relationship with Baxter. Discuss the validity of Baxter's defense. Are there any other defenses that Baxter might assert to avoid liability? Discuss fully. **(See page 151.)**

Business Case Problems

7–4. Defenses to Product Liability. Brandon Stroud was driving a golf car made by Textron, Inc., to transport guests at Christmas party. The golf car did not have lights, but Textron did not warn against using it on public roads at night. When Stroud attempted to cross a road at 8:30 P.M., his golf car was struck by a vehicle driven by Joseph Thornley. Stroud was killed. His estate filed a suit against Textron, alleging strict product liability and product liability based on negligence. The charge was that the golf car was defective and unreasonably dangerous. What defense might Textron assert? Explain. [*Moore v. Barony House Restaurant, LLC*, 382 S.C. 35, 674 S.E.2d 500 (S.C.App. 2009)] **(See page 151.)**

7–5. Product Misuse. Five-year-old Cheyenne Stark was riding in the backseat of her parents' Ford Taurus. Cheyenne was not sitting in a booster seat. Instead, she was using a seatbelt designed by Ford, but was wearing the shoulder belt behind her back. The car was involved in a collision. As a result, Cheyenne suffered a spinal cord injury and was paralyzed from the waist down. The family filed a suit against Ford Motor Co., alleging that the seatbelt was defectively designed. Could Ford successfully claim that Cheyenne had misused the seatbelt? Why or why not? [*Stark v. Ford Motor Co.*, 693 S.E.2d 253 (N.C.App. 2010)] **(See page 151.)**

7–6. Design Defects. Yun Tung Chow tried to unclog a floor drain in the kitchen of the restaurant where he worked. He used a drain cleaner called Lewis Red Devil Lye that contained crystalline sodium hydroxide. The product label said to wear eye protection, to put one tablespoon of lye directly into the drain, and to keep one's face away from

the drain because there could be dangerous backsplash. Without eye protection, Chow mixed three tablespoons of lye in a can and poured that mixture down the drain while bending over it. Liquid splashed back into his face, causing injury. He brought a product liability suit based on inadequate warnings and design defect. The trial court granted summary judgment to the manufacturer, and Chow appealed. An expert for Chow stated that the product was defective because it had a tendency to backsplash. Is that a convincing argument? Why or why not? [*Yun Tung Chow v. Reckitt & Coleman, Inc.*, 69 A.D.3d 413, 891 N.Y.S.2d 402 (N.Y.A.D. 1 Dept. 2010)] **(See page 146.)**

7–7. Strict Product Liability. David Dobrovolny bought a new Ford F-350 pickup truck. A year later, the truck spontaneously caught fire in Dobrovolny's driveway. The truck was destroyed, but no other property was damaged, and no one was injured. Dobrovolny filed a suit in a Nebraska state court against Ford Motor Co. on a theory of strict product liability to recover the cost of the truck. Nebraska limits the application of strict product liability to situations involving personal injuries. Is Dobrovolny's claim likely to succeed? Why or why not? Is there another basis for liability on which he might recover? Explain. [*Dobrovolny v. Ford Motor Co.*, 281 Neb. 86, 793 N.W.2d 445 (2011)] **(See page 143.)**

7–8. BUSINESS CASE PROBLEM WITH SAMPLE ANSWER: Product Liability.

While driving on Interstate 40 in North Carolina, Carroll Jett became distracted by a texting system in the cab of his tractor-trailer truck. He smashed into several vehicles that were slowed or stopped in

front of him, injuring Barbara and Michael Durkee and others. The injured motorists filed a suit in a federal district court against Geologic Solutions, Inc., the maker of the texting system, alleging product liability. Was the accident caused by Jett's inattention or the texting device? Should a manufacturer be required to design a product that is incapable of distracting a driver? Discuss. [Durkee v. Geologic Solutions, Inc., 2013 WL 14717 (4th Cir. 2013)] **(See page 142.)**

• For a sample answer to Problem 7–8, go to Appendix F at the end of this text.

7–9. A QUESTION OF ETHICS: Dangerous Products.

 *Susan Calles lived with her four daughters—Amanda, age eleven; Victoria, age five; and Jenna and Jillian, age three. In March 1998, Calles bought an Aim N Flame utility lighter, which she stored on the top shelf of her kitchen cabinet. A trigger can ignite the Aim N Flame after an "ON/OFF" switch is slid to the "on" position. On the night of March 31, Calles and Victoria left to get videos. Jenna and Jillian were in bed, and Amanda was watching television. Calles returned to find fire trucks and emergency vehicles around her home. Robert Finn, a fire investigator, determined that Jenna had started a fire using the lighter. Jillian suffered smoke inhalation, was hospitalized, and died on April 21. Calles filed a suit in an Illinois state court against Scripto-Tokai Corp., which distributed the Aim N Flame, and others. In her suit, which was grounded, in part, in strict liability claims, Calles alleged that the lighter was an "unreasonably dangerous product." Scripto filed a motion for summary judgment. [Calles v. Scripto-Tokai Corp., 224 Ill.2d 247, 864 N.E.2d 249, 309 Ill. Dec. 383 (2007)] **(See page 145.)***

(a) A product is "unreasonably dangerous" when it is dangerous beyond the expectation of the ordinary consumer. Whose expectation—Calles's or Jenna's—applies? Does the lighter pass this test? Explain.

(b) Calles presented evidence as to the likelihood and seriousness of injury from lighters that do not have child-safety devices. Scripto argued that the Aim N Flame is an alternative source of fire and is safer than a match. Calles admitted that she knew the dangers presented by lighters in the hands of children. Scripto admitted that it had been a defendant in several suits for injuries under similar circumstances. How should the court rule? Why?

Legal Reasoning Group Activity

7–10. Product Liability. Bret D'Auguste was an experienced skier when he rented equipment to ski at Hunter Mountain Ski Bowl in New York. When D'Auguste entered an extremely difficult trail, he noticed immediately that the surface consisted of ice with almost no snow. He tried to exit the steeply declining trail by making a sharp right turn, but in the attempt, his left ski snapped off. D'Auguste lost his balance, fell, and slid down the mountain, striking his face and head against a fence along the trail. According to a report by a rental shop employee, one of the bindings on D'Auguste's skis had a "cracked heel housing." D'Auguste filed a lawsuit against the bindings' manufacturer on a theory of strict product liability. The manufacturer filed a motion for summary judgment. **(See page 142.)**

(a) The first group will take the position of the manufacturer and develop an argument why the court should *grant* the summary judgment motion and dismiss the strict product liability claim.

(b) The second group will take the position of D'Auguste and formulate a basis for why the court should *deny* the motion and allow the strict product liability claim.

CHAPTER 8
INTELLECTUAL PROPERTY RIGHTS

Intellectual property is any property that results from intellectual, creative processes—that is to say, the products of an individual's mind. Although it is an abstract term for an abstract concept, intellectual property is nonetheless familiar to almost everyone. The apps for your iPhone and iPad, the movies you see, and the music you listen to are all forms of intellectual property. More than two hundred years ago, the framers of the U.S. Constitution recognized the importance of protecting creative works in Article I, Section 8 (see Appendix B). Statutory protection of these rights began in the 1940s and continues to evolve to meet the needs of modern society.

Of significant concern to businesspersons is the need to protect their rights in intellectual property, which in today's world may exceed the value of physical property, such as machines and buildings. Consider, for instance, the importance of intellectual property rights to technology companies, such as Apple, Inc. Intellectual property rights can be a company's most valuable assets, which is why Apple sued rival Samsung Electronics Company. Apple claimed that Samsung's Galaxy line of mobile phones and tablets (those that run Google's Android software) copied the look, design, and user interface of Apple's iPhone and iPad. Although Apple is one of Samsung's biggest customers and buys many of its components from Samsung, Apple must also protect its iPhone and iPad revenues from competing Android products. You will read about the verdict in this case on page 163.

SECTION 1
TRADEMARKS AND RELATED PROPERTY

A **trademark** is a distinctive mark, motto, device, or implement that a manufacturer stamps, prints, or otherwise affixes to the goods it produces so that they can be identified on the market and their origins made known. In other words, a trademark is a source indicator. At common law, the person who used a symbol or mark to identify a business or product was protected in the use of that trademark. Clearly, by using another's trademark, a business could lead consumers to believe that its goods were made by the other business. The law seeks to avoid this kind of confusion. In this section, we examine various aspects of the law governing trademarks.

In the following classic case concerning Coca-Cola, the defendants argued that the Coca-Cola trademark was entitled to no protection under the law because the term did not accurately represent the product.

CLASSIC CASE 8.1

The Coca-Cola Co. v. The Koke Co. of America
Supreme Court of the United States, 254 U.S. 143, 41 S.Ct. 113, 65 L.Ed.189 (1920).

COMPANY PROFILE   John Pemberton, an Atlanta pharmacist, invented a caramel-colored, carbonated soft drink in 1886. His bookkeeper, Frank Robinson, named the beverage Coca-Cola after two of the ingredients, coca leaves and kola nuts. Asa Candler bought the Coca-Cola Company

CASE 8.1 CONTINUED

(**www.coca-colacompany.com**) in 1891, and within seven years, he had made the soft drink available throughout the United States, as well as in parts of Canada and Mexico. Candler continued to sell Coke aggressively and to open up new markets, reaching Europe before 1910. In doing so, however, he attracted numerous competitors, some of which tried to capitalize directly on the Coke name.

BACKGROUND AND FACTS   The Coca-Cola Company sought to enjoin (prevent) the Koke Company of America and other beverage companies from, among other things, using the word Koke for their products. The Koke Company of America and other beverage companies contended that the Coca-Cola trademark was a fraudulent representation and that Coca-Cola was therefore not entitled to any help from the courts. The Koke Company and the other defendants alleged that the Coca-Cola Company, by its use of the Coca-Cola name, represented that the beverage contained cocaine (from coca leaves), which it no longer did. The trial court granted the injunction against the Koke Company, but the appellate court reversed the lower court's ruling. Coca-Cola then appealed to the United States Supreme Court.

IN THE LANGUAGE OF THE COURT
Mr. Justice *HOLMES* delivered the opinion of the Court.

* * * *

* * * Before 1900 the beginning of [Coca-Cola's] good will was more or less helped by the presence of cocaine, a drug that, like alcohol or caffeine or opium, may be described as a deadly poison or as a valuable [pharmaceutical item, depending on the speaker's purposes]. The amount seems to have been very small,[a] but it may have been enough to begin a bad habit and after the Food and Drug Act of June 30, 1906, if not earlier, long before this suit was brought, it was eliminated from the plaintiff's compound.

* * * Since 1900 the sales have increased at a very great rate corresponding to a like increase in advertising. The name now characterizes a beverage to be had at almost any soda fountain. It means a single thing coming from a single source, and well known to the community. It hardly would be too much to say that the drink characterizes the name as much as the name the drink. In other words *Coca-Cola probably means to most persons the plaintiff's familiar product to be had everywhere rather than a compound of particular substances.* * * * Before this suit was brought the plaintiff had advertised to the public that it must not expect and would not find cocaine, and had eliminated everything tending to suggest cocaine effects except the name and the picture of [coca] leaves and nuts, which probably conveyed little or nothing to most who saw it. It appears to us that it would be going too far to deny the plaintiff relief against a palpable [readily evident] fraud because possibly here and there an ignorant person might call for the drink with the hope for incipient cocaine intoxication. The plaintiff's position must be judged by the facts as they were when the suit was begun, not by the facts of a different condition and an earlier time. [Emphasis added.]

DECISION AND REMEDY   *The district court's injunction was allowed to stand. The competing beverage companies were enjoined from calling their products* Koke.

IMPACT OF THIS CASE ON TODAY'S LAW   *In this early case, the United States Supreme Court made it clear that trademarks and trade names (and nicknames for those marks and names, such as the nickname "Coke" for "Coca-Cola") that are in common use receive protection under the common law. This holding is significant historically because it is the predecessor to the federal statute later passed to protect trademark rights—the Lanham Act of 1946, to be discussed next. In many ways, this act represented a codification of common law principles governing trademarks.*

WHAT IF THE FACTS WERE DIFFERENT?   *Suppose that Coca-Cola had been trying to make the public believe that its product contained cocaine. Would the result in this case likely have been different? Why or why not?*

---

a. In reality, until 1903 the amount of active cocaine in each bottle of Coke was equivalent to one "line" of cocaine.

Statutory Protection of Trademarks

Statutory protection of trademarks and related property is provided at the federal level by the Lanham Act of 1946.[1] The Lanham Act was enacted, in part, to protect manufacturers from losing business to rival companies that used confusingly similar trademarks.

The Lanham Act incorporates the common law of trademarks and provides remedies for owners of trademarks who wish to enforce their claims in federal court. Many states also have trademark statutes.

TRADEMARK DILUTION In 1995, Congress amended the Lanham Act by passing the Federal Trademark Dilution Act,[2] which allowed trademark owners to bring suits in federal court for trademark **dilution.** In 2006, Congress further amended the law on trademark dilution by passing the Trademark Dilution Revision Act (TDRA).[3]

Under the TDRA, to state a claim for trademark dilution, a plaintiff must prove the following:

1. The plaintiff owns a famous mark that is distinctive.
2. The defendant has begun using a mark in commerce that allegedly is diluting the famous mark.
3. The similarity between the defendant's mark and the famous mark gives rise to an *association* between the marks.
4. The association is likely to impair the distinctiveness of the famous mark or harm its reputation.

Trademark dilution laws protect "distinctive" or "famous" trademarks (such as Rolls Royce, McDonald's, and Apple) from certain unauthorized uses even when the use is on noncompeting goods or is unlikely to confuse. More than half of the states have also enacted trademark dilution laws.

SIMILAR MARKS MAY CONSTITUTE TRADEMARK DILUTION Note that a famous mark may be diluted by the use of an *identical* mark or by the use of a *similar* mark.[4] A similar mark is more likely to lessen the value of a famous mark when the companies using the marks provide related goods or compete against each other in the same market.

▶ **Case in Point 8.1** Samantha Lundberg opened "Sambuck's Coffeehouse," in Astoria, Oregon, even though she knew that "Starbucks" is one of the largest coffee chains in the nation. When Starbucks Corporation filed a dilution lawsuit, the federal court ruled that use of the "Sambuck's" mark constituted trademark dilution because it created confusion for consumers. Not only was there a "high degree" of similarity between the marks, but also both companies provided coffee-related services and marketed their services through "stand-alone" retail stores. Therefore, the use of the similar mark (Sambuck's) reduced the value of the famous mark (Starbucks).[5] ◀

Trademark Registration

Trademarks may be registered with the state or with the federal government. To register for protection under federal trademark law, a person must file an application with the U.S. Patent and Trademark Office in Washington, D.C. Under current law, a mark can be registered (1) if it is currently in commerce or (2) if the applicant intends to put it into commerce within six months.

In special circumstances, the six-month period can be extended by thirty months. Thus, the applicant would have a total of three years from the date of notice of trademark approval to make use of the mark and file the required use statement. Registration is postponed until the mark is actually used.

During this waiting period, any applicant can legally protect his or her trademark against a third party who previously has neither used the mark nor filed an application for it. Registration is renewable between the fifth and sixth years after the initial registration and every ten years thereafter (every twenty years for those trademarks registered before 1990).

Trademark Infringement

Registration of a trademark with the U.S. Patent and Trademark Office gives notice on a nationwide basis that the trademark belongs exclusively to the registrant. The registrant is also allowed to use the symbol ® to indicate that the mark has been registered. Whenever that trademark is copied to a substantial degree or used in its entirety by another, intentionally or unintentionally, the trademark has been *infringed* (used without authorization).

---

1. 15 U.S.C. Sections 1051–1128.

2. 15 U.S.C. Section 1125.

3. Pub. L. No. 103-312, 120 Stat. 1730 (2006).

4. See *Louis Vuitton Malletier S.A. v. Haute Diggity Dog, LLC,* 507 F.3d 252 (4th Cir. 2007); and *Moseley v. V Secret Catalogue, Inc.,* 537 U.S. 418, 123 S.Ct. 1115, 155 L.Ed.2d 1 (2003).

5. *Starbucks Corp. v. Lundberg,* 2005 WL 3183858 (D.Or. 2005).

When a trademark has been infringed, the owner of the mark has a cause of action against the infringer. To succeed in a trademark infringement action, the owner must show that the defendant's use of the mark created a likelihood of confusion about the origin of the defendant's goods or services. The owner need not prove that the infringer acted intentionally or that the trademark was registered (although registration does provide proof of the date of inception of the trademark's use).

The most commonly granted remedy for trademark infringement is an *injunction* to prevent further infringement. Under the Lanham Act, a trademark owner that successfully proves infringement can recover actual damages, plus the profits that the infringer wrongfully received from the unauthorized use of the mark. A court can also order the destruction of any goods bearing the unauthorized trademark. In some situations, the trademark owner may also be able to recover attorneys' fees.

Distinctiveness of the Mark

A trademark must be sufficiently distinctive to enable consumers to identify the manufacturer of the goods easily and to distinguish between those goods and competing products.

STRONG MARKS Fanciful, arbitrary, or suggestive trademarks are generally considered to be the most distinctive (strongest) trademarks. Marks that are fanciful, arbitrary, or suggestive are protected as inherently distinctive without demonstrating secondary meaning. These marks receive automatic protection because they serve to identify a particular product's source, as opposed to describing the product itself.

Fanciful and Arbitrary Trademarks. Fanciful trademarks are inherently distinctive and include invented words, such as "Xerox" for one manufacturer's copiers and "Google" for search engines. Arbitrary trademarks are those that use common words in an uncommon way that is nondescriptive, such as "Dutch Boy" as a name for paint.

Even a single letter used in a particular style can be an arbitrary trademark. ▶ **Case in Point 8.2** Sports entertainment company ESPN sued Quiksilver, Inc., a maker of youth-oriented clothing, alleging trademark infringement. ESPN claimed that Quiksilver's clothing had used the stylized "X" mark that ESPN uses in connection with the "X Games" (extreme action sports competitions). Quiksilver filed counterclaims for trademark infringement and dilution, arguing that it had a long history of using the stylized X on its products.

ESPN created the X Games in the mid-1990s, and Quiksilver has been using the X mark since 1994. ESPN asked the court to dismiss Quiksilver's counterclaims, but the court refused, holding that the X on Quiksilver's clothing is clearly an arbitrary mark. The court found that the two Xs are "similar enough that a consumer might well confuse them."[6] ◀

Suggestive Trademarks. Suggestive trademarks indicate something about a product's nature, quality, or characteristics, without describing the product directly. These marks require imagination on the part of the consumer to identify the characteristic. For example, "Dairy Queen" suggests an association between its products and milk, but it does not directly describe ice cream.

"Blu-ray" is a suggestive mark that is associated with the high-quality, high-definition video contained on a particular optical data storage disc. Although blue-violet lasers are used to read *blu-ray* discs, the term *blu-ray* does not directly describe the disc.

SECONDARY MEANING Descriptive terms, geographic terms, and personal names are not inherently distinctive and do not receive protection under the law until they acquire a secondary meaning. A secondary meaning may arise when customers begin to associate a specific term or phrase (such as *London Fog*) with specific trademarked items (coats with "London Fog" labels) made by a particular company.

▶ **Case in Point 8.3** Frosty Treats, Inc., sells frozen desserts out of ice cream trucks. The video game series Twisted Metal depicts an ice cream truck with a clown character on it that is similar to the clowns on Frosty Treats' trucks. In the last game of the series, the truck bears the label "Frosty Treats." Frosty sued the video game maker for trademark infringement. The court, however, held that "Frosty Treats" is a descriptive term and is not protected by trademark law unless it has acquired a secondary meaning.

To establish secondary meaning, Frosty Treats would have had to show that the public recognized its trademark and associated it with a single source. Because Frosty Treats failed to do so, the court entered a judgment in favor of the video game producer.[7] ◀

---

6. *ESPN, Inc. v. Quiksilver, Inc.,* 586 F.Supp.2d 219 (S.D.N.Y. 2008).
7. *Frosty Treats, Inc., v. Sony Computer Entertainment America, Inc.,* 426 F.3d 1001 (8th Cir. 2005).

Once a secondary meaning is attached to a term or name, a trademark is considered distinctive and is protected. Even a color can qualify for trademark protection, as did the color schemes used by some state university sports teams, including Ohio State University and Louisiana State University.[8]

GENERIC TERMS Generic terms that refer to an entire class of products, such as *bicycle* and *computer,* receive no protection, even if they acquire secondary meanings. A particularly thorny problem arises when a trademark acquires generic use. For instance, *aspirin* and *thermos* were originally the names of trademarked products, but today the words are used generically. Other trademarks that have acquired generic use are *escalator, trampoline, raisin bran, dry ice, lanolin, linoleum, nylon,* and *cornflakes.*

Service, Certification, and Collective marks

A **service mark** is essentially a trademark that is used to distinguish the *services* (rather than the products) of one person or company from those of another. For example, each airline has a particular mark or symbol associated with its name. Titles and character names used in radio and television are frequently registered as service marks.

Other marks protected by law include certification marks and collective marks. A **certification mark** is used by one or more persons, other than the owner, to certify the region, materials, mode of manufacture, quality, or other characteristic of specific goods or services. Certification marks include "Good Housekeeping Seal of Approval" and "UL Tested."

When used by members of a cooperative, association, or other organization, a certification mark is referred to as a **collective mark.** Collective marks appear at the ends of motion picture credits to indicate the various associations and organizations that participated in the making of the films. The union marks found on the tags of certain products are also collective marks.

Trade Dress

The term **trade dress** refers to the image and overall appearance of a product. Trade dress is a broad concept and can include either all or part of the total image or overall impression created by a product or its packaging.

▶ **Example 8.4** The distinctive decor, menu, layout, and style of service of a particular restaurant may be regarded as trade dress. Trade dress can also include the layout and appearance of a catalogue, the use of a lighthouse as part of the design of a golf hole, the fish shape of a cracker, or the G-shaped design of a Gucci watch. ◀

Basically, trade dress is subject to the same protection as trademarks. In cases involving trade dress infringement, as in trademark infringement cases, a major consideration is whether consumers are likely to be confused by the allegedly infringing use.

Counterfeit Goods

Counterfeit goods copy or otherwise imitate trademarked goods, but they are not the genuine trademarked goods. The importation of goods that bear counterfeit (fake) trademarks poses a growing problem for U.S. businesses, consumers, and law enforcement. In addition to the negative financial effects on legitimate businesses, certain counterfeit goods, such as pharmaceuticals and nutritional supplements, can present serious public health risks.

Although Congress has enacted statutes against counterfeit goods (discussed next), the United States cannot prosecute foreign counterfeiters because our national laws do not apply to them. Instead, one effective tool that U.S. officials use to combat online sales of counterfeit goods is to obtain a court order to close down the domain names of Web sites that sell such goods.

▶ **Example 8.5** In 2012, U.S. agents shut down 101 domain names on the Monday after Thanksgiving ("Cyber Monday," the online version of "Black Friday," the day after Thanksgiving when the holiday shopping season begins). Although the criminal enterprises may continue selling counterfeit versions of brand-name products under different domain names, shutting down the Web sites, particularly on key shopping days, prevents some counterfeit goods from entering the United States. ◀

THE STOP COUNTERFEITING IN MANUFACTURED GOODS ACT The Stop Counterfeiting in Manufactured Goods Act[9] (SCMGA) was enacted to combat counterfeit goods. The act makes it a crime to traffic inten-

---

8. *Board of Supervisors of Louisiana State University v. Smack Apparel Co.,* 438 F.Supp.2d 653 (E.D.La. 2006). See also *Abraham v. Alpha Chi Omega,* 781 F.Supp.2d 396 (N.D.Tex. 2011).

9. Pub. L. No. 109-181 (2006), which amended 18 U.S.C. Sections 2318–2320.

tionally in or attempt to traffic in counterfeit goods or services, or to knowingly use a counterfeit mark on or in connection with goods or services.

Before this act, the law did not prohibit the creation or shipment of counterfeit labels that were not attached to any product. Therefore, counterfeiters would make labels and packaging bearing another's trademark, ship the labels to another location, and then affix them to an inferior product to deceive buyers. The SCMGA closed this loophole by making it a crime to knowingly traffic in counterfeit labels, stickers, packaging, and the like, regardless of whether the items are attached to any goods.

PENALTIES FOR COUNTERFEITING Persons found guilty of violating the SCMGA may be fined up to $2 million or imprisoned for up to ten years (or more if they are repeat offenders). If a court finds that the statute was violated, it must order the defendant to forfeit the counterfeit products (which are then destroyed), as well as any property used in the commission of the crime. The defendant must also pay restitution to the trademark holder or victim in an amount equal to the victim's actual loss.

▶ **Case in Point 8.6** Wajdi Beydoun pleaded guilty to conspiring to import cigarette-rolling papers from Mexico that were falsely marked as "Zig-Zags" and selling them in the United States. The court sentenced Beydoun to prison and ordered him to pay $566,267 in restitution. On appeal, the court affirmed the prison sentence but reversed the restitution because the amount exceeded the actual loss suffered by the legitimate sellers of Zig-Zag rolling papers.[10] ◀

The United States has also joined with other nations in a new international agreement aimed at combating counterfeiting (see the discussion on page 173).

Trade Names

Trademarks apply to *products*. A **trade name** indicates part or all of a business's name, whether the business is a sole proprietorship, a partnership, or a corporation. Generally, a trade name is directly related to a business and its goodwill.

A trade name may be protected as a trademark if the trade name is also the name of the company's trademarked product—for example, Coca-Cola. Unless it is also used as a trademark or service mark, a trade name cannot be registered with the federal government. Trade names are protected under the common law,

but only if they are unusual or fancifully used. The word *Safeway,* for example, was sufficiently fanciful to obtain protection as a trade name for a grocery chain.

Licensing

One way to avoid litigation and still make use of another's trademark or other form of intellectual property is to obtain a license to do so. A **license** in this context is an agreement, or contract, permitting the use of a trademark, copyright, patent, or trade secret for certain purposes. The party that owns the intellectual property rights and issues the license is the *licensor,* and the party obtaining the license is the *licensee.*

A license grants only the rights expressly described in the license agreement. A licensor might, for example, allow the licensee to use the trademark as part of its company or domain name, but not otherwise use the mark on any products or services. Disputes frequently arise over licensing agreements, particularly when the license involves Internet uses.

▶ **Case in Point 8.7** George V Restauration S.A. and others owned and operated the Buddha Bar Paris, a restaurant with an Asian theme in Paris, France. One of the owners allowed Little Rest Twelve, Inc., to use the Buddha Bar trademark and its associated concept in New York City under the name *Buddha Bar NYC.* Little Rest paid royalties for its use of the Buddha Bar mark and advertised Buddha Bar NYC's affiliation with Buddha Bar Paris, a connection also noted on its Web site and in the media.

When a dispute arose, the owners of Buddha Bar Paris withdrew their permission for Buddha Bar NYC's use of their mark, but Little Rest continued to use it. The owners of the mark filed a suit in a New York state court against Little Rest. The court granted an injunction to prevent Little Rest from using the mark.[11] ◀

SECTION 2
PATENTS

A **patent** is a grant from the government that gives an inventor the exclusive right to make, use, or sell his or her invention for a period of twenty years. Patents for designs, as opposed to those for inventions, are given for a fourteen-year period. The applicant must

10. *United States v. Beydoun,* 469 F.3d 102 (5th Cir. 2006).

11. *George V Restauration S.A. v. Little Rest Twelve, Inc.,* 58 A.D.3d 428, 871 N.Y.S.2d 65 (2009).

demonstrate to the satisfaction of the U.S. Patent and Trademark Office that the invention, discovery, process, or design is novel, useful, and not obvious in light of current technology.

Until recently, U.S. patent law differed from the laws of many other countries because the first person to invent a product obtained the patent rights rather than the first person to file for a patent. It was often difficult to prove who invented an item first, however, which prompted Congress to change the system in 2011 by passing the America Invents Act.[12] Now the first person to file an application for a patent on a product or process will receive patent protection. In addition, the new law established a nine-month limit for challenging a patent on any ground.

The period of patent protection begins on the date the patent application is filed, rather than when the patent is issued, which may sometimes be years later. After the patent period ends (either fourteen or twenty years later), the product or process enters the public domain, and anyone can make, sell, or use the invention without paying the patent holder.

Searchable Patent Databases

A significant development relating to patents is the availability online of the world's patent databases. The Web site of the U.S. Patent and Trademark Office (**www.uspto.gov**) provides searchable databases covering U.S. patents granted since 1976. The Web site of the European Patent Office (**www.epo.org**) provides online access to 50 million patent documents in more than seventy nations through a searchable network of databases.

Businesses use these searchable databases in many ways. Because patents are valuable assets, businesses may need to perform patent searches to list or inventory their assets. Patent searches may also be conducted to study trends and patterns in a specific technology or to gather information about competitors in the industry.

What Is Patentable?

Under federal law, "[w]hoever invents or discovers any new and useful process, machine, manufacture, or composition of matter, or any new and useful improvement thereof, may obtain a patent therefor,

subject to the conditions and requirements of this title."[13] Thus, to be patentable, the applicant must prove that the invention, discovery, process, or design is *novel, useful,* and *not obvious* (in light of current technology).

In sum, almost anything is patentable, except the laws of nature, natural phenomena, and abstract ideas (including algorithms[14]). Even artistic methods and works of art, certain business processes, and the structures of storylines are patentable, provided that they are novel and not obvious.[15]

Plants that are reproduced asexually (by means other than from seed), such as hybrid or genetically engineered plants, are patentable in the United States, as are genetically engineered (or cloned) microorganisms and animals. ▶ **Case in Point 8.8** Monsanto, Inc., sells its patented genetically modified (GM) seeds to farmers as a way to achieve higher yields from crops using fewer pesticides. It requires farmers who buy GM seeds to sign licensing agreements promising to plant the seeds for only one crop and to pay a technology fee for each acre planted. To ensure compliance, Monsanto has many full-time employees whose job is to investigate and prosecute farmers who use the GM seeds illegally. Monsanto has filed nearly 150 lawsuits against farmers in the United States and has been awarded more than $15 million in damages (not including out-of-court settlement amounts).[16] ◀

Patent Infringement

If a firm makes, uses, or sells another's patented design, product, or process without the patent owner's permission, that firm commits the tort of patent infringement. Patent infringement may occur even though the patent owner has not put the patented product into commerce. Patent infringement may also occur even though not all features or parts of a product are copied. (To infringe the patent on a process, however, all steps or their equivalent must be copied.)

---

12. The full title of this law is the Leahy-Smith America Invents Act, Pub. L. No. 112-29 (2011), which amended 35 U.S.C. Sections 1, 41, and 321.

13. 35 U.S.C. Section 101.

14. An *algorithm* is a step-by-step procedure, formula, or set of instructions for accomplishing a specific task. An example is the set of rules used by a search engine to rank the listings contained within its index in response to a query.

15. For a United States Supreme Court case discussing the obviousness requirement, see *KSR International Co. v. Teleflex, Inc.,* 550 U.S. 398, 127 S.Ct. 1727, 167 L.Ed.2d 705 (2007).

16. See, for example, *Monsanto Co. v. Bowman,* 657 F.3d 1341 (Fed.Cir. 2011); and *Monsanto Co. v. Scruggs,* 2009 WL 1228318 (Fed.Cir. 2009).

PATENT INFRINGEMENT SUITS AND HIGH-TECH COMPANIES Obviously, companies that specialize in developing new technology stand to lose significant profits if someone "makes, uses, or sells" devices that incorporate their patented inventions. Because these firms are the holders of numerous patents, they are frequently involved in patent infringement lawsuits (as well as other types of intellectual property disputes).

Many companies that make and sell electronics and computer software and hardware are based in foreign nations (for example, Samsung Electronics Company is a Korean firm). Foreign firms can apply for and obtain U.S. patent protection on items that they sell within the United States. Similarly, U.S. firms can obtain protection in foreign nations where they sell goods.

Limitations on Exported Software. The United States Supreme Court has narrowly construed patent infringement as it applies to exported software. As a general rule, under U.S. law, no patent infringement occurs when a patented product is made and sold in another country.

▶ **Case in Point 8.9** AT&T Corporation holds a patent on a device used to digitally encode, compress, and process recorded speech. AT&T brought an infringement case against Microsoft Corporation, which admitted that its Windows operating system incorporated software code that infringed on AT&T's patent.

The case reached the United States Supreme Court on the question of whether Microsoft's liability extended to computers made in another country. The Court held that it did not. Microsoft was liable only for infringement in the United States and not for the Windows-based computers produced in foreign locations. The Court reasoned that Microsoft had not "supplied" the software for the computers but had only electronically transmitted a master copy, which the foreign manufacturers copied and loaded onto the computers.[17] ◀

Apple, Inc. v. Samsung Electronics Company. As mentioned in the chapter introduction, Apple sued Samsung alleging that Samsung's Galaxy mobile phones and tablets that use Google's HTC Android operating system infringe on Apple's patents. Apple has design patents that cover the graphical user interface (the display of icons on the home screen), the device's shell, and the screen and button design. Apple also has patents that cover the way information is displayed on iPhones and other devices, the way windows pop open, and the way information is scaled and rotated.

In 2012, a jury issued a verdict in favor of Apple and awarded more than $1 billion in damages—one of the largest awards ever made in a patent case (a judge later ruled that part of the damages had been incorrectly calculated, however).[18] The jury found that Samsung had willfully infringed five of Apple's patents. The case provides an important precedent for Apple in its legal battles against Android devices made by other companies worldwide. Nevertheless, litigation between the two companies has continued.

Remedies for Patent Infringement

If a patent is infringed, the patent holder may sue for relief in federal court. The patent holder can seek an injunction against the infringer and can also request damages for royalties and lost profits. In some cases, the court may grant the winning party reimbursement for attorneys' fees and costs. If the court determines that the infringement was willful, the court can triple the amount of damages awarded (treble damages).

In the past, permanent injunctions were routinely granted to prevent future infringement. In 2006, however, the United States Supreme Court ruled that patent holders are not automatically entitled to a permanent injunction against future infringing activities. The courts have discretion to decide whether equity requires it. According to the Court, a patent holder must prove that it has suffered irreparable injury and that the public interest would not be disserved by a permanent injunction.[19] This decision gives courts discretion to decide what is equitable in the circumstances and allows them to consider what is in the public interest rather than just the interests of the parties.

▶ **Case in Point 8.10** In the first case applying this rule, a court found that although Microsoft had infringed on the patent of a small software company, the latter was not entitled to an injunction. According to the court, the small company was not irreparably harmed and could be adequately compensated by monetary damages. Also, the public might suffer negative effects from an injunction because the

---

17. *Microsoft Corp. v. AT&T Corp.,* 550 U.S. 437, 127 S.Ct. 1746, 167 L.Ed.2d 737 (2007).

18. *Apple, Inc. v. Samsung Electronics Co.,* CV 11-1846 and CV 12-0630 (N.D.Cal. August 24, 2012). In 2013, a judge ruled that part of the damages awarded were incorrectly calculated and excessive, invalidating approximately $450.5 million of the jury's award. The judge ordered a new trial to determine the appropriate amount of damages. *Apple, Inc. v. Samsung Electronics Co.,* ___ F.Supp.2d ___, 2013 WL 772525 (N.D.Cal. 2013).

19. *eBay, Inc. v. MercExchange, LLC,* 547 U.S. 388, 126 S.Ct. 1837, 164 L.Ed.2d 641 (2006).

infringement involved part of Microsoft's widely used Office Suite software.[20] ◀

SECTION 3
COPYRIGHTS

A **copyright** is an intangible property right granted by federal statute to the author or originator of a literary or artistic production of a specified type. The Copyright Act of 1976,[21] as amended, governs copyrights. Works created after January 1, 1978, are automatically given statutory copyright protection for the life of the author plus 70 years. For copyrights owned by publishing houses, the copyright expires 95 years from the date of publication or 120 years from the date of creation, whichever comes first. For works by more than one author, the copyright expires 70 years after the death of the last surviving author.[22]

Copyrights can be registered with the U.S. Copyright Office (**www.copyright.gov**) in Washington, D.C. A copyright owner no longer needs to place the symbol © or the term *Copr.* or *Copyright* on the work to have the work protected against infringement. Chances are that if somebody created it, somebody owns it.

Generally, copyright owners are protected against the following:

1. Reproduction of the work.
2. Development of derivative works.
3. Distribution of the work.
4. Public display of the work.

What Is Protected Expression?

Works that are copyrightable include books, records, films, artworks, architectural plans, menus, music videos, product packaging, and computer software. To be protected, a work must be "fixed in a durable medium" from which it can be perceived, reproduced, or communicated. Protection is automatic. Registration is not required.

Section 102 of the Copyright Act explicitly states that it protects original works that fall into one of the following categories:

1. Literary works (including newspaper and magazine articles, computer and training manuals, catalogues, brochures, and print advertisements).
2. Musical works and accompanying words (including advertising jingles).
3. Dramatic works and accompanying music.
4. Pantomimes and choreographic works (including ballets and other forms of dance).
5. Pictorial, graphic, and sculptural works (including cartoons, maps, posters, statues, and even stuffed animals).
6. Motion pictures and other audiovisual works (including multimedia works).
7. Sound recordings.
8. Architectural works.

SECTION 102 EXCLUSIONS It is not possible to copyright an *idea*. Section 102 of the Copyright Act specifically excludes copyright protection for any "idea, procedure, process, system, method of operation, concept, principle, or discovery, regardless of the form in which it is described, explained, illustrated, or embodied." Thus, anyone can freely use the underlying ideas or principles embodied in a work.

What is copyrightable is the particular way in which an idea is *expressed*. Whenever an idea and an expression are inseparable, the expression cannot be copyrighted. Generally, anything that is not an original expression will not qualify for copyright protection. Facts widely known to the public are not copyrightable. Page numbers are not copyrightable because they follow a sequence known to everyone. Mathematical calculations are not copyrightable.

COMPILATIONS OF FACTS Unlike ideas, *compilations* of facts are copyrightable. Under Section 103 of the Copyright Act, a compilation is "a work formed by the collection and assembling of preexisting materials or data that are selected, coordinated, or arranged in such a way that the resulting work as a whole constitutes an original work of authorship."

The key requirement in the copyrightability of a compilation is originality. If the facts are selected, coordinated, or arranged in an original way, they can qualify for copyright protection. Therefore, the White Pages of a telephone directory do not qualify for copyright protection because they simply list alphabetically names and telephone numbers. The Yellow Pages of a directory can be copyrightable, provided the information is selected, coordinated, or arranged in an original way. Similarly, a compilation of infor-

---

20. *Z4 Technologies, Inc. v. Microsoft Corp.*, 434 F.Supp.2d 437 (E.D.Tex. 2006).
21. 17 U.S.C. Sections 101 *et seq.*
22. These time periods reflect the extensions of the length of copyright protection enacted by Congress in the Copyright Term Extension Act of 1998, 17 U.S.C. Section 302. The United States Supreme Court upheld the constitutionality of the act in 2003. See *Eldred v. Ashcroft*, 537 U.S. 186, 123 S.Ct. 769, 154 L.Ed.2d 683 (2003).

mation about yachts listed for sale has qualified for copyright protection.[23]

Copyright Infringement

Whenever the form or expression of an idea is copied, an infringement of copyright has occurred. The reproduction does not have to be exactly the same as the original, nor does it have to reproduce the original in its entirety. If a substantial part of the original is reproduced, the copyright has been infringed.

In the following case, rapper Curtis Jackson—better known as "50 Cent"—was the defendant in a suit that claimed his album *Before I Self–Destruct,* and the companion film of the same name, infringed the copyright of Shadrach Winstead's book, *The Preacher's Son—But the Streets Turned Me into a Gangster.*

---

23. *BUC International Corp. v. International Yacht Council, Ltd.,* 489 F.3d 1129 (11th Cir. 2007).

CASE ANALYSIS

Case 8.2   Winstead v. Jackson
United States Court of Appeals, Third Circuit, 2013 WL 139622 (2013).

IN THE LANGUAGE OF THE COURT
PER CURIAM. [By the Whole Court]

* * * *

* * * Winstead filed his * * * complaint in the United States District Court for the District of New Jersey, claiming that Jackson's album/CD and film derived their contents from, and infringed the copyright of, his book.

* * * *

* * * The District Court dismissed Winstead's * * * complaint * * * , concluding that Jackson * * * did not improperly copy protected aspects of Winstead's book.

* * * *

Winstead appeals.

* * * *

Here, it is not disputed that Winstead is the owner of the copyrighted property * * * . However, *not all copying is copyright infringement, so even if actual copying is proven, the court must decide, by comparing the allegedly infringing work with the original work, whether the copying was unlawful. Copying may be proved inferentially by showing that the allegedly infringing work is substantially similar to the copyrighted work.* A court compares the allegedly infringing work with the original work, and considers whether a "lay-observer" would believe that the copying was of protectable aspects of the copyrighted work. The inquiry involves distinguishing between the author's expression and the idea or theme that he or she seeks to convey or explore, because the former is protected and the latter is not. The court must determine whether the allegedly infringing work is similar because it appropriates the unique expressions of the original work, or merely because it contains elements that would be expected when two works express the same idea or explore the same theme. [Emphasis added.]

* * * A lay observer would not believe that Jackson's album/CD and film copied protectable aspects of Winstead's book. Jackson's album/CD is comprised of 16 individual songs, which explore drug-dealing, guns and money, vengeance, and other similar clichés of hip hop gangsterism. Jackson's fictional film is the story of a young man who turns to violence when his mother is killed in a drive-by shooting. The young man takes revenge by killing the man who killed his mother, and then gets rich by becoming an "enforcer" for a powerful criminal. He takes up with a woman who eventually betrays him, and is shot to death by her boyfriend, who has just been released from prison. The movie ends with his younger brother vowing to seek vengeance. Winstead's book purports to be autobiographical and tells the story of a young man whose beloved father was a Bishop in the church. The protagonist was angry as a child because his stepmother abused him, but he found acceptance and self-esteem on the streets of Newark because he was physically powerful. He earned money robbing and beating people, went to jail, returned to crime upon his release, and then made even more money. The protagonist discusses his time at Rahway State Prison in great and compelling detail. The story ends when the protagonist learns that his father has passed away; he conveys his belief that this tragedy has led to his redemption, and he hopes that others might learn from his mistakes.

* * * Although Winstead's book and Jackson's works share similar themes and setting, the story of an angry and wronged protagonist who turns to a life of violence and crime

CASE 8.2 CONTINUES ▶

CASE 8.2 CONTINUED

has long been a part of the public domain [and is therefore not protected by copyright law]. Winstead argues * * * that a protagonist asking for God's help when his father dies, cutting drugs with mixing agents to maximize profits, and complaining about relatives who are addicts and steal the product, are protectable, but these things are not unique. To the extent that Jackson's works contain these elements, they are to be expected when two works express the same idea about "the streets" or explore the same theme. Winstead argues that not every protagonist whose story concerns guns, drugs, and violence in an urban setting winds up in prison or loses a parent, but this argument only serves to illustrate an important difference between his book and Jackson's film. Jackson's protagonist never spends any time in prison, whereas Winstead's protagonist devotes a considerable part of his story to his incarcerations.

In addition, Winstead's book and Jackson's works are different with respect to character, plot, mood, and sequence of events. Winstead's protagonist embarks on a life of crime at a very young age, but is redeemed by the death of his beloved father. Jackson's protagonist turns to crime when he is much older and only after his mother is murdered. He winds up dead at a young age, unredeemed. Winstead's book is hopeful; Jackson's film is characterized * * * by moral apathy. It is true that both works involve the loss of a parent and the protagonist's recognition of the parent's importance in his life, but nowhere does Jackson appropriate anything unique about Winstead's expression of this generic topic.

Winstead contends that direct phrases from his book appear in Jackson's film. * * * He emphasizes these phrases: "Yo, where is my money at," "I would never have done no shit like that to you," "my father, my strength was gone," "he was everything to me," and "I did not know what to do," but, like the phrases "putting the work in," "get the dope, cut the dope," "let's keep it popping," and "the strong take from the weak but the smart take from everybody," they are either common in general or common with respect to hip hop culture, and do not enjoy copyright protection. The average person reading or listening to these phrases in the context of an overall story or song would not regard them as unique and protectable. Moreover, words and short phrases do not enjoy copyright protection. The similarity between Winstead's book and the lyrics to Jackson's songs on the album/CD is even more tenuous. "Stretching the dope" and "bloodshot red eyes" are common phrases that do not enjoy copyright protection. A side-by-side comparison of Winstead's book and the lyrics from Jackson's album/CD do not support a claim of copyright infringement.

For the foregoing reasons, we will affirm the order of the District Court dismissing [Winstead's] complaint.

LEGAL REASONING QUESTIONS

1. Which expressions of an original work are protected by copyright law?

2. Is all copying copyright infringement? If not, what is the test for determining whether a creative work has been unlawfully copied?

3. How did the court in this case determine whether the defendant's work infringed on the plaintiff's copyright?

4. Is a claim of copyright infringement supported if two works share similar themes and setting, as well as words and short phrases? Explain.

REMEDIES FOR COPYRIGHT INFRINGEMENT Those who infringe copyrights may be liable for damages or criminal penalties. These range from actual damages or statutory damages, imposed at the court's discretion, to criminal proceedings for willful violations.

Actual damages are based on the harm caused to the copyright holder by the infringement, while statutory damages, not to exceed $150,000, are provided for under the Copyright Act. Criminal proceedings may result in fines and/or imprisonment. A court can also issue a permanent injunction against a defendant when the court deems it necessary to prevent future copyright infringement.

▶ **Case in Point 8.11** Rusty Carroll operated an online term paper business, R2C2, Inc., that offered up to 300,000 research papers for sale at nine Web sites. Individuals whose work was posted on these Web sites without their permission filed a lawsuit against Carroll for copyright infringement. Because Carroll had repeatedly failed to comply with court orders regarding discovery, the court found that the copyright infringement was likely to continue unless an injunction was issued. The court therefore issued a permanent injunction prohibiting Carroll and R2C2 from selling any term paper without sworn documentary evidence that the paper's author had given permission.[24] ◄

THE "FAIR USE" EXCEPTION An exception to liability for copyright infringement is made under the "fair use" doctrine. In certain circumstances, a person or organization can reproduce copyrighted material without paying royalties (fees paid to the copyright holder for the privilege of reproducing the copyrighted material). Section 107 of the Copyright Act provides as follows:

> [T]he fair use of a copyrighted work, including such use by reproduction in copies or phonorecords or by any other means specified by [Section 106 of the Copyright Act], for purposes such as criticism, comment, news reporting, teaching (including multiple copies for classroom use), scholarship, or research, is not an infringement of copyright. In determining whether the use made of a work in any particular case is a fair use the factors to be considered shall include—
>
> (1) the purpose and character of the use, including whether such use is of a commercial nature or is for nonprofit educational purposes;
> (2) the nature of the copyrighted work;
> (3) the amount and substantiality of the portion used in relation to the copyrighted work as a whole; and
> (4) the effect of the use upon the potential market for or value of the copyrighted work.

WHAT IS FAIR USE? Because these guidelines are very broad, the courts determine whether a particular use is fair on a case-by-case basis. Thus, anyone who reproduces copyrighted material may be committing a violation. In determining whether a use is fair, courts have often considered the fourth factor to be the most important.

► **Case in Point 8.12** BMG Music Publishing, an owner of copyrighted music, granted a license to Leadsinger, Inc., a manufacturer of karaoke devices. The license gave Leadsinger permission to reproduce the sound recordings, but not to reprint the song lyrics, which appeared at the bottom of a TV screen when the karaoke device was used.

BMG demanded that Leadsinger pay a "lyric reprint" fee and a "synchronization" fee. Leadsinger refused to pay, claiming that its use of the lyrics was educational and thus did not constitute copyright infringement under the fair use exception. A federal appellate court disagreed. The court held that Leadsinger's display of the lyrics was not a fair use because it would have a negative effect on the value of the copyrighted work.[25] ◄

The First Sale Doctrine

Section 109(a) of the Copyright Act provides that "the owner of a particular copy or phonorecord lawfully made under [the Copyright Act], or any person authorized by such owner, is entitled, without the authority of the copyright owner, to sell or otherwise dispose of the possession of that copy or phonorecord." This rule is known as the first sale doctrine.

Under this doctrine, once a copyright owner sells or gives away a particular copy of a work, the copyright owner no longer has the right to control the distribution of that copy. Thus, for example, a person who buys a copyrighted book can sell it to someone else.

In 2011, a court held that the first sale doctrine also applies to a person who receives promotional CDs, such as a music critic or radio programmer. ► **Case in Point 8.13** Universal Music Group (UMG) regularly ships promotional CDs to people in the music industry. Troy Augusto obtained some of these promotional CDs from various sources and sold them through online auction sites. UMG filed a copyright infringement lawsuit. Augusto argued that the music company had given up its right to control further distribution of the CDs under the first sale doctrine. Ultimately, a federal appellate court held in favor of Augusto. The promotional CDs were dispatched to the recipients without any prior arrangement as to those particular copies. Therefore, the court concluded that UMG had conveyed title of the copyrighted promotional CDs to the recipients.[26] ◄

In 2012, the United States Supreme Court heard the appeal of a case involving the resale of textbooks on eBay. To read about the Court's decision in this important case, see this chapter's *Insight into the Global Environment* feature on the following page.

Copyright Protection for Software

In 1980, Congress passed the Computer Software Copyright Act, which amended the Copyright Act of 1976 to include computer programs in the list of

---

24. *Weidner v. Carroll*, 2010 WL 310310 (S.D.Ill. 2010).

25. *Leadsinger, Inc. v. BMG Music Publishing*, 512 F.3d 522 (9th Cir. 2008).
26. *UMG Recordings, Inc. v. Augusto*, 628 F.3d 1175 (9th Cir. 2011).

INSIGHT INTO THE GLOBAL ENVIRONMENT
Is It Legal to Resell Textbooks Purchased Abroad?

Students and professors alike complain about the high price of college textbooks. Some enterprising students have found that if they purchase textbooks printed abroad, they can sometimes save enough to justify the shipping charges. Textbook prices are lower in other countries because (1) production costs are lower there and (2) average incomes are also lower, so students are unable to pay the higher prices that U.S. students face. (Also, neither students nor professors abroad have the full range of paper and digital supplements that are offered with most textbooks in the U.S.)

A Cornell University Student Starts a Side Business

Supap Kirtsaeng, a citizen of Thailand, started his studies at Cornell University in 1997 and then went on to a Ph.D. program at the University of Southern California. He enlisted friends and family in Thailand to buy copies of textbooks there and ship them to him in the United States. To pay for his education, Kirtsaeng resold the textbooks on eBay, where he eventually made about $100,000. John Wiley & Sons, Inc., which had printed eight of those textbooks in Asia, sued Kirtsaeng in federal district court for copyright infringement under Section 602(a)(1) of the Copyright Act. Wiley claimed that it is impermissible to import a work "without the authority of the owner." Kirtsaeng's defense was that Section 109(a) of the Copyright Act allows the first purchaser-owner of a book to sell or otherwise dispose of it without the copyright owner's permission. Kirtsaeng did not prevail.[a]

Kirtsaeng Appeals the Verdict

Kirtsaeng appealed to the U.S. Court of Appeals for the Second Circuit, but the court upheld the lower court's judgment.[b] The majority held that the first sale doctrine of the Copyright Act refers specifically to works that are manufactured in the United States. Therefore, the doctrine does not apply to textbooks printed and sold abroad, and then resold in the United States. Kirtsaeng appealed to the United States Supreme Court.

The Supreme Court Weighs In

The Supreme Court had to decide this question: Can any copy of a book or CD or DVD that was legally produced abroad, acquired abroad, and then imported into the United States be resold in the United States without the copyright owner's permission? The answer to this question has implications for discount sellers, such as Costco, and online businesses, such as eBay and Google, all of which offer "good" prices on many products that were made abroad.

The Supreme Court ruled that in Kirtsaeng's favor, reversing the appellate court's decision.[c] The majority of the Court ruled that the first sale doctrine applies, even when the good was purchased abroad: " [T]he common-law history of the 'first-sale' doctrine . . . favors a non-geographical interpretation. We . . . doubt that Congress would have intended to create the practical copyright-related harms with which a geographical interpretation would threaten ordinary scholarly, artistic, commercial activities . . . ." As it turned out, much of the Court's decision concerned the potential consequences of what might occur if the Court did not reverse the appellate decision. Allowing that decision to stand would have meant that one "could prevent a buyer from domestically selling or even giving away copies of a video game made in Japan, a film made in Germany or a dress (with a design copyright) made in China."

LEGAL CRITICAL THINKING
INSIGHT INTO THE SOCIAL ENVIRONMENT

What options do textbook publishers face given this Supreme Court decision?

a. *John Wiley & Sons, Inc. v. Kirtsaeng,* 93 U.S.P.Q.2d 1432 (S.D.N.Y. 2009).
b. *John Wiley & Sons, Inc. v. Kirtsaeng,* 654 F.3d 210 (2d Cir. 2011).
c. *Kirtsaeng v. John Wiley & Sons, Inc.,* ___ U.S. ___, 133 S.Ct. 1351, ___ L.Ed.2d ___ (2013).

creative works protected by federal copyright law.[27] Generally, copyright protection extends to those parts of a computer program that can be read by humans, such as the "high-level" language of a source code.

Protection also extends to the binary-language object code, which is readable only by the computer, and to such elements as the overall structure, sequence, and organization of a program.

Not all aspects of software are protected, however. Courts typically have not extended copyright protec-

27. Pub. L. No. 96-517 (1980), amending 17 U.S.C. Sections 101, 117.

tion to the "look and feel"—the general appearance, command structure, video images, menus, windows, and other screen displays—of computer programs. ▶ **Example 8.14** MiTek develops a software program for laying out wood trusses (used in construction). Another company comes out with a different program that includes similar elements, such as the menu and submenu command tree-structures. MiTek cannot successfully sue for copyright infringement because the command structure of software is not protected. ◀ (Note that copying the "look and feel" of another's product may be a violation of trade dress or trademark laws, however.)

As will be explored in Chapter 9, technology has vastly increased the potential for copyright infringement via the Internet.

SECTION 4
TRADE SECRETS

The law of trade secrets protects some business processes and information that are not, or cannot be, patented, copyrighted, or trademarked against appropriation by competitors. A **trade secret** is basically information of commercial value, such as customer lists, plans, and research and development. Trade secrets may also include pricing information, marketing methods, production techniques, and generally anything that makes an individual company unique and that would have value to a competitor.

Unlike copyright and trademark protection, protection of trade secrets extends both to ideas and to their expression. (For this reason, and because there are no registration or filing requirements for trade secrets, trade secret protection may be well suited for software.) Of course, the secret formula, method, or other information must be disclosed to some persons, particularly to key employees. Businesses generally attempt to protect their trade secrets by having all employees who use a process or information agree in their contracts, or in confidentiality agreements, never to divulge it.

State and Federal Law on Trade Secrets

Under Section 757 of the *Restatement of Torts*, those who disclose or use another's trade secret, without authorization, are liable to that other party if:

1. They discovered the secret by improper means, or
2. Their disclosure or use constitutes a breach of a duty owed to the other party.

Stealing confidential business data by industrial espionage, such as by tapping into a competitor's computer, is a theft of trade secrets without any contractual violation and is actionable in itself.

Although trade secrets have long been protected under the common law, today most states' laws are based on the Uniform Trade Secrets Act,[28] which has been adopted in forty-seven states. Additionally, the Economic Espionage Act[29] (to be discussed in Chapter 10) makes the theft of trade secrets a federal crime.

Trade Secrets in Cyberspace

Computer technology is undercutting many business firms' ability to protect their confidential information, including trade secrets. For example, a dishonest employee could e-mail trade secrets in a company's computer to a competitor or a future employer. If e-mail is not an option, the employee might walk out with the information on a flash drive.

A former employee's continued use of a Twitter account after leaving the company may provide grounds for a suit alleging misappropriation of trade secrets. ▶ **Case in Point 8.15** Noah Kravitz worked for a company called PhoneDog for four years as a product reviewer and video blogger. PhoneDog provided him with the Twitter account "@PhoneDog_Noah." Kravitz's popularity grew, and he had approximately 17,000 followers by the time he quit. PhoneDog requested that Kravitz stop using the Twitter account. Although Kravitz changed his handle to "@noahkravitz," he continued to use the account. PhoneDog subsequently sued Kravitz for misappropriation of trade secrets, among other things. Kravitz moved for a dismissal, but the court found that the complaint adequately stated a cause of action for misappropriation of trade secrets and allowed the suit to continue.[30] ◀

For a comprehensive summary of trade secrets and the other forms of intellectual property discussed in this chapter, see Exhibit 8–1 on the following page.

---

28. The Uniform Trade Secrets Act, as drafted by the National Conference of Commissioners on Uniform State Laws (NCCUSL), can be found at **uniformlaws.org**.
29. 18 U.S.C. Sections 1831–1839.
30. *PhoneDog v. Kravitz,* 2011 WL 5415612 (N.D.Cal. 2011). See also *Mintel Learning Technology, Inc. v. Ambrow Education Holding Ltd.,* 2012 WL 762126 (N.D.Cal. 2012).

EXHIBIT 8-1 **Forms of Intellectual Property**

Form	Definition	How Acquired	Duration	Remedy for Infringement
Patent	A grant from the government that gives an inventor exclusive rights to an invention.	By filing a patent application with the U.S. Patent and Trademark Office and receiving its approval.	Twenty years from the date of the application; for design patents, fourteen years.	Monetary damages, including royalties and lost profits, *plus* attorneys' fees. Damages may be tripled for intentional infringements.
Copyright	The right of an author or originator of a literary or artistic work, or other production that falls within a specified category, to have the exclusive use of that work for a given period of time.	Automatic (once the work or creation is put in tangible form). Only the *expression* of an idea (and not the idea itself) can be protected by copyright.	For authors: the life of the author, plus 70 years. For publishers: 95 years after the date of publication or 120 years after creation.	Actual damages plus profits received by the party who infringed *or* statutory damages under the Copyright Act, *plus* costs and attorneys' fees in either situation.
Trademark (service mark and trade dress)	Any distinctive word, name, symbol, or device (image or appearance), or combination thereof, that an entity uses to distinguish its goods or services from those of others. The owner has the exclusive right to use that mark or trade dress.	1. At common law, ownership created by use of the mark. 2. Registration with the appropriate federal or state office gives notice and is permitted if the mark is currently in use or will be within the next six months.	Unlimited, as long as it is in use. To continue notice by registration, the owner must renew by filing between the fifth and sixth years, and thereafter, every ten years.	1. Injunction prohibiting the future use of the mark. 2. Actual damages plus profits received by the party who infringed (can be increased under the Lanham Act). 3. Destruction of articles that infringed. 4. *Plus* costs and attorneys' fees.
Trade Secret	Any information that a business possesses and that gives the business an advantage over competitors (including formulas, lists, patterns, plans, processes, and programs).	Through the originality and development of the information and processes that constitute the business secret and are unknown to others.	Unlimited, so long as not revealed to others. Once revealed to others, it is no longer a trade secret.	Monetary damages for misappropriation (the Uniform Trade Secrets Act also permits punitive damages if willful), *plus* costs and attorneys' fees.

SECTION 5

INTERNATIONAL PROTECTION FOR INTELLECTUAL PROPERTY

For many years, the United States has been a party to various international agreements relating to intellectual property rights. For instance, the Paris Convention of 1883, to which about 173 countries are signatory, allows parties in one country to file for patent and trademark protection in any of the other member countries. Other international agreements in this area include the Berne Convention, the Trade-Related Aspects of Intellectual Property Rights (known as the TRIPS agreement), the Madrid Protocol, and the Anti-Counterfeiting Trade Agreement.

The Berne Convention

Under the Berne Convention of 1886, if a U.S. citizen writes a book, every country that has signed the convention must recognize the U.S. author's copyright in the book. Also, if a citizen of a country that has not signed the convention first publishes a book in one of the 165 countries that have signed, all other countries that have signed the convention must recognize that author's copyright. Copyright notice is not needed to gain protection under the Berne Convention for works published after March 1, 1989.

This convention and other international agreements have given some protection to intellectual property on a worldwide level. None of them, however, has been as significant and far reaching in scope as the TRIPS agreement, discussed in the next subsection.

In 2011, the European Union agreed to extend the period of royalty protection for musicians from fifty years to seventy years. This decision aids major record labels as well as performers and musicians who previously faced losing royalties from sales of their older recordings. The profits of musicians and record companies have been shrinking in recent years because of the sharp decline in sales of compact discs and the rise in illegal downloads.

In the following case, the United States Supreme Court had to decide if Congress had exceeded its authority under the U.S. Constitution when it enacted a law that restored copyright protection to many foreign works that were already in the public domain. (*Public domain* means that rights to certain intellectual property, such as songs and other published works, belong to everyone and are not protected by copyright or patent laws.)

CASE 8.3

Golan v. Holder

Supreme Court of the United States, ___ U.S. ___, 132 S.Ct. 873, 181 L.Ed.2d 835 (2012).

BACKGROUND AND FACTS   The United States joined the Berne Convention in 1989, but it failed to give foreign copyright holders the same protections enjoyed by U.S. authors. Contrary to the Berne Convention, the United States did not protect any foreign work that had already entered the public domain.

In 1994, Congress enacted the Uruguay Round Agreements Act (URAA), which "restored" copyright protection for many foreign works that were already in the public domain. The URAA put foreign and domestic works on the same footing, allowing their copyrights to extend for the same number of years. Lawrence Golan, along with a group of musicians, conductors, and publishers, filed a suit against Eric Holder, in his capacity as the U.S. attorney general. These individuals had enjoyed free access to foreign works in the public domain before the URAA's enactment. They claimed that the URAA violated the copyright clause of the U.S. Constitution and thus that Congress had exceeded its constitutional authority in passing the URAA.

A federal appellate court held that Congress did not violate the copyright clause by passing the URAA. The petitioners appealed. The United States Supreme Court granted *certiorari* to resolve the matter.

 IN THE LANGUAGE OF THE COURT
Justice *GINSBURG* delivered the opinion of the Court.

* * * *

* * * The Constitution states that "Congress shall have Power . . . to promote the Progress of Science . . . by securing for limited Times to Authors . . . the exclusive Right to their . . . Writings." Petitioners [Golan and others] find in this grant of authority an impenetrable [impassable] barrier to the extension of copyright protection to authors whose writings, for whatever reason, are in the public domain. We see no such barrier in the text of the Copyright Clause * * * .

* * * *

The text of the Copyright Clause does not exclude application of copyright protection to works in the public domain. * * * Petitioners' contrary argument relies primarily on the Constitution's confinement of a copyright's lifespan to a "limited Tim[e]." "Removing works from the public domain," they contend, "violates the 'limited times' restriction by turning a

CASE 8.3 CONTINUES ➡

CASE 8.3 CONTINUED   fixed and predictable period into one that can be reset or resurrected at any time, even after it expires."

Our decision in [a prior case] is largely dispositive [capable of settling a dispute] of petitioners' limited-time argument.[a] There we addressed the question of whether Congress violated the Copyright Clause when it extended, by 20 years, the terms of existing copyrights. Ruling that Congress acted within constitutional bounds, we declined to infer from the text of the Copyright Clause "the command that a time prescription, once set, becomes forever 'fixed' or 'inalterable.'" *"The word 'limited,' we observed, "does not convey a meaning so constricted." Rather, the term is best understood to mean "confine[d] within certain bounds," "restrain[ed]," or "circumscribed."* The construction petitioners tender closely resembles the definition rejected in *Eldred* [the prior case] and is similarly infirm [weak]. [Emphasis added.]

* * * *

* * * In aligning the United States with other nations bound by the Berne Convention, and thereby according equitable treatment to once disfavored foreign authors, Congress can hardly be charged with a design to move stealthily toward a regime of perpetual copyrights.

DECISION AND REMEDY *The United States Supreme Court affirmed the federal appellate court's ruling that the URAA does not violate the U.S. Constitution's copyright clause. Thus, Golan and the others could no longer use, without permission, any of the foreign works that were previously in the public domain. By passing the URAA in the United States, Congress, in effect, took those works out of the public domain and extended copyright protection to them. Henceforth, U.S. copyright and patent laws cover all such foreign intellectual property.*

THE GLOBAL DIMENSION *What does the Court's decision in this case mean for copyright holders in the United States who want copyright protection in other countries? Will other nations be more or less inclined to protect U.S. authors? Explain.*

THE ECONOMIC DIMENSION *Why did a group of musicians, conductors, publishers, and others file this suit? What did they hope to gain by a decision in their favor?*

---

a. See *Eldred v. Ashcroft*, 537 U.S. 186, 123 S.Ct. 769, 154 L.Ed.2d 683 (2003).

The TRIPS Agreement

Representatives from more than one hundred nations signed the TRIPS agreement in 1994. The agreement established, for the first time, standards for the international protection of intellectual property rights, including patents, trademarks, and copyrights for movies, computer programs, books, and music. The TRIPS agreement provides that each member country of the World Trade Organization must include in its domestic laws broad intellectual property rights and effective remedies (including civil and criminal penalties) for violations of those rights.

Generally, the TRIPS agreement forbids member nations from discriminating against foreign owners of intellectual property rights (in the administration, regulation, or adjudication of such rights). In other words, a member nation cannot give its own nationals (citizens) favorable treatment without offering the same treatment to nationals of all other member countries. ▶ **Example 8.16** A U.S. software manufacturer brings a suit for the infringement of intellectual property rights under Germany's national laws. Because Germany is a member of the TRIPS agreement, the U.S. manufacturer is entitled to receive the same treatment as a German manufacturer. ◀

Each member nation must also ensure that legal procedures are available for parties who wish to bring actions for infringement of intellectual property rights. Additionally, a related document established a mechanism for settling disputes among member nations.

The Madrid Protocol

In the past, one of the difficulties in protecting U.S. trademarks internationally was the time and expense required to apply for trademark registration in foreign countries. The filing fees and procedures for trademark registration vary significantly among individual countries. The Madrid Protocol, which was signed into law in 2003, may help to resolve these problems.

The Madrid Protocol is an international treaty that has been signed by eighty-six countries. Under its provisions, a U.S. company wishing to register its trademark abroad can submit a single application and designate other member countries in which the company would like to register its mark. The treaty was designed to reduce the costs of international trademark protection by more than 60 percent.

Although the Madrid Protocol may simplify and reduce the cost of trademark registration in foreign countries, it remains to be seen whether it will provide significant benefits to trademark owners. Even with an easier registration process, there are still questions as to whether all member countries will enforce the law and protect the mark.

The Anti-Counterfeiting Trade Agreement

In 2011 Australia, Canada, Japan, Korea, Morocco, New Zealand, Singapore, and the United States signed the Anti-Counterfeiting Trade Agreement (ACTA), an international treaty to combat global counterfeiting and piracy. The members of the European Union, Mexico, Switzerland, and other nations that support ACTA are still developing domestic procedures to comply with its provisions. Once a nation has adopted appropriate procedures, it can ratify the treaty.

PROVISIONS AND GOALS The goals of the treaty are to increase international cooperation, facilitate the best law enforcement practices, and provide a legal framework to combat counterfeiting. The treaty will have its own governing body.

ACTA applies not only to counterfeit physical goods, such as medications, but also to pirated copyrighted works being distributed via the Internet. The idea is to create a new standard of enforcement for intellectual property rights that goes beyond the TRIPS agreement and encourages international cooperation and information sharing among signatory countries.

BORDER SEARCHES Under ACTA, member nations are required to establish border measures that allow officials, on their own initiative, to search commercial shipments of imports and exports for counterfeit goods. The treaty neither requires nor prohibits random border searches of electronic devices, such as laptops, tablet devices, and smartphones, for infringing content. If border authorities reasonably believe that any goods in transit are counterfeit, the treaty allows them to keep the suspect goods unless the owner proves that the items are authentic and noninfringing.

The treaty allows member nations, in accordance with their own laws, to order online service providers to furnish information about (including the identity of) suspected trademark and copyright infringers.

Reviewing: Intellectual Property Rights

Two computer science majors, Trent and Xavier, have an idea for a new video game, which they propose to call "Hallowed." They form a business and begin developing their idea. Several months later, Trent and Xavier run into a problem with their design and consult a friend, Brad, who is an expert in designing computer source codes. After the software is completed but before Hallowed is marketed, a video game called Halo 2 is released for both the Xbox and the Playstation systems. Halo 2 uses source codes similar to those of Hallowed and imitates Hallowed's overall look and feel, although not all the features are alike. Using the information presented in the chapter, answer the following questions.

1. Would the name *Hallowed* receive protection as a trademark or as trade dress? Explain.
2. If Trent and Xavier had obtained a patent on Hallowed, would the release of Halo 2 have infringed on their patent? Why or why not?
3. Based only on the facts described above, could Trent and Xavier sue the makers of Halo 2 for copyright infringement? Why or why not?
4. Suppose that Trent and Xavier discover that Brad took the idea of Hallowed and sold it to the company that produced Halo 2. Which type of intellectual property issue does this raise?

DEBATE THIS . . . *Congress has amended copyright law several times so that copyright holders now have protection for many decades. Was Congress right in extending these copyright time periods?*

Terms and Concepts

certification mark 160
collective mark 160
copyright 164
dilution 158

intellectual property 156
license 161
patent 161
service mark 160

trade dress 160
trade name 161
trade secret 169
trademark 156

ExamPrep

Issue Spotters

1. Roslyn is a food buyer for Organic Cornucopia Food Company when she decides to go into business for herself as Roslyn's Kitchen. She contacts Organic's suppliers, offering to buy their entire harvest for the next year, and Organic's customers, offering to sell her products for less than her ex-employer. Has Roslyn violated any of the intellectual property rights discussed in this chapter? Explain. **(See page 169.)**

2. Global Products develops, patents, and markets software. World Copies, Inc., sells Global's software without the maker's permission. Is this patent infringement? If so, how might Global save the cost

of suing World for infringement and at the same time profit from World's sales? **(See page 162.)**

• Check your answers to the Issue Spotters against the answers provided in Appendix E at the end of this text.

Before the Test

Go to **www.cengagebrain.com**, enter the ISBN 9781285185248, and click on "Find" to locate this text-book's Web site. Then, click on "Access Now" under "Study Tools," and select Chapter 8 at the top. There, you will find a Practice Quiz that you can take to assess your mastery of the concepts in this chapter, as well as Flash-cards and a Glossary of important terms.

Business Scenarios

8–1. Fair Use. Professor Wise is teaching a summer seminar in business torts at State University. Several times during the course, he makes copies of relevant sections from business law texts and distributes them to his students. Wise does not realize that the daughter of one of the textbook authors is a member of his seminar. She tells her father about Wise's copying activities, which have taken place without her father's or his publisher's permission. Her father sues Wise for copyright infringement. Wise claims protection under the fair use doctrine. Who will prevail? Explain. **(See page 167.)**

8–2. Patent Infringement. John and Andrew Doney invented a hard-bearing device for balancing rotors. Although they obtained a patent for their invention from the U.S. Patent and Trademark Office, it was never used as an automobile wheel balancer. Some time later, Exetron Corp. produced an automobile wheel balancer that used a hard-bearing device with a support plate similar to that of the Doneys' device. Given that the Doneys had not used their device for automobile wheel balancing, does Exetron's use of a similar device infringe on the Doneys' patent? Why or why not? **(See page 162.)**

Business Case Problems

8–3. Trade Secrets. Briefing.com offers Internet-based analyses of investment opportunities to investors. Richard Green is the company's president. One of Briefing.com's competitors is StreetAccount, LLC (limited liability company), whose owners include Gregory Jones and Cynthia Dietzmann. Jones worked for Briefing.com for six years until he quit in March 2003 and was a member of its board of directors until April 2003. Dietzmann worked for Briefing.com for seven years until she quit in March 2003. As Briefing.com employees, Jones and Dietzmann had access to confidential

business data. For instance, Dietzmann developed a list of contacts through which Briefing.com obtained market information to display online. When Dietzmann quit, she did not return all of the contact information to the company. Briefing.com and Green filed a suit in a federal district court against Jones, Dietzmann, and StreetAccount, alleging that they had appropriated these data and other "trade secrets" to form a competing business. What are trade secrets? Why are they protected? Under what circumstances is a party liable at common law for their appropriation? How should these principles apply in this case? [*Briefing.com v. Jones,* 2006 WY 16, 126 P.3d 928 (2006)] **(See page 169.)**

8–4. Licensing. Redwin Wilchcombe composed, performed, and recorded a song called *Tha Weedman* at the request of Lil Jon, a member of Lil Jon & the East Side Boyz (LJESB), for LJESB's album *Kings of Crunk*. Wilchcombe was not paid, but was given credit on the album as a producer. After the album had sold 2 million copies, Wilchcombe filed a suit against LJESB, alleging copyright infringement. The defendants claimed that they had a license to use the song. Do the facts support this claim? Explain. [*Wilchcombe v. TeeVee Toons, Inc.,* 555 F.3d 949 (11th Cir. 2009)] **(See page 161.)**

8–5. BUSINESS CASE PROBLEM
WITH SAMPLE ANSWER: Trade Secrets.

 Jesse Edwards, an employee of Carbon Processing and Reclamation, LLC (CPR), put unmarked boxes of company records in his car. Edwards's wife, Channon, who suspected him of hiding financial information from her, gained access to the documents. William Jones, the owner of CPR, filed a suit, contending that Channon's unauthorized access to the files was a theft of trade secrets. Could the information in the documents be trade secrets? Should liability be imposed? Why or why not? [Jones v. Hamilton, *53 So.3d 134 (Ala.Civ.App. 2010)*] **(See page 169.)**

• **For a sample answer to Problem 8–5, go to Appendix F at the end of this text.**

8–6. Spotlight on Macy's—Copyright Infringement. United

 Fabrics International, Inc., bought a fabric design from an Italian designer and registered a copyright to it with the U.S. Copyright Office. When Macy's, Inc., began selling garments with a similar design, United filed a copyright infringement suit against Macy's. Macy's argued that United did not own a valid copyright to the design and so could not claim infringement. Does United have to prove that the copyright is valid to establish infringement? Explain. [*United Fabrics International, Inc. v. C&J Wear, Inc.,* 630 F.3d 1255 (9th Cir. 2011)] **(See page 165.)**

8–7. Theft of Trade Secrets. Hanjuan Jin, a citizen of the People's Republic of China, began working at Motorola in 1998. She worked as a software engineer in a division that created proprietary standards for cellular communications. In 2004 and 2005, contrary to Motorola's policies, Jin also began working as a consultant for Lemko Corp. Lemko introduced Jin to Sun Kaisens, a Chinese software company. During 2005, Jin returned to Beijing on several occasions and began working with Sun Kaisens and with the Chinese military. The following year, she started corresponding with Sun Kaisens's management about a possible full-time job in China. During this period, she took several medical leaves of absence from Motorola. In February 2007, after one of these medical leaves, she returned to Motorola.

During the next several days at Motorola, she accessed and downloaded thousands of documents on her personal laptop as well as on pen drives. On the following day, she attempted to board a flight to China but was randomly searched by U.S. Customs and Border Protection officials at Chicago's O'Hare International Airport. Ultimately, U.S. officials discovered the downloaded Motorola documents. Are there any circumstances under which Jin could avoid being prosecuted for theft of trade secrets? If so, what are these circumstances? Discuss fully. [*United States v. Hanjuan Jin,* 833 F.Supp.2d 977 (N.D.Ill. 2012)] **(See page 169.)**

8–8. Copyright Infringement. SilverEdge Systems Software hired Catherine Conrad to perform a singing telegram. SilverEdge arranged for James Bendewald to record Conrad's performance of her copyrighted song to post on its Web site. Conrad agreed to wear a microphone to assist in the recording, told Bendewald what to film, and asked for an additional fee only if SilverEdge used the video for a commercial purpose. Later, the company chose to post a video of a different performer's singing telegram instead. Conrad filed a suit in a federal district court against SilverEdge and Bendewald for copyright infringement. Are the defendants liable? Explain. [*Conrad v. Bendewald,* 2013 WL 310194 (7th Cir. 2013)] **(See page 165.)**

8–9. A QUESTION OF ETHICS: Copyright Infringement.

 Custom Copies, Inc., prepares and sells coursepacks, which contain compilations of readings for college courses. A teacher selects the readings and delivers a syllabus to the copy shop, which obtains the materials from a library, copies them, and binds the copies. Blackwell Publishing, Inc., which owns the copyright to some of the materials, filed a suit, alleging copyright infringement. [Blackwell Publishing, Inc. v. Custom Copies, Inc., *2006 WL 1529503 (N.D.Fla. 2006)*] **(See page 165.)**

(a) Custom Copies argued, in part, that creating and selling did not "distribute" the coursepacks. Does a copy shop violate copyright law if it only copies materials for coursepacks? Does the copying fall under the "fair use" exception? Should the court grant the defendant's motion? Why or why not?

(b) What is the potential impact if copies of a book or journal are created and sold without the permission of, and the payment of royalties or a fee to, the copyright owner? Explain.

8–10. SPECIAL CASE ANALYSIS: Copyright Infringement.

 Go to Case Analysis Case 8.2, *Winstead v. Jackson,* on pages 165 and 166. Read the excerpt and answer the following questions. **(See page 165.)**

(a) Issue: This case focused on an allegation of copyright infringement involving what parties and which creative works?

(b) **Rule of Law:** What is the test for determining whether a creative work infringes the copyright of another work?

(c) **Applying the Rule of Law:** How did the court determine whether the claim of copyright infringement was supported in this case?

(d) **Conclusion:** Was the defendant liable for copyright infringement? Why or why not?

Legal Reasoning Group Activity

8–11. Patents. After years of research, your company develops a product that might revolutionize the green (environmentally conscious) building industry. The product is made from relatively inexpensive and widely available materials combined in a unique way that can substantially lower the heating and cooling costs of residential and commercial buildings. The company has registered the trademark it intends to use on the product, and has filed a patent application with the U.S. Patent and Trademark Office. **(See page 161.)**

(a) One group should provide three reasons why this product does or does not qualify for patent protection.

(b) Another group should develop a four-step procedure for how your company can best protect its intellectual property rights (trademark, trade secret, and patent) and prevent domestic and foreign competitors from producing counterfeit goods or cheap knockoffs.

(c) Another group should list and explain three ways your company can utilize licensing.

CHAPTER 9

INTERNET LAW, SOCIAL MEDIA, AND PRIVACY

The Internet has changed our lives and our laws. Technology has put the world at our fingertips and now allows even the smallest business to reach customers around the globe. At the same time, the Internet presents a variety of challenges for the law. Courts are often in uncharted waters when deciding disputes that involve the Internet, social media, and online privacy. There may not be any common law precedents for judges to rely on when resolving a case. Long-standing principles of justice may be inapplicable. New rules are evolving, as we discuss in this chapter, but often not as quickly as technology.

SECTION 1
INTERNET LAW

A number of laws specifically address issues that arise only on the Internet. Three such issues are unsolicited e-mail, domain names, and cybersquatting, as we discuss here. We also discuss how the law is dealing with problems of trademark infringement and dilution online.

Spam

Businesses and individuals alike are targets of **spam.**[1] Spam is the unsolicited "junk e-mail" that floods virtual mailboxes with advertisements, solicitations, and other messages. Considered relatively harmless in the early days of the Internet, by 2013 spam accounted for roughly 75 percent of all e-mails.

STATE REGULATION OF SPAM In an attempt to combat spam, thirty-six states have enacted laws that prohibit or regulate its use. Many state laws that regulate spam require the senders of e-mail ads to instruct the recipients on how they can "opt out" of further e-mail ads from the same sources. For instance, in some states, an unsolicited e-mail must include a toll-free phone number or return e-mail address that the recipient can use to ask the sender to send no more unsolicited e-mails.

THE FEDERAL CAN-SPAM ACT In 2003, Congress enacted the Controlling the Assault of Non-Solicited Pornography and Marketing (CAN-SPAM) Act.[2] The legislation applies to any "commercial electronic mail messages" that are sent to promote a commercial product or service. Significantly, the statute preempts state antispam laws except for those provisions in state laws that prohibit false and deceptive e-mailing practices.

Generally, the act permits the sending of unsolicited commercial e-mail but prohibits certain types of spamming activities. Prohibited activities include the use of a false return address and the use of false, misleading, or deceptive information when sending e-mail. The statute also prohibits the use of "dictionary attacks"—sending messages to randomly generated e-mail addresses—and the "harvesting" of e-mail addresses from Web sites through the use of specialized software.

▶ **Example 9.1** Federal officials arrested Robert Alan Soloway, considered to be one of the world's most prolific spammers. Soloway, known as the "Spam King," had been using *botnets* (automated spamming networks) to send out hundreds of millions of unwanted e-mails. In 2008, Soloway pleaded guilty to mail fraud, spam, and failure to pay taxes. ◀

Arresting prolific spammers, however, has done little to curb spam, which continues to flow at a rate of 70 billion messages per day.

THE U.S. SAFE WEB ACT After the CAN-SPAM Act of 2003 prohibited false and deceptive e-mails originating in the United States, spamming from servers

---

1. The term *spam* is said to come from the lyrics of a Monty Python song that repeats the word *spam* over and over.

2. 15 U.S.C. 7701 *et seq.*

located in other nations increased. These cross-border spammers generally were able to escape detection and legal sanctions because the Federal Trade Commission (FTC) lacked the authority to investigate foreign spamming.

Congress sought to rectify the situation by enacting the U.S. Safe Web Act (also known as the Undertaking Spam, Spyware, and Fraud Enforcement with Enforcers Beyond Borders Act).[3] The act allows the FTC to cooperate and share information with foreign agencies in investigating and prosecuting those involved in spamming, spyware, and various Internet frauds and deceptions.

The Safe Web Act also provides a "safe harbor" for **Internet service providers (ISPs)**—that is, organizations that provide access to the Internet. The safe harbor gives ISPs immunity from liability for supplying information to the FTC concerning possible unfair or deceptive conduct in foreign jurisdictions.

Domain Names

As e-commerce expanded worldwide, one issue that emerged involved the rights of a trademark owner to use the mark as part of a domain name. A **domain name** is part of an Internet address, such as "**cengage.com**."

STRUCTURE OF DOMAIN NAMES Every domain name ends with a generic top-level domain (TLD), which is the part of the name to the right of the period that often indicates the type of entity that operates the site. For instance, *com* is an abbreviation for *commercial*, and *edu* is short for *education*.

The second-level domain (SLD)—the part of the name to the left of the period—is chosen by the business entity or individual registering the domain name. Competition for SLDs among firms with similar names and products has led to numerous disputes. By using an identical or similar domain name, parties have attempted to profit from a competitor's **goodwill** (the nontangible value of a business). For instance, a party might use a similar domain name to sell pornography, offer for sale another party's domain name, or otherwise infringe on others' trademarks.

DISTRIBUTION SYSTEM The Internet Corporation for Assigned Names and Numbers (ICANN), a nonprofit corporation, oversees the distribution of domain names and operates an online arbitration system. Due to numerous complaints, ICANN completely overhauled the domain name distribution system.

In 2012, ICANN started selling new generic top-level domain names (gTLDs) for an initial price of $185,000 plus an annual fee of $25,000. Whereas TLDs were limited to only a few terms (such as "com," "net," and "org"), gTLDs can take any form. By 2013, many companies and corporations had acquired gTLDs based on their brands, such as .aol, .bmw, .canon, .gap, .target, .toyota, and .walmart. Some companies have numerous gTLDs. Google's gTLDs, for instance, include .android, .bing, .chrome, .gmail, .goog, and .YouTube.

Cybersquatting

One of the goals of the new gTLD system is to alleviate the problem of *cybersquatting*. **Cybersquatting** occurs when a person registers a domain name that is the same as, or confusingly similar to, the trademark of another and then offers to sell the domain name back to the trademark owner.

▶ **Case in Point 9.2** Apple, Inc., has repeatedly sued cybersquatters that registered domain names similar to its products, such as iphone4s.com and ipods.com. In 2012, Apple won a judgment in litigation at the World Intellectual Property Organization (WIPO—see Chapter 24) against a company that was squatting on the domain name iPhone5.com.[4] ◀

ANTICYBERSQUATTING LEGISLATION Because cybersquatting has led to so much litigation, Congress enacted the Anticybersquatting Consumer Protection Act (ACPA),[5] which amended the Lanham Act—the federal law protecting trademarks, discussed in Chapter 8. The ACPA makes cybersquatting illegal when both of the following are true:

1. The name is identical or confusingly similar to the trademark of another.
2. The one registering, trafficking in, or using the domain name has a "bad faith intent" to profit from that trademark.

THE ONGOING PROBLEM OF CYBERSQUATTING Despite the ACPA, cybersquatting continues to present a problem for businesses, largely because more TLDs and gTLDs are now available and many more companies are registering domain names. Indeed, domain name registrars have proliferated. Registrar compa-

---

3. Pub. L. No. 109-455, 120 Stat. 3372 (2006), codified in various sections of 15 U.S.C. and 12 U.S.C. Section 3412.

4. WIPO Case No. D2012-0951.
5. 15 U.S.C. Section 1129.

nies charge a fee to businesses and individuals to register new names and to renew annual registrations (often through automated software). Many of these companies also buy and sell expired domain names.

All domain name registrars are supposed to relay information about these transactions to ICANN and other companies that keep a master list of domain names, but this does not always occur. The speed at which domain names change hands and the difficulty in tracking mass automated registrations have created an environment where cybersquatting can flourish.

▶ **Case in Point 9.3**   OnNet USA, Inc., owns the English-language rights to 9Dragons, a game with a martial arts theme, and operates a Web site for its promotion. When a party known as "Warv0x" began to operate a pirated version of the game at Play9D.com, OnNet filed an action under the ACPA in a federal court. OnNet was unable to obtain contact information for the owner of Play9D.com through its Australian domain name registrar, however, and thus could not complete service of process (see Chapter 3). Therefore, the federal court allowed OnNet to serve the defendant by publishing a notice of the suit in a newspaper in Gold Coast, Australia.[6] ◀

TYPOSQUATTING   Cybersquatters have also developed new tactics, such as **typosquatting,** or registering a name that is a misspelling of a popular brand, such as googl.com or appple.com. Because many Internet users are not perfect typists, Web pages using these misspelled names receive a lot of traffic.

More traffic generally means increased profit (advertisers often pay Web sites based on the number of unique visits, or hits), which in turn provides incentive for more cybersquatters. Also, if the misspelling is significant, the trademark owner may have difficulty proving that the name is identical or confusingly similar to the trademark of another as the ACPA requires.

Cybersquatting is costly for businesses, which must attempt to register all variations of a name to protect their domain name rights from would-be cybersquatters and typosquatters. Large corporations may have to register thousands of domain names across the globe just to protect their basic brands and trademarks.

APPLICABILITY AND SANCTIONS OF THE ACPA   The ACPA applies to all domain name registrations of trademarks. Successful plaintiffs in suits brought under the act can collect actual damages and profits, or they can elect to receive statutory damages ranging from $1,000 to $100,000.

Although some companies have been successful suing under the ACPA, there are roadblocks to pursuing such lawsuits. Some domain name registrars offer privacy services that hide the true owners of Web sites, making it difficult for trademark owners to identify cybersquatters. Thus, before bringing a suit, a trademark owner has to ask the court for a subpoena to discover the identity of the owner of the infringing Web site. Because of the high costs of court proceedings, discovery, and even arbitration, many disputes over cybersquatting are settled out of court.

Meta Tags

Search engines compile their results by looking through a Web site's key-word field. As noted in Chapter 4, *meta tags* are key words that are inserted into the HTML (hypertext markup language) code to tell Internet browsers specific information about a Web page. Meta tags increase the likelihood that a site will be included in search engine results, even though the site may have nothing to do with the key words. Using this same technique, one site may appropriate the key words of other sites with more frequent hits so that the appropriating site will appear in the same search engine results as the more popular sites.

Using another's trademark in a meta tag without the owner's permission, however, normally constitutes trademark infringement. Some uses of another's trademark as a meta tag may be permissible if the use is reasonably necessary and does not suggest that the owner authorized or sponsored the use.

▶ **Case in Point 9.4**   Farzad and Lisa Tabari are auto brokers—the personal shoppers of the automotive world. They contact authorized dealers, solicit bids, and arrange for customers to buy from the dealer offering the best combination of location, availability, and price. The Tabaris offered this service at the Web sites **buy-a-lexus.com** and **buyorleaselexus.com**. Toyota Motor Sales U.S.A., Inc., the exclusive distributor of Lexus vehicles and the owner of the Lexus mark, objected to the Tabaris' practices. The Tabaris removed Toyota's photographs and logo from their site and added a disclaimer in large type at the top, but they refused to give up their domain names. Toyota sued for infringement. The court forced the Tabaris to stop using any "domain name, service mark, trademark,

---

6. *OnNet USA, Inc. v. Play9D.com,* ___F.Supp.2d ___, 2013 WL 120319 (N.D.Cal. 2013).

trade name, meta tag or other commercial indication of origin that includes the mark LEXUS."[7] ◄

Trademark Dilution in the Online World

As discussed in Chapter 8, trademark *dilution* occurs when a trademark is used, without authorization, in a way that diminishes the distinctive quality of the mark.

Unlike trademark infringement, a claim of dilution does not require proof that consumers are likely to be confused by a connection between the unauthorized use and the mark. For this reason, the products involved need not be similar, as the following *Spotlight Case* illustrates.

---

7. *Toyota Motor Sales, U.S.A., Inc. v. Tabari*, 610 F.3d 171 (9th Cir. 2011).

SPTLIGHT on Internet Porn

Case 9.1 Hasbro, Inc. v. Internet Entertainment Group, Ltd.
United States District Court, Western District of Washington, ___ F.Supp.2d ___ (1996).

BACKGROUND AND FACTS In 1949, Hasbro, Inc.—then known as the Milton Bradley Company—published its first version of Candy Land, a children's board game. Hasbro is the owner of the trademark "Candy Land," which has been registered with the U.S. Patent and Trademark Office since 1951. Over the years, Hasbro has produced several versions of the game, including Candy Land puzzles, a travel version, a computer game, and a handheld electronic version. In the mid-1990s, Brian Cartmell and his employer, the Internet Entertainment Group, Ltd., used the term *candyland.com* as a domain name for a sexually explicit Internet site. Anyone who performed an online search using the word *candyland* was directed to this adult Web site. Hasbro filed a trademark dilution claim in a federal court, seeking a permanent injunction to prevent the defendants from using the Candy Land trademark.

IN THE LANGUAGE OF THE COURT
DWYER, U.S. District Judge

* * * *

2. Hasbro has demonstrated a probability of proving that defendants Internet Entertainment Group, Ltd., Brian Cartmell and Internet Entertainment Group, Inc. (collectively referred to as "defendants") have been diluting the value of Hasbro's CANDY LAND mark by using the name CANDYLAND to identify a sexually explicit Internet site, and by using the name string "candyland.com" as an Internet domain name which, when typed into an Internet-connected computer, provides Internet users with access to that site.
* * * *

4. Hasbro has shown that defendants' use of the CANDY LAND name and the domain name candyland.com in connection with their Internet site is causing irreparable injury to Hasbro.

5. *The probable harm to Hasbro from defendants' conduct outweighs any inconvenience that defendants will experience if they are required to stop using the CANDYLAND name.* [Emphasis added.]
* * * *

THEREFORE, IT IS HEREBY ORDERED that Hasbro's motion for preliminary injunction is granted.

DECISION AND REMEDY *The federal district court granted Hasbro an injunction against the defendants, agreeing that the domain name* candyland *was "causing irreparable injury to Hasbro." The judge ordered the defendants to immediately remove all content from the* candyland.com *Web site and to stop using the Candy Land mark.*

CASE 9.1 CONTINUED **THE ECONOMIC DIMENSION** *How can companies protect themselves from others who create Web sites that have similar domain names, and what limits each company's ability to be fully protected?*

WHAT IF THE FACTS WERE DIFFERENT? *Suppose that the site using* candyland.com *had not been sexually explicit but had sold candy. Would the result have been the same? Explain.*

Licensing

Recall from Chapter 8 that a company may permit another party to use a trademark (or other intellectual property) under a license. A licensor might grant a license allowing its trademark to be used as part of a domain name, for example.

Indeed, licensing is ubiquitous in the online world. When you download an application on your smartphone, tablet, or other mobile device, for instance, you are typically entering into to a license agreement. You are obtaining only a *license* to use that app and not ownership rights in it. Apps published on Google Play, for instance, may use its licensing service to prompt users to agree to a license at the time of installation and use. Licensing agreements frequently include restrictions that prohibit licensees from sharing the file and using it to create similar software applications. The license may also limit the use of the application to a specific device or give permission to the user for a certain time period. For further discussion of licensing and e-contracts, see Chapter 12.

SECTION 2
COPYRIGHTS IN DIGITAL INFORMATION

Copyright law is probably the most important form of intellectual property protection on the Internet. This is because much of the material on the Internet (including software and database information) is copyrighted, and in order to transfer that material online, it must be "copied." Generally, whenever a party downloads software or music into a computer's random access memory, or RAM, without authorization, a copyright is infringed. Technology has vastly increased the potential for copyright infringement.

▶ **Case in Point 9.5** In one case, a rap song that was included in the sound track of a movie had used only a few seconds from the guitar solo of another's copyrighted sound recording without permission. Nevertheless, a federal court held that digitally sampling a copyrighted sound recording of any length constitutes copyright infringement.[8] ◀

Some other federal courts have not found that digital sampling is always illegal. Some courts have allowed the defense of fair use (see Chapter 8), while others have not. ▶ **Example 9.6** Hip hop stars Jay-Z and Kanye West were sued for digitally sampling music by soul musician Syl Johnson. Given the uncertain outcome of the litigation, they ended up settling the suit in 2012 for an undisclosed amount. ◀

Initially, criminal penalties for copyright violations could be imposed only if unauthorized copies were exchanged for financial gain. Yet much piracy of copyrighted materials online was "altruistic" in nature— unauthorized copies were made simply to be shared with others. Then, Congress amended the law and extended criminal liability for the piracy of copyrighted materials to persons who exchange unauthorized copies of copyrighted works without realizing a profit.

Digital Millennium Copyright Act

In 1998, Congress passed further legislation to protect copyright holders—the Digital Millennium Copyright Act (DMCA).[9] The DMCA gave significant protection to owners of copyrights in digital information. Among other things, the act established civil and criminal penalties for anyone who circumvents (bypasses) encryption software or other technological antipiracy protection. Also prohibited are the manufacture, import, sale, and distribution of devices or services for circumvention.

The DMCA provides for exceptions to fit the needs of libraries, scientists, universities, and others. In general, the law does not restrict the "fair use" of circumvention methods for educational and other noncommercial purposes. For instance, circumvention is allowed to test computer security, to conduct encryption research, to protect personal privacy, and

---

8. *Bridgeport Music, Inc. v. Dimension Films,* 410 F.3d 792 (6th Cir. 2005).
9. 17 U.S.C. Sections 512, 1201–1205, 1301–1332; and 28 U.S.C. Section 4001.

to enable parents to monitor their children's use of the Internet. The exceptions are to be reconsidered every three years.

The DMCA also limits the liability of Internet service providers (ISPs). Under the act, an ISP is not liable for copyright infringement by its customer *unless* the ISP is aware of the subscriber's violation. An ISP may be held liable only if it fails to take action to shut down the subscriber after learning of the violation. A copyright holder must act promptly, however, by pursuing a claim in court, or the subscriber has the right to be restored to online access.

MP3 and File-Sharing Technology

Soon after the Internet became popular, a few enterprising programmers created software to compress large data files, particularly those associated with music. The best-known compression and decompression system is MP3, which enables music fans to download songs or entire CDs onto their computers or onto portable listening devices, such as iPods. The MP3 system also made it possible for music fans to access other fans' files by engaging in file-sharing via the Internet.

METHODS OF FILE-SHARING File-sharing is accomplished through **peer-to-peer (P2P) networking.** The concept is simple. Rather than going through a central Web server, P2P networking uses numerous personal computers (PCs) that are connected to the Internet. Individuals on the same network can access files stored on one another's PCs through a **distributed network.** Parts of the network may be distributed all over the country or the world, which offers an unlimited number of uses. Persons scattered throughout the country or the world can work together on the same project by using file-sharing programs.

A newer method of sharing files via the Internet is **cloud computing,** which is essentially a subscription-based or pay-per-use service that extends a computer's software or storage capabilities. Cloud computing can deliver a single application through a browser to multiple users. Alternatively, cloud computing might be a utility program to pool resources and provide data storage and virtual servers that can be accessed on demand. Amazon, Facebook, Google, IBM, and Sun Microsystems are using and developing more cloud computing services.

SHARING STORED MUSIC FILES When file-sharing is used to download others' stored music files, copyright issues arise. Recording artists and their labels stand to lose large amounts of royalties and revenues if relatively few digital downloads or CDs are purchased and then made available on distributed networks. Anyone can get the music for free on these networks.

▶ **Case in Point 9.7** The issue of file-sharing infringement has been the subject of an ongoing debate since the highly publicized cases against two companies (Napster, Inc. and Grokster, Ltd.) that created software used for copyright infringement. In the first case, Napster operated a Web site with free software that enabled users to copy and transfer MP3 files via the Internet. Firms in the recording industry sued Napster. Ultimately, the court held that Napster was liable for contributory and vicarious[10] (indirect) copyright infringement.

As technology evolved, Grokster, Ltd., and several other companies created and distributed new types of file-sharing software. This software did not maintain a central index of content, but allowed P2P network users to share stored music files. The court held that because the companies distributed file-sharing software "with the object of promoting its use to infringe the copyright," they were liable for the resulting acts of infringement by the software's users.[11] ◀

In the following case, a group of recording companies sued an Internet user who had downloaded a number of copyrighted songs from the Internet. The user then shared the audio files with others via a P2P network. One of the issues before the court was whether the user was an "innocent infringer." In other words, was she innocent of copyright infringement because she was unaware that the works were copyrighted?

---

10. *Vicarious (indirect) liability* exists when one person is subject to liability for another's actions. A common example occurs in the employment context, when an employer is held vicariously liable by third parties for torts committed by employees in the course of their employment.

11. *A&M Records, Inc. v. Napster, Inc.,* 239 F.3d 1004 (9th Cir. 2001); and *Metro-Goldwyn-Mayer Studios, Inc. v. Grokster, Ltd.,* 545 U.S. 913, 125 S.Ct. 2764, 162 L.Ed.2d 781 (2005). Grokster, Ltd., later settled this dispute out of court and stopped distributing its software.

CASE 9.2

Maverick Recording Co. v. Harper

United States Court of Appeals, Fifth Circuit, 598 F.3d 193 (2010).

COMPANY PROFILE Recording star Madonna, others in the music business, and Time Warner created Maverick Records in 1992. Initially, the company saw great success with Alanis Morissette, The Prodigy, Candlebox, and the Deftones. It also created the sound track for the movie *The Matrix*. In a dispute over management of the company, Madonna and another co-owner were bought out. Today, Maverick is a wholly owned subsidiary of Warner Music Group.

BACKGROUND AND FACTS Maverick Recording Company and several other music-recording firms (the plaintiffs) hired MediaSentry to investigate the infringement of their copyrights over the Internet. During its investigation, MediaSentry discovered that Whitney Harper was using a file-sharing program to share digital audio files with other users of a peer-to-peer network. The shared audio files included a number of the plaintiffs' copyrighted works. The plaintiffs brought an action in a federal court against Harper for copyright infringement. They sought $750 per infringed work, the minimum amount of damages set forth in Section 504(c)(1) of the Copyright Act.

Harper asserted that her infringement was "innocent" and that therefore Section 504(c)(2) of the Copyright Act should apply. That section provides that when an infringer was not aware, and had no reason to believe, that his or her acts constituted copyright infringement, "the court in its discretion may reduce the award of statutory damages to a sum of not less than $200." The trial court granted summary judgment for the plaintiffs on the issue of copyright infringement and enjoined Harper from further downloading and sharing of copyrighted works. The court, however, awarded the plaintiffs only $200 for each infringed work. Both parties appealed. Harper claimed that there was insufficient evidence of copyright infringement. The plaintiffs argued that the district court had erred by failing to rule out the innocent infringer defense as a matter of law.

IN THE LANGUAGE OF THE COURT
Edith *BROWN CLEMENT,* Circuit Judge:

* * * *

The uncontroverted [undisputed] evidence is more than sufficient to compel a finding that Harper had downloaded the files: there was no evidence from which a fact-finder could draw a reasonable inference that Harper had *not* downloaded them or that they were something other than audio files. * * * The district court properly rejected Harper's argument that the evidence of infringement was insufficient. * * * *

* * * The district court held that there was a genuine issue of material fact as to whether Harper was an innocent infringer. * * * Harper averred [asserted] in an affidavit that she did not understand the nature of file-sharing programs and that she believed that listening to music from file-sharing networks was akin to listening to a noninfringing Internet radio station. The district court ruled that this assertion created a triable [capable of being tried before a judge or a jury] issue as to whether Harper's infringement was "innocent" under [Section 504(c)(2) of the Copyright Act].

* * * We hold that the defense was unavailable to her as a matter of law. *The innocent infringer defense is limited by [Section 402(d) of the Copyright Act]: with one exception not relevant here, when a proper copyright notice "appears on the published * * * phonorecords to which a defendant * * * had access, then no weight shall be given to such a defendant's interposition of a defense based on innocent infringement in mitigation of actual or statutory damages."* [Emphasis added.]

CASE 9.2 CONTINUES ➡

The district court acknowledged that Plaintiffs provided proper notice on each of the published phonorecords from which the audio files were taken. * * * Harper contended only that she was too young and naive to understand that the copyrights on published music applied to downloaded music.

These arguments are insufficient to defeat the interposition [interference] of the [Section 402(d)] limitation on the innocent infringer defense. Harper's reliance on her own understanding of copyright law—or lack thereof—is irrelevant in the context of [Section 402(d)]. *The plain language of the statute shows that the infringer's knowledge or intent does not affect its application. Lack of legal sophistication cannot overcome a properly asserted [Section 402(d)] limitation to the innocent infringer defense.* [Emphasis added.]

* * * *

In short, the district court found a genuine issue of fact as to whether Harper intended to infringe Plaintiffs' copyrights, but that issue was not material: [Section 402(d)] forecloses, as a matter of law, Harper's innocent infringer defense. Because the defense does not apply, Plaintiffs are entitled to statutory damages. And because Plaintiffs requested the minimum statutory damages under [Section 504(c)(1)], Harper's culpability is not an issue and there are no issues left for trial. Plaintiffs must be awarded statutory damages of $750 per infringed work.

DECISION AND REMEDY *The U.S. Court of Appeals for the Fifth Circuit affirmed the trial court's finding of copyright liability, reversed its finding that the innocent infringer defense presented an issue for trial, and remanded the case for further proceedings consistent with the court's opinion. The appellate court concluded that the district court had erred by awarding damages of $200 per infringement because Harper was not an innocent infringer.*

THE ETHICAL DIMENSION *In this and other cases involving similar rulings, the courts have held that when the published phonorecordings from which audio files were taken contained copyright notices, the innocent infringer defense does not apply. It is irrelevant that the notice is not provided in the online file. Is this fair? Explain.*

MANAGERIAL IMPLICATIONS *Owners and managers of firms in the business of recording and distributing music face a constant challenge in protecting their copyrights. This is particularly true for audio files in the online environment, where Internet users can easily download a copyrighted song and make it available to P2P file-sharing networks. Among other things, this means that recording companies must be ever vigilant in searching the Web to find infringing uses of any works distributed online. Today, it is not uncommon for companies to hire antipiracy firms to investigate the illegal downloading of their copyrighted materials.*

DVDs AND FILE-SHARING File-sharing also creates problems for the motion picture industry, which loses significant amounts of revenue annually as a result of pirated DVDs. Numerous Web sites offer software that facilitates the illegal copying of movies, such as BitTorrent, which enables users to download high-quality files from the Internet.

▶ **Case in Point 9.8** TorrentSpy, a popular BitTorrent indexing Web site, enabled users to locate and exchange files. The Motion Picture Association of America (MPAA) and Columbia Pictures, Inc., brought a lawsuit against the operators of TorrentSpy for facilitating copyright infringement. The MPAA also claimed that the operators had destroyed evidence that would reveal the identity of individual infringers. The operators had ignored a court order to keep server logs of the Internet addresses of people who facilitated the trading of files via the site. Because TorrentSpy's operators had willfully destroyed evidence, a federal court found in favor of the MPAA and ordered the defendants to pay a judgment of $111 million.[12] ◀

SECTION 3
SOCIAL MEDIA

Social media provide a means by which people can create, share, and exchange ideas and comments via the Internet. Social networking sites, such as Facebook, Google+, MySpace, LinkedIn, Pinterest, and Tumblr, have become ubiquitous. Studies show that Internet users spend more time on social networks than at any other sites. The amount of time people spend accessing social networks on their smartphones and other

---

12. *Columbia Pictures Industries, v. Bunnell,* 2007 WL 4877701 (C.D.Cal. 2007).

mobile devices has increased every year (by nearly 37 percent in 2012 alone).

▶ **Example 9.9** Facebook, which was launched in 2004, had more than a billion active users by 2013. Individuals of all ages use Facebook to maintain social contacts, update friends on events, and distribute images to others. Facebook members often share common interests based on their school, location, or recreational affiliation, such as a sports team. ◀

Legal Issues

The emergence of Facebook and other social networking sites has created a number of legal and ethical issues for businesses. For instance, a firm's rights in valuable intellectual property may be infringed if users post trademarked images or copyrighted materials on these sites without permission.

Social media posts now are routinely included in discovery in litigation (see Chapter 3) because they can provide damaging information that establishes a person's intent or what she or he knew at a particular time. Like e-mail, posts on social networks can be the smoking gun that leads to liability.

Tweets and other social media posts can also be used to reduce damages awards. ▶ **Example 9.10** Omeisha Daniels sued for injuries she sustained in a car accident. She claimed that her injuries made it impossible for her to continue working as a hairstylist. The jury originally awarded her $237,000, but when the jurors saw Daniels's tweets and photographs of her partying in New Orleans and vacationing on the beach, they reduced the damages to $142,000. ◀

CRIMINAL INVESTIGATIONS Law enforcement uses social media to detect and prosecute criminals. ▶ **Example 9.11** A nineteen-year-old posts a message on Facebook bragging about how drunk he was on New Year's Eve and apologizing to the owner of the parked car that he hit. The next day, police officers arrest him for drunk driving and leaving the scene of an accident. ◀

ADMINISTRATIVE AGENCIES Federal regulators also use social media posts in their investigations into illegal activities. ▶ **Example 9.12** Reed Hastings, the top executive of Netflix, stated on Facebook that Netflix subscribers had watched a billion hours of video the previous month. This prompted a federal agency investigation. Because such a statement is considered to be material information to investors, it must be disclosed to all investors at the same time under securities law. ◀

The decision in a hearing before an administrative law judge can turn on the content of two Facebook posts, as occurred in the following case.

CASE ANALYSIS

Case 9.3 In re O'Brien
Superior Court of New Jersey, Appellate Division, 2013 WL 132508 (2013).

IN THE LANGUAGE OF THE COURT
PER CURIAM.
* * * *

[Jennifer] O'Brien has been employed as a teacher in the [City of Paterson, New Jersey] schools since March 1998. She has a master's degree in education, and certifications as an elementary school teacher and supervisor.

* * * In December 2010, O'Brien was assigned to teach the first grade [at School No. 21].

* * * There were twenty-three students in O'Brien's first-grade class. Almost all were six years old. All were either Latino or African-American.

On March 28, 2011, O'Brien posted two statements on Facebook, an Internet social-networking site. The first statement was, "I'm not a teacher—I'm a warden for future criminals!" The second statement was, "They had a scared straight program in school—why couldn't I bring first graders?"

* * * *

On March 30, 2011, [Frank Puglise, the principal of School No. 21] confronted O'Brien about the postings.

According to Puglise, O'Brien insisted that she did not intend her comments to be offensive, but she was otherwise unrepentant [unapologetic]. O'Brien was suspended * * *, pending a complete investigation.

News of O'Brien's Facebook postings spread quickly throughout the district. * * * Two angry parents went to Puglise's office to express their outrage. One parent threatened to remove her child from the school. According to Puglise, the school received at least a dozen irate phone calls. * * * There was a protest outside

CASE 9.3 CONTINUES ▶

the school, attended by twenty to twenty-five persons.

The following day, reporters and camera crews from major news organizations descended upon the school and remained there until late in the afternoon. A larger-than-usual crowd attended the Home-School Council meeting that evening, and the meeting was principally devoted to the Facebook postings. Parents expressed their outrage concerning the postings, and Puglise reassured the attendees that O'Brien had been removed from the classroom.

On April 14, 2011, the deputy superintendent of schools filed a complaint against O'Brien, charging her with conduct unbecoming a teacher.

The charges were filed with the Commissioner of Education * * * , and the matter was referred to the Office of Administrative Law for a hearing before an Administrative Law Judge (ALJ).
* * * *

On October 31, 2011, the ALJ issued her initial decision. The ALJ rejected O'Brien's contention that her comments were protected by the First Amendment to the United States Constitution. The ALJ wrote that O'Brien's remarks were not addressing a matter of public concern, but were "a personal expression" of dissatisfaction with her job.

The ALJ also wrote that * * * her right to express her views was outweighed by the district's need to operate its schools efficiently. The ALJ stated that:

> An Internet social-networking site such as Facebook is a questionable place to begin an earnest conversa-

tion about an important school issue such as classroom discipline. More to the point, a description of first-grade children as criminals with their teacher as their warden is intemperate and vituperative [insulting]. It becomes impossible for parents to cooperate with or have faith in a teacher who insults their children and trivializes legitimate educational concerns on the internet.

The ALJ added that, while First Amendment protections do not generally rise or fall on the public reactions to a person's statements, "in a public school setting thoughtless words can destroy the partnership between home and school that is essential to the mission of the schools."

The ALJ found that evidence supported the charges of conduct unbecoming a teacher. The ALJ determined that the evidence established that O'Brien failed to maintain a safe, caring, nurturing, educational environment * * * . The ALJ additionally determined that O'Brien breached her duty as a professional teacher * * * . In addition, the ALJ found that O'Brien's conduct endangered the mental well-being of the students.

The ALJ also determined O'Brien's actions warranted her removal * * * . The ALJ wrote,

> If this was an aberrational [not normal] lapse in judgment, a reaction to an unusually bad day, I would have expected to have heard more genuine and passionate contrition in O'Brien's testimony. I needed to hear that she was terribly sorry she had insulted her young students; that she loved being their teacher; and that she wanted desperately to return to the classroom. I heard nothing of the

sort. Rather, I came away with the impression that O'Brien remained somewhat befuddled by the commotion she had created, and that while she continued to maintain that her conduct was not inappropriate, she was sorry others thought differently.

The ALJ observed that, with some sensitivity training, and after some time to "reflect," O'Brien might successfully return to the classroom. The ALJ concluded, however, that O'Brien's relationship with the Paterson school community had been irreparably damaged, "not because the community thinks so, but because O'Brien fails to understand why it does." The ALJ ordered O'Brien's removal from her tenured position.

* * * The Acting Commissioner issued a final decision * * * . *The Acting Commissioner concluded that O'Brien's Facebook postings were not constitutionally protected; the evidence established that O'Brien engaged in conduct unbecoming a teacher; and removal was the appropriate penalty.* This appeal followed. [Emphasis added.]
* * * *

We * * * affirm the Acting Commissioner's final determination substantially for the reasons stated by the ALJ and the Acting Commissioner in their decisions.
* * * *

* * * We are satisfied that, in determining the appropriate penalty, the ALJ and Acting Commissioner considered all relevant factors and reasonably concluded that the seriousness of O'Brien's conduct warranted her removal from her tenured position in the district.

Affirmed.

LEGAL REASONING QUESTIONS

1. Certain interests of public employees and their employer are balanced to determine whether the First Amendment protects an employee's Facebook posts. What are those interests?

2. What did O'Brien do that constituted conduct unbecoming a tenured teacher?

3. What penalty did the administrative law judge impose? Why?

4. Would the outcome have been different if O'Brien had apologized? Discuss.

EMPLOYERS' SOCIAL MEDIA POLICIES Employees who use social media in a way that violates their employer's stated policies may be disciplined or fired from their jobs. (Many large corporations have established specific guidelines on creating a social media policy in the workplace.) Courts and employment agencies usually uphold an employer's right to terminate a person based on his or her violation of a social media policy.

▶ **Case in Point 9.13**   Virginia Rodriquez worked for Wal-Mart Stores, Inc., for almost twenty years and had been promoted to management. Then she was disciplined for violating the company's policies by having a fellow employee use Rodriquez's password to alter the price of an item that she purchased. Under Wal-Mart's rules, another violation within a year would mean termination. Nine months later, on Facebook, Rodriquez publicly chastised employees under her supervision for calling in sick to go to a party. The posting violated Wal-Mart's "Social Media Policy," which was "to avoid public comment that adversely affects employees." Wal-Mart terminated Rodriquez. She filed a lawsuit, alleging discrimination, but the court issued a summary judgment in Wal-Mart's favor.[13] ◀ Note, however, that employees' posts on social media may be protected under labor law, as discussed in Chapter 5.

The Electronic Communications Privacy Act

The Electronic Communications Privacy Act (ECPA)[14] amended federal wiretapping law to cover electronic forms of communications. Although Congress enacted the ECPA many years before social media networks existed, it nevertheless applies to communications through social media.

The ECPA prohibits the intentional interception of any wire, oral, or electronic communication. It also prohibits the intentional disclosure or use of the information obtained by the interception.

EXCLUSIONS Excluded from the ECPA's coverage are any electronic communications through devices that an employer provides for its employee to use "in the ordinary course of its business." Consequently, if a company provides the electronic device (cell phone, laptop, tablet) to the employee for ordinary business use, the company is not prohibited from intercepting business communications made on it.

This "business-extension exception" to the ECPA permits employers to monitor employees' electronic communications made in the ordinary course of business. It does not, however, permit employers to monitor employees' personal communications. Another exception allows an employer to avoid liability under the act if the employees consent to having their electronic communications monitored by the employer.

STORED COMMUNICATIONS Part of the ECPA is known as the Stored Communications Act (SCA).[15] The SCA prohibits intentional and unauthorized access to *stored* electronic communications and sets forth criminal and civil sanctions for violators. A person can violate the SCA by intentionally accessing a stored electronic communication. The SCA also prevents "providers" of communication services (such as cell phone companies and social media networks) from divulging private communications to certain entities and individuals.

▶ **Case in Point 9.14**   Two restaurant employees, Brian Pietrylo and Doreen Marino, were fired after their manager uncovered their password-protected MySpace group. The group's communications, stored on MySpace's Web site, contained sexual remarks about customers and management, and comments about illegal drug use and violent behavior. One employee said the group's purpose was to "vent about any BS we deal with out of work without any outside eyes spying on us." The restaurant learned about the private MySpace group when a hostess showed it to a manager who requested access. The hostess was not explicitly threatened with termination but feared she would lose her job if she did not comply. The court allowed the employees' SCA claim, and the jury awarded them $17,003 in compensatory and punitive damages.[16] ◀

Protection of Social Media Passwords

In recent years, employees and applicants for jobs or colleges have sometimes been asked to divulge their social media passwords. Employers and schools have sometimes looked at an individual's Facebook or other account to see if it included controversial postings such as racially discriminatory remarks or photos

---

13. *Rodriquez v. Wal-Mart Stores, Inc.,* ___F.Supp.2d __, 2013 WL 102674 (N.D.Tex. 2013).
14. 18 U.S.C. Sections 2510–2521.

15. 18 U.S.C. Sections 2701–2711.
16. *Pietrylo v. Hillstone Restaurant Group,* 2009 WL 3128420 (D.N.J. 2009).

of drug parties. Such postings can have a negative effect on a person's prospects even though they were made years earlier or have been taken out of context.

By 2013, four states (California, Illinois, Maryland, and Michigan) had enacted legislation to protect individuals from having to disclose their social media passwords. Each state's law is slightly different. Some states, such as Michigan, prohibit employers from taking adverse action against an employee or job applicant based on what the person has posted online. Michigan's law also applies to e-mail and cloud storage accounts. The federal government is also considering legislation that would prohibit employers and schools from demanding passwords to social media accounts.

Even if legislation is passed, however, it will not completely prevent employers and others from taking actions against a person based on his or her social network postings. Management and human resources personnel are unlikely to admit that they looked at someone's Facebook page and that it influenced their decision. How would a person who does not get a job be able to prove that she or he was rejected because the employer accessed social media? Also, the employer or school may use private browsing, which enables people to keep their Web browsing activities confidential.

Company-wide Social Media Networks

Many companies, including Dell, Inc., and Nikon Instruments, form their own internal social media networks. Software companies offer a variety of systems, including Salesforce.com's Chatter, Microsoft's Yammer, and Cisco Systems' WebEx Social. Posts on these internal networks are quite different from the typical posts on Facebook, LinkedIn, and Twitter. Employees use these intranets to exchange messages about topics related to their work such as deals that are closing, new products, production flaws, how a team is solving a problem, and the details of customer orders. Thus, the tone is businesslike.

PROTECTION OF TRADE SECRETS An important advantage to using an internal system for employee communications is that the company can better protect its trade secrets. The company usually decides which employees can see particular intranet files and which employees will belong to each specific "social" group within the company. Companies providing internal social media networks often keep the resulting data on their own servers in secure "clouds."

OTHER ADVANTAGES Internal social media systems also offer additional benefits such as real-time information about important issues, such as production glitches. Additionally, posts can include tips on how to best sell new products or deal with difficult customers, as well as information about competitors' products and services.

Another major benefit of intranets is a significant reduction in the use of e-mail. Rather than wasting fellow employees' time reading mass e-mailings, workers can post messages or collaborate on presentations via the company's social network.

SECTION 4
ONLINE DEFAMATION

Cyber torts are torts that arise from online conduct. One of the most prevalent cyber torts is online defamation. Recall from Chapter 6 that defamation is wrongfully hurting a person's reputation by communicating false statements about that person to others. Because the Internet enables individuals to communicate with large numbers of people simultaneously (via a blog or tweet, for instance), online defamation has become a problem in today's legal environment.

▶ **Example 9.15** Courtney Love was sued for defamation based on remarks she posted about fashion designer Dawn Simorangkir on Twitter. Love claimed that her statements were opinion (rather than statements of fact, as required) and therefore were not actionable as defamation. Nevertheless, Love ended up paying $430,000 to settle the case out of court. ◀

Identifying the Author of Online Defamation

An initial issue raised by online defamation is simply discovering who is committing it. In the real world, identifying the author of a defamatory remark generally is an easy matter. Suppose, though, that a business firm has discovered that defamatory statements about its policies and products are being posted in an online forum. Such forums allow anyone—customers, employees, or crackpots—to complain about a firm that they dislike while remaining anonymous.

Therefore, a threshold barrier to anyone who seeks to bring an action for online defamation is discovering the identity of the person who posted the defamatory message. An Internet service provider (ISP) can disclose personal information about its customers only when ordered to do so by a court. Consequently, businesses and individuals are increasingly bringing lawsuits against "John Does" (John Doe, Jane Doe, and the like are fictitious names used in lawsuits when the identity of a party is not known or when a party wishes to conceal his or her name for privacy reasons). Then, using the authority of the courts, the plaintiffs can obtain from the ISPs the identity of the persons responsible for the defamatory messages.

Liability of Internet Service Providers

Recall from the discussion of defamation in Chapter 6 that normally one who repeats or otherwise republishes a defamatory statement is subject to liability as if he or she had originally published it. Thus, newspapers, magazines, and television and radio stations are subject to liability for defamatory content that they publish or broadcast, even though the content was prepared or created by others.

Applying this rule to cyberspace, however, raises an important issue: Should ISPs be regarded as publishers and therefore be held liable for defamatory messages that are posted by their users in online forums or other arenas?

GENERAL RULE The Communications Decency Act (CDA) states that "[n]o provider or user of an interactive computer service shall be treated as the publisher or speaker of any information provided by another information content provider."[17] Thus, under the CDA, ISPs usually are treated differently from publishers in print and other media and are not liable for publishing defamatory statements that come from a third party.

EXCEPTIONS Although the courts generally have construed the CDA as providing a broad shield to protect ISPs from liability for third party content, some courts have started establishing some limits to this immunity. ▶ **Case in Point 9.16** Roommate.com, LLC, operates an online roommate-matching Web site that helps individuals find roommates based on their descriptions of themselves and their room-

mate preferences. Users respond to a series of online questions, choosing from answers in drop-down and select-a-box menus.

Some of the questions asked users to disclose their sex, family status, and sexual orientation—which is not permitted under the federal Fair Housing Act. When a nonprofit housing organization sued Roommate.com, the company claimed it was immune from liability under the CDA. A federal appellate court disagreed and ruled that Roommate.com was not immune from liability. Roommate.com was ordered to pay nearly $500,000 for prompting discriminatory preferences from users and matching users based on these criteria in violation of federal law.[18] ◀

SECTION 5

PRIVACY

Facebook, Google, and Yahoo have all been accused of violating users' privacy rights. As discussed in Chapter 4, the courts have held that the right to privacy is guaranteed by the Bill of Rights, and some state constitutions guarantee it as well. To maintain a suit for the invasion of privacy, though, a person must have a reasonable expectation of privacy in the particular situation (see Chapter 6). People clearly have a reasonable expectation of privacy when they enter their personal banking or credit-card information online. They also have a reasonable expectation that online companies will follow their own privacy policies. But it is probably not reasonable to expect privacy in statements made on Twitter.

Sometimes, people are confused and mistakenly believe that they are making statements or posting photos in a private forum. ▶ **Example 9.17** Randi Zuckerberg, the older sister of Mark Zuckerberg (the founder of Facebook), used a mobile app called "Poke" to post a "private" photo on Facebook of their family gathering during the holidays. Poke allows the sender to decide how long the photo can be seen by others. Facebook allows users to configure their privacy settings to limit access to photos, which Randi thought she had done. Nonetheless, the photo showed up in the Facebook feed of Callie Schweitzer, who then put it on Twitter where it eventually went viral. Schweitzer apologized and removed the photo, but it had already gone public for the world to see. ◀

---

17. 47 U.S.C. Section 230.

18. *Fair Housing Council of San Fernando Valley v. Roommate.com, LLC,* 666 F.3d 1216 (9th Cir. 2012).

Data Collection and Cookies

Whenever a consumer purchases items from an online retailer, such as Amazon.com, or a retailer that sells both offline and online, such as Best Buy, the retailer collects information about the consumer. **Cookies** are invisible files that computers, smartphones, and other mobile devices create to track a user's Web browsing activities. Cookies provide detailed information to marketers about an individual's behavior and preferences, which is then used to personalize online services.

Over time, the retailer can amass considerable data about a person's shopping habits. Does collecting this information violate a consumer's right to privacy? Should retailers be able to pass on the data they have collected to their affiliates? Should they be able to use the information to predict what a consumer might want and then create online "coupons" customized to fit the person's buying history?

▶ **Example 9.18** Facebook, Inc., recently settled a lawsuit over its use of a targeted advertising technique called "Sponsored Stories." An ad would display a Facebook friend's name, profile picture, and a statement that the friend "likes" the company sponsoring the advertisement, alongside the company's logo. A group of plaintiffs filed suit, claiming that Facebook had used their pictures for advertising without their permission. When a federal court refused to dismiss the case, Facebook agreed to settle. ◀

Internet Companies' Privacy Policies

The Federal Trade Commission (FTC) investigates consumer complaints of privacy violations. The FTC has forced many companies, including Google, Facebook, Twitter, and MySpace, to enter a consent decree that gives the FTC broad power to review their privacy and data practices. It can then sue companies that violate the terms of the decree.

▶ **Example 9.19** In 2012, Google settled a suit brought by the FTC alleging that it had misused data from Apple's Safari users. Google allegedly had used cookies to trick the Safari browser on iPhones and iPads so that Google could monitor users who had blocked such tracking. This violated the consent decree with the FTC. Google agreed to pay $22.5 million to settle the suit without admitting liability. ◀

Facebook has faced a number of complaints about its privacy policy and has changed its policy several times to satisfy its critics and ward off potential government investigations. Other companies, including mobile app developers, have also changed their privacy policies to provide more information to consumers. Consequently, it is frequently the companies, rather than courts or legislatures, that are defining the privacy rights of their online users.

The Consumer Privacy Bill of Rights

To protect consumers' personal information, the Obama administration has proposed a consumer privacy bill of rights (see Exhibit 9–1 below). The goal is to ensure that personal information is safe online.

If this proposed privacy bill of rights becomes law, retailers will have to change some of their procedures. Retailers will have to give customers better choices about what data are collected and how the data are used for marketing. They may also have to take into account consumers' expectations about how their information will be used once it is collected.

EXHIBIT 9–1 The Proposed Consumer Privacy Bill of Rights

1. Individual Control—Consumers have a right to exercise control over what personal data organizations collect from them and how they use it.

2. Transparency—Consumers have the right to easily understandable information about privacy and security practices.

3. Respect for Context—Consumers have a right to expect that organizations will collect, use, and disclose personal data in ways that are consistent with the context in which consumers provide the data.

4. Security—Consumers have the right to secure and responsible handling of personal data.

5. Access and Accuracy—Consumers have a right to access and correct personal data in usable formats, in a manner that is appropriate to the sensitivity of the data and the risk of adverse consequences to consumers if the data are inaccurate.

6. Focus Collection—Consumers have a right to reasonable limits on the personal data that companies collect and retain.

7. Accountability—Consumers have a right to have personal data handled by companies with appropriate measures in place to assure that they adhere to the Consumer Privacy Bill of Rights.

Reviewing: Internet Law, Social Media, and Privacy

While he was in high school, Joel Gibb downloaded numerous songs to his smartphone from an unlicensed file-sharing service. He used portions of the copyrighted songs when he recorded his own band and posted videos on YouTube and Facebook. Gibb also used BitTorrent to download several movies from the Internet. Now he has applied to Boston University. The admissions office has requested access to his Facebook password, and he has complied. Using the information presented in the chapter, answer the following questions.

1. What laws, if any, did Gibb violate by downloading the music and videos from the Internet?
2. Was Gibb's use of portions of copyrighted songs in his own music illegal? Explain.
3. Can individuals legally post copyrighted content on their Facebook pages? Why or why not?
4. Did Boston University violate any laws when it asked Joel to provide his Facebook password? Explain.

DEBATE THIS ... *Internet service providers should be subject to the same defamation laws as newspapers, magazines, and television and radio stations.*

Terms and Concepts

cookie 190
cloud computing 182
cyber tort 188
cybersquatting 178

distributed network 182
domain name 178
goodwill 178
Internet service provider (ISP) 178

peer-to-peer (P2P) networking 182
social media 184
spam 177
typosquatting 179

ExamPrep

Issue Spotters

1. Karl self-publishes a cookbook titled *Hole Foods,* in which he sets out recipes for donuts, Bundt cakes, tortellini, and other foods with holes. To publicize the book, Karl designs the Web site **holefoods.com**. Karl appropriates the key words of other cooking and cookbook sites with more frequent hits so that **holefoods.com** will appear in the same search engine results as the more popular sites. Has Karl done anything wrong? Explain. **(See page 181.)**

2. Eagle Corporation began marketing software in 2001 under the mark "Eagle." In 2013, Eagle.com, Inc., a different company selling different products, begins to use *eagle* as part of its URL and registers it as a domain

name. Can Eagle Corporation stop this use of *eagle?* If so, what must the company show? **(See page 180.)**

• Check your answers to the Issue Spotters against the answers provided in Appendix E at the end of this text.

Before the Test

Go to **www.cengagebrain.com**, enter the ISBN 9781285185248, and click on "Find" to locate this textbook's Web site. Then, click on "Access Now" under "Study Tools," and select Chapter 9 at the top. There, you will find a Practice Quiz that you can take to assess your mastery of the concepts in this chapter, as well as Flashcards and a Glossary of important terms.

Business Scenarios

9–1. Domain Names. Tony owns Antonio's, a pub in a small town in Iowa. Universal Dining, Inc., opens a chain of pizza parlors in California called "Antonio's." Without Tony's consent, Universal uses "antoniosincalifornia" as part of the domain name for the chain's Web site. Has Universal committed trademark dilution or any other violation of the law? Explain. **(See page 178.)**

9–2. Internet Service Providers. CyberConnect, Inc., is an Internet service provider (ISP). Pepper is a CyberConnect subscriber. Market Reach, Inc., is an online advertising company. Using sophisticated software, Market Reach directs its ads to those users most likely to be interested in a particular product. When Pepper receives one of the ads, she objects to the content. Further, she claims that CyberConnect should pay damages for "publishing" the ad. Is the ISP regarded as a publisher and therefore liable for the content of Market Reach's ad? Why or why not? **(See page 178.)**

9–3. Privacy. SeeYou, Inc., is an online social network. SeeYou's members develop personalized profiles to interact and share information—photos, videos, stories, activity updates, and other items—with other members. Members post the information that they want to share and decide with whom they want to share it. SeeYou launched a program to allow members to share with others what they do elsewhere online. For example, if a member rents a movie through Netflix, SeeYou will broadcast that information to everyone in the member's online network. How can SeeYou avoid complaints that this program violates its members' privacy? **(See page 189.)**

Business Case Problems

9–4. Copyrights in Digital Information. When she was in college, Jammie Thomas-Rasset wrote a case study on Napster, the online peer-to-peer (P2P) file-sharing network, and knew that it was shut down because it was illegal. Later, Capitol Records, Inc., which owns the copyrights to a large number of music recordings, discovered that "tereastarr"—a user name associated with Thomas-Rasset's Internet protocol address—had made twenty-four songs available for distribution on KaZaA, another P2P network. Capitol notified Thomas-Rasset that she had been identified as engaging in the unauthorized trading of music. She replaced the hard drive on her computer with a new drive that did not contain the songs in dispute. Is Thomas-Rasset liable for copyright infringement? Explain. [*Capitol Records, Inc. v. Thomas-Rasset*, 692 F.3d 899 (8th Cir. 2012)] **(See page 182.)**

9–5. Domain Names. Austin Rare Coins, Inc., buys and sells rare coins, bullion, and other precious metals through eight Web sites with different domain names. An unknown individual took control of Austin's servers and transferred the domain names to another registrant without Austin's permission. The new registrant began using the domain names to host malicious content—including hate letters to customers and fraudulent contact information—and to post customers' credit-card numbers and other private information, thereby tarnishing Austin's goodwill. Austin filed a suit in a federal district court against the new registrant under the Anticybersquatting Consumer Protection Act. Is Austin entitled to a transfer of the domain names? Explain. [*Austin Rare Coins, Inc. v. Acoins.com*, __ F.Supp.2d __, 2013 WL 85142 (E.D.Va. 2013)] **(See page 178.)**

9–6. BUSINESS CASE PROBLEM WITH SAMPLE ANSWER: Privacy.

 Using special software, South Dakota law enforcement officers found a person who appeared to possess child pornography at a specific Internet protocol address. The officers subpoenaed Midcontinent Communications, the service that assigned the address, for the personal information of its subscriber. With this information, the officers obtained a search warrant for the residence of John Rolfe, where they found a laptop that contained child pornography. Rolfe argued that the subpoenas violated his "expectation of privacy." Did Rolfe have a privacy interest in the information obtained by the subpoenas issued to Midcontinent? Discuss. [State of South Dakota v. Rolfe, 825 N.W.2d 901 (S.Dak. 2013)] **(See page 189.)**

- **For a sample answer to Problem 9–6, go to Appendix F at the end of this text.**

9–7. File-Sharing. Dartmouth College professor M. Eric Johnson, in collaboration with Tiversa, Inc., a company that monitors peer-to-peer networks to provide security services, wrote an article titled "Data Hemorrhages in the Health-Care Sector." In preparing the article, Johnson and Tiversa searched the networks for data that could be used to commit medical or financial identity theft. They found a document that contained the Social Security numbers, insurance information, and treatment codes for patients of LabMD, Inc. Tiversa notified LabMD of the find in order to solicit its business. Instead of hiring Tiversa, however, LabMD filed a suit in a federal district court against the company, alleging trespass, conversion, and violations of federal statutes. What do these facts indicate about the security of private information? Explain. How should the court rule? [*LabMD, Inc. v. Tiversa, Inc.,* 2013 WL 425983 (11th Cir. 2013)] **(See page 182.)**

9–8. A QUESTION OF ETHICS: Criminal Investigations.

 After the unauthorized release and posting of classified U.S. government documents to WikiLeaks. org, allegedly involving Bradley Manning, a U.S. Army private first class, the U.S. government began a criminal investigation. The government obtained a court order to require Twitter, Inc., to turn over subscriber information and communications to and from the e-mail addresses of Birgitta Jonsdottir and others. The court sealed the order and the other documents in the case, reasoning that "there exists no *right to public notice of all the types of documents filed in a . . . case." Jonsdottir and the others appealed this decision. [In re Application of the United States of America for an Order Pursuant to 18 U.S.C. Section 2703(d), 707 F.3d 283 (4th Cir. 2013)]* **(See page 185.)**

(a) Why would the government want to "seal" the documents of an investigation? Why would the individuals under investigation want those documents to be "unsealed"? What factors should be considered in striking a balance between these competing interests?

(b) How does law enforcement use social media to detect and prosecute criminals? Is this use of social media an unethical invasion of individuals' privacy? Discuss.

Legal Reasoning Group Activity

9–9. File-Sharing. James, Chang, and Sixta are roommates. They are music fans and frequently listen to the same artists and songs. They regularly exchange MP3 music files that contain songs from their favorite artists. **(See page 182.)**

(a) One group of students will decide whether the fact that the roommates are transferring files among themselves for no monetary benefit precludes them from being subject to copyright law.

(b) The second group will consider an additional fact. Each roommate regularly buys CDs and rips them to his or her hard drive. Then the roommate gives the CDs to the other roommates to do the same.

CHAPTER 10

CRIMINAL LAW AND CYBER CRIME

Criminal law is an important part of the legal environment of business. Various sanctions are used to bring about a society in which individuals engaging in business can compete and flourish. These sanctions include damages for various types of tortious conduct (see Chapters 6 and 7), damages for breach of contract (to be discussed in Chapter 19), and the equitable remedies discussed in Chapter 1. Additional sanctions are imposed under criminal law. Indeed, many statutes regulating business provide for criminal as well as civil penalties.

In this chapter, after explaining some essential differences between criminal law and civil law, we look at how crimes are classified and at the elements that must be present for criminal liability to exist. We then examine the various categories of crimes, the defenses that can be raised to avoid criminal liability, and the rules of criminal procedure.

We conclude the chapter with a discussion of crimes that occur in cyberspace, which are often called *cyber crimes*. Cyber attacks are becoming all too common—even e-mail and data of government agencies and former U.S. presidents have been hacked. Smartphones are being infected by malicious software, which puts users' data at risk, as you will read in a feature later in this chapter.

CIVIL LAW AND CRIMINAL LAW

Recall from Chapter 1 that *civil law* pertains to the duties that exist between persons or between persons and their governments. Criminal law, in contrast, has to do with crime. A **crime** can be defined as a wrong against society set forth in a statute and punishable by a fine and/or imprisonment—or, in some cases, death.

As mentioned in Chapter 1, because crimes are *offenses against society as a whole*, they are prosecuted by a public official, such as a district attorney (D.A.) or an attorney general (A.G.), not by the victims. Once a crime has been reported, the D.A.'s office decides whether to file criminal charges and to what extent to pursue the prosecution or carry out additional investigation.

Key Differences between Civil Law and Criminal Law

Because the state has extensive resources at its disposal when prosecuting criminal cases, there are numerous procedural safeguards to protect the rights of defendants. We look here at one of these safeguards—the higher burden of proof that applies in a criminal case—as well as the harsher sanctions for criminal acts compared with those for civil wrongs. Exhibit 10–1 on the following page summarizes these and other key differences between civil law and criminal law.

BURDEN OF PROOF In a civil case, the plaintiff usually must prove his or her case by a *preponderance of the evidence.* Under this standard, the plaintiff must convince the court that based on the evidence presented by both parties, it is more likely than not that the plaintiff's allegation is true.

In a criminal case, in contrast, the state must prove its case **beyond a reasonable doubt.** If the jury views the evidence in the case as reasonably permitting either a guilty or a not guilty verdict, then the jury's verdict must be not guilty. In other words, the government (prosecutor) must prove beyond a reasonable doubt that the defendant has committed every essential element of the offense with which she or he is charged.

If the jurors are not convinced of the defendant's guilt beyond a reasonable doubt, they must find

EXHIBIT 10-1 Key Differences between Civil Law and Criminal Law

Issue	Civil Law	Criminal Law
Party who brings suit	The person who suffered harm.	The state.
Wrongful act	Causing harm to a person or to a person's property.	Violating a statute that prohibits some type of activity.
Burden of proof	Preponderance of the evidence.	Beyond a reasonable doubt.
Verdict	Three-fourths majority (typically).	Unanimous (almost always).
Remedy	Damages to compensate for the harm or a decree to achieve an equitable result.	Punishment (fine, imprisonment, or death).

the defendant not guilty. Note also that in a criminal case, the jury's verdict normally must be unanimous—agreed to by all members of the jury—to convict the defendant.[1] (In a civil trial by jury, in contrast, typically only three-fourths of the jurors need to agree.)

CRIMINAL SANCTIONS The sanctions imposed on criminal wrongdoers are also harsher than those applied in civil cases. Remember from Chapter 6 that the purpose of tort law is to enable a person harmed by a wrongful act to obtain compensation from the wrongdoer, rather than to punish the wrongdoer. In contrast, criminal sanctions are designed to punish those who commit crimes and to deter others from committing similar acts in the future.

Criminal sanctions include fines as well as the much harsher penalty of the loss of one's liberty by incarceration in a jail or prison. Most criminal sanctions also involve probation and sometimes require performance of community service, completion of an educational or treatment program, or payment of restitution. The harshest criminal sanction is, of course, the death penalty.

Civil Liability for Criminal Acts

Some torts, such as assault and battery, provide a basis for a criminal prosecution as well as a civil action in tort. ▶ **Example 10.1** Jonas is walking down the street, minding his own business, when a person attacks him. In the ensuing struggle, the attacker stabs Jonas several times, seriously injuring him. A police officer restrains and arrests the assailant. In this situation, the attacker may be subject both to criminal prosecution by the state and to a tort lawsuit brought by Jonas to obtain compensation for his injuries. ◀

Exhibit 10–2 on the following page illustrates how the same wrongful act can result in both a civil (tort) action and a criminal action against the wrongdoer.

Classification of Crimes

Depending on their degree of seriousness, crimes are classified as felonies or misdemeanors. **Felonies** are serious crimes punishable by death or by imprisonment for more than one year.[2] Many states also define different degrees of felony offenses and vary the punishment according to the degree.[3] For instance, most jurisdictions punish a burglary that involves forced entry into a home at night more harshly than a burglary that involves breaking into a nonresidential building during the day.

Misdemeanors are less serious crimes, punishable by a fine or by confinement for up to a year. **Petty offenses** are minor violations, such as jaywalking or violations of building codes, considered to be a subset of misdemeanors. Even for petty offenses, however, a guilty party can be put in jail for a few days, fined, or both, depending on state or local law. Whether a crime is a felony or a misdemeanor can determine in which court the case is

---

1. A few states allow jury verdicts that are not unanimous. Arizona, for example, allows six of eight jurors to reach a verdict in criminal cases. Louisiana and Oregon have also relaxed the requirement of unanimous jury verdicts.

2. Some states, such as North Carolina, consider felonies to be punishable by incarceration for at least two years.

3. Although the American Law Institute issued the Model Penal Code in 1962, it is not a uniform code, and each state has developed its own set of laws governing criminal acts. Thus, types of crimes and prescribed punishments may differ from one jurisdiction to another.

EXHIBIT 10-2 Civil (Tort) Lawsuit and Criminal Prosecution for the Same Act

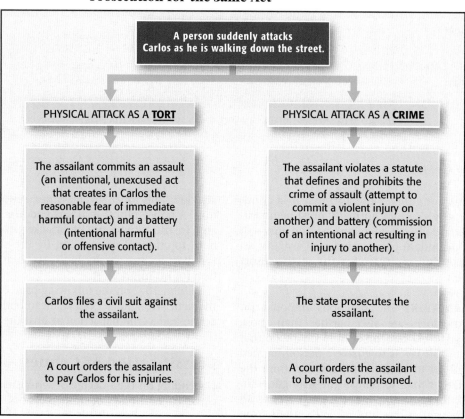

tried and, in some states, whether the defendant has a right to a jury trial.

SECTION 2
CRIMINAL LIABILITY

The following two elements normally must exist *simultaneously* for a person to be convicted of a crime:

1. The performance of a prohibited act *(actus reus)*.
2. A specified state of mind, or intent, on the part of the actor *(mens rea)*.

The Criminal Act

Every criminal statute prohibits certain behavior. Most crimes require an act of *commission*—that is, a person must *do* something in order to be accused of a

crime. In criminal law, a prohibited act is referred to as the ***actus reus,***[4] or guilty act. In some instances, an act of omission can be a crime, but only when a person has a legal duty to perform the omitted act, such as filing a tax return.

The *guilty act* requirement is based on one of the premises of criminal law—that a person should be punished for harm done to society. For a crime to exist, the guilty act must cause some harm to a person or to property. Thinking about killing someone or about stealing a car may be morally wrong, but the thoughts do no harm until they are translated into action.

Of course, a person can be punished for *attempting* murder or robbery, but normally only if he or she has taken substantial steps toward the criminal objective. Additionally, the person must have specifically

---

4. Pronounced *ak*-tuhs *ray*-uhs.

intended to commit the crime to be convicted of an attempt.

State of Mind

A wrongful mental state, or **mens rea,**[5] also is typically required to establish criminal liability. The required mental state, or intent, is indicated in the applicable statute or law. Murder, for example, involves the guilty act of killing another human being, and the guilty mental state is the desire, or intent, to take another's life. For theft, the guilty act is the taking of another person's property. The mental state involves both the awareness that the property belongs to another and the desire to deprive the owner of it.

RECKLESSNESS A court can also find that the required mental state is present when a defendant's acts are reckless or criminally negligent. A defendant is *criminally reckless* if he or she consciously disregards a substantial and unjustifiable risk.

▶ **Example 10.2** A fourteen-year-old New Jersey girl posts a Facebook message saying that she is going to launch a terrorist attack on her high school and asking if anyone wants to help. The police arrest the girl for the crime of making a terrorist threat. The statute requires the intent to commit an act of violence with "the intent to terrorize" or "in reckless disregard of the risk of causing" terror or inconvenience. Although the girl argues that she had no intent to cause harm, the police can prosecute her under the "reckless disregard" part of the statute. ◀

CRIMINAL NEGLIGENCE *Criminal negligence* involves the mental state in which the defendant takes an unjustified, substantial, and foreseeable risk that results in harm. A defendant can negligent even if she or he was not actually aware of the risk but *should have been aware* of it.[6]

A homicide is classified as *involuntary manslaughter* when it results from an act of criminal negligence and there is no intent to kill. ▶ **Example 10.3** Dr. Conrad Murray, the personal physician of pop star Michael Jackson, was convicted of involuntary manslaughter in 2011 for prescribing the drug that led to Jackson's sudden death in 2009. Murray had given Jackson propofol, a powerful anesthetic normally used in surgery, as a sleep aid on the night of his death, even though he knew that Jackson had already taken other sedatives. ◀

STRICT LIABILITY AND OVERCRIMINALIZATION An increasing number of laws and regulations impose criminal sanctions for strict liability crimes. Strict liability crimes are offenses that do not require a wrongful mental state to establish criminal liability.

Federal Crimes. The federal criminal code now lists more than four thousand criminal offenses, many of which do not require a specific mental state. There are also at least ten thousand federal rules that can be enforced through criminal sanctions, and many of these rules do not require intent.

▶ **Example 10.4** Eddie Leroy Anderson, a retired logger and former science teacher, and his son went digging for arrowheads near a campground in Idaho. They did not realize that they were on federal land and that it is a felony to remove artifacts from federal land without a permit. Although the crime carries as much as two years in prison, father and son pleaded guilty, and each received a sentence of probation and a $1,500 fine. ◀

Strict liability crimes are particularly common in environmental laws, laws aimed at combatting illegal drugs, and other laws affecting public health, safety, and welfare. Under federal law, for example, tenants can be evicted from public housing if a member of the household or a guest used illegal drugs. The eviction can occur regardless of whether the tenant knew or should have known about the drug activity.[7]

State Crimes. Many states have also enacted laws that punish behavior as criminal without the need to show criminal intent. ▶ **Example 10.5** In Arizona, a hunter who shoots an elk outside the area specified by the hunting permit has committed a crime. The hunter can be convicted of the crime regardless of her or his intent or knowledge of the law. ◀

Overcriminalization. Proponents of strict liability criminal laws argue that they are necessary to protect the public and the environment. Critics say laws that criminalize conduct without any required intent have led to *overcriminalization,* or the use of criminal law as

---

5. Pronounced *mehns ray*-uh.
6. Model Penal Code Section 2.02(2)(d).

7. See, for example, *Department of Housing and Urban Development v. Rucker,* 535 U.S. 125, 122 S.Ct. 1230, 152 L.Ed.2d 258 (2002).

the main tool to solve social problems, such as illegal drug use. They argue that when the requirement of intent is removed, people are more likely to commit crimes unknowingly—and perhaps even innocently. When an honest mistake can lead to a criminal conviction, the idea that crimes are a wrong against society is undermined.

Corporate Criminal Liability

A corporation is a legal entity created under the laws of a state. At one time, it was thought that a corporation could not incur criminal liability because, although a corporation is a legal person, it can act only through its agents (corporate directors, officers, and employees). Therefore, the corporate entity itself could not "intend" to commit a crime. Over time, this view has changed. Obviously, corporations cannot be imprisoned, but they can be fined or denied certain legal privileges (such as necessary licenses).

LIABILITY OF THE CORPORATE ENTITY Today, corporations normally are liable for the crimes committed by their agents and employees within the course and scope of their employment.[8] For liability to be imposed, the prosecutor generally must show that the corporation could have prevented the act or that a supervisor authorized or had knowledge of the act. In addition, corporations can be criminally liable for failing to perform specific duties imposed by law (such as duties under environmental laws or securities laws).

▶ **Case in Point 10.6** A prostitution ring, the Gold Club, was operating out of some motels in West Virginia. A motel manager, who was also a corporate officer, gave discounted rates to Gold Club prostitutes, and they paid him in cash. The corporation received a portion of the funds generated by the Gold Club's illegal operations. A jury found that the corporation was criminally liable because a supervisor within the corporation—the motel manager—had knowledge of the prostitution and the corporation had allowed it to continue.[9] ◀

LIABILITY OF THE CORPORATE OFFICERS AND DIRECTORS Corporate directors and officers are personally liable for the crimes they commit, regardless of whether the crimes were committed for their private benefit or on the corporation's behalf. Additionally, corporate directors and officers may be held liable for the actions of employees under their supervision. Under the *responsible corporate officer* doctrine, a court may impose criminal liability on a corporate officer who participated in, directed, or merely knew about a given criminal violation.

▶ **Case in Point 10.7** The Roscoe family owned the Customer Company, which operated an underground storage tank that leaked gasoline. An employee, John Johnson, reported the leak to the state environmental agency, and the Roscoes hired an environmental services firm to clean up the spill. The clean-up did not occur immediately, however. The state sent many notices to John Roscoe, a corporate officer, warning him that the company was violating federal and state environmental laws. Roscoe gave the letters to Johnson, who passed them on to the environmental services firm, but the spill was not cleaned up.

The state eventually filed criminal charges against the corporation and the Roscoes individually. They were convicted under the responsible corporate officer doctrine. The Roscoes were in positions of responsibility, they had influence over the corporation's actions, and their failure to act constituted a violation of environmental laws.[10] ◀

SECTION 3
TYPES OF CRIMES

Federal, state, and local laws provide for the classification and punishment of hundreds of thousands of different criminal acts. Generally, though, criminal acts can be grouped into five broad categories: violent crime (crimes against persons), property crime, public order crime, white-collar crime, and organized crime. Note also that many crimes may be committed in cyberspace, as well as the physical world. When they occur in the virtual world, we

---

8. See Model Penal Code Section 2.07.
9. As a result of the convictions, the motel manager was sentenced to fifteen months in prison, and the corporation was ordered to forfeit the motel property. *United States v. Singh*, 518 F.3d 236 (4th Cir. 2008).

10. The Roscoes and the corporation were sentenced to pay penalties of $2,493,250. *People v. Roscoe*, 169 Cal.App.4th 829, 87 Cal.Rptr.3d 187 (3 Dist. 2008).

refer to them as cyber crimes, as discussed later in the chapter.

Violent Crime

Certain crimes are called *violent crimes,* or crimes against persons, because they cause others to suffer harm or death. Murder is a violent crime. So is sexual assault, or rape. **Robbery**—defined as the taking of money, personal property, or any other article of value from a person by means of force or fear—is also a violent crime. Typically, states have more severe penalties for *aggravated robbery*—robbery with the use of a deadly weapon.

Assault and battery, which were discussed in Chapter 6 in the context of tort law, are also classified as violent crimes. ▶ **Example 10.8** Former rap star Flavor Flav (whose real name is William Drayton) was arrested in Las Vegas in 2012 on assault and battery charges. During an argument with his fiancée, Drayton allegedly threw her to the ground and then grabbed two kitchen knives and chased her son. ◀

Each violent crime is further classified by degree, depending on the circumstances surrounding the criminal act. These circumstances include the intent of the person committing the crime and whether a weapon was used. For crimes other than murder, the level of pain and suffering experienced by the victim is also a factor.

Property Crime

The most common type of criminal activity is property crime, in which the goal of the offender is some form of economic gain or the damaging of property. Robbery is a form of property crime, as well as a violent crime, because the offender seeks to gain the property of another. We look here at a number of other crimes that fall within the general category of property crime. (Note also that many types of cyber crime, discussed later in this chapter, are forms of property crime as well.)

BURGLARY Traditionally, **burglary** was defined as breaking and entering the dwelling of another at night with the intent to commit a felony. This definition was aimed at protecting an individual's home and its occupants. Most state statutes have eliminated some of the requirements found in the common law definition. The time of day at which the breaking and entering occurs, for example, is usually immaterial. State statutes frequently omit the element of breaking, and some states do not require that the building be a dwelling. When a deadly weapon is used in a burglary, the perpetrator can be charged with *aggravated burglary* and punished more severely.

LARCENY Under the common law, the crime of **larceny** involved the unlawful taking and carrying away of someone else's personal property with the intent to permanently deprive the owner of possession. Put simply, larceny is stealing, or theft. Whereas robbery involves force or fear, larceny does not. Therefore, picking pockets is larceny, not robbery. Similarly, taking company products and supplies home for personal use without permission is larceny. (Note that a person who commits larceny generally can also be sued under tort law because the act of taking possession of another's property involves a trespass to personal property.)

Most states have expanded the definition of property that is subject to larceny statutes. Stealing computer programs may constitute larceny even though the "property" is not physical (see the discussion of computer crime later in this chapter). So, too, can the theft of natural gas or Internet and television cable service.

OBTAINING GOODS BY FALSE PRETENSES Obtaining goods by means of false pretenses is a form of theft that involves trickery or fraud, such as using someone else's credit-card number without permission to purchase an iPad. Statutes dealing with such illegal activities vary widely from state to state. They often apply not only to property, but also to services and cash.

Sometimes, a statute consolidates the crime of obtaining goods by false pretenses with other property offenses, such as larceny and embezzlement, into a single crime called simply "theft." Under such a statute, it is not necessary for a defendant to be charged specifically with larceny, embezzlement, or obtaining goods by false pretenses. *Petty theft* is the theft of a small quantity of cash or low-value goods. *Grand theft* is the theft of a larger amount of cash or higher-value property. In the following case, the sales manager of a sports vehicle dealership was charged under a state statute with grand theft.

CASE ANALYSIS

Case 10.1 People v. Whitmer

Court of Appeal of California, Second District, Division 4, 213 Cal.App.4th 122, 152 Cal.Rptr.3d 216 (2013).

IN THE LANGUAGE OF THE COURT
MANELLA, J. [Judge]

* * * *

Jerome Gilding owned Temple City Power Sports, a business located in San Gabriel [California] that sold and serviced motorcycles, motorized dirt bikes [all terrain vehicles (ATVs)], and jet skis.

Customers of the dealership negotiated purchases with salespersons. The dealership made sales to customers who entered into financing agreements or paid with credit cards. In such cases, after the salesperson reached an agreement with the customer regarding an item and the manner of payment, the transaction was referred to the sales manager for approval. If approved, the transaction was sent to the dealership finance department, which collected the information necessary to process the financing agreement or credit card sale. When the dealership sold an item to a customer who failed to make the loan payments or used a bad credit card, the dealership incurred a "charge back," that is, took responsibility for the loss on the transaction. * * * To prevent charge backs, the dealership's policy was to require customers to make purchases in person and to present two forms of identification.

Ordinarily, when credit card purchases were made, the card was swiped through a credit card machine, which instantaneously sent information regarding the purchase to the pertinent bank. An approval or denial was received from the bank within a few seconds. In contrast, if the machine was set for an "offline" * * * sale, the machine recorded the transaction but sent no information to the bank. As a result, no immediate credit approval or denial was generated; instead, information regarding the transaction was transmitted to the bank at the end of the business day. Gilding did not permit offline sales.

Associated with each vehicle sold by the dealership is a document known as the "manufacturer certificate of origin" (MSO). The vehicle's original MSO can be used to establish title to the vehicle in other states and countries. The dealership retained the original MSO after a sale unless the vehicle was sold to an out-of-state purchaser or transferred to another dealer. The dealership had contractual obligations to several manufacturers not to sell vehicles for exportation outside the United States.

In 2009 [Jeffrey Whitmer] was the dealership's sales manager, and Alex Barrera was employed as a salesperson. Eric Van Hek worked in the financial department until August or September 2009, when he was replaced by Richard Carlos. In late August or early September 2009, Gilding told [Whitmer] not to deal with Mordichi Mor, who had engaged in a fraudulent transaction at the dealership in 2008.

* * * *

* * * In the fall of 2009, * * * after meeting with Mordichi [Whitmer] directed Carlos to process sales transactions involving customers Carlos had never met * * * . Whenever the transaction involved a credit card [Whitmer] told Carlos to process it as an offline sale. Carlos prepared the paperwork for each transaction and gave it to [Whitmer] who returned the documents to him with the customer's signature. [Whitmer] directed other employees to deliver the purchased vehicles to Mordichi's home.

* * * *

[At Whitmer's request] Angela Wilcox, a dealership employee, * * * gave [Whitmer] original MSOs from the dealership's files related to deals [Whitmer] arranged with Mor.

* * * In mid-December 2009, a credit card company told [Gilding] that credit card usage had increased at the dealership, and that he should expect charge backs. He initiated an inquiry that uncovered 20 potentially fraudulent sales of motorcycles, motorized dirt bikes, ATVs, and recreational vehicles at the dealership from August 4 to December 8, 2009. Barrera was the salesperson in all the sales, each of which involved one of seven purported buyers. * * * The dealership incurred a charge back on each sale ranging from $9,100 to $21,479.80, resulting in losses exceeding $250,000. In addition, the original MSOs for the vehicles in the dealership's files had been replaced by copies, even though the transactions were not of the type that required the dealership to transfer the original MSO to the purchaser.

Shortly after Gilding discovered the potential fraud, Barrera stopped appearing for work.

Later, [local] Police Department Detective Armando Valenzuela determined that the identification information provided for the buyers on the sales documents was false, and that the existence of the buyers could not be established. He also discovered that several of the vehicles had been shipped to Israel.

On February 16, 2010, Detective Valenzuela * * * arrested [Whitmer, who was charged with twenty counts of grand theft. A jury in a California state court convicted him on all counts. He appealed to a state intermediate appellate court, contending that he was unlawfully convicted.]

* * * We will affirm the convictions if there is substantial evidence to support a finding that each act of grand theft qualified as an independent offense.

CASE 10.1 CONTINUED

We conclude that the record discloses evidence sufficient to establish that appellant was properly convicted of 20 counts of grand theft. Each transaction involved a different vehicle. The 20 transactions occurred on 13 different dates. With the exception of two dates, whenever more than one transaction occurred on a single date, the transactions involved distinct fictitious buyers. On the two dates a fictitious buyer purportedly bought more than one vehicle, the transactions involved separate paperwork and documentation. This constituted substantial evidence that the 20 transactions constitute distinct offenses.

* * * In sum, appellant was properly convicted under the 20 counts of grand theft.

* * * *

* * * Appellant argues there was no direct evidence that he intentionally participated in the fraud activities related to the taking of each vehicle. *Appellant's argument misapprehends our role in reviewing the record for substantial evidence. We do not engage in independent factfinding, but instead affirm the jury's determinations if they are supported by any logical inferences grounded in the evidence.* [Emphasis added.]

There was ample evidence that appellant directly perpetrated the thefts. * * * Appellant authorized the offline credit card sales and other violations of dealership policies, obtained the false signatures from the fictitious buyers on the sales documents, and arranged for the delivery of the vehicles. Furthermore, * * * appellant admitted that Mor had "gotten the ball rolling" on the thefts, that Van Hek had instructed appellant how to do offline transactions, and that appellant had participated for "personal gain." This evidence was sufficient to establish that appellant supervised and directed the thefts within the dealership.

* * * *

* * * The judgment is affirmed.

LEGAL REASONING QUESTIONS

1. What is the definition of the crime of obtaining goods by false pretenses? Do the facts in this case satisfy that definition? Explain.
2. Besides the defendant, who may have committed a crime in this case?
3. How might the dealership have prevented the crimes in this case?
4. Why do some states combine larceny, embezzlement, and obtaining goods by false pretenses into a single crime called theft? Discuss.

RECEIVING STOLEN GOODS It is a crime to receive goods that a person knows or should have known were stolen or illegally obtained. To be convicted, the recipient of such goods need not know the true identity of the owner or the thief, and need not have paid for the goods. All that is necessary is that the recipient knows or should know that the goods are stolen, which implies an intent to deprive the true owner of those goods.

ARSON The willful and malicious burning of a building (and, in some states, vehicles and other items of personal property) is the crime of **arson.** At common law, arson applied only to burning down another person's house. The law was designed to protect human life. Today, arson statutes have been extended to cover the destruction of any building, regardless of ownership, by fire or explosion.

Every state has a special statute that covers the act of burning a building for the purpose of collecting insurance. (Of course, the insurer need not pay the claim when insurance fraud is proved.)

FORGERY The fraudulent making or altering of any writing (including electronic records) in a way that changes the legal rights and liabilities of another is **forgery.** ▶ **Example 10.9** Without authorization, Severson signs Bennett's name to the back of a check made out to Bennett and attempts to cash it. Severson is committing forgery. ◀ Forgery also includes changing trademarks, falsifying public records, counterfeiting, and altering a legal document.

Public Order Crime

Historically, societies have always outlawed activities that are considered contrary to public values and morals. Today, the most common public order crimes include public drunkenness, prostitution, gambling, and illegal drug use. These crimes are sometimes referred to as *victimless crimes* because they normally harm only the offender. From a broader perspective, however, they are deemed detrimental to society as a whole because they may create an environment that gives rise to property and violent crimes.

▶ **Example 10.10**   A man flying from Texas to California on a commercial airliner becomes angry and yells obscenities at a flight attendant when a beverage cart strikes his knee. After the pilot diverts the plane and makes an unscheduled landing at a nearby airport, police remove the passenger and arrest him. If the man is later found guilty of the public order crime of interfering with a flight crew, he may be sentenced to more than two years in prison. ◀

White-Collar Crime

Crimes occurring in the business context are popularly referred to as *white-collar crimes,* although this is not an official legal term. Ordinarily, **white-collar crime** involves an illegal act or series of acts committed by an individual or business entity using some nonviolent means to obtain a personal or business advantage.

Usually, this kind of crime takes place in the course of a legitimate business occupation. Corporate crimes fall into this category. Certain property crimes, such as larceny and forgery, may also be white-collar crimes if they occur within the business context. The crimes discussed next normally occur only in the business context.

EMBEZZLEMENT   When a person who is entrusted with another person's property fraudulently appropriates it, **embezzlement** occurs. Typically, embezzlement is carried out by an employee who steals funds. Banks are particularly prone to this problem, but embezzlement can occur in any firm. Embezzlement is not larceny because the wrongdoer does not *physically* take the property from the possession of another, and it is not robbery because no force or fear is used. The intent to return the embezzled property—or its actual return—is not a defense to the crime of embezzlement.

Embezzlement occurs whether the embezzler takes the funds directly from the victim or from a third person. If the financial officer of a large corporation pockets checks from third parties that were given to her to deposit into the corporate account, she is embezzling.

Frequently, an embezzler takes a relatively small amount at one time but does so repeatedly over a long period. This might be done by underreporting income or deposits and embezzling the remaining amount or by creating fictitious persons or accounts and writing checks to them from the corporate account. Even an employer's failure to remit state withholding taxes that were collected from employee wages can constitute embezzlement.

MAIL AND WIRE FRAUD   Among the most potent weapons against white-collar criminals are the federal laws that prohibit mail fraud[11] and wire fraud.[12] These laws make it a federal crime to devise any scheme that uses U.S. mail, commercial carriers (FedEx, UPS), or wire (telegraph, telephone, television, the Internet, e-mail) with the intent to defraud the public. These laws are often applied when persons send out advertisements or e-mails with the intent to fraudulently obtain cash or property by false pretenses.

▶ **Case in Point 10.11**   Cisco Systems, Inc., offers a warranty program to authorized resellers of Cisco parts. Iheanyi Frank Chinasa and Robert Kendrick Chambliss devised a scheme to intentionally defraud Cisco with respect to this program and obtain replacement parts to which they were not entitled. The two men planned and used specific language in numerous e-mails and Internet service requests that they sent to Cisco to convince Cisco to ship them new parts via commercial carriers. Ultimately, Chinasa and Chambliss were convicted of mail and wire fraud, and conspiracy to commit mail and wire fraud.[13] ◀

The maximum penalty under these statutes is substantial. Persons convicted of mail, wire, and Internet fraud may be imprisoned for up to twenty years and/or fined. If the violation affects a financial institution or involves fraud in connection with emergency disaster-relief funds, the violator may be fined up to $1 million, imprisoned for up to thirty years, or both.

BRIBERY   The crime of bribery involves offering to give something of value to a person in an attempt to influence that person, who is usually, but not always, a public official, to act in a way that serves a private interest. Three types of bribery are considered crimes: bribery of public officials, commercial bribery, and bribery of foreign officials. As an element of the crime of bribery, intent must be present and proved. The bribe itself can be anything the recipient considers to be valuable. Realize that the *crime of bribery occurs when the bribe is offered*—it is not required that the bribe be accepted. *Accepting a bribe* is a separate crime.

Commercial bribery involves corrupt dealings between private persons or businesses. Typically, people make commercial bribes to obtain proprietary information, cover up an inferior product, or secure

---

11. The Mail Fraud Act of 1990, 18 U.S.C. Sections 1341–1342.
12. 18 U.S.C. Section 1343.
13. *United States v. Chinasa,* 789 F.Supp.2d 691 (E.D.Va. 2011). See also *United States v. Lyons,* 569 F.3d 995 (9th Cir. 2009).

new business. Industrial espionage sometimes involves commercial bribes. ▶ **Example 10.12**   Kent Peterson works at the firm of Jacoby & Meyers. He offers to pay Laurel, an employee in a competing firm, to give him that firm's trade secrets and pricing schedules. Peterson has committed commercial bribery. ◀ So-called kickbacks, or payoffs for special favors or services, are a form of commercial bribery in some situations.

BANKRUPTCY FRAUD   Federal bankruptcy law allows individuals and businesses to be relieved of oppressive debt through bankruptcy proceedings. Numerous white-collar crimes may be committed during the many phases of a bankruptcy action. A creditor may file a false claim against the debtor, which is a crime. Also, a debtor may fraudulently transfer assets to favored parties before or after the petition for bankruptcy is filed. For instance, a company-owned automobile may be "sold" at a bargain price to a trusted friend or relative. Closely related to the crime of fraudulent transfer of property is the crime of fraudulent concealment of property, such as the hiding of gold coins.

INSIDER TRADING   An individual who obtains "inside information" about the plans of a publicly listed corporation can often make stock-trading profits by purchasing or selling corporate securities based on this information. *Insider trading* is a violation of securities law. Basically, securities law prohibits a person who possesses inside information and has a duty not to disclose it to outsiders from trading on that information. A person may not profit from the purchase or sale of securities based on inside information until the information is made available to the public.

THEFT OF TRADE SECRETS AND OTHER INTELLECTUAL PROPERTY   As discussed in Chapter 8, trade secrets constitute a form of intellectual property that for many businesses can be extremely valuable. The Economic Espionage Act[14] makes the theft of trade secrets a federal crime. The act also makes it a federal crime to buy or possess another person's trade secrets, knowing that the trade secrets were stolen or otherwise acquired without the owner's authorization.

Violations of the Economic Espionage Act can result in steep penalties: imprisonment for up to ten years and a fine of up to $500,000. A corporation or other organization can be fined up to $5 million. Additionally, the law provides that any property

acquired as a result of the violation, such as airplanes and automobiles, is subject to criminal forfeiture, or seizure by the government. Similarly, any property used in the commission of the violation, such as servers and other electronic devices, is subject to forfeiture. A theft of trade secrets conducted via the Internet, for instance, could result in the forfeiture of every computer or other device used to commit or facilitate the violation as well as any assets gained.

Organized Crime

White-collar crime takes place within the confines of the legitimate business world. *Organized crime,* in contrast, operates *illegitimately* by, among other things, providing illegal goods and services. Traditionally, the preferred markets for organized crime have been gambling, prostitution, illegal narcotics, and loan sharking (lending funds at higher-than-legal interest rates), along with more recent ventures into counterfeiting and credit-card scams.

MONEY LAUNDERING   The profits from organized crime and illegal activities amount to billions of dollars a year. These profits come from illegal drug transactions and, to a lesser extent, from racketeering, prostitution, and gambling. Under federal law, banks, savings and loan associations, and other financial institutions are required to report currency transactions involving more than $10,000. Consequently, those who engage in illegal activities face difficulties in depositing their cash profits from illegal transactions.

As an alternative to storing cash from illegal transactions in a safe-deposit box, wrongdoers and racketeers launder "dirty" money through legitimate business to make it "clean." **Money laundering** is engaging in financial transactions to conceal the identity, source, or destination of illegally gained funds. ▶ **Example 10.13**   Leo Harris, a successful drug dealer, becomes a partner with a restaurateur. Little by little, the restaurant shows increasing profits. As a partner in the restaurant, Harris is able to report the "profits" of the restaurant as legitimate income on which he pays federal and state taxes. He can then spend those funds without worrying that his lifestyle may exceed the level possible with his reported income. ◀

RACKETEERING   To curb the entry of organized crime into the legitimate business world, Congress enacted the Racketeer Influenced and Corrupt

---

14. 18 U.S.C. Sections 1831–1839.

Organizations Act (RICO).[15] The statute makes it a federal crime to:

1. Use income obtained from racketeering activity to purchase any interest in an enterprise.
2. Acquire or maintain an interest in an enterprise through racketeering activity.
3. Conduct or participate in the affairs of an enterprise through racketeering activity.
4. Conspire to do any of the preceding activities.

Broad Application of RICO. The broad language of RICO has allowed it to be applied in cases that have little or nothing to do with organized crime. RICO incorporates by reference twenty-six separate types of federal crimes and nine types of state felonies.[16] If a person commits two of these offenses, he or she is guilty of "racketeering activity."

Under the criminal provisions of RICO, any individual found guilty is subject to a fine of up to $25,000 per violation, imprisonment for up to twenty years, or both. Additionally, any assets (property or cash) that were acquired as a result of the illegal activity or that were "involved in" or an "instrumentality of" the activity are subject to government forfeiture.

Civil Liability. In the event of a RICO violation, the government can seek civil penalties. The government can seek the divestiture of a defendant's interest in a business or the dissolution of the business. (Divestiture refers to the taking of possession—or forfeiture—of the defendant's interest and its subsequent sale.)

Moreover, in some cases, the statute allows private individuals to sue violators and potentially recover three times their actual losses (treble damages), plus attorneys' fees, for business injuries caused by a RICO violation. This is perhaps the most controversial aspect of RICO and one that continues to cause debate in the nation's federal courts. The prospect of receiving treble damages in civil RICO lawsuits has given plaintiffs a financial incentive to pursue businesses and employers for violations.

See *Concept Summary 10.1* on the following page for a review of the different types of crimes.

---

15. 18 U.S.C. Sections 1961–1968.
16. See 18 U.S.C. Section 1961(1)(A). The crimes listed in this section include murder, kidnapping, gambling, arson, robbery, bribery, extortion, money laundering, securities fraud, counterfeiting, dealing in obscene matter, dealing in controlled substances (illegal drugs), and a number of others.

DEFENSES TO CRIMINAL LIABILITY

Persons charged with crimes may be relieved of criminal liability if they can show that their criminal actions were justified under the circumstances. In certain situations, the law may also allow a person to be excused from criminal liability because she or he lacks the required mental state. We look at several defenses to criminal liability here.

Note that procedural violations (such as obtaining evidence without a valid search warrant) may also operate as defenses. Evidence obtained in violation of a defendant's constitutional rights may not be admitted in court. If the evidence is suppressed, then there may be no basis for prosecuting the defendant.

Justifiable Use of Force

Probably the best-known defense to criminal liability is **self-defense.** Other situations, however, also justify the use of force: the defense of one's dwelling, the defense of other property, and the prevention of a crime. In all of these situations, it is important to distinguish between deadly and nondeadly force. *Deadly force* is likely to result in death or serious bodily harm. *Nondeadly force* is force that reasonably appears necessary to prevent the imminent use of criminal force.

Generally speaking, people can use the amount of nondeadly force that seems necessary to protect themselves, their dwellings, or other property, or to prevent the commission of a crime. Deadly force can be used in self-defense only when the defender *reasonably believes* that imminent death or grievous bodily harm will otherwise result. In addition, normally the attacker must be using unlawful force, and the defender must not have initiated or provoked the attack.

Many states are expanding the situations in which the use of deadly force can be justified. Florida, for instance, allows the use of deadly force to prevent the commission of a "forcible felony," including robbery, carjacking, and sexual battery.

Necessity

Sometimes, criminal defendants can be relieved of liability by showing **necessity**—that a criminal act was necessary to prevent an even greater harm. ▶ **Example 10.14** Jake Trevor is a convicted felon and, as such, is legally prohibited from possessing a

CONCEPT SUMMARY 10.1
Types of Crimes

CRIME CATEGORY	DEFINITION AND EXAMPLES
Violent Crime	1. *Definition*—Crime that causes others to suffer harm or death. 2. *Examples*—Murder, assault and battery, sexual assault (rape), and robbery.
Property Crime	1. *Definition*—Crime in which the goal of the offender is some form of economic gain or the damaging of property; the most common form of crime. 2. *Examples*—Burglary, larceny, arson, receiving stolen goods, forgery, and obtaining goods by false pretenses.
Public Order Crime	1. *Definition*—Crime that is contrary to public values and morals. 2. *Examples*—Public drunkenness, prostitution, gambling, and illegal drug use.
White-Collar Crime	1. *Definition*—An illegal act or series of acts committed by an individual or business entity using some nonviolent means to obtain a personal or business advantage; usually committed in the course of a legitimate occupation. 2. *Examples*—Embezzlement, mail and wire fraud, bribery, bankruptcy fraud, insider trading, and the theft of intellectual property.
Organized Crime	1. *Definition*—A form of crime conducted by groups operating illegitimately to satisfy the public's demand for illegal goods and services (such as gambling and illegal narcotics). 2. *Money laundering*—Passing "dirty" money (obtained through criminal activities, such as illegal drug trafficking) through legitimate enterprises so as to "launder" it (make it appear to be legitimate income). 3. *RICO*—The Racketeer Influenced and Corrupt Organizations Act (RICO) makes it a federal crime to (a) use income obtained from racketeering activity to purchase any interest in an enterprise, (b) acquire or maintain an interest in an enterprise through racketeering activity, (c) conduct or participate in the affairs of an enterprise through racketeering activity, or (d) conspire to do any of the preceding activities. RICO provides for both civil and criminal liability.

firearm. While he and his wife are in a convenience store, a man draws a gun, points it at the cashier, and demands all the cash in the register. Afraid that the man will start shooting, Trevor grabs the gun and holds onto it until police arrive. In this situation, if Trevor is charged with possession of a firearm, he can assert the defense of necessity. ◄

Insanity

A person who suffers from a mental illness may be incapable of the state of mind required to commit a crime. Thus, insanity may be a defense to a criminal charge. Note that an insanity defense does not enable a person to avoid imprisonment. It simply means that if the defendant successfully proves insanity, she or he will be placed in a mental institution.

▶ **Example 10.15** James Holmes opened fire with an automatic weapon in a crowded Colorado movie theater during the screening of *The Dark Knight Rises*, killing twelve people and injuring more than fifty. Holmes had been a graduate student until he suffered from mental health problems. Before the incident, he had no criminal history. Holmes's attorneys are expected to assert the defense of insanity to try to avoid a possible death penalty. If the defense is successful, Holmes will be confined to a mental institution, rather than a prison. ◄

MODEL PENAL CODE The courts have had difficulty deciding what the test for legal insanity should be. Federal courts and some states use the substantial-capacity test set forth in the Model Penal Code:

A person is not responsible for criminal conduct if at the time of such conduct as a result of mental disease or defect he or she lacks substantial capacity either to appreciate the wrongfulness of his [or her] conduct or to conform his [or her] conduct to the requirements of the law.

M'NAGHTEN AND OTHER STATE RULES Some states use the *M'Naghten* test.[17] Under this test, a person is not responsible if, at the time of the offense, he or she did not know the nature and quality of the act or did not know that the act was wrong. Other states use the irresistible-impulse test. A person operating under an irresistible impulse may know an act is wrong but cannot refrain from doing it. Under any of these tests, proving insanity is extremely difficult. For this reason, the insanity defense is rarely used and usually is not successful. Four states have abolished the insanity defense.

Mistake

Everyone has heard the saying "Ignorance of the law is no excuse." Ordinarily, ignorance of the law or a mistaken idea about what the law requires is not a valid defense. A *mistake of fact,* however, as opposed to a *mistake of law,* can excuse criminal responsibility if it negates the mental state necessary to commit a crime.

▶ **Example 10.16** Oliver Wheaton mistakenly walks off with Julie Tyson's briefcase. If Wheaton genuinely thought that the case was his, there is no theft. Theft requires knowledge that the property belongs to another. (If Wheaton's act causes Tyson to incur damages, however, she may sue him in a civil action for trespass to personal property or conversion—torts that were discussed in Chapter 6.) ◀

Duress

Duress exists when the *wrongful threat* of one person induces another person to perform an act that he or she would not otherwise have performed. In such a situation, duress is said to negate the mental state necessary to commit a crime because the defendant was forced or compelled to commit the act.

Duress can be used as a defense to most crimes except murder. Both the definition of duress and the types of crimes that it can excuse vary among the states, however. Generally, to successfully assert duress as a defense, the defendant must reasonably have believed that he or she was in immediate danger,

and the jury (or judge) must conclude that the defendant's belief was reasonable.

Entrapment

Entrapment is a defense designed to prevent police officers or other government agents from enticing persons to commit crimes in order to later prosecute them for those crimes. In the typical entrapment case, an undercover agent *suggests* that a crime be committed and somehow pressures or induces an individual to commit it. The agent then arrests the individual for the crime.

For entrapment to be considered a defense, both the suggestion and the inducement must take place. The defense is not intended to prevent law enforcement agents from setting a trap for an unwary criminal. Rather, its purpose is to prevent them from pushing the individual into a criminal act. The crucial issue is whether the person who committed a crime was predisposed to commit the illegal act or did so only because the agent induced it.

Statute of Limitations

With some exceptions, such as the crime of murder, statutes of limitations apply to crimes just as they do to civil wrongs. In other words, the state must initiate criminal prosecution within a certain number of years. If a criminal action is brought after the statutory time period has expired, the accused person can raise the statute of limitations as a defense.

The running of the time period in a statute of limitations may be *tolled*—that is, suspended or stopped temporarily—if the defendant is a minor or is not in the jurisdiction. When the defendant reaches the age of majority or returns to the jurisdiction, the statutory time period begins to run again.

Immunity

Accused persons are understandably reluctant to give information if it will be used to prosecute them, and they cannot be forced to do so. The privilege against **self-incrimination** is guaranteed by a clause in the Fifth Amendment to the U.S. Constitution. The clause reads "nor shall [any person] be compelled in any criminal case to be a witness against himself."

When the state wishes to obtain information from a person accused of a crime, the state can grant *immunity* from prosecution. Alternatively, the state

---

17. A rule derived from *M'Naghten's* Case, 8 Eng.Rep. 718 (1843).

can agree to prosecute the accused for a less serious offense in exchange for the information. Once immunity is given, the person has an absolute privilege against self-incrimination and therefore can no longer refuse to testify on Fifth Amendment grounds.

Often, a grant of immunity from prosecution for a serious crime is part of the **plea bargaining** between the defending and prosecuting attorneys. The defendant may be convicted of a lesser offense, while the state uses the defendant's testimony to prosecute accomplices for serious crimes carrying heavy penalties.

SECTION 5
CRIMINAL PROCEDURES

Criminal law brings the force of the state, with all of its resources, to bear against the individual. Criminal procedures are designed to protect the constitutional rights of individuals and to prevent the arbitrary use of power on the part of the government.

The U.S. Constitution provides specific safeguards for those accused of crimes. The United States Supreme Court has ruled that most of these safeguards apply not only in federal court but also in state courts by virtue of the due process clause of the Fourteenth Amendment. These protections include the following:

1. The Fourth Amendment protection from unreasonable searches and seizures.
2. The Fourth Amendment requirement that no warrant for a search or an arrest be issued without probable cause.
3. The Fifth Amendment requirement that no one be deprived of "life, liberty, or property without due process of law."
4. The Fifth Amendment prohibition against **double jeopardy** (trying someone twice for the same criminal offense).[18]
5. The Fifth Amendment requirement that no person be required to be a witness against (incriminate) himself or herself.

6. The Sixth Amendment guarantees of a speedy trial, a trial by jury, a public trial, the right to confront witnesses, and the right to a lawyer at various stages in some proceedings.
7. The Eighth Amendment prohibitions against excessive bail and fines and against cruel and unusual punishment.

Fourth Amendment Protections

The Fourth Amendment protects the "right of the people to be secure in their persons, houses, papers, and effects." Before searching or seizing private property, normally law enforcement officers must obtain a **search warrant**—an order from a judge or other public official authorizing the search or seizure.

Advances in technology allow the authorities to track phone calls and vehicle movements with greater ease and precision. Nevertheless, the use of such technology can still constitute a search within the meaning of the Fourth Amendment. ▶ **Case in Point 10.17** Antoine Jones owned and operated a nightclub. Police suspected that he was also trafficking in narcotics. As part of their investigation, police obtained a warrant to attach a Global Positioning System (GPS) to his wife's car. Although the warrant specified that the GPS had to be attached within ten days, officers did not attach it until eleven days later.

Law enforcement then tracked the vehicle's movement for about a month, eventually arresting Jones for possession and intent to distribute cocaine. Jones was convicted. He appealed, arguing that police did not have a warrant for the GPS tracking. The United States Supreme Court held that the attachment of a GPS tracking device to a suspect's vehicle constitutes a Fourth Amendment search. The Court did not rule on whether the search in this case was unreasonable and required a warrant, however, and allowed Jones's conviction to stand.[19] ◀

PROBABLE CAUSE To obtain a search warrant, law enforcement officers must convince a judge that they have reasonable grounds, or **probable cause,** to believe a search will reveal a specific illegality. Probable cause requires the officers to have trustworthy evidence that would convince a reasonable person that the proposed search or seizure is more likely justified than not.

---

18. The prohibition against double jeopardy means that once a criminal defendant is found not guilty of a particular crime, the government may not indict that person again and retry him or her for the same crime. The prohibition does not preclude the crime victim from bringing a *civil* suit against that same person to recover damages, however. Additionally, a state's prosecution of a crime will not prevent a separate federal prosecution of the same crime, and vice versa.

19. *United States v. Jones,* __ U.S. __, 132 S.Ct. 945, 181 L.Ed.2d 911 (2012).

SCOPE OF WARRANT The Fourth Amendment prohibits general warrants. It requires a particular description of what is to be searched or seized. General searches through a person's belongings are impermissible. The search cannot extend beyond what is described in the warrant. Although search warrants require specificity, if a warrant is issued for a person's residence, items in that residence may be searched even if they do not belong to that individual.

In the following case, police officers obtained a search warrant and conducted a search for weapons in the home of a suspect's foster mother. A judge later ruled that the warrant was not supported by probable cause, and the homeowners sued individual police officers for executing an illegal search warrant.

CASE 10.2

Messerschmidt v. Millender
Supreme Court of the United States, ___ U.S. ___, 132 S.Ct. 1235, 182 L.Ed.2d 47 (2012).

BACKGROUND AND FACTS The Los Angeles County Sheriff's Department was protecting a woman from Jerry Ray Bowen, when he tried to kill her with a shotgun. The woman told the police that she and Bowen used to date, that Bowen was a gang member, and that she thought Bowen was staying at the home of Augusta Millender, his former foster mother. After investigating the incident further, the police prepared a warrant to search the home for all guns and gang-related material, and a magistrate approved it.

When the police, including Curt Messerschmidt, served the search warrant, they discovered that Bowen was not at the home, but they searched it anyway. The homeowners sued individual police officers in federal court for subjecting them to an illegal search. A federal appellate court held that the police lacked probable cause for such a broad search and that the police officers could be held personally liable. The police officers appealed. The United States Supreme Court granted *certiorari* to determine whether the police officers were immune from personal liability.

IN THE LANGUAGE OF THE COURT
Chief Justice *ROBERTS* delivered the opinion of the Court.

* * * *

The validity of the warrant is not before us. The question instead is whether Messerschmidt and [the other officers] are entitled to immunity from damages, even assuming that the warrant should not have been issued.

"The doctrine of qualified immunity protects government officials 'from liability for civil damages insofar as their conduct does not violate clearly established statutory or constitutional rights of which a reasonable person would have known.'" * * * "Whether an official protected by qualified immunity may be held personally liable for an allegedly unlawful official action generally turns on the 'objective legal reasonableness' of the action * * *."

Where the alleged Fourth Amendment violation involves a search or seizure pursuant to a warrant, the fact that a neutral magistrate has issued a warrant is the clearest indication that the officers acted in an objectively reasonable manner * * *. "Nonetheless, * * * we have recognized an exception allowing suit when 'it is obvious that no reasonably competent officer would have concluded that a warrant should issue.'" [Emphasis added.]

Our precedents make clear, however, that the threshold for establishing this exception is a high one, and it should be. * * * As we explained in [another case], "in the ordinary case, an officer cannot be expected to question the magistrate's probable-cause determination" because "it is the magistrate's responsibility to determine whether the officer's allegations establish probable cause and, if so, to issue a warrant comporting in form with the requirements of the Fourth Amendment."

DECISION AND REMEDY *The United States Supreme Court reversed the decision of the federal appellate court. It held that Messerschmidt and the other police officers were immune from personal liability.*

THE LEGAL ENVIRONMENT DIMENSION *How would police officers behave if they could always be held personally liable for executing unconstitutional warrants? Would they be more or less inclined to apply for and execute search warrants? Explain.*

CASE 10.2 CONTINUED

MANAGERIAL IMPLICATIONS *The principles of this case would also apply in the context of searches of businesses. Businesses may be subject to warrantless administrative searches. Evidence gleaned from a search conducted in reasonable reliance on information that later proves to have been false may still be admissible in court in a case against the business.*

The Exclusionary Rule

Under what is known as the **exclusionary rule,** any evidence obtained in violation of the constitutional rights spelled out in the Fourth, Fifth, and Sixth Amendments generally is not admissible at trial. All evidence derived from the illegally obtained evidence is known as the "fruit of the poisonous tree," and such evidence normally must also be excluded from the trial proceedings. For instance, if a confession is obtained after an illegal arrest, the arrest is the "poisonous tree," and the confession, if "tainted" by the arrest, is the "fruit."

The purpose of the exclusionary rule is to deter police from conducting warrantless searches and engaging in other misconduct. The rule can sometimes lead to injustice, however. If the evidence of a defendant's guilt was obtained improperly (without a valid search warrant, for instance), it normally cannot be used against the defendant in court.

The *Miranda* Rule

An important question many courts faced in the 1950s and 1960s was not whether suspects had constitutional rights—that was not in doubt—but how and when those rights could be exercised. Could the right to be silent (under the Fifth Amendment's protection against self-incrimination) be exercised during pretrial interrogation proceedings or only during the trial? Were confessions obtained from suspects admissible in court if the suspects had not been advised of their right to remain silent and other constitutional rights?

To clarify these issues, the United States Supreme Court issued a landmark decision in 1966 in *Miranda v. Arizona,* which we present here. Today, the procedural rights required by the Court in this case are familiar to almost every American.

CLASSIC CASE 10.3

Miranda v. Arizona
Supreme Court of the United States, 384 U.S. 436, 86 S.Ct. 1602, 16 L.Ed.2d 694 (1966).

BACKGROUND AND FACTS   On March 13, 1963, Ernesto Miranda was arrested at his home for the kidnapping and rape of an eighteen-year-old woman. Miranda was taken to a Phoenix, Arizona, police station and questioned by two officers. Two hours later, the officers emerged from the interrogation room with a written confession signed by Miranda. A paragraph at the top of the confession stated that the confession had been made voluntarily, without threats or promises of immunity, and "with full knowledge of my legal rights, understanding any statement I make may be used against me."

Miranda was never advised that he had a right to remain silent and a right to have a lawyer present. The confession was admitted into evidence at his trial, and Miranda was convicted and sentenced to prison for twenty to thirty years. Miranda appealed, claiming that he had not been informed of his constitutional rights. The Supreme Court of Arizona held that Miranda's constitutional rights had not been violated and affirmed his conviction. The *Miranda* case was subsequently reviewed by the United States Supreme Court.

 IN THE LANGUAGE OF THE COURT
Mr. Chief Justice *WARREN* delivered the opinion of the Court.

The cases before us raise questions which go to the roots of our concepts of American criminal jurisprudence; the restraints society must observe consistent with the Federal Constitution in prosecuting individuals for crime.

CASE 10.3 CONTINUES ➡

CASE 10.3 CONTINUED

* * * *

At the outset, if a person in custody is to be subjected to interrogation, he must first be informed in clear and unequivocal terms that he has the right to remain silent.

* * * *

The warning of the right to remain silent must be accompanied by the explanation that anything said can and will be used against the individual in court. This warning is needed in order to make him aware not only of the privilege, *but also of the consequences of forgoing it.* [Emphasis added.]

The circumstances surrounding in-custody interrogation can operate very quickly to overbear the will of one merely made aware of his privilege by his interrogators. Therefore the right to have counsel present at the interrogation is indispensable to the protection of the Fifth Amendment privilege under the system we delineate today.

* * * *

In order fully to apprise a person interrogated of the extent of his rights under this system then, it is necessary to warn him not only that he has the right to consult with an attorney, but also that if he is indigent [without funds] a lawyer will be appointed to represent him. * * * The warning of a right to counsel would be hollow if not couched in terms that would convey to the indigent—the person most often subjected to interrogation—the knowledge that he too has a right to have counsel present.

DECISION AND REMEDY *The United States Supreme Court held that Miranda could not be convicted of the crime on the basis of his confession because his confession was inadmissible as evidence. For any statement made by a defendant to be admissible, the defendant must be informed of certain constitutional rights prior to police interrogation. If the accused waives his or her rights to remain silent and to have counsel present, the government must demonstrate that the waiver was made knowingly, voluntarily, and intelligently.*

IMPACT OF THIS CASE ON TODAY'S LAW *Despite considerable criticism and later attempts to overrule the* Miranda *decision through legislation, the requirements stated in this case continue to provide the benchmark by which criminal procedures are judged today. Police officers routinely advise suspects of their "Miranda rights" on arrest. When Ernesto Miranda himself was later murdered, the suspected murderer was "read his* Miranda *rights."*

THE GLOBAL DIMENSION *The right to remain silent has long been a legal hallmark in Great Britain as well as in the United States. In 1994, however, the British Parliament passed an act that provides that a criminal defendant's silence may be interpreted as evidence of his or her guilt. British police officers are now required, when making an arrest, to inform the suspect, "You do not have to say anything. But if you do not mention now something which you later use in your defense, the court may decide that your failure to mention it now strengthens the case against you. A record will be made of everything you say, and it may be given in evidence if you are brought to trial." Should U.S. law also be changed to allow a defendant's silence during questioning to be considered as an indication of guilt? Why or why not?*

Exceptions to the *Miranda* Rule

Although the Supreme Court's decision in the *Miranda* case was controversial, it has survived several attempts by Congress to overrule it. Over time, however, the Supreme Court has made a number of exceptions to the *Miranda* ruling. For instance, the Court has recognized a "public safety" exception that allows certain statements to be admitted even if the defendant was not given *Miranda* warnings. A defendant's statements that reveal the location of a weapon would be admissible under this exception.

Additionally, a suspect must unequivocally and assertively ask to exercise her or his right to counsel in order to stop police questioning. Saying, "Maybe I should talk to a lawyer" during an interrogation after being taken into custody is not enough.

Criminal Process

As mentioned earlier in this chapter, a criminal prosecution differs significantly from a civil case in several respects. These differences reflect the desire to safeguard the rights of the individual against the state. Exhibit 10–3 below summarizes the major steps in processing a criminal case. We now discuss three phases of the criminal process—arrest, indictment or information, and trial—in more detail.

ARREST Before a warrant for arrest can be issued, there must be probable cause to believe that the individual in question has committed a crime. As discussed earlier in this chapter, *probable cause* can

be defined as a substantial likelihood that the person has committed or is about to commit a crime. Note that probable cause involves a likelihood, not just a possibility. Arrests can be made without a warrant if there is no time to get one, but the action of the arresting officer is still judged by the standard of probable cause.

INDICTMENT OR INFORMATION Individuals must be formally charged with having committed specific

EXHIBIT 10-3 Major Procedural Steps in a Criminal Case

ARREST

BOOKING

INITIAL APPEARANCE
The defendant appears before the judge and is informed of the charges and of his or her rights. A lawyer may be appointed for the defendant. The judge sets bail (conditions under which a suspect can obtain release pending disposition of the case).

GRAND JURY
A grand jury determines if there is probable cause to believe that the defendant committed the crime. The federal government and about half of the states require grand jury indictments for at least some felonies.

PRELIMINARY HEARING
In a court proceeding, a prosecutor presents evidence, and the judge determines if there is probable cause to hold the defendant over for trial.

INDICTMENT
An *indictment* is a written document issued by the grand jury to formally charge the defendant with a crime.

INFORMATION
An *information* is a formal criminal charge made by the prosecutor.

ARRAIGNMENT
The defendant is brought before the court, informed of the charges, and asked to enter a plea. Usually, the prosecutor will attempt to get the defendant to enter into a plea bargain at this stage. Most defendants plead guilty to a lesser offense or receive a reduced sentence for their crime without ever proceeding to trial.

TRIAL
The trial can be either a jury trial or a bench trial. (In a bench trial, there is no jury, and the judge decides questions of fact as well as questions of law.) If the verdict is "guilty," the judge sets a date for the sentencing. Everyone convicted of a crime has the right to an appeal.

crimes before they can be brought to trial. If issued by a grand jury, such a charge is called an **indictment.**[20] A **grand jury** does not determine the guilt or innocence of an accused party. Rather, its function is to hear the state's evidence and to determine whether a reasonable basis (probable cause) exists for believing that a crime has been committed and that a trial ought to be held.

Usually, grand juries are called in cases involving serious crimes, such as murder. For lesser crimes, an individual may be formally charged with a crime by an **information,** or criminal complaint. An information will be issued by a government prosecutor if the prosecutor determines that there is sufficient evidence to justify bringing the individual to trial.

TRIAL At a criminal trial, the accused person does not have to prove anything. The entire burden of proof is on the prosecutor (the state). As mentioned earlier, the prosecution must show that, based on all the evidence, the defendant's guilt is established *beyond a reasonable doubt.* If there is reasonable doubt as to whether a criminal defendant committed the crime with which she or he has been charged, then the verdict must be "not guilty." A verdict of "not guilty" is not the same as stating that the defendant is innocent. It merely means that not enough evidence was properly presented to the court to prove guilt beyond a reasonable doubt.

Courts have complex rules about what types of evidence may be presented and how the evidence may be brought out in criminal cases, especially in jury trials. These rules are designed to ensure that evidence presented at trials is relevant, reliable, and not prejudicial toward the defendant.

Federal Sentencing Guidelines

The Sentencing Reform Act created the U.S. Sentencing Commission, which performs the task of standardizing sentences for *federal* crimes. The commission's guidelines establish a range of possible penalties for each federal crime. Originally, the guidelines were mandatory, in that the judge was required to select a sentence from within the set range and was not allowed to deviate from it.

PROBLEMS WITH CONSTITUTIONALITY In 2005, the United States Supreme Court held that certain provisions of the federal sentencing guidelines were unconstitutional. ▶ **Case in Point 10.18** Freddie Booker

was arrested with 92.5 grams of crack cocaine in his possession. Booker admitted to police that he had sold an additional 566 grams of crack cocaine, but he was never charged with, or tried for, possession of this additional quantity. Nevertheless, under the federal sentencing guidelines the judge was required to sentence Booker to twenty-two years in prison. The Court ruled that this sentence was unconstitutional because a jury did not find beyond a reasonable doubt that Booker had possessed the additional 566 grams of crack.[21] ◀

Essentially, the Court's ruling changed the federal sentencing guidelines from mandatory to advisory. Depending on the circumstances of the case, a federal trial judge may now depart from the guidelines if she or he believes that it is reasonable to do so.

FACTORS THAT INCREASE CRIMINAL PENALTIES Sentencing guidelines still exist and provide for enhanced punishment for certain types of crimes. Penalties can be enhanced for white-collar crimes, violations of the Sarbanes-Oxley Act (mentioned in Chapter 5), and violations of securities laws.[22]

The sentencing judge must take into account the various sentencing factors that apply to an individual defendant before concluding that a particular sentence is reasonable. When the defendant is a business firm, these factors include the company's history of past violations, management's cooperation with federal investigators, and the extent to which the firm has undertaken specific programs and procedures to prevent criminal activities by its employees.

SECTION 6
CYBER CRIME

The U.S. Department of Justice broadly defines **computer crime** as any violation of criminal law that involves knowledge of computer technology for its perpetration, investigation, or prosecution. Many computer crimes fall under the broad label of **cyber crime,** which describes any criminal activity occurring via a computer in the virtual community of the Internet.

---

20. Pronounced in-*dyte*-ment.

21. *United States v. Booker,* 543 U.S. 220, 125 S.Ct. 738, 160 L.Ed.2d 621 (2005).
22. The sentencing guidelines were amended in 2003, as required under the Sarbanes-Oxley Act of 2002, to impose stiffer penalties for corporate securities fraud.

Most cyber crimes are simply existing crimes, such as fraud and theft of intellectual property, in which the Internet is the instrument of wrongdoing. ▶ **Example 10.19** Richard O'Dwyer ran TVShack.net, a Web site with links directing users to copyrighted TV shows and movies. U.S. authorities seized his .net domain name, claiming that the site was nothing more than a search engine for pirated content. O'Dwyer simply moved the site to a .cc domain over which the United States apparently has no authority. ◀

Here we look at several types of activities that constitute cyber crimes against persons or property. (Of course, just as computers and the Internet have expanded the scope of crime, they have also provided new ways of detecting and combatting crime. For instance, police are using social media as an investigative tool, as discussed in Chapter 9.)

Cyber Fraud

As pointed out in Chapter 6, fraud is any misrepresentation knowingly made with the intention of deceiving another and on which a reasonable person would and does rely to her or his detriment. **Cyber fraud** is fraud committed over the Internet.

ONLINE AUCTION FRAUD Online auction fraud, in its most basic form, is a simple process. A person puts up an expensive item for auction, on either a legitimate or a fake auction site, and then refuses to send the product after receiving payment. Or, as a variation, the wrongdoer may send the purchaser an item that is worth less than the one offered in the auction.

The larger online auction sites, such as eBay, try to protect consumers against such schemes by providing warnings about deceptive sellers or offering various forms of insurance. It is nearly impossible to completely block fraudulent auction activity on the Internet, however. Because users can assume multiple identities, it is very difficult to pinpoint fraudulent sellers—they will simply change their screen names with each auction.

ONLINE RETAIL FRAUD Somewhat similar to online auction fraud is online retail fraud, in which consumers pay directly (without bidding) for items that are never delivered. As with other forms of online fraud, it is difficult to determine the actual extent of online sales fraud, but anecdotal evidence suggests that it is a substantial problem. ▶ **Case in Point 10.20** Jeremy Jaynes grossed more than $750,000 per week selling nonexistent or

worthless products such as "penny stock pickers" and "Internet history erasers." By the time he was arrested, he had amassed an estimated $24 million from his various fraudulent schemes.[23] ◀

Cyber Theft

In cyberspace, thieves are not subject to the physical limitations of the "real" world. A thief can steal data stored in a networked computer with Internet access from anywhere on the globe. Only the speed of the connection and the thief's computer equipment limit the quantity of data that can be stolen.

IDENTITY THEFT Not surprisingly, there has been a marked increase in identity theft in recent years. **Identity theft** occurs when the wrongdoer steals a form of identification—such as a name, date of birth, or Social Security number—and uses the information to access the victim's financial resources.

The Internet has provided even easier access to private data, as we discussed in Chapter 9. Frequent Web surfers surrender a wealth of information about themselves without knowing it. Most Web sites use "cookies" to collect data on those who visit their sites. Web browsers often store information such as the consumer's name and e-mail address. Finally, every time a purchase is made online, the item is linked to the purchaser's name.

PHISHING A distinct form of identity theft known as **phishing** has added a different wrinkle to the practice. In a phishing attack, the perpetrator "fishes" for financial data and passwords from consumers by posing as a legitimate business, such as a bank or credit-card company. The "phisher" sends an e-mail asking the recipient to update or confirm vital information, often with the threat that an account or some other service will be discontinued if the information is not provided. Once the unsuspecting individual enters the information, the phisher can use it to masquerade as that person or to drain his or her bank or credit account. ▶ **Example 10.21** Customers of Wachovia Bank (now owned by Wells Fargo) received official-looking e-mails telling them to type in personal information on a Web form to complete a mandatory installation of a new Internet security certificate. But the Web site was bogus. When people filled out the forms, their

---

23. *Jaynes v. Commonwealth of Virginia*, 276 Va.App. 443, 666 S.E.2d 303 (2008).

computers were infected and funneled their data to a computer server. The cyber criminals then sold the data. ◄

EMPLOYMENT FRAUD Cyber criminals also look for victims at online job-posting sites. Claiming to be an employment officer in a well-known company, the criminal sends bogus e-mail messages to job seekers. The messages ask the unsuspecting job seekers to reveal enough information to allow for identity theft. As the unemployment rate has remained high, cyber criminals have found many opportunities for employment fraud.

▶ **Example 10.22**   The job site Monster.com once asked 4.5 million users to change their passwords. Cyber thieves had broken into its databases and stolen user identities, passwords, and other data in one of Britain's largest cyber theft cases. ◄

CREDIT-CARD NUMBERS Companies take risks by storing their online customers' credit-card numbers. Although the consumer can make a purchase more quickly without entering a lengthy card number, the electronic warehouses that store the numbers are targets for cyber thieves. Stolen credit-card numbers are much more likely to hurt merchants and credit-card issuers (such as banks) than consumers. In most situations, the legitimate holders of credit cards are not held responsible for the costs of purchases made with a stolen number.

Hacking

A **hacker** is someone who uses one computer to break into another. The danger posed by hackers has increased significantly because of **botnets,** or networks of computers that have been appropriated by hackers without the knowledge of their owners. A hacker may secretly install a program on thousands, if not millions, of personal computer "robots," or "bots," that allows him or her to forward transmissions to an even larger number of systems.

▶ **Example 10.23**   When a hacker broke into Sony Corporation's PlayStation 3 video gaming and entertainment networks, the company had to temporarily shut down its online services. This single hacking incident affected more than 100 million online accounts that provide gaming, chat, and music streaming services. ◄

MALWARE Botnets are one of the latest forms of **malware**, a term that refers to any program that is harmful to a computer or, by extension, a computer user. A **worm,** for example, is a software program that is capable of reproducing itself as it spreads from one computer to the next.

▶ **Example 10.24**   Within three weeks, the computer worm called "Conflicker" spread to more than a million personal computers around the world. It was transmitted to some computers through the use of Facebook and Twitter. This worm also infected servers and devices plugged into infected computers, via USB ports, such as iPads, iPhones, and flash drives. ◄

A **virus,** another form of malware, is also able to reproduce itself, but must be attached to an "infested" host file to travel from one computer network to another. For instance, hackers are now capable of corrupting banner ads that use Adobe's Flash Player. When an Internet user clicks on the banner ad, a virus is installed. Worms and viruses can be programmed to perform a number of functions, such as prompting host computers to continually "crash" and reboot, or otherwise infect the system. (For a discussion of how malware is now affecting smartphones, see this chapter's *Insight into the Global Environment* feature on the following page.)

SERVICE-BASED HACKING Today, many companies offer "software as a service." Instead of buying software to install on a computer, the user connects to Web-based software. The user can write e-mails, edit spreadsheets, or perform other tasks using his or her Web browser. Cyber criminals have adapted this distribution method to provide "crimeware as a service."

A would-be thief no longer has to be a computer hacker to create a botnet, or steal banking information and credit-card numbers. He or she can rent the online services of cyber criminals to do the work for a small price. Fake security software (also known as scareware) is a common example. The thief can even target individual groups, such as U.S. physicians or British attorneys.

CYBERTERRORISM Cyberterrorists, as well as hackers, may target businesses. The goals of a hacking operation might include a wholesale theft of data, such as a merchant's customer files, or the monitoring of a computer to discover a business firm's plans and transactions. A cyberterrorist might also want to insert false codes or data. For instance, the processing control

INSIGHT INTO THE GLOBAL ENVIRONMENT
Even Smartphones Are Vulnerable to International Cyber Attacks

Recent statistics show that the number of bank robberies occurring annually is on the decline. Criminals have learned that it is easier, less risky, and more profitable to steal via the Internet. Advances in the speed and use of the Internet have fostered the growth of a relatively new criminal industry that uses malware to conduct espionage and profit from crime.

Who Are the Creators of Malware?

While any smart teenager can buy prepackaged hacking software on the Internet, the malware that businesses and governments are worried about is much more sophisticated. There is evidence that malware that can be used for international diplomatic espionage as well as industrial espionage is most often developed by so-called cyber mercenaries. According to Steve Sachs of the cyber security firm FireEye, "There are entire little villages dedicated to malware in Russia, villages in China, very sophisticated, very organized, very well-funded."

Flame Malware

The most sophisticated globally created and propagated malware has been labeled Flame. Flame was discovered in 2012, although experts believe that it was lying dormant in thousands of computers worldwide for at least five years.

Flame can record screen shots, keyboard strokes, network traffic, and audio. It can also record Skype conversations. It can even turn infected computers into Bluetooth beacons, which can then attempt to download contact information from nearby Bluetooth-enabled devices.

The Malware Can Infect Smartphones

Many smartphone owners are unaware that their Apple, Nokia, and Microsoft Windows mobile phones can be infected with Flame malware or variants of it without

their knowledge. The information that is hacked from smartphones can then be sent on to a series of command-and-control servers and ultimately to members of international criminal gangs.

Once a computer or smartphone is infected with this malware, all information in the device can be transferred. Additionally, files can be deleted, and furthermore, files that have been erased on hard drives can be resurrected. This malware has been responsible for stealing e-mail databases from Microsoft's e-mail program Outlook and has even been able to capture e-mail from remote servers.[a] Until recently, most attacks involved diplomatic espionage, but cyber technicians at large business enterprises are now worried that industrial espionage may be taking place. In fact, an extensive hacking operation was uncovered in 2013 that was linked to a Chinese military unit (the "Comment Crew"). The wide-ranging cyber attacks involved the theft of hundreds of terabytes of data and intellectual property of more than 140 corporations in twenty different industries. The goal of the attacks was to help Chinese companies better compete against U.S. and foreign firms.[b]

LEGAL CRITICAL THINKING
INSIGHT INTO THE TECHNOLOGICAL ENVIRONMENT

What entities might pay "cyber mercenaries" to create some of the malware described in this feature?

---

a. Mark Stevens, "CWI Cryptanalyst Discovers New Cryptographic Attack Variant in Flame Spy Malware," June 7, 2012, **www.cwi.nl/news/2012**.

b. David E. Sanger, David Barboza, and Nicole Perlroth, "Chinese Army Unit Is Seen as Tied to Hacking Against U.S.," **www.nytimes.com/2013**.

---

system of a food manufacturer could be changed to alter the levels of ingredients so that consumers of the food would become ill.

A cyberterrorist attack on a major financial institution, such as the New York Stock Exchange or a large bank, could leave securities or money markets in flux and seriously affect the daily lives of millions of citizens. Similarly, any prolonged disruption of computer, cable, satellite, or telecommunications sys-

tems due to the actions of expert hackers would have serious repercussions on business operations—and national security—on a global level.

Prosecuting Cyber Crime

Cyber crime has raised new issues in the investigation of crimes and the prosecution of offenders. Determining the "location" of a cyber crime and identifying a criminal in cyberspace present significant challenges for law enforcement.

JURISDICTION AND IDENTIFICATION CHALLENGES A threshold issue is, of course, jurisdiction. Jurisdiction is normally based on physical geography, as discussed in Chapter 2. Each state and nation has jurisdiction, or authority, over crimes committed within its boundaries. But geographic boundaries simply do not apply in cyberspace. A person who commits an act against a business in California, where the act is a cyber crime, might never have set foot in California but might instead reside in New York, or even in Canada, where the act may not be a crime.

Identifying the wrongdoer can also be difficult. Cyber criminals do not leave physical traces, such as fingerprints or DNA samples, as evidence of their crimes. Even electronic "footprints" can be hard to find and follow. For instance, e-mail may be sent through a remailer, an online service that guarantees that a message cannot be traced to its source.

For these reasons, laws written to protect physical property are often difficult to apply in cyberspace. Nonetheless, governments at both the state and the federal level have taken significant steps toward controlling cyber crime. California, for instance, which has the highest identity theft rate in the nation, has established a new eCrime unit to investigate and prosecute cyber crimes. Other states, including Florida, Louisiana, and Texas, also have special law enforcement units that focus solely on Internet crimes.

THE COMPUTER FRAUD AND ABUSE ACT Perhaps the most significant federal statute specifically addressing cyber crime is the Counterfeit Access Device and Computer Fraud and Abuse Act.[24] This act is commonly known as the Computer Fraud and Abuse Act (CFAA).

Among other things, the CFAA provides that a person who accesses a computer online, without authority, to obtain classified, restricted, or protected data (or attempts to do so) is subject to criminal prosecution. Such data could include financial and credit records, medical records, legal files, military and national security files, and other confidential information. The data can be located in government or private computers. The crime has two elements: accessing a computer without authority and taking the data.

This theft is a felony if it is committed for a commercial purpose or for private financial gain, or if the value of the stolen data (or computer time) exceeds $5,000. Penalties include fines and imprisonment for up to twenty years. A victim of computer theft can also bring a civil suit against the violator to obtain damages, an injunction, and other relief.

---

24. 18 U.S.C. Section 1030.

Reviewing: Criminal Law and Cyber Crime

Edward Hanousek worked for Pacific & Arctic Railway and Navigation Company (P&A) as a roadmaster of the White Pass & Yukon Railroad in Alaska. Hanousek was responsible "for every detail of the safe and efficient maintenance and construction of track, structures and marine facilities of the entire railroad," including special projects. One project was a rock quarry, known as "6-mile," above the Skagway River. Next to the quarry, and just beneath the surface, ran a high-pressure oil pipeline owned by Pacific & Arctic Pipeline, Inc., P&A's sister company. When the quarry's backhoe operator punctured the pipeline, an estimated 1,000 to 5,000 gallons of oil were discharged into the river. Hanousek was charged with negligently discharging a harmful quantity of oil into a navigable water of the United States in violation of the criminal provisions of the Clean Water Act (CWA). Using the information presented in the chapter, answer the following questions.

1. Did Hanousek have the required mental state (*mens rea*) to be convicted of a crime? Why or why not?
2. Which theory discussed in the chapter would enable a court to hold Hanousek criminally liable for violating the statute if he participated in, directed, or merely knew about the specific violation?
3. Could the backhoe operator who punctured the pipeline also be charged with a crime in this situation? Explain.

4. Suppose that at trial, Hanousek argued that he should not be convicted because he was not aware of the requirements of the CWA. Would this defense be successful? Why or why not?

DEBATE THIS . . . *Because of overcriminalization, particularly by the federal government, Americans may be breaking the law regularly without knowing it. Should Congress rescind many of the more than four thousand federal crimes now on the books?*

Terms and Concepts

actus reus 196	exclusionary rule 209	necessity 204
arson 201	felony 195	petty offense 195
beyond a reasonable doubt 194	forgery 201	phishing 213
botnet 214	grand jury 212	plea bargaining 207
burglary 199	hacker 214	probable cause 207
computer crime 212	identity theft 213	robbery 199
crime 194	indictment 212	search warrant 207
cyber crime 212	information 212	self-defense 204
cyber fraud 213	larceny 199	self-incrimination 206
double jeopardy 207	malware 214	virus 214
duress 206	*mens rea* 197	white-collar crime 202
embezzlement 202	misdemeanor 195	worm 214
entrapment 206	money laundering 203	

ExamPrep

Issue Spotters

1. Dana takes her roommate's credit card without permission, intending to charge expenses that she incurs on a vacation. Her first stop is a gas station, where she uses the card to pay for gas. With respect to the gas station, has she committed a crime? If so, what is it? **(See page 199.)**

2. Without permission, Ben downloads consumer credit files from a computer belonging to Consumer Credit Agency. He then sells the data to Dawn. Has Ben committed a crime? If so, what is it? **(See page 216.)**

- **Check your answers to the Issue Spotters against the answers provided in Appendix E at the end of this text.**

Before the Test

Go to **www.cengagebrain.com**, enter the ISBN 9781285185248, and click on "Find" to locate this textbook's Web site. Then, click on "Access Now" under "Study Tools," and select Chapter 10 at the top. There, you will find a Practice Quiz that you can take to assess your mastery of the concepts in this chapter, as well as Flashcards and a Glossary of important terms.

Business Scenarios

10–1. Types of Cyber Crimes. The following situations are similar, but each represents a variation of a particular crime. Identify the crime and point out the differences in the variations. **(See page 213.)**

(a) Chen, posing fraudulently as Diamond Credit Card Co., sends an e-mail to Emily, stating that the company has observed suspicious activity in her account and has frozen the account. The e-mail asks her to reregister her credit-card number and password to reopen the account.

(b) Claiming falsely to be Big Buy Retail Finance Co., Conner sends an e-mail to Dino, asking him to confirm or update his personal security information to prevent his Big Buy account from being discontinued.

(c) Felicia posts her résumé on GotWork.com, an online job-posting site, seeking a position in business and managerial finance and accounting. Hayden, who misrepresents himself as an employment officer with International Bank & Commerce Corp., sends her an e-mail asking for more personal information.

10–2. Property Crimes. Which, if any, of the following crimes necessarily involves illegal activity on the part of more than one person? **(See page 202.)**

(a) Bribery.

(b) Forgery.

(c) Embezzlement.

(d) Larceny.

(e) Receiving stolen property.

10–3. Cyber Scam. Kayla, a student at Learnwell University, owes $20,000 in unpaid tuition. If Kayla does not pay the tuition, Learnwell will not allow her to graduate. To obtain the funds to pay the debt, she sends e-mails to people that she does not personally know asking for financial help to send Milo, her disabled child, to a special school. In reality, Kayla has no children. Is this a crime? If so, which one? **(See page 213.)**

Business Case Problems

10–4. Cyber Crime. Jiri Klimecek was a member of a group that overrode copyright protection in movies, video games, and software, and made them available for download online. Klimecek bought and installed hardware and software to set up a computer server and paid half of the monthly service charges to connect the server to the Internet. He knew that users around the world could access the server to upload and download copyrighted works. He obtained access to Czech movies and music to make them available. Klimecek was indicted in a federal district court for copyright infringement. He claimed that he did not understand the full scope of the operation. Did Klimecek commit a crime? If so, was he a "minor participant" entitled to a reduced sentence? Explain. [*United States v. Klimecek*, ___F.3d ___ (7th Cir. 2009)] **(See page 212.)**

10–5. Fourth Amendment. Three police officers, including Maria Trevizo, were on patrol in Tucson, Arizona, near a neighborhood associated with the Crips gang, when they pulled over a car with suspended registration. Each officer talked to one of the three occupants. Trevizo spoke with Lemon Johnson, who was wearing clothing consistent with Crips membership. Visible in his jacket pocket was a police scanner, and he said that he had served time in prison for burglary. Trevizo asked him to get out of the car and patted him down "for officer safety." She found a gun. Johnson was charged in an Arizona state court with illegal possession of a weapon. What standard should apply to an officer's patdown of a passenger during a traffic stop? Should a search warrant be required? Could a search proceed solely on the basis of probable cause? Would a reasonable suspicion short of probable cause be sufficient? Discuss. [*Arizona v. Johnson*, 555 U.S. 323, 129 S.Ct. 781, 172 L.Ed.2d 694 (2009)] **(See page 207.)**

10–6. Searches. Charles Byrd was in a minimum-security jail awaiting trial. A team of sheriff's deputies took several inmates into a room for a strip search without any apparent justification. Byrd was ordered to remove all of his clothing except his boxer shorts. A female deputy searched Byrd while several male deputies watched. One of the male deputies videotaped the search. Byrd filed a suit against the sheriff's department. Did the search violate Byrd's rights? Discuss. [*Byrd v. Maricopa County Sheriff's Department*, 629 F.3d. 1135 (9th Cir. 2011)] **(See page 207.)**

10–7. Credit-Card Theft. Jacqueline Barden was shopping for school clothes with her children when her purse and automobile were taken. In Barden's purse were her car keys, credit and debit cards for herself and her children, as well as the children's Social Security cards and birth certificates needed for enrollment at school. Immediately after the purse and car were stolen, Rebecca Mary Turner attempted to use Barden's credit card at a local Exxon gas station, but the card was declined. The gas station attendant recognized Turner because she had previously written bad checks and used credit cards that did not belong to her.

Turner was later arrested while attempting to use one of Barden's checks to pay for merchandise at a Wal-Mart—where the clerk also recognized Turner from prior criminal activity. Turner claimed that she had not stolen Barden's purse or car, and that a friend had told her he had some checks and credit cards and asked her to try using them at Wal-Mart. Turner was convicted at trial. She appealed, claiming that there was insufficient evidence that she committed credit- and debit-card theft. Was the evidence sufficient to uphold her conviction? Why or why not? [*Turner v. State of Arkansas*, 2012 Ark.App. 150 (2012)] **(See page 202.)**

10–8. BUSINESS CASE PROBLEM WITH SAMPLE ANSWER: Criminal Liability.
 During the morning rush hour, David Green threw bottles and plates from a twenty-sixth-floor hotel balcony overlooking Seventh Avenue in New York City. A video of the incident also showed him doing cartwheels while holding a beer bottle and sprinting toward the balcony while holding a glass steadily in his hand. When he saw police on the street below and on the roof of the

CHAPTER 10 Criminal Law and Cyber Crime **219**

building across the street, he suspended his antics but resumed tossing objects off the balcony after the police left. He later admitted that he could recall what he had done, but claimed to have been intoxicated and said his only purpose was to amuse himself and his friends. Did Green have the mental state required to establish criminal liability? Discuss. [State of New York v. Green, *104 A.D.3d 126, 958 N.Y.S.2d 138 (1 Dept. 2013)]* **(See page 197.)**

• For a sample answer to Problem 10–8, go to Appendix F at the end of this text.

10–9. A QUESTION OF ETHICS: Identity Theft.

 Twenty-year-old Davis Omole had good grades in high school, where he played on the football and chess teams, and went on to college. Omole worked at a cell phone store where he stole customers' personal information. He used the stolen identities to create a hundred different accounts on eBay, and held more than three hundred auctions listing for sale items that he did not own (including cell phones, plasma televisions, and stereos). From these auctions, he collected $90,000. To avoid getting caught, he continuously closed and opened the eBay accounts, activated and deactivated cell phone and e-mail accounts, and changed mailing addresses and post office boxes. Omole, who had previously been convicted in a state court for Internet fraud, was convicted in a federal district court of identity theft and wire fraud. [United States v. Omole, *523 F.3d 691 (7th Cir. 2008)]* **(See page 213.)**

(a) Omole displayed contempt for the court and ridiculed his victims, calling them stupid for having been cheated. What does this behavior suggest about Omole's ethics?

(b) Under federal sentencing guidelines, Omole could have been imprisoned for more than eight years. He received only three years, however, two of which comprised the mandatory sentence for identity theft. Was this sentence too lenient? Explain.

Legal Reasoning Group Activity

10–10. Cyber Crime. Cyber crime costs consumers millions of dollars per year, and it costs businesses, including banks and other credit-card issuers, even more. Nonetheless, when cyber criminals are caught and convicted, they are rarely ordered to pay restitution or sentenced to long prison terms. **(See page 212.)**

(a) One group should argue that stiffer sentences would reduce the amount of cyber crime.

(b) A second group should determine how businesspersons can best protect themselves from cyber crime and avoid the associated costs.

UNIT TWO Focus on Ethics

Ethics and Torts and Crimes

Ethical and legal concepts are often closely intertwined. This is because the common law, as it evolved in England and then in America, reflected society's values and customs. This connection between law and ethics is clearly evident in the area of tort law, which provides remedies for harms caused by actions that society has deemed wrongful. Criminal law is also rooted in common law concepts of right and wrong behavior, although common law concepts governing criminal acts are now expressed in, or replaced by, federal, state, and local criminal statutes. The number of torts and crimes has continued to expand as new ways to commit wrongs have been discovered.

The laws governing torts, crimes, and intellectual property—the areas of law covered in this unit—constitute an important part of the legal environment of business. In each of these areas, new legal (and ethical) challenges have emerged as a result of developments in technology. In this *Focus on Ethics* feature, we look at the ethical dimensions of selected topics discussed in the preceding chapters, including some issues that are unique to the cyber age.

Privacy Rights in an Online World

Privacy rights are protected under constitutional law, tort law, and various federal and state statutes. How to protect privacy rights in the online world, though, has been a recurring problem over the past decade. One difficulty is that individuals today often are not even aware that information about their personal lives and preferences is being collected by Internet companies and other online users. Nor do they know how that information will be used.

As discussed in Chapter 9, "cookies" installed in computers may allow users' Web movements to be tracked. Many e-mail services, such as Google's Gmail, automatically scan and save information about users. Persons who purchase goods from online merchants or auctions inevitably must reveal some personal information, often including their credit-card numbers.

In addition, many goods purchased today use radio-frequency identification (RFID) tags to transmit information. Such tags are frequently included in automobiles, clothing, and cell phones. For instance, clothing manufacturers may use RFID tags to track merchandise and see which products are being sold through which retailers. Health-care facilities, hospitals, libraries, museums, and schools may also use RFID tags. The possibility that these tags may be used to read information linked to a person without her or his consent raises privacy concerns.

The Increased Value of Personal Information

One of the major concerns of consumers in recent years has been the collection and sale of their personal information— sometimes even by third parties with whom the consumers have never had dealings. This information has become increasingly valuable to online marketers, who are willing to pay a high price to those who collect and sell it.

Because of consumers' concerns—and the possibility of lawsuits based on privacy laws—businesses marketing goods online need to exercise care. Today, many online businesses create and post on their Web sites a privacy policy disclosing how any information obtained from their customers will be used.

Privacy Rights in the Workplace

Another area of concern is the extent to which employees' privacy rights should be protected in the workplace. Traditionally, employees have been afforded a certain "zone of privacy" in the workplace. For example, the courts have concluded that employees have a reasonable expectation of privacy with respect to personal items contained in their desks or in their lockers. Should this zone of privacy extend to personal e-mail sent via the employer's server or social media posts made via a smartphone that the employer provided? This question and others relating to employee privacy rights should be considered by employers today given the increased use of the Internet and social media by employees.

LEGAL REASONING

1. *Some observers maintain that privacy rights are quickly becoming a thing of the past. In your opinion, is it possible to protect privacy rights in today's online world? Why or why not?*

Should Civil Liberties Be Sacrificed to Control Crime and Terrorist Activities in the Cyber Age?

The very real and substantial threat posed by criminal conspirators and terrorists today has raised some important questions about what methods should be used to combat them. In 2012, for instance, the movie *Zero Dark Thirty* raised the question of whether it is ever acceptable for the United States to use torture to obtain information about terrorists.

Similarly, as criminals and terrorists use the Internet to communicate and even to recruit new members, the question arises as to whether it is possible to control many types of crime and terrorist activities without sacrificing some civil liberties. Should the U.S. government actively monitor e-mail, social media, and other electronic communications of particular users or groups?

Traditionally, Americans rejected any attempt by the government to monitor Internet use to detect criminal conspiracies or terrorist activities. Immediately after the terrorist attacks of 2001, however, Americans seemed more willing to trade off some of their civil liberties for greater national security. The USA Patriot Act (see Chapter 4) gave law enforcement personnel more authority to conduct electronic surveillance, such as monitoring Web sites and e-mail exchanges. Today, though,

UNIT TWO Focus on Ethics

Ethics and Torts and Crimes, *Continued*

many complain that this legislation has gone too far in curbing traditional civil liberties guaranteed by the U.S. Constitution.

LEGAL REASONING

2. *Many believe that the federal government should not be allowed to monitor the Internet activities and e-mail exchanges of its citizens without obtaining a warrant. Yet others maintain that in some situations, when time is of the essence, such monitoring may be necessary to keep Americans safe from terrorists. Where should the line be drawn between justifiable and unjustifiable governmental interference with American citizens' civil liberties? Discuss fully.*

Global Companies and Censorship Issues—Google China

Doing business on a global level can sometimes involve serious ethical challenges. Consider the ethical firestorm that erupted when Google, Inc., decided to market "Google China" (**Google.cn**) in 2006. This version of Google's widely used search engine was tailored to the Chinese government's censorship requirements.

In China, Web sites that offer pornography, criticism of the government, or information on sensitive topics, such as the Tiananmen Square massacre in 1989, are censored—that is, they cannot be accessed by Web users. Government agencies enforce the censorship and encourage citizens to inform on one another. Thousands of Web sites are shut down each year, and the sites' operators are subject to potential imprisonment.

The Chinese government insists that in restricting access to certain Web sites, it is merely following the lead of other national governments, which also impose controls on information access. As an example, it cites France, which bans access to any Web sites selling or displaying Nazi paraphernalia. The United States itself prohibits the dissemination of certain types of materials, such as child pornography, over the Internet. Furthermore, the U.S. government monitors Web sites and e-mail communications to protect against terrorist threats. How, ask Chinese officials, can other nations point their fingers at China for engaging in a common international practice?

Censorship—The Lesser of Two Evils?

Human rights groups came out strongly against Google's decision, maintaining that the company was seeking profits in a lucrative marketplace at the expense of assisting the Chinese Communist Party in suppressing free speech. Google defended its actions by pointing out that its Chinese search engine at least lets users know which sites are being censored. Google China includes the links to censored sites, but when a user tries to access a link, the program states that it is not accessible.

Google claimed that its approach was essentially the "lesser of two evils": if U.S. companies did not cooperate with

the Chinese government, Chinese residents would have less user-friendly Internet access. Moreover, Google asserted that providing Internet access, even if censored, is a step toward more open access in the future because technology is, in itself, a revolutionary force.

China's Cyberattack and Google's Response

Google's attitude changed when it discovered that its software had been the target of a cyberattack that apparently originated in China. David Drummond, senior vice president of corporate development and Google's chief legal officer, informed the public about the attack in an article on the official Google blog on January 12, 2010. Drummond described the attack as "highly sophisticated" and said that it was not limited to Google—some twenty other large companies were similarly targeted. Drummond believed the goal of the attackers was to access the Gmail accounts of Chinese human rights activists. Google also discovered that the accounts of dozens of human rights advocates in the United States, China, and Europe had routinely been accessed by third parties.

Drummond said that the attacks and the surveillance that the investigation uncovered led Google to announce a change in its China policy: "We have decided we are no longer willing to continue censoring our results on **Google.cn** . . . . We recognize that this may well mean having to shut down **Google.cn**."[1] In 2010, Google stopped operating **Google.cn** and automatically redirected users to its Hong Kong servers at **Google.com.hk** for search services in Chinese.

Although the Chinese government censors results on Google's Hong Kong servers, it nonetheless found Google's auto-redirect policy unacceptable and threatened to revoke Google's license. Then Google again revised its policy so that it no longer auto-redirects Chinese users to the Hong Kong servers. Instead, Google directs Chinese users to a Web page at which they must elect to use the Hong Kong servers. In addition, Google reopened Google China to host minimal searches for content that does not require censorship, such as for maps, music, and translation services.

Proponents of human rights applauded Google's efforts to avoid censorship of its search content, but others are not so sure. If Google and similar companies refuse to cooperate with governments that engage in censorship, will this transform the World Wide Web? Will the information highway of the future be forced to stop at national borders?

LEGAL REASONING

3. *Do companies that do business on a global level, such as Google, have an ethical duty to foreign citizens not to suppress*

---

1. David Drummond, "A New Approach to China," *The Official Google Blog*, January 12, 2010.

FOCUS ON ETHICS CONTINUES ▶

free speech? Is it ever acceptable for these companies to censor the information that they provide in other nations at the request of a foreign government? Explain your answer.

Do Gun Makers Have a Duty to Warn?

One of the big issues in today's legal environment is how tort law principles apply to harms (injury or death) caused by guns. Many negligence lawsuits have been filed across the nation against gun manufacturers. Plaintiffs often claim that gun makers have a duty to warn users of their products of the dangers associated with gun use. Would it be fair to impose such a requirement on gun manufacturers? Some say no, because such dangers are open and obvious. (Recall from Chapter 6 that, generally, there is no duty to warn of open and obvious dangers.) Others contend that warnings could prevent numerous gun accidents.

State courts addressing this issue have generally ruled that manufacturers have no duty to warn users of the obvious risks associated with gun use. For example, New York's highest court held that a gun manufacturer's duty of care does not extend to those who are injured by the illegal use of handguns.[2] Some courts, however, have held that gun makers whose marketing or sales practices cause a large influx of guns into the illegal secondary market could be liable under a public nuisance theory.[3] Other courts have allowed plaintiffs to sue for negligence when guns are sold to a straw purchaser (a person pretending to be a legitimate buyer) and then distributed to criminals.[4]

LEGAL REASONING

4. *In your opinion, should gun manufacturers have a duty to warn gun users of the dangers of using guns? Would such a warning be effective in preventing gun-related violence? Discuss.*

Trademark Protection versus Free Speech Rights

Another legal issue pits the rights of trademark owners against the right to free speech. The question is whether a company's ownership rights in a trademark used as a domain name outweigh the free speech rights of those who use a similar domain name to criticize or parody the company. A common tactic of those critical of a company's goods or services is to add the word *sucks* or *stinks* (or some other disparaging term) to the trademark owner's domain name.

A number of companies have sued the owners of such sites for trademark infringement in the hope that a court or an arbitrating panel will order the site owner to cease using the domain name. To date, though, companies have had little success pursuing this alternative. After all, one of the primary reasons trademarks are protected under U.S. law is to prevent customers from becoming confused about the origin of the goods for sale—and a "sucks" site certainly does not create such confusion.

Furthermore, U.S. courts and arbitrators give extensive protection to free speech rights, including the right to express opinions about companies and their products.[5] Even international arbitration panels, when hearing disputes between U.S. parties, give significant weight to U.S. constitutional law protecting speech.[6]

Trade Secrets versus Free Speech Rights

Another ongoing issue with ethical dimensions involves the point at which free speech rights come into conflict with the right of copyright holders to protect their property by using encryption technology. This issue came before the California Supreme Court in the case of *DVD Copy Control Association v. Bunner.*[7]

Trade associations in the movie industry sued an Internet Web site operator who had posted the code of a computer program that cracked technology used to encrypt DVDs. This posed a significant threat to the movie industry because, by using the code-cracking software, users would be able to duplicate the copyrighted movies stored on the DVDs.

In their suit, the trade associations claimed that the Web site operator had misappropriated trade secrets. The defendant argued that software programs designed to break encryption programs were a form of constitutionally protected speech. When the case reached the California Supreme Court, the court held that although the First Amendment applies to computer code, computer code is not a form of "pure speech," and the courts can therefore protect it to a lesser extent. The court reinstated a trial court order that enjoined (prevented) the Web site operator from continuing to post the code.

LEGAL REASONING

5. *Generally, do you believe that the law has struck a fair balance between the rights of intellectual property owners and the rights of the public? Why or why not?*

2. *Hamilton v. Beretta U.S.A. Corp.,* 96 N.Y.2d 222, 750 N.E.2d 1055, 727 N.Y.S.2d 7 (2001). See also, *Williams v. Beesmiller, Inc.,* 962 N.Y.S.2d 834, 103 A.D.3d 1191 (2013).

3. *City of New York v. Beretta U.S.A. Corp.,* 524 F.3d 384 (2d Cir. 2008); *Gilland v. Sportsmen's Outpost, Inc.,* 2011 WL 2479693 (Conn.Super. 2011); and *Illeto v. Glock, Inc.,* 349 F.3d 1191 (9th Cir. 2003).

4. *Williams v. Beemiller, Inc.,* 962 N.Y.S.2d 834, 103 A.D.3d 1191 (2013); and *Smith v. Atlantic Gun & Tackle, Inc.,* 376 F.Supp.2d 291 (E.D.N.Y. 2005).

5. Many businesses have concluded that although they cannot control what people say about them, they can make it more difficult for it to be said. Today, businesses commonly register such insulting domain names before the cyber-gripers themselves can register them.

6. See, for example, *Sutherland Institute v. Continuative, LLC,* WIPO Arbitration and Mediation Center, Case No. D2009-0893.

7. 31 Cal.4th 864, 4 Cal.Rptr.3d 69 (2003). See also *VI 4D, LLP v. Crucians in Focus, Inc.,* 2012 WL 6757243 (VI Super. 2012).

Unit Three

Contracts
and E-Contracts

Contents

CHAPTER 11
NATURE AND TERMINOLOGY

The noted legal scholar Roscoe Pound once said that "[t]he social order rests upon the stability and predictability of conduct, of which keeping promises is a large item."[1] Contract law deals with, among other things, the formation and keeping of promises. A **promise** is a declaration by a person (the *promisor*) to do or not to do a certain act. As a result, the person to whom the promise is made (the *promisee*) has a right to expect or demand that something either will or will not happen in the future.

Like other types of law, contract law reflects our social values, interests, and expectations at a given point in time. It shows, for instance, to what extent our society allows people to make promises or commitments that are legally binding. It distinguishes between promises that create only *moral* obligations (such as a promise to take a friend to lunch) and promises that are legally binding (such as a promise to pay for merchandise purchased).

Contract law also demonstrates which excuses our society accepts for breaking certain types of promises. In addition, it indicates which promises are considered to be contrary to public policy—against the interests of society as a whole—and therefore legally invalid. When the person making a promise is a child or is mentally incompetent, for example, a question will arise as to whether the promise should be enforced. Resolving such questions is the essence of contract law.

---

1. Roscoe Pound, *Jurisprudence*, Vol. 3 (St. Paul, Minn.: West Publishing Co., 1959), p. 162.

SECTION 1
AN OVERVIEW OF CONTRACT LAW

Before we look at the numerous rules that courts use to determine whether a particular promise will be enforced, it is necessary to understand some fundamental concepts of contract law. In this section, we describe the sources and general function of contract law and introduce the objective theory of contracts.

Sources of Contract Law

The common law governs all contracts except when it has been modified or replaced by statutory law, such as the Uniform Commercial Code (UCC),[2] or by administrative agency regulations. Contracts relating to services, real estate, employment, and insurance, for instance, generally are governed by the common law of contracts. (For a sample contract with an explanation of its terms, see the *Appendix to Chapter 19: Reading and Analyzing Contracts*.)

Contracts for the sale and lease of goods, however, are governed by the UCC—to the extent that the UCC has modified general contract law. The relationship between general contract law and the law governing sales and leases of goods will be explored in detail in Chapter 20. In the discussion of general contract law that follows, we indicate in footnotes the areas in which the UCC has significantly altered common law contract principles.

The Function of Contract Law

No aspect of modern life is entirely free of contractual relationships. You acquire rights and obligations, for example, when you borrow funds, buy or lease a house, obtain insurance, and purchase goods or services. Contract law is designed to provide stability and predictability, as well as certainty, for both buyers and sellers in the marketplace.

---

2. See Chapters 1 and 20 for further discussions of the significance and coverage of the UCC. The UCC is presented in Appendix C at the end of this book.

Contract law assures the parties to private agreements that the promises they make will be enforceable. Clearly, many promises are kept because the parties involved feel a moral obligation to keep them or because keeping a promise is in their mutual self-interest. The **promisor** (the person making the promise) and the **promisee** (the person to whom the promise is made) may also decide to honor their agreement for other reasons. In business agreements, the rules of contract law are often followed to avoid potential disputes.

By supplying procedures for enforcing private contractual agreements, contract law provides an essential condition for the existence of a market economy. Without a legal framework of reasonably assured expectations within which to make long-run plans, businesspersons would be able to rely only on the good faith of others. Duty and good faith are usually sufficient to obtain compliance with a promise. When price changes or adverse economic factors make compliance costly, however, these elements may not be enough. Contract law is necessary to ensure compliance with a promise or to entitle the innocent party to some form of relief.

The Definition of a Contract

A **contract** is "a promise or a set of promises for the breach of which the law gives a remedy, or the performance of which the law in some way recognizes as a duty."[3] Put simply, a contract is an agreement that can be enforced in court. It is formed by two or more parties who agree to perform or to refrain from performing some act now or in the future.

Generally, contract disputes arise when there is a promise of future performance. If the contractual promise is not fulfilled, the party who made it is subject to the sanctions of a court (see Chapter 19). That party may be required to pay damages for failing to perform the contractual promise. In a few instances, the party may be required to perform the promised act.

[3.] *Restatement (Second) of Contracts,* Section 1. As mentioned in Chapter 1, *Restatements of the Law* are scholarly books that restate the existing common law principles distilled from court opinions as a set of rules on a particular topic. Courts often refer to the *Restatements* for guidance. The *Restatement of the Law of Contracts* was compiled by the American Law Institute in 1932. The *Restatement,* which is now in its second edition (a third edition is being drafted), will be referred to throughout the following chapters on contract law.

The Objective Theory of Contracts

In determining whether a contract has been formed, the element of intent is of prime importance. In contract law, intent is determined by what is called the **objective theory of contracts,** not by the personal or subjective intent, or belief, of a party. (We will also look at the objective theory of contracts in Chapter 12, in the context of contract formation.)

FACTS AS INTERPRETED BY A REASONABLE PERSON The theory is that a party's intention to enter into a legally binding agreement, or contract, is judged by outward, objective facts. The facts are as interpreted by a *reasonable* person, rather than by the party's own secret, subjective intentions. Objective facts may include:

1. What the party said when entering into the contract.
2. How the party acted or appeared (intent may be manifested by conduct as well as by oral or written words).
3. The circumstances surrounding the transaction.

▶ **Case in Point 11.1** Linear Technology Corporation (LTC) makes and sells integrated circuits for use in cell phones and computers. LTC sued its competitor, Micrel, Inc., for infringement of a patent on a particular chip. In its defense, Micrel claimed that LTC's patent was invalid because LTC had offered to sell the chip commercially before the date on which it could be legally sold. The issue was whether LTC had entered into sales contracts when it solicited input on pricing and accepted distributors' purchase orders using a "will advise" procedure before the critical date. The court ruled that under the objective theory of contracts, no reasonable customer could interpret LTC's requests for information about pricing and potential orders as an offer that could bind LTC to a sale. Therefore, LTC did not violate the ban on sales and could continue its suit against Micrel for patent infringement.[4] ◀

UNDERLYING MOTIVE NOT IMPORTANT A party may have many reasons for entering into an agreement—obtaining real property, goods, or services, for example, and profiting from the deal. Any of these purposes may provide a motivation for performing the contract. In the following case, however, one party failed to perform and claimed that he had not intended to enter into the contract when he signed it.

[4.] *Linear Technology Corp. v. Micrel, Inc.,* 275 F.3d 1040 (Fed.Cir. 2001).

CASE ANALYSIS

Case 11.1   Pan Handle Realty, LLC v. Olins
Appellate Court of Connecticut, 140 Conn.App. 556, 59 A.3d 842 (2013).

IN THE LANGUAGE OF THE COURT
SHELDON, J. [Judge]

* * * *

* * * The plaintiff is a Connecticut limited liability company [a form of business organization] * * * , which constructed a luxury home at 4 Pan Handle Lane in Westport [Connecticut] (the property). * * * The defendant [Robert Olins] expressed an interest in leasing the property from the plaintiff for a period of one year. In pursuit of that interest, he submitted an application proposing to rent the property from the plaintiff at the rate of $12,000 per month, together with an accompanying financial statement. The plaintiff responded to the defendant's proposal by preparing a draft lease for his review, which the defendant promptly forwarded to his attorney.

On January 17, 2009, the defendant and his real estate agent, Laura Sydney, met with Irwin Stillman, then acting as the plaintiff's representative, to discuss the draft lease (January 17 meeting). At that meeting, the defendant and Irwin Stillman agreed to several revisions to the draft lease that had been proposed by the defendant's attorney, then incorporated the revisions into the lease and signed it. The resulting lease, which was dated January 19, 2009, specified a lump sum annual rent of $138,000. At the time of the signing, the defendant gave the plaintiff a postdated check for $138,000 * * * . The lease agreement required the plaintiff to make certain modifications to the property prior to the occupancy date, including the removal of all of the furnishings from the leased premises.

On January 21, 2009, the plaintiff's real estate broker informed it that, according to Sydney, the defendant planned to move into the property

on January 28, 2009. The next day, the defendant requested information from the plaintiff for his renter's insurance policy, which the plaintiff duly provided. By that time, the plaintiff had also completed the modifications requested by the defendant at the January 17 meeting and agreed to in the lease agreement, including the removal of the furniture. The defendant's check, which was postdated January 26, 2009, was deposited by the plaintiff on that date.

The following day, however, Citibank advised the plaintiff that the defendant had issued a stop payment order on his postdated rental check and explained that the check would not be honored. The plaintiff subsequently received a letter from the defendant's attorney stating that "[the defendant] is unable to pursue any further interest in the property." Thereafter, the plaintiff made substantial efforts to secure a new tenant for the property, listing the property with a real estate broker, advertising its availability and expending $80,000 to restage it. Although, by these efforts, the plaintiff generated several offers to lease the property, it was never able to find a qualified tenant, or, for that reason, to enter into an acceptable lease agreement with anyone for all or any part of the one year period of the defendant's January 19, 2009 lease.

Thereafter, on March 6, 2009, the plaintiff filed this action [in a Connecticut state court], alleging that the defendant had breached an enforceable lease agreement. The plaintiff further alleged that, despite its efforts to mitigate [lessen] its damages, it had sustained damages as a result of the defendant's breach, including unpaid rental payments it was to have received under the lease, brokerage commissions it incurred to rent the

property again and the cost of modifications to the property that were completed at the defendant's request.

* * * The court issued a memorandum of decision resolving the merits of the case in favor of the plaintiff (May 11 decision). In that decision, the court found, more particularly, that the plaintiff had met its burden of proving that the parties had entered into an enforceable lease agreement, that the defendant had breached that agreement, and that the breach had caused the plaintiff damages in lost rent and utility bills incurred during the lease period * * * . On the basis of these findings, the court awarded the plaintiff compensatory damages in the amount of $146,000—$138,000 in unpaid rent for the term of the lease and $8,000 in utility fees incurred by the plaintiff during the lease period—plus interest, and attorney's fees.

* * * This appeal followed.

* * * *

The defendant's * * * claim on appeal is that the court improperly determined that the parties entered into a valid lease agreement. The defendant contends that because "material terms were still being negotiated and various issues were unresolved," there was no meeting of the minds, which is required to form a contract.

* * * *

In order for an enforceable contract to exist, the court must find that the parties' minds had truly met. * * * *If there has been a misunderstanding between the parties, or a misapprehension by one or both so that their minds have never met, no contract has been entered into by them and the court will not make for them a contract which they themselves did not make.* [Emphasis added.]

There was evidence in the record to support the court's finding that the parties entered into a valid lease agree-

CASE 11.1 CONTINUED

ment because there was a true meeting of the parties' minds as to the essential terms of the agreement. Prior to the January 17 meeting, the plaintiff had provided the defendant with a draft lease agreement, which the defendant had forwarded to his attorney for review. The defendant testified that at the January 17 meeting, he and the plaintiff's representative discussed the revisions proposed by the defendant's attorney, made the revisions and signed the lease. It was then that the defendant tendered a check, postdated to the start of the lease period, on which he noted payment for a one-year lease of the premises.

There is no evidence in the record to support the defendant's conten-

tion that he did not intend to be bound by the lease when he signed it or that terms of the lease were still being negotiated at that time. Pursuant to the lease, the plaintiff was obligated to make modifications to the premises and the defendant was required to tender a security deposit [and] procure renter's insurance * * * . The defendant's apparent unilateral change of heart regarding the lease agreement does not negate the parties' prior meeting of the minds that occurred at the time the lease was executed. There is ample evidence in the record evincing [showing] the intent of the parties to be bound by the lease when they signed it and, thus, to support the court's find-

ing that "the lease agreement was a valid and binding contract which the defendant * * * has breached."

* * * *

* * * As in any other contract action the measure of damages is that the award should place the injured party in the same position as he would have been in had the contract been fully performed. * * * As a consequence, the unpaid rent * * * may be used by the court in computing the losses suffered by the plaintiff by reason of the defendant's breach of contract of lease.

* * * *

The judgment is affirmed.

LEGAL REASONING QUESTIONS

1. What is the objective theory of contracts?
2. How did the objective theory of contracts affect the result in this case? Explain.
3. The defendant never moved into the house. Why then did the court find that he breached the lease?
4. On finding that the defendant breached the lease, what did the court impose as a sanction? How was this determined?

SECTION 2
ELEMENTS OF A CONTRACT

The many topics that will be discussed in the following chapters on contract law require an understanding of the basic elements of a valid contract and the way in which a contract is created. It is also necessary to understand the types of circumstances in which even legally valid contracts will not be enforced.

Requirements of a Valid Contract

The following list briefly describes the four requirements that must be met before a valid contract exists. If any of these elements is lacking, no contract will have been formed. (Each requirement will be explained more fully in subsequent chapters.)

1. *Agreement.* An agreement to form a contract includes an *offer* and an *acceptance*. One party must offer to enter into a legal agreement, and another party must accept the terms of the offer.
2. *Consideration.* Any promises made by the parties to the contract must be supported by legally sufficient and bargained-for *consideration* (something of value received or promised, such as money, to convince a person to make a deal).
3. *Contractual capacity.* Both parties entering into the contract must have the contractual *capacity* to do so. The law must recognize them as possessing characteristics that qualify them as competent parties.
4. *Legality.* The contract's purpose must be to accomplish some goal that is legal and not against public policy.

Defenses to the Enforceability of a Contract

Even if all of the requirements listed above are satisfied, a contract may be unenforceable if the following requirements are not met. These requirements typically are raised as *defenses* to the enforceability of an otherwise valid contract.

1. *Voluntary consent.* The consent of both parties must be voluntary. For instance, if a contract was formed as a result of fraud, undue influence, mistake, or duress, the contract may not be enforceable (see Chapter 15).
2. *Form.* The contract must be in whatever form the law requires. Some contracts must be in writing to be enforceable (see Chapter 16).

SECTION 3

TYPES OF CONTRACTS

There are many types of contracts. They are categorized based on legal distinctions as to their formation, performance, and enforceability.

Contract Formation

Contracts can be classified according to how and when they are formed. Exhibit 11–1 below shows three such classifications, and the following subsections explain them in greater detail.

BILATERAL VERSUS UNILATERAL CONTRACTS Every contract involves at least two parties. The **offeror** is the party making the offer. The **offeree** is the party to whom the offer is made. Whether the contract is classified as *bilateral* or *unilateral* depends on what the offeree must do to accept the offer and bind the offeror to a contract.

Bilateral Contracts. If the offeree can accept simply by promising to perform, the contract is a **bilateral contract.** Hence, a bilateral contract is a "promise for a promise." No performance, such as payment of funds or delivery of goods, need take place for a bilateral contract to be formed. The contract comes into existence at the moment the promises are exchanged. (An example of a bilateral contract appears in the *Appendix to Chapter 19.*)

▶ **Example 11.2** Javier offers to buy Ann's smartphone for $200. Javier tells Ann that he will give her the $200 for the smartphone next Friday, when he gets paid. Ann accepts Javier's offer and promises to give him the smartphone when he pays her on Friday. Javier and Ann have formed a bilateral contract. ◀

Unilateral Contracts. If the offer is phrased so that the offeree can accept the offer only by completing the contract performance, the contract is a **unilateral contract.** Hence, a unilateral contract is a "promise for an act."[5] In other words, a unilateral contract is formed not at the moment when promises are exchanged but at the moment when the contract is *performed.* ▶ **Example 11.3** Reese says to Celia, "If you drive my car from New York to Los Angeles, I'll give you $1,000." Only on Celia's completion of the act—bringing the car to Los Angeles—does she fully accept Reese's offer to pay $1,000. If she chooses not to accept the offer to drive the car to Los Angeles, there are no legal consequences. ◀

Contests, lotteries, and other competitions involving prizes are examples of offers to form unilateral

---

5. The phrase *unilateral contract,* if read literally, is a contradiction in terms. A contract cannot be one sided because, by definition, an agreement implies the existence of two or more parties.

EXHIBIT 11–1 Classifications Based on Contract Formation

CONTRACT FORMATION		
BILATERAL A promise for a promise	**FORMAL** Requires a special form for creation	**EXPRESS** Formed by words
UNILATERAL A promise for an act	**INFORMAL** Requires no special form for creation	**IMPLIED** Formed by the conduct of the parties

contracts. If a person complies with the rules of the contest—such as by submitting the right lottery number at the right place and time—a unilateral contract is formed. The organization offering the prize is then bound to a contract to perform as promised in the offer. If the person fails to comply with the contest rules, however, no binding contract is formed. (See this chapter's *Insight into Ethics* feature below for a discussion of whether a company can change a contest prize from what it originally advertised.)

Revocation of Offers for Unilateral Contracts. A problem arises in unilateral contracts when the promisor attempts to *revoke* (cancel) the offer after the promisee has begun performance but before the act has been completed. ▶ **Example 11.4** Seiko offers to buy Jin's sailboat, moored in San Francisco, on delivery of the boat to Seiko's dock in Newport Beach, three hundred miles south of San Francisco. Jin rigs the boat and sets sail. Shortly before his arrival at Newport Beach, Jin receives a message from Seiko withdrawing her offer. Seiko's offer was for a unilateral contract, which could be accepted only by Jin's delivery of the sailboat at her dock. ◀

In contract law, offers are normally *revocable* (capable of being taken back, or canceled) until accepted. Under the traditional view of unilateral contracts, Seiko's revocation would terminate the offer. Because of the harsh effect on the offeree of the revocation of an offer to form a unilateral contract, the modern-day view is different. Today, once performance has been *substantially* undertaken, the offeror cannot revoke the offer. Thus, in *Example 11.4* above, even though Jin has not yet accepted the offer by complete performance, Seiko is normally prohibited from revoking it. Jin can deliver the boat and bind Seiko to the contract.

FORMAL VERSUS INFORMAL CONTRACTS Another classification system divides contracts into formal contracts and informal contracts. **Formal contracts** are contracts that require a special form or method of creation (formation) to be enforceable.[6] One example is *negotiable instruments,* which include checks, drafts,

---

6. See *Restatement (Second) of Contracts,* Section 6, which explains that formal contracts include (1) contracts under seal, (2) recognizances, (3) negotiable instruments, and (4) letters of credit.

INSIGHT INTO ETHICS
Can a Company That Sponsors a Contest Change the Prize from What It Originally Offered?

Courts have historically treated contests as unilateral contracts, which typically cannot be modified by the offeror after the offeree has begun to perform. But this principle may not always apply to contest terms or advertisements.

John Rogalski entered a poker tournament conducted by Little Poker League, LLC (LPL).The tournament lasted several months as players competed for spots in a winner-take-all final event. During the final event, Rogalski and the other contestants signed a "World Series of Poker (WSOP) Agreement," which stated that LPL would pay the $10,000 WSOP entry fee on the winner's behalf and provide $2,500 for travel-related expenses. The agreement also stated that if the winner did not attend the WSOP, he or she would relinquish the WSOP seat and return the expense money to LPL.

Rogalski won and took the $2,500 for travel expenses, but did not attend the WSOP. He then filed a suit for $10,000 against LPL, arguing that it had advertised that the winner could choose to receive the cash value of the prizes ($12,500) instead of going to the WSOP. Rogalski claimed that, by participating in the tournament, he had accepted the advertised offer to take the cash in lieu of entering the WSOP. He further claimed that the later agreement was an invalid contract modification. LPL filed a counterclaim to recover the $2,500 in expenses. The court ruled in favor of LPL, finding that the contract was not formed when Rogalski began participating in the contest. Rather, it was formed when he signed the WSOP agreement. Under the contest rules as stated in the WSOP agreement, Rogalski had to return the $2,500 of expenses to LPL.[a]

LEGAL CRITICAL THINKING
INSIGHT INTO THE SOCIAL ENVIRONMENT
Why would a company that changes its advertised prizes have to worry about its reputation?

---

a. *Rogalski v. Little Poker League, LLC,* 2011 WL 589636 (Minn.App. 2011).

promissory notes, bills of exchange, and certificates of deposit. Negotiable instruments are formal contracts because, under the Uniform Commercial Code (UCC), a special form and language are required to create them.

Letters of credit, which are frequently used in international sales contracts (see Chapter 24), are another type of formal contract. Letters of credit are agreements to pay contingent on the purchaser's receipt of invoices and *bills of lading* (documents evidencing receipt of, and title to, goods shipped).

Informal contracts (also called *simple contracts*) include all other contracts. No special form is required (except for certain types of contracts that must be in writing), as the contracts are usually based on their substance rather than their form. Typically, businesspersons put their contracts in writing to ensure that there is some proof of a contract's existence should disputes arise.

EXPRESS VERSUS IMPLIED CONTRACTS Contracts may also be categorized as *express* or *implied*. In an **express contract,** the terms of the agreement are fully and explicitly stated in words, oral or written. A signed lease for an apartment or a house is an express written contract. If one classmate calls another on the phone and agrees to buy her textbooks from last semester for $300, an express oral contract has been made.

A contract that is implied from the conduct of the parties is called an **implied contract** (or sometimes an *implied-in-fact contract*). This type of contract differs from an express contract in that the conduct of the parties, rather than their words, creates and defines the terms of the contract.

Requirements for Implied Contracts. For an implied contract to arise, certain requirements must be met. Normally, if the following conditions exist, a court will hold that an implied contract was formed:

1. The plaintiff furnished some service or property.
2. The plaintiff expected to be paid for that service or property, and the defendant knew or should have known that payment was expected.
3. The defendant had a chance to reject the services or property and did not.

▶ **Example 11.5** Oleg, a small-business owner, needs an accountant to complete his tax return. He drops by a local accountant's office, explains his situation to the accountant, and learns what fees she charges. The next day, he returns and gives the receptionist all of the necessary documents to com-

plete his return. Then he walks out without saying anything further to the accountant. In this situation, Oleg has entered into an implied contract to pay the accountant the usual fees for her services. The contract is implied because of Oleg's conduct and hers. She expects to be paid for completing the tax return, and by bringing in the records she will need to do the job, Oleg has implied an intent to pay her. ◀

Contracts with Express and Implied Terms. Note that a contract may be a mixture of an express contract and an implied contract. In other words, a contract may contain some express terms, while others are implied. During the constructions of a home, for instance, the homeowner often asks the builder to make changes in the original specifications.

▶ **Case in Point 11.6** Lamar Hopkins hired Uhrhahn Construction & Design, Inc., for several projects in building his home. For each project, the parties signed a written contract that was based on a cost estimate and specifications and that required changes to the agreement to be in writing. While the work was in progress, however, Hopkins repeatedly asked Uhrhahn to deviate from the contract specifications, which Uhrhahn did. None of these requests was made in writing.

One day, Hopkins asked Uhrhahn to use Durisol blocks instead of the cinder blocks specified in the original contract, indicating that the cost would be the same. Uhrhahn used the Durisol blocks but demanded extra payment when it became clear that the Durisol blocks were more complicated to install. Although Hopkins had paid for the other deviations from the contract that he had orally requested, he refused to pay Uhrhahn for the substitution of the Durisol blocks. Uhrhahn sued for breach of contract. The court found that Hopkins, through his conduct, had waived the provision requiring written contract modification and created an implied contract to pay the extra cost of installing the Durisol blocks.[7] ◀

Contract Performance

Contracts are also classified according to the degree to which they have been performed. A contract that has been fully performed on both sides is called an **executed contract.** A contract that has not been fully performed by the parties is called an **executory contract.** If one party has fully performed but the

---

7. *Uhrhahn Construction & Design, Inc. v. Hopkins,* 179 P.3d 808 (Utah App. 2008).

other has not, the contract is said to be executed on the one side and executory on the other, but the contract is still classified as executory.

▶ **Example 11.7** Jackson, Inc., agreed to buy ten tons of coal from the Northern Coal Company. Northern delivered the coal to Jackson's steel mill, where it is being burned. At this point, the contract is executed on the part of Northern and executory on Jackson's part. After Jackson pays Northern, the contract will be executed on both sides. ◀

Contract Enforceability

A **valid contract** has the elements necessary to entitle at least one of the parties to enforce it in court. Those elements, as mentioned earlier, consist of (1) an agreement (offer and acceptance) (2) supported by legally sufficient consideration (3) made by parties who have the legal capacity to enter into the contract, and (4) a legal purpose.

As you can see in Exhibit 11–2 below, valid contracts may be enforceable, voidable, or unenforceable. Additionally, a contract may be referred to as a *void contract*. We look next at the meaning of the terms *voidable, unenforceable,* and *void* in relation to contract enforceability.

VOIDABLE CONTRACTS A **voidable contract** is a valid contract but one that can be avoided at the option of one or both of the parties. The party having the option can elect either to avoid any duty to perform or to *ratify* (make valid) the contract. If the

contract is avoided, both parties are released from it. If it is ratified, both parties must fully perform their respective legal obligations.

As you will read in Chapter 14, contracts made by minors generally are voidable at the option of the minor (with certain exceptions). Contracts made by mentally incompetent persons and intoxicated persons may also be voidable. Additionally, contracts entered into under fraudulent conditions are voidable at the option of the defrauded party. Contracts entered into under legally defined duress or undue influence are also voidable (see Chapter 15).

UNENFORCEABLE CONTRACTS An **unenforceable contract** is one that cannot be enforced because of certain legal defenses against it. It is not unenforceable because a party failed to satisfy a legal requirement of the contract. Rather, it is a valid contract rendered unenforceable by some statute or law. For instance, certain contracts must be in writing (see Chapter 16), and if they are not, they will not be enforceable except in certain exceptional circumstances.

VOID CONTRACTS A **void contract** is no contract at all. The terms *void* and *contract* are contradictory. None of the parties have any legal obligations if a contract is void. A contract can be void because one of the parties was determined by a court to mentally incompetent, for instance, or because the purpose of the contract was illegal (see Chapter 14).

To review the various types of contracts, see *Concept Summary 11.1* on the following page.

EXHIBIT 11–2 Enforceable, Voidable, Unenforceable, and Void Contracts

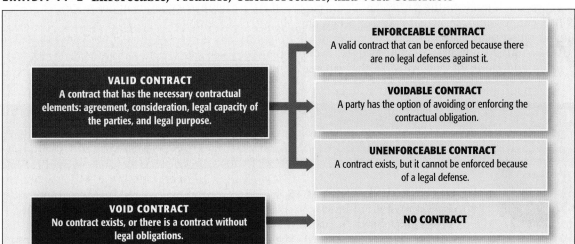

CONCEPT SUMMARY 11.1
Types of Contracts

ASPECT	DEFINITION
Formation	1. *Bilateral*—A promise for a promise. 2. *Unilateral*—A promise for an act (acceptance is the completed performance of the act). 3. *Formal*—Requires a special form for creation. 4. *Informal*—Requires no special form for creation. 5. *Express*—Formed by words (oral, written, or a combination). 6. *Implied*—Formed by the conduct of the parties.
Performance	1. *Executed*—A fully performed contract. 2. *Executory*—A contract not fully performed.
Enforceability	1. *Valid*—The contract has the necessary contractual elements: agreement (offer and acceptance), consideration, legal capacity of the parties, and legal purpose. 2. *Voidable*—One party has the option of avoiding or enforcing the contractual obligation. 3. *Unenforceable*—A contract exists, but it cannot be enforced because of a legal defense. 4. *Void*—No contract exists, or there is a contract without legal obligations.

SECTION 4
QUASI CONTRACTS

Quasi contracts, or contracts *implied in law,* are not actual contracts. Express contracts and implied contracts are actual or true contracts formed by the words or actions of the parties. The word *quasi* is Latin for "as if" or "analogous to." Quasi contracts are not true contracts because they do not arise from any agreement, express or implied, between the parties themselves. Rather, quasi contracts are fictional contracts that courts can impose on the parties "as if" the parties had entered into an actual contract. They are equitable rather than legal contracts.

Usually, quasi contracts are imposed to avoid the *unjust enrichment* of one party at the expense of another. The doctrine of unjust enrichment is based on the theory that individuals should not be allowed to profit or enrich themselves inequitably at the expense of others. When the court imposes a quasi contract, a plaintiff may recover in ***quantum meruit,***[8] a Latin phrase meaning "as much as he or she deserves." *Quantum meruit* essentially describes the extent of compensation owed under a contract implied in law.

In the following case, the parties did not have an express contract, but one party enjoyed the benefits of the other party's services. The court had to decide if the parties had a quasi contract.

---

8. Pronounced *kwahn*-tuhm *mehr*-oo-wit.

CASE 11.2

Seawest Services Association v. Copenhaver
Court of Appeals of Washington, 166 Wash.App. 1006 (2012).

BACKGROUND AND FACTS Seawest Services Association owned and operated a water distribution system that served homes both inside and outside a housing development. Seawest had two classes of members. "Full members" owned property in the housing development, and "limited members" received water services for homes outside the development. Both full and limited members paid water bills and, as necessary, assessments for work performed on the water system. In 2001, the

CASE 11.2 CONTINUED

Copenhavers purchased a home outside the housing development. They did not have an express contract with Seawest, but they paid water bills for eight years and paid one $3,950 assessment for water system upgrades. In 2009, a dispute arose between the parties, and the Copenhavers began refusing to pay their water bills and assessments. Seawest sued the Copenhavers in a Washington state court. The trial court found that the Copenhavers were limited members of Seawest and thus were liable for the unpaid water bills and assessments. The Copenhavers appealed.

 IN THE LANGUAGE OF THE COURT
LAU, J. [Judge]

* * * *

* * * *The essential elements of unjust enrichment are " 'a benefit conferred upon the defendant by the plaintiff; an appreciation or knowledge by the defendant of the benefit; and the acceptance or retention by the defendant under such circumstances as to make it inequitable for the defendant to retain the benefit without the payment of its value.' "* [Emphasis added.]

Undisputed evidence * * * shows that the Copenhavers * * * have utilized the Seawest system and have paid, without objection until litigation ensued, all water use, water maintenance, and assessment base charges to Seawest.

* * * *

* * * The Copenhavers would be unjustly enriched if they could retain benefits provided by Seawest without paying for them. The Copenhavers obtained property that carried with it a water share. They knew that no property owner is entitled to receive water without membership in Seawest.

We conclude that the undisputed record supports a contract implied in law.

DECISION AND REMEDY *The Washington appellate court affirmed the trial court's judgment. It held that the Copenhavers were liable to Seawest because the parties had a quasi contract.*

THE ETHICAL DIMENSION *In recognizing quasi contracts, does the law try to correct for unethical behavior? Why or why not?*

THE ECONOMIC DIMENSION *Could the Copenhavers have successfully argued that by forcing them to pay a price to which they had not agreed, Seawest was unjustly enriched at their expense?*

Limitations on Quasi-Contractual Recovery

Although quasi contracts exist to prevent unjust enrichment, the party obtaining the enrichment is not held liable in some situations. In general, a party who has conferred a benefit on someone else unnecessarily or as a result of misconduct or negligence cannot invoke the principle of quasi contract. The enrichment in those situations will not be considered "unjust."

▶ **Case in Point 11.8** Qwest Wireless, LLC, provides wireless phone services in Arizona and thirteen other states. Qwest marketed and sold handset insurance to its customers, although it did not have a license to sell insurance in Arizona or in any other state. Patrick and Vicki Van Zanen sued Qwest for unjust enrichment based on its receipt of sales commissions for the handset insurance. The court agreed

that Qwest had violated the insurance-licensing statute. Nevertheless, the court found that the commissions did not constitute unjust enrichment because the customers had, in fact, received the insurance. Qwest had not retained a benefit (the commissions) without paying for it (providing insurance).[9] ◀

When an Actual Contract Exists

The doctrine of quasi contract generally cannot be used when there is an *actual contract* that covers the matter in controversy. A remedy already exists if a party is unjustly enriched as a result of a breach of contract: the nonbreaching party can sue the breaching party for breach of contract.

▶ **Example 11.9** Fung contracts with Cameron to deliver a furnace to a building owned by Grant. Fung

---

9. *Van Zanen v. Qwest Wireless, LLC,* 522 F.3d 1127 (10th Cir. 2008).

delivers the furnace, but Cameron never pays Fung. Grant has been unjustly enriched in this situation, to be sure. Fung, however, cannot recover from Grant in quasi contract because Fung had an actual contract with Cameron. Fung already has a remedy—he can sue for breach of contract to recover the price of the furnace from Cameron. The court does not need to impose a quasi contract in this situation to achieve justice. ◄

SECTION 5
INTERPRETATION OF CONTRACTS

Sometimes, parties agree that a contract has been formed but disagree on its meaning or legal effect. One reason this may happen is that one of the parties is not familiar with the legal terminology used in the contract. To an extent, *plain language* laws (enacted by the federal government and a majority of the states) have helped to avoid this difficulty. Sometimes, though, a dispute may arise over the meaning of a contract simply because the rights or obligations under the contract are not expressed clearly—no matter how "plain" the language used.

In this section, we look at some common law rules of contract interpretation. These rules, which have evolved over time, provide the courts with guidelines for deciding disputes over how contract terms or provisions should be interpreted. Exhibit 11–3 below provides a brief graphic summary of how these rules are applied.

The Plain Meaning Rule

When a contract's writing is clear and unequivocal, a court will enforce it according to its obvious terms. The meaning of the terms must be determined from the *face of the instrument*—from the written document alone. This is sometimes referred to as the *plain meaning rule*.

The words—and their plain, ordinary meaning—determine the intent of the parties at the time that they entered into the contract. A court is bound to give effect to the contract according to this intent. The importance of each word or phrase in a contract is discussed further in the *Appendix to Chapter 19: Reading and Analyzing Contracts*.

AMBIGUITY A court will consider a contract to be ambiguous (unclear) in the following situations:

1. When the intent of the parties cannot be determined from the contract's language.
2. When the contract lacks a provision on a disputed term.
3. When a term is susceptible to more than one interpretation.
4. When there is uncertainty about a provision.

EXTRINSIC EVIDENCE If a contract term is ambiguous, a court can consider *extrinsic evidence* (evidence outside the contract), or it may interpret the ambiguity against the party who drafted the term. **Extrinsic evidence** is any evidence not contained in the document itself—such as the testimony of parties and witnesses, additional agreements or communications, or other relevant information.

EXHIBIT 11-3 **Rules of Contract Interpretation**

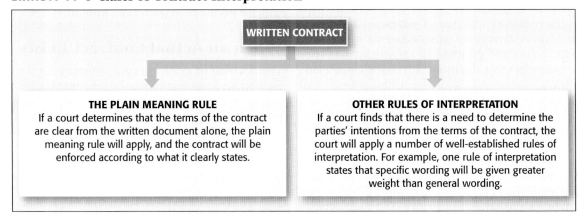

WRITTEN CONTRACT

THE PLAIN MEANING RULE
If a court determines that the terms of the contract are clear from the written document alone, the plain meaning rule will apply, and the contract will be enforced according to what it clearly states.

OTHER RULES OF INTERPRETATION
If a court finds that there is a need to determine the parties' intentions from the terms of the contract, the court will apply a number of well-established rules of interpretation. For example, one rule of interpretation states that specific wording will be given greater weight than general wording.

The admissibility of extrinsic evidence can significantly affect the court's interpretation of ambiguous contractual provisions and thus the outcome of litigation. When a contract is clear and unambiguous, a court cannot consider extrinsic evidence. The following case illustrates these points.

SP TLIGHT on Columbia Pictures

Case 11.3   Wagner v. Columbia Pictures Industries, Inc.
California Court of Appeal, Second District, 146 Cal.App.4th 586, 52 Cal.Rptr.3d 898 (2007).

BACKGROUND AND FACTS Actor Robert Wagner entered into an agreement with Spelling-Goldberg Productions (SGP) "relating to *Charlie's Angels* (herein called the 'series')." The contract entitled Wagner to 50 percent of the net profits that SGP received from broadcasting the series and from all ancillary, music, and subsidiary rights in connection with the series. SGP hired Ivan Goff and Ben Roberts to write the series, under a contract subject to the Writers Guild of America Minimum Basic Agreement (MBA).[a] The MBA stipulates that the writer of a television show retains the right to make and market films based on the material, subject to the producer's right to buy this right if the writer decides to sell it within five years.

The first *Charlie's Angels* episode aired in 1976. In 1982, SGP sold its rights to the series to Columbia Pictures Industries, Inc. Thirteen years later, Columbia bought the movie rights to the material from Goff's and Roberts's heirs. In 2000 and 2003, Columbia produced and distributed two *Charlie's Angels* films. Wagner filed a suit in a California state court against Columbia, claiming a share of the profits from the films. The court granted Columbia's motion for summary judgment. Wagner appealed to a state intermediate appellate court.

IN THE LANGUAGE OF THE COURT
JOHNSON, Acting P.J. [Presiding Judge]

* * * *

Wagner contends the "subsidiary rights" provision in the agreement with SGP entitles him * * * to 50 percent of the net profits from the two "Charlie's Angels" films.

* * * *

Wagner introduced evidence of the history of the negotiations underlying the "Charlie's Angels" contract in support of his [contention].

This history begins with a contract the Wagners [Wagner and his wife, Natalie Wood] entered into with SGP to star in a television movie-of-the-week, "Love Song." As compensation for Wagner and Wood acting in "Love Song," SGP agreed to pay them a fixed amount plus one-half the net profits * * * .

* * * *

In the * * * "Love Song" contract net profits were not limited to monies received "for the right to exhibit the Photoplay." Instead they were defined as the net of "all monies received by Producer as consideration for the right to exhibit the Photoplay, and exploitation of all ancillary, music and subsidiary rights in connection therewith."

* * * *

Wagner's argument is simple and straightforward. The net profits provision in the "Love Song" agreement was intended to give the Wagners a one-half share in the net profits received by SGP "from all sources" without limitation as to source or time. The "Charlie's Angels" agreement was based on the "Love Song" agreement and defines net profits in identical language. Therefore, the "Charlie's Angels" agreement should also be interpreted as providing the Wagners with a 50 percent share in SGP's income "from all sources" without limitation

---

a. The Writers Guild of America is an association of screen and television writers that negotiates industry-wide agreements with motion picture and television producers.

CASE 11.3 CONTINUES ▶

as to source or time. Since Columbia admits it stands in SGP's shoes with respect to SGP's obligations under the "Charlie's Angels" agreement, Columbia is obligated to pay Wagner * * * 50 percent of the net profits derived from the "Charlie's Angels" movies.
* * * *

The problem with Wagner's extrinsic evidence is that it does not explain the ["Charlie's Angels"] contract language, it contradicts it. *Under the parol evidence rule,[b] extrinsic evidence is not admissible to contradict express terms in a written contract or to explain what the agreement was. The agreement is the writing itself. Parol evidence cannot be admitted to show intention independent of an unambiguous written instrument.* [Emphasis added.]

Even if the Wagners and SGP intended the Wagners would share in the net profits "from any and all sources" they did not say so in their contract. What they said in their contract was the Wagners would share in "all monies actually received by Producer, as consideration for the right to exhibit photoplays of the series, and from the exploitation of all ancillary, music and subsidiary rights in connection therewith." For a right to be "subsidiary" or "ancillary," meaning supplementary or subordinate, there must be a primary right to which it relates. The only primary right mentioned in the contract is "the right to exhibit photoplays of the series." Thus the Wagners were entitled to share in the profits from the exploitation of the movie rights to "Charlie's Angels" if those rights were exploited by Columbia as ancillary or subsidiary rights of its primary "right to exhibit photoplays of the series" but not if those rights were acquired by Columbia independently from its right to exhibit photoplays.

DECISION AND REMEDY   *The state intermediate appellate court affirmed the lower court's summary judgment in favor of Columbia. The contract "unambiguously" stated the conditions under which the parties were to share the films' profits, and those conditions had not occurred.*

WHAT IF THE FACTS WERE DIFFERENT?   *How might the result in this case have been different if the court had admitted Wagner's evidence of the "Love Song" contract?*

THE LEGAL ENVIRONMENT DIMENSION   *Under what circumstances would Wagner have been entitled to a share of the profits from the* Charlie's Angels *movies even though the evidence of the* Love Song *contract was irrelevant?*

---

b. The *parol evidence rule* prohibits the parties from introducing in court evidence of an oral agreement that contradicts the written terms of a contract (see Chapter 16).

Other Rules of Interpretation

Generally, a court will interpret the language to give effect to the parties' intent as *expressed in their contract*. This is the primary purpose of the rules of interpretation—to determine the parties' intent from the language used in their agreement and to give effect to that intent. A court normally will not make or remake a contract, nor will it interpret the language according to what the parties *claim* their intent was when they made it.

RULES THE COURTS USE   The courts use the following rules in interpreting contractual terms:

1. As far as possible, a reasonable, lawful, and effective meaning will be given to all of a contract's terms.

2. A contract will be interpreted as a whole. Individual, specific clauses will be considered subordinate to the contract's general intent. All writings that are a part of the same transaction will be interpreted together.

3. Terms that were the subject of separate negotiation will be given greater consideration than standardized terms and terms that were not negotiated separately.

4. A word will be given its ordinary, commonly accepted meaning, and a technical word or term will be given its technical meaning, unless the parties clearly intended something else.

5. Specific and exact wording will be given greater consideration than general language.

6. Written or typewritten terms will prevail over preprinted ones.

7. Because a contract should be drafted in clear and unambiguous language, a party who uses ambiguous expressions is held to be responsible for the ambiguities. Thus, when the language has more than one meaning, it will be interpreted against the party who drafted the contract.

8. Evidence of *usage of trade, course of dealing,* and *course of performance* may be admitted to clarify the meaning of an ambiguously worded contract. (These terms will be defined and discussed in more detail in Chapter 20.)

EXPRESS TERMS USUALLY GIVEN THE MOST WEIGHT Express terms (terms expressly stated in the contract) are given the greatest weight, followed by course of performance, course of dealing, and custom and usage of trade—in that order. When considering custom and usage, a court will look at the trade customs and usage common to the particular business or industry and to the locale in which the contract was made or is to be performed.

▶ **Case in Point 11.10** Jessica Robbins bought a house in Tennessee. U.S. Bank financed the purchase, and Tennessee Farmers Mutual Insurance Company issued the homeowner's insurance policy. The policy included a clause that promised payment to the bank unless the house was lost due to an "increase in hazard" that the bank knew about but did not tell the insurer. When Robbins fell behind on her mortgage payments, the bank started foreclosure proceedings. No one told the insurer. Robbins filed for bankruptcy, which postponed foreclosure.

Meanwhile, the house was destroyed in a fire. The bank filed a claim under the policy, but the insurer refused to pay because it had not been told by the bank of an "increase in hazard"—the foreclosure. The bank then filed a lawsuit. The court found that the plain meaning of the words "increase in hazard" in the policy referred to physical conditions on the property that posed a risk, not to events such as foreclosure. Thus, the bank was not required to notify the insurer under the terms of the policy, and the lack of notice did not invalidate the coverage.[10] ◀

---

10. *U.S. Bank, N.A. v. Tennessee Farmers Mutual Insurance Co.*, 277 S.W.3d 381 (Tenn.Sup.Ct. 2009).

Reviewing: Nature and Terminology

Mitsui Bank hired Ross Duncan as a branch manager in one of its Southern California locations. At that time, Duncan received an employee handbook informing him that Mitsui would review his performance and salary level annually. In 2012, Mitsui decided to create a new lending program to help financially troubled businesses stay afloat. It hired Duncan to be the credit development officer (CDO) and gave him a written compensation plan. Duncan's compensation was to be based on the program's success and involved a bonus and commissions based on the volume of new loans and sales. The written plan also stated, "This compensation plan will be reviewed and potentially amended after one year and will be subject to such review and amendment annually thereafter."

Duncan's efforts as CDO were successful, and the business-lending program he developed grew to represent 25 percent of Mitsui's business in 2013 and 40 percent in 2014. Nevertheless, Mitsui refused to give Duncan a raise in 2013. Mitsui also amended his compensation plan to significantly reduce his compensation and to change his performance evaluation schedule to every six months. When he had still not received a raise by 2014, Duncan resigned as CDO and filed a lawsuit alleging breach of contract. Using the information presented in the chapter, answer the following questions.

1. What are the four requirements of a valid contract?
2. Did Duncan have a valid contract with Mitsui for employment as CDO? If so, was it a bilateral or a unilateral contract?
3. What are the requirements of an implied contract?
4. Can Duncan establish an implied contract based on the employment manual or the written compensation plan? Why or why not?

DEBATE THIS ... *Companies should be able to make or break employment contracts whenever and however they wish.*

Terms and Concepts

bilateral contract 228	informal contract 230	quasi contract 232
contract 225	objective theory of contracts 225	unenforceable contract 231
executed contract 230	offeree 228	unilateral contract 228
executory contract 230	offeror 228	valid contract 231
express contract 230	promise 224	void contract 231
extrinsic evidence 235	promisee 225	voidable contract 231
formal contract 229	promisor 225	
implied contract 230	*quantum meruit* 232	

ExamPrep

Issue Spotters

1. Joli receives a letter from Kerin saying that he has a book at a certain price. Joli signs and returns the letter to Kerin. When Kerin delivers the book, Joli sends it back, claiming that they do not have a contract. Kerin claims they do. What standard determines whether these parties have a contract? **(See page 225.)**

2. Dyna tells Ed that she will pay him $1,000 to set fire to her store so that she can collect under a fire insurance policy. Ed sets fire to the store, but Dyna refuses to pay. Can Ed recover? Why or why not? **(See page 231.)**

• Check your answers to the Issue Spotters against the answers provided in Appendix E at the end of this text.

Before the Test

Go to **www.cengagebrain.com**, enter the ISBN 9781285185248, and click on "Find" to locate this textbook's Web site. Then, click on "Access Now" under "Study Tools," and select Chapter 11 at the top. There, you will find a Practice Quiz that you can take to assess your mastery of the concepts in this chapter, as well as Flashcards and a Glossary of important terms.

Business Scenarios

11–1. Unilateral Contract. Rocky Mountain Races, Inc., sponsors the "Pioneer Trail Ultramarathon" with an advertised first prize of $10,000. The rules require the competitors to run 100 miles from the floor of Blackwater Canyon to the top of Pinnacle Mountain. The rules also provide that Rocky reserves the right to change the terms of the race at any time. Monica enters the race and is declared the winner. Rocky offers her a prize of $1,000 instead of $10,000. Did Rocky and Monica have a contract? Explain. **(See page 228.)**

11–2. Implied Contract. Janine was hospitalized with severe abdominal pain and placed in an intensive care unit. Her doctor told the hospital personnel to order around-the-clock nursing care for Janine. At the hospital's request, a nursing services firm, Nursing Services Unlimited, provided two weeks of in-hospital care and, after Janine was sent home, an additional two weeks of at-home care. During the at-home period of care, Janine was fully aware that she was receiving the benefit of the nursing services. Nursing Services later billed Janine $4,000 for the nursing care, but Janine refused to pay on the ground that she had never contracted for the services, either orally or in writing. In view of the fact that no express contract was ever formed, can Nursing Services recover the $4,000 from Janine? If so, under what legal theory? Discuss. **(See page 230.)**

11–3. Contract Classification. For employment with the Firestorm Smokejumpers—a crew of elite paratroopers who parachute into dangerous situations to fight fires—applicants must complete a series of tests. The crew chief sends the most qualified applicants a letter stating that they will be admitted to Firestorm's training sessions if they pass a medical exam. Jake Kurzyniec receives the letter and passes the exam, but a new crew chief changes the selection process and rejects him. Is there a contract between Kurzyniec and Firestorm? If there is a contract, what type of contract is it? **(See page 228.)**

Business Case Problems

11–4. Spotlight on Taco Bell—Implied Contract. Thomas Rinks and Joseph Shields developed Psycho Chihuahua, a caricature of a Chihuahua dog with a "do-not-back-down" attitude. They promoted and marketed the character through their company, Wrench, L.L.C. Ed Alfaro and Rudy Pollak, representatives of Taco Bell Corp., learned of Psycho Chihuahua and met with Rinks and Shields to talk about using the character as a Taco Bell "icon." Wrench sent artwork, merchandise, and marketing ideas to Alfaro, who promoted the character within Taco Bell. Alfaro asked Wrench to propose terms for Taco Bell's use of Psycho Chihuahua. Taco Bell did not accept Wrench's terms, but Alfaro continued to promote the character within the company. Meanwhile, Taco Bell hired a new advertising agency, which proposed an advertising campaign involving a Chihuahua. When Alfaro learned of this proposal, he sent the Psycho Chihuahua materials to the agency. Taco Bell made a Chihuahua the focus of its marketing but paid nothing to Wrench. Wrench filed a suit against Taco Bell in a federal court claiming that it had an implied contract with Taco Bell and that Taco Bell breached that contract. Do these facts satisfy the requirements for an implied contract? Why or why not? [*Wrench, L.L.C. v. Taco Bell Corp.*, 256 F.3d 446 (6th Cir. 2001), cert. denied, 534 U.S. 1114, 122 S.Ct. 921, 151 L.Ed.2d 805 (2002)] **(See page 230.)**

11–5. Quasi Contract. Kim Panenka asked to borrow $4,750 from her sister, Kris, to make a mortgage payment. Kris deposited a check for that amount into Kim's bank account. Hours later, Kim asked to borrow another $1,100. Kris took a cash advance on her credit card and deposited this amount into Kim's account. When Kim did not repay the amounts, Kris filed a suit, arguing that she had "loaned" Kim the money. Can the court impose a contract between the sisters? Explain. [*Panenka v. Panenka*, 331 Wis.2d 731, 795 N.W.2d 493 (2011)] **(See page 232.)**

11–6. Interpretation of Contracts. Lisa and Darrell Miller had a son, Landon. When the Millers divorced, they entered into a "Joint Plan" (JP). Under the JP, Darrell agreed to "begin setting funds aside for Landon to attend college." After Landon's eighteenth birthday, Lisa asked a court to order Darrell to pay the boy's college expenses based on the JP. Darrell contended that the JP was not clear on this point. Do the rules of contract interpretation support Lisa's request or Darrell's contention? Explain. [*Miller v. Miller*, 1 So.3d 815 (La.App. 2009)] **(See page 234.)**

11–7. BUSINESS CASE PROBLEM
WITH SAMPLE ANSWER: Quasi Contract.

 Robert Gutkowski, a sports marketing expert, met numerous times with George Steinbrenner, the owner of the New York Yankees, to discuss the Yankees Entertainment and Sports Network (YES). Gutkowski was paid as a consultant. Later, he filed a suit, seeking an ownership share in YES. There was no written contract for the share, but he claimed that there were discussions about his being a part owner. Does Gutkowski have a valid claim for

payment? Discuss. [Gutkowski v. Steinbrenner, *680 F. Supp.2d 602 (S.D.N.Y. 2010)]* **(See page 232.)**

- **For a sample answer to Problem 11–7, go to Appendix F at the end of this text.**

11–8. Implied Contracts. Ralph Ramsey insured his car with Allstate Insurance Co. He also owned a house on which he maintained a homeowner's insurance policy with Allstate. Bank of America had a mortgage on the house and paid the insurance premiums on the homeowner's policy from Ralph's account. After Ralph died, Allstate canceled the car insurance. Ralph's son Douglas inherited the house. The bank continued to pay the premiums on the homeowner's policy, but from Douglas's account, and Allstate continued to renew the insurance. When a fire destroyed the house, Allstate denied coverage, however, claiming that the policy was still in Ralph's name. Douglas filed a suit in a federal district court against the insurer. Was Allstate liable under the homeowner's policy? Explain. [*Ramsey v. Allstate Insurance Co.*, 2013 WL 467327 (6th Cir. 2013)] **(See page 230.)**

11–9. A QUESTION OF ETHICS: Unilateral Contracts.

 International Business Machines Corp. (IBM) hired Niels Jensen in 2000 as a software sales representative. According to the brochure on IBM's "Sales Incentive Plan" (SIP), "the more you sell, the more earnings for you." But "the SIP program does not constitute a promise by IBM. IBM reserves the right to modify the program at any time." Jensen was given a "quota letter" that said he would be paid $75,000 as a base salary and, if he attained his quota, an additional $75,000 as incentive pay. Jensen closed a deal worth more than $24 million to IBM. When IBM paid him less than $500,000 as a commission, Jensen filed a suit. He argued that the SIP was a unilateral offer that became a binding contract when he closed the sale. [Jensen v. International Business Machines Corp., *454 F.3d 382 (4th Cir. 2006)]* **(See page 228.)**

(a) Would it be fair to the employer for the court to hold that the SIP brochure and the quota letter created a unilateral contract if IBM did not *intend* to create such a contract? Would it be fair to the employee to hold that *no* contract was created? Explain.

(b) The "Sales Incentives" section of IBM's brochure included a clause providing that "management will decide if an adjustment to the payment is appropriate" when an employee closes a large transaction. Does this affect your answers to the above questions? From an ethical perspective, would it be fair to hold that a contract exists despite these statements? Why or why not?

Legal Reasoning Group Activity

11–10. Contracts. Review the basic requirements for a valid contract listed at the beginning of this chapter. Now consider the relationship created when a student enrolls in a college or university. **(See page 227.)**

(a) One group should analyze and discuss whether a contract has been formed between the student and the college or university.

(b) A second group should assume that there is a contract and explain whether it is bilateral or unilateral.

CHAPTER 12

AGREEMENT IN TRADITIONAL AND E-CONTRACTS

Contract law developed over time to meet society's need to know with certainty what kinds of promises, or contracts, will be enforced and the point at which a valid and binding contract is formed. For a contract to be considered valid and enforceable, the requirements listed in Chapter 11 must be met. In this chapter, we look closely at the first of these requirements, *agreement.*

Agreement is required to form a contract, whether it is formed in the traditional way (on paper) or online. In today's world, many contracts are formed via the Internet—even from smartphones, tablets, and other mobile devices. We discuss online offers and acceptances and examine some laws that have been created to apply to electronic contracts, or *e-contracts,* in the latter part of this chapter.

AGREEMENT

An essential element for contract formation is **agreement**—the parties must agree on the terms of the contract and manifest to each other their *mutual assent* (agreement) to the same bargain. Ordinarily, agreement is evidenced by two events: an *offer* and an *acceptance.* One party offers a certain bargain to another party, who then accepts that bargain.

The agreement does not necessarily have to be in writing. Both parties, however, must manifest their assent, or voluntary consent, to the same bargain. Once an agreement is reached, if the other elements of a contract (consideration, capacity, and legality—discussed in subsequent chapters) are present, a valid contract is formed. Generally, the contract creates enforceable rights and duties between the parties.

Because words often fail to convey the precise meaning intended, the law of contracts generally adheres to the *objective theory of contracts,* as discussed in Chapter 11. Under this theory, a party's words and conduct are held to mean whatever a reasonable person in the offeree's position would think they meant.

Requirements of the Offer

An **offer** is a promise or commitment to do or refrain from doing some specified action in the future. As mentioned in Chapter 11, the parties to a contract are the *offeror,* the one who makes an offer or proposal to another party, and the *offeree,* the one to whom the offer or proposal is made. Under the common law, three elements are necessary for an offer to be effective:

1. The offeror must have a serious intention to become bound by the offer.
2. The terms of the offer must be reasonably certain, or definite, so that the parties and the court can ascertain the terms of the contract.
3. The offer must be communicated to the offeree.

Once an effective offer has been made, the offeree's acceptance of that offer creates a legally binding contract (providing the other essential elements for a valid and enforceable contract are present).

INTENTION The first requirement for an effective offer is a serious intent on the part of the offeror. Serious intent is not determined by the subjective intentions, beliefs, and assumptions of the offeror. Rather, it is determined by what a reasonable person in the offeree's position would conclude that the offeror's words and actions meant. Offers made in obvious anger, jest, or undue excitement do not meet the serious-and-objective-intent test because a reasonable person would realize that a serious offer was not being made. Because these offers are not effective, an offeree's acceptance does not create an agreement.

▶ **Example 12.1**   Linda and Dena ride to school each day in Dena's new automobile, which has a market value of $20,000. One cold morning, they get into the car, but the car will not start. Dena yells in anger, "I'll sell this car to anyone for $500!" Linda drops $500 on Dena's lap. A reasonable person—taking into consideration Dena's frustration and the obvious difference in value between the market price of the car and the proposed purchase price—would realize that Dena's offer was not made with serious and objective intent. No agreement is formed. ◀

In the classic case presented next, the court considered whether an offer made "after a few drinks" met the serious-and-objective-intent requirement.

CLASSIC CASE 12.1

Lucy v. Zehmer
Supreme Court of Appeals of Virginia, 196 Va. 493, 84 S.E.2d 516 (1954).

BACKGROUND AND FACTS   W. O. Lucy, the plaintiff, filed a suit against A. H. and Ida Zehmer, the defendants, to compel the Zehmers to transfer title of their property, known as the Ferguson Farm, to the Lucys (W. O. and his wife) for $50,000, as the Zehmers had allegedly agreed to do. Lucy had known A. H. Zehmer for fifteen or twenty years and for the last eight years or so had been anxious to buy the Ferguson Farm from him. One night, Lucy stopped to visit the Zehmers in the combination restaurant, filling station, and motor court they operated. While there, Lucy tried to buy the Ferguson Farm once again. This time he tried a new approach. According to the trial court transcript, Lucy said to Zehmer, "I bet you wouldn't take $50,000 for that place." Zehmer replied, "Yes, I would too; you wouldn't give fifty." Throughout the evening, the conversation returned to the sale of the Ferguson Farm for $50,000. All the while, the men continued to drink whiskey and engage in light conversation.

Eventually, Lucy enticed Zehmer to write up an agreement to the effect that the Zehmers would sell the Ferguson Farm to Lucy for $50,000 complete. Later, Lucy sued Zehmer to compel him to go through with the sale. Zehmer argued that he had been drunk and that the offer had been made in jest and hence was unenforceable. The trial court agreed with Zehmer, and Lucy appealed.

IN THE LANGUAGE OF THE COURT
BUCHANAN, J. [Justice] delivered the opinion of the court.
* * * *

In his testimony, Zehmer claimed that he "was high as a Georgia pine," and that the transaction "was just a bunch of two doggoned drunks bluffing to see who could talk the biggest and say the most." That claim is inconsistent with his attempt to testify in great detail as to what was said and what was done.
* * * *

The appearance of the contract, the fact that it was under discussion for forty minutes or more before it was signed; Lucy's objection to the first draft because it was written in the singular, and he wanted Mrs. Zehmer to sign it also; the rewriting to meet that objection and the signing by Mrs. Zehmer; the discussion of what was to be included in the sale, the provision for the examination of the title, the completeness of the instrument that was executed, the taking possession of it by Lucy with no request or suggestion by either of the defendants that he give it back, are facts which furnish persuasive evidence that the execution of the contract was a serious business transaction rather than a casual, jesting matter as defendants now contend.
* * * *

In the field of contracts, as generally elsewhere, *we must look to the outward expression of a person as manifesting his intention rather than to his secret and unexpressed intention.* The law imputes to a person an intention corresponding to the reasonable meaning of his words and acts. [Emphasis added.]

CASE 12.1 CONTINUES ▶

* * * *

Whether the writing signed by the defendants and now sought to be enforced by the complainants was the result of a serious offer by Lucy and a serious acceptance by the defendants, or was a serious offer by Lucy and an acceptance in secret jest by the defendants, in either event it constituted a binding contract of sale between the parties.

DECISION AND REMEDY *The Supreme Court of Appeals of Virginia determined that the writing was an enforceable contract and reversed the ruling of the lower court. The Zehmers were required by court order to follow through with the sale of the Ferguson Farm to the Lucys.*

IMPACT OF THIS CASE ON TODAY'S LAW *This is a classic case in contract law because it illustrates so clearly the objective theory of contracts with respect to determining whether a serious offer was intended. Today, the courts continue to apply the objective theory of contracts and routinely cite* Lucy v. Zehmer *as a significant precedent in this area.*

WHAT IF THE FACTS WERE DIFFERENT? *Suppose that the day after Lucy signed the purchase agreement for the farm, he decided that he did not want it after all, and Zehmer sued Lucy to perform the contract. Would this change in the facts alter the court's decision that Lucy and Zehmer had created an enforceable contract? Why or why not?*

SITUATIONS WHEN INTENT MAY BE LACKING The concept of intention can be further clarified through an examination of types of statements that are *not* offers. We look at these expressions and statements in the subsections that follow.

Expressions of Opinion. An expression of opinion is not an offer. It does not indicate an intention to enter into a binding agreement.

▶ **Case in Point 12.2** George Hawkins took his son to McGee, a physician, and asked McGee to operate on the son's hand. McGee said that the boy would be in the hospital three or four days and that the hand would *probably* heal a few days later. The son's hand did not heal for a month, but the father did not win a suit for breach of contract. The court held that McGee had not made an offer to heal the son's hand in a few days. He had merely expressed an opinion as to when the hand would heal.[1] ◀

Statements of Future Intent. A statement of an intention to do something in the future is not an offer. ▶ **Example 12.3** Samir says, "I *plan* to sell my stock in Novation, Inc., for $150 per share." If John "accepts" and tenders the $150 per share for the stock, no contract is created. Samir has merely expressed his intention to enter into a future contract for the sale of the stock. No contract is formed because a reasonable person would conclude that

Samir was only *thinking about* selling his stock, not *promising* to sell it. ◀

Preliminary Negotiations. A request or invitation to negotiate is not an offer. It only expresses a willingness to discuss the possibility of entering into a contract. Statements such as "Will you sell Blythe Estate?" or "I wouldn't sell my car for less than $5,000" are examples. A reasonable person in the offeree's position would not conclude that these statements indicated an intention to enter into a binding obligation.

Likewise, when the government or private firms require construction work, they invite contractors to submit bids. The *invitation* to submit bids is not an offer, and a contractor does not bind the government or private firm by submitting a bid. (The bids that the contractors submit are offers, however, and the government or private firm can bind the contractor by accepting the bid.)

Advertisements. In general, advertisements (including representations made in mail-order catalogues, price lists, and circulars) are treated not as offers to contract but as invitations to negotiate.[2] ▶ **Case in Point 12.4** An advertisement on the *Science NOW* Web site asked readers to submit "news tips," which the organization would investigate for possible inclusion in its magazine or on the Web site. Erik Trell, a professor and physician, submitted a manu-

---

1. *Hawkins v. McGee*, 84 N.H. 114, 146 A. 641 (1929).

2. *Restatement (Second) of Contracts*, Section 26, Comment b.

script in which he claimed to have solved a famous mathematical problem.

When *Science NOW* did not publish the solution, Trell filed a lawsuit for breach of contract. He claimed that the *Science NOW* ad was an offer, which he had accepted by submitting his manuscript. The court dismissed Trell's suit, holding that the ad was not an offer, but merely an invitation to offer. Responses to the ad were not acceptances. Trell's submission of the manuscript for publication was the offer, which *Science NOW* did not accept.[3] ◄

Price lists are another form of invitation to negotiate or trade. A seller's price list is not an offer to sell at that price. It merely invites the buyer to offer to buy at that price. In fact, the seller usually puts "prices subject to change" on the price list. Only in rare circumstances will a price quotation be construed as an offer.

Although most advertisements and price lists are treated as invitations to negotiate, this does not mean that they can never be an offer. On some occasions, courts have construed advertisements to be offers because the ads contained definite terms that invited acceptance (such as an ad offering a reward for the return of a lost dog).

Online Auctions. The most familiar type of auction today takes place on the Internet. Online auction sites, such as eBay, eBid, and WebStore, provide a forum for buyers and sellers to find or sell almost anything. Like advertisements and price lists, "offers" to sell an item on these sites generally are treated as invitations to negotiate. Unlike live auctions (discussed next), online auctions are automated. Buyers can enter incremental bids on an item (without approving each price increase) up to a specified amount or without a limit, if they want to be assured of making the winning bid.

Live Auctions. In a live auction, a seller "offers" goods for sale through an auctioneer, but this is not an offer to form a contract. Rather, it is an invitation asking bidders to submit offers. In the context of an auction, a bidder is the offeror, and the auctioneer is the offeree. The offer is accepted when the auctioneer strikes the hammer. Before the fall of the hammer, a bidder may revoke (take back) her or his bid, or the auctioneer may reject that bid or all bids. Typically, an auctioneer will reject a bid that is below the price the seller is willing to accept.

When the auctioneer accepts a higher bid, he or she rejects all previous bids. Because rejection terminates an offer (as will be discussed later), those bids represent offers that have been terminated. Thus, if the highest bidder withdraws her or his bid before the hammer falls, none of the previous bids is reinstated. If the bid is not withdrawn or rejected, the contract is formed when the auctioneer announces, "Going once, going twice, sold!" (or something similar) and lets the hammer fall.

Auctions with and without Reserve. Auctions traditionally have been referred to as either "with reserve" or "without reserve." In an auction with reserve, the seller (through the auctioneer) may withdraw the goods at any time before the auctioneer closes the sale by announcement or by the fall of the hammer.

All auctions are assumed to be auctions with reserve unless the terms of the auction are explicitly stated to be *without reserve*. In an auction without reserve, the goods cannot be withdrawn by the seller and must be sold to the highest bidder. In auctions with reserve, the seller may reserve the right to confirm or reject the sale even after "the hammer has fallen." In this situation, the seller is obligated to notify those attending the auction that sales of goods made during the auction are not final until confirmed by the seller.[4]

Agreements to Agree. Traditionally, agreements to agree—that is, agreements to agree to the material terms of a contract at some future date—were not considered to be binding contracts. The modern view, however, is that agreements to agree may be enforceable agreements (contracts) if it is clear that the parties intended to be bound by the agreements. In other words, under the modern view the emphasis is on the parties' intent rather than on form.

► **Case in Point 12.5** After a person was injured and nearly drowned on a water ride at one of its amusement parks, Six Flags, Inc., filed a lawsuit against the manufacturer that had designed the ride. The defendant manufacturer claimed that the parties did not have a binding contract but had only engaged in preliminary negotiations that were never formalized in a construction contract. The court, however, held that the evidence was sufficient to show an intent to be bound. The evidence included a faxed document specifying the details of the water ride, along with the parties' subsequent actions (beginning

---

3. *Trell v. American Association for the Advancement of Science,* ___ F.Supp.2d ___ (W.D.N.Y. 2007).

4. These rules apply under both the common law of contracts and the Uniform Commercial Code (UCC)—see UCC 2–328.

construction and handwriting notes on the fax). The manufacturer was required to provide insurance for the water ride at Six Flags. Its insurer was required to defend Six Flags in the personal-injury lawsuit that arose out of the incident.[5] ◄

Preliminary Agreements. Increasingly, the courts are holding that a preliminary agreement constitutes a binding contract if the parties have agreed on all essential terms and no disputed issues remain to be resolved. In contrast, if the parties agree on certain major terms but leave other terms open for further negotiation, a preliminary agreement is not binding. The parties are bound only in the sense that they have committed themselves to negotiate the undecided terms in good faith in an effort to reach a final agreement.

In the following *Spotlight Case*, the dispute was over an agreement to settle a case during the trial. One party claimed that the agreement formed via e-mail was binding. The other party claimed the e-mail exchange was merely an agreement to work out the terms of a settlement in the future. Can an exchange of e-mails create a complete and unambiguous agreement?

---

5. *Six Flags, Inc. v. Steadfast Insurance Co.,* 474 F.Supp.2d 201 (D.Mass. 2007).

SP TLIGHT on Amazon.com

Case 12.2   Basis Technology Corp. v. Amazon.com, Inc.
Appeals Court of Massachusetts, 71 Mass.App.Ct. 29, 878 N.E.2d 952 (2008).

BACKGROUND AND FACTS   Basis Technology Corporation created software and provided technical services for a Japanese-language Web site belonging to Amazon.com, Inc. The agreement between the two companies allowed for separately negotiated contracts for additional services that Basis might provide to Amazon. At the end of 1999, Basis and Amazon entered into stock-purchase agreements. Later, Amazon objected to certain actions related to the securities that Basis sold. Basis sued Amazon for various claims involving these securities and for failing to pay for services performed by Basis that were not included in the original agreement. During the trial, the two parties appeared to reach an agreement to settle out of court via a series of e-mail exchanges outlining the settlement. When Amazon reneged, Basis served a motion to enforce the proposed settlement. The trial judge entered a judgment against Amazon, which appealed.

IN THE LANGUAGE OF THE COURT
SIKORA, J. [Judge]

* * * *

* * * On the evening of March 23, after the third day of evidence and after settlement discussions, Basis counsel sent an e-mail with the following text to Amazon counsel:

> [Amazon counsel]—This e-mail confirms the essential business terms of the settlement between our respective clients * * *. Basis and Amazon agree that they promptly will take all reasonable steps to memorialize in a written agreement, to be signed by individuals authorized by each party, the terms set forth below, as well as such other terms that are reasonably necessary to make these terms effective.
> * * * *
> [Amazon counsel], please contact me first thing tomorrow morning if this e-mail does not accurately summarize the settlement terms reached earlier this evening.
> See you tomorrow morning when we report this matter settled to the Court.

At 7:26 A.M. on March 24, Amazon counsel sent an e-mail with a one-word reply: "correct." Later in the morning, in open court and on the record, both counsel reported the result of a settlement without specification of the terms.

On March 25, Amazon's counsel sent a facsimile of the first draft of a settlement agreement to Basis's counsel. The draft comported with all the terms of the e-mail exchange, and added some implementing and boilerplate [standard contract provisions] terms.

CASE 12.2 CONTINUED

* * * *

[Within a few days, though,] the parties were deadlocked. On April 21, Basis served its motion to enforce the settlement agreement. Amazon opposed. * * * The motion and opposition presented the issues whether the e-mail terms were sufficiently complete and definite to form an agreement and whether Amazon had intended to be bound by them.

* * * *

We examine the text of the terms for the incompleteness and indefiniteness charged by Amazon. *Provisions are not ambiguous simply because the parties have developed different interpretations of them.* [Emphasis added.]

* * * *

We must interpret the document as a whole. In the preface to the enumerated terms, Basis counsel stated that the "e-mail confirms the essential business terms of the settlement between our respective clients," and that the parties "agree that they promptly will take all reasonable steps to memorialize" those terms. Amazon counsel concisely responded, "correct." Thus the "essential business terms" were resolved. The parties were proceeding to "memorialize" or record the settlement terms, not to create them.

* * * *

To ascertain intent, a court considers the words used by the parties, the agreement taken as a whole, and surrounding facts and circumstances. The essential circumstance of this disputed agreement is that it concluded a trial.

* * * As the trial judge explained in her memorandum of decision, she "terminated" the trial; she did not suspend it for exploratory negotiations. She did so in reliance upon the parties' report of an accomplished agreement for the settlement of their dispute.

* * * *

In sum, the deliberateness and the gravity attributable to a report of a settlement, especially during the progress of a trial, weigh heavily as circumstantial evidence of the intention of a party such as Amazon to be bound by its communication to the opposing party and to the court.

DECISION AND REMEDY   *The Appeals Court of Massachusetts affirmed the trial court's finding that Amazon intended to be bound by the terms of the March 23 e-mail. That e-mail constituted a complete and unambiguous statement of the parties' desire to be bound by the settlement terms.*

WHAT IF THE FACTS WERE DIFFERENT?   *Suppose that the attorneys for both sides had simply had a phone conversation that included all of the terms to which they actually agreed in their e-mail exchanges. Would the court have ruled differently? Why or why not?*

THE LEGAL ENVIRONMENT DIMENSION   *What does the result in this case suggest that a businessperson should do before agreeing to a settlement of a legal dispute?*

DEFINITENESS OF TERMS The second requirement for an effective offer involves the definiteness of its terms. An offer must have reasonably definite terms so that a court can determine if a breach has occurred and give an appropriate remedy.[6] The specific terms required depend, of course, on the type of contract. Generally, a contract must include the following terms, either expressed in the contract or capable of being reasonably inferred from it:

1. The identification of the parties.
2. The identification of the object or subject matter of the contract (also the quantity, when appropriate), including the work to be performed, with specific identification of such items as goods, services, and land.
3. The consideration to be paid.
4. The time of payment, delivery, or performance.

An offer may invite an acceptance to be worded in such specific terms that the contract is made definite. ▶ **Example 12.6** Nintendo of America, Inc.,

---

6. *Restatement (Second) of Contracts,* Section 33.

contacts your Play 2 Win Games store and offers to sell "from one to twenty-five Nintendo 3DS gaming systems for $75 each. State number desired in acceptance." You agree to buy twenty systems. Because the quantity is specified in the acceptance, the terms are definite, and the contract is enforceable. ◀

When the parties have clearly manifested an intent to form a contract, courts sometimes are willing to supply a missing term in a contract, especially a sales contract.[7] But a court will not rewrite a contract if the parties' expression of intent is too vague or uncertain to be given any precise meaning.

COMMUNICATION The third requirement for an effective offer is communication—the offer must

---

7. See UCC 2–204. Note that Article 2 of the UCC specifies different rules relating to the definiteness of terms used in a contract for the sale of goods. In essence, Article 2 modifies general contract law by requiring *less* specificity.

be communicated to the offeree. Ordinarily, one cannot agree to a bargain without knowing that it exists. ▶ **Example 12.7** Tolson advertises a reward for the return of her lost cat. Dirk, not knowing of the reward, finds the cat and returns it to Tolson. Usually, Dirk cannot recover the reward because an essential element of a reward contract is that the one who claims the reward must have known it was offered. A few states would allow recovery of the reward, but not on contract principles. Dirk would be allowed to recover on the basis that it would be unfair to deny him the reward just because he did not know about it. ◀

In the following case, a woman hit by a bus signed documents that clearly released her claims against the bus company in exchange for the payment of $1 million from the company's insurer. Did the documents have to be delivered to the company or its insurer for the release and settlement to be binding?

CASE ANALYSIS

Case 12.3 Gyabaah v. Rivlab Transportation Corp.

New York Supreme Court, Appellate Division, First Department, 102 A.D.3d 451, 958 N.Y.S.2d 109 (2013).

IN THE LANGUAGE OF THE COURT
*TOM, J.P. [Judge Presiding],
ANDRIAS, RENWICK, DEGRASSE,
ABDUS-SALAAM, JJ. [Judges]*

* * * *

[Adwoa Gyabaah was hit by a bus owned by Rivlab Transportation Corporation. She retained attorney Jeffrey Aronsky to represent her in negotiations with Rivlab, its insurer National Casualty Company, and their attorneys. Gyabaah agreed to pay Aronsky a contingency fee of one-third of the amount of her recovery. Aronsky] commenced this personal injury action on plaintiff's behalf on August 25, 2010 [against Rivlab]. By letter to Aronsky dated October 1, 2010, defendant's carrier tendered its $1 million policy limits for purposes of settlement. Aronsky explained the proposal to plaintiff who, at that time, chose to accept the settlement.

Accordingly, plaintiff executed a general release on October 5, 2010 * * *. Aronsky advised plaintiff that he would hold the release pending receipt of * * * advice from plaintiff as to whether she preferred to have the settlement structured [paid over a period of time rather than in one lump sum].

By December 9, 2010, plaintiff had retained new counsel, Kenneth A. Wilhelm, Esq. [Esquire]. On that date, Wilhelm advised Aronsky that plaintiff did not wish to settle the case or have the release sent to defendant. Aronsky moved the court below for an order enforcing what he contended was a $1 million settlement and setting his firm's contingency fee at one-third of the recovery pursuant to plaintiff's retainer agreement. In making his motion, Aronsky did not allege that acceptance of the offer was ever communicated to defendant or

its carrier. This omission is fatal to Aronsky's claim of a settlement for reasons that follow. Aronsky maintained that "plaintiff's signing of the General Release constituted a binding legal contract." The court denied the motion and vacated the release in what it perceived to be the interest of justice.

* * * The application of contract law * * * required the denial of Aronsky's motion. A general release is governed by principles of contract law. * * * *It is essential in any bilateral contract that the fact of acceptance be communicated to the offeror. Therefore, this action was not settled because the executed release was never forwarded to defendant nor was acceptance of the offer otherwise communicated to defendant or its carrier.* This record does not contain a single affidavit by anyone asserting that either occurred. * * * We do not share the * * * view that an October 6,

2010 letter from defendant's counsel to Aronsky "evidenced" an agreement to settle. Defense counsel's statement in the letter that he was "advised" of a settlement does not suffice as evidence that such a settlement was effected. * * * Because there has been no settlement, the amount of Aronsky's fee should be determined upon the disposition of this action [as a percentage of the fee recovered by the Wilhelm firm based on the *pro rata* share of the work the two attorneys performed in obtaining the recovery]. [Emphasis added.]

* * * We see no need for a hearing to determine whether Aronsky was discharged for cause. The record discloses that plaintiff has not made a *prima facie* showing of any cause for Aronsky's discharge. Plaintiff stated in her affidavit that she signed the release * * * because she felt "pressured" to do so. Plaintiff made no mention of what the pressure consisted of or, more importantly, what professional misconduct, if any, brought it about. To be sure, a hearing was not warranted by plaintiff's untenable [indefensible] argument that Aronsky disobeyed her instructions by making the instant motion albeit [although] after he had already been discharged as her attorney.

[The order of the lower court denying Aronsky's motion insofar as it sought to enforce a purported settlement and set Aronsky's fee accordingly is affirmed.]

LEGAL REASONING QUESTIONS

1. Why did the court conclude that the parties in this case were not bound by the settlement and release documents signed by Gyabaah?

2. Why did Aronsky fail to deliver the signed documents to Rivlab or its insurer?

3. What is the most likely reason that Gyabaah did not wish to settle the case with Rivlab or its insurer according to their terms?

4. If Aronsky had informed Rivlab or its insurer that Gyabaah had agreed to the settlement, would her later "change of heart" have been sufficient to set aside the agreement?

Termination of the Offer

The communication of an effective offer to an offeree gives the offeree the power to transform the offer into a binding, legal obligation (a contract) by an acceptance. This power of acceptance does not continue forever, though. It can be terminated either by action of the parties or by operation of law.

TERMINATION BY ACTION OF THE PARTIES An offer can be terminated by action of the parties in any of three ways: by revocation, by rejection, or by counteroffer.

Revocation. The offeror's act of withdrawing (revoking) an offer is known as **revocation.** Unless an offer is irrevocable, the offeror usually can revoke the offer, as long as the revocation is communicated to the offeree before the offeree accepts. Revocation may be accomplished by either of the following:

1. Express repudiation of the offer (such as "I withdraw my previous offer of October 17").

2. Performance of acts that are inconsistent with the existence of the offer and are made known to the offeree (for instance, selling the offered property to another person in the presence of the offeree).

In most states, a revocation becomes effective when the offeree or the offeree's *agent* (a person acting on behalf of the offeree) actually receives it. Therefore, a revocation sent via FedEx on April 1 and delivered at the offeree's residence or place of business on April 3 becomes effective on April 3.

An offer made to the general public can be revoked in the same manner that the offer was originally communicated. ▶ **Example 12.8** An electronics retailer offers a $10,000 reward to anyone who provides information leading to the arrest of the individuals who broke into its store. The offer is published on the Web sites and in the printed editions of three local papers and of four papers in nearby communities. To revoke the offer, the retailer must publish the revocation in all seven papers in which it published the offer. ◀

Irrevocable Offers. Although most offers are revocable, some can be made irrevocable—that is, they cannot be revoked. Increasingly, courts refuse to allow an offeror to revoke an offer when the offeree has changed position because of justifiable reliance on the offer. (The courts apply the doctrine of *detrimental reliance,* or *promissory estoppel,* which will be discussed in Chapter 13.) In some circumstances, "firm offers" made by merchants may also be considered irrevocable—see the discussion of a "merchant's firm offer" in Chapter 20.

Another form of irrevocable offer is an **option contract.** An option contract is created when an offeror promises to hold an offer open for a specified period of time in return for a payment (consideration) given by the offeree. An option contract takes away the offeror's power to revoke the offer for the period of time specified in the option.

Option contracts are frequently used in conjunction with the sale or lease of real estate. ▶ **Example 12.9** Tyrell agrees to lease a house from Jackson, the property owner. The lease contract includes a clause stating that Tyrell is paying an additional $15,000 for an option to purchase the property within a specified period of time. If Tyrell decides not to purchase the house after the specified period has lapsed, he loses the $15,000, and Jackson is free to sell the property to another buyer. ◀

Rejection. If the offeree rejects the offer—by words or by conduct—the offer is terminated. Any subsequent attempt by the offeree to accept will be construed as a new offer, giving the original offeror (now the offeree) the power of acceptance. Like a revocation, a rejection of an offer is effective only when it is actually received by the offeror or the offeror's agent.

Merely inquiring about an offer does not constitute rejection. When the offeree merely inquires as to the "firmness" of the offer, there is no reason to presume that he or she intends to reject it. ▶ **Example 12.10** Raymond offers to buy Francie's iPhone 5 for $200, and Francie responds, "Is that your best offer?" or "Will you pay me $275 for it?" A reasonable person would conclude that Francie did not reject the offer but merely made an inquiry about it. She can still accept and bind Raymond to the $200 purchase price. ◀

Counteroffer. A **counteroffer** is a rejection of the original offer and the simultaneous making of a new offer. ▶ **Example 12.11** Burke offers to sell his home to Lang for $270,000. Lang responds, "Your price is too high. I'll offer to purchase your house for $250,000." Lang's response is called a counteroffer because it rejects Burke's offer to sell at $270,000 and creates a new offer by Lang to purchase the home at a price of $250,000. ◀

At common law, the **mirror image rule** requires the offeree's acceptance to match the offeror's offer exactly—to mirror the offer. Any change in, or addition to, the terms of the original offer automatically terminates that offer and substitutes the counteroffer. The counteroffer, of course, need not be accepted, but if the original offeror does accept the terms of the counteroffer, a valid contract is created.[8]

TERMINATION BY OPERATION OF LAW The power of the offeree to transform the offer into a binding, legal obligation can be terminated by operation of law through the occurrence of any of the following events:

1. Lapse of time.
2. Destruction of the specific subject matter of the offer.
3. Death or incompetence of the offeror or the offeree.
4. Supervening illegality of the proposed contract. (A statute or court decision that makes an offer illegal automatically terminates the offer.)

Lapse of Time. An offer terminates automatically by law when the period of time *specified in the offer* has passed. If the offer states that it will be left open until a particular date, then the offer will terminate at midnight on that day. If the offer states that it will be open for a number of days, this time period normally begins to run when the offeree *receives* the offer (not when it is formed or sent).

If the offer does not specify a time for acceptance, the offer terminates at the end of a *reasonable* period of time. What constitutes a reasonable period of time depends on the subject matter of the contract, business and market conditions, and other relevant circumstances. An offer to sell farm produce, for example, will terminate sooner than an offer to sell farm equipment because farm produce is perishable. Produce is also subject to greater fluctuations in market value.

Destruction of the Subject Matter. An offer is automatically terminated if the specific subject matter of the offer (such as a smartphone or a house) is destroyed before the offer is accepted.[9] ▶ **Example 12.12** John-

---

8. The mirror image rule has been greatly modified in regard to sales contracts. Section 2–207 of the UCC provides that a contract is formed if the offeree makes a definite expression of acceptance (such as signing the form in the appropriate location), even though the terms of the acceptance modify or add to the terms of the original offer (see Chapter 20).

9. *Restatement (Second) of Contracts,* Section 36.

son offers to sell his prize greyhound to Rizzo. If the dog dies before Rizzo can accept, the offer is automatically terminated. Johnson does not have to tell Rizzo that the animal has died for the offer to terminate. ◄

Death or Incompetence of the Offeror or Offeree. An offeree's power of acceptance is terminated when the offeror or offeree dies or is legally incapacitated—*unless the offer is irrevocable.* ▶ **Example 12.13** Sybil Maven offers to sell commercial property to Westside Investment for $2 million. In June, Westside pays Maven $5,000 in exchange for her agreement to hold the offer open for ten months (forming an option contract). If Maven dies in July, her offer is not terminated because it is irrevocable. Westside can purchase the property anytime within the ten-month period. ◄

A revocable offer is personal to both parties and cannot pass to the heirs, guardian, or estate of either party. This rule applies whether or not the other party had notice of the death or incompetence.

Supervening Illegality of the Proposed Contract. A statute or court decision that makes an offer illegal automatically terminates the offer.[10] ▶ **Example 12.14** Lee offers to lend Kim $10,000 at an annual interest rate

---
10. *Restatement (Second) of Contracts,* Section 36.

of 15 percent. Before Kim can accept the offer, a law is enacted that prohibits interest rates higher than 12 percent. Lee's offer is automatically terminated. (If the statute is enacted after Kim accepts the offer, a valid contract is formed, but the contract may still be unenforceable—see Chapter 14.) ◄

Concept Summary 12.1 below provides a review of the ways in which an offer can be terminated.

Acceptance

Acceptance is a voluntary act by the offeree that shows assent (agreement) to the terms of an offer. The offeree's act may consist of words or conduct. The acceptance must be unequivocal and must be communicated to the offeror. Generally, only the person to whom the offer is made or that person's agent can accept the offer and create a binding contract.

UNEQUIVOCAL ACCEPTANCE To exercise the power of acceptance effectively, the offeree must accept unequivocally. This is the *mirror image rule* previously discussed. An acceptance may be unequivocal even though the offeree expresses dissatisfaction with the contract. For instance, "I accept the offer, but can you give me a better price?" is an effective acceptance.

CONCEPT SUMMARY 12.1
Methods by Which an Offer Can Be Terminated

BY ACTION OF THE PARTIES—

1. *Revocation*—Unless the offer is irrevocable, it can be revoked at any time before acceptance without liability. Revocation is not effective until received by the offeree or the offeree's agent. Some offers, such as a merchant's firm offer and option contracts, are irrevocable. Also, in some situations, an offeree's detrimental reliance or partial performance will cause a court to rule that the offeror cannot revoke the offer.
2. *Rejection*—Accomplished by words or actions that demonstrate a clear intent not to accept the offer; not effective until received by the offeror or the offeror's agent.
3. *Counteroffer*—A rejection of the original offer and the making of a new offer.

BY OPERATION OF LAW—

1. *Lapse of time*—The offer terminates at the end of the time period specified in the offer or, if no time period is stated in the offer, at the end of a reasonable time period.
2. *Destruction of the subject matter*—When the specific subject matter of the offer is destroyed before the offer is accepted, the offer automatically terminates.
3. *Death or incompetence of the offeror or offeree*—If the offeror or offeree dies or becomes incompetent, this offer terminates (unless the offer is irrevocable).
4. *Supervening illegality*—When a statute or court decision makes the proposed contract illegal, the offer automatically terminates.

An acceptance cannot impose new conditions or change the terms of the original offer. If it does, the acceptance may be considered a counteroffer, which is a rejection of the original offer. For instance, the statement "I accept the offer but only if I can pay on ninety days' credit" is a counteroffer and not an unequivocal acceptance.

Certain terms, when included in an acceptance, will not change the offer sufficiently to constitute rejection. ▶ **Example 12.15** In response to an art dealer's offer to sell a painting, the offeree, Ashton Gibbs, replies, "I accept. Please send a written contract." Gibbs is requesting a written contract but is not making it a condition for acceptance. Therefore, the acceptance is effective without the written contract. In contrast, if Gibbs replies, "I accept *if* you send a written contract," the acceptance is expressly conditioned on the request for a writing, and the statement is not an acceptance but a counteroffer. (Notice how important each word is!)[11] ◀

SILENCE AS ACCEPTANCE Ordinarily, silence cannot constitute acceptance, even if the offeror states, "By your silence and inaction, you will be deemed to have accepted this offer." An offeree should not be obligated to act affirmatively to reject an offer when no consideration (nothing of value) has passed to the offeree to impose such a duty.

In some instances, however, the offeree does have a duty to speak and her or his silence or inaction will operate as an acceptance. Silence may constitute an acceptance in the following circumstances:

1. When an offeree takes the benefit of offered services even though he or she had an opportunity to reject them and knew that they were offered with the expectation of compensation. ▶ **Example 12.16** John is a student who earns extra income by washing store windows. John taps on the window of a store, catches the attention of the store's manager, and points to the window and raises his cleaner, signaling that he will be washing the window. The manager does nothing to stop him. Here, the store manager's silence constitutes an acceptance, and an implied contract is created. The store is bound to pay a reasonable value for John's work. ◀
2. When the offeree has had prior dealings with the offeror. For instance, a merchant routinely receives shipments from a certain supplier and

always notifies that supplier when defective goods are rejected. The merchant's silence regarding a particular shipment (failure to reject the goods) will constitute acceptance.

COMMUNICATION OF ACCEPTANCE In a bilateral contract, acceptance is in the form of a promise (not performance). Because bilateral contracts are formed when the promise is made (rather than when the act is performed), communication of acceptance is necessary. Communication of acceptance may not be necessary if the offer dispenses with the requirement, however, or if the offer can be accepted by silence.

▶ **Case in Point 12.17** Powerhouse Custom Homes, Inc., owed $95,260.42 to 84 Lumber Company under a credit agreement. When Powerhouse failed to pay, 84 Lumber filed a suit to collect. During mediation, the parties agreed to a deadline for objections to whatever agreement they might reach. If there were no objections, the agreement would be binding. Powerhouse then offered to pay less than the amount owed, and 84 Lumber did not respond. Powerhouse argued that 84 Lumber accepted the offer by not objecting to it within the deadline. The court, however, held that for a contract to be formed, an offer must be accepted unequivocally. Although Powerhouse had made an offer of a proposed settlement, 84 Lumber did not communicate its acceptance. Thus, the court reasoned that the parties did not reach an agreement on the proposed settlement.[12] ◀

Because a unilateral contract calls for the full performance of some act, acceptance is usually evident, and notification is therefore unnecessary. Nevertheless, exceptions do exist, such as when the offeror requests notice of acceptance or has no way of determining whether the requested act has been performed.

MODE AND TIMELINESS OF ACCEPTANCE In bilateral contracts, acceptance must be timely. The general rule is that acceptance in a bilateral contract is timely if it is made before the offer is terminated. Problems may arise, though, when the parties involved are not dealing face to face. In such situations, the offeree should use an authorized mode of communication.

The Mailbox Rule. Acceptance takes effect, thus completing formation of the contract, at the time the offeree sends or delivers the communication via the mode expressly or impliedly authorized by the offeror. This is the so-called **mailbox rule,** also called the

---

11. As noted in footnote 8, in regard to sales contracts, the UCC provides that an acceptance may still be valid even if some terms are added. The new terms are simply treated as proposed additions to the contract.

12. *Powerhouse Custom Homes, Inc. v. 84 Lumber Co.,* 307 Ga.App. 605, 705 S.E.2d 704 (2011).

deposited acceptance rule, which the majority of courts follow. Under this rule, if the authorized mode of communication is the mail, then an acceptance becomes valid when it is dispatched (placed in the control of the U.S. Postal Service)—*not* when it is received by the offeror. (Note, however, that if the offer stipulates when acceptance will be effective, then the offer will not be effective until the time specified.)

The mailbox rule does not apply to instantaneous forms of communication, such as when the parties are dealing face to face, by telephone, by fax, and usually by e-mail. Under the Uniform Electronic Transactions Act (UETA—discussed later in this chapter), e-mail is considered sent when it either leaves the control of the sender or is received by the recipient. This rule takes the place of the mailbox rule when the parties have agreed to conduct transactions electronically and allows an e-mail acceptance to become effective when sent.

Authorized Means of Acceptance. A means of communicating acceptance can be expressly authorized by the offeror or impliedly authorized by the facts and circumstances of the situation.[13] An acceptance sent by means not expressly or impliedly authorized normally is not effective until it is received by the offeror.

When an offeror specifies how acceptance should be made (for example, by overnight delivery), *express authorization* is said to exist. The contract is not formed unless the offeree uses that specified mode of acceptance. Moreover, both offeror and offeree are bound in contract the moment this means of acceptance is employed. ▶ **Example 12.18** Motorola Mobility, Inc., offers to sell 144 Atrix 4G smartphones and 72 Lapdocks to Call Me Plus phone stores. The offer states that Call Me Plus must accept the offer via FedEx overnight delivery. The acceptance is effective (and a binding contract is formed) the moment that Call Me Plus gives the overnight envelope containing the acceptance to the FedEx driver. ◀

If the offeror does not expressly authorize a certain mode of acceptance, then acceptance can be made by *any reasonable means.*[14] Courts look at the prevailing business usages and the surrounding circumstances to determine whether the mode of acceptance used was reasonable. Usually, the offeror's choice of a particular means in making the offer implies that the offeree can use the *same or a faster means* for acceptance. Thus, if

the offer is made via Priority U.S. mail, it would be reasonable to accept the offer via Priority mail or by a faster method, such as signed scanned documents sent as attachments via e-mail or overnight delivery.

Substitute Method of Acceptance. Sometimes, the offeror authorizes a particular method of acceptance, but the offeree accepts by a different means. In that situation, the acceptance may still be effective if the substituted method serves the same purpose as the authorized means.

The acceptance by a substitute method is not effective on dispatch, though, and no contract will be formed until the acceptance is received by the offeror. For instance, an offer specifies acceptance by FedEx overnight delivery, but the offeree instead accepts by overnight delivery from another carrier. The substitute method of acceptance will still be effective, but the contract will not be formed until the offeror receives it.

SECTION 2
AGREEMENT IN E-CONTRACTS

Numerous contracts are formed online. Electronic contracts, or **e-contracts,** must meet the same basic requirements (agreement, consideration, contractual capacity, and legality) as paper contracts. Disputes concerning e-contracts, however, tend to center on contract terms and whether the parties voluntarily agreed to those terms.

Online contracts may be formed not only for the sale of goods and services but also for *licensing.* As mentioned in Chapter 9, the purchase of software generally involves a license, or a right to use the software, rather than the passage of title (ownership rights) from the seller to the buyer. ▶ **Example 12.19** Galynn downloads an app on her iPad that enables her to work on spreadsheets. During the transaction, she has to select "I agree" several times to indicate that she understands that she is purchasing only the right to use the software under specific terms. After she agrees to these terms (the licensing agreement), she can use the application. ◀

Online Offers

Sellers doing business via the Internet can protect themselves against contract disputes and legal liability by creating offers that clearly spell out the terms

---

13. *Restatement (Second) of Contracts,* Section 30, provides that an offer invites acceptance "by any medium reasonable in the circumstances," unless the offer specifies the means of acceptance.
14. *Restatement (Second) of Contracts,* Section 30. This is also the rule under UCC 2–206(1)(a).

that will govern their transactions if the offers are accepted. All important terms should be conspicuous and easy to view.

DISPLAYING THE OFFER The seller's Web site should include a hypertext link to a page containing the full contract so that potential buyers are made aware of the terms to which they are assenting. The contract generally must be displayed online in a readable format, such as a twelve-point typeface.

All provisions should be reasonably clear.
▶ **Example 12.20** Netquip sells a variety of heavy equipment, such as trucks and trailers, on its Web site. Because Netquip's pricing schedule is very complex, the schedule must be fully provided and explained on the Web site. In addition, the terms of the sale (such as any warranties and the refund policy) must be fully disclosed. ◀

PROVISIONS TO INCLUDE An important rule to keep in mind is that the offeror (the seller) controls the offer and thus the resulting contract. The seller should therefore anticipate the terms he or she wants to include in a contract and provide for them in the offer. In some instances, a standardized contract form may suffice. At a minimum, an online offer should include the following provisions:

1. *Acceptance of terms.* A clause that clearly indicates what constitutes the buyer's agreement to the terms of the offer, such as a box containing the words "I accept" that the buyer can click. (Mechanisms for accepting online offers will be discussed in detail later in the chapter.)
2. *Payment.* A provision specifying how payment for the goods (including any applicable taxes) must be made.
3. *Return policy.* A statement of the seller's refund and return policies.
4. *Disclaimer.* Disclaimers of liability for certain uses of the goods. For example, an online seller of business forms may add a disclaimer that the seller does not accept responsibility for the buyer's reliance on the forms rather than on an attorney's advice.
5. *Limitation on remedies.* A provision specifying the remedies available to the buyer if the goods are found to be defective or if the contract is otherwise breached. Any limitation of remedies should be clearly spelled out.
6. *Privacy policy.* A statement indicating how the seller will use the information gathered about the buyer.

7. *Dispute resolution.* Provisions relating to dispute settlement, such as an arbitration clause or a *forum-selection clause* (discussed next).

DISPUTE-SETTLEMENT PROVISIONS Online offers frequently include provisions relating to dispute settlement. For example, the offer might include an arbitration clause specifying that any dispute arising under the contract will be arbitrated in a designated forum.

Forum-Selection Clause. Many online contracts contain a **forum-selection clause** indicating the forum, or location (such as a court or jurisdiction), in which contract disputes will be resolved. As discussed in Chapter 2, significant jurisdictional issues may arise when parties are at a great distance, as they often are when they form contracts via the Internet. A forum-selection clause will help to avert future jurisdictional problems and also help to ensure that the seller will not be required to appear in court in a distant state.

▶ **Case in Point 12.21** Before advertisers can place ads through Google, Inc., they must agree to certain terms that are displayed in an online window. These terms include a forum-selection clause, which provides that any dispute is to be "adjudicated in Santa Clara County, California." Lawrence Feldman, who advertised through Google, complained that he was overcharged and filed a lawsuit against Google in a federal district court in Pennsylvania. The court held that Feldman had agreed to the forum-selection clause in Google's online contract and transferred the case to a court in Santa Clara County.[15] ◀

Choice-of-Law Clause. Some online contracts may also include a *choice-of-law clause* specifying that any contract dispute will be settled according to the law of a particular jurisdiction, such as a state or country. As will be discussed in Chapter 24, choice-of-law clauses are particularly common in international contracts, but they may also appear in e-contracts to specify which state's laws will govern in the United States.

Online Acceptances

The *Restatement (Second) of Contracts,* which, as noted earlier, is a compilation of common law contract principles, states that parties may agree to a contract "by written or spoken words or by other action or by failure

---

15. *Feldman v. Google, Inc.,* 513 F.Supp.2d 229 (E.D.Pa. 2007).

to act."[16] The Uniform Commercial Code (UCC), which governs sales contracts, has a similar provision. Section 2–204 of the UCC states that any contract for the sale of goods "may be made in any manner sufficient to show agreement, including conduct by both parties which recognizes the existence of such a contract."

CLICK-ON AGREEMENTS The courts have used the *Restatement* and UCC provisions to conclude that a binding contract can be created by conduct. This includes the act of clicking on a box indicating "I accept" or "I agree" to accept an online offer. The agreement resulting from such an acceptance is often called a **click-on agreement** (sometimes referred to as a *click-on license* or *click-wrap agreement*). Exhibit 12–1 below shows a portion of a typical click-on agreement that accompanies a software package.

Generally, the law does not require that the parties have read all of the terms in a contract for it to be effective. Therefore, clicking on a box that states "I agree" to certain terms can be enough. The terms may be contained on a Web site through which the buyer is obtaining goods or services. They may also appear on a screen when software is loaded from a CD-ROM or DVD or downloaded from the Internet.

▶ **Case in Point 12.22** The "Terms of Use" that govern Facebook users' accounts include a forum-selection clause that provides for the resolution of all disputes in a court in Santa Clara County, California. To sign up for a Facebook account, a person must click on a box indicating that he or she has agreed to this term.

Mustafa Fteja was an active user of facebook.com when his account was disabled. He sued Facebook in a federal court in New York, claiming that it had disabled his Facebook page without justification and for discriminatory reasons. Facebook filed a motion to transfer the case to California under the forum-selection clause. The court found that the clause in Facebook's online contract was binding and transferred the case. When Fteja clicked on the button to accept the "Terms of Use" and become a Facebook user, he agreed to resolve all disputes with Facebook in Santa Clara County, California.[17] ◀

SHRINK-WRAP AGREEMENTS With a **shrink-wrap agreement** (or *shrink-wrap license*),

the terms are expressed inside the box in which the goods are packaged. (The term *shrink-wrap* refers to the plastic that covers the box.) Usually, the party who opens the box is told that she or he agrees to the terms by keeping whatever is in the box. Similarly, when a purchaser opens a software package, he or she agrees to abide by the terms of the limited license agreement.

▶ **Example 12.23** Ava orders a new iMac from Big Dog Electronics, which ships it to her. Along with the iMac, the box contains an agreement setting forth the terms of the sale, including what remedies are available. The document also states that Ava's retention of the iMac for longer than thirty days will be construed as an acceptance of the terms. ◀

In most instances, a shrink-wrap agreement is not between a retailer and a buyer, but between the manufacturer of the hardware or software and the ultimate buyer-user of the product. The terms generally concern warranties, remedies, and other issues associated with the use of the product.

Shrink-Wrap Agreements and Enforceable Contract Terms. In some cases, the courts have enforced the terms of shrink-wrap agreements in the same way as the terms of other contracts. These courts have reasoned that by including the terms with the product, the seller proposed a contract. The buyer could accept this contract by using the product after having an opportunity to read the terms. Thus, a buyer's failure to object to terms contained within a shrink-wrapped software package may constitute an acceptance of the terms by conduct.

EXHIBIT 12–1 A Click-On Agreement Sample

This exhibit illustrates an online offer to form a contract. To accept the offer, the user simply scrolls down the page and clicks on the "I Accept" button.

16. *Restatement (Second) of Contracts,* Section 19.
17. *Fteja v. Facebook, Inc.,* 841 F.Supp.2d 829 (S.D.N.Y. 2012).

Shrink-Wrap Terms That May Not Be Enforced. Sometimes, however, the courts have refused to enforce certain terms included in shrink-wrap agreements because the buyer did not expressly consent to them. An important factor is when the parties formed their contract.

If a buyer orders a product over the telephone, for instance, and is not informed of an arbitration clause or forum-selection clause at that time, the buyer clearly has not expressly agreed to these terms. If the buyer discovers the clauses *after* the parties entered into a contract, a court may conclude that those terms were proposals for additional terms and were not part of the contract.

BROWSE-WRAP TERMS Like the terms of click-on agreements, **browse-wrap terms** can occur in transactions conducted over the Internet. Unlike click-on agreements, however, browse-wrap terms do not require Internet users to assent to the terms before downloading or using certain software. In other words, a person can install the software without clicking "I agree" to the terms of a license. Browse-wrap terms are often unenforceable because they do not satisfy the agreement requirement of contract formation.[18]

▶ **Example 12.24** BrowseNet Corporation provides free downloadable software called "QuickLoad" on its Web site. Users must indicate, by clicking on a designated box, that they wish to obtain it. On the Web site's download page is a reference to a license agreement that users can view only by scrolling to the next screen. In other words, the user does not have to agree to the terms of the license before downloading the software. One of the license terms requires all disputes to be submitted to arbitration in California. If a user sues BrowseNet in Washington state, the arbitration clause might not be enforceable because users were not required to indicate their assent to the agreement. ◀

E-Signature Technologies

Today, numerous technologies allow electronic documents to be signed. An **e-signature** has been defined as "an electronic sound, symbol, or process attached to or logically associated with a record and executed or adopted by a person with the intent to sign the record."[19] Thus, e-signatures include encrypted digital signatures, names (intended as signatures) at the end of e-mail messages, and clicks on a Web page if the click includes some means of identification.

Federal Law on E-Signatures and E-Documents

In 2000, Congress enacted the Electronic Signatures in Global and National Commerce Act (E-SIGN Act),[20] which provides that no contract, record, or signature may be "denied legal effect" solely because it is in electronic form. In other words, under this law, an electronic signature is as valid as a signature on paper, and an e-document can be as enforceable as a paper one.

For an e-signature to be enforceable, the contracting parties must have agreed to use electronic signatures. For an electronic document to be valid, it must be in a form that can be retained and accurately reproduced.

The E-SIGN Act does not apply to all types of documents. Contracts and documents that are exempt include court papers, divorce decrees, evictions, foreclosures, health-insurance terminations, prenuptial agreements, and wills. Also, the only agreements governed by the UCC that fall under this law are those covered by Articles 2 and 2A (sales and lease contracts) and UCC 1–107 and 1–206. Despite these limitations, the E-SIGN Act significantly expanded the possibilities for contracting online.

Partnering Agreements

One way that online sellers and buyers can prevent disputes over signatures in their e-contracts, as well as disputes over the terms and conditions of those contracts, is to form partnering agreements. In a **partnering agreement,** a seller and a buyer who frequently do business with each other agree in advance on the terms and conditions that will apply to all transactions subsequently conducted electronically. The partnering agreement can also establish special access and identification codes to be used by the parties when transacting business electronically.

A partnering agreement reduces the likelihood that disputes will arise under the contract because the parties have agreed in advance to the terms and conditions that will accompany each sale. Furthermore, if a dispute does arise, a court or arbitration forum will be able to refer to the partnering agreement when determining the parties' intent.

---

18. See, for example, *Jesmer v. Retail Magic, Inc.,* 863 N.Y.S.2d 737 (2008).
19. This definition is from the Uniform Electronic Transactions Act, which will be discussed later in this chapter.

20. 15 U.S.C. Sections 7001 *et seq.*

THE UNIFORM ELECTRONIC TRANSACTIONS ACT

Although most states have laws governing e-signatures and other aspects of electronic transactions, these laws vary. In an attempt to create more uniformity among the states, in 1999 the National Conference of Commissioners on Uniform State Laws and the American Law Institute promulgated the Uniform Electronic Transactions Act (UETA). The UETA has been adopted, at least in part, by forty-eight states. Among other things, the UETA declares that a signature may not be denied legal effect or enforceability solely because it is in electronic form.

The primary purpose of the UETA is to remove barriers to e-commerce by giving the same legal effect to electronic records and signatures as is given to paper documents and signatures. As mentioned earlier, the UETA broadly defines an *e-signature* as "an electronic sound, symbol, or process attached to or logically associated with a record and executed or adopted by a person with the intent to sign the record."[21] A **record** is "information that is inscribed on a tangible medium or that is stored in an electronic or other medium and is retrievable in perceivable [visual] form."[22]

The Scope and Applicability of the UETA

The UETA does not create new rules for electronic contracts but rather establishes that records, signatures, and contracts may not be denied enforceability solely due to their electronic form. The UETA does not apply to all writings and signatures. It covers only electronic records and electronic signatures *relating to a transaction*. A *transaction* is defined as an interaction between two or more people relating to business, commercial, or governmental activities.[23]

The act specifically does not apply to wills or testamentary trusts or to transactions governed by the UCC (other than those covered by Articles 2 and 2A).[24] In addition, the provisions of the UETA allow the states to exclude its application to other areas of law.

---

21. UETA 102(8).
22. UETA 102(15).
23. UETA 2(12) and 3.
24. UETA 3(b).

The UETA does not apply to a transaction unless each of the parties has previously agreed to conduct transactions by electronic means. The agreement need not be explicit, however. It can be implied by the conduct of the parties and the surrounding circumstances, such as negotiating a contract via e-mail.[25] The parties can agree to opt out of all or some of the terms of the UETA, but if they do not, then the UETA terms will govern their electronic transactions.

The Federal E-SIGN Act and the UETA

Congress passed the E-SIGN Act in 2000, a year after the UETA was presented to the states for adoption. Thus, a significant issue was to what extent the federal E-SIGN Act preempted the UETA as adopted by the states.

The E-SIGN Act[26] refers explicitly to the UETA and provides that if a state has enacted the uniform version of the UETA, it is not preempted by the E-SIGN Act. In other words, if the state has enacted the UETA without modification, state law will govern. The problem is that many states have enacted nonuniform (modified) versions of the UETA, usually to exclude other areas of state law from the UETA's terms. The E-SIGN Act specifies that those exclusions will be preempted to the extent that they are inconsistent with the E-SIGN Act's provisions.

The E-SIGN Act explicitly allows the states to enact alternative requirements for the use of electronic records or electronic signatures. Generally, however, the requirements must be consistent with the provisions of the E-SIGN Act, and the state must not give greater legal status or effect to one specific type of technology. Additionally, if a state enacts alternative requirements after the E-SIGN Act was adopted, the state law must specifically refer to the E-SIGN Act. The relationship between the UETA and the E-SIGN Act is illustrated in Exhibit 12–2 on the following page.

Signatures on Electronic Records

Under the UETA, if an electronic record or signature is the act of a particular person, the record or signature may be attributed to that person. If a person types her or his name at the bottom of an e-mail purchase order, for instance, that name would qualify as a "signature." The signature would therefore be attributed to the person whose name appeared.

---

25. UETA 5(b), and Comment 4B.
26. 15 U.S.C. Section 7002(2)(A)(i).

EXHIBIT 12-2 The E-SIGN Act and the UETA

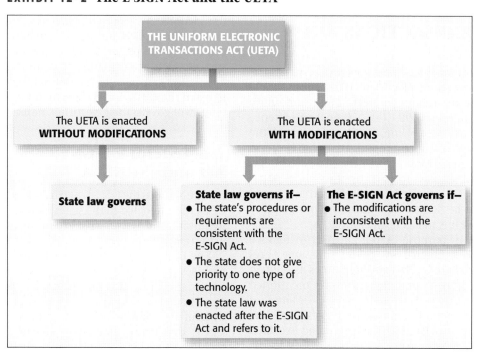

The UETA does not contain any express provisions about what constitutes fraud or whether an agent is authorized to enter a contract. Under the UETA, other state laws control if any issues relating to agency, authority, forgery, or contract formation arise. If existing state law requires a document to be notarized, the UETA provides that this requirement is satisfied by the electronic signature of a notary public or other person authorized to verify signatures.

The Effect of Errors

The UETA encourages, but does not require, the use of security procedures (such as encryption) to verify changes to electronic documents and to correct errors. It does this by providing a benefit to parties who have agreed to a security procedure. If one of the parties does not detect an error because he or she did not follow the procedure, the other party can legally avoid the effect of the change or error. When the parties have not agreed to use a security procedure, then other state laws (including contract law governing mistakes—see Chapter 15) will determine the effect of the error.

To avoid the effect of errors, a party must promptly notify the other party of the error and of her or his intent not to be bound by the error. In addition, the party must take reasonable steps to return any benefit received: parties cannot avoid a transaction if they have benefited.

Timing

An electronic record is considered *sent* when it is properly directed to the intended recipient in a form readable by the recipient's computer system. Once the electronic record leaves the control of the sender or comes under the control of the recipient, the UETA deems it to have been sent. An electronic record is considered *received* when it enters the recipient's processing system in a readable form—*even if no individual is aware of its receipt.*

SECTION 4
INTERNATIONAL TREATIES AFFECTING E-CONTRACTS

Today, much of the e-commerce conducted on a worldwide basis involves buyers and sellers from the United States. The preeminence of U.S. law in this area is likely to be challenged in the future, however, as Internet use continues to expand worldwide. Already, several international organizations have created their own regulations for global Internet transactions.

The United Nations Convention on the Use of Electronic Communications in International Contracts improves commercial certainty by determining an Internet user's location for legal purposes. The convention also establishes standards for creating functional equivalence between electronic communications and paper documents. The convention also provides that e-signatures will be treated as the equivalent of signatures on paper documents.

Another treaty relevant to e-contracts is the Hague Convention on the Choice of Court Agreements. Although it does not specifically mention e-commerce, this convention provides more certainty regarding jurisdiction and recognition of judgments by other nations' courts, thereby facilitating both offline and online transactions.

Reviewing: Agreement in Traditional and E-Contracts

Shane Durbin wanted to have a recording studio custom-built in his home. He sent invitations to a number of local contractors to submit bids on the project. Rory Amstel submitted the lowest bid, which was $20,000 less than any of the other bids Durbin received. Durbin called Amstel to ascertain the type and quality of the materials that were included in the bid and to find out if he could substitute a superior brand of acoustic tiles for the same bid price. Amstel said he would have to check into the price difference. The parties also discussed a possible start date for construction. Two weeks later, Durbin changed his mind and decided not to go forward with his plan to build a recording studio. Amstel filed a suit against Durbin for breach of contract. Using the information presented in the chapter, answer the following questions.

1. Did Amstel's bid meet the requirements of an offer? Explain.
2. Was there an acceptance of the offer? Why or why not?
3. Suppose that the court determines that the parties did not reach an agreement. Further suppose that Amstel, in anticipation of building Durbin's studio, had purchased materials and refused other jobs so that he would have time in his schedule for Durbin's project. Under what theory discussed in the chapter might Amstel attempt to recover these costs?
4. How is an offer terminated? Assuming that Durbin did not inform Amstel that he was rejecting the offer, was the offer terminated at any time described here? Explain.

DEBATE THIS . . . *The terms and conditions in click-on agreements are so long and detailed that no one ever reads the agreements. Therefore, the act of clicking on "I agree" is not really an acceptance.*

Terms and Concepts

acceptance 249
agreement 240
browse-wrap terms 254
click-on agreement 253
counteroffer 248
e-contract 251

e-signature 254
forum-selection clause 252
mailbox rule 250
mirror image rule 248
offer 240
option contract 248

partnering agreement 254
record 255
revocation 247
shrink-wrap agreement 253

ExamPrep

Issue Spotters

1. Fidelity Corporation offers to hire Ron to replace Monica, who has given Fidelity a month's notice of intent to quit. Fidelity gives Ron a week to decide whether to accept. Two days later, Monica decides not to quit and signs an employment contract with Fidelity for another year. The next day, Monica tells Ron of the new contract. Ron immediately faxes a formal letter of acceptance to Fidelity. Do Fidelity and Ron have a contract? Why or why not? **(See page 247.)**

2. Applied Products, Inc., does business with Beltway Distributors, Inc., online. Under the Uniform Electronic Transactions Act, what determines the effect of the electronic documents evidencing the parties' deal? Is a party's "signature" necessary? Explain. **(See page 255.)**

• **Check your answers to the Issue Spotters against the answers provided in Appendix E at the end of this text.**

Before the Test

Go to **www.cengagebrain.com**, enter the ISBN 9781285185248, and click on "Find" to locate this textbook's Web site. Then, click on "Access Now" under "Study Tools," and select Chapter 12 at the top. There, you will find a Practice Quiz that you can take to assess your mastery of the concepts in this chapter, as well as Flashcards and a Glossary of important terms.

Business Scenarios

12–1. Agreement. Ball e-mails Sullivan and inquires how much Sullivan is asking for a specific forty-acre tract of land Sullivan owns. Sullivan responds, "I will not take less than $60,000 for the forty-acre tract as specified." Ball immediately sends Sullivan a fax stating, "I accept your offer for $60,000 for the forty-acre tract as specified." Discuss whether Ball can hold Sullivan to a contract for the sale of the land. **(See page 242.)**

12–2. Offer and Acceptance. Schmidt, the owner of a small business, has a large piece of used farm equipment for sale. He offers to sell the equipment to Barry for $10,000. Discuss the legal effects of the following events on the offer: **(See page 249.)**

(a) Schmidt dies prior to Barry's acceptance, and at the time he accepts, Barry is unaware of Schmidt's death.

(b) The night before Barry accepts, fire destroys the equipment.

(c) Barry pays $100 for a thirty-day option to purchase the equipment. During this period, Schmidt dies, and later Barry accepts the offer, knowing of Schmidt's death.

(d) Barry pays $100 for a thirty-day option to purchase the equipment. During this period, Barry dies, and Barry's estate accepts Schmidt's offer within the stipulated time period.

12–3. Online Acceptance. Anne is a reporter for *Daily Business Journal,* a print publication consulted by investors and other businesspersons. She often uses the Internet to perform research for the articles that she writes for the publication. While visiting the Web site of Cyberspace Investments Corp., Anne reads a pop-up window that states, "Our business newsletter, *E-Commerce Weekly,* is available at a one-year subscription rate of $5 per issue. To subscribe, enter your e-mail address below and click 'SUBSCRIBE.' By subscribing, you agree to the terms of the subscriber's agreement. To read this agreement, click 'AGREEMENT.' " Anne enters her e-mail address, but does not click on "AGREEMENT" to read the terms. Has Anne entered into an enforceable contract to pay for *E-Commerce Weekly?* Explain. **(See page 252.)**

Business Case Problems

12–4. Spotlight on Crime Stoppers—Communication. The

Baton Rouge Crime Stoppers (BCS) offered a reward for information about the "South Louisiana Serial Killer." The information was to be provided via a hot line. Dianne Alexander had survived an attack by a person suspected of being the killer. She identified a suspect in a police photo lineup and later sought to collect the reward. BCS refused to pay because she did not provide information to them

via the hot line. Did Alexander comply with the terms of the offer? Explain. [*Alexander v. Lafayette Crime Stoppers, Inc.,* 38 So.3d 282 (La.App. 3 Dist. 2010) **(See page 246.)**

12–5. BUSINESS CASE PROBLEM WITH SAMPLE ANSWER: Offer and Acceptance.

While gambling at Prairie Meadows Casino, Troy Blackford became angry and smashed a slot machine. He was banned from the premises. Despite the ban, he later gambled at the casino and won $9,387. When he tried to collect his winnings, the casino refused to pay. Blackford filed a suit for breach of contract, arguing that he and the casino had a contract because he had accepted its offer to gamble. Did the casino and Blackford have a contract? Discuss. [Blackford v. Prairie Meadows Racetrack and Casino, 778 N.W.2d 184 (Sup.Ct. Iowa 2010)] **(See page 240.)**

- For a sample answer to Problem 12–5, go to Appendix F at the end of this text.

12–6. Shrink-Wrap Agreements. TracFone Wireless, Inc., sells phones and wireless service. The phones are sold for less than their cost, which TracFone recoups by selling prepaid airtime for their use on its network. Software in the phones prohibits their use on other networks. The phones are sold subject to the condition that the buyer agrees "not to tamper with or alter the software." This is printed on the packaging. Bequator Corp. bought at least 18,616 of the phones, disabled the software so that they could be used on other networks, and resold them. Is Bequator liable for breach of contract? Explain. [TracFone Wireless, Inc. v. Bequator Corp., __ F.Supp.2d __ (S.D.Fla. 2011)] **(See page 253.)**

12–7. Online Acceptances. Heather Reasonover opted to try Internet service from Clearwire Corp. Clearwire sent her a confirmation e-mail that included a link to its Web site. Clearwire also sent her a modem. In the enclosed written materials, at the bottom of a page, in small type was the Web site URL. When Reasonover plugged in the modem, an "I accept terms" box appeared. Without clicking on the box, Reasonover quit the page. A clause in Clearwire's "Terms of Service," accessible only through its Web site, required its subscribers to submit any dispute to arbitration. Is Reasonover bound to this clause? Why or why not? [Kwan v. Clearwire Corp., 2012 WL 32380 (W.D.Wash. 2012)] **(See page 252.)**

12–8. Acceptance. Judy Olsen, Kristy Johnston, and their mother, Joyce Johnston, owned seventy-eight acres of real property on Eagle Creek in Meagher County, Montana. When Joyce died, she left her interest in the property to Kristy. Kristy wrote to Judy, offering to buy Judy's interest or to sell her own interest to Judy. The letter said to "please respond to Bruce Townsend." In a letter to Kristy— not to Bruce—Judy accepted Kristy's offer to sell her interest. By that time, however, Kristy had made the same offer to sell her interest to their brother Dave, and he had accepted. Did Judy and Kristy have an enforceable binding contract? Or did Kristy's offer specifying one exclusive mode of acceptance mean that Judy's reply was not effective? Discuss. [Olsen v. Johnston, 368 Mont. 347, __ P.3d __, (2013)] **(See page 249.)**

12–9. A QUESTION OF ETHICS: E-Contract Disputes.

 Dewayne Hubbert, Elden Craft, Chris Grout, and Rhonda Byington bought computers from Dell Corp. through its Web site. Before buying, Hubbert and the others configured their own computers. To make a purchase, each buyer completed forms on five Web pages. On each page, Dell's "Terms and Conditions of Sale" were accessible by clicking on a blue hyperlink. A statement on three of the pages read, "All sales are subject to Dell's Term[s] and Conditions of Sale," but a buyer was not required to click an assent to the terms to complete a purchase. The terms were also printed on the backs of the invoices and on separate documents contained in the shipping boxes with the computers. Among those terms was a "Binding Arbitration" clause.

The computers contained Pentium 4 microprocessors, which Dell advertised as the fastest, most powerful Intel Pentium processors then available. In 2002, Hubbert and the others filed a suit in an Illinois state court against Dell, alleging that this marketing was false, misleading, and deceptive. The plaintiffs claimed that the Pentium 4 microprocessor was slower and less powerful, and provided less performance, than either a Pentium III or an AMD Athlon, and at a greater cost. Dell asked the court to compel arbitration. [Hubbert v. Dell Corp., 359 Ill.App.3d 976, 835 N.E.2d 113, 296 Ill.Dec. 258 (5 Dist. 2005)] **(See page 251.)**

(a) Should the court enforce the arbitration clause in this case? If you were the judge, how would you rule on this issue?

(b) Do you think shrink-wrap, click-on, and browse-wrap terms impose too great a burden on purchasers? Why or why not?

(c) An ongoing complaint about shrink-wrap, click-on, and browse-wrap terms is that sellers (often large corporations) draft them and buyers (typically individual consumers) do not read them. Should purchasers be bound in contract by terms that they have not even read? Why or why not?

Legal Reasoning Group Activity

12–10. E-Contracts. To download a specific application (app) to your smartphone or tablet device, usually you have to check a box indicating that you agree to the company's terms and conditions. Most individuals do so without ever reading those terms and conditions. Print out a specific set of terms and conditions from a downloaded app to use in this assignment. **(See page 251.)**

(a) One group will determine which of these terms and conditions are favorable to the company.

(b) Another group will determine which of these terms and conditions conceivably will be favorable to the individual.

(c) A third group will determine which terms and conditions, on net, favor the company too much.

CHAPTER 13

CONSIDERATION

The fact that a promise has been made does not mean the promise can or will be enforced. Under Roman law, a promise was not enforceable without a *causa*—that is, a reason for making the promise that was also deemed to be a sufficient reason for enforcing it.

Under the common law, a primary basis for the enforcement of promises is consideration. **Consideration** usually is defined as the value (such as cash) given in return for a promise (in a bilateral contract) or in return for a performance (in a unilateral contract). As long as consideration is present, the courts generally do not interfere with contracts based on the amount of consideration paid.

It is up to the contracting parties to determine how much their bargain is worth. Therefore, courts normally enforce a player's contract with a sports team, even if the player does not perform as well as expected or is injured and unable to play. Consequently, no matter how well or how poorly baseball player Prince Fielder performs, his $214 million contract with the Detroit Tigers is enforceable during its nine-year period.

SECTION 1
ELEMENTS OF CONSIDERATION

Often, consideration is broken down into two parts: (1) something of *legally sufficient value* must be given in exchange for the promise, and (2) there must be a *bargained-for* exchange.

Legally Sufficient Value

To be legally sufficient, consideration must be something of value in the eyes of the law. The "something of legally sufficient value" may consist of the following:

1. A promise to do something that one has no prior legal duty to do.
2. The performance of an action that one is otherwise not obligated to undertake.
3. The refraining from an action that one has a legal right to undertake (called a **forbearance**).

Consideration in bilateral contracts normally consists of a promise in return for a promise, as explained in Chapter 11. In a contract for the sale of goods, for instance, the seller promises to ship specific goods to the buyer, and the buyer promises to pay for those goods. Each of these promises constitutes consideration for the contract.

In contrast, unilateral contracts involve a promise in return for a performance. ▶ **Example 13.1** Anita says to her neighbor, "When you finish painting the garage, I will pay you $800." Anita's neighbor paints the garage. The act of painting the garage is the consideration that creates Anita's contractual obligation to pay her neighbor $800. ◀

What if, in return for a promise to pay, a person refrains from pursuing harmful habits (a forbearance), such as the use of tobacco and alcohol? Does such forbearance constitute legally sufficient consideration? This was the issue before the court in the following classic case concerning consideration.

CLASSIC CASE 13.1

Hamer v. Sidway
Court of Appeals of New York, Second Division, 124 N.Y. 538, 27 N.E. 256 (1891).

BACKGROUND AND FACTS   William E. Story, Sr., was the uncle of William E. Story II. In the presence of family members and others, the uncle promised to pay his nephew $5,000 ($76,000 in today's dollars) if he would refrain from drinking, using tobacco, swearing, and playing cards or billiards for money until he reached the age of twenty-one. (Note that in 1869, when this contract was formed, it was legal in New York to drink and play cards for money before the age of twenty-one.)

The nephew agreed and fully performed his part of the bargain. When he reached the age of twenty-one, he wrote and told his uncle that he had kept his part of the agreement and was therefore entitled to $5,000. The uncle wrote a letter back indicating that he was pleased with his nephew's performance and saying "you shall have five thousand dollars, as I promised you." The uncle also said that the $5,000 was in the bank and that the nephew could "consider this money on interest." The nephew left the $5,000 in the care of his uncle where it would earn interest under the terms and conditions of the letter.

The uncle died about twelve years later without having paid his nephew any part of the $5,000 and interest. The executor of the uncle's estate (Sidway, the defendant in this action) claimed that there had been no valid consideration for the promise. Sidway refused to pay the $5,000 (plus interest) to Hamer, a third party to whom the nephew had transferred his rights in the note. The court reviewed the case to determine whether the nephew had given valid consideration under the law.

IN THE LANGUAGE OF THE COURT
PARKER, J. [Justice]

* * * *

* * * Courts will not ask whether the thing which forms the consideration does in fact benefit the promisee or a third party, or is of any substantial value to any one. It is enough that something is promised, done, forborne, or suffered by the party to whom the promise is made as consideration for the promise made to him. *In general a waiver of any legal right at the request of another party is a sufficient consideration for a promise.* Any damage, or suspension, or forbearance of a right will be sufficient to sustain a promise. * * * Now, applying this rule to the facts before us, the promisee used tobacco, occasionally drank liquor, and he had a legal right to do so. That right he abandoned for a period of years upon the strength of the promise of the testator [his uncle] that for such forbearance he would give him $5,000. We need not speculate on the effort which may have been required to give up the use of those stimulants. It is sufficient that he restricted his lawful freedom of action within certain prescribed limits upon the faith of his uncle's agreement * * *. [Emphasis added.]

DECISION AND REMEDY   *The court ruled that the nephew had provided legally sufficient consideration by giving up smoking, drinking, swearing, and playing cards or billiards for money until he reached the age of twenty-one. Therefore, he was entitled to the funds.*

IMPACT OF THIS CASE ON TODAY'S LAW   *Although this case was decided more than a century ago, the principles enunciated by the court remain applicable to contracts formed today, including online contracts. For a contract to be valid and binding, consideration must be given, and that consideration must be something of legally sufficient value.*

WHAT IF THE FACTS WERE DIFFERENT?   *If the nephew had not had a legal right to engage in the behavior that he agreed to forgo, would the result in this case have been different? Explain.*

Bargained-for Exchange

The second element of consideration is that it must provide the basis for the bargain struck between the contracting parties. The item of value must be given or promised by the promisor (offeror) in return for the promisee's promise, performance, or promise of performance.

This element of bargained-for exchange distinguishes contracts from gifts. ▶ **Example 13.2** Sheng-Li says to his son, "In consideration of the fact that you are not as wealthy as your brothers, I will pay you $5,000." The fact that the word *consideration* is used does not, by itself, mean that consideration has been given. Indeed, Sheng-Li's promise is not enforceable because the son does not have to do anything in order to receive the $5,000 promised. Because the son does not need to give Sheng-Li something of legal value in return for his promise, there is no bargained-for exchange. Rather, Sheng-Li has simply stated his motive for giving his son a gift. ◀

SECTION 2

ADEQUACY OF CONSIDERATION

Adequacy of consideration involves how much consideration is given. Essentially, adequacy of consideration concerns the fairness of the bargain.

The General Rule

On the surface, when the items exchanged are of unequal value, fairness would appear to be an issue. In general, however, a court will not question the adequacy of consideration based solely on the comparative value of the things exchanged.

In other words, the determination of whether consideration exists does not depend on a comparison of the values of the things exchanged. Something need not be of direct economic or financial value to be considered legally sufficient consideration. In many situations, the exchange of promises and potential benefits is deemed to be sufficient consideration.

Under the doctrine of freedom of contract, courts leave it up to the parties to decide what something is worth, and parties are usually free to bargain as they wish. If people could sue merely because they had entered into an unwise contract, the courts would be overloaded with frivolous suits.

When Voluntary Consent May Be Lacking

When there is a large disparity in the amount or value of the consideration exchanged, it may raise a red flag for a court to look more closely at the bargain. Shockingly inadequate consideration can indicate that fraud, duress, or undue influence was involved. It may also cause a judge to question whether the contract is so one sided that it is *unconscionable*,[1] a concept that will be discussed further in Chapter 14.

For instance, an experienced appliance dealer induces a consumer to sign a contract written in complicated legal language. If the contract requires the consumer to pay twice the market value of the appliance, the disparity in value may indicate that the sale involved undue influence or fraud. A judge would thus want to make sure that the person voluntarily entered into this agreement.

SECTION 3

AGREEMENTS THAT LACK CONSIDERATION

Sometimes, one of the parties (or both parties) to an agreement may think that consideration has been exchanged when in fact it has not. Here, we look at some situations in which the parties' promises or actions do not qualify as contractual consideration.

Preexisting Duty

Under most circumstances, a promise to do what one already has a legal duty to do does not constitute legally sufficient consideration. The preexisting legal duty may be imposed by law or may arise out of a previous contract. A sheriff, for instance, has a duty to investigate crime and to arrest criminals. Hence, a sheriff cannot collect a reward for providing information leading to the capture of a criminal.

Likewise, if a party is already bound by contract to perform a certain duty, that duty cannot serve as consideration for a second contract. ▶ **Example 13.3** Ajax Contractors begins construction on a seven-story office building and after three months demands an extra $75,000 on its contract. If the extra $75,000 is not paid, the contractor will stop working. The owner of the land, finding no one else to complete the construction, agrees to pay the extra $75,000. The agreement

---

1. Pronounced un-*kon*-shun-uh-bul.

is unenforceable because it is not supported by legally sufficient consideration. Ajax Contractors had a preexisting contractual duty to complete the building. ◀

UNFORESEEN DIFFICULTIES The rule regarding preexisting duty is meant to prevent extortion and the so-called holdup game. Nonetheless, if, during performance of a contract, extraordinary difficulties arise that were totally unforeseen at the time the contract was formed, a court may allow an exception to the rule. The key is whether the court finds the modification is fair and equitable in view of circumstances not anticipated by the parties when the contract was made.[2]

Suppose that in *Example 13.3*, Ajax Contractors had asked for the extra $75,000 because it encountered a rock formation that no one knew existed. If the landowner agrees to pay the extra $75,000 to excavate the rock and the court finds that it is fair to do so, Ajax Contractors can enforce the agreement. If rock formations are common in the area, however, the court may determine that the contractor should have known of the risk. In that situation, the court may choose to apply the preexisting duty rule and prevent Ajax Contractors from obtaining the extra $75,000.

RESCISSION AND NEW CONTRACT The law recognizes that two parties can mutually agree to rescind, or cancel, their contract, at least to the extent that it is *executory* (still to be carried out). **Rescission**[3] is the unmaking of a contract so as to return the parties to the positions they occupied before the contract was made.

Sometimes, parties rescind a contract and make a new contract at the same time. When this occurs, it is often difficult to determine whether there was consideration for the new contract, or whether the parties had a preexisting duty under the previous contract. If a court finds there was a preexisting duty, then the new contract will be invalid because there was no consideration.

Past Consideration

Promises made in return for actions or events that have already taken place are unenforceable. These promises lack consideration in that the element of bargained-for exchange is missing. In short, you can bargain for something to take place now or in the future but not for something that has already taken place. Therefore, **past consideration** is no consideration.

▶ **Case in Point 13.4** Jamil Blackmon became friends with Allen Iverson when Iverson was a high school student who showed tremendous promise as an athlete. One evening, Blackmon suggested that Iverson use "The Answer" as a nickname in the summer league basketball tournaments. Blackmon said that Iverson would be "The Answer" to all of the National Basketball Association's woes. Later that night, Iverson said that he would give Blackmon 25 percent of any proceeds from the merchandising of products that used "The Answer" as a logo or a slogan. Because Iverson's promise was made in return for past consideration, it was unenforceable. In effect, Iverson stated his intention to give Blackmon a gift.[4] ◀

In a variety of situations, an employer will often ask an employee to sign a *noncompete agreement*, also called a *covenant not to compete*. Under such an agreement, the employee agrees not to compete with the employer for a certain period of time after the employment relationship ends. When a current employee is required to sign a noncompete agreement, his or her employment is not sufficient consideration for the agreement because the individual is already employed. To be valid, the agreement requires new consideration.

In the following case, the court had to decide if new consideration supported a noncompete agreement between physicians and a medical clinic.

---

2. *Restatement (Second) of Contracts,* Section 73.
3. Pronounced reh-*sih*-zhen.

4. *Blackmon v. Iverson,* 324 F.Supp.2d 602 (E.D.Pa. 2003).

CASE ANALYSIS

Case 13.2 Baugh v. Columbia Heart Clinic, P.A.[a]
Court of Appeals of South Carolina, 402 S.C. 1, 738, S.E.2d 480 (2013).

IN THE LANGUAGE OF THE COURT
THOMAS, J. [Judge]

* * * *

Columbia Heart [Clinic, P.A., in Columbia, South Carolina] is a corporate medical practice that provides comprehensive cardiology services. Its physicians are all cardiologists.

---

a. *P.A.* means "Professional Organization."

CASE 13.2 CONTINUES ▶

J. Kevin Baugh, M.D., and Barry J. Feldman, M.D., * * * are cardiologists who had been shareholders and employees of Columbia Heart since before 2000.

* * * *

When [Baugh and Feldman] became shareholders, they each entered employment agreements that forfeited money payable to them upon termination if they competed with Columbia Heart in Lexington and Richland Counties within a year. These agreements contained no other provisions that discouraged competition, and their consideration was a compensation system.

In 2004, Columbia Heart's shareholders embarked on the construction of a new medical office building in Lexington County through a limited liability company (the LLC). The LLC was almost entirely owned by the shareholder-physicians of Columbia Heart. * * * Each member of the LLC signed personal obligations on the project debt in proportion to their equity [ownership share] in the LLC. Because of (1) the investment and liabilities undertaken by Columbia Heart's shareholders as members of the LLC and (2) a recent departure of a large number of Columbia Heart physicians, Columbia Heart sought to bind its shareholder-physicians more tightly to the medical practice. Thus, in July 2004 Columbia Heart's shareholder-physicians entered into * * * [non-compete] agreements.

* * * *

* * * Article 5 [of the agreements] says the following:

Physician, in the event of termination * * * for any reason, during the twelve (12) month period immediately following the date of termination * * * shall not Compete * * * with Columbia Heart.

Section 5.2 defines specific terms "for purposes of Article 5":

"Compete" means directly or indirectly, on his own behalf or on behalf of any other Person, other than at the direction of Columbia Heart and on behalf of Columbia Heart: (A) organizing or owning any interest in a business which engages in the Business in the Territory; (B) engaging in the Business in the Territory; and (C) assisting any Person (as director, officer, employee, agent, consultant, lender, lessor or otherwise) to engage in the Business in the Territory.

"Business" is defined as "the practice of medicine in the field of cardiology." "Territory" is defined as "the area within a twenty (20) mile radius of any Columbia Heart office at which Physician routinely provided services during the year prior to the date of termination."

No separate monetary consideration was paid to any shareholder-physician to sign the Agreements, nor did the Agreements change the [established] compensation system.

* * * *

Columbia Heart opened a new office in the LLC's building in December 2005. In April 2006, [Baugh and Feldman] left Columbia Heart.

Within a month after departing, [Baugh and Feldman] opened a new practice, Lexington Heart Clinic, where they treated patients in cardiology and hired a number of Columbia Heart's administrative and medical support staff. Lexington Heart was on the same campus as Columbia Heart's Lexington office, separated by an approximate distance of 300 yards. Columbia Heart's * * * office closed in September 2006 because of fiscal unsustainability.

[Baugh and Feldman] filed suit against Columbia Heart [in a South Carolina state court] * * * seeking * * * a ruling that the Agreements contain unenforceable non-competition provisions.

The trial court * * * held the Agreements' non-competition provisions unenforceable * * * . This appeal followed.

* * * *

[Baugh and Feldman] contend * * * that the Agreements are unenforceable because they are not supported by new consideration. We disagree.

*When a covenant not to compete is entered into after the inception of employment, separate consideration, in addition to continued * * * employment, is necessary in order for the covenant to be enforceable. There is no consideration when the contract containing the covenant is exacted after several years' employment and the employee's duties and position are left unchanged.* [Emphasis added.]

[Baugh and Feldman] executed the Agreements after they became employed by Columbia Heart, and the Agreements did not change the general compensation system agreed to by the parties under their prior employment contracts. However, * * * Article 4 of the Agreements provides the following:

Physician shall be paid Five Thousand and No/100 Dollars ($5,000.00) per month for each of the twelve (12) months following termination, so long as the Physician is not in violation of Article 5 of this Agreement.

This language established that Columbia Heart promised to pay [Baugh and Feldman] each * * * a total of $60,000 over twelve months after termination so long as they did not violate the non-competition provision in Article 5. * * * Consequently, the Agreements are supported by new consideration.

* * * *

We reverse the trial court's finding that the non-competition provisions in Article 5 and Article 4 are unenforceable.

CASE 13.2 CONTINUED

LEGAL REASONING QUESTIONS

1. What is consideration?

2. When a noncompete agreement is entered into *before* employment, would additional compensation (beyond the basic salary for the position) constitute sufficient consideration for the agreement? Why or why not?

3. When a noncompete agreement is entered into *after* employment has begun, would continued employment constitute sufficient consideration for the agreement? Explain.

4. In this case, did the court hold that the noncompete agreement at the heart of the dispute was supported by consideration? Why or why not?

Illusory Promises

If the terms of the contract express such uncertainty of performance that the promisor has not definitely promised to do anything, the promise is said to be *illusory*—without consideration and unenforceable. A promise is illusory when it fails to bind the promisor.

▶ **Example 13.5** The president of Tuscan Corporation says to her employees, "If profits continue to be high, everyone will get a 10 percent bonus at the end of the year—if management agrees." This is an *illusory promise,* or no promise at all, because performance depends solely on the discretion of the president (management). There is no bargained-for consideration. The statement indicates only that management may or may not do something in the future. Therefore, even though the employees work hard and profits remain high, the company is not obligated to pay the bonus now or later. ◀

OPTION-TO-CANCEL CLAUSES Sometimes, option-to-cancel clauses in contracts present problems in regard to consideration. When the promisor has the option to cancel the contract before performance has begun, the promise is illusory. ▶ **Example 13.6** Abe contracts to hire Chris for one year at $5,000 per month, reserving the right to cancel the contract at any time. On close examination of these words, you can see that Abe has not actually agreed to hire Chris, as Abe could cancel without liability before Chris started performance. This contract is therefore illusory.

But if Abe instead reserves the right to cancel the contract at any time *after* Chris has begun performance by giving Chris *thirty days' notice,* the promise is not illusory. Abe, by saying that he will give Chris

thirty days' notice, is relinquishing the opportunity (legal right) to hire someone else instead of Chris for a thirty-day period. If Chris works for one month and Abe then gives him thirty days' notice, Chris has an enforceable claim for two months' salary ($10,000). ◀

REQUIREMENTS AND OUTPUT CONTRACTS Problems with consideration may also arise in other types of contracts because of uncertainty of performance. Uncertain performance is characteristic of requirements and output contracts, for instance. In a *requirements contract,* a buyer and a seller agree that the buyer will purchase from the seller all of the goods of a designated type that the buyer needs, or requires. In an *output contract,* the buyer and seller agree that the buyer will purchase from the seller all of what the seller produces, or the seller's output. These types of sales contracts will be discussed further in Chapter 20.

Concept Summary 13.1 on the following page provides a convenient summary of the main aspects of consideration.

SECTION 4
SETTLEMENT OF CLAIMS

Businesspersons and others often enter into contracts to settle legal claims. It is important to understand the nature of consideration given in these kinds of settlement agreements, or contracts. Claims are commonly settled through an *accord and satisfaction,* in which a debtor offers to pay a lesser amount than the creditor purports to be owed. Claims may also be settled by the signing of a *release* or a *covenant not to sue.*

CONCEPT SUMMARY 13.1
Consideration

Elements of Consideration	Consideration is the value given in exchange for a promise. A contract cannot be formed without sufficient consideration. Consideration is often broken down into two elements: 1. *Legal value*—Something of legally sufficient value must be given in exchange for a promise. This may consist of a promise, a performance, or a forbearance. 2. *Bargained-for exchange*—There must be a bargained-for exchange.
Adequacy of Consideration	Adequacy of consideration relates to how much consideration is given and whether a fair bargain was reached. Courts will inquire into the adequacy of consideration (if the consideration is legally sufficient) only when fraud, undue influence, duress, or the lack of a bargained-for exchange may be involved.
Agreements That Lack Consideration	Consideration is lacking in the following situations: 1. *Preexisting duty*—Consideration is not legally sufficient if one is either by law or by contract under a *preexisting duty* to perform the action being offered as consideration for a new contract. 2. *Past consideration*—Actions or events that have already taken place do not constitute legally sufficient consideration. 3. *Illusory promises*—When the nature or extent of performance is too uncertain, the promise is rendered illusory and unenforceable.

Accord and Satisfaction

In an **accord and satisfaction,** a debtor offers to pay, and a creditor accepts, a lesser amount than the creditor originally claimed was owed. The *accord* is the agreement. In the accord, one party undertakes to give or perform, and the other to accept, in satisfaction of a claim, something other than that on which the parties originally agreed. *Satisfaction* is the performance (usually payment) that takes place after the accord is executed.

A basic rule is that there can be no satisfaction unless there is first an accord. For accord and satisfaction to occur, the amount of the debt *must be in dispute.*

LIQUIDATED DEBTS If a debt is *liquidated,* accord and satisfaction cannot take place. A **liquidated debt** is one whose amount has been ascertained, fixed, agreed on, settled, or exactly determined. ▶ **Example 13.7** Barbara Kwan signs an installment loan contract with her bank. In the contract, Kwan agrees to pay a set rate of interest on a specified amount of borrowed funds at monthly intervals for two years. Because both parties know the precise amount of the total obligation, it is a liquidated debt. ◀

In the majority of states, acceptance of a lesser sum than the entire amount of a liquidated debt is *not* sat- isfaction, and the balance of the debt is still legally owed. The reason for this rule is that the debtor has given no consideration to satisfy the obligation of paying the balance to the creditor. The debtor had a preexisting legal obligation to pay the entire debt. (Of course, even with liquidated debts, creditors often do negotiate debt settlement agreements with debtors for a lesser amount than was originally owed. Creditors sometimes even forgive or write off a liquidated debt as uncollectable.)

UNLIQUIDATED DEBTS An **unliquidated debt** is the opposite of a liquidated debt. The amount of the debt is *not* settled, fixed, agreed on, ascertained, or determined, and reasonable persons may differ over the amount owed. In these circumstances, acceptance of a lesser sum operates as satisfaction, or discharge, of the debt because there is valid consideration. The parties give up a legal right to contest the amount in dispute.

Release

A **release** is a contract in which one party forfeits the right to pursue a legal claim against the other party. It bars any further recovery beyond the terms stated in the release.

A release will generally be binding if it meets the following requirements:

1. The agreement is made in good faith (honesty).
2. The release contract is in a signed writing (required in many states).
3. The contract is accompanied by consideration.[5]

Clearly, an individual is better off knowing the extent of his or her injuries or damages before signing a release. ▶ **Example 13.8**   Lupe's car is damaged in an automobile accident caused by Dexter's negligence. Dexter offers to give her $3,000 if she will release him from further liability resulting from the accident. Lupe agrees and signs the release.

If Lupe later discovers that it will cost $4,200 to repair her car, she cannot recover the additional amount from Dexter. Lupe is limited to the $3,000 specified in the release. Lupe and Dexter both volun-

tarily agreed to the terms in the release, which was in a signed writing, and sufficient consideration was present. The consideration was the legal right Lupe forfeited to sue to recover damages, should they be more than $3,000, in exchange for Dexter's promise to give her $3,000. ◀

Covenant Not to Sue

Unlike a release, a **covenant not to sue** does not always bar further recovery. The parties simply substitute a contractual obligation for some other type of legal action based on a valid claim. Suppose in *Example 13.8* above, that Lupe agrees with Dexter not to sue for damages in a tort action if he will pay for the damage to her car. If Dexter fails to pay for the repairs, Lupe can bring an action against him for breach of contract.

As the following case illustrates, a covenant not to sue can form the basis for a dismissal of the claims of either party to the covenant.

---

5. Under the Uniform Commercial Code (UCC), a written, signed waiver or renunciation by an aggrieved party discharges any further liability for a breach, even without consideration.

SP TLIGHT on Nike

Case 13.3   Already, LLC v. Nike, Inc.

Supreme Court of the United States, __ U.S. __, 133 S.Ct. 721, 184 L.Ed.2d 553 (2013).

BACKGROUND AND FACTS   Nike, Inc., designs, makes, and sells athletic footwear, including a line of shoes known as "Air Force 1." Already, LLC, also designs and markets athletic footwear, including the "Sugar" and "Soulja Boy" lines. Nike filed a suit in a federal district court against Already, alleging that Soulja Boys and Sugars infringed the Air Force 1 trademark. Already filed a counterclaim, contending that the Air Force 1 trademark was invalid. While the suit was pending, Nike issued a covenant not to sue, promising not to raise any trademark claims against Already or any affiliated entity based on Already's existing footwear designs, or any future Already designs that constituted a "colorable imitation" of Already's current products. Nike then filed a motion to dismiss its own claims and to dismiss Already's counterclaim. Already opposed the dismissal of its counterclaim, but the court granted Nike's motion. The U.S. Court of Appeals for the Second Circuit affirmed. Already appealed to the United States Supreme Court.

   IN THE LANGUAGE OF THE COURT
Chief Justice *ROBERTS* delivered the opinion of the Court.
     * * * *

* * * A defendant cannot automatically moot a case simply by ending its unlawful conduct once sued. Otherwise, a defendant could engage in unlawful conduct, stop when sued to have the case declared moot [of no legal relevance], then pick up where he left off, repeating this cycle until he achieves all his unlawful ends. Given this concern, * * * *a defendant claiming that its voluntary compliance moots a case bears the formidable burden of showing that it is absolutely clear the allegedly wrongful behavior could not reasonably be expected to recur.* [This is the voluntary cessation test. Emphasis added.]
     * * * *

We begin our analysis with the terms of the covenant:

CASE 13.3 CONTINUES ▶

CASE 13.3 CONTINUED

[Nike] unconditionally and irrevocably covenants to refrain from making *any* claim(s) or demand(s) * * * against Already or *any* of its * * * related business entities * * * [including] distributors * * * and employees of such entities and *all* customers * * * on account of any *possible* cause of action based on or involving trademark infringement * * * relating to the NIKE Mark based on the appearance of *any* of Already's current and/or previous footwear product designs, and *any* colorable imitations thereof, regardless of whether that footwear is produced * * * or otherwise used in commerce.

The breadth of this covenant suffices to meet the burden imposed by the voluntary cessation test.

In addition, Nike originally argued that the Sugars and Soulja Boys infringed its trademark; in other words, Nike believed those shoes were "colorable imitations" of the Air Force 1s. Nike's covenant now allows Already to produce all of its existing footwear designs—including the Sugar and Soulja Boy—and any "colorable imitation" of those designs. * * * It is hard to imagine a scenario that would potentially infringe Nike's trademark and yet not fall under the covenant. Nike, having taken the position in court that there is no prospect of such a shoe, would be hard pressed to assert the contrary down the road. If such a shoe exists, the parties have not pointed to it, there is no evidence that Already has dreamt of it, and we cannot conceive of it. It sits, as far as we can tell, on a shelf between Dorothy's ruby slippers and Perseus's winged sandals.

* * * *

* * * Given the covenant's broad language, and given that Already has asserted no concrete plans to engage in conduct not covered by the covenant, we can conclude the case is moot because the challenged conduct cannot reasonably be expected to recur.

DECISION AND REMEDY *The United States Supreme Court affirmed the judgment of the lower court. Under the covenant not to sue, Nike could not file a claim for trademark infringement against Already, and Already could not assert that Nike's trademark was invalid.*

THE ECONOMIC DIMENSION *Why would any party agree to a covenant not to sue?*

THE LEGAL ENVIRONMENT DIMENSION *Which types of contracts are similar to a covenant not to sue? Explain.*

SECTION 5

EXCEPTIONS TO THE CONSIDERATION REQUIREMENT

There are some exceptions to the rule that only promises supported by consideration are enforceable. The following types of promises may be enforced despite the lack of consideration:

1. Promises that induce detrimental reliance, under the doctrine of *promissory estoppel*.
2. Promises to pay debts that are barred by a statute of limitations.
3. Promises to make charitable contributions.

Promissory Estoppel

Sometimes, individuals rely on promises to their detriment, and their reliance may form a basis for a court to infer contract rights and duties. Under the doctrine of **promissory estoppel** (also called *detrimental reliance*), a person who has reasonably and substantially relied on the promise of another may be able to obtain some measure of recovery.

Promissory estoppel is applied in a wide variety of contexts in which a promise is otherwise unenforceable, such as when a promise made *without consideration*. Under this doctrine, a court may enforce an otherwise unenforceable promise to avoid the injustice that would otherwise result.

REQUIREMENTS TO STATE A CLAIM For the promissory estoppel doctrine to be applied, the following elements are required:

1. There must be a clear and definite promise.
2. The promisor should have expected that the promisee would rely on the promise.
3. The promisee reasonably relied on the promise by acting or refraining from some act.
4. The promisee's reliance was definite and resulted in substantial detriment.

5. Enforcement of the promise is necessary to avoid injustice.

If these requirements are met, a promise may be enforced even though it is not supported by consideration.[6] In essence, the promisor will be **estopped** (prevented) from asserting the lack of consideration as a defense.

Promissory estoppel is similar in some ways to the doctrine of quasi contract that was discussed in Chapter 11. In both situations, a court, acting in the interests of equity, imposes contract obligations on the parties to prevent unfairness even though no actual contract exists. The difference is that with quasi contract, no promise was made at all. In contrast, with promissory estoppel, a promise was made and relied on, but it was unenforceable.

APPLICATION OF THE DOCTRINE Promissory estoppel was originally applied to situations involving gifts (I promise to pay you $1,000 a week so that you will not have to work) and donations to charities (I promise to contribute $50,000 a year to the Raising Giants orphanage). Later, courts began to apply the doctrine to avoid inequity or hardship in other situations, including business transactions, some employment relationships, and even disputes among family members.

▶ **Case in Point 13.9** Jeffrey and Kathryn Dow own 125 acres of land in Corinth, Maine. The Dows regarded the land as their children's heritage, and the subject of the children's living on the land was often discussed within the family. With the Dows' permission, their daughter Teresa installed a mobile home and built a garage on the land. After Teresa married Jarrod Harvey, the Dows agreed to finance the construction of a house on the land for the couple. When Jarrod died in a motorcycle accident, however, Teresa financed the house with his life insurance proceeds. The construction cost about $200,000. Her father, Jeffrey, performed a substantial amount of carpentry and other work on the house.

Teresa then asked her parents for a deed to the property so that she could obtain a mortgage. They refused. Teresa sued her parents for promissory estoppel. Maine's highest court ruled in favor of Teresa's promissory estoppel claim. The court reasoned that the Dows' support and encouragement of their daughter's construction of a house on the land "conclusively demonstrated" their intent to transfer. For years, they had made general promises to convey the

land to their children, including Teresa. Teresa had reasonably relied on their promise in financing construction of a house to her detriment ($200,000). The court concluded that enforcing the promise was the only way to avoid injustice in this situation.[7] ◀

Promises to Pay Debts Barred by a Statute of Limitations

Statutes of limitations in all states require a creditor to sue within a specified period to recover a debt. If the creditor fails to sue in time, recovery of the debt is barred by the statute of limitations.

A debtor who promises to pay a previous debt even though recovery is barred by the statute of limitations makes an enforceable promise. *The promise needs no consideration.* (Some states, however, require that it be in writing.) In effect, the promise extends the limitations period, and the creditor can sue to recover the entire debt or at least the amount promised. The promise can be implied if the debtor acknowledges the barred debt by making a partial payment.

Charitable Subscriptions

A charitable subscription is a promise to make a donation to a religious, educational, or charitable institution. Traditionally, such promises were unenforceable because they are not supported by legally sufficient consideration. A gift, after all, is the opposite of bargained-for consideration. The modern view, however, is to make exceptions to the general rule by applying the doctrine of promissory estoppel.

▶ **Example 13.10** A church solicits and receives pledges (commitments to contribute funds) from church members to erect a new church building. On the basis of these pledges, the church purchases land, hires architects, and makes other contracts that change its position. Because of the church's detrimental reliance, a court may enforce the pledges under the theory of promissory estoppel. Alternatively, a court may find consideration in the fact that each promise was made in reliance on the other promises of support or that the church trustees, by accepting the subscriptions, impliedly promised to complete the proposed undertaking. ◀

6. *Restatement (Second) of Contracts,* Section 90.

7. *Harvey v. Dow,* 2011 ME 4, 11 A.3d 303 (2011).

Reviewing: Consideration

John operates a motorcycle repair shop from his home but finds that his business is limited by the small size of his garage. Driving by a neighbor's property, he notices a for-sale sign on a large, metal-sided garage. John contacts the neighbor and offers to buy the building, hoping that it can be dismantled and moved to his own property. The neighbor accepts John's payment and makes a generous offer in return: if John will help him dismantle the garage, which will take a substantial amount of time, he will help John reassemble it after it has been transported to John's property. They agree to have the entire job completed within two weeks. John spends every day for a week working with his neighbor to disassemble the building. In his rush to acquire a larger workspace, he turns down several lucrative repair jobs. Once the disassembled building has been moved to John's property, however, the neighbor refuses to help John reassemble it as he originally promised. Using the information presented in the chapter, answer the following questions.

1. Are the basic elements of consideration present in the neighbor's promise to help John reassemble the garage? Why or why not?
2. Suppose that the neighbor starts to help John but then realizes that, because of the layout of John's property, putting the building back together will take much more work than dismantling it took. Under which principle discussed in the chapter might the neighbor be allowed to ask for additional compensation?
3. What if John's neighbor made his promise to help reassemble the garage at the time he and John were moving it to John's property, saying, "Since you helped me take it down, I will help you put it back up." Would John be able to enforce this promise? Why or why not?
4. Under what doctrine discussed in the chapter might John seek to recover the profits he lost when he turned down repair jobs for one week?

DEBATE THIS . . . *Courts should not be able to rule on the adequacy of consideration. A deal is a deal.*

Terms and Concepts

accord and satisfaction 266
consideration 260
covenant not to sue 267
estopped 269

forbearance 260
liquidated debt 266
past consideration 263
promissory estoppel 268

release 266
rescission 263
unliquidated debt 266

ExamPrep

Issue Spotters

1. In September, Sharyn agrees to work for Totem Productions, Inc., at $500 a week for a year beginning January 1. In October, Sharyn is offered the same work at $600 a week by Umber Shows, Ltd. When Sharyn tells Totem about the other offer, they tear up their contract and agree that Sharyn will be paid $575. Is the new contract binding? Explain. **(See page 263.)**

2. Before Maria starts her first year of college, Fred promises to give her $5,000 when she graduates. She goes to college, borrowing and spending far more than $5,000. At the beginning of the spring semester of her senior year, she reminds Fred of the promise. Fred sends her a note that says, "I revoke the promise." Is Fred's promise binding? Explain. **(See page 268.)**

• Check your answers to the Issue Spotters against the answers provided in Appendix E at the end of this text.

Before the Test

Go to **www.cengagebrain.com**, enter the ISBN 9781285185248, and click on "Find" to locate this text-book's Web site. Then, click on "Access Now" under "Study Tools," and select Chapter 13 at the top. There, you will find a Practice Quiz that you can take to assess your mastery of the concepts in this chapter, as well as Flashcards and a Glossary of important terms.

Business Scenarios

13–1. Preexisting Duty. Tabor is a buyer of file cabinets manufactured by Martin. Martin's contract with Tabor calls for delivery of fifty file cabinets at $40 per cabinet in five equal installments. After delivery of two installments (twenty cabinets), Martin informs Tabor that because of inflation, Martin is losing money and will promise to deliver the remaining thirty cabinets only if Tabor will pay $50 per cabinet. Tabor agrees in writing to do so. Discuss whether Martin can legally collect the additional $100 on delivery to Tabor of the next installment of ten cabinets. **(See page 262.)**

13–2. Consideration. Daniel, a recent college graduate, is on his way home for the Christmas holidays from his new job. He gets caught in a snowstorm and is taken in by an elderly couple, who provide him with food and shelter. After the snowplows have cleared the road, Daniel proceeds home. Daniel's father, Fred, is most appreciative of the elderly couple's action and in a letter promises to pay them $500. The elderly couple, in need of funds, accept Fred's offer. Then, because of a dispute between Daniel and Fred, Fred refuses to pay the elderly couple the $500. Discuss whether the couple can hold Fred liable in contract for the services rendered to Daniel. **(See page 260.)**

13–3. Illusory Promises. Costello hired Sagan to drive his racing car in a race. Sagan's friend Gideon promised to pay Sagan $3,000 if she won the race. Sagan won the race, but Gideon refused to pay. Gideon contended that no legally binding contract had been formed because he had received no consideration from Sagan in exchange for his promise to pay the $3,000. Sagan sued Gideon for breach of contract, arguing that winning the race was the consideration given in exchange for Gideon's promise to pay the $3,000. What rule of law discussed in this chapter supports Gideon's claim? **(See page 265.)**

13–4. Accord and Satisfaction. Merrick grows and sells blueberries. Maine Wild Blueberry Co. agreed to buy all of Merrick's crop under a contract that left the price unliquidated. Merrick delivered the berries, but a dispute arose over the price. Maine Wild sent Merrick a check with a letter stating that the check was the "final settlement." Merrick cashed the check but filed a suit for breach of contract, claiming that he was owed more. What will the court likely decide in this case? Why? **(See page 266.)**

Business Case Problems

13–5. Past Consideration. Access Organics, Inc., hired Andy Hernandez to sell organic produce. Later, Hernandez signed an agreement not to compete with Access for two years following the termination of his employment. He did not receive a pay increase or any other new benefits in return for signing the agreement. When Access encountered financial trouble, Hernandez left and began to compete with his former employer. Access filed a lawsuit against Hernandez. Is the noncompete agreement enforceable? Discuss. [*Access Organics, Inc. v. Hernandez,* 341 Mont. 73, 175 P.3d 899 (2008)] **(See page 263.)**

13–6. BUSINESS CASE PROBLEM WITH SAMPLE ANSWER: Rescission.

 Farrokh and Scheherezade Sharabianlou signed a purchase agreement to buy a building owned by Berenstein Associates for $2 million. They deposited $115,000 toward the purchase. Before the deal closed, an environmental assessment of the property indicated the presence of chemicals used in dry cleaning. This sub- *stantially reduced the property's value. Do the Sharabianlous have a good argument for the return of their deposit and rescission of the contract? Explain your answer. [Sharabianlou v. Karp, 181 Cal.App.4th 1133, 105 Cal.Rptr.3d 300 (1st Dist. 2010)]* **(See page 263.)**

• **For a sample answer to Problem 13–6, go to Appendix F at the end of this text.**

13–7. Statute of Limitations. Leonard Kranzler loaned Lewis Saltzman $100,000. Saltzman made fifteen payments on the loan, but this did not repay the entire amount. More than ten years after the date of the loan, but less than two years after the date of the last payment, Kranzler filed a suit against Saltzman to recover the outstanding balance. Saltzman claimed that the suit was barred by a ten-year statute of limitations. Does Kranzler need to prove a new promise with new consideration to collect the unpaid debt? Explain. [*Kranzler v. Saltzman,* 407 Ill. App.3d 24, 942 N.E.2d 722, 347 Ill.Dec. 519 (1 Dist. 2011)] **(See page 269.)**

13–8. Consideration. On Brenda Sniezek's first day of work for the Kansas City Chiefs Football Club, she signed a document that purported to compel arbitration of any disputes that she might have with the Chiefs. In the document, Sniezek agreed to comply at all times with and be bound by the constitution and bylaws of the National Football League (NFL). She agreed to refer all disputes to the NFL Commissioner for a binding decision. On the Commissioner's decision, she agreed to release the Chiefs and others from any related claims. Nowhere in the document did the Chiefs agree to do anything. Was there consideration for the arbitration provision? Explain. [*Sniezek v. Kansas City Chiefs Football Club*, __ S.W.3e __, 2013 WL 661632 (Mo.App. W.D. 2013)] **(See page 260.)**

13–9. A QUESTION OF ETHICS: Promissory Estoppel.

 Claudia Aceves borrowed from U.S. Bank to buy a home. Two years later, she could no longer afford the monthly payments. The bank notified her that it planned to foreclose (take possession of and sell) on her home. Aceves filed for bankruptcy. The bank offered to modify Aceves's mortgage if she would forgo bankruptcy. She agreed. Once she withdrew the filing, however, the bank foreclosed. [Aceves v. U.S. Bank, N.A., 192 Cal.App.4th 218, 120 Cal.Rptr.3d 507 (2 Dist. 2011)] **(See page 268.)**

(a) Could Aceves succeed on a claim of promissory estoppel? Why or why not?

(b) Did Aceves or U.S. Bank behave unethically? Discuss.

Legal Reasoning Group Activity

13–10. Preexisting Duty. Melissa Faraj owns a lot and wants to build a house according to a particular set of plans and specifications. She solicits bids from building contractors and receives three bids: one from Carlton for $160,000, one from Feldberg for $158,000, and one from Siegel for $153,000. She accepts Siegel's bid. One month after beginning construction of the house, Siegel contacts Faraj and tells her that because of inflation and a recent price hike for materials, he will not finish the house unless Faraj agrees to pay an extra $13,000. Faraj reluctantly agrees to pay the additional sum. **(See page 262.)**

(a) One group will discuss whether a contractor can ever raise the price of completing construction based on inflation and the rising cost of materials.

(b) A second group will assume that after the house is finished, Faraj refuses to pay the extra $13,000. The group will decide whether Faraj is legally required to pay this additional amount.

(c) A third group will discuss the types of extraordinary difficulties that could arise during construction that would justify a contractor charging more than the original bid.

CHAPTER 14
CAPACITY AND LEGALITY

In addition to agreement and consideration, for a contract to be deemed valid, the parties to the contract must have **contractual capacity**—the legal ability to enter into a contractual relationship. Courts generally presume the existence of contractual capacity, but in some situations, as when a person is young or mentally incompetent, capacity may be lacking or questionable. Similarly, contracts calling for the performance of an illegal act are illegal and thus void—they are not contracts at all. In this chapter, we examine contractual capacity and some aspects of illegal bargains.

Realize that capacity and legality are not inherently related other than that they are both contract requirements. We treat these topics in one chapter merely for convenience and reasons of space.

SECTION 1
CONTRACTUAL CAPACITY

Historically, the law has given special protection to those who bargain with the inexperience of youth and those who lack the degree of mental competence required by law. A person who has been determined by a court to be mentally incompetent, for instance, cannot form a legally binding contract with another party. In other situations, a party may have the capacity to enter into a valid contract but also have the right to avoid liability under it. Minors—or *infants,* as they are commonly referred to in legal terminology—usually are not legally bound by contracts. In this section, we look at the effect of youth, intoxication, and mental incompetence on contractual capacity.

Minors

Today, in almost all states, the **age of majority** (when a person is no longer a minor) for contractual purposes is eighteen years.[1] In addition, some states provide for the termination of minority on marriage.

Minority status may also be terminated by a minor's **emancipation,** which occurs when a child's parent or legal guardian relinquishes the legal right to exercise control over the child. Normally, minors who leave home to support themselves are considered emancipated. Several jurisdictions permit minors themselves to petition a court for emancipation. For business purposes, a minor may petition a court to be treated as an adult.

The general rule is that a minor can enter into any contract that an adult can, except contracts prohibited by law for minors (for example, the purchase of tobacco or alcoholic beverages). A contract entered into by a minor, however, is voidable at the option of that minor, subject to certain exceptions. To exercise the option to avoid a contract, a minor need only manifest (clearly show) an intention not to be bound by it. The minor "avoids" the contract by disaffirming it.

DISAFFIRMANCE The legal avoidance, or setting aside, of a contractual obligation is referred to as **disaffirmance.** To disaffirm, a minor must express his or her intent, through words or conduct, not to be bound to the contract. The minor must disaffirm the entire contract, not merely a portion of it. For instance, the minor cannot decide to keep part of the goods purchased under a contract and return the remaining goods.

▶ **Case in Point 14.1** Fifteen-year-old Morgan Kelly was a cadet in her high school's Navy Junior

---

1. The age of majority may still be twenty-one for other purposes, such as the purchase and consumption of alcohol.

Reserve Officer Training Corps. As part of the program, she visited a U.S. Marine Corps training facility. To enter the camp, she was required to sign a waiver that exempted the Marines from all liability for any injuries arising from her visit. While participating in activities on the camp's confidence-building course, Kelly fell from the "Slide for Life" and suffered serious injuries. She filed a suit to recover her medical costs. The Marines asserted that she had signed their waiver of liability. Kelly claimed that she had disaffirmed the waiver when she filed suit. The court ruled in Kelly's favor. Liability waivers are generally enforceable contracts, but a minor can avoid a contract by disaffirming it.[2] ◄

Note that an adult who enters into a contract with a minor cannot avoid his or her contractual duties on the ground that the minor can do so. Unless the minor exercises the option to disaffirm the contract, the adult party normally is bound by it. On disaffirming a contract, a minor can recover any property that he or she transferred to the adult as consideration, even if the property is in the possession of a third party.[3]

Must Be within a Reasonable Time. A contract can ordinarily be disaffirmed at any time during minority[4] or for a reasonable period after reaching majority. What constitutes a "reasonable" time may vary. If an individual fails to disaffirm an executed contract (fully performed) within a reasonable time after reaching the age of majority, a court will likely hold that the contract has been ratified (*ratification* will be discussed shortly).

Minor's Obligations on Disaffirmance. Although all states' laws permit minors to disaffirm contracts (with certain exceptions), states differ on the extent of a minor's obligations on disaffirmance. Courts in most states hold that the minor need only return the goods (or other consideration) subject to the contract, provided the goods are in the minor's possession or control. Even if the minor returns damaged goods, the minor often is entitled to disaffirm the contract and obtain a full refund of the purchase price.

Courts in a growing number of states place an additional duty on the minor to restore the adult party to

the position she or he held before the contract was made. These courts may hold a minor responsible for damage, ordinary wear and tear, and depreciation of goods that the minor used prior to disaffirmance.

▶ **Case in Point 14.2** Sixteen-year-old Joseph Dodson bought a pickup truck from a used-car dealer. Although the truck developed mechanical problems nine months later, Dodson continued to drive it until it stopped running. Then Dodson disaffirmed the contract and attempted to return the truck to the dealer for a full refund. When the dealer refused to accept the pickup or refund the purchase price, Dodson filed a suit. Ultimately, the Tennessee Supreme Court allowed Dodson to disaffirm the contract but required him to compensate the seller for the depreciated value—not the purchase price—of the pickup.[5] ◄

EXCEPTIONS TO A MINOR'S RIGHT TO DISAFFIRM State courts and legislatures have carved out several exceptions to the minor's right to disaffirm. Marriage contracts and contracts to enlist in the armed services, for instance, cannot be avoided for public-policy reasons. Some contracts may not be disaffirmed for other reasons, including those discussed here.

Misrepresentation of Age. Ordinarily, minors can disaffirm contracts even when they have misrepresented their age (claimed to be twenty-one years old when they were not). Nevertheless, a growing number of states have enacted laws to prohibit disaffirmance in such situations. In some states, misrepresentation of age is enough to prevent disaffirmance. Other states prohibit disaffirmance by minors who misrepresented their age while engaged in business as an adult.

Contracts for Necessaries. A minor who enters into a contract for necessaries may disaffirm the contract but remains liable for the reasonable value of the goods. **Necessaries** are basic needs, such as food, clothing, shelter, and medical services. What is a necessary for one minor, however, may be a luxury for another, depending on the minors' customary living standard. Contracts for necessaries are enforceable only to the level of value needed to maintain the minor's standard of living.

RATIFICATION In contract law, **ratification** is the act of accepting and giving legal force to an obligation

2. *Kelly v. United States,* 809 F.Supp.2d 429 (E.D.N.C. 2011).
3. Section 2–403(1) of the Uniform Commercial Code (UCC) allows an exception if the third party is a "good faith purchaser for value." See Chapter 20.
4. In some states, however, a minor who enters into a contract for the sale of land cannot disaffirm the contract until she or he reaches the age of majority.
5. *Dodson v. Shrader,* 824 S.W.2d 545 (Tenn.Sup.Ct. 1992) is a seminal case on this subject. See also *Restatement (Third) of Restitution,* Sections 16 and 33.

that previously was not enforceable. A minor who has reached the age of majority can ratify a contract expressly or impliedly. *Express* ratification takes place when the individual, on reaching the age of majority, states orally or in writing that he or she intends to be bound by the contract. *Implied* ratification takes place when the minor, on reaching the age of majority, indicates an intent to abide by the contract.

▶ **Example 14.3** Lin enters into a contract to sell her laptop to Andrew, a minor. If, on reaching the age of majority, Andrew e-mails Lin stating that he still agrees to buy the laptop, he has *expressly* ratified the contract. If, instead, Andrew takes possession of the laptop as a minor and continues to use it well after reaching the age of majority, he has *impliedly* ratified the contract. ◀

If a minor fails to disaffirm a contract within a reasonable time after reaching the age of majority, then the court must determine whether the conduct constitutes ratification or disaffirmance. Generally, courts presume that executed contracts (fully performed) are ratified and that executory contracts (not yet fully performed by both parties) are disaffirmed.

PARENTS' LIABILITY As a general rule, parents are not liable for contracts made by minor children acting on their own. As a consequence, businesses ordinarily require parents to cosign any contract made with a minor. The parents then become personally obligated under the contract to perform the conditions of the contract, even if their child avoids liability. (Parents can sometimes be held liable for a minor's torts, however, depending on state law.)

Concept Summary 14.1 below reviews the rules relating to contracts by minors.

Intoxication

Intoxication is a condition in which a person's normal capacity to act or think is inhibited by alcohol or some other drug. A contract entered into by an intoxicated person can be either voidable or valid (and thus enforceable).[6]

If the person was sufficiently intoxicated to lack mental capacity, then the agreement may be voidable even if the intoxication was purely voluntary. If, despite intoxication, the person understood the legal consequences of the agreement, the contract will be enforceable.

Courts look at objective indications of the intoxicated person's condition to determine if he or she possessed or lacked the required capacity. It is difficult to prove that a person's judgment was so severely impaired that he or she could not comprehend the legal consequences of entering into a contract. Therefore, courts rarely permit contracts to be avoided due to intoxication.

DISAFFIRMANCE If a contract is voidable because one party was intoxicated, that person has the option of disaffirming it while intoxicated and for a reasonable time after becoming sober. The person claiming intoxication typically must be able to return all

---

6. Note that if an alcoholic makes a contract while sober, there is no lack of capacity. See *Wright v. Fisher,* 32 N.W. 605 (Mich. 1887).

CONCEPT SUMMARY 14.1
Contracts by Minors

CONCEPT	DESCRIPTION
General Rule	Contracts entered into by minors are *voidable* at the option of the minor.
Rules of Disaffirmance	A minor may disaffirm the contract at any time while still a minor and within a reasonable time after reaching the age of majority. Most states do not require restitution.
Exceptions to Basic Rules of Disaffirmance	1. *Misrepresentation of age (or fraud)*—In many jurisdictions, misrepresentation of age prohibits the right of disaffirmance. 2. *Necessaries*—Minors remain liable for the reasonable value of necessaries (goods and services). 3. *Ratification*—After reaching the age of majority, a person can ratify a contract that he or she formed as a minor, thereby becoming fully liable for it.

consideration received unless the contract involved necessaries. Contracts for necessaries are voidable, but the intoxicated person is liable in quasi contract for the reasonable value of the consideration received (see Chapter 13).

RATIFICATION An intoxicated person, after becoming sober, may ratify a contract expressly or impliedly, just as a minor may do on reaching majority. Implied ratification occurs when a person enters into a contract while intoxicated and fails to disaffirm the contract within a *reasonable* time after becoming sober. Acts or conduct inconsistent with an intent to disaffirm—such as the continued use of property purchased under a voidable contract—will also ratify the contract.

See *Concept Summary 14.2* below for a review of the rules relating to contracts by intoxicated persons.

Mental Incompetence

Contracts made by mentally incompetent persons can be void, voidable, or valid. We look here at the circumstances that determine when each of these classifications applies.

WHEN THE CONTRACT WILL BE VOID If a court has previously determined that a person is mentally incompetent, any contract made by that person is *void*—no contract exists. On determining that someone is mentally incompetent, the court appoints a guardian to represent the individual. Only the guardian can enter into binding legal obligations on behalf of the mentally incompetent person.

WHEN THE CONTRACT WILL BE VOIDABLE If a court has not previously judged a person to be mentally incompetent but the person was incompetent at the time the contract was formed, the contract may be voidable. A contract is *voidable* if the person did not know he or she was entering into the contract or lacked the mental capacity to comprehend its nature, purpose, and consequences. In such situations, the contract is voidable (or can be ratified) at the option of the mentally incompetent person but not at the option of the other party.

▶ **Example 14.4** Larry agrees to sell his stock in Google, Inc., to Sergey for substantially less than its market value. At the time of the deal, Larry is confused about the purpose and details of the transaction, but he has not been declared incompetent. Nonetheless, if a court finds that Larry did not understand the nature and consequences of the contract due to a lack of mental capacity, he can avoid the sale. ◀

WHEN THE CONTRACT WILL BE VALID A contract entered into by a mentally incompetent person (whom a court has not previously declared incompetent) may also be *valid* if the person had capacity *at the time the contract was formed*. Some people who are incompetent due to age or illness have *lucid intervals*—temporary periods of sufficient intelligence, judgment, and will. During such intervals, they will be considered to have legal capacity to enter into contracts.

See *Concept Summary 14.3* on the following page for a review of the rules relating to contracts entered into by mentally incompetent persons.

CONCEPT SUMMARY 14.2
Contracts by Intoxicated Persons

CONCEPT	DESCRIPTION
General Rules	If a person was sufficiently intoxicated to lack the mental capacity to comprehend the legal consequences of entering into the contract, the contract may be *voidable* at the option of the intoxicated person. If, despite intoxication, the person understood these legal consequences, the contract will be enforceable.
Disaffirmance	An intoxicated person may disaffirm the contract at any time while intoxicated and for a reasonable time after becoming sober but must make full restitution. Contracts for necessaries are voidable, but the intoxicated person is liable for the reasonable value of the goods or services.
Ratification	After becoming sober, a person can ratify a contract that she or he formed while intoxicated, thereby becoming fully liable for it.

CONCEPT SUMMARY 14.3
Contracts by Mentally Incompetent Persons

CONCEPT	DESCRIPTION
Void	If a court has declared a person to be mentally incompetent and has appointed a legal guardian, any contract made by that person is void from the outset.
Voidable	If a court has *not* declared a person mentally incompetent, but that person lacked the capacity to comprehend the subject matter, nature, and consequences of the agreement, then the contract is voidable at that person's option.
Valid	If a court has *not* declared a person mentally incompetent and that person was able to understand the nature and effect of the contract at the time it was formed, then the contract is valid and enforceable.

SECTION 2
LEGALITY

Legality is the fourth requirement for a valid contract to exist. For a contract to be valid and enforceable, it must be formed for a legal purpose. A contract to do something that is prohibited by federal or state statutory law is illegal and, as such, void from the outset and thus unenforceable. Additionally, a contract to commit a tortious act—such as an agreement to engage in fraudulent misrepresentation (see Chapter 6)—is contrary to public policy and therefore illegal and unenforceable.

Contracts Contrary to Statute

Statutes often set forth rules specifying which terms and clauses may be included in contracts and which are prohibited. We now examine several ways in which contracts may be contrary to statute and thus illegal.

CONTRACTS TO COMMIT A CRIME Any contract to commit a crime is in violation of a statute. Thus, a contract to sell illegal drugs in violation of criminal laws is unenforceable, as is a contract to cover up a corporation's violation of the Dodd-Frank Wall Street Reform and Consumer Protection Act. Similarly, a contract to smuggle undocumented workers from another country into the United States for an employer is illegal, as is a contract to dump hazardous waste in violation of environmental laws.

Sometimes, the object or performance of a contract is rendered illegal by a statute *after* the parties entered into the contract. In that situation, the contract is considered to be discharged by law. (See the discussion of impossibility or impracticability of performance in Chapter 18.)

USURY Almost every state has a statute that sets the maximum rate of interest that can be charged for different types of transactions, including ordinary loans. A lender who makes a loan at an interest rate above the lawful maximum commits **usury.** Although usurious contracts are illegal, most states simply limit the interest that the lender may collect on the contract to the lawful maximum interest rate in that state. In a few states, the lender can recover the principal amount of the loan but no interest.

Usury statutes place a ceiling on allowable rates of interest, but states can make exceptions to facilitate business transactions. For instance, many states exempt corporate loans from the usury laws, and nearly all states allow higher interest rate loans for borrowers who could not otherwise obtain funds. In reaction to the latest economic recession, the federal government placed some restrictions on the interest rates and fees that banks and credit-card companies can legally charge consumers.[7]

GAMBLING Gambling is the creation of risk for the purpose of assuming it. Any scheme that involves the distribution of property by chance among persons who have paid valuable consideration for the opportunity (chance) to receive the property is gambling. Traditionally, the states have deemed gambling

---

7. The Credit Card Accountability, Responsibility, and Disclosure Act of 2009, Pub. L. No. 111-24, 123 Stat. 1734.

contracts illegal and thus void. It is sometimes difficult, however, to distinguish a gambling contract from the risk sharing inherent in almost all contracts.

All states have statutes that regulate gambling, and many states allow certain forms of gambling, such as betting on horse races, poker machines, and charity-sponsored bingo. In addition, nearly all states allow state-operated lotteries as well as gambling on Native American reservations. Even in states that permit certain types of gambling, though, courts often find that gambling contracts are illegal.

▶ **Case in Point 14.5** Video poker machines are legal in Louisiana, but their use requires the approval of the state video gaming commission. Gaming Venture, Inc., did not obtain this approval before agreeing with Tastee Restaurant Corporation to install poker machines in some of its restaurants. For this reason, when Tastee allegedly reneged on the deal by refusing to install the machines, a state court held that their agreement was an illegal gambling contract and therefore void.[8] ◀

---

8. *Gaming Venture, Inc. v. Tastee Restaurant Corp.*, 996 So.2d 515 (La.App. 5 Cir. 2008).

LICENSING STATUTES All states require members of certain professions—including physicians, lawyers, real estate brokers, accountants, architects, electricians, and stockbrokers—to have licenses. Some licenses are obtained only after extensive schooling and examinations, which indicate to the public that a special skill has been acquired. Others require only that the applicant be of good moral character and pay a fee.

Whether a contract with an unlicensed person is legal and enforceable depends on the purpose of the licensing statute. If the statute's purpose is to protect the public from unauthorized practitioners (such as unlicensed attorneys and electricians, for instance), then a contract involving an unlicensed practitioner is generally illegal and unenforceable. If the statute's purpose is merely to raise government revenues, however, a court may enforce the contract and fine the unlicensed person.

Can a member of a profession who is licensed in one jurisdiction recover on a contract to perform professional services in another jurisdiction? What if the contract was the result of a winning entry in an international competition? In the following case, the court had to answer these questions.

CASE 14.1

Sturdza v. United Arab Emirates
District of Columbia Court of Appeals, 11 A.3d 251 (2011).

BACKGROUND AND FACTS The United Arab Emirates (UAE) held a competition for the design of a new embassy in Washington, D.C. At the conclusion of the competition, the UAE informed Elena Sturdza—an architect licensed in Maryland and Texas but not in the District of Columbia—that she had won. Sturdza and the UAE began to negotiate a contract. For two years, they exchanged proposals. Then, without explanation, the UAE stopped communicating with Sturdza. No contract between the UAE and Sturdza was ever signed. Later, Sturdza learned that the UAE had contracted with a District of Columbia architect, Angelos Demetriou, to use his design for its embassy. Sturdza filed suit against the UAE for breach of contract, claiming that Demetriou's design copied many of the features that were hallmarks of her design. The district court issued a summary judgment in the UAE's favor. Sturdza appealed.

IN THE LANGUAGE OF THE COURT
GLICKMAN, Associate Judge:

* * * *

* * * Sturdza argues that the District's architectural licensing statute should not be construed to apply to architects who submit plans in the District in international architectural design competitions. According to Sturdza, "it is plain" that the consumer protection concerns underlying the licensure requirement do not apply to such competitions, because the purpose of the law is merely to protect "ordinary local DC consumers against fraudulent practices and representations by persons holding themselves out as experts."

We are not persuaded by Sturdza's argument. It is not "plain" to us that the public welfare rationale for licensing architects is inapplicable to international competitions to design buildings such as the UAE embassy. For the safety and well-being of those who work in and visit such buildings, and of neighboring property owners, we would suppose the District has every reason to insist that the architects who design them and oversee their construction be qualified, and hence licensed, to do so.

But even if we were prepared to agree with Sturdza on these matters, her argument founders on the plain language of the statute. The licensing requirement for the practice of architecture in the District is categorical. It contains no exemption for international design competitions; indeed, it admits of no exception based on the type of client or architectural service rendered. *We must apply the statute as it is written and not create* ad hoc [for the particular case at hand] *exceptions by judicial decree based on nebulous policy considerations.* [Emphasis added.]

* * * *

* * * *A contract made in violation of a licensing statute that is designed to protect the public will usually be considered void and unenforceable* * * * . Although the operation of this rule may appear to be harsh and disproportionate in some cases, we have uniformly rejected appeals to deviate from or mitigate it; the potential unfair applications of the rule at the margins have not persuaded us to sacrifice the benefits of a clear-cut, unmistakable requirement, with equally clear consequences for noncompliance, in this area of consumer protection. * * * One who engages in the practice of architecture in this jurisdiction without having secured the necessary District of Columbia license is barred from recovering for his or her services in an action for breach of contract. [Emphasis added.]

DECISION AND REMEDY *The District of Columbia Court of Appeals held that an architect cannot recover on a contract to perform architectural services in the District of Columbia if he or she lacks a District of Columbia license. There is no exception for international design competitions.*

THE GLOBAL DIMENSION *The architectural services at the center of this case were to be performed for a foreign embassy. Should the court have made an exception for such a situation? Why or why not?*

THE LEGAL ENVIRONMENT DIMENSION *Should restrictions on the enforcement of contracts with unlicensed practitioners extend beyond the performance of professional services to include negotiations to provide the services? Discuss.*

Contracts Contrary to Public Policy

Although contracts involve private parties, some are not enforceable because of the negative impact they would have on society. These contracts are said to be *contrary to public policy.* Examples include a contract to commit an immoral act, such as selling a child, and a contract that prohibits marriage. We look here at certain types of business contracts that are often found to be against public policy.

CONTRACTS IN RESTRAINT OF TRADE Contracts in restraint of trade (anticompetitive agreements) usually adversely affect the public policy that favors competition in the economy. Typically, such contracts also violate one or more federal or state antitrust statutes.[9]

An exception is recognized when the restraint is reasonable and is contained in an ancillary (secondary or subordinate) clause in a contract. Such restraints often are included in contracts for the sale of an ongoing business and employment contracts.

Covenants Not to Compete and the Sale of an Ongoing Business. Many contracts involve a type of restraint called a **covenant not to compete,** or a restrictive covenant (promise). A covenant not to compete may be created when a seller of a store agrees not to open a new store in a certain geographic area surrounding the old business. The agreement enables the purchaser to buy, and the seller to sell, the goodwill and reputation of an ongoing business without having to worry that the seller will open a competing business a block away. Provided the restrictive covenant is reasonable and is an ancillary part of the sale of an ongoing business, it is enforceable.

---

9. Federal statutes include the Sherman Antitrust Act, the Clayton Act, and the Federal Trade Commission Act.

Covenants Not to Compete in Employment Contracts. Sometimes, agreements not to compete (also referred to as *noncompete agreements*) are included in employment contracts. People in middle- or upper-level management positions commonly agree not to work for competitors or not to start competing businesses for a specified period of time after termination of employment. (For an example of such a noncompete clause, see paragraph 9 of the sample contract in the appendix following Chapter 19.)

Such agreements are legal in most states so long as the specified period of time (of restraint) is not excessive in duration and the geographic restriction is reasonable. What constitutes a reasonable time period may be shorter in the online environment than in conventional employment contracts because the restrictions apply worldwide.

To be reasonable, a restriction on competition must protect a legitimate business interest and must not be any greater than necessary to protect that interest. ▶ **Case in Point 14.6** Safety and Compliance Management, Inc. (SCMI), provides drug- and alcohol-testing services. When SCMI hired Angela to pick up test specimens, she signed a covenant not to compete "in any area of SCMI business." Angela later quit SCMI's employ to work in a hospital where she sometimes collected patient specimens. SCMI claimed this was a breach of their noncompete agreement. A court ruled that the covenant was unreasonable because it imposed a greater restriction on Angela than necessary to protect SCMI.[10] ◀

The contract in the following *Spotlight Case* provided an exclusive license to open and operate comedy clubs under a certain famous trademark. It included a covenant not to compete. The question was whether the restraint was reasonable.

---

10. *Stultz v. Safety and Compliance Management, Inc.,* 285 Ga.App.799, 648 S.E.2d 129 (2007).

SP●TLIGHT on the Improv

Case 14.2   Comedy Club, Inc. v. Improv West Associates
United States Court of Appeals, Ninth Circuit, 553 F.3d 1277 (2009).

BACKGROUND AND FACTS Improv West Associates is the founder of the Improv Comedy Club and owner of the "Improv" trademark. Comedy Club, Inc. (CCI), owns and operates restaurants and comedy clubs. Improv West granted CCI an exclusive license to open four Improv clubs per year in 2001, 2002, and 2003. Their agreement prohibited CCI from opening any non-Improv comedy clubs "in the contiguous United States" until 2019. When CCI failed to open eight clubs by the end of 2002, Improv West commenced arbitration. In 2005, the arbitrator found that CCI had forfeited its right to open Improv clubs but that the parties' agreement had not terminated and the covenant not to compete was enforceable. Therefore, CCI could not open any new comedy clubs for the agreement's duration. A federal district court confirmed the award, and CCI appealed.

IN THE LANGUAGE OF THE COURT
GOULD, Circuit Judge:

* * * *

The basic outline of what the arbitrator did, terminating an exclusive right to open Improv clubs nationwide, because of contractually inadequate performance contrary to the agreed schedule, while keeping in force the restrictive covenant makes sense in so far as CCI should not have an exclusive license on Improv clubs absent complying with designated performance. And so long as CCI was running some Improv clubs, a restrictive covenant to some degree could protect Improv West from damage caused by improper competition. Because we cannot say that there is no basis in the record for the arbitrator's decision, we hold that the arbitrator's award is not completely irrational.

* * * *

CCI's "business" is operating full-service comedy clubs. CCI currently operates at least seven Improv clubs. As interpreted by the arbitrator, the * * * covenant not to compete applies geographically to the contiguous United States, and does not end until 2019. Thus, the covenant not to compete has dramatic geographic and temporal [time-related] scope. Combined with the arbitrator's ruling that CCI forfeited its rights to use the Improv marks license in any new location, the practical effect of the arbitrator's award * * * is that for more than fourteen years the entire contiguous United States comedy club market, except for CCI's current Improv clubs, is off limits to CCI. This forecloses competition in a substantial share of the comedy club business.

* * * *

* * * *The economic restraint of [this covenant] on competition is too broad to be countenanced [tolerated]* * * * . *The covenant not to compete must be more narrowly tailored to relate to the areas in which CCI is operating Improv clubs under the license agreement.* [Emphasis added.]

However, we do not void the entire * * * covenant not to compete. * * * We weigh CCI's right to operate its business against Improv West's interest to protect and maintain its trademark, trade name and goodwill. This balance tilts in favor of Improv West with regard to counties where CCI is operating an Improv club.

Therefore, we hold that the district court should vacate [set aside] the arbitrator's [award] as to any county where CCI does not currently operate an Improv club, but uphold [the covenant] in those counties where CCI currently operates Improv clubs. Nationwide CCI may open and operate non-Improv comedy clubs in all those counties where it does not currently operate an Improv club. However, CCI may not open or operate any non-Improv clubs in those counties where it currently owns or operates Improv clubs.

DECISION AND REMEDY *The federal appellate court reversed part of the lower court's confirmation of the award and remanded the case. A covenant not to compete in the comedy club business for fourteen years in forty-eight states is too broad to be enforced.*

THE ETHICAL DIMENSION *Should any companies or subsidiaries affiliated with CCI be subject to the covenant not to compete? Would it be unethical to impose such a requirement? Discuss.*

THE LEGAL ENVIRONMENT DIMENSION *Why would a business such as Improv West include a covenant not to compete in an agreement such as the contract at issue in this case? Explain.*

Enforcement Problems. The laws governing the enforceability of covenants not to compete vary significantly from state to state. In some states, including Texas, such a covenant will not be enforced unless the employee has received some benefit in return for signing the noncompete agreement. This is true even if the covenant is reasonable as to time and area. If the employee receives no benefit, the covenant will be deemed void. California prohibits altogether the enforcement of covenants not to compete.

Occasionally, depending on the jurisdiction, courts will *reform* covenants not to compete. If a covenant is found to be unreasonable in time or geographic area, the court may convert the terms into reasonable ones and then enforce the reformed covenant. Such court actions present a problem, though, in that the judge implicitly becomes a party to the contract. Consequently, courts usually resort to con-

tract **reformation** only when necessary to prevent undue burdens or hardships.

UNCONSCIONABLE CONTRACTS OR CLAUSES A court ordinarily does not look at the fairness or equity of a contract (or inquire into the adequacy of consideration, as discussed in Chapter 13). Persons are assumed to be reasonably intelligent, and the courts will not come to their aid just because they have made an unwise or foolish bargain.

In certain circumstances, however, bargains are so oppressive that the courts relieve innocent parties of part or all of their duties. Such bargains are deemed **unconscionable**[11] because they are so unscrupulous or grossly unfair as to be "void of conscience."

---

11. Pronounced un-*kon*-shun-uh-bul.

The Uniform Commercial Code (UCC) incorporates the concept of unconscionability in its provisions with regard to the sale and lease of goods.[12] A contract can be unconscionable on either procedural or substantive grounds, as discussed in the following subsections and illustrated graphically in Exhibit 14–1 below.

Procedural Unconscionability. *Procedural* unconscionability often involves inconspicuous print, unintelligible language ("legalese"), or the lack of an opportunity to read the contract or ask questions about its meaning. This type of unconscionability typically arises when a party's lack of knowledge or understanding of the contract terms deprived him or her of any meaningful choice.

Procedural unconscionability can also occur when there is such disparity in bargaining power between the two parties that the weaker party's consent is not voluntary. This type of situation often involves an *adhesion* contract (see Chapter 15), which is a contract written exclusively by one party and presented to the other on a take-it-or-leave-it basis.[13] In other words, the party to whom the contract is presented (usually a buyer or borrower) has no opportunity to negotiate its terms. Not all adhesion contracts are unconscionable, only those that unreasonably favor the drafter.[14]

Substantive Unconscionability. *Substantive* unconscionability occurs when contracts, or portions of contracts, are oppressive or overly harsh. Courts generally focus on provisions that deprive one party of the benefits of the agreement or leave that party without a remedy for nonperformance by the other.

Substantive unconscionability can arise in a wide variety of business contexts. For instance, a contract clause that gives the business entity free access to the courts but requires the other party to arbitrate any dispute with the firm may be unconscionable.[15] Similarly, contracts drafted by cell phone providers and insurance companies have been found substantively unconscionable when they included provisions that were overly harsh or one sided.[16]

EXCULPATORY CLAUSES Often closely related to the concept of unconscionability are **exculpatory**

---

12. See UCC 2–302 and 2A–719.

13. For a classic case involving an adhesion contract, see *Henningsen v. Bloomfield Motors, Inc.*, 32 N.J. 358, 161 A.2d 69 (1960).

14. See, for example, *Thibodeau v. Comcast Corp.*, 2006 PA Super. 346, 912 A.2d 874 (2006).

15. See, for example, *Wisconsin Auto Title Loans, Inc. v. Jones*, 290 Wis.2d 514, 714 N.W.2d 155 (2006).

16. See, for example, *Gatton v. T-Mobile USA, Inc.*, 152 Cal.App.4th 571, 61 Cal.Rptr.3d 344 (2007); *Kinkel v. Cingular Wireless, LLC,* 223 Ill.2d 1, 857 N.E.2d 250, 306 Ill.Dec. 157 (2006); and *Aul v. Golden Rule Insurance Co.*, 737 N.W.2d 24 (Wis.App. 2007).

EXHIBIT 14–1 Unconscionability

UNCONSCIONABLE CONTRACT OR CLAUSE
This is a contract or clause that is void for reasons of public policy.

PROCEDURAL UNCONSCIONABILITY
This occurs if a contract is entered into, or a term becomes part of the contract, because of a party's lack of knowledge or understanding of the contract or the term.

SUBSTANTIVE UNCONSCIONABILITY
This exists when a contract, or one of its terms, is oppressive or overly harsh.

FACTORS THAT COURTS CONSIDER
- Is the print inconspicuous?
- Is the language unintelligible?
- Did one party lack an opportunity to ask questions about the contract?
- Was there a disparity of bargaining power between the parties?

FACTORS THAT COURTS CONSIDER
- Does a provision deprive one party of the benefits of the agreement?
- Does a provision leave one party without a remedy for nonperformance by the other?

clauses, which release a party from liability in the event of monetary or physical injury *no matter who is at fault.* Indeed, courts sometimes refuse to enforce such clauses on the ground that they are unconscionable.

Often Violate Public Policy. Most courts view exculpatory clauses with disfavor. Exculpatory clauses found in rental agreements for commercial property are frequently held to be contrary to public policy, and such clauses are almost always unenforceable in residential property leases. Courts also usually hold that exculpatory clauses are against public policy in the employment context. Thus, employers frequently cannot enforce exculpatory clauses in contracts with employees or independent contractors (see Chapter 32) to avoid liability for work-related injuries.

▶ **Case in Point 14.7** Speedway SuperAmerica, LLC, hired Sebert Erwin to work for its convenience stores. The company required Erwin, who had an eighth-grade education, to sign a contract stating that he was not an employee and had no right to workers' compensation. The contract also included a clause under which Erwin promised not to hold Speedway liable for anything that happened to him while working for the company. When Erwin was later injured on the job and sued Speedway for damages, the court held that the exculpatory clause was invalid because it was against public policy.[17] ◀

When Courts Will Enforce Exculpatory Clauses. Courts do enforce exculpatory clauses if they are reasonable, do not violate public policy, and do not protect parties from liability for intentional misconduct. The language used must not be ambiguous, and the parties must have been in relatively equal bargaining positions.

Businesses such as health clubs, racetracks, amusement parks, skiing facilities, horse-rental operations, golf-cart concessions, and skydiving organizations frequently use exculpatory clauses to limit their liability for patrons' injuries. Because these services are not essential, the companies offering them have no relative advantage in bargaining strength, and anyone contracting for their services does so voluntarily. Courts also may enforce reasonable exculpatory clauses in loan documents, real estate contracts, and trust agreements.

In the following case, the court considered whether an exculpatory clause that released "any Event sponsors and their agents and employees" from liability for future negligence was ambiguous.

---

17. *Speedway SuperAmerica, LLC v. Erwin,* 250 S.W.3d 339 (Ky. 2008).

CASE ANALYSIS

Case 14.3 Holmes v. Multimedia KSDK, Inc.

Missouri Court of Appeals, Eastern District, Division Two, ___ S.W.3d ___, 2013 WL 150809 (2013).

IN THE LANGUAGE OF THE COURT
Kathianne *KNAUP CRANE,* Presiding Judge.

* * * *

* * * On or about May 12, 2009, plaintiff Colleen M. Holmes signed and dated an Entry Form for the 2009 Susan G. Komen Race for the Cure (the Event) to be held on Saturday, June 13, 2009 [in St. Louis, Missouri]. The one-page entry form contained a section titled, "RACE WAIVER AND RELEASE." This section contained the following language:

* * * I understand that my consent to these provisions is given in consideration for being permit-

ted to participate in this Event. I further understand that I may be removed from this competition if I do not follow all the rules of this Event. I am a voluntary participant in this Event, and in good physical condition. I know that this Event is a potentially hazardous activity and I hereby voluntarily assume full and complete responsibility for, and the risk of, any injury or accident that may occur during my participation in this Event or while on the premises of this Event. I * * * hereby release and hold harmless and covenant not to file suit against The Susan G. Komen Breast Cancer Foundation, Inc., * * * D/B/A Susan G. Komen for the Cure, The St. Louis Affiliate of The Susan G. Komen Breast Cancer

Foundation * * * , their Affiliates and any affiliated Individuals, any Event sponsors and their agents and employees, and all other persons or entities associated with this Event (collectively, the "Releasees") for any injury or damages I might suffer in connection with my participation in this Event or while on the premises of this Event. This release applies to any and all loss, liability, or claims I may have arising out of my participation in this Event, including but not limited to, personal injury or damage suffered by me or others, whether such losses, liabilities, or claims be caused by falls, contact with and/or the actions of other participants, contact with fixed or non-fixed objects, contact with animals, conditions of

CASE 14.3 CONTINUES ➡

CASE 14.3 CONTINUED

the premises of the Event, negligence of the Releasees, risks not known to me or not reasonably foreseeable at this time, or otherwise.

On June 1, 2009, defendant Multimedia KSDK, Inc. (KSDK) executed a Race Sponsorship Agreement with the St. Louis Affiliate of the Event. This agreement governed the terms of KSDK's sponsorship of the Event in 2009. KSDK, as an Event sponsor, agreed to, and did, broadcast the Event. Defendants Lynn Beall and Michael Shipley, KSDK employees, were involved in arranging the live coverage.

On February 23, 2011, Mrs. Holmes and her husband, Rick W. Holmes (collectively, plaintiffs) filed a lawsuit in the Circuit Court of the City of St. Louis. Plaintiffs alleged that while Mrs. Holmes was a participant in the Event, she was caused to trip and fall over an audio-visual box, and she sustained injuries. Plaintiffs alleged that the audio-visual box was owned and operated by KSDK and was placed on the ground without barricades or warnings in a high pedestrian traffic area.

The circuit court entered summary judgment in defendants' favor on the grounds that plaintiffs' claims were barred by the language of the release, the release was not ambiguous, and the release applied to defendants. Plaintiffs appeal.

* * * *

[The plaintiffs] on appeal claim the release is ambiguous. Whether a release is ambiguous is a question of law. Interpretation of a release or settlement agreement is governed by the same principles as any other contract. * * * *Contract terms are ambiguous only*

if the language may be given more than one reasonable interpretation. Simply because parties disagree over the meaning of a contract does not mean that it is ambiguous. [Emphasis added.]

* * * *

* * * Plaintiffs assert that the trial court erred in entering summary judgment because the release was ambiguous in that it did not clearly and explicitly set forth the individuals and entities it purported to release from liability. We disagree.

The release described the individuals and entities to be released in the following language:

> The St. Louis Affiliate of Susan G. Komen for the Cure, their affiliates, and any affiliated individuals, any Event sponsors and their agents and employees, and all other persons or entities associated with this Event.

Plaintiffs argue that the * * * language is ambiguous because it does not specifically name the individuals and entities being released. They contend that such specificity is required in a prospective release.

We have routinely held that the word "any" when used with a class in a release is all-inclusive, it excludes nothing, and it is not ambiguous. * * * *A release that releases claims against "any and all persons" is unambiguous and enforceable to bar claims against third parties who were not parties to the release, and it is not necessary that the release identify those persons by name or otherwise.* Thus, * * * the release of "any Event sponsors" unambiguously releases all Event sponsors without exclusion, and it is not necessary that each sponsor be named. [Emphasis added.]

However, plaintiffs argue that this reasoning does not apply to the use of "any" with classes of persons in a prospective release for future acts of negligence because courts require more specificity in a prospective release. We disagree.

Public policy disfavors but *does not prohibit* releases of future negligence. * * * To be enforceable in Missouri, exculpatory clauses must contain clear, unambiguous, unmistakable, and conspicuous language in order to release a party from his or her own future negligence. The exculpatory language must effectively notify a party that he or she is releasing the other party from claims arising from the other party's own negligence. * * * The words "negligence" or "fault" or their equivalents must be used conspicuously so that a clear and unmistakable waiver and shifting of risk occurs. There must be no doubt that a reasonable person agreeing to an exculpatory clause actually understands what future claims he or she is waiving.

* * * *

* * * [It is] not required that for a release of liability for future negligence to be effective, it must identify every individual sought to be released by name.

The release of "any Event sponsors and their agents and employees" from liability for future negligence clearly releases all Event sponsors and their agents and employees without exclusion. It is not ambiguous because it does not name each individual Event sponsor it purported to release from liability.

* * * *

The judgment of the trial court is affirmed.

LEGAL REASONING QUESTIONS

1. When do courts enforce exculpatory clauses?

2. What are the specific requirements for an exculpatory clause to be enforceable in Missouri?

3. Was the exculpatory clause at issue in this case enforceable? Why or why not?

4. When Holmes signed the release on May 12, KSDK had not yet become a sponsor of the event. Did this fact render the clause unenforceable? Explain.

DISCRIMINATORY CONTRACTS Contracts in which a party promises to discriminate on the basis of race, color, national origin, religion, gender, age, or disability are contrary to both statute and public policy. They are also unenforceable.[18] For instance, if a property owner promises in a contract not to sell the property to a member of a particular race, the contract is unenforceable. The public policy underlying these prohibitions is very strong, and the courts are quick to invalidate discriminatory contracts.

Exhibit 14–2 below illustrates the types of contracts that may be illegal because they are contrary to statute or public policy.

Effect of Illegality

In general, an illegal contract is void—that is, the contract is deemed never to have existed, and the courts will not aid either party. In most illegal contracts, both parties are considered to be equally at fault—*in pari delicto*.[19] If the contract is executory

18. The major federal statute prohibiting discrimination is the Civil Rights Act of 1964, 42 U.S.C. Sections 2000e–2000e-17.
19. Pronounced in-*pah*-ree deh-*lick*-tow.

(not yet fulfilled), neither party can enforce it. If it has been executed, neither party can recover damages.

The courts are usually not concerned if one wrong-doer in an illegal contract is unjustly enriched at the expense of the other—except under certain circumstances. The main reason for this hands-off attitude is the belief that a plaintiff who has broken the law by entering into an illegal bargain should not be allowed to obtain help from the courts. Another justification is the hoped-for deterrent effect: a plaintiff who suffers a loss because of an illegal bargain will presumably be deterred from entering into similar illegal bargains in the future.

There are exceptions to the general rule that neither party to an illegal bargain can sue for breach and neither party can recover for performance rendered. We look at these exceptions next.

JUSTIFIABLE IGNORANCE OF THE FACTS When one of the parties is relatively innocent (has no reason to know that the contract is illegal), that party can often recover any benefits conferred in a partially executed contract. In this situation, the courts will not enforce the contract but will allow the parties to return to their original positions.

EXHIBIT 14–2 Contract Legality

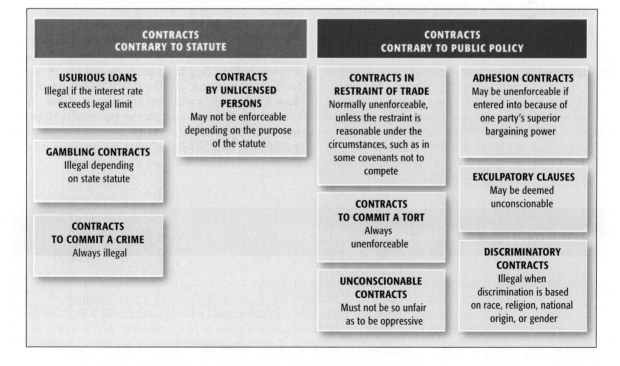

A court may sometimes permit an innocent party who has fully performed under the contract to enforce the contract against the guilty party. ▶ **Example 14.8** A trucking company contracts with Gillespie to carry crates filled with goods to a specific destination for the normal fee of $5,000. The trucker delivers the crates and later finds out that they contained illegal goods. Although the law specifies that the shipment, use, and sale of the goods were illegal, the trucker, being an innocent party, can still legally collect the $5,000 from Gillespie. ◀

MEMBERS OF PROTECTED CLASSES When a statute is clearly designed to protect a certain class of people, a member of that class can enforce a contract in violation of the statute even though the other party cannot. ▶ **Example 14.9** Statutes prohibit certain employees (such as flight attendants and pilots) from working more than a certain number of hours per month. An employee who is required to work more than the maximum can recover for those extra hours of service. ◀

Other examples of statutes designed to protect a particular class of people are state statutes that regulate the sale of insurance. If an insurance company violates a statute when selling insurance, the purchaser can still enforce the policy and recover from the insurer.

WITHDRAWAL FROM AN ILLEGAL AGREEMENT If the illegal part of a bargain has not yet been performed, the party rendering performance can withdraw from the contract and recover the performance or its value. ▶ **Example 14.10** Sam and Jim decide to wager (illegally) on the outcome of a boxing match. Each deposits cash with a stakeholder, who agrees to pay the winner of the bet. At this point, each party has performed part of the agreement, but the illegal element of the agreement will not occur until the funds are paid to the winner. Before that payment occurs, either party is entitled to withdraw from the bargain by giving notice of repudiation to the stakeholder. ◀

CONTRACT ILLEGAL THROUGH FRAUD, DURESS, OR UNDUE INFLUENCE Often, one party to an illegal contract is more at fault than the other. When one party uses fraud, duress, or undue influence to induce another party to enter into an illegal bargain, the second party will be allowed to recover for the performance or its value.

SEVERABLE, OR DIVISIBLE, CONTRACTS A contract that is *severable,* or divisible, consists of distinct parts that can be performed separately, with separate consideration provided for each part. With an *indivisible* contract, in contrast, complete performance by each party is essential, even if the contract contains a number of seemingly separate provisions.

If a contract is divisible into legal and illegal portions, a court may enforce the legal portion but not the illegal one, so long as the illegal portion does not affect the essence of the bargain. This approach is consistent with the courts' basic policy of enforcing the legal intentions of the contracting parties whenever possible.

▶ **Example 14.11** Cole signs an employment contract that includes an overly broad and thus illegal covenant not to compete. In that situation, a court might allow the employment contract to be enforceable but reform the unreasonably broad covenant by converting its terms into reasonable ones. Alternatively, the court could declare the covenant illegal (and thus void) and enforce the remaining employment terms. ◀ (A contract might include a clause stating that the parties intend the contract terms to be enforced to "the fullest extent possible." Such a clause indicates that the parties regard their contract as divisible and, in the event of a dispute, want the court to strike out the illegal terms and enforce the rest. For an example, see the *Appendix to Chapter 19: Reading and Analyzing Contracts.*)

Reviewing: Capacity and Legality

Renee Beaver started racing go-karts competitively in 2012, when she was fourteen. Many of the races required her to sign an exculpatory clause to participate, which she or her parents regularly signed. In 2014, right before her sixteenth birthday, she participated in the annual Elkhart Grand Prix, a series of races in Elkhart, Indiana. During the event in which she drove, a piece of foam padding used as a course barrier was torn from its base and ended up on the track. A portion of the padding struck Beaver in the head, and another portion was thrown into oncoming traffic, causing a multikart collision during which she sustained severe injuries. Beaver filed an action against the race organizers for negligence. The race organizers could not locate the exculpatory clause that Beaver had supposedly signed. The organizers argued that she must have signed one to enter the race, but even if she had not signed one, her actions showed her intent to be bound by its terms. Using the information presented in the chapter, answer the following questions.

1. Did Beaver have the contractual capacity to enter a contract with an exculpatory clause? Why or why not?
2. Assuming that Beaver did, in fact, sign the exculpatory clause, did she later disaffirm or ratify the contract? Explain.
3. Now assume that Beaver stated that she was eighteen years old at the time that she signed the exculpatory clause. How might this affect Beaver's ability to disaffirm or ratify the contract?
4. If Beaver did not actually sign the exculpatory clause, could a court conclude that she impliedly accepted its terms by participating in the race? Why or why not?

DEBATE THIS . . . *After agreeing to an exculpatory clause or purchasing some item, such as a computer, minors often seek to avoid the contracts. Today's minors are far from naïve and should not be allowed to avoid their contractual obligations.*

Terms and Concepts

age of majority 273
contractual capacity 273
covenant not to compete 279
disaffirmance 273

emancipation 273
exculpatory clause 282
necessaries 274
ratification 274

reformation 281
unconscionable 281
usury 277

ExamPrep

Issue Spotters

1. Joan, who is sixteen years old, moves out of her parents' home and signs a one-year lease for an apartment at Kenwood Apartments. Joan's parents tell her that she can return to live with them at any time. Unable to pay the rent, Joan moves back to her parents' home two months later. Can Kenwood enforce the lease against Joan? Why or why not? **(See page 273.)**

2. Sun Airlines, Inc., prints on its tickets that it is not liable for any injury to a passenger caused by the airline's negligence. If the cause of an accident is found to be the airline's negligence, can it use the

clause as a defense to liability? Why or why not? **(See page 282.)**

• Check your answers to the Issue Spotters against the answers provided in Appendix E at the end of this text.

Before the Test

Go to **www.cengagebrain.com**, enter the ISBN 9781285185248, and click on "Find" to locate this textbook's Web site. Then, click on "Access Now" under "Study Tools," and select Chapter 14 at the top. There, you will find a Practice Quiz that you can take to assess your mastery of the concepts in this chapter, as well as Flashcards and a Glossary of important terms.

Business Scenarios

14–1. Covenants Not to Compete. A famous New York City hotel, Hotel Lux, is noted for its food as well as its luxury accommodations. Hotel Lux contracts with a famous chef, Chef Perlee, to become its head chef at $30,000 per month. The contract states that should Perlee leave the employment of Hotel Lux for any reason, he will not work as a chef for any hotel or restaurant in New York, New Jersey, or Pennsylvania for a period of one year. During the first six months of the contract, Hotel Lux heavily advertises Perlee as its head chef, and business at the hotel is excellent. Then a dispute arises between the hotel's management and Perlee, and Perlee terminates his employment. One month later, he is hired by a famous New Jersey restaurant just across the New York state line. Hotel Lux learns of Perlee's employment through a large advertisement in a New York City newspaper. It seeks to enjoin (prevent) Perlee from working in that restaurant as a chef for one year. Discuss how successful Hotel Lux will be in its action. **(See page 279.)**

14–2. Capacity. Joanne is a seventy-five-year-old widow who survives on her husband's small pension. Joanne has become increasingly forgetful, and her family worries that she may have Alzheimer's disease (a brain disorder that seriously affects a person's ability to carry out daily activities). No physician has diagnosed her, however, and no court has ruled on Joanne's legal competence. One day while she is out shopping, Joanne stops by a store that is having a sale on pianos and enters into a fifteen-year installment contract to buy a grand piano. When the piano arrives the next day, Joanne seems confused and repeatedly asks the delivery person why a piano is being delivered. Joanne claims that she does not recall buying a piano. Explain whether this contract is void, voidable, or valid. Can Joanne avoid her contractual obligation to buy the piano? If so, how? **(See page 273.)**

14–3. Licensing Statutes. State X requires that persons who prepare and serve liquor in the form of drinks at commercial establishments be licensed by the state to do so. The only requirement for obtaining a yearly license is that the person be at least twenty-one years old. Mickey, aged thirty-five, is hired as a bartender for the Southtown Restaurant. Gerald, a staunch alumnus of a nearby university, brings twenty of his friends to the restaurant to celebrate a football victory one afternoon. Gerald orders four rounds of drinks, and the bill is nearly $600. When he learns that Mickey has failed to renew his bartender's license, Gerald refuses to pay, claiming that the contract is unenforceable. Discuss whether Gerald is correct. **(See page 278.)**

Business Case Problems

14–4. Spotlight on Arbitration Clauses—Unconscionable Contracts or Clauses. Roberto Basulto and Raquel Gonzalez, who did not speak English, responded to an ad on Spanish-language television sponsored by Hialeah Automotive, LLC, which does business as Potamkin Dodge. Potamkin's staff understood that Basulto and Gonzalez did not speak or read English and conducted the entire transaction in Spanish. They explained the English-language contract, but did not explain an accompanying arbitration agreement. This agreement limited the amount of damages that the buyers could seek in court to less than $5,000, but did not limit Potamkin's right to pursue greater damages. Basulto and Gonzalez bought a Dodge Caravan and signed the contract in blank (meaning that some parts were left blank). Potamkin later filled in a lower trade-in allowance than agreed and refused to change it. The buyers returned the van—having driven it a total of seven miles—and asked for a return of their trade-in vehicle, but it had been sold. The buyers filed a suit in a Florida state court against Potamkin. The dealer sought arbitration. Was the arbitration agreement unconscionable? Why or why not? [*Hialeah Automotive, LLC v. Basulto*, 156 Fla. 92, 22 So.3d 586 (3 Dist. 2009)] **(See page 281.)**

**14–5. BUSINESS CASE PROBLEM
WITH SAMPLE ANSWER: Unconscionable Contracts or Clauses.**
 Geographic Expeditions, Inc. (GeoEx), which guided climbs up Mount Kilimanjaro, required climbers to sign a release to participate in an expedition. The form mandated the arbitration of any dispute in San Francisco and limited damages to the cost of the trip. GeoEx told climbers that the terms were nonnegotiable and were the same as terms imposed by other travel firms. Jason Lhotka died on a GeoEx climb. His mother filed a suit against GeoEx. GeoEx sought arbitration. Was the arbitration clause unconscionable? Why or why not? [*Lhotka v. Geographic Expeditions, Inc.,* 181 Cal.App.4th 816, 104 Cal.Rptr.3d 844 (1 Dist. 2010)] **(See page 281.)**

- **For a sample answer to Problem 14–5, go to Appendix F at the end of this text.**

14–6. Mental Incompetence. Dorothy Drury suffered from dementia and chronic confusion. When she became unable to manage her own affairs, including decisions about medical and financial matters, her son Eddie arranged for her move to an assisted living facility. During admission, she signed a residency agreement, which included an arbitration clause. After she sustained injuries in a fall at the facility, a suit was filed to recover damages. The facility asked the court to compel arbitration. Was Dorothy bound to the residency agreement? Discuss. [*Drury v. Assisted Living Concepts, Inc.,* 245 Or.App. 217, 262 P.3d 1162 (2011)] **(See page 276.)**

14–7. Licensing Statutes. PEMS Co. International, Inc., agreed to find a buyer for Rupp Industries, Inc., for a commission of 2 percent of the purchase price, which was to be paid by the buyer. Using PEMS's services, an investment group bought Rupp for $20 million and changed its name to Temp-Air, Inc. PEMS asked Temp-Air to pay a commission on the sale. Temp-Air refused, arguing that PEMS acted as a broker in the deal without a license. The applicable statute defines a broker as any person who deals with the sale of a business. If this statute was intended to protect the public, can PEMS collect its commission? Explain. [*PEMS Co. International, Inc. v. Temp-Air, Inc.,* __ N.W.2d __ (Minn.App. 2011)] **(See page 278.)**

14–8. Minors. D.V.G. (a minor) was injured in a one-car auto accident in Hoover, Alabama. The vehicle was covered by an insurance policy issued by Nationwide Mutual Insurance Co. Stan Brobston, D.V.G.'s attorney, accepted Nationwide's offer of $50,000 on D.V.G.'s behalf. Before the settlement could be submitted to an Alabama state court for approval, D.V.G. died from injuries received in a second, unrelated auto accident. Nationwide argued that it was not bound to the settlement because a minor lacks the capacity to contract and so cannot enter into a binding settlement without court approval. Should Nationwide be bound to the settlement? Why or why not? [*Nationwide Mutual Insurance Co. v. Wood,* __ So.3d __, 2013 WL 646468 (Ala. 2013)] **(See page 273.)**

14–9. A QUESTION OF ETHICS: Covenants Not to Compete.

 Brendan Coleman created and marketed Clinex, a software billing program. Later, Retina Consultants, P.C., a medical practice, hired Coleman as a software engineer. Together, they modified the Clinex program to create Clinex-RE. Coleman signed an agreement to the effect that he owned Clinex, Retina owned Clinex-RE, and he would not market Clinex in competition with Clinex-RE. After Coleman quit Retina, he withdrew funds from a Retina bank account and marketed both forms of the software to other medical practices. At trial, the court entered a judgment enjoining (preventing) Coleman from marketing the software that was in competition with the software he had developed for Retina Consultants. The court also obligated Coleman to return the funds taken from the company's bank account. Coleman appealed. [*Coleman v. Retina Consultants, P.C.,* 286 Ga. 317, 687 S.E.2d 457 (2009)] **(See page 279.)**

(a) Should the court uphold the noncompete clause? If so, why? If not, why not?

(b) Should the court require Coleman to return the funds he withdrew from the company's accounts? Discuss fully.

(c) Did Coleman's behavior after he left the company influence the court's decision? Explain your answer.

Legal Reasoning Group Activity

14–10. Covenants Not to Compete. Assume that you are part of a group of executives at a large software corporation. The company is considering whether to incorporate covenants not to compete into its employment contracts. You know that there are some issues with the enforceability of these covenants and want to make an informed decision. **(See page 279.)**

(a) One group should make a list of what interests are served by enforcing covenants not to compete.

(b) A second group should create a list of what interests are served by refusing to enforce covenants not to compete.

(c) A third group should discuss whether a court should reform (and then enforce) a covenant not to compete that it determines is illegal, and create an argument for and against reformation.

CHAPTER 15

MISTAKES, FRAUD, AND VOLUNTARY CONSENT

An otherwise valid contract may still be unenforceable if the parties have not genuinely agreed to its terms. As mentioned in Chapter 11, a lack of *voluntary consent* (assent) can be used as a defense to the contract's enforceability.

Voluntary consent may be lacking because of a mistake, misrepresentation, undue influence, or duress—in other words, because there is no true "meeting of the minds." Generally, a party who demonstrates that he or she did not truly agree to the terms of a contract has a choice. The party can choose either to carry out the contract or to rescind (cancel) it and thus avoid the entire transaction. In this chapter, we examine the kinds of factors that may indicate a lack of voluntary consent.

SECTION 1
MISTAKES

We all make mistakes, so it is not surprising that mistakes are made when contracts are formed. In certain circumstances, contract law allows a contract to be avoided on the basis of mistake. It is important to distinguish between *mistakes of fact* and *mistakes of value or quality.* Only a mistake of fact makes a contract voidable. Also, the mistake must involve some *material fact*—a fact that a reasonable person would consider important when determining his or her course of action.

▶ **Example 15.1** Sung buys a violin from Bev for $250. Although the violin is very old, neither party believes that it is valuable. Later, however, an antiques dealer informs the parties that the violin is rare and worth thousands of dollars. Here, both parties were mistaken, but the mistake is a mistake of *value* rather than a mistake of *fact* that warrants contract rescission. Therefore, Bev cannot rescind the contract. ◀

Mistakes of fact occur in two forms—*bilateral* and *unilateral.* A unilateral mistake is made by only *one* of the parties. A bilateral, or mutual, mistake is made by *both* of the contracting parties. We look next at these two types of mistakes and illustrate them graphically in Exhibit 15–1 on the following page.

Unilateral Mistakes of Fact

A unilateral mistake is made by only one of the parties. In general, a unilateral mistake does not give the mistaken party any right to relief from the contract. Normally, the contract is enforceable.

▶ **Example 15.2** Elena intends to sell her jet ski for $2,500. When she learns that Chin is interested in buying a used jet ski, she sends him an e-mail offering to sell the jet ski to him. When typing the e-mail, however, she mistakenly keys in the price of $1,500. Chin immediately sends Elena an e-mail reply accepting her offer. Even though Elena intended to sell her personal jet ski for $2,500, she has made a unilateral mistake and is bound by the contract to sell it to Chin for $1,500. ◀

This general rule has at least two exceptions.[1] The contract may be enforceable if:

1. The *other* party to the contract knows or should have known that a mistake of fact was made.

2. The error was due to a substantial mathematical mistake in addition, subtraction, division, or multiplication and was made inadvertently and without gross (extreme) negligence. If, for instance, a contractor's bid was significantly low because he or she made a mistake in addition when totaling

---
1. The *Restatement (Second) of Contracts,* Section 153, liberalizes the general rule to take into account the modern trend of allowing avoidance even though only one party has been mistaken.

EXHIBIT 15-1 Mistakes of Fact

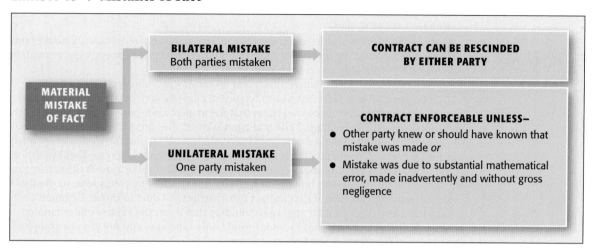

the estimated costs, any contract resulting from the bid normally may be rescinded.

Of course, in both situations, the mistake must still involve some material fact.

Bilateral (Mutual) Mistakes of Fact

A bilateral mistake is a "mutual misunderstanding concerning a basic assumption on which the contract was made."[2] When both parties are mistaken about

---
2. *Restatement (Second) of Contracts,* Section 152.

the same material fact, the contract can be rescinded by either party.

A word or term in a contract may be subject to more than one reasonable interpretation. If the parties to the contract attach materially different meanings to the term, a court may allow the contract to be rescinded because there has been no true "meeting of the minds."

In the following case, the court had to grapple with the question of whether a mutual mistake of fact had occurred.

CASE 15.1

L&H Construction Co. v. Circle Redmont, Inc.

District Court of Appeal of Florida, Fifth District, 55 So.3d 630 (2011).

BACKGROUND AND FACTS L&H Construction Company was a general contractor involved in the renovation of the Thomas Edison historic site in West Orange, New Jersey, for the National Park Service. L&H contracted with Circle Redmont, Inc., which is based in Melbourne, Florida, to make a cast-iron staircase and a glass flooring system. Redmont's original proposal was to "engineer, fabricate, and install" the staircase and flooring system.

During negotiations, however, installation and its costs were cut from the deal. In the final agreement, payment was due on "Supervision of Installation" instead of "Completion of Installation." Nevertheless, the final agreement stated that Redmont would "engineer, fabricate, and install." Later, Redmont claimed that this was a mistake. L&H insisted that installation was included. L&H filed a suit in a Florida state court against Redmont. The court found that the word *install* in the phrase "engineer, fabricate, and install" was the result of a mutual mistake. L&H appealed.

CASE 15.1 CONTINUES ▶

CASE 15.1 CONTINUED

IN THE LANGUAGE OF THE COURT
PER CURIAM. [By the Whole Court]
* * * *

A mistake is mutual when the parties agree to one thing and then, due to either a scrivener's error [an error made by the person copying the document] or inadvertence [carelessness], express something different in the written instrument. [Emphasis added.]

Clearly, the final contract between L&H and Redmont was ambiguous. While the final * * * proposal stated that Redmont was to "engineer, fabricate and install" the staircase and flooring system, [the agreement also] states that the final $40,000 progress payment was "Due upon Supervision of Installation." The trial court allowed the parties to present some parol evidence to establish the parties' true intent and subsequently found the contract contained a mutual mistake as to whether Redmont was to install, or merely supervise, the installation of the product. This was an issue that could have been decided for or against either party and we cannot say the trial court's findings of fact were unsupported by competent, substantial evidence. Although the face of the contract clearly reflected a duty to install, Redmont's witnesses' testimony supported the trial court's finding that it was the express understanding between Redmont and L&H that Redmont would only supervise, and not provide complete installation of the staircase and flooring system.

Redmont's witnesses testified that L&H knew that installation was being deleted as a means of saving money for L&H. Redmont's installation supervisor testified that the final * * * proposal was specifically worked up to schedule the progress payments toward the end of the job pursuant to L&H's president's request, and that L&H had decided that it wanted only installation supervision, and the contract price reflected installation supervision, not complete installation. Redmont's [chief financial officer] further testified that L&H was aware that Redmont was not going to install the product "because L&H's president had asked us to take the installation out to save money." Moreover, Redmont's president testified that he spoke directly with L&H's president regarding Redmont's supervision of installation and it was decided that Redmont would only provide installation supervision. * * * Redmont's president also reiterated [repeated] that he had direct conversations with L&H's president where he said, "Fred, how can we save me some money here and what can we do." The weight to be given to the testimony turned on the witnesses' credibility, a matter exclusively within the trial court's province.

DECISION AND REMEDY *A state intermediate appellate court upheld the lower court's finding that the use of the word* install *in the parties' agreement was a mutual mistake. The appellate court reversed the lower court's final judgment in Redmont's favor on other grounds, however.*

WHAT IF THE FACTS WERE DIFFERENT? *Suppose that Redmont had intentionally misled L&H to believe that installation was included in the price. Would the court's decision on the mutual mistake issue have been different? Discuss.*

THE ECONOMIC DIMENSION *The parties performed as agreed, with Redmont working on schedule and L&H making timely payments, until the issue of installation arose. Assuming that no further disputes arose, what might be the appropriate remedy?*

Mistakes of Value

If a mistake concerns the future market value or quality of the object of the contract, the mistake is one of *value*, and the contract normally is enforceable. The reason for this is that value is variable. Depending on the time, place, and other circumstances, the same item may be worth considerably different amounts.

When parties form a contract, their agreement establishes the value of the object of their transaction—for the moment. Each party is considered to have assumed the risk that the value will change in the future or prove to be different from what he or she thought. Without this rule, almost any party who did not receive what she or he considered a fair bargain could argue mistake.

SECTION 2
FRAUDULENT MISREPRESENTATION

Although fraud is a tort (see Chapter 6), it also affects the authenticity of the innocent party's consent to the contract. When an innocent party is fraudulently induced to enter into a contract, the contract normally can be avoided because that party has not *voluntarily* consented to its terms.[3] Ordinarily, the innocent party can either rescind the contract and be restored to her or his original position or enforce the contract and seek damages for any harms resulting from the fraud.

Generally, fraudulent misrepresentation refers only to misrepresentation that is consciously false and is intended to mislead another. The person making the fraudulent misrepresentation knows or believes that the assertion is false or knows that she or he does not have a basis (stated or implied) for the assertion.[4] Typically, fraudulent misrepresentation consists of the following elements:

1. A misrepresentation of a material fact must occur.
2. There must be an intent to deceive.
3. The innocent party must justifiably rely on the misrepresentation.
4. To collect damages, a party must have been harmed as a result of the misrepresentation.

Misrepresentation Has Occurred

The first element of proving fraud is to show that misrepresentation of a material fact has occurred. This misrepresentation can occur by words or actions. For instance, the statement "This sculpture was created by Michelangelo" is a misrepresentation of fact if another artist sculpted the statue. Similarly, if a customer asks to see only paintings by the decorative artist Paul Wright and the gallery owner immediately leads the customer over to paintings that were not done by Wright, the owner's actions can be a misrepresentation.

MISREPRESENTATION BY CONDUCT Misrepresentation also occurs when a party takes specific action to conceal a fact that is material to the contract.[5] Therefore, if a seller, by her or his actions, prevents a buyer from learning of some fact that is material to the contract, such behavior constitutes misrepresentation by conduct.

▶ **Case in Point 15.3** Actor Tom Selleck contracted to purchase a horse named Zorro for his daughter from Dolores Cuenca. Cuenca acted as though Zorro was fit to ride in competitions, when in reality the horse suffered from a medical condition. Selleck filed a lawsuit against Cuenca for wrongfully concealing the horse's condition and won. A jury awarded Selleck more than $187,000 for Cuenca's misrepresentation by conduct.[6] ◀

STATEMENTS OF OPINION Statements of opinion and representations of future facts (predictions) generally are not subject to claims of fraud. Every person is expected to exercise care and judgment when entering into contracts. The law will not come to the aid of one who simply makes an unwise bargain. Statements such as "This land will be worth twice as much next year" or "This car will last for years and years" are statements of opinion, not fact. Contracting parties should recognize them as opinions and not rely on them. A fact is objective and verifiable, whereas an opinion is usually subject to debate.

Nevertheless, in certain situations, such as when a naïve purchaser relies on an opinion from an expert, the innocent party may be entitled to rescission or reformation. (As discussed in Chapter 14, *reformation* occurs when a court alters the terms of a contract to prevent undue hardships or burdens.)

▶ **Case in Point 15.4** In a classic case, an instructor at an Arthur Murray dance school told Audrey Vokes, a widow without family, that she had the potential to become an accomplished dancer. The instructor sold her 2,302 hours of dancing lessons for a total amount of $31,090.45 (equivalent to $142,000 in 2014). When it became clear to Vokes that she did not, in fact, have the potential to be an excellent dancer, she sued the school for fraudulent misrepresentation. The court held that because the dance school had superior knowledge about a person's dance potential, the instructor's statements could be considered statements of fact rather than opinion.[7] ◀

MISREPRESENTATION OF LAW Misrepresentation of law *ordinarily* does not entitle a party to relief from a contract. ▶ **Example 15.5** Camara has a parcel of property that she is trying to sell to Pike. Camara knows that a local ordinance prohibits the construction

---

3. *Restatement (Second) of Contracts*, Sections 163 and 164.
4. *Restatement (Second) of Contracts*, Section 162.
5. *Restatement (Second) of Contracts*, Section 160.

6. *Selleck v. Cuenca*, Case No. GIN056909, North County of San Diego, California, decided September 9, 2009.
7. *Vokes v. Arthur Murray, Inc.*, 212 So.2d 906 (Fla.App. 1968).

of anything higher than three stories on the property. Nonetheless, she tells Pike, "You can build a condominium a hundred stories high on this land if you want to." Pike buys the land and later discovers that Camara's statement was false. Normally, Pike cannot avoid the contract because people are assumed to know state and local laws. ◄

Exceptions to this rule occur when the misrepresenting party is in a profession that is known to require greater knowledge of the law than the average citizen possesses. For instance, if Camara, in *Example 15.5* above, had been a lawyer or a real estate broker, her willful misrepresentation of the area's zoning laws probably would have constituted fraud.

MISREPRESENTATION BY SILENCE   Ordinarily, neither party to a contract has a duty to come forward and disclose facts. Therefore, courts typically do not set aside contracts because a party did not volunteer pertinent information.   ▶ **Example 15.6**   Jim is selling a car that has been in an accident and has been repaired.

He does not need to volunteer this information to a potential buyer. If, however, the purchaser asks Jim if the car has had extensive bodywork and he lies, he has committed a fraudulent misrepresentation. ◄

In general, if a seller knows of a serious potential problem that the buyer cannot reasonably be expected to discover, the seller may have a duty to speak. Generally, the seller must disclose only **latent defects**—that is, defects that could not readily be ascertained. Because a buyer of a house could easily discover the presence of termites through an inspection, for instance, termites may not qualify as a latent defect. Also, when the parties are in a *fiduciary relationship*—one of trust, such as partners, physician and patient, or attorney and client—they have a duty to disclose material facts. Failure to do so may constitute fraud.

In the following case, a real estate investor claimed that misrepresentation by silence had occurred when a seller of property failed to disclose material facts about its value.

CASE 15.2

Fazio v. Cypress/GR Houston I, LP
Court of Appeals of Texas, First Division, ___ S.W.3d ___ (2012).

BACKGROUND AND FACTS   Peter Fazio began talks with Cypress/GR Houston I, LP, to buy retail property whose main tenant was a Garden Ridge store. In performing a background investigation, Fazio and his agents became concerned about Garden Ridge's financial health. Nevertheless, after being assured that Garden Ridge had a positive financial outlook, Fazio sent Cypress a letter of intent to buy the property for $7.67 million "based on the currently reported absolute net income of $805,040." Cypress then agreed to provide all information in its possession, but it failed to disclose that:

1. A consultant for Garden Ridge had recently requested a $240,000 reduction in the annual rent as part of a restructuring of the company's real estate leases.
2. Cypress's bank was so concerned about Garden Ridge's financial health that it had required a personal guaranty of the property's loan.

The parties entered into a purchase agreement, but Garden Ridge went into bankruptcy shortly after the deal closed. Fazio sued Cypress for fraud after he was forced to sell the property for only $3.75 million. A jury found in Fazio's favor, but the trial court awarded judgment *n.o.v.* ("notwithstanding the verdict"— see Chapter 3) to Cypress. Fazio appealed.

   IN THE LANGUAGE OF THE COURT
Evelyn V. *KEYES*, Justice.

* * * *

We * * * *hold that Fazio's claims clearly fall within the category of claims for which an action for fraudulent inducement lies.* [Emphasis added.]

Cypress knew from the express representation in the LOI [letter of intent] that Fazio was willing to pay the requested purchase price of $7,667,000 for the Property "based on the currently reported absolute net income of $805,040." It further knew that this income was generated by rental income received from Garden Ridge. Fazio agreed in the LOI to conduct due diligence [background investigation], and, in accepting the LOI, Cypress agreed to "provide Buyer with all information in [its] possession * * * ." Fazio, an experienced real estate investor, and his experienced agents conducted reasonable due diligence before Fazio signed the Purchase Agreement, including requesting and reviewing all economic information about the Property in Cypress's possession. When Fazio discovered disturbing information about Garden Ridge in the financial statements provided to him, he conducted further investigations with both Garden Ridge and Cypress. He was repeatedly assured that all was well and that Garden Ridge anticipated strong sales * * * .

A reasonable person in Fazio's position would clearly have attached importance to the facts that approximately eight months before he purchased the Property in September 2003, Garden Ridge had retained [a consultant] to assist it in restructuring and renegotiating Garden Ridge's real estate leases; [the consultant] had prepared a letter for Garden Ridge to send to landlords; a copy of that letter, stating that Garden Ridge was restructuring and that as part of its restructuring it needed to reduce its occupancy costs at certain stores, including the Garden Ridge store on the Property, was sent to Cypress's President, Maguire, on March 5, 2003; and [the consultant] had contacted Cypress's Director of Finance and others at Cypress on at least three other occasions to discuss the proposed rent relief, seeking an annual rent reduction of 30% for the Property, or $241,512.

A reasonable real estate investor who had signed an LOI to purchase the Property for $7,667,000 on September 2, 2003 would also attach importance to and be induced to act on the information that, on August 14, 2003, Cypress's lender, Guaranty Bank, had requested that Cypress's President execute a personal guaranty of the balance of $4,500,000 on the $5,704,000 loan secured by the Property because the bank was concerned about Garden Ridge's financial condition.

* * * We * * * hold that Cypress's active concealment of this material information, which it was under a duty to disclose as financial information material to the real estate transaction in its possession, was fraudulent as a matter of law.

DECISION AND REMEDY   *The Texas appellate court reversed the trial court and held that Cypress was liable to Fazio for fraud.*

THE ETHICAL DIMENSION   *Was Cypress's conduct unethical? Why or why not?*

THE SOCIAL DIMENSION   *What does the decision in this case suggest to sellers of commercial real estate and others who engage in business negotiations?*

Intent to Deceive

The second element of fraud is knowledge on the part of the misrepresenting party that facts have been falsely represented. This element, normally called **scienter**,[8] or "guilty knowledge," signifies that there was an *intent to deceive*. *Scienter* clearly exists if a party knows a fact is not as stated. *Scienter* also exists if a party makes a statement that he or she believes is not true or makes a statement recklessly, without regard to whether it is true or false. Finally, this element is met if a party says or implies that a statement is made on some basis, such as personal knowledge or personal investigation, when it is not.

▶ **Case in Point 15.7**   Robert Sarvis applied for a position as a business law professor two weeks after

his release from prison. On his résumé, he said that he had been a corporate president for fourteen years and had taught business law at another college. After he was hired, his probation officer alerted the school to Sarvis's criminal history. The school immediately fired him. When Sarvis sued the school for breach of his employment contract, the court concluded that by not disclosing his history, Sarvis clearly exhibited an intent to deceive and that the school had justifiably relied on his misrepresentations. Therefore, the school could rescind Sarvis's employment contract.[9] ◀

INNOCENT MISREPRESENTATION   If a person makes a statement that she or he believes to be true but that actually misrepresents material facts, the person is

---

8. Pronounced sy-*en*-ter.

9. *Sarvis v. Vermont State Colleges,* 172 Vt. 76, 772 A.2d 494 (2001).

guilty only of an **innocent misrepresentation**, not of fraud. When an innocent misrepresentation occurs, the aggrieved party can rescind the contract but usually cannot seek damages. ▶ **Example 15.8** Parris tells Roberta that a tract of land contains 250 acres. Parris is mistaken—the tract contains only 215 acres—but Parris had no knowledge of the mistake. Roberta relies on the statement and contracts to buy the land. Even though the misrepresentation is innocent, Roberta can avoid the contract if the misrepresentation is material. ◀

NEGLIGENT MISREPRESENTATION Sometimes, a party will make a misrepresentation through carelessness, believing the statement is true. If the party did not exercise reasonable care in uncovering or disclosing the facts or use the skill and competence that her or his business or profession requires, the misrepresentation may constitute **negligent misrepresentation.** For instance, an operator of a weight scale certifies the weight of Sneed's commodity, even though the scale's accuracy has not been checked for more than three years.

In almost all states, such negligent misrepresentation is equal to *scienter,* or knowingly making a misrepresentation. In effect, negligent misrepresentation is treated as fraudulent misrepresentation, even though the misrepresentation was not purposeful. In negligent misrepresentation, culpable ignorance of the truth supplies the intention to mislead, even if the defendant can claim, "I didn't know."

Reliance on the Misrepresentation

The third element of fraud is reasonably *justifiable reliance* on the misrepresentation of fact. The deceived party must have a justifiable reason for relying on the misrepresentation. Also, the misrepresentation must be an important factor (but not necessarily the sole factor) in inducing the deceived party to enter into the contract.

Reliance is not justified if the innocent party knows the true facts or relies on obviously extravagant statements (such as, "this pickup truck will get fifty miles to the gallon"). ▶ **Example 15.9** Meese, a securities broker, offers to sell BIM stock to Packer. Meese assures Packer that BIM shares are blue chip securities—that is, they are stable, have limited risk, and yield a good return on investment over time. In reality, Meese knows nothing about the quality of BIM stock and does not believe the truth of what he is saying. Thus, Meese's statement is an intentional misrepresentation of a material fact. If Packer is induced by Meese's statement to enter into a contract to buy the stock, he probably can avoid the contract. Packer justifiably relied on his broker's misrepresentation of material fact. ◀

The same rule applies to defects in property sold. If the defects would be obvious on inspection, the buyer cannot justifiably rely on the seller's representations. If the defects are hidden or latent, as previously discussed, the buyer is justified in relying on the seller's statements.

In the following case, the receiver for a car wash assured the buyer that the property would be "appropriately winterized," but it was not. Was the buyer justified in relying on the seller's representations? (A *receiver,* also called a *trustee,* is an independent, impartial party appointed by a bankruptcy court to manage property in bankruptcy and dispose of it in an orderly manner for the benefit of the creditors.)

CASE ANALYSIS

Case 15.3 Cronkelton v. Guaranteed Construction Services, LLC
Court of Appeals of Ohio, Third District, ___ N.E.2d ___, 2013 WL 428734, 2013-Ohio-328 (2013).

IN THE LANGUAGE OF THE COURT
PRESTON, P.J. [Presiding Judge]

* * * *

The case before this Court stems from a real estate transaction for a foreclosed car wash in Bellefontaine, Ohio. [A court had appointed Patrick Shivley to be a receiver for the protection of the property, which was offered for sale by Huntington Bank. Clifford] Cronkelton filed a complaint against appellants [Guaranteed Construction Services, LLC, and Shivley] in the Logan County Court of Common Pleas following his purchase of the car wash. Cronkelton asserted * * * fraud.

* * * *

* * * The trial court held a jury trial on the fraud claim. The jury returned a verdict for Cronkelton.

* * * The trial court filed its judgment entry recording the jury's verdict for Cronkelton and awarding Cronkelton $43,671 in compensatory damages, $66,000 in punitive dam-

CASE 15.2 CONTINUED

ages, and $30,000 for attorney fees. [Guaranteed Construction Services and Shivley filed an appeal.]

* * * *

* * * [At the trial] Cronkelton testified that he first inspected the foreclosed car wash at the end of November 2009. At that time, Cronkelton tested the equipment and knew that some of the pieces of equipment were fully functioning and some were not. * * * Shortly thereafter, Cronkelton called Shivley to discuss the winterization of the property. Cronkelton testified:

so I called him, said, hey, it's going to freeze here this week. * * * It's supposed to get down to like ten degrees, have you got it winterized, you know. If it's not winterized, I'm not interested in the property. If it freezes, I'm not interested in the property at all. And he guaranteed me. He said, no, it will be taken care of. We don't have a problem. That's my job as receiver. I'll take care of it.

After the phone call, Shivley sent Cronkelton an e-mail dated December 7, 2009 that stated:

As per our phone conversation Guaranteed [Construction Services] will winterize the Car Wash with the anticipation of reopening the wash in the near future. Within this Winterization we will put antifreeze and secure floor heating as well as blow water out of all lines in self serve bays as well as empty tanks, etc. We will leave the heat on at a minimal level in the pump room. * * * We will complete all of this on Wednesday, December 9, 2009.

[Guaranteed Construction hired Strayer Company to winterize the property. But on December 10, Strayer's owner sent a memo to Guaranteed Construction and Shivley stating that the building was not designed to be winterized and that the only way to avoid problems was to leave the heat on. Shivley knew Huntington Bank had shut off the heat because the property was not generating income. In March 2010, Shivley informed Huntington of damage to the property as a result of freezing. Shivley did not share any of this information with Cronkelton.]

Cronkelton testified that they closed on the property in June and he received the keys at that time. Cronkelton testified that he immediately went to the property:

I opened the door, and the huge canisters that I was telling you about were all busted. The tops had been exploded off the top of them. * * * You could see pipes that were bursted * * * . So it was clear at that time that this whole thing had froze up, and the extent of the damage could not even be, you know, detailed at that point.

* * * *

* * * Appellants argue Cronkelton unjustifiably relied on Shivley's statements about the car wash's condition because Cronkelton had the opportunity to inspect the property prior to closing.

* * * *

* * * Whether or not reliance on a material misrepresentation was justified under the facts of a case is a question for the trier of fact. Consequently, we must determine whether the jury's decision is supported by competent, credible evidence.

In the present case, it is undisputed that the damage caused by freezing was open and obvious upon inspection, that Cronkelton did inspect the property in November 2009, and that he could have inspected the property again before signing the purchase agreement. Cronkelton testified regarding why he did not inspect the property after November 2009:

* * * [Shivley] wrote me this e-mail, guaranteed me it was taken care of in detail what he was going to do, so I had no reason. And because * * * he was appointed by the Court, I don't know how much more I could have done to know that I could trust him.

* * * The jury found that Cronkelton had reasonably relied on Shivley's representations.

The jury's finding was supported by competent, credible evidence. * * * *When determining whether reliance is justifiable, courts consider the various circumstances involved, such as the nature of the transaction, the form and materiality of the transaction, the form and materiality of the representation, the relationship of the parties, the respective intelligence, experience, age, and mental and physical condition of the parties, and their respective knowledge and means of knowledge.* [Emphasis added.]

Cronkelton relied on representations made by Shivley * * *. As a receiver, Shivley had a fiduciary duty to the assets under his control. Under the circumstances of this case, Cronkelton had a reasonable basis to believe that Shivley, who was acting as an arm of the court, would take the promised steps to winterize the property.

* * * *

* * * We affirm the judgment of the trial court.

LEGAL REASONING QUESTIONS

1. What is a receiver? What are a receiver's duties?

2. In evaluating a claim of fraud, what factors does a court consider in determining whether reliance was justifiable?

3. In this case, what did the jury find with respect to the plaintiff's claim of reliance? What was the appellate court's opinion of this finding?

4. Did Shivley's misrepresentations rise to the level of fraud? Explain.

Injury to the Innocent Party

Most courts do not require a showing of injury when the action is to rescind the contract. These courts hold that because rescission returns the parties to the positions they held before the contract was made, a showing of injury to the innocent party is unnecessary.

In contrast, to recover damages caused by fraud, proof of harm is universally required. The measure of damages is ordinarily equal to the property's value had it been delivered as represented, less the actual price paid for the property. (What if someone pretends to be someone else online? Can the victim of the hoax prove injury sufficient to recover for fraudulent misrepresentation? See this chapter's *Insight into Social Media* feature on the following page for a discussion of this topic.)

Additionally, because fraud actions necessarily involve wrongful conduct, courts may also award *punitive damages,* or *exemplary damages.* As discussed in Chapter 6, punitive damages are intended to punish the defendant and are granted to a plaintiff over and above compensation for the proved, actual loss. Because of the potential for punitive damages, which normally are not available in contract actions, plaintiffs often include a claim for fraudulent misrepresentation in their contract disputes.

SECTION 3
UNDUE INFLUENCE

Undue influence arises from relationships in which one party can greatly influence another party, thus overcoming that party's free will. A contract entered into under excessive or undue influence lacks voluntary consent and is therefore voidable.[10]

One Party Dominates the Other

In various types of relationships, one party may have the opportunity to dominate and unfairly influence another party. Minors and elderly people, for instance, are often under the influence of guardians (persons who are legally responsible for another). If a guardian induces a young or elderly ward (a person whom the guardian looks after) to enter into a contract that benefits the guardian, the guardian may have exerted undue influence. Undue influence can arise from a number of fiduciary relationships, such as physician-patient, parent-child, husband-wife, or guardian-ward situations.

The essential feature of undue influence is that the party being taken advantage of does not, in reality, exercise free will in entering into a contract. It is not enough that a person is elderly or suffers from some physical or mental impairment. There must be clear and convincing evidence that the person did not act out of her or his free will.[11] Similarly, the existence of a fiduciary relationship alone is insufficient to prove undue influence.[12]

A Presumption of Undue Influence in Certain Situations

When the dominant party in a fiduciary relationship (such as the one between an attorney and a client) benefits from that relationship, a presumption of undue influence arises. The dominant party (the attorney) must exercise the utmost good faith in dealing with the other party. When a contract enriches the dominant party, the court will often *presume* that the contract was made under undue influence.

▶ **Example 15.10** Erik is the guardian for Kinsley, his ward. On her behalf, he enters into a contract from which he benefits financially. If Kinsley challenges the contract, the court will likely presume that the guardian has taken advantage of his ward. To rebut (refute) this presumption, Erik has to show that he made full disclosure to Kinsley and that consideration was present. He must also show that Kinsley received, if available, independent and competent advice before completing the transaction. Unless the presumption can be rebutted, the contract will be rescinded. ◀

SECTION 4
DURESS

Agreement to the terms of a contract is not voluntary if one of the parties is *forced* into the agreement. The use of threats to force a party to enter into a contract is referred to as *duress.* In addition, blackmail or extortion to induce consent to a contract constitutes duress. Duress is both a defense to the enforcement of a contract and a ground for the rescission of a contract.

The Threatened Act Must Be Wrongful or Illegal

To establish duress, there must be proof of a threat to do something that the threatening party has

---

10. *Restatement (Second) of Contracts,* Section 177.

11. See, for example, *Bailey v. Turnbow,* 273 Va. 262, 639 S.E.2d 291 (2007); and *Hooten v. Jensen,* 94 Ark.App. 130, 227 S.W.3d 431 (2006).
12. See, for example, *Landers v. Sgouros,* 224 S.W.3d 651 (Mo.App. 2007); and *Ware v. Ware,* 161 P.3d 1188 (Alaska 2007).

INSIGHT INTO SOCIAL MEDIA
"Catfishing": Is That Online "Friend" Who You Think It Is?

When you are communicating with a person you have met only online, how do you know that person is who she or he purports to be? After all, the person could turn out to be a "catfish." The term comes from *Catfish*, a 2010 film about a fake online persona.

According to a story told in the film, when live cod were shipped long distances, they were inactive and their flesh became mushy. When catfish were added to the tanks, the cod swam around and stayed in good condition. At the end of the film, a character says of the creator of the fake persona, "There are those people who are catfish in life. And they keep you on your toes. They keep you guessing, they keep you thinking, they keep you fresh."

Catfishing Makes National Headlines

Catfishing made headlines in 2012 when a popular Notre Dame football star supposedly fell victim to it. Linebacker Manti Te'o said that his girlfriend Lennay Kekua, a student at Stanford, had died of leukemia after a near-fatal car accident. Although Kekua had Facebook and Twitter accounts and Te'o had communicated with her online and by telephone for several years, reporters could find no evidence of her existence. Te'o later claimed that he had been a victim of a catfishing hoax. Others suggested that his friends created the persona and her tragic death to provide an inspirational story what would increase Te'o's chances of winning the Heisman trophy.

Is Online Fraudulent Misrepresentation Actionable?

Some victims of catfishing have turned to the courts, but they have had little success. A few have attempted to sue Internet service providers for allowing fake personas, but the courts have generally dismissed these suits.[a] Laws in some states make it a crime to impersonate someone online, but these laws generally do not apply to those who create totally fake personas.

Attempts to recover damages for fraudulent misrepresentation have generally failed to meet the requirement that there must be proof of actual injury. For instance, Paula Bonhomme developed an online romantic relationship with a man called Jesse. Jesse was actually a woman named Janna St. James, who also communicated with Bonhomme using her own name and pretending to be a friend of Jesse's.

St. James created a host of fictional characters, including an ex-wife and a son for Jesse. Bonhomme in turn sent gifts totaling more than $10,000 to Jesse and the other characters. After being told by St. James that Jesse had attempted suicide, Bonhomme suffered such emotional distress that she incurred more than $5,000 in bills for a therapist. Eventually, she was told that Jesse had died of liver cancer. When Bonhomme finally learned the truth, she suffered additional emotional distress, resulting in more expenses for a therapist and lost earnings due to her "affected mental state."

Although Bonhomme had incurred considerable expenses, the Illinois Supreme Court ruled that she could not bring a suit for fraudulent misrepresentation. The case involved only a "purely personal relationship" without any "commercial, transactional, or regulatory component." Bonhomme and St. James "were not engaged in any kind of business dealings or bargaining." Therefore, the truth of representations "made in the context of purely private personal relationships is simply not something the state regulates or in which the state possesses any kind of valid public policy interest."[b]

LEGAL CRITICAL THINKING
INSIGHT INTO THE LEGAL ENVIRONMENT

So far, victims of catfishing have had little success in the courts. Under what circumstances might a person be able to collect damages for fraudulent misrepresentation involving online impersonation?"

---

a. See, for example, *Robinson v. Match.com, LLC,* 2012 WL 3263992 (N.D.Tex. 2012).

b. *Bonhomme v. St. James,* 970 N.E.2d 1 (Ill. 2012).

---

no right to do. Generally, for duress to occur, the threatened act must be wrongful or illegal, and it must render the person incapable of exercising free will. A threat to exercise a legal right, such as the right to sue someone, ordinarily does not constitute duress.

▶ **Example 15.11** Joan accidentally drives into Olin's car at a stoplight. Joan has no automobile insurance, but she has substantial assets. At the scene, Olin claims to have suffered whiplash and tells Joan that he will agree not to file a lawsuit against her if she pays him $5,000. Joan initially refuses, but Olin says,

"If you don't pay me $5,000 right now, I'm going to sue you for $25,000." Joan then gives Olin a check for $5,000 to avoid the lawsuit. The next day, Joan stops payment on the check. When Olin later sues to enforce their oral settlement agreement for $5,000, Joan claims duress as a defense to its enforcement. In this situation, because Olin had a right to sue Joan, his threat to sue her does not constitute duress. A court normally would not consider the threat of a civil suit to be duress. ◄

Economic Duress

Economic need generally is not sufficient to constitute duress, even when one party exacts a very high price for an item that the other party needs. If the party exacting the price also creates the need, however, *economic duress* may be found.

▶ **Example 15.12** The Internal Revenue Service (IRS) assesses a large tax and penalty against Weller. Weller retains Eyman, the accountant who prepared the tax returns on which the assessment was based, to challenge the assessment. Two days before the deadline for filing a reply with the IRS, Eyman declines to represent Weller unless he signs a very expensive contingency-fee agreement for the services.

In this situation, a court might find that the agreement was unenforceable because of economic duress. Although Eyman has threatened only to withdraw his services, something that he is legally entitled to do, he is responsible for delaying the withdrawal until two days before the IRS deadline. It would be impossible at that late date to obtain adequate representation elsewhere. Therefore, Weller could argue that he was forced either to sign the contract or to lose his right to challenge the IRS assessment. ◄

SECTION 5

ADHESION CONTRACTS AND UNCONSCIONABILITY

Questions concerning voluntary consent may arise when the terms of a contract are dictated by a party with overwhelming bargaining power and the signer must agree to those terms or go without the commodity or service in question. As explained in Chapter 14, **adhesion contracts** are written *exclusively* by one party and presented to the other party on a take-it-or-leave-it basis. These contracts often use standard forms, which give the adhering party no opportunity to negotiate the contract terms.

Standard-Form Contracts

Standard-form contracts often contain fine-print provisions that shift a risk ordinarily borne by one party to the other. A variety of businesses use such contracts. Life insurance policies, residential leases, loan agreements, and employment agency contracts are often standard-form contracts. To avoid enforcement of the contract or of a particular clause, the plaintiff normally must show that the contract or particular term is *unconscionable*.

▶ **Case in Point 15.13** Sherry Simpson signed a standard-form contract with Addy's Harbor Dodge, a car dealership, when she traded in her automobile for a new vehicle. Above the signature line was a statement indicating that there were additional terms and conditions on the opposite page. Simpson did not read these terms, which contained an arbitration clause that also limited the damages she could recover in the event of a dispute.

Simpson later filed a lawsuit, claiming that Addy's had misrepresented the trade-in value of her vehicle, artificially increased the purchase price, and failed to provide all promised rebates. Addy's filed a motion to compel arbitration, which the court denied. The court refused to enforce the arbitration provision on the ground that it was unconscionable. Not only was it oppressive, one sided, and inconspicuous, but it also required Simpson to give up remedies that were available under the state statute.[13] ◄

Unconscionability and the Courts

Technically, unconscionability under Section 2–302 of the Uniform Commercial Code (UCC) applies only to contracts for the sale of goods. Many courts, however, have broadened the concept and applied it in other situations.

Although unconscionability was discussed in Chapter 14, it is important to note here that the UCC gives courts a great degree of discretion to invalidate or strike down a contract or clause as being unconscionable. As a result, some states have *not* adopted Section 2–302 of the UCC. In those states, the legislature and the courts prefer to rely on traditional notions of fraud, undue influence, and duress.

See *Concept Summary 15.1* on the following page for a review of all of the factors that may indicate a lack of voluntary consent.

---

13. *Simpson v. MSA of Myrtle Beach, Inc.*, 373 S.C. 15, 644 S.E.2d 663 (2007).

CONCEPT SUMMARY 15.1
Voluntary Consent

PROBLEMS OF ASSENT	RULE
Mistakes	1. *Bilateral (mutual) mistake*—If both parties are mistaken about a material fact, such as the identity of the subject matter, either party can avoid the contract. If the mistake relates to the value or quality of the subject matter, either party can enforce the contract. 2. *Unilateral mistake*—Generally, the mistaken party is bound by the contract, unless the other party knows or should have known of the mistake, or the mistake is an inadvertent mathematical error in addition, subtraction, or the like that is committed without gross negligence.
Fraudulent Misrepresentation	The elements of fraudulent misrepresentation are: 1. A misrepresentation of a material fact has occurred. 2. There has been an intent to deceive. 3. The innocent party has justifiably relied on the misrepresentation. 4. To collect damages, a party must have been harmed as a result of the misrepresentation.
Undue Influence and Duress	1. *Undue influence*—Arises from special relationships, such as fiduciary relationships, in which one party's free will has been overcome by the undue influence of another. Usually, the contract is voidable. 2. *Duress*—Defined as the use of threats to force a party to enter into a contract out of fear; for example, the threat of violence or economic pressure. The party forced to enter into the contract can rescind the contract.
Adhesion Contracts and Unconscionability	Concerns one-sided bargains in which one party has substantially superior bargaining power and can dictate the terms of a contract. Unconscionability typically occurs as a result of the following: 1. *Standard-form contracts*—In which a fine-print provision purports to shift a risk normally borne by one party to the other (for example, a liability disclaimer). 2. *Take-it-or-leave-it adhesion contracts*—In which the buyer has no choice but to agree to the seller's dictated terms if the buyer is to procure certain goods or services.

Reviewing: Mistakes, Fraud, and Voluntary Consent

Chelene had been a caregiver for Marta's eighty-year-old mother, Janis, for nine years. Shortly before Janis passed away, Chelene convinced her to buy Chelene's house for Marta. The elderly woman died before the papers were signed, however. Four months later, Marta used her inheritance to buy Chelene's house without having it inspected. The house was built in the 1950s, and Chelene said it was in "perfect condition." Nevertheless, one year after the purchase, the basement started leaking. Marta had the paneling removed from the basement walls and discovered that the walls were bowed inward and cracked. Marta then had a civil engineer inspect the basement walls, and he found that the cracks had been caulked and painted over before the paneling was installed. He concluded that the "wall failure" had existed "for at least thirty years" and that the basement walls were "structurally unsound." Using the information presented in the chapter, answer the following questions.

1. Can Marta obtain rescission of the contract based on undue influence? If the sale to Janis had been completed before her death, could Janis have obtained rescission based on undue influence? Explain.
2. Can Marta sue Chelene for fraudulent misrepresentation? Why or why not? What element(s) might be lacking?

Continued

3. Now assume that Chelene knew that the basement walls were cracked and bowed and that she had hired someone to install paneling before she offered to sell the house. Did she have a duty to disclose this defect to Marta? Could a court find that Chelene's silence in this situation constituted misrepresentation? Explain.

4. If Chelene knew about the problem with the walls but did not know that the house was structurally unsound, could she be liable for negligent misrepresentation? Why or why not?

5. Can Marta avoid the contract on the ground that both parties made a mistake about the condition of the house? Explain.

DEBATE THIS... *The concept of* caveat emptor *("let the buyer beware") should be applied to all sales, including those of real property.*

Terms and Concepts

adhesion contract 300	latent defects 294	*scienter* 295
innocent misrepresentation 296	negligent misrepresentation 296	voluntary consent 290

ExamPrep

Issue Spotters

1. In selling a house, Matt tells Ann that the wiring, fixtures, and appliances are of a certain quality. Matt knows nothing about the quality, but it is not as specified. Ann buys the house. On learning the true quality, Ann confronts Matt. He says he wasn't trying to fool her, he was only trying to make a sale. Can she rescind the deal? Why or why not? **(See page 295.)**

2. Elle, an accountant, certifies several audit reports for Flite Corporation, her client, knowing that Flite intends to use the reports to obtain loans from Good Credit Company (GCC). Elle believes that the reports are true and does not intend to deceive GCC, but she does not check the reports before certifying them. Can Elle be held liable to GCC? Why or why not? **(See page 296.)**

- Check your answers to the Issue Spotters against the answers provided in Appendix E at the end of this text.

Before the Test

Go to **www.cengagebrain.com**, enter the ISBN 9781285185248, and click on "Find" to locate this textbook's Web site. Then, click on "Access Now" under "Study Tools," and select Chapter 15 at the top. There, you will find a Practice Quiz that you can take to assess your mastery of the concepts in this chapter, as well as Flashcards, and a Glossary of important terms.

Business Scenarios

15–1. Undue Influence. Juan is an elderly man who lives with his nephew, Samuel. Juan is totally dependent on Samuel's support. Samuel tells Juan that unless he transfers a tract of land he owns to Samuel for a price 35 percent below its market value, Samuel will no longer support and take care of him. Juan enters into the contract. Discuss fully whether Juan can set aside this contract. **(See page 298.)**

15–2. Fraudulent Misrepresentation. Grano owns a forty-room motel on Highway 100. Tanner is interested in purchasing the motel. During the course of negotiations, Grano tells Tanner that the motel netted $30,000 during the previous year and that it will net at least $45,000 the next year. The motel books, which Grano turns over to Tanner before the purchase, clearly show that Grano's motel netted only $15,000 the previous year. Also, Grano fails to tell Tanner that a bypass to Highway 100 is being planned that will redirect most traffic away from the front of the motel. Tanner purchases the motel. During the first year under Tanner's operation, the motel nets only $18,000. At this time, Tanner learns of the motel's previous low profits and the planned bypass. Tanner wants Grano to return the purchase price. Discuss fully Tanner's probable success in getting his funds back. **(See page 293.)**

15–3. Voluntary Consent. Discuss whether either of the following contracts will be unenforceable on the ground that voluntary consent is lacking:

(a) Simmons finds a stone in his pasture that he believes to be quartz. Jenson, who also believes that the stone is quartz, contracts to purchase it for $10. Just before delivery, the stone is discovered to be a diamond worth $1,000. **(See page 292.)**

(b) Jacoby's barn is burned to the ground. He accuses Goldman's son of arson and threatens to have the prosecutor bring a criminal action unless Goldman agrees to pay him $5,000. Goldman agrees to pay. **(See page 298.)**

Business Case Problems

15–4. Fraudulent Misrepresentation. Peggy Williams helped eighty-seven-year-old Melvin Kaufman care for Elsie Kaufman, his wife and Williams's great aunt, for several years before her death. Melvin then asked Williams to "take care of him the rest of his life." He conveyed his house to her for "Ten and No/100 Dollars ($10.00), and other good and valuable consideration," according to the deed, and executed a power of attorney in her favor. When Melvin returned from a trip to visit his brother, however, Williams had locked him out of the house. He filed a suit in a Texas state court, alleging fraud. He claimed that he had deeded the house to her in exchange for her promise of care, but that she had not taken care of him and had not paid him the ten dollars. Williams admitted that she had not paid the ten dollars, but argued that she had made no such promise, that Melvin had given her the house when he had been unable to sell it, and that his trip had been intended as a move. Do these facts show fraud? If so, what would be the appropriate remedy? Explain. [*Williams v. Kaufman,* 275 S.W.3d 637 (Tex.App.—Beaumont 2009)] **(See page 293.)**

15–5. BUSINESS CASE PROBLEM
WITH SAMPLE ANSWER: Fraudulent Misrepresentation.

Ricky and Sherry Wilcox hired Esprit Log and Timber Frame Homes to build a log house, which the Wilcoxes intended to sell. They paid Esprit $125,260 for materials and services. They eventually sold the home for $1,620,000 but sued Esprit due to construction delays. The logs were supposed to arrive at the construction site precut and predrilled, but that did not happen. So it took five extra months to build the house while the logs were cut and drilled one by one. The Wilcoxes claimed that the interest they paid on a loan for the extra construction time cost them about $200,000. The jury agreed and awarded them that much in damages, plus $250,000 in punitive damages and $20,000 in attorneys' fees. Esprit appealed, claiming that the evidence did not support the verdict because the Wilcoxes had sold the house for a good price. Is Esprit's argument credible? Why or why not? How should the court rule? [Esprit Log and

Timber Frame Homes, Inc. v. Wilcox, *302 S.E.2d 550, 691 S.E.2d 344 (2010)]* **(See page 293.)**

• **For a sample answer to Problem 15–5, go to Appendix F at the end of this text.**

15–6. Mutual Mistake. When Steven Simkin divorced Laura Blank, they agreed to split their assets equally. They owned an account with Bernard L. Madoff Investment Securities estimated to be worth $5.4 million. Simkin kept the account and paid Blank more than $6.5 million—including $2.7 million to offset the amount of the funds that they believed were in the account. Later, they learned that the account actually contained no funds due to its manager's fraud. Could their agreement be rescinded on the basis of a mistake? Discuss. [*Simkin v. Blank,* 80 A.D.3d 401, 915 N.Y.S.2d 47 (1 Dept. 2011)] **(See page 291.)**

15–7. Misrepresentation. Charter One Bank owned a fifteen-story commercial building. A fire inspector told Charter that the building's drinking-water and fire-suppression systems were linked. Without disclosing this information, Charter sold the building to Northpoint Properties, Inc. Northpoint spent $280,000 to repair the water and fire-suppression systems and filed a suit against Charter One. Is the seller liable for not disclosing the building's defects? Discuss. [*Northpoint Properties, Inc. v. Charter One Bank,* 2011-Ohio-2512 (Ohio App. 8 Dist. 2011)] **(See page 293.)**

15–8. Standard-Form Contracts. David Desgro hired Paul Pack to inspect a house that Desgro wanted to buy. Pack had Desgro sign a standard-form contract that included a twelve-month limit for claims based on the agreement. Pack reported that the house had no major problems, but after Desgro bought it, he discovered issues with the plumbing, insulation, heat pump, and floor support. Thirteen months after the inspection, Desgro filed a suit in a Tennessee state court against Pack. Was Desgro's complaint filed too late, or was the contract's twelve-month limit unenforceable? Discuss. [*Desgro v. Pack,* __ So.3d __, 2013 WL 84899 (Tenn.App. 2013)] **(See page 300.)**

15–9. A QUESTION OF ETHICS: Mistake.

On behalf of BRJM, LLC, Nicolas Kepple offered Howard Engelsen $210,000 for a parcel of land known as lot five on the north side of Barnes Road in Stonington, Connecticut. Engelsen's company, Output Systems, Inc., owned the land. Engelsen had the lot surveyed and obtained an appraisal. The appraiser valued the property at $277,000, after determining that it was 3.0 acres in size and thus could not be subdivided because it did not meet the town's minimum legal requirement of 3.7 acres for subdivision. Engelsen responded to Kepple's offer with a counteroffer of $230,000, which Kepple accepted. On May 3, 2002, the parties signed a contract. When Engelsen refused to go through with the deal, BRJM filed a suit in a Connecticut state court against Output, seeking specific performance and other relief. The defendant asserted the defense of mutual mistake on at least two grounds. [BRJM, LLC v. Output Systems, Inc., 100 Conn.App. 153, 917 A.2d 605 (2007)] **(See page 290.)**

(a) In the counteroffer, Engelsen asked Kepple to remove from their contract a clause requiring written confirmation of the availability of a "free split," which meant that the property could be subdivided without the town's prior approval. Kepple agreed. After signing the contract, Kepple learned that the property was *not* entitled to a free split. Would this circumstance qualify as a mistake on which the defendant could avoid the contract? Discuss.

(b) After signing the contract, Engelsen obtained a second appraisal that established the size of lot five as 3.71 acres, which meant that it could be subdivided, and valued the property at $490,000. Can the defendant avoid the contract on the basis of a mistake in the first appraisal? Explain.

Legal Reasoning Group Activity

15–10. Fraudulent Misrepresentation. Radiah Givens was involved romantically with Joseph Rosenzweig. She moved into an apartment on which he made the down payment. She signed the mortgage, but he made the payments and paid household expenses. They later married. She had their marriage annulled, however, when she learned that he was married to someone else. Rosenzweig then filed a suit against her to collect on the mortgage. **(See page 293.)**

(a) The first group should decide whether Rosenzweig committed fraud.

(b) The second group should evaluate whether Rosenzweig's conduct was deceitful, and if so, whether his deceitfulness should affect the decision in this case.

(c) The third group should consider how fraud is related to ethics. Can a contracting party act ethically and still commit fraud? How?

CHAPTER 16

THE WRITING REQUIREMENT AND ELECTRONIC RECORDS

A contract that is otherwise valid may still be unenforceable if it is not in the proper form. Certain types of contracts are required to be in writing or evidenced by a memorandum or electronic record (*record* was defined in Chapter 12). The writing requirement does not mean that an agreement must be a formal written contract. An exchange of e-mails that evidences the parties' agreement usually is sufficient, provided that they are "signed," or agreed to, by the party against whom enforcement is sought.

In this chapter, we examine the kinds of contracts that require a writing and some exceptions to the writing requirement. We also discuss the *parol evidence rule,* which courts follow when determining whether evidence that is extraneous, or external, to written contracts may be admissible at trial. Though not inherently related to the writing requirement, the parol evidence rule has general application in contract law.

WRITING REQUIREMENT: THE STATUTE OF FRAUDS

Every state has a statute that stipulates what types of contracts must be in writing. We refer to such a statute as the **Statute of Frauds.** The origins of these statutes can be traced to early English law.

Origins of the Statute

At early common law, parties to a contract were not allowed to testify if a dispute arose. This led to the practice of hiring third party witnesses. As early as the seventeenth century, the English recognized that this practice created many problems and enacted a statute to help deal with them.

The statute, passed by the English Parliament in 1677, was known as "An Act for the Prevention of Frauds and Perjuries." The act established that certain types of contracts, to be enforceable, had to be evidenced by a writing and signed by the party against whom enforcement was sought. The primary purpose of the statute was to ensure that, for certain types of contracts, there was reliable evidence of the contracts and their terms.

State Legislation

Today, although each state has a statute modeled after the English act, the statutes vary slightly from state to state. All states require certain types of contracts to be in writing or evidenced by a written memorandum or an electronic record. In addition, the party or parties against whom enforcement is sought must have signed the contract, unless certain exceptions apply (as discussed later in this chapter). Recall from Chapter 12 that in the context of electronic communications, a party's name typed at the bottom of an e-mail can qualify as a signature.

The actual name of the Statute of Frauds is misleading because the statute does not apply to fraud. Rather, it denies enforceability to certain contracts that do not comply with its writing requirements. The primary purpose of the statute is to prevent harm to innocent parties by requiring written evidence of agreements concerning important transactions. A contract that is oral when it is required to be in writing is normally voidable by a party who later does not wish to follow through with the agreement.

SECTION 2
CONTRACTS THAT REQUIRE A WRITING

The following types of contracts are generally required to be in writing or evidenced by a written memorandum or electronic record:

1. Contracts involving interests in land.
2. Contracts that cannot *by their terms* be performed within one year from the day after the date of formation.
3. Collateral, or secondary, contracts, such as promises to answer for the debt or duty of another and promises by the administrator or executor of an estate to pay a debt of the estate personally—that is, out of her or his own pocket.
4. Promises made in consideration of marriage.
5. Under the Uniform Commercial Code (UCC—see Chapter 20), contracts for the sale of goods priced at $500 or more.

Contracts Involving Interests in Land

A contract calling for the sale of land is not enforceable unless it is in writing or evidenced by a written memorandum. Land is *real property* and includes all physical objects that are permanently attached to the soil, such as buildings, fences, trees, and the soil itself.

The Statute of Frauds operates as a *defense* to the enforcement of an oral contract for the sale of land. ▶ **Example 16.1** Skylar contracts orally to sell his property in Fair Oaks to Beth. If he later decides not to sell, under most circumstances, Beth cannot enforce the contract. ◀

The Statute of Frauds also requires written evidence of contracts for the transfer of other interests in land, such as mortgage agreements and leases. Similarly, an agreement that includes an option to purchase real property must be in writing for the option to be enforced.

Generally, for a land sale contract to be enforceable under the Statute of Frauds, the contract must describe the property being transferred with sufficient certainty for it to be identified. Whether a contract for the sale of land met this requirement was at issue in the following case.

CASE ANALYSIS

Case 16.1 Salim v. Solaiman
Court of Appeals of Georgia, 302 Ga.App. 607, 691 S.E.2d 389 (2010).

IN THE LANGUAGE OF THE COURT
ADAMS, Judge.

* * * *

Mohammad Salim bought * * * a convenience store and gas station * * *. He made some improvements to the property and then offered it for sale. Talat Solaiman and Sabina Chowdhury approached Salim about buying the property in December 2006. After negotiating a purchase price of $975,000, the parties signed a handwritten document memorial-izing the terms of the agreement and on December 26, signed a more formal, typewritten "Purchase and Sale Agreement" prepared by Solaiman and Chowdhury.

The typed agreement * * * described [the property] simply as "the property and business (known as BP Food Mart) located at 199 Upper Riverdale Road, Jonesboro, GA 30236." The agreement set a closing date of January 5, 2007 and required Solaiman and Chowdhury to pay a $25,000 "security deposit" to be applied toward the down payment. But the agreement did not specify what would happen to the security deposit in the event the sale failed to close.

* * * Solaiman and Chowdhury conducted due diligence [investigation], including visiting the store and speaking to store clerks, vendors and customers. They also ordered a title search on the property and paid $2,000 for an application to renew the store's alcoholic beverage license in their name.

* * * The closing did not occur on January 5. And after receiving the title report in mid-January, Solaiman and Chowdhury decided that they no longer wanted to buy the property.

They notified Salim of their decision and asked for reimbursement of the security deposit and the alcohol license renewal fee. * * * Salim refused to repay the funds, and Solaiman and Chowdhury filed this action [for breach of contract] in December 2007.

The trial court issued judgment in favor of Solaiman and Chowdhury after finding the parties' purchase agreement to be unenforceable because "it does not sufficiently describe the real property to be purchased."

* * * *

The requirement that a contract to purchase real property include an adequate property description arises under the Statute of Frauds. To comply with the Statute, an agreement for the sale of land *must be in writing and must provide a sufficiently definite description of the property to be sold. Specifically, such a contract must describe the property * * * with the same degree of certainty as that required in a deed conveying realty."* The property description must demonstrate "with sufficient certainty" the grantor's intention with regard to the quantity and location of the land to be conveyed, "so that its identification is practicable * * * ." To be enforceable, therefore, the purchase agreement in this case was required to either "describe the particular tract or provide a key by which it may be located with the aid of extrinsic [outside] evidence." To suffice as a key, the description "must open the door to extrinsic evidence which leads unerringly to the land in question." But if the words in the agreement, "when aided by extrinsic evidence, fail to locate and identify a certain tract of land, the description fails and the instrument is void." [Emphasis added.]

The property description contained in the four corners of the purchase agreement clearly fails to identify the land at issue with the requisite certainty as it merely provides a street address.

* * * *

Accordingly, we affirm the trial court's holding that the parties' purchase agreement was void for lack of an adequate property description.

LEGAL REASONING QUESTIONS

1. Why was Salim arguing that the contract should be deemed enforceable when he was being sued for breach of contract?

2. What might Salim have done to ensure that the sales contract would be enforceable?

3. Why does the Statute of Frauds require that a contract for a sale of land include a sufficiently definite description of the property?

4. If the contract had contained a sufficient description of the property, would the court likely have forced Solaiman and Chowdhury to go through with the purchase? Explain.

The One-Year Rule

Contracts that cannot, *by their own terms*, be performed within one year *from the day after* the contract is formed must be in writing to be enforceable.[1] The reason for this rule is that the parties' memory of their contract's terms is not reliable for longer than a year.

TIME PERIOD STARTS THE DAY AFTER THE CONTRACT IS FORMED The one-year period begins to run *the day after the contract is made.* ▶ **Example 16.2** Superior University forms a contract with Kimi San stating that San will teach three courses in history during the coming academic year (September 15 through June 15). If the contract is formed in March, it must be in writing to be enforceable—because it cannot be performed within one year. If the contract is not formed until July, however, it does not have to be in writing to be enforceable—because it can be performed within one year. ◀

MUST BE OBJECTIVELY IMPOSSIBLE TO PERFORM WITHIN ONE YEAR The test for determining whether an oral contract is enforceable under the one-year rule is whether performance is *possible* within one year. It does not matter whether the agreement is *likely* to be performed during that period.

When performance of a contract is objectively impossible during the one-year period, the oral contract will be unenforceable. ▶ **Example 16.3** A contract to provide five crops of tomatoes to be grown on a specific farm in Illinois would be objectively impossible to perform within one year. No farmer in Illinois can grow five crops of tomatoes in a single year. ◀

If performance is possible within one year under the contract's terms, the contract does not "fall

---

1. *Restatement (Second) of Contracts,* Section 130.

within" or "under" the Statute of Frauds and need not be in writing. ▶ **Example 16.4** Janine enters a contract to provide security services for a warehouse for as long as the warehouse needs them. The contract could be fully performed within a year because the warehouse could go out of business within twelve months. Therefore, the contract need not be in writing to be enforceable. ◀ Similarly, an oral contract for lifetime employment does not fall within the Statute of Frauds because an employee can die within a year, so the contract can be performed within one year.[2]

Exhibit 16–1 below graphically illustrates the one-year rule.

Collateral Promises

A **collateral promise,** or secondary promise, is one that is ancillary (subsidiary) to a principal transaction or primary contractual relationship. In other words, a collateral promise is one made by a third party to assume the debts or obligations of a primary party to a contract if that party does not perform. Any collateral promise of this nature falls under the Statute of Frauds and therefore must be in writing to be enforceable.

To understand this concept, it is important to distinguish between primary and secondary promises and obligations.

PRIMARY OBLIGATIONS A primary obligation is a third party's promise to pay another person's debt (or

---

2. See, for example, *Gavegnano v. TLT Construction Corp.,* 67 Mass.App. Ct. 1102, 851 N.E.2d 1133 (2006).

other obligation) that is not conditioned on the person's failure to pay (or perform). As a general rule, a contract in which a party assumes a primary obligation does not need to be in writing to be enforceable. ▶ **Example 16.5** Nigel tells Leanne Lu, an orthodontist, that he will pay for the services provided for Nigel's niece. Because Nigel has assumed direct financial responsibility for his niece's debt, this is a primary obligation and need not be in writing to be enforceable. ◀

SECONDARY OBLIGATIONS A secondary obligation is a promise to pay another's debt only if that party fails to pay. ▶ **Example 16.6** Kareem's mother borrows $10,000 from the Medford Trust Company on a promissory note payable in six months. Kareem promises the bank officer handling the loan that he will pay the $10,000 *if his mother does not pay the loan on time.* Kareem, in this situation, becomes what is known as a *guarantor* on the loan. He is guaranteeing to the bank (the creditor) that he will pay the loan if his mother fails to do so. This kind of collateral promise must be in writing to be enforceable. ◀

Exhibit 16–2 on the following page illustrates the concept of a collateral promise. (Notice that the bottom arrow says "Promises to Answer for A's Debt." It does not say "Promises to Pay.")

AN EXCEPTION—THE "MAIN PURPOSE" RULE An oral promise to answer for the debt of another is covered by the Statute of Frauds *unless* the guarantor's main purpose in incurring a secondary obligation is to secure a personal benefit. This type of contract need

---

EXHIBIT 16–1 The One-Year Rule

Under the Statute of Frauds, contracts that by their terms are impossible to perform within one year from the day after the date of contract formation must be in writing to be enforceable. Put another way, if it is at all possible to perform an oral contract within one year from the day after the contract is made, the contract will fall outside the Statute of Frauds and be enforceable.

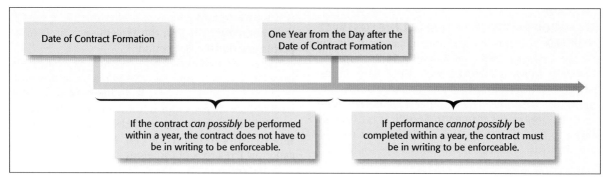

EXHIBIT 16-2 Collateral Promises

A collateral (secondary) promise is one made by a third party (C, in this exhibit) to a creditor (B, in this exhibit) to pay the debt of another (A, in this exhibit), who is primarily obligated to pay the debt. Under the Statute of Frauds, collateral promises must be in writing to be enforceable.

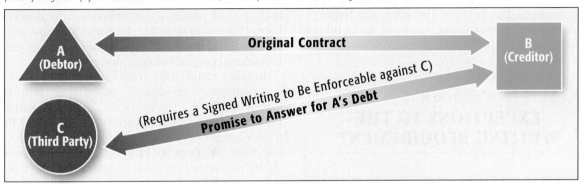

not be in writing.[3] The assumption is that a court can infer from the circumstances of a particular case whether the "leading objective" of the guarantor was to secure a personal benefit. In this situation, the guarantor is, in effect, answering for (guaranteeing) her or his own debt.

▶ **Example 16.7**   Carlie Braswell contracts with Custom Manufacturing Company to have some machines custom-made for her factory. She promises Newform Supply, Custom's supplier, that if Newform continues to deliver the materials to Custom for the production of the custom-made machines, she will guarantee payment. This promise need not be in writing, even though the effect may be to pay the debt of another. This is because Braswell's main purpose in forming the contract is to secure a benefit for herself. ◀

Another typical application of the main purpose rule occurs when one creditor guarantees a debtor's debt to another creditor to forestall litigation. A creditor might do this because it allows the debtor to remain in business long enough to generate profits sufficient to pay *both* creditors. In this situation, the guaranty does not need to be in writing to be enforceable.

Promises Made in Consideration of Marriage

A unilateral promise to make a monetary payment or to give property in consideration of a promise

to marry must be in writing. In other words, if a mother promises to pay a man $20,000 if he marries her daughter, that promise must be in writing to be enforceable. ▶ **Example 16.8**   Evan promises to buy Celeste a house in Maui if she marries him. Celeste would need written evidence of Evan's promise to enforce it. ◀

The same rule applies to **prenuptial agreements**—agreements made before marriage that define each partner's ownership rights in the other partner's property. Prenuptial agreements must be in writing to be enforceable. ▶ **Example 16.9**   Before marrying country singer Keith Urban, actress Nicole Kidman entered into a prenuptial agreement with him. Kidman agreed that if the couple divorced, she would pay Urban $640,000 for every year they had been married, unless Urban had relapsed and used drugs again. In that event, he would receive nothing. ◀

Contracts for the Sale of Goods

The Uniform Commercial Code (UCC) includes Statute of Frauds provisions that require written evidence or an electronic record of a contract for the sale of goods priced at $500 or more. (This low threshold amount may be increased in the future.)

A writing that will satisfy the UCC requirement need only state the quantity term (such as 6,000 boxes of cotton gauze, for instance). The contract will not be enforceable for any quantity greater than that set forth in the writing. Other agreed-on terms can be omitted or even stated imprecisely in the writing, as long as they adequately reflect both parties' intentions.

---

3. *Restatement (Second) of Contracts,* Section 116.

A written memorandum or series of communications evidencing a contract will suffice, provided that the writing is signed by the party against whom enforcement is sought. The writing normally need not designate the buyer or the seller, the terms of payment, or the price. Requirements of the Statute of Frauds under the UCC will be discussed in more detail in Chapter 20.

SECTION 3
EXCEPTIONS TO THE WRITING REQUIREMENT

Exceptions to the writing requirement are made in certain circumstances. We describe those situations here.

Partial Performance

When a contract has been partially performed and the parties cannot be returned to their positions prior to the contract, a court may grant *specific performance*. Specific performance is an equitable remedy that requires performance of the contract according to its precise terms (see Chapter 19).

Courts may grant specific performance of an oral contract to transfer an interest in land that has been partially performed. Partial performance can arise when the purchaser has paid part of the price, taken possession of the property, and made permanent improvements to it. Whether a court will enforce an oral contract usually is determined by the degree of harm that would be suffered if the court chose *not* to enforce the oral contract. The parties still must prove that an oral contract existed, however.

In some states, mere reliance on certain types of oral contracts is enough to remove them from the Statute of Frauds.[4] Under the UCC, an oral contract for the sale of goods is enforceable to the extent that a seller accepts payment or a buyer accepts delivery of the goods.[5] ▶ **Example 16.10** Cooper orders twenty chairs from an online seller. After ten chairs have been delivered and accepted, Cooper repudiates (denies the existence of) the contract. In that situation, the seller can enforce the contract (and obtain payment) to the extent of the ten chairs already accepted by Cooper. ◀

Partial performance is an unmistakable indication that one party believes there is a contract. In the following case, the court considered whether by accepting that performance, the other party indicated that it also understood that a contract was in effect.

---

4. *Restatement (Second) of Contracts,* Section 129.
5. UCC 2–201(3)(c). See Chapter 20.

CASE 16.2

NYKCool A.B. v. Pacific Fruit, Inc.
United States Court of Appeals, Second Circuit, 2013 WL 163621 (2013).

COMPANY PROFILE   NYKCool A.B., based in Stockholm, Sweden, provides maritime transportation for hire. It is a subsidiary of NYKReefers Limited, which operates as a subsidiary of Nippon Yusen Kabushiki Kaisha, one of the world's largest shipping companies. NYKCool has a fleet of more than fifty ships and offices in Argentina, Brazil, Chile, Ecuador, Japan, New Zealand, South Africa, the United Kingdom, and the United States. NYKCool focuses on transporting perishables, especially fruit. To reduce the number of empty containers, the firm disperses its large fleet around the globe in cost-efficient patterns and carries other cargoes on its vessels' return trips.

BACKGROUND AND FACTS   Pacific Fruit, Inc., exports cargo from Ecuador. NYKCool and Pacific entered into a written contract with a two-year duration, under which NYKCool agreed to transport weekly shipments of bananas from Ecuador to California and Japan. At the end of the period, the parties agreed to extend the deal. Due to a disagreement over one of the terms, a new contract was never signed, but the parties' trade continued. After nearly four more years of performance between 2005 and 2008, a dispute arose over unused cargo capacity and unpaid freight charges. An arbitration panel of the Society of Maritime Arbitrators found that Pacific Fruit was liable to NYKCool for $8,787,157 for breach of contract. NYKCool filed a petition in a federal district court to confirm the award. Pacific Fruit appealed the judgment in NYKCool's favor, contending that the arbitration panel "manifestly disregarded" the law when it concluded that the parties had an enforceable contract.

CASE 16.2 CONTINUED

IN THE LANGUAGE OF THE COURT
Robert A. *KATZMANN*, Barrington D. *PARKER* and Richard C. *WESLEY*, Circuit Judges.
* * * *

On appeal, Pacific Fruit first contends that the arbitration panel manifestly disregarded the New York contract law by concluding that Pacific Fruit * * * entered into an oral contract with NYKCool, under which NYKCool agreed to transport weekly shipments of [Pacific Fruit's] bananas from Ecuador to California and Japan for the period between 2005 and 2008. In order to vacate an arbitration award for manifest disregard of the law, a court must conclude that the arbitrator knew of the relevant legal principle, appreciated that this principle controlled the outcome of the disputed issue, and nonetheless willfully flouted the governing law by refusing to apply it. This rigorous standard ensures that awards are vacated on grounds of manifest disregard only in those exceedingly rare instances where some egregious [shocking] impropriety on the part of the arbitrator is apparent. As such, the standard essentially bars review of whether an arbitrator misconstrued a contract.

Here, we detect no manifest disregard of the law in the arbitration panel's conclusion that the parties had entered into a binding oral contract for the period between 2005 and 2008. In particular, we agree with the panel's conclusion that *the parties' substantial partial performance on the contract weighs strongly in favor of contract formation.* It is undisputed that in 2005 and 2006 NYKCool transported 30 million boxes of cargo for [Pacific Fruit] on over 100 voyages, for which it received $70 million dollars in payments even though there was no written contract in place. Moreover, *the parties' behavior during 2005 and 2006 strongly suggests that they believed themselves subject to a binding agreement.* Notably, the parties engaged in extensive renegotiation of the terms of the contract when [Pacific Fruit] began facing difficulties meeting its cargo commitments. In these circumstances, the panel cannot be said to have engaged in egregious impropriety in concluding that the parties intended to enter a binding oral agreement. [Emphasis added.]
* * * *

For the foregoing reasons, the Order of the district court confirming the arbitration award is hereby AFFIRMED.

DECISION AND REMEDY *The U.S. Court of Appeals for the Second Circuit affirmed the judgment of the lower court. The appellate court reasoned that "the parties' substantial partial performance on the contract weighs strongly in favor of contract formation."*

THE LEGAL ENVIRONMENT DIMENSION *What circumstance in this case demonstrates most strongly that Pacific did not truly believe that it did not have a contract with NYKCool? Explain.*

THE ECONOMIC DIMENSION *How can a carrier avoid losses under a contract that obligates it only to transport cargo one way and not on the return voyage?*

Admissions

If a party against whom enforcement of an oral contract is sought "admits" under oath that a contract for sale was made, the contract will be enforceable.[6] The party's admission can occur at any stage of the court proceedings, such as during a deposition or other discovery, pleadings, or testimony.

If a party admits a contract subject to the UCC, it is enforceable, but only to the extent of the quantity admitted.[7] ▶ **Example 16.11** Rachel, the president of Bistro Corporation, admits under oath that an oral agreement was made with Commercial Kitchens, Inc., to buy certain equipment for $10,000. A court will enforce the agreement only to the extent admitted ($10,000), even if Commercial Kitchens claims that the agreement involved $20,000 worth of equipment. ◀

6. *Restatement (Second) of Contracts,* Section 133.

7. UCC 2–201(3)(b).

Promissory Estoppel

An oral contract that would otherwise be unenforceable under the Statute of Frauds may be enforced in some states under the doctrine of promissory estoppel. Recall from Chapter 13 that if a person justifiably relies on another's promise to his or her detriment, a court may *estop* (prevent) the promisor from denying that a contract exists. Section 139 of the *Restatement (Second) of Contracts* provides that in these circumstances, an oral promise can be enforceable notwithstanding the Statute of Frauds.

For the promise to be enforceable, the promisee must have justifiably relied on it to her or his detriment, and the reliance must have been foreseeable to the person making the promise. In addition, there must be no way to avoid injustice except to enforce the promise. (Note the similarities between promissory estoppel and the doctrine of partial performance discussed previously. Both require reasonable reliance and operate to estop a party from claiming that no contract exists.)

Special Exceptions under the UCC

Special exceptions to the writing requirement apply to sales contracts. Oral contracts for customized goods may be enforced in certain circumstances. Another exception has to do with oral contracts *between merchants* that have been confirmed in a written memorandum. We will examine these exceptions in more detail in Chapter 20, when we discuss the UCC's Statute of Frauds provisions.

Exhibit 16–3 below graphically summarizes the types of contracts that fall under the Statute of Frauds and the various exceptions that apply.

SECTION 4
SUFFICIENCY OF THE WRITING

A written contract will satisfy the writing requirement, as will a written memorandum or an electronic record that evidences the agreement and is signed by the party against whom enforcement is sought. The signature need not be placed at the end of the document but can be anywhere in the writing. A signature can consist of a typed name (as discussed in Chapter 12) or even just initials rather than the full name.

What Constitutes a Writing?

A writing can consist of any order confirmation, invoice, sales slip, check, fax, or e-mail—or such items in combination. The written contract need not consist of a single document in order to constitute an enforceable contract. One document may incorporate another document by expressly referring to it. Several documents may form a single contract if they are physically attached, such as by staple, paper clip, or glue. Several documents may form a single contract even if they are only placed in the same envelope.

▶ **Example 16.12**   Simpson orally agrees to sell some land next to a shopping mall to Terro Properties. Simpson gives Terro an unsigned memo that contains

EXHIBIT 16–3 Business Contracts and the Writing Requirement

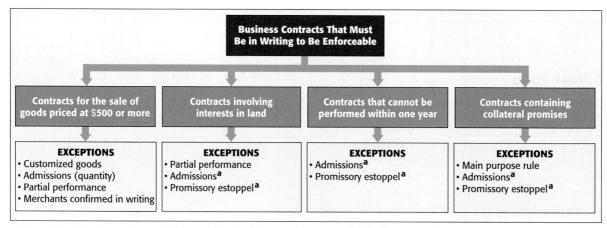

a. Some states follow Section 133 (on admissions) and Section 139 (on promissory estoppel) of the *Restatement (Second) of Contracts.*

a legal description of the property, and Terro gives Simpson an unsigned first draft of their real estate contract. Simpson sends Terro a signed letter that refers to the memo and to the first and final drafts of the contract. Terro sends Simpson an unsigned copy of the final draft of the contract with a signed check stapled to it. Together, the documents can constitute a writing sufficient to satisfy the writing requirement and bind both parties to the terms of the contract. ◄

What Must Be Contained in the Writing?

A memorandum or note evidencing the oral contract need only contain the essential terms of the contract, not every term. There must, of course, also be some indication that the parties voluntarily agreed to the terms. As mentioned earlier, under the UCC, a writing evidencing a contract for the sale of goods need only state the quantity and be signed by the party against whom enforcement is sought.

Under most state laws, the writing must also name the parties and identify the subject matter, the consideration, and the essential terms with reasonable certainty. In addition, contracts for the sale of land often are required to state the price and describe the property with sufficient clarity to allow them to be determined without reference to outside sources.

Note that because only the party against whom enforcement is sought must have signed the writing, a contract may be enforceable by one of its parties but not by the other. In the following case, the plaintiff sought to enforce a written contract that was missing the signatures of the parties against whom enforcement was being sought.

CASE 16.3

Beneficial Homeowner Service Corporation v. Steele

Supreme Court of New York, Suffolk County, 30 Misc.3d 1208(A) (2011).

BACKGROUND AND FACTS   Beneficial Homeowner Service Corporation filed a suit in a New York state court against Stephen and Susan Steele to foreclose on a mortgage. (A mortgage is a written instrument that gives a creditor an interest in property that the debtor provides as security for the payment of the loan. In a foreclosure, the lender repossesses and sells the property that secured the loan.) Beneficial (the lender) claimed that the loan was secured by real property in East Hampton, New York. Beneficial sought $91,614.34 in unpaid principal, plus interest. The lender, based on its assertion that both Stephen and Susan Steele had signed the loan agreement, filed a motion for summary judgment. Among the documents that Beneficial filed with the court was a copy of the loan agreement. There were two problems—the agreement identified Stephen Steele as the sole obligor (the party owing the obligation), and it had not been signed.

IN THE LANGUAGE OF THE COURT
Jeffrey Arlen *SPINNER*, J. [Judge]

* * * *

This Court must question how, under the circumstances presented here, Plaintiff can, with unbridled temerity [unchecked audacity], demand enforcement of the Loan Agreement against Defendant STEPHEN STEELE, who has not executed that instrument and against Defendant SUSAN STEELE, who is not even a party to that agreement. * * * This posture by Plaintiff strains credulity and causes the Court to seriously question Plaintiff's good faith in commencing this action.

Distilled to its essence, a mortgage is a conveyance of an interest in land that is expressly intended to constitute security for some obligation, most commonly an indebtedness. *It follows logically then that in order for a mortgage to be valid and subsisting, there must be an underlying obligation that is to be secured by an interest in the real property* * * * . Here, the Loan Agreement that has been presented to the Court facially appears to run counter to New York's Statute of Frauds. Since there has been presented to this Court no valid underlying obligation and no further explanation, the mortgage appears to fail as a matter of law. [Emphasis added.]

CASE 16.3 CONTINUES ▶

This situation is all the more disturbing when it is considered that the sworn statements contained in both the Complaint and the Affidavit in Support Of the Motion for Summary Judgment expressly and falsely assert that Defendant SUSAN STEELE executed the Loan Agreement. This is compounded by the sworn statement of Shana Richmond, Plaintiff's foreclosure specialist, * * * which contains the same painfully obvious misstatements of fact.

* * * Where a party comes before the Court and is shown to have acted in a manner which is offensive to good conscience, fairness and justice, that party will be completely without recourse in a court of equity, no matter what his legal rights may be.

DECISION AND REMEDY *The court denied Beneficial's motion for summary judgment. Because a mortgage involves a transfer of real property, it and its underlying obligation must be in writing to satisfy the Statute of Frauds. To be enforceable, the writings must be signed by the party against whom enforcement is sought. The court ordered a hearing to determine whether, in presenting the unsigned document, Beneficial had acted in good faith.*

WHAT IF THE FACTS WERE DIFFERENT? *Suppose that at the hearing, the Steeles admit they had an obligation to pay the outstanding loan amount. Would the result be different? Explain.*

THE ECONOMIC DIMENSION *Why might Beneficial have tried to enforce an unsigned document?*

SECTION 5
THE PAROL EVIDENCE RULE

Sometimes, a written contract does not include—or contradicts—an oral understanding reached by the parties before or at the time of contracting. For instance, a landlord might tell a person who agrees to rent an apartment that cats are allowed, whereas the lease contract clearly states that no pets are permitted. In deciding such disputes, the courts look to a common law rule governing the admissibility in court of oral evidence, or *parol evidence.*

Under the **parol evidence rule,** if a court finds that a written contract represents the complete and final statement of the parties' agreement, it will not allow either party to present parol evidence. *Parol evidence* is testimony or other evidence of communications between the parties that is not contained in the contract itself. A party normally cannot present evidence of the parties' prior negotiations, prior agreements, or contemporaneous (happening at the same time) oral agreements if that evidence contradicts or varies the terms of the written contract.[8]

▶ **Example 16.13** TKTS, Inc., sends Gwen an offer to sell season tickets to the Dallas Cowboys football games in Cowboys Stadium. Prices and seat locations are indicated in diagrams in a brochure that accompanies the offer. Gwen responds, listing her seat prefer-ence. TKTS sends her the tickets, along with a different diagram showing seat locations. Also enclosed is a document that reads, "This is the entire agreement of the parties," which Gwen signs and returns. When Gwen goes to the first game, she discovers that her seat is not where she expected, based on the brochure. Under the parol evidence rule, however, the brochure is not part of the parties' agreement. The document that Gwen signed was identified as the parties' entire contract. Therefore, she cannot introduce in court any evidence of prior negotiations or agreements that contradict or vary the contract's terms. ◀

Exceptions to the Parol Evidence Rule

Because of the rigidity of the parol evidence rule, the courts have created the following exceptions:

1. *Contracts subsequently modified.* Evidence of any subsequent modification (oral or written) of a written contract can be introduced in court. Oral modifications may not be enforceable under the Statute of Frauds, however (for instance, a modification that increases the price of the goods being sold to more than $500). Also, oral modifications will not be enforceable if the original contract provides that any modification must be in writing.[9]

2. *Voidable or void contracts.* Oral evidence can be introduced in all cases to show that the contract

---

8. *Restatement (Second) of Contracts,* Section 213.

9. UCC 2–209(2), (3).

was voidable or void (for example, induced by mistake, fraud, or misrepresentation). The reason is simple: if deception led one of the parties to agree to the terms of a written contract, oral evidence attesting to the fraud should not be excluded. Courts frown on bad faith and are quick to allow such evidence when it establishes fraud. *Contracts containing ambiguous terms.* When the terms of a written contract are ambiguous and require interpretation, evidence is admissible to show the meaning of the terms. ▶ **Case in Point 16.14** Pamela Watkins bought a home from Sandra Schexnider. Their agreement stated that Watkins would make payments on the mortgage until the note was paid in full, when "the house" would become hers. The agreement also stipulated that she would pay for insurance on "the property." The home was destroyed in a hurricane, and the insurance proceeds satisfied (paid off) the mortgage. Watkins claimed that she owned the land, but Schexnider argued that she had sold only the house. The court found that because "the house" term in the contract was ambiguous, parol evidence was admissible. The court also concluded that the parties intended to transfer ownership of both the house and the land, and ordered that title to the property be transferred to Watkins.[10] ◀

3. *Incomplete contracts.* When the written contract is incomplete in that it lacks one or more of the essential terms, the courts allow additional evidence to "fill in the gaps."

4. *Prior dealing, course of performance, or usage of trade.* Under the UCC, evidence can be introduced to explain or supplement a written contract by showing a prior dealing, course of performance, or usage of trade.[11] This is because when buyers and sellers deal with each other over extended periods of time, certain customary practices develop. These practices are often overlooked in writing the contract, so courts allow the introduction of evidence to show how the parties have acted in the past. Usage of trade—practices and customs generally followed in a particular industry—can also shed light on the meaning of certain contract provisions. Thus, evidence of trade usage may be admissible. We will discuss these terms in further detail in Chapter 20, in the context of sales contracts.

5. *Contracts subject to an orally agreed-on condition precedent.* As you will read in Chapter 18, sometimes the parties agree that a condition must be fulfilled before a party is required to perform the contract. This is called a *condition precedent.* If the parties have orally agreed on a condition precedent that does not conflict with the terms of their written agreement, a court may allow parol evidence to prove the oral condition. The parol evidence rule does not apply here because the existence of the entire written contract is subject to an orally agreed-on condition. Proof of the condition does not alter or modify the written terms but affects the *enforceability* of the written contract.

6. *Contracts with an obvious or gross clerical (or typographic) error that clearly would not represent the agreement of the parties.* Parol evidence is admissible to correct an obvious typographic error. ▶ **Example 16.15** Davis agrees to lease office space from Stone Enterprises for $3,000 per month. The signed written lease provides for a monthly payment of $300 rather than the $3,000 agreed to by the parties. Because the error is obvious, Stone Enterprises would be allowed to admit parol evidence to correct the mistake. ◀

Integrated Contracts

In determining whether to allow parol evidence, courts consider whether the written contract is intended to be the complete and final statement of the terms of the agreement. If it is, the contract is referred to as an **integrated contract,** and extraneous evidence (evidence from outside the contract) is excluded. For an example of an integration clause within a contract, see Paragraph 19 of the sample contract in the *Appendix to Chapter 19: Reading and Analyzing Contracts.*

An integrated contract can be either completely or partially integrated. If it contains all of the terms of the parties' agreement, it is completely integrated. If it contains only some of the terms that the parties agreed on and not others, it is partially integrated. If the contract is only partially integrated, evidence of consistent additional terms is admissible to supplement the written agreement.[12] Note that for both completely and partially integrated contracts, courts exclude any evidence that *contradicts* the writing and allow parol evidence only to add to the terms of a partially integrated contract. Exhibit 16–4 on the following page illustrates the relationship between integrated contracts and the parol evidence rule.

---

10. *Watkins v. Schexnider,* 31 So.3d 609 (La.App. 3 Cir. 2010).
11. UCC 1–205, 2–202.

12. *Restatement (Second) of Contracts,* Section 216; and UCC 2–202.

EXHIBIT 16–4 The Parol Evidence Rule

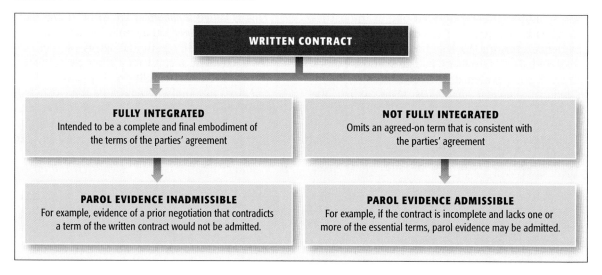

SECTION 6
THE STATUTE OF FRAUDS IN THE INTERNATIONAL CONTEXT

As you will read in Chapter 20, the Convention on Contracts for the International Sale of Goods (CISG) governs international sales contracts between citizens of countries that have ratified the convention (agreement). Article 11 of the CISG does not incorporate any Statute of Frauds provisions. Rather, it states that a "contract for sale need not be concluded in or evidenced by writing and is not subject to any other requirements as to form."

Article 11 accords with the legal customs of most nations, which no longer require contracts to meet certain formal or writing requirements to be enforceable. Ironically, even England, the nation that created the original Statute of Frauds in 1677, has repealed all of it except the provisions relating to collateral promises and to transfers of interests in land. Many other countries that once had such statutes have also repealed all or parts of them. Some countries, such as France, have never required certain types of contracts to be in writing.

Reviewing: The Writing Requirement and Electronic Records

Charter Golf, Inc., manufactures and sells golf apparel and supplies. Ken Odin had worked as a Charter sales representative for six months when he was offered a position with a competing firm. Charter's president, Jerry Montieth, offered Odin a 10 percent commission "for the rest of his life" if Ken would turn down the offer and stay with Charter. He also promised that Odin would not be fired unless he was dishonest. Odin turned down the competitor's offer and stayed with Charter. Three years later, Charter fired Odin for no reason. Odin sued, alleging breach of contract. Using the information presented in the chapter, answer the following questions.

1. Would a court likely decide that Odin's employment contract falls within the Statute of Frauds? Why or why not?
2. Assume that the court does find that the contract falls within the Statute of Frauds and that the state in which the court sits recognizes every exception to the Statute of Frauds discussed in the chapter. What exception provides Odin with the best chance of enforcing the oral contract in this situation?

3. Now suppose that Montieth had taken out a pencil, written "10 percent for life" on the back of a register receipt, and handed it to Odin. Would this satisfy the Statute of Frauds? Why or why not?
4. Assume that Odin had signed a written employment contract at the time he was hired to work for Charter, but it was not completely integrated. Would a court allow Odin to present parol evidence of Montieth's subsequent promises?

DEBATE THIS . . . *Many countries have eliminated the Statute of Frauds except for sales of real estate. The United States should do the same.*

Terms and Concepts

collateral promise 308

integrated contract 315

parol evidence rule 314

prenuptial agreement 309

Statute of Frauds 305

ExamPrep

Issue Spotters

1. GamesCo orders $800 worth of game pieces from Midstate Plastic, Inc. Midstate delivers, and GamesCo pays for $450 worth. GamesCo then says it wants no more pieces from Midstate. GamesCo and Midstate have never dealt with each other before and have nothing in writing. Can Midstate enforce a deal for $350 more? Explain your answer. **(See page 309.)**
2. Paula orally agrees to work with Next Corporation in New York City for two years. Paula moves her family and begins work. Three months later, Paula is fired for no stated cause. She sues for reinstatement and back pay. Next Corporation argues that there is no written contract between them. What will the court say? **(See page 312.)**

• **Check your answers to the Issue Spotters against the answers provided in Appendix E at the end of this text.**

Before the Test

Go to **www.cengagebrain.com**, enter the ISBN 9781285185248, and click on "Find" to locate this textbook's Web site. Then, click on "Access Now" under "Study Tools," and select Chapter 16 at the top. There, you will find a Practice Quiz that you can take to assess your mastery of the concepts in this chapter, as well as Flashcards and a Glossary of important terms

Business Scenarios

16–1. The One-Year Rule. On May 1, by telephone, Yu offers to hire Benson to perform personal services. On May 5, Benson returns Yu's call and accepts the offer. Discuss fully whether this contract falls under the Statute of Frauds in the following circumstances: **(See page 307.)**

(a) The contract calls for Benson to be employed for one year, with the right to begin performance immediately.
(b) The contract calls for Benson to be employed for nine months, with performance of services to begin on September 1.

(c) The contract calls for Benson to submit a written research report, with a deadline of two years for submission.

16–2. Collateral Promises. Mallory promises a local hardware store that she will pay for a lawn mower that her brother is purchasing on credit if the brother fails to pay the debt. Must this promise be in writing to be enforceable? Why or why not? **(See page 308.)**

Business Case Problems

16–3. The Parol Evidence Rule. Evangel Temple Assembly of God leased a facility from Wood Care Centers, Inc., to house evacuees who had lost their homes in Hurricane

Katrina. One clause in the lease contract said that Evangel could terminate the lease at any time by giving Wood Care notice and paying 10 percent of the balance remaining on the lease. Another clause stated that if the facility was not given a property tax exemption (as a church), Evangel had the option to terminate the lease without making the 10 percent payment. Nine months later, the last of the evacuees left the facility, and Evangel notified Wood Care that it would end the lease. Wood Care demanded the 10 percent payment. Is parol evidence admissible to interpret this lease? Why or why not? [*Wood Care Centers, Inc. v. Evangel Temple Assembly of God of Wichita Falls*, 307 S.W.3d 816 (Tex.App.—Fort Worth 2010)] **(See page 314.)**

16–4. Sufficiency of the Writing. Newmark & Co. Real Estate, Inc., contacted 2615 East 17 Street Realty, LLC, to lease certain real property on behalf of a client. Newmark e-mailed the landlord a separate agreement for the payment of Newmark's commission. The landlord e-mailed it back with a separate demand to pay the commission in installments. Newmark revised the agreement and e-mailed a final copy to the landlord. Does the agreement qualify as a writing under the Statute of Frauds? Explain. [*Newmark & Co. Real Estate, Inc. v. 2615 East 17 Street Realty, LLC*, 80 A.D.3d 476, 914 N.Y.S.2d 162 (1 Dept. 2011)] **(See page 312.)**

16–5. BUSINESS CASE PROBLEM
WITH SAMPLE ANSWER: The Parol Evidence Rule.

 *Rimma Vaks and her husband, Steven Mangano, executed a written contract with Denise Ryan and Ryan Auction Co. to auction their furnishings. The six-page contract provided a detailed summary of the parties' agreement. It addressed the items to be auctioned, how reserve prices would be determined, and the amount of Ryan's commission. When a dispute arose between the parties, Vaks and Mangano sued Ryan for breach of contract. Vaks and Mangano asserted that, before they executed the contract, Ryan made various oral representations that were inconsistent with the terms of their written agreement. Assuming that their written contract was valid, can Vaks and Mangano recover for breach of an oral contract? Why or why not? [*Vaks v. Ryan, 2012 WL 194398 (Mass.App. 2012)]* **(See page 314.)**

- **For a sample answer to Problem 16–5, see Appendix F at the end of this text.**

16–6. Promises Made in Consideration of Marriage. After twenty-nine years of marriage, Robert and Mary Lou Tuttle were divorced. They admitted in court that before they were married, they had signed a prenuptial agreement. They agreed that the agreement had stated that each would keep his or her own property and anything derived from that property. Robert came into the marriage owning farmland while Mary Lou owned no real estate. During the marriage, ten different parcels of land, totaling about six hundred acres, were acquired, and two corporations, Tuttle Grain, Inc., and Tuttle Farms, Inc., were formed. A copy of the prenuptial agreement could not be found. Can the court enforce the agreement without a writing? Why or why not? [*In re Marriage of Tuttle*, 2013 WL 164035 (Ill. App. 5 Dist. 2013)] **(See page 309.)**

16–7. A QUESTION OF ETHICS: The Parol Evidence Rule.

 *Robert Shelborne asked attorney William Williams to represent him in a deal with Robert Tundy. Shelborne expected to receive $31 million and agreed to pay Williams a fee of $1 million. Tundy said that a tax of $100,000 would have to be paid for Shelborne to receive the $31 million. Shelborne asked James Parker to loan him $50,000. Parker, Shelborne, and Williams wired the funds to Tundy. They never heard from him again. No $31 million was transferred. Shelborne then disappeared. Parker filed a suit against Williams, alleging breach of contract. Parker offered as evidence a recording of a phone conversation in which Williams guaranteed Shelborne's loan. [*Parker v. Williams, 977 So.2d 476 (Ala. 2007)]* **(See page 314.)**

(a) Is the court likely to rule in Parker's favor on the contract claim? Why or why not? Does Williams have a defense under the Statute of Frauds?

(b) The sham deal at the center of this case is known to law enforcement authorities as advance fee fraud, or a "419 scam." The victim is promised a transfer of funds from an overpaid contract, or some other suspect source, but is asked to pay a tax or other fee first. Among the parties in this case, who, if anyone, behaved ethically? Discuss.

Legal Reasoning Group Activity

16–8. The Writing Requirement. Jason Novell, doing business as Novell Associates, hired Barbara Meade to work for him. The parties orally agreed on the terms of employment, including payment of a share of the company's income to Meade, but they did not put anything in writing. Two years later, Meade quit. Novell then told Meade that she was entitled to $9,602—25 percent of the difference between the accounts receivable and the accounts payable as of Meade's last day of work. Meade disagreed and demanded more than $63,500—25 percent of the revenue from all invoices, less the cost of materials and outside processing, for each of the years that she had worked

for Novell. Meade filed a lawsuit against Novell for breach of contract. **(See page 305.)**

(a) The first group should decide whether the parties had an enforceable contract.

(b) The second group should decide whether that the parties' oral agreement falls within any exception to the Statute of Frauds

(c) The third group should discuss how the lawsuit would be affected if Novell admitted that the parties had an oral contract under which Meade was entitled to 25 percent of the difference between accounts receivable and payable as of the day Meade quit.

CHAPTER 17
THIRD PARTY RIGHTS

Once it has been determined that a valid and legally enforceable contract exists, attention can turn to the rights and duties of the parties to the contract. A contract is a private agreement between the parties who have entered into it, and traditionally these parties alone have rights and liabilities under the contract. This principle is referred to as **privity of contract** (see Chapter 7). A *third party*—one who is not a direct party to a particular contract—normally does not have rights under that contract.

There are exceptions to the rule of privity of contract. For instance, as discussed in Chapter 7, privity of contract is not required to recover damages under product liability laws. Hence, a person injured by a defective product can still recover damages even though she or he was not the buyer of the product. In this chapter, we look at two other exceptions. One exception allows a party to a contract to transfer the rights or duties arising from the contract to another person through an *assignment* (of rights) or a *delegation* (of duties). The other exception involves a *third party beneficiary contract*—a contract in which the parties to the contract intend that the contract benefit a third party.

SECTION 1
ASSIGNMENTS AND DELEGATIONS

In a bilateral contract, the two parties have corresponding rights and duties. One party has a *right* to require the other to perform some task, and the other has a *duty* to perform it. The transfer of contractual *rights* to a third party is known as an **assignment.** The transfer of contractual *duties* to a third party is known as a **delegation.** An assignment or a delegation occurs *after* the original contract was made.

Assignments

Assignments are important because they are used in many types of business financing. Banks, for instance, frequently assign their rights to receive payments under their loan contracts to other firms, which pay for those rights. If Tia obtains a loan from a bank, she may later receive a notice from the bank stating that it has transferred (assigned) its rights to receive payments on the loan to another firm. When it is time to repay the loan, Tia must make the payments to that other firm.

Financial institutions that make *mortgage* loans (loans to enable prospective home buyers to purchase land or a home) often assign their rights to collect the mortgage payments to a third party, such as PNC Mortgage. Following the assignment, the home buyers are notified that they must make future payments not to the bank that loaned them the funds but to the third party. Billions of dollars change hands daily in the business world in the form of assignments of rights in contracts. If it were not possible to transfer contractual rights, many businesses could not continue to operate.

THE EFFECT OF AN ASSIGNMENT In an assignment, the party assigning the rights to a third party is known as the **assignor,**[1] and the party receiving the rights is the **assignee.**[2] Other traditional terms used to describe the parties in assignment relationships are **obligee** (the person to whom a duty, or obligation, is owed) and **obligor** (the person who is obligated to perform the duty).

Extinguishes the Rights of the Assignor. When rights under a contract are assigned unconditionally, the

---

1. Pronounced uh-*sye*-nore.
2. Pronounced uh-*sye*-nee.

rights of the assignor are extinguished.[3] The third party (the assignee) has a right to demand performance from the other original party to the contract. The assignee takes only those rights that the assignor originally had, however.

▶ **Example 17.1** Brower is obligated by contract to pay Horton $1,000. Brower is the obligor because she owes an obligation, or duty, to Horton. Horton is the obligee, the one to whom the obligation, or duty, is owed. If Horton then assigns his right to receive the $1,000 to Kuhn, Horton is the assignor and Kuhn is the assignee. Kuhn now becomes the obligee because Brower owes Kuhn the $1,000. Here, a valid assignment of a debt exists. Kuhn (the assignee-obligee) is entitled to enforce payment in court if Brower (the obligor) does not pay him the $1,000. ◀ These concepts are illustrated in Exhibit 17–1 on the following page.

In the following case, a lender assigned its rights to loan payments from a borrower. The court had to decide whether the borrower owed the payments to the assignee.

---

3. *Restatement (Second) of Contracts,* Section 317.

CASE 17.1

Hosch v. Colonial Pacific Leasing Corp.

Court of Appeals of Georgia, 113 Ga.App. 873, 722 S.E.2d 778 (2012).

BACKGROUND AND FACTS Edward Hosch entered into four loan agreements with Citicapital Commercial Corporation to finance the purchase of heavy construction equipment. A few months later, Citicapital merged into Citicorp Leasing, Inc., which was then renamed GE Capital Commercial, Inc. One year later, GE Capital assigned the loans to Colonial Pacific Leasing Corporation. When Hosch defaulted on the loans, Colonial provided a notice of default and demanded payment. Hosch failed to repay the loans, so Colonial sued to collect the amount due. The trial court granted summary judgment to Colonial and entered final judgment against Hosch. On appeal, Hosch argued that there was insufficient evidence that the loans had been assigned to Colonial.

IN THE LANGUAGE OF THE COURT
McFADDEN, Judge.

* * * *

Hosch contends that the trial court erred in granting Colonial's motion for summary judgment because there is no evidence that the contracts were assigned to Colonial. However, the contention is refuted by the record, which includes affidavits of a GE litigation specialist, a written assignment and other documents establishing that Hosch's four loans were assigned to Colonial. Hosch has presented no contradictory evidence showing that the loans were not assigned to Colonial, and instead submitted his own affidavit stating that he had not been notified of any such assignment. However, the loan agreements expressly provide that the lender may transfer or assign any or all of its rights under the agreements without notice to or the consent of Hosch.

"A party may assign to another a contractual right to collect payment, including the right to sue to enforce the right. But an assignment must be in writing in order for the contractual right to be enforceable by the assignee." Because the record, as noted above, contains a written assignment of the loans to Colonial, as well as other evidence of the assignment, the trial court did not err in granting summary judgment to Colonial. [Emphasis added.]

DECISION AND REMEDY *The Georgia appellate court found sufficient evidence that GE Capital had assigned the loans to Colonial. It therefore affirmed the trial court's judgment for Colonial.*

THE LEGAL ENVIRONMENT DIMENSION *Do borrowers benefit from the fact that lenders may freely assign their rights under loan agreements? If so, how?*

WHAT IF THE FACTS WERE DIFFERENT? *Suppose that Hosch had sold the equipment financed by the loans from Citicapital to a third party. Would Hosch still have been liable to Colonial Pacific? Why or why not?*

EXHIBIT 17-1 Assignment Relationships

In the assignment relationship illustrated here, Horton assigns his *rights* under a contract that he made with Brower to a third party, Kuhn. Horton thus becomes the *assignor* and Kuhn the *assignee* of the contractual rights. Brower, the *obligor,* now owes performance to Kuhn instead of Horton. Horton's original contract rights are extinguished after assignment.

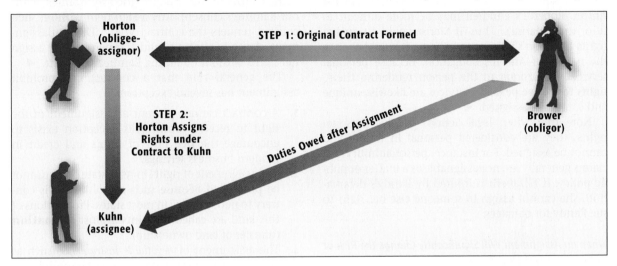

Assignee's Rights Are Subject to the Same Defenses. The assignee's rights are subject to the defenses that the obligor has against the assignor. In other words, the assignee obtains only those rights that the assignor originally had.

▶ **Example 17.2** In *Example 17.1,* Brower owes Horton the $1,000 under a contract in which Brower agreed to buy Horton's 15-inch MacBook Pro laptop. When Brower decided to purchase the laptop, she relied on Horton's fraudulent misrepresentation that the MacBook had retina display. When Brower discovers that it does not have this feature, she tells Horton that she is going to return the laptop to him and cancel the contract. Even though Horton has assigned his "right" to receive the $1,000 to Kuhn, Brower need not pay Kuhn the $1,000. Brower can raise the defense of Horton's fraudulent misrepresentation to avoid payment. ◀

Form of the Assignment. In general, an assignment can take any form, oral or written. Naturally, it is more difficult to prove that an oral assignment occurred, so it is advisable to put all assignments in writing. Of course, assignments covered by the Statute of Frauds—such as an assignment of an interest in land—must be in writing to be enforceable. In addition, most states require contracts for the assignment of wages to be in writing.[4]

4. See, for example, California Labor Code Section 300. There are other assignments that must be in writing as well.

RIGHTS THAT CANNOT BE ASSIGNED As a general rule, all rights can be assigned. Exceptions are made, however, under certain circumstances. Some of these exceptions are listed below and described in more detail in the following subsections:

1. The assignment is prohibited by statute.
2. The contract is personal.
3. The assignment significantly changes the risk or duties of the obligor.
4. The contract prohibits assignment.

When a Statute Prohibits Assignment. When a statute expressly prohibits assignment of a particular right, that right cannot be assigned. ▶ **Example 17.3** Quincy is an employee of Specialty Travel, Inc. Specialty is an employer bound by workers' compensation statutes in this state, and thus Quincy is a covered employee. Quincy is injured on the job and begins to collect monthly workers' compensation checks. In need of a loan, Quincy borrows from Draper, assigning to Draper all of her future workers' compensation benefits. A state statute prohibits the assignment of *future* workers' compensation benefits, and thus such rights cannot be assigned. ◀

When a Contract Is Personal in Nature. If a contract is for personal services, the rights under the contract normally cannot be assigned unless all that remains is a monetary payment.[5] ▶ **Example 17.4** Anton signs a contract to be a tutor for Marisa's children. Marisa then attempts to assign to Roberto her right to Anton's services. Roberto cannot enforce the contract against Anton. Roberto's children may be more difficult to tutor than Marisa's. Thus, if Marisa could assign her rights to Anton's services to Roberto, it would change the nature of Anton's obligation. Because personal services are unique to the person rendering them, rights to receive personal services are likewise unique and cannot be assigned. ◀

Note that when legal actions involve personal rights, they are considered personal in nature and cannot be assigned. For instance, personal-injury tort claims generally are nonassignable as a matter of public policy. If Elizabeth is injured by Randy's defamation, she cannot assign to someone else her right to sue Randy for damages.

When an Assignment Will Significantly Change the Risk or Duties of the Obligor. A right cannot be assigned if the assignment will significantly increase or alter the risks to or the duties of the obligor (the party owing performance under the contract).[6] ▶ **Example 17.5** Larson owns a hotel. To insure it, he takes out a policy with Southeast Insurance. The policy insures against fire, theft, floods, and vandalism. Larson attempts to assign the insurance policy to Hewitt, who also owns a hotel.

The assignment is ineffective because it substantially alters Southeast Insurance's *duty of performance*. An insurance company evaluates the particular risk of a certain party and tailors its policy to fit that risk. If the policy is assigned to a third party, the insurance risk is materially altered because the insurance company may have no information on the third party. Therefore, the assignment will not operate to give Hewitt any rights against Southeast Insurance. ◀

When the Contract Prohibits Assignment. When a contract specifically stipulates that a right cannot be assigned, then *ordinarily* it cannot be assigned. (For an example of a contract that prohibits assignment by one party, see Paragraph 12 of the sample contract in the *Appendix to Chapter 19: Reading and Analyzing Contracts*.) Note that restraints on the power to assign operate only against the parties themselves. They do not prohibit an assignment by operation of law, such as an assignment pursuant to bankruptcy or death.

Whether an *antiassignment clause* is effective depends, in part, on how it is phrased. A contract that states that *any* assignment is void effectively prohibits any assignment. ▶ **Example 17.6** Ramirez agrees to build a house for Carmen. Their contract states "This contract cannot be assigned by Carmen without Ramirez's consent. Any assignment without such consent renders the contract void." This antiassignment clause is effective, and Carmen cannot assign her rights without obtaining Ramirez's consent. ◀

The general rule that a contract can prohibit assignment has several exceptions:

1. A contract cannot prevent an assignment of the right to receive funds. This exception exists to encourage the free flow of funds and credit in modern business settings.
2. The assignment of rights in real estate often cannot be prohibited because such a prohibition is contrary to public policy in most states. Prohibitions of this kind are called restraints against **alienation** (transfer of land ownership).
3. The assignment of *negotiable instruments* (such as checks and promissory notes) cannot be prohibited.
4. In a contract for the sale of goods, the right to receive damages for breach of contract or payment of an account owed may be assigned even though the sales contract prohibits such an assignment.[7]

NOTICE OF ASSIGNMENT Once a valid assignment of rights has been made, the assignee (the third party to whom the rights have been assigned) should notify the obligor (the one owing performance) of the assignment. For instance, in *Example 17.1* on page 320, when Horton assigns to Kuhn his right to receive the $1,000 from Brower, Kuhn should notify Brower, the obligor, of the assignment.

Giving notice is not legally necessary to establish the validity of the assignment: an assignment is effective immediately, whether or not notice is given. Two major problems arise, however, when notice of the assignment is not given to the obligor:

1. *Priority issues.* If the assignor assigns the same right to two different persons, the question arises as to which one has priority—that is, which one has the right to the performance by the obligor. The rule most often observed in the United States is that the first assignment in time is the first in right. Nevertheless, some states follow the English rule, which basically gives priority to the first assignee who gives notice. ▶ **Example 17.7** Jason owes Alexis $5,000 under a contract. Alexis first assigns the claim to Carmen, who does not give notice to

---

5. *Restatement (Second) of Contracts*, Sections 317 and 318.
6. Section 2–210(2) of the Uniform Commercial Code (UCC).

7. UCC 2–210(2).

Jason, and then assigns it to Dorman, who notifies Jason. In most states, Carmen would have priority because the assignment to her was first in time. In some states, however, Dorman would have priority because he gave first notice. ◄

2. *Potential for discharge by performance to the wrong party.* Until the obligor has notice of an assignment, the obligor can discharge his or her obligation by performance to the assignor (the obligee). Performance by the obligor to the assignor (obligee) constitutes a discharge to the assignee. Once the obligor receives proper notice, however, only performance to the assignee can discharge the obligor's obligations.

▶ **Example 17.8** Recall that Alexis, the obligee in *Example 17.7*, assigned to Carmen her right to collect $5,000 from Jason, and Carmen did not give notice to Jason. Jason subsequently pays Alexis the $5,000. Although the assignment was valid, Jason's payment to Alexis is a discharge of the debt. Carmen's failure to notify Jason of the assignment causes her to lose the right to collect the $5,000 from Jason. (Note that Carmen still has a claim against Alexis for the $5,000.) If Carmen had given Jason notice of the assignment, however, Jason's payment to Alexis would not have discharged the debt. ◄

In the following case, the parties disputed whether the right to buy advertising space in publications at a steep discount was validly assigned from the original owner to companies that he later formed.

SPOTLIGHT on *PC Magazine*

Case 17.2   Gold v. Ziff Communications Co.
Appellate Court of Illinois, First District, 322 Ill.App.3d 32, 748 N.E.2d 198, 254 Ill.Dec. 752 (2001).

BACKGROUND AND FACTS Ziff Communications Company, a publisher of specialty magazines, bought *PC Magazine* from its founder, Anthony Gold, for more than $10 million. As part of the deal, Ziff gave Gold or a company that he owned and controlled "ad/list rights"—rights to advertise at an 80 percent discount on a limited number of pages in Ziff publications and free use of Ziff's subscriber lists. In 1983, Gold formed Software Communications, Inc. (SCI), a mail-order software business that he wholly owned, to use the ad/list rights. In 1987 and 1988, he formed two new mail-order companies, Hanson & Connors, Inc., and PC Brand, Inc. Gold told Ziff that he was allocating his ad/list rights to Hanson & Connors, which took over most of SCI's business, and to PC Brand, of which Gold owned 90 percent. Ziff's other advertisers complained about this "allocation."

Ziff refused to run large ads for Hanson & Connors or to release its subscriber lists to the company. Ziff also declared PC Brand ineligible for the ad discount because it "was not controlled by Gold." Gold and his companies filed a suit in an Illinois state court against Ziff, alleging breach of contract. The court ordered Ziff to pay the plaintiffs more than $88 million in damages and interest. Ziff appealed to an intermediate state appellate court, arguing, in part, that Gold had not properly assigned the ad/list rights to Hanson & Connors and PC Brand.

IN THE LANGUAGE OF THE COURT
Justice *COUSINS* delivered the opinion of the court.

* * * *

Ziff * * * argues that Gold never properly reassigned his rights under the amended ad/list agreement from SCI to PC Brand and Hanson. We agree with plaintiffs that assignments can be implied from circumstances. *No particular mode or form* * * * *is necessary to effect a valid assignment, and any acts or words are sufficient which show an intention of transferring or appropriating the owner's interest.* [Emphasis added.]

In the instant case, it is undisputed that Gold owned 100% of SCI. In a letter dated May 13, 1988, Gold, as president of SCI, instructed Ziff that he was allocating the ad/list rights to Hanson and PC Brand. Additionally, SCI stopped using the ad/list rights when PC Brand and

CASE 17.2 CONTINUES ▶

CASE 17.2 CONTINUED Hanson were formed. * * * Gold's behavior toward his companies and his conduct toward the obligor, Ziff, implied that the ad/list rights were assigned to PC Brand and Hanson.

DECISION AND REMEDY *The state intermediate appellate court affirmed the lower court's decision that the rights had been properly assigned. The appellate court remanded the case for a new trial on the amount of the damages, however.*

THE SOCIAL DIMENSION *Would the assignments in this case have been valid if Gold had not notified Ziff? Why or why not?*

THE ECONOMIC DIMENSION *How might Ziff have effectively avoided both this dispute with Gold and complaints from its other advertisers?*

Delegations

Just as a party can transfer rights through an assignment, a party can also transfer duties. Duties are not assigned, however, they are *delegated*. The party delegating the duties is the **delegator,** and the party to whom the duties are delegated is the **delegatee.** Normally, a delegation of duties does not relieve the delegator of the obligation to perform in the event that the delegatee fails to do so.

No special form is required to create a valid delegation of duties. As long as the delegator expresses an intention to make the delegation, it is effective. The del-

egator need not even use the word *delegate*. Exhibit 17–2 below illustrates delegation relationships.

DUTIES THAT CANNOT BE DELEGATED As a general rule, any duty can be delegated. There are, however, some exceptions to this rule. Delegation is prohibited in the circumstances discussed next.

When the Duties Are Personal in Nature. When special trust has been placed in the obligor or when performance depends on the personal skill or talents of the obligor, contractual duties cannot be delegated. ▶ **Example 17.9** O'Brien, who is impressed with

---

EXHIBIT 17–2 Delegation Relationships

In the delegation relationship illustrated here, Brower delegates her *duties* under a contract that she made with Horton to a third party, Kuhn. Brower thus becomes the *delegator* and Kuhn the *delegatee* of the contractual duties. Kuhn now owes performance of the contractual duties to Horton. Note that a delegation of duties normally does not relieve the delegator (Brower) of liability if the delegatee (Kuhn) fails to perform the contractual duties.

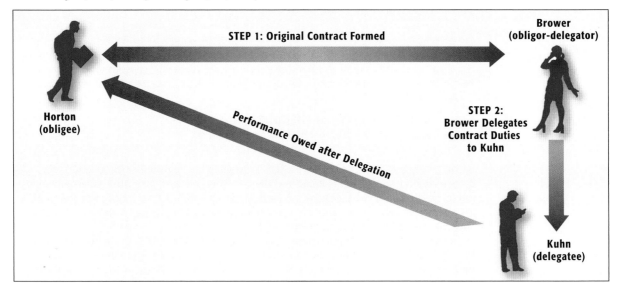

STEP 1: Original Contract Formed

Brower (obligor-delegator)

Horton (obligee)

Performance Owed after Delegation

STEP 2: Brower Delegates Contract Duties to Kuhn

Kuhn (delegatee)

Brodie's ability to perform veterinary surgery, contracts with Brodie to have her perform surgery on O'Brien's prize-winning stallion in July. Brodie later decides that she would rather spend the summer at the beach, so she delegates her duties under the contract to Lopez, who is also a competent veterinary surgeon. The delegation is not effective without O'Brien's consent, no matter how competent Lopez is, because the contract is for *personal* performance.

In contrast, nonpersonal duties may be delegated. Assume that Brodie contracts with O'Brien to pick up and deliver a large horse trailer to O'Brien's property. Brodie delegates this duty to Lopez, who owns a towing business. This delegation is effective because the performance required is of a *routine* and *nonpersonal* nature. ◄

When Performance by a Third Party Will Vary Materially from That Expected by the Obligee. When performance by a third party will vary materially from that expected by the obligee under the contract, contractual duties cannot be delegated. ► **Example 17.10** Jared, a wealthy investor, established the company Heaven Sent to provide grants of capital to struggling but potentially successful businesses. Jared contracted with Merilyn, whose judgment Jared trusted, to select the recipients of the grants. Later, Merilyn delegated this duty to Donald. Jared did not trust Donald's ability to select worthy recipients. This delegation is not effective because it materially alters Jared's expectations under the contract with Merilyn. ◄

When the Contract Prohibits Delegation. When the contract expressly prohibits delegation by including an *antidelegation clause,* the duties cannot be delegated. ► **Example 17.11**   Stark, Ltd., contracts with Belisario, a certified public accountant, to perform its annual audits for five years. The contract prohibits delegation. Belisario cannot delegate the duty to perform the audit to another accountant—not even an accountant at the same firm. ◄

EFFECT OF A DELEGATION If a delegation of duties is enforceable, the obligee must accept performance from the delegatee. ► **Example 17.12**   Bryan has a duty to pick up and deliver metal fabrication equipment to Alicia's property. Bryan delegates his duty to Liam. In this situation, Alicia (the obligee) must accept performance from Liam (the delegatee) because the delegation is effective. ◄ The obligee can legally refuse performance from the delegatee only if the duty is one that cannot be delegated.

As noted, a valid delegation of duties does not relieve the delegator of obligations under the contract. Although there are many exceptions, the general rule today is that the obligee can sue both the delegatee and the delegator. ► **Example 17.13**   In *Example 17.12,* if Liam (the delegatee) fails to perform, Bryan (the delegator) is still liable to Alicia (the obligee to whom performance is owed). The obligee can also hold the delegatee liable if the delegatee made a promise of performance that will directly benefit the obligee. For instance, if Liam promised Bryan in a contract to deliver the equipment to Alicia's property but fails to do so, Alicia can sue Bryan, Liam, or both. ◄

Concept Summary 17.1 on the following page outlines the basic principles of the laws governing assignments and delegations.

Assignment of "All Rights"

When a contract provides for an "assignment of all rights," this wording may create both an assignment of rights and a delegation of duties.[8] Typically, this occurs when general words are used, such as "I assign the contract" or "I assign all my rights under the contract." A court normally will construe such words as implying both an assignment of rights and a delegation of any duties of performance. Thus, the assignor remains liable if the assignee fails to perform the contractual obligations.

[handwritten margin note: also mean / delegate duties]

SECTION 2
THIRD PARTY BENEFICIARIES

Another exception to the doctrine of privity of contract arises when the contract is intended to benefit a third party. When the original parties to the contract agree that the contract performance should be rendered to or directly benefit a third person, the third person becomes an *intended* **third party beneficiary** of the contract. As the **intended beneficiary** of the contract, the third party has legal rights and can sue the promisor directly for breach of the contract.

Who Is the Promisor?

Who, though, is the promisor? In a bilateral contract, both parties to the contract make promises that can be enforced, so the court has to determine which party

---

8. *Restatement (Second) of Contracts,* Section 328; UCC 2–210(3), (4).

CONCEPT SUMMARY 17.1
Assignments and Delegations

Which Rights Can Be Assigned, and Which Duties Can Be Delegated?	All rights can be assigned *unless:* 1. A statute expressly prohibits assignment. 2. The contract is for personal services. 3. The assignment will materially alter the obligor's risk or duties. 4. The contract prohibits assignment.	All duties can be delegated *unless:* 1. Performance depends on the obligor's personal skills or talents or special trust has been placed in the obligor. 2. Performance by a third party will materially vary from that expected by the obligee. 3. The contract prohibits delegation.
What If the Contract Prohibits Assignment or Delegation?	No rights can be assigned *except:* 1. Rights to receive funds. 2. Ownership rights in real estate. 3. Rights to negotiable instruments. 4. Rights to damages for breach of a sales contract or payments under a sales contract.	No duties can be delegated.
What Is the Effect on the Original Party's Rights?	On a valid assignment, effective immediately, the original party (assignor) no longer has any rights under the contract.	On a valid delegation, if the delegatee fails to perform, the original party (delegator) is liable to the obligee (who may also hold the delegatee liable).

made the promise that benefits the third party. That person is the promisor. In effect, allowing a third party to sue the promisor directly circumvents the "middle person" (the promisee) and thus reduces the burden on the courts. Otherwise, the third party would sue the promisee, who would then sue the promisor.

▶ **Case in Point 17.14** The classic case that gave third party beneficiaries the right to bring a suit directly against a promisor was decided in 1859. The case involved three parties—Holly, Lawrence, and Fox. Holly had borrowed $300 from Lawrence. Shortly thereafter, Holly loaned $300 to Fox, who in return promised Holly that he would pay Holly's debt to Lawrence on the following day. When Lawrence failed to obtain the $300 from Fox, he sued Fox to recover the funds. The court had to decide whether Lawrence could sue Fox directly (rather than suing Holly). The court held that when "a promise [is] made for the benefit of another, he for whose benefit it is made may bring an action for its breach."[9] ◀

Types of Intended Beneficiaries

The law distinguishes between *intended* beneficiaries and *incidental* beneficiaries. Only intended beneficiaries acquire legal rights in a contract.

CREDITOR BENEFICIARY One type of intended beneficiary is a *creditor beneficiary.* Like the plaintiff in *Case in Point 17.14,* a creditor beneficiary benefits from a contract in which one party (the promisor) promises another party (the promisee) to pay a debt that the promisee owes to a third party (the creditor beneficiary).

▶ **Case in Point 17.15** Autumn Allan owned a condominium unit in a Texas complex located directly beneath a condo unit owned by Aslan Koraev. Over the course of two years, Allan's unit suffered eight incidents of water and sewage incursion as a result of plumbing problems and misuse of appliances in Koraev's unit. Allan sued Koraev for breach of contract and won.

Koraev appealed, arguing that he had no contractual duty to Allan. The court found that Allan was an intended third party beneficiary of the contract between Koraev and the condominium owners' association. Because the governing documents stated that each owner had to comply strictly with their provisions, failure to comply created grounds for an action by the condominium association or an aggrieved (wronged) owner. Here, Allan was clearly an aggrieved owner and could sue Koraev directly for his failure to perform his contract duties to the condominium association.[10] ◀

---

9. *Lawrence v. Fox,* 20 N.Y. 268 (1859).

10. *Allan v. Nersesova,* 307 S.W.3d 564 (Tx.App.—Dallas 2010).

DONEE BENEFICIARY Another type of intended beneficiary is a *donee beneficiary.* When a contract is made for the express purpose of giving a *gift* to a third party, the third party (the donee beneficiary) can sue the promisor directly to enforce the promise.[11]

The most common donee beneficiary contract is a life insurance contract. ▶ **Example 17.16**   Ang (the promisee) pays premiums to Standard Life, a life insurance company. Standard Life (the promisor) promises to pay a certain amount upon Ang's death to anyone Ang designates as a beneficiary. The designated beneficiary is a donee beneficiary under the life insurance policy and can enforce the promise made by the insurance company to pay her or him on Ang's death. ◀

Most third party beneficiaries do not fit neatly into either the creditor beneficiary or the donee beneficiary category. Thus, the modern view adopted by the *Restatement (Second) of Contracts* does not draw clear lines between the types of intended beneficiaries. Today, courts frequently distinguish only between *intended beneficiaries* (who can sue to enforce contracts made for their benefit) and *incidental beneficiaries* (who cannot sue, as will be discussed shortly).

When the Rights of an Intended Beneficiary Vest

An intended third party beneficiary cannot enforce a contract against the original parties until the rights of the third party have *vested,* which means the rights have taken effect and cannot be taken away. Until these rights have vested, the original parties to the contract—the promisor and the promisee—can modify or rescind the contract without the consent of the third party.

When do the rights of third parties vest? The majority of courts hold that the rights vest when any of the following occurs:

1. The third party materially changes his or her position in justifiable reliance on the promise.
2. The third party brings a lawsuit on the promise.
3. The third party demonstrates her or his consent to the promise at the request of the promisor or promisee, such as by sending a letter or e-mail indicating that she or he is aware of and consents to a contract formed for her or his benefit.[12]

If the contract expressly reserves to the contracting parties the right to cancel, rescind, or modify the contract, the rights of the third party beneficiary are subject to any changes that result. If the original contract reserves the right to revoke the promise or change the beneficiary, the vesting of the third party's rights does not terminate that power.[13] In most life insurance contracts, for instance, the policyholder reserves the right to change the designated beneficiary.

Incidental Beneficiaries

Sometimes, a third person receives a benefit from a contract even though that person's benefit is not the reason the contract was made. Such a person is known as an **incidental beneficiary.** Because the benefit is *unintentional,* an incidental beneficiary cannot sue to enforce the contract.

▶ **Case in Point 17.17**   Spectators at the infamous boxing match in which Mike Tyson was disqualified for biting his opponent's ear sued Tyson and the fight's promoters for a refund on the basis of breach of contract. The spectators claimed that they were third party beneficiaries of the contract between Tyson and the fight's promoters. The court, however, held that the spectators could not sue because they were not in contractual privity with the defendants. Any benefits they received from the contract were incidental to the contract, and according to the court, the spectators got what they paid for: "the right to view whatever event transpired."[14] ◀

Intended versus Incidental Beneficiaries

In determining whether a third party beneficiary is an intended or an incidental beneficiary, the courts focus on intent, as expressed in the contract language and implied by the surrounding circumstances. Any beneficiary who is not deemed an intended beneficiary is considered incidental. Exhibit 17–3 on the following page illustrates the distinction between intended beneficiaries and incidental beneficiaries.

Although no single test can embrace all possible situations, courts often apply the *reasonable person* test: Would a reasonable person in the position of the beneficiary believe that the promisee intended to confer on the beneficiary the right to enforce the contract? In addition, the presence of one or more of

---

11. This principle was first enunciated in *Seaver v. Ransom,* 224 N.Y. 233, 120 N.E. 639 (1918).
12. *Restatement (Second) of Contracts,* Section 311.

13. Defenses against third party beneficiaries are given in the *Restatement (Second) of Contracts,* Section 309.
14. *Castillo v. Tyson,* 268 A.D.2d 336, 701 N.Y.S.2d 423 (Sup.Ct.App.Div. 2000).

EXHIBIT 17-3   Third Party Beneficiaries

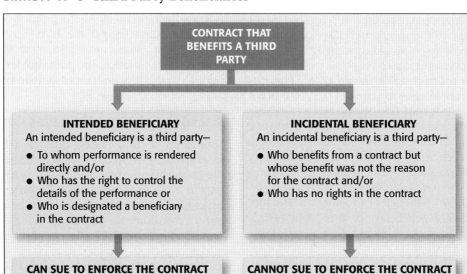

the following factors strongly indicates that the third party is an intended beneficiary to the contract:

1. Performance is rendered directly to the third party.
2. The third party has the right to control the details of performance.

3. The third party is expressly designated as a beneficiary in the contract.

In the following case, a subcontractor argued that it was a third party beneficiary of a contract between a general contractor and a public entity.

CASE ANALYSIS

Case 17.3   Lake County Grading Co. v. Village of Antioch

Appellate Court of Illinois, Second District, 2013 IL App (2d) 120474, 368 Ill.App.3d 831, 985 N.E.2d 638 (2013).

IN THE LANGUAGE OF THE COURT
Presiding Justice *BURKE* delivered the judgment of the court, with opinion:
* * * *

This action arises from construction work performed in two residential subdivisions in Antioch, [Illinois,] commonly known as the NeuHaven Subdivision and the Clublands Subdivision. Pursuant to the contract, Neumann [Homes, Inc.,] agreed to construct certain public improvements for the Village [of Antioch's]

benefit. Thereafter, Neumann and plaintiff [Lake County Grading Company] entered into agreements for plaintiff to perform certain grading work required under the contract. * * * Plaintiff completed the work in compliance with the contract but was not paid in full for its services.
* * * *

Neumann was unable to complete the improvements or to pay plaintiff in full. On November 1, 2007, Neumann declared bankruptcy.

Plaintiff filed a * * * complaint [in an Illinois state court] seeking to

recover payment [as a third party beneficiary] from the Village [for breach of contract].

* * * Specifically, plaintiff alleged that Section 1 of the Bond Act [30 Illinois Compiled Statutes 550/1] and Section 3.2(a) of the contract conferred third-party beneficiary status upon plaintiff. Plaintiff alleged that the Village has breached its duty to require from Neumann a * * * payment bond for the benefit of plaintiff.

* * * The trial court granted plaintiff summary judgment * * * . The Village timely appeals.

* * * *

An individual not a party to a contract may only enforce the contract's rights when the contract's original parties intentionally entered into the contract for the direct benefit of the individual. There is a strong presumption that the parties to a contract intend that the contract's provisions apply only to them, and not to third parties. Without contract language, the contracting parties' knowledge, expectation, or even intention that others will benefit from their agreement is not enough to overcome the presumption that the contract was intended for the direct benefit of the parties.

A person's status as a third-party beneficiary turns on whether the contract language shows such an intent of the contracting parties. *The contract language must show that the contract was made for the direct, not merely incidental, benefit of the third party. Such an intention must be shown by an express provision in the contract identifying the third-party beneficiary by name or by description of a class to which the third party belongs.* If a contract makes no mention of the plaintiff or the class to which he belongs, he is not a third-party beneficiary of the contract. [Emphasis added.]

Plaintiff qualifies as a third-party beneficiary. The payment bond requirement found in Section 1 of the Bond Act is read into a public works contract between a public entity and a general contractor. Specifically, Section 1 states that, as part of its agreement with the general contractor, the public entity "shall require every contractor for the work to furnish, supply and deliver a bond," and the bond shall be conditioned for the completion of the contract, for the payment of material used in the work, and for all labor performed in the work, including work completed by subcontractors.

* * * The Village violated Section 1, and thus breached the contract, when it failed to require Neumann to procure such a payment bond.

A subcontractor is a third-party beneficiary of a contract between a public entity and a general contractor because, as a policy matter, it would be meaningless here to read the Bond Act requirements into the general contract without reading in third-party rights to enforce that statute.

Moreover, consistent with the payment bond provision, Section 3.2(a) of the contract provides that "the Village agrees that Neumann shall construct the public improvements using subcontractors and materialmen selected from time to time by Neumann in Neumann's sole discretion." The payment bond provision read into the contract as well as Section 3.2(a) of the contract itself show the intent of Neumann and the Village to make plaintiff a third-party beneficiary.

* * * *

We hold that the Village breached the contract when it failed to require Neumann to furnish a payment bond for the benefit of subcontractors. Section 1 of the Bond Act requires the general contractor to post a payment bond, and that requirement is read into a public construction contract precisely to give the subcontractor a remedy; thus a payment bond became a term of the contract between Neumann and the Village. As a direct third-party beneficiary, plaintiff had the right to sue on the contract.

* * * *

For the reasons stated, the summary judgment entered in favor of plaintiff is affirmed.

LEGAL REASONING QUESTIONS

1. What do courts focus on when determining whether a third party beneficiary is an intended or an incidental beneficiary?
2. What right does the status of an intended beneficiary confer on a third party to a contract?
3. In this case, did the court conclude that the plaintiff was an intended or an incidental third party beneficiary? Why?
4. Did the plaintiff obtain the remedy that it sought in this case? Explain.

Reviewing: Third Party Rights

Myrtle Jackson owns several commercial buildings that she leases to businesses, one of which is a restaurant. The lease states that tenants are responsible for securing all necessary insurance policies but the landlord is obligated to keep the buildings in good repair. The owner of the restaurant, Joe McCall, tells his restaurant manager to purchase insurance, but the manager never does so. Jackson tells her son-in-law,

Continued

Rob Dunn, to perform any necessary maintenance for the buildings. Dunn knows that the ceiling in the restaurant needs repair but fails to do anything about it.

One day a customer, Ian Faught, is dining in the restaurant when a chunk of the ceiling falls on his head and fractures his skull. Faught files suit against the restaurant and discovers that there is no insurance policy in effect. Faught then files a suit against Jackson. He argues that he is an intended third party beneficiary of the lease provision requiring the restaurant to carry insurance and thus can sue Jackson for failing to enforce that provision. Using the information presented in the chapter, answer the following questions.

1. Can Jackson delegate her duty to maintain the buildings to Dunn? Why or why not?
2. Who can be held liable for Dunn's failure to fix the ceiling, Jackson or Dunn? Why?
3. Was Faught an intended third party beneficiary of the lease between Jackson and McCall? Why or why not?
4. Suppose that Jackson tells Dan Stryker, a local builder to whom she owes $50,000, that he can collect the rents from the buildings' tenants until the debt is satisfied. Is this a valid assignment? Why or why not?

DEBATE THIS . . . *As a matter of public policy, personal-injury tort claims cannot be assigned. This public policy is wrong and should be changed.*

Terms and Concepts

alienation 322	delegation 319	obligor 319
assignee 319	delegator 324	privity of contract 319
assignment 319	incidental beneficiary 327	third party beneficiary 325
assignor 319	intended beneficiary 325	
delegatee 324	obligee 319	

ExamPrep

Issue Spotters

1. Brian owes Jeff $100. Ed tells Brian to give him the $100 and he will pay Jeff. Brian gives Ed the $100. Ed never pays Jeff. Can Jeff successfully sue Ed for the $100? Why or why not? **(See page 325.)**

2. Eagle Company contracts to build a house for Frank. The contract states that "any assignment of this contract renders the contract void." After Eagle builds the house, but before Frank pays, Eagle assigns its right to payment to Good Credit Company. Can Good Credit enforce the contract against Frank? Why or why not? **(See page 322.)**

• **Check your answers to the Issue Spotters against the answers provided in Appendix E at the end of this text.**

Before the Test

Go to **www.cengagebrain.com**, enter the ISBN 9781285185248, and click on "Find" to locate this textbook's Web site. Then, click on "Access Now" under "Study Tools," and select Chapter 17 at the top. There, you will find a Practice Quiz that you can take to assess your mastery of the concepts in this chapter, as well as Flashcards and a Glossary of important terms.

Business Scenarios

17–1. Third Party Beneficiary. Alexander has been accepted as a freshman at a college two hundred miles from his home for the fall semester. Alexander's wealthy uncle, Michael, decides to give Alexander a car for Christmas. In November, Michael makes a contract with Jackson Auto Sales to purchase a new car for $18,000 to be delivered to Alexander just before the Christmas holidays, in mid-December. The title to the car is to be in Alexander's name.

Michael pays the full purchase price, calls Alexander and tells him about the gift, and takes off for a six-month vacation in Europe. Is Alexander an intended third party beneficiary of the contract between Michael and Jackson Auto Sales? Suppose that Jackson Auto Sales never delivers the car to Alexander. Does Alexander have the right to sue Jackson Auto Sales for breaching its contract with Michael? Explain. **(See page 325.)**

17–2. Assignment. Five years ago, Hensley purchased a house. At that time, being unable to pay the full purchase price, she borrowed funds from Thrift Savings and Loan, which in turn took a mortgage at 6.5 percent interest on the house. The mortgage contract did not prohibit the assignment of the mortgage. Then Hensley secured a new job in another city and sold the house to Sylvia. The purchase price included payment to Hensley of the value of her equity and the assumption of the mortgage debt still owed to Thrift. At the time the contract between Hensley and Sylvia was made, Thrift did not know about or consent to the sale. On the basis of these facts, if Sylvia defaults in making the mortgage payments to Thrift, what are Thrift's rights? Discuss. **(See page 319.)**

17–3. Assignment. Marsala, a college student, signs a one-year lease agreement that runs from September 1 to August 31. The lease agreement specifies that the lease cannot be assigned without the landlord's consent. In late May, Marsala decides not to go to summer school and assigns the balance of the lease (three months) to a close friend, Fred. The landlord objects to the assignment and denies Fred access to the apartment. Marsala claims that Fred is financially sound and should be allowed the full rights and privileges of an assignee. Discuss fully who is correct, the landlord or Marsala. **(See page 319.)**

17–4. Delegation. Inez has a specific set of plans to build a sailboat. The plans are detailed, and any boatbuilder can construct the boat. Inez secures bids, and the low bid is made by the Whale of a Boat Corp. Inez contracts with Whale to build the boat for $4,000. Whale then receives unexpected business from elsewhere. To meet the delivery date in the contract with Inez, Whale delegates its obligation to build the boat, without Inez's consent, to Quick Brothers, a reputable boatbuilder. When the boat is ready for delivery, Inez learns of the delegation and refuses to accept delivery, even though the boat is built to her specifications. Discuss fully whether Inez is obligated to accept and pay for the boat. Would your answer be any different if Inez had not had a specific set of plans but had instead contracted with Whale to design and build a sailboat for $4,000? Explain. **(See page 319.)**

Business Case Problems

17–5. Spotlight on Drug Testing—Third Party Beneficiary. Bath Iron Works (BIW) offered a job to Thomas Devine, contingent on Devine's passing a drug test. The testing was conducted by NorDx, a subcontractor of Roche Biomedical Laboratories. When NorDx found that Devine's urinalysis showed the presence of opiates, a result confirmed by Roche, BIW refused to offer Devine permanent employment. Devine sued Roche, claiming that the ingestion of poppy seeds can yield a positive result and that he tested positive only because of his daily consumption of poppy seed muffins. Devine argued that he was a third party beneficiary of the contract between his prospective employer (BIW) and NorDx (Roche). Is Devine an intended third party beneficiary of the BIW–NorDx contract? Why or why not? Do drug-testing labs have a duty to the persons being tested to exercise reasonable care in conducting the tests? Explain. [*Devine v. Roche Biomedical Laboratories*, 659 A.2d 868 (Me. 1995)] **(See page 325.)**

17–6. Assignment. Senna Hills, Ltd., granted Southern Union Co. the right to distribute propane in a residential subdivision developed by Senna in exchange for a fee. Under their agreement, Senna's "right to receive a Fee shall continue for so long as the Propane System is owned by Southern Union." The agreement also allowed Southern Union to assign the distribution right. Later, Sonterra Energy Corp. bought the distribution system and was assigned the distribution right, but did not pay the fee to Senna. Did Sonterra breach the propane service agreement? Why or why not? [*Senna Hills, Ltd. v. Sonterra Energy Corp.*, __ S.W.3d __ (Tex.App.—Austin 2010)] **(See page 319.)**

17–7. BUSINESS CASE PROBLEM WITH SAMPLE ANSWER: Duties That Cannot Be Delegated.

Bruce Albea Contracting, Inc., was the general contractor on a state highway project. Albea subcontracted the asphalt work to APAC-Southeast, Inc. Their contract prohibited any delegation without Albea's consent. In midproject, APAC delegated its duties to Matthews Contracting Co. Although Albea allowed Matthews to finish the work, Albea did not pay APAC for its work on the project. Albea argued that APAC had violated the antidelegation clause, rendering their contact void. Is Albea correct? Explain. [Western Surety Co. v. APAC-Southeast, Inc., *302 Ga.App. 654, 691 S.E.2d 234 (2010)*] **(See page 324.)**

• **For a sample answer to Problem 17–7, go to Appendix F at the end of this text.**

17–8. Notice of Assignment. Arnold Kazery was the owner of a hotel leased to George Wilkinson. The lease included renewal options of ten years each. When Arnold transferred his interest in the property to his son, Sam, no one notified Wilkinson. For the next twenty years, Wilkinson paid the rent to Arnold and renewed the lease by notice to Arnold. When Wilkinson wrote to Arnold that he was exercising another option to renew, Sam filed a suit against him, claiming that the lease was void. Did Wilkinson give proper notice to renew? Discuss. [*Kazery v. Wilkinson*, 52 So.3d 1270 (Miss.App. 2011)] **(See page 322.)**

17–9. Third Party Beneficiary. David and Sandra Dess contracted with Sirva Relocation, LLC, to assist in selling their home. In their contract, the Desses agreed to disclose all information about the property on which Sirva "and other prospective buyers may rely in deciding whether and on what terms to purchase the Property." The Kincaids contracted with Sirva to buy the house. After the closing, they discovered dampness in the walls, defective and rotten windows, mold, and other undisclosed problems. Can the Kincaids bring an action against the Desses for breach of their contract with Sirva? Why or why not? [*Kincaid v. Dess*, 298 P.3d 358 (2013)] **(See page 325.)**

17–10. A QUESTION OF ETHICS: Assignment and Delegation.

 Premier Building & Development, Inc., entered a listing agreement giving Sunset Gold Realty, LLC, the exclusive right to find a tenant for some commercial property. The terms of the listing agreement stated that it was binding on both parties and "their . . .

assigns." Premier Building did not own the property at the time, but had the option to purchase it. To secure financing for the project, Premier Building established a new company called Cobblestone Associates. Premier Building then bought the property and conveyed it to Cobblestone the same day. Meanwhile, Sunset Gold found a tenant for the property, and Cobblestone became the landlord. Cobblestone acknowledged its obligation to pay Sunset Gold for finding a tenant, but it later refused to pay Sunset Gold's commission. Sunset Gold then sued Premier Building and Cobblestone for breach of the listing agreement. [Sunset Gold Realty, LLC v. Premier Building & Development, Inc., 36 A.3d 243 (Conn.App.Ct. 2012)] **(See page 319.)**

(a) Is Premier Building relieved of its contractual duties if it assigned the contract to Cobblestone? Why or why not?

(b) Given that Sunset Gold performed its obligations under the listing agreement, did Cobblestone behave unethically in refusing to pay Sunset Gold's commission? Why or why not?

Legal Reasoning Group Activity

17–11. Assignment. The Smiths buy a house. They borrow 80 percent of the purchase price from the local ABC Savings and Loan. Before they make their first payment, ABC transfers the right to receive mortgage payments to Citibank. **(See page 319.)**

(a) The first group will outline what would happen if the Smiths continue to make all their payments to ABC Savings and Loan because ABC never notified them of the assignment.

(b) The second group will describe what would happen if the Smiths were notified by ABC of the assignment, but continued to make payments to ABC.

(c) A third group will determine what would happen if the Smiths fail to make any payments on the loan. Which financial institution would have the right to repossess their house?

CHAPTER 18

PERFORMANCE AND DISCHARGE IN TRADITIONAL AND E-CONTRACTS

Just as rules are necessary to determine when a legally enforceable contract exists, so also are they required to determine when one of the parties can justifiably say, "I have fully performed, so I am now discharged from my obligations under this contract." The legal environment of business requires the identification of some point at which the parties can reasonably know that their duties have ended.

The most common way to **discharge,** or terminate, one's contractual duties is by the **performance** of those duties. For example, a buyer and seller enter into an agreement via e-mail for the sale of a 2014 Lexus for $42,000. This contract will be discharged by performance when the buyer pays $42,000 to the seller and the seller transfers possession of the Lexus to the buyer.

The duty to perform under any contract (including e-contracts) may be *conditioned* on the occurrence or nonoccurrence of a certain event, or the duty may be *absolute*. In the first part of this chapter, we look at conditions of performance and the degree of performance required. We then examine some other ways in which a contract can be discharged, including discharge by agreement of the parties and discharge by operation of law.

CONDITIONS

In most contracts, promises of performance are not expressly conditioned or qualified. Instead, they are *absolute promises.* They must be performed, or the parties promising the acts will be in breach of contract.

▶ **Example 18.1** Paloma Enterprises contracts to sell a truckload of organic produce to Tran for $10,000. The parties' promises are unconditional: Paloma will deliver the produce to Tran, and Tran will pay $10,000 to Paloma. The payment does not have to be made if the produce is not delivered. ◀

In some situations, however, performance is contingent on the occurrence or nonoccurrence of a certain event. A **condition** is a qualification in a contract based on a possible future event. The occurrence or nonoccurrence of the event will trigger the performance of a legal obligation or terminate an existing obligation under a contract.[1] If the condi-

tion is not satisfied, the obligations of the parties are discharged.

Three types of conditions can be present in contracts: conditions *precedent,* conditions *subsequent,* and *concurrent* conditions. Conditions are also classified as *express* or *implied.*

Conditions Precedent

A condition that must be fulfilled before a party's performance can be required is called a **condition precedent.** The condition precedes the absolute duty to perform. Life insurance contracts frequently specify that certain conditions, such as passing a physical examination, must be met before the insurance company will be obligated to perform under the contract.

In addition, many contracts are conditioned on an independent appraisal of value. ▶ **Example 18.2** Restoration Motors offers to buy Charlie's 1960 Cadillac limousine only if an expert appraiser estimates that it can be restored for less than a certain price. Thus, the parties' obligations are conditioned on the outcome of the appraisal. If the condition is not satisfied—that is, if the appraiser

---

1. The *Restatement (Second) of Contracts,* Section 224, defines a condition as "an event, not certain to occur, which must occur, unless its nonoccurrence is excused, before performance under a contract becomes due."

deems the cost to be above that price—their obligations are discharged. ◄

Sometimes, a lease of real property includes an option to buy that property. The lease in the following case required timely rent payments as a condition of exercising such an option, but the lessee (the tenant) often failed to make the payments on time. The court had to decide whether the lessee could still exercise the option even though it had not strictly complied with the condition precedent.

CASE 18.1

Pack 2000, Inc. v. Cushman
Appellate Court of Connecticut, 126 Conn.App. 339, 11 A.3d 181 (2011).

COMPANY PROFILE The first Midas muffler repair shop opened in Macon, Georgia, in 1956. Within ten years, Midas had added shock absorber services and expanded beyond the United States into the European market. By 1986, Midas had added brake services and opened shops around the world. Today, with more than 1,700 locations, Midas is a leader in muffler and exhaust services. It also offers comprehensive auto programs for tires, maintenance, and commercial fleet services. Recently, the company has renewed its focus on its franchise and real estate businesses.

BACKGROUND AND FACTS Eugene Cushman agreed to transfer two Midas muffler shops to Pack 2000, Inc. The deal included leases for the real estate on which the shops were located. Each lease provided Pack with an option to buy the leased real estate subject to certain conditions. Pack was to pay rent by the first day of each month, make payments on the notes by the eighth day of each month, and pay utilities and other accounts on time. Pack, however, was often late in making these payments. The utility and phone companies threatened to cut off services, an insurance company canceled Pack's liability coverage, and other delinquencies prompted collection calls and letters. When Pack sought to exercise the options to buy the real estate, Cushman responded that Pack had not complied with the conditions. Pack filed a suit in a Connecticut state court against Cushman, seeking specific performance of the options. The court rendered a judgment in Pack's favor. Cushman appealed.

IN THE LANGUAGE OF THE COURT
LAVERY, J. [Judge]

* * * *

When a lease provides the lessee with the option to purchase realty subject to certain terms and conditions, the right of the lessee to exercise the option is contingent on the lessee's strict compliance with those terms and conditions.

* * * *

The defendant claims that the plaintiff has lost its right to exercise the options at issue because it has not strictly complied with the conditions precedent to the defendant's duty to perform. A condition precedent is a fact or event which the parties intend must exist or take place before there is a right to performance. * * * *Whether the performance of a certain act by a party to a contract is a condition precedent to the duty of the other party to act depends on the intent of the parties as expressed in the contract and read in the light of the circumstances surrounding the execution of the instrument.* [Emphasis added.]

In the present case, the two lease agreements provide that the defendant's duty to perform under the terms of the options is conditioned on the plaintiff's "compliance with the terms and conditions of the Lease, the Letter of Intent, and Management Agreement * * * ." Additionally, the management agreement provides that the plaintiff must be in "full compliance with the management agreement" in order to exercise the options to purchase the defendant's realty. Under the terms of these agreements, the plaintiff is required to make periodic payments to the defendant and to certain third parties by specified deadlines. We conclude, therefore, that the plaintiff's right to exercise the options is subject to a condition precedent—namely, the timely submission of the aforementioned payments.

CASE 18.1 CONTINUED

Upon our review of the record, we find ample support for the * * * finding that the plaintiff was often late in making the required payments. Accordingly, * * * the plaintiff did not strictly comply with the terms and conditions of its agreements with the defendant. We conclude, therefore, that the plaintiff did not have the right to exercise the options to purchase the defendant's realty because the plaintiff was not in strict compliance with the contracts that set forth the terms of the options.

DECISION AND REMEDY *A state intermediate appellate court reversed the lower court's judgment and remanded the case for the entry of a judgment for the defendant. A party retains its right to exercise an option to buy real estate only by strict compliance with the conditions precedent to its exercise of the option. In this case, the plaintiff did not strictly comply with those conditions.*

WHAT IF THE FACTS WERE DIFFERENT? *Suppose that Pack had late payments. Would the result in this case have been different? Explain.*

THE ECONOMIC DIMENSION *Why are rent and other payments due under a lease subject to strict time deadlines?*

Conditions Subsequent

When a condition operates to terminate a party's absolute promise to perform, it is called a **condition subsequent.** The condition follows, or is subsequent to, the time that the absolute duty to perform arose. If the condition occurs, the party's duty to perform is discharged. ▶ **Example 18.3** A law firm hires Julie Mendez, a recent law school graduate. Their contract provides that the firm's obligation to continue employing Mendez is discharged if Mendez fails to pass the bar exam by her second attempt. This is a condition subsequent because a failure to pass the exam—and thus to obtain a license to practice law—would discharge a duty (employment) that has already arisen. ◀

Generally, conditions precedent are common, and conditions subsequent are rare. The *Restatement (Second) of Contracts* does not use the terms *condition subsequent* and *condition precedent* but refers to both simply as conditions.[2]

Concurrent Conditions

When each party's performance is conditioned on the other party's performance or tender of performance (offer to perform), **concurrent conditions** are present. These conditions exist only when the contract expressly or impliedly calls for the parties to perform their respective duties *simultaneously.*

▶ **Example 18.4** If Janet Feibush promises to pay for goods when Hewlett-Packard delivers them, the parties' promises to perform are mutually dependent. Feibush's duty to pay for the goods does not become absolute until Hewlett-Packard either delivers or tenders the goods. Likewise, Hewlett-Packard's duty to deliver the goods does not become absolute until Feibush tenders or actually makes payment. Therefore, neither can recover from the other for breach without first tendering performance. ◀

Express and Implied Conditions

Conditions can also be classified as express or implied in fact. *Express conditions* are provided for by the parties' agreement. Although no particular words are necessary, express conditions are normally prefaced by the words *if, provided, after,* or *when.*

▶ **Case in Point 18.5** Alejandro Alvarado's automobile insurance policy stated that, if he was involved in an accident, he must cooperate with the insurance company in the defense of any claim or lawsuit. Alvarado was involved in an accident and was sued for negligence. He notified the insurance company, but then failed to cooperate in his defense and did not appear in court for the trial. Although Alvarado was found to have been negligent, the insurance company was not liable for the damages awarded. The court found that the cooperation clause was a condition precedent to coverage under the policy. Therefore, because Alvarado did

---

2. *Restatement (Second) of Contracts,* Section 224.

not cooperate with the insurer, the accident was not covered by the policy.[3] ◄

Implied conditions are understood to be part of the agreement, but they are not found in the express language of the agreement. Courts may imply conditions from the purpose of the contract or from the intent of the parties. Conditions are often implied when they are necessarily inherent in the actual performance of the contract.

SECTION 2
DISCHARGE BY PERFORMANCE

The great majority of contracts are discharged by performance. The contract comes to an end when both parties fulfill their respective duties by performing the acts they have promised.

Performance can also be accomplished by *tender*. **Tender** is an unconditional offer to perform by a person who is ready, willing, and able to do so. Therefore, a seller who places goods at the disposal of a buyer has tendered delivery and can demand payment. A buyer who offers to pay for goods has tendered payment and can demand delivery of the goods.

Once performance has been tendered, the party making the tender has done everything possible to carry out the terms of the contract. If the other party then refuses to perform, the party making the tender can sue for breach of contract. There are two basic types of performance—*complete performance* and *substantial performance*.

Complete Performance

When a party performs exactly as agreed, there is no question as to whether the contract has been performed. When a party's performance is perfect, it is said to be complete. Normally, conditions expressly stated in a contract must fully occur in all respects for complete performance (strict performance) of the contract to take place. Any deviation breaches the contract and discharges the other party's obligations to perform.

Most construction contracts, for instance, require the builder to meet certain specifications. If the specifications are conditions, complete performance is required to avoid material breach (*material breach* will be discussed shortly). If the conditions are met, the other party to the contract must then fulfill her or his obligation to pay the builder.

If the parties to the contract did not expressly make the specifications a condition, however, and the builder fails to meet the specifications, performance is not complete. What effect does such a failure have on the other party's obligation to pay? The answer is part of the doctrine of *substantial performance*.

Substantial Performance

A party who in good faith performs substantially all of the terms of a contract can enforce the contract against the other party under the doctrine of substantial performance. The basic requirements for performance to qualify as substantial performance are as follows:

1. The party must have performed in good faith. Intentional failure to comply with the contract terms is a breach of the contract.
2. The performance must not vary greatly from the performance promised in the contract. An omission, variance, or defect in performance is considered minor if it can easily be remedied by compensation (monetary damages).
3. The performance must create substantially the same benefits as those promised in the contract.

Courts decide whether the performance was substantial on a case-by-case basis, examining all of the facts of the particular situation. ► **Case in Point 18.6** Wisconsin Electric Power Company (WEPCO) contracted with Union Pacific Railroad to transport coal to WEPCO from mines in Colorado. The contract required WEPCO to notify Union Pacific monthly of how many tons of coal (below a specified maximum) it wanted to have shipped the next month. Union Pacific was to make "good faith reasonable efforts" to meet the schedule.

The contract also required WEPCO to supply the railcars. When WEPCO did not supply the railcars, Union Pacific used its own railcars and delivered 84 percent of the requested coal. In this situation, a federal court held that the delivery of 84 percent of the contracted amount constituted substantial performance.[4] ◄

EFFECT ON DUTY TO PERFORM If performance is substantial, the other party's duty to perform remains absolute (except that the party can sue for damages due to the minor deviations). In other words, the parties must continue performing under the contract (for instance, making payment to the party who substantially per-

---

3. *Progressive County Mutual Insurance Co. v. Trevino,* 202 S.W.3d 811 (Tex. App.—San Antonio 2006).

4. *Wisconsin Electric Power Co. v. Union Pacific Railroad Co.,* 557 F.3d 504 (7th Cir. 2009).

formed). If performance is not substantial, there is a *material breach* (to be discussed shortly), and the non-breaching party is excused from further performance.

MEASURE OF DAMAGES Because substantial performance is not perfect, the other party is entitled to damages to compensate for the failure to comply with the contract. The measure of the damages is the cost to bring the object of the contract into compliance with its terms, if that cost is reasonable under the circumstances.

If the cost is unreasonable, the measure of damages is the difference in value between the performance that was rendered and the performance that would have been rendered if the contract had been performed completely.

The following case is a classic illustration that there is no exact formula for deciding when a contract has been substantially performed.

CLASSIC CASE 18.2

Jacob & Youngs v. Kent
Court of Appeals of New York, 230 N.Y. 239, 129 N.E. 889 (1921).

BACKGROUND AND FACTS The plaintiff, Jacob & Youngs, Inc., was a builder that had contracted with George Kent to construct a country residence for him. A specification in the building contract required that "all wrought-iron pipe must be well galvanized, lap welded pipe of the grade known as 'standard pipe' of Reading manufacture." Jacob & Youngs installed substantially similar pipe that was not of Reading manufacture. When Kent became aware of the difference, he ordered the builder to remove all of the plumbing and replace it with the Reading type. To do so would have required removing finished walls that encased the plumbing—an expensive and difficult task. The builder explained that the plumbing was of the same quality, appearance, value, and cost as Reading pipe. When Kent refused to pay the $3,483.46 still owed for the work, Jacob & Youngs sued to compel payment. The trial court ruled in favor of Kent. The plaintiff appealed, and the appellate court reversed the trial court's decision. Kent then appealed to the Court of Appeals of New York, the state's highest court.

 IN THE LANGUAGE OF THE COURT
CARDOZO, Justice.

* * * *

* * * The courts never say that one who makes a contract fills the measure of his duty by less than full performance. They do say, however, that *an omission, both trivial and innocent, will sometimes be atoned [compensated] for by allowance of the resulting damage, and will not always be the breach of a condition[.]* [Emphasis added.]

* * * Where the line is to be drawn between the important and the trivial cannot be settled by a formula. * * * *We must weigh the purpose to be served, the desire to be gratified, the excuse for deviation from the letter, [and] the cruelty of enforced adherence. Then only can we tell whether literal fulfillment is to be implied by law as a condition.* [Emphasis added.]

* * * We think the measure of the allowance is not the cost of replacement, which would be great, but the difference in value, which would be either nominal or nothing. * * * The owner is entitled to the money which will permit him to complete, unless the cost of completion is grossly and unfairly out of proportion to the good to be attained.

DECISION AND REMEDY *New York's highest court affirmed the appellate court's decision, holding that Jacob & Youngs had substantially performed the contract.*

IMPACT OF THIS CASE ON TODAY'S LAW *At the time of the* Jacob & Youngs *case, some courts did not apply the doctrine of substantial performance to disputes involving breaches of contract. This landmark decision contributed to a developing trend toward equity and fairness in those circumstances. Today, an unintentional and trivial deviation from the terms of a contract will not prevent its enforcement but will permit an adjustment in the value of its performance.*

THE LEGAL ENVIRONMENT DIMENSION *The New York Court of Appeals found that Jacob & Youngs had substantially performed the contract. To what, if any, remedy was Kent entitled?*

Performance to the Satisfaction of Another

Contracts often state that completed work must personally satisfy one of the parties or a third person. The question then is whether this satisfaction becomes a condition precedent, requiring actual personal satisfaction or approval for discharge, or whether the performance need only satisfy a *reasonable person* (substantial performance).

WHEN THE CONTRACT IS PERSONAL When the subject matter of the contract is *personal,* the obligation is conditional, and performance must actually satisfy the party specified in the contract. For instance, contracts for portraits, works of art, and tailoring are considered personal because they involve matters of personal taste. Therefore, only the personal satisfaction of the party fulfills the condition—unless a court finds that the party is expressing dissatisfaction simply to avoid payment or otherwise is not acting in good faith.

REASONABLE PERSON STANDARD Most other contracts need to be performed only to the satisfaction of a reasonable person unless they *expressly state otherwise.* When the subject matter of the contract is mechanical, courts are more likely to find that the performing party has performed satisfactorily if a reasonable person would be satisfied with what was done. ▶ **Example 18.7** Mason signs a contract with Jen to mount a new heat pump on a concrete platform to her satisfaction. Such a contract normally need only be performed to the satisfaction of a reasonable person. ◀

When contracts require performance to the satisfaction of a third party with superior knowledge or training in the subject matter—such as a supervising engineer—the courts are divided. A majority of courts require the work to be satisfactory to a reasonable person, but some courts require the personal satisfaction of the third party designated in the contract. (Again,

the personal judgment must be made honestly, or the condition will be excused.)

Material Breach of Contract

A **breach of contract** is the nonperformance of a contractual duty. The breach is *material* when performance is not at least substantial.[5] As mentioned earlier, when there is a material breach, the nonbreaching party is excused from the performance of contractual duties. That party can also sue the breaching party for damages resulting from the breach.

▶ **Example 18.8** When country singer Garth Brooks's mother died, he donated $500,000 to a hospital in his hometown to build a new women's health center named after his mother. After several years passed and the health center was not built, Brooks demanded a refund. The hospital refused, claiming that while it had promised to honor his mother in some way, it did not promise to build a women's health center. Brooks sued for breach of contract. A jury determined that the hospital's failure to build a women's health center and name it after Brooks's mother was a material breach of the contract. The jury awarded Brooks $500,000 in actual damages for the contract breach—plus another $500,000 because it found the hospital guilty of reckless disregard and intentionally acting with malice toward others. ◀

MATERIAL VERSUS MINOR BREACH If the breach is *minor* (not material), the nonbreaching party's duty to perform can sometimes be suspended until the breach has been remedied, but the duty to perform is not entirely excused. Once the minor breach has been cured, the nonbreaching party must resume performance of the contractual obligations.

Both parties in the following case were arguably in breach of their contract. Which party's breach was material?

---

5. *Restatement (Second) of Contracts,* Section 241.

CASE ANALYSIS

Case 18.3   Kohel v. Bergen Auto Enterprises, L.L.C.
Superior Court of New Jersey, Appellate Division, 2013 WL 439970 (2013).

IN THE LANGUAGE OF THE COURT
PER CURIAM.
* * * *

On May 24, 2010, plaintiffs Marc and Bree Kohel entered into a sales contract with defendant Bergen Auto Enterprises, L.L.C. d/b/a Wayne Mazda

Inc. (Wayne Mazda), for the purchase of a used 2009 Mazda. Plaintiffs agreed to pay $26,430.22 for the Mazda and were credited $7,000 as a trade-in, for their 2005 Nissan Altima. As plaintiffs still owed $8,118.28 on the Nissan, Wayne Mazda assessed plaintiffs a net pay-off of this amount and agreed to remit the balance due to satisfy the outstanding lien.

Plaintiffs took possession of the Mazda with temporary plates and left the Nissan with defendant. A few days later, a representative of defendant advised plaintiffs that the Nissan's vehicle identification tag (VIN tag) was missing. The representative claimed it was unable to sell the car and offered to rescind the transaction. Plaintiffs refused.

When the temporary plates on the Mazda expired on June 24, 2010, defendant refused to provide plaintiffs with the permanent plates they had paid for. In addition, defendant refused to pay off plaintiffs' outstanding loan on the Nissan, as they had agreed. As a result, plaintiffs were required to continue to make monthly payments on both the Nissan and the Mazda.

On July 28, 2010, plaintiffs filed a complaint in [a New Jersey state court] against Wayne Mazda * * * . Plaintiffs alleged breach of contract.
* * * *

On February 2, 2012, the court rendered an oral decision finding

that there was a breach of contract by Wayne Mazda * * * . On February 17, 2012, the court entered judgment in the amount of $5,405.17 in favor of plaintiffs against Wayne Mazda. [The defendant appealed to a state intermediate appellate court.]
* * * *

Defendant argues that plaintiffs' delivery of the Nissan without a VIN tag was, itself, a breach of the contract of sale and precludes a finding that defendant breached the contract. However, the trial court found that plaintiffs were not aware that the Nissan lacked a VIN tag when they offered it in trade. Moreover, defendant's representatives examined the car twice before accepting it in trade and did not notice the missing VIN until they took the car to an auction where they tried to sell it. *There is a material distinction in plaintiffs' conduct, which the court found unintentional, and defendant's refusal to release the permanent plates for which the plaintiffs had paid, an action the court concluded was done to maintain "leverage."* [Emphasis added.]

* * * The evidence * * * indicated that * * * the problem with the missing VIN tag could be rectified. Marc Kohel applied and paid for a replacement VIN tag at Meadowlands

[Nissan for $35.31]. While he initially made some calls to Meadowlands, he did not follow up in obtaining the VIN tag after the personnel at Wayne Mazda began refusing to take his calls.

* * * The court concluded that "Wayne Mazda didn't handle this as—as adroitly [skillfully] as they could * * * ." Kevin DiPiano, identified in the complaint as the owner and/or CEO of Wayne Mazda, would not even take [the plaintiffs'] calls to discuss this matter. The court found:

> Mr. DiPiano could have been a better businessman, could have been a little bit more compassionate or at least responsive, you know? He was not. He acted like he didn't care. That obviously went a long way to infuriate the plaintiffs. I don't blame them for being infuriated.

* * * *

* * * Here, plaintiffs attempted to remedy the VIN tag issue but this resolution was frustrated by defendant's unreasonable conduct. We thus reject defendant's argument that plaintiffs' failure to obtain the replacement VIN tag amounted to a repudiation of the contract.
* * * *

Affirmed.

LEGAL REASONING QUESTIONS

1. What is a *material* breach of contract? When a material breach occurs, what are the nonbreaching party's options?

2. What is a *minor* breach of contract? When a minor breach occurs, is the nonbreaching party excused from performance? Explain.

3. In this case, what were the defendant's main arguments that the plaintiffs should not have been granted relief for Wayne Mazda's breach?

4. Was there a difference in the degree to which the plaintiffs and the defendant failed to perform the contract? Explain. Which party was in material breach?

DISCHARGES NONBREACHING PARTY FROM FURTHER PERFORMANCE Any breach entitles the nonbreaching party to sue for damages, but only a material breach discharges the nonbreaching party from the contract. The policy underlying these rules allows a contract to go forward when only minor problems

occur but allows it to be terminated if major difficulties arise.

▶ **Case in Point 18.9** Su Yong Kim sold an apartment building with substandard plumbing that violated the city's housing code. The contract stated that Kim would have the plumbing fixed (brought up to code) within eight months. A year later, Kim still had not made the necessary repairs, so the buyers stopped making the payments due under the contract. A court found that Kim's failure to make the required repairs was a material breach because it defeated the purpose of the contract—to lease the building to tenants. Because Kim's breach was material, the buyers were no longer obligated to continue making payments under the contract.[6] ◄

Anticipatory Repudiation

Before either party to a contract has a duty to perform, one of the parties may refuse to carry out his or her contractual obligations. This is called **anticipatory repudiation**[7] of the contract.

REPUDIATION IS A MATERIAL BREACH When an anticipatory repudiation occurs, it is treated as a material breach of the contract, and the nonbreaching party is permitted to bring an action for damages immediately. The nonbreaching party can file suit even though the scheduled time for performance under the contract may still be in the future. Until the nonbreaching party treats an early repudiation as a breach, however, the repudiating party can retract her or his anticipatory repudiation by proper notice and restore the parties to their original obligations.[8]

An anticipatory repudiation is treated as a present, material breach for two reasons. First, the nonbreaching party should not be required to remain ready and willing to perform when the other party has already repudiated the contract. Second, the nonbreaching party should have the opportunity to seek a similar contract elsewhere and may have a duty to do so to minimize his or her loss.[9]

ANTICIPATORY REPUDIATION AND MARKET PRICES Quite often, anticipatory repudiation occurs when performance of the contract would be extremely unfavorable to one of the parties because of a sharp fluctuation in market prices.

▶ **Example 18.10** Mobile X enters into an e-contract to manufacture and sell 100,000 cell phones to Best Com, a global telecommunications company.

Delivery is to be made two months from the date of the contract. One month later, three inventory suppliers raise their prices to Mobile X. Because of these higher prices, Mobile X stands to lose $500,000 if it sells the cell phones to Best Com at the contract price. Mobile X immediately sends an e-mail to Best Com, stating that it cannot deliver the 100,000 cell phones at the contract price. Even though you may sympathize with Mobile X, its e-mail is an anticipatory repudiation of the contract. Best Com can treat the repudiation as a material breach and immediately pursue remedies, even though the contract delivery date is still a month away. ◄

Time for Performance

If no time for performance is stated in the contract, a *reasonable time* is implied.[10] If a specific time is stated, the parties must usually perform by that time. Unless time is expressly stated to be vital, though, a delay in performance will not destroy the performing party's right to payment.[11]

When time is expressly stated to be "of the essence" or vital, the parties normally must perform within the stated time period because the time element becomes a condition. Even when the contract states that time is of the essence, a court may find that a party who fails to complain about the other party's delay has waived the breach of the time provision.

SECTION 3
DISCHARGE BY AGREEMENT

Any contract can be discharged by agreement of the parties. The agreement can be contained in the original contract, or the parties can form a new contract for the express purpose of discharging the original contract.

Discharge by Mutual Rescission

As mentioned in previous chapters, *rescission* is the process by which a contract is canceled or terminated and the parties are returned to the positions they occupied prior to forming it. For **mutual rescission** to take place, the parties must make another agreement that also satisfies the legal requirements for a contract. There must be an *offer*, an *acceptance*, and

6. *Kim v. Park,* 192 Or.App. 365, 86 P.3d 63 (2004).
7. *Restatement (Second) of Contracts,* Section 253; Section 2–610 of the Uniform Commercial Code (UCC).
8. See UCC 2–611.
9. The doctrine of anticipatory repudiation first arose in the landmark case of *Hochster v. De La Tour,* 2 Ellis and Blackburn Reports 678 (1853). An English court recognized the delay and expense inherent in a rule requiring a nonbreaching party to wait until the time of performance before suing on an anticipatory repudiation.
10. See UCC 2–204.
11. See, for example, *Manganaro Corp. v. Hitt Contracting, Inc.,* 193 F.Supp.2d 88 (D.D.C. 2002).

consideration. Ordinarily, if the parties agree to rescind the original contract, their promises not to perform the acts stipulated in the original contract will be legal consideration for the second contract (the rescission).

Agreements to rescind most executory contracts (in which neither party has performed) are enforceable, even if the agreement is made orally and even if the original agreement was in writing. Under the Uniform Commercial Code (UCC), however, agreements to rescind a sales contract must be in writing (or contained in an electronic record) when the contract requires a written rescission.[12] Agreements to rescind contracts involving transfers of realty also must be evidenced by a writing or record.

When one party has fully performed, an agreement to cancel the original contract normally will *not* be enforceable unless there is additional consideration. Because the performing party has received no consideration for the promise to call off the original bargain, additional consideration is necessary to support a rescission contract.

Discharge by Novation

A contractual obligation may also be discharged through novation. A **novation** occurs when both of the parties to a contract agree to substitute a third party for one of the original parties. The requirements of a novation are as follows:

1. A previous valid obligation.
2. An agreement by all parties to a new contract.
3. The extinguishing of the old obligation (discharge of the prior party).
4. A new contract that is valid.

▶ **Example 18.11** Union Corporation contracts to sell its pharmaceutical division to British Pharmaceuticals, Ltd. Before the transfer is completed, Union, British Pharmaceuticals, and a third company, Otis Chemicals, execute a new agreement to transfer all of British Pharmaceuticals' rights and duties in the transaction to Otis Chemicals. As long as the new contract is supported by consideration, the novation will discharge the original contract (between Union and British Pharmaceuticals) and replace it with the new contract (between Union and Otis Chemicals). ◀

A novation expressly or impliedly revokes and discharges a prior contract. The parties involved may expressly state in the new contract that the old contract is now discharged. If the parties do not expressly discharge the old contract, it will be impliedly discharged if the new contract's terms are inconsistent with the old contract's terms. It is this immediate discharge of the prior contract that distinguishes a novation from both an accord and satisfaction, which will be discussed shortly, and an assignment of all rights, discussed in Chapter 17.

Discharge by Settlement Agreement

A compromise, or settlement agreement, that arises out of a genuine dispute over the obligations under an existing contract will be recognized at law. The agreement will be substituted as a new contract and will either expressly or impliedly revoke and discharge the obligations under the prior contract. In contrast to a novation, a substituted agreement does not involve a third party. Rather, the two original parties to the contract form a different agreement to substitute for the original one.

Discharge by Accord and Satisfaction

As discussed in Chapter 13, in an accord and satisfaction, the parties agree to accept performance that is different from the performance originally promised. An *accord* is a contract to perform some act to satisfy an existing contractual duty that is not yet discharged.[13] A *satisfaction* is the performance of the accord agreement. An accord and its satisfaction discharge the original contractual obligation.

Once the accord has been made, the original obligation is merely suspended until the accord agreement is fully performed. If it is not performed, the obligee (the one to whom performance is owed) can file a lawsuit based on the original obligation or the accord.

▶ **Example 18.12** Fahreed has a judgment against Ling for $8,000. Later, both parties agree that the judgment can be satisfied by Ling's transfer of his automobile to Fahreed. This agreement to accept the auto in lieu of $8,000 in cash is the accord. If Ling transfers the car to Fahreed, the accord is fully performed, and the debt is discharged. If Ling refuses to transfer the car, the accord is breached. Because the original obligation was merely suspended, Fahreed can sue Ling to enforce the original judgment for $8,000 in cash or bring an action for breach of the accord. ◀

---

12. UCC 2–209(2), (4).

13. *Restatement (Second) of Contracts*, Section 281.

SECTION 4
DISCHARGE BY OPERATION OF LAW

Under specified circumstances, contractual duties may be discharged by operation of law. These circumstances include material alteration of the contract, the running of the statute of limitations, bankruptcy, and the impossibility or impracticability of performance.

Material Alteration of the Contract

To discourage parties from altering written contracts, the law allows an innocent party to be discharged when the other party has materially altered a written contract without consent. For instance, a party alters a material term of a contract, such as the stated quantity or price, without the knowledge or consent of the other party. In this situation, the party who was unaware of the alteration can treat the contract as discharged or terminated.

Statutes of Limitations

As mentioned earlier in this text, statutes of limitations restrict the period during which a party can sue on a particular cause of action. After the applicable limitations period has passed, a suit can no longer be brought. The limitations period for bringing suits for breach of oral contracts usually is two to three years, and for written or otherwise recorded contracts, four to five years. Parties generally have ten to twenty years to file for recovery of amounts awarded in judgments, depending on state law.

Lawsuits for breach of a contract for the sale of goods generally must be brought within four years after the cause of action has accrued.[14] By their original agreement, the parties can reduce this four-year period to not less than one year, but they cannot agree to extend it.

Bankruptcy

A proceeding in bankruptcy attempts to allocate the debtor's assets to the creditors in a fair and equitable fashion. Once the assets have been allocated, the debtor receives a **discharge in bankruptcy.** A discharge in bankruptcy ordinarily prevents the creditors from enforcing most of the debtor's contracts. Partial payment of a debt *after* discharge in bankruptcy will not revive the debt.

Impossibility of Performance

After a contract has been made, supervening events (such as a fire) may make performance impossible in an objective sense. This is known as **impossibility of performance** and can discharge a contract.[15] The doctrine of impossibility of performance applies only when the parties could not have reasonably foreseen, at the time the contract was formed, the event that rendered performance impossible. Performance may also become so difficult or costly due to some unforeseen event that a court will consider it commercially unfeasible, or impracticable, as will be discussed later in the chapter.

Objective impossibility ("It can't be done") must be distinguished from *subjective impossibility* ("I'm sorry, I simply can't do it"). An example of subjective impossibility occurs when a party cannot deliver goods on time because of freight car shortages or cannot make payment on time because the bank is closed. In effect, in each of these situations the party is saying, "It is impossible for *me* to perform," not "It is impossible for *anyone* to perform." Accordingly, such excuses do not discharge a contract, and the nonperforming party is normally held in breach of contract.

WHEN PERFORMANCE IS IMPOSSIBLE Three basic types of situations may qualify as grounds for the discharge of contractual obligations based on impossibility of performance:[16]

1. *When one of the parties to a personal contract dies or becomes incapacitated prior to performance.*
   ▶ **Example 18.13** Frederic, a famous dancer, contracts with Ethereal Dancing Guild to play a leading role in its new ballet. Before the ballet can be performed, Frederic becomes ill and dies. His personal performance was essential to the completion of the contract. Thus, his death discharges the contract and his estate's liability for his nonperformance. ◀

2. *When the specific subject matter of the contract is destroyed.*

---

14. Section 2–725 of the UCC contains this four-year limitation period. A cause of action for a sales contract generally accrues when the breach occurs, even if the aggrieved party is not aware of the breach. A breach of warranty normally occurs when the seller delivers the goods to the buyer.

15. *Restatement (Second) of Contracts,* Section 261.
16. *Restatement (Second) of Contracts,* Sections 262–266; UCC 2–615.

▶ **Example 18.14** A-1 Farm Equipment agrees to sell Gunther the green tractor on its lot and promises to have the tractor ready for Gunther to pick up on Saturday. On Friday night, however, a truck veers off the nearby highway and smashes into the tractor, destroying it beyond repair. Because the contract was for this specific tractor, A-1's performance is rendered impossible owing to the accident. ◀

3. *When a change in law renders performance illegal.*
   ▶ **Example 18.15** Hopper contracts with Playlist, Inc., to create a Web site through which users can post and share movies, music, and other forms of digital entertainment. Hopper goes to work. Before the site is operational, however, Congress passes the No Online Piracy in Entertainment (NOPE) Act. The NOPE Act makes it illegal to operate a Web site on which copyrighted works are posted without the copyright owners' consent. In this situation, the contract is discharged by operation of law. The purpose of the contract has been rendered illegal, and contract performance is objectively impossible. ◀

TEMPORARY IMPOSSIBILITY An occurrence or event that makes performance temporarily impossible operates to suspend performance until the impossibility ceases.

Performance Normally Is Only Delayed. Once the temporary event ends, the parties ordinarily must perform the contract as originally planned. ▶ **Case in Point 18.16** Keefe Hurwitz contracted to sell his home in Louisiana to Wesley and Gwendolyn Payne for $241,500. Four days later, Hurricane Katrina made landfall and caused extensive damage to the house. Hurwitz refused to pay the cost ($60,000) for the necessary repairs before the deal closed. The Paynes filed a lawsuit to enforce the contract at the agreed-on price. Hurwitz argued that Hurricane Katrina had made it impossible for him to perform and had discharged his duties under the contract. The court, however, ruled that Hurricane Katrina had caused only a temporary impossibility. Hurwitz was required to pay for the necessary repairs and to perform the contract as written. He could not obtain a higher purchase price to offset the cost of the repairs.[17] ◀

Performance Can Be Discharged. Sometimes, the lapse of time and the change in circumstances surrounding the contract make it substantially more burdensome for the parties to perform the promised acts. In that situation,

the contract is discharged. ▶ **Case in Point 18.17** In 1942, actor Gene Autry was drafted into the U.S. Army. Being drafted rendered his contract with a Hollywood movie company temporarily impossible to perform, and it was suspended until the end of World War II in 1945. When Autry got out of the army, the purchasing power of the dollar had declined so much that performance of the contract would have been substantially burdensome to him. Therefore, the contract was discharged.[18] ◀

It can be difficult to predict how a court will—or should—rule on whether performance is impossible in a particular situation, as discussed in this chapter's *Insight into Ethics* feature on the following page.

Commercial Impracticability

Courts may also excuse parties from their performance when it becomes much more difficult or expensive than the parties originally contemplated at the time the contract was formed. For someone to invoke the doctrine of **commercial impracticability** successfully, however, the anticipated performance must become *significantly* difficult or costly.[19]

The added burden of performing not only must be extreme but also *must not have been known by the parties when the contract was made.* In one classic case, for example, a court held that a contract could be discharged because a party would otherwise have to pay ten times more than the original estimate to excavate a certain amount of gravel.[20]

Frustration of Purpose

Closely allied with the doctrine of commercial impracticability is the doctrine of **frustration of purpose.** In principle, a contract will be discharged if supervening circumstances make it impossible to attain the purpose both parties had in mind when they made the contract. As with commercial impracticability and impossibility, the supervening event must not have been reasonably foreseeable at the time the contract was formed.

There are some differences between the doctrines, however. Commercial impracticability usually involves an event that increases the cost or difficulty of performance. In contrast, frustration of purpose typically involves an event that decreases the value of what a party receives under the contract. [21]

See Exhibit 18–1 on the following page for a summary of the ways in which a contract can be discharged.

---

17. *Payne v. Hurwitz,* 978 So.2d 1000 (La.App. 1st Cir. 2008).

18. *Autry v. Republic Productions,* 30 Cal.2d 144, 180 P.2d 888 (1947).
19. *Restatement (Second) of Contracts,* Section 264.
20. *Mineral Park Land Co. v. Howard,* 172 Cal. 289, 156 P. 458 (1916).
21. See, for example, *East Capitol View Community Development Corp. v. Robinson,* 941 A.2d 1036 (D.C.App. 2008).

INSIGHT INTO ETHICS
When Is Impossibility of Performance a Valid Defense?

The doctrine of impossibility of performance is applied only when the parties could not have reasonably foreseen, at the time the contract was formed, the event or events that rendered performance impossible. In some cases, the courts may seem to go too far in holding that the parties should have foreseen certain events or conditions. Thus, the parties cannot avoid their contractual obligations under the doctrine of impossibility of performance.

Actually, courts today are more likely to allow parties to raise this defense than courts in the past, which rarely excused parties from performance under the impossibility doctrine. Indeed, until the latter part of the nineteenth century, courts were reluctant to discharge a contract even when performance appeared to be impossible.

Generally, the courts must balance the freedom of parties to contract (and thereby assume the risks involved) against the injustice that may result when certain contractual obligations are enforced. If the courts allowed parties to raise impossibility of performance as a defense to contractual obligations more often, freedom of contract would suffer.

LEGAL CRITICAL THINKING

INSIGHT INTO THE SOCIAL ENVIRONMENT

Why might those entering into contracts be worse off in the long run if the courts increasingly accept impossibility of performance as a defense?

EXHIBIT 18-1 Contract Discharge

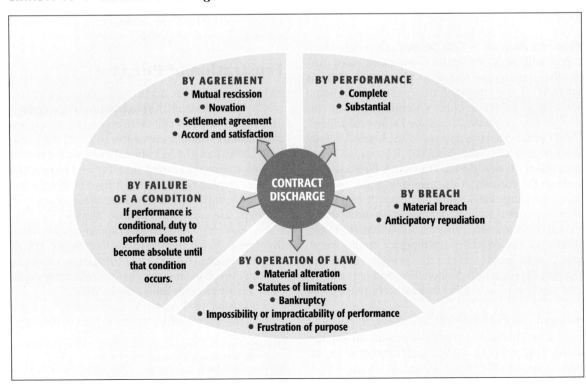

Reviewing: Performance and Discharge in Traditional and E-Contracts

Val's Foods signs a contract to buy 1,500 pounds of basil from Sun Farms, a small organic herb grower, as long as an independent organization inspects the crop and certifies that it contains no pesticide or herbicide residue. Val's has a contract with several restaurant chains to supply pesto and intends to use Sun Farms' basil in the pesto to fulfill these contracts. While Sun Farms is preparing to harvest the basil, an unexpected hailstorm destroys half the crop. Sun Farms attempts to purchase additional basil from other farms, but it is late in the season and the price is twice the normal market price. Sun Farms is too small to absorb this cost and immediately notifies Val's that it will not fulfill the contract. Using the information presented in the chapter, answer the following questions.

1. Suppose that the basil does not pass the chemical-residue inspection. Which concept discussed in the chapter might allow Val's to refuse to perform the contract in this situation?
2. Under which legal theory or theories might Sun Farms claim that its obligation under the contract has been discharged by operation of law? Discuss fully.
3. Suppose that Sun Farms contacts every basil grower in the country and buys the last remaining chemical-free basil anywhere. Nevertheless, Sun Farms is able to ship only 1,475 pounds to Val's. Would this fulfill Sun Farms' obligations to Val's? Why or why not?
4. Now suppose that Sun Farms sells its operations to Happy Valley Farms. As a part of the sale, all three parties agree that Happy Valley will provide the basil as stated under the original contract. What is this type of agreement called?

DEBATE THIS . . . *The doctrine of commercial impracticability should be abolished.*

Terms and Concepts

anticipatory repudiation 340	condition precedent 333	impossibility of performance 342
breach of contract 338	condition subsequent 335	mutual rescission 340
commercial impracticability 343	discharge 333	novation 341
concurrent conditions 335	discharge in bankruptcy 342	performance 333
condition 333	frustration of purpose 343	tender 336

ExamPrep

Issue Spotters

1. Ready Foods contracts to buy two hundred carloads of frozen pizzas from Stealth Distributors. Before Ready or Stealth starts performing, can the parties call off the deal? What if Stealth has already shipped the pizzas? Explain your answers. **(See page 341.)**
2. C&D Services contracts with Ace Concessions, Inc., to service Ace's vending machines. Later, C&D wants Dean Vending Services to assume the duties under a new contract. Ace consents. What type of agreement is this? Are Ace's obligations discharged? Why or why not? **(See page 341.)**

• Check your answers to the Issue Spotters against the answers provided in Appendix E at the end of this text.

Before the Test

Go to **www.cengagebrain.com**, enter the ISBN 9781285185248, and click on "Find" to locate this textbook's Web site. Then, click on "Access Now" under "Study Tools," and select Chapter 18 at the top. There, you will find a Practice Quiz that you can take to assess your mastery of the concepts in this chapter, as well as Flashcards and a Glossary of important terms.

Business Scenarios

18–1. Conditions of Performance. The Caplans contract with Faithful Construction, Inc., to build a house for them for $360,000. The specifications state "all plumbing bowls and fixtures . . . to be Crane brand." The Caplans leave on vacation, and during their absence, Faithful is unable to buy and install Crane plumbing fixtures. Instead, Faithful installs Kohler brand fixtures, an equivalent in the industry. On completion of the building contract, the Caplans inspect the work, discover the substitution, and refuse to accept the house, claiming Faithful has breached the conditions set forth in the specifications. Discuss fully the Caplans' claim. **(See page 333.)**

18–2. Discharge by Agreement. Junior owes creditor Iba $1,000, which is due and payable on June 1. Junior has been in a car accident, has missed a great deal of work, and consequently will not have the funds on June 1. Junior's father, Fred, offers to pay Iba $1,100 in four equal installments if Iba will discharge Junior from any further liability on the debt. Iba accepts. Is this transaction a novation or an accord and satisfaction? Explain. **(See page 341.)**

18–3. Impossibility of Performance. In the following situations, certain events take place after the contracts are formed. Discuss which of these contracts are discharged because the events render the contracts impossible to perform. **(See page 342.)**

(a) Jimenez, a famous singer, contracts to perform in your nightclub. He dies prior to performance.

(b) Raglione contracts to sell you her land. Just before title is to be transferred, she dies.

(c) Oppenheim contracts to sell you one thousand bushels of apples from her orchard in the state of Washington. Because of a severe frost, she is unable to deliver the apples.

(d) Maxwell contracts to lease a service station for ten years. His principal income is from the sale of gasoline. Because of an oil embargo by foreign oil-producing nations, gasoline is rationed, cutting sharply into Maxwell's gasoline sales. He cannot make his lease payments.

18–4. Implied Conditions. Heublein, Inc., makes wines and distilled spirits. Tarrant Distributors, Inc., agreed to distribute Heublein brands. When problems arose, the parties entered mediation. Under a settlement agreement, Heublein agreed to pay Tarrant the amount of its "net loss" as determined by Coopers & Lybrand, an accounting firm, according to a specified formula. The parties agreed that Coopers & Lybrand's calculation would be "final and binding." Heublein disagreed with Coopers & Lybrand's calculation, however, and refused to pay. The parties asked a court to rule on the dispute. Heublein argued that the settlement agreement included an implied condition precedent that Coopers & Lybrand would correctly apply the specified formula before Heublein would be obligated to pay. Tarrant pointed to the clause stating that the calculation would be "final and binding." With whom will the court agree, and why? **(See page 336.)**

Business Case Problems

18–5. Condition Precedent. Just Homes, LLC (JH), hired Mike Building & Contracting, Inc., to do $1.35 million worth of renovation work on three homes. Community Preservation Corporation (CPC) supervised Mike's work on behalf of JH. The contract stated that in the event of a dispute, JH would have to obtain the project architect's certification to justify terminating Mike. As construction progressed, relations between Mike and CPC worsened. At a certain point in the project, Mike requested partial payment, and CPC recommended that JH not make it. Mike refused to continue work without further payment. JH evicted Mike from the project. Mike sued for breach of contract. JH contended that it had the right to terminate the contract due to CPC's negative reports and Mike's failure to agree with the project's engineer. Mike moved for summary judgment for the amounts owed for work performed. Mike claimed that JH had not fulfilled the condition precedent—JH never obtained the project architect's certification for Mike's termination. Which of the two par-

ties involved breached the contract? Explain your answer. [*Mike Building & Contracting, Inc. v. Just Homes, LLC*, 27 Misc.3d 833, 901 N.Y.S.2d 458 (2010)] **(See page 333.)**

18–6. BUSINESS CASE PROBLEM
WITH SAMPLE ANSWER: Conditions of Performance.

James Maciel leased an apartment in Regent Village, a university-owned housing facility for Regent University (RU) students in Virginia Beach, Virginia. The lease ran until the end of the fall semester. Maciel had an option to renew the lease semester by semester as long as he maintained his status as an RU student. When Maciel completed his coursework for the spring semester, he told RU that he intended to withdraw. The university told him that he could stay in the apartment until May 31, the final day of the spring semester. Maciel asked for two additional weeks, but the university denied the request. On June 1, RU changed the locks on the apartment. Maciel entered through a window and e-mailed the university that he planned to stay "for another one

or two weeks." When he was charged with trespassing, Maciel argued that he had "legal authority" to occupy the apartment. Was Maciel correct? Explain. [Maciel v. Commonwealth, __ S.E.2d __ (Va.App. 2011)] **(See page 333.)**

• For a sample answer to Problem 18–6, go to Appendix F at the end of this text.

18–7. Material Breach. The Northeast Independent School District in Bexar County, Texas, hired STR Constructors, Ltd., to renovate a middle school. STR subcontracted the tile work in the school's kitchen to Newman Tile, Inc. (NTI). The project had already fallen behind schedule. As a result, STR allowed other workers to walk over and damage the newly installed tile before it had cured, forcing NTI to constantly redo its work. Despite NTI's requests for payment, STR remitted only half the amount due under their contract. When the school district refused to accept the kitchen, including the tile work, STR told NTI to quickly make the repairs. A week later, STR terminated their contract. Did STR breach the contract with NTI? Explain. [*STR Constructors, Ltd. v. Newman Tile, Inc.*, __ S.W.3d __, 2013 WL 632969 (Tex.App.—El Paso 2013)] **(See page 338.)**

18–8. A QUESTION OF ETHICS: Conditions.

King County, Washington, hired Frank Coluccio Construction Co. (FCCC) to act as general contractor for a public works project involving the construction of a small utility tunnel under the Duwamish Waterway. FCCC hired Donald B. Murphy Contractors, Inc. (DBM), as a subcontractor. DBM was responsible for constructing an access shaft at the eastern end of the tunnel. Problems arose during construction, including a "blow-in" of the access shaft that caused it to fill with water, soil, and debris. FCCC and DBM incurred substantial expenses from the repairs and delays. Under the project contract, King County was supposed to buy an insurance policy to "insure against physical loss or damage by perils included under an 'All-Risk' Builder's Risk policy." Any claim under this policy was to be filed through the insured. King County, which had general property damage insurance, did not obtain an all-risk builder's risk policy. For the losses attributable to the blow-in, FCCC and DBM submitted builder's risk claims, which the

county denied. FCCC filed a suit in a Washington state court against King County, alleging, among other claims, breach of contract. [Frank Coluccio Construction Co. v. King County, *136 Wash.App. 751, 150 P.3d 1147 (Div. 1 2007)*] **(See page 333.)**

(a) King County's property damage policy specifically excluded, at the county's request, coverage of tunnels. The county drafted its contract with FCCC to require the all-risk builder's risk policy and authorize itself to "sponsor" claims. When FCCC and DBM filed their claims, the county secretly colluded with its property damage insurer to deny payment. What do these facts indicate about the county's ethics and legal liability in this situation?

(b) Could DBM, as a third party to the contract between King County and FCCC, maintain an action on the contract against King County? Discuss.

(c) All-risk insurance is a promise to pay on the "fortuitous" happening of a loss or damage from any cause except those that are specifically excluded. Payment usually is not made on a loss that, at the time the insurance was obtained, the claimant subjectively knew would occur. If a loss results from faulty workmanship on the part of a contractor, should the obligation to pay under an all-risk policy be discharged? Explain.

18–9. SPECIAL CASE ANALYSIS: Material Breach.

Go to Case Analysis Case 18.3, *Kohel v. Bergen Auto Enterprises, L.L.C.*, on pages 338 and 339. Read the excerpt and answer the following questions.

(a) **Issue:** This case involved allegations of breach of contract involving which parties and for what actions?

(b) **Rule of Law:** What is the difference between a *material* breach and a *minor* breach of contract?

(c) **Applying the Rule of Law:** How did the court determine which party was in material breach of the contract in this case?

(d) **Conclusion:** Was the defendant liable for breach? Why or why not?

Legal Reasoning Group Activity

18–10. Anticipatory Repudiation. ABC Clothiers, Inc., has a contract with Taylor & Sons, a retailer, to deliver one thousand summer suits to Taylor's place of business on or before May 1. On April 1, Taylor receives a letter from ABC informing him that ABC will not be able to make the delivery as scheduled. Taylor is very upset, as he had planned a big ad campaign. **(See page 340.)**

(a) The first group will discuss whether Taylor can immediately sue ABC for breach of contract (on April 2).

(b) Now suppose that Taylor's son, Tom, tells his father that they cannot file a lawsuit until ABC actually fails to deliver the suits on May 1. The second group will decide who is correct, Taylor senior or Tom.

(c) Assume that Taylor & Sons can either file immediately or wait until ABC fails to deliver the goods. The third group will evaluate which course of action is better, given the circumstances.

CHAPTER 19

BREACH OF CONTRACT AND REMEDIES

When one party breaches a contract, the other party—the nonbreaching party—can choose one or more of several remedies. (Does changing terms of service on a social networking site constitute a breach of contract? See this chapter's *Insight into Social Media* feature on page 350 for a look at this issue.) A *remedy* is the relief provided for an innocent party when the other party has breached the contract. It is the means employed to enforce a right or to redress an injury.

The most common remedies available to a nonbreaching party include damages, *rescission* and *restitution, specific performance,* and *reformation.* As discussed in Chapter 1, a distinction is made between *remedies at law* and *remedies in equity.* Today, the remedy at law normally is monetary damages, which are discussed in the first part of this chapter. Equitable remedies include rescission and restitution, specific performance, and reformation, all of which will be examined later in the chapter. Usually, a court will not award an equitable remedy unless the remedy at law is inadequate.

SECTION 1
DAMAGES

A breach of contract entitles the nonbreaching party to sue for monetary damages. As discussed in Chapter 6, tort law damages are designed to compensate a party for harm suffered as a result of another's wrongful act. In the context of contract law, damages compensate the nonbreaching party for the loss of the bargain. Often, courts say that innocent parties are to be placed in the position they would have occupied had the contract been fully performed.[1]

Realize at the outset, though, that collecting damages through a court judgment requires litigation, which can be expensive and time consuming. Also keep in mind that court judgments are often difficult to enforce, particularly if the breaching party does not have sufficient assets to pay the damages awarded (as discussed in Chapter 3). For these reasons, most parties settle their lawsuits for damages (or other remedies) prior to trial.

Types of Damages

There are four broad categories of damages:

1. Compensatory (to cover direct losses and costs).

2. Consequential (to cover indirect and foreseeable losses).
3. Punitive (to punish and deter wrongdoing).
4. Nominal (to recognize wrongdoing when no monetary loss is shown).

Compensatory and punitive damages were discussed in Chapter 6 in the context of tort law. Here, we look at these types of damages, as well as consequential and nominal damages, in the context of contract law.

COMPENSATORY DAMAGES Damages that compensate the nonbreaching party for the *loss of the bargain* are known as *compensatory damages.* These damages compensate the injured party only for damages actually sustained and proved to have arisen directly from the loss of the bargain caused by the breach of contract. They simply replace what was lost because of the wrong or damage and, for this reason, are often said to "make the person whole."

Can an award of damages for a breach of contract elevate the nonbreaching party to a better position than he or she would have been in if the contract had not been breached? That was the question in the following case.

---

1. *Restatement (Second) of Contracts,* Section 347.

CASE ANALYSIS

Case 19.1 Hallmark Cards, Inc. v. Murley

United States Court of Appeals, Eighth Circuit, 703 F.3d 456 (2013).

IN THE LANGUAGE OF THE COURT

BYE, Circuit Judge.

* * * *

[Janet] Murley served as [Hallmark Cards, Inc.'s] vice-president of marketing from 1999 to 2002. In this capacity, she was responsible for product and business development, advertising, and research, and had access to confidential information including Hallmark's business plans, market research, and financial information. In 2002, Hallmark eliminated Murley's position as part of a corporate restructuring. Murley and Hallmark entered into a negotiated separation agreement which laid out the terms of Murley's departure. Pursuant to the agreement, Murley agreed not to work in the greeting card or gift industry for a period of eighteen months, solicit Hallmark employees, disclose or use any proprietary or confidential information, or retain any business records or documents relating to Hallmark. She also agreed to release Hallmark from any claims arising from her termination. In exchange, Hallmark offered Murley a $735,000 severance payment, eighteen months of paid COBRA benefits, executive outplacement services, and paid tax preparation for two years.

In 2006, after the expiration of her non-compete agreement, Murley accepted a consulting assignment with Recycled Paper Greetings ("RPG") for $125,000. Murley admits that in the course of that assignment, she disclosed to RPG confidential Hallmark information including slides from Hallmark's business model redesign, information regarding Hallmark's consumer buying process, and long-term industry analysis gathered from Hallmark's market research. Hallmark was unaware of Murley's disclosures until 2009, when RPG was purchased by American Greetings. Prior to the closing of that sale, American Greetings contacted Hallmark to arrange a third-party review of RPG's records to ensure none of Hallmark's confidential information was contained therein. The third-party reviewer uncovered a number of Hallmark's documents in the records and alerted Hallmark to its findings.

On May 14, 2009, Hallmark filed suit [in a federal district court] against Murley, alleging breach of contract.

Hallmark sought damages of $860,000, consisting of the $735,000 severance payment it made to Hurley under the parties' 2002 agreement and the $125,000 Murley received from RPG in exchange for her consulting services. * * * The jury returned a verdict in Hallmark's favor and awarded it exactly $860,000 in damages.

* * * This appeal followed.

* * * *

With respect to the $735,000, Murley contends Hallmark was not entitled to a return of its full payment under the parties' separation agreement because Murley fulfilled several material terms of that agreement (e.g., the release of liability and non-compete provisions). Under the circumstances, we cannot characterize the jury's reimbursement of Hallmark's original payment under the separation agreement as grossly excessive or glaringly unwarranted by the evidence. Hallmark's terms under the separation agreement clearly indicated its priority in preserving confidentiality. At trial, Hallmark presented ample evidence that Murley not only retained but disclosed Hallmark's confidential materials to a competitor in violation of the terms and primary purpose of that agreement. Thus, the jury's determination that Hallmark was entitled to a full refund of its $735,000 is not against the weight of the evidence.

With respect to the remaining $125,000 of the jury award, Murley argues Hallmark can claim no entitlement to her compensation by RPG for consulting services unrelated to Hallmark. We agree. *In an action for breach of contract, a plaintiff may recover the benefit of his or her bargain as well as damages naturally and proximately caused by the breach and damages that could have been reasonably contemplated by the defendant at the time of the agreement.* Moreover, the law cannot elevate the non-breaching party to a better position than she would have enjoyed had the contract been completed on both sides. By awarding Hallmark more than its $735,000 severance payment, the jury award placed Hallmark in a better position than it would find itself had Murley not breached the agreement. The jury's award of the $125,000 payment by RPG was, therefore, improper. We vacate the award and remand for the district court to reduce the fee award appropriately. [Emphasis added.]

* * * *

* * * So modified, the judgment will stand affirmed.

LEGAL REASONING QUESTIONS

1. What are compensatory damages? What is the standard measure of compensatory damages?

2. In this case, what was the basis for Hallmark's suit against Murley? How much did Hallmark seek to recover in the form of damages?

CASE 19.1 CONTINUES ▶

CASE 19.1 CONTINUED

3. What were Murley's arguments against the amount of damages that Hallmark requested?

4. Did the court award Hallmark the amount that it sought in damages? Why or why not?

Standard Measure. The standard measure of compensatory damages is the difference between the value of the breaching party's promised performance under the contract and the value of her or his actual performance. This amount is reduced by any loss that the injured party has avoided, however.

INSIGHT INTO SOCIAL MEDIA
Was Instagram's Revision of Its Terms of Service a Breach of Contract?

In 2012, Facebook acquired the social networking site Instagram for $715 million. Instagram is a photo-sharing service that also allows users to add filters and effects to the photos.

The Terms of Service Are a Contract

When you use social media or other services on the Internet or download an app for your mobile devices, you normally have to indicate that you accept the terms of service associated with that service or app. Of course, users rarely, if ever, actually read those terms. They simply click on "accept" and start using the service. By clicking on "accept," however, those users are entering into a contract.

Instagram Changes Its Terms of Service

In 2013, to the consternation of a number of users, Instagram changed its terms of service to give it the right and ability to transfer and otherwise use user content on the site, apparently without compensation. The new terms also limited users' ability to bring class-action lawsuits against Instagram, limited the damages they could recover to $100, and required arbitration of any disputes.

Lucy Funes, an Instagram user in California, filed a class-action lawsuit on behalf of herself and other users, claiming breach of contract and breach of the covenant of good faith and fair dealing that a contract implies.[a] Although Instagram subsequently modified the language that appeared to give it the right to use users' photos without compensation, it retained other controversial terms, including the mandatory arbitration clause and a provision allowing it to place ads in conjunction with user content.

Instagram Seeks Dismissal of the Lawsuit

While Funes is contending that Instagram breached their contract by changing its terms of service, Instagram argues that Funes cannot claim breach of contract. The reason is that she—and other users—were given thirty days' notice before the new terms of service took effect. Because Funes continued to use her account after that thirty-day period, Instagram maintains that, in effect, she agreed to the new terms.

Behind the Change in Terms of Service

In revising its terms of service, Instagram, or rather its new owner Facebook, was trying to monetize, or find a way to make revenue, from the many users of its site. A challenge for Facebook is how to translate its billions of users into profits. This challenge has become particularly acute for Facebook since its initial public offering in 2012. Now that it is a public company, Facebook must answer to its shareholders.

Facebook has faced a number of class-action lawsuits, including an ongoing suit for $15 billion from users who claim that Facebook has been "improperly tracking the Internet use of its members even after they have logged out of their accounts." As Facebook tries to increase its profits to please its shareholders, it is likely to face even more lawsuits from users who resent the company's efforts to monetize the content on its site.

LEGAL CRITICAL THINKING
INSIGHT INTO THE ETHICAL ENVIRONMENT

Within Instagram's current terms of service there is a statement, "We may not always identify paid services, sponsored content, or commercial communications as such." Is it ethical for Instagram to act this way? Discuss.

---

a. *Funes v. Instagram, Inc.,* 3:12-CV06482-WHA (N.D.Cal. 2012).

▶ **Example 19.1** Randall contracts to perform certain services exclusively for Hernandez during the month of March for $4,000. Hernandez cancels the contract and is in breach. Randall is able to find another job during March but can earn only $3,000. He can sue Hernandez for breach and recover $1,000 as compensatory damages. Randall can also recover from Hernandez the amount that he spent to find the other job. ◀

Expenses that are caused directly by a breach of contract—such as those incurred to obtain performance from another source—are known as **incidental damages.** Note that the measure of compensatory damages often varies by type of contract. Certain types of contracts deserve special mention.

Sale of Goods. In a contract for the sale of goods, the usual measure of compensatory damages is an amount equal to the difference between the contract price and the market price.[2] ▶ **Example 19.2** Medik Laboratories contracts to buy ten model UTS network servers from Cal Industries for $4,000 each. Cal Industries, however, fails to deliver the ten servers to Medik. The market price of the servers at the time Medik learns of the breach is $4,500. Therefore, Medik's measure of damages is $5,000 (10 × $500), plus any incidental damages (expenses) caused by the breach. ◀

When the buyer breaches and the seller has not yet produced the goods, compensatory damages normally equal lost profits on the sale, not the difference between the contract price and the market price.

Sale of Land. Ordinarily, because each parcel of land is unique, the remedy for a seller's breach of a contract for a sale of real estate is specific performance. The buyer is awarded the parcel of property for which she or he bargained (*specific performance* will be discussed more fully later in this chapter). When the buyer is the party in breach, the measure of damages is typically the difference between the contract price and the market price of the land. The same measure is used when specific performance is not available (because the seller has sold the property to someone else, for example). The majority of states follow this rule.

A minority of states follow a different rule when the seller breaches the contract and the breach is not

deliberate (intentional).[3] These states limit the prospective buyer's damages to a refund of any down payment made plus any expenses incurred (such as fees for title searches, attorneys, and escrows). Thus, the minority rule effectively returns purchasers to the positions they occupied prior to the sale, rather than giving them the benefit of the bargain.

Construction Contracts. The measure of damages in a building or construction contract varies depending on which party breaches and when the breach occurs.

1. *Breach by owner.* The owner may breach at three different stages—before performance has begun, during performance, or after performance has been completed. If the owner breaches *before performance has begun,* the contractor can recover only the profits that would have been made on the contract (that is, the total contract price less the cost of materials and labor).

   If the owner breaches *during performance,* the contractor can recover the profits plus the costs incurred in partially constructing the building. If the owner breaches *after the construction has been completed,* the contractor can recover the entire contract price, plus interest.

2. *Breach by contractor.* When the construction contractor breaches the contract—either by failing to begin construction or by stopping work partway through the project—the measure of damages is the cost of completion. The cost of completion includes reasonable compensation for any delay in performance. If the contractor finishes late, the measure of damages is the loss of use.

3. *Breach by both owner and contractor.* When the performance of both parties—the construction contractor and the owner—falls short of what their contract required, the courts attempt to strike a fair balance in awarding damages.

▶ **Case in Point 19.3** Jamison Well Drilling, Inc., contracted to drill a well for Ed Pfeifer for $4,130. Jamison drilled the well and installed a storage tank. The well did not comply with state health department requirements, however, and failed repeated tests for bacteria. The health department ordered the well to be abandoned and sealed. Pfeifer used the storage tank but paid Jamison nothing. Jamison filed a suit to

---

2. More specifically, the amount is the difference between the contract price and the market price at the time and place at which the goods were to be delivered or tendered. See Sections 2–708 and 2–713 of the Uniform Commercial Code (UCC).

3. "Deliberate" breaches include the seller's failure to convey (transfer title to) the land because the market price has gone up. "Nondeliberate" breaches include the seller's failure to convey the land because of a problem with the title, such as the discovery of an unknown *easement* that gives another party a right of use over the property.

EXHIBIT 19-1 Measurement of Damages—Breach of Construction Contracts

Party in Breach	Time of Breach	Measurement of Damages
Owner	Before construction has begun.	Profits (contract price less cost of materials and labor).
Owner	During construction.	Profits, plus costs incurred up to time of breach.
Owner	After construction is completed.	Full contract price, plus interest.
Contractor	Before construction has begun.	Cost in excess of contract price to complete work.
Contractor	Before construction is completed.	Generally, all costs incurred by owner to complete.

recover. The court held that Jamison was entitled to $970 for the storage tank but was not entitled to the full contract price because the well was not usable.[4] ◄

The rules concerning the measurement of damages in breached construction contracts are summarized in Exhibit 19–1 above.

Construction Contracts and Economic Waste. If the contractor substantially performs, a court may use the cost-of-completion formula, but only if requiring completion will not entail unreasonable economic waste. *Economic waste* occurs when the cost of repairing or completing the performance as required by the contract greatly outweighs the benefit to the owner.

▶ **Example 19.4** Halverson Contracting discovers that it will cost $20,000 to move a large coral rock eleven inches as specified in the contract. Changing the rock's position will alter the appearance of the project only slightly. In this situation, a court would likely conclude that full completion would involve economic waste. Thus, the contractor will not be required to incur addition $20,000 in expenses to complete performance. ◄

CONSEQUENTIAL DAMAGES Foreseeable damages that result from a party's breach of contract are called **consequential damages,** or *special damages.* They

---

4. *Jamison Well Drilling, Inc. v. Pfeifer,* 2011 Ohio 521 (2011).

differ from compensatory damages in that they are caused by special circumstances beyond the contract itself. They flow from the consequences, or results, of a breach. When a seller fails to deliver goods, knowing that the buyer is planning to use or resell those goods immediately, a court may award consequential damages for the loss of profits from the planned resale.

▶ **Example 19.5** Marty contracts to buy a certain quantity of Quench, a specialty sports drink, from Nathan. Nathan knows that Marty has contracted with Ruthie to resell and ship the Quench within hours of its receipt. The beverage will then be sold to fans attending the Super Bowl. Nathan fails to timely deliver the Quench. Marty can recover the consequential damages—the loss of profits from the planned resale to Ruthie—caused by the nondelivery. (If Marty purchases Quench from another vender, he can also recover compensatory damages for the difference between the contract price and the market price.) ◄

For the nonbreaching party to recover consequential damages, the breaching party must have known (or had reason to know) that special circumstances would cause the nonbreaching party to suffer an additional loss. This rule was enunciated in the following classic case. In reading this decision, it is helpful to understand that in the mid-nineteenth century, large flour mills customarily kept more than one main crankshaft on hand in the event that one broke and had to be repaired.

CLASSIC CASE 19.2

Hadley v. Baxendale
Court of Exchequer, 156 Eng.Rep. 145 (1854).

BACKGROUND AND FACTS The Hadleys (the plaintiffs) ran a flour mill in Gloucester, England. The main crankshaft attached to the steam engine in the mill broke, causing the mill to shut down. The crankshaft had to be sent to a foundry located in Greenwich so that a new shaft could be made to fit the other parts of the engine. Baxendale, the defendant, was a common carrier that transported the shaft

CASE 19.2 CONTINUED

from Gloucester to Greenwich. The freight charges were collected in advance, and Baxendale promised to deliver the shaft the following day. It was not delivered for a number of days, however. As a consequence, the mill was closed for several days. The Hadleys sued to recover the profits lost during that time. Baxendale contended that the loss of profits was "too remote" to be recoverable. The court held for the plaintiffs, and the jury was allowed to take into consideration the lost profits. The defendant appealed.

IN THE LANGUAGE OF THE COURT
ALDERSON, J. [Judge]

* * * *

* * * Where two parties have made a contract which one of them has broken, the damages which the other party ought to receive in respect of such breach of contract should be such as may fairly and reasonably be considered either arising naturally, [that is,] according to the usual course of things, from such breach of contract itself, or such as may reasonably be supposed to have been in the contemplation of both parties, at the time they made the contract, as the probable result of the breach of it. Now, if the special circumstances under which the contract was actually made were communicated by the plaintiffs to the defendants, and thus known to both parties, the damages resulting from the breach of such a contract, *which they would reasonably contemplate,* would be the amount of injury which would ordinarily follow from a breach of contract under these special circumstances so known and communicated.
* * * Now, in the present case, if we are to apply the principles above laid down, we find that the only circumstances here communicated by the plaintiffs to the defendants at the time the contract was made, were, that the article to be carried was the broken shaft of a mill, and that the plaintiffs were the millers of that mill. * * * Special circumstances were here never communicated by the plaintiffs to the defendants. It follows, therefore, that the loss of profits here cannot reasonably be considered such a consequence of the breach of contract as could have been fairly and reasonably contemplated by both the parties when they made this contract. [Emphasis added.]

DECISION AND REMEDY *The Court of Exchequer ordered a new trial. According to the court, to collect consequential damages, the plaintiffs would have to have given express notice of the special circumstances that caused the loss of profits.*

IMPACT OF THIS CASE ON TODAY'S LAW *This case established the rule that consequential damages are awarded only for injuries that the defendant could reasonably have foreseen as a probable result of the usual course of events following a breach. Today, the rule enunciated by the court in this case still applies. To recover consequential damages, the plaintiff must show that the defendant had reason to know or foresee that a particular loss or injury would occur.*

THE E-COMMERCE DIMENSION *If a Web merchant loses business due to a computer system's failure that can be attributed to malfunctioning software, can the merchant recover the lost profits from the software maker? Explain.*

PUNITIVE DAMAGES Punitive damages generally are not awarded in lawsuits for breach of contract. Because punitive damages are designed to punish a wrongdoer and set an example to deter similar conduct in the future, they have no legitimate place in contract law. A contract is simply a civil relationship between the parties. The law may compensate one party for the loss of the bargain—no more and no less. When a person's actions cause both a breach of contract and a tort (such as fraud), punitive damages may be available. Overall, though, punitive damages are almost never available in contract disputes.

NOMINAL DAMAGES When no actual damage or financial loss results from a breach of contract and only a technical injury is involved, the court may award **nominal damages** to the innocent party. Awards of nominal damages are often small, such as one dollar, but they do establish that the defendant acted wrongfully. Most lawsuits for nominal damages are brought as a matter of principle under the theory that a breach has occurred and some damages must be imposed regardless of actual loss.

▶ **Example 19.6** Jackson contracts to buy potatoes from Stanley at fifty cents a pound. Stanley breaches the contract and does not deliver the potatoes. In the meantime, the price of potatoes has fallen. Jackson is able to buy them in the open market at half the price he contracted for with Stanley. He is clearly better off because of Stanley's breach. Thus, because Jackson sustained only a technical injury and suffered no monetary loss, he is likely to be awarded only nominal damages if he brings a suit for breach of contract. ◀

Mitigation of Damages

In most situations, when a breach of contract occurs, the innocent injured party is held to a duty to mitigate, or reduce, the damages that he or she suffers. Under this doctrine of **mitigation of damages,** the duty owed depends on the nature of the contract.

RENTAL AGREEMENTS Some states require a landlord to use reasonable means to find a new tenant if a tenant abandons the premises and fails to pay rent. If an acceptable tenant is found, the landlord is required to lease the premises to this tenant to mitigate the damages recoverable from the former tenant.

The former tenant is still liable for the difference between the amount of the rent under the original lease and the rent received from the new tenant. If the landlord has not taken reasonable steps to find a new tenant, a court will likely reduce any award made by the amount of rent the landlord could have received had he or she done so.

EMPLOYMENT CONTRACTS In the majority of states, a person whose employment has been wrongfully terminated owes a duty to mitigate the damages suffered because of the employer's breach of the employment contract. In other words, a wrongfully terminated employee has a duty to take a similar job if one is available. If the employee fails to do this, the damages awarded will be equivalent to the person's former salary less the income he or she would have received in a similar job obtained by reasonable means.

The employer has the burden of proving that such a job existed and that the employee could have been hired. Normally, the employee is under no duty to take a job of a different type and rank.

Liquidated Damages versus Penalties

A **liquidated damages** provision in a contract specifies that a certain dollar amount is to be paid in the event of a *future* default or breach of contract. (*Liquidated* means determined, settled, or fixed.)

Liquidated damages differ from penalties. Although a **penalty** also specifies a certain amount to be paid in the event of a default or breach of contract, it is designed to penalize the breaching party, not to make the innocent party whole. Liquidated damages provisions usually are enforceable. In contrast, if a court finds that a provision calls for a penalty, the agreement as to the amount will not be enforced, and recovery will be limited to actual damages.

ENFORCEABILITY To determine if a particular provision is for liquidated damages or for a penalty, a court must answer two questions:

1. When the contract was entered into, was it apparent that damages would be difficult to estimate in the event of a breach?
2. Was the amount set as damages a reasonable estimate and not excessive?[5]

If the answers to both questions are yes, the provision normally will be enforced. If either answer is no, the provision usually will not be enforced.

▶ **Case in Point 19.7** James Haber contracted with B-Sharp Musical Productions, Inc., to provide a particular band to perform at his son's bar mitzvah for $30,000. The contract contained a liquidated damages clause under which if Haber canceled within ninety days of the date of the bar mitzvah, he would still owe $30,000 to B-Sharp. If he canceled more than ninety days beforehand, Haber would owe B-Sharp half of that amount ($15,000).

Haber canceled less than ninety days before the bar mitzvah and refused to pay B-Sharp the $25,000 balance due under the contract. B-Sharp sued. The court held that the liquidated damages clause was enforceable. The court reasoned that the expense and possibility of rebooking a canceled performance could not be determined at the time of contracting and that the clause provided a reasonable amount of damages.[6] ◀

---

5. *Restatement (Second) of Contracts,* Section 356(1).
6. *B-Sharp Musical Productions, Inc. v. Haber,* 27 Misc.3d 41, 899 N.Y.S.2d 792 (2010).

LIQUIDATED DAMAGES COMMON IN CERTAIN CONTRACTS Liquidated damages provisions are frequently used in construction contracts. For instance, a provision requiring a construction contractor to pay $300 for every day he or she is late in completing the project is a liquidated damages provision.

Such provisions are also common in contracts for the sale of goods.[7] In addition, contracts with entertainers and professional athletes often include liquidated damages provisions. ▶ **Example 19.8** A television network settled its contract dispute with *Tonight Show* host Conan O'Brien for $33 million. The amount of the settlement was somewhat less than the $40 million O'Brien could have received under a liquidated damages clause in his contract. ◀

SECTION 2
EQUITABLE REMEDIES

Sometimes, damages are an inadequate remedy for a breach of contract. In these situations, the nonbreaching party may ask the court for an equitable remedy. Equitable remedies include rescission and restitution, specific performance, and reformation.

Rescission and Restitution

As discussed in Chapter 18, *rescission* is essentially an action to undo, or terminate, a contract—to return the contracting parties to the positions they occupied prior to the transaction.[8] When fraud, a mistake, duress, undue influence, misrepresentation, or lack of capacity to contract is present, unilateral rescission is available. Rescission may also be available by statute.[9] The failure of one party to perform entitles the other party to rescind the contract. The rescinding party must give prompt notice to the breaching party.

RESTITUTION Generally, to rescind a contract, both parties must make **restitution** to each other by

returning goods, property, or funds previously conveyed.[10] If the property or goods can be returned, they must be. If the goods or property have been consumed, restitution must be made in an equivalent dollar amount.

Essentially, restitution involves the plaintiff's recapture of a benefit conferred on the defendant that has unjustly enriched her or him. ▶ **Example 19.9** Katie contracts with Mikhail to design a house for her. Katie pays Mikhail $9,000 and agrees to make two more payments of $9,000 (for a total of $27,000) as the design progresses. The next day, Mikhail calls Katie and tells her that he has taken a position with a large architectural firm in another state and cannot design the house. Katie decides to hire another architect that afternoon. Katie can obtain restitution of the $9,000. ◀

RESTITUTION IS NOT LIMITED TO RESCISSION CASES Restitution may be appropriate when a contract is rescinded, but the right to restitution is not limited to rescission cases. Because an award of restitution basically returns something to its rightful owner, a party can seek restitution in actions for breach of contract, tort actions, and other types of actions.

Restitution can be obtained when funds or property have been transferred by mistake or because of fraud or incapacity. Similarly, restitution might be available when there has been misconduct by a party in a confidential or other special relationship. Even in criminal cases, a court can order restitution of funds or property obtained through embezzlement, conversion, theft, or copyright infringement.

Specific Performance

The equitable remedy of **specific performance** calls for the performance of the act promised in the contract. This remedy is attractive to a nonbreaching party because it provides the exact bargain promised in the contract. It also avoids some of the problems inherent in a suit for damages, such as collecting a judgment and arranging another contract. In addition, the actual performance may be more valuable than the monetary damages.

Normally, however, specific performance will not be granted unless the party's legal remedy (monetary damages) is inadequate.[11] For this reason, contracts for the sale of goods rarely qualify for specific performance. The legal remedy—monetary damages—is ordinarily

---

7. Section 2–718(1) of the UCC specifically authorizes the use of liquidated damages provisions.

8. The rescission discussed here is *unilateral* rescission, in which only one party wants to undo the contract. In mutual rescission, which was discussed in Chapter 18, both parties agree to undo the contract. Mutual rescission discharges the contract. Unilateral rescission generally is available as a remedy for breach of contract.

9. Many states have statutes allowing individuals who enter "home solicitation contracts" to rescind those contracts within three business days for any reason. See, for example, California Civil Code Section 1689.5.

10. *Restatement (Second) of Contracts,* Section 370.

11. *Restatement (Second) of Contracts,* Section 359.

adequate in such situations because substantially identical goods can be bought or sold in the market. Only if the goods are unique will a court grant specific performance. For instance, paintings, sculptures, or rare books or coins are so unique that monetary damages will not enable a buyer to obtain substantially identical substitutes in the market.

SALE OF LAND A court may grant specific performance to a buyer in an action for a breach of contract involving the sale of land. In this situation, the legal remedy of monetary damages may not compensate the buyer adequately because every parcel of land is unique: the same land in the same location obviously cannot be obtained elsewhere. Only when specific performance is unavailable (such as when the seller has sold the property to someone else) will monetary damages be awarded instead.

▶ **Case in Point 19.10** Howard Stainbrook entered into a contract to sell Trent Low forty acres of mostly timbered land for $45,000. Low agreed to pay for a survey of the property and other costs in addition to the price. He gave Stainbrook a check for $1,000 to show his intent to fulfill the contract. One month later, Stainbrook died. His son David became the executor of the estate. After he discovered that the timber on the property was worth more than $100,000, David asked Low to withdraw his offer to buy the forty acres. Low refused and filed a suit against David seeking specific performance of the contract. The court found that because Low had substantially performed his obligations under the contract and offered to perform the rest, he was entitled to specific performance.[12] ◀

CONTRACTS FOR PERSONAL SERVICES Contracts for personal services require one party to work personally for another party. Courts generally refuse to grant specific performance of personal-service contracts because to order a party to perform personal services against his or her will amounts to a type of involuntary servitude.[13]

Moreover, the courts do not want to monitor contracts for personal services, which usually require the exercise of personal judgment or talent. ▶ **Example 19.11** Nicole contracts with a surgeon to perform surgery to remove a tumor on her brain. If he refuses, the court would not compel (nor would Nicole want) the surgeon to perform under those circumstances. A court cannot ensure meaningful performance in such a situation.[14] ◀

If a contract is not deemed personal, the remedy at law of monetary damages may be adequate if substantially identical service (such as lawn mowing) is available from other persons.

Reformation

Reformation is an equitable remedy used when the parties have *imperfectly* expressed their agreement in writing. Reformation allows a court to rewrite the contract to reflect the parties' true intentions.

Exhibit 19–2 on the following page graphically summarizes the remedies, including reformation, that are available to the nonbreaching party.

WHEN FRAUD OR MUTUAL MISTAKE IS PRESENT Courts order reformation most often when fraud or mutual mistake (for example, a clerical error) is present. Typically, a party seeks reformation so that some other remedy may then be pursued.

▶ **Example 19.12** If Carson contracts to buy a forklift from Yoshie but their contract mistakenly refers to a crane, a mutual mistake has occurred (see Chapter 15). Accordingly, a court can reform the contract so that it conforms to the parties' intentions and accurately refers to the forklift being sold. ◀

WRITTEN CONTRACT INCORRECTLY STATES THE PARTIES' ORAL AGREEMENT A court will also reform a contract when two parties enter into a binding oral contract but later make an error when they attempt to put the terms into writing. Normally, a court will allow into evidence the correct terms of the oral contract, thereby reforming the written contract.

COVENANTS NOT TO COMPETE Courts also may reform contracts when the parties have executed a written covenant not to compete (discussed in Chapter 14). If the covenant is for a valid and legitimate purpose (such as the sale of a business) but the area or time restraints of the covenant are unreasonable, reformation may occur. Some courts will reform the restraints by making them reasonable and then

---

12. *Stainbrook v. Low*, 842 N.E.2d 386 (Ind.App. 2006).

13. Involuntary servitude, or slavery, is contrary to the public policy expressed in the Thirteenth Amendment to the U.S. Constitution. A court can, however, enter an order (injunction) prohibiting a person who breached a personal-service contract from engaging in similar contracts for a period of time in the future.

14. Similarly, courts often refuse to order specific performance of construction contracts because courts are not set up to operate as construction supervisors or engineers.

EXHIBIT 19-2 Remedies for Breach of Contract

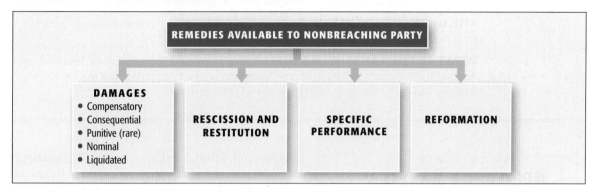

REMEDIES AVAILABLE TO NONBREACHING PARTY

DAMAGES
- Compensatory
- Consequential
- Punitive (rare)
- Nominal
- Liquidated

RESCISSION AND RESTITUTION

SPECIFIC PERFORMANCE

REFORMATION

will enforce the entire contract as reformed. Other courts, however, will throw out the entire restrictive covenant as illegal.

In the following case, a physician claimed that the covenant not to compete he signed was unreasonable and should therefore be declared illegal.

CASE 19.3

Emerick v. Cardiac Study Center, Inc.
166 Wash.App. 1039 (2012).

BACKGROUND AND FACTS Cardiac Study Center is a medical practice group of approximately fifteen cardiologists. In 2002, Cardiac hired Dr. Robert Emerick as an employee. In 2004, Emerick became a shareholder of Cardiac. He signed a shareholder agreement and an employment contract that included a covenant not to compete. Under the covenant, any physician who left the group would have to promise not to practice competitively in the surrounding area for a period of five years. In 2005, patients and other medical providers began to complain to Cardiac about Emerick's conduct. Some physicians stopped referring patients to Cardiac as a result. Finally, Cardiac terminated Emerick's employment in 2009. Emerick sued Cardiac seeking a declaration that the covenant not to compete was unenforceable. He prevailed at trial, and Cardiac appealed.

IN THE LANGUAGE OF THE COURT
ARMSTRONG, P.J. [Presiding Judge]

* * * *

* * * *Courts will enforce a covenant not to compete if it is reasonable and lawful.* We test reasonableness by asking (1) whether the restraint is necessary to protect the employer's business or goodwill, (2) whether it imposes on the employee any greater restraint than is reasonably necessary to secure the employer's business or goodwill, and (3) whether enforcing the covenant would injure the public through loss of the employee's service and skill to the extent that the court should not enforce the covenant, [that is,] whether it violates public policy. [Emphasis added.]

* * * Specifically, an employer has a "legitimate interest in protecting its existing client base" and in prohibiting the employee from taking its clients.

* * * Cardiac provided Emerick with an immediate client base and established referral sources when he moved to the area. Moreover, Emerick had access to Cardiac's business model and goodwill. These are all protectable business interests that the trial court should have considered in assessing the covenant's enforceability.

CASE 19.3 CONTINUES ▶

DECISION AND REMEDY *The state appellate court ruled in favor of Cardiac Study Center. The court reversed and remanded the trial court's decision and held that the covenant not to compete was reasonable.*

THE GLOBAL DIMENSION *Should an employer be able to restrict a former employee from engaging in a competing business on a global level? Why or why not?*

WHAT IF THE FACTS WERE DIFFERENT? *Suppose that Emerick had authored a nationally published book,* How to Avoid Cardiac Surgery through Diet and Exercise. *Could Cardiac have blocked the book's distribution in Cardiac's area based on the covenant not to compete?*

SECTION 3
RECOVERY BASED ON QUASI CONTRACT

In some situations, when no actual contract exists, a court may step in to prevent one party from being unjustly enriched at the expense of another party. As discussed in Chapter 11, quasi contract is a legal theory under which an obligation is imposed in the absence of an agreement.

The legal obligation arises because the law considers that the party accepting the benefits has made an implied promise to pay for them. Generally, when one party has conferred a benefit on another party, justice requires that the party receiving the benefit pay the reasonable value for it. The party conferring the benefit can recover in *quantum meruit,* which means "as much as he or she deserves."

When Quasi Contract Is Used

Quasi contract allows a court to act as if a contract exists when there is no actual contract or agreement between the parties. A court can also use this theory when the parties entered into a contract, but it is unenforceable for some reason.

Quasi-contractual recovery is often granted when one party has partially performed under a contract that is unenforceable. It provides an alternative to suing for damages and allows the party to recover the reasonable value of the partial performance. Depending on the case, the amount of the recovery may be measured either by the benefit received or by the detriment suffered.

▶ **Example 19.13** Ericson contracts to build two oil derricks for Petro Industries. The derricks are to be built over a period of three years, but the parties do not make a written contract. Thus, the writing requirement will bar enforcement of the contract.[15] After Ericson completes one derrick, Petro Industries informs him that it will not pay for the derrick. Ericson can sue Petro Industries under the theory of quasi contract. ◀

The Requirements of Quasi Contract

To recover under the theory of quasi contract, the party seeking recovery must show the following:

1. The party has conferred a benefit on the other party.
2. The party conferred the benefit with the reasonable expectation of being paid.
3. The party did not act as a volunteer in conferring the benefit.
4. The party receiving the benefit would be unjustly enriched if allowed to retain the benefit without paying for it.

Applying these requirements to *Example 19.13* above, Ericson can sue in quasi contract because all of the conditions for quasi-contractual recovery have been fulfilled. Ericson conferred a benefit on Petro Industries by building the oil derrick. Ericson built the derrick with the reasonable expectation of being paid. He was not intending to act as a volunteer. The derrick conferred an obvious benefit on Petro Industries. Petro Industries would be unjustly enriched if it was allowed to keep the derrick without paying Ericson for the work. Therefore, Ericson should be able to recover in *quantum meruit* the reasonable value of the oil derrick that was built, which is ordinarily equal to its fair market value.

Concept Summary 19.1 on the following page reviews all of the equitable remedies, including quasi

---

15. Contracts that by their terms cannot be performed within one year must be in writing to be enforceable (see Chapter 16).

CONCEPT SUMMARY 19.1
Equitable Remedies

REMEDY	DESCRIPTION
Rescission and Restitution	1. *Rescission*—A remedy whereby a contract is canceled and the parties are restored to the original positions that they occupied prior to the transaction. 2. *Restitution*—When a contract is rescinded, both parties must make restitution to each other by returning the goods, property, or funds previously conveyed.
Specific Performance	An equitable remedy calling for the performance of the act promised in the contract. Only available when monetary damages would be inadequate—such as in contracts for the sale of land or unique goods—and never available in personal-service contracts.
Reformation	An equitable remedy allowing a contract to be reformed, or rewritten, to reflect the parties' true intentions. Available when an agreement is imperfectly expressed in writing, such as when a mutual mistake has occurred.
Recovery Based on Quasi Contract	An equitable theory under which a party who confers a benefit on another with the reasonable expectation of being paid can seek a court order for the fair market value of the benefit conferred.

contract, that may be available in the event that a contract is breached.

SECTION 4
WAIVER OF BREACH

Under certain circumstances, a nonbreaching party may be willing to accept a defective performance of the contract. This knowing relinquishment of a legal right (that is, the right to require satisfactory and full performance) is called a **waiver.**

Consequences of a Waiver of Breach

When a waiver of a breach of contract occurs, the party waiving the breach cannot take any later action on it. In effect, the waiver erases the past breach, and the contract continues as if the breach had never occurred. Of course, the waiver of breach of contract extends only to the matter waived and not to the whole contract.

Reasons for Waiving a Breach

Businesspersons often waive breaches of contract to obtain whatever benefit is still possible out of the contract. For instance, a seller contracts with a buyer to deliver to the buyer ten thousand tons of coal on or before November 1. The contract calls for the buyer to pay by November 10 for coal delivered. Because of a coal miners' strike, coal is hard to find. The seller breaches the contract by not tendering delivery until November 5. The buyer will likely choose to waive the seller's breach, accept delivery of the coal, and pay as contracted.

Waiver of Breach and Subsequent Breaches

Ordinarily, a waiver by a contracting party will not operate to waive subsequent, additional, or future breaches of contract. This is always true when the subsequent breaches are unrelated to the first breach. ▶ **Example 19.14** Ashton owns a multimillion-dollar apartment complex that is under construction. Ashton allows the contractor to complete a stage of construction late. By doing so, Ashton waives his right to sue for the delay. Ashton does not, however, waive the right to sue for failure to comply with engineering specifications on the same job. ◀

PATTERN-OF-CONDUCT EXCEPTION A waiver can extend to subsequent defective performance if a reasonable person would conclude that similar defective performance in the future will be acceptable. Therefore, a *pattern of conduct* that waives a number of successive breaches will operate as a continued waiver. To change this result, the nonbreaching party should give notice to the breaching party that full performance will be required in the future.

EFFECT ON THE CONTRACT The party who has rendered defective or less-than-full performance remains liable for the damages caused by the breach of contract. In effect, the waiver operates to keep the contract going. The waiver prevents the nonbreaching party from declaring the contract at an end or rescinding the contract. The contract continues, but the nonbreaching party can recover damages caused by the defective or less-than-full performance.

SECTION 5
CONTRACT PROVISIONS LIMITING REMEDIES

A contract may include provisions stating that no damages can be recovered for certain types of breaches or that damages will be limited to a maximum amount. The contract may also provide that the only remedy for breach is replacement, repair, or refund of the purchase price. The contract may also provide that one party can seek injunctive relief if the other party breaches the contract (for an example, see Paragraph 11 in *Appendix to Chapter 19: Reading and Analyzing Contracts,* following this chapter). Provisions stating that no damages can be recovered are called *exculpatory clauses* (see Chapter 14). Provisions that affect the availability of certain remedies are called *limitation-of-liability clauses.*

The UCC Allows Sales Contracts to Limit Remedies

The Uniform Commercial Code (UCC) provides that in a contract for the sale of goods, remedies can be limited. We will examine the UCC provisions on limited remedies in Chapter 22, in the context of the remedies available on the breach of a contract for the sale or lease of goods.[16]

Enforceability of Limitation-of-Liability Clauses

Whether a limitation-of-liability clause in a contract will be enforced depends on the type of breach that is excused by the provision. Normally, a provision excluding liability for fraudulent or intentional injury will not be enforced. Likewise, a clause excluding liability for illegal acts, acts that are contrary to public policy, or violations of law will not be enforced. A clause that excludes liability for negligence may be enforced in some situations when the parties have roughly equal bargaining positions.

▶ **Case in Point 19.15** Engineering Consulting Services, Ltd. (ECS), contracted with RSN Properties, Inc, a real estate developer. ECS was to perform soil studies for $2,200 and render an opinion on the use of septic systems in a particular subdivision being developed. A clause in the contract limited ECS's liability to RSN to the value of the engineering services or the sum of $50,000, whichever was greater.

ECS concluded that most of the lots were suitable for septic systems, so RSN proceeded with the development. RSN constructed the roads and water lines to the subdivision in reliance on ECS's conclusions, which turned out to be incorrect. RSN sued ECS for breach of contract and argued that the limitation of liability was against public policy and unenforceable. The court, however, enforced the limitation-of-liability clause as "a reasonable allocation of risks in an arm's-length business transaction."[17] ◀

---
16. See UCC 2–719(1).
17. *RSN Properties, Inc. v. Engineering Consulting Services, Ltd.,* 301 Ga.App. 52, 686 S.E.2d 853 (2009).

Reviewing: Breach of Contract and Remedies

Kyle Bruno enters a contract with X Entertainment to be a stuntman in a movie. Bruno is widely known as the best motorcycle stuntman in the business, and the movie to be produced, *Xtreme Riders,* has numerous scenes involving high-speed freestyle street-bike stunts. Filming is set to begin August 1 and end by December 1 so that the film can be released the following summer. Both parties to the contract have stipulated that the filming must end on time to capture the profits from the summer movie market. The contract states that Bruno will be paid 10 percent of the net proceeds from the movie for his stunts.

The contract also includes a liquidated damages provision, which specifies that if Bruno breaches the contract, he will owe X Entertainment $1 million. In addition, the contract includes a limitation-of-liability clause stating that if Bruno is injured during filming, X Entertainment's liability is limited to nominal damages. Using the information presented in the chapter, answer the following questions.

1. One day, while Bruno is preparing for a difficult stunt, he gets into an argument with the director and refuses to perform any stunts at all. Can X Entertainment seek specific performance of the contract? Why or why not?
2. Suppose that while performing a high-speed wheelie on a motorcycle, Bruno is injured by the intentionally reckless act of an X Entertainment employee. Will a court be likely to enforce the limitation-of-liability clause? Why or why not?
3. What factors would a court consider to determine whether the $1 million liquidated damages provision constitutes valid damages or is a penalty?
4. Suppose that there was no liquidated damages provision (or the court refused to enforce it) and X Entertainment breached the contract. The breach caused the release of the film to be delayed until after summer. Could Bruno seek consequential (special) damages for lost profits from the summer movie market in that situation? Explain.

DEBATE THIS . . . *Courts should always uphold limitation-of-liability clauses, whether or not the two parties to the contract had equal bargaining power.*

Terms and Concepts

consequential damages 352
incidental damages 351
liquidated damages 354
mitigation of damages 354

nominal damages 353
penalty 354
reformation 356
restitution 355

specific performance 355
waiver 359

ExamPrep

Issue Spotters

1. Greg contracts to build a storage shed for Haney, who pays Greg in advance, but Greg completes only half the work. Haney pays Ipswich $500 to finish the shed. If Haney sues Greg, what would be the measure of recovery? **(See page 348.)**
2. Lyle contracts to sell his ranch to Marley, who is to take possession on June 1. Lyle delays the transfer until August 1. Marley incurs expenses in providing for cattle that he bought for the ranch. When they made the contract, Lyle had no reason to know of the cattle. Is Lyle liable for Marley's expenses in providing for the cattle? Why or why not? **(See page 352.)**

• Check your answers to the Issue Spotters against the answers provided in Appendix E at the end of this text.

Before the Test

Go to **www.cengagebrain.com**, enter the ISBN 9781285185248, and click on "Find" to locate this textbook's Web site. Then, click on "Access Now" under "Study Tools," and select Chapter 19 at the top. There, you will find a Practice Quiz that you can take to assess your mastery of the concepts in this chapter, as well as Flashcards and a Glossary of important terms.

Business Scenarios

19–1. Liquidated Damages. Cohen contracts to sell his house and lot to Windsor for $100,000. The terms of the contract call for Windsor to pay 10 percent of the purchase price as a

deposit toward the purchase price, or a down payment. The terms further stipulate that if the buyer breaches the contract, Cohen will retain the deposit as liquidated damages.

Windsor pays the deposit, but because her expected financing of the $90,000 balance falls through, she breaches the contract. Two weeks later Cohen sells the house and lot to Ballard for $105,000. Windsor demands her $10,000 back, but Cohen refuses, claiming that Windsor's breach and the contract terms entitle him to keep the deposit. Discuss who is correct. **(See page 354.)**

19–2. Specific Performance. In which of the following situations would specific performance be an appropriate remedy? Discuss fully. **(See page 355.)**

(a) Thompson contracts to sell her house and lot to Cousteau. Then, on finding another buyer willing to pay a higher purchase price, she refuses to deed the property to Cousteau.

(b) Amy contracts to sing and dance in Fred's nightclub for one month, beginning May 1. She then refuses to perform.

(c) Hoffman contracts to purchase a rare coin owned by Erikson, who is breaking up his coin collection. At the last minute, Erikson decides to keep his coin collection intact and refuses to deliver the coin to Hoffman.

(d) ABC Corp. has three shareholders: Panozzo, who owns 48 percent of the stock; Chang, who owns another 48 percent; and Ryan, who owns 4 percent. Ryan contracts to sell her 4 percent to Chang. Later, Ryan refuses to transfer the shares to Chang.

Business Case Problems

19–3. Quasi Contract. Middleton Motors, Inc., a struggling Ford dealership in Madison, Wisconsin, sought managerial and financial assistance from Lindquist Ford, Inc., a successful Ford dealership in Bettendorf, Iowa. While the two dealerships negotiated the terms for the services and a cash infusion, Lindquist sent Craig Miller, its general manager, to assume control of Middleton. After about a year, the parties had not agreed on the terms, Lindquist had not invested any funds, Middleton had not made a profit, and Miller was fired without being paid. Lindquist and Miller filed a suit in a federal district court against Middleton based on quasi contract, seeking to recover Miller's pay for his time. What are the requirements to recover on a theory of quasi contract? Which of these requirements is most likely to be disputed in this case? Why? [*Lindquist Ford, Inc. v. Middleton Motors, Inc.*, 557 F.3d 469 (7th Cir. 2009)] **(See page 358.)**

19–4. Liquidated Damages and Penalties. Planned Pethood Plus, Inc., is a veterinarian-owned clinic. It borrowed $389,000 from KeyBank at an interest rate of 9.3 percent per year for ten years. The loan had a "prepayment penalty" clause that clearly stated that if the loan was repaid early, a specific formula would be used to assess a lump-sum payment to extinguish the obligation. The sooner the loan was paid off, the higher the prepayment penalty. After a year, the veterinarians decided to pay off the loan. KeyBank invoked a prepayment penalty of $40,525.92, which was equal to 10.7 percent of the balance due. The veterinarians sued, contending that the prepayment requirement was unenforceable because it was a penalty. The bank countered that the amount was not a penalty but liquidated damages and that the sum was reasonable. The trial court agreed with the bank, and the veterinarians appealed. Was the loan's prepayment charge reasonable, and should it have been enforced? Why or why not? [*Planned Pethood Plus, Inc. v. KeyCorp, Inc.*, 228 P.3d 262 (Colo.App. 2010)] **(See page 354.)**

19–5. Measure of Damages. Before buying a house, Dean and Donna Testa hired Ground Systems, Inc. (GSI), to inspect the sewage and water disposal system. GSI reported a split system with a watertight septic tank, a wastewater tank, a distribution box, and a leach field. The Testas bought the house. Later, Dean saw that the system was not as GSI described—there was no distribution box or leach field, and there was only one tank, which was not watertight. The Testas arranged for the installation of a new system and sold the house. Assuming that GSI is liable for breach of contract, what is the measure of damages? [*Testa v. Ground Systems, Inc.*, 206 N.J. 330, 20 A.3d 435 (App.Div. 2011)] **(See page 348.)**

19–6. BUSINESS CASE PROBLEM WITH SAMPLE ANSWER: Consequential Damages.

 After submitting the high bid at a foreclosure sale, David Simard entered into a contract to purchase real property in Maryland for $192,000. Simard defaulted (failed to pay) on the contract. A state court ordered the property to be resold at Simard's expense, as required by state law. The property was then resold for $163,000, but the second purchaser also defaulted on his contract. The court then ordered a second resale, resulting in a final price of $130,000. Assuming that Simard is liable for consequential damages, what is the extent of his liability? Is he liable for losses and expenses related to the first resale? If so, is he also liable for losses and expenses related to the second resale? Why or why not? [Burson v. Simard, 35 A.3d 1154 (Md. 2012)] **(See page 352.)**

- For a sample answer to Problem 19–6, go to Appendix F at the end of this text.

19–7. Liquidated Damages. Cuesport Properties, LLC, sold a condominium in Anne Arundel County, Maryland, to Critical Developments, LLC. As part of the sale, Cuesport agreed to build a wall between Critical Developments' unit and an adjacent unit within thirty days of closing. If Cuesport failed to do so, it was to pay $126 per day until completion. This was an estimate of the amount of rent that Critical Developments would lose until the wall was finished and the unit could be rented. Actual damages were otherwise difficult to estimate at the time of the contract. The wall was built on time, but without a county permit, and it did not comply with the county building code. Critical Developments did not modify the wall to comply with the code until 260 days after the date of the contract deadline for completion of the wall. Does Cuesport have to pay Critical Developments $126 for each of the 260 days? Explain. [*Cuesport Properties, LLC v. Critical Developments, LLC,* 209 Md.App. 607, 61 A.3d 91 (2013)] **(See page 354.)**

19–8. A QUESTION OF ETHICS: Remedies.

On a weekday, Tamara Cohen, a real estate broker, showed a townhouse owned by Ray and Harriet Mayer to Jessica Seinfeld, the wife of comedian Jerry Seinfeld. On the weekend, when Cohen was unavailable because her religious beliefs prevented her from working, the Seinfelds revisited the townhouse on their own and agreed to buy it. The contract stated that the "buyers will pay buyer's real estate broker's fees." [Cohen v. Seinfeld, 15 Misc.3d 1118(A), 839 N.Y.S.2d 432 (Sup. 2007)] **(See page 355.)**

(a) Is Cohen entitled to payment even though she was not available to show the townhouse to the Seinfelds on the weekend? Explain.

(b) What obligation do parties involved in business deals owe to each other with respect to their religious beliefs? How might the situation in this case have been avoided?

Legal Reasoning Group Activity

19–9. Breach and Remedies. Frances Morelli agreed to sell Judith Bucklin a house in Rhode Island for $177,000. The sale was supposed to be closed by September 1, when the parties were to exchange the deed for the price. The contract included a provision that "if Seller is unable to convey good, clear, insurable, and marketable title, Buyer shall have the option to: (a) accept such title as Seller is able to convey without reduction of the Purchase Price, or (b) cancel this Agreement and receive a return of all Deposits."

An examination of the public records revealed that the house did not have marketable title. Bucklin offered Morelli additional time to resolve the problem, and the closing did not occur as scheduled. Morelli decided "the deal is over" and offered to return the deposit. Bucklin refused and, in mid-October, decided to exercise her option to accept the house without marketable title. She notified Morelli, who did not respond. She then filed a lawsuit against Morelli in a state court.

(a) One group will discuss whether Morelli breached the contract and will decide in whose favor the court should rule.

(b) A second group will assume that Morelli did breach the contract and will determine what the appropriate remedy is in this situation.

APPENDIX TO CHAPTER 19

READING AND ANALYZING CONTRACTS

As the text and cases in this unit have indicated, businesses use contracts to make their transactions more predictable. Contracts allow parties to clarify their obligations in great detail. Businesses also use contracts to resolve anticipated problems or conflicts and to clarify responsibility in the event of a breach. An understanding of what is in a typical contract is crucial to using contracts effectively.

Being able to read and understand a contract takes some practice, however. Contract terms often are highly technical and complex, and sometimes the vocabulary and phrasing can be unfamiliar. Nevertheless, businesspersons need to be able to understand the meaning of various contract provisions so that they will know what their business's obligations and rights are under the contract.

Reading a Contract

A contract is generally intended to serve two purposes:

1. To achieve some commercial purpose—such as, a sale of goods, a lease of property, or an employment agreement.
2. To prevent future conflict by clarifying the obligations and rights of the parties.

Parties should address the details of the business agreement and also should think strategically about how a conflict should be resolved if something goes awry.

Different types of contracts will have different provisions. Sales contracts should contain information on the products being sold, the quantity, the price, and delivery terms. Employment contracts may contain information on the term of employment, employment duties, confidentiality and nondisclosure of the employer's documents and information, and restrictions on competing with the employer after leaving the position.

Although standard forms exist for many types of contracts, the parties to a particular contract may have specific requirements and thus may need to tailor the contract to fit their transaction. A larger transaction or more specialized goods or real estate will require a more specific and probably a longer contract. For example, a sales contract between Airbus and American Airlines for the sale of an Airbus S.A.S. plane was more than 109 pages, not counting the eleven exhibits that followed the main contract.[1]

Regardless of the specificity of the contract provisions, it is important for a businessperson to read and evaluate the responsibilities or commitments of both parties to the contract. Sometimes, a single word or phrase can make an enormous difference. For example, a rental contract for a house may state that the owner is responsible for any plumbing issues, or it may specify that the renter is the responsible party. If a plumber has to be called to deal with clogged pipes on a holiday, that single phrase in the contract will determine who has to pay the plumber's very high holiday rates.

---

1. "Sample Business Contracts," *Onecle.com,* July 14, 2012.

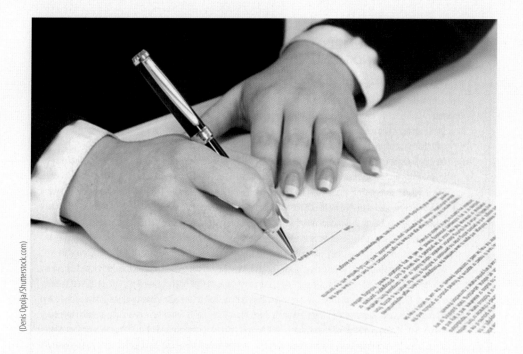

(Denis Opolja/Shutterstock.com)

Contract Analysis Exercise

The sample contract on pages 366–369 is based on an actual employment-related contract between a company called Boulder Dry and its chief financial officer (CFO). As you read the contract, think about the following questions:

1. Which party seems to have had the stronger bargaining position, and why?
2. Which specific provisions favor the employer?
3. Which specific provisions favor the employee?
4. The parties' main intentions in signing this contract were to protect the firm's confidential information and to explain how the CFO could use that information. Which provisions are related to those two purposes?
5. Which provisions seem entirely unrelated to the main purposes? Why are these other provisions included in the contract? What do they do for the parties?
6. What terms in the contract do you find difficult to understand?
7. As a potential employee being asked to sign this agreement, what concerns might you have?
8. If after one year the employee resigns from Boulder Dry, what provisions of this contract should the employee have reviewed before resigning because they would affect his or her future? When leaving the company, what actions would the employee take to ensure that he or she was in compliance with all obligations?

SEE SAMPLE CONTRACT ON THE FOLLOWING PAGES.

EMPLOYEE NONCOMPETITION
AND NONDISCLOSURE AGREEMENT

In consideration of my employment or continued employment, with Boulder Dry (the "Company"), and the compensation received from the Company, I hereby agree as follows:

1. *Proprietary Information and Inventions:* I understand and acknowledge that:

   A. The Company is engaged in research, development, production, marketing, and servicing. I am expected to make new contributions and inventions of value to the Company as part of my employment.

   B. My employment creates a relationship of trust between the Company and me with respect to information that may be made known to me or learned by me during my employment.

   C. The Company possesses information that has been discovered or developed by the Company that has commercial value to the Company and is treated by the Company as confidential. All such information is hereinafter called "Proprietary Information," which term shall include, but shall not be limited to, systems, processes, data, computer programs, discoveries, marketing plans, strategies, forecasts, new products, unpublished financial statements, licenses, and customer and supplier lists. The term "Proprietary Information" shall not include any of the foregoing that is in the public domain.

   D. All existing confidential lists of customers of the Company, and all confidential lists of customers developed during my employment, are the sole and exclusive property of the Company and I shall not have any right, title, or interest therein.

2. *Ownership of Proprietary Information:* All Proprietary Information shall be the sole property of the Company, including patents, copyrights, and trademarks. I hereby assign to the Company any rights I may have or acquire in such Proprietary Information. Both during and after my employment, I will keep in strictest confidence and trust all Proprietary Information. I will not use or disclose any Proprietary Information without the written consent of the Company, except as may be necessary in performing my duties as a Company employee.

3. *Commitment to Company and Other Employment:* During my employment, I will devote substantially all of my time to the Company, and I will not, without the Company's prior written consent, engage in any employment or business other than for the Company.

4. *Documentation:* Upon the termination of my employment, I will deliver to the Company all documents, computer programs, data, and other materials of any nature pertaining to my work with the Company. I will not take any originals or reproductions of the foregoing that are embodied in a tangible medium of expression.

5. *Disclosure of Inventions:* I will promptly disclose to the Company all discoveries, designs, inventions, blueprints, computer programs, and data ("Inventions") made by me, either alone or jointly with others, during my employment. Inventions include by definition those things that are related to the business of the Company or that result from the use of property owned, leased, or contracted for by the Company.

6. *Ownership of Inventions:* All Inventions shall be the sole property of the Company, and the Company shall be the sole owner of all patents, copyrights, trademarks, and other rights. I assign to the Company any rights I may have or acquire in such Inventions. I shall assist the Company to obtain and enforce patents, copyrights, trademarks, and other rights and protections relating to Inventions. This obligation shall continue beyond the termination of my employment, but the Company shall compensate me at a reasonable rate after my termination.

7. *Other Agreements:* I represent and warrant that this Agreement and the performance of it do not breach any other agreement to which I am a party. I have not entered into and shall not enter into any agreement in conflict with this Agreement.

8. *Use of Confidential Information of Other Persons:* I have not brought and will not bring with me to the Company any materials or documents of an employer or a former employer that are not generally available to the public. If I desire or need to use any materials from a prior employer, I will obtain express written authorization from such employer.

9. *Restrictive Covenant:* I hereby acknowledge my possession of Proprietary Information and the highly competitive nature of the business of the Company. I will not, during my employment and for three (3) years following my termination, directly or indirectly engage in any competitive business or assist others in engaging in any competitive business. I understand that this Section is not meant to prevent me from earning a living. It does intend to prevent any competitive business from gaining any unfair advantage from my knowledge of Proprietary Information. I understand that by making my new employer aware of the provisions of this Section 9, that employer can take such action as to avoid my breaching the provisions hereof and to indemnify me in the event of a breach.

COMMENTS TO CONTRACT PARAGRAPHS

Paragraph 1A. This is essentially a broad description of the employee's role at the company and explains why this agreement is necessary. Often, a clause like this precedes a statement indicating that the employer gets to keep any value that the employee adds to the firm.

Paragraph 1B. This paragraph establishes that a relationship of trust and confidence exists between employer and employee. Through this clause, both parties are agreeing they owe duties to each other related to information that benefits the company. The clause implies that that there will be negative consequences for the employee if he or she breaks that relationship.

Paragraph 1C. This paragraph establishes what the term "Proprietary Information" means. In contracts, terms that are capitalized and placed in quotation marks (sometimes in parentheses as well) are called "defined terms." Whenever the term "Proprietary Information" appears throughout the rest of the contract, it will have the definition set out in this paragraph. The definition is extremely broad and captures almost any intellectual property, data, and similar items. The contract asserts that this information is important to the business and gives the company some strategic advantage.

Paragraph 1D. This clause clarifies that customer lists belong to the employer even if the employee develops or expands the lists in some way. This may become important if the employee leaves the company because the clause clarifies that the employee may not recruit or "steal" customers.

Paragraph 2. Here, we see the defined term "Proprietary Information" again. This paragraph documents that the employer owns all Proprietary Information, as defined, even if it was created by the employee. Further, the employee agrees to give the employer any legal rights that the employee may obtain to any Proprietary Information.

Paragraph 3. In this clause, the employee promises that he or she will work full time for the employer and will not take any additional employment without the employer's permission.

Paragraph 4. This clause further asserts that the company takes the confidential nature of the Proprietary Information seriously. Here, the employee promises that if he or she leaves the company's employment, he or she will turn over any work-related material to the company.

Paragraph 5. If the employee creates something of any kind at work, he or she must tell the employer about it, and the employer will receive any disclosures confidentially. The contract goes out of its way to ensure that almost anything the employee invents at work or that is related to work fits under this paragraph. Such items are given a new term called "Inventions." Note that the definition of inventions includes the same items that are in the definition of Proprietary Information as well as some additional ones. The paragraphs discussing Proprietary Information deal with information that the company already possesses and will continue to possess and that the employee will access or need. This paragraph expands the obligations of the employee to what could be called new proprietary information, defined as "Inventions."

Paragraph 6. Just as the employee agreed to give any right in already existing information (such as a modified customer list) to the employer, here the employee promises to give all legal rights to inventions to the employer. In addition, because the rights may originally belong to the employee, the employee promises to help the employer secure any rights or protections necessary to increase the value of the invention. This obligation to help the employer continues to exist after the employee leaves the firm, and the employer agrees to pay for the work required in that situation. The employer is making sure that it can keep anything the employee invents during work time or with company resources.

Paragraph 7. The employer wants to ensure that this contract does not conflict with any others the employee may have already signed. Here, the employee affirms that he or she has made no conflicting agreements. The clause implies that the employee will be responsible for any consequences that arise from such conflicts.

Paragraph 8. The employer does not want to become involved in a dispute with another company by hiring this employee. In this clause, the employee states that he or she is not bringing the employer any confidential information belonging to someone else.

Paragraph 9. This paragraph is a covenant not to compete, one of the most important provisions from the perspective of the employee. Employers worry that former employees will join a rival company and take their information and expertise with them. A covenant not to compete helps prevent that from happening. In short, a covenant not to compete prohibits an employee from working for a competing business for a specified time. This covenant applies regardless of whether the employee leaves the company or is terminated. Covenants not to compete have to be carefully drafted. A court will not enforce a covenant that is too broad in its coverage or that lasts for too long. Three years, the length of this covenant not to compete, is not unduly long. If the covenant is challenged, however, the employer will have to show that this length of time was necessary to protect its business interests. Employees do not appreciate covenants not to compete, but find that they are an inevitable part of employment in information-sensitive industries.

10. ***Agreement Not to Solicit Customers:*** During the course of my employment and for a period of three (3) years following my termination, I will not attempt to solicit any person, firm, or corporation that has been a customer account of the Company.

11. ***Remedies:*** I acknowledge that a remedy at law for any breach or threatened breach of the provisions of this Agreement would be inadequate. I therefore agree that the Company shall be entitled to injunctive relief in addition to any other available rights and remedies in case of any such breach or threatened breach. Nothing contained herein shall be construed as prohibiting the Company from pursuing any other remedies available for any such breach or threatened breach.

12. ***Assignment:*** This Agreement and the rights and obligations of the parties hereto shall bind and inure to the benefit of any successor(s) of the Company, whether by reorganization, merger, consolidation, sale of assets, or otherwise. Neither this Agreement nor any rights or benefits hereunder may be assigned by me.

13. ***Interpretation:*** It is the desire and intent of the parties hereto that the provisions of this Agreement shall be enforced to the fullest extent permissible. Accordingly, if any provision of this Agreement shall be adjudicated to be invalid or unenforceable, such provision shall be deemed deleted. Such deletion will apply only to the deleted provision in the particular jurisdiction in which such adjudication is made. If any provision contained herein shall be held to be excessively broad as to duration, geographical scope, activity, or subject, it shall be construed by limiting and reducing it so as to be enforceable.

14. ***Notices:*** All notices pursuant to this Agreement shall be given by personal delivery or by certified mail, return receipt requested. Notices to the Employee shall be addressed to the Employee at the address of record with the Company. Notices to the Company shall be addressed to its principal office. The date of personal delivery or the date of mailing any such notice shall be deemed to be the date of delivery thereof.

15. ***Waivers:*** Any waiver of breach of any provision of this Agreement shall not thereby be deemed a waiver of any preceding or succeeding breach of the same or any other provision of this Agreement.

16. ***Headings:*** The headings of the sections hereof are inserted for convenience only and shall not be deemed to constitute a part hereof nor to affect the meaning hereof.

17. ***Governing Law:*** This Agreement shall be governed by and construed and enforced in accordance with the laws of the State of New Hampshire.

18. ***No Employment Agreement:*** I acknowledge that this Agreement does not constitute an employment agreement. This Agreement shall be binding upon me regardless of whether my employment shall continue for any length of time and whether my employment is terminated for any reason whatsoever. This is true whether my employment is terminated by the Company or by me.

19. ***Complete Agreement, Amendments, and Prior Agreements:*** The foregoing is the entire agreement of the parties with respect to the subject matter hereof and may not be amended, supplemented, canceled, or discharged except by written instrument executed by both parties hereto. This Agreement supersedes any and all prior agreements between the parties hereto with respect to the matters covered hereby.

Date: _____ Employee: _____

Accepted and agreed to as of this date by Company:

Date: _____ By: _____

Name: _____

Title: _____

Paragraph 10. Similar to a covenant not to compete, this clause prohibits an employee from soliciting the company's customers during his or her employment or for up to three years afterward. Without such protection, an employer would be vulnerable to any former employee taking customer lists and using them to solicit customers at a new employer or at his or her own business.

Paragraph 11. This paragraph allows the employer to seek injunctive relief against the employee, should it be necessary. Here, the employee agrees that the employer not only may seek monetary damages from the employee in the event that this agreement is breached but may also prohibit him or her from engaging in whatever behavior violates the contract. Recall that typically the first line of remedies is damages to compensate for injury. Here the parties are acknowledging in advance (for the benefit of any court that later is involved) that the harm caused by a breach of the contract cannot be compensated or corrected with monetary damages.

Paragraph 12. Companies change, and so do their owners. This paragraph states that the contract will survive even if ownership of the company changes due to a merger, reorganization, or other reason. The employee cannot avoid this contract simply because the owner that signed the agreement later sells the company to someone else. This paragraph and many of the subsequent paragraphs are often referred to as "boilerplate language," meaning provisions that appear in some form in many contracts. They are included because conflicts have arisen over these points in the past and courts have interpreted contracts without this language in a way that the parties want to avoid. Boilerplate language can be very dangerous because parties may see the headings and not read further because the language is similar from contract to contract. But boilerplate language can make a difference in which party later wins a dispute (because the language spells out the law that will be used to interpret the contract, where a case must be brought, the proper way to give notice of changes, and the like).

Paragraph 13. Employers know that even the most carefully drafted agreements can sometimes be rendered unenforceable by a reviewing court. Laws change over time, and so do attitudes toward contract terms. This paragraph states that if part of this contract is rendered unenforceable for some reason, the rest of the contract will survive intact (that is, the unenforceable part of the contract is severable). The paragraph specifically references the covenant not to compete and the prohibition against solicitation. If a court rejects those terms as too broad in scope or too lengthy, the parties agree that the court should adjust the clause in order to make it enforceable under the law.

Paragraph 14. This paragraph deals with notices. If the employer or the employee wants to communicate about the contract, the communication must be sent by personal delivery or registered/certified mail. Note that this means that an e-mail is not sufficient notice under this agreeement.

Paragraph 15. This paragraph is meant to protect the employer. Sometimes, through generosity or neglect, employers fail to enforce every clause of a contract. For example, an employer may allow a former employee to start a competing business earlier than the contract states or permit an employee to take a second job. This paragraph ensures that if the employer allows some action that is prohibited in the contract, that does not mean that the contract term is waived forever. Just because the employer does not fully enforce the contract every time does not necessarily mean the employer is barred from doing so in the future.

Paragraph 16. This clause is meant to clarify that the headings are just headings and do not change the interpretation of the language in the paragraphs or the overall meaning of the contract.

Paragraph 17. This contract will be interpreted using the law of the state of New Hampshire. It is likely that the employer selected New Hampshire for some particular reason. Typically, an employer chooses a state where the law provides the most benefits for the employer. For example, employers typically choose the law of a particular state because it is their geographic home state and the employer's lawyers are familiar with its law. Employers may also choose a legal jurisdiction because its laws create a climate that is more favorable to the employer than the employee.

Paragraph 18. In this paragraph, the employee acknowledges that this contract is about nondisclosure of information and does not constitute an employment agreement that promises any length of service or any promise of continued employment.

Paragraph 19. This paragraph states that this contract is the complete agreement between the employer and the employee. Any other side agreements, e-mails, conversations, or other communications are irrelevant. The employee cannot rely on a manager's promise of a particular salary or terms of a covenant not to compete. This agreement is the final statement of the relationship between the employer and the employee.

UNIT THREE **Focus on Ethics**

Contract Law and the Application of Ethics

Generally, a responsible business manager will evaluate a business transaction on the basis of three criteria—legality, profitability, and ethics (see Chapter 5). But what does acting ethically mean in the area of contracts? If you enter into a contract with an individual who fails to look after her or his own interests, is that your fault? Should you be doing something about it? If the contract happens to be to your advantage and to the other party's detriment, do you have a responsibility to correct the situation?

Suppose that your neighbor puts a "For sale" sign on her car and offers to sell it for $6,000. You learn that she is moving to another state and needs the extra cash to help finance the move. You know that she could easily get $10,000 for the car, and you consider purchasing it and then reselling it at a profit. But you also discover that your neighbor is completely unaware that she has priced the car significantly below its *Blue Book* value. Are you ethically obligated to tell her that she is essentially giving away $4,000 if she sells you the car for only $6,000?

This kind of situation, transplanted into the world of commercial transactions, raises an obvious question: At what point should the sophisticated businessperson cease looking after his or her own economic welfare and become "his or her brother's keeper," so to speak?

Freedom of Contract and Freedom from Contract

The answer to the question just raised is not simple. On the one hand, a common ethical assumption in our society is that individuals should be held responsible for the consequences of their own actions, including their contractual promises. This principle is expressed in the legal concept of freedom of contract. On the other hand, another common assumption in our society is that individuals should not harm one another by their actions. This is the basis of both tort law and criminal law.

In the area of contract law, ethical behavior often involves balancing these principles. In the above example, if you purchased the car and your neighbor later learned its true value and sued you for the difference, very likely no court of law would find that the contract should be rescinded. At times, however, courts will hold that the principle of freedom *of* contract should give way to the principle of freedom *from* contract, a doctrine based on the assumption that people should not be harmed by the actions of others. We look next at some examples of situations in which parties to contracts may be excused from performance under their contracts to prevent injustice.

Impossibility of Performance The doctrine of impossibility of performance is based to some extent on the ethical question of whether one party should suffer economic loss when it is impossible to perform a contract. The rule that one is "bound by his or her contracts" is not followed when performance becomes impossible.

The doctrine, however, is applied only when the parties themselves did not consciously assume the risk of the events that rendered performance impossible. Furthermore, this doctrine rests on the assumption that the party claiming the defense of impossibility has acted ethically.

A contract is discharged, for example, if it calls for the delivery of a particular car and, through no fault of either party, this car is stolen and completely demolished in an accident. Yet the doctrine would not excuse performance if the party who agreed to sell the car caused its destruction by her or his negligence.

Before the late nineteenth century, courts were reluctant to discharge a contract even when performance was literally impossible. Just as society's ethics changes with the passage of time, however, the law also changes to reflect society's new perceptions of ethical behavior.[1]

Today, courts are much more willing to discharge a contract when its performance has become literally impossible. Holding a party in breach of contract, when performance has become impossible through no fault of that party, no longer coincides with society's notions of fairness.

LEGAL REASONING

1. *Suppose that you contract to purchase steel at a fixed price per ton. Before the contract is performed, a lengthy steelworkers' strike causes the price of steel to triple from the price specified in the contract. If you demand that the supplier fulfill the contract, the supplier will go out of business. What are your ethical obligations in this situation? What are your legal rights?*

Unconscionability The doctrine of unconscionability is a good example of how the law attempts to enforce ethical behavior. Under this doctrine, a contract may be deemed to be so unfair to one party as to be unenforceable—even though that party voluntarily agreed to the contract's terms. Unconscionable action, like unethical action, defies precise definition. Information about the particular facts and specific circumstances surrounding the contract is essential. For example, a court might find that a contract made with a marginally literate consumer was unfair and unenforceable but might uphold the same contract made with a major business firm.

Section 2–302 of the Uniform Commercial Code (to be discussed in Unit Four), incorporates the common law concept of unconscionability. Similarly, it does not define the concept with any precision. Rather, it leaves it to the courts to determine when a contract is so one sided and unfair to one party as to be unconscionable and thus unenforceable.

Usually, courts will do all that they can to save contracts rather than render them unenforceable. Only in extreme situations, as when a contract or clause is so one sided as to "shock the conscience" of the court, will a court hold a contract or contractual clause unconscionable.

---

1. A leading English case in which the court held that a defendant was discharged from the duty to perform due to impossibility of performance is *Taylor v. Caldwell*, 122 Eng.Rep. 309 (K.B. [King's Bench] 1863).

Exculpatory Clauses In some situations, courts have also refused to enforce exculpatory clauses on the ground that they are unconscionable or contrary to public policy. An *exculpatory clause* attempts to excuse a party from liability in the event of monetary or physical injury, no matter who is at fault. In some situations, such clauses are upheld.

Nonessential Services. Generally, the law permits parties to assume, by express agreement, the risks inherent in certain nonessential activities. For example, a health club can require its members to sign a clause releasing the club from any liability for injuries the members might incur while using the club's equipment and facilities. Likewise, an exculpatory clause releasing a ski resort from liability for skiing accidents would likely be enforced.[2] In such situations, exculpatory clauses make it possible for a firm's owner to stay in business—by shifting some of the liability risks from the business to the customer.

Disparities in Bargaining Power. Nonetheless, some jurisdictions take a dubious view of exculpatory clauses, particularly when the agreement is between parties with unequal bargaining power, such as a landlord and a tenant or an employer and an employee. Frequently, courts will hold that an exculpatory clause that attempts to exempt an employer from *all* liability for negligence toward its employees is against public policy and thus void.[3]

The courts reason that disparity in bargaining power and economic necessity force the employee to accept the employer's terms. Also, if a plaintiff can prove that an exculpatory clause is ambiguous, the courts generally will not enforce the clause.[4]

LEGAL REASONING

2. *In determining whether an exculpatory clause should be enforced, why does it matter whether the contract containing the clause involves essential services (such as transportation) or nonessential services (such as skiing or other leisure-time activities)?*

Covenants Not to Compete

In today's complicated, technological business world, knowledge learned on the job, including trade secrets, has become a valuable commodity. To prevent this knowledge from falling into the hands of competitors, more and more employers are requiring their employees to sign covenants not to compete. The increasing number of lawsuits over noncompete clauses in employment contracts has caused many courts to reconsider the reasonableness of these covenants.

Generally, the courts have few problems with enforcing a covenant not to compete that is ancillary to the sale of a business as long as the covenant's terms are reasonable. After all, part of what is being sold is the business's reputation and goodwill. If, after the sale, the seller opens a competing business nearby, the value of the original business to the purchaser could be greatly diminished.

More difficult for the courts is determining whether covenants not to compete in the employment context should be enforced. Often, this determination involves balancing the interests of the employer against the interests of the employee. Employers have a legitimate interest in protecting their trade secrets and customer lists. At the same time, employees should not be unreasonably restricted in their ability to work in their chosen profession or trade.

Jurisdictional Differences in Enforcement Jurisdictions vary in their approach to covenants not to compete. Many jurisdictions will enforce noncompete covenants in the employment context if both of the following are true.

1. The limitations placed on an employee are reasonable as to time and geographic area.
2. The limitations do not impose a greater restraint than necessary to protect the goodwill or other business interests of the employer.[5]

In a number of jurisdictions, if a court finds that a restraint in a noncompete covenant is not reasonable in light of the circumstances, it will reform the unreasonable provision and then enforce it. A court might, for instance, rewrite an unreasonable restriction by reducing the time period during which a former employee cannot compete from three years to one year. The court would then enforce the reformed agreement.[6]

Other jurisdictions are not so "employer friendly" and refuse to enforce unreasonable covenants. Under California law, covenants not to compete are illegal, as are a number of other types of agreements that have a similar effect.[7] Other western states also tend to regard noncompete covenants with suspicion. For example, courts in Washington State refuse to reform noncompete covenants that are unreasonable and lacking in consideration.[8] Courts in Arizona and Texas have reached similar conclusions.[9]

2. *Myers v. Lutsen Mountains Corp.,* 587 F.3d 891 (8th Cir. 2009).
3. See, for example, *Wallace v. Busch Entertainment Corp., City of Santa Barbara v. Superior Court,* 62 Cal.Rptr.3d 527, 161 P.3d 1095 (2007).
4. See, for example, *Tatman v. Space Coast Kennel Club, Inc.,* 27 So.3d 108 (Fla.App. 5 Dist., 2010).
5. See *Drummond American, LLC v. Share Corp.,* 692 F.Supp.2d 650 (E.D.Tex., 2010); and *TEKsystems, Inc. v. Bolton,* 2010 WL 447782(D.Md. 2010).
6. See, for example, *Estee Lauder Companies v. Batra,* 430 F.Supp.2d 158 (S.D.N.Y. 2006).
7. See, for example, *SriCom, Inc. v. Ebis Logic, Inc.,* 2012 WL 4051222 (N.D.Ca l. 2012); and *Thomas Weisel Partners, LLC v. BNP Paribas,* 2010 WL 1267744(N.D.Cal. 2010).]
8. See, for example, *International Paper Co. v. Stuit,* 2012 WL 187143 (W.D.Wash. 2012); and *EEOC v. Fry's Electronics, Inc.,* 2011 WL 666328 (W.D.Wash. 2011).
9. *Philipello v. Taylor,* 2012 WL 1435171 (Tex.App.—Waco 2012); and *Varsity Gold, Inc. v. Porzio,* 202 Ariz. 355, 45 P.3d 352 (2002).

FOCUS ON ETHICS CONTINUES ➧

Do Noncompete Covenants Stifle Innovation? One of the reasons that the courts usually look closely at covenants not to compete and evaluate them on a case-by-case basis is the strong public policy favoring competition in this country. Some scholars claim that covenants not to compete, regardless of how reasonable they are, may stifle competition and innovation.

Consider, for example, the argument put forth some years ago by Ronald Gilson, a Stanford University professor of law and business. He contended that California's prohibition on covenants not to compete helped to explain why technological innovation and economic growth skyrocketed in California's Silicon Valley in the late 1990s, while technological development along Massachusetts's Route 128 languished during the same time period. According to Gilson, the different legal rules regarding covenants not to compete in California and Massachusetts were a "critical" factor in explaining why one area saw so much innovation and transfer of technology knowledge and the other area did not.[10]

LEGAL REASONING

3. *Employers often include covenants not to compete in employment contracts to protect their trade secrets. What effect, if any, will the growth in e-commerce have on the reasonableness of covenants not to compete?*

Oral Contracts and Promissory Estoppel

Oral contracts are made every day. Many—if not most—of them are carried out, and no problems arise. Occasionally, however, oral contracts are not performed, and one party decides to sue the other. Sometimes, to prevent injustice, the courts will enforce oral contracts under the theory of promissory estoppel.

Ethical standards certainly underlie this doctrine, under which a person who has reasonably relied on the promise of another to his or her detriment can often obtain some measure of recovery. Essentially, promissory estoppel allows a variety of oral promises to be enforced even though they lack what is formally regarded as consideration.

An oral promise made by an insurance agent to a business owner, for example, may be binding if the owner relies on that promise to her or his detriment. Employees who rely to their detriment on an employer's promise may be able to recover damages under the doctrine of promissory estoppel. If a subcontractor fails to complete specific work at a certain price as promised, the contractor whose bid was based on that promise may be able to recover on the basis of promissory estoppel. These are but a few of the many examples in which the courts,

---

10. Ronald J. Gilson, "The Legal Infrastructure of High Technology Industrial Districts: Silicon Valley, Route 128, and Covenants Not to Compete," *New York University Law Review* (June 1999): 575–579.

in the interests of fairness and justice, have estopped a promisor from denying that a contract existed.

Oral Contracts and the Writing Requirement

The courts sometimes use the theory of promissory estoppel to remove a contract from the writing requirement, thereby making oral contracts enforceable. As you learned in Chapter 16, the Statute of Frauds was originally enacted in England in 1677.

Before the Statute of Frauds was passed, English courts had enforced oral contracts on the strength of oral testimony by witnesses. It was not too difficult to evade justice by procuring "convincing" witnesses to support the claim that a contract had been created and then breached. Moreover, seventeenth-century English courts did not allow oral testimony to be given by the parties to a lawsuit—or by any parties with an interest in the litigation, such as husbands or wives. Only written evidence or the testimony of third parties could be used in actions for breach of contract. These constraints enhanced the possibility of fraud.

Detrimental Reliance Under the Statute of Frauds, if a contract is oral when it is required to be in writing, it will not, as a rule, be enforced by the courts. An exception to this rule is made if a party has reasonably relied, to his or her detriment, on the oral contract. Enforcing an oral contract on the basis of a party's reliance arguably undercuts the essence of the Statute of Frauds. The reason that such an exception is made is to prevent the statute—which was created to prevent injustice—from being used to promote injustice. Nevertheless, this use of the doctrine is controversial—as is the Statute of Frauds itself.

Criticisms of the Statute of Frauds Since its inception more than three hundred years ago, the Statute of Frauds has been criticized by some. They point out that although the statute was created to protect the innocent, it can also be used as a technical defense by a party breaching a genuine, mutually agreed-on oral contract that happens to fall under the statute. For this reason, some legal scholars believe the act has caused more injustice than it has prevented. Thus, exceptions are sometimes made—such as under the doctrine of promissory estoppel—to prevent unfairness and inequity. Generally, the courts are slow to apply the statute if doing so will result in obvious injustice. In some instances, this has required a good deal of inventiveness on the part of the courts.

LEGAL REASONING

4. *Many countries have no Statute of Frauds, and even England, the country that created the original act, has repealed it. Should the United States do likewise? What are some of the costs and benefits to society of the Statute of Frauds?*

BUSINESS LAW

CLARKSON · MILLER · CROSS

UNIT FOUR

DOMESTIC AND INTERNATIONAL SALES AND LEASE CONTRACTS

CONTENTS

CHAPTER 20

THE FORMATION OF SALES AND LEASE CONTRACTS

When we turn to contracts for the sale and lease of goods, we move away from common law principles and into the area of statutory law. State statutory law governing sales and lease transactions is based on the uniform Commercial code (UCC), which, as mentioned in Chapter 1, has been adopted as law by all of the states.[1] Of all the attempts to produce a uniform body of laws relating to commercial transactions in the United States, none has been as successful as the UCC.

We open this chapter with a discussion of the UCC's Article 2 (on sales) and Article 2A (on leases) as a background to the topic of this chapter, which is the formation of contracts for the sale and lease of goods. The goal of the UCC is to simplify and to streamline commercial transactions. The UCC allows parties to form sales and lease contracts, including those entered into online, without observing the same degree of formality used in forming other types of contracts. We look at the important issue of whether online sales can be taxed in this chapter's *Insight into E-Commerce* feature.

Today, businesses often engage in sales and lease transactions on a global scale. Because international sales transactions are increasingly commonplace, we conclude the chapter with an examination of the United Nations Convention on Contracts for the International Sale of Goods (CISG), which governs international sales contracts. The CISG is a model uniform law that applies only when a nation has adopted it, just as the UCC applies only to the extent that it has been adopted by a state.

---

1. Louisiana has not adopted Articles 2 and 2A, however.

SECTION 1
THE UNIFORM COMMERCIAL CODE

In the early years of this nation, sales law varied from state to state, and this lack of uniformity complicated the formation of multistate sales contracts. The problems became especially troublesome in the late nineteenth century as multistate contracts became the norm. For this reason, numerous attempts were made to produce a uniform body of laws relating to commercial transactions. The National Conference of Commissioners on Uniform State Laws (NCCUSL) drafted two uniform ("model") acts that were widely adopted by the states: the Uniform Negotiable Instruments Law (1896) and the Uniform Sales Act (1906). Several other proposed uniform acts followed, although most were not as widely adopted.

In the 1940s, the NCCUSL recognized the need to integrate the half dozen or so uniform acts covering commercial transactions into a single, comprehensive body of statutory law. The NCCUSL developed the Uniform Commercial Code (UCC) to serve that purpose. First issued in 1949, the UCC facilitates commercial transactions by making the laws governing sales and lease contracts clearer, simpler, and more readily applicable to the numerous difficulties that can arise during such transactions.

Comprehensive Coverage of the UCC

The UCC is the single most comprehensive codification of the broad spectrum of laws involved in a total commercial transaction. The UCC views the entire "commercial transaction for the sale of and payment for goods" as a single legal occurrence having numerous facets. The articles and sections of the UCC are periodically revised or supplemented to clarify certain aspects or to establish new rules as needed when the business environment changes.

You can gain an idea of the UCC's comprehensiveness by looking at the titles of the articles of the UCC in Appendix C. As you will note, Article 1, titled General Provisions, sets forth definitions and general principles applicable to commercial transactions. For instance, there is an obligation to perform in "good faith" all contracts falling under the UCC [UCC 1–304]. Article 1 thus provides the basic groundwork for the remaining articles, each of which focuses on a particular aspect of commercial transactions.

Does the duty of good faith and fair dealing apply to contracts other than contracts for sales of goods? That question arose in the following case.

CASE ANALYSIS

Case 20.1   Amaya v. Brater
Court of Appeals of Indiana, 981 N.E.2d 1235 (2013).

IN THE LANGUAGE OF THE COURT
CRONE, Judge.

* * * *

* * * In the spring of 2010, [Peter] Amaya, an Ohio resident, was a third-year medical student at Indiana University School of Medicine [IUSM] located in Indianapolis. He was attending medical school on scholarship. On March 29, 2010, Amaya sat for a combined mini-block examination consisting of Introduction to Clinical Medicine II, Pharmacology, and Pathology. Three professors, Drs. [Joseph] DiMicco, [Klaus] Hilgarth, and [Kathleen] Prag, each observed Amaya during the examination and concluded that he was cheating by looking at the paper of the student to his right. On March 30, 2010, Dr. DiMicco confronted Amaya with his observations, and Amaya denied cheating on the mini-block examination. On April 5, 2010, Dr. Hilgarth confronted Amaya with his observations and explained to Amaya that his behavior of looking into the workspace of the student to his right gave the appearance of cheating. Amaya denied that he cheated or that he engaged in any behavior that gave the appearance of cheating. Amaya maintained that he was merely looking over and up at the clock on the right-hand wall of the testing room.
* * * *

* * * On August 18, 2010, Dean [Craig] Brater advised Amaya that he * * * was dismissed from Indiana University School of Medicine.

* * * Amaya filed a * * * complaint [in an Indiana state court against the dean and IUSM, alleging] breach of contract and * * * breach of good faith and fair dealing.

* * * The trial court * * * granted IUSM's motion for summary judgment.

* * * Amaya now appeals.
* * * *

* * * Amaya raises two separate theories of liability against IUSM: (1) breach of contract, and (2) breach of the duty of good faith and fair dealing. * * * A separate cause of action for alleged breach of duty of good faith and fair dealing is inapposite [unsuitable] here. *The duty of good faith and fair dealing is a concept created by the Uniform Commercial Code and restricted to contracts for the sale of goods* * * *. Accordingly, the sole issue for our determination on appeal is whether the trial court erred when it entered summary judgment on Amaya's claim for breach of contract. [Emphasis added.]

* * * The legal relationship between a student and a university [is] one of implied contract.

* * * The courts' approach has been similar to that used with contracts conditioned upon the satisfaction of one party. The university requires that the student's academic performance be satisfactory to the university in its honest judgment.
* * * *

IUSM's *Student Handbook* provides that the [Student Promotions Committee (SPC)] is appointed by the dean to monitor student academic and professional standards as determined by the faculty. Section V(F), entitled "Dismissal," provides that "a student may be required to meet with the SPC to show cause why he/she should not be dismissed from school when he/she * * * has been cited for lack of acceptable academic ethics or professional behavior." The designated evidence indicates that three faculty members observed Amaya cheating during the mini-block examination. Amaya was informed of these observations and was requested to prepare for a * * * hearing before the SPC. Amaya appeared before the SPC and presented a PowerPoint presentation. He also tendered voluminous written material, including photographs, field studies, experts' reports, timelines, and statistical analysis. Following Amaya's presentation, the SPC tabled its vote in order to further deliberate and thoroughly review Amaya's information. The SPC also asked for written submissions from the three faculty members and from Amaya.

CASE 20.1 CONTINUES ▶

Thereafter, Amaya was informed that a subcommittee of the SPC had conducted field tests to determine the validity of the information he had submitted. Considering the results of those field tests as well as the written responses to additional questions, the SPC determined that the evidence supported the charge of cheating. Amaya was granted his request for a reconsideration hearing as provided by section VI of the *Student Handbook*. When the SPC declined to reverse its decision, Amaya was then afforded the opportunity to meet with the dean for further review as provided for in the *Student Handbook*. After considering all the evidence presented, the Dean determined that dismissal was warranted.

* * * IUSM's conclusion that Amaya failed to maintain acceptable professional standards was a rational determination arrived at after much deliberation and after Amaya had numerous opportunities to be heard.

* * * *

* * * We affirm the trial court's entry of summary judgment.

LEGAL REASONING QUESTIONS

1. What is the duty of good faith and fair dealing (see page 381)?
2. To what type of contracts does the duty apply?
3. What type of contract was at the center of this case?
4. Did the court conclude that the duty of good faith and fair dealing applied in this case? Why or why not?

A Single, Integrated Framework for Commercial Transactions

The UCC attempts to provide a consistent and integrated framework of rules to deal with all the phases *ordinarily arising* in a commercial sales transaction from start to finish. For an example how several articles of the UCC can apply to a single commercial transaction, see Exhibit 20–1 on the following page.

SECTION 2
THE SCOPE OF ARTICLES 2 (SALES) AND 2A (LEASES)

Article 2 of the UCC sets forth the requirements for *sales contracts*, as well as the duties and obligations of the parties involved in the sales contract. Article 2A covers similar issues for *lease contracts*. Bear in mind, however, that the parties to sales or lease contracts are free to agree to terms different from those stated in the UCC.

Article 2—The Sale of Goods

Article 2 of the UCC (as adopted by state statutes) governs **sales contracts,** or contracts for the sale of goods. To facilitate commercial transactions, Article 2

modifies some of the common law contract requirements that were discussed in the previous chapters.

To the extent that it has not been modified by the UCC, however, the common law of contracts also applies to sales contracts. In other words, the common law requirements for a valid contract—agreement consideration, capacity, and legality—that were discussed in previous chapters are also applicable to sales contracts.

In general, the rule is that whenever a conflict arises between a common law contract rule and the state statutory law based on the UCC, the UCC controls. Thus, when a UCC provision addresses a certain issue, the UCC rule governs. When the UCC is silent, the common law governs.

The relationship between general contract law and the law governing sales of goods is illustrated in Exhibit 20–2 on the following page.

In regard to Article 2, keep two points in mind.

1. Article 2 deals with the sale of *goods*. It does not deal with real property (real estate), services, or intangible property such as stocks and bonds. Thus, if the subject matter of a dispute is goods, the UCC governs. If it is real estate or services, the common law applies.
2. In some situations, the rules can vary depending on whether the buyer or the seller is a *merchant*.

We look now at how the UCC defines a *sale, goods,* and *merchant status*.

EXHIBIT 20-1   How Several Articles of the UCC Can Apply to a Single Transaction

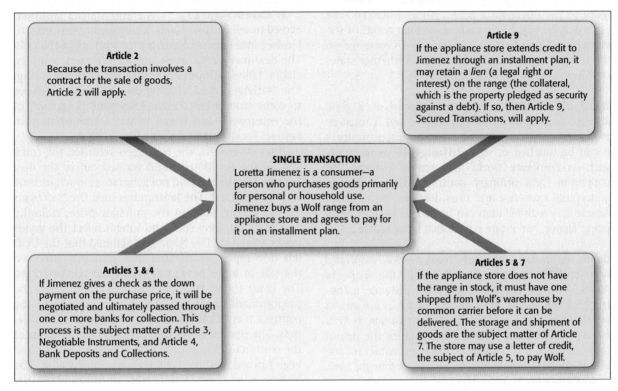

Article 2
Because the transaction involves a contract for the sale of goods, Article 2 will apply.

Article 9
If the appliance store extends credit to Jimenez through an installment plan, it may retain a *lien* (a legal right or interest) on the range (the collateral, which is the property pledged as security against a debt). If so, then Article 9, Secured Transactions, will apply.

SINGLE TRANSACTION
Loretta Jimenez is a consumer—a person who purchases goods primarily for personal or household use. Jimenez buys a Wolf range from an appliance store and agrees to pay for it on an installment plan.

Articles 3 & 4
If Jimenez gives a check as the down payment on the purchase price, it will be negotiated and ultimately passed through one or more banks for collection. This process is the subject matter of Article 3, Negotiable Instruments, and Article 4, Bank Deposits and Collections.

Articles 5 & 7
If the appliance store does not have the range in stock, it must have one shipped from Wolf's warehouse by common carrier before it can be delivered. The storage and shipment of goods are the subject matter of Article 7. The store may use a letter of credit, the subject of Article 5, to pay Wolf.

EXHIBIT 20-2   The Law Governing Contracts

This exhibit graphically illustrates the relationship between general contract law and statutory law (UCC Articles 2 and 2A) governing contracts for the sale and lease of goods. Sales contracts are not governed exclusively by Article 2 of the UCC but are also governed by general contract law whenever it is relevant and has not been modified by the UCC.

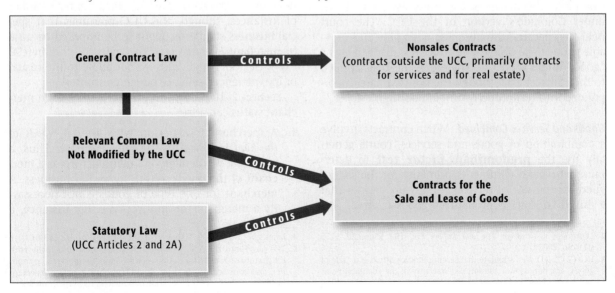

General Contract Law — Controls → **Nonsales Contracts** (contracts outside the UCC, primarily contracts for services and for real estate)

Relevant Common Law Not Modified by the UCC — Controls →

Statutory Law (UCC Articles 2 and 2A) — Controls → **Contracts for the Sale and Lease of Goods**

WHAT IS A SALE? The UCC defines a **sale** as "the passing of title [evidence of ownership rights] from the seller to the buyer for a price" [UCC 2–106(1)]. The price may be payable in cash or in other goods or services. (See this chapter's *Insight into E-Commerce* on the following page for a discussion of whether states can impose taxes on online sales.)

WHAT ARE GOODS? To be characterized as a *good,* an item of property must be *tangible,* and it must be *movable.* **Tangible property** has physical existence—it can be touched or seen. **Intangible property**—such as corporate stocks and bonds, patents and copyrights, and ordinary contract rights—has only conceptual existence and thus does not come under Article 2. A *movable* item can be carried from place to place. Hence, real estate is excluded from Article 2.

Goods Associated with Real Estate. Goods *associated* with real estate often do fall within the scope of Article 2, however [UCC 2–107]. For instance, a contract for the sale of minerals, oil, or gas is a contract for the sale of goods if *severance, or separation, is to be made by the seller.* Similarly, a contract for the sale of growing crops or timber to be cut is a contract for the sale of goods *regardless of who severs them from the land.*
▶ **Case in Point 20.1** Homeowners in Colorado installed underground radiant heating systems to warm indoor flooring or melt snow and ice under driveways and sidewalks. The systems began to leak as a result of the hardening of a hose called Entran II. The homeowners sued Goodyear Tire and Rubber Company, the maker of the hose, asserting claims under Colorado's version of the UCC. The court held that because the hose was a tangible and movable good at the time the contract was made, it was a "good" under the UCC. Therefore, the UCC applied to the contract even though the hose was later incorporated into real property (under flooring).[2] ◀

Goods and Services Combined. When contracts involve a combination of goods and services, courts generally use the **predominant-factor test** to determine whether a contract is primarily for the sale of goods or the sale of services.[3] If a court decides that a mixed contract is primarily a goods contract, *any*

dispute, even a dispute over the services portion, will be decided under the UCC.
▶ **Case in Point 20.2** Gene and Martha Jannusch agreed to sell Festival Foods, a concessions business, to Lindsey and Louann Naffziger for a price of $150,000. The deal included a truck, a trailer, freezers, roasters, chairs, tables, a fountain service, signs, and lighting. The Naffzigers paid $10,000 down with the balance to come from a bank loan. They took possession of the equipment and began to use it immediately in Festival Foods operations at various events.

After six events, the Naffzigers returned the truck and all the equipment, and wanted out of the deal because the business did not generate as much income as they expected. The Jannusches sued the Naffzigers for the balance due on the purchase price, claiming that the Naffzigers could no longer reject the goods under the UCC. The Naffzigers claimed that the UCC did not apply because the deal primarily involved the sale of a business rather than the sale of goods. The court found that the UCC governed under the predominant-factor test. The primary value of the contract was in the goods, not the value of the business. The parties had agreed on the essential terms of the contract (such as the price). Thus, a contract had been formed, and the Naffzigers had breached it. The Naffzigers took possession and control of all of the physical aspects of the business. Therefore, they had no right to return them.[4] ◀

WHO IS A MERCHANT? Article 2 governs the sale of goods in general. It applies to sales transactions between all buyers and sellers. In a limited number of instances, though, the UCC presumes that special business standards ought to be imposed because of merchants' relatively high degree of commercial expertise.[5] Such standards do not apply to the casual or inexperienced seller or buyer (consumer).

Section 2–104 sets forth three ways in which merchant status can arise:

1. A merchant is a person who *deals in goods of the kind* involved in the sales contract. Thus, a retailer, a wholesaler, or a manufacturer is a merchant of the goods sold in his or her business. A merchant for one type of goods is not necessarily a merchant for another type. For instance, a

---

2. *Loughridge v. Goodyear Tire and Rubber Co.,* 192 F.Supp.2d 1175 (D.Colo. 2002).
3. UCC 2–314(1) does stipulate that serving food or drinks is a "sale of goods" for purposes of the implied warranty of merchantability, as will be discussed in Chapter 23. The UCC also specifies that selling unborn animals or rare coins qualifies as a "sale of goods."

4. *Jannusch v. Naffziger,* 379 Ill.App.3d 381, 883 N.E.2d 711 (2008).
5. The provisions that apply only to merchants deal principally with the Statute of Frauds, firm offers, confirmatory memoranda, warranties, and contract modification. These special rules reflect expedient business practices commonly known to merchants in the commercial setting. They will be discussed later in this chapter.

INSIGHT INTO E-COMMERCE
Taxing Web Purchases

In 1992, the United States Supreme Court ruled that an individual state cannot compel an out-of-state business that lacks a substantial physical presence within that state to collect and remit state taxes.[a] Although Congress has the power to pass legislation requiring out-of-state corporations to collect and remit state sales taxes, it has not yet done so. Thus, only online retailers that also have a physical presence within a state must collect state taxes on any Web sales made to residents of that state. (State residents are supposed to self-report their purchases and pay use taxes to the state, which they rarely do.)

Redefining Physical Presence

Several states have found a way to collect taxes on Internet sales made to state residents by out-of-state corporations—by redefining *physical presence*. In 2008, New York changed its tax laws in this manner. Now, an online retailer that pays any party within New York to solicit business for its products is considered a physical presence in the state and must collect state taxes. Since then, at least seventeen other states have made similar changes in their laws in an effort to increase their revenues by collecting sales tax from online retailers.

These new laws, often called the "Amazon tax" because they are largely aimed at Amazon.com, affect all online sellers, including Overstock.com and Drugstore.com. These tax laws especially affect those retailers that pay affiliates to direct traffic to their Web sites. These laws allow states to tax online commerce even though, to date, Congress has explicitly chosen not to tax Internet sales.

Local Governments Sue Online Travel Companies

Travelocity, Priceline.com, Hotels.com, and Orbitx.com are online travel companies (OTCs) that offer, among other things, hotel booking services. By 2013, more than twenty cities, including Atlanta, Charleston, Philadelphia, and San Antonio, had filed suits claiming that the OTCs owed taxes on hotel reservations that they had booked. All of the cities involved in the suits impose a hotel occupancy tax, which is essentially a sales tax.

Initially, some cities won their cases, but more recently, they have been losing in court.[b] As of 2013, the OTCs had prevailed in fifteen of nineteen cases nationwide.

The Market Place Fairness Act

By the time you read this, online sales taxes may have become a reality for every online business that has annual revenues in excess of $1 million. For several years now, legislation called the Market Place Fairness Act has been introduced in the U.S. Senate. The act would allow states to collect sales taxes from online retailers for transactions within the state.

There are several problems with such legislation. The current tax system involves 9,600 taxing jurisdictions. Even one zip code may cover multiple taxing entities such as different cities and counties. Just consider that the Dallas–Fort Worth airport includes six separate taxing jurisdictions. Current software solutions for retailers that allow them to collect and remit sales taxes for different jurisdictions are extremely costly to install and operate. Overstock.com, for example, spent $1.3 million to add just one state to its sales tax collection system.

LEGAL CRITICAL THINKING
INSIGHT INTO ETHICS

Some argue that if online retailers are required to collect and pay sales taxes in jurisdictions in which they have no physical presence, they have no democratic way to fight high taxes in those places. Is this an instance of taxation without representation? Discuss.

---

a. *Quill Corp. v. North Dakota*, 504 U.S. 298, 112 S.Ct. 1904, 119 L.Ed.2d 91 (1992).

b. *Travelscape, LLC v. South Carolina Department of Revenue*, 391 S.C. 89, 705 S.E.2d 28 (2011).

---

sporting goods retailer is a merchant when selling tennis rackets but not when selling a used computer.

2. A merchant is a person who, by occupation, holds himself or herself out as having knowledge and skill unique to the practices or goods involved in the transaction. This broad definition may include banks or universities as merchants.

3. A person who *employs a merchant as a broker, agent, or other intermediary* has the status of merchant in that transaction. Hence, if an art collector hires a broker to purchase or sell art for

her, the collector is considered a merchant in the transaction.

In summary, a person is a **merchant** when she or he, acting in a mercantile capacity, possesses or uses an expertise specifically related to the goods being sold. This basic distinction is not always clear-cut. For instance, state courts appear to be split on whether farmers should be considered merchants.

Article 2A—Leases

Leases of personal property (goods such as automobiles and industrial equipment) have become increasingly common. In this context, a lease is a transfer of the right to possess and use goods for a period of time in exchange for payment. Article 2A of the UCC was created to fill the need for uniform guidelines in this area.

Article 2A covers any transaction that creates a lease of goods or a sublease of goods [UCC 2A–102, 2A–103(1)(k)]. Article 2A is essentially a repetition of Article 2, except that it applies to leases of goods rather than sales of goods and thus varies to reflect differences between sales and lease transactions. (Note that Article 2A is not concerned with leases of real property, such as land or buildings.)

DEFINITION OF A LEASE AGREEMENT Article 2A defines a **lease agreement** as a lessor's and lessee's bargain with respect to the lease of goods, as found in their language and as implied by other circumstances [UCC 2A–103(1)(k)]. A **lessor** is one who transfers the right to the possession and use of goods under a lease [UCC 2A–103(1)(p)]. A **lessee** is one who acquires the right to the possession and use of goods under a lease [UCC 2A–103(1)(o)]. In other words, the lessee is the party who is leasing the goods from the lessor.

Article 2A applies to all types of leases of goods. Special rules apply to certain types of leases, however, including consumer leases and finance leases.

CONSUMER LEASES A *consumer lease* involves three elements:

1. A lessor who regularly engages in the business of leasing or selling.
2. A lessee (except an organization) who leases the goods "primarily for a personal, family, or household purpose."

3. Total lease payments that are less than $25,000 [UCC 2A–103(1)(e)].

To ensure special protection for consumers, certain provisions of Article 2A apply only to consumer leases. For instance, one provision states that a consumer may recover attorneys' fees if a court determines that a term in a consumer lease contract is unconscionable [UCC 2A–108(4)(a)].

FINANCE LEASES A *finance lease* involves a lessor, a lessee, and a supplier. The lessor buys or leases goods from the supplier and leases or subleases them to the lessee [UCC 2A–103(1)(g)]. Typically, in a finance lease, the lessor is simply financing the transaction. ▶ **Example 20.3** Marlin Corporation wants to lease a crane for use in its construction business. Marlin's bank agrees to purchase the equipment from Jenco, Inc., and lease the equipment to Marlin. In this situation, the bank is the lessor-financer, Marlin is the lessee, and Jenco is the supplier. ◀

Article 2A, unlike ordinary contract law, makes the lessee's obligations under a finance lease irrevocable and independent from the financer's obligations [UCC 2A–407]. In other words, the lessee must perform and continue to make lease payments even if the leased equipment turns out to be defective. The lessee must look almost entirely to the supplier for any recovery.
▶ **Example 20.4** McKessen Company obtains surgical ophthalmic equipment from a manufacturer and leases it to Vasquez for use at his medical eye center. When the equipment turns out to be defective, Vasquez stops making the lease payments. McKessen sues. Because the lease clearly qualifies as a finance lease under Article 2A, a court would hold in favor of McKessen. Vasquez is obligated to make all payments due under the lease regardless of the condition or performance of the leased equipment. Vasquez can sue the manufacturer of the defective equipment, however. ◀

SECTION 3
THE FORMATION OF SALES AND LEASE CONTRACTS

In regard to the formation of sales and lease contracts, the UCC modifies the common law in several ways. We look here at how Articles 2 and 2A of the UCC modify common law contract rules. Remember, though, that parties to sales and lease contracts are basically free to establish whatever terms they wish.

The UCC comes into play when the parties either fail to provide certain terms in their contract or wish to change the effect of the UCC's terms in the contract's application. The UCC makes this very clear by its repeated use of such phrases as "unless the parties otherwise agree" and "absent a contrary agreement by the parties."

Offer

In general contract law, the moment a definite offer is met by an unqualified acceptance, a binding contract is formed. In commercial sales transactions, the verbal exchanges, correspondence, and actions of the parties may not reveal exactly when a binding contractual obligation arises. The UCC states that an agreement sufficient to constitute a contract can exist even if the moment of its making is undetermined [UCC 2–204(2), 2A–204(2)].

OPEN TERMS According to general contract law, an offer must be definite enough for the parties (and the courts) to ascertain its essential terms when it is accepted. In contrast, the UCC states that a sales or lease contract will not fail for indefiniteness even if one or more terms are left open as long as *both* of the following are true:

1. The parties intended to make a contract.
2. There is a reasonably certain basis for the court to grant an appropriate remedy [UCC 2–204(3), 2A–204(3)].

The UCC provides numerous *open-term* provisions (discussed next) that can be used to fill the gaps in a contract. Thus, if a dispute occurs, all that is necessary to prove the existence of a contract is an indication (such as a purchase order) that there is a contract. Missing terms can be proved by evidence, or a court can presume that the parties intended whatever is reasonable under the circumstances.

Keep in mind, though, that if too many terms are left open, a court may find that the parties did not intend to form a contract. Also, the *quantity* of goods involved usually must be expressly stated in the contract. If the quantity term is left open, the courts will have no basis for determining a remedy.

Open Price Term. If the parties have not agreed on a price, the court will determine a "reasonable price at the time for delivery" [UCC 2–305(1)]. If either the

buyer or the seller is to determine the price, the price is to be decided in good faith [UCC 2–305(2)]. Under the UCC, *good faith* means honesty in fact and the observance of reasonable commercial standards of fair dealing in the trade [UCC 2–103(1)(b)]. The concepts of *good faith* and *commercial reasonableness* permeate the UCC.

Sometimes, the price fails to be set through the fault of one of the parties. In that situation, the other party can treat the contract as canceled or determine a reasonable price. ▶ **Example 20.5** Perez and Merrick enter into a contract for the sale of goods and agree that Perez will determine the price. Perez refuses to specify the price. Merrick can either treat the contract as canceled or set a reasonable price [UCC 2–305(3)]. ◀

Open Payment Term. When the parties do not specify payment terms, payment is due at the time and place at which the buyer is to receive the goods [UCC 2–310(a)]. The buyer can tender payment using any commercially normal or acceptable means, such as a check or credit card. If the seller demands payment in cash, however, the buyer must be given a reasonable time to obtain it [UCC 2–511(2)]. This is especially important when the contract states a definite and final time for performance.

▶ **Case in Point 20.6** Max Alexander agreed to purchase hay from Wagner's farm. Alexander left his truck and trailer at the farm for the seller to load the hay. Nothing was said about when payment was due, and the parties were unaware of the UCC's rules. When Alexander came back to get the hay, a dispute broke out. Alexander claimed that he had been given less hay than he had ordered and argued that he did not have to pay at that time. Wagner refused to release the hay (or the vehicles on which the hay was loaded) until Alexander paid for it. Eventually, Alexander jumped into his truck and drove off without paying for the hay—for which he was later prosecuted for the crime of theft (see Chapter 10). Because the parties had failed to specify when payment was due, UCC 2–310(a) controlled, and payment was due at the time Alexander picked up the hay.[6] ◀

Open Delivery Term. When no delivery terms are specified, the buyer normally takes delivery at the seller's place of business [UCC 2–308(a)]. If the seller has no place of business, the seller's residence is used. When goods are located in some other place and both parties

---

6. *State v. Alexander*, 186 Or.App. 600, 64 P.3d 1148 (2003).

know it, delivery is made there. If the time for shipment or delivery is not clearly specified in the sales contract, then the court will infer a "reasonable" time for performance [UCC 2–309(1)].

Duration of an Ongoing Contract. A single contract might specify successive performances but not indicate how long the parties are required to deal with each other. In this situation, either party may terminate the ongoing contractual relationship. Nevertheless, principles of good faith and sound commercial practice call for reasonable notification before termination so as to give the other party sufficient time to seek a substitute arrangement [UCC 2–309(2), (3)].

Options and Cooperation with Regard to Performance. When the contract contemplates shipment of the goods but does not specify the shipping arrangements, the *seller* has the right to make these arrangements in good faith, using commercial reasonableness in the situation [UCC 2–311].

When a sales contract omits terms relating to the assortment of goods, the *buyer* can specify the assortment. ▶ **Example 20.7** Petry Drugs agrees to purchase one thousand toothbrushes from Marconi's Dental Supply. The toothbrushes come in a variety of colors, but the contract does not specify color. Petry, the buyer, has the right to take six hundred blue toothbrushes and four hundred green ones if it wishes. Petry, however, must exercise good faith and commercial reasonableness in making the selection [UCC 2–311]. ◀

REQUIREMENTS AND OUTPUT CONTRACTS Normally, as mentioned earlier, if the parties do not specify a quantity, no contract is formed. A court will have no basis for determining a remedy because there is almost no way to determine objectively what is a reasonable quantity of goods for someone to buy. (In contrast, a court can objectively determine a reasonable price for particular goods by looking at the market for like goods.) The UCC recognizes two exceptions to this rule in requirements and output contracts [UCC 2–306(1)].

Requirements Contracts. Requirements contracts are common in the business world and normally are enforceable. In a **requirements contract,** the buyer agrees to purchase and the seller agrees to sell all or up to a stated amount of what the buyer requires.

▶ **Example 20.8** Newport Cannery forms a contract with Victor Tu. The cannery agrees to purchase from Tu, and Tu agrees to sell to the cannery, all of the

green beans that the cannery requires during the following summer. ◀ There is implicit consideration in a requirements contract because the buyer (the cannery, in *Example 20.8*) gives up the right to buy from any other seller, and this forfeited right creates a legal detriment (consideration).

If, however, the buyer promises to purchase only if he or she *wishes* to do so, the promise is illusory (without consideration) and unenforceable by either party.[7] Similarly, if the buyer reserves the right to buy the goods from someone other than the seller, the promise is unenforceable (illusory) as a requirements contract.

Output Contracts. In an **output contract,** the seller agrees to sell and the buyer agrees to buy all or up to a stated amount of what the seller *produces.* ▶ **Example 20.9** Ruth Sewell has planted two acres of organic tomatoes. Bella Union, a local restaurant, agrees to buy all of the tomatoes that Sewell produces that year to use at the restaurant. ◀ Again, because the seller essentially forfeits the right to sell goods to another buyer, there is implicit consideration in an output contract.

The UCC imposes a *good faith limitation* on requirements and output contracts. The quantity under such contracts is the amount of requirements or the amount of output that occurs during a *normal* production period. The actual quantity purchased or sold cannot be unreasonably disproportionate to normal or comparable prior requirements or output [UCC 2–306(1)].

MERCHANT'S FIRM OFFER Under regular contract principles, an offer can be revoked at any time before acceptance. The major common law exception is an *option contract* (discussed in Chapter 12), in which the offeree pays consideration for the offeror's irrevocable promise to keep the offer open for a stated period. The UCC creates a second exception for *firm offers* made by a merchant concerning the sale or lease of goods (regardless of whether or not the offeree is a merchant).

When a Merchant's Firm Offer Arises. A **firm offer** arises when a merchant-offeror gives *assurances in a signed writing* that the offer will remain open. The merchant's firm offer is irrevocable without the neces-

---

7. See, for example, *In re Anchor Glass Container Corp.,* 345 Bankr. 765 (M.D.Fla. 2006).

sity of consideration[8] for the stated period or, if no definite period is stated, a reasonable period (neither to exceed three months) [UCC 2–205, 2A–205].

▶ **Example 20.10** Osaka, a used-car dealer, e-mails a letter to Gomez on January 1, stating, "I have a used 2013 Toyota RAV4 on the lot that I'll sell you for $22,000 any time between now and January 31." This e-mail creates a firm offer, and Osaka will be liable for breach of contract if he sells the RAV4 to another person before January 31. ◀

Requirements for a Firm Offer. To qualify as a firm offer, the offer must be:

1. *Written* (or electronically recorded, such as in an e-mail).
2. *Signed* by the offeror.[9]

When a firm offer is contained in a form contract prepared by the offeree, the offeror must also sign a separate assurance of the firm offer. The requirement of a separate signature ensures that the offeror will be made aware of the firm offer.

For instance, an offeree might respond to an initial offer by sending its own form contract containing a clause stating that the offer will remain open for three months. If the firm offer is buried amid copious language on the last page of the offeree's form contract, the offeror may inadvertently sign the contract without realizing that it contains a firm offer. This would defeat the purpose of the rule—which is to give effect to a merchant's *deliberate* intent to be bound to a firm offer.

Acceptance

Acceptance of an offer to buy, sell, or lease goods generally may be made in any reasonable manner and by any reasonable means. The UCC permits acceptance of an offer to buy goods "either by a prompt *promise* to ship or by the prompt or current shipment of conforming or nonconforming goods" [UCC 2–206(1)(b)]. *Conforming goods* accord with the contract's terms, whereas *nonconforming goods* do not.

The prompt shipment of nonconforming goods constitutes both an acceptance, which creates a contract, and a breach of that contract. This rule does not apply if the seller **seasonably** (within a reasonable amount of time) notifies the buyer that the nonconforming ship-

ment is offered only as an *accommodation,* or as a favor. The notice of accommodation must clearly indicate to the buyer that the shipment does not constitute an acceptance and that, therefore, no contract has been formed.

▶ **Example 20.11** McFarren Pharmacy orders five cases of Johnson & Johnson 3-by-5-inch gauze pads from H.T. Medical Supply, Inc. If H.T. ships five cases of Xeroform 3-by-5-inch gauze pads instead, the shipment acts as both an acceptance of McFarren's offer and a *breach* of the resulting contract. McFarren may sue H.T. for any appropriate damages. If, however, H.T. notifies McFarren that the Xeroform gauze pads are being shipped *as an accommodation*—because H.T. has only Xeroform pads in stock—the shipment will constitute a counteroffer, not an acceptance. A contract will be formed only if McFarren accepts the Xeroform gauze pads. ◀

COMMUNICATION OF ACCEPTANCE Under the common law, because a unilateral offer invites acceptance by performance, the offeree need not notify the offeror of performance unless the offeror would not otherwise know about it. In other words, a unilateral offer can be accepted by beginning performance.

The UCC is more stringent than the common law in this regard because it requires notification. Under the UCC, if the offeror is not notified within a reasonable time that the offeree has accepted the contract by beginning performance, then the offeror can treat the offer as having lapsed before acceptance [UCC 2–206(2), 2A–206(2)].

ADDITIONAL TERMS Recall from Chapter 12 that under the common law, the mirror image rule requires that the terms of the acceptance exactly match those of the offer. ▶ **Example 20.12** Aldrich e-mails an offer to sell twenty Samsung Galaxy model 7.0 tablets to Beale. If Beale accepts the offer but changes it to require model 8.9 tablets, then there is no contract. ◀

To avoid these problems, the UCC dispenses with the mirror image rule. Under the UCC, a contract is formed if the offeree's response indicates a *definite* acceptance of the offer, *even if the acceptance includes terms additional to or different from those contained in the offer* [UCC 2–207(1)]. Whether the additional terms become part of the contract depends, in part, on whether the parties are nonmerchants or merchants.

Rules When One Party or Both Parties Are Nonmerchants. If one (or both) of the parties is a *nonmerchant,* the contract is formed according to the terms of the original

---

8. If the offeree pays consideration, then an option contract (not a merchant's firm offer) is formed.
9. *Signed* includes any symbol executed or adopted by a party with a present intention to authenticate a writing [UCC 1–201(37)]. A complete signature is not required.

offer and does not include any of the additional terms in the acceptance [UCC 2–207(2)].

▶ **Case in Point 20.13** OfficeSupplyStore.com sells office supplies on the Web. Employees of the Kansas City School District in Missouri ordered $17,642.54 worth of office supplies—without the authority or approval of their employer—from the Web site. The invoices accompanying the goods contained a *forum-selection clause* (see Chapter 12) that required all disputes to be resolved in California.

When the goods were not paid for, Office Supply filed suit in California. The Kansas City School District objected, arguing that the forum-selection clause was not binding. The court held that the forum-selection clause was not part of the parties' contract. The clause was an additional term included in the invoices delivered to a nonmerchant buyer (the school district) with the purchased goods. Therefore, the clause did not become part of the contract unless the buyer expressly agreed, which did not happen in this case.[10] ◀

Rules When Both Parties Are Merchants. The drafters of the UCC created a special rule for merchants to avoid

---

10. *OfficeSupplyStore.com v. Kansas City School Board,* 334 S.W.3d 574 (Kan. 2011).

the "battle of the forms," which occurs when two merchants exchange separate standard forms containing different contract terms.

Under UCC 2–207(2), in contracts *between merchants,* the additional terms *automatically* become part of the contract *unless* one of the following conditions arises:

1. The original offer expressly limited acceptance to its terms.
2. The new or changed terms materially alter the contract.
3. The offeror objects to the new or changed terms within a reasonable period of time.

When determining whether an alteration is material, courts consider several factors. Generally, if the modification does not involve any unreasonable element of surprise or hardship for the offeror, a court will hold that the modification did not materially alter the contract. Courts also consider the parties' prior dealings.

In the following case, a party conditioned its acceptance of an offer on the other parties' agreement to additional terms by a specific date. When the parties agreed to the most important terms after the deadline, the court had to decide if there was an enforceable contract.

CASE 20.2

WPS, Inc. v. Expro Americas, LLC
Court of Appeals of Texas, First District, 369 S.W.3d 384 (2012).

BACKGROUND AND FACTS In April 2006, WPS, Inc., submitted a formal proposal to manufacture equipment for Expro Americas, LLC, and Surface Production Systems, Inc. (SPS). Expro and SPS then submitted two purchase orders. WPS accepted the first purchase order in part, and it accepted the second order conditionally. Among other things, WPS required that, by April 28, 2006, Expro and SPS give their "full release to proceed" and agree to "pay all valid costs associated with any order cancellation." The parties' negotiations continued, and Expro and SPS eventually submitted a third purchase order on May 9, 2006.

The third purchase order did not comply with all of WPS's requirements, but it did give WPS full permission to proceed and agreed that Expro and SPS would pay all cancellation costs. With Expro and SPS's knowledge, WPS then began work under the third purchase order. Expro and SPS soon canceled the order, however, so WPS sent them an invoice charging them for the cancellation costs. At trial, the jury and court concluded that there was a contract and found in WPS's favor. Expro and SPS appealed.

 IN THE LANGUAGE OF THE COURT
Terry *JENNINGS,* Justice.

* * * *

* * * WPS replied with a conditional acceptance of the second purchase order. WPS also stated that its conditional acceptance depended upon the receipt of a revised purchase order by April 28, 2006. Although it is undisputed that Expro * * * and SPS did not issue a revised purchase order by this date, the evidence * * * reveals that the parties continued their discus-

CASE 20.2 CONTINUED

sions and negotiations over those matters that had yet to be resolved. * * * *The parties operated as if they had additional time to resolve the outstanding differences.* [Emphasis added.]

Expro * * * and SPS submitted their revised third purchase order on May 9, 2006, agreeing in writing to virtually all the matters that had remained unresolved to that date. * * * Most importantly, Expro * * * and SPS provided * * * a "full release to proceed" and agreed to "pay all valid costs associated with any order cancellation." In his testimony, [SPS's vice president] conceded that *the term "Release to Proceed" "basically means that one party is in agreement," authorizing the other party to go forward.* * * * WPS had previously sought the release to proceed so that it could "diligently" perform its obligations under the contract. The jury could have reasonably concluded that WPS, having now obtained the release * * * and * * * [the] promise to pay cancellation charges * * *, was contractually obligated to perform and meet the delivery date. [Emphasis added.]

DECISION AND REMEDY *The Texas appellate court found that WPS had a contract with Expro and SPS. It affirmed the lower court's judgment for WPS.*

THE LEGAL ENVIRONMENT DIMENSION *In allowing a party to condition its acceptance on additional terms, does contract law make negotiations more or less efficient? Explain your answer.*

THE ECONOMIC DIMENSION *Why would a manufacturer like WPS want its purchase orders to include terms such as those at issue in this case? Why would a buyer like Expro or SPS want to exclude such terms?*

Conditioned on Offeror's Assent. Regardless of merchant status, the UCC provides that the offeree's response cannot be construed as an acceptance if it contains additional or different terms and is expressly *conditioned* on the offeror's assent to those terms [UCC 2–207(1)].

▶ **Example 20.14** Philips offers to sell Hundert 650 pounds of turkey thighs at a specified price and with specified delivery terms. Hundert responds, "I accept your offer for 650 pounds of turkey thighs *on the condition that you agree to give me ninety days to pay for them.*" Hundert's response will be construed not as an acceptance but as a counteroffer, which Philips may or may not accept. ◀

Additional Terms May Be Stricken. The UCC provides yet another option for dealing with conflicting terms in the parties' writings. Section 2–207(3) states that conduct by both parties that recognizes the existence of a contract is sufficient to establish a contract for sale even though the writings of the parties do not otherwise establish a contract. In this situation, "the terms of the particular contract will consist of those terms on which the writings of the parties agree, together with any supplementary terms incorporated under any other provisions of this Act." In a dispute over contract terms, this provision allows a court simply to strike from the contract those terms on which the parties do not agree.

▶ **Example 20.15** SMT Marketing orders goods over the phone from Brigg Sales, Inc., which ships the goods to SMT with an acknowledgment form (confirming the order). SMT accepts and pays for the goods. The parties' writings do not establish a contract, but there is no question that a contract exists. If a dispute arises over the terms, such as the extent of any warranties, UCC 2–207(3) provides the governing rule. ◀

As noted previously, the fact that a merchant's acceptance frequently contains terms that add to or even conflict with those of the offer is often referred to as the "battle of the forms." Although the UCC tries to eliminate this battle, the problem of differing contract terms still arises in commercial settings, particularly when standard forms (for placing and confirming orders) are used.

Consideration

The common law rule that a contract requires consideration also applies to sales and lease contracts. Unlike the common law, however, the UCC does not require a contract modification to be supported by new consideration. The UCC states that an agreement modifying a contract for the sale or lease of goods "needs no consideration to be binding" [UCC 2–209(1), 2A–208(1)]. Of course, any contract modification must be made in good faith [UCC 1–304].

In some situations, an agreement to modify a sales or lease contract without consideration must be in writing to be enforceable. For instance, if the contract itself specifies that any changes to the contract must be in a signed writing, only those changes agreed to in a signed writing are enforceable.

Sometimes, when a consumer (nonmerchant) is buying goods from a merchant-seller, the merchant supplies a form that contains a prohibition against oral modification. In those situations, the consumer must sign a separate acknowledgment of the clause for it to be enforceable [UCC 2–209(2), 2A–208(2)]. Also, any modification that makes a sales contract come under Article 2's writing requirement (its Statute of Frauds, discussed next) usually requires a writing (or electronic record) to be enforceable.

The Statute of Frauds

The UCC contains Statute of Frauds provisions covering sales and lease contracts. Under these provisions, sales contracts for goods priced at $500 or more and lease contracts requiring total payments of $1,000 or more must be in writing to be enforceable [UCC 2–201(1), 2A–201(1)]. (These low threshold amounts may eventually be raised.)

SUFFICIENCY OF THE WRITING A writing, e-mail, or other electronic record will be sufficient to satisfy the UCC's Statute of Fraud as long as it:

1. Indicates that the parties intended to form a contract.
2. Is signed by the party (or agent of the party) against whom enforcement is sought. (Remember that a typed name can qualify as a signature on an electronic record, as discussed in Chapter 9.)

The contract normally will not be enforceable beyond the quantity of goods shown in the writing, however. All other terms can be proved in court by oral testimony. For leases, the writing must reasonably identify and describe the goods leased and the lease term.

SPECIAL RULES FOR CONTRACTS BETWEEN MERCHANTS The UCC provides a special rule for merchants in sales transactions (there is no corresponding rule that applies to leases under Article 2A). Merchants can satisfy the Statute of Frauds if, after the parties have agreed orally, one of the merchants sends a signed written (or electronic) confirmation to the other merchant within a reasonable time.

The communication must indicate the terms of the agreement, and the merchant receiving the confirmation must have reason to know of its contents. Unless the merchant who receives the confirmation gives written notice of objection to its contents within ten days after receipt, the writing is sufficient against the receiving merchant, even though she or he has not signed it [UCC 2–201(2)].

▶ **Example 20.16** Alfonso is a merchant-buyer in Cleveland. He contracts over the telephone to purchase $6,000 worth of spare aircraft parts from Goldstein, a merchant-seller in New York City. Two days later, Goldstein e-mails a signed confirmation detailing the terms of the oral contract, and Alfonso subsequently receives it. Alfonso does not notify Goldstein in writing (or e-mail) that he objects to the contents of the confirmation within ten days of receipt. Therefore, Alfonso cannot raise the Statute of Frauds as a defense against the enforcement of the oral contract. ◀

EXCEPTIONS The UCC defines three exceptions to the writing requirements of the Statute of Frauds. An oral contract for the sale of goods priced at $500 or more or the lease of goods involving total payments of $1,000 or more will be enforceable despite the absence of a writing in the circumstances described next [UCC 2–201(3), 2A–201(4)].

Specially Manufactured Goods. An oral contract for the sale or lease of custom-made goods will be enforceable if:

1. The goods are *specially manufactured* for a particular buyer or specially manufactured or obtained for a particular lessee.
2. The goods are *not suitable for resale or lease* to others in the ordinary course of the seller's or lessor's business.
3. The seller or lessor has *substantially started to manufacture* the goods or has made commitments for the manufacture or procurement of the goods.

In these situations, once the seller or lessor has taken action, the buyer or lessee cannot repudiate the agreement claiming the Statute of Frauds as a defense.

▶ **Example 20.17** Womach orders custom window treatments to use at a day spa business for $6,000 from Hunter Douglas. The contract is oral. When Hunter Douglas manufactures the window coverings and tenders delivery to Womach, she refuses to pay for them, even though the job has been completed on time. Womach claims that she is not liable because the contract was oral. If the unique style, size, and color of the window treatments make it improbable that Hunter Douglas can find another buyer, Womach is liable to Hunter Douglas. ◄

Admissions. An oral contract for the sale or lease of goods is enforceable if the party against whom enforcement is sought admits in pleadings, testimony, or other court proceedings that a sales or lease contract was made. In this situation, the contract will be enforceable even though it was oral, but enforceability will be limited to the quantity of goods admitted.

► **Case in Point 20.18** Gerald Lindgren, a farmer, agreed by phone to sell his crops to Glacial Plains Cooperative. The parties reached four oral agreements: two for the delivery of soybeans and two for the delivery of corn. Lindgren made the soybean deliveries and part of the first corn delivery, but he sold the rest of his corn to another dealer. Glacial Plains bought corn elsewhere, paying a higher price, and then sued Lindgren for breach of contract. In papers filed with the court, Lindgren acknowledged his oral agreements with Glacial Plains and admitted that he did not fully perform. The court applied the admissions exception and held that the four agreements were enforceable.[11] ◄

Partial Performance. An oral contract for the sale or lease of goods is enforceable if payment has been made and accepted or goods have been received and accepted. This is the "partial performance" exception. The oral contract will be enforced at least to the extent that performance actually took place.

► **Case in Point 20.19** Quality Pork International formed an oral contract with Rupari Food Services, Inc., which buys food products and sells them to retail operations. Quality was to ship three orders of pork to Star Food Processing, Inc., and Rupari was to pay for the products. Quality shipped the goods to Star and sent invoices to Rupari. Rupari billed Star for all three orders but paid Quality only for the first two. Quality filed a suit against Rupari to recover $44,051.98, the cost of the third order.

Rupari argued that because the parties did not have a written agreement, there was no enforceable contract. The court held that even though Rupari had not signed a written contract or purchase order, it had accepted the goods and partially performed the contract by paying for the first two shipments. Rupari's conduct was sufficient to prove the existence of a con-

tract, and the court required Rupari to pay for the last shipment.[12] ◄

The exceptions just discussed and other ways in which sales law differs from general contract law are summarized in Exhibit 20–3 on the following page.

Parol Evidence

Recall from Chapter 16 that parol evidence consists of evidence outside the contract such as evidence of the parties' prior negotiations, prior agreements, or contemporaneous (simultaneous) oral agreements. When a contract completely sets forth all the terms and conditions agreed to by the parties and is intended as a final statement of their agreement, it is considered fully *integrated* (see Chapter 16). The terms of a **fully integrated contract** cannot be contradicted by evidence of any prior agreements or contemporaneous oral agreements.

If, however, the writing contains some of the terms the parties agreed on but not others, then the contract is not fully integrated. When a court finds that a contract is *not fully integrated,* then the court may allow evidence of *consistent additional terms* to explain or supplement the terms in the contract. The court may also allow the parties to submit evidence of *course of dealing, usage of trade,* or *course of performance* [UCC 2–202, 2A–202].

COURSE OF DEALING AND USAGE OF TRADE Under the UCC, the meaning of any agreement, evidenced by the language of the parties and by their actions, must be interpreted in light of commercial practices and other surrounding circumstances. In interpreting a commercial agreement, a court will assume that the course of dealing between the parties and the general usage of trade were taken into account when the agreement was phrased.

Course of Dealing. A **course of dealing** is a sequence of actions and communications between the parties to a particular transaction that establishes a common basis for their understanding [UCC 1–303(b)]. A course of dealing is restricted to the sequence of conduct between the parties in their transactions prior to the agreement.

Under the UCC, a course of dealing between the parties is relevant in ascertaining the meaning of the parties' agreement. It "may give particular meaning

---

11. *Glacial Plains Cooperative v. Lindgren,* 759 N.W.2d 661 (Min.App. 2009).

12. *Quality Pork International v. Rupari Food Services, Inc.,* 267 Neb. 474, 675 N.W.2d 642 (2004).

EXHIBIT 20-3 Major Differences between Contract Law and Sales Law

	Contract Law	Sales Law
Contract Terms	Contract must contain all material terms.	Open terms are acceptable if parties intended to form a contract, but the contract is not enforceable beyond quantity term.
Acceptance	Mirror image rule applies. If additional terms are added in acceptance, a counteroffer is created.	Additional terms will not negate acceptance unless acceptance is expressly conditioned on assent to the additional terms.
Contract Modification	Modification requires consideration.	Modification does not require consideration.
Irrevocable Offers	Option contracts (with consideration).	Merchants' firm offers (without consideration).
Statute of Frauds Requirements	All material terms must be included in the writing.	Writing is required only for sale of goods priced at $500 or more, but the contract is not enforceable beyond the quantity specified. Merchants can satisfy the writing by a confirmation evidencing their agreement. *Exceptions:* 1. Specially manufactured goods. 2. Admissions by party against whom enforcement is sought. 3. Partial performance.

to specific terms of the agreement, and may supplement or qualify the terms of the agreement" [UCC 1–303(d)].

Usage of Trade. Any practice or method of dealing that is so regularly observed in a place, vocation, or trade as to justify an expectation by the parties that it will be observed in their transaction is a **usage of trade** [UCC 1–303(c)].

▶ **Example 20.20** Phat Khat Loans, Inc., hires Fleet Title Review Company to search the public records for prior claims on potential borrrowers' assets. Fleet's invoice states, "Liability limited to amount of fee." In the title search industry, liability limits are common. After conducting many searches for Phat Khat, Fleet reports that there are no claims with respect to Main Street Autos. Phat Khat loans $100,000 to Main, with payment guaranteed by Main's assets. When Main defaults on the loan, Phat Khat learns that another lender has priority to Main's assets under a previous claim. If Phat Khat sues Fleet Title for breach of contract, Fleet's liability will normally be limited to the amount of its fee. The statement in the invoice was part of the contract between Phat Khat and Fleet, according to the usage of trade in the industry and the parties' course of dealing. ◀

COURSE OF PERFORMANCE The conduct that occurs under the terms of a particular agreement is called a **course of performance** [UCC 1–303(a)]. Presumably, the parties themselves know best what they meant by their words. Thus, the course of performance actually carried out under the parties' agreement is the best indication of what they meant [UCC 2–208(1), 2A–207(1)].

▶ **Example 20.21** Janson's Lumber Company contracts with Lopez to sell Lopez a specified number of two-by-fours. The lumber in fact does not measure exactly 2 inches by 4 inches but rather 1⅞ inches by 3¾ inches. Janson's agrees to deliver the lumber in five deliveries, and Lopez, without objection, accepts the lumber in the first three deliveries. On the fourth delivery, however, Lopez objects that the two-by-fours do not measure precisely 2 inches by 4 inches.

The course of performance in this transaction—that is, the fact that Lopez accepted three deliveries without objection under the agreement—is relevant in determining that here a "two-by-four" actually means a "1⅞-by-3¾." Janson's can also prove that two-by-fours need not be exactly 2 inches by 4 inches by applying usage of trade, course of dealing, or both. Janson's can, for example, show that in previous transactions, Lopez took 1⅞-inch-by-3¾-inch lumber without objection. In addition, Janson's can show that in the trade, two-by-fours are commonly 1⅞ inches by 3¾ inches. ◀

RULES OF CONSTRUCTION The UCC provides *rules of construction* for interpreting contracts. Express terms, course of performance, course of dealing, and usage of trade are to be construed to be consistent with each other whenever reasonable. When such a construction is unreasonable, however, the UCC establishes the following order of priority [UCC 1–303(e), 2–208(2), 2A–207(2)]:

1. Express terms.
2. Course of performance.
3. Course of dealing.
4. Usage of trade.

Unconscionability

As discussed in Chapters 14 and 15, an unconscionable contract is one that is so unfair and one sided that it would be unreasonable to enforce it. The UCC allows a court to evaluate a contract or any clause in a contract, and if the court deems it to have been unconscionable *at the time it was made,* the court can do any of the following [UCC 2–302, 2A–108]:

1. Refuse to enforce the contract.
2. Enforce the remainder of the contract without the unconscionable part.
3. Limit the application of the unconscionable term to avoid an unconscionable result.

The following classic case illustrates an early application of the UCC's unconscionability provisions.

CLASSIC CASE 20.3

Jones v. Star Credit Corp.
Supreme Court of New York, Nassau County, 59 Misc.2d 189, 298 N.Y.S.2d 264 (1969).

BACKGROUND AND FACTS The Joneses agreed to purchase a freezer for $900 as the result of a salesperson's visit to their home. Tax and financing charges raised the total price to $1,234.80. At trial, the freezer was found to have a maximum retail value of approximately $300. The Joneses, who had made payments totaling $619.88, brought a suit in a New York state court to have the purchase contract declared unconscionable under the UCC.

 IN THE LANGUAGE OF THE COURT
Sol M. *WACHTLER,* Justice.

＊ ＊ ＊ ＊

＊ ＊ ＊ [Section 2–302 of the UCC] authorizes the court to find, as a matter of law, that a contract or a clause of a contract was "unconscionable at the time it was made," and upon so finding the court may refuse to enforce the contract, excise the objectionable clause or limit the application of the clause to avoid an unconscionable result.

＊ ＊ ＊ ＊

＊ ＊ ＊ The question which presents itself is whether or not, under the circumstances of this case, the sale of a freezer unit having a retail value of $300 for $900 ($1,439.69 including credit charges and $18 sales tax) is unconscionable as a matter of law.

Concededly, deciding [this case] is substantially easier than explaining it. No doubt, the mathematical disparity between $300, which presumably includes a reasonable profit margin, and $900, which is exorbitant on its face, carries the greatest weight. Credit charges alone exceed by more than $100 the retail value of the freezer. These alone may be sufficient to sustain the decision. Yet, a caveat [warning] is warranted lest we reduce the import of Section 2–302 solely to a mathematical ratio formula. It may, at times, be that; yet it may also be much more. The very limited financial resources of the purchaser, known to the sellers at the time of the sale, is entitled to weight in the balance. Indeed, the value disparity itself leads inevitably to the felt conclusion that knowing advantage was taken of the plaintiffs. In addition, *the meaningfulness of choice essential to the making of a contract can be negated by a gross inequality of bargaining power.* [Emphasis added.]

＊ ＊ ＊ ＊

CASE 20.3 CONTINUES ➡

* * * The defendant has already been amply compensated. In accordance with the statute, the application of the payment provision should be limited to amounts already paid by the plaintiffs and the contract be reformed and amended by changing the payments called for therein to equal the amount of payment actually so paid by the plaintiffs.

DECISION AND REMEDY *The court held that the contract was not enforceable and reformed the contract so that no further payments were required.*

IMPACT OF THIS CASE ON TODAY'S LAW *This early classic case illustrates the approach that many courts take today when deciding whether a sales contract is unconscionable—an approach that focuses on "excessive" price and unequal bargaining power. Most of the litigants who have used UCC 2–302 successfully could demonstrate* both *an absence of meaningful choice and that the contract terms were unreasonably favorable to the other party.*

THE SOCIAL DIMENSION *Why would the seller's knowledge of the buyers' limited resources support a finding of unconscionability?*

Concept Summary 20.1 on the next page reviews the concepts and rules related to the formation of sales and lease contracts.

SECTION 4
CONTRACTS FOR THE INTERNATIONAL SALE OF GOODS

International sales contracts between firms or individuals located in different countries may be governed by the 1980 United Nations Convention on Contracts for the International Sale of Goods (CISG). The CISG governs international contracts only if the countries of the parties to the contract have ratified the CISG and if the parties have not agreed that some other law will govern their contract. As of 2013, the CISG had been adopted by seventy-eight countries, including the United States, Canada, some Central and South American countries, China, most European nations, Japan, and Mexico. That means that the CISG is the uniform international sales law of countries that account for more than two-thirds of all global trade. (For an example of an international sales contract, see the appendix to this chapter.)

Essentially, the CISG is to international sales contracts what Article 2 of the UCC is to domestic sales contracts. In domestic transactions, the UCC applies when the parties to a contract for a sale of goods have failed to specify in writing some important term, such as the price or delivery. Similarly, whenever the parties to international transactions have failed to spec-

ify in writing the precise terms of a contract, the CISG will be applied.

Unlike the UCC, *the CISG does not apply to consumer sales.* Neither the UCC nor the CISG applies to contracts for services.

A Comparison of CISG and UCC Provisions

The provisions of the CISG, although similar for the most part to those of the UCC, differ from them in some respects. If the CISG and the UCC conflict, the CISG applies (because it is a treaty of the U.S. national government and therefore is supreme—see the discussion of the supremacy clause in Chapter 4).

The major differences between the CISG and the UCC in regard to contract formation concern the mirror image rule, irrevocable offers, the Statute of Frauds, and the time of contract formation. We discuss these differences in the subsections that follow. CISG provisions relating to risk of loss, performance, remedies, and warranties will be discussed in the following chapters as those topics are examined.

THE MIRROR IMAGE RULE Under the UCC, a definite expression of acceptance that contains additional terms can still result in the formation of a contract, unless the additional terms are conditioned on the assent of the offeror. In other words, the UCC does away with the mirror image rule in domestic sales contracts.

Article 19 of the CISG provides that a contract can be formed even though the acceptance contains additional terms, unless the additional terms materially

---

CONCEPT SUMMARY 20.1

The Formation of Sales and Lease Contracts

CONCEPT	DESCRIPTION
Offer and Acceptance	1. *Offer—* a. Not all terms have to be included for a contract to be formed. b. The price does not have to be included for a contract to be formed. c. Particulars of performance can be left open. d. An offer by a merchant in a signed writing with assurances that the offer will not be withdrawn is irrevocable without consideration (for up to three months). 2. *Acceptance—* a. Acceptance may be made by any reasonable means of communication. It is effective when dispatched. b. The acceptance of a unilateral offer can be made by a promise to ship or by the shipment of conforming or nonconforming goods. c. Acceptance by performance requires notice within a reasonable time. Otherwise, the offer can be treated as lapsed. d. A definite expression of acceptance creates a contract even if the terms of the acceptance modify the terms of the offer.
Consideration	A modification of a contract for the sale of goods does not require consideration.
Requirements under the Statute of Frauds	1. All contracts for the sale of goods priced at $500 or more must be in writing. A writing is sufficient as long as it indicates a contract between the parties and is signed by the party against whom enforcement is sought. A contract is not enforceable beyond the quantity shown in the writing. 2. When written confirmation of an oral contract between merchants is not objected to in writing by the receiver within ten days, the oral contract is enforceable. 3. Exceptions to the requirement of a writing exist in the following situations: a. When the oral contract is for specially manufactured or obtained goods not suitable for resale or lease to others and the seller or lessor has made commitments for the manufacture or procurement of the goods. b. If the defendant admits in pleadings, testimony, or other court proceedings that an oral contract for the sale or lease of goods was made, then the contract will be enforceable to the extent of the quantity of goods admitted. c. The oral agreement will be enforceable to the extent that payment has been received and accepted or to the extent that goods have been received and accepted.
Parol Evidence Rule	1. The terms of a clearly and completely worded written contract cannot be contradicted by evidence of prior agreements or contemporaneous oral agreements. 2. Evidence is admissible to clarify the terms of a writing in the following situations: a. If the contract terms are ambiguous. b. If evidence of course of dealing, usage of trade, or course of performance is necessary to learn or to clarify the intentions of the parties to the contract.

---

alter the contract. Under the CISG, however, the definition of a "material alteration" includes almost any change in the terms. If an additional term relates to payment, quality, quantity, price, time and place of delivery, extent of one party's liability to the other, or the settlement of disputes, the CISG considers the added term a material alteration. In effect, then, the CISG requires that the terms of the acceptance mirror those of the offer.

Therefore, as a practical matter, businesspersons undertaking international sales transactions should not use the sale or purchase forms that they customarily use for transactions within the United States. Instead, they should draft specific forms to suit the needs of the particular transaction.

IRREVOCABLE OFFERS UCC 2–205 provides that a merchant's firm offer is irrevocable, even without consideration, if the merchant gives assurances in a signed writing. In contrast, under the CISG, an offer can become irrevocable without a signed writing. Article 16(2) of the CISG provides that an offer will be irrevocable if:

1. The offeror states orally that the offer is irrevocable.
2. The offeree reasonably relies on the offer as being irrevocable.

In both of these situations, the offer will be irrevocable even without a writing and without consideration.

THE WRITING REQUIREMENT As discussed previously, the UCC has a Statute of Frauds provision. UCC 2–201 requires contracts for the sale of goods priced at $500 or more to be evidenced by a written or electronic record signed by the party against whom enforcement is sought.

Article 11 of the CISG, however, states that a contract of sale "need not be concluded in or evidenced by writing and is not subject to any other requirements as to form. It may be proved by any means, including witnesses." Article 11 of the CISG accords with the legal customs of most nations, which no longer require contracts to meet certain formal or writing requirements to be enforceable.

TIME OF CONTRACT FORMATION Under the common law of contracts and the UCC, an acceptance is effective on dispatch, so a contract is created when the acceptance is transmitted. Under the CISG, in contrast, a contract is created not at the time the acceptance is transmitted but only on its *receipt* by the offeror. (The offer becomes *irrevocable,* however, when the acceptance is sent.)

Article 18(2) states that an acceptance by return promise (a unilateral contract—see Chapter 11) "becomes effective at the moment the indication of assent reaches the offeror." Under Article 18(3), the offeree may also bind the offeror by performance even without giving any notice to the offeror. The acceptance becomes effective "at the moment the act is performed." Thus, it is the offeree's reliance, rather than the communication of acceptance to the offeror, that creates the contract.

Special Provisions in International Contracts

Language and legal differences among nations can create various problems for parties to international contracts when disputes arise. It is possible to avoid these problems by including in a contract special provisions relating to choice of language, choice of forum, choice of law, and the types of events that may excuse the parties from performance.

CHOICE OF LANGUAGE A deal struck between a U.S. company and a company in another country frequently involves two languages. One party may not understand complex contractual terms that are written in the other party's language. Translating the terms poses its own problems, as typically many phrases are not readily translatable into another language.

To make sure that no disputes arise out of this language problem, an international sales contract should include a **choice-of-language clause,** designating the official language by which the contract will be interpreted in the event of disagreement. The clause might also specify that the agreement is to be translated into, say, Spanish, and that the translation is to be approved by both parties so that they can rely on it. If arbitration is anticipated, an additional clause must be added to indicate the official language that will be used at the arbitration proceeding.

CHOICE OF FORUM A forum-selection clause designates the forum (place, or court) in which any disputes that arise under the contract will be litigated. Including a forum-selection clause in an international contract is especially important because when several countries are involved, litigation may be sought in courts in different nations. There are no universally accepted rules regarding the jurisdiction of a particular court over subject matter or parties to a dispute, although the adoption of the 2005 Choice of Court Convention helps resolve certain issues.

A forum-selection clause should indicate the specific court that will have jurisdiction. The forum does not necessarily have to be within the geographic boundaries of either party's nation.

Under certain circumstances, a forum-selection clause will not be valid. Specifically, if the clause denies one party an effective remedy, or is the product of fraud or unconscionable conduct, the clause will not be enforced. Similarly, if the designated forum causes substantial inconvenience to one of the parties, or violates public policy, the clause may not be enforced.

CHOICE OF LAW A contractual provision designating the applicable law, called a **choice-of-law clause,** is typically included in every international contract. At common law (and in European civil law systems—

see Chapter 24), parties are allowed to choose the law that will govern their contractual relationship.

There must normally be some connection between the chosen law and the contracting parties to show that the parties are not merely trying to avoid the laws of their own jurisdictions. ▶ **Example 20.22** A U.S. automaker contracts with a German company. The parties cannot choose the law of China to govern their agreement if neither the contract nor the parties have anything to do with China. The choice of Chinese law in that situation might reflect an attempt to avoid consumer, environmental, or employment laws that would otherwise apply to the transaction. ◀

Under the UCC, parties may choose the law that will govern the contract as long as the choice is "reasonable." Article 6 of the CISG, however, imposes no limitation on the parties in their choice of what law will govern the contract. The 1986 Hague Convention on the Law Applicable to Contracts for the International Sale of Goods—often referred to as the Choice-of-Law Convention—allows unlimited autonomy in the choice of law. Whenever a choice of law is not specified in a contract, the Hague Convention indicates that the law of the country where the seller's place of business is located will govern.

FORCE MAJEURE CLAUSE Every contract, and particularly those involving international transactions, should have a ***force majeure* clause.** The meaning of the French term *force majeure* is "impossible or irresistible force"—sometimes loosely defined as "an act of God." *Force majeure* clauses commonly stipulate that in addition to acts of God, a number of other eventualities (such as governmental orders or regulations, embargoes, or extreme shortages of materials) may excuse a party from liability for nonperformance.

Reviewing: The Formation of Sales and Lease Contracts

Guy Holcomb owns and operates Oasis Goodtime Emporium, an adult entertainment establishment. Holcomb wanted to create an adult Internet system for Oasis that would offer customers adult theme videos and "live" chat room programs using performers at the club. On May 10, Holcomb signed a work order authorizing Thomas Consulting Group (TCG) "to deliver a working prototype of a customer chat system, demonstrating the integration of live video and chatting in a Web browser." In exchange for creating the prototype, Holcomb agreed to pay TCG $64,697. On May 20, Holcomb signed an additional work order in the amount of $12,943 for TCG to install a customized firewall system. The work orders stated that Holcomb would make monthly installment payments to TCG, and both parties expected the work would be finished by September.

Due to unforeseen problems largely attributable to system configuration and software incompatibility, the project required more time than anticipated. By the end of the summer, the Web site was still not ready, and Holcomb had fallen behind in his payments to TCG. TCG threatened to cease work and file a suit for breach of contract unless the bill was paid. Rather than make further payments, Holcomb wanted to abandon the Web site project. Using the information presented in the chapter, answer the following questions.

1. Would a court be likely to decide that the transaction between Holcomb and TCG was covered by the Uniform Commercial Code (UCC)? Why or why not?
2. Would a court be likely to consider Holcomb a merchant under the UCC? Why or why not?
3. Did the parties have a valid contract under the UCC? Were any terms left open in the contract? If so, which terms? How would a court deal with open terms?
4. Suppose that Holcomb and TCG meet in October in an attempt to resolve their problems. At that time, the parties reach an oral agreement that TCG will continue to work without demanding full payment of the past due amounts and Holcomb will pay TCG $5,000 per week. Assuming the contract falls under the UCC, is the oral agreement enforceable? Why or why not?

DEBATE THIS ... *The UCC should require the same degree of definiteness of terms, especially with respect to price and quantity, as contract law does.*

Terms and Concepts

choice-of-language clause 392

choice-of-law clause 392

course of dealing 387

course of performance 388

firm offer 382

force majeure clause 393

fully integrated contract 387

intangible property 378

lease agreement 380

lessee 380

lessor 380

merchant 380

output contract 382

predominant-factor test 378

requirements contract 382

sale 378

sales contract 376

seasonably 383

tangible property 378

usage of trade 388

ExamPrep

Issue Spotters

1. E-Design, Inc., orders 150 computer desks. Fav-O-Rite Supplies, Inc., ships 150 printer stands. Is this an acceptance of the offer or a counteroffer? If it is an acceptance, is it a breach of the contract? Why or why not? What if Fav-O-Rite told E-Design it was sending the printer stands as "an accommodation"? **(See page 383.)**

2. Truck Parts, Inc. (TPI), often sells supplies to United Fix-It Company (UFC), which services trucks. Over the phone, they negotiate for the sale of eighty-four sets of tires. TPI sends a letter to UFC detailing the terms and two weeks later ships the tires. Is there an enforce-able contract between them? Why or why not? **(See page 386.)**

- Check your answers to the Issue Spotters against the answers provided in Appendix E at the end of this text.

Before the Test

Go to **www.cengagebrain.com**, enter the ISBN 9781285185248, and click on "Find" to locate this text-book's Web site. Then, click on "Access Now" under "Study Tools," and select Chapter 20 at the top. There, you will find a Practice Quiz that you can take to assess your mastery of the concepts in this chapter, as well as Flashcards and a Glossary of important terms.

Business Scenarios

20–1. The Statute of Frauds. Fresher Foods, Inc., orally agreed to purchase one thousand bushels of corn for $1.25 per bushel from Dale Vernon, a farmer. Fresher Foods paid $125 down and agreed to pay the remainder of the purchase price on delivery, which was scheduled for one week later. When Fresher Foods tendered the balance of $1,125 on the scheduled day of delivery and requested the corn, Vernon refused to deliver it. Fresher Foods sued Vernon for damages, claiming that Vernon had breached their oral contract. Can Fresher Foods recover? If so, to what extent? **(See page 386.)**

20–2. Additional Terms. Strike offers to sell Bailey one thousand shirts for a stated price. The offer declares that shipment will be made by Dependable Truck Line. Bailey replies, "I accept your offer for one thousand shirts at the price quoted. Delivery to be by Yellow Express Truck Line." Both Strike and Bailey are merchants. Three weeks later, Strike ships the shirts by Dependable Truck Line, and Bailey refuses to accept delivery. Strike sues for breach of contract. Bailey claims that there never was a contract because his reply, which included a modification of carriers, did not constitute an acceptance. Bailey further claims that even if there had been a contract, Strike would have been in breach because Strike shipped the shirts by Dependable, contrary to the contract terms. Discuss fully Bailey's claims. **(See page 383.)**

Business Case Problems

20–3. Spotlight on Goods and Services—The Statute of Frauds.

 Fallsview Glatt Kosher Caterers ran a business that provided travel packages, including food, entertainment, and lectures on religious subjects, to customers during the Passover holiday at a New York resort. Willie Rosenfeld verbally agreed to pay Fallsview $24,050 for the Passover package for himself and his family. Rosenfeld did not appear at the resort and never paid the amount owed. Fallsview sued Rosenfeld for breach of contract. Rosenfeld claimed that the contract was unenforceable because it was not in writing and violated the UCC's Statute of Frauds. Is the contract valid? Explain. [*Fallsview Glatt Kosher Caterers, Inc. v. Rosenfeld*, 794 N.Y.S.2d 790 (N.Y.Super. 2005)] **(See page 386.)**

20–4. BUSINESS CASE PROBLEM
WITH SAMPLE ANSWER: Additional Terms.

 B.S. International, Ltd. (BSI), makes costume jewelry. JMAM, LLC, is a wholesaler of costume jewelry. JMAM sent BSI a letter with the terms for orders, including the necessary procedure for obtaining credit for items that customers rejected. The letter stated, "By signing below, you agree to the terms." Steven Baracsi, BSI's owner, signed the letter and returned it. For six years, BSI made jewelry for JMAM, which resold it. Items rejected by customers were sent back to JMAM, but were never returned to BSI. BSI filed a suit against JMAM, claiming $41,294.21 for the unreturned items. BSI showed the court a copy of JMAM's terms. Across the bottom had been typed a "PS" requiring the return of rejected merchandise. Was this "PS" part of the contract? Discuss. [B.S. International, Ltd. v. JMAM, LLC, 13 A.3d 1057 (R.I. 2011)] **(See page 383.)**

- **For a sample answer to Problem 20–4, go to Appendix F at the end of this text.**

20–5. Partial Performance and the Statute of Frauds. After a series of e-mails, Jorge Bonilla, the sole proprietor of a printing company in Uruguay, agreed to buy a used printer from Crystal Graphics Equipment, Inc., in New York. Crystal Graphics, through its agent, told Bonilla that the printing press was fully operational, contained all of its parts, and was in excellent condition except for some damage to one of the printing towers. Bonilla paid $95,000. Crystal Graphics sent him a signed, stamped invoice reflecting this payment. The invoice was dated six days after Bonilla's conversation with the agent. When the printing press arrived, Bonilla discovered that it was missing parts and was damaged. Crystal Graphics sent replacement parts, but they did not work. Ultimately, Crystal Graphics was never able to make the printer operational. Bonilla sued, alleging breach of contract, breach of the implied covenant of good faith and fair dealing, breach of express warranty, and breach of implied warranty. Crystal Graphics claimed that the contract was not enforceable because it did not satisfy the Statute of Frauds. Can Crystal Graphics prevail on this basis? Why or why not? [*Bonilla v. Crystal Graphics Equipment, Inc.*, 2012 WL 360145 (S.D.Fla. 2012)] **(See page 386.)**

20–6. The Statute of Frauds. Kendall Gardner agreed to buy from B&C Shavings, a specially built shaving mill to pro-

duce wood shavings for poultry processors. B&C faxed an invoice to Gardner reflecting a purchase price of $86,200, with a 30 percent down payment and the "balance due before shipment." Gardner paid the down payment. B&C finished the mill and wrote Gardner a letter telling him to "pay the balance due or you will lose the down payment." By then, Gardner had lost his customers for the wood shavings, could not pay the balance due, and asked for the return of his down payment. Did these parties have an enforceable contract under the Statute of Frauds? Explain. [*Bowen v. Gardner*, 2013 Ark.App. 52, __ S.W.3d __ (2013)] **(See page 386.)**

20–7. A QUESTION OF ETHICS: Contract Terms.

 Daniel Fox owned Fox & Lamberth Enterprises, Inc., a kitchen and bath remodeling business, in Dayton, Ohio. Fox leased a building from Carl and Bellulah Hussong. Craftsmen Home Improvement, Inc., also remodeled baths and kitchens. When Fox planned to close his business, Craftsmen expressed an interest in buying his showroom assets. Fox set a price of $50,000. Craftsmen's owners agreed and gave Fox a list of the desired items and "A Bill of Sale" that set the terms for payment. The parties did not discuss Fox's arrangement with the Hussongs, but Craftsmen expected to negotiate a new lease and extensively modified the premises, including removing some of the displays to its own showroom. When the Hussongs and Craftsmen could not agree on new terms, Craftsmen told Fox that the deal was off. [Fox & Lamberth Enterprises, Inc. v. Craftsmen Home Improvement, Inc., __ Ohio App.3d __, __ N.E.2d __ (2 Dist. 2006)] **(See page 386.)**

(a) In Fox's suit in an Ohio state court for breach of contract, Craftsmen raised the Statute of Frauds as a defense. What are the requirements of the Statute of Frauds? Did the deal between Fox and Craftsmen meet these requirements? Did it fall under one of the exceptions? Explain.

(b) Craftsmen also claimed that the predominant factor of its agreement with Fox was a lease for the Hussongs' building. What is the "predominant-factor" test? Does it apply here? In any event, is it fair to hold a party to a contract to buy a business's assets when the buyer cannot negotiate a favorable lease of the premises on which the assets are located? Discuss.

Legal Reasoning Group Activity

20–8. Parol Evidence. Mountain Stream Trout Co. agreed to buy "market size" trout from trout grower Lake Farms, LLC. Their five- year contract did not define *market size*. At the time, in the trade, *market size* referred to fish of one-pound live weight. After three years, Mountain Stream began taking fewer, smaller deliveries of larger fish, claiming that *market size* varied according to whatever its customers demanded and that its customers now demanded larger fish. Lake Farms filed a suit for breach of contract. **(See page 387.)**

(a) The first group will decide whether parol (outside) evidence is admissible to explain the terms of this contract. Are there any exceptions that could apply?

(b) A second group will determine the impact of course of dealing and usage of trade on the interpretation of contract terms.

(c) A third group will discuss how parties to a commercial contract can avoid the possibility that a court will interpret the contract terms in accordance with trade usage.

An Example of a Contract for the International Sale of Coffee

①

OVERLAND COFFEE IMPORT CONTRACT
OF THE
GREEN COFFEE ASSOCIATION
OF

②

NEW YORK CITY, INC.*

Contract Seller's No.: **504617**
Buyer's No.: **P9264**
Date: **10/11/15**

SOLD BY: **XYZ Co.**
TO: **Starbucks**

③

QUANTITY: **Five Hundred** (**500**) Tons of (Bags) **Mexican** coffee
weighing about **152.117 lbs.** per bag.

PACKAGING: Coffee must be packed in clean sound bags of uniform size made of sisal, henequen, jute, burlap, or similar woven material, without inner lining or outer covering of any material properly sewn by hand and/or machine. Bulk shipments are allowed if agreed by mutual consent of Buyer and Seller.

④

DESCRIPTION: **High grown Mexican Altura**

⑤

PRICE: At **Ten/$10.00 dollars** U.S. Currency, per **lb.** net, (U.S. Funds)
Upon delivery in Bonded Public Warehouse at **Laredo, TX**
(City and State)

⑥

PAYMENT: **Cash against warehouse receipts**

Bill and tender to DATE when all import requirements and governmental regulations have been satisfied, and coffee delivered or discharged (as per contract terms). Seller is obliged to give the Buyer two (2) calendar days free time in Bonded Public Warehouse following but not including date of tender.

⑦

ARRIVAL: During **December** via **truck**
(Period) (Method of Transportation)
from **Mexico** for arrival at **Laredo, TX, USA**
(Country of Exportation) (Country of Importation)
Partial shipments permitted.

⑧

ADVICE OF ARRIVAL: Advice of arrival with warehouse name and location, together with the quantity, description, marks and place of entry, must be transmitted directly, or through Seller's Agent/Broker, to the Buyer or his Agent/ Broker. Advice will be given as soon as known but not later than the fifth business day following arrival at the named warehouse. Such advice may be given verbally with written confirmation to be sent the same day.

⑨

WEIGHTS: (1) DELIVERED WEIGHTS: Coffee covered by this contract is to be weighed at location named in tender. Actual tare to be allowed.
(2) SHIPPING WEIGHTS: Coffee covered by this contract is sold on shipping weights. Any loss in weight exceeding **1/2** percent at location named in tender is for account of Seller at contract price.
(3) Coffee is to be weighed within fifteen (15) calendar days after tender. Weighing expenses, if any, for account of **Seller** (Seller or Buyer)

⑩

MARKINGS: Bags to be branded in English with the name of Country of Origin and otherwise to comply with laws and regulations of the Country of Importation, in effect at the time of entry, governing marking of import merchandise. Any expense incurred by failure to comply with these regulations to be borne by Exporter/Seller.

⑪

RULINGS: The "Rulings on Coffee Contracts" of the Green Coffee Association of New York City, Inc., in effect on the date this contract is made, is incorporated for all purposes as a part of this agreement, and together herewith, constitute the entire contract. No variation or addition hereto shall be valid unless signed by the parties to the contract.
Seller guarantees that the terms printed on the reverse hereof, which by reference are made a part hereof, are identical with the terms as printed in By-Laws and Rules of the Green Coffee Association of New York City, Inc., heretofore adopted.
Exceptions to this guarantee are:

ACCEPTED:
XYZ Co.

BY _____*DM*_____ Seller
Agent

Starbucks

BY _____ Buyer
Agent

COMMISSION TO BE PAID BY:
Seller

ABC Brokerage

Broker(s)

⑫

⑬

When this contract is executed by a person acting for another, such person hereby represents that he is fully authorized to commit his principal.

* Reprinted with permission of The Green Coffee Association of New York City, Inc.

ersstock.com/Sergii Figurnyi)

1 This is a contract for a sale of coffee to be *imported* internationally. If the parties have their principal places of business located in different countries, the contract may be subject to the United Nations Convention on Contracts for the International Sale of Goods (CISG). If the parties' principal places of business are located in the United States, the contract may be subject to the Uniform Commercial Code (UCC).

2 Quantity is one of the most important terms to include in a contract. Without it, a court may not be able to enforce the contract. See Chapter 20.

3 Weight per unit (bag) can be exactly stated or approximately stated. If it is not so stated, usage of trade in international contracts determines standards of weight.

4 Packaging requirements can be conditions for acceptance and payment. Bulk shipments are not permitted without the consent of the buyer.

5 A description of the coffee and the "Markings" constitute express warranties. Warranties in contracts for domestic sales of goods are discussed generally in Chapter 23. International contracts rely more heavily on descriptions and models or samples.

6 Under the UCC, parties may enter into a valid contract even though the price is not set. Under the CISG, a contract must provide for an exact determination of the price.

7 The terms of payment may take one of two forms: credit or cash. Credit terms can be complicated. A cash term can be simple, and payment can be made by any means acceptable in the ordinary course of business (for example, a personal check or a letter of credit). If the seller insists on actual cash, the buyer must be given a reasonable time to get it. See Chapter 22.

8 *Tender* means the seller has placed goods that conform to the contract at the buyer's disposition. What constitutes a valid tender is explained in Chapter 21. This contract requires that the coffee meet all import regulations and that it be ready for pickup by the buyer at a "Bonded Public Warehouse." (A *bonded warehouse* is a place in which goods can be stored without payment of taxes until the goods are removed.)

9 The delivery date is significant because, if it is not met, the buyer may hold the seller in breach of the contract. Under this contract, the seller is given a "period" within which to deliver the goods, instead of a specific day. The seller is also given some time to rectify goods that do not pass inspection (see the "Guarantee" clause on page two of the contract). For a discussion of the remedies of the buyer and seller, see Chapter 22.

10 As part of a proper tender, the seller (or its agent) must inform the buyer (or its agent) when the goods have arrived at their destination.

11 In some contracts, delivered and shipping weights can be important. During shipping, some loss can be attributed to the type of goods (spoilage of fresh produce, for example) or to the transportation itself. A seller and buyer can agree on the extent to which either of them will bear such losses.

12 Documents are often incorporated in a contract by reference, because including them word for word can make a contract difficult to read. If the document is later revised, the entire contract might have to be reworked. Documents that are typically incorporated by reference include detailed payment and delivery terms, special provisions, and sets of rules, codes, and standards.

13 In international sales transactions, and for domestic deals involving certain products, brokers are used to form the contracts. When so used, the brokers are entitled to a commission.

(Continued)

An Example of a Contract for the International Sale of Coffee

TERMS AND CONDITIONS

(14) ARBITRATION: All controversies relating to, in connection with, or arising out of this contract, its modification, making or the authority or obligations of the signatories hereto, and whether involving the principals, agents, brokers, or others who actually subscribe hereto, shall be settled by arbitration in accordance with the "Rules of Arbitration" of the Green Coffee Association of New York City, Inc., as they exist at the time of the arbitration (including provisions as to payment of fees and expenses). Arbitration is the sole remedy hereunder, and it shall be held in accordance with the law of New York State, and judgment of any award may be entered in the courts of that State, or in any other court of competent jurisdiction. All notices or judicial service in reference to arbitration or enforcement shall be deemed given if transmitted as required by the aforesaid rules.

(15) GUARANTEE: (a) If all or any of the coffee is refused admission into the country of importation by reason of any violation of governmental laws or acts, which violation existed at the time the coffee arrived at Bonded Public Warehouse, seller is required, as to the amount not admitted and as soon as possible, to deliver replacement coffee in conformity to all terms and conditions of this contract, excepting only the Arrival terms, but not later than thirty (30) days after the date of the violation notice. Any payment made and expenses incurred for any coffee denied entry shall be refunded within ten (10) calendar days of denial of entry, and payment shall be made for the replacement delivery in accordance with the terms of this contract. Consequently, if Buyer removes the coffee from the Bonded Public Warehouse, Seller's responsibility as to such portion hereunder ceases.

(b) Contracts containing the overstamp "No Pass-No Sale" on the face of the contract shall be interpreted to mean: If any or all of the coffee is not admitted into the country of Importation in its original condition by reason of failure to meet requirements of the government's laws or Acts, the contract shall be deemed null and void as to that portion of the coffee which is not admitted in its original condition. Any payment made and expenses incurred for any coffee denied entry shall be refunded within ten (10) calendar days of denial of entry.

(16) CONTINGENCY: This contract is not contingent upon any other contract.

(17) CLAIMS: Coffee shall be considered accepted as to quality unless within *fifteen* (15) calendar days after delivery at Bonded Public Warehouse or within *fifteen* (15) calendar days after all Government clearances have been received, whichever is later, either:

(a) Claims are settled by the parties hereto, or,

(b) Arbitration proceedings have been filed by one of the parties in accordance with the provisions hereof.

(c) If neither (a) nor (b) has been done in the stated period or if any portion of the coffee has been removed from the Bonded Public Warehouse before representative sealed samples have been drawn by the Green Coffee Association of New York City, Inc., in accordance with its rules, Seller's responsibility for quality claims ceases for that portion so removed.

(d) Any question of quality submitted to arbitration shall be a matter of allowance only, unless otherwise provided in the contract.

(18) DELIVERY: (a) No more than three (3) chops may be tendered for each lot of 250 bags.

(b) Each chop of coffee tendered is to be uniform in grade and appearance. All expense necessary to make coffee uniform shall be for account of seller.

(c) Notice of arrival and/or sampling order constitutes a tender, and must be given not later than the fifth business day following arrival at Bonded Public Warehouse stated on the contract.

INSURANCE: Seller is responsible for any loss or damage, or both, until Delivery and Discharge of coffee at the Bonded Public Warehouse in the Country of Importation.

All Insurance Risks, costs and responsibility are for Seller's Account until Delivery and Discharge of coffee at the Bonded Public Warehouse in the Country of Importation.

Buyer's insurance responsibility begins from the day of importation or from the day of tender, whichever is later.

(19) FREIGHT: Seller to provide and pay for all transportation and related expenses to the Bonded Public Warehouse in the Country of Importation.

(20) EXPORT DUTIES/TAXES: Exporter is to pay all Export taxes, duties or other fees or charges, if any, levied because of exportation.

IMPORT DUTIES/TAXES: Any Duty or Tax whatsoever, imposed by the government or any authority of the Country of Importation, shall be borne by the Importer/Buyer.

(21) INSOLVENCY OR FINANCIAL FAILURE OF BUYER OR SELLER: If, at any time before the contract is fully executed, either party hereto shall meet with creditors because of inability generally to make payment of obligations when due, or shall suspend such payments, fail to meet his general trade obligations in the regular course of business, shall file a petition in bankruptcy or, for an arrangement, shall become insolvent, or commit an act of bankruptcy, then the other party may at his option, expressed in writing, declare the aforesaid to constitute a breach and default of this contract, and may, in addition to other remedies, decline to deliver further or make payment or may sell or purchase for the defaulter's account, and may collect damage for any injury or loss, or shall account for the profit, if any, occasioned by such sale or purchase.

This clause is subject to the provisions of (11 USC 365 (e) 1) if invoked.

(22) BREACH OR DEFAULT OF CONTRACT: In the event either party hereto fails to perform, or breaches or repudiates this agreement, the other party shall subject to the specific provisions of this contract be entitled to the remedies and relief provided for by the Uniform Commercial Code of the State of New York. The computation and ascertainment of damages, or the determination of any other dispute as to relief, shall be made by the arbitrators in accordance with the Arbitration Clause herein.

Consequential damages shall not, however, be allowed.

(23)

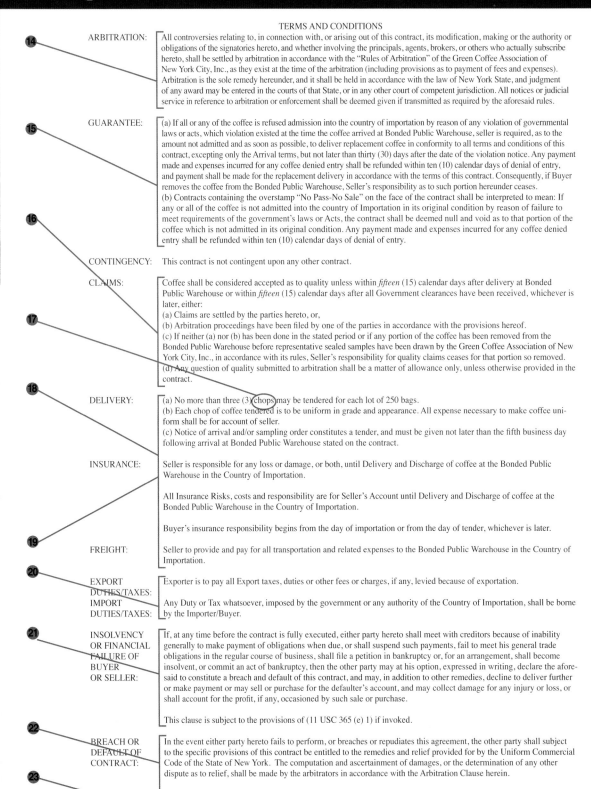

An Example of a Contract for the International Sale of Coffee

⑭ Arbitration is the settling of a dispute by submitting it to a disinterested party (other than a court), which renders a decision. The procedures and costs can be provided for in an arbitration clause or incorporated through other documents. To enforce an award rendered in an arbitration, the winning party can "enter" (submit) the award in a court "of competent jurisdiction." For a general discussion of arbitration and other forms of dispute resolution (other than courts), see Chapter 2.

⑮ When goods are imported internationally, they must meet certain import requirements before being released to the buyer. See Chapter 24. Because of this, buyers frequently want a guaranty clause that covers the goods not admitted into the country and that either requires the seller to replace the goods within a stated time or allows the contract for those goods not admitted to be void.

⑯ In the "Claims" clause, the parties agree that the buyer has a certain time within which to reject the goods. The right to reject is a right by law and does not need to be stated in a contract. If the buyer does not exercise the right within the time specified in the contract, the goods will be considered accepted. See Chapter 22.

⑰ Many international contracts include definitions of terms so that the parties understand what they mean. Some terms are used in a particular industry in a specific way. Here, the word *chop* refers to a unit of like-grade coffee beans. The buyer has a right to inspect ("sample") the coffee. If the coffee does not conform to the contract, the seller must correct the nonconformity. See Chapter 22.

⑱ The "Delivery," "Insurance," and "Freight" clauses, with the "Arrival" clause on page one of the contract, indicate that this is a destination contract. The seller has the obligation to deliver the goods to the destination, not simply deliver them into the hands of a carrier. Under this contract, the destination is a "Bonded Public Warehouse" in a specific location. The seller bears the risk of loss until the goods are delivered at their destination. Typically, the seller will have bought insurance to cover the risk. See Chapter 21 for a discussion of delivery terms and the risk of loss.

⑲ Delivery terms are commonly placed in all sales contracts. Such terms determine who pays freight and other costs and, in the absence of an agreement specifying otherwise, who bears the risk of loss. International contracts may use these delivery terms, or they may use INCOTERMS, which are published by the International Chamber of Commerce. For example, the INCOTERM DDP (delivered duty paid) requires the seller to arrange shipment, obtain and pay for import or export permits, and get the goods through customs to a named destination.

⑳ Exported and imported goods are subject to duties, taxes, and other charges imposed by the governments of the countries involved. International contracts spell out who is responsible for these charges.

㉑ This clause protects a party if the other party should become financially unable to fulfill the obligations under the contract. Thus, if the seller cannot afford to deliver, or the buyer cannot afford to pay, for the stated reasons, the other party can consider the contract breached. This right is subject to "11 USC 365(e)(1)," which refers to a specific provision of the U.S. Bankruptcy Code dealing with executory contracts.

㉒ In the "Breach or Default of Contract" clause, the parties agree that the remedies under this contract are the remedies (except for consequential damages) provided by the UCC, as in effect in the state of New York. The amount and "ascertainment" of damages, as well as other disputes about relief, are to be determined by arbitration. Breach of contract and contractual remedies in general are explained in Chapter 22. Arbitration is discussed in Chapter 2.

㉓ Three clauses frequently included in international contracts (see Chapter 20) are omitted here. There is no choice-of-language clause designating the official language to be used in interpreting the contract terms. There is no choice-of-forum clause designating the place in which disputes will be litigated, except for arbitration (law of New York State). Finally, there is no *force majeure* clause relieving the sellers or buyers from nonperformance due to events beyond their control.

CHAPTER 21

TITLE, RISK, AND INSURABLE INTEREST

Before the creation of the Uniform Commercial Code (UCC), *title*—the right of ownership—was the central concept in sales law. Title controlled all issues of rights and remedies of the parties to a sales contract. There were numerous problems with this concept, however. Anything can happen between the time a contract is signed and the time the goods are transferred to the buyer's or lessee's possession. It was frequently difficult to determine when title actually passed from the seller to the buyer.

Therefore, it was also difficult to predict which party a court would decide had title at the time of a loss.

Because of such problems, the UCC divorced the question of title as completely as possible from the question of the rights and obligations of buyers, sellers, and third parties (such as subsequent purchasers, creditors, or the tax collector). Nevertheless, in some situations, title is still relevant under the UCC, and the UCC has special rules for assigning title. These rules will be discussed in the sections that follow. In

most situations, however, the UCC has replaced the concept of title with three other concepts: identification, risk of loss, and insurable interest.

In lease contracts, of course, the lessor-owner of the goods retains title. Hence, the UCC's provisions relating to passage of title do not apply to leased goods. Other concepts discussed in this chapter, though, including identification, risk of loss, and insurable interest, relate to lease contracts as well as to sales contracts.

IDENTIFICATION

Before any interest in specific goods can pass from the seller or lessor to the buyer or lessee, the goods must be (1) in existence and (2) identified as the specific goods designated in the contract [UCC 2–105(2)]. **Identification** takes place when specific goods are designated as the subject matter of a sales or lease contract.

Title and risk of loss cannot pass to the buyer from the seller unless the goods are identified to the contract. (As mentioned, title to leased goods remains with the lessor—or, if the owner is a third party, with that party.) Identification is significant because it gives the buyer or lessee the right to insure (or to have an insurable interest in) the goods and the right to recover from third parties who damage the goods.

The parties can agree in their contract on when identification will take place (although it will not effectively pass title and risk of loss to the buyer on

future goods, such as unborn cattle). If the parties do not so specify, however, the UCC provisions discussed here determine when identification takes place [UCC 2–501(1), 2A–217].

Existing Goods

If the contract calls for the sale or lease of specific and ascertained goods that are already in existence, identification takes place at the time the contract is made.
▶ **Example 21.1** Litco Company contracts to lease a fleet of five cars designated by their vehicle identification numbers (VINs). Because the cars are identified by their VINs, identification has taken place, and Litco acquires an insurable interest in the cars at the time of contracting. ◀

Future Goods

Any goods that are not in existence at the time of contracting are known as future goods. If a sale or lease involves unborn animals to be born within twelve months after contracting, identification takes place when the animals are conceived.

If a sale involves crops that are to be harvested within twelve months (or the next harvest season occurring after contracting, whichever is longer), identification takes place when the crops are planted. Otherwise, identification takes place when the crops begin to grow. (See this chapter's *Insight into the Global Environment* feature below for a discussion of how contracts for agricultural products can benefit the environment.)

In a sale or lease of any other future goods, identification occurs when the seller or lessor ships, marks, or otherwise designates the goods as those to which the contract refers. ▶ **Case in Point 21.2** Gordon Bonner contracted with Ronnie Carman to build a forty-six-foot motorboat for $278,950. The contract required progress payments but did not contain any specific provisions regarding delivery (which, as you will read shortly, can determine when title to the goods passes to the buyer). After nearly three years, with the boat still not completed, Carman filed for bankruptcy. The bankruptcy trustee wanted to sell the unfinished boat to pay Carman's creditors, but Bonner claimed that the boat—which was still on Carman's business premises—was his.

The court held that under the UCC, the boat constituted future goods because it did not exist at the time the contract was signed. In addition, title had not passed to Bonner because the boat had not been identified to the contract. The boat could have been identified by listing its hull number in the contract or by later marking or designating it as Bonner's, but no such steps were taken. Therefore, the bankruptcy trustee could sell the boat and distribute the funds to Carman's creditors.[1] ◀

---

1. *In re Carman,* 399 Bankr. 158 (D.Md. 2009). For another case in which a boat was held to be future goods, see *Gonsalves v. Montgomery,* 2006 WL 2711540 (N.D.Cal. 2006).

INSIGHT INTO THE GLOBAL ENVIRONMENT
Contracts with Fair Trade Pricing Can Promote Environmental Sustainability

Most sales contracts have price terms that are mutually agreed to by the buyer and seller. But sales contracts can do more than that. Thanks to the Fair Trade movement, they can also benefit poor farmers in developing nations and can promote environmentally sustainable farming practices.

The Fair Trade Movement

The Fair Trade movement originated during the 1980s. Today, the Fair Trade Labelling Organizations International determines minimum "fair prices that ensure that small producers can earn a living wage." It urges importers to pay these fair prices for the products they obtain.

Under the Fair Trade system, low-income farmers and artisans in developing countries form alliances with importers and marketers in western Europe and North America. Participants must agree to certain basic principles:

- Producers must receive a stable minimum price for their products.
- Producers will not use forced or child labor.
- Production methods will be environmentally friendly.

When these standards are met, international certification bodies allow the products to carry a Fair Trade logo, such as the well-known label borne by some coffee imported into the United States. Retailers are free to charge any price they wish, but because they necessarily pay more for Fair Trade products, they pass on the higher costs to their customers.

The Fair Trade Sustainability Alliance

The Fair Trade Sustainability Alliance (FairTSA), a nonprofit organization that promotes socially responsible development in emerging countries, has taken the Fair Trade concept to another level. FairTSA attempts to ensure that the community development associated with its work is accountable and sustainable. In addition to promoting sustainable development, FairTSA monitors suppliers and certifies those that practice ethical and accountable supply chain management.

FairTSA will certify a producer of any type of agricultural products. To win certification, a producer must accept professional standards and be open for audits and inspections.

LEGAL CRITICAL THINKING

INSIGHT INTO ETHICS

Why might marketing managers of large retail companies, particularly grocery chains, want to purchase Fair Trade products?

Goods That Are Part of a Larger Mass

Goods that are part of a larger mass are identified when the goods are marked, shipped, or somehow designated by the seller or lessor as the particular goods to pass under the contract. ▶ **Example 21.3** A buyer orders 10,000 pairs of men's jeans from a lot that contains 90,000 articles of clothing for men, women, and children. Until the seller separates the 10,000 pairs of men's jeans from the other items, title and risk of loss remain with the seller. ◀

A common exception to this rule involves fungible goods. **Fungible goods** are goods that are alike naturally, by agreement, or by trade usage. Typical examples include specific grades or types of wheat, petroleum, and cooking oil, which usually are stored in large containers. If the owners of these goods hold title as *tenants in common* (owners with an undivided share of the whole), a seller-owner can pass title and risk of loss to the buyer without actually separating the goods. The buyer replaces the seller as an owner in common [UCC 2–105(4)].

▶ **Example 21.4** Alvarez, Braudel, and Carpenter are farmers. They deposit, respectively, 5,000 bushels, 3,000 bushels, and 2,000 bushels of grain of the same grade and quality in a grain elevator. The three become owners in common, with Alvarez owning 50 percent of the 10,000 bushels, Braudel 30 percent,

and Carpenter 20 percent. Alvarez contracts to sell her 5,000 bushels of grain to Treyton. Because the goods are fungible, she can pass title and risk of loss to Treyton without physically separating the 5,000 bushels. Treyton now becomes an owner in common with Braudel and Carpenter. ◀

SECTION 2
WHEN TITLE PASSES

Once goods exist and are identified, the provisions of UCC 2–401 apply to the passage of title. In nearly all subsections of UCC 2–401, the words "unless otherwise explicitly agreed" appear, meaning that any explicit understanding between the buyer and the seller determines when title passes.

Without an explicit agreement to the contrary, *title passes to the buyer at the time and the place the seller performs by delivering the goods* [UCC 2–401(2)]. ▶ **Example 21.5** Joshua buys cattle at a livestock auction. Title will pass when the cattle are physically delivered to him (unless, of course, the parties agree otherwise). ◀

If a seller gives up possession or control of goods, but keeps a "certificate of origin" supposedly showing ownership, has there been a delivery sufficient to pass title? That was the question in the following case.

CASE 21.1

United States v. 2007 Custom Motorcycle
United States District Court, District of Arizona, ___ F.Supp.2d ___ (2011).

BACKGROUND AND FACTS Timothy Allen commissioned a custom motorcycle from Indy Route 66 Cycles, Inc. Indy built the motorcycle and issued a "Certificate of Origin." Two years later, federal law enforcement officers arrested Allen on drug charges and seized his home and other property. The officers also seized the Indy-made motorcycle from the garage at the home of Allen's sister, Tena. The government alleged that the motorcycle was subject to forfeiture as the proceeds of drug trafficking. Indy filed a claim against the government, arguing that it owned the motorcycle, as evidenced by the "Certificate of Origin," which the company still possessed. Indy claimed that it had been keeping the motorcycle in storage. The government filed a motion to strike the claim, asserting that title to the motorcycle had passed when it was delivered to Allen.

 IN THE LANGUAGE OF THE COURT
Frederick J. *MARTONE,* Judge.

* * * *

The only * * * question is whether claimant [Indy] can show an * * * ownership interest based on the Certificate of Origin.

CASE 21.1 CONTINUED

Under Indiana law, the question of motor vehicle ownership is governed by the sales provisions of Indiana's Uniform Commercial Code ("UCC"). Although the government challenges the current significance of the Certificate of Origin, it does not dispute that claimant owned the motorcycle before selling it to Allen. With respect to the alleged sale, the government relies on [Indiana Code Section 26-1-2-401(2), Indiana's version of UCC 2–401(2)],

> Unless otherwise explicitly agreed, title passes to the buyer at the time and place at which the seller completes his performance with reference to the physical delivery of the goods.

Claimant does not dispute that this provision applies, and it does not contend that it agreed to different terms with Allen. *Therefore, claimant's standing turns on whether it delivered the motorcycle to Allen.* [Emphasis added.]

On this point, the government first offers an affidavit by claimant's former vice president, Vince Ballard, stating that the motorcycle was "built and delivered on or about 4/30/2007." Ballard also referred to the Certificate of Origin, which purported to transfer the motorcycle from "Route Sixty Six Motorcycle Co." to the company's retail division as a "distributor or dealer," on April 30, 2007. He went on to state that Allen did not pay for the motorcycle and referred to the * * * claimant storing the motorcycle starting on April 30, 2007. The affidavit is inconclusive. It implies that claimant delivered the motorcycle to Allen, and it asserts that claimant kept the motorcycle in storage.

Nevertheless, it is undisputed that the motorcycle was found in Allen's sister's garage two years later, which strongly indicates that claimant delivered it to Allen. Claimant offers no explanation for how the motorcycle ended up with Allen's sister when it was allegedly in storage. * * * Under the circumstances, we grant the government's motion to strike the claim * * * for lack of standing.

DECISION AND REMEDY   *The district court issued a ruling in the government's favor and granted the motion to strike Indy's claim. The seller had given up possession of the goods to the buyer. This was sufficient to pass title even though the seller had kept a "Certificate of Origin." As a consequence, the cycle was subject to forfeiture as the proceeds of drug trafficking.*

WHAT IF THE FACTS WERE DIFFERENT?   *Suppose that Indy had given the "Certificate of Origin" to Allen and had kept the motorcycle. Would the result have been different? Explain.*

THE LEGAL ENVIRONMENT DIMENSION   *Should the passage of title be tied so closely to the possession of the goods? Discuss.*

Shipment and Destination Contracts

Unless otherwise agreed, delivery arrangements can determine when title passes from the seller to the buyer. In a **shipment contract,** the seller is required or authorized to ship goods by carrier, such as a trucking company. Under a shipment contract, the seller is required only to deliver the goods into the hands of a carrier, and title passes to the buyer at the time and place of shipment [UCC 2–401(2)(a)]. Generally, *all contracts are assumed to be shipment contracts if nothing to the contrary is stated in the contract.*

In a **destination contract,** the seller is required to deliver the goods to a particular destination, usually directly to the buyer, but sometimes to another party designated by the buyer. Title passes to the buyer when the goods are *tendered* at that destination [UCC 2–401(2)(b)]. As you will read in Chapter 22, *tender of delivery* occurs when the seller places or holds conforming goods at the buyer's disposal (with any necessary notice), enabling the buyer to take possession [UCC 2–503(1)].

Delivery without Movement of the Goods

Sometimes, a sales contract does not call for the seller to ship or deliver the goods (such as when the buyer is to pick up the goods). In that situation, the passage of title depends on whether the seller must deliver a **document of title,** such as a bill of lading or a warehouse receipt, to the buyer. A *bill of lading*[2] is a receipt for goods that is signed by a carrier and serves as a contract for the transportation of the goods. A *warehouse receipt* is a receipt issued by a warehouser for goods stored in a warehouse.

WHEN A TITLE DOCUMENT IS REQUIRED When a title document is required, title passes to the buyer *when and where the document is delivered*. Thus, if the goods are stored in a warehouse, title passes to the buyer when the appropriate documents are delivered to the buyer. The goods never move. In fact, the buyer can choose to leave the goods at the same warehouse for a period of time, and the buyer's title to those goods will be unaffected.

WHEN A TITLE DOCUMENT IS NOT REQUIRED When no document of title is required and the goods are identified to the contract, title passes at the time and place the sales contract is made. If the goods have not been identified, title does not pass until identification occurs.

▶ **Example 21.6** Juarez sells lumber to Bodan. They agree that Bodan will pick up the lumber at the yard. If the lumber has been identified (segregated, marked, or in any other way distinguished from all other lumber), title passes to Bodan when the contract is signed. If the lumber is still in large storage bins at the mill, title does not pass to Bodan until the particular pieces of lumber to be sold under this contract are identified [UCC 2–401(3)]. ◀

Sales or Leases by Nonowners

Problems occur when persons who acquire goods with imperfect titles attempt to sell or lease them. Sections 2–402 and 2–403 of the UCC deal with the rights of two parties who lay claim to the same goods sold with imperfect titles. Generally, a buyer acquires at least whatever title the seller has to the goods sold.

These same UCC sections also protect lessees. Obviously, a lessee does not acquire whatever title the lessor has to the goods. Rather, the lessee acquires a right to possess and use the goods—that is, a *leasehold interest*. A lessee acquires whatever leasehold interest the lessor has or has the power to transfer, subject to the lease contract [UCC 2A–303, 2A–304, 2A–305].

VOID TITLE A buyer may unknowingly purchase goods from a seller who is not the owner of the goods. If the seller is a thief, the seller's title is *void*—legally, no title exists. Thus, the buyer acquires no title, and the real owner can reclaim the goods from the buyer. If the goods were leased instead, the same result would occur because the lessor would have no leasehold interest to transfer.

▶ **Example 21.7** If Saki steals a valuable necklace owned by Shannon, Saki has a *void title* to that necklace. If Saki sells the necklace to Valdez, Shannon can reclaim it from Valdez even though Valdez acted in good faith and honestly was not aware that the necklace was stolen. (Note that Valdez may file a tort claim against Saki under these circumstances, but here we are only discussing title to the goods.) ◀ Article 2A contains similar provisions for leases.

VOIDABLE TITLE A seller has a *voidable title* to goods obtained by fraud, paid for with a check that was later dishonored, purchased from a minor, or purchased on credit when the seller was **insolvent.** (Under the UCC, insolvency occurs when a person ceases to pay debts in the ordinary course of business, cannot pay debts as they become due, or is insolvent under federal bankruptcy law [UCC 1–201(23)].)

Good Faith Purchasers. In contrast to a seller with void title, a seller with voidable title has the power to transfer good title to a good faith purchaser for value. A **good faith purchaser** is one who buys without knowledge of circumstances that would make an ordinary person inquire about the validity of the seller's title to the goods. One who purchases *for value* gives legally sufficient consideration (value) for the goods purchased. The original owner normally cannot recover goods from a good faith purchaser for value [UCC 2–403(1)].[3]

If the buyer is not a good faith purchaser for value, the actual owner can reclaim the goods from the buyer (or from the seller, if the goods are still in the seller's possession). Exhibit 21–1 on the following page illustrates these concepts.

Voidable Title and Leases. The same rules apply in situations involving leases. A lessor with voidable title has the power to transfer a valid leasehold interest to a good faith lessee for value. The real owner cannot recover the goods, except as permitted by the terms of the lease. The real owner can, however, receive all

---

2. The term *bill of lading* has been used by international carriers for many years. It derives from *bill*, which historically referred to a schedule of costs for services, and the verb *to lade*, which means to load cargo onto a ship or other form of transportation.

3. The real owner could sue the person who initially obtained voidable title to the goods.

EXHIBIT 21–1 Void and Voidable Titles

If goods are transferred from their owner to another by theft, the thief acquires no ownership rights. Because the thief's title is *void,* a later buyer can acquire no title, and the owner can recover the goods. If the transfer occurs by fraud, the transferee acquires a *voidable* title. A later good faith purchaser for value can acquire good title, and the original owner cannot recover the goods.

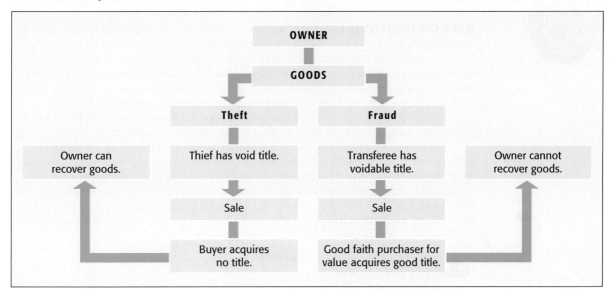

proceeds arising from the lease. The owner can also obtain a transfer of the rights that the lessor had under the lease, including the right to the return of the goods when the lease expires [UCC 2A–305(1)].

THE ENTRUSTMENT RULE Entrusting goods to a merchant *who deals in goods of that kind* gives the merchant the power to transfer all rights to *a buyer in the ordinary course of business* [UCC 2–403(2)]. This is known as the **entrustment rule.** Entrusting includes both turning over the goods to the merchant and leaving purchased goods with the merchant for later delivery or pickup [UCC 2–403(3)]. Article 2A provides a similar rule for leased goods [UCC 2A–305(2)]. Under the UCC, a person is a **buyer in the ordinary course of business** if:

1. She or he buys goods in good faith (honestly).
2. The goods are purchased without knowledge that the sale violates the rights of another person in the goods.
3. The goods are purchased in the ordinary course from a merchant (other than a pawnbroker) in the business of selling goods of that kind.
4. The sale to that person comports with the usual or customary practices in the kind of business in which the seller is engaged [UCC 1–201(9)].

The entrustment rule basically allows innocent buyers to obtain legitimate title to goods purchased from merchants even if the merchants do not have good title. ▶ **Example 21.8** Jan leaves her watch with a jeweler to be repaired. The jeweler sells both new and used watches. The jeweler sells Jan's watch to Kim, a customer who is unaware that the jeweler has no right to sell it. Kim, as a good faith buyer, gets good title against Jan's claim of ownership.[4] Kim, however, obtains only those rights held by the person entrusting the goods (Jan).

Now suppose that Jan had stolen the watch from Greg and left it with the jeweler to be repaired. The jeweler then sold it to Kim. Kim would obtain good title against Jan, who entrusted the watch to the jeweler, but not against Greg (the real owner), who neither entrusted the watch to Jan nor authorized Jan to entrust it. ◀

A nonowner's sale of *Red Elvis,* an artwork by Andy Warhol, was at the center of the dispute over title in the following case.

---

4. Jan can sue the jeweler for the tort of conversion (or trespass to personal property) to obtain damages equivalent to the cash value of the watch (see Chapter 6).

Case 21.2 Lindholm v. Brant
Supreme Court of Connecticut, 283 Conn. 65, 925 A.2d 1048 (2007).

BACKGROUND AND FACTS In 1987, Kerstin Lindholm of Greenwich, Connecticut, bought a silkscreen by Andy Warhol titled *Red Elvis* from Anders Malmberg, a Swedish art dealer, for $300,000. In 1998, Lindholm loaned *Red Elvis* to the Guggenheim Museum in New York City for an exhibition to tour Europe. Peter Brant, who was on the museum's board of trustees and also a Greenwich resident, believed that Lindholm was the owner. Stellan Holm, a Swedish art dealer who had bought and sold other Warhol works with Brant, told him, however, that Malmberg had bought it and would sell it for $2.9 million. Malmberg refused Brant's request to provide a copy of an invoice between Lindholm and himself on the ground that such documents normally and customarily are not disclosed in art deals.

To determine whether Malmberg had good title, Brant hired an attorney to search the Art Loss Register (an international database of stolen and missing artworks) and other sources. No problems were found, but Brant was cautioned that this provided only "minimal assurances." Brant's attorney drafted a formal contract, which conditioned payment on the delivery of *Red Elvis* to a warehouse in Denmark. The exchange took place in April 2000.[a] Lindholm filed a suit in a Connecticut state court against Brant, alleging conversion, among other things. The court issued a judgment in Brant's favor. Lindholm appealed to the Connecticut Supreme Court.

IN THE LANGUAGE OF THE COURT
SULLIVAN, J. [Justice]

* * * *

* * * "A person buys goods in the ordinary course if the sale to the person comports with the usual or customary practices in the kind of business in which the seller is engaged or with the seller's own usual or customary practices * * *" [according to Connecticut General Statutes Annotated Section 42a-1-201(9), (Connecticut's version of UCC 1–201(9)]. *A person buys goods in good faith if there is "honesty in fact and the observance of reasonable commercial standards of fair dealing" in the conduct or transaction concerned* [under Section 42a-1-201(20)]. [Emphasis added.]

We are required, therefore, to determine whether the defendant followed the usual or customary practices and observed reasonable commercial standards of fair dealing in the art industry in his dealings with Malmberg. * * * The defendant presented expert testimony that the vast majority of art transactions, in which the buyer has no reason for concern about the seller's ability to convey good title, are "completed on a handshake and an exchange of an invoice." It is not customary for sophisticated buyers and sellers to obtain a signed invoice from the original seller to the dealer prior to a transaction, nor is it an ordinary or customary practice to request the underlying invoice or corroborating information as to a dealer's authority to convey title. Moreover, it is not customary to approach the owner of an artwork if the owner regularly worked with a particular art dealer because any inquiries about an art transaction customarily are presented to the art dealer rather than directly to the [owner]. *It is customary to rely upon representations made by respected dealers regarding their authority to sell works of art.* A dealer customarily is not required to present an invoice establishing when and from whom he bought the artwork or the conditions of the purchase. [Emphasis added.]

We are compelled to conclude, however, that the sale from Malmberg to the defendant was unlike the vast majority of art transactions. * * * Under such circumstances, a

---

a. Unaware of this deal, Lindholm accepted a Japanese buyer's offer of $4.6 million for *Red Elvis*. The funds were wired to Malmberg, who kept them. Lindholm filed a criminal complaint against Malmberg in Sweden. In 2003, a Swedish court convicted Malmberg of "gross fraud embezzlement." The court awarded Lindholm $4.6 million and other relief.

CASE 21.2 CONTINUED handshake and an exchange of invoice is not sufficient to confer status as a buyer in the ordinary course.

* * * *

* * * A merchant buyer has a heightened duty of inquiry when a reasonable merchant would have doubts or questions regarding the seller's authority to sell. * * * In the present case, the defendant had concerns about Malmberg's ability to convey good title to *Red Elvis* because he believed that Lindholm might have had a claim to the painting. The defendant also was concerned that Malmberg had not yet acquired title to the painting * * * .

Because of his concern that Lindholm might make a claim to *Red Elvis,* the defendant took the extraordinary step of hiring counsel to conduct an investigation and to negotiate a formal contract of sale on his behalf. * * * Such searches typically are not conducted during the course of a normal art transaction and, therefore, provided the defendant with at least some assurance that Lindholm had no claims to the painting.

Moreover, * * * both Malmberg and Holm had reputations as honest, reliable, and trustworthy art dealers. * * * The defendant had little reason to doubt Malmberg's claim that he was the owner of *Red Elvis,* and any doubts that he did have reasonably were allayed [reduced] by relying on Holm's assurances that Malmberg had bought the painting from the plaintiff * * * .

The defendant's concerns were further allayed when Malmberg delivered *Red Elvis* to a * * * warehouse in Denmark, the delivery location the parties had agreed to in the contract of sale. At the time of the sale, the painting was on loan to the Guggenheim, whose policy it was to release a painting on loan only to the true owner, or to someone the true owner had authorized to take possession. * * * We conclude that these steps were sufficient to conform to reasonable commercial standards for the sale of artwork under the circumstances and, therefore, that the defendant had status as a buyer in the ordinary course of business.

DECISION AND REMEDY *The Connecticut Supreme Court affirmed the judgment of the lower court. The state supreme court concluded that "on the basis of all the circumstances surrounding this sale," Brant was a buyer in the ordinary course of business and, therefore, took all rights to Red Elvis under UCC 2–403(2).*

THE ETHICAL DIMENSION *How did the "usual and customary" methods of dealing in the art business help Malmberg deceive the other parties in this case? What additional steps might those parties have taken to protect themselves from such deceit?*

THE GLOBAL DIMENSION *Considering the international locales in this case, why was Lindholm able to bring an action against Brant in Connecticut?*

SECTION 3
RISK OF LOSS

At the various stages of a sale or lease transaction, the question may arise as to who bears the risk of loss. In other words, who suffers the financial loss if the goods are damaged, destroyed, or lost in transit? Under the UCC, risk of loss does not necessarily pass with title. When risk of loss passes from a seller or lessor to a buyer or lessee is generally determined by the contract between the parties.

Sometimes, the contract states expressly when the risk of loss passes. At other times, it does not, and a court must interpret the existing terms to determine whether the risk has passed. When no provision in the contract indicates when risk passes, the UCC provides special rules, based on delivery terms, to guide the courts.

Like risk of loss, the risk of liability that arises from the goods does not necessarily require the passage of title. And like risk of loss, when this risk passes from a seller to a buyer is generally determined by the contract between the parties, as in the following case.

CASE ANALYSIS

Case 21.3 Person v. Bowman

Court of Appeals of Washington, 2013 WL 663726 (2013).

IN THE LANGUAGE OF THE COURT
WORSWICK, C.J. [Chief Judge]

* * * *

On April 18, 2009, [Diana] Person was injured when she was thrown from a horse-drawn buggy at Summit Stables in Puyallup [Washington]. She was riding in the buggy while Alex Herring was operating it. The horse pulling the buggy, Toby, was the subject of a purchase agreement Alex's mother, Tammy Herring, and Stacy Bowman executed on October 4, 2006. The agreement, entitled "Bill of Sale—Purchase Agreement," defines Herring as the "BUYER" and [Stacy and Gregory Bowman, who together owned Summit Stables] as the "SELLER". It provided that Herring would make a $300 down payment and then monthly payments in an amount "to be determined" until she paid $2,200 in total for Toby. It required Herring to keep Toby at Summit Stables until she paid off the balance. And, it required Herring to pay a boarding fee and be responsible for any incidental costs such as veterinary, farrier, and training expenses. The Bowmans would provide Toby's registration papers to Herring only when she paid in full. Finally, the contract contained the following clause: "By signing below the buyer acknowledges this Sale Is Final and they have purchased the horse."

According to Herring, until she paid the purchase price in full, she considered Toby a rented horse. Stacy Bowman acknowledged * * * that the agreement with Herring was akin to "a lease to own the horse." She admitted that she may have used the word "lease" in talking

to Herring, but explained, "I could have because she didn't outright own the horse yet." Herring made the final payment for Toby over seven months after the accident. * * * Person, who frequented and volunteered at the stable, thought that Herring had leased Toby.

[Person and her husband Robert filed a suit in a Washington state court against the Bowmans to recover for Person's injuries. From a judgment in the defendants' favor, the Persons appealed.]

* * * *

The Persons argue that the trial court erred when it found that Herring owned Toby * * * . The Persons contend that Herring had not yet assumed ownership of Toby but, instead, was * * * leasing him, and, as a result, the Bowmans [are] liable.

* * * *

* * * The trial court ruled that the purchase agreement between the Bowmans and Herring established, as a matter of law, that Herring owned Toby and, as such, that liability rested solely with Alex Herring.

* * * *

Washington follows the objective manifestation theory of contract interpretation, under which courts try to ascertain the parties' intent by focusing on the objective manifestations of the agreement, rather than on the unexpressed subjective intent of the parties. [Emphasis added.]

* * * Looking at the contract * * * makes it clear that Herring owned Toby. The title of the agreement, the use of BUYER and SELLER, and the buyer's responsibility to board the horse and pay all incidental expenses all show ownership responsibility. While the contract

requires keeping the horse at the stable, making timely payments, not removing the horse without permission, and it gives the seller the right to terminate the contract upon default, these provisions give the seller recourse should it have to recover the horse. In other words, these provisions act as the seller's security interest, protecting the seller until it no longer has a risk of loss.

* * * *

* * * Evidence presented to the trial court consisted of Herring's assertions that she did not own Toby at the time of the accident and did not believe she would own him until she paid the full contract price. It consisted of Person's belief that Toby was a leased horse. And it consisted of statements [by] Stacy Bowman * * * using the word "lease," equating the situation as "a lease to own the horse," and acknowledging that she may have used the word "lease" in talking to Herring.

But none of these statements demonstrates that the parties intended to lease Toby. Each statement acknowledges that the Bowmans retained a security interest in Toby and that Herring would not own Toby free and clear or have the right to remove him from the stable until she made her final payment. *While Herring's subjective belief may have been that she did not own Toby and that this was a lease-like agreement, the parties' objective manifestations are consistent with this being a sale not a lease.* [Emphasis added.]

We affirm.

CASE 21.3 CONTINUED

LEGAL REASONING QUESTIONS

1. What did the contract between Herring and the Bowmans require Herring to do? What is the significance of these provisions?

2. On the issue of liability, in whose favor did the court rule? Why?

3. What theory of contract interpretation supported the court's reasoning?

4. If the agreement between Herring and the Bowmans had been a lease, would the result have been the same? Explain.

Delivery with Movement of the Goods—Carrier Cases

When the contract involves movement of the goods via a common carrier but does not specify when risk of loss passes, the courts first look for specific delivery terms in the contract. The terms that have traditionally been used in contracts within the United States are listed and defined in Exhibit 21–2 below. *Unless the parties agree otherwise,* these terms will determine which party will pay the costs of delivering the goods and who will bear the risk of loss. If the contract does not include these terms, then the courts must decide whether the contract is a shipment or a destination contract.

SHIPMENT CONTRACTS In a shipment contract, the seller or lessor is required or authorized to ship goods by carrier, but is not required to deliver them to a particular destination. The risk of loss in a shipment contract passes to the buyer or lessee when the goods are delivered to the carrier [UCC 2–509(1)(a), 2A–219(2)(a)].

▶ **Example 21.9** Pitman, a seller in Texas, sells five hundred cases of grapefruit to a buyer in New York, F.O.B. Houston (free on board in Houston). This term means that the buyer pays the transportation charges from Houston—see Exhibit 21–2 below. The contract authorizes shipment by carrier. It does not require that the seller tender the grapefruit in New York. Risk passes to the buyer when conforming goods are properly placed in the possession of the carrier. If the goods are damaged in transit, the loss is the buyer's. (Actually, buyers have recourse against carriers, subject to certain limitations, and they usually insure the goods from the time the goods leave the seller.) ◀

DESTINATION CONTRACTS In a destination contract, the risk of loss passes to the buyer or lessee when the goods are tendered to the buyer or lessee at the specified destination [UCC 2–509(1)(b), 2A–219(2)(b)]. In *Example 21.9* above, if the contract had been a destination contract, F.O.B. New York, risk of loss during transit to New York would have been the seller's. Risk of loss would not have passed to the buyer until the carrier tendered the grapefruit to the buyer in New York.

Whether a contract is a shipment contract or a destination contract can have significant consequences for the parties. When an agreement is ambiguous as to whether it is a shipment or a destination contract,

EXHIBIT 21–2 Contract Terms—Definitions

The contract terms listed and defined in this exhibit help to determine which party will bear the costs of delivery and when risk of loss will pass from the seller to the buyer.

F.O.B. (free on board)—Indicates that the selling price of goods includes transportation costs to the specific F.O.B. place named in the contract. The seller pays the expenses and carries the risk of loss to the F.O.B. place named [UCC 2–319(1)]. If the named place is the place from which the goods are shipped (for example, the seller's city or place of business), the contract is a shipment contract. If the named place is the place to which the goods are to be shipped (for example, the buyer's city or place of business), the contract is a destination contract.

F.A.S. (free alongside)—Requires that the seller, at his or her own expense and risk, deliver the goods alongside the carrier before risk passes to the buyer [UCC 2–319(2)]. An F.A.S. contract is essentially an F.O.B. contract for ships.

C.I.F. or **C.&F.** (cost, insurance, and freight or just cost and freight)—Requires, among other things, that the seller "put the goods in possession of a carrier" before risk passes to the buyer [UCC 2–320(2)]. (These are basically pricing terms, and the contracts remain shipment contracts, not destination contracts.)

Delivery ex-ship (delivery from the carrying vessel)—Means that risk of loss does not pass to the buyer until the goods are properly unloaded from the ship or other carrier [UCC 2–322].

courts normally will presume that it is a shipment contract. Thus, the parties must use clear and explicit language to overcome this presumption and create a destination contract.

Delivery without Movement of the Goods

The UCC also addresses situations in which the contract does not require the goods to be shipped or moved. Frequently, the buyer or lessee is to pick up the goods from the seller or lessor, or the goods are to be held by a bailee. A **bailment** is a temporary delivery of personal property, without passage of title, into the care of another, called a *bailee*. Under the UCC, a bailee is a party who—by a bill of lading, warehouse receipt, or other document of title—acknowledges possession of goods and/or contracts to deliver them. For instance, a warehousing company or a trucking company may be a bailee.[5]

GOODS HELD BY THE SELLER When the seller keeps the goods for pickup, a document of title usually is not used. If the seller is not a merchant, the risk of loss to goods held by the seller passes to the buyer on *tender of delivery* [UCC 2–509(3)]. Thus, the seller bears the risk of loss until he or she makes the goods available to the buyer and notifies the buyer that the goods are ready to be picked up.

Merchants. If the seller is a merchant, risk of loss to goods held by the seller passes to the buyer when the buyer *actually takes physical possession of the goods* [UCC 2–509(3)]. In other words, the merchant bears the risk of loss between the time the contract is formed and the time the buyer picks up the goods.

▶ **Case in Point 21.10** Henry Ganno purchased a twelve-foot beam at a lumberyard. The lumberyard loaded the beam onto Ganno's truck, but did not tie it down (it was policy not to secure loads for customers). After he drove onto the highway, the beam fell out of Ganno's truck, and he was injured while trying to retrieve it. Ganno sued the lumberyard for negligence, but the court held that Ganno—not the lumberyard—bore the risk of loss and injury after he left the lumberyard's premises. Once the truck was loaded, the risk of loss passed to Ganno under the UCC because he had taken physical possession of the goods.[6] ◀

---

5. The law requires bailees to take appropriate care of the bailed goods.
6. *Ganno v. Lanoga Corp.,* 119 Wash.App. 310, 80 P.3d 180 (2003).

Leases. Except in a finance lease (in which the lessor acquires goods to supply the lessee—see Chapter 20), the lessor normally retains the risk of loss [UCC 2A–219]. If a lease contract provides that risk of loss is to pass to the lessee but does not specify when, then it depends on whether the lessor is a merchant. If the lessor is a merchant, the risk of loss passes to the lessee on the lessee's receipt of the goods. If the lessor is not a merchant, the risk passes to the lessee on tender of delivery (when goods are made available for pickup) [UCC 2A–219(2)(c)].

▶ **Example 21.11** Erikson Crane leases a helicopter from Jevis, Ltd., which is in the business of renting aircraft. While Erikson's pilot is on the way to Idaho to pick up the helicopter, the helicopter is damaged during an unexpected storm. In this situation, Jevis is a merchant-lessor, so it bears the risk of loss to the leased helicopter until Erikson takes possession of the helicopter. ◀

GOODS HELD BY A BAILEE When a bailee is holding goods that are to be delivered under a contract without being moved, the goods are usually represented by a document of title. The title document may be written or evidenced by an electronic record.

Negotiability of Title Document. A document of title is either *negotiable* or *nonnegotiable,* depending on whether the transferee is a buyer or lessee, and how it is transferred. Negotiable and nonnegotiable documents may transfer different rights to the goods that the documents cover.

With a negotiable document of title, a party can transfer the rights by signing and delivering, or in some situations simply delivering, the document. The rights to the goods—free of any claims against the party that issued the document—pass with the document to the transferee. With a nonnegotiable document of title, the transferee obtains only the rights goods that the party transferring it had, subject to any prior claims.

When Risk of Loss Passes. When goods are held by a bailee, risk of loss passes to the buyer when one of the following occurs:

1. The buyer receives a negotiable document of title for the goods.
2. The bailee acknowledges the buyer's right to possess the goods.
3. The buyer receives a nonnegotiable document of title, *and* the buyer has had a *reasonable time* to present the document to the bailee and demand

the goods. If the bailee refuses to honor the document, the risk of loss remains with the seller [UCC 2–503(4)(b), 2–509(2)].

With respect to leases, if goods held by a bailee are to be delivered without being moved, the risk of loss passes to the lessee on acknowledgment by the bailee of the lessee's right to possession of the goods [UCC 2A–219(2)(b)].

Concept Summary 21.1 below reviews the rules for when title and risk of loss pass to the buyer or lessee when the seller or lessor is not required to ship or deliver the goods.

Conditional Sales

Buyers and sellers sometimes form sales contracts that are conditioned either on the buyer's approval of the goods or on the buyer's resale of the goods. The UCC states that (unless otherwise agreed) if the goods are for the buyer to use, the transaction is a *sale on approval*. If the goods are for the buyer to resell, the transaction is a *sale or return*.

SALE ON APPROVAL When a seller offers to sell goods to a buyer and permits the buyer to take the goods on a trial basis, a **sale on approval** is made. The goods are delivered primarily so that the prospective buyer can use the goods and be convinced of their appearance or performance. The term *sale* here is misleading, however, because only an *offer* to sell has been made, along with a bailment created by the buyer's possession.

Title and risk of loss (from causes beyond the buyer's control) remain with the seller until the buyer accepts (approves) the offer. Acceptance can be made expressly or by any act inconsistent with the *trial purpose* or the seller's ownership (such as reselling the goods). Thus, the buyer's decision not to return the goods within the trial period will be considered acceptance. If the buyer does not wish to accept, the buyer must notify the seller, and the return is made at the seller's expense and risk [UCC 2–327(1)]. Goods held on approval are not subject to the claims of the buyer's creditors until acceptance.

▶ **Example 21.12** Brad orders a Bowflex Tread-Climber online, and the manufacturer allows him to try it risk-free for thirty days. If Brad decides to keep the TreadClimber, then the sale is complete, but if he returns it within thirty days, there will be no sale and he will not be charged. If Brad files for bankruptcy within the thirty-day period and still has the TreadClimber in his possession, his creditors may not

CONCEPT SUMMARY 21.1
Delivery without Movement of the Goods

CONCEPT	DESCRIPTION

Goods Not Represented by a Document of Title	Unless otherwise agreed, if the goods are not represented by a document of title, title and risk pass as follows:
	1. Title passes on the formation of the contract [UCC 2–401(3)(b)].
	2. Risk of loss passes to the buyer or lessee:
	  a. if the seller or lessor is a merchant, risk passes on the buyer's or lessee's *receipt* of the goods.
	  b. If the seller or lessor is a nonmerchant, risk passes to the buyer or lessee on the seller's or lessor's *tender* of delivery of the goods [UCC 2–509(3), 2A–219(2)(c)].

Goods Represented by a Document of Title	Unless otherwise agreed, if the goods are represented by a document of title, title and risk pass to the buyer when any of the following occurs: 1. The buyer receives a negotiable document of title for the goods. 2. The bailee acknowledges the buyer's right to possess the goods. 3. The buyer receives a nonnegotiable document of title or a writing (record) directing the bailee to hand over the goods, and the buyer has had a reasonable time to present the document to the bailee and demand the goods [UCC 2–503(4)(b), 2–509(2)].
Leased Goods Held by a Bailee	If leased goods held by a bailee are to be delivered without being moved, the risk of loss passes to the lessee on acknowledgment by the bailee of the lessee's right to possession of the goods [UCC 2A–219(2)(b)].

yet attach (seize) the TreadClimber because he has not accepted it. ◄

SALE OR RETURN In a **sale or return,** in contrast, the sale is completed, but the buyer has an option to return the goods and undo the sale. Sale-or-return contracts often arise when a merchant purchases goods primarily for resale. The merchant has the right to return part or all of the goods in lieu of payment if the goods fail to be resold. Basically, a sale or return is a sale of goods in the present that may be undone at the buyer's option within a specified time period.
▶ **Example 21.13** Freedom Press, a publisher, delivers forty cases of a best-selling book to Powell's Books, a retailer. If Freedom Press agrees that Powell's can return any unsold copies of the books at the end of a year, the transaction is a sale or return. ◄

Because the buyer receives possession at the time of the sale, title and risk of loss pass to the buyer and remain with the buyer unless the goods are returned within the time period specified. If the buyer decides to return the goods within this time period, the return is made at the buyer's risk and expense. Goods held under a sale-or-return contract are subject to the claims of the buyer's creditors while they are in the buyer's possession.

Risk of Loss When a Sales or Lease Contract Is Breached

When a sales or lease contract is breached, the transfer of risk operates differently depending on which party breaches. Generally, the party in breach bears the risk of loss.

WHEN THE SELLER OR LESSOR BREACHES If the goods are so nonconforming that the buyer has the right to reject them, the risk of loss does not pass to the buyer. ▶ **Example 21.14** Lowe's orders stainless steel refrigerators from Whirlpool, F.O.B. Whirlpool's plant. Whirlpool ships white refrigerators instead. The white refrigerators (nonconforming goods) are damaged in transit. The risk of loss falls on Whirlpool. Had it shipped stainless steel refrigerators (conforming goods) instead, the risk would have fallen on Lowe's [UCC 2–510(1)]. ◄

With nonconforming goods, the risk of loss does not pass to the buyer until either:

1. The defects are *cured* (that is, the goods are repaired, replaced, or discounted in price by the seller—see Chapter 22).

2. The buyer accepts the goods in spite of their defects (thus waiving the right to reject).

When Acceptance Is Revoked. If a buyer accepts a shipment of goods and later discovers a defect, acceptance can be revoked. The revocation allows the buyer to pass the risk of loss back to the seller, at least to the extent that the buyer's insurance does not cover the loss [UCC 2–510(2)].

Leases. Article 2A provides a similar rule for leases. If the tender or delivery of goods is so nonconforming that the lessee has the right to reject them, the risk of loss remains with the lessor (or the supplier) until cure or acceptance [UCC 2A–220(1)(a)]. If the lessee accepts the goods and then rightfully revokes acceptance, the risk of loss passes back to the lessor to the extent that the lessee's insurance does not cover the loss [UCC 2A–220(1)(b)].

WHEN THE BUYER OR LESSEE BREACHES The general rule is that when a buyer or lessee breaches a contract, the risk of loss *immediately shifts* to the buyer or lessee. This rule has three important limitations [UCC 2–510(3), 2A–220(2)]:

1. The seller or lessor must have already identified the contract goods.
2. The buyer or lessee bears the risk for only a *commercially reasonable time* after the seller or lessor has learned of the breach.
3. The buyer or lessee is liable only to the extent of any deficiency in the seller's or lessor's insurance coverage.

See *Concept Summary 21.2* on the following page for a review of the rules on who bears the risk of loss when a contract is breached.

SECTION 4
INSURABLE INTEREST

Parties to sales and lease contracts often obtain insurance coverage to protect against damage, loss, or destruction of goods. Any party purchasing insurance, however, must have a sufficient interest in the insured item to obtain a valid policy. Insurance laws—not the UCC—determine sufficiency. The UCC is helpful, though, because it contains certain rules regarding insurable interests in goods.

CONCEPT SUMMARY 21.2
Risk of Loss When a Sales or Lease Contract Is Breached

CONCEPT	DESCRIPTION
When the Seller or Lessor Breaches the Contract	If the seller or lessor breaches by tendering nonconforming goods that the buyer or lessee has a right to reject, the risk of loss does not pass to the buyer or lessee until the defects are cured or the buyer accepts the goods (thus waiving the right to reject) [UCC 2–510(1), 2A–220(1)].
When the Buyer or Lessee Breaches the Contract	If the buyer or lessee breaches the contract, the risk of loss to identified goods immediately shifts to the buyer or lessee. Limitations to this rule are as follows [UCC 2–510(3), 2A–220(2)]: 1. The seller or lessor must have already identified the contract goods. 2. The buyer or lessee bears the risk for only a commercially reasonable time after the seller or lessor has learned of the breach. 3. The buyer or lessee is liable only to the extent of any deficiency in the seller's or lessor's insurance coverage.

Insurable Interest of the Buyer or Lessee

A buyer or lessee has an **insurable interest** in *identified goods*. The moment the contract goods are identified by the seller or lessor, the buyer or lessee has a property interest in them. That interest allows the buyer or lessee to obtain the necessary insurance coverage for those goods even before the risk of loss has passed [UCC 2–501(1), 2A–218(1)]. Identification can be made at any time and in any manner agreed to by the parties.

When the parties do not explicitly agree on identification in their contract, then the UCC provisions on identification discussed on page 400 of this chapter apply. Buyers obtain an insurable interest in crops at the time of identification. ▶ **Example 21.15** In March, a farmer sells a cotton crop that she hopes to harvest in October. If the contract does not specify otherwise, the buyer acquires an insurable interest in the crop when it is planted because the goods (the cotton crop) are identified to the sales contract at that time [UCC 2–501(1)(c)]. ◀

Insurable Interest of the Seller or Lessor

A seller has an insurable interest in goods as long as he or she retains title to the goods. Even after title passes to a buyer, a seller who has a *security interest* (a right to secure payment) in the goods still has an insurable interest and can insure the goods [UCC 2–501(2)].

Thus, both the buyer and the seller can have an insurable interest in identical goods at the same time. Of course, the buyer or seller must sustain an actual loss to have the right to recover from an insurance company. In regard to leases, the lessor retains an insurable interest in leased goods unless the lessee exercises an option to buy, in which event the risk of loss passes to the lessee [UCC 2A–218(3)].

Reviewing: Title, Risk, and Insurable Interest

In December, Mendoza agreed to buy the broccoli grown on one hundred acres of Willow Glen's one-thousand-acre broccoli farm. The sales contract specified F.O.B. Willow Glen's field by Falcon Trucking. The broccoli was to be planted in February and harvested in March of the following year. Using the information presented in the chapter, answer the following questions.

Continued

1. At what point is a crop of broccoli identified to the contract under the Uniform Commercial Code? Why is identification significant?
2. When does title to the broccoli pass from Willow Glen to Mendoza under the contract terms? Why?
3. Suppose that while in transit, Falcon's truck overturns and spills the entire load. Who bears the loss, Mendoza or Willow Glen?
4. Suppose that instead of buying fresh broccoli, Mendoza had contracted with Willow Glen to purchase one thousand cases of frozen broccoli from Willow Glen's processing plant. The highest grade of broccoli is packaged under the "FreshBest" label, and everything else is packaged under the "FamilyPac" label. Further suppose that although the contract specified that Mendoza was to receive FreshBest broccoli, Falcon Trucking delivered FamilyPac broccoli to Mendoza. If Mendoza refuses to accept the broccoli, who bears the loss?

DEBATE THIS . . . *The distinction between shipment and destination contracts for the purpose of deciding who will bear the risk of loss should be eliminated in favor of a rule that always requires the buyer to obtain insurance for the goods being shipped.*

Terms and Concepts

bailment 410
buyer in the ordinary course of business 405
destination contract 403
document of title 403

entrustment rule 405
fungible goods 402
good faith purchaser 404
identification 400
insolvent 404

insurable interest 413
sale on approval 411
sale or return 412
shipment contract 403

ExamPrep

Issue Spotters

1. Adams Textiles in Kansas City sells certain fabric to Silk & Satin Stores in Oklahoma City. Adams packs the fabric and ships it by rail to Silk. While the fabric is in transit across Kansas, a tornado derails the train and shreds and scatters the fabric across miles of cornfields. What are the consequences if Silk bore the risk? If Adams bore the risk? **(See page 413.)**

2. Karlin takes her television set for repair to Orken, a merchant who sells new and used television sets. By accident, one of Orken's employees sells the set to Grady, an innocent purchaser-customer, who takes possession. Karlin wants her set back from Grady. If

Karlin files a lawsuit, will she prevail? Why or why not? **(See page 404.)**

• **Check your answers to the Issue Spotters against the answers provided in Appendix E at the end of this text.**

Before the Test

Go to **www.cengagebrain.com**, enter the ISBN 9781285185248, and click on "Find" to locate this textbook's Web site. Then, click on "Access Now" under "Study Tools," and select Chapter 21 at the top. There, you will find a Practice Quiz that you can take to assess your mastery of the concepts in this chapter, as well as Flashcards, and a Glossary of important terms.

Business Scenarios

21–1. Risk of Loss. Mackey orders from Pride one thousand cases of Greenie brand peas from lot A at list price to be shipped F.O.B. Pride's city via Fast Freight Lines. Pride receives the order and immediately sends Mackey an acceptance of the order with a promise to ship promptly. Pride later separates the one thousand cases of Greenie

peas and prints Mackey's name and address on each case. The peas are placed on Pride's dock, and Fast Freight is notified to pick up the shipment. The night before the pickup by Fast Freight, through no fault of Pride's, a fire destroys the one thousand cases of peas. Pride claims that title passed to Mackey at the time the contract was made and that risk of loss passed to Mackey when the goods were marked with Mackey's name and address. Discuss Pride's contentions. **(See page 407.)**

21–2. Risk of Loss. On May 1, Sikora goes into Carson's retail clothing store to purchase a suit. Sikora finds a suit he likes for $190 and buys it. The suit needs alterations. Sikora is to pick up the altered suit at Carson's store on May 10. Consider the following separate sets of circumstances: **(See page 407.)**

(a) One of Carson's major creditors obtains a judgment on the debt Carson owes and has the court issue a writ of execution (a court order to seize a debtor's property to satisfy a debt) to collect on that judgment all clothing in Carson's possession. Discuss Sikora's rights in the suit under these circumstances.

(b) On May 9, through no fault of Carson's, the store burns down, and all contents are a total loss. Between Carson and Sikora, who suffers the loss of the suit destroyed by the fire? Explain.

21–3. Sale or Return. Zeke, who sells lawn mowers, tells Stasio, a regular customer, about a special promotional campaign. On receipt of a $50 down payment, Zeke will sell Stasio a new Universal lawn mower for $200, even though it normally sells for $350. Zeke also says that if Stasio does not like the performance of the lawn mower, he can return it within thirty days, and Zeke will refund the $50 down payment. Stasio pays the $50 and takes the mower. On the tenth day, the lawn mower is stolen through no fault of Stasio's. Stasio calls Zeke and demands the return of his $50. Zeke claims that Stasio should suffer the risk of loss and that he still owes Zeke $150 for the rest of the purchase price. Discuss who is correct, Stasio or Zeke. **(See page 412.)**

Business Case Problems

21–4. Delivery without Movement of the Goods. Aleris International, Inc., signed a contract to buy a John Deere loader from Holt Equipment Co. The agreement provided that "despite physical delivery of the equipment, title shall remain in the seller until" Aleris paid the full price. The next month, Aleris filed for bankruptcy. Holt filed a claim with the court to repossess the loader. Holt asserted that it was the owner. Who is entitled to the loader, and why? [*In re Aleris International, Ltd.*, __ Bankr. __ (D.Del. 2011)] **(See page 403.)**

21–5. Goods Held by the Seller or Lessor. Douglas Singletary bought a manufactured home from Andy's Mobile Home and Land Sales. The contract stated that the buyer accepted the home "as is where is." Singletary paid the full price, and his crew began to ready the home to relocate it to his property. The night before the home was to be moved, however, it was destroyed by fire. Who suffered the loss? Explain. [*Singletary, III v. P&A Investments, Inc.*, 712 S.E.2d 681 (N.C.App. 2011)] **(See page 410.)**

21–6. BUSINESS CASE PROBLEM WITH SAMPLE ANSWER: Passage of Title.

 Kenzie Godfrey, a college student majoring in physics, was a passenger in a taxi when it collided with a car driven by Dawn Altieri. Altieri had originally leased the car from G.E. Capital Auto Lease, Inc. By the time of the accident, she had bought it, but she had not fully paid for it or completed the transfer-of-title paperwork. Godfrey suffered a brain injury and sought to recover damages from the owner of the car that Altieri was driving. Who had title to the car at the time of the accident? Explain. [Godfrey v. G.E. Capital Auto Lease, Inc., 89 A.D.3d 471, 933 N.Y.S.2d 208 (1 Dept. 2011)] **(See page 403.)**

• **For a sample answer to Problem 21–6, go to Appendix F at the end of this text.**

21–7. Risk of Loss. Ethicon, Inc., a pharmaceutical company, entered into an agreement with UPS Supply Chain Solutions, Inc., to transport pharmaceuticals. Under a contract with UPS's subsidiary, Worldwide Dedicated Services, Inc., (WDS), the drivers were provided by International Management Services Co. (IMSCO). During the transport of a shipment from Ethicon's facility in Texas to buyers "F.O.B. Tennessee," one of the trucks collided with a concrete barrier near Little Rock, Arkansas, and caught fire, damaging the goods. Who was liable for the loss? Why? [*Royal & Sun Alliance Insurance, PLC v. International Management Services Co.*, 703 F.3d 604 (2d Cir. 2013)] **(See page 407.)**

21–8. A QUESTION OF ETHICS: Void and Voidable Titles.

 Kenneth West agreed to sell his car, a 1975 Corvette, to a man representing himself as Robert Wilson. In exchange for a cashier's check, West signed over the Corvette's title to Wilson and gave him the car. Ten days later, when West learned that the cashier's check was a forgery, he filed a stolen vehicle report with the police. The police could not immediately locate Wilson or the Corvette, however, and the case grew cold. Nearly two and a half years later, the police found the Corvette in the possession of Tammy Roberts, who also had the certificate of title. She said that she had bought the car from her brother, who had obtained it through an ad in a newspaper. West filed a suit in a Colorado state court against Roberts to reclaim the car. The court applied Colorado Revised Statutes Section 4-2-403 (Colorado's version of Section 2–403 of the Uniform Commercial Code) to determine the vehicle's rightful owner. [West v. Roberts, 143 P.3d 1037 (Colo. 2006)] **(See page 404.)**

(a) Under UCC 2–403, what title, if any, to the Corvette did "Wilson" acquire? What was the status of Roberts's title, if any, assuming that she bought the car without knowledge of circumstances that would make a person of ordinary prudence inquire about the validity of the seller's title? In whose favor should the court rule? Explain.

(b) If the original owner of a vehicle relinquishes it due to fraud, should he or she be allowed to recover the vehicle from a good faith purchaser? If not, which party or parties might the original owner sue for recovery? What is the ethical principle underlying your answer to these questions? Discuss.

21–9. SPECIAL CASE ANALYSIS: Risk of Loss.

Go to Case Analysis Case 21.3, *Person v. Bowman,* on page 408. Read the excerpt and answer the following questions.

(a) **Issue:** What document was at the center of this case?

(b) **Rule of Law:** What determines when the risk of loss passes from a seller to a buyer? Does this also determine when the risk of liability from use of the goods passes from the seller to the buyer?

(c) **Applying the Rule of Law:** How did the objective theory of contract interpretation affect the court's reasoning in this case?

(d) **Conclusion:** Whom did the court determine was liable? Why?

Legal Reasoning Group Activity

21–10. Shipment Contracts. Professional Products, Inc. (PPI), bought three pallets of computer wafers from Omneon Video Graphics. (A computer wafer is a thin, round slice of silicon from which microchips are made.) Omneon agreed to ship the wafers to the City University of New York "FOB Omneon's dock." Shipment was arranged through Haas Industries, Inc. The "conditions of carriage" on the back of the bill of lading stated that Haas's liability for lost goods was limited to fifty cents per pound. When the shipment arrived, it included only two pallets. **(See page 403.)**

(a) The first group will determine who suffers the loss in this situation.

(b) The second group will discuss whether it is it fair for a carrier to limit its liability for lost goods.

CHAPTER 22

PERFORMANCE AND BREACH OF SALES AND LEASE CONTRACTS

The performance that is required of the parties under a sales or lease contract consists of the duties and obligations each party has under the terms of the contract. The basic obligation of the seller or lessor is to transfer and deliver the goods as stated in the contract, and the basic duty of the buyer or lessee is to accept and pay for the goods.

Keep in mind that "duties and obligations" under the terms of the contract include those specified by the agreement, by custom, and by the Uniform Commercial Code (UCC). Thus, parties to a sales or lease contract may be bound not only by terms they expressly agreed on, but also by terms implied by custom, such as a customary method of weighing or measuring particular goods.

Sometimes, circumstances make it difficult for a person to carry out the promised performance, leading to a breach of the contract. When a breach occurs, the aggrieved (wronged) party looks for remedies—which we examine in the second half of the chapter. Note that in contrast to the common law of contracts, remedies under the UCC are *cumulative* in nature—meaning that the aggrieved party is not limited to one exclusive remedy.

SECTION 1
PERFORMANCE OBLIGATIONS

As discussed in previous chapters, the obligations of good faith and commercial reasonableness underlie every sales and lease contract.

The UCC's Good Faith Provision

The UCC's good faith provision, which can never be disclaimed, reads as follows: "Every contract or duty within this Act imposes an obligation of good faith in its performance or enforcement" [UCC 1–304]. *Good faith* means honesty in fact. For a merchant, it means honesty in fact and the observance of reasonable commercial standards of fair dealing in the trade [UCC 2–103(1)(b)]. In other words, merchants are held to a higher standard of performance or duty than are nonmerchants.

Good Faith and Contract Performance

The principle of good faith applies to both parties and provides a framework for the entire agreement. If a sales contract leaves open some particulars of performance, for instance, the parties must exercise good faith and commercial reasonableness when later specifying the details. The *Focus on Ethics* feature at the end of this unit explores the ethical implications of the UCC's good faith standard.

In performing a sales or lease contract, the basic obligation of the seller or lessor is to *transfer and deliver conforming goods*. The basic obligation of the buyer or lessee is to *accept and pay for conforming goods* in accordance with the contract [UCC 2–301, 2A–516(1)]. Overall performance of a sales or lease contract is controlled by the agreement between the parties. When the contract is unclear and disputes arise, the courts look to the UCC and impose standards of good faith and commercial reasonableness.

SECTION 2
OBLIGATIONS OF THE SELLER OR LESSOR

As stated, the basic duty of the seller or lessor is to deliver the goods called for under the contract to the buyer or lessee.

Tender of Delivery

Goods that conform to the contract description in every way are called **conforming goods.** To fulfill the contract, the seller or lessor must either deliver or tender delivery of conforming goods to the buyer or lessee. **Tender of delivery** occurs when the seller or lessor makes conforming goods available and gives the buyer or lessee whatever notification is reasonably necessary to enable the buyer or lessee to take delivery [UCC 2–503(1), 2A–508(1)].

Tender must occur at a *reasonable hour* and in a *reasonable manner.* For example, a seller cannot call the buyer at 2:00 A.M. and say, "The goods are ready. I'll give you twenty minutes to get them." Unless the parties have agreed otherwise, the goods must be tendered for delivery at a reasonable hour and kept available for a reasonable time to enable the buyer to take possession [UCC 2–503(1)(a)].

Normally, all goods called for by a contract must be tendered in a single delivery—unless the parties have agreed on delivery in several lots or *installments* (to be discussed shortly) [UCC 2–307, 2–612, 2A–510]. ▶ **Example 22.1** An order for 1,000 Under Armour men's shirts cannot be delivered two shirts at a time. If, however, the parties agree that the shirts will be delivered in four orders of 250 each as they are produced (for summer, fall, winter, and spring inventory), then tender of delivery may occur in this manner. ◀

Place of Delivery

The buyer and seller (or lessor and lessee) may agree that the goods will be delivered to a particular destination where the buyer or lessee will take possession. If the contract does not indicate where the goods will be delivered, then the place for delivery will be one of the following:

1. The *seller's place of business.*
2. The *seller's residence,* if the seller has no business location [UCC 2–308(a)].
3. The *location of the goods,* if both parties know at the time of contracting that the goods are located somewhere other than the seller's business [UCC 2–308(b)].

▶ **Example 22.2** Li Wan and Boyd both live in San Francisco. In San Francisco, Li Wan contracts to sell Boyd five used trucks, which both parties know are located in a Chicago warehouse. If nothing more is specified in the contract, the place of delivery for the trucks is Chicago. Li Wan may tender delivery by giving Boyd either a negotiable or a nonnegotiable document of title. Alternatively, Li Wan may obtain the bailee's (warehouser's) acknowledgment that Boyd is entitled to possession.[1] ◀

Delivery via Carrier

In many instances, it is clear from the surrounding circumstances or delivery terms in the contract (such as F.O.B. or F.A.S. terms; see Exhibit 21–2) that the parties intended the goods to be moved by a carrier. In carrier contracts, the seller fulfills the obligation to deliver the goods through either a shipment contract or a destination contract.

SHIPMENT CONTRACTS Recall from Chapter 21 that a *shipment contract* requires or authorizes the seller to ship goods by a carrier, rather than to deliver them at a particular destination [UCC 2–319, 2–509(1)(a)]. Under a shipment contract, unless otherwise agreed, the seller must do the following:

1. Place the goods into the hands of the carrier.
2. Make a contract for their transportation that is reasonable according to the nature of the goods and their value. (For example, certain types of goods need refrigeration in transit.)
3. Obtain and promptly deliver or tender to the buyer any documents necessary to enable the buyer to obtain possession of the goods from the carrier.
4. Promptly notify the buyer that shipment has been made [UCC 2–504].

If the seller does not make a reasonable contract for transportation or notify the buyer of the shipment, the buyer can reject the goods, but only if a *material loss* or a *significant delay* results. ▶ **Example 22.3** Zigi's Organic Fruits sells strawberries to Lozier under a shipment contract. If Zigi's does not arrange for refrigerated transportation and the berries spoil during transport, a material loss will likely result because Lozier will be unable to sell them. ◀ (Of course, the parties are free to make agreements that alter the UCC's rules and allow the buyer to reject goods for other reasons.)

DESTINATION CONTRACTS In a *destination contract,* the seller agrees to deliver conforming goods to the

---

1. Unless the buyer objects, the seller may also tender delivery by instructing the bailee in a writing (record) to release the goods to the buyer without the bailee's acknowledgment of the buyer's rights [UCC 2–503(4)]. Risk of loss, however, does not pass until the buyer has had a reasonable amount of time in which to present the document or the instructions. See Chapter 21.

buyer at a particular destination. The goods must be tendered at a reasonable hour and held at the buyer's disposal for a reasonable length of time. The seller must also give the buyer appropriate notice and any necessary documents to enable the buyer to obtain delivery from the carrier [UCC 2–503].

The Perfect Tender Rule

As previously noted, the seller or lessor has an obligation to ship or tender *conforming goods,* which the buyer or lessee is then obligated to accept and pay for according to the terms of the contract [UCC 2–507].

Under the common law, the seller was obligated to deliver goods that conformed with the terms of the contract in every detail. This is called the **perfect tender rule.**

The UCC preserves the perfect tender doctrine. It states that if goods or tender of delivery fails *in any respect* to conform to the contract, the buyer or lessee may accept the goods, reject the entire shipment, or accept part and reject part [UCC 2–601, 2A–509].

The corollary to this rule is that if the goods conform in every respect, the buyer or lessee does not have a right to reject the goods, as the following case illustrates.

CASE ANALYSIS

Case 22.1   Wilson Sporting Goods Co. v. U.S. Golf and Tennis Centers, Inc.

Court of Appeals of Tennessee, 2012 WL 601804 (2012).

IN THE LANGUAGE OF THE COURT
Charles D. *SUSANO,* Jr., J.
[Judge]

* * * *

[U.S. Golf & Tennis Centers, Inc. (the Company), and its owners, Arthur and Louise Bell, operate] two retail sporting goods stores specializing in the sale of golf and tennis equipment: one in Tennessee and the one in Ohio. * * * The Company agreed to purchase from Wilson [Sporting Goods Company] 4,000 units of second-hand golf balls at a unit price of $5.00—a unit being two dozen golf balls. Thus, the Company purchased 96,000 golf balls for a total price of $20,000. The order was shipped * * * with half of the shipment being received at the Ohio store and the other half being delivered to the Tennessee store. It is undisputed that the shipment conformed in quantity and quality to the specifications of the parties' contract.

When Wilson filed suit in [a Tennessee state court against U.S. Golf] the $20,000 balance on the contract was past due and owing.

The record reflects a series of fax communications between Mr. Bell and Wilson * * * in which Mr. Bell repeatedly sought written confirmation that the Company had received the "lowest price" for the golf balls. In its faxes, Wilson confirmed that the Company received the lowest price "that Wilson offered to any one in the market." The communications ended with Wilson seeking "prompt payment," and with Mr. Bell, apparently unsatisfied with Wilson's responses, seeking authorization to return the shipment to Wilson.

In answer to Wilson's suit, the defendants alleged breach of contract in that Wilson had "misrepresented the price of the goods at issue. * * * Before delivery the defendants heard that in fact Wilson had sold the product for $2.00 per dozen. * * * Accordingly, there was never a meeting of the minds as to the amount that would be charged."

[After a trial, the court entered a judgment in favor of Wilson for $33,099.28, including interest, attorneys' fees, and other expenses. The defendants appealed.]

* * * *

The defendants contend that they were legally entitled to cancel the subject contract and that, therefore, the trial court erred in upholding the contract and awarding Wilson a judgment for $33,099.28.

* * * The defendants point, in particular, to Tennessee Code Section 47–2–601 [Tennessee's version of UCC 2–601] which provides, in relevant part, that *"if the goods or the tender of delivery fail in any respect to conform to the contract,"* the buyer may, among other options, *"reject the whole * * * ."* From the defendants' point of view, the goods in this case failed to conform to the contract because, according to the defendants, Wilson charged the defendants a higher price for the goods than that agreed upon. The defendants assert that Mr. Bell, acting upon behalf of the Company, was thus entitled to and did in fact reject the shipment. The defendants argue that once they rejected the goods, they were entitled to cancel the contract pursuant to Tennessee Code Section 47–2–711 [Tennessee's version of UCC 2–711]. That section provides as follows:

CASE 22.1 CONTINUES ➡

CASE 22.1 CONTINUED

"Where * * * the buyer rightfully rejects * * * , the buyer may cancel." [Emphasis added.]

* * * Wilson responds that the goods in no way failed to conform to the contract, and that there was no rejection * * * of the goods by the Company. Accordingly, Wilson concludes that the Code sections relied upon by the defendants do not apply to permit the defendants to cancel the contract. In a word, Wilson is correct.

Nothing in the evidence before us shows or even suggests that the defendants ever rejected delivery of the shipment of the golf balls or that [they] ever had the right to do so. *The defendants do not dispute that*

the product received by the Company conformed to the contract with respect to quantity and quality. Their sole contention at trial was that the price charged was not the lowest available price, as contemplated by the contract. The trial court, however, found that the parties had a contract for an agreed total purchase price of $20,000, and that "the lowest price for the specific goods ordered and received was confirmed." * * * In addition to the fact that the contract's terms regarding price are clear, there is nothing in the record to contradict Wilson's confirmations to Mr. Bell that the defendants did receive the lowest price offered

to anyone for the goods received. [Emphasis added.]

In summary, the cited UCC provisions regarding rejection * * * and cancellation do not apply in this case where the trial court properly found that the seller, [that is,] Wilson, fully performed, but the buyer, the Company, failed to make any payments. As discussed, the agreed contract terms, including purchase price, were clear. The trial court did not err in upholding the contract and holding the defendants liable for the goods received.

* * * *

The judgment of the trial court is affirmed.

LEGAL REASONING QUESTIONS

1. What is the perfect tender rule?
2. According to the UCC, what are a buyer's options if the goods do *not* conform to the contract? Does a buyer have those same options if the goods conform in every respect? Explain.
3. In this case, what provision in the parties' contract was at the heart of their dispute?
4. What did the court rule on the dispute between these parties? Why?

Exceptions to the Perfect Tender Rule

Because of the rigidity of the perfect tender rule, several exceptions to the rule have been created, some of which we discuss here.

AGREEMENT OF THE PARTIES Exceptions to the perfect tender rule may be established by agreement. If the parties have agreed, for instance, that defective goods or parts will not be rejected if the seller or lessor is able to repair or replace them within a reasonable period of time, the perfect tender rule does not apply.

CURE The UCC does not specifically define the term **cure,** but it refers to the right of the seller or lessor to repair, adjust, or replace defective or nonconforming goods [UCC 2–508, 2A–513].

The seller or lessor has a right to attempt to "cure" a defect when the following are true:

1. A delivery is rejected because the goods were nonconforming.

2. The time for performance has not yet expired.
3. The seller or lessor provides timely notice to the buyer or lessee of the intention to cure.
4. The cure can be made *within the contract time for performance.*

Reasonable Grounds. Once the time for performance under the contract has expired, the seller or lessor no longer has a right to cure. Nevertheless, the seller or lessor can still cure if he or she has *reasonable grounds to believe that the nonconforming tender will be acceptable to the buyer or lessee* [UCC 2–508(2), 2A–513(2)].

▶ **Example 22.4** In the past, EZ Office Supply has frequently accepted blue pens when the seller, Baxter's Wholesale, did not have black pens in stock. In this context, Baxter's has reasonable grounds to believe that EZ will again accept such a substitute. Even if EZ rejected the substituted goods on one particular occasion, Baxter's has reasonable grounds to believe that blue pens will be acceptable. Therefore, if EZ indicates that it will not accept blue pens, Baxter's normally will have a reasonable time to obtain and tender black pens. ◀

A seller or lessor will sometimes tender nonconforming goods with some type of price allowance (discount). A discounted price can serve as the "reasonable grounds" to believe that the buyer or lessee will accept the nonconforming tender.

Limits Right to Reject Goods. The right to cure substantially restricts the right of the buyer or lessee to reject goods. To reject, the buyer or lessee must inform the seller or lessor of the particular defect. If the defect is not disclosed, the buyer or lessee cannot later assert the defect as a defense if the defect is one that the seller or lessor could have cured. Generally, buyers and lessees must act in good faith and state specific reasons for refusing to accept goods [UCC 2–605, 2A–514].

SUBSTITUTION OF CARRIERS Sometimes, an agreed-on manner of delivery (such as the use of a particular carrier to transport the goods) becomes impracticable or unavailable through no fault of either party. In that situation, if a commercially reasonable substitute is available, this substitute performance is sufficient tender to the buyer and must be used [UCC 2–614(1)]. The seller or lessor is required to arrange for a substitute carrier and normally is responsible for any additional shipping costs (unless the contract states otherwise).

▶ **Example 22.5**   A sales contract calls for a large generator to be shipped by Mac's Trucking on or before June 1. The contract terms clearly state the importance of the delivery date. The employees of Mac's go on strike. The seller must make a reasonable substitute tender, by another trucking company or perhaps by rail, if it is available. ◀

INSTALLMENT CONTRACTS An **installment contract** is a single contract that requires or authorizes delivery in two or more separate lots to be accepted and paid for separately. With an installment contract, a buyer or lessee can reject an installment *only if the nonconformity substantially impairs the value* of the installment and cannot be cured [UCC 2–307, 2–612(2), 2A–510(1)]. If the buyer or lessee fails to notify the seller or lessor of the rejection, however, and subsequently accepts a nonconforming installment, the contract is reinstated [UCC 2–612(3), 2A–510(2)].

Unless the contract provides otherwise, the entire installment contract is breached only when one or more nonconforming installments *substantially* impair the value of the *whole contract*. ▶ **Example 22.6**   A contract calls for the parts of a machine to be delivered in installments. The first part is necessary for the operation of the machine, but when it is delivered, it is irreparably defective. The failure of this first installment will be a breach of the whole contract because the machine will not operate without the first part.

Suppose that, instead, the contract had called for twenty carloads of plywood and only 6 percent of one carload had deviated from the thickness specifications in the contract. It is unlikely that a court would find that a defect in 6 percent of one installment substantially impaired the value of the whole contract. ◀

The point to remember is that the UCC significantly alters the right of the buyer or lessee to reject the entire contract if the contract requires delivery to be made in several installments. The UCC strictly limits rejection to instances of *substantial* nonconformity.

COMMERCIAL IMPRACTICABILITY As discussed in Chapter 18, occurrences unforeseen by either party when a contract was made may make performance commercially impracticable. When this occurs, the perfect tender rule no longer applies. The seller or lessor must, however, notify the buyer or lessee as soon as practicable that there will be a delay or nondelivery.

▶ **Example 22.7**   Houston Oil Company, which receives its oil from the Middle East, has a contract to supply Northwest Fuels with one hundred thousand barrels of oil. Because of an oil embargo by the Organization of Petroleum Exporting Countries, Houston is unable to secure oil from the Middle East or any other source to meet the terms of the contract. This situation comes fully under the commercial impracticability exception to the perfect tender doctrine. ◀

An Unforeseeable Contingency. The doctrine of commercial impracticability does not extend to problems that could have been foreseen—such as an increase in cost resulting from inflation. The nonoccurrence of the contingency must have been a basic assumption on which the contract was made [UCC 2–615, 2A–405].

Can unanticipated increases in a seller's costs that make performance "impracticable" constitute a valid defense to performance on the basis of commercial impracticability? The court dealt with this question in the following classic case.

CLASSIC CASE 22.2

Maple Farms, Inc. v. City School District of Elmira
Supreme Court of New York, 76 Misc.2d 1080, 352 N.Y.S.2d 784 (1974).

BACKGROUND AND FACTS On June 15, 1973, Maple Farms, Inc., formed an agreement with the city school district of Elmira, New York, to supply the school district with milk for the 1973–1974 school year. The agreement was in the form of a requirements contract, under which Maple Farms would sell to the school district all the milk the district required at a fixed price. The specified price was the June market price of milk. By December 1973, the price of raw milk had increased by 23 percent over the price specified in the contract.

This meant that if the terms of the contract were fulfilled, Maple Farms would lose $7,350. Because it had similar contracts with other school districts, Maple Farms stood to lose a great deal if it was held to the price stated in the contracts. The school district refused to release Maple Farms from its contract. Therefore, Maple Farms brought an action in a New York state court for a declaratory judgment (a determination of the parties' rights under a contract). Maple Farms contended that when the parties formed their contract, they had not contemplated such a substantial increase in the price of raw milk. Given the increased price, performance of the contract was commercially impracticable.

IN THE LANGUAGE OF THE COURT
Charles B. *SWARTWOOD*, Justice.

* * * *

* * * [The doctrine of commercial impracticability requires first that] a contingency—something unexpected—must have occurred. Second, the risk of the unexpected occurrence must not have been allocated either by agreement or by custom.

* * * Here we find that the contingency causing the increase of the price of raw milk was not totally unexpected. The price from the low point in the year 1972 to the price on the date of the award of the contract in June 1973 had risen nearly 10%. And *any businessman should have been aware of the general inflation in this country during the previous years* * * * . [Emphasis added.]

* * * Here the very purpose of the contract was to guard against fluctuation of price of half pints of milk as a basis for the school budget. Surely had the price of raw milk fallen substantially, the defendant could not be excused from performance. We can reasonably assume that the plaintiff had to be aware of escalating inflation. It is chargeable with knowledge of the substantial increase of the price of raw milk from the previous year's low. * * * It nevertheless entered into this agreement with that knowledge. It did not provide in the contract any exculpatory clause to excuse it from performance in the event of a substantial rise in the price of raw milk. On these facts the risk of a substantial or abnormal increase in the price of raw milk can be allocated to the plaintiff.

DECISION AND REMEDY *The New York trial court ruled that inflation and fluctuating prices did not render performance impracticable in this case and granted summary judgment in favor of the school district.*

IMPACT OF THIS CASE ON TODAY'S LAW *This classic case illustrates the UCC's commercial impracticability doctrine as courts still apply it today. Under this doctrine, increased cost alone does not excuse performance unless the rise in cost is due to some unforeseen contingency that alters the essential nature of the performance.*

WHAT IF THE FACTS WERE DIFFERENT? *Suppose that the court had ruled in the plaintiff's favor. How might that ruling have affected the plaintiff's contracts with other parties?*

Partial Performance. Sometimes, the unforeseen event only *partially* affects the capacity of the seller or lessor to perform. Therefore, the seller or lessor can *partially* fulfill the contract but cannot tender total performance. In this event, the seller or les-sor is required to distribute any remaining goods or deliveries fairly and reasonably among the parties to whom it is contractually obligated to deliver the goods [UCC 2–615(b), 2A–405(b)]. The buyer or lessee must receive notice of the allocation and has the right to accept or reject it [UCC 2–615(c), 2A–405(c)].

▶ **Example 22.8**   A Florida orange grower, Best Citrus, Inc., contracts to sell this season's crop to a number of customers, including Martin's grocery chain. Martin's contracts to purchase two thousand crates of oranges. Best Citrus has sprayed *some* of its orange groves with a chemical called Karmoxin. The U.S. Department of Agriculture discovers that persons who eat products sprayed with Karmoxin may develop cancer and issues an order prohibiting the sale of these products. Best Citrus picks all the oranges not sprayed with Karmoxin, but the quantity is insufficient to meet all the contracted-for deliveries. In this situation, Best Citrus is required to allocate its production. It notifies Martin's that it cannot deliver the full quantity specified in the contract and indicates the amount it will be able to deliver. Martin's can either accept or reject the allocation, but Best Citrus has no further contractual liability. ◀

DESTRUCTION OF IDENTIFIED GOODS   Sometimes, an unexpected event, such as a fire, totally destroys goods through no fault of either party before risk passes to the buyer or lessee. In such a situation, *if the goods were identified at the time the contract was formed,* the parties are excused from performance [UCC 2–613, 2A–221]. If the goods are only partially destroyed, however, the buyer or lessee can inspect them and either treat the contract as void or accept the damaged goods with a reduction in the contract price.

▶ **Example 22.9**   Atlas Sporting Equipment agrees to lease to River Bicycles sixty bicycles of a particular model that has been discontinued. No other bicycles of that model are available. River specifies that it needs the bicycles to rent to tourists. Before Atlas can deliver the bicycles, they are destroyed by a fire. In this situation, Atlas is not liable to River for failing to deliver the bicycles. Through no fault of either party, the goods were destroyed before the risk of loss passed to the lessee. The loss was total, so the contract is avoided. Clearly, Atlas has no obligation to tender the bicycles, and River has no obligation to make the lease payments for them. ◀

ASSURANCE AND COOPERATION   Two other exceptions to the perfect tender doctrine apply equally to both parties to sales and lease contracts: the right of assurance and the duty of cooperation.

The Right of Assurance.   The UCC provides that if one party has "reasonable grounds" to believe that the other party will not perform, the first party may *in*

writing "demand adequate assurance of due performance" from the other party. Until such assurance is received, the first party may "suspend" further performance without liability. What constitutes "reasonable grounds" is determined by commercial standards. If such assurances are not forthcoming within a reasonable time (not to exceed thirty days), the failure to respond may be treated as a repudiation of the contract [UCC 2–609, 2A–401].

▶ **Case in Point 22.10**   Two companies that made road-surfacing materials, Koch Materials and Shore Slurry Seal, Inc., entered into a contract. Koch obtained a license to use Novachip, a special material made by Shore, and Shore agreed to buy all of its asphalt from Koch for the next seven years. A few years into the contract term, Shore notified Koch that it planned to sell its assets to Asphalt Paving Systems, Inc. Koch demanded assurances that Asphalt Paving would continue the deal, but Shore refused to provide assurances. The court held that Koch could treat Shore's failure to give assurances as a repudiation and sue Shore for breach of contract.[2] ◀

The Duty of Cooperation.   Sometimes, the performance of one party depends on the cooperation of the other. The UCC provides that when cooperation is not forthcoming, the other party can suspend performance without liability and hold the uncooperative party in breach or proceed to perform the contract in any reasonable manner [UCC 2–311(3)].

▶ **Example 22.11**   Aman is required by contract to deliver 1,200 LG washing machines to various locations in California on or before October 1. Frieda, the buyer, is to specify the locations for delivery. Aman repeatedly requests the delivery locations, but Frieda does not respond. The washing machines are ready for shipment on October 1, but Frieda still refuses to give Aman the delivery locations. If Aman does not ship on October 1, he cannot be held liable. Aman is excused for any resulting delay of performance because of Frieda's failure to cooperate. ◀

SECTION 3
OBLIGATIONS OF THE BUYER OR LESSEE

The main obligation of the buyer or lessee under a sales or lease contract is to pay for the goods tendered in accordance with the contract. Once the seller or

---

2. *Koch Materials Co. v. Shore Slurry Seal, Inc.,* 205 F.Supp.2d 324 (D.N.J. 2002).

lessor has adequately tendered delivery, the buyer or lessee is obligated to accept the goods and pay for them according to the terms of the contract.

Payment

In the absence of any specific agreements, the buyer or lessee must make payment at the time and place the goods are *received* [UCC 2–310(a), 2A–516(1)]. When a sale is made on credit, the buyer is obligated to pay according to the specified credit terms (for example, 60, 90, or 120 days), not when the goods are received. The credit period usually begins on the *date of shipment* [UCC 2–310(d)]. Under a lease contract, a lessee must make the lease payment that was specified in the contract [UCC 2A–516(1)].

Payment can be made by any means agreed on between the parties—cash or any other method generally acceptable in the commercial world. If the seller demands cash, the seller must permit the buyer reasonable time to obtain it [UCC 2–511].

Right of Inspection

Unless the parties otherwise agree, or for C.O.D. (collect on delivery) transactions, the buyer or lessee has an absolute right to inspect the goods before making payment. This right allows the buyer or lessee to verify that the goods tendered or delivered conform to the contract. If the goods are not as ordered, the buyer or lessee has no duty to pay. *An opportunity for inspection is therefore a condition precedent to the right of the seller or lessor to enforce payment* [UCC 2–513(1), 2A–515(1)].

Inspection can take place at any reasonable place and time and in any reasonable manner. Generally, what is reasonable is determined by custom of the trade, past practices of the parties, and the like. The buyer bears the costs of inspecting the goods but can recover the costs from the seller if the goods do not conform and are rejected [UCC 2–513(2)].

Acceptance

After having had a reasonable opportunity to inspect the goods, the buyer or lessee can demonstrate acceptance in any of the following ways:

1. The buyer or lessee indicates (by words or conduct) to the seller or lessor that the goods are conforming or that he or she will retain them in spite of their nonconformity [UCC 2–606(1)(a), 2A–515(1)(a)].

2. The buyer or lessee *fails to reject* the goods within a reasonable period of time [UCC 2–602(1), 2–606(1)(b), 2A–515(1)(b)].

3. In sales contracts, the buyer will be deemed to have accepted the goods if he or she *performs any act inconsistent with the seller's ownership.* For instance, any use or resale of the goods—except for the limited purpose of testing or inspecting the goods—generally constitutes an acceptance [UCC 2–606(1)(c)].

Partial Acceptance

If some of the goods delivered do not conform to the contract and the seller or lessor has failed to cure, the buyer or lessee can make a *partial* acceptance [UCC 2–601(c), 2A–509(1)]. The same is true if the nonconformity was not reasonably discoverable before acceptance. (In the latter situation, the buyer or lessee may be able to revoke the acceptance, as will be discussed later in this chapter.)

A buyer or lessee cannot accept less than a single commercial unit, however. The UCC defines a *commercial unit* as a unit of goods that, by commercial usage, is viewed as a "single whole" for purposes of sale and that cannot be divided without materially impairing the character of the unit, its market value, or its use [UCC 2–105(6), 2A–103(1)(c)]. A commercial unit can be a single article (such as a machine), a set of articles (such as a suite of furniture), a quantity (such as a bale, a gross, or a carload), or any other unit treated in the trade as a single whole.

See *Concept Summary 22.1* on the following page for a review of the obligations of both parties to a sales or lease contract.

SECTION 4
ANTICIPATORY REPUDIATION

What if, before the time for contract performance, one party clearly communicates to the other the intention *not* to perform? As discussed in Chapter 18, such an action is a breach of the contract by *anticipatory repudiation.*

Suspension of Performance Obligations

When anticipatory repudiation occurs, the nonbreaching party has a choice of two responses:

CONCEPT SUMMARY 22.1
Performance of Sales and Lease Contracts

CONCEPT	DESCRIPTION
Obligations of the Seller or Lessor	1. The seller or lessor must tender *conforming* goods to the buyer or lessee at a *reasonable hour* and in a *reasonable manner.* Under the perfect tender doctrine, the seller or lessor must tender goods that conform exactly to the terms of the contract [UCC 2–503(1), 2A–508(1)]. 2. If the seller or lessor tenders nonconforming goods and the buyer or lessee rejects them, the seller or lessor may *cure* (repair or replace the goods) within the contract time for performance [UCC 2–508(1), 2A–513(1)]. Even if the time for performance under the contract has expired, the seller or lessor has a reasonable time to substitute conforming goods without liability if the seller or lessor has reasonable grounds to believe the nonconforming tender will be acceptable to the buyer or lessee [UCC 2–508(2), 2A–513(2)]. 3. If the agreed-on means of delivery becomes impracticable or unavailable, the seller must substitute an alternative means (such as a different carrier) if a reasonable one is available [UCC 2–614(1)]. 4. If a seller or lessor tenders nonconforming goods in any one installment under an installment contract, the buyer or lessee may reject the installment only if the nonconformity substantially impairs its value and cannot be cured. The entire installment contract is breached only when one or more installments *substantially* impair the value of the *whole* contract [UCC 2–612, 2A–510]. 5. When performance becomes commercially impracticable owing to circumstances unforeseen when the contract was formed, the perfect tender rule no longer applies [UCC 2–615, 2A–405].
Obligations of the Buyer or Lessee	1. On tender of delivery by the seller or lessor, the buyer or lessee must pay for the goods at the time and place the goods are *received,* unless the sale is made on credit. Payment can be made by any method generally acceptable in the commercial world, but the seller can demand cash [UCC 2–310, 2–511]. 2. Unless otherwise agreed or in C.O.D. shipments, the buyer or lessee has an absolute right to inspect the goods before acceptance [UCC 2–513(1), 2A–515(1)]. 3. The buyer or lessee can manifest acceptance of delivered goods in words or by conduct, such as by failing to reject the goods after having had a reasonable opportunity to inspect them. A buyer will be deemed to have accepted goods if he or she performs any act inconsistent with the seller's ownership [UCC 2–606(1), 2A–515(1)].

---

1. Treat the repudiation as a final breach by pursuing a remedy.
2. Wait to see if the repudiating party will decide to honor the contract despite the avowed intention to renege [UCC 2–610, 2A–402].

In either situation, the nonbreaching party may suspend performance.

A Repudiation May Be Retracted

The UCC permits the breaching party to "retract" his or her repudiation (subject to some limitations). This can be done by any method that clearly indicates the party's intent to perform. Once retraction is made, the rights of the repudiating party under the contract are reinstated. There can be no retraction, however, if since the time of the repudiation the other party has canceled or materially changed position or otherwise indicated that the repudiation is final [UCC 2–611, 2A–403].

▶ **Example 22.12** On April 1, Cora Lyn, who owns a small inn, purchases a suite of furniture from Tom Horton, proprietor of Horton's Furniture Warehouse. The contract states that "delivery must be made on or before May 1." On April 10, Horton informs Lyn that he cannot make delivery until May 10 and asks her to consent to the modified delivery date.

In this situation, Lyn has two options. She can either treat Horton's notice of late delivery as a final breach of contract and pursue a remedy or agree to the later delivery date. Suppose that Lyn does neither for two weeks. On April 24, Horton informs Lyn that he will be able to deliver the furniture by May 1 after all. In effect, Horton has retracted his repudiation, reinstating the rights and obligations of the parties under the original contract. Note that if Lyn had told Horton that she was canceling the contract after he repudiated, he would not have been able to retract his repudiation. ◄

SECTION 5

REMEDIES OF THE SELLER OR LESSOR

When the buyer or lessee is in breach, the seller or lessor has numerous remedies under the UCC. Generally, the remedies available to the seller or lessor depend on the circumstances existing at the time of the breach. The most pertinent considerations are which party has possession of the goods, whether the goods are in transit, and whether the buyer or lessee has rejected or accepted the goods.

When the Goods Are in the Possession of the Seller or Lessor

Under the UCC, if the buyer or lessee breaches the contract before the goods have been delivered, the seller or lessor has the right to pursue the following remedies:

1. Cancel (rescind) the contract.
2. Resell the goods and sue to recover damages.
3. Sue to recover the purchase price or lease payments due.
4. Sue to recover damages for the buyer's nonacceptance of goods.

THE RIGHT TO CANCEL THE CONTRACT If the buyer or lessee breaches the contract, the seller or lessor can choose to simply cancel the contract [UCC 2–703(f), 2A–523(1)(a)]. The seller or lessor must notify the buyer or lessee of the cancellation, and at that point all remaining obligations of the seller or lessor are discharged. The buyer or lessee is not discharged from all remaining obligations, however. She or he is in breach, and the seller or lessor can pursue remedies available under the UCC for breach.

THE RIGHT TO WITHHOLD DELIVERY In general, sellers and lessors can withhold delivery or discontinue performance of their obligations under sales or lease contracts when the buyers or lessees are in breach. This is true whether a buyer or lessee has wrongfully rejected or revoked acceptance of contract goods (discussed later in this chapter), failed to make a payment, or repudiated the contract [UCC 2–703(a), 2A–523(1) (c)]. The seller or lessor can also refuse to deliver the goods to a buyer or lessee who is insolvent (unable to pay debts as they become due) unless the buyer or lessee pays in cash [UCC 2–702(1), 2A–525(1)].

THE RIGHT TO RESELL OR DISPOSE OF THE GOODS When a buyer or lessee breaches or repudiates the contract while the seller or lessor is in possession of the goods, the seller or lessor can resell or dispose of the goods. The seller can retain any profits made as a result of the sale and can hold the buyer or lessee liable for any loss [UCC 2–703(d), 2–706(1), 2A–523(1)(e), 2A–527(1)].

The seller must give the original buyer reasonable notice of the resale, unless the goods are perishable or will rapidly decline in value [UCC 2–706(2), (3)]. The resale can be private or public, and the goods can be sold as a unit or in parcels. A good faith purchaser at the resale takes the goods free of any of the rights of the original buyer [UCC 2–706(5)].

When the Goods Are Unfinished. When the goods contracted for are unfinished at the time of the breach, the seller or lessor can do either of the following:

1. Cease manufacturing the goods and resell them for scrap or salvage value.
2. Complete the manufacture and resell or dispose of the goods, and hold the buyer or lessee liable for any deficiency.

In choosing between these two alternatives, the seller or lessor must exercise reasonable commercial judgment in order to mitigate the loss and obtain maximum value from the unfinished goods [UCC 2–704(2), 2A–524(2)]. Any resale of the goods must be made in good faith and in a commercially reasonable manner.

When the Resale Price Is Insufficient. In sales transactions, the seller can recover any deficiency between the resale price and the contract price. The seller can also recover *incidental damages* (see Chapter 19), defined as the costs to the seller resulting from the breach [UCC 2–706(1), 2–710].

In lease transactions, the lessor may lease the goods to another party and recover damages from the original lessee. Damages include any unpaid lease payments up to the beginning date of the lease term under the new lease. The lessor can also recover any deficiency between the lease payments due under the original lease contract and those under the new lease contract, along with incidental damages [UCC 2A–527(2)].

THE RIGHT TO RECOVER THE PURCHASE PRICE OR LEASE PAYMENTS DUE Under the UCC, an unpaid seller or lessor can bring an action to recover the purchase price or the payments due under the lease contract, plus incidental damages [UCC 2–709(1), 2A–529(1)]. If a seller or lessor is unable to resell or dispose of the goods and sues for the contract price or lease payments due, the goods must be held for the buyer or lessee. The seller or lessor can resell the goods at any time before collecting the judgment from the buyer or lessee. If the goods are resold, the net proceeds from the sale must be credited to the buyer or lessee because of the duty to mitigate damages.

▶ **Example 22.13**   Southern Realty contracts with Gem Point, Inc., to purchase one thousand pens with Southern Realty's name inscribed on them. Gem Point tenders delivery of the pens, but Southern Realty wrongfully refuses to accept them. In this situation, Gem Point can bring an action for the purchase price because it delivered conforming goods, and Southern Realty refused to accept or pay for the goods. Gem Point obviously cannot resell the pens inscribed with the buyer's business name, so this situation falls under UCC 2–709. Gem Point is required to make the pens available for Southern Realty, but can resell them (in the event that it can find a buyer) at any time prior to collecting the judgment from Southern Realty. ◀

THE RIGHT TO RECOVER DAMAGES FOR THE BUYER'S NONACCEPTANCE If a buyer or lessee repudiates a contract or wrongfully refuses to accept the goods, a seller or lessor can bring an action to recover the damages sustained. Ordinarily, the amount of damages equals the difference between the contract price or lease payments and the market price or lease payments at the time and place of tender of the goods, plus incidental damages [UCC 2–708(1), 2A–528(1)].

When the ordinary measure of damages is inadequate to put the seller or lessor in as good a position as the buyer's or lessee's performance would have, the UCC provides an alternative. In that situation, the proper measure of damages is the lost profits of the seller or lessor, including a reasonable allowance for overhead and other expenses [UCC 2–708(2), 2A–528(2)].

When the Goods Are in Transit

When the seller or lessor has delivered the goods to a carrier or a bailee but the buyer or lessee has not yet received them, the goods are said to be *in transit*.

EFFECT OF INSOLVENCY AND BREACH If the seller or lessor learns that the buyer or lessee is insolvent, the seller or lessor can stop the delivery of the goods still in transit, regardless of the quantity of goods shipped. A different rule applies if the buyer or lessee is in breach but is not insolvent. In this situation, the seller or lessor can stop the goods in transit only if the quantity shipped is at least a carload, a truckload, a planeload, or a larger shipment [UCC 2–705(1), 2A–526(1)].

▶ **Example 22.14**   Arturo Ortega orders a truckload of lumber from Timber Products, Inc., to be shipped to Ortega six weeks later. Ortega, who has not paid Timber Products for a past shipment, promises to pay the debt immediately and to pay for the current shipment as soon as it is received. After the lumber has been shipped, a bankruptcy court judge notifies Timber Products that Ortega has filed a petition in bankruptcy and listed Timber Products as one of his creditors. If the goods are still in transit, Timber Products can stop the carrier from delivering the lumber to Ortega. ◀

REQUIREMENTS FOR STOPPING DELIVERY To stop delivery, the seller or lessor must *timely notify* the carrier or other bailee that the goods are to be returned or held for the seller or lessor. If the carrier has sufficient time to stop delivery, the goods must be held and delivered according to the instructions of the seller or lessor. The seller or lessor is liable to the carrier for any additional costs incurred [UCC 2–705(3), 2A–526(3)].

The seller or lessor has the right to stop delivery of the goods under UCC 2–705(2) and 2A–526(2) until the time when:

1. The buyer or lessee receives the goods.
2. The carrier or the bailee acknowledges the rights of the buyer or lessee in the goods (by reshipping or holding the goods for the buyer or lessee, for example).
3. A negotiable document of title covering the goods has been properly transferred to the buyer in a

sales transaction, giving the buyer ownership rights in the goods [UCC 2–705(2)].

Once the seller or lessor reclaims the goods in transit, she or he can pursue the remedies allowed to sellers and lessors when the goods are in their possession.

When the Goods Are in the Possession of the Buyer or Lessee

When the buyer or lessee breaches the contract while the goods are in his or her possession, the seller or lessor can sue. The seller or lessor can recover the purchase price of the goods or the lease payments due, plus incidental damages [UCC 2–709(1), 2A–529(1)].

In some situations, a seller may also have a right to reclaim the goods from the buyer. For instance, in a sales contract, if the buyer has received the goods on credit and the seller discovers that the buyer is insolvent, the seller can demand the return of the goods [UCC 2–702(2)]. Ordinarily, the demand must be made within ten days of the buyer's receipt of the goods.[3] The seller's right to reclaim the goods is subject to the rights of a good faith purchaser or other subsequent buyer in the ordinary course of business who purchases the goods from the buyer before the seller reclaims them.

In regard to lease contracts, if the lessee is in default (fails to make payments that are due, for instance), the lessor may reclaim the leased goods that are in the lessee's possession [UCC 2A–525(2)].

SECTION 6
REMEDIES OF THE BUYER OR LESSEE

When the seller or lessor breaches the contract, the buyer or lessee has numerous remedies available under the UCC. Like the remedies available to sellers and lessors, the remedies available to buyers and lessees depend on the circumstances existing at the time of the breach. Relevant factors include whether the seller has refused to deliver conforming goods or delivered nonconforming goods.

---

3. The seller can demand and reclaim the goods at any time, though, if the buyer misrepresented his or her solvency in writing within three months prior to the delivery of the goods.

When the Seller or Lessor Refuses to Deliver the Goods

If the seller or lessor refuses to deliver the goods to the buyer or lessee, the basic remedies available to the buyer or lessee include the right to:

1. Cancel (rescind) the contract.
2. Obtain goods that have been paid for if the seller or lessor is insolvent.
3. Sue to obtain specific performance if the goods are unique or if damages are an inadequate remedy.
4. Buy other goods (obtain *cover*—defined on page 429) and recover damages from the seller.
5. Sue to obtain identified goods held by a third party (*replevy* goods—defined on page 429).
6. Sue to obtain damages.

THE RIGHT TO CANCEL THE CONTRACT   When a seller or lessor fails to make proper delivery or repudiates the contract, the buyer or lessee can cancel, or rescind, the contract. The buyer or lessee is relieved of any further obligations under the contract but retains all rights to other remedies against the seller or lessor [UCC 2–711(1), 2A–508(1)(a)]. (The right to cancel the contract is also available to a buyer or lessee who has rightfully rejected goods or revoked acceptance, as will be discussed shortly.)

THE RIGHT TO OBTAIN THE GOODS UPON INSOLVENCY   If a buyer or lessee has partially or fully paid for goods that are in the possession of a seller or lessor who becomes insolvent, the buyer or lessee can obtain the goods. The seller or lessor must have become insolvent within ten days after receiving the first payment, and the goods must be identified to the contract. To exercise this right, the buyer or lessee must pay the seller or lessor any unpaid balance of the purchase price or lease payments [UCC 2–502, 2A–522].

THE RIGHT TO OBTAIN SPECIFIC PERFORMANCE   A buyer or lessee can obtain specific performance if the goods are unique or the remedy at law (monetary damages) is inadequate [UCC 2–716(1), 2A–521(1)]. Ordinarily, an award of damages is sufficient to place a buyer or lessee in the position she or he would have occupied if the seller or lessor had fully performed.

When the contract is for the purchase of a particular work of art or a similarly unique item, however, damages may not be sufficient. Under these circumstances, equity requires that the seller or lessor perform exactly by delivering the particular goods identified to the contract (the remedy of specific performance).

▶ **Case in Point 22.15**   Together, Doreen Houseman and Eric Dare bought a house and a pedigreed dog. When the couple separated, they agreed that Dare would keep the house (and pay Houseman for her interest in it) and that Houseman would keep the dog. Houseman allowed Dare to take the dog for visits, but after one visit, Dare kept the dog. Houseman filed a lawsuit seeking specific performance of their agreement. The court found that because pets have special subjective value to their owners, a dog can be considered a unique good. Thus, an award of specific performance was appropriate.[4] ◀

THE RIGHT OF COVER   In certain situations, buyers and lessees can protect themselves by obtaining **cover**— that is, by buying or leasing substitute goods for those that were due under the contract. This option is available when the seller or lessor repudiates the contract or fails to deliver the goods, or when a buyer or lessee has rightfully rejected goods or revoked acceptance.

In purchasing or leasing substitute goods, the buyer or lessee must act in good faith and without unreasonable delay [UCC 2–712, 2A–518]. The buyer or lessee can recover from the seller or lessor:

1. The difference between the cost of cover and the contract price (or lease payments).
2. Incidental damages that resulted from the breach.
3. *Consequential damages* to compensate for indirect losses (such as lost profits) resulting from the breach that were reasonably foreseeable at the time of contract formation. The amount of consequential damages is reduced by any amount the buyer or lessee saved as a result of the breach (such as when a buyer obtains cover without having to pay delivery charges that were part of the original sales contract).

Buyers and lessees are not required to cover, and failure to do so will not bar them from using any other remedies available under the UCC. A buyer or lessee who fails to cover, however, risks collecting a lower amount of consequential damages. A court may reduce the consequential damages by the amount of the loss that could have been avoided had the buyer or lessee purchased or leased substitute goods.

THE RIGHT TO REPLEVY GOODS   Buyers and lessees also have the right to replevy goods. **Replevin**[5] is an action to recover identified goods in the hands of a party who is unlawfully withholding them. Under the UCC, a buyer or lessee can replevy goods identified to the contract if the seller or lessor has repudiated or breached the contract. To maintain an action to replevy goods, buyers and lessees must usually show that they were unable to cover for the goods after making a reasonable effort [UCC 2–716(3), 2A–521(3)].

THE RIGHT TO RECOVER DAMAGES   If a seller or lessor repudiates the contract or fails to deliver the goods, the buyer or lessee can sue for damages. For the buyer, the measure of recovery is the difference between the contract price and the market price of the goods at the time the buyer *learned* of the breach. For the lessee, the measure is the difference between the lease payments and the lease payments that could be obtained for the goods at the time the lessee learned of the breach.

The market price or market lease payments are determined at the place where the seller or lessor was supposed to deliver the goods. The buyer or lessee can also recover incidental and consequential damages less the expenses that were saved as a result of the breach [UCC 2–713, 2A–519].

▶ **Case in Point 22.16**   Les Entreprises Jacques Defour & Fils, Inc., contracted to buy a thirty-thousand-gallon industrial tank from Dinsick Equipment Corporation for $70,000. Les Entreprises hired Xaak Transport, Inc., to pick up the tank, but when Xaak arrived at the pickup location, there was no tank. Les Entreprises paid Xaak $7,459 for its services and filed a suit against Dinsick. The court awarded compensatory damages of $70,000 for the tank and incidental damages of $7,459 for the transport. To establish a breach of contract requires an enforceable contract, substantial performance by the nonbreaching party, a breach by the other party, and damages. In this case, Les Entreprises agreed to buy a tank and paid the price. Dinsick failed to tender or deliver the tank, or to refund the price. The shipping costs were a necessary part of performance, so this was a reasonable expense.[6] ◀

When the Seller or Lessor Delivers Nonconforming Goods

When the seller or lessor delivers nonconforming goods, the buyer or lessee has several remedies available under the UCC.

4. *Houseman v. Dare,* 405 N.J.Super. 538, 966 A.2d 24 (2009).
5. Pronounced ruh-*pleh*-vun, derived from the Old French word *plevir,* meaning "to pledge."
6. *Les Enterprises Jacques Defour & Fils, Inc. v. Dinsick Equipment Corp.,* 2011 WL 307501(N.D.Ill. 2011).

THE RIGHT TO REJECT THE GOODS If either the goods or their tender fails to conform to the contract in any respect, the buyer or lessee can reject all of the goods or any commercial unit of the goods [UCC 2–601, 2A–509]. On rejecting the goods, the buyer or lessee may obtain cover or cancel the contract, and may seek damages just as if the seller or lessor had refused to deliver the goods. (See the earlier discussion of these remedies.)

▶ **Case in Point 22.17** Jorge Jauregui contracted to buy a new Kawai RX5 piano for $24,282 from Bobb's Piano Sales & Service, Inc. When the piano was delivered with "unacceptable damage," Jauregui rejected it and filed a lawsuit for breach of contract. The court ruled that Bobb's had breached the contract by delivering nonconforming goods. Jauregui was entitled to damages equal to the contract price with interest, plus the sales tax, delivery charge, and attorneys' fees.[7] ◀

Timeliness and Reason for Rejection Are Required. The buyer or lessee must reject the goods within a reasonable amount of time after delivery or tender of delivery and must seasonably (timely) notify the seller or lessor [UCC 2–602(1), 2A–509(2)]. If the buyer or lessee fails to reject the goods within a reasonable amount of time, acceptance will be presumed.

When rejecting goods, the buyer or lessee must also designate defects that are ascertainable by reasonable inspection. Failure to do so precludes the buyer or lessee from using such defects to justify rejection or to establish breach when the seller or lessor could have cured the defects if they had been disclosed seasonably [UCC 2–605, 2A–514].

Duties of Merchant-Buyers and Lessees When Goods Are Rejected. Sometimes, a *merchant-buyer or lessee* rightfully rejects goods, and the seller or lessor has no agent or business at the place of rejection. In that situation, the merchant-buyer or lessee has a good faith obligation to follow any reasonable instructions received from the seller or lessor with respect to the goods [UCC 2–603, 2A–511]. The buyer or lessee is entitled to be reimbursed for the care and cost entailed in following the instructions. The same requirements apply if the buyer or lessee rightfully revokes her or his acceptance of the goods at some later time [UCC 2–608(3), 2A–517(5)]. (Revocation of acceptance will be discussed shortly.)

If no instructions are forthcoming and the goods are perishable or threaten to decline in value quickly, the buyer or lessee can resell the goods. The buyer or lessee must exercise good faith and can take appropriate reimbursement and a selling commission (not to exceed 10 percent of the gross proceeds) from the proceeds [UCC 2–603(1), (2); 2A–511(1)]. If the goods are not perishable, the buyer or lessee may store them for the seller or lessor or reship them to the seller or lessor [UCC 2–604, 2A–512].

REVOCATION OF ACCEPTANCE Acceptance of the goods precludes the buyer or lessee from exercising the right of rejection, but it does not necessarily prevent the buyer or lessee from pursuing other remedies. In certain circumstances, a buyer or lessee is permitted to *revoke* his or her acceptance of the goods.

Acceptance of a lot or a commercial unit can be revoked if the nonconformity *substantially* impairs the value of the lot or unit *and* if one of the following factors is present:

1. Acceptance was based on the reasonable assumption that the nonconformity would be cured, and it has not been cured within a reasonable period of time [UCC 2–608(1)(a), 2A–517(1)(a)].
2. The failure of the buyer or lessee to discover the nonconformity was reasonably induced by either the difficulty of discovery before acceptance or by assurances made by the seller or lessor [UCC 2–608(1)(b), 2A–517(1)(b)].

Revocation of acceptance is not effective until notice is given to the seller or lessor. Notice must occur within a reasonable time after the buyer or lessee either discovers or *should have discovered* the grounds for revocation. Additionally, revocation must occur before the goods have undergone any substantial change (such as spoilage) not caused by their own defects [UCC 2–608(2), 2A–517(4)]. Once acceptance is revoked, the buyer or lessee can pursue remedies, just as if the goods had been rejected.

THE RIGHT TO RECOVER DAMAGES FOR ACCEPTED GOODS A buyer or lessee who has accepted nonconforming goods may also keep the goods and recover damages [UCC 2–714(1), 2A–519(3)]. To do so, the buyer or lessee must notify the seller or lessor of the breach within a reasonable time after the defect was or should have been discovered. Failure to give notice of the defects (breach) to the seller or lessor bars the buyer or lessee from pursuing any remedy [UCC 2–607(3), 2A–516(3)]. In addition, the par-

---

7. *Jauregui v. Bobb's Piano Sales & Service, Inc.*, 922 So.2d 303 (Fla.App. 2006).

ties to a sales or lease contract can insert into the contract a provision requiring the buyer or lessee to give notice of any defects in the goods within a pre-scribed period.

When the goods delivered are not as promised, the measure of damages equals the difference between the value of the goods as accepted and their value if they had been delivered as warranted, unless special circumstances show proximately caused damages of a different amount [UCC 2–714(2), 2A–519(4)]. The

buyer or lessee is also entitled to incidental and conse-quential damages when appropriate [UCC 2–714(3), 2A–519]. With proper notice to the seller or lessor, the buyer or lessee can also deduct all or any part of the damages from the price or lease payments still due under the contract [UCC 2–717, 2A–516(1)].

Is two years after a sale of goods a reasonable time period in which to discover a defect in those goods and notify the seller of a breach? That was the ques-tion in the following case.

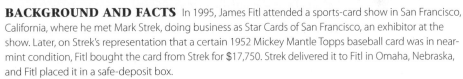

SP TLIGHT on Baseball Cards

Case 22.3   Fitl v. Strek
Supreme Court of Nebraska, 269 Neb. 51, 690 N.W.2d 605 (2005).

BACKGROUND AND FACTS In 1995, James Fitl attended a sports-card show in San Francisco, California, where he met Mark Strek, doing business as Star Cards of San Francisco, an exhibitor at the show. Later, on Strek's representation that a certain 1952 Mickey Mantle Topps baseball card was in near-mint condition, Fitl bought the card from Strek for $17,750. Strek delivered it to Fitl in Omaha, Nebraska, and Fitl placed it in a safe-deposit box.

In May 1997, Fitl sent the card to Professional Sports Authenticators (PSA), a sports-card grading service. PSA told Fitl that the card was ungradable because it had been discolored and doctored. Fitl complained to Strek, who replied that Fitl should have initiated a return of the card within "a typical grace period for the unconditional return of a card, . . . 7 days to 1 month" of its receipt. In August, Fitl sent the card to ASA Accugrade, Inc. (ASA), another grading service, for a second opinion of the value. ASA also concluded that the card had been refinished and trimmed. Fitl filed a suit in a Nebraska state court against Strek, seeking damages. The court awarded Fitl $17,750, plus his court costs. Strek appealed to the Nebraska Supreme Court.

IN THE LANGUAGE OF THE COURT
WRIGHT, J. [Judge]

* * * *

Strek claims that the [trial] court erred in determining that notification of the defective condition of the baseball card 2 years after the date of purchase was timely pursuant to [UCC] 2–607(3)(a).

* * * The [trial] court found that Fitl had notified Strek within a reasonable time after discovery of the breach. Therefore, our review is whether the [trial] court's finding as to the reasonableness of the notice was clearly erroneous.

Section 2–607(3)(a) states: "Where a tender has been accepted * * * the buyer must within a reasonable time after he discovers or should have discovered any breach notify the seller of breach or be barred from any remedy." [Under UCC 1–204(2)] *"what is a reasonable time for taking any action depends on the nature, purpose and circumstances of such action."* [Emphasis added.]

The notice requirement set forth in Section 2–607(3)(a) serves three purposes.

* * * The most important one is to enable the seller to make efforts to cure the breach by making adjustments or replacements in order to minimize the buyer's damages and the seller's liability. A second policy is to provide the seller a reasonable opportunity to learn the facts so that he may adequately prepare for negotiation and defend himself in a suit. A third policy

CASE 22.3 CONTINUES ▶

* * * is the same as the policy behind statutes of limitation: to provide a seller with a terminal point in time for liability.

* * * *A party is justified in relying upon a representation made to the party as a positive statement of fact when an investigation would be required to ascertain its falsity.* In order for Fitl to have determined that the baseball card had been altered, he would have been required to conduct an investigation. We find that he was not required to do so. Once Fitl learned that the baseball card had been altered, he gave notice to Strek. [Emphasis added.]

* * * One of the most important policies behind the notice requirement * * * is to allow the seller to cure the breach by making adjustments or replacements to minimize the buyer's damages and the seller's liability. However, even if Fitl had learned immediately upon taking possession of the baseball card that it was not authentic and had notified Strek at that time, there is no evidence that Strek could have made any adjustment or taken any action that would have minimized his liability. In its altered condition, the baseball card was worthless.

* * * Earlier notification would not have helped Strek prepare for negotiation or defend himself in a suit because the damage to Fitl could not be repaired. Thus, the policies behind the notice requirement, to allow the seller to correct a defect, to prepare for negotiation and litigation, and to protect against stale claims at a time beyond which an investigation can be completed, were not unfairly prejudiced by the lack of an earlier notice to Strek. Any problem Strek may have had with the party from whom he obtained the baseball card was a separate matter from his transaction with Fitl, and an investigation into the source of the altered card would not have minimized Fitl's damages.

DECISION AND REMEDY *The state supreme court affirmed the decision of the lower court. Under the circumstances, notice of a defect in the card two years after its purchase was reasonable. The buyer had reasonably relied on the seller's representation that the card was "authentic" (which it was not), and when the defects were discovered, the buyer had given timely notice.*

WHAT IF THE FACTS WERE DIFFERENT? *Suppose that Fitl and Strek had included in their deal a written clause requiring Fitl to give notice of any defect in the card within "7 days to 1 month" of its receipt. Would the result have been different? Why or why not?*

THE LEGAL ENVIRONMENT DIMENSION *What might a court award to a buyer who prevails in a dispute such as the one in this case?*

SECTION 7
ADDITIONAL PROVISIONS AFFECTING REMEDIES

The parties to a sales or lease contract can vary their respective rights and obligations by contractual agreement. For instance, a seller and buyer can expressly provide for remedies in addition to those provided in the UCC. They can also specify remedies in lieu of those provided in the UCC (including liquidated damages clauses—see Chapter 19), or they can change the measure of damages. A seller can provide that the buyer's only remedy on the seller's breach will be repair or replacement of the item. Alternatively, the seller can limit the buyer's remedy to return of the goods and refund of the purchase price.

In sales and lease contracts, an agreed-on remedy is in addition to those provided in the UCC unless the parties expressly agree that the remedy is exclusive of all others [UCC 2–719(1), 2A–503(1),(2)].

Exclusive Remedies

If the parties state that a remedy is *exclusive*, then it is the sole (only) remedy. ▶ **Example 22.18** Standard Tool Company agrees to sell a pipe-cutting machine to United Pipe & Tubing Corporation. The contract limits United's remedy exclusively to repair or replacement of any defective parts. Thus, repair or replacement of defective parts is the buyer's only remedy under this contract. ◀

When circumstances cause an exclusive remedy to fail in its essential purpose, however, it is no longer exclusive, and the buyer or lessee may pursue other remedies available under the UCC [UCC 2–719(2), 2A–503(2)]. In *Example 22.18*, suppose that Standard Tool Company was unable to repair a defective part, and no replacement parts were available. In this situa- tion, because the exclusive remedy failed in its essen- tial purpose (to provide recovery), the buyer could pursue other remedies available under the UCC. (See the *Managerial Strategy* feature below for guidelines on what to do when a contract is breached.)

MANAGERIAL STRATEGY

Facing a Breach of Contract

A contract for the sale of goods has been breached. Can the dispute be settled without a trip to court? The answer, of course, depends on the willingness of the parties to agree on an appropriate remedy.

A Store Policy against Refunds

As the manager of a retail outlet, you may wish to establish a policy of not providing refunds. Instead, you will offer only to repair or replace items that are defective. Does this mean that you will never have to provide a refund if a cus- tomer purchases a good (or service) that turns out to be defective and cannot be repaired? That was the question facing a court in New York when a store cited its no-refund policy in declining to provide a dissatisfied customer with a full refund.

Sarah Milligan purchased a wig from Shuly Wigs, Inc., but discovered that the wig was defective. Shuly twice tried to repair the wig, but both attempts failed. Milligan purchased another wig and asked Shuly for a refund. When Shuly refused, Milligan sued. A small claims court ruled in Milligan's favor. On appeal, the reviewing court af- firmed the ruling. The court observed that when "a vendor prohibits refunds and limits the purchaser's remedies to repair or replacement of its goods, the remedy fails of its essential purpose if a delay or failure adequately to repair or replace the goods in a reasonable time deprives the plaintiff of a substantial benefit of her bargain."[a]

Contractual Clauses Concerning Applicable Remedies

Often, the parties to sales and lease contracts agree in advance in their contracts on what remedies will be applicable in the event of a breach. This may take the form of a contract provision restricting or expanding remedies available under Section 2–719 of the Uniform Commercial Code (UCC). Such clauses help to reduce uncertainty and the necessity for costly litigation.

When the Contract Is Silent on Applicable Remedies

If your agreement does not cover a breach and you are the nonbreaching party, the UCC gives you a variety of alterna- tives. You need to determine the available remedies, ana- lyze them, rank them in order of priority, and then predict how successful you might be in pursuing each remedy if you decide to go to court. Before going to court, however, consider the position of the breaching party to determine if you can negotiate a settlement.

For example, when defective goods are delivered and accepted, usually it is preferable for the buyer and seller to reach an agreement on a reduced purchase price. Practi- cally speaking, though, the buyer may be unable to obtain a partial refund from the seller. In this situation, UCC 2–717 allows the buyer to give notice of the intention to deduct the damages from any part of the purchase price not yet paid. If you are a buyer who has accepted defective goods and has not yet paid in full, you may wish to exercise your rights under UCC 2–717 and deduct appropriate damages from your final payment. Remember that most breaches of contract do not end up in court—they are settled beforehand.

MANAGERIAL IMPLICATIONS

Of course, the best way to avoid having to go to court to settle a dispute about a breached contract is to specify in the contract itself what remedies will be available to each party in the event of a breach. Nothing in the UCC prevents parties from expanding the remedies available under it, as UCC 2–719 points out. In general, the more clearly remedies for breach are outlined in a sales contract, the less chance there will be a lawsuit.

BUSINESS QUESTIONS

1. *Under what circumstances is a negotiated settlement for a breach preferable to litigation?*

2. *Assume that you are in a dispute over a breach of contract and you discover that the contract does not explicitly mention any remedies. What do you do now?*

---

a. *Milligan v. Shuly Wigs, Inc.,* 34 Misc.3d. 128(A), 941 N.Y.S.2d 539 (2011).

Consequential Damages

As discussed earlier, consequential damages are special damages that compensate for indirect losses (such as lost profits) resulting from a breach of contract that were reasonably foreseeable. Under the UCC, parties to a contract can limit or exclude consequential damages, provided the limitation is not unconscionable.

When the buyer or lessee is a consumer, any limitation of consequential damages for personal injuries resulting from consumer goods is *prima facie* (presumed to be) unconscionable. The limitation of consequential damages is not necessarily unconscionable when the loss is commercial in nature—for example, lost profits and property damage [UCC 2–719(3), 2A–503(3)].

Statute of Limitations

An action for breach of contract under the UCC must be commenced *within four years after the cause of action accrues* [UCC 2–725(1)]. This means that a buyer or lessee must file the lawsuit within four years after the breach occurs.[8] The parties can agree in their contract to reduce this period to not less than one year, but cannot extend it beyond four years [UCC 2–725(1), 2A–506(1)].

If a buyer or lessee has accepted nonconforming goods, that party has a reasonable time to notify the seller or lessor of the breach. Failure to provide notice will bar the buyer or lessee from pursuing any remedy [UCC 2–607(3) (a), 2A–516(3)].

SECTION 8
DEALING WITH INTERNATIONAL CONTRACTS

Buyers and sellers (or lessees and lessors) engaged in international business transactions may be separated by thousands of miles. Therefore, special precautions are often taken to ensure performance under international contracts. Sellers and lessors want to avoid delivering goods for which they might not be paid. Buyers and lessees desire the assurance that sellers and lessors will not be paid until there is evidence

---

8. For breach of warranty, to be discussed in Chapter 23, the cause of action arises when the seller or lessor delivers the contracted goods [UCC 2–725(2), 2A–506(2)]. Thus, the buyer or lessee has four years from the delivery date to file a suit for breach of warranty.

that the goods have been shipped. Thus, **letters of credit** frequently are used to facilitate international business transactions.

Letter-of-Credit Transactions

In a simple letter-of-credit transaction, the *issuer* (a bank or other financial institution) agrees to issue a letter of credit and to ascertain whether the *beneficiary* (seller or lessor) performs certain acts. In return, the *account party* (buyer or lessee) promises to reimburse the issuer for the amount paid to the beneficiary. The transaction may also involve an *advising bank* that transmits information and a *paying bank* that expedites payment under the letter of credit. See Exhibit 22–1 on the following page for an illustration of a letter-of-credit transaction.

PAYMENT UNDER A LETTER OF CREDIT Under a letter of credit, the issuer is bound to pay the beneficiary (seller or lessor) when the beneficiary has complied with the terms and conditions of the letter of credit. The letter of credit assures the beneficiary of payment at the same time as it assures the account party (buyer or lessee) of performance. Typically, a letter of credit will require that the beneficiary deliver a *bill of lading* (the carrier's contract) to prove that shipment has been made.

THE VALUE OF A LETTER OF CREDIT The basic principle behind letters of credit is that payment is made against the documents presented by the beneficiary and not against the facts that the documents purport to reflect. Thus, in a letter-of-credit transaction, the issuer (bank) does not police the underlying contract. The letter of credit is independent of the underlying contract between the buyer and the seller. Eliminating the need for the bank (issuer) to inquire into whether actual contractual conditions have been satisfied greatly reduces the costs of letters of credit. Moreover, the use of a letter of credit protects both buyers and sellers.

Remedies for Breach of International Sales Contracts

The United Nations Convention on Contracts for the International Sale of Goods (CISG) provides international sellers and buyers with remedies very similar to those available under the UCC. Article 74 of the CISG provides for money damages, including foresee-

EXHIBIT 22–1 A Letter-of-Credit Transaction

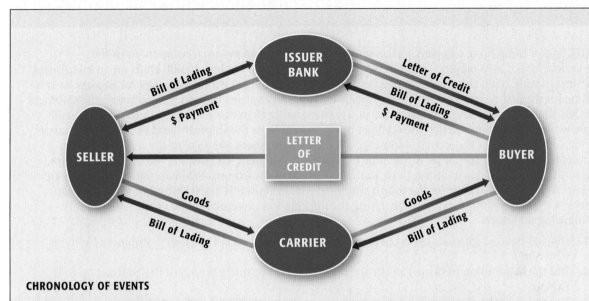

CHRONOLOGY OF EVENTS

1. Buyer contracts with issuer bank to issue a letter of credit. This sets forth the bank's obligation to pay on the letter of credit and buyer's obligation to pay the bank.

2. Letter of credit is sent to seller informing seller that on compliance with the terms of the letter of credit (such as presentment of necessary documents—in this example, a bill of lading), the bank will issue payment for the goods.

3. Seller delivers goods to carrier and receives a bill of lading.

4. Seller delivers the bill of lading to issuer bank and, if the document is proper, receives payment.

5. Issuer bank delivers the bill of lading to buyer.

6. Buyer delivers the bill of lading to carrier.

7. Carrier delivers the goods to buyer.

8. Buyer settles with issuer bank.

able consequential damages, on a contract's breach. As under the UCC, the measure of damages normally is the difference between the contract price and the market price of the goods.

Under Article 49, the buyer is permitted to avoid obligations under the contract if the seller breaches the contract or fails to deliver the goods during the time specified in the contract or later agreed on by the parties. Similarly, under Article 64, the seller can avoid obligations under the contract if the buyer breaches the contract, fails to accept delivery of the goods, or fails to pay for the goods.

The CISG also allows for specific performance as a remedy under Article 28, which provides that "one party is entitled to require performance of any obligation by the other party." Nevertheless, a court may grant specific performance under Article 28 only if it would do so "under its own [national] law." As already discussed, U.S. courts normally grant specific performance only if no adequate remedy at law (monetary damages) is available and the goods are unique in nature. In other countries, such as Germany, however, specific performance is a commonly granted remedy for breach of contract.

Reviewing: Performance and Breach of Sales and Lease Contracts

GFI, Inc., a Hong Kong company, makes audio decoder chips, an essential component in the manufacture of MP3 players. Egan Electronics contracts with GFI to buy 10,000 chips on an installment contract, with 2,500 chips to be shipped every three months, F.O.B. Hong Kong, via Air Express. At the time for the first delivery, GFI delivers only 2,400 chips but explains to Egan that although the shipment is less than 5 percent short, the chips are of a higher quality than those specified in the contract and are worth 5 percent more than the contract price. Egan accepts the shipment and pays GFI the contract price. At the time for the second shipment, GFI makes a shipment identical to the first. Egan again accepts and pays for the chips. At the time for the third shipment, GFI ships 2,400 of the same chips, but this time GFI sends them via Hong Kong Air instead of Air Express. While in transit, the chips are destroyed. When it is time for the fourth shipment, GFI again sends 2,400 chips, but this time Egan rejects the chips without explanation. Using the information presented in the chapter, answer the following questions.

1. Did GFI have a legitimate reason to expect that Egan would accept the fourth shipment? Why or why not?
2. Did the substitution of carriers in the third shipment constitute a breach of the contract by GFI? Explain.
3. Suppose that the silicon used for the chips becomes unavailable for a period of time. Consequently, GFI cannot manufacture enough chips to fulfill the contract, but does ship as many as it can to Egan. Under what doctrine might a court release GFI from further performance of the contract?
4. Under the UCC, does Egan have a right to reject the fourth shipment? Why or why not?

DEBATE THIS ... *If a contract specifies a particular carrier, then the shipper must use that carrier or be in breach of the contract—no exceptions should ever be allowed.*

Terms and Concepts to Review

conforming goods 418	installment contract 421	replevin 429
cover 429	letter of credit 434	tender of delivery 418
cure 420	perfect tender rule 419	

ExamPrep

Issue Spotters

1. Country Fruit Stand orders eighty cases of peaches from Downey Farms. Without stating a reason, Downey delivers thirty cases instead of eighty at the wrong time. Does Country have the right to reject the shipment? Explain. **(See page 419.)**

2. Brite Images agrees to sell Poster Planet five thousand posters of celebrities, to be delivered on May 1. On April 1, Brite repudiates the contract. Poster Planet informs Brite that it expects delivery. Can Poster Planet sue Brite without waiting until May 1? Why or why not? **(See page 424.)**

• **Check your answers to the Issue Spotters against the answers provided in Appendix E at the end of this text.**

Before the Test

Go to **www.cengagebrain.com**, enter the ISBN 9781285185248, and click on "Find" to locate this textbook's Web site. Then, click on "Access Now" under "Study Tools," and select Chapter 22 at the top. There, you will find a Practice Quiz that you can take to assess your mastery of the concepts in this chapter, as well as Flashcards and a Glossary of important terms.

Business Scenarios

22–1. Anticipatory Repudiation. Moore contracted in writing to sell her 2012 Hyundai Santa Fe to Hammer for $16,500. Moore agreed to deliver the car on Wednesday, and Hammer promised to pay the $16,500 on the following Friday. On Tuesday, Hammer informed Moore that he would not be buying the car after all. By Friday, Hammer had changed his mind again and tendered $16,500 to Moore. Moore, although she had not sold the car to another party, refused the tender and refused to deliver. Hammer claimed that Moore had breached their contract. Moore contended that Hammer's repudiation released her from her duty to perform under the contract. Who is correct, and why? **(See page 424.)**

22–2. Remedies of the Buyer or Lessee. Lehor collects antique cars. He contracts to purchase spare parts for a 1938 engine from Beem. These parts are not made anymore and are scarce. To obtain the contract with Beem, Lehor agrees to pay 50 percent of the purchase price in advance. Lehor sends the payment on May 1, and Beem receives it on May 2. On May 3, Beem, having found another buyer willing to pay substantially more for the parts, informs Lehor that he will not deliver as contracted. That same day, Lehor learns that Beem is insolvent. Discuss fully any possible remedies available to Lehor to enable him to take possession of these parts. **(See page 428.)**

Business Case Problems

22–3. Spotlight on Revocation of Acceptance—Remedies of the

Buyer. L.V.R.V., Inc., sells recreational vehicles (RVs) in Las Vegas, Nevada, as Wheeler's Las Vegas RV. In September 1997, Wheeler's sold a Santara RV made by Coachmen Recreational Vehicle Co. to Arthur and Roswitha Waddell. The Waddells hoped to spend two or three years driving around the country, but almost immediately—and repeatedly—they experienced problems with the RV. Its entry door popped open. Its cooling and heating systems did not work properly. Its batteries did not maintain a charge. Most significantly, its engine overheated when ascending a moderate grade. The Waddells brought it to Wheeler's service department for repairs. Over the next year and a half, the RV spent more than seven months at Wheeler's. In March 1999, the Waddells filed a complaint in a Nevada state court against the dealer to revoke their acceptance of the RV. What are the requirements for a buyer's revocation of acceptance? Were the requirements met in this case? In whose favor should the court rule? Why? [*Waddell v. L.V.R.V., Inc.*, 122 Nev. 15, 125 P.3d 1160 (2006)] **(See page 428.)**

22–4. Obligations of the Seller. Flint Hills Resources, LP, a crude oil refiner, agreed to buy "approximately 1,000 barrels per day" of Mexican natural gas condensate from JAG Energy, Inc., an oil broker. Four months into the contract, Pemex, the only authorized seller of freshly extracted Mexican condensate, warned Flint Hills that some companies might be selling stolen Mexican condensate. Fearing potential criminal liability, Flint Hills refused to accept more deliveries from JAG without proof of the title to its product. JAG promised to forward documents showing its chain of title. After several weeks, when JAG did not produce the documents, Flint Hills canceled their agreement. JAG filed a suit in a federal district court against Flint Hills, alleging breach of contract. Did Flint Hills have a right to demand assurance of JAG's title to its product? If so, did Flint Hills act reasonably in exercising that right? Explain. [*Flint Hills Resources LP v. Jag Energy, Inc.*, 559 F.3d 373 (5th Cir. 2009)] **(See page 417.)**

22–5. Breach and Damages. Utility Systems of America, Inc., was doing roadwork when Chad DeRosier, a nearby landowner, asked Utility to dump 1,500 cubic yards of fill onto his property. Utility agreed but exceeded DeRosier's request by dumping 6,500 cubic yards. Utility offered to remove the extra fill for $9,500. DeRosier paid a different contractor $46,629 to remove the fill and do certain other work. He then filed a suit against Utility. Because Utility charged nothing for the fill, was there a breach of contract? If so, would the damages be greater than $9,500? Could consequential damages be justified? Discuss. [*DeRosier v. Utility Systems of America, Inc.*, 780 N.W.2d 1 (Minn.App. 2010)] **(See page 429.)**

22–6. Right of Inspection. Jessie Romero offered to deliver two trade-in vehicles—a 2003 Mitsubishi Montero SP and a 2002 Chevrolet Silverado pickup—to Scoggin-Dickey Chevrolet Buick, Inc., in exchange for a 2006 Silverado pickup. Scoggin-Dickey agreed. The parties negotiated a price, including a value for the trade-in vehicles, plus cash. Romero paid the cash and took the new Silverado. On inspecting the trade-in vehicles, however, Scoggin-Dickey found that they had little value. The dealer repossessed the Silverado. Did the dealership have the right to inspect the goods and reject them when it did? Why or why not? [*Romero v. Scoggin-Dickey Chevrolet Buick, Inc.*, __ S.W.3d __ (Tex.Civ.App.—Amarillo 2010)] **(See page 424.)**

22–7. The Right to Recover Damages. Woodridge USA Properties, L.P., bought eighty-seven commercial truck trailers from Southeast Trailer Mart, Inc. (STM). Gerald McCarty, an independent sales agent who arranged the deal, showed Woodridge the documents of title. They did not indicate that Woodridge was the buyer. Woodridge asked McCarty to sell the trailers, and within three months they were sold, but McCarty did not give the proceeds to Woodridge. Woodridge—without mentioning the title documents—asked STM to refund the contract price. STM refused. Does Woodridge have a right to recover damages from STM? Explain. [*Woodridge USA Properties, L.P. v. Southeast Trailer Mart, Inc.*, __ F.3d __ (11th Cir. 2011)] **(See page 429.)**

22–8. BUSINESS CASE PROBLEM
WITH SAMPLE ANSWER: Nonconforming Goods.

Padma Paper Mills, Ltd., converts waste paper into usable paper. In 2007, Padma entered into a contract with Universal Exports, Inc., under which Universal Exports certified that it would ship white envelope cuttings, and Padma paid $131,000 for the paper. When the shipment arrived, however, Padma discovered that Universal Exports had sent multicolored paper plates and other brightly colored paper products. Padma accepted the goods but notified Universal Exports that they did not conform to the contract. Can Padma recover even though it accepted the goods knowing that they were nonconforming? If so, how? [Padma Paper Mills, Ltd. v. Universal Exports, Inc., *34 Misc.3d 1236(A) (N.Y.Sup. 2012)]* **(See page 430.)**

- **For a sample answer for Problem 22–8, go to Appendix F at the end of this text.**

22–9. A QUESTION OF ETHICS: Revocation of Acceptance.

Scotwood Industries, Inc., sells calcium chloride flake for use in ice melt products. Between July and September 2004, Scotwood delivered thirty-seven shipments of flake to Frank Miller & Sons, Inc.

After each delivery, Scotwood billed Miller, which paid thirty-five of the invoices and processed 30 to 50 percent of the flake. In August, Miller began complaining about the product's quality. Scotwood assured Miller that it would remedy the situation. Finally, in October, Miller told Scotwood, "This is totally unacceptable. We are willing to discuss Scotwood picking up the material." Miller claimed that the flake was substantially defective because it was chunked. Calcium chloride maintains its purity for up to five years, but if it is exposed to and absorbs moisture, it chunks and becomes unusable. Scotwood sued to collect payment on the unpaid invoices. In response, Miller filed a counterclaim in a federal district court for breach of contract, seeking to recover based on revocation of acceptance, among other things. [Scotwood Industries, Inc. v. Frank Miller & Sons, Inc., *435 F.Supp.2d 1160 (D.Kan. 2006)]* **(See page 430.)**

(a) What is revocation of acceptance? How does a buyer effectively exercise this option? Do the facts in this case support this theory as a ground for Miller to recover damages? Why or why not?

(b) Is there an ethical basis for allowing a buyer to revoke acceptance of goods and recover damages? If so, is there an ethical limit to this right? Discuss.

Legal Reasoning Group Activity

22–10. Performance Obligations. Kodiak agrees to sell 1,000 espresso machines to Lin to be delivered on May 1. Due to a strike during the last week of April, there is a temporary shortage of delivery vehicles. Kodiak can deliver the espresso makers 200 at a time over a period of ten days, with the first delivery on May 1. **(See page 417.)**

(a) The first group will determine if Kodiak has the right to deliver the goods in five lots. What happens if Lin objects to delivery in lots?

(b) A second group will analyze whether the doctrine of commercial impracticability applies to this scenario, and if it does, what the result will be.

CHAPTER 23
WARRANTIES

Most goods are covered by some type of warranty designed to protect buyers. In sales and lease law, a warranty is an assurance or guarantee by the seller or lessor about the quality and features of the goods being sold or leased.

The Uniform Commercial Code (UCC) has numerous rules governing product warranties as they occur in sales and lease contracts. Articles 2 (on sales) and 2A (on leases) designate several types of warranties that can arise in a sales or lease contract, including warranties of title, express warranties, and implied warranties. In this chapter, we discuss these types of warranties as well as a federal statute that is designed to prevent deception and make warranties more understandable.

Because a warranty imposes a duty on the seller or lessor, a breach of warranty is a breach of the seller's or lessor's promise. Assuming that the parties have not agreed to limit or modify the remedies available, if the seller or lessor breaches a warranty, the buyer or lessee can sue to recover damages from the seller or lessor. Under some circumstances, a breach of warranty can allow the buyer or lessee to rescind (cancel) the agreement.

SECTION 1
WARRANTIES OF TITLE

Under the UCC, three types of title warranties—*good title, no liens,* and *no infringements*—can automatically arise in sales and lease contracts [UCC 2–312, 2A–211]. Normally, a seller or lessor can disclaim or modify these title warranties only by including *specific language* in the contract. For example, sellers may assert that they are transferring only such rights, title, and interest as they have in the goods.

Good Title

In most sales, sellers warrant that they have good and valid title to the goods sold and that the transfer of the title is rightful [UCC 2–312(1)(a)]. If the buyer subsequently learns that the seller did not have valid title to the goods that were purchased, the buyer can sue the seller for breach of this warranty.

▶ **Example 23.1** Alexis steals two iPads from Camden and sells them to Emma, who does not know that they are stolen. If Camden discovers that Emma has the iPads, then he has the right to reclaim them from her. When Alexis sold Emma the iPads, Alexis *automatically* warranted to Emma that the title conveyed was valid and that its transfer was rightful. Because a thief has no title to stolen goods, Alexis breached the warranty of title imposed by UCC 2–312(1)(a) and became liable to Emma for appropriate damages. (See Chapter 21 for a detailed discussion of sales by nonowners.) ◀

No Liens

A second warranty of title protects buyers and lessees who are *unaware* of any encumbrances (claims, charges, or liabilities—usually called *liens*[1]) against goods at the time the contract is made [UCC 2–312(1)(b), 2A–211(1)].

This warranty protects buyers who, for instance, unknowingly purchase goods that are subject to a creditor's security interest. (A *security interest* in this context is an interest in the goods that secures payment or performance of an obligation.) If a creditor legally repossesses the goods from a buyer *who had no actual knowledge of the security interest,* the buyer can recover from the seller for breach of warranty.

---

1. Pronounced *leens.*

(In contrast, a buyer who has *actual knowledge of a security interest* has no recourse against a seller.)

▶ **Example 23.2** Henderson buys a used boat from Loring for cash. A month later, Barish proves that she has a valid security interest in the boat and that Loring, who has missed five payments, is in default. Barish then repossesses the boat from Henderson. Henderson demands his cash back from Loring. Under Section 2–312(1)(b), Henderson has legal grounds to recover from Loring because the seller of goods warrants that the goods are delivered free from any security interest or other lien of which the buyer has no knowledge. ◀

Article 2A affords similar protection for lessees. Section 2A–211(1) provides that during the term of the lease, no claim of any third party will interfere with the lessee's enjoyment of the leasehold interest.

No Infringements

A third type of warranty of title arises automatically when the seller or lessor is a merchant. A merchant-seller or lessor warrants that the buyer or lessee takes the goods *free of infringements* from any copyright, trademark, or patent claims of a third person[2] [UCC 2–312(3), 2A–211(2)].

NOTICE REQUIRED IN SALES CONTRACTS If the buyer is subsequently sued by a third party holding copyright, trademark, or patent rights in the goods, then this warranty is breached. The buyer *must notify the seller* of the litigation within a reasonable time to enable the seller to decide whether to defend the lawsuit. The seller then decides whether to defend the buyer and bear all expenses in the action.

If the seller agrees in a writing (or record) to defend and to pay the expenses, then the buyer must turn over control of the litigation to the seller. Otherwise, the buyer is barred from any remedy against the seller for liability established by the litigation [UCC 2–607(3)(b), 2–607(5)(b)]. Thus, if a buyer wins at trial but did not notify the seller of the litigation, the buyer cannot sue the seller to recover the expenses of the lawsuit.

NOTICE IN LEASE CONTRACTS In situations that involve leases rather than sales, Article 2A provides

---

2. Recall from Chapter 20 that a *merchant* is defined in UCC 2–104(1) as a person who deals in goods of the kind involved in the sales contract or who, by occupation, presents himself or herself as having knowledge or skill peculiar to the goods involved in the transaction.

for the same notice of infringement litigation [UCC 2A–516(3)(b), 2A–516(4)(b)]. After being notified of the lawsuit, the lessor (or supplier, in a finance lease) who agrees to pay all expenses can demand that the lessee turn over the control of the litigation. Failure to provide notice normally bars any subsequent remedy against the lessor for liability established by the litigation.

There is an exception for leases to individual consumers for personal, family, or household purposes. A consumer who fails to notify the lessor within a reasonable time does not lose his or her remedy against the lessor for whatever liability is established in the litigation [UCC 2A–516(3)(b)].

EXPRESS WARRANTIES

A seller or lessor can create an **express warranty** by making representations concerning the quality, condition, description, or performance potential of the goods.

Statements That Create Express Warranties

Under UCC 2–313 and 2A–210, express warranties arise when a seller or lessor indicates any of the following:

1. That the goods conform to any *affirmation* (declaration that something is true) *of fact* or *promise* that the seller or lessor makes to the buyer or lessee about the goods. Such affirmations or promises are usually made during the bargaining process. ▶ **Example 23.3** D. J. Vladick, a salesperson at Home Depot, tells a customer, "These drill bits will *easily* penetrate stainless steel—and without dulling." Vladick's statement is an express warranty. ◀

2. That the goods conform to any *description* of them. ▶ **Example 23.4** A label reads "Crate contains one Kawasaki 750 4X4 ATV," and a contract calls for the delivery of a "wool coat." Both statements create express warranties that the content of the goods sold conforms to the description. ◀

3. That the goods conform to any *sample or model* of the goods shown to the buyer or lessee. ▶ **Example 23.5** Melissa Faught orders a stainless steel 5500 Super Angel juicer for $1,100 after

seeing a dealer demonstrate its use at a raw foods health fair. The Super Angel is shipped to her. When the juicer arrives, it is an older model, not the 5500 model. This is a breach of an express warranty because the dealer warranted that the juicer would be the same model used in the demonstration. ◀

Express warranties can be found in a seller's or lessor's advertisement, brochure, or promotional materials, in addition to being made orally or in an express warranty provision in a sales or lease contract.

Basis of the Bargain

To create an express warranty, a seller or lessor does not have to use formal words such as *warrant* or *guarantee*. It is only necessary that a reasonable buyer or lessee would regard the representation as being part of the basis of the bargain [UCC 2–313(2), 2A–210(2)].

The UCC does not explicitly define the phrase "basis of the bargain." Generally, it means that the buyer or lessee must have relied on the representation at the time of entering into the agreement. Therefore, a court must determine in each case whether a representation was made at such a time and in such a way that it induced the buyer or lessee to enter into the contract.

Statements of Opinion and Value

Only statements of fact create express warranties. A seller or lessor who makes a statement that merely relates to the value or worth of the goods, or states an opinion about or recommends the goods, does not create an express warranty [UCC 2–313(2), 2A–210(2)].

▶ **Example 23.6**   A car salesperson claims that "this is the best used car to come along in years. It has four new tires and a 250-horsepower engine just rebuilt this year." The seller has made several *affirmations of fact* that can create a warranty. The automobile has an engine. It is a 250-horsepower engine and was rebuilt this year. There are four tires on the car and the tires are new. The seller's *opinion* that the vehicle is "the best used car to come along in years," however, is known as "puffery" and creates no warranty. (*Puffery* is an expression of opinion by a seller or lessor that is not made as a representation of fact.) ◀

A statement about the value of the goods, such as "this is worth a fortune" or "anywhere else you'd pay $10,000 for it," usually does not create a warranty.

OPINIONS BY EXPERTS   Ordinarily, statements of opinion do not create warranties. If the seller or lessor is an expert, however, and gives an opinion as an expert to a layperson, then a warranty may be created. ▶ **Example 23.7**   Stephen is an art dealer and an expert in seventeenth-century paintings. If Stephen tells Lauren, a purchaser, that in his opinion a particular painting is by Rembrandt, Stephen has warranted the accuracy of his opinion. ◀

REASONABLE RELIANCE   It is not always easy to determine whether a statement constitutes an express warranty or puffery. The reasonableness of the buyer's or lessee's reliance appears to be the controlling criterion in many cases. ▶ **Example 23.8**   A salesperson's statements that a ladder will "never break" and will "last a lifetime" are so clearly improbable that they do not create a warranty. No reasonable buyer would rely on such statements. ◀

Additionally, the context in which a statement is made may be relevant in determining the reasonableness of a buyer's or lessee's reliance. A reasonable person is more likely to rely on a written statement made in an advertisement than on a statement made orally by a salesperson.

▶ **Case in Point 23.9**   A tobacco farmer read an advertisement for Chlor-O-Pic, a chemical fumigant. The ad stated that, if applied as directed, Chlor-O-Pic would give "season-long control with application in fall, winter, or spring" against black shank disease, a fungal disease that destroys tobacco crops. The farmer bought Chlor-O-Pic and applied it as directed to his tobacco crop. Nonetheless, the crop developed black shank disease. The farmer sued the manufacturer of Chlor-O-Pic, arguing that he had purchased the product in reliance on a "strong promise" of "season-long control." The court found that the manufacturer's strong promise had created an express warranty and that the farmer was entitled to the value of the damaged crop.[3] ◀

SECTION 3
IMPLIED WARRANTIES

An **implied warranty** is one that *the law derives* by inference from the nature of the transaction or the relative situations or circumstances of the parties.

---

3. *Triple E, Inc. v. Hendrix & Dail, Inc.*, 344 S.C. 186, 543 S.E.2d 245 (2001). See also *Nomo Agroindustrial Sa De CV v. Enza Zaden North America, Inc.*, 492 F.Supp.2d 1175 (D.Ariz. 2007).

Under the UCC, merchants impliedly warrant that the goods they sell or lease are merchantable and, in certain circumstances, fit for a particular purpose. In addition, an implied warranty may arise from a course of dealing or usage of trade. We examine these three types of implied warranties in the following subsections.

Implied Warranty of Merchantability

Every sale or lease of goods made by a merchant who deals in goods of the kind sold or leased automatically gives rise to an **implied warranty of merchantability** [UCC 2–314, 2A–212]. Thus, a merchant who is in the business of selling ski equipment makes an implied warranty of merchantability every time he sells a pair of skis. A neighbor selling her skis at a garage sale does not (because she is not in the business of selling goods of this type).

MERCHANTABLE GOODS To be *merchantable,* goods must be "reasonably fit for the ordinary purposes for which such goods are used." They must be of at least average, fair, or medium-grade quality. The quality must be comparable to quality that will pass without objection in the trade or market for goods of the same description.

To be merchantable, the goods must also be adequately packaged and labeled, and they must conform to the promises or affirmations of fact made on the container or label, if any. Of course, merchants are not absolute insurers against *all* accidents arising in connection with the goods. A bar of soap is not unmerchantable merely because a user could slip and fall by stepping on it.

The warranty of merchantability may be breached even though the merchant did not know or could not have discovered that a product was defective (not merchantable). ▶ **Example 23.10** Christine contracts to purchase a log home package from Milde, a log home dealer. The dealer provides the logs and other materials and constructs the home. Immediately after Christine moves into the house, she finds that when it rains, water seeps through the exterior walls, staining and discoloring the interior walls. The problem occurs because a defective waterproofing product was used on the logs. Even though Milde did not know that the product was defective, he can be held liable because the waterproofing product was not reasonably fit for its ordinary purpose—that is, making the house waterproof. ◀

If the buyer of a product that requires a significant number of repairs sells the item before filing a complaint against its manufacturer, is the sale evidence of the product's merchantability? That was the question in the following case.

SPOTLIGHT on DaimlerChrysler

Case 23.1 Shoop v. DaimlerChrysler Corp.
Appellate Court of Illinois, First District, 371 Ill.App.3d 1058, 864 N.E.2d 785, 309 Ill.Dec. 544 (2007).

COMPANY PROFILE In 1920, Walter Chrysler, the head of manufacturing operations for General Motors Corporation(GMC), was dissatisfied with its management and quit. He took over Maxwell Motor Company and renamed it Chrysler Corporation. For most of its history, Chrysler ranked third in vehicle sales among the "Big 3" U.S. automakers—GMC, Ford Motor Company, and Chrysler. In 1998, the German company Daimler-Benz AG, maker of Mercedes-Benz vehicles, bought Chrysler and created DaimlerChrysler AG. The new entity proved less successful than its investors had hoped, and in 2007, Chrysler was sold to Cerberus Capital Management, which renamed it Chrysler, LLC (**www.chrysler.com**). Its vehicles are made and sold under the Chrysler, Dodge, Jeep, and Mopar brands.

BACKGROUND AND FACTS In April 2002, Darrell Shoop bought a 2002 Dodge Dakota truck for $28,000 from Dempsey Dodge in Chicago, Illinois. DaimlerChrysler Corporation had manufactured the Dakota. Problems with the truck arose almost immediately. Defects in the engine, suspension, steering, transmission, and other components required repairs twelve times within the first eighteen months, including at least five times for the same defect, which remained uncorrected. In May 2005, after having driven the Dakota 39,000 miles, Shoop accepted $16,500 for the trade-in value of the truck as part of a purchase of a new vehicle. At the time, a comparable vehicle in average condition would have had an average trade-in value of $14,425 and an average retail value of $17,225. Shoop filed a suit in an Illinois state court against DaimlerChrysler, alleging, among other things, a breach of the implied warranty of merchantability. DaimlerChrysler countered, in part, that Shoop's sale of the Dakota was evidence of its merchantability. The court issued a summary judgment in DaimlerChrysler's favor. Shoop appealed to a state intermediate appellate court.

IN THE LANGUAGE OF THE COURT
Justice *MURPHY* delivered the opinion of the court.

* * * *

Under Section 2–314(c)(2) of the UCC, a product breaches the implied warranty of merchantability if it is not fit for the ordinary purposes for which such goods are used. With regard to automobiles, fitness for the ordinary purpose of driving implies that the vehicle should be in a safe condition and substantially free from defects. *Breach of an implied warranty of merchantability may also occur where the warrantor has unsuccessfully attempted to repair or replace defective parts.* Whether an implied warranty has been breached is a question of fact. [Emphasis added.]

Defendant contends that the Dakota was fit for the ordinary purpose of driving because plaintiff drove it daily for more than three years after purchase and traded it in for its fair market value. * * * A *prima facie* case [legally sufficient case] that a product was defective and that the defect existed when it left the manufacturer's control is made by proof that in the absence of abnormal use or reasonable secondary causes the product failed to perform in the manner reasonably to be expected in light of its nature and intended function. [In a previous case, the] court found that the only defect of any consequence, a jerking transmission, was remedied, and the plaintiff failed to exclude the buildup of moisture or other materials as a reasonable cause of the problem. Here, however, plaintiff's complaint specifically eliminated any abnormal uses and secondary causes as the source of the defects in the vehicle.

In [a different case], the court rejected the defendant's argument that the implied warranty of merchantability was not breached when the plaintiff drove the vehicle for almost 100,000 miles because the testimony established that the plaintiff had the vehicle serviced no less than six times. In addition, in [another case], the court held that the jury could have concluded that a defective paint job on a new car rendered it unmerchantable as a new car, and in [a fourth case] a question of fact existed as to whether the plaintiff's car was in a safe condition and substantially free of defects when an expert testified that poor gas mileage was consistent with a number of defects.

The amended complaint alleged that plaintiff began experiencing problems with the Dakota's engine, suspension and steering, transmission, and other components of the truck soon after he took possession. Plaintiff was required to take the truck to a Chrysler dealership 12 times within 18 months for repairs, and he alleged that defendant was unable to cure the defects after a reasonable number of attempts. When [Shoop's witness Thomas] Walters test drove the Dakota, he experienced a loping or jerking sensation when he braked at very low speeds. Furthermore, at highway speeds, a steering wheel shimmy with additional vibration was also present when he braked. He also noticed an intermittent single pop noise from the front suspension when he turned left into plaintiff's driveway. Therefore, a genuine issue of material fact existed as to whether defendant breached the implied warranty of merchantability.

DECISION AND REMEDY *The state intermediate appellate court concluded that "a genuine issue of material fact existed as to whether [DaimlerChrysler] breached the implied warranty of merchantability." The court reversed the lower court's summary judgment and remanded the case for trial.*

THE ETHICAL DIMENSION *Should Shoop's trade-in of the Dakota preclude his recovery in this case? Why or why not?*

THE LEGAL ENVIRONMENT DIMENSION *If Shoop is allowed to recover damages for breach of warranty, what should be the measure of those damages?*

MERCHANTABLE FOOD The serving of food or drink to be consumed on or off the premises is also treated as a sale of goods and subject to the implied warranty of merchantability [UCC 2–314(1)]. "Merchantable" food is food that is fit to eat.

Courts generally determine whether food is fit to eat on the basis of consumer expectations. Consumers should reasonably expect to find on occasion bones in fish fillets, cherry pits in cherry pie, a nutshell in a package of shelled nuts, and the like—because such substances are natural to the ingredients or the finished food product. In contrast, consumers would not reasonably expect to find an inchworm in a can of peas or a piece of glass in a soft drink—because these substances are *not* natural to the food product.

In the following classic case, the court had to determine whether one should reasonably expect to find a fish bone in fish chowder.

CLASSIC CASE 23.2

Webster v. Blue Ship Tea Room, Inc.

Supreme Judicial Court of Massachusetts, 347 Mass. 421 198 N.E.2d 309 (1964).

BACKGROUND AND FACTS Blue Ship Tea Room, Inc., was located in Boston in an old building overlooking the ocean. Webster, who had been born and raised in New England, went to the restaurant and ordered fish chowder. The chowder was milky in color. After three or four spoonfuls, she felt something lodged in her throat. As a result, she underwent two esophagoscopies (procedures in which a telescope-like instrument is used to look into the throat). In the second esophagoscopy, a fish bone was found and removed. Webster filed a suit against the restaurant in a Massachusetts state court for breach of the implied warranty of merchantability. The jury rendered a verdict for Webster, and the restaurant appealed to the state's highest court.

IN THE LANGUAGE OF THE COURT
REARDON, Justice.

[The plaintiff] ordered a cup of fish chowder. Presently, there was set before her "a small bowl of fish chowder." * * * After 3 or 4 [spoonfuls] she was aware that something had lodged in her throat because she "couldn't swallow and couldn't clear her throat by gulping and she could feel it." This misadventure led to two esophagoscopies at the Massachusetts General Hospital, in the second of which, on April 27, 1959, a fish bone was found and removed. The sequence of events produced injury to the plaintiff which was not insubstantial.

We must decide whether a fish bone lurking in a fish chowder, about the ingredients of which there is no other complaint, constitutes a breach of implied warranty under applicable provisions of the Uniform Commercial Code * * * . As the judge put it in his charge [jury instruction], "Was the fish chowder fit to be eaten and wholesome? * * * Nobody is claiming that the fish itself wasn't wholesome. * * * But the bone of contention here—I don't mean that for a pun—but was this fish bone a foreign substance that made the fish chowder unwholesome or not fit to be eaten?"

     * * * *

[We think that it] is not too much to say that a person sitting down in New England to consume a good New England fish chowder embarks on a gustatory [taste-related] adventure which may entail the removal of some fish bones from his bowl as he proceeds. We are not inclined to tamper with age-old recipes by any amendment reflecting the plaintiff's view of the effect of the Uniform Commercial Code upon them. We are aware of the heavy body of case law involving foreign substances in food, but we sense a strong distinction between them and those relative to unwholesomeness of the food itself, [such as] tainted mackerel, and a fish bone in a fish chowder. * * * We consider that the joys of life in New England include the ready availability of fresh fish chowder. We should be prepared to cope with the hazards of fish bones, the occasional presence of which in chowders is, it seems to us, to be anticipated, and which, in the light of a hallowed tradition, do not impair their fitness or merchantability.

CASE 23.2 CONTINUED

DECISION AND REMEDY *The Supreme Judicial Court of Massachusetts "sympathized with a plaintiff who has suffered a peculiarly New England injury" but entered a judgment for the defendant, Blue Ship Tea Room. A fish bone in fish chowder is not a breach of the implied warranty of merchantability.*

IMPACT OF THIS CASE ON TODAY'S LAW *This classic case, phrased in memorable language, was an early application of the UCC's implied warranty of merchantability to food products. The case established the rule that consumers should expect to find, on occasion, elements of food products that are natural to the product (such as fish bones in fish chowder). Courts today still apply this rule.*

THE E-COMMERCE DIMENSION *If Webster had made the chowder herself from a recipe that she had found on the Internet, could she have successfully brought an action against its author for a breach of the implied warranty of merchantability? Explain.*

Implied Warranty of Fitness for a Particular Purpose

The **implied warranty of fitness for a particular purpose** arises in the sale or lease of goods when a seller or lessor (merchant or nonmerchant) knows *both* of the following:

1. The particular purpose for which a buyer or lessee will use the goods.
2. That the buyer or lessee is relying on the skill and judgment of the seller or lessor to select suitable goods [UCC 2–315, 2A–213].

PARTICULAR VERSUS ORDINARY PURPOSE A "particular purpose" of the buyer or lessee differs from the "ordinary purpose for which goods are used" (merchantability). Goods can be merchantable but unfit for a particular purpose.

▶ **Example 23.11** Shakira needs a gallon of paint to match the color of her living room walls—a light shade somewhere between coral and peach. She takes a sample to Sherwin-Williams and requests a gallon of paint of that color. Instead, the salesperson gives her a gallon of bright blue paint. Here, the salesperson has not breached any warranty of implied merchantability—the bright blue paint is of high quality and suitable for interior walls. The salesperson has breached an implied warranty of fitness for a particular purpose, though, because the paint is not the right color for Shakira's purpose (to match her living room walls). ◀

KNOWLEDGE AND RELIANCE REQUIREMENTS A seller or lessor need not have actual knowledge of the buyer's or lessee's particular purpose. It is sufficient if a seller or lessor "has reason to know" the purpose. For an implied warranty to be created, however, the buyer or lessee must have *relied* on the skill or judgment of the seller or lessor in selecting or furnishing suitable goods. Moreover, the seller or lessor must have reason to know that the buyer or lessee is relying on her or his judgment or skill.

▶ **Example 23.12** Carlos Fuentes tells Tyrone, a salesperson at GamerPC, that he is looking to buy a new PC, such as the Cyberpower Black Pearl or Velocity Raptor Signature Edition, to use for gaming. Fuentes's statement implies that he needs a PC with a video card that is capable of running fast-paced video games with detailed graphics. Tyrone recommends and sells Carlos a computer that does not have a video card and is too slow to run such video games. By doing so, Tyrone has breached the implied warranty of fitness for a particular purpose. ◀

Warranties Implied from Prior Dealings or Trade Custom

Implied warranties can also arise (or be excluded or modified) as a result of course of dealing or usage of trade [UCC 2–314(3), 2A–212(3)]. Without evidence to the contrary, when both parties to a sales or lease contract have knowledge of a well-recognized trade custom, the courts will infer that both parties intended for that custom to apply to their contract.

▶ **Example 23.13** Industry-wide custom is to lubricate a new car before it is delivered. If a dealer fails to lubricate a car, the dealer can be held liable to a buyer for damages resulting from the breach of an implied warranty. (This, of course, would also be negligence on the part of the dealer.) ◀

Lemon Laws

Purchasers of defective automobiles—called "lemons"—may have remedies in addition to those offered by the UCC. All of the states and the District of Columbia have enacted *lemon laws*.

Basically, state lemon laws provide remedies to consumers who buy automobiles that repeatedly fail to meet standards of quality and performance because they are "lemons." Although lemon laws vary by state, typically they apply to automobiles under warranty that are defective in a way that significantly affects the vehicle's value or use. Lemon laws do not necessarily cover used-car purchases (unless the car is covered by a manufacturer's extended warranty) or vehicles that are leased.[4]

SELLER HAS HAD OPPORTUNITY TO REMEDY DEFECT Generally, the seller or manufacturer is given a number of opportunities to remedy the defect (usually four). If the seller fails to cure the problem despite a reasonable number of attempts (as specified by state law), the buyer is entitled to a new car, replacement of defective parts, or return of all consideration paid. Buyers who prevail in a lemon-law dispute may also be entitled to reimbursement of their attorneys' fees.

ARBITRATION OFTEN REQUIRED In most states, lemon laws require the owner of the vehicle to notify the dealer or manufacturer of the problem and to provide the dealer or manufacturer with an opportunity to solve it. If the problem remains, the owner must then submit complaints to the arbitration program specified in the manufacturer's warranty before taking the case to court.

Decisions by arbitration panels are binding on the manufacturer—that is, cannot be appealed by the manufacturer to the courts—but usually are not binding on the purchaser. Most major automobile companies operate their own arbitration panels. All arbitration boards must meet state and/or federal standards of impartiality, and some states have established mandatory government-sponsored arbitration programs for lemon-law disputes.

Magnuson-Moss Warranty Act

The Magnuson-Moss Warranty Act of 1975[5] was designed to prevent deception in warranties by making them easier to understand.

APPLIES ONLY TO CONSUMER TRANSACTIONS The Magnuson-Moss Warranty Act modifies UCC warranty rules to some extent when *consumer* transactions are involved. The UCC, however, remains the primary codification of warranty rules for commercial transactions.

Under the Magnuson-Moss Act, no seller is *required* to give a written warranty for consumer goods sold. If a seller chooses to make an express written warranty, however, and the cost of the consumer goods is more than $25, the warranty must be labeled as either "full" or "limited."

A *full warranty* requires free repair or replacement of any defective part. If the product cannot be repaired within a reasonable time, the consumer has the choice of a refund or a replacement without charge. A full warranty can be for an unlimited or limited time period, such as a "full twelve-month warranty." A *limited warranty* is one in which the buyer's recourse is limited in some fashion, such as to replacement of an item. The fact that only a limited warranty is being given must be conspicuously stated.

REQUIRES CERTAIN DISCLOSURES The Magnuson-Moss Act further requires the warrantor to make certain disclosures fully and conspicuously in a single document in "readily understood language." The seller must disclose the name and address of the warrantor, specifically what is warranted, and the procedures for enforcing the warranty. The seller must also clarify that the buyer has legal rights and explain limitations on warranty relief.

See *Concept Summary 23.1* on the following page for a review of the various types of warranties.

See *Concept Summary 23.1* on the following page for a review of the various types of warranties.

SECTION 4
OVERLAPPING WARRANTIES

Sometimes, two or more warranties are made in a single transaction. An implied warranty of merchantability, an implied warranty of fitness for a particular purpose, or both can exist in addition to an express warranty. ▶ **Example 23.14** A sales contract for a new car states that "this car engine is warranted to be free from defects for 36,000 miles or thirty-six months, whichever occurs first." This statement creates an express warranty against all defects, as well as an implied warranty that the car will be fit for normal use. ◀

When the Warranties Are Consistent

The rule under the UCC is that express and implied warranties are construed as *cumulative* if they are consistent with one another [UCC 2–317, 2A–215].

---

4. Note that in some states, such as California, these laws may extend beyond automobile purchases and apply to other consumer goods.
5. 15 U.S.C. Sections 2301–2312.

CONCEPT SUMMARY 23.1
Types of Warranties

CONCEPT	DESCRIPTION
Warranties of Title	The UCC provides for the following warranties of title [UCC 2–312, 2A–211]: 1. *Good title*—A seller warrants that he or she has the right to pass good and rightful title to the goods. 2. *No liens*—A seller warrants that the goods sold are free of any encumbrances (claims, charges, or liabilities—usually called *liens*). A lessor warrants that the lessee will not be disturbed in her or his possession of the goods by the claims of a third party. 3. *No infringements*—A merchant-seller warrants that the goods are free of infringement claims (claims that a patent, trademark, or copyright has been infringed) by third parties. Lessors make similar warranties.
Express Warranties	An express warranty arises under the UCC when a seller or lessor indicates any of the following as part of the sale or bargain [UCC 2–313, 2A–210]: 1. An affirmation of fact or promise. 2. A description of the goods. 3. A sample or model shown as conforming to the contract goods.
Implied Warranty of Merchantability	When a seller or lessor is a merchant who deals in goods of the kind sold or leased, the seller or lessor warrants that the goods sold or leased are properly packaged and labeled, are of proper quality, and are reasonably fit for the ordinary purposes for which such goods are used [UCC 2–314, 2A–212].
Implied Warranty of Fitness for a Particular Purpose	An implied warranty of fitness for a particular purpose arises when the buyer's or lessee's purpose or use is known by the seller or lessor, and the buyer or lessee purchases or leases the goods in reliance on the seller's or lessor's selection [UCC 2–315, 2A–213].
Other Implied Warranties	Other implied warranties can arise as a result of course of dealing or usage of trade [UCC 2–314(3), 2A–212(3)].
Magnuson-Moss Warranty Act	An express written warranty covering consumer goods priced at more than $25, *if made,* must be labeled as either a full warranty or a limited warranty. A full warranty requires free repair or replacement of defective parts and refund or replacement for goods that cannot be repaired in a reasonable time. A limited warranty is one in which the buyer's recourse is limited in some fashion, such as to replacement of an item. Sellers must make certain disclosures to buyers and must state any limitations on a warranty clearly, conspicuously, and in readily understood language.

In other words, courts interpret two or more warranties as being in agreement with each other unless this construction is unreasonable. If it is unreasonable for the two warranties to be consistent, then the court looks at the intention of the parties to determine which warranty is dominant.

Conflicting Warranties

If the warranties are *inconsistent*, the courts usually apply the following rules to interpret which warranty is most important:

1. *Express* warranties displace inconsistent *implied* warranties, except implied warranties of fitness for a particular purpose.
2. Samples take precedence over inconsistent general descriptions.
3. Exact or technical specifications displace inconsistent samples or general descriptions.

▶ **Example 23.15** Innova, Ltd., leases a high-speed server from Vernon Sources. The contract contains an express warranty concerning the speed of the CPU and the application programs that the server is capable of running. Innova does not realize that the speed expressly warranted in the contract is insufficient for its needs until it tries to run the software and the server slows to a crawl.

Because Innova made it clear that it was leasing the server to perform certain tasks, Innova files an action against Vernon for breach of the implied warranty of fitness for a particular purpose. In this situation, Innova normally will prevail. Although the express warranty on CPU speed takes precedence over the implied warranty of merchantability, it normally does not take precedence over an implied warranty of fitness for a particular purpose. ◀

SECTION 5
WARRANTY DISCLAIMERS AND LIMITATIONS ON LIABILITY

The UCC generally permits warranties to be disclaimed or limited by specific and unambiguous language, provided that this is done in a manner that protects the buyer or lessee from surprise. Because each type of warranty is created in a different way, the manner in which a seller or lessor can disclaim warranties varies with the type of warranty.

Express Warranties

A seller or lessor can disclaim all oral express warranties by including in the contract a written (or an electronically recorded) disclaimer. The disclaimer must be in language that is clear and conspicuous, and called to a buyer's or lessee's attention [UCC 2–316(1), 2A–214(1)]. This allows the seller or lessor to avoid false allegations that oral warranties were made, and it ensures that only representations made by properly authorized individuals are included in the bargain.

Note, however, that a buyer or lessee must be made aware of any warranty disclaimers or modifications *at the time the contract is formed.* In other words, the seller or lessor cannot modify any warranties or disclaimers made during the bargaining process without the consent of the buyer or lessee.

Implied Warranties

Generally, unless circumstances indicate otherwise, the implied warranties of merchantability and fitness are disclaimed by an expression such as "as is" or "with all faults." Both parties must be able to clearly understand from the language used that there are no implied warranties [UCC 2–316(3)(a), 2A–214(3)(a)]. (Note, however, that some states have passed consumer protection statutes that forbid "as is" sales or make it illegal to disclaim warranties of merchantability on consumer goods.)

▶ **Case in Point 23.16** Mandy Morningstar advertised a "lovely, eleven-year-old mare" with extensive jumping ability for sale. After examining the horse twice, Sue Hallett contracted to buy the horse. She signed a contract that described the horse as an eleven-year-old mare and as being sold "as is." Shortly after the purchase, a veterinarian determined that the horse was actually sixteen years old and in no condition for jumping. Hallett stopped payment, and Morningstar filed a lawsuit for breach of contract.

The court held that the statement in the contract describing the horse as eleven years old constituted an express warranty, which Morningstar had breached. Although the "as is" clause effectively disclaimed any implied warranties (of merchantability and fitness for a particular purpose, such as jumping), the court ruled that it did not disclaim the express warranty concerning the horse's age.[6] ◀

In the following case, the court explained the rationale behind the effect of an "as is" clause.

---

6. *Morningstar v. Hallett,* 858 A.2d 125 (Pa.Super.Ct. 2004).

CASE ANALYSIS

Case 23.3 Roberts v. Lanigan Auto Sales
Court of Appeals of Kentucky, __ S.W.3d __, 2013 WL 44020 (2013).

IN THE LANGUAGE OF THE COURT
VANMETER, Judge:

* * * *

* * * [Evan] Roberts purchased a used vehicle from Lanigan [Auto Sales] in September 2009. Roberts and Lanigan executed a purchase contract, which contained a clause stating the

vehicle is "sold as is * * * without any guarantee express or implied." Following the purchase, Roberts independently obtained a report which indicated that the vehicle had previ-

CASE 23.3 CONTINUED

ously been involved in an accident and suffered damage to the undercarriage of the vehicle.

Roberts filed the underlying action [in a Kentucky state court] alleging that Lanigan * * * committed fraud by omitting, suppressing, and concealing the vehicle's prior damage and accident history in order to induce Roberts into purchasing the vehicle. Lanigan maintained it never represented that the vehicle had not been damaged or involved in a wreck and filed a * * * motion to dismiss the action for failure to state a claim upon which relief can be granted. * * * The trial court * * * dismissed Roberts' action on the basis that the purchase contract, which contained the express term "sold as is," barred his action for fraud. This appeal followed.

On appeal, Roberts argues the trial court erred by dismissing his action because the "sold as is" clause in the purchase contract did not bar his action for fraud. We disagree.

* * * *

[Kentucky Revised Statute] 355.2–316 [Kentucky's version of UCC 2–316] seeks to provide a structure for construing both oral representations and written disclaimers within an agreement for the sale of goods. To carry out that purpose, the statute provides that, "unless the circumstances indicate otherwise, all implied warranties are excluded by expressions like 'as is,' 'with all faults' or other language which in common understanding calls the buyer's attention to the exclusion of warranties."

* * * An "as is" clause in a sales contract is understood to mean that the buyer takes the entire risk as to the quality of the goods involved. * * * A valid "as is" agreement prevents a buyer from holding a seller liable if the thing sold turns out to be worth less than the price paid, because it is impossible for the buyer's injury on account of this disparity to have been caused by the seller and the sole cause of the buyer's injury is the buyer himself or herself. Thus, by agreeing to purchase something "as is," a buyer agrees to make his or her own appraisal of the bargain and to accept the risk that he or she may be wrong, and the seller gives no assurances, express or implied, concerning the value or condition of the thing sold. [Emphasis added.]

In an action for fraud, a party must prove by clear and convincing evidence that (1) the seller made a material misrepresentation to the buyer, (2) which was false, (3) known by the seller to be false, (4) made with the intent to be relied upon, (5) was reasonably relied upon and (6) caused injury. Here, Roberts executed a written sales contract which stated the car was "sold as is" and acknowledging, "I hereby make this purchase knowingly without any guarantee expressed or implied by this dealer or his agent." * * * The effect of the "sold as is" clause is to shift the assumption of risk regarding the value or condition of the vehicle to Roberts despite any express or implied warranties that were made by Lanigan. Since the only claimed injury concerns the value or condition of the car sold, and because the sole cause of such an injury is the buyer himself, Roberts is unable to prove that the seller's representation caused the injury. Furthermore, by agreeing to buy the vehicle "as is," Roberts agreed to make his own assessment of the condition of the vehicle in spite of Lanigan's representations. Thus, he cannot later claim that he reasonably relied on those representations when agreeing to purchase the vehicle.

This is not to say that an "as is" clause bars any claim of fraud; when circumstances indicate otherwise, express or implied warranties may not be disclaimed by a written contract. Different circumstances could support an action for fraud despite an "as is" clause when the injury results in consequential damages, [that is,] injury to a person or property as a result of a breach of warranty, rather than an injury as a result of decreased value of the goods. Our holding here merely follows the rationale that an "as is" clause transfers the risk to the buyer that the condition or value of the goods is not what the seller represents. In accordance with that rationale, the trial court did not err by dismissing Roberts' action.

The order of the [trial court] is affirmed.

LEGAL REASONING QUESTIONS

1. What language in a sales contract excludes all implied warranties?
2. How does an "as is" clause in a sales contract affect the bargain between the buyer and the seller?
3. Does an "as is" clause in a sales contract bar all claims of fraud? Explain.
4. In this case, what did the court rule on the effect of the "as is" clause? Why?

DISCLAIMER OF THE IMPLIED WARRANTY OF MERCHANTABILITY To specifically disclaim an implied warranty of merchantability, a seller or lessor must mention the word *merchantability*. The disclaimer need not be written, but if it is, the writing (or record) must be conspicuous [UCC 2–316(2), 2A–214(4)].

Under the UCC, a term or clause is conspicuous when it is written or displayed in such a way that a reasonable person would notice it. Conspicuous terms include words set in capital letters, in a larger font size, or in a different color so as to be set off from the surrounding text.

DISCLAIMER OF THE IMPLIED WARRANTY OF FITNESS To disclaim an implied warranty of fitness for a particular purpose, the disclaimer must be in a writing (or record) and must be conspicuous. The writing does not have to mention the word *fitness*. It is sufficient if, for instance, the disclaimer states, "There are no warranties that extend beyond the description on the face hereof.

Buyer's or Lessee's Examination or Refusal to Inspect

If a buyer or lessee examines the goods (or a sample or model) as fully as desired, *there is no implied warranty with respect to defects that a reasonable examination would reveal or defects that are found on examination* [UCC 2–316(3)(b), 2A–214(2)(b)]. Also, if a buyer or lessee refuses to examine the goods on the seller's or lessor's request that he or she do so, there is no implied warranty with respect to reasonably evident defects.

▶ **Example 23.17** Janna buys a table at Gershwin's Home Store. No express warranties are made. Gershwin asks Janna to inspect the table before buying it, but she refuses. Had Janna inspected the table, she would have noticed that one of its legs was obviously cracked, which made it unstable. Janna takes the table home and sets a lamp on it. The table later collapses, and the lamp starts a fire that causes

significant damage. Janna normally will not be able to hold Gershwin's liable for breach of the warranty of merchantability because she refused to examine the table as Gershwin requested. Janna therefore assumed the risk that the table was defective. ◀

Warranty Disclaimers and Unconscionability

The UCC sections dealing with warranty disclaimers do not refer specifically to unconscionability as a factor. Ultimately, however, the courts will test warranty disclaimers with reference to the UCC's unconscionability standards [UCC 2–302, 2A–108]. Factors such as lack of bargaining position, "take-it-or-leave-it" choices, and a buyer's or lessee's failure to understand or know of a warranty disclaimer will be relevant to the issue of unconscionability.

Statutes of Limitations

As discussed in Chapter 22, a cause of action for breach of contract under the UCC must be commenced within four years after the breach occurs (unless the parties agree to a shorter period). An action for breach of warranty accrues when the seller or lessor *tenders* delivery, even if the buyer or lessee is unaware of the breach at that time [UCC 2–725(2), 2A–506(2)]. In addition, the nonbreaching party usually must notify the breaching party within a reasonable time after discovering the breach or be barred from pursuing any remedy [UCC 2–607(3)(a), 2A–516(3)].

Reviewing: Warranties

Shalene Kolchek bought a Great Lakes spa from Val Porter, a dealer who was selling spas at the state fair. Porter told Kolchek that Great Lakes spas were "top of the line" and "the Cadillac of spas" and indicated that the spa she was buying was "fully warranted for three years." Kolchek signed an installment contract. Then, Porter handed her the manufacturer's paperwork and arranged for the spa to be delivered and installed for her. Three months later, Kolchek noticed that one corner of the spa was leaking onto her new deck and causing damage. She complained to Porter, but he did nothing about the problem. Kolchek's family continued to use the spa. Using the information presented in the chapter, answer the following questions.

1. Did Porter's statement that the spa was "top of the line" and "the Cadillac of spas" create any type of warranty? Why or why not?
2. If the paperwork provided to Kolchek after her purchase indicated that the spa had no warranty, would this be an effective disclaimer under the Uniform Commercial Code? Explain.
3. Can Kolchek sue Porter for breach of the implied warranty of merchantability because the spa leaked? Explain.

4. Suppose that one year later, Pacific Credit Union contacted Kolchek and claimed that it had a security interest in the spa. Would this be a breach of any of the title warranties discussed in the chapter? Explain.

DEBATE THIS... *No express warranties should be created by the oral statements made by salespersons about a product.*

Terms and Concepts

express warranty 440

implied warranty 441

implied warranty of fitness for a particular purpose 445

implied warranty of merchantability 442

ExamPrep

Issue Spotters

1. General Construction Company (GCC) tells Industrial Supplies, Inc., that it needs an adhesive to do a particular job. Industrial provides a five-gallon bucket of a certain brand. When it does not perform to GCC's specifications, GCC sues Industrial, which claims, "We didn't expressly promise anything." What should GCC argue? **(See page 445.)**

2. Stella bought a cup of coffee at the Roasted Bean Drive-Thru. The coffee had been heated to 190 degrees and consequently had dissolved the inside of the cup. When Stella lifted the lid, the cup collapsed, spilling the contents on her lap. To recover for third-degree burns on her thighs, Stella filed a suit against the Roasted Bean. Can Stella recover for breach of the implied warranty of merchantability? Why or why not? **(See page 442.)**

- **Check your answers to the Issue Spotters against the answers provided in Appendix E at the end of this text.**

Before the Test

Go to **www.cengagebrain.com**, enter the ISBN 9781285185248, and click on "Find" to locate this textbook's Web site. Then, click on "Access Now" under "Study Tools," and select Chapter 23 at the top. There, you will find a Practice Quiz that you can take to assess your mastery of the concepts in this chapter, as well as Flashcards and a Glossary of important terms.

Business Scenarios

23–1. Implied Warranties. Moon, a farmer, needs to install a two-thousand-pound piece of equipment in his barn. This will require lifting the equipment thirty feet up into a hayloft. Moon goes to Davidson Hardware and tells Davidson that he needs some heavy-duty rope to be used on his farm. Davidson recommends a one-inch-thick nylon rope, and Moon purchases two hundred feet of it. Moon ties the rope around the piece of equipment; puts the rope through a pulley; and, with a tractor, lifts the equipment off the ground. Suddenly, the rope breaks. The equipment crashes to the ground and is severely damaged. Moon files a suit against Davidson for breach of the implied warranty of fitness for a particular pur-

pose. Discuss how successful Moon will be in his suit. **(See page 441.)**

23–2. Warranty Disclaimers. Tandy purchased a washing machine from Marshall Appliances. The sales contract included a provision explicitly disclaiming all express or implied warranties, including the implied warranty of merchantability. The disclaimer was printed in the same size and color as the rest of the contract. The machine never functioned properly. Tandy sought a refund of the purchase price, claiming that Marshall had breached the implied warranty of merchantability. Can Tandy recover the purchase price, notwithstanding the warranty disclaimer in the contract? Explain. **(See page 448.)**

Business Case Problems

23–3. BUSINESS CASE PROBLEM WITH SAMPLE ANSWER: Express Warranties.

 Videotape is recorded magnetically. The magnetic particles that constitute the recorded image are bound to the tape's polyester base. The binder that holds the particles to the base breaks down

over time. This breakdown, which is called sticky shed syndrome, causes the image to deteriorate. The Walt Disney Co. made many of its movies available on tape. Buena Vista Home Entertainment, Inc., sold the tapes, which it described as part of a "Gold Collection" or "Masterpiece Collection." The advertising included such statements as "Give Your

Children the memories of a lifetime—Collect Each Timeless Masterpiece!" and "Available for a Limited Time Only!" Charmaine Schreib and others who bought the tapes filed a suit in an Illinois state court against Disney and Buena Vista, alleging, among other things, breach of warranty. The plaintiffs claimed that the defendants' marketing promised the tapes would last for generations. In reality, the tapes were as subject to sticky shed syndrome as other tapes. Did the ads create an express warranty? In whose favor should the court rule on this issue? Explain. [Schreib v. The Walt Disney Co., __ N.E.2d __, 2006 WL 573008 (Ill.App. 1 Dist. 2006)] **(See page 440.)**

- **For a sample answer to Problem 23–3, go to Appendix F at the end of this text.**

23–4. Implied Warranties. Peter and Tanya Rothing operated Diamond R Stables near Belgrade, Montana, where they bred, trained, and sold horses. Arnold Kallestad owned a ranch in Gallatin County, Montana, where he grew hay and grain, and raised Red Angus cattle. For more than twenty years, Kallestad had sold between three hundred and one thousand tons of hay annually, sometimes advertising it for sale in the Bozeman Daily Chronicle. In 2001, the Rothings bought hay from Kallestad for $90 a ton. They received delivery on April 23. In less than two weeks, at least nine of the Rothings' horses exhibited symptoms of poisoning that was diagnosed as botulism. Before the outbreak was over, nineteen animals had died. Robert Whitlock, associate professor of medicine and the director of the Botulism Laboratory at the University of Pennsylvania, concluded that Kallestad's hay was the source. The Rothings filed a suit in a Montana state court against Kallestad, claiming, in part, breach of the implied warranty of merchantability. Kallestad asked the court to dismiss this claim on the ground that, if botulism had been present, it had been in no way foreseeable. Should the court grant this request? Why or why not? [Rothing v. Kallestad, 337 Mont. 193, 159 P.3d 222 (2007)] **(See page 441.)**

23–5. Spotlight on Apple—Implied Warranties. Alan Vitt purchased an iBook G4 laptop computer from Apple, Inc. Shortly after the one-year warranty expired, the laptop failed to work due to a weakness in the product manufacture. Vitt sued Apple, arguing that the laptop should have lasted "at least a couple of years," which Vitt believed was a reasonable consumer expectation for a laptop. Vitt claimed that Apple's descriptions of the laptop as "durable," "rugged," "reliable," and "high performance" were affirmative statements concerning the quality and performance of the laptop, which Apple did not meet. How should the court rule? Why? [Vitt v. Apple Computer, Inc., 2012 WL 627702 (9th Cir. 2011)] **(See page 441.)**

23–6. Implied Warranties. Bariven, S.A., agreed to buy 26,000 metric tons of powdered milk for $123.5 million from Absolute Trading Corp. to be delivered in shipments from China to Venezuela. After the first three shipments, China halted dairy exports due to the presence of melamine in some products. Absolute assured Bariven that its milk was safe, and when China resumed dairy exports, Absolute delivered sixteen more shipments. Tests of samples of the milk revealed that it contained dangerous levels of melamine. Did Absolute breach any implied warranties? Discuss. [Absolute Trading Corp. v. Bariven S.A., 2013 WL 49735 (11th Cir. 2013)] **(See page 441.)**

23–7. A QUESTION OF ETHICS: Lemon Laws.

 Randal Schweiger bought a 2008 Kia Spectra EX from Kia Motors America, Inc., for his stepdaughter, April Kirichkow. The cost was $17,231, plus sales tax, fees, and other items. April had trouble starting the car. The Kia dealership replaced different parts of the motor several times, but was unable to fix the problem. Schweiger sought a refund under the state's lemon law. When they could not agree on the amount, Schweiger filed a suit in a Wisconsin state court against Kia. From a judgment in Schweiger's favor, Kia appealed. [Schweiger v. Kia Motors America, Inc., __ Wis.2d __, __ N.W.2d __, 2013 WL 1149765 (2013)] **(See page 445.)**

(a) Kia offered a refund of $3,306.24. Should this offer bar Schweiger's claim for a refund? Why or why not?

(b) Schweiger claimed that Kia's offer did not include the $1,301 cost of a service contract. Kia argued that the "payoff to the lender" of $13,060.16, which Schweiger agreed was the correct amount, "would by definition refund the cost of the service contract." The court found "no logical basis" for this argument. Is it ethical for a party to argue a position for which there is no logical basis? Discuss.

Legal Reasoning Group Activity

23–8. Warranties. Milan purchased saffron extract, marketed as "America's Hottest New Way to a Flat Belly," online from Dr. Chen. The Web site stated that recently published studies showed a significant weight loss (more than 25 percent) for people who used pure saffron extract as a supplement without diet and exercise. Dr. Chen said that the saffron suppresses appetite by increasing levels of serotonin, which reduces emotional eating. Milan took the extract as directed without any resulting weight loss. **(See page 440.)**

(a) The first group will determine whether Dr. Chen's Web site made any express warranty on the saffron extract or its effectiveness in causing weight loss.

(b) The second group will discuss whether the implied warranty of merchantability applies to the purchase of weight-loss supplements.

(c) The third group will decide if Dr. Chen's sale of saffron extract breached the implied warranty of fitness for a particular purpose.

CHAPTER 24

INTERNATIONAL LAW IN A GLOBAL ECONOMY

International business transactions are not unique to the modern world. Commerce has always crossed national borders. What is new in our day is the dramatic growth in world trade and the emergence of a global business community. Exchanges of goods, services, and ideas (intellectual property) on a global level are now routine. Therefore, students of business law and the legal environment should be familiar with the laws pertaining to international business transactions.

Laws affecting the international legal environment of business include both international law and national law. **International law** can be defined as a body of law—formed as a result of international customs, treaties, and organizations—that governs relations among or between nations.

International law may be public, creating standards for the nations themselves. It may also be private, establishing international standards for private transactions that cross national

borders. (Can officials legally search electronic devices, including laptops and smartphones, of persons who cross national borders? See this chapter's *Insight into the Global Environment* feature on the following page for the answer.) **National law** is the law of a particular nation, such as Brazil, Germany, Japan, or the United States. In this chapter, we examine how both international law and national law frame business operations in the global context.

SECTION 1
INTERNATIONAL LAW

The major difference between international law and national law is that government authorities can enforce national law. What government, however, can enforce international law? By definition, a *nation* is a sovereign entity—which means that there is no higher authority to which that nation must submit.
▶ **Example 24.1** In February 2013, North Korea performed its third underground nuclear weapons test in violation of United Nations Security Council resolutions. Although world leaders uniformly condemned North Korea's action, the United Nations had no ready means of enforcing its resolutions. ◀

If a nation violates an international law and persuasive tactics fail, other countries or international organizations have no recourse except to take coercive actions. Coercive actions might include economic sanctions, severance of diplomatic relations, boycotts, and, as a last resort, war against the violating nation.

International law attempts to reconcile each country's need to be the final authority over its own

affairs with the desire of nations to benefit economically from trade and harmonious relations with one another. Sovereign nations can, and do, voluntarily agree to be governed in certain respects by international law, usually for the purpose of facilitating international trade and commerce. As a result, a body of international law has evolved.

Sources of International Law

Basically, there are three sources of international law: international customs, treaties and international agreements, and international organizations and conferences. We look at each of these sources here.

INTERNATIONAL CUSTOMS One important source of international law consists of the international customs that have evolved among nations in their relations with one another. Article 38(1) of the Statute of the International Court of Justice refers to an international custom as "evidence of a general practice accepted as law." The legal principles and doctrines that you will read about shortly are rooted in international customs and traditions that have evolved over time in the international arena.

INSIGHT INTO THE GLOBAL ENVIRONMENT
Border Searches of Your Electronic Devices

Every year, tens of millions of travelers arrive at U.S. borders where they are subject to a search. Of these travelers, about 12 million undergo a secondary screening, and approximately five thousand of these screenings involve an electronic device. About three hundred devices—computers, BlackBerrys, tablets, and smartphones—are sent to the Immigration and Customs Enforcement forensics laboratory in Fairfax, Virginia, for further examination.

The U.S. government has historically had a broad power to search travelers and their property when they enter this country. That power includes the right to inspect papers and other physical documents in the possession of anyone entering the United States, including U.S. citizens.

A Legal Challenge to Extensive Searches of Electronic Devices

Increasingly, however, instead of being carried in physical form, documents are carried on the hard drives of laptop computers, in tablets, or in smartphones. Indeed, a person might have thousands and thousands of photos, e-mails, video clips, and documents on the hard drive of a laptop. Does the government's power to conduct border searches give it the right to rummage through all of the data on an electronic device? Several recent lawsuits have raised this issue.

When Pascal Abidor, a Ph.D. student who has dual U.S. and French citizenship, traveled by train from Canada to New York, U.S. Customs and Border Control agents pulled him aside and required him to log on to his computer. They then examined much of its contents. Abidor was released after a few hours, but the Department of Homeland Security kept his laptop for eleven days. Abidor challenged the search. His complaint alleged:

> [A government policy that authorizes] the suspicionless search of the contents of Americans' laptops, cell phones, cameras, and other electronic devices at the international border . . . violates the constitutional rights of American citizens to keep the private and expressive details of their lives, as well as sensitive information obtained or created in the course of their work, free from unwarranted government scrutiny.

Although the lawsuit was filed several years ago, as we go to press, there is no information available on the verdict.[a]

Protecting Attorney-Client Privilege

Border searches present a special problem for attorneys because they have a duty to protect the attorney-client privilege by preventing anyone, including the government, from client communications. To avoid this problem, attorneys should never keep client files on a digital device that they are taking abroad. If the attorneys will need the files during the trip abroad, they can be put on a server in the "cloud."

LEGAL CRITICAL THINKING
INSIGHT INTO THE TECHNOLOGICAL ENVIRONMENT

What are some steps that businesspersons can take to avoid any issues at the border with respect to the contents of their electronic devices?

---

a. *Abidor v. Napolitano,* 10-cv-04059-ERK (E.D.N.Y.).

TREATIES AND INTERNATIONAL AGREEMENTS Treaties and other explicit agreements between or among foreign nations provide another important source of international law. A **treaty** is an agreement or contract between two or more nations that must be authorized and ratified by the supreme power of each nation. Under Article II, Section 2, of the U.S. Constitution, the president has the power "by and with the Advice and Consent of the Senate, to make Treaties, provided two-thirds of the Senators present concur."

A *bilateral* agreement, as the term implies, is an agreement formed by two nations to govern their commercial exchanges or other relations with one another. A *multilateral* agreement is formed by several nations. For instance, regional trade associations such as the Andean Community, the Association of Southeast Asian Nations, and the European Union are the result of multilateral trade agreements.

INTERNATIONAL ORGANIZATIONS The term **international organization** generally refers to an organization composed mainly of officials of member nations and usually established by treaty. The United States is a member of more than one hundred multilateral and bilateral organizations, including at least twenty through the United Nations.

Adopt Resolutions. These organizations adopt resolutions, declarations, and other types of standards that often require nations to behave in a particular manner. The General Assembly of the United Nations, for instance, has adopted numerous nonbinding resolutions and declarations that embody principles of international law. Disputes with respect to these resolutions and declarations may be brought before the International Court of Justice. That court, however, normally has authority to settle legal disputes only when nations voluntarily submit to its jurisdiction.

Create Uniform Rules. The United Nations Commission on International Trade Law has made considerable progress in establishing uniformity in international law as it relates to trade and commerce. One of the commission's most significant creations to date is the 1980 Convention on Contracts for the International Sale of Goods (CISG).

Recall from Chapters 20 through 22 that the CISG is similar to Article 2 of the Uniform Commercial Code in that it is designed to settle disputes between parties to sales contracts. It spells out the duties of international buyers and sellers that will apply if the parties have not agreed otherwise in their contracts. The CISG governs only sales contracts between trading partners in nations that have ratified the CISG, however.

Common Law and Civil Law Systems

Companies operating in foreign nations are subject to the laws of those nations. In addition, international disputes are often resolved through the court systems of foreign nations. Therefore, businesspersons should understand that legal systems around the globe generally are divided into *common law* and *civil law* systems. Exhibit 24–1 below lists some of the nations that use civil law systems and some that use common law systems.

EXHIBIT 24–1 The Legal Systems of Selected Nations

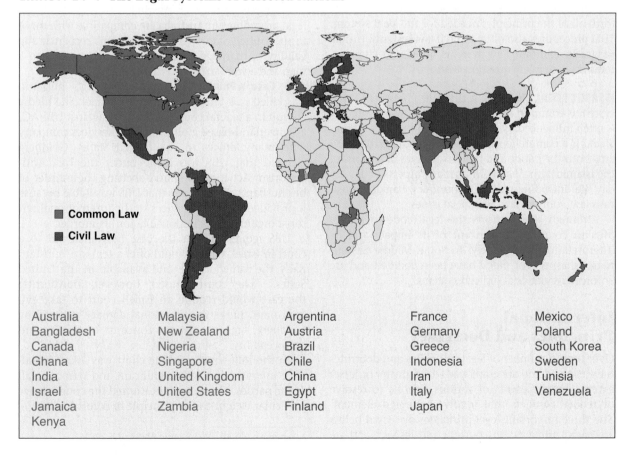

■ Common Law
■ Civil Law

Australia	Malaysia	Argentina	France	Mexico
Bangladesh	New Zealand	Austria	Germany	Poland
Canada	Nigeria	Brazil	Greece	South Korea
Ghana	Singapore	Chile	Indonesia	Sweden
India	United Kingdom	China	Iran	Tunisia
Israel	United States	Egypt	Italy	Venezuela
Jamaica	Zambia	Finland	Japan	
Kenya				

COMMON LAW SYSTEMS As discussed in Chapter 1, in a common law system, the courts independently develop the rules governing certain areas of law, such as torts and contracts. These common law rules apply to all areas not covered by statutory law. Although the common law doctrine of *stare decisis* obligates judges to follow precedential decisions in their jurisdictions, courts may modify or even overturn precedents when deemed necessary.

CIVIL LAW SYSTEMS In contrast to common law countries, most European nations, as well as nations in Latin America, Africa, and Asia, base their legal systems on Roman civil law, or "code law." The term *civil law,* as used here, refers not to civil as opposed to criminal law but to *codified* law—an ordered grouping of legal principles enacted into law by a legislature or other governing body.

In a **civil law system,** the primary source of law is a statutory code. Courts interpret the code and apply the rules to individual cases, but courts may not depart from the code and develop their own laws. Judicial precedents are not binding, as they are in a common law system. In theory, the law code sets forth all of the principles needed for the legal system. Trial procedures also differ in civil law systems. Unlike judges in common law systems, judges in civil systems often actively question witnesses.

ISLAMIC LEGAL SYSTEMS A third, less prevalent, legal system is common in Islamic countries, where the law is often influenced by *sharia,* the religious law of Islam. *Sharia* is a comprehensive code of principles that governs both the public and the private lives of persons of the Islamic faith. *Sharia* directs many aspects of day-to-day life, including politics, economics, banking, business law, contract law, and social issues.

Although *sharia* affects the legal codes of many Muslim countries, the extent of its impact and its interpretation vary widely. In some Middle Eastern nations, aspects of *sharia* have been codified and are enforced by national judicial systems.

International Principles and Doctrines

Over time, a number of legal principles and doctrines have evolved and are employed—to a greater or lesser extent—by the courts of various nations to resolve or reduce conflicts that involve a foreign element. The three important legal principles discussed below are based primarily on courtesy and respect, and are applied in the interests of maintaining harmonious relations among nations.

One way to understand two of these principles—*comity* and the *act of state doctrine*—is to consider the relationships among the states in our federal form of government. Each state honors (gives "full faith and credit" to) the contracts, property deeds, wills, and other legal obligations formed in other states, as well as judicial decisions with respect to such obligations. On a global basis, nations similarly attempt to honor judgments rendered in other countries when it is feasible to do so. Of course, in the United States the states are constitutionally required to honor other states' actions, whereas international law does not *require* nations to honor the actions of other nations.

THE PRINCIPLE OF COMITY The principle of **comity** basically refers to legal reciprocity. One nation will defer and give effect to the executive, legislative, and judicial acts of another country, as long as the acts are consistent with the law and public policy of the accommodating nation. For instance, a U.S. court ordinarily will recognize and enforce a default judgment (see Chapter 3) from an Australian court because the legal procedures in Australia are compatible with those in the United States. Nearly all nations recognize the validity of marriage decrees (at least those between a man and a woman) issued in another country.

▶ **Case in Point 24.2** Karen Goldberg's husband was killed in a terrorist bombing in Israel. She filed a lawsuit in a federal court in New York against UBS AG, a Switzerland-based global financial services company with many offices in the United States. Goldberg claimed that UBS was liable under the U.S. Anti-Terrorism Act for aiding and abetting the murder of her husband. She argued that UBS was liable because it provided financial services to the international terrorist organizations responsible for his murder.

UBS requested that the case be transferred to a court in Israel, which would offer a remedy "substantially the same" as the one available in the United States. The court refused, however. Transferring the case would require an Israeli court to take evidence and judge the emotional damage suffered by Goldberg, "raising distinct concerns of comity and enforceability."[1] ◀

In the following case, the court was asked to balance interests that were significant and serious to all of the parties. The defendant wanted the court to give particular weight to the principle of comity.

---

1. *Goldberg v. UBS AG,* 690 F.Supp.2d 92 (E.D.N.Y. 2010).

CASE ANALYSIS

Case 24.1   Linde v. Arab Bank, PLC[a]

United States Court of Appeals, Second Circuit, 706 F.3d 92 (2013).

IN THE LANGUAGE OF THE COURT
Susan L. *CARNEY*, Circuit Judge:

This case concerns claims brought by victims and families of victims of terrorist attacks committed in Israel between 1995 and 2004 [during a period commonly referred to as the Second Intifada]. Proceeding under the Anti-Terrorism Act [ATA] and the Alien Tort Claims Act, plaintiffs [filed a suit in a federal district court to] seek monetary damages from Arab Bank, PLC ("Arab Bank" or the "Bank"), a large bank headquartered in Jordan, with branches in New York, throughout the Middle East, and around the world. According to plaintiffs, Arab Bank provided financial services and support to terrorists during this period, facilitating the attacks that caused them grave harm.
* * * *

This appeal is brought by defendant Arab Bank from the District Court's orders imposing sanctions.

That order was entered following the Bank's repeated failures, over several years and despite multiple discovery orders, to produce certain documents relevant to plaintiffs' case. The Bank argues that the documents are covered by foreign bank secrecy laws such that their disclosure would subject the Bank to criminal prosecution and other penalties in several foreign jurisdictions. The sanctions order takes the form of a jury instruction that would permit—but not require—the jury to infer from the Bank's failure to produce these documents that the Bank provided financial services to designated foreign terrorist organizations, and did so knowingly.
* * * *

The District Court carefully explained its decision to impose this sanction. It noted that many of the documents that plaintiffs had already obtained tended to support the inference that Arab Bank knew that its services benefited terrorists. According to the District Court, these documents included * * * documents from Arab Bank's Lebanon branch that suggested * * * Arab Bank officials approved the transfer of funds into an account at that branch despite the fact that the transfers listed known terrorists as beneficiaries. As a consequence of the evidentiary gap created by Arab Bank's non-disclosure, the court reasoned, plaintiffs would be "hard-pressed to show that * * * these transfers were not approved by mistake, but instead are representative of numerous other transfers to terrorists." The permissive inference instruction will, according to the District Court, help to rectify this evidentiary imbalance.
* * * *

* * * Arab Bank * * * filed [a] petition for mandamus [an order from a federal appellate court to a district court correcting an erroneous order under circumstances amounting to a clear abuse of discretion by the district court].
* * * *

Arab Bank argues that the District Court's decisions ordering production and imposing sanctions should be vacated because they offend international comity. This argument derives from the notion that the sanctions force foreign authorities either to waive enforcement of their bank secrecy laws or to enforce those laws, and in so doing create an allegedly devastating financial liability for the leading financial institution in their region. The Bank asserts, further, that international comity principles merit special weight here because the District Court's decisions affect the United States' interests in combating terrorism and pertain to a region of the world pivotal to United States foreign policy.

* * * The [District] Court expressly noted that it had "considered the interests of the United States and the foreign jurisdictions whose foreign bank secrecy laws are at issue."

Additionally, international comity calls for more than an examination of only some of the interests of some foreign states. Rather, the concept of international comity requires a particularized analysis of the respective interests of the foreign nation and the requesting nation. In other words, the analysis invites a weighing of all of the relevant interests of all of the nations affected by the court's decision. * * * The District Court recognized the legal conflict faced by Arab Bank and the comity interests implicated by the bank secrecy laws. But [the Court] also observed—and properly so—that Jordan and Lebanon have expressed a strong interest in deterring the financial support of terrorism, and that these interests have often outweighed the enforcement of bank secrecy laws, even in the view of the foreign states. Moreover, * * * the District Court took into account the United States' interests in the effective prosecution of civil claims under the ATA [Anti-Terrorism Act]. This type of holistic, multi-factored analysis does not so obviously offend international comity so as to support issuance of a writ of mandamus. [Emphasis added.]
* * * *

* * * We find no clear abuse of discretion in the District Court's

---

a. *PLC* stands for "public liability company," which is a publicly traded company in England and Ireland. This business form is the equivalent to a publicly traded corporation in the United States.

CASE 24.1 CONTINUES ▶

CASE 24.1 CONTINUED

conclusion that the interests of other sovereigns in enforcing bank secrecy laws are outweighed by the need to impede terrorism financing as embod-

ied in the tort remedies provided by U.S. civil law and the stated commitments of the foreign nations.

* * * *

* * * The Bank's petition for a writ of *mandamus* is DENIED.

LEGAL REASONING QUESTIONS

1. How is the principle of comity applied?
2. What considerations can take precedence over comity?
3. What interests were at stake in the dispute at the heart of this case?
4. Did this court apply the principle of comity? Why or why not?

THE ACT OF STATE DOCTRINE The **act of state doctrine** provides that the judicial branch of one country will not examine the validity of public acts committed by a recognized foreign government within the latter's own territory.

▶ **Case in Point 24.3** Spectrum Stores, Inc., a gasoline retailer in the United States, filed a lawsuit in a U.S. court against Citgo Petroleum Corporation, which is owned by the government of Venezuela. Spectrum alleged that Citgo had conspired with other oil companies in Venezuela and Saudi Arabia to limit production of crude oil and thereby fix the prices of petroleum products sold in the United States. Because Citgo is owned by a foreign government, the U.S. court dismissed the case under the act of state doctrine. A government controls the natural resources, such as oil reserves, within its territory. A U.S. court will not rule on the validity of a foreign government's acts within its own territory [2] ◀

When a Foreign Government Takes Private Property. The act of state doctrine can have important consequences for individuals and firms doing business with, and investing in, other countries. This doctrine is frequently employed in cases involving expropriation or confiscation.

Expropriation occurs when a government seizes a privately owned business or privately owned goods for a proper public purpose and awards just compensation. When a government seizes private property for an illegal purpose and without just compensation, the taking is referred to as a **confiscation.** The line between these two forms of taking is sometimes blurred because of differing interpretations of what is illegal and what constitutes just compensation.

▶ **Example 24.4** Flaherty, Inc., a U.S. company, owns a mine in Brazil. The government of Brazil seizes the mine for public use and claims that the profits Flaherty has already realized from the mine constitute just compensation. Flaherty disagrees, but the act of state doctrine may prevent the company's recovery in a U.S. court. ◀ Note that in a case alleging that a foreign government has wrongfully taken the plaintiff's property, the defendant government has the burden of proving that the taking was an expropriation, not a confiscation.

Doctrine May Immunize a Foreign Government's Actions. When applicable, both the act of state doctrine and the doctrine of *sovereign immunity,* which we discuss next, tend to shield foreign nations from the jurisdiction of U.S. courts. As a result, firms or individuals who own property overseas generally have little legal protection against government actions in the countries where they operate.

THE DOCTRINE OF SOVEREIGN IMMUNITY When certain conditions are satisfied, the doctrine of **sovereign immunity** exempts foreign nations from the jurisdiction of the U.S. courts. In 1976, Congress codified this rule in the Foreign Sovereign Immunities Act (FSIA).[3]

The FSIA exclusively governs the circumstances in which an action may be brought in the United States against a foreign nation, including attempts to attach a foreign nation's property. Because the law is jurisdictional in nature, a plaintiff generally has the burden of showing that a defendant is not entitled to sovereign immunity.

When a Foreign State Will Not Be Immune. Section 1605 of the FSIA sets forth the major exceptions to the jurisdictional immunity of a foreign state. A foreign state is not immune from the jurisdiction of U.S. courts in the following situations:

---

2. *Spectrum Stores, Inc. v. Citgo Petroleum Corp.,* 632 F.3d 938 (5th Cir. 2011).

3. 28 U.S.C. Sections 1602–1611.

1. When the foreign state has waived its immunity either explicitly or by implication.
2. When the foreign state has engaged in commercial activity within the United States or in commercial activity outside the United States that has "a direct effect in the United States."
3. When the foreign state has committed a tort in the United States or has violated certain international laws.

Application of the Act. When courts apply the FSIA, questions frequently arise as to whether an entity is a "foreign state" and what constitutes a "commercial activity." Under Section 1603 of the FSIA, a *foreign state* includes both a political subdivision of a foreign state and an instrumentality (department or agency of any branch of a government) of a foreign state.

Section 1603 broadly defines a *commercial activity* as a regular course of commercial conduct, transaction, or act that is carried out by a foreign state within the United States. Section 1603, however, does not describe the particulars of what constitutes a commercial activity. Thus, the courts are left to decide whether a particular activity is governmental or commercial in nature.

SECTION 2
DOING BUSINESS INTERNATIONALLY

A U.S. domestic firm can engage in international business transactions in a number of ways. The simplest way is for U.S. firms to **export** their goods and services to foreign markets. Alternatively, a U.S. firm can establish foreign production facilities to be closer to the foreign market or markets in which its products are sold. The advantages may include lower labor costs, fewer government regulations, and lower taxes and trade barriers. A domestic firm can also obtain revenues by licensing its technology to an existing foreign company or by selling franchises to overseas entities.

Exporting

Exporting can take two forms: direct exporting and indirect exporting. In *direct exporting,* a U.S. company signs a sales contract with a foreign purchaser that provides for the conditions of shipment and payment for the goods. (International contracts for the purchase and sale of goods, as well as the use of letters of credit to make payments, were discussed in Chapters 20 through 22.)

If sufficient business develops in a foreign country, a U.S. company may establish a specialized marketing organization there by appointing a foreign agent or a foreign distributor. This is called *indirect exporting.*

When a U.S. firm wishes to limit its involvement in an international market, it will typically establish an *agency relationship* with a foreign firm. The foreign firm then acts as the U.S. firm's agent and can enter contracts in the foreign location on behalf of the principal (the U.S. company).

DISTRIBUTORSHIPS When a foreign country represents a substantial market, a U.S. firm may wish to appoint a distributor located in that country. The U.S. firm and the distributor enter into a **distribution agreement.** This is a contract setting out the terms and conditions of the distributorship, such as price, currency of payment, guarantee of supply availability, and method of payment. Disputes concerning distribution agreements may involve jurisdictional or other issues, as well as contract law.

THE NATIONAL EXPORT INITIATIVE Although the United States is one of the world's major exporters, exports make up a much smaller share of annual output in the United States than they do in our most important trading partners. In the past, the United States has not promoted exports as actively as many other nations have.

In an effort to increase U.S. exports, the Obama administration created the National Export Initiative (NEI) with a goal of doubling U.S. exports by 2015. Some commentators believe that another goal of the NEI is to reduce outsourcing—the practice of having manufacturing or other activities performed in lower-wage countries such as China and India.

Export Promotion. An important component of the NEI is the Export Promotion Cabinet, which includes officials from sixteen government agencies and departments. All cabinet members must submit detailed plans to the president, outlining the steps that they will take to increase U.S. exports.

The U.S. Commerce Department plays a leading role in the NEI, and hundreds of its trade experts serve as advocates to help some twenty thousand U.S. companies increase their export sales. In addition, the Commerce Department and other Export Promotion Cabinet members work to promote U.S. exports in the high-growth developing markets of Brazil, China, and India. The members also identify market opportunities in fast-growing sectors, such as environmental goods and services, biotechnology, and renewable energy.

Increased Export Financing. Under the NEI, the Export-Import Bank of the United States increased the financing that it makes available to small and medium-sized businesses by 50 percent. In the initial phase, the bank added hundreds of new small-business clients that sell a wide variety of products, from sophisticated polymers to date palm trees and nanotechnology-based cosmetics.

Manufacturing Abroad

An alternative to direct or indirect exporting is the establishment of foreign manufacturing facilities. Typically, U.S. firms establish manufacturing plants abroad when they believe that by doing so they will reduce costs. Costs for labor, shipping, and raw materials may be lower in foreign nations, which can enable the business to compete more effectively in foreign markets.

Foreign firms have done the same in the United States. Sony, Nissan, and other Japanese manufacturers have established U.S. plants to avoid import duties that the U.S. Congress may impose on Japanese products entering this country.

LICENSING A U.S. firm may license a foreign manufacturing company to use its copyrighted, patented, or trademarked intellectual property or trade secrets. Basically, licensing allows the foreign firm to use an established brand name for a fee. A licensing agreement with a foreign-based firm is much the same as any other licensing agreement (see Chapters 8, 9, and 12). Its terms require a payment of royalties on some basis—such as so many cents per unit produced or a certain percentage of profits from units sold in a particular geographic territory.

▶ **Example 24.5** The Coca-Cola Bottling Company licenses firms worldwide to use (and keep confidential) its secret formula for the syrup used in its soft drink. In return, the company receives a percentage of the income gained from the sale of Coca-Cola by those firms. ◀

The firm that receives the license can take advantage of an established reputation for quality. The firm that grants the license receives income from the for-

eign sales of its products and also establishes a global reputation. Once a firm's trademark is known worldwide, the demand for other products manufactured or sold by that firm may increase—obviously, an important consideration.

FRANCHISING Franchising is a well-known form of licensing and is evident the world over. The owner of a trademark, trade name, or copyright (the franchisor) licenses another (the franchisee) to use the mark, name, or copyright, under certain conditions or limitations, in the selling of goods or services. Franchising allows the franchisor to maintain greater control over the business operation than is possible with most other licensing agreements. In return, the franchisee pays a fee, usually based on a monthly percentage of gross or net sales. Examples of international franchises include Holiday Inn and Hertz.

INVESTING IN A WHOLLY OWNED SUBSIDIARY OR A JOINT VENTURE Another way to expand into a foreign market is to establish a wholly owned subsidiary firm in a foreign country. In many European countries, a subsidiary would likely take the form of a *société anonyme* (S.A.), which is similar to a U.S. corporation. In German-speaking nations, it would be called an *Aktiengesellschaft* (A.G.). When a wholly owned subsidiary is established, the parent company remains in the United States. The parent maintains complete ownership of all of the facilities in the foreign country, as well as total authority and control over all phases of the operation.

A U.S. firm can also expand into international markets through a *joint venture*. In a joint venture, the U.S. company owns only part of the operation. The rest is owned either by local owners in the foreign country or by another foreign entity. All of the firms involved in a joint venture share responsibilities, as well as profits and liabilities.

SECTION 3
REGULATION OF SPECIFIC BUSINESS ACTIVITIES

Doing business abroad can affect the economies, foreign policies, domestic politics, and other national interests of the countries involved. For this reason, nations impose laws to restrict or facilitate international business. Controls may also be imposed by international agreements.

Investment Protections

Firms that invest in foreign nations face the risk that the foreign government may expropriate the investment property. Expropriation, as mentioned earlier in this chapter, occurs when property is taken and the owner is paid just compensation for what is taken. This generally does not violate accepted principles of international law.

Confiscating property without compensation (or without adequate compensation), in contrast, normally violates international law. Few remedies are available for confiscation of property by a foreign government. Claims are often resolved by lump-sum settlements after negotiations between the United States and the taking nation.

Because the possibility of confiscation may deter potential investors, many countries guarantee compensation to foreign investors if their property is taken. A guaranty can be in the form of national constitutional or statutory laws or provisions in international treaties. As further protection for foreign investments, some countries provide insurance for their citizens' investments abroad.

Export Controls

Article I, Section 9, of the U.S. Constitution provides that "No Tax or Duty shall be laid on Articles exported from any State." Thus, Congress cannot impose any export taxes.

Congress can, however, use a variety of other devices to restrict or encourage exports, including the following:

1. *Export quotas.* Congress sets export quotas on various items, such as grain being sold abroad.
2. *Restrictions on technology exports.* Under the Export Administration Act of 1979,[4] the flow of technologically advanced products and technical data can be restricted.
3. *Incentives and subsidies.* The United States (and other nations) also uses incentives and subsidies to stimulate other exports and thereby aid domestic businesses. ▶ **Example 24.6** Under the Export Trading Company Act of 1982,[5] U.S.

banks are encouraged to invest in export trading companies, which are formed when exporting firms join together to export a line of goods. The Export-Import Bank of the United States provides financial assistance, primarily in the form of credit guaranties given to commercial banks that in turn lend funds to U.S. exporting companies. ◀

Import Controls

All nations have restrictions on imports, and the United States is no exception. Restrictions include strict prohibitions, quotas, and tariffs.

PROHIBITED GOODS Under the Trading with the Enemy Act of 1917,[6] no goods may be imported from nations that have been designated enemies of the United States. Other laws prohibit the importation of illegal drugs, books that urge insurrection against the United States,[7] and agricultural products that pose dangers to domestic crops or animals.

The importation of goods that infringe U.S. patents is also prohibited. The International Trade Commission is the government agency that investigates allegations that imported goods infringe U.S. patents and imposes penalties if necessary.

▶ **Case in Point 24.7** Fuji Photo Film Company owned numerous patents for disposable cameras, including the plastic shell covering. Jazz Photo Corporation collected used plastic shells in the United States, shipped them abroad to have new film inserted, and imported the refurbished shells back into the United States for sale. The International Trade Commission (ITC) determined that Jazz's resale of shells originally sold outside the United States infringed Fuji's patents. The ITC ordered Jazz to stop the imports. When Jazz imported and sold 27 million more refurbished shells, Fuji complained to the ITC, which fined Jazz more than $13.5 million.[8] ◀

QUOTAS AND TARIFFS Limits on the amounts of goods that can be imported are known as **quotas.** At one time, the United States had legal quotas on the number of automobiles that could be imported from Japan. Today, Japan "voluntarily" restricts the number of automobiles exported to the United States.

---

4. 50 U.S.C. Sections 2401–2420.
5. 15 U.S.C. Sections 4001, 4003.
6. 12 U.S.C. Section 95a.
7. Because numerous resources that advocate the overthrow of the U.S. government are available on the Internet, this prohibition against importing books that urge insurrection is rather meaningless.
8. *Fuji Photo Film Co. v. International Trade Commission,* 474 F.3d 1281 (Fed.Cir. 2007).

Tariffs are taxes on imports. A tariff is usually a percentage of the value of the import, but it can be a flat rate per unit (such as per barrel of oil). Tariffs raise the prices of imported goods, causing some consumers to purchase domestically manufactured goods instead of imports.

POLITICAL FACTORS Sometimes, countries impose tariffs on goods from a particular nation in retaliation for political acts. ▶ **Example 24.8** In 2009, Mexico imposed tariffs of 10 to 20 percent on ninety products exported from the United States in retaliation for the Obama administration's cancellation of a cross-border trucking program. The program had been instituted to comply with a provision in the North American Free Trade Agreement (to be discussed shortly) that called for Mexican trucks to eventually be granted full access to U.S. highways.

U.S. truck drivers opposed the program, however, and consumer protection groups claimed that the Mexican trucks posed safety issues. Because the Mexican tariffs were imposed on $2.4 billion of U.S. goods annually, in 2011 President Barack Obama negotiated a deal that allowed Mexican truckers to enter the United States. In exchange, Mexico agreed to suspend half of the tariffs immediately and the remainder when the first Mexican hauler complied with the new U.S. requirements. ◀

ANTIDUMPING DUTIES The United States has laws specifically directed at what it sees as unfair international trade practices. **Dumping,** for example, is the sale of imported goods at "less than fair value." *Fair value* is usually determined by the price of the goods in the exporting country. Foreign firms that engage in dumping in the United States hope to undersell U.S. businesses and obtain a larger share of the U.S. market. To prevent this, an extra tariff—known as an *antidumping duty*—may be assessed on the imports.

Two U.S. government agencies are instrumental in imposing antidumping duties: the International Trade Commission (ITC) and the International Trade Administration (ITA). The ITC assesses the effects of dumping on domestic businesses and then makes recommendations to the president concerning temporary import restrictions.

The ITA, which is part of the Department of Commerce, decides whether imports were sold at less than fair value. The ITA's determination establishes the amount of antidumping duties, which are set to equal the difference between the price charged in the United States and the price charged in the export-

ing country. A duty may be retroactive to cover past dumping.

Minimizing Trade Barriers

Restrictions on imports are also known as *trade barriers*. The elimination of trade barriers is sometimes seen as essential to the world's economic well-being. Most of the world's leading trading nations are members of the World Trade Organization (WTO), which was established in 1995 to minimize trade barriers among nations.

Each member country of the WTO is required to grant **normal trade relations (NTR) status** (formerly known as *most-favored-nation status*) to other member countries. This means that each member is obligated to treat other members at least as well as it treats the country that receives its most favorable treatment with regard to imports or exports. Various regional trade agreements and associations also help to minimize trade barriers between nations.

THE EUROPEAN UNION (EU) The European Union (EU) arose out of the 1957 Treaty of Rome, which created the Common Market, a free trade zone comprising the nations of Belgium, France, Italy, Luxembourg, the Netherlands, and West Germany. Today, the EU is a single integrated trading unit made up of twenty-seven European nations.

The EU has gone a long way toward creating a new body of law to govern all of the member nations—although some of its efforts to create uniform laws have been confounded by nationalism. Its governing authorities issue regulations, or directives, that define EU law in various areas, such as environmental law, product liability, anticompetitive practices, and corporations. The directives normally are binding on all member countries.

THE NORTH AMERICAN FREE TRADE AGREEMENT (NAFTA) The North American Free Trade Agreement (NAFTA) created a regional trading unit consisting of Canada, Mexico, and the United States. The goal of NAFTA was to eliminate tariffs among these three nations on substantially all goods by reducing the tariffs incrementally over a period of time.

NAFTA gives the three countries a competitive advantage by retaining tariffs on goods imported from countries outside the NAFTA trading unit. Additionally, NAFTA provides for the elimination of barriers that traditionally have prevented the cross-border movement of services, such as financial and transportation services. NAFTA also attempts to eliminate citizenship requirements for the licensing of accountants, attorneys, physicians, and other professionals.

THE CENTRAL AMERICA–DOMINICAN REPUBLIC–UNITED STATES FREE TRADE AGREEMENT (CAFTA-DR)

The Central America–Dominican Republic–United States Free Trade Agreement (CAFTA-DR) was formed by Costa Rica, the Dominican Republic, El Salvador, Guatemala, Honduras, Nicaragua, and the United States. Its purpose is to reduce trade tariffs and improve market access among all of the signatory nations, including the United States. Legislatures from all seven countries have approved the CAFTA-DR, despite significant opposition in certain nations.

THE REPUBLIC OF KOREA–UNITED STATES FREE TRADE AGREEMENT (KORUS FTA)

In 2011, the United States ratified its first free trade agreement with South Korea—the Republic of Korea–United States Free Trade Agreement (KORUS FTA). The treaty's provisions will eliminate 95 percent of each nation's tariffs on industrial and consumer exports within five years.

KORUS is the largest free trade agreement that the United States has entered into since NAFTA. It is expected to boost U.S. exports by more than $10 billion a year and will benefit U.S. automakers, farmers, ranchers, and manufacturers by enabling them to compete in new markets.

Also in 2011, Congress ratified free trade agreements with Colombia and Panama. The Colombian trade agreement includes a provision requiring an exchange of tax information, and the Panama bill incorporates assurances on labor rights. The treaties are expected to increase U.S. exports and reduce prices for consumers. The Obama administration hopes that the agreements will also provide impetus for negotiations of the trans-Pacific trade initiative, aimed at increasing exports to Japan and other Asian nations.

SECTION 4
INTERNATIONAL DISPUTE RESOLUTION

International contracts frequently include arbitration clauses. By means of such clauses, the parties agree in advance to be bound by the decision of a specified third party in the event of a dispute, as discussed in Chapter 3.

The New York Convention

The United Nations Convention on the Recognition and Enforcement of Foreign Arbitral Awards (often referred to as the New York Convention) assists in the enforcement of arbitration clauses, as do provisions in specific treaties among nations. Basically, the convention requires courts in nations that have signed it to honor private agreements to arbitrate and recognize arbitration awards made in other contracting states. The New York Convention has been implemented in nearly one hundred countries, including the United States.

Under the New York Convention, a court will compel the parties to arbitrate their dispute if all of the following are true:

1. There is a written (or recorded) agreement to arbitrate the matter.
2. The agreement provides for arbitration in a convention signatory nation.
3. The agreement arises out of a commercial legal relationship.
4. One party to the agreement is not a U.S. citizen. In other words, both parties cannot be U.S. citizens.

In the following case, the parties had agreed to arbitrate any disputes in Guernsey, which is a British Crown dependency in the English Channel. The court had to decide whether the agreement was enforceable even though one party was a U.S. company and the other party may have had its principal place of business in the United States.

CASE 24.2

S & T Oil Equipment & Machinery, Ltd. v. Juridica Investments, Ltd.
United States Court of Appeals, Fifth Circuit, 2012 WL 28242 (2012).

BACKGROUND AND FACTS Juridica Investments, Ltd. (JIL), entered into a financing contract with S & T Oil Equipment & Machinery, Ltd., a U.S. company. The contract included an arbitration provision stating that any disputes would be arbitrated "in St. Peter Port, Guernsey, Channel Islands." The contract

CASE 24.2 CONTINUES ▶

CASE 24.2 CONTINUED also stated that it was executed in Guernsey and would be fully performed there. When a dispute arose between the parties, JIL initiated arbitration in Guernsey. Nevertheless, S & T filed a suit in federal district court in the United States. When JIL filed a motion to dismiss in favor of arbitration, the court granted the motion and compelled arbitration under the Convention on the Recognition and Enforcement of Foreign Arbitral Awards. S & T appealed.

IN THE LANGUAGE OF THE COURT
PER CURIAM: [By the Whole Court]

* * * *

The parties dispute whether the fourth * * * factor [that one party is not an American citizen] is satisfied in this case. In considering this fourth factor, courts must ask the following: Is a party to the agreement not an American citizen or does the commercial relationship have some reasonable relation with one or more foreign states? If either question is answered in the affirmative, then the fourth * * * factor is satisfied.

* * * *

*Although it is not absolutely clear where JIL has its principal place of business, it is evident that the commercial relationship between S & T and JIL has some reasonable relation with one or more foreign states. Even if JIL's principal place of business is in the United States, the * * * agreement's arbitral clause can still be enforceable under the Convention if the legal relationship between JIL and S & T involved* "property abroad, envisages performance or enforcement abroad, or has some other reasonable relation with one or more foreign states." *As we stated in [another case], this reasonable relation with a foreign state must be* "independent of the arbitral clause itself." [Emphasis added.]

Here, it is evident that the legal relationship between JIL and S & T envisaged performance abroad. The * * * agreement specifically states that it was executed in Guernsey and would be performed by JIL "exclusively and wholly in and from Guernsey." Indeed, pursuant to the terms of the * * * agreement, JIL performed part of the agreement abroad when it wired funds from Guernsey to cover * * * legal fees and costs * * * .

Given these facts, it is evident that the commercial relationship between S & T and JIL has some reasonable relation with one or more foreign states that is independent of the arbitral clause itself. As such, the fourth * * * factor is satisfied in this case. The district court therefore did not err in compelling arbitration.

DECISION AND REMEDY *The U.S. Court of Appeals for the Fifth Circuit held that arbitration was required under the Convention on the Recognition and Enforcement of Foreign Arbitral Awards. It therefore affirmed the district court's judgment compelling arbitration.*

THE GLOBAL DIMENSION *What would happen if Congress did not require a reasonable relationship with a foreign state for arbitration agreements between U.S. citizens doing business abroad? Would there be more or fewer agreements to arbitrate disputes abroad?*

THE TECHNOLOGICAL DIMENSION *How might these parties have avoided the time and expense of settling their dispute in a foreign jurisdiction?*

Effect of Choice-of-Law and Choice-of-Forum Clauses

If a sales contract does not include an arbitration clause, litigation may occur. When the contract contains forum-selection and choice-of-law clauses (see Chapter 20), the lawsuit will be heard by a court in the specified forum and decided according to that forum's law.

▶ **Case in Point 24.9** Intermax Trading Corporation, a New York firm, contracted to act as the North American sales agent for Garware Polyester, Ltd., based in Mumbai, India. The parties executed a series of contracts with provisions stating that the courts of Mumbai, India, would have exclusive jurisdiction over any disputes relating to the agreements. When Intermax fell behind in its payments to Garware, Garware filed a lawsuit in a U.S. court to collect the balance due. Garware claimed that the forum-selection clause did not apply to sales of warehoused goods, but the court sided with Intermax. Because the forum-selection clause was valid and enforceable, Garware had to bring its complaints against Intermax in a court in India.[9] ◀

If the contract does not specify a forum and choice of law, proceedings will be more complex and legally uncertain. Litigation may take place in two or more countries, with each country applying its own choice-of-law rules to determine the substantive law that will be applied to the particular transactions. Even if a plaintiff wins a favorable judgment in its own country, there is no way to predict whether courts in the defendant's country will enforce the judgment.

SECTION 5
U.S. LAWS IN A GLOBAL CONTEXT

The globalization of business raises questions about the extraterritorial application of a nation's laws—that is, the effect of the country's laws outside its boundaries. To what extent do U.S. domestic laws apply to other nations' businesses? To what extent do U.S. domestic laws apply to U.S. firms doing business abroad? Here, we discuss the extraterritorial application of certain U.S. laws, including antitrust laws, tort laws, and laws prohibiting employment discrimination.

U.S. Antitrust Laws

U.S. antitrust laws have a wide application. They may *subject* firms in foreign nations to their provisions, as well as *protect* foreign consumers and competitors from violations committed by U.S. citizens. Section 1 of the Sherman Act—the most important U.S. antitrust law—provides for the extraterritorial effect of the U.S. antitrust laws.

The United States is a major proponent of free competition in the global economy. Thus, any conspiracy that has a *substantial effect* on U.S. commerce is within the reach of the Sherman Act. The law applies even if the violation occurs outside the United States, and foreign governments as well as businesses can be sued for violations. Before U.S. courts will exercise jurisdiction and apply antitrust laws, however, it

must be shown that the alleged violation had a substantial effect on U.S. commerce.

▶ **Example 24.10** An investigation by the U.S. government revealed that a Tokyo-based auto-parts supplier, Furukawa Electric Company, and its executives conspired with competitors in an international price-fixing agreement (an agreement to set prices). The agreement lasted more than ten years and resulted in automobile manufacturers paying noncompetitive higher prices for parts in cars sold to U.S. consumers. Because the conspiracy had a substantial effect on U.S. commerce, the United States had jurisdiction to prosecute the case. In 2011, Furukawa agreed to plead guilty and pay a $200 million fine. The Furukawa executives from Japan also agreed to serve up to eighteen months in a U.S. prison and to cooperate fully with the ongoing investigation. ◀

International Tort Claims

The international application of tort liability is growing in significance and controversy. An increasing number of U.S. plaintiffs are suing foreign (or U.S.) entities for torts that these entities have allegedly committed overseas. Often, these cases involve human rights violations by foreign governments. The Alien Tort Claims Act (ATCA),[10] allows even foreign citizens to bring civil suits in U.S. courts for injuries caused by violations of the law of nations or a treaty of the United States.

Since 1980, foreign plaintiffs have increasingly used this act to bring actions against companies operating in nations such as Colombia, Ecuador, Egypt, Guatemala, India, Indonesia, Nigeria, and Saudi Arabia. Some of these cases have involved alleged environmental destruction. Others have involved human rights violations.[11] In addition, mineral companies in Southeast Asia have been sued for collaborating with oppressive government regimes.

In the following *Spotlight Case,* the United States Supreme Court considers the parameters of the ATCA (which the Court refers to as the Alien Tort Statute, or ATS). The question is whether the statute allows courts to recognize a cause of action for violations of the law of nations occurring within the territory of a sovereign other than the United States.

9. *Garware Polyester, Ltd. v. Intermax Trading Corp.,* 2001 WL 1035134 (S.D.N.Y. 2001).

10. 28 U.S.C. Section 1350.
11. See, for example, *Khulumani v. Barclay National Bank, Ltd.,* 504 F.3d 254 (2007), in which plaintiffs claimed that hundreds of corporations allegedly "aided and abetted" the government of South Africa in maintaining its apartheid (racially discriminatory) regime.

SP TLIGHT on International Torts

Case 24.3   Kiobel v. Royal Dutch Petroleum Co.
Supreme Court of the United States, ___ U.S. ___, 133 S.Ct. 1659, ___ L.Ed. ___ (2013).

BACKGROUND AND FACTS Shell Petroleum Development Company of Nigeria, Ltd. (SPDC), a Nigerian firm, engaged in oil exploration and production in Ogoniland, Nigeria. When some Ogoni residents protested the environmental effects of SPDC's practices, the Nigerian government violently suppressed the demonstrations. Some protesters who were granted political asylum in the United States filed a suit in a federal district court against Royal Dutch Petroleum Company (a Dutch firm and one of SPDC's parent companies) under the Alien Tort Statute (ATS). The petitioners alleged that the respondents aided and abetted Nigerian military and police atrocities, which violated the law of nations. The court dismissed parts of the complaint. On appeal, the U.S. Court of Appeals for the Second Circuit dismissed the entire complaint. The petitioners appealed.

IN THE LANGUAGE OF THE COURT
Chief Justice *ROBERTS* delivered the opinion of the Court.

* * * *

* * * A canon of statutory interpretation known as the presumption against extraterritorial application * * * provides that when a statute gives no clear indication of an extraterritorial application, it has none and reflects *the presumption that United States law governs domestically but does not rule the world.* [Emphasis added.]

This presumption serves to protect against unintended clashes between our laws and those of other nations [that] could result in international discord.

* * * *

Petitioners contend that even if the presumption applies, the text, history, and purposes of the ATS rebut it for causes of action brought under that statute.

[But] nothing in the text of the statute suggests that Congress intended causes of action recognized under it to have extraterritorial reach. *The ATS covers actions by aliens for violations of the law of nations, but that does not imply extraterritorial reach—such violations affecting aliens can occur either within or outside the United States.* [Emphasis added.]

* * * *

Nor does the historical background against which the ATS was enacted overcome the presumption * * * . When Congress passed the ATS, three principal offenses against the law of nations had been identified * * * : violation of safe conducts, infringement of the rights of ambassadors, and piracy.

* * * *

* * * Prominent contemporary examples [of the first two offenses that occurred in the United States] provide no support for the proposition that Congress expected causes of action to be brought under the statute for violations of the law of nations occurring abroad.

* * * Piracy typically occurs on the high seas, beyond the territorial jurisdiction of the United States or any other country.

Applying U.S. law to pirates, however, does not typically impose the sovereign will of the United States onto conduct occurring within the territorial jurisdiction of another sovereign, and therefore carries less direct foreign policy consequences.

* * * *

Finally, there is no indication that the ATS was passed to make the United States a uniquely hospitable forum for the enforcement of international norms. * * * Indeed, the parties offer no evidence that any nation, meek or mighty, presumed to do such a thing.

DECISION AND REMEDY *The United States Supreme Court affirmed the lower court's judgment. The presumption against extraterritoriality applies to claims under the ATS, nothing in the statute rebuts that presumption, and all the conduct about which the petitioners complained took place outside the United States.*

THE LEGAL ENVIRONMENT DIMENSION *What are the ramifications for the respondents of the ruling in this case?*

THE GLOBAL DIMENSION *If the Court had adopted the petitioners' view, how might U.S. citizens have been affected?*

Antidiscrimination Laws

As you probably already know, federal laws in the United States prohibit discrimination on the basis of race, color, national origin, religion, gender, age, and disability. These laws, as they affect employment relationships, generally apply extraterritorially.

▶ **Example 24.11** The Age Discrimination in Employment Act protects U.S. employees working abroad for U.S. employers. The Americans with Disabilities Act, which requires employers to accommodate the needs of workers with disabilities, also applies to U.S. nationals working abroad for U.S. firms. ◀

In addition, the major U.S. law regulating employment discrimination—Title VII of the Civil Rights Act of 1964—also applies extraterritorially to all U.S. employees working for U.S. employers abroad. Generally, U.S. employers must abide by U.S. discrimination laws unless to do so would violate the laws of the country where their workplaces are located. This "foreign laws exception" allows employers to avoid being subjected to conflicting laws.

Reviewing: International Law in a Global Economy

Robco, Inc., was a Florida arms dealer. The armed forces of Honduras contracted to purchase weapons from Robco over a six-year period. After the government was replaced and a democracy installed, the Honduran government sought to reduce the size of its military, and its relationship with Robco deteriorated. Honduras refused to honor the contract and purchase the inventory of arms, which Robco could sell only at a much lower price. Robco filed a suit in a federal district court in the United States to recover damages for this breach of contract by the government of Honduras. Using the information presented in the chapter, answer the following questions.

1. Should the Foreign Sovereign Immunities Act (FSIA) preclude this lawsuit? Why or why not?
2. Does the act of state doctrine bar Robco from seeking to enforce the contract? Explain.
3. Suppose that prior to this lawsuit, the new government of Honduras had enacted a law making it illegal to purchase weapons from foreign arms dealers. What doctrine of deference might lead a U.S. court to dismiss Robco's case in that situation?
4. Now suppose that the U.S. court hears the case and awards damages to Robco, but the government of Honduras has no assets in the United States that can be used to satisfy the judgment. Under which doctrine might Robco be able to collect the damages by asking another nation's court to enforce the U.S. judgment?

DEBATE THIS . . . *The U.S. federal courts are accepting too many lawsuits initiated by foreigners that concern matters not relevant to this country.*

Terms and Concepts

act of state doctrine 458

civil law system 456

comity 456

confiscation 458

distribution agreement 459

dumping 462

export 459

expropriation 458

international law 453

international organization 454

national law 453

normal trade relations (NTR) status 462

quota 461

sovereign immunity 458

tariff 462

treaty 454

ExamPrep

Issue Spotters

1. Café Rojo, Ltd., an Ecuadoran firm, agrees to sell coffee beans to Dark Roast Coffee Company, a U.S. firm. Dark Roast accepts the beans but refuses to pay. Café Rojo sues Dark Roast in an Ecuadoran court and is awarded damages, but Dark Roast's assets are in the United States. Under what circumstances would a U.S. court enforce the judgment of the Ecuadoran court? **(See page 456.)**

2. Gems International, Ltd., is a foreign firm that has a 12 percent share of the U.S. market for diamonds. To capture a larger share, Gems offers its products at a below-cost discount to U.S. buyers (and inflates the prices in its own country to make up the difference).

How can this attempt to undersell U.S. businesses be defeated? **(See page 462.)**

- **Check your answers to the Issue Spotters against the answers provided in Appendix E at the end of this text.**

Before the Test

Go to **www.cengagebrain.com**, enter the ISBN 9781285185248, and click on "Find" to locate this textbook's Web site. Then, click on "Access Now" under "Study Tools," and select Chapter 24 at the top. There, you will find a Practice Quiz that you can take to assess your mastery of the concepts in this chapter, as well as Flashcards and a Glossary of important terms.

Business Scenarios

24–1. Doing Business Internationally. Macrotech, Inc., develops an innovative computer chip and obtains a patent on it. The firm markets the chip under the trade-marked brand name "Flash." Macrotech wants to sell the chip to Nitron, Ltd., in Pacifica, a foreign country. Macrotech is concerned, however, that after an initial purchase, Nitron will duplicate the chip, pirate it, and sell the pirated version to computer manufacturers in Pacifica. To avoid this possibility, Macrotech could establish its own manufacturing facility in Pacifica, but it does not want to do this. How can Macrotech, without establishing a manufacturing facility in Pacifica, protect Flash from being pirated by Nitron? **(See page 459.)**

24–2. Dumping. The U.S. pineapple industry alleged that producers of canned pineapple from the Philippines were selling their canned pineapple in the United States for less than its fair market value (dumping). The Philippine producers also exported other products, such as pineapple juice and juice concentrate. These products used separate parts of the same fresh pineapple, so they shared raw material costs with the canned fruit, according to the producers' own financial records. To determine fair value and antidumping duties, the pineapple industry argued that a court should calculate the Philippine producers' cost of

production and allocate a portion of the shared fruit costs to the canned fruit. The result of this allocation showed that more than 90 percent of the canned fruit sales were below the cost of production. Is this a reasonable approach to determining the production costs and fair market value of canned pineapple in the United States? Why or why not? **(See page 462.)**

24–3. Sovereign Immunity. Taconic Plastics, Ltd., is a manufacturer incorporated in Ireland with its principal place of business in New York. Taconic enters into a contract with a German firm, Werner Voss Architects and Engineers, acting as an agent for the government of Saudi Arabia. The contract calls for Taconic to supply special material for tents designed to shelter religious pilgrims visiting holy sites in Saudi Arabia. Most of the material is made in, and shipped from, New York. The German company does not pay Taconic and files for bankruptcy. Taconic files a suit in a U.S. court against the government of Saudi Arabia, seeking to collect $3 million. The defendant files a motion to dismiss the suit based on the doctrine of sovereign immunity. Under what circumstances does this doctrine apply? What are its exceptions? Should this suit be dismissed? Explain. **(See page 458.)**

Business Case Problems

24–4. Dumping. Nuclear power plants use low-enriched uranium (LEU) as a fuel. LEU consists of feed uranium enriched by energy to a certain assay—the percentage of the isotope necessary for a nuclear reaction. The amount of energy required is described by an industry standard as a "separative work unit" (SWU). A nuclear utility may buy LEU from an enricher, or the utility may provide an enricher with feed uranium and pay for the SWUs necessary to produce LEU. Under an SWU contract, the LEU returned to the utility may not be exactly the uranium the utility provided. This is because feed uranium is fungible and trades like a commodity (such as wheat or corn), and profitable enrichment requires the constant processing of undifferentiated stock. Foreign enrichers, including Eurodif, S.A., allegedly exported LEU to the United States and sold it for "less than fair value." Did this constitute dumping? Explain. If so, what could be done to prevent it? [*United States v. Eurodif, S.A.,* 555 U.S. 305, 129 S.Ct. 878, 172 L.Ed.2d 679 (2009)] **(See page 462.)**

24–5. International Agreements and Jurisdiction. U.S. citizens who were descendants of victims of the Holocaust (the mass murder of 6 million Jews by the Nazis during World War II) in Europe filed a claim for breach of contract in the United States against an Italian insurance company, Assicurazioni Generali, S.P.A. (Generali). Before the Holocaust, the plaintiffs' ancestors had purchased insurance policies from Generali, but Generali refused to pay them benefits under the policies. Due to certain agreements among nations after World War II, such lawsuits could not be filed for many years. In 2000, however, the United States agreed that Germany could establish a foundation—the International Commission on Holocaust-Era Insurance Claims, or ICHEIC—that would compensate victims who had suffered losses at the hands of the Germans during the war. Whenever a German company was sued in a U.S. court based on a Holocaust-era claim, the U.S. government would inform the court that the matter should be referred to the ICHEIC as the exclusive forum and remedy for the resolution. There was no such agreement with Italy, however, so the federal district court dismissed the suit. The plaintiffs appealed. Did the plaintiffs have to take their claim to the ICHEIC rather than sue in a U.S. court? Why or why not? [*In re Assicurazioni Generali, S.P.A.,* 592 F.3d 113 (2d Cir. 2010)] **(See page 458.)**

24–6. BUSINESS CASE PROBLEM WITH SAMPLE ANSWER: Sovereign Immunity.

 Bell Helicopter Textron, Inc., designs, makes, and sells helicopters with distinctive and famous trade dress that identifies them as Bell aircraft. Bell also owns the helicopters' design patents. Bell's Model 206 Series includes the Jet Ranger. Thirty-six years after Bell developed the Jet Ranger, the Islamic Republic of Iran began to make and sell counterfeit Model 206 Series helicopters and

parts. Iran's counterfeit versions—the Shahed 278 and the Shahed 285—used Bell's trade dress (see Chapter 8). The Shahed aircraft was promoted at an international air show in Iran to aircraft customers. Bell filed a suit in a U.S. district court against Iran, alleging violations of trademark and patent laws. Is Iran—a foreign nation—exempt in these circumstances from the jurisdiction of U.S. courts? Explain. [Bell Helicopter Textron, Inc. v. Islamic Republic of Iran, 764 F.Supp.2d 122 (D.D.C. 2011)] **(See page 458.)**

• For a sample answer to Problem 24–6, go to Appendix F at the end of this text.

24–7. Commercial Activity Exception. Technology Incubation and Entrepreneurship Training Society (TIETS) entered into a joint-venture agreement with Mandana Farhang and M.A. Mobile to develop and market certain technology for commercial purposes. Farhang and M.A. Mobile filed a suit in a federal district court in California, where they both were based, alleging claims under the joint-venture agreement and a related nondisclosure agreement. The parties agreed that TIETS was a "foreign state" covered by the Foreign Sovereign Immunities Act (FSIA) because it was a part of the Indian government. Nevertheless, Farhang and M.A. Mobile argued that TIETS did not enjoy sovereign immunity because it had engaged in a commercial activity that has a direct effect in the United States. Could TIETS still be subject to the jurisdiction of U.S. courts under the commercial activities exception even though the joint venture was to take place outside the United States? If so, how? [*Farhang v. Indian Institute of Technology,* 2012 WL113739 (N.D.Cal. 2012)] **(See page 458.)**

24–8. Sovereign Immunity. In 1954, the government of Bolivia began expropriating land from Francisco Loza for public projects, including an international airport. The government directed the payment of compensation in exchange for at least some of his land. But the government never paid the full amount. Decades later, his heirs, Genoveva and Marcel Loza, who were both U.S. citizens, filed a suit in a federal district court in the United States against the government of Bolivia, seeking damages for the taking. Can the court exercise jurisdiction? Explain. [*Santivanez v. Estado Plurinacional de Bolivia,* 2013 WL 879983 (11th Cir. 2013)] **(See page 458.)**

24–9. A QUESTION OF ETHICS: Terrorism.

 On December 21, 1988, Pan Am Flight 103 exploded 31,000 feet in the air over Lockerbie, Scotland, killing all 259 passengers and crew on board and 11 people on the ground. Among those killed was Roger Hurst, a U.S. citizen. An investigation determined that a portable radio-cassette player packed in a brown Samsonite suitcase smuggled onto the plane was the source of the explosion. The explosive device was constructed with a digital timer specially made for, and bought by, Libya.

Abdel Basset Ali Al-Megrahi, a Libyan government official and an employee of the Libyan Arab Airline (LAA), was convicted by the Scottish High Court of Justiciary on criminal charges that he planned and executed the bombing in association with members of the Jamahiriya Security Organization (JSO) (an agency of the Libyan government that performed security and intelligence functions) or the Libyan military. Members of the victims' families filed a suit in a U.S. district court against the JSO, the LAA, Al-Megrahi, and others. The plaintiffs claimed violations of U.S. federal law, including the Anti-Terrorism Act, and state law, including the intentional infliction of emotional distress. [Hurst v. Socialist People's Libyan Arab Jamahiriya, 474 F.Supp.2d 19 (D.D.C. 2007)] **(See page 458.)**

(a) Under what doctrine, codified in which federal statute, might the defendants claim to be immune from the jurisdiction of a U.S. court? Should this law include an exception for "state-sponsored terrorism"? Why or why not?

(b) The defendants agreed to pay $2.7 billion, or $10 million per victim, to settle all claims for "compensatory death damages." The families of eleven victims, including Hurst, were excluded from the settlement because they were "not wrongful death beneficiaries under applicable state law." These plaintiffs continued the suit. The defendants filed a motion to dismiss. Should the motion be granted on the ground that the settlement bars the plaintiffs' claims? Explain.

Legal Reasoning Group Activity

24–10. Globalization. Assume that you are manufacturing iPad accessories and that your business is becoming more successful. You are now considering expanding operations into another country. **(See page 459.)**

(a) One group will explore the costs and benefits of advertising on the Internet.

(b) Another group will consider whether to take in a partner from a foreign nation and will explain the benefits and risks of having a foreign partner.

(c) A third group will discuss what problems may arise if you want to manufacture in a foreign location.

UNIT FOUR Focus on Ethics

Domestic and International Sales and Lease Contracts

Transactions involving the sale or lease of goods make up a great deal of the business activity in the commercial and manufacturing sectors of our economy. Articles 2 and 2A of the Uniform Commercial Code (UCC) govern the sale or lease of goods in every state except Louisiana. Many of the UCC's provisions express our ethical standards.

Good Faith and Commercial Reasonableness

The concepts of good faith and commercial reasonableness permeate the UCC and help to prevent unethical behavior by businesspersons. These two key concepts are read into every contract and impose certain duties on all parties. Additionally, reasonableness in the formation, performance, and termination of contracts underlies almost all of the UCC's provisions.

As an example, consider the UCC's approach to open terms. Section 2–311(1) states that when a term is to be specified by one of the parties, "any such specification must be made in within limits set by commercial reasonableness." The requirement of commercial reasonableness means that the term subsequently supplied by one party should not come as a surprise to the other. The party filling in the missing term may not use the opportunity to take advantage of the other party. For instance, the party may not add a term that will be beneficial to himself or herself (and detrimental to the other party) and then demand that the other party perform the contract.

Under the UCC, the party filling in the missing term is not allowed to deviate from what is commercially reasonable in the context of the transaction. Courts frequently look to course of dealing, usage of trade, and the surrounding circumstances in determining what is commercially reasonable in a given situation.

LEGAL REASONING

1. *How can a court objectively measure good faith and commercial reasonableness?*

Good Faith in Output and Requirements Contracts The obligation of good faith is particularly important in so-called output and requirements contracts. UCC 2–306 states that "quantity" in these contracts "means such actual output or requirements as may occur in good faith." For example, Mandrow's Machines, which assembles personal computers, has a requirements contract with Advanced Tech Circuit Boards, under which Advanced Tech is to supply Mandrow's with all of the circuit boards it needs. If Mandrow's suddenly quadruples the size of its business, it cannot insist that Advanced Tech supply all of its requirements, as specified in the original contract.

As another example, assume that the market price of the goods subject to a requirements contract rises rapidly and

dramatically because of an extreme shortage of materials necessary to their production. The buyer could claim that she needs all of the seller's output and buy the entire output at the contract price (which is substantially below the market price). Then, the buyer could turn around and sell the goods that she does not need at the higher market price. Under the UCC, this type of unethical behavior is prohibited, even though the buyer in this instance has not technically breached the contract.

Bad Faith Not Required for Breach A party can breach the obligation of good faith under the UCC even if the party did not show "bad faith"—that is, even when there is no proof that the party was dishonest. For example, a large manufacturer of recreational boats, Genmar Holdings, Inc., purchased Horizon, a small company that produced a particular type of fishing boat. At the time of the purchase, Genmar promised that Horizon boats would be the company's "champion" and vowed to keep Horizon's key employees on as managers. The contract required Genmar to pay Horizon a lump sum in cash and also to pay "earn-out consideration" under a specified formula for five years. The "earn-out" amount would depend on the number of Horizon brand boats sold and on annual gross revenues.

One year after the sale, Genmar renamed the Horizon brand boats "Nova" and told employees to give priority to producing Genmar brand boats over the Nova boats. Because the Genmar boats were more difficult and time consuming to make than the Nova boats, gross revenues and production decreased, and Genmar was not required to pay the "earn-out" amounts. Eventually, Genmar fired the former Horizon employees and stopped manufacturing the Nova boats entirely. The former employees filed a suit alleging that Genmar had breached the implied covenant of good faith and fair dealing. Genmar argued that it could not have violated good faith because there was no proof that it had engaged in fraud, deceit, or misrepresentation. The court held for the plaintiffs, however, and the decision was affirmed on appeal.[1] It is possible for a party to breach its good faith obligations under the UCC even if the party did not engage in fraud, deceit, or misrepresentation.

Commercial Reasonableness Under the UCC, the concept of good faith is closely linked to commercial reasonableness. All commercial actions—including the performance and enforcement of contract obligations—must display commercial reasonableness. A merchant is expected to act in a reasonable manner according to reasonable commercial customs. The reliance of the UCC's drafters on commercial customs, or usage of trade, as a guideline to reasonable behavior in a given trade or

---

1. *O'Tool v. Genmar Holdings, Inc.,* 387 F.3d 1188 (10th Cir. 2004).

FOCUS ON ETHICS CONTINUES ▶

industry indicates the importance of good faith and commercial reasonableness in sales law.

The concept of commercial reasonableness is clearly expressed in the doctrine of commercial impracticability, which is related to the common law doctrine of impossibility of performance. Under the commercial impracticability doctrine, a party's nonperformance of a contractual obligation may be excused when performance of the contract becomes impracticable because of unforeseen circumstances. The courts make clear, however, that performance will not be excused under this doctrine unless the nonperforming party has made every reasonable effort to fulfill his or her obligations.

LEGAL REASONING

2. *Generally, the courts determine what constitutes "reasonable" behavior in disputes between contract parties over whether a party has demonstrated commercial reasonableness. Should the UCC be more specific in defining what will be deemed reasonable in particular circumstances so that the courts do not have to decide the issue? Why or why not?*

The Concept of the Good Faith Purchaser

The concept of the good faith purchaser reflects the UCC's emphasis on protecting innocent parties. Suppose, for example, that you innocently and in good faith purchase a boat for a fair market price from someone who appears to have good title. Under the UCC, you are protected from the possibility that the real owner—from whom the seller may have fraudulently obtained the boat—will later appear and demand his boat back. (Note that nothing prevents the true owner from bringing suit against the party who defrauded him.)

Ethical questions arise, though, when both parties to a dispute over title to goods are good faith purchasers. For example, suppose that a car dealer purchases a used car in good faith for value and sells it to a customer, also a good faith purchaser. If it turns out that there was actually a lien on the vehicle and the true owner claims title to the car, which of these two good faith purchasers should lose out? Here, a court would likely look to trade usage for guidance. In one case involving this situation, the court noted that in the used-car industry, it is customary for the seller to reimburse the buyer when the seller cannot deliver good title to a vehicle. According to the court, this custom is consistent with public policy. Car dealers are better able than buyers to investigate irregularities in title, so the risk of forged title documents "can and should be borne by dealers rather than purchasers."[2]

Another ethical issue is raised when the purchaser of goods is not quite so innocent. Suppose that the purchaser

has reason to suspect that the seller may not have good title to the goods being sold but nonetheless goes ahead with the transaction because it is a "good deal." Has this buyer crossed the boundary that separates the good faith purchaser from one who purchases in bad faith? This boundary is important in the law of sales because the UCC will not be a refuge for those who purchase in bad faith. The term *good faith purchaser* means just that—one who purchases goods without knowing, or having any reason to know, that there is anything shady or illegal about the deal.

LEGAL REASONING

3. *Why does the UCC protect innocent persons (good faith purchasers) who buy goods from sellers with voidable title but not innocent persons who buy goods from sellers with void title?*

Unconscionability

The doctrine of unconscionability is a good example of how the law attempts to enforce ethical behavior. This doctrine suggests that some contracts may be so unfair to one party as to be unenforceable, even though that party originally agreed to the contract's terms. Under UCC Section 2–302, a court will consider a contract's fairness and may hold that the contract or a clause in it was unconscionable at the time the contract was made. If a court makes such a determination, it may refuse to enforce the contract, enforce the contract without the unconscionable clause, or limit the clause's application so as to avoid an unconscionable result.

The Test for Unconscionability The UCC does not define the term *unconscionability*. The drafters of the UCC, however, have added explanatory comments to the relevant sections, and these comments serve as guidelines for applying the UCC. Comment 1 to Section 2–302 discusses the basic test for unconscionability. The test is whether, under the circumstances existing at the time of the contract's formation, the clause in question was so one sided as to be unconscionable. This test is to be applied against the general commercial background of the contract.

Unconscionability—A Case Example In one case applying Section 2–302, a New York appellate court held that an arbitration clause was unconscionable and refused to enforce it. Gateway 2000, Inc., which sold computers and software directly to consumers, included an arbitration clause in its retail agreements. The clause specified that any dispute arising out of the contract had to be arbitrated in Chicago, Illinois, in accordance with the arbitration rules of the International Chamber of Commerce (ICC).

A number of consumers who had purchased Gateway products became incensed when they learned that the ICC

---

2. *Superior, Inc. v. Arrington,* 2009 Ark.App. 875 (2009).

rules required advance fees of $4,000 (more than the cost of most Gateway products). Furthermore, the $2,000 registration fee was nonrefundable—even if the consumer prevailed at the arbitration. Additionally, the consumers would have to pay travel expenses to Chicago. In the class-action litigation against Gateway that followed, the New York court agreed with the consumers that the "egregiously [flagrantly] oppressive" arbitration clause was unconscionable. The clause barred consumers from resorting to the courts and made arbitration financially prohibitive, leaving consumers "with no forum at all in which to resolve a dispute."[3]

Warranties

A seller or lessor has not only a legal obligation to provide safe products but also an ethical one. When faced with the possibility of increasing safety at no extra cost, every ethical businessperson will certainly opt for a safer product. An ethical issue arises, however, when producing a safer product means higher costs. To some extent, our warranty laws serve to protect consumers from sellers who may be tempted to neglect ethical concerns if what they are doing is both legal and profitable.

Express and Implied Warranties The UCC recognizes both express and implied warranties. Under UCC 2–314 and 2A–212, goods sold by a merchant or leased by a lessor must be fit for the ordinary purposes for which such goods are used, be of proper quality, and be properly labeled and packaged.

The UCC injects greater fairness into contractual situations by recognizing descriptions as express warranties. Hence, a seller or lessor of goods may be held to have breached a contract if the goods fail to conform to the description. In this way, the UCC acknowledges that a buyer or lessee may often reasonably believe that a seller or lessor is warranting his or her product, even though the word *warrant* or *guarantee* was not used. Thus, the law imposes an ethical obligation on sellers and lessors in a statutory form.

Warranty Disclaimers The UCC requirement that warranty disclaimers be sufficiently conspicuous to catch the eye of a reasonable purchaser is based on the ethical premise that sellers of goods should not take advantage of unwary consumers. Buyers may not always read the "fine print" on standard purchase order forms. As discussed in Chapter 23, if a seller's or lessor's warranty disclaimer fails to meet the specific requirements imposed by the UCC, the warranties will not be effectively disclaimed. Before the UCC was adopted by the states, purchasers of automobiles frequently signed standard-form purchase agreements drafted by the auto manufacturer without learning the meaning of all the fine print until later.

Freedom of Contract versus Freedom from Contract— Revisited Although freedom of contract reflects a basic ethical principle in our society, courts have made it clear that when such freedom leads to gross unfairness, it should be curbed. (Several examples of the exceptions to freedom of contract that courts will make were offered in the *Focus on Ethics* feature at the end of Unit Three.)

Nonetheless, before the UCC was in effect, courts generally would not intervene in cases involving warranty disclaimers in fine print or otherwise "hidden" in a standard purchase order form. Exceptions were made only when the resulting unfairness "shocked the conscience" of the court. By establishing specific requirements for warranty disclaimers, the UCC has made dealing fairly with buyers and lessees—already an ethical obligation of all sellers and lessors—a legal obligation as well.

Today, if a warranty disclaimer unfairly "surprises" a purchaser or a lessee, chances are that the disclaimer was not sufficiently conspicuous. In this situation, the unfairness of the bargain need not be so great as to "shock the court's conscience" before a remedy will be granted.

LEGAL REASONING

4. *Review the UCC provisions that apply to the topics discussed in Chapters 20 through 23. Discuss fully how various UCC provisions, excluding the provisions discussed above, reflect social values and ethical standards.*

International Transactions

Conducting business internationally presents unique challenges including, at times, ethical challenges. This is understandable, given that laws and cultures vary from one country to another. Consider the role of women.

In the United States, equal employment opportunity is a fundamental public policy. This policy is clearly expressed in Title VII of the Civil Rights Act of 1964, which prohibits discrimination against women in the employment context. Some other countries, however, largely reject any professional role for women. Consequently, U.S. women conducting business transactions in those countries may encounter difficulties. For example, when the World Bank sent a delegation that included women to negotiate with the Central Bank of Korea, the Koreans were surprised and offended. They thought that the presence of women meant that the negotiations were not being taken seriously.

There are also some important ethical differences among nations. In Islamic countries, for example, the consumption of

---

3. *Brower v. Gateway 2000, Inc.*, 246 A.D.2d 246, 676 N.Y.S.2d 569 (1998). See also *DeFontes v. Dell, Inc.*, 984 A.2d 1061 (R.I. 2009).

FOCUS ON ETHICS CONTINUES ➡

alcohol and certain foods is forbidden by the Islamic religion. Thus, it would be thoughtless and imprudent to invite a Saudi Arabian business contact out for a drink.

Additionally, in many foreign nations, gift giving is a common practice between contracting companies or between companies and government officials. To Americans, such gift giving may look suspiciously like an unethical (and possibly illegal) bribe. This cultural difference has been an important source of friction in international business, particularly since the U.S. Congress passed the Foreign Corrupt Practices Act in 1977 (discussed in Chapters 5 and 10). This act prohibits U.S.

business firms from offering certain side payments to foreign officials to secure favorable contracts.

LEGAL REASONING

5. *Should U.S. firms doing business internationally send female employees to foreign nations that reject any role for women in business? Why or why not? How can a U.S. company accommodate the culture of foreign nations and still treat its own employees equally?*

UNIT FIVE

NEGOTIABLE INSTRUMENTS

CONTENTS

CHAPTER 25

THE FUNCTION AND CREATION OF NEGOTIABLE INSTRUMENTS

Most commercial transactions that take place in the modern business world would be inconceivable without negotiable instruments. A **negotiable instrument** is a signed writing (or electronic record) that contains an unconditional promise or order to pay an exact amount, either on demand or at a specific future time.

A negotiable instrument can function as a substitute for cash or as an extension of credit. The checks that you write are negotiable instruments that act as substitutes for cash. The promissory note that you probably signed to obtain an educational loan is a negotiable instrument that functions as an extension of credit.

For a negotiable instrument to operate *practically* as either a substitute for cash or a credit device, or both, it is essential that the instrument be *easily transferable without danger of being uncollectible*. This is a fundamental function of negotiable instruments. Each rule described in the following pages can be examined in light of this function.

The law governing negotiable instruments grew out of commercial necessity. In the medieval world, mer-chants developed their own set of rules, which eventually became known as the *Lex Mercatoria* (Law Merchant). The Law Merchant was later codified in England and is the forerunner of Article 3 of the Uniform Commercial Code (UCC). Article 3 imposes special requirements for the form and content of negotiable instruments, and also governs their negotiation, or transfer. Article 4 of the UCC, which governs bank depos-its and collections, will be covered in Chapter 28. Revised Articles 3 and 4 are included in their entirety in Appendix C.

SECTION 1
TYPES OF NEGOTIABLE INSTRUMENTS

UCC 3–104(b) defines an *instrument* as a "negotiable instrument."[1] For that reason, whenever the term *instrument* is used in this book, it refers to a negotiable instrument. Negotiable instruments are also some-times referred to as *commercial paper*.

The UCC specifies four types of negotiable instru-ments: *drafts*, *checks*, *notes*, and *certificates of deposit* (CDs). These instruments, which are summarized briefly in Exhibit 25–1 on the following page, fre-quently are divided into two classifications: *orders to pay* (drafts and checks) and *promises to pay* (promis-

sory notes and CDs). We will discuss both classifica-tions in the following subsections.

Negotiable instruments may also be classified as either demand instruments or time instruments. A *demand instrument* is payable on demand—that is, it is payable immediately after it is issued and thereaf-ter for a reasonable period of time.[2] **Issue** is "the first delivery of an instrument by the maker or drawer . . . for the purpose of giving rights on the instrument to any person" [UCC 3–105]. All checks are demand instruments because, by definition, they must be payable on demand. A *time instrument* is payable at a future date.

---

1. Note that all of the references to Article 3 of the UCC in this chapter are to the 1990 version of Article 3, which has been adopted by al-most all of the states.

2. "A promise or order is 'payable on demand' if it (i) states that it is payable on demand or at sight, or otherwise indicates that it is pay-able at the will of the holder, or (ii) does not state any time of pay-ment" [UCC 3–108(a)]. The UCC defines a *holder* as "the person in possession of a negotiable instrument that is payable either to bearer or to an identified person [who] is the person in possession" [UCC 1–201(21)(A)]. The term *bearer* will be defined later in this chapter.

EXHIBIT 25–1 Basic Types of Negotiable Instruments

Instruments	Characteristics	Parties
ORDERS TO PAY Draft	An order by one person to another person or to bearer [UCC 3–104(e)].	*Drawer*—The person who signs or makes the order to pay [UCC 3–103(a)(3)].
Check	A draft drawn on a bank and payable on demand [UCC 3–104(f)].ª (With certain types of checks, such as cashier's checks, the bank is both the drawer and the drawee—see Chapter 28 for details.)	*Drawee*—The person to whom the order to pay is made [UCC 3–103(a)(2)]. *Payee*—The person to whom payment is ordered.
PROMISES TO PAY Promissory note	A promise by one party to pay money to another party or to bearer [UCC 3–104(e)].	*Maker*—The person who promises to pay [UCC 3–103(a)(5)].
Certificate of deposit	A note made by a bank acknowledging a deposit of funds made payable to the holder of the note [UCC 3–104(j)].	*Payee*—The person to whom the promise is made.

a. Under UCC 4–105(1), banks include savings banks, savings and loan associations, credit unions, and trust companies (organizations that perform the fiduciary functions of trusts and agencies).

Drafts and Checks (Orders to Pay)

A **draft** is an unconditional written order that involves *three parties*. The party creating the draft (the **drawer**) orders another party (the **drawee**) to pay money, usually to a third party (the **payee**). The most common type of draft is a check, but drafts other than checks may be used in commercial transactions.

TIME DRAFTS AND SIGHT DRAFTS A *time draft* is payable at a definite future time. A *sight draft* (or demand draft) is payable on sight—that is, when it is presented to the drawee (usually a bank or financial institution) for payment. A sight draft may be payable on acceptance.

Acceptance is the drawee's written promise to pay the draft when it comes due. Usually, an instrument is accepted by writing the word *accepted* across its face, followed by the date of acceptance and the signature of the drawee. A draft can be both a time and a sight draft. Such a draft is payable at a stated time after sight. An example would be a draft that states that it is payable ninety days after sight.

Exhibit 25–2 on the following page shows a typical time draft. For the drawee to be obligated to honor the order, the drawee must be obligated to the drawer either by agreement or through a debtor-creditor relationship. ▶ **Example 25.1** On January 16, OurTown Real Estate orders $1,000 worth of office supplies from Eastman Supply Company, with

payment due April 16. Also on January 16, OurTown sends Eastman a draft drawn on its account with the First National Bank of Whiteacre as payment. In this scenario, the drawer is OurTown, the drawee is OurTown's bank (First National Bank of Whiteacre), and the payee is Eastman Supply Company. First National Bank is obligated to honor the draft because of its account agreement with OurTown Real Estate. ◀

TRADE ACCEPTANCES A trade acceptance is a type of draft that is frequently used in the sale of goods. In a **trade acceptance,** the seller of the goods is both the drawer and the payee. The buyer to whom credit is extended is the drawee. Essentially, the draft orders the buyer to pay a specified amount to the seller, usually at a stated time in the future.

▶ **Example 25.2** Jackson Street Bistro buys its restaurant supplies from Osaka Industries. When Jackson requests supplies, Osaka creates a draft ordering Jackson to pay Osaka for the supplies within ninety days and sends it along with the supplies. When the supplies arrive, Jackson accepts the draft by signing its face and is then obligated to make the payment. This signed draft is a trade acceptance and can be sold to a third party if Osaka needs cash before the payment is due. (Osaka would sell the draft through the *commercial money market*—the market that businesses use for short-term borrowing.) ◀

EXHIBIT 25-2 A Typical Time Draft

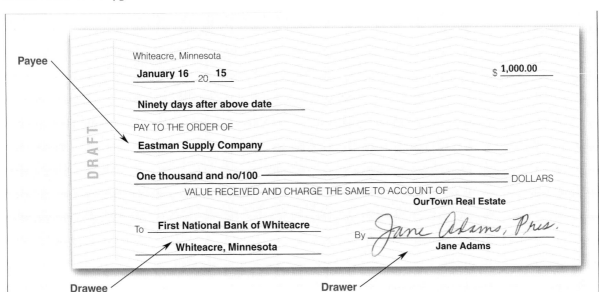

When a draft orders the buyer's bank to pay, it is called a **banker's acceptance.** Banker's acceptances are commonly used in international trade.

CHECKS As mentioned, the most commonly used type of draft is a **check.** (Although fewer checks are written today and most transactions are electronic, checks are still more common than promissory notes or other types of negotiable instruments.) The writer of the check is the drawer, the bank on which the check is drawn is the drawee, and the person to whom the check is made payable is the payee.

Checks are demand instruments because they are payable on demand. For a discussion of how payments made via smartphones can replace checks and also promote sustainability, see this chapter's *Insight into E-Commerce* feature on page 480.

Checks will be discussed more fully in Chapter 28, but it should be noted here that with certain types of checks, such as *cashier's checks,* the bank is both the drawer and the drawee. The bank customer purchases a cashier's check from the bank by paying the amount of the check and indicating to whom the check should be made payable. The bank, not the customer, is the drawer of the check, as well as the drawee. A cashier's check functions the same as cash because the bank has committed itself to paying the stated amount on demand.

Promissory Notes (Promises to Pay)

A **promissory note** is a written promise made by one person (the **maker** of the promise) to pay another (usually a payee) a specified sum. A promissory note, which is often referred to simply as a *note,* can be made payable at a definite time or on demand. It can name a specific payee or merely be payable to bearer (bearer instruments will be discussed later in this chapter).

▶ **Example 25.3** On April 30, Laurence and Margaret Roberts, who are called co-makers, sign a writing unconditionally promising to pay "to the order of" the First National Bank of Whiteacre $3,000 (with 8 percent interest) on or before June 29. This writing is a promissory note. ◀ A typical promissory note is shown in Exhibit 25–3 on page 481.

Of course, a promissory note is not a debt—it is only the evidence of a debt. But does the loss of a note affect the rights of the owner? That was the question in the following case.

CASE 25.1

Silicon Valley Bank v. Miracle Faith World Outreach, Inc.

Appellate Court of Connecticut, 140 Conn.App. 827, 60 A.3d 343 (2013).

COMPANY PROFILE Miracle Faith World Outreach, Inc., a Connecticut religious corporation, was founded by Bobby and Christine Davis in 1964. The Miracle Faith World Outreach Church started with prayer meetings in Christine's mother's home in Stamford. As its numbers grew, the church expanded first into the basement of a three-family house and later into churches in Springdale and Stamford before buying a new facility in Monroe. The twenty-acre property included a two-story church building and a fellowship hall totaling more than twenty thousand square feet.

BACKGROUND AND FACTS Miracle Faith World Outreach borrowed $1,962,000 to buy the buildings and land in Monroe, and signed a note payable to Silicon Valley Bank in Santa Clara, California. In the seventh year of the note's ten-year term, with more than $1,600,000 owing on the principal and almost $60,000 owing on unpaid interest, Miracle Faith defaulted. Silicon Valley filed an action in a Connecticut state court to foreclose. Eugene Wong, an associate at the bank, provided the court with only a copy of the note. Wong said that he had looked for the original at several of the bank's offices and at a third-party storage facility, but was unable to find it. On appeal from a judgment in the bank's favor, Miracle Faith argued that "the court abused its discretion by determining that the plaintiff was the owner and holder of the note" even though the bank could produce only a copy.

IN THE LANGUAGE OF THE COURT
BEACH, J. [Judge]

* * * *

*A bill or note is not a debt; it is only primary evidence of a debt; and where this is lost, impaired or destroyed bona fide, it may be supplied by secondary evidence * * * . The loss of a bill or note alters not the rights of the owner, but merely renders secondary evidence necessary and proper.* [Emphasis added.]

The Uniform Commercial Code * * * addresses situations * * * where the instrument sought to be enforced is unavailable, by creating an exception to the general rule that one must hold an instrument in order to enforce its payment. General Statutes Section 42a–3–309(a) [Connecticut's version of UCC 3–309(a)] provides:

"A person not in possession of an instrument is entitled to enforce the instrument if (i) the person was in possession of the instrument and entitled to enforce it when loss of possession occurred, (ii) the loss of possession was not the result of a transfer by the person or a lawful seizure, and (iii) the person cannot reasonably obtain possession of the instrument because the instrument was destroyed, its whereabouts cannot be determined, or it is in the wrongful possession of an unknown person or a person that cannot be found or is not amenable to service of process."

Here, the court found that the plaintiff had sustained its burden of showing that the note was lost and that the copy it produced was authentic.

The plaintiff established that it had entered into a transaction including a promissory note secured by a mortgage, a term loan agreement, and a mortgage with the defendant. Wong testified that ordinarily the original note would have been kept in the plaintiff's California headquarters. After a period of time, it would have been sent to a third-party storage facility. Wong testified that he checked "all the places where the note could possibly be," but he was unable to locate it. Although the original was lost, a copy of the note had been kept in the plaintiff's credit file for the subject loan. Although the defendant takes issue with the admission of the copy of the note, it does not claim that the copy was in any way inaccurate. The court, therefore, did not abuse its discretion in admitting a copy of the note.

DECISION AND REMEDY *A state intermediate appellate court concluded that the lower court did not abuse its discretion in admitting a copy of the note and affirmed the judgment. A note is not a debt—it is*

CASE 25.1 CONTINUES ➧

CASE 25.1 CONTINUED *only evidence of a debt—and its loss does not alter the rights of the owner. The bank showed that the note was lost and that the copy it produced was authentic.*

THE LEGAL ENVIRONMENT DIMENSION *Wong testified that he had looked for the note at a third-party storage facility. If the note had been found there, would that mean that the note had been "transferred" to the facility, making the storage company the holder of the instrument? Explain.*

THE TECHNOLOGICAL DIMENSION *If a note is the best primary evidence of the existence of a debt, what might be the best evidence of the amount of the debt and the interest calculation?*

COMMONLY ASSIGNED Promissory notes are commonly assigned (negotiated, or transferred) from one lender, or payee, to another. Assignment does not affect the maker's obligation to pay the note as promised. ▶ **Case in Point 25.4** Joseph Cotton borrowed funds from a bank for his education and signed a promissory note for their repayment. The bank assigned the note to the U.S. Department of Education, and Cotton failed to pay the debt. The government then obtained a court order allowing it to garnish (take a percentage of) Cotton's wages and his federal income tax refund.

INSIGHT INTO E-COMMERCE
Smartphone-Based Payment Systems

In 2009, customers at certain Starbucks locations in New York, San Francisco, and Seattle found that they could download an iPhone app to pay for their cappuccinos. Once the app is downloaded, the customer pays by simply flashing a bar code that appears on the iPhone's screen. By 2013, more than seven thousand Starbucks locations were accepting payments from all types of smartphone-based operating systems.

The Competition Will Become Fierce

The promise of a "mobile or digital wallet" is becoming a reality. Banks, credit-card issuers, and, of course, AT&T, T-Mobile, and Verizon Wireless want to be part of the smartphone payment system revolution. All wireless carriers have agreements with American Express, Discovery, MasterCard, and Visa. In fact, Visa has its own e-wallet service.

Mobile payments can take many forms. American Express's digital payment system, Serve, allows person-to-person payments over mobile phones. Some merchants that already accept American Express cards accept payments via mobile phones. Bank of America, JPMorgan Chase, and Wells Fargo have created ClearXchange, which allows bank customers to make person-to-person payments using mobile phone numbers.

Linking Digital Wallets to Other Apps on a Smartphone

According to those in this burgeoning field, the Holy Grail is a link from a digital wallet to another app within a single smartphone. Google, for example, is combining its Google Wallet with its Google Offers (a discount-deal app). Presumably, when more app-enabled "stores" are linked to digital wallets within smartphones, mobile payment systems will grow rapidly. Today, mobile pay volume is only about $150 billion, but that is expected to explode as the mass market adopts these systems.

Cutting Down on Resource Use and Sustainability

Approximately 70 billion checks are written and processed each year in the United States. All of these checks are written on paper, and some of them are transported in physical form for long distances within the U.S. banking system—a process that requires airplane and truck fuel. Thus, whenever we make payments by some electronic means instead of by checks, trees do not have to be cut down to make paper, and fossil fuels do not have to be used to transport the checks. Many people, especially younger ones, have already embraced online shopping and electronic banking. The increased use of smartphone-based payment system is just another step toward sustainability.

LEGAL CRITICAL THINKING
INSIGHT INTO TECHNOLOGY

Does having a digital wallet in an iPhone, Android-based phone, or other smartphone entail more or fewer security risks than carrying a physical wallet with cash and credit cards? Explain.

EXHIBIT 25-3 A Typical Promissory Note

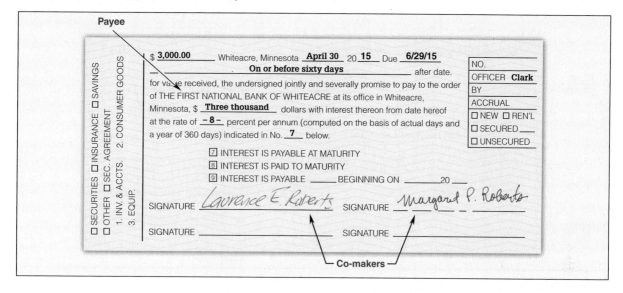

Cotton filed a lawsuit seeking to avoid payment and claiming that he had not signed any document promising to pay the government. The court found that the signature on Cotton's employment records matched the one on the bank's note, which had been validly assigned to the government. Thus, the government was entitled to enforce the note.[3] ◀

USED AS A CREDIT DEVICE Promissory notes are used in a variety of credit transactions. Often, a promissory note will carry the name of the transaction involved. ▶ **Example 25.5** A note may be secured by personal property, such as an automobile. This type of note is referred to as a *collateral note* because property pledged as security for the satisfaction of a debt is called *collateral*.[4] A note payable in installments, such as installment payments for a large-screen 3D LCD television over a twelve-month period, is called an *installment note*. ◀

Certificates of Deposit (Promises to Pay)

A **certificate of deposit (CD)** is a type of note issued when a party deposits funds with a bank, and the bank promises to repay the funds, with interest, on a certain

date [UCC 3–104(j)]. The bank is the maker of the note, and the depositor is the payee. ▶ **Example 25.6** On February 15, Sara Levin deposits $5,000 with the First National Bank of Whiteacre. The bank promises to repay the $5,000, plus 3.25 percent annual interest, on August 15. ◀ Exhibit 25–4 on the following page shows a typical small CD.

Because CDs are time deposits, the purchaser-payee typically is not allowed to withdraw the funds before the date of maturity (except in limited circumstances, such as disability or death). If a payee wants to access the funds before to the maturity date, he or she can sell (negotiate) the CD to a third party. Certificates of deposit in small denominations (for amounts up to $100,000) are often sold by savings and loan associations, savings banks, commercial banks, and credit unions.

SECTION 2

REQUIREMENTS FOR NEGOTIABILITY

For an instrument to be negotiable, it must meet the following requirements:

1. Be in writing.
2. Be signed by the maker or the drawer.
3. Be an unconditional promise or order to pay.
4. State a fixed amount of money.
5. Be payable on demand or at a definite time.
6. Be payable to order or to bearer.

---

3. *Cotton v. U.S. Department of Education,* 2006 WL 3313753 (M.D.Fla. 2006).
4. To minimize the risk of loss when making a loan, a creditor often requires the debtor to provide some *collateral,* or security, beyond a promise that the debt will be repaid. When this security takes the form of personal property (such as a motor vehicle), the creditor has an interest in the property known as a *security interest.* Security interests will be discussed in detail in Chapter 30.

EXHIBIT 25-4 A Typical Small Certificate of Deposit

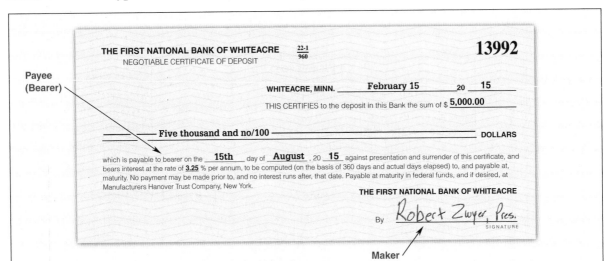

Written Form

Negotiable instruments must be in written form (but may be evidenced by an electronic record) [UCC 3–103(a)(6), (9)].[5] Clearly, an oral promise can create the danger of fraud or make it difficult to determine liability.

1. The writing must be on material that lends itself to *permanence*. Promises carved in blocks of ice or inscribed in the sand or on other impermanent surfaces would not qualify as negotiable instruments. The UCC nevertheless gives considerable leeway as to what can be a negotiable instrument. ▶ **Example 25.7** Checks and notes have been written on napkins, menus, tablecloths, shirts, and a variety of other materials. Courts will enforce negotiable instruments written on these odd types of materials. ◀

2. The writing must also have *portability*. Although the UCC does not explicitly state this requirement, if an instrument is not movable, it obviously cannot meet the requirement that it be freely transferable. ▶ **Example 25.8** Cullen writes on the side of a cow, "I, Cullen, promise to pay $500 to the order of Merrill." Technically, this would meet the requirements of a negotiable instrument—except for portability. Because a cow cannot easily be transferred in the ordinary course of business, the "instrument" is nonnegotiable. ◀

Signatures

For an instrument to be negotiable, it must be signed by (1) the maker if it is a note or a certificate of deposit or (2) the drawer if it is a draft or a check [UCC 3–103(a)(3), (5)]. If a person signs an instrument as an authorized *agent* (agency is discussed in Chapters 32 and 33) for the maker or drawer, the maker or drawer has effectively signed the instrument [UCC 3–402]. (Agents' signatures will be discussed in Chapter 27.)

SIGNATURE REQUIREMENTS The UCC is quite lenient with regard to what constitutes a signature. Nearly any symbol executed or adopted by a person with the intent to authenticate a written or electronic document can be a **signature** [UCC 1–201(37)]. A signature can be made by a device, such as a rubber stamp, or a thumbprint, and can consist of any name, including a trade or assumed name, or a word, mark, or symbol [UCC 3–401(b)]. If necessary, parol evidence (discussed in Chapter 16) is admissible to identify the signer. When the signer is identified, the signature becomes effective.

Although there are almost no limitations on the manner in which a signature can be made, one

---

5. Under the Uniform Electronic Transactions Act (UETA), discussed in Chapter 12, an electronic record may be sufficient to constitute a negotiable instrument (see UETA Section 16). A small number of states have also adopted amendments to Article 3 that explicitly authorize electronic negotiable instruments.

should be careful about receiving an instrument that has been signed in an unusual way. Oddities on a negotiable instrument can open the door to disputes and lead to litigation. Furthermore, an unusual signature clearly will decrease the *marketability* of an instrument because it creates uncertainty.

PLACEMENT OF THE SIGNATURE The location of the signature on the document is unimportant, although the usual place is the lower right-hand corner. ▶ **Example 25.9** A *handwritten* statement on the body of the instrument, such as "I, Kammie Orlik, promise to pay Janis Tan," is sufficient to act as a signature. ◀

Unconditional Promise or Order to Pay

The terms of the promise or order must be included in the writing on the face of a negotiable instrument. The terms must also be *unconditional*—that is, they cannot be conditioned on the occurrence or nonoccurrence of some other event or agreement [UCC 3–104(a)].

PROMISES For an instrument to be negotiable, it must contain an express promise or order to pay. ▶ **Example 25.10** Kyra executes a promissory note that says "I promise to pay Alvarez $1,000 on demand for the purchase of these goods." These words satisfy the promise-to-pay requirement. ◀

A mere acknowledgment of the debt, such as an I.O.U. ("I owe you"), might logically *imply* a promise, but it is *not* sufficient under the UCC. This is because the UCC requires that a promise be an *affirmative* (express) undertaking [UCC 3–103(a)(9)]. In contrast, if such words as "to be paid on demand" or "due on demand" are added to an I.O.U., the need for an express promise is satisfied.

A certificate of deposit is exceptional in this respect. No express promise is required in a CD because the bank's acknowledgment of the deposit and the other terms of the instrument clearly indicate a promise by the bank to repay the sum of money [UCC 3–104(j)].

ORDERS An *order* is associated with three-party instruments, such as checks, drafts, and trade acceptances. An order directs a third party to pay the instrument as drawn. In the typical check, for instance, the word *pay* (to the order of a payee) is a command to the drawee bank to pay the check when presented, and thus it is an order.

A command, such as "pay," is mandatory even if it is accompanied by courteous words, as in "Please pay" or "Kindly pay." Generally, the language used must indicate that a command, or order, is being given. Stating "I wish you would pay" does not fulfill this requirement.

An order may be addressed to one person or to more than one person, either jointly ("to A *and* B") or alternatively ("to A *or* B") [UCC 3–103(a)(6)]. (The effect of naming alternative or joint payees will be discussed in Chapter 26.)

UNCONDITIONALITY OF THE PROMISE OR ORDER Only *unconditional* promises or orders can be negotiable [UCC 3–104(a)]. A promise or order is conditional (and *not* negotiable) if it states *any* of the following:

1. An express condition to payment.
2. That the promise or order is subject to or governed by another writing (or record).
3. That the rights or obligations with respect to the promise or order are stated in another writing or record.

A mere *reference* to another writing or record, however, does not of itself make the promise or order conditional [UCC 3–106(a)]. For instance, including the phrase "as per contract" or "This debt arises from the sale of goods X and Y" does not render an instrument nonnegotiable. Similarly, a statement in the instrument that payment can be made only out of a particular fund or source will not render the instrument nonnegotiable [UCC 3–106(b)(ii)]. ▶ **Example 25.11** The terms of Biggs's note state that payment will be made out of the proceeds of next year's cotton crop. This term does not make the note nonnegotiable—although the payee of such a note may find the note commercially unacceptable and refuse to take it. ◀

If the payment is to be made from a fund that does not yet exist, however, or is conditioned on the occurrence of some future event, the instrument will be nonnegotiable. ▶ **Example 25.12** Duffy's note promises to pay Sherman from the trust account that Duffy will establish when he receives the proceeds from his father's estate. This promise is conditional, and the note is nonnegotiable. ◀

A Fixed Amount of Money

Negotiable instruments must state with certainty a fixed amount of money to be paid at the time the instrument is payable [UCC 3–104(a)]. This requirement ensures that the value of the instrument can be determined with clarity and certainty.

FIXED AMOUNT The term *fixed amount* (sometimes called *sum certain*) means that the amount must be ascertainable from the face of the instrument. Interest may be stated as a fixed or variable rate. A demand note payable with 10 percent interest meets the requirement of a fixed amount because its amount can be determined at the time it is payable [UCC 3–104(a)].

The rate of interest may also be determined with reference to information that is not contained in the instrument itself but is described by it, such as a formula or a source [UCC 3–112(b)]. For instance, an instrument that is payable at the *legal rate of interest* (a rate of interest fixed by statute) is negotiable. Mortgage notes tied to a variable rate of interest (a rate that fluctuates as a result of market conditions) are also negotiable.

PAYABLE IN MONEY UCC 3–104(a) provides that a fixed amount is to be *payable in money*. The UCC defines money as "a medium of exchange authorized or adopted by a domestic or foreign government as a part of its currency" [UCC 1–201(24)]. Gold is not a medium of exchange adopted by the U.S. government, so a note made payable in gold is nonnegotiable. An instrument payable in the United States with a face amount stated in a foreign currency can be paid in the foreign money or in the equivalent in U.S. dollars [UCC 3–107].

Payable on Demand or at a Definite Time

A negotiable instrument must "be payable on demand or at a definite time" [UCC 3–104(a)(2)]. To determine the value of a negotiable instrument, it is necessary to know when the maker, drawee, or *acceptor* is required to pay. (An **acceptor** is a drawee who has accepted, or agreed to pay, an instrument when it is presented later for payment.) It is also necessary to know when the obligations of secondary parties, such as *indorsers*,[6] will arise.

Furthermore, it is necessary to know when an instrument is due in order to calculate when the statute of limitations may apply [UCC 3–118(a)]. Finally, with an interest-bearing instrument, it is necessary to know the exact interval during which the interest will accrue to determine the instrument's value at the present time.

PAYABLE ON DEMAND Instruments that are payable on demand include those that contain the words "Payable at sight" or "Payable upon presentment." **Presentment** occurs when a demand to either pay or accept an instrument is made by or on behalf of a person entitled to enforce the instrument [UCC 3–501]. In other words, presentment occurs when a person brings the instrument to the appropriate party for payment or acceptance.

The very nature of the instrument may indicate that it is payable on demand. For instance, a check, by definition, is payable on demand [UCC 3–104(f)]. If no time for payment is specified and the person responsible for payment must pay on the instrument's presentment, the instrument is payable on demand [UCC 3–108(a)].

In the following case, the issue before the court was whether a promissory note was a demand note.

---

6. We should note that because the UCC uses the spelling *indorse* (*indorsement*, and the like), rather than the more common spelling *endorse* (*endorsement*, and the like), we adopt the UCC's spelling here and in other chapters in this text. Indorsers will be discussed in Chapter 26.

CASE ANALYSIS

Case 25.2 Reger Development, LLC v. National City Bank
United States Court of Appeals, Seventh Circuit, 592 F.3d 759 (2010).

IN THE LANGUAGE OF THE COURT
FLAUM, Circuit Judge.

* * * *

* * * Plaintiff-appellant Reger Development, LLC * * * is an Illinois limited liability company involved in real estate development. Kevin Reger is Reger Development's principal and sole member. Defendant-appellee National City Bank * * * had lent money to Reger Development for several previous projects. In June 2007, National City offered the company a line of credit to fund potential development opportunities. * * * Reger Development then executed the form contract, which was structured as a promissory note ("Note") * * * .

The main question in this case is whether the Note entitles National City to demand payment from Reger Development at will. * * * [One of the contract clauses reads, in part:]

PAYMENT: Borrower will pay this loan in full immediately upon Lender's demand.
* * * *

The Note [continues on] to reference payment on lender's demand several times in other provisions.

* * * [About a year later, National City asked Reger Development to pay down some of the loan and] notified appellant that it would be reducing the amount of cash available through the line of credit * * * .

Kevin Reger "expressed surprise" about these developments and asked if National City would call the line of credit if Reger Development did not agree to the requests. The bank acknowledged that Reger Development was not in default but stated that "there is a possibility that we may demand payment of the line."

Reger Development then filed a complaint in Illinois state court accusing National City of breaching the terms of the Note. * * * Appellee removed the case to the Northern District of Illinois under diversity jurisdiction and then successfully moved to dismiss the complaint for failure to state a cause of action under which relief could be granted. * * * Reger Development [appealed].
* * * *

While Illinois law generally holds that "a covenant of fair dealing and good faith is implied into every contract absent express disavowal," *the duty to act in good faith does not apply to lenders seeking payment on demand notes*. In light of this controlling law, appellant's complaint appears vacuous [lacking in content]. Reger Development's allegations are "that National City breached the Contract Documents by arbitrarily and capriciously (1) demanding payment under the Line of Credit even though Reger Development was in good standing and (2) unilaterally changing and attempting to change the fundamental terms of the Contract Documents without Reger Development's consent." Reger Development [points] to several provisions in the Note that it believes to be fundamentally inconsistent with the nature of a demand instrument. These include * * * the prepayment clause, which allows the borrower to pay down "all or a portion of the amount owed earlier than it is due;" and the clause that grants National City the right to access the borrower's financial information. Reger Development describes the latter as a "financial insecurity" provision that conditions the right to demand payment on some economic cause. [Emphasis added.]

We are not persuaded by the suggestion that these references * * * somehow overpower the repeated, explicit contract language setting forth the lender's right to demand payment at any time. A bank that wishes to call the Note can specify some future date on which it needs payment as a "due date." Failure to pay at that point in time, as well as failure to make monthly interest payments required by the Note, would constitute default, but *the mere use of the terms "due date" or "default" would not alter the nature of the agreement.* * * * The language merely reinforces National City's right to collect scheduled monthly interest payments and does not deviate from the structure of a demand note. [Emphasis added.]
* * * *

For the foregoing reasons, we AFFIRM the district court's grant of National City's motion to dismiss the Reger Development complaint.

LEGAL REASONING QUESTIONS

1. In its opinion, the court pointed out that "the duty to act in good faith does not apply to lenders seeking payment on demand notes." Why not?
2. If National City had demanded "payment of the line" instead of just indicating that there was a possibility it might do so in the future, would the outcome of this case have been any different? Explain.
3. Why might a creditor such as National City Bank prefer a note that is payable on demand?
4. Why might a debtor such as Reger Development agree to a note that includes a term making it payable on demand?

PAYABLE AT A DEFINITE TIME If an instrument is not payable on demand, to be negotiable it must be payable at a definite time. An instrument is payable at a definite time if it states *any* of the following:

1. That it is payable on a specified date.
2. That it is payable within a definite period of time (such as thirty days) after being presented for payment.
3. That it is payable on a date or time readily ascertainable at the time the promise or order is issued [UCC 3–108(b)].

The maker or drawee is under no obligation to pay until the specified date.

When an instrument is payable by the maker or drawer *on or before* a stated date, it is clearly payable at a definite time. The maker or drawer has the *option* of paying before the stated maturity date, but the payee can still rely on payment being made by the maturity date. The option to pay early does not violate the definite-time requirement. ▶ **Example 25.13** Ari gives Ernesto an instrument dated May 1, 2015, that indicates on its face that it is payable *on or before* May 1, 2016. This instrument satisfies the definite-time requirement. ◀

In contrast, an instrument that is undated and made payable "one month after date" is clearly non-negotiable. There is no way to determine the maturity date from the face of the instrument. Whether the time period is a month or a year, if the date is uncertain, the instrument is not payable at a definite time. ▶ **Example 25.14** An instrument that states, "One year after the death of my grandfather, Jerome Adams, I promise to pay $5,000 to the order of Lucy Harmon. [Signed] Jacqueline Wells," is nonnegotiable. The date that the instrument becomes payable is uncertain. ◀

ACCELERATION CLAUSE An **acceleration clause** allows a payee or other holder of a time instrument to demand payment of the entire amount due, with interest, if a certain event occurs, such as a default in payment of an installment when due. (A **holder** is any person in possession of a negotiable instrument that is payable either to the bearer or to an identified person that is the person in possession [UCC 1–201(20)].)

▶ **Example 25.15** Marta lends $1,000 to Ruth, who makes a negotiable note promising to pay $100 per month for eleven months. The note contains an acceleration provision that permits Marta or any holder to immediately demand all the payments plus the interest owed to date if Ruth fails to pay an installment in any given month. Ruth fails to make the third payment. Marta accelerates the unpaid balance, and the note becomes due and payable in full. Ruth owes Marta the remaining principal plus any unpaid interest to that date. ◀

Under the UCC, instruments that include acceleration clauses are negotiable for two reasons: (1) The exact value of the instrument can be ascertained. (2) The instrument will be payable on a specified date if the event allowing acceleration does not occur [UCC 3–108(b)(ii)]. Thus, the specified date is the outside limit used to determine the value of the instrument.

EXTENSION CLAUSE The reverse of an acceleration clause is an **extension clause,** which allows the date of maturity to be extended into the future [UCC 3–108(b)(iii), (iv)]. To keep the instrument negotiable,

the interval of the extension must be specified if the right to extend the time of payment is given to the maker or the drawer of the instrument. If, however, the holder of the instrument can extend the time of payment, the extended maturity date need not be specified.

▶ **Example 25.16** Alek executes a note that reads, "The maker has the right to postpone the time of payment of this note beyond its definite maturity date of January 1, 2016. This extension, however, shall be for no more than a reasonable time." A note with this language is not negotiable because it does not satisfy the definite-time requirement. The right to extend is the maker's, and the maker has not indicated when the note will become due after the extension.

In contrast, suppose that Alek's note reads, "The holder of this note at the date of maturity, January 1, 2016, can extend the time of payment until the following June 1 or later, if the holder so wishes." This note is a negotiable instrument. The length of the extension does not have to be specified because the option to extend is solely that of the holder. After January 1, 2016, the note is, in effect, a demand instrument. ◀

Payable to Order or to Bearer

Because one of the functions of a negotiable instrument is to serve as a substitute for cash, freedom to transfer is essential. To ensure a proper transfer, the instrument must be "payable to order or to bearer" at the time it is issued or first comes into the possession of the holder [UCC 3–104(a)(1)]. An instrument is not negotiable unless it meets this requirement.

ORDER INSTRUMENTS An **order instrument** is an instrument that is payable (1) "to the order of an identified person" or (2) "to an identified person or order" [UCC 3–109(b)]. An identified person is the person "to whom the instrument is initially payable" as determined by the intent of the maker or drawer [UCC 3–110(a)]. The identified person, in turn, may transfer the instrument to whomever he or she wishes.

Thus, the maker or drawer is agreeing to pay either the person specified on the instrument or whomever that person might designate. In this way, the instrument retains its transferability. ▶ **Example 25.17** An instrument states, "Payable to the order of James Yung" or "Pay to James Yung or order." Clearly, the maker or drawer has indicated that payment will be made to Yung or to whomever Yung designates. The instrument is negotiable. ◀

Note that with order instruments, the person specified must be identified with *certainty* because the transfer of an order instrument requires the indorsement, or signature, of the payee. An *indorsement* is a signature placed on an instrument, such as on the back of a check, generally for the purpose of transferring one's ownership rights in the instrument. Indorsements will be discussed at length in Chapter 26. An order instrument made "Payable to the order of my nicest cousin," for instance, is not negotiable because it does not clearly specify the payee.

BEARER INSTRUMENTS A **bearer instrument** is an instrument that does not designate a specific payee [UCC 3–109(a)]. The term **bearer** refers to a person in possession of an instrument that is payable to bearer or indorsed in blank (with a signature only, as will be discussed in Chapter 26) [UCC 1–201(5), 3–109(a),

3–109(c)]. This means that the maker or drawer agrees to pay anyone who presents the instrument for payment.

Any instrument containing terms such as the following is a bearer instrument:

1. "Payable to the order of bearer."
2. "Payable to Simon Reed or bearer."
3. "Payable to bearer."
4. "Pay cash."
5. "Pay to the order of cash."

The bearer instrument at the center of the following case was a *gambling marker*—that is, a credit instrument that allows a gambler to receive tokens or chips from a casino based on a prior credit application. The question before the court was whether the gambling marker was negotiable.

SP TLIGHT on Casino Markers

Case 25.3 Las Vegas Sands, LLC v. Nehme
United States Court of Appeals, Ninth Circuit, 632 F.3d 526 (2011).

BACKGROUND AND FACTS Amine Nehme, a California resident, applied for credit at the Venetian Resort Hotel Casino in Las Vegas, Nevada. Nehme was granted $500,000 in credit. He soon accrued more than $1.2 million in gambling debts to the Venetian, which he paid. About a year later, Nehme deposited $1,000 with the Venetian and signed a gambling marker for $500,000. Typically, a gambling marker is dated, includes the gambler's name and that of his or her bank and the bank account number, and states "Pay to the Order of [the casino's name]."

In this case, though, the line following "Pay to the Order of" was apparently left blank, which made the marker a bearer instrument. Nehme quickly lost $500,000 gambling and left the casino. The Venetian presented the marker for payment to Bank of America, Nehme's bank, which returned it for insufficient funds. The casino's owner, Las Vegas Sands, LLC, applied Nehme's deposit against the marker and filed a suit against him to recover the remainder—$499,000—plus interest, claiming that he had failed to pay a negotiable instrument. A federal district court issued a summary judgment in the Venetian's favor. Nehme appealed.

 IN THE LANGUAGE OF THE COURT
BEA, Circuit Judge:

* * * *

The * * * claim in the Venetian's complaint against Nehme is for failure to pay the marker.
* * * *

* * * Subsection 6 of [Nevada Revised Statutes Section 104.3104, Nevada's version of UCC 3–104] provides that "an order that meets all of the requirements of subsection 1 * * * and otherwise falls within the definition of 'check' in subsection 6 is a negotiable instrument and a check." In pertinent part, *subsection 1 defines a negotiable instrument as "an unconditional * * * order to pay a fixed amount of money * * * if it * * * is payable on demand or at a definite time; and * * * does not state any other undertaking by the person promising or ordering payment to do any act*

CASE 25.3 CONTINUES ▶

CASE 25.3 CONTINUED   *in addition to the payment of money.*" One definition of a check in subsection 6 is a "draft * * * payable on demand and drawn on a bank." [Emphasis added.]

Here, the marker is a negotiable instrument and a check because it provides a mechanism for payment of $500,000 from Bank of America to the order of the Venetian [as the holder], is signed by Nehme, and is payable on demand because it states no time or date of payment. On the face of the marker, the order is unconditional and states no undertakings by Nehme other than to pay a specific sum of money. The marker therefore was valid and enforceable as a negotiable instrument under Nevada law. The Venetian presented the marker to Bank of America for payment, and the marker was returned for insufficient funds. Thus, the Venetian has a right to enforce the marker against Nehme unless Nehme can establish a defense to liability.

DECISION AND REMEDY *The U.S. Court of Appeals for the Ninth Circuit agreed with the lower court that the marker was a negotiable instrument. The appellate court reversed the lower court's judgment, however, and remanded the case for a trial to determine whether Nehme could establish a defense to liability on other grounds.*

WHAT IF THE FACTS WERE DIFFERENT? *Suppose that the marker had stated "Payable to the Order of the Venetian." Could the casino have transferred it for collection? If so, how?*

THE ECONOMIC DIMENSION *What is the advantage to the Venetian of the court's holding that Nehme's marker is a negotiable instrument?*

Can Be Payable to Nonexistent Person. In addition, an instrument that "indicates that it is not payable to an identified person" is a bearer instrument [UCC 3–109(a)(3)]. Thus, an instrument that is "payable to X" can be negotiated as a bearer instrument, as though it were payable to cash. Similarly, an instrument that is "payable to Captain America" is negotiable as a bearer instrument because it is obvious that it is payable to a *nonexistent person.*

Cannot Be Payable to Nonexistent Organization. The UCC does not accept an instrument issued to a *nonexistent organization* as payable to bearer, however [UCC 3–109, Comment 2]. Therefore, an instrument "payable to the order of the Camrod Company," if no such company exists, would not be a bearer instrument or an order instrument. In fact, the instrument would not qualify as a negotiable instrument.

See *Concept Summary 25.1* for a convenient review of the basic rules governing negotiability.

SECTION 3
FACTORS THAT DO NOT AFFECT NEGOTIABILITY

Certain ambiguities or omissions will not affect the negotiability of an instrument. Article 3's rules for interpreting ambiguous terms include the following:

1. Unless the date of an instrument is necessary to determine a definite time for payment, the fact that an instrument is undated does not affect its negotiability. A typical example is an undated check, which is still negotiable. If a check is not dated, under the UCC its date is the date of its issue, meaning the date on which the drawer first delivers the check to another person to give that person rights on the check [UCC 3–113(b)].

2. Antedating or postdating an instrument does not affect its negotiability [UCC 3–113(a)]. *Antedating* occurs when a party puts a date on an instrument that precedes the actual calendar date. *Postdating* occurs when a party puts a date on an instrument that is after the actual date. ▶ **Example 25.18** Crenshaw draws a check on his account at First Bank, payable to Sirah Imports. He postdates the check by fifteen days. Sirah Imports can immediately negotiate the check, and, unless Crenshaw tells First Bank otherwise, the bank can charge the amount of the check to Crenshaw's account [UCC 4–401(c)]. ◀

3. Handwritten terms outweigh typewritten and printed terms (preprinted terms on forms, for example), and typewritten terms outweigh printed terms [UCC 3–114]. ▶ **Example 25.19** Like most checks, your check is printed "Pay to the order of" followed by a blank line. In handwriting, you insert in the blank "Anita Delgado or bearer." The

CONCEPT SUMMARY 25.1
Requirements for Negotiability

REQUIREMENTS	BASIC RULES
Must Be in Writing UCC 3–103(6), (9)	A writing can be on anything that is readily transferable and that has a degree of permanence.
Must Be Signed by the Maker or Drawer UCC 1–201(37) UCC 3–103(a)(3), (5) UCC 3–401(b) UCC 3–402	1. The signature can be anywhere on the face of the instrument. 2. It can be in any form (such as a word, mark, or rubber stamp) that purports to be a signature and authenticates the writing. 3. A signature may be made in a representative capacity.
Must Be a Definite Promise or Order UCC 3–103(a)(6), (9) UCC 3–104(a)	1. A promise must be more than a mere acknowledgment of a debt. 2. The words "I/We promise" or "Pay" meet this criterion.
Must Be Unconditional UCC 3–106	1. Payment cannot be expressly conditional on the occurrence of an event. 2. Payment cannot be made subject to or governed by another agreement.
Must Be an Order or Promise to Pay a Fixed Amount UCC 3–104(a) UCC 3–107 UCC 3–112(b)	An amount may be considered a fixed sum even if payable in installments, with a fixed or variable rate of interest, or at a foreign exchange rate.
Must Be Payable in Money UCC 3–104(a)	Any medium of exchange recognized as the currency of a government is money.
Must Be Payable on Demand or at a Definite Time UCC 3–104(a)(2) UCC 3–108(a), (b), (c)	1. Any instrument that is payable on sight, presentment, or issue or that does not state any time for payment is a demand instrument. 2. An instrument is still payable at a definite time, even if it is payable on or before a stated date or within a fixed period after sight or if the drawer or maker has the option to extend the time for a definite period. 3. Acceleration clauses do not affect the negotiability of the instrument.
Must Be Payable to Order or to Bearer UCC 3–104(a)(1) UCC 3–109 UCC 3–110(a)	1. An order instrument must identify the payee with reasonable certainty. 2. An instrument whose terms indicate payment to no particular person is payable to bearer.

handwritten terms will outweigh the printed form (an order instrument), and the check will be a bearer instrument. ◀

4. Words outweigh figures unless the words are ambiguous [UCC 3–114]. This rule becomes important when the numerical amount and the written amount on a check differ. ▶ **Example 25.20** Rizzo issues a check payable to Reliable Appliance Company. For the amount, she fills in the number "$100" but writes out the words "One thousand

and 00/100" dollars. The check is payable in the amount of $1,000. ◀

5. When an instrument simply states "with interest" and does not specify a particular interest rate, the interest rate is the *judgment rate of interest* [UCC 3–112(b)]. The judgment rate of interest refers to the rate of interest fixed by statute that applies to a monetary judgment awarded by a court.

6. A check is negotiable even if there is a notation on it stating that it is "nonnegotiable" or "not

governed by Article 3." Any other instrument, however, can be made nonnegotiable by the maker's or drawer's conspicuously noting on it that it is "nonnegotiable" or "not governed by Article 3" [UCC 3–104(d)].

Reviewing: The Function and Creation of Negotiable Instruments

Robert Durbin, a student, borrowed funds from a bank for his education and signed a promissory note for their repayment. The bank lent the funds under a federal program designed to assist students at postsecondary institutions. Under this program, repayment ordinarily begins nine to twelve months after the student borrower fails to carry at least one-half of the normal full-time course load at his or her school. The federal government guarantees that the note will be fully repaid. If the student defaults on the repayment, the lender presents the current balance—principal, interest, and costs—to the government. When the government pays the balance, it becomes the lender, and the borrower owes the government directly. After Durbin defaulted on his note, the government paid the lender the balance due and took possession of the note. Durbin then refused to pay the government, claiming that the government was not the holder of the note. The government filed a suit in a federal district court against Durbin to collect the amount due. Using the information presented in the chapter, answer the following questions.

1. Using the categories discussed in the chapter, what type of negotiable instrument was the note that Durbin signed (an order to pay or a promise to pay)? Explain.
2. Suppose that the note did not state a specific interest rate but instead referred to a statute that established the maximum interest rate for government-guaranteed school loans. Would the note fail to meet the requirements for negotiability in that situation? Why or why not?
3. For the government to be a holder, which method must have been used to transfer the instrument from the bank to the government?
4. Suppose that, in court, Durbin argues that because the school closed down before he could finish his education, there was a failure of consideration: he did not get something of value in exchange for his promise to pay. Assuming that the government is a holder of the promissory note, would this argument likely be successful against it? Why or why not?

DEBATE THIS . . . *Congress should pass a law disallowing all negotiable instruments that are not written on paper.*

Terms and Concepts

acceleration clause 486	draft 477	negotiable instrument 476
acceptance 477	drawee 477	order instrument 486
acceptor 484	drawer 477	payee 477
banker's acceptance 478	extension clause 486	presentment 484
bearer 487	holder 486	promissory note 478
bearer instrument 487	issue 476	signature 482
certificate of deposit (CD) 481	maker 478	trade acceptance 477
check 478		

ExamPrep

Issue Spotters

1. Sasha owes $600 to Yale, who asks Sasha to sign an instrument for the debt. Suppose that each of the following is included on that instrument: "I.O.U. $600," "I promise to pay $600," or an instruction to Sasha's bank stating, "I wish you would pay $600 to Yale." Which of these phrases would prevent the instrument's negotiability? Why? **(See page 483.)**

2. Marit worked for Town & Garden, a landscape design service, owned by Donald. Marit signed a note payable to Donald to become a co-owner of Town & Garden. The note, which was undated, required installment payments, but Donald never asked for them. Is Marit's note a demand note? Explain. **(See page 484.)**

- **Check your answers to the Issue Spotters against the answers provided in Appendix E at the end of this text.**

Before the Test

Go to **www.cengagebrain.com**, enter the ISBN 9781285185248, and click on "Find" to locate this textbook's Web site. Then, click on "Access Now" under "Study Tools," and select Chapter 25 at the top. There, you will find a Practice Quiz that you can take to assess your mastery of the concepts in this chapter, as well as Flashcards and a Glossary of important terms.

Business Scenarios

25–1. Negotiable Instruments. Sabrina Runyan writes the following note on a sheet of paper: "I, the undersigned, do hereby acknowledge that I owe Leo Woo one thousand dollars, with interest, payable out of the proceeds of the sale of my horse, Lightning, next month. Payment is to be made on or before six months from date." Discuss specifically why this is not a negotiable instrument. **(See page 481.)**

25–2. Negotiability. Juan Sanchez writes the following note on the back of an envelope: "I, Juan Sanchez, promise to pay Kathy Martin or bearer $500 on demand." Is this a negotiable instrument? Discuss fully. **(See page 481.)**

25–3. Promissory Notes. A college student, Austin Keynes, wished to purchase a new entertainment system from Friedman Electronics, Inc. Because Keynes did not have the cash to pay for the entertainment system, he offered to sign a note promising to pay $150 per month for the next six months. Friedman Electronics, eager to sell the system to Keynes, agreed to accept the promissory note, which read, "I, Austin Keynes, promise to pay to Friedman Electronics or its order the sum of $150 per month for the next six months." The note was signed by Austin Keynes. A week later, Friedman Electronics, which was badly in need of cash, signed the back of the note and sold it to the First National Bank of Halston. Give the specific designation of each of the three parties on this note. **(See page 478.)**

25–4. Bearer Instruments. Adam's checks are imprinted with the words "Pay to the order of" followed by a blank. Adam fills in an amount on one of the checks and signs it, but he does not write anything in the blank following the phrase "Pay to the order of." Adam gives this check to Beth. On another check, Adam writes in the blank "Carl or bearer." Which, if either, of these checks is a bearer instrument, and why? **(See page 487.)**

Business Case Problems

25–5. Negotiability. In September 2001, Cory Babcock and Honest Air Conditioning & Heating, Inc., bought a new 2001 Chevrolet Corvette from Cox Chevrolet in Sarasota, Florida. Their retail installment sales contract (RISC) required monthly payments until $52,516.20 was paid. The RISC imposed many other conditions on the buyers and seller with respect to the payment for, and handling of, the Corvette. Cox assigned the RISC to General Motors Acceptance Corp. (GMAC). In August 2002, the buyers sold the car to Florida Auto Brokers, which agreed to pay the balance due on the RISC. The check to GMAC for this amount was dishonored for insufficient funds, however, after the vehicle's title had been forwarded. GMAC filed a suit in a Florida state court against Honest Air and Babcock, seeking $35,815.26 as damages for breach of contract. The defendants argued that the RISC was a negotiable instrument. A ruling in their favor on this point would reduce any damages due GMAC to less than the Corvette's current value. What are the requirements for an instrument to be negotiable? Does the RISC qualify? Explain. [*General Motors Acceptance Corp. v. Honest Air Conditioning & Heating, Inc.*, 933 So.2d 34 (Fla.App. 2 Dist. 2006)] **(See page 481.)**

25–6. Negotiability. Michael Scotto borrowed $2,970 from Cindy Vinueza. Both of their signatures appeared at the bottom of a note that stated, "I Michael Scotto owe Cindy Vinueza $2,970 (two thousand and nine-hundred & seventy dollars) & agree to pay her back in full. Signed on this 26th day of September 2009." More than a year later, Vinueza filed a suit against Scotto to recover on the note. Scotto admitted that he had borrowed the funds, but he contended—without proof—that he had paid Vinueza in full. Is this note negotiable? Which party is likely to prevail? Why? [*Vinueza v. Scotto*, 30 Misc.3d 1229, 924 N.Y.S.2d 312 (1 Dist. 2011)] **(See page 481.)**

25–7. BUSINESS CASE PROBLEM WITH SAMPLE ANSWER: Payable on Demand or at a Definite Time.

 *Abby Novel signed a handwritten note that read, "Glen Gallwitz 1-8-2002 loaned me $5,000 at 6 percent interest a total of $10,000.00." The note did not state a time for repayment. Novel used the funds to manufacture and market a patented jewelry display design. More than seven years after Novel signed the note, Gallwitz filed a suit to recover the stated amount. Novel claimed that she did not have to pay because the note was not negotiable—it was incomplete. Is she correct? Explain. [*Gallwitz v. Novel, 2011-Ohio-297 (5 Dist. 2011)]* **(See page 484.)**

• **For a sample answer to Problem 25–7, go to Appendix F at the end of this text.**

25–8. Bearer Instruments. Eligio Gaitan borrowed the funds to buy real property in Downers Grove, Illinois, and signed a note payable to Encore Credit Corp. Encore indorsed the note in blank. Later, when Gaitan defaulted on the payments, an action to foreclose on the property was filed in an Illinois state court by U.S. Bank, N.A. The note was in the bank's possession, but there was no evidence that the note had been transferred or negotiated to the bank. Can U.S. Bank enforce payment of the note? Why or why not? [*U.S. Bank National Association v. Gaitan,* 2013 IL App (2d) 120105-U, 2013 WL 160378 (2013)] **(See page 487.)**

25–9. A QUESTION OF ETHICS: Promissory Notes.

 *In November 2000, Monay Jones signed a promissory note in favor of a mortgage company in the amount of $261,250, using the deed to her home in Denver, Colorado, as collateral. Fifth Third Bank soon became the holder of the note. After Jones defaulted on the payment, in September 2001 she and the bank agreed to raise the note's balance to $280,231.23. She again defaulted. In November, the bank received a check from a third party as payment on Jones's note. It was the bank's policy to refuse personal checks in payoff of large debts. The bank representative who worked on Jones's account noted receipt of the check in the bank's records and forwarded it to the "payoff department." A week later, the bank discovered that the check had been lost without having been posted to Jones's account or submitted for payment. The bank notified Jones, and both parties searched, without success, for a copy of the check or evidence of the identity of its maker, the drawee bank, or the amount. In late 2002, the bank filed a suit in a Colorado state court to foreclose on Jones's home. She insisted that the note had been paid in full by a cashier's check issued by an Arkansas bank at the request of her deceased aunt. [*Fifth Third Bank v. Jones, 168 P.3d 1 (Colo.App. 2007)]* **(See page 478.)**

(a) What evidence supports a finding that Jones gave the bank a check? Does it seem more likely that the check was a cashier's check or a personal check? Would it be fair for a court to find that the check had paid the note in full?

(b) Under UCC 3–310, if a cashier's check or other certified check "is taken for an obligation, the obligation is discharged." The bank argued that it had not "taken [Jones's check] for an obligation" because the bank's internal administrative actions were still pending when the check was lost. Would it be fair for the court to rule in the bank's favor based on this argument? Why or why not?

Legal Reasoning Group Activity

25–10. Requirements for Negotiability. Peter Gowin was an employee of a granite countertop business owned by Joann Stathis. In November 2015, Gowin signed a promissory note agreeing to pay $12,500 in order to become a co-owner of the business. The note was dated January 15, 2015 (ten months before it was signed) and required him to make installment payments starting in February 2015. Stathis told Gowin not to worry about the note and never requested any payments. Gowin continued to work at the business until 2017, when he quit, claiming that he owned half of the business. Stathis argued that Gowin was not a co-owner because he had never paid the $12,500 into the business. **(See page 481.)**

(a) The first group will formulate an argument in favor of Stathis that Gowin did not own any interest in the business because he had never paid the $12,500.

(b) The second group will evaluate the strength of Gowin's argument. Gowin claimed that because compliance with the stated dates was impossible, the note effectively did not state a date for its payment and therefore was a demand note under UCC 3–108(a). Because no demand for payment had been made, Gowin argued that his obligation to pay had not arisen and the termination of his ownership interest in the granite business was improper.

CHAPTER 26

TRANSFERABILITY AND HOLDER IN DUE COURSE

Once issued, a negotiable instrument can be transferred to others by *assignment* or by *negotiation*. Recall from Chapter 17 that an assignment is a transfer of rights under a contract. Under contract law principles, a transfer by assignment to an assignee gives the assignee only those rights that the assignor possessed. Any defenses that can be raised against an assignor can normally be raised against the assignee. This same rule applies when a negotiable instrument, such as a promissory note, is transferred by assignment to an assignee: the assignee receives only those rights in the instrument that the assignor had prior to the assignment.

In contrast, when an instrument is transferred by **negotiation,** the Uniform Commercial Code (UCC) provides that the transferee (the person to whom the instrument is transferred) becomes a *holder* [UCC 3–201(a)]. A holder receives, at the very least, the rights of the previous possessor [UCC 3–203(b), 3–305]. But unlike an assignment, a transfer by negotiation can make it possible for a holder to receive *more* rights in the instrument than the prior possessor had [UCC 3–305]. A holder who receives greater rights is known as a *holder in due course,* a concept we discuss in this chapter. First, though, we look at the requirements for negotiation and examine the various types of *indorsements* that are used when order instruments are negotiated.

SECTION 1
NEGOTIATION

As just described, negotiation is the transfer of an instrument in such form that the transferee becomes a holder. There are two methods of negotiating an instrument so that the receiver becomes a holder. The method used depends on whether the instrument is an *order instrument* or a *bearer instrument.*

Negotiating Order Instruments

An order instrument contains the name of a payee capable of indorsing, as in "Pay to the order of Jamie Fowler." If an instrument is an order instrument, it is negotiated by delivery with any necessary indorsements (*indorsements* will be discussed shortly). ▶ **Example 26.1** Welpac Corporation issues a payroll check "to the order of Elliot Goodseal." Goodseal takes the check to the bank, signs his name on the back (an indorsement), gives it to the teller (a delivery), and receives cash. Goodseal has negotiated the check to the bank [UCC 3–201(b)]. ◀

Negotiating order instruments requires both delivery and indorsement. If Goodseal had taken the check to the bank and delivered it to the teller without signing it, the transfer would not qualify as a negotiation. In that situation, the transfer would be treated as an assignment, and the bank would become an assignee rather than a holder. In fact, whenever a transfer fails to qualify as a negotiation because it fails to meet one or more of the requirements of a negotiable instrument, it is treated as an assignment.

Negotiating Bearer Instruments

If an instrument is payable to bearer, it is negotiated by delivery—that is, by transfer into another person's possession. Indorsement is not necessary [UCC 3–201(b)]. The use of bearer instruments thus involves a greater risk of loss or theft than the use of order instruments. ▶ **Example 26.2** Alonzo Cruz writes a check payable to "cash," thus creating a bearer instrument. Cruz then hands the check to Blaine Parrington (a delivery). Parrington puts the check in his wallet, which is subsequently stolen. The thief now has possession of the check. At this point, the thief has no rights in the check. If the thief "delivers" the check to an innocent third person, however, negotiation will be complete. All rights to the check will pass *absolutely* to that third person, and Parrington will lose all right to recover the proceeds of the check from that person [UCC 3–306]. Of course, Parrington can recover his funds from the thief—if the thief can be found. ◄

SECTION 2
INDORSEMENTS

An indorsement is required whenever an order instrument is negotiated. An **indorsement** is a signature with or without additional words or statements. It is most often written on the back of the instrument itself. If there is no room on the instrument, the indorsement can be written on a separate piece of paper (called an *allonge*) that is firmly affixed to the instrument, such as with staples. A paper firmly attached to a negotiable instrument is part of the instrument [UCC 3–204(a)].

A person who transfers a note or a draft by signing (indorsing) it and delivering it to another person is an **indorser.** The person to whom the check is indorsed and delivered is the **indorsee.** ▶ **Example 26.3** Luisa Perez receives a graduation check for $100. She can transfer the check to her mother (or to anyone) by signing it on the back. Luisa is an indorser. If Luisa indorses the check by writing "Pay to Avery Perez," Avery Perezis the indorsee. ◄

There are four main categories of indorsements: blank, special, qualified, and restrictive. Note that a single indorsement may have characteristics of more than one category. In other words, these categories are not mutually exclusive.

Blank Indorsements

A **blank indorsement** does not specify a particular indorsee and can consist of a mere signature [UCC 3–205(b)]. ▶ **Example 26.4** A check payable "to the order of Mark Deitsch" can be indorsed in blank simply by writing Deitsch's signature on the back of the check. ◄ Exhibit 26–1 below shows a blank indorsement.

EXHIBIT 26–1 A Blank Indorsement

An order instrument indorsed in blank becomes a bearer instrument and can be negotiated by delivery alone [UCC 3–205(b)]. In other words, as will be discussed later, a blank indorsement converts an order instrument to a bearer instrument, which anybody can cash. ▶ **Example 26.5** Rita Chou indorses in blank a check payable to her order and then loses it on the street. If Schaefer finds the check, he can sell it to Duncan for value without indorsing it. This constitutes a negotiation because Schaefer has made delivery of a bearer instrument (which was an order instrument until it was indorsed in blank). ◄

Does an instrument that requires an indorsement for negotiation need to contain the written signature of an individual's name? That was the question in the following case.

CASE 26.1

In re Bass
Supreme Court of North Carolina, 738 S.E.2d 173 (2013).

BACKGROUND AND FACTS Tonya Bass signed a note with Mortgage Lenders Network USA, Inc., to borrow $139,988, repayable with interest in monthly installments of $810.75, to buy a house in Durham County, North Carolina. The note was transferred by stamped imprints to Emax Financial Group LLC, then to Residential Funding Corporation, and finally to U.S. Bank N.A. When Bass stopping paying on

CASE 26.1 CONTINUED

the note, U.S. Bank filed an action in a North Carolina state court to foreclose. The court issued an order permitting the foreclosure to proceed, and Bass appealed. She argued that the stamp transferring the note from Mortgage Lenders to Emax was invalid because it was not accompanied by a signature. A state intermediate appellate court issued a decision in Bass's favor based on the lack of a "proper indorsement." U.S. Bank appealed.

 IN THE LANGUAGE OF THE COURT
MARTIN, Justice.

* * * *

The UCC defines "signature" broadly, as "any symbol executed or adopted with present intention to adopt or accept a writing." The official comment explains that

> as the term "signed" is used in the Uniform Commercial Code, a complete signature is not necessary. The symbol may be printed, stamped or written; it may be by initials or by thumbprint. It may be on any part of the document and in appropriate cases may be found in a billhead or letterhead. No catalog of possible situations can be complete and the court must use common sense and commercial experience in passing upon these matters. The question always is whether the symbol was executed or adopted by the party with present intention to adopt or accept the writing.

Thus, the UCC does not limit a signature to a long-form writing of an individual person's name. Under this broad definition, the authenticating intent is sufficiently shown by the fact that the name of a party is written on the line which calls for the name of that party. Even if there might be some irregularities in the signature, the necessary intent can still be found based on the signature itself and other attendant circumstances. [Emphasis added.]

* * * [Bass] asserts the stamp by Mortgage Lenders does not qualify as an indorsement under [North Carolina General Statutes (N.C.G.S.)] Section 25–3–204(a) [North Carolina's version of UCC 3–204(a)]. She [contends] that an indorsement must include some representation of an individual signature to be valid.

The contested stamp indicates on its face an intent to transfer the debt from Mortgage Lenders to Emax:

> Pay to the order of:
> Emax Financial Group, LLC
> without recourse
> By: Mortgage Lenders Network USA, Inc.

In addition, the stamp appears on the page of the Note where other, uncontested indorsements were placed. We also observe that the original Note was indeed transferred in accordance with the stamp's clear intent. The stamp evidences that it was executed or adopted by the party with present intention to adopt or accept the writing. Under the broad definition of "signature" and the accompanying official comment, the stamp by Mortgage Lenders constitutes a signature.

* * * With no unambiguous evidence indicating the signature was made for any other purpose, the stamp was an indorsement that transferred the Note from Mortgage Lenders to Emax.

DECISION AND REMEDY   *The North Carolina Supreme Court reversed the decision of the lower court and held that U.S. Bank was the holder of the note. The indorsements on the note unambiguously indicated the intent of each creditor to transfer the note to a succeeding lender and finally to U.S. Bank.*

THE LEGAL ENVIRONMENT DIMENSION   *Even though forged or unauthorized signatures on negotiable instruments are uncommon, should U.S. Bank have had to prove that the indorsements on this note were valid and authorized? Why or why not?*

THE ECONOMIC DIMENSION   *How does the presumption that an indorsement is legitimate "without unambiguous evidence to the contrary" protect the transferability of a negotiable instrument?*

Special Indorsements

A **special indorsement** contains the signature of the indorser and identifies the person to whom the indorser intends to make the instrument payable—that is, it names the indorsee [UCC 3–205(a)].
▶ **Example 26.6** Words such as "Pay to the order of Russell Clay" or "Pay to Russell Clay," followed by the signature of the indorser, are sufficient to identify the indorsee. ◀ When an instrument is indorsed in this way, it is an order instrument.

To avoid the risk of loss from theft, a holder may convert a blank indorsement to a special indorsement by writing, above the signature of the indorser, words identifying the indorsee [UCC 3–205(c)]. This changes the bearer instrument back to an order instrument. ▶ **Example 26.7** A check is made payable to Hal Cohen. He signs his name on the back of the check—a blank indorsement—and negotiates the check by delivering it to William Hunter. Hunter is not able to cash the check immediately but wants to avoid any risk should he lose the check. He therefore writes "Pay to William Hunter" above Cohen's blank indorsement. In this manner, Hunter has converted Cohen's blank indorsement into a special indorsement. Further negotiation now requires William Hunter's indorsement, plus delivery. ◀ Exhibit 26–2 below shows a special indorsement.

EXHIBIT 26-2 A Special Indorsement

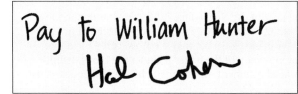

Qualified Indorsements

Generally, an indorser, *merely by indorsing,* impliedly promises to pay the holder, or any subsequent indorser, the amount of the instrument in the event that the drawer or maker defaults on the payment [UCC 3–415(a)]. Usually, then, indorsements are *unqualified indorsements.* In other words, the indorser is guaranteeing payment of the instrument in addition to transferring title to it.

An indorser who does not wish to be liable on an instrument can use a **qualified indorsement** to disclaim this liability [UCC 3–415(b)]. The nota-tion "without recourse" is commonly used to create a qualified indorsement.
▶ **Example 26.8** A check is made payable to the order of Sarah Jacobs. Sarah wants to negotiate the check to Allison Jong but does not want to assume liability for the check's payment. Sarah could create a qualified indorsement by indorsing the check as follows: "Pay to Allison Jong, without recourse, [signed] Sarah Jacobs" (see Exhibit 26–3 below). ◀

EXHIBIT 26-3 A Qualified Indorsement

Pay to Allison Jong, without recourse
Sarah Jacobs

THE EFFECT OF QUALIFIED INDORSEMENTS Qualified indorsements are often used by persons (agents—see Chapter 32) acting in a representative capacity. For instance, insurance agents sometimes receive checks payable to them that are really intended as payment to the insurance company. The agent is merely indors-ing the payment through to the insurance company and should not be required to make good on a check if it is later dishonored. The "without recourse" indorsement relieves the agent from any liability on the check.

If the instrument is dishonored, the holder can-not recover from the agent who indorsed "without recourse" unless the indorser breached one of the transfer warranties that will be discussed in Chapter 27. These warranties relate to good title, authorized signa-ture, no material alteration, and other requirements.

SPECIAL VERSUS BLANK QUALIFIED INDORSEMENTS A qualified indorsement ("without recourse") can be accompanied by either a special indorsement or a blank indorsement. In either situation, the instru-ment still transfers title and can be further negotiated.

A special qualified indorsement includes the name of the indorsee as well as the words "without recourse," as shown in Exhibit 26–3 above. The special indorsement makes the instrument an order instru-ment, and it requires an indorsement, plus delivery, for negotiation.

A blank qualified indorsement ("without recourse, [signed] Jennie Cole") makes the instrument a bearer instrument, and only delivery is required for negotiation. ▶ **Case in Point 26.9**   Chester Crow executed a promissory note payable "to the order of The First National Bank of Shreveport or bearer." More than ten years later, Credit Recoveries, Inc., filed a suit alleging that Crow still owed $7,222.57 on the note. Crow claimed that the bank had canceled the note. On the back of the note was the following qualified indorsement: "Pay to the Order of Credit Recoveries, Inc., without recourse [signed, the Vice President of the bank]." A state appellate court held that because

the note was made payable to bearer (or to the bank), it was bearer paper and could have been transferred by mere delivery to Credit Recoveries. Any later indorsement did not change the fact that Credit Recoveries had title to, and was a holder of, the note. Therefore, Crow still owed the balance of the note.[1] ◀

The following case illustrates the effect of a blank qualified indorsement.

---

1. *Credit Recoveries, Inc. v. Crow,* 862 So.2d 1146 (La.App. 2 Cir. 2003).

CASE ANALYSIS

Case 26.2   Hammett v. Deutsche Bank National Co.
United States District Court, Eastern District of Virginia, 2010 WL 1225849 (2010).

IN THE LANGUAGE OF THE COURT
Liam *O'GRADY,* District Judge.

* * * *

On October 6, 2005 Plaintiffs [Vernon Hammett and others] purchased a residential property in Alexandria. As part of that transaction, Plaintiffs executed a promissory note (the "Note") in the amount of $475,000 and a deed of trust[a] (the "Deed") securing the note in favor of Encore Credit Corporation ("Encore").

The Note was presented to the Court with an attached "allonge"[b] which contains a blank endorsement which reads: "Pay To The Order Of ____ Without Recourse Encore Credit Corp. A California Corporation." Defendants [Deutsche Bank National

Company and others] are now in possession of the Note.

At some point after executing the Note and the Deed, Plaintiffs "refused" to continue paying on their obligation under the Note. Defendants then initiated foreclosure proceedings[c] on the Property. Defendant Deutsche Bank * * * subsequently purchased the property at the foreclosure sale * * * .

* * * *

Plaintiffs filed their Complaint on September 8, 2009 in the Circuit Court for Fairfax County, Virginia. Defendants then removed the action to this Court and filed motions to dismiss on January 13, 2010 and February 25, 2010, respectively.

* * * *

Plaintiffs allege that the entities which foreclosed on their home are not entitled as a matter of law to do so. Specifically, Plaintiffs allege that "Defendants have no legal or equitable right or interest in the Promissory Note and/or the Deed of Trust * * * . However, nothing in Plaintiffs' conclusory [convincing, but not defini-

tive] allegations provides a plausible basis for relief after considering the settled law of negotiable instruments or the enforcement of a deed of trust securing notes after their negotiation.

Under Virginia law, *the holder of an instrument or a nonholder in possession of the instrument with the same rights as the holder may enforce the instrument. Further, an individual may be "entitled to enforce the instrument even though the person is not the owner of the instrument or is in wrongful possession of the instrument."* An individual becomes the "holder" of an instrument through the process of negotiation, and if "an instrument is payable to an identified person, negotiation requires transfer of possession of the instrument and its endorsement by the holder." On the other hand, *if an instrument has a blank endorsement, it is considered "payable to bearer," and it may be negotiated by transfer of possession alone.* In this case, the face of the Note shows that the Note has a blank endorsement. Accordingly, it may be negotiated by a simple change in possession and enforced by its current possessor, Deutsche Bank. [Emphasis added.]

Further, absent a contrary provision, notes are generally freely

---

a. As you will read in Chapter 49, a *deed* is a document by which real property, or realty, is transferred from one party to another. With a *deed of trust,* a type of instrument in use in some states, legal title to real property is held by one or more trustees. A deed of trust is used to secure the repayment of funds or to meet some other condition.

b. An *allonge* (pronounced uh-*long*) is a piece of paper firmly attached to a negotiable instrument, on which indorsements can be made if there is no room on the instrument.

c. Mortgages and foreclosure proceedings will be discussed in Chapter 30.

CASE 26.2 CONTINUES ▶

CASE 26.2 CONTINUED

transferable, and the transferee retains the right to enforce the instrument. The explicit terms of the Note at issue here indicate that it is freely transferable. ("I understand that the Lender may transfer this Note. The Lender or anyone who takes this Note by transfer and who is entitled to receive payments under this Note is called the Note Holder").

By their own allegations, Plaintiffs admit they "refused to pay" on the Note. * * * "To permit the parties to the [instrument] to object to its payment, on any of the grounds stated, would greatly impair the negotiability of bills and notes[,] their most distinguishing, most useful, and most valued feature."

* * * *

Plaintiffs' Complaint fails to state a plausible basis on which relief may be granted. * * * Accordingly, this case is dismissed.

LEGAL REASONING QUESTIONS

1. How do the requirements for negotiation of an instrument with a blank qualified indorsement, as was used in this case, differ from those for negotiation of an instrument with a special qualified indorsement?

2. Suppose that the indorsement at issue in this case had been written on a separate document that was not firmly affixed to the note. Would this document have constituted an allonge? Would Deutsche Bank be entitled to enforce the note? Explain.

3. The court's opinion in this case indicates that indorsing a note "without recourse" does not undercut its negotiability. What effect does this type of indorsement have?

4. What is the most significant feature of a negotiable instrument according to the court in this case? How would a decision in the plaintiffs' favor have affected this feature?

Restrictive Indorsements

A **restrictive indorsement** requires the indorsee to comply with certain instructions regarding the funds involved but does not prohibit further negotiation of the instrument [UCC 3–206(a)]. Although most indorsements are nonrestrictive, many forms of restrictive indorsements exist, including those discussed here.

INDORSEMENTS TO PAY ONLY A NAMED PAYEE An indorsement such as "Pay to Julie Diaz only, [signed] Thomas Fasulo" does not destroy negotiability. Diaz can negotiate the paper to a holder just as if it had read "Pay to Julie Diaz, [signed] Thomas Fasulo" [UCC 3–206(a)]. If the holder gives value, this type of restrictive indorsement has the same legal effect as a special indorsement.

CONDITIONAL INDORSEMENTS When payment depends on the occurrence of some event specified in the indorsement, the instrument has a conditional indorsement [UCC 3–204(a)]. ▶ **Example 26.10** Keenan Barton indorses a check as follows: "Pay to Lars Johansen if he completes the renovation of my kitchen by June 1, 2015, [signed] Keenan Barton." Barton has created a conditional indorsement. ◀

Article 3 states that an indorsement conditioning the right to receive payment "does not affect the right of the indorsee to enforce the instrument" [UCC 3–206(b)]. A person paying or taking an instrument for value (*taking for value* will be discussed later in the chapter) can disregard the condition without liability.

The effect of a conditional indorsement, which appears on the back of an instrument, differs from the effect of conditional language that appears on the *face* (front) of an instrument. As noted, conditional instruments do not prevent further negotiation. In contrast, an instrument with conditional language on its face is not negotiable, because it does not meet the requirement that a negotiable instrument must contain an unconditional promise to pay.

INDORSEMENTS FOR DEPOSIT OR COLLECTION A common type of restrictive indorsement makes the indorsee (almost always a bank) a collecting agent of the indorser [UCC 3–206(c)]. In particular, the indorsements "For deposit only" and "For collection only" have the effect of locking the instrument into the bank collection process. Only a bank can acquire the rights of a holder following one of these indorsements until the item has been specially indorsed by a bank to a person who is not a bank [UCC 3–206(c), 4–201(b)]. A bank's liability for payment of an instrument with a restrictive indorsement of this kind will be discussed in Chapter 27.

Exhibit 26–4 on the next page illustrates this type of indorsement on a check payable and issued to Marcel Dumont.

EXHIBIT 26-4 "For Deposit Only" and "For Collection Only" Indorsements

> For deposit only
> Marcel Dumont

or

> For collection only
> Marcel Dumont

TRUST (AGENCY) INDORSEMENTS Indorsements to persons who are to hold or use the funds for the benefit of the indorser or a third party are called **trust indorsements** (also known as *agency indorsements*) [UCC 3–206(d), (e)]. ▶ **Example 26.11** Raj Gupta asks his accountant, Stephanie Malik, to pay some bills for him while he is out of the country. Gupta indorses his payroll check to Stephanie Malik "as agent for Raj Gupta." This trust (agency) indorsement obligates Malik to use the funds only for the benefit of Gupta. ◀

The result of a trust indorsement is that legal rights in the instrument are transferred to the original indorsee. If the original indorsee pays or applies the proceeds consistently with the indorsement, the indorsee is a holder and can become a holder in due course (a status that will be described shortly). Sample trust (agency) indorsements are shown in Exhibit 26–5.

EXHIBIT 26-5 Trust (Agency) Indorsements

> Pay to Stephanie Malik
> as Agent for Raj Gupta
> Raj Gupta

or

> Pay to Ellen Cook
> in trust for Roger Callahan
> Roger Callahan

The fiduciary restrictions—restrictions mandated by a relationship involving trust and loyalty—on the instrument do not reach beyond the original indorsee [UCC 3–206(d), (e)]. Any subsequent purchaser can qualify as a holder in due course unless he or she has actual notice that the instrument was negotiated in breach of a fiduciary duty.

For a synopsis of the various indorsements and the consequences of using each type, see *Concept Summary 26.1* on the following page.

How Indorsements Can Convert Order Instruments to Bearer Instruments and Vice Versa

Earlier we saw that order instruments and bearer instruments are negotiated differently. The method used for negotiation depends on the character of the instrument *at the time the negotiation takes place.* Indorsement can convert an order instrument into a bearer instrument. For instance, a check originally payable to "cash" but subsequently indorsed with the words "Pay to Arnold" must be negotiated as an order instrument (by indorsement and delivery), even though it was previously a bearer instrument [UCC 3–205(a)].

As mentioned earlier, an instrument payable to the order of a named payee and indorsed in blank becomes a bearer instrument [UCC 3–205(b)]. ▶ **Example 26.12** A check is made payable to the order of Jessie Arnold. Arnold indorses it by signing her name on the back. The instrument, which is now a bearer instrument, can be negotiated by delivery without indorsement. Arnold can negotiate the check to whomever she wishes merely by delivery, and that person can negotiate by delivery without indorsement. If Arnold loses the check after she indorses it, anyone who finds the check can negotiate it further. ◀

Similarly, a bearer instrument can be converted into an order instrument through indorsement. ▶ **Example 26.13** Jessie Arnold takes the check that she indorsed in blank (now a bearer instrument) and negotiates it, by delivery, to Jonas Tolling. Tolling indorses the check "Pay to Mark Hyatt, [signed] Jonas Tolling." By adding this special indorsement, Tolling has converted the check into an order instrument. The check can be further negotiated only by indorsement (by Mark Hyatt) and delivery [UCC 3–205(b)]. ◀ Exhibit 26–6 on the next page illustrates how an indorsement can convert an order instrument into a bearer instrument and vice versa.

EXHIBIT 26–6 **Converting an Order Instrument to a Bearer Instrument and Vice Versa**

Indorsement Converting an Order Instrument to a Bearer Instrument

A check payable to the order of Jessie Arnold is an order instrument. Arnold indorses the check in blank (by simply signing her name), thus converting the instrument to a bearer instrument, and delivers the check to Jonas Tolling.

Indorsement Converting a Bearer Instrument to an Order Instrument

Jonas Tolling adds a special indorsement and negotiates the check to Mark Hyatt. The special indorsement, because it makes the instrument payable to a specific indorsee (Mark Hyatt), converts the bearer instrument back into an order instrument. To negotiate the instrument further, Mark Hyatt must indorse and deliver the instrument.

CONCEPT SUMMARY 26.1

Types of Indorsements and Their Effect

TYPE OF INDORSEMENT	DESCRIPTION	EXAMPLES	LEGAL EFFECT
Blank Indorsements	Indorser does not identify the person to whom the instrument is payable; can consist of a mere signature.	"Elana Guiterrez" "Mark Deitsch"	Creates a bearer instrument, which can be negotiated by delivery alone.
Special Indorsements	Indorser identifies the person to whom the instrument is payable.	"Pay to the order of Russell Clay" "Pay to William Hunter"	Creates an order instrument. Negotiation requires indorsement and delivery.
Qualified Indorsements	Indorser includes words indicating that he or she is not guaranteeing or assuming liability for payment.	"Without recourse, Elana Guitterez" (blank qualified indorsement) "Pay to Allison Jong without recourse, Sarah Jacobs" (special qualified indorsement, which creates an order instrument)	Relieves indorser of any liability for payment of the instrument; frequently used by agents or others acting on behalf of another.
Restrictive Indorsements	Indorser includes specific instructions regarding the funds involved or states a condition to the right of the indorsee to receive payment.	"For deposit only" "For collection only"	Only a bank can become a holder of instruments that are indorsed for deposit or collection.
		"Pay to Stephanie Malik as agent for Raj Gupta" "Pay to Ellen Cook in trust for Roger Callahan"	In a trust indorsement, the third party agent or trustee has the rights of a holder but has fiduciary duties to use the funds consistently with the indorsement.

SECTION 3
MISCELLANEOUS INDORSEMENT PROBLEMS

Of course, a significant problem occurs when an indorsement is forged or unauthorized. The UCC rules concerning unauthorized or forged signatures and indorsements will be discussed in Chapter 27 in the context of signature liability. These rules will be examined again in Chapter 28 in the context of the bank's liability for payment of an instrument containing an unauthorized signature. Here we look at some other difficulties that may arise with indorsements.

Misspelled Names

An indorsement should be identical to the name that appears on the instrument. A payee or indorsee whose name is misspelled can indorse with the misspelled name, the correct name, or both [UCC 3–204(d)]. ▶ **Example 26.14** Marley Ellison receives a check payable to the order of Mary Ellison. She can indorse the check either "Marley Ellison" or "Mary Ellison." ◀ The usual practice is to indorse with the name as it appears on the instrument followed by the correct name.

Instruments Payable to Entities

A negotiable instrument can be drawn payable to an entity such as an estate, a partnership, or an organization. In this situation, an authorized representative of the entity can negotiate the instrument. ▶ **Example 26.15** A check states "Pay to the order of the Red Cross." An authorized representative of the Red Cross can negotiate this check. ◀

Similarly, negotiable paper can be payable to a public officer. For instance, checks reading "Pay to the order of the County Tax Collector" or "Pay to the order of Larry White, Receiver of Taxes" can be negotiated by whoever holds the office [UCC 3–110(c)].

Alternative or Joint Payees

An instrument payable to two or more persons *in the alternative* (for instance, "Pay to the order of Ying or Tuan") requires the indorsement of only one of the payees [UCC 3–110(d)]. If, however, an instrument is made payable to two or more persons *jointly* (such as,

"Pay to the order of Bridgette and Tony Van Horn"), all of the payees' indorsements are necessary for negotiation.

IF THE INSTRUMENT IS AMBIGUOUS If an instrument payable to two or more persons does not clearly indicate whether it is payable in the alternative or payable jointly, then "the instrument is payable to the persons alternatively" [UCC 3–110(d)]. The same principles apply to special indorsements that identify more than one person to whom the indorser intends to make the instrument payable [UCC 3–205(a)].

▶ **Case in Point 26.16** Hyatt Corporation hired Skyscraper Building Maintenance, LLC, to perform maintenance. Skyscraper asked Hyatt to make checks for the services payable to Skyscraper and J&D Financial Corporation. Two of the checks issued by Hyatt were made payable to "J&D Financial Corp. Skyscraper Building Maint." Parties listed in this manner—without an "and" or "or" between them—are referred to as *stacked payees*. The checks were indorsed only by Skyscraper and negotiated by a bank.

J&D and Hyatt filed a lawsuit against the bank claiming that the checks were payable *jointly* and thus required indorsement by both payees. The bank argued that the checks were payable to J&D and Skyscraper *alternatively*. The court found that the bank was not liable. A check payable to stacked payees is ambiguous and thus payable *alternatively,* with indorsement by only one of the payees, under UCC 3–110(d).[2] ◀

SUSPENSION OF THE DRAWER'S OBLIGATION When a drawer gives one alternative or joint payee a check, the drawer's obligation on the check to other payees is suspended [UCC 3–310(b)(1)]. The payee who has possession of the check holds it for the benefit of all of the payees. In other words, the drawer has no obligation to make sure that the funds are allocated or distributed among the joint payees.

▶ **Case in Point 26.17** Vernon and Shirley Graves owned a building that they leased to John and Tamara Johnson to use for their towing business. The Johnsons insured the property and business through Westport Insurance Company. When a fire destroyed the building, Westport Insurance agreed to pay $98,000 in three payments with the checks co-payable to Johnson's Towing and Vernon Graves. Westport issued two checks, for $30,000 and $29,000,

---

2. *Hyatt Corp. v. Palm Beach National Bank,* 840 So.2d 300 (Fla.App. 2003).

and delivered them to Graves. A third check was given to the Johnsons, but they did not remit the funds to the Graveses, who subsequently filed a lawsuit against the Johnsons and Westport. The court dismissed the lawsuit, holding that the parties had agreed that the insurance company would issue the checks to joint payees and that Westport had complied with this agreement. Once Westport sent the checks to one of the joint payees, its obligation to the other joint payees was suspended until the check was either paid or dishonored.[3] ◄

SECTION 4
HOLDER IN DUE COURSE (HDC)

One of the important distinctions in the law governing negotiable instruments is that between a holder and a *holder in due course* (HDC). Often, whether a holder is entitled to obtain payment will depend on whether she or he is an HDC.

Holder versus Holder in Due Course

When an instrument is transferred, an ordinary holder obtains only those rights that the transferor had in the instrument, as mentioned previously.

In this respect, a holder has the same status as an assignee (see Chapter 17). Like an assignee, a holder normally is subject to the same defenses that could be asserted against the transferor.

In contrast, a **holder in due course (HDC)** takes an instrument *free* of most of the defenses and claims that could be asserted against the transferor. An HDC is a holder who meets certain acquisition requirements (to be discussed shortly) and therefore receives a higher level of protection from defenses and claims asserted by other parties.

▶ **Example 26.18** Shanna Morrison buys a BMW X3 SUV for her business from Heritage Motors in Irvine, California, signing a promissory note for $40,000 as part of the deal. Heritage negotiates the note to Apollo Financial Services, which promises to pay Heritage for it in six months. During the next two months, Morrison has significant problems with the SUV and sues Heritage for fraud and breach of con-

tract. She also refuses to make further payments on the note.

Whether Apollo can hold Morrison liable on the note depends on whether it has met the requirements for HDC status. If Apollo has met these requirements and thus has HDC status, it is entitled to payment on the note. If Apollo has not met these requirements, it has the status of an ordinary holder, and Morrison's defense against payment to Heritage will also be effective against Apollo. ◄

Requirements for HDC Status

The basic requirements for attaining HDC status are set forth in UCC 3–302. An HDC must first be a holder of a negotiable instrument and must have taken the instrument (1) for value, (2) in good faith, and (3) without notice that it is defective (such as when the instrument is overdue, dishonored, irregular, or incomplete). We now examine each of these requirements.

TAKING FOR VALUE An HDC must have given value for the instrument [UCC 3–302(a)(2)(i), 3–303]. A person who receives an instrument as a gift or inherits it has *not* met the requirement of value. In these situations, the person normally becomes an ordinary holder and does not possess the rights of an HDC.

Under UCC 3–303(a), a holder takes an instrument for value if the holder has done any of the following:

1. Performed the promise for which the instrument was issued or transferred.
2. Acquired a security interest or other lien in the instrument, excluding a lien obtained by a judicial proceeding (see Chapters 29 and 30).
3. Taken the instrument in payment of, or as security for, a preexisting obligation (sometimes called an **antecedent claim**). ▶ **Example 26.19** Zon owes Dwyer $2,000 on a past-due account. Zon negotiates a $2,000 note signed by Gordon to Dwyer. If Dwyer accepts it to discharge the overdue account balance, Dwyer has given value for the instrument. ◄
4. Given a negotiable instrument as payment. ▶ **Example 26.20** Justin issued a $5,000 negotiable promissory note to Paige. The note is due six months from the date issued. Paige needs cash and does not want to wait until the maturity date to collect. She negotiates the note to her friend

3. *Graves v. Johnson*, 862 N.E.2d 716 (Ind.App. 2007).

Lexi, who pays $2,000 in cash and writes Paige a check—a negotiable instrument—for the balance of $3,000. Lexi has given full value for the note by paying $2,000 in cash and issuing Paige the check for $3,000. ◄

5. Given an irrevocable commitment (such as a letter of credit, described in Chapter 22) as payment.

Value Is Distinguishable from Consideration. The concept of value in the law of negotiable instruments is not the same as the concept of consideration in the law of contracts. Although a promise to give value in the future is valid consideration to support a contract, it does not constitute sufficient value to make the promisor an HDC. If a person promises to perform or give value in the future, that person is not an HDC.

A holder takes an instrument for value *only to the extent that the promise has been performed* [UCC 3–303(a)(1)]. Therefore, in *Example 26.18* on page 502, Apollo Financial Services is not an HDC because it did not take the instrument (Morrison's note) for value—it has not yet paid Heritage Motors for the note. Thus, Morrison's defense of breach of contract is valid against Apollo as well as against Heritage. If Apollo had paid Heritage for the note at the time of transfer (given value), it would be an HDC and could have held Morrison liable on the note even though Morrison has a valid defense against Heritage. Exhibit 26–7 below illustrates these concepts.

Exceptions. In a few situations, the holder may pay for the instrument but does not acquire HDC status. For instance, when the instrument is purchased at a judicial sale, such as a bankruptcy or creditor's sale, the holder will not be an HDC. Similarly, if the instrument is acquired as a result of taking over a trust or estate (as administrator), or as part of a corporate purchase of assets, the holder will have only the rights of an ordinary holder [UCC 3–302(c)].

TAKING IN GOOD FAITH The second requirement for HDC status is that the holder must take the instrument in *good faith* [UCC 3–302(a)(2)(ii)]. This means that the holder must have acted honestly in the process of acquiring the instrument. UCC 3–103(a)(4) defines *good faith* as "honesty in fact and the observance of reasonable commercial standards of fair dealing" [UCC 3–103(a)(4)].

The good faith requirement applies only to the *holder*. It is immaterial whether the transferor acted in good faith. Thus, even a person who takes a negotiable instrument from a thief may become an HDC if the person acquired the instrument in good faith and had no reason to be suspicious of the transaction. The purchaser must honestly believe that the instrument was not defective, however. If a person purchases a $10,000 note for $300 from a stranger on a street corner, the issue of good faith can be raised on the grounds of both the suspicious circumstances and the grossly inadequate consideration (value).

In the following case, the court had to determine whether a check had been accepted in good faith.

EXHIBIT 26–7 Taking for Value

By exchanging defective goods (a BMW X3 SUV) for the note, Heritage Motors breached its contract with Morrison. Morrison could assert this defense if Heritage presented the note to her for payment. Heritage exchanged the note for Apollo Financial Services' promise to pay in six months, however. Because Apollo did not take the note for value, it is not a holder in due course. Thus, Morrison can assert against Apollo the defense of Heritage's breach when Apollo submits the note to Morrison for payment. In contrast, if Apollo had taken the note for value, Morrison could not assert that defense and would be liable to pay the note.

(Yuri Arcurs/Shutterstock.com) (Tupungato/Shutterstock.com) (wavebreakmedia/Shutterstock.com)

SP TLIGHT on Holder in Due Course

Case 26.3 Georg v. Metro Fixtures Contractors, Inc.
Supreme Court of Colorado, 178 P.3d 1209 (2008).

BACKGROUND AND FACTS Cassandra Demery worked as a bookkeeper at Clinton Georg's business, Freestyle, until Georg discovered that she had embezzled more than $200,000 and had failed to pay $240,000 in state and federal taxes owed by Freestyle. Georg fired Demery and said that if she did not repay the embezzled funds, he would notify the authorities.

Demery went to work as a bookkeeper for Metro Fixtures, a company owned by her parents. Without authorization, she wrote a check to Freestyle for $189,000 out of Metro's account and deposited it to Freestyle's checking account. She told Georg that the check was a loan to her from her family to enable her to repay him. Georg used the funds to pay his back taxes.

Two years later, Metro discovered Demery's theft and sued Georg and Freestyle for *conversion* (see Chapter 6) because Demery had no authority to take the funds. The trial court held that Freestyle was a holder in due course (HDC) and granted summary judgment. Metro appealed. The appeals court reversed, holding that because Demery had deposited the check directly into Freestyle's account, Freestyle could not have been an HDC, as it never had actual possession of the check. Georg and Freestyle appealed.

IN THE LANGUAGE OF THE COURT
HOBBS, Justice.

* * * *

A check is a negotiable instrument. The holder in due course doctrine is designed to encourage the transfer and usage of checks and facilitate the flow of capital. *An entity may qualify as a holder in due course even if the instrument at issue may have passed through the hands of a thief.* [Emphasis added.] A holder in due course must meet five conditions: (1) be a holder; (2) of a negotiable instrument who took it; (3) for value; (4) in good faith; (5) without notice of certain problems with the instrument.

To be a holder one must meet two conditions * * * : (1) he or she must have possession (2) of an instrument drawn, issued, or indorsed to him or her. Possession is an element designed to prevent two or more claimants from qualifying as holders who could take free of the other party's claim of ownership. With rare exceptions, those claiming to be holders have physical ownership of the instrument in question.

An otherwise authorized signature on a negotiable instrument is not converted into an unauthorized forgery when an agent, authorized to sign negotiable instruments in his principal's name, abuses that authority by negotiating the instrument to a holder in due course for the agent's own personal benefit.

Section 4–201(a) [of Colorado's UCC statute] states that a collecting bank "is an agent or sub-agent of the owner of the item." Further, the statute states, "This provision applies regardless of the form of indorsement or lack of indorsement * * *." A check payable to a party and deposited in that party's account makes the party the "owner" of the check under the UCC. Further, the [well-known] treatise on the UCC speaks to a collecting bank as an agent for the owner's possession:

> Sometimes the one claiming to be a holder in due course will not have possession of the instrument at the time of the suit. When a collecting bank holds the check, the solution is simple for section 4-201 makes that bank the agent of the owner of the check. *Under traditional analysis, the agent's possession would be the owner's possession and thus the owner would have "possession."*

Thus, there are circumstances wherein requiring actual physical possession of the instrument would be problematic and constructive possession applies. *Nevertheless, a determination of constructive possession should occur only when delivery is clearly for an identifiable person under circumstances excluding any other party as a holder in due course.* [Emphasis added.]

* * * *

CASE 26.3 CONTINUED   Colorado's UCC intends to promote reliability on issued instruments, not to undermine their efficacy by placing the burden on the person to whom it is issued to determine a check's validity. Metro's recourse is not against Freestyle, but rather against its agent employee for breaching her fiduciary duty to the company.

Having reviewed the holder in due course elements in light of the undisputed facts of the case, we determine that Freestyle was a holder with constructive possession of a negotiable instrument, which was given for value and taken in good faith without notice of a forgery or an unauthorized signature. Accordingly, we reverse the judgment of the court of appeals and remand with directions that the court of appeals return this case to the district court for entry of judgment in favor of Freestyle.

DECISION AND REMEDY *The Colorado Supreme Court reinstated the verdict of the trial court and held that Freestyle had received the check in good faith, not knowing it involved theft. Demery was the wrong-doer in this case, and either Metro or Freestyle would have to absorb the loss. Because Freestyle had no reason to know of the theft and Metro did not take steps to prevent it, the loss should fall on Metro.*

WHAT IF THE FACTS WERE DIFFERENT? *Suppose that Demery had gone to work for a company with which she had no relationship and had stolen funds from it to pay Georg. Would Georg then be the more innocent party? Why or why not?*

THE ETHICAL DIMENSION *Since Georg knew that Demery had previously embezzled funds from Freesytle when she was an employee, shouldn't he have been suspicious about the source of the funds that Demery was using to repay Freestyle? Why did the court conclude that Freestyle acted in good faith in accepting the check?*

TAKING WITHOUT NOTICE The final requirement for HDC status concerns notice of defects. A person cannot be an HDC if she or he knows or has reason to know that the instrument is defective in any one of the following ways [UCC 3–302(a)]:

1. It is overdue.
2. It has been dishonored.
3. It is part of a series in which at least one instrument has an uncured (uncorrected) default.
4. The instrument contains an unauthorized signature or has been altered.
5. There is a defense against the instrument or a claim to the instrument.
6. The instrument is so incomplete or irregular as to call into question its authenticity.

What Constitutes Notice? Under UCC 1–201(25), a person is considered to have notice if she or he has any one of the following:

1. Has actual knowledge of the defect.
2. Has received a notice or notification about the defect (such as a letter from a bank identifying the serial numbers of stolen bearer instruments).
3. Has reason to know that a defect exists, given all the facts and circumstances known at the time in question.

The holder must also have received the notice "at a time and in a manner that gives a reasonable opportunity to act on it" [UCC 3–302(f)]. A purchaser's knowledge of certain facts, such as insolvency proceedings against the maker or drawer of the instrument, does not constitute notice that the instrument is defective [UCC 3–302(b)].

Overdue Demand Instruments. What constitutes notice that an instrument is overdue depends on whether it is a demand instrument (payable on demand) or a time instrument (payable at a definite time).

A purchaser has notice that a *demand instrument* is overdue in two situations. One situation occurs when a person takes a demand instrument knowing that demand has been made.

The other situation occurs when a person takes a demand instrument an unreasonable length of time after its date. For a check, a "reasonable time" is ninety days after the date of the check. For all other demand instruments, what will be considered a reasonable time depends on the circumstances [UCC 3–304(a)].

Overdue Time Instruments. Normally, a *time instrument* is overdue on the day after its due date. Anyone who takes a time instrument after the due date is on notice that it is overdue [UCC 3–304(b)].[4] Therefore, if a promissory note due on May 15 is purchased on May 16, the purchaser will be an ordinary holder, not an HDC. If an instrument states that it is "Payable in thirty days," counting begins the day after the instrument is dated. For instance, a note dated December 1 that is payable in thirty days is due by midnight on December 31. If the payment date falls on a Sunday or holiday, the instrument is payable on the next business day.

A series of notes issued at the same time with successive maturity dates is overdue when any note in the series is overdue. This serves to notify prospective purchasers that they cannot qualify as HDCs [UCC 3–302(a)(2)(iii)].

If the principal is to be paid in installments, the default or nonpayment of any one installment will make the instrument overdue and provide notice to prospective purchasers of the default. The instrument will remain overdue until the default is cured [UCC 3–304(b)(1)]. An instrument does not become overdue if there is a default on a payment of interest only, however [UCC 3–304(c)]. For this reason, most installment notes provide that any payment will be applied first to interest and then the balance will be applied to the principal. This serves as notice that any installment payment for less than the full amount results in a default on an installment payment toward the principal.

Dishonored Instruments. An instrument is *dishonored* when the party to whom the instrument is presented refuses to pay it. If a holder knows or has reason to know that an instrument has been dishonored, the holder is on notice and cannot claim HDC status [UCC 3–302(a)(2)]. Thus, a person who takes a check clearly stamped "insufficient funds" is put on notice. Conversely, if a person purchasing an instrument does not know and has no reason to know that it has been dishonored, the person is *not* put on notice and therefore can become an HDC.

▶ **Example 26.21** Lucinda Gonzalez holds a demand note dated September 1 on Apex, Inc., a local business firm. On September 17, she demands payment, and Apex refuses (that is, dishonors the instrument). On September 22, Gonzalez negotiates the note to Brenner, a purchaser who lives in another

state. Brenner does not know, and has no reason to know, that the note has been dishonored. Because Brenner is *not* put on notice, Brenner can become an HDC. ◀

Notice of Claims or Defenses. A holder cannot become an HDC if he or she has notice of any claim to the instrument or defense against it [UCC 3–302(a)(2)(v), (vi)]. A purchaser has notice if the claims or defenses are apparent on the face of the instrument or if the purchaser otherwise had reason to know of them from facts surrounding the transaction.[5] For instance, a potential purchaser who knows that the maker of a note has breached the underlying contract with the payee cannot thereafter purchase the note as an HDC.

Knowledge of one defense precludes a holder from asserting HDC status in regard to all other defenses.
▶ **Example 26.22** James Wu, knowing that the note he has taken has a forged indorsement, presents it to the maker for payment. The maker refuses to pay on the ground of breach of the underlying contract. The maker can assert this defense against Wu even though Wu had no knowledge of the breach. Wu's knowledge of the forgery prevents him from being an HDC in any circumstances. ◀

Incomplete Instruments. A purchaser cannot become an HDC of an instrument so incomplete on its face that an element of negotiability is lacking (for example, the amount is not filled in) [UCC 3–302(a)(1)]. Minor omissions (such as the omission of the date— see Chapter 25) are permissible because these do not call into question the validity of the instrument [UCC 3–113(b)].

Similarly, when a person accepts an instrument that has been completed without knowing that it was incomplete when issued, the person can take it as an HDC [UCC 3–115(b), 3–302(a)(1)]. Even if an instrument that is originally incomplete is later completed in an unauthorized manner, an HDC can still enforce the instrument as completed [UCC 3–407(c)].

▶ **Example 26.23** Peyton asks Brittany to buy a textbook for him when she goes to the campus book-

---

4. A time instrument also becomes overdue the day after an accelerated due date, unless the purchaser has no reason to know that the due date has been accelerated [UCC 3–302(a)(2)(iii), 3–304(b)(3)].

5. If an instrument contains a statement required by a statute or an administrative rule to the effect that the rights of a holder or transferee are subject to the claims or defenses that the issuer could assert against the original payee, the instrument is negotiable. There cannot be an HDC of the instrument, however. See UCC 3–106(d) and the discussion of federal limitations on HDC rights in Chapter 27.

store. Peyton writes a check payable to the campus store, leaves the amount blank, and tells Brittany to fill in the price of the textbook. The cost of the textbook is $85. If Brittany fills in the check for $150 before she gets to the bookstore, the bookstore cashier sees only a properly completed instrument. Therefore, because the bookstore had no notice that the check was incomplete when it was issued, the bookstore can take the check for $150 and become an HDC. (Material alterations will be discussed in Chapter 27.) ◄

Irregular Instruments. Any irregularity on the face of an instrument (such as an obvious forgery or alteration) that calls into question its validity or ownership will bar HDC status. In addition, any irregularity that creates an ambiguity as to the party to pay prevents a holder from becoming an HDC.

A difference between the handwriting used in the body of a check and that used in the signature will not by itself make an instrument irregular. Nor will antedating or postdating a check or stating the amount in digits but failing to write out the numbers. Visible evidence that a maker's or drawer's signature is forged, however, will disqualify a purchaser from HDC status.

Nevertheless, a good forgery of a signature or a careful alteration can go undetected by reasonable examination. In that situation, the purchaser can qualify as an HDC [UCC 3–302(a)(1)]. Losses that result from well-crafted forgeries usually fall on the party to whom the forger transferred the instrument (assuming, of course, that the forger cannot be found). Typically, this means the bank that accepts a check despite evidence on the check's face that it is irregular will bear the loss if the check later turns out to be forged.

SECTION 5
HOLDER THROUGH AN HDC

A person who does not qualify as an HDC but who derives his or her title through an HDC can acquire the rights and privileges of an HDC. This rule, which is sometimes called the **shelter principle,** is set out in UCC 3–203(b):

Transfer of an instrument, whether or not the transfer is a negotiation, vests in the transferee any right of the transferor to enforce the instrument, including any right as a holder in due course, but the transferee cannot acquire rights of a holder in due course by a transfer, directly or indirectly, from a holder in due course if the transferee engaged in fraud or illegality affecting the instrument.

The Purpose of the Shelter Principle

The shelter principle extends the benefits of HDC status and is designed to aid the HDC in readily disposing of the instrument. Anyone, no matter how far removed from an HDC, who can ultimately trace her or his title back to an HDC comes within the shelter principle. The idea is based on the legal theory that the transferee of an instrument receives at least the rights that the transferor had. By extending the benefits of HDC status, the shelter principle promotes the marketability and free transferability of negotiable instruments.

Limitations on the Shelter Principle

There are some limitations on the shelter principle. If a holder participated in fraud or illegality affecting the instrument, that holder is not allowed to improve her or his status by repurchasing the instrument from a later HDC. Similarly, a holder who had notice of a claim or defense against an instrument cannot gain HDC status by later reacquiring the instruments from HDCs [UCC 3–203(b)].

▶ **Example 26.24** Matthew and Carla collaborate to defraud Dina. Dina is induced to give Carla a negotiable note payable to Carla's order. Carla then specially indorses the note for value to Ling, an HDC. Matthew and Carla split the proceeds. Ling negotiates the note to Stuart, another HDC. Stuart then negotiates the note for value to Matthew. Matthew, even though he obtained the note through an HDC, is not a holder through an HDC because he participated in the original fraud and can never acquire HDC rights in this note. ◄

See *Concept Summary 26.2* on the following page for a review of the requirements for HDC status.

CONCEPT SUMMARY 26.2
Rules and Requirements for HDC Status

BASIC REQUIREMENTS	RULES
Must Be a *Holder*	A *holder* is defined as a person in possession of an instrument "if the instrument is payable to bearer or, in the cases of an instrument payable to an identified person, if the identified person is in possession" [UCC 1–201(20)].
Must Take *for Value*	A holder gives *value* by doing any of the following [UCC 3–303]: 1. Performing the promise for which the instrument was issued or transferred. 2. Acquiring a security interest or other lien in the instrument (other than a lien obtained by a judicial proceeding). 3. Taking the instrument in payment of, or as security for, an antecedent debt. 4. Giving a negotiable instrument as payment. 5. Giving an irrevocable commitment as payment.
Must Take *in Good Faith*	*Good faith* is defined for purposes of revised Article 3 as "honesty in fact and the observance of reasonable commercial standards of fair dealing" [UCC 3–103(a)(4)].
Must Take *without Notice*	A holder must not be *on notice* that the instrument is defective in any of the following ways [UCC 3–302, 3–304]: 1. The instrument is overdue. 2. The instrument has been dishonored. 3. There is an uncured (uncorrected) default with respect to another instrument issued as part of the same series. 4. The instrument contains an unauthorized signature or has been altered. 5. There is a defense against the instrument or a claim to the instrument. 6. The instrument is so irregular or incomplete as to call into question its authenticity.
Shelter Principle— Holder through a Holder in Due Course	A holder who cannot qualify as an HDC has the rights of an HDC if he or she derives title through an HDC [UCC 3–203(b)].

Reviewing: Transferability and Holder in Due Course

The Brown family owns several companies, including the J. H. Stevedoring Company and Penn Warehousing and Distribution, Inc. Many aspects of the companies' operations and management are intertwined. Dennis Bishop worked for J. H. and Penn for more than ten years until by 2013, he had become the financial controller at J. H. His responsibilities included approving invoices for payment and reconciling the corporate checkbook. In December 2014, Bishop began stealing from Penn and J. H. by writing checks on the corporate accounts and using the funds for his own benefit (committing the crime of embezzlement). Several members of the Brown family signed the checks for Bishop without hesitation because he was a longtime, trusted employee. Over the next two years, Bishop embezzled $1,209,436. He used $670,632 to buy horses from the Fasig-Tipton Company and Fasig-Tipton Midlantic, Inc., with Penn and J. H. checks made payable to those firms. When Bishop's fraud was revealed, J. H. and Penn filed a suit in a federal district court against the Fasig-Tipton firms (the defendants) to recover the amounts of the checks made payable to them. Using the information presented in the chapter, answer the following questions.

1. What method was most likely used to negotiate the instruments described here?
2. Suppose that all of the checks issued to the defendants were made payable to "Fasig-Tipton Co., Fasig-Tipton Midlantic, Inc." Under the Uniform Commercial Code, were the instruments payable jointly or in the alternative? Why is this significant?
3. Do the defendants in this situation (the two Fasig-Tipton firms) meet the requirements of an HDC? Why or why not?
4. In whose favor should the court rule, and why?

DEBATE THIS ... *We should eliminate the status of holder in due course for those who possess negotiable instruments.*

Terms and Concepts

antecedent claim 502	indorsement 494	restrictive indorsement 498
blank indorsement 494	indorser 494	shelter principle 507
holder in due course (HDC) 502	negotiation 493	special indorsement 496
indorsee 494	qualified indorsement 496	trust indorsement 499

ExamPrep

Issue Spotters

1. Kurt receives from Nabil a check that is made out "Pay to the order of Kurt." Kurt turns it over and writes on the back, "Pay to Adam. [Signed] Kurt." What type of indorsement is this? What effect does this indorsement have on whether the check is considered an order instrument or a bearer instrument? Explain. **(See page 493.)**

2. Ben contracts with Amy to fix her roof. Amy writes Ben a check, but Ben never makes the repairs. Carl knows Ben breached the contract, but cashes the check anyway. Can Carl become an HDC? Why or why not? **(See page 502.)**

• **Check your answers to the Issue Spotters against the answers provided in Appendix E at the end of this text.**

Before the Test

Go to **www.cengagebrain.com**, enter the ISBN 9781285185248, and click on "Find" to locate this textbook's Web site. Then, click on "Access Now" under "Study Tools," and select Chapter 26 at the top. There, you will find a Practice Quiz that you can take to assess your mastery of the concepts in this chapter, as well as Flashcards and a Glossary of important terms.

Business Scenarios

26–1. Indorsements. A check drawn by Cullen for $500 is made payable to the order of Jordan and issued to Jordan. Jordan owes his landlord $500 in rent and transfers the check to his landlord with the following indorsement: "For rent paid, [signed] Jordan." Jordan's landlord has contracted to have Deborah do some landscaping on the property. When Deborah insists on immediate payment, the landlord transfers the check to Deborah without indorsement. Later, to pay for some palm trees purchased from Better-Garden Nursery, Deborah transfers the check with the following indorsement: "Pay to Better-Garden Nursery,

without recourse, [signed] Deborah." Better-Garden Nursery sends the check to its bank indorsed "For deposit only, [signed] Better-Garden Nursery." **(See page 494.)**

(a) Classify each of these indorsements.
(b) Was the transfer from Jordan's landlord to Deborah, without indorsement, an assignment or a negotiation? Explain.

26–2. Holder in Due Course. Through negotiation, Emilio has received from dishonest payees two checks with the following histories:

(a) The drawer issued a check to the payee for $9. The payee cleverly altered the numeral amount on the check from $9 to $90 and the written word from "nine" to "ninety."

(b) The drawer issued a check to the payee without filling in the amount. The drawer authorized the payee to fill in the amount for no more than $90. The payee filled in the amount of $900.

Discuss whether Emilio, by giving value to the payees, can qualify as a holder in due course of these checks. **(See page 502.)**

26–3. Negotiation. Bertram writes a check for $200 payable to "cash." He puts the check in his pocket and drives to the bank to cash the check. As he gets out of his car in the bank's parking lot, the check slips out of his pocket and falls to the pavement. Jerrod walks by moments later, picks up the check, and later that day delivers it to Amber, to whom he owes $200. Amber indorses the check "For deposit only, [signed] Amber Dowel" and deposits it into her checking account. In light of these circumstances, answer the following questions:

(a) Is the check a bearer instrument or an order instrument?

(b) Did Jerrod's delivery of the check to Amber constitute a valid negotiation? Why or why not?

(c) What type of indorsement did Amber make?

(d) Does Bertram have a right to recover the $200 from Amber? Explain. **(See page 493.)**

Business Case Problems

26–4. Alternative or Joint Payees. Hartford Mutual Insurance Co. issued a check for $60,150 payable to "Andrew Michael Bogdan, Jr., Crystal Bogdan, Oceanmark Bank FSB, Goodman-Gable-Gould Company." The check was to pay a claim related to the Bogdans' commercial property. Besides the Bogdans, the payees were the mortgage holder (Oceanmark) and the insurance agent who adjusted the claim. The Bogdans and the agent indorsed the check and cashed it at Provident Bank of Maryland. Meanwhile, Oceanmark sold the mortgage to Pelican National Bank, which asked Provident to pay it the amount of the check. Provident refused. Pelican filed a suit in a Maryland state court against Provident, arguing that the check had been improperly negotiated. Was this check payable jointly or in the alternative? Whose indorsements were required to cash it? In whose favor should the court rule? Explain. [*Pelican National Bank v. Provident Bank of Maryland*, 381 Md. 327, 849 A.2d 475 (2004)] **(See page 501.)**

26–5. Holder in Due Course. American International Group, Inc. (AIG), an insurance company, issued a check to Jermielem Merriwether in connection with a personal-injury matter. Merriwether presented the check to A-1 Check Cashing Emporium for payment. A-1's clerk forgot to have Merriwether sign the check. When he could not reach Merriwether and ask him to come back to A-1 to sign the check, the clerk printed Merriwether's name on the back and deposited the check for collection. When the check was not paid, A-1 sold it to Robert Triffin, who is in the business of buying dishonored checks. When Triffin could not get the check honored, he sued AIG, contending that he, through A-1, had the right to collect on the check as a holder in due course (HDC). The trial court rejected that claim. Triffin appealed. On what basis could he claim HDC status? [*Triffin v. American International Group, Inc.*, ___ A.2d ___ (N.J.Super. 2008)] **(See page 502.)**

26–6. Transfer and Holder in Due Course. Germanie Fequiere executed and delivered a promissory note in the principal amount of $240,000 to BNC Mortgage. As security for the note, Fequiere executed and delivered a mortgage on real property. BNC indorsed the promissory note in blank. Later, Chase Home Finance, LLC, became the holder in due course of the note and holder of the mortgage. When Fequiere failed to make payments on the note, Chase sought to foreclose on the property. Fequiere asserted that Chase could not foreclose on the property because the mortgage on the property had not been properly transferred from BNC to Chase. Assuming that is true, does it mean that Chase, as holder of the negotiable note, cannot foreclose on the collateral (the property secured by the mortgage)? Explain your answer. [*Chase Home Finance, LLC v. Fequiere*, 119 Conn.App. 570, 989 A.2d 606 (2010)] **(See page 502.)**

26–7. BUSINESS CASE PROBLEM WITH SAMPLE ANSWER: Negotiation.

 *Sandra Ford signed a note and a mortgage on her home in Westwood, New Jersey, to borrow $403,750 from Argent Mortgage Co. Argent transferred the note and mortgage to Wells Fargo Bank, N.A., without indorsement. The following spring, Ford stopped making payments on the note. Wells Fargo filed a suit in a New Jersey state court against Ford to foreclose on the mortgage. Ford asserted that Argent had committed fraud in connection with the note by providing misleading information and charging excessive fees. Ford contended that Wells Fargo was subject to these defenses because the bank was not a holder in due course of the note. Was the transfer of the note from Argent to Wells Fargo a negotiation or an assignment? What difference does it make? If Argent indorsed the note to Wells Fargo now, would the bank's status change? Discuss. [Wells Fargo Bank, N.A. v. Ford, 418 N.J.Super. 592, 15 A.3d 327 (App.Div. 2011)] **(See page 494.)**

- **For a sample answer to Problem 26–7, go to Appendix F at the end of this text.**

26–8. Indorsements. Angela Brock borrowed $544,000 and signed a note payable to Amerifund Mortgage Services, LLC, to buy a house in Silver Spring, Maryland. The note was indorsed in blank and transferred several times "without recourse" before Brock fell behind on the payments. On behalf of Deutsche Bank National Trust Co., BAC Home Loans Servicing LP initiated foreclosure. Brock filed an action in a Maryland state court to block it, arguing that BAC could not foreclose because Deutsche Bank, not BAC, owned the note. Can BAC enforce the note? Explain. [*Deutsche Bank National Trust Co. v. Brock,* 430 Md. 714, 63 A.3d 40 (2013)] **(See page 494.)**

26–9. A QUESTION OF ETHICS: Indorsements.

 As an assistant comptroller for Interior Crafts, Inc., in Chicago, Illinois, Todd Leparski was authorized to receive checks from Interior's customers and deposit the checks into Interior's account. Over a period of five months, Leparski stole more than $500,000 from Interior by indorsing the checks "Interior Crafts—For Deposit Only" but then depositing some of them into his own account at Marquette Bank. Leparski used an automated teller machine owned by Pan American Bank to make the deposits into Marquette. Marquette alerted Interior, which was able to recover about $250,000 from Leparski. Interior also recovered $250,000 under its policy with American Insurance Co. To collect the rest of the missing funds, Interior filed a suit in an Illinois state court against Leparski and the banks. The court ruled in favor of Interior, and Pan American appealed to a state intermediate appellate court. [Interior Crafts, Inc. v. Leparski, 366 Ill.App.3d 1148, 853 N.E.2d 1244, 304 Ill.Dec. 878 (3 Dist. 2006)] **(See page 494.)**

(a) What type of indorsement is "Interior Crafts—For Deposit Only"? What is the obligation of a party that receives a check with this indorsement? Does the fact that Interior authorized Leparski to indorse its checks but not to deposit those checks into his own account absolve Pan American of liability? Explain.

(b) From an ethical perspective, how might a business firm such as Interior discourage an employee's thievery such as Leparski's acts in this case? Discuss.

Legal Reasoning Group Activity

26–10. Holder in Due Course. Celine issues a ninety-day negotiable promissory note payable to the order of Hayden. The amount of the note is left blank, pending a determination of the amount that Hayden will need to purchase a used car for Celine. Celine authorizes any amount not to exceed $2,000. Hayden, without authority, fills in the note in the amount of $5,000 and thirty days later sells the note to First National Bank of Oklahoma for $4,850. Hayden does not buy the car and leaves the state. First National Bank has no knowledge that the instrument was incomplete when issued or that Hayden had no authority to complete the instrument in the amount of $5,000. **(See page 502.)**

(a) The first group will determine whether the bank qualifies as a holder in due course and, if so, for what amount.

(b) The second group will decide what would happen if Hayden had sold the note to a stranger in a bar for $500. Would the stranger qualify as a holder in due course? Explain.

CHAPTER 27

LIABILITY, DEFENSES, AND DISCHARGE

Liability on a negotiable instrument can arise either from a person's signature on the instrument (*signature liability*) or from the warranties that are implied when the person presents the instrument for negotiation (*warranty liability*). A person who signs a negotiable instrument is potentially liable for payment of the amount stated on the instrument. Unlike signature liability, warranty liability does not require a signature and extends to both signers and nonsigners. A breach of warranty can occur when the instrument is transferred or presented for payment.

This chapter focuses on the liability *of the instrument itself or the warranties connected with the transfer or presentment of the instrument,* as opposed to the liability on any underlying contract. Suppose that Donna agrees to buy one thousand backup hard drives from Luis and issues a check to Luis in payment.

The liability discussed in this chapter does not relate directly to the contract (for instance, whether the hard drives are of proper quality or fit for their intended purpose). Instead, the chapter discusses the liability connected with the *check* (such as what recourse Luis will have if Donna's bank refuses to pay the check due to insufficient funds in her account or her order to stop payment on the check).

SECTION 1

SIGNATURE LIABILITY

The key to liability on a negotiable instrument is a signature. As discussed in Chapter 25, the Uniform Commercial Code (UCC) broadly defines a signature to include any name, word, mark, or symbol that is executed or adopted by a person [UCC 1–201(37), 3–401(b)].

The general rule is that every party, except a qualified indorser,[1] who signs a negotiable instrument is either primarily or secondarily liable for payment of that instrument when it comes due. A person is *not* liable on an instrument unless he or she has signed it personally or through an authorized representative (agent) [UCC 3–401(a)].

Primary Liability

Primary liability is unconditional. A person who is primarily liable on a negotiable instrument is absolutely required to pay the instrument—unless, of course, he or she has a valid defense to payment. Liability is immediate when the instrument is signed or issued. No action by the holder of the instrument is required. Only *makers* and *acceptors* of instruments are primarily liable [UCC 3–412, 3–413].

MAKERS The maker of a promissory note unconditionally promises to pay the note according to its terms. It is the maker's promise to pay that renders the instrument negotiable. Even if the promissory note was incomplete at the time the maker signed it, the maker is still obligated to pay. The maker must pay it according to either its stated terms or terms that were agreed on and later filled in to complete the instrument [UCC 3–115, 3–407, 3–412].

▶ **Example 27.1** Tristan executes a preprinted promissory note to Sharon, without filling in the due-date blank. If Sharon does not complete the form by

---

1. A qualified indorser—one who indorses "without recourse"—undertakes no obligation to pay [UCC 3–415(b)]. A qualified indorser merely assumes warranty liability, which will be discussed later in this chapter.

adding the date, the note will be payable on demand. If Sharon subsequently writes in a due date that Tristan authorized, the note is payable on the stated due date. In either situation, Tristan (the maker) is obligated to pay the note. (Note that if Sharon fills in a date that Tristan did not authorize, Tristan can claim a defense to payment—material alteration, which will be discussed later in this chapter.) ◄

ACCEPTORS An *acceptor* is a drawee, such as a bank, that promises to pay an instrument when it is presented later for payment, as mentioned in Chapter 25. Once a drawee *accepts* a draft (usually by writing "accepted" across its face and signing it), the drawee is obligated to pay the draft when it is presented for payment [UCC 3–409(a)]. The drawee's acceptance is a promise to pay that places the drawee in almost the same position as the maker of a promissory note [UCC 3–413]. Failure to pay an accepted draft when presented leads to primary signature liability for the drawee-acceptor.

Secondary Liability

Drawers and *indorsers* are secondarily liable. On a negotiable instrument, secondary liability is *contingent liability*. In other words, a drawer or an indorser will be liable *only if* the party that is primarily responsible for paying the instrument refuses to do so—that is, **dishonors** the instrument.

On drafts and checks, a drawer's secondary liability does not arise until the drawee fails to pay or to accept the instrument, whichever is required. With regard to promissory notes, an indorser's secondary liability does not arise until the maker, who is primarily liable, has defaulted on the instrument [UCC 3–412, 3–415].

Thus, dishonor of an instrument triggers the liability of parties who are secondarily liable on the instrument—that is, the drawer and *unqualified* indorsers.
▶ **Example 27.2** Nina Lee writes a check for $1,000 on her account at Western Bank payable to the order of Rick Carerra. Carerra indorses and delivers the check, for value, to Eric Deere. Deere deposits the check into his account at Universal Bank, but the bank returns the check to Deere marked "insufficient funds," thus dishonoring the check. The question for Deere is whether the drawer (Lee) or the drawee-indorser (Carerra) can be held liable on the check after the bank has dishonored it. The answer to the question depends on whether certain conditions (outlined next) for secondary liability have been satisfied. ◄

Parties are secondarily liable on a negotiable instrument *only if* the following events occur:[2]

1. The instrument is properly and timely presented.
2. The instrument is dishonored.
3. Timely notice of dishonor is given to the secondarily liable party.[3]

PROPER PRESENTMENT As discussed in Chapter 25, *presentment* occurs when a person presents an instrument either to the party liable on the instrument for payment or to a drawee for acceptance. The UCC requires that a holder present the instrument to the appropriate party, in a timely fashion, and give reasonable identification if requested [UCC 3–414(f), 3–415(e), 3–501].

The party to whom the instrument must be presented depends on the type of instrument involved. A note or certificate of deposit (CD) must be presented to the maker for payment. A draft is presented to the drawee for acceptance, payment, or both. A check is presented to the drawee (bank) for payment [UCC 3–501(a), 3–502(b)].

Presentment can be made by any commercially reasonable means, including oral, written, or electronic communication [UCC 3–501(b)]. Ordinarily, it is effective when the demand for payment or acceptance is received. (If presentment takes place after an established cutoff hour, however, it may be treated as occurring on the next business day.)

TIMELY PRESENTMENT Timeliness is important for proper presentment [UCC 3–414(f), 3–415(e), 3–501(b)(4)]. Failure to present an instrument on time is a common reason for improper presentment and can lead to unqualified indorsers being discharged from secondary liability. A reasonable time for presentment is determined by the nature of the instrument, any usage of banking or trade, and the facts of the particular case.

If the instrument is payable on demand, the holder should present it for payment or acceptance within a reasonable time. The holder of a domestic check must present that check for payment or collection within

---

2. An instrument can be drafted to include a waiver of the presentment and notice of dishonor requirements [UCC 3–504]. Presume, for simplicity's sake, that such waivers have *not* been incorporated into the instruments described in this chapter.
3. These requirements are necessary for a secondarily liable party to have *signature* liability on a negotiable instrument, but not for a secondarily liable party to have *warranty* liability (discussed later in this chapter).

thirty days of its *date* to make the drawer secondarily liable. With respect to indorsers, the holder must present a check within thirty days after its indorsement to make the indorser secondarily liable [UCC 3–414(f), 3–415(e)].

The time for proper presentment for different types of instruments is shown in Exhibit 27–1 below.

DISHONOR As mentioned previously, an instrument is dishonored when the required payment or acceptance is refused or cannot be obtained within the prescribed time. An instrument is also dishonored when the required presentment is excused (as it would be, for instance, if the maker had died) and the instrument is not properly accepted or paid [UCC 3–502(e), 3–504].

In the following situations, a delay in payment or a refusal to pay an instrument will not dishonor the instrument:

1. When presentment is made after an established cutoff hour (not earlier than 2:00 P.M.), a bank can postpone payment until the following business day without dishonoring the instrument [UCC 3–501(b)(4)].

2. When the holder refuses to exhibit the instrument, to give reasonable identification, or to sign a receipt for the payment on the instrument, a bank's refusal to pay does not dishonor the instrument [UCC 3–501(b)(2)].

3. When an instrument is returned because it lacks a proper indorsement, the instrument is not dishonored [UCC 3–501(b)(3)(i)].

PROPER NOTICE Once an instrument has been dishonored, proper notice must be given to secondary parties (drawers and indorsers) for them to be held liable. ▶ **Example 27.3** Oman writes a check on his account at People's Bank payable to Bea. Bea indorses the check in blank and cashes it at Midwest Grocery, which transfers it to People's Bank for payment. If People's Bank refuses to pay it, Midwest must timely notify Bea to hold her liable. ◀

Notice can be given in any reasonable manner, including an oral, written, or electronic communication, as well as notice written or stamped on the instrument itself [UCC 3–503(b)].[4] If the party giving notice is a bank, it must give any necessary notice before its midnight deadline (midnight of the next banking day after receipt) [UCC 3–503(c)]. Notice by any party other than a bank must be given within thirty days following the day of dishonor or the day on which the person who is secondarily liable received notice of dishonor [UCC 3–503(c)].

Accommodation Parties

An **accommodation party** is one who signs an instrument for the purpose of lending his or her name as credit to another party on the instrument [UCC 3–419(a)]. Banks may require an accommodation party—a cosigner—to secure against nonpayment of a negotiable instrument. A parent who cosigns a promissory note with her or his son or daughter, for instance, is an accommodation party, and the child (the maker) is the accommodated party.

ACCOMMODATION MAKERS If the accommodation party signs on behalf of the *maker,* he or she is an *accommodation maker* and is primarily liable on the instrument. ▶ **Example 27.4** Alex takes out a loan to purchase a car, and his uncle cosigns the note. The uncle becomes primarily liable on the instrument. In

---

4. Written notice is preferable because a secondary party may claim that an oral notice was never received. Also, to give proper notice of the dishonor of a foreign draft (a draft drawn in one country and payable in another country), a formal notice called a *protest* is required [UCC 3–505(b)].

EXHIBIT 27–1 Time for Proper Presentment

Type of Instrument	For Acceptance	For Payment
Time	On or before due date.	On due date.
Demand	Within a reasonable time (after date of issue or after secondary party becomes liable on the instrument).	Within a reasonable time.
Check	Not applicable.	Within thirty days of its date, to hold drawer secondarily liable. Within thirty days of indorsement, to hold indorser secondarily liable.

other words, Alex's uncle is guaranteeing payment, and the bank can seek payment directly from the uncle. ◄

ACCOMMODATION INDORSERS If the accommodation party signs on behalf of a *payee or other holder* (usually to make the instrument more marketable), she or he is an *accommodation indorser.* As an indorser, she or he is secondarily liable. ▶ **Example 27.5** Frank Huston applies to Northeast Bank for a $20,000 loan to start a small business. Huston's lender (who has possession of the note) asks Susan Smith, who has invested in Huston's business, to sign the note. In this situation, Smith is an indorser and thus has secondary liability—that is, the lender must pursue Huston first before seeking payment from Smith. If Smith ends up paying the amount due on the note, she has a right to reimbursement from Huston (the accommodated party) [UCC 3–419(e)]. ◄

Authorized Agents' Signatures

The general law of agency, covered in Chapters 32 and 33, applies to negotiable instruments. Questions often arise as to the liability on an instrument signed by an agent. An **agent** is a person who agrees to represent or act for another, called the **principal.**

Agents can sign negotiable instruments, just as they can sign contracts, and thereby bind their principals [UCC 3–401(a)(ii), 3–402(a)]. Without such a rule, all corporate commercial business would stop, as every corporation can and must act through its agents. Certain requirements must be met, however, before the principal becomes liable on the instrument. A basic requirement to hold the principal liable on the instrument is that the agent must be *authorized* to sign the instrument on the principal's behalf.

LIABILITY OF THE PRINCIPAL Generally, an authorized agent binds a principal on an instrument if the agent *clearly names* the principal in the signature (in handwriting, or by some mark or symbol). In this situation, the UCC presumes that the signature is authorized and genuine [UCC 3–308(a)]. The agent can add his or her own name, but if the signature shows clearly that it is made on behalf of a specific principal, the agent is not liable on the instrument [UCC 3–402(b)(1)].
▶ **Example 27.6** Either of the following signatures by Sandra Binney as agent for Bob Aronson will bind Aronson on the instrument:

1. Aronson, by Binney, agent.
2. Aronson.

If Binney (the agent) signs just her own name, however, she will be personally liable to a holder in due course (HDC) who has no notice of her agency status. ◄

An agent can escape liability to ordinary holders if the agent proves that the original parties did not intend the agent to be liable on the instrument [UCC 3–402(a), (b)(2)].[5] In either situation, the principal is bound if the party entitled to enforce the instrument can prove the agency relationship.

LIABILITY OF THE AGENT An authorized agent may be held personally liable on a negotiable instrument in the following three situations.

1. When the agent signs his or her own name on the instrument with no indication of agency status, an HDC can hold the agent personally liable as noted above.
2. When the agent signs in both the agent's name and the principal's name but nothing on the instrument indicates the agency relationship, the agent may be liable. (Thus, in *Example 27.6,* if Binney signed the instrument "Sandra Binney, Bob Aronson" or "Aronson, Binney," she may be held personally liable because it is not clear that there is an agency relationship.)
3. When the agent indicates his or her agency status in signing a negotiable instrument but fails to name the principal (such as, "Sandra Binney, agent"), the agent may be liable [UCC 3–402(b)(2)].

Obviously, to protect against potential liability, an authorized agent should disclose on the instrument the identity of the principal and also indicate that the agent is signing in a representative capacity.
▶ **Case in Point 27.7** Hugh Caraway was the president of Internacional Realty, Inc. When Internacional hired Land Design Studio to landscape an apartment complex, Caraway signed a promissory note as "Hugh Caraway, Internacional Realty, Inc." When Internacional did not make any payments on the note, Land Design filed a suit against both Caraway and Internacional. Caraway claimed that he had signed the note as an agent and should not be personally liable for the debt. The court ruled that Caraway was personally liable on the note because there was no indication that he was signing as an agent for Internacional.[6] ◄

---

5. See UCC 3–402, Comment 1.
6. *Caraway v. Land Design Studio,* 47 S.W.3d 696 (Tex.App.—Austin 2001).

CHECKS SIGNED BY AGENTS An important exception to the rules on agent liability is made for checks that are signed by agents. If an agent signs his or her own name on a *check that is payable from the account of the principal,* and the principal is identified on the check, the agent will not be personally liable on the check [UCC 3–402(c)]. ▶ **Example 27.8** Sandra Binney, who is *authorized* to draw checks on Aronson Company's account, signs a check that is preprinted with Aronson Company's name. The signature reads simply "Sandra Binney." In this situation, Binney will not be personally liable on the check. ◀

In the following case, an agent signed his own name to a check that was preprinted with the name of the principal. The court had to determine whether the agent was personally liable.

CASE 27.1

Jeanmarie v. Peoples
Court of Appeal of Louisiana, Fourth Circuit, 34 So.3d 945 (2010).

BACKGROUND AND FACTS On August 26, 2005, Anthony and Alcibia Jeanmarie sold property located in New Orleans to Melanie Murray. As part of the transaction, Encore Credit Corporation provided two loans to Murray, for $104,000 and $26,000. Murray secured each loan with a mortgage (mortgages will be discussed in Chapter 30) in favor of Encore. Mark Peoples, through his company, Pyramid Title, LLC, handled the closing of the sale. At the closing, a check was drawn on the Pyramid escrow account[a] in the sum of $110,303.86, payable to the Jeanmaries.

The Jeanmaries deposited the check in their account, but two days later the check was returned because there were insufficient funds in Pyramid's escrow account to cover the check. According to Peoples, one reason for the insufficient funds was that Encore Credit had not "timely funded" the $26,000 loan, which would normally be in the account. The Jeanmaries filed an action in a Louisiana state court, seeking payment from both Pyramid Title, LLC, and Peoples personally.

Peoples contended that he should not be held liable because he had signed the Pyramid check to the Jeanmaries in his representative capacity. The trial court held for the Jeanmaries. Peoples and Pyramid appealed.

IN THE LANGUAGE OF THE COURT
Joan Bernard *ARMSTRONG,* Chief Judge.

* * * *

The record contains an undisputed copy of the check in question. It bears the title, "Pyramid Title LLC Escrow Account." Mr. Peoples does not contest the fact that the check bears his signature upon the line entitled "Authorized Signature." [Louisiana's equivalent to UCC 3–402] concerning signatures affixed in a representative capacity provides as follows:

§ 3–402. Signature by representative
* * * *

(c) *If a representative signs the name of the representative as drawer of a check without indication of the representative status and the check is payable from an account of the represented person who is identified on the check, the signer is not liable on the check if the signature is an authorized signature of the represented person.* [Emphasis added.]

Comment No. 3 of the Uniform Commercial Code found under [Louisiana's equivalent to UCC 3–402] shows that [the section] quoted above is the paragraph applicable to the fact situation found in the instant case:

3. Subsection (c) * * * states that if the check identifies the represented person, the agent who signs on the signature line does not have to indicate agency status. Virtually all checks used today

---

a. Until a sale of real property, or real estate, is finalized (closed), funds paid by the buyer to the seller, such as a down payment, as well as funds to be paid to the seller by a financing institution, are typically held in an *escrow account.* The concept of escrow and the utilization of escrow accounts in the sale of real property will be discussed in Chapter 49.

CASE 27.1 CONTINUED   are in personalized form that identify the person on whose account the check is drawn. In this case, nobody is deceived into thinking that the person signing the check is meant to be liable.

In the instant case, the check clearly identifies the represented person at the top in bold-face and a large font as Pyramid Title LLC * * * .

The signature line is entitled, "AUTHORIZED SIGNATURE," a designation not typically found on personal checks. It is patent [obvious] on the face of the check that Mark Peoples signed as the authorized signatory for Pyramid Title and not in his personal capacity * * * . There is nothing subtle, obscure or ambiguous about this.

DECISION AND REMEDY *The Louisiana appellate court held that it was clear from the face of the instrument that Peoples had signed the check in his representative capacity and thus was not personally liable on the instrument. The court vacated the trial court's ruling on this issue and remanded the case for further proceedings consistent with its opinion.*

WHAT IF THE FACTS WERE DIFFERENT? *Suppose that the name* Pyramid Title, LLC, *had not been included on the face of the check. Would Peoples have been personally liable for payment of the check in that situation? Why or why not?*

THE ECONOMIC DIMENSION *Should Encore Credit Corporation's failure to "timely fund" the $26,000 loan be taken into consideration by the court when determining whether Peoples could be held personally liable on the check? Discuss fully.*

Unauthorized Signatures

Unauthorized signatures arise in two situations:

1. When a person forges another person's name on a negotiable instrument.
2. When an agent who lacks the authority signs an instrument on behalf of a principal.

THE GENERAL RULE The general rule is that an unauthorized signature is wholly inoperative and will not bind the person whose name is signed or forged. ▶ **Example 27.9** Parker finds Dolby's checkbook lying in the street, writes out a check to himself, and forges Dolby's signature. Banks normally have a duty to determine whether a person's signature on a check is forged. If a bank fails to determine that Dolby's signature is not genuine and cashes the check for Parker, the bank will generally be liable to Dolby for the amount. ◀ (The liability of banks for paying instruments with forged signatures will be discussed further in Chapter 28.)

Similarly, if an agent lacks the authority to sign the principal's name or has exceeded the authority given by the principal, the signature does not bind the principal but will bind the "unauthorized signer" [UCC 3–403(a)]. ▶ **Example 27.10** Maya Campbell is the principal, and Lena Shem is her agent. Shem, without authority, signs a promissory note as follows: "Maya Campbell, by Lena Shem, agent."

Because Maya Campbell's "signature" is unauthorized, Campbell cannot be held liable, but Shem is liable to a holder of the note. This would be true even if Shem had signed the note "Maya Campbell," without indicating any agency relationship. In either situation, the unauthorized signer, Shem, is liable on the instrument. ◀

EXCEPTIONS TO THE GENERAL RULE There are two exceptions to the general rule that an unauthorized signature will not bind the person whose name is signed:

1. *Ratification.* When the person whose name is signed *ratifies* (affirms) the signature, he or she will be bound [UCC 3–403(a)]. The parties involved need not be principal and agent for this section of the UCC to apply. For instance, a mother may ratify her daughter's forgery of the mother's signature so that the daughter will not be prosecuted for forgery.

   A person can ratify an unauthorized signature either expressly (by affirming the signature) or impliedly (by other conduct, such as keeping any benefits received in the transaction or failing to repudiate the signature).
2. *Negligence.* When the negligence of the person whose name was forged substantially contributed to the forgery, a court may not allow the person to

deny the effectiveness of an unauthorized signature [UCC 3–115, 3–406, 4–401(d)(2)].

▶ **Example 27.11**   Rob, the owner of a business, leaves his signature stamp and a blank check on an office counter. An employee uses the stamp to fill in the check and cashes it. Rob can be estopped (prevented), on the basis of his negligence, from denying liability for payment of the check. Whatever loss occurs, however, may be allocated between certain parties on the basis of *comparative negligence* [UCC 3–406(b)]. If Rob can demonstrate that the bank was negligent in paying the check, a court may require the bank to bear a portion of the loss. (The liability of the parties in this type of situation will be discussed further in Chapter 28.) ◀

WHEN THE HOLDER IS A HOLDER IN DUE COURSE   A person who forges a check or signs an instrument without authorization can be held personally liable for payment by a holder in due course, or HDC [UCC 3–403(a)]. This is true even if the name of the person signing the instrument without authorization does not appear on the instrument.

▶ **Example 27.12**   If Michel Vuillard signs "Paul Richman" without Richman's authorization, Vuillard is personally liable just as if he had signed his own name. Vuillard's liability is limited, however, to persons who in good faith pay the instrument or take it for value. A holder who knew the signature was unauthorized would not qualify as an HDC (because of the good faith requirement) and thus could not recover from Vuillard on the instrument. (The defenses that are effective against ordinary holders versus HDCs will be discussed in detail later in this chapter.) ◀

Special Rules for Unauthorized Indorsements

Generally, when an indorsement is forged or unauthorized, the burden of loss falls on the first party to take the instrument with the forged or unauthorized indorsement. The reason for this general rule is that the first party to take an instrument is in the best position to prevent the loss.

▶ **Example 27.13**   Jen Nilson steals a check drawn on Universal Bank and payable to the order of Inga Leed. Nilson indorses the check "Inga Leed" and presents the check to Universal Bank for payment. The bank, without asking Nilson for identification, pays the check, and Nilson disappears. In this situation, Leed will not be liable on the check. because her

indorsement was forged. The bank will bear the loss, which it might have avoided if it had asked Nilson for identification. ◀

This general rule has two important exceptions. These exceptions arise when an indorsement is made by an *imposter* or by a *fictitious payee*.

IMPOSTER RULE   An **imposter** is one who, through deception, induces a maker or drawer to issue an instrument in the name of an impersonated payee. The imposter may carry out the deception by her or his personal appearance or by use of the mails, Internet, telephone, or other communication.

Focus Is on the Maker's or Drawer's Intent.   If the maker or drawer believes the imposter to be the named payee at the time of issue, the imposter's indorsement is not treated as unauthorized when the instrument is transferred to an innocent party. This is because the maker or drawer *intended* the imposter to receive the instrument.

In these situations, the unauthorized indorsement of a payee's name can be as effective as if the real payee had signed. The UCC's *imposter rule* provides that an imposter's indorsement will be effective—that is, not a forgery—insofar as the drawer or maker is concerned [UCC 3–404(a)].

Comparative Negligence Applies.   The comparative negligence standard mentioned previously also applies to situations involving imposters [UCC 3–404(d)]. Thus, if a bank fails to exercise ordinary care in cashing a check made out to an imposter, the drawer may be able to recover a portion of the loss from the bank.

▶ **Example 27.14**   Carol impersonates Donna and induces Edward to write a check payable to the order of Donna. Carol, continuing to impersonate Donna, negotiates the check to First National Bank as payment on her loan there. As the drawer of the check, Edward is liable for its amount to First National. If the bank failed to use due care when taking the check from Carol, however, Edward may be able to recover a portion of his loss from First National. ◀

FICTITIOUS PAYEES   When a person causes an instrument to be issued to a payee who will have *no interest* in the instrument, the payee is referred to as a **fictitious payee.** A fictitious payee can be a person or firm that does not truly exist, or it may be an identifiable party that will not acquire any interest in the instrument.

Payee's Indorsement Not Treated as a Forgery. Under the UCC's *fictitious payee rule,* the payee's indorsement is not treated as a forgery, and an innocent holder can hold the maker or drawer liable on the instrument [UCC 3–404(b), 3–405]. Basically, the loss falls on the maker or drawer of the instrument rather than on the third party that accepts it or on the bank that cashes it.

Typical Incidents. Fictitious payees most often arise in two situations:

1. When a dishonest employee deceives the employer into signing an instrument payable to a party with no right to receive payment on the instrument.
2. When a dishonest employee or agent has the authority to issue an instrument on behalf of the employer and issues a check to a party who has no interest in the instrument.

▶ **Case in Point 27.15** Braden Furniture Company gave its bookkeeper, Bonnie Manning, general authority to access the company's accounting program and create checks. Over the course of seven years, Manning created more than two hundred unauthorized checks, totaling $470,000, which she deposited in her own account at Union State Bank. Braden Furniture was not a customer of Union State Bank.

The majority of the checks did not identify a payee (the payee line on the check was left blank). Braden Furniture (the drawer) sued Union State Bank for the loss, claiming that the bank was negligent in accepting and paying the blank checks. The court, however, held that the fictitious payee rule applied. Therefore, under Alabama's version of the UCC, the loss fell on Braden Furniture, not on Union State Bank.[7] ◀

For a synopsis of the rules relating to signature liability, see *Concept Summary 27.1* on the following page.

SECTION 2
WARRANTY LIABILITY

In addition to the signature liability, transferors make certain implied warranties regarding the instruments that they are negotiating. Warranty liability arises even when a transferor does not indorse (sign) the instrument [UCC 3–416, 3–417].

Warranty liability is particularly important when a holder cannot hold a party liable on her or his signa-

ture, such as when a person delivers a bearer instrument. *Unlike secondary signature liability, warranty liability is not subject to the conditions of proper presentment, dishonor, or notice of dishonor.*

Warranties fall into two categories: those that arise from the *transfer* of a negotiable instrument and those that arise on *presentment.* Both transfer and presentment warranties attempt to shift liability back to the wrongdoer or to the person who dealt face to face with the wrongdoer and thus was in the best position to prevent the wrongdoing.

Transfer Warranties

A person who transfers an instrument *for consideration* makes the following five **transfer warranties** to all subsequent transferees and holders who take the instrument in good faith [UCC 3–416] (with some exceptions, as will be discussed shortly):

1. The transferor is entitled to enforce the instrument.
2. All signatures are authentic and authorized.
3. The instrument has not been altered.
4. The instrument is not subject to a defense or claim of any party that can be asserted against the transferor.
5. The transferor has no knowledge of any bankruptcy proceedings against the maker, the acceptor, or the drawer of the instrument.[8]

Note that for transfer warranties to arise, an instrument *must be transferred for consideration.* ▶ **Example 27.16** Quality Products Corporation sells goods to Royal Retail Stores and receives in payment Royal Retail's promissory note. Quality then sells the note, for value, to Superior Finance Company. In this situation, the instrument has been transferred for consideration. ◀

PARTIES TO WHOM WARRANTY LIABILITY EXTENDS
The manner of transfer and the type of negotiation that are used determine how far a transfer warranty will run and whom it will cover. Transfer of an order instrument by indorsement and delivery extends warranty liability to any subsequent holder who takes the instrument in good faith. The warranties of a person who, for

---

7. *Braden Furniture Co. v. Union State Bank,* 109 So.3d 625 (Ala. 2012).

8. A 2002 amendment to UCC 3–416(a) adds a sixth warranty. It involves "a remotely created consumer item," such as an electronic check, drawn on a customer's account, which is not created by the payor bank and does not contain the drawer's handwritten signature. This amendment has been adopted in only a few states. Under this amendment, a bank that accepts and pays the instrument warrants to the next bank in the collection chain that the consumer authorized the item in that amount.

CONCEPT SUMMARY 27.1
Signature Liability

CONCEPT	DESCRIPTION

Primary and Secondary Liability	Every party (except a qualified indorser) who signs a negotiable instrument is either primarily or secondarily liable for payment of the instrument when it comes due.
	1. *Primary liability*—Makers and acceptors are primarily liable [UCC 3–409, 3–412, 3–413].
	2. *Secondary liability*—Drawers and indorsers are secondarily liable [UCC 3–414, 3–415, 3–501, 3–502, 3–503]. Parties who are secondarily liable on an instrument promise to pay on that instrument only if the following events occur:
	  a. The instrument is properly and timely presented.
	  b. The instrument is dishonored.
	  c. Timely notice of dishonor is given.

Accommodation Parties	An *accommodation party* is one who signs an instrument for the purpose of lending his or her name as credit to another party on the instrument [UCC 3–419]. Accommodation *makers* are primarily liable; accommodation *indorsers* are secondarily liable.
Agents' Signatures	An *agent* is a person who agrees to represent or act for another, called the *principal*. Agents can sign negotiable instruments and thereby bind their principals. Liability on the instrument depends on whether the agent is authorized and on whether the agent's representative capacity and the principal's identity are both indicated on the instrument [UCC 3–401, 3–402, 3–403]. Agents need not indicate their representative capacity on *checks*—provided the checks clearly identify the principal and are drawn on the principal's account.
Unauthorized Signatures	An unauthorized signature is wholly inoperative as the signature of the person whose name is signed *unless*: 1. The person whose name is signed ratifies (affirms) it or is precluded from denying it [UCC 3–115, 3–403, 3–406, 4–401]. 2. The instrument has been negotiated to a holder in due course [UCC 3–403].
Special Rules for Unauthorized Indorsements	An unauthorized indorsement will not bind the maker or drawer of the instrument except in the following circumstances: 1. When an imposter induces the maker or drawer of an instrument to issue it to the imposter *(imposter rule)* [UCC 3–404(a)]. 2. When a person causes an instrument to be issued to a payee who will have *no interest* in the instrument *(fictitious payee rule)* [UCC 3–404(b), 3–405].

---

consideration, transfers *without indorsement* (by delivery of a bearer instrument), however, will extend only to the immediate transferee [UCC 3–416(a)].

▶ **Example 27.17** Wylie forges Kim's name as a maker of a promissory note. The note is made payable to Wylie. Wylie indorses the note in blank, negotiates it for consideration to Bret, and then leaves the country. Bret, without indorsement, delivers the note for consideration to Fern. Fern, also without indorsement, delivers the note for consideration to Rick. On Rick's presentment of the note to Kim, the forgery is discovered. Rick can hold Fern (the immediate transferor) liable for breach of the warranty that all signatures are genuine. Rick cannot hold Bret liable because Bret is not Rick's immedi-

ate transferor. Rather, Bret is a prior nonindorsing transferor.

Note that if Wylie had added a special indorsement ("Payable to Bret") instead of a blank indorsement, the instrument would have remained an order instrument. In that situation, Bret would have had to indorse the instrument to negotiate it to Fern, and his transfer warranties would extend to all subsequent holders, including Rick. This example shows the importance of the distinction between transfer by indorsement and delivery (of an order instrument) and transfer by delivery only, without indorsement (of a bearer instrument). ◀

For a synopsis of the rules on transfer warranty liability, see *Concept Summary 27.2* on the following page.

CONCEPT SUMMARY 27.2
Transfer Warranty Liability for Transferors Who Receive Consideration

TRANSFERORS	TRANSFEREES TO WHOM WARRANTIES EXTEND IF CONSIDERATION IS RECEIVED
Indorsers Who Receive Consideration	Five transfer warranties extend to *all* subsequent holders: 1. The transferor is entitled to enforce the instrument. 2. All signatures are authentic and authorized. 3. The instrument has not been altered. 4. The instrument is not subject to a defense or claim of any party that can be asserted against the transferor. 5. The transferor has no knowledge of insolvency proceedings against the maker, acceptor, or drawer of the instrument.
Nonindorsers Who Receive Consideration	Same as for indorsers, but warranties extend *only* to the *immediate transferee*.

RECOVERY FOR BREACH OF WARRANTY A transferee or holder who takes an instrument in good faith can sue on the basis of breach of a warranty as soon as he or she has reason to know of the breach [UCC 3–416(d)]. Notice of a claim for breach of warranty must be given to the warrantor within thirty days after the transferee or holder has reason to know of the breach and the identity of the warrantor [UCC 3–416(c)]. Failure to give notice relieves the warrantor from liability for any loss caused by a delay.

The transferee or holder can recover damages for the breach in an amount equal to the loss suffered (but not more than the amount of the instrument), plus expenses and any loss of interest caused by the breach [UCC 3–416(b)].

These warranties can be disclaimed with respect to any instrument except a check [UCC 3–416(c)]. In the check-collection process, discussed in Chapter 28, banks rely on these warranties. For all other instruments, the immediate parties can agree to a disclaimer, and an indorser can disclaim by including in the indorsement such words as "without warranties."

Presentment Warranties

Any person who presents an instrument for payment or acceptance makes the following **presentment warranties** to any other person who in good faith pays or accepts the instrument [UCC 3–417(a), (d)]:

1. The person obtaining payment or acceptance is entitled to enforce the instrument or is authorized to obtain payment or acceptance on behalf of a person who is entitled to enforce the instrument. (This is, in effect, a warranty that there are no missing or unauthorized indorsements.)
2. The instrument has not been altered.
3. The person obtaining payment or acceptance has no knowledge that the signature of the drawer of the instrument is unauthorized.[9]

GOAL IS TO PROTECT TRANSFEREE These warranties are referred to as *presentment warranties* because they protect the person to whom the instrument is presented. They often have the effect of shifting liability back to the party that was in the best position to prevent the wrongdoing.

LIMITATIONS The second and third warranties do not apply to makers, acceptors, and drawers. It is assumed that a drawer or a maker will recognize his or her own signature and that a maker or an acceptor will recognize whether an instrument has been materially altered.

Presentment warranties cannot be disclaimed with respect to checks. Moreover, a claim for breach must be given to the warrantor within thirty days after the claimant knows or has reason to know of the breach and the identity of the warrantor. If the claim is made after thirty days, the warrantor is not liable for any loss caused by the delay [UCC 3–417(e)].

---

9. As discussed in Footnote 8, the 2002 amendments to Article 3 of the UCC provide additional protection for "a remotely created consumer item," such as a check drawn on a personal account that the account holder authorized over the phone but did not physically sign.

SECTION 3
DEFENSES AND LIMITATIONS

Depending on whether a holder or a holder in due course (HDC)—or a holder through an HDC—makes the demand for payment, certain defenses can bar collection from persons who would otherwise be liable on an instrument. There are two general categories of defenses—*universal defenses* and *personal defenses*. Both are discussed below and summarized in Exhibit 27–2 below.

Universal Defenses

Universal defenses (also called *real defenses*) are valid against *all* holders, including HDCs and holders through HDCs. Universal defenses include those listed below and described in the following subsections.

1. Forgery of a signature on the instrument.
2. Fraud in the execution.
3. Material alteration.
4. Discharge in bankruptcy.
5. Minority.
6. Illegality, mental incapacity, and extreme duress.

FORGERY A forged signature will not bind the person whose name is used. Thus, when a person forges an instrument, the person whose name is forged has no liability to pay any holder or any HDC the value of the forged instrument. If the person whose name is forged ratifies (approves or validates) the signature, however, he or she may be liable. Similarly, a maker or drawer who is barred from denying a forgery (because it was made possible by his or her negligence, for instance) may also be held liable [UCC 3–401(a), 3–403(a)].

FRAUD IN THE EXECUTION If a person is deceived into signing a negotiable instrument by being told that it is something else (such as a receipt), *fraud in the execution* (or inception) is committed against the signer [UCC 3–305(a)(1)(iii)]. ▶ **Example 27.18** Connor, a salesperson, asks Javier, a customer, to sign a paper, which Connor says is a receipt for the delivery of goods that Javier is picking up from the store. In fact, the paper is a promissory note, but Javier is unfamiliar with the English language and does not realize this. In this situation, even if the note is negotiated to an HDC, Javier has a valid defense against payment. ◀

This defense cannot be raised, however, if a reasonable inquiry would have revealed the nature and terms of the instrument. Thus, the signer's age, experience, and intelligence are relevant because they frequently determine whether the signer should have understood the nature of the transaction before signing.

EXHIBIT 27–2 Defenses against Liability on Negotiable Instruments

UNIVERSAL (REAL) DEFENSES	PERSONAL (LIMITED) DEFENSES
Valid against all holders, including holders in due course	**Valid against ordinary holders but not against holders in due course**
1. Forgery.	1. Breach of contract (including breach of contract warranties).
2. Fraud in the execution.	2. Lack or failure of consideration.
3. Material alteration.	3. Fraud in the inducement (ordinary fraud).
4. Discharge in bankruptcy.	4. Illegality, mental incapacity, or duress, if the contract is voidable.
5. Minority, if the contract is voidable.	5. Previous payment or cancellation of the instrument.
6. Illegality, mental incapacity, or duress, if the contract is void under state law.	6. Unauthorized completion of an incomplete instrument and nondelivery of the instrument.

MATERIAL ALTERATION An alteration is *material* if it changes the contract terms between two parties *in any way.* Examples include any unauthorized addition of words or numbers or other changes to complete an incomplete instrument that affect the obligation of a party to the instrument [UCC 3–407(a)]. Making any change in the amount, the date, or the rate of interest—even if the change is only one penny, one day, or 1 percent—is material.

It is not a material alteration, however, to correct the maker's address or to draw a red line across the instrument to indicate that an auditor has checked it. It is also not a material alteration to change the figures on a check so that they agree with the written amount. If the alteration is not material, any holder is entitled to enforce the instrument according to its original terms.

A Complete or Partial Defense. Material alteration is a *complete defense* against an ordinary holder but only a *partial defense* against an HDC. An ordinary holder can recover nothing on an instrument that has been materially altered [UCC 3–407(b)]. In contrast, when an original term, such as the amount payable, has been *altered,* an HDC can enforce the instrument against the maker or drawer according to the original terms but not for the altered amount [UCC 3–407(c)(i)].

Note that if an alteration is readily apparent (such as a number changed on the face of a check), then obviously the holder has notice of some defect or defense. Thus, the holder cannot be an HDC (and therefore cannot enforce the instrument) [UCC 3–302(a)(1), (2)(iv)].

An HDC Can Enforce an Incomplete Instrument That Was Subsequently Altered. If an instrument was originally incomplete and was later completed in an unauthorized manner, alteration can no longer be claimed as a defense against an HDC [UCC 3–407(b), (c)]. The HDC can enforce the instrument as completed because a drawer or maker who issued an incomplete instrument normally will be held responsible for such an alteration. A drawer or maker could have avoided the alteration by the exercise of greater care in completing the instrument.

DISCHARGE IN BANKRUPTCY Discharge in bankruptcy (see Chapter 31) is an absolute defense on any instrument regardless of the status of the holder [UCC 3–305(a)(1)(iv)]. This defense exists because the purpose of bankruptcy is to finally settle all of the insolvent party's debts.

MINORITY Minority, or infancy, is a universal defense only to the extent that state law recognizes it as a defense to a simple contract. Because state laws on minority vary, so do determinations of whether minority is a universal defense against an HDC [UCC 3–305(a)(1)(i)]. (See Chapter 14 for further discussion of the contractual liability of minors.)

ILLEGALITY Certain types of illegality constitute universal defenses, whereas others are personal defenses. If a statute provides that an illegal transaction is void, then the defense is universal—that is, absolute against both an ordinary holder and an HDC. If the law merely makes the instrument voidable, then the illegality is a personal defense against an ordinary holder, but not against an HDC [UCC 3–305(a)(1)(ii)].

MENTAL INCAPACITY If a court has declared a person to be mentally incompetent, then any instrument issued by that person is void. The instrument is void *ab initio* (from the beginning) and unenforceable by any holder or HDC [UCC 3–305(a)(1)(ii)]. Mental incapacity in these circumstances is a universal defense. If a court has not declared a person to be mentally incompetent, then mental incapacity operates as a personal defense against ordinary holders but not against HDCs.

EXTREME DURESS When a person signs and issues a negotiable instrument under such extreme duress as an immediate threat of force or violence (for instance, at gunpoint), the instrument is void and unenforceable by any holder or HDC [UCC 3–305(a)(1)(ii)]. (Ordinary duress is a defense against ordinary holders but not against HDCs.)

Personal Defenses

Personal defenses (sometimes called *limited defenses*) are used to avoid payment to an ordinary holder of a negotiable instrument. They are not a defense against an HDC or a holder through an HDC. Personal defenses include the following:

1. Breach of contract or breach of warranty.
2. Lack or failure of consideration.
3. Fraud in the inducement (ordinary fraud).
4. Illegality.
5. Mental incompetence.
6. Ordinary duress or undue influence rendering the contract voidable [UCC 3–305(a)(1)(ii)].
7. Discharge by previous payment or cancellation [UCC 3–601(b), 3–602(a), 3–603, 3–604].

8. Unauthorized completion of an incomplete instrument [UCC 3–115, 3–302, 3–407, 4–401(d)(2)].
9. Nondelivery of the instrument [UCC 1–201(14), 3–105(b), 3–305(a)(2)].

BREACH OF CONTRACT OR BREACH OF WARRANTY A breach of the underlying contract for which the negotiable instrument was issued is a personal defense. If a breach occurs, the maker of a note can refuse to pay it, or the drawer of a check can order his or her bank to stop payment on the check. Breach of warranty can also be claimed as a defense to liability on the instrument.

▶ **Example 27.19** Elias purchases two dozen pairs of athletic shoes from De Soto. The shoes are to be delivered in six weeks. Elias gives De Soto a promissory note for $1,000, which is the price of the shoes. The shoes arrive, but many of them are discolored, and the soles of several pairs are coming apart. Elias has a defense to liability on the note on the basis of breach of contract and breach of warranty. (Recall from Chapter 23 that a seller impliedly promises that the goods being sold are at least merchantable.) ◀

If, however, the note is no longer in the hands of the payee-seller (De Soto) but is presented for payment by an HDC, the result is different. The maker-buyer (Elias) in that situation will not be able to plead breach of contract or warranty as a defense against liability on the note. ◀

LACK OR FAILURE OF CONSIDERATION The absence of consideration (value) may be a successful defense in some instances [UCC 3–303(b), 3–305(a)(2)]. ▶ **Example 27.20** Tony gives Cleo, as a gift, a note that states, "I promise to pay you $100,000," and Cleo accepts the note. No consideration is given in return for Tony's promise, and a court will not enforce the promise. ◀

Similarly, if delivery of goods becomes impossible, a party who has issued a draft or note under the contract has a defense for not paying it. Thus, in *Example 27.19,* if the shoes were lost in an accident and delivery became impossible, De Soto could not subsequently enforce Elias's promise to pay the $1,000 promissory note. If the note was in the hands of an HDC, however, Elias's defense would not be available against the HDC.

In the following case, a party asserted lack of consideration as a defense for not paying a promissory note.

CASE ANALYSIS

Case 27.2   Mills v. Chauvin

Supreme Court of New York, Appellate Division, Third Department, 103 A.D.3d 1041, 962 N.Y.S.2d 412 (2013).

IN THE LANGUAGE OF THE COURT
PER CURIAM.

* * * *

Plaintiff, Gregory Mills, and defendant, Robert Chauvin, are two experienced attorneys who shared both a friendship and a professional/business relationship. Those longstanding relationships deteriorated and gave rise to this action.

* * * *

* * * The parties formed a partnership and took ownership of a commercial office building located on Crescent Road in the Town of Clifton Park, Saratoga County. * * * After Chauvin decided, for a variety of reasons, that he no longer wished

to maintain his ownership of the Crescent Road property, the parties agreed that Mills would purchase Chauvin's one-half interest in such property and they executed a purchase and sale agreement establishing a purchase price of $261,176.67 and a closing date.

* * * *

Chauvin was an investor in the Amelia Village [real estate development] project [in Virginia]. Over a course of time, Mills made multiple monetary payments to Chauvin—totaling $395,750—which Chauvin claims were investments in the project and Mills claims were loans. Ultimately, Mills requested that Chauvin return the payments he had advanced. In connection therewith,

Chauvin executed a promissory note * * * that obligated him to pay Mills $395,750. However, Chauvin later challenged the validity of the promissory note and claimed that Mills was not entitled to a return of his investments.

* * * *

Mills subsequently filed [a] complaint [in a New York state court against Chauvin] to recover the payments Mills had made with respect to the Amelia Village project, based upon claims of breach of contract and unjust enrichment, respectively.

* * * *

The action proceeded to a nonjury trial * * *. At the conclusion thereof, Supreme Court [the trial court] found * * * that the promissory note was

CASE 27.2 CONTINUED

valid and enforceable and that Mills was entitled to recover pursuant to its terms. Chauvin now appeals from the judgment entered upon that decision.

* * * *

* * * Initially, we reject Chauvin's claim that Supreme Court erred in concluding that the * * * promissory note was enforceable. Chauvin does not dispute that Mills had previously paid him $395,750 in connection with the Amelia Village project, that he signed the promissory note promising to repay that amount to Mills, or that he tendered the note to Mills for the purpose of providing documentation to Mills' lending institution in support of Mills' application for financing of the purchase of the Crescent Road property. Instead, Chauvin claims that the promissory note was not enforceable because it was not given to secure a debt and, therefore, lacked consideration.

In this regard, Mills testified that * * * the parties * * * agreed that Chauvin would repay Mills all of the money that Mills had contributed to the Amelia Village project and that the promissory note confirmed their agreement. On the other hand, Chauvin claims that the payments that Mills made to the Amelia Village project were investments that could not be returned when Mills withdrew from that project, and that the promissory note was not intended to be a promise of repayment.

* * * *

The record amply supports Supreme Court's finding that the consideration for the promissory note was the $395,750 that Mills had provided to Chauvin in connection with the Amelia Village project and that the promissory note represented security for Chauvin's antecedent obligation to repay such funds.

The note itself—which was drafted by Chauvin, signed by him, notarized and transmitted to Mills clearly states that it was executed in return for a loan received by Chauvin and contained an unconditional promise or order to pay a sum certain in money. In addition, Mills took the note as a holder in due course. Based upon our independent evaluation of the evidence and, giving due deference to the trial court's credibility determinations concerning witnesses, we conclude that Supreme Court's determination that Chauvin failed to establish a bona fide defense of lack of consideration is supported by the record. [Emphasis added.]

* * * *

ORDERED that the order and judgments are affirmed, with costs to plaintiff.

LEGAL REASONING QUESTIONS

1. If the court had accepted Chauvin's claim that Mills's funds represented an investment, would the result in this case have been different? Explain.

2. Do the facts in this case support the court's conclusion that Mills took Chauvin's note as an HDC? Why or why not?

3. How did Mills's status as an HDC affect Chauvin's asserted defense?

4. In whose favor did the court ultimately rule? Why?

FRAUD IN THE INDUCEMENT (ORDINARY FRAUD) A person who issues a negotiable instrument based on false statements by the other party will be able to avoid payment on that instrument, unless the holder is an HDC. ▶ **Example 27.21** Weston agrees to purchase Sharla's used tractor for $26,500. Sharla, knowing her statements are false, tells Weston that the tractor is in good working order and that it has been used for only one harvest. In addition, she tells Weston that she owns the tractor free and clear of all claims.

Weston pays Sharla $4,500 in cash and issues a negotiable promissory note for the balance. As it turns out, Sharla still owes the original seller $10,000 on the purchase of the tractor, and the tractor is subject to a valid security interest (discussed in Chapter 30). In addition, the tractor has been used in three harvests, and its brakes need repair.

In this situation, Weston can refuse to pay the note if it is held by an ordinary holder. If, however, Sharla has negotiated the note to an HDC, Weston must pay the HDC. Of course, Weston can then sue Sharla to recover the funds. ◀

ILLEGALITY As mentioned, if a statute provides that an illegal transaction is voidable, the defense is personal. For example, some states make contracts in restraint of trade voidable. Thus, an instrument given in payment of a contract to restrain trade in those states is voidable and operates as a personal defense (only against ordinary holders).

MENTAL INCAPACITY If a maker or drawer issues a negotiable instrument while mentally incompetent but before a court has declared him or her to be so, the instrument is voidable. In this situation, mental incapacity serves as a personal defense (only against ordinary holders).

Federal Limitations on the Rights of HDCs

The federal government limits the rights of HDCs in certain circumstances because of the harsh effects that the HDC rules can sometimes have on consumers. Under the HDC doctrine, a consumer who purchased a defective product (such as a defective automobile) would continue to be liable to HDCs even if the consumer returned the defective product to the retailer.

▶ **Example 27.22** To buy a used truck with a one-year warranty, Brian pays $5,000 down and signs a promissory note to the dealer for the remaining $15,000. The truck turns out to be defective, but the dealer has already sold the note to an HDC. Thus, even if Brian returns the truck to the dealer, the HDC doctrine would mean that he remains liable to the HDC for $15,000 because his claim of breach of warranty is a personal defense. ◀

To protect consumers who purchase defective products, the Federal Trade Commission (FTC) adopted Rule 433, which effectively abolished the HDC doctrine in consumer transactions.[10]

FTC RULE 433 FTC Rule 433 severely limits the rights of HDCs that purchase instruments arising out of *consumer credit* transactions. The rule applies to consumers who purchase goods or services for personal, family, or household use using a consumer credit contract. The regulation prevents a consumer from being required to make payment for a defective product to a third party HDC who has acquired a promissory note that formed part of the consumer's contract with the dealer who sold the defective good.

Rule 433 requires the following provision to be included in boldface type in a consumer credit contract:

NOTICE
ANY HOLDER OF THIS CONSUMER CREDIT CONTRACT IS SUBJECT TO ALL CLAIMS AND DEFENSES WHICH THE DEBTOR COULD ASSERT AGAINST THE SELLER OF GOODS OR SERVICES OBTAINED PURSUANT HERETO OR WITH THE PROCEEDS HEREOF. RECOVERY HEREUNDER BY THE DEBTOR SHALL NOT EXCEED AMOUNTS PAID BY THE DEBTOR HEREUNDER.

EFFECT OF THE RULE When a negotiable instrument contains the required notice, a consumer can bring any defense that she or he has against the seller of a product against a subsequent holder as well. In essence, FTC Rule 433 places an HDC of the instrument in the position of a contract assignee.

The rule makes the buyer's duty to pay conditional on the seller's full performance of the contract. It also clearly reduces the degree of transferability of negotiable instruments resulting from consumer credit contracts. An instrument that contains this notice or a similar statement required by law remains negotiable, but there cannot be an HDC of such an instrument [UCC 3–106(d)].

There is a loophole, however, in that FTC Rule 433 does not prohibit third parties from purchasing notes or credit contracts that do *not* contain the required notice. So, if a third party purchases an instrument arising from a consumer credit transaction that lacks the notice, that third party normally is not subject to the buyer's defenses against the seller. Thus, some consumers remain unprotected by the FTC rule.[11]

SECTION 4
DISCHARGE

Discharge from liability on an instrument can come from payment, cancellation, or material alteration. Discharge can also occur if a party reacquires an instrument, if a holder impairs another party's right of recourse, or if a holder surrenders collateral without consent.

Discharge by Payment or Tender of Payment

All parties to a negotiable instrument will be discharged when the party primarily liable on it pays to a holder the full amount due [UCC 3–602, 3–603].[12]

---

10. 16 C.F.R. Section 433.2. The rule was enacted in 1976 pursuant to the FTC's authority under the Federal Trade Commission Act, 15 U.S.C. Sections 41–58.

11. A 2002 amendment to UCC 3–305(e) closes this loophole, but only a minority of the states have adopted the amendment. The amendment makes a third party holder in possession of a note or other instrument that was supposed to include this notice subject to a buyer's defenses against a seller even if the instrument did not include the notice.

12. This is true even if the payment is made with knowledge of a claim to the instrument by another person unless the payor knows that "payment is prohibited by injunction or similar process of a court of competent jurisdiction" or, in most situations, "the party making payment accepted, from a person having a claim to the instrument, indemnity against loss resulting from refusal to pay the person entitled to enforce the instrument" [UCC 3–602(a), (b)(1)].

The liability of all parties is also discharged when the drawee of an unaccepted draft or check makes payment in good faith to the holder.

Payment by any other party (for instance, an indorser) discharges only the liability of that party and subsequent parties. The party making such a payment still has the right to recover on the instrument from any prior parties.[13]

GOOD FAITH REQUIRED A party will not be discharged if that party knowingly (in bad faith) pays a holder who acquired the instrument by theft or who obtained the instrument from someone else who acquired it by theft [UCC 3–602(b)(2)]. An exception to this rule is made if the person has the rights of an HDC.

TENDER OF PAYMENT Sometimes, a tender (offer) of payment is made to a person entitled to enforce the instrument, and the tender is refused. In that situation, the rights of indorsers and accommodation parties to seek reimbursement are impaired (impairment of the right of recourse is discussed shortly). Therefore, the indorsers and accommodation parties are discharged to the extent of the amount of the tender [UCC 3–603(b)].

When a tender of payment of the amount due on an instrument is made to a person entitled to enforce the instrument, the obligation to pay interest after the date of tender is discharged [UCC 3–603(c)].

Discharge by Cancellation or Surrender

Intentional cancellation of an instrument discharges the liability of all parties [UCC 3–604]. Destruction or mutilation of a negotiable instrument is considered cancellation only if it is done with the intention of eliminating obligation on the instrument [UCC 3–604(a)(i)]. Thus, if an instrument is destroyed or mutilated by accident, the instrument is not discharged, and the original terms can be established by parol evidence [UCC 3–309].

Any of the following acts—if done by the holder with the intent to cancel the obligation—will discharge liability:

1. Writing "Paid" across the face of an instrument.
2. Intentionally tearing up an instrument.
3. Crossing out a party's signature. Doing this will discharge that party's liability and the liability of subsequent indorsers who have already signed the instrument.
4. Surrendering the instrument (such as a promissory note) to the party to be discharged.

▶ **Case in Point 27.23** Edith Mark bought a Ford pickup and signed a loan contract and promissory note with Huntington National Bank to finance the purchase. She had made twenty of the sixty-six payments required on the loan when she received the original agreement, stamped "PAID," in the mail, along with the title certificate. Mark stopped making payments on the loan, and the bank filed a lawsuit. Mark argued that the note had been discharged by surrender, but the bank claimed that the documents were returned to her due to an inadvertent clerical error. The court held that because the bank did not intend to discharge the note when it returned the documents to Mark, the surrender did not constitute a valid cancellation of the note.[14] ◀

Discharge by Material Alteration

Materially altering an instrument may discharge the liability of all parties, as previously discussed [UCC 3–407(b)]. (An HDC may be able to enforce a materially altered instrument against its maker or drawer according to the instrument's *original* terms, however.)

Discharge by Reacquisition

The reacquisition of an instrument by a person that held it previously discharges all intervening indorsers against subsequent holders who do not qualify as HDCs [UCC 3–207]. Of course, the person reacquiring the instrument may be liable to subsequent holders if the instrument is dishonored.

Discharge by Impairment of Recourse

Discharge can also occur when a party's right of recourse is impaired [UCC 3–605]. A *right of recourse* is a right to seek reimbursement. Ordinarily, when a holder collects the amount of an instrument from an

---

13. Under the 2002 amendment to UCC 3–602(b), when a party entitled to enforce an instrument transfers it without giving notice to the parties obligated to pay it, and one of those parties pays the transferor, that payment is effective. For example, Roberto borrows $5,000 from Consumer Finance Company on a note payable to the lender. Consumer Finance transfers the note to Delta Investment Corporation but continues to collect payments from Roberto. Under this amendment, those payments effectively discharge Roberto to the extent of their amount.

14. *Huntington National Bank v. Mark,* 2004 WL 1627029 (Ohio App. 2004).

indorser, the indorser has a right of recourse against prior indorsers, the maker or drawer, and accommodation parties.

If the holder has adversely affected the indorser's right to seek reimbursement from these other parties, however, the indorser is not liable on the instrument (to the extent that the indorser's right of recourse is impaired). This occurs when, for example, the holder releases or agrees not to sue a party against whom the indorser has a right of recourse. It also occurs when a holder agrees to an extension of the instrument's due date or to some other material modification that results in a loss to the indorser with respect to the right of recourse [UCC 3–605(c), (d)].[15]

Discharge by Impairment of Collateral

Sometimes, a party to an instrument gives collateral as security that her or his performance will occur.

---

15. The 2002 amendments to UCC 3–605 essentially apply the principles of suretyship and guaranty (to be discussed in Chapter 29) to circumstances involving the impairment of the right of recourse of "secondary obligors." These obligors include indorsers and accommodation parties. Amended UCC 3–605(a) differs from these principles, however, in that the release of a principal obligor by a person entitled to enforce a check grants a complete discharge to an indorser of the check without requiring proof of harm.

When a holder "impairs the value" of that collateral without the consent of the parties who would benefit from the collateral in the event of nonpayment, those parties to the instrument are discharged to the extent of the impairment [UCC 3–605(e), (f)].

▶ **Example 27.24** Jerome and Myra sign a note as co-makers, putting up Jerome's property as collateral. The note is payable to Montessa. Montessa is required by law to file a *financing statement* (discussed in Chapter 30) with the state to put others on notice of her interest in Jerome's property as collateral for the note. If Montessa fails to file the financing statement and Jerome goes through bankruptcy and the property is sold to pay other debts, Jerome will be unable to pay anything on the note. By not filing the financing statement, Montessa has impaired the value of the collateral to Myra, who is discharged to the extent of that impairment.

In other words, when Jerome goes through bankruptcy, Montessa's earlier failure to file the statement prevents her from taking possession of the collateral, selling it, and crediting the amount owed on the note. Myra, as co-maker, is then responsible only for any remaining indebtedness, instead of the entire unpaid balance. Thus, Myra is discharged to the extent that the proceeds from the sale of the collateral would have discharged her liability on the note. ◀

Reviewing: Liability, Defenses, and Discharge

Nancy Mahar was the office manager at Golden Years Nursing Home, Inc. She was given a signature stamp to issue checks to the nursing home's employees for up to $100 as advances on their pay. The checks were drawn on Golden Years' account at First National Bank. Over a seven-year period, Mahar wrote a number of checks to employees exclusively for the purpose of embezzling funds for herself. She forged the employees' indorsements on the checks, signed her name as a second indorser, and deposited the checks in her personal account at Star Bank. The employees whose names were on the checks never actually requested them. When the scheme was uncovered, Golden Years filed a suit against Mahar, Star Bank, and others to recover the funds. Using the information presented in the chapter, answer the following questions.

1. With regard to signature liability, which provision of the Uniform Commercial Code (UCC) discussed in this chapter applies to this scenario?
2. What is the rule set forth by that provision?
3. Under the UCC, which party, Golden Years or Star Bank, must bear the loss in this situation? Why?
4. Based on these facts, describe any transfer or presentment warranties that Mahar may have violated.

DEBATE THIS . . . *Because signature stamps create so many opportunities for embezzlement, they should be banned.*

Terms and Concepts

accommodation party 514

agent 515

dishonor 513

fictitious payee 518

imposter 518

personal defense 523

presentment warranty 521

principal 515

transfer warranty 519

universal defense 522

ExamPrep

Issue Spotters

1. Rye signs corporate checks for Suchin Corporation. Rye writes a check payable to U-All Company, even though Suchin does not owe U-All anything. Rye signs the check, forges U-All's indorsement, and cashes the check at Viceroy Bank, the drawee. Does Suchin have any recourse against the bank for the payment? Why or why not? **(See page 518.)**

2. Skye asked Jim to buy a textbook for her at the campus bookstore. Skye wrote a check payable to the bookstore and left the amount blank for Jim to fill in the price of the book. The cost of the book was $100. Jim filled in the check for $200 before he got to the bookstore. The clerk at the bookstore took the check for $200 and gave Jim the book, plus $100 in cash. Was the bookstore a holder in due course on Skye's check? **(See page 527.)**

- Check your answers to the Issue Spotters against the answers provided in Appendix E at the end of this text.

Before the Test

Go to **www.cengagebrain.com**, enter the ISBN 9781285185248, and click on "Find" to locate this textbook's Web site. Then, click on "Access Now" under "Study Tools," and select Chapter 27 at the top. There, you will find a Practice Quiz that you can take to assess your mastery of the concepts in this chapter, as well as Flashcards and a Glossary of important terms.

Business Scenarios

27–1. Material Alteration. Williams purchased a used car from Stein for $1,000. Williams paid for the car with a check (written in pencil) payable to Stein for $1,000. Stein, through careful erasures and alterations, changed the amount on the check to read $10,000 and negotiated the check to Boz. Boz took the check for value, in good faith, and without notice of the alteration and thus met the Uniform Commercial Code's requirements for the status of a holder in due course. Can Williams successfully raise the universal (real) defense of material alteration to avoid payment on the check? Explain. **(See page 523.)**

27–2. Signature Liability. Waldo makes out a negotiable promissory note payable to the order of Grace. Grace indorses the note by writing on it "Without recourse, Grace" and transfers the note for value to Adam. Adam, in need of cash, negotiates the note to Keith by indorsing it with the words "Pay to Keith, Adam." On the due date, Keith presents the note to Waldo for payment, only to learn that Waldo has filed for bankruptcy and will have all debts (including the note) discharged. Discuss fully whether Keith can hold Waldo, Grace, or Adam liable on the note. **(See page 512.)**

27–3. Defenses. Niles sold Kennedy a small motorboat for $1,500, maintaining to Kennedy that the boat was in excellent condition. Kennedy gave Niles a check for $1,500, which Niles indorsed and gave to Frazier for value. When Kennedy took the boat for a trial run, she discovered that the boat leaked, needed to be painted, and required a new motor. Kennedy stopped payment on her check, which had not yet been cashed. Niles has disappeared. Can Frazier recover from Kennedy as a holder in due course? Discuss. **(See page 522.)**

Business Case Problems

27–4. BUSINESS CASE PROBLEM WITH SAMPLE ANSWER: Defenses.

 Thomas Klutz obtained a franchise from Kahala Franchise Corp. to operate a Samurai Sam's restaurant. Under their agreement, Klutz could transfer the franchise only if he obtained Kahala's approval and paid a transfer fee. Without telling Kahala, Klutz sold the restaurant to William Thorbecke. Thorbecke signed a note for the price. When Kahala learned of the deal, the franchisor told Thorbecke to stop using the Samurai Sam's name. Thorbecke stopped paying on the note, and Klutz filed a claim for the unpaid amount. In defense, Thorbecke asserted breach *of contract and fraud. Are these defenses effective against Klutz? Explain. [Kahala Franchise Corp. v. Hit Enterprises, LLC, 159 Wash.App. 1013 (Div. 2 2011)]* **(See page 522.)**

- **For a sample answer to Problem 27–4, go to Appendix F at the end of this text.**

27–5. Defenses. Damion and Kiya Carmichael took out a loan from Ameriquest Mortgage Co. to refinance their mortgage. They signed a note to make monthly payments on the loan. Later, Deutsche Bank National Trust Co. acquired the note. The Carmichaels stopped making payments and filed for bankruptcy. Deutsche asked the court to foreclose on the mortgage. The Carmichaels asserted that they had been fraudulently induced to make the loan and sign the note. Was the bank free of this defense? Explain. *[In re Carmichael, 443 Bankr. 698 (E.D.Pa. 2011)]* **(See page 522.)**

27–6. Unauthorized Indorsements. Angela Brock borrowed $544,000 and signed a note payable to Amerifund Mortgage Services, LLC, to buy a house in Silver Spring, Maryland. The note was indorsed in blank and transferred several times "without recourse" before Brock fell behind on the payments. On behalf of Deutsche Bank National Trust Co., BAC Home Loans Servicing LP initiated foreclosure. Brock filed an action in a Maryland state court to block it, arguing that BAC could not foreclose because Deutsche Bank, not BAC, owned the note. Can BAC enforce the note? Explain. *[Deutsche Bank National Trust Co. v. Brock, 63 A.3d 40 (Md. 2013)]* **(See page 518.)**

27–7. SPECIAL CASE ANALYSIS: Defenses.

Go to Case Analysis Case 27.2, *Mills v. Chauvin,* on pages 524 and 525. Read the excerpt and answer the following questions.

(a) **Issue:** What document was at the center of the dispute in this case?

(b) **Rule of Law:** What are the elements of consideration? What are the requirements for attaining the status of a holder in due course (HDC)?

(c) **Applying the Rule of Law:** Did the document at the center of the dispute in this case satisfy the elements of consideration? Did the party in possession of the document take it as an HDC? Explain.

(d) **Conclusion:** Who did the court determine was liable? Why?

27–8. A QUESTION OF ETHICS: Primary and Secondary Liability.

Clarence Morgan, Jr., owned Easy Way Automotive, a car dealership in D'Lo, Mississippi. Easy Way sold a truck to Loyd Barnard, who signed a note for the amount of the price payable to Trustmark National Bank in six months. Before the note came due, Barnard returned the truck to Easy Way, which sold it to another buyer. Using some of the proceeds from the second sale, Easy Way sent a check to Trustmark to pay Barnard's note. Meanwhile, Barnard obtained another truck from Easy Way, financed through another six-month note payable to Trustmark. After eight of these deals, some of which involved more than one truck, an Easy Way check to Trustmark was dishonored. In a suit in a Mississippi state court, Trustmark sought to recover the amounts of two of the notes from Barnard. Trustmark had not secured titles to two of the trucks covered by the notes, however, and this complicated Barnard's efforts to reclaim the vehicles from the later buyers. [Trustmark National Bank v. Barnard, 930 So.2d 1281 (Miss.App. 2006)] **(See page 512.)**

(a) On what basis might Barnard be liable on the Trustmark notes? Would he be primarily or secondarily liable? Could this liability be discharged on the theory that Barnard's right of recourse had been impaired when Trustmark did not secure titles to the trucks covered by the notes? Explain.

(b) Easy Way's account had been subject to other recent overdrafts, and a week after the check to Trustmark was returned for insufficient funds, Morgan committed suicide. At the same time, Barnard was unable to obtain a mortgage because the unpaid notes affected his credit rating. How do the circumstances of this case underscore the importance of practicing business ethics?

Legal Reasoning Group Activity

27–9. Agents' Signatures. Robert Helmer and Percy Helmer, Jr., were authorized signatories on the corporate checking account of Event Marketing, Inc. The Helmers signed a check drawn on Event Marketing's account and issued to Rummel Technologies, Inc. (RTI), in the amount of $84,965. The check was signed on July 13, 2015, but dated August 14. When RTI presented the check for payment, it was dishonored due to insufficient funds. RTI filed a suit in a Georgia state court against the Helmers to collect the amount of the check. **(See page 515.)**

(a) The first group will determine whether an authorized signatory on a corporate account can be held personally liable for corporate checks returned for insufficient funds.

(b) The second group will decide if the Helmers were personally liable on Event Marketing's check in this situation.

CHAPTER 28

BANKING IN THE DIGITAL AGE

Checks are the most common type of negotiable instruments regulated by the Uniform Commercial Code (UCC). Checks are convenient to use because they serve as a substitute for cash. To be sure, most students today tend to use debit cards rather than checks for many retail transactions. Not only do debit cards now account for more retail payments than checks, but payments are increasingly being made via smartphones, iPads, and other mobile devices. Nonetheless, commercial checks remain an integral part of the U.S. economic system.

Articles 3 and 4 of the UCC govern issues relating to checks. As discussed in the preceding chapters, Article 3 sets forth the requirements for all negotiable instruments, including checks. Article 4 establishes a framework for deposit and checking agreements between a bank and its customers. Article 4 also governs the relationships of banks with one another as they process checks for payment. A check therefore may fall within the scope of Article 3 and yet be subject to the provisions of Article 4 while in the course of collection. If a conflict arises between Articles 3 and 4, Article 4 controls [UCC 4–102(a)].

In this chapter, we first identify the legal characteristics of checks and the legal duties and liabilities that arise when a check is issued. Then we examine the check-collection process, electronic checks and funds, and other aspects of banking in the digital age.

SECTION 1
CHECKS

As explained in Chapter 25, a **check** is a special type of draft that is drawn on a bank, ordering the bank to pay a fixed amount of money on demand [UCC 3–104(f)]. Article 4 defines a *bank* as "a person engaged in the business of banking, including a savings bank, savings and loan association, credit union or trust company" [UCC 4–105(1)]. If any other institution (such as a brokerage firm) handles a check for payment or for collection, then the check is not covered by Article 4.

Recall from the preceding chapters that a person who writes a check is called the *drawer*. The drawer is usually a depositor in the bank on which the check is drawn. The person to whom the check is payable is the *payee*. The bank or financial institution on which the check is drawn is the *drawee*. Thus, if Anne Tomas writes a check on her checking account to pay her college tuition, she is the drawer, her bank is the drawee, and her college is the payee.

Between the time that a check is drawn and the time it reaches the drawee, the effectiveness of the check may be altered in some way. For instance, the account on which the check is drawn may no longer have sufficient funds to pay the check, or the drawer may have died. To avoid such problems, a payee may insist on payment by an instrument that has already been accepted by the drawee, such as a cashier's check, a traveler's check, or a certified check.

Cashier's Checks

Checks are usually three-party instruments, but on some checks, the bank serves as both the drawer *and* the drawee. For example, when a bank draws a check on itself, the check is called a **cashier's check** and is a negotiable instrument on issue (see Exhibit 28–1 on the following page) [UCC 3–104(g)]. Normally, a cashier's check indicates a specific payee. In effect, with a cashier's check, the bank assumes responsibility for paying the check, thus making the check more readily acceptable as a substitute for cash.

▶ **Example 28.1** Blake needs to pay a moving company $8,000 for moving his household goods to his new home in another state. The moving company requests payment in the form of a cashier's check.

EXHIBIT 28-1 A Cashier's Check

Blake goes to a bank (he need not have an account at the bank) and purchases a cashier's check, payable to the moving company, in the amount of $8,000. Blake has to pay the bank the $8,000 for the check, plus a small service fee. He then gives the check to the moving company. ◄

Cashier's checks are commonly used in business to pay for real estate transactions or to make tax payments because payment is immediately credited (the payee need not wait to see if the check "clears"). Except in very limited circumstances, the issuing bank *must* honor its cashier's checks when they are presented for payment.

If a bank wrongfully dishonors a cashier's check, a holder can recover from the bank all expenses incurred, interest, and consequential damages [UCC 3–411]. This same rule applies if a bank wrongfully dishonors a certified check (to be discussed shortly) or a *teller's check*. (A *teller's check* is similar to a cashier's check except that usually it is drawn by a bank on another bank [UCC 3–104(h)]. A teller's check may be used when a person withdraws funds from one bank to transfer to an account at another bank.)

Traveler's Checks

A **traveler's check** is an instrument that is payable on demand, drawn on or payable at a financial institution (such as a bank), and designated as a traveler's

check. The issuing institution is directly obligated to accept and pay its traveler's check according to the check's terms.

Traveler's checks are designed to be a safe substitute for cash when a person is on vacation or traveling and are issued for a fixed amount, such as $20, $50, or $100. The purchaser is required to sign the check at the time it is purchased and again at the time it is used [UCC 3–104(i)]. Today, instead of issuing traveler's checks, most major banks purchase and issue American Express traveler's checks for their customers (see Exhibit 28–2 on the following page).

Certified Checks

A **certified check** is a check that has been *accepted* by the bank on which it is drawn [UCC 3–409(d)]. When a drawee bank *certifies* (accepts) a check, it immediately charges the drawer's account with the amount of the check and transfers those funds to its own certified-check account. In effect, the bank is agreeing in advance to accept that check when it is presented for payment and to make payment from those funds reserved in the certified-check account. Essentially, certification prevents the bank from denying liability. It is a promise that sufficient funds are on deposit and *have been set aside* to cover the check.

To certify a check, the bank writes or stamps the word *certified* on the face of the check and typically

EXHIBIT 28-2   An American Express Traveler's Check

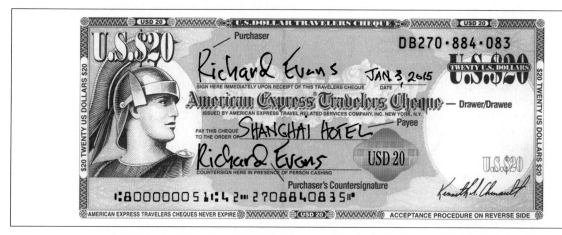

writes the amount that it will pay.[1] Either the drawer or the holder (payee) of a check can request certification, but the drawee bank is not required to certify a check. A bank's refusal to certify a check is not a dishonor of the check [UCC 3–409(d)]. Once a check is certified, the drawer and any prior indorsers are completely discharged from liability on the check [UCC 3–414(c), 3–415(d)]. Only the certifying bank is required to pay the instrument.

SECTION 2
THE BANK-CUSTOMER RELATIONSHIP

The bank-customer relationship begins when the customer opens a checking account and deposits funds that the bank will use to pay for checks written by the customer. Essentially, three types of relationships come into being, as discussed next.

Creditor-Debtor Relationship

A creditor-debtor relationship is created between a customer and a bank when, for example, the customer makes cash deposits into a checking account. When a customer makes a deposit, the customer becomes a creditor, and the bank a debtor, for the amount deposited.

Agency Relationship

An agency relationship also arises between the customer and the bank when the customer writes a check on his or her account. In effect, the customer is ordering the bank to pay the amount specified on the check to the holder when the holder presents the check to the bank for payment. In this situation, the bank becomes the customer's agent and is obligated to honor the customer's request.

Similarly, when the customer deposits a check into his or her account, the bank, as the customer's agent, is obligated to collect payment on the check from the bank on which the check was drawn. Thus, when checking account funds are transferred among different banks, each bank acts as the collection agent for its customers [UCC 4–201(a)].

Contractual Relationship

Whenever a bank-customer relationship is established, certain contractual rights and duties arise. The contractual rights and duties of the bank and the customer depend on the nature of the transaction. These rights and duties are discussed in detail in the following pages.

SECTION 3
THE BANK'S DUTY TO HONOR CHECKS

When a banking institution provides checking services, it agrees to honor the checks written by its customers, with the usual stipulation that sufficient

---

1. If the certification does not state an amount, and the amount is later increased and the instrument negotiated to a holder in due course (HDC), the certifying bank must pay the amount of the instrument when it was taken by the HDC.

funds must be available in the account to pay each check. When a drawee bank *wrongfully* fails to honor a check, it is liable to its customer for damages resulting from its refusal to pay [UCC 4–402(b)]. The customer does not have to prove that the bank breached its contractual commitment or was negligent.

The customer's agreement with the bank includes a general obligation to keep sufficient funds on deposit to cover all checks written. The customer is liable to the payee or to the holder of a check in a civil suit if a check is dishonored for insufficient funds. If intent to defraud can be proved, the customer can also be subject to criminal prosecution for writing a bad check.

When the bank properly dishonors a check for insufficient funds, it has no liability to the customer. The bank may rightfully refuse payment on a customer's check in other circumstances as well. Here, we examine the rights and duties of both the bank and its customers in specific situations.

The following case began when a bank customer was erroneously accused of criminal conduct when she attempted to cash a check. The court had to determine whether the customer could bring a lawsuit for wrongful dishonor even though the check in question had been drawn on an account in the bank's name.

CASE ANALYSIS

Case 28.1 Afiriyie v. Bank of America, N.A.
Superior Court of New Jersey, Appellate Division, 2013 WL 451895 (2013).

IN THE LANGUAGE OF THE COURT
PER CURIAM.

* * * *

In 2006, plaintiff Ama B. Afiriyie opened checking and savings accounts with defendant Bank of America ("BOA") as well as a secured credit card account for which she paid a security deposit of $300.

On March 8, 2007, plaintiff received a check from BOA, dated March 5, 2007, in the amount of $300. The check came with an attached "stub," explaining that the check represented "a credit balance refund" from her BOA account. Plaintiff called the toll-free number on the check stub and inquired about why the check had been issued and whether it was "good." She was told by a representative from BOA that the check was valid and could be cashed at any BOA branch. The representative explained that the check had been issued as a result of plaintiff's secured credit card account being upgraded to "unsecured" status.

* * * On March 8, 2007, plaintiff entered a BOA banking office located at the Pathmark Supermarket in South Orange [New Jersey].

Plaintiff proceeded to a teller window * * * and handed over * * * the check, asking that it be cashed. The teller * * * looked to [Diane Lowe, the bank manager] for assistance.

* * * *

* * * Lowe [did not ask Afiriyie whether she was a customer of the bank but] asked her where she had gotten the check. Plaintiff replied that BOA had issued it, and Lowe responded that the bank does not issue checks like this.

* * * *

[Lowe walked to her office and called BOA.] She then advised plaintiff that she was attempting to verify the check but had not been able to do so. Therefore, Lowe could not cash the check, and she was not allowed to give the check back.

* * * *

[Lowe called the South Orange Police Department. When the police arrived,] she asserted that plaintiff had attempted to cash a check that she believed to be fraudulent.

* * * *

[Afiriyie was arrested and charged with forgery and attempted theft by deception. Ultimately, the charges were

dismissed. Later, Afiriyie filed a suit in a New Jersey state court against BOA and Lowe. The defendants filed motions for summary judgment, which the court denied. After a trial, a jury awarded Afiriyie $710,000 in damages.]

* * * The court granted a new trial [on the ground] that the $710,000 award * * * shocked the judge's conscience, representing recovery far beyond what a reasonable factfinder could determine.

* * * Defendants [appealed] from the denial of their pretrial motions for summary judgment.

* * * *

In the complaint, plaintiff alleged wrongful dishonor of a negotiable instrument contrary to N.J.S.A. [New Jersey Statutes Annotated] 12A:4–402 [New Jersey's version of UCC 4–402].

* * * *

* * * The statute addresses wrongful dishonor of checks payable from a customer's own account.

The parties dispute whether * * * the check at issue was payable from an account of plaintiff. The facts of this case are somewhat unusual in this regard.

CASE 28.1 CONTINUED

The summary judgment record shows that plaintiff opened a secured credit card account with BOA, making a $300 deposit that the bank held pursuant to the terms of a secured credit card agreement [in a "collateral account"].

The record therefore shows that the money in the account originated with plaintiff and was being held to secure her own account. * * * BOA exercised control over the money. BOA ultimately determined that plaintiff was entitled to receive the money in refund of her security deposit. In addition, the check by which BOA refunded the security deposit was drawn on an account in BOA's name. Yet the problem for BOA is that the correspondence from the bank to plaintiff dated March 5, 2007 enclosing the $300

check refers to the bank account as her account.

*In light of this correspondence from the bank, it is reasonable to regard the refund check in this case * * * as the functional equivalent of funds coming from plaintiff's own account. * * * We conclude that the distinctive circumstances of this matter can support plaintiff's statutory claim for wrongful dishonor.* [Emphasis added.]

Defendants alternatively contend that there was no wrongful dishonor under the UCC because, under N.J.S.A. 12A: 3–501(b)(4) [New Jersey's version of UCC 3–501(b)(4)] BOA had until the day after plaintiff came to the bank to process her request for payment. That argument does not work here because defendants' actions are inconsistent with the benign [harmless] ordinary process-

ing of a check. During the interval between plaintiff's presentment of the check and BOA's ultimate authentication of it, Lowe called the police and plaintiff was arrested and charged with forgery and attempted theft by deception. Viewing the facts in a light most favorable to plaintiff, Lowe told the police that the check was fraudulent and the police arrested and charged plaintiff based upon Lowe's statements. *BOA cannot, on the one hand, cause plaintiff to be arrested for attempting to pass a fraudulent check, and, on the other hand, claim that they never dishonored that check.* [Emphasis added.]

* * * *

In sum, the trial court did not err in declining to grant summary judgment dismissing plaintiff's statutory claim of wrongful dishonor.

LEGAL REASONING QUESTIONS

1. Why did the bank argue that UCC 4–402 did not apply in this case? What did the court decide on this issue?

2. On what basis did the court reason that the bank may have wrongfully dishonored the check?

3. During the trial, Lowe admitted that she made a mistake when she did not ask Afiriyie whether she was a bank customer. How might this simple question have changed the facts?

4. Besides asking Afiriyie whether she was a bank customer, what other steps might Lowe have taken to avoid the dispute in this case?

Overdrafts

When the bank receives an item properly payable from its customer's checking account but the account contains insufficient funds to cover the amount of the check, the bank has two options. It can either dishonor the item, or it can pay the item and charge the customer's account, thus creating an **overdraft** [UCC 4–401(a)]. The bank can subtract the difference (plus a service charge) from the customer's next deposit because the check carries with it an enforceable implied promise to reimburse the bank.

With a joint account, however, the bank cannot automatically hold any joint-account owner liable for payment of an overdraft. A joint-account owner is not liable for an overdraft unless he or she either signed the check or benefited from the proceeds of the check [UCC 4–401(b)]. ▶ **Example 28.2** Aaron and Sarah are married and have a joint bank account. Aaron

writes a check to pay the electric bill for their apartment. If the check results in an overdraft, both Aaron and Sarah will be liable, because both obviously benefited from having electricity in their apartment. ◀

A bank can expressly agree with a customer to accept overdrafts through what is sometimes called an "overdraft protection agreement." If such an agreement is formed, any failure of the bank to honor a check because it would create an overdraft breaches this agreement and is treated as a wrongful dishonor [UCC 4–402(a), (b)].

Postdated Checks

A bank may charge a postdated check against a customer's account unless the customer notifies the bank, in a timely manner, not to pay the check until the stated date. (Indeed, banks typically ignore the dates on checks and treat them as demand instruments unless a customer has notified the bank that a check was postdated.) The notice of postdating must be given in time to allow the bank to act on the notice before committing itself to pay on the check.

The UCC states that the bank should treat the notice like a stop-payment order (to be discussed shortly). If the bank fails to act on the customer's notice and charges the customer's account before the date on the postdated check, the bank may be liable for any damages incurred by the customer. Damages include those that result from the dishonor of checks that are subsequently presented for payment and are dishonored for insufficient funds [UCC 4–401(c)].

Stale Checks

Commercial banking practice regards a check that is presented for payment more than six months from its date as a **stale check.** A bank is not obligated to pay an uncertified check presented more than six months from its date [UCC 4–404]. When receiving a stale check for payment, the bank has the option of paying or not paying the check. If a bank pays a stale check in good faith without consulting the customer, the bank has the right to charge the customer's account for the amount of the check.

Stop-Payment Orders

A **stop-payment order** is an order by a customer to her or his bank not to pay a certain check.[2] Only a customer or a "person authorized to draw on the account" can order the bank not to pay the check when it is presented for payment [UCC 4–403(a)]. A customer has no right to stop payment on a check that has already been certified (or accepted) by a bank, however.

CUSTOMER MUST HAVE LEGITIMATE REASON The customer-drawer must have a *valid legal ground* for issuing a stop-payment order, or the holder can sue the customer-drawer for payment. A person who wrongfully stops payment on a check will be liable to the payee for the amount of the check. The person may also may be liable for consequential damages incurred by the payee as a result of the wrongful stop-payment order.

REASONABLE TIME AND MANNER The customer-drawer must issue the stop-payment order within a reasonable time and in a reasonable manner to permit the bank to act on it [UCC 4–403(a)]. Most banks allow stop-payment orders to be submitted electronically via the bank's Web site. A written or electronic stop-payment order is effective for six months, at which time it must be renewed in writing [UCC 4–403(b)]. Although a stop-payment order can be given orally over the phone, it is binding on the bank for only fourteen calendar days unless confirmed in writing (or record).[3]

BANK'S LIABILITY FOR WRONGFUL PAYMENT If the bank pays the check in spite of a stop-payment order, the bank will be obligated to recredit the customer's account. In addition, if the bank's payment over a stop-payment order causes subsequent checks written on the drawer's account to "bounce," the bank will be liable for the resultant costs the drawer incurs. The bank is liable only for the amount of the actual loss suffered by the drawer because of the wrongful payment, however [UCC 4–403(c)].

▶ **Example 28.3** Mike Murano orders one hundred cell phones from Advanced Communications, Inc., at $50 each. Murano pays in advance for the phones with a check for $5,000. Later that day, Advanced Communications tells Murano that it will not deliver the phones as arranged. Murano immediately calls the bank and stops payment on the check. Two days later, in spite of this stop-payment order, the bank inadvertently honors Murano's check to Advanced Communications for the undelivered phones. The bank will be liable to Murano for the full $5,000.

The result would be different, however, if Advanced Communications had delivered and Murano had accepted ninety-nine phones. Because Murano would have owed Advanced Communications $4,950 for the goods delivered, Murano's actual loss would be only $50. Consequently, the bank would be liable to Murano for only $50. ◀

Incompetence or Death of a Customer

Neither the incompetence nor the death of a customer revokes a bank's authority to pay an item until the bank knows of the situation and has had reason-

---

2. Note that although this discussion focuses on checks, the right to stop payment is not limited to checks. It extends to any item payable by any bank. See Official Comment 3 to UCC 4–403.

3. Some states do not recognize oral stop-payment orders. The orders must be in writing.

able time to act on the notice [UCC 4–405]. Thus, if, at the time a check is issued or its collection is undertaken, a bank does not know that the customer who wrote the check has been declared incompetent or died, the bank can pay without incurring liability. Without this provision, banks would constantly be required to verify the continued competence and life of their drawers.

Even when a bank knows of the death of its customer, for ten days after the *date of death* it can pay or certify checks drawn on or before the date of death. An exception to the rule is made if a person claiming an interest in the account of the deceased customer, such as an heir or an executor of the estate (see Chapter 51), orders the bank to stop payment.

Forged Drawers' Signatures

When a bank pays a check on which the drawer's signature is forged, generally the bank suffers the loss.[4] A bank may be able to recover at least some of the loss from the customer, however, if the customer's negligence substantially contributed to the forgery. A bank may also obtain partial recovery from the forger of the check (if he or she can be found) or from the holder who presented the check for payment (if the holder knew that the signature was forged).

THE GENERAL RULE A forged signature on a check has no legal effect as the signature of a drawer [UCC 3–403(a)]. For this reason, banks require a signature card from each customer who opens a checking account. Signature cards allow a bank to verify whether the signatures on its customers' checks are genuine.

The general rule is that the bank must recredit the customer's account when it pays on a forged signature. (Banks today normally verify signatures only on checks that exceed a certain threshold, such as $2,500 or some higher amount. Even though a bank sometimes incurs liability costs when it has paid forged checks, the costs of verifying the signature on every check would be much higher.)

Note that a bank may contractually shift to the customer the risk of forged checks created electronically or by the use of nonmanual signatures. For instance, the contract might stipulate that the customer is solely responsible for maintaining security over any signature stamp.

CUSTOMER NEGLIGENCE When a customer's negligence substantially contributes to a forgery, the bank normally will *not* be obligated to recredit the customer's account for the amount of the check [UCC 3–406(a)]. The customer's liability may be reduced, however, by the amount of the loss caused by negligence on the part of the bank (or other "person") in paying the instrument or taking it for value [UCC 3–406(b)].

▶ **Case in Point 28.4** Kenneth Wulf worked for Auto-Owners Insurance Company for ten years. During that time, Wulf opened a checking account at Bank One in the name of "Auto-Owners, Kenneth B. Wulf." Over a period of eight years, he deposited $546,000 worth of checks that he had stolen from Auto-Owners and indorsed with a stamp that read "Auto-Owners Insurance Deposit Only." When the scam was finally discovered, Auto-Owners sued Bank One for negligence.

The insurance company claimed that the bank should not have allowed Wulf to open an account in Auto-Owners' name without proof that he was authorized to do so. The court ruled in favor of the bank, though, finding that Bank One's conduct was not a substantial factor in bringing about the loss. The negligence of Auto-Owners (the customer) contributed substantially to its own losses. Therefore, the bank did not have to recredit the customer's account.[5] ◀

Timely Examination of Bank Statements Required. Banks typically send or provide online monthly statements that detail the activity in their customers' checking accounts. In the past, banks routinely included the canceled checks themselves (or copies of them) with the statement.

Today, most banks simply provide the customer with information (check number, amount, and date of payment) on the statement that will allow the customer to reasonably identify each check that the bank has paid [UCC 4–406(a), (b)]. If the bank retains the canceled checks, it must keep the checks—or legible images of them—for seven years [UCC 4–406(b)]. The customer may obtain a copy of a canceled check from the bank during this period of time.

The customer has a duty to promptly examine bank statements (and canceled checks or copies, if they are included) with reasonable care and to report any alterations or forged signatures [UCC 4–406(c)]. The customer is also obligated to report any alteration

---

4. Each year, check fraud costs banks many billions of dollars—perhaps equivalent to the combined losses from credit-card fraud, theft from automated teller machines, and armed robberies.

5. *Auto-Owners Insurance Co. v. Bank One*, 879 N.E.2d 1086 (Ind.Sup.Ct. 2008).

or apparent forgery in the signatures of indorsers (to be discussed shortly). If the customer fails to fulfill her or his duty and the bank suffers a loss as a result, the customer will be liable for the loss [UCC 4–406(d)].

Consequences of Failure to Detect Forgeries. Sometimes, the same wrongdoer forges the customer's signature on a series of checks. To recover for all of the forged items, the customer must discover and report the first forged check to the bank within thirty calendar days of the receipt or availability of the bank statement [UCC 4–406(d)(2)]. Failure to notify the bank within this time period discharges the bank's liability for all forged checks that it pays prior to notification.

▶ **Case in Point 28.5** Joseph Montanez, an employee at Espresso Roma Corporation, used stolen software and blank checks to generate company checks on his home computer. The series of forged checks spanned a period of more than two years and totaled more than $330,000. When the bank statements containing the forged checks arrived in the mail, Montanez removed the checks so that the forgeries would go undetected.

Eventually, Espresso Roma discovered the forgeries and asked the bank to recredit its account. When the bank refused, litigation ensued. The court held that the bank was not liable for the forged checks because Espresso Roma had failed to report the first forgeries within thirty days, as required by the UCC.[6] ◀

Negligence and the Bank's Duty of Care. In one situation, a bank customer can escape liability, at least in part, for failing to notify the bank of forged or altered checks within the required thirty-day period. When the customer can prove that the bank was also negligent—that is, that the bank failed to exercise ordinary care—then the bank, too, will be liable. The loss will be allocated between the bank and the customer on the basis of comparative negligence [UCC 4–406(e)].

The UCC defines *ordinary care* as the "observance of reasonable commercial standards, prevailing in the area in which [a] person is located, with respect to the business in which that person is engaged" [UCC 3–103(a)(7)]. As mentioned earlier, it is customary in the banking industry to examine signatures only on checks that exceed a certain amount. Thus, if a bank fails to examine a signature on a particular check, the

bank has not necessarily breached its duty to exercise ordinary care.

One-Year Time Limit. Regardless of the degree of care exercised by the customer or the bank, the UCC places an absolute time limit on the liability of a bank for paying a check with a customer's forged signature. A customer who fails to report a forged signature within one year from the date that the statement was made available for inspection loses the legal right to have the bank recredit her or his account [UCC 4–406(f)]. The parties can also agree in their contract to a lower time limit, but the UCC stipulates that the bank has no liability on forged instruments after one year.

OTHER PARTIES FROM WHOM THE BANK MAY RECOVER As noted earlier, a forged signature on a check has no legal effect as the signature of a drawer. Instead, the person who forged the signature is liable [UCC 3–403(a)]. Therefore, when a bank pays a check on which the drawer's signature is forged, the bank has a right to recover from the party who forged the signature (if he or she can be found).

The bank may also have a right to recover from a party who transferred a check bearing a forged drawer's signature and received payment. (Transfer warranties were discussed in Chapter 27). This right is limited, however, in that the bank cannot recover from a person who took the check in good faith and for value. A bank also cannot recover from a person who in good faith changed position in reliance on the payment or acceptance [UCC 3–418(c)].

Checks Bearing Forged Indorsements

A bank that pays a customer's check bearing a forged indorsement must recredit the customer's account or be liable to the customer (drawer) for breach of contract. ▶ **Example 28.6** Cameron issues a $500 check "to the order of Sophia Alonzo." Margo steals the check, forges Alonzo's indorsement, and cashes the check. When the check reaches Cameron's bank, the bank pays it and debits Cameron's account. The bank must recredit Cameron's account for the $500 because it failed to carry out Cameron's order to pay "to the order of Sophia Alonzo" [UCC 4–401(a)]. Of course, Cameron's bank can in turn recover—for breach of warranty (see Chapter 27)—from the bank that cashed the check when Margo presented it [UCC 4–207(a)(2)]. ◀

6. *Espresso Roma Corp. v. Bank of America, N.A.*, 100 Cal.App.4th 525, 124 Cal.Rptr.2d 549 (2002).

Eventually, *the loss usually falls on the first party to take the instrument bearing the forged indorsement* because a forged indorsement does not transfer title. Thus, whoever takes an instrument with a forged indorsement cannot become a holder.

The customer, in any event, has a duty to report forged indorsements promptly. The bank is relieved of liability if the customer fails to report the forged indorsements within three years of receiving the bank statement that contained the forged items [UCC 4–111].[7]

In the following case, a bank changed its statutory duties concerning forged indorsements by contract. The court had to decide whether to follow the UCC or enforce the contract as written.

---

7. This is a general statute of limitations for all actions under Article 4. It provides that any lawsuit must be brought within three years of the time that the cause of action arises.

CASE 28.2

Michigan Basic Property Insurance Association v. Washington
Court of Appeals of Michigan, 2012 WL 205753 (2012).

BACKGROUND AND FACTS The Michigan Basic Property Insurance Association (MBP) issued a check from its account with Fifth Third Bank to Joyce Washington, Countrywide Home Loans, and T & C Federal Credit Union as co-payees. Shortly afterward, Washington indorsed the check herself by signing all three payees' names. When the check reached Fifth Third, it notified MBP of the payment through a daily account statement. MBP did not object, so Fifth Third withdrew the money from MBP's account. Afterward, Fifth Third also sent information about the check in a monthly account statement, and MBP still failed to object even though the account agreement required it to provide prompt notice of any forgeries. MBP was forced to issue a second check to Countrywide, so it sued Fifth Third and sought to have its account recredited. The trial court found that Fifth Third was liable to MBP, and another party appealed on MBP's behalf.

IN THE LANGUAGE OF THE COURT
PER CURIAM.

* * * *

* * * A bank may only deduct "properly payable" items from its customer's account and should use due care at the time of presentment to mitigate its losses.

* * * *

* * * *"If an instrument is payable to 2 or more persons not alternatively, it is payable to all of them and may be negotiated, discharged, or enforced only by all of them."* To "negotiate" the check, each joint payee must "endorse" it. If a joint payee's endorsement signature is missing or forged, the endorsement is incomplete and the check is not "properly payable." [Emphasis added.]

The subject check was endorsed in the name of all three named payees: Washington, Countrywide, and T & C. * * * [T]here is no [evidence disputing] that at least two of those endorsements were forged by Washington * * *. The obviously forged endorsements rendered the check not "properly payable" under the UCC.

As a general rule, a bank that pays funds from a customer's account based on a check with forged endorsements must recredit or reimburse those funds to the customer's account.

* * * *

While Fifth Third would be liable to reimburse MBP's account under the UCC, the parties' actions are also governed by the account contract * * * . The UCC allows individuals to contractually alter UCC requirements.

* * * *

* * * Fifth Third provides daily and monthly statements to MBP from which MBP can detect any abnormal activity. If MBP fails to use ordinary care to review the statements and notify Fifth Third within 30 days of any discrepancy or forgery, the burden of loss is contractually shifted to MBP. The contract also creates a strict assumption of liability by MBP for "any improper endorsements by payees."

CASE 28.2 CONTINUES ▶

CASE 28.2 CONTINUED

* * * *

* * * Fifth Third's statutory liability was eliminated by the parties' contractual agreement that MBP would bear the loss incurred from "improper endorsements by payees" and would provide notice of any discrepancies within 30 days of the relevant account statement. The subject check bore such an improper endorsement and MBP did not provide the required notice, precluding its claim for reimbursement * * * .

DECISION AND REMEDY *The Michigan appellate court reversed the trial court's judgment and held that Fifth Third was not liable to MBP.*

THE LEGAL ENVIRONMENT DIMENSION *As a practical matter, does it make sense for the customer to bear primary responsibility for discovering instances of fraud? Which party is in a better position to detect any irregularities? Why?*

THE SOCIAL DIMENSION *What reasonable steps could MBP have taken to have prevented its loss?*

Altered Checks

The customer's instruction to the bank is to pay the exact amount on the face of the check to the holder. The bank has an implicit duty to examine checks before making final payments. If it fails to detect an alteration, it is liable to its customer for the loss because it did not pay as the customer ordered.

The bank's loss is the difference between the original amount of the check and the amount actually paid. ▶ **Example 28.7** Hailey Lyonne writes a check for $11 that is increased to $111. Lyonne's account will be charged $11 (the amount the customer ordered the bank to pay). The bank will normally be responsible for the remaining $100 [UCC 4–401(d)(1)]. ◀

CUSTOMER NEGLIGENCE As in a situation involving a forged drawer's signature, a customer's negli-

gence can shift the loss when payment is made on an altered check (unless the bank was also negligent). For instance, a person may carelessly write a check and leave large gaps around the numbers and words where additional numbers and words can be inserted (see Exhibit 28–3 below).

Similarly, a person who signs a check and leaves the dollar amount for someone else to fill in is barred from protesting when the bank unknowingly and in good faith pays whatever amount is shown [UCC 4–401(d)(2)]. Finally, if the bank can trace its loss on successive altered checks to the customer's failure to discover the initial alteration, then the bank can reduce its liability for reimbursing the customer's account [UCC 4–406].

In every situation involving a forged drawer's signature or an alteration, a bank must observe reasonable commercial standards of care in paying on

EXHIBIT 28-3 A Poorly Filled-Out Check

a customer's checks [UCC 4–406(e)]. The customer's contributory negligence can be asserted only if the bank has exercised ordinary care.

OTHER PARTIES FROM WHOM THE BANK MAY RECOVER The bank is entitled to recover the amount of loss (including expenses) from the transferor who presented the check for payment. A transferor, by presenting a check for payment, warrants that the check has not been altered.

There are two exceptions to this rule. First, if the bank is also the drawer (as it is on a cashier's check), it cannot recover from the presenting party if the party is a holder in due course (HDC) acting in good faith [UCC 3–417(a)(2), 4–208(a)(2)]. The reason is that an instrument's drawer is in a better position than an HDC to know whether the instrument has been altered.

Second, an HDC who presents a certified check for payment in good faith does not warrant to the check's certifier that the check was not altered before the HDC acquired it [UCC 3–417(a)(2), 4–208(a)(2)]. ▶ **Example 28.8** Alan, the drawer, draws a check for $500 payable to Rhea, the payee. Rhea alters the amount to $5,000. National City Bank, the drawee, certifies the check for $5,000. Rhea negotiates the check to Jordan, an HDC. The drawee bank pays Jordan $5,000. On discovering the mistake, the bank cannot recover from Jordan the $4,500 paid by mistake, even though the bank was not in a superior position to detect the alteration. This result is in accord with the purpose of certification, which is to obtain the definite obligation of a bank to honor a definite instrument. ◀

For a synopsis of the rules governing the honoring of checks, see *Concept Summary 28.1* below.

CONCEPT SUMMARY 28.1
Honoring Checks

SITUATION	BASIC RULES
Wrongful Dishonor [UCC 4–402]	The bank is liable to its customer for actual damages proved if it wrongfully dishonors a check due to its own mistake.
Overdraft [UCC 4–401]	The bank has a right to charge a customer's account for any item properly payable, even if the charge results in an overdraft.
Postdated Check [UCC 4–401]	The bank may charge a postdated check against a customer's account, unless the customer notifies the bank of the postdating in time to allow the bank to act on the notice before the bank commits itself to pay on the check.
Stale Check [UCC 4–404]	The bank is not obligated to pay an uncertified check presented more than six months after its date, but the bank may do so in good faith without liability.
Stop-Payment Order [UCC 4–403]	The customer (or a "person authorized to draw on the account") must institute a stop-payment order in time for the bank to have a reasonable opportunity to act. A customer has no right to stop payment on a check that has been certified or accepted by the bank, however, and can be held liable for stopping payment on any check without a valid legal ground.
Death or Incompetence of a Customer [UCC 4–405]	So long as the bank does not know of the death or incompetence of a customer, the bank can pay an item without liability. Even with knowledge of a customer's death, a bank can honor or certify checks (in the absence of a stop-payment order) for ten days after the date of the customer's death.
Forged Signature or Alteration [UCC 4–406]	The customer has a duty to examine account statements with reasonable care on receipt and to notify the bank promptly of any unauthorized signatures or alterations. The customer's failure to report promptly an unauthorized signature or alteration will discharge the bank's liability—unless the bank failed to exercise reasonable care (and then the bank may be responsible for some portion of the loss). The customer is prevented from holding the bank liable after one year for unauthorized customer signatures or alterations and after three years for unauthorized indorsements.

SECTION 4
THE BANK'S DUTY TO ACCEPT DEPOSITS

A bank has a duty to its customer to accept the customer's deposits of cash and checks. When checks are deposited, the bank must make the funds represented by those checks available within certain time frames. A bank also has a duty to collect payment on any checks payable or indorsed to its customer and deposited by the customer into his or her account. Cash deposits made in U.S. currency are received into the customer's account without being subject to further collection procedures.

Availability Schedule for Deposited Checks

The Expedited Funds Availability Act (EFAA)[8] and Regulation CC[9] (the regulation implementing the act) establish when funds from deposited checks must be made available to the customer. The rules are as follows:

1. Any local check (drawn on a bank in the same area) deposited must be available for withdrawal by check or as cash within one business day from the date of deposit.
2. For nonlocal checks, the funds must be available for withdrawal within not more than five business days.
3. Under the Check Clearing in the 21st Century Act[10] (Check 21, which will be discussed shortly), a bank must credit a customer's account as soon as the bank receives the funds.
4. For cash deposits, wire transfers, and government checks, funds must be available on the next business day.
5. The first $100 of any deposit must be available for cash withdrawal on the opening of the *next business day* after deposit.

A different availability schedule applies to deposits made at *nonproprietary* automated teller machines (ATMs). These are ATMs that are not owned or operated by the bank receiving the deposits. Basically, a five-day hold is permitted on all deposits, including cash deposits, made at nonproprietary ATMs. Other exceptions also exist. For instance, a banking institution has eight days to make funds available in new accounts (those open less than thirty days).

Before the EFAA was enacted, a bank could wait for a sometimes lengthy period before making deposited funds available to the customer. Some commentators argue that making funds available more quickly has encouraged fraud. See this chapter's *Insight into Ethics* feature on the following page for a discussion of this issue.

Interest-Bearing Accounts

Under the Truth-in-Savings Act (TISA)[11] and Regulation DD,[12] the act's implementing regulation, banks must pay interest based on the full balance of a customer's interest-bearing account each day. ▶ **Example 28.9** Nigel has an interest-bearing checking account with First National Bank. Nigel keeps a $500 balance in the account for most of the month but withdraws all but $50 the day before the bank posts the interest. The bank cannot pay interest on just the $50. The interest must be adjusted to account for the entire month, including those days when Nigel's balance was higher. ◀

Before opening a deposit account, new customers must be provided certain information, including the following:

1. The minimum balance required to open an account and to be paid interest.
2. The interest, stated in terms of the annual percentage yield on the account.
3. How interest is calculated.
4. Any fees, charges, and penalties and how they are calculated.

Also, under the TISA and Regulation DD, a customer's monthly statement must disclose the interest earned on the account, any fees that were charged, how the fees were calculated, and the number of days that the statement covers.

The Traditional Collection Process

Usually, deposited checks involve parties who do business at different banks, but sometimes checks are written between customers of the same bank. Either situation brings into play the bank collection process as it operates under Article 4 of the UCC. The

---

8. 12 U.S.C. Sections 4001–4010.
9. 12 C.F.R. Sections 229.1–229.42.
10. 12 U.S.C. Sections 5001–5018.

---

11. 12 U.S.C. Sections 4301–4313.
12. 12 C.F.R. Sections 230.1–230.9.

INSIGHT INTO ETHICS
Expedited Funds and an Increase in Check Fraud

Since the Expedited Funds Availability Act (EFAA) was enacted in 1987, millions of people have fallen prey to various types of check fraud. In a common scam, the fraudsters contact an individual—usually via e-mail—and say that they will send that person a check for a certain amount if he or she agrees to wire some of the funds back to them, typically to cover "fees and taxes." The victim receives a check and deposits it in his or her account. A day or so later, when the law says the funds must be made available, the victim confirms that the funds are in his or her bank account, and wires the requested amount back to the fraudsters.

Unfortunately, by the time the bank discovers the check is a fake and notifies the customer, he or she has already sent thousands of dollars to the fraudsters. Because the check was counterfeit, the bank has no liability on it, and the loss falls to the customer. The incidence of these scams is increasing, largely because the fraudsters know that the law requires U.S. banks to make the funds available soon after checks are deposited even if those checks later prove to be counterfeit. (For a case involving this type of scam, see *Case 28.3* on page 545.)

Moreover, technology has improved fraudsters' ability to create checks that look real. Although the EFAA was intended to protect bank customers, it now appears to be having the opposite effect—making them a target for increased fraud.

LEGAL CRITICAL THINKING
INSIGHT INTO THE BUSINESS ENVIRONMENT

Why would banks say that they are worse off because of the EFAA?

---

check-collection process described in the following subsections has been modified as the banking industry continues to implement Check 21, which will be discussed shortly.

DESIGNATIONS OF BANKS The first bank to receive a check for payment is the **depositary bank.**[13] For instance, when a person deposits a tax-refund check from the Internal Revenue Service into a personal checking account at the local bank, that bank is the depositary bank.

The bank on which a check is drawn (the drawee bank) is called the **payor bank.** Any bank except the payor bank that handles a check during some phase of the collection process is a **collecting bank.** Any bank except the payor bank or the depositary bank to which an item is transferred in the course of this collection process is called an **intermediary bank.**

BANKS MAY HAVE MORE THAN ONE ROLE During the collection process, any bank can take on one or more of the various roles of depositary, payor, collecting, or intermediary bank. ▶ **Example 28.10** Brooke, a buyer in New York, writes a check on her New York bank and sends it to David, a seller in San Francisco. David deposits the check in his San Francisco bank account.

David's bank is both a *depositary bank* and a *collecting bank.* Brooke's bank in New York is the *payor bank.* As the check travels from San Francisco to New York, any *collecting bank* handling the item in the collection process (other than the ones acting as depositary bank and payor bank) is also called an *intermediary bank.* ◀

Exhibit 28–4 on the following page illustrates how various banks function in the check-collection process.

CHECK COLLECTION BETWEEN CUSTOMERS OF THE SAME BANK An item that is payable by the depositary bank that receives it (which in this situation is also the payor bank) is called an "on-us item." Usually, a bank issues a "provisional credit" for on-us items within the same day. If the bank does not dishonor the check by the opening of the second banking day following its receipt, the check is considered paid [UCC 4–215(e)(2)].

CHECK COLLECTION BETWEEN CUSTOMERS OF DIFFERENT BANKS Once a depositary bank receives a check, it must arrange to present the check, either directly or through intermediary banks, to the appropriate payor bank.

---

13. All definitions in this section are found in UCC 4–105. The terms *depositary* and *depository* have different meanings in the banking context. A depository bank is a *physical place* (a bank or other institution) in which deposits or funds are held or stored.

EXHIBIT 28-4 The Check-Collection Process

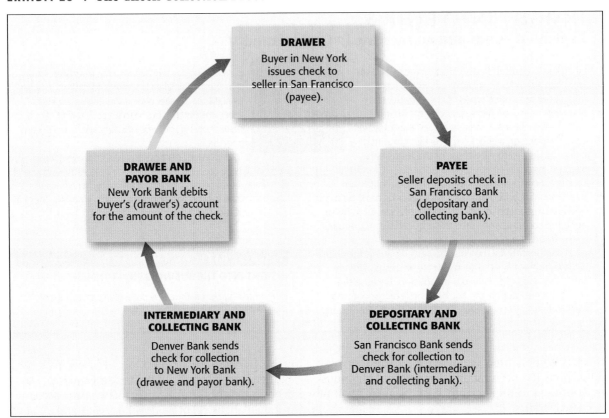

Deadline Is Midnight of the Next Banking Day. Each bank in the collection chain must pass the check on before midnight of the next banking day following its receipt [UCC 4–202(b)].[14] A "banking day" is any part of a day on which the bank is open to carry on substantially all of its banking functions.

Thus, if only a bank's drive-through facilities are open, a check deposited on Saturday will not trigger a bank's midnight deadline until the following Monday. When the check reaches the payor bank, that bank is liable for the face amount of the check, unless the payor bank dishonors the check or returns it by midnight of the next banking day following receipt [UCC 4–302].[15]

Deferred Posting after Cutoff Hour. Because of this deadline and because banks need to maintain an even work flow in the many items they handle daily, the UCC permits what is called *deferred posting.* According to UCC 4–108, "a bank may fix an afternoon hour of 2:00 P.M. or later as a cutoff hour for the handling of money and items and the making of entries on its books."

Any checks received after that hour "may be treated as being received at the opening of the next banking day." Thus, if a bank's "cutoff hour" is 3:00 P.M., a check received by a payor bank at 4:00 P.M. on Monday will be deferred for posting until Tuesday. In this situation, the payor bank's deadline will be midnight Wednesday.

The provisional credit mentioned earlier also applies to checks presented to one bank for collection from another. As the number of banks in the collection chain increases, so does the time before the credit becomes final and the check is considered paid, as occurred in the following case.

---

14. A bank may take a "reasonably longer time" in certain circumstances, such as a power failure that disrupts the bank's computer system [UCC 4–202(b)].

15. Most checks are cleared by a computerized process, and communication and computer facilities may fail because of electrical outages, equipment malfunction, or other conditions. If such conditions arise and a bank fails to meet its midnight deadline, the bank is "excused" from liability if the bank has exercised "such diligence as the circumstances require" [UCC 4–109(d)].

CASE 28.3

Cumis Mutual Insurance Society, Inc. v. Rosol
Superior Court of New Jersey, Appellate Division, 2011 WL 589397 (2011).

BACKGROUND AND FACT   Mizek Rosol, a resident of New Jersey, received an e-mail message from someone he did not know, offering to pay a 10 percent fee if he would receive checks, deposit them, and transfer the funds to others. Rosol opened a new account at Polish & Slavic Federal Credit Union (PSFCU) and deposited a cashier's check for $9,800 issued by a credit union in Florida. Three days later, he deposited a check for $45,000 drawn on a Canadian bank. Within a week, PSFCU told him that payment on the first check had been "stopped" but did not disclose that the check was fraudulent. PSFCU issued a provisional credit to Rosol's account for the amount of the Canadian check. A PSFCU employee told Rosol that "these monies were collected and in his account." Rosol transferred $36,240 to a party in Japan and $4,500 to someone in Great Britain. Ten days later, PSFCU told Rosol that the Canadian check had been dishonored and demanded that he repay the transferred funds. He refused. PSFCU filed a claim with its insurer, Cumis Mutual Insurance Society, Inc. Cumis paid the claim and filed a suit in a New Jersey state court against Rosol to recover the amount. The court issued a summary judgment in Cumis's favor. Rosol appealed.

IN THE LANGUAGE OF THE COURT
PER CURIAM.

* * * *

The relationship between a collecting bank, such as PSFCU, and the owner of a negotiable instrument, such as Rosol, is governed by the provisions of [New Jersey Statutes Annotated] N.J.S.A. 12A:4-201(a) [New Jersey's version of UCC 2–401(a)]. That statute provides, in applicable part, as follows:

> a. Unless a contrary intent clearly appears and before the time that a settlement given by a collecting bank for an item is or becomes final, the bank, with respect to the item, is an agent or sub-agent of the owner of the item and any settlement given for the item is provisional. * * * Any rights of the owner to proceeds of the item are subject to rights of a collecting bank, such as those resulting from outstanding advances on the item and rights of recoupment.

A straightforward application of the language of the governing statute to the facts of this case supports the result reached by the [lower court]. Rosol deposited a check, drawn on a foreign bank, for collection. PSFCU credited the amount of the check to his account prior to final settlement. Rosol drew on those funds. The check was subsequently dishonored, also prior to final settlement. *Consequently, pursuant to the statute, the credit to Rosol's account was "provisional" and PSFCU had a "right of recoupment."* [Emphasis added.]

* * * *

Rosol * * * contends that, had he been advised that the first check was "fraudulent," as opposed to just "stopped," he would not have transferred funds from the account. Given the nature of the transactions Rosol was engaged in, we question whether Rosol's position is reasonable. We also observe that the assertion [statement] is inconsistent with his position that he was told the second check had actually cleared. In any event, while we do not find that argument sufficient in itself to preclude his liability under N.J.S.A. 12A:4-201(a), the state of his knowledge about the first check may inform the [trial court's] view, one way or another, on the issue of whether he acted reasonably in relying on any representations that may have been made by PSFCU's employees.

DECISION AND REMEDY   *A state intermediate appellate court reversed the lower court's judgment and remanded the case because "there were genuine issues of material fact precluding summary judgment." If PSFCU reasonably led Rosol to believe that the Canadian check had been finally credited to his account, the credit union could not rely on UCC 2–401(a) to recover the transferred funds.*

CASE 28.3 CONTINUES ➧

THE ETHICAL DIMENSION *In what ways was Rosol's apparent motive similar to the most common reason that ethical problems occur in business?*

THE LEGAL ENVIRONMENT DIMENSION *How do the rules concerning liability on a forged drawer's signature apply to the circumstances in this case? Explain.*

HOW THE FEDERAL RESERVE SYSTEM CLEARS CHECKS The **Federal Reserve System** is a network of twelve district banks, which are located around the country and headed by the Federal Reserve Board of Governors. Most banks in the United States have Federal Reserve accounts. The Federal Reserve System simplifies the check-collection process by acting as a **clearinghouse**—a place where banks exchange checks and drafts drawn on each other and settle daily balances.

▶ **Example 28.11** Tami Moy who lives in Cleveland, Ohio, writes a check to Jeanne Sutton of Boston, Massachusetts. When Jeanne receives the check in the mail, she deposits it in her bank. Her bank then deposits the check in the Federal Reserve Bank of Boston, which transfers it to the Federal Reserve Bank of Cleveland. That Federal Reserve bank then sends the check to Moy's bank, which deducts the amount of the check from Moy's account. ◀

ELECTRONIC CHECK PRESENTMENT In the past, most checks were processed manually and physically transported to each bank in the collection chain. The employees of each bank in the chain had to handle each check that passed through the bank for collection or payment. Today, most checks are processed electronically—a practice that has been facilitated by Check 21 (to be discussed next).

Whereas manual check processing can take days, *electronic check presentment* can be done on the day of the deposit. With electronic check presentment, items are encoded with information (such as the amount of the check) that is read and processed by other banks' computers. In some situations, a check may be retained at its place of deposit, and only its image or description is presented for payment [UCC 4–110].

A bank that encodes information on an item after the item has been issued warrants to any subsequent bank or payor that the encoded information is correct [UCC 4–209]. This is also true for a bank that retains an item and presents an image or description of the item for payment.

Regulation CC provides that a returned check must be encoded with the routing number of the depositary bank, the amount of the check, and other information. The regulation further states that a check must still be returned within the deadlines required by the UCC.

Check Clearing and the Check 21 Act

To streamline the check-collection process and to improve the overall efficiency of the nation's payment system, Congress passed the Check Clearing in the 21st Century Act (Check 21). Check 21 is a federal law and applies to all financial institutions, other businesses, and individuals in the United States.

Before the implementation of Check 21, banks had to present the original paper check for payment in the absence of an agreement for presentment in some other form. Check 21 has changed the situation by creating a new negotiable instrument called a **substitute check.** Although the act does not require banks to change their current check-collection practices, its creation of substitute checks facilitates the use of electronic check processing.

SUBSTITUTE CHECKS A substitute check is a paper reproduction of the front and back of an original check that contains all of the same information required on checks for automated processing. Banks create a substitute check from a digital image of an original check. Financial institutions that exchange digital images of checks do not have to send the original paper checks. They can simply transmit the information electronically and replace the original checks with the substitute checks. Banks that do not exchange checks electronically are required to accept substitute checks in the same way that they accept original checks.

By eliminating the original check after a substitute check is created, the financial system can prevent the check from being paid twice and reduce the expense of paper storage and retrieval. Nevertheless, at least for quite a while, not all checks will be converted to substitute checks. Thus, if a bank returns canceled checks to deposit holders at the end of each month, some of those returned checks may be substitute checks, and some may be original canceled paper checks.

FASTER ACCESS TO FUNDS The Expedited Funds Availability Act (discussed previously) requires the Federal Reserve Board to revise the availability schedule for funds from deposited checks to correspond to reductions in check-processing time. Therefore, as the speed of check processing increases under Check 21, the Federal Reserve Board will reduce the maximum time that a bank can hold funds from deposited checks before making them available to the depositor.

Thus, account holders will have faster access to their deposited funds, but they will also have less *float time*—the time between when a check is written and when the amount is actually deducted from the account. Consequently, account holders who plan to cover their checks after writing them may experience unexpected overdrafts.

SECTION 5
ELECTRONIC FUND TRANSFERS

By utilizing computer technology in the form of electronic fund transfer systems, banking institutions no longer have to move mountains of paperwork to process fund transfers. An **electronic fund transfer (EFT)** is a transfer of funds made by the use of an electronic terminal, a telephone, a computer, or magnetic tape.

The law governing EFTs depends on the type of transfer involved. Consumer fund transfers are governed by the Electronic Fund Transfer Act (EFTA).[16] Commercial fund transfers are governed by Article 4A of the UCC.

Although electronic banking offers numerous benefits, it also poses difficulties on occasion. It is difficult to issue stop-payment orders with electronic banking. Also, fewer records are available to prove or disprove that a transaction took place, and the possibilities for tampering with a person's private banking information have increased.

Types of EFT Systems

Most banks offer EFT services to their customers. The following are the most common types of EFT systems used by bank customers:

1. *Automated teller machines* (ATMs)—The machines are connected online to the bank's computers.

---

16. 15 U.S.C. Sections 1693–1693r. The EFTA amended Title IX of the Consumer Credit Protection Act.

A customer inserts a plastic card (called an ATM or debit card) issued by the bank and keys in a *personal identification number* (PIN) to access her or his accounts and conduct banking transactions.
2. *Point-of-sale systems*—Online terminals allow consumers to transfer funds to merchants to pay for purchases using a debit card.
3. *Direct deposits and withdrawals*—Customers can authorize the bank to allow another party, such as the government or an employer, to make direct deposits into their accounts. Similarly, a customer can ask the bank to make automatic payments to a third party at regular, recurrent intervals from the customer's funds (insurance premiums or loan payments, for example).
4. *Internet payment systems*—Most financial institutions permit their customers to access the institution's computer system via the Internet and direct a transfer of funds between accounts or pay a particular bill. Payments can be made on a one-time or a recurring basis.

Consumer Fund Transfers

The Electronic Fund Transfer Act (EFTA) provides a basic framework for the rights, liabilities, and responsibilities of users of EFT systems. The act gave the Federal Reserve Board authority to issue rules and regulations to help implement the act's provisions. The Federal Reserve Board's implemental regulation is called **Regulation E.**

The EFTA governs financial institutions that offer electronic transfers of funds involving customer accounts. The types of accounts covered include checking accounts, savings accounts, and any other asset accounts established for personal, family, or household purposes. Telephone transfers are covered by the EFTA only if they are made in accordance with a prearranged plan under which periodic or recurring transfers are contemplated.

DISCLOSURE REQUIREMENTS The EFTA is essentially a disclosure law benefiting consumers. The act requires financial institutions to inform consumers of their rights and responsibilities, including those listed here, with respect to EFT systems.

1. The bank must provide a monthly statement for every month in which there is an electronic transfer of funds. The statement must show the amount and date of the transfer, the names of the retailers or other third parties involved, the location or identification of the terminal, and the fees.

2. If a customer's debit card is lost or stolen and used without her or his permission, the customer shall be required to pay no more than $50. The customer, however, must notify the bank of the loss or theft within two days of learning about it. Otherwise, the customer's liability increases to $500. The customer may be liable for more than $500 if she or he does not report the unauthorized use within sixty days after it appears on the customer's statement. (If a customer voluntarily gives her or his debit card to another, who then uses it improperly, the protections just mentioned do not apply.)

3. The customer must discover any error on the monthly statement within sixty days and notify the bank. The bank then has ten days to investigate and must report its conclusions to the customer in writing. If the bank takes longer than ten days, it must return the disputed amount to the customer's account until it finds the error. If there is no error, the customer is required to return the funds to the bank.

4. The bank must furnish receipts for transactions made through computer terminals, but it is not obligated to do so for telephone transfers.

UNAUTHORIZED TRANSFERS Because of the vulnerability of EFT systems to fraudulent activities, the EFTA clearly defined what constitutes an unauthorized transfer. Under the act, a transfer is unauthorized if all of the following conditions are met:

1. It is initiated by a person who has no actual authority to initiate the transfer.
2. The consumer receives no benefit from it.
3. The consumer did not furnish the person "with the card, code, or other means of access" to his or her account.

VIOLATIONS AND DAMAGES Unauthorized access to an EFT system constitutes a federal felony, and those convicted may be fined up to $10,000 and sentenced to as long as ten years in prison. Banks must strictly comply with the terms of the EFTA and are liable for any failure to adhere to its provisions.

For a bank's violation of the EFTA, a consumer may recover both actual damages (including attorneys' fees and costs) and punitive damages of not less than $100 and not more than $1,000.[17] Failure to investigate an error in good faith makes the bank liable for

treble damages (three times the amount of damages). Even when a customer has sustained no actual damage, the bank may be liable for legal costs and punitive damages if it fails to follow the proper procedures outlined by the EFTA for error resolution.

Commercial Fund Transfers

Funds are also transferred electronically "by wire" between commercial parties. In fact, the dollar volume of payments made by wire transfer is more than $1 trillion a day—an amount that far exceeds the dollar volume of payments made by other means. The two major wire payment systems are the Federal Reserve wire transfer network (Fedwire) and the New York Clearing House Interbank Payments Systems (CHIPS).

Commercial wire transfers are governed by Article 4A of the UCC, which has been adopted by most of the states. Article 4A uses the term *funds transfer* rather than *wire transfer* to describe the overall payment transaction. The full text of Article 4A is presented in Appendix C.

▶ **Example 28.12** Jellux, Inc., owes $5 million to Perot Corporation. Instead of sending Perot a check or some other instrument that would enable Perot to obtain payment, Jellux instructs its bank, North Bank, to credit $5 million to Perot's account in South Bank. North Bank debits Jellux's North Bank account and wires $5 million to South Bank with instructions to credit $5 million to Perot's South Bank account. In more complex transactions, additional banks would be involved. ◀

SECTION 6
E-MONEY AND ONLINE BANKING

Electronic payments (e-payments) have the potential to replace *physical* cash—coins and paper currency—with *virtual* cash in the form of electronic impulses. This is the unique promise of **digital cash,** or **e-money,** which consists of funds stored on microchips in laptops, smartphones, tablets, and other devices.

Online banking has become commonplace in today's world. In a few minutes, anybody with the proper software can access his or her account, transfer funds, write "checks," pay bills, monitor investments, and even buy and sell stocks.

---

17. In a class-action suit, up to $500,000 or 1 percent of the institution's net worth can be awarded as punitive damages.

Forms of E-Money

The simplest kind of e-money system uses *stored-value cards*. These are plastic cards embossed with magnetic strips containing magnetically encoded data. In some applications—for instance, gift cards for retailers such as Home Depot or Starbucks—a stored-value card can be used only to purchase goods and services offered by the specific card issuer.

Smart cards are plastic cards containing computer microchips that can hold much more information than magnetic strips can. A smart card carries and processes security programming. This capability gives smart cards a technical advantage over stored-value cards. The microprocessors on smart cards can also authenticate the validity of transactions. Retailers can program electronic cash registers to confirm the authenticity of a smart card by examining a unique digital signature stored on its microchip. (Digital signatures were mentioned in Chapter 12.)

Privacy Protection

Relatively few laws directly apply to the security of e-money payment information and e-money issuers' financial records. The Electronic Communications Privacy Act[18] (ECPA, which was discussed in Chapter 9) might apply to e-money transactions. The ECPA prohibits any person from knowingly divulging to any other person the contents of an electronic communication while it is being transmitted or stored.

E-MONEY ISSUERS' FINANCIAL RECORDS Under the Right to Financial Privacy Act of 1978,[19] a financial institution may not give financial information about an individual to a federal agency unless the person explicitly consents. If the person does not consent, a federal agency normally must obtain a warrant to access his or her financial records. A digital cash issuer may be subject to this act if that issuer is deemed to be (1) a bank by virtue of its holding customer funds or (2) any entity that issues a physical card similar to a credit or debit card.

CONSUMER FINANCIAL DATA In 1999, Congress passed the Financial Services Modernization Act,[20] also known as the Gramm-Leach-Bliley Act, in an attempt to delineate how financial institutions can treat customer data. In general, the act and its rules[21] place restrictions and obligations on financial institutions to protect consumer data and privacy. All financial institutions must provide their customers with information on their privacy policies and practices. No financial institution can disclose nonpublic personal information about a consumer to an unaffiliated third party unless the act's disclosure and opt-out requirements are met.

---

18. 18 U.S.C. Sections 2510–2521.

19. 12 U.S.C. Sections 3401 *et seq.*
20. 12 U.S.C. Sections 24a, 248b, 1820a, 1828b, and others.
21. 12 C.F.R. Part 40.

Reviewing: Banking in the Digital Age

RPM Pizza, Inc., issued a check for $96,000 to Systems Marketing for an advertising campaign. A few days later, RPM decided not to go through with the deal and placed a written stop-payment order on the check. RPM and Systems had no further contact for many months. Three weeks after the stop-payment order expired, however, Toby Rierson, an employee at Systems, cashed the check. Bank One Cambridge, RPM's bank, paid the check with funds from RPM's account. Because of the amount of the check and because it was more than six months old (stale), the bank should have verified the signature on the check according to standard banking procedures and the bank's own policies. Bank One did not do so, however. RPM filed a suit in a federal district court against Bank One to recover the amount of the check. Using the information presented in the chapter, answer the following questions.

1. How long is a written stop-payment order effective? What else could RPM have done to prevent this check from being cashed?
2. What would happen if it turned out that RPM did not have a legitimate reason for stopping payment on the check?

3. What are a bank's obligations with respect to stale checks? Should Bank One have contacted RPM before paying the check? Why or why not?
4. Assume that Rierson's indorsement on the check was a forgery. Would a court be likely to hold the bank liable for the amount of the check because it failed to verify the signature on the check? Why or why not?

DEBATE THIS . . . *To reduce fraud, checks that utilize mechanical or electronic signature systems should not be honored.*

Terms and Concepts

cashier's check 531

certified check 532

check 531

clearinghouse 546

collecting bank 543

depositary bank 543

digital cash 548

electronic fund transfer (EFT) 547

e-money 548

Federal Reserve System 546

intermediary bank 543

overdraft 535

payor bank 543

Regulation E 547

smart card 549

stale check 536

stop-payment order 536

substitute check 546

traveler's check 532

ExamPrep

Issue Spotters

1. Lyn writes a check for $900 to Mac, who indorses the check in blank and transfers it to Nan. She presents the check to Omega Bank, the drawee bank, for payment. Omega does not honor the check. Is Lyn liable to Nan? Could Lyn be subject to criminal prosecution? Why or why not? **(See page 533.)**

2. Roni writes a check for $700 to Sela. Sela indorses the check in blank and transfers it to Titus, who alters the check to read $7,000 and presents it to Union Bank, the drawee, for payment. The bank cashes it. Roni discovers the alteration and sues the bank. How much, if anything, can Roni recover? From whom can the bank recover this amount? **(See page 540.)**

• **Check your answers to the Issue Spotters against the answers provided in Appendix E at the end of this text.**

Before the Test

Go to **www.cengagebrain.com**, enter the ISBN 9781285185248, and click on "Find" to locate this textbook's Web site. Then, click on "Access Now" under "Study Tools," and select Chapter 28 at the top. There, you will find a Practice Quiz that you can take to assess your mastery of the concepts in this chapter, as well as Flashcards and a Glossary of important terms.

Business Scenarios

28–1. Forged Signatures. Roy Supply, Inc., and R. M. R. Drywall, Inc., had checking accounts at Wells Fargo Bank. Both accounts required all checks to carry two signatures—that of Edward Roy and that of Twila June Moore, both of whom were executive officers of both companies. Between January 2009 and March 2010, the bank honored hundreds of checks on which Roy's signature was forged by Moore. On January 31, 2011, Roy and the two corporations notified the bank of the forgeries and then filed a suit in a California state court against the bank, alleging

negligence. Who is liable for the amounts of the forged checks? Why? **(See page 537.)**

28–2. Customer Negligence. Gary goes grocery shopping and carelessly leaves his checkbook in his shopping cart. His checkbook, with two blank checks remaining, is stolen by Dolores. On May 5, Dolores forges Gary's name on a check for $10 and cashes the check at Gary's bank, Citizens Bank of Middletown. Gary has not reported the loss of his blank checks to his bank. On June 1, Gary receives his monthly bank statement and copies of canceled checks from Citizens Bank, including the forged check, but he does not examine the canceled checks. On June 20, Dolores forges Gary's last check. This check is for $1,000 and is cashed at Eastern City Bank, a bank with which Dolores has previously done business. Eastern City Bank puts the check through the collection process, and Citizens Bank honors it. On July 1, on receipt of his bank statement and canceled checks covering June transactions, Gary discovers both forgeries and immediately notifies Citizens Bank. Dolores cannot be found. Gary claims that Citizens Bank must recredit his account for both checks, as his signature was forged. Discuss fully Gary's claim. **(See page 537.)**

Business Case Problems

28–3. Spotlight on Embezzlement—Forged Drawers' Signatures.

In December 1999, Spacemakers of America, Inc., hired Jenny Triplett as a bookkeeper. Triplett was responsible for maintaining the company checkbook and reconciling it with the monthly statements from SunTrust Bank. She also handled invoices from vendors. Spacemakers' president, Dennis Rose, reviewed the invoices and signed the checks to pay them, but no other employee checked Triplett's work.

By the end of her first full month of employment, Triplett had forged six checks totaling more than $22,000, all payable to Triple M Entertainment, which was not a Spacemakers vendor. By October 2000, Triplett had forged fifty-nine more checks, totaling more than $475,000. A SunTrust employee became suspicious of an item that required sight inspection under the bank's fraud detection standards, which exceeded those of other banks in the area. Triplett was arrested. Spacemakers filed a suit in a Georgia state court against SunTrust. The bank filed a motion for summary judgment. On what basis could the bank avoid liability? In whose favor should the court rule, and why? [*Spacemakers of America, Inc. v. SunTrust Bank*, 271 Ga.App. 335, 609 S.E.2d 683 (2005)] **(See page 537.)**

28–4. Bank's Duty to Honor Checks. Sheila Bartell was arrested on various charges related to burglary, the possession for sale of methamphetamine, and other crimes. She pleaded guilty in a California state court to some charges in exchange for the dismissal of others and an agreement to reimburse the victims. The victims included "Rita E.," who reported that her checkbook had been stolen and her signature forged on three checks totaling $590. Wells Fargo Bank had "covered" the checks and credited her account, however, so the court ordered Bartell to pay the bank. Bartell appealed, arguing that the bank was not entitled to restitution. What principles apply when a person forges a drawer's signature on a check? Is the bank entitled to recover from the defendant? Explain. [*People v. Bartell*, 170 Cal.App.4th 1258, 88 Cal.Rptr.3d 844 (3 Dist. 2009)] **(See page 533.)**

28–5. Forged Drawers' Signatures. Debbie Brooks and Martha Tingstrom lived together. Tingstrom handled their finances. For five years, Brooks did not look at any statements concerning her accounts. When she finally reviewed the statements, she discovered that Tingstrom had taken $85,500 through Brooks's checking account with Transamerica Financial Advisors. Tingstrom had forged Brooks's name on six checks paid between one and two years earlier. Another year passed before Brooks filed a suit against Transamerica. Who is most likely to suffer the loss for the checks paid with Brooks's forged signature? Why? [*Brooks v. Transamerica Financial Advisors*, 57 So.3d 1153 (La.App. 2 Cir. 2011)] **(See page 537.)**

28–6. BUSINESS CASE PROBLEM WITH SAMPLE ANSWER: Honoring Checks.

*Adley Abdulwahab (Wahab) opened an account on behalf of W Financial Group, LLC, with Wells Fargo Bank. Wahab was one of three authorized signers on the account. Five months later, Wahab withdrew $1,701,250 from W Financial's account to buy a cashier's check payable to Lubna Lateef. Wahab visited a different Wells Fargo branch and deposited the check into the account of CA Houston Investment Center, LLC. Wahab was the only authorized signer on this account. Lateef never received or indorsed the check. W Financial filed a suit to recover the amount. Applying the rules for payment on a forged indorsement, who is liable? Explain. [Jones v. Wells Fargo Bank, 666 F.3d 955 (5th Cir. 2012)] **(See page 533.)***

• **For a sample answer to Problem 28–6, go to Appendix F at the end of this text.**

28–7. Consumer Fund Transfers. Stephen Patterson held an account with Suntrust Bank in Alcoa, Tennessee. Juanita Wehrman—with whom Patterson was briefly involved in a romantic relationship—stole his debit card and used it for sixteen months (well beyond the length of their relationship) to make unauthorized purchases in excess of $30,000. When Patterson learned what was happening, he closed his account. The bank refused to reimburse him more than $677.46—the amount of unauthorized transactions that occurred within sixty days of the transmittal of the bank statement that revealed the first unauthorized transaction. Is the bank's refusal justifiable? Explain. [*Patterson v. Suntrust Bank*, __ S.W.3d __, 2013 WL 139315 (Tenn.App. 2013)] **(See page 547.)**

28–8. A QUESTION OF ETHICS: Forged Drawer's Signature.

From the 1960s, James Johnson served as Bradley Union's personal caretaker and assistant, and was authorized by Union to handle his banking transactions. Louise Johnson, James's wife, wrote checks

on Union's checking account to pay his bills, normally signing the checks "Brad Union." Branch Banking & Trust Co. (BB&T) managed Union's account. In December 2000, on the basis of Union's deteriorating mental and physical condition, a North Carolina state court declared him incompetent. Douglas Maxwell was appointed as Union's guardian. Maxwell "froze" Union's checking account and asked BB&T for copies of the canceled checks, which were provided by July 2001. Maxwell believed that Union's signature on the checks had been forged. In August 2002, Maxwell contacted BB&T, which refused to recredit Union's account. Maxwell filed a suit on Union's behalf in a North Carolina state court against BB&T. [Union v. Branch Banking & Trust Co., *176 N.C.App. 711, 627 S.E.2d 276 (2006)]* **(See page 537.)**

(a) Before Maxwell's appointment, BB&T sent monthly statements and canceled checks to Union, and Johnson reviewed them, but no unauthorized signatures were ever reported. On whom can liability be imposed in the case of a forged drawer's signature on a check? What are the limits set by Section 4–406(f) of the Uniform Commercial Code? Should Johnson's position, Union's incompetence, or Maxwell's appointment affect the application of these principles? Explain.

(b) Why was this suit brought against BB&T? Is BB&T liable? If not, who is? Why? Regardless of any violations of the law, did anyone act unethically in this case? If so, who and why?

Legal Reasoning Group Activity

28–9. Bank's Duty to Honor Checks. On January 5, Brian drafts a check for $3,000 drawn on Southern Marine Bank and payable to his assistant, Shanta. Brian puts last year's date on the check by mistake. On January 7, before Shanta has had a chance to go to the bank, Brian is killed in an automobile accident. Southern Marine Bank is aware of Brian's death. On January 10, Shanta presents the check to the bank, and the bank honors the check by payment to Shanta. Later, Brian's widow, Joyce, claims that because the bank knew of Brian's death and also because the check was by date over one year old, the bank acted wrongfully when it paid Shanta. Joyce, as executor of Brian's estate and sole heir by his will, demands that Southern Marine Bank recredit Brian's estate for the check paid to Shanta. **(See page 533.)**

(a) The first group will determine whether the bank acted wrongfully by honoring Brian's check and paying Shanta.

(b) The second group will assess whether Joyce has a valid claim against Southern Marine Bank for the amount of the check paid to Shanta.

(c) A third group will assume that the check Brian drafted was on his business account rather than on his personal bank account and that he had two partners in the business. Would a business partner be in a better position to force Southern Marine Bank to recredit Brian's account than his widow? Why or why not?

UNIT FIVE Focus on Ethics

Negotiable Instruments

Articles 3 and 4 of the Uniform Commercial Code (UCC), which deal with negotiable instruments, constitute an important part of the law governing commercial transactions. These articles reflect several fundamental ethical principles. One basic principle is that individuals should be protected against harm caused by the misuse of negotiable instruments. Another principle—one that underlies the entire concept of negotiable instruments—is that the laws governing the instruments' use should be practical and reasonable to encourage the free flow of commerce.

Here, we look first at some of the ethical implications of the concept of a holder in due course (HDC). We then examine some other ethical issues that frequently arise in relation to negotiable instruments.

Ethics, the HDC Concept, and *Ort v. Fowler*

The drafters of Article 3 did not create the HDC concept out of thin air. Indeed, under the common law, courts had often restricted the extent to which defenses could successfully be raised against a good faith holder of a negotiable instrument. As an example, consider a classic 1884 case, *Ort v. Fowler*.[1]

Case Background Ort, a farmer, was working alone in his field one day, when he was approached by a stranger who claimed to be the statewide agent for a manufacturer of iron posts and wire fencing. The two men conversed for some time, and eventually the stranger persuaded the farmer to act as an area representative for the manufacturer. The stranger then completed two documents for Ort to sign, telling him that they were identical copies of an agreement in which Ort agreed to represent the manufacturer.

Because the farmer did not have his glasses with him and could read only with great difficulty, he asked the stranger to read the document to him. The stranger then purported to do so, not mentioning that the document was a promissory note. Both men signed each document. The stranger later negotiated the promissory note he had fraudulently obtained from Ort to a party that today we would refer to as an HDC. When this party brought suit against him, Ort attempted to defend on the basis of fraud in the execution.

The Court's Decision The Kansas court that decided the issue entertained three possible views. One was that because Ort never *intended* to execute a note, he should not be held liable for doing so. A second view was that the jury should decide, as a question of fact, whether Ort was guilty of negligence under the circumstances. The third view was that Ort's action in signing a promissory note solely in reliance on a stranger's assurances that it was a different instrument constituted negligence. After all, Ort possessed all his faculties and was able to read the English language.

---

1. 31 Kan. 478, 2 P. 580 (1884).

This third view was the one adopted by the court in 1884. The court held that Ort's negligence had contributed to the fraud and that such negligence precluded Ort from raising fraud as a defense against payment on the note. Today, the UCC expresses essentially the same reasoning: fraud is a defense against an HDC only if the injured party signed the instrument "with neither knowledge nor a reasonable opportunity to learn of its character or its essential terms" [UCC 3–305(a)(1)(iii)].

The Reasoning of the HDC Concept Although it may seem unfair that the consequences of another's fraud should fall on an innocent victim, the UCC assumes that it would be even less fair to deny payment to an HDC. The reasoning behind this assumption is that an HDC, as a third party, is less likely to have been responsible for—or to have had an opportunity to protect against—the fraud in the underlying transaction.

In general, the HDC doctrine, like other sections of the UCC, reflects the philosophy that when two or more innocent parties are at risk, the burden should fall on the party that was in the best position to prevent the loss. For businesspersons, the HDC doctrine means that they should exercise caution when they issue and accept commercial paper in order to protect against the risk of loss through fraud.

LEGAL REASONING

1. *What do you think would result if the law was changed to allow personal defenses to be successfully raised against HDCs? Who would lose, and who would gain? How would such a change in the law affect the flow of commerce in this country?*

Good Faith in Negotiable Instruments Law

Clearly, the principle of good faith reflects ethical principles. The most notable application of the good faith requirement in negotiable instruments law is, of course, the HDC doctrine. Traditionally, to acquire the protected status of an HDC, a holder must have acquired an instrument in good faith. Other transactions subject to Articles 3 and 4 also require good faith—as, indeed, do all transactions governed by the UCC.

The Importance of Good Faith A party that acts in bad faith may be precluded from seeking shelter under UCC provisions that would otherwise apply, such as the fictitious payee rule or the imposter rule. Cases often turn on whether a party exercised good faith, as a case decided by Maryland's courts illustrates.

American General Financial Services, Inc., a bank, was contacted by telephone by a man who said he was Ronald E. Wilder—although later it was discovered that he was an imposter. The man wanted to obtain a loan for $20,000 to

FOCUS ON ETHICS CONTINUES ▶

renovate his property and supplied Wilder's personal information and copies of his tax returns to complete the loan application. American General ran a credit check on Wilder and, finding that he had excellent credit, approved an $18,000 loan. The imposter then came to the bank, presented a driver's license with his photo and Ronald Wilder's personal information to a bank employee, and obtained the check.

Later that day, the imposter took the $18,000 check to a check-cashing business, State Security Check Cashing, Inc., to cash it. He presented the same false identification that he had used at the bank. A State Security employee examined the check and reviewed the loan documents before giving the man the face value of the check (less State Security's fee). The day after the check was negotiated, the real Ronald E. Wilder informed American General that someone had fraudulently applied for a loan in his name. When he learned about the check written to the imposter, Wilder placed a stop-payment order on the check. American General then refused to pay State Security, which sued to recover for payment of the check's proceeds to the imposter.

The court had to decide which party—the bank or the check-cashing company—was liable for the amount of the check. Good faith was the controlling issue. American General claimed that State Security had not taken the check in good faith, because "suspicious circumstances" surrounded the transaction. After all, reasonable persons do not cash $18,000 loan checks at check-cashing establishments, which charge very high fees ($900 in this case). The bank argued that State Security should have taken additional steps to verify the check or at least have waited until the check cleared before disbursing the funds. The trial court agreed: State Security was in the best position to prevent the loss and should not have immediately paid out the funds. Because State Security had not exercised good faith or due care, it was not an HDC and was precluded from asserting the imposter rule.

State Security appealed, and the reviewing court reversed. The appellate court found that the bank had not shown that State Security had failed to exercise good faith when it cashed the check in reliance on the same documents that the bank had seen. This meant that State Security was an HDC and that the imposter rule applied. Therefore, the appellate court ruled that American General was liable for the $18,000.[2]

How Should Good Faith Be Tested? There has long been a division of opinion as to how good faith should be measured or tested. At one end of the spectrum of views is the position that the test of good faith should be subjective in nature. In other words, as long as a person acts honestly, no matter how negligent or foolish the conduct may be, that person is

acting in good faith. At the other end of the spectrum is the "objective" test of good faith. Under this test, honesty in itself is not enough. A party must also act reasonably under the circumstances.

Over time, the pendulum seems to have swung from one end of the spectrum to the other. When the UCC was initially drafted, the definition of *good faith* set forth in UCC 1–201(19) established a subjective test for good faith. It defined good faith as "honesty in fact in the conduct or transaction concerned." The only UCC article that incorporated a more objective test for good faith was Article 2. Section 2–103(1)(b) defined good faith as both honesty in fact *and* the observance of reasonable commercial standards of fair dealing in the trade. Under this test, a person who acts honestly in fact but does not observe reasonable commercial standards of fair dealing will not meet the good faith requirement. This more objective measure of good faith has since been incorporated into other articles of the UCC, including Articles 3, 4, and 4A.

Criticisms of the Objective Standard Some critics claim that while the subjective test of "honesty in fact" is manageable, the objective test that requires the "observance of reasonable commercial standards" opens the door to potentially endless litigation. After all, it is difficult to determine what is commercially reasonable in a given context until you hear what others in that commercial situation have to say. Thus, parties to a dispute can nearly always make some kind of good faith argument, and any time the issue is raised, litigation can result.

How Good Faith Standards Can Affect HDC Status Whether the objective or the subjective standard of good faith is used has considerable impact on HDC status, as an example will illustrate. Mitchell was a farmer who operated a multistate farming operation on leased property. Runnells, a grain broker, had sold Mitchell's 2001 grain crop. Mitchell instructed Runnells to use the crop proceeds to draw checks payable to Mitchell's various landlords in fulfillment of his rent obligations. The checks totaled more than $153,000. The landlords accepted the checks in payment of the farmer's rent. They were completely unaware that Mitchell had already pledged the proceeds from the sale of his crops as collateral for a loan from Agriliance (security interests will be discussed in Chapter 29). Agriliance filed a lawsuit in a federal court against Runnells and the various landlords for conversion (wrongful taking of personal property—see Chapter 6).

According to the UCC, an HDC takes a negotiable instrument free of any claim to the instrument, including claims of prior secured parties. Thus, the outcome of the case depended on whether Runnells and the landlords were HDCs. Under the subjective standard, the landlords were HDCs because they took the checks without actual knowledge of Agriliance's claim to the crop proceeds. The objective standard, however, dictated a different result. Because farmers commonly use

2. *State Security Check Cashing, Inc. v. American General Financial Services, Inc.,* 409 Md. 81, 972 A.2d 882 (2009).

their crops as collateral for loans, the court held that reasonable commercial standards of fair dealing required Mitchell's creditors (Runnells and the landlords) to search the public records. Such a search would have revealed the existence of Agriliance's prior secured claim. Runnells and the landlords could not be HDCs in this case because they failed to meet the objective standard of good faith. The court, therefore, ruled that Agriliance was entitled to the crop proceeds.[3]

LEGAL REASONING

2. *Because the UCC offers special protection to HDCs, innocent makers of notes or drawers of checks in fraudulent transactions often have no legal recourse. From an ethical standpoint, how could you justify to the "losers" in such situations the provisions of the UCC that fail to protect them? Can you think of a way in which such problems could be handled more fairly or ethically than they are under the UCC?*

Efficiency versus Due Care

A major problem faced by today's banking institutions is how to verify customer signatures on the billions of checks that are processed by the banking system each month. If a bank fails to verify a signature on a check it receives for payment and the check turns out to be forged, the bank will normally be held liable to its customer for the amount paid. But how can banks possibly examine, item by item, each signature on every check that they pay?

3. *Agriliance, L.L.C. v. Runnells Grain Elevator, Inc.,* 272 F.Supp.2d 800 (S.D. Iowa 2003).

The banks' solution to this problem is simply to not examine all signatures. Instead, computers are programmed to verify signatures only on checks exceeding a certain threshold amount, such as $2,500 or perhaps some higher figure. Checks for less than the threshold amount are selected for signature verification only on a random basis. In other words, serious attention is restricted to serious matters. As a result, many, if not most, checks are paid without signature verification. This practice, which has become an acceptable standard in today's banking industry, is economically efficient for banks. Even though liability costs are sometimes incurred—when forged checks are paid—the total costs involved in verifying the authenticity of each and every signature would be far higher.

Some people have argued that banks using such procedures are not exercising due care in handling their customers' accounts. Under the UCC, banks are held to a standard of "ordinary care." At one time in the banking industry, ordinary care was generally interpreted to mean that a bank had a duty to inspect *all* signatures on checks. But what constitutes ordinary care in today's world? Does a bank exercise ordinary care if it follows the prevailing industry practice of examining signatures on only a few, randomly selected checks payable for under a certain amount? Or does ordinary care still mean that a bank should examine each signature?

LEGAL REASONING

3. *Do you think that the UCC's provisions have struck an appropriate balance between the interests of banks and those of bank customers? Why or why not?*

BUSINESS LAW

CLARKSON · MILLER · CROSS

UNIT SIX

CREDITORS' RIGHTS AND BANKRUPTCY

CONTENTS

CHAPTER 29

CREDITORS' RIGHTS AND REMEDIES

Normally, creditors have no problem collecting the debts owed to them. When disputes arise over the amount owed, however, or when the debtor simply cannot or will not pay, what happens? What remedies are available to creditors when a debtor **defaults** (fails to pay as promised)? In this chapter, we focus on some basic laws that assist the debtor and creditor in resolving their dispute without resorting to bankruptcy (see Chapter 31). In Chapter 30, we will discuss the remedies that are available only to secured creditors under Article 9 of the Uniform Commercial Code (UCC). *Secured creditors* are those whose loans are supported or backed by *collateral,* which is specific property that the borrower pledges to ensure repayment.

LAWS ASSISTING CREDITORS

Both the common law and statutory laws other than Article 9 of the UCC create various rights and remedies for creditors. We discuss here some of these rights and remedies, including liens, garnishment, and creditors' composition agreements.

Liens

A **lien** is an encumbrance on (claim against) property to satisfy a debt or protect a claim for the payment of a debt. Liens may arise under the common law (usually by possession of the property) or under statutory law. Statutory liens include *mechanic's liens,* whereas *artisan's liens* were recognized at common law. *Judicial liens* may be used by a creditor to collect on a debt before or after a judgment is entered by a court.

Liens are a very important tool for creditors because they generally take priority over other claims against the same property (priority of claims will be discussed in depth in Chapter 30). In fact, mechanic's and artisan's liens normally take priority over creditors who have a *perfected* security interest in the property. (As you will read in Chapter 30, a creditor who has perfected a security interest in property—by filing a financing statement, for example—usually prevails against other parties with an interest in the same property, except for certain lienholders.)

MECHANIC'S LIENS Sometimes, a person who has contracted for labor, services, or materials to be furnished for making improvements on real property does not immediately pay for the improvements. When that happens, the creditor can place a **mechanic's lien** on the property.

Real Property Secures the Debt. A mechanic's lien creates a special type of debtor-creditor relationship in which the real estate itself becomes security for the debt. ▶ **Example 29.1** Kirk contracts to paint Tanya's house for an agreed-on price to cover labor and materials. If Tanya refuses to pay or pays only a portion of the charges after the work is completed, a mechanic's lien against the property can be created. Kirk is then a lienholder, and the real property is encumbered (burdened) with the mechanic's lien for the amount owed.

If Tanya does not pay the lien, the property can be sold to satisfy the debt. Tanya must be given notice of the *foreclosure* (the process by which the creditor legally takes the debtor's property to satisfy a debt, discussed later in this chapter) and sale in advance, however. ◀

Governed by State Law. State law governs the procedures that must be followed to create a mechanic's (or other statutory) lien. Generally, the lienholder must file a written notice of lien within a specific time period (usually within 60 to 120 days) from the last date that material or labor was provided. If the property owner fails to pay the debt, the lienholder is entitled to foreclose on the real estate and to sell it to satisfy the debt. The sale proceeds are used to pay the debt and the costs of the legal proceedings. The surplus, if any, is paid to the former owner.

In the following case, the owner of the property on which a contractor was attempting to foreclose a mechanic's lien claimed to be wholly unaware of any work done by the contractor. Could this prevent the foreclosure?

CASE 29.1

BHP Land Services, Inc. v. Seymour
Superior Court of Connecticut, 2011 WL 1106031 (2011).

BACKGROUND AND FACTS Jean Seymour lives in Barkhamsted, Connecticut. She owns a house, a horse barn, and eighteen to nineteen acres of pastureland in Enfield. Jean's daughter Jennifer lives on the Enfield property, which she calls the RoundTuit Ranch, where she boards, trains, and sells horses. Jean pays the property tax and the mortgage but does not participate in the RoundTuit business. Jennifer does not pay rent, but pays the costs of the business, including snow plowing and house repairs. Jennifer hired BHP Land Services, Inc., to remove tree stumps and grade two acres for $2,450 per acre. When the work was done, Jennifer paid the bill. The next year, she hired BHP to stump, clear, and level another nine acres at the same per acre price. When Jennifer did not pay the bill, BHP filed a suit in a Connecticut state court against Jean, who responded that she never authorized the work.

 IN THE LANGUAGE OF THE COURT
KLACZAK, Lawrence C., J.T.R. [Judge Trial Referee[a]]

* * * *

In this case the plaintiff in its [complaint] seeks to foreclose a mechanic's lien on a parcel of property known as 100 Fletcher Road, Enfield, Connecticut.
* * * *

A mechanic's lien is available to one who has a claim for services rendered for the improvement of a plot of land. The owner of the land upon which improvement is made, or someone having authority, must have consented to the services having been rendered. [Emphasis added.]
* * * *

Jean Seymour had given her daughter apparent carte blanche authority to operate the ranch as she saw fit * * * when this clearing work was done. Any improvements to the property inured [came in effect] to Jean's benefit as the record owner. Jennifer also acted as her mother's agent when they appeared at [the Enfield] Inland Wetland Agency regarding the grading, clearing and seeding project on the property.

Clearly, on that occasion, Jean represented that Jennifer could act as her agent and, further, she (Jean), was obviously aware that work was expected to be done which would enhance the property. The Court concludes that Jean permitted Jennifer to act as the agent of the property owner. Jennifer had the authority to do work on the property without any authorization from Jean and she had unfettered authority to act as the agent of the owner.

The complaint sufficiently alleges * * * facts to substantiate an order to foreclose the mechanic's lien, and the evidence as discussed herein supports the Court's finding.
* * * *

Judgment shall enter against the defendant in the amount of $26,250, which was the * * * price for the work done.

DECISION AND REMEDY *The court found that Jennifer Seymour had the authority to act as her mother's agent (see Chapter 32) and have work done on the property. Therefore, the court issued a judgment in BHP's favor and ordered a hearing to determine the terms of the foreclosure, as well as its fees and costs.*

---

a. A judge trial referee is a judge who has been designated by the chief justice of the Connecticut Supreme Court to hear a certain case.

CASE 29.1 CONTINUES ▶

CASE 29.1 CONTINUED   **THE ECONOMIC DIMENSION** *What should Jean do next—appeal the court's decision, settle with BHP for the amount of the judgment, or go through the foreclosure process? Explain.*

                        THE LEGAL ENVIRONMENT DIMENSION *When no actual contract exists, under what theory may a court step in to prevent a property owner from being unjustly enriched by the services of a contractor?*

ARTISAN'S LIENS When a debtor fails to pay for labor and materials furnished for the repair or improvement of personal property, a creditor can recover payment through an **artisan's lien.**

Lienholder Must Retain Possession. In contrast to a mechanic's lien, an artisan's lien is *possessory*. The lienholder ordinarily must have retained possession of the property and have expressly or impliedly agreed to provide the services on a cash, not a credit, basis. The lien remains in existence as long as the lienholder maintains possession, and the lien is terminated once possession is *voluntarily* surrendered—unless the surrender is only temporary.[1]

▶ **Example 29.2** MacKenzie takes a sapphire necklace that she inherited to a jewelry store to have it made into a ring and set of earrings. The store's owner agrees to reset the sapphires into custom jewelry for $4,000. MacKenzie comes to pick up the jewelry but refuses to pay the $4,000 she owes. The jeweler can assert an artisan's lien on the jewelry in his possession until MacKenzie pays. If the jeweler gives the jewelry to MacKenzie (without requiring full payment), the lien disappears. ◀

Priority over Other Creditors' Claims. As mentioned, artisan's liens usually take priority over other creditors' claims to the same property.[2] ▶ **Case in Point 29.3** Erie Power Technologies, Inc., hired Shaw Group to design and fabricate heat recovery steam generators for Erie's power plant. Erie delivered the necessary materials for the development of the generators and made several payments to Shaw as the work progressed. Shaw completed the fabrication of the materials in its possession, but Erie made no further payments and filed for bankruptcy.

Under Erie's bankruptcy reorganization plan (see Chapter 31), it was required to pay Shaw $320,000 for completing the generators. Erie then filed a lawsuit to recover that payment, claiming that those funds should have gone to other secured creditors who had priority over Shaw. The court held that Shaw had a common law artisan's lien in the goods that it possessed and had added value to them. Because the artisan's lien took priority over the claims of other secured creditors, the court granted a summary judgment in favor of Shaw.[3] ◀

Foreclosure on Personal Property Possible. Modern statutes permit the holder of an artisan's lien to foreclose and sell the property subject to the lien to satisfy the debt. As with a mechanic's lien, the lienholder is required to give notice to the owner of the property before the foreclosure and sale. The sale proceeds are used to pay the debt and the costs of the legal proceedings, and the surplus, if any, is paid to the former owner.

JUDICIAL LIENS When a debt is past due, a creditor can bring a legal action against the debtor to collect the debt. If the creditor is successful in the action, the court awards the creditor a judgment against the debtor (usually for the amount of the debt plus any interest and legal costs incurred in obtaining the judgment). Frequently, however, the creditor is unable to collect the awarded amount.

To ensure that a judgment in the creditor's favor will be collectible, the creditor may request that certain nonexempt property of the debtor be seized to satisfy the debt. (As will be discussed later in this chapter, under state or federal statutes, some kinds of property are exempt from attachment by creditors.) A court's order to seize the debtor's property is known as a *writ of attachment* if it is issued prior to a judgment in the creditor's favor. If the order is issued after a judgment, it is referred to as a *writ of execution.*

Writ of Attachment. In the context of judicial liens, **attachment** refers to a court-ordered seizure and

---

1. Involuntary surrender of possession by a lienholder, such as when a police officer seizes goods from a lienholder, does not terminate the lien.
2. An artisan's lien has priority over a filed statutory lien (such as a title lien on an automobile or a lien filed under Article 9 of the UCC) and a bailee's lien (such as a storage lien).

3. *In re Erie Power Technologies, Inc.,* 364 Bankr. 896 (W.D.Pa. 2007).

taking into custody of property before a judgment is obtained on a past-due debt. (As you will read in Chapter 30, attachment means something different in the context of secured transactions.[4]) Because attachment is a *prejudgment* remedy, it occurs either at the time a lawsuit is filed or immediately afterward.

A creditor must comply with the specific state's statutory restrictions and requirements. Under the due process clause of the Fourteenth Amendment to the U.S. Constitution, the debtor must be given notice and an opportunity to be heard (see Chapter 4).The creditor must have an enforceable right to payment of the debt under law and must follow certain procedures. Otherwise, the creditor can be liable for damages for wrongful attachment.

The typical procedure for attachment is as follows:

1. The creditor files with the court an *affidavit* (a written statement, made under oath) stating that the debtor has failed to pay and indicating the statutory grounds under which attachment is sought.
2. The creditor must post a bond to cover at least the court costs, the value of the property attached, and the value of the loss of use of that property suffered by the debtor.
3. When the court is satisfied that all the requirements have been met, it issues a **writ of attachment,** which directs the sheriff or other officer to seize the debtor's nonexempt property. If the creditor prevails at trial, the seized property can be sold to satisfy the judgment.

Writ of Execution. If a creditor wins a judgment against a debtor and the debtor will not or cannot pay the amount due, the creditor can request a **writ of execution** from the court. A writ of execution is an order that directs the sheriff to seize (levy) and sell any of the debtor's nonexempt real or personal property. The writ applies only to property that is within the court's geographic jurisdiction (usually the county in which the courthouse is located).

The proceeds of the sale are used to pay the judgment, accrued interest, and costs of the sale. Any excess is paid to the debtor. The debtor can pay the judgment and redeem the nonexempt property at any time before the sale takes place. (Because of exemption laws and bankruptcy laws, however, many judgments are practically uncollectible.)

Garnishment

An order for **garnishment** permits a creditor to collect a debt by seizing property of the debtor (such as wages or funds in a bank account) that is being held by a third party. As a result of a garnishment proceeding, the debtor's employer may be ordered by the court to turn over a portion of the debtor's wages to pay the debt.

▶ **Case in Point 29.4** Helen Griffin failed to pay a debt she owed to Indiana Surgical Specialists. When Indiana Surgical filed a lawsuit to collect, the court issued a judgment in favor of Indiana Surgical and a garnishment order to withhold the appropriate amount from Griffin's earnings until her debt was paid. At the time, Griffin was working as an independent contractor (see Chapter 34 for a discussion of independent-contractor status) driving for a courier service. She claimed that her wages could not be garnished because she was not an employee. The court held that payments for the services of an independent contractor fall within the definition of earnings and can be garnished.[5] ◀

Many types of property can be garnished, including tax refunds, pensions, and trust funds—so long as the property is not exempt from garnishment and is in the possession of a third party.

PROCEDURES Garnishment can be a prejudgment remedy, requiring a hearing before a court, but it is most often a postjudgment remedy. State law governs garnishment actions, so the specific procedures vary from state to state. According to the laws in many states, the judgment creditor needs to obtain only one order of garnishment, which will then apply continuously to the judgment debtor's wages until the entire debt is paid. In other states, the judgment creditor must go back to court for a separate order of garnishment for each pay period.

LAWS LIMITING THE AMOUNT OF WAGES SUBJECT TO GARNISHMENT Both federal and state laws limit the amount that can be taken from a debtor's weekly take-home pay through garnishment proceedings.[6] Federal law provides a minimal framework to protect debtors from losing all their income to pay judgment debts.[7] State laws also provide dollar exemptions, and

---

5. *Indiana Surgical Specialists v. Griffin,* 867 N.E.2d 260 (Ind.App. 2007).
6. A few states (for example, Texas) do not permit garnishment of wages by private parties except under a child-support order.
7. For example, the federal Consumer Credit Protection Act, 15 U.S.C. Sections 1601–1693r, provides that a debtor can retain either 75 percent of his or her disposable earnings per week or an amount equivalent to thirty hours of work paid at federal minimum wage rates, whichever is greater.

---

4. In secured transactions, *attachment* refers to the process through which a security interest becomes effective and enforceable against a debtor with respect to the debtor's collateral [UCC 9–203].

these amounts are often larger than those provided by federal law.

Under federal law, an employer cannot dismiss an employee because his or her wages are being garnished.

Creditors' Composition Agreements

Creditors may contract with the debtor for discharge of the debtor's liquidated debts (debts that are definite, or fixed, in amount) on payment of a sum less than that owed. These agreements are referred to as **creditors' composition agreements** (or *composition agreements*) and usually are held to be enforceable unless they are formed under duress.

SECTION 2
MORTGAGES

When individuals purchase real property, they typically borrow from a financial institution part or all of the funds needed to pay the purchase price. A **mortgage** is a written instrument that gives the creditor an interest in, or lien on, the debtor's real property as security for payment of a debt. The creditor is the *mortgagee,* and the debtor is the *mortgagor.* (For a discussion of some questionable lending practices in the mortgage industry in recent years, see this chapter's *Insight into Ethics* feature below.)

INSIGHT INTO ETHICS
Reverse Redlining in the Mortgage Market

In December 2011, Bank of America reached a settlement with the U.S. Department of Justice. It agreed to pay $335 million to compensate 200,000 borrowers who allegedly were discriminated against by Countrywide Financial. Bank of America acquired Countrywide in 2008 when Countrywide was collapsing under its burden of bad loans. The Justice Department alleged that Countrywide had engaged in reverse redlining.

First, There Was Redlining

For decades, the mortgage lending industry was accused of *redlining*—that is, drawing a red line on a map around poorer neighborhoods and refusing to offer mortgages to borrowers, often members of minority groups, who wished to purchase homes in those areas. In 1977, Congress passed the Community Reinvestment Act to require lenders to make mortgages more readily obtainable in redlined areas. Nonetheless, in the mid-1990s African American and Hispanic applicants for mortgages were still being rejected at a rate 1.6 times higher than white applicants with similar credit histories. Under the Clinton administration (1993–2001), organizations in redlined areas increasingly pressured banks to make more loans available. The lenders responded with *reverse redlining.*

Then, Reverse Redlining Became Profitable

Reverse redlining is the opposite of redlining—instead of denying mortgages to members of minority groups, lend-

ers targeted them. During the housing boom, lenders aggressively marketed their *subprime mortgages* in poorer areas. (Subprime mortgages are higher-risk loans given to borrowers with poor credit scores who cannot qualify for standard mortgages.) Wells Fargo, for instance, enlisted pastors in churches in African American communities to offer wealth-building seminars. The bank would make a donation to the church for every new mortgage application it received.

Why were lenders suddenly so interested in these borrowers? The answer is that subprime mortgages carry much higher interest rates than standard mortgages and are usually accompanied by higher up-front fees. In many instances, the Justice Department asserted, mortgage companies pushed African American and Hispanic borrowers into high-cost subprime mortgages even when they could qualify for standard mortgages. Other borrowers were given mortgages that they would not be able to pay— the lender pocketed the fees and sold the worthless mortgages to investors. As a result of such practices, minority groups have incurred a disproportionate percentage of foreclosures.

LEGAL CRITICAL THINKING
INSIGHT INTO DIVERSITY

To what extent do lending institutions have a moral duty to extend loans to lower-income individuals?

Typically, as part of the mortgage loan, borrowers make a **down payment** (the part of the purchase price that is paid up front in cash). Lenders offer various types of mortgages to meet the needs of different borrowers, but a basic distinction is whether the interest rate is fixed or variable.

Fixed-Rate Mortgages

A *fixed-rate mortgage* has a fixed, or unchanging, rate of interest, so the payments remain the same for the duration of the loan. Lenders determine the interest rate for a standard fixed-rate mortgage loan based on a variety of factors, including the borrower's credit history, credit score, income, and debts. For a borrower to qualify, lenders typically require that the monthly mortgage payment (including principal, interest, taxes, and insurance) not exceed 28 percent of the person's monthly gross income.

Adjustable-Rate Mortgages

The rate of interest paid by the borrower changes periodically with an *adjustable-rate mortgage (ARM)*. Typically, the initial interest rate for an ARM is set at a relatively low fixed rate for a specified period, such as a year or three years. After that time, the interest rate adjusts annually or by some other period, such as biannually or monthly. The interest rate adjustment is calculated by adding a certain number of percentage points (called the margin) to an index rate (one of various government interest rates).

ARMs contractually shift the risk that the interest rate will change from the lender to the borrower. Borrowers will have lower initial payments if they are willing to assume the risk of interest rate changes.

Creditor Protection

When creditors extend mortgages, they are advancing a significant amount of funds for a number of years. Consequently, creditors take a number of steps to protect their interest, including the following:

1. *Requiring mortgage insurance.* One precaution is to require debtors to obtain private mortgage insurance if they do not make a down payment of at least 20 percent of the purchase price. For instance, if a borrower makes a down payment of only 5 percent of the purchase price, the creditor might require insurance covering 15 percent of the cost. Then, if the debtor defaults, the credi-

tor repossesses the house and receives reimbursement from the insurer for the covered portion of the loan.
2. *Recording the mortgage.* The creditor will record the mortgage with the appropriate office in the county where the property is located. Recording ensures that the creditor is officially on record as holding an interest in the property. In essence, recording a mortgage perfects the lender's security interest in the property (see Chapter 30). A lender that fails to record a mortgage could find itself in the position of an unsecured creditor.
3. *Including contract provisions.* Creditors also include provisions in the mortgage contract that are aimed at protecting their investment. For instance, many lenders include a **prepayment penalty** clause, which requires the borrower to pay a penalty if the mortgage is repaid in full within a certain period. A prepayment penalty helps to protect the lender should the borrower refinance within a short time after obtaining a mortgage. Creditors frequently also require the debtor to maintain homeowner's insurance (see Chapter 50) on the mortgaged property.

Mortgage Foreclosure

If the homeowner *defaults,* or fails to make the mortgage payments, the lender has the right to foreclose on the mortgaged property. **Foreclosure** is the legal process by which the lender repossesses and auctions off the property that has secured the loan.

Foreclosure is expensive and time consuming, though. It generally benefits neither the borrowers, who lose their homes, nor the lenders, which face the prospect of losses on their loans. Therefore, both lenders and borrowers are motivated to avoid foreclosure proceedings if possible.

WAYS TO AVOID FORECLOSURE There are several possible methods of avoiding foreclosure. If the borrower might be able to make payments in the future, the lender may grant a **forbearance,** which is a postponement of part or all of the payments on a loan for a limited time. This option works well when the debtor can solve the problem by securing a new job, selling the property, or finding another acceptable solution.

The borrower and the lender may also enter into a **workout agreement**—a contract that describes their respective rights and responsibilities as they try to resolve the default without proceeding to foreclosure. Usually, the lender agrees to delay seeking foreclosure in exchange for the borrower providing additional financial information that might be used to modify the mortgage.

When a borrower is unable to make mortgage payments, a lender may agree to a **short sale**—that is, a sale of the property for less than the balance due on the mortgage loan. Typically, the borrower has to show some hardship, such as the loss of job, a decline in the value of the home, a divorce, or a death in the household. The lender often has approval rights in a short sale, so the sale process may take much longer than an ordinary real estate transaction.

FORECLOSURE PROCEDURE If all efforts to find another solution fail, the lender will proceed to foreclosure. The lender must strictly comply with the state statute governing foreclosures. Many problems arose in the last ten years because lenders, facing a record number of foreclosures during the recession, had difficulty complying with the required statutory formalities.

To bring a foreclosure action, a bank must have standing to sue. In the following case, the court had to decide whether a bank could foreclose a mortgage even though the bank could not prove when it became the owner of the borrower's promissory note.

CASE ANALYSIS

Case 29.2   McLean v. JPMorgan Chase Bank, N.A.
District Court of Appeal of Florida, Fourth District, 79 So.2d 170 (2012).

IN THE LANGUAGE OF THE COURT
PER CURIAM.
* * * *

On May 11, 2009, Chase filed a * * * mortgage foreclosure action [in a Florida state court] against * * * Robert McLean. The complaint generally alleged that McLean had defaulted under the note and mortgage, and that Chase was "the legal and/or equitable owner and holder of the Note and Mortgage and has the right to enforce the loan documents." * * * [The complaint] alleged that Chase "is not in possession of the subject Promissory Note and * * * cannot reasonably obtain possession of said Note because it is lost, stolen, or destroyed." The copy of the mortgage attached to the complaint stated that the lender was American Brokers Conduit and that the mortgagee was MERS [Mortgage Electronic Registration Systems, Inc.].

McLean filed a motion to dismiss, which the trial court denied * * * . However, in the order denying McLean's motion to dismiss, the trial court ordered Chase to file and

serve within fifteen days "a copy of the assignment by which it obtained its rights and standing to proceed in this cause * * * ." In compliance with the trial court's order, Chase filed an Assignment of Mortgage, which reflected that MERS assigned the mortgage to Chase. However, the Assignment of Mortgage was signed by MERS representatives on May 14, 2009, three days *after* Chase filed the instant foreclosure complaint.
* * * *

Subsequently, Chase filed the original note and mortgage * * * . The original note bore a special endorsement, stating: "Pay to the Order of JPMorgan Chase Bank, N.A., as Trustee Without Recourse By: American Brokers Conduit." The endorsement to the note was not dated.

Chase filed a motion for summary judgment, as well as an affidavit in support of summary judgment. The affidavit, which was executed by a representative of American Home Mortgage Servicing after the lawsuit was filed, set forth the amounts due and owing under the loan. The affi-

davit further stated that Chase "is the holder and owner" of the mortgage originally given by Robert McLean to MERS. However, the affidavit did not specifically state when Chase became the owner of the note and mortgage, nor did the affidavit indicate that Chase was the owner of the note and mortgage before suit was filed. In fact, the affidavit failed to mention any endorsement of the note to Chase. Following a hearing on Chase's motion for summary judgment, the trial court entered a final judgment of foreclosure in favor of Chase. McLean appealed.
* * * *

A crucial element in any mortgage foreclosure proceeding is that the party seeking foreclosure must demonstrate that it has standing to foreclose. [Emphasis added.]
* * * *

* * * [A] party's standing is determined at the time the lawsuit was filed. Stated another way, *the plaintiff's lack of standing at the inception of the case is not a defect that may be cured by the acquisition of standing after the case is filed. Thus, a party is not permitted to*

establish the right to maintain an action retroactively by acquiring standing to file a lawsuit after the fact. [Emphasis added.]

* * * *

In the present case, as is common in recent foreclosure cases, Chase did not attach a copy of the original note to its complaint, but instead brought a count to re-establish a lost note. Later, however, Chase filed * * * the original promissory note, which bore a special endorsement in favor of Chase. [Thus,] * * * it obtained standing to foreclose, at least at some point.

Nonetheless, the record evidence is insufficient to demonstrate that Chase had standing to foreclose *at*

the time the lawsuit was filed. The mortgage was assigned to Chase three days after Chase filed the instant foreclosure complaint. While the original note contained an undated special endorsement in Chase's favor, the affidavit filed in support of summary judgment did not state when the endorsement was made to Chase. Furthermore, the affidavit, which was dated after the lawsuit was filed, did not specifically state when Chase became the owner of the note, nor did the affidavit indicate that Chase was the owner of the note before suit was filed.

We therefore reverse the summary judgment and corresponding final judgment of foreclosure. On remand,

in order for Chase to be entitled to summary judgment, it must show * * * that it was the holder of the note on the date the complaint was filed ([that is,] that the note was endorsed to Chase on or before the date the lawsuit was filed). By contrast, if the evidence shows that the note was endorsed to Chase after the lawsuit was filed, then Chase had no standing at the time the complaint was filed, in which case the trial court should dismiss the instant lawsuit and Chase must file a new complaint.

Reversed and Remanded for further proceedings consistent with this opinion.

LEGAL REASONING QUESTIONS

1. Why did the appellate court reverse the judgment of the lower court in this case? What did the appellate court suggest that the lower court do?

2. How might Chase establish its standing to foreclose at the time the complaint was filed?

3. If Chase cannot prove that it owned the note at the time of its complaint, what will happen next? Will Chase prevail? Why or why not?

4. Why do states require strict compliance with the provisions of their foreclosure laws, such as the requirement in this case that the lender own the note at the time of the complaint?

REDEMPTION RIGHTS Every state allows a defaulting borrower to redeem the property before the foreclosure sale by paying the full amount of the debt, plus any interest and costs that have accrued. This is known as the **right of redemption.** The idea behind this right is that it is only fair for the borrower to have a chance to regain possession after default.

Some states even allow a borrower to repurchase property *after* a judicial foreclosure—called a *statutory right of redemption.* Generally, the borrower may exercise this right for up to one year from the time the house is sold at a foreclosure sale.[8] The borrower may retain possession of the property after the foreclosure sale until the statutory redemption period ends. If the borrower does not exercise the right of redemption,

the new buyer receives title to and possession of the property.

Concept Summary 29.1 on the following page provides a synopsis of the remedies available to creditors.

SECTION 3
SURETYSHIP AND GUARANTY

When a third person promises to pay a debt owed by another in the event that the debtor does not pay, either a *suretyship* or a *guaranty* relationship is created. Exhibit 29–1 on page 567 illustrates these relationships. The third person's creditworthiness becomes the security for the debt owed.

Suretyship and guaranty provide creditors with the right to seek payment from the third party if the primary debtor, or *principal,* defaults on her or his

---

8. Some states do not allow a borrower to waive the statutory right of redemption. This means that a buyer at auction must wait one year to obtain title to, and possession of, a foreclosed property.

CONCEPT SUMMARY 29.1
Remedies Available to Creditors

REMEDY	DESCRIPTION

Liens	1. *Mechanic's lien*—A lien placed on an owner's real estate for labor, services, or materials furnished for improvements made to the realty.
	2. *Artisan's lien*—A lien placed on an owner's personal property for labor performed or value added to that property.
	3. *Judicial liens*—
	   a. Writ of attachment—A court-ordered seizure of property prior to a court's final determination of the creditor's rights to the property. Creditors must strictly comply with applicable state statutes to obtain a writ of attachment.
	   b. Writ of execution—A court order directing the sheriff to seize (levy) and sell a debtor's nonexempt real or personal property to satisfy a court's judgment in the creditor's favor.

Garnishment	A collection remedy that allows the creditor to attach a debtor's funds (such as wages owed or bank accounts) and property that are held by a third person.
Creditors' Composition Agreement	A contract between a debtor and her or his creditors by which the debtor's debts are discharged by payment of a sum less than the amount that is actually owed.
Mortgage Foreclosure	On the debtor's default, the entire mortgage debt is due and payable, allowing the creditor to foreclose on the realty by selling it to satisfy the debt.

obligations. At common law, there were significant differences in the liability of a surety and a guarantor, as discussed in the following subsections. Today, however, the distinctions outlined here have been abolished in some states.

Suretyship

A contract of strict **suretyship** is a promise made by a third person to be responsible for the debtor's obligation. It is an express contract between the **surety** (the third party) and the creditor.

In the strictest sense, the surety is primarily liable for the debt of the principal. The creditor can demand payment from the surety from the moment the debt is due and that the creditor need not exhaust all legal remedies against the principal debtor before holding the surety responsible for payment.

▶ **Example 29.5**   Roberto Delmar wants to obtain a loan from the bank to buy a used car. Because Roberto is still in college, the bank will not lend him the funds without a cosigner. Roberto's father, José Delmar, who has dealt with the bank before, agrees to cosign (add his signature to) the note, thereby becoming a surety and thus jointly liable for payment of the debt. When José Delmar cosigns the note, he becomes primarily liable to the bank. On the note's due date, the bank can seek payment from either Roberto or José Delmar, or both jointly. ◀

Guaranty

With a suretyship arrangement, the surety is *primarily* liable for the debtor's obligation. With a guaranty arrangement, the **guarantor**—the third person making the guaranty—is *secondarily* liable.

LIABILITY ARISES WHEN DEBTOR DEFAULTS The guarantor can be required to pay the obligation *only after the principal debtor defaults,* and usually only after the creditor has made an attempt to collect from the debtor. The guaranty contract terms determine the extent and time of the guarantor's liability.

▶ **Example 29.6**   BX Enterprises, a small corporation, needs to borrow funds to meet its payroll. BX's president is Dawson, a wealthy businessperson who owns 70 percent of the company. The bank is skeptical about the creditworthiness of BX and requires Dawson to sign an agreement making herself personally liable for payment if BX does not pay off the loan. As a guarantor of the loan, Dawson cannot be held liable until BX is in default. ◀

EXHIBIT 29–1 Suretyship and Guaranty Parties

In a suretyship or guaranty arrangement, a third party promises to be responsible for a debtor's obligations. A third party who agrees to be responsible for the debt even if the primary debtor does not default is known as a *surety*. A third party who agrees to be *secondarily* responsible for the debt—that is, responsible only if the primary debtor defaults—is known as a *guarantor*. As noted in Chapter 16, normally a promise of guaranty (a collateral, or secondary, promise) must be in writing to be enforceable.

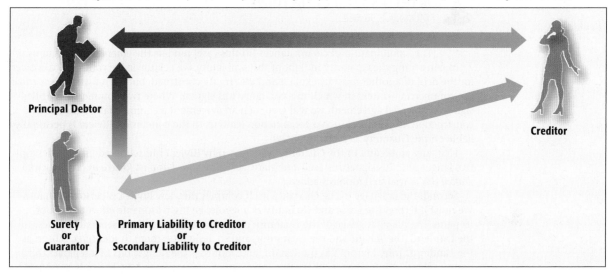

Principal Debtor

Creditor

Surety or Guarantor } **Primary Liability to Creditor or Secondary Liability to Creditor**

WRITING OR RECORD REQUIRED Under the Statute of Frauds, a guaranty contract between the guarantor and the creditor must be in writing (or electronically recorded) to be enforceable unless the *main purpose* exception (discussed in Chapter 16) applies.[9] Under the

common law, a suretyship agreement did not need to be in writing to be enforceable, and oral surety agreements were sufficient. Today, however, some states require a writing (or electronic record) to enforce a suretyship.

In the following *Spotlight Case*, the issue was whether a guaranty of a lease signed by the president of a corporation was enforceable against the officer personally, although he claimed to have signed the guaranty only as a representative of the corporation.

---

9. Briefly, the main purpose exception provides that if the main purpose of the guaranty agreement is to benefit the guarantor, then the contract need not be in writing to be enforceable.

SPOTLIGHT on Personal Guaranties

Case 29.3 Wilson Court Limited Partnership v. Tony Maroni's, Inc.
Supreme Court of Washington, 134 Wash.2d 692, 952 P.2d 590 (1998).

BACKGROUND AND FACTS Tony Riviera founded Tony Maroni's, Inc., to sell Tony Maroni's Famous Gourmet Pizza in Seattle, Washington. Tony Maroni's, Inc., agreed to lease retail space owned by Wilson Court Limited Partnership. Riviera, Tony Maroni's president, signed the lease for 1,676 square feet of space for a sixty-month term. When he signed the lease, Riviera also signed a guaranty agreement that was incorporated by reference into the lease.

On the signature line of the guaranty, Riviera wrote "President" after his name. The guaranty did not specifically identify who was bound, referring only to "the undersigned" or "Guarantor." Riviera also signed the lease in a representative capacity, but the lease clearly indicated that only Tony Maroni's was bound by

CASE 29.3 CONTINUES ▶

CASE 29.3 CONTINUED its terms. When Tony Maroni's defaulted on the lease, Wilson filed a suit in a Washington state court against Tony Maroni's, Riviera, and others. Riviera asserted, in part, that he was not personally liable on the guaranty because he signed only in his capacity as a corporate officer. The court issued a summary judgment in favor of Wilson. Riviera appealed to the Washington Supreme Court.

 IN THE LANGUAGE OF THE COURT
TALMADGE, Justice.

* * * *

* * * [The] combination of circumstances [in this case] renders the Guaranty ambiguous.

In construing the Guaranty in light of this ambiguity, we acknowledge contracts to answer for the debt of another must be explicit and are strictly construed, but we must also recognize the commercial context in which this Guaranty was signed. Where two commercial entities sign a commercial agreement, we will give such an agreement a commercially reasonable construction. In this case, such a construction leads us to the conclusion Riviera is personally liable on the Guaranty as a matter of law.

First, any ambiguity in the Guaranty was created by Riviera himself in adding the descriptive language to his signature. *Such ambiguity will be construed against Riviera as the party who drafted this language.* [Emphasis added.]

Second, the language of the Guaranty itself compels the view Riviera is personally liable. We must interpret the Lease and Guaranty as a whole, giving reasonable effect to each of its parts. The plain language of the Guaranty clearly contemplates three separate entities, the Landlord, the Tenant and the Guarantor, and so designates them. It identifies Wilson as the Landlord, Tony Maroni's as the Tenant, and addresses the obligations of a separate third party, referred to interchangeably as the undersigned or Guarantor. * * * The only reasonable interpretation of these provisions is that the Landlord, Tenant and undersigned/Guarantor are three separate and distinct entities. If Riviera signed the Guaranty only in his representative capacity, Tony Maroni's would be both Tenant and Guarantor, rendering the Guaranty provisions absurd.

Moreover, the Guaranty language stands in stark contrast to the language of the Lease where a corporate obligation was unambiguously contemplated. Riviera signed the Lease as president of Tony Maroni's to bind the company. No such intent can be gleaned from the Guaranty.

Third, the very nature of a guaranty is such that Riviera created personal liability by his signature.

* * * *

Riviera is an experienced businessperson with prior experience in commercial leasing who dealt directly with Wilson in securing the Lease. There is no evidence or assertion of any improper conduct by Wilson. Given the commercial sophistication of the parties, the circumstances under which the Guaranty was entered into, and the nature of the Guaranty, a commercially reasonable approach to this case requires us * * * to hold Riviera personally liable under the Guaranty.

DECISION AND REMEDY *The Washington Supreme Court affirmed the judgment of the lower court. The president was personally liable because otherwise the corporation would be the guarantor of its own lease. This would be commercially unreasonable because, as a matter of law, a party cannot be the guarantor of its own contract.*

WHAT IF THE FACTS WERE DIFFERENT? *Suppose that the parties had carefully read the contract before they signed it. If they had been sure that the agreement stated what they intended and if everything discussed was in writing, how might the outcome of this case have been different?*

THE ECONOMIC DIMENSION *Why would a landlord, a lender, or any creditor require a guaranty?*

Actions That Release the Surety and the Guarantor

Basically, the same actions will release a surety or a guarantor from an obligation. In general, the same rules apply to both sureties and guarantors. So, for simplicity, this subsection and the following subsections will refer just to sureties.

MATERIAL MODIFICATION Making any material modification to the terms of the original contract—without the surety's consent—will discharge the surety's obligation. (The extent to which the surety is discharged depends on whether he or she was compensated and to what extent he or she suffered a loss from the modification. For example, a father who receives no consideration in return for acting as a surety on his daughter's loan will be completely discharged if the loan contract is modified without his consent.)

SURRENDER OF PROPERTY If a creditor surrenders the collateral to the debtor or impairs the collateral without the surety's consent, these acts can reduce the obligation of the surety. If the creditor's actions reduce the value of the property used as collateral, the surety is released to the extent of any loss suffered.

PAYMENT OR TENDER OF PAYMENT Naturally, any payment of the principal obligation by the debtor or by another person on the debtor's behalf will discharge the surety from the obligation. Even if the creditor refused to accept payment of the principal debt when it was tendered, the obligation of the surety can be discharged (if the creditor knew about the suretyship).

Defenses of the Surety and the Guarantor

Generally, the surety or guarantor can also assert any of the defenses available to the principal debtor to avoid liability on the obligation to the creditor. A few exceptions do exist, however. They apply to both sureties and guarantors, but again, for simplicity, we refer just to sureties.

INCAPACITY AND BANKRUPTCY Incapacity and bankruptcy are personal defenses, which can be asserted only by the person who is affected. Therefore, the surety cannot assert the principal debtor's incapac-

ity or bankruptcy as a defense. A surety may assert his or her own incapacity or bankruptcy as a defense, however.

STATUTE OF LIMITATIONS The surety cannot assert the statute of limitations as a defense. (In contrast, the principal debtor can claim the statute of limitations as a defense to payment.)

FRAUD If the creditor fraudulently induced the person to act as a surety on the debt, the surety or guarantor can assert fraud as a defense. In most states, the creditor has a legal duty to inform the surety, before the formation of the suretyship contract, of material facts known by the creditor that would substantially increase the surety's risk. Failure to so inform may constitute fraud and renders the suretyship obligation voidable.

Rights of the Surety and the Guarantor

When the surety or guarantor pays the debt owed to the creditor, he or she acquires certain rights, as discussed next. Again, for simplicity, the discussion refers just to sureties.

THE RIGHT OF SUBROGATION The surety has the legal **right of subrogation.** Simply stated, this means that any right that the creditor had against the debtor now becomes the right of the surety. Included are creditor rights in bankruptcy, rights to collateral possessed by the creditor, and rights to judgments obtained by the creditor. In short, the surety now stands in the shoes of the creditor and may pursue any remedies that were available to the creditor against the debtor.

▶ **Case in Point 29.7** Guerrero Brothers, Inc. (GBI), contracted with the Public School System (PSS) to build a high school. Century Insurance Company (CIC) agreed to provide GBI with the required payment and performance bonds on the project. Thus, CIC acted as a surety of GBI's performance and promised to finish the project if GBI defaulted.

Four years after construction began, PSS canceled GBI's contract, and CIC fulfilled GBI's obligations by finishing construction of the school. Numerous disputes arose, and litigation ensued. Ultimately, PSS agreed to pay GBI $500,000 in contract funds. CIC then filed an action against GBI and PSS to recover the $867,000 it claimed PSS owed it for finishing the school. The court found that CIC, as a performing surety, was entitled to the remaining contract funds through the right of subrogation. It had performed GBI's obligations and therefore stepped into GBI's shoes and had the right to obtain payment from PSS.[10] ◄

THE RIGHT OF REIMBURSEMENT The surety or guarantor has a **right of reimbursement** from the debtor. Basically, the surety is entitled to receive from the debtor all outlays made on behalf of the suretyship arrangement. Such outlays can include expenses incurred as well as the actual amount of the debt paid to the creditor.

THE RIGHT OF CONTRIBUTION Two or more sureties are called **co-sureties.** When a co-surety pays more than her or his proportionate share on a debtor's default, she or he is entitled to recover from the other co-sureties the amount paid above that surety's obligation. This is the **right of contribution.** Generally, a co-surety's liability either is determined by agreement or, in the absence of agreement, is set at the maximum liability under the suretyship contract.

▶ **Example 29.8** Yasser and Itzhak, two co-sureties, are obligated under a suretyship contract to guarantee Jules's debt. Itzhak's maximum liability is $15,000, and Yasser's is $10,000. Jules owes $10,000 and is in default. Itzhak pays the creditor the entire $10,000.

In the absence of an agreement to the contrary, Itzhak can recover $4,000 from Yasser. The amount of the debt that Yasser agreed to cover ($10,000) is divided by the total amount that he and Itzhak together agreed to cover ($25,000). The result is multiplied by the amount of the default, yielding the amount that Yasser owes—$10,000 ÷ $25,000 × $10,000 = $4,000. ◄

SECTION 4
PROTECTION FOR DEBTORS

The law protects debtors as well as creditors. Certain property of the debtor, for example, is exempt under state law from creditors' actions. Consumer protection statutes (see Chapter 44) also protect debtors' rights. Of course, bankruptcy laws, which will be discussed in Chapter 31, are designed specifically to assist debtors in need of help.

---

10. *Century Insurance Co. v. Guerrero Brothers, Inc.,* 2010 WL 997112 (N.Mariana Islands 2010).

In most states, certain types of real and personal property are exempt from execution or attachment. State exemption statutes usually include both real and personal property.

Exempted Real Property

Probably the most familiar exemption is the **homestead exemption.** Each state permits the debtor to retain the family home, either in its entirety or up to a specified dollar amount, free from the claims of unsecured creditors or trustees in bankruptcy.

THE GENERAL RULE The purpose of the homestead exemption is to ensure that the debtor will retain some form of shelter. (Note that federal bankruptcy law places a cap on the amount that debtors filing bankruptcy can claim is exempt under their states' homestead exemption—see Chapter 31 for details.)

▶ **Example 29.9** Vince Beere owes Chris Veltman $40,000. The debt is the subject of a lawsuit, and the court awards Veltman a judgment of $40,000 against Beere. Beere's homestead is valued at $50,000, and the homestead exemption is $25,000. There are no outstanding mortgages or other liens on his homestead. To satisfy the judgment debt, Beere's family home is sold at public auction for $45,000. The proceeds of the sale are distributed as follows:

1. Beere is given $25,000 as his homestead exemption.
2. Veltman is paid $20,000 toward the judgment debt, leaving a $20,000 deficiency judgment (that is, "leftover debt") that can be satisfied from any other nonexempt property (personal or real) that Beere may own, if permitted by state law. ◄

LIMITATIONS In a few states, statutes allow the homestead exemption only if the judgment debtor has a family. If a judgment debtor does not have a family, a creditor may be entitled to collect the full amount realized from the sale of the debtor's home. In addition, the homestead exemption interacts with other areas of law and can sometimes operate to cancel out a portion of a lien on a debtor's real property.

▶ **Case in Point 29.10** Antonio Stanley purchased a modular home from Yates Mobile Services Corporation. When Stanley failed to pay the purchase price of the modular home, Yates obtained a judicial lien against Stanley's property in the amount of $165,138. Stanley then filed for bankruptcy and asserted the homestead exemption. The court found that Stanley was entitled to avoid the lien to the extent that it impaired his exemption. Using a bankruptcy law formula, the court determined that the total impairment was $143,639 and that Stanley could avoid paying this amount to Yates. Thus, Yates was left with a judicial lien on Stanley's home in the amount of $21,499.[11] ◄

Exempted Personal Property

Personal property that is most often exempt from satisfaction of judgment debts includes the following:

---

11. *In re Stanley,* 2010 WL 2103441 (M.D.N.C. 2010).

1. Household furniture up to a specified dollar amount.
2. Clothing and certain personal possessions, such as family pictures or a Bible.
3. A vehicle (or vehicles) for transportation (at least up to a specified dollar amount).
4. Certain classified animals, usually livestock but including pets.
5. Equipment that the debtor uses in a business or trade, such as tools or professional instruments, up to a specified dollar amount.

Reviewing: Creditors' Rights and Remedies

Air Ruidoso, Ltd., operated a commuter airline and air charter service between Ruidoso, New Mexico, and airports in Albuquerque and El Paso. Executive Aviation Center, Inc., provided services for airlines at the Albuquerque International Airport. When Air Ruidoso failed to pay more than $10,000 that it owed on its account for fuel, oil, and oxygen, Executive Aviation took possession of Air Ruidoso's plane, claiming that it had a lien on the plane. Using the information presented in the chapter, answer the following questions.

1. Can Executive Aviation establish an artisan's lien on the plane? Why or why not?
2. Suppose that Executive Aviation files a lawsuit in court against Air Ruidoso for the $10,000 past-due debt. What two methods discussed in this chapter would allow the court to order the seizure of Air Ruidoso's plane to satisfy the debt?
3. Suppose that Executive Aviation discovers that Air Ruidoso has sufficient assets in one of its bank accounts to pay the past-due amount. How might Executive Aviation attempt to obtain access to these funds?
4. Suppose that a clause in the contract between Air Ruidoso and Executive Aviation provides that "if the airline becomes insolvent, Braden Fasco, the chief executive officer of Air Ruidoso, agrees to cover its outstanding debts." Is this a suretyship or a guaranty agreement?

DEBATE THIS . . . *Because writs of attachment are a prejudgment remedy for nonpayment of a debt, they are unfair and should be abolished.*

Terms and Concepts

artisan's lien 560
attachment 560
co-surety 570
creditors' composition agreement 562
default 558
down payment 563
forbearance 563
foreclosure 563
garnishment 561

guarantor 566
homestead exemption 570
lien 558
mechanic's lien 558
mortgage 562
prepayment penalty 563
right of contribution 570
right of redemption 565
right of reimbursement 570

right of subrogation 569
short sale 564
surety 566
suretyship 566
workout agreement 563
writ of attachment 561
writ of execution 561

ExamPrep

Issue Spotters

1. Jorge contracts with Larry of Midwest Roofing to fix Jorge's roof. Jorge pays half of the contract price in advance. Larry and Midwest complete the job, but Jorge refuses to pay the rest of the price. What can Larry and Midwest do? **(See page 558.)**

2. Alyssa owes Don $5,000 and refuses to pay. Don obtains a garnishment order and serves it on Alyssa's employer. If the employer complies with the order and Alyssa stays on the job, is one order enough to garnish all of Alyssa's wages for each pay period until the debt is paid? Explain. **(See page 561.)**

- Check your answers to the Issue Spotters against the answers provided in Appendix E at the end of this text.

Before the Test

Go to **www.cengagebrain.com**, enter the ISBN 9781285185248, and click on "Find" to locate this textbook's Web site. Then, click on "Access Now" under "Study Tools," and select Chapter 29 at the top. There, you will find a Practice Quiz that you can take to assess your mastery of the concepts in this chapter, as well as Flashcards and a Glossary of important terms.

Business Scenarios

29–1. Liens. Karen and Gerald Bladavich own property in South Dakota that they lease to Wyoming Alaska Corp. (WACO) for use as a gas station and convenience store. The lease obligates the Bladavichs to pay for repairs, but WACO is authorized to make necessary repairs. After seventeen years, the property was run-down. The store's customers were tripping over chunks of concrete in the parking lot. An underground gasoline storage tank was leaking. The store's manager hired Cortez Construction, Inc., to install a new tank and make other repairs. The Bladavichs saw the new tank sitting on the property before the work began. When WACO paid only a small portion of the cost, Cortez filed a mechanic's lien and asked a court to foreclose on the property. The Bladavichs disputed the lien, arguing that they had not requested the work. What is the purpose of a mechanic's lien? Should property owners who do not contract for improvements be liable for the cost under such a lien? Discuss. **(See page 558.)**

29–2. Liens. Kanahara is employed part-time by the Cross-Bar Packing Corp. and earns take-home pay of

$400 per week. He is $2,000 in debt to the Holiday Department Store for goods purchased on credit over the past eight months. Most of this property is nonexempt and is now in Kanahara's apartment. Kanahara is in default on his payments to Holiday. Holiday learns that Kanahara has a girlfriend in another state and that he plans to give her most of this property for Christmas. Discuss what actions are available to and should be taken by Holiday to collect the debt owed by Kanahara. **(See page 558.)**

29–3. Liens. Nabil is the owner of a relatively old home valued at $105,000. The home's electrical system is failing and the wiring needs to be replaced. He contracts with Kandhari Electrical to replace the electrical system. Kandhari performs the repairs, and on June 1 submits a bill of $10,000 to Nabil. Because of financial difficulties, Nabil does not pay the bill. Nabil's only asset is his home, but his state's homestead exemption is $60,000. Discuss fully Kandhari's remedies in this situation. **(See page 558.)**

Business Case Problems

29–4. BUSINESS CASE PROBLEM WITH SAMPLE ANSWER: Guaranty.

 Majestic Group Korea, Ltd., borrowed $1.5 million from Overseas Private Investment Corp. (OPIC) to finance a Ruby Tuesday's restaurant. Nam Koo Kim, the sole owner of Majestic, and his spouse, Hee Sun Kim, signed personal guaranties for full payment of the loan. Majestic defaulted. OPIC filed a suit against the Kims to recover. Hee claimed that she did not understand the extent of her liability when she signed the guaranty. Was Hee liable for the debt? Explain. [Overseas Private Investment Corp. v. Kim, 69 A.D.3d 1185, 895 N.Y.S.2d 217 (2010)] **(See page 566.)**

- For a sample answer to Problem 29–4, go to Appendix F at the end of this text.

29–5. Protection for Debtors. Bill and Betty Ma owned half of a two-unit residential building. Betty lived in the unit, but Bill did not. To collect a judgment against the Mas, Mei-Fang Zhang obtained a writ of execution directing the sheriff to seize and sell the building. State law allowed a $100,000 homestead exemption if the debtor lived in the home and $175,000 if the debtor was also disabled and "unable to engage in gainful employment." Bill argued that he could not work because of "gout and dizziness." How much of an exemption are the Mas entitled to have? Why? [*Zhang v. Tse,* ___ F.Supp.2d ___ (N.D.Cal. 2011)] **(See page 570.)**

29–6. Foreclosure on Mortgages and Liens. LaSalle Bank loaned $8 million to Cypress Creek 1, LP, to build an apartment complex. The loan was secured by a mortgage. Cypress Creek hired contractors to provide concrete work, plumbing, carpentry, and other construction services. Cypress Creek went bankrupt, owing LaSalle $3 million. The contractors recorded mechanic's liens when they did not get paid for their work. The property was sold to LaSalle at a sheriff's sale for $1.3 million. The contractors claimed that they should be paid the amounts they were owed out of the $1.3 million and that the mechanic's liens should be satisfied before any funds were distributed to LaSalle for its mortgage. The trial court distributed the $1.3 million primarily to LaSalle, with only a small fraction going to the contractors. Do the liens come before the mortgage in priority of payment? Discuss. [*LaSalle Bank National Association v. Cypress Creek 1, LP,* 242 Ill.2d 231, 950 N.E.2d 1109 (2011)] **(See page 563.)**

29–7. Guaranty. Timothy Martinez, owner of Koenig & Vits, Inc. (K&V), guaranteed K&V's debt to Community Bank & Trust. The guaranty stated that the bank was not required to seek payment of the debt from any other source before enforcing the guaranty. K&V defaulted. Through a Wisconsin state court, the bank sought payment of $536,739.40, plus interest at the contract rate of 7.5 percent, from Martinez. Martinez argued that the bank could not enforce his guaranty while other funds were available to satisfy K&V's debt. For example, the debt might be paid out of the proceeds of a sale of corporate assets. Is this an effective defense to a guaranty? Why or why not? [*Community Bank & Trust v. Koenig & Vits, Inc.,* 346 Wis.2d 279 (Wis.App. 2013)] **(See page 566.)**

29–8. A QUESTION OF ETHICS: Guaranty.

 73-75 Main Avenue, LLC, agreed to lease a portion of the commercial property at 73 Main Avenue, Norwalk, Connecticut, to PP Door Enterprise, Inc. Nan Zhang, as manager of PP Door, signed the lease agreement. The lessor required the principal officers of PP

Door to execute personal guaranties. In addition, the principal officers agreed to provide the lessor with credit information. Apparently, both the lessor and the principals of PP Door signed the lease and guaranty agreements that were sent to PP Door's office. When PP Door failed to make monthly payments, 73-75 Main Avenue filed a suit against PP Door and its owner Li. At trial, Li testified that she was the sole owner of PP Door but denied that Zhang was its manager. She also denied signing the guaranty agreement. She claimed that she had signed the credit authorization form because Zhang had told her he was too young to have good credit. Li claimed to have no knowledge of the lease agreement. She did admit, however, that she had paid the rent. She claimed that Zhang had been in a car accident and had asked her to help pay his bills, including the rent at 73 Main Avenue. Li further testified that she did not see the name PP Door on the storefront of the leased location. [73-75 Main Avenue, LLC v. PP Door Enterprise Inc., *120 Conn.App. 150, 991 A.2d 650 (2010)]* **(See page 566.)**

(a) Li argued that she was not liable on the lease agreement because Zhang was not authorized to bind her to the lease. Do the facts support Li? Why or why not?

(b) Li claimed that the guaranty for rent was not enforceable against her. Why might the court agree?

29–9. SPECIAL CASE ANALYSIS: Foreclosure.

 Go to Case Analysis Case 29.2, *McLean v. JPMorgan Chase Bank, N.A.* on pages 564 and 565. Read the excerpt and answer the following questions.

(a) **Issue:** The dispute in this case focused on an attempt to enforce an unpaid note. Who argued that the note should not be enforced, and on what ground?

(b) **Rule of Law:** What must a party prove at the time that a complaint is filed to be entitled to enforce a note?

(c) **Applying the Rule of Law:** How did the court apply the rule of law to the circumstances in this case?

(d) **Conclusion:** After applying the rule of law to the case, what did the court conclude? Who benefited from this decision?

Legal Reasoning Group Activity

29–10. Attachment. Brent Avery, on behalf of his law firm—The Law Office of Brent Avery—contracted with Marlin Broadcasting to air commercials on KRTV, a local radio station. Avery, who was the sole member of his firm, helped to create the ads, which solicited direct contact with "defense attorney Brent Avery," featured his voice, and repeated his name and experience to make potential clients familiar with him. When KRTV was not paid for the broadcasts, Marlin filed a lawsuit against Avery and his firm, alleging an outstanding balance of $35,250.

Pending the court's hearing of the suit, Marlin filed a request for a writ of attachment. Marlin offered in evidence

the parties' contracts, the ads' transcripts, and KRTV's invoices. Avery contended that he could not be held personally liable for the cost of the ads. Marlin countered that the ads unjustly enriched Avery by conferring a personal benefit on him to Marlin's detriment. **(See page 560.)**

(a) The first group will decide what the purpose of attachment is and explain it.

(b) The second group will outline what a creditor must prove to obtain a writ of attachment.

(c) The third group will determine whether Marlin Broadcasting is entitled to attachment in this scenario.

CHAPTER 30

SECURED TRANSACTIONS

Whenever the payment of a debt is guaranteed, or *secured,* by personal property owned or held by the debtor, the transaction becomes known as a **secured transaction.** The concept of the secured transaction is as basic to modern business practice as the concept of credit. Logically, sellers and lenders do not want to risk nonpayment, so they usually will not sell goods or lend funds unless the promise of payment is somehow guaranteed. Indeed, business as we know it could not exist without laws permitting and governing secured transactions.

Article 9 of the Uniform Commercial Code (UCC) governs secured transactions in personal property. Personal property includes accounts, agricultural liens, and *chattel paper* (any documents or records evidencing a debt secured by personal property). It also includes commercial assignments of $1,000 or more, *fixtures* (certain property that is attached to land), instruments, and other types of intangible property, such as patents. Article 9 does not cover creditor tools such as liens and mortgages on real property (see Chapter 29).

SECTION 1
THE TERMINOLOGY OF SECURED TRANSACTIONS

In every state, the UCC's terminology is now uniformly used in all documents that involve secured transactions. The following is a brief summary of the UCC's definitions of terms relating to secured transactions:

1. A **secured party** is any creditor who has a *security interest* in the debtor's *collateral.* This creditor can be a seller, a lender, a cosigner, or even a buyer of accounts or chattel paper [UCC 9–102(a)(72)].
2. A **debtor** is the party who *owes payment* or other performance of a secured obligation [UCC 9–102(a)(28)].
3. A **security interest** is the interest in the collateral (such as personal property, fixtures, or accounts) that *secures payment or performance* of an obligation [UCC 1–201(37)].
4. A **security agreement** is an *agreement* that creates or provides for a security interest [UCC 9–102(a)(73)].
5. **Collateral** is the *subject* of the *security interest* [UCC 9–102(a)(12)].
6. A **financing statement**—referred to as the UCC-1 form—is the *instrument normally filed to give public notice to third parties* of the secured party's security interest [UCC 9–102(a)(39)].

Together, these basic definitions form the concept under which a debtor-creditor relationship becomes a secured transaction relationship (see Exhibit 30–1 on the following page).

SECTION 2
CREATION OF A SECURITY INTEREST

A creditor has two main concerns if the debtor *defaults:* (1) Can the debt be satisfied through the possession and (usually) sale of the collateral? (2) Will the creditor have priority over any other creditors or buyers who may have rights in the same collateral? These two concerns are met through the creation and perfection of a security interest. We begin by examining how a security interest is created.

Basic Requirements

To become a secured party, the creditor must obtain a security interest in the collateral of the debtor. Three requirements must be met for a creditor to have an enforceable security interest:

1. Unless the creditor has possession of the collateral, there must be a written or authenticated security agreement that clearly describes the col-

EXHIBIT 30-1 Secured Transactions—Concept and Terminology

In a security agreement, a debtor and a creditor agree that the creditor will have a security interest in collateral in which the debtor has rights. In essence, the collateral secures the loan and ensures the creditor of payment should the debtor default.

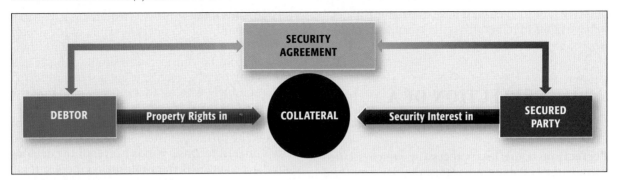

lateral subject to the security interest and is signed or authenticated by the debtor.

2. The secured party must give the debtor something of value.

3. The debtor must have rights in the collateral.

Once these requirements have been met, the creditor's rights are said to *attach* to the collateral. **Attachment** gives the creditor an enforceable security interest in the collateral [UCC 9–203].[1]

▶ **Example 30.1** To furnish his new office suite, Abdul applies for a credit card at an office supply store. The application contains a clause stating that the store will retain a security interest in the goods that he buys with the card until he has paid for the goods in full. This application would be considered a *written security agreement,* which is the first requirement for an enforceable security interest. The goods that Abdul buys with the card are the *something of value* from the secured party (the second requirement). His ownership interest in those goods is the *right* that he has in them (the third requirement). Thus, the requirements for an enforceable security interest are met. When Abdul buys something with the card, the store's rights attach to the purchased goods. ◀

Written or Authenticated Security Agreement

When the collateral is *not* in the possession of the secured party, the security agreement must be either

written or *authenticated,* and it must describe the collateral. **Authentication** means to sign, execute, or adopt any symbol on an electronic record that verifies that the person signing has the intent to adopt or accept the record [UCC 9–102(a)(7)].

If the security agreement is in writing or authenticated, *only the debtor's signature or authentication* is required to create the security interest. The reason authentication is acceptable is to provide for electronic filing (the filing process will be discussed later).

A security agreement must contain a description of the collateral that reasonably identifies it. Generally, such phrases as "all the debtor's personal property" or "all the debtor's assets" would *not* constitute a sufficient description [UCC 9–108(c)].

Secured Party Must Give Value

The secured party must give something of value to the debtor. Under the UCC, value can include a binding commitment to extend credit and, in general, any consideration sufficient to support a simple contract [UCC 1–204]. Normally, the value given by a secured party involves a direct loan or a commitment to sell goods on credit.

Debtor Must Have Rights in the Collateral

The debtor must have rights in the collateral. That is, the debtor must have some ownership interest or right to obtain possession of that collateral. The debtor's rights can represent either a current or a future legal interest in the collateral.

---

1. As was mentioned in Chapter 29, the term *attachment* has a different meaning in secured transactions than it does in the context of judicial liens. In judicial liens, attachment refers to a court-ordered seizure and taking into custody of property prior to the securing of a court judgment for a past-due debt.

For instance, a retailer-debtor can give a secured party a security interest not only in existing inventory owned by the retailer but also in *future* inventory that he or she will acquire. (A common misconception is that the debtor must have title to the collateral to have rights in it, but this is not a requirement.)

SECTION 3
PERFECTION OF A SECURITY INTEREST

Perfection is the legal process by which secured parties protect themselves against the claims of third parties who may wish to have their debts satisfied out of the same collateral. Whether a secured party's security interest is perfected or unperfected can have serious consequences for the secured party if, for example, the debtor defaults on the debt or files for bankruptcy.

What if the debtor has borrowed from two different creditors and used the same property as collateral for both loans? If the debtor defaults on both loans, which of the two creditors has first rights to the collateral? In this situation, the creditor with a perfected security interest will prevail.

Perfection usually is accomplished by filing a financing statement. In some circumstances, however, a security interest becomes perfected even though no financing statement is filed.

Perfection by Filing

The most common means of perfection is by filing a *financing statement* with the office of the appropriate government official. A financing statement gives public notice to third parties of the secured party's security interest. The security agreement itself can also be filed to perfect the security interest. The financing statement must provide the names of the debtor and the secured party, and it must indicate the collateral covered by the financing statement.

A uniform financing statement form (see Exhibit 30–2 on the next page) is used in all states [UCC 9–521]. Communication of the financing statement to the appropriate filing office, together with payment of the correct filing fee, or the acceptance of the financing statement by the filing officer constitutes a filing [UCC 9–516(a)]. The filing can be accomplished electronically [UCC 9–102(a)(18)]. Once completed, filings are indexed by the name of the debtor so that they can be located by subse-

quent searches. A financing statement may be filed even before a security agreement is made or a security interest attaches [UCC 9–502(d)].

THE DEBTOR'S NAME The UCC requires that a financing statement be filed under the name of the debtor [UCC 9–502(a)(1)]. Slight variations in names normally will not be considered misleading if a search of the filing office's records, using a standard search engine routinely used by that office, would find the filings [UCC 9–506(c)].[2]

If the debtor is identified by the correct name at the time the financing statement is filed, the secured party's interest retains its priority even if the debtor's name later changes. Because most states use electronic filing systems, UCC 9–503 sets out detailed rules for determining when the debtor's name as it appears on a financing statement is sufficient.

1. *Corporations.* For corporations, which are organizations that have registered with the state, the debtor's name on the financing statement must be "the name of the debtor indicated on the public record of the debtor's jurisdiction of organization" [UCC 9–503(a)(1)].
2. *Trusts.* If the debtor is a trust or a trustee for property held in trust (see Chapter 51), the financing statement must disclose this information and provide the trust's name as specified in its official documents [UCC 9–503(a)(3)].
3. *Individuals and organizations.* For all others, the financing statement must disclose "the individual or organizational name of the debtor" [UCC 9–503(a)(4)(A)]. The word *organization* includes unincorporated associations, such as clubs and some churches, as well as joint ventures and general partnerships. If an organizational debtor does not have a group name, the names of the individuals in the group must be listed.
4. *Trade names.* In general, it is not sufficient to provide only the debtor's trade name (or fictitious name), when the business is not organized as a corporation or other entity that is distinct from the owner [UCC 9–503(c)]. In other words, listing the debtor as Pete's Plumbing would not be sufficient for perfection. The financing statement must also include the owner-debtor's actual name—Pete Hanson. The reason for this rule is to ensure that the debtor's name on a financing statement is one

---

2. If the name listed in the financing statement is so inaccurate that a search using the standard search engine will not find the debtor's name, the financing statement is deemed seriously misleading under UCC 9–506. See also UCC 9–507, which governs the effectiveness of financing statements found to be seriously misleading.

EXHIBIT 30-2   **The Uniform Financing Statement**

UCC FINANCING STATEMENT

FOLLOW INSTRUCTIONS (front and back) CAREFULLY

A. NAME & PHONE OF CONTACT AT FILER [optional]

B. SEND ACKNOWLEDGMENT TO: (Name and Address)

THE ABOVE SPACE IS FOR FILING OFFICE USE ONLY

1. DEBTOR'S EXACT FULL LEGAL NAME   insert only one debtor name (1a or 1b) - do not abbreviate or combine names

1a. ORGANIZATION'S NAME			

OR

1b. INDIVIDUAL'S LAST NAME	FIRST NAME	MIDDLE NAME	SUFFIX

1c. MAILING ADDRESS	CITY	STATE	POSTAL CODE	COUNTRY

1d. **SEE INSTRUCTIONS**	ADD'L INFO RE ORGANIZATION DEBTOR	1e. TYPE OF ORGANIZATION	1f. JURISDICTION OF ORGANIZATION	1g. ORGANIZATIONAL ID #, if any ☐ NONE

2. ADDITIONAL DEBTOR'S EXACT FULL LEGAL NAME - insert only one debtor name (2a or 2b)   do not abbreviate or combine names

2a. ORGANIZATION'S NAME			

OR

2b. INDIVIDUAL'S LAST NAME	FIRST NAME	MIDDLE NAME	SUFFIX

2c. MAILING ADDRESS	CITY	STATE	POSTAL CODE	COUNTRY

2d. **SEE INSTRUCTIONS**	ADD'L INFO RE ORGANIZATION DEBTOR	2e. TYPE OF ORGANIZATION	2f. JURISDICTION OF ORGANIZATION	2g. ORGANIZATIONAL ID #, if any ☐ NONE

3. SECURED PARTY'S NAME (or NAME of TOTAL ASSIGNEE of ASSIGNOR S/P)   insert only one secured party name (3a or 3b)

3a. ORGANIZATION'S NAME			

OR

3b. INDIVIDUAL'S LAST NAME	FIRST NAME	MIDDLE NAME	SUFFIX

3c. MAILING ADDRESS	CITY	STATE	POSTAL CODE	COUNTRY

4. This FINANCING STATEMENT covers the following collateral:

5. ALTERNATIVE DESIGNATION [if applicable]:	☐ LESSEE/LESSOR	☐ CONSIGNEE/CONSIGNOR	☐ BAILEE/BAILOR	☐ SELLER/BUYER	☐ AG. LIEN	☐ NON-UCC FILING

6. ☐ This FINANCING STATEMENT is to be filed [for record] (or recorded) in the REAL ESTATE RECORDS. Attach Addendum [if applicable]	7. Check to REQUEST SEARCH REPORT(S) on Debtor(s) [ADDITIONAL FEE] [optional]	☐ All Debtors	☐ Debtor 1	☐ Debtor 2

8. OPTIONAL FILER REFERENCE DATA

FILING OFFICE COPY — UCC FINANCING STATEMENT (FORM UCC1) (REV. 05/22/02) that prospective lenders can locate and recognize in future searches.

CHANGES IN THE DEBTOR'S NAME If the debtor's name changes, the financing statement remains effective for collateral the debtor acquired before or within four months after the name change. Unless an amendment to the financing statement is filed within this four-month period, collateral acquired by the debtor after the four-month period is unperfected [UCC 9–507(b) and (c)].

A one-page uniform financing statement amendment form is available for filing name changes and for other purposes (see the discussion of amendments later in this chapter) [UCC 9–521].

DESCRIPTION OF THE COLLATERAL Both the security agreement and the financing statement must describe the collateral in which the secured party has a security interest. The security agreement must describe the collateral because no security interest in goods can exist unless the parties agree on which goods are subject to the security interest.

The financing statement must also describe the collateral to provide public notice of the fact that certain goods of the debtor are subject to a security interest. Other parties who might later wish to lend funds to the debtor or buy the collateral can thus learn of the

security interest by checking with the office in which a financing statement would be filed. For land-related security interests, a legal description of the realty is also required [UCC 9–502(b)].

Level of Detail Can Vary. Sometimes, the descriptions in the two documents vary. The description in the security agreement must be more precise than the description in the financing statement, which is allowed to be more general. ▶ **Example 30.2** A security agreement for a commercial loan to a manufacturer of automotive parts may list all of the manufacturer's equipment subject to the loan by serial number. The financing statement, in contrast, may simply state "all equipment owned or hereafter acquired." ◀

General Descriptions Allowed in Financing Statements. The UCC permits broad, general descriptions in the financing statement, such as "all assets" or "all personal property." Usually, if a financing statement accurately describes the agreement between the secured party and the debtor, the description is sufficient [UCC 9–504].

In the following case, a secured party filed a financing statement claiming a security interest in livestock. The court had to decide if the secured party had perfected her security interest even though the collateral could not be identified by the security agreement alone.

CASE 30.1

In re Baker
United States Bankruptcy Court, Northern District of New York, 465 Bankr. 359 (2012).

BACKGROUND AND FACTS In 2006, Jeanne Angell sold fifty-eight dairy cows to Richard and Amanda Baker. Angell gave the Bakers a certificate of registration for each cow. Each certificate gave the cow's name, provided a diagram with the animal's distinctive markings, and identified Angell as a former owner. In 2008, the parties executed a security agreement, and Angell attempted to perfect her security interest by filing a financing statement. Both documents identified the cows by name and by their ear tag identification numbers. The Bakers then sold twenty-two of the cows at auction, and Angell was entitled to the proceeds because they still owed her for the cows. Sixteen of the cows, however, either did not have ear tags or had tag numbers that did not match the financing statement. The auction company therefore identified the cows using their names, which appeared on both the certificates and the financing statement, and the diagrams on the certificates. The Bakers later filed for bankruptcy. The bankruptcy trustee argued that Angell had not perfected her security interest because the financing statement did not describe the cows in sufficient detail.

 IN THE LANGUAGE OF THE COURT
Diane *DAVIS*, Bankruptcy Judge.

* * * *

* * * Uniform Commercial Code Section 9–108 * * * states that a "description of personal * * * property is sufficient, whether or not it is specific, it if reasonably identifies what is described" such that the "identity of the collateral is objectively determinable." * * * "Generally, a financing statement sufficiently indicates collateral claimed to be covered by [the statement] * * * if it provides notice that a person may have a security interest in the collateral claimed." *Thus, the theory underpinning the financing statement is one of inquiry notice, and the test is one of reasonable identification, which this Court must now construe in practice.* [Emphasis added.]

* * * *

"A financing statement imposes a duty on third parties to inquire of the parties concerned to learn the identity of specific property covered, and thus to charge the third party with knowledge of whatever facts a reasonable inquiry would have revealed." Trustee submits that the collateral in this case was described with such particularity that no further inquiry would have been required of a third party. Given the character of the collateral at issue and the almost certain loss of ear tags, the Court is unconvinced. At a minimum, the third party would have been placed on notice that Defendant claimed a security interest in a certain number of cows. Cows are not fungible; they are identifiable by a number of methods, including ear tag designation, breed, lot number, brand, unique permanent markings, and/or registration certificate.

While Defendant's use of the ear tag identification numbers was, as of the time of filing, inaccurate, both the Certificates and the [financing statement] included the name of each cow in addition to an ear tag designation. Given this information, [the Bakers], Defendant, and/or a third party would have been able to readily and easily ascertain which cows were covered by Defendant's security interest. [The auction company], with the aid of the Certificates, did just that by comparing the names on the [financing statement] to the names and diagrams on the respective Certificate for each cow. Accordingly, Defendant's [financing statement] was effective to perfect Defendant's secured interest in the sixteen cows, irrespective of the erroneous or outdated ear tag designations.

DECISION AND REMEDY *The bankruptcy court determined that Angell was entitled to the proceeds from the auction. It held that the trustee could not invalidate Angell's security interest.*

THE LEGAL ENVIRONMENT DIMENSION *Do the UCC's rules concerning collateral descriptions encourage parties to enter security agreements? Why or why not?*

WHAT IF THE FACTS WERE DIFFERENT? *Suppose that Angell had listed only the cows' names and not their ear-tag designations. Would the result have been different? Explain.*

WHERE TO FILE In most states, a financing statement must be filed centrally in the appropriate state office, such as the office of the secretary of state, in the state where the debtor is located. An exception occurs when the collateral consists of timber to be cut, fixtures, or items to be extracted—such as oil, coal, gas, and minerals [UCC 9–301(3) and (4), 9–502(b)]. In those circumstances, the financing statement is filed in the county where the collateral is located.

The state in which a financing statement should be filed depends on the debtor's location, not the location of the collateral [UCC 9–301]. The debtor's location is determined as follows [UCC 9–307]:

1. For an *individual debtor,* it is the state of the debtor's principal residence.

2. For an organization registered with the state, such as a corporation, it is the state in which the organization is registered. Thus, if a debtor is incorporated in Delaware and has its chief executive office in New York, a secured party would file the financing statement in Delaware because that is where the debtor's business is registered.

3. For *all other entities,* it is the state in which the business is located or, if the debtor has more than one office, the place from which the debtor manages its business operations and affairs.

CONSEQUENCES OF AN IMPROPER FILING Any improper filing renders the secured party's interest unperfected and reduces the secured party's claim in bankruptcy to that of an unsecured creditor. For instance, if the debtor's name is incorrect or if the collateral is not sufficiently described on the financing statement, the filing may not be effective.

▶ **Case in Point 30.3** Corona Fruits & Veggies, Inc., loaned funds to Juarez, a strawberry farmer. The documents set out Juarez's full name, but Juarez generally went by the name "Munoz" and signed the documents "Armando Munoz." Corona filed financing statements that identified the debtor as "Armando Munoz." Later, in December, Juarez contracted to sell strawberries to Frozsun Foods, Inc., which filed a financing statement that identified the debtor as "Armando Juarez."

By the next July, Juarez owed Corona $230,482.52 and Frozsun $19,648.52. When Juarez did not repay his debts, Corona and Frozsun filed a suit against him. The court concluded that the identification of the debtor as "Armando Munoz" in Corona's financing statement was seriously misleading. Frozsun's interest thus took priority because its financing statement was recorded properly.[3] ◀

The UCC financing statement (see Exhibit 30–2 on page 577) includes a section for listing an "Additional Debtor." Is it misleading to include the names of additional debtors on an attached list but not refer to that list in the financing statement? The court in the following case considered this question.

_____

3. *Corona Fruits & Veggies, Inc. v. Frozsun Foods, Inc.,* 143 Cal.App.4th 319, 48 Cal.Rptr.3d 868 (2006).

CASE 30.2

In re Camtech Precision Manufacturing, Inc.
United States Bankruptcy Court, Southern District of Florida, 443 Bankr. 190 (2011).

BACKGROUND AND FACTS Camtech Precision Manufacturing, Inc., makes precision parts and assemblies for aerospace and defense customers. Camtech is a subsidiary of R&J National Enterprises, Inc. (R&J). R&J had a nearly $4 million line of credit with Regions Bank in 2010. Regions Bank filed a series of financing statements with the appropriate state offices in Florida and New York to perfect security interests in the assets of R&J and its related companies. All of the statements were filed on the Uniform Commercial Code financing statement form used in all states. The forms listed R&J as the debtor in the "Debtor" box and Avstar Aircraft Accessories, Inc., another R&J subsidiary, as an additional debtor in the "Additional Debtor" box.

Neither box, however, indicated that there were more debtors. Attached to each form was a sheet of plain paper that listed Camtech Precision Manufacturing, Inc., and Avstar Fuel Systems, Inc., as additional debtors. In 2010, R&J and the others filed a petition in a federal bankruptcy court to declare bankruptcy (see Chapter 31). A committee of the companies' unsecured creditors asked the court to rule that Regions' statements failed to perfect the bank's security interest in the assets of Camtech and Avstar Fuel.

IN THE LANGUAGE OF THE COURT
Paul G. *HYMAN*, Chief Judge.

* * *

As a general rule, minor errors in a UCC financing statement do not affect the effectiveness of the financing statement, unless the errors render the document seriously misleading. Based upon the undisputed fact that * * * searches of New York and Florida records failed to disclose a financing statement naming Regions as a secured creditor of Camtech or Avstar Fuel, Plaintiff argues that the subject UCCs are seriously misleading and ineffective to perfect Regions' asserted security interest. The Court agrees. While Regions' UCCs contain the statutorily required information and the correct names of the Debtors, the Court finds that the manner in which this information was provided for Camtech and Avstar Fuel made the UCCs seriously misleading as to these additional Debtors. [Emphasis added.]

Both New York and Florida have approved standard national and/or state forms for listing additional debtors. Regions concedes that it did not use an approved additional party form when listing Camtech and Avstar Fuel as additional debtors. * * * Had the additional debtor information been submitted using an approved standard form which is readily available

CASE 30.2 CONTINUED online, or had there been a direction in the additional debtor box on the first page of the [Uniform Commercial Code Financing Statement] form to look at the attachment for additional debtor information, the result here would be different.

* * * *

* * * Regions' unapproved attachment did not contain any "fields" corresponding to the * * * additional party form, nor did it contain any additional debtor "boxes" in which to list the names of the additional debtors. Listing the additional debtors names elsewhere on an unapproved attachment is irrelevant. This error was compounded by the fact that there was no direction in the additional debtor box on the first page of each [statement] to look at the attachment listing additional debtors. * * * The Court finds that listing additional debtors on an unapproved attachment which wasn't referenced in the additional debtor box on the first page of Regions' UCCs was an error and an omission that made the financing statements seriously misleading as to Camtech and Avstar Fuel.

DECISION AND REMEDY *The court found that Regions' statements were seriously misleading and ineffective to perfect security interests in the assets of Camtech and Avstar Fuel. Because Regions failed to perfect its security interests, the bank was an unsecured creditor with respect to the companies' assets.*

WHAT IF THE FACTS WERE DIFFERENT? *Suppose that searches of the Florida and New York records had revealed that Regions was a secured creditor of Camtech and Avstar Fuel. Would the result have been different in this case? Explain.*

THE ECONOMIC DIMENSION *Why did Camtech and Avstar Fuel's unsecured creditors ask the court to rule that Regions's interest in the debtors' assets was also unsecured?*

Perfection without Filing

In two types of situations, security interests can be perfected without filing a financing statement. The first occurs when the collateral is transferred into the possession of the secured party.

The second occurs when the security interest is one of a limited number under the UCC that can be perfected on attachment (without a filing and without possession of the goods) [UCC 9–309]. The phrase *perfected on attachment* means that these security interests are automatically perfected at the time of their creation. Two of the most common security interests that are perfected on attachment are a *purchase-money security interest* in consumer goods (defined and explained shortly) and an assignment of a beneficial interest in a estate of a deceased person [UCC 9–309(1), (13)].

Where or how to perfect a security interest sometimes depends on the classification or definition of the collateral. Collateral is generally divided into two classifications: *tangible collateral* (collateral that can be seen, felt, and touched) and *intangible collateral* (collateral that consists of or generates rights). Exhibit 30–3 on the following page summarizes the various classifications of collateral and the methods of perfecting a security interest in collateral falling within each of those classifications.[4]

PERFECTION BY POSSESSION In the past, one of the most frequently used means of obtaining financing under the common law was to **pledge** certain collateral as security for the debt and transfer the collateral into the creditor's possession. When the debt was paid, the collateral was returned to the debtor. Although the debtor usually entered into a written security agreement, oral security agreements were also enforceable as long as the secured party possessed the collateral.

Article 9 of the UCC retained the common law pledge and the principle that the security agreement need not be in writing to be enforceable if the collateral is transferred to the secured party [UCC 9–310, 9–312(b), 9–313]. ▶ **Example 30.4** Sheila needs cash to pay for a medical procedure. She obtains a loan for $4,000 from Trent. As security on the loan, she gives him a promissory note on which she is the payee. Even though the agreement to hold the note

---

4. There are additional classifications, such as agricultural liens, commercial tort claims, and investment property. For definitions of these types of collateral, see UCC 9–102(a)(5), (a)(13), and (a)(49).

EXHIBIT 30–3 Types of Collateral and Methods of Perfection

Tangible Collateral		Method of Perfection
All things that are movable at the time the security interest attaches (such as livestock) or that are attached to the land, including timber to be cut and growing crops.		
1. Consumer Goods [UCC 9–301, 9–303, 9–309(1), 9–310(a), 9–313(a)]	Goods used or bought primarily for personal, family, or household purposes—for example, household furniture [UCC 9–102(a)(23)].	For purchase-money security interest, attachment (that is, the creation of a security interest) is sufficient. For boats, motor vehicles, and trailers, filing or compliance with a certificate-of-title statute is required. For other consumer goods, general rules of filing or possession apply.
2. Equipment [UCC 9–301, 9–310(a), 9–313(a)]	Goods bought for or used primarily in business (and not part of inventory or farm products)—for example, a delivery truck [UCC 9–102(a)(33)].	Filing or (rarely) possession by secured party.
3. Farm Products [UCC 9–301, 9–310(a), 9–313(a)]	Crops (including aquatic goods), livestock, or supplies produced in a farming operation—for example, ginned cotton, milk, eggs, and maple syrup [UCC 9–102(a)(34)].	Filing or (rarely) possession by secured party.
4. Inventory [UCC 9–301, 9–310(a), 9–313(a)]	Goods held by a person for sale or under a contract of service or lease; raw materials held for production and work in progress [UCC 9–102(a)(48)].	Filing or (rarely) possession by secured party.
5. Accessions [UCC 9–301, 9–310(a), 9–313(a)]	Personal property that is so attached, installed, or fixed to other personal property (goods) that it becomes a part of these goods—for example, a DVD player installed in an automobile [UCC 9–102(a)(1)].	Filing or (rarely) possession by secured party (same as personal property being attached).
Intangible Collateral		Method of Perfection
Nonphysical property that exists only in connection with something else.		
1. Chattel Paper [UCC 9–301, 9–310(a), 9–312(a), 9–313(a), 9–314(a)]	A writing or writings (record or records) that evidence both a monetary obligation and a security interest in goods and software used in goods—for example, a security agreement or a security agreement and promissory note. *Note:* If the record or records consist of information stored in an electronic medium, the collateral is called *electronic chattel paper.* If the information is inscribed on a tangible medium, it is called *tangible chattel paper* [UCC 9–102(a)(11), (a)(31), and (a)(78)].	Filing or possession or control by secured party.
2. Instruments [UCC 9–301, 9–309(4), 9–310(a), 9–312(a) and (e), 9–313(a)]	A negotiable instrument, such as a check, note, certificate of deposit, draft, or other writing that evidences a right to the payment of money and is not a security agreement or lease but rather a type that can ordinarily be transferred (after indorsement, if necessary) by delivery [UCC 9–102(a)(47)].	Except for temporary perfected status, filing or possession. For the sale of promissory notes, perfection can be by attachment (automatically on the creation of the security interest).
3. Accounts [UCC 9–301, 9–309(2) and (5), 9–310(a)]	Any right to receive payment for the following: (a) any property, real or personal, sold, leased, licensed, assigned, or otherwise disposed of, including intellectual licensed property; (b) services rendered or to be rendered, such as contract rights; (c) policies of insurance; (d) secondary obligations incurred; (e) use of a credit card; (f) winnings of a government-sponsored or government-authorized lottery or other game of chance; and (g) health-care insurance receivables, defined as an interest or claim under a policy of insurance to payment for health-care goods or services provided [UCC 9–102(a)(2) and (a)(46)].	Filing required except for certain assignments that can be perfected by attachment (automatically on the creation of the security interest).

EXHIBIT 30-3 Types of Collateral and Methods of Perfection, *Continued*

Intangible Collateral		Method of Perfection
4. Deposit Accounts [UCC 9–104, 9–304, 9–312(b), 9–314(a)]	Any demand, time, savings, passbook, or similar account maintained with a bank [UCC 9–102(a)(29)].	Perfection by control, such as when the secured party is the bank in which the account is maintained or when the parties have agreed that the secured party can direct the disposition of funds in a particular account.
5. General Intangibles [UCC 9–301, 9–309(3), 9–310(a) and (b)(8)]	Any personal property (or debtor's obligation to make payments on such) other than that defined above [UCC 9–102(a)(42)], including software that is independent from a computer or other good [UCC 9–102(a)(44), (a)(61), and (a)(75)].	Filing only (for copyrights, with the U.S. Copyright Office), except a sale of a payment intangible by attachment (automatically on the creation of the security interest).

as collateral was oral, Trent has a perfected security interest. He does not need to file a financing statement because he has possession of the note. No other creditor of Sheila's can attempt to recover the promissory note from Trent in payment for other debts. ◄

For most collateral, possession by the secured party is impractical because then the debtor cannot use or derive income from the property to pay off the debt. ▶ **Example 30.5** Jason, a farmer, takes out a loan to finance the purchase of a corn harvester and uses the equipment as collateral. Clearly, the purpose of the purchase would be defeated if Jason transferred the collateral into the creditor's possession because he would not be able to use the equipment to harvest his corn. ◄ Certain items, however, such as stocks, bonds, negotiable instruments, and jewelry, are commonly transferred into the creditor's possession when they are used as collateral for loans.

PERFECTION BY ATTACHMENT—THE PURCHASE-MONEY SECURITY INTEREST IN CONSUMER GOODS

Under the UCC, fourteen types of security interests are perfected automatically at the time they are created [UCC 9–309]. The most common is the **purchase-money security interest (PMSI)** in *consumer goods* (items bought primarily for personal, family, or household purposes).

A PMSI in consumer goods is created when a seller or lender agrees to extend credit to a buyer for part or all of the purchase price of the goods in a sales transaction. The entity that extends the credit and obtains the PMSI can be either the seller (a store, for instance) or a financial institution that lends the

buyer the funds with which to purchase the goods [UCC 9–102(a)(2)].

Automatic Perfection. A PMSI in consumer goods is perfected automatically at the time of a credit sale— that is, at the time the PMSI is created. The seller in this situation does not need to do anything more to perfect her or his interest.

▶ **Example 30.6** Jami purchases a Whirlpool washer and dryer from West Coast Appliance for $2,500. Unable to pay the entire amount in cash, Jami signs a purchase agreement to pay $1,000 down and $100 per month until the balance, plus interest, is fully paid. West Coast Appliance is to retain a security interest in the appliances until full payment has been made. Because the security interest was created as part of the purchase agreement with a consumer, it is a PMSI, and West Coast Appliance's security interest is automatically perfected. ◄

Exceptions to Automatic Perfection. There are two exceptions to the rule of automatic perfection for PMSIs:

1. Certain types of security interests that are subject to other federal or state laws may require additional steps to be perfected [UCC 9–311]. Many jurisdictions, for instance, have certificate-of-title statutes that establish perfection requirements for security interests in certain goods, including automobiles, trailers, boats, mobile homes, and farm tractors.

   ▶ **Example 30.7** Martin Sedek purchases a boat at a Florida dealership. Florida has a certificate-of-title statute. Sedek obtains financing for his purchase through General Credit

Corporation. General Credit Corporation will need to file a certificate of title with the appropriate state official to perfect the PMSI. ◄

2. PMSIs in nonconsumer goods, such as a business's inventory or livestock, are not automatically perfected [UCC 9–324]. These types of PMSIs will be discussed later in this chapter in the context of priorities.

Effective Time Duration of Perfection

A financing statement is effective for five years from the date of filing [UCC 9–515]. If a **continuation statement** is filed *within six months prior* to the expiration date, the effectiveness of the original statement is continued for another five years. The continuation period starts with the expiration date of the first five-year period [UCC 9–515(d), (e)]. The effectiveness of the statement can be continued in the same manner indefinitely. Any attempt to file a continuation statement outside the six-month window will render the continuation ineffective, and

the perfection will lapse at the end of the five-year period.

If a financing statement lapses, the security interest that had been perfected by the filing now becomes unperfected. A purchaser for value can take the property that was used as collateral as if the security interest had never been perfected [UCC 9–515(c)].

For a synopsis of the rules for creating and perfecting a security interest, see *Concept Summary 30.1* below.

SECTION 4
THE SCOPE OF A SECURITY INTEREST

As previously mentioned, a security interest can cover property in which the debtor has ownership or possessory rights in the present or in the future. Therefore, security agreements can cover the proceeds of the sale of collateral, after-acquired property, and future advances, as discussed next.

CONCEPT SUMMARY 30.1
Creating and Perfecting a Security Interest

CONCEPT	DESCRIPTION
Creating a Security Interest	1. Unless the creditor has possession of the collateral, there must be a written or authenticated security agreement signed or authenticated by the debtor and describing the collateral subject to the security interest. 2. The secured party must give value to the debtor. 3. The debtor must have rights in the collateral—some ownership interest or right to obtain possession of the specified collateral.

Perfecting a Security Interest	1. *Perfection by filing*—The most common method of perfection is by filing a financing statement containing the names of the secured party and the debtor and indicating the collateral covered by the financing statement.
	  a. Communication of the financing statement to the appropriate filing office, together with the correct filing fee, constitutes a filing.
	  b. The financing statement must be filed under the name of the debtor. Fictitious (trade) names normally are not sufficient.
	2. *Perfection without filing*—
	  a. By transfer of collateral—The debtor can transfer possession of the collateral to the secured party. For example, a *pledge* is this type of transfer.
	  b. By attachment—A limited number of security interests are perfected by attachment, such as a purchase-money security interest (PMSI) in consumer goods. If the secured party has a PMSI in consumer goods (bought for personal, family, or household purposes), the secured party's security interest is perfected automatically.

Proceeds

Proceeds are the cash or property received when collateral is sold or disposed of in some other way [UCC 9–102(a)(64)]. A security interest in the collateral gives the secured party a security interest in the proceeds acquired from the sale of that collateral.

▶ **Example 30.8** People's Bank has a perfected security interest in the inventory of a retail seller of heavy farm machinery. The retailer sells a tractor out of this inventory to Jacob Lamensdorf, who is by definition *a buyer in the ordinary course of business* (this term will be discussed later in the chapter). Lamensdorf agrees, in a security agreement, to make monthly payments to the retailer for a period of twenty-four months. If the retailer goes into default on the loan from the bank, the bank is entitled to the remaining payments Lamensdorf owes to the retailer as proceeds. ◀

A security interest in proceeds perfects automatically on the *perfection* of the secured party's security interest in the original collateral and remains perfected for twenty days after the debtor receives the proceeds. One way to extend the twenty-day automatic perfection period is to provide for such extended coverage in the original security agreement [UCC 9–315(c), (d)]. This is typically done when the collateral is the type that is likely to be sold, such as a retailer's inventory of tablets or smartphones, for example. The UCC also permits a security interest in identifiable cash proceeds to remain perfected after twenty days [UCC 9–315(d)(2)].

After-Acquired Property

After-acquired property is property that the debtor acquired after the execution of the security agreement. The security agreement may provide for a security interest in after-acquired property, such as a debtor's inventory [UCC 9–204(1)]. A secured party whose security interest is in existing inventory knows that the debtor will sell that inventory, thereby reducing the collateral subject to the security interest.

Generally, the debtor will purchase new inventory to replace the inventory sold. The secured party wants this newly acquired inventory to be subject to the original security interest. Thus, the after-acquired property clause continues the secured party's claim to any inventory acquired thereafter. (This is not to say that the original security interest will take priority over the rights of all other creditors with regard to this after-acquired inventory, as will be discussed later.)

▶ **Example 30.9** Amato buys factory equipment from Bronson on credit, giving as security an interest in all of her equipment—both what she is buying and what she already owns. The security agreement with Bronson contains an after-acquired property clause. Six months later, Amato pays cash to another seller of factory equipment for additional equipment. Six months after that, Amato goes out of business before she has paid off her debt to Bronson. Bronson has a security interest in all of Amato's equipment, even the equipment bought from the other seller. ◀

Future Advances

Often, a debtor will arrange with a bank to have a *continuing line of credit* under which the debtor can borrow funds intermittently. Advances against lines of credit can be subject to a properly perfected security interest in certain collateral.

The security agreement may provide that any future advances made against that line of credit are also subject to the security interest in the same collateral [UCC 9–204(c)]. Future advances need not be of the same type or otherwise related to the original advance to benefit from this type of **cross-collateralization.**[5] Cross-collateralization occurs when an asset that is not the subject of a loan is used to collateralize that loan.

▶ **Example 30.10** Stroh is the owner of a small manufacturing plant with equipment valued at $1 million. He has an immediate need for $40,000 of working capital, so he obtains a loan from Midwestern Bank and signs a security agreement, putting up all of his equipment as security. The bank properly perfects its security interest. The security agreement provides that Stroh can borrow up to $500,000 in the future, using the same equipment as collateral for any future advances. In this situation, Midwestern Bank does not have to execute a new security agreement and perfect a security interest in the collateral each time an advance is made, up to a cumulative total of $500,000. For priority purposes, each advance is perfected as of the date of the *original* perfection. ◀

The Floating-Lien Concept

A security agreement that provides for a security interest in proceeds, in after-acquired property, or in collateral subject to future advances by the secured party (or in all three) is often characterized as a **floating lien.** This type of security interest continues in the collateral or proceeds even if the collateral is sold, exchanged, or disposed of in some other way.

---

5. See Official Comment 5 to UCC 9–204.

A FLOATING LIEN IN INVENTORY Floating liens commonly arise in the financing of inventories. A creditor is not interested in specific pieces of inventory, which are constantly changing, so the lien "floats" from one item to another, as the inventory changes.

▶ **Example 30.11** Cascade Sports, Inc., an Oregon corporation, operates as a cross-country ski dealer and has a line of credit with Portland First Bank to finance its inventory of cross-country skis. Cascade and Portland First enter into a security agreement that provides for coverage of proceeds, after-acquired inventory, present inventory, and future advances. Portland First perfects its security interest in the inventory by filing centrally with the office of the secretary of state in Oregon. One day, Cascade sells a new pair of the latest cross-country skis and receives a used pair in trade. That same day, Cascade purchases two new pairs of cross-country skis from a local manufacturer for cash. Later that day, to meet its payroll, Cascade borrows $8,000 from Portland First Bank under the security agreement.

Portland First has a perfected security interest in the used pair of skis under the proceeds clause, has a perfected security interest in the two new pairs of skis purchased from the local manufacturer under the after-acquired property clause, and has the new amount of funds advanced to Cascade secured on all of the above collateral by the future-advances clause. All of this is accomplished under the original perfected security interest. The various items in the inventory have changed, but Portland First still has a perfected security interest in Cascade's inventory. Hence, it has a floating lien in the inventory. ◀

A FLOATING LIEN IN A SHIFTING STOCK OF GOODS The concept of the floating lien can also apply to a shifting stock of goods. The lien can start with raw materials, follow them as they become finished goods and inventories, and continue as the goods are sold and are turned into accounts receivable, chattel paper, or cash.

SECTION 5
PRIORITIES

When more than one party claims an interest in the same collateral, which has priority? The UCC sets out detailed rules to answer this question. Although in many situations the party who has a perfected security interest will have priority, there are exceptions that give priority rights to another party, such as a buyer in the ordinary course of business.

General Rules of Priority

The basic rule is that when more than one security interest has been perfected in the same collateral, the first security interest to be perfected (or filed) has priority over any security interests that are perfected later. If only one of the conflicting security interests has been perfected, then that security interest has priority. If none of the security interests have been perfected, then the first security interest that attaches has priority.

The UCC's rules of priority can be summarized as follows:

1. *Perfected security interest versus unsecured creditors and unperfected security interests.* When two or more parties have claims to the same collateral, a perfected secured party's interest has priority over the interests of most other parties [UCC 9–322(a)(2)]. This includes priority to the proceeds from a sale of collateral resulting from a bankruptcy (giving the perfected secured party rights superior to those of the bankruptcy trustee, as will be discussed in Chapter 31).
2. *Conflicting perfected security interests.* When two or more secured parties have perfected security interests in the same collateral, generally the first to perfect (by filing or taking possession of the collateral) has priority [UCC 9–322(a)(1)].
3. *Conflicting unperfected security interests.* When two conflicting security interests are unperfected, the first to attach (be created) has priority [UCC 9–322(a)(3)]. This is sometimes called the "first-in-time" rule.

▶ **Case in Point 30.12** Ag Venture Financial Services, Inc., made multiple loans to a family-owned dairy farm, Montagne Heifers, Inc. (MHI). Michael Montagne owned the business, and his wife and son were shareholders and employees. In 2005, MHI executed a promissory note and security agreement in favor of Ag Venture, which listed all of MHI's accounts, equipment, farm products, inventory, livestock, and proceeds as collateral. In 2006, Montagne and his wife separated, and he signed a separation agreement that gave her some funds and certain parcels of land.

In 2007, Montagne gave his son a promissory note for $100,000 in exchange for his shares in MHI. The note listed all of MHI's equipment, inventory, livestock, and proceeds as collateral.

Also in 2007, Montagne sold a herd of dairy cows for $500,000 and gave his former wife a check for $240,000. In 2008, Montagne filed a petition for bankruptcy, and a dispute arose over which party (Ag Venture, Montagne's son, or Montagne's former wife) was entitled to the proceeds from the 2007 sale of the cows. The court held that because Ag Venture's security interest in the proceeds was the first in time to *attach* (it was created in 2005), Ag Venture had first priority to the proceeds.[6] ◄

Exceptions to the General Priority Rules

Under some circumstances, on the debtor's default, the perfection of a security interest will not protect a secured party against certain other third parties having claims to the collateral. For example, the UCC provides that in some instances a PMSI, properly perfected,[7] will prevail over another security interest in after-acquired collateral, even though the other was perfected first.

BUYERS IN THE ORDINARY COURSE OF BUSINESS
Under the UCC, a person who buys "in the ordinary course of business" takes the goods free from any security interest created by the seller *even if the security interest is perfected and the buyer knows of its existence* [UCC 9–320(a)]. In other words, a buyer in the ordinary course will have priority even if a previously perfected security interest exists as to the goods. The rationale for this rule is obvious: if buyers could not obtain the goods free and clear of any security interest the merchant had created, for example, in inventory, the free flow of goods in the marketplace would be hindered.

As mentioned in Chapter 21, a *buyer in the ordinary course of business* is a person who in good faith, and without knowledge that the sale violates the rights of another in the goods, buys in the ordinary course from a person in the business of selling goods of that kind [UCC 1–201(9)]. Note that the buyer can know about the existence of a perfected security interest, so long as he or she does not know that buying the goods violates the rights of any third party.

▶ **Example 30.13** Dubbs Auto grants a security interest in its inventory to Heartland Bank for a

$300,000 line of credit. Heartland perfects its security interest by filing financing statements with the appropriate state offices. Dubbs uses $9,000 of its credit to buy two used trucks and delivers the certificates of title, which designate Dubbs as the owner, to Heartland. Later, Dubbs sells one of the trucks to Shea Murdoch and another to Michael Laxton. National City Bank finances both purchases. New certificates of title designate the buyers as the owners and Heartland as the "first lienholder," but Heartland receives none of the funds from the sales. If Heartland sues National City, claiming that its security interest in the vehicles takes priority, it will lose. Because Murdoch and Laxton are buyers in the ordinary course of business, Heartland's security interest in the motor vehicles was extinguished when the vehicles were sold to them. ◄

PMSI IN GOODS OTHER THAN INVENTORY AND LIVESTOCK
An important exception to the first-in-time rule involves certain types of collateral, such as equipment, that is not inventory (or livestock) and in which one of the secured parties has a perfected PMSI [UCC 9–324(a)]. ▶ **Example 30.14** Piper Sandoval borrows funds from West Bank, signing a security agreement in which she puts up all of her present and after-acquired equipment as security. On May 1, West Bank perfects this security interest (which is not a PMSI). On July 1, Sandoval purchases a new piece of equipment from Zylex Company on credit, signing a security agreement. The delivery date for the new equipment is August 1.

Zylex thus has a PMSI in the new equipment (which is not part of its inventory), but the PMSI is not in consumer goods and thus is not automatically perfected. If Sandoval defaults on her payments to both West Bank and Zylex, which of them has priority with regard to the new piece of equipment? Generally, West Bank would have priority because its interest perfected first in time. In this situation, however, as long as Zylex perfected its PMSI in the new equipment within twenty days after Sandoval took possession on August 1, Zylex has priority. ◄

PMSI IN INVENTORY
Another important exception to the first-in-time rule has to do with security interests in inventory. A perfected PMSI in inventory has priority over a conflicting security interest in the same inventory. To maintain this priority, the holder of the PMSI must notify the holder of the conflicting security interest on or before the time the debtor takes possession of the inventory [UCC 9–324(b)].

▶ **Example 30.15** On May 1, SNS Electronics borrows funds from Key Bank. SNS signs a security

---

6. *In re Montagne*, 417 Bankr. 214 (D.Vt. 2009).
7. Recall that, with some exceptions (such as motor vehicles), a PMSI in *consumer goods* is automatically perfected—no filing is necessary. A PMSI that is *not* in consumer goods must still be perfected, however.

agreement that puts up all of its present inventory and any after-acquired inventory as collateral. Key Bank perfects its interest (not a PMSI) on that date. On June 10, SNS buys new inventory from Martin, Inc., a manufacturer, to use for its Fourth of July sale. SNS makes a down payment for the new inventory and signs a security agreement giving Martin a PMSI in the new inventory as collateral for the remaining debt. Martin delivers the inventory to SNS on June 28, but SNS's Fourth of July sale is a disaster, and most of its inventory remains unsold. In August, SNS defaults on its payments to both Key Bank and Martin.

Does Key Bank or Martin have priority with respect to the new inventory delivered to SNS on June 28? If Martin has not perfected its security interest by June 28, Key Bank's after-acquired collateral clause has priority because it was the first to be perfected (on May 1). If, however, Martin has perfected *and* gives proper notice of its security interest to Key Bank before SNS takes possession of the goods on June 28, Martin has priority. ◄

BUYERS OF THE COLLATERAL The UCC recognizes that there are certain types of buyers whose interest in purchased goods could conflict with those of a perfected secured party on the debtor's default. These include buyers in the ordinary course of business (as discussed), as well as buyers of farm products, instruments, documents, or securities. The UCC sets down special rules of priority for these types of buyers.

Exhibit 30–4 on the following page describes the various rules regarding the priority of claims to a debtor's collateral.

SECTION 6
RIGHTS AND DUTIES OF DEBTORS AND CREDITORS

The security agreement itself determines most of the rights and duties of the debtor and the secured party. The UCC, however, imposes some rights and duties that are applicable in the absence of a valid security agreement that states the contrary.

Information Requests

At the time of filing, a secured party can also furnish a *copy* of the financing statement and request that the filing officer note the file number, date, and hour of the original filing on the copy [UCC 9–523(a)]. The filing officer must send this copy to the person designated by the secured party or to the debtor, if the debtor makes the request.

The filing officer must also give information to a person who is contemplating obtaining a security interest from a prospective debtor [UCC 9–523(c), (d)]. If requested, the filing officer must issue a certificate (for a fee) that provides information on possible perfected financing statements with respect to the named debtor.

Release, Assignment, and Amendment

A secured party can release all or part of any collateral described in the financing statement, thereby terminating its security interest in that collateral. The release is recorded by filing a uniform amendment form [UCC 9–512, 9–521(b)].

A secured party can also assign all or part of the security interest to a third party (the assignee). The assignee becomes the secured party of record if the assignment is filed by use of a uniform amendment form [UCC 9–514, 9–521(a)].

If the debtor and the secured party agree, they can amend the filing—to add or substitute new collateral, for example—by filing a uniform amendment form that indicates the file number of the initial financing statement [UCC 9–512(a)]. The amendment does not extend the time period of perfection, but if new collateral is added, the perfection date (for priority purposes) for the new collateral begins on the date the amendment is filed [UCC 9–512(b), (c)].

Confirmation or Accounting Request by Debtor

The debtor may believe that the amount of the unpaid debt or the list of the collateral subject to the security interest is inaccurate. The debtor has the right to request a confirmation of the unpaid debt or list of collateral [UCC 9–210]. The debtor is entitled to one request without charge every six months.

The secured party must comply with the debtor's confirmation request by authenticating and sending to the debtor an accounting within fourteen days after the request is received. Otherwise, the secured party can be held liable for any loss suffered by the debtor, plus $500 [UCC 9–210, 9–625(f)].

EXHIBIT 30–4 Priority of Claims to a Debtor's Collateral

Parties	Priority
Perfected Secured Party versus Unsecured Parties and Creditors	A perfected secured party's interest has priority over the interests of most other parties, including unsecured creditors, unperfected secured parties, subsequent lien creditors, trustees in bankruptcy, and buyers who do not purchase the collateral in the ordinary course of business.
Perfected Secured Party versus Perfected Secured Party	Between two perfected secured parties in the same collateral, the general rule is that the first in time of perfection is the first in right to the collateral [UCC 9–322(a)(1)].
Perfected Secured Party versus Perfected PMSI	A PMSI, even if second in time of perfection, has priority providing that the following conditions are met: 1. *Other collateral*—A PMSI has priority, providing it is perfected within twenty days after the debtor takes possession [UCC 9–324(a)]. 2. *Inventory*—A PMSI has priority if it is perfected and proper written or authenticated notice is given to the other security-interest holder on or before the time the debtor takes possession [UCC 9–324(b)]. 3. *Software*—Applies to a PMSI in software only if used in goods subject to a PMSI. If the goods are inventory, priority is determined the same as for inventory. If they are not, priority is determined as for goods other than inventory [UCC 9–103(c), 9–324(f)].

Perfected Secured Party versus Purchaser of Debtor's Collateral	1. *Buyer of goods in the ordinary course of the seller's business*—Buyer prevails over a secured party's security interest, even if perfected and even if the buyer knows of the security interest [UCC 9–320(a)].
	2. *Buyer of consumer goods purchased outside the ordinary course of business*—Buyer prevails over a secured party's interest, even if perfected by attachment, providing the buyer purchased as follows:
	  a. For value.
	  b. Without actual knowledge of the security interest.
	  c. For use as a consumer good.
	  d. Prior to the secured party's perfection by *filing* [UCC 9–320(b)].
	3. *Buyer of chattel paper*—Buyer prevails if the buyer:
	  a. Gave new value in making the purchase.
	  b. Took possession in the ordinary course of the buyer's business.
	  c. Took without knowledge of the security interest [UCC 9–330].
	4. *Buyer of instruments, documents, or securities*—Buyer who is a holder in due course, a holder to whom negotiable documents have been duly negotiated, or a bona fide purchaser of securities has priority over a previously perfected security interest [UCC 9–330(d), 9–331(a)].
	5. *Buyer of farm products*—Buyer from a farmer takes free and clear of perfected security interests unless, where permitted, a secured party files centrally an effective financing statement (EFS) or the buyer receives proper notice of the security interest before the sale.

Unperfected Secured Party versus Unsecured Creditor	An unperfected secured party prevails over unsecured creditors and creditors who have obtained judgments against the debtor but who have not begun the legal process to collect on those judgments [UCC 9–201(a)].

Termination Statement

When the debtor has fully paid the debt, if the secured party perfected the security interest by filing, the debtor is entitled to have a termination statement filed. Such a statement demonstrates to the public that the filed perfected security interest has been terminated [UCC 9–513].

Whenever consumer goods are involved, the secured party *must* file a termination statement (or, alternatively, a release) within one month of the final payment or within twenty days of receiving the debtor's authenticated demand, whichever is earlier [UCC 9–513(b)].

When the collateral is not consumer goods, the secured party is not required to file or to send a termination statement—unless the debtor demands one [UCC 9–513(c)]. Whenever a secured party fails to file or send the termination statement as requested, the debtor can recover $500 plus any additional loss suffered [UCC 9–625(e)(4), (f)].

SECTION 7
DEFAULT

Article 9 defines the rights, duties, and remedies of the secured party and of the debtor on the debtor's default. If the secured party fails to comply with his or her duties, the debtor is afforded particular rights and remedies under the UCC.

What Constitutes Default

What constitutes *default* is not always clear. In fact, Article 9 does not define the term. Consequently, parties are encouraged in practice—and by the UCC—to include in their security agreements the standards under which their rights and duties will be measured [UCC 9–601, 9–603]. In so doing, parties can stipulate the conditions that will constitute a default. Often, these critical terms are shaped by creditors themselves with an attempt to provide the maximum protection possible.

The parties cannot agree to waive or alter certain UCC provisions, however, such as those involving the debtor's right to an accounting or disposition of collateral [UCC 9–602]. In addition, the terms may not run counter to the UCC's provisions regarding good faith and unconscionability.

Any breach of the terms of the security agreement can constitute default. Nevertheless, default occurs most commonly when the debtor fails to meet the scheduled payments that the parties have agreed on or when the debtor becomes bankrupt.

Basic Remedies

The rights and remedies of secured parties under Article 9 are *cumulative* [UCC 9–601(c)]. Therefore, if a creditor is unsuccessful in enforcing rights by one method, she or he can pursue another method. Generally, a secured party's remedies can be divided into the two basic categories discussed next.

REPOSSESSION OF THE COLLATERAL—THE SELF-HELP REMEDY On the debtor's default, a secured party can take possession (peacefully or by court order) of the collateral covered by the security agreement [UCC 9–609(b)]. This provision, because it occurs without the use of the judicial process, is often referred to as the "self-help" provision of Article 9.

The UCC does not define what constitutes *peaceful possession,* however. The general rule is that the collateral has been taken peacefully if the secured party has taken it without committing (1) trespass onto land, (2) assault and/or battery, or (3) breaking and entering.

On taking possession, the secured party may either retain the collateral for satisfaction of the debt [UCC 9–620] or resell the goods and apply the proceeds toward the debt [UCC 9–610].

JUDICIAL REMEDIES Alternatively, a secured party can relinquish the security interest and use any judicial remedy available, such as obtaining a judgment on the underlying debt, followed by execution and levy [UCC 9–601(a)]. (**Execution** is the implementation of a court's decree or judgment. **Levy** is the obtaining of funds by legal process through the seizure and sale of nonexempt property, usually done after a writ of execution has been issued. This writ was discussed in Chapter 29.)

▶ **Example 30.16** Gillian loans funds to Blum to buy a car, using the car as collateral. Blum fails to repay the loan. Gillian can sue Blum for the funds. If that proves unsuccessful, she can repossess the car. In other words, Gillian's attempt to sue Blum does not prevent her from repossessing the car if the suit does not result in satisfaction of the debt. ◀

Disposition of Collateral

Once default has occurred and the secured party has obtained possession of the collateral, the secured party can:

1. Retain the collateral in full or partial satisfaction of the debt (subject to limitations, discussed next).
2. Sell, lease, license, or otherwise dispose of the collateral in any commercially reasonable manner and apply the proceeds toward satisfaction of the debt [UCC 9–602(7), 9–603, 9–610(a), 9–613, 9–620]. Any sale is always subject to procedures established by state law.

RETENTION OF COLLATERAL BY THE SECURED PARTY Parties are sometimes better off if they do not sell the collateral. Therefore, the UCC generally allows secured parties to choose not to sell the collateral. A secured party may retain the collateral unless it consists of consumer goods and the debtor has paid 60 percent or more of the purchase price in a PMSI or debt in a non-PMSI (as will be discussed shortly) [UCC 9–620(e)].

This general right to retain the collateral is subject to several limitations.

Notice Requirements. The secured party must notify the debtor of its proposal to retain the collateral. Notice is required unless the debtor has signed a statement renouncing or modifying her or his rights *after default* [UCC 9–620(a), 9–621].

If the collateral is consumer goods, the secured party does not need to give any other notice. In all other situations, the secured party must also send notice to any other secured party from whom the secured party has received notice of a claim of interest in the collateral in question. The secured party must also send notice to any *junior lienholder* who held a security interest (or statutory lien) in the collateral ten days before the debtor consented to the retention [UCC 9–621]. (A **junior lienholder** is a person holding a lien that is subordinate to one or more other liens on the same property.)

Objections. If, within twenty days after the notice is sent, the secured party receives an objection from the debtor or other party who was notified, the secured party must sell or otherwise dispose of the collateral. (Disposition procedures will be discussed shortly). If no written (or recorded) objection is received, the secured party may retain the collateral in full or partial satisfaction of the debtor's obligation [UCC 9–620(a), 9–621].

CONSUMER GOODS When the collateral is consumer goods and the debtor has paid 60 percent of the purchase price on a PMSI or loan amount, the secured party must sell or otherwise dispose of the repossessed collateral within ninety days [UCC 9–620(e), (f)]. Failure to comply opens the secured party to an action for conversion or other liability under UCC 9–625(b) and (c). A secured party will not be liable, however, if the consumer-debtor signed a written statement *after default* renouncing or modifying the right to demand the sale of the goods [UCC 9–624].

DISPOSITION OF COLLATERAL BY THE SECURED PARTY A secured party who does not choose to retain the collateral or who is required to sell it must dispose of it in a *commercially reasonable* manner. The secured

party must notify the debtor and other specified parties in writing ahead of time about the sale or disposition of the collateral. Notification is not required if the collateral is perishable, will decline rapidly in value, or is of a type customarily sold on a recognized market [UCC 9–611(b), (c)].[8]

Sale Can Be Public or Private. The UCC allows substantial flexibility with regard to disposition. The sale can be public or private. The collateral can be disposed of in its present condition or following any commercially reasonable preparation or processing [UCC 9–610(a)]. The secured party may purchase the collateral at a public sale, but normally not at a private sale [UCC 9–610(c)].

Must Be Commercially Reasonable. Every aspect of the disposition's method, manner, time, and place must be *commercially reasonable* [UCC 9–610(b)]. If the secured party does not dispose of the collateral in a commercially reasonable manner, the price paid for the collateral at the sale may be negatively affected. In that situation, a court can reduce the amount of any deficiency that the debtor owes to the secured party [UCC 9–626(a)(3)].

Although the purpose of requiring a commercially reasonable disposition is to obtain a satisfactory price, the courts look at many factors to determine reasonableness. ▶ **Case in Point 30.17** Shannon Hicklin bought a used Ford Explorer under an installment sales contract. When she fell three payments behind—still owing $5,741.65—Onyx Acceptance Corporation repossessed the car and sold it for $1,500 at a private auction. After deducting the costs of repossession and sale, there was a deficiency under the contract of $5,018.88. Onyx filed a suit to collect this amount from Hicklin.

Onyx claimed that the sale was commercially reasonable because the auction price ($1,500) was more than 50 percent of the estimated market value ($2,335). The court, however, found that the price alone was not enough to prove reasonableness. Onyx needed to show that every aspect of the sale was conducted in a commercially reasonable manner. Alternatively, under UCC 9–627(b)(3), Onyx could show that the sale conformed with the reasonable commercial practices among dealers in that type of property. Because Onyx did not do either, it could not collect any deficiency from Hicklin.[9] ◀

---

8. The debtor may waive the right to receive a notice of disposition, but only after default [UCC 9–624(a)].
9. *Hicklin v. Onyx Corp.*, 970 A.2d 244 (Del.Sup.Ct. 2009).

In the following case, two defaulting debtors alleged that their creditor's sale of the debtors' shares of stock was commercially unreasonable. The debt- ors contended that a different type of sale or a different "inducement" might have attracted a higher price.

CASE ANALYSIS

Case 30.3   Smith v. Firstbank Corp.
Court of Appeals of Michigan, 2013 WL 951377 (2013).

COMPANY PROFILE   Since its founding in Jackson, Michigan, in 1900, Sparton Corporation has designed, developed, and manufactured electronic and electromechanical devices. From prototype through shipment, Sparton has worked with diverse companies in the aerospace, medical, defense, security, navigation, exploration, and industrial markets. Today, Sparton is headquartered in Schaumburg, Illinois. It has more than 1,300 employees and maintains production facilities in the United States and in Vietnam.

IN THE LANGUAGE OF THE COURT
PER CURIAM.

* * * *

The facts in this secured transactions case are not in dispute. Plaintiffs [Bradley Smith, on his own behalf and on behalf of the John J. Smith Revocable Living Trust] borrowed funds from [defendant Firstbank Corporation] in 2002; the notes to defendant were secured with pledges of Sparton Corporation stock as well as other collateral. Plaintiffs defaulted on these loans. Eventually, after many modifications and extensions, defendant took possession of the pledged shares of Sparton stock. Shortly thereafter, defendant sold the stock in two private transactions: on January 12, 2010, it sold 602,170 shares to a brokerage firm at $4.84 per share, and on February 19, 2010, it sold 450,000 shares to a brokerage firm at $5.05 per share. The parties agree that the closing price for Sparton stock on the New York Stock Exchange on both sale dates was $6.05 per share.

Defendant then released the remaining collateral to plaintiffs and remitted to plaintiffs by cashier's check the excess funds collected in the private sales. The value of the collateral retained by plaintiffs was over five million dollars.

Plaintiffs filed suit [in a Michigan state court] against defendant, alleging that the sales violated defendant's contractual duties to plaintiffs because they were "commercially unreasonable" * * * . Defendant moved the trial court for summary disposition [judgment]. * * * The trial court issued an Opinion and Order granting defendant's motion * * * . This appeal followed.

* * * *

At issue in the instant case is the secured party's disposition of collateral after the debtors' default. Defendant, the secured party, was authorized by MCL [Michigan Compiled Laws] 440.9609 [Michigan's version of UCC 9–609] to take possession of the collateral following plaintiffs' default. The parties agree that plaintiffs defaulted in the instant case, and that defendant was within its rights to take possession of the pledged shares.

MCL 440.9610 [Michigan's version of UCC 9–610] governs the disposition of collateral after default, and provides in relevant part: * * *

Every aspect of a disposition of collateral, including the method, manner, time, place, and other terms, must be commercially reasonable.

Further, MCL 440.9627 [Michigan's version of UCC 9–627] provides guidance for determination of whether the disposition of collat- eral was commercially reasonable, and provides in relevant part: * * *

The fact that a greater amount could have been obtained by a collec- tion, enforcement, disposition, or acceptance at a different time or in a different method from that selected by the secured party is not of itself sufficient to preclude the secured party from establishing that the col- lection, enforcement, disposition, or acceptance was made in a commer- cially reasonable manner.

* * * *

* * * *The circumstances surrounding previous sales of Sparton stock on the public market, and concerns about what public sales would do to the share price, rendered defendant's choice to sell in private transactions reasonable. * * * In* 2008, Wachovia [Bank] sold approxi- mately 400,000 shares of Sparton to satisfy plaintiff Smith's debts. The sale required 18 separate transactions over a two-month period; during that period the share price declined by almost 50 percent. * * * *It was not commercially unreasonable for defendant to seek a private sale to avoid this risk.* [Emphasis added.]

Plaintiffs further argue, however, that even if defendant's choice to con- duct a private, bulk sale was reasonable, the manner in which it conducted the private sale was not. * * * The record does not support this contention. An e-mail from Rick Barratt, agent of defendant, to Oberon Securities indi- cated that, in addition to requesting that Oberon bring them a buyer, defen- dant * * * "directed [our investment banker] to bring similar type offers to us as well." In addition, defendant's

Chief Executive Officer testified * * * that "discounts in large transactions, in thinly traded stocks, were common" and that he was advised by employees of Oberon Securities that selling a "block this large would require a discount of 15 to 20 percent."

The evidence thus does not support the contention that defendant did not seek multiple offers or seek to get the best price for the stock. Rather, the evidence shows that defendant * * *

received one offer for Smith's stock, at a discount. Rather than risk public sales and a repeat of what happened in 2008, defendant made the sale. In fact, plaintiffs' contention that defendant did not attempt to garner the best sale price it could is contradicted by the fact that defendant was able to sell the second block of shares (the shares pledged by the trust) for 21 cents more per share, notwithstanding that the closing price for Sparton was exactly

the same on the day of both the first and second sales.

* * * *

* * * Although plaintiffs speculate that public sales would have resulted in a higher price, or that the private buyer could have been induced to pay a higher price, speculation and conjecture are insufficient to allow an opposing party to survive a motion for summary disposition.

Affirmed.

LEGAL REASONING QUESTIONS

1. What type of property was at the center of the dispute in this case? How did that property become involved in the dispute?

2. On what ground did the plaintiffs argue that the bank should not have been granted a summary judgment?

3. Why does collateral have to be disposed of in a commercially reasonable manner? Is price alone enough to prove reasonableness? Why or why not?

4. What factors did the court look at to determine reasonableness in this case? How did the court rule on the issue in this case?

PROCEEDS FROM DISPOSITION Proceeds from the disposition of collateral after default on the underlying debt are distributed in the following order:

1. Reasonable expenses incurred by the secured party in repossessing, storing, and reselling the collateral.
2. Balance of the debt owed to the secured party.
3. Junior lienholders who have made written or authenticated demands.
4. Any surplus to the debtor, unless the collateral consists of accounts, payment intangibles, promissory notes, or chattel paper [UCC 9–608(a); 9–615(a), (e)].

NONCASH PROCEEDS Whenever the secured party receives noncash proceeds from the disposition of collateral after default, the secured party must make a value determination and apply this value in a commercially reasonable manner [UCC 9–608(a)(3), 9–615(c)].

DEFICIENCY JUDGMENT Often, after proper disposition of the collateral, the secured party still has not collected all that the debtor owes. Unless otherwise agreed, the debtor normally is liable for any deficiency,

and the creditor can obtain a **deficiency judgment** from a court to collect the deficiency. Practically speaking, though, debtors who have defaulted on a loan rarely have the cash to pay any deficiency.

Note, however, that if the underlying transaction is a sale of accounts, chattel paper, or promissory notes, the debtor is *not* liable for any deficiency. As noted above, the debtor is also not entitled to any surplus from the disposition of these types of collateral, unless that right is granted by the security agreement [UCC 9–615(e)].

REDEMPTION RIGHTS The debtor or any other secured party can exercise the right of *redemption* of the collateral. Redemption may occur at any time before the secured party disposes of the collateral, enters into a contract for its disposition, or discharges the debtor's obligation by retaining the collateral. To redeem the collateral, the debtor or other secured party must tender the entire obligation that is owed, plus any reasonable expenses and attorneys' fees incurred by the secured party in retaking and maintaining the collateral [UCC 9–623].

Concept Summary 30.2 on the following page provides a review of the secured party's remedies on the debtor's default.

CONCEPT SUMMARY 30.2

Remedies of the Secured Party on the Debtor's Default

CONCEPT	DESCRIPTION

Repossession of the Collateral	The secured party may take possession (peacefully or by court order) of the collateral covered by the security agreement and then pursue one of two alternatives:
	1. Retain the collateral (unless the collateral is consumer goods and the debtor has paid 60 percent of the selling price on a PMSI or 60 percent of the debt on a non-PMSI). To retain the collateral, the secured party must—
	  a. Give notice to the debtor if the debtor has not signed a statement renouncing or modifying his or her rights after default. With consumer goods, no other notice is necessary.
	  b. Send notice to any other secured party who has given written or authenticated notice of a claim to the same collateral or who has filed a security interest or a statutory lien ten days before the debtor consented to the retention. If an objection is received within twenty days from the debtor or any other secured party given notice, the creditor must dispose of the collateral according to the requirements of UCC 9–602, 9–603, 9–610, and 9–613. Otherwise, the creditor may retain the collateral in full or partial satisfaction of the debt.
	2. Dispose of the collateral in accordance with the requirements of UCC 9–602(7), 9–603, 9–610(a), and 9–613. To do so, the secured party must—
	  a. Dispose of (sell, lease, or license) the goods in a commercially reasonable manner.
	  b. Notify the debtor and (except in sales of consumer goods) other identified persons, including those who have given notice of claims to the collateral to be sold (unless the collateral is perishable or will decline rapidly in value).
	  c. Apply the proceeds in the following order:
	    (1) Expenses incurred by the secured party in repossessing, storing, and reselling the collateral.
	    (2) The balance of the debt owed to the secured party.
	    (3) Junior lienholders who have made written or authenticated demands.
	    (4) Surplus to the debtor (unless the collateral consists of accounts, payment intangibles, promissory notes, or chattel paper).

Judicial Remedies	The secured party may relinquish the security interest and proceed with any judicial remedy available, such as obtaining a judgment on the underlying debt, followed by execution and levy on the nonexempt assets of the debtor.

Reviewing: Secured Transactions

Paul Barton owned a small property-management company, doing business as Brighton Homes. In October, Barton went on a spending spree. First, he bought a Bose surround-sound system for his home from KDM Electronics. The next day, he purchased a Wilderness Systems kayak and roof rack from Outdoor Outfitters, and the day after that he bought a new Toyota 4-Runner financed through Bridgeport Auto. Two weeks later, Barton purchased six new iMac computers for his office, also from KDM Electronics. Barton bought each of these items under an installment sales contract. Six months later, Barton's property-management business was failing, and he could not make the payments due on any of these purchases and thus defaulted on the loans. Using the information presented in the chapter, answer the following questions.

1. For which of Barton's purchases (the surround-sound system, the kayak, the 4-Runner, and the six iMacs) would the creditor need to file a financing statement to perfect its security interest?
2. Suppose that Barton's contract for the office computers mentioned only the name *Brighton Homes.* What would be the consequences if KDM Electronics filed a financing statement that listed only Brighton Homes as the debtor's name?
3. Which of these purchases would qualify as a PMSI in consumer goods?
4. Suppose that after KDM Electronics repossesses the surround-sound system, it decides to keep the system rather than sell it. Can KDM do this under Article 9? Why or why not?

DEBATE THIS... *A financing statement that does not have the debtor's exact name should still be effective because creditors should always be protected when debtors default.*

Terms and Concepts

after-acquired property 585
attachment 575
authentication 575
collateral 574
continuation statement 584
cross-collateralization 585
debtor 574
deficiency judgment 593

execution 590
financing statement 574
floating lien 585
junior lienholder 591
levy 590
perfection 576
pledge 581

proceeds 585
purchase-money security
  interest (PMSI) 583
secured party 574
secured transaction 574
security agreement 574
security interest 574

ExamPrep

Issue Spotters

1. Nero needs $500 to buy textbooks and other supplies. Olivia agrees to loan Nero $500, accepting Nero's computer as collateral. They put their agreement in writing. How can Olivia let other creditors know of her interest in the computer? **(See page 576.)**
2. Liberty Bank loans Michelle $5,000 to buy a car, which is used as collateral to secure the loan. After repaying less than 50 percent of the loan, Michelle defaults. Liberty could repossess and keep the car, but the bank does not want it. What are the alternatives? **(See page 591.)**

• Check your answers to the Issue Spotters against the answers provided in Appendix E at the end of this text.

Before the Test

Go to **www.cengagebrain.com**, enter the ISBN 9781285185248, and click on "Find" to locate this textbook's Web site. Then, click on "Access Now" under "Study Tools," and select Chapter 30 at the top. There, you will find a Practice Quiz that you can take to assess your mastery of the concepts in this chapter, as well as Flashcards and a Glossary of important terms.

Business Scenarios

30–1. Priorities. Redford is a seller of electric generators. He purchases a large quantity of generators from a manufacturer, Mallon Corp., by making a down payment and signing an agreement to make the balance of payments over a period of time. The agreement gives Mallon Corp. a security interest in the generators and the proceeds. Mallon Corp. properly files a financing statement on its security interest. Redford receives the generators and immediately sells one of them to Garfield on an installment contract, with payment to be made in twelve equal installments. At the time of the sale, Garfield knows of Mallon's security interest. Two months later, Redford goes into default on his payments to Mallon. Discuss Mallon's rights against Garfield in this situation. **(See page 586.)**

30–2. Perfection of a Security Interest. Marsh has a prize horse named Arabian Knight. Marsh is in need of working capital. She borrows $50,000 from Mendez, who takes possession of Arabian Knight as security for the loan. No written agreement is signed. Discuss whether, in the absence of a written agreement, Mendez has a security interest in Arabian Knight. If Mendez does have a security interest, is it a perfected security interest? Explain. **(See page 576.)**

30–3. The Scope of a Security Interest. Edward owned a retail sporting goods shop. A new ski resort was being constructed in his area, and to take advantage of the potential business, Edward decided to expand his operations. He borrowed a large sum from his bank, which took a security interest in his present inventory and any after-acquired inventory as collateral for the loan. The bank properly perfected the security interest by filing a financing statement. Edward's business was profitable, so he doubled his inventory. A year later, just a few months after the ski resort had opened, an avalanche destroyed the ski slope and lodge. Edward's business consequently took a turn for the worse, and he defaulted on his debt to the bank. The bank then sought possession of his entire inventory, even though the inventory was now twice as large as it had been when the loan was made. Edward claimed that the bank had rights to only half of his inventory. Is Edward correct? Explain. **(See page 584.)**

Business Case Problems

30–4. Spotlight on Radio Shack—Priorities. In June 1995, Michael and Debra Boudreaux, doing business as D&J Enterprises, Inc., bought a retail electronics store operated under a franchise from Radio Shack. The Boudreauxes borrowed from Cabool State Bank to pay for the business and signed loan documents and a financing statement, which identified the Boudreauxes as "Debtors." Elsewhere on the financing statement, the bank identified "D&J Enterprises, Inc., Radio Shack, Dealer, Debra K. Boudreaux, Michael C. Boudreaux" as "Debtors." The statement covered, in part, the store inventory.

Before the end of the year, the Boudreauxes changed the name of their business to Tri-B Enterprises, Inc. In January 1998, the store closed. The next month, Radio Shack terminated the franchise and, despite the lack of a security interest, took possession of the inventory, claiming the Boudreauxes and Tri-B owed Radio Shack $6,394.73. The bank filed a suit in a Missouri state court against Radio Shack, claiming a perfected security interest in the inventory with priority over Radio Shack's claim. Did the bank's security interest take priority over Radio Shack's claim? Why or why not? [*Cabool State Bank v. Radio Shack,* 65 S.W.3d 613 (Mo.App. 2002)] **(See page 586.)**

30–5. Default. Primesouth Bank issued a loan to Okefenokee Aircraft, Inc. (OAI), to buy a plane. OAI executed a note in favor of Primesouth in the amount of $161,306.25 plus interest. The plane secured the note. When OAI defaulted, Primesouth repossessed the plane. Instead of disposing of the collateral and seeking a deficiency judgment, however, the bank retained possession of the plane and filed a suit in a Georgia state court against OAI to enforce the note. OAI did not deny that it had defaulted on the note or dispute the amount due. Instead, OAI argued that Primesouth Bank was not acting in a commercially reasonable manner. According to OAI, the creditor must sell the collateral and apply the proceeds against the debt. What is a secured creditor's obligation in these circumstances? Can the creditor retain the collateral and seek a judgment for the amount of the underlying debt, or is a sale required? Discuss. [*Okefenokee Aircraft, Inc. v. Primesouth Bank,* 296 Ga.App. 782, 676 S.E.2d 394 (2009)] **(See page 590.)**

30–6. Disposition of Collateral. PRA Aviation, LLC, borrowed $3 million from Center Capital Corp. to buy a Gates Learjet 55B. Center perfected a security interest in the plane. Later, PRA defaulted on the loan, and Center obtained possession of the jet. The market, design, and mechanical condition of similar aircraft were reviewed to estimate the jet's value at $1.45 million. The jet was marketed in trade publications, on the Internet, and by direct advertising to select customers for $1.595 million. There were three offers. Center sold the jet to the high bidder for $1.3 million. Was the sale commercially reasonable? Explain. [*Center Capital Corp. v. PRA Aviation, LLC,* 2011 WL 867516 (E.D.Pa. 2011)] **(See page 590.)**

30–7. BUSINESS CASE PROBLEM
WITH SAMPLE ANSWER: Perfecting a Security Interest.

 Thomas Tille owned M.A.T.T. Equipment Co. To operate the business, Tille borrowed funds from Union Bank. For each loan, Union filed a financing statement that included Tille's signature and address, the bank's address, and a description of the collateral. The first loan covered all of Tille's equipment, including "any after-acquired property." The second loan covered a truck crane "whether owned now or acquired later." The third loan covered a "Bobcat mini-excavator." Did these financing statements perfect Union's security interests? Explain. [Union Bank Co. v. Heban, *2012-Ohio-30 (Ohio App. 2012)]* **(See page 576.)**

• **For a sample answer for Problem 30–7, go to Appendix F at the end of this text.**

30–8. Disposition of Collateral. With a loan of 1.4 million euros from Barclays Bank, PLC, Thomas Poynter bought a yacht. The loan agreement gave Barclays multiple stand-alone options on default. One option required the lender to give ten days' advance notice of a sale. A different option permitted the lender to avoid this requirement. When Poynter did not repay the loan, Barclays repossessed the yacht, notified Poynter that it would be sold—but did not specify a date, time, or place—and sold the yacht two months later. The sale price was less than Poynter owed, and Barclays filed a suit in a federal district court for the deficiency. Is Barclays entitled to collect even though it did not give Poynter ten days' advance notice of the sale? Explain. [*Barclays Bank PLC v. Poynter*, 710 F.3d 16 (1st Cir. 2013)] **(See page 590.)**

30–9. A QUESTION OF ETHICS: Priorities.

In 1995, Mark Denton cosigned a $101,250 loan issued by the First Interstate Bank (FIB) in Missoula, Montana, to Denton's friend Eric Anderson. Denton's business assets—a mini-warehouse operation—secured the loan. On his own, Anderson obtained a $260,000 U.S. Small Business Administration (SBA) loan from FIB at the same time. The purpose of both loans was to buy logging equipment so that Anderson could start a business. In 1997, the business failed. As a consequence, FIB repossessed and sold the equipment and applied the proceeds to the SBA loan. FIB then asked Denton to pay the other loan's outstanding balance ($98,460), plus interest. When Denton refused, FIB initiated proceedings to obtain his business assets. Denton filed a suit in a Montana state court against FIB, claiming, in part, that Anderson's equipment was the collateral for the loan that FIB was attempting to collect from Denton. [Denton v. First Interstate Bank of Commerce, 2006 MT 193, 333 Mont. 169, 142 P.3d 797 (2006)] **(See page 586.)**

(a) Denton's assets served as the security for Anderson's loan because Anderson had nothing to offer. When the loan was obtained, Dean Gillmore, FIB's loan officer, explained to them that if Anderson defaulted, the proceeds from the sale of the logging equipment would be applied to the SBA loan first. Under these circumstances, is it fair to hold Denton liable for the unpaid balance of Anderson's loan? Why or why not?

(b) Denton argued that the loan contract was unconscionable and constituted a "contract of adhesion." What makes a contract unconscionable? Did the transaction between the parties in this case qualify? What is a "contract of adhesion"? Was this deal unenforceable on that basis? Explain.

Legal Reasoning Group Activity

30–10. Security Interests. Nick Sabol, doing business in the recording industry as Sound Farm Productions, applied to Morton Community Bank for a $58,000 loan to expand his business. Besides the loan application, Sabol signed a promissory note that referred to the bank's rights in "any collateral." Sabol also signed a letter authorizing Morton Community Bank to execute, file, and record all financing statements, amendments, and other documents required by Article 9 to establish a security interest in his state. Sabol did not sign any other documents, including the financing statement, which contained a description of the collateral. Two years later, without having repaid the loan, Sabol filed for bankruptcy. The bank claimed a security interest in Sabol's sound equipment. **(See page 574.)**

(a) The first group will list all the requirements of an enforceable security interest and explain why each of these elements is necessary.

(b) The second group will determine if Morton Community Bank had a valid security interest.

(c) The third group will discuss whether a bank should be able to execute financing statements on a debtor's behalf without the debtor being present or signing them. Are there are any drawbacks to this practice? Explain.

CHAPTER 31

BANKRUPTCY LAW

Many people in today's economy are struggling to pay their debts. In the old days, debtors were punished and sometimes even sent to prison for failing to pay what they owed. Today, the law provides debtors with numerous rights, some of which were discussed in Chapters 29 and 30. In this chapter, we look at *bankruptcy*—the last resort in resolving debtor-creditor problems.

The right to petition for bankruptcy relief under federal law is an essential aspect of our capitalistic society, in which individuals and businesses have great opportunities for financial success but may also encounter financial difficulties. Therefore, every businessperson should have some understanding of this topic. In this chapter, you will learn about the bankruptcy process. You will also read about how bankruptcy courts are using the Web and social media to communicate with the public.

SECTION 1

THE BANKRUPTCY CODE

Bankruptcy relief is provided under federal law. Although state laws may play a role in bankruptcy proceedings, particularly state laws governing property, the governing law is based on federal legislation.

Article I, Section 8, of the U.S. Constitution gave Congress the power to establish "uniform laws on the subject of bankruptcies throughout the United States." Federal bankruptcy legislation was first enacted in 1898 and since then has undergone several modifications, most recently in the 2005 Bankruptcy Reform Act.[1] Federal bankruptcy laws (as amended) are called the Bankruptcy Code or, more simply, the Code.

Goals of Bankruptcy Law

Bankruptcy law in the United States has two main goals:

1. To protect a debtor by giving him or her a fresh start without creditors' claims.
2. To ensure equitable treatment of creditors who are competing for a debtor's assets.

Thus, the law attempts to balance the rights of the debtor and of the creditors.

Although the twin goals of bankruptcy remain the same, the balance between them shifted somewhat after the 2005 reform legislation. That law was enacted, in part, because of the growing concern that the law allowed too many debtors to avoid paying their debts. Thus, one of the major goals of the reforms was to require more consumers to pay as many of their debts as they possibly could instead of having those debts fully extinguished in bankruptcy.

Bankruptcy Courts

Bankruptcy proceedings are held in federal bankruptcy courts, which are under the authority of U.S. district courts. Rulings from bankruptcy courts can be appealed to the district courts. The bankruptcy court holds the proceedings required to administer the estate of the debtor in bankruptcy (the *estate* consists of the debtor's assets, as will be discussed shortly). For a discussion of how bankruptcy courts are adapting to the use of social media, see this chapter's *Insight into Social Media* feature on the following page.

Bankruptcy court judges are appointed for terms of fourteen years. A bankruptcy court can conduct a jury trial if the appropriate district court has authorized it and the parties to the bankruptcy consent. Bankruptcy courts follow the Federal Rules of

---

1. The full title of the act was the Bankruptcy Abuse Prevention and Consumer Protection Act of 2005, Pub. L. No. 109-8, 119 Stat. 23 (April 20, 2005).

INSIGHT INTO SOCIAL MEDIA
Live Chatting with Your State's Bankruptcy Court

Chatting on social media has become a way of life for most younger people in this country and elsewhere. Online chats preceded social media and are still used at retail Web sites. Today, some tech-savvy employees at bankruptcy courts are using the retail online chat model to answer questions about bankruptcy.

Arizona Was First to Use Live Chats

The U.S. Bankruptcy Court for the District of Arizona started live chatting several years ago. It added live chat to its Web site as part of a strategic initiative to educate the public about bankruptcy. Rather than leaving voice messages, people who access the court's Web site can send and receive text messages via an easy-to-use chat box. The court's goal is to respond to a live chat request within thirty seconds.

In 2011, New Mexico became the second state to add online chatting to its bankruptcy court's Web site. Nevada followed with its live chat in 2012.

The courts that have adopted online chatting average about ten chats a day. Most chats last less than ten minutes.

Who Uses Bankruptcy Court Chat Rooms?

At first, only individuals interested in filing for bankruptcy without an attorney used the live chat services. When paralegals learned that they could get quick answers to their questions online, they also began to use the services.

Then, during the real estate meltdown of the last few years, many real estate lawyers expanded into the area of bankruptcy law, often as a way to help their clients avoid foreclosure through bankruptcy filings. Many of these lawyers also have used live chat to expand their knowledge of bankruptcy law.

The Courts and Facebook

In this age of expanding social media, many courts have created their own Facebook pages. For example, the New Jersey Supreme Court, Superior Court, and Tax Court have a Facebook page that covers all three courts.

Increasingly, bankruptcy courts are posting announcements on their Facebook pages. Anyone who has signed up for Facebook can readily find announcements from the U.S. Bankruptcy Court for the Southern District of Mississippi. Information from the bankruptcy courts for Hawaii, New Mexico, Rhode Island, and Riverside, California, also is available on Facebook.

LEGAL CRITICAL THINKING
INSIGHT INTO TECHNOLOGY

Are there any downsides to live chats with bankruptcy courts? If so, what are they?

Bankruptcy Procedure rather than the Federal Rules of Civil Procedure (discussed in Chapter 3).

Types of Bankruptcy Relief

The Bankruptcy Code is contained in Title 11 of the *United States Code* and has eight chapters. Chapters 1, 3, and 5 of the Code contain general definitional provisions, as well as provisions governing case administration, creditors, the debtor, and the estate. These three chapters normally apply to all kinds of bankruptcies.

Four chapters of the Code set forth the most important types of relief that debtors can seek:

1. Chapter 7 provides for **liquidation** proceedings (the selling of all nonexempt assets and the distribution of the proceeds to the debtor's creditors).

2. Chapter 11 governs reorganizations.
3. Chapter 12 (for family farmers and family fishermen) and 13 (for individuals) provide for the adjustment of debts by persons with regular incomes.[2]

Note that a debtor (except for a municipality) need not be insolvent[3] to file for bankruptcy relief under the Bankruptcy Code. Anyone obligated to a creditor can declare bankruptcy.

---

2. There are no Chapters 2, 4, 6, 8, or 10 in Title 11. Such "gaps" are not uncommon in the *United States Code*. They occur because chapter numbers (or other subdivisional unit numbers) are sometimes reserved for future use when a statute is enacted. (A gap may also appear if a law has been repealed.)

3. The inability to pay debts as they become due is known as *equitable* insolvency. *Balance sheet* insolvency, which exists when a debtor's liabilities exceed assets, is not the test. Thus, debtors whose cash-flow problems become severe may petition for bankruptcy voluntarily or be forced into involuntary bankruptcy even though their assets far exceed their liabilities.

Special Requirements for Consumer-Debtors

A **consumer-debtor** is a debtor whose debts result primarily from the purchase of goods for personal, family, or household use. The Bankruptcy Code requires that the clerk of the court give all consumer-debtors written notice of the general purpose, benefits, and costs of each chapter under which they might proceed. In addition, the clerk must provide consumer-debtors with information on the types of services available from credit counseling agencies.

SECTION 2
LIQUIDATION PROCEEDINGS

Liquidation under Chapter 7 of the Bankruptcy Code is probably the most familiar type of bankruptcy proceeding and is often referred to as an *ordinary,* or *straight, bankruptcy.* Put simply, a debtor in a liquidation bankruptcy turns all assets over to a **bankruptcy trustee,** a person appointed by the court to manage the debtor's funds. The trustee sells the nonexempt assets and distributes the proceeds to creditors. With certain exceptions, the remaining debts are then **discharged** (extinguished), and the debtor is relieved of the obligation to pay the debts.

Any "person"—defined as including individuals, partnerships, and corporations[4]—may be a debtor in a liquidation proceeding. A husband and wife may file jointly for bankruptcy under a single petition. Railroads, insurance companies, banks, savings and loan associations, investment companies licensed by the Small Business Administration, and credit unions *cannot* be debtors in a liquidation bankruptcy, however. Other chapters of the Bankruptcy Code or other federal or state statutes apply to them.

A straight bankruptcy can be commenced by the filing of either a voluntary or an involuntary **petition in bankruptcy**—the document that is filed with a bankruptcy court to initiate bankruptcy proceedings. If a debtor files the petition, the bankruptcy is voluntary. If one or more creditors file a petition to force the debtor into bankruptcy, the bankruptcy is involuntary. We discuss both voluntary and involuntary bankruptcy proceedings under Chapter 7 in the following subsections.

---
4. The definition of *corporation* includes unincorporated companies and associations. It also covers labor unions.

Voluntary Bankruptcy

To bring a voluntary petition in bankruptcy, the debtor files official forms designated for that purpose in the bankruptcy court. The law now requires that *before* debtors can file a petition, they must receive credit counseling from an approved nonprofit agency within the 180-day period preceding the date of filing. Debtors filing a Chapter 7 petition must include a certificate proving that they have received individual or group counseling from an approved agency within the last 180 days (roughly six months).

A consumer-debtor who is filing for liquidation bankruptcy must confirm the accuracy of the petition's contents. The debtor must also state in the petition, at the time of filing, that he or she understands the relief available under other chapters of the Code and has chosen to proceed under Chapter 7.

Attorneys representing the consumer-debtors must file an affidavit stating that they have informed the debtors of the relief available under each chapter of the Bankruptcy Code. In addition, the attorneys must reasonably attempt to verify the accuracy of the consumer-debtors' petitions and schedules (described below). Failure to do so is considered perjury.

CHAPTER 7 SCHEDULES The voluntary petition must contain the following schedules:

1. A list of both secured and unsecured creditors, their addresses, and the amount of debt owed to each.
2. A statement of the financial affairs of the debtor.
3. A list of all property owned by the debtor, including property that the debtor claims is exempt.
4. A list of current income and expenses.
5. A certificate of credit counseling (as discussed previously).
6. Proof of payments received from employers within sixty days prior to the filing of the petition.
7. A statement of the amount of monthly income, itemized to show how the amount is calculated.
8. A copy of the debtor's federal income tax return for the most recent year ending immediately before the filing of the petition.

The official forms must be completed accurately, sworn to under oath, and signed by the debtor. To conceal assets or knowingly supply false information on these schedules is a crime under the bankruptcy laws.

With the exception of tax returns, failure to file the required schedules within forty-five days after the filing of the petition (unless an extension is granted) will result in an automatic dismissal of the petition. The debtor has up to seven days before the date of the first creditors' meeting to provide a copy of the most recent tax returns to the trustee.

TAX RETURNS DURING BANKRUPTCY In addition, a debtor may be required to file a tax return at the end of each tax year while the case is pending and to provide a copy to the court. This may be done at the request of the court or of the **U.S. trustee**—a government official who performs administrative tasks that a bankruptcy judge would otherwise have to perform.

Any *party in interest* (a party, such as a creditor, who has a valid interest in the outcome of the proceedings) may make this request as well. Debtors may also be required to file tax returns during Chapter 11 and 13 bankruptcies.

SUBSTANTIAL ABUSE—MEANS TEST In the past, a bankruptcy court could dismiss a Chapter 7 petition for relief (discharge of debts) if the use of Chapter 7 would constitute a "substantial abuse" of bankruptcy law. Today, the law provides a *means test* to determine a debtor's eligibility for Chapter 7.

The purpose of the test is to keep upper-income people from abusing the bankruptcy process by filing for Chapter 7, as was thought to have happened in the past. The test forces more people to file for Chapter 13 bankruptcy rather than have their debts discharged under Chapter 7.

The Basic Formula. A debtor wishing to file for bankruptcy must complete the means test to determine whether she or he qualifies for Chapter 7. The debtor's average monthly income in recent months is compared with the median income in the geographic area in which the person lives. (The U.S. Trustee Program provides these data at its Web site.) If the debtor's income is below the median income, the debtor usually is allowed to file for Chapter 7 bankruptcy, as there is no presumption of bankruptcy abuse.

Applying the Means Test to Future Disposable Income. If the debtor's income is above the median income, then further calculations must be made to determine whether the person will have sufficient disposable income in the future to repay at least some of his or her unsecured debts. *Disposable income* is calculated by subtracting living expenses and secured debt payments, such as mortgage payments, from monthly income.

In making this calculation, the debtor's recent monthly income is presumed to continue for the next sixty months. Living expenses are the amounts allowed under formulas used by the Internal Revenue Service (IRS). The IRS allowances include modest allocations for food, clothing, housing, utilities, transportation (including a car payment), health care, and other necessities. (The U.S. Trustee Program's Web site also provides these amounts.) The allowances do not include expenditures for items such as cell phones and cable television service.

Can the Debtor Afford to Pay Unsecured Debts? Once future disposable income has been estimated, that amount is used to determine whether the debtor will have income that could be applied to unsecured debts. The courts may also consider the debtor's bad faith or other circumstances indicating abuse.

▶ **Case in Point 31.1** At thirty-three years old, Lisa Hebbring owned a home and a car, but had $11,124 in credit-card debt. Hebbring was earning $49,000 per year when she filed for Chapter 7 bankruptcy. Her petition listed monthly net income of $2,813 and expenditures of $2,897, for a deficit of $84.

In calculating her income, Hebbring excluded a $313 monthly deduction for contributions to retirement plans. The U.S. trustee filed a motion to dismiss Hebbring's petition due to substantial abuse, claiming that the retirement contributions should be disallowed. The court agreed and dismissed the Chapter 7 petition. Because Hebbring's retirement contributions were not reasonably necessary based on her age and financial circumstances, the court found that she was capable of paying her unsecured debts.[5] ◀

ADDITIONAL GROUNDS FOR DISMISSAL As already noted, a court can dismiss a debtor's voluntary petition for Chapter 7 relief for substantial abuse or for failing to provide the necessary documents within the specified time.

In addition, a court might dismiss a Chapter 7 in two other situations. First, if the debtor has been convicted of a violent crime or a drug-trafficking offense, the victim can file a motion to dismiss the voluntary petition.[6] Second, if the debtor fails to pay postpetition domestic-support obligations (which include child and spousal support), the court may dismiss the debtor's petition.

---

5. *Hebbring v. U.S. Trustee,* 463 F.3d 902 (9th Cir. 2006).
6. Note that the court may not dismiss a case on this ground if the debtor's bankruptcy is necessary to satisfy a claim for a domestic-support obligation.

ORDER FOR RELIEF If the voluntary petition for bankruptcy is found to be proper, the filing of the petition will itself constitute an **order for relief.** (An order for relief is a court's grant of assistance to a petitioner.) Once a consumer-debtor's voluntary petition has been filed, the trustee and creditors must be given notice of the order for relief by mail not more than twenty days after entry of the order.

Involuntary Bankruptcy

An involuntary bankruptcy occurs when the debtor's creditors force the debtor into bankruptcy proceedings. An involuntary case cannot be filed against a charitable institution or a farmer (an individual or business that receives more than 50 percent of gross income from farming operations).

An involuntary petition should not be used as an everyday debt-collection device, and the Code provides penalties for the filing of frivolous petitions against debtors. If the court dismisses an involuntary petition, the petitioning creditors may be required to pay the costs and attorneys' fees incurred by the debtor in defending against the petition. If the petition was filed in bad faith, damages can be awarded for injury to the debtor's reputation. Punitive damages may also be awarded.

REQUIREMENTS For an involuntary action to be filed, the following requirements must be met:

1. If the debtor has twelve or more creditors, three or more of these creditors having unsecured claims totaling at least $15,325 must join in the petition.
2. If a debtor has fewer than twelve creditors, one or more creditors having a claim totaling $15,325 or more may file.[7]

ORDER FOR RELIEF If the debtor challenges the involuntary petition, a hearing will be held, and the bankruptcy court will enter an order for relief if it finds either of the following:

1. The debtor is not paying debts as they come due.
2. A general receiver, assignee, or custodian took possession of, or was appointed to take charge of, substantially all of the debtor's property within 120 days before the filing of the petition.

If the court grants an order for relief, the debtor will be required to supply the same information in the bankruptcy schedules as in a voluntary bankruptcy.

Automatic Stay

The moment a petition, either voluntary or involuntary, is filed, an **automatic stay,** or suspension, of all actions by creditors against the debtor or the debtor's property normally goes into effect. In other words, once a petition has been filed, creditors cannot contact the debtor by phone or mail or start any legal proceedings to recover debts or to repossess property. (In some circumstances, a secured creditor or other party in interest may petition the bankruptcy court for relief from the automatic stay, as will be discussed shortly.)

If a creditor *knowingly* violates the automatic stay (a willful violation), any injured party, including the debtor, is entitled to recover actual damages, costs, and attorneys' fees, and may be awarded punitive damages as well. Until the bankruptcy proceeding is closed or dismissed, the automatic stay prohibits a creditor from taking any act to collect, assess, or recover a claim against the debtor that arose before the filing of the petition.

▶ **Case in Point 31.2** Stefanie Kuehn filed for bankruptcy. When she requested a transcript from the university at which she obtained her master's degree, the university refused because she owed more than $6,000 in tuition. Kuehn complained to the court. The court ruled that the university violated the automatic stay by refusing to provide a transcript because it was attempting to collect an unpaid tuition debt.[8] ◀

THE ADEQUATE PROTECTION DOCTRINE Underlying the Code's automatic-stay provision for a secured creditor is a concept known as *adequate protection.* The **adequate protection doctrine,** among other things, protects secured creditors from losing their security as a result of the automatic stay.

The bankruptcy court can provide adequate protection by requiring the debtor or trustee to make periodic cash payments or a one-time cash payment. The court can also require the debtor or trustee to provide additional collateral or replacement liens to the extent that the stay may actually cause the value of the property to decrease.

EXCEPTIONS TO THE AUTOMATIC STAY The Code provides the following exceptions to the automatic stay:

1. Collection efforts can continue for domestic-support obligations, which include any debt owed to or recoverable by a spouse, a former spouse, a

---

7. 11 U.S.C. Section 303. The amounts stated in this chapter are in accordance with those computed on April 1, 2013.

8. *In re Kuehn,* 563 F.3d 289 (7th Cir. 2009).

child of the debtor, that child's parent or guardian, or a governmental unit.

2. Proceedings against the debtor related to divorce, child custody or visitation, domestic violence, and support enforcement are not stayed.

3. Investigations by a securities regulatory agency (see Chapter 42) can continue.

4. Certain statutory liens for property taxes are not stayed.

REQUESTS FOR RELIEF FROM THE AUTOMATIC STAY A secured creditor or other party in interest can petition the bankruptcy court for relief from the automatic stay. If a creditor or other party requests relief from the stay, the stay will automatically terminate sixty days after the request, unless the court grants an extension[9] or the parties agree otherwise.

SECURED PROPERTY The automatic stay on secured property terminates forty-five days after the creditors' meeting (to be discussed shortly). The stay terminates unless the debtor redeems or reaffirms certain debts (*reaffirmation* will be discussed later in this chapter). In other words, the debtor cannot keep the secured property (such as a financed automobile), even if she or he continues to make payments on it, without reinstating the rights of the secured party to collect on the debt.

BAD FAITH If the debtor had two or more bankruptcy petitions dismissed during the prior year, the Code presumes bad faith. In such a situation, the automatic stay does *not* go into effect until the court determines that the petition was filed in good faith.

In addition, the automatic stay on secured debts (see Chapter 30) will terminate thirty days after the petition is filed if the debtor filed a bankruptcy petition that was dismissed within the prior year. Any party in interest can request that the court extend the stay by showing that the filing is in good faith.

Estate in Bankruptcy

On the commencement of a liquidation proceeding under Chapter 7, an *estate in bankruptcy* (sometimes called an *estate in property*) is created. The estate consists of all the debtor's interests in property currently held, wherever located. The estate in bankruptcy includes all of the following:

1. *Community property* (property jointly owned by a husband and wife in certain states—see Chapter 49).

2. Property transferred in a transaction voidable by the trustee.

3. Proceeds and profits from the property of the estate.

Certain after-acquired property—such as gifts, inheritances, property settlements (from divorce), and life insurance death proceeds—to which the debtor becomes entitled *within 180 days after filing* may also become part of the estate.

Generally, though, the filing of a bankruptcy petition fixes a dividing line. Property acquired prior to the filing of the petition becomes property of the estate, and property acquired after the filing of the petition, except as just noted, remains the debtor's.

The Bankruptcy Trustee

Promptly after the order for relief in the liquidation proceeding has been entered, a trustee is appointed. The basic duty of the trustee is to collect the debtor's available estate and reduce it to cash for distribution, preserving the interests of both the debtor and the unsecured creditors. The trustee is held accountable for administering the debtor's estate.

To enable the trustee to accomplish this duty, the Code gives the trustee certain powers, stated in both general and specific terms. These powers must be exercised within two years of the order for relief.

DUTIES FOR MEANS TESTING The trustee is required to promptly review all materials filed by the debtor to determine if there is substantial abuse. Within ten days after the first meeting of the creditors (discussed shortly), the trustee must file a statement indicating whether the case is presumed to be an abuse under the means test. The trustee must provide a copy of this statement to all creditors within five days.

When there is a presumption of abuse, the trustee must either file a motion to dismiss the petition (or convert it to a Chapter 13 case) or file a statement explaining why a motion would not be appropriate. If the debtor owes a domestic-support obligation (such as child support), the trustee must provide written notice of the bankruptcy to the claim holder (a former spouse, for instance).

THE TRUSTEE'S POWERS The trustee has the power to require persons holding the debtor's property at the time the petition is filed to deliver the property

---

9. The court might grant an extension, for example, on a motion by the trustee that the property is of value to the estate.

to the trustee.[10] To enable the trustee to implement this power, the Code provides that the trustee has rights *equivalent* to those of certain other parties, such as a creditor who has a judicial lien. This power of a trustee, which is equivalent to that of a lien creditor, is known as *strong-arm power.*

In addition, the trustee has specific *powers of avoidance*. They enable the trustee to set aside (avoid) a sale or other transfer of the debtor's property and take the property back for the debtor's estate. These powers apply to voidable rights available to the debtor, preferences, and fraudulent transfers by the debtor. Each power is discussed in more detail below. In addition, a trustee can avoid certain statutory liens (creditors' claims against the debtor's property).

The debtor shares most of the trustee's avoidance powers. Thus, if the trustee does not take action to enforce one of the rights just mentioned, the debtor in a liquidation bankruptcy can enforce that right. [11]

VOIDABLE RIGHTS A trustee steps into the shoes of the debtor. Thus, any reason that a debtor can use to obtain the return of her or his property can be used by the trustee as well. These grounds include fraud, duress, incapacity, and mutual mistake.

▶ **Example 31.3** Ben sells his boat to Tara. Tara gives Ben a check, knowing that she has insufficient funds in her bank account to cover the check. Tara has committed fraud. Ben has the right to avoid that transfer and recover the boat from Tara. If Ben files for bankruptcy relief under Chapter 7, the trustee can exercise the same right to recover the boat from Tara, and the boat becomes a part of the debtor's estate. ◀

PREFERENCES A debtor is not permitted to transfer property or to make a payment that favors—or gives a **preference** to—one creditor over others. The trustee is allowed to recover payments made both voluntarily and involuntarily to one creditor in preference over another.

To have made a recoverable preferential payment, an *insolvent* debtor must have transferred property, for a *preexisting* debt, within *ninety days* before the filing of the bankruptcy petition. The transfer must have

given the creditor more than the creditor would have received as a result of the bankruptcy proceedings. The Code presumes that a debtor is insolvent during the ninety-day period before filing a petition.

If a **preferred creditor** (one who has received a preferential transfer from the debtor) has sold the property to an innocent third party, the trustee cannot recover the property from the innocent party. The preferred creditor, however, generally *can* be held accountable for the value of the property.

Preferences to Insiders. Sometimes, the creditor receiving the preference is an insider. An **insider** is an individual, partner, partnership, corporation, or officer or director of a corporation (or a relative of one of these) who has a close relationship with the debtor. In this situation, the avoidance power of the trustee extends to transfers made within *one year* before filing. (If the transfer was fraudulent, as will be discussed shortly, the trustee can avoid transfers made within *two years* before filing.)

If the transfer occurred before the ninety-day period, however, the trustee must prove that the debtor was insolvent when the transfer occurred or that it was made to or for the benefit of an insider.

Transfers That Do Not Constitute Preferences. Not all transfers are preferences. To be a preference, the transfer must be made for something other than current consideration.

Most courts generally assume that payment for services rendered *within fifteen days* before the payment is not a preference. If a creditor receives payment in the ordinary course of business from an individual or business debtor, such as payment of last month's cell phone bill, the bankruptcy trustee cannot recover the payment.

To be recoverable, a preference must be a transfer for an antecedent (preexisting) debt, such as a year-old landscaping bill. In addition, the Code permits a consumer-debtor to transfer any property to a creditor up to a total value of $6,225 without the transfer's constituting a preference. Payment of domestic-support debts does not constitute a preference.

FRAUDULENT TRANSFERS The trustee may avoid fraudulent transfers or obligations if they (1) were made within two years prior to the filing of the petition or (2) were made with actual intent to hinder, delay, or defraud a creditor. ▶ **Example 31.4** April is planning to petition for bankruptcy, so she sells

---

10. Usually, though, the trustee takes constructive, rather than actual, possession of the debtor's property. For example, to obtain control of a debtor's business inventory, a trustee might change the locks on the doors to the business and hire a security guard.

11. Under a Chapter 11 bankruptcy (to be discussed later), for which no trustee other than the debtor generally exists, the debtor has the same avoidance powers as a trustee under Chapter 7. Under Chapters 12 and 13 (also to be discussed later), a trustee must be appointed.

her gold jewelry, worth $10,000, to a friend for $500. The friend agrees that in the future he will "sell" the jewelry back to April for the same amount. This is a fraudulent transfer that the trustee can undo. ◄

Transfers made for less than reasonably equivalent consideration are also vulnerable if the debtor thereby became insolvent or was left engaged in business with an unreasonably small amount of capital. When a fraudulent transfer is made outside the Code's two-year limit, creditors may seek alternative relief under state laws. Some state laws may allow creditors to recover transfers made up to three years before the filing of a petition.

Exemptions

As just described, the trustee takes control of the debtor's property in a Chapter 7 bankruptcy, but an individual debtor is entitled to exempt (exclude) certain property from the bankruptcy. The Bankruptcy Code exempts the following property:[12]

1. Up to $22,975 in equity in the debtor's residence and burial plot (the homestead exemption).
2. Interest in a motor vehicle up to $3,675.
3. Interest, up to $550 for a particular item, in household goods and furnishings, wearing apparel, appliances, books, animals, crops, and musical instruments (the aggregate total of all items is limited, however, to $12,250).
4. Interest in jewelry up to $1,550.
5. Interest in any other property up to $1,225, plus any unused part of the $22,975 homestead exemption up to $11,500.
6. Interest in any tools of the debtor's trade up to $2,300.
7. A life insurance contract owned by the debtor (other than a credit life insurance contract).
8. Certain interests in accrued dividends and interest under, or loan value of, life insurance contracts owned by the debtor, not to exceed $12,250.
9. Professionally prescribed health aids.
10. The right to receive Social Security and certain welfare benefits, alimony and support, certain retirement funds and pensions, and education savings accounts held for specific periods of time.
11. The right to receive certain personal-injury and other awards up to $22,975.

Individual states have the power to pass legislation precluding debtors from using the federal exemptions within the state. A majority of the states have done this. In those states, debtors may use only state, not federal, exemptions. In the rest of the states, an individual debtor (or a husband and wife filing jointly) may choose either the exemptions provided under state law or the federal exemptions.

The Homestead Exemption

The Bankruptcy Code limits the amount of equity that can be claimed under the homestead exemption. In general, if the debtor acquired the homestead within three and a half years preceding the date of filing, the maximum equity exempted is $155,675, even if state law would permit a higher amount.

In addition, the state homestead exemption is available only if the debtor has lived in a state for two years before filing the bankruptcy petition. Furthermore, a debtor who has violated securities laws, been convicted of a felony, or engaged in certain other intentional misconduct may not be permitted to claim the homestead exemption.

Creditors' Meeting

Within a reasonable time after the order for relief has been granted (not more than forty days), the trustee must call a meeting of the creditors listed in the schedules filed by the debtor. The bankruptcy judge does not attend this meeting. The debtor is required to attend (unless excused by the court) and to submit to examination under oath by the creditors and the trustee. At the meeting, the trustee ensures that the debtor is aware of the potential consequences of bankruptcy and of his or her ability to file for bankruptcy under a different chapter of the Bankruptcy Code.

Creditors' Claims

To be entitled to receive a portion of the debtor's estate, each creditor normally files a *proof of claim* with the bankruptcy court clerk within ninety days of the creditors' meeting.[13] A proof of claim is necessary if there is any dispute concerning the claim. The

---

12. The dollar amounts stated in the Bankruptcy Code are adjusted automatically every three years on April 1 based on changes in the Consumer Price Index. The adjusted amounts are rounded to the nearest $25. The amounts stated in this chapter are in accordance with those computed on April 1, 2013.

---

13. This ninety-day rule applies in Chapter 12 and Chapter 13 bankruptcies as well.

proof of claim lists the creditor's name and address, as well as the amount that the creditor asserts is owed to the creditor by the debtor.

When the debtor has no assets—called a "no-asset case"—creditors are notified of the debtor's petition for bankruptcy but are instructed not to file a claim. In no-asset cases, the unsecured creditors will receive no payment, and most, if not all, of these debts will be discharged.

Distribution of Property

The Code provides specific rules for the distribution of the debtor's property to secured and unsecured creditors. If any amount remains after the priority classes of creditors have been satisfied, it is turned over to the debtor. Exhibit 31–1 below illustrates the collection and distribution of property in most voluntary bankruptcies.

DISTRIBUTION TO SECURED CREDITORS The rights of perfected secured creditors were discussed in Chapter 30. The Code requires that consumer-debtors file a statement of intention with respect to the secured collateral. They can choose to pay off the debt and redeem the collateral, claim it is exempt, reaffirm the debt and continue making payments, or surrender the property to the secured party.

If the collateral is surrendered to the secured party, the secured creditor can enforce the security interest.

The secured party can either (1) accept the property in full satisfaction of the debt or (2) sell the collateral and use the proceeds to pay off the debt. Thus, the secured party has priority over unsecured parties as to the proceeds from the disposition of the collateral. Should the collateral be insufficient to cover the secured debt owed, the secured creditor becomes an unsecured creditor for the difference.

DISTRIBUTION TO UNSECURED CREDITORS Bankruptcy law establishes an order of priority for classes of debts owed to *unsecured* creditors, and they are paid in the order of their priority. Each class must be fully paid before the next class is entitled to any of the remaining proceeds.

If there are insufficient proceeds to pay fully all the creditors in a class, the proceeds are distributed *proportionately* to the creditors in that class, and classes lower in priority receive nothing.

In almost all Chapter 7 bankruptcies, the funds will be insufficient to pay all creditors. The order of priority among classes of unsecured creditors is as follows (some of these classes involve cases against bankrupt businesses):

1. Claims for domestic-support obligations, such as child support and alimony.
2. Administrative expenses, including court costs, trustee fees, and attorneys' fees.
3. In an involuntary bankruptcy, expenses incurred by the debtor in the ordinary course of business.

EXHIBIT 31–1 Collection and Distribution of Property in Most Voluntary Bankruptcies

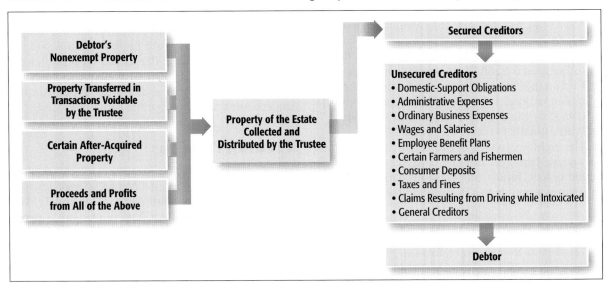

4. Unpaid wages, salaries, and commissions earned within ninety days of the filing of the petition. The amount is capped for each claimant.
5. Unsecured claims for contributions to be made to employee benefit plans. The amount is capped for each claimant.
6. Consumer deposits given to the debtor before the petition was filed. The amount is capped for each claimant.
7. Certain taxes and penalties due to government units, such as income and property taxes.
8. Claims for death or personal injury resulting from the unlawful operation of a motor vehicle.
9. Claims of general creditors.

If any amount remains after the priority classes of creditors have been satisfied, it is turned over to the debtor.

Discharge

From the debtor's point of view, the primary purpose of liquidation is to obtain a fresh start through a discharge of debts. Certain debts, however, are not dischargeable in bankruptcy. Also, certain debtors may not qualify to have all debts discharged in bankruptcy. These situations are discussed next.

EXCEPTIONS TO DISCHARGE Claims that are not dischargeable in bankruptcy include the following:

1. Claims for back taxes accruing within two years prior to bankruptcy.
2. Claims for amounts borrowed by the debtor to pay federal taxes or any nondischargeable taxes.[14]
3. Claims against property or funds obtained by the debtor under false pretenses or by false representations.
4. Claims by creditors who were not notified of the bankruptcy. These claims did not appear on the schedules the debtor was required to file.
5. Claims based on fraud[15] or misuse of funds by the debtor while acting in a fiduciary capacity or claims involving the debtor's embezzlement or larceny.

6. Domestic-support obligations and property settlements as provided for in a separation agreement or divorce decree.
7. Claims for amounts due on a retirement account loan.
8. Claims based on willful or malicious conduct by the debtor toward another or the property of another.
9. Certain government fines and penalties.
10. Student loans, unless payment of the loans imposes an undue hardship on the debtor and the debtor's dependents. (For an example of what constitutes undue hardship, see *Case in Point 31.5* below.)
11. Consumer debts of more than $650 for luxury goods or services owed to a single creditor incurred within ninety days of the order for relief.
12. Cash advances totaling more than $925 that are extensions of open-end consumer credit obtained by the debtor within seventy days of the order for relief.
13. Judgments against a debtor as a result of the debtor's operation of a motor vehicle while intoxicated.
14. Fees or assessments arising from property in a homeowners' association, as long as the debtor retained an interest in the property.
15. Taxes with respect to which the debtor failed to provide required or requested tax documents.

▶ **Case in Point 31.5** Keldric Mosley incurred student loans while attending Alcorn State University and then joined the U.S. Army Reserve Officers' Training Corps. He was injured during training and resigned from the Corps because of medical problems related to his injuries. Mosley worked briefly for several employers, but depressed and physically limited by his injuries, he was unable to keep any of the jobs. A federal bankruptcy court granted him a discharge under Chapter 7, but it did not include the student loans.

Mosley became homeless and had a monthly income of only $210 in disability benefits, but he still owed $45,000 in student loans. He asked the bankruptcy court to reopen his case and discharge his student loans based on undue hardship. The court held that Mosley's medical problems, lack of skills, and "dire living conditions" made it unlikely that he would be able to hold a job and repay the loans. The court therefore discharged the debt, reasoning that Mosley could not maintain a minimal standard of living if forced to repay the loans.[16] ◀

---

14. Taxes accruing within three years prior to bankruptcy are nondischargeable, including federal and state income taxes, employment taxes, taxes on gross receipts, property taxes, excise taxes, customs duties, and any other taxes for which the government claims the debtor is liable in some capacity. See 11 U.S.C. Sections 507(a)(8) and 523(a)(1).

15. Even if a debtor who is sued for fraud settles the lawsuit, the settlement agreement may not be discharged in bankruptcy because of the underlying fraud. See *Archer v. Warner*, 538 U.S. 314, 123 S.Ct. 1462, 155 L.Ed.2d 454 (2003).

---

16. *In re Mosley*, 494 F.3d 1320 (11th Cir. 2007).

OBJECTIONS TO DISCHARGE In addition to the exceptions to discharge previously discussed, a bankruptcy court may also deny the discharge based on the debtor's *conduct.* Grounds for denial of discharge of the debtor include the following:

1. The debtor's concealment or destruction of property with the intent to hinder, delay, or defraud a creditor.
2. The debtor's fraudulent concealment or destruction of financial records.
3. The grant of a discharge to the debtor within eight years before the petition was filed.
4. The debtor's failure to complete the required consumer education course.
5. Proceedings in which the debtor could be found guilty of a felony (basically, a court may not discharge any debt until the completion of felony proceedings against the debtor).

When a discharge is denied under any of these circumstances, the debtor's assets are still distributed to the creditors. After the bankruptcy proceeding, however, the debtor remains liable for the unpaid portion of all claims.

EFFECT OF A DISCHARGE The primary effect of a discharge is to void, or set aside, any judgment on a discharged debt and prohibit any action to collect a discharged debt. A discharge does not affect the liability of a co-debtor.

REVOCATION OF DISCHARGE A discharge may be revoked (taken back) within one year if it is discovered that the debtor acted fraudulently or dishonestly during the bankruptcy proceeding. If revocation occurs, a creditor whose claim was not satisfied in the distribution of the debtor's property can proceed with his or her claim against the debtor.

Reaffirmation of Debt

An agreement to pay a debt dischargeable in bankruptcy is called a **reaffirmation agreement.** A debtor may wish to pay a debt—for example, a debt owed to a family member, physician, bank, or some other creditor—even though the debt could be discharged in bankruptcy. Also, as noted previously, a debtor cannot retain secured property while continuing to pay without entering into a reaffirmation agreement.

PROCEDURES To be enforceable, reaffirmation agreements must be made before the debtor is granted a discharge. The agreement must be signed and filed with the court. Court approval is required unless the debtor is represented by an attorney during the negotiation of the reaffirmation and submits the proper documents and certifications. Even when the debtor is represented by an attorney, court approval may be required if it appears that the reaffirmation will result in undue hardship to the debtor.

When court approval is required, a separate hearing will take place. The court will approve the reaffirmation only if it finds that the agreement will not result in undue hardship to the debtor and that the reaffirmation is consistent with the debtor's best interests.

REQUIRED DISCLOSURES To discourage creditors from engaging in abusive reaffirmation practices, the law provides specific language for disclosures that must be given to debtors entering into reaffirmation agreements. Among other things, these disclosures explain that the debtor is not required to reaffirm any debt. They also inform the debtor that liens on secured property, such as mortgages and cars, will remain in effect even if the debt is not reaffirmed.

The reaffirmation agreement must disclose the amount of the debt reaffirmed, the rate of interest, the date payments begin, and the right to rescind. The disclosures also caution the debtor: "Only agree to reaffirm a debt if it is in your best interest. Be sure you can afford the payments you agree to make."

The original disclosure documents must be signed by the debtor, certified by the debtor's attorney, and filed with the court at the same time as the reaffirmation agreement. A reaffirmation agreement that is not accompanied by the original signed disclosures will not be effective.

SECTION 3
REORGANIZATIONS

The type of bankruptcy proceeding most commonly used by corporate debtors is the Chapter 11 *reorganization.* In a reorganization, the creditors and the debtor formulate a plan under which the debtor pays a portion of the debts and is discharged of the remainder. The debtor is allowed to continue in business. Although this type of bankruptcy is generally a corporate reorganization, any debtor (except a stockbroker or a commodities broker) who is eligible for Chapter 7 relief is eligible for relief under Chapter 11. Railroads are also eligible.

Congress has established a "fast-track" Chapter 11 procedure for small-business debtors whose liabilities do not exceed $2.49 million and who do not own or manage real estate. The fast track enables a debtor to avoid the appointment of a creditors' committee and also shortens the filing periods and relaxes certain other requirements. Because the process is shorter and simpler, it is less costly.

The same principles that govern the filing of a liquidation (Chapter 7) petition apply to reorganization (Chapter 11) proceedings. The case may be brought either voluntarily or involuntarily. The automatic-stay provisions and its exceptions (such as substantial abuse), as well as the adequate protection doctrine apply in reorganizations.

Workouts

In some instances, to avoid bankruptcy proceedings, creditors may prefer private, negotiated adjustments of creditor-debtor relations, also known as **workouts.** Often, these out-of-court workouts are much more flexible and thus more conducive to a speedy settlement. Speed is critical because delay is one of the most costly elements in any bankruptcy proceeding. Another advantage of workouts is that they avoid the various administrative costs of bankruptcy proceedings.

Best Interests of the Creditors

Once a petition for Chapter 11 bankruptcy has been filed, a bankruptcy court, after notice and a hearing, can dismiss or suspend all proceedings at any time if dismissal or suspension would better serve the interests of the creditors. The Code also allows a court, after notice and a hearing, to dismiss a case under reorganization "for cause" when there is no reasonable likelihood of rehabilitation. Similarly, a court can dismiss when there is an inability to effect a plan or an unreasonable delay by the debtor that may harm the interests of creditors. A debtor whose petition is dismissed for these reasons can file a subsequent Chapter 11 petition in the future, however.[17]

Debtor in Possession

On entry of the order for relief, the debtor generally continues to operate the business as a **debtor in possession (DIP).** The court, however, may appoint a trustee (often referred to as a *receiver*) to operate the debtor's business if gross mismanagement of the business is shown or if appointing a trustee is in the best interests of the estate.

The DIP's role is similar to that of a trustee in a liquidation.[18] The DIP is entitled to avoid preferential payments made to creditors and fraudulent transfers of assets. The DIP has the power to decide whether to cancel or assume obligations under prepetition executory contracts (those that are not yet performed) or unexpired leases. The DIP can also exercise a trustee's strong-arm powers.

Creditors' Committees

As soon as practicable after the entry of the order for relief, a creditors' committee of unsecured creditors is appointed.[19] This committee is often composed of the biggest suppliers to the business. The committee may consult with the trustee or the DIP concerning the administration of the case or the formulation of the plan. Additional creditors' committees may be appointed to represent special interest creditors.

Generally, no orders affecting the estate will be entered without the consent of the committee or after a hearing in which the judge is informed of the committee's position. As mentioned earlier, businesses with debts of less than $2.49 million that do not own or manage real estate can avoid creditors' committees. In these cases, orders can be entered without a committee's consent.

The Reorganization Plan

A reorganization plan to rehabilitate the debtor is a plan to conserve and administer the debtor's assets in the hope of an eventual return to successful operation and solvency. The plan must be fair and equitable and must do the following:

1. Designate classes of claims and interests.
2. Specify the treatment to be afforded to the classes of creditors. (The plan must provide the same treatment for all claims in a particular class.)
3. Provide an adequate means for the plan's execution. (Individual debtors are required to utilize postpetition assets as necessary to execute the plan.)
4. Provide for payment of tax claims over a five-year period.

---

17. See 11 U.S.C. Section 1112(b).

18. 11 U.S.C. Section 544(a).
19. If the debtor has filed a reorganization plan accepted by the creditors, the trustee may decide not to call a meeting of the creditors.

FILING THE PLAN Only the debtor may file a plan within the first 120 days after the date of the order for relief. This period may be extended, but not beyond eighteen months from the date of the order for relief. If the debtor does not meet the 120-day deadline or obtain an extension, and if the debtor fails to procure the required creditor consent (discussed next) within 180 days, any party may propose a plan. If a small-business debtor chooses to avoid a creditors' committee, the time for the debtor's filing is 180 days.

ACCEPTANCE OF THE PLAN Once the plan has been developed, it is submitted to each class of creditors for acceptance. For the plan to be adopted, each class must accept it. A class has accepted the plan when a majority of the creditors, representing two-thirds of the amount of the total claim, vote to approve it.

The plan need not provide for full repayment to unsecured creditors. Instead, creditors receive a percentage of each dollar owed to them by the debtor.

CONFIRMATION OF THE PLAN Confirmation is conditioned on the debtor's certifying that all postpetition domestic-support obligations have been paid in full. Even when all classes of creditors accept the plan, the court may refuse to confirm it if it is not "in the best interests of the creditors." For small-business debtors, if the plan meets the listed requirements, the court must confirm the plan within forty-five days (unless this period is extended).

The plan can be modified on the request of the debtor, the DIP, the trustee, the U.S. trustee, or a holder of an unsecured claim. If an unsecured creditor objects to the plan, specific rules apply to the value of property to be distributed under the plan. Tax claims must be paid over a five-year period.

Even if only one class of creditors has accepted the plan, the court may still confirm the plan under the Code's so-called **cram-down provision.** In other words, the court may confirm the plan over the objections of a class of creditors. Before the court can exercise this right of cram-down confirmation, it must be demonstrated that the plan does not discriminate unfairly against any creditors and is fair and equitable.

DISCHARGE The plan is binding on confirmation. Nevertheless, the law provides that confirmation of a plan does not discharge an individual debtor. *For individual debtors, the plan must be completed before discharge will be granted,* unless the court orders oth-

erwise. For all other debtors, the court may order discharge at any time after the plan is confirmed.

The debtor is given a reorganization discharge from all claims not protected under the plan. This discharge does not apply to any claims that would be denied discharge under liquidation.

BANKRUPTCY RELIEF UNDER CHAPTER 13 AND CHAPTER 12

In addition to bankruptcy relief through liquidation and reorganization, the Code also provides for individuals' repayment plans (Chapter 13) and family-farmer and family-fisherman debt adjustments (Chapter 12).

Individuals' Repayment Plans

Chapter 13 of the Bankruptcy Code provides for "Adjustment of Debts of an Individual with Regular Income." Individuals (not partnerships or corporations) with regular income who owe fixed (liquidated) unsecured debts of less than $383,175 or fixed secured debts of less than $1,149,525 may take advantage of bankruptcy repayment plans.

Among those eligible are salaried employees and sole proprietors, as well as individuals who live on welfare, Social Security, fixed pensions, or investment income. Many small-business debtors have a choice of filing under either Chapter 11 or Chapter 13. Repayment plans offer some advantages because they are less expensive and less complicated than reorganization or liquidation proceedings.

FILING THE PETITION A Chapter 13 repayment plan case can be initiated only by the debtor's filing of a voluntary petition or by court conversion of a Chapter 7 petition (because of a finding of substantial abuse under the means test, for example). Certain liquidation and reorganization cases may be converted to repayment plan cases with the consent of the debtor.[20]

A trustee, who will make payments under the plan, must be appointed. On the filing of a repayment plan petition, the automatic stay previously discussed takes effect. Although the stay applies to all or part of the debtor's consumer debt, it does not apply to

---

20. A Chapter 13 repayment plan may be converted to a Chapter 7 liquidation at the request of the debtor or, under certain circumstances, by a creditor "for cause." A Chapter 13 case may be converted to a Chapter 11 case after a hearing.

any business debt incurred by the debtor or to any domestic-support obligations.

GOOD FAITH REQUIREMENT The Bankruptcy Code imposes the requirement of good faith on a debtor at both the time of the filing of the petition and the time of the filing of the plan. The Code does not define good faith, but if the circumstances on the whole indicate bad faith, a court can dismiss a debtor's Chapter 13 petition.

▶ **Case in Point 31.6** Roger and Pauline Buis formed an air show business, Otto Airshows, that included a helicopter decorated as "Otto the Clown." After a competitor won a defamation lawsuit against the Buises and Otto Airshows, the Buises stopped doing business as Otto Airshows.

The Buises formed a new firm, Prop and Rotor Aviation, Inc., and leased the Otto equipment to it.

Within a month, they filed a bankruptcy petition under Chapter 13. The plan and the schedules failed to mention the lawsuit, the equipment lease, and several other items. The court therefore dismissed the Buises' petition due to bad faith. The debtors had not included all of their assets and liabilities on their initial petition, and they had timed its filing to avoid payment on the defamation judgment.[21] ◀

In determining whether a Chapter 13 plan was proposed in good faith, should the bankruptcy court consider whether the debtor included his Social Security income in the amount of disposable income available for payment of unsecured creditors? That was the issue in the following case.

---

21. *In re Buis,* 337 Bankr. 243 (N.D.Fla. 2006).

CASE ANALYSIS

Case 31.1 *In re* Welsh

United States Court of Appeals, Ninth Circuit, 711 F.3d 1120 (2013).

IN THE LANGUAGE OF THE COURT
RIPPLE, Senior Circuit Judge:
* * * *

[David and Sharon Welsh] filed a voluntary Chapter 13 petition [in a federal bankruptcy court]. Their required schedules revealed the following assets: a home in Missoula, Montana, valued at $400,000, encumbered by a secured claim of $330,593.66; a Ford F-250 valued at $10,000, encumbered by a secured claim of $18,959; a 2006 Subaru Outback valued at of $9,500, encumbered by a secured claim of $12,211; a 2005 Toyota Matrix valued at $2,200, encumbered by a secured claim of $1,996; a 2005 Airstream trailer valued at $23,000, encumbered by a secured claim of $39,000; and two 2007 Honda ATVs each valued at $2,700, encumbered by secured claims of $3,065 and $4,500. In addition to their secured debts, the schedules revealed unsecured claims totaling approximately $180,500, the largest of which were their daughter's

student loan debt in the amount of $60,000 and a joint debt owed to Bank of America on a line of credit in the amount of $50,000.

Mrs. Welsh is employed as a nurse and reported on Schedule I a monthly income of $6,975.40. She also draws a pension of $1,100 per month. Mr. Welsh is retired, but listed a monthly income of $358.03 from wages, salary and commissions, as well as Social Security income in the amount of $1,165.

Because their income exceeds the median for the state of Montana, the debtors calculated their disposable income according to the means test. * * * They listed their current monthly income as $8,116.31; their current monthly income did not include Mr. Welsh's Social Security income of $1,165 because Social Security income is excluded from the current monthly income calculation. After deducting future payments on secured claims, the debtors were left with a disposable income of $218.12 per month.

The Welshes proposed a plan that provided for payments of $125 per month to unsecured creditors for the first thirty months of the plan. After their vehicle loans were paid, the payments would increase to $500 per month for the last thirty months of the plan. The proposed plan would pay off approximately $14,700 of the debtors' $180,500 unsecured debt.

The [Bankruptcy] Trustee objected on the ground that the debtors had not proposed their plan in good faith * * * because [they failed] to commit one hundred percent of their disposable income to the plan.
* * * *

The bankruptcy court * * * rejected the Trustee's argument.

[On the Trustee's appeal] the [Bankruptcy Appellate Panel (BAP) for the Ninth Circuit] affirmed the bankruptcy court's judgment.
* * * *

In this appeal, the Trustee * * * maintains that, in determining whether the Welshes proposed their Chapter 13

CASE 31.1 CONTINUES ▶

CASE 31.1 CONTINUED

plan in good faith, the bankruptcy court * * * should have considered Mr. Welsh's Social Security income.

* * * *

In 2005, Congress * * * enacted the Bankruptcy Abuse Prevention and Consumer Protection Act ("BAPCPA"). The good faith requirement * * * remained the same, but there were significant changes with respect to the calculation of disposable income. Before the BAPCPA, bankruptcy judges had authority to determine a debtor's ability to pay based on the individual circumstances of each case and each debtor. Congress replaced this discretion with a detailed, mechanical means test, which requires debtors with above-median income to calculate their "disposable income" by subtracting specific expenses from "current monthly income," as defined by the Bankruptcy Code. For our purposes, several elements of this calculation are important. *The debtor begins with his "current monthly income," which, by definition, explicitly "excludes benefits received under the Social Security Act."* The debtor then subtracts living expenses based on the Internal Revenue Service's "Collection

Financial Standards," a detailed series of averages for living expenses that the Service uses to calculate necessary expenditures for delinquent taxpayers. The debtor also subtracts his averaged payments to secured creditors due during the following sixty months. [Emphasis added.]

As is the case here, the manner in which the means test calculates "disposable income" may underestimate the amount of actual funds that a taxpayer has available to pay unsecured creditors. A debtor who receives Social Security income * * * does not have to account for that income when calculating "disposable income" according to the means test. * * * The result may be that * * * little "disposable income," as that figure is calculated, remains to pay unsecured creditors.

* * * *

Here, the Trustee does not contend, of course, that the calculation of disposable income should have incorporated Social Security income; the statutory language is clearly to the contrary. Instead, he concedes that disposable income was calculated correctly under the BAPCPA, but nevertheless maintains that the Welshes'

failure to dedicate Mr. Welsh's Social Security income to the payment of unsecured creditors requires a conclusion that the plan was not proposed in good faith * * * . We cannot conclude, however, that a plan prepared completely in accordance with the very detailed calculations that Congress set forth is not proposed in good faith. To hold otherwise would be to allow the bankruptcy court to substitute its judgment of how much and what kind of income should be dedicated to the payment of unsecured creditors for the judgment of Congress. Such an approach would not only flout the express language of Congress, but also one of Congress's purposes in enacting the BAPCPA, namely to reduce the amount of discretion that bankruptcy courts previously had over the calculation of an above-median debtor's income and expenses.

* * * *

We conclude that Congress's adoption of the BAPCPA forecloses a court's consideration of a debtor's Social Security income * * * as part of the inquiry into good faith * * * . We therefore affirm the judgment of the BAP.

LEGAL REASONING QUESTIONS

1. What Bankruptcy Code requirements were at the center of this case?
2. On what ground did the trustee contend that the debtors had not proposed their Chapter 13 plan in good faith?
3. How did the court rule with respect to the trustee's argument? Why?
4. In evaluating a debtor's petition, what factors should be part of a good faith analysis? Should consideration of the calculation of disposable income play a role? Why or why not?

THE REPAYMENT PLAN A plan of rehabilitation by repayment must provide for the following:

1. The turning over to the trustee of such future earnings or income of the debtor as is necessary for execution of the plan.
2. Full payment through deferred cash payments of all claims entitled to priority, such as taxes.[22]

3. Identical treatment of all claims within a particular class. (The Code permits the debtor to list co-debtors, such as guarantors or sureties, as a separate class.)

The repayment plan may provide either for payment of all obligations in full or for payment of a lesser amount. The debtor must begin making payments under the proposed plan within thirty days after the plan has been filed and must continue to make "timely" payments from her or his disposable

---

22. As with a Chapter 11 reorganization plan, full repayment of all claims is not always required.

income. If the debtor fails to make timely payments or to commence payments within the thirty-day period, the court can convert the case to a liquidation (Chapter 7) bankruptcy or dismiss the petition.

In putting together a repayment plan, a debtor must apply the means test to identify the amount of disposable income that will be available to repay creditors. The debtor is allowed to deduct certain expenses from monthly income to arrive at this amount. Can a debtor who owns a car outright claim costs of car ownership as an expense? That was the issue in the following case.

CASE 31.2

Ransom v. FIA Card Services, N.A.
Supreme Court of the United States, __ U.S. ___, 131 S.Ct. 716, 178 L.Ed.2d 603 (2011).

BACKGROUND AND FACTS Jason Ransom filed a petition in a federal bankruptcy court to declare bankruptcy under Chapter 13. Among his assets, Ransom reported a Toyota Camry that he owned free of any debt. In listing monthly expenses for the means test, he claimed a car-ownership deduction of $471 and a separate $388 deduction for car-operating costs. Based on his means-test calculations, Ransom proposed a five-year plan that would repay about 25 percent of his unsecured debt. He listed FIA Card Services, N.A., as an unsecured creditor. FIA objected to Ransom's plan, arguing that he should not have claimed the car-ownership allowance because he did not make payments on his car. The court agreed with FIA and issued a decision in its favor. A Bankruptcy Appellate Panel and the U.S. Court of Appeals for the Ninth Circuit affirmed the decision. Ransom appealed to the United States Supreme Court.

 IN THE LANGUAGE OF THE COURT
Justice *KAGAN* delivered the opinion of the Court.
* * * *

[Under the Bankruptcy Code] a debtor may claim not all, but only "applicable" expense amounts * * * .
* * * *

What makes an expense amount "applicable" * * * (appropriate, relevant, suitable, or fit) is most naturally understood to be its correspondence to an individual debtor's financial circumstances. * * * A debtor may claim a deduction * * * only if that deduction is appropriate for him. And a deduction is so appropriate * * * only if the debtor will incur that kind of expense during the life of the plan.

If Congress had * * * omitted the term "applicable" * * * all debtors would be eligible to claim a deduction for each category [listed in the tables of standardized expense amounts that a debtor can claim as reasonable living expenses and shielded from creditors]. Interpreting the statute to require a threshold determination of eligibility ensures that the term "applicable" carries meaning, as each word in a statute should.

This reading draws support from the statute's context and purpose. The Code initially defines a debtor's disposable income as his "current monthly income * * * less amounts reasonably necessary to be expended." The statute then instructs that "amounts reasonably necessary to be expended * * * shall be determined in accordance with" the means test. Because Congress intended the means test to approximate the debtor's reasonable expenditures on essential items, a debtor should be required to qualify for a deduction by actually incurring an expense in the relevant category.

Finally, consideration of the [Bankruptcy Code's] purpose strengthens our reading of the term "applicable." *Congress designed the means test to measure debtors' disposable income and, in that way, to ensure that they repay creditors the maximum they can afford. This purpose is best achieved by interpreting the means test, consistent with the statutory text, to reflect a debtor's ability to afford repayment.* [Emphasis added.]
* * * *

Because Ransom owns his vehicle free and clear of any encumbrance, he incurs no expense in the "Ownership Costs" category * * * . Accordingly, the car-ownership expense amount is not "applicable" to him.

CASE 31.2 CONTINUES ▶

CASE 31.2 CONTINUED

DECISION AND REMEDY *The United States Supreme Court affirmed the lower court's decision. A debtor who does not make loan or lease payments may not take a car-ownership deduction. In Ransom's case, the ultimate result was that confirmation of his repayment plan was denied. (Confirmation of repayment plans is discussed below.)*

THE ECONOMIC DIMENSION *Should debtors with older vehicles be allowed to take an additional deduction for operating expenses? Explain.*

THE CULTURAL DIMENSION *What argument might be made in favor of allowing a debtor who lives outside an area with mass transit to claim a deduction in the "Ownership Costs" category for a car that he or she owns free and clear?*

Length of the Plan. The length of the payment plan can be three or five years, depending on the debtor's family income. If the debtor's family income is greater than the median family income in the relevant geographic area under the means test, the term of the proposed plan must be for five years.[23] The term may not exceed five years.

Confirmation of the Plan. After the plan is filed, the court holds a confirmation hearing, at which interested parties (such as creditors) may object to the plan. The hearing must be held at least twenty days, but no more than forty-five days, after the meeting of the creditors. The debtor must have filed all prepetition tax returns and paid all postpetition domestic-support obligations before a court will confirm any plan.

The court will confirm a plan with respect to each claim of a secured creditor under any of the following circumstances:

1. If the secured creditors have accepted the plan.
2. If the plan provides that secured creditors retain their liens until there is payment in full or until the debtor receives a discharge.

---

23. See 11 U.S.C. Section 1322(d) for details on when the court will find that the Chapter 13 plan should extend to a five-year period.

3. If the debtor surrenders the property securing the claims to the creditors.

In addition, for a motor vehicle purchased within 910 days before the petition is filed, the plan must provide that a creditor with a purchase-money security interest (PMSI—discussed in Chapter 30) retains its lien until the entire debt is paid. For PMSIs on other personal property, the payment plan must cover debts incurred within a one-year period preceding the filing.

DISCHARGE After the debtor has completed all payments, the court grants a discharge of all debts provided for by the repayment plan. Generally, all debts are dischargeable except the following:

1. Allowed claims not provided for by the plan.
2. Certain long-term debts provided for by the plan.
3. Certain tax claims and payments on retirement accounts.
4. Claims for domestic-support obligations.
5. Debts related to injury or property damage caused while driving under the influence of alcohol or drugs.

In the following case, the issue before the United States Supreme Court was whether the discharge of certain student loan debt had been rendered void by a legal error on the part of the bankruptcy court.

CASE 31.3

United Student Aid Funds, Inc. v. Espinosa
Supreme Court of the United States, 559 U.S. 260, 130 S.Ct. 1367, 176 L.Ed.2d 158 (2010).

BACKGROUND AND FACTS Francisco Espinosa filed a petition for an individual repayment plan under Chapter 13 of the Bankruptcy Code. His plan proposed to pay only the principal of his student loan debt and to discharge the interest on the loan. United Student Aid Funds, Inc. (the creditor), had notice of the plan and did not object. Without finding that payment of the interest would cause undue

CASE 31.3 CONTINUED

hardship (as required under the Code), the court confirmed the plan. Years later, however, United filed a motion under Federal Rule of Civil Procedure 60(b)(4) asking the bankruptcy court to rule that its order confirming the plan was void because the order was issued in violation of the laws and rules governing bankruptcy. The court denied United's petition and ordered the creditor to cease its collection efforts. United appealed, and the case ultimately reached the United States Supreme Court.

IN THE LANGUAGE OF THE COURT
Justice *THOMAS* delivered the opinion of the Court.

* * * *

A discharge under Chapter 13 "is broader than the discharge received in any other chapter." Chapter 13 nevertheless restricts or prohibits entirely the discharge of certain types of debts. As relevant here, [Section] 1328(a) [of the Bankruptcy Code] provides that when a debtor has completed the repayments required by a confirmed plan, a bankruptcy court "shall grant the debtor a discharge of all debts provided for by the plan or disallowed under Section 502 of this title, except," *inter alia* [among others], "any debt * * * of the kind specified in [Section] 523(a)(8). [That section], in turn, specifies certain student loan debts "unless excepting such debt from discharge * * * would impose an undue hardship on the debtor and the debtor's dependents." * * * *[The] Bankruptcy Rules require a party seeking to determine the dischargeability of a student loan debt to commence an adversary proceeding by serving a summons and complaint on affected creditors.* We must decide whether the Bankruptcy Court's order confirming Espinosa's plan is "void" under Federal Rule of Civil Procedure 60(b)(4) because the Bankruptcy Court confirmed the plan without complying with these requirements. [Emphasis added.]

The Bankruptcy Court's order confirming Espinosa's proposed plan was a final judgment, from which United did not appeal. * * * Rule 60(b)(4)—the provision under which United brought this motion—authorizes the court to relieve a party from a final judgment if "the judgment is void."

* * * *

"A judgment is not void * * * simply because it is or may have been erroneous." Similarly, a motion under Rule 60(b)(4) is not a substitute for a timely appeal. Instead, Rule 60(b)(4) applies only in the rare instance where a judgment is premised either on a certain type of jurisdictional error or on a violation of due process that deprives a party of notice or the opportunity to be heard.

* * * *

Unable to demonstrate a jurisdictional error or a due process violation, United and the Government, as *amicus* [friend of the court], urge us to expand the universe of judgment defects that support Rule 60(b)(4) relief. Specifically, they contend that the Bankruptcy Court's confirmation order is void because the court lacked statutory authority to confirm Espinosa's plan absent a finding of undue hardship.

* * * *

*Given the Code's clear * * * requirement for an undue hardship determination, the Bankruptcy Court's failure to find undue hardship before confirming Espinosa's plan was a legal error. But the order remains enforceable and binding on United because United had notice of the error and failed to object or timely appeal.* [Emphasis added.]

United's response—that it had no obligation to object to Espinosa's plan until Espinosa served it with the summons and complaint the Bankruptcy Rules require—is unavailing [fails to achieve the desired result]. Rule 60(b)(4) does not provide a license for litigants to sleep on their rights. United had actual notice of the filing of Espinosa's plan, its contents, and the Bankruptcy Court's subsequent confirmation of the plan. In addition, United filed a proof of claim regarding Espinosa's student loan debt, thereby submitting itself to the Bankruptcy Court's jurisdiction with respect to that claim. United therefore forfeited its arguments regarding the validity of service or the adequacy of the Bankruptcy Court's procedures by failing to raise a timely objection in that court.

CASE 31.3 CONTINUES ➡

CASE 31.3 CONTINUED **DECISION AND REMEDY** *The United States Supreme Court affirmed the judgment of the lower court. The bankruptcy court's order confirming Espinosa's Chapter 13 repayment plan was not void, and the student loan debt was thus discharged.*

THE ETHICAL DIMENSION *At one point, United argued that if the Court failed to declare the bankruptcy court's order void, it would encourage dishonest debtors to abuse the Chapter 13 process. How might such abuse occur? Discuss whether the possibility of such abuse should affect the Court's decision.*

MANAGERIAL IMPLICATIONS *Business owners and managers should be aware that courts generally have little sympathy for those who "sleep on their rights." In this case, the creditor could have objected to the plan, but it did not. The creditor also could have appealed the confirmation order, but it did not. Only years later did the creditor seek to have the confirmation order declared void. If a client or other debtor petitions for bankruptcy relief, businesspersons should protect their rights by responding promptly to any notices received from the debtor or the bankruptcy court.*

Family Farmers and Fishermen

To help relieve economic pressure on small farmers, Congress created Chapter 12 of the Bankruptcy Code. In 2005, Congress extended this protection to family fishermen, modified its provisions somewhat, and made it a permanent chapter in the Bankruptcy Code (previously, the statutes authorizing Chapter 12 had to be periodically renewed by Congress).

DEFINITIONS For purposes of Chapter 12, a *family farmer* is one whose gross income is at least 50 percent farm dependent and whose debts are at least 50 percent farm related. The total debt for a family farmer must not exceed $4,031,575. A partnership or closely held corporation (see Chapter 39) at least 50 percent owned by the farm family can also qualify as a family farmer.[24]

A *family fisherman* is defined as one whose gross income is at least 50 percent dependent on commercial fishing operations[25] and whose debts are at least 80 percent related to commercial fishing. The total debt for a family fisherman must not exceed $1,868,200. As with family farmers, a partnership or closely held corporation can also qualify.

FILING THE PETITION The procedure for filing a family-farmer or family-fisherman bankruptcy plan is very similar to the procedure for filing a repayment plan under Chapter 13. The debtor must file a plan not later than ninety days after the order for relief. The filing of the petition acts as an automatic stay against creditors' and co-obligors' actions against the estate.

A farmer or fisherman who has already filed a reorganization or repayment plan may convert it to a Chapter 12 plan. The debtor may also convert a Chapter 12 plan to a liquidation plan.

CONTENT AND CONFIRMATION OF THE PLAN The content of a plan under Chapter 12 is basically the same as that of a Chapter 13 repayment plan. Generally, the plan must be confirmed or denied within forty-five days of filing.

Court confirmation of the plan is the same as for a repayment plan. The plan must provide for payment of secured debts at the value of the collateral. If the secured debt exceeds the value of the collateral, the remaining debt is unsecured.

For unsecured debtors, the plan must be confirmed if either (1) the value of the property to be distributed under the plan equals the amount of the claim or (2) the plan provides that all of the debtor's disposable income to be received in a three-year period (or longer, by court approval) will be applied to making payments. Disposable income is all income received less amounts needed to support the farmer or fisherman and his or her family and to continue the farming or commercial fishing operation. Completion of payments under the plan discharges all debts provided for by the plan.

See *Concept Summary 31.1* on the facing page for a comparison of bankruptcy procedures under Chapters 7, 11, 12, and 13.

---

24. Note that for a corporation or partnership to qualify under Chapter 12, at least 80 percent of the value of the firm's assets must consist of assets related to the farming operation.
25. Commercial fishing operations include catching, harvesting, or raising fish, shrimp, lobsters, urchins, seaweed, shellfish, or other aquatic species or products.

CONCEPT SUMMARY 31.1
Forms of Bankruptcy Relief Compared

ISSUE	CHAPTER 7	CHAPTER 11	CHAPTERS 12 AND 13
Purpose	Liquidation.	Reorganization.	Adjustment.
Who Can Petition	Debtor (voluntary) or creditors (involuntary).	Debtor (voluntary) or creditors (involuntary).	Debtor (voluntary) only.
Who Can Be a Debtor	Any "person" (including partnerships, corporations, and municipalities) except railroads, insurance companies, banks, savings and loan institutions, investment companies licensed by the Small Business Administration, and credit unions. Farmers and charitable institutions cannot be involuntarily petitioned. If the court finds the petition to be a substantial abuse of the use of Chapter 7, the debtor may be required to convert to a Chapter 13 repayment plan.	Any debtor eligible for Chapter 7 relief. Railroads are also eligible. Individuals have specific rules and limitations.	*Chapter 12*—Any family farmer (one whose gross income is at least 50 percent farm dependent and whose debts are at least 50 percent farm related) or family fisherman (one whose gross income is at least 50 percent dependent on commercial fishing operations and whose debts are at least 80 percent related to commercial fishing) or any partnership or closely held corporation at least 50 percent owned by a family farmer or fisherman, when total debt does not exceed a specified amount ($4,031,575 for farmers and $1,868,200 for fishermen). *Chapter 13*—Any individual (not partnerships or corporations) with regular income who owes fixed (liquidated) unsecured debts of less than $383,175 or fixed secured debts of less than $1,149,525.
Procedure Leading to Discharge	Nonexempt property is sold, and the proceeds are distributed (in order) to priority groups. Dischargeable debts are terminated.	Plan is submitted. If the plan is approved and followed, debts are discharged.	Plan is submitted and must be approved if the value of the property to be distributed equals the amount of the claims or if the debtor turns over disposable income for a three-year or five-year period. If the plan is followed, debts are discharged.
Advantages	On liquidation and distribution, most debts are discharged, and the debtor has an opportunity for a fresh start.	Debtor continues in business. Creditors can either accept the plan, or it can be "crammed down" on them. The plan allows for the reorganization and liquidation of debts over the plan period.	Debtor continues in business or possession of assets. If the plan is approved, most debts are discharged after the plan period.

Reviewing: Bankruptcy Law

Three months ago, Janet Hart's husband of twenty years died of cancer. Although he had medical insurance, he left Janet with outstanding medical bills of more than $50,000. Janet has worked at the local library for the past ten years, earning $1,500 per month. Since her husband's death, Janet also receives $1,500 in Social Security benefits and $1,100 in life insurance proceeds every month, for a total monthly income of $4,300. After she pays the mortgage payment of $1,500 and the amounts due on other debts, Janet has barely enough left to buy groceries for her family (she has two teenage daughters at home). She decides to file for Chapter 7 bankruptcy, hoping for a fresh start. Using the information presented in the chapter, answer the following questions.

1. What must Janet do *before* filing a petition for relief under Chapter 7?
2. How much time does Janet have after filing the bankruptcy petition to submit the required schedules? What happens if Janet does not meet the deadline?
3. Assume that Janet files a petition under Chapter 7. Further assume that the median family income in the geographic area in which Janet lives is $49,300. What steps would a court take to determine whether Janet's petition is presumed to be "substantial abuse" using the means test?
4. Suppose that the court determines that no *presumption* of substantial abuse applies in Janet's case. Nevertheless, the court finds that Janet does have the ability to pay at least a portion of the medical bills out of her disposable income. What would the court likely order in that situation?

DEBATE THIS . . . *Rather than being allowed to file Chapter 7 bankruptcy petitions, individuals and couples should always be forced to make an effort to pay off their debts through Chapter 13.*

Terms and Concepts

adequate protection doctrine 602

automatic stay 602

bankruptcy trustee 600

consumer-debtor 600

cram-down provision 610

debtor in possession (DIP) 609

discharge 600

insider 604

liquidation 599

order for relief 602

petition in bankruptcy 600

preference 604

preferred creditor 604

reaffirmation agreement 608

U.S. trustee 601

workout 609

ExamPrep

Issue Spotters

1. After graduating from college, Tina works briefly as a salesperson before filing for bankruptcy. Tina's petition states that her only debts are student loans, taxes accruing within the last year, and a claim against her based on her misuse of customers' funds during her employment. Are these debts dischargeable in bankruptcy? Explain. **(See page 607.)**

2. Ogden is a vice president of Plumbing Service, Inc. (PSI). On May 1, Ogden loans PSI $10,000. On June 1, the firm repays the loan. On July 1, PSI files for bankruptcy. Quentin is appointed trustee. Can Quentin re-cover the $10,000 paid to Ogden on June 1? Why or why not? **(See page 604.)**

• Check your answers to the Issue Spotters against the answers provided in Appendix E at the end of this text.

Before the Test

Go to **www.cengagebrain.com**, enter the ISBN 9781285185248, and click on "Find" to locate this textbook's Web site. Then, click on "Access Now" under "Study Tools," and select Chapter 31 at the top. There, you will find a Practice Quiz that you can take to assess your mastery of the concepts in this chapter, as well as Flashcards and a Glossary of important terms.

Business Scenarios

31–1. Voluntary versus Involuntary Bankruptcy. Burke has been a rancher all her life, raising cattle and crops. Her ranch is valued at $500,000, almost all of which is exempt under state law. Burke has eight creditors and a total indebtedness of $70,000. Two of her largest creditors are Oman ($30,000 owed) and Sneed ($25,000 owed). The other six creditors have claims of less than $5,000 each. A drought has ruined all of Burke's crops and forced her to sell many of her cattle at a loss. She cannot pay off her creditors. **(See page 600.)**

(a) Under the Bankruptcy Code, can Burke, with a $500,000 ranch, voluntarily petition herself into bankruptcy? Explain.

(b) Could either Oman or Sneed force Burke into involuntary bankruptcy? Explain.

31–2. Preferences. Peaslee is not known for his business sense. He started a greenhouse and nursery business two years ago, and because of his lack of experience, he soon was in debt to a number of creditors. On February 1, Peaslee borrowed $5,000 from his father to pay some of these creditors. On May 1, Peaslee paid back the $5,000, depleting his working capital. One creditor, the Cool Springs Nursery Supply Corp., had extended credit to Peaslee on numerous purchases. Cool Springs pressured Peaslee for payment, and on July 1, Peaslee paid Cool Springs half the amount owed. On September 1, Peaslee voluntarily petitioned himself into bankruptcy. The trustee in bankruptcy claims that both Peaslee's father and Cool Springs must turn over to the debtor's estate the amounts Peaslee paid to them. Discuss fully the trustee's claims. **(See page 604.)**

31–3. Distribution of Property. Montoro petitioned himself into voluntary bankruptcy. There were three major claims against his estate. One was made by Carlton, a friend who held Montoro's negotiable promissory note for $2,500. Another was made by Elmer, Montoro's employee who claimed that Montoro owed him three months' back wages of $4,500. The last major claim was made by the United Bank of the Rockies on an unsecured loan of $5,000. In addition, Dietrich, an accountant retained by the trustee, was owed $500, and property taxes of $1,000 were owed to Rock County. Montoro's nonexempt property was liquidated, with proceeds of $5,000. Discuss fully what amount each party will receive, and why. **(See page 606.)**

Business Case Problems

31–4. Discharge in Bankruptcy. Caroline McAfee loaned $400,000 to Carter Oaks Crossing. Joseph Harman, president of Carter Oaks Crossing, signed a promissory note providing that the company would repay the amount with interest in installments beginning in 1999 and ending by 2006. Harman signed a personal guaranty for the note. Carter Oaks Crossing defaulted on the note, so McAfee sued Harman for payment under the guaranty. Harman moved for summary judgment on the ground that McAfee's claim against him had been discharged in his Chapter 7 bankruptcy case, filed after 1999 but before the default on the note. The guaranty was not listed among Harman's debts in the bankruptcy filing. Would the obligation under the guaranty have been discharged in bankruptcy, as Harman claimed? Why or why not? [*Harman v. McAfee*, 302 Ga.App. 698, 691 S.E.2d 586 (2010)] **(See page 607.)**

31–5. Discharge in Bankruptcy. Monica Sexton filed a petition for Chapter 13 reorganization. One of her creditors was Friedman's Jewelers. Her petition misclassified Friedman's claim as $800 of unsecured debt. Within days, Friedman's filed proof of a secured claim for $300 and an unsecured claim for $462. Eventually, Friedman's was sent payments of about $300 by check. None of the checks were cashed. By then, Friedman's had filed its own petition under Chapter 11, Bankruptcy Receivables Management (BRM) had bought Friedman's unpaid accounts, and the checks had not been forwarded. Sexton received a discharge on the completion of her plan. BRM was not notified. BRM wrote to Sexton's attorney to ask about the status of her case, but received no response. BRM demanded that Sexton surrender the collateral on its claim. Sexton asked the court to impose sanctions on BRM for violating the discharge order. Was Sexton's debt to Friedman's dischargeable? Should BRM be sanctioned? Discuss. [*In re Sexton*, __ Bankr. __ (E.D.N.C. 2011)] **(See page 608.)**

**31–6. BUSINESS CASE PROBLEM
WITH SAMPLE ANSWER: Automatic Stay.**

 Michelle Gholston leased a Chevy Impala from EZ Auto Van Rentals. In November 2011, Gholston filed for bankruptcy. Around November 21, the bankruptcy court notified EZ Auto of Gholston's bankruptcy and the imposition of an automatic stay. Nevertheless, because Gholston had fallen behind on her payments, EZ Auto repossessed the vehicle on November 28. Gholston's attorney then reminded EZ Auto about the automatic stay, but the company failed to return the car. As a result of the car's repossession, Gholston suffered damages that included emotional distress, lost wages, attorneys' fees, and car rental expenses. Can Gholston recover from EZ Auto? Why or why not? [In re Gholston, ___ Bankr.___, 2012 WL 639288 (M.D.Fla. 2012)] **(See page 602.)**

- **For a sample answer to Problem 31–6, go to Appendix F at the end of this text.**

31–7. Discharge in Bankruptcy. Like many students, Barbara Hann financed her education partially through loans. These loans included three federally insured Stafford Loans of $7,500 each ($22,500 in total). Hann believed that she repaid the loans, but when later, she filed a Chapter 13 petition, Educational Credit Management Corp. (ECMC) filed an unsecured proof of claim based on the loans. Hann objected. At a hearing at which ECMC failed to appear, Hann submitted correspondence from the lender that indicated the loans had been paid. The court entered an order sustaining Hann's objection. Despite the order, can ECMC resume its effort to collect on Hann's loans? Explain. [*In re Hann,* 711 F.3d 235 (1st Cir. 2013)] **(See page 607.)**

31–8. A QUESTION OF ETHICS: Discharge in Bankruptcy.

 In October 1994, Charles Edwards formed ETS Payphones, Inc., to sell and lease pay phones as investment opportunities—an investor would buy a phone from ETS, which would lease it back. ETS *promised returns of 14 to 15 percent but consistently sustained losses. To meet its obligations to existing investors, ETS had to continually attract new investors. Eventually, ETS*
defrauded thousands of investors of more than $300 million. Edwards transferred the funds from ETS to himself. In 2000, ETS filed a petition in a federal bankruptcy court to declare bankruptcy. Darryl Laddin was appointed trustee. On the debtor's behalf, Laddin filed a suit against Reliance Trust Co. and others. He alleged, among other things, that the defendants helped defraud investors by "ignoring the facts" and "funneling" the investors' funds to ETS, causing it to "incur millions of dollars in additional debt." Laddin sought treble (triple) damages. [Official Committee of Unsecured Creditors of PSA, Inc. v. Edwards, 437 F.3d 1145 (11th Cir. 2006)] **(See page 607.)**

(a) The defendants argued, in part, that the doctrine of *in pari delicto,* which provides that a wrongdoer may not profit from his or her wrongful acts, barred Laddin's claim. Who should be considered ethically responsible for the investors' losses? Explain.

(b) Laddin contended that his actions, as trustee on behalf of the debtor, should not be subject to the *in pari delicto* doctrine because it depends on the "personal malfeasance of the individual seeking to recover." The defendants filed a motion to dismiss Laddin's complaint. Should the court rule in favor of Laddin or the defendants? Why?

Legal Reasoning Group Activity

31–9. Discharge in Bankruptcy. Cathy Coleman took out loans to complete her college education. After graduation, Coleman was irregularly employed as a teacher before filing a petition in a federal bankruptcy court under Chapter 13. The court confirmed a five-year plan under which Coleman was required to commit all of her disposable income to paying the student loans. Less than a year later, when Coleman was laid off, she still owed more than $100,000 to Educational Credit Management Corp. Coleman asked the court to discharge the debt on the ground that it would be an undue hardship for her to pay it. **(See page 607.)**

(a) The first group will determine when a debtor normally is entitled to a discharge under Chapter 13.

(b) The second group will discuss whether student loans are dischargeable, and when "undue hardship" is a legitimate ground for an exception.

(c) The third group will outline the goals of bankruptcy law and make an argument, based on these facts and principles, in support of Coleman's request.

UNIT SIX Focus on Ethics

Creditors' Rights and Bankruptcy

We have certainly come a long way from the period in our history when debtors' prisons existed. Today, debtors are in a much more favorable position—they can file for protection under bankruptcy law. Indeed, after the Bankruptcy Reform Act of 1978 was passed, some claimed that we had gone too far toward protecting debtors and had made it too easy for them to avoid paying what they legally owed.

Critics of the 2005 Bankruptcy Reform Act were concerned that the pendulum had swung too far in the opposite direction—favoring creditors' interests and making it too difficult for debtors to obtain a fresh start. Clearly, it is hard to protect the rights of both debtors and creditors at the same time, and laws governing debtor-creditor relationships have traditionally been perceived, by one group or another, as being unfair.

Attempts to balance the rights of both debtors and creditors necessarily raise questions of fairness and justice. In this *Focus on Ethics* feature, we look at several aspects of debtor-creditor relationships that frequently involve issues of fairness. We also examine the ethical ramifications of the bankruptcy reform legislation for debtors and creditors.

LEGAL REASONING

1. *Do you think that the law favors debtors at the expense of creditors or vice versa? Is there any way to achieve a better balance between the interests of creditors and those of debtors?*

"Self-Help" Repossession

Section 9–503 of the Uniform Commercial Code (UCC) states that "[u]nless otherwise agreed, a secured party has on default the right to take possession of the collateral. In taking possession, a secured party may proceed without judicial process if this can be done without breach of the peace." The underlying rationale for this "self-help" provision of Article 9 is that it simplifies the process of repossession for creditors and reduces the burden on the courts. Because the UCC does not define "breach of the peace," however, it is not always easy to predict what behavior will constitute such a breach.

One problem is that the debtor may not realize what is happening when agents of the creditor show up to repossess the collateral. Often, to avoid a confrontation with the debtor, a secured creditor will arrange to have the collateral repossessed during the night or in the early morning, when the debtor is likely to be asleep. But a debtor who awakens in the night and sees his or her car being towed away may not realize that it is being repossessed.

At the same time, repossession can be risky for the creditor. If the repossession results in a breach of the peace, the creditor may be liable for substantial damages. Inevitably, repossession attempts will occasionally result in confrontations with the debtor. Indeed, some contend that the self-help provision encourages violence by providing an incentive for debtors

to incite creditors to breach the peace, which may entitle the debtors to damages.

LEGAL REASONING

2. *So long as there is no breach of the peace, a lender may repossess goods on the debtor's default under the self-help provision of the UCC's Article 9. Do you think that debtors have a right to be told in advance about a planned repossession? Some observers argue that the self-help remedy under Article 9 should be abolished. Do you agree? Why or why not?*

Ethics and Bankruptcy

As we have discussed, the first goal of bankruptcy law is to provide relief and protection to debtors. Society generally has concluded that everyone should be given the chance to start over. But how far should society go in allowing debtors to avoid obligations that they voluntarily incurred?

Consider the concept of bankruptcy from the creditor's perspective. The creditor has transferred purchasing power from herself or himself to the debtor. That transfer of purchasing power represents a transfer of an asset for an asset. The debtor obtains the asset of funds, goods, or services, and the creditor obtains the asset of a *secured* or *unsecured* legal obligation to repay.

Once the debtor is in bankruptcy, voluntarily or involuntarily, the creditor's asset generally has a diminished value. Indeed, in many circumstances, that asset has no value. Yet the easier it becomes for debtors to discharge their debts under bankruptcy laws, the greater will be the incentive for debtors to use such laws to avoid paying amounts that are legally owed.

Clearly, bankruptcy law is a balancing act between providing a second chance for debtors and ensuring that creditors are given reasonable protection. Understandably, ethical issues arise in the process.

LEGAL REASONING

3. *Is it unethical to avoid paying one's debts by going into bankruptcy? Does a person have a moral responsibility to pay his or her debts? Discuss.*

Bankruptcy and Economics

When the number of bankruptcies increases, creditors incur higher risks in making loans—because bankruptcy shifts the cost of the debt from the debtor to the creditor. To compensate for these higher risks, creditors take one or more of the following actions: increase the interest rates charged to everyone, require additional security (collateral), or become more selective in granting credit.

FOCUS ON ETHICS CONTINUES ▶

621

Thus, with more lenient bankruptcy laws, debtors who find themselves in bankruptcy will be better off, but debtors who will never be in bankruptcy will be worse off. Ethical concerns regarding this trade-off must be matched with the economic concerns of other groups of individuals affected by the law, especially in the economic environment after the latest economic recession.

Consequences of Bankruptcy Under bankruptcy law, filing for personal bankruptcy (particularly under Chapter 7) has become more difficult. Although less stigma is attached to bankruptcy today than in previous years, bankruptcy is never easy for debtors. Many debtors feel a sense of shame and failure when they petition for bankruptcy. After all, bankruptcy is a matter of public record, and there is no way to avoid a certain amount of publicity. In one case, a couple who filed for Chapter 7 bankruptcy wanted to use their attorney's mailing address in another town on their bankruptcy schedules in an effort to prevent an elderly parent and one of their employers from learning about the bankruptcy. The court, however, held that debtors are not entitled to be protected from publicity surrounding the filing of their cases.[1]

A court in another case held that the public interest in information involving a particular bankruptcy debtor (Gitto Global Corporation) was important enough to justify disclosing a previously sealed report from a bankruptcy examiner. In essence, the court gave the media access to the bankruptcy examiner's report on the misconduct of more than 120 individuals at the debtor company.[2]

Bankruptcy also has other consequences for debtors, including blemished credit ratings and higher interest charges for new debts, such as those incurred through the purchase of cars or homes. Some private employers may even refuse to hire a job applicant who has filed for bankruptcy.[3]

---

1. *In the Matter of Laws,* 223 Bankr. 714 (D.Neb. 1998).
2. *In re Gitto Global Corp.,* 422 F.3d 1 (D.Mass. 2005).
3. See, for example, *In re Potter,* 431 Bankr. 894 (S.D.Tex. 2010).

Thus, bankruptcy can have adverse effects for both debtors and creditors. Because of the consequences of bankruptcy, debtors do not always get the fresh start promised by bankruptcy law. At the same time, creditors rarely are able to recover all that is owed them once a debtor petitions for bankruptcy.

LEGAL REASONING

4. *Are borrowers better off as a result of the bankruptcy reform legislation? Why or why not?*

Investment Risk Management and Bankruptcy In the years leading up to the recession, many investors opted to invest most or all of their funds in risky propositions that promised to yield ultra-high returns. Rather than simply seeking a healthy profit, these investors were looking for extraordinary gains. Too often, they were so certain of success that they failed to manage the risk of investment by diversifying their portfolios or holding some funds in reserve. Many were so overconfident that they borrowed additional funds to invest. When the recession hit, however, those risky investments came crashing down, and many investors were left unable to pay their debts and had to file for bankruptcy.

The combination of overdependence on credit and overconfidence in investments helped bring on the global economic crisis from which the United States has not yet fully recovered. What these investors lacked was a sense of self-sufficiency and a clear understanding of the importance of minimizing debt. A person or firm that minimizes debt and is financially self-reliant will be less affected by fluctuations in the market or difficulties in obtaining credit—and thus will be less likely to be bankrupted in a recession.

LEGAL REASONING

5. *How does minimizing business or personal debt help prevent bankruptcies in a recession?*

BUSINESS LAW

CLARKSON · MILLER · CROSS

CHAPTER 32

AGENCY FORMATION AND DUTIES

One of the most common, important, and pervasive legal relationships is that of **agency.** In an agency relationship involving two parties, one of the parties, called the *agent,* agrees to represent or act for the other, called the *principal.* The principal has the right to control the agent's conduct in matters entrusted to the agent. By using agents, a principal can conduct multiple business operations simultaneously in various locations. Thus,

for example, contracts that bind the principal can be made at different places with different persons at the same time.

A familiar example of an agent is a corporate officer who serves in a representative capacity for the owners of the corporation. In this capacity, the officer has the authority to bind the principal (the corporation) to a contract. In fact, agency law is essential to the existence and operation of a corporate entity because only through its agents

can a corporation function and enter into contracts.

Most employees are also considered to be agents of their employers. Thus, some of the concepts of employment law that you will learn about in Chapters 34 and 35 are based on agency law. Indeed, agency relationships permeate the business world. For that reason, an understanding of the law of agency is crucial to understanding business law.

SECTION 1
AGENCY RELATIONSHIPS

Section 1(1) of the *Restatement (Third) of Agency*[1] defines *agency* as "the fiduciary relation [that] results from the manifestation of consent by one person to another that the other shall act in his [or her] behalf and subject to his [or her] control, and consent by the other so to act." In other words, in a principal-agent relationship, the parties have agreed that the agent will act *on behalf and instead of* the principal in negotiating and transacting business with third parties.

The term **fiduciary** is at the heart of agency law. This term can be used both as a noun and as an adjective. When used as a noun, it refers to a person having a duty created by his or her undertaking to act primarily for another's benefit in matters connected with the undertaking. When used as an adjective, as in the phrase *fiduciary relationship,* it means that the relationship involves trust and confidence.

Agency relationships commonly exist between employers and employees. Agency relationships may

sometimes also exist between employers and independent contractors who are hired to perform special tasks or services.

Employer-Employee Relationships

Normally, all employees who deal with third parties are deemed to be agents. A salesperson in a department store, for instance, is an agent of the store's owner (the principal) and acts on the owner's behalf. Any sale of goods made by the salesperson to a customer is binding on the principal. Similarly, most representations of fact made by the salesperson with respect to the goods sold are binding on the principal.

Because employees who deal with third parties generally are deemed to be agents of their employers, agency law and employment law overlap considerably. Agency relationships, though, as will become apparent, can exist outside an employer-employee relationship, and thus agency law has a broader reach than employment law does.

Employment laws (state and federal) apply only to the employer-employee relationship. Thus, statutes that govern Social Security, withholding taxes, workers' compensation, unemployment compensation, and workplace safety apply only when an employer-

---

1. The *Restatement (Third) of Agency* is an authoritative summary of the law of agency and is often referred to by judges in their decisions and opinions.

employee relationship exists (see Chapter 34). Similarly, laws that prohibit employment discrimination (see Chapter 35) apply only to employers and employees. *These laws do not apply to an independent contractor.*

Employer–Independent Contractor Relationships

Independent contractors are not employees because, by definition, those who hire them have no control over the details of their work performance. Section 2 of the *Restatement (Third) of Agency* defines an **independent contractor** as follows:

> [An independent contractor is] a person who contracts with another to do something for him [or her] but who is not controlled by the other nor subject to the other's right to control with respect to his [or her] physical conduct in the performance of the undertaking. He [or she] may or may not be an agent.

Building contractors and subcontractors are independent contractors. A property owner who hires a contractor and subcontractors to complete a project does not control the details of the way they perform their work. Truck drivers who own their vehicles and hire out on a per-job basis are independent contractors, but truck drivers who drive company trucks on a regular basis usually are employees.

The relationship between a principal and an independent contractor may or may not involve an agency relationship. To illustrate: A homeowner who hires a real estate broker to sell her house has not only contracted with an independent contractor (the broker) but also established an agency relationship for the specific purpose of selling the property. Another example is an insurance agent, who is both an independent contractor and an agent of the insurance company for which he sells policies. (Note that an insurance *broker*, in contrast, normally is an agent of the person obtaining insurance and not of the insurance company.)

Determination of Employee Status

The courts are frequently asked to determine whether a particular worker is an employee or an independent contractor. How a court decides this issue can have a significant effect on the rights and liabilities of the parties. For instance, employers are required to pay certain taxes, such as Social Security and unemployment taxes, for employees but not for independent contractors.

CRITERIA USED BY THE COURTS In deciding whether a worker is categorized as an employee or an independent contractor, courts often consider the following questions:

1. *How much control does the employer exercise over the details of the work?* If the employer exercises considerable control over the details of the work and the day-to-day activities of the worker, this indicates employee status. This is perhaps the most important factor weighed by the courts in determining employee status.
2. *Is the worker engaged in an occupation or business distinct from that of the employer?* If so, this points to independent-contractor, not employee, status.
3. *Is the work usually done under the employer's direction or by a specialist without supervision?* If the work is usually done under the employer's direction, this indicates employee status.
4. *Does the employer supply the tools at the place of work?* If so, this indicates employee status.
5. *For how long is the person employed?* If the person is employed for a long period of time, this indicates employee status.
6. *What is the method of payment—by time period or at the completion of the job?* Payment by time period, such as once every two weeks or once a month, indicates employee status.
7. *What degree of skill is required of the worker?* If a great degree of skill is required, this may indicate that the person is an independent contractor hired for a specialized job and not an employee.

Disputes Involving Employment Law. Sometimes, workers may benefit from having employee status—for tax purposes and to be protected under certain employment laws, for example. As mentioned earlier, federal statutes governing employment discrimination apply only when an employer-employee relationship exists. Protection under employment-discrimination statutes provides a significant incentive for workers to claim that they are employees rather than independent contractors.

▶ **Case in Point 32.1** A Puerto Rican television station, WIPR, contracted with Victoria Alberty-Vélez to cohost a television show. Alberty signed a new contract for each episode and was committed to work for WIPR only during the filming of the episodes. WIPR paid her a lump sum for each contract and did not withhold any taxes.

When Alberty became pregnant, WIPR stopped contracting with her. She filed a lawsuit claiming

[handwritten: can proceed w/ discrimination if employee, cannot if contractor]

[handwritten top right: employer can mean many things]

that WIPR was discriminating against her in violation of federal antidiscrimination laws, but the court found in favor of WIPR. Because the parties had used repeated fixed-length contracts and had described Alberty as an independent contractor on tax documents, she could not maintain an employment-discrimination suit.[2] ◄

Disputes Involving Tort Liability. Whether a worker is an employee or an independent contractor can also affect the employer's liability for the worker's actions.

▶ **Case in Point 32.2** El Palmar Taxi, Inc., requires its drivers to supply their own cabs, which must display El Palmar's logo. The drivers pay gas, maintenance, and insurance costs, and a fee to El Palmar. They are expected to comply with the law, including licensing regulations, but they can work when they want for as long as they want. Mario Julaju drove a taxi under

[handwritten: degree of control]

a contract with El Palmar that described him as an independent contractor.

El Palmar sent Julaju to pick up Maria Lopez and her children. During the ride, Julaju's cab collided with a truck. To recover for their injuries, the Lopezes sued El Palmar. The employer argued that it was not liable because Julaju was an independent contractor. The court held in favor of El Palmar. An employer normally is not responsible for the actions of an independent contractor with whom the employer contracts. Here, the employment contract had clearly specified that Julaju was an independent contractor, and there were no facts indicating that he was an employee (or that the employer controlled his activities).[3] ◄

In the following case, the court had to determine the status of an auto service company and its tow truck driver who assaulted the passenger of a vehicle the company had been hired to tow.

---

2. *Alberty-Vélez v. Corporación de Puerto Rico para la Difusión Pública,* 361 F.3d 1 (1st Cir. 2004).

3. *Lopez v. El Palmar Taxi, Inc.,* 297 Ga.App. 121, 676 S.E.2d 460 (2009).

CASE 32.1

Coker v. Pershad

Superior Court of New Jersey, Appellate Division, 2013 WL 1296271 (2013).

BACKGROUND AND FACTS AAA North Jersey, Inc., contracted with Five Star Auto Service to perform towing and auto repair services for AAA. Terence Pershad, the driver of a tow truck for Five Star, responded to a call to AAA for assistance by the driver of a car involved in an accident in Hoboken, New Jersey. Pershad got into a fight with Nicholas Coker, a passenger in the car, and assaulted Coker with a knife. Coker filed a suit in a New Jersey state court against Pershad, Five Star, and AAA. The court determined that Pershad was Five Star's employee and that Five Star was an independent contractor, not AAA's employee. Thus, AAA was "not responsible for the alleged negligence of its independent contractor, defendant Five Star, in hiring Mr. Pershad." Five Star entered into a settlement with Coker. Coker appealed the ruling in AAA's favor.

IN THE LANGUAGE OF THE COURT
PER CURIAM.

* * * *

The important difference between an employee and an independent contractor is that one who hires an independent contractor has no right of control over the manner in which the work is to be done. [Emphasis added.]

* * * *

* * * Plaintiff [Coker] argues AAA controlled the means and method of the work performed by Five Star. * * * Factors * * * [that] determine whether a principal maintains the right of control over an individual or a corporation claimed to be an independent contractor [include]:

(a) the extent of control which, by the agreement, the master may exercise over the details of the work;

(b) whether or not the one employed is engaged in a distinct occupation or business;

(c) the kind of occupation, with reference to whether, in the locality, the work is usually done under the direction of the employer or by a specialist without supervision;

CASE 32.1 CONTINUED

(d) the skill required in the particular occupation;
(e) whether the employer or the workman supplies the * * * tools * * * ;
(f) the length of time for which the person is employed * * * .

Applying these factors to the facts of this case, it is clear AAA did not control the manner and means of Five Star's work. The Agreement specifically stated Five Star was an independent contractor. Five Star purchased its own trucks and any other necessary equipment. AAA assigned jobs to Five Star and Five Star completed the work without any further supervision by AAA. Five Star chose the employees to send on towing calls and the trucks and equipment the employees would use.

Five Star was also in business for itself and performed auto repair services for principals and customers other than AAA. Five Star hired and fired its own employees * * * .

* * * *

Plaintiff also argues Five Star should be considered to be controlled by AAA because "providing towing and other roadside assistance is arguably the focus of the regular business of AAA." * * * [But] AAA is an automobile club that provides a wide variety of services to its members. It contracts with numerous service providers, such as gas stations, motels and other businesses, to provide these services. Thus, AAA is not solely in the towing business.

* * * AAA had used Five Star to provide towing services for approximately eight years and there is nothing in the record to demonstrate it lacked the skill needed to provide these services.

DECISION AND REMEDY *A state intermediate appellate court affirmed the lower court's ruling. AAA could not be held liable for the actions of Five Star, its independent contractor, because "AAA did not control the manner and means of Five Star's work."*

THE LEGAL ENVIRONMENT DIMENSION *Five Star's contract with AAA required Five Star to be available to provide service for AAA members. Does this support Coker's argument that Five Star was AAA's employee? Why or why not?*

MANAGERIAL IMPLICATIONS *When an employment contract clearly designates one party as an independent contractor, the relationship between the parties is presumed to be that of employer and independent contractor. But this is only a presumption. Evidence can be introduced to show that the employer exercised sufficient control to establish the other party as an employee. The Internal Revenue Service is increasingly pursuing employers that it claims have wrongly classified employees as independent contractors. Thus, from a tax perspective, business managers need to ensure that all independent contractors fully control their own work.*

CRITERIA USED BY THE IRS The Internal Revenue Service (IRS) has established its own criteria for determining whether a worker is an independent contractor or an employee. The most important factor is the degree of control the business exercises over the worker.

The IRS tends to closely scrutinize a firm's classification of its workers because, as mentioned, employers can avoid certain tax liabilities by hiring independent contractors instead of employees. Even when a firm has classified a worker as an independent contractor, the IRS may decide that the worker is actually an employee.

If the IRS decides that an employee is misclassified, the employer will be responsible for paying any applicable Social Security, withholding, and unemployment taxes. Microsoft Corporation, for instance, was once ordered to pay back payroll taxes for hundreds of temporary workers who had contractually agreed to work for Microsoft as independent contractors.[4]

EMPLOYEE STATUS AND "WORKS FOR HIRE" Under the Copyright Act, any copyrighted work created by an employee within the scope of her or his employment at the request of the employer is a "work for hire." The employer owns the copyright to the work. In contrast, when an employer hires an independent contractor—a freelance artist, writer, or computer programmer, for example—the independent contractor normally owns the copyright. An exception is made if the parties agree in writing that the work is a "work

---

4. *Vizcaino v. U.S. District Court for the Western District of Washington,* 173 F.3d 713 (9th Cir. 1999).

for hire" and the work falls into one of nine specific categories, including audiovisual and other works.

▶ **Case in Point 32.3**   Artisan House, Inc., hired a professional photographer, Steven H. Lindner, owner of SHL Imaging, Inc., to take pictures of its products for the creation of color slides to be used by Artisan's sales force. Lindner controlled his own work and carefully chose the lighting and angles used in the photographs. When Artisan published the photographs in a catalogue and brochures without Lindner's permission, SHL filed a lawsuit for copyright infringement. Artisan claimed that its publication of the photographs was authorized because they were works for hire. The court, however, decided that SHL was an independent contractor and owned the copyright to the photographs. Because SHL had not given Artisan permission (a license) to reproduce the photographs in other publications, Artisan was liable for copyright infringement.[5] ◀

SECTION 2
FORMATION OF THE AGENCY RELATIONSHIP

Agency relationships normally are *consensual*—that is, they come about by voluntary consent and agreement between the parties. Generally, the agreement need not be in writing,[6] and consideration is not required.

A person must have contractual capacity to be a principal.[7] Those who cannot legally enter into contracts directly should not be allowed to do so indi-

rectly through an agent. Any person can be an agent, however, regardless of whether he or she has the capacity to contract (including minors).

An agency relationship can be created for any legal purpose. An agency relationship created for a purpose that is illegal or contrary to public policy is unenforceable. ▶ **Example 32.4**   Archer (as principal) contracts with Burke (as agent) to sell illegal narcotics. The agency relationship is unenforceable because selling illegal narcotics is a felony and is contrary to public policy. If Burke sells the narcotics and keeps the profits, Archer cannot sue to enforce the agency agreement. ◀

An agency relationship can arise in four ways: by agreement of the parties, by ratification, by estoppel, and by operation of law.

Agency by Agreement

Most agency relationships are based on an express or implied agreement that the agent will act for the principal and that the principal agrees to have the agent so act. An agency agreement can take the form of an express written contract or be created by an oral agreement. ▶ **Example 32.5**   Rees asks Grace, a gardener, to contract with others for the care of his lawn on a regular basis. If Grace agrees, an agency relationship exists between Reese and Grace for the lawn care. ◀

An agency agreement can also be implied by conduct. ▶ **Example 32.6**   A hotel expressly allows only Boris Renke to park cars, but Renke has no employment contract there. The hotel's manager tells Renke when to work, as well as where and how to park the cars. The hotel's conduct manifests a willingness to have Renke park its customers' cars, and Renke can infer from the hotel's conduct that he has authority to act as a parking valet. Thus, there is an implied agreement that Renke is an agent of the hotel and provides valet parking services for hotel guests. ◀

At issue in the following case was whether an agency relationship arose when a man, who was being hospitalized, asked his wife to sign the admissions papers for him.

---

5. *SHL Imaging, Inc. v. Artisan House, Inc.*, 117 F.Supp.2d 301 (S.D.N.Y. 2000).
6. There are two main exceptions to the statement that agency agreements need not be in writing: (1) Under the *equal dignity rule* (discussed in the next chapter), an agreement must be in writing if it empowers the agent to enter into a contract that the Statute of Frauds requires to be in writing. (2) An agreement that gives an agent power of attorney must also be in writing.
7. Note that some states allow a minor to be a principal. When a minor is permitted to be a principal, any resulting contracts will be voidable by the minor principal but *not* by the adult third party.

CASE 32.2

Laurel Creek Health Care Center v. Bishop
Court of Appeals of Kentucky, 2010 WL 985299 (2010).

BACKGROUND AND FACTS   Gilbert Bishop was admitted to Laurel Creek Health Care Center suffering from various physical ailments. During an examination, Bishop told Laurel Creek staff that he could not use his hands well enough to write or hold a pencil, but he was otherwise found to be mentally

CASE 32.2 CONTINUED   competent. Bishop's sister, Rachel Combs, testified that when she arrived at the facility, she offered to sign the admissions forms. Laurel Creek employees told her, however, that it was their policy to have the patient's spouse sign the admissions papers if the patient was unable to do so. Combs also testified that Gilbert asked her to get his wife, Anna, so that she could sign his admissions papers.

Combs then brought Anna to the hospital, and Anna signed the admissions paperwork, which contained a provision for mandatory arbitration. Subsequently, Bishop went into cardiopulmonary arrest and died. Following his death, Bishop's family brought an action in a Kentucky state court against Laurel Creek for negligence. Laurel Creek asked the trial court to order the parties to proceed to arbitration in accordance with the mandatory arbitration provision contained in the admissions paperwork signed by Anna. The trial court denied the request on the ground that Anna was not Bishop's agent and had no legal authority to make decisions for him. Laurel Creek appealed.

 IN THE LANGUAGE OF THE COURT
LAMBERT, Judge.

* * * *

Laurel Creek first argues that this is a case of actual agency and that Anna Bishop had actual authority as Gilbert's agent to sign the admissions paperwork and is therefore bound by the arbitration agreement therein.

* * * *

We agree with Laurel Creek that Gilbert created an actual agency relationship between him and his wife. According to his sister, Rachel, Gilbert specifically asked that his wife be brought to the nursing home so that she could sign the admissions documents for him, and Anna acted upon that delegation of authority and signed the admissions papers. This is consistent with the creation of actual authority as described in the *Restatement (Third) of Agency,* [Section] 2.01, Comment c (2006). The *Restatement* explains the rationale for the creation of actual agency in three steps. *First, "the principal manifests assent to be affected by the agent's action."* In the instant case, Gilbert asked that Anna come to the hospital to sign the papers for him. *Second, "the agent's actions establish the agent's consent to act on the principal's behalf."* Here, Anna signed all the admissions papers per her husband's request and therefore consented to act on Gilbert's behalf. *Third, by acting within such authority, the agent affects the principal's legal relations with third parties.* Clearly here, Anna's actions affected Gilbert's relations with Laurel Creek, a third party. [Emphasis added.]

* * * *

* * * The evidence indicates that Gilbert indicated to Laurel Creek that he was physically incapable of signing the documents but was of sound mental capacity and wanted his wife to sign the documents on his behalf. When Gilbert communicated this to his sister, and the sister brought Anna in to sign the documents, Gilbert created an agency relationship upon which Laurel Creek relied.

DECISION AND REMEDY   *The Kentucky Court of Appeals reversed the trial court's judgment and remanded the case for further proceedings consistent with its opinion. An actual agency relationship between Bishop and his wife, Anna, had been formed, and the trial court had erred when it found otherwise.*

THE ECONOMIC DIMENSION   *Which party benefited from the court's ruling? Why?*

THE LEGAL ENVIRONMENT DIMENSION   *Laurel Creek argued that even if there was no actual agency relationship, an implied agency relationship existed. Is this argument valid? Why or why not?*

Agency by Ratification

On occasion, a person who is in fact not an agent (or who is an agent acting outside the scope of her or his authority) may make a contract on behalf of another (a principal). If the principal approves or affirms that contract by word or by action, an agency relationship is created by *ratification*. Ratification involves a question of intent, and intent can be expressed by either words or conduct. The basic requirements for ratification will be discussed in Chapter 33.

Agency by Estoppel

Sometimes, a principal causes a third person to believe that another person is the principal's agent, and the third person acts to his or her detriment in reasonable reliance on that belief. When this occurs, the principal is "estopped to deny" (prevented from denying) the agency relationship. An agency by estoppel arises when the principal's actions have created the *appearance* of an agency that does not in fact exist.

THE THIRD PARTY'S RELIANCE MUST BE REASONABLE
The third person must prove that he or she *reasonably* believed that an agency relationship existed, however.[8] Facts and circumstances must show that an ordinary, prudent person familiar with business practice and custom would have been justified in concluding that the agent had authority.

▶ **Case in Point 32.7** Marsha and Jerry Wiedmaier owned Wiedmaier, Inc., a corporation that operated a truck stop. Their son, Michael, did not own any interest in the corporation but had worked at the truck stop as a fuel operator. Michael decided to form his own business called Extreme Diecast, LLC. To obtain a line of credit with Motorsport Marketing, Inc., which sells racing memorabilia, Michael asked his mother to sign the credit application form.

After Marsha had signed as "Secretary-Owner" of Wiedmaier, Inc., Michael added his name to the list of corporate owners and faxed the form to Motorsport. Later, when Michael stopped making payments on the merchandise he had ordered, Motorsport sued Wiedmaier, Inc., for the unpaid balance. The court ruled that Michael was an apparent agent of Wiedmaier, Inc., because the credit application had caused Motorsport to reasonably believe that Michael was acting as Wiedmaier's agent in ordering merchandise.[9] ◀

CREATED BY THE PRINCIPAL'S CONDUCT Note that the acts or declarations of a purported *agent* in and of themselves do not create an agency by estoppel. Rather, it is the deeds or statements of the *principal* that create an agency by estoppel. Thus, in *Case in Point 32.7,* if Marsha Wiedmaier had not signed the credit application on behalf of the principal-corporation, then Motorsport would not have been justified in believing that Michael was Wiedmaier's agent.

---

8. These concepts also apply when a person who is in fact an agent undertakes an action that is beyond the scope of her or his authority, as will be discussed in Chapter 33.
9. *Motorsport Marketing, Inc. v. Wiedmaier, Inc.,* 195 S.W.3d 492 (Mo.App. 2006).

Agency by Operation of Law

The courts may find an agency relationship in the absence of a formal agreement in other situations as well. This may occur in family relationships, such as when one spouse purchases certain basic necessaries and charges them to the other spouse's account. The courts often rule that a spouse is liable for payment for the necessaries because of either a social policy or a legal duty to supply necessaries to family members.

Agency by operation of law may also occur in emergency situations. If an agent cannot contact the principal and failure to act would cause the principal substantial loss, the agent may take steps beyond the scope of her or his authority. For example, a railroad engineer may contract on behalf of his or her employer for medical care for an injured motorist hit by the train.

Concept Summary 32.1 on the following page reviews the various ways that agencies are formed.

SECTION 3

DUTIES OF AGENTS AND PRINCIPALS

Once the principal-agent relationship has been created, both parties have duties that govern their conduct. As discussed previously, the principal-agent relationship is *fiduciary*—based on trust. In a fiduciary relationship, each party owes the other the duty to act with the utmost good faith. In this section, we examine the various duties of agents and principals.

Agent's Duties to the Principal

Generally, the agent owes the principal five duties— performance, notification, loyalty, obedience, and accounting.

PERFORMANCE An implied condition in every agency contract is the agent's agreement to use reasonable diligence and skill in performing the work. When an agent fails to perform his or her duties, liability for breach of contract may result.

Standard of Care. The degree of skill or care required of an agent is usually that expected of a reasonable person under similar circumstances. Generally, this is interpreted to mean ordinary care. If an agent has represented herself or himself as possessing special skills,

---

CONCEPT SUMMARY 32.1
Formation of the Agency Relationship

METHOD OF FORMATION	DESCRIPTION
By Agreement	The agency relationship is formed through express consent (oral or written) or implied by conduct.
By Ratification	The principal either by act or by agreement ratifies the conduct of a person who is not in fact an agent.
By Estoppel	The principal causes a third person to believe that another person is the principal's agent, and the third person acts to his or her detriment in reasonable reliance on that belief.
By Operation of Law	The agency relationship is based on a social or legal duty (such as the need to support family members) or formed in emergency situations when the agent is unable to contact the principal and failure to act outside the scope of the agent's authority would cause the principal substantial loss.

---

however, the agent is expected to exercise the degree of skill claimed. Failure to do so constitutes a breach of the agent's duty.

Gratuitous Agents. Not all agency relationships are based on contract. In some situations, an agent acts gratuitously—that is, without payment. A gratuitous agent cannot be liable for breach of contract because there is no contract. He or she is subject only to tort liability. Once a gratuitous agent has begun to act in an agency capacity, he or she has the duty to continue to perform in that capacity. A gratuitous agent must perform in an acceptable manner and is subject to the same standards of care and duty to perform as other agents.

▶ **Example 32.8**   Bower's friend Alcott is a real estate broker. Alcott offers to sell Bower's vacation home at no charge. If Alcott never attempts to sell the home, Bower has no legal cause of action to force her to do so. If Alcott does attempt to sell the home to Friedman, but then performs so negligently that the sale falls through, Bower can sue Alcott for negligence. ◀

NOTIFICATION An agent is required to notify the principal of all matters that come to her or his attention concerning the subject matter of the agency. This is the *duty of notification,* or the duty to inform.

▶ **Example 32.9**   Perez, an artist, is about to negotiate a contract to sell a series of paintings to Barber's Art Gallery for $25,000. Perez's agent learns that Barber is insolvent and will be unable to pay for the paintings. The agent has a duty to inform Perez of

Barber's insolvency because it is relevant to the subject matter of the agency, which is the sale of Perez's paintings. ◀

Generally, the law assumes that the principal is aware of any information acquired by the agent that is relevant to the agency—regardless of whether the agent actually passes on this information to the principal. It is a basic tenet of agency law that notice to the agent is notice to the principal.

LOYALTY Loyalty is one of the most fundamental duties in a fiduciary relationship. Basically, the agent has the duty to act *solely for the benefit of his or her principal* and not in the interest of the agent or a third party. For instance, an agent cannot represent two principals in the same transaction unless both know of the dual capacity and consent to it.

Maintain Confidentiality. The duty of loyalty also means that any information or knowledge acquired through the agency relationship is confidential. It is a breach of loyalty to disclose such information either during the agency relationship or after its termination. Typical examples of confidential information are trade secrets and customer lists compiled by the principal.

Actions Must Benefit the Principal. The agent's loyalty must be undivided. The agent's actions must be strictly for the benefit of the principal and must not result in any secret profit for the agent.

▶ **Case in Point 32.10**   Don Cousins contracted with Leo Hodgins, a real estate agent, to negotiate the purchase of an office building. While working for Cousins, Hodgins discovered that the property owner would sell the building only as a package deal with another parcel. Hodgins therefore bought the two properties intending to resell the building to Cousins. When Cousins found out, he sued.

The court held that Hodgins had breached his fiduciary duties. As a real estate agent, Hodgins had a duty to communicate all offers to his principal and not to secretly purchase the property and then resell

it to his principal. Hodgins was required to act in Cousins's best interests and could only become the purchaser in this situation with Cousins's knowledge and approval.[10] ◄

In the following case, an employer alleged that a former employee had breached his duty of loyalty by planning a competing business while still working for the employer.

---

10. *Cousins v. Realty Ventures, Inc.,* 844 So.2d 860 (La.App. 5 Cir. 2003).

CASE ANALYSIS

Case 32.3 Taser International, Inc. v. Ward
Court of Appeals of Arizona, Division 1, 224 Ariz. 389, 231 P.3d 921 (2010).

IN THE LANGUAGE OF THE COURT
PORTLEY, Judge.

* * * *

Taser International develops and manufactures electronic control devices, commonly called stun guns, and accessories for electronic control devices, including a personal video and audio recording device called TASER CAM. Taser sells its products to the military, law enforcement, corrections, private security, and the general public.

[Steve] Ward was employed full-time with Taser from January 1, 2004, to July 24, 2007, and served as Taser's vice president of marketing during the time relevant to this appeal. He was an at-will employee,[a] and he did not sign any employment contract, non-compete agreement, or non-disclosure agreement.

* * * *

In December 2006, Ward began exploring whether he could personally develop the concept of an eyeglass-mounted camera. He sought

legal advice about whether he could permissibly develop such a camera independent of Taser, and hired patent counsel to conduct a patent search on the idea.

Between April 2007 and his resignation approximately four months later, Ward shifted his exploration to the concept of a clip-on camera device, after learning that the eyeglass-mounted concept was already patent protected. He directed patent counsel to conduct a patent search on the modified idea. He communicated with JAM-Proactive, a product development company, about the design and development of a clip-on camera device, and he received a detailed product development proposal from JAM-Proactive on June 12, 2007. Prior to his resignation, Ward planned to leave Taser to form a new business, and completed substantial work on a business plan to develop, market, and sell a clip-on camera device.

Ward resigned on July 24, 2007. * * * He formed Vievu LLC on August 23, 2007, and Vievu now markets a clip-on camera device to general consumers and law enforcement. Ten months after Ward resigned, Taser announced the AXON, a product that provides an audio-video record of an incident from the visual perspective of the person involved.

[Taser filed a suit against Ward in an Arizona state court alleging, among other things, that Ward had breached his duty of loyalty to Taser. Taser moved for summary judgment in its favor, which the court granted. Ward appealed.]

* * * *

"In Arizona, an employee/agent owes his or her employer/principal a fiduciary duty." *"It is too plain to need discussion that an agent is under the duty to act with entire good faith and loyalty for the furtherance of the interests of his principal in all matters concerning or affecting the subject of his agency, and if he fails to do so, he is responsible to his principal for any loss resulting therefrom."* [Emphasis added.]

One aspect of this broad principle is that an employee is precluded from actively competing with his or her employer during the period of employment.

Although an employee may not compete prior to termination, "[the employee] may take action [during employment], not otherwise wrongful, to prepare for competition following termination of the agency relationship." Preparation cannot take the form of "acts in direct competition with the employer's business."

The line separating mere preparation from active competition may be difficult

---

a. As you will read in Chapter 34, *employment at will* is a common law doctrine under which either party may terminate an employment relationship at any time for any reason, unless a contract specifies otherwise.

to discern in some cases, and we must "focus on the nature of the defendant's preparations to compete." [Emphasis added.]

＊＊＊＊

It is undisputed that, prior to his resignation, Ward did not solicit or recruit any Taser employees, distributors, customers, or vendors; he did not buy, sell, or incorporate any business; he did not acquire office space or other general business services; he did not contact or enter into any agreements with suppliers or manufacturers for his proposed clip-on camera; and he did not sell any products. However, Ward did begin developing a business plan, counseled with several attorneys, explored and abandoned the concept of an eyeglass-mounted camera device, and engaged, to some extent, in the exploration and development of a clip-on camera device.

Ward argues that his pre-termination activities did not constitute active competition but were merely lawful preparation for a future business venture. Taser contends, however, that "this case is not about just investigating computer software, acquiring a line of credit, securing office space, or getting prices on telephones ＊＊＊ [but] about developing a rival design during employment, knowing full well TASER has sold such a device and continues to develop a second-generation product."

Upon review, we agree with Ward that certain of his pre-termination activities are qualitatively different than "direct competition" and cannot form the basis for liability.

＊＊＊＊

However, assuming Taser was engaged in the research and development of a recording device during Ward's employment, assuming Ward

knew or should have known of those efforts, and assuming Taser's device would compete with Ward's concept, substantial design and development efforts by Ward during his employment would constitute direct competition with the business activities of Taser and would violate his duty of loyalty. In the context of a business which engages in research, design, development, manufacture, and marketing of products, we cannot limit "competition" to just actual sales of competing products.

Summary judgment on this theory is nevertheless improper because a genuine issue of material fact exists as to the extent of Ward's pre-termination design and development efforts.

＊＊＊＊

For the foregoing reasons, we reverse the grant of summary judgment entered in favor of Taser ＊＊＊ and remand for further proceedings.

LEGAL REASONING QUESTIONS

1. Why was it unclear whether Ward's pretermination actions constituted direct competition with his employer or were mere planning activities?
2. Suppose that Ward's planning and development efforts were focused on a product that would in no way compete with Taser's products. Would such efforts have breached his duty of loyalty to Taser in any way? Explain fully.
3. Are there other duties to his employer that Ward might have breached in addition to the duty of loyalty as Taser alleged here? Discuss.
4. If the judgment in the case on remand is again in Taser's favor, what might be an appropriate remedy?

OBEDIENCE When acting on behalf of the principal, an agent has a duty to follow all lawful and clearly stated instructions of the principal. Any deviation from such instructions is a violation of this duty.

During emergency situations, however, when the principal cannot be consulted, the agent may deviate from the instructions without violating this duty. Whenever instructions are not clearly stated, the agent can fulfill the duty of obedience by acting in good faith and in a manner reasonable under the circumstances.

ACCOUNTING Unless the agent and principal agree otherwise, the agent must keep and make available to the principal an account of all property and funds

received and paid out on the principal's behalf. This includes gifts from third parties in connection with the agency. For instance, a gift from a customer to a salesperson for prompt deliveries made by the salesperson's firm, in the absence of a company policy to the contrary, belongs to the firm.

The agent has a duty to maintain a separate account for the principal's funds and must not intermingle these funds with the agent's personal funds. If a licensed professional (such as an attorney) violates this duty, he or she may be subject to disciplinary proceedings carried out by the appropriate regulatory institution (such as the state bar association). Of course, the professional will also be liable to the principal (the professional's client) for failure to account.

Principal's Duties to the Agent

The principal also has certain duties to the agent. These duties relate to compensation, reimbursement and indemnification, cooperation, and safe working conditions.

COMPENSATION In general, when a principal requests certain services from an agent, the agent reasonably expects payment. The principal therefore has a duty to pay the agent for services rendered. For instance, when an accountant or an attorney is asked to act as an agent, an agreement to compensate the agent for this service is implied.

The principal also has a duty to pay that compensation in a timely manner. Unless the agency relationship is gratuitous and the agent does not act in exchange for payment, the principal must pay the agreed-on value for the agent's services. If no amount has been expressly agreed on, then the principal owes the agent the customary compensation for such services.

REIMBURSEMENT AND INDEMNIFICATION The principal has a duty to reimburse the agent for any funds disbursed at the principal's request. The principal must also reimburse the agent for any necessary expenses incurred in the course of the reasonable performance of her or his agency duties.[11] Agents cannot recover for expenses incurred as a result of their own misconduct or negligence, though.

Subject to the terms of the agency agreement, the principal has the duty to *indemnify* (compensate) an agent for liabilities incurred because of authorized and lawful acts and transactions. For instance, if the agent, on the principal's behalf, forms a contract with a third party, and the principal fails to perform the contract, the third party may sue the agent for damages. In this situation, the principal is obligated to compensate the agent for any costs incurred by the agent as a result of the principal's failure to perform the contract.

Additionally, the principal must indemnify the agent for the value of benefits that the agent confers on the principal. The amount of indemnification usually is specified in the agency contract. If it is not, the courts will look to the nature of the business and the type of loss to determine the amount. Note that this rule applies to acts by gratuitous agents as well.

---

11. This principle applies to acts by gratuitous agents as well. If a finder of a dog that becomes sick takes the dog to a veterinarian and pays the veterinarian's fees, the gratuitous agent is entitled to be reimbursed by the dog's owner.

COOPERATION A principal has a duty to cooperate with the agent and to assist the agent in performing his or her duties. The principal must do nothing to prevent that performance.

For instance, when a principal grants an agent an exclusive territory, the principal creates an **exclusive agency,** in which the principal cannot compete with the agent or appoint or allow another agent to compete. If the principal does so, he or she violates the exclusive agency and is exposed to liability for the agent's lost profits.

▶ **Example 32.11** River City Times Company (the principal) grants Emir (the agent) the right to sell its newspapers at a busy downtown intersection to the exclusion of all other vendors. This creates an exclusive territory within which only Emir has the right to sell those newspapers. If River City Times allows another vendor to sell its papers in that area, Emir can sue for lost profits. ◀

SAFE WORKING CONDITIONS The common law requires the principal to provide safe working premises, equipment, and conditions for all agents and employees. The principal has a duty to inspect working areas and to warn agents and employees about any unsafe situations. When the agent is an employee, the employer's liability is frequently covered by state workers' compensation insurance. In addition, federal and state statutes often require the employer to meet certain safety standards (see Chapter 34).

SECTION 4
RIGHTS AND REMEDIES OF AGENTS AND PRINCIPALS

In general, for every duty of the principal, the agent has a corresponding right, and vice versa. When one party to the agency relationship violates his or her duty to the other party, the remedies available to the nonbreaching party arise out of contract and tort law. These remedies include monetary damages, termination of the agency relationship, an injunction, and required accountings.

Agent's Rights and Remedies against the Principal

The agent has the right to be compensated, to be reimbursed and indemnified, and to have a safe working environment. An agent also has the right to perform agency duties without interference by the principal.

TORT AND CONTRACT REMEDIES Remedies of the agent for breach of duty by the principal follow normal contract and tort remedies. ▶ **Example 32.12** Aaron Hart, a builder who has just constructed a new house, contracts with a real estate agent, Fran Boller, to sell the house. The contract calls for the agent to have an exclusive ninety-day listing and to receive 6 percent of the selling price when the home is sold. Boller holds several open houses and shows the home to a number of potential buyers.

One month before the ninety-day listing terminates, Hart agrees to sell the house to another buyer—not one to whom Boller has shown the house—after the ninety-day listing expires. Hart and the buyer agree that Hart will reduce the price of the house by 3 percent because he will sell it directly and thus will not have to pay Boller's commission. In this situation, if Boller learns of Hart's actions, she can terminate the agency relationship and sue Hart for damages, including the 6 percent commission she should have earned on the sale of the house. ◀

DEMAND FOR AN ACCOUNTING An agent can also withhold further performance and demand that the principal give an accounting. For instance, a sales agent may demand an accounting if the agent and principal disagree on the amount of commissions the agent should have received for sales made during a specific period of time.

NO RIGHT TO SPECIFIC PERFORMANCE When the principal-agent relationship is not contractual, the agent has no right to specific performance. An agent can recover for past services and future damages but cannot force the principal to allow him or her to continue acting as an agent.

Principal's Rights and Remedies against the Agent

In general, a principal has contract remedies for an agent's breach of fiduciary duties. The principal also has tort remedies if the agent engages in misrepresentation, negligence, deceit, libel, slander, or trespass. In addition, any breach of a fiduciary duty by an agent may justify the principal's termination of the agency. The main actions available to the principal are constructive trust, avoidance, and indemnification.

CONSTRUCTIVE TRUST Anything that an agent obtains by virtue of the employment or agency relationship belongs to the principal. An agent commits a breach of fiduciary duty if he or she secretly retains benefits or profits that, by right, belong to the principal. ▶ **Example 32.13** Lee, a purchasing agent for Metcalf, receives cash rebates from a customer. If Lee keeps the rebates for himself, he violates his fiduciary duty to his principal, Metcalf. On finding out about the cash rebates, Metcalf can sue Lee and recover them. ◀

AVOIDANCE When an agent breaches the agency agreement or agency duties under a contract, the principal has a right to avoid any contract entered into with the agent. This right of avoidance is at the election of the principal.

INDEMNIFICATION In certain situations, when a principal is sued by a third party for an agent's negligent conduct, the principal can sue the agent for indemnification—that is, for an equal amount of damages. The same holds true if the agent violates the principal's instructions.

▶ **Example 32.14** Parker (the principal) owns a used-car lot where Moore (the agent) works as a salesperson. Parker tells Moore to make no warranties for the used cars. Moore is eager to make a sale to Walters, a customer, and adds a 50,000-mile warranty for the car's engine. Parker may still be liable to Walters for engine failure, but if Walters sues Parker, Parker normally can then sue Moore for indemnification for violating his instructions. ◀

Sometimes, it is difficult to distinguish between instructions of the principal that limit an agent's authority and those that are merely advice. ▶ **Example 32.15** Gutierrez (the principal) owns an office supply company, and Logan (the agent) is the manager. Gutierrez tells Logan, "Don't purchase any more inventory this month." Gutierrez goes on vacation. A large order comes in from a local business, and the inventory on hand is insufficient to meet it. What is Logan to do? In this situation, Logan probably has the inherent authority to purchase more inventory despite Gutierrez's command. It is unlikely that Logan would be required to indemnify Gutierrez in the event that the local business subsequently canceled the order. ◀

Reviewing: Agency Formation and Duties

James Blatt hired Marilyn Scott to sell insurance for the Massachusetts Mutual Life Insurance Company. Their contract stated, "Nothing in this contract shall be construed as creating the relationship of employer and employee." The contract was terminable at will by either party. Scott financed her own office and staff, was paid according to performance, had no taxes withheld from her checks, and could legally sell products of Massachusetts Mutual's competitors. Blatt learned that Scott was simultaneously selling insurance for Perpetual Life Insurance Corporation, one of Massachusetts Mutual's fiercest competitors. Blatt therefore withheld client contact information from Scott that would have assisted her insurance sales for Massachusetts Mutual. Scott complained to Blatt that he was inhibiting her ability to sell insurance for Massachusetts Mutual. Blatt subsequently terminated their contract. Scott filed a suit in a New York state court against Blatt and Massachusetts Mutual. Scott claimed that she had lost sales for Massachusetts Mutual—and her commissions—as a result of Blatt's withholding contact information from her. Using the information presented in the chapter, answer the following questions.

1. Who is the principal and who is the agent in this scenario? By which method was an agency relationship formed between Scott and Blatt?
2. What facts would the court consider most important in determining whether Scott was an employee or an independent contractor?
3. How would the court most likely rule on Scott's employee status? Why?
4. Which of the four duties that Blatt owed Scott in their agency relationship has probably been breached?

DEBATE THIS . . . *All works created by independent contractors should be considered works for hire under copyright law.*

Terms and Concepts

agency 624
exclusive agency 634

fiduciary 624

independent contractor 625

ExamPrep

Issue Spotters

1. Winona contracted with XtremeCast, a broadcast media firm, to cohost an Internet-streaming sports program. Winona and XtremeCast signed a new contract for each episode. In each contract, Winona agreed to work a certain number of days for a certain salary. During each broadcast, Winona was free to improvise her performance. She had no other obligation to work for XtremeCast. Was Winona an independent contractor? **(See page 625.)**

2. Dimka Corporation wants to build a new mall on a specific tract of land. Dimka contracts with Nadine to buy the property. When Nadine learns of the difference between the price that Dimka is willing to pay and the price at which the owner is willing to sell, she wants to buy the land and sell it to Dimka herself. Can she do this? Discuss. **(See page 631.)**

- **Check your answers to the Issue Spotters against the answers provided in Appendix E at the end of this text.**

Before the Test

Go to **www.cengagebrain.com**, enter the ISBN 9781285185248, and click on "Find" to locate this textbook's Web site. Then, click on "Access Now" under "Study Tools," and select Chapter 32 at the top. There, you will find a Practice Quiz that you can take to assess your mastery of the concepts in this chapter, as well as Flashcards and a Glossary of important terms.

Business Scenarios

32–1. Agency Formation. Paul Gett is a well-known, wealthy financial expert living in the city of Torris. Adam Wade, Gett's friend, tells Timothy Brown that he is Gett's agent for the purchase of rare coins. Wade even shows Brown a local newspaper clipping mentioning Gett's interest in coin collecting. Brown, knowing of Wade's friendship with Gett, contracts with Wade to sell a rare coin valued at $25,000 to Gett. Wade takes the coin and disappears with it. On the payment due date, Brown seeks to collect from Gett, claiming that Wade's agency made Gett liable. Gett does not deny that Wade was a friend, but he claims that Wade was never his agent. Discuss fully whether an agency was in existence at the time the contract for the rare coin was made. **(See page 628.)**

32–2. Duty of Loyalty. Peter hires Alice as an agent to sell a piece of property he owns. The price is to be at least $30,000. Alice discovers that the fair market value of Peter's property is actually at least $45,000 and could be higher because a shopping mall is going to be built nearby. Alice forms a real estate partnership with her cousin Carl. Then she prepares for Peter's signature a contract for the sale of the property to Carl for $32,000. Peter signs the contract. Just before closing and passage of title, Peter learns about the shopping mall and the increased fair market value of his property. Peter refuses to deed the property to Carl. Carl claims that Alice, as Peter's agent, solicited a price above that agreed on when the agency was created and that the contract is therefore binding and enforceable. Discuss fully whether Peter is bound to this contract. **(See page 631.)**

32–3. Employee versus Independent Contractor. Stephen Hemmerling was a driver for the Happy Cab Co. Hemmerling paid certain fixed expenses and abided by a variety of rules relating to the use of the cab, the hours that could be worked, and the solicitation of fares, among other things. Rates were set by the state. Happy Cab did not withhold taxes from Hemmerling's pay. While driving the cab, Hemmerling was injured in an accident and filed a claim for workers' compensation benefits in a state court. Such benefits are not available to independent contractors. On what basis might the court hold that Hemmerling was an employee? Explain. **(See page 625.)**

Business Case Problems

32–4. Spotlight on Agency—Independent Contractors. Frank Frausto delivered newspapers under a renewable six-month contract called a "Delivery Agent Agreement." The agreement identified Frausto as an independent contractor. The company collected payment from customers and took complaints about delivery. Frausto was given the route for his paper delivery and was required to deliver the paper within a certain time period each day. Frausto delivered the papers using his own vehicle and had to provide proof of insurance to the company. The company provided health and disability insurance but did not withhold taxes from Frausto's weekly income. One morning, Frausto was delivering papers and collided with Santiago on his motorcycle. Santiago filed a negligence action against Frausto and the newspaper company. The newspaper company argued that it should not be liable because Frausto was an independent contractor. What was the result? Why? [*Santiago v. Phoenix Newspapers, Inc.,* 794 P.2d 138 (Ariz. 1990)] **(See page 625.)**

32–5. Agency Formation. Ford Motor Credit Co. is a subsidiary of Ford Motor Co. with its own offices, officers, and directors. Ford Credit buys contracts and leases of automobiles entered into by dealers and consumers. Ford Credit also provides inventory financing for dealers' purchases of Ford and non-Ford vehicles and makes loans to Ford and non-Ford dealers. Dealers and consumers are not required to finance their purchases or leases of Ford vehicles through Ford Credit. Ford Motor is not a party to the agreements between Ford Credit and its customers and does not directly receive any payments under those agreements. Also, Ford Credit is not subject to any agreement with Ford Motor "restricting or conditioning" its ability to finance the dealers' inventories or the consumers' purchases or leases of vehicles. A number of plaintiffs filed a product liability suit in a Missouri state court against Ford Motor. Ford Motor claimed that the court did not have venue. The plaintiffs asserted that Ford Credit, which had an office in the jurisdiction, acted as Ford's "agent for the transaction of its usual and customary business" there. Is Ford Credit an agent of Ford Motor? Discuss. [*State ex rel. Ford Motor Co. v. Bacon,* 63 S.W.3d 641 (Mo. 2002)] **(See page 628.)**

32–6. Agency by Ratification. Wesley Hall, an independent contractor managing property for Acree Investments, Ltd., lost control of a fire he had set to clear ten acres of Acree land. The runaway fire burned seventy-eight acres of Earl Barrs's property. Russell Acree, one of the owners of Acree Investments, had previously owned the ten acres, but he had put it into the company and was no longer the principal owner. Hall had worked for Russell Acree in the past and had told the state forestry department that he was burning the land for Acree. Barrs sued Russell Acree for the acts of his agent, Hall. In his suit,

Barrs noted that Hall had been an employee of Russell Acree, Hall had talked about burning the land "for Acree," and Russell Acree had apologized to Barrs for the fire. Barrs also pointed out that Acree Investments had not been identified as the principal property owner until Barrs filed his lawsuit. Barrs argued that those facts were sufficient to create an agency by ratification to impose liability on Russell Acree. Was Barrs's agency by ratification claim valid? Why or why not? [*Barrs v. Acree*, 691 S.E.2d 575 (Ga.App. 2010)] **(See page 629.)**

32–7. BUSINESS CASE PROBLEM
WITH SAMPLE ANSWER: Employment Relationships.

William Moore owned Moore Enterprises, a whole-sale tire business. William's son, Jonathan, worked as a Moore Enterprises employee while he was in high school. Later, Jonathan started his own busi-ness, called Morecedes Tire. Morecedes regrooved tires and sold them to businesses, including Moore Enterprises. A decade after Jonathan started Morecedes, William offered him work with Moore Enterprises. On the first day, William told Jonathan to load certain tires on a trailer but did not tell him how to do it. Was Jonathan an independent contractor? Discuss. [Moore v. Moore, 152 Idaho 245, 269 P.3d 802 (2011)] **(See page 625.)**

- **For a sample answer to Problem 32–7, go to Appendix F at the end of this text.**

32–8. Agent's Duties to Principal. William and Maxine Miller were shareholders of Claimsco International, Inc. They filed a suit against the other shareholders, Michael Harris and Kenneth Hoxie, and the accountant who worked for all of them—John Verchota. The Millers alleged that Verchota had breached a duty that he owed them. They claimed that at Harris's instruction, Verchota had adjusted Claimsco's books to maximize the Millers' financial lia-bilities, falsely reflect income to them without actually transferring that income, and unfairly disadvantage them compared to the other shareholders. Which duty are the Millers referring to? If the allegations can be proved, did

Verchota breach this duty? Explain. [*Miller v. Harris*, 2013 IL App (2d) 120512, 985 N.E.2d 671 (Ill.App. 2 Dist. 2013)] **(See page 630.)**

32–9. A QUESTION OF ETHICS: Agency Formation and Duties.

Western Fire Truck, Inc., contracted with Emergency One, Inc. (EO), to be its exclusive dealer in Colorado and Wyoming through December 2003. James Costello, a Western salesperson, was authorized to order EO vehicles for his customers. Without informing Western, Costello e-mailed EO about Western's difficulties in obtaining cash to fund its operations. He asked about the viability of Western's contract and his possible employment with EO. On EO's request, and in disregard of Western's instructions, Costello sent some payments for EO vehicles directly to EO. In addition, Costello, with EO's help, sent a competing bid to a potential Western customer. EO's representative e-mailed Costello, "You have my permission to kick [Western's] ass." In April 2002, EO terminated its contract with Western, and, after reviewing Costello's e-mail, fired Costello. Western filed a suit in a Colorado state court, alleging that Costello breached his duty as an agent and that EO aided and abetted the breach. [Western Fire Truck, Inc. v. Emergency One, Inc., 134 P.3d 570 (Colo. App. 2006)] **(See page 628.)**

(a) Was there an agency relationship between Western and Costello? Western required monthly reports from its sales staff, but Costello did not report regu-larly. Does this indicate that Costello was not West-ern's agent? In determining whether an agency rela-tionship exists, is the right to control or the fact of control more important? Explain.

(b) Did Costello owe Western a duty? If so, what was the duty? Did Costello breach it? If so, how?

(c) A Colorado state statute allows a court to award pu-nitive damages in "circumstances of fraud, malice, or willful and wanton conduct." Did any of these circum-stances exist in this case? Should punitive damages be assessed against either defendant? Why or why not?

Legal Reasoning Group Activity

32–10. Agent's Duties to Principal. John Warren wanted to buy a condominium in California. Hildegard Merrill was the agent for the seller. Because Warren's credit rating was poor, Merrill told him he needed a co-borrower to obtain a mortgage at a reasonable rate. Merrill said that her daughter Charmaine would "go on title" until the loan and sale were complete if Warren would pay her $10,000. Merrill also offered to defer her commission on the sale as a loan to Warren so that he could make a 20 percent down payment on the property. He agreed to both plans.

Merrill secured the mortgage in Charmaine's name alone by misrepresenting her daughter's address, business,

and income. To close the sale, Merrill had Warren remove his name from the title to the property. In October, War-ren moved into the condominium, repaid Merrill the amount of her deferred commission, and began paying the mortgage. Within a few months, Merrill had Warren evicted. Warren subsequently filed a suit against Merrill and Charmaine. **(See page 630.)**

(a) The first group will determine who among these par-ties was in an agency relationship.

(b) The second group will discuss the basic duty that an agent owes a principal and decide whether that duty was breached here.

CHAPTER 33

AGENCY LIABILITY TO THIRD PARTIES AND TERMINATION

I n the discussion of agency in the previous chapter, we focused on how the relationship between a principal and an agent is formed and the duties of the principal and agent in that relationship. This chapter deals with another important aspect of agency law—the liability of principals and agents to third parties.

We look first at the liability of principals for contracts formed by agents with third parties. Generally, the liability of the principal will depend on whether the agent was authorized to form the contract. The second part of the chapter deals with an agent's liability to third parties in contract and tort, and the principal's liability to third parties because of an agent's torts. The chapter concludes with a discussion of how agency relationships are terminated.

SECTION 1
SCOPE OF AGENT'S AUTHORITY

The liability of a principal to third parties with whom an agent contracts depends on whether the agent had the authority to enter into legally binding contracts on the principal's behalf. An agent's authority can be either *actual* (express or implied) or *apparent*. If an agent contracts outside the scope of his or her authority, the principal may still become liable by ratifying the contract.

Express Authority

Express authority is authority declared in clear, direct, and definite terms. Express authority can be given orally or in writing.

THE EQUAL DIGNITY RULE In most states, the **equal dignity rule** requires that if the contract being executed is or must be in writing, then the agent's authority must also be in writing. Failure to comply with the equal dignity rule can make a contract voidable *at the option of the principal*. The law regards the contract at that point as a mere offer. If the principal decides to accept the offer, the acceptance must be ratified, or affirmed, in writing (or in an electronic record).

▶ **Example 33.1** Paloma (the principal) orally asks Austin (the agent) to sell a ranch that Paloma owns. Austin finds a buyer and signs a sales contract (a contract for an interest in realty must be in writing) on behalf of Paloma to sell the ranch. The buyer cannot enforce the contract unless Paloma subsequently ratifies Austin's agency status *in writing*. Once the sales contract is ratified, either party can enforce rights under the contract. ◀

Modern business practice allows several exceptions to the equal dignity rule:

1. An executive officer of a corporation normally can conduct *ordinary* business transactions without obtaining written authority from the corporation (see Chapters 39 and 40).
2. When the agent acts in the presence of the principal, the rule does not apply.
3. When the agent's act of signing is merely a formality, then the agent does not need written authority to sign. ▶ **Example 33.2** Sandra Healy (the principal) negotiates a contract but is called out of town the day it is to be signed. If Healy orally authorizes Santini to sign, the oral authorization is sufficient. ◀

POWER OF ATTORNEY Giving an agent a **power of attorney** confers express authority.[1] The power of attorney is a written document and is usually notarized. (A document is notarized when a **notary public**—a public official authorized to attest to the

---

1. An agent who holds a power of attorney is called an *attorney-in-fact* for the principal. The holder does not have to be an attorney-at-law (and often is not).

authenticity of signatures—signs and dates the document and imprints it with her or his seal of authority.) Most states have statutory provisions for creating a power of attorney.

A power of attorney can be *special* (permitting the agent to perform specified acts only), or it can be *general* (permitting the agent to transact all business for the principal). Because of the extensive authority granted to an agent by a general power of attorney (see Exhibit 33–1 below), it should be used with great caution and usually only in exceptional circumstances. Ordinarily, a power of attorney terminates

EXHIBIT 33–1 A Sample General Power of Attorney

GENERAL POWER OF ATTORNEY

Know All Men by These Presents:

That I, _____ , hereinafter referred to as PRINCIPAL, in the County of _____
State of _____ , do(es) appoint _____ as my true and lawful attorney.

In principal's name, and for principal's use and benefit, said attorney is authorized hereby;

(1) To demand, sue for, collect, and receive all money, debts, accounts, legacies, bequests, interest, dividends, annuities, and demands as are now or shall hereafter become due, payable, or belonging to principal, and take all lawful means, for the recovery thereof and to compromise the same and give discharges for the same;

(2) To buy and sell land, make contracts of every kind relative to land, any interest therein or the possession thereof, and to take possession and exercise control over the use thereof;

(3) To buy, sell, mortgage, hypothecate, assign, transfer, and in any manner deal with goods, wares and merchandise, choses in action, certificates or shares of capital stock, and other property in possession or in action, and to make, do, and transact all and every kind of business of whatever nature;

(4) To execute, acknowledge, and deliver contracts of sale, escrow instructions, deeds, leases including leases for minerals and hydrocarbon substances and assignments of leases, covenants, agreements and assignments of agreements, mortgages and assignments of mortgages, conveyances in trust, to secure indebtedness or other obligations, and assign the beneficial interest thereunder, subordinations of liens or encumbrances, bills of lading, receipts, evidences of debt, releases, bonds, notes, bills, requests to reconvey deeds of trust, partial or full judgments, satisfactions of mortgages, and other debts, and other written instruments of whatever kind and nature, all upon such terms and conditions as said attorney shall approve.

GIVING AND GRANTING to said attorney full power and authority to do all and every act and thing whatsoever requisite and necessary to be done relative to any of the foregoing as fully to all intents and purposes as principal might or could do if personally present.

All that said attorney shall lawfully do or cause to be done under the authority of this power of attorney is expressly approved.

Dated: _____   /s/_____

State of _____   ⎫ SS.
    County of _____   ⎬
On _____ , before me, the undersigned, a Notary Public in and for said
State, personally appeared _____

known to me to be the person _____ whose name _____ subscribed
to the within instrument and acknowledged that _____ executed the same.

Witness my hand and official seal.   (Seal) _____
                                                      Notary Public in and for said State.

on the incapacity or death of the person giving the power.[2]

Implied Authority

An agent has the **implied authority** to do what is reasonably necessary to carry out express authority and accomplish the objectives of the agency. Authority can also be implied by custom or inferred from the position the agent occupies. (For a discussion of what happens when an employee-agent makes unauthorized use of the employer's computer data, see this chapter's *Insight into Ethics* feature below.)

▶ **Example 33.3** Archer is employed by Packard Grocery to manage one of its stores. Packard has not expressly stated that Archer has authority to contract with third persons. Nevertheless, authority to manage a business implies authority to do what is reasonably required (as is customary or can be inferred from a manager's position) to operate the business. This includes forming contracts to hire employees, to buy merchandise and equipment, and to advertise the products sold in the store. ◀

---

2. A *durable* power of attorney, however, continues to be effective despite the principal's incapacity. An elderly person, for example, might grant a durable power of attorney to provide for the handling of property and investments or specific health-care needs should he or she become incompetent (see Chapter 51).

INSIGHT INTO ETHICS
The Ethical and Legal Implications of Breaching Company Policy on the Use of Electronic Data

Suppose that an employee-agent who is authorized to access company trade secrets contained in computer files takes those secrets to a competitor for whom the employee is about to begin working. Clearly, the agent has violated the ethical—and legal—duty of loyalty to the principal. Does this breach of loyalty mean that the employee's act of accessing the trade secrets was unauthorized?

The question has significant implications for both parties. If the act was unauthorized, the employee will be subject to state and federal laws prohibiting unauthorized access to computer information and data, including the Computer Fraud and Abuse Act (CFAA, discussed in Chapter 10). If the act was authorized, these laws will not apply.

Does Exceeding Authorized Access to a Company's Database Violate the Law?

David Nosal once worked for Korn/Ferry and had access to the company's confidential database. When he left, he encouraged several former colleagues who still worked there to join him in starting a competing firm. He asked them to access Korn/Ferry's database and download source lists, names, and client contact information before they quit. The employees had authority to access the database, but Korn/Ferry's policy forbade disclosure of confidential information.

The government filed charges against Nosal and his colleagues for violating the CFAA, among other things.

A Court Rules That Violating an Employer's Use Restrictions Is Not a Crime

The U.S. Court of Appeals for the Ninth Circuit refused to find that the defendants had violated the CFAA. The court ruled that the phrase "exceed authorized access" in the CFAA refers to restrictions on access, not restrictions on use. The court reasoned that Congress's intent in enacting the CFAA was to prohibit people from hacking into computers without authorization.

The court also stated that the CFAA should not be used to criminally prosecute persons who use data in an unauthorized or unethical way. The court pointed out that "adopting the government's interpretation would turn vast numbers of teens and pre-teens into juvenile delinquents—and their parents and teachers into delinquency contributors." Furthermore, "the effect this broad construction of the CFAA has on workplace conduct pales by comparison with its effect on everyone else who uses a computer, smart-phone, iPad, Kindle, Nook, X-box, Blu-Ray player or any other Internet-enabled device."[a]

LEGAL CRITICAL THINKING
INSIGHT INTO THE LEGAL ENVIRONMENT

If an employee accesses Facebook at work even though personal use of a workplace computer is against the employer's stated policies, can the employee be criminally prosecuted? Why or why not?

---

a. *United States. v. Nosal,* 675 F.3d 854 (9th Cir. 2012).

Note, however, that an agent's implied authority cannot contradict his or her express authority. Thus, if a principal has limited an agent's express authority, then the fact that the agent customarily would have such authority is irrelevant. ▶ **Example 33.4** Juanita Alvarez is the owner of six Baja Tacos restaurants. Alvarez (the principal) strictly forbids the managers (agents) of her taco shops from entering into contracts to hire additional workers. Therefore, the fact that managers customarily would have authority to hire employees is immaterial. ◀

Apparent Authority

Actual authority (express or implied) arises from what the principal makes clear *to the agent*. Apparent authority, in contrast, arises from what the principal causes a third party to believe. An agent has **apparent authority** when the principal, by either word or action, causes a *third party* reasonably to believe that the agent has authority to act,

even though the agent has no express or implied authority.

A PATTERN OF CONDUCT Apparent authority usually comes into existence through a principal's pattern of conduct over time. ▶ **Example 33.5** Bailey is a traveling salesperson with the authority to solicit orders for the goods of Carlon Industries (the principal). Because she does not carry any goods with her, she normally would not have the implied authority to collect payments from customers on Carlon's behalf.

Suppose that Bailey does accept payments from Jayco Enterprises, however, and submits them to Carlon's accounting department for processing. If Carlon does nothing to stop Bailey from continuing this practice, a pattern develops over time. Thus, the principal confers apparent authority on Bailey to accept payments from Jayco. ◀

At issue in the following *Spotlight Case* was whether the manager of a horse breeding operation had the authority to bind the farm's owner in a contract guaranteeing breeding rights.

Case 33.1   Lundberg v. Church Farm, Inc.
Court of Appeals of Illinois, 502 N.E.2d 806, 151 Ill.App.3d (1986).

BACKGROUND AND FACTS Gilbert Church owned a horse breeding farm managed by Herb Bagley. Advertisements for the breeding rights to one of Church Farm's stallions, Imperial Guard, directed all inquiries to "Herb Bagley, Manager." Vern and Gail Lundberg bred Thoroughbred horses. The Lundbergs contacted Bagley and executed a preprinted contract giving them breeding rights to Imperial Guard "at Imperial Guard's location," subject to approval of the mares by Church. Bagley handwrote a statement on the contract that guaranteed the Lundbergs "six live foals in the first two years." He then signed it "Gilbert G. Church by H. Bagley."

The Lundbergs bred four mares, which resulted in one live foal. Church then moved Imperial Guard from Illinois to Oklahoma. The Lundbergs sued Church for breaching the contract by moving the horse. Church claimed that Bagley was not authorized to sign contracts for Church or to change or add terms, but only to present preprinted contracts to potential buyers. Church testified that although Bagley was his farm manager and the contact person for breeding rights, Bagley had never before modified the preprinted forms or signed Church's name on these contracts. The jury found in favor of the Lundbergs and awarded $147,000 in damages. Church appealed.

IN THE LANGUAGE OF THE COURT
Justice *UNVERZAGT* delivered the opinion of the court.
* * * *

* * * Defendant contends that plaintiffs have failed to establish that Bagley had apparent authority to negotiate and sign the Lundberg contract for Church Farm * * *.

*The party asserting an agency has the burden of proving its existence * * * but may do so by inference and circumstantial evidence. * * * Additionally, an agent may bind his principal by acts which the principal has not given him actual authority to perform, but which he appears authorized to* *perform.* * * * An agent's apparent authority is that authority which "the principal knowingly permits the agent to assume or which he holds his agent out as possessing. It is the authority that a reasonably prudent man, exercising diligence and discretion, in view of the principal's conduct, would naturally suppose the agent to possess." [Emphasis added.]

Plaintiffs produced evidence at trial that Gil Church approved the Imperial Guard advertisement listing Herb Bagley as Church Farm's manager, and directing all inquiries to him. Church also permitted Bagley to live on the farm and to handle its daily operations. Bagley was the only person available to visitors to the farm. Bagley answered Church Farm's phone calls, and there was a preprinted signature line for him on the breeding rights package.

The conclusion is inescapable that Gil Church affirmatively placed Bagley in a managerial position giving him complete control of Church Farm and its dealings with the public. We believe that this is just the sort of "holding out" of an agent by a principal that justifies a third person's reliance on the agent's authority.

We cannot accept defendant's contention that the Lundbergs were affirmatively obligated to seek out Church to ascertain the actual extent of Bagley's authority. Where an agent has apparent authority to act, the principal will be liable in spite of any undisclosed limitations the principal has placed on that authority.

DECISION AND REMEDY *The state appellate court affirmed the lower court's judgment in favor of the Lundbergs for $147,000. Because Church allowed circumstances to lead the Lundbergs to believe Bagley had the authority, Church was bound by Bagley's actions.*

THE LEGAL ENVIRONMENT DIMENSION *The court held that Church had allowed the Lundbergs to believe that Bagley was his agent. What steps could Church have taken to protect himself against a finding of apparent authority?*

THE ETHICAL DIMENSION *Does a principal have an ethical responsibility to inform an unaware third party that an apparent agent does not in fact have the authority to act on the principal's behalf?*

APPARENT AUTHORITY AND ESTOPPEL A court can apply the doctrine of agency by estoppel (discussed in Chapter 32) when a principal has given a third party reason to believe that an agent has authority to act. If the third party honestly relies on the principal's representations to his or her detriment, the principal may be *estopped* (prevented) from denying that the agent had authority.

▶ **Case in Point 33.6** Francis Azur was president and chief executive officer of ATM Corporation of America. Michelle Vanek, Azur's personal assistant at ATM, reviewed his credit-card statements, among other duties. For seven years, Vanek took unauthorized cash advances from Azur's credit-card account with Chase Bank. The charges appeared on at least sixty-five monthly statements. When Azur discovered Vanek's fraud, he fired her and closed the account. He filed a suit against Chase, arguing that the bank should not have allowed Vanek to take cash advances. The court concluded that Azur (the principal) had given the bank reason to believe that Vanek (the agent) had authority. Therefore, Azur was estopped (prevented) from denying Vanek's authority.[3] ◀

---

3. *Azur v. Chase Bank, USA, N.A.*, 601 F.3d 212 (3d Cir. 2010).

Emergency Powers

When an unforeseen emergency demands action by the agent to protect or preserve the property and rights of the principal, but the agent is unable to communicate with the principal, the agent has emergency power.

▶ **Example 33.7** Rob Fulsom is an engineer for Pacific Drilling Company. While Fulsom is acting within the scope of his employment, he is severely injured in an accident at an oil rig many miles from home.

Acosta, the rig supervisor, directs Thompson, a physician, to give medical aid to Fulsom and to charge Pacific for the medical services. Acosta, an agent, has no express or implied authority to bind the principal, Pacific Drilling, for Thompson's medical services. Because of the emergency situation, however, the law recognizes Acosta as having authority to act appropriately under the circumstances. ◀

Ratification

Ratification occurs when the principal affirms, or accepts responsibility for, an agent's *unauthorized* act. When ratification occurs, the principal is bound to the agent's act, and the act is treated as if it had been authorized by the principal *from the outset*. Ratification can be either express or implied.

If the principal does not ratify the contract, the principal is not bound, and the third party's agreement with the agent is viewed as merely an unaccepted offer. Because the third party's agreement is an unaccepted offer, the third party can revoke it at any time, without liability, before the principal ratifies the contract. The agent, however, may be liable to the third party for misrepresenting her or his authority.

The requirements for ratification can be summarized as follows:

1. The agent must have acted on behalf of an identified principal who subsequently ratifies the action.
2. The principal must know all of the material facts involved in the transaction. If a principal ratifies a contract without knowing all of the facts, the principal can rescind (cancel) the contract.[4]
3. The principal must affirm the agent's act in its entirety.
4. The principal must have the legal capacity to authorize the transaction at the time the agent engages in the act and at the time the principal ratifies. The third party must also have the legal capacity to engage in the transaction.
5. The principal's affirmation (ratification) must occur before the third party withdraws from the transaction.
6. The principal must observe the same formalities when ratifying the act as would have been required to authorize it initially.

Concept Summary 33.1 on the next page summarizes the rules concerning an agent's authority to bind the principal and a third party.

SECTION 2
LIABILITY FOR CONTRACTS

Liability for contracts formed by an agent depends on how the principal is classified and on whether the actions of the agent were authorized or unauthorized. Principals are classified as disclosed, partially disclosed, or undisclosed.[5]

1. A **disclosed principal** is a principal whose identity is known by the third party at the time the contract is made by the agent.
2. A **partially disclosed principal** is a principal whose identity is not known by the third party. Nevertheless, the third party knows that the agent is or *may* be acting for a principal at the time the contract is made. ▶ **Example 33.8** Eileen has contracted with a real estate agent to sell certain property. She wishes to keep her identity a secret, but the agent makes it clear to potential buyers of the property that the agent is acting in an agency capacity. In this situation, Eileen is a partially disclosed principal. ◀
3. An **undisclosed principal** is a principal whose identity is totally unknown by the third party. In addition, the third party has no knowledge that the agent is acting in an agency capacity at the time the contract is made.

Authorized Acts

If an agent acts within the scope of her or his authority, normally the principal is obligated to perform the contract regardless of whether the principal was disclosed, partially disclosed, or undisclosed.

Whether the *agent may also be held liable* under the contract, however, depends on the disclosed, partially disclosed, or undisclosed status of the principal.

DISCLOSED OR PARTIALLY DISCLOSED PRINCIPAL A disclosed or partially disclosed principal is liable to a third party for a contract made by the agent. If the principal is disclosed, the agent has no contractual liability for the nonperformance of the principal or the third party. If the principal is partially disclosed, in most states the agent is also treated as a party to the contract, and the third party can hold the agent liable for contractual nonperformance.[6]

▶ **Case in Point 33.9** Walgreens leased commercial property at a mall owned by Kedzie Plaza Associates. Kedzie used Taxman Corporation, a property management company. Taxman signed the lease with Walgreens on behalf of the principal, Kedzie. The lease required the landlord to keep the sidewalks free of snow and ice. Therefore, Taxman, on behalf of Kedzie, contracted with another company to remove ice and snow from the sidewalks surrounding the Walgreens store.

When a Walgreens employee slipped on ice outside the store and was injured, she sued Taxman, among others, for negligence. Because the identity of the principal (Kedzie) was fully disclosed in the snow-removal contract, however, the court ruled that the agent, Taxman, could not be held liable. Taxman did

---

4. If the third party has changed position in reliance on the apparent contract, however, the principal can rescind but must reimburse the third party for any costs.
5. *Restatement (Third) of Agency,* Section 1.04(2).

6. *Restatement (Third) of Agency,* Section 6.02.

CONCEPT SUMMARY 33.1
Authority of an Agent to Bind the Principal and a Third Party

AUTHORITY OF AGENT	DEFINITION	EFFECT ON PRINCIPAL AND THIRD PARTY
Express Authority	Authority expressly given by the principal to the agent.	Principal and third party are bound in contract.
Implied Authority	Authority implied (1) by custom, (2) from the position in which the principal has placed the agent, or (3) because such authority is necessary if the agent is to carry out expressly authorized duties and responsibilities.	Principal and third party are bound in contract.
Apparent Authority	Authority created when the conduct of the principal leads a third party to believe that the principal's agent has authority.	Principal and third party are bound in contract.
Unauthorized Acts	Acts committed by an agent that are outside the scope of his or her express, implied, or apparent authority.	Principal and third party are not bound in contract—*unless* the principal ratifies prior to the third party's withdrawal.

not assume a contractual obligation to remove the snow but merely retained a contractor to do so on behalf of the owner.[7] ◄

UNDISCLOSED PRINCIPAL When neither the fact of an agency relationship nor the identity of the principal is disclosed, the undisclosed principal is bound to perform just as if the principal had been fully disclosed at the time the contract was made.

When a principal's identity is undisclosed and the agent is forced to pay the third party, the agent is entitled to be *indemnified* (compensated) by the principal. The principal had a duty to perform, even though his or her identity was undisclosed,[8] and failure to do so will make the principal ultimately liable. Once the undisclosed principal's identity is revealed, the third

party generally can elect to hold either the principal or the agent liable on the contract.

Conversely, the undisclosed principal can require the third party to fulfill the contract, *unless* one of the following is true:

1. The undisclosed principal was expressly excluded as a party in the written contract.
2. The contract is a negotiable instrument signed by the agent with no indication of signing in a representative capacity.[9]
3. The performance of the agent is personal to the contract, thus allowing the third party to refuse the principal's performance.

In the following case, three parties involved in an auto sales transaction were embroiled in a dispute over who was liable when the car's engine caught fire.

7. *McBride v. Taxman Corp.*, 327 Ill.App.3d 992, 765 N.E.2d 51 (2002).
8. If the agent is a gratuitous agent, and the principal accepts the benefits of the agent's contract with a third party, then the principal will be liable to the agent on the theory of quasi contract (see Chapter 11).
9. Under the Uniform Commercial Code (UCC), only the agent is liable if the instrument neither names the principal nor shows that the agent signed in a representative capacity [UCC 3–402(b)(2)].

CASE 33.2

Williams v. Pike
Court of Appeal of Louisiana, Second Circuit, 58 So.3d 525 (2011).

BACKGROUND AND FACTS Bobby Williams bought a car for $3,000 at Sherman Henderson's auto repair business in Monroe, Louisiana. Although the car's owner was Joe Pike, the owner of Justice Wrecker Service, Henderson negotiated the sale, accepted Williams's payment, and gave him two receipts.

CASE 33.2 CONTINUES ➡

CASE 33.2 CONTINUED

Williams drove the car to Memphis, Tennessee, where his daughter was a student. Three days after the sale, the car began to emit smoke and flames from under the hood. Williams extinguished the blaze and contacted Henderson. The next day, Williams's daughter had the vehicle towed at her expense to her apartment's parking lot, from which it was soon stolen. Williams filed a suit in a Louisiana state court against Pike and Henderson. The court awarded Williams $2,000, plus the costs of the suit, adding that if Williams had returned the car, it would have awarded him the entire price. Pike and Henderson appealed.

IN THE LANGUAGE OF THE COURT
DREW, J. [Judge]

* * * *

Pike, the owner of Justice Wrecker Service, obtained a permit to sell the car issued by the state. That permit shows Justice Wrecker to be the owner, not Henderson. The car was displayed for sale at Henderson's business and Henderson facilitated the sale, though he argues his lack of ownership * * * should protect him from a judgment.

The defendants [also] state that Williams did not prove the amount to which he was entitled as to a reduced price. They allege that this "small fire" should not have entitled Williams to a $2,000 reduction in the price.

Williams responds that the judgment should be affirmed because the car purchased from Pike did not serve the purpose for which it was intended. Plaintiff provided notice to both defendants because Henderson was acting as agent for Pike.

Henderson's agency relationship properly puts him in court as a defendant. Henderson negotiated and completed the sale to Williams and did not make abundantly clear to Williams that Henderson was acting for Pike. Williams testified at the time of purchase he was unaware of Pike, while Henderson testified he mentioned Pike to Williams at the time of sale. In Williams' view, he had a cause of action against Henderson for breach of the implied warranty of the vehicle, since Henderson held himself out as owner of the car and did not disclose to Williams this * * * relationship with Pike. [Emphasis added.]

Factors in calculating the reduction in purchase price include loss of use of the car, inconvenience caused by the seller's failure to correct the defect, and amount of payments made. Here, Williams paid $3,000 for a car which he used only three days. His daughter had to pay to have the car towed and had to travel to Louisiana for the trial. The $2,000 award was appropriate and within the trial court's great discretion. We cannot improve upon the trial court's decision here.

DECISION AND REMEDY *A state intermediate appellate court affirmed the ruling of the lower court, including its judgment and the assessment of costs against both defendants. The appellate court added the costs of the appeal to this amount. Both Pike and Henderson—the undisclosed principal and his agent—were liable to Williams.*

WHAT IF THE FACTS WERE DIFFERENT? *Suppose that Henderson had fully disclosed the fact of his agency relationship and the identity of his principal. Would the result have been different? Why or why not?*

THE LEGAL ENVIRONMENT DIMENSION *Is Henderson entitled to be compensated by Pike for any portion of the judgment that he pays to Williams? Explain.*

Unauthorized Acts

If an agent has no authority but nevertheless contracts with a third party, the *principal* cannot be held liable on the contract. It does not matter whether the principal was disclosed, partially disclosed, or undisclosed. The *agent* is liable, however.

▶ **Example 33.10** Chu signs a contract for the purchase of a truck, purportedly acting as an agent under authority granted by Navarro. In fact, Navarro has not given Chu any such authority. Navarro refuses to pay for the truck, claiming that Chu had no authority to purchase it. The seller of the truck is entitled to hold Chu liable for payment. ◀

IMPLIED WARRANTY If the principal is disclosed or partially disclosed, and the agent contracts with a third party without authorization, the agent is liable to the third party who relied on the agency status. The agent's liability here is based on his or her breach of the *implied warranty of authority,* not on the breach of the contract itself.[10] An agent impliedly warrants that he or she has the authority to enter a contract on behalf of the principal.

▶ **Example 33.11** Pinnell, a reclusive artist, hires Auber to solicit offers for particular paintings from various galleries, but does not authorize her to enter into sales agreements. Olaf, a gallery owner, offers to buy two of Pinnell's paintings for an upcoming show. If Auber draws up a sales contract with Olaf, she impliedly warrants that she has the authority to enter into sales contracts on behalf of Pinnell. If Pinnell does not agree to ratify Auber's sales contract, Olaf cannot hold Pinnell liable, but he can hold Auber liable for breaching the implied warranty of authority. ◀

THIRD PARTY'S KNOWLEDGE Note that if the third party knows at the time the contract is made that the agent does not have authority, then the agent is not liable. Similarly, if the agent expressed to the third party *uncertainty* as to the extent of her or his authority, the agent is not personally liable.

Actions by E-Agents

Although in the past standard agency principles applied only to *human* agents, today these same agency principles also apply to e-agents. An electronic agent, or **e-agent,** is a semiautonomous computer program that is capable of executing specific tasks. For instance, software that can search through many databases and retrieve only relevant information for the user is an e-agent.

The Uniform Electronic Transactions Act (UETA), which was discussed in Chapter 12, sets forth provisions relating to the principal's liability for the actions of e-agents. According to Section 15 of the UETA, e-agents can enter into binding agreements on behalf of their principals—at least, in those states that have adopted the act. Thus, if consumers place an order over the Internet, and the company (principal) takes the order via an e-agent, the company cannot later claim that it did not receive the order.

The UETA also stipulates that if an e-agent does not provide an opportunity to prevent errors at the time of the transaction, the other party to the transaction can avoid the transaction. Therefore, if an e-agent

fails to provide an on-screen confirmation of a purchase or sale, the other party can avoid the effect of any errors. ▶ **Example 33.12** Bigelow wants to purchase three copies of three different books (a total of nine items). The e-agent mistakenly records an order for thirty-three of a single book and does not provide an on-screen verification of the order. If thirty-three books are then sent to Bigelow, he can avoid the contract to purchase them. ◀

SECTION 3
LIABILITY FOR TORTS AND CRIMES

Obviously, any person, including an agent, is liable for his or her own torts and crimes. Whether a principal can also be held liable for an agent's torts and crimes depends on several factors, which we examine here. In some situations, a principal may be held liable not only for the torts of an agent but also for torts committed by an independent contractor.

Principal's Tortious Conduct

A principal who acts through an agent may be liable for harm resulting from the principal's own negligence or recklessness. Thus, a principal may be liable if he or she gives improper instructions, authorizes the use of improper materials or tools, or establishes improper rules that result in the agent's committing a tort.

▶ **Example 33.13** Parker knows that Audrey's driver's license has been suspended but nevertheless tells her to use the company truck to deliver some equipment to a customer. If someone is injured as a result, Parker will be liable for his own negligence in instructing Audrey to drive without a valid license. ◀

Principal's Authorization of Agent's Tortious Conduct

Similarly, a principal who authorizes an agent to commit a tort may be liable to persons or property injured thereby, because the act is considered to be the principal's. ▶ **Example 33.14** Pedro directs his agent, Andy, to cut the corn on specific acreage, which neither of them has the right to do. The harvest is therefore a trespass (a tort), and Pedro is liable to the owner of the corn. ◀

---

10. The agent is not liable on the contract because the agent was never intended personally to be a party to the contract.

Note that an agent acting at the principal's direction can be liable as a *tortfeasor* (one who commits a wrong, or tort), along with the principal, for committing the tortious act even if the agent was unaware that the act was wrong. Assume in *Example 33.14* that Andy, the agent, did not know that Pedro lacked the right to harvest the corn. Andy can still be held liable to the owner of the field for damages, along with Pedro, the principal.

Liability for Agent's Misrepresentation

A principal is exposed to tort liability whenever a third person sustains a loss due to the agent's misrepresentation. The principal's liability depends on whether the agent was actually or apparently authorized to make representations and whether the representations were made within the scope of the agency. The principal is always directly responsible for an agent's misrepresentation made within the scope of the agent's authority.

▶ **Example 33.15** Ainsley is a demonstrator for Pavlovich's products. Pavlovich sends Ainsley to a home show to demonstrate the products and to answer questions from consumers. Pavlovich has given Ainsley authority to make statements about the products. If Ainsley makes only true representations, all is fine. But if he makes false claims, Pavlovich will be liable for any injuries or damages sustained by third parties in reliance on Ainsley's false representations. ◀

APPARENT IMPLIED AUTHORITY When a principal has placed an agent in a position of apparent authority—making it possible for the agent to defraud a third party—the principal may also be liable for the agent's fraudulent acts. For instance, partners in a partnership generally have the apparent implied authority to act as agents of the firm, as will be discussed in Chapter 37. Thus, if one of the partners commits a tort or a crime, the partnership itself—and often the other partners personally—can be held liable for the loss.

▶ **Case in Point 33.16** Selheimer & Company, a securities broker-dealer that operated as a partnership, provided various financial services. The managing partner, Perry Selheimer, embezzled funds that clients had turned over to the firm for investment. After Selheimer was convicted, other partners in the firm claimed that they were not liable for losses resulting from his illegal activities. The court, however, held that Selheimer had apparent implied authority to act in the ordinary course of the partnership's business. Thus, the firm, as principal, was liable, and under the law of partnerships the personal assets of the individual partners could be used to cover the firm's liability.[11] ◀

INNOCENT MISREPRESENTATION Tort liability based on fraud requires proof that a material misstatement was made knowingly and with the intent to deceive. An agent's *innocent* misstatements in a contract or warranty transaction can also provide grounds for the third party's rescission of the contract and the award of damages. Justice dictates that when a principal knows that an agent is not accurately advised of facts but does not correct either the agent's or the third party's impressions, the principal is responsible. The point is that the principal is always directly responsible for an agent's misrepresentation made within the scope of authority.

Liability for Agent's Negligence

Under the doctrine of ***respondeat superior*** (a Latin term meaning "let the master respond),"[12] a principal may also be liable for harm that his or her agent causes to a third party. This doctrine imposes **vicarious liability,** or indirect liability, on an employer that is similar to strict liability (see Chapter 7), in that both are imposed regardless of fault. Under this doctrine, the employer is liable for torts committed by an employee acting within the course or scope of employment. (Of course, the employee is also liable for any torts that she or he commits.)

Third parties injured through the negligence of an employee can sue either that employee or the employer, if the employee's negligent conduct occurred while the employee was acting within the scope of employment. ▶ **Case in Point 33.17** Aegis Communications hired Southwest Desert Images (SDI) to provide landscaping services for its property. An herbicide sprayed by SDI employee David Hoggatt entered the Aegis building through the air-conditioning system and caused Catherine Warner, an Aegis employee, to suffer a heart attack. Warner sued SDI and Hoggatt for negligence, but the lower court dismissed the suit against Hoggatt. On appeal,

---

11. *In re Selheimer & Co.,* 319 Bankr. 395 (E.D.Pa. 2005).
12. Pronounced ree-*spahn*-dee-uht soo-*peer*-ee-your. The doctrine of *respondeat superior* applies not only to employer-employee relationships but also to other principal-agent relationships in which the principal has the right of control over the agent.

the court found that Hoggatt was also liable. An agent is not excused from responsibility for tortious conduct just because he is working for a principal. Both the agent and the principal are liable.[13] ◀

THE DOCTRINE OF RESPONDEAT SUPERIOR At early common law, a servant (employee) was viewed as the master's (employer's) property. The master was deemed to have absolute control over the servant's acts and was held strictly liable for them, no matter how carefully the master supervised the servant. Although employers today are not masters of their employees, control is still a central concept to liability.

Underlying Rationale. The rationale for the doctrine of *respondeat superior* is based on the social duty that requires every person to manage his or her affairs so as not to injure another. This duty applies even when a person acts through an agent (controls the conduct of another).

Public Policy. Generally, public policy requires that an injured person be afforded effective relief, and a business enterprise is usually better able to provide that relief than is an individual employee. Employers normally carry liability insurance to cover any damages awarded as a result of such lawsuits. They are also able to spread the cost of risk over the entire business enterprise.

The courts have applied the doctrine of *respondeat superior* for nearly two centuries. It continues to have practical implications in all situations involving principal-agent (employer-employee) relationships.

---

13. *Warner v. Southwest Desert Images, LLC,* 218 Ariz. 121, 180 P.3d 986 (2008).

Today, the small-town grocer with one clerk and the multinational corporation with thousands of employees are equally subject to the doctrine. (Keep this principle in mind when you read Chapters 34 and 35.)

DETERMINING THE SCOPE OF EMPLOYMENT The key to determining whether a principal may be liable for the torts of an agent under the doctrine of *respondeat superior* is whether the torts are committed within the scope of the agency or employment. Courts may consider the following factors in determining whether a particular act occurred within the course and scope of employment:

1. Whether the employee's act was authorized by the employer.
2. The time, place, and purpose of the act.
3. Whether the act was one commonly performed by employees on behalf of their employers.
4. The extent to which the employer's interest was advanced by the act.
5. The extent to which the private interests of the employee were involved.
6. Whether the employer furnished the means or instrumentality (for example, a truck or a machine) by which an injury was inflicted.
7. Whether the employer had reason to know that the employee would perform the act in question and whether the employee had done it before.
8. Whether the act involved the commission of a serious crime.

Whether a real estate salesperson's actions in connection with certain real estate transactions fell within the salesperson's scope of employment was at issue in the following case.

CASE ANALYSIS

Case 33.3   Auer v. Paliath
Court of Appeals of Ohio, Second District, 2013 -Ohio- 391, 986 N.E.2d 1052, (2013).

IN THE LANGUAGE OF THE COURT
FROELICH, J. [Judge]
* * * *

Torri Auer [a California resident] brought suit [in an Ohio state court] against real estate salesperson Jamie Paliath, real estate broker Keller

Williams Home Town Realty, and others based on alleged fraud by Paliath in the sale of several rental properties [in Dayton, Ohio] to Auer * * * . After a jury trial * * * , Paliath was found liable to Torri Auer in the amount of $135,200 for fraud in the inducement of Auer's purchases of the

properties. * * * The jury also awarded $135,200 to Auer from Home Town Realty, based on the broker's vicarious liability for Paliath's actions in connection with Auer's purchases of the properties.

Home Town Realty appeals from the trial court's judgment.

CASE 33.3 CONTINUES ▶

* * * *

* * * Under [Ohio Revised Code (R.C.) Section 4735.01] the term "real estate broker" includes "any person, partnership, association, limited liability company, limited liability partnership, or corporation * * * who for another * * * and who for a fee, commission, or other valuable consideration" engages in various activities regarding real estate, including selling, purchasing, leasing, renting, listing, auctioning, buying, managing, and advertising real estate. A real estate salesperson generally means "any person associated with a licensed real estate broker to do or to deal with any acts or transactions set out or comprehended by the definition of a real estate broker, for compensation or otherwise."

Under R.C. Section 4735.21, no real estate salesperson may collect any money in connection with any real estate transaction, except as in the name of and with the consent of the licensed real estate broker under whom the salesperson is licensed.

* * * *

* * * A real estate broker will be held vicariously liable for intentional torts committed by salesmen acting within the scope of their authority. Vicarious liabil-ity is appropriate because a real estate salesman has no independent status or right to conclude a sale and can only function through the broker with whom he is associated. A salesman is required to be under the supervision of a licensed broker in all of his activities related to real estate transactions. [Emphasis added.]

* * * *

* * * When a real estate salesperson acts in the name of a real estate broker in connection with the type of real estate transaction for which he or she was hired and the broker collects a commission for the transaction, the salesperson's actions in connection with that real estate transaction are within the scope of the salesperson's employment, as a matter of law.

In this case, Paliath contracted with Home Town Realty as a real estate salesperson to assist clients with the purchase and sale of real estate. Paliath advised and assisted Auer in the purchase of the * * * properties, and her fraudulent conduct involved misrepresentations regarding those properties.

Reviewing the properties separately, the evidence at trial established that Home Town Realty was listed as the real estate broker on the purchase contract, the agency disclosure statement, and the settlement statement for the Belton Street sale. Home Town Realty received a commission check of $180 from the title company that conducted the closing. Based on this evidence, it was established, as a matter of law, that Paliath acted within the scope of her employment as a real estate salesperson with Home Town Realty in relation to Auer's purchase of the Belton property.

Similarly, Paliath's actions with respect to the 1111–1115 Richmond Avenue properties were taken as a real estate salesperson assisting Auer with the purchase of the properties. Home Town was listed as a broker on the purchase contract, the agency disclosure statement, and the settlement statement for 1111 Richmond Avenue, and it received a commission of $2,400 following the closing. * * * The evidence thus demonstrated, as a matter of law, that Paliath was acting in the scope of her employment regarding the sale of 1111 Richmond Avenue.

* * * *

* * * The trial court's judgment will be affirmed.

LEGAL REASONING QUESTIONS

1. What conduct was at the center of the dispute in this case?
2. Who did the plaintiff allege was liable for this conduct? Which of these parties was the principal, and which was the agent?
3. What factors did the court apply to determine liability in this case?
4. How did the court rule on the question of vicarious liability?

THE DISTINCTION BETWEEN A "DETOUR" AND A "FROLIC" A useful insight into the concept of "scope of employment" may be gained from Judge Baron Parke's classic distinction between a "detour" and a "frolic" in the case of *Joel v. Morison* (1834).[14] In this case, the English court held that if a servant merely took a detour from his master's business, the master will be responsible. If, however, the servant was on a "frolic of his own" and not in any way "on his master's business," the master will not be liable.

▶ **Example 33.18** Mandel, a traveling salesperson, while driving his employer's vehicle to call on a customer, decides to stop at the post office—which is one block off his route—to mail a personal letter. As Mandel approaches the post office, he negligently runs into a parked vehicle owned by Chan. In this sit-

---

14. 6 Car. & P. 501, 172 Eng.Rep. 1338 (1834).

uation, because Mandel's detour from the employer's business is not substantial, he is still acting within the scope of employment, and the employer is liable.

The result would be different, though, if Mandel had decided to pick up a few friends for drinks in another city and in the process had negligently run his vehicle into Chan's. In that circumstance, the departure from the employer's business would be substantial, and the employer normally would not be liable to Chan for damages. Mandel would be considered to have been on a "frolic" of his own. ◀

EMPLOYEE TRAVEL TIME An employee going to and from work or to and from meals usually is considered to be outside the scope of employment. In contrast, all travel time of traveling salespersons or others whose jobs require travel is normally considered to be within the scope of employment for the duration of the business trip, including the return trip home.

NOTICE OF DANGEROUS CONDITIONS The employer is charged with knowledge of any dangerous conditions discovered by an employee and pertinent to the employment situation. ▶ **Example 33.19** Brad, a maintenance employee in an apartment building, notices a lead pipe protruding from the ground in the building's courtyard. Brad neglects either to fix the pipe or to inform his employer of the danger. John trips on the pipe and is injured.

The employer is charged with knowledge of the dangerous condition regardless of whether Brad actually informed the employer. That knowledge is imputed to the employer by virtue of the employment relationship. ◀

Liability for Agent's Intentional Torts

Most intentional torts that individuals commit have no relation to their employment, and their employers will not be held liable. Nevertheless, under the doctrine of *respondeat superior,* the employer can be liable for intentional torts that an employee commits within the course and scope of employment. For instance, an employer is liable when an employee (such as a "bouncer" at a nightclub or a security guard at a department store) commits the tort of assault and battery or false imprisonment while acting within the scope of employment.

In addition, an employer who knows or should know that an employee has a propensity for committing tortious acts is liable for the employee's acts even if they would not ordinarily be considered within the scope of employment. ▶ **Example 33.20** Chaz, the owner of the Comedy Club, hires Alec as a bouncer for the club even though he knows that Alec has a history of arrests for criminal assault and battery. In this situation, Chaz may be liable if Alec viciously attacks a customer in the parking lot after hours. ◀

An employer is also liable for permitting an employee to engage in reckless actions that can injure others. ▶ **Example 33.21** The owner of Bates Trucking observes an employee smoking while filling containerized trucks with highly flammable liquids. Failure to stop the employee will cause the employer to be liable for any injuries that result if a truck explodes. ◀ Needless to say, most employers purchase liability insurance to cover their potential liability for employee conduct in many situations (see Chapter 50).

Liability for Independent Contractor's Torts

Generally, an employer is not liable for physical harm caused to a third person by the negligent act of an independent contractor in the performance of the contract. This is because the employer does not have *the right to control* the details of an independent contractor's performance.

Courts make an exception to this rule when the contract involves unusually hazardous activities, such as blasting operations, the transportation of highly volatile chemicals, or the use of poisonous gases. In these situations, strict liability (discussed in Chapter 7) is imposed, so an employer cannot be shielded from liability merely by using an independent contractor.

Liability for Agent's Crimes

An agent is liable for his or her own crimes. A principal or employer normally is *not* liable for an agent's crime even if the crime was committed within the scope of authority or employment. An exception to this rule is made when the principal or employer participated in the crime by conspiracy or other action.

Also, in some jurisdictions, a principal may be liable under specific statutes if an agent, in the course and scope of employment, violates certain regulations. For instance, a principal might be liable for an agent's violation of sanitation rules or regulations governing prices, weights, and the sale of liquor.

SECTION 4
TERMINATION OF AN AGENCY

Agency law is similar to contract law in that both an agency and a contract may be terminated *by an act of the parties or by operation of law*. Once the relationship between the principal and the agent has ended, the agent no longer has the right (*actual* authority) to bind the principal. For an agent's *apparent* authority to be terminated, though, third persons may also need to be notified that the agency has been terminated.

Termination by Act of the Parties

An agency relationship may be terminated by act of the parties in any of the following ways:

1. *Lapse of time.* When an agency agreement specifies the time period during which the agency relationship will exist, the agency ends when that time period expires. If no definite time is stated, then the agency continues for a reasonable time and can be terminated at will by either party. What constitutes a reasonable time depends on the circumstances and the nature of the agency relationship.

2. *Purpose achieved.* If an agent is employed to accomplish a particular objective, such as the purchase of breeding stock for a cattle rancher, the agency automatically ends after the cattle have been purchased. If more than one agent is employed to accomplish the same purpose, such as the sale of real estate, the first agent to complete the sale automatically terminates the agency relationship for all the others.

3. *Occurrence of a specific event.* When an agency relationship is to terminate on the happening of a certain event, the agency automatically ends when the event occurs. ▶ **Example 33.22** If Posner appoints Rubik to handle her business affairs while she is away, the agency automatically terminates when Posner returns. ◀

4. *Mutual agreement.* The parties to an agency can cancel (rescind) their contract by mutually agreeing to terminate the agency relationship, even if it was for a specific (longer) duration.

5. *Termination by one party.* As a general rule, either party can terminate the agency relationship. The act of termination is called *revocation* if done by

the principal and *renunciation* if done by the agent. Although both parties may have the *power* to terminate the agency, they may not possess the right and therefore may be liable for breach of contract or *wrongful termination*.

WRONGFUL TERMINATION Wrongful termination can subject the canceling party to a lawsuit for breach of contract. ▶ **Example 33.23** Rawlins has a one-year employment contract with Munro to act as agent in return for $65,000. Although Munro has the *power* to discharge Rawlins before the contract period expires, if he does so, he can be sued for breaching the contract because he had no *right* to terminate the agency. ◀

Even in an agency at will—in which either party may terminate at any time—the principal who wishes to terminate must give the agent *reasonable* notice. The notice must be at least sufficient to allow the agent to recoup his or her expenses and, in some situations, to make a normal profit.

AGENCY COUPLED WITH AN INTEREST A special rule applies to an *agency coupled with an interest*. In an **agency coupled with an interest,** the agent has some legal right to (an interest in) the property that is the subject of the agency. For instance, a principal might provide inventory for the agent to sell and then to keep the profits. Because the agent has an additional interest in the property beyond the normal commission for selling it, the agent's position cannot be terminated until the agent's interest ends.

This type of agency is not an agency in the usual sense because it is created for the agent's benefit instead of for the principal's benefit. ▶ **Example 33.24** Julie borrows $5,000 from Rob, giving Rob some of her jewelry and signing a letter authorizing him to sell the jewelry as her agent if she fails to repay the loan. After Julie receives the $5,000 from Rob, she attempts to revoke his authority to sell the jewelry as her agent. Julie will not succeed in this attempt because a principal cannot revoke an agency created for the agent's benefit. ◀

An agency coupled with an interest should not be confused with a situation in which the agent merely derives proceeds or profits from the sale of the subject matter. Many agents are paid a commission for their services, but the agency relationship involved does not constitute an agency coupled with an interest. For instance, a real estate agent who merely receives a commission from the sale of real property does not have a beneficial interest in the property itself.

NOTICE OF TERMINATION When the parties terminate an agency, it is the principal's duty to inform any third parties who know of the existence of the agency that it has been terminated. No particular form is required for notice of termination of the principal-agent relationship to be effective. The principal can personally notify the agent, or the agent can learn of the termination through some other means.

Although an agent's actual authority ends when the agency is terminated, an agent's *apparent authority* continues until the third party receives notice (from any source) that such authority has been terminated. ▶ **Example 33.25** Manning bids on a shipment of steel, and Stone is hired as an agent to arrange transportation for the shipment. When Stone learns that Manning has lost the bid, Stone's authority to make the transportation arrangement terminates. ◀

If the principal knows that a third party has dealt with the agent, the principal is expected to notify that person *directly*. For third parties who have heard about the agency but have not yet dealt with the agent, *constructive notice* is sufficient.[15] If the agent's authority is written, however, normally it must be revoked in writing (unless the written document contained an expiration date).

Termination by Operation of Law

Certain events terminate agency authority automatically because their occurrence makes it impossible for the agent to perform or improbable that the principal would continue to want performance. We look at these events here. Note that when an agency terminates by operation of law, there is no duty to notify third persons—unless the agent's authority is coupled with an interest.

1. *Death or insanity.* The general rule is that the death or insanity of either the principal or the agent automatically and immediately terminates an ordinary agency relationship.[16] Knowledge of the death or insanity is not required. ▶ **Example 33.26** Grey sends Bosley to Japan to purchase a rare book. Before Bosley makes the purchase, Grey dies. Bosley's agent status is terminated at the moment of Grey's death, even though Bosley does not know that Grey has died. ◀

   (Some states, however, have enacted statutes that change the common law rule to require an agent's knowledge of the principal's death before termination.)

2. *Impossibility.* When the specific subject matter of an agency is destroyed or lost, the agency terminates. ▶ **Example 33.27** Tsang employs Arnez to sell Tsang's house. Prior to any sale, the house is destroyed by fire. Arnez's agency and authority to sell the house terminate. ◀ Similarly, when it is impossible for the agent to perform the agency lawfully because of a change in the law, the agency terminates.

3. *Changed circumstances.* Sometimes, an event occurs that has such an unusual effect on the subject matter of the agency that the agent can reasonably infer that the principal will not want the agency to continue. In such situations, the agency terminates. ▶ **Example 33.28** Baird hires Joslen to sell a tract of land for $40,000. Subsequently, Joslen learns that there is oil under the land and that the land is therefore worth $1 million. The agency and Joslen's authority to sell the land for $40,000 are terminated. ◀

4. *Bankruptcy.* If either the principal or the agent petitions for bankruptcy, the agency is *usually* terminated. In certain circumstances, such as when the agent's financial status is irrelevant to the purpose of the agency, the agency relationship may continue. *Insolvency* (the inability to pay debts when they come due or when liabilities exceed assets), as distinguished from bankruptcy, does not necessarily terminate the relationship.

5. *War.* When the principal's country and the agent's country are at war with each other, the agency is terminated. In this situation, the agency is automatically suspended or terminated because there is no way to enforce the legal rights and obligations of the parties.

See *Concept Summary 33.2* on the following page for a synopsis of the rules governing the termination of an agency.

---

15. With *constructive notice* of a fact, knowledge of the fact is imputed by law to a person if he or she could have discovered the fact by proper diligence. Constructive notice is often accomplished by publication in a newspaper.

16. An exception to this rule exists in the bank-customer relationship. A bank, as agent, can continue to exercise specific types of authority even after the customer's death or insanity, and can continue to pay checks drawn by the customer for ten days after death (see Chapter 28).

CONCEPT SUMMARY 33.2
Termination of an Agency

METHOD OF TERMINATION	RULES	TERMINATION OF AGENT'S AUTHORITY
Act of the Parties		
1. Lapse of time.	Automatic at end of the stated time.	
2. Purpose achieved.	Automatic on the completion of the purpose.	
3. Occurrence of a specific event.	Normally automatic on the happening of the event.	**Notice to Third Parties Required—** 1. Direct to those who have dealt with agency. 2. Constructive to all others.
4. Mutual agreement.	Mutual consent required.	
5. At the option of one party (revocation, if by principal, renunciation, if by agent).	Either party normally has a right to terminate the agency but may lack the power to do so, which can lead to liability for breach of contract.	
Operation of Law		
1. Death or insanity.	Automatic on the death or insanity of either the principal or the agent (except when the agency is coupled with an interest).	
2. Impossibility— destruction of the specific subject matter.	Applies any time the agency cannot be performed because of an event beyond the parties' control.	
3. Changed circumstances.	Events so unusual that it would be inequitable to allow the agency to continue to exist.	**No Notice Required—** Automatic on the happening of the event.
4. Bankruptcy.	Bankruptcy petition (not mere insolvency) usually terminates the agency.	
5. War between principal's country and agent's country.	Automatically suspends or terminates agency—no way to enforce legal rights.	

Reviewing: Agency Liability to Third Parties and Termination

Lynne Meyer, on her way to a business meeting and in a hurry, stopped at a Buy-Mart store for a new car charger for her smartphone. There was a long line at one of the checkout counters, but a cashier, Valerie Watts, opened another counter and began loading the cash drawer. Meyer told Watts that she was in a hurry and asked Watts to work faster. Instead, Watts slowed her pace. At this point, Meyer hit Watts.

It is not clear whether Meyer hit Watts intentionally or, in an attempt to retrieve the car charger, hit her inadvertently. In response, Watts grabbed Meyer by the hair and hit her repeatedly in the back of the head, while Meyer screamed for help. Management personnel separated the two women and questioned them about the incident. Watts was immediately fired for violating the store's no-fighting policy. Meyer subsequently sued Buy-Mart, alleging that the store was liable for the tort (assault and battery) committed by its employee. Using the information presented in the chapter, answer the following questions.

1. Under what doctrine discussed in this chapter might Buy-Mart be held liable for the tort committed by Watts?
2. What is the key factor in determining whether Buy-Mart is liable under this doctrine?
3. How is Buy-Mart's potential liability affected by whether Watts's behavior constituted an intentional tort or a tort of negligence?
4. Suppose that when Watts applied for the job at Buy-Mart, she disclosed in her application that she had previously been convicted of felony assault and battery. Nevertheless, Buy-Mart hired Watts as a cashier. How might this fact affect Buy-Mart's liability for Watts's actions?

DEBATE THIS ... *The doctrine of* respondeat superior *should be modified to make agents solely liable for their tortious (wrongful) acts committed within the scope of employment.*

Terms and Concepts

agency coupled with an interest 652	express authority 639	ratification 643
apparent authority 642	implied authority 641	*respondeat superior* 648
disclosed principal 644	notary public 639	undisclosed principal 644
e-agent 647	partially disclosed principal 644	vicarious liability 648
equal dignity rule 639	power of attorney 639	

ExamPrep

Issue Spotters

1. Davis contracts with Estee to buy a certain horse on her behalf. Estee asks Davis not to reveal her identity. Davis makes a deal with Farmland Stables, the owner of the horse, and makes a down payment. Estee does not pay the rest of the price. Farmland Stables sues Davis for breach of contract. Can Davis hold Estee liable for whatever damages he has to pay? Why or why not? **(See page 645.)**
2. Vivian, owner of Wonder Goods Company, employs Xena as an administrative assistant. In Vivian's absence, and without authority, Xena represents herself as Vivian and signs a promissory note in Vivian's name. In what circumstance is Vivian liable on the note? **(See page 646.)**

- Check your answers to the Issue Spotters against the answers provided in Appendix E at the end of this text.

Before the Test

Go to **www.cengagebrain.com**, enter the ISBN 9781285185248, and click on "Find" to locate this textbook's Web site. Then, click on "Access Now" under "Study Tools," and select Chapter 33 at the top. There, you will find a Practice Quiz that you can take to assess your mastery of the concepts in this chapter, as well as Flashcards and a Glossary of important terms.

Business Scenarios

33–1. Unauthorized Acts. Janell Arden is a purchasing agent-employee for the A&B Coal Supply partnership. Arden has authority to purchase the coal needed by A&B to satisfy the needs of its customers. While Arden is leaving a coal mine from which she has just purchased a large quantity of coal, her car breaks down. She walks into a small roadside grocery store for help. While there, she encounters Will Wilson, who owns 360 acres back in the mountains with all mineral rights. Wilson, in need of cash, offers to sell Arden the property for $1,500 per acre.

On inspection of the property, Arden forms the opinion that the subsurface contains valuable coal deposits. Arden contracts to purchase the property for A&B Coal Supply, signing the contract "A&B Coal Supply, Janell Arden, agent." The closing date is August 1. Arden takes the contract to the partnership. The managing partner is furious, as A&B is not in the property business. Later, just before closing, both Wilson and the partnership learn that the value of the land is at least $15,000 per acre. Discuss the rights of A&B and Wilson concerning the land contract. **(See page 646.)**

33–2. Ratification by Principal. Springer was a political candidate running for Congress. He was operating on a tight budget and instructed his campaign staff not to purchase any campaign materials without his explicit authorization. In spite of these instructions, one of his campaign workers ordered Dubychek Printing Co. to print some promotional materials for Springer's campaign. When the printed materials arrived, Springer did not return them but instead used them during his campaign. When Springer failed to pay for the materials, Dubychek sued for recovery of the price. Springer contended that he was not liable on the sales contract because he had not authorized his agent to purchase the printing services. Dubychek argued that the campaign worker was Springer's agent and that the worker had authority to make the printing contract. Additionally, Dubychek claimed that even if the purchase was unauthorized, Springer's use of the materials constituted ratification of his agent's unauthorized purchase. Is Dubychek correct? Explain. **(See page 643.)**

33–3. Respondeat Superior. ABC Tire Corp. hires Arnez as a traveling salesperson and assigns him a geographic area and time schedule in which to solicit orders and service customers. Arnez is given a company car to use in covering the territory. One day, Arnez decides to take his personal car to cover part of his territory. It is 11:00 A.M., and Arnez has just finished calling on all customers in the city of Tarrytown. His next appointment is at 2:00 P.M. in the city of Austex, twenty miles down the road. Arnez starts out for Austex, but halfway there he decides to visit a former college roommate who runs a farm ten miles off the main highway. Arnez is enjoying his visit with his former roommate when he realizes that it is 1:45 P.M. and that he will be late for the appointment in Austex. Driving at a high speed down the country road to reach the main highway, Arnez crashes his car into a tractor, severely injuring Thomas, the driver of the tractor. Thomas claims that he can hold ABC Tire Corp. liable for his injuries. Discuss fully ABC's liability in this situation. **(See page 648.)**

Business Case Problems

33–4. Undisclosed Principal. Homeowners Jim and Lisa Criss hired Kevin and Cathie Pappas, doing business as Outside Creations, to undertake a landscaping project. Kevin signed the parties' contract as "Outside Creations Rep." The Crisses made payments on the contract with checks payable to Kevin, who deposited them in his personal account—there was no Outside Creations account. Later, alleging breach of contract, the Crisses filed a suit in a Georgia state court against the Pappases. The defendants contended that they could not be liable because the contract was not with them personally. They claimed that they were the agents of Forever Green Landscaping and Irrigation, Inc., which had been operating under the name "Outside Creations" at the time of the contract and had since filed for bankruptcy. The Crisses pointed out that the name "Forever Green" was not in the contract. Can the Pappases be liable on this contract? Why or why not? [*Pappas v. Criss*, 296 Ga.App. 803, 676 S.E.2d 21 (2009)] **(See page 645.)**

33–5. Liability Based on Actual or Apparent Authority. Summerall Electric Co. and other subcontractors were hired by National Church Services, Inc. (NCS), which was the general contractor on a construction project for the Church of God at Southaven. As work progressed, payments from NCS to the subcontractors were late and eventually stopped altogether. The church had paid NCS in full for the entire project beforehand, but apparently NCS had mismanaged the project. When payments from NCS stopped, the subcontractors filed *mechanic's liens* (see Chapter 29) for the value of the work they had performed but for which they had not been paid. The subcontractors sued the church, contending that it was liable for the payments because NCS was its agent on the basis of either actual or apparent authority. Was NCS an agent for the church, thereby making the church liable to the subcontractors? Explain your reasoning. [*Summerall Electric Co. v. Church of God at Southaven*, 25 So.3d 1090 (App.Miss. 2010)] **(See page 642.)**

33–6. Disclosed Principal. To display desserts in restaurants, Mario Sclafani ordered refrigeration units from Felix Storch, Inc. Felix faxed a credit application to Sclafani. The application was faxed back with a signature that appeared to be Sclafani's. Felix delivered the units. When they were not paid for, Felix filed a suit against Sclafani to collect. Sclafani denied that he had seen the application or signed it. He testified that he referred all credit questions to "the girl in the office." Who was the principal? Who was the agent? Who is liable on the contract? Explain. [*Felix Storch, Inc. v. Martinucci Desserts USA, Inc.*, 30 Misc.2d 1217, 924 N.Y.S.2d 308 (Suffolk Co. 2011)] **(See page 644.)**

33–7. BUSINESS CASE PROBLEM
WITH SAMPLE ANSWER: Liability for Contracts.

 Thomas Huskin and his wife entered into a contract to have their home remodeled by House Medic Handyman Service. Todd Hall signed the contract as an authorized representative of House Medic. It turned out that House Medic was a fictitious name for Hall Hauling, Ltd. The contract did not indicate this, however, and Hall did not inform the Huskins about Hall Hauling. When a contract dispute later arose, the Huskins sued Todd Hall personally for breach of contract. Can Hall be held personally liable? Why or why not? [Huskin v. Hall, *2012 WL 553136 (Ohio Ct.App. 2012)*] **(See page 644.)**

- **For a sample answer to Problem 33–7, go to Appendix F at the end of this text.**

33–8. Agent's Authority.
Basic Research, L.L.C., advertised its products on television networks owned by Rainbow Media Holdings, Inc., through an ad agency, Icebox Advertising, Inc. As Basic's agent, Icebox had the express authority to buy ads from Rainbow on Basic's behalf, but the authority was limited to buying ads with cash in advance. Despite this limit, Rainbow sold ads to Basic through Icebox on credit. Basic paid Icebox for the ads, but Icebox did not pass all of the payments on to Rainbow. Icebox filed for bankruptcy. Can Rainbow recoup the unpaid amounts from Basic? Explain. [*American Movie Classics v. Rainbow Media Holdings*, 2013 WL 323229 (10th Cir. 2013)] **(See page 639.)**

33–9. A QUESTION OF ETHICS: Power of Attorney.

 Warren Davis lived with Renee Brandt in a house that Davis owned in Virginia Beach, Virginia. At Davis's request, attorney Leigh Ansell prepared, and Davis acknowledged, a durable power of attorney appointing Ansell to act as Davis's attorney-in-fact. Ansell was authorized to sign "any . . . instrument of . . . deposit" and "any contract . . . relating to . . . personal property." Ansell could act "in any circumstances as fully and effectively as I could do as part of my normal, everyday business affairs if acting personally." A few days later, at Davis's direction, Ansell prepared, and Davis signed, a will that gave Brandt the right to occupy, rent-free, the house in which she and Davis lived "so long as she lives in the premises." The will's other chief beneficiaries were Davis's daughters, Sharon Jones and Jody Clark. According to Ansell, Davis intended to "take care of [Brandt] outside of this will" and asked Ansell to designate Brandt the beneficiary "payable on death" (POD) of Davis's $250,000 certificate of deposit (CD). The CD had no other named beneficiary. Less than two months later, Davis died. A suit between Brandt and Davis's daughters ensued in a Virginia state court. [Jones v. Brandt, *645 S.E.2d 312 (Va. 2007)*] **(See page 639.)**

(a) Should the language in a power of attorney be interpreted broadly or strictly? Why?

(b) In this case, did Ansell have the authority under the power of attorney to change the beneficiary of Davis's CD? Explain.

(c) Ansell advised Davis by letter that he had complied with the instruction to designate Brandt the beneficiary of the CD. Davis made no objection. Based on these facts, what theory might apply to validate the designation?

Legal Reasoning Group Activity

33–10. Liability for Independent Contractor's Torts. Dean Brothers Corp. owns and operates a steel drum manufacturing plant. Lowell Wyden, the plant superintendent, hired Best Security Patrol, Inc. (BSP), a security company, to guard Dean property and "deter thieves and vandals." Some BSP security guards, as Wyden knew, carried firearms. Pete Sidell, a BSP security guard, was not certified as an armed guard but nevertheless came to work with his gun (in a briefcase).

While working at the Dean plant on October 31, 2014, Sidell fired his gun at Tyrone Gaines, in the belief that Gaines was an intruder. The bullet struck and killed Gaines. Gaines's mother filed a lawsuit claiming that her son's death was the result of BSP's negligence, for which Dean was responsible. **(See page 647.)**

(a) The first group will determine what the plaintiff's best argument is to establish that Dean is responsible for BSP's actions.

(b) The second group will discuss Dean's best defense and formulate arguments in support of it.

CHAPTER 34

EMPLOYMENT, IMMIGRATION, AND LABOR LAW

Until the early 1900s, most employer-employee relationships were governed by the common law. Even today, under the common law *employment-at-will doctrine*, private employers have considerable freedom to hire and fire workers at will, regardless of the employees' performance.

In addition, however, numerous statutes and administrative agency regulations now govern the workplace.

Thus, to a large extent, statutory law has displaced common law doctrines. In this chapter and the next, we look at the most significant laws regulating employment relationships.

In this chapter, we discuss federal statutes that regulate various aspects of the workplace, including employee wages, hours, medical leave, safety, and pension and health plans. We consider employee privacy rights and such issues as the use of electronic

monitoring by employers and drug testing.

We also examine immigration law, a topic of special importance to employers in our diverse society. We conclude the chapter with coverage of labor laws, which continue to have an impact on the employment environment. As you will read in this chapter's *Managerial Strategy* feature, rules that arise in the context of labor unions sometimes can apply to *all* employees, not just to union workers.

SECTION 1

EMPLOYMENT AT WILL

Employment relationships have traditionally been governed by the common law doctrine of **employment at will.** Under this doctrine, either party may terminate the employment relationship at any time and for any reason, unless doing so violates an employee's statutory or contractual rights.

Today, the majority of U.S. workers continue to have the legal status of "employees at will." In other words, this common law doctrine is still in widespread use, and only one state (Montana) does not apply it.

Nonetheless, federal and state statutes governing employment relationships prevent the doctrine from being applied in a number of circumstances. An employer may not fire an employee if doing so would violate a federal or state statute, such as one prohibiting employment discrimination (see Chapter 35).

Note that the distinction made under agency law (discussed in Chapter 32) between employee status and independent-contractor status is important here. The employment laws that will be discussed in this chapter and in Chapter 35 apply only to the

employer-employee relationship. They do not apply to independent contractors.

Exceptions to the Employment-at-Will Doctrine

Because of the harsh effects of the employment-at-will doctrine for employees, courts have carved out various exceptions to it. These exceptions are based on contract theory, tort theory, and public policy.

EXCEPTIONS BASED ON CONTRACT THEORY Some courts have held that an *implied* employment contract exists between the employer and the employee. If the employee is fired outside the terms of the implied contract, he or she may succeed in an action for breach of contract even though no written employment contract exists.

▶ **Example 34.1** BDI Enterprise's employment manual and personnel bulletin both state that, as a matter of policy, workers will be dismissed only for good cause. Jing Chin is an employee at BDI. If Chin reasonably expects BDI to follow this policy, a court may find that there is an implied contract based on the terms stated in the manual and bulletin. ◀ Generally, the key consideration in determining whether an employment manual creates an implied contractual obligation is the employee's reasonable expectations.

Courts in a few states have gone further and held that all employment contracts contain an implied covenant of good faith. This means that both sides promise to abide by the contract in good faith. If an employer fires an employee for an arbitrary or unjustified reason, the employee can claim that the employer breached the covenant of good faith and violated the contract.

EXCEPTIONS BASED ON TORT THEORY In some situations, the discharge of an employee may give rise to an action for wrongful discharge under tort theories. Abusive discharge procedures may result in a lawsuit for intentional infliction of emotional distress or defamation.

In addition, some courts have permitted workers to sue under the tort theory of fraud when an employer made false promises to a prospective employee. ▶ **Example 34.2** Goldfinch Consulting, Inc., induces Brianna to leave a lucrative job and move to another state by offering her "a long-term job with a thriving business." In fact, Goldfinch is not only having significant financial problems but is also planning a merger that will result in the elimination of the position offered to Brianna. If she takes the job in reliance on Goldfinch's representations and is fired shortly thereafter, Brianna may be able to bring an action against the employer for fraud. ◀

EXCEPTIONS BASED ON PUBLIC POLICY The most common exception to the employment-at-will doc-

trine is made on the basis that the employer's reason for firing the employee violates a fundamental public policy of the jurisdiction. Generally, the courts require that the public policy involved be expressed clearly in the statutory law governing the jurisdiction.

The public-policy exception may apply to an employee who is discharged for **whistleblowing**—that is, telling government authorities, upper-level managers, or the media that her or his employer is engaged in some unsafe or illegal activity.

▶ **Case in Point 34.3** Rebecca Wendeln was the staff coordinator at a nursing home. She discovered that a patient at the home had been improperly moved and had been injured as a result. Wendeln reported the incident to state authorities, as she was required to do by state law. Her supervisor was angry about the report, and Wendeln was fired shortly thereafter. When Wendeln sued, the court held that although she was an employee at will, she was protected in this instance from retaliatory firing because a clear mandate of public policy had been violated.[1] ◀ (Normally, whistleblowers seek protection from retaliatory discharge under federal and state statutes, such as the Whistleblower Protection Act of 1989.[2])

In the following case, an employer fired an employee after he complained about how his supervisor performed her job. The court had to decide whether the employee was protected by the employer's whistleblower policy even though it was implemented after he was hired.

---

1. *Wendeln v. The Beatrice Manor, Inc.,* 271 Neb. 373, 712 N.W.2d 226 (2006).
2. 5 U.S.C. Section 1201.

CASE 34.1

Waddell v. Boyce Thompson Institute for Plant Research, Inc.
Supreme Court of New York, Appellate Division, 92 A.D.3d 1172, 940 N.Y.S.2d 331 (2012).

BACKGROUND AND FACTS Donald Waddell worked as a business office supervisor for the Boyce Thompson Institute for Plant Research. Waddell did not have an employment contract for a fixed term. The Institute's employee manual said that his job was "terminable at the will of either the employee or [the Institute], at any time, with or without cause." Several months after hiring Waddell, the Institute implemented a whistleblower policy designed to encourage "the highest standards of financial reporting and lawful and ethical behavior." The whistleblower policy stated that the Institute would not retaliate against an employee for making a complaint "in good faith pursuant to this policy."

Beginning in May 2010, Waddell repeatedly complained that his supervisor, Sophia Darling, needed to file certain financial documents more promptly. In August 2010, Darling fired Waddell, telling him that his disrespectful and insubordinate conduct violated the Institute's Code of Conduct. Waddell then sued the

CASE 34.1 CONTINUES ▶

CASE 34.1 CONTINUED Institute, and the trial court held that he failed to state a proper claim for breach of an implied contract. Waddell appealed.

IN THE LANGUAGE OF THE COURT
PETERS, J.P. [Justice Presiding]

* * * *

* * * *It is well settled that, "absent an agreement establishing a fixed duration, an employment relationship is presumed to be a hiring at will, terminable at any time by either party."* This presumption may be rebutted by proof establishing that "the employer made the employee aware of its express written policy limiting its right of discharge and that the employee detrimentally relied on that policy in accepting the employment." Notably, "the requirements for such an implied contract of employment have been strictly construed, and the successful plaintiff must sustain an 'explicit and difficult pleading burden.' " [Emphasis added.]

* * * We find that plaintiff has failed to state a cause of action for breach of an implied contract. It is undisputed that the Whistleblower Policy had not been implemented until several months after plaintiff began employment with defendant. As such, [the trial court] correctly found that the essential element of detrimental reliance in accepting employment was lacking. Further, plaintiff did not allege that he forsook any other employment opportunities in reliance upon defendant's Whistleblower Policy or because of what he believed to be defendant's termination policy. Nor is the quality of plaintiff's service relevant in determining whether the presumption of at-will employment has been overcome. * * * Accordingly, plaintiff's claim for breach of an implied employment contract was properly dismissed.

DECISION AND REMEDY *The New York appellate court found that Waddell did not state a proper claim for breach of contract. It therefore affirmed the judgment for the Institute.*

THE LEGAL ENVIRONMENT DIMENSION *If Waddell had been allowed to bring a claim for breach of contract, how might his supervisor, Sophia Darling, have defended her conduct? Explain your answer.*

THE ETHICAL DIMENSION *Is the at-will employment doctrine fair to employees? Why or why not?*

Wrongful Discharge

Whenever an employer discharges an employee in violation of an employment contract or a statutory law protecting employees, the employee may bring an action for **wrongful discharge.** Even if an employer's actions do not violate any express employment contract or statute, the employer may still be subject to liability under a common law doctrine, such as a tort theory or agency. For instance, if an employer discharges a female employee while publicly disclosing private facts about her sex life to her co-workers, the employee could bring a wrongful discharge suit based on an invasion of privacy (see Chapter 6).

SECTION 2
WAGES, HOURS, AND LAYOFFS

In the 1930s, Congress enacted several laws to regulate the wages and working hours of employees, including the following:

1. The Davis-Bacon Act[3] requires contractors and subcontractors working on federal government construction projects to pay "prevailing wages" to their employees.
2. The Walsh-Healey Act[4] applies to U.S. government contracts. It requires that a minimum wage, as well as overtime pay at 1.5 times regular pay rates, be paid to employees of manufacturers or suppliers entering into contracts with agencies of the federal government.
3. The Fair Labor Standards Act (FLSA)[5] extended wage-hour requirements to cover all employers engaged in interstate commerce or in producing goods for interstate commerce, plus selected other types of businesses. The FLSA, as amended, provides the most comprehensive federal regulation of wages and hours today.

---

3. 40 U.S.C. Sections 276a–276a-5.
4. 41 U.S.C. Sections 35–45.
5. 29 U.S.C. Sections 201–260.

Child Labor

The FLSA prohibits oppressive child labor. Children under fourteen years of age are allowed to do only certain types of work, such as deliver newspapers, work for their parents, and be employed in entertainment and (with some exceptions) agriculture. Children aged fourteen and fifteen are allowed to work, but not in hazardous occupations. There are also numerous restrictions on how many hours per day and per week children can work.

Working times and hours are not restricted for persons between the ages of sixteen and eighteen, but they cannot be employed in hazardous jobs. None of these restrictions apply to those over the age of eighteen.

Minimum Wages

The FLSA provides that a **minimum wage** of $7.25 per hour must be paid to employees in covered industries (by the time you read this text, the minimum wage may be higher). Congress periodically revises this minimum wage. Additionally, many states have minimum wages. When the state minimum wage is greater than the federal minimum wage, the employee is entitled to the higher wage.

When an employee receives tips while on the job, the employer is required to pay only $2.13 an hour in direct wages—if that amount, plus the tips received, equals at least the federal minimum wage. If an employee's tips and direct wages do not equal the federal minimum wage, the employer must make up the difference. If employers pay at least the federal minimum wage, the FLSA allows them to take employee tips and make other arrangements for their distribution.

Overtime Provisions and Exemptions

Under the FLSA, any employee who works more than forty hours per week must be paid no less than 1.5 times her or his regular pay for all hours over forty. The FLSA overtime provisions apply only after an employee has worked more than forty hours per *week,* so employees who work ten hours a day, four days per week, are not entitled to overtime pay.

Certain employees—usually administrative, executive, and professional employees, as well as outside salespersons and computer programmers—are exempt from the FLSA's overtime provisions. Employers are not required to pay overtime wages to exempt employees. An employer can voluntarily pay overtime to ineligible employees but cannot waive or reduce the overtime requirements of the FLSA.

EXECUTIVE EMPLOYEES An executive employee is one whose primary duty is management. An employee's primary duty is determined by what he or she does that is of principal value to the employer, not by how much time the employee spends doing particular tasks. An employer cannot deny overtime wages based only on an employee's job title, however, and must be able to show that the employee's primary duty qualifies her or him for an exemption.[6]

▶ **Case in Point 34.4** Kevin Keevican, a manager at a Starbucks store, worked seventy hours a week for $650 to $800, a 10 to 20 percent bonus, and paid sick leave. Keevican (and other former managers) filed a claim against Starbucks for unpaid overtime. Keevican claimed that he had spent 70 to 80 percent of his time waiting on customers and thus was not an executive employee. The court, however, found that Keevican was "the single highest-ranking employee" in his particular store. He was responsible on site for that store's day-to-day overall operations. Because his primary duty was managerial, Starbucks was not required to pay overtime.[7] ◀

ADMINISTRATIVE EMPLOYEES To qualify under the administrative employee exemption, the employee must be paid a salary, not hourly wages, and have a primary duty directly related to management or the employer's general business operations. In addition, the employee's primary duty must include the exercise of discretion and independent judgment with respect to matters of significance.

▶ **Case in Point 34.5** Patty Lee Smith was a pharmaceutical sales representative at Johnson and Johnson (J&J). She traveled to ten physicians' offices a day to promote the benefits of J&J's drug Concerta. Smith's work was unsupervised, she controlled her own schedule, and she received a salary of $66,000. When she filed a claim for overtime pay, the court held that she was an administrative employee and therefore exempt from the FLSA's overtime provisions.[8] ◀

---

6. See, for example, *Slusser v. Vantage Builders, Inc.,* 576 F.Supp.2d 1207 (D.N.M. 2008).
7. *Mims v. Starbucks Corp.,* 2007 WL 10369 (S.D.Tex. 2007).
8. *Smith v. Johnson and Johnson,* 593 F.3d 280 (3d Cir. 2010).

Layoffs

During the latest economic recession, millions of workers were laid off from their jobs as companies reduced costs by restructuring their operations and downsizing their workforces. In this section, we discuss the laws pertaining to employee layoffs, an area that is increasingly the subject of litigation.

THE WORKER ADJUSTMENT AND RETRAINING NOTIFICATION ACT The Worker Adjustment and Retraining Notification (WARN) Act[9] applies to employers with at least one hundred full-time employees. It requires an employer to provide sixty days' notice before implementing a mass layoff or closing a plant that employs more than fifty full-time workers. A mass layoff is a layoff of at least one-third of the full-time employees at a particular job site.

Notification Requirements. Employers must provide advance notice of the layoff to the affected workers *or* their representative (if the workers are members of a labor union). Employers must also notify state and local government authorities so that they can provide resources, such as job training, to displaced workers. Any part-time and seasonal employees who are being laid off must be notified, even though these workers do not count in determining whether the act's provisions are triggered. Even companies that anticipate filing for bankruptcy normally must provide notice under the WARN Act before implementing a mass layoff.

Remedies for Violations. If sued, an employer that orders a mass layoff or plant closing in violation of the WARN Act can be fined up to $500 for each day of the violation. Employees can recover back pay for each day of the violation (up to sixty days), plus reasonable attorneys' fees. An employee can also recover benefits under an employee benefit plan, including the cost of medical expenses that would have been covered by the plan.

Because the WARN Act applies to large employers that lay off thousands of workers, lawsuits can be expensive. The amount that an employer must pay grows larger each day and is multiplied by the number of employees involved in the suit.

STATE LAWS MAY ALSO REQUIRE LAYOFF NOTICES Many states also have statutes requiring employers to provide notice before initiating mass layoffs. These laws may have requirements different from and even stricter than those in the WARN Act. In New York, for instance, companies with fifty or more employees must provide ninety days' notice before any layoff that affects twenty-five or more full-time employees.

SECTION 3
FAMILY AND MEDICAL LEAVE

In 1993, Congress passed the Family and Medical Leave Act (FMLA)[10] to allow employees to take time off work for family or medical reasons. A majority of the states also have legislation allowing for family or medical leave. Many employers maintain private family-leave plans for their workers. The FMLA does not supersede any state or local law that provides more generous family- or medical-leave protection. Additional categories of FMLA leave were created in 2009 for military caregivers and for qualifying exigencies that arise due to military service.

Coverage and Application

The FMLA requires employers that have fifty or more employees to provide an employee with up to twelve weeks of unpaid family or medical leave during any twelve-month period. The FMLA expressly covers private and public (government) employees who have worked for their employers for at least a year.

An eligible employee may take up to *twelve weeks of leave* within a twelve-month period for any of the following reasons:

1. To care for a newborn baby within one year of birth.
2. To care for an adopted or foster child within one year of the time the child is placed with the employee.
3. To care for the employee's spouse, child, or parent who has a serious health condition.
4. If the employee suffers from a serious health condition and is unable to perform the essential functions of her or his job.
5. For any qualifying exigency (nonmedical emergency) arising out of the fact that the employee's spouse, son, daughter, or parent is a covered mili-

---

9. 29 U.S.C. Sections 2101 *et seq.*

10. 29 U.S.C. Sections 2601, 2611–2619, 2651–2654.

tary member on active duty.[11] For instance, an employee can take leave to arrange for child care or to deal with financial or legal matters when a spouse is being deployed to Korea.

In addition, an employee may take up to *twenty-six weeks of military caregiver leave* within a twelve-month period to care for a family member with a serious injury or illness incurred as a result of military duty.[12]

Benefits and Protections

When an employee takes FMLA leave, the employer must continue the worker's health-care coverage on the same terms as if the employee had continued to work. On returning from FMLA leave, most employees must be restored to their original position or to a comparable position (with nearly equivalent pay and benefits, for example). An important exception allows the employer to avoid reinstating a *key employee*—defined as an employee whose pay falls within the top 10 percent of the firm's workforce.

Violations

An employer that violates the FMLA can be required to provide various remedies, including the following:

1. Damages to compensate the employee for lost wages and benefits, denied compensation, and actual monetary losses (such as the cost of providing for care of a family member). Compensatory damages are available up to an amount equivalent to the employee's wages for twelve weeks.
2. Job reinstatement.
3. Promotion, if a promotion has been denied.

A successful plaintiff is also entitled to court costs and attorneys' fees. If bad faith on the part of the employer is shown, the plaintiff can receive twice the amount of damages awarded by the judge or jury. Supervisors can also be held personally liable, as employers, for violations of the act.

Employers generally are required to notify employees when an absence will be counted against FMLA leave. If an employer fails to provide such notice, and the employee consequently incurs costs or is otherwise harmed because he or she did not receive notice, the employer may be sanctioned.[13]

---

11. 29 C.F.R. Section 825.126.
12. 29 C.F.R. Section 825.200.
13. *Ragsdale v. Wolverine World Wide, Inc.,* 535 U.S. 81, 122 S.Ct. 1155, 152 L.Ed.2d 167 (2002).

SECTION 4
WORKER HEALTH AND SAFETY

Under the common law, employees who were injured on the job had to file lawsuits against their employers to obtain recovery. Today, numerous state and federal statutes protect employees from the risk of accidental injury, death, or disease resulting from their employment.

The Occupational Safety and Health Act

At the federal level, the primary legislation protecting employees' health and safety is the Occupational Safety and Health Act,[14] which is administered by the Occupational Safety and Health Administration (OSHA). The act imposes on employers a general duty to keep the workplace safe.

To this end, OSHA has established specific safety standards that employers must follow depending on the industry. For instance, OSHA regulations require the use of safety guards on certain mechanical equipment and set maximum levels of exposure to substances in the workplace that may be harmful to a worker's health.

NOTICES, RECORDS, AND REPORTS The act requires that employers post certain notices in the workplace, maintain specific records, and submit reports. Employers with eleven or more employees are required to keep occupational injury and illness records for each employee. Each record must be made available for inspection when requested by an OSHA compliance officer.

Whenever a work-related injury or disease occurs, employers must make reports directly to OSHA. If an employee dies or three or more employees are hospitalized because of a work-related incident, the employer must notify the OSHA within eight hours. A company that fails to do so will be fined. Following the incident, a complete inspection of the premises is mandatory.

INSPECTIONS OSHA compliance officers may enter and inspect the facilities of any establishment covered by the Occupational Safety and Health Act. Employees may also file complaints of violations. Under the act,

---

14. 29 U.S.C. Sections 553, 651–678.

an employer cannot discharge an employee who files a complaint or who, in good faith, refuses to work in a high-risk area if bodily harm or death might result.

State Workers' Compensation Laws

State **workers' compensation laws** establish an administrative procedure for compensating workers injured on the job. Instead of suing, an injured worker files a claim with the state agency or board that administers local workers' compensation claims.

Most workers' compensation statutes are similar. No state covers all employees. Typically, domestic workers, agricultural workers, temporary employees, and employees of common carriers (companies that provide transportation services to the public) are excluded, but minors are covered.

Usually, the statutes allow employers to purchase insurance from a private insurer or a state fund to pay workers' compensation benefits in the event of a claim. Most states also allow employers to be *self-insured*—that is, employers that show an ability to pay claims do not need to buy insurance.

WORKERS' COMPENSATION REQUIREMENTS In general, the only requirements to recover benefits under state workers' compensation laws are:

1. The existence of an employment relationship.
2. An *accidental* injury that *occurred on the job or in the course of employment,* regardless of fault. (An injury that occurs while an employee is commuting to or from work usually is not covered because it did not occur on the job or in the course of employment.)

An injured employee must notify her or his employer promptly (usually within thirty days of the accident). Generally, an employee must also file a workers' compensation claim within a certain period (sixty days to two years) from the time the injury is first noticed, rather than from the time of the accident.

WORKERS' COMPENSATION VERSUS LITIGATION If an employee accepts workers' compensation benefits, he or she may not sue for injuries caused by the employer's negligence. By barring lawsuits for negligence, workers' compensation laws also prevent employers from avoiding liability by using defenses, such as contributory negligence or assumption of risk. A worker

may sue an employer who *intentionally* injures the worker, however.

INCOME SECURITY

Federal and state governments participate in insurance programs designed to protect employees and their families from the financial impact of retirement, disability, death, hospitalization, and unemployment. The key federal law on this subject is the Social Security Act.[15]

Social Security

The Social Security Act provides for old-age (retirement), survivors', and disability insurance. The act is therefore often referred to as OASDI. Both employers and employees must "contribute" under the Federal Insurance Contributions Act (FICA)[16] to help pay for benefits that will partially make up for the employees' loss of income on retirement.

The basis for the employee's and the employer's contribution is the employee's annual wage base—the maximum amount of the employee's wages that is subject to the tax. The employer withholds the employee's FICA contribution from the employee's wages and then matches this contribution.

The annual wage base is adjusted each year as needed to take into account the rising cost of living. In 2013, employers were required to withhold 6.2 percent of each employee's wages, up to a maximum wage base of $113,700, and to match this contribution.

Retired workers are eligible to receive monthly payments from the Social Security Administration, which administers the Social Security Act. Social Security benefits are fixed by statute but increase automatically with increases in the cost of living.

Medicare

Medicare is a federal government health-insurance program administered by the Social Security Administration for people sixty-five years of age and older and for some under age sixty-five who are disabled. It originally had two parts, one pertaining to

15. 42 U.S.C. Sections 301–1397e.
16. 26 U.S.C. Sections 3101–3125.

hospital costs and the other to nonhospital medical costs, such as visits to physicians' offices.

ADDITIONAL COVERAGE OPTIONS Medicare now offers additional coverage options and a prescription-drug plan. People who have Medicare hospital insurance can obtain additional federal medical insurance if they pay small monthly premiums.

TAX CONTRIBUTIONS Like Social Security, Medicare is funded by "contributions" from the employer and the employee, but there is no cap on the amount of wages subject to the Medicare tax. In 2013, both the employer and the employee were required to pay 1.45 percent of *all* wages and salaries to finance Medicare.

Thus, for Social Security and Medicare together, in 2013 the employer and employee each paid 7.65 percent of the first $113,700 of income (6.2 percent for Social Security + 1.45 percent for Medicare), for a combined total of 15.3 percent. In addition, all wages and salaries above $113,700 were taxed at a combined (employer and employee) rate of 2.9 percent for Medicare.[17] Self-employed persons pay both the employer and the employee portions of the Social Security and Medicare taxes.

In addition, as of 2013, a Medicare tax of 3.8 percent is applied to all investment income for single wage earners making more than $200,000 and married couples making more than $250,000.

Private Pension Plans

The major federal statute that regulates employee retirement plans is the Employee Retirement Income Security Act (ERISA).[18] Its provisions governing employers who have private pension funds for their employees are enforced by the U.S. Department of Labor.

ERISA created the Pension Benefit Guaranty Corporation (PBGC), an independent federal agency, to provide timely and uninterrupted payment of voluntary private pension benefits. The pension plans pay annual insurance premiums (at set rates adjusted for inflation) to the PBGC, which then pays benefits to participants in the event that a plan is unable to do so.

ERISA does *not* require an employer to establish a pension plan. When a plan exists, however, ERISA provides standards for its management. ERISA

also imposes detailed record-keeping and reporting requirements.

VESTING A key provision of ERISA concerns vesting. **Vesting** gives an employee a legal right to receive pension benefits at some future date when she or he stops working. Before ERISA was enacted, some employees who had worked for companies for as long as thirty years received no pension benefits when their employment terminated because those benefits had not vested.

ERISA establishes complex vesting rules. Generally, however, all of an employee's contributions to a pension plan vest immediately, and the employee's rights to the employer's contributions vest after five years of employment.

INVESTMENT OF PENSION FUNDS In an attempt to prevent mismanagement of pension funds, ERISA established rules on how they must be invested. Managers must choose investments cautiously and must diversify the plan's investments to minimize the risk of large losses.

Unemployment Insurance

The Federal Unemployment Tax Act (FUTA)[19] created a state-administered system that provides unemployment compensation to eligible individuals who have lost their jobs. The FUTA and state laws require employers that fall under the provisions of the act to pay unemployment taxes at regular intervals. The proceeds from these taxes are then paid out to qualified unemployed workers.

To be eligible for unemployment compensation, a worker must be willing and able to work. Workers who have been fired for misconduct or who have voluntarily left their jobs are not eligible for benefits. Normally, workers must be actively seeking employment to continue receiving benefits. Temporary measures recently enacted in response to persistent high unemployment rates also allow some jobless persons to retain unemployment benefits while pursuing additional education and training.

COBRA

Federal law also enables employees to continue health-care coverage after their jobs have been terminated and they are no longer eligible for group

---

17. As a result of the Health Care and Education Reconciliation Act of 2010, Medicare tax rates will rise, and the applicable compensation base will include more than just salary incomes.
18. 29 U.S.C. Sections 1001 *et seq.*

19. 26 U.S.C. Sections 3301–3310.

health-insurance plans. The Consolidated Omnibus Budget Reconciliation Act (COBRA)[20] prohibits an employer from eliminating a worker's medical, vision, or dental insurance on the voluntary or involuntary termination of the worker's employment.

Employers, with some exceptions, must inform employees of COBRA's provisions when they face termination or a reduction of hours that would affect their eligibility for coverage under the plan. Only workers fired for gross misconduct are excluded. An employer that does not comply with COBRA risks substantial penalties, such as a tax of up to 10 percent of the annual cost of the group plan or $500,000, whichever is less.

PROCEDURES A worker has sixty days (from the date that the group coverage would stop) to decide whether to continue with the employer's group insurance plan. If the worker chooses to discontinue the coverage, the employer has no further obligation.

If the worker chooses to continue coverage, the employer is obligated to keep the policy active for up to eighteen months (twenty-nine months if the worker is disabled). The coverage must be the same as that provided to the worker prior to the termination or reduction of work. If family members were originally included, COBRA prohibits their exclusion.

PAYMENT Generally, an employer can require the employee to pay all of the premiums, plus a 2 percent administrative charge. If the worker fails to pay the premiums, becomes eligible for Medicare, or obtains coverage under another plan (or if the employer completely eliminates its group plan), the employer is relieved of further responsibility.

Employer-Sponsored Group Health Plans

The Health Insurance Portability and Accountability Act (HIPAA),[21] discussed in Chapter 4, also affects employer-sponsored group health plans. HIPAA does not require employers to provide health insurance, but it does establish requirements for those that do. Under HIPAA, employers must give credit to employees for previous health coverage (including COBRA coverage) to decrease any waiting period before their coverage becomes effective.

In addition, HIPAA restricts the manner in which employers collect, use, and disclose the health infor-

mation of employees and their families. Employers must train employees, designate privacy officials, and distribute privacy notices to ensure that employees' health information is not disclosed to unauthorized parties.

Failure to comply with HIPAA regulations can result in civil penalties of up to $100 per person per violation (with a cap of $25,000 per year). The employer is also subject to criminal prosecution for certain types of HIPAA violations and can face up to $250,000 in criminal fines and imprisonment for up to ten years if convicted.

Affordable Care Act

Under the Affordable Care Act[22] (ACA, commonly referred to as Obamacare), most employers with fifty or more full-time employees are required to offer health-insurance benefits. There is no requirement to provide health benefits if fewer than fifty people are employed. Any business offering health benefits to its employees (even if not legally required to do so) may be eligible for tax credits of up to 35 percent to offset the costs.

An employer who fails to provide health benefits as required under the statute can be fined up to $2,000 for each employee after the first thirty people. (This is known as the 50/30 rule: employers with fifty employees must provide insurance, and those failing to do so will be fined for each employee after the first thirty.) An employer who offers a plan that costs an employee more than 9.5 percent of the employee's income may receive a penalty of $3,000.

Employers will be fined for failing to provide benefits only if one of their employees receives a federal subsidy to buy health insurance through a state health-insurance exchange. The act established state exchanges to provide a marketplace for business owners and individuals to compare premiums and purchase policies.

SECTION 6

EMPLOYEE PRIVACY RIGHTS

In the last thirty years, concerns about the privacy rights of employees have arisen as employers purportedly use invasive tactics to monitor and screen

---

20. 29 U.S.C. Sections 1161–1169.
21. 29 U.S.C. Sections 1181 *et seq.*

22. Pub. L. 111-148, 124 Stat. 119, Mar. 23, 2010, codified in various sections of 42 U.S.C.

workers. Perhaps the greatest privacy concern in employment today involves electronic monitoring of employees' activities.

Electronic Monitoring

More than half of employers engage in some form of electronic monitoring of their employees. Many employers review employees' e-mail, blogs, instant messages, and tweets, as well as their social media, smartphone, and Internet use. Employers may also video their employees at work, record and listen to their telephone conversations and voice mail, and read their text messages and social media posts.

EMPLOYEE PRIVACY PROTECTION Employees of private (nongovernment) employers have some privacy protection under tort law (see Chapter 6) and state constitutions. In addition, state and federal statutes may limit an employer's conduct in certain respects. For instance, as discussed in Chapter 9, the Electronic Communications Privacy Act prohibits employers from intercepting an employee's personal electronic communications unless they are made on devices and systems furnished by the employer. Nonetheless, employers do have considerable leeway to monitor employees in the workplace.

Private employers generally are free to use filtering software (discussed in Chapter 4) to block access to certain Web sites, such as sites containing sexually explicit images. The First Amendment's protection of free speech prevents only *government employers* from restraining speech by blocking Web sites.

WAS THERE A REASONABLE EXPECTATION OF PRIVACY? When determining whether an employer should be held liable for violating an employee's privacy rights, the courts generally weigh the employer's interests against the employee's reasonable expectation of privacy. Normally, if employees have been informed that their communications are being monitored, they cannot reasonably expect those interactions to be private. Also, if the employer provided the e-mail system or blog that the employee used for communications, a court will typically hold that the employee did not have a reasonable expectation of privacy.

If employees are *not* informed that certain communications are being monitored, however, the employer may be held liable for invading their privacy. Most employers that engage in electronic monitoring notify their employees about the monitoring.

Nevertheless, a general policy may not sufficiently protect an employer who monitors forms of communications that the policy fails to mention. For instance, notifying employees that their e-mails and phone calls may be monitored does not necessarily protect an employer who monitors social media posts or text messages.

Other Types of Monitoring

In addition to monitoring their employees' online activities, employers also engage in other types of employee screening and monitoring. The practices discussed next have often been challenged as violations of employee privacy rights.

LIE-DETECTOR TESTS At one time, many employers required employees or job applicants to take polygraph examinations (lie-detector tests). Today, the Employee Polygraph Protection Act[23] generally prohibits employers from requiring employees or job applicants to take lie-detector tests or suggesting or requesting that they do so. The act also restricts employers' ability to use or ask about the results of any lie-detector test or to take any negative employment action based on the results.

Certain employers are exempt from these prohibitions. Federal, state, and local government employers, and certain security service firms, may conduct polygraph tests. In addition, companies that manufacture and distribute controlled substances may perform lie-detector tests. Other employers may use polygraph tests when investigating losses attributable to theft, including embezzlement and the theft of trade secrets.

DRUG TESTING In the interests of public safety and to reduce unnecessary costs, many employers, including the government, require their employees to submit to drug testing.

Public Employers. Government (public) employers are constrained in drug testing by the Fourth Amendment to the U.S. Constitution, which prohibits unreasonable searches and seizures (see Chapter 4). Drug testing of public employees is allowed by statute for transportation workers. Courts normally uphold drug testing of certain employees when drug use in a particular job may threaten public safety. Also, when there is a reasonable basis for suspecting public employees of

---

23. 29 U.S.C. Sections 2001 *et seq.*

drug use, courts often find that drug testing does not violate the Fourth Amendment.

Private Employers. The Fourth Amendment does not apply to drug testing conducted by private employers. Hence, the privacy rights and drug testing of private-sector employees are governed by state law, which varies from state to state. Many states have statutes that allow drug testing by private employers but put restrictions on when and how the testing may be performed. A collective bargaining agreement (discussed later in this chapter) may also provide protection against (or authorize) drug testing.

The permissibility of a private employee's drug test often hinges on whether the employer's testing was reasonable. Random drug tests and even "zero-tolerance" policies (which deny a "second chance" to employees who test positive for drugs) have been held to be reasonable.[24]

Many workers at U.S. government facilities are employees of private contractors, not of the government. Until recently, these workers generally were not subject to the drug testing and background checks that are applied to federal government employees. In the following case, several contract workers claimed that their privacy rights had been violated by new standards that required them to submit to background checks.

---

24. See *CITGO Asphalt Refining Co. v. Paper, Allied-Industrial, Chemical, and Energy Workers International Union Local No. 2-991*, 385 F.3d 809 (3d Cir. 2004).

CASE 34.2

National Aeronautics and Space Administration v. Nelson
Supreme Court of the United States, __ U.S. __, 131 S.Ct. 746, 178 L.Ed.2d 667 (2011).

COMPANY PROFILE *The National Aeronautics and Space Administration (NASA) is an independent federal agency charged with planning and conducting "space activities." One of NASA's facilities is the Jet Propulsion Laboratory (JPL), which develops and runs most U.S. unmanned space missions— from the* Explorer 1 *satellite in 1958 to the Mars rovers of this century. The JPL is owned by NASA but is operated by the California Institute of Technology and is staffed exclusively by contract employees.*

BACKGROUND AND FACTS In 2007, under newly implemented standards, contract employees with long-term access to federal facilities were ordered to complete a standard background check. The National Agency Check with Inquiries (NACI) performs background checks for the government. The NACI is designed to obtain information on such issues as counseling and treatment, as well as mental and financial stability. Robert Nelson and other JPL employees filed a lawsuit in a federal district court against NASA, claiming that the NACI violated their privacy rights. The court denied the plaintiffs' request to prohibit use of the NACI, but the U.S. Court of Appeals for the Ninth Circuit reversed this decision. NASA appealed to the United States Supreme Court, arguing that the Privacy Act of 1974 provides sufficient protection for employees' privacy. This act allows the government to retain information only for "relevant and necessary" purposes, requires written consent before the information may be disclosed, and imposes criminal liability for violations.

IN THE LANGUAGE OF THE COURT
Justice *ALITO* delivered the opinion of the Court.

Respondents in this case, federal contract employees at a Government laboratory, claim that two parts of a standard employment background investigation violate their rights * * * . Respondents challenge a section of a form questionnaire that asks employees about treatment or counseling for recent illegal-drug use. They also object to certain open-ended questions on a form sent to employees' designated references.
* * * *

*We will assume for present purposes that the Government's challenged inquiries implicate a privacy interest of constitutional significance. We hold, however, that, whatever the scope of this interest, it does not prevent the Government from asking reasonable questions * * * in an employment background investigation that is subject to the Privacy Act's safeguards against public disclosure.* [Emphasis added.]

CASE 34.2 CONTINUED

* * * *

* * * The questions challenged by respondents are part of a standard employment background check of the sort used by millions of private employers. The Government itself has been conducting employment investigations since the earliest days of the Republic. Since 1871, the President has enjoyed statutory authority to ascertain the fitness of applicants for the civil service as to age, health, character, knowledge and ability for the employment sought and that [statute] appears to have been regarded as a codification of established practice. Standard background investigations similar to those at issue here became mandatory for all candidates for the federal civil service in 1953. And the particular investigations challenged in this case arose from a decision to extend that requirement to federal contract employees requiring long-term access to federal facilities.

As this long history suggests, the Government has an interest in conducting basic employment background checks. Reasonable investigations of applicants and employees aid the Government in ensuring the security of its facilities and in employing a competent, reliable workforce.

DECISION AND REMEDY *The United States Supreme Court reversed the judgment of the lower court and remanded the case. The NACI does not violate an individual's right to privacy because its inquiries are reasonable and the Privacy Act protects against the disclosure of private information.*

WHAT IF THE FACTS WERE DIFFERENT? *Suppose that after the decision in this case, a JPL employee refused to cooperate in an NACI background check. What would be the most likely consequences?*

THE LEGAL ENVIRONMENT DIMENSION *The U.S. Constitution does not explicitly mention a general right to privacy. From what sources does the Court infer this right? (Hint: See the section on "Privacy Rights" in Chapter 4.)*

GENETIC TESTING A serious privacy issue arose when some employers began conducting genetic testing of employees or prospective employees in an effort to identify individuals who might develop significant health problems in the future. To prevent the improper use of genetic information by employers and health-insurance providers, in 2008 Congress passed the Genetic Information Nondiscrimination Act (GINA).[25]

Under GINA, employers cannot make decisions about hiring, firing, job placement, or promotion based on the results of genetic testing. GINA also prohibits group health plans and insurers from denying coverage or charging higher premiums based solely on a genetic predisposition to develop a disease in the future.

SECTION 7
IMMIGRATION LAW

The United States did not have any laws restricting immigration until the late nineteenth century. Today, the most important laws affecting the employment

relationship are the Immigration Reform and Control Act (IRCA) of 1986[26] and the Immigration Act of 1990.[27]

Immigration law has become increasingly important in recent years. An estimated 12 million undocumented immigrants now live in the United States, many of whom came to find jobs. Because U.S. employers face serious penalties if they hire undocumented workers, it is necessary for businesspersons to have an understanding of immigration laws.

The Immigration Reform and Control Act

When the IRCA was enacted in 1986, it provided amnesty to certain groups of aliens living illegally in the United States at the time. It also established a system that sanctions employers that hire immigrants who lack work authorization.

The IRCA makes it illegal to hire, recruit, or refer for a fee someone not authorized to work in this country. Through Immigration and Customs Enforcement officers, the federal government conducts random

---

25. 26 U.S.C. Section 9834; 42 U.S.C. Sections 300gg-53, 1320d-9, 2000ff-1 to 2000ff-11.

26. 29 U.S.C. Section 1802.
27. This act amended various provisions of the Immigration and Nationality Act of 1952, 8 U.S.C. Sections 1101 *et seq.*

compliance audits and engages in enforcement actions against employers who hire undocumented workers.

I-9 EMPLOYMENT VERIFICATION To comply with IRCA requirements, an employer must perform **I-9 verifications** for new hires, including those hired as "contractors" or "day workers" if they work under the employer's direct supervision. The employer must complete Form I-9, Employment Eligibility Verification, which is available from U.S. Citizenship and Immigration Services,[28] for each worker *within three days* of his or her commencement of employment. The three-day period allows the employer to check the form's accuracy and to review and verify documents establishing the prospective worker's identity and eligibility for employment in the United States.

Documentation. The employer must declare, under penalty of perjury, that an employee produced documents establishing his or her identity and legal employability. Acceptable documents include a U.S. passport establishing the person's citizenship or a document authorizing a foreign citizen to work in the United States, such as a permanent resident card or an *Alien Registration Receipt* (discussed on the next page).

Legal Actions. Most legal actions alleging violations of I-9 rules are brought against employees. An employee must state on the I-9 form that she or he is a U.S. citizen or otherwise authorized to work in the United States. If the employee enters false information on the form or presents false documentation, the employer can fire the worker, who then may be subject to deportation. Nevertheless, employers must be honest when verifying an employee's documentation: if an employer "should have known" that the worker was unauthorized, the employer has violated the rules.

ENFORCEMENT U.S. Immigration and Customs Enforcement (ICE) is the largest investigative arm of the U.S. Department of Homeland Security. ICE has a general inspection program that conducts random compliance audits. Other audits may occur if the agency receives a written complaint alleging that an employer has committed violations. Government inspections include a review of an employer's file of I-9 forms. The government does not need a subpoena or a warrant to conduct such an inspection.

If an investigation reveals a possible violation, ICE will bring an administrative action and issue a Notice of Intent to Fine, which sets out the charges against the employer. The employer has a right to a hearing on the enforcement action if it files a request within thirty days. This hearing is conducted before an *administrative law judge* (see Chapters 1 and 43), and the employer has a right to counsel and to *discovery* (see Chapter 3). The typical defense in such actions is good faith or substantial compliance with the documentation provisions.

PENALTIES An employer who violates the law by hiring an unauthorized worker is subject to substantial penalties. The employer can be fined up to $2,200 for each unauthorized employee for a first offense, $5,000 per employee for a second offense, and up to $11,000 for subsequent offenses.

Employers who have engaged in a "pattern or practice of violations" are subject to criminal penalties, which include additional fines and imprisonment for up to ten years. A company may also be barred from future government contracts.

In determining the penalty, ICE considers the seriousness of the violation (such as intentional falsification of documents) and the employer's past compliance. ICE regulations also identify factors that will mitigate or aggravate the penalty under certain circumstances, such as whether the employer cooperated in the investigation or is a small business.

The Immigration Act

Often, U.S. businesses find that they cannot hire sufficient domestic workers with specialized skills. For this reason, U.S. immigration laws have long made provisions for businesses to hire specially qualified foreign workers. The Immigration Act of 1990 placed caps on the number of visas (entry permits) that can be issued to immigrants each year.

Most temporary visas are set aside for workers who can be characterized as "persons of extraordinary ability," members of the professions holding advanced degrees, or other skilled workers and professionals. To hire such an individual, an employer must submit a petition to U.S. Citizenship and Immigration Services, which determines whether the job candidate meets the legal standards. Each visa is for a specific job, and there are legal limits on the employee's ability to switch jobs once he or she is in the United States.

---

28. U.S. Citizenship and Immigration Services is a federal agency that is part of the U.S. Department of Homeland Security.

I-551 ALIEN REGISTRATION RECEIPTS A company seeking to hire a noncitizen worker may do so if the worker is self-authorized. This means that the worker either is a lawful permanent resident or has a valid temporary Employment Authorization Document. A lawful permanent resident can prove his or her status to an employer by presenting an **I-551 Alien Registration Receipt,** known as a green card, or a properly stamped foreign passport.

Many immigrant workers are not already self-authorized, and an employer that wishes to hire them can attempt to obtain labor certification, or green cards, for them. To gain authorization for hiring a foreign worker, the employer must show that no U.S. worker is qualified, willing, and able to take the job. Approximately fifty thousand new green cards are issued each year. A green card can be obtained only for a person who is being hired for a permanent, full-time position. (A separate authorization system provides for the temporary entry and hiring of non-immigrant visa workers.)

The government has detailed regulations governing the advertising of positions as well as the certification process.[29] Any U.S. applicants who meet the stated job qualifications must be interviewed for the position. The employer must also be able to show that the qualifications required for the job are a business necessity.

THE H-1B VISA PROGRAM The most common and controversial visa program today is the H-1B visa system. To obtain an H1-B visa, the potential employee must be qualified in a "specialty occupation," which is defined as involving highly specialized knowledge and the attainment of a bachelor's or higher degree or its equivalent. Individuals with H-1B visas can stay in the United States for three to six years and work only for the sponsoring employer.

The recipients of these visas include many high-tech workers, such as computer programmers and electronics specialists. A maximum of sixty-five thousand H-1B visas are set aside each year for new immigrants. That limit is typically reached within the first few weeks of the year. Consequently, many companies, such as Microsoft, continue to lobby Congress to expand the number of H-1B visas available to immigrants. These companies contend that the H-1B system is keeping some of the world's brightest scientific and engineering minds out of the United States.

In 2013, frustrated by the shortage of visas, several Silicon Valley entrepreneurs started a colony of foreign-born individuals who live and work on a cruise ship stationed in international waters off the coast of California. The ship, called *Blueseed,* stays outside U.S. jurisdiction so that its residents can start or work for companies near Silicon Valley without having to obtain H-1B visas.

LABOR CERTIFICATION Before submitting an H-1B application, an employer must file a Labor Certification application on a form known as ETA 9035. The employer must agree to provide a wage level at least equal to the wages offered to other individuals with similar experience and qualifications. The employer must also show that the hiring will not adversely affect other workers similarly employed. The employer is required to inform U.S. workers of the intent to hire a foreign worker by posting the form. The U.S. Department of Labor reviews the applications and may reject them for omissions or inaccuracies.

H-2, O, L, AND E VISAS Other specialty temporary visas are available for other categories of employees. H-2 visas provide for workers performing agricultural labor of a seasonal nature. O visas provide entry for persons who have "extraordinary ability in the sciences, arts, education, business or athletics which has been demonstrated by sustained national or international acclaim." L visas allow a company's foreign managers or executives to work inside the United States. E visas permit the entry of certain foreign investors or entrepreneurs.

State Immigration Legislation

Until 2010, immigration and the treatment of illegal immigrants were governed exclusively by federal laws. Then Arizona enacted a law that required Arizona law enforcement officials to identify, charge, and potentially deport immigrants living in Arizona who are there illegally. Among other things, that law required immigrants to carry their papers at all times and allowed police to check a person's immigration status during any law enforcement action.

PREEMPTION ISSUES The federal government, however, insisted that federal immigration laws preempt state legislation. The United States Supreme Court ruled on the legality of the Arizona law in 2012. By that time, several other states had passed similar legislation.

---

29. The most relevant regulations can be found at 20 C.F.R. Section 655 (for temporary employment) and 20 C.F.R. Section 656 (for permanent employment).

In the *Arizona v. United States*[30] case, the Supreme Court upheld the controversial "show-me-your-papers" provision that requires police to check the immigration status of persons stopped for another violation. All other provisions of Arizona's law were struck down because they were preempted by federal laws.

THE FUTURE OF STATE LEGISLATION The Supreme Court's decision does not prohibit states from enacting laws related to immigration, but it does set some limits. States are prohibited from making it a crime for immigrants not to carry their registration documents or for those without work permits to seek employment.

States also cannot authorize law enforcement to arrest anyone based solely on a reasonable suspicion that the person is in the country illegally. States can, however, require individuals to show documentation of their immigration status to law enforcement when requested to do so during a lawful stop for other reasons.

SECTION 8
LABOR UNIONS

In the 1930s, in addition to the wage and hour laws discussed earlier, Congress enacted several other laws regulating employment relationships. These laws protect employees' rights to join labor unions, to bargain with management over the terms and conditions of employment, and to conduct strikes.

Federal Labor Laws

Federal labor laws governing union-employer relations have developed considerably since the first law was enacted in 1932. Initially, the laws were concerned with protecting the rights and interests of workers. Subsequent legislation placed some restraints on unions and granted rights to employers. We look here at four major federal statutes regulating union-employer relations.

NORRIS-LAGUARDIA ACT Congress protected peaceful strikes, picketing, and boycotts in 1932 in the Norris-LaGuardia Act.[31] The statute restricted the power of federal courts to issue injunctions against unions engaged in peaceful strikes. In effect, this act declared a national policy permitting employees to organize.

NATIONAL LABOR RELATIONS ACT One of the foremost statutes regulating labor is the National Labor Relations Act (NLRA) of 1935.[32] This act established the rights of employees to engage in collective bargaining and to strike.

The act also specifically defined a number of employer practices as unfair to labor:

1. Interference with the efforts of employees to form, join, or assist labor organizations or to engage in concerted activities for their mutual aid or protection.
2. An employer's domination of a labor organization or contribution of financial or other support to it.
3. Discrimination in the hiring of or the awarding of tenure to employees for reason of union affiliation.
4. Discrimination against employees for filing charges under the act or giving testimony under the act.
5. Refusal to bargain collectively with the duly designated representative of the employees.

The National Labor Relations Board. The NLRA also created the National Labor Relations Board (NLRB) to oversee union elections and to prevent employers from engaging in unfair and illegal union activities and unfair labor practices. (To learn how recent NLRB rulings have affected social media policies, see this chapter's *Managerial Strategy* feature on the next page.)

The NLRB has the authority to investigate employees' charges of unfair labor practices and to file complaints against employers in response to these charges. When violations are found, the NLRB may issue a **cease-and-desist order** compelling the employer to stop engaging in the unfair practices. Cease-and-desist orders can be enforced by a federal appellate court if necessary. After the NLRB rules on claims of unfair labor practices, its decision may be appealed to a federal court.

▶ **Case in Point 34.6** Roundy's, Inc., which operates a chain of stores in Wisconsin, became involved in a dispute with a local construction union. When union members started distributing "extremely unflattering" flyers outside the stores, Roundy's ejected them from the property. The NLRB filed a complaint against Roundy's for unfair labor practices. An administrative law judge ruled that Roundy's had violated the law by discriminating against the union, and a

---

30. ___ U.S. ___, 132 S.Ct. 2492, 183 L.Ed.2d 351 (2012).
31. 29 U.S.C. Sections 101–110, 113–115.

32. 20 U.S.C. Sections 151–169.

MANAGERIAL STRATEGY

Many Companies Have to Revise Their Social Media Policies

Over the past few years, many companies have created social media policies for their employees. For example, Costco's policy used to read as follows:

> "Any communication transmitted, stored or displayed electronically must comply with the policies outlined in the Costco Employee Agreement. Employees should be aware that statements posted electronically that damage the company, defame any individual or damage any person's reputation, or violate the policies outlined in the Costco Employee Agreement, may be subject to discipline up to and including termination of employment."

Since a ruling by the National Labor Relations Board (NLRB) in 2012, however, many companies have had to revise their policies.

The NLRB Rules on Protected "Concerted Activities"

Section 7 of the National Labor Relations Act states: "Employees shall have the right to self-organization, to form, join, or assist labor organizations . . . and to engage in other *concerted activities* for the purpose of collective bargaining or *other mutual aid or protection.*" [Emphasis added.]

When employees challenged Costco's social media policy, the NLRB found that the policy violated the National Labor Relations Act because it was overly broad and did not specifically reference Section 7 activity. The ruling stated: "The broad prohibition against making statements that 'damage the company, defame any individual or damage any person's reputation' clearly encompasses concerted communications protesting the Respondent's [Costco's] treatment of its employees."[a]

The NLRB Continues to Strike Down Broad Prohibitions in Social Media Policies

Since the ruling on Costco's social media policy, the NLRB has struck down similar policies at several companies,

including EchoStar Technologies and Dish Network. The NLRB's general counsel has also issued three reports concluding that many companies' social media policies illegally restrict workers' exercise of their rights.

In one case, Karl Knauz BMW, a car dealership, had told its employees to always be "polite and friendly to our customers, vendors, and suppliers, as well as to your fellow employees." The NLRB found that this policy, like the one at Costco, was "unlawful because employees would reasonably construe its broad prohibition against disrespectful conduct and language which injures the image or reputation of the dealership" as encompassing Section 7 activity. In other words, the policy was overly broad because it could apply to discussions in which employees objected to their working conditions and sought the support of others in improving those conditions—which are protected activities.[b]

MANAGERIAL IMPLICATIONS

All companies that have social media policies should include a statement that any employee communications protected by Section 7 of the National Labor Relations Act are excluded from those policies. Companies can no longer have a policy that states that all social media posts must be "completely accurate and not misleading" because such a policy would be considered overbroad. Note also that companies cannot require their employees to report any unusual or inappropriate internal social media activity.

BUSINESS QUESTIONS

1. *Employees meeting around the water cooler or coffee machine have always had the right to discuss work-related matters. Is a social media outlet simply a digital water cooler? Why or why not?*

2. *If your company instituted a policy stating that employees should "think carefully about 'friending' co-workers," would that policy be lawful? Why or why not?*

---

a. *Costco Wholesale Corporation and United Food and Commercial Workers Union, Local 371,* Case 34-CA-01242, September 7, 2012, decision and order from NLRB (available at www.nlrb.gov/case/34–CA-012421).

b. www.nlrb.gov/category/case-number/13-CA-046452.

---

federal appellate court affirmed. It is an unfair labor practice for an employer to prohibit union members from distributing flyers outside a store when it allows nonunion members to do so.[33] ◄

---

33. *Roundy's, Inc. v. NLRB,* 647 F.3d 638 (7th Cir. 2012).

Good Faith Bargaining. Under the NLRA, employers and unions have a duty to bargain in good faith. Bargaining over certain subjects is mandatory, and a party's refusal to bargain over these subjects is an unfair labor practice that can be reported to the NLRB. In one case, for example, an employer was required to bargain with the union over the use of hidden video surveillance cameras.[34]

Workers Protected by the NLRA. To be protected under the NLRA, an individual must be an employee or a job applicant (otherwise, the NLRA's ban on discrimination in regard to hiring would mean little). Additionally, the United States Supreme Court has held that individuals who are hired by a union to organize a company (union organizers) are to be considered employees of the company for NLRA purposes.[35]

LABOR-MANAGEMENT RELATIONS ACT The Labor-Management Relations Act (LMRA or Taft-Hartley Act) of 1947[36] was passed to proscribe certain unfair union practices, such as the *closed shop*. A **closed shop** is a firm that requires union membership as a condition of employment.

Although the act made the closed shop illegal, it preserved the legality of the union shop. A **union shop** is a firm that does not require union membership as a prerequisite for employment but can, and usually does, require that workers join the union after a specified amount of time on the job.

The LMRA also prohibited unions from refusing to bargain with employers, engaging in certain types of picketing, and *featherbedding* (causing employers to

hire more employees than necessary). In addition, the act allowed individual states to pass their own **right-to-work laws**—laws making it illegal for union membership to be required for *continued* employment in any establishment. Thus, union shops are technically illegal in the twenty-four states that have right-to-work laws.

LABOR-MANAGEMENT REPORTING AND DISCLOSURE ACT The Labor-Management Reporting and Disclosure Act (LMRDA)[37] established an employee bill of rights and reporting requirements for union activities. The act regulates unions' internal business procedures, including elections. For instance, the LMRDA requires unions to hold regularly scheduled elections of officers using secret ballots. Former convicts are prohibited from holding union office. Moreover, union officials are accountable for union property and funds. Members have the right to attend and to participate in union meetings, to nominate officers, and to vote in most union proceedings.

The act also outlawed **hot-cargo agreements,** in which employers voluntarily agree with unions not to handle, use, or deal in goods of other employers produced by nonunion employees.

The LMRDA holds union officers to a high standard of responsibility and ethical conduct in administering the affairs of their union. This standard was at the core of the dispute in the following case.

34. *National Steel Corp. v. NLRB*, 324 F.3d 928 (7th Cir. 2003).
35. *NLRB v. Town & Country Electric, Inc.*, 516 U.S. 85, 116 S.Ct. 450, 133 L.Ed.2d 371 (1995).
36. 29 U.S.C. Sections 141 *et seq.*
37. 29 U.S.C. Sections 401 *et seq.*

CASE ANALYSIS

Case 34.3 Services Employees International Union v. National Union of Healthcare Workers
United States Court of Appeals, Ninth Circuit, 711 F.3d 970 (2013).

IN THE LANGUAGE OF THE COURT
TALLMAN, Circuit Judge:

* * * *

The Services Employees International Union ("SEIU") consists of 2.2 million members who work in healthcare, public services, and property services. United Health Workers ("UHW") is one of many "local" unions affiliated with SEIU [and represents] approximately 150,000 healthcare workers in California.

* * * The SEIU constitution vests SEIU's International Executive Board with authority regarding alignment and jurisdiction of local unions like UHW.

* * * *

* * * The international union intended to move 150,000 long-term care workers from three separate unions, including some 65,000 from UHW, into a new local union chartered by SEIU.

* * * *

* * * The SEIU constitution grants SEIU the authority to place a local union into trusteeship "to protect the interests of the membership" from local union malfeasance.

* * * *

The SEIU International Executive Board [gave] UHW until January 27, 2009, to confirm in writing that it would not oppose the creation of the new long-term care workers union. The UHW would not so promise, and

CASE 34.3 CONTINUED

SEIU placed UHW into trusteeship on January 27, 2009.

* * * *

* * * UHW officials sought to create an ungovernable situation for trustees appointed to administer UHW by: (1) blocking access to UHW buildings to prevent the SEIU-appointed trustees from entering; (2) removing UHW property from UHW buildings, including office equipment, computers, and employee grievance files; [and] (3) instructing lower-level UHW officials and rank-and-file members not to recognize the authority of the trustees.

At the same time, the [UHW officials], while still on the UHW payroll, began to create and promote [a] new union.

Within a week after the trusteeship was announced, the * * * [UHW officials] had created the National Union of Healthcare Workers ("NUHW").

* * * *

[SEIU filed a suit in a federal district court against the NUHW and the UHW officials] for breach of fiduciary duties. * * * The jury returned a verdict awarding damages against the individual defendants * * *, and the district court entered judgment against the defendants. [The defendants appealed.]

* * * *

Under Section 501 of the Labor Management Reporting and Disclosure Act ("LMRDA"), officers of labor unions are held to the highest standards of responsibility and ethical conduct in administering the affairs of the union. [Emphasis added.]

The UHW defendants posit that they owed this duty to only the rank-and-file members of their local union. Because they subjectively believed their actions assisted those members by establishing a more democratic union with localized control, they maintain they have done no wrong under Section 501. Their argument ignores the fact that they diverted union resources to weaken their own union and form a rival union merely because they did not agree with the constitutionally permissible decision of the international union. *Because no construction of the LMRDA allows such conduct based merely on the defendants' subjective motives, we reject the defendants' argument.* [Emphasis added.]

The SEIU Executive Committee, under the authority given to it by both its constitution and the UHW constitution, carefully considered and adopted a measure it believed would better serve its members. The UHW officers disagreed, which they may do, and they voiced their opposition, which they also may do. What they may not do under the law is use their union's resources to actively obstruct implementation of the final decision.

* * * *

The judgment of liability was properly entered when a correctly instructed jury, on a sufficient factual record, found the defendants in breach of their fiduciary duties under Section 501 of the LMRDA.

AFFIRMED.

LEGAL REASONING QUESTIONS

1. What standard was at the core of the dispute in this case?
2. To whom was this standard owed, according to the United Health Workers (the defendants)?
3. Under this standard, what could the defendants do and what could they not do, according to the court?
4. How did the court rule on the dispute in this case? Why?

Union Organization

Typically, the first step in organizing a union at a particular firm is to have the workers sign authorization cards. An **authorization card** usually states that the worker desires to have a certain union, such as the United Auto Workers, represent the workforce. If a majority of the workers sign authorization cards, the union organizers (unionizers) present the cards to the employer and ask for formal recognition of the union.

The employer is not required to recognize the union at this point in the process, but it may do so voluntarily on a showing of majority support. (Under proposed legislation, the employer would have to recognize the union as soon as a majority of the workers had signed authorization cards—without holding an election, as described next.)[38]

UNION ELECTIONS If the employer refuses to voluntarily recognize the union after a majority of the workers sign authorization cards, the union organizers present the cards to the NLRB with a petition for an election. If less than 50 percent of the workers sign the cards, the unionizers may still petition for an election. For an election to be held, they must demonstrate that at least 30 percent of the workers to be represented support a union or an election on unionization.

---

38. If the proposed Employee Free Choice Act (or Card Check Bill) ever becomes law, some of the information here may change.

The proposed union must represent an *appropriate bargaining unit.* Not every group of workers can form a single union. One key requirement to being an appropriate bargaining unit is a *mutuality of interest* among all the workers to be represented by the union. Factors considered in determining whether there is a mutuality of interest include the *similarity of the jobs* of all the workers to be unionized and their physical location.

If all of these requirements are met, an election is held. The NLRB supervises the election and ensures secret voting and voter eligibility. If the proposed union receives majority support in a fair election, the NLRB certifies the union as the bargaining representative for the employees.

UNION ELECTION CAMPAIGNS Many disputes between labor and management arise during union election campaigns. Generally, the employer has control over unionizing activities that take place on company property and during working hours. Thus, the employer may limit the campaign activities of union supporters as long as the employer has a legitimate business reason for doing so. The employer may also reasonably limit the times and places that union solicitation occurs, provided that the employer is not discriminating against the union.

▶ **Example 34.7** A union is seeking to organize clerks at a department store owned by Amanti Enterprises. Amanti can prohibit all union solicitation in areas of the store open to the public because the unionizing activities could interfere with the store's business. It can also restrict union-related activities to coffee breaks and lunch hours. If Amanti allows solicitation for charitable causes in the workplace, however, it may not prohibit union solicitation. ◀

An employer may campaign among its workers against the union, but the NLRB carefully monitors and regulates the tactics used by management. If the employer issued threats ("If the union wins, you'll all be fired") or engaged in other unfair labor practices, the NLRB may certify the union even though it lost the election. Alternatively, the NLRB may ask a court to order a new election.

Collective Bargaining

If the NLRB certifies the union, the union becomes the *exclusive bargaining representative* of the workers. The central legal right of a union is to engage in collective bargaining on the members' behalf. **Collective bargaining** is the process by which labor and management negotiate the terms and conditions of employment.

NEGOTIATING TERMS AND CONDITIONS Wages, hours of work, and certain other conditions of employment may be discussed during collective bargaining sessions. For instance, subjects for negotiation may include workplace safety, employee discounts, healthcare plans, pension funds, and apprentice and scholarship programs.

Management need not bargain over a decision to shut down certain facilities. It must bargain, however, over the economic consequences of this decision. Thus, issues such as *severance pay* (pay given to an employee on termination) in the event of plant shutdown or rights of transfer to other plants are considered mandatory subjects of collective bargaining.

GOOD FAITH Both the employer and the union must negotiate in good faith and make a reasonable effort to come to an agreement. They are not obligated to reach an agreement, but they must at least try to reach a compromise.

Although good faith is a matter of subjective intent, a party's actions can be used to evaluate the party's good or bad faith. Excessive delaying tactics may be proof of bad faith, as is insistence on obviously unreasonable contract terms. The following actions constitute bad faith in bargaining:

1. Rejecting a proposal without offering a counterproposal.
2. Engaging in a campaign among workers to undermine the union.
3. Unilaterally changing wages or terms and conditions of employment during the bargaining process.
4. Constantly shifting positions on disputed contract terms.
5. Sending bargainers who lack authority to commit the company to a contract.

If an employer (or a union) refuses to bargain in good faith without justification, it has committed an unfair labor practice, and the other party may petition the NLRB for an order requiring good faith bargaining.

Strikes

Even when labor and management have bargained in good faith, they may be unable to reach a final agreement. When extensive collective bargaining has been conducted and an impasse results, the union may call a strike against the employer to pressure it into making concessions. In a **strike,** the unionized employees leave their jobs and refuse to work. The workers also typically picket the workplace, walking or standing outside the facility with signs stating their complaints.

A strike is an extreme action. Striking workers lose their rights to be paid, and management loses production and may lose customers when orders cannot be filled. Labor law regulates the circumstances and conduct of strikes. Most strikes take the form of "economic strikes," which are initiated because the union wants a better contract. ▶ **Example 34.8**   The Chicago Teachers Union engaged in an economic strike in 2012 after contract negotiations with the school district failed to bring an agreement on pay and performance. Classes were canceled for 350,000 public school students during the strike. ◀

THE RIGHT TO STRIKE The right to strike is guaranteed by the NLRA, within limits. Strike activities, such as picketing, are protected by the free speech guarantee of the First Amendment to the U.S. Constitution. Persons who are not employees have a right to participate in picketing an employer.

The NLRA also gives workers the right to refuse to cross a picket line of fellow workers who are engaged in a lawful strike. Employers are permitted to hire replacement workers to substitute for the striking workers.

ILLEGAL STRIKES In the following situations, the conduct of the strikers may cause the strikes to be illegal:

1. *Violent strikes.* The use of violence (including the threat of violence) against management employees or substitute workers is illegal.
2. *Massed picketing.* If the strikers form a barrier and deny management or other nonunion workers access to the plant, the strike is illegal.
3. *Sit-down strikes.* Strikes in which employees simply stay in the plant without working are illegal.
4. *No-strike clause.* A strike may be illegal if it contravenes a no-strike clause that was in the previous collective bargaining agreement between the employer and the union.
5. *Secondary boycotts.* A **secondary boycott** is an illegal strike that is directed against someone other than the strikers' employer, such as the companies that sell materials to the employer. ▶ **Example 34.9**   The unionized workers of SemiCo go out on strike. To increase their economic leverage, the workers picket the leading suppliers and customers of SemiCo in an attempt to hurt the company's business. SemiCo is considered the primary employer, and its suppliers and customers are considered secondary employers. Picketing of the suppliers or customers is a secondary boycott, which was made illegal by the Labor-Management Relations Act. ◀
6. *Wildcat strikes.* A wildcat strike occurs when a small number of workers, perhaps dissatisfied with a union's representation, call their own strike. The union is the exclusive bargaining representative of a group of workers, and only the union can call a strike. Therefore, a wildcat strike, unauthorized by the certified union, is illegal.

STRIKERS' RIGHTS AFTER A STRIKE ENDS An important issue concerns the rights of strikers after a strike ends. In a typical economic strike, the employer has a right to hire permanent replacements during the strike. The employer need not terminate the replacement workers when the strikers seek to return to work. In other words, striking workers are not guaranteed the right to return to their jobs after the strike if satisfactory replacement workers have been found.

If the employer has not hired replacement workers to fill the strikers' positions, however, then the employer must rehire economic strikers to fill any vacancies. Employers may not discriminate against former economic strikers, and those who are rehired retain their seniority rights. Different rules apply when a union strikes because the employer has engaged in unfair labor practices. In this situation, the employer may still hire replacements but must give the strikers back their jobs once the strike is over.

Lockouts

Lockouts are the employer's counterpart to the workers' right to strike. A **lockout** occurs when the employer shuts down to prevent employees from working. Lockouts usually are used when the employer believes that a strike is imminent. A lockout may be a legal employer response when a union and an employer have reached a stalemate in collective bargaining.

▶ **Example 34.10**   In 2011, the owners of the National Football League (NFL) teams imposed a lockout on the NFL players' union after negotiations on a new collective bargaining agreement broke down. The NFL owners had proposed to reduce players' salaries and extend the season by two games because of decreased profits due to the struggling economy. When the lockout was imposed, the union requested decertification, which cleared the way for a group of players to file an antitrust lawsuit (see Chapter 46). A settlement was reached before the start of the 2011 football season. The players accepted 3 percent less of the revenue generated (47 percent rather than 50 percent) in exchange for better working conditions and

more retirement benefits. The owners agreed to keep the same number of games per season. ◄

Some lockouts are illegal, however. An employer may not use a lockout as a tool to break the union and pressure employees into decertification. An employer must be able to show some economic justification.

Reviewing: Employment, Immigration, and Labor Law

Rick Saldona began working as a traveling salesperson for Aimer Winery in 2008. Sales constituted 90 percent of Saldona's work time. Saldona worked an average of fifty hours per week but received no overtime pay. In June 2014, Saldona's new supervisor, Caesar Braxton, claimed that Saldona had been inflating his reported sales calls and required Saldona to submit to a polygraph test. Saldona reported Braxton to the U.S. Department of Labor, which prohibited Aimer from requiring Saldona to take a polygraph test for this purpose.

In August 2014, Saldona's wife, Venita, fell from a ladder and sustained a head injury while employed as a full-time agricultural harvester. Saldona presented Aimer's Human Resources Department with a letter from his wife's physician indicating that she would need daily care for several months, and Saldona took leave until December 2014. Aimer had sixty-three employees at that time. When Saldona returned to Aimer, he was informed that his position had been eliminated because his sales territory had been combined with an adjacent territory. Using the information presented in the chapter, answer the following questions.

1. Would Saldona have been legally entitled to receive overtime pay at a higher rate? Why or why not?
2. What is the maximum length of time Saldona would have been allowed to take leave to care for his injured spouse?
3. Under what circumstances would Aimer have been allowed to require an employee to take a polygraph test?
4. Would Aimer likely be able to avoid reinstating Saldona under the *key employee* exception? Why or why not?

DEBATE THIS . . . *The U.S. labor market is highly competitive, so state and federal laws that require overtime pay are unnecessary and should be abolished.*

Terms and Concepts

ExamPrep

Issue Spotters

1. Erin, an employee of Fine Print Shop, is injured on the job. For Erin to obtain workers' compensation, does her injury have to have been caused by Fine Print's negligence? Does it matter whether the action causing the injury was intentional? Explain. **(See page 664.)**

2. Onyx applies for work with Precision Design Company, which tells her that it requires union membership as a condition of employment. She applies for work with Quality Engineering, Inc., which does not require union membership as a condition of employment but requires employees to join a union after six months on the job. Are these conditions legal? Why or why not? **(See page 674.)**

- **Check your answers to the Issue Spotters against the answers provided in Appendix E at the end of this text.**

Before the Test

Go to **www.cengagebrain.com**, enter the ISBN 9781285185248, and click on "Find" to locate this textbook's Web site. Then, click on "Access Now" under "Study Tools," and select Chapter 34 at the top. There, you will find a Practice Quiz that you can take to assess your mastery of the concepts in this chapter, as well as Flashcards and a Glossary of important terms.

Business Scenarios

34–1. Unfair Labor Practices. Consolidated Stores is undergoing a unionization campaign. Prior to the union election, management states that the union is unnecessary to protect workers. Management also provides bonuses and wage increases to the workers during this period. The employees reject the union. Union organizers protest that the wage increases during the election campaign unfairly prejudiced the vote. Should these wage increases be regarded as an unfair labor practice? Discuss. **(See page 676.)**

34–2. Wrongful Discharge. Denton and Carlo were employed at an appliance plant. Their job required them to perform occasional maintenance work while standing on a wire mesh twenty feet above the plant floor. Other employees had fallen through the mesh, and one of them had been killed by the fall. When their supervisor told them to perform tasks that would likely involve walking on the mesh, Denton and Carlo refused because they feared they might suffer bodily injury or death. Because they refused to do the requested work, the two employees were fired from their jobs. Was their discharge wrongful? If so, under what federal employment law? To what federal agency or department should they turn for assistance? **(See page 660.)**

Business Case Problems

34–3. Employment at Will. Thomas Ellis signed an agreement with the BlueSky Charter School to serve as its director for one year, from July 1 to June 30. A sentence in bold type stated that the employment was "at will." The agreement included a provision for automatic annual renewal unless the school's board acted before April 15. On May 7, the board terminated the arrangement. Was Ellis an at-will employee? If so, what effect did this status have on the board's authority to terminate his employment? [*Ellis v. BlueSky Charter School*, __ N.W.2d __ (Mn.App. 2010)] **(See page 658.)**

34–4. Minimum Wage. Misty Cumbie worked as a waitress at the Vita Café in Portland, Oregon. The café was owned and operated by Woody Woo, Inc. Woody Woo paid its servers an hourly wage that was higher than the state's minimum wage, but the servers were required to contribute their tips to a "tip pool." Approximately one-third of the tip-pool funds went to the servers, and the rest was distributed to kitchen staff members, who otherwise rarely received tips for their services. Did this tip-pooling arrangement violate the minimum wage provisions of the Fair Labor Standards Act? Explain.

[*Cumbie v. Woody Woo, Inc.*, 596 F.3d 577 (9th Cir. 2010)] **(See page 661.)**

34–5. Unfair Labor Practices. The Laborers' International Union of North America, Local 578, and Shaw Stone & Webster Construction, Inc., agreed on a provision in their collective bargaining agreement that required all employees to pay dues to the union. Sebedeo Lopez went to work for Shaw Stone without paying the union dues. When the union pressed the company to fire him, Lopez agreed to pay. The union continued to demand his discharge, however, and Shaw Stone fired him. Was the union guilty of unfair labor practices? Why or why not? [*Laborers' International Union of North America, Local 578 v. National Labor Relations Board*, 594 F.3d 732 (10th Cir. 2010)] **(See page 676.)**

34–6. BUSINESS CASE PROBLEM WITH SAMPLE ANSWER: Workers' Compensation.

As a safety measure, Dynea USA, Inc., required an employee, Tony Fairbanks, to wear steel-toed boots. One of the boots caused a sore on Fairbanks's leg. The skin over the sore broke, and

within a week, Fairbanks was hospitalized with a methicillin-resistant staphylococcus aureus (MRSA) infection. He filed a workers' compensation claim. Dynea argued that the MRSA bacteria that caused the infection had been on Fairbanks's skin before he came to work. What are the requirements to recover workers' compensation benefits? Does this claim qualify? Explain. [Dynea USA, Inc. v. Fairbanks, 241 Or.App. 311, 250 P.3d 389 (2011)] **(See page 664.)**

- **For a sample answer to Problem 34–6, go to Appendix F at the end of this text.**

34–7. Exceptions to the Employment-at-Will Doctrine. Li Li worked for Packard Bioscience, and Mark Schmeizl was her supervisor. In March 2000, Schmeizl told Li to call Packard's competitors, pretend to be a potential customer, and request "pricing information and literature." Li refused to perform the assignment. She told Schmeizl that she thought the work was illegal and recommended that he contact Packard's legal department. Although a lawyer recommended against the practice, Schmeizl insisted that Li perform the calls. Moreover, he later wrote negative performance reviews because she was unable to get the requested information when she called competitors and identified herself as a Packard employee. On June 1, 2000, Li was terminated on Schmeizl's recommendation. Can Li bring a claim for wrongful discharge? Why or why not? [*Li v. Canberra Industries*, 39 A.3d 789 (Conn.App. 2012)] **(See page 658.)**

34–8. Collective Bargaining. SDBC Holdings, Inc., acquired Stella D'oro Biscuit Co., a bakery in New York City. At the time, a collective bargaining agreement existed between Stella D'oro and Local 50, Bakery, Confectionary, Tobacco Workers and Grain Millers International Union. During negotiations to renew the agreement, Stella D'oro refused to give the union a copy of the company's financial statement. Stella D'oro did allow Local 50 to examine and take notes on the financial statement and offered the union an opportunity to make its own copy. Did Stella D'oro engage in an unfair labor practice? Discuss. [*SDBC Holdings, Inc. v. National Labor Relations Board*, 711 F.3d 281 (2d Cir. 2013)] **(See page 676.)**

34–9. A QUESTION OF ETHICS: Workers' Compensation Law.

In 1999, after working for Atchison Leather Products, Inc., in Kansas for ten years, Beverly Tull began to complain of hand, wrist, and shoulder pain. Atchison recommended that she contact a certain physician, who in April 2000 diagnosed the condition as carpal tunnel syndrome "severe enough" for surgery. In August, Tull filed a claim with the state workers' compensation board. Because Atchison changed workers' compensation insurance companies every year, a dispute arose as to which company should pay Tull's claim. Fearing liability, no insurer would authorize treatment, and Tull was forced to delay surgery until December. The board granted her temporary total disability benefits for the subsequent six weeks that she missed work. On April 23, 2002, Berger Co. bought Atchison. The new employer adjusted Tull's work so that it was less demanding and stressful, but she continued to suffer pain. In July, a physician diagnosed her condition as permanent. The board granted her permanent partial disability benefits. By May 2005, the bickering over the financial responsibility for Tull's claim involved five insurers—four of which had each covered Atchison for a single year and one of which covered Berger. [Tull v. Atchison Leather Products, Inc., 37 Kan.App.2d 87, 150 P.3d 316 (2007)] **(See page 664.)**

(a) When an injured employee files a claim for workers' compensation, a proceeding is held to assess the injury and determine the amount of compensation. Should a dispute between insurers over the payment of the claim be resolved in the same proceeding? Why or why not?

(b) The board designated April 23, 2002, as the date of Tull's injury. What is the reason for determining the date of a worker's injury? Should the board in this case have selected this date or a different date? Why?

(c) How should the board assess liability for the payment of Tull's medical expenses and disability benefits? Would it be appropriate to impose joint and several liability on the insurers (holding each of them responsible for the full amount of damages), or should the individual liability of each of them be determined? Explain.

Legal Reasoning Group Activity

34–10. Immigration. Nicole Tipton and Sadik Seferi owned and operated a restaurant in Iowa. Acting on a tip from the local police, agents of Immigration and Customs Enforcement executed search warrants at the restaurant and at an apartment where some restaurant workers lived. The agents discovered six undocumented aliens working at the restaurant and living together. When the I-9 forms for the restaurant's employees were reviewed, none were found for the six aliens. They were paid in cash while other employees were paid by check. Tipton and Seferi were charged with hiring and harboring undocumented aliens. **(See page 669.)**

(a) The first group will develop an argument that Tipton and Seferi were guilty of hiring and harboring illegal aliens.

(b) The second group will assess whether Tipton and Seferi can assert a defense by claiming that they did not know that the workers were unauthorized aliens.

CHAPTER 35

EMPLOYMENT DISCRIMINATION AND DIVERSITY

Out of the 1960s civil rights movement to end racial and other forms of discrimination grew a body of law protecting employees against discrimination in the workplace. Legislation, judicial decisions, and administrative agency actions restrict employers from discriminating against workers on the basis of race, color, religion, national origin, gender, age, or disability. A class of persons defined by one or more of these criteria is known as a **protected class.**

Several federal statutes prohibit **employment discrimination** against

members of protected classes. The most important statute is Title VII of the Civil Rights Act of 1964.[1] Title VII prohibits employment discrimination on the basis of race, color, religion, national origin, and gender. The Age Discrimination in Employment Act of 1967[2] and the Americans with Disabilities Act of 1990[3] prohibit discrimination on the basis of age and disability, respectively. The protections afforded under these laws also extend to U.S. citizens who are working

abroad for U.S. firms or for companies that are controlled by U.S. firms (see Chapter 24).

This chapter focuses on the kinds of discrimination prohibited by these federal statutes. Note, however, that discrimination against employees on the basis of any of the above-mentioned criteria may also violate state human rights statutes or other state laws prohibiting discrimination. By encouraging employment of members of protected classes, these laws also promote diversity in the workplace.

---

1. 42 U.S.C. Sections 2000e–2000e-17.
2. 29 U.S.C. Sections 621–634.
3. 42 U.S.C. Sections 12102–12118.

TITLE VII OF THE CIVIL RIGHTS ACT OF 1964

Title VII of the Civil Rights Act of 1964 and its amendments prohibit job discrimination against employees, applicants, and union members on the basis of race, color, national origin, religion, and gender at any stage of employment. It prohibits discrimination in the hiring process, discipline procedures, discharge, promotion, and benefits.

Title VII applies to employers with fifteen or more employees, labor unions with fifteen or more members, labor unions that operate hiring halls (to which members go regularly to be assigned jobs as they become available), employment agencies, and state and local governing units or agencies. The United States Supreme Court has ruled that an employer with fewer than fifteen employees is not automati-

cally shielded from a lawsuit filed under Title VII.[4] In addition, the act prohibits discrimination in most federal government employment. When Title VII applies to the employer, any employee—including an undocumented (alien) worker—can bring an action for employment discrimination.

The Equal Employment Opportunity Commission

The Equal Employment Opportunity Commission (EEOC) monitors compliance with Title VII. An employee alleging discrimination must file a claim with the EEOC before a lawsuit can be brought against the employer. The EEOC may investigate the dispute and attempt to obtain the parties' voluntary consent to an out-of-court settlement. If a voluntary

---

4. *Arbaugh v. Y&H Corp.*, 546 U.S. 500, 126 S.Ct. 1235, 163 L.Ed.2d 1097 (2006).

agreement cannot be reached, the EEOC may file a suit against the employer on the employee's behalf.

The EEOC does not investigate every claim of employment discrimination. Generally, it takes only "priority cases," such as cases that affect many workers and those involving retaliatory discharge (firing an employee in retaliation for submitting a claim to the EEOC). If the EEOC decides not to investigate a claim, the employee may bring his or her own lawsuit against the employer.

Limitations on Class Actions

In 2011, the United States Supreme Court limited the rights of employees to bring discrimination claims against their employer as a group, or class. The decision did not affect the rights of individual employees to sue under Title VII, however.

▶ **Case in Point 35.1**   A group of female employees sued Wal-Mart, the nation's largest private employer. The employees alleged that store managers who had discretion over pay and promotions were biased against women and disproportionately favored men. The Supreme Court ruled in favor of Wal-Mart, effectively blocking the class action (a lawsuit in which a small number of plaintiffs sue on behalf of a larger group). The Court held that the women had failed to prove a company-wide policy of discrimination that had a common effect on all women included in the class. Therefore, they could not maintain a class action.[5] ◀

Intentional and Unintentional Discrimination

Title VII of the Civil Rights Act of 1964 prohibits both intentional and unintentional discrimination.

---

5. *Wal-Mart Stores, Inc. v. Dukes*, ___ U.S. ___, 131 S.Ct. 2541, 180 L.Ed.2d 374 (2011).

INTENTIONAL DISCRIMINATION Intentional discrimination by an employer against an employee is known as **disparate-treatment discrimination.** Because intent may sometimes be difficult to prove, courts have established certain procedures for resolving disparate-treatment cases.

▶ **Example 35.2**   Samantha applies for employment with a construction firm and is rejected. If she sues on the basis of disparate-treatment discrimination in hiring, she must show that:

1. She is a member of a protected class.
2. She applied and was qualified for the job in question.
3. She was rejected by the employer.
4. The employer continued to seek applicants for the position or filled the position with a person not in a protected class.

If Samantha can meet these relatively easy requirements, she has made out a ***prima facie* case** of illegal discrimination. This means that she has met her initial burden of proof and will win unless the employer can present a legally acceptable defense. (Defenses to claims of employment discrimination will be discussed later in this chapter.)

The burden then shifts to the employer-defendant, who must articulate a legal reason for not hiring the plaintiff. For instance, the employer might say that Samantha was not hired because she lacked sufficient experience or training. To prevail, the plaintiff must then show that the employer's reason is a *pretext* (not the true reason) and that discriminatory intent actually motivated the employer's decision. ◀

In the following case, the trial court assumed that the plaintiff had established a *prima facie* case of discrimination before considering the defendant's evidence of a nondiscriminatory reason for its decision to discharge the plaintiff. The reviewing court had to consider whether to uphold the trial court's finding.

CASE ANALYSIS

Case 35.1   Dees v. United Rentals North America, Inc.
United States Court of Appeals, Ninth Circuit, 2013 WL 28405 (2013).

COMPANY PROFILE   *United Rentals North America, Inc., rents, sells, and services equipment for underground construction, temporary power, climate control, disaster recovery,* *and more. Since its founding in 1997, United Rentals has grown to become the world's largest rental equipment provider, with more than $7 billion of inventory available at more than* *830 locations and online. The company's customer base includes construction and industrial companies, government agencies, local governments, and individual homeowners.*

CASE 35.1 CONTINUED

 **IN THE LANGUAGE
OF THE COURT**
PER CURIAM.
* * * *

In * * * 2006 [Ellis Dees, an African American, applied] to United Rentals for employment at its Gulfport, Mississippi location, and was offered a service technician position in St. Rose, Louisiana. Branch Manager Mike Sauve made the decision to make the offer, which Dees accepted.

Although the first two years of Dees' employment in St. Rose went smoothly, United Rentals contends that his attitude and work performance deteriorated beginning in 2009. Specifically, it alleges that he began, with increasing frequency, to mark equipment as fit to be rented even though it was not in working order. Dees' managers—Sauve and Lee Vincent—coached him when these incidents occurred, and noted them in his 2009 mid-year and full-year performance reviews. Dees was also given written warnings in August 2009, October 2009, February 2010, and March 2010. Dees was given a "final written warning" on March 4, 2010, advising him that "the next incident will result in immediate termination." Following a further incident six days later, Sauve and Vincent told Dees that he was fired. Dees was sixty-two years old at the time.

Dees filed a charge with the Equal Employment Opportunity Commission, alleging employment discrimination based on his race and age [in violation of Title VII of the Civil Rights Act and the Age Discrimination in Employment Act (ADEA)]. After receiving a "right to sue" notice, he filed suit in [a federal district court]. United Rentals filed a motion for summary judgment, which the district court granted * * * . Dees timely appealed.

* * * *

* * * [Under Title VII or the ADEA] Dees first must make a *prima facie* case of discrimination based on age or race. To establish a *prima facie* case, Dees must show that he: (1) was a member of a protected group; (2) qualified for the position in question; (3) was subjected to an adverse employment action; and (4) received less favorable treatment due to his membership in the protected class than did other similarly situated employees who were not members of the protected class, under nearly identical circumstances.

If Dees makes a prima facie *case, the burden then shifts to United Rentals to articulate a legitimate, non-discriminatory reason for firing him.* If it does so, Dees must, as to his Title VII claim, offer sufficient evidence to create a genuine issue of material fact either (1) that United Rentals' reason is not true, but is instead a pretext for discrimination * * * ; or (2) that United Rentals' reason, while true, is only one of the reasons for its conduct, and another motivating factor is Dees' protected characteristic. [Emphasis added.]

* * * *

The district court assumed, without deciding, that Dees established a *prima facie* case of discrimination under Title VII and the ADEA. The district court * * * determined that United Rentals had provided extensive evidence of a legitimate, non-discriminatory reason for Dees' termination—namely, unsatisfactory job performance. * * * The burden shifted back to Dees to produce evidence that United Rentals' reason was a pretext for discrimination. The district court concluded that Dees had only made conclusory [conclusive] allegations that he was discriminated against.

* * * *

His termination notice states that he was terminated for failing to follow United Rentals' policy of ensuring that the batteries in rental equipment were in good working order prior to delivery of the equipment.

* * * Dees has presented nothing to tie United Rentals' final termination decision to a discriminatory motive. * * * Dees himself describes United Rentals as motivated by an "I ain't missing no rents" philosophy that encouraged renting out equipment regardless of its readiness. No evidence shows that United Rentals' philosophy also included discriminating against African Americans or senior workers. Similarly, no evidence demonstrates that United Rentals' decision to discharge Dees was motivated by his race or age. * * * Dees' subjective belief that United Rentals discriminated against him is clearly insufficient to demonstrate pretext.

* * * *

For the reasons set forth above, we AFFIRM the district court's grant of summary judgment in United Rentals' favor.

LEGAL REASONING QUESTIONS

1. How did the court treat Dees's attempt to establish a *prima facie* case of employment discrimination?
2. On what did both the trial court and the appellate court focus their analysis?
3. What did the plaintiff fail to do in submitting his side of the case? How did this failure affect his claims?
4. If Dees had been laid off due to a reduction in force of all workers whose performance did not meet the defendant's standards, would the result in this case have been different? Explain.

UNINTENTIONAL DISCRIMINATION Employers often use interviews and tests to choose from among a large number of applicants for job openings. Minimum educational requirements are also common. Some employer practices, such as those involving educational requirements, may have an unintended discriminatory impact on a protected class.

Disparate-impact discrimination occurs when a protected group of people is adversely affected by an employer's practices, procedures, or tests, even though they do not appear to be discriminatory. In a disparate-impact discrimination case, the complaining party must first show statistically (using the methods discussed next) that the employer's practices, procedures, or tests are discriminatory in effect. Once the plaintiff has made out a *prima facie* case, the burden of proof shifts to the employer to show that the practices or procedures in question were justified.

There are two ways of proving that disparate-impact discrimination exists.

Pool of Applicants. A plaintiff can prove a disparate impact by comparing the employer's workforce to the pool of qualified individuals available in the local labor market. The plaintiff must show that (1) as a result of educational or other job requirements or hiring procedures, (2) the percentage of nonwhites, women, or members of other protected classes in the employer's workforce (3) does not reflect the percentage of that group in the pool of qualified applicants. If the plaintiff can show a connection between the practice and the disparity, he or she has made out a *prima facie* case and need not provide evidence of discriminatory intent.

Rate of Hiring. A plaintiff can also prove disparate-impact discrimination by comparing the *selection rates* of whites and nonwhites (or members of another protected class), regardless of the racial balance in the employer's workforce. When an educational or other job requirement or hiring procedure excludes members of a protected class from an employer's workforce at a substantially higher rate than for nonmembers, discrimination occurs.

Under EEOC guidelines, a selection rate for a protected class that is less than four-fifths, or 80 percent, of the rate for the group with the highest rate of hiring generally will be regarded as evidence of disparate impact. ▶ **Example 35.3** One hundred white applicants take an employment test, and fifty pass the test and are hired. One hundred minority group applicants take the test, and twenty pass the employment test and are hired. Because twenty is less than four-fifths (80 percent) of fifty, the test would be considered discriminatory under the EEOC guidelines. ◀

Discrimination Based on Race, Color, and National Origin

Title VII prohibits employers from discriminating against employees or job applicants on the basis of race, color, or national origin. Race is interpreted broadly to apply to the ancestry or ethnic characteristics of a group of persons, such as Native Americans. National origin refers to discrimination based on a person's birth in another country or his or her ancestry or culture, such as Hispanic. (For a discussion of whether employers can legally discriminate against employees based on their appearance, see this chapter's *Insight into Ethics* on the following page.)

If an employer's standards or policies for selecting or promoting employees have a discriminatory effect on employees or job applicants in these protected classes, then a presumption of illegal discrimination arises. To avoid liability, the employer must show that its standards or policies have a substantial, demonstrable relationship to realistic qualifications for the job in question.

▶ **Case in Point 35.4** Jiann Min Chang was an instructor at Alabama Agricultural and Mechanical University (AAMU). When AAMU terminated his employment, Chang filed a lawsuit claiming discrimination based on national origin. Chang established a *prima facie* case because he (1) was a member of a protected class, (2) was qualified for the job, (3) suffered an adverse employment action, and (4) was replaced by someone outside his protected class (a non-Asian instructor). When the burden of proof shifted to the employer, however, AAMU showed that Chang had argued with a vice president and refused to comply with her instructions. The court ruled that the university had not renewed Chang's contract for a legitimate reason—insubordination—and therefore was not liable for unlawful discrimination.[6] ◀

REVERSE DISCRIMINATION Note that Title VII also protects against *reverse discrimination*—that is, discrimination against majority group individuals, such as white males. ▶ **Case in Point 35.5** An African American woman fired four white men from their

---

6. *Jiann Min Chang v. Alabama Agricultural and Mechanical University,* 2009 WL 3403180 (11th Cir. 2009).

INSIGHT INTO ETHICS
Appearance-Based Discrimination

Research has shown that short men make statistically less income than tall men. It has also shown that compared with attractive individuals, less attractive people generally receive poorer performance reviews, lower salaries, and smaller damages awards if they win lawsuits. Should something be done about this?

Can "Lookism" Be Prohibited?

Although there is certainly evidence that appearance-based discrimination exists in the workplace and elsewhere, it is not so clear that it can be prohibited. In the 1970s, Michigan decided to do something about "lookism" and passed a law barring various kinds of appearance-based discrimination.[a] Whether because of the cost or the difficulty of proving this type of discrimination, however, only a few lawsuits based on the law have been filed each year. At least six cities have similar laws, but these laws also have not given rise to many lawsuits.

Federal and state laws prohibit discrimination against people who are clinically obese, but discrimination against those who are merely overweight is usually not illegal. Given that one study found that more than 40 percent of overweight women felt stigmatized by their employers, this remains a serious problem.

A Double Standard for Grooming

Women sometimes complain that they are held to different grooming standards in the workplace than their male counterparts. A female bartender at a casino in Nevada brought a lawsuit after she was fired for not complying with rules that required her to wear makeup and teased hair while male bartenders were just told to "look neat." The court ruled, however, that these allegations were not enough to outweigh an at-will employment contract.[b]

At the same time, women in senior management positions find that they can look "too sexy." A few years ago, a Citibank employee made headlines when she claimed that she was fired for her excessive sexiness, which supposedly distracted her male co-workers.

LEGAL CRITICAL THINKING
INSIGHT INTO SOCIAL MEDIA

The majority of workers today post photographs of themselves, their families, and their friends on Facebook and other social media. How might this practice affect appearance-based discrimination in the workplace?

---

a. Michigan Compiled Laws Section 37.2202.

b. *Jespersen v. Harrah's Operating Co.*, 444 F.3d 1104 (9th Cir. 2006).

---

management positions at a school district. She claimed that the terminations were part of a reorganization plan to cut costs in the department. The men sued for (reverse) racial discrimination and won. They were awarded nearly $3 million in damages.[7] ◀

In 2009, the United States Supreme Court issued a decision that has had a significant impact on disparate-impact and reverse discrimination litigation. ▶ **Case in Point 35.6** The fire department in New Haven, Connecticut, administered a test to identify which firefighters were eligible for promotions. No African Americans and only two Hispanic firefighters passed the test. Fearing that it would be sued for racial discrimination if it used the test results for promotions, the city refused to use the results.

The white firefighters (and one Hispanic) who had passed the test then sued the city, claiming reverse discrimination. The Supreme Court held that the city's actions were not justified. Mere fear of litigation was not a sufficient reason for the city to discard its test results.[8] The city subsequently certified the test results and promoted all the firefighters involved in the lawsuit. ◀

POTENTIAL SECTION 1981 CLAIMS Victims of racial or ethnic discrimination may also have a cause of action under 42 U.S.C. Section 1981. This section, which was enacted as part of the Civil Rights Act of 1866 to protect the rights of freed slaves, prohibits discrimination on the basis of race or ethnicity in the formation

---

7. *Johnston v. School District of Philadelphia*, 2006 WL 999966 (E.D.Pa. 2006). The damages awarded by a jury were reduced slighted by the appellate court.

8. *Ricci v. DeStefano*, 557 U.S. 557, 129 S.Ct. 2658, 174 L.Ed.2d 490 (2009).

or enforcement of contracts. Because employment is often a contractual relationship, Section 1981 can provide an alternative basis for a plaintiff's action and is potentially advantageous because it does not place a cap on damages.

Discrimination Based on Religion

Title VII of the Civil Rights Act of 1964 also prohibits government employers, private employers, and unions from discriminating against persons because of their religion. Employers cannot treat their employees more or less favorably based on their religious beliefs or practices and cannot require employees to participate in any religious activity (or forbid them from participating in one).

▶ **Example 35.7**   Jason Sewell claims that his employer, a car dealership, fired him for not attending the weekly prayer meetings of dealership employees. If the dealership does require its employees to attend prayer gatherings and fired Sewell for not attending, he has a valid claim of religious discrimination. ◀

REASONABLE ACCOMMODATION   An employer must "reasonably accommodate" the religious practices of its employees, unless to do so would cause undue hardship to the employer's business. An employee's religion might prohibit her or him from working on a certain day of the week, for instance, or at a certain type of job. The employer must make a reasonable attempt to accommodate the employee's sincerely held religious belief. Reasonable accommodation is required even if the belief is not based on the doctrines of a traditionally recognized religion, such as Christianity or Judaism, or of a denomination, such as Baptist.

UNDUE HARDSHIP   A reasonable attempt to accommodate does not necessarily require the employer to make every change an employee requests or to make a permanent change for an employee's benefit. An employer is not required to make an accommodation that would cause the employer undue hardship.

▶ **Case in Point 35.8**   Miguel Sánchez-Rodríguez sold cell phones at kiosks in shopping malls for AT&T in Puerto Rico. After six years, Sánchez informed his supervisors that he had become a Seventh Day Adventist and could no longer work on Saturdays for religious reasons. AT&T responded that his position required rotating Saturday shifts and that his inability to work on Saturdays would cause it hardship.

As a reasonable accommodation, the company suggested that Sánchez swap schedules with others and offered him two other positions that would not require work on Saturdays. Sánchez was unable to find workers to swap shifts with him, however, and declined the other jobs because they would result in less income (no commissions). He began missing work on Saturdays. After a time, AT&T indicated that it would discipline him for any additional Saturdays that he missed. Eventually, he was placed on active disciplinary status. Sánchez resigned and filed a religious discrimination lawsuit. The court found in favor of AT&T, and a federal appellate court affirmed. The company had made adequate efforts at accommodation by allowing Sánchez to swap shifts and offering him other positions that did not require work on Saturdays.[9] ◀

Discrimination Based on Gender

Under Title VII and other federal acts, employers are forbidden from discriminating against employees on the basis of gender. Employers are prohibited from classifying or advertising jobs as male or female unless the employer can prove that the gender of the applicant is essential to the job. Employers also cannot have separate male and female seniority lists or refuse to promote employees based on their gender.

GENDER MUST BE A DETERMINING FACTOR   Generally, to succeed in a suit for gender discrimination, a plaintiff must demonstrate that gender was a determining factor in the employer's decision to hire, fire, or promote him or her. Typically, this involves looking at all of the surrounding circumstances.

▶ **Case in Point 35.9**   Wanda Collier worked for Turner Industries Group, LLC, in the maintenance department. She complained to her supervisor that Jack Daniell, the head of the department, treated her unfairly. Her supervisor told her that Daniell had a problem with her gender and was harder on women. The supervisor talked to Daniell about Collier's complaint, but did not take any disciplinary action.

A month later, Daniell confronted Collier, pushing her up against a wall and berating her. After this incident, Collier filed a formal complaint and kept a male co-worker with her at all times. A month later, she was fired. She subsequently filed a lawsuit alleging gender discrimination. The court allowed Collier's clam to go to a jury because there was suf-

---

9. *Sánchez-Rodríguez v. AT&T Mobility Puerto Rico, Inc.*, 673 F.3d 1 (1st Cir. 2012).

ficient evidence that gender was a determining factor in Daniell's conduct.[10] ◄

PREGNANCY DISCRIMINATION The Pregnancy Discrimination Act[11] amended Title VII and expanded the definition of gender discrimination to include discrimination based on pregnancy. Women affected by pregnancy, childbirth, or related medical conditions must be treated—for all employment-related purposes, including the receipt of benefits under employee benefit programs—the same as other persons not so affected but similar in ability to work.

WAGE DISCRIMINATION Several laws prohibit employers from engaging in gender-based wage discrimination. The Equal Pay Act[12] requires equal pay for male and female employees working at the same establishment doing similar work (a barber and a hair stylist, for example).

To determine whether the Equal Pay Act has been violated, a court will look to the primary duties of the two jobs—the job content rather than the job description controls.[13] If a court finds that the wage differential is due to "any factor other than gender," such as a seniority or merit system, then it does not violate the Equal Pay Act.

In 2009, Congress enacted the Lilly Ledbetter Fair Pay Act, which made discriminatory wages actionable under federal law regardless of when the discrimination began.[14] This act countered a previous decision by the United States Supreme Court that had limited the time period in which plaintiffs could file a wage-discrimination complaint to 180 days after the employer's decision.[15] Today, if a plaintiff continues to work for the employer while receiving discriminatory wages, the time period for filing a complaint is practically unlimited.

Constructive Discharge

The majority of Title VII complaints involve unlawful discrimination in decisions to hire or fire employees. In some situations, however, employees who leave their jobs voluntarily can claim that they were "constructively discharged" by the employer. **Constructive discharge** occurs when the employer causes the employee's working conditions to be so intolerable that a reasonable person in the employee's position would feel compelled to quit.

PROVING CONSTRUCTIVE DISCHARGE The employee must present objective proof of intolerable working conditions, which the employer knew or had reason to know about yet failed to correct within a reasonable time period. Courts generally also require the employee to show causation—that the employer's unlawful discrimination caused the working conditions to be intolerable. Put a different way, the employee's resignation must be a foreseeable result of the employer's discriminatory action. Courts weigh the facts on a case-by-case basis.

Employee demotion is one of the most frequently cited reasons for a finding of constructive discharge, particularly when the employee was subjected to humiliation. ▶ **Example 35.10** Khalil's employer humiliates him by informing him in front of his co-workers that he is being demoted to an inferior position. Khalil's co-workers then continually insult him, harass him, and make derogatory remarks to him about his national origin (he is from Iran). The employer is aware of this discriminatory treatment but does nothing to remedy the situation, despite repeated complaints from Khalil. After several months, Khalil quits his job and files a Title VII claim. In this situation, Khalil would likely have sufficient evidence to maintain an action for constructive discharge in violation of Title VII. ◄

APPLIES TO ALL TITLE VII DISCRIMINATION Plaintiffs can use constructive discharge to establish any type of discrimination claims under Title VII, including race, color, national origin, religion, gender, and pregnancy, but it is most commonly asserted in cases involving sexual harassment. Constructive discharge may also be used in cases involving discrimination based on age or disability (discussed later in this chapter).

When constructive discharge is claimed, the employee can pursue damages for loss of income, including back pay. These damages ordinarily are not available to an employee who left a job voluntarily.

Sexual Harassment

Title VII also protects employees against **sexual harassment** in the workplace. Sexual harassment can take two forms:

10. *Collier v. Turner Industries Group, LLC,* 797 F.Supp.2d 1029 (D. Idaho 2011).
11. 42 U.S.C. Section 2000e(k).
12. 29 U.S.C. Section 206(d).
13. For an illustration of the factors courts consider in wage-discrimination claims under the Equal Pay Act, see *Beck-Wilson v. Principi,* 441 F.3d 353 (6th Cir. 2006).
14. Pub. L. No. 111-2, 123 Stat. 5 (January 5, 2009), amending 42 U.S.C. Section 2000e-5[e].
15. *Ledbetter v. Goodyear Tire Co.,* 550 U.S. 618, 127 S.Ct. 2162, 167 L.Ed.2d 982 (2007).

1. *Quid pro quo* harassment occurs when sexual favors are demanded in return for job opportunities, promotions, salary increases, or other benefits. *Quid pro quo* is a Latin phrase that is often translated as "something in exchange for something else."

2. *Hostile-environment* harassment occurs when a pattern of sexually offensive conduct runs throughout the workplace and the employer has not taken steps to prevent or discourage it. In the words of the United States Supreme Court, hostile-environment harassment exists when "the workplace is permeated with discriminatory intimidation, ridicule, and insult, that is sufficiently severe or pervasive to alter the conditions of the victim's employment and create an abusive working environment."[16]

The courts determine whether the sexually offensive conduct was sufficiently severe or pervasive to create a hostile environment on a case-by-case basis. Typically, a single incident of sexually offensive conduct is not enough to permeate the work environment (although there have been exceptions when the conduct was particularly objectionable).[17]

If the employee who is alleging sexual harassment has signed an employment contract containing an arbitration clause (see Chapter 3), she or he will most likely be required to arbitrate the claim.[18] In other words, the dispute will not be litigated in court.

HARASSMENT BY SUPERVISORS For an employer to be held liable for a supervisor's sexual harassment, the supervisor normally must have taken a *tangible employment action* against the employee. A **tangible employment action** is a significant change in employment status or benefits, such as when an employee is fired, refused a promotion, demoted, or reassigned to a position with significantly different responsibilities. Only a supervisor, or another person acting with the authority of the employer, can cause this sort of harm. A constructive discharge also qualifies as a tangible employment action.[19]

THE *ELLERTH/FARAGHER* AFFIRMATIVE DEFENSE In 1998, the United States Supreme Court issued several important rulings that have had a lasting impact on cases involving alleged sexual harassment by supervisors.[20] The Court held that an employer (a city) was liable for a supervisor's harassment of employees even though the employer was unaware of the behavior. Although the city had a written policy against sexual harassment, it had not distributed the policy to its employees and had not established any complaint procedures for employees who felt that they had been sexually harassed. In another case, the Court held that an employer can be liable for a supervisor's sexual harassment even though the employee does not suffer adverse job consequences.

The Court's decisions in these cases established what has become known as the *Ellerth/Faragher* affirmative defense to charges of sexual harassment. The defense has two elements:

1. The employer must have taken reasonable care to prevent and promptly correct any sexually harassing behavior (by establishing effective harassment policies and complaint procedures, for instance).

2. The plaintiff-employee must have unreasonably failed to take advantage of preventive or corrective opportunities provided by the employer to avoid harm.

An employer that can prove both elements normally will not be liable for a supervisor's harassment.

RETALIATION BY EMPLOYERS Employers sometimes retaliate against employees who complain about sexual harassment or other Title VII violations. Retaliation can take many forms. An employer might demote or fire the person, or otherwise change the terms, conditions, and benefits of employment. Title VII prohibits retaliation, and employees can sue their employers when it occurs.

In a *retaliation claim,* an individual asserts that she or he has suffered harm as a result of making a charge, testifying, or participating in a Title VII investigation or proceeding. Plaintiffs do not have to prove that the challenged action adversely affected their workplace or employment. Instead, plaintiffs must show that the action would likely have dissuaded a reasonable worker from making or supporting a charge of discrimination.

Title VII's retaliation protection extends to an employee who speaks out about discrimination

---

16. *Harris v. Forklift Systems,* 510 U.S. 17, 114 S.Ct. 367, 126 L.Ed.2d 295 (1993). See also *Baker v. Via Christi Regional Medical Center,* 491 F.Supp.2d 1040 (D.Kan. 2007).

17. See, for example, *Pomales v. Celulares Telefonica, Inc.,* 447 F.3d 79 (1st Cir. 2006); and *Fontanez-Nunez v. Janssen Ortho, LLC,* 447 F.3d 50 (1st Cir. 2006).

18. See, for example, *EEOC v. Cheesecake Factory, Inc.,* 2009 WL 1259359 (D.Ariz. 2009).

19. See, for example, *Pennsylvania State Police v. Suders,* 542 U.S. 129, 124 S.Ct. 2342, 159 L.Ed.2d 204 (2004).

20. *Burlington Industries, Inc. v. Ellerth,* 524 U.S. 742, 118 S.Ct. 2257, 141 L.Ed.2d 633 (1998); and *Faragher v. City of Boca Raton,* 524 U.S. 775, 118 S.Ct. 2275, 141 L.Ed.2d 662 (1998).

against another employee during an employer's internal investigation.[21] The Supreme Court has also held that Title VII protected an employee who was fired after his fiancée filed a gender discrimination claim against their employer.[22]

In the following case, a law professor lost her job after she complained about comments made by her dean and colleagues. The court had to decide whether she had been retaliated against for engaging in protected conduct.

---

21. *Crawford v. Metropolitan Government of Nashville and Davidson County, Tennessee,* 555 U.S. 271, 129 S.Ct. 846, 172 L.Ed.2d 650 (2009).
22. See *Thompson v. North American Stainless, LP,* ___ U.S. ___, 131 S.Ct. 863, 178 L.Ed.2d 694 (2011).

CASE 35.2

Morales-Cruz v. University of Puerto Rico
United States Court of Appeals, First Circuit, 676 F.3d 220 (2012).

BACKGROUND AND FACTS In 2003, Myrta Morales-Cruz began a tenure-track teaching position at the University of Puerto Rico School of Law. During Morales-Cruz's probationary period, one of her colleagues in a law school clinic had an affair with one of their students that resulted in a pregnancy. In 2008, Morales-Cruz wanted the university's administrative committee to approve a one-year extension for her tenure review. The law school's dean asked Morales-Cruz about her colleague's affair and criticized her for failing to report it. He later recommended granting the extension but called Morales-Cruz "insecure," "immature," and "fragile." Similarly, a law school committee recommended granting the extension. Nevertheless, a dissenting professor commented that in dealing with her colleague's affair, Morales-Cruz had shown poor judgment, exhibited "personality flaws," and demonstrated that she had trouble with "complex and sensitive" situations.

Morales-Cruz soon learned about the dean's and the dissenting professor's comments and complained in writing to the university's chancellor. As a result, the dean then recommended denying the one-year extension, and the administrative committee ultimately did just that. When her employment was terminated, Morales-Cruz sued the university under Title VII. Among other things, she asserted that the dean had retaliated against her for complaining to the chancellor. The district court found that Morales-Cruz had not stated a proper retaliation claim under Title VII.

IN THE LANGUAGE OF THE COURT
SELYA, Circuit Judge.

* * * *

The amended complaint alleges that various officials described the plaintiff as "fragile," "immature," "unable to handle complex and sensitive issues," * * * and exhibiting "lack of judgment." These descriptors are admittedly unflattering—but they are without exception gender-neutral. All of them apply equally to persons of either gender * * * .

* * * *

* * * Title VII makes it unlawful for an employer to take materially adverse action against an employee "because he has opposed any practice made an unlawful employment practice by this subchapter." *To state a cause of action under this portion of the statute, the pleading must contain plausible allegations indicating that the plaintiff opposed a practice prohibited by Title VII and suffered an adverse employment action as a result of that opposition.* [Emphasis added.]

The plaintiff alleges that she was retaliated against for writing to the Chancellor to complain about the "discriminatory" comments made in the course of her request for an extension. In support of this allegation, she points out that after she sent her letter the Dean reversed his position on her extension. This construct suffers from a fatal flaw: her factual allegations do not support a reasonable inference that she was engaging in protected conduct when she opposed the remarks made.

CASE 35.2 CONTINUES ▶

CASE 35.2 CONTINUED * * * The facts alleged * * * provide no reasonable basis for inferring that the comments cited reflected gender-based discrimination. Those comments were unarguably gender-neutral and do not afford an objectively reasonable foundation for a retaliation action.

DECISION AND REMEDY *The appellate court held that Morales-Cruz could not bring a retaliation claim under Title VII. It therefore affirmed the district court's judgment for the University of Puerto Rico.*

THE ETHICAL DIMENSION *Could Morales-Cruz's dean have had legitimate reasons for changing his mind about the one-year extension? If so, what might they have been?*

THE LEGAL ENVIRONMENT DIMENSION *What steps should employers take to reduce the likelihood that supervisors will retaliate against employees who make or support discrimination claims?*

HARASSMENT BY CO-WORKERS AND OTHERS When the harassment of co-workers, rather than supervisors, creates a hostile working environment, an employee may still have a cause of action against the employer. Normally, though, the employer will be held liable only if it knew or should have known about the harassment and failed to take immediate remedial action.

Occasionally, a court may also hold an employer liable for harassment by *nonemployees* if the employer knew about the harassment and failed to take corrective action. ▶ **Example 35.11** Jordan, who owns and manages a Great Bites restaurant, knows that one of his regular customers, Dean, repeatedly harasses Kaylia, a waitress. If Jordan does nothing and permits the harassment to continue, he may be liable under Title VII even though Dean is not an employee of the restaurant. ◀

SAME-GENDER HARASSMENT In *Oncale v. Sundowner Offshore Services, Inc.,*[23] the United States Supreme Court held that Title VII protection extends to individuals who are sexually harassed by members of the same gender. Proving that the harassment in same-gender cases is "based on sex" can be difficult, though. It is easier to establish a case of same-gender harassment when the harasser is homosexual.[24]

SEXUAL ORIENTATION HARASSMENT Federal law (Title VII) does not prohibit discrimination or harassment based on a person's sexual orientation. Nonetheless, a growing number of states have enacted laws that prohibit sexual orientation discrimination in

private employment.[25] Some states, such as Michigan, explicitly prohibit discrimination based on a person's gender identity or expression. Many companies have also voluntarily established nondiscrimination policies that include sexual orientation.

Online Harassment

Employees' online activities can create a hostile working environment in many ways. Racial jokes, ethnic slurs, or other comments contained in e-mail, texts, blogs, and social media can lead to a claim of hostile-environment harassment or other forms of discrimination. A worker who regularly sees sexually explicit images on a co-worker's computer screen may find the images offensive and claim that they create a hostile working environment.

Nevertheless, employers may be able to avoid liability for online harassment by taking prompt remedial action.

Remedies under Title VII

Employer liability under Title VII may be extensive. If the plaintiff successfully proves that unlawful discrimination occurred, he or she may be awarded reinstatement, back pay, retroactive promotions, and damages.

Compensatory damages are available only in cases of intentional discrimination. Punitive damages may be recovered against a private employer only if the employer acted with malice or reckless indifference to an individual's rights. The statute limits the total amount of compensatory and punitive damages that plaintiffs can recover from specific employers,

---

23. 523 U.S. 75, 118 S.Ct. 998, 140 L.Ed.2d 207 (1998).

24. See, for example, *Tepperwien v. Entergy Nuclear Operations, Inc.,* 606 F.Supp.2d 427 (S.D.N.Y. 2009).

25. See, for example, 775 Illinois Compiled Statutes 5/1–103.

depending on the size of the employer. For instance, there is a $50,000 cap on damages from employers with one hundred or fewer employees.

SECTION 2

DISCRIMINATION BASED ON AGE

Age discrimination is potentially the most widespread form of discrimination because anyone—regardless of race, color, national origin, or gender—could be a victim at some point in life. The Age Discrimination in Employment Act[26] (ADEA), as amended, prohibits employment discrimination on the basis of age against individuals forty years of age or older. The act also prohibits mandatory retirement for nonmanagerial workers.

The United States Supreme Court has ruled that the ADEA encompasses not only claims of age discrimination, but also claims of retaliation for complaining about age discrimination.[27] Thus, the ADEA protects federal and private-sector employees from retaliation based on age-related complaints.

For the act to apply, an employer must have twenty or more employees, and the employer's business activities must affect interstate commerce. The EEOC administers the ADEA, but the act also permits private causes of action against employers for age discrimination.

---

26. 29 U.S.C. Sections 621–634.
27. *Gomez-Perez v. Potter,* 553 U.S. 474, 128 S.Ct. 1931, 170 L.Ed.2d 887 (2008).

Procedures under the ADEA

The burden-shifting procedure under the ADEA differs from the procedure under Title VII as a result of a 2009 United States Supreme Court decision, which dramatically changed the burden of proof in age discrimination cases.[28] As explained earlier, if the plaintiff in a Title VII case can show that the employer was motivated, at least in part, by unlawful discrimination, the burden of proof shifts to the employer to articulate a legitimate nondiscriminatory reason for the challenged action. Thus, in cases in which the employer has a "mixed motive" for discharging an employee, the employer has the burden of proving its reason was legitimate.

Under the ADEA, in contrast, a plaintiff must show that the unlawful discrimination was not just *a* reason but *the* reason for the adverse employment action. In other words, the employee has the burden of establishing *but for* causation—that is, "but for" the employee's age, the action would not have been taken.

Thus, to establish a *prima facie* case, the plaintiff must show that she or he (1) was a member of the protected age group, (2) was qualified for the position from which she or he was discharged, and (3) was discharged because of age discrimination. Then the burden shifts to the employer. If the employer offers a legitimate reason for its action, the plaintiff must show that the stated reason is only a pretext for the employer's decision. The following case illustrates this process.

---

28. *Gross v. FBL Financial Services, Inc.,* 557 U.S. 167, 129 S.Ct. 2343, 174 L.Ed.2d 119 (2009).

CASE 35.3

Mora v. Jackson Memorial Foundation, Inc.
United States Court of Appeals, Eleventh Circuit, 597 F.3d 1201 (2010).

BACKGROUND AND FACTS Josephine Mora, a fund-raiser for Jackson Memorial Foundation, Inc., was sixty-two years old when the foundation's chief executive officer (CEO) fired her, citing errors and issues with professionalism. Mora filed a suit against the foundation, alleging age discrimination. She asserted that when she was fired, the CEO told her, "I need someone younger I can pay less." She had a witness who heard that statement and also heard the CEO say that Mora was "too old to be working here anyway." The foundation moved for summary judgment, arguing that Mora was fired chiefly because she was incompetent. The district court granted the motion, and Mora appealed.

   IN THE LANGUAGE OF THE COURT
PER CURIAM. [By the Whole Court]

★ ★ ★ ★

CASE 35.3 CONTINUES ▶

CASE 35.3 CONTINUED

After Plaintiff [Mora] appealed, the Supreme Court, in *Gross v. FBL Financial Services, Inc.,*[a] clarified the nature of ADEA claims. The Supreme Court concluded that ADEA claims are not subject to the burden-shifting protocol set forth for Title VII suits in *Price Waterhouse v. Hopkins.*[b] The ADEA requires that "age [be] the reason that the employer decided to act." *Because an ADEA plaintiff must establish "but for" causality, no "same decision" affirmative defense [the argument that the same decision—to fire someone, for example—would have been made regardless of the alleged discrimination] can exist: the employer either acted "because of" the plaintiff's age or it did not.* [Emphasis added.]

Because the Supreme Court has excluded the whole idea of a "mixed motive" ADEA claim—and the corresponding "same decision" defense—we need not consider the district court's analysis of Defendant's [the foundation's] affirmative defense. Instead, * * * we look to determine whether a material factual question exists on this record about whether Defendant discriminated against her. We say "Yes."

* * * *

A plaintiff in an ADEA claim may "establish a claim of illegal age discrimination through either direct evidence or circumstantial evidence." Plaintiff's testimony that Rodriguez [the CEO] fired her because she was "too old" was substantiated by the affidavits of two other employees of Defendant. Rodriguez and Quevedo [another employee] testified that no such comments were made * * * .

The resolution of this case depends on whose account of the pertinent conversations a jury would credit. We conclude that a reasonable juror could accept that Rodriguez made the discriminatory-sounding remarks and that the remarks are sufficient evidence of a discriminatory motive which was the "but for" cause of Plaintiff's dismissal. Summary judgment for Defendant was therefore incorrect.

We have considered cases factually similar to Plaintiff's. In [one case], we concluded that statements from a county official who "didn't want to hire any old pilots" were direct evidence of discrimination * * * . In [another case], we likewise concluded that an employer's statement that he wanted "aggressive, young men like himself to be promoted" was circumstantial evidence of discrimination.

While these cases were litigated under the now-defunct ADEA mixed motive theory, they remain instructive. Plaintiff's situation is similar. A reasonable juror could find that Rodriguez's statements should be taken at face value and that he fired Plaintiff because of her age.

DECISION AND REMEDY *The U.S. Court of Appeals for the Eleventh Circuit vacated (set aside) the decision of the trial court and remanded the case for further proceedings. Because there was a "disputed question of material fact" as to whether the plaintiff had been fired because of her age, the defendant was not entitled to summary judgment.*

THE ETHICAL DIMENSION *Is the court's decision in this case fair to employers? Why or why not?*

MANAGERIAL IMPLICATIONS *Business owners and supervisory personnel should be careful to avoid statements regarding an employee's age that may sound discriminatory. If the employee later has to be dismissed due to poor performance, comments about his or her age may become the basis for an age discrimination lawsuit.*

---

a. 557 U.S. 167, 129 S.Ct. 2343, 174 L.Ed.2d 119 (2009).
b. 490 U.S. 228, 109 S.Ct. 1775, 104 L.Ed.2d 268 (1989).

Replacing Older Workers with Younger Workers

Numerous age discrimination cases have been brought against employers who, to cut costs, replaced older, higher-salaried employees with younger, lower-salaried workers. Whether a firing is discriminatory or simply part of a rational business decision to prune the company's ranks is not always clear.

A plaintiff must prove that the discharge was motivated by age bias. The plaintiff does not need to prove that she or he was replaced by a person "outside the protected class" (under the age of forty years), as long as the replacement worker is younger than the plaintiff. Nevertheless, the bigger the age gap, the more likely the plaintiff will succeed in showing age discrimination.

State Employees Not Covered by the ADEA

Generally, the states are immune under the Eleventh Amendment from lawsuits brought by private individuals in federal court—unless a state consents to the suit. This immunity stems from the United States Supreme Court's interpretation of the Eleventh Amendment (see Appendix B).

State immunity under the Eleventh Amendment is not absolute, however. In some situations, such as when fundamental rights are at stake, Congress has the power to abrogate (abolish) state immunity to private suits through legislation that unequivocally shows Congress's intent to subject states to private suits.[29]

Generally, though, the Court has found that state employers are immune from private suits brought by employees under the ADEA (for age discrimination), the Americans with Disabilities Act (for disability-based discrimination),[30] and the Fair Labor Standards Act.[31] As explained in Chapter 34, state employers are not immune from the requirements of the Family and Medical Leave Act.[32]

SECTION 3
DISCRIMINATION BASED ON DISABILITY

The Americans with Disabilities Act (ADA) of 1990[33] prohibits disability-based discrimination in all workplaces with fifteen or more workers. An exception is state government employers, who are generally immune under the Eleventh Amendment, as just discussed. Basically, the ADA requires that employers "reasonably accommodate" the needs of persons with disabilities unless to do so would cause the employer to suffer an "undue hardship." The ADA Amendments Act[34] broadened the coverage of the ADA's protections, as discussed shortly.

Procedures under the ADA

To prevail on a claim under the ADA, a plaintiff must show that he or she (1) has a disability, (2) is otherwise qualified for the employment in question, and (3) was excluded from the employment solely because of the disability. As in Title VII cases, the plaintiff must pursue the claim through the EEOC before filing an action in court for a violation of the ADA.

The EEOC may decide to investigate and perhaps even sue the employer on behalf of the employee. The EEOC can bring a suit on behalf of the employee under the ADA even if the employee signed an arbitration agreement with the employer.[35] If the EEOC decides not to sue, then the employee may do so.

Plaintiffs in lawsuits brought under the ADA may seek many of the same remedies that are available under Title VII. These include reinstatement, back pay, a limited amount of compensatory and punitive damages (for intentional discrimination), and certain other forms of relief. Repeat violators may be ordered to pay fines of up to $100,000.

What Is a Disability?

The ADA is broadly drafted to cover persons with physical or mental impairments that "substantially limit" their everyday activities. Specifically, the ADA defines a *disability* as including any of the following:

1. A physical or mental impairment that substantially limits one or more of the major life activities of the affected individual.
2. A record of having such an impairment.
3. Being regarded as having such an impairment.

TYPES OF DISABILITY Health conditions that have been considered disabilities under federal law include blindness, alcoholism, heart disease, cancer, muscular dystrophy, cerebral palsy, paraplegia, diabetes, acquired immune deficiency syndrome (AIDS), testing positive for the human immunodeficiency virus

---

29. *Tennessee v. Lane,* 541 U.S. 509, 124 S.Ct. 1978, 158 L.Ed.2d 820 (2004).
30 *Board of Trustees of the University of Alabama v. Garrett,* 531 U.S. 356, 121 S.Ct. 955, 148 L.Ed.2d 866 (2001).
31. *Alden v. Maine,* 527 U.S. 706, 119 S.Ct. 2240, 144 L.Ed.2d 636 (1999).
32. *Nevada Department of Human Resources v. Hibbs,* 538 U.S. 721, 123 S.Ct. 1972, 155 L.Ed.2d 953 (2003).
33. 42 U.S.C. Sections 12103–12118.

34. 42 U.S.C. Sections 12103 and 12205a.
35. This was the Supreme Court's ruling in *EEOC v. Waffle House, Inc.,* 534 U.S. 279, 122 S.Ct. 754, 151 L.Ed.2d 755 (2002).

(HIV, the virus that causes AIDS), and morbid obesity (which exists when an individual's weight is twice the normal weight for his or her height).

The ADA includes a separate provision that prevents employers from taking adverse employment actions based on stereotypes or assumptions about individuals who associate with people who have disabilities.[36] An employer cannot, for instance, refuse to hire the parent of a child with a disability based on the assumption that the person will miss work too often or be unreliable.[37]

CORRECTABLE CONDITIONS At one time, the courts focused on whether a person had a disability *after* the use of corrective devices or medication. A person with severe myopia (nearsightedness), which can be corrected with lenses, for instance, did not qualify as having a disability because that individual's major life activities were not substantially impaired.

In 2008, Congress amended the ADA to strengthen its protections and prohibit employers from considering mitigating measures or medications when determining if an individual has a disability. Disability is now determined on a case-by-case basis. A condition may fit the definition of disability in one set of circumstances, but not in another.

Reasonable Accommodation

The ADA does not require that employers accommodate the needs of job applicants or employees with disabilities who are not otherwise qualified for the work. If a job applicant or an employee with a disability, with reasonable accommodation, can perform essential job functions, however, the employer must make the accommodation.

Required modifications may include installing ramps for a wheelchair, establishing flexible working hours, creating or modifying job assignments, and designing or improving training materials and procedures. Generally, employers should give primary consideration to employees' preferences in deciding what accommodations should be made.

UNDUE HARDSHIP Employers who do not accommodate the needs of persons with disabilities must demonstrate that the accommodations would cause *undue hardship* in terms of being significantly difficult or expensive for the employer. Usually, the courts decide

whether an accommodation constitutes an undue hardship on a case-by-case basis.

▶ **Example 35.12** Bryan Lockhart, who uses a wheelchair, works for a cell phone company that provides parking for its employees. Lockhart informs his supervisor that the parking spaces are so narrow that he is unable to extend the ramp on his van that allows him to get in and out of the vehicle. Lockhart therefore requests that the company reasonably accommodate his needs by paying a monthly fee for him to use a larger parking space in an adjacent lot. In this situation, a court would likely find that it would *not* be an undue hardship for the employer to pay for additional parking for Lockhart. ◀

JOB APPLICATIONS AND PHYSICAL EXAMS Employers must modify their job-application and selection process so that those with disabilities can compete for jobs with those who do not have disabilities. For instance, a job announcement might be modified to allow applicants to respond by e-mail or letter, as well as by telephone, so that it does not discriminate against potential applicants with hearing impairments.

Employers are restricted in the kinds of questions they may ask on job-application forms and during preemployment interviews. In addition, employers cannot require persons with disabilities to submit to preemployment physicals unless such exams are required of all other applicants. An employer can disqualify the applicant only if the medical problems discovered during a preemployment physical would make it impossible for the applicant to perform the job.

▶ **Example 35.13** Abba Freight Systems runs a trucking operation. When filling the position of delivery truck driver, Abba cannot screen out all applicants who are unable to meet the U.S. Department of Transportation's hearing standard. Abba would first have to prove that drivers who are deaf are not qualified to perform the essential job function of driving safely and pose a higher risk of accidents than drivers who are not deaf.[38] ◀

SUBSTANCE ABUSERS Drug addiction is considered a disability under the ADA because it is a substantially limiting impairment. The act does not protect individuals who are actually using illegal drugs, however. Instead, the ADA protects only persons with *former* drug addictions—those who have completed or are now in a supervised drug-rehabilitation program.

36. 42 U.S.C. Section 12112(b)(4).
37. See, for example, *Francin v. Mosby, Inc.*, 248 S.W.3d 619 (Mo. 2008).
38. See, for example, *Bates v. United Parcel Service, Inc.*, 465 F.3d 1069 (9th Cir. 2006).

Individuals who have used drugs casually in the past also are not protected under the act. They are not considered addicts and therefore do not have a disability (addiction).

People suffering from alcoholism are protected by the ADA. Employers cannot legally discriminate against employees simply because they suffer from alcoholism. Of course, employers can prohibit the use of alcohol in the workplace and require that employees not be under the influence of alcohol while working. Employers can also fire or refuse to hire a person who is an alcoholic if (1) he or she poses a *substantial risk of harm* either to himself or herself or to others, and (2) the risk cannot be reduced by reasonable accommodation.

HEALTH-INSURANCE PLANS Workers with disabilities must be given equal access to any health insurance provided to other employees. An employer can put a limit, or cap, on health-care payments under its group health policy, however, as long as the cap is applied equally to all insured employees and does not discriminate on the basis of disability. Whenever a group health-care plan makes a disability-based distinction in its benefits, the plan violates the ADA. (An exception exists if the employer can justify its actions under the business necessity defense, as discussed in the next section).

SECTION 4
DEFENSES TO EMPLOYMENT DISCRIMINATION

The first line of defense for an employer charged with employment discrimination is to assert that the plaintiff has failed to meet his or her initial burden of proving that discrimination occurred. As noted, plaintiffs bringing age discrimination claims may find it difficult to meet this initial burden because they must prove that age discrimination was the reason for their employer's decision.

Once a plaintiff succeeds in proving that discrimination occurred, the burden shifts to the employer to justify the discriminatory practice. Possible justifications include that the discrimination was the result of a business necessity, a bona fide occupational qualification, or a seniority system. In some situations, as noted earlier, an effective antiharassment policy and prompt remedial action when harassment occurs may shield employers from liability for sexual harassment under Title VII.

Business Necessity

An employer may defend against a claim of disparate-impact (unintentional) discrimination by asserting that a practice that has a discriminatory effect is a **business necessity.** ▶ **Example 35.14** Jiffy Mart requires its employees to have a high school diploma. If this requirement is shown to have a discriminatory effect, Jiffy might argue that a high school education is necessary for workers to perform the job at a required level of competence. If Jiffy can demonstrate to the court's satisfaction that a definite connection exists between a high school education and job performance, then Jiffy normally will succeed in this business necessity defense. ◀

Bona Fide Occupational Qualification

Another defense applies when discrimination against a protected class is essential to a job—that is, when a particular trait is a **bona fide occupational qualification (BFOQ).** Race, color, and national origin, however, can never be BFOQs.

Generally, courts have restricted the BFOQ defense to instances in which the employee's gender or religion is essential to the job. ▶ **Example 35.15** Urban Minx, a women's clothing store, might legitimately hire only female salespersons if part of a salesperson's job involves assisting clients in the store's dressing rooms. Similarly, the Federal Aviation Administration can legitimately impose age limits for airline pilots—but an airline cannot impose weight limits only on female flight attendants. ◀

Seniority Systems

An employer with a history of discrimination may have no members of protected classes in upper-level positions. Even if the employer now seeks to be unbiased, it may face a lawsuit from members of protected classes claiming that they should be promoted ahead of schedule to compensate for past discrimination. If no present intent to discriminate is shown, however, and if promotions or other job benefits are distributed according to a fair **seniority system** (in which workers with more years of service are promoted first or laid off last), the employer normally has a good defense against the suit.

According to the United States Supreme Court, this defense may also apply to claims of discrimination under the ADA. ▶ **Case in Point 35.16** A baggage handler who had injured his back requested an assignment to a mailroom position at U.S. Airways, Inc. The airline refused to give the employee the position because another employee had seniority. The Court sided with U.S. Airways. If an employee with a disability requests an accommodation that conflicts with an employer's seniority system, the accommodation generally will not be considered "reasonable" under the ADA.[39] ◄

After-Acquired Evidence of Employee Misconduct

In some situations, employers have attempted to avoid liability for employment discrimination on the basis of "after-acquired evidence"—that is, evidence that the employer discovers after a lawsuit is filed—of an employee's misconduct. ▶ **Example 35.17** An employer fires a worker, Ravi, who then sues the employer for employment discrimination. During pretrial investigation, the employer learns that Ravi made material misrepresentations on his employment application—misrepresentations that, had the employer known about them, would have served as a ground to fire the individual. ◄

According to the United States Supreme Court, after-acquired evidence of wrongdoing cannot be used to shield an employer entirely from liability for employment discrimination. It may, however, be used to limit the amount of damages for which the employer is liable.[40]

SECTION 5
AFFIRMATIVE ACTION

Federal statutes and regulations providing for equal opportunity in the workplace were designed to reduce or eliminate discriminatory practices with respect to hiring, retaining, and promoting employees. **Affirmative action** programs go a step further and attempt to "make up" for past patterns of discrimination by giving members of protected classes preferential treatment in hiring or promotion.

These programs also promote diversity in schools and workplaces. During the 1960s, all federal and state government agencies, private companies that contracted to do business with the federal government, and institutions that received federal funding were required to implement affirmative action policies.

Title VII of the Civil Rights Act of 1964 neither requires nor prohibits affirmative action. Thus, most private companies and organizations have not been required to implement affirmative action policies, though many have done so voluntarily. Affirmative action programs have been controversial, however, particularly when they result in reverse discrimination against members of a majority group, such as white males.

Constitutionality of Affirmative Action Programs

Because of their inherently discriminatory nature, affirmative action programs may violate the equal protection clause of the Fourteenth Amendment to the U.S. Constitution. The United States Supreme Court has held that any federal, state, or local government affirmative action program that uses racial or ethnic classifications as the basis for making decisions is subject to strict scrutiny by the courts.[41] Recall from Chapter 4 that strict scrutiny is the highest standard, which means that most programs do not survive a court's analysis under this test.

Today, an affirmative action program normally is constitutional only if it attempts to remedy past discrimination and does not make use of quotas or preferences. Furthermore, once such a program has succeeded in the goal of remedying past discrimination, it must be changed or dropped.

Affirmative Action in Schools

Most of the affirmative action cases that have reached the United States Supreme Court in the last twenty years have involved university admissions programs and schools, rather than business employers.

RACE AS A "PLUS" FACTOR Generally, the Court has found that a school admissions policy that *automatically* awards minority group applicants a specified number of points violates the equal protection clause.[42] A school can, however, "consider race or ethnicity more flexibly as a 'plus' factor in the context of individu-

---

39. *U.S. Airways, Inc. v. Barnett,* 535 U.S. 391, 122 S.Ct. 1516, 152 L.Ed.2d 589 (2002).
40. *McKennon v. Nashville Banner Publishing Co.,* 513 U.S. 352, 115 S.Ct. 879, 130 L.Ed.2d 852 (1995). See also *EEOC v. Dial Corp.,* 469 F.3d 735 (8th Cir. 2006).
41. See the landmark decision in *Adarand Constructors, Inc. v. Peña,* 515 U.S. 200, 115 S.Ct. 2097, 132 L.Ed.2d 158 (1995).
42. *Gratz v. Bollinger,* 539 U.S. 244, 123 S.Ct. 2411, 156 L.Ed.2d 257 (2003).

alized consideration of each and every applicant."[43] In other words, it is unconstitutional for schools to apply a mechanical formula that gives "diversity bonuses" based on race or ethnicity.

▶ **Case in Point 35.18** School districts in Seattle, Washington, and Jefferson County, Kentucky, adopted plans that relied on race to assign certain children to schools. The Seattle plan classified children as "white" or "nonwhite" and used racial classifications as a "tie-breaker" to determine which school students would attend. The school district in Jefferson County classified students as "black" or "other" to assign children to elementary schools.

Parent groups filed lawsuits claiming that the racial preferences violated the equal protection clause. The United States Supreme Court held that the school districts had failed to show that the use of racial classifications in their student assignment plans was

necessary to achieve their stated goal of racial diversity. Hence, the affirmative action programs of both school districts were unconstitutional.[44] ◀

A CHANGE ON THE HORIZON The Supreme Court's view of race-conscious admission policies might be changing. At the time this book went to press, the Court had not yet issued its widely anticipated ruling in the case of *Fisher v. University of Texas*.[45] The case involved Abigail Fisher, a white woman who claimed that her rights to equal protection had been violated when she was denied admission to the University of Texas. The university's affirmative action program followed the guidelines previously set forth by the Court and did not apply a mechanical formula but considered race merely as a plus factor.

---

43. *Grutter v. Bollinger,* 539 U.S. 306, 123 S.Ct. 2325, 156 L.Ed.2d 304 (2003).

44. The Court consolidated the two cases and issued one opinion for both. See *Parents Involved in Community Schools v. Seattle School District No. 1,* 551 U.S. 701, 127 S.Ct. 2738, 168 L.Ed.2d 508 (2007).
45. The Supreme Court granted *certiorari* at 132 S.Ct. 1536 (2012).

Reviewing: Employment Discrimination and Diversity

Amaani Lyle, an African American woman, was hired by Warner Brothers Television Productions to be a scriptwriters' assistant for the writers of *Friends,* a popular, adult-oriented television series. One of her essential job duties was to type detailed notes for the scriptwriters during brainstorming sessions in which they discussed jokes, dialogue, and story lines. The writers then combed through Lyle's notes after the meetings for script material. During these meetings, the three male scriptwriters told lewd and vulgar jokes and made sexually explicit comments and gestures. They often talked about their personal sexual experiences and fantasies, and some of these conversations were then used in episodes of *Friends*.

During the meetings, Lyle never complained that she found the writers' conduct offensive. After four months, Lyle was fired because she could not type fast enough to keep up with the writers' conversations during the meetings. She filed a suit against Warner Brothers, alleging sexual harassment and claiming that her termination was based on racial discrimination. Using the information presented in the chapter, answer the following questions.

1. Would Lyle's claim of racial discrimination be for intentional (disparate-treatment) or unintentional (disparate-impact) discrimination? Explain.
2. Can Lyle establish a *prima facie* case of racial discrimination? Why or why not?
3. When Lyle was hired, she was told that typing speed was extremely important to the position. At the time, she maintained that she could type eighty words per minute, so she was not given a typing test. It later turned out that Lyle could type only fifty words per minute. What impact might typing speed have on Lyle's lawsuit?
4. Lyle's sexual-harassment claim is based on the hostile working environment created by the writers' sexually offensive conduct at meetings that she was required to attend. The writers, however, argue that their behavior was essential to the "creative process" of writing for *Friends,* a show that routinely

Continued

contained sexual innuendos and adult humor. Which defense discussed in the chapter might Warner Brothers assert using this argument?

DEBATE THIS ... *Members of minority groups and women have made enough economic progress in the last several decades that they no longer need special legislation to protect them.*

Terms and Concepts

affirmative action 696

bona fide occupational
 qualification (BFOQ) 695

business necessity 695

constructive discharge 687

disparate-impact discrimination 684

disparate-treatment discrimination 682

employment discrimination 681

prima facie case 682

protected class 681

seniority system 695

sexual harassment 687

tangible employment action 688

ExamPrep

Issue Spotters

1. Ruth is a supervisor for a Subs & Suds restaurant. Tim is a Subs & Suds employee. The owner announces that some employees will be discharged. Ruth tells Tim that if he has sex with her, he can keep his job. Is this sexual harassment? Why or why not? **(See page 687.)**

2. Koko, a person with a disability, applies for a job at Lively Sales Corporation for which she is well qualified, but she is rejected. Lively continues to seek applicants and eventually fills the position with a person who does not have a disability. Could Koko succeed in a suit against Lively for discrimination? Explain. **(See page 693.)**

• **Check your answers to the Issue Spotters against the answers provided in Appendix E at the end of this text.**

Before the Test

Go to **www.cengagebrain.com**, enter the ISBN 9781285185248, and click on "Find" to locate this textbook's Web site. Then, click on "Access Now" under "Study Tools," and select Chapter 35 at the top. There, you will find a Practice Quiz that you can take to assess your mastery of the concepts in this chapter, as well as Flashcards and a Glossary of important terms.

Business Scenarios

35–1. Title VII Violations. Discuss fully whether either of the following actions would constitute a violation of Title VII of the 1964 Civil Rights Act, as amended: **(See page 681.)**

 (a) Tennington, Inc., is a consulting firm and has ten employees. These employees travel on consulting jobs in seven states. Tennington has an employment record of hiring only white males.

 (b) Novo Films is making a movie about Africa and needs to employ approximately one hundred extras for this picture. To hire these extras, Novo advertises in all major newspapers in Southern California. The ad states that only African Americans need apply.

35–2. Religious Discrimination. Gina Gomez, a devout Roman Catholic, worked for Sam's Department Stores,

Inc., in Phoenix, Arizona. Sam's considered Gomez a productive employee because her sales exceeded $200,000 per year. At the time, the store gave its managers the discretion to grant unpaid leave to employees but prohibited vacations or leave during the holiday season—October through December. Gomez felt that she had a "calling" to go on a "pilgrimage" in October to Bosnia where some persons claimed to have had visions of the Virgin Mary. The Catholic Church had not designated the site an official pilgrimage site, the visions were not expected to be stronger in October, and tours were available at other times. The store managers denied Gomez's request for leave, but she had a nonrefundable ticket and left anyway. Sam's terminated her employment, and she could not find another job. Can Gomez establish a *prima facie* case of religious discrimination? Explain. **(See page 686.)**

Business Case Problems

35–3. Spotlight on Title VII of the Civil Rights Act of 1964—

Discrimination Based on Gender. Burlington Coat Factory Warehouse, Inc., had a dress code that required male salesclerks to wear business attire consisting of slacks, shirt, and a necktie. Female salesclerks, by contrast, were required to wear a smock so that customers could readily identify them. Karen O'Donnell and other female employees refused to wear the smock. Instead they reported to work in business attire and were suspended. After numerous suspensions, the female employees were fired for violating Burlington's dress code policy. All other conditions of employment, including salary, hours, and benefits, were the same for female and male employees. Was the dress code policy discriminatory? Why or why not? [*O'Donnell v. Burlington Coat Factory Warehouse, Inc.,* 656 F.Supp. 263 (S.D. Ohio 1987)] **(See page 686.)**

35–4. Discrimination Based on Gender. Brenda Lewis had been employed for two years at Heartland Inns of America, LLC, and gradually worked her way up the management ladder. Lewis, who described herself as a tomboy, was commended for her good work. When she moved to a different Heartland hotel, the director of operations, Barbara Cullinan, told one of the owners that Lewis was not a "good fit" for the front desk because she was not feminine enough. Cullinan told various people that the hotel wanted "pretty" girls at the front desk. Cullinan then informed Lewis that her hiring had not been done properly and that she would need to undergo another interview. Soon after the interview, Cullinan fired Lewis. The reason given in a letter was that Lewis was hostile during the interview. Lewis sued Heartland for gender discrimination based on unlawful gender stereotyping. The district court dismissed the suit. Lewis appealed. Does her claim fall under Title VII's prohibition against discrimination based on gender? Why or why not? [*Lewis v. Heartland Inns of America, LLC,* 591 F.3d 1033 (8th Cir. 2010)] **(See page 686.)**

35–5. BUSINESS CASE PROBLEM WITH SAMPLE ANSWER: Retaliation by Employers.

Entek International hired Shane Dawson, a male homosexual. Some of Dawson's co-workers, including his supervisor, made derogatory comments about his sexual orientation. Dawson's work deteriorated. He filed a complaint with Entek's human resources department. Two days later, he was fired. State law made it unlawful for an employer to discriminate against an individual based on sexual orientation. Could Dawson establish a claim for retaliation? Explain. [Dawson v. Entek International, *630 F.3d 928 (9th Cir. 2011)*] **(See page 688.)**

• **For a sample answer to Problem 35–5, go to Appendix F at the end of this text.**

35–6. Sexual Harassment by Co-Worker. Billie Bradford worked for the Kentucky Department of Community Based Services (DCBS). One of Bradford's co-workers, Lisa Stander, routinely engaged in extreme sexual behavior (such as touching herself and making crude comments) in Bradford's presence. Bradford and others regularly complained about Stander's conduct to their supervisor, Angie Taylor. Rather than resolve the problem, Taylor nonchalantly told Stander to stop, encouraged Bradford to talk to Stander, and suggested that Stander was just having fun. Assuming that Bradford was subjected to a hostile work environment, could DCBS be liable? Why or why not? [*Bradford v. Department of Community Based Services,* 2012 WL 360032 (E.D.Ky. 2012)] **(See page 687.)**

35–7. Age Discrimination. Beginning in 1986, Paul Rangel was a sales professional for the pharmaceutical company sanofi-aventis U.S. LLC (S-A). Rangel had satisfactory performance reviews until 2006, when S-A issued new "Expectations" guidelines with sales call quotas and other standards that he failed to meet. After two years of negative performance reviews, Rangel—who was then more than forty years old—was terminated as part of a nationwide reduction in force of all sales professionals who had not met the "Expectations" guidelines, including younger workers. Did S-A engage in age discrimination? Discuss. [*Rangel v. sanofi aventis U.S. LLC,* 2013 WL 142040 (10th Cir. 2013)] **(See page 691.)**

35–8. SPECIAL CASE ANALYSIS: Employment Discrimination.

Go to Case Analysis Case 35.1, *Dees v. United Rentals North America, Inc.,* on pages 682 and 683. Read the excerpt and answer the following questions.

(a) **Issue:** What conduct on the part of the plaintiff and what action on the part of the defendant were at the center of the dispute in this case?

(b) **Rule of Law:** Once a *prima facie* case of employment discrimination has been established, as the case moves forward, who must prove what, and who must respond with evidence of what else?

(c) **Applying the Rule of Law:** What was the court's evaluation of the parties' allegations and evidence in this case?

(d) **Conclusion:** In whose favor did the court rule? Why?

35–9. A QUESTION OF ETHICS: Discrimination Based on Disability.

Titan Distribution, Inc., employed Quintak, Inc., to run its tire mounting and distribution operation in Des Moines, Iowa. Robert Chalfant worked for Quintak as a second shift supervisor at Titan. He suffered a heart attack in 1992 and underwent heart bypass surgery in 1997. He also had arthritis. In July 2002, Titan

decided to fire Quintak. Chalfant applied to work at Titan. On his application, he described himself as disabled. After a physical exam, Titan's physician concluded that Chalfant could work in his current capacity, and he was notified that he would be hired. Despite the notice, Nadis Barucic, a Titan employee, wrote "not pass px" at the top of Chalfant's application, and he was not hired. He took a job with AMPCO Systems, a parking ramp management company. This work involved walking up to five miles a day and lifting more weight than he had at Titan. In September, Titan eliminated its second shift. Chalfant filed a suit in a federal district court against Titan, in part, under the Americans with Disabilities Act (ADA). Titan argued that it had not hired Chalfant because he did not pass the physical, *but no one—including Barucic—could explain why she had written "not pass px" on his application. Later, Titan claimed that Chalfant was not hired because the entire second shift was going to be eliminated. [Chalfant v. Titan Distribution, Inc., 475 F.3d 982 (8th Cir. 2007)]* **(See page 693.)**

(a) What must Chalfant establish to make his case under the ADA? Can he meet these requirements? Explain.

(b) In employment-discrimination cases, punitive damages can be appropriate when an employer acts with malice or reckless indifference toward an employee's protected rights. Would an award of punitive damages to Chalfant be appropriate in this case? Discuss.

Legal Reasoning Group Activity

35–10. Racial Discrimination. Two African American plaintiffs sued the producers of the reality television series *The Bachelor* and *The Bachelorette* for racial discrimination. The plaintiffs claimed that the shows have never featured persons of color in the lead roles. The plaintiffs also alleged that the producers failed to provide people of color who auditioned for the lead roles with the same opportunities to compete as white people who auditioned. **(See page 682.)**

(a) The first group will assess whether the plaintiffs can establish a *prima facie* case of disparate-treatment (intentional) discrimination.

(b) The second group will consider whether the plaintiffs can establish disparate-impact discrimination.

(c) The third group will assume that the plaintiffs established a *prima facie* case and that the burden has shifted to the employer to articulate a legal reason for not hiring the plaintiffs. What legitimate reasons might the employer assert for not hiring the plaintiffs in this situation? Should the law require television producers to hire persons of color for lead roles in reality television shows? Discuss.

Ethical principles—and challenging ethical issues—pervade the areas of agency and employment. As you read in Chapter 32, when one person agrees to act on behalf of another, as an agent does in an agency relationship, both that person and the principal assume certain ethical responsibilities and duties. In essence, agency law gives legal force to the ethical duties arising in an agency relationship. Although agency law also focuses on the rights of agents and principals, those rights are framed by the concept of duty—that is, an agent's duty becomes a right for the principal, and vice versa. Significantly, many of the duties of the principal and agent are negotiable. When they form their contract, the principal and the agent can extend or abridge many of the ordinary duties owed in such a relationship.

Employees who deal with third parties are also deemed to be agents and thus share the ethical (and legal) duties imposed under agency law. It is not always possible for an employee to negotiate favorable employment terms, however. Often, a person who is offered a job must either accept the job on the employer's terms or look elsewhere for a position. Although numerous federal and state statutes protect employees, in some situations employees still have little recourse against their employers. At the same time, employers complain that statutes regulating employment relationships impose so many requirements that they find it hard to exercise a reasonable amount of control over their workplaces.

The Agent's Duty to the Principal

The principal-agent relationship is based on trust. Because of the nature of this relationship, which we call a fiduciary relationship, an agent is considered to owe certain duties to the principal. These duties include being loyal and obedient, informing the principal of important facts concerning the agency, accounting to the principal for property or funds received, and performing with reasonable diligence and skill.

The ethical conduct expected of an agent has evolved into rules that, if breached, cause the agent to be held legally liable. Thus, an agent may not represent two principals in the same transaction, make a secret profit from the agency relationship, or fail to disclose his or her interest in property being purchased by the principal.

Does an Agent Also Have a Duty to Society? A question that sometimes arises is whether an agent's obligation includes a duty to society as well as to the principal.

Consider, for example, the situation faced by an employee who knows that her employer is engaging in an unethical—or even illegal—practice, such as marketing an unsafe product. Does the employee's duty to the principal include keeping silent about this practice, which may harm users of the product? Does the employee have a duty to protect consumers by disclosing this information to the public, even if she loses her job as a result? Some scholars have argued that many of the greatest evils in the past thirty years were carried out in the name of duty to the principal.

LEGAL REASONING

1. *How much obedience and loyalty does an agent-employee owe to an employer? What if the employer engages in an activity—or requests that the employee engage in an activity—that violates the employee's ethical standards but does not necessarily violate any public policy or law? In this situation, does an employee's duty to abide by her or his own ethical standards override the employee's duty of loyalty to the employer?*

Does an Agent's Breach of Loyalty Terminate the Agent's Authority? Several cases in recent years have involved employee-agents who breached the duty of loyalty by taking their employer's trade secrets to a competitor. The employees obtained the secrets from computer files that they were authorized to access. The question for the courts is whether the act of accessing the trade secrets was unauthorized because of the employees' breach of loyalty. If the accessing was unauthorized, the employees could be subject to severe penalties under statutes prohibiting unauthorized access to computer data.

To date, most courts have ruled that an agent's authority continues, even though there was a breach of loyalty. In one case, for example, three employees of Lockheed Martin Corporation copied confidential information and trade secrets from Lockheed's computer network onto compact discs and BlackBerries (personal digital assistants). Lockheed had authorized the employee-agents to access these files but was understandably upset when the three resigned and went to work for a competitor, taking the trade secrets with them. Lockheed sued the former employees under the Computer Fraud and Abuse Act (discussed in Chapter 10), arguing that they had accessed the data without authorization. The federal district court, however, held that the individuals did not lose their authorization to access the computer network when they breached the duty of loyalty. Therefore, the court dismissed the case.[1]

LEGAL REASONING

2. *When an agent acts in violation of his or her ethical or legal duty to the principal, should that action terminate the agent's authority to act on behalf of the principal? Why or why not?*

---

1. *Lockheed Martin Corp. v. Speed,* 2006 WL 2683058 (M.D.Fla. 2006). See also *Clarity Services, Inc. v. Barney,* 698 F.Supp.2d 1309 (M.D.Fla. 2010).

FOCUS ON ETHICS CONTINUES ➡

UNIT SEVEN Focus on Ethics

Agency and Employment, *Continued*

The Principal's Duty to the Agent

Just as agents owe certain duties to their principals, so do principals owe duties to their agents, such as compensation and reimbursement for job-related expenses. Principals also owe their agents a duty of cooperation. One might expect principals to cooperate with their agents out of self-interest, but this does not always happen. Suppose that a principal hires an agent on commission to sell a building, and the agent puts considerable time and expense into finding a buyer. If the principal changes his mind and decides to retain the building, he may try to prevent the agent from completing the sale. Is such an action ethical? Does it violate the principal's duty of cooperation? What alternatives would the principal have?

Although a principal is legally obligated to fulfill certain duties to the agent, these duties do not include any specific duty of loyalty. Some argue that employers' failure to be loyal to their employees has resulted in a reduction in employee loyalty to employers. After all, why should an employee be loyal to an employer's interests over the years when the employee knows that the employer has no corresponding legal duty to be loyal to the employee's interests? Employers who do show a sense of loyalty toward their employees—for example, by not laying off longtime employees when business is slow or replacing them with younger workers at lower cost—base that loyalty primarily on ethical, not legal, considerations.

Respondeat Superior

Agency relationships have ethical ramifications for third parties as well as for agents and principals. A legal concept that addresses the effect of agency relationships on third parties is the doctrine of *respondeat superior*. This doctrine raises a significant ethical question: Why should innocent employers be required to assume responsibility for the tortious, or wrongful, actions of their agent-employees? One reason has to do with the courts' perception that when one of two innocent parties must suffer a loss, the party in the better position to prevent that loss should bear the burden. Thus, because the employer has more control over an employee's behavior than a third party does, the employer should bear the cost of that behavior.

Another reason is that the employer is assumed to be better able to pay for any damage incurred by a third party. One of our society's shared beliefs is that an injured party should be afforded the most effective relief possible. Thus, even though an employer may be entirely innocent, the employer has "deeper pockets" than the employee and will be more likely to have the funds necessary to make the injured party whole.

LEGAL REASONING

3. *If an agent-employee injures a third party during the course of employment, the doctrine of* respondeat superior *applies. The employer may be held liable for the employee's action*

even though the employer did not authorize the action and was not even aware of it. Is it fair to hold the employer liable in this situation? Would it be more equitable if the employee alone was held liable for his or her tortious actions to third parties, even when the actions were committed within the scope of employment?

Immigration Reform

Unauthorized workers make up 5 percent of the total U.S. workforce and 12 percent of the workers in the construction industry. Not long ago, the federal government significantly stepped up enforcement actions (raids) to combat the growing number of unauthorized immigrants. The raids targeted workers in many industries, including food-processing and packaging firms, contractors (landscape, cleaning, and janitorial services), construction firms, temporary employment services, and fast-food restaurants. Often, the unauthorized workers were performing jobs that no one else wanted because the jobs paid low wages or involved substandard conditions.

As a result of these raids, many immigrant workers were detained and deported, their families were torn apart, the businesses for which they worked were disrupted, and some managers faced prison terms. The impact of these raids on immigrants—in a nation founded by immigrants—has led many U.S. citizens to believe that reforming the immigration laws is a moral imperative. Many believe that it is unethical to imprison and deport these impoverished and unrepresented workers—who often were already being exploited by their U.S. employers.

When President Barack Obama took office, he promised to reform immigration law. The goal was to decrease bureaucracy, increase efficiency, and boost the number of immigrant workers with legal status in the United States. Nevertheless, Congress has not yet reached a consensus on the specific changes necessary. The comprehensive immigration reforms suggested by a bipartisan group of senators in early 2013 were quickly rejected.[2]

LEGAL REASONING

4. *How should immigration law be reformed? Does the United States have any ethical duties to undocumented aliens who come here to work? How can the law be fair and balance the rights of immigrants, their families, the companies that employ them, and U.S. citizens?*

Problems with I-9 Verification

Verifying a person's eligibility to work in the United States can be a complicated and costly process for employers. The most recent I-9 form (see Chapter 34) specifies the documents that

---

2. The Border Security, Economic Opportunity, and Immigration Modernization Act of 2013, Senate Bill 744.

an employer may accept to verify employment eligibility and identification.

At the same time, it is illegal for an employer to discriminate against foreign-born workers by requiring them to provide a driver's license or Social Security card to prove their identity. If an employer relies on the documents a worker provides to prove identity and eligibility (such as a school photo identification card) and these documents later prove to be fraudulent or invalid, the employer can be sanctioned for hiring a person that the employer "should have known" was unauthorized.

Thus, employers are forced to choose between violating antidiscrimination laws and risking sanctions for violating immigration laws. It is an ethical dilemma with no easy answer.

Discrimination against Transgender Persons

Although some states have laws that specifically ban discrimination based on gender identity, most courts have held that federal law (Title VII, discussed in Chapter 35) does *not* protect transgender persons from discrimination. The situation may be changing, however, now that one federal court has extended Title VII protection against gender discrimination to transsexuals.

Diane Schroer (previously David Schroer) was born male but always identified with the female gender. Schroer, who has master's degrees in history and international relations, served twenty-five years in the military and was a commander of special forces. After retiring with top-secret clearance, Schroer applied for a terrorism specialist position at the Library of Congress. At the job interview, Schroer dressed as a man and received the highest interview score of all eighteen candidates. The selection committee unanimously voted to offer the job to Schroer.

Schroer then met with her future supervisor, and explained that she had been diagnosed with gender identity disorder and was planning to have sex reassignment surgery. The next day, the Library of Congress withdrew its offer to hire Schroer. When Schroer sued alleging gender discrimination, the Library claimed that it had withdrawn its offer because Schroer was untrustworthy and would be unable to receive the needed security clearance.

The court, however, found that these reasons were pretexts (excuses) and ruled in favor of Schroer. The court held that the Library had refused to hire Schroer because her appearance and background did not comport with the selection committee's stereotypes about how women and men should act and appear. The court concluded that the revocation of the job offer violated Title VII and constituted discrimination "because of sex" even though Title VII does not include transsexuals as a protected class. Schroer was awarded nearly $500,000 in back pay and damages.[3]

LEGAL REASONING

5. *Should the law prohibit discrimination against transgender persons? Why or why not?*

---

3. *Schroer v. Billington,* 577 F.Supp.2d 293 (D.D.C. 2008). See also *Glenn v. Brumby,* 724 F.Supp.2d 1284 (N.D.Ga. 2010).

BUSINESS LAW

CLARKSON · MILLER · CROSS

Unit Eight

BUSINESS ORGANIZATIONS

Contents

CHAPTER 36

SOLE PROPRIETORSHIPS AND FRANCHISES

One of the goals of many business students is to become an **entrepreneur,** one who initiates and assumes the financial risk of a new business enterprise and undertakes to provide or control its management. One of the first decisions an entrepreneur must make is which form of business organization will be most appropriate for the new endeavor.

In selecting an organizational form, the entrepreneur will consider a number of factors, including (1) ease of creation, (2) the liability of the owners, (3) tax considerations, and (4) the ability to raise capital. Keep these factors in mind as you read this unit and learn about the various forms of business organization. You may find it helpful to refer to Exhibit 41–4 in Chapter 41, which compares the major business forms in use today. Remember,

too, in considering these business forms that the primary motive of an entrepreneur is to make profits.

Traditionally, entrepreneurs have used three major business forms—the sole proprietorship, the partnership, and the corporation. In this chapter, we examine sole proprietorships and also look at franchises. Although the franchise is not strictly speaking a business organizational form, it is widely used today by entrepreneurs.

SECTION 1
SOLE PROPRIETORSHIPS

The simplest form of business is a **sole proprietorship.** In this form, the owner is the business. Thus, anyone who does business without creating a separate business organization has a sole proprietorship. More than two-thirds of all U.S. businesses are sole proprietorships. They are usually small enterprises—about 99 percent of the sole proprietorships in the United States have revenues of less than $1 million per year. Sole proprietors can own and manage any type of business from an informal, home-office or Web-based undertaking to a large restaurant or construction firm.

Advantages of the Sole Proprietorship

A major advantage of the sole proprietorship is that the proprietor owns the entire business and receives all of the profits (because she or he assumes all of the risk). In addition, starting a sole proprietorship is often easier and less costly than starting any other kind of business, as few legal formalities are required.

Generally, no documents need to be filed with the government to start a sole proprietorship.[1]

FLEXIBILITY This form of business organization also offers more flexibility than does a partnership or a corporation. The sole proprietor is free to make any decision he or she wishes concerning the business—such as whom to hire, when to take a vacation, and what kind of business to pursue.

The sole proprietor can sell or transfer all or part of the business to another party at any time and does not need approval from anyone else. (In contrast, approval is typically required from partners in a partnership and from shareholders in a corporation.)

Sometimes, a sole proprietor can even benefit in a lawsuit from the fact that the business is indistinguishable from the owner. ▶ **Case in Point 36.1** James Ferguson operated "Jim's 11-E Auto Sales" as a sole proprietorship and obtained insurance from Consumers Insurance Company. The policy was issued to "Jim Ferguson, Jim's 11-E Auto Sales." Later,

---

1. Although starting a sole proprietorship involves fewer legal formalities than other business organizational forms, even a small sole proprietorship may need to comply with zoning requirements, obtain a state business license, and the like.

Ferguson bought a motorcycle in his own name, intending to repair and sell it through his dealership. One day when he was riding the motorcycle, he was struck by a car and seriously injured.

When Ferguson sued Consumers Insurance, the insurer argued that because Ferguson bought the motorcycle in his own name and was riding it at the time of the accident, it was his personal vehicle and was not covered under the dealership's policy. The court, however, held that the policy covered Ferguson's injuries. "Because the business is operated as a sole proprietorship, Jim Ferguson and 'Jim's 11-E Auto Sales' are one and the same."[2] ◄

TAXES A sole proprietor pays only personal income taxes (including Social Security and Medicare taxes— see Chapter 34) on the business's profits, which are

reported as personal income on the proprietor's personal income tax return. Sole proprietors are also allowed to establish certain retirement accounts that are tax-exempt until the funds are withdrawn.

Disadvantages of the Sole Proprietorship

The major disadvantage of the sole proprietorship is that the proprietor alone bears the burden of any losses or liabilities incurred by the business enterprise. In other words, the sole proprietor has unlimited liability, or legal responsibility, for all obligations that arise in doing business. Any lawsuit against the business or its employees can lead to unlimited personal liability for the owner of a sole proprietorship.

The personal liability of the owner of a sole proprietorship was at issue in the following case.

2. *Ferguson v. Jenkins,* 204 S.W.3d 779 (Tenn.App. 2006).

CASE 36.1

Quality Car & Truck Leasing, Inc. v. Sark

Court of Appeals of Ohio, Fourth District, 2013 -Ohio- 44, 2013 WL 139359 (2013).

BACKGROUND AND FACTS Michael Sark operated a logging business as a sole proprietorship. To acquire equipment for the business, Sark and his wife, Paula, borrowed funds from Quality Car & Truck Leasing, Inc. When his business encountered financial difficulties, Sark became unable to pay his creditors, including Quality. The Sarks sold their house (valued at $203,500) to their son, Michael, Jr., for one dollar but continued to live in it. Three months later, Quality obtained a judgment in an Ohio state court against the Sarks for $150,481.85 and then filed a claim to set aside the transfer of the house to Michael, Jr., as a fraudulent conveyance. From a decision in Quality's favor, the Sarks appealed, arguing that they did not intend to defraud Quality and that they were not actually Quality's debtors.

 IN THE LANGUAGE OF THE COURT
KLINE, J. [Judge]

* * * *

The trial court found that summary judgment was proper under [Ohio Revised Code (R.C.) Section] 1336.04(A)(2)(a). That statute provides as follows:

> A transfer made or an obligation incurred by a debtor is fraudulent as to a creditor, whether the claim of the creditor arose before or after the transfer was made or the obligation was incurred, if the debtor made the transfer or incurred the obligation * * * without receiving a reasonably equivalent value in exchange for the transfer or obligation, and * * * the debtor was engaged or was about to engage in a business or a transaction for which the remaining assets of the debtor were unreasonably small in relation to the business or transaction.

The trial court found "that Michael Senior and Paula made a transfer without the exchange of reasonably equivalent value and that the debtor was engaged or was about to engage in a business * * * transaction for which the remaining assets of the debtor were unreasonably small in relation to the business or transaction."

* * * The Sarks argue that summary judgment was not proper because there is a genuine issue of material fact regarding whether they intended to defraud Quality Leasing. The Sarks'

CASE 36.1 CONTINUES ➡

argument fails because intent is not relevant to an analysis under R.C. Section 1336.04(A)(2)(a). *A creditor does not need to show that a transfer was made with intent to defraud in order to prevail under R.C. Section 1336.04(A)(2)(a). Thus, the Sarks cannot defeat summary judgment by showing that they did not act with fraudulent intent when Michael Senior and Paula transferred the Property to Michael Junior.* [Emphasis added.]

The Sarks also claim that summary judgment was improper because there is an issue of fact regarding whether Michael Senior and Paula are actually Quality Leasing's debtors. Michael Senior apparently returned the equipment that secured the debts owed to Quality Leasing. According to the Sarks, Quality Leasing's appraisals of the equipment showed that the value of the equipment would be enough to satisfy the debts.

The Sarks' argument, however, does not address the fact that they are clearly judgment debtors to Quality Leasing and that the judgment has not been satisfied. * * * The Sarks have not challenged the validity of the judgment against them nor have they shown that the judgment has been satisfied. Thus, there is no genuine issue of material fact regarding whether Paula and Michael Senior are debtors to Quality Leasing.

In conclusion, there is no genuine issue as to any material fact. Quality Leasing is entitled to judgment as a matter of law.

DECISION AND REMEDY *A state intermediate appellate court affirmed the lower court's judgment in Quality's favor. "Reasonable minds can come to only one conclusion, and that conclusion is adverse to the Sarks," said the court. The Sarks "are clearly judgment debtors to Quality Leasing and . . . the judgment has not been satisfied."*

THE ECONOMIC DIMENSION *What might the Sarks have done to avoid this dispute, as well as the loss of their home and their apparently declining business?*

THE ETHICAL DIMENSION *Why did the Sarks take the unethical step of fraudulently conveying their home to their son? What should they have done instead?*

PERSONAL ASSETS AT RISK Creditors can pursue the owner's personal assets to satisfy any business debts. Although sole proprietors may obtain insurance to protect the business, liability can easily exceed policy limits. This unlimited liability is a major factor to be considered in choosing a business form.

▶ **Example 36.2** Sheila Fowler operates a golf shop near a world-class golf course as a sole proprietorship. One of Fowler's employees fails to secure a display of golf clubs. They fall on Dean Maheesh, a professional golfer, and seriously injure him. If Maheesh sues Fowler's shop and wins, Fowler's personal liability could easily exceed the limits of her insurance policy. Fowler could lose not only her business, but also her house, car, and any other personal assets that can be attached to pay the judgment. ◀

LACK OF CONTINUITY The sole proprietorship also has the disadvantage of lacking continuity after the death of the proprietor. When the owner dies, so does the business—it is automatically dissolved. Another disadvantage is that in raising capital, the proprietor

is limited to his or her personal funds and funds from any loans that he or she can obtain for the business.

SECTION 2
FRANCHISES

Instead of setting up a sole proprietorship to market their own products or services, many entrepreneurs opt to purchase a franchise. A **franchise** is an arrangement in which the owner of intellectual property—such as a trademark, a trade name, or a copyright—licenses others to use it in the selling of goods or services. A **franchisee** (a purchaser of a franchise) is generally legally independent of the **franchisor** (the seller of the franchise). At the same time, the franchisee is economically dependent on the franchisor's integrated business system.

In other words, a franchisee can operate as an independent businessperson but still obtain the advantages of a regional or national organization. Today, franchising companies and their franchisees account for a significant portion of all retail sales in this country. Well-known franchises include McDonald's, 7-Eleven, and Holiday Inn. Franchising has also become a popular way for businesses to expand their operations internationally without violating the legal restrictions that many nations impose on foreign ownership of businesses.

Types of Franchises

Many different kinds of businesses now sell franchises, and numerous types of franchises are available. Generally, though, franchises fall into one of three classifications: distributorships, chain-style business operations, and manufacturing arrangements.

DISTRIBUTORSHIP In a *distributorship,* a manufacturer (the franchisor) licenses a dealer (the franchisee) to sell its product. Often, a distributorship covers an exclusive territory. Automobile dealerships and beer distributorships are common examples.

▶ **Example 36.3** Black Butte Beer Company distributes its brands of beer through a network of authorized wholesale distributors, each with an assigned territory. Marik signs a distributorship contract for the area from Gainesville to Ocala, Florida. If the contract states that Marik is the exclusive distributor in that area, then no other franchisee may distribute Black Butte beer in that region. ◀

CHAIN-STYLE BUSINESS OPERATION In a *chain-style business operation,* a franchise operates under a franchisor's trade name and is identified as a member of a select group of dealers that engage in the franchisor's business. The franchisee is generally required to follow standardized or prescribed methods of operation. Often, the franchisor insists that the franchisee maintain certain standards of performance.

In addition, the franchisee may be required to obtain materials and supplies exclusively from the franchisor. McDonald's and most other fast-food chains are examples of this type of franchise. Chain-style franchises are also common in service-related businesses, including real estate brokerage firms, such as Century 21, and tax-preparing services, such as H&R Block, Inc.

MANUFACTURING ARRANGEMENT In a *manufacturing,* or *processing-plant, arrangement,* the franchisor transmits to the franchisee the essential ingredients or formula to make a particular product. The franchisee then markets the product either at wholesale or at retail in accordance with the franchisor's standards. Examples of this type of franchise include Pepsi-Cola and other soft-drink bottling companies.

Laws Governing Franchising

Because a franchise relationship is primarily a contractual relationship, it is governed by contract law. If the franchise exists primarily for the sale of products manufactured by the franchisor, the law governing sales contracts as expressed in Article 2 of the Uniform Commercial Code applies (see Chapters 20 through 23).

Additionally, the federal government and most states have enacted laws governing certain aspects of franchising. Generally, these laws are designed to protect prospective franchisees from dishonest franchisors and to prevent franchisors from terminating franchises without good cause.

FEDERAL REGULATION OF FRANCHISES The federal government regulates franchising through laws that apply to specific industries and through the Franchise Rule, created by the Federal Trade Commission (FTC).

Industry-Specific Standards. Congress has enacted laws that protect franchisees in certain industries, such as automobile dealerships and service stations. These laws protect the franchisee from unreasonable demands and bad faith terminations of the franchise by the franchisor.

An automobile manufacturer–franchisor cannot make unreasonable demands of dealer-franchisees or set unrealistically high sales quotas. If an automobile manufacturer–franchisor terminates a franchise because of a dealer-franchisee's failure to comply with unreasonable demands, the manufacturer may be liable for damages.[3]

Similarly, federal law prescribes the conditions under which a franchisor of service stations can terminate the franchise.[4] Federal antitrust laws (discussed in Chapter 46) also apply in certain circumstances to prohibit certain types of anticompetitive agreements.

---

3. Automobile Dealers' Franchise Act of 1965, also known as the Automobile Dealers' Day in Court Act, 15 U.S.C. Sections 1221 *et seq.*
4. Petroleum Marketing Practices Act (PMPA) of 1979, 15 U.S.C. Sections 2801 *et seq.* See Case Analysis 36.2 on pages 713 and 714.

The Franchise Rule. The FTC's Franchise Rule requires franchisors to disclose certain material facts that a prospective franchisee needs in order to make an informed decision concerning the purchase of a franchise.[5] The Franchise Rule requires the following:

1. *Written (or electronically recorded) disclosures.* The franchisor must make numerous disclosures, such as the range of goods and services included and the value and estimated profitability of the franchise. Disclosures can be in writing or done electronically online. Prospective franchisees must be able to download or save all electronic disclosure documents.

2. *Reasonable basis for any representations.* To prevent deception, all representations made to a prospective franchisee must have a reasonable basis at the time they are made.

3. *Projected earnings figures.* If a franchisor provides projected earnings figures, the franchisor must indicate whether the figures are based on actual data or hypothetical examples. (The Franchise Rule does not require franchisors to provide potential earnings figures, however, as discussed in the *Insight into Ethics* feature on the following page.)

4. *Actual data.* If a franchisor makes sales or earnings projections based on actual data for a specific franchise location, the franchisor must disclose the number and percentage of its existing franchises that have achieved this result.

5. *Explanation of terms.* Franchisors are also required to explain termination, cancellation, and renewal provisions of the franchise contract to potential franchisees before the agreement is signed.

Those who violate the Franchise Rule are subject to substantial civil penalties, and the FTC can sue on behalf of injured parties to recover damages.

STATE REGULATION OF FRANCHISING State legislation varies but often is aimed at protecting franchisees from unfair practices and bad faith terminations by franchisors.

State Disclosures. Approximately fifteen states have laws similar to the federal rules that require franchisors to provide presale disclosures to prospective franchisees.[6] Many state laws also require that a disclosure document (known as the Franchise Disclosure Document, or FDD) be registered or filed with a state official. State laws may also require that a franchisor submit advertising aimed at prospective franchisees to the state for approval.

To protect franchisees, a state law might require the disclosure of information such as the actual costs of operation, recurring expenses, and profits earned, along with facts substantiating these figures. State deceptive trade practices acts (see Chapter 44) may also apply and prohibit certain types of actions by franchisors.

May Require Good Cause to Terminate the Franchise. To protect franchisees against arbitrary or bad faith terminations, state law may prohibit termination without "good cause" or require that certain procedures be followed in terminating a franchise. ▶ **Case in Point 36.4** FMS, Inc., entered into a franchise agreement with Samsung Construction Equipment North America to become an authorized dealership selling Samsung construction equipment. Then Samsung sold its equipment business to Volvo Construction Equipment North America, Inc., which was to continue selling Samsung brand equipment.

Later, Volvo rebranded the construction equipment under its own name and canceled FMS's franchise. FMS sued, claiming Volvo had terminated the franchise without "good cause" in violation of state law. Because Volvo was no longer manufacturing the Samsung brand equipment, however, the court found that Volvo had good cause to terminate FMS's franchise. If Volvo had continued making the Samsung equipment, though, it could not have terminated the franchise.[7] ◀

The Franchise Contract

The franchise relationship is defined by the contract between the franchisor and the franchisee. The franchise contract specifies the terms and conditions of the franchise and spells out the rights and duties of the franchisor and the franchisee.

If either party fails to perform its contractual duties, that party may be subject to a lawsuit for breach of contract. Furthermore, if a franchisee is induced to enter into a franchise contract by the franchisor's fraudulent misrepresentation, the franchisor may be liable for damages. Generally, statutes and the case law governing franchising tend to emphasize the

---

5. 16 C.F.R. Section 436.1.

6. These states include California, Hawaii, Illinois, Indiana, Maryland, Michigan, Minnesota, New York, North Dakota, Oregon, Rhode Island, South Dakota, Virginia, Washington, and Wisconsin.

7. *FMS, Inc. v. Volvo Construction Equipment North America, Inc.,* 557 F.3d 758 (7th Cir. 2009).

INSIGHT INTO ETHICS
Should Franchisors Have to Give
Prospective Franchisees Information about Potential Earnings?

Entrepreneurs who are thinking about investing in a franchise almost invariably ask, "How much will I make?" Surprisingly, current law does not require franchisors to provide any information about the earnings potential of a franchise.

Voluntary Disclosure of Earnings Data

Franchisors can voluntarily choose to provide projected earnings in their disclosures but are not required to do so. If franchisors do include earnings data, they must indicate whether these figures are actual or hypothetical and have a reasonable basis for these claims. About 75 percent of franchisors choose *not* to provide information about earnings potential.

Franchisee Complaints

The failure of the FTC's Franchise Rule to require disclosure of earnings potential has led to many complaints from franchisees. After all, some franchisees invest their life savings in franchises that ultimately fail because of unrealistic earnings expectations. Moreover, the franchisee may be

legally obliged to continue paying the franchisor even when the business is not turning a profit.

For instance, Thomas Anderson asked the franchisor, Rocky Mountain Chocolate Factory, Inc. (RMCF), and five of its franchisees for earnings information before he entered into a franchise agreement, but he did not receive any data. Although his chocolate franchise failed to become profitable, a court ordered Anderson and his partner to pay $33,109 in past due royalties and interest to RMCF (plus court costs and expenses).[a]

LEGAL CRITICAL THINKING
INSIGHT INTO THE BUSINESS ENVIRONMENT

If the law required franchisors to provide estimates of potential earnings, would there be more or less growth in the number of franchises? Explain your answer.

a. *Rocky Mountain Chocolate Factory, Inc. v. SDMS, Inc.,* 2009 WL 579516 (D.Colo. 2009).

importance of good faith and fair dealing in franchise relationships.

Because each type of franchise relationship has its own characteristics, franchise contracts tend to differ. Nonetheless, certain major issues typically are addressed in a franchise contract. We look at some of them next.

PAYMENT FOR THE FRANCHISE The franchisee ordinarily pays an initial fee or lump-sum price for the franchise license (the privilege of being granted a franchise). This fee is separate from the various products that the franchisee purchases from or through the franchisor. The franchise agreement may also require the franchisee to pay a percentage of the franchisor's advertising costs and certain administrative expenses.

In some industries, the franchisor relies heavily on the initial sale of the franchise for realizing a profit. In other industries, the continued dealing between the parties brings profit to both. Generally, the franchisor receives a stated percentage of the annual (or monthly) sales or volume of business done by the franchisee.

BUSINESS PREMISES The franchise agreement may specify whether the premises for the business must be leased or purchased outright. Sometimes, a building must be constructed to meet the terms of the agreement. The agreement will specify whether the franchisor or the franchisee is responsible for supplying equipment and furnishings for the premises.

LOCATION OF THE FRANCHISE Typically, the franchisor determines the territory to be served. Some franchise contracts give the franchisee exclusive rights, or "territorial rights," to a certain geographic area. Other franchise contracts, while defining the territory allotted to a particular franchise, either specifically state that the franchise is nonexclusive or are silent on the issue of territorial rights.

Many franchise cases involve disputes over territorial rights, and the implied covenant of good faith and fair dealing often comes into play in this area of franchising. If the franchise contract does not grant the franchisee exclusive territorial rights and the franchisor allows a competing franchise to be established nearby, the franchisee may suffer a significant loss in profits. In this situation, a court may hold that the franchisor breached an implied covenant of good faith and fair dealing.

BUSINESS ORGANIZATION   The franchisor may require that the business use a particular organizational form and capital structure. The franchise agreement may also set out standards such as sales quotas and record-keeping requirements. Additionally, a franchisor may retain stringent control over the training of personnel involved in the operation and over administrative aspects of the business.

QUALITY CONTROL   The day-to-day operation of the franchise business normally is left up to the franchisee. Nonetheless, the franchise agreement may specify that the franchisor will provide some degree of supervision and control so that it can protect the franchise's name and reputation.

Means of Control.   When the franchise prepares a product, such as food, or provides a service, such as motel accommodations, the contract often states that the franchisor will establish certain standards for the facility. Typically, the contract will state that the franchisor is permitted to make periodic inspections to ensure that the standards are being maintained.

As a means of controlling quality, franchise agreements also typically limit the franchisee's ability to sell the franchise to another party. ▶ **Example 36.5** Mark Keller, Inc., an authorized Jaguar franchise, contracts to sell its dealership to Henrique Autos West. A Jaguar franchise generally cannot be sold without Jaguar Cars' permission. Prospective franchisees must meet Jaguar's customer satisfaction standards. If Henrique Autos fails to meet those standards, Jaguar can refuse to allow the sale and can terminate the franchise.[8] ◀

Degree of Control.   As a general rule, the validity of a provision permitting the franchisor to establish and enforce certain quality standards is unquestioned. The franchisor has a legitimate interest in maintaining the quality of the product or service to protect its name and reputation.

If a franchisor exercises too much control over the operations of its franchisees, however, the franchisor risks potential liability. A franchisor may occasionally be held liable—under the doctrine of *respondeat*

superior (see Chapter 33)—for the tortious acts of the franchisees' employees.

PRICING ARRANGEMENTS   Franchises provide the franchisor with an outlet for the firm's goods and services. Depending on the nature of the business, the franchisor may require the franchisee to purchase certain supplies from the franchisor at an established price.[9] A franchisor cannot, however, set the prices at which the franchisee will resell the goods because such price setting may be a violation of state or federal antitrust laws, or both. A franchisor can suggest retail prices but cannot mandate them.

SECTION 3
FRANCHISE TERMINATION

The duration of the franchise is a matter to be determined between the parties. Sometimes, a franchise relationship starts with a short trial period, such as a year, so that the franchisee and the franchisor can determine whether they want to stay in business with each another. Other times, the duration of the franchise contract correlates with the term of the lease for the business premises, and both are renewable at the end of that period.

Grounds for Termination Set by Franchise Contract

Usually, the franchise agreement specifies that termination must be "for cause" and then defines the grounds for termination. Cause might include, for instance, the death or disability of the franchisee, insolvency of the franchisee, breach of the franchise agreement, or failure to meet specified sales quotas.

NOTICE REQUIREMENTS   Most franchise contracts provide that notice of termination must be given. If no set time for termination is specified, then a reasonable time, with notice, is implied. A franchisee must be given reasonable time to wind up the business— that is, to do the accounting and return the copyright or trademark or any other property of the franchisor.

---

8. For example, see *Midwest Automotive III, LLC v. Iowa Department of Transportation*, 646 N.W.2d 417 (Iowa 2002).

9. Although a franchisor can require franchisees to purchase supplies from it, requiring a franchisee to purchase exclusively from the franchisor may violate federal antitrust laws (see Chapter 46).

OPPORTUNITY TO CURE A BREACH A franchise agreement may state that the franchisee may attempt to cure an ordinary, curable breach within a certain period of time after notice so as to postpone, or even avoid, the termination of the contract. Even when a contract contains a notice-and-cure provision, however, a franchisee's breach of the duty of honesty and fidelity may be enough to allow the franchisor to terminate the franchise.

▶ **Case in Point 36.6** Pilot Air Freight Corporation is a franchisor that moves freight through its network of operations at airports and other sites. LJL Transportation, Inc., was a franchisee. The franchise agreement required LJL to assign all shipments to the Pilot network. The agreement also provided that "Pilot shall allow Franchisee an opportunity to cure a default within ninety (90) days of receipt of written notice." After eight years as a Pilot franchisee, LJL began to divert shipments to Northeast Transportation, a competing service owned by LJL's owners. Pilot then terminated the franchise agreement. LJL filed a lawsuit claiming that it should be allowed to cure its breach, but the court ruled in favor of Pilot. A franchise agreement may be terminated immediately when there is a material breach so serious that it goes directly to the heart and essence of the contract.[10] ◀

---

10. *LJL Transportation, Inc. v. Pilot Air Freight Corp.*, 599 Pa. 546, 962 A.2d 639 (Pa.Sup.Ct. 2009).

Wrongful Termination

Because a franchisor's termination of a franchise often has adverse consequences for the franchisee, much franchise litigation involves claims of wrongful termination. Generally, the termination provisions of contracts are more favorable to the franchisor than to the franchisee. This means that the franchisee, who normally invests a substantial amount of time and financial resources in making the franchise operation successful, may receive little or nothing for the business on termination. The franchisor owns the trademark and hence the business.

It is in this area that statutory and case law become important. The federal and state laws discussed earlier attempt, among other things, to protect franchisees from the arbitrary or unfair termination of their franchises by the franchisors.

In the following case, a group of service-station franchisees claimed that their franchisor had violated the Petroleum Marketing Practices Act (PMPA) of 1979, which limits the circumstances in which petroleum franchisors may terminate a franchise. The franchisees contended that changes in the rental provisions of the franchise contract had effectively increased their fuel costs, thereby "constructively" (in effect) terminating the franchises. The franchisees, however, had continued to operate their service stations. Under the PMPA, must a franchisee abandon its franchise in order to recover for constructive termination? That was the issue facing the United States Supreme Court.

CASE ANALYSIS

Case 36.2   Mac's Shell Service, Inc. v. Shell Oil Products Co.
Supreme Court of the United States, 559 U.S. 175, 130 S.Ct. 1251, 176 L.Ed.2d 36 (2010).

IN THE LANGUAGE OF THE COURT
Justice *ALITO* delivered the opinion of the Court.

* * * *

This litigation involves a dispute between Shell Oil Company (Shell), a petroleum franchisor, and several Shell franchisees in Massachusetts. Pursuant to their franchise agreements with Shell, each franchisee was

required to pay Shell monthly rent for use of the service-station premises. For many years, Shell offered the franchisees a rent subsidy that reduced the monthly rent by a set amount for every gallon of motor fuel a franchisee sold above a specified threshold. Shell renewed the subsidy annually through notices that "explicitly provided for cancellation [of the rent subsidy] with thirty days' notice."

Nonetheless, Shell representatives made various oral representations to the franchisees "that the subsidy or something like it would always exist."

In 1998, Shell joined with two other oil companies to create Motiva Enterprises LLC (Motiva), a joint venture that combined the companies' petroleum-marketing operations in the eastern United States. Shell assigned to Motiva its rights

CASE 36.2 CONTINUES ▶

and obligations under the relevant franchise agreements. * * * Effective January 1, 2000, Motiva ended the volume-based rent subsidy, thus increasing the franchisees' rent.

In July 2001, sixty-three Shell franchisees (hereinafter dealers) filed suit against Shell and Motiva in Federal District Court. Their complaint alleged that Motiva's discontinuation of the rent subsidy constituted a breach of contract under state law. Additionally, the dealers asserted [a claim] under the PMPA [Petroleum Marketing Practices Act]. * * * They maintained that Shell and Motiva, by eliminating the rent subsidy, had "constructively terminated" their franchises in violation of the Act.

After a two-week trial involving eight of the dealers, the jury found against Shell and Motiva on all claims. Both before and after the jury's verdict, Shell and Motiva moved for judgment as a matter of law on the dealers' [PMPA claim]. They argued that they could not be found liable for constructive termination under the Act because none of the dealers had abandoned their franchises in response to Motiva's elimination of the rent subsidy— something Shell and Motiva said was a necessary element of any constructive termination claim. * * * The District Court denied [the motion], and Shell and Motiva appealed. [The U.S. Court of Appeals for the First Circuit affirmed the district court's judgment, and Shell and Motiva appealed to the United States Supreme Court.]
* * * *

The * * * question we are asked to decide is whether a service-station franchisee may recover for constructive termination under the PMPA when the franchisor's allegedly wrongful conduct did not force the

franchisee to abandon its franchise. *For the reasons that follow, we conclude that a necessary element of any constructive termination claim under the Act is that the franchisor's conduct forced an end to the franchisee's use of the franchisor's trademark, purchase of the franchisor's fuel, or occupation of the franchisor's service station.* [Emphasis added.]

When given its ordinary meaning, the text of the PMPA prohibits only that franchisor conduct that has the effect of ending a franchise. As relevant here, the Act provides that "no franchisor * * * may * * * terminate any franchise," except for an enumerated reason and after providing written notice.

The word "terminate" ordinarily means "put an end to." * * * The object of the verb "terminate" is the noun "franchise," a term the Act defines as "any contract" for the provision of one (or more) of the three elements of a typical petroleum franchise. Thus, when given its ordinary meaning, the Act is violated only if an agreement for the use of a trademark, purchase of motor fuel, or lease of a premises is "put [to] an end" * * * . Conduct that does not force an end to the franchise, in contrast, is not prohibited by the Act's plain terms.
* * * *

Requiring franchisees to abandon their franchises before claiming constructive termination is also consistent with the general understanding of the doctrine of constructive termination. As applied in analogous legal contexts—both now and at the time Congress enacted the PMPA—*a plaintiff must actually sever a particular legal relationship in order to maintain a claim for constructive termination.* For example, courts have long recognized a theory of constructive discharge in the field of employment

law. Similarly, landlord-tenant law has long recognized the concept of constructive eviction. The general rule under that doctrine is that a tenant must actually move out in order to claim constructive eviction. [Emphasis added.]

As generally understood in these and other contexts, a termination is deemed "constructive" because it is the plaintiff, rather than the defendant, who formally puts an end to the particular legal relationship— not because there is no end to the relationship at all. There is no reason why a different understanding should apply to constructive termination claims under the PMPA. At the time when it enacted the statute, Congress presumably was aware of how courts applied the doctrine of constructive termination in these analogous legal contexts. And in the absence of any contrary evidence, we think it reasonable to interpret the Act in a way that is consistent with this well-established body of law.
* * * *

We therefore hold that a necessary element of any constructive termination claim under the PMPA is that the complained-of conduct forced an end to the franchisee's use of the franchisor's trademark, purchase of the franchisor's fuel, or occupation of the franchisor's service station. Because none of the dealers in this litigation abandoned any element of their franchise operations in response to Motiva's elimination of the rent subsidy, they cannot maintain a constructive termination claim on the basis of that conduct.
* * * *

The judgment of the Court of Appeals is reversed * * * . The cases are remanded for further proceedings consistent with this opinion.

It is so ordered.

LEGAL REASONING QUESTIONS

1. Why might a franchisor want to terminate a franchise? Why might a franchisee want to continue its association with a franchisor?

2. In this case, if Shell Oil Products Company wanted to terminate the plaintiffs' franchises, why didn't Shell simply notify the franchisees that the franchises were terminated effective immediately?

3. The PMPA regulates only the circumstances in which service-station franchisors may terminate a franchise or decline to renew a franchise relationship. Are there any reasons why Congress might have limited the scope of the PMPA to just these two aspects of franchising? Explain.

4. Suppose that some of the service-station franchisees, on the expiration of their contracts with Shell, signed a renewal agreement with Motiva, even though the franchisees believed that the rental terms of the new agreement were unacceptable. Given the Court's reasoning on the issue of constructive termination, would the franchisees have been be likely to succeed in a suit against the franchisor for "constructive nonrenewal" of the franchise agreement? Why or why not?

The Importance of Good Faith and Fair Dealing

Generally, both statutory law and case law emphasize the importance of good faith and fair dealing in terminating a franchise relationship. In determining whether a franchisor has acted in good faith when terminating a franchise agreement, the courts usually try to balance the rights of both parties.

▶ **Case in Point 36.7**   Chic Miller's Chevrolet is a General Motors Corporation (GM) dealership. Chic Miller's entered into lending agreements, commonly known as floor plan financing, to enable it to buy new vehicles from GM. At first, the dealership had floor plan financing through GM, but then it switched to Chase Manhattan Bank. Later, Chase declined to provide further financing, and Chic Miller's was unable to obtain a loan from any other lender, including GM. Under the franchise's "Dealer Sales and Service Agreement," GM could terminate a dealership for "Failure of Dealer to maintain the line of credit." GM therefore terminated Chic Miller's franchise. Chic Miller's sued, claiming that GM had failed to act in good faith in terminating the franchise, but the court held in GM's favor. GM had good cause to terminate the dealership because Chic Miller's failed to maintain floor plan financing, which was a material requirement under the franchise agreement.[11]   ◀

If a court perceives that a franchisor has arbitrarily or unfairly terminated a franchise, the franchisee will be provided with a remedy for wrongful termination. If a franchisor's decision to terminate a franchise was made in the normal course of business, however, and reasonable notice of termination was given, a court will be less likely to consider the termination wrongful. The importance of good faith and fair dealing in a franchise relationship is underscored by the consequences of the franchisor's acts in the following case.

---

11. *Chic Miller's Chevrolet, Inc. v. General Motors, Inc.,* 352 F.Supp.2d 251 (D.Conn. 2005).

SP TLIGHT on Holiday Inns

Case 36.3   Holiday Inn Franchising, Inc. v. Hotel Associates, Inc.

Court of Appeals of Arkansas, 2011 Ark.App. 147, 382 S.W.3d 6 (2011).

BACKGROUND AND FACTS Buddy House was in the construction business in Arkansas and Texas. For decades, he collaborated on projects with Holiday Inn Franchising, Inc. Their relationship was characterized by good faith—many projects were undertaken without written contracts. At Holiday Inn's request, House inspected a hotel in Wichita Falls, Texas, to estimate the cost of getting it into shape.

CASE 36.3 CONTINUES ▶

CASE 36.3 CONTINUED

Holiday Inn wanted House to renovate the hotel and operate it as a Holiday Inn. House estimated that recovering the cost of renovation would take him more than ten years, so he asked for a franchise term longer than Holiday Inn's usual ten years. Holiday Inn refused, but said that if the hotel was run "appropriately," the term would be extended at the end of ten years. House bought the hotel, renovated it, and operated it as Hotel Associates, Inc. (HAI), generating substantial profits. He refused offers to sell it for as much as $15 million.

Before the ten years had passed, Greg Aden, a Holiday Inn executive, developed a plan to license a different local hotel as a Holiday Inn instead of renewing House's franchise license. Aden stood to earn a commission from licensing the other hotel. No one informed House of Aden's plan. When the time came, HAI applied for an extension of its franchise, and Holiday Inn asked for major renovations. HAI spent $3 million to comply with this request. Holiday Inn did not renew HAI's license, however, but instead granted a franchise to the other hotel. HAI sold its hotel for $5 million and filed a suit in an Arkansas state court against Holiday Inn, asserting fraud. The court awarded HAI compensatory and punitive damages. Holiday Inn appealed.

IN THE LANGUAGE OF THE COURT
Raymond R. *ABRAMSON,* Judge.

* * * *

Generally, a mere failure to volunteer information does not constitute fraud. But *silence can amount to actionable fraud in some circumstances where the parties have a relation of trust or confidence, where there is inequality of condition and knowledge, or where there are other attendant circumstances.* [Emphasis added.]

In this case, substantial evidence supports the existence of a duty on Holiday Inn's part to disclose the Aden [plan] to HAI. Buddy House had a long-term relationship with Holiday Inn characterized by honesty, trust, and the free flow of pertinent information. He testified that [Holiday Inn's] assurances at the onset of licensure [the granting of the license] led him to believe that he would be relicensed after ten years if the hotel was operated appropriately. Yet, despite Holiday Inn's having provided such an assurance to House, it failed to apprise House of an internal business plan * * * that advocated licensure of another facility instead of the renewal of his license. *A duty of disclosure may exist where information is peculiarly within the knowledge of one party and is of such a nature that the other party is justified in assuming its nonexistence.* Given House's history with Holiday Inn and the assurance he received, we are convinced he was justified in assuming that no obstacles had arisen that jeopardized his relicensure. [Emphasis added.]

Holiday Inn asserts that it would have provided Buddy House with the Aden [plan] if he had asked for it. But, Holiday Inn cannot satisfactorily explain why House should have been charged with the responsibility of inquiring about a plan that he did not know existed. Moreover, several Holiday Inn personnel testified that Buddy House in fact should have been provided with the Aden plan. Aden himself stated that * * * House should have been given the plan. * * * In light of these circumstances, we see no ground for reversal on this aspect of HAI's cause of action for fraud.

DECISION AND REMEDY *The state intermediate appellate court affirmed the lower court's judgment and its award of compensatory damages. The appellate court increased the amount of punitive damages, however, citing Holiday Inn's "degree of reprehensibility."*

THE LEGAL ENVIRONMENT DIMENSION *Why should House and HAI have been advised of Holiday Inn's plan to grant a franchise to a different hotel in their territory?*

THE ECONOMIC DIMENSION *A jury awarded HAI $12 million in punitive damages. The court reduced this award to $1 million, but the appellate court reinstated the original award. What is the purpose of punitive damages? Did Holiday Inn's conduct warrant this award? Explain.*

Reviewing: Sole Proprietorships and Franchises

Carlos Del Rey decided to open a Mexican fast-food restaurant and signed a franchise contract with a national chain called La Grande Enchilada. The contract required the franchisee to strictly follow the franchisor's operating manual and stated that failure to do so would be grounds for terminating the franchise contract. The manual set forth detailed operating procedures and safety standards, and provided that a La Grande Enchilada representative would inspect the restaurant monthly to ensure compliance. Nine months after Del Rey began operating his restaurant, a spark from the grill ignited an oily towel in the kitchen. No one was injured, but by the time firefighters were able to put out the fire, the kitchen had sustained extensive damage. The cook told the fire department that the towel was "about two feet from the grill" when it caught fire. This was in compliance with the franchisor's manual that required towels be placed at least one foot from the grills. Nevertheless, the next day La Grande Enchilada notified Del Rey that his franchise would terminate in thirty days for failure to follow the prescribed safety procedures. Using the information presented in the chapter, answer the following questions.

1. What type of franchise was Del Rey's La Grande Enchilada restaurant?
2. If Del Rey operates the restaurant as a sole proprietorship, who bears the loss for the damaged kitchen? Explain.
3. Assume that Del Rey files a lawsuit against La Grande Enchilada, claiming that his franchise was wrongfully terminated. What is the main factor that a court would consider in determining whether the franchise was wrongfully terminated?
4. Would a court be likely to rule that La Grande Enchilada had good cause to terminate Del Rey's franchise in this situation? Why or why not?

DEBATE THIS . . . *All franchisors should be required by law to provide a comprehensive estimate of the profitability of a prospective franchise based on the experiences of their existing franchisees.*

Terms and Concepts

entrepreneur 706

franchise 708

franchisee 708

franchisor 708

sole proprietorship 706

ExamPrep

Issue Spotters

1. Frank plans to open a sporting goods store and to hire Gogi and Hap. Frank will invest only his own funds. He expects that he will not make a profit for at least eighteen months and will make only a small profit in the three years after that. He hopes to expand eventually. Would a sole proprietorship be an appropriate form for Frank's business? Why or why not? **(See page 706.)**

2. Anchor Bottling Company and U.S. Beverages, Inc. (USB), enter into a franchise agreement that states the franchise may be terminated at any time "for cause." Anchor fails to meet USB's specified sales quota. Does this constitute "cause" for termination? Why or why not? **(See page 712.)**

• **Check your answers to the Issue Spotters against the answers provided in Appendix E at the end of this text.**

Before the Test

Go to **www.cengagebrain.com**, enter the ISBN 9781285185248, and click on "Find" to locate this textbook's Web site. Then, click on "Access Now" under "Study Tools," and select Chapter 36 at the top. There, you will find a Practice Quiz that you can take to assess your mastery of the concepts in this chapter, as well as Flashcards and a Glossary of important terms.

Business Scenarios

36–1. Franchising. Maria, Pablo, and Vicky are recent college graduates who would like to go into business for themselves. They are considering purchasing a franchise. If they enter into a franchising arrangement, they would have the support of a large company that could answer any questions they might have. Also, a firm that has been in business for many years would be experienced in dealing with some of the problems that novice businesspersons might encounter. These and other attributes of franchises can lessen some of the risks of the marketplace. What other aspects of franchising—positive and negative—should Maria, Pablo, and Vicky consider before committing themselves to a particular franchise? **(See page 708.)**

36–2. Control of a Franchise. National Foods, Inc., sells franchises to its fast-food restaurants, known as Chicky–D's.

Under the franchise agreement, franchisees agree to hire and train employees strictly according to Chicky-D's standards. Chicky-D's regional supervisors are required to approve all job candidates before they are hired and all general policies affecting those employees. Chicky-D's reserves the right to terminate a franchise for violating the franchisor's rules. In practice, however, Chicky-D's regional supervisors routinely approve new employees and individual franchisees' policies. After several incidents of racist comments and conduct by Tim, a recently hired assistant manager at a Chicky-D's, Sharon, a counterperson at the restaurant, resigns. Sharon files a suit in a federal district court against National. National files a motion for summary judgment, arguing that it is not liable for harassment by franchise employees. Will the court grant National's motion? Why or why not? **(See page 712.)**

Business Case Problems

36–3. Spotlight on McDonald's—Franchise Termination. J.C.,

Inc., had a franchise agreement with McDonald's Corp to operate McDonald's restaurants in Lancaster, Ohio. The agreement required J.C. to make monthly payments of certain percentages of the gross sales to McDonald's. If any payment was more than thirty days late, McDonald's had the right to terminate the franchise. The agreement also stated that even if McDonald's accepted a late payment, that would not "constitute a waiver of any subsequent breach." McDonald's sometimes accepted J.C.'s late payments, but when J.C. defaulted on the payments in July 2010, McDonald's gave notice of thirty days to comply or surrender possession of the restaurants. J.C. missed the deadline. McDonald's demanded that J.C. vacate the restaurants, but J.C. refused. McDonald's alleged that J.C. had violated the franchise agreement. J.C. claimed that McDonald's had breached the implied covenant of good faith and fair dealing. Which party should prevail and why? [*McDonald's Corp. v. C.B. Management Co.,*13 F.Supp.2d 705 (N.D.Ill. 1998)] **(See page 712.)**

36–4. Franchise Disclosure. Peaberry Coffee, Inc., owned and operated about twenty company stores in the Denver area. The company began a franchise program and prepared a disclosure document as required by the Federal Trade Commission (FTC). Peaberry sold ten franchises, and each franchisee received a disclosure document. Later, when the franchises did not do well, the franchisees sued Peaberry, claiming that its FTC disclosure document had been fraudulent. Specifically, the franchisees claimed that Peaberry had not disclosed that most of the company stores were unprofitable and that its parent company had suffered significant financial losses over the years. In addition, Peaberry had included in the franchisees' informa-

tion packets, an article from the *Denver Business Journal* in which an executive had said that Peaberry was profitable. The FTC disclosure document had also contained an exculpatory clause (see Chapter 14), which said the buyers should not rely on any material that was not in the franchise contract itself. Can a franchisor disclaim the relevance of the information it provides to franchisees? Why or why not? [*Colorado Coffee Bean, LLC v. Peaberry Coffee, Inc.,* 251 P.3d 9 (Colo.App. 2010)] **(See page 710.)**

36–5. The Franchise Contract. Kubota Tractor Corp. makes farm, industrial, and outdoor equipment. Its franchise contracts allow Kubota to enter into dealership agreements with "others at any location." Kejzar Motors, Inc., is a Kubota dealer in Nacogdoches and Jasper, Texas. These two Kejzar stores operate as one dealership with two locations. Kubota granted a dealership to Michael Hammer in Lufkin, Texas, which lies between Kejzar's two store locations. Kejzar filed a suit in a Texas state court against Kubota. Kejzar asked for an injunction to prevent Kubota from locating a dealership in the same market area. Kejzar argued that the new location would cause it to suffer a significant loss of profits. Which party in a franchise relationship typically determines the territory served by a franchisee? Which legal principles come into play in this area? How do these concepts most likely apply in this case? Discuss. [*Kejzar Motors, Inc. v. Kubota Tractor Corp.,* 334 S.W.3d 351 (Tex.App.—Tyler 2011)] **(See page 710.)**

36–6. BUSINESS CASE PROBLEM WITH SAMPLE ANSWER: Franchise Termination.

George Oshana and GTO Investments, Inc., operated a Mobil gas station franchise in Itasca, Illinois. In 2010, Oshana and GTO became involved in a rental dispute with Buchanan Energy, to which Mobil had assigned the lease. In November 2011,

Buchanan terminated the franchise because Oshana and GTO had failed to pay the rent. Oshana and GTO, however, alleged that they were "ready, willing, and able to pay the rent" but that Buchanan failed to accept their electronic fund transfer. Have Oshana and GTO stated a claim for wrongful termination of their franchise? Why or why not? [*Oshana v. Buchanan Energy, 2012 WL 426921 (N.D.Ill. 2012)*] **(See page 713.)**

• For a sample answer to Problem 36–6, go to Appendix F at the end of this text.

36–7. Quality Control. JTH Tax, Inc., doing business as Liberty Tax Service, provides tax preparation and related loan services through company-owned and franchised stores. Liberty's agreement with its franchisees reserved the right to control their ads. In operations manuals, Liberty provided step-by-step instructions, directions, and limitations regarding the franchisees' ads and retained the right to unilaterally modify the steps at any time. The California attorney general filed a suit in a California state court against Liberty, alleging that its franchisees had used misleading or deceptive ads regarding refund anticipation loans and e-refund checks. Can Liberty be held liable? Discuss. [*People v. JTH Tax, Inc., 212 Cal.App.4th 1219, 151 Cal.Rptr.3d 728 (1 Dist. 2013)*] **(See page 712.)**

36–8. A QUESTION OF ETHICS: Sole Proprietorship.

In August 2004, Ralph Vilardo contacted Travel Center, Inc., in Cincinnati, Ohio, to buy a trip to Florida in December for his family to celebrate his fiftieth wedding anniversary. Vilardo paid $6,900

to David Sheets, the sole proprietor of Travel Center. Vilardo also paid $195 to Sheets for a separate trip to Florida in February 2005. Sheets assured Vilardo that everything was set, but in fact no arrangements were made. Later, two unauthorized charges for travel services totaling $1,182.35 appeared on Vilardo's credit-card statement. Vilardo filed a suit in an Ohio state court against Sheets and his business, alleging, among other things, fraud and violations of the state consumer protection law. Vilardo served Sheets and Travel Center with copies of the complaint, the summons, a request for admissions, and other documents filed with the court, including a motion for summary judgment. Each of these filings asked for a response within a certain time period. Sheets responded once on his own behalf with a denial of all of Vilardo's claims. Travel Center did not respond. [*Vilardo v. Sheets, 2006 WL 1843585 (12 Dist. 2006)*] **(See page 706.)**

(a) Almost four months after Vilardo filed his complaint, Sheets decided that he was unable to adequately represent himself and retained an attorney, who asked the court for more time. Should the court grant this request? Why or why not? Ultimately, what should the court rule?

(b) Sheets admitted that Travel Center, Inc., was a sole proprietorship. He also argued that liability might be imposed on his business but not on himself. How would you rule with respect to this argument? Why? Would there be anything unethical about allowing Sheets to avoid liability on this basis? Explain.

Legal Reasoning Group Activity

36–9. Franchise Termination. Walid Elkhatib, an Arab American, bought a Dunkin' Donuts franchise in Illinois. Ten years later, Dunkin' Donuts began offering breakfast sandwiches with bacon, ham, or sausage through its franchises. Elkhatib refused to sell these items at his store on the ground that his religion forbade the handling of pork. Elkhatib then opened a second franchise, at which he also refused to sell pork products.

The next year, at both locations, Elkhatib began selling meatless sandwiches. He also opened a third franchise. When he proposed to relocate this franchise, Dunkin' Donuts refused to approve the new location and informed him that it would not renew any of his franchise agreements because he did not carry the full sandwich line.

Elkhatib filed a lawsuit against Dunkin' Donuts. **(See page 712.)**

(a) The first group will argue on behalf of Elkhatib that Dunkin' Donuts wrongfully terminated his franchises.

(b) The second group will take the side of Dunkin' Donuts and justify its decision to terminate the franchises.

(c) The third group will assess whether Dunkin' Donuts acted in good faith in its relationship with Elkhatib. Also, consider whether Dunkin' Donuts should be required to accommodate Elkhatib's religious beliefs and allow him not to serve pork in these three locations.

CHAPTER 37

PARTNERSHIPS AND LIMITED LIABILITY PARTNERSHIPS

H istorically, two or more persons entering into business together have most commonly organized their business as a partnership or a corporation. A *partnership* arises from an agreement, express or implied, between two or more persons to carry on a business for a profit. Partners are co-owners of the business and have joint control over its operation and the right to share in its profits. In this chapter, we

examine several forms of partnership. (Corporations will be discussed in Chapters 39 through 41.)

We begin with an examination of traditional partnerships, or *general partnerships,* and the rights and duties of partners in this business entity.

We then examine some special forms of partnerships known as *limited partnerships* and *limited liability partnerships,* which receive different treatment under the law.

Although general partnerships are less common today than in the past, the limited liability forms of partnership are quite prevalent. Accountants, attorneys, and architects frequently organize as limited liability partnerships. DLA Piper, the second-largest U.S. law firm, for instance, is structured as two limited liability partnerships— DLA Piper U.S., LLP, and DLA Piper International, LLP—both run by a single management board.

SECTION 1
BASIC PARTNERSHIP CONCEPTS

Partnerships are governed both by common law concepts—in particular, those relating to agency—and by statutory law. As in so many other areas of business law, the National Conference of Commissioners on Uniform State Laws has drafted uniform laws for partnerships, and these have been widely adopted by the states.

Agency Concepts and Partnership Law

When two or more persons agree to do business as partners, they enter into a special relationship with one another. To an extent, their relationship is similar to an agency relationship because each partner is deemed to be the agent of the other partners and of the partnership. The agency concepts that were discussed in Chapters 32 and 33 thus apply—specifically, the imputation of knowledge of, and responsibility for, acts carried out within the scope of the partnership

relationship. In their relationships with one another, partners, like agents, are bound by fiduciary ties.

In one important way, however, partnership law differs from agency law. The partners in a partnership agree to commit funds or other assets, labor, and skills to the business with the understanding that profits and losses will be shared. Thus, each partner has an *ownership interest* in the firm. In a nonpartnership agency relationship, the agent usually does not have an ownership interest in the business and is not obligated to bear a portion of ordinary business losses.

The Uniform Partnership Act

The Uniform Partnership Act (UPA) governs the operation of partnerships *in the absence of express agreement* and has done much to reduce controversies in the law relating to partnerships. A majority of the states have enacted the most recent version of the UPA (as amended in 1997) to provide limited liability for partners in a limited liability partnership.[1] We therefore

---

1. At the time this book went to press, more than two-thirds of the states, as well as the District of Columbia, Puerto Rico, and the U.S. Virgin Islands, had adopted the UPA with the 1997 amendments.

base our discussion of the UPA in this chapter on the 1997 version of the act and refer to older versions of the UPA in footnotes when appropriate.

Definition of a Partnership

The UPA defines a **partnership** as "an association of two or more persons to carry on as co-owners a business for profit" [UPA 101(6)]. Note that the UPA's definition of *person* includes corporations, so a corporation can be a partner in a partnership [UPA 101(10)]. The *intent* to associate is a key element of a partnership, and one cannot join a partnership unless all other partners consent [UPA 401(i)].

Essential Elements of a Partnership

Conflicts sometimes arise over whether a business enterprise is a legal partnership, especially when there is no formal, written partnership agreement. To determine whether a partnership exists, courts usually look for the following three essential elements, which are implicit in the UPA's definition:

equal right

1. A sharing of profits or losses.
2. A joint ownership of the business.
3. An equal right to be involved in the management of the business.

If the evidence in a particular case is insufficient to establish all three factors, the UPA provides a set of guidelines to be used.

THE SHARING OF PROFITS AND LOSSES The sharing of both profits and losses from a business creates a presumption (legal inference) that a partnership exists. ▶ **Example 37.1** Syd and Drake start a business that sells fruit smoothies near a college campus. They open a joint bank account from which they pay for supplies and expenses, and they share the proceeds (and losses) that the smoothie stand generates. If a conflict arises as to their business relationship, a court will assume that a partnership exists unless the parties prove otherwise. ◀

A court will not presume that a partnership exists, however, if shared profits were received as payment of any of the following [UPA 202(c)(3)]:

1. A debt by installments or interest on a loan.
2. Wages of an employee or for the services of an independent contractor.
3. Rent to a landlord.

4. An annuity to a surviving spouse or representative of a deceased partner.
5. A sale of the **goodwill** (the valuable reputation of a business viewed as an intangible asset) of a business or property.

▶ **Example 37.2** Mason Snopel owes a creditor, Alice Burns, $5,000 on an unsecured debt. They agree that Mason will pay 10 percent of his monthly business profits to Alice until the loan with interest has been repaid. Although Mason and Alice are sharing profits from the business, they are not presumed to be partners. ◀

JOINT PROPERTY OWNERSHIP Joint ownership of property does not in and of itself create a partnership [UPA 202(c)(1) and (2)]. The parties' intentions are key. ▶ **Example 37.3** Chiang and Burke jointly own farmland and lease it to a farmer for a share of the profits from the farming operation in lieu of fixed rental payments. This arrangement normally would not make Chiang, Burke, and the farmer partners. ◀

Entity versus Aggregate

At common law, a partnership was treated only as an aggregate of individuals and never as a separate legal entity. Thus, at common law a lawsuit could never be brought by or against the firm in its own name. Each individual partner had to sue or be sued.

Today, in contrast, a majority of the states follow the UPA and treat a partnership as an entity for most purposes. For instance, a partnership usually can sue or be sued, collect judgments, and have all accounting performed in the name of the partnership entity [UPA 201, 307(a)].

As an entity, a partnership may hold the title to real or personal property in its name rather than in the names of the individual partners. Additionally, federal procedural laws permit the partnership to be treated as an entity in suits in federal courts and bankruptcy proceedings.

Tax Treatment of Partnerships

Modern law does treat a partnership as an aggregate of the individual partners rather than a separate legal entity in one situation—for federal income tax purposes. The partnership is a pass-through entity and not a taxpaying entity. A **pass-through entity** is a business entity that has no tax liability—the entity's income is passed through to the owners of the entity, who pay income taxes on it.

Thus, the income or losses the partnership incurs are "passed through" the entity framework and attributed to the partners on their individual tax returns. The partnership itself pays no taxes and is responsible only for filing an **information return** with the Internal Revenue Service.

A partner's profit from the partnership (whether distributed or not) is taxed as individual income to the individual partner. Similarly, partners can deduct a share of the partnership's losses on their individual tax returns (in proportion to their partnership interests).

SECTION 2

PARTNERSHIP
FORMATION AND OPERATION

As a general rule, agreements to form a partnership can be *oral, written,* or *implied by conduct.* Some partnership agreements, however, such as one authorizing partners to transfer interests in real property, must be in writing (or in an electronic record) to be legally enforceable (see Chapter 16).

A partnership agreement, also known as **articles of partnership,** can include almost any terms that the parties wish, unless they are illegal or contrary to public policy or statute [UPA 103]. The terms commonly included in a partnership agreement are listed in Exhibit 37–1 on the facing page.

The rights and duties of partners are governed largely by the specific terms of their partnership agreement. In the absence of provisions to the contrary in the partnership agreement, the law imposes certain rights and duties, as discussed in the following subsections. The character and nature of the partnership business generally influence the application of these rights and duties.

Duration of the Partnership

The partnership agreement can specify the duration of the partnership by stating that it will continue until a designated date or until the completion of a particular project. This is called a *partnership for a term.* Generally, withdrawal from a partnership for a term prematurely (before the expiration date) constitutes a breach of the agreement, and the responsible partner can be held liable for any resulting losses [UPA 602(b)(2)]. If no fixed

duration is specified, the partnership is a *partnership at will,* which means that the partnership can be dissolved at any time.

Partnership by Estoppel

Occasionally, persons who are not partners nevertheless hold themselves out as partners and make representations that third parties rely on in dealing with them.

LIABILITY IMPOSED When a third person has reasonably and detrimentally relied on the representation that a nonpartner was part of a partnership, a court may conclude that a **partnership by estoppel** exists and impose liability—but not partnership *rights*—on the alleged partner. Similarly, a partnership by estoppel may be imposed when a partner represents, expressly or impliedly, that a nonpartner is a member of the firm.

NONPARTNER AGENTS When a partnership by estoppel is deemed to exist, the nonpartner is regarded as an agent whose acts are binding on the partnership [UPA 308].

▶ **Case in Point 37.4** Jackson Paper Manufacturing Company makes paper that is used by Stonewall Packaging, LLC. Jackson and Stonewall have officers and directors in common, and they share employees, property, and equipment. In reliance on Jackson's business reputation, Best Cartage, Inc., agreed to provide transportation services for Stonewall and bought thirty-seven tractor-trailers to use in fulfilling the contract. Best provided the services until Stonewall terminated the agreement.

Best filed a suit for breach of contract against Stonewall and Jackson, seeking $500,678 in unpaid invoices and consequential damages of $1,315,336 for the tractor-trailers it had purchased. Best argued that Stonewall and Jackson had a partnership by estoppel. The court agreed, finding that "defendants combined labor, skills, and property to advance their alleged business partnership." Jackson had negotiated the agreement on Stonewall's behalf, and a news release stated that Jackson had sought tax incentives for Stonewall. Jackson also had bought real estate, equipment, and general supplies for Stonewall with no expectation of payment from Stonewell to Jackson. This was sufficient to prove a partnership by estoppel.[2] ◀

---

2. *Best Cartage, Inc. v. Stonewall Packaging, LLC,* 727 S.E.2d 291 (N.C.App. 2012).

EXHIBIT 37-1 Common Terms Included in a Partnership Agreement

Term	Description
Basic Structure	1. Name of the partnership. 2. Names of the partners. 3. Location of the business and the state law under which the partnership is organized. 4. Purpose of the partnership. 5. Duration of the partnership.
Capital Contributions	1. Amount of capital that each partner is contributing. 2. The agreed-on value of any real or personal property that is contributed instead of cash. 3. How losses and gains on contributed capital will be allocated, and whether contributions will earn interest.
Sharing of Profits and Losses	1. Percentage of the profits and losses of the business that each partner will receive. 2. When distributions of profit will be made and how net profit will be calculated.
Management and Control	1. How management responsibilities will be divided among the partners. 2. Name(s) of the managing partner or partners, and whether other partners have voting rights.
Accounting and Partnership Records	1. Name of the bank in which the partnership will maintain its business and checking accounts. 2. Statement that an accounting of partnership records will be maintained and that any partner or her or his agent can review these records at any time. 3. The dates of the partnership's fiscal year (if used) and when the annual audit of the books will take place.
Dissociation and Dissolution	1. Events that will cause the dissociation of a partner or dissolve the partnership, such as the retirement, death, or incapacity of any partner. 2. How partnership property will be valued and apportioned on dissociation and dissolution. 3. Whether an arbitrator will determine the value of partnership property on dissociation and dissolution and whether that determination will be binding.
Arbitration	1. Whether arbitration is required for any dispute relating to the partnership agreement.

Rights of Partners

The rights of partners in a partnership relate to the following areas: management, interest in the partnership, compensation, inspection of books, accounting, and property.

MANAGEMENT RIGHTS In a general partnership, all partners have equal rights in managing the partnership [UPA 401(f)]. Unless the partners agree otherwise, each partner has one vote in management matters *regardless of the proportional size of his or her interest in the firm.* In a large partnership, partners often agree to delegate daily management responsibilities to a management committee made up of one or more of the partners.

For Ordinary Decisions. The majority rule controls decisions on ordinary matters connected with partnership business, unless otherwise specified in the agreement. Decisions that significantly affect the nature of the partnership or that are outside the ordinary course of the partnership business, however, require the *unanimous* consent of the partners [UPA 301(2), 401(i), 401(j)].

When Unanimous Consent May Be Required. Unanimous consent is likely to be required for any decision to:

1. Alter the essential nature of the firm's business as expressed in the partnership agreement.
2. Change the capital structure of the partnership.
3. Amend the terms of the partnership agreement.
4. Admit a new partner.
5. Engage in a completely new business.
6. Assign partnership property to a trust for the benefit of creditors, or allow a creditor to enter a judgment against the partnership, for an agreed sum, without the use of legal proceedings.
7. Dispose of the partnership's *goodwill* (defined on page 721).
8. Submit partnership claims to arbitration.

9. Undertake any act that would make further conduct of the partnership business impossible.

INTEREST IN THE PARTNERSHIP Each partner is entitled to the proportion of business profits and losses that is specified in the partnership agreement. If the agreement does not apportion profits (indicate how the profits will be shared), the UPA provides that profits will be shared equally. If the agreement does not apportion losses, losses will be shared in the same ratio as profits [UPA 401(b)].

▶ **Example 37.5** Rimi and Brett form a partnership. The partnership agreement provides for capital contributions of $60,000 from Rimi and $40,000 from Brett, but it is silent as to how they will share profits or losses. In this situation, they will share both profits and losses equally. If their partnership agreement had provided that they would share profits in the same ratio as capital contributions, however, 60 percent of the profits would go to Rimi, and 40 percent would go to Brett. If the agreement was silent as to losses, losses would be shared in the same ratio as profits (60 percent and 40 percent, respectively). ◀

COMPENSATION Devoting time, skill, and energy to partnership business is a partner's duty and generally is not a compensable service. Rather, as mentioned, a partner's income from the partnership takes the form of a distribution of profits according to the partner's share in the business.

Partners can, of course, agree otherwise. For instance, the managing partner of a law firm often receives a salary—in addition to her or his share of profits—for performing special administrative or managerial duties.

INSPECTION OF THE BOOKS Partnership books and records must be kept accessible to all partners. Each partner has the right to receive (and the corresponding duty to produce) full and complete information concerning the conduct of all aspects of partnership business [UPA 403]. Each firm retains books for recording and securing such information. Partners contribute the information, and a bookkeeper typically has the duty to preserve it.

The partnership books must be kept at the firm's principal business office (unless the partners agree otherwise). Every partner is entitled to inspect all books and records on demand and can make copies of the materials. The personal representative of a deceased partner's estate has the same right of access to partnership books and records that the decedent would have had [UPA 403].

ACCOUNTING OF PARTNERSHIP ASSETS OR PROFITS An accounting of partnership assets or profits is required to determine the value of each partner's share in the partnership. An accounting can be performed voluntarily, or it can be compelled by court order. Under UPA 405(b), a partner has the right to bring an action for an accounting during the term of the partnership, as well as on the partnership's dissolution and winding up.

PROPERTY RIGHTS Property acquired *by* a partnership is the property of the partnership and not of the partners individually [UPA 203]. Partnership property includes all property that was originally contributed to the partnership and anything later purchased by the partnership or in the partnership's name (except in rare circumstances) [UPA 204].

A partner may use or possess partnership property only on behalf of the partnership [UPA 401(g)]. A partner is *not* a co-owner of partnership property and has no right to sell, mortgage, or transfer partnership property to another [UPA 501].[3]

In other words, partnership property is owned by the partnership as an entity and not by the individual partners. Thus, partnership property cannot be used to satisfy the personal debt of an individual partner. That partner's creditor, however, can petition a court for a **charging order** to attach the partner's *interest* in the partnership to satisfy the partner's obligation [UPA 502]. A partner's interest in the partnership includes her or his proportionate share of the profits and losses and the right to receive distributions. (A partner can also assign her or his right to a share of the partnership profits to another to satisfy a debt.)

Duties and Liabilities of Partners

The duties and liabilities of partners are derived from agency law. Each partner is an agent of every other partner and acts as both a principal and an agent in any business transaction within the scope of the partnership agreement.

Each partner is also a general agent of the partnership in carrying out the usual business of the firm "or

---

3. Under the previous version of the UPA, partners were *tenants in partnership*. This meant that every partner was a co-owner with all other partners of the partnership property. The current UPA does not recognize this concept.

business of the kind carried on by the partnership" [UPA 301(1)]. Thus, every act of a partner concerning partnership business and "business of the kind" and every contract signed in the partnership's name bind the firm.

FIDUCIARY DUTIES The fiduciary duties that a partner owes to the partnership and the other partners are the duty of care and the duty of loyalty [UPA 404(a)]. Under the UPA, a partner's *duty of care* is limited to refraining from "grossly negligent or reckless conduct, intentional misconduct, or a knowing violation of law" [UPA 404(c)].[4] A partner is not liable

---

4. The previous version of the UPA touched only briefly on the duty of loyalty and left the details of the partners' fiduciary duties to be developed under the law of agency.

to the partnership for simple negligence or honest errors in judgment in conducting partnership business.

The *duty of loyalty* requires a partner to account to the partnership for "any property, profit, or benefit" derived by the partner in the conduct of the partnership's business or from the use of its property. A partner must also refrain from competing with the partnership in business or dealing with the firm as an adverse party [UPA 404(b)].

The duty of loyalty can be breached by self-dealing, misusing partnership property, disclosing trade secrets, or usurping a partnership business opportunity. The following case is a classic example.

CLASSIC CASE 37.1

Meinhard v. Salmon
Court of Appeals of New York, 249 N.Y. 458, 164 N.E. 545 (1928).

BACKGROUND AND FACTS Walter Salmon negotiated a twenty-year lease for the Hotel Bristol in New York City. To pay for the conversion of the building into shops and offices, Salmon entered into an agreement with Morton Meinhard to assume half of the cost. They agreed to share the profits and losses from the *joint venture* (a type of business organization similar to a partnership—see Chapter 38), but Salmon was to have the sole power to manage the building. Less than four months before the end of the lease term, the building's owner, Elbridge Gerry, approached Salmon about a project to raze the converted structure, clear five adjacent lots, and construct a single building across the whole property. Salmon agreed and signed a new lease in the name of his own business, Midpoint Realty Company, without telling Meinhard. When Meinhard learned of the deal, he filed a suit in a New York state court against Salmon. The court ruled in Meinhard's favor, and Salmon appealed.

IN THE LANGUAGE OF THE COURT
CARDOZO, C.J. [Chief Justice]

* * * *

Joint adventurers, like copartners, owe to one another, while the enterprise continues, the duty of the finest loyalty. Many forms of conduct permissible in a work-a-day world for those acting at arm's length are forbidden to those bound by fiduciary ties. * * * Not honesty alone, but the punctilio [strictness in observance of details] of an honor the most sensitive, is then the standard of behavior. As to this there has developed a tradition that is unbending and inveterate [entrenched]. Uncompromising rigidity has been the attitude of courts * * * when petitioned to undermine the rule of undivided loyalty.

* * * The trouble about [Salmon's] conduct is that he excluded his coadventurer from any chance to compete, from any chance to enjoy the opportunity for benefit.

* * * The very fact that Salmon was in control with exclusive powers of direction charged him the more obviously with the duty of disclosure, [because] only through disclosure could opportunity be equalized.

* * * Authority is, of course, abundant that one partner may not appropriate to his own use a renewal of a lease, though its term is to begin at the expiration of the partnership. The lease at hand with its many changes is not strictly a renewal. Even so, the standard of loyalty for those in trust relations is without the fixed divisions of a graduated scale. * * * *A man obtaining [an] * * * opportunity * * * by the position he occupies as a partner is bound by his obligation to his*

CASE 37.1 CONTINUES ➡

CASE 37.1 CONTINUED

copartners in such dealings not to separate his interest from theirs, but, if he acquires any benefit, to communicate it to them. Certain it is also that there may be no abuse of special opportunities growing out of a special trust as manager or agent. [Emphasis added.]

* * * Very likely [Salmon] assumed in all good faith that with the approaching end of the venture he might ignore his coadventurer and take the extension for himself. He had given to the enterprise time and labor as well as money. He had made it a success. Meinhard, who had given money, but neither time nor labor, had already been richly paid. * * * [But] Salmon had put himself in a position in which thought of self was to be renounced, however hard the abnegation [self-denial]. He was much more than a coadventurer. He was a managing coadventurer. For him and for those like him the rule of undivided loyalty is relentless and supreme.

DECISION AND REMEDY *The Court of Appeals of New York held that Salmon breached his fiduciary duty by failing to inform Meinhard of the business opportunity and secretly taking advantage of it himself. The court granted Meinhard an interest "measured by the value of half of the entire lease."*

WHAT IF THE FACTS WERE DIFFERENT? *Suppose that Salmon had disclosed Gerry's proposal to Meinhard, who had said that he was not interested. Would the result in this case have been different? Explain.*

IMPACT OF THIS CASE ON TODAY'S LAW *This classic case involved a joint venture, not a partnership. At the time, a member of a joint venture had only the duty to refrain from actively subverting the rights of the other members. The decision in this case imposed the highest standard of loyalty on joint-venture members. The duty is now the same in both joint ventures and partnerships. The eloquent language in this case that describes the standard of loyalty is frequently quoted approvingly by courts in cases involving partnerships.*

BREACH AND WAIVER OF FIDUCIARY DUTIES A partner's fiduciary duties may not be waived or eliminated in the partnership agreement. In fulfilling them, each partner must act consistently with the obligation of good faith and fair dealing [UPA 103(b), 404(d)]. The agreement can specify acts that the partners agree will violate a fiduciary duty.

Note that a partner may pursue his or her own interests without automatically violating these duties [UPA 404(e)]. The key is whether the partner has disclosed the interest to the other partners. ▶ **Example 37.6** Jayne Trell, a partner at Jacoby & Meyers, owns a shopping mall. Trell may vote against a partnership proposal to open a competing mall, provided that she has fully disclosed her interest in the existing shopping mall to the other partners at the firm. ◀ A partner cannot make secret profits or put self-interest before his or her duty to the interest of the partnership, however.

AUTHORITY OF PARTNERS The UPA affirms general principles of agency law that pertain to a partner's authority to bind a partnership in contract. A partner may also subject the partnership to tort liability under agency principles. When a partner is carrying on partnership business with third parties in the usual way, apparent authority exists, and both the partner and the firm share liability.

If a partner acts within the scope of her or his authority, the partnership is legally bound to honor the partner's commitments to third parties. The partnership will not be liable, however, if the third parties *know* that the partner has no such authority.

Limitations on Authority. A partnership may limit a partner's capacity to act as the firm's agent or transfer property on its behalf by filing a "statement of partnership authority" in a designated state office [UPA 105, 303]. Such limits on a partner's authority normally are effective only with respect to third parties who are notified of the limitation. (An exception is made in real estate transactions when the statement has been recorded with the appropriate state office—see Chapter 49.)

The Scope of Implied Powers. The agency concepts relating to apparent authority, actual authority, and ratification that were discussed in Chapter 33 also apply to partnerships. The extent of *implied authority* *generally is broader for partners than for ordinary agents,* however.

In an ordinary partnership, the partners can exercise all implied powers reasonably necessary and customary to carry on that particular business. Some customarily implied powers include the authority to make warranties on goods in the sales business and the power to enter into contracts consistent with the firm's regular course of business.

▶ **Example 37.7** Jamie Schwab is a partner in a firm that operates a retail tire store. He regularly promises that "each tire will be warranted for normal wear for 40,000 miles." Because Schwab has authority to make warranties, the partnership is bound to honor the warranty. Schwab would not, however, have the authority to sell the partnership's office equipment or other property without the consent of all of the other partners. ◀

LIABILITY OF PARTNERS One significant disadvantage associated with a traditional partnership is that the partners are *personally* liable for the debts of the partnership. Moreover, in most states, the liability is essentially unlimited because the acts of one partner in the ordinary course of business subject the other partners to personal liability [UPA 305].

Joint Liability. At one time, each partner in a partnership generally was jointly liable for the partnership's obligations. **Joint liability** means that a third party must sue all of the partners as a group, but each partner can be held liable for the full amount.[5]

If, for instance, a third party sued one partner on a partnership contract, that partner has the right to demand that the other partners be sued with her or him. In fact, if the third party does not name all of the partners in the lawsuit, the assets of the partnership cannot be used to satisfy the judgment. With joint liability, the partnership's assets must be exhausted before creditors can reach the partners' individual assets.[6]

Joint and Several Liability. In the majority of the states, under UPA 306(a), partners are both jointly and severally (separately, or individually) liable for all partnership obligations, including contracts, torts, and breaches of trust. **Joint and several liability**

means that a third party has the option of suing all of the partners together (jointly) or one or more of the partners separately (severally).

All partners in a partnership can be held liable even if a particular partner did not participate in, know about, or ratify the conduct that gave rise to the cause of action. Normally, though, the partnership's assets must be exhausted before a creditor can enforce a judgment against a partner's separate assets [UPA 307(d)].

A judgment against one partner severally (separately) does not extinguish the others' liability. (Similarly, a release of one partner does not discharge the partners' several liability.) Those not sued in the first action normally may be sued subsequently, unless the court in the first action held that the partnership was in no way liable. If a plaintiff is successful in a suit against a partner or partners, he or she may collect on the judgment only against the assets of those partners named as defendants.

Indemnification. With joint and several liability, a partner who commits a tort can be required to indemnify (reimburse) the partnership for any damages it pays. Indemnification will typically be granted *unless* the tort was committed in the ordinary course of the partnership's business.

▶ **Case in Point 37.8** Nicole Moren was a partner in Jax Restaurant. After work one day, Moren was called back to the restaurant to help in the kitchen. She brought her two-year-old son, Remington, and placed him on the kitchen counter. While she was making pizzas, Remington reached into the dough press. His hand was crushed, causing permanent injuries. Through his father, Remington filed a suit against the partnership for negligence.

The partnership filed a complaint against Moren, arguing that it was entitled to indemnification from her for her negligence. The court held in favor of Moren and ordered the partnership to pay damages to Remington. Moren was not required to indemnify the partnership because her negligence occurred in the ordinary course of the partnership's business.[7] ◀

Liability of Incoming Partners. A partner newly admitted to an existing partnership is not personally liable for any partnership obligations incurred before the person became a partner [UPA 306(b)]. In other words, the new partner's liability to existing creditors

---

5. Under the prior version of the UPA, which is still in effect in a few states, partners were subject to joint liability on partnership debts and contracts, but not on partnership debts arising from torts.

6. For a case applying joint liability to a partnership, see *Shar's Cars, LLC v. Elder,* 97 P.3d 724 (Utah App. 2004).

7. *Moren v. Jax Restaurant,* 679 N.W.2d 165 (Minn.App. 2004).

of the partnership is limited to her or his capital contribution to the firm.

▶ **Example 37.9** Smartclub, an existing partnership with four members, admits a new partner, Alex Jaff. He contributes $100,000 to the partnership. Smartclub has debts amounting to $600,000 at the time Jaff joins the firm. Although Jaff's capital contribution of $100,000 can be used to satisfy Smartclub's obligations, Jaff is not personally liable for partnership debts incurred before he became a partner. Thus, his personal assets cannot be used to satisfy the partnership's preexisting debt.

If, however, the partnership incurs additional debts after Jaff becomes a partner, he will be personally liable for those amounts, along with all the other partners. ◀

SECTION 3

DISSOCIATION OF A PARTNER

Dissociation occurs when a partner ceases to be associated in the carrying on of the partnership business. Although a partner always has the *power* to dissociate from the firm, he or she may not have the *right* to dissociate.

Dissociation normally entitles the partner to have his or her interest purchased by the partnership. It also terminates the partner's actual authority to act for the partnership and to participate in running its business. The partnership may continue to do business without the dissociated partner.[8]

Events That Cause Dissociation

Under UPA 601, a partner can be dissociated from a partnership in any of the following ways:

1. By the partner's voluntarily giving notice of an "express will to withdraw." (When a partner gives notice of intent to withdraw, the remaining partners must decide whether to continue the partnership business. If they decide not to continue, the voluntary dissociation of a partner will dissolve the firm [UPA 801(1)].)

2. By the occurrence of an event specified in the partnership agreement.

3. By a unanimous vote of the other partners under certain circumstances, such as when a partner transfers substantially all of her or his interest in the partnership, or when it becomes unlawful to carry on partnership business with that partner.

4. By order of a court or arbitrator if the partner has engaged in wrongful conduct that affects the partnership business. The court may order dissociation if a partner breached the partnership agreement, violated a duty owed to the partnership or the other partners, or engaged in conduct that makes it "not reasonably practicable to carry on the business in partnership with the partner" [UPA 601(5)].

5. By the partner's declaring bankruptcy, assigning his or her interest in the partnership for the benefit of creditors, or becoming physically or mentally incapacitated, or by the partner's death.

Wrongful Dissociation

As mentioned, a partner has the power to dissociate from a partnership at any time, but if she or he lacks the right to dissociate, then the dissociation is considered wrongful under the law [UPA 602]. When a partner's dissociation breaches a partnership agreement, for instance, it is wrongful.

▶ **Example 37.10** Jenkins & Whalen's partnership agreement states that it is a breach of the agreement for any partner to assign partnership property to a creditor without the consent of the other partners. If Kenzie, a partner, makes such an assignment, she has not only breached the agreement but has also wrongfully dissociated from the partnership. ◀

A partner who wrongfully dissociates is liable to the partnership and to the other partners for damages caused by the dissociation. This liability is in addition to any other obligation of the partner to the partnership or to the other partners.

Effects of Dissociation

Dissociation (rightful or wrongful) terminates some of the rights of the dissociated partner, requires that the partnership purchase his or her interest, and alters the liability of the parties to third parties.

RIGHTS AND DUTIES On a partner's dissociation, his or her right to participate in the management and conduct of the partnership business terminates [UPA 603]. The partner's duty of loyalty also ends. A partner's duty of care continues only with respect to

---

8. Under the previous version of the UPA, when a partner withdrew from a partnership, the partnership was considered dissolved, and the business had to end. The new UPA dramatically changed the law governing partnership breakups by no longer requiring that a partnership end if one partner dissociates.

events that occurred before dissociation, unless the partner participates in winding up the partnership's business (discussed shortly).

▶ **Example 37.11**   Debbie Pearson, a partner who leaves the accounting firm Bubb & Flint, can immediately compete with that firm for new clients. She must exercise care in completing ongoing client transactions, however. Pearson must also account to Bubb & Flint for any fees received from the old clients based on those transactions. ◀

BUYOUTS After a partner's dissociation, his or her interest in the partnership must be purchased according to the rules in UPA 701. The **buyout price** is based on the amount that would have been distributed to the partner if the partnership had been wound up on the date of dissociation. Offset against the price are amounts owed by the partner to the partnership, including damages for wrongful dissociation.

▶ **Case in Point 37.12**   Wilbur and Dee Warnick and their son Randall bought a ranch for $335,000 and formed a partnership to operate it. The partners' initial capital contributions totaled $60,000, of which Randall paid 34 percent. Over the next twenty years, each partner contributed funds to the operation and received cash distributions from the partnership. In 1999, Randall dissociated from the partnership.

When the parties could not agree on a buyout price, Randall filed a lawsuit. The court awarded Randall $115,783.13—the amount of his cash contributions, plus 34 percent of the increase in the value of the partnership's assets above all partners' cash contributions. Randall's parents appealed, arguing that $50,000 should be deducted from the appraised value of the assets for the estimated expenses of selling them. The court affirmed the buyout price, however, because "purely hypothetical costs of sale are not a required deduction in valuing partnership assets" to determine a buyout price.[9] ◀

LIABILITY TO THIRD PARTIES For two years after a partner dissociates from a continuing partnership, the partnership may be bound by the acts of the dissociated partner based on apparent authority [UPA 702]. In other words, if a third party reasonably believed at the time of a transaction that the dissociated partner was still a partner, the partnership may be liable. Also, a dissociated partner may be liable for partnership obligations entered into during a two-year period following dissociation [UPA 703].

---

9. *Warnick v. Warnick,* 2006 WY 58, 133 P.3d 997 (2006).

To avoid this possible liability, a partnership should notify its creditors, customers, and clients of a partner's dissociation. In addition, either the partnership or the dissociated partner can file a statement of dissociation in the appropriate state office to limit the dissociated partner's authority to ninety days after the filing [UPA 704]. Filing this statement helps to minimize the firm's potential liability for the former partner and vice versa.

SECTION 4
PARTNERSHIP TERMINATION

The same events that cause dissociation can result in the end of the partnership if the remaining partners no longer wish to (or are unable to) continue the partnership business. Only certain departures of a partner will end the partnership, though, and generally the partnership can continue if the remaining partners consent [UPA 801].

The termination of a partnership is referred to as **dissolution**, which essentially means the commencement of the winding up process. **Winding up** is the actual process of collecting, liquidating, and distributing the partnership assets.

Dissolution

Dissolution of a partnership generally can be brought about by acts of the partners, by operation of law, or by judicial decree [UPA 801]. Any partnership (including one for a fixed term) can be dissolved by the partners' agreement.

If the partnership agreement states that it will dissolve on a certain event, such as a partner's death or bankruptcy, then the occurrence of that event will dissolve the partnership. A partnership for a fixed term or a particular undertaking is dissolved by operation of law at the expiration of the term or on the completion of the undertaking.

ILLEGALITY OR IMPRACTICALITY Any event that makes it unlawful for the partnership to continue its business will result in dissolution [UPA 801(4)]. Under the UPA, a court may order dissolution when it becomes obviously impractical for the firm to continue—for instance, if the business can only be operated at a loss [UPA 801(5)]. Even when one partner has brought a court action seeking to dissolve a partnership, the partnership continues to exist until it is legally dissolved by the court or by the parties' agreement.[10]

---

10. See, for example, *Curley v. Kaiser,* 112 Conn.App. 213, 962 A.2d 167 (2009).

In the following case, a family partnership began to experience serious problems because of a dispute between two partners. The court had to decide whether it could be judicially dissolved because its economic purpose was being frustrated.

CASE 37.2

Russell Realty Associates v. Russell

Supreme Court of Virginia, 724 S.E.2d 690 (2012).

BACKGROUND AND FACTS In 1978, members of the Russell family began operating Russell Realty Associates (RRA) as a partnership. Eddie Russell enjoyed decision-making authority over the partnership's business, which involved buying, holding, leasing, and selling investment properties. After several years, Eddie and his sister, Nina Russell, became involved in several heated disputes over whether to develop or sell particular properties and whether and how to include Nina's son in the partnership.

Nina began to routinely question Eddie's business decisions. She insisted on recording business meetings and editing the partnership's official minutes. Because of their disagreements, RRA experienced two years of delays relating to zoning approval and appraisals before it could sell one piece of property. It also was unable to accept an attractive offer for another property. Despite the siblings' disputes, RRA continued to profit and make distributions to its partners. Nevertheless, in 2008, Eddie filed a complaint seeking a judicial dissolution of the partnership. The circuit court granted the dissolution, and Nina appealed.

IN THE LANGUAGE OF THE COURT
OPINION BY Senior Justice Elizabeth B. *LACY.*

* * * *

* * * *[Under the Virginia Code, a partnership may be dissolved if]*

a. The economic purpose of the partnership is likely to be unreasonably frustrated; [or]
* * * *

c. It is not otherwise reasonably practicable to carry on the partnership business in conformity with the partnership agreement. [Emphasis added.]

* * * *

The purpose of RRA was to acquire, hold, invest in, and lease and sell investment properties. The partners' expectations for realizing these purposes included not only expectations of economic success, but also the ability to undertake these activities in an efficient and productive manner to maximize return to the partnership. The record shows, however, that not only did significant distrust and disagreement exist between the partners, but as relevant here, this relationship frustrated the ability of the Partnership to take advantage of a lucrative offer for the sale of [one piece of] property and to secure certain zoning and appraisals for [another] property in a timely manner. The record also demonstrates that the disruptive relationship between the partners has resulted in the Partnership incurring substantial added costs relating to the conduct, recording, and transcribing of meetings and minutes of the Partnership meetings, as well as the costs incurred in addressing litigation filed or threatened to be filed aside from the instant case.

This record further shows that, despite the provision of the Partnership Agreement giving Eddie decision-making authority, the relationship between the partners imposed additional and unnecessary economic costs on the Partnership in a number of ways including preventing the Partnership from taking advantage of and conducting its business in a timely and efficient manner. The relationship also imposed significant additional costs in terms of the time spent resolving issues directly and indirectly affecting the purposes of the Partnership. The relationship between the partners has deteriorated over the years and nothing in the record suggests

CASE 37.2 CONTINUED

that it will improve. For these reasons, we conclude that the record supports the circuit court's holding that the economic purpose of the Partnership is likely to be unreasonably frustrated.

DECISION AND REMEDY *The Virginia Supreme Court held that Russell Realty could be judicially dissolved. It therefore affirmed the decision of the circuit court.*

THE ETHICAL DIMENSION *Does the judicial power to dissolve partnerships encourage partners to be more respectful toward each other? Why or why not?*

THE LEGAL ENVIRONMENT DIMENSION *Eddie petitioned for the dissolution of Russell Realty rather than dissociating from the firm because the partnership agreement prohibited the withdrawal of any partner. How might Eddie have divested himself of his interest in the firm without petitioning for its dissolution?*

GOOD FAITH Each partner must exercise good faith when dissolving a partnership. Some state statutes allow partners injured by another partner's bad faith to file a tort claim for wrongful dissolution of a partnership.

▶ **Case in Point 37.13** Attorneys Randall Jordan and Mary Helen Moses formed a two-member partnership. Although the partnership was for an indefinite term, Jordan ended the partnership three years later and asked the court for declarations concerning the partners' financial obligations. Moses, who had objected to ending the partnership, filed a claim against Jordan for wrongful dissolution and for appropriating $180,000 in fees that should have gone to the partnership. Ultimately, the court held in favor of Moses.

A claim for wrongful dissolution of a partnership may be based on the excluded partner's loss of "an existing, or continuing, business opportunity" or of income and material assets. Because Jordan had attempted to appropriate partnership assets through dissolution, Moses could sue for wrongful dissolution.[11] ◀

Winding Up and Distribution of Assets

After dissolution, the partnership continues for the limited purpose of winding up the business. The partners cannot create new obligations on behalf of the partnership. They have authority only to complete transactions begun but not finished at the time of dissolution and to wind up the business of the partnership [UPA 803, 804(1)].

DUTIES AND COMPENSATION *Winding up* includes collecting and preserving partnership assets, discharging liabilities (paying debts), and accounting to each partner for the value of his or her interest in the partnership. Partners continue to have fiduciary duties to one another and to the firm during this process.

UPA 401(h) provides that a partner is entitled to compensation for services in winding up partnership affairs above and apart from his or her share in the partnership profits. A partner may also receive reimbursement for expenses incurred in the process.

CREDITORS' CLAIMS Both creditors of the partnership and creditors of the individual partners can make claims on the partnership's assets. In general, partnership creditors share proportionately with the partners' individual creditors in the partners' assets, which include their interests in the partnership. A partnership's assets are distributed according to the following priorities [UPA 807]:

1. Payment of debts, including those owed to partner and nonpartner creditors.
2. Return of capital contributions and distribution of profits to partners.[12]

If the partnership's liabilities are greater than its assets, the partners bear the losses—in the absence of a contrary agreement—in the same proportion in which they shared the profits (rather than, for example, in proportion to their contributions to the partnership's capital).

---

11. *Jordan v. Moses*, 291 Ga. 39, 727 S.E.2d 469 (2012).

12. Under the previous version of the UPA, creditors of the partnership had priority over creditors of the individual partners. Also, in distributing partnership assets, third party creditors were paid before partner creditors, and capital contributions were returned before profits.

Partnership Buy-Sell Agreements

Before entering into a partnership, partners should agree on how the assets will be valued and divided in the event that the partnership dissolves. A **buy-sell agreement,** sometimes called simply a *buyout agreement,* provides for one or more partners to buy out the other or others, should the situation warrant.

Agreeing beforehand on who buys what, under what circumstances, and, if possible, at what price may eliminate costly negotiations or litigation later. Alternatively, the agreement may specify that one or more partners will determine the value of the interest being sold and that the other or others will decide whether to buy or sell.

Under UPA 701(a), if a partner's dissociation does not result in a dissolution of the partnership, a buy-out of the partner's interest is mandatory. The UPA contains an extensive set of buyout rules that apply when the partners do not have a buyout agreement. Basically, a withdrawing partner receives the same amount through a buyout that he or she would receive if the business were winding up [UPA 701(b)].

In the following case, one of the three partners in an agricultural partnership died. Despite provisions in the partnership agreement that required its dissolution on a certain date or on a partner's death, whichever came first, the remaining partners did not dissolve the firm and did not liquidate the assets.

CASE ANALYSIS

Case 37.3 Estate of Webster v. Thomas

Appellate Court of Illinois, Fifth District, 2013 IL App (5th) 120121-U, 2013 WL 164041 (2013).

IN THE LANGUAGE OF THE COURT
Justice *WEXSTTEN* delivered the opinion of the court:

* * * *

Clyde L. Webster, Jr., who formed T & T Agri-Partners Company with partners [James] Theis and [Larry] Thomas, died September 18, 2002. The T & T Agri-Partners Company owns approximately 180 acres of farmland in Christian County [Illinois] subject to mortgage liability to the Rochester State Bank and/or Farm Credit Services of Central Illinois. This farmland constitutes T & T Agri-Partners Company's only asset.

The September 1, 1997, partnership agreement executed by Clyde, Theis, and Thomas * * * issued 180 partnership units, with Thomas holding 40 (22.2%), Theis holding 80 (44.5%), and Clyde holding 60 (33.3%). The partnership agreement further provided as follows: * * *

Unless extended by the written consent of those Partners whose combined ownership interest equals at least one hundred twenty (120)

Partnership units, the Partnership shall continue until the first to occur of January 31, 2010 A.D., or the earlier dissolution of the Partnership.

* * * *

* * * If a Partner dies, the Partnership will be dissolved, unless those Partners owning at least one hundred twenty (120) Partnership units including the personal representative of the deceased Partner's estate * * * vote to continue the Partnership within one hundred twenty (120) days of the date of the deceased Partner's death.

Upon dissolution, the assets of the Partnership shall be liquidated and distributed. * * *

Any Partner who shall violate any of the terms of this Agreement * * * shall indemnify and hold harmless the Partnership, and all other Partners from any and all * * * losses, * * * including but not limited to attorneys' fees.

On October 14, 2008, [the Estate of Webster through its personal representative Joseph Webster (the plaintiff)] filed its complaint [in an Illinois state circuit court] against [Theis, Thomas, and the partnership

(the defendants)]. The plaintiff's complaint sought a declaratory judgment ordering the partnership assets to be distributed based upon the then-current value of the acreage.

* * * *

On December 9, 2009, the circuit court entered an order granting summary judgment on * * * the plaintiff's complaint. [But the defendants did not liquidate the partnership, and the case went to trial.]

* * * *

On September 2, 2011, after the * * * trial, the circuit court entered its order, finding that the partnership expired by its terms on January 31, 2010, and despite demand by the plaintiff, the partnership had failed and refused to liquidate the assets and disburse funds to the plaintiff according to * * * the partnership agreement. The circuit court thereby ordered the defendants to liquidate the partnership.

* * * *

The circuit court further * * * ordered [the defendants to pay] reasonable attorney fees and costs incurred by the plaintiff.

CASE 37.3 CONTINUED

* * * On March 8, 2012, the defendants filed a notice of appeal [arguing that the circuit court erred in ordering them to pay the plaintiff's attorney fees].

* * * *

The partnership agreement clearly provided that upon Clyde's death and the partners' failure to vote to continue the partnership, the partnership dissolved. Pursuant to the plain language of the partnership agreement, the assets upon dissolution were to be liquidated and distributed by paying the partners in proportion to their capital accounts. Yet, the defendants failed to do so. [Emphasis added.]

On December 9, 2009, seven years after Clyde's death, the circuit court entered summary judgment on * * * the plaintiff's complaint and construed the partnership agreement by determining that upon dissolution, which occurred at Clyde's death on September 18, 2002, and as a result of the remaining partners not agreeing to continue partnership, the assets of the partnership were to be liquidated and distributed * * * *. Again, however, despite the agreement's language and despite the circuit court's order, the defendants failed to liquidate the partnership assets. In failing to do so, they violated the partnership agreement and were liable for the plaintiff's attorney fees pursuant to the same agreement.

* * * *

* * * The judgment of the * * * court of Christian County is affirmed.

LEGAL REASONING QUESTIONS

1. What did the partnership agreement at the center of this case require on the death of a partner and the dissolution of the firm?
2. What conduct by which parties triggered this litigation?
3. On what did the court base its order regarding attorneys' fees?
4. What might the defendants have done to avoid the dispute that arose from the circumstances of this case?

SECTION 5

LIMITED LIABILITY PARTNERSHIPS

The **limited liability partnership (LLP)** is a hybrid form of business designed mostly for professionals who normally do business as partners in a partnership. Almost all of the states have enacted LLP statutes.

The major advantage of the LLP is that it allows a partnership to continue as a pass-through entity for tax purposes but limits the personal liability of the partners. The LLP is especially attractive for professional service firms and family businesses. All of the "Big Four" accounting firms—the four largest international accountancy and professional services firms—are organized as LLPs, including Ernst & Young, LLP, and PricewaterhouseCoopers, LLP.

Formation of an LLP

LLPs must be formed and operated in compliance with state statutes, which may include provisions of the UPA. The appropriate form must be filed with a central state agency, usually the secretary of state's office, and the business's name must include either "Limited Liability Partnership" or "LLP" [UPA 1001, 1002]. An LLP must file an annual report with the state to remain qualified as an LLP in that state [UPA 1003].

In most states, it is relatively easy to convert a traditional partnership into an LLP because the firm's basic organizational structure remains the same. Additionally, all of the statutory and common law rules governing partnerships still apply (apart from those modified by the LLP statute). Normally, LLP statutes are simply amendments to a state's already existing partnership law.

Liability in an LLP

An LLP allows professionals, such as attorneys and accountants, to avoid personal liability for the malpractice of other partners. A partner in an LLP is still liable for her or his own wrongful acts, such as negligence, however. Also liable is the partner who supervised the individual who committed a wrongful act. (This generally is true for all types of partners and partnerships, not just LLPs.)

▶ **Example 37.14** Five lawyers operate a law firm as an LLP. One of the attorneys, Dan Kolcher, is sued for malpractice and loses. The firm's malpractice insurance is insufficient to pay the judgment. If the firm had been organized as a traditional (general) partnership, the personal assets of the other attorneys could be used to satisfy the obligation. Because the firm is organized as an LLP, however, no other partner at the law firm can be held *personally* liable for Kolcher's malpractice, unless she or he acted as Kolcher's supervisor. In the absence of a supervisor, only Kolcher's personal assets can be used to satisfy the judgment. ◄

Although LLP statutes vary from state to state, generally each state statute limits the liability of partners in some way. For instance, Delaware law protects each innocent partner from the "debts and obligations of the partnership arising from negligence, wrongful acts, or misconduct." The UPA more broadly exempts partners from personal liability for any partnership obligation, "whether arising in contract, tort, or otherwise" [UPA 306(c)].

LIABILITY FROM STATE TO STATE When an LLP formed in one state wants to do business in another state, it may be required to register in the second state—for example, by filing a statement of foreign qualification [UPA 1102]. Because state LLP statutes are not uniform, a question sometimes arises as to which law applies if the LLP statutes in the two states provide different liability protection. Most states apply the law of the state in which the LLP was formed, even when the firm does business in another state, which is also the rule under UPA 1101.

SHARING LIABILITY AMONG PARTNERS When more than one partner in an LLP is negligent, there is a question as to how liability should be shared. Some states provide for proportionate liability—that is, for separate determinations of the negligence of the partners.

▶ **Example 37.15** Accountants Zach and Lyla are partners in an LLP, with Zach supervising Lyla. Lyla negligently fails to file a tax return for a client, Centaur Tools. Centaur files a suit against Zach and Lyla. Under a proportionate liability statute, Zach will be liable for no more than his portion of the responsibility for the missed tax deadline. In a state that does not allow for proportionate liability, Zach can be held liable for the entire loss. ◄

Family Limited Liability Partnerships

A **family limited liability partnership (FLLP)** is a limited liability partnership in which the partners are related to each other—for example, as spouses,

parents and children, siblings, or cousins. A person acting in a fiduciary capacity for persons so related can also be a partner. All of the partners must be natural persons or persons acting in a fiduciary capacity for the benefit of natural persons.

Probably the most significant use of the FLLP form of business organization is in agriculture. Family-owned farms sometimes find this form to their benefit. The FLLP offers the same advantages as other LLPs with certain additional advantages, such as, in Iowa, an exemption from real estate transfer taxes when partnership real estate is transferred among partners.[13]

LIMITED PARTNERSHIPS

We now look at a business organizational form that limits the liability of *some* of its owners—the **limited partnership (LP).** Limited partnerships originated in medieval Europe and have been in existence in the United States since the early 1800s. Limited partnerships differ from traditional (general) partnerships in several ways.

A limited partnership consists of at least one **general partner** and one or more **limited partners.** A general partner assumes management responsibility for the partnership and has full responsibility for the partnership and for all its debts. A limited partner contributes cash or other property and owns an interest in the firm but is not involved in management responsibilities and is not personally liable for partnership debts beyond the amount of his or her investment. A limited partner can forfeit limited liability by taking part in the management of the business. A comparison of traditional partnerships and limited partnerships appears in Exhibit 37–2 on the facing page.[14]

Most states and the District of Columbia have adopted the Revised Uniform Limited Partnership Act (RULPA), which we refer to in the following discussion. A minority of states have adopted some amendments that were proposed in 2001 to make the RULPA more flexible.

must be truly silent

---

13. Iowa Statutes Section 428A.2.
14. Under the UPA, a general partnership can be converted into a limited partnership and vice versa [UPA 902, 903]. The UPA also provides for the merger of a general partnership with one or more general or limited partnerships [UPA 905].

EXHIBIT 37–2 A Comparison of General Partnerships and Limited Partnerships

Characteristic	General Partnership (UPA)	Limited Partnership (RULPA)
Creation	By agreement of two or more persons to carry on a business as co-owners for profit.	By agreement of two or more persons to carry on a business as co-owners for profit. Must include one or more general partners and one or more limited partners. Filing of a certificate with the secretary of state is required.
Sharing of Profits and Losses	By agreement. In the absence of agreement, profits are shared equally by the partners, and losses are shared in the same ratio as profits.	Profits are shared as required in the certificate agreement, and losses are shared likewise, up to the amount of the limited partners' capital contributions. In the absence of a provision in the certificate agreement, profits and losses are shared on the basis of percentages of capital contributions.
Liability	Unlimited personal liability of all partners.	Unlimited personal liability of all general partners; limited partners liable only to the extent of their capital contributions.
Capital Contribution	No minimum or mandatory amount; set by agreement.	Set by agreement.
Management	By agreement. In the absence of agreement, all partners have an equal voice.	Only the general partner (or the general partners). Limited partners have no voice or else are subject to liability as general partners (but only if a third party has reason to believe that the limited partner is a general partner). A limited partner may act as an agent or employee of the partnership and vote on amending the certificate or on the sale or dissolution of the partnership.
Duration	Terminated by agreement of the partners, but can continue to do business even when a partner dissociates from the partnership.	Terminated by agreement in the certificate or by retirement, death, or mental incompetence of a general partner in the absence of the right of the other general partners to continue the partnership. Death of a limited partner does not terminate the partnership, unless he or she is the only remaining limited partner.
Distribution of Assets on Liquidation— Order of Priorities	1. Payment of debts, including those owed to partner and nonpartner creditors. 2. Return of capital contributions and distribution of profit to partners.	1. Outside creditors and partner creditors. 2. Partners and former partners entitled to distributions of partnership assets. 3. Unless otherwise agreed, return of capital contributions and distribution of profit to partners.

Formation of a Limited Partnership

In contrast to the informal, private, and voluntary agreement that usually suffices for a traditional partnership, the formation of a limited partnership is a public and formal proceeding that must follow statutory requirements. Not only must a limited partnership have at least one general partner and one limited partner, but the partners must also sign a **certificate of limited partnership.**

Like *articles of incorporation* (see Chapter 39), this certificate must include certain information such as the name, mailing address, and capital contribution of each general and limited partner. The certificate must be filed with the designated state official—under the RULPA, the secretary of state. The certificate is usually open to public inspection.

Liabilities of Partners in a Limited Partnership

General partners, unlike limited partners, are personally liable to the partnership's creditors. Thus, at least one general partner is necessary in a limited partnership so that someone has personal liability. This policy can be circumvented in states that allow a corporation to be the general partner in a partnership. Because the corporation has limited liability by virtue of corporation statutes, if a corporation is the general partner, no one in the limited partnership has personal liability.

The liability of a limited partner, as mentioned, is limited to the capital that she or he contributes or agrees to contribute to the partnership [RULPA 502]. Limited partners enjoy this limited liability only so long as they do not participate in management [RULPA 303].

A limited partner who participates in management will be just as liable as a general partner to any creditor who transacts business with the limited partnership. Liability arises when the creditor believes, based on the limited partner's conduct, that the limited partner is a general partner [RULPA 303]. The extent of review and advisement that a limited partner can engage in before being exposed to liability is not always clear, though.

Rights and Duties in a Limited Partnership

With the exception of the right to participate in management, limited partners have essentially the same rights as general partners. Limited partners have a right of access to the partnership's books and to information regarding partnership business.

On dissolution of the partnership, limited partners are entitled to a return of their contributions in accordance with the partnership certificate [RULPA 201(a)(10)]. They can also assign their interests subject to the certificate [RULPA 702, 704]. In addition, limited partners can sue an outside party on behalf of the firm if the general partners with authority to do so have refused to file suit [RULPA 1001].

Dissociation and Dissolution

A general partner has the power to voluntarily dissociate, or withdraw, from a limited partnership unless the partnership agreement specifies otherwise. A limited partner theoretically can withdraw from the partnership by giving six months' notice unless the partnership agreement specifies a term, as most do. Also, some states have passed laws prohibiting the withdrawal of limited partners.

EVENTS THAT CAUSE DISSOCIATION In a limited partnership, a general partner's voluntary dissociation from the firm normally will lead to dissolution *unless* all partners agree to continue the business. Similarly, the bankruptcy, retirement, death, or mental incompetence of a general partner will cause the dissociation of that partner and the dissolution of the limited partnership unless the other members agree to continue the firm [RULPA 801].

Bankruptcy of a limited partner, however, does not dissolve the partnership unless it causes the bankruptcy of the firm. Death or an assignment of the interest of a limited partner does not dissolve a limited partnership [RULPA 702, 704, 705]. A limited partnership can be dissolved by court decree [RULPA 802].

DISTRIBUTION OF ASSETS On dissolution, creditors' claims, including those of partners who are creditors, take first priority. After that, partners and former partners receive unpaid distributions of partnership assets. Unless otherwise agreed, they are also entitled to a return of their contributions in the proportions in which the partners share in distributions [RULPA 804].

VALUATION OF ASSETS Disputes commonly arise about how the partnership's assets should be valued and distributed and whether the business should be sold. ▶ **Case in Point 37.16** Actor Kevin Costner was a limited partner in Midnight Star Enterprises, LP, which runs a casino, bar, and restaurant in South Dakota. There were two other limited partners, Carla and Francis Caneva, who owned a small percentage of the partnership (3.25 units each) and received salaries for managing its operations. Another company owned by Costner, Midnight Star Enterprises, Limited (MSEL), was the general partner. Costner thus controlled a majority of the partnership (93.5 units).

When communications broke down between the partners, MSEL asked a court to dissolve the partnership. MSEL's accountant determined that the firm's fair market value was $3.1 million. The Canevas presented evidence that a competitor would buy the business for $6.2 million. The Canevas wanted the court to force Costner to either buy the business for that price within ten days or sell it on the open market to the highest bidder. Ultimately, the state's highest court held in favor of Costner. A partner cannot force the sale of a limited partnership when the other partners want to continue the business. The court also accepted the $3.1 million buyout price of MSEL's accountant and ordered Costner to pay the Canevas the value of their 6.5 partnership units.[15] ◀

---

15. *In re Dissolution of Midnight Star Enterprises, LP,* 2006 SD 98, 724 N.W.2d 334 (N.D.Sup.Ct. 2006).

Limited Liability Limited Partnerships

A **limited liability limited partnership (LLLP)** is a type of limited partnership. An LLLP differs from a limited partnership in that a general partner in an LLLP has the same liability as a limited partner in a limited partnership. In other words, the liability of all partners is limited to the amount of their investments in the firm.

A few states provide expressly for LLLPs.[16] In states that do not provide for LLLPs but do allow for limited partnerships and limited liability partnerships, a limited partnership should probably still be able to register with the state as an LLLP.

---

16. See, for example, Colorado Revised Statutes Annotated Section 7-62-109. Other states that provide for LLLPs include Delaware, Florida, Georgia, Kentucky, Maryland, Nevada, Texas, and Virginia.

Reviewing: Partnerships and Limited Liability Partnerships

Grace Tarnavsky and her sons, Manny and Jason, bought a ranch known as the Cowboy Palace in March 2009, and the three verbally agreed to share the business for five years. Grace contributed 50 percent of the investment, and each son contributed 25 percent. Manny agreed to handle the livestock, and Jason agreed to handle the bookkeeping. The Tarnavskys took out joint loans and opened a joint bank account into which they deposited the ranch's proceeds and from which they made payments for property, cattle, equipment, and supplies. In September 2013, Manny severely injured his back while baling hay and became permanently unable to handle livestock. Manny therefore hired additional laborers to tend the livestock, causing the Cowboy Palace to incur significant debt. In September 2014, Al's Feed Barn filed a lawsuit against Jason to collect $32,400 in unpaid debts. Using the information presented in the chapter, answer the following questions.

1. Was this relationship a partnership for a term or a partnership at will?
2. Did Manny have the authority to hire additional laborers to work at the ranch after his injury? Why or why not?
3. Under the current UPA, can Al's Feed Barn bring an action against Jason individually for the Cowboy Palace's debt? Why or why not?
4. Suppose that after his back injury in 2013, Manny sent his mother and brother a notice indicating his intent to withdraw from the partnership. Can he still be held liable for the debt to Al's Feed Barn? Why or why not?

DEBATE THIS . . . *A partnership should automatically end when one partner dissociates from the firm.*

Terms and Concepts

articles of partnership 722
buyout price 729
buy-sell agreement 732
certificate of limited partnership 735
charging order 724
dissociation 728
dissolution 729
family limited liability
   partnership (FLLP) 734

general partner 734
goodwill 721
information return 722
joint and several liability 727
joint liability 727
limited liability limited
   partnership (LLLP) 737
limited liability partnership (LLP) 733

limited partner 734
limited partnership (LP) 734
partnership 721
partnership by estoppel 722
pass-through entity 721
winding up 729

ExamPrep

Issue Spotters

1. Darnell and Eliana are partners in D&E Designs, an architectural firm. When Darnell dies, his widow claims that as Darnell's heir, she is entitled to take his place as Eliana's partner or to receive a share of the firm's assets. Is she right? Why or why not? **(See page 728.)**

2. Finian and Gloria are partners in F&G Delivery Service. When business is slow, without Gloria's knowledge, Finian leases the delivery vehicles as moving vans. Because the vehicles would otherwise be sitting idle in a parking lot, can Finian keep the income resulting from the leasing of the delivery vehicles? Explain your answer. **(See page 726.)**

• Check your answers to the Issue Spotters against the answers provided in Appendix E at the end of this text.

Before the Test

Go to **www.cengagebrain.com**, enter the ISBN 9781285185248, and click on "Find" to locate this textbook's Web site. Then, click on "Access Now" under "Study Tools," and select Chapter 37 at the top. There, you will find a Practice Quiz that you can take to assess your mastery of the concepts in this chapter, as well as Flashcards and a Glossary of important terms.

Business Scenarios

37–1. Partnership Formation. Daniel is the owner of a chain of shoe stores. He hires Rubya to be the manager of a new store, which is to open in Grand Rapids, Michigan. Daniel, by written contract, agrees to pay Rubya a monthly salary and 20 percent of the profits. Without Daniel's knowledge, Rubya represents himself to Classen as Daniel's partner and shows Classen the agreement to share profits. Classen extends credit to Rubya. Rubya defaults. Discuss whether Classen can hold Daniel liable as a partner. **(See page 722.)**

37–2. Dissolution of a Limited Partnership. Dorinda, Luis, and Elizabeth form a limited partnership. Dorinda is a general partner, and Luis and Elizabeth are limited partners. Consider the separate events below, and discuss fully whether each event constitutes a dissolution of the limited partnership. **(See page 736.)**

(a) Luis assigns his partnership interest to Ashley.

(b) Elizabeth is petitioned into involuntary bankruptcy.

(c) Dorinda dies.

37–3. Distribution of Partnership Assets. Shawna and David formed a partnership. At the time of the partnership's formation, Shawna's capital contribution was $10,000, and David's was $15,000. Later, Shawna made a $10,000 loan to the partnership when it needed working capital. The partnership agreement provided that profits were to be shared with 40 percent for Shawna and 60 percent for David. The partnership was dissolved after David's death. At the end of the dissolution and the winding up of the partnership, the partnership's assets were $50,000, and the partnership's debts were $8,000. Discuss fully how the assets should be distributed. **(See page 731.)**

Business Case Problems

37–4. Limited Partnership. James Carpenter contracted with Austin Estates, LP, to buy property in Texas. Carpenter asked Sandra McBeth to invest in the deal. He admitted that a dispute had arisen with the city of Austin over water for the property, but he assured her that it would not be a significant obstacle. McBeth agreed to invest $800,000 to hold open the option to buy the property. She became a limited partner in StoneLake Ranch, LP. Carpenter acted as the firm's general partner. Despite his assurances to McBeth, the purchase was delayed due to the water dispute. Unable to complete the purchase in a timely manner, Carpenter paid the $800,000 to Austin Estates without notifying McBeth. Later, Carpenter and others—excluding McBeth—bought the property and sold it at a profit. McBeth filed a suit in a Texas state court against Carpenter. What is the nature of the fiduciary duty that a general partner owes a limited partner? Did Carpenter breach that duty in this case? Explain. [*McBeth v. Carpenter*, 565 F.3d 171 (5th Cir. 2009)] **(See page 734.)**

37–5. Partnership Dissolution. George Chaney and William Dickerson were partners in Bowen's Mill Landing, which purchased a large piece of land in the 1980s. The partners had planned to develop the property, but nothing was ever done. Chaney died in 1990, and his wife inherited his interest. When she died in 2004, her two sons, John and Dewey Lynch, inherited the half-interest in the partnership. Dickerson died in 1995, and his daughter, Billie Thompson, inherited his half-interest. In 2006, the Lynches filed a petition for partition, asking that a commission be appointed to make a fair division of the land, giving the Lynches half and Thompson half. In 2007, the commission reported on how to divide the land into two parts. Thompson objected that the land belonged to Bowen's Mill Landing and could not be divided. The trial court ordered Thompson to "effectuate the dissolution of any partnership entity and . . . to wind up the business and affairs of any partnership" so that the land could be divided. Thompson appealed. Can the court order the partnership to dissolve? Why or why not? [*Thompson v. Lynch*, 990 A.2d 432 (Sup.Ct.Del. 2010)] **(See page 729.)**

37–6. Fiduciary Duties of Partners. Karl Horvath, Hein Rüsen, and Carl Thomas formed a partnership, HRT Enterprises, to buy a manufacturing plant. Rüsen and Thomas leased the plant to their own company, Merkur Steel. Merkur then sublet the premises to other companies owned by Rüsen and Thomas. The rent that these companies paid to Merkur was higher than the rent that Merkur paid to HRT. Rüsen and Thomas did not tell Horvath about the subleases. Did Rüsen and Thomas breach their fiduciary duties to HRT and Horvath? Discuss. [*Horvath v. HRT Enterprises*, 489 Mich.App. 992, 800 N.W.2d 595 (2011)] **(See page 725.)**

37–7. BUSINESS CASE PROBLEM WITH SAMPLE ANSWER: Partnership Formation.

 Patricia Garcia and Bernardo Lucero were in a romantic relationship. While they were seeing each other, Garcia and Lucero acquired an electronics service center, paying $30,000 apiece. Two years later, they purchased an apartment complex. The property was deeded to Lucero, but neither Garcia nor Lucero made a down payment. The couple considered both properties to be owned "50/50," and they agreed to share profits, losses, and management rights. When the couple's romantic relationship ended, Garcia asked a court to declare that she had a partnership with Lucero. In court, Lucero argued that the couple did not have a written partnership agreement. Did they have a partnership? Why or why not? [*Garcia v. Lucero*, 366 S.W.3d 275 (Tex.App. 2012)] **(See page 722.)**

• For a sample answer to Problem 37–7, go to Appendix F at the end of this text.

37–8. Winding Up and Distribution of Assets. Dan and Lori Cole operated a Curves franchise exercise facility in Angola, Indiana, as a partnership. The firm leased commercial space from Flying Cat, LLC, for a renewable three-year term and renewed the lease for a second three-year term. But two years after the renewal, the Coles divorced. By the end of the second term, Flying Cat was owed more than $21,000 on the lease. Without telling the landlord about the divorce, Lori signed another extension. More rent went unpaid. Flying Cat obtained a judgment in an Indiana state court against the partnership for almost $50,000. Can Dan be held liable? Why or why not? [*Curves for Women Angola v. Flying Cat, LLC*, 983 N.E.2d 629 (Ind. App. 2013)] **(See page 731.)**

37–9. A QUESTION OF ETHICS: Wrongful Dissociation.

 Elliot Willensky and Beverly Moran formed a partnership to buy, renovate, and sell a house. Moran agreed to finance the effort, which was to cost no more than $60,000. Willensky agreed to oversee the work, which was to be done in six months. Willensky lived in the house during the renovation. As the project progressed, Willensky incurred excessive and unnecessary expenses, misappropriated funds for his personal use, did not pay bills on time, and did not keep Moran informed of the costs. More than a year later, the renovation was still not completed, and Willensky walked off the project. Moran completed the renovation, which ultimately cost $311,222, and sold the house. Moran then sued to dissolve the partnership and recover damages from Willensky for breach of contract and wrongful dissociation. [*Moran v. Willensky*, 395 S.W.3d 651 (Tenn.Ct.App. 2010)] **(See page 728.)**

(a) Moran alleged that Willensky had wrongfully dissociated from the partnership. When did this dissociation occur? Why was his dissociation wrongful?

(b) Which of Willensky's actions simply represent unethical behavior or bad management, and which constitute a breach of the agreement?

Legal Reasoning Group Activity

37–10. Liability of Partners. At least six months before the Summer Olympic Games in Atlanta, Georgia, Stafford Fontenot and four others agreed to sell Cajun food at the games and began making preparations. On May 19, the group (calling themselves "Prairie Cajun Seafood Catering of Louisiana") applied for a business license from the county health department. Later, Ted Norris sold a mobile kitchen to them for $40,000. They gave Norris an $8,000 check drawn on the "Prairie Cajun Seafood Catering of Louisiana" account and two promissory notes, one for $12,000 and the other for $20,000. The notes, which were dated June 12, listed only Fontenot "d/b/a Prairie Cajun Seafood" as the maker (*d/b/a* is an abbreviation for "doing business as").

On July 31, Fontenot and his friends signed a partnership agreement, which listed specific percentages of profits and losses. They drove the mobile kitchen to Atlanta, but business was "disastrous." When the notes were not paid, Norris filed a suit in a Louisiana state court against Fontenot, seeking payment. **(See page 727.)**

(a) The first group will discuss the elements of a partnership and determine whether a partnership exists among Fontenot and the others.

(b) The second group will determine who can be held liable on the notes and why.

CHAPTER 38

OTHER ORGANIZATIONAL FORMS FOR SMALL BUSINESSES

The U.S. Small Business Administration (SBA) reports that small businesses employ half of all private-sector employees in the country. In addition, small businesses generate more than half of the nation's gross domestic product, hire 43 percent of high-tech workers, and obtain a disproportionate number of patents. Nevertheless, more than half of small businesses fail within four years—in part, because of a lack of understanding of legal issues and how to respond to them.

We have already discussed sole proprietorships, partnerships, and several forms of limited partnerships in previous chapters. Here, we examine a relatively new form of business organization called the *limited liability company (LLC),* which has become the organizational form of choice among many small businesses.

In this chapter, we look in detail at the LLC and its advantages and disadvantages. We also discuss the operation and management options in an LLC.

Next, we consider a variety of other special business forms, including joint ventures, syndicates, joint stock companies, business trusts, and cooperatives. These business forms can be used by businesses of any size, but several of them are—like LLCs—especially attractive to small businesses. We conclude the chapter with a discussion of factors that anyone starting a small business should consider, including organizational forms, protection of intellectual property, and financing.

SECTION 1
THE LIMITED LIABILITY COMPANY

A **limited liability company (LLC)** is a hybrid that combines the limited liability aspects of a corporation and the tax advantages of a partnership. The LLC has been available for only a few decades, but it has become the preferred structure for many small businesses.

LLCs are governed by state statutes, which vary from state to state. In an attempt to create more uniformity, the National Conference of Commissioners on Uniform State Laws issued the Uniform Limited Liability Company Act (ULLCA). Less than one-fifth of the states have adopted it, though. Thus, the law governing LLCs remains far from uniform.

Some provisions are common to most state statutes, however, and we base our discussion of LLCs in this section on these common elements.

The Nature of the LLC

LLCs share many characteristics with corporations. Like corporations, LLCs must be formed and operated in compliance with state law. Like the shareholders of a corporation, the owners of an LLC, who are called **members,** enjoy limited liability [ULLCA 303].[1]

LIMITED LIABILITY OF MEMBERS Members of LLCs are shielded from personal liability in many situations, even sometimes when sued by employees of the firm. ▶ **Case in Point 38.1** Penny McFarland was the activities director at a retirement community in Virginia that was owned by an LLC. Her supervisor told her to take the residents outside for a walk when the temperature was 95 degrees. McFarland complained to the state health department and was fired

---

1. Members of an LLC can also bring derivative actions, which you will read about in Chapter 40, on behalf of the LLC [ULLCA 101]. As with a corporate shareholder's derivative suit, any damages recovered go to the LLC, not to the members personally.

from her job. She sued a number of managers and members of the LLC for wrongful discharge.

The court held that under Virginia state law, members, managers, and agents of an LLC are not responsible for its liabilities "solely" by virtue of their status. Only those who "have played a key role in contributing to the company's tortious conduct" can be part of a wrongful discharge claim. The court therefore dismissed the action against all but one defendant.[2] ◄

---

2. *McFarland v. Virginia Retirement Services of Chesterfield, LLC*, 477 F.Supp.2d 727 (2007).

LIABILITY UNDER THE ALTER-EGO THEORY Sometimes, when a corporation is deemed to be merely an "alter ego" of the shareholder-owner, a court will *pierce the corporate veil* and hold the shareholder-owner personally liable (see Chapter 39). A court may apply the alter-ego theory when a shareholder commingles personal and corporate funds or fails to observe required corporate formalities.

Whether the alter-ego theory should be applied to an LLC was at issue in the following case.

CASE ANALYSIS

Case 38.1   ORX Resources, Inc. v. MBW Exploration, LLC
Court of Appeal of Louisiana, Fourth Circuit, 32 So.3d 931 (2010).

IN THE LANGUAGE OF THE COURT
Charles R. *JONES,* Judge.

* * * *

On January 16, 2003, ORX [Resources, Inc.,] entered into the "Clovelly Purchase Agreement" with Coastline Oil & Gas, Inc. Pursuant to this Agreement, ORX purchased certain oil, gas and mineral leases/interests in a tract of land located in Lafourche Parish, known as the "Clovelly Prospect." ORX partnered with other entities, including MBW [Exploration, LLC], to share in the expense and potential profits of the venture to explore and develop the Clovelly Prospect. The partnering parties entered into a Joint Operating Agreement ("JOA") and the Clovelly Prospect Participation Agreement ("Participation Agreement"). Mr. [Mark] Washauer signed these documents in October of 2003 and December of 2004, respectively, on behalf of MBW, in his capacity as a "Managing Member." However, MBW did not come into existence until July of 2005, when its articles of organization were filed with the Louisiana Secretary of State.

The JOA provided that ORX was to serve as the "Operator" drilling a well within the Clovelly Prospect. It further provided that the nonoperating working interest partners, like MBW, would pay their proportionate share of the costs in exchange for a corresponding working interest ownership share in the Clovelly Prospect. The drilled well was governed by the Participation Agreement, which provided that MBW had a working interest in the Clovelly Prospect whereby MBW would share in 2.5% of the costs incurred, and would gain a proportionate share of the returns, if any, produced by the well.

Later, ORX submitted an Authorization for Expenditure ("AFE") to MBW for approval, which Mr. Washauer signed in his own name. Additionally, he paid MBW's participation fee with a check drawn from the account of another entity, MBW Properties, LLC.

In 2006, ORX, as the well Operator, began planning the Allain LeBreton Well No. 2 in the Clovelly Prospect, ("the Well"), which was the "initial well" called for in the Participation Agreement. * * * Mr. Washauer paid the full amount of

MBW's share of an ORX cash call invoice of $59,325 with a personal check.

The well proved to be unsuccessful, and was ultimately plugged. MBW's unpaid share of expenses for said project amounted to $84,220.01, for which ORX demanded payment via correspondence, but to no avail. As a result, ORX filed suit for breach of contract against both MBW and Mr. Washauer ("the Appellants").

* * * [The trial court—a state district court—determined that Washauer operated MBW as his alter ego and allowed ORX to pierce the veil of the LLC. The court granted summary judgment in favor of ORX, holding that Washauer and MBW were liable, jointly and severally, to ORX in the amount of $84,220.01.] The Appellants timely filed [an] appeal from this judgment.

* * * *

We first address whether the district court erred in ruling that the alter ego theory of the corporate veil piercing applied to Louisiana limited liability companies.

* * * *

The provisions of La. R.S. [Louisiana Revised Statutes]

CASE 38.1 CONTINUES ➤

CASE 38.1 CONTINUED

12:1320(D) provide for the piercing of an LLC's veil when the situation so warrants.

* * * *

* * * *Piercing the veil of an LLC is justified to prevent the use of the LLC form to defraud creditors.* Under our * * * review, we find that the district court did not err in determining that the alter ego theory of corporate veil piercing applies to a Louisiana limited liability company, under the facts of this case, where it appears that Mr. Washauer used MBW as a shell and tried to avoid paying a legitimate debt of the LLC. [Emphasis added.]

* * * *

The Louisiana Supreme Court has identified *five nonexclusive factors to be used in determining whether to apply the*

alter ego doctrine: [commingling of corporate and shareholder funds; failure to follow statutory formalities for incorporating and transacting corporate affairs; undercapitalization; failure to provide separate bank accounts and bookkeeping records; and failure to hold regular shareholder and director meetings]. [Emphasis added.]

* * * *

In applying [these] factors, * * * we find that Mr. Washauer's activities on behalf of MBW do merit the piercing of the veil of this LLC. Commingling of the LLC's funds occurred with the funds of Mr. Washauer and a separate company of his. This commingling occurred because MBW was undercapitalized and did not have a separate bank account to transact its own

affairs. Furthermore, at the time MBW began contracting with ORX, it was not yet recognized as an LLC by the Louisiana Secretary of State. Lastly, while LLCs are not bound by corporate laws to hold regular meetings, the fact that MBW has not had a meeting in over a year further evidences that Mr. Washauer was operating MBW at his leisure and direction. Thus, we find that the district court did not err in determining that MBW was being operated as the alter ego of Mr. Washauer under the [above-mentioned] factors, and therefore, he can be held personally liable jointly and solidarily [severally] with MBW.

For the foregoing reasons,* * * the judgment of the district court is affirmed * * * .

LEGAL REASONING QUESTIONS

1. One of the advantages of the LLC is that its members enjoy limited personal liability for the company's obligations. In view of this fact, does the possibility that a court may hold an LLC member personally liable for the LLC's debts reduce the utility of the LLC form of business organization? Explain.

2. What does *jointly* and *severally* mean in terms of liability? Would ORX prefer that Washauer and MBW be held personally liable jointly and severally or that Washauer alone be held personally liable? Explain.

3. How might members of LLCs avoid the liability to which Washauer was subject in this case?

4. MBW appears to have been a one-member LLC. If the firm had had more members, how might that have affected the result in this case?

OTHER SIMILARITIES TO CORPORATIONS Another similarity between corporations and LLCs is that LLCs are legal entities apart from their owners. As a legal person, the LLC can sue or be sued, enter into contracts, and hold title to property [ULLCA 201]. The terminology used to describe LLCs formed in other states or nations is also similar to that used in corporate law. For instance, an LLC formed in one state but doing business in another state is referred to in the second state as a *foreign LLC*.

The Formation of the LLC

LLCs are creatures of statute and thus must follow state statutory requirements. To form an LLC, **articles of organization** must be filed with a cen-

tral state agency—usually the secretary of state's office [ULLCA 202].[3]

CONTENTS OF THE ARTICLES Typically, the articles of organization must include the name of the business, its principal address, the name and address of a registered agent, the members' names, and how the LLC will be managed [ULLCA 203]. The business's name must include the words *Limited Liability Company* or the initials *LLC* [ULLCA 105(a)]. Although a majority of the states permit one-member LLCs, some states require at least two members.

---

3. In addition to requiring articles of organization to be filed, a few states require that a notice of the intention to form an LLC be published in a local newspaper.

PREFORMATION CONTRACTS Businesspersons sometimes enter into contracts on behalf of a business organization that is not yet formed. As you will read in Chapter 39, persons who are forming a corporation may enter into contracts during the process of incorporation but before the corporation becomes a legal entity. These contracts are referred to as *preincorporation contracts*. Once the corporation is formed and adopts the preincorporation contracts (by means of a *novation*, discussed in Chapter 18), it can enforce the contract terms.

In dealing with the preorganization contracts of LLCs, courts may apply the well-established principles of corporate law relating to preincorporation contracts. ▶ **Case in Point 38.2** 607 South Park, LLC, entered into an agreement to sell a hotel to 607 Park View Associates, Ltd., which then assigned the rights to the purchase to another company, 02 Development, LLC. At the time, 02 Development did not yet exist—it was legally created several months later. 607 South Park subsequently refused to sell the hotel to 02 Development, and 02 Development sued for breach of the purchase agreement.

A California appellate court ruled that LLCs should be treated the same as corporations with respect to preorganization contracts. Although 02 Development did not exist when the agreement was executed, once it came into existence, it could enforce any preorganization contract made on its behalf.[4] ◀

Jurisdictional Requirements

As we have seen, LLCs and corporations share several characteristics, but a significant difference between these organizational forms involves federal jurisdictional requirements. Under the federal jurisdiction statute, a corporation is deemed to be a citizen of the state where it is incorporated and maintains its principal place of business. The statute does not mention the state citizenship of partnerships, LLCs, and other unincorporated associations, but the courts have tended to regard these entities as citizens of every state of which their members are citizens.

The state citizenship of an LLC may come into play when a party sues the LLC based on diversity of citizenship. Remember from Chapter 2 that when parties to a lawsuit are from different states and the amount in controversy exceeds $75,000, a federal court can

exercise diversity jurisdiction. *Total* diversity of citizenship must exist, however.

▶ **Example 38.3** Jen Fong, a citizen of New York, wishes to bring a suit against Skycel, an LLC formed under the laws of Connecticut. One of Skycel's members also lives in New York. Fong will not be able to bring a suit against Skycel in federal court on the basis of diversity jurisdiction because the defendant LLC is also a citizen of New York. The same would be true if Fong was bringing a suit against multiple defendants and one of the defendants lived in New York. ◀

Advantages of the LLC

The LLC offers many advantages to businesspersons, which is why this form of business organization has become increasingly popular.

LIMITED LIABILITY A key advantage of the LLC is that the liability of members is limited to the amount of their investments. Although the LLC as an entity can be held liable for any loss or injury caused by the wrongful acts or omissions of its members, the members themselves generally are not personally liable.

FLEXIBILITY IN TAXATION Another advantage of the LLC is its flexibility in regard to taxation. An LLC that has *two or more members* can choose to be taxed as either a partnership or a corporation. As will be discussed in Chapter 39, a corporate entity must pay income taxes on its profits, and the shareholders pay personal income taxes on profits distributed as dividends. An LLC that wants to distribute profits to its members may prefer to be taxed as a partnership to avoid the "double taxation" that is characteristic of the corporate entity.

Unless an LLC indicates that it wishes to be taxed as a corporation, the Internal Revenue Service (IRS) automatically taxes it as a partnership. This means that the LLC, as an entity, pays no taxes. Rather, as in a partnership, profits are "passed through" the LLC to the members, who then personally pay taxes on the profits. If an LLC's members want to reinvest profits in the business rather than distribute the profits to members, however, they may prefer to be taxed as a corporation. Corporate income tax rates may be lower than personal tax rates. Part of the attractiveness of the LLC is this flexibility with respect to taxation.

An LLC that has only *one member* cannot be taxed as a partnership. For federal income tax purposes, one-member LLCs are automatically taxed as sole

---

4. *02 Development, LLC v. 607 South Park, LLC,* 159 Cal.App.4th 609, 71 Cal.Rptr.3d 608 (2008).

proprietorships unless they indicate that they wish to be taxed as corporations. With respect to state taxes, most states follow the IRS rules.

MANAGEMENT AND FOREIGN INVESTORS Another advantage of the LLC for businesspersons is the flexibility it offers in terms of business operations and management—as will be discussed shortly. Foreign investors are allowed to become LLC members, so organizing as an LLC can enable a business to attract investors from other countries.

Disadvantages of the LLC

The main disadvantage of the LLC is that state LLC statutes are not uniform. Therefore, businesses that operate in more than one state may not receive consistent treatment in these states.

Generally, most states apply to a foreign LLC (an LLC formed in another state) the law of the state where the LLC was formed. Difficulties can arise, though, when one state's court must interpret and apply another state's laws.

SECTION 2

LLC MANAGEMENT AND OPERATION

The members of an LLC have considerable flexibility in managing and operating the business. Here, we discuss management options, fiduciary duties owed, and the operating agreement and general operating procedures of LLCs.

Management of an LLC

Basically, LLC members have two options for managing the firm. It can be either a "member-managed" LLC or a "manager-managed" LLC. Most state LLC statutes and the ULLCA provide that unless the articles of organization specify otherwise, an LLC is assumed to be member managed [ULLCA 203(a)(6)].

In a *member-managed* LLC, all of the members participate in management, and decisions are made by majority vote [ULLCA 404(a)]. In a *manager-managed* LLC, the members designate a group of persons to manage the firm. The management group may consist of only members, both members and nonmembers, or only nonmembers.

Fiduciary Duties

Under the ULLCA, managers in a manager-managed LLC owe fiduciary duties (the duty of loyalty and the duty of care) to the LLC and its members [ULLCA 409(a), 409(h)]. (As you will read in Chapter 39, this same rule applies in corporate law—corporate directors and officers owe fiduciary duties to the corporation and its shareholders.) Because not all states have adopted the ULLCA, though, some state statutes provide that managers owe fiduciary duties only to the LLC and not to the LLC's members. Although to whom the duty is owed may seem insignificant at first glance, it can have a dramatic effect on the outcome of litigation.

In Alabama, where the following case arose, managers owe fiduciary duties to the LLC and to its members.

CASE 38.2

Polk v. Polk
Court of Civil Appeals of Alabama, 70 So.3d 363 (2011).

BACKGROUND AND FACTS Leslie Polk and his children, Yurii and Dusty Polk and Lezanne Proctor, formed Polk Plumbing, LLC, in Alabama. Leslie, Dusty, and Yurii performed commercial plumbing work, and Lezanne, an accountant, maintained the financial records and served as the office manager. After a couple of years, Yurii quit the firm. Eighteen months later, Leslie "fired" Dusty and Lezanne. He denied them access to the LLC's books and offices but continued to operate the business.

Dusty and Lezanne filed a suit in an Alabama state court against Leslie, claiming breach of fiduciary duty. The court submitted the claim to a jury with the instruction that in Alabama employment relationships are "at will" (see Chapter 34). The court also told the jury that it could not consider the plaintiffs' "firing" as part of their claim. The jury awarded Dusty and Lezanne one dollar each in damages. They appealed,

CASE 38.2 CONTINUED   arguing that the judge's instructions to the jury were prejudicial—that is, that the instructions had substantially affected the outcome of the trial.

 IN THE LANGUAGE OF THE COURT
MOORE, Judge.

* * * *

In this case, Dusty and Lezanne served as managers of the LLC. The LLC's Operating Agreement * * * provided that the Members may elect one or more of the Members to serve as Managers of the Company for the purpose of handling the day to day details of the Company. * * * The Managers shall serve for a period of one year or until their replacement or recall is voted by a majority of the Members.

Based on the evidence presented at trial showing that the parties continued to act as managers of the LLC after the first year of operation, the foregoing contractual provision guaranteed that Dusty and Lezanne would remain managers until replaced or recalled by a vote of the majority of the members. Hence, their employment as managers of the LLC was not at will and the trial court erred in instructing the jury that it was. [Emphasis added.]

The trial court further erred in not allowing the jury to consider the circumstances of Dusty and Lezanne's "firing" as part of their breach-of-fiduciary-duty claim. * * * The record contains no evidence indicating that a vote was ever held to recall or replace Dusty and Lezanne. Rather, as Leslie testified, he simply acted in disregard of the terms of the Operating Agreement and instead rested on his right as the patriarch of the family to "fire" Dusty and Lezanne for, in his opinion, not working enough. Hence, * * * Leslie did not have the authority under the Operating Agreement to terminate the management positions of Dusty and Lezanne in the manner in which he did.

* * * *

By failing to instruct the jury that it also could consider Leslie's "firing" of Dusty and Lezanne as evidence in support of their breach-of-fiduciary-duty claim, we conclude that the trial court probably injuriously affected substantial rights of Dusty and Lezanne.

* * * *

Had the jury properly considered all the evidence supporting their breach-of-fiduciary-duty claim, it might have concluded that a higher amount of compensatory damages and possibly even punitive damages should have been awarded to Dusty and Lezanne.

DECISION AND REMEDY *A state intermediate appellate court reversed the lower court's judgment on the claim for breach of fiduciary duty and remanded the case for a new trial. The lower court committed reversible error by instructing the jury that Dusty and Lezanne's employment as managers was at will and by failing to instruct the jury that it could consider their "firing" as evidence in support of their claim.*

WHAT IF THE FACTS WERE DIFFERENT? *Suppose that Leslie owned a majority of Polk Plumbing. Could his "firing" of Dusty and Lezanne still be considered as evidence of a breach of fiduciary duty? Explain.*

THE LEGAL ENVIRONMENT DIMENSION *Under what circumstances might the employment-at-will doctrine apply to the members of an LLC?*

The LLC Operating Agreement

The members of an LLC can decide how to operate the various aspects of the business by forming an **operating agreement** [ULLCA 103(a)]. In many states, an operating agreement is not required for an LLC to exist, and if there is one, it need not be in writing. Generally, though, LLC members should protect their interests by creating a written operating agreement.

Operating agreements typically contain provisions relating to the following areas:

1. Management and how future managers will be chosen or removed. (Although most LLC statutes are silent on this issue, the ULLCA provides that

members may choose and remove managers by majority vote [ULLCA 404(b)(3)].)

2. How profits will be divided.
3. How membership interests may be transferred.
4. Whether the dissociation of a member, such as by death or departure, will trigger dissolution of the LLC.
5. Whether formal members' meetings will be held.
6. How voting rights will be apportioned. (If the agreement does not cover voting, LLC statutes in most states provide that voting rights are apportioned according to each member's capital contributions.[5] Some states provide that, in the absence of an agreement to the contrary, each member has one vote.)

STATE STATUTES FILL IN GAPS If the agreement does not cover a topic, such as how profits will be divided, the state LLC statute will govern. Most LLC statutes provide that if the members have not specified how profits will be divided, they will be divided equally among the members.

PARTNERSHIP LAW MAY APPLY If a dispute arises and the state's LLC statute does not cover the issue, courts sometimes apply the principles of partnership law. ▶ **Case in Point 38.4** Clifford Kuhn, Jr., and Joseph Tumminelli formed Touch of Class Limousine Service as an LLC. They did not create a written operating agreement but orally agreed that Kuhn would provide the financial backing and that Tumminelli would manage the day-to-day operations. Tumminelli embezzled $283,000 from the company after cashing customers' checks at Quick Cash, Inc., a local check-cashing service.

Kuhn sued Tumminelli and Quick Cash to recover the embezzled funds. He argued that Quick Cash was liable because Tumminelli did not have the authority to cash the company's checks. The court, however, held that in the absence of a written operating agreement to the contrary, a member of an LLC, like a partner in a partnership, has the authority to cash a firm's checks. Therefore, Kuhn's claim against Quick Cash was dismissed.[6] ◀

---

5. In contrast, partners in a partnership generally have equal rights in management and equal voting rights unless they specify otherwise in their partnership agreement (see Chapter 37).
6. *Kuhn v. Tumminelli,* 366 N.J.Super. 431, 841 A.2d 496 (2004).

DISSOCIATION AND DISSOLUTION OF AN LLC

Recall from Chapter 37 that in a partnership, *dissociation* occurs when a partner ceases to be associated in the carrying on of the partnership business. The same concept applies to LLCs. A member of an LLC has the *power* to dissociate from the LLC at any time, but he or she may not have the *right* to dissociate.

Under the ULLCA, the events that trigger a member's dissociation from an LLC are similar to the events causing a partner to be dissociated under the Uniform Partnership Act (UPA). These include voluntary withdrawal, expulsion by other members or by court order, incompetence, and death. Generally, if a member dies or otherwise dissociates from an LLC, the other members may continue to carry on the LLC business, unless the operating agreement provides otherwise.

Effect of Dissociation

When a member dissociates from an LLC, he or she loses the right to participate in management and the right to act as an agent for the LLC. The member's duty of loyalty to the LLC also terminates, and the duty of care continues only with respect to events that occurred before dissociation. Generally, the dissociated member also has a right to have his or her interest in the LLC bought out by the other members. The LLC's operating agreement may contain provisions establishing a buyout price, but if it does not, the member's interest is usually purchased at a fair value. In states that have adopted the ULLCA, the LLC must purchase the interest at fair value within 120 days after the dissociation.

If the member's dissociation violates the LLC's operating agreement, it is considered legally wrongful, and the dissociated member can be held liable for damages caused by the dissociation. ▶ **Example 38.5** Chadwick and Barrow are members in an LLC. Chadwick manages the accounts, and Barrow, who has many connections in the community and is a skilled investor, brings in the business. If Barrow wrongfully dissociates from the LLC, the LLC's business will suffer, and Chadwick can hold Barrow liable for the loss of business resulting from her withdrawal. ◀

Dissolution

Regardless of whether a member's dissociation was wrongful or rightful, normally the dissociated member has no right to force the LLC to dissolve. The remaining members can opt either to continue or to dissolve the business.

Members can also stipulate in their operating agreement that certain events will cause dissolution, or they can agree that they have the power to dissolve the LLC by vote. As with partnerships, a court can order an LLC to be dissolved in certain circumstances. For instance, a court might order dissolution when the members have engaged in illegal or oppressive conduct, or when it is no longer feasible to carry on the business.

In the following case, the court had to decide whether an LLC could be dissolved because continuing the business was impracticable.

CASE 38.3

Venture Sales, LLC v. Perkins
Supreme Court of Mississippi, 86 So. 3d 910 (2012).

BACKGROUND AND FACTS   Walter Perkins, Gary Fordham, and David Thompson formed Venture Sales, LLC, to develop a subdivision in Petal, Mississippi. All three members contributed land and funds to Venture Sales, resulting in total holdings of 466 acres of land and about $158,000 in cash.

Perkins was an assistant coach for the Cleveland Browns, so he trusted Fordham and Thompson to develop the property. Over a decade later, however, Fordham and Thompson still had not done anything with the property, although they had developed at least two other subdivisions in the area. Fordham and Thompson said that they did not know when they could develop the property and that they had been unable to get the additional $8 million they needed to proceed. Fordham and Thompson suggested selling the property, but Perkins did not agree with the proposed listing price of $3.5 million. Perkins then sought a judicial dissolution of Venture Sales in Mississippi state court. The trial court ordered the company dissolved. Fordham, Thompson, and Venture Sales appealed.

 IN THE LANGUAGE OF THE COURT
WALLER, Chief Justice, for the Court.

* * * *

* * * [Under the Mississippi Code, an LLC may be dissolved if it] is not reasonably practicable to carry on the business in conformity with the certificate of formation or the limited liability company agreement * * * .

* * * *

While no definitive, widely accepted test or standard exists for determining "reasonable practicability," it is clear that *when a limited liability company is not meeting the economic purpose for which it was established, dissolution is appropriate. In making this determination, we must first look to the company's operating agreement to determine the purpose for which the company was formed.* [Emphasis added.]

Venture Sales' operating agreement states that the company's purpose is "to initially acquire, *develop and sale* [sic] *commercial and residential properties* near Petal, Forrest County, Mississippi." At trial, Fordham admitted that the company was formed for the purpose of acquiring and developing property. Yet, more than ten years after Venture Sales was formed with Perkins as a member, the property remains completely undeveloped. Fordham and Thompson have offered a number of reasons why development has been delayed to this point. [Emphasis in original.]

* * * *

Despite [the] alleged hindrances, Fordham and Thompson have, during this ten-year period, successfully formed two other LLCs and have developed at least two other subdivisions with around 200 houses, collectively, within twenty-five miles of the subject property. More importantly, though, Fordham and Thompson presented no evidence that Venture Sales would be able to develop the land as intended within the foreseeable future. When asked by the trial court when Venture Sales might be able to begin developing as it had planned,

CASE 38.3 CONTINUES ➡

CASE 38.3 CONTINUED Fordham could not say. Fordham and Thompson admitted that it would take around $8 million to "kick off" construction of the subdivision as planned, and the [trial court] found that Venture Sales was currently unable to get additional bank loans or other funding needed to begin development.

   * * * *

  Fordham and Thompson claim that Perkins has blocked Venture Sales from taking advantage of certain "business opportunities," such as selling the property at a reduced price of $3.5 million * * * . However, these "business opportunities" were merely ideas from Fordham about how to make use of the property. * * * As discussed above, they presented no evidence that Venture Sales could develop the property, which is the purpose for which the company was formed.

DECISION AND REMEDY *The Mississippi Supreme Court held that Venture Sales could be judicially dissolved. It therefore affirmed the decision of the trial court.*

THE LEGAL ENVIRONMENT DIMENSION *Would dissolution be appropriate if the parties had formed a partnership rather than an LLC? Explain your answer.*

MANAGERIAL IMPLICATIONS *To avoid the type of dispute in which the members of Venture Sales became embroiled, the managers of an LLC or other business organization should take care to act on the firm's "economic purpose" within a reasonable time. To ensure that they will be able to do so, the managers should draw up plans and determine the full cost of the project. They should also ascertain how the needed funds will be obtained. If bank loans or other funding will not be available, as occurred in this case, the LLC should require a higher level of contributions from its members to ensure that there will be sufficient funds to complete the project successfully.*

Winding Up

When an LLC is dissolved, any members who did not wrongfully dissociate may participate in the winding up process. To wind up the business, members must collect, liquidate, and distribute the LLC's assets.

  Members may preserve the assets for a reasonable time to optimize their return, and they continue to have the authority to perform reasonable acts in conjunction with winding up. In other words, the LLC will be bound by the reasonable acts of its members during the winding up process.

  Once all of the LLC's assets have been sold, the proceeds are distributed to pay off debts to creditors first (including debts owed to members who are creditors of the LLC). The members' capital contributions are returned next, and any remaining amounts are then distributed to members in equal shares or according to their operating agreement.

SECTION 4
SPECIAL BUSINESS FORMS

In addition to the LLC and the other traditional business forms discussed in this unit, several other forms can be used to organize a business. Many of these special business forms, such as joint ventures and syndicates, are particularly attractive to small businesses. For the most part, they are hybrid organizations—that is, they combine features of other organizational forms such as partnerships and corporations.

Joint Venture

In a **joint venture,** two or more persons or business entities combine their efforts or their property for a single transaction or project or a related series of transactions or projects. Unless otherwise agreed, joint venturers share profits and losses equally and have an equal voice in controlling the project. For instance, when several contractors combine their resources to build and sell houses in a single development, their relationship is a joint venture.

  Joint ventures range in size from very small activities to multimillion-dollar joint actions carried out by some of the world's largest corporations. Large organizations often form joint ventures with other enterprises to produce new products or services. ▶ **Example 38.6** Intel Corporation and Micron Technology, Inc., formed a joint venture to manufacture NAND flash memory. NAND is a data-storage chip widely used in digital cameras, cell phones, and portable music players. ◀

SIMILARITIES TO PARTNERSHIPS A joint venture resembles a partnership and is taxed like a partnership. For this reason, most courts apply the same principles to joint ventures as they apply to partnerships. Joint venturers owe each other the same fiduciary duties, including the duty of loyalty, that partners owe each other. Thus, if one of the venturers secretly buys land that was to be acquired by the joint venture, the other joint venturers may be awarded damages for the breach of loyalty.

Liability and Management Rights. A joint venturer can be held personally liable for the venture's debts (because joint venturers share profits and losses). Like partners, joint venturers have equal rights to manage the activities of the enterprise, but they can agree to give control of the operation to one of the members.

Authority to Enter Contracts. Joint venturers also have authority as agents to enter into contracts for the business that will bind the joint venture. ▶ **Case in Point 38.7** Murdo Cameron developed components for replicas of vintage P-51 Mustang planes. Cameron and Douglas Anderson agreed in writing to collaborate on the design and manufacture of two P-51s, one for each of them.

Without Cameron's knowledge, Anderson borrowed funds from SPW Associates, LLP, to finance the construction, using the first plane as security for the loan. After Anderson built one plane, he defaulted on the loan. SPW filed a lawsuit to obtain possession of the aircraft. The court ruled that Anderson and Cameron had entered into a joint venture and that the plane was the venture's property. Under partnership law, partners have the power as agents to bind the partnership. Because this principle applies to joint ventures, Anderson had the authority to grant SPW a security interest in the plane, and SPW was entitled to take possession of the plane.[7] ◀

DIFFERENCES FROM PARTNERSHIPS Joint ventures also differ from partnerships in several important ways. The members of a joint venture have less implied and apparent authority than the partners in a partnership. In part, this reduced authority is because a joint venture is typically created for a single project or series of transactions, whereas a partnership usually (though not always) involves an ongoing business. As

discussed in Chapter 37, each partner is treated as an agent of the other partners.

Because the activities of a joint venture are more limited than the business of a partnership, the members of a joint venture are presumed to have less power to bind their co-venturers. In *Case in Point 38.7*, for instance, if Anderson's loan agreement with SPW had not been directly related to the business of building vintage planes, the court might have concluded that Anderson lacked the authority to bind the joint venture. Also, unlike most partnerships, a joint venture normally terminates when the project or transaction for which it was formed is completed.

Syndicate

In a **syndicate,** or *investment group,* several individuals or firms join together to finance a particular project, such as the construction of a shopping center or the purchase of a professional basketball franchise. The form of such entities varies considerably. A syndicate may be organized as a corporation or as a general or limited partnership. In some instances, the members do not have a legally recognized business arrangement but merely purchase and own property jointly.

Joint Stock Company

A **joint stock company** is a true hybrid of a partnership and a corporation. It has many characteristics of a corporation in that (1) its ownership is represented by transferable shares of stock, (2) it is managed by directors and officers of the company or association, and (3) it can have a perpetual existence.

Most of its other features, however, are more characteristic of a partnership, and it generally is treated as a partnership. Like a partnership, a joint stock company is formed by agreement (not statute). Property usually is held in the names of the owners, who are called shareholders, and they have personal liability. In a joint stock company, however, shareholders are not considered to be agents of each other, as they would be in a true partnership.

Business Trust

A **business trust** is created by a written trust agreement that sets forth the interests of the beneficiaries and the obligations and powers of the trustees. The business trust form of organization was started in

---

7. *SPW Associates, LLP v. Anderson,* 2006 ND 159, 718 N.W.2d 580 (N.D.Sup.Ct. 2006).

Massachusetts in an attempt to obtain the limited liability advantage of corporate status. Legal ownership and management of the trust's property stay with one or more of the trustees, and the profits are distributed to the beneficiaries.

A business trust resembles a corporation in many respects. Beneficiaries of the trust, for instance, are not personally responsible for the trust's debts or obligations. In fact, in a number of states, business trusts must pay corporate taxes.

Cooperative

A **cooperative** is an association that is organized to provide an economic service to its members (or shareholders). It may or may not be incorporated. Most cooperatives are organized under state statutes for cooperatives, general business corporations, or LLCs.

The cooperative form of business is generally adopted by groups of individuals who wish to pool their resources to gain some advantage in the marketplace. *Consumer purchasing co-ops* are formed to obtain lower prices through quantity discounts. *Seller marketing co-ops* are formed to control the market and thereby enable members to sell their goods at higher prices. Co-ops range in size from small, local consumer cooperatives to national businesses such as Ace Hardware and Land O'Lakes, a well-known producer of dairy products.

INCORPORATED CO-OPS Generally, an incorporated cooperative will distribute dividends, or profits, to its owners on the basis of their transactions with the cooperative rather than on the basis of the amount of capital they contributed. Members of incorporated cooperatives have limited liability, as do shareholders of corporations and members of LLCs.

UNINCORPORATED CO-OPS Cooperatives that are not incorporated are often treated like partnerships. The members have joint liability for the cooperative's acts.

See *Concept Summary 38.1* below for a review of the types of special business forms discussed in this chapter.

SECTION 5
GENERAL CONSIDERATIONS FOR SMALL BUSINESS

In the earliest stages, a small business may operate as a sole proprietorship, which requires few legal formalities. The law considers all new, single-owner businesses to be sole proprietorships, unless the owner affirmatively adopts some other form.

Once business is under way, however, the sole proprietorship form may become problematic if additional investors are needed or the personal financial risks of the business become too great. The owner and any additional investors will then want to establish a more formal organization, such as a limited partnership (LP), a limited liability partnership (LLP), a limited liability company (LLC), or a corporation.

CONCEPT SUMMARY 38.1
Special Business Forms

CONCEPT	DESCRIPTION
Joint Venture	An organization created by two or more persons in contemplation of a limited activity or a single transaction; similar to a partnership in many respects.
Syndicate	An investment group that undertakes to finance a particular project; may be organized as a corporation or as a general or limited partnership.
Joint Stock Company	A business form similar to a corporation in some respects (transferable shares of stock, management by directors and officers, perpetual existence) but otherwise resembling a partnership.
Business Trust	A business form created by a written trust agreement that sets forth the interests of the beneficiaries and the obligations and powers of the trustee(s). A business trust is similar to a corporation in many respects. Beneficiaries are not personally liable for the debts or obligations of the business trust.
Cooperative	An association organized to provide an economic service, without profit, to its members. A cooperative can take the form of a corporation or a partnership.

Each business form has its own advantages and disadvantages. Factors to consider when choosing a business form include liability, taxation, continuity of life, and the legal formalities and costs associated with organizing the business. Small businesses also need to consider employment laws, applicable environmental or health regulations, licensing requirements, zoning codes, and intellectual property rights. Of course, they also need to protect their hard-earned profits from cyber thieves. See this chapter's *Managerial Strategy* feature below for a discussion of new developments in this area.

MANAGERIAL STRATEGY

Small-Business Owners Now Have Recourse When Cyber Thieves Empty Their Bank Accounts

Between 150 and 200 cyber attacks on business organizations occur every day. Most of these attacks are initiated by cyber thieves in other countries, especially China and Russia. Thirty percent of the attacks are aimed at small businesses (those with fewer than 250 employees).

Who Is Responsible for the Loss due to a Fraudulent Fund Transfer?

If cyber thieves cause you, an individual, to lose the funds in your bank account, usually your bank is responsible for the loss. The laws that protect individuals' bank accounts do not extend to small businesses, however. Nevertheless, some recent court decisions have allowed businesses to recover from their banks when their funds were fraudulently transferred.

In 2009, an employee at Experi-Metal, Inc., received an e-mail containing a link to a Web page with a Comerica Bank business connect form. Knowing that Comerica was the company's bank, the employee followed a further link and filled in the requested information. Experi-Metal had just been the victim of a phishing attack—the most common method used by cyber thieves to obtain the information needed for fraudulent fund transfers. Within minutes, cyber thieves transferred almost $2 million from Experi-Metal's account to bank accounts in China, Estonia, and Russia.

Experi-Metal sued Comerica, arguing, among other things, that the bank had not observed good faith when it accepted the online command for the wire transfers. Ultimately, the court found that the bank's employees had failed to meet reasonable commercial standards of fair dealing in not questioning the unusual size of the transfers and their destinations.[a]

A Small Business Wins an Appeal

Pacto Construction Company did its banking with Ocean Bank (later acquired by People's United Bank). In 2009, cyber thieves installed malware in Pacto's computers. The malware recorded the keystrokes of Pacto's employees, thereby enabling the thieves to obtain the answers to the security questions posed by Ocean Bank for wire transfers. Over a five-day period, Ocean Bank approved wire transfers from Pacto's account for hundreds of thousands of dollars. The funds were sent to numerous individuals, none of whom had ever done business with Pacto. Although the bank's high-risk alert system indicated that the transfers might be fraudulent, the bank continued to allow them. Pacto sued the bank to recover its lost funds, but a U.S. district court ruled against Pacto.

On appeal, however, the reviewing court agreed with Pacto that Ocean Bank had not monitored the transactions effectively and should have notified Pacto before allowing them to be completed. These failures and others "rendered Ocean Bank's security procedures commercially unreasonable."[b]

MANAGERIAL IMPLICATIONS

Small-business owners now have some recourse if cyber thieves steal funds from their bank accounts. Nonetheless, small-business owners are well advised to be aware of potential cyber threats when they use banks' security procedures. Even though precedent makes recovery of funds stolen by cyber thieves now possible, few small companies have the resources to pursue a lawsuit against their banks.

BUSINESS QUESTIONS

1. Might there be any repercussions against small businesses because of recent decisions in their favor in cases involving cyber theft?

2. Why is it so difficult for banks to recover funds stolen online from their small-business customers?

---

a. *Experi-Metal, Inc. v. Comerica Bank,* 2011 WL 2433383 (E.D.Mich. 2011).

b. *Pacto Construction Co. v. People's United Bank, d/b/a Ocean Bank,* 684 F.3d 197 (1st Cir. 2012).

Limitations on Liability

A key consideration in starting a business is whether the business form chosen will limit the owner's personal liability for business debts and obligations. If you form a limited liability entity, you normally can avoid personal liability if, say, a customer slips and breaks his ankle in your store, sues, and is awarded damages by a court. Although the business entity may be liable for damages, you and the other owners normally will not be personally liable beyond the extent of your contributions to the firm. Legal limited liability generally is necessary for those who wish to raise outside capital.

Corporate business forms offer limited liability to the shareholder-owners. In a traditional partnership, however, there is no limited liability. Each partner is personally liable for the debts and obligations of the partnership. In a limited partnership, the limited partners have limited liability, but there must be at least one general partner who remains personally liable for the partnership's obligations.

Today, all states permit businesspersons to conduct their business operations as LLCs, and most states provide for limited liability partnership (LLPs) (see Chapter 37). These increasingly popular business forms also offer the advantage of limited personal liability for business debts and obligations.

MAINTAIN INSURANCE Note that limited personal liability does not obviate the need to obtain insurance for significant business liability risks (see Chapter 50). Limited liability organizations protect only personal assets, and a substantial uninsured liability can bankrupt the business and cause the owners to lose their entire investments.

CONDUCT OF OWNERS Moreover, limited personal liability may be lost by contract. For instance, when an individual personally guarantees payment of a business loan, the individual is personally liable for the business's obligation. In addition, if a small-business owner fails to comply with the rules for a business form, such as by commingling personal and business funds, the business can lose its shield from personal liability (see the discussion of *piercing the corporate veil* in Chapter 39).

Tax Considerations

Taxes are another critical factor to be considered in choosing a small-business form. A sole proprietorship is not a separate legal entity, and the owner pays taxes on business income as an individual. All revenues are taxable, but business expenses can be deducted, so the owner is taxed only once on the business's profits.

All corporations must pay certain state and local taxes, but the key consideration involves corporate income taxes. As mentioned earlier, the corporate form entails *double taxation*. The company pays a corporate income tax on its profits, and the shareholder-owners also pay individual income tax on any distributions of the remaining profits that they receive from the corporation. Double taxation is limited to distributions of profits, though, so corporations are taxed only once on retained earnings. (See Chapter 39 for a complete discussion of corporate taxation).

Partnerships, LLCs, LLPs, and S corporations (see Chapter 39) avoid double taxation and provide for "pass-through" taxation—that is, profits are passed through to the partners, members, or owners and are taxed only on their individual returns, not at the business level.

Continuity of Life

Continuity of life is another concern in selecting a business form. A business should prepare for the possibility that an owner may die, resign, be expelled, or become incapacitated. Corporations have continuity of life—that is, they survive their owners—except in the unusual event that the corporate documents provide otherwise. Normally, on the death of a corporate shareholder-owner, that shareholder's ownership interest simply passes to his or her heirs.

In many states, a partnership will not terminate on the death or withdrawal of a partner, unless the partners have expressly provided otherwise. (In those states that have not adopted the most recent version of the Uniform Partnership Act, however, the death of a partner will automatically dissolve the partnership—see Chapter 37.) By definition, a sole proprietorship terminates with the death of the sole proprietor.

Legal Formality and Expense

Additionally, businesspersons need to consider the legal formalities and expenses involved in starting a business. The requirements and costs associated with forming and operating as a corporation can be considerable. The expense of establishing an LLP may also be significant. For these reasons, some individuals initially operate their businesses as sole proprietorships or traditional partnerships. By doing so, they run considerable financial risk because of the personal liability associated with each of these business forms. Start-up formalities and costs generally are less extensive for LLCs than for corporations or limited partnerships.

Requirements for All Business Forms

Any business, whatever its form, has to meet a variety of legal requirements, which typically relate to the following:

1. Business name registration.
2. Occupational licensing.
3. State tax registration (for instance, to obtain permits for collecting and remitting sales taxes).
4. Health and environmental permits.
5. Zoning and building codes.
6. Import/export regulations.

If the business has employees, the owner must also comply with a host of laws governing the workplace (see Chapters 34 and 35). Some small businesses that have only a few employees are exempted from certain laws. For instance, recent health-care legislation imposes a fine on employers that do not provide health insurance for their employees. Companies with fewer than fifty employees, however, are exempt from this requirement. Moreover, small businesses that help pay for employees' insurance are eligible for tax credits under the legislation.

Converting an LLC into a Corporation

If a small business begins as an LLC and thrives, the owners may wish to convert it to a corporation. By incorporating, the larger business can attract more outside capital with public offerings of its equity. Because the company will likely be retaining its earnings to fund future growth, rather than distributing them to the owners, it will not experience the double-taxation disadvantage of the corporate form. In addition, the corporate structure facilitates the use of equity-based employee incentive plans, such as grants of stock options, and a more expansive management structure.

If the LLC agreement does not provide otherwise, this conversion may require the unanimous consent of the members. The LLC must then file articles of dissolution with the state. The members will agree on a process to assign ownership interests in the new corporation by shareholdings. Then, they will go about forming the successor corporation.

Protecting Intellectual Property

Protecting rights in intellectual property is the central concern for some businesses. For instance, software companies depend on their copyrights and patents to protect their investments in the research and development required to create new programs.

Without copyright or patent protection, a competitor or a customer could simply copy the software. Laws governing rights in intellectual property were discussed in detail in Chapter 8. Here, we examine some aspects of intellectual property law that individuals should consider at the outset of any business venture.

TRADEMARKS Choosing a trademark or service mark and making sure that it can be protected under trademark law can be crucial to the success of a new business venture. A factor to consider in choosing a name for your business entity is whether you will use your business name as a trademark.

If you decide to use your business (trade) name as a trademark, then you need to follow the principles of trademark law. The general rule is that your trademark cannot be the same as another's mark or so similar that confusion might result.

Registration. Historically, the first business that actually used a trademark in the marketplace owned it. Today, for national trademark protection, the business must be the first to register the trademark with the U.S. Patent and Trademark Office (PTO) in Washington, D.C. First use still takes some precedence over federal registration, however.

Suppose that you have used a particular trademark for two years but have not registered the mark with the PTO. If another company then registers the same mark with the PTO, you will probably have the traditional common law right to continue using that mark, but only in the geographic region in which you have been operating. Outside that region, the federal registrant will own the mark.

Use of Symbols. After registering your trademark, you must protect it. If your mark is federally registered, you may use the symbol ® with your mark. This well-known symbol puts others on notice of your registration and helps to prevent trademark infringement.

Even if you have not registered, you can use the symbol ™ with your mark.

Five years after you initially register your mark, you should renew your registration with the PTO. Thereafter, you can renew at ten-year intervals. Filing for renewal informs the PTO that your mark is still in use and ensures that others cannot contest its validity.

TRADE SECRETS Much of the value of a business may lie in its trade secrets. As discussed in Chapter 8, trade secrets are business secrets that have value and might be appropriated by another company, such as a competitor. Trade secrets may include information concerning product development, production processes and techniques, or customer lists. Preserving the secrecy of the information is necessary for legal protections.

As a practical matter, trade secrets must be divulged to key employees. Thus, any business runs the risk that those employees might disclose the secrets to competitors—or even set up competing businesses themselves. Generally, protecting against the possibility that valuable trade secrets will fall into the hands of others, especially competitors, presents an ongoing challenge for businesses, including new enterprises.

Nondisclosure and Noncompete Agreements. To protect their trade secrets, companies may require employees who have access to trade secrets to agree in their employment contracts never to divulge those secrets. A small business may also choose to include a covenant not to compete in an employment contract. A noncompete covenant will help to protect against the possibility that a key employee will go to work for a competitor or set up a competing business—situations in which the company's trade secrets will likely be disclosed.

Misappropriation. As discussed in Chapter 8, trade secrets are protected under the common law.[8] Thus, a company can sue an individual or a firm that has misappropriated its trade secrets. ▶ **Example 38.8** Two engineers, Gavin LaRue and Kaoru Matsuo, develop new software for their company, Tanaka Enterprises, LLP, in Chicago. Six months later, LaRue and Matsuo leave to work at KCI Technologies, LLC, a New York firm, where they develop a similar product. Tanaka sues. In this situation, a court may find that LaRue and Matsuo misappropriated Tanaka's trade secrets. ◀

---

8. The theft of trade secrets is also a federal crime under the Economic Espionage Act of 1996 (see Chapter 10).

SECTION 6
FINANCIAL CAPITAL

Raising financial capital is critical to the growth of most small businesses. In the early days of a business, the sole proprietor or partners may be able to contribute sufficient capital, but if the business becomes successful, more funds may be needed. The owner or owners may want to raise capital from external sources to expand the business. One way to do this is to borrow funds. Another is to exchange equity (ownership rights) in the company in return for funds, either through private arrangements or through public stock offerings.

Loans

A small business may find it beneficial to obtain a bank loan because raising capital in this way allows the founder to retain full ownership and control of the business. Note, though, that the bank may place some restrictions on future business decisions as a condition of granting the loan.

In addition, bank loans may not be available for some businesses. Banks are usually reluctant to lend significant sums to businesses that are not yet established. Even if a bank is willing to make such a loan, the bank may require personal guaranty contracts from the owners, putting their personal assets at risk (see Chapter 29).

Loans with desirable terms may be available from the U.S. Small Business Administration (SBA). One SBA program provides loans of up to $25,000 to businesspersons who are women, low-income individuals, or members of minority groups. Be aware that the SBA requires business owners to put some of their own funds at risk in the business.

Some entrepreneurs have even used their credit cards to obtain initial capital. In addition, many states offer small-business grants to individuals starting a business.

Venture Capital

As will be discussed in Chapter 39, many new businesses raise needed capital by exchanging equity in the firm for venture capital. In other words, an outsider contributes funds in exchange for an ownership interest in the company. **Venture capitalists,** often organized into major firms, seek out promising enterprises and fund them in exchange for equity stakes.

Akin to venture capitalists are *angels*—that is, individuals who typically invest somewhat smaller sums in new businesses.

THE PROS AND CONS OF VENTURE CAPITAL FINANCING

In addition to providing needed financing, venture capitalists offer other advantages for businesses. Venture capitalists are often experienced managers who can provide invaluable assistance to entrepreneurs with respect to strategic business decisions, marketing, and important business contacts. Obtaining this assistance may be crucial to a new company's success.

The disadvantage is that a venture capitalist with a substantial equity stake will demand a corresponding degree of operational control over the company and a similar proportion of future profits.

REQUIRES A BUSINESS PLAN

To attract outside venture capital, you will need a **business plan** that describes the company, its products, and its anticipated future performance. The plan should be relatively concise (typically fewer than fifty pages). After considering your plan, a venture capitalist may decide to investigate your venture further. This step may require you to disclose trade secrets, and you should insist that the potential investor sign a confidentiality agreement. If all goes well, you will then negotiate the terms of financing. A key point to be negotiated is how much ownership and control the venture capitalist will receive in exchange for the capital contribution.

Crowdfunding

Although venture capitalists are a source of financing for young companies, there are not enough venture capitalists to fund all of the small businesses looking for help. Now, start-ups that are unable to attract venture capitalists have a new way to obtain funding—crowdfunding.

Crowdfunding is a cooperative activity in which people network and pool funds and other resources via the Internet to assist a cause or invest in a venture. Sometimes, crowdfunding is used to raise funds for charitable purposes, such as disaster relief, but increasingly it is being used to finance budding entrepreneurs. Several rock bands have financed tours in this way, and now ventures of all kinds are trying to raise funds through crowdfunding.

SPECIALIZED CROWDFUNDING SITES In a very short time, crowdfunding Web sites have proliferated. They offer partial ownership of start-ups in exchange for cash investments. At first, there were mostly general-purpose sites, such as Profounder.com and Startup Addict, but now the sites have become specialized. If you are interested only in new mobile apps, for example, you can go to the Apps Funder (**www.appsfunder.com**).

As you might imagine, many of the apps are games, but this site also has a serious side. For instance, one new app that was funded involves sharing music scores. Another site, NewJelly (**www.newjelly.com**), raises funds for "dream" projects for artists and filmmakers.

LESS REGULATION ENCOURAGES CROWDFUNDING Crowdfunding has taken off in many other countries, including France and Germany. Other countries' investor protection laws and regulations are often less stringent than U.S. laws, so many future crowdfunding sites are likely to be based abroad.

In 2012, President Barack Obama signed the JOBS Act (the acronym stands for "Jump-start Our Business Start-ups"), which relieved some of the regulatory burdens that you will read about in Chapter 42. Before this legislation, start-ups could look for financing only from investors who were "accredited," meaning that they had investment experience and a high net worth. If companies sought investment funds from the general public, they had to meet expensive and lengthy disclosure requirements. Under the new legislation, investing in start-ups has become more accessible to so-called nonaccredited investors.

Reviewing: Other Organizational Forms for Small Businesses

The city of Papagos, Arizona, had a deteriorating bridge in need of repair on a prominent public roadway. The city posted notices seeking proposals for an artistic bridge design and reconstruction. Davidson Masonry, LLC, which was owned and managed by Carl Davidson and his wife, Marilyn Rowe, decided to submit a bid to create a decorative concrete structure that incorporated artistic metalwork.

Continued

They contacted Shana Lafayette, a local sculptor who specialized in large-scale metal creations, to help them design the bridge. The city selected their bridge design and awarded them the contract for a commission of $184,000. Davidson Masonry and Lafayette then entered into an agreement to work together on the bridge project. Davidson Masonry agreed to install and pay for concrete and structural work, and Lafayette agreed to install the metalwork at her expense. They agreed that overall profits would be split, with 25 percent going to Lafayette and 75 percent going to Davidson Masonry. Lafayette designed numerous metal sculptures of trout that were incorporated into colorful decorative concrete forms designed by Rowe, while Davidson performed the structural engineering. The group worked together successfully until the completion of the project. Using the information presented in the chapter, answer the following questions.

1. Would Davidson Masonry automatically be taxed as a partnership or a corporation?
2. Is Davidson Masonry member managed or manager managed?
3. When Davidson Masonry and Lafayette entered an agreement to work together, what kind of special business form was created? Explain.
4. Suppose that during construction, Lafayette had entered into an agreement to rent space in a warehouse that was close to the bridge so that she could work on her sculptures near the site where they would eventually be installed. She entered into the contract without the knowledge or consent of Davidson Masonry. In this situation, would a court be likely to hold that Davidson Masonry was bound by the contract that Lafayette entered? Why or why not?

DEBATE THIS . . . *Because LLCs are essentially just partnerships with limited liability for members, all partnership laws should apply.*

Terms and Concepts

articles of organization 742	crowdfunding 755	member 740
business plan 755	joint stock company 749	operating agreement 745
business trust 749	joint venture 748	syndicate 749
cooperative 750	limited liability company (LLC) 740	venture capitalist 754

ExamPrep

Issue Spotters

1. Gabriel, Harris, and Ida are members of Jeweled Watches, LLC. What are their options with respect to the management of their firm? **(See page 744.)**

2. Greener Delivery Company and Hiway Trucking, Inc., form a business trust. Insta Equipment Company and Jiffy Supply Corporation form a joint stock company. Kwik Mart, Inc., and Luscious Produce, Inc., form an incorporated cooperative. What do these forms of business organization have in common? **(See page 749.)**

- **Check your answers to the Issue Spotters against the answers provided in Appendix E at the end of this text.**

Before the Test

Go to **www.cengagebrain.com**, enter the ISBN 9781285185248, and click on "Find" to locate this textbook's Web site. Then, click on "Access Now" under "Study Tools," and select Chapter 38 at the top. There, you will find a Practice Quiz that you can take to assess your mastery of the concepts in this chapter, as well as Flashcards and a Glossary of important terms.

Business Scenarios

38–1. Limited Liability Companies. John, Lesa, and Tabir form a limited liability company. John contributes 60 percent of the capital, and Lesa and Tabir each contribute 20 percent. Nothing is decided about how profits will be divided. John assumes that he will be entitled to 60 percent of the profits, in accordance with his contribution. Lesa and Tabir, however, assume that the profits will be divided equally. A dispute over the profits arises, and ultimately a court has to decide the issue. What law will the court apply? In most states, what will result? How could this dispute have been avoided in the first place? Discuss fully. **(See page 742.)**

38–2. Special Business Forms. Bateson Corp. is considering entering into two contracts—one with a joint stock company that distributes home products east of the Mississippi River and the other with a business trust formed by a number of sole proprietors who are sellers of home products on the West Coast. Both contracts will require Bateson to make large capital outlays in order to supply the businesses with restaurant equipment. In both business organizations, at least two shareholders or beneficiaries are personally wealthy, but both organizations have limited financial resources. The owner-managers of Bateson are not familiar with either form of business organization. Because each form resembles a corporation, they are concerned about potential limits on liability in the event that either business organization breaches the contract by failing to pay for the equipment. Discuss fully Bateson's concern. **(See page 749.)**

Business Case Problems

38–3. Joint Venture. Holiday Isle Resort & Marina, Inc., operated four restaurants, five bars, and various food kiosks at its resort in Islamorada, Florida. Holiday entered into a "joint-venture agreement" with Rip Tosun to operate a fifth restaurant called "Rip's—A Place for Ribs." The agreement gave Tosun authority over the employees and "full authority as to the conduct of the business." It also prohibited Tosun from competing with Rip's without Holiday's approval but did not prevent Holiday from competing. Later, Tosun sold half of his interest in Rip's to Thomas Hallock. Soon, Tosun and Holiday opened the Olde Florida Steakhouse next to Rip's. Holiday stopped serving breakfast at Rip's and diverted employees and equipment from Rip's to the Steakhouse, which then started offering breakfast. Hallock filed a suit in a Florida state court against Holiday. Did Holiday breach the joint-venture agreement? Did it breach the duties that joint venturers owe each other? Explain. [*Hallock v. Holiday Isle Resort & Marina, Inc.*, 4 So.3d 17 (Fla.App. 3 Dist. 2009)] **(See page 748.)**

38–4. Limited Liability Companies. Coco Investments, LLC, and other investors participated in a condominium conversion project to be managed by Zamir Manager River Terrace, LLC. The participants entered into a new LLC agreement for the project. The investors subsequently complained that Zamir had failed to disclose its plans for dramatic changes involving higher-than-expected construction costs and delays, had failed to provide financial information, and had restructured loans in a manner that allowed Zamir representatives to avoid personal liability. The investors sued Zamir on various grounds, including breach of contract and breach of fiduciary duty. Zamir moved for summary judgment. How should the court rule? Explain. [*Coco Investments, LLC v. Zamir Manager River Terrace, LLC*, 26 Misc.3d 1231 (N.Y.Sup. 2010)] **(See page 744.)**

38–5. LLC Dissolution. Walter Van Houten and John King formed 1545 Ocean Avenue, LLC, with each managing 50 percent of the business. Its purpose was to renovate an existing building and construct a new commercial building. Van Houten and King quarreled over many aspects of the work on the properties. King claimed that Van Houten paid the contractors too much for the work performed. As the projects neared completion, King demanded that the LLC be dissolved and that Van Houten agree to a buyout. Because the parties could not agree on a buyout, King sued for dissolution. The trial court enjoined (prevented) further work on the projects until the dispute was settled. As the ground for dissolution, King cited the fights over management decisions. There was no claim of fraud or frustration of purpose. The trial court ordered that the LLC be dissolved, and Van Houten appealed. Should either of the owners be forced to dissolve the LLC before the completion of its purpose—that is, before the building projects are finished? Explain. [*In re 1545 Ocean Avenue, LLC*, 893 N.Y.S.2d 590 (N.Y.A.D. 2 Dept. 2010)] **(See page 746.)**

38–6. BUSINESS CASE PROBLEM WITH SAMPLE ANSWER: LLC Operation.

 After Hurricane Katrina, James Williford, Patricia Mosser, Marquetta Smith, and Michael Floyd formed Bluewater Logistics, LLC, to bid on construction contracts. Under Mississippi law, every member of a member-managed LLC is entitled to participate in managing the business. The operating agreement provided for a "super majority" 75 percent vote to remove a member "under

any other circumstances that would jeopardize the company status" as a contractor. After Bluewater had completed more than $5 million in con- tracts, Smith told Williford that she, Mosser, and Floyd were exercising their "super majority" vote to fire him. No reason was provided. Williford sued Bluewater and the other members. Did Smith, Mosser, and Floyd breach the state LLC statute, their fiduciary duties, or the Bluewater operating agreements? Discuss. [Bluewater Logistics, LLC v. Williford, 55 So.3d 148 (Miss. 2011)] **(See page 744.)**

• **For a sample answer to Problem 38–6, go to Appendix F at the end of this text.**

38–7. Jurisdictional Requirements. Fadal Machining Centers, LLC, and MAG Industrial Automation Centers, LLC, sued a New Jersey–based corporation, Mid-Atlantic CNC, Inc., in federal district court. Ten percent of MAG was owned by SP MAG Holdings, a Delaware LLC. SP MAG had six members, including a Delaware limited partnership called Silver Point Capital Fund and a Delaware LLC called SPCP Group III. In turn, Silver Point and SPCP Group had a com- mon member, Robert O'Shea, who was a New Jersey citizen. Assuming that the amount in controversy exceeds $75,000, does the district court have diversity jurisdiction? Why or why not? [*Fadal Machining Centers, LLC v. Mid-Atlantic CNC, Inc.,* 2012 WL 8669 (9th Cir. 2012)] **(See page 743.)**

38–8. A QUESTION OF ETHICS: Limited Liability Companies.

Blushing Brides, LLC, a publisher of wedding planning magazines in Columbus, Ohio, opened an account with Gray Printing Co. in July 2000. On behalf of Blushing Brides, Louis Zacks, the firm's member-manager, signed a credit agreement that identified the firm as the "purchaser" and required payment within thirty days. Despite the agreement, Blushing Brides typically took up to six months to pay the full amount for its orders. Gray printed and shipped 10,000 copies of a fall/winter 2001 issue for Blushing Brides but had not been paid when the firm ordered 15,000 copies of a spring/summer 2002 issue. Gray refused to print the new order without an assurance of payment. On May 22, Zacks signed a promissory note payable to Gray within thirty days for $14,778, plus interest at 6 percent per year. Gray printed the new order but by October had been paid only $7,500. Gray filed a suit in an Ohio state court against Blushing Brides and Zacks to collect the balance. [Gray Printing Co. v. Blushing Brides, LLC, 2006 WL 832587 (Ohio App. 2006)] **(See page 744.)**

(a) Under what circumstances is a member of an LLC liable for the firm's debts? In this case, is Zacks personally liable under the credit agreement for the unpaid amount on Blushing Brides' account? Did Zacks's promissory note affect the parties' liability on the account? Explain.

(b) Should a member of an LLC assume an ethical responsibility to meet the obligations of the firm? Discuss.

(c) Gray shipped only 10,000 copies of the spring/summer 2002 issue of Blushing Brides' magazine, waiting for the publisher to identify a destination for the other 5,000 copies. The magazine had a retail price of $4.50 per copy. Did Gray have a legal or ethical duty to "mitigate the damages" by attempting to sell or otherwise distribute these copies itself? Why or why not?

38–9. SPECIAL CASE ANALYSIS:
Limited Liability Companies.

Go to Case Analysis Case 38.1, *ORX Resources, Inc. v. MBW Exploration, LLC,* on pages 741 and 742. Read the excerpt and answer the following questions.

(a) **Issue:** What was the main issue in this case?

(b) **Rule of Law:** What rule of law did the court apply?

(c) **Applying the Rule of Law:** How did the court apply the rule of law to the facts of this case?

(d) **Conclusion:** What was the court's conclusion?

Legal Reasoning Group Activity

38–10. Fiduciary Duties in LLCs. Newbury Properties Group owns, manages, and develops real property. Jerry Stoker and the Stoker Group, Inc. (the Stokers), also develop real property. Newbury entered into agreements with the Stokers concerning a large tract of property in Georgia. The parties formed Bellemare, LLC, to develop various parcels of the tract for residential purposes. The operating agreement of Bellemare indicated that "no Member shall be accountable to the LLC or to any other Member with respect to any other business or activity even if the business or activity competes with the LLC's business." Later, when the Newbury group contracted with other parties to develop parcels within the tract in competition with Bellemare, LLC, the Stokers sued, alleging breach of fiduciary duty. **(See page 744.)**

(a) The first group will discuss and outline the fiduciary duties that the members of an LLC owe to each other.

(b) The second group will determine whether the terms of an operating agreement can alter these fiduciary duties.

(c) The last group will decide in whose favor the court should rule in this situation.

CHAPTER 39

CORPORATE FORMATION AND FINANCING

The corporation is a creature of statute. A corporation is an artificial being, existing only in law and neither tangible nor visible. Its existence generally depends on state law, although some corporations, especially public organizations, are created under federal law. Each state has its own body of corporate law, and these laws are not entirely uniform.

The Model Business Corporation Act (MBCA) is a codification of modern corporation law that has been influential in shaping state corporation statutes. Today, the majority of state statutes are guided by the most recent version of the MBCA, often referred to as the Revised Model Business Corporation Act (RMBCA).

Keep in mind, however, that there is considerable variation among the laws of states that have used the MBCA or the RMBCA as a basis for their statutes. In addition, several states do not follow either act. Consequently, individual state corporation laws should be relied on to determine corporate law rather than the MBCA or RMBCA.

THE NATURE AND CLASSIFICATION OF CORPORATIONS

A corporation is a legal entity created and recognized by state law. This business entity can have one or more owners (called shareholders), and it operates under a name distinct from the names of its owners. The owners may be individuals, or *natural persons* (as opposed to the artificial *legal person* of the corporation), or other businesses. Although the corporation substitutes itself for its shareholders when conducting corporate business and incurring liability, its authority to act and the liability for its actions are separate and apart from the individuals who own it.

A corporation is recognized as a "person," and it enjoys many of the same rights and privileges under state and federal law that U.S. citizens enjoy. For instance, corporations possess the same right of access to the courts as citizens and can sue or be sued. The constitutional guarantees of due process, free speech, and freedom from unreasonable searches and seizures also apply to corporations.

Corporate Personnel

In a corporation, the responsibility for the overall management of the firm is entrusted to a *board of directors,* whose members are elected by the shareholders. The board of directors makes the policy decisions and hires *corporate officers* and other employees to run the daily business operations of the corporation.

When an individual purchases a share of stock in a corporation, that person becomes a shareholder and an owner of the corporation. Unlike the partners in a partnership, the body of shareholders can change constantly without affecting the continued existence of the corporation.

A shareholder can sue the corporation, and the corporation can sue a shareholder. Additionally, under certain circumstances, a shareholder can sue on behalf of a corporation. The rights and duties of corporate directors, officers, and shareholders will be examined in Chapter 40.

The Limited Liability of Shareholders

One of the key advantages of the corporate form is the limited liability of its owners. Normally, corporate shareholders are not personally liable for the obligations of the corporation beyond the extent of their investments.

In certain limited situations, however, a court can *pierce the corporate veil* (see page 771) and impose liability on shareholders for the corporation's obligations. Additionally, creditors often will not extend credit to small companies unless the shareholders assume personal liability, as guarantors, for corporate obligations.

Corporate Earnings and Taxation

When a corporation earns profits, it can either pass them on to shareholders in the form of **dividends** or retain them as profits. These **retained earnings,** if invested properly, will yield higher corporate profits in the future and thus cause the price of the company's stock to rise. Individual shareholders can then reap the benefits of these retained earnings in the capital gains that they receive when they sell their stock.

CORPORATE TAXATION Whether a corporation retains its profits or passes them on to the shareholders as dividends, those profits are subject to income tax by various levels of government. Failure to pay taxes can lead to severe consequences. The state can suspend the entity's corporate status until the taxes are paid or even dissolve the corporation for failing to pay taxes. (Businesses today, including corporations, may also be required to collect state sales taxes on goods or services sold via the Internet, as discussed in the *Insight into E-Commerce* feature in Chapter 20.)

Another important aspect of corporate taxation is that corporate profits can be subject to double taxation. The company pays tax on its profits. Then, if the profits are passed on to the shareholders as dividends, the shareholders must also pay income tax on them (unless the dividends represent distributions of capital). The corporation normally does not receive a tax deduction for dividends it distributes. This double-taxation feature is one of the major disadvantages of the corporate form.

HOLDING COMPANIES Some U.S. corporations use holding companies to reduce or defer their U.S. income taxes. At its simplest, a **holding company** (sometimes referred to as a *parent company*) is a company whose business activity consists of holding shares in another company. Typically, the holding company is established in a low-tax or no-tax offshore jurisdiction, such as the Cayman Islands, Dubai, Hong Kong, Luxembourg, Monaco, or Panama.

Sometimes, a U.S. corporation sets up a holding company in a low-tax offshore environment and then transfers its cash, bonds, stocks, and other investments to the holding company. In general, any profits received by the holding company on these investments are taxed at the rate of the offshore jurisdiction where the company is registered. In other words, holding company profits are not taxed at the rates applicable to the parent company or its shareholders in their country of residence. Thus, deposits of cash, for instance, may earn interest that is taxed at only a minimal rate.

Once the profits are brought "onshore," though, they are taxed at the federal corporate income tax rate, and any payments received by the shareholders are also taxable at the full U.S. rates.

Tort Liability

A corporation is liable for the torts committed by its agents or officers within the course and scope of their employment. This principle applies to a corporation exactly as it applies to the ordinary agency relationships discussed in Chapter 33. It follows the doctrine of *respondeat superior.*

The following case arose from a fraudulent scheme perpetrated by the officer of an investment firm through a separate investment fund that the officer controlled and managed. When investors in the fund filed a suit to recover the funds they had lost, the court had to determine whether the corporate employer of the officer could be liable for his actions.

CASE ANALYSIS

Case 39.1   Belmont v. MB Investment Partners, Inc.
United States Court of Appeals, Third Circuit, 708 F.3d 470 (2013).

IN THE LANGUAGE OF THE COURT
JORDAN, Circuit Judge.
* * * *

[Mark] Bloom formed North Hills [L.P.] in 1997, as an enhanced stock index fund based on various stock indices. Bloom was the sole principal and managing member of North Hills Management, LLC, the general partner of North Hills, and he had sole authority over the selection of the

CASE 39.1 CONTINUED

fund's investments. * * * Between 2001 and 2007, Bloom raised approximately $30 million from 40 to 50 investors for the North Hills fund. He claimed that North Hills consistently generated investment returns of 10–15 percent per year without significant risk.

In fact, however, North Hills was a Ponzi scheme that Bloom used to finance his lavish personal lifestyle, and, over time, he diverted at least $20 million from North Hills for his own personal use. Bloom used those funds to acquire multiple apartments and homes, furnishings, luxury cars and boats, and jewelry, and to fund parties and travel.

* * * *

Bloom operated North Hills the entire time that he was an executive of [MB Investment Partners, Inc.] He made no attempt, while working at MB, to conceal his activities related to North Hills. Investments in North Hills were administered by Bloom and other MB personnel, using MB's offices, computers, filing facilities, and office equipment. MB support staff sometimes carried out tasks related to North Hills.

MB officers and directors were aware that Bloom was operating North Hills while he was also working as an investment adviser at MB.

* * * During the period of the North Hills fraud, MB did not have in place basic compliance procedures employed throughout the investment advising industry to identify and prevent fraud and self-dealing by MB employees and affiliates. Compliance weaknesses permitted Bloom to avoid required disclosures to MB about North Hills as a personal investment vehicle. *MB officers and directors failed to make basic inquiries about Bloom's operation of North Hills, and did not collect any information on North Hills or monitor sales of investments in North Hills to MB's own customers.* [Emphasis added.]

* * * *

* * * In 2008, * * * two large investors in North Hills requested a full redemption of their investments. By that time, most of the money that had been invested in North Hills was gone * * * . [Bloom] was arrested on February 25, 2009, and he was terminated by MB that same day.

* * * *

The Investors filed their * * * Complaint in this action on October 28, 2009 * * * , alleging * * * fraud * * * on the part of Bloom * * * and MB.

* * * *

* * * On January 5, 2012, the District Court granted summary judgment to [MB]. * * * On February 17, 2012, the Court entered a default judgment against Bloom and in favor of the Investors in the amount of approximately $5.7 million.

* * * This timely appeal followed.

* * * *

* * * Bloom's violations * * * are beyond dispute, and the Investors argue that those violations may be imputed to MB as his employer.

* * * *The fraud of an officer of a corporation is imputed to the corporation when the officer's fraudulent contact was (1) in the course of his employment, and (2) for the benefit of the corporation.* This is true even if the officer's conduct was unauthorized, effected for his own benefit but clothed with apparent authority of the corporation, or contrary to instructions. The underlying reason is that a corporation can speak and act only through its agents and so must be accountable for any acts committed by one of its agents within his actual or apparent scope of authority and while transacting corporate business. [Emphasis added.]

* * * *

* * * We therefore conclude that imputation may be appropriate in this case, if the Investors can prove that the manner in which Bloom marketed North Hills to them while he was working for MB, and the apparent benefit to MB, made it appear that he marketed North Hills within the scope of his authority as a senior executive of MB.

* * * *

For the foregoing reasons, we * * * will vacate the grant of summary judgment to MB * * * , and we will remand this case for a trial with respect to those claims against MB.

LEGAL REASONING QUESTIONS

1. What is the imputation doctrine? What public-policy reasons support imputing the fraud of a corporate officer to the corporation?

2. What circumstances in this case suggest that MB should be held liable for Bloom's fraud?

3. What conditions did the court place on the application of the imputation doctrine in this case?

4. MB, which was already in financial distress, had to cease operations as a result of Bloom's fraud. How might MB have discovered the fraud before it grew so large as to have such dire effects?

Criminal Acts

Under modern criminal law (see Chapter 10), a corporation may also be held liable for the criminal acts of its agents and employees, provided the punishment is one that can be applied to the corporation. Although corporations cannot be imprisoned, they can be fined. (Of course, corporate directors and officers can be imprisoned, and some have been in recent years.) In addition, under sentencing guidelines for crimes committed by corporate employees (white-collar crimes), corporate lawbreakers can face fines amounting to hundreds of millions of dollars.[1]

▶ **Case in Point 39.1** Brian Gauthier drove a dump truck for Angelo Todesca Corporation. The truck was missing its back-up alarm, but Angelo allowed Gauthier to continue driving it. At a worksite, Gauthier backed up to dump a load and struck and killed a police officer who was directing traffic. The state charged Angelo and Gauthier with the crime of vehicular homicide.

Angelo argued that a corporation could not be guilty of vehicular homicide because it cannot operate a vehicle. The court ruled that if an employee commits a crime "while engaged in corporate business that the employee has been authorized to conduct," the corporation can be held liable for the crime. Hence, the court held that Angelo Todesca Corporation was liable for Gauthier's negligent operation of its truck, which resulted in a person's death.[2] ◀

Classification of Corporations

Corporations can be classified in several ways. The classification of a corporation normally depends on its location, purpose, and ownership characteristics, as described in the following subsections.

DOMESTIC, FOREIGN, AND ALIEN CORPORATIONS A corporation is referred to as a **domestic corporation** by its home state (the state in which it incorporates). A corporation formed in one state but doing business in another is referred to in the second state as a **foreign corporation.** A corporation formed in another country (say, Mexico) but doing business in the United States is referred to in the United States as an **alien corporation.**

A corporation does not have an automatic right to do business in a state other than its state of incorporation. In some instances, it must obtain a *certificate of authority* in any state in which it plans to do business. Once the certificate has been issued, the corporation generally can exercise in that state all of the powers conferred on it by its home state. If a foreign corporation does business in a state without obtaining a certificate of authority, the state can impose substantial fines and sanctions on that corporation.

Note that most state statutes specify certain activities, such as soliciting orders via the Internet, that are not considered "doing business" within the state. Thus, a foreign corporation normally does not need a certificate of authority to sell goods or services via the Internet or by mail.

PUBLIC AND PRIVATE CORPORATIONS A **public corporation** is a corporation formed by the government to meet some political or governmental purpose. Cities and towns that incorporate are common examples. In addition, many federal government organizations, such as the U.S. Postal Service, the Tennessee Valley Authority, and AMTRAK, are public corporations.

Note that a public corporation is not the same as a *publicly held* corporation. A **publicly held corporation** (often called a *public company*) is any corporation whose shares are publicly traded in a securities market, such as the New York Stock Exchange or the NASDAQ (an electronic stock exchange founded by the National Association of Securities Dealers).

In contrast to public corporations (*not* public companies), private corporations are created either wholly or in part for private benefit—that is, for profit. Most corporations are private. Although they may serve a public purpose, as a public electric or gas utility does, they are owned by private persons rather than by a government.[3]

NONPROFIT CORPORATIONS Corporations formed for purposes other than making a profit are called *nonprofit* or *not-for-profit* corporations. Private hospitals, educational institutions, charities, and religious organizations, for example, are frequently organized as nonprofit corporations. The nonprofit corporation is a convenient form of organization that allows various groups to own property and to form contracts without exposing the individual members to personal liability.

CLOSE CORPORATIONS Most corporate enterprises in the United States fall into the category of close corporations. A **close corporation** is one whose shares are held by members of a family or by relatively few persons. Close corporations are also referred to as *closely held, family,* or *privately held* corporations. Usually, the members of the small group constituting the shareholders of a close corporation are personally known to each other. Because the number of shareholders is so small, there is no trading market for the shares.

---

1. Note that the Sarbanes-Oxley Act of 2002 (see Chapter 5) stiffened the penalties for certain types of corporate crime and ordered the U.S. Sentencing Commission to revise the sentencing guidelines accordingly.

2. *Commonwealth v. Angelo Todesca Corp.*, 446 Mass. 128, 842 N.E.2d 930 (2006).

3. The United States Supreme Court first recognized the property rights of private corporations and clarified the distinction between public and private corporations in the landmark case *Trustees of Dartmouth College v. Woodward,* 17 U.S. (4 Wheaton) 518, 4 L.Ed. 629 (1819).

In practice, a close corporation is often operated like a partnership. Some states have enacted special statutory provisions that apply to these corporations and allow them to depart significantly from certain formalities required by traditional corporation law.[4]

Additionally, the RMBCA gives a close corporation considerable flexibility in determining its rules of operation [RMBCA 7.32]. If all of a corporation's shareholders agree in writing, the corporation can operate without directors and bylaws. In addition, the corporation can operate without annual or special shareholders' or directors' meetings, stock certificates, or formal records of shareholders' or directors' decisions.[5]

Management of Close Corporations. Management of a close corporation resembles that of a sole proprietorship or a partnership, in that a single shareholder or a tightly knit group of shareholders usually hold the positions of directors and officers. As a corporation, however, the firm must meet all specific legal requirements set forth in state statutes.

To prevent a majority shareholder from dominating the company, a close corporation may require that more than a simple majority of the directors approve any action taken by the board. Typically, this would apply only to extraordinary actions, such as changing the amount of dividends or dismissing an employee-shareholder, and not to ordinary business decisions.

Transfer of Shares in Close Corporations. By definition, a close corporation has a small number of shareholders. Thus, the transfer of one shareholder's shares to someone else can cause serious management problems. The other shareholders may find themselves required to share control with someone they do not know or like.

4. For example, in some states (such as Maryland), a close corporation need not have a board of directors.
5. Shareholders cannot agree, however, to eliminate certain rights of shareholders, such as the right to inspect corporate books and records or the right to bring *derivative actions* (lawsuits on behalf of the corporation—see Chapter 40).

▶ **Example 39.2** Three brothers, Terry, Damon, and Henry Johnson, are the only shareholders of Johnson's Car Wash, Inc. Terry and Damon do not want Henry to sell his shares to an unknown third person. To avoid this situation, the corporation could restrict the transferability of shares to outside persons. Shareholders could be required to offer their shares to the corporation or the other shareholders before selling them to an outside purchaser.

In fact, a few states have statutes that prohibit the transfer of close corporation shares unless certain persons—including shareholders, family members, and the corporation—are first given the opportunity to purchase the shares for the same price. ◀

Shareholder Agreement to Restrict Stock Transfers. Control of a close corporation can also be stabilized through the use of a *shareholder agreement*. A shareholder agreement can provide for proportional control when one of the original shareholders dies. The decedent's shares of stock in the corporation would be divided in such a way that the proportionate holdings of the survivors, and thus their proportionate control, would be maintained.

Agreements between shareholders can also restrict the transfer of a close corporation's stock in other ways. For instance, shareholders might agree that existing shareholders will have an option to purchase stock before it is sold or transferred to an outside party.

Misappropriation of Close Corporation Funds. Sometimes, a majority shareholder in a close corporation takes advantage of his or her position and misappropriates company funds. In such situations, the normal remedy for the injured minority shareholders is to have their shares appraised and to be paid the fair market value for them.

In the following case, a minority shareholder alleged that the majority shareholders paid themselves excessive compensation in breach of their fiduciary duty.

CASE 39.2

Rubin v. Murray
Appeals Court of Massachusetts, 79 Mass.App.Ct. 64, 943 N.E.2d 949 (2011).

BACKGROUND AND FACTS Olympic Adhesives, Inc., makes and sells industrial adhesives. John Murray, Stephen Hopkins, and Paul Ryan were the controlling shareholders of the company, as well as officers, directors, and employees. Merek Rubin was a minority shareholder. Murray, Hopkins, and Ryan

CASE 39.2 CONTINUES ▶

were paid salaries. Under Olympic's profit-sharing plan, one-third of its net operating income was paid into a fund that was distributed to employees, including Murray, Hopkins, and Ryan.

Twice a year, Murray, Hopkins, and Ryan also paid themselves additional compensation—a percentage of the net profits after profit sharing, allocated according to their stock ownership. Over a fifteen-year period, the percentage grew from 75 percent to between 92 and 98 percent. During this time, the additional compensation totaled nearly $15 million. Rubin filed a suit in a Massachusetts state court against Murray, Hopkins, and Ryan, alleging that they had paid themselves excessive compensation and deprived him of his share of Olympic's profits in violation of their fiduciary duty to him as a minority shareholder. The court ordered the defendants to repay Olympic nearly $6 million to be distributed among its shareholders. The defendants appealed.

 IN THE LANGUAGE OF THE COURT
KATZMANN, J. [Judge]

* * * *

[The trial] judge undertook to determine the reasonable compensation for top executives in a firm of Olympic's size and character, in order to determine the excess amounts that should be returned to the corporation. The defendants claim that the judge relied on speculative and insufficient evidence in determining what amounts constituted their reasonable compensation for the relevant years.

* * * *A salary must bear a reasonable relation to the officer's ability and to the quantity and quality of the services he renders. In addition, compensation may be based to some extent on the profits resulting from their efforts.* [Emphasis added.]

* * * *

* * * The judge, relying on evidence that officer compensation fell between approximately four percent to seven percent of net sales for comparable companies * * *, and adding his own success premium based on the individual defendants' significant abilities and contributions, determined that fair and reasonable compensation for them was approximately ten percent of Olympic's average annual net sales. *Determining reasonable compensation based on a percentage of net profits, with his own adjustments for performance, was a permissible exercise of the judge's discretion.* This amount the judge then confirmed with evidence of the average compensation for top officers in comparable firms. [Emphasis added.]

* * * The judge could appropriately take into account that Murray, Olympic's president and treasurer, was vague in identifying a basis for determining distribution of additional compensation among the individual defendants and, when pressed by the judge, testified that Olympic used no numerical factors to set or apportion the additional compensation. The judge found it significant that amounts paid to the individual defendants in additional compensation corresponded to the percentage of their stock ownership, rather than to any enumerated performance factors bearing on the distribution, and he was entitled to reject Murray's explanation that the correlation was just a coincidence.

DECISION AND REMEDY *A state intermediate appellate court affirmed the lower court's judgment. The appellate court concluded that the findings as to the amounts that constituted reasonable compensation for the defendants were based on sufficient evidence and were not clearly erroneous.*

WHAT IF THE FACTS WERE DIFFERENT? *Suppose that Murray could have pinpointed a job-related basis for the distribution of the net profits among the defendants. Would the result have been different? Explain.*

THE ECONOMIC DIMENSION *What are the tax consequences of passing corporate profits on to shareholders as dividends?*

S CORPORATIONS A close corporation that meets the qualifying requirements specified in Subchapter S of the Internal Revenue Code can choose to operate as an **S corporation.** (A corporation will automatically be taxed under Subchapter C unless it elects S corporation status.) If a corporation has S corporation status, it can avoid the imposition of income taxes at the corporate level while retaining many of the advantages of a corporation, particularly limited liability.

Important Requirements. Among the numerous requirements for S corporation status, the following are the most important:

1. The corporation must be a domestic corporation.
2. The corporation must not be a member of an affiliated group of corporations.
3. The shareholders of the corporation must be individuals, estates, or certain trusts and tax-exempt organizations.
4. The corporation must have no more than one hundred shareholders.
5. The corporation must have only one class of stock, although all shareholders do not need to have the same voting rights.
6. No shareholder of the corporation may be a nonresident alien.

Effect of S Election. An S corporation is treated differently than a regular corporation for tax purposes. An S corporation is taxed like a partnership, so the corporate income passes through to the shareholders, who pay personal income tax on it. This treatment enables the S corporation to avoid the double taxation imposed on regular corporations.

In addition, the shareholders' tax brackets may be lower than the tax bracket that the corporation would have been in if the tax had been imposed at the corporate level. The resulting tax saving is particularly attractive when the corporation wants to accumulate earnings for some future business purpose. If the corporation has losses, the S election allows the shareholders to use the losses to offset other income. Nevertheless, because the limited liability company (see Chapter 38) and the limited liability partnership (see Chapter 37) offer similar tax advantages and greater flexibility, the S corporation has lost much of its appeal.

PROFESSIONAL CORPORATIONS Professionals such as physicians, lawyers, dentists, and accountants can incorporate. Professional corporations are typically identified by the letters *P.C.* (professional corporation), *S.C.* (service corporation), or *P.A.* (professional association).

In general, the laws governing the formation and operation of professional corporations are similar to those governing ordinary business corporations.

There are some differences in terms of liability, however, because the shareholder-owners are professionals who are held to a higher standard of conduct.

For liability purposes, some courts treat a professional corporation somewhat like a partnership and hold each professional liable for any malpractice committed within the scope of the business by the others in the firm. With the exception of malpractice or a breach of duty to clients or patients, a shareholder in a professional corporation generally cannot be held liable for the torts committed by other professionals at the firm.

BENEFIT CORPORATIONS A growing number of states have enacted legislation that creates a new corporate form called a *benefit corporation*. A **benefit corporation** is a for-profit corporation that seeks to have a material positive impact on society and the environment. Benefit corporations differ from traditional corporations in the following three ways:

1. *Purpose.* Although the corporation is designed to make a profit, its purpose is to benefit the public as a whole (rather than just to provide long-term shareholder value, as in ordinary corporations). The directors of a benefit corporation must, during the decision-making process, consider the impact of their decisions on society and the environment.
2. *Accountability.* Shareholders of a benefit corporation determine whether the company has achieved a material positive impact. Shareholders also have a right of private action, called a *benefit enforcement proceeding,* enabling them to sue the corporation if it fails to pursue or create public benefit.
3. *Transparency.* A benefit corporation must issue an annual benefit report on its overall social and environmental performance that uses a recognized third-party standard to assess its performance. The report must be delivered to the shareholders and posted on a public Web site.

See *Concept Summary 39.1* on the following page for a review of the ways in which corporations are classified.

SECTION 2
CORPORATE FORMATION

Many Fortune 500 companies started as sole proprietorships or partnerships and then converted to corporate entities as the businesses grew and needed to

---

CONCEPT SUMMARY 39.1
Classification of Corporations

CLASSIFICATION	DESCRIPTION
Domestic, Foreign, and Alien Corporations	A corporation is referred to as a *domestic corporation* in its home state (the state in which it incorporates). A corporation is referred to as a *foreign corporation* by any state that is not its home state. A corporation is referred to as an *alien corporation* if it originates in another country but does business in the United States.
Public and Private Corporations	A *public corporation* is formed by a government (for example, a city, town, or public project). A *private corporation* is formed wholly or in part for private benefit. Most corporations are private corporations.
Nonprofit Corporation	A corporation formed without a profit-making purpose (for example, charitable, educational, and religious organizations and hospitals).
Close Corporation	A corporation that is owned by a family or a relatively small number of individuals. Because the number of shareholders is small and the transfer of shares is usually restricted, the shares are not traded in a public securities market. (Sometimes called a closely held corporation.)
S Corporation	A small domestic corporation (must have no more than one hundred shareholders) that, under Subchapter S of the Internal Revenue Code, is given special tax treatment. S corporations allow shareholders to enjoy the limited legal liability of the corporate form but avoid its double-taxation feature. (Shareholders pay taxes on the income at personal income tax rates, and the S corporation is not taxed separately.)
Professional Corporation	A corporation formed by professionals (for instance, physicians or lawyers) to obtain the advantages of incorporation (such as tax benefits and limited liability). A professional corporation functions like an ordinary corporation but is treated differently in terms of liability. Courts may treat the shareholders like partners with regard to malpractice liability.
Benefit Corporation	A type of corporation designed for businesses that want to consider society and the environment in addition to profit. Shareholders have a right to sue the corporation in enforcement proceedings if it fails to benefit the public. The corporation must issue annual benefit reports.

---

obtain additional capital by issuing shares of stock. Incorporating a business is much simpler today than it was twenty years ago, and many states allow businesses to incorporate via the Internet. Here, we examine the process by which a corporation comes into existence. (Corporate financing will be discussed later in this chapter.)

Promotional Activities

In the past, preliminary steps were taken to organize and promote the business prior to incorporating. Contracts were made with investors and others on behalf of the future corporation. Today, due to the relative ease of forming a corporation in most states, persons incorporating their business rarely, if ever, engage in preliminary promotional activities.

Nevertheless, it is important for businesspersons to understand that they are personally liable for all preincorporation contracts made with investors, accountants, or others on behalf of the future corporation. Personal liability continues until the newly formed corporation assumes liability for the preincorporation contracts through a *novation* (see Chapter 18).

▶ **Example 39.3** Jade Sorrel contracts with an accountant, Ray Cooper, to provide tax advice for a proposed corporation, Blackstone, Inc. Cooper provides the services to Sorrel, knowing that the corporation has not yet been formed. Once Blackstone, Inc., is formed, Cooper sends an invoice to the corporation and to Sorrel personally, but the bill is not paid. Because Sorrel is personally liable for the preincorporation contract, Cooper can sue Sorrel for breach of the contract. Cooper cannot seek to hold Blackstone, Inc., liable unless he has entered into a contract with the corporation through a novation. ◀

Incorporation Procedures

Exact procedures for incorporation differ among states, but the basic steps are as follows: (1) select a state of incorporation, (2) secure the corporate name, (3) prepare the articles of incorporation, and (4) file the articles of incorporation with the secretary of state. These steps are discussed in more detail in the following subsections.

SELECT THE STATE OF INCORPORATION The first step in the incorporation process is to select a state in which to incorporate. Because state laws differ, individuals may look for the states that offer the most advantageous tax or incorporation provisions. Another consideration is the fee that a particular state charges to incorporate, as well as the annual fees and the fees for specific transactions (such as stock transfers).

Delaware has historically had the least restrictive laws and provisions that favor corporate management. Consequently, many corporations, including a number of the largest, have incorporated there. Delaware's statutes permit firms to incorporate in that state and conduct business and locate their operating headquarters elsewhere. Most other states now permit this as well.

Note, though, that close corporations, particularly those of a professional nature, generally incorporate in the state where their principal shareholders live and work. For reasons of convenience and cost, businesses often choose to incorporate in the state in which most of the corporation's business will be conducted.

SECURE THE CORPORATE NAME The choice of a corporate name is subject to state approval to ensure against duplication or deception. State statutes usually require that the secretary of state run a check on the proposed name in the state of incorporation.

Some states require that the persons incorporating a firm run a check on the proposed name at their own expense. A check can often be made via the Internet. If a firm is likely to do business in other states—or over the Internet—the incorporators should check existing corporate names in those states as well.

Once cleared, a name can be reserved for a short time, for a fee, pending the completion of the articles of incorporation. All states require the corporation's name to include the word *Corporation (Corp.), Incorporated (Inc.), Company (Co.),* or *Limited (Ltd.)*.[6]

---

6. Failure to use one of these abbreviations to disclose corporate status may be grounds for holding an individual incorporator liable for corporate contracts under agency law (see Chapter 33).

First Check Available Domain Names. All corporations need to have an online presence to compete effectively in today's business climate. The corporate name should be one that can be used as the business's Internet domain name. Therefore, it is advisable to check what domain names are available *before* securing a corporate name with the state.

Incorporators can do this by going to one of the many companies that issue domain names, such as Network Solutions (**www.whois.com/whois**), and finding out if the preferred name is available. If another business is using that name, the incorporators can select an alternative name that can be used as the business's URL, and then seek approval from the state for the name.

Trade Name Disputes. A new corporation's name cannot be the same as (or deceptively similar to) the name of an existing corporation doing business within the same state. If a firm does business under a name that is the same as or deceptively similar to an existing company's name, it may be liable for trade name infringement (see Chapter 8).

▶ **Example 39.4** An existing corporation is named Digital Synergy, Inc. The state is not likely to allow a new corporation to use the name Digital Synergy Company. That name is deceptively similar to the first and could cause confusion. The use of too similar a name could also transfer part of the goodwill established by the first corporate user to the second, thus infringing on the first company's trademark rights. ◀

PREPARE THE ARTICLES OF INCORPORATION The primary document needed to incorporate a business is the **articles of incorporation** (for an example, see Exhibit 39–1 on the next page). The articles include basic information about the corporation and serve as a primary source of authority for its future organization and business functions. The person or persons who execute (sign) the articles are the *incorporators*.

Generally, the articles of incorporation *must* include the following information [RMBCA 2.02].

1. The name of the corporation.
2. The number of shares the corporation is authorized to issue.
3. The name and street address of the corporation's initial registered agent and registered office.
4. The name and address of each incorporator.

EXHIBIT 39-1 Sample Articles of Incorporation

ARTICLE ONE The name of the corporation is _____.

ARTICLE TWO The period of its duration is _____ (may be a number of years or until a certain date).

ARTICLE THREE The purpose (or purposes) for which the corporation is organized is (are) _____
_____
_____.

ARTICLE FOUR The aggregate number of shares that the corporation shall have the authority to issue is _____ with
the par value of _____ dollar(s) each (or without par value).

ARTICLE FIVE The corporation will not commence business until it has received for the issuance of its shares
consideration of the value of $1,000 (can be any sum not less than $1,000).

ARTICLE SIX The address of the corporation's registered office is _____,
and the name of its registered agent at such address is _____
_____.

ARTICLE SEVEN The number of initial directors is _____, and the names and addresses of the directors are
_____
_____.

ARTICLE EIGHT The names and addresses of the incorporators are

(Name)	(Address)	(Signature)
(Name)	(Address)	(Signature)
(Name)	(Address)	(Signature)

Sworn to on _____ by the above-named incorporators.
        (Date)

Notary Public
_____

(Notary Seal)

In addition, the articles *may* set forth other information, such as the names and addresses of the initial members of the board of directors, and the duration and purpose of the corporation.

Articles of incorporation vary widely depending on the jurisdiction and the size and type of the corporation. Frequently, the articles do not provide much detail about the firm's operations, which are spelled out in the company's **bylaws** (internal rules of management adopted by the corporation at its first organizational meeting).

Shares of the Corporation. The articles must specify the number of shares of stock the corporation is authorized to issue [RMBCA 2.02(a)]. For instance, a company might state that the aggregate number of shares that the corporation has the authority to issue is five thousand. Large corporations often state a par value for each share, such as $.20 per share, and specify the various types or classes of stock authorized for issuance (see the discussion of *common* and *preferred stock* later in this chapter).

Sometimes, the articles set forth the capital structure of the corporation and other relevant information. To allow for the raising of additional capital in the future, the articles of incorporation often authorize many more shares of stock than will initially be issued.

Registered Office and Agent. The corporation must indicate the location and street address of its registered office within the state. Usually, the registered office is also the principal office of the corporation.

The corporation must also give the name and address of a specific person who has been designated as an *agent*. The registered agent is the person who can receive legal documents (such as orders to appear in court) on behalf of the corporation.

Incorporators. Each incorporator must be listed by name and address. The incorporators need not have any interest at all in the corporation, and sometimes signing the articles is their only duty. Many states do not have residency or age requirements for incorporators. It can be as few as one or as many as three. Incorporators frequently participate in the first organizational meeting of the corporation.

Duration and Purpose. A corporation has perpetual existence unless the articles state otherwise. The RMBCA does not require a specific statement of purpose to be included in the articles. A corporation can be formed for any lawful purpose.

Some incorporators choose to specify the intended business activities (such as "to engage in the production and sale of agricultural products"). It is increasingly common, though, for the articles to include only a general statement of purpose. The articles may indicate that the corporation is organized for "any legal business." By not mentioning specifics, the corporation avoids the need for future amendments to the corporate articles [RMBCA 2.02(b)(2)(i), 3.01].

Internal Organization. The articles can describe the corporation's internal management structure, although this usually is included in the bylaws adopted after the corporation is formed. The articles of incorporation commence the corporation, whereas the bylaws are formed after commencement by the board of directors. Bylaws cannot conflict with the incorporation statute or the articles of incorporation [RMBCA 2.06].

Under the RMBCA, shareholders may amend or repeal the bylaws. The board of directors may also amend or repeal the bylaws unless the articles of incorporation or state statutory provisions reserve this power to the shareholders exclusively [RMBCA 10.20].

The bylaws typically describe such matters as voting requirements for shareholders, the election of the board of directors, and the methods of replacing directors. Bylaws also frequently outline the manner and time of holding shareholders' and board meetings (these corporate activities will be discussed in Chapter 40).

FILE THE ARTICLES WITH THE STATE   Once the articles of incorporation have been prepared and signed, they are sent to the appropriate state official, usually the secretary of state, along with the required filing fee. In most states, the secretary of state then stamps the articles "Filed" and returns a copy of the articles to the incorporators. Once this occurs, the corporation officially exists.

First Organizational Meeting to Adopt Bylaws

After incorporation, the first organizational meeting must be held. Usually, the most important function of this meeting is the adoption of bylaws, which, as mentioned, are the internal rules of management for the corporation. If the articles of incorporation named the initial board of directors, then the directors, by majority vote, call the meeting to adopt the bylaws and complete the company's organization.

If the articles did not name the directors (as is typical), then the incorporators hold the meeting to elect the directors and adopt bylaws. The incorporators may also complete the routine business of incorporation (such as authorizing the issuance of shares and hiring employees) at this meeting. The business transacted depends on the requirements of the state's corporation statute, the nature of the corporation, the provisions made in the articles, and the desires of the incorporators.

Improper Incorporation

The procedures for incorporation are very specific. If they are not followed precisely, others may be able to challenge the existence of the corporation. Errors in incorporation procedures can become important when, for instance, a third party who is attempting to enforce a contract or bring a suit for a tort injury learns of them.

DE JURE CORPORATIONS   If a corporation has substantially complied with all conditions precedent to incorporation, the corporation is said to have *de jure* (rightful and lawful) existence. In most states and under RMBCA 2.03(b), the secretary of state's filing of the articles of incorporation is conclusive proof that all mandatory statutory provisions have been met [RMBCA 2.03(b)].

Sometimes, the incorporators fail to comply with all statutory mandates. If the defect is minor, such as an incorrect address listed on the articles of incorporation, most courts will overlook the defect and find that a corporation (*de jure*) exists.

DE FACTO CORPORATIONS If the defect in formation is substantial, however, such as a corporation's failure to hold an organizational meeting to adopt bylaws, the outcome will vary depending on the jurisdiction. Some states, including Mississippi, New York, Ohio, and Oklahoma, still recognize the common law doctrine of *de facto* corporation.[7] In those states, the courts will treat a corporation as a legal corporation despite the defect in its formation if the following three requirements are met:

1. A state statute exists under which the corporation can be validly incorporated.
2. The parties have made a good faith attempt to comply with the statute.
3. The parties have already undertaken to do business as a corporation.

Many state courts, however, have interpreted their states' version of the RMBCA as abolishing the common law doctrine of *de facto* corporations. These states include Alaska, Arizona, Minnesota, New Mexico, Oregon, South Dakota, Tennessee, Utah, and Washington, as well as the District of Columbia. In those jurisdictions, if there is a substantial defect in complying with the incorporation statute, the corporation does not legally exist, and the incorporators are personally liable.

Corporation by Estoppel

Sometimes, a business association holds itself out to others as being a corporation when it has made no attempt to incorporate. In those situations, the firm normally will be estopped (prevented) from denying corporate status in a lawsuit by a third party. The estoppel doctrine most commonly applies when a third party contracts with an entity that claims to be a corporation but has not filed articles of incorporation. It may also apply when a third party contracts with a person claiming to be an agent of a corporation that does not in fact exist.

When justice requires, courts in some states will treat an alleged corporation as if it were an actual corporation for the purpose of determining the rights and liabilities in particular circumstances.[8] Recognition of corporate status does not extend beyond the resolution of the problem at hand.

▶ **Case in Point 39.5** W.P. Media, Inc., and Alabama MBA, Inc., agreed to form a wireless Internet services company. W.P. Media was to create a wireless network, and Alabama MBA was to contribute the capital. Hugh Brown signed the parties' contract on behalf of Alabama MBA as the chair of its board. At the time, however, Alabama MBA's articles of incorporation had not yet been filed. Brown filed the articles of incorporation the following year. Later, Brown and Alabama MBA filed a suit alleging that W.P. Media had breached their contract by not building the wireless network. The Supreme Court of Alabama held that because W.P. Media had treated Alabama MBA as a corporation, W.P. Media was estopped from denying Alabama MBA's corporate existence.[9] ◀

SECTION 3
CORPORATE POWERS

When a corporation is created, the express and implied powers necessary to achieve its purpose also come into existence. The express powers of a corporation are found in its articles of incorporation, in the law of the state of incorporation, and in the state and federal constitutions.

Corporate bylaws and the resolutions of the corporation's board of directors also establish the express powers of the corporation. Because state corporation statutes frequently provide default rules that apply if the company's bylaws are silent on an issue, it is important that the bylaws set forth the specific operating rules of the corporation. In addition, after the bylaws are adopted, the corporation's board of directors will pass resolutions that also grant or restrict corporate powers.

The following order of priority is used if a conflict arises among the various documents involving a corporation:

1. The U.S. Constitution.
2. State constitutions.

---

7. See, for example, *In re Hausman,* 13 N.Y.3d 408, 921 N.E.2d 191, 893 N.Y.S.2d 499 (2009).

8. Some states have expressly rejected the common law theory of corporation by estoppel, finding that it is inconsistent with their statutory law. Other states have abolished only the doctrines of *de facto* and *de jure* corporations. See, for example, *Stone v. Jetmar Properties, LLC,* 733 N.W.2d 480 (Minn.App. 2007).

9. *Brown v. W.P. Media, Inc.,* 17 So.3d 1167 (2009).

3. State statutes.
4. The articles of incorporation.
5. Bylaws.
6. Resolutions of the board of directors.

Implied Powers

When a corporation is created, certain implied powers arise. In the absence of express constitutional, statutory, or other prohibitions, the corporation has the implied power to perform all acts reasonably necessary to accomplish its corporate purposes. For this reason, a corporation has the implied power to borrow funds within certain limits, lend funds, and extend credit to those with whom it has a legal or contractual relationship.

To borrow funds, the corporation acts through its board of directors to authorize the loan. Most often, the president or chief executive officer (see Chapter 40) of the corporation will execute the necessary documents on behalf of the corporation. Corporate officers such as these have the implied power to bind the corporation in matters directly connected with the *ordinary* business affairs of the enterprise.

There is a limit to what a corporate officer can do, though. A corporate officer does not have the authority to bind the corporation to an action that will greatly affect the corporate purpose or undertaking, such as the sale of substantial corporate assets.

Ultra Vires Doctrine

The term *ultra vires* means "beyond the power." In corporate law, acts of a corporation that are beyond its express or implied powers are *ultra vires* acts.

WHEN A CORPORATION'S ACTIONS EXCEED ITS STATED PURPOSE In the past, most cases dealing with *ultra vires* acts involved contracts made for unauthorized purposes. Now, however, most private corporations are organized for "any legal business" and do not state a specific purpose, so the *ultra vires* doctrine has declined in importance.

Today, cases that allege *ultra vires* acts usually involve nonprofit corporations or municipal (public) corporations. ▶ **Case in Point 39.6** Four men formed a nonprofit corporation to create the Armenian Genocide Museum & Memorial (AGM&M). The bylaws appointed them as trustees (similar to corporate directors) for life. One of the trustees, Gerard L. Cafesjian, became the chair and president of AGM&M.

Eventually, the relationship among the trustees deteriorated, and Cafesjian resigned.

The corporation then brought a suit claiming that Cafesjian had engaged in numerous *ultra vires* acts, self-dealing, and mismanagement. Although the bylaws required an 80 percent affirmative vote of the trustees to take action, Cafesjian had taken many actions without the board's approval. He had also entered into contracts for real estate transactions in which he had a personal interest. Because Cafesjian had taken actions that exceeded his authority and had failed to follow the rules set forth in the bylaws for board meetings, the court ruled that the corporation could go forward with its suit.[10] ◀

REMEDIES FOR *ULTRA VIRES* ACTS Under Section 3.04 of the RMBCA, the shareholders can seek an injunction from a court to prevent (or stop) the corporation from engaging in *ultra vires* acts. The attorney general in the state of incorporation can also bring an action to obtain an injunction against the *ultra vires* transactions or to seek dissolution of the corporation. The corporation or its shareholders (on behalf of the corporation) can seek damages from the officers and directors who were responsible for the *ultra vires* acts.

SECTION 4
PIERCING THE CORPORATE VEIL

Occasionally, the owners use a corporate entity to perpetrate a fraud, circumvent the law, or in some other way accomplish an illegitimate objective. In these situations, the courts will ignore the corporate structure and **pierce the corporate veil,** exposing the shareholders to personal liability [RMBCA 2.04].

Generally, courts pierce the veil when the corporate privilege is abused for personal benefit or when the corporate business is treated so carelessly that it is indistinguishable from that of a controlling shareholder. When the facts show that great injustice would result from the use of a corporation to avoid individual responsibility, a court will look behind the corporate structure to the individual shareholders.

---

10. *Armenian Assembly of America, Inc. v. Cafesjian*, 692 F.Supp.2d 20 (D.C. 2010).

Factors That Lead Courts to Pierce the Corporate Veil

The following are some of the factors that frequently cause the courts to pierce the corporate veil:

1. A party is tricked or misled into dealing with the corporation rather than the individual.
2. The corporation is set up never to make a profit or always to be insolvent, or it is too "thinly" capitalized. That is, it has insufficient capital at the time it is formed to meet its prospective debts or potential liabilities.
3. The corporation is formed to evade an existing legal obligation.
4. Statutory corporate formalities, such as holding required corporation meetings, are not followed.
5. Personal and corporate interests are mixed together, or **commingled,** to such an extent that the corporation has no separate identity.

Although state corporation codes usually do not prohibit a shareholder from lending funds to her or his corporation, courts will scrutinize the transaction closely if the loan comes from an officer, director, or majority shareholder. Loans from persons who control the corporation must be made in good faith and for fair value.

A Potential Problem for Close Corporations

The potential for corporate assets to be used for personal benefit is especially great in a close corporation, in which the shares are held by a single person or by only a few individuals, usually family members. In such a situation, the separate status of the corporate entity and the sole shareholder (or family-member shareholders) must be carefully preserved.

Certain practices invite trouble for the one-person or family-owned (close) corporation, including any of the following:

1. The commingling of corporate and personal funds.
2. The failure to hold board of directors' meetings and record the minutes.
3. The shareholders' continuous personal use of corporate property (for instance, company-owned vehicles).

In the following case, when a close corporation failed to pay its legal fees, its attorneys sought to hold the shareholders personally liable. The court had to decide whether to pierce the corporate veil.

CASE 39.3

Brennan's, Inc. v. Colbert
Court of Appeal of Louisiana, 85 So. 3d 787 (2012).

BACKGROUND AND FACTS Pip, Jimmy, and Theodore Brennan are brothers and shareholders of Brennan's, Inc., which owns and operates New Orleans's famous Brennan's Restaurant. In 1998, the Brennan brothers retained attorney Edward Colbert and his firm, Kenyon & Kenyon, L.L.P., to represent Brennan's, Inc., in a dispute with another family member. All bills were sent to Brennan's, Inc., and the payments came from the company's checking accounts.

As a close corporation, Brennan's, Inc., did not hold formal corporate meetings with agendas and minutes, but it did maintain corporate books, hold corporate bank accounts, and file corporate tax returns. In 2005, Brennan's, Inc., sued Colbert and his law firm for legal malpractice. In its answer, Kenyon & Kenyon demanded unpaid legal fees both from Brennan's, Inc., and from the Brennan brothers personally. The trial court found that the Brennan brothers could not be held personally liable. Kenyon & Kenyon appealed. The law firm argued that the court should pierce the corporate veil because Brennan's, Inc., did not observe corporate formalities and because the Brennan brothers did not honor their promises to pay their legal bills.

 IN THE LANGUAGE OF THE COURT
Daniel L. *DYSART,* Judge.

* * * *

As a general rule, a corporation is a distinct legal entity, separate from the individuals who compose it, thus insulating the shareholders from personal liability.

There are limited exceptions where the court may ignore the corporate fiction and find the shareholders personally liable for the debts of a corporation. One of those exceptions is where

CASE 39.3 CONTINUED

the corporation is found to be the "alter ego" of the shareholder. It usually involves situations where fraud or deceit has been practiced by the shareholder through the corporation. Another basis is where the shareholders disregard the corporate formalities to the extent that the corporation and the shareholders are no longer distinct entities.

* * * *

Absent fraud, malfeasance or criminal wrongdoing, courts have been reluctant to hold a shareholder personally liable for corporate obligations. When a party seeks to pierce the corporate veil, the totality of the circumstances is determinative. [Emphasis added.]

* * * *

The Kenyon firm was aware of the nature of the operation of Brennan's, Inc., * * * prior to being retained. The client was Brennan's, Inc., bills were sent to Brennan's, Inc., and payments were paid with checks from the Brennan's, Inc., bank accounts. * * * Brennan's, Inc., maintained its own accounting records and filed its own tax returns. * * * The Kenyon firm acknowledged that Brennan's, Inc., *acting through its shareholders,* promised to make good on the debt. [Emphasis in original.]

There is no evidence that the Brennan brothers ever agreed to bind themselves personally for any debt incurred in connection with the legal services provided by the Kenyon firm. There is no written retention agreement between the corporation and the Kenyon firm, nor is there a written guaranty from any of the brothers.

The Kenyon firm admits that there is no requirement for small, [close] corporations to operate with the formality usually expected of larger corporations. The Kenyon firm has failed to establish that the lack of corporate formalities, particularly meetings, agendas and minutes, is sufficient to pierce the corporation veil. Brennan's, Inc., at all times since its inception has maintained corporate books, corporate bank accounts, and has filed corporate tax returns.

* * * *

The Kenyon firm has not proven that any of the Brennan brothers made promises to pay the firm's bills without the intent to pay them. * * * *If a broken promise to pay was sufficient to establish fraud, then every lawsuit against a corporation for a debt would automatically allow for the piercing of the corporate veil. Clearly, a juridical entity such as a corporation can only speak through its shareholders.* [Emphasis added.]

DECISION AND REMEDY   *The Louisiana appellate court held that Kenyon & Kenyon could not hold the Brennan brothers personally liable by piercing the corporate veil. The court therefore affirmed the trial court's judgment for the Brennan brothers.*

THE ETHICAL DIMENSION   *Should the Brennan brothers be held personally liable because they misled their attorneys? Why or why not?*

THE ECONOMIC DIMENSION   *Do corporations benefit from shareholders' limited liability? If so, how?*

The Alter-Ego Theory

Sometimes, courts pierce the corporate veil under the theory that the corporation was not operated as a separate entity, but was just another side (or alter ego) of the individual or group that actually controlled the corporation. This is called the alter-ego theory, which was discussed in the context of limited liability companies in Chapter 38.

The alter-ego theory is applied when a corporation is so dominated and controlled by an individual or group that the separate identities of the person (or group) and the corporation are no longer distinct.

Courts use the alter-ego theory to avoid injustice or fraud that would result if wrongdoers were allowed to hide behind the protection of limited liability. ▶ **Case in Point 39.7**   Harvey and Barbara Jacobson owned Aqua Clear Technologies, Inc., which installed and serviced home water-softening systems. The Jacobsons consistently took funds out of the business for their personal expenses, including payments for their home, cars, health-insurance premiums, and credit cards.

Three weeks after Aqua filed a bankruptcy petition, Harvey formed another corporation called

Discount Water Services, Inc. Discount appropriated Aqua's equipment and inventory (without buying it) and continued to service water-softening systems for Aqua's customers, even using the same phone number. The trustee appointed to Aqua's bankruptcy case sought to recover Aqua's assets on the ground that Discount was Aqua's alter ego. The court ruled that Discount was simply a continuation of Aqua's business (its alter ego) under a new name, and therefore held Discount liable for the claims asserted against Aqua in bankruptcy (totaling $108,732.64).[11] ◄

SECTION 5
CORPORATE FINANCING

Corporations are financed by the issuance and sale of corporate **securities,** which include stocks and bonds. **Stocks,** or *equity securities,* represent the purchase of ownership in the business firm. **Bonds** (debentures), or *debt securities,* represent the borrowing of funds by firms (and governments).

Of course, not all debt is in the form of debt securities. For instance, some debt is in the form of accounts payable and notes payable, which typically are short-term debts. Bonds are simply a way for corporations to split up their long-term debt so that it can be more easily marketed.

Bonds

Bonds are issued by business firms and by governments at all levels as evidence of the funds they are borrowing from investors. Bonds normally have a designated *maturity date*—the date when the principal, or face amount, of the bond (or loan) is returned to the investor. They are sometimes referred to as *fixed-income securities* because their owners (that is, the creditors) receive fixed-dollar interest payments, usually semiannually, during the period of time prior to maturity.

Because debt financing represents a legal obligation of the corporation, various features and terms of a particular bond issue are specified in a lending agreement, called a **bond indenture.** A corporate trustee, often a commercial bank trust department, represents the collective well-being of all bondholders in ensuring that the corporation meets the terms

of the bond issue. The bond indenture specifies the maturity date of the bond and the pattern of interest payments until maturity.

Stocks

Issuing stocks is another way for corporations to obtain financing [RMBCA 6.01]. The ways in which stocks differ from bonds are summarized in Exhibit 39–2 on the top of the next page.

Exhibit 39–3 on the following page offers a summary of the types of stocks issued by corporations. The two major types are *common stock* and *preferred stock.*

COMMON STOCK The true ownership of a corporation is represented by **common stock.** Common stock provides a proportionate interest in the corporation with regard to (1) control, (2) earnings, and (3) net assets. A shareholder's interest is generally in proportion to the number of shares he or she owns out of the total number of shares issued.

Voting Rights. Any person who purchases common stock acquires voting rights—one vote per share held. Voting rights in a corporation apply to the election of the firm's board of directors and to any proposed changes in the ownership structure of the firm. For instance, a holder of common stock generally has the right to vote in a decision on a proposed merger, as mergers can change the proportion of ownership. State corporation law specifies the types of actions for which shareholder approval must be obtained.

Earnings. Firms are not obligated to return a principal amount per share to each holder of common stock because no firm can ensure that the market price per share of its common stock will not decline over time. The issuing firm also does not have to guarantee a dividend. Indeed, some corporations never pay dividends.

Holders of common stock are investors who assume a *residual* position in the overall financial structure of the business. In terms of receiving returns on their investments, they are last in line. They are entitled to the earnings that are left after federal and state taxes are paid and after preferred stockholders, bondholders, suppliers, employees, and other groups have been paid. Once those groups are paid, however, the owners of common stock may be entitled to *all* the remaining earnings. (The board of directors nor-

---
11. *In re Aqua Clear Technologies, Inc.,* 361 Bankr. 567 (S.D.Fla. 2007).

EXHIBIT 39-2 How Do Stocks and Bonds Differ?

Stocks	Bonds
1. Stocks represent ownership.	1. Bonds represent debt.
2. Stocks (common) do not have a fixed dividend rate.	2. Interest on bonds must always be paid, whether or not any profit is earned.
3. Stockholders can elect the board of directors, which controls the corporation.	3. Bondholders usually have no voice in or control over management of the corporation.
4. Stocks do not have a maturity date. The corporation usually does not repay the stockholder.	4. Bonds have a maturity date, when the corporation is to repay the bondholder the face value of the bond.
5. All corporations issue or offer to sell stocks. This is the usual definition of a corporation.	5. Corporations do not necessarily issue bonds.
6. Stockholders have a claim against the property and income of the corporation after all creditors' claims have been met.	6. Bondholders have a claim against the property and income of the corporation that must be met before the claims of stockholders.

mally is not under any duty to declare the remaining earnings as dividends, however.)

PREFERRED STOCK **Preferred stock** is an equity security with *preferences*. Usually, this means that holders of preferred stock have priority over holders of common stock as to dividends and payment on dissolution of the corporation. The preferences must be stated in the articles of incorporation. Holders of preferred stock may or may not have the right to vote.

Preferred stock is not included among the liabilities of a business because it is equity. Like other equity securities, preferred shares have no fixed maturity date on which the firm must pay them off. Although firms occasionally buy back preferred stock, they are not legally obligated to do so.

Holders of preferred stock are investors who have assumed a rather cautious position. They have a stronger position than common shareholders with respect to dividends and claims on assets, but they do not share in the full prosperity of the firm if its earnings grow over time. Preferred stockholders do receive fixed dividends periodically, however, and they may benefit to some extent from changes in the market price of the shares.

EXHIBIT 39-3 Types of Stocks

Type	Definition
Common Stock	Voting shares that represent ownership interest in a corporation. Common stock has the lowest priority with respect to payment of dividends and distribution of assets on the corporation's dissolution.
Preferred Stock	Shares of stock that have priority over common-stock shares as to payment of dividends and distribution of assets on dissolution. Dividend payments are usually a fixed percentage of the face value of the share. Preferred shares may or may not be voting shares.
Cumulative Preferred Stock	Preferred shares on which required dividends not paid in a given year must be paid in a subsequent year before any common-stock dividends can be paid.
Participating Preferred Stock	Preferred shares entitling the owner to receive (1) the preferred-stock dividend and (2) additional dividends after the corporation has paid dividends on common stock.
Convertible Preferred Stock	Preferred shares that, under certain conditions, can be converted into a specified number of common shares either in the issuing corporation or, sometimes, in another corporation.
Redeemable, or Callable, Preferred Stock	Preferred shares issued with the express condition that the issuing corporation has the right to repurchase the shares as specified.

Venture Capital and Private Equity Capital

Corporations traditionally obtain financing through issuing and selling securities (stocks and bonds) in the capital market. Many investors do not want to purchase stock in a business that lacks a track record, however, and banks generally are reluctant to extend loans to high-risk enterprises. Numerous corporations fail because they are undercapitalized. Therefore, to obtain sufficient financing, many entrepreneurs seek alternative financing.

VENTURE CAPITAL Start-up businesses and high-risk enterprises often obtain venture capital financing. As discussed in Chapter 38, *venture capital* is capital provided to new businesses by professional, outside investors, usually in exchange for an ownership interest in the business.

Venture capital investments are high risk—the investors must be willing to lose their invested funds—but offer the potential for well-above-average returns at some point in the future. Many Internet-based companies, such as Google and Amazon, were initially financed by venture capital.

PRIVATE EQUITY CAPITAL Private equity firms obtain their capital from wealthy investors in private markets. The firms use their **private equity capital** to invest in existing corporations. Usually, a private equity firm buys an entire corporation and may later reorganize it as a publicly held corporation. Sometimes, divisions of the purchased company are sold off to pay down debt.

Ultimately, the private equity firm may sell shares in the reorganized (and perhaps more profitable) company to the public in an *initial public offering* (usually called an IPO—see Chapter 42). In this way, the private equity firm can make profits by selling its shares in the company to the public.

Reviewing: Corporate Formation and Financing

William Sharp was the sole shareholder and manager of Chickasaw Club, Inc., an S corporation that operated a popular nightclub of the same name in Columbus, Georgia. Sharp maintained a corporate checking account but paid the club's employees, suppliers, and entertainers in cash out of the club's proceeds. Sharp owned the property on which the club was located. He rented it to the club but made mortgage payments out of the club's proceeds and often paid other personal expenses with Chickasaw corporate funds.

At 12:45 A.M. on July 31, eighteen-year-old Aubrey Lynn Pursley, who was already intoxicated, entered the Chickasaw Club. A city ordinance prohibited individuals under the age of twenty-one from entering nightclubs, but Chickasaw employees did not check Pursley's identification to verify her age. Pursley drank more alcohol at Chickasaw and was visibly intoxicated when she left the club at 3:00 A.M. with a beer in her hand. Shortly afterward, Pursley lost control of her car, struck a tree, and was killed. Joseph Dancause, Pursley's stepfather, filed a tort lawsuit in a Georgia state court against Chickasaw Club, Inc., and William Sharp, seeking damages. Using the information presented in the chapter, answer the following questions.

1. Under what theory might the court in this case make an exception to the limited liability of shareholders and hold Sharp personally liable for the damages? What factors would be relevant to the court's decision?
2. Suppose that Chickasaw's articles of incorporation failed to describe the corporation's purpose or management structure as required by state law. Would the court be likely to rule that Sharp is personally liable to Dancause on that basis? Why or why not?
3. Suppose that the club extended credit to its regular patrons in an effort to maintain a loyal clientele, although neither the articles of incorporation nor the corporate bylaws authorized this practice. Would the corporation likely have the power to engage in this activity? Explain.

4. How would the court classify the Chickasaw Club corporation—domestic or foreign, public or private? Why?

DEBATE THIS ... *The sole shareholder of an S corporation should not be able to avoid liability for the torts of her or his employees.*

Terms and Concepts

alien corporation 762	common stock 774	public corporation 762
articles of incorporation 767	dividends 760	publicly held corporation 762
benefit corporation 765	domestic corporation 762	retained earnings 760
bond 774	foreign corporation 762	S corporation 764
bond indenture 774	holding company 760	securities 774
bylaws 768	pierce the corporate veil 771	stock 774
close corporation 762	preferred stock 775	*ultra vires* 771
commingle 772	private equity capital 776	

ExamPrep

Issue Spotters

1. Northwest Brands, Inc., is a small business incorporated in Minnesota. Its one class of stock is owned by twelve members of a single family. Ordinarily, corporate income is taxed at the corporate and shareholder levels. Is there a way for Northwest Brands to avoid this double taxation? Explain your answer. **(See page 764.)**

2. The incorporators of Consumer Investments, Inc., want their new corporation to have the authority to transact nearly any conceivable type of business. Can they grant this authority to their firm? If so, how? If not, why not? **(See page 772.)**

• **Check your answers to the Issue Spotters against the answers provided in Appendix E at the end of this text.**

Before the Test

Go to **www.cengagebrain.com**, enter the ISBN 9781285185248, and click on "Find" to locate this textbook's Web site. Then, click on "Access Now" under "Study Tools," and select Chapter 39 at the top. There, you will find a Practice Quiz that you can take to assess your mastery of the concepts in this chapter, as well as Flashcards and a Glossary of important terms.

Business Scenarios

39–1. Incorporation. Jonathan, Gary, and Ricardo are active members of a partnership called Swim City. The partnership manufactures, sells, and installs outdoor swimming pools in the states of Arkansas and Texas. The partners want to continue to be active in management and to expand the business into other states as well. They are also concerned about rather large recent judgments entered against swimming pool companies throughout the United States. Based on these facts only, discuss whether the partnership should incorporate. **(See page 759.)**

39–2. Preincorporation. Cummings, Okawa, and Taft are recent college graduates who want to form a corporation to manufacture and sell digital tablets. Peterson tells

them he will set in motion the formation of their corporation. First, Peterson makes a contract with Owens for the purchase of a piece of land for $20,000. Owens does not know of the prospective corporate formation at the time the contract is signed. Second, Peterson makes a contract with Babcock to build a small plant on the property being purchased. Babcock's contract is conditional on the corporation's formation. Peterson secures all necessary subscription agreements and capitalization, and he files the articles of incorporation. **(See page 776.)**

(a) Discuss whether the newly formed corporation, Peterson, or both are liable on the contracts with Owens and Babcock.

(b) Discuss whether the corporation is automatically liable to Babcock on formation.

39–3. Corporate Powers. Oya Paka and two business associates formed a corporation called Paka Corp. for the purpose of selling computer services. Oya, who owned 50 percent of the corporate shares, served as the corporation's president. Oya wished to obtain a personal loan from her bank for $250,000, but the bank required the note to be cosigned by a third party. Oya cosigned the note in the name of the corporation. Later, Oya defaulted on the note, and the bank sued the corporation for payment. The corporation asserted, as a defense, that Oya had exceeded her authority when she cosigned the note on behalf of the corporation. Had she? Explain. **(See page 770.)**

Business Case Problems

39–4. Spotlight on Smart Inventions—Piercing the Corporate Veil. Thomas Persson and Jon Nokes founded Smart Inventions, Inc., to market household consumer products. The success of their first product, the Smart Mop, continued with later products, which were sold through infomercials and other means. Persson and Nokes were the firm's officers and equal shareholders. Persson was responsible for product development, and Nokes was in charge of day-to-day operations. By 1998, they had become dissatisfied with each other's efforts. Nokes represented the firm as financially "dying," "in a grim state, . . . worse than ever," and offered to buy all of Persson's shares for $1.6 million. Persson accepted. On the day that they signed the agreement to transfer the shares, Smart Inventions began marketing a new product—the Tap Light. It was an instant success, generating millions of dollars in revenues. In negotiating with Persson, Nokes had intentionally kept the Tap Light a secret. Persson sued Smart Inventions, asserting fraud and other claims. Under what principle might Smart Inventions be liable for Nokes's fraud? Is Smart Inventions liable in this case? Explain. [*Persson v. Smart Inventions, Inc.*, 125 Cal.App.4th 1141, 23 Cal. Rptr.3d 335 (2 Dist. 2005)] **(See page 771.)**

39–5. Improper Incorporation. Denise Rubenstein and Christopher Mayor agreed to form Bayshore Sunrise Corp. (BSC) in New York to rent certain premises and operate a laundromat. BSC entered into a twenty-year commercial lease with Bay Shore Property Trust on April 15. Mayor signed the lease as the president of BSC, but the articles of incorporation were not filed until the next day—April 16. Three years later, BSC defaulted on the lease, which resulted in its termination. Rubenstein and BSC sued Mayor, his brother-in-law Thomas Castellano, and Planet Laundry, Inc., claiming wrongful interference with a contractual relationship. The plaintiffs alleged that Mayor and Castellano conspired to squeeze Rubenstein out of BSC and arranged the default on the lease so that Mayor and Castellano could form and operate their own business, Planet Laundry, at the same address. The defendants argued that they could not be liable on the plaintiffs' claim because there had never been an enforceable lease—BSC lacked the capacity to enter into contracts on April 15. What theory might Rubenstein and BSC assert to refute this argument? Discuss. [*Rubenstein v. Mayor*, 41 A.D.3d 826, 839 N.Y.S.2d 170 (2 Dept. 2007)] **(See page 769.)**

39–6. Piercing the Corporate Veil. Smith Services, Inc., a trucking business owned by Tony Smith, charged its fuel purchases to an account at Laker Express. When Smith Services was not paid on several contracts, it ceased doing business and was dissolved. Smith continued to provide trucking services, however, as a sole proprietor. Laker Express sought to recover Smith Services' unpaid fuel charges, which amounted to about $35,000, from Smith. He argued that he was not personally liable for a corporate debt. Should the court pierce the corporate veil? Explain. [*Bear, Inc. v. Smith*, 303 S.W.3d 137 (Ky.App. 2010)] **(See page 771.)**

39–7. BUSINESS CASE PROBLEM WITH SAMPLE ANSWER: Close Corporations. *Mark Burnett and Kamran Pourgol were the only shareholders in a corporation that built and sold a house. When the buyers discovered that the house exceeded the amount of square footage allowed by the building permit, Pourgol agreed to renovate the house to conform to the permit. No work was done, however, and Burnett filed a suit against Pourgol. Burnett claimed that, without his knowledge, Pourgol had submitted incorrect plans to obtain the building permit, misrepresented the extent of the renovation, and failed to fix the house. Was Pourgol guilty of misconduct? If so, how might it have been avoided? Discuss. [Burnett v. Pourgol, 83 A.D.3d 756, 921 N.Y.S.2d 280 (2 Dept. 2011)]* **(See page 772.)**

- For a sample answer to Problem 39–7, go to Appendix F at the end of this text.

39–8. Piercing the Corporate Veil. In 1997, Leon Greenblatt, Andrew Jahelka, and Richard Nichols incorporated Loop Corp. with only $1,000 of capital. Three years later, Banco Panamericano, Inc., which was run entirely by Greenblatt and owned by a Greenblatt family trust, extended a large line of credit to Loop. Loop's subsidiaries then participated in the credit, giving $3 million to Loop while acquiring a security interest in Loop itself. Loop then opened an account with Wachovia Securities, LLC, to buy stock shares using credit provided by Wachovia. When the stock values plummeted, Loop owed Wachovia $1.89 million.

Loop also defaulted on its loan from Banco, but Banco agreed to lend Loop millions of dollars more. Rather than repay Wachovia with the influx of funds, Loop gave the funds to closely related entities and "compensated" Nichols and Jahelka without issuing any W-2 forms (forms reporting compensation to the Internal Revenue Service). The evidence also showed that Loop made loans to other related entities and shared office space, equipment, and telephone and fax numbers with related entities. Loop also moved employees among related entities, failed to file its tax returns on time (or sometimes at all), and failed to follow its own bylaws. In a lawsuit brought by Wachovia, can the court hold Greenblatt, Jahelka, and Nichols personally liable by piercing the corporate veil? Why or why not? [*Wachovia Securities, LLC v. Banco Panamericano, Inc.,* 674 F.3d 743 (9th Cir. 2012)] **(See page 771.)**

39–9. A QUESTION OF ETHICS: Improper Incorporation.

 Mike Lyons incorporated Lyons Concrete, Inc., in Montana, but did not file its first annual report, so the state involuntarily dissolved the firm in 1996. Unaware of the dissolution, Lyons continued to do business as Lyons Concrete. In 2003, he signed a written contract with William Weimar to form and pour a certain amount of concrete on Weimar's property in Lake County for $19,810. Weimar was in a rush to complete the entire project, and he and Lyons orally agreed to additional work on a time-and-materials basis. When scheduling conflicts arose, Weimar had his own employees set some of the forms, which proved deficient. Weimar also directed Lyons to pour concrete in the rain, which undercut its quality. In mid-project, Lyons submitted an invoice for $14,389, which Weimar paid. After the work was complete, Lyons sent Weimar an invoice for $25,731, but he refused to pay, claiming that the $14,389 covered everything. To recover the unpaid amount, Lyons filed a mechanic's lien as "Mike Lyons d/b/a Lyons Concrete, Inc." against Weimar's property. Weimar filed a suit in a Montana state court to strike the lien, and Lyons filed a counterclaim to reassert it. [*Weimar v. Lyons, 338 Mont. 242, 164 P.3d 922 (2007)*] **(See page 769.)**

(a) Before the trial, Weimar asked for a change of venue on the ground that a sign on the courthouse lawn advertised "Lyons Concrete." How might the sign affect a trial on the parties' dispute? Should the court grant this request? Why or why not?

(b) Weimar asked the court to dismiss the counterclaim on the ground that the state had dissolved Lyons Concrete in 1996. Lyons immediately filed new articles of incorporation for "Lyons Concrete, Inc." Under what doctrine might the court rule that Weimar could not deny the existence of Lyons Concrete? What ethical values underlie this doctrine? Should the court make this ruling? Explain.

(c) At the trial, Weimar argued, in part, that there was no "fixed price" contract between the parties and that even if there were, the poor quality of the work, which required repairs, amounted to a breach, excusing Weimar's further performance. Should the court rule in Weimar's favor on this basis? Why or why not?

Legal Reasoning Group Activity

39–10. Corporate versus LLC Form of Business. Although a limited liability company (LLC—see Chapter 38) may be the best organizational form for most businesses, a significant number of firms may be better off as a corporation or some other form of organization. **(See page 759.)**

(a) The first group will outline several reasons why a firm might be better off as a corporation than as an LLC.

(b) The second group will discuss the differences between corporations and LLCs in terms of their management structure.

CHAPTER 40

CORPORATE DIRECTORS, OFFICERS, AND SHAREHOLDERS

A corporation joins together the efforts and resources of a large number of individuals for the purpose of producing greater returns than those persons could have obtained individually. Corporate directors, officers, and shareholders all play different roles within the corporate entity.

Sometimes, actions that may benefit the corporation as a whole do not coincide with the separate interests of the individuals making up the corporation. In such situations, it is important to know the rights and duties of all participants in the corporate enterprise. This chapter focuses on these rights and duties and the ways in which conflicts among corporate participants are resolved.

SECTION 1

ROLE OF DIRECTORS AND OFFICERS

The board of directors is the ultimate authority in every corporation. Directors have responsibility for all policymaking decisions necessary to the management of all corporate affairs. Additionally, the directors must act as a body in carrying out routine corporate business. The board selects and removes the corporate officers, determines the capital structure of the corporation, and declares dividends. Each director has one vote, and customarily the majority rules. The general areas of responsibility of the board of directors are shown in Exhibit 40–1 on the following page.

Directors are sometimes inappropriately characterized as *agents* because they act on behalf of the corporation. No individual director, however, can act as an agent to bind the corporation. As a group, directors collectively control the corporation in a way that no agent is able to control a principal. In addition, although directors occupy positions of trust and control over the corporation, they are not *trustees* because they do not hold title to property for the use and benefit of others.

Few qualifications are required for directors. Only a handful of states impose minimum age and residency requirements. A director may be a shareholder, but that is not necessary (unless the articles of incorporation or bylaws require ownership interest).

Election of Directors

Subject to statutory limitations, the number of directors is set forth in the corporation's articles or bylaws. Historically, the minimum number of directors has been three, but today many states permit fewer. Normally, the incorporators appoint the first board of directors at the time the corporation is created, or the directors are named in the articles of incorporation. The initial board serves until the first annual shareholders' meeting. Subsequent directors are elected by a majority vote of the shareholders.

A director usually serves for a term of one year—from annual meeting to annual meeting. Most state statutes permit longer and staggered terms. A common practice is to elect one-third of the board members each year for a three-year term. In this way, there is greater management continuity.

REMOVAL OF DIRECTORS A director can be removed *for cause*—that is, for failing to perform a required duty—either as specified in the articles or bylaws or by shareholder action. The board of directors may also have the power to remove a director for cause, subject to shareholder review. In most states, a director cannot be removed without cause unless the shareholders have reserved the right to do so at the time of election.

VACANCIES ON THE BOARD Vacancies occur on the board if a director dies or resigns or when a new position is created through amendment of the articles or

EXHIBIT 40-1 Directors' Management Responsibilities

Authorize Major Corporate Policy Decisions	Select and Remove Corporate Officers and Other Managerial Employees, and Determine Their Compensation	Make Financial Decisions
Examples: • Oversee major contract negotiations and management-labor negotiations. • Initiate negotiations on the sale or lease of corporate assets outside the regular course of business. • Decide whether to pursue new product lines or business opportunities.	*Examples:* • Search for and hire corporate executives and determine the elements of their compensation packages, including stock options. • Supervise managerial employees and make decisions regarding their termination.	*Examples:* • Make decisions regarding the issuance of authorized shares and bonds. • Decide when to declare dividends to be paid to shareholders.

bylaws. In these situations, either the shareholders or the board itself can fill the vacant position, depending on state law or on the provisions of the bylaws.

Note, however, that even when an election appears to be authorized by the bylaws, a court can invalidate the results if the directors were attempting to manipulate the election in order to reduce the shareholders' influence. ▶ **Case in Point 40.1** The bylaws of Liquid Audio, Inc., authorized a board of five directors. Two directors were elected each year. Another company offered to buy all of Liquid Audio's stock, but the board rejected this offer.

To prevent the shareholders from electing new directors who would allow the sale, the directors amended the bylaws. The amendment increased the number of directors to seven, thereby diminishing the shareholders' influence in the upcoming election. The shareholders filed an action challenging the election. The court ruled that the directors' action was illegal because they had attempted to diminish the shareholders' right to vote effectively in an election of directors.[1] ◀

Compensation of Directors

In the past, corporate directors were rarely compensated. Today, directors are often paid at least nominal sums and may receive more substantial compensation in large corporations because of the time, work, effort, and especially risk involved.

Most states permit the corporate articles or bylaws to authorize compensation for directors. In fact, the Revised Model Business Corporation Act (RMBCA)

states that unless the articles or bylaws provide otherwise, the board itself may set the directors' compensation [RMBCA 8.11]. Directors also receive indirect benefits, such as business contacts and prestige, and other rewards, such as stock options.

In many corporations, directors are also chief corporate officers (president or chief executive officer, for example) and receive compensation in their managerial positions. A director who is also an officer of the corporation is referred to as an **inside director,** whereas a director who does not hold a management position is an **outside director.** Typically, a corporation's board of directors includes both inside and outside directors.

Board of Directors' Meetings

The board of directors conducts business by holding formal meetings with recorded minutes. The dates of regular meetings are usually established in the articles or bylaws or by board resolution, and ordinarily no further notice is required.

Special meetings can be called, with notice sent to all directors. Most states today allow directors to participate in board of directors' meetings from remote locations via telephone, Web conferencing, or Skype, provided that all the directors can simultaneously hear each other during the meeting [RMBCA 8.20].

QUORUM OF DIRECTORS Unless the articles of incorporation or bylaws specify a greater number, a majority of the board of directors normally constitutes a *quorum* [RMBCA 8.24]. (A **quorum** is the minimum number of members of a body of officials or other group that must be present for business to be validly transacted.) Some state statutes specifically allow

---

1. *MM Companies, Inc. v. Liquid Audio, Inc.,* 813 A.2d 1118 (Del.Sup.Ct. 2003).

corporations to set a quorum at less than a majority but not less than one-third of the directors.[2]

VOTING Once a quorum is present, the directors transact business and vote on issues affecting the corporation. Each director present at the meeting has one vote.[3] Ordinary matters generally require a simple majority vote, but certain extraordinary issues may require a greater-than-majority vote.

Committees of the Board of Directors

When a board of directors has a large number of members and must deal with myriad complex business issues, meetings can become unwieldy. Therefore, the boards of large, publicly held corporations typically create committees of directors and delegate certain tasks to these committees. By focusing on specific subjects, committees can increase the efficiency of the board.

Two common types of committees are the *executive committee* and the *audit committee*. An executive committee handles interim management decisions between board meetings. It is limited to dealing with ordinary business matters, though, and does not have the power to declare dividends, amend the bylaws, or authorize the issuance of stock. The Sarbanes-Oxley Act requires all publicly held corporations to have an audit committee. The audit committee is responsible for the selection, compensation, and oversight of the independent public accountants that audit the firm's financial records.

Rights of Directors

A corporate director must have certain rights to function properly in that position.

RIGHT TO PARTICIPATION The *right to participation* means that directors are entitled to participate in all board of directors' meetings and have a right to be notified of these meetings. Because the dates of regular board meetings are usually specified in the bylaws, no notice of these meetings is required. If special meetings are called, however, notice is required unless waived by the director [RMBCA 8.23].

RIGHT OF INSPECTION A director also has a *right of inspection,* which means that each director can access the corporation's books and records, facilities, and premises. Inspection rights are essential for directors to make informed decisions and to exercise the necessary supervision over corporate officers and employees. This right of inspection is almost absolute and cannot be restricted (by the articles, bylaws, or any act of the board of directors).

RIGHT TO INDEMNIFICATION When a director becomes involved in litigation by virtue of her or his position or actions, the director may also have a *right to indemnification* (reimbursement) for the legal costs, fees, and damages incurred. Most states allow corporations to indemnify and purchase liability insurance for corporate directors [RMBCA 8.51].

Corporate Officers and Executives

Corporate officers and other executive employees are hired by the board of directors. At a minimum, most corporations have a president, one or more vice presidents, a secretary, and a treasurer. In most states, an individual can hold more than one office, such as president and secretary, and can be both an officer and a director of the corporation.

In addition to carrying out the duties articulated in the bylaws, corporate and managerial officers act as agents of the corporation. Therefore, the ordinary rules of agency (discussed in Chapters 32 and 33) normally apply to their employment.

Corporate officers and other high-level managers are employees of the company, so their rights are defined by employment contracts. Nevertheless, the board of directors normally can remove a corporate officer at any time with or without cause. If the directors remove an officer in violation of the terms of an employment contract, however, the corporation may be liable for breach of contract.

For a synopsis of the roles of directors and officers, see *Concept Summary 40.1* on the following page.

SECTION 2

DUTIES AND LIABILITIES OF DIRECTORS AND OFFICERS

The duties of corporate directors and officers are similar because both groups are involved in decision making and are in positions of control. Directors and

---

2. See, for example, Delaware Code Annotated Title 8, Section 141(b); and New York Business Corporation Law Section 707.

3. Except in Louisiana, which allows a director to vote by proxy under certain circumstances.

CONCEPT SUMMARY 40.1
Roles of Directors and Officers

ASPECT	DESCRIPTION
Election of Directors	The incorporators usually appoint the first board of directors. Thereafter, shareholders elect the directors. Directors usually serve a one-year term, although the term can be longer. Few qualifications are required. A director can be a shareholder but is not required to be. Compensation usually is specified in the corporate articles or bylaws.
Board of Directors' Meetings	The board of directors conducts business by holding formal meetings with recorded minutes. The dates of regular meetings are usually established in the corporate articles or bylaws. Special meetings can be called, with notice sent to all directors. Usually, a quorum is a majority of the corporate directors. Once a quorum is present, each director has one vote, and the majority normally rules in ordinary matters.
Rights of Directors	Directors' rights include the rights of participation, inspection, compensation, and indemnification.
Board of Directors' Committees	Directors may appoint committees and delegate some of their responsibilities to the committees and to corporate officers and executives. For example, directors commonly appoint an *executive committee,* which handles ordinary, interim management decisions between board of directors' meetings. Directors may also appoint an *audit committee* to hire and supervise the independent public accountants who audit the corporation's financial records.
Role of Corporate Officers and Executives	The board of directors normally hires the corporate officers and other executive employees. In most states, a person can hold more than one office and can be both an officer and a director of a corporation. The rights of corporate officers and executives are defined by employment contracts.

---

officers are considered to be fiduciaries of the corporation because their relationship with the corporation and its shareholders is one of trust and confidence. As fiduciaries, directors and officers owe ethical—and legal—duties to the corporation and the shareholders as a whole. These fiduciary duties include the duty of care and the duty of loyalty.

Duty of Care

Directors and officers must exercise due care in performing their duties. The standard of *due care* has been variously described in judicial decisions and codified in many state corporation codes. Generally, it requires a director or officer to:

1. Act in good faith (honestly).
2. Exercise the care that an ordinarily prudent (careful) person would exercise in similar circumstances.
3. Do what she or he believes is in the best interests of the corporation [RMBCA 8.30(a), 8.42(a)].

If directors or officers fail to exercise due care and the corporation or its shareholders suffer harm as a result, the directors or officers can be held liable for negligence (unless the *business judgment rule* applies, as will be discussed shortly).

DUTY TO MAKE INFORMED DECISIONS Directors and officers are expected to be informed on corporate matters and to conduct a reasonable investigation of the situation before making a decision. This means that they must do what is necessary to be adequately informed: attend meetings and presentations, ask for information from those who have it, read reports, and review other written materials. In other words, directors and officers must investigate, study, and discuss matters and evaluate alternatives before making a decision. They cannot decide on the spur of the moment without adequate research.

Although directors and officers are expected to act in accordance with their own knowledge and training, they are also normally entitled to rely on information given to them by certain other persons. Under the laws of most states and Section 8.30(b) of the RMBCA, such persons include competent officers or employees, professionals such as attorneys and accountants, and committees of the board of directors (on which the director does not serve). The reliance must be in good faith to insulate a director from liability if the information later proves to be inaccurate or unreliable.

DUTY TO EXERCISE REASONABLE SUPERVISION
Directors are also expected to exercise a reasonable amount of supervision when they delegate work to corporate officers and employees. ▶ **Example 40.2** Dale, a corporate bank director, fails to attend any board of directors' meetings for five years. In addition, Dale never inspects any of the corporate books or records and generally fails to supervise the activities of the bank president and the loan committee. Meanwhile, Brennan, the bank president, who is a corporate officer, makes various improper loans and permits large overdrafts. In this situation, Dale (the corporate director) can be held liable to the corporation for losses resulting from the unsupervised actions of the bank president and the loan committee. ◀

DISSENTING DIRECTORS Directors are expected to attend board of directors' meetings, and their votes should be entered into the minutes. Sometimes, an individual director disagrees with the majority's vote (which becomes an act of the board of directors). Unless a dissent is entered in the minutes, the director is presumed to have assented. If the directors are later held liable for mismanagement as a result of a decision, dissenting directors are rarely held individually liable to the corporation. For this reason, a director who is absent from a given meeting sometimes registers a dissent with the secretary of the board regarding actions taken at the meeting.

The Business Judgment Rule

Directors and officers are expected to exercise due care and to use their best judgment in guiding corporate management, but they are not insurers of business success. Under the **business judgment rule,** a corporate director or officer will not be liable to the corporation or to its shareholders for honest mistakes of judgment and bad business decisions.

Courts give significant deference to the decisions of corporate directors and officers, and consider the reasonableness of a decision at the time it was made, without the benefit of hindsight. Thus, corporate decision makers are not subjected to second-guessing by shareholders or others in the corporation.

WHEN THE RULE APPLIES The business judgment rule will apply as long as the director or officer:

1. Took reasonable steps to become informed about the matter.
2. Had a rational basis for her or his decision.
3. Did not have a conflict of interest between her or his personal interest and that of the corporation.

PROVIDES BROAD PROTECTIONS The business judgment rule provides broad protections to corporate decision makers. In fact, unless there is evidence of bad faith, fraud, or a clear breach of fiduciary duties, most courts will apply the rule and protect directors and officers who make bad business decisions from liability for those choices.

▶ **Case in Point 40.3** After a foreign firm announced its intention to acquire Lyondell Chemical Company, Lyondell's directors did nothing to prepare for a possible merger. They failed to research Lyondell's market value and made no attempt to seek out other potential buyers. The $13 billion cash merger was negotiated and finalized in less than a week—and the directors met for only seven hours to discuss it. Shareholders sued, claiming that the directors had breached their fiduciary duties by failing to maximize the sale price of the corporation. The Delaware Supreme Court ruled that the directors were protected by the business judgment rule.[4] ◀

Duty of Loyalty

Loyalty can be defined as faithfulness to one's obligations and duties. In the corporate context, the duty of loyalty requires directors and officers to subordinate their personal interests to the welfare of the corporation. For instance, a director should not oppose a transaction that is in the corporation's best interest simply because pursuing it may cost the director his or her position.

Directors cannot use corporate funds or confidential corporate information for personal advantage and must refrain from self-dealing. Cases dealing with the duty of loyalty typically involve one or more of the following:

1. Competing with the corporation.
2. Usurping (taking personal advantage of) a corporate opportunity.
3. Pursuing an interest that conflicts with that of the corporation.
4. Using information that is not available to the public to make a profit trading securities (see the discussion of *insider trading* in Chapter 42).

4. *Lyondell Chemical Co. v. Ryan,* 970 A.2d 235 (Del.Sup. 2009).

5. Authorizing a corporate transaction that is detrimental to minority shareholders.
6. Selling control over the corporation.

The following classic case illustrates the conflict that can arise between a corporate official's personal interest and his or her duty of loyalty.

CLASSIC CASE 40.1

Guth v. Loft, Inc.
Supreme Court of Delaware, 23 Del.Ch. 255, 5 A.2d 503 (1939).

BACKGROUND AND FACTS In 1930, Charles Guth became the president of Loft, Inc., a candy-and-restaurant chain. Guth and his family also owned Grace Company, which made syrups for soft drinks. Coca-Cola Company supplied Loft with cola syrup. Unhappy with what he felt was Coca-Cola's high price, Guth entered into an agreement with Roy Megargel to acquire the trademark and formula for Pepsi-Cola and form Pepsi-Cola Corporation. Neither Guth nor Megargel could finance the new venture, however, and Grace Company was insolvent.

Without the knowledge of Loft's board, Guth used Loft's capital, credit, facilities, and employees to further the Pepsi enterprise. At Guth's direction, a Loft employee made the concentrate for the syrup, which was sent to Grace to add sugar and water. Loft charged Grace for the concentrate but allowed forty months' credit. Grace charged Pepsi for the syrup but also granted substantial credit. Grace sold the syrup to Pepsi's customers, including Loft, which paid on delivery or within thirty days. Loft also paid for Pepsi's advertising. Finally, with profits declining as a result of switching from Coca-Cola, Loft filed a suit in a Delaware state court against Guth, Grace, and Pepsi, seeking their Pepsi stock and an accounting. The court entered a judgment in the plaintiff's favor. The defendants appealed to the Delaware Supreme Court.

IN THE LANGUAGE OF THE COURT
LAYTON, Chief Justice, delivering the opinion of the court:

* * * *

Corporate officers and directors are not permitted to use their position of trust and confidence to further their private interests. * * * They stand in a fiduciary relation to the corporation and its stockholders. A public policy, existing through the years, and derived from a profound knowledge of human characteristics and motives, has established *a rule that demands of a corporate officer or director, peremptorily [not open for debate] and inexorably [unavoidably], the most scrupulous observance of his duty, not only affirmatively to protect the interests of the corporation committed to his charge, but also to refrain from doing anything that would work injury to the corporation * * *.* The rule that requires an undivided and unselfish loyalty to the corporation demands that there shall be no conflict between duty and self-interest. [Emphasis added.]

* * * *

* * * *If there is presented to a corporate officer or director a business opportunity which the corporation is financially able to undertake [that] is * * * in the line of the corporation's business and is of practical advantage to it * * * and, by embracing the opportunity, the self-interest of the officer or director will be brought into conflict with that of his corporation, the law will not permit him to seize the opportunity for himself.* * * * In such circumstances, * * * the corporation may elect to claim all of the benefits of the transaction for itself, and the law will impress a trust in favor of the corporation upon the property, interests and profits so acquired. [Emphasis added.]

* * * *

* * * The appellants contend that no conflict of interest between Guth and Loft resulted from his acquirement and exploitation of the Pepsi-Cola opportunity [and] that the acquisition did not place Guth in competition with Loft * * * . [In this case, however,] Guth was Loft, and Guth was Pepsi. He absolutely controlled Loft. His authority over Pepsi was supreme. As Pepsi, he created and controlled the supply of Pepsi-Cola syrup, and he determined the price and the terms. What he offered, as Pepsi, he had the power, as Loft, to accept. Upon any consideration of human characteristics and motives, he created a conflict between self-interest

CASE 40.1 CONTINUES ▶

and duty. He made himself the judge in his own cause. * * * Moreover, a reasonable probability of injury to Loft resulted from the situation forced upon it. Guth was in the same position to impose his terms upon Loft as had been the Coca-Cola Company.

* * * The facts and circumstances demonstrate that Guth's appropriation of the Pepsi-Cola opportunity to himself placed him in a competitive position with Loft with respect to a commodity essential to it, thereby rendering his personal interests incompatible with the superior interests of his corporation; and this situation was accomplished, not openly and with his own resources, but secretly and with the money and facilities of the corporation which was committed to his protection.

DECISION AND REMEDY *The Delaware Supreme Court upheld the judgment of the lower court. The state supreme court was "convinced that the opportunity to acquire the Pepsi-Cola trademark and formula, goodwill and business belonged to [Loft], and that Guth, as its President, had no right to appropriate the opportunity to himself."*

WHAT IF THE FACTS WERE DIFFERENT? *Suppose that Loft's board of directors had approved Pepsi-Cola's use of its personnel and equipment. Would the court's decision have been different? Discuss.*

IMPACT OF THIS CASE ON TODAY'S LAW *This early Delaware decision was one of the first to set forth a test for determining when a corporate officer or director has breached the duty of loyalty. The test has two basic parts: Was the opportunity reasonably related to the corporation's line of business, and was the corporation financially able to undertake the opportunity? The court also considered whether the corporation had an interest or expectancy in the opportunity and recognized that when the corporation had "no interest or expectancy, the officer or director is entitled to treat the opportunity as his own."*

Conflicts of Interest

Corporate directors often have many business affiliations, and a director may sit on the board of more than one corporation. Of course, directors are precluded from entering into or supporting businesses that operate in direct competition with corporations on whose boards they serve. Their fiduciary duty requires them to make a full disclosure of any potential conflicts of interest that might arise in any corporate transaction [RMBCA 8.60].

Sometimes, a corporation enters into a contract or engages in a transaction in which an officer or director has a personal interest. The director or officer must make a *full disclosure* of the nature of the conflicting interest and all facts pertinent to the transaction, and must abstain from voting on the proposed transaction. Otherwise, directors would be prevented from ever having financial dealings with the corporations they serve.

▶ **Example 40.4** Ballo Corporation needs office space. Stephanie Colson, one of its five directors, owns the building adjoining the corporation's headquarters. Colson can negotiate a lease for the space to Ballo if she fully discloses her conflicting interest and

any facts known to her about the proposed transaction to Ballo and the other four directors. If the lease arrangement is fair and reasonable, Colson abstains from voting on it, and the other members of the corporation's board of directors unanimously approve it, the contract is valid. ◀

Liability of Directors and Officers

Directors and officers are exposed to liability on many fronts. They can be held liable for negligence in certain circumstances, as previously discussed. They may also be held liable for the crimes and torts committed by themselves or by corporate employees under their supervision, as discussed in Chapters 10, 33, and 39. (See this chapter's *Insight into Ethics* on the following page for a discussion of how one federal statute makes lying a crime.)

Additionally, if shareholders perceive that the corporate directors are not acting in the best interests of the corporation, they may sue the directors, in what is called a *shareholder's derivative suit,* on behalf of the corporation. (This type of action will be discussed later in this chapter, in the context of shareholders'

INSIGHT INTO ETHICS
When Is Lying a Federal Crime?

The federal government defines and prosecutes almost 4,500 crimes. In addition to prosecuting defendants for allegedly committing these crimes, the government can also charge them with lying about their actions. Under Section 1001 of Title 18 of the *United States Code,* any person convicted of knowingly and willfully making "any material false, fictitious or fraudulent statements or misrepresentations" can be fined or imprisoned or both. When prosecutors do not have enough evidence to charge someone with the underlying crime, they may still bring charges under Section 1001 if the person made any false statements in interviews.

A Costly Phone Interview

In 2004, attorney Melissa Ann Mahler was interviewed by phone by an official at the Securities and Exchange Commission. She made a false statement about a securities transaction in her personal brokerage account. Ultimately, a court determined that she had violated Section 1001. The court suspended Mahler's attorney's license, sentenced her to two years on probation, fined her $2,500, and ordered her to perform a hundred hours of community service.[a]

Whistling at a Whale Can Be Dangerous

Nancy Black, a marine biologist who operates a whale-watching boat company in California, also ran afoul of Section 1001. When a humpback whale appeared near one of her boats, the captain of the boat whistled at the whale, hoping that the sound would intrigue the whale and cause it to come closer. Regulators investigated whether the whistling constituted harassment of a whale, which is a federal crime.

Prosecutors have not charged Black with whale harassment. Instead, she has been charged with lying about the

incident by supplying the regulators with a video that had been edited to delete material that Black thought was not relevant. In an interview, she commented, "I wasn't charged with anything about the dealings with the humpback. So why would they charge me with lying about it? It makes no sense."[b]

What Constitutes a Lie under Section 1001?

The courts have interpreted Section 1001 as encompassing almost any statement made to a federal official. The statement may be oral or in writing. The person making it need not be under oath, and the government does not have to have warned the person that any falsehood could have very serious consequences.

Although the lie has to be "material," any statement that has a "natural tendency to influence, or [is] capable of influencing, the decision of the decision-making body to which it is addressed" is considered material.[c] In other words, the federal government does not have to show that the falsehood actually influenced or misled anyone.

Consider a not too far-fetched example. Suppose that you fill out your time sheets at work inaccurately by listing more hours than you actually worked and occasionally complete a time sheet for a day that you did not work. If your employer has to submit employees' time sheets to a federal regulatory agency, you could ultimately be held criminally liable for lying.

LEGAL CRITICAL THINKING

INSIGHT INTO THE SOCIAL ENVIRONMENT
Many businesspersons believe that the federal government's power under Section 1001 is almost without limits. What ethical issues are at stake here?

---

a. *Matter of Mahler,* 94 A.D.3d 114, 939 N.Y.S.2d 900 (2012). See also *In re Simels,* 94 A.D.3d 108, 940 N.Y.S. 2d 577 (2012).

b. " 'Lying' Is a Handy Charge for the U.S. Government," *Wall Street Journal,* April 11, 2012.

c. *United States v. Gaudin,* 515 U.S. 506,115 S.Ct. 2310, 132 L.Ed.2d 444 (1995).

---

rights.) Directors and officers can also be held personally liable under a number of statutes, such as statutes enacted to protect consumers or the environment (see Chapters 44 and 45).

See *Concept Summary 40.2* on the following page for a review of the duties and liabilities of directors and officers.

SECTION 3
THE ROLE OF SHAREHOLDERS

The acquisition of a share of stock makes a person an owner and a shareholder in a corporation. Shareholders thus own the corporation. Although

---

CONCEPT SUMMARY 40.2
Duties and Liabilities of Directors and Officers

ASPECT	DESCRIPTION
Duties of Directors and Officers	1. *Duty of care*—Directors and officers are obligated to act in good faith, to use prudent business judgment in the conduct of corporate affairs, and to act in the corporation's best interests. If a director or officer fails to exercise this duty of care, he or she may be answerable to the corporation and to the shareholders for breaching the duty. The *business judgment rule* immunizes a director from liability for a corporate decision as long as it was within the power of the corporation and the authority of the director to make and was an informed, reasonable, and loyal decision. 2. *Duty of loyalty*—Directors and officers have a fiduciary duty to subordinate their own interests to those of the corporation in matters relating to the corporation. 3. *Conflicts of interest*—To fulfill their duty of loyalty, directors and officers must make a full disclosure of any potential conflicts between their personal interests and those of the corporation.
Liability of Directors and Officers	Corporate directors and officers are personally liable for their own torts and crimes (when not protected under the business judgment rule). Additionally, they may be held personally liable for the torts and crimes committed by corporate personnel under their direct supervision (see Chapters 6, 10, 33, and 39). They may also be held personally liable for violating certain statutes, such as environmental and consumer protection laws, and can sometimes be sued by shareholders for mismanaging the corporation.

---

they have no legal title to corporate property, such as buildings and equipment, they do have an equitable (ownership) interest in the firm.

As a general rule, shareholders have no responsibility for the daily management of the corporation, although they are ultimately responsible for choosing the board of directors, which does have such control. Ordinarily, corporate officers and other employees owe no direct duty to individual shareholders (unless some contract or special relationship exists between them in addition to the corporate relationship).

The duty of officers and directors is to act in the best interests of the corporation and its shareholder-owners *as a whole*. In turn, as you will read later in this chapter, controlling shareholders owe a fiduciary duty to minority shareholders.

Shareholders' Powers

Shareholders must approve fundamental changes affecting the corporation before the changes can be implemented. Hence, shareholder approval normally is required to amend the articles of incorporation or bylaws, to conduct a merger or dissolve the corporation, and to sell all or substantially all of the corporation's assets. Some of these powers are subject to

prior board approval. Shareholder approval may also be requested (though it is not required) for certain other actions, such as to approve an independent auditor.

Shareholders also have the power to vote to elect or remove members of the board of directors. As described earlier, the first board of directors is either named in the articles of incorporation or chosen by the incorporators to serve until the first shareholders' meeting. From that time on, selection and retention of directors are exclusively shareholder functions.

Directors usually serve their full terms. If the shareholders judge them unsatisfactory, they are simply not reelected. Shareholders have the inherent power, however, to remove a director from office *for cause* (breach of duty or misconduct) by a majority vote.[5] As noted earlier in this chapter, some state statutes (and some articles of incorporation) permit removal of directors without cause by the vote of a majority of the shareholders entitled to vote.[6]

---

5. A director can often demand court review of removal for cause, however.
6. Most states allow *cumulative voting* for directors (described later in the chapter). If cumulative voting is authorized, a director may not be removed if the number of votes against removal would be sufficient to elect a director under cumulative voting. See, for example, California Corporations Code Section 303A. See also Section 8.08(c) of the RMBCA.

Shareholders' Meetings

Shareholders' meetings must occur at least annually. In addition, special meetings can be called to deal with urgent matters.

NOTICE OF MEETINGS A corporation must notify its shareholders of the date, time, and place of an annual or special shareholders' meeting at least ten days, but not more than sixty days, before the meeting date [RMBCA 7.05].[7] (The date and time of the annual meeting can be specified in the bylaws.) Notice of a special meeting must include a statement of the purpose of the meeting, and business transacted at the meeting is limited to that purpose.

The RMBCA does not specify how the notice must be given (such as by mail, e-mail, or social media), but most corporations specify in their bylaws the acceptable methods of notifying shareholders about meetings. Also, some states' incorporation statutes outline the means of notice that a corporation can use in that jurisdiction. For instance, in Alaska, notice may be given in person, by mail, or by fax, e-mail, blog, or Web post—as long as the shareholder has agreed to that electronic method.[8]

PROXIES It usually is not practical for owners of only a few shares of stock of publicly traded corporations to attend a shareholders' meeting. Therefore, the law allows stockholders to appoint another person as their agent to vote their shares at the meeting. The signed appointment form or electronic transmission authorizing an agent to vote the shares is called a **proxy** (from the Latin *procurare*, meaning "to manage or take care of").

Management often solicits proxies, but any person can do so to concentrate voting power. Groups of shareholders have used proxies as a device for taking over a corporation (corporate takeovers will be discussed in Chapter 41). Proxies normally are revocable (can be withdrawn), unless they are specifically designated as irrevocable and coupled with an interest. A proxy is coupled with an interest when, for instance, the person receiving the proxies from shareholders has agreed to buy their shares. Under RMBCA 7.22(c), proxies are valid for eleven months, unless the proxy agreement mandates a longer period.

SHAREHOLDER PROPOSALS When shareholders want to change a company policy, they can put their ideas up for a shareholder vote. They do this by submitting a shareholder proposal to the board of directors and asking the board to include the proposal in the proxy materials that are sent to all shareholders before meetings.

The Securities and Exchange Commission (SEC) regulates the purchase and sale of securities, as you will read in Chapter 42. The SEC has special provisions relating to proxies and shareholder proposals. SEC Rule 14a-8 provides that all shareholders who own stock worth at least $1,000 are eligible to submit proposals for inclusion in corporate proxy materials. The corporation is required to include information on whatever proposals will be considered at the shareholders' meeting along with proxy materials. Only those proposals that relate to significant policy considerations, not ordinary business operations, must be included.

ELECTRONIC PROXY MATERIALS In the past, corporations had to send large packets of paper documents to shareholders, but today, the SEC requires all publicly held companies to distribute electronic proxy (e-proxy) materials.[9] Although the law requires proxy materials to be posted online, public companies may still choose among several options—including paper documents or a DVD sent by mail—for actually delivering the materials to shareholders.

If a company wishes to distribute proxy materials only via the Internet, it can choose the notice-and-access delivery option. Under this model, the corporation posts the proxy materials on a Web site and notifies the shareholders that the proxy materials are available online. If a shareholder requests paper proxy materials, the company must send them within three business days. Shareholders can permanently elect to receive all future proxy materials on paper or by e-mail with electronic links.

Shareholder Voting

Shareholders exercise ownership control through the power of their votes. Corporate business matters are presented in the form of resolutions, which shareholders vote to approve or disapprove. Unless there is a provision to the contrary, each common shareholder is entitled to one vote per share, although the voting techniques discussed next enhance the power of the shareholder's vote.

---

7. The shareholder can waive the requirement of notice by signing a waiver form [RMBCA 7.06]. A shareholder who does not receive notice but who learns of the meeting and attends without protesting the lack of notice is said to have waived notice by such conduct.

8. Alaska Statutes Section 10.06.410 Notice of Shareholders' Meetings.

9. 17 C.F.R. Parts 240, 249, and 274.

The articles of incorporation can exclude or limit voting rights, particularly for certain classes of shares. For instance, owners of preferred shares are usually denied the right to vote [RMBCA 7.21]. If a state statute requires specific voting procedures, the corporation's articles or bylaws must be consistent with the statute.

QUORUM REQUIREMENTS For shareholders to act during a meeting, a quorum must be present. Generally, a quorum exists when shareholders holding more than 50 percent of the outstanding shares are present, but state laws often permit the articles of incorporation to set higher or lower quorum requirements. In some states, obtaining the unanimous written consent of shareholders is a permissible alternative to holding a shareholders' meeting [RMBCA 7.25].

Once a quorum is present, voting can proceed. A straight majority vote of the shares represented at the meeting is usually required to pass resolutions. ▶ **Example 40.5** Novo Pictures, Inc., has 10,000 outstanding shares of voting stock. Its articles of incorporation set the quorum at 50 percent of outstanding shares and provide that a majority vote of the shares present is necessary to pass ordinary mat-

ters. Therefore, for this firm, a quorum of stockholders representing 5,000 outstanding shares must be present to conduct business at the shareholders' meeting. If exactly 5,000 shares are represented at the meeting, a vote of at least 2,501 of those shares is needed to pass a resolution. If 6,000 shares are represented, a vote of 3,001 will be necessary. ◀

At times, more than a simple majority vote will be required either by statute or by the articles of incorporation. Extraordinary corporate matters, such as a merger, a consolidation, or dissolution of the corporation (see Chapter 41), require a higher percentage (more than a majority) of all corporate shares entitled to vote [RMBCA 7.27].

The corporation in the following case had eighty-four shares of voting common stock outstanding. The shareholder-appellee owned twenty shares, he and his estranged wife jointly held another sixteen shares, and three different individuals owned sixteen shares each. At a shareholders' meeting, the appellee was the only shareholder present in person. Another shareholder (not the wife) was present by proxy. Could the shares held jointly by the appellee and his wife be counted for purposes of a quorum?

CASE ANALYSIS

Case 40.2 Case v. Sink & Rise, Inc.
Supreme Court of Wyoming, 2013 WY 19, 297 P.3d 762 (2013).

IN THE LANGUAGE OF THE COURT
HILL, Justice.

This case involves a dispute over corporate action during a shareholder meeting of Appellee Sink & Rise, Inc., (Sink & Rise) a Wyoming corporation. Appellee James Caleb Case (Cale Case) was the only shareholder present at the meeting. He concluded that a quorum existed and thus voted on and passed several resolutions. Cale Case also elected himself and another shareholder as the directors of the corporation, and replaced his estranged wife, Appellant Shirley Case, as the corporation's secretary.

Shirley Case took issue with her estranged husband's actions during

the shareholder meeting and filed a complaint in [a Wyoming state] district court to set aside the corporate action that occurred at the shareholder meeting. * * * The district court concluded that the resolutions were passed with requisite authority and thus they were not set aside after trial. This appeal followed.

* * * *

* * * Shirley Case argues that because her estranged husband was not entitled to vote the jointly held shares, those same shares could not be counted for quorum purposes. She reasons that because she was absent from the meeting and because only shares "entitled to vote" are to be counted in establishing a quorum, the shares in question were essentially useless at the meeting.

* * * We find the answer in the Sink & Rise corporate documents, and within Wyoming law. First, we reiterate the [district court's] characterization of the stock as being owned by husband and wife with rights of survivorship. We agree with the district court's further classification of the stock as creating a presumption of tenancy by the entirety under Wyoming law. As tenants by the entirety, each owns an undivided 100% interest in the 16 shares.

In an estate of the entirety, the husband and the wife during their joint lives each owns, not a part, or a separate or a separable interest, but the whole. [Emphasis added.]

To further help us in our consideration, we turn to the corporate documents.

CASE 40.2 CONTINUED

* * * Sink & Rise's bylaws * * * define what constitutes a "quorum," and relate the corporation's rule on voting shares:

6. *Quorum*. A majority of the outstanding shares entitled to vote, represented in person or by proxy, shall constitute a quorum at a meeting of Shareholders. If a quorum is present, the affirmative vote of the majority of shares entitled to vote at the meeting shall be the act of the Shareholders. * * *

7. *Voting of Shares*. * * * Each outstanding share is entitled to vote the number of shares owned by him/her on each matter submitted to a vote at a meeting of Shareholders. * * *

According to the bylaws, for the corporation to count shares in determining a

quorum, the shares must be (1) entitled to vote, and (2) represented in person or by proxy. From our reading of the corporate documents, and because the joint stock was held by husband and wife as tenants by the entirety, we conclude that the shares held jointly by Cale Case and Shirley Case were "entitled to vote" at the meeting. Cale Case represented the stock in person, as required by the bylaws. [Emphasis added.]

As the district court noted, and the parties agree here, the joint stock in question cannot be, and was not, voted without agreement between Cale Case and Shirley Case. * * * [But] the fact that Cale Case and Shirley Case must agree on how to vote the

stock before it can actually be voted does not strip it of its voting privileges. Cale Case did not attempt to vote the stock at the meeting, but instead considered it only for quorum purposes.

Sink & Rise's bylaws do not prevent stock owned by a husband and wife as tenants by the entirety * * * from being counted for purposes of a quorum if represented in person. The stock in question was represented in person by Cale Case at the * * * shareholder meeting, and it was properly counted to establish a quorum.
* * * *

We affirm the district court's decision.

LEGAL REASONING QUESTIONS

1. How many shareholders were present at the shareholders' meeting that gave rise to the dispute in this case?

2. How did the court "characterize" and "classify" the shares of stock that Cale and Shirley Case held jointly?

3. According to the court, how many shares were represented at the shareholders' meeting? Was a quorum present? Explain.

4. Were the shares that Cale owned jointly with Shirley voted at the meeting? How did the jointly owned shares affect the business conducted? Explain.

VOTING LISTS The corporation prepares the voting list before each shareholders' meeting. Ordinarily, only persons whose names appear on the corporation's stockholder records as owners are entitled to vote.[10]

The voting list contains the name and address of each shareholder as shown on the corporate records on a given cutoff date, or *record date*. (Under RMBCA 7.07, the bylaws or board of directors may fix a record date that is as much as seventy days before the meeting.) The voting list also includes the number of voting shares held by each owner. The list is usually kept at the corporate headquarters and must be made available for shareholder inspection [RMBCA 7.20].

CUMULATIVE VOTING Most states permit, and many require, shareholders to elect directors by *cumulative*

voting, a voting method designed to allow minority shareholders to be represented on the board of directors.[11]

Formula. With cumulative voting, each shareholder is entitled to a total number of votes equal to the number of board members to be elected multiplied by the number of voting shares that the shareholder owns. The shareholder can cast all of these votes for one candidate or split them among several nominees for director. All nominees stand for election at the same time. When cumulative voting is not required by statute or under the articles, the entire board can be elected by a majority of shares at a shareholders' meeting.

---

10. When the legal owner is deceased, bankrupt, mentally incompetent, or in some other way under a legal disability, his or her vote can be cast by a person designated by law to control and manage that owner's property.

11. See, for example, California Corporations Code Section 708. Some states, such as Nebraska, require cumulative voting in their state constitutions. Under RMBCA 7.28, no cumulative voting rights exist unless the articles of incorporation so provide.

How Cumulative Voting Works. Cumulative voting can best be understood by example. ▶ **Example 40.6** A corporation has 10,000 shares issued and outstanding. The minority shareholders hold 3,000 shares, and the majority shareholders hold the other 7,000 shares. Three members of the board are to be elected. The majority shareholders' nominees are Alvarez, Beasley, and Caravel. The minority shareholders' nominee is Dovrik. Can Dovrik be elected to the board by the minority shareholders?

If cumulative voting is allowed, the answer is yes. The minority shareholders have 9,000 votes among them (the number of directors to be elected times the number of shares, or 3 × 3,000 = 9,000 votes). All of these votes can be cast to elect Dovrik. The majority shareholders have 21,000 votes (3 × 7,000 = 21,000 votes), but these votes must be distributed among their three nominees.

The principle of cumulative voting is that no matter how the majority shareholders cast their 21,000 votes, they will not be able to elect all three directors if the minority shareholders cast all of their 9,000 votes for Dovrik, as illustrated in Exhibit 40–2 below. ◀

SHAREHOLDER VOTING AGREEMENTS Before a shareholders' meeting, a group of shareholders can create a *shareholder voting agreement* by agreeing in writing to vote their shares together in a specified manner. Such agreements usually are held to be valid and enforceable. Nevertheless, corporate managers must be careful that such agreements do not constitute a breach of their fiduciary duties.

▶ **Case in Point 40.7** Several shareholders of Cryo-Cell International, Inc., mounted a proxy contest in an effort to replace the board of directors. Another stockholder, Andrew Filipowski, agreed to support management in exchange for being included in management's slate of directors. The company's chief executive officer, Mercedes Walton, secretly promised Filipowski that if management's slate won, the board of directors would add another board seat to be filled by a Filipowski designee.

After management won the election, Walton prepared to add Filipowski's designee to the board. When the dissident shareholders challenged the election results, the court held that the board's actions and Walton's secret agreement constituted serious breaches of fiduciary duty that tainted the election. The court therefore ordered a new election to be held.[12] ◀

VOTING TRUST Another voting technique is for shareholders to enter into a *voting trust*. (A shareholder can also appoint a voting agent and vote by proxy, as mentioned previously.) A **voting trust** is an agreement (a trust contract) under which a shareholder assigns the right to vote his or her shares to a trustee, usually for a specified period of time. The trustee is then responsible for voting the shares on behalf of all the shareholders in the trust. The shareholder retains all rights of ownership (for example, the right to receive dividend payments) except the power to vote the shares [RMBCA 7.30].

SECTION 4
RIGHTS OF SHAREHOLDERS

Shareholders possess numerous rights. A significant right—the right to vote their shares—has already been discussed. We look at some additional rights of shareholders in the following subsections.

Stock Certificates

In the past, corporations commonly issued **stock certificates** that evidenced ownership of a specified number of shares in the corporation. Only a few jurisdictions still require physical stock certificates, and shareholders there have the right to demand that the corporation issue certificates (or replace those that

---

12. *Portnoy v. Cryo-Cell International, Inc.,* 940 A.2d 43 (Del.Ch. 2008).

EXHIBIT 40–2 Results of Cumulative Voting

Ballot	Majority Shareholder Votes			Minority Shareholder Votes	Directors Elected
	Alvarez	*Beasley*	*Caravel*	*Dovrik*	
1	10,000	10,000	1,000	9,000	Alvarez, Beasley, Dovrik
2	9,001	9,000	2,999	9,000	Alvarez, Beasley, Dovrik
3	6,000	7,000	8,000	9,000	Beasley, Caravel, Dovrik

were lost or destroyed). Stock is intangible personal property, however, and the ownership right exists independently of the certificate itself.

In most states and under RMBCA 6.26, a board of directors may provide that shares of stock will be uncertificated, or "paperless"—that is, no actual, physical stock certificates will be issued. When shares are uncertificated, the corporation may be required to send each shareholder a letter or some other form of notice that contains the same information that traditionally appeared on the face of stock certificates. Notice of shareholders' meetings, dividends, and operational and financial reports are all distributed according to the recorded ownership listed in the corporation's books.

Preemptive Rights

Sometimes, the articles of incorporation grant preemptive rights to shareholders. With **preemptive rights,** a shareholder receives a preference over all other purchasers to subscribe to or purchase a prorated share of a new issue of stock. In other words, the shareholder can purchase a percentage of the new shares that is equal to his or her current percentage of ownership in the corporation.

Under RMBCA 6.30, preemptive rights do not exist unless provided for in the articles of incorporation. Generally, preemptive rights apply only to additional, newly issued stock sold for cash, and the preemptive rights must be exercised within a specific time period, which is usually thirty days.

ALLOW A SHAREHOLDER TO MAINTAIN PROPORTIONATE INTEREST Preemptive rights allow each shareholder to maintain her or his proportionate control, voting power, or financial interest in the corporation. ▶ **Example 40.8** Tron Corporation authorizes and issues 1,000 shares of stock, and Omar Loren purchases 100 shares, making him the owner of 10 percent of the company's stock. Subsequently, Tron, by vote of its shareholders, authorizes the issuance of another 1,000 shares (by amending the articles of incorporation). This increases its capital stock to a total of 2,000 shares.

If preemptive rights have been provided, Loren can purchase one additional share of the new stock being issued for each share he already owns—or 100 additional shares. Thus, he will own 200 of the 2,000 shares outstanding, and his relative position as a shareholder will be maintained. If preemptive rights are not provided, his proportionate control and vot-

ing power will be diluted from that of a 10 percent shareholder to that of a 5 percent shareholder because the additional 1,000 shares were issued. ◀

IMPORTANT IN CLOSE CORPORATIONS Preemptive rights are most important in close corporations because each shareholder owns a relatively small number of shares but controls a substantial interest in the corporation. Without preemptive rights, it would be possible for a shareholder to lose his or her proportionate control over the firm. Nevertheless, preemptive rights can hinder a corporation from raising capital from new, outside investors who can provide needed expertise as well as capital.

Stock Warrants

Stock warrants are rights to buy stock at a stated price by a specified date that are given by the company. Usually, when preemptive rights exist and a corporation is issuing additional shares, it gives its shareholders stock warrants. Warrants are often publicly traded on securities exchanges.

Dividends

As mentioned in Chapter 39, a **dividend** is a distribution of corporate profits or income *ordered by the directors* and paid to the shareholders in proportion to their respective shares in the corporation. Dividends can be paid in cash, property, stock of the corporation that is paying the dividends, or stock of other corporations.[13]

State laws vary, but each state determines the general circumstances and legal requirements under which dividends are paid. State laws also control the sources of revenue to be used. Only certain funds are legally available for paying dividends. Depending on state law, dividends may be paid from the following sources:

1. *Retained earnings.* All states allow dividends to be paid from the undistributed net profits earned by the corporation, including capital gains from the sale of fixed assets. As mentioned in Chapter 39, the undistributed net profits are called *retained earnings.*
2. *Net profits.* A few states allow dividends to be issued from current net profits without regard to deficits in prior years.

---

13. On one occasion, a distillery declared and paid a dividend in bonded whiskey.

3. *Surplus.* A number of states allow dividends to be paid out of any kind of surplus. For instance, earned surplus is the sum of a company's net profits over a period of time. It increases by the amount of each year's net income after dividend payments. Earned surplus is not extra cash, but shareholder equity. A company's board of directors may choose to pay dividends from the surplus or to use it for some other corporate purpose (such as for acquisitions).

ILLEGAL DIVIDENDS Sometimes, dividends are improperly paid from an unauthorized account, or their payment causes the corporation to become insolvent. Generally, shareholders must return illegal dividends only if they knew that the dividends were illegal when the payment was received (or if the dividends were paid when the corporation was insolvent). Whenever dividends are illegal or improper, the board of directors can be held personally liable for the amount of the payment.

THE DIRECTORS' FAILURE TO DECLARE A DIVIDEND
When directors fail to declare a dividend, shareholders can ask a court to compel the directors to meet and declare a dividend. To succeed, the shareholders must show that the directors have acted so unreasonably in withholding the dividend that their conduct is an abuse of their discretion.

Often, a corporation accumulates large cash reserves for a legitimate corporate purpose, such as expansion or research. The mere fact that the firm has sufficient earnings or surplus available to pay a dividend normally is not enough to compel the directors to distribute funds that, in the board's opinion, should not be distributed.[14] The courts are reluctant to interfere with corporate operations and will not compel directors to declare dividends unless abuse of discretion is clearly shown.

Inspection Rights

Shareholders in a corporation enjoy both common law and statutory inspection rights. The RMBCA provides that every shareholder is entitled to examine specified corporate records, including voting lists [RMBCA 7.20, 16.02]. The shareholder may inspect in person, or an attorney, accountant, or other authorized assistant can do so as the shareholder's agent.

PROPER PURPOSE A shareholder only has a right to inspect and copy corporate books and records for a *proper purpose*, however, and the request to inspect must be made in advance. A shareholder who is denied the right of inspection can seek a court order to compel the inspection.

▶ **Case in Point 40.9** Jeffrey Hagen was a minority shareholder of Distributed Solutions, Inc. (DSI). Craig Johnson, the majority shareholder, sold DSI's payroll services to himself and set up another payroll services company. Johnson told Hagen that he was dissolving DSI because it conducted no business and had no future prospects. Hagen asked to inspect the corporate records so that he could determine DSI's financial condition, the value of its stock, and whether any misconduct had occurred. Johnson refused to permit an inspection. A court found that Hagen had shown a proper purpose and allowed him access to DSI's records.[15] ◄

POTENTIAL FOR ABUSE The power of inspection is fraught with potential abuses, and the corporation is allowed to protect itself from them. For instance, a shareholder can properly be denied access to corporate records to prevent harassment or to protect trade secrets or other confidential corporate information.[16] In some states, a shareholder must have held her or his shares for a minimum period of time immediately preceding the demand to inspect or must hold a certain percentage of outstanding shares.

Transfer of Shares

Corporate stock represents an ownership right in intangible personal property. The law generally recognizes the right of an owner to transfer property to another person unless there are valid restrictions on its transferability. Restrictions on the transfer of shares in a close corporation usually are valid.

When shares are transferred, a new entry is made in the corporate stock book to indicate the new owner. Until the corporation is notified and the entry is complete, all rights—including voting rights, notice of shareholders' meetings, and the right to dividend distributions—remain with the current record owner.

---

14. A striking exception to this rule was made in *Dodge v. Ford Motor Co.*, 204 Mich. 459, 170 N.W. 668 (1919), when Henry Ford, the president and major stockholder of Ford Motor Company, refused to declare a dividend notwithstanding the firm's large capital surplus. The court, holding that Ford had abused his discretion, ordered the company to declare a dividend.

15. *Hagen v. Distributed Solutions, Inc.*, 328 Ill.App.3d 132, 764 N.E.2d 1141, 262 Ill.Dec. 24 (1 Dist. 2002).

16. See, for example, *Disney v. Walt Disney Co.*, 857 A.2d 444 (Del.Ch. 2004).

Rights on Dissolution

When a corporation is dissolved and its outstanding debts and the claims of its creditors have been satisfied, there may be assets remaining. The remaining assets are distributed to the shareholders in proportion to the percentage of shares owned by each shareholder.

The articles of incorporation may provide that certain classes of preferred stock will be given priority. If no class of stock has been given preference in the distribution of assets, all of the stockholders share the remaining assets. (See Chapter 41 for a full discussion of the process of dissolution, including the circumstances under which shareholders may petition a court to have the corporation dissolved.)

The Shareholder's Derivative Suit

When the corporation is harmed by the actions of a third party, the directors can bring a lawsuit in the name of the corporation against that party. If the corporate directors fail to bring a lawsuit, shareholders can do so "derivatively" in what is known as a **shareholder's derivative suit.**

Before shareholders can bring a derivative suit, they must submit a written demand to the corporation, asking the board of directors to take appropriate action [RMBCA 7.40]. The directors then have ninety days in which to act. Only if they refuse to do so can the derivative suit go forward.

WHEN ACTS OF DIRECTORS AND OFFICERS CAUSE HARM TO THE CORPORATION The right of shareholders to bring a derivative action is especially important when the wrong suffered by the corporation results from the actions of the corporate directors and officers. For obvious reasons, the directors and officers would probably be unwilling to take any action against themselves.

Nevertheless, a court will dismiss a derivative suit if a majority of the directors or an independent panel determines in good faith that the lawsuit is not in the best interests of the corporation [RMBCA 7.44].

ANY DAMAGES AWARDED GO TO THE CORPORATION When shareholders bring a derivative suit, they are not pursuing rights or benefits for themselves personally but are acting as guardians of the corporate entity. Therefore, if the suit is successful, any damages recovered normally go into the corporation's treasury, not to the shareholders personally.[17]

In the following case, a minority shareholder alleged that a corporation's directors had breached their fiduciary duty by denying him the benefits of his ownership interest. The court had to decide whether the shareholder could bring an individual claim rather than a derivative suit.

---

17. The shareholders may be entitled to reimbursement for reasonable expenses of the derivative lawsuit, including attorneys' fees.

CASE 40.3

McCann v. McCann
Supreme Court of Idaho, 152 Idaho 809, 275 P.3d 824 (2012).

BACKGROUND AND FACTS In the 1970s, William McCann gave each of his sons, Bill and Ron, roughly one-third of the shares of his close corporation, McCann Ranch and Livestock Company. The remaining shares eventually went to a trust for William's wife, Gertrude. When William died, Bill became the corporation's president and chief executive officer. McCann Ranch went to great lengths to provide for Gertrude, giving her about 75 percent of its net income. Bill also received a raise, and soon afterward he began making payments to Gertrude's account. In 2008, Ron filed a direct (nonderivative) lawsuit alleging that the corporation's directors had breached the fiduciary duty they owed him as a minority shareholder. According to the complaint, the directors subjected Ron to a "squeeze-out" designed to deprive him of the benefits of being a shareholder. Ron claimed that the directors refused to give him a corporate job or board membership, failed to pay him dividends, and deprived him of other income through a series of business decisions that benefited only Bill and Gertrude. The district court granted judgment for the defendants, finding that Ron had essentially filed a derivative suit without making a written demand on the corporation. Ron appealed.

CASE 40.3 CONTINUES ▶

CASE 40.3 CONTINUED

IN THE LANGUAGE OF THE COURT
BURDICK, Chief Justice.

* * * *

* * * "In Idaho a director has a fiduciary responsibility to both the corporation and to shareholders." * * *

* * * *

"A well-recognized exception to the rule that a shareholder must bring a derivative action for claims alleging injury to the corporation is that in a [close] corporation a minority shareholder may bring a direct action, rather than a derivative action, if the shareholder alleges harm to himself distinct from that suffered by other shareholders of the corporation or breach of a special duty owed by the defendant to the shareholder." [Emphasis added.]

* * * *

* * * Ron alleges that the Respondents engaged in a squeeze-out by: (1) not paying dividends despite sufficient cash flow; (2) not providing corporate employment to Ron; (3) not providing board membership to Ron; (4) authorizing phony transactions to Gertrude to avoid any benefit to Ron; (5) frustrating the intent of the founder of the Corporation to provide an actual financial benefit to Ron; and (6) making management decisions that allow all of the cash flow to be obtained solely for the benefit of Bill and Gertrude at the expense of Ron.

* * * *

Many of the actions undertaken by the Corporation, in and of themselves, are legitimate uses of corporate power and discretion. Regardless of his ownership interest, Ron is not entitled to a seat on the board of directors. Nor is he entitled to corporate employment. Nor is there evidence he is entitled to a dividend. By themselves, any payments from the Corporation do not harm Ron any more than they harm the other shareholders. However, they may be used as facts to support a squeeze-out.

* * * *

In this light, the actions of the Corporation and its directors have an effect on Ron above and beyond the effect of every other shareholder. Each of these transactions hurts Ron specifically.

The Corporation went to great lengths to provide Gertrude with the money she needed. However, because the Corporation did not use an alternate and less harmful means of providing for Gertrude, it may be argued that the transactions were not made in good faith. The Corporation could have issued a dividend that would benefit all shareholders. Instead, Ron lost his voice in corporate decisions, his corporate employment, and received no meaningful benefit from his ownership stake.

DECISION AND REMEDY *The Idaho Supreme Court held that Ron could bring a direct suit alleging that the corporation's directors had breached their fiduciary duty. It therefore reversed the district court's decision, granting judgment to the defendants.*

THE ETHICAL DIMENSION *If this case proceeds to trial, how might the directors try to defend their decisions? What rule concerning director liability might protect them? Explain your answer.*

THE LEGAL ENVIRONMENT DIMENSION *Can Ron initiate an action to dissolve the McCann Ranch corporation? Why or why not?*

SECTION 5
DUTIES AND LIABILITIES OF SHAREHOLDERS

One of the hallmarks of the corporate form of organization is that shareholders are not personally liable for the debts of the corporation. If the corporation fails, the shareholders can lose their investments, but that generally is the limit of their liability. As discussed in Chapter 39, in certain instances of fraud, undercapitalization, or careless observance of corporate formalities, a court will pierce the corporate veil (disregard the corporate entity) and hold the shareholders individually liable. But these situations are the exception, not the rule.

A shareholder can also be personally liable in certain other rare instances. One relates to illegal dividends, which were discussed previously. Another relates to *watered stock*. Still another concerns the duties majority shareholders owe to minority shareholders.

Concept Summary 40.3 below reviews the role, rights, and liability of shareholders in a corporation.

Watered Stock

When a corporation issues shares for less than their fair market value, the shares are referred to as **watered stock.**[18] Usually, the shareholder who receives watered stock must pay the difference to the corporation (the shareholder is personally liable). In some states, the shareholder who receives watered stock may be liable to creditors of the corporation for unpaid corporate debts.

▶ **Example 40.10** During the formation of a corporation, Gomez, one of the incorporators, transfers his property, Sunset Beach, to the corporation

---

18. The phrase *watered stock* was originally used to describe cattle that were kept thirsty during a long drive and then were allowed to drink large quantities of water just before their sale. The increased weight of the watered stock allowed the seller to reap a higher profit.

for 10,000 shares of stock at a par value of $100 per share for a total price of $1 million. After the property is transferred and the shares are issued, Sunset Beach is carried on the corporate books at a value of $1 million.

On appraisal, it is discovered that the market value of the property at the time of transfer was only $500,000. The shares issued to Gomez are therefore watered stock, and he is liable to the corporation for the difference between the value of the shares and the value of the property. ◀

Duties of Majority Shareholders

In some instances, a majority shareholder is regarded as having a fiduciary duty to the corporation and to the minority shareholders. This duty occurs when a single shareholder (or a few shareholders acting in concert) owns a sufficient number of shares to exercise *de facto* (actual) control over the corporation. In these situations, the majority shareholder owes a fiduciary duty to the minority shareholders.

When a majority shareholder breaches her or his fiduciary duty to a minority shareholder, the minority shareholder can sue for damages. A breach of

---

CONCEPT SUMMARY 40.3
Role, Rights, and Liability of Shareholders

ASPECT	DESCRIPTION
Shareholders' Powers	Shareholders' powers include approval of all fundamental changes affecting the corporation and election of the board of directors.
Shareholders' Meetings	Shareholders' meetings must occur at least annually, and special meetings can be called when necessary. Notice of the time and place of a meeting (and its purpose, if the meeting is specially called) must be sent to shareholders. A minimum number of shareholders (quorum) must be present to vote.
Shareholders' Rights	Shareholders have numerous rights, which may include the following: 1. Voting rights. 2. Preemptive rights (depending on the corporate articles). 3. The right to receive dividends (at the discretion of the directors). 4. The right to inspect the corporate records. 5. The right to transfer shares (this right may be restricted in close corporations). 6. The right to receive a share of corporate assets when the corporation is dissolved. 7. The right to sue on behalf of the corporation (bring a shareholder's derivative suit) when the directors fail to do so.
Shareholders' Liability	Shareholders may be liable for watered stock. In certain situations, majority shareholders may be regarded as having a fiduciary duty to minority shareholders and will be liable if that duty is breached.

fiduciary duties by those who control a close corporation normally constitutes what is known as *oppressive conduct*. A common example of a breach of fiduciary duty occurs when the majority shareholders "freeze out" the minority shareholders and exclude them from certain benefits of participating in the firm.

▶ **Case in Point 40.11** Brodie, Jordan, and Barbuto formed a close corporation to operate a machine shop. Each owned one-third of the shares in the company, and all three were directors. Brodie served as the corporate president for twelve years but thereafter met with the other shareholders only a few times a year.

After disagreements arose, Brodie asked the company to purchase his shares, but his requests were refused. A few years later, Brodie died, and his wife inherited his shares in the company. Jordan and Barbuto refused to perform a valuation of the company, denied her access to the corporate information she requested, did not declare any dividends, and refused to elect her as a director. In this situation, a court found that the majority shareholders had violated their fiduciary duty to Brodie's wife.[19] ◀

19. *Brodie v. Jordan,* 447 Mass. 866, 857 N.E.2d 1076 (2006).

Reviewing: Corporate Directors, Officers, and Shareholders

David Brock is on the board of directors of Firm Body Fitness, Inc., which owns a string of fitness clubs in New Mexico. Brock owns 15 percent of the Firm Body stock and is also employed as a tanning technician at one of the fitness clubs. After the January financial report showed that Firm Body's tanning division was operating at a substantial net loss, the board of directors, led by Marty Levinson, discussed the possibility of terminating the tanning operations. Brock successfully convinced a majority of the board that the tanning division was necessary to market the clubs' overall fitness package. By April, the tanning division's financial losses had risen. The board hired a business analyst, who conducted surveys and determined that the tanning operations did not significantly increase membership.

A shareholder, Diego Peñada, discovered that Brock owned stock in Sunglow, Inc., the company from which Firm Body purchased its tanning equipment. Peñada notified Levinson, who privately reprimanded Brock. Shortly thereafter, Brock and Mandy Vail, who owned 37 percent of the Firm Body stock and also held shares of Sunglow, voted to replace Levinson on the board of directors. Using the information presented in the chapter, answer the following questions.

1. What duties did Brock, as a director, owe to Firm Body?
2. Does the fact that Brock owned shares in Sunglow establish a conflict of interest? Why or why not?
3. 3Suppose that Firm Body brought an action against Brock claiming that he had breached the duty of loyalty by not disclosing his interest in Sunglow to the other directors. What theory might Brock use in his defense?
4. Now suppose that Firm Body did not bring an action against Brock. What type of lawsuit might Peñada be able to bring based on these facts?

DEBATE THIS ... *Because most shareholders never bother to vote for directors, shareholders have no real control over corporations.*

Terms and Concepts

business judgment rule 784	preemptive rights 793	stock certificate 792
dividend 793	proxy 789	stock warrant 793
inside director 781	quorum 781	voting trust 792
outside director 781	shareholder's derivative suit 795	watered stock 797

ExamPrep

Issue Spotters

1. Wonder Corporation has an opportunity to buy stock in XL, Inc. The directors decide that instead of Wonder buying the stock, the directors will buy it. Yvon, a Wonder shareholder, learns of the purchase and wants to sue the directors on Wonder's behalf. Can she do it? Explain. **(See page 795.)**

2. Nico is Omega Corporation's majority shareholder. He owns enough stock in Omega that if he were to sell it, the sale would be a transfer of control of the firm. Discuss whether Nico owes a duty to Omega or the minority shareholders in selling his shares. **(See page 797.)**

- **Check your answers to the Issue Spotters against the answers provided in Appendix E at the end of this text.**

Before the Test

Go to **www.cengagebrain.com**, enter the ISBN 9781285185248, and click on "Find" to locate this textbook's Web site. Then, click on "Access Now" under "Study Tools," and select Chapter 40 at the top. There, you will find a Practice Quiz that you can take to assess your mastery of the concepts in this chapter, as well as Flashcards and a Glossary of important terms.

Business Scenarios

40–1. Conflicts of Interest. Oxy Corp. is negotiating with Wick Construction Co. for the renovation of Oxy's corporate headquarters. Wick, the owner of Wick Construction Co., is also one of the five members of Oxy's board of directors. The contract terms are standard for this type of contract. Wick has previously informed two of the other directors of his interest in the construction company. Oxy's board approves the contract by a three-to-two vote, with Wick voting with the majority. Discuss whether this contract is binding on the corporation. **(See page 786.)**

40–2. Liability of Directors. AstroStar, Inc., has approximately five hundred shareholders. Its board of directors consists of three members—Eckhart, Dolan, and Macero. At a regular board meeting, the board selects Galiard as president of the corporation by a two-to-one vote, with Eckhart dissenting. The minutes of the meeting do not register Eckhart's dissenting vote. Later, an audit reveals that Galiard is a former convict and has embezzled $500,000 from the corporation that is not covered by insurance. Can the corporation hold directors Eckhart, Dolan, and Macero personally liable? Discuss. **(See page 786.)**

40–3. Rights of Shareholders. Lucia has acquired one share of common stock of a multimillion-dollar corporation with more than 500,000 shareholders. Lucia's ownership interest is so small that she is not sure what her rights are as a shareholder. For example, she wants to know whether this one share entitles her to (a) attend and vote at shareholders' meetings, (b) inspect the corporate books, and (c) receive yearly dividends. Discuss Lucia's rights in these three matters. **(See page 792.)**

Business Case Problems

40–4. Duties of Directors and Officers. First Niles Financial, Inc., is a company whose sole business is to own and operate a bank, Home Federal Savings and Loan Association of Niles, Ohio. First Niles's directors included bank officers William Stephens, Daniel Csontos, and Lawrence Safarek; James Kramer, president of an air-conditioning company that serviced the bank; and Ralph Zuzolo, whose law firm served the bank and whose title company participated in most of its real estate deals. First Niles's board put the bank up for sale and received three bids. Farmers National Bank Corp. stated that it would not retain the board. Cortland Bancorp indicated that it would terminate the directors but consider them for future service. First Financial Corp. said nothing about the directors. The board did not pursue Farmers' offer, failed to timely respond to Cortland's request, and rejected First Financial's bid. Leonard Gantler and other First Niles shareholders filed a suit in a Delaware state court against Stephens and the others. What duties do directors and officers owe to a corporation and its shareholders? How might those duties have been breached here? Discuss. [*Gantler v. Stephens*, 965 A.2d 695 (Del.Sup.Ct. 2009)] **(See page 782.)**

40–5. Fiduciary Duty of Officers. Designer Surfaces, Inc., supplied countertops to homeowners who shopped at stores such as Lowe's and Costco. The homeowners paid the store, which then contracted with Designer to fabricate and install the countertops. Designer bought materials from Arizona Tile, LLC, on an open account. Designer's only known corporate officers were Howard Berger and John McCarthy. Designer became insolvent and could not pay Arizona Tile for all the materials it had purchased, including materials for which Designer had already received payment from the retail stores. Arizona Tile sued Designer and won a default judgment, but the company had no funds. Arizona Tile then sued Berger and McCarthy personally for diverting company funds that Designer had received in trust for payment to Arizona Tile. Arizona Tile argued that the use of the funds for other purposes was a breach of fiduciary duty. Berger and McCarthy argued that corporate law imposed neither a fiduciary duty on corporate officers nor personal liability for breach of a duty to suppliers of materials. Which argument is more credible and why? [*Arizona Tile, LLC v. Berger*, 223 Ariz. 491, 224 P.3d 988 (Ariz.App. 2010)] **(See page 782.)**

40–6. BUSINESS CASE PROBLEM
WITH SAMPLE ANSWER: Rights of Shareholders.

Stanka Woods is the sole member of Hair Ventures, LLC. Hair Ventures owns 3 million shares of stock in Biolustré Inc. For several years, Woods and other Biolustré shareholders did not receive notice of shareholders' meetings or financial reports. On learning that Biolustré planned to issue more stock, Woods, through Hair Ventures, demanded to see Biolustré's books and records. Biolustré asserted that the request was not for a proper purpose. Does Woods have a right to inspect Biolustré's books and records? If so, what are the limits? Do any of those limits apply in this case? Explain. [Biolustré Inc. v. Hair Ventures, LLC, 2011 WL 540054 (Tex.App.—San Antonio 2011)] **(See page 792.)**

- For a sample answer to Problem 40–6, go to Appendix F at the end of this text.

40–7. Duty of Loyalty.
Kids International Corp. produced children's wear for Wal-mart and other retailers. Gila Dweck was a Kids director and its chief executive officer. Because she felt that she was not paid enough for the company's success, she started Success Apparel to compete with Kids. Success operated out of Kids' premises, used its employees, borrowed on its credit, took advantage of its business opportunities, and capitalized on its customer relationships. As an "administrative fee," Dweck paid Kids 1 percent of Success's total sales. Did Dweck breach any fiduciary duties? Explain. [*Dweck v. Nasser*, 2012 WL 3194069 (Del.Ch. 2012)] **(See page 784.)**

40–8. A QUESTION OF ETHICS: Duties of Directors and Officers.

New Orleans Paddlewheels, Inc. (NOP), is a Louisiana corporation formed in 1982 when James Smith, Sr., and Warren Reuther were its only shareholders, with each holding 50 percent of the stock. NOP is part of a sprawling enterprise of tourism and hospitality companies in New Orleans. The positions on the board of each company were split equally between the Smith and Reuther families. At Smith's request, his son James Smith, Jr. (JES), became involved in the businesses. In 1999, NOP's board elected JES as president, to be in charge of day-to-day operations, and Reuther is chief executive officer (CEO), to be in charge of marketing and development. Over the next few years, animosity developed between Reuther and JES. In October 2001, JES terminated Reuther as CEO and denied him access to the offices and books of NOP and the other companies, literally changing the locks on the doors. At the next meetings of the boards of NOP and the overall enterprise, deadlock ensued, with the directors voting along family lines on every issue. Complaining that the meetings were a "waste of time," JES began to run the entire enterprise by taking advantage of an unequal balance of power on the companies' executive committees. In NOP's subsequent bankruptcy proceeding, Reuther filed a motion for the appointment of a trustee to formulate a plan for the firm's reorganization, alleging, among other things, misconduct by NOP's management. [In re New Orleans Paddlewheels, Inc., 350 Bankr. 667 (E.D.La. 2006)] **(See page 782.)**

(a) Was Reuther legally entitled to have access to the books and records of NOP and the other companies? JES maintained, among other things, that NOP's books were "a mess." Was JES's denial of that access unethical? Why or why not?

(b) How would you describe JES's attempt to gain control of NOP and the other companies? Were his actions devious and self-serving in the pursuit of personal gain or legitimate and reasonable in the pursuit of a business goal? Discuss.

Legal Reasoning Group Activity

40–9. Shareholders' Duties.
Milena Weintraub and Larry Griffith were shareholders in Grand Casino, Inc., which operated a casino in South Dakota. Griffith owned 51 percent of the stock and Weintraub 49 percent. Weintraub managed the casino, which Griffith typically visited once a week. At the end of 2012, an accounting audit showed that the cash on hand was less than the amount posted in the casino's books. Later, more shortfalls were discovered. In October 2014, Griffith did a complete audit. Weintraub was unable to account for $200,500 in missing cash. Griffith then kept all of the casino's most recent profits, including Weintraub's $90,447.20 share, and, without telling Weintraub, sold the casino for $400,000 and kept all of the proceeds.

Weintraub filed a suit against Griffith, asserting a breach of fiduciary duty. Griffith countered with evidence of Weintraub's misappropriation of corporate cash. **(See page 796.)**

(a) The first group will discuss the duties that these parties owed to each other, and determine whether Weintraub or Griffith, or both, breached those duties.

(b) The second group will decide how this dispute should be resolved and who should pay what to whom to reconcile the finances.

(c) A third group will discuss whether Weintraub or Griffin violated any ethical duties to each other or to the corporation.

A corporation may grow simply by reinvesting retained earnings in more equipment or by hiring more employees. A corporation may also extend its operations by combining with another corporation through a merger, a consolidation, or a share exchange. In addition, a corporation may purchase the assets of, or a controlling interest in, another corporation.

This chapter examines each of these types of corporate expansion. We look at how each type of transaction is carried out and whether the approval of the shareholders and the board of directors is required. We also consider the rights of shareholders who object to the proposed transaction.

In the latter part of the chapter, we discuss dissolution and winding up—the processes by which a corporation terminates its existence. Dissolution may come about either voluntarily or involuntarily. We will look at some typical reasons for dissolution and at the methods used in the termination process.

This chapter concludes with a brief comparison of the major forms of business organization discussed in Chapters 36 through 41. We present a summary of the advantages and disadvantages of each business form.

SECTION 1
MERGER, CONSOLIDATION, AND SHARE EXCHANGE

The terms *merger* and *consolidation* traditionally referred to two legally distinct proceedings. Today, however, people commonly use the term *consolidation* to refer to all types of combinations, including mergers (discussed below) and acquisitions (discussed later in this chapter).

Whether a combination is a merger, a consolidation, or a share exchange, the rights and liabilities of shareholders, the corporation, and the corporation's creditors are the same. Note also that the power to merge, consolidate, and exchange shares is conferred by statute, and thus state law establishes the specific procedures.

Merger

A **merger** involves the legal combination of two or more corporations. After a merger, only one of the corporations continues to exist. ▶ **Example 41.1** Corporation A and Corporation B decide to merge. They agree that A will absorb B. Therefore, after the merger, B ceases to exist as a separate entity, and A continues as the **surviving corporation.** ◀ Exhibit 41–1 below graphically illustrates this process.

ONE OF THE FIRMS SURVIVES After the merger, Corporation A is recognized as a single corporation possessing all of the rights, privileges, and powers of itself and B. It automatically acquires all of B's property and assets without the necessity of a formal transfer. Corporation A also becomes liable for all of B's debts

EXHIBIT 41–1 Merger

Corporation A and Corporation B decide to merge. They agree that A will absorb B, so after the merger, B no longer exists as a separate entity, and A continues as the surviving corporation.

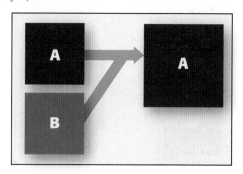

and obligations. Finally, Corporation A's articles of incorporation are deemed amended to include any changes that are stated in the **articles of merger** (a document, filed with the secretary of state, that sets forth the terms and conditions of the merger).

IT INHERITS LEGAL RIGHTS AND OBLIGATIONS In a merger, the surviving corporation inherits the disappearing corporation's preexisting legal rights. Thus, in *Example 41.1*, if Corporation B had a right of action against a third party under tort or property law, Corporation A can bring a suit after the merger to recover B's damages.

Consolidation

In a **consolidation,** two or more corporations combine in such a way that each corporation ceases to exist and a new one emerges. ▶ **Example 41.2**   Corporation A and Corporation B consolidate to form an entirely new organization, Corporation C. In the process, A and B both terminate, and C comes into existence as a new entity. ◀ Exhibit 41–2 below graphically illustrates this process.

A NEW CORPORATION IS FORMED The results of a consolidation are similar to those of a merger—only one company remains—but it is a completely new entity (the *consolidated corporation*). Corporation C is recognized as a new corporation and a single entity, while A and B cease to exist.

IT INHERITS ALL RIGHTS AND LIABILITIES OF BOTH PREDECESSORS Corporation C (the *consolidated corporation*) inherits all of the rights, privileges, and powers previously held by A and B. Title to any property and

---

EXHIBIT 41–2   Consolidation

Corporation A and Corporation B consolidate to form an entirely new organization, Corporation C. In the process, A and B terminate, and C comes into existence.

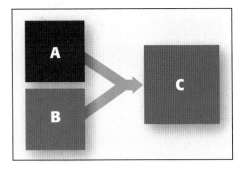

---

assets owned by A and B passes to C without a formal transfer. C assumes liability for all debts and obligations owed by A and B. The *articles of consolidation* take the place of A's and B's original corporate articles and are thereafter regarded as C's corporate articles.

When a merger or a consolidation takes place, the surviving corporation or newly formed corporation will issue shares or pay some fair consideration to the shareholders of the corporation or corporations that cease to exist. True consolidations have become less common among for-profit corporations because it is often advantageous for one of the firms to survive. In contrast, nonprofit corporations and associations may prefer consolidation because it suggests a new beginning in which neither of the two initial entities is dominant.

Share Exchange

In a **share exchange,** some or all of the shares of one corporation are exchanged for some or all of the shares of another corporation, but both corporations continue to exist. Share exchanges are often used to create *holding companies* (companies that own part or all of other companies' outstanding stock—see Chapter 39).

If one corporation owns *all* of the shares of another corporation, it is referred to as the **parent corporation,** and the wholly owned company is the **subsidiary corporation.** ▶ **Example 41.3**   UAL Corporation is a large holding company that owns United Airlines. UAL is the parent corporation, and United Airlines is the subsidiary. ◀

Merger, Consolidation, and Share Exchange Procedures

All states have statutes authorizing mergers, consolidations, and share exchanges for domestic (in-state) and foreign (out-of-state) corporations. The procedures vary somewhat among jurisdictions.

In some states, a consolidation resulting in an entirely new corporation simply follows the initial incorporation procedures discussed in Chapter 39, whereas other business combinations must follow the procedures outlined below.

The Revised Model Business Corporation Act (RMBCA) sets forth the following basic requirements [RMBCA 11.01–11.07]:

1. The board of directors of *each* corporation involved must approve the merger or share exchange plan.

2. The plan must specify any terms and conditions of the merger. It also must state how the value of the shares of each merging corporation will be determined and how they will be converted into shares or other securities, cash, property, or additional interests in another corporation.

3. The majority of the shareholders of *each* corporation must vote to approve the plan at a shareholders' meeting. If any class of stock is entitled to vote as a separate group, the majority of each separate voting group must approve the plan. As mentioned in Chapter 40, frequently a corporation's articles of incorporation or bylaws require approval by more than a majority once a quorum is present. In addition, some state statutes require the approval of two-thirds of the outstanding shares of voting stock (not just the shareholders present at the meeting), and others require a four-fifths approval.

4. Once the plan is approved by the directors and the shareholders of both corporations, the surviving corporation files the plan (articles of merger, consolidation, or share exchange) with the appropriate official, usually the secretary of state.

5. When state formalities are satisfied, the state issues a certificate of merger to the surviving corporation or a certificate of consolidation to the newly consolidated corporation.

Short-Form Mergers

RMBCA 11.04 provides a simplified procedure for the merger of a substantially owned subsidiary corporation into its parent corporation. Under these provisions, a **short-form merger**—also referred to as a **parent-subsidiary merger**—can be accomplished *without* the approval of the shareholders of either corporation.

The short-form merger can be used only when the parent corporation owns at least 90 percent of the outstanding shares of each class of stock of the subsidiary corporation. Once the board of directors of the parent corporation approves the plan, it is filed with the state, and copies are sent to each shareholder of record in the subsidiary corporation.

Shareholder Approval

As mentioned, except in a short-form merger, the shareholders of both corporations must approve a merger or other plan of consolidation. Shareholders invest in a corporation with the expectation that the board of directors will manage the enterprise and make decisions on *ordinary* business matters. For *extraordinary* matters, normally both the board of directors and the shareholders must approve the transaction.

Mergers and other combinations are extraordinary business matters, meaning that the board of directors must normally obtain the shareholders' approval and provide appraisal rights (discussed next). Amendments to the articles of incorporation and the dissolution of the corporation also generally require shareholder approval.

Sometimes, a transaction can be structured in such a way that shareholder approval is not required, but if the shareholders challenge the transaction, a court might require shareholder approval. For this reason, the board of directors may request shareholder approval even when it might not be legally required.

Appraisal Rights

What if a shareholder disapproves of a merger or a consolidation but is outvoted by the other shareholders? The law will not force a dissenting shareholder to become an unwilling shareholder in a corporation that is new or different from the one in which the shareholder originally invested.

Thus, the law gives dissenting shareholders a statutory right to be paid the fair value of the shares they held on the date of the merger or consolidation. This right is referred to as the shareholder's **appraisal right.** It extends to mergers, consolidations, share exchanges, and sales of substantially all of the corporate assets. The "fair value of the shares" normally is the value on the day prior to the date on which the vote was taken [RMBCA 13.21].

So long as the transaction does not involve fraud or other illegal conduct, appraisal rights are the exclusive remedy for a shareholder who is dissatisfied with the price received for the stock. Each state establishes the procedures for asserting appraisal rights in that jurisdiction.

Appraisal rights can be particularly important in a short-form merger because the minority stockholders do not receive advance notice of the merger, the directors do not consider or approve it, and there is no vote. Appraisal rights are often the only recourse available to shareholders who object to parent-subsidiary mergers.

SECTION 2
PURCHASE OF ASSETS

When a corporation acquires all or substantially all of the assets of another corporation by direct purchase, the purchasing, or acquiring, corporation simply extends its ownership and control over more assets. Because no change in the legal entity occurs, the *acquiring corporation* usually does not need to obtain shareholder approval for the purchase.[1]

In contrast, the corporation that is *selling* all of its assets is substantially changing its business position and perhaps its ability to carry out its corporate purposes. For that reason, the corporation whose assets are being sold must obtain approval from both its board of directors and its shareholders [RMBCA 12.02]. In most states and under RMBCA 13.02, dissenting shareholders of the selling corporation can demand appraisal rights.

Government Restrictions

Both the U.S. Department of Justice and the Federal Trade Commission have guidelines that significantly constrain and often prohibit mergers that could result from a purchase of assets. (These guidelines are part of the federal antitrust laws that will be discussed in Chapter 46.)

Successor Liability in Purchases of Assets

Generally, a corporation that purchases the assets of another corporation is not automatically responsible for the liabilities of the selling corporation. Exceptions to this rule are made in certain circumstances, however.

In any of the following situations, the acquiring corporation will be held to have assumed *both* the assets and the liabilities of the selling corporation:

1. When the purchasing corporation impliedly or expressly assumes the seller's liabilities.
2. When the sale transaction is, in effect, a merger or consolidation of the two companies.[2]
3. When the purchaser continues the seller's business and retains the same shareholders, directors, and officers.
4. When the sale is entered into fraudulently for the purpose of escaping liability.

The following case involved a purchase of corporate assets in which the purchasing corporation agreed to assume the seller's liabilities. The court had to decide whether the liabilities being assumed were limited to those that existed on the closing date or included liabilities that arose after the closing date.

---

1. Shareholder approval may be required in a few situations. If the acquiring corporation plans to pay for the assets with its stock but not enough authorized unissued shares are available, then the shareholders must approve the issuance of additional shares. Shareholder approval is also needed if the acquiring corporation's stock is traded on a national stock exchange and the corporation will be issuing a significant number of shares.

2. See, for example, *Cargo Partner AG v. Albatrans, Inc.,* 352 F.3d 41 (2d Cir. 2003), applying New York law on *de facto* mergers; and *Village Builders 96, LP v. U.S. Laboratories, Inc.,* 121 Nev. 261, 112 P.3d 1082 (2005).

CASE ANALYSIS

Case 41.1   American Standard, Inc. v. OakFabco, Inc.
Court of Appeals of New York, 14 N.Y.3d 399, 901 N.Y.S.2d 572 (2010).

IN THE LANGUAGE OF THE COURT
SMITH, J. [Judge]
* * * *

In 1970, American Standard, Inc. sold its Kewanee Boiler division to Kewanee Boiler Corp., now known as OakFabco, Inc. (OakFabco). The parties entered an asset purchase and sale agreement.

The agreement said that OakFabco would purchase "Kewanee Assets" subject to "Kewanee Liabilities." The term "Kewanee Liabilities" was defined as "all the debts, liabilities, obligations and commitments (fixed or contingent) connected with or attributable to Kewanee existing and outstanding at the Closing Date."

The boilers manufactured by Kewanee had been insulated with asbestos, and as a result many tort claims were brought in the years and decades following the purchase of the business. Some of those claims were brought by plaintiffs who had suffered injuries after the closing of the transaction, allegedly attributable to boilers manufactured and

CASE 41.1 CONTINUED

sold before the closing. In this declaratory judgment action brought by American Standard [in a New York state court] against OakFabco, the issue is whether liabilities for such injuries were among the "Kewanee Liabilities" that OakFabco assumed.

[The trial] court held that these liabilities were assumed by OakFabco, and entered a declaratory judgment accordingly. [A state intermediate appellate court] affirmed * * *. We granted leave to appeal.

* * * *

American Standard's position—that OakFabco assumed all tort liabilities arising out of boilers manufactured by the Kewanee Boiler division, whether the injury was suffered before or after American Standard sold the division—is strongly supported by the purpose of the transaction, as described in the agreement itself: *It was a purchase and sale of substantially all the assets of the Kewanee Boiler business "subject to all debts, liabilities, and obligations connected with or attributable to such business and operations."* Nothing in the nature of the transaction suggests that the parties intended OakFabco, which got all the assets, to escape any

of the related obligations. [Emphasis added.]

OakFabco, however, argues that the definition of "Kewanee Liabilities"—the liabilities OakFabco assumed—is less broad than the purpose of the transaction would imply. It stresses the words "existing and outstanding" in the definition— "all the debts, liabilities, obligations and commitments * * * existing and outstanding at the Closing Date." According to OakFabco, a tort claim cannot be "existing and outstanding" before the tort plaintiff has been injured, because until then it is not possible for a tort lawsuit to be brought.

* * * *

That there was no such intention is made clear by a clause in the agreement relating to certain obligations owed to the boiler division's customers. The agreement said that the buyer would deliver at the closing:

An executed undertaking wherein the Buyer will assume and agree to pay, and defend and hold Seller harmless against, all Kewanee Liabilities, including, by way of specification but not limitation, the following:

* * * *

(iii) warranty, service, repair and return obligations of Kewanee and other claims and complaints arising out of or in connection with any products manufactured, sold, leased or installed by Kewanee on or prior to the Closing Date.

This language clearly meant that the buyer would deal with any problems customers had after the closing date with boilers that had been installed previously. It would have been absurd for OakFabco to tell a customer whose boiler failed after the closing that, since the customer's claim was not "existing and outstanding" on the closing date, it was not OakFabco's problem. By including warranty, service, repair and return claims of this kind in the definition of "Kewanee Liabilities," the parties demonstrated that they were not reading the words "existing and outstanding" as OakFabco would have us read them. [Emphasis added.]

We therefore agree with the [lower court] that the liabilities assumed by OakFabco include claims brought by tort claimants injured after the closing date by boilers installed before that date.

Accordingly, the order of the [lower court] should be * * * affirmed.

LEGAL REASONING QUESTIONS

1. Generally, a corporation that purchases the assets of another is not automatically responsible for the liabilities of the selling corporation, with some exceptions. Which exception applied to this case? Explain.

2. How does this case illustrate the kinds of problems that can arise over contract interpretation?

3. Why is an acquiring corporation shouldered with the liabilities of an acquired corporation when the acquirer was most likely not involved in the circumstances that gave rise to the liabilities?

4. How might the Internet prevent a prospective acquiring company from unknowingly assuming the liabilities in a purchase of assets?

SECTION 3
PURCHASE OF STOCK

An alternative to the purchase of another corporation's assets is the purchase of a substantial number of the voting shares of its stock. This enables the acquiring corporation to control the **target corporation** (the corporation being acquired). The process of acquiring control over a corporation in this way is commonly referred to as a corporate **takeover.**

Tender Offers

In seeking to purchase the stock of the target corporation, the acquiring corporation deals directly with the target's shareholders by making a *tender offer*. A **tender offer** is a proposal to buy shares of stock from a target corporation's shareholders either for cash or for some type of corporate security of the acquiring company. The tender offer can be conditioned on the receipt of a specified number of outstanding shares by a certain date.

As a means of inducing shareholders to accept the offer, the tender price offered generally is higher than the market price of the target's stock before the tender offer was announced. ▶ **Example 41.4** In a merger of two Fortune 500 pharmaceutical companies, Pfizer, Inc., paid $68 billion to acquire its rival, Wyeth. Wyeth shareholders reportedly received approximately $50.19 per share (part in cash and part in Pfizer stock), which amounted to a 15 percent premium over the market price of the stock. ◀

Application of Securities Laws

Federal securities laws strictly control the terms, duration, and circumstances under which most tender offers are made. In addition, many states have passed antitakeover statutes.

Generally, the offering corporation does not need to notify the Securities and Exchange Commission (SEC) or the target corporation's management until after the tender offer is made. The offeror must then disclose to the SEC the source of the funds used in the offer, the purpose of the offer, and the acquiring corporation's plans for the firm if the takeover is successful.

Responses to Tender Offers

A firm may respond to a tender offer in numerous ways. If the target firm's board of directors views the tender offer as favorable, the board will recommend that the shareholders accept it. Frequently, though, the target corporation's management opposes the proposed takeover. This is referred to as a *hostile takeover.*

To resist a takeover, a target company may make a *self-tender,* in which it offers to acquire stock from its own shareholders and thereby retain corporate control. The target corporation may also engage in a media campaign to persuade its shareholders that the tender offer is not in their best interests. Another possible defense is for the target firm to issue additional stock, thereby increasing the number of shares that the acquiring corporation must purchase to gain control. Several other tactics to resist a takeover are described in Exhibit 41–3 below.

Concept Summary 41.1 on the following page reviews all of the ways in which a corporation may expand its operations.

EXHIBIT 41-3 The Terminology of Takeover Defenses

Term	Definition
Crown Jewel	When threatened with a takeover, management makes the company less attractive to the raider by selling the company's most valuable asset (the "crown jewel") to a third party.
Golden Parachute	When a takeover is successful, top management usually is changed. With this in mind, a company may establish special termination or retirement benefits that must be paid to top managers if they are "retired." In other words, a departing high-level manager's parachute will be "golden" when he or she is forced to "bail out" of the company.
Greenmail	To regain control, a target company may pay a higher-than-market price to repurchase all of the stock that the acquiring corporation bought. When a takeover is attempted through a gradual accumulation of target stock rather than a tender offer, the intent may be to induce the target company to buy back the shares at a premium price—a concept similar to blackmail.
Pac-Man	Named after the Atari video game, this is an aggressive defense in which the target corporation attempts its own takeover of the acquiring corporation.
Poison Pill	The target corporation issues to its stockholders rights to purchase additional shares at low prices when there is a takeover attempt. This makes the takeover undesirably or even prohibitively expensive for the acquiring corporation.
White Knight	The target corporation solicits a merger with a third party, which then makes a better (often simply a higher) tender offer to the target's shareholders. The third party that "rescues" the target is the "white knight."

CONCEPT SUMMARY 41.1
Methods of Expanding
Corporate Operations and Interests

METHOD	DESCRIPTION
Merger and Consolidation	1. *Merger*—The legal combination of two or more corporations, with the result that the surviving corporation acquires all of the assets and obligations of the other corporation, which then ceases to exist.
	2. *Consolidation*—The legal combination of two or more corporations, with the result that each corporation ceases to exist and a new one emerges. The new corporation assumes all of the assets and obligations of the former corporations.
	3. *Share exchange*—A form of business combination in which some or all of the shares of one corporation are exchanged for some or all of the shares of another corporation, but both firms continue to exist.
	4. *Procedure*—Determined by state statutes. Basic requirements are the following:
	a. The board of directors of each corporation involved must approve the plan of merger, consolidation, or share exchange.
	b. The shareholders of each corporation must approve the merger or other consolidation plan at a shareholders' meeting.
	c. Articles of merger or consolidation (the plan) must be filed, usually with the secretary of state.
	d. The state issues a certificate of merger (or consolidation) to the surviving (or newly consolidated) corporation.
	5. *Short-form merger (parent-subsidiary merger)*—When the parent corporation owns at least 90 percent of the outstanding shares of each class of stock of the subsidiary corporation, shareholder approval is not required for the two firms to merge.
	6. *Appraisal rights*—Statutory rights of dissenting shareholders to receive the fair value for their shares when a merger or consolidation takes place. If the shareholder and the corporation do not agree on the fair value, a court will determine it.
Purchase of Assets	A purchase of assets occurs when one corporation acquires all or substantially all of the assets of another corporation.
	1. *Acquiring corporation*—The acquiring (purchasing) corporation is not required to obtain shareholder approval. The corporation is merely increasing its assets, and no fundamental business change occurs.
	2. *Acquired corporation*—The acquired (purchased) corporation is required to obtain the approval of both its directors and its shareholders for the sale of its assets because the sale will substantially change the corporation's business position.
Purchase of Stock	A purchase of stock occurs when one corporation acquires a substantial number of the voting shares of the stock of another (target) corporation.
	1. *Tender offer*—A public offer to all shareholders of the target corporation to purchase their stock at a price generally higher than the market price of the target stock prior to the announcement of the tender offer. Federal and state securities laws strictly control the terms, duration, and circumstances under which most tender offers are made.
	2. *Target responses*—The ways in which target corporations respond to takeover bids include self-tender (the target firm's offer to acquire its own shareholders' stock) and numerous other strategies (see Exhibit 41–3).

Takeover Defenses and Directors' Fiduciary Duties

As mentioned, the board of directors of the target corporation often opposes the takeover. Clearly, board members have an interest in keeping their jobs and control, but they also have a fiduciary duty to the corporation and its shareholders to act in the best interests of the company.

In a hostile takeover attempt, sometimes directors' duties of care and loyalty collide with their self-interest. Then the shareholders, who would have received a premium for their shares as a result of the takeover, file lawsuits. Such lawsuits frequently allege that the directors breached their fiduciary duties in defending against the tender offer.

BUSINESS JUDGMENT RULE Courts apply the *business judgment rule* (see Chapter 40) when analyzing whether the directors acted reasonably in resisting the takeover attempt. The directors must show that they had reasonable grounds to believe that the tender offer posed a danger to the corporation's policies and effectiveness.

RATIONAL RESPONSE In addition, the board's response must have been rational in relation to the threat posed.[3]

---

3. For a landmark Delaware Supreme Court case applying the business judgment rule to hostile takeovers, see *Unocal Corp. v. Mesa Petroleum Co.,* 493 A.2d 946 (Del.Sup.Ct. 1985). See also *Shaper v. Bryan,* 371 Ill. App.3d 1079, 864 N.E.2d 876, 309 Ill.Dec. 635 (2007).

Basically, the defensive tactics used must have been reasonable, and the board of directors must have been trying to protect the corporation and its shareholders from a perceived danger. If the directors' actions were reasonable under the circumstances, then they are not liable for breaching their fiduciary duties.

One technique to avoid takeovers is the poison pill defense (see Exhibit 41–3). With this defensive measure, a board gives shareholders the right to buy additional shares at low prices. The right is triggered when a party acquires a certain proportion of the target corporation's stock—often between 15 and 20 percent. (This party, of course, does not have the right to purchase shares at a discount.) With more shares outstanding, the acquiring party's interest is diluted. The tactic is meant to make a takeover too expensive for the acquiring party.

▶ **Example 41.5** In 2012, Netflix, Inc., used the poison pill defense to effectively block a takeover attempt by billionaire investor Carl Icahn. Netflix gave its shareholders the right to acquire more stock if any individual acquires more than 10 percent of the company. Consequently, Icahn was able to acquire only 9.98 percent of the shares. ◀

In the following case, shareholders claimed that the directors had breached their fiduciary duties in their use of a poison pill defense.

CASE 41.2

Air Products and Chemicals, Inc. v. Airgas, Inc.
Court of Chancery of Delaware, 16 A.3d 48 (2011).

BACKGROUND AND FACTS Air Products and Chemicals, Inc., which provides gases and chemicals for industrial uses, made a tender offer of $70 per share for all of the shares of Airgas, Inc. The Airgas board of directors, which had expressed the view that the company's stock was worth at least $78 per share, rejected the offer as "clearly inadequate." The board took defensive measures to block the bid, including a poison pill that would be triggered if any party acquired 15 percent of the Airgas stock. Air Products and some Airgas shareholders filed a suit in a Delaware state court against Airgas, seeking an order to compel the board to remove the poison pill and allow the Airgas shareholders to decide whether to accept Air Products' offer. The shareholders alleged that the board had breached its fiduciary duties.

IN THE LANGUAGE OF THE COURT
CHANDLER, Chancellor

* * * *

Now, having thoroughly read, reviewed, and reflected upon all of the evidence presented to me, and having carefully considered the arguments made by counsel, I conclude that the Airgas board * * * has not breached its fiduciary duties owed to the Airgas stockholders. I find

CASE 41.2 CONTINUED

that the board has acted in good faith and in the honest belief that the Air Products offer, at $70 per share, is inadequate.

*Inadequate price has become a form of substantive coercion * * * . That is, the idea that Airgas's stockholders will disbelieve the board's views on value * * * and so they may mistakenly tender into an inadequately priced offer. Substantive coercion has been clearly recognized by [the Delaware] Supreme Court as a valid threat.* [Emphasis added.]

* * * *

* * * A board that has a good faith, reasonable basis to believe a bid is inadequate may block that bid using a poison pill, irrespective of stockholders' desire to accept it. [Emphasis added.]

Here, * * * the Airgas board has demonstrated that it has a reasonable basis for sustaining its long-term corporate strategy—the Airgas board is independent, and has relied on the advice of three different outside independent financial advisors in concluding that Air Products' offer is inadequate. Air Products' own three nominees who were elected to the Airgas board have joined wholeheartedly in the Airgas board's determination, and when the Airgas board met to consider the $70 "best and final" offer, it was one of those Air Products Nominees who said, "We have to protect the pill." Indeed, one of Air Products' own directors conceded at trial that the Airgas board members had acted within their fiduciary duties in their desire to "hold out for the proper price," and that if an offer was made for Air Products that he considered to be unfair to the stockholders of Air Products * * * he would likewise use every legal mechanism available to hold out for the proper price as well. Under Delaware law, the Airgas directors have complied with their fiduciary duties.

DECISION AND REMEDY *The court dismissed the shareholders' claims. The power to defeat an inadequate tender offer lies with the board of the target corporation. In this case, the Airgas board identified a valid threat—the allegedly inadequate price of Air Products' offer, coupled with the fact that a majority of Airgas's shareholders would likely accept it. The board responded reasonably and did not breach its fiduciary duties to shareholders.*

WHAT IF THE FACTS WERE DIFFERENT? *Suppose that the Airgas board had opposed the takeover in order to perpetuate the directors' own corporate power, and not to preserve shareholder value. Would the result have been different? Explain.*

THE SOCIAL DIMENSION *One reason for using a poison pill defense is to gain time for the shareholders of a target corporation to obtain the information they need to make an informed decision about a tender offer. How much time is enough?*

SECTION 4
TERMINATION

The termination of a corporation's existence has two phases—dissolution and winding up. **Dissolution** is the legal death of the artificial "person" of the corporation. *Winding up* is the process by which corporate assets are *liquidated,* or converted into cash and distributed among creditors and shareholders according to specific rules of preference.[4]

Voluntary Dissolution

State corporation statutes establish the procedures required for the voluntary dissolution of a corporation. Basically, there are two possible methods of voluntarily dissolving a corporation:

1. By the shareholders' unanimous vote to initiate dissolution proceedings (in some states).
2. By a proposal of the board of directors that is submitted to the shareholders at a shareholders' meeting.

ARTICLES OF DISSOLUTION When a corporation is dissolved voluntarily, the corporation must file *articles of dissolution* with the state and notify its creditors of

---

4. Some prefer to call this phase *liquidation,* but we use the term *winding up* to mean all acts needed to bring the legal and financial affairs of the business to an end, including liquidating the assets and distributing them among creditors and shareholders. See RMBCA 14.05.

the dissolution. The corporation must also establish a date (at least 120 days after the date of dissolution) by which all claims against the corporation must be received [RMBCA 14.06].

NOTICE TO CREDITORS A corporation's creditors want to be notified when the firm is dissolved so that they can file claims for payment. If a corporation's assets are liquidated without notice to a party who has a claim against the firm, shareholders of the former corporation can be held personally liable for the debt.

▶ **Case in Point 41.6** Christine Parent leased an automobile from Amity Autoworld, Ltd. Soon after that, Amity sold all of its automobile-franchising assets to another company named Atlantic. A month later, Parent made a claim for damages against Amity. She then filed a small claims action against Amity and obtained a $2,643 judgment, but she was unable to collect the amount because Amity had been sold to Atlantic.

Amity's principal shareholder and chief executive officer, John Staluppi, was the son of Atlantic's principal shareholder. Therefore, Parent filed a claim against Staluppi personally. A state court ruled that because Amity was liquidated and dissolved without any notice to creditors, those creditors (including Parent) could hold Amity's principal shareholder, Staluppi liable.[5] ◀

Involuntary Dissolution

Because corporations are creatures of statute, the state can also dissolve a corporation in certain circumstances. The secretary of state or the state attorney general can bring an action to dissolve a corporation that has failed to pay its annual taxes or to submit required annual reports [RMBCA 14.20]. A state court can also dissolve a corporation for making fraudulent misrepresentations to the state during incorporation or for engaging in mismanagement [RMBCA 14.30].

In some circumstances, a shareholder or a group of shareholders may petition a court to have the corporation dissolved. The RMBCA permits any shareholder to initiate an action for dissolution in any of the following circumstances [RMBCA 14.30]:

1. The directors are deadlocked in the management of corporate affairs, the shareholders are unable to break the deadlock, and the corporation is suf-

fering irreparable injury as a result or is about to do so.
2. The acts of the directors or those in control of the corporation are illegal, oppressive, or fraudulent.
3. Corporate assets are being misapplied or wasted.
4. The shareholders are deadlocked in voting power and have failed, for a specified period (usually two annual meetings), to elect successors to directors whose terms have expired or would have expired with the election of successors.

▶ **Case in Point 41.7** Mt. Princeton Trout Club, Inc. (MPTC), was formed to own land in Colorado and to provide recreational benefits to its shareholders. The articles of incorporation prohibited MPTC from selling or leasing any of its property without the approval of a majority of the directors. Nevertheless, MPTC officers entered into leases and contracts to sell corporate property without even notifying the directors. When a shareholder petitioned for dissolution, the court dissolved MPTC based on a finding that its officers had engaged in illegal, oppressive, and fraudulent conduct.[6] ◀

Winding Up

When dissolution takes place by voluntary action, the members of the board of directors act as trustees of the corporate assets. As trustees, they are responsible for winding up the affairs of the corporation for the benefit of corporate creditors and shareholders. This responsibility makes the board members personally liable for any breach of their fiduciary trustee duties.

When the dissolution is involuntary—or if board members do not wish to act as trustees of the assets—the court will appoint a **receiver** to wind up the corporate affairs and liquidate corporate assets. Courts may also appoint a receiver when shareholders or creditors can show that the board of directors should not be permitted to act as trustees of the corporate assets.

On dissolution, the liquidated assets are first used to pay creditors. Any remaining assets are distributed to shareholders according to their respective stock rights. Preferred stock has priority over common stock. Generally, the preferences are stated in the corporate articles.

---

5. *Parent v. Amityworld, Ltd.*, 15 Misc.3d 633, 832 N.Y.S.2d 775 (2007).

6. *Colt v. Mt. Princeton Trout Club, Inc.*, 78 P.3d 1115 (Colo.App. 2003).

SECTION 5
MAJOR BUSINESS FORMS COMPARED

As mentioned in Chapter 36, when deciding which form of business organization to choose, businesspersons normally consider several factors, including ease of creation, the liability of the owners, tax considerations, and the ability to raise capital. Each major form of business organization offers distinct advantages and disadvantages with respect to these and other factors.

Exhibit 41–4 below and on the next page summarizes the essential advantages and disadvantages of each of the forms of business organization discussed in Chapters 36 through 41.

EXHIBIT 41–4 Major Forms of Business Compared

Characteristic	Sole Proprietorship	Partnership	Corporation
Method of Creation	Created at will by owner.	Created by agreement of the parties.	Authorized by the state under the state's corporation law.
Legal Position	Not a separate entity; owner is the business.	A general partnership is a separate legal entity in most states.	Always a legal entity separate and distinct from its owners—a legal fiction for the purposes of owning property and being a party to litigation.
Liability	Unlimited liability.	Unlimited liability.	Limited liability of shareholders— shareholders are not liable for the debts of the corporation.
Duration	Determined by owner; automatically dissolved on owner's death.	Terminated by agreement of the partners, but can continue to do business even when a partner dissociates from the partnership.	Can have perpetual existence.
Transferability of Interest	Interest can be transferred, but individual's proprietorship then ends.	Although partnership interest can be assigned, assignee does not have full rights of a partner.	Shares of stock can be transferred.
Management	Completely at owner's discretion.	Each partner has a direct and equal voice in management unless expressly agreed otherwise in the partnership agreement.	Shareholders elect directors, who set policy and appoint officers.
Taxation	Owner pays personal taxes on business income.	Each partner pays pro rata share of income taxes on net profits, whether or not they are distributed.	Double taxation—corporation pays income tax on net profits, with no deduction for dividends, and shareholders pay income tax on disbursed dividends they receive.
Organizational Fees, Annual License Fees, and Annual Reports	None or minimal.	None or minimal.	All required.
Transaction of Business in Other States	Generally no limitation.	Generally no limitation.[a]	Normally must qualify to do business and obtain certificate of authority.

a. A few states have enacted statutes requiring that foreign partnerships qualify to do business there.

Continued

EXHIBIT 41-4 Major Forms of Business Compared—Continued

Charactistic	Limited Partnership	Limited Liability Company	Limited Liability Partnership
Method of Creation	Created by agreement to carry on a business for profit. At least one party must be a general partner and the other(s) limited partner(s). Certificate of limited partnership is filed. Charter must be issued by the state.	Created by an agreement of the member-owners of the company. Articles of organization are filed. Charter must be issued by the state.	Created by agreement of the partners. A statement of qualification for the limited liability partnership is filed.
Legal Position	Treated as a legal entity.	Treated as a legal entity.	Generally, treated same as a general partnership.
Liability	Unlimited liability of all general partners. Limited partners are liable only to the extent of capital contributions.	Member-owners' liability is limited to the amount of capital contributions or investments.	Varies, but under the Uniform Partnership Act, liability of a partner for acts committed by other partners is limited.
Duration	By agreement in certificate, or by termination of the last general partner (retirement, death, and the like) or last limited partner.	Unless a single-member LLC, can have perpetual existence (same as a corporation).	Remains in existence until cancellation or revocation.
Transferability of Interest	Interest can be assigned (same as a general partnership), but if assignee becomes a member with consent of other partners, certificate must be amended.	Member interests are freely transferable.	Interest can be assigned same as in a general partnership.
Management	General partners have equal voice or by agreement. Limited partners may not retain limited liability if they actively participate in management.	Member-owners can fully participate in management or can designate a group of persons to manage on behalf of the members.	Same as a general partnership.
Taxation	Generally taxed as a partnership.	LLC is not taxed, and members are taxed personally on profits "passed through" the LLC.	Same as a general partnership.
Organizational Fees, Annual License Fees, and Annual Reports	Organizational fee required; usually not others.	Organizational fee required. Others vary with states.	Fees are set by each state for filing statements of qualification, statements of foreign qualification, and annual reports.
Transaction of Business in Other States	Generally no limitations.	Generally no limitations, but may vary depending on state.	Must file a statement of foreign qualification before doing business in another state.

Reviewing: Mergers and Takeovers

In November 2012, Mario Bonsetti and Rico Sanchez incorporated Gnarly Vulcan Gear, Inc. (GVG), to manufacture windsurfing equipment. Bonsetti owned 60 percent and Sanchez owned 40 percent of the corporation's stock, and both men served on the board of directors. In January 2014, Hula Boards, Inc., owned solely by Mai Jin Li, made a public offer to Bonsetti and Sanchez to buy GVG stock. Hula offered

30 percent more than the market price per share for the GVG stock, and Bonsetti and Sanchez each sold 20 percent of their stock to Hula. Jin Li became the third member of the GVG board of directors. In April 2015, an irreconcilable dispute arose between Bonsetti and Sanchez over design modifications of their popular Baked Chameleon board. Sanchez and Jin Li voted to merge GVG with Hula Boards under the latter name, despite Bonsetti's dissent. Gnarly Vulcan Gear was dissolved, and production of the Baked Chameleon ceased. Using the information presented in the chapter, answer the following questions.

1. What rights does Bonsetti have (in most states) as a minority shareholder dissenting to the merger of GVG and Hula Boards?
2. Could the parties have used a short-form merger procedure in this situation? Why or why not?
3. What is the term used for Hula's offer to purchase GVG stock? By what method did Hula acquire control over GVG?
4. Suppose that after the merger, a person who was injured on a Baked Chameleon board sued Hula (the surviving corporation). Can Hula be held liable for an injury? Why or why not?

DEBATE THIS ... *Corporate law should be altered to prohibit incumbent management from using most of the legal methods available for fighting takeovers.*

Terms and Concepts

appraisal right 803
articles of merger 802
consolidation 802
dissolution 809
merger 801

parent corporation 802
parent-subsidiary merger 803
receiver 810
share exchange 802
short-form merger 803

subsidiary corporation 802
surviving corporation 801
takeover 805
target corporation 805
tender offer 806

ExamPrep

Issue Spotters

1. Macro Corporation and Micro Company combine, and a new organization, MM, Inc., takes their place. What is the term for this type of combination? What happens to the assets, property, and liabilities of Micro? **(See page 802.)**
2. Peppertree, Inc., hired Robert McClellan, a licensed contractor, to repair a condominium complex that was damaged in an earthquake. McClellan completes the work, but Peppertree fails to pay. McClellan is awarded $181,000 in an arbitration proceeding. Peppertree then forms another corporation and transfers all of its assets to the new corporation without notifying McClellan. Can McClellan hold Peppertree's

shareholders personally liable for the debt? Why or why not? **(See page 804.)**

• Check your answers to the Issue Spotters against the answers provided in Appendix E at the end of this text.

Before the Test

Go to **www.cengagebrain.com**, enter the ISBN 9781285185248, and click on "Find" to locate this text-book's Web site. Then, click on "Access Now" under "Study Tools," and select Chapter 41 at the top. There, you will find a Practice Quiz that you can take to assess your mastery of the concepts in this chapter, as well as Flashcards and a Glossary of important terms.

Business Scenarios

41–1. Corporate Merger. Alir owns 10,000 shares of Ajax Corp. Her shares represent a 10 percent ownership in Ajax. Zeta Corp. is interested in acquiring Ajax in a

merger, and the board of directors of each corporation has approved the merger. The shareholders of Zeta have already approved the acquisition, and Ajax has called for a shareholders' meeting to approve the merger. Alir disapproves of the merger and does not want to accept Zeta shares for the Ajax shares she holds. The market price of Ajax shares is $20 per share the day before the shareholder vote and drops to $16 on the day the shareholders of Ajax approve the merger. Discuss Alir's rights in this matter, beginning with the notice of the proposed merger. **(See page 801.)**

41–2. Purchase of Assets. Paradise Pools, Inc. (PPI) entered into a contract with Vittorio, LLP, to build a pool as part of a hotel being developed by Takahashi Development. PPI built the pool, but Vittorio, the general contractor, defaulted on other parts of the project. Takahashi completed the construction itself. Litigation followed and Takahashi was awarded $18,656 against PPI. Meanwhile, Paradise Corp. (PC) was incorporated with the same management as PPI, but different shareholders. PC acquired PPI's assets in 2014, without assuming its liabilities, and soon became known as "Paradise Pools and Spas." Takahashi sought to obtain a writ of garnishment against PC to enforce the judgment against PPI. Is PC liable for PPI's obligation to Takahashi? Why or why not? **(See page 804.)**

41–3. Corporate Takeover. Alitech Corp. is a small midwestern business that owns a valuable patent. Alitech has approximately a thousand shareholders with 100,000 authorized and outstanding shares. Block Corp. would like to have the use of the patent, but Alitech refuses to give Block a license. Block has tried to acquire Alitech by purchasing Alitech's assets, but Alitech's board of directors has refused to approve the acquisition. Alitech's shares are selling for $5 per share. Discuss how Block Corp. might proceed to gain the control and use of Alitech's patent. **(See page 805.)**

Business Case Problems

41–4. Successor Liability. General Star Indemnity Co. agreed to insure Indianapolis Racing League race cars against damage during on-track accidents. General Star deposited $400,000 with G Force, LLC (GFCO), a Colorado firm, to enable it to buy and provide parts for damaged cars without delay. GFCO agreed to return any unspent funds. Near the end of the season, Elan Motorsports Technologies acquired GFCO and incorporated G Force, LLC, in Georgia (GFGA). GFCO ceased to exist. GFGA renewed the arrangement with General Star and engaged in the same operations as GFCO, but Elan employees conducted GFGA's business at Elan's offices. In 2002, Elan assumed ownership of GFGA's assets and continued the business. Elan also assumed GFGA's liabilities, except for the obligation to return General Star's unspent funds. General Star filed a suit in a Georgia state court against Elan, seeking to recover its deposit. What is the rule concerning the liability of a corporation that buys the assets of another? Are there exceptions? Which principles apply in this case? Explain. [*General Star Indemnity Co. v. Elan Motorsports Technologies, Inc.,* 356 F.Supp.2d 1333 (N.D.Ga. 2004)] **(See page 804.)**

41–5. Dissolution. Clara Mahaffey operated Mahaffey's Auto Salvage, Inc., in Dayton, Ohio, as a sole proprietorship. In 1993, Kenneth Stumpff and Mahaffey's son, Richard Harris, joined the firm. Stumpff ran the wrecker and bought the vehicles for salvage. Harris handled the day-to-day operations and the bookkeeping. They became the company's equal 50 percent shareholders on Mahaffey's death in 2002. Harris, who inherited the land on which the firm was located, increased the rent to $1,500 per month. Within two years of Mahaffey's death, and without consulting Stumpff, Harris raised the rent to $2,500. Stumpff's wife died, and he took a leave of absence, during which the company paid him $2,500 a month and provided health insurance. After two years, Harris stopped the payments, discontinued the health benefits, and fired Stumpff, threatening to call the police if he came on the premises. Stumpff withdrew $16,000 from the firm's account, leaving a balance of $113. Harris offered to buy Stumpff's interest in the business, but Stumpff refused and filed a suit in an Ohio state court against Harris. A state statute permits the dissolution of a corporation if the owners are deadlocked in its management. Should the court order the dissolution of Mahaffey's? Why or why not? [*Stumpff v. Harris,* 2006 WL 2640232 (Ohio App. 2006)] **(See page 809.)**

41–6. Successor Liability. In 2004, the Watergate Hotel in Washington, D.C., obtained a loan from PB Capital. At this time, hotel employees were represented by a union (see Chapter 34), and under a collective bargaining agreement, the hotel agreed to make contributions to an employees' pension fund run by the union. In 2007, the hotel was closed due to poor business, although the owner stated that the hotel would reopen in 2010. Despite this expectation, PB Capital—which was still owed $40 million by the hotel owner—instituted foreclosure proceedings (see Chapter 29). At the foreclosure sale, PB Capital bought the hotel and reopened it under new management and with a new workforce. The union sued PB Capital, contending that it should pay $637,855 owed by the previous owner into the employees' pension fund. Should PB Capital, as the hotel's new owner, have to incur the previous owner's obligation to pay into the pension fund under the theory of successor liability? Why or why not? [*Board of Trustees of Unite Here Local 25 v. MR Watergate, LLC,* 677 F.Supp.2d 229 (D.D.C. 2010)] **(See page 804.)**

41-7. BUSINESS CASE PROBLEM
WITH SAMPLE ANSWER: Purchase of Assets.

Grand Adventures Tour & Travel Publishing Corp. (GATT) provided travel services. Duane Boyd, a former GATT director, incorporated Interline Travel & Tour, Inc. At a public sale, Interline bought GATT's assets. Interline moved into GATTs office building, hired former GATT employees, and began to serve GATT's customers. A GATT creditor, Call Center Technologies, Inc., filed an action to collect the unpaid amount on a contract with GATT from Interline. Is Interline liable? Why or why not? [Call Center Technologies, Inc. v. Grand Adventures Tour & Travel Publishing Corp., *635 F.3d 48 (2d Cir. 2011)]* **(See page 804.)**

- For a sample answer to Problem 41-7, go to Appendix F at the end of this text.

41-8. A QUESTION OF ETHICS: Purchase of Stock.

Topps Co. makes baseball and other cards, including the Pokemon collection, and distributes Bazooka bubble gum and other confections. Arthur Shorin, the son of Joseph Shorin, one of Topps's founders and the inspiration for "Bazooka Joe" (a character in the comic strip wrapped around each piece of gum), worked for Topps for fifty years and had served as its board chair and chief executive officer since 1980. Shorin's son-in-law, Scott Silverstein, served as Topps's president and chief operating officer. When Topps's financial performance began to lag, the board considered selling the company. Michael Eisner (formerly head of Disney Studios) offered to pay $9.75 per share and to retain Topps's management in a merger with his company. Upper Deck Co., Topps's chief competitor in the sports-card business, offered $10.75 per share but did not offer to retain the managers. Topps demanded that Upper Deck not reveal its bid publicly, but Topps publicized the offer, without accurately representing Upper Deck's interest and disparaging its seriousness. Upper Deck asked Topps to allow it to tell its side of events and to make a tender offer to Topps's shareholders. Topps refused and scheduled a shareholder vote on the Eisner offer. Topps's shareholders filed a suit in a Delaware state court against their firm, asking the court to prevent the vote. [In re Topps Co. Shareholders Litigation, 926 A.2d 58 (Del.Ch. 2007)] **(See page 805.)**

(a) The shareholders contended that Topps's conduct had "tainted the vote." What factors support this contention? How might these factors affect the vote?

(b) Why might Topps's board and management be opposed to either of the offers for the company? Is this opposition ethical? Should the court enjoin (prevent) the scheduled vote? Explain.

Legal Reasoning Group Activity

41-9. Mergers and Acquisitions. Angie Jolson is the chair of the board of directors of Artel, Inc., and Sam Douglas is the chair of the board of directors of Fox Express, Inc. Jolson and Douglas meet to consider the possibility of combining their corporations and activities into a single corporate entity. They consider two alternative courses of action: Artel could acquire all of the stock and assets of Fox Express, or the corporations could combine to form a new corporation, called A&F Enterprises, Inc. Both Jolson and Douglas are concerned about the necessity of a formal transfer of property, liability for existing debts, and the need to amend the articles of incorporation. **(See page 801.)**

(a) The first group will identify the first proposed combination and outline its legal effect on the transfer of property, the liabilities of the combined corporations, and the need to amend the articles of incorporation.

(b) The second group will do the same for the second proposed combination—determine what it is called and describe its legal effect on the transfer of property, the liabilities of the combined corporations, and the need to amend the articles of incorporation.

CHAPTER 42

SECURITIES LAW AND CORPORATE GOVERNANCE

After the stock market crash of October 29, 1929, and the ensuing economic depression, Congress enacted legislation to regulate securities markets. The result was the Securities Act of 1933[1] and the Securities Exchange Act of 1934.[2] Both acts were designed to provide investors with more information to help them make buying and selling decisions about securities and to prohibit deceptive, unfair, and manipulative practices.

Securities generally include any instruments evidencing corporate ownership (stock) or debts (bonds).

Today, the sale and transfer of securities are heavily regulated by federal and state statutes and by government agencies. Moreover, the Securities and Exchange Commission has implemented new regulations since Congress passed the Dodd-Frank Wall Street Reform and Consumer Protection Act[3] in reaction to the latest economic reces-

sion. This chapter discusses the nature of federal securities regulation and its effect on the business world.

We also discuss corporate governance and the Sarbanes-Oxley Act, which significantly affects certain types of securities transactions. In the concluding pages of this chapter, we look at how securities laws are being adapted to the online environment.

---

1. 15 U.S.C. Sections 77a–77aa.
2. 15 U.S.C. Sections 78a–78mm.

3. Pub. L. No. 111–203, July 21, 2010, 124 Stat. 1376; 12 U.S.C. Sections 5301 *et seq.*

SECTION 1
THE SECURITIES AND EXCHANGE COMMISSION

The Securities Exchange Act of 1934 created the Securities and Exchange Commission (SEC) as an independent regulatory agency. The SEC administers the Securities Act of 1933 and the 1934 act. The SEC also plays a key role in interpreting the provisions of these acts (and their amendments) and in creating regulations governing the purchase and sale of securities. The basic functions of the SEC are as follows:

1. Interprets federal securities laws and investigates securities law violations.
2. Issues new rules and amends existing rules.
3. Oversees the inspection of securities firms, brokers, investment advisers, and ratings agencies.
4. Oversees private regulatory organizations in the securities, accounting, and auditing fields.
5. Coordinates U.S. securities regulation with federal, state, and foreign authorities.

Updating the Regulatory Process

The SEC is working to make the regulatory process more efficient and more relevant to today's securities trading practices. To this end, the SEC has embraced modern technology and communications methods, especially the Internet, more completely than many other federal agencies have. For instance, the agency now requires companies to file certain information electronically so that it can be posted on the SEC's EDGAR (Electronic Data Gathering, Analysis, and Retrieval) database.

In addition, the SEC now requires companies to make disclosures about the potential impacts of climate change on their future profitability.[4] For instance, companies should disclose estimates for any material capital expenditures for pollution-control facilities and risk factors relating to existing or pending environmental legislation.

---

4. 17 C.F.R. Parts 211, 231, and 241.

The SEC's Expanding Regulatory Powers

Since the SEC's creation, its regulatory functions have gradually been increased by legislation granting it authority in different areas. For instance, to further curb securities fraud, Congress enacted the Securities Enforcement Remedies and Penny Stock Reform Act of 1990.[5] This act expanded the SEC's enforcement options and allowed SEC administrative law judges to hear cases involving more types of alleged securities law violations, such as fraudulent financial reporting and financial fraud. The Securities Acts Amendments of 1990 authorized the SEC to seek sanctions against those who violate foreign securities laws.[6]

The National Securities Markets Improvement Act of 1996 expanded the power of the SEC to exempt persons, securities, and transactions from the requirements of the securities laws.[7] The Sarbanes-Oxley Act of 2002, which you will read about later in this chapter, further expanded the authority of the SEC and required the SEC to adopt new rules.

SECTION 2
THE SECURITIES ACT OF 1933

The Securities Act of 1933 governs initial sales of stock by businesses. The act was designed to prohibit various forms of fraud and to stabilize the securities industry by requiring that investors receive financial and other significant information concerning the securities being offered for public sale. Basically, the purpose of this act is to require disclosure. The 1933 act provides that all securities transactions must be registered with the SEC unless they are specifically exempt from the registration requirements.

What Is a Security?

Section 2(1) of the Securities Act of 1933 contains a broad definition of securities, which generally include the following:[8]

1. Instruments commonly known as securities, such as preferred and common stocks, treasury stocks, bonds, debentures, and stock warrants.

2. Any interests commonly known as securities, such as stock options, puts, calls, or other types of privilege on a security or on the right to purchase a security or a group of securities in a national security exchange.
3. Notes, instruments, or other evidence of indebtedness, including certificates of interest in a profit-sharing agreement and certificates of deposit.
4. Any fractional undivided interest in oil, gas, or other mineral rights.
5. Investment contracts, which include interests in limited partnerships and other investment schemes.

THE *HOWEY* TEST In interpreting the 1933 act, the United States Supreme Court has held that an **investment contract** is any transaction in which a person (1) invests (2) in a common enterprise (3) reasonably expecting profits (4) derived *primarily* or *substantially* from others' managerial or entrepreneurial efforts. Known as the *Howey* test, this definition continues to guide the determination of what types of contracts can be considered securities.[9]

▶ **Case in Point 42.1**   Alpha Telcom sold, installed, and maintained pay-phone systems. The company guaranteed buyers of the systems a 14 percent annual return. Alpha was operating at a net loss, however, and continually borrowed funds to pay investors the fixed rate of return it had promised. Eventually, the company filed for bankruptcy, and the SEC brought an action alleging that Alpha had violated the Securities Act of 1933. A federal court concluded that the pay-phone program was a security because it involved an investment contract.[10] ◀

MANY TYPES OF SECURITIES For our purposes, it is convenient to think of securities in their most common form—stocks and bonds issued by corporations. Bear in mind, though, that securities can take many forms, including interests in whiskey, cosmetics, worms, beavers, boats, vacuum cleaners, muskrats, and cemetery lots. Almost any stake in the ownership or debt of a company can be considered a security. Investment contracts in condominiums, franchises, limited partnerships in real estate, and oil or gas or other mineral rights have qualified as securities.

9. *SEC v. W. J. Howey Co.,* 328 U.S. 293, 66 S.Ct. 1100, 90 L.Ed. 1244 (1946).
10. *SEC v. Alpha Telcom, Inc.,* 187 F.Supp.2d 1250 (2002). See also *SEC v. Edwards,* 540 U.S. 389, 124 S.Ct. 892, 157 L.Ed.2d 813 (2004), in which the United States Supreme Court held that an investment scheme offering contractual entitlement to a fixed rate of return can be an investment contract and therefore can be considered a security under federal law.

5. 15 U.S.C. Section 77g.
6. 15 U.S.C. Section 78a.
7. 15 U.S.C. Sections 77z-3, 78mm.
8. 15 U.S.C. Section 77b(1). Amendments in 1982 added stock options.

Registration Statement

Section 5 of the Securities Act of 1933 broadly provides that if a security does not qualify for an exemption, that security must be *registered* before it is offered to the public. Issuing corporations must file a *registration statement* with the SEC and must provide all investors with a *prospectus*. A **prospectus** is a disclosure document that describes the security being sold, the financial operations of the issuing corporation, and the investment or risk attaching to the security. The prospectus also serves as a selling tool for the issuing corporation.

The SEC now allows an issuer to deliver its prospectus to investors electronically via the Internet.[11] In principle, the registration statement and the prospectus supply sufficient information to enable unsophisticated investors to evaluate the financial risk involved.

CONTENTS OF THE REGISTRATION STATEMENT The registration statement must be written in plain English and fully describe the following:

1. The securities being offered for sale, including their relationship to the registrant's other capital securities.
2. The corporation's properties and business (including a financial statement certified by an independent public accounting firm).
3. The management of the corporation, including managerial compensation, stock options, pensions, and other benefits. Any interests of directors or officers in any material transactions with the corporation must be disclosed.
4. How the corporation intends to use the proceeds of the sale.
5. Any pending lawsuits or special risk factors.

All companies, both domestic and foreign, must file their registration statements electronically so that they can be posted on the SEC's EDGAR database (mentioned previously) and investors can access the information via the Internet. The EDGAR database includes material on *initial public offerings* (IPOs), proxy statements, corporations' annual reports, registration statements, and other documents that have been filed with the SEC.

REGISTRATION PROCESS The registration statement does not become effective until it has been reviewed and approved by the SEC (unless it is filed by a *well-known seasoned issuer,* as will be discussed shortly). The 1933 act restricts the types of activities that an issuer can engage in at each stage of the registration process. If an issuer violates these restrictions, investors can rescind their contracts to purchase the securities.

Prefiling Period. During the *prefiling period* (before the registration statement is filed), the issuer normally cannot sell or offer to sell the securities. Once the registration statement has been filed, a waiting period begins while the SEC reviews the registration statement for completeness.[12]

Waiting Period. During the waiting period, the securities can be offered for sale but cannot be sold by the issuing corporation. Only certain types of offers are allowed. All issuers can distribute a *preliminary prospectus,*[13] which contains most of the information that will be included in the final prospectus but often does not include a price.

Most issuers can also use a *free-writing prospectus* during this period (although some inexperienced issuers will need to file a preliminary prospectus first). A **free-writing prospectus** is any type of written, electronic, or graphic offer that describes the issuer or its securities and includes a legend indicating that the investor may obtain the prospectus at the SEC's Web site.

Posteffective Period. Once the SEC has reviewed and approved the registration statement and the waiting period is over, the registration is effective, and the *posteffective period* begins. The issuer can now offer and sell the securities without restrictions.

If the company issued a preliminary or free-writing prospectus to investors, it must provide those investors with a final prospectus either before or at the time they purchase the securities. The issuer can require investors to download the final prospectus from a Web site if it notifies them of the appropriate Internet address.

---

11. Basically, an electronic prospectus must meet the same requirements as a printed prospectus. The SEC rules address situations in which the graphics, images, or audio files in or accompanying a printed prospectus cannot be reproduced in an electronic form. 17 C.F.R. Section 232.304.

12. The waiting period must last at least twenty days but always extends much longer because the SEC inevitably requires numerous changes and additions to the registration statement.

13. A preliminary prospectus may also be called a *red herring prospectus.* The name comes from the legend printed in red across the prospectus stating that the registration has been filed but has not become effective.

Well-Known Seasoned Issuers

A *well-known seasoned issuer* (WKSI) is a firm that has issued at least $1 billion in securities in the last three years or has at least $700 million of value of outstanding stock in the hands of the public. WKSIs can file registration statements the day they announce a new offering and are not required to wait for SEC review and approval. They can also use a free-writing prospectus at any time, even during the prefiling period.

Exempt Securities and Transactions

Certain types of securities are exempt from the registration requirements of the Securities Act of 1933. These securities—which generally can also be resold without being registered—are summarized under the heading "Exempt Securities" in Exhibit 42–1 on the following page.[14] The exhibit also lists and describes certain transactions that are exempt from registration requirements under various SEC regulations.

The transaction exemptions are the most important because they are very broad and can enable an issuer to avoid the high cost and complicated procedures associated with registration. Because the coverage of the exemptions overlaps somewhat, an offering may qualify for more than one. Therefore, many sales occur without registration. Even when a transaction is exempt from the registration requirements, the offering is still subject to the antifraud provisions of the 1933 act (as well as those of the 1934 act, to be discussed later in this chapter).

REGULATION A OFFERINGS An exemption from registration is available for an issuer's offerings that do not exceed $5 million in securities during any twelve-month period.[15] Under Regulation A,[16] the issuer must file with the SEC a notice of the issue and an offering circular, which must also be provided to investors before the sale. This process is much less expensive than the procedures associated with full registration.

Testing the Waters. Companies are allowed to "test the waters" for potential interest before preparing the offering circular. To *test the waters* means to determine potential interest without actually selling any securities or requiring any commitment from those who express interest. Small-business issuers can also use an integrated registration and reporting system that requires simpler forms than the full registration system.

Using the Internet. Some companies have sold their securities via the Internet using Regulation A. ▶ **Example 42.2**　The Spring Street Brewing Company was the first company to sell securities via an online initial public offering (IPO). Spring Street raised about $1.6 million—without having to pay any commissions to brokers or underwriters. ◀

Such online IPOs are particularly attractive to small companies and start-up ventures that may find it difficult to raise capital from institutional investors or through underwriters. By making the offering online, the company can avoid both commissions and the costly and time-consuming filings required for a traditional IPO under federal and state law.

SMALL OFFERINGS—REGULATION D　The SEC's Regulation D contains several exemptions from registration requirements (Rules 504, 504a, 505, and 506) for offers that either involve a small dollar amount or are made in a limited manner.

Rule 504.　Rule 504 is the exemption used by most small businesses.　It provides that noninvestment company offerings up to $1 million in any twelve-month period are exempt.[17] Noninvestment companies are firms that are not engaged primarily in the business of investing or trading in securities. (In contrast, an **investment company** is a firm that buys a large portfolio of securities and professionally manages it on behalf of many smaller shareholders/owners. A **mutual fund** is a well-known type of investment company.)

▶ **Example 42.3**　Zeta Enterprises is a limited partnership that develops commercial property. Zeta intends to offer $600,000 of its limited partnership interests for sale between June 1 and next May 31 of the next year. The buyers will become limited partners in Zeta. Because an interest in a limited partnership meets the definition of a security (discussed earlier in this chapter), this offering would be subject to the registration and prospectus requirements of the Securities Act of 1933.

---

14. 15 U.S.C. Section 77c.
15. 15 U.S.C. Section 77c(b).
16. 17 C.F.R. Sections 230.251–230.263.

---

17. 17 C.F.R. Section 230.504. Small businesses in California may also be exempt under SEC Rule 1001. California's rule permits limited offerings of up to $5 million *per transaction*, if they satisfy certain conditions.

EXHIBIT 42–1 Exemptions for Securities Offerings under the 1933 Securities Act

Under Rule 504, however, the sales of Zeta's interests are exempt from these requirements because Zeta is a noninvestment company making an offering of less than $1 million in a given twelve-month period. Therefore, Zeta can sell its interests without filing a registration statement with the SEC or issuing a prospectus to any investor. ◀

Rule 505. Another exemption is available under Rule 505 for private, noninvestment company offerings up to $5 million in any twelve-month period. Under this exemption, the offer may be made to an unlimited number of *accredited investors* and up to thirty-five unaccredited investors. **Accredited investors** include banks, insurance companies, investment companies, employee benefit plans, the issuer's executive officers and directors, and persons whose income or net worth exceeds a certain threshold.

The SEC must be notified of the sales, and precautions must be taken because these *restricted securities* may be resold only by registration or in an exempt transaction. No general solicitation or advertising is allowed. The issuer must provide any unaccredited investors with disclosure documents that generally are the same as those used in registered offerings.

Rule 506—Private Placement Exemption. Rule 506

exempts private, noninvestment company offerings in unlimited amounts that are not generally solicited or advertised. This exemption is often referred to as the *private placement exemption* because it exempts "transactions not involving any public offering."[18] There can be an unlimited number of accredited investors and up to thirty-five unaccredited investors. To qualify for the exemption, the issuer must believe that each unaccredited investor has sufficient knowledge or experience in financial matters to be capable of evaluating the investment's merits and risks.[19]

The private placement exemption is perhaps the most important exemption for firms that want to raise funds through the sale of securities without registering them. ▶ **Example 42.4** Citco Corporation needs to raise capital to expand its operations. Citco decides to make a private $10 million offering of its common stock directly to two hundred accredited investors and a group of thirty highly sophisticated, but unaccredited, investors. Citco provides all of these investors with a prospectus and material information about the firm, including its most recent financial statements.

As long as Citco notifies the SEC of the sale, this offering will likely qualify as an exempt transaction under Rule 506. The offering is nonpublic and not generally advertised. There are fewer than thirty-five unaccredited investors, and each of them possesses sufficient knowledge and experience to evaluate the risks involved. The issuer has provided all purchasers with the material information. Thus, Citco will *not* be required to comply with the registration requirements of the Securities Act of 1933. ◀

RESALES AND SAFE HARBOR RULES Most securities can be resold without registration. The Securities Act of 1933 provides exemptions for resales by most persons other than issuers or underwriters. The average

investor who sells shares of stock need not file a registration statement with the SEC.

Resales of restricted securities acquired under Rule 505 or Rule 506, however, trigger the registration requirements *unless the party selling them complies with Rule 144 or Rule 144A*. These rules are sometimes referred to as safe harbors.

Rule 144. Rule 144 exempts restricted securities from registration on resale if all of the following conditions are met:

1. There is adequate current public information about the issuer. ("Adequate current public information" refers to the reports that certain companies are required to file under the Securities Exchange Act of 1934.)
2. The person selling the securities has owned them for at least six months if the issuer is subject to the reporting requirements of the 1934 act.[20] If the issuer is not subject to the 1934 act's reporting requirements, the seller must have owned the securities for at least one year.
3. The securities are sold in certain limited amounts in unsolicited brokers' transactions.
4. The SEC is notified of the resale.[21]

Rule 144A. Securities that at the time of issue were not of the same class as securities listed on a national securities exchange or quoted in a U.S. automated inter-dealer quotation system may be resold under Rule 144A.[22] They may be sold only to a qualified institutional buyer (an institution, such as an insurance company or a bank, that owns and invests at least $100 million in securities). The seller must take reasonable steps to ensure that the buyer knows that the seller is relying on the exemption under Rule 144A.

Violations of the 1933 Act

It is a violation of the Securities Act of 1933 to intentionally defraud investors by misrepresenting or omitting facts in a registration statement or prospectus. Liability is also imposed on those who are negligent

---

18. 15 U.S.C. Section 77d(2).

19. 17 C.F.R. Section 230.506.

20. Before 2008, when amendments to Rule 144 became effective, the holding period for restricted securities was one year if the issuer was subject to the reporting requirements of the 1934 act. See the revised SEC Rules and Regulations at 72 Federal Rules 71546-01, 2007 WL 4368599, Release No. 33-8869. This reduced holding period allows nonpublic issuers to raise capital electronically from private and overseas sources more quickly.

21. 17 C.F.R. Section 230.144.

22. 17 C.F.R. Section 230.144A.

in not discovering the fraud. Selling securities before the effective date of the registration statement or under an exemption for which the securities do not qualify results in liability.

REMEDIES Criminal violations are prosecuted by the U.S. Department of Justice. Violators may be fined up to $10,000, imprisoned for up to five years, or both.

The SEC is authorized to impose civil sanctions against those who willfully violate the 1933 act. It can request an injunction to prevent further sales of the securities involved or ask a court to grant other relief, such as ordering a violator to refund profits. Private parties who purchase securities and suffer harm as a result of false or omitted statements or other violations may bring a suit in a federal court to recover their losses and additional damages.

DEFENSES There are three basic defenses to charges of violations under the 1933 act. A defendant can avoid liability by proving any of the following:

1. The statement or omission was not material.
2. The plaintiff knew about the misrepresentation at the time the stock was purchased.
3. The defendant exercised *due diligence* in preparing the registration and reasonably believed at the time that the statements were true.

The due diligence defense is the most important because it can be asserted by any defendant, except the issuer of the stock. The defendant must prove that she or he reasonably believed, at the time the registration statement became effective, that the statements in it were true and there were no omissions of material facts.

The following case involved allegations of omissions of material information from an issuing company's registration statement. The defendants contended that the omissions were not material.

CASE 42.1

Litwin v. Blackstone Group, LP
United States Court of Appeals, Second Circuit, 634 F.3d 706 (2011).

BACKGROUND AND FACTS Blackstone Group, LP, manages investments. Its corporate private equity division accounts for nearly 40 percent of the assets under the company's management. In preparation for an initial public offering (IPO), Blackstone filed a registration statement with the Securities and Exchange Commission (SEC). At the time, corporate private equity's investments included FGIC Corporation and Freescale Semiconductor, Inc. FGIC insured investments in subprime mortgages. Before the IPO, FGIC's customers began to suffer large losses. By the time of the IPO, this situation was generating substantial losses for FGIC and, in turn, for Blackstone.

Meanwhile, Freescale had recently lost an exclusive contract to make wireless 3G chipsets for Motorola, Inc. (its largest customer). Blackstone's registration statement did not mention the impact on its revenue of the investments in FGIC and Freescale. Martin Litwin and others who invested in the IPO filed a suit in a federal district court against Blackstone and its officers, alleging material omissions from the statement. Blackstone filed a motion to dismiss, which the court granted. The plaintiffs appealed.

IN THE LANGUAGE OF THE COURT
STRAUB, Circuit Judge:

* * * *

Materiality is an inherently fact-specific finding that is satisfied when a plaintiff alleges a statement or omission that a reasonable investor would have considered significant in making investment decisions. * * * However, it is not necessary to assert that the investor would have acted differently if an accurate disclosure was made. Rather, when a district court is presented with a motion [to dismiss] a complaint may not properly be dismissed on the ground that the alleged misstatements or omissions are not material unless they are so obviously unimportant to a reasonable investor that reasonable minds could not differ on the question of their importance. [Emphasis added.]

In this case, the key information that plaintiffs assert should have been disclosed is whether, and to what extent, the particular known trend, event, or uncertainty might have

CASE 42.1 CONTINUED been reasonably expected to materially affect Blackstone's investments. * * * Plaintiffs are not seeking the disclosure of the mere fact of Blackstone's investment in FGIC, of the downward trend in the real estate market, or of Freescale's loss of its exclusive contract with Motorola. Rather, plaintiffs claim that Blackstone was required to disclose the manner in which those then- known trends, events, or uncertainties might reasonably be expected to materially impact Blackstone's future revenues.

* * * The question, of course, is not whether a loss in a particular investment's value will merely affect revenues, because * * * it will almost certainly have some effect. *The relevant question is whether Blackstone reasonably expects the impact to be material.* [Emphasis added.]

* * * Because Blackstone's Corporate Private Equity segment plays such an important role in Blackstone's business and provides value to all of its other asset management and financial advisory services, a reasonable investor would almost certainly want to know information related to that segment that Blackstone reasonably expects will have a material adverse effect on its future revenues. Therefore, the alleged * * * omissions relating to FGIC and Freescale were plausibly material.

DECISION AND REMEDY *The U.S. Court of Appeals for the Second Circuit vacated the lower court's dismissal and remanded the case. The plaintiffs had provided sufficient allegations that Blackstone had omitted material information that it was required to disclose under the securities laws for the case to go to trial.*

THE LEGAL ENVIRONMENT DIMENSION *Litwin alleged that Blackstone had negligently omitted material information from the registration statement. What will he and the others have to show to prove their case?*

THE ECONOMIC DIMENSION *Blackstone raised more than $4.5 billion through the IPO. Blackstone officers received nearly all of the net proceeds. If the company had disclosed the omitted information in its registration statement, how might these results have been different?*

SECTION 3
THE SECURITIES EXCHANGE ACT OF 1934

The Securities Exchange Act of 1934 provides for the regulation and registration of securities exchanges, brokers, dealers, and national securities associations, such as the National Association of Securities Dealers (NASD). Unlike the 1933 act, which is a one-time disclosure law, the 1934 act provides for continuous periodic disclosures by publicly held corporations to enable the SEC to regulate subsequent trading.

The Securities Exchange Act of 1934 applies to companies that have assets in excess of $10 million and five hundred or more shareholders. These corporations are referred to as *Section 12 companies* because they are required to register their securities under Section 12 of the 1934 act. Section 12 companies are required to file reports with the SEC annually and quarterly, and sometimes even monthly if specified events occur (such as a merger).

The act also authorizes the SEC to engage in market surveillance to deter undesirable market practices such as fraud, market manipulation, and misrepresentation. In addition, the act provides for the SEC's regulation of proxy solicitations for voting (discussed in Chapter 40).

Section 10(b), SEC Rule 10b-5, and Insider Trading

Section 10(b) is one of the more important sections of the Securities Exchange Act of 1934. This section prohibits the use of any manipulative or deceptive mechanism in violation of SEC rules and regulations. Among the rules that the SEC has promulgated pursuant to the 1934 act is **SEC Rule 10b-5,** which prohibits the commission of fraud in connection with the purchase or sale of any security.

SEC Rule 10b-5 applies to almost all cases concerning the trading of securities, whether on organized exchanges, in over-the-counter markets, or in private transactions. Generally, the rule covers just about any form of security. The securities need not be registered under the 1933 act for the 1934 act to apply.

Private parties can sue for securities fraud under the 1934 act and SEC rules. The basic elements of a securities fraud action are as follows:

1. A *material misrepresentation* (or omission) in connection with the purchase and sale of securities.
2. *Scienter* (a wrongful state of mind).
3. *Reliance* by the plaintiff on the material misrepresentation.
4. An *economic loss.*
5. *Causation,* meaning that there is a causal connection between the misrepresentation and the loss.

INSIDER TRADING One of the major goals of Section 10(b) and SEC Rule 10b-5 is to prevent **insider trading,** which occurs when persons buy or sell securities on the basis of information that is not available to the public. Corporate directors, officers, and others, such as majority shareholders, often have advance inside information that can affect the future market value of the corporate stock. Obviously, if they act on this information, their positions give them a trading advantage over the general public and other shareholders.

The 1934 Securities Exchange Act defines inside information. It also extends liability to those who take advantage of such information in their personal transactions when they know that the information is unavailable to those with whom they are dealing. Section 10(b) of the 1934 act and SEC Rule 10b-5 apply to anyone who has access to or receives information of a nonpublic nature on which trading is based—not just to corporate "insiders."

DISCLOSURE UNDER SEC RULE 10B-5 Any material omission or misrepresentation of material facts in connection with the purchase or sale of a security may violate Section 10(b) of the 1934 act and SEC Rule 10b-5. The key to liability (which can be civil or criminal) is whether the information omitted or misrepresented is *material.*

The following are some examples of material facts calling for disclosure under SEC Rule 10b-5:

1. Fraudulent trading in the company stock by a broker-dealer.
2. A dividend change (whether up or down).
3. A contract for the sale of corporate assets.
4. A new discovery, a new process, or a new product.
5. A significant change in the firm's financial condition.
6. Potential litigation against the company.

Note that any one of these facts, by itself, is not automatically considered material. Rather, it will be regarded as a material fact only if it is significant enough that it would likely affect an investor's decision as to whether to purchase or sell the company's securities.

▶ **Example 42.5** Zilotek, Inc., is the defendant in a class-action product liability suit that its attorney believes the company will lose. The attorney has advised Zilotek's directors, officers, and accountants that the company will likely have to pay a substantial damages award. Zilotek plans to make a $5 million offering of newly issued stock before the date when the trial is expected to end. Zilotek's potential liability and the financial consequences to the firm are material facts that must be disclosed because they are significant enough to affect an investor's decision as to whether to purchase the stock. ◀

The case that follows is a classic decision interpreting materiality under SEC Rule 10b-5.

CLASSIC CASE 42.2

SEC v. Texas Gulf Sulphur Co.
United States Court of Appeals, Second Circuit, 401 F.2d 833 (1968).

BACKGROUND AND FACTS Texas Gulf Sulphur Company (TGS) conducted aerial geophysical surveys over more than 15,000 square miles of eastern Canada. The operations indicated concentrations of commercially exploitable minerals. At one site near Timmins, Ontario, TGS drilled a hole that appeared to yield a core with an exceedingly high mineral content. The company did not disclose the results of the core sample to the public. After learning of the sample, TGS officers and employees made substantial purchases of TGS's stock or accepted stock options (rights to purchase stock). Further drilling, however, was necessary to establish whether there was enough ore to be mined commercially. Several months later, TGS

CASE 42.2 CONTINUED

announced that the strike was expected to yield at least 25 million tons of ore. Subsequently, the price of TGS stock rose substantially. The Securities and Exchange Commission (SEC) brought a suit against the officers and employees of TGS for violating SEC Rule 10b-5. The officers and employees argued that the information on which they had traded had not been material at the time of their trades because the mine had not then been commercially proved. The trial court held that most of the defendants had not violated SEC Rule 10b-5, and the SEC appealed.

 IN THE LANGUAGE OF THE COURT
WATERMAN, Circuit Judge.

* * * *

* * * Whether facts are material within Rule 10b-5 when the facts relate to a particular event and are undisclosed by those persons who are knowledgeable thereof *will depend at any given time upon a balancing of both the indicated probability that the event will occur and the anticipated magnitude of the event in light of the totality of the company activity.* Here, * * * knowledge of the possibility, which surely was more than marginal, of the existence of a mine of the vast magnitude indicated by the remarkably rich drill core located rather close to the surface (suggesting mineability by the less expensive openpit method) within the confines of a large anomaly (suggesting an extensive region of mineralization) might well have affected the price of TGS stock and would certainly have been an important fact to a reasonable, if speculative, investor in deciding whether he should buy, sell, or hold. [Emphasis added.]

* * * *

* * * A major factor in determining whether the * * * discovery was a material fact is the importance attached to the drilling results by those who knew about it. * * * The timing by those who knew of it of their stock purchases * * *—purchases in some cases by individuals who had never before purchased * * * TGS stock—virtually compels the inference that the insiders were influenced by the drilling results.

DECISION AND REMEDY *The appellate court ruled in favor of the SEC. All of the trading by insiders who knew of the mineral find before its true extent had been publicly announced violated SEC Rule 10b-5.*

WHAT IF THE FACTS WERE DIFFERENT? *Suppose that further drilling had revealed that there was not enough ore at this site for it to be mined commercially. Would the defendants still have been liable for violating SEC Rule 10b-5? Why or why not?*

IMPACT OF THIS CASE ON TODAY'S LAW *This landmark case affirmed the principle that the test of whether information is "material," for SEC Rule 10b-5 purposes, is whether it would affect the judgment of reasonable investors. The corporate insiders' purchases of stock and stock options indicated that they were influenced by the drilling results and that the information about the drilling results was material. The courts continue to cite this case when applying SEC Rule 10b-5 to cases of alleged insider trading.*

OUTSIDERS AND SEC RULE 10B-5 The traditional insider-trading case involves true insiders—corporate officers, directors, and majority shareholders who have access to (and trade on) inside information. Increasingly, however, liability under Section 10(b) of the 1934 act and SEC Rule 10b-5 has been extended to include certain "outsiders"—those who trade on inside information acquired indirectly. Two theories have been developed under which outsiders may be held liable for insider trading: the *tipper/tippee theory* and the *misappropriation theory.*

Tipper/Tippee Theory. Anyone who acquires inside information as a result of a corporate insider's breach of his or her fiduciary duty can be liable under SEC Rule 10b-5. This liability extends to **tippees** (those who receive "tips" from insiders) and even remote tippees (tippees of tippees).

The key to liability under this theory is that the inside information must be obtained as a result of someone's breach of a fiduciary duty to the corporation whose shares are traded. The tippee is liable only if the following requirements are met:

1. There is a breach of a duty not to disclose inside information.
2. The disclosure is made in exchange for personal benefit.
3. The tippee knows (or should know) of this breach and benefits from it.[23]

Misappropriation Theory. Liability for insider trading may also be established under the misappropriation theory. This theory holds liable an individual who wrongfully obtains (misappropriates) inside information and trades on it for her or his personal gain because the individual basically stole information rightfully belonging to another.

The misappropriation theory has been controversial because it significantly extends the reach of SEC Rule 10b-5 to outsiders who ordinarily would *not* be deemed fiduciaries of the corporations in whose stock they trade. It is not always wrong to disclose material, nonpublic information about a company to a person who would not otherwise be privy to it. Nevertheless, a person who obtains the information and trades securities on it can be held liable.

▶ **Case in Point 42.6** Patricia Rocklage was the wife of Scott Rocklage, the CEO of Cubist Pharmaceuticals, Inc. Scott had sometimes disclosed material, nonpublic information about Cubist to Patricia. She had always kept the information confidential. When Scott told Patricia that one of Cubist's key drugs had failed its clinical trial, however, Patricia informed her brother, William Beaver, who owned Cubist stock. Beaver sold his Cubist shares and tipped his friend David Jones, who sold his shares. When Cubist publicly announced the trial results, the price of its stock dropped. Beaver and Jones avoided significant losses by selling when they did. The SEC filed a lawsuit against Patricia, Beaver, and Jones. The court found all three defendants guilty of insider trading under the misappropriation theory.[24] ◀

Insider Reporting and Trading—Section 16(b)

Section 16(b) of the 1934 act provides for the recapture by the corporation of all profits realized by certain insiders on any purchase and sale or sale and purchase of the corporation's stock within any six-

month period. It is irrelevant whether the insider actually uses inside information—*all such short-swing profits must be returned to the corporation.*

In this context, insiders means officers, directors, and large stockholders of Section 12 corporations (those owning 10 percent of the class of equity securities registered under Section 12 of the 1934 act).[25] To discourage such insiders from using nonpublic information about their companies to their personal benefit in the stock market, they must file reports with the SEC concerning their ownership and trading of the corporation's securities.

Section 16(b) applies not only to stock but also to warrants, options, and securities convertible into stock. In addition, the courts have fashioned complex rules for determining profits. Note that the SEC exempts a number of transactions under Rule 16b-3.[26] For all of these reasons, corporate insiders should seek the advice of competent counsel before trading in the corporation's stock. Exhibit 42–2 on the following page compares the effects of SEC Rule 10b-5 and Section 16(b).

The Private Securities Litigation Reform Act

The disclosure requirements of SEC Rule 10b-5 had the unintended effect of deterring the disclosure of forward-looking information. To understand why, consider the following situation. ▶ **Example 42.7** QT Company announces that it projects that its earnings in a future time period will be a certain amount, but the forecast turns out to be wrong. The earnings are in fact much lower, and the price of the company's stock is affected—negatively. The shareholders then bring a class-action suit against the company, alleging that the directors violated SEC Rule 10b-5 by disclosing misleading financial information. ◀

In an attempt to rectify this problem and promote disclosure, Congress passed the Private Securities Litigation Reform Act (PSLRA) of 1995. Among other things, the PSLRA provides a "safe harbor" for publicly held companies that make forward-looking statements, such as financial forecasts. Those who make such statements are protected against liability for securities fraud if they include "meaningful cautionary statements identifying important factors that

23. See, for example, *Chiarella v. United States,* 445 U.S. 222, 100 S.Ct. 1108, 63 L.Ed.2d 348 (1980); and *Dirks v. SEC,* 463 U.S. 646, 103 S.Ct. 3255, 77 L.Ed.2d 911 (1983).
24. *SEC v. Rocklage,* 470 F.3d 1 (1st Cir. 2006).
25. 15 U.S.C. Section 78*l.* Note that Section 403 of the Sarbanes-Oxley Act of 2002 shortened the reporting deadlines specified in Section 16(b).
26. 17 C.F.R. Section 240.16b-3.

EXHIBIT 42–2 Comparison of Coverage, Application, and Liability under SEC Rule 10b-5 and Section 16(b)

Area of Comparison	SEC Rule 10b-5	Section 16(b)
What is the subject matter of the transaction?	Any security (does not have to be registered).	Any security (does not have to be registered).
What transactions are covered?	Purchase or sale.	Short-swing purchase and sale or short-swing sale and purchase.
Who is subject to liability?	Almost anyone with inside information under a duty to disclose—including officers, directors, controlling shareholders, and tippees.	Officers, directors, and certain shareholders who earn 10 percent or more.
Is omission or misrepresentation necessary for liability?	Yes.	No.
Are there any exempt transactions?	No.	Yes, there are a number of exemptions.
Who may bring an action?	A person transacting with an insider, the SEC, or a purchaser or seller damaged by a wrongful act.	A corporation or a shareholder by derivative action.

could cause actual results to differ materially from those in the forward-looking statement."[27]

The PSLRA also affected the level of detail required in securities fraud complaints. Plaintiffs must specify each misleading statement and say how it led them to a mistaken belief.

Regulation of Proxy Statements

Section 14(a) of the Securities Exchange Act of 1934 regulates the solicitation of proxies (see Chapter 40) from shareholders of Section 12 companies. The SEC regulates the content of proxy statements. Whoever solicits a proxy must fully and accurately disclose in the proxy statement all of the facts that are pertinent to the matter on which the shareholders are to vote. SEC Rule 14a-9 is similar to the antifraud provisions of SEC Rule 10b-5. Remedies for violations are extensive, ranging from injunctions to prevent a vote from being taken to monetary damages.

Violations of the 1934 Act

As mentioned earlier, violations of Section 10(b) of the Securities Exchange Act of 1934 and SEC Rule 10b-5, including insider trading, may lead to both criminal and civil liability.

27. 15 U.S.C. Sections 77z-2, 78u-5.

***SCIENTER* REQUIREMENT** For either criminal or civil sanctions to be imposed, however, *scienter* must exist—that is, the violator must have had an intent to defraud or knowledge of his or her misconduct (see Chapter 15). *Scienter* can be proved if it is shown that the defendant made false statements or wrongfully failed to disclose material facts.

In some situations, *scienter* can even be proved by showing that the defendant was consciously reckless as to the truth or falsity of his or her statements. ▶ **Case in Point 42.8** Alvin Gebhart and Jack Archer started a business venture purchasing mobile home parks (MHPs) from owners and converting them to resident ownership. They formed MHP Conversions, LP, to facilitate the conversion process and issue promissory notes that were sold to investors to raise funds for the purchases.

Archer ran the MHP program, and Gebhart sold the promissory notes. Gebhart sold nearly $2.4 million in MHP promissory notes to clients, who bought the notes based on Gebhart's positive statements about the investment. During the time Gebhart was selling the notes, however, he never actually looked into the finances of the MHP program. He relied entirely on information that Archer gave him, some of which was not true. When Gebhart was later sued for securities fraud, a federal appellate court concluded that there was sufficient evidence of *scienter*. Gebhart knew that he had no knowledge of the financial affairs of MHP, and he had been consciously reckless as to the truth or falsity of his statements about investing in MHP.[28] ◄

In the complaint, the plaintiff must state facts giving rise to an inference of *scienter* at least as

likely as any plausible opposing inference. Opposing inferences and their proof were at issue in the following case.

---

28. *Gebhart v. SEC,* 595 F.3d 1034 (9th Cir. 2010).

CASE ANALYSIS

Case 42.3 City of Livonia Employees' Retirement System and Local 295/Local 851 v. Boeing Co.

United States Court of Appeals, Seventh Circuit, 711 F.3d 754 (2013).

**IN THE LANGUAGE
OF THE COURT**
POSNER, Circuit Judge.
* * * *

* * * On April 21 [2009] Boeing [Company] performed a stress test on the wings of its new 787-8 Dreamliner, a plane that had not yet flown. The wings failed the test * * * . Yet Boeing announced on May 3 that "all structural tests required on the static airframe prior to first flight are complete" and that "the initial results of the test are positive" * * * . The implication was that the plane was on track for its "First Flight," which had been scheduled for June 30.

In mid-May, after making some changes in the design * * * , Boeing conducted another test. Although the plane failed that test too, [Boeing's chief executive officer James] McNerney stated publicly that he thought the plane would fly in June. Later [the head of Boeing's commercial aircraft division Scott] Carson told [the media] that the Dreamliner "definitely will fly" this month (June).

* * * Yet on June 23, * * * Boeing announced that the First Flight of the Dreamliner had been canceled because, Carson explained, of an "anomaly" revealed by the * * * tests. He said that Boeing had hoped to be able to solve the problem in time for a First Flight in June, but had been unable to do so. In fact the First Flight did not take place until December 2009.

When Boeing announced the cancellation of the First Flight, it

also announced that the cancellation would cause a delay of unspecified length in the delivery of the Dreamliner, which many airlines had already ordered. In the two days after these announcements, Boeing's stock price dropped by more than 10 percent. * * * Persons who bought Boeing stock between the tests and the announcements of the cancellation and of the delay in delivery and who therefore lost money when the price dropped [filed a suit in a federal district court against Boeing and its officers, alleging violations of Section 10(b) and Rule 10b-5].

The district judge dismissed the * * * complaint. [The plaintiffs appealed.]

There is no securities fraud by hindsight. The law does not require public disclosure of mere risks of failure. No prediction—even a prediction that the sun will rise tomorrow—has a 100 percent probability of being correct. The future is shrouded in uncertainty. If a mistaken prediction is deemed a fraud, there will be few predictions, including ones that are well grounded, as no one wants to be held hostage to an unknown future. [Emphasis added.]

Any sophisticated purchaser of a product that is still on the drawing boards knows, moreover, that its market debut may be delayed, or indeed that the project may be abandoned before it yields salable product. The purchasers of the Dreamliner protected themselves against the possibility of delay in delivery by reserving the right to cancel their orders; there

are no allegations regarding cancellation penalties, or for that matter penalties imposed on Boeing for delivery delays. And therefore * * * the defendants * * * had, so far as appears, little incentive to delay the announcement of the postponement.

Without a motive to commit securities fraud, businessmen are unlikely to commit it. A more plausible inference than that of fraud is that the defendants, unsure whether they could fix the problem by the end of June, were reluctant to tell the world "we have a problem and maybe it will cause us to delay the First Flight and maybe not, but we're working on the problem and we hope we can fix it in time to prevent any significant delay, but we can't be sure, so stay tuned." There is a difference * * * between a duty of truthfulness and a duty of candor, or between a lie and reticence [uncommunicativeness]. There is no duty of total corporate transparency—no rule that every hitch or glitch, every pratfall [embarrassing mistake], in a company's operations must be disclosed in real time, forming a running commentary, a baring of the corporate innards, day and night. [Emphasis added.]
* * * *

* * * The * * * complaint alleged [that] what McNerney and Carson knew about the likely postponement of the First Flight * * * was confirmed by "internal e-mails" of Boeing. The reference to internal e-mails implied that someone inside Boeing was aiding the plaintiffs. But as no such

CASE 42.3 CONTINUED

person was identified, the judge could not determine whether such e-mails * * * existed.

Allegations * * * merely implying unnamed confidential sources of damaging information require a

heavy discount. The sources may be ill-informed, may be acting from spite rather than knowledge, may be misrepresented, may even be nonexistent * * * . The district judge therefore rightly refused to give any weight to

the "internal e-mails" to which the complaint referred.

* * * *

The judgment dismissing the suit is affirmed.

LEGAL REASONING QUESTIONS

1. Which *pleading* (a document filed with the court—see Chapter 2) was at the center of the dispute in this case?
2. What must this pleading state in a suit alleging violations of Section 10(b) and Rule 10b-5?
3. Did the court conclude that the pleading here met this requirement? Why or why not?
4. If a pleading does not meet this requirement, should the court impose sanctions on the lawyers who filed it? Discuss.

SCIENTER NOT REQUIRED FOR SECTION 16(B) VIOLATIONS Violations of Section 16(b) include the sale by insiders of stock acquired less than six months before the time of sale (or less than six months after the sale, if selling short—that is, selling securities that one does not yet own). These violations are subject to civil sanctions. Liability under Section 16(b) is strict liability. Neither *scienter* nor negligence is required.

CRIMINAL PENALTIES For violations of Section 10(b) and Rule 10b-5, an individual may be fined up to $5 million, imprisoned for up to twenty years, or both. A partnership or a corporation may be fined up to $25 million. Under Section 807 of the Sarbanes-Oxley Act of 2002, for a *willful* violation of the 1934 act the violator can be imprisoned for up to twenty-five years (in addition to being subject to a fine).

For a defendant to be convicted in a criminal prosecution under the securities laws, there can be no reasonable doubt that the defendant knew he or she was acting wrongfully. In other words, a jury is not allowed merely to speculate that the defendant may have acted willfully. ▶ **Case in Point 42.9** Martha Stewart, founder of a well-known media and homemaking empire, was charged with intentionally deceiving investors based on statements she made at a conference. In 2001, Stewart's stockbroker allegedly informed Stewart that the head of ImClone Systems, Inc., was selling his shares in that company. Stewart then sold her ImClone shares. The next day, ImClone announced that the U.S. Food and Drug Administration had failed to approve Erbitux, the company's greatly anticipated medication.

After the government began investigating Stewart's ImClone trades, she publicly stated that she had pre-

viously instructed her stockbroker to sell her ImClone stock if the price fell to $60 per share. The government prosecutor claimed that Stewart's statement showed she had the intent to deceive investors. The court, however, acquitted Stewart on this charge because "to find the essential element of criminal intent beyond a reasonable doubt, a rational juror would have to speculate."[29] ◀

CIVIL SANCTIONS The SEC can also bring a civil action against anyone who purchases or sells a security while in the possession of material nonpublic information in violation of the 1934 act or SEC rules.[30] The violation must occur through the use of a national securities exchange or a broker or dealer.[31]

A court can assess a penalty amounting to as much as triple the profits gained or the loss avoided by the guilty party.[32] The Insider Trading and Securities Fraud Enforcement Act enlarged the class of persons who may be subject to civil liability for insider trading. This act also gave the SEC authority to offer monetary rewards to informants.[33]

Private parties may also sue violators of Section 10(b) and Rule 10b-5. A private party can obtain rescission (cancellation) of a contract to buy securities or damages to the extent of the violator's illegal profits. Those found liable have a right to seek contribution from those who share responsibility for the violations,

29. *United States v. Stewart,* 305 F.Supp.2d 368 (S.D.N.Y. 2004). (Stewart was later convicted on other charges relating to her ImClone trading that did not require proof of intent.)
30. 15 U.S.C. Section 78u(d)(2)(A).
31. Transactions pursuant to a public offering by an issuer of securities are excepted.
32. 15 U.S.C. Section 78u(d)(2)(C).
33. 15 U.S.C. Section 78u-1.

including accountants, attorneys, and corporations. (The liability of accountants and attorneys for violations of the securities laws is discussed in Chapter 47.) For violations of Section 16(b), a corporation can bring an action to recover the short-swing profits.

SECTION 4

STATE SECURITIES LAWS

Today, every state has its own corporate securities laws, or **blue sky laws,** that regulate the offer and sale of securities within its borders. (The phrase *blue sky laws* comes from a 1917 United States Supreme Court decision. The Court stated that the purpose of such laws was to prevent "speculative schemes which have no more basis than so many feet of 'blue sky.'")[34] Article 8 of the Uniform Commercial Code also imposes various requirements relating to the purchase and sale of securities.

Requirements

Typically, state laws have disclosure requirements and antifraud provisions, many of which are patterned after Section 10(b) of the Securities Exchange Act of 1934 and SEC Rule 10b-5. State laws also provide for the registration of securities offered or issued for sale within the state and impose disclosure requirements.

Methods of registration, required disclosures, and exemptions from registration vary among states. Unless an exemption from registration is applicable, issuers must register or qualify their stock with the appropriate state official, often called a *corporations commissioner.* Additionally, most state securities laws regulate securities brokers and dealers.

Concurrent Regulation

State securities laws apply mainly to intrastate transactions. Since the adoption of the 1933 and 1934 federal securities acts, the state and federal governments have regulated securities concurrently. Issuers must comply with both federal and state securities laws, and exemptions from federal law are not exemptions from state laws.

The dual federal and state system has not always worked well, particularly during the early 1990s,

when the securities markets underwent considerable expansion. Today, many of the duplicate regulations have been eliminated, and the SEC has exclusive power to regulate most national securities activities. The National Conference of Commissioners on Uniform State Laws also substantially revised the Uniform Securities Act in 2002 to coordinate state and federal securities regulation and enforcement efforts. Seventeen states have adopted the most recent version of the Uniform Securities Act.[35]

SECTION 5

CORPORATE GOVERNANCE

Corporate governance can be narrowly defined as the relationship between a corporation and its shareholders. Defined more broadly, corporate governance specifies the rights and responsibilities among different corporate participants (including stakeholders) and spells out the rules and procedures for making decisions on corporate affairs. Regardless of the way it is defined, effective corporate governance requires more than just compliance with laws and regulations.

Effective corporate governance is essential in large corporations because corporate ownership (by shareholders) is separated from corporate control (by officers and managers). Under these circumstances, officers and managers may attempt to advance their own interests at the expense of the shareholders. The well-publicized corporate scandals in the early 2000s clearly illustrate the reasons for concern about managerial opportunism. Indeed, corporate governance has become an issue of concern for corporate entities around the world. With the globalization of business, a corporation's bad acts (or lack of control systems) can have far-reaching consequences.

Attempts at Aligning the Interests of Officers with Those of Shareholders

Some corporations have sought to align the financial interests of their officers with those of the company's

---

34. *Hall v. Geiger-Jones Co.,* 242 U.S. 539, 37 S.Ct. 217, 61 L.Ed. 480 (1917).

35. At the time this book went to press, the Uniform Securities Act had been adopted in Georgia, Hawaii, Idaho, Indiana, Iowa, Kansas, Maine, Michigan, Minnesota, Mississippi, Missouri, New Mexico, Oklahoma, South Carolina, South Dakota, Vermont, and Wisconsin, as well as in the U.S. Virgin Islands. You can find current information on state adoptions at www.uniformlaws.org.

shareholders by providing the officers with **stock options,** which enable them to purchase shares of the corporation's stock at a set price. When the market price rises above that level, the officers can sell their shares for a profit. Because a stock's market price generally increases as the corporation prospers, the options give the officers a financial stake in the corporation's well being and supposedly encourage them to work hard for the benefit of the shareholders.

Options have turned out to be an imperfect device for providing effective governance, however. Executives in some companies have "cooked" the company's books in order to keep share prices high so that they could sell their stock for a profit. Executives in other corporations have experienced no losses when share prices dropped because their options were "repriced" so that they did not suffer from the share price decline. Thus, although stock options theoretically can motivate officers to protect shareholder interests, stock option plans have sometimes become a way for officers to take advantage of shareholders.

With stock options generally failing to work as planned, there has been an outcry for more "outside" directors (those with no formal employment affiliation with the company). The theory is that independent directors will more closely monitor the actions of corporate officers. Hence, today we see more boards with outside directors. Note, though, that outside directors may not be truly independent of corporate officers. They may be friends or business associates of the leading officers.

The Goal Is to Promote Accountability

Effective corporate governance standards are designed to address problems such as those briefly discussed above and to motivate officers to make decisions that promote the financial interests of the company's shareholders. Generally, corporate governance entails corporate decision-making structures that monitor employees (particularly officers) to ensure that they are acting for the benefit of the shareholders. Thus, corporate governance involves, at a minimum:

1. The audited reporting of financial conditions at the corporation so that managers can be evaluated.
2. Legal protections for shareholders so that violators of the law who attempt to take advantage of shareholders can be punished for misbehavior and victims can recover damages for any associated losses.

THE COMPANY BENEFITS Effective corporate governance can have considerable practical significance. Firms that are more accountable to shareholders typically report higher profits, higher sales growth, higher firm value, and other economic advantages. Thus, a corporation with better corporate governance and greater accountability to investors may also have a higher valuation than a corporation that is less concerned about governance. Corporations that promote diversity in the workplace, and especially in management, may similarly experience increased profits, growth, and value.

GOVERNANCE AND CORPORATE LAW State corporation statutes set up the legal framework for corporate governance. Under the corporate law of Delaware, where most major companies incorporate, all corporations must have certain structures of corporate governance in place. The most important structure, of course, is the board of directors because the board makes the major decisions about the future of the corporation.

THE BOARD OF DIRECTORS Under corporate law, a corporation must have a board of directors elected by the shareholders. Almost anyone can become a director, though some organizations, such as the New York Stock Exchange, require certain standards of service for directors of their listed corporations.

Directors are responsible for ensuring that the corporation's officers are operating wisely and in the exclusive interest of shareholders. Directors receive reports from the officers and give them managerial directions. In reality, though, corporate directors devote a relatively small amount of time to monitoring officers.

Ideally, shareholders would monitor the directors' supervision of the officers. In practice, however, it can be difficult for shareholders to monitor directors and hold them responsible for corporate failings. Although the directors can be sued if they fail to do their jobs effectively, directors are rarely held personally liable.

THE COMPENSATION COMMITTEE An important committee of the board of directors, mentioned in Chapter 40, is the *compensation committee*, which determines the compensation to be paid to the company's officers. As part of this process, the committee must assess the officers' performance and design a compensation system that will best align the officers' interests with those of the shareholders.

The Sarbanes-Oxley Act of 2002

As discussed in Chapter 5, Congress passed the Sarbanes-Oxley Act in 2002 in response to a series of corporate scandals. The act addresses certain issues relating to corporate governance. Generally, the act attempts to increase corporate accountability by imposing strict disclosure requirements and harsh penalties for violations of securities laws. Among other things, the act requires chief corporate executives to take personal responsibility for the accuracy of financial statements and reports that are filed with the SEC.

Additionally, the act requires that certain financial and stock-transaction reports be filed with the SEC earlier than was required under the previous rules. The act also created a new entity, called the Public Company Accounting Oversight Board, which regulates and oversees public accounting firms. Other provisions of the act established private civil actions and expanded the SEC's remedies in administrative and civil actions.

Because of the importance of this act for corporate leaders and for those dealing with securities transactions, we present excerpts and explanatory comments in Appendix D at the end of this text. We also highlight some of its key provisions relating to corporate accountability in Exhibit 42–3 on the next page.

MORE INTERNAL CONTROLS AND ACCOUNTABILITY

The Sarbanes-Oxley Act also introduced direct *federal* corporate governance requirements for public companies (companies whose shares are traded in the public securities markets). The law addressed many of the corporate governance procedures just discussed and created new requirements in an attempt to make the system work more effectively. The requirements deal with independent monitoring of company officers by both the board of directors and auditors.

Sections 302 and 404 of the Sarbanes-Oxley Act require high-level managers (the most senior officers) to establish and maintain an effective system of internal controls. Moreover, senior management must reassess the system's effectiveness annually. Some companies had to take expensive steps to bring their internal controls up to the new federal standards. These include "disclosure controls and procedures" to ensure that company financial reports are accurate and timely and to document financial results prior to reporting. After the act was passed, hundreds of companies reported that they had identified and corrected shortcomings in their internal control systems.

EXEMPTIONS FOR SMALLER COMPANIES

The act initially required all public companies to have an independent auditor file a report with the SEC on management's assessment of internal controls. Congress, however, enacted an exemption for smaller companies in 2010 in an effort to reduce compliance costs. Public companies with a market capitalization, or public float, of less than $75 million no longer need to have an auditor report on management's assessment of internal controls.

CERTIFICATION AND MONITORING REQUIREMENTS

Section 906 of the Sarbanes-Oxley Act requires that chief executive officers and chief financial officers certify the accuracy of the information in the corporate financial statements. These corporate officers are subject to both civil and criminal penalties for violations of this section. This requirement makes the officers directly accountable for the accuracy of their financial reporting and precludes any "ignorance defense" if shortcomings are later discovered.

The act also includes requirements to improve directors' monitoring of officers' activities. All members of a publicly traded corporation's audit committee, which oversees the corporation's accounting and financial reporting processes, must be outside directors. (The New York Stock Exchange has a similar rule that also extends to the board's compensation committee, which monitors and determines the compensation of the company's officers.)

The audit committee must have a written charter that sets out its duties and provides for performance appraisal. At least one "financial expert" must serve on the audit committee, which must hold executive meetings without company officers being present. The audit committee must also establish procedures to encourage whistleblowers (see Chapter 34) to report violations. In addition to reviewing the internal controls, the committee also monitors the actions of the outside auditor.

SECTION 6

ONLINE SECURITIES FRAUD

A major problem facing the SEC today is how to enforce the antifraud provisions of the securities laws in the online environment. In 1999, in the first cases involving illegal online securities offerings, the SEC filed suit against three individuals for illegally offer-

EXHIBIT 42-3 Some Key Provisions of the Sarbanes-Oxley Act Relating to Corporate Accountability

Certification Requirements—Under Section 906 of the Sarbanes-Oxley Act, the chief executive officers (CEOs) and chief financial officers (CFOs) of most major companies listed on public stock exchanges must certify financial statements that are filed with the SEC. CEOs and CFOs have to certify that filed financial reports "fully comply" with SEC requirements and that all of the information reported "fairly represents in all material respects, the financial conditions and results of operations of the issuer."

Under Section 302 of the act, CEOs and CFOs of reporting companies are required to certify that a signing officer reviewed each quarterly and annual filing with the SEC and that none contained untrue statements of material fact. Also, the signing officer or officers must certify that they have established an internal control system to identify all material information and that any deficiencies in the system were disclosed to the auditors.

Effectiveness of Internal Controls on Financial Reporting—Under Section 404(a), all public companies are required to assess the effectiveness of their internal control over financial reporting. Section 404(b) requires independent auditors to report on management's assessment of internal controls, but companies with a public float of less than $75 million are exempted from this requirement.

Loans to Directors and Officers—Section 402 prohibits any reporting company, as well as any private company that is filing an initial public offering, from making personal loans to directors and executive officers (with a few limited exceptions, such as for certain consumer and housing loans).

Protection for Whistleblowers—Section 806 protects "whistleblowers"—employees who report ("blow the whistle" on) securities violations by their employers—from being fired or in any way discriminated against by their employers.

Blackout Periods—Section 306 prohibits certain types of securities transactions during "blackout periods"—periods during which the issuer's ability to purchase, sell, or otherwise transfer funds in individual account plans (such as pension funds) is suspended.

Enhanced Penalties for—

- *Violations of Section 906 Certification Requirements*—A CEO or CFO who certifies a financial report or statement filed with the SEC knowing that the report or statement does not fulfill all of the requirements of Section 906 will be subject to criminal penalties of up to $1 million in fines, ten years in prison, or both. *Willful* violators of the certification requirements may be subject to $5 million in fines, twenty years in prison, or both.

- *Violations of the Securities Exchange Act of 1934*—Penalties for securities fraud under the 1934 act were also increased (as discussed earlier in this chapter). Individual violators may be fined up to $5 million, imprisoned for up to twenty years, or both. *Willful* violators may be imprisoned for up to twenty-five years in addition to being fined.

- *Destruction or Alteration of Documents*—Anyone who alters, destroys, or conceals documents or otherwise obstructs any official proceeding will be subject to fines, imprisonment for up to twenty years, or both.

- *Other Forms of White-Collar Crime*—The act stiffened the penalties for certain criminal violations, such as federal mail and wire fraud, and ordered the U.S. Sentencing Commission to revise the sentencing guidelines for white-collar crimes (see Chapter 6).

Statute of Limitations for Securities Fraud—Section 804 provides that a private right of action for securities fraud may be brought no later than two years after the discovery of the violation or five years after the violation, whichever is earlier.

ing securities on an Internet auction site.[36] In essence, all three indicated that their companies would soon go public and attempted to sell unregistered securities via the Web auction site. All of these actions were in violation of Sections 5, 17(a)(1), and 17(a)(3) of the 1933 Securities Act.

Since then, the SEC has brought a variety of Internet-related fraud cases and regularly issues interpretive releases to explain how securities laws apply in the online environment.

---

36. *In re Davis,* SEC Administrative File N.o. 3-10080 (October 20, 1999); *In re Haas,* SEC Administrative File No. 3-10081 (October 20, 1999); and *In re Sitaras,* SEC Administrative File No. 3-10082 (October 20, 1999).

Online Investment Scams

As discussed in Chapter 10, the Internet has created a new vehicle for criminals to use to commit fraud and provided them with new ways of targeting innocent investors. The criminally inclined can use spam, online newsletters and bulletin boards, chat rooms, blogs, social media, and tweets to spread false information and perpetrate fraud. For a relatively small cost, criminals can even build sophisticated Web pages to facilitate their investment scams.

FRAUDULENT E-MAIL There are countless variations of investment scams, but they almost always promise spectacular returns for small investments. A person might receive spam e-mail that falsely claims that a home business can "turn $5 into $60,000 in just three to six weeks." Although most people today are dubious of the bogus claims made in spam messages, such offers can appear more attractive during times of economic recession. Often, investment scams are simply the electronic version of pyramid schemes in which the participants attempt to profit solely by recruiting new participants.

ONLINE INVESTMENT NEWSLETTERS AND FORUMS
Hundreds of online investment newsletters provide free information on stocks. Legitimate online newsletters can help investors gather valuable information, but some online newsletters are used for fraud.

The law allows companies to pay people who write these newsletters to tout their securities, but the newsletters are required to disclose who paid for the advertising. Many fraudsters either fail to disclose or lie about who paid them. Thus, an investor reading an online newsletter may believe that the information is unbiased, when in fact the fraudsters will directly profit by convincing investors to buy or sell particular stocks.

The same deceptive tactics can be used on online bulletin boards (such as newsgroups and usenet groups), blogs, and social networking sites, including Twitter. While hiding their true identity, fraudsters may falsely pump up a company or reveal some "inside" information about a new product or lucrative contract to convince people to invest. By using multiple aliases on an online forum, a single person can easily create the illusion of widespread interest in a small stock.

Ponzi Schemes

Although securities fraud is increasingly occurring online, schemes conducted primarily offline have not disappeared. In recent years, the SEC has filed an increasing number of enforcement actions against perpetrators of *Ponzi schemes* (see Chapter 10).

Since 2010, the SEC has brought more than a hundred enforcement actions against nearly two hundred individuals and two hundred and fifty entities for carrying out Ponzi schemes. It has also barred more than sixty-five persons from working in the securities industry.

OFFSHORE FRAUD Ponzi schemes sometimes target U.S. residents and convince them to invest in offshore companies or banks. ▶ **Case in Point 42.10** In 2012, Texas billionaire R. Allen Stanford, of the Stanford Financial Group, was convicted for orchestrating a $7 billion scheme to defraud more than five thousand investors. Stanford had advised clients to buy certificates of deposit with improbably high interest rates from his Antigua-based Stanford International Bank. Although some early investors were paid returns from the funds provided by later investors, Stanford used $1.6 billion of the funds for personal purchases. He also falsified financial statements that were filed with the SEC and reportedly paid more than $100,000 in bribes to an Antigua official to ensure that the bank would not be audited.[37] ◀

"RISK-FREE" FRAUD Another type of online fraud scheme offers risk-free or low-risk investments to lure investors. ▶ **Case in Point 42.11** Michael C. Regan used his firm, Regan & Company, to fraudulently obtain at least $15.9 million from dozens of investors by selling securities in his River Stream Fund. Regan told investors that he had a "proven track record" of successful securities trading. He showed them false account statements and tax returns that listed artificially high account balances.

In reality, Regan was not a registered investment adviser, had not traded any securities for several years, and had suffered substantial losses on investments he did make. Regan promised investors returns averaging 20 percent with minimal risk to their principal and claimed to be using an investment strategy based on "short-term price trends." He used less than half of the funds entrusted to him for trading purposes and spent at least $2.4 million for his personal and family expenses. In 2009, the SEC filed a complaint alleging that Regan and his company had engaged in a multimillion-dollar Ponzi scheme. Regan agreed to settle the case and return more than $8.7 million (plus interest) of the wrongfully acquired funds.[38] ◀

37. *United States v. Stanford,* 860 F.Supp.2d 371 (S.D.Tex. 2012).
38. You can read the SEC's complaint against Regan at www.sec.gov/litigation/complaints/2009/comp21102.pdf.

Reviewing: Securities Law and Corporate Governance

Dale Emerson served as the chief financial officer for Reliant Electric Company, a distributor of electricity serving portions of Montana and North Dakota. Reliant was in the final stages of planning a takeover of Dakota Gasworks, Inc., a natural gas distributor that operated solely within North Dakota. Emerson went on a weekend fishing trip with his uncle, Ernest Wallace. Emerson mentioned to Wallace that he had been putting in a lot of extra hours at the office planning a takeover of Dakota Gasworks. When he returned from the fishing trip, Wallace purchased $20,000 worth of Reliant stock. Three weeks later, Reliant made a tender offer to Dakota Gasworks stockholders and purchased 57 percent of Dakota Gasworks stock. Over the next two weeks, the price of Reliant stock rose 72 percent before leveling out. Wallace then sold his Reliant stock for a gross profit of $14,400. Using the information presented in the chapter, answer the following questions.

1. Would registration with the SEC be required for Dakota Gasworks securities? Why or why not?
2. Did Emerson violate Section 10(b) of the Securities Exchange Act of 1934 and SEC Rule 10b-5? Why or why not?
3. What theory or theories might a court use to hold Wallace liable for insider trading?
4. Under the Sarbanes-Oxley Act of 2002, who would be required to certify the accuracy of the financial statements Reliant filed with the SEC?

DEBATE THIS . . . *Insider trading should be legalized.*

Terms and Concepts

accredited investor 820	investment company 819	SEC Rule 10b-5 823
blue sky laws 830	investment contract 817	securities 816
corporate governance 830	mutual fund 819	stock option 831
free-writing prospectus 818	prospectus 818	tippee 825
insider trading 824		

ExamPrep

Issue Spotters

1. When a corporation wishes to issue certain securities, it must provide sufficient information for an unsophisticated investor to evaluate the financial risk involved. Specifically, the law imposes liability for making a false statement or omission that is "material." What sort of information would an investor consider material? **(See page 824.)**

2. Lee is an officer of Magma Oil, Inc. Lee knows that a Magma geologist has just discovered a new deposit of oil. Can Lee take advantage of this information to buy and sell Magma stock? Why or why not? **(See page 824.)**

- Check your answers to the Issue Spotters against the answers provided in Appendix E at the end of this text.

Before the Test

Go to **www.cengagebrain.com**, enter the ISBN 9781285185248, and click on "Find" to locate this textbook's Web site. Then, click on "Access Now" under "Study Tools," and select Chapter 42 at the top. There, you will find a Practice Quiz that you can take to assess your mastery of the concepts in this chapter, as well as Flashcards and a Glossary of important terms.

Business Scenarios

42–1. Registration Requirements. Estrada Hermanos, Inc., a corporation incorporated and doing business in Florida, decides to sell $1 million worth of its common stock to the public. The stock will be sold only within the state of Florida. José Estrada, the chair of the board, says the offering need not be registered with the Securities and Exchange Commission. His brother, Gustavo, disagrees. Who is right? Explain. **(See page 818.)**

42–2. Registration Requirements. Huron Corp. has 300,000 common shares outstanding. The owners of these outstanding shares live in several different states. Huron has decided to split the 300,000 shares two for one. Will Huron Corp. have to file a registration statement and prospectus on the 300,000 new shares to be issued as a result of the split? Explain. **(See page 818.)**

42–3. Insider Trading. David Gain was the chief executive officer (CEO) of Forest Media Corp., which became inter-ested in acquiring RS Communications, Inc. To initiate negotiations, Gain met with RS's CEO, Gill Raz, on Friday, July 12. Two days later, Gain phoned his brother Mark, who bought 3,800 shares of RS stock on the following Monday. Mark discussed the deal with their father, Jordan, who bought 20,000 RS shares on Thursday. On July 25, the day before the RS bid was due, Gain phoned his parents' home, and Mark bought another 3,200 RS shares. The same routine was followed over the next few days, with Gain periodically phoning Mark or Jordan, both of whom continued to buy RS shares. Forest's bid was refused, but on August 5, RS announced its merger with another company. The price of RS stock rose 30 percent, increasing the value of Mark and Jordan's shares by $664,024 and $412,875, respectively. Did Gain engage in insider trading? What is required to impose sanctions for this offense? Could a court hold Gain liable? Why or why not? **(See page 824.)**

Business Case Problems

42–4. Violations of the 1934 Act. To comply with accounting principles, a company that engages in software develop-ment must either "expense" the cost (record it immedi-ately on the company's financial statement) or "capitalize" it (record it as a cost incurred in increments over time). If the project is in the pre- or post-development stage, the cost must be expensed. Otherwise it may be capitalized. Capitalizing a cost makes a company look more profitable in the short term. Digimarc Corp., which provides secure personal identification documents, announced that it had improperly capitalized software development costs over at least the previous eighteen months. The errors resulted in $2.7 million in overstated earnings, requiring a restate-ment of prior financial statements. Zucco Partners, LLC, which had bought Digimarc stock within the relevant period, filed a suit in a federal district court against the firm. Zucco claimed that it could show that there had been disagreements within Digimarc over its accounting. Is this sufficient to establish a violation of SEC Rule 10b-5? Why or why not? [*Zucco Partners, LLC v. Digimarc Corp.*, 552 F.3d 981 (9th Cir. 2009)] **(See page 827.)**

42–5. Insider Trading. Jabil Circuit, Inc., is a publicly traded electronics and technology company headquartered in St. Petersburg, Florida. In 2008, a group of shareholders who had owned Jabil stock from 2001 to 2007 sued the com-pany and its auditors, directors, and officers for insider trading. Jabil's compensation for executives included stock options. Some stock options were backdated to a point in time when the stock price was lower, making the options worth more to certain company executives. Backdating is legal as long as it is reported, but Jabil did not report that backdating had occurred. Thus, expenses were under-stated and net income was overstated by millions of dol-lars. The shareholders claimed that by rigging the value of the stock options by backdating, the executives had engaged in insider trading. The shareholders also asserted that there was a pattern of stock sales by executives before unfavorable news about the company was reported to the public. The shareholders, however, had no specific infor-mation about these stock trades or when (or even if) a particular executive was aware of any accounting errors related to backdating. Were the shareholders' allegations sufficient to assert that insider trading had occurred under SEC Rule 10b-5? Why or why not? [*Edward J. Goodman Life Income Trust v. Jabil Circuit, Inc.*, 594 F.3d 783 (11th Cir. 2010)] **(See page 824.)**

42–6. BUSINESS CASE PROBLEM WITH SAMPLE ANSWER: Violations of the 1934 Act.

Matrixx Initiatives, Inc., makes and sells over-the-counter pharmaceutical products. Its core brand is Zicam, which accounts for 70 percent of its sales. Matrixx received reports that some consumers had lost their sense of smell (a condition called anosmia) *after using Zicam Cold Remedy. Four product liability suits were filed against Matrixx, seeking damages for anosmia. In public statements relating to revenues and product safety, however, Matrixx did not reveal this information. James Siracusano and other Matrixx investors filed a suit in a federal district court against the company and its executives under Section 10(b) of the Securities Exchange Act of 1934 and SEC Rule 10b-5, claiming that the statements were misleading because they did not disclose the information regarding the product liability suits. Matrixx argued that to be material, information must consist of a statistically significant number of adverse events*

that require disclosure. Because Siracusano's claim did not allege that Matrixx knew of a statistically significant number of adverse events, the company contended that the claim should be dismissed. What is the standard for materiality in this context? Should Siracusano's claim be dismissed? Explain. [Matrixx Initiatives, Inc. v. Siracusano, __ U.S. __, 131 S.Ct. 1309, 179 L.Ed.2d 398 (2011)] **(See page 827.)**

- **For a sample answer to Problem 42–6, go to Appendix F at the end of this text.**

42–7. Disclosure under SEC Rule 10b-5. Dodona I, LLC, invested $4 million in two securities offerings from Goldman, Sachs & Co. The investments were in collateralized debt obligations (CDOs). Their value depended on residential mortgage-backed securities (RMBS), whose value in turn depended on the performance of subprime residential mortgages. Before marketing the CDOs, Goldman had noticed several "red flags" relating to investments in the subprime market, in which it had invested heavily. To limit its risk, Goldman began betting against subprime mortgages, RMBS, and CDOs, including the CDOs it had sold to Dodona. In an internal e-mail, one Goldman official commented that the company had managed to "make some lemonade from some big old lemons." Nevertheless, Goldman's marketing materials provided only boilerplate statements about the risks of investing in the securities. The CDOs were later downgraded to junk status, and Dodona suffered a major loss while Goldman profited. Assuming that Goldman did not affirmatively misrepresent any facts about the CDOs, can Dodona still recover under SEC Rule 10b-5? If so, how? [*Dodona I, LLC v. Goldman, Sachs & Co.,* 847 F.Supp.2d 624 (S.D.N.Y. 2012)] **(See page 823.)**

42–8. A QUESTION OF ETHICS: Violations of the 1934 Act.

Melvin Lyttle told John Montana and Paul Knight about a "Trading Program" that purportedly would buy and sell securities in deals that were fully insured, as well as monitored and controlled by the

Federal Reserve. Without checking the details or even verifying whether the Program existed, Montana and Knight, with Lyttle's help, began to sell interests in the Program to investors. For a minimum investment of $1 million, the investors were promised extraordinary rates of return—from 10 percent to as much as 100 percent per week—without risk. They were told, among other things, that the Program would "utilize banks that can ensure full bank integrity of The Transaction whose undertaking[s] are in complete harmony with international banking rules and protocol and who guarantee maximum security of a Funder's Capital Placement Amount." Nothing was required but the investors' funds and their silence—the Program was to be kept secret. Over a four-month period in 1999, Montana raised approximately $23 million from twenty-two investors. The promised gains did not accrue, however. Instead, Montana, Lyttle, and Knight depleted investors' funds in high-risk trades or spent the funds on themselves. [SEC v. Montana, 464 F.Supp.2d 772 (S.D.Ind. 2006)] **(See page 827.)**

(a) The Securities and Exchange Commission (SEC) filed a suit in a federal district court against Montana and the others, seeking an injunction, civil penalties, and refund of profits with interest. The SEC alleged, among other things, violations of Section 10(b) of the Securities Exchange Act of 1934 and SEC Rule 10b-5. What is required to establish such violations? Describe how and why the facts in this case meet, or fail to meet, these requirements.

(b) It is often remarked, "There's a sucker born every minute!" Does that phrase describe the Program's investors? Ultimately, about half of the investors recouped the amount they invested. Should the others be considered at least partly responsible for their own losses? Why or why not?

Legal Reasoning Group Activity

42–9. Violations of Securities Laws. Karel Svoboda, a credit officer for Rogue Bank, evaluated and approved his employer's extensions of credit to clients. These responsibilities gave Svoboda access to nonpublic information about the clients' earnings, performance, acquisitions, and business plans from confidential memos, e-mail, and other sources. Svoboda devised a scheme with Alena Robles, an independent accountant, to use this information to trade securities. Pursuant to their scheme, Robles traded in the securities of more than twenty different companies and profited by more than $2 million. Svoboda also executed trades for his own profit of more than $800,000, despite their agreement that Robles would do all of the trading. Aware that their scheme violated

Rogue Bank's policy, they attempted to conduct their trades to avoid suspicion. When the bank questioned Svoboda about his actions, he lied, refused to cooperate, and was fired. **(See page 824.)**

(a) The first group will determine whether Svoboda or Robles committed any crimes.

(b) The second group will decide whether Svoboda or Robles is subject to civil liability. If so, who could file a suit and on what ground? What are the possible sanctions?

(c) A third group will identify any defenses that Svoboda or Robles could raise and determine their likelihood of success.

UNIT EIGHT Focus on Ethics

Business Organizations

Every now and then, scandals in the business world rock the nation. Certainly, this was true in the first decade of the 2000s when the activities of Enron Corporation, WorldCom, and a number of other companies came to light. As noted in this unit, Congress responded to public outcry by passing the Sarbanes-Oxley Act. That act imposed stricter requirements on corporations with respect to accounting practices and statements made in documents filed with the Securities and Exchange Commission (SEC).

The lesson for the business world is, of course, that if business leaders do not behave ethically (and legally), the government will create new laws and regulations that force them to do so. We offered suggestions on how business decision makers can create an ethical workplace in Chapter 5. Here, we look at selected areas in which the relationships within specific business organizational forms may raise ethical issues.

The Emergence of Corporate Governance

The well-publicized corporate abuses of the last decade provided the impetus for businesspersons to create their own internal rules for corporate governance (discussed in Chapter 42). Examples of these abuses make it clear why such rules are needed. In a few situations, officers have blatantly stolen from the corporation and its shareholders. More frequently, though, officers have received excessive benefits, or "perks," because of their position. To illustrate: Tyco International bought a $6,000 shower curtain and a $15,000 umbrella stand for its chief executive officer's apartment.

Corporate officers may be given numerous benefits, which they may or may not deserve. On several occasions, a leading corporate officer has received compensation of $50 million or more in a year when the company's share price actually declined. Even if corporate officers are scrupulously honest and have modest personal tastes, their behavior may still raise concerns: they may not be good managers, and they may make incompetent corporate decisions. They may be a little lazy and fail to do the hard work necessary to investigate the corporation's alternatives. Sometimes, officers may simply fail to appreciate the concerns of shareholders on certain matters, such as maximizing short-term versus long-term results.

Corporate governance controls are meant to ensure that officers receive only the benefits they earn. Governance monitors the actions taken by officers to make sure they are wise and in the best interests of the company. In this way, the corporation can be confident that it is acting ethically toward its shareholders.

Fiduciary Duties Revisited

The law of agency, as outlined in Chapters 32 and 33, permeates nearly all relationships within any partnership or corporation. An important duty that arises in the law of agency, and applies to all partners and corporate directors, officers, and management personnel, is the duty of loyalty. As caretakers of the shareholders' wealth, corporate directors and officers also have a fiduciary duty to exercise care when making decisions affecting the corporate enterprise.

The Duty of Loyalty Every individual has personal interests, which may at times conflict with the interests of the partnership or corporation with which he or she is affiliated. In particular, partners or corporate officers and directors may face a conflict between personal interests and the interests of the business entity.

Acquiring Assets. Corporate officers and directors may find themselves in a position to acquire assets that would also benefit the corporation if acquired in the corporation's name. If an officer does purchase the asset without offering the opportunity to the corporation, however, she or he may be liable for usurping a corporate opportunity.[1]

Disclosure. Most courts also hold that a corporate officer or director has a fiduciary duty to disclose improper conduct to the corporation. For example, a leading case on the issue involved Thomas Coughlin, a top executive in theft prevention at Wal-Mart. He had held several other high-level positions prior to becoming a member of the board of directors. When he retired, Coughlin signed an agreement and release of claims with Wal-Mart under which he was to receive millions of dollars in benefits over the years.

Then Wal-Mart discovered that Coughlin, before his retirement, had abused his position of authority. He had conspired with subordinates to misappropriate hundreds of thousands of dollars in property and cash through various fraudulent schemes. Wal-Mart sued Coughlin alleging that he had breached his fiduciary duty of loyalty by failing to disclose his misconduct before entering a self-dealing contract.

Ultimately, the Supreme Court of Arkansas agreed and held that the director's fiduciary duty obligated him to divulge material facts of *past* fraud to the corporation before entering the contract. The court stated, "We are persuaded, in addition, that the majority view is correct, which is that the failure of a fiduciary to disclose material facts of his fraudulent conduct to his corporation prior to entering into a self-dealing contract with that corporation will void that contract."[2]

The Duty of Care In addition to the duty of loyalty, every corporate director or officer owes a duty of care. *Due care* means

---

1. For a landmark case on this issue, see *Guth v. Loft, Inc.,* 5 A.2d 503 (Del. 1939), presented as Case 40.1 in Chapter 40.
2. *Wal-Mart Stores, Inc. v. Coughlin,* 369 Ark. 365, 255 S.W.3d 424 (2007). See also *Blankenship v. USA Truck, Inc.,* 601 F.3d 852 (8th Cir. 2010), interpreting Arkansas law by applying the *Wal-Mart* case; and *Mazak Corp. v. King,* 2012 WL 3590817 (6th Cir. 2012), in which a federal court recognized that the *Wal-Mart* case stated the rule in the majority of states.

838

that officers and directors must keep themselves informed and make businesslike judgments. Officers have a duty to disclose material information that shareholders need for competent decision making.

Some courts have even suggested that corporate directors have a duty to detect and "ferret out" wrongdoing within the corporation.[3] In fact, a number of courts applying Delaware law have recognized that directors may be held liable for failing to exercise proper oversight.[4] For example, one Delaware court held that shareholders of Citigroup, Inc., could sue the directors and officers for failure to exercise due care to adequately protect the corporation from exposure to the subprime lending market.[5] Corporate law also creates other structures to protect shareholder interests, such as the right to inspect books and records.

Although traditionally the duty of care did not require directors to monitor the behavior of corporate employees to detect and prevent wrongdoing, the tide may be changing. The corporate sentencing guidelines give courts the power to impose substantial penalties on corporations and corporate directors for criminal wrongdoing. Moreover, since the Sarbanes-Oxley Act required the sentencing commission to revise these guidelines, the penalties for white-collar crimes, such as federal mail and wire fraud, have increased dramatically. The guidelines allow these penalties to be mitigated, though, if a company can show that it has an effective compliance program in place to detect and prevent wrongdoing by corporate personnel.

LEGAL REASONING

1. *Three decades ago, corporations and corporate directors were rarely prosecuted for crimes, and penalties for corporate crimes were relatively light. Today, this is no longer true. Under the corporate sentencing guidelines, corporate wrongdoers can receive substantial penalties. Do these developments mean that corporations are committing more crimes today than in the past? Will stricter laws be effective in curbing corporate criminal activity? How can a company avoid liability for crimes committed by its employees?*

Fiduciary Duties to Creditors It is a long-standing principle that corporate directors ordinarily owe fiduciary duties only to a corporation's shareholders. Directors who have favored the interests of other corporate "stakeholders," such as creditors, over those of the shareholders have been held liable for breaching these duties.

The picture changes, however, when a corporation approaches insolvency. At this point, the shareholders' equity interests in the corporation may be worthless, while the interests of creditors become paramount. In this situation, do the fiduciary duties of loyalty and care extend to the corporation's creditors as well as to the shareholders?

The answer to this question, according to some courts, is yes. In one case, a Delaware court held that when a corporation is on the brink of insolvency, the directors assume a fiduciary duty to other stakeholders that sustain the corporate entity, including creditors.[6] When a corporation is insolvent, courts may require directors to consider the best interests of the whole corporate enterprise, including all its constituent groups, and not to give preference to the interests of any one group.[7]

LEGAL REASONING

2. *Do you agree that when a corporation is approaching insolvency, the directors' fiduciary obligations should extend to the corporation's creditors as well as to the shareholders? Why or why not?*

Corporate Blogs and Tweets and Securities Fraud

In the fast-paced world of securities trading, there is a great demand for the latest information about companies, earnings, and market conditions. Corporations have adapted to technology by establishing Web sites and blogs, and by using other social and online media, such as Twitter and online shareholder forums. Nearly 20 percent of Fortune 500 companies sponsor blogs. Corporations that use the Internet to distribute information about the company to investors, however, need to make sure that they comply with the regulations issued by the SEC. The SEC treats statements by employees in online media, such as blogs and Twitter, the same as any other company statements for purposes of federal securities laws.

"Tweets" That Contain Financial Information Some corporate blogs include links to corporate employees' Twitter accounts so that readers can communicate directly with, and get updates from, the individual who posted the information. For example, when eBay, Inc., launched its corporate blog, it hired Richard Brewer-Hay, a seasoned blogger, to report online. He began tweeting about eBay's quarterly earnings and what took place at Silicon Valley technology conferences.

3. *In re China Agritech, Inc. Shareholder Derivative Litigation,* 2013 WL 2181514 (Del.Ch. 2013); and *In re Caremark International, Inc. Derivative Litigation,* 698 A.2d 959 (Del.Ch. 1996).

4. See, for example, *McCall v. Scott,* 239 F.3d 808 (6th Cir. 2001); *Guttman v. Huang,* 823 A.2d 492 (Del.Ch. 2003); *Landy v. D'Alessandro,* 316 F.Supp.2d 49 (D.Mass. 2004); and *Miller v. U.S. Foodservice, Inc.,* 361 F.Supp.2d 470 (D.Md. 2005).

5. *In re Citigroup, Inc. Shareholder Derivative Litigation,* 964 A.2d 106 (Del.Ch. 2009).

6. *Credit Lyonnais Bank Nederland N.V. v. Pathe Communications Corp.,* 1991 WL 277613 (Del.Ch. 1991). See also *Production Resources Group, LLC v. NCT Group, Inc.,* 863 A.2d 772 (Del.Ch. 2004); and *In re USDigital, Inc.,* 443 Bankr. 22 (D.Del. 2011).

7. See *Berg & Berg Enterprises, LLC v. Boyle,* 178 Cal.App.4th 1020, 100 Cal.Rptr.3d 875 (2009); *In re Moeller,* 466 Bankr. 525 (S.D.Cal. 2012); and *Scouler & Co., LLC v. Schwartz,* 2012 WL 1502762 (N.D.Cal. 2012).

FOCUS ON ETHICS CONTINUES ➤

UNIT EIGHT Focus on Ethics

Business Organizations, *Continued*

Brewer-Hay's tweets won him a following, but then eBay's lawyers required him to include a regulatory disclaimer with certain posts to avoid problems with the SEC. Many of his followers were disappointed by the company's oversight, which put an end to his spontaneous, personal, and informal style. Brewer-Hay's tweets on financial matters became much more reserved and often simply repeated eBay executives' statements verbatim.[8]

The SEC Provides Guidance The reaction of eBay's lawyers to Brewer-Hay's tweets was prompted in part by an interpretive release that the SEC issued in August 2008. The SEC generally embraces new technology and encourages companies to use electronic communication methods. The SEC noted that "the use of the Internet has grown such that, for some companies in certain circumstances, posting of the information on the company's Web site, in and of itself, may be a sufficient method of public disclosure."

The release also addressed company-sponsored blogs, electronic shareholders' forums, and other "interactive Web site features." The SEC acknowledged that blogs and other interactive Web features are a useful means of ongoing communications among companies, their clients, investors, shareholders, and stakeholders.

The SEC cautioned, though, that all communications made by or on behalf of a company are subject to the antifraud provisions of federal securities laws. "While blogs or forums can be informal and conversational in nature, statements made there . . . will not be treated differently from other company statements." In addition, the release stated that companies cannot require investors to waive protections under federal securities laws as a condition of participating in a blog or forum. (The release also cautioned companies that they can, in some situations, be liable for providing hyperlinks to third party information or inaccurate summaries of financial information on their Web sites.)[9]

LEGAL REASONING

3. *When a company's executives offer opinions about the firm's financial status and future business prospects through blogs, social media, and other Internet forums, the SEC can hold the company liable for violating securities laws. Is this fair to investors who want to hear the straight scoop from the firm's executives? What arguments can you make in favor of this restriction? What arguments can you make against it?*

---

8. Cari Tuna, "Corporate Blogs and 'Tweets' Must Keep SEC in Mind," *online.wsj.com*, April 27, 2009.

9. SEC Release Nos. 34–58288, IC–28351, File No.S7–23–08. Commission Guidance on the Use of Company Web Sites.

BUSINESS LAW

CLARKSON · MILLER · CROSS

CHAPTER 43

ADMINISTRATIVE AGENCIES

Government agencies established to administer the law have a great impact on the day-to-day operations of businesses. In its early years, the United States had a simple, nonindustrial economy with little regulation. As the economy has grown and become more complex, the size of government has also increased, and so has the number of administrative agencies.

In some instances, new agencies have been created in response to a crisis. In the wake of the financial crisis

that led to the latest economic recession, for instance, Congress enacted the Dodd-Frank Wall Street Reform and Consumer Protection Act. Among other things, this statute created the Financial Stability Oversight Council to identify and respond to emerging risks in the financial system. It also created the Consumer Financial Protection Bureau (CFPB) in an attempt to protect consumers from abusive practices by financial institutions. The CFPB supervises the activities of banks and nonbanks offering

consumer financial products, mortgage lenders, and credit-card companies.

As the number of agencies has multiplied, so have the rules, orders, and decisions that they issue. Today, there are rules covering almost every aspect of a business's operations. These regulations make up the body of *administrative law*. You were introduced briefly to some of the main principles of administrative law in Chapter 1. In the following pages, we will look at these principles in much greater detail.

SECTION 1
THE PRACTICAL SIGNIFICANCE OF ADMINISTRATIVE LAW

Unlike statutory law, administrative law is created by administrative agencies, not by legislatures, but it is nevertheless of paramount significance for businesses. When Congress—or a state legislature—enacts legislation, it typically adopts a rather general statute and leaves its implementation to an administrative agency. The agency then creates the detailed rules and regulations necessary to carry out the statute. The administrative agency, with its specialized personnel, has the time, resources, and expertise to make the detailed decisions required for regulation.

Administrative Agencies Exist at All Levels of Government

Administrative agencies are spread throughout the government. At the federal level, the Securities and Exchange Commission regulates a firm's capital structure and financing, as well as its financial reporting.

The National Labor Relations Board oversees relations between a firm and any unions with which it may deal. The Equal Employment Opportunity Commission also regulates employer-employee relationships. The Environmental Protection Agency and the Occupational Safety and Health Administration affect the way a firm manufactures its products, and the Federal Trade Commission influences the way it markets those products.

There are administrative agencies at the state and local levels as well. Commonly, a state agency (such as a state pollution-control agency) is created as a parallel to a federal agency (such as the Environmental Protection Agency). Just as federal statutes take precedence over conflicting state statutes, so do federal agency regulations take precedence over conflicting state regulations. Because the rules of state and local agencies vary widely, we focus here exclusively on federal administrative law.

Agencies Provide a Comprehensive Regulatory Scheme

Often, administrative agencies at various levels of government work together and share the responsibil-

ity of creating and enforcing particular regulations.
▶ **Example 43.1** When Congress enacted the Clean Air Act (to be discussed in Chapter 45), it provided only general directions for the prevention of air pollution. The specific pollution-control requirements imposed on business are almost entirely the product of decisions made by the Environmental Protection Agency (EPA). Moreover, the EPA works with parallel environmental agencies at the state level to analyze existing data and determine the appropriate pollution-control standards. ◀

Legislation and regulations have significant benefits—in the example of the Clean Air Act, a cleaner environment than existed in decades past. At the same time, these benefits entail considerable costs for business. The EPA has estimated the costs of compliance with the Clean Air Act at many tens of billions of dollars yearly. Although the agency has calculated that the overall benefits of its regulations often exceed their costs, the burden on business is substantial. Business therefore has a strong incentive to try to influence the regulatory environment through lobbying.

SECTION 2
AGENCY CREATION AND POWERS

Congress creates federal administrative agencies. By delegating some of its authority to make and implement laws, Congress can indirectly monitor a particular area in which it has passed legislation. Delegation enables Congress to avoid becoming bogged down in the details relating to enforcement—details that are often best left to specialists.

To create an administrative agency, Congress passes **enabling legislation,** which specifies the name, purposes, functions, and powers of the agency being created. Federal administrative agencies can exercise only those powers that Congress has delegated to them in enabling legislation. Through similar enabling acts, state legislatures create state administrative agencies.

An agency's enabling statute defines its legal authority. An agency cannot regulate beyond the powers granted by the statute, and it may be required to take some regulatory action by the terms of that statute. When regulated groups oppose a rule adopted by an agency, they often bring a lawsuit arguing that the rule was not authorized by the enabling statute

and is therefore void. Conversely, a group may file a suit claiming that an agency has illegally *failed* to pursue regulation required by the enabling statute.

Enabling Legislation—An Example

Congress created the Federal Trade Commission (FTC) by enacting the Federal Trade Commission Act of 1914.[1] The act prohibits unfair methods of competition and deceptive trade practices. It also describes the procedures that the FTC must follow to charge persons or organizations with violations of the act, and it provides for judicial review of agency orders. The act grants the FTC the power to do the following:

1. Create "rules and regulations for the purpose of carrying out the Act."
2. Conduct investigations of business practices.
3. Obtain reports from interstate corporations concerning their business practices.
4. Investigate possible violations of federal antitrust statutes. (The FTC shares this task with the Antitrust Division of the U.S. Department of Justice—see Chapter 46.)
5. Publish findings of its investigations.
6. Recommend new legislation.
7. Hold trial-like hearings to resolve certain trade disputes that involve FTC regulations or federal antitrust laws.

The FTC is composed of five members. Each is appointed by the president, with the advice and consent of the Senate, for a term of seven years. The president designates one of the commissioners to be the chair.

Types of Agencies

As discussed in Chapter 1, there are two basic types of administrative agencies: executive agencies and independent regulatory agencies. Federal *executive agencies* include the cabinet departments of the executive branch, which assist the president in carrying out executive functions, and the subagencies within the cabinet departments. The Occupational Safety and Health Administration, for example, is a subagency within the U.S. Department of Labor. Executive agencies usually have a single administrator, director, or secretary who is appointed by the president to oversee the agency and can be removed by the president at any time. Exhibit 43–1 on the following page lists the

---

1. 15 U.S.C. Sections 41–58.

EXHIBIT 43-1 Executive Departments and Important Subagencies

Department and Date Formed	Selected Subagencies
State (1789)	Passport Office; Bureau of Diplomatic Security; Foreign Service; Bureau of Human Rights and Humanitarian Affairs; Bureau of Consular Affairs; Bureau of Intelligence and Research
Treasury (1789)	Internal Revenue Service; U.S. Mint
Interior (1849)	U.S. Fish and Wildlife Service; National Park Service; Bureau of Indian Affairs; Bureau of Land Management
Justice (1870)[a]	Federal Bureau of Investigation; Drug Enforcement Administration; Bureau of Prisons; U.S. Marshals Service
Agriculture (1889)	Soil Conservation Service; Agricultural Research Service; Food Safety and Inspection Service; Forest Service
Commerce (1913)[b]	Bureau of the Census; Bureau of Economic Analysis; Minority Business Development Agency; U.S. Patent and Trademark Office; National Oceanic and Atmospheric Administration
Labor (1913)[b]	Occupational Safety and Health Administration; Bureau of Labor Statistics; Employment Standards Administration; Office of Labor-Management Standards; Employment and Training Administration
Defense (1949)[c]	National Security Agency; Joint Chiefs of Staff; Departments of the Air Force, Navy, Army; service academies
Housing and Urban Development (1965)	Office of Community Planning and Development; Government National Mortgage Association; Office of Fair Housing and Equal Opportunity
Transportation (1967)	Federal Aviation Administration; Federal Highway Administration; National Highway Traffic Safety Administration; Federal Transit Administration
Energy (1977)	Office of Civilian Radioactive Waste Management; Office of Nuclear Energy; Energy Information Administration
Health and Human Services (1980)[d]	Food and Drug Administration; Centers for Medicare and Medicaid Services; Centers for Disease Control and Prevention; National Institutes of Health
Education (1980)[d]	Office of Special Education and Rehabilitation Services; Office of Elementary and Secondary Education; Office of Postsecondary Education; Office of Vocational and Adult Education
Veterans Affairs (1989)	Veterans Health Administration; Veterans Benefits Administration; National Cemetery System
Homeland Security (2002)	U.S. Citizenship and Immigration Services; Directorate of Border and Transportation Services; U.S. Coast Guard; Federal Emergency Management Agency

a. Formed from the Office of the Attorney General (created in 1789).
b. Formed from the Department of Commerce and Labor (created in 1903).
c. Formed from the Department of War (created in 1789) and the Department of the Navy (created in 1798).
d. Formed from the Department of Health, Education, and Welfare (created in 1953).

cabinet departments and some of their most important subagencies.

Independent regulatory agencies are outside the federal executive departments (those headed by a cabinet secretary). Examples of independent agencies include the Federal Trade Commission and the Securities and Exchange Commission (SEC).

Rather than having a single person as its head, an independent agency usually is run by a commission or board made up of several members, one of whom serves as the agency's chair. Commissioners or board members typically serve for fixed terms and cannot be removed without just cause. The SEC has five commissioners who serve for five-year terms that are staggered so that one term ends on June 5 of every year. The SEC's commissioners oversee its four divisions and nineteen offices. Selected independent regulatory agencies, as well as their principal functions, are listed in Exhibit 43–2 below.

Agency Powers and the Constitution

Administrative agencies occupy an unusual niche in the U.S. legal scheme because they exercise powers that normally are divided among the three branches of government. Agencies' powers include functions associated with the legislature *(rulemaking)*, the executive branch *(enforcement)*, and the courts *(adjudication)*.

The constitutional principle of *checks and balances* allows each branch of government to act as a check on the actions of the other two branches. Furthermore, the U.S. Constitution authorizes only the legislative branch to create laws. Yet administrative agencies, to

which the Constitution does not specifically refer, can make **legislative rules,** or *substantive rules,* that are as legally binding as laws that Congress passes.

Administrative agencies also issue **interpretive rules,** which simply declare policy and do not affect legal rights or obligations. ▶ **Example 43.2** The Equal Employment Opportunity Commission periodically issues interpretive rules indicating how it plans to interpret the provisions of certain statutes, such as the Americans with Disabilities Act (see Chapter 35). These informal rules provide enforcement guidelines for agency officials. ◀

THE DELEGATION DOCTRINE Courts generally hold that Article I of the U.S. Constitution is the basis for all administrative law. Section 1 of that article grants all legislative powers to Congress and requires Congress to oversee the implementation of all laws. Article I, Section 8, gives Congress the power to make all laws necessary for executing its specified powers.

EXHIBIT 43–2 Selected Independent Regulatory Agencies

Name and Date Formed	Principal Duties
Federal Reserve System Board of Governors (the Fed)—1913	Determines policy with respect to interest rates, credit availability, and the money supply. The Federal Reserve became involved in various "bailouts" in the financial sector, including a "conservatorship" of two large mortgage institutions (Fannie Mae and Freddie Mac) and control of the world's largest insurance company, AIG.
Federal Trade Commission (FTC)—1914	Prevents businesses from engaging in unfair trade practices; stops the formation of monopolies in the business sector; protects consumer rights.
Securities and Exchange Commission (SEC)—1934	Regulates the nation's stock exchanges, in which shares of stock are bought and sold; enforces the securities laws, which require full disclosure of the financial profiles of companies that wish to sell stock and bonds to the public.
Federal Communications Commission (FCC)—1934	Regulates all communications by telegraph, cable, telephone, radio, satellite, and television.
National Labor Relations Board (NLRB)—1935	Protects employees' rights to join unions and bargain collectively with employers; attempts to prevent unfair labor practices by both employers and unions.
Equal Employment Opportunity Commission (EEOC)—1964	Works to eliminate discrimination in employment based on religion, gender, race, color, disability, national origin, or age; investigates claims of discrimination.
Environmental Protection Agency (EPA)—1970	Undertakes programs aimed at reducing air and water pollution; works with state and local agencies to help fight environmental hazards. (It has recently been suggested that its status be elevated to that of a department.)
Nuclear Regulatory Commission (NRC)—1975	Ensures that electricity-generating nuclear reactors in the United States are built and operated safely; regularly inspects operations of such reactors.

The courts interpret these passages as establishing the **delegation doctrine.** This doctrine holds that Article I grants Congress the authority to delegate some of its power by establishing administrative agencies to create rules for implementing those laws.

The three branches of government exercise certain controls over agency powers and functions, as discussed next, but in many ways administrative agencies function independently. For this reason, administrative agencies, which constitute the **bureaucracy,** are sometimes referred to as the fourth branch of the U.S. government.

EXECUTIVE CONTROLS The executive branch of government exercises control over agencies both through the president's power to appoint federal officers and through the president's veto power. The president may veto enabling legislation passed by Congress or congressional attempts to modify an existing agency's authority.

LEGISLATIVE CONTROLS Congress exercises authority over agency powers through legislation. Congress gives power to an agency through enabling legislation and can take power away—or even abolish an agency altogether—through subsequent legislation. Legislative authority is required to fund an agency, and enabling legislation usually sets certain time and monetary limits on the funding of particular programs. Congress can always revise these limits.

In addition to its power to create and fund agencies, Congress has the authority to investigate the implementation of its laws and the agencies that it has created. Congress also has the power to "freeze" the enforcement of most federal regulations before the regulations take effect. (Another legislative check on agency actions is the Administrative Procedure Act, discussed shortly.)

JUDICIAL CONTROLS The judicial branch exercises control over agency powers through the courts' review of agency actions. As you will read in the next section, the Administrative Procedure Act provides for judicial review of most agency decisions. Agency actions are not automatically subject to judicial review, however. The party seeking court review must first exhaust all administrative remedies under what is called the *exhaustion doctrine.*

In other words, the complaining party normally must have gone through the administrative process (from complaint to hearing to final agency order, which will be discussed later in this chapter) before

seeking court review.[2] ▶ **Example 43.3** The Federal Trade Commission (FTC) claims that Sysco Industries used deceptive advertising and orders it to run new ads correcting the misstatements. Sysco contends that its ads were not deceptive. Under the exhaustion doctrine, Sysco must go through the entire FTC process before it can bring a suit against the FTC in court to challenge the order. (The ajudication process used by administrative agencies is described later in this chapter.) ◀

THE ADMINISTRATIVE PROCEDURE ACT

All federal agencies must follow specific procedural requirements when fulfilling their three basic functions of rulemaking, enforcement, and adjudication. In this section, we focus on agency rulemaking (enforcement and adjudication will be discussed in a later section of this chapter).

Sometimes, Congress specifies certain procedural requirements in an agency's enabling legislation. In the absence of any directives from Congress concerning a particular agency procedure, the Administrative Procedure Act (APA) of 1946[3] applies.

The Arbitrary and Capricious Test

One of Congress's goals in enacting the APA was to provide for more judicial control over administrative agencies. To that end, the APA provides that courts should "hold unlawful and set aside" agency actions found to be "arbitrary, capricious, an abuse of discretion, or otherwise not in accordance with law."[4] Under this standard, parties can challenge regulations as contrary to law or as so irrational that they are arbitrary and capricious.

There is no precise definition of what makes a rule arbitrary and capricious, but the standard includes factors such as whether the agency has done any of the following:

1. Failed to provide a rational explanation for its decision.
2. Changed its prior policy without justification.
3. Considered legally inappropriate factors.

2. The plaintiff must also have *standing to sue* the agency—see Chapter 2.
3. 5 U.S.C. Sections 551–706.
4. 5 U.S.C. Section 706(2)(A).

4. Entirely failed to consider a relevant factor.
5. Rendered a decision plainly contrary to the evidence.

In the following case, the United States Supreme Court considered the application of the arbitrary and capricious standard.

CASE ANALYSIS

Case 43.1   Federal Communications Commission v. Fox Television Stations, Inc.

Supreme Court of the United States, 556 U.S. 502, 129 S.Ct. 1800, 173 L.Ed.2d 738 (2009).

IN THE LANGUAGE OF THE COURT
Justice *SCALIA* delivered the opinion of the Court.
* * * *

The Communications Act of 1934 established a system of limited-term broadcast licenses subject to various "conditions" * * * .

* * * [These conditions include] the indecency ban—the statutory proscription [prohibition] against "utter[ing] any obscene, indecent, or profane language by means of radio communication"—which Congress has instructed the [Federal Communications] Commission to enforce * * * .
* * * *

The Commission first invoked the statutory ban on indecent broadcasts in 1975, declaring a daytime broadcast of George Carlin's "Filthy Words" monologue actionably indecent. At that time, the Commission announced the definition of indecent speech that it uses to this day, prohibiting "language that describes, in terms patently offensive as measured by contemporary community standards for the broadcast medium, sexual or excretory activities or organs, at times of the day when there is a reasonable risk that children may be in the audience."
* * * *

Over a decade later, the Commission emphasized that the "full context" in which particular materials appear is "critically important," but that a few "principal" factors guide the inquiry, such as the

"explicitness or graphic nature" of the material, the extent to which the material "dwells on or repeats" the offensive material, and the extent to which the material was presented to "pander," to "titillate," or to "shock." * * * "Where sexual or excretory references have been made once or have been passing or fleeting in nature, this characteristic has tended to weigh against a finding of indecency."

In 2004, the Commission took one step further by declaring for the first time that a nonliteral (expletive) use of the F- and S-Words could be actionably indecent, even when the word is used only once. The first order to this effect dealt with an NBC broadcast of the Golden Globe Awards, in which the performer Bono [lead singer of the rock group U-2] commented, "This is really, really, f***ing brilliant."
* * * *

The order acknowledged that "prior Commission and staff action have indicated that isolated or fleeting broadcasts of the 'F-Word' * * * are not indecent or would not be acted upon." It explicitly ruled that "any such interpretation is no longer good law."

[The present case] concerns utterances in two live broadcasts aired by Fox Television Stations, Inc., * * * prior to the Commission's Golden Globes Order. The first occurred during the 2002 Billboard Music Awards, when the singer Cher exclaimed, "I've also had critics for the last 40 years saying that I was on my way out every year. Right. So f*** 'em." The second involved a segment of the

2003 Billboard Music Awards, [when Nicole Richie asked] the audience, "Why do they even call it 'The Simple Life?' Have you ever tried to get cow s*** out of a Prada purse? It's not so f***ing simple."

On March 15, 2006, the Commission released Notices of Apparent Liability for a number of broadcasts that the Commission deemed actionably indecent, including the two described above.
* * * *

* * * In the Commission's view, "granting an automatic exemption for 'isolated or fleeting' expletives unfairly forces viewers (including children)" to take "the first blow" and would allow broadcasters "to air expletives at all hours of a day so long as they did so one at a time."

Fox [appealed] to the Second Circuit [Court of Appeals] for review of the [order] * * * . The Court of Appeals reversed the agency's order, finding the Commission's reasoning inadequate under the Administrative Procedure Act. * * * We granted *certiorari*.
* * * *

The Administrative Procedure Act, which sets forth the full extent of judicial authority to review executive agency action for procedural correctness, permits (insofar as relevant here) the setting aside of agency action that is "arbitrary" or "capricious." *Under what we have called this "narrow" standard of review, we insist that an agency "examine the relevant data and articulate*

CASE 43.1 CONTINUES ▶

CASE 43.1 CONTINUED

a satisfactory explanation for its action."
We have made clear, however, that "a
court is not to substitute its judgment for
that of the agency," and should "uphold
a decision of less than ideal clarity if
the agency's path may reasonably be
discerned." [Emphasis added.]

In overturning the Commission's judgment, the Court of Appeals here relied in part on Circuit precedent requiring a more substantial explanation for agency action that changes prior policy. The Second Circuit has interpreted the Administrative Procedure Act and our opinion in [a previous case] as requiring agencies to make clear "why the original reasons for adopting the [displaced] rule or policy are no longer dispositive [a deciding factor]" as well as "why the new rule effectuates the statute as well as or better than the old rule." The Court of Appeals for the District of Columbia Circuit has similarly indicated that a court's standard of review is "heightened somewhat" when an agency reverses course.

We find no basis in the Administrative
Procedure Act or in our opinions for a
requirement that all agency change be
subjected to more searching review. The
Act mentions no such heightened stan-
dard. [Emphasis added.]

To be sure, the requirement that an agency provide reasoned explanation for its action would ordinarily demand that it display awareness that it *is* changing position. An agency may not, for example, depart from a prior policy *sub silentio* [under silence, without any notice of the change] or simply disregard rules that are still on the books. And of course the agency must show that there are good reasons for the new policy. But it need not demonstrate to a court's satisfaction that the reasons for the new policy are *better* than the reasons for the old one; it suffices that the new policy is permissible under the statute, that there are good reasons for it, and that the agency *believes* it to be better.

* * * *

Judged under the above-described standards, the Commission's new enforcement policy and its order finding the broadcasts actionably indecent were neither arbitrary nor capricious. First, the Commission forthrightly acknowledged that its recent actions have broken new ground, taking account of inconsistent "prior Commission and staff action" and explicitly disavowing them as "no longer good law." * * * There is no doubt that the Commission knew it was making a change. That is why it declined to assess penalties * * * .

Moreover, the agency's reasons for expanding the scope of its enforcement activity were entirely rational. It was certainly reasonable to determine that it made no sense to distinguish between literal and nonliteral uses of offensive words, requiring repetitive use to render only the latter indecent. * * * It is surely rational (if not inescapable) to believe that a safe harbor for single words would "likely lead to more widespread use of the offensive language."

* * * *

The judgment of the United States Court of Appeals for the Second Circuit is reversed, and the case is remanded for further proceedings consistent with this opinion.[a]

LEGAL REASONING QUESTIONS

1. Today, children are likely exposed to indecent language in various media far more often than they were in the 1970s, when the Federal Communications Commission (FCC) first began to sanction indecent speech. Does this mean that we need more stringent—or less stringent—regulation of broadcasts? Explain.

2. Technological advances have made it easier for broadcasters to "bleep out" offending words in the programs that they air. Does this development support a more stringent—or less stringent—enforcement policy by the FCC? Explain.

3. Should an administrative agency be locked into its first interpretation of a statute? Why or why not?

4. In the ruling that the Supreme Court reviewed in this case, did the U.S. Court of Appeals for the Second Circuit reject the FCC's reasons for its actions because the court disagreed with those reasons? Explain.

a. On remand, the U.S. Court of Appeals for the Second Circuit ruled that the FCC's indecency policies were unconstitutionally vague and violated the broadcast network's First Amendment rights. See *Fox Television Stations, Inc. v. Federal Communications Commission,* 613 F.3d 317 (2010).

Rulemaking

Today, the major function of an administrative agency is **rulemaking**—the formulation of new regulations, or rules. The APA defines a *rule* as "an agency statement of general or particular applicability and future effect designed to implement, interpret, or prescribe law and policy."[5]

Regulations are sometimes said to be *legislative* because, like statutes, they have a binding effect.

5. 5 U.S.C. Section 551(4).

Thus, violators of agency rules may be punished. Because agency rules have such significant legal force, the APA established procedures for agencies to follow in creating rules. Many rules must be adopted using the APA's *notice-and-comment rulemaking* procedure.

Notice-and-comment rulemaking involves three basic steps: notice of the proposed rulemaking, a comment period, and the final rule. The APA recognizes some limited exceptions to these procedural requirements, but they are seldom invoked. If the required procedures are violated, the resulting rule may be invalid.

The impetus for rulemaking may come from various sources, including Congress, the agency itself, or private parties, who may petition an agency to begin a rulemaking (or repeal a rule). For example, environmental groups have petitioned for stricter air-pollution controls to combat emissions that may contribute to climate change.

NOTICE OF THE PROPOSED RULEMAKING When a federal agency decides to create a new rule, the agency publishes a notice of the proposed rulemaking proceedings in the *Federal Register*. The *Federal Register* is a daily publication of the executive branch that prints government orders, rules, and regulations. The notice states where and when the proceedings will be held, the agency's legal authority for making the rule (usually its enabling legislation), and the terms or subject matter of the proposed rule.

The APA requires an agency to make available to the public certain information, such as the key scientific data underlying the proposal. The proposed rule is also often reported by the news media and published in the trade journals of the industries that will be affected.

COMMENT PERIOD Following the publication of the notice of the proposed rulemaking proceedings, the agency must allow ample time for persons to comment in writing on the proposed rule. The purpose of this comment period is to give interested parties the opportunity to express their views on the proposed rule in an effort to influence agency policy. Anyone can submit comments in writing or, if a hearing is held, orally. All comments are logged in and become a public record that others can examine.

The agency need not respond to all comments, but it must respond to any significant comments that bear directly on the proposed rule. The agency responds by either modifying its final rule or explain-

ing, in a statement accompanying the final rule, why it did not make any changes. In some circumstances, particularly when less formal procedures are used, an agency may accept comments after the comment period is closed.

THE FINAL RULE After the agency reviews the comments, it drafts the final rule and publishes it in the *Federal Register*. The final rule must contain a "concise general statement of . . . basis and purpose" that describes the reasoning behind the rule.[6]

Binding Effect. The final rule may modify the terms of the proposed rule in light of the public comments, but if substantial changes are made, a new proposal and a new opportunity for comment are required. The final rule is later compiled along with the rules and regulations of other federal administrative agencies in the *Code of Federal Regulations*. Final rules have binding legal effect unless the courts later overturn them and for this reason are considered legislative rules.

Failure to Follow Rulemaking Procedures. If an agency failed to follow proper rulemaking procedures when it issued the final rule, however, the rule may not be binding. ▶ **Case in Point 43.4** Members of the Hemp Industries Association (HIA) manufacture and sell food products made from hemp seed and oil. These products contain only trace amounts of tetrahydrocannabinol (THC, a component of marijuana) and are nonpsychoactive—that is, they do not affect a person's mind or behavior. In 2001, the U.S. Drug Enforcement Administration (DEA) published an interpretive rule declaring that "any product that contains any amount of THC is a Schedule I controlled substance [a drug whose availability is restricted by law]."

Subsequently, without following formal rulemaking procedures, the DEA declared that two legislative rules relating to products containing natural THC were final. These rules effectively banned the possession and sale of the food products of the HIA's members. The HIA petitioned for court review, arguing that the DEA rules should not have been enforced. A federal appellate court agreed and ruled in favor of the HIA. The DEA should have held hearings on the record concerning the rules, invited public comment, and then issued formal rulings on each finding, conclusion, and exception. Because the DEA did

---

6. 5 U.S.C. Section 555(c).

not follow its formal rulemaking procedures, the rules were not enforceable.[7] ◄

Informal Agency Actions

Rather than take the time to conduct notice-and-comment rulemaking, agencies have increasingly been using more informal methods of policymaking, such as issuing interpretive rules and guidance documents. As mentioned, *legislative rules* are substantive in that they affect legal rights, whereas *interpretive rules* simply declare policy and do not affect legal rights or obligations. Agencies also issue various other materials, such as guidance documents, which advise the public on the agencies' legal and policy positions.

Informal agency actions are exempt from the APA's requirements because they do not establish legal rights. A party cannot be directly prosecuted for violating an interpretive rule or a guidance document. Nevertheless, an informal action can be important because it warns regulated entities that the agency may engage in formal rulemaking if they ignore its informal policymaking.

SECTION 4
JUDICIAL DEFERENCE TO AGENCY DECISIONS

When asked to review agency decisions, courts historically granted deference (significant weight) to the agency's judgment, often citing the agency's great expertise in the subject area of the regulation. This deference seems especially appropriate when applied to an agency's analysis of factual questions, but should it also extend to an agency's interpretation of its own legal authority? In *Chevron U.S.A., Inc. v. Natural Resources Defense Council,* Inc.,[8] the United States Supreme Court held that it should, thereby creating a standard of broadened deference to agencies on questions of legal interpretation.

The Holding of the *Chevron* Case

At issue in the *Chevron* case was whether the courts should defer to an agency's interpretation of a statute giving it authority to act. The Environmental Protection Agency (EPA) had interpreted the phrase "stationary source" in the Clean Air Act as referring to an entire manufacturing plant, and not to each facility within a plant. The agency's interpretation enabled it to adopt the so-called bubble policy, which allowed companies to offset increases in emissions in part of a plant with decreases elsewhere in the plant. This interpretation reduced the pollution-control compliance costs faced by manufacturers. An environmental group challenged the legality of the EPA's interpretation.

The Supreme Court held that the courts should defer to an agency's interpretation of *law* as well as fact. The Court found that the agency's interpretation of the statute was reasonable and upheld the bubble policy. The Court's decision in the *Chevron* case created a new standard for courts to use when reviewing agency interpretations of law. This standard involves the following two questions:

1. Did Congress directly address the issue in dispute in the statute? If so, the statutory language prevails.
2. If the statute is silent or ambiguous, is the agency's interpretation "reasonable"? If it is, a court should uphold the agency's interpretation even if the court would have interpreted the law differently.

When Courts Will Give *Chevron* Deference to Agency Interpretation

The notion that courts should defer to agencies on matters of law was controversial. Under the holding of the *Chevron* case, when the meaning of a particular statute's language is unclear and an agency interprets it, the court must follow the agency's interpretation as long as it is reasonable. This led to considerable discussion and litigation to test the boundaries of the *Chevron* holding. For instance, are courts required to give deference to all agency interpretations or only to those that result from adjudication or formal rulemaking procedures? Are informal agency interpretations issued through opinion letters and internal memoranda also entitled to deference?

▶ **Case in Point 43.5** The U.S. Customs Service is authorized to classify imported goods and determine the tariff (tax) imposed on them. "Ruling letters" set tariff classifications for particular imports. Mead Corporation imported "daily planners," which had been tariff-free for several years. The Customs Service issued a ruling letter reclassifying them as "bound diaries," which were subject to a tariff. Mead brought a law-

---

7. *Hemp Industries Association v. Drug Enforcement Administration,* 357 F.3d 1012 (9th Cir. 2004).
8. 467 U.S. 837, 104 S.Ct. 2778, 81 L.Ed.2d 694 (1984).

suit claiming that the ruling letter should not receive *Chevron* deference because it was not put into effect pursuant to notice-and-comment rulemaking. When the case reached the United States Supreme Court, the Court agreed that the ruling letter was *not* entitled to *Chevron* deference. For agencies to be assured of such judicial deference, they must meet the formal legal standards for notice-and-comment rulemaking.[9] ◄

9. *United States v. Mead Corporation,* 533 U.S. 218, 121 S.Ct. 2164, 150 L.Ed.2d 292 (2001).

In the following case, a medical educational foundation challenged an agency regulation that required it to deduct Social Security contributions from the wages of physicians who were participating in its hospital residency program. The Supreme Court had to decide if the "full-time employee" rule enacted by the Treasury Department was entitled to *Chevron* deference.

CASE 43.2

Mayo Foundation for Medical Education and Research v. United States
Supreme Court of the United States, 562 U.S. ___, 131 S.Ct. 704, 178 L.Ed.2d 588 (2011).

BACKGROUND AND FACTS The Mayo Foundation for Medical Education and Research (Mayo) offers residency programs to physicians who have graduated from medical school and seek additional instruction in a chosen specialty. Although the resident physicians participate in some formal educational activities, they spend fifty to eighty hours a week caring for patients. As discussed in Chapter 34, the Federal Insurance Contributions Act (FICA) requires employees and employers to pay Social Security taxes on all wages employees receive. FICA, however, excludes from its definition of *employment* any "service performed in the employ of . . . a school, college, or university . . . if such service is performed by a student who is enrolled and regularly attending classes at [the school]."[a]

From 1951 to 2004, the Treasury Department construed the student exception as exempting students who work for their schools "as an incident to and for the purpose of pursuing a course of study." In late 2004, the department issued new regulations providing that the services of an employee who is normally scheduled to work forty or more hours per week "are not incident to and for the purpose of pursuing a course of study." As an example, the rule stated that a medical resident whose normal schedule requires him or her to perform services forty or more hours per week is not a student. Mayo filed a suit in a federal district court, which held that this rule was invalid. The U.S. Court of Appeals for the Eighth Circuit reversed the trial court's ruling, concluding that the department's regulation was a permissible interpretation of an ambiguous statute. Mayo appealed to the United States Supreme Court.

  IN THE LANGUAGE OF THE COURT
Chief Justice *ROBERTS* delivered the opinion of the Court.
* * * *

* * * Mayo's residency programs, which usually last three to five years, train doctors primarily through hands-on experience. * * * In 2005, Mayo paid its residents annual "stipends" ranging between $41,000 and $56,000 and provided them with health insurance, malpractice insurance, and paid vacation time.

Mayo residents also take part in "a formal and structured educational program." Residents are assigned textbooks and journal articles to read and are expected to attend weekly lectures and other conferences.
* * * *

a. See U.S.C. Section 3121(b).

CASE 43.2 CONTINUES ▶

On December 21, 2004, the [Treasury] Department adopted an amended rule prescribing that an employee's service is "incident" to his studies only when "the educational aspect of the relationship between the employer and the employee, as compared to the service aspect of the relationship, [is] predominant." * * * The amended provision clarifies that the Department's analysis "is not affected by the fact that the services performed . . . may have an educational, instructional, or training aspect."

* * * *

We begin our analysis with the first step of the two-part framework announced in *Chevron*, and ask whether Congress has "directly addressed the precise question at issue." We agree with the Court of Appeals that Congress has not done so. The statute does not define the term "student," and does not otherwise attend to the precise question whether medical residents are subject to FICA.

* * * *

* * * Such an ambiguity would lead us inexorably [impossible to prevent] to *Chevron* step two, under which we may not disturb an agency rule unless it is " 'arbitrary or capricious in substance, or manifestly contrary to the statute.' "

* * * *

* * * The Department issued the full-time employee rule pursuant to the explicit authorization to "prescribe all needful rules and regulations for the enforcement" of the Internal Revenue Code. *The Department issued the full-time employee rule only after notice-and-comment procedures, again a consideration identified in our precedents as a "significant" sign that a rule merits* Chevron *deference.* [Emphasis added.]

* * * *

The full-time employee rule easily satisfies the second step of Chevron, *which asks whether the Department's rule is a "reasonable interpretation" of the enacted text.* To begin, Mayo accepts that "the 'educational aspect of the relationship between the employer and the employee, as compared to the service aspect of the relationship, [must] be predominant' " in order for an individual to qualify for the exemption. Mayo objects, however, to the Department's conclusion that residents who work more than 40 hours per week categorically cannot satisfy that requirement. Because residents' employment is itself educational, Mayo argues, the hours a resident spends working make him "more of a student, not less of one." [Emphasis added.]

We disagree. Regulation, like legislation, often requires drawing lines. Mayo does not dispute that the Treasury Department reasonably sought a way to distinguish between workers who study and students who work. Focusing on the hours an individual works and the hours [she or] he spends in studies is a perfectly sensible way of accomplishing that goal.

* * * The Department reasonably determined that taxing residents under FICA would further the purpose of the Social Security Act. * * * Although Mayo contends that medical residents have not yet begun their "working lives" because they are not "fully trained," the Department certainly did not act irrationally in concluding that these doctors * * * are the kind of workers that Congress intended to both contribute to and benefit from the Social Security system.

DECISION AND REMEDY *The United States Supreme Court affirmed the decision of the appellate court, holding that the Treasury Department's full-time employee rule was valid. The Court found that the number of hours worked was a reasonable way to distinguish between workers who studied and students who worked. Therefore, the rule easily satisfied the* Chevron *standard.*

THE ETHICAL DIMENSION *A number of students work full time for their school to pay for their education. Is it fair to require them to pay FICA taxes when they would not have to do so if they worked only thirty hours per week? Explain.*

THE LEGAL ENVIRONMENT DIMENSION *Would the United States Supreme Court have deferred to the Treasury Department's full-time employee regulation even if it had disagreed with the rule? Why or why not?*

SECTION 5
ENFORCEMENT AND ADJUDICATION

Although rulemaking is the most prominent agency activity, enforcement of the rules is also critical. Often, an agency itself enforces its rules. It identifies alleged violators and pursues civil remedies against them in a proceeding held by the agency rather than in federal court, although the agency's determinations are reviewable in court.

Investigation

After final rules are issued, agencies conduct investigations to monitor compliance with those rules or with the requirements of the enabling statute. A typical agency investigation of this kind might begin when a citizen reports a possible violation to the agency.

Many agency rules also require considerable compliance reporting from regulated entities, and such a report may trigger an enforcement investigation. For example, environmental regulators often require reports of emissions, and the Occupational Safety and Health Administration (OSHA) requires companies to report any work-related deaths.

INSPECTIONS AND TESTS Many agencies gather information through on-site inspections. Sometimes, inspecting an office, a factory, or some other business facility is the only way to obtain the evidence needed to prove a regulatory violation. Administrative inspections and tests cover a wide range of activities, including safety inspections of underground coal mines, safety tests of commercial equipment and automobiles, and environmental monitoring of factory emissions.

An agency may also ask a firm or individual to submit certain documents or records to the agency for examination. For instance, the Federal Trade Commission often asks to inspect corporate records for compliance.

Normally, business firms comply with agency requests to inspect facilities or business records because it is in any firm's interest to maintain a good relationship with regulatory bodies. In some instances, however, such as when a firm thinks an agency's request is unreasonable and may be detrimental to the firm's interest, the firm may refuse to comply with the request. In such situations, an agency may resort to the use of a subpoena or a search warrant.

SUBPOENAS There are two basic types of subpoenas. The subpoena *ad testificandum*[10] ("to testify") is an ordinary subpoena. It is a writ, or order, compelling a witness to appear at an agency hearing. The subpoena *duces tecum*[11] ("bring it with you") compels an individual or organization to hand over books, papers, records, or documents to the agency. An administrative agency may use either type of subpoena to obtain testimony or documents.

There are limits on the information that an agency can demand. To determine whether an agency is abusing its discretion in its pursuit of information as part of an investigation, a court may consider such factors as the following:

1. *The purpose of the investigation.* An investigation must have a legitimate purpose. Harassment is an example of an improper purpose. An agency may not issue an administrative subpoena to inspect business records if the agency's motive is to harass or pressure the business into settling an unrelated matter.
2. *The relevance of the information being sought.* Information is relevant if it reveals that the law is being violated or if it assures the agency that the law is not being violated.
3. *The specificity of the demand for testimony or documents.* A subpoena must, for example, adequately describe the material being sought.
4. *The burden of the demand on the party from whom the information is sought.* In responding to a request for information, a party must bear the costs of, for example, copying the documents that must be handed over. A business generally is not required to reveal its trade secrets, however.

SEARCHES DURING SITE INSPECTIONS As mentioned, agency investigations often involve on-site inspections. For instance, the Environmental Protection Agency (EPA) frequently conducts inspections to enforce environmental laws. The EPA may inspect a site to determine if hazardous wastes are being stored properly or to sample a facility's wastewater to ensure that it complies with the Clean Water Act. Usually, companies do not resist such inspections, although in some circumstances they may do so.

SEARCH WARRANTS The Fourth Amendment protects against unreasonable searches and seizures by

---

10. Pronounced ad tes-te-fe-*kan*-dum.
11. Pronounced *doo*-suhs *tee*-kum.

requiring in most instances that a search warrant be obtained before a physical search for evidence is conducted. An agency typically must obtain a search warrant that directs law enforcement officials to search a specific place for a specific item and present it to the agency.

Agencies can conduct warrantless searches in several situations. Warrants are not required to conduct searches in certain highly regulated industries. Firms that sell firearms or liquor, for instance, are automatically subject to inspections without warrants. Sometimes, a statute permits warrantless searches of certain types of hazardous operations, such as coal mines or liquid propane retailers. Also, a warrantless inspection in an emergency situation is normally considered reasonable.

Adjudication

After an investigation reveals a suspected violation, an agency may begin to take administrative action against an individual or organization. Most administrative actions are resolved through negotiated settlements at their initial stages, without formal **adjudication** (the process of resolving a dispute by presenting evidence and arguments before a neutral decision maker).

NEGOTIATED SETTLEMENTS Depending on the agency, negotiations may involve a simple conversation or a series of informal conferences. Whatever form the negotiations take, their purpose is to rectify the problem to the agency's satisfaction and eliminate the need for additional proceedings.

Settlement is an appealing option to firms for two reasons: to avoid appearing uncooperative and to avoid the expense involved in formal adjudication proceedings and in possible later appeals. Settlement is also an attractive option for agencies. To conserve their resources and avoid formal actions, administrative agencies devote a great deal of effort to giving advice and negotiating solutions to problems.

FORMAL COMPLAINTS If a settlement cannot be reached, the agency may issue a formal complaint against the suspected violator. ▶ **Example 43.6** The Environmental Protection Agency (EPA) finds that Acme Manufacturing, Inc., is polluting groundwater in violation of federal pollution laws. The EPA issues a complaint against Acme in an effort to bring the plant into compliance with federal regulations. This complaint is a public document, and a press release may

accompany it. Acme will respond by filing an answer to the EPA's allegations. If Acme and the EPA cannot agree on a settlement, the case will be adjudicated. ◀

Agency adjudication may involve a trial-like arbitration procedure before an **administrative law judge (ALJ).** The Administrative Procedure Act (APA) requires that before the hearing takes place, the agency must issue a notice that includes the facts and law on which the complaint is based, the legal authority for the hearing, and its time and place. The administrative adjudication process is described next and illustrated graphically in Exhibit 43–3 below.

THE ROLE OF THE ADMINISTRATIVE LAW JUDGE An ALJ presides over the hearing and has the power to

EXHIBIT 43-3 The Process of Formal Administrative Adjudication administer oaths, take testimony, rule on questions of evidence, and make determinations of fact. The law requires an ALJ to be an unbiased adjudicator (judge), even though the ALJ actually works for the agency prosecuting the case (in *Example 43.6,* the EPA). There are no juries in administrative hearings. The ALJ assumes the role of a judge and jury in a trial.

Certain safeguards prevent bias on the part of the ALJ and promote fairness in the proceedings. For instance, the APA requires that the ALJ be separate from an agency's investigative and prosecutorial staff. The APA also prohibits *ex parte* (private) communications between the ALJ and any party to an agency proceeding, such as the EPA or the manufacturer. Finally, provisions of the APA protect the ALJ from agency disciplinary actions unless the agency can show good cause for such an action.

HEARING PROCEDURES Hearing procedures vary widely from agency to agency. Administrative agencies generally exercise substantial discretion over the type of procedure that will be used. Frequently, disputes are resolved through informal adjudication proceedings. ▶ **Example 43.7** The Federal Trade Commission (FTC) charges Good Foods, Inc., with deceptive advertising. Representatives of Good Foods and the FTC, their counsel, and the ALJ meet at a table in a conference room to resolve the dispute informally. ◀

A formal adjudicatory hearing, in contrast, resembles a trial in many respects. Prior to the hearing, the parties are permitted to undertake discovery—involving depositions, interrogatories, and requests for documents or other information, as described in Chapter 3. The discovery process usually is not quite as extensive as it would be in a court proceeding. The hearing itself must comply with the procedural requirements of the APA and must also meet the constitutional standards of due process. During the hearing, the parties may give testimony, present other evidence, and cross-examine adverse witnesses.

A significant difference between a trial and an administrative agency hearing, though, is that normally much more information, including hearsay (secondhand information), can be introduced as evidence during an administrative hearing. The burden of proof in an enforcement proceeding is placed on the agency.

AGENCY ORDERS Following a hearing, the ALJ renders an **initial order,** or decision, on the case. Either party can appeal the ALJ's decision to the board or commission that governs the agency. If Acme in *Example 43.6* above is dissatisfied with the ALJ's decision, it can appeal the decision to the EPA. If Acme is dissatisfied with the commission's decision, it can appeal the decision to a federal court of appeals.

If no party appeals the case, the ALJ's decision becomes the **final order** of the agency. The ALJ's decision also becomes final if a party appeals and the commission and the court decline to review the case. If a party appeals and the case is reviewed, the final order comes from the commission's decision or (if that decision is appealed to a federal appellate court) that of the reviewing court.

In the following case, a federal appeals court reviewed the Drug Enforcement Administration's denial of a university professor's application to register to cultivate marijuana.

CASE 43.3

Craker v. Drug Enforcement Administration
United States Court of Appeals, First Circuit, 714 F.3d 17 (2013).

BACKGROUND AND FACTS Dr. Lyle Craker, a professor in the University of Massachusetts's Department of Plant, Soil and Insect Sciences, applied to the Drug Enforcement Administration (DEA) for permission to register to manufacture marijuana for clinical research. He stated that "a second source of plant material is needed to facilitate privately funded Food and Drug Administration (FDA)-approved research into medical uses of marijuana, ensuring a choice of sources and an adequate supply of quality, research-grade marijuana for medicinal applications." An administrative law judge recommended that Craker's application be granted, but a DEA Deputy Administrator issued an order denying his application.

CASE 43.3 CONTINUES ▶

Under the DEA's interpretation, the Controlled Substances Act (CSA) requires an applicant to prove both that effective controls against diversion of the marijuana for unapproved purposes are in place and that its supply and the competition to supply it are inadequate. The Administrator determined that the professor did not prove that effective controls against the marijuana's diversion were in place or that supply and competition were inadequate. Craker petitioned the U.S. Court of Appeals for the First Circuit to review the order.

 IN THE LANGUAGE OF THE COURT
HOWARD, Circuit Judge.

* * *

Since 1968, the National Center for Natural Products Research ("NCNPR") at the University of Mississippi has held the necessary registration and a government contract to grow marijuana for research purposes. The contract is administered by the National Institute on Drug Abuse ("NIDA"), a component of the National Institutes of Health ("NIH"), which, in turn, is a component of the [U.S.] Department of Health and Human Services ("HHS"). The contract is opened for competitive bidding every five years. The NCNPR is the only entity registered by the DEA to manufacture marijuana.

* * * *

Dr. Craker's argument with respect to competition is essentially that there cannot be "adequately competitive conditions" when there is only one manufacturer of marijuana.

The Administrator * * * observed that NIDA had provided marijuana manufactured by the University of Mississippi either at cost or free to researchers, and that Dr. Craker had made no showing of how he could provide it for less * * * . Additionally, the Administrator noted that Dr. Craker is free to bid on the contract when it comes up for renewal.

*We see nothing improper in the Administrator's approach. The [CSA's] term "adequately competitive conditions" is not necessarily as narrow as the petitioner suggests. * * * That the current regime may not be the most competitive situation possible does not render it "inadequate."* [Emphasis added.]

* * * *

In finding that Dr. Craker failed to demonstrate that the current supply of marijuana was not adequate and uninterrupted, the Administrator observed that there were over 1,000 kilograms of marijuana in NIDA possession, an amount which far exceeds present research demands and "any foreseeable" future demand. Dr. Craker does not dispute this finding, or that the current amount is more than ninety times the amount he proposes to supply. Instead, he argues that the adequacy of supply must not be measured against NIDA-approved research, but by whether the supply is adequate to supply projects approved by the FDA. But even if we were to accept his premise—which we don't—Dr. Craker fails to demonstrate that the supply is inadequate for those needs, either. He merely states that certain projects were rejected as "not bona-fide" by NIDA, a claim which does not address the adequacy of supply. The fact that Dr. Craker disagrees with the method by which marijuana research is approved does not undermine the substantial evidence that supports the Administrator's conclusion.

DECISION AND REMEDY *The U.S. Court of Appeals for the First Circuit denied Craker's petition to review the agency's order "because the Administrator's interpretation of the CSA is permissible and her findings are reasonable and supported by the evidence."*

THE ECONOMIC DIMENSION *Why should a court wait to review an agency's order until the order has gone through the entire procedural process and can be considered final?*

THE LEGAL ENVIRONMENT DIMENSION *Under what standard does a court defer to an agency's interpretation of a statute? Did the court in this case appear to have applied that standard to the DEA's interpretation of the Controlled Substances Act? Discuss.*

PUBLIC ACCOUNTABILITY

As a result of growing public concern over the powers exercised by administrative agencies, Congress passed several laws to make agencies more accountable through public scrutiny. Here, we discuss the most significant of these laws.

Freedom of Information Act

Enacted in 1966, the Freedom of Information Act (FOIA)[12] requires the federal government to disclose certain records to any person or entity on written request, even if no reason is given for the request. All federal government agencies must make their records available electronically on the Internet and in other electronic formats.

The FOIA exempts certain types of records, such as those pertaining to national security, and those containing information that is confidential or personal. For other records, though, a request that complies with the FOIA procedures need only contain a reasonable description of the information sought. An agency's failure to comply with an FOIA request can be challenged in a federal district court. The media, industry trade associations, public-interest groups, and even companies seeking information about competitors rely on these FOIA provisions to obtain information from government agencies.

Government in the Sunshine Act

Congress passed the Government in the Sunshine Act,[13] or open meeting law, in 1976. It requires that "every portion of every meeting of an agency" be open to "public observation." The act also requires the establishment of procedures to ensure that the public is provided with adequate advance notice of scheduled meetings and agendas. Like the FOIA, the Sunshine Act contains certain exceptions. Closed meetings are permitted when (1) the subject of the meeting concerns accusing any person of a crime, (2) an open meeting would frustrate the implementation of agency actions, or (3) the subject of the meeting involves matters relating to future litigation or rulemaking. Courts interpret these exceptions to allow open access whenever possible.

Regulatory Flexibility Act

Concern over the effects of regulation on the efficiency of businesses, particularly smaller ones, led Congress to pass the Regulatory Flexibility Act[14] in 1980. Under this act, whenever a new regulation will have a "significant impact upon a substantial number of small entities," the agency must conduct a regulatory flexibility analysis. The analysis must measure the cost that the rule would impose on small businesses and consider less burdensome alternatives. The act also contains provisions to alert small businesses—through advertising in trade journals, for example—about forthcoming regulations. The act reduces some record-keeping burdens for small businesses, especially with regard to hazardous waste management.

Small Business Regulatory Enforcement Fairness Act

The Small Business Regulatory Enforcement Fairness Act (SBREFA)[15] allows Congress to review new federal regulations for at least sixty days before they take effect. This period gives opponents of the rules time to present their arguments to Congress.

The SBREFA also authorizes the courts to enforce the Regulatory Flexibility Act. This helps to ensure that federal agencies, such as the Internal Revenue Service, will consider ways to reduce the economic impact of new regulations on small businesses. Federal agencies are required to prepare guides that explain in plain English how small businesses can comply with federal regulations.

The SBREFA also set up the Office of the National Ombudsman at the Small Business Administration to receive comments from small businesses about their dealings with federal agencies. Based on these comments, Regional Small Business Fairness Boards rate the agencies and publicize their findings.

---

12. 5 U.S.C. Section 552.
13. 5 U.S.C. Section 552b.

14. 5 U.S.C. Sections 601–612.
15. 5 U.S.C. Sections 801 *et seq.*

Reviewing: Administrative Agencies

Assume that the Securities and Exchange Commission (SEC) has a rule that it will enforce statutory provisions prohibiting insider trading only when the insiders make monetary profits for themselves. Then the SEC makes a new rule, declaring that it will now bring enforcement actions against individuals for insider trading even if the individuals did not personally profit from the transactions. In making the new rule, the SEC does not conduct a rulemaking procedure but simply announces its decision. A stockbrokerage firm objects and says that the new rule was unlawfully developed without opportunity for public comment. The brokerage firm challenges the rule in an action that ultimately is reviewed by a federal appellate court. Using the information presented in the chapter, answer the following questions.

1. Is the SEC an executive agency or an independent regulatory agency? Does it matter to the outcome of this dispute? Explain.
2. Suppose that the SEC asserts that it has always had the statutory authority to pursue persons for insider trading regardless of whether they personally profited from the transactions. This is the only argument the SEC makes to justify changing its enforcement rules. Would a court be likely to find that the SEC's action was arbitrary and capricious under the Administrative Procedure Act (APA)? Why or why not?
3. Would a court be likely to give *Chevron* deference to the SEC's interpretation of the law on insider trading?
4. Now assume that a court finds that the new rule is merely "interpretive." What effect would this determination have on whether the SEC had to follow the APA's rulemaking procedures?

DEBATE THIS . . . *Because an administrative law judge (ALJ) acts as both judge and jury, there should always be at least three ALJs in each administrative hearing.*

Terms and Concepts

adjudication 854
administrative law judge (ALJ) 854
bureaucracy 846
delegation doctrine 846
enabling legislation 843
final order 855
initial order 855
interpretive rule 845
legislative rule 845
notice-and-comment rulemaking 849
rulemaking 848

ExamPrep

Issue Spotters

1. The U.S. Department of Transportation (DOT) sometimes hears an appeal from a party whose contract with the DOT has been canceled. An administrative law judge (ALJ), who works for the DOT, hears this appeal. What safeguards promote the ALJ's fairness? **(See page 855.)**
2. Techplate Corporation learns that a federal administrative agency is considering a rule that will have a negative impact on the firm's ability to do business. Does the firm have any opportunity to express its opinion about the pending rule? Explain. **(See page 849.)**

• **Check your answers to the Issue Spotters against the answers provided in Appendix E at the end of this text.**

Before the Test

Go to **www.cengagebrain.com**, enter the ISBN 9781285185248, and click on "Find" to locate this textbook's Web site. Then, click on "Access Now" under "Study Tools," and select Chapter 43 at the top. There, you will find a Practice Quiz that you can take to assess your mastery of the concepts in this chapter, as well as Flashcards and a Glossary of important terms.

Business Scenarios

43–1. Rulemaking and Adjudication Powers. For decades, the Federal Trade Commission (FTC) resolved fair trade and advertising disputes through individual adjudications. In the 1960s, the FTC began promulgating rules that defined fair and unfair trade practices. In cases involving violations of these rules, the due process rights of participants were more limited and did not include cross-examination. Although anyone charged with violating a rule would receive a full adjudication, the legitimacy of the rule itself could not be challenged in the adjudication. Furthermore, a party charged with violating a rule was almost certain to lose the adjudication. Affected parties complained to a court, arguing that their rights before the FTC were unduly limited by the new rules. What would the court examine to determine whether to uphold the new rules? **(See page 848.)**

43–2. Informal Rulemaking. Assume that the Food and Drug Administration (FDA), using proper procedures, adopts a rule describing its future investigations. This new rule covers all future circumstances in which the FDA wants to regulate food additives. Under the new rule, the FDA is not to regulate food additives without giving food companies an opportunity to cross-examine witnesses. Later, the FDA wants to regulate methylisocyanate, a food additive. The FDA undertakes an informal rulemaking procedure, without cross-examination, and regulates methylisocyanate. Producers protest, saying that the FDA promised them the opportunity for cross-examination. The FDA responds that the Administrative Procedure Act does not require such cross-examination and that it is free to withdraw the promise made in its new rule. If the producers challenge the FDA in court, on what basis would the court rule in their favor? Explain. **(See page 848.)**

Business Case Problems

43–3. Investigation. Riverdale Mills Corp. makes plastic-coated steel wire products using a water-based cleaning process that generates acidic and alkaline wastewater. To meet federal clean-water requirements, Riverdale has a system within its plant to treat the water. It then flows through a pipe that opens into a manhole-covered test pit outside the plant in full view of Riverdale's employees. Three hundred feet away, the pipe merges into the public sewer system. The Environmental Protection Agency (EPA) sent agents to inspect the plant. Without a search warrant and without Riverdale's consent, the agents took samples from the test pit. Based on the samples, Riverdale and James Knott, the company's owner, were charged with criminal violations of the federal Clean Water Act. The defendants sued the EPA agents and others, alleging violations of the Fourth Amendment. What right does the Fourth Amendment provide in this context? Should the agents be held liable? Why or why not? [*Riverdale Mills Corp. v. Pimpare*, 392 F.3d 55 (1st Cir. 2004)] **(See page 853.)**

43–4. Rulemaking. The Investment Company Act prohibits a mutual fund from engaging in certain transactions when there may be a conflict of interest between the manager of the fund and its shareholders. Under rules issued by the Securities and Exchange Commission (SEC), however, a fund that meets certain conditions may engage in an otherwise prohibited transaction. In June 2004, the SEC added two new conditions. A year later, the SEC reconsidered the new conditions in terms of the costs that they would impose on the funds. Within eight days, and without asking for public input, the SEC readopted the conditions. The Chamber of Commerce of

the United States asked a federal appellate court to review the new rules. The Chamber argued that in readopting the rules, the SEC relied on materials not in the "rulemaking record" without providing an opportunity for public comment. The SEC countered that the information was otherwise "publicly available." In adopting a rule, should an agency consider information that is not part of the rulemaking record? Why or why not? [*Chamber of Commerce of the United States v. Securities and Exchange Commission*, 443 F.3d 890 (D.C.Cir. 2006)] **(See page 848.)**

43–5. BUSINESS CASE PROBLEM WITH SAMPLE ANSWER: Agency Powers.

 A well-documented rise in global temperatures has coincided with a significant increase in the concentration of carbon dioxide in the atmosphere. Some scientists believe that the two trends are related, because when carbon dioxide is released into the atmosphere, it produces a greenhouse effect, trapping solar heat. Under the Clean Air Act (CAA), the Environmental Protection Agency (EPA) is authorized to regulate "any" air pollutants "emitted into . . . the ambient air" that in its "judgment cause, or contribute to, air pollution." A group of private organizations asked the EPA to regulate carbon dioxide and other "greenhouse gas" emissions from new motor vehicles. The EPA refused, stating, among other things, that Congress last amended the CAA in 1990 without authorizing new, binding auto emissions limits. The petitioners—nineteen states, including Massachusetts, and others—brought a lawsuit asking a court to review the EPA's denial. Did the EPA have the authority to regulate greenhouse gas emissions from new motor vehicles? If so, was its stated reason for refusing to do so consistent with that authority? Discuss. [Massachusetts v.

Environmental Protection Agency, *549 U.S. 497, 127 S.Ct. 1438, 167 L.Ed.2d 248 (2007)]* **(See page 845.)**

- **For a sample answer to Problem 43–5, go to Appendix F at the end of this text.**

43–6. Judicial Deference. After Dave Conley died of lung cancer, his widow filed for benefits under the Black Lung Benefits Act. To qualify for benefits under the act, exposure to coal dust must have been a substantial contributing factor to a person's death. Conley had been a coal miner, but he had also been a longtime smoker. At the benefits hearing, a physician testified that coal dust was a substantial factor in Conley's death. No evidence was presented to support this conclusion, however. The administrative law judge awarded benefits. On appeal, should a court defer to this decision? Discuss. [*Conley v. National Mines Corp.*, 595 F.3d 297 (6th Cir. 2010)] **(See page 850.)**

43–7. Arbitrary and Capricious Test. Michael Manin, an airline pilot, was twice convicted of disorderly conduct, a minor misdemeanor. To renew his flight certification with the National Transportation Safety Board (NTSB), Manin filed an application that asked him about his criminal history. He did not disclose his two convictions. When these came to light more than ten years later, Manin argued that he had not known that he was required to report convictions for minor misdemeanors. The NTSB's policy was to consider an applicant's understanding of what information a question sought before determining whether an answer was false. But without explanation, the agency departed from this policy, refused to consider Manin's argument, and revoked his certification. Was this action arbitrary or capricious? Explain. [*Manin v. National Transportation Safety Board*, 627 F.3d 1239 (D.C.Cir. 2011)] **(See page 846.)**

43–8. A QUESTION OF ETHICS: Rulemaking.

*To ensure highway safety and protect driver health, Congress charged federal agencies with regulating the hours of service of commercial motor vehicle operators. Between 1940 and 2003, the regula-*tions that applied to long-haul truck drivers were mostly unchanged. (Long-haul drivers are those who operate beyond a 150-mile radius of their base.) In 2003, the Federal Motor Carrier Safety Administration (FMCSA) revised the regulations significantly, increasing the number of daily and weekly hours that drivers could work. The agency had not considered the impact of the changes on the health of the drivers, however, and the revisions were overturned. The FMCSA then issued a notice that it would reconsider the revisions and opened them up for public comment. The agency analyzed the costs to the industry and the crash risks due to driver fatigue under different options and concluded that the safety benefits of not increasing the hours were less than the economic costs. In 2005, the agency issued a rule that was nearly identical to the 2003 version. Public Citizen, Inc., and others, including the Owner-Operator Independent Drivers Association, asked the U.S. Court of Appeals for the District of Columbia Circuit to review the 2005 rule as it applied to long-haul drivers. [Owner-Operator Independent Drivers Association, Inc. v. Federal Motor Carrier Safety Administration, 494 F.3d 188 (D.C.Cir. 2007)]* **(See page 848.)**

(a) The FMCSA's cost-benefit analysis included new methods that were not disclosed to the public in time for comments. Was this unethical? Should the agency have disclosed the new methodology sooner? Why or why not?

(b) The FMCSA created a graph to show the risk of a crash as a function of the time a driver spent on the job. The graph plotted the first twelve hours of a day individually, but the rest of the time was depicted with an aggregate figure at the seventeenth hour. This made the risk at those hours appear to be lower. Is it unethical for an agency to manipulate data? Explain.

Legal Reasoning Group Activity

43–9. Investigation. Maureen Droge was a flight attendant for United Air Lines, Inc. (UAL). After being assigned to work in Paris, France, she became pregnant. Because UAL does not allow its flight attendants to fly during their third trimester of pregnancy, Droge was placed on involuntary leave. She applied for temporary disability benefits through the French social security system. Her request was denied because UAL does not contribute to the French system on behalf of its U.S.-based flight attendants. Droge filed a charge of discrimination with the U.S. Equal Employment Opportunity Commission (EEOC), alleging that UAL had discriminated against her and other Americans. The EEOC issued a subpoena, asking UAL to detail all benefits received by all UAL employees living outside the United States. UAL refused to provide the information on the ground that it was irrelevant and compliance would be unduly burdensome. The EEOC filed a suit in a federal district court against UAL. **(See page 853.)**

(a) The first group will decide whether the court should enforce the subpoena, and explain why.

(b) The second group will discuss whether the EEOC should be able to force a U.S. company that is operating overseas to provide the same (disability) benefits to employees located there as it does to employees in the United States. Should UAL be required to contribute to the French social security system for employees who reside in France?

CHAPTER 44
CONSUMER LAW

All statutes, agency rules, and common law judicial decisions that serve to protect the interests of consumers are classified as **consumer law.** Traditionally, in disputes involving consumers, it was assumed that the freedom to contract carried with it the obligation to live by the deal made. Over time, this attitude has changed considerably.

Today, countless federal and state laws attempt to protect consumers from unfair trade practices, unsafe products, discriminatory or unreasonable credit requirements, and other problems related to consumer transactions. Nearly every agency and department of the federal government has an office of consumer affairs, and most states have one or more such offices to help consumers. Also, typically the attorney general's office assists consumers at the state level.

In recent years, there has been a renewed interest in attempting to protect consumers in their dealings with credit-card companies, financial institutions, and insurance companies. Congress has enacted new credit-card regulations and financial reforms to regulate the nation's largest banks. Congress has also enacted health-care reforms and revised food safety laws.

In this chapter, we examine some of the major laws and regulations protecting consumers, focusing primarily on federal legislation. Realize, though, that state laws often provide more sweeping and significant protections for the consumer than do federal laws. Exhibit 44–1 on the next page indicates many of the areas of consumer law that are regulated by federal statutes.

DECEPTIVE ADVERTISING

The Federal Trade Commission Act[1] (mentioned in Chapter 43) created the Federal Trade Commission (FTC) to carry out the broadly stated goal of preventing unfair and deceptive trade practices, including deceptive advertising.

A Reasonable Consumer Would Be Misled

Generally, **deceptive advertising** occurs if a reasonable consumer would be misled by the advertising claim. Vague generalities and obvious exaggerations are permissible. These claims are known as *puffery*. When a claim takes on the appearance of literal authenticity, however, it may create problems.

CLAIMS THAT APPEAR TO BE BASED ON FACTUAL EVIDENCE Advertising that *appears* to be based on factual evidence but in fact is not reasonably supported by some evidence will be deemed deceptive. ▶ **Case in Point 44.1** MedLab, Inc., advertised that its weight-loss supplement ("The New Skinny Pill") would cause users to lose substantial amounts of weight rapidly. The ads claimed that "clinical studies prove" that people who take the pill lose "as much as 15 to 18 pounds per week and as much as 50 percent of all excess weight in just 14 days, without dieting or exercising." The FTC sued MedLab for deceptive advertising.

An expert hired by the FTC to evaluate the claim testified that to lose this much weight, "a 200-pound individual would need to run between 57 and 68 miles every day"—the equivalent of more than two marathons per day. The court concluded that the advertisement was false and misleading, granted the FTC a summary judgment, and issued a permanent injunction to stop MedLab from running the ads.[2] ◀

---

1. 15 U.S.C. Sections 41–58.

2. *Federal Trade Commission v. MedLab, Inc,* 615 F.Supp.2d 1068 (N.D.Cal. 2009).

EXHIBIT 44-1 Selected Areas of Consumer Law Regulated by Statutes

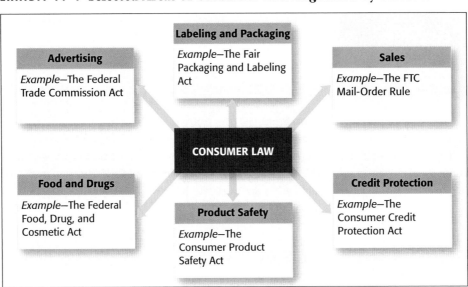

Advertising

Example—The Federal Trade Commission Act

Labeling and Packaging

Example—The Fair Packaging and Labeling Act

Sales

Example—The FTC Mail-Order Rule

CONSUMER LAW

Food and Drugs

Example—The Federal Food, Drug, and Cosmetic Act

Product Safety

Example—The Consumer Product Safety Act

Credit Protection

Example—The Consumer Credit Protection Act

CLAIMS BASED ON HALF-TRUTHS Some advertisements contain "half-truths," meaning that the presented information is true but incomplete and therefore leads consumers to a false conclusion. ▶ **Example 44.2** The maker of Campbell's soups advertised that "most" Campbell's soups are low in fat and cholesterol and thus helpful in fighting heart disease. What the ad did not say was that many Campbell's soups are high in sodium and that high-sodium diets may increase the risk of heart disease. Hence, the FTC ruled that Campbell's claims were deceptive. ◀

Advertising that contains an endorsement by a celebrity may be deemed deceptive if the celebrity does not actually use the product.

Bait-and-Switch Advertising

The FTC has issued rules that govern specific advertising techniques. One of the most important rules is contained in the FTC's "Guides Against Bait Advertising."[3] The rule seeks to prevent **bait-and-switch advertising**—that is, advertising a very low price for a particular item that will likely be unavailable to the consumer, who will then be encouraged to purchase a more expensive item.

The low price is the "bait" to lure the consumer into the store. The salesperson is instructed to "switch" the consumer to a different, more expensive item. Under the

FTC guidelines, bait-and-switch advertising occurs if the seller refuses to show the advertised item, fails to have a reasonable quantity of the item in stock, fails to promise to deliver the advertised item within a reasonable time, or discourages employees from selling the item.

Online Deceptive Advertising

Deceptive advertising occurs in the online environment as well as offline. The FTC actively monitors online advertising and has identified hundreds of Web sites that have made false or deceptive claims for products ranging from medical treatments for various diseases to exercise equipment and weight-loss aids.

The FTC has issued guidelines to help online businesses comply with existing laws prohibiting deceptive advertising.[4] These guidelines include three basic requirements:

1. All ads—both online and offline—must be truthful and not misleading.
2. The claims made in an ad must be substantiated—that is, advertisers must have evidence to back up their claims.
3. Ads cannot be unfair, which the FTC defines as "likely to cause substantial consumer injury that consumers could not reasonably avoid and that

---

3. 16 C.F.R. Part 238.

4. "Advertising and Marketing on the Internet: Rules of the Road," www.ftc.com, December 2000.

is not outweighed by the benefit to consumers or competition."

CLEAR AND CONSPICUOUS DISCLOSURE
In addition, the guidelines call for "clear and conspicuous" disclosure of any qualifying or limiting information. The overall impression of the ad is important in meeting this requirement. The FTC suggests that advertisers should assume that consumers will not read an entire Web page.

Therefore, to satisfy the "clear and conspicuous" requirement, the disclosure should be placed as close as possible to the claim being qualified or be included within the claim itself. If such placement is not feasible, the next-best location is on a section of the page to which a consumer can easily scroll. Generally, hyperlinks to a disclosure are recommended only for lengthy disclosures or for disclosures that must be repeated in several locations on the Web page.

SPAM ADVERTISING
As discussed in Chapter 9, Congress passed the federal CAN-SPAM Act to combat the problems associated with unsolicited commercial e-mails, commonly referred to as spam. Many states have also passed consumer protection laws that regulate deceptive online advertising. In the following case, an e-mail service provider claimed that an online marketing company had violated a California statute that prohibited deceptive content in e-mail advertising. The court had to decide whether the CAN-SPAM Act preempted the state statute (preemption was discussed in Chapter 4).

CASE 44.1

Hypertouch, Inc. v. ValueClick, Inc.
California Court of Appeal, Second District, 192 Cal.App.4th 805, 123 Cal.Rptr.3d 8 (2011).

BACKGROUND AND FACTS Hypertouch, Inc., provides e-mail service to customers located inside and outside California. ValueClick, Inc., and its subsidiaries provide online marketing services to third party advertisers that promote retail products. ValueClick contracts with these advertisers to place offers on its Web sites. ValueClick also contracts with affiliates that send out commercial e-mail advertisements. The advertisements include links redirecting consumers to promotions on ValueClick's Web sites.

If a consumer clicks through an e-mail advertisement and participates in a promotional offer, the affiliate that sent the initial e-mail is compensated for generating a customer "lead." The affiliate, rather than ValueClick, controls the content and subject lines of the e-mails. Hypertouch filed a complaint against ValueClick, its subsidiaries, and others for violating a California state statute that prohibits e-mail advertising that contains deceptive content and headings. The trial court held that the federal CAN-SPAM Act preempts the California statute and granted a summary judgment in favor of ValueClick. Hypertouch appealed.

IN THE LANGUAGE OF THE COURT
ZELON, J. [Judge]

* * * *

A determination whether Hypertouch's claims are preempted by federal law requires an analysis of both section 17529.5 [the California statute] and the CAN-SPAM Act.

* * * *

In 2003, the California Legislature passed Senate Bill 186, which imposed broad restrictions on advertising in unsolicited commercial e-mail advertisements sent from or to a computer within California. * * * The Legislature concluded that, to effectively regulate the abuses associated with spam, it was necessary to target not only the entities that send unsolicited commercial e-mail advertisements, but also the advertisers whose products and services are promoted in those e-mails[.]

Like several other California consumer protection statutes targeting deceptive advertising practices, section 17529.5 dispenses with many of the elements associated with common law fraud, which normally requires the plaintiff to prove "(a) [a] misrepresentation . . .; (b) knowledge of falsity (or *'scienter'*); (c) intent to defraud, [that is,] to induce reliance; (d) justifiable reliance; and (e) resulting damage."

CASE 44.1 CONTINUES ▶

CASE 44.1 CONTINUED

* * * *

The CAN-SPAM Act includes a provision that expressly preempts state statutes that regulate the use of commercial e-mail "except to the extent that any such statute . . . prohibits falsity or deception in any portion of a commercial [e-mail]." * * * [The legislative history indicates that the act] was intended "to implement 'one national standard' " regarding the content of commercial e-mail because "the patchwork of state laws had proven ineffective."

The legislative history also makes clear, however, that the Act's preemption provision was largely intended to target state statutes imposing content requirements on commercial e-mails, while leaving states free to regulate the use of deceptive practices in commercial e-mails in whatever manner they chose.

* * * *

The [preemption] clause does not reference either fraud or the common law, but rather permits any state law that prohibits " 'falsity and deception in any portion of a commercial electronic mail message.' " Congress "is certainly familiar with the word 'fraud' and choose[es] not to use it; the words 'falsity or deception' suggest broader application."

* * * [Furthermore,] at the time the CAN-SPAM Act was passed, Congress was aware that many states imposed liability for deceptive commercial e-mails without requiring reliance or other elements of common law fraud. Despite this knowledge, Congress chose not to use the word "fraud" in the savings [preemption] provision, thereby suggesting that it intended the phrase "falsity or deception" to have a broader application.

* * * *

Rather than broadening the scope of prohibited content in commercial e-mail, California's decision to dispense with the elements of common law fraud was intended to create a more effective mechanism for eradicating the use of deceptive commercial e-mails. Section 17529.5 seeks to accomplish this goal in two ways. *First, the statute permits a recipient of a deceptive commercial e-mail to bring suit regardless of whether they were actually misled or harmed by the deceptive message.* This ensures that the use of deceptive e-mail will not go unpunished merely because it failed to mislead its targets. Second, imposing strict liability on the advertisers who benefit from (and are the ultimate cause of) deceptive e-mails, forces those entities to take a more active role in supervising the complex web of affiliates who are promoting their products. [Emphasis added.]

* * * *

*The numerous subject lines at issue in this suit contain a wide variety of different statements. Some simply state that the recipient of the e-mail can get a free gift ("Get a $300 gift card FREE" * * *), others suggest that the recipient can obtain something free for doing a particular task ("Let us know your opinion and win a free gift card") * * * .* [Emphasis added.]

[ValueClick has] made no effort to explain why a reasonable trier of fact could not conclude that many of the subject lines at issue here, such as those offering a free gift card with no qualifying language, would be likely to mislead a reasonable person. Instead, it targets isolated e-mails in the record, such as one e-mail with the subject line "GAP Promotion," and argues that those particular e-mails are, as a matter of law, not deceptive. Regardless of whether Respondent [ValueClick] is correct that the isolated e-mails it cites are not likely to mislead the recipient, that alone does not entitle it to summary judgment on [Hypertouch's claims.]

DECISION AND REMEDY *The state appellate court held that California's antispam statute is not preempted by the federal CAN-SPAM Act, which exempts state laws that prohibit falsity or deception in commercial e-mail. The court therefore reversed the lower court's decision and remanded the case for trial.*

THE E-COMMERCE DIMENSION *Describe some ways in which the subject line of an e-mail advertisement might be deceptive.*

MANAGERIAL IMPLICATIONS *Business owners and managers who engage in e-mail advertising or contract with online marketing companies for that purpose need to be aware of and comply with the applicable state laws. The online marketing company in this case claimed that it was not responsible for the deceptive content of the advertising because it did not send or initiate the e-mails—that was done by the affili-*

CASE 44.1 CONTINUED

ates—and it did not know that the e-mails were deceptive. The state court rejected this argument, however, finding that California's law applies more broadly to any entity that advertises in deceptive e-mails. This holding will aid plaintiffs who sue under California's antispam statute. It may also persuade courts in other states to apply the same reasoning and broadly interpret their state laws against deceptive online advertising.

Federal Trade Commission Actions

The FTC receives complaints from many sources, including competitors of alleged violators, consumers, trade associations, Better Business Bureaus, and government organizations and officials. When the agency receives numerous and widespread complaints about a particular problem, it will investigate.

FORMAL COMPLAINT If the FTC concludes that a given advertisement is unfair or deceptive, it drafts a formal complaint, which is sent to the alleged offender. The company may agree to settle the complaint without further proceedings. If not, the FTC can conduct a hearing in which the company can present its defense (see Chapter 43).

FTC ORDERS If the FTC succeeds in proving that an advertisement is unfair or deceptive, it usually issues a **cease-and-desist order** requiring the company to stop the challenged advertising. In some circumstances, it may also impose a sanction known as **counteradvertising.** This requires the company to advertise anew—in print, on the Internet, on radio, and on television—to inform the public about the earlier misinformation. The FTC sometimes institutes a **multiple product order,** which requires a firm to stop false advertising for all of its products, not just the product involved in the original action.

RESTITUTION POSSIBLE When a company's deceptive ad leads to wrongful payments by consumers, the FTC may seek other remedies, including restitution. ▶ **Case in Point 44.3** Verity International, Ltd., billed phone-line subscribers who accessed certain online pornography sites at the rate for international calls to Madagascar. When consumers complained about the charges, Verity told them that the charges were valid and had to be paid, or the consumers would face further collection actions. A federal appellate court held that this representation of "uncontestability" was deceptive and a violation of the FTC Act. The court

ordered Verity to pay nearly $18 million in restitution to consumers.[5] ◀

Telemarketing and Fax Advertising

The Telephone Consumer Protection Act (TCPA)[6] prohibits telephone solicitation using an automatic telephone dialing system or a prerecorded voice. In addition, most states have statutes regulating telephone solicitation. The TCPA also makes it illegal to transmit ads via fax without first obtaining the recipient's permission. (Similar issues have arisen with respect to spam e-mail—see Chapter 9.)

STATUTORY REMEDIES The Federal Communications Commission (FCC) enforces the TCPA. The FCC imposes substantial fines ($11,000 each day) on companies that violate the junk fax provisions of the act and even fined one company as much as $5.4 million.[7] The TCPA also gives consumers a right to sue for either $500 for each violation of the act or for the actual monetary losses resulting from a violation, whichever is greater. If a court finds that a defendant willfully or knowingly violated the act, the court has the discretion to treble (triple) the amount of damages awarded.

FRAUDULENT TELEMARKETING The Telemarketing and Consumer Fraud and Abuse Prevention Act[8] directed the FTC to establish rules governing telemarketing and to bring actions against fraudulent telemarketers.

The FTC's Telemarketing Sales Rule (TSR)[9] requires a telemarketer to identify the seller's name, describe

---

5. *Federal Trade Commission v. Verity International, Ltd.,* 443 F.3d 48 (2d Cir. 2006).
6. 47 U.S.C. Sections 227 *et seq.*
7. See *Missouri ex rel. Nixon v. American Blast Fax, Inc.,* 323 F.3d 649 (8th Cir. 2003); *cert.* denied, 540 U.S. 1104, 124 S.Ct. 1043, 157 L.Ed.2d 888 (2004).
8. 15 U.S.C. 6101–6108.
9. 16 C.F.R. Sections 310.1–310.8.

the product being sold, and disclose all material facts related to the sale (such as the total cost of the goods being sold). The TSR makes it illegal for telemarketers to misrepresent information or facts about their goods or services. A telemarketer must also remove a consumer's name from its list of potential contacts if the customer so requests.

An amendment to the TSR established the national Do Not Call Registry. Telemarketers must refrain from calling those consumers who have placed their names on the list. Significantly, the TSR applies to any offer made to consumers in the United States—even if the offer comes from a foreign firm. Thus, the TSR helps to protect consumers from illegal cross-border telemarketing operations.

SECTION 2
LABELING AND PACKAGING LAWS

A number of federal and state laws deal specifically with the information given on labels and packages. In general, labels must be accurate, and they must use words that are easily understood by the ordinary consumer. In some instances, labels must specify the raw materials used in the product, such as the percentage of cotton, nylon, or other fiber used in a garment. In other instances, the products must carry a warning, such as those required on cigarette packages and advertising.[10]

Fuel Economy Labels on Automobiles

The Energy Policy and Conservation Act of 1975[11] requires automakers to attach an information label to every new car. The label must include the Environmental Protection Agency's fuel economy estimate for the vehicle. In the following case, the buyer of a new car complained that the vehicle had failed to achieve the fuel economy estimate advertised in the automaker's brochure and listed on the label.

---

10. 15 U.S.C. Sections 1331–1341.
11. 49 U.S.C. Section 32908(b)(1).

SP TLIGHT on Honda

Case 44.2   Paduano v. American Honda Motor Co.
California Court of Appeal, Fourth District, 169 Cal.App.4th 1453, 88 Cal.Rptr.3d 90 (2009).

BACKGROUND AND FACTS In 2004, Gaetano Paduano bought a new Honda Civic Hybrid in California. The information label on the car stated that the fuel economy estimates from the Environmental Protection Agency (EPA) were forty-seven miles per gallon (mpg) for city driving and forty-eight mpg for highway driving. Honda's sales brochure added, "Just drive the Hybrid like you would a conventional car and save on fuel bills." Paduano soon became frustrated with the car's fuel economy, which was less than half of the EPA's estimate. When American Honda Motor Company refused to repurchase the vehicle, Paduano filed a suit in a California state court against the automaker, alleging deceptive advertising in violation of the state's Consumer Legal Remedies Act and Unfair Competition Law. Honda argued that the federal Energy Policy and Conservation Act (EPCA), which prescribed the EPA's fuel economy estimate, preempted Paduano's claims (see Chapter 4). The court issued a summary judgment in Honda's favor. Paduano appealed to a state intermediate appellate court.

 IN THE LANGUAGE OF THE COURT
AARON, J. [Judge]

* * * *

The basic rules of preemption are not in dispute: *Under the supremacy clause of the United States Constitution, Congress has the power to preempt state law concerning matters that lie within the authority of Congress. In determining whether federal law preempts state law, a court's task is*

CASE 44.2 CONTINUED

to discern congressional intent. Congress's express intent in this regard will be found when Congress explicitly states that it is preempting state authority. [Emphasis added.]
* * * *

Honda * * * argues that [the EPCA] prevents Paduano from pursuing his * * * claims. That provision states in pertinent part,

When a requirement under [the EPCA] is in effect, a State or a political subdivision of a State may adopt or enforce a law or regulation on disclosure of fuel economy or fuel operating costs for an automobile covered by [the EPCA] only if the law or regulation is identical to that requirement.

* * * Honda goes on to assert that "Paduano's deceptive advertising and misrepresentation claims would impose *non* identical disclosure requirements."

Contrary to Honda's characterization * * * , Paduano's claims are based on statements Honda made in its advertising brochure to the effect that one may drive a Civic Hybrid in the same manner as one would a conventional car, and need not do anything "special," in order to achieve the beneficial fuel economy of the EPA estimates. * * * Paduano is challenging * * * Honda's * * * commentary in which it alludes to those estimates in a manner that may give consumers the misimpression that they will be able to achieve mileage close to the EPA estimates while driving a Honda hybrid in the same manner as they would a conventional vehicle. Paduano does not seek to require Honda to provide "additional alleged facts" regarding the Civic Hybrid's fuel economy, as Honda suggests, but rather, seeks to prevent Honda from making misleading claims about how easy it is to achieve better fuel economy. Contrary to Honda's assertions, if Paduano were to prevail on his claims, Honda would not have to do anything differently with regard to its disclosure of the EPA mileage estimates.
* * * *

* * * Allowing states to regulate false advertising and unfair business practices may further the goals of the EPCA, and we reject Honda's claim.

DECISION AND REMEDY *The state intermediate appellate court concluded that federal law did not preempt Paduano's claims concerning Honda's advertising. The court reversed the lower court's judgment and remanded the case.*

THE ETHICAL DIMENSION *Suppose that the defendant automaker had opposed this action solely to avoid paying damages to the purchaser of a car that had proved to be a "lemon." Would this have been unethical? Explain.*

THE LEGAL ENVIRONMENT DIMENSION *What does the interpretation of the law in this case suggest to businesspersons who sell products labeled with statements mandated by federal or state law?*

Food Labeling

Because the quality and safety of food are so important to consumers, several statutes deal specifically with food labeling. The Fair Packaging and Labeling Act requires that food product labels identify (1) the product, (2) the net quantity of the contents (and, if the number of servings is stated, the size of a serving), (3) the manufacturer, and (4) the packager or distributor. The act includes additional requirements concerning descriptions on packages, savings claims, components of nonfood products, and standards for the partial filling of packages.

NUTRITIONAL CONTENT OF FOOD PRODUCTS Food products must bear labels detailing the nutritional content, including the number of calories and the amounts of various nutrients that the food contains. The Nutrition Labeling and Education Act[12] requires standard nutrition facts (including the amount and type of fat that the food contains) to be listed on food labels and regulates the use of such terms as *fresh* and *low fat*.

The U.S. Food and Drug Administration (FDA) and the U.S. Department of Agriculture (USDA) are the

---

12. 21 U.S.C. Section 343.1.

primary agencies that issue regulations on food labeling. These rules are published in the *Federal Register* and updated annually. For instance, labels on fresh meats, vegetables, and fruits must indicate where the food originated so that consumers can know whether their food was imported.

CALORIC CONTENT OF RESTAURANT FOODS The health-care reforms enacted by Congress in 2010 included provisions aimed at combating obesity in the United States. All restaurant chains with twenty or more locations are required to post the caloric content of the foods on their menus so that customers will know how many calories they are eating.[13] Foods offered through vending machines must also be labeled so that their caloric content is visible to would-be purchasers.

In addition, restaurants must post guidelines on the number of calories that an average person requires daily so that customers can determine what portion of a day's calories a particular food will provide. The hope is that consumers, armed with this information, will consider the number of calories when they make their food choices. The federal law on menu labeling supersedes all state and local laws already in existence.

SECTION 3
SALES

A number of statutes protect consumers by requiring the disclosure of certain terms in sales transactions and providing rules governing unsolicited merchandise and home or door-to-door sales, mail-order sales, and referral sales. The FTC has regulatory authority in this area, as do other federal agencies.

The Federal Reserve Board of Governors, for instance, has issued a regulation that governs credit provisions associated with sales contracts (Regulation Z[14]—discussed later in this chapter). Many states and the FTC have **"cooling-off" laws** that permit the buyers of goods sold door to door to cancel their contracts within three business days. The FTC rule further requires that consumers be notified in Spanish of this right if the oral negotiations for the sale were in that language.

Telephone and Mail-Order Sales

The FTC Mail or Telephone Order Merchandise Rule amended the FTC Mail-Order Rule.[15] The rule provides specific protections for consumers who purchase goods over the phone, through the mail, by fax, or via the Internet (whether by smartphone, tablet device, or personal computer). Merchants must ship orders within the time promised in their advertisements and notify consumers when orders cannot be shipped on time. The rule also requires merchants to issue a refund within a specified period of time when a consumer cancels an order.

In addition, under the Postal Reorganization Act,[16] a consumer who receives *unsolicited* merchandise sent by U.S. mail can keep it, throw it away, or dispose of it in any manner that she or he sees fit. The recipient will not be obligated to the sender.

Online Sales

The FTC and other federal agencies have brought numerous enforcement actions against those who perpetrate online fraud (see the discussion of wire fraud in Chapter 10). Nonetheless, protecting consumers from fraudulent and deceptive sales practices conducted via the Internet has proved to be a challenging task.

Faced with economic recession, job losses, mounting debt, and dwindling savings, many consumers are looking for any source of income. The number of consumers who have fallen prey to Internet fraud has grown in recent years. Complaints to the FTC about sales of fraudulent business opportunities, such as work-at-home offers and real estate systems, nearly tripled from 2008 to 2013. About 10 percent of U.S. adults claim to have been victims of online fraud.

SECTION 4
PROTECTION OF HEALTH AND SAFETY

Labeling and packaging laws (discussed earlier) promote consumer health and safety. Nevertheless, there is a significant distinction between regulating the information dispensed about a product and regulating the actual content of the product. The classic example is tobacco products. Tobacco companies

---

13. See Section 4205 of the Patient Protection and Affordable Care Act, Pub. L. No. 111-148, 124 Stat. 119 (March 23, 2010).

14. 12 C.F.R. Sections 226.1–226.30.

15. 16 C.F.R. Sections 435.1–435.2.

16. 39 U.S.C. Section 3009.

must label their products to warn consumers about the health hazards associated with their use, but the sale of tobacco products has not been subjected to significant restrictions. Here, we examine various laws that regulate the actual products made available to consumers.

The Federal Food, Drug, and Cosmetic Act

The most important federal legislation regulating food and drugs is the Federal Food, Drug, and Cosmetic Act (FDCA).[17] The act protects consumers against adulterated (contaminated) and misbranded foods and drugs.

FOOD SAFETY The FDCA establishes food standards, specifies safe levels of potentially hazardous food additives, and provides classifications of foods and food advertising. Most of these statutory requirements are monitored and enforced by the Food and Drug Administration (FDA).

Tainted Foods. In recent years, many people in the United States have contracted food poisoning from eating foods that were contaminated—often with salmonella or E. coli bacteria. There have been high-profile recalls of peanut products, eggs, and beef. Tainted cantaloupes killed thirty-three people.

Modernization Legislation. In 2011, Congress enacted the Food Safety Modernization Act (FSMA)[18] to provide greater government control over the U.S. food safety system. The FSMA gives the FDA authority to directly recall any food products that it suspects are tainted (rather than relying on the producers to recall items).

The act requires any person who manufactures, processes, packs, distributes, receives, holds, or imports food products to pay a fee and register with the U.S. Department of Health and Human Services. (There are some exceptions for small farmers.) The act also requires owners and operators of facilities to analyze and identify food safety hazards, implement preventive controls, monitor effectiveness, and take corrective actions.

The FSMA also places more restrictions on importers of food and requires them to verify that imported

foods meet U.S. safety standards. In 2013, the FDA proposed new rules to implement the FSMA, but these rules have not been finalized. Given that some members of the food industry have expressed concerns about aspects of the proposed rules, it may be several years before final rules implementing the FSMA are in place.

DRUGS The FDA also has the responsibility of ensuring that drugs are safe and effective before they are marketed to the public. Because the FDA must ensure the safety of new medications, there is always a delay before drugs are available to the public and this sometimes leads to controversy.

▶ **Case in Point 44.4** A group of citizens petitioned the FDA to allow everyone access to Plan B—the morning-after birth control pill—without a prescription. The FDA denied the petition and continued to require women under the age of seventeen to obtain a prescription. The group appealed to a federal district court, claiming that the prescription requirement can delay access to the pill. The pill should be taken as soon as possible after sexual intercourse, preferably within twenty-four hours. The court ruled in favor of the plaintiffs and ordered the FDA to make the morning-after pill available to people of any age without a prescription. Shortly after the decision in 2013, the FDA changed its policy to allow anyone to obtain the morning after pill without a prescription.[19] ◀

The Consumer Product Safety Act

In 1972, the Consumer Product Safety Act[20] created the first comprehensive scheme of regulation over matters of consumer safety. The act also established the Consumer Product Safety Commission (CPSC), which has far-reaching authority over consumer safety.

THE CPSC'S AUTHORITY The CPSC conducts research on the safety of individual consumer products and maintains a clearinghouse on the risks associated with various products. The Consumer Product Safety Act authorizes the CPSC to do the following:

1. Set safety standards for consumer products.
2. Ban the manufacture and sale of any product that the commission believes poses an "unreasonable risk" to consumers. (Products banned by the CPSC have included various types of fireworks, cribs,

17. 21 U.S.C. Sections 301–393.
18. Pub. L. No. 111-353, 124 Stat. 3885 (January 4, 2011). This statute affected numerous parts of Title 21 of the U.S.C.

19. *Tummino v. Hamburg,* ___ F.Supp.2d ___, 2013 WL 1348656 (E.D.N.Y. 2013). An appeal was filed in this case.
20. 15 U.S.C. Sections 2051–2083.

and toys, as well as many products containing asbestos or vinyl chloride.)

3. Remove from the market any products it believes to be imminently hazardous. The CPSC frequently works in conjunction with manufacturers to voluntarily recall defective products from stores.
   ▶ **Example 44.5** In cooperation with the CPSC, Kolcraft Enterprises, Inc., recalled one million infant play yards because of a defective latch that could cause a rail to fall, posing a risk to children. ◀
4. Require manufacturers to report on any products already sold or intended for sale if the products have proved to be hazardous.
5. Administer other product-safety legislation, including the Child Protection and Toy Safety Act of 1969[21] and the Federal Hazardous Substances Act of 1960.[22]

NOTIFICATION REQUIREMENTS The Consumer Product Safety Act requires the distributors of consumer products to notify the CPSC immediately if they receive information that a product "contains a defect which . . . creates a substantial risk to the public" or "an unreasonable risk of serious injury or death."
  ▶ **Case in Point 44.6** A company that sold juicers received twenty-three letters from customers complaining that during operation the juicer had suddenly exploded, sending pieces of glass and razor-sharp metal across the room. The government sued the company because it had waited more than six months before notifying the CPSC. The court held that the company had violated that law and ordered it to pay damages.[23] ◀

Health-Care Reforms

In 2010, the health-care reforms enacted by Congress went into effect and gave Americans new rights and benefits with regard to health care.[24] By 2014, these laws prohibited certain insurance company practices, such as denying coverage for preexisting conditions.

EXPANDED COVERAGE FOR CHILDREN AND SENIORS The reforms expanded access to health care by enabling

more children to obtain health-insurance coverage. In addition, the reforms allowed young adults (under age twenty-six) to remain on their parents' health insurance. The act also ended lifetime and most annual limits on care, and gave patients access to recommended preventive services (such as cancer screening, vaccinations, and well-baby checks) without cost. Medicare recipients now receive a 50 percent discount on name-brand drugs, and the gap in Medicare's prescription drug coverage will be eliminated by 2020.

CONTROLLING COSTS OF HEALTH INSURANCE In an attempt to control the rising costs of health insurance, the law places restrictions on insurance companies. Insurance companies must spend at least 85 percent of all premium dollars collected from large employers (80 percent of the premiums collected from individuals and small employers) on benefits and quality improvement. If insurance companies do not meet these goals, they must provide rebates to consumers. Additionally, states can require insurance companies to justify their premium increases to be eligible to participate in the new health-insurance exchanges.

SECTION 5
CREDIT PROTECTION

Credit protection is one of the more important aspects of consumer protection legislation. Nearly 80 percent of U.S. consumers have credit cards, and most carry a balance on these cards—a total of about $2.5 trillion of debt nationwide. The Consumer Financial Protection Bureau (CFPB—see Chapter 43) is the agency dedicated to overseeing the practices of banks, mortgage lenders, and credit-card companies.[25]

The Truth-in-Lending Act

A key statute regulating the credit and credit-card industries is the Truth-in-Lending Act (TILA), the name commonly given to Title I of the Consumer Credit Protection Act, as amended.[26] The TILA is basically a *disclosure law*. It is administered by the Federal Reserve Board and requires sellers and lenders to disclose credit terms or loan terms so that individuals can shop around for the best financing arrangements.

21. 15 U.S.C. Section 1262(e).
22. 15 U.S.C. Sections 1261–1273.
23. *United States v. Mirama Enterprises, Inc.*, 185 F.Supp.2d 1148 (S.D.Cal. 2002).
24. Patient Protection and Affordable Health Care Act of 2010, Pub. L. No.111-148, 124 Stat. 119 (March 23, 2010); and the Health Care and Education Reconciliation Act of 2010, Pub. L. No. 111-152, 124 Stat. 1029 (March 30, 2010).

25. Title 10 of the Restoring American Financial Stability Act of 2010, S.B. 3217, April 15, 2010.
26. 15 U.S.C. Sections 1601–1693r.

TILA requirements apply only to persons who, in the ordinary course of business, lend funds, sell on credit, or arrange for the extension of credit. Thus, sales or loans made between two consumers do not come under the protection of the act. Additionally, this law protects only debtors who are natural persons (as opposed to the artificial "person" of a corporation). It does not extend to other legal entities.

DISCLOSURE REQUIREMENTS The disclosure requirements are contained in **Regulation Z,** issued by the Federal Reserve Board of Governors. If the contracting parties are subject to the TILA, the requirements of Regulation Z apply to any transaction involving an installment sales contract that calls for payment to be made in more than four installments.

Transactions subject to Regulation Z typically include installment loans, retail and installment sales, car loans, home-improvement loans, and certain real estate loans if the amount of financing is less than $25,000.

Under the provisions of the TILA, all of the terms of a credit instrument must be clearly and conspicuously disclosed. A lender must disclose the annual percentage rate (APR), finance charge, amount financed, and total payments (the sum of the amount loaned, plus any fees, finance charges, and interest at the end of the loan). The TILA provides for contract rescission (cancellation) if a creditor fails to follow the *exact* procedures required by the act.[27]

EQUAL CREDIT OPPORTUNITY Congress enacted the Equal Credit Opportunity Act (ECOA)[28] as an amendment to the TILA. The ECOA prohibits the denial of credit solely on the basis of race, religion, national origin, color, gender, marital status, or age. The act also prohibits credit discrimination on the basis of whether an individual receives certain forms of income, such as public-assistance benefits.

Under the ECOA, a creditor may not require a cosigner on a credit instrument if the applicant qualifies under the creditor's standards of creditworthiness for the amount and terms of the credit request. ▶ **Case in Point 44.7** Tonja, an African American, applied for financing with a used-car dealer. The dealer looked at Tonja's credit report and, without submitting the application to the lender, decided that she would not qualify.

Instead of informing Tonja that she did not qualify, the dealer told her that she needed a cosigner on the loan to purchase the car. She filed a complaint. A federal appellate court ruled that the dealer qualified as a creditor in this situation because the dealer unilaterally denied the credit. Thus, the dealer could be held liable under the ECOA.[29] ◀

CREDIT-CARD RULES The TILA also contains provisions regarding credit cards. One provision limits the liability of a cardholder to $50 per card for unauthorized charges made before the creditor is notified that the card has been lost. If a consumer receives an *unsolicited* credit card in the mail that is later stolen, the company that issued the card cannot charge the consumer for any unauthorized charges.

Another provision requires credit-card companies to disclose the balance computation method that is used to determine the outstanding balance and to state when finance charges begin to accrue. Other provisions set forth procedures for resolving billing disputes with the credit-card company. These procedures are used if, for example, a cardholder thinks that an error has occurred in billing or wishes to withhold payment for a faulty product purchased by credit card.

AMENDMENTS TO CREDIT-CARD RULES Amendments to the TILA's credit-card rules that became effective in 2010 added the following protections:

1. A company may not retroactively increase the interest rates on existing card balances unless the account is sixty days delinquent.
2. A company must provide forty-five days' advance notice to consumers before changing its credit-card terms.
3. Monthly bills must be sent to cardholders twenty-one days before the due date.
4. The interest rate charged on a customer's credit-card balance may not be increased except in specific situations, such as when a promotional rate ends.
5. A company may not charge over-limit fees except in specified situations.
6. When the customer has balances at different interest rates, payments in excess of the minimum amount due must be applied first to the balance with the highest rate (for instance, a higher interest rate is commonly charged for cash advances).

---

27. Note, however, that amendments to the TILA enacted in 1995 prevent borrowers from rescinding loans because of minor clerical errors in closing documents [15 U.S.C. Sections 1605, 1631, 1635, 1640, and 1641].
28. 15 U.S.C. Sections 1691–1691f.
29. *Treadway v. Gateway Chevrolet Oldsmobile, Inc.,* 362 F.3d 971 (7th Cir. 2004).

7. A company may not compute finance charges based on the previous billing cycle (a practice known as double-cycle billing, which hurts consumers because they are charged interest for the previous cycle even though they have paid the bill in full).

The Fair Credit Reporting Act

The Fair Credit Reporting Act (FCRA)[30] protects consumers against inaccurate credit reporting and requires that lenders and other creditors report correct, relevant, and up-to-date information. The act provides that consumer credit reporting agencies may issue credit reports to users only for specified purposes. Legitimate purposes include the extension of credit, the issuance of insurance policies, and in response to the consumer's request.

CONSUMER NOTIFICATION AND INACCURATE INFORMATION Any time a consumer is denied credit or insurance on the basis of her or his credit report, the consumer must be notified of that fact. The notice must include the name and address of the credit reporting agency that issued the report. The same notice must be sent to consumers who are charged more than others ordinarily would be for credit or insurance because of their credit reports.

Under the FCRA, consumers may request the source of any information used by the credit agency, as well as the identity of anyone who has received an agency's report. Consumers are also permitted to access the information about them contained in a credit reporting agency's files. If a consumer discovers that an agency's files contain inaccurate information, he or she should report the problem to the agency.

On the consumer's written (or electronic) request, the agency must conduct a systematic examination of its records. Any unverifiable or erroneous information must be deleted within a reasonable period of time.

REMEDIES FOR VIOLATIONS A credit reporting agency that fails to comply with the act is liable for actual damages, plus additional damages not to exceed $1,000 and attorneys' fees.[31] Creditors and other companies that use information from credit reporting agencies may also be liable for violations of the FCRA. The United States Supreme Court held that

an insurance company's failure to notify new customers that they were paying higher insurance rates as a result of their credit scores was a *willful* violation of the FCRA.[32]

▶ **Case in Point 44.8** Branch Banking & Trust Company of Virginia (BB&T) gave Rex Saunders an auto loan but failed to give him a payment coupon book and refused his attempts to make payments on the loan. In fact, BB&T told him that it had not extended a loan to him. Eventually, BB&T discovered its mistake and demanded full payment, plus interest and penalties.

When payment was not immediately forthcoming, BB&T declared that Saunders was in default. It then repossessed the car and forwarded adverse credit information about Saunders to credit reporting agencies, without noting that Saunders disputed the information. Saunders filed a lawsuit alleging violations of the FCRA and was awarded $80,000 in punitive damages. An appellate court found that the damages award was reasonable, given BB&T's willful violation.[33] ◀

The Fair and Accurate Credit Transactions Act

Congress passed the Fair and Accurate Credit Transactions (FACT) Act in an effort to combat identity theft (discussed in Chapter 10).[34] The act established a national fraud alert system. Consumers who suspect that they have been or may be victimized by identity theft can place an alert on their credit files. When a consumer establishes that identify theft has occurred, the credit reporting agency must stop reporting allegedly fraudulent account information.

The act also requires the major credit reporting agencies to provide consumers with free copies of their own credit reports every twelve months. Another provision requires account numbers on credit-card receipts to be truncated (shortened). Merchants, employees, or others who may have access to the receipts no longer have the consumers' names and full credit-card numbers. Financial institutions must work with the FTC to identify "red flag" indicators of identity theft and to develop rules for the disposal of sensitive credit information.

30. 15 U.S.C. Sections 1681–1681t.
31. 15 U.S.C. Section 1681n.

32. *Safeco Insurance. Co. of America v. Burr,* 551 U.S. 47, 127 S.Ct. 2201, 167 L.Ed.2d 1045 (2007).
33. *Saunders v. Branch Banking & Trust Co. of Virginia,* 526 F.3d 142 (4th Cir. 2008).
34. Pub. L. No. 108-159, 117 Stat. 1952 (December 4, 2003).

The Fair Debt Collection Practices Act

The Fair Debt Collection Practices Act (FDCPA)[35] attempts to curb perceived abuses by collection agencies. The act applies only to specialized debt-collection agencies and attorneys who regularly attempt to collect debts on behalf of someone else, usually for a percentage of the amount owed. Creditors attempting to collect debts are not covered by the act unless, by misrepresenting themselves, they cause debtors to believe they are collection agencies. A debt collector who fails to comply with the act is liable for actual damages, plus additional damages not to exceed $1,000[36] and attorneys' fees.

PROHIBITED DEBT-COLLECTION TACTICS Under the FDCPA, a collection agency may not do any of the following:

1. Contact the debtor at the debtor's place of employment if the debtor's employer objects.
2. Contact the debtor at inconvenient or unusual times (for example, at three o'clock in the morning) or at any time, if the debtor is being represented by an attorney.
3. Contact third parties other than the debtor's parents, spouse, or financial adviser about payment of a debt unless a court authorizes such action.
4. Harass or intimidate the debtor (by using abusive language or threatening violence, for example) or make false or misleading statements (such as posing as a police officer).
5. Communicate with the debtor at any time after receiving notice that the debtor is refusing to pay the debt, except to advise the debtor of further action to be taken by the collection agency.

NOTIFICATION AND BONA FIDE ERRORS The FDCPA also requires a collection agency to include a **validation notice** whenever it initially contacts a debtor for payment of a debt or within five days of that initial contact. The notice must state that the debtor has thirty days in which to dispute the debt and to request a written verification of the debt from the collection agency.

Debt collectors who violate the act are exempt from liability if they can show that the violation was not intentional and "resulted from a bona fide error notwithstanding the maintenance of procedures reasonably adapted to avoid any such error." The "bona fide error" defense typically has been applied to mistakes of fact or clerical errors. Should the defense also apply to mistakes of law? In other words, if a debt collector violates the act because of a mistaken interpretation of the legal requirements of the FDCPA, can the debt collector avoid liability under the act? That was the issue in the following case.

---

35. 15 U.S.C. Section 1692.
36. According to the U.S. Court of Appeals for the Sixth Circuit, the $1,000 limit on damages applies to each lawsuit, not to each violation. See *Wright v. Finance Service of Norwalk, Inc.*, 22 F.3d 647 (6th Cir. 1994).

CASE ANALYSIS

Case 44.3   Jerman v. Carlisle, McNellie, Rini, Kramer & Ulrich, LPA

Supreme Court of the United States, 559 U.S. 573, 130 S.Ct. 1605, 176 L.Ed.2d 519 (2010).

IN THE LANGUAGE OF THE COURT
Justice *SOTOMAYOR* delivered the opinion of the Court.
* * * *

Respondents in this case are a law firm, Carlisle, McNellie, Rini, Kramer & Ulrich, L.P.A., [Legal Professional Association], and one of its attorneys, Adrienne S. Foster (collectively Carlisle). In April 2006, Carlisle filed a complaint in Ohio state court on behalf of a client, Countrywide Home Loans, Inc. Carlisle sought foreclosure of a mortgage held by Countrywide in real property owned by petitioner Karen L. Jerman. The complaint included a "Notice," later served on Jerman, stating that the mortgage debt would be assumed to be valid unless Jerman disputed it in writing. Jerman's lawyer sent a letter disputing the debt, and Carlisle sought verification from Countrywide. When Countrywide acknowledged that Jerman had, in fact, already paid the debt in full, Carlisle withdrew the foreclosure lawsuit.

CASE 44.3 CONTINUES ➡

CASE 44.3 CONTINUED

Jerman then filed her own lawsuit seeking * * * damages under the FDCPA [Fair Debt Collection Practices Act], contending that Carlisle violated [the act] by stating that her debt would be assumed valid unless she disputed it in writing. While acknowledging a division of authority on the question, the District Court held that Carlisle had violated [the act] by requiring Jerman to dispute the debt in writing. The court ultimately granted summary judgment to Carlisle, however, concluding that Section 1692k(c) [of the FDCPA] shielded it from liability because the violation was not intentional, resulted from a bona fide error, and occurred despite the maintenance of procedures reasonably adapted to avoid any such error. The Court of Appeals for the Sixth Circuit affirmed. Acknowledging that the Courts of Appeals are divided regarding the scope of the bona fide error defense, and that the "majority view is that the defense is available for clerical and factual errors only," the Sixth Circuit nonetheless held that Section 1692k(c) extends to "mistakes of law."

* * * *

The parties disagree about whether a "violation" resulting from a debt collector's misinterpretation of the legal requirements of the FDCPA can ever be "not intentional" under 1692k(c). Jerman contends that when a debt collector intentionally commits the act giving rise to the violation (here, sending a notice that included the "in writing" language), a misunderstanding about what the Act requires cannot render the violation "not intentional," given the general rule that mistake or ignorance of law is no defense. Carlisle and the dissent, in contrast, argue that nothing in the statutory text excludes legal errors from the category of "bona

fide error[s]" covered by 1692k(c) and note that the Act refers not to an unintentional "act" but rather an unintentional "violation." The latter term, they contend, evinces [makes clear] Congress' intent to impose liability only when a party knows its conduct is unlawful. Carlisle urges us, therefore, to read 1692k(c) to encompass "all types of error," including mistakes of law.

We decline to adopt the expansive reading of Section 1692k(c) that Carlisle proposes. *We have long recognized the "common maxim, familiar to all minds, that ignorance of the law will not excuse any person, either civilly or criminally." Our law is therefore no stranger to the possibility that an act may be "intentional" for purposes of civil liability, even if the actor lacked actual knowledge that her conduct violated the law.* [Emphasis added.]

* * * When Congress has intended to provide a mistake-of-law defense to civil liability, it has often done so more explicitly than here. In particular, the FTC [Federal Trade Commission] Act's administrative-penalty provisions—which * * * Congress expressly incorporated into the FDCPA—apply only when a debt collector acts with "actual knowledge or knowledge fairly implied on the basis of objective circumstances" that its action was "prohibited by [the FDCPA]." Given the absence of similar language in Section 1692k(c), it is a fair inference that Congress chose to permit injured consumers to recover actual damages, costs, fees, and modest statutory damages for "intentional" conduct, including violations resulting from mistaken interpretation of the FDCPA, while reserving the more onerous penalties of the FTC Act for debt collectors whose intentional actions also reflected "knowledge fairly implied on

the basis of objective circumstances" that the conduct was prohibited.

* * * *

We draw additional support for the conclusion that bona fide errors in Section 1692k(c) do not include mistaken interpretations of the FDCPA from the requirement that a debt collector maintain "procedures reasonably adapted to avoid any such error." The dictionary defines "procedure" as "a series of steps followed in a regular orderly definite way." In that light, the statutory phrase is more naturally read to apply to processes that have mechanical or other such "regular orderly" steps to avoid mistakes—for instance, the kind of internal controls a debt collector might adopt to ensure its employees do not communicate with consumers at the wrong time of day or make false representations as to the amount of a debt. * * * We do not dispute that some entities may maintain procedures to avoid legal errors. But legal reasoning is not a mechanical or strictly linear process. For this reason, we find * * * that the broad statutory requirement of procedures reasonably designed to avoid "any" bona fide error indicates that the relevant procedures are ones that help to avoid errors like clerical or factual mistakes. Such procedures are more likely to avoid error than those applicable to legal reasoning, particularly in the context of a comprehensive and complex federal statute such as the FDCPA that imposes open-ended prohibitions on, *inter alia* [among other things], "false, deceptive," or "unfair" practices.

* * * *

For the reasons discussed above, the judgment of the United States Court of Appeals for the Sixth Circuit is reversed, and the case is remanded for further proceedings consistent with this opinion.

LEGAL REASONING QUESTIONS

1. One of the concerns raised by Carlisle was that if attorneys could be held liable for their reasonable misinterpretations of the FDCPA's requirements, there would be a "flood of lawsuits" against creditors' attorneys by plaintiffs seeking damages and attorneys' fees. Should this concern have any bearing on the outcome of this case? Why or why not?

CASE 44.3 CONTINUED

2. Jerman's attorneys contended that if the Court agreed with Carlisle's argument (that the bona fide error defense included errors in legal interpretation), ethical debt collectors would be placed at a disadvantage. Why would this be?

3. Suppose that instead of serving notice to Jerman in writing, Carlisle had simply told her that her debt would be assumed to be valid unless she disputed it in writing. Would the result have been different? Explain.

4. How might the ruling in this case affect other collection agencies?

Reviewing: Consumer Law

Leota Sage saw a local motorcycle dealer's newspaper advertisement offering a MetroRider EZ electric scooter for $1,699. When she went to the dealership, however, she learned that the EZ model had been sold out. The salesperson told Sage that he still had the higher-end MetroRider FX model in stock for $2,199 and would sell her one for $1,999. Sage was disappointed but decided to purchase the FX model. When Sage said that she wished to purchase the scooter on credit, she was directed to the dealer's credit department. As she filled out the credit forms, the clerk told Sage, who is an Asian American, that she would need a cosigner to obtain a loan. Sage could not understand why she would need a cosigner and asked to speak to the store manager. The manager apologized, told her that the clerk was mistaken, and said that he would "speak to" the clerk about that. The manager completed Sage's credit application, and Sage then rode the scooter home. Seven months later, Sage received a letter from the manufacturer informing her that a flaw had been discovered in the scooter's braking system and that the model had been recalled. Using the information presented in the chapter, answer the following questions.

1. Did the dealer engage in deceptive advertising? Why or why not?

2. Suppose that Sage had ordered the scooter through the dealer's Web site but the dealer was unable to deliver it by the date promised. What would the FTC have required the merchant to do in that situation?

3. Assuming that the clerk required a cosigner based on Sage's race or gender, what act prohibits such credit discrimination?

4. What organization has the authority to ban the sale of scooters based on safety concerns?

DEBATE THIS . . . *Laws against bait-and-switch advertising should be abolished because no consumer is ever forced to buy anything.*

Terms and Concepts

bait-and-switch advertising 862	"cooling-off" laws 868	multiple product order 865
cease-and-desist order 865	counteradvertising 865	Regulation Z 871
consumer law 861	deceptive advertising 861	validation notice 873

ExamPrep

Issue Spotters

1. United Pharmaceuticals, Inc., believes that it has developed a new drug that will be effective in the treatment of patients with AIDS. The drug has had only limited testing, but United wants to make the drug widely available as soon as possible. To market the drug, what must United prove to the U.S. Food and Drug Administration? **(See page 869.)**

2. Gert buys a notebook computer from EZ Electronics. She pays for it with her credit card. When the computer proves defective, she asks EZ to repair or replace it, but EZ refuses. What can Gert do? **(See page 871.)**

• Check your answers to the Issue Spotters against the answers provided in Appendix E at the end of this text.

Before the Test

Go to **www.cengagebrain.com**, enter the ISBN 9781285185248, and click on "Find" to locate this textbook's Web site. Then, click on "Access Now" under "Study Tools," and select Chapter 44 at the top. There, you will find a Practice Quiz that you can take to assess your mastery of the concepts in this chapter, as well as Flashcards and a Glossary of important terms.

Business Scenarios

44–1. Unsolicited Merchandise. Andrew, a resident of California, received an advertising circular in the U.S. mail announcing a new line of regional cookbooks distributed by the Every-Kind Cookbook Co. Andrew didn't want any books and threw the circular away. Two days later, Andrew received in the mail an introductory cookbook entitled *Lower Mongolian Regional Cookbook,* as announced in the circular, on a "trial basis" from Every-Kind. Andrew was not interested but did not go to the trouble to return the cookbook. Every-Kind demanded payment of $20.95 for the *Lower Mongolian Regional Cookbook.* Discuss whether Andrew can be required to pay for the book. **(See page 868.)**

44–2. Credit-Card Rules. Maria Ochoa receives two new credit cards on May 1. She has solicited one of them from Midtown Department Store, and the other arrives unsolicited from High-Flying Airlines. During the month of May, Ochoa makes numerous credit-card purchases from Midtown Department Store, but she does not use the High-Flying Airlines card. On May 31, a burglar breaks into Ochoa's home and steals both credit cards, along with other items. Ochoa notifies the Midtown Department Store of the theft on June 2, but she fails to notify High-Flying Airlines. Using the Midtown credit card, the burglar makes a $500 purchase on June 1 and a $200 purchase on June 3. The burglar then charges a vacation flight on the High-Flying Airlines card for $1,000 on June 5. Ochoa receives the bills for these charges and refuses to pay them. Discuss Ochoa's liability for the charges. **(See page 871.)**

Business Case Problems

44–3. Spotlight on McDonald's—Food Labeling. McDonald's Corp.'s Happy Meal® meal selection consists of an entrée, a small order of french fries, a small drink, and a toy. In the early 1990s, McDonald's began to aim its Happy Meal marketing at children aged one to three. In 1995, McDonald's began making nutritional information for its food products available in documents known as "McDonald's Nutrition Facts." Each document lists the food items that the restaurant serves and provides a nutritional breakdown, but the Happy Meal is not included. Marc Cohen filed a suit in an Illinois state court, alleging, among other things, that McDonald's had violated a state law prohibiting consumer fraud and deceptive business practices by failing to adhere to the Nutrition Labeling and Education Act (NLEA) of 1990. The NLEA sets out different requirements for products specifically intended for children under the age of four—generally, the products' labels cannot declare the percent of daily value of nutritional components. Would this requirement be readily understood by a consumer who is not familiar with nutritional standards? Why or why not? Should a state court impose such regulations? Explain. [*Cohen v. McDonald's Corp.*, 347 Ill.App.3d 627, 808 N.E.2d 1, 283 Ill.Dec. 451 (1 Dist. 2004)] **(See page 867.)**

44–4. Debt Collection. 55th Management Corp. in New York City owns residential property that it leases to various tenants. In June 2000, claiming that one of the tenants, Leslie Goldman, owed more than $13,000 in back rent, 55th retained Jeffrey Cohen, an attorney, to initiate nonpayment proceedings. Cohen filed a petition in a New York state court against Goldman, seeking recovery of the unpaid rent and at least $3,000 in attorneys' fees. After receiving notice of the petition, Goldman filed a suit in a federal district court against Cohen. Goldman contended that the notice of the petition constituted an initial contact that, under the Fair Debt Collection Practices Act (FDCPA), required a validation notice. Because Cohen did not give Goldman a validation notice at the time or within five days of the notice of the petition, Goldman argued that Cohen was in violation of the FDCPA. Should the filing of a suit in a state court be considered "communication," requiring a debt collector to provide a validation notice under the FDCPA? Why or why not? [*Goldman v. Cohen,* 445 F.3d 152 (2d Cir. 2006)] **(See page 873.)**

44–5. Food Labeling. The Nutrition Labeling and Education Act (NLEA) requires packaged food to have a "Nutrition Facts" panel that sets out "nutrition information," including "the total number of calories" per serving. Before the 2010 health-care reforms enacted provisions on menu labeling (see page 868), restaurants were exempt from this requirement. The NLEA also regulated nutritional content claims, such as "low sodium," that a purveyor might choose to add to a label. The NLEA permitted a state or city to require restaurants to disclose nutrition information about the food they serve, but expressly preempted state or local attempts to regulate nutritional content claims. New York City Health Code Section 81.50 requires 10 percent of the restaurants in the city, including McDonald's, Burger King, and KFC, to post calorie content information on their menus. The New York State Restaurant Association (NYSRA) filed a suit in a federal district court, contending that the NLEA preempts Section 81.50. (Under the U.S. Constitution, state or local laws that conflict with federal laws are preempted.) Was the NYSRA correct? Explain. *[New York State Restaurant Association v. New York City Board of Health*, 556 F.3d 114 (2d Cir. 2009)] **(See page 867.)**

44–6. Deceptive Advertising. Brian Cleary and Rita Burke filed a suit against cigarette maker Philip Morris USA, Inc., seeking class-action status for a claim of deceptive advertising. Cleary and Burke claimed that "light" cigarettes, such as Marlboro Lights, were advertised as safer than regular cigarettes, even though the health effects are the same. They contended that the tobacco companies concealed the true nature of light cigarettes. Philip Morris correctly claimed that it was authorized by the government to advertise cigarettes, including light cigarettes. Assuming that is true, should the plaintiffs still be able to bring a deceptive advertising claim against the tobacco company? Why or why not? *[Cleary v. Philip Morris USA, Inc.*, 683 F.Supp.2d 730 (N.D.Ill. 2010)] **(See page 861.)**

**44–7. BUSINESS CASE PROBLEM
WITH SAMPLE ANSWER: Fair Debt-Collection Practices.**

 Bank of America hired Atlantic Resource Management, LLC, to collect a debt from Michael E. Engler. Atlantic called Engler's employer and asked his supervisor about the company's policy concerning the execution of warrants. It then told the supervisor that, to stop the process, Engler needed to call Atlantic

about "Case Number 37291 NY0969" during the first three hours of his next shift. When Engler's supervisor told him about the call, Engler feared that he might be arrested, and he experienced discomfort, embarrassment, and emotional distress at work. Can Engler recover under the Fair Debt Collection Practices Act? Why or why not? *[Engler v. Atlantic Resource Management, LLC*, 2012 WL 464728 (W.D.N.Y. 2012)] **(See page 873.)**

- For a sample answer to Problem 44–7, go to Appendix F at the end of this text.

44–8. A QUESTION OF ETHICS: Fair Debt-Collection Practices.

 Barry Sussman graduated from law school, but also served time in prison for attempting to collect debts by posing as an FBI agent. He theorized that if a debt-collection business collected only debts that it owned as a result of buying checks written on accounts with insufficient funds (NSF checks), it would not be subject to the Federal Debt Collection Practices Act (FDCPA). Sussman formed Check Investors, Inc., to act on his theory. Check Investors bought more than 2.2 million NSF checks, with an estimated face value of about $348 million, for pennies on the dollar. Check Investors added a fee of $125 or $130 (more than the legal limit in most states) to the face amount of each check and aggressively pursued its drawer to collect. The firm's employees were told to accuse drawers of being criminals and to threaten them with arrest and prosecution. The threats were false. Check Investors never took steps to initiate a prosecution. The employees contacted the drawers' family members and used "saturation phoning"—phoning a drawer numerous times in a short period. They used abusive language, referring to drawers as "deadbeats," "retards," "thieves," and "idiots." Between January 2000 and January 2003, Check Investors netted more than $10.2 million from its efforts. [Federal Trade Commission v. Check Investors, Inc., 502 F.3d 159 (3d Cir. 2007)] **(See page 873.)**

(a) The Federal Trade Commission filed a suit in a federal district court against Check Investors and others, alleging, in part, violations of the FDCPA. Was Check Investors a "debt collector," collecting "debts," within the meaning of the FDCPA? If so, did its methods violate the FDCPA? Were its practices unethical? What might Check Investors argue in its defense? Discuss.

(b) Are "deadbeats" the primary beneficiaries of laws such as the FDCPA? If not, how would you characterize debtors who default on their obligations?

Legal Reasoning Group Activity

44–9. Consumer Protections. Many states have enacted laws that go even further than federal law to protect consumers. These laws vary tremendously from state to state.

(a) The first group will decide whether having different laws is fair to sellers who may be prohibited from engaging in a practice in one state that is legal in another.

(b) The second group will consider how these different laws might affect a business.

(c) A third group will determine whether is it fair that residents of one state have more protection than residents of another.

CHAPTER 45
ENVIRONMENTAL LAW

C oncern over the degradation of the environment
has increased over time in
response to the environmental effects
of population growth, urbanization, and
industrialization. Environmental protection is not without a price, however. For
many businesses, the costs of complying with environmental regulations are

high, and for some they may seem too
high. A constant tension exists between
the desire to increase profits and
productivity and the need to protect the
environment.

In this chapter, we discuss
environmental law, which consists
of all laws and regulations designed to
protect and preserve our environmental

resources. To a great extent, environmental law consists of statutes passed
by federal, state, or local governments
and regulations issued by administrative agencies. Before examining
statutory and regulatory environmental
laws, however, we look at the remedies
against environmental pollution that
are available under the common law.

SECTION 1
COMMON LAW ACTIONS

Common law remedies against environmental pollution originated centuries ago in England. Those
responsible for operations that created dirt, smoke,
noxious odors, noise, or toxic substances were sometimes held liable under common law theories of
nuisance or negligence. Today, injured individuals
continue to rely on the common law to obtain damages and injunctions against business polluters.

Nuisance

Under the common law doctrine of **nuisance,** persons may be held liable if they use their property
in a manner that unreasonably interferes with others' rights to use or enjoy their own property. Courts
typically balance the harm caused by the pollution
against the costs of stopping it.

Courts have often denied injunctive relief on the
ground that the hardships that would be imposed on
the polluter and on the community are greater than
the hardships suffered by the plaintiff. ▶ **Example
45.1** Hewitt's factory causes neighboring landowners to suffer from smoke, soot, and vibrations.
If the factory is the core of the local economy, a
court may leave it in operation and award mone-

tary damages to the injured parties. Damages can
include compensation for the decline in the value
of their property caused by Hewitt's operation. ◀

To obtain relief from pollution under the nuisance
doctrine, a property owner may have to identify a distinct harm separate from that affecting the general
public. This harm is referred to as a "private" nuisance.
Under the common law, individuals were denied
standing (access to the courts—see Chapter 2) unless
they suffered a harm distinct from that suffered by the
public at large. Some states still require this. A public
authority (such as a state's attorney general), however,
can sue to stop a "public" nuisance.

Negligence and Strict Liability

An injured party may sue a business polluter in tort
under the negligence and strict liability theories discussed in Chapters 6 and 7. A negligence action is
based on a business's alleged failure to use reasonable care toward a party whose injury was foreseeable
and was caused by the lack of reasonable care. For
instance, employees might sue an employer whose
failure to use proper pollution controls contaminated
the air, causing the employees to suffer respiratory illnesses. Lawsuits for personal injuries caused by exposure to a toxic substance, such as asbestos, radiation,
or hazardous waste, have given rise to a growing body
of tort law known as **toxic torts.**

Businesses that engage in ultrahazardous activities— such as the transportation of radioactive materials—are strictly liable for any injuries the activities cause. In a strict liability action, the injured party does not have to prove that the business failed to exercise reasonable care.

SECTION 2

FEDERAL, STATE, AND LOCAL REGULATIONS

All levels of government in the United States regulate some aspect of the environment. In this section, we look at some of the ways in which the federal, state, and local governments control business activities and land use in the interests of environmental preservation and protection.

State and Local Regulations

In addition to the federal regulations to be discussed shortly, many states have enacted laws to protect the environment. State laws may restrict a business's discharge of chemicals into the air or water or regulate its disposal of toxic wastes. States may also regulate the disposal or recycling of other wastes, including glass, metal, plastic containers, and paper. Additionally, states may restrict emissions from motor vehicles.

City, county, and other local governments also regulate some aspects of the environment. For instance, local zoning laws may be designed to inhibit or regulate the growth of cities and suburbs or to protect the natural environment. In the interest of safeguarding the environment, such laws may prohibit certain land uses. Even when zoning laws permit a business's proposed development, the plans may have to be altered to lessen the development's impact on the environment. In addition, cities and counties may impose rules regulating methods of waste removal, the appearance of buildings, the maximum noise level, and other aspects of the local environment.

State and local regulatory agencies also play a significant role in implementing federal environmental legislation. Typically, the federal government relies on state and local governments to enforce federal environmental statutes and regulations such as those regulating air quality.

Federal Regulations

Congress has passed a number of statutes to control the impact of human activities on the environment.

Exhibit 45–1 on the next page lists and summarizes the major federal environmental statutes discussed in this chapter. Most of these statutes are designed to address pollution in the air, water, or land. Some specifically regulate toxic chemicals, including pesticides, herbicides, and hazardous wastes.

ENVIRONMENTAL REGULATORY AGENCIES The primary federal agency regulating environmental law is the Environmental Protection Agency (EPA), which was created in 1970 to coordinate federal environmental responsibilities. Other federal agencies with authority for regulating specific environmental matters include the Department of the Interior, the Department of Defense, the Department of Labor, the Food and Drug Administration, and the Nuclear Regulatory Commission. All federal agencies must take environmental factors into consideration when making significant decisions. In addition, as mentioned, state and local agencies play an important role in enforcing federal environmental legislation.

Most federal environmental laws provide that citizens can sue to enforce environmental regulations if government agencies fail to do so—or to limit enforcement actions if agencies go to far in their actions. Typically, a threshold hurdle in such suits is meeting the requirements for standing to sue (see Chapter 2).

ENVIRONMENTAL IMPACT STATEMENTS The National Environmental Policy Act of 1969[1] requires that an **environmental impact statement (EIS)** be prepared for every major federal action that significantly affects the quality of the environment. An EIS must analyze the following:

1. The impact on the environment that the action will have.
2. Any adverse effects on the environment and alternative actions that might be taken.
3. Any irreversible effects the action might generate.

An action qualifies as "major" if it involves a substantial commitment of resources (monetary or otherwise). An action is "federal" if a federal agency has the power to control it. ▶ **Example 45.2** Development of a ski resort by a private developer on federal land may require an EIS. Construction or operation of a nuclear plant, which requires a federal permit, or creation of a dam as part of a federal project requires an EIS. ◀

If an agency decides that an EIS is unnecessary, it must issue a statement supporting this conclusion.

---

1. 42 U.S.C. Sections 4321–4370d.

EXHIBIT 45-1 Major Federal Environmental Statutes

Popular Name	Purpose	Statute Reference
Rivers and Harbors Appropriations Act (1899)	To prohibit ships and manufacturers from discharging and depositing refuse in navigable waterways.	33 U.S.C. Sections 401–418.
Federal Insecticide, Fungicide, and Rodenticide Act (1947)	To control the use of pesticides and herbicides.	7 U.S.C. Sections 136–136y.
Federal Water Pollution Control Act (1948)	To eliminate the discharge of pollutants from major sources into navigable waters.	33 U.S.C. Sections 1251–1387.
Clean Air Act (1963, 1970)	To control air pollution from mobile and stationary sources.	42 U.S.C. Sections 7401–7671q.
National Environmental Policy Act (1969)	To limit environmental harm from federal government activities.	42 U.S.C. Sections 4321–4370d.
Ocean Dumping Act (1972)	To prohibit the dumping of radiological, chemical, and biological warfare agents and high-level radioactive waste into the ocean.	16 U.S.C. Sections 1401–1445.
Endangered Species Act (1973)	To protect species that are threatened with extinction.	16 U.S.C. Sections 1531–1544.
Safe Drinking Water Act (1974)	To regulate pollutants in public drinking water systems.	42 U.S.C. Sections 300f–300j-25.
Resource Conservation and Recovery Act (1976)	To establish standards for hazardous waste disposal.	42 U.S.C. Sections 6901–6986.
Toxic Substances Control Act (1976)	To regulate toxic chemicals and chemical compounds.	15 U.S.C. Sections 2601–2692.
Comprehensive Environmental Response, Compensation, and Liability Act (1980)	To regulate the clean-up of hazardous waste–disposal sites.	42 U.S.C. Sections 9601–9675.
Oil Pollution Act (1990)	To establish liability for the clean-up of navigable waters after oil spills.	33 U.S.C. Sections 2701–2761.
Small Business Liability Relief and Brownfields Revitalization Act (2002)	To allow developers who comply with state voluntary clean-up programs to avoid federal liability for the properties that they decontaminate and develop.	42 U.S.C. Section 9628.

Private individuals, consumer interest groups, businesses, and others who believe that a federal agency's activities threaten the environment often use EISs as a means to challenge those activities.

SECTION 3
AIR POLLUTION

Federal involvement with air pollution goes back to the 1950s and 1960s, when Congress authorized funds for air-pollution research and enacted the Clean Air Act.[2] The Clean Air Act, as amended, provides the

---

2. 42 U.S.C. Sections 7401–7671q.

basis for issuing regulations to control multistate air pollution. It covers both mobile sources (such as automobiles and other vehicles) and stationary sources (such as electric utilities and industrial plants) of pollution.

Mobile Sources

Regulations governing air pollution from automobiles and other mobile sources specify pollution standards and establish time schedules for meeting the standards. The EPA periodically updates the pollution standards in light of new developments and data, usually reducing the amount of emissions allowed.

REDUCING EMISSIONS The Obama administration has announced a long-term goal of reducing emissions, including those from cars and sport utility vehicles, by 80 percent by 2050. In 2010, the administration ordered the EPA to develop national standards regulating fuel economy and emissions for medium- and heavy-duty trucks starting with 2014 models.

GREENHOUSE GASES A growing concern among many scientists and others around the world is that greenhouse gases, such as carbon dioxide (CO_2), are contributing to global warming and climate change. The Clean Air Act, as amended, however, does not specifically mention CO_2 emissions. Therefore, until 2009, the EPA did not regulate CO_2 emissions from motor vehicles.

▶ **Case in Point 45.3** Environmental groups and several states, including Massachusetts, sued the EPA in an effort to force the agency to regulate CO_2 emissions. When the case reached the United States Supreme Court, the EPA argued that the plaintiffs lacked standing because global warming has widespread effects and thus an individual plaintiff could not show the particularized harm required for standing. Furthermore, the agency maintained that it did not have authority under the Clean Air Act to address global climate change and regulate CO_2.

The Court, however, ruled that Massachusetts had standing because its coastline, including state-owned lands, faced an imminent threat from rising sea levels purportedly caused by global warming. The Court also held that the Clean Air Act's broad definition of "air pollutant" gives the EPA authority to regulate CO_2 and requires the EPA to regulate any air pollutants that might "endanger public health or welfare." Accordingly, the Court ordered the EPA to determine whether CO_2 was a pollutant that endangered public health.[3] ◀ The EPA later concluded that greenhouse gases, including CO_2 emissions, do constitute a public danger.

Stationary Sources

The Clean Air Act also authorizes the EPA to establish air-quality standards for stationary sources (such as manufacturing plants) but recognizes that the primary responsibility for implementing these standards rests with state and local governments. The standards are aimed at controlling hazardous air pollutants—

those likely to cause death or a serious, irreversible, or incapacitating condition, such as cancer or neurological or reproductive damage.

The EPA sets primary and secondary levels of ambient standards—that is, maximum permissible levels of certain pollutants—and the states formulate plans to achieve those standards. Different standards apply depending on whether the sources of pollution are located in clean areas or polluted areas and whether they are existing sources or major new sources.

HAZARDOUS AIR POLLUTANTS The Clean Air Act requires the EPA to list all hazardous air pollutants (HAPs) on a prioritized schedule. In all, nearly two hundred substances—including asbestos, benzene, beryllium, cadmium, mercury, and vinyl chloride—have been classified as hazardous. They are emitted from stationary sources by a variety of business activities, including smelting (melting ore to produce metal), dry cleaning, house painting, and commercial baking.

MAXIMUM ACHIEVABLE CONTROL TECHNOLOGY Instead of establishing specific emissions standards for each hazardous air pollutant, the Clean Air Act requires major new sources[4] to use pollution-control equipment that represents the *maximum achievable control technology,* or MACT, to reduce emissions. The EPA issues guidelines as to what equipment meets this standard.[5]

Violations of the Clean Air Act

For violations of emission limits under the Clean Air Act, the EPA can assess civil penalties of up to $25,000 per day. Additional fines of up to $5,000 per day can be assessed for other violations, such as failure to maintain the required records. To penalize those who find it more cost-effective to violate the act than to comply with it, the EPA is authorized to impose a penalty equal to the violator's economic benefits from noncompliance. Persons who provide information about violators may be paid up to $10,000. Private citizens can also sue violators.

Those who knowingly violate the act may be subject to criminal penalties, including fines of up to

---

3. *Massachusetts v. Environmental Protection Agency,* 549 U.S. 497, 127 S.Ct. 1438, 167 L.Ed.2d 248 (2007).

4. The term *major new sources* is defined to include existing sources modified by a change in a method of operation that increases emissions.
5. The EPA has also issued rules to regulate hazardous air pollutants emitted by landfills. See 40 C.F.R. Sections 60.750–60.759.

$1 million and imprisonment for up to two years (for false statements or failure to report violations). Corporate officers are among those who may be subject to these penalties.

SECTION 4
WATER POLLUTION

Water pollution stems mostly from industrial, municipal, and agricultural sources. Pollutants entering streams, lakes, and oceans include organic wastes, heated water, sediments from soil runoff, nutrients (including fertilizers and human and animal wastes), and toxic chemicals and other hazardous substances.

Federal regulations governing water pollution can be traced back to the Rivers and Harbors Appropriations Act of 1899.[6] These regulations prohibited ships and manufacturers from discharging or depositing refuse in navigable waterways without a permit.[7] In 1948, Congress passed the Federal Water Pollution Control Act (FWPCA),[8] but its regulatory system and enforcement powers proved to be inadequate.

The Clean Water Act

In 1972, amendments to the FWPCA—known as the Clean Water Act (CWA)—established the following goals: (1) make waters safe for swimming, (2) protect fish and wildlife, and (3) eliminate the discharge of pollutants into the water. The CWA also set specific schedules, which were extended by amendment in 1977 and by the Water Quality Act of 1987.[9] Under these schedules, the EPA limits the discharge of various types of pollutants based on the technology available for controlling them.

FOCUS ON POINT-SOURCE EMISSIONS The CWA established a permit system, called the National Pollutant Discharge Elimination System (NPDES), for regulating discharges from "point sources" of pollution, which include industrial, municipal (such as pipes and sewage treatment plants), and agricultural facilities.[10] Under this system, any point source emitting pollutants into water must have a permit. Pollution not from point sources, such as runoff from small farms, is not subject to much regulation. NPDES permits can be issued by the EPA and authorized state agencies and Indian tribes, but only if the discharge will not violate water-quality standards. NPDES permits must be reissued every five years. Although initially the NPDES system focused mainly on industrial wastewater, it was later expanded to cover stormwater discharges.

In practice, the permit system under the CWA includes the following elements:

1. National effluent (pollution) standards set by the EPA for each industry.
2. Water-quality standards set by the states under EPA supervision.
3. A *discharge permit* program that sets water-quality standards to limit pollution.
4. Special provisions for toxic chemicals and for oil spills.
5. Construction grants and loans from the federal government for *publicly owned treatment works,* primarily sewage treatment plants.

STANDARDS FOR EQUIPMENT Regulations generally specify that the *best available control technology,* or BACT, be installed. The EPA issues guidelines as to what equipment meets this standard. Essentially, the guidelines require the most effective pollution-control equipment available.

New sources must install BACT equipment before beginning operations. Existing sources are subject to timetables for the installation of BACT equipment and must immediately install equipment that utilizes the *best practical control technology,* or BPCT. The EPA also issues guidelines as to what equipment meets this standard.

The EPA must take into account many factors when issuing and updating its rules. Some provisions of the CWA instruct the EPA to weigh the cost of the technology required relative to the benefits achieved. The provision that covers power plants, however, neither requires nor prohibits a cost-benefit analysis. The question in the following case was whether the EPA could base its decision on such an analysis anyway.

---

6. 33 U.S.C. Sections 401–418..

7. The term *navigable waters* is interpreted today as including intrastate lakes and streams used by interstate travelers and industries, as well as coastal and freshwater wetlands.

8. 33 U.S.C. Sections 1251–1387.

9. This act amended 33 U.S.C. Section 1251.

10. 33 U.S.C. Section 1342.

CASE 45.1

Entergy Corp. v. Riverkeeper, Inc.
Supreme Court of the United States, 556 U.S. 208, 129 S.Ct. 1498, 173 L.Ed.2d 369 (2009).

BACKGROUND AND FACTS As part of its implementation of the Clean Water Act, the Environmental Protection Agency (EPA) has developed two sets of rules that apply to the cooling systems of power plants. Phase I rules require new power plants to restrict their inflow of water "to a level commensurate with that which can be attained by a closed-cycle recirculating cooling water system." Phase II rules apply "national performance standards" to more than five hundred existing plants but do not require closed-cycle cooling systems. The EPA found that converting these facilities to closed-cycle operations would cost $3.5 billion per year. The facilities would then produce less power while burning the same amount of coal. Moreover, other technologies can attain nearly the same results as closed-cycle systems. Phase II rules also allow a variance from the national performance standards if a facility's cost of compliance "would be significantly greater than the benefits." Environmental organizations, including Riverkeeper, Inc., challenged the Phase II regulations, arguing that existing plants should be required to convert to closed-cycle systems. The U.S. Court of Appeals for the Second Circuit issued a ruling in the plaintiffs' favor. Power-generating companies, including Entergy Corporation, appealed to the United States Supreme Court.

IN THE LANGUAGE OF THE COURT
Justice *SCALIA* delivered the opinion of the Court.

* * * *

In setting the Phase II national performance standards and providing for site-specific cost-benefit variances, the EPA relied on its view that [the] "best technology available" standard permits consideration of the technology's costs and of the relationship between those costs and the environmental benefits produced.

* * * The "best" technology—that which is "most advantageous"—may well be the one that produces the most of some good, here a reduction in adverse environmental impact. But "best technology" may also describe the technology that most efficiently produces some good. *In common parlance one could certainly use the phrase "best technology" to refer to that which produces a good at the lowest per-unit cost, even if it produces a lesser quantity of that good than other available technologies.* [Emphasis added.]

* * * This latter reading is [not] precluded by the statute's use of the phrase "for minimizing adverse environmental impact." *Minimizing * * * is a term that admits of degree and is not necessarily used to refer exclusively to the "greatest possible reduction."* [Emphasis added.]

Other provisions in the Clean Water Act also suggest the agency's interpretation. When Congress wished to mandate the greatest feasible reduction in water pollution, it did so in plain language: The provision governing the discharge of toxic pollutants into the Nation's waters requires the EPA to set "effluent limitations which shall require the elimination of discharges of all pollutants * * * ." The less ambitious goal of "minimizing adverse environmental impact" suggests, we think, that the agency retains some discretion to determine the extent of reduction that is warranted under the circumstances. That determination could plausibly involve a consideration of the benefits derived from reductions and the costs of achieving them.

* * * [Under other Clean Water Act provisions that impose standards on sources of pollution,] the EPA is instructed to consider, among other factors, "the total cost of application of technology in relation to the * * * benefits to be achieved."

* * * *

This * * * comparison of * * * statutory factors * * * leads us to the conclusion that it was well within the bounds of reasonable interpretation for the EPA to conclude that cost-benefit analysis is not categorically forbidden.

* * * *

CASE 45.1 CONTINUES ➡

CASE 45.1 CONTINUED   While not conclusive, it surely tends to show that the EPA's current practice is a reasonable and hence legitimate exercise of its discretion to weigh benefits against costs that the agency has been proceeding in essentially this fashion for over 30 years.

DECISION AND REMEDY *The United States Supreme Court concluded that the EPA permissibly relied on a cost-benefit analysis to set national performance standards and to allow for variances from those standards as part of the Phase II regulations. The Court reversed the lower court's judgment and remanded the case.*

THE ETHICAL DIMENSION *In this case, aquatic organisms were most directly at risk. Is it acceptable to apply cost-benefit analyses to situations in which the lives of people are directly affected? Explain.*

THE GLOBAL DIMENSION *In analyzing the costs and benefits of an action that affects the environment, should a line be drawn at a nation's borders? Why or why not?*

WETLANDS The CWA prohibits the filling or dredging of **wetlands** unless a permit is obtained from the Army Corps of Engineers. The EPA defines *wetlands* as "those areas that are inundated or saturated by surface or ground water at a frequency and duration sufficient to support . . . vegetation typically adapted for life in saturated soil conditions."

Wetlands are thought to be vital to the ecosystem because they filter streams and rivers and provide habitat for wildlife. In the past, the EPA's broad interpretation of what constituted a wetland generated substantial controversy. In recent years, the courts have considerably scaled back the CWA's protection of wetlands.[11]

In the following case, the court had to deal with the meaning of *wetlands* and whether the term included saturated land adjacent to *navigable-in-fact waters*—that is, waters that are navigable in their natural or unimproved condition and used as highways of commerce.

---

11. See, for example, *Rapanos v. United States,* 547 U.S. 715, 126 S.Ct. 2208, 165 L.Ed.2d 159 (2006).

CASE ANALYSIS

Case 45.2   United States v. Lucas
United States Court of Appeals, Fifth District, 516 F.3d 316 (2008).

IN THE LANGUAGE OF THE COURT
Patrick E. *HIGGINBOTHAM,* Circuit Judge.

* * * *

Robert J. Lucas owned Big Hill Acres, Inc. (BHA, Inc.) and Consolidated Investments, Inc. Through these companies, he acquired Big Hill Acres (BHA), a large parcel of land in Jackson County, Mississippi, approximately eight miles from the Gulf of Mexico. He subdivided the property and sold mobile home lots under long-term installment plans. The property was not connected to a central municipal waste system, and County law required Lucas to certify and install individual septic systems on each lot before they could establish electric hook-ups or sell the lots. In Jackson County, septic systems must be approved by an engineer with the Mississippi Department of Health (MDH) or by an independent licensed engineer. Lucas initially hired an MDH engineer to approve septic systems, but MDH withdrew many of its initial approvals when it found that the lots were on saturated soils. Lucas then hired a private licensed engineer, M. E. Thompson, Jr., to approve and certify the septic systems. Robbie Lucas Wrigley, Lucas's daughter, advertised the lots, showed them to prospective buyers, and leased them.

The [U.S.] Army Corps of Engineers, the EPA [Environmental Protection Agency], the MDH, and the Mississippi Department of Environmental Quality (DEQ) became concerned that Defendants were selling house lots and installing septic systems on wetlands. These agencies

CASE 45.2 CONTINUED

issued several cease and desist orders against Lucas and Thompson, and the EPA sent letters to residents and organized a meeting of the residents to warn them of lot conditions and to tell them where wetlands were located on the property. It also met with BHA's counsel to attempt to designate the areas where they would allow development. These efforts were not fully successful.

The Government filed a forty-one–count indictment against Defendants * * * , charging filling of wetlands without a Section 404 permit from the [U.S. Army] Corps [of Engineers], failing to obtain Section 402 National Pollutant Discharge Elimination System (NPDES) Permits for the septic tanks, mail fraud, and conspiracy to commit mail fraud and to violate Sections 402 and 404 of the CWA [Clean Water Act]. * * * A jury convicted Defendants on all counts, and the court * * * sentenced Lucas, Wrigley, and Thompson to prison terms; placed BHA, Inc., and Consolidated Investments on probation; and ordered all Defendants to pay restitution, special assessments, and fines.

The first and overarching [dominant] question is jurisdiction—whether the jury was properly required to find that the property at issue was subject to the CWA. * * * The instructions stated in relevant part,

* * * *

The term *wetlands* means those areas that are inundated or saturated by surface or groundwater at a frequency and duration sufficient to support, and that under normal circumstances do support, a prevalence of vegetation typically adapted for life in saturated soil conditions * * * . * * * Wetlands that are waters of the United States are protected by the Clean Water Act. *Wetlands are considered waters of the United States if they are adjacent to a navigable body of open water. Wetlands are adjacent to a navigable body of water if there is a significant nexus [connection] between the wetlands in question and a navigable-in-fact waterway.* Some of the factors which you may wish to consider in determining whether there is a significant nexus include, but are not limited to: * * * flow rate of surface waters from the wetlands into a navigable body of water * * * when, or to what extent, contaminants from the wetlands have or will affect a navigable body of water * * * . [Emphasis added.]

Defendants argue that the court erred in not including their requested language that:

* * * adjacency implicates a "significant nexus" between the water in question and the navigable-in-fact waterway. If the government fails to prove beyond a reasonable doubt that the wetlands at issue in this case are in fact navigable or truly adjacent to [that is,] lying near, close, contiguous, or adjoining a navigable waterway, you must find the defendants not guilty * * * .

* * * *

* * * *A district court abuses its discretion in omitting a requested jury instruction only if the requested language "(1) is substantively correct; (2) is not substantially covered in the charge given to the jury; and (3) concerns an important point in the trial * * * ."* [Emphasis added.]

The court's instructions were not in error, nor was the court's omission of Defendants' requested instructions. * * * The instructions substantially covered Defendants' requested instructions by requiring adjacency as defined by a significant nexus.

* * * *

The government has shown that there is a significant nexus between the wetlands on Big Hill Acres and navigable-in-fact waters. * * * The surface from the Big Hill Acres site drains in three directions. The western portions of the site drain into Bayou Costapia. Bayou Costapia empties into the Tchoutacabouffa River, which then empties into the Gulf of Mexico. The central portions of the Big Hill Acres development drained through tributaries into Old Fort Bayou Creek. And Old Fort Bayou Creek connects to Old Fort Bayou, which is a protected coastal preserve emptying into the Gulf of Mexico. And the eastern portions drain into the headwaters of Little Bluff Creek, which then connects to Bluff Creek, which flows into the Pascagoula River and on to the Gulf of Mexico. The court did not abuse its discretion in giving the CWA instructions.

LEGAL REASONING QUESTIONS

1. Suppose that during most of the year, there was a solid strip of land around the property in question that was never under water or saturated. Would the outcome of this case have been the same? Why or why not?

2. According to the judge, what three characteristics of jury instructions does a federal appellate court examine to determine whether a district court has abused its discretion in omitting a requested jury instruction? Which of these three characteristics was at issue in this case?

3. Would the court have ruled differently if the water from the wetlands had drained or flowed directly into international or foreign waters rather than into the waters of the United States? Discuss.

4. Does it seem appropriate to sentence businesspersons to prison for violations of the Clean Water Act?

VIOLATIONS OF THE CLEAN WATER ACT Because point-source water pollution control is based on a permit system, the permits are the key to enforcement. States have primary responsibility for enforcing the permit system, subject to EPA monitoring.

Discharging emissions into navigable waters without a permit, or in violation of pollution limits under a permit, violates the CWA. Violators are subject to a variety of civil and criminal penalties.

Depending on the violation, civil penalties range from $10,000 to $25,000 per day, but not more than $25,000 per violation. Lying about a violation is more serious than admitting the truth about improper discharges.

Criminal penalties, which apply only if a violation was intentional, range from a fine of $2,500 per day and imprisonment for up to one year to a fine of $1 million and fifteen years' imprisonment. Injunctive relief and damages can also be imposed. The polluting party can be required to clean up the pollution or pay for the cost of doing so.

In the following case, landowners filed a lawsuit challenging an EPA order finding that they had violated the CWA. The United States Supreme Court had to decide whether the federal courts could review the EPA's decision.

CASE 45.3

Sackett v. Environmental Protection Agency
Supreme Court of the United States, ___ U.S. ___, 132 S.Ct. 1367, 182 L.Ed.2d 367 (2012).

BACKGROUND AND FACTS To build a home in Idaho, Michael and Chantell Sackett filled part of their residential lot with dirt and rock. A few months later, they received a compliance order from the Environmental Protection Agency (EPA). The order asserted that, because their property was near a major lake, the Sacketts had polluted wetlands in violation of the Clean Water Act. The order required the Sacketts to restore their property immediately, and they faced heavy fines of $75,000 a day. The Sacketts requested a hearing with the EPA. When a hearing was denied, they sued the EPA in federal district court, asserting, among other things, that the compliance order was "arbitrary and capricious" under the Administrative Procedure Act (APA). The district court found that it could not review the EPA's compliance order. On appeal, a federal appellate court affirmed, concluding that the Sacketts had to wait for the EPA to bring an enforcement action against them. The United States Supreme Court granted *certiorari* to resolve the matter.

IN THE LANGUAGE OF THE COURT
Justice *SCALIA* delivered the opinion of the Court.

* * * *

* * * The APA * * * provides for judicial review of "final agency action for which there is no other adequate remedy in a court." We consider first whether the compliance order is final agency action. There is no doubt it is agency action, which the APA defines as including even a "failure to act." But is it *final?* It has all of the hallmarks of APA finality that our opinions establish. Through the order, the EPA " 'determined' " " 'rights or obligations.' " By reason of the order, the Sacketts have the legal obligation to "restore" their property according to an agency-approved Restoration Work Plan, and must give the EPA access to their property and to "records and documentation related to the conditions at the Site." Also, " 'legal consequences . . . flow' " from issuance of the order. * * * The order exposes the Sacketts to double penalties in a future enforcement proceeding. [Emphasis in original.]

The issuance of the compliance order also marks the " 'consummation' " of the agency's decision-making process. As the Sacketts learned when they unsuccessfully sought a hearing, * * * [the] compliance order * * * [was] not subject to further agency review.

The APA's judicial review provision also requires that the person seeking APA review of final agency action have "no other adequate remedy in a court[.]" In Clean Water Act enforcement cases, judicial review ordinarily comes by way of a civil action brought by the EPA * * * .

CASE 45.3 CONTINUED But the Sacketts cannot initiate that process, and each day they wait for the agency to drop the hammer, they accrue * * * an additional $75,000 in potential liability.
* * * *

* * * Compliance orders * * * can obtain quick remediation through voluntary compliance. The Government warns that the EPA is less likely to use the orders if they are subject to judicial review. That may be true—but it will be true for all agency actions subjected to judicial review. * * * *There is no reason to think that the Clean Water Act was uniquely designed to enable the strong-arming of regulated parties into "voluntary compliance" without the opportunity for judicial review* * * * . Compliance orders will remain an effective means of securing prompt voluntary compliance in those many cases where there is no substantial basis to question their validity. [Emphasis added.]

DECISION AND REMEDY *The United States Supreme Court held that the Sacketts could challenge the EPA's compliance order in federal court. The Court reversed the judgment of the federal appellate court.*

THE LEGAL ENVIRONMENT DIMENSION *What does the Court's decision in this case mean for people and businesses that face compliance orders? Are they more or less likely to acquiesce to orders they find objectionable? Why?*

THE ENVIRONMENTAL DIMENSION *Is it appropriate to impose significant fines on citizens when they violate environmental laws? Discuss.*

Drinking Water

The Safe Drinking Water Act[12] requires the EPA to set maximum levels for pollutants in public water systems. Public water systems operators must come as close as possible to meeting the EPA's standards by using the best available technology that is economically and technologically feasible.

The act, as amended, also requires each supplier of drinking water to send every household it supplies with water an annual statement describing the source of its water. The statement must also disclose the level of any contaminants contained in the water, and any possible health concerns associated with the contaminants.

Ocean Dumping

The Marine Protection, Research, and Sanctuaries Act of 1972[13] (popularly known as the Ocean Dumping Act) regulates the transportation and dumping of material (pollutants) into ocean waters. It prohibits the ocean dumping of any radiological, chemical, and biological warfare agents and high-level radioactive waste.

The act also established a permit program for transporting and dumping other materials, and designated certain areas as marine sanctuaries. Each violation of any provision or permit requirement in the Ocean Dumping Act may result in a civil penalty of up to $50,000. A knowing violation is a criminal offense that may result in a $50,000 fine, imprisonment for not more than a year, or both. A court may also grant an injunction to prevent an imminent or continuing violation.

Oil Pollution

When more than 10 million gallons of oil leaked into Alaska's Prince William Sound from the *Exxon Valdez* supertanker in 1989, Congress responded and passed the Oil Pollution Act.[14] (At that time, the *Exxon Valdez* disaster was the worst oil spill in U.S. history, but the BP oil spill in the Gulf of Mexico in 2010 surpassed it.)

Under this act, any oil facility, oil shipper, vessel owner, or vessel operator that discharges oil into navigable waters or onto an adjoining shore may be liable for clean-up costs, as well as damages. In addition, the polluter can be ordered to pay for damage to natural resources, private property, and the local economy, including the increased cost of providing public services. The party held responsible for the clean-up

---

12. 42 U.S.C. Sections 300f to 300j-25.
13. 16 U.S.C. Sections 1401–1445.

14. 33 U.S.C. Sections 2701–2761.

costs can bring a civil suit for contribution from other potentially liable parties.

SECTION 5
TOXIC CHEMICALS

Originally, most environmental clean-up efforts were directed toward reducing smog and making water safe for fishing and swimming. Today, control of toxic chemicals used in agriculture and in industry has become increasingly important.

Pesticides and Herbicides

The Federal Insecticide, Fungicide, and Rodenticide Act (FIFRA) of 1947[15] regulates pesticides and herbicides. Pesticides and herbicides must be (1) registered before they can be sold, (2) certified and used only for approved applications, and (3) used in limited quantities when applied to food crops.

EPA ACTIONS The EPA can cancel or suspend registration of substances that are identified as harmful. The EPA can also inspect factories where the chemicals are made. A substance is deemed harmful if human exposure to the substance, including exposure through eating food, results in a risk of one in a million (or higher) of developing cancer.[16]

VIOLATIONS AND PENALTIES It is a violation of FIFRA to sell a pesticide or herbicide that is either unregistered or has had its registration canceled or suspended. It is also a violation to sell a pesticide or herbicide with a false or misleading label, or to destroy or deface any labeling required under the act. For instance, it is an offense to sell a substance that has a chemical strength different from the concentration declared on the label.

Penalties for commercial dealers include imprisonment for up to one year and a fine of up to $25,000 (producers can be fined up to $50,000). Farmers and other private users of pesticides or herbicides who violate the act are subject to a $1,000 fine and incarceration for up to thirty days. Note that a state can also regulate the sale and use of federally registered pesticides.

▶ **Case in Point 45.4** The EPA conditionally registered Strongarm, a weed-killing pesticide. Dow Agrosciences, LLC, sold Strongarm to Texas pea-

nut farmers. When the farmers applied it, however, Strongarm damaged their crops and failed to control the growth of weeds. The farmers sued Dow for violations of Texas law, but the lower courts ruled that FIFRA preempted their claims. The farmers appealed to the United States Supreme Court. The Court held that under a specific provision of FIFRA, a state can regulate the sale and use of federally registered pesticides so long as the regulation does not permit anything that FIFRA prohibits.[17] ◀

Toxic Substances

The Toxic Substances Control Act[18] regulates chemicals and chemical compounds that are known to be toxic—such as asbestos and polychlorinated biphenyls, popularly known as PCBs. The act also controls the introduction of new chemical compounds by requiring investigation of any possible harmful effects from these substances.

The regulations authorize the EPA to require that manufacturers, processors, and other entities planning to use chemicals first determine their effects on human health and the environment. The EPA can regulate substances that may pose an imminent hazard or an unreasonable risk of injury to health or the environment. The EPA may require special labeling, limit the use of a substance, set production quotas, or prohibit the use of a substance altogether.

SECTION 6
HAZARDOUS WASTES

Some industrial, agricultural, and household wastes pose more serious threats than others. If not properly disposed of, these toxic chemicals may present a substantial danger to human health and the environment. If released into the environment, they may contaminate public drinking water resources.

Resource Conservation and Recovery Act

The Resource Conservation and Recovery Act (RCRA)[19] was passed in response to growing concern about the effects of hazardous waste materials on the environ-

---

15. 7 U.S.C. Sections 136–136y.
16. 21 U.S.C. Section 346a.
17. *Bates v. Dow Agrosciences, LLC,* 544 U.S. 431, 125 S.Ct. 1788, 161 L.Ed.2d 687 (2005).
18. 15 U.S.C. Sections 2601–2692.
19. 42 U.S.C. Sections 6901–6986.

ment. The RCRA required the EPA to establish regulations to determine which forms of solid waste should be considered hazardous and to establish regulations to monitor and control hazardous waste disposal.

The act also requires all producers of hazardous waste materials to label and package properly any hazardous waste to be transported. The RCRA was amended in 1984 and 1986 to decrease the use of land containment in the disposal of hazardous waste and to require smaller generators of hazardous waste to comply with the act.

Under the RCRA, a company may be assessed a civil penalty of up to $25,000 for each violation.[20] The penalty is based on the seriousness of the violation, the probability of harm, and the extent to which the violation deviates from RCRA requirements. Criminal penalties include fines of up to $50,000 for each day of violation, imprisonment for up to two years (in most instances), or both. Criminal fines and the time of imprisonment can be doubled for certain repeat offenders.

Superfund

In 1980, Congress passed the Comprehensive Environmental Response, Compensation, and Liability Act (CERCLA),[21] commonly known as Superfund. The basic purpose of Superfund is to regulate the clean-up of disposal sites in which hazardous waste is leaking into the environment.

CERCLA, as amended, has four primary elements:

1. It established an information-gathering and analysis system that enables the government to identify chemical dump sites and determine the appropriate action.
2. It authorized the EPA to respond to hazardous substance emergencies and to arrange for the clean-up of a leaking site directly if the persons responsible for the problem fail to clean up the site.
3. It created a Hazardous Substance Response Trust Fund (also called *Superfund*) to pay for the clean-up of hazardous sites using funds obtained through taxes on certain businesses.
4. It allowed the government to recover the cost of clean-up from the persons who were (even remotely) responsible for hazardous substance releases.

POTENTIALLY RESPONSIBLE PARTIES Superfund provides that when a release or a threatened release of hazardous chemicals from a site occurs, the following persons may be held responsible for cleaning up the site:

1. The person who generated the wastes disposed of at the site.
2. The person who transported the waste to the site.
3. The person who owned or operated the site at the time of the disposal.
4. The current owner or operator.

A person falling within one of these categories is referred to as a **potentially responsible party (PRP).** If the PRPs do not clean up the site, the EPA can clean up the site and recover the clean-up costs from the PRPs.

Strict Liability of PRPs. Superfund imposes strict liability on PRPs, and that liability cannot be avoided through transfer of ownership. Thus, selling a site where hazardous wastes were disposed of does not relieve the seller of liability, and the buyer also becomes liable for the clean-up. Liability also extends to businesses that merge with or buy corporations that have violated CERCLA. Although a parent corporation is not automatically liable for the violations of its subsidiary, it can be held liable if the subsidiary was merely a shell company or if the parent corporation participated in or controlled the facility.[22]

Joint and Several Liability. Liability under Superfund is usually joint and several. In other words, a PRP who generated *only a fraction of the hazardous waste* disposed of at a site may nevertheless be liable for *all* of the clean-up costs. CERCLA authorizes a party who has incurred clean-up costs to bring a "contribution action" against any other person who is liable or potentially liable for a percentage of the costs.

MINIMIZING LIABILITY One way for a business to minimize its potential liability under Superfund is to conduct environmental compliance audits of its own operations regularly. A business can perform internal investigations of its own operations and property to determine whether any environmental hazards exist.

The EPA encourages companies to conduct self-audits and promptly detect, disclose, and correct wrongdoing. Companies that do so are subject to lighter penalties

20. 42 U.S.C. Section 6928(a).
21. 42 U.S.C. Sections 9601–9675.

22. The landmark case establishing the liability of a parent corporation under CERCLA is *United States v. Bestfoods,* 524 U.S. 51, 118 S.Ct. 1876, 141 L.Ed.2d 43 (1998).

(fines may be reduced as much as 75 percent) for violations of environmental laws. Under EPA guidelines, the EPA will waive all fines if a small company corrects environmental violations within 180 days after being notified of the violations (or 360 days if pollution-prevention techniques are involved). The policy does not apply to criminal violations of environmental laws, though, or to violations that pose a significant threat to public health, safety, or the environment.

DEFENSES There are a few defenses to liability under CERCLA. The most important is the innocent landowner defense.[23] Under this defense, an innocent property owner may be able to avoid liability by showing that he or she had no contractual or employment

relationship with the person who released the hazardous substance on the land. Thus, if the party who disposed of the substances transferred the property by contract to the current owner, the defense normally will not be available.

To assert the defense, the landowner must be able to show that at the time the property was acquired, she or he had no reason to know that hazardous substances had been disposed of on it. The landowner must also show that at the time of the purchase, she or he undertook all appropriate investigation into the previous ownership and uses of the property to determine whether there was reason to be concerned about hazardous substances. In effect, this defense protects only property owners who took precautions and investigated the possibility of environmental hazards at the time they bought the property.

---

23. 42 U.S.C. Section 9601(35)(B).

Reviewing: Environmental Law

Residents of Lake Caliopa, Minnesota, began noticing an unusually high number of lung ailments among their population. A group of concerned local citizens pooled their resources and commissioned a study of the frequency of these health conditions per capita in Lake Caliopa as compared with national averages. The study concluded that asthma, bronchitis, and emphysema occurred four to seven times more frequently among residents of Lake Caliopa than in the population nationwide. During the study period, citizens began expressing concerns about the large volumes of smog emitted by the Cotton Design apparel manufacturing plant on the outskirts of town. The plant had opened its production facility two miles east of town beside the Tawakoni River in 1999 and employed seventy full-time workers.

Just downstream on the Tawakoni River, the city of Lake Caliopa operated a public water works facility, which supplied all city residents with water. The Minnesota Pollution Control Agency required Cotton Design to install new equipment to control air and water pollution. Later, citizens sued Cotton Design for various respiratory ailments allegedly caused or compounded by smog from Cotton Design's factory. Using the information presented in the chapter, answer the following questions.

1. Under the common law, what would each plaintiff be required to identify in order to be given relief by the court?
2. Are air-quality regulations typically overseen by federal, state, or local governments?
3. What standard for limiting emissions into the air does Cotton Design's pollution-control equipment have to meet?
4. What information must the city send to every household that it supplies with water?

DEBATE THIS . . . *The courts should reject all cases in which the wetlands in question do not consist of actual bodies of water that exist during the entire year.*

Terms and Concepts

environmental impact
  statement (EIS) 879
environmental law 878

nuisance 878
potentially responsible party (PRP) 889

toxic tort 878
wetlands 884

ExamPrep

Issue Spotters

1. Resource Refining Company's plant emits smoke and fumes. Resource's operation includes a short railway system, and trucks enter and exit the grounds continuously. Constant vibrations from the trains and trucks rattle nearby residential neighborhoods. The residents sue Resource. Are there any reasons why the court might refuse to issue an injunction against Resource's operation? Explain. **(See page 878.)**

2. ChemCorp generates hazardous wastes from its operations. Disposal Trucking Company transports those wastes to Eliminators, Inc., which owns a site for hazardous waste disposal. Eliminators sells the property on which the disposal site is located to

Fluid Properties, Inc. If the Environmental Protection Agency cleans up the site, from whom can it recover the cost? **(See page 889.)**

• Check your answers to the Issue Spotters against the answers provided in Appendix E at the end of this text.

Before the Test

Go to **www.cengagebrain.com**, enter the ISBN 9781285185248, and click on "Find" to locate this textbook's Web site. Then, click on "Access Now" under "Study Tools," and select Chapter 45 at the top. There, you will find a Practice Quiz that you can take to assess your mastery of the concepts in this chapter, as well as Flashcards and a Glossary of important terms.

Business Scenarios

45–1. Clean Air Act. Current scientific knowledge indicates that there is no safe level of exposure to a cancer-causing agent. In theory, even one molecule of such a substance has the potential for causing cancer. Section 112 of the Clean Air Act requires that all cancer-causing substances be regulated to ensure a margin of safety. Some environmental groups have argued that all emissions of such substances must be eliminated if a margin of safety is to be reached. Such a total elimination would likely shut down many major U.S. industries. Should the Environmental Protection Agency totally eliminate all emissions of cancer-causing chemicals? Discuss. **(See page 880.)**

45–2. Environmental Laws. Fruitade, Inc., is a processor of a soft drink called Freshen Up. Fruitade uses returnable bottles, which it cleans with a special acid to allow for further beverage processing. The acid is diluted with water and then allowed to pass into a navigable stream. Fruitade

crushes its broken bottles and throws the crushed glass into the stream. Discuss fully any environmental laws that Fruitade has violated. **(See page 882.)**

45–3. Environmental Laws. Moonbay is a home-building corporation that primarily develops retirement communities. Farmtex owns a number of feedlots in Sunny Valley. Moonbay purchased 20,000 acres of farmland in the same area and began building and selling homes on this acreage. In the meantime, Farmtex continued to expand its feedlot business, and eventually only 500 feet separated the two operations. Because of the odor and flies from the feedlots, Moonbay found it difficult to sell the homes in its development. Moonbay wants to enjoin (prevent) Farmtex from operating its feedlot in the vicinity of the retirement home development. Under what common law theory would Moonbay file this action? Has Farmtex violated any federal environmental laws? Discuss. **(See page 878.)**

Business Case Problems

45–4. Environmental Impact Statement. The fourth largest crop in the United States is alfalfa, of which 5 percent is exported to Japan. RoundUp Ready alfalfa is genetically engineered to resist glyphosate, the active ingredient in the herbicide RoundUp. The U.S. Department of

Agriculture (USDA) regulates genetically engineered agricultural products through the Animal and Plant Health Inspection Service (APHIS). APHIS concluded that RoundUp Ready alfalfa does not have any harmful health effects on humans or livestock and deregulated it.

Geertson Seed Farms and others filed a suit in a federal district court against Mike Johanns (then the secretary of the USDA) and others, asserting that APHIS's decision required the preparation of an environmental impact statement (EIS). The plaintiffs argued, among other things, that the introduction of RoundUp Ready alfalfa might significantly decrease the availability of or even eliminate, all nongenetically engineered varieties. The plaintiffs were concerned that the RoundUp Ready alfalfa might contaminate standard alfalfa because alfalfa is pollinated by bees, which can travel as far as two miles from a pollen source. If contamination occurred, farmers would not be able to market "contaminated" varieties as "organic," which would affect the sales of "organic" livestock and exports to Japan, which does not allow the import of glyphosate-resistant alfalfa. Should an EIS be prepared in this case? Why or why not? [*Geertson Seed Farms v. Johanns,* __ F.Supp.2d __ (N.D.Cal. 2007)] **(See page 879.)**

45–5. BUSINESS CASE PROBLEM
WITH SAMPLE ANSWER: Environmental Impact Statement.

 The U.S. National Park Service (NPS) manages the Grand Canyon National Park in Arizona under a management plan that is subject to periodic review. In 2006, after nine years of background work and the completion of a comprehensive environmental impact statement, the NPS issued a new management plan for the park. The plan allowed for the continued use of rafts on the Colorado River, which runs through the Grand Canyon. The number of rafts was limited, however. Several environmental groups criticized the plan because they felt that it still allowed too many rafts on the river. The groups asked a federal appellate court to overturn the plan, claiming that it violated the wilderness status of the national park. When can a federal court overturn a determination by an agency such as the NPS? Explain. [River Runners for Wilderness v. Martin, 593 F.3d 1064 (9th Cir. 2010)] **(See page 879.)**

- **For a sample answer to Problem 45–5, go to Appendix F at the end of this text.**

45–6. Superfund. A by-product of phosphate fertilizer production is pyrite waste, which contains arsenic and lead. From 1884 to 1906, seven phosphate fertilizer plants operated on a forty-three-acre site in Charleston, South Carolina. Planters Fertilizer & Phosphate Co. bought the site in 1906 and continued to make fertilizer. In 1966, Planters sold the site to Columbia Nitrogen Corp. (CNC), which also operated the fertilizer plants. In 1985, CNC sold the site to James

Holcombe and J. Henry Fair. Holcombe and Fair subdivided and sold the site to Allwaste Tank Cleaning Inc., Robin Hood Container Express, the city of Charleston, and Ashley II of Charleston, Inc. Ashley spent almost $200,000 cleaning up the contaminated soil. Who can be held liable for the cost? Why? [*PCS Nitrogen Inc. v. Ashley II of Charleston LLC,* 714 F.3d 161 (4th Cir. 2013)] **(See page 889.)**

45–7. A QUESTION OF ETHICS: Clean Air Act.

 In the Clean Air Act, Congress allowed California, which has particular problems with clean air, to adopt its own standard for emissions from cars and trucks. California's standard is subject to the approval of the Environmental Protection Agency (EPA) based on certain criteria. Congress also allowed other states to adopt California's standard after the EPA's approval. In 2004, in an effort to address global warming, the California Air Resources Board amended the state's standard to attain "the maximum feasible and cost-effective reduction of GHG [greenhouse gas] emissions from motor vehicles." The regulation, which applies to new passenger vehicles and light-duty trucks for 2009 and later, imposes decreasing limits on emissions of carbon dioxide through 2016. While EPA approval was pending, Vermont and other states adopted similar standards. Green Mountain Chrysler Plymouth Dodge Jeep and other auto dealers, automakers, and associations of automakers filed a suit in a federal district court against George Crombie (then the secretary of the Vermont Agency of Natural Resources) and others, seeking relief from the state regulations. [Green Mountain Chrysler Plymouth Dodge Jeep v. Crombie, 508 F.Supp.2d 295 (D.Vt. 2007)] **(See page 880.)**

(a) Under the Environmental Policy and Conservation Act (EPCA) of 1975, the National Highway Traffic Safety Administration sets fuel economy standards for new cars. The plaintiffs argued, among other things, that the EPCA, which prohibits states from adopting separate fuel economy standards, preempts Vermont's GHG regulation. Do the GHG rules equate to the fuel economy standards? Discuss.

(b) Do Vermont's rules tread on the efforts of the federal government to address global warming internationally? Who should regulate GHG emissions? The federal government? The state governments? Both? Neither? Why?

(c) The plaintiffs claimed that they would go bankrupt if they were forced to adhere to the state's GHG standards. Should they be granted relief on this basis? Does history support their claim? Explain.

Legal Reasoning Group Activity

45–8. Clean-Up Costs. It has been estimated that for every dollar spent cleaning up hazardous waste sites, administrative agencies spend seven dollars in overhead. **(See page 889.)**

(a) The first group will list and explain possible ways to trim these administrative costs.

(b) The second group will evaluate whether the laws pertaining to hazardous waste clean-up can or should be changed to reduce the costs to government.

CHAPTER 46
ANTITRUST LAW

After the Civil War (1861–1865), the American public became increasingly concerned about declining competition in the marketplace. Large corporate enterprises were attempting to reduce or eliminate competition by legally tying themselves together in *business trusts* (see Chapter 38).

The most famous trust was the Standard Oil trust of the late 1800s. Its participants transferred their stock to a trustee who then fixed prices, controlled production, and established exclusive geographic markets for all of the oil companies that were members of the trust. Some observers began to argue that the trust wielded so much economic power that corporations

outside the trust could not compete effectively.

Eventually, legislation began to be enacted at both the state and the federal level to rein in the trusts. Hence, the laws that regulate economic competition in the United States today are still referred to as **antitrust laws.** At the national level, antitrust legislation began when Congress passed the Interstate Commerce Act[1] in 1887, followed by the Sherman Antitrust Act[2] in 1890. In 1914, Congress passed the Clayton Act[3] and the Federal Trade Commission Act[4] to further curb anti-

---

1. 49 U.S.C. Sections 501–526
2. 15 U.S.C. Sections 1–7.
3. 15 U.S.C. Sections 12–27.
4. 15 U.S.C. Sections 41–58a.

competitive or unfair business practices. This chapter examines these major antitrust statutes, focusing particularly on the Sherman Act and the Clayton Act, as amended, and the types of activities they prohibit.

As you read the chapter, remember that the purpose of antitrust legislation was—and still is—to foster competition. Behind the laws lies our society's belief that competition leads to lower prices, better products, a wider selection of goods, and more product information. This is why the U.S. government is concerned about the pricing of e-books, as you will read later in this chapter.

THE SHERMAN ANTITRUST ACT

The author of the Sherman Antitrust Act of 1890, Senator John Sherman, was the brother of the famed Civil War general and a recognized financial authority. He had been concerned for years about what he saw as diminishing competition within U.S. industry and the emergence of monopolies. He told Congress that the Sherman Act "does not announce a new principle of law, but applies old and well-recognized principles of the common law."[5]

Indeed, not only the legislation that Sherman proposed but subsequent antitrust laws as well were the direct descendants of common law actions intended

---

5. 21 *Congressional Record* 2456 (1890).

to limit **restraints of trade** (agreements between firms that have the effect of reducing competition in the marketplace). The common law was not always consistent, however, and had not been effective in curbing the trusts. Therefore, in 1890 Congress passed "An Act to Protect Trade and Commerce against Unlawful Restraints and Monopolies"—more commonly referred to as the Sherman Antitrust Act, or simply the Sherman Act.

Major Provisions of the Sherman Act

Sections 1 and 2 contain the main provisions of the Sherman Act:

1. Every contract, combination in the form of trust or otherwise, or conspiracy, in restraint of trade

or commerce among the several States, or with foreign nations, is hereby declared to be illegal [and is a felony punishable by fine and/or imprisonment].

2. Every person who shall monopolize, or attempt to monopolize, or combine or conspire with any other person or persons, to monopolize any part of the trade or commerce among the several States, or with foreign nations, shall be deemed guilty of a felony [and is similarly punishable].

Differences between Section 1 and Section 2

These two sections of the Sherman Act are quite different. Section 1 requires two or more persons, as a person cannot contract, combine, or conspire alone. Thus, the essence of the illegal activity is *the act of joining together*. Section 2, though, can apply either to one person or to two or more persons because it refers to "every person." Thus, unilateral conduct can result in a violation of Section 2.

The cases brought to the courts under Section 1 of the Sherman Act differ from those brought under Section 2. Section 1 cases are often concerned with whether an agreement (written or oral) leads to a restraint of trade. Section 2 cases deal with the structure of a monopoly that exists in the marketplace. The term **monopoly** generally is used to describe a market in which there is a single seller or a very limited number of sellers. Whereas Section 1 focuses on agreements that are restrictive—that is, agreements that have a wrongful purpose—Section 2 looks at the so-called misuse of **monopoly power** in the marketplace.

Monopoly power exists when a firm has an extreme amount of **market power**—the ability to affect the market price of its product. Both Section 1 and Section 2 seek to curtail market practices that result in undesired monopoly pricing and output behavior. For a case to be brought under Section 2, however, the "threshold" or "necessary" amount of monopoly power must already exist.

Jurisdictional Requirements

The Sherman Act applies only to restraints that have a significant impact on interstate commerce. Courts have generally held that any activity that substantially affects interstate commerce falls within the scope of the Sherman Act. As will be discussed later

in this chapter, the Sherman Act also extends to U.S. nationals abroad that are engaged in activities that affect U.S. foreign commerce.

Federal courts have exclusive jurisdiction over antitrust cases brought under the Sherman Act. State laws regulate local restraints on competition, and state courts can decide claims brought under those laws.

SECTION 2
SECTION 1 OF THE SHERMAN ACT

The underlying assumption of Section 1 of the Sherman Act is that society's welfare is harmed if rival firms are permitted to join in an agreement that consolidates their market power or otherwise restrains competition. The types of trade restraints that Section 1 of the Sherman Act prohibits generally fall into two broad categories: *horizontal restraints* and *vertical restraints*, both of which will be discussed shortly. First, though, we look at the rules that the courts may apply when assessing the anticompetitive impact of alleged restraints of trade.

Per Se Violations versus the Rule of Reason

Some restraints are so substantially anticompetitive that they are deemed ***per se* violations**—illegal *per se* (inherently)—under Section 1. Other agreements, however, even though they result in enhanced market power, do not *unreasonably* restrain trade and are therefore lawful. Using the **rule of reason,** the courts analyze anticompetitive agreements that allegedly violate Section 1 of the Sherman Act to determine whether they actually constitute reasonable restraints of trade.

RATIONALE FOR THE RULE OF REASON The need for a rule-of-reason analysis of some agreements in restraint of trade is obvious. If the rule of reason had not been developed, almost any business agreement could conceivably be held to violate the Sherman Act.

FACTORS THAT COURTS CONSIDER When analyzing an alleged Section 1 violation under the rule of reason, a court will consider the following factors:

1. The purpose of the agreement.
2. The parties' ability to implement the agreement to achieve that purpose.

3. The effect or potential effect of the agreement on competition.
4. Whether the parties could have relied on less restrictive means to achieve their purpose.

▶ **Case in Point 46.1** The National Football League (NFL) includes thirty-two separately owned professional football teams. Each team has its own name, colors, and logo, and owns related intellectual property that it markets through National Football League Properties (NFLP). Until 2000, the NFLP granted nonexclusive licenses to a number of vendors, permitting them to manufacture and sell apparel bearing NFL team insignias. American Needle, Inc., was one of those licensees.

In late 2000, the teams authorized the NFLP to grant exclusive licenses. The NFLP granted Reebok International, Ltd., an exclusive ten-year license to manufacture and sell trademarked headwear for all thirty-two teams. It then declined to renew American Needle's nonexclusive license. American Needle sued, claiming that the NFL teams, the NFLP, and Reebok had violated Section 1 of the Sherman Act. The United States Supreme Court agreed. The Court concluded that the agreement among the NFL teams to license their intellectual property exclusively through the NFLP to Reebok constituted concerted activity.[6] ◀

Horizontal Restraints

The term **horizontal restraint** is encountered frequently in antitrust law. A horizontal restraint is any agreement that in some way restrains competition between rival firms competing in the same market.

PRICE FIXING Any **price-fixing agreement**—an agreement among competitors to fix prices—constitutes a *per se* violation of Section 1. The agreement on price need not be explicit. As long as it restricts output or artificially fixes price, it violates the law.

▶ **Case in Point 46.2** Independent oil producers in Texas and Louisiana were caught between falling demand due to the great depression of the 1930s and increasing supply from newly discovered oil fields in the region. In response to these conditions, a group of the major refining companies agreed to buy "distress" gasoline (excess supplies) from the independents so as to dispose of it in an "orderly manner." Although there was no explicit agreement as to price, it was

clear that the purpose of the agreement was to limit the supply of gasoline on the market and thereby raise prices.

There may have been good reasons for the agreement. Nonetheless, the United States Supreme Court recognized the potentially adverse effects that such an agreement could have on open and free competition. The Court held that the reasonableness of a price-fixing agreement is never a defense. Any agreement that restricts output or artificially fixes price is a *per se* violation of Section 1.[7] ◀

Price Fixing and E-Books. The U.S. government actively pursues companies that it suspects of being involved in price-fixing cartels (groups). ▶ **Example 46.3** In 2012, the U.S. Justice Department filed a lawsuit against five major book publishers and Apple, Inc., charging that they had conspired to fix the prices of e-books. The five publishers and Apple allegedly were concerned that competition among e-book sellers—such as Amazon—had reduced the price of e-books to $9.99 per e-book, which cut into their retail profit margins. The companies allegedly worked together to raise retail e-book prices and eliminate price competition (and the price of e-books did go up). All five of the book publishers subsequently settled with the Justice Department. Apple continued to dispute the government's allegations. Apple lost the case and is appealing. ◀

Price Fixing and Drug Manufacturers. Price-fixing accusations are also frequently made against drug manufacturers. ▶ **Case in Point 46.4** The manufacturer of the prescription drug Cardizem CD, which can help prevent heart attacks, was about to lose its patent on the drug. Another company had developed a generic version in anticipation of the patent's expiration. After the two firms became involved in litigation over the patent, the original manufacturer agreed to pay the second company $40 million per year not to market the generic version until their dispute was resolved. This agreement was held to be a *per se* violation of the Sherman Act because it restrained competition between rival firms and delayed the entry of generic versions of Cardizem into the market.[8] ◀

GROUP BOYCOTTS A **group boycott** is an agreement by two or more sellers to refuse to deal with

---

6. *American Needle, Inc. v. National Football League,* 560 U.S. 183, 130 S.Ct. 2201, 176 L.Ed.2d 947 (2010).

7. *United States v. Socony-Vacuum Oil Co.,* 310 U.S. 150, 60 S.Ct. 811, 84 L.Ed. 1129 (1940).
8. *In re Cardizem CD Antitrust Litigation,* 332 F.3d 896 (6th Cir. 2003).

(boycott) a particular person or firm. Because they involve concerted action, group boycotts have been held to constitute *per se* violations of Section 1 of the Sherman Act.

To prove a violation of Section 1, the plaintiff must demonstrate that the boycott or joint refusal to deal was undertaken with the intention of eliminating competition or preventing entry into a given market. Although most boycotts are illegal, a few, such as group boycotts against a supplier for political reasons, may be protected under the First Amendment right to freedom of expression.

HORIZONTAL MARKET DIVISION It is a *per se* violation of Section 1 of the Sherman Act for competitors to divide up territories or customers. ▶ **Example 46.5** Alred Office Supply, Belmont Business, and Carlson's, Inc., compete against each other in the states of Kansas, Nebraska, and Oklahoma. They agree that Alred will sell products only in Kansas, Belmont will sell only in Nebraska, and Carlson's will sell only in Oklahoma. This concerted action reduces the firms' marketing costs and allows all three (assuming there is no other competition) to raise the price of the goods sold in their respective states—a *per se* violation of Section 1.

The same violation would take place if the three firms agreed to divide up their territories by customers. For example, Alred might sell only to institutional purchasers (such as governments and schools) in all three states, Belmont only to wholesalers, and Carlson only to retailers. ◀

TRADE ASSOCIATIONS Businesses in the same general industry or profession frequently organize trade associations to pursue common interests. A trade association may engage in various joint activities, such as exchanging information, representing the members' business interests before governmental bodies, and conducting advertising campaigns. Trade associations also frequently are involved in setting regulatory standards to govern the industry or profession.

Generally, the rule of reason is applied to many of these horizontal actions. If a court finds that a trade association practice or agreement that restrains trade is nonetheless sufficiently beneficial both to the association and to the public, it may deem the restraint reasonable.

In *concentrated industries,* however, trade associations can be, and have been, used as a means to facilitate anticompetitive actions, such as fixing prices or allocating markets. A **concentrated industry** is one in which either a single firm or a small number of firms control a large percentage of market sales. When trade association agreements have substantially anticompetitive effects, a court will consider them to be in violation of Section 1 of the Sherman Act.

JOINT VENTURES Joint ventures (see Chapter 38) undertaken by competitors are also subject to antitrust laws. If a joint venture does not involve price fixing or market divisions, the agreement will be analyzed under the rule of reason. Whether the joint undertaking violates Section 1 will then depend on the factors stated earlier in this chapter. A court will look at the venture's purpose, the potential benefits relative to the likely harms, and whether there are less restrictive alternatives for achieving the same goals.

Vertical Restraints

A **vertical restraint** of trade results from an agreement between firms at different levels in the manufacturing and distribution process. In contrast to horizontal relationships, which occur at the same level of operation, vertical relationships encompass the entire chain of production.

The chain of production normally includes the purchase of inventory, basic manufacturing, distribution to wholesalers, and eventual sale of a product at the retail level. For some products, these distinct phases are carried on by different firms. In other instances, a single firm carries out two or more of the separate functional phases. Such enterprises are said to be **vertically integrated firms.**

Even though firms operating at different functional levels are not in direct competition with one another, they are in competition with other firms. Thus, agreements between firms standing in a vertical relationship may affect competition. Some vertical restraints are *per se* violations of Section 1. Others are judged under the rule of reason.

TERRITORIAL OR CUSTOMER RESTRICTIONS In arranging for the distribution of its products, a manufacturing firm often wishes to insulate dealers from direct competition with other dealers selling its products. To do so, the manufacturer may institute territorial restrictions or attempt to prohibit wholesalers or retailers from reselling the products to certain classes of buyers, such as competing retailers.

May Have Legitimate Purpose. A firm may have legitimate reasons for imposing such territorial or customer restrictions. For instance, an electronics manufacturer may wish to prevent a dealer from reducing costs and undercutting rivals by offering its products without promotion or customer service. In this situation, the cost-cutting dealer reaps the benefits (sales of the product) paid for by other dealers who undertake promotion and arrange for customer service. By not providing customer service (and relying on a nearby dealer to provide these services), the cost-cutting dealer may also harm the manufacturer's reputation.

Judged under the Rule of Reason. Territorial and customer restrictions were once considered *per se* violations of Section 1,[9] but in 1977, the United States Supreme Court held that they should be judged under the rule of reason. ▶ **Case in Point 46.6** GTE Sylvania, Inc., a manufacturer of television sets, limited the number of retail franchises that it granted in any given geographic area. It also required each franchisee to sell only Sylvania products from the location at which it was franchised. Sylvania retained sole discretion to increase the number of retailers in an area.

When Sylvania decided to open a new franchise, it terminated the franchise of Continental T.V., Inc., an existing franchisee in that area that would have been in competition with the new franchise. Continental filed a lawsuit claiming that Sylvania's vertically restrictive franchise system violated Section 1 of the Sherman Act. The United States Supreme Court found that "vertical restrictions promote interbrand competition by allowing the manufacturer to achieve cer-

tain efficiencies in the distribution of his products." Therefore, Sylvania's vertical system, which was not price restrictive, did not constitute a *per se* violation of Section 1 of the Sherman Act.[10] ◀

The decision in the *Continental* case marked a definite shift from rigid characterization of territorial and customer restrictions to a more flexible, economic analysis of these vertical restraints under the rule of reason. This rule is still applied in most vertical restraint cases.

RESALE PRICE MAINTENANCE AGREEMENTS An agreement between a manufacturer and a distributor or retailer in which the manufacturer specifies what the retail prices of its products must be is known as a **resale price maintenance agreement.** Such agreements were once considered to be *per se* violations of Section 1 of the Sherman Act. In 1997, however, the United States Supreme Court ruled that *maximum* resale price maintenance agreements should be judged under the rule of reason.[11] The setting of a maximum price that retailers and distributors can charge for a manufacturer's products may sometimes increase competition and benefit consumers.

The question before the United States Supreme Court in the following case was whether *minimum* resale price maintenance agreements should be treated as *per se* violations.

---

9. See *United States v. Arnold, Schwinn & Co.,* 388 U.S. 365, 87 S.Ct. 1856, 18 L.Ed.2d 1249 (1967).

10. *Continental T.V., Inc. v. GTE Sylvania, Inc.,* 433 U.S. 36, 97 S.Ct. 2549, 53 L.Ed.2d 568 (1977).

11. *State Oil Co. v. Khan,* 522 U.S. 3, 118 S.Ct. 275, 139 L.Ed.2d 199 (1997).

CASE ANALYSIS

Case 46.1   Leegin Creative Leather Products, Inc. v. PSKS, Inc.

Supreme Court of the United States, 551 U.S. 877, 127 S.Ct. 2705, 168 L.Ed.2d 623 (2007).

IN THE LANGUAGE OF THE COURT
Justice *KENNEDY* delivered the opinion of the Court.

* * * *

Petitioner, Leegin Creative Leather Products, Inc. (Leegin), designs, manufactures, and distributes leather goods and accessories. In 1991, Leegin

began to sell [products] under the brand name "Brighton."

Respondent, PSKS, Inc. (PSKS), operates Kay's Kloset, a women's apparel store in Lewisville, Texas. * * * It first started purchasing Brighton goods from Leegin in 1995.

* * * *

In December 2002, Leegin discovered Kay's Kloset had been marking

down Brighton's entire line by 20 percent. * * * Leegin stopped selling [Brighton products] to the store.

PSKS sued Leegin in the United States District Court for the Eastern District of Texas. It alleged, among other claims, that Leegin had violated the antitrust laws by "enter[ing] into agreements with retailers to charge only those prices fixed by Leegin."

CASE 46.1 CONTINUES ▶

CASE 46.1 CONTINUED

* * * [The court] entered judgment against Leegin in the amount of $3,975,000.80.

The [U.S.] Court of Appeals for the Fifth Circuit affirmed. * * * We granted *certiorari* * * * .

* * * *

The rule of reason is the accepted standard for testing whether a practice restrains trade in violation of [Section] 1 [of the Sherman Act].

* * * *

*Resort to per se rules is confined to restraints * * * that would always or almost always tend to restrict competition and decrease output. To justify a per se prohibition a restraint must have manifestly anticompetitive effects, and lack * * * any redeeming virtue.* [Emphasis added.]

As a consequence, the *per se* rule is appropriate only after courts have had considerable experience with the type of restraint at issue, and only if courts can predict with confidence that it would be invalidated in all or almost all instances under the rule of reason.

* * * *

The reasoning of the Court's more recent jurisprudence has rejected the rationales on which [the application of the *per se* rule to minimum resale price maintenance agreements] was based. * * * [These rationales were] based on formalistic legal doctrine rather than demonstrable economic effect.

* * * Furthermore [the Court] treated vertical agreements a manufacturer makes with its distributors as analogous to a horizontal combination among competing distributors. * * * Our recent cases formulate antitrust principles in accordance with the appreciated differences in economic effect between vertical and horizontal agreements * * * .

* * * *

The justifications for vertical price restraints are similar to those for other vertical restraints. *Minimum resale price maintenance can stimulate interbrand competition * * * by reducing intrabrand competition * * * .* The promotion of interbrand competition is important because the primary purpose of the antitrust laws is to protect this type of competition. * * * *Resale price maintenance also has the potential to give consumers more options so that they can choose among low-price, low-service brands; high-price, high-service brands; and brands that fall in between.* [Emphasis added.]

* * * *

While vertical agreements setting minimum resale prices can have procompetitive justifications, they may have anticompetitive effects in other cases; and unlawful price fixing, designed solely to obtain monopoly profits, is an ever present temptation.

* * * *

Notwithstanding the risks of unlawful conduct, it cannot be stated with any degree of confidence that resale price maintenance always or almost always tends to restrict competition and decrease output. Vertical agreements establishing minimum resale prices can have either procompetitive or anticompetitive effects, depending upon the circumstances in which they are formed. * * * As the *[per se]* rule would proscribe a significant amount of procompetitive conduct, these agreements appear ill suited for *per se* condemnation.

* * * *

The judgment of the Court of Appeals is reversed, and the case is remanded for proceedings consistent with this opinion.

LEGAL REASONING QUESTIONS

1. Should the Court have applied the doctrine of *stare decisis* to hold that minimum resale price maintenance agreements are still subject to the *per se* rule? Why or why not?

2. What factors might the courts consider in applying the rule of reason to minimum resale price maintenance agreements?

3. In what ways do minimum resale price maintenance agreements facilitate interbrand competition?

4. In general, how are the interests of manufacturers, retailers, and consumers aligned—and in conflict—with respect to a product's profit margin? (A product's profit margin is the difference between the price a manufacturer charges retailers and the price retailers charge consumers.)

SECTION 3

SECTION 2 OF THE SHERMAN ACT

Section 1 of the Sherman Act proscribes certain concerted, or joint, activities that restrain trade. In contrast, Section 2 condemns "every person who shall monopolize, or attempt to monopolize." Thus, two distinct types of behavior are subject to sanction under Section 2: *monopolization* and *attempts to monopolize.*

One tactic that may be involved in either offense is predatory pricing. **Predatory pricing** occurs when one firm (the predator) attempts to drive its competitors from the market by selling its product at prices substantially *below* the normal costs of production. Once the competitors are eliminated, the predator presumably will raise its prices far above their competitive levels to recapture its losses and earn higher profits.

Monopolization

The United States Supreme Court has defined **monopolization** as involving the following two elements:

1. The possession of monopoly power in the relevant market.
2. "The willful acquisition or maintenance of the power as distinguished from growth or development as a consequence of a superior product, business acumen, or historic accident."[12]

To establish a violation of Section 2, a plaintiff must prove both of these elements—monopoly power and an *intent* to monopolize.

MONOPOLY POWER The Sherman Act does not define *monopoly*. In economic theory, monopoly refers to

control of a specific market by a single entity. It is well established in antitrust law, however, that a firm may be a monopolist even though it is not the sole seller in a market.

Additionally, size alone does not determine whether a firm is a monopoly. ▶ **Example 46.7** A "mom and pop" grocery located in the isolated town of Happy Camp, Idaho, is a monopolist if it is the only grocery serving that particular market. Size in relation to the market is what matters because monopoly involves the power to affect prices. ◀

Monopoly power may be proved by direct evidence that the firm used its power to control prices and restrict output.[13] Usually, though, there is not enough evidence to show that the firm intentionally controlled prices, so the plaintiff has to offer indirect, or circumstantial, evidence of monopoly power. To prove monopoly power indirectly, the plaintiff must show that the firm has a dominant share of the relevant market and that there are significant barriers for new competitors entering that market.

In the following case, the court had to decide whether there was sufficient evidence to show that a company possessed monopoly power in the relevant market.

12. *United States v. Grinnell Corp.*, 384 U.S. 563, 86 S.Ct. 1698, 16 L.Ed.2d 778 (1966).

13. See, for example, *Broadcom Corp. v. Qualcomm, Inc.*, 501 F.3d 297 (3d Cir. 2007).

CASE 46.2

E.I. DuPont de Nemours and Co. v. Kolon Industries
United States Court of Appeals, Fourth Circuit, 637 F.3d 435 (2011).

COMPANY PROFILE DuPont was founded in 1802 as a gunpowder manufacturer. Today, it operates in ninety countries in the fields of agriculture, apparel, communications, electronics, home construction, nutrition, and transportation. It recently made a major investment in a biodegradable ingredient used in cosmetics, liquid detergents, and antifreeze.

BACKGROUND AND FACTS DuPont manufactures and sells para-aramid fiber, which is a complex synthetic fiber used to make body armor, fiber-optic cables, and tires, among other things. Although several companies around the world manufacture this fiber, only three sell into the U.S. market—DuPont (based in the United States), Teijin (based in the Netherlands), and Kolon Industries, Inc. (based in Korea). DuPont is the industry leader, producing more than 70 percent of all para-aramid fibers purchased in the United States. In 2009, DuPont brought a lawsuit against Kolon for misappropriation of trade secrets.

Kolon counterclaimed that DuPont had monopolized and attempted to monopolize the para-aramid market in violation of Section 2 of the Sherman Act. Kolon claimed that DuPont had illegally used multiyear supply agreements for all of its high-volume para-aramid fiber customers. Under the agreements, the customers were required to purchase between 80 and 100 percent of their para-aramid needs from DuPont. Kolon alleged that those agreements removed substantial commercial opportunities from competition and limited other para-aramid fiber producers' ability to compete. On DuPont's motion, a federal district court dismissed Kolon's counterclaim, finding that Kolon had failed to sufficiently plead (demonstrate) unlawful exclusionary conduct. Kolon appealed to the U.S. Court of Appeals for the Fourth Circuit.

CASE 46.2 CONTINUES ▶

CASE 46.2 CONTINUED

IN THE LANGUAGE OF THE COURT
James *WYNN*, United States Circuit Judge.
* * * *

* * * *To prove a Section 2 monopolization offense, a plaintiff must establish two elements: (1) the possession of monopoly power; and (2) willful acquisition or maintenance of that power—as opposed to simply superior products or historic accidents. An attempted monopolization offense consists of: (1) the use of anticompetitive conduct; (2) with specific intent to monopolize; and (3) a dangerous probability of success.* [Emphasis added.]
* * * *

* * * To run afoul of Section 2, a defendant must be guilty of illegal conduct "to foreclose competition, to gain a competitive advantage, or to destroy a competitor." Conduct that might otherwise be lawful may be impermissibly exclusionary under antitrust law when practiced by a monopolist. Indeed, "a monopolist is not free to take certain actions that a company in a competitive * * * market may take, because there is no market constraint on a monopolist's behavior." And although not *per se* illegal, exclusive dealing arrangements can constitute an improper means of acquiring or maintaining a monopoly.
* * * *

Here, the district court assumed that Kolon adequately pled possession of monopoly power. That assumption was correct, given that Kolon pled, among other things, that: numerous barriers to entry into the U.S. para-aramid fiber market exist and supply is low; DuPont has long dominated the U.S. para-aramid fiber market; and DuPont currently controls over 70 percent of that market, [that is,] that "DuPont's market share remains greater than 70% of all sales by purchase volume of para-aramid fiber in the United States."
* * * *

* * * Kolon complained that "because DuPont's supply contracts severely restricted access to customers and preclude effective competition, DuPont's conduct has had a direct, substantial, and adverse effect on competition. And DuPont's anticompetitive conduct has allowed it to control output and increase prices for para-aramid fiber in the United States." And "by precluding Kolon from competition for these customers when demand for para-aramid fibers has significantly increased and supply is low, DuPont's conduct has constrained the only potential entrant to the United States in decades from effectively entering the market, reducing if not practically eliminating additional competition, as well as preserving and growing DuPont's monopoly position." These allegations are sufficient to withstand a motion to dismiss.

DECISION AND REMEDY   *The federal appellate court reversed the district court's decision. The appellate court found that Kolon had alleged sufficient facts to show that DuPont's behavior violated the prohibition against monopolization and attempted monopolization in Section 2 of the Sherman Act.*

WHAT IF THE FACTS WERE DIFFERENT?   *Suppose that DuPont had 45 percent of the market and Kolon and numerous other competitors had the remaining 55 percent. Would the appellate court have ruled the same way? Why or why not?*

MANAGERIAL IMPLICATIONS   *Kolon's success in raising antitrust issues against a major supplier of a particular product in the United States can give some hope to other companies that are attempting to expand their market share against a dominant competitor. In other words, managers who see competitive opportunities, even though their companies have only a very small market share, may be able to resort to the courts to prevent the dominant company or companies from acting in anticompetitive ways.*

RELEVANT MARKET Before a court can determine whether a firm has a dominant market share, it must define the relevant market. The relevant market consists of two elements: (1) a relevant product market and (2) a relevant geographic market.

Relevant Product Market. The relevant product market includes all products that, although produced by different firms, have identical attributes, such as sugar. It also includes products that are reasonably interchangeable for the purpose for which they are produced. Products will be considered reasonably interchangeable if consumers treat them as acceptable substitutes.[14]

Establishing the relevant product market is often the key issue in monopolization cases because the way the market is defined may determine whether a firm has monopoly power. By defining the product market narrowly, the degree of a firm's market power is enhanced.

▶ **Case in Point 46.8**   Whole Foods Market, Inc., wished to acquire Wild Oats Markets, Inc., its main competitor in nationwide high-end organic food supermarkets. The Federal Trade Commission (FTC) filed a Section 2 claim against Whole Foods to prevent the merger. The FTC argued that the relevant product market consisted of only "premium natural and organic supermarkets" rather than all supermarkets, as Whole Foods maintained. An appellate court accepted the FTC's narrow definition of the relevant market and remanded the case to the lower court to decide what remedies were appropriate, as the merger had already taken place. Whole Foods later entered into a settlement with the FTC under which it was required to divest (sell or give up control over) thirteen stores, most of which were formerly Wild Oats outlets.[15] ◀

Relevant Geographic Market.   The second component of the relevant market is the geographic extent of the market in which the firm and its competitors sell the product or services. For products that are sold nationwide, the geographic boundaries of the market can encompass the entire United States.

If transportation costs are significant or a producer and its competitors sell in only a limited area (one in which customers have no access to other sources of the product), then the geographic market is limited to that area. A national firm may thus compete in several distinct areas and have monopoly power in one geographic area but not in another.

Generally, the geographic market is that section of the country within which a firm can increase its price a bit without attracting new sellers or without losing many customers to alternative suppliers outside that area. Of course, the Internet is changing perceptions of the size and limits of a geographic market. It may become difficult to perceive any geographic market

as local, except for products that are not easily transported, such as concrete.

THE INTENT REQUIREMENT   Monopoly power, in and of itself, does not constitute the offense of monopolization under Section 2 of the Sherman Act. The offense also requires an *intent* to monopolize.

Why Intent Is Required.   A dominant market share may be the result of good business judgment or the development of a superior product. It may simply be the result of a historical accident. In these situations, the acquisition of monopoly power is not an antitrust violation. Indeed, it would be contrary to society's interest to condemn every firm that acquired a position of power because it was well managed and efficient and marketed a product desired by consumers.

Inferred from Anticompetitive Conduct.   If a firm possesses market power as a result of carrying out some purposeful act to acquire or maintain that power through anticompetitive means, then it is in violation of Section 2. In most monopolization cases, intent may be inferred from evidence that the firm had monopoly power and engaged in anticompetitive behavior.

▶ **Case in Point 46.9**   When Navigator, the first popular graphical Internet browser, was introduced, Microsoft perceived a threat to its dominance of the operating-system market. Microsoft developed a competing browser, Internet Explorer (IE), and then began to require computer makers that wanted to install the Windows operating system to install IE and exclude Navigator. Microsoft included codes in Windows that would cripple the operating system if IE was deleted and paid Internet service providers to distribute IE and exclude Navigator.

Because of this pattern of exclusionary conduct, a court found that Microsoft was guilty of monopolization. The court reasoned that Microsoft's pattern of conduct could be rational only if the firm knew that it possessed monopoly power.[16] ◀

UNILATERAL REFUSALS TO DEAL   As discussed previously, joint refusals to deal (group boycotts) are subject to close scrutiny under Section 1 of the Sherman Act. A single manufacturer acting unilaterally, though,

---

14. See, for example, *Linzer Products Corp. v. Sekar,* 499 F.Supp.2d 540 (S.D.N.Y. 2007); and *HDC Medical, Inc. v. Minntech Corp.,* 474 F.3d 543 (8th Cir. 2007).

15. *Federal Trade Commission v. Whole Foods Market, Inc.,* 548 F.3d 1028 (D.C.Cir. 2008); and 592 F.Supp.2d 107 (D.D.C. 2009).

16. *United States v. Microsoft Corp.,* 253 F.3d 34 (D.C.Cir. 2001). Microsoft has faced numerous antitrust claims and has settled a number of lawsuits in which it was accused of antitrust violations and anticompetitive tactics.

normally is free to deal, or not to deal, with whomever it wishes.[17]

Nevertheless, in some instances, a unilateral refusal to deal will violate Section 2 of the Sherman Act. These instances occur only if (1) the firm refusing to deal has—or is likely to acquire—monopoly power and (2) the refusal is likely to have an anticompetitive effect on a particular market.

▶ **Case in Point 46.10** Aspen Skiing Company, the owner of three of the four major ski areas in Aspen, Colorado, refused to continue its participation in a jointly offered "all Aspen" lift ticket. The United States Supreme Court ruled that the owner's refusal to cooperate with its smaller competitor was a violation of Section 2 of the Sherman Act. Because the company owned three-fourths of the local ski areas, it had monopoly power, and thus its unilateral refusal had an anticompetitive effect on the market.[18] ◀

Attempts to Monopolize

Section 2 also prohibits **attempted monopolization** of a market, which requires proof of the following three elements:

1. Anticompetitive conduct.
2. The specific intent to exclude competitors and garner monopoly power.
3. A "dangerous" probability of success in achieving monopoly power. The probability cannot be dangerous unless the alleged offender possesses some degree of market power.[19]

As mentioned earlier, predatory pricing is a form of anticompetitive conduct that, in theory, could be used by firms that are attempting to monopolize. (Predatory pricing may also lead to claims of price discrimination, to be discussed shortly.)

Predatory bidding involves the acquisition and use of *monopsony power,* which is market power on the *buy* side of a market. This may occur when a buyer bids up the price of an input too high for its competitors to pay, causing them to leave the market. The predatory bidder may then attempt to drive down input prices so that it can reap above-competitive profits and recoup any losses it suffered in bidding up the prices. The United States Supreme Court has held that the antitrust test that applies to claims of predatory pricing also applies to claims of predatory bidding.[20]

SECTION 4
THE CLAYTON ACT

In 1914, Congress enacted the Clayton Act. The act was aimed at specific anticompetitive or monopolistic practices that the Sherman Act did not cover. The substantive provisions of the act—set out in Sections 2, 3, 7, and 8—deal with four distinct forms of business behavior, which are declared illegal but not criminal. For each provision, the act states that the behavior is *illegal only if it tends to substantially lessen competition or to create monopoly power.*

Section 2—Price Discrimination

Section 2 of the Clayton Act prohibits **price discrimination,** which occurs when a seller charges different prices to competing buyers for identical goods or services. Congress strengthened this section by amending it with the passage of the Robinson-Patman Act in 1936.

As amended, Section 2 prohibits price discrimination that cannot be justified by differences in production costs, transportation costs, or cost differences due to other reasons. In short, a seller is prohibited from charging one buyer a lower price than it charges that buyer's competitor.

REQUIRED ELEMENTS To violate Section 2, the seller must be engaged in interstate commerce, the goods must be of like grade and quality, and the goods must have been sold to two or more purchasers. In addition, the effect of the price discrimination must be to substantially lessen competition, tend to create a monopoly, or otherwise injure competition. Without proof of an actual injury resulting from the price discrimination, the plaintiff cannot recover damages.

Note that price discrimination claims can arise from discounts, offsets, rebates, or allowances given

---

17. For a classic case in this area, see *United States v. Colgate & Co.,* 250 U.S. 300, 39 S.Ct. 465, 63 L.Ed. 992 (1919). See also *Pacific Bell Telephone Co. v. Linkline Communications, Inc.,* 555 U.S. 438, 129 S.Ct. 1109, 172 L.Ed.2d 836 (2009).

18. *Aspen Skiing Co. v. Aspen Highlands Skiing Corp.,* 472 U.S. 585, 105 S.Ct. 2847, 86 L.Ed.2d 467 (1985). See also *America Channel, LLC v. Time Warner Cable, Inc.,* 2007 WL 142173 (D.Minn. 2007).

19. See, for example, *Nobody in Particular Presents, Inc. v. Clear Channel Communications, Inc.,* 311 F.Supp.2d 1048 (D.Colo. 2004); and *City of Moundridge, Kansas v. Exxon Mobil Corp.,* 471 F.Supp.2d 20 (D.D.C. 2007).

20. *Weyerhaeuser Co. v. Ross-Simmons Hardwood Lumber Co.,* 549 U.S. 312, 127 S.Ct. 1069, 166 L.Ed.2d 911 (2007).

to one buyer over another. Moreover, giving favorable credit terms, delivery, or freight charges to some buyers, but not others, can also lead to allegations of price discrimination. For example, when a seller offers goods to different customers at the same price but includes free delivery for certain buyers, it may violate Section 2 in some circumstances.

DEFENSES There are several statutory defenses to liability for price discrimination.

1. *Cost justification.* If the seller can justify the price reduction by demonstrating that a particular buyer's purchases saved the seller costs in producing and selling the goods, the seller will not be liable for price discrimination.
2. *Meeting a competitor's prices.* If the seller charged the lower price in a good faith attempt to meet an equally low price of a competitor, the seller will not be liable for price discrimination. ▶ **Case in Point 46.11** Water Craft was a retail dealership of Mercury Marine outboard motors. On discovering that Mercury was selling its outboard motors at a substantial discount to Water Craft's largest competitor, Water Craft filed a price discrimination lawsuit against Mercury. Mercury Marine was able show that the discounts were made in good faith to meet the low price charged by another manufacturer of marine motors. Therefore, the court found that the "meeting competition defense" applied.[21] ◀
3. *Changing market conditions.* A seller may lower its price on an item in response to changing conditions affecting the market for or the marketability of the goods concerned. Sellers are allowed to readjust their prices to meet the realities of the market without liability for price discrimination. Thus, if an advance in technology makes a particular product less marketable than it was previously, a seller can lower the product's price.

Section 3—Exclusionary Practices

Under Section 3 of the Clayton Act, sellers or lessors cannot sell or lease goods "on the condition, agreement or understanding that the . . . purchaser or lessee thereof shall not use or deal in the goods . . . of a competitor or competitors of the seller." In effect, this section prohibits two types of vertical agreements involving exclusionary practices—exclusive-dealing contracts and tying arrangements.

EXCLUSIVE-DEALING CONTRACTS A contract under which a seller forbids a buyer to purchase products from the seller's competitors is called an **exclusive-dealing contract.** A seller is prohibited from making an exclusive-dealing contract under Section 3 if the effect of the contract is "to substantially lessen competition or tend to create a monopoly."

In the past, courts were more inclined to find that exclusive-dealing contracts substantially lessened competition. ▶ **Case in Point 46.12** In one classic case, Standard Oil Company, the largest gasoline seller in the nation in the late 1940s, made exclusive-dealing contracts with independent stations in seven western states. The contracts involved 16 percent of all retail outlets, whose sales were approximately 7 percent of all retail sales in that market. The United States Supreme Court ruled that the market was substantially concentrated because the seven largest gasoline suppliers all used exclusive-dealing contracts with their independent retailers and together controlled 65 percent of the market.

Looking at market conditions after the arrangements were instituted, the Court found that market shares were extremely stable and that entry into the market was apparently restricted. Thus, the Court held that the Clayton Act had been violated because competition was "foreclosed in a substantial share" of the relevant market.[22] ◀

In recent years, however, a number of decisions have called into doubt the Supreme Court's holding in *Case in Point 46.12*. Today, it is clear that to violate antitrust law, an exclusive-dealing agreement (or a tying arrangement, discussed next) must qualitatively and substantially harm competition. To prevail, a plaintiff must present affirmative evidence that the performance of the agreement will foreclose competition and harm consumers.

TYING ARRANGEMENTS When a seller conditions the sale of a product (the tying product) on the buyer's agreement to purchase another product (the tied product) produced or distributed by the same seller, a **tying arrangement** results. The legality of a tying arrangement (or *tie-in sales agreement*) depends on several factors, such as the purpose of the agreement. Courts also focus on the agreement's likely effect on

21. *Water Craft Management, LLC v. Mercury Marine,* 457 F.3d 484 (5th Cir. 2006).

22. *Standard Oil Co. of California v. United States,* 337 U.S. 293, 69 S.Ct. 1051, 93 L.Ed. 1371 (1949).

competition in the relevant markets (the market for the tying product and the market for the tied product).

▶ **Example 46.13** Morshigi Precision, Inc., manufactures laptop hardware and provides repair service for the hardware. Morshigi also makes and markets software, but the company will provide support for buyers of the software only if they also buy its hardware service. This is a tying arrangement. Depending on the purpose of the agreement and the effect of the agreement on competition in the market for the two products, the agreement may be illegal. ◀

Section 3 of the Clayton Act has been held to apply only to commodities, not to services. Tying arrangements, however, can also be considered agreements that restrain trade in violation of Section 1 of the Sherman Act. Thus, cases involving tying arrangements of services have been brought under Section 1 of the Sherman Act. Although earlier cases condemned tying arrangements as illegal *per se,* courts now evaluate tying agreements under the rule of reason.[23]

Section 7—Mergers

Under Section 7 of the Clayton Act, a person or business organization cannot hold stock or assets in more than one business when "the effect . . . may be to substantially lessen competition." Section 7 is the statutory authority for preventing mergers that could result in monopoly power or a substantial lessening of competition in the marketplace. Section 7 applies to both horizontal and vertical mergers, as discussed in the following subsections.

A crucial consideration in most merger cases is **market concentration.** Determining market concentration involves allocating percentage market shares among the various companies in the relevant market. When a small number of companies share a large part of the market, the market is concentrated. ▶ **Example 46.14** If the four largest grocery stores in Chicago accounted for 80 percent of all retail food sales, the market clearly would be concentrated in those four firms. If one of these stores absorbed the assets and liabilities of another, so the other ceased to exist, the resulting merger would further concentrate the market and possibly diminish competition. ◀

Competition is not necessarily diminished solely as a result of market concentration, however. Courts will consider other factors in determining if a merger violates Section 7. One factor of particular importance is whether the merger will make it more difficult for *potential* competitors to enter the relevant market.

HORIZONTAL MERGERS Mergers between firms that compete with each other in the same market are called **horizontal mergers.** If a horizontal merger creates an entity with a significant market share, the merger may be considered illegal because it increases market concentration. The Federal Trade Commission (FTC) and the U.S. Department of Justice (DOJ) have established guidelines for determining which mergers will be challenged.[24]

When analyzing the legality of a horizontal merger, the courts consider three additional factors. The first factor is the overall concentration of the relevant market. The second is the relevant market's history of tending toward concentration. The final factor is whether the merger is apparently designed to establish market power or restrict competition.

VERTICAL MERGERS A **vertical merger** occurs when a company at one stage of production acquires a company at a higher or lower stage of production. An example of a vertical merger is a company merging with one of its suppliers or retailers. Whether a vertical merger will be deemed illegal generally depends on several factors, such as whether the merger creates a single firm that controls an undue percentage share of the relevant market.

The courts also analyze whether the merger results in a significant increase in the concentration of firms in that market, barriers to entry into the market, and the apparent intent of the merging parties. If a merger does not prevent competitors of either of the merging firms from competing in a segment of the market, the merger will not be condemned as foreclosing competition and thus is legal.

Section 8—Interlocking Directorates

Section 8 of the Clayton Act deals with *interlocking directorates*—that is, the practice of having individuals serve as directors on the boards of two or more competing companies simultaneously. Specifically,

---

23. The United States Supreme Court held that the rule of reason applies to tying arrangements in *Illinois Tool Works, Inc. v. Independent Ink, Inc.,* 547 U.S. 28, 126 S.Ct. 1281, 164 L.Ed.2d 26 (2006). This decision was the first time the Court recognized that tying arrangements can have legitimate business justifications.

24. These guidelines include a formula for assessing the degree of concentration in the relevant market called the *Herfindahl-Hirschman Index* (HHI). The HHI was revised in 2010 and is available at **www. justice.gov/atr/public/guidelines/hmg-2010.html**.

no person may be a director for two or more competing corporations at the same time if either of the corporations has capital, surplus, or undivided profits aggregating more than $28,883,000 or competitive sales of $2,888,300 or more. The Federal Trade Commission adjusts these threshold amounts each year. (The amounts given here are those announced by the commission in 2013.)

SECTION 5
ENFORCEMENT AND EXEMPTIONS

The federal agencies that enforce the federal antitrust laws are the U.S. Department of Justice (DOJ) and the Federal Trade Commission (FTC), which was established by the Federal Trade Commission Act of 1914. Section 5 of that act condemns all forms of anticompetitive behavior that are not covered under other federal antitrust laws.

Agency Actions

Only the DOJ can prosecute violations of the Sherman Act, which can be either criminal or civil offenses. Violations of the Clayton Act are not crimes, but the act can be enforced by either the DOJ or the FTC through civil proceedings.

The DOJ or the FTC may ask the courts to impose various remedies, including **divestiture** (making a company give up one or more of its operations) and dissolution. A meatpacking firm, for instance, might be forced to divest itself of control or ownership of butcher shops.

The FTC has sole authority to enforce violations of Section 5 of the Federal Trade Commission Act. FTC actions are effected through administrative orders, but if a firm violates an FTC order, the FTC can seek court sanctions for the violation.

The president, of course, plays a role in establishing enforcement policies at the agencies. The Obama administration—much like the European Union—has vigorously enforced antitrust regulations in recent years.

Private Actions

A private party who has been injured as a result of a violation of the Sherman Act or the Clayton Act can sue for **treble damages** (three times the actual damages suffered) and attorneys' fees. In some instances, private parties may also seek injunctive relief to prevent antitrust violations.

REQUIRED ELEMENTS A party wishing to sue under the Sherman Act must prove that:

1. The antitrust violation either caused or was a substantial factor in causing the injury that was suffered.
2. The unlawful actions of the accused party affected business activities of the plaintiff that were protected by the antitrust laws.

PROOF OF ILLEGALITY Additionally, the United States Supreme Court has held that to pursue antitrust lawsuits, private parties must present some evidence suggesting that an illegal agreement was made. ▶ **Case in Point 46.15** A group of subscribers to local telephone and high-speed Internet services filed a class-action lawsuit against several regional telecommunication companies (including Bell Atlantic). The plaintiffs claimed that the companies had conspired with one another and engaged in *parallel conduct*—offering similar services and pricing—over a period of years to prevent other companies from entering the market and competing.

The United States Supreme Court dismissed the case, finding that "without more, parallel conduct does not suggest conspiracy." A bare assertion of conspiracy is not enough to allow an antitrust lawsuit to go forward. The Court noted that more specificity is necessary to avoid potentially "massive" discovery costs, which are especially likely to occur when the suit is brought by a large class of plaintiffs.[25] ◀

Exemptions from Antitrust Laws

There are many legislative and constitutional limitations on antitrust enforcement. Most of the statutory and judicially created exemptions to the antitrust laws apply in such areas as labor, insurance, and foreign trade (see Exhibit 46–1 on the following page).

One of the most significant exemptions covers joint efforts by businesspersons to obtain legislative, judicial, or executive action. Under this exemption, for example, DVD producers can jointly lobby Congress to change the copyright laws without being held liable for attempting to restrain trade. Another exemption covers professional baseball teams.

---

25. *Bell Atlantic Corp. v. Twombly,* 550 U.S. 544, 127 S.Ct. 1955, 167 L.Ed.2d 929 (2007).

EXHIBIT 46-1 Exemptions to Antitrust Enforcement

Exemption	Source and Scope
Labor	Clayton Act—Permits unions to organize and bargain without violating antitrust laws and specifies that strikes and other labor activities normally do not violate any federal law.
Agricultural associations	Clayton Act and Capper-Volstead Act of 1922—Allow agricultural cooperatives to set prices.
Fisheries	Fisheries Cooperative Marketing Act of 1976—Allows the fishing industry to set prices.
Insurance companies	McCarran-Ferguson Act of 1945—Exempts the insurance business in states in which the industry is regulated.
Exporters	Webb-Pomerene Act of 1918—Allows U.S. exporters to engage in cooperative activity to compete with similar foreign associations. Export Trading Company Act of 1982—Permits the U.S. Department of Justice to exempt certain exporters.
Professional baseball	The United States Supreme Court has held that professional baseball is exempt because it is not "interstate commerce."[a]
Oil marketing	Interstate Oil Compact of 1935—Allows states to set quotas on oil to be marketed in interstate commerce.
Defense activities	Defense Production Act of 1950—Allows the president to approve, and thereby exempt, certain activities to further the military defense of the United States.
Small businesses' cooperative research	Small Business Administration Act of 1958—Allows small firms to undertake cooperative research.
State actions	The United States Supreme Court has held that actions by a state are exempt if the state clearly articulates and actively supervises the policy behind its action.[b]
Regulated industries	Industries (such as airlines) are exempt when a federal administrative agency (such as the Federal Aviation Administration) has primary regulatory authority.
Businesspersons' joint efforts to seek government action	Cooperative efforts by businesspersons to obtain legislative, judicial, or executive action are exempt unless it is clear that an effort is "objectively baseless" and is an attempt to make anticompetitive use of government processes.[c]

a. *Federal Baseball Club of Baltimore, Inc. v. National League of Professional Baseball Clubs,* 259 U.S. 200, 42 S.Ct. 465, 66 L.Ed. 898 (1922). A federal district court has held that this exemption applies only to the game's reserve system. (Under the reserve system, teams hold players' contracts for the players' entire careers. The reserve system generally is being replaced by the free agency system.) See *Piazza v. Major League Baseball,* 831 F.Supp. 420 (E.D.Pa. 1993).
b. See *Parker v. Brown,* 317 U.S. 341, 63 S.Ct. 307, 87 L.Ed. 315 (1943).
c. *Eastern Railroad Presidents Conference v. Noerr Motor Freight, Inc.,* 365 U.S. 127, 81 S.Ct. 523, 5 L.Ed.2d 464 (1961); and *United Mine Workers of America v. Pennington,* 381 U.S. 657, 89 S.Ct. 1585, 14 L.Ed.2d 626 (1965). These two cases established the exception often referred to as the *Noerr-Pennington* doctrine.

SECTION 6

U.S. ANTITRUST LAWS IN THE GLOBAL CONTEXT

U.S. antitrust laws have a broad application. Not only may persons in foreign nations be subject to their provisions, but the laws may also be applied to protect foreign consumers and competitors from violations committed by U.S. business firms. Consequently, *foreign persons,* a term that by definition includes foreign governments, may sue under U.S. antitrust laws in U.S. courts.

The Extraterritorial Application of U.S. Antitrust Laws

Section 1 of the Sherman Act provides for the extraterritorial effect of the U.S. antitrust laws. The United States is a major proponent of free competition in the global economy, and thus any conspiracy that has a *substantial effect* on U.S. commerce is within the reach of the Sherman Act. The violation may even occur outside the United States, and foreign governments as well as individuals can be sued for violation of U.S. antitrust laws.

Before U.S. courts will exercise jurisdiction and apply antitrust laws, it must be shown that the alleged violation had a substantial effect on U.S. commerce. U.S. jurisdiction is automatically invoked, however, when a *per se* violation occurs.

If a domestic firm, for example, joins a foreign cartel to control the production, price, or distribution of goods, and this cartel has a *substantial effect* on U.S. commerce, a *per se* violation may exist. Hence, both the domestic firm and the foreign cartel could be sued

for violation of the U.S. antitrust laws. Likewise, if a foreign firm doing business in the United States enters into a price-fixing or other anticompetitive agreement to control a portion of U.S. markets, a *per se* violation may exist.

In the following case, the court had to decide whether an alleged anticompetitive conspiracy had a substantial effect on U.S. commerce.

CASE 46.3

Carrier Corp. v. Outokumpu Oyj
United States Court of Appeals, Sixth Circuit, 673 F.3d 430 (2012).

BACKGROUND AND FACTS Carrier Corporation is a U.S. firm that manufactures air-conditioning and refrigeration (ACR) equipment. To make these products, Carrier uses ACR copper tubing bought from Outokumpu Oyj, a Finnish company. Carrier is one of the world's largest purchasers of ACR copper tubing. The Commission of the European Communities (EC) found that Outokumpu had conspired with other companies to fix ACR tubing prices in Europe. Carrier then filed a suit in a U.S. court, alleging that the cartel had also conspired to fix prices in the United States by agreeing that only Outokumpu would sell ACR tubing in the U.S. market. The district court dismissed Carrier's claim for lack of jurisdiction. Carrier appealed.

 IN THE LANGUAGE OF THE COURT
Karen Nelson *MOORE*, Circuit Judge.

* * * *

Carrier's complaint describes, in some detail, an elaborate worldwide conspiracy in which the U.S. market for ACR copper tubing was assigned to Outokumpu. Furthermore, *Carrier alleges that this conspiracy caused the price of goods purchased within the United States to increase, which in turn caused a direct antitrust injury.* In support of these allegations, the complaint references numerous specific dates during which the * * * cartel met and the various agreements its members entered into. *Assuming that these allegations are true, as we must, we conclude that Carrier has met any applicable requirement that it allege a [substantial] effect on U.S. commerce.* [Emphasis added.]

Outokumpu, which attached the full EC decision to its motion to dismiss, counters that many of the details contained in the complaint are drawn from [an] EC * * * decision that found no evidence that the cartel's focus extended beyond Europe. * * * As a consequence, Outokumpu argues that any details regarding specific meetings and agreements occurring during the [cartel] meetings are of no assistance to Carrier because they relate only to a European conspiracy.

We are [not] persuaded by this argument. * * * The EC * * * decision clearly states that "insofar as the activities of the cartel relate to sales in countries that are not members of the Community * * * they lie outside the scope of this Decision." Thus, any silence on the part of the EC decision as to U.S. markets may simply reflect the limited scope of the decision.

* * * *

Furthermore, Carrier offers additional circumstantial allegations that corroborate its claim that the market-allocation scheme extended to the United States. Although Carrier's complaint provides numerous circumstantial allegations, of particular interest is its claim that [Outokumpu's competitors] initially refrained from aggressively competing for Carrier's U.S. business until 2003, and then suddenly began doing so at that time. It is true that the mere fact that competitors do not intrude upon one another's markets does not necessarily mean

CASE 46.3 CONTINUES ▸

CASE 46.3 CONTINUED that an illegal market-allocation scheme is taking place. When two companies refrain from entering a market and then suddenly do so after a cartel dissolves, however, there are good grounds for suspicion.

DECISION AND REMEDY *The federal appellate court found that the district court had jurisdiction over Carrier's Sherman Act claims. It therefore reversed the district court's judgment for the defendants.*

THE LEGAL ENVIRONMENT DIMENSION *When this case proceeds, should the district court apply the rule of reason? Why or why not?*

WHAT IF THE FACTS WERE DIFFERENT? *Suppose that Carrier had engaged in anticompetitive conduct that affected Outokumpu. Discuss fully whether the foreign firm would be protected from illegal competition by the U.S. firm.*

The Application of Foreign Antitrust Laws

Large U.S. companies increasingly need to worry about the application of foreign antitrust laws as well. The European Union (EU), in particular, has stepped up its enforcement actions against antitrust violators in recent years.

EUROPEAN UNION ENFORCEMENT The EU's laws promoting competition are stricter in many respects than those of the United States and define more conduct as anticompetitive. The EU actively pursues antitrust violators, especially individual companies and cartels that allegedly engage in monopolistic conduct. ▶ **Example 46.16** The EU fined Intel, Inc., the world's largest semiconductor chip maker, $1.44 billion in an antitrust case. According to European regulators, Intel offered computer manufacturers and retailers price discounts and marketing subsidies if they agreed to buy Intel's chips rather than the chips produced by Intel's main competitor in Europe. The EU has also fined Microsoft Corporation more than $2 billion in the last ten years for anticompetitive conduct. ◀

INCREASED ENFORCEMENT IN ASIA AND LATIN AMERICA Many other nations also have laws that promote competition and prohibit trade restraints. For instance, Japanese antitrust laws forbid unfair trade practices, monopolization, and restrictions that unreasonably restrain trade. China's antitrust rules restrict monopolization and price fixing (although the Chinese government may set prices on exported goods without violating these rules). Indonesia, Malaysia, South Korea, and Vietnam all have statutes protecting competition. Argentina, Brazil, Chile, Peru, and several other Latin American countries have adopted modern antitrust laws as well.

Most of the antitrust laws apply extraterritorially, as U.S. antitrust laws do. This means that a U.S. company may be subject to another nation's antitrust laws if the company's conduct has a substantial effect on that nation's commerce. For instance, South Korea once fined Intel $25 million for antitrust violations, and Japan settled an antitrust case against Intel.

Reviewing: Antitrust Law

The Internet Corporation for Assigned Names and Numbers (ICANN) is a nonprofit entity that organizes Internet domain names. It is governed by a board of directors elected by various groups with commercial interests in the Internet. One of ICANN's functions is to authorize an entity to serve as a registry for certain "Top Level Domains" (TLDs). ICANN and VeriSign entered into an agreement that authorized VeriSign to serve as a registry for the ".com" TLD and provide registry services in accordance with ICANN's specifications. VeriSign complained that ICANN was restricting the services that it could make available as a registrar and blocking new services, imposing unnecessary conditions on those services, and setting the prices at which the services were offered. VeriSign claimed that ICANN's control of the registry services for domain names violated Section 1 of the Sherman Act. Using the information presented in the chapter, answer the following questions.

1. Should ICANN's actions be judged under the rule of reason or be deemed *per se* violations of Section 1 of the Sherman Act? Why?
2. Should ICANN's actions be viewed as a horizontal or a vertical restraint of trade? Why?
3. Does it matter that ICANN's directors are chosen by groups with a commercial interest in the Internet? Explain.
4. If the dispute is judged under the rule of reason, what might be ICANN's defense for having a standardized set of registry services that must be used?

DEBATE THIS . . . *The Internet and the rise of e-commerce have rendered our current antitrust concepts and laws obsolete.*

Terms and Concepts

antitrust law 893	market power 894	restraint of trade 893
attempted monopolization 902	monopolization 899	rule of reason 894
concentrated industry 896	monopoly 894	treble damages 905
divestiture 905	monopoly power 894	tying arrangement 903
exclusive-dealing contract 903	*per se* violation 894	vertical merger 904
group boycott 895	predatory pricing 898	vertical restraint 896
horizontal merger 904	price discrimination 902	vertically integrated firm 896
horizontal restraint 895	price-fixing agreement 895	
market concentration 904	resale price maintenance agreement 897	

ExamPrep

Issue Spotters

1. Under what circumstances would Pop's Market, a small store in a small, isolated town, be considered a monopolist? If Pop's is a monopolist, is it in violation of Section 2 of the Sherman Act? Why or why not? **(See page 899.)**

2. Maple Corporation conditions the sale of its syrup on the buyer's agreement to buy Maple's pancake mix. What factors would a court consider to decide whether this arrangement violates the Clayton Act? **(See page 903.)**

- Check your answers to the Issue Spotters against the answers provided in Appendix E at the end of this text.

Before the Test

Go to **www.cengagebrain.com**, enter the ISBN 9781285185248, and click on "Find" to locate this textbook's Web site. Then, click on "Access Now" under "Study Tools," and select Chapter 46 at the top. There, you will find a Practice Quiz that you can take to assess your mastery of the concepts in this chapter, as well as Flashcards and a Glossary of important terms.

Business Scenarios

46–1. Group Boycott. Jorge's Appliance Corp. was a new retail seller of appliances in Sunrise City. Because of its innovative sales techniques and financing, Jorge's caused the appliance department of No-Glow Department Store, a large chain store with a great deal of buying power, to lose a substantial amount of sales. No-Glow told a number of appliance manufacturers from whom it made large-volume purchases that if they continued to sell to Jorge's, No-Glow would stop buying from them. The manufacturers immediately stopped selling appliances to Jorge's.

Jorge's filed a suit against No-Glow and the manufacturers, claiming that their actions constituted an antitrust violation. No-Glow and the manufacturers were able to prove that Jorge's was a small retailer with a small market share. They claimed that because the relevant market was not substantially affected, they were not guilty of restraint of trade. Discuss fully whether there was an antitrust violation. **(See page 895.)**

46–2. Antitrust Laws. Allitron, Inc., and Donovan, Ltd., are interstate competitors selling similar appliances, principally in the states of Illinois, Indiana, Kentucky, and Ohio. Allitron and Donovan agree that Allitron will no longer sell in Indiana and Ohio and that Donovan will no longer sell in Illinois and Kentucky. Have Allitron and Donovan violated any antitrust laws? If so, which law? Explain. **(See page 896.)**

Business Case Problems

46–3. Tying Arrangement. John Sheridan owned a Marathon gas station franchise. He sued Marathon Petroleum Co. under Section 1 of the Sherman Act and Section 3 of the Clayton Act, charging it with illegally tying the processing of credit-card sales to the gas station. As a condition of obtaining a Marathon dealership, dealers had to agree to let the franchisor process credit cards. They could not shop around to see if credit-card processing could be obtained at a lower price from another source. The district court dismissed the case for failure to state a claim. Sheridan appealed. Is there a tying arrangement? If so, does it violate the law? Explain. [*Sheridan v. Marathon Petroleum Co.*, 530 F.3d 590 (7th Cir. 2008)] **(See page 903.)**

46–4. Monopolization. When Deer Valley Resort Co. (DVRC) was developing its ski resort in the Wasatch Mountains near Park City, Utah, it sold parcels of land in the resort village to third parties. Each sales contract reserved the right of approval over the conduct of certain businesses on the property, including ski rentals. For fifteen years, DVRC permitted Christy Sports, LLC, to rent skis in competition with DVRC's ski rental outlet. When DVRC opened a new midmountain ski rental outlet, it revoked Christy's permission to rent skis. This meant that most skiers who flew into Salt Lake City and shuttled to Deer Valley had few choices: they could carry their ski equipment with them on their flights, take a shuttle into Park City and look for cheaper ski rentals there, or rent from DVRC. Christy filed a suit in a federal district court against DVRC. Was DVRC's action an attempt to monopolize in violation of Section 2 of the Sherman Act? Why or why not? [*Christy Sports, LLC v. Deer Valley Resort Co.*, 555 F.3d 1188 (10th Cir. 2009)] **(See page 899.)**

46–5. Price Fixing. Together, EMI, Sony BMG Music Entertainment, Universal Music Group Recordings, Inc., and Warner Music Group Corp. produced, licensed, and distributed 80 percent of the digital music sold in the United States. The companies formed MusicNet to sell music to online services that sold the songs to consumers. MusicNet required all of the services to sell the songs at the same price and subject to the same restrictions. Digitization of music became cheaper, but MusicNet did not change its prices. Did MusicNet violate the antitrust

laws? Explain. [*Starr v. Sony BMG Music Entertainment*, 592 F.3d 314 (2d Cir. 2010)] **(See page 895.)**

46–6. BUSINESS CASE PROBLEM WITH SAMPLE ANSWER: Price Discrimination.

 Dayton Superior Corp. sells its products in interstate commerce to several companies, including Spa Steel Products, Inc. The purchasers often compete directly with each other for customers. From 2005 to 2007, one of Spa Steel's customers purchased Dayton Superior's products from two of Spa Steel's competitors. According to the customer, Spa Steel's prices were always 10 to 15 percent higher for the same products. As a result, Spa Steel lost sales to at least that customer and perhaps others. Spa Steel wants to sue Dayton Superior for price discrimination. Which requirements for such a claim under Section 2 of the Clayton Act does Spa Steel satisfy? What additional facts will it need to prove? [Dayton Superior Corp. v. Spa Steel Products, Inc., 2012 WL 113663 (N.D.N.Y. 2012)] **(See page 902.)**

- **For a sample answer to Problem 46–6, go to Appendix F at the end of this text.**

46–7. SPECIAL CASE ANALYSIS: Resale Price Maintenance Agreements.

 Go to Case Analysis Case 46.1, *Leegin Creative Leather Products, Inc. v. PSKS, Inc.*, on pages 897 and 898. Read the excerpt and answer the following questions.

(a) **Issue:** The dispute in this case was between which parties and turned on what legal issue?

(b) **Rule of Law:** In resolving this dispute, what common law rule did the Court overturn, and what rule did the Court create to replace this rejected precedent?

(c) **Applying the Rule of Law:** What reasons did the Court give to justify its change in the law, and how did the new rule apply in this case?

(d) **Conclusion:** In whose favor did the Court rule and why?

46–8. A QUESTION OF ETHICS: Section 1 of the Sherman Act.

 In the 1990s, DuCoa, L.P., made choline chloride, a B-complex vitamin essential for the growth and development of animals. DuCoa, Bioproducts, Inc., and Chinook Group, Ltd., each had one-third of the

U.S. market for choline chloride. To stabilize the market and keep the price of the vitamin higher than it would otherwise have been, the companies agreed to fix the price and allocate market share by deciding which of them would offer the lowest price to each customer. At times, however, the companies disregarded the agreement. During an increase in competitive activity in August 1997, Daniel Rose became president of DuCoa. The next month, a subordinate advised him of the conspiracy. By February 1998, Rose had begun to implement a strategy to persuade DuCoa's competitors to rejoin the conspiracy. By April, the three companies had reallocated their market shares and increased their prices. In June, the U.S. Department of Justice began to investigate allegations of price fixing in the vitamin market. Ultimately, a federal district court convicted Rose of conspiracy to violate

Section 1 of the Sherman Act. [United States v. Rose, 449 F.3d 627 (5th Cir. 2006)] **(See page 894.)**

(a) The court "enhanced" Rose's sentence to thirty months' imprisonment, one year of supervised release, and a $20,000 fine based, among other things, on his role as "a manager or supervisor" in the conspiracy. Rose appealed this enhancement to the U.S. Court of Appeals for the Fifth Circuit. Was it fair to increase Rose's sentence on this ground? Why or why not?

(b) Was Rose's participation in the conspiracy unethical? If so, how might Rose have behaved ethically instead? If not, could any of the participants' conduct be considered unethical? Explain.

Legal Reasoning Group Activity

46–9. Antitrust Violations. Residents of the city of Madison, Wisconsin, became concerned about overconsumption of liquor near the campus of the University of Wisconsin (UW). The city initiated a new policy, imposing conditions on area bars to discourage reduced-price "specials" that were believed to encourage high-volume and dangerous drinking. In 2012, the city began to draft an ordinance to ban all drink specials. Bar owners responded by announcing that they had "voluntarily" agreed to discontinue drink specials on Friday and Saturday nights after 8:00 P.M. The city put its ordinance on hold. Several

UW students filed a lawsuit against the local bar owners association, alleging violations of antitrust law.

(a) The first group will identify the grounds on which the plaintiffs might base their claim for relief and formulate an argument on behalf of the plaintiffs.

(b) The second group will determine whether the defendants are exempt from the antitrust laws.

(c) The third group will decide how the court should rule in this dispute and provide reasons for the ruling.

CHAPTER 47

PROFESSIONAL LIABILITY AND ACCOUNTABILITY

Professionals, such as accountants, attorneys, physicians, and architects, are increasingly faced with the threat of liability. In part, this is because the public has become more aware that professionals are required to deliver competent services and adhere to certain standards of performance within their professions.

The failure of several major companies and leading public accounting firms in the past twenty years has focused attention on the importance of abiding by professional account-

ing standards. Numerous corporations and former corporations—from American International Group (AIG), the world's largest insurance company, to HealthSouth, Goldman Sachs, Lehman Brothers, Tyco International, and India-based Satyam Computer Services—have been accused of engaging in accounting fraud. These companies may have reported fictitious revenues, concealed liabilities or debts, or artificially inflated their assets.

Considering the many potential sources of legal liability that they face,

accountants, attorneys, and other professionals should be very aware of their legal obligations. In this chapter, we look at the potential liability of professionals under both the common law and statutory law. We also discuss issues that professionals should consider when using cloud computing for storing client information and data in this chapter's *Managerial Strategy* feature. The chapter concludes with a brief examination of the relationships of professionals, particularly accountants and attorneys, with their clients.

POTENTIAL LIABILITY TO CLIENTS

Under the common law, professionals may be liable to clients for breach of contract, negligence, or fraud.

Liability for Breach of Contract

Accountants and other professionals face liability under the common law for any breach of contract. A professional owes a duty to her or his client to honor the terms of their contract and to perform the contract within the stated time period. If the professional fails to perform as agreed in the contract, then she or he has breached the contract, and the client has the right to recover damages from the professional.

Damages include expenses incurred by the client to hire another professional to provide the contracted-for services and any other reasonable and foreseeable losses that arise from the professional's breach. For instance, if the client had to pay liquidated damages

or penalties for failing to meet deadlines, the court may order the professional to pay an equivalent amount in damages to the client.

Liability for Negligence

Accountants and other professionals may also be held liable for negligence in the performance of their services. Recall from Chapter 6 that to establish negligence, the plaintiff must prove four elements: duty, breach, causation, and damages. These elements must be proved in negligence cases against professionals, which often focus on the standard of care exercised by the professional.

All professionals are subject to the standards of conduct and the ethical codes established by their profession, by state statutes, and by judicial decisions. They are also governed by the contracts they enter into with their clients.

In performing their contracts, professionals must exercise the established standards of care, knowledge, and judgment generally accepted by members of their professional group. How do those standards apply when a professional stores confidential client information and other data on the cloud? See the

Managerial Strategy feature below for a discussion of this issue.

MANAGERIAL STRATEGY

Professionals' Responsibilities for Protecting Data in the Cloud

To achieve both cost savings and better security, more and more attorneys and accountants are storing their data, including confidential client information, on the cloud. Sometimes, professionals assume that once their data have migrated to the cloud, they no longer have to be concerned with keeping the information secure. But cloud computing is simply the virtualization of the computing process. It's analogous to outsourcing infrastructure technology. In other words, the professional is still ultimately responsible for the information.

Attorneys' Ethical Obligations with Stored Information

Attorneys' obligations for their clients' information are spelled out in the American Bar Association's Model Rules of Professional Conduct, which serve as the basis for the ethics rules for attorneys adopted by most states. Comment 17 to Model Rule 1.6 states, "The lawyer must take reasonable precautions to prevent the [client's] information from coming into the hands of unintended recipients." Thus, lawyers have an ethical duty to safeguard confidential client information, whether it is stored as documents in a filing cabinet or as electromagnetic impulses on a hard server that might be located anywhere—even in another country.

Note that Rule 1.6 does not require an attorney to *guarantee* that a breach of confidentiality will never occur. Certainly, it is harder to maintain control over information stored on the cloud. Although the attorney "owns" the data, he or she may not even know the location of the computer where the information is stored. Furthermore, a provider of cloud computing services may move data from one server to another. Nevertheless, attorneys should be aware of jurisdictional issues and make sure that their cloud computing provider is complying with data protection regulations and privacy notification requirements wherever the provider's servers are located.

Litigation Issues

The problems presented by e-discovery become even more complex when information is stored in the cloud. Not only will adequate data maps have to be readily available during discovery and subsequent litigation, but the

attorney will have to ascertain who will have access to sensitive information.

Attorneys must be particularly careful to avoid *spoliation,* or the negligent altering or destruction of evidence relevant to the litigation. Preserving information in the cloud can be more difficult if the data are spread across multiple physical storage sites. Sometimes, attorneys can be required to isolate the relevant data within their cloud computing provider's cloud resources.

Accountants Face Similar Issues

Like attorneys, accountants are legally obligated to keep client information secure and confidential. Because accountants have access to their clients' financial records and personal financial information, identity theft is a major concern. Accountants should remember that when they move confidential client information to the cloud, they are moving it to the Internet with all the potential security problems that entails.

Other issues may arise as well. If an accountant has to change cloud computing service providers, can she or he assume that all the information will be transmitted to the new provider? An accountant should also consider what will happen in the event that confidential client information is lost. What form of disaster recovery is available? Before an emergency occurs, the accountant should determine whether there are backup storage facilities also located in the cloud.

MANAGERIAL IMPLICATIONS

Professionals' risks from cloud computing are the same as those that all users face—Internet-facilitated breaches due to malware and hackers, and the possibility of government surveillance. All of these issues must be considered when signing a contract with a cloud computing service.

BUSINESS QUESTIONS

1. To what extent must professionals reveal to their clients where confidential data are stored?

2. To what extent should professionals create their own backup data storage systems?

ACCOUNTANT'S DUTY OF CARE Accountants play a major role in a business's financial system. Accountants have the expertise and experience necessary to establish and maintain accurate financial records, and to design, control, and audit record-keeping systems. They also prepare reliable statements that reflect an individual's or a business's financial status, give tax advice, and prepare tax returns.

Generally, an accountant must possess the skills that an ordinarily prudent accountant would have and must exercise the degree of care that an ordinarily prudent accountant would exercise. The level of skill expected of accountants and the degree of care that they should exercise in performing their services are reflected in the standards discussed next.

GAAP and GAAS. In the performance of their services, accountants must comply with **generally accepted accounting principles (GAAP)** and **generally accepted auditing standards (GAAS).** The Financial Accounting Standards Board (FASB, usually pronounced "faz-bee") determines what accounting conventions, rules, and procedures constitute GAAP at a given point in time. GAAS are standards concerning an auditor's professional qualities and the judgment that he or she exercises in auditing financial records. The American Institute of Certified Public Accountants established GAAS.

A violation of GAAP and GAAS is considered *prima facie* evidence of negligence on the part of the accountant. Compliance with GAAP and GAAS, however, does not *necessarily* relieve an accountant from potential legal liability. An accountant may be held to a higher standard of conduct established by state statutes and by judicial decisions.

Usually, though, if an accountant conforms to generally accepted standards and acts in good faith, she or he normally will not be held liable to the client for a mistake in judgment. Although the United States has used the GAAP standards for many years, they are now being replaced by global accounting rules.

Global Accounting Rules. In 2008, the Securities and Exchange Commission (SEC) unanimously approved a plan to require U.S. companies to use global accounting rules, known as **International Financial Reporting Standards (IFRS).** These rules, which are established by the London-based International Accounting Standards Board, are being phased in and will be required for all financial reports filed with the SEC.[1]

The SEC decided to replace the rules-based GAAP with the principles-based IFRS for several reasons. GAAP rules are very detailed and fill nearly 25,000 pages. The IFRS are simpler, more straightforward, and shorter—filling only 2,500 pages—and they focus more on general principles than on specific rules. Consequently, companies should find it less difficult to comply with the IFRS.

In addition, having uniform accounting rules that apply to all nations makes sense in a global economy. The members of the European Union and 113 other nations—including nearly all of the United States' trading partners—already use the IFRS.

Discovering Improprieties. An accountant is not required to discover every impropriety, **defalcation**[2] (embezzlement), or fraud in a client's books. If, however, an impropriety goes undiscovered because of the accountant's negligence or failure to perform an express or implied duty, the accountant will be liable for any resulting losses suffered by the client. Therefore, an accountant who uncovers suspicious financial transactions and fails to investigate the matter fully or to inform the client of the discovery can be held liable to the client for the resulting loss.

Audits, Qualified Opinions, and Disclaimers. One of the more important tasks that an accountant may perform for a business is an audit. An *audit* is a systematic inspection, by analyses and tests, of a business's financial records. An accountant qualified to perform audits is often called an **auditor.**

The purpose of an audit is to provide the auditor with evidence to support an opinion on the reliability of the business's financial statements. A normal audit is not intended to uncover fraud or other misconduct. Nevertheless, an accountant may be liable for failing to detect misconduct if a normal audit would have revealed it. Also, if the auditor agreed to examine the records for evidence of fraud or other obvious misconduct and then failed to detect it, he or she may be liable. After performing an audit, the auditor issues an opinion letter stating whether, in his or her opinion, the financial statements fairly present the business's financial position.

Qualified Opinions and Disclaimers. In issuing an opinion letter, an auditor may *qualify* the opinion or include a disclaimer. In a disclaimer, the auditor basi-

---

1. The smallest publicly reporting companies are set to make the transition to IFRS by 2016.

2. This term, pronounced deh-ful-*kay*-shun, is derived from the Latin *de* ("off") and *falx* ("sickle"—a tool for cutting grain or tall grass). In law, the term refers to the act of a defaulter or of an embezzler. As used here, it means embezzlement.

cally is stating that she or he does not have sufficient information to issue an opinion. A qualified opinion or a disclaimer must be specific and identify the reason for the qualification or disclaimer. The auditor cannot include a general statement disclaiming any liability for false or misleading financial statements.

▶ **Example 47.1** Richard Zehr performs an audit of Lacey Corporation's financial statements. In the opinion letter, Zehr qualifies his opinion by stating that there is uncertainty about how a lawsuit against the firm will be resolved. In this situation, Zehr will not be liable if the outcome of the suit is unfavorable for the firm. Zehr could still be liable, however, if he failed to discover other problems that an audit in compliance with GAAS and IFRS would have revealed. ◀

Unaudited Financial Statements. Sometimes, accountants are hired to prepare unaudited financial statements. (A financial statement is considered unaudited if incomplete auditing procedures have been used in its preparation or if insufficient procedures have been used to justify an opinion.)

Accountants may be subject to liability for failing, in accordance with standard accounting procedures, to designate a balance sheet as "unaudited." An accountant will also be held liable for failure to disclose to a client any facts or circumstances that give reason to believe that misstatements have been made or that a fraud has been committed.

Defenses to Negligence. If an accountant is found guilty of negligence, the client can collect damages for losses that arose from the accountant's negligence. An accountant facing a negligence claim, however, has several possible defenses, including the following:

1. The accountant was not negligent.
2. If the accountant was negligent, this negligence was not the proximate cause of the client's losses (see *Case in Point 47.2* below).
3. The client was also negligent (depending on whether the state applies contributory negligence or comparative negligence—see Chapter 6).

▶ **Case in Point 47.2** Coopers & Lybrand, LLP, provided accounting services for Oregon Steel Mills (OSM), Inc. Coopers advised OSM to report a certain transaction as a $12.3 million gain on its financial statements. Later, when OSM planned to make a public offering of its stock, the SEC reviewed its financial statements. The SEC concluded that the accounting treatment of the transaction was incorrect, and required OSM to correct its statements.

Because of the delay, the public offering did not occur on May 2, when OSM's stock was selling for $16 per share, but on June 13, when, due to unrelated factors, the price was $13.50. OSM filed a lawsuit against Coopers claiming that the negligent accounting resulted in the stock's being sold at a lower price. The court held, however, that although the accountant's negligence had delayed the stock offering, the negligence was not the proximate cause of the decline in the stock price. Thus, Coopers could not be held liable for damages based on the price decline.[3] ◀

ATTORNEY'S DUTY OF CARE The conduct of attorneys is governed by rules established by each state and by the American Bar Association's Model Rules of Professional Conduct. All attorneys owe a duty to provide competent and diligent representation. Attorneys are required to be familiar with well-settled principles of law applicable to a case and to find relevant law that can be discovered through a reasonable amount of research. The lawyer must also investigate and discover facts that could materially affect the client's legal rights.

Normally, an attorney's performance is expected to be that of a reasonably competent general practitioner of ordinary skill, experience, and capacity. An attorney who holds himself or herself out as having expertise in a particular area of law (such as intellectual property), is held to a higher standard of care in that area of law than attorneys without such knowledge.

Misconduct. Typically, state rules of professional conduct for attorneys provide that committing a criminal act that reflects adversely on the person's "honesty or trustworthiness, or fitness as a lawyer" is professional misconduct. The rules often further provide that a lawyer should not engage in conduct involving "dishonesty, fraud, deceit, or misrepresentation." Under these rules, state authorities can discipline attorneys for many types of misconduct.

▶ **Case in Point 47.3** Michael Inglimo, who was licensed to practice law in Wisconsin, occasionally used marijuana with a person who later became his client in a criminal case. After the trial, the client claimed that Inglimo had been high on drugs during the trial and had not adequately represented him. Two years later, Inglimo was convicted for misdemeanor possession of marijuana. State authorities also discovered that Inglimo had written several checks for personal expenses out of his client trust account,

---

3. *Oregon Steel Mills, Inc. v. Coopers & Lybrand, LLP,* 336 Or. 329, 83 P.3d 322 (2004).

commingled client funds, and engaged in other trust account violations.

The state initiated disciplinary proceedings to have Inglimo's license to practice law suspended. Inglimo argued that he should not be suspended because his misconduct was related to his past use of controlled substances and he no longer used drugs. The court, however, concluded that the suspension was necessary to protect the public in light of Inglimo's "disturbing pattern of disregard" for his professional obligations.[4] ◀

Liability for Malpractice. When an attorney fails to exercise reasonable care and professional judgment,

---

4. *In re Disciplinary Proceedings against Inglimo,* 2007 WI 126, 305 Wis.2d 71, 740 N.W.2d 125 (2007).

she or he breaches the duty of care and can be held liable for *malpractice* (professional negligence).

In malpractice cases—as in all cases involving allegations of negligence—the plaintiff must prove that the attorney's breach of the duty of care actually caused the plaintiff to suffer some injury. ▶ **Example 47.4** Attorney Karen Boehmer allows the statute of limitations to lapse on a claim of Beth Curl, a client. In this situation, Boehmer can be held liable for malpractice because Curl can no longer pursue her claim and has lost a potential award of damages. ◀

Allegations of malpractice gave rise to the following case.

CASE 47.1

Kelley v. Buckley
Court of Appeals of Ohio, Eighth District, 193 Ohio App.3d 11, 2011 Ohio 1362 (2011).

BACKGROUND AND FACTS Attorneys Michael Kelley and James Ferraro founded Kelley & Ferraro, LLP (K&F), an Ohio law firm. When Kelley died, his widow, Lynn Kelley, contacted lawyer Brent Buckley of Buckley King, LPA, who had drafted the K&F partnership agreement. The agreement provided that on Michael's death, Lynn was to be paid 40 percent of the firm's gross revenues. Buckley King had recently been retained by Ferraro to represent his interests in any dispute with Michael's estate, however, and Brent Buckley himself advised Lynn, the executor of the estate, to settle with Ferraro quickly.

Despite Lynn's repeated requests, Buckley did not give her a copy of the partnership agreement. Meanwhile, she became embroiled in litigation with lawyer John Sivinski, who had worked for K&F and claimed a share of Michael's profits. Buckley King represented Ferraro and K&F in this dispute and withheld copies of an employment contract between K&F and Sivinski. When Lynn eventually obtained a copy of Sivinski's contract, it revealed that his claim against the estate was fraudulent. She then filed a suit in an Ohio state court against Brent Buckley and Buckley King, alleging malpractice. The court issued a summary judgment in favor of Buckley and the firm. Lynn appealed.

IN THE LANGUAGE OF THE COURT
Colleen Conway *COONEY,* J. [Judge]

* * * *

Buckley argues they did not breach any duty of care owed to Michael Kelley when they negotiated the K&F partnership agreement on Michael Kelley's behalf * * * because Michael Kelley limited the scope of their representation on that undertaking.

* * * *

[This] defense is dependent upon the hearsay statements of the late Michael Kelley. * * * *A decedent's declarations are only admissible to rebut testimony of an adverse party * * * for the benefit of the executor or other representative of a decedent's estate [the person who died] and [are] not available to a party opposing the decedent. * * * Thus, Buckley may not rely on Michael Kelley's hearsay statements* * * *. [Emphasis added.]

* * * *

There is a genuine issue of material fact as to whether * * * Buckley created the Sivinski contracts that became the subject of litigation against Lynn Kelley and whether [he] could have swiftly ended that litigation by producing the second Sivinski contract. * * * Based on the

CASE 47.1 CONTINUED

conflicting evidence in the record, we find the trial court erred in finding no genuine issues of fact on these very serious allegations.

* * * *

Buckley contends that Lynn Kelley consented to the Buckley Firm's representation of Ferraro and K&F in her claims against them. However, the record contains no written consent to that effect * * * .

* * * *

Buckley argues Lynn Kelley's legal malpractice claims fail because she failed to demonstrate a genuine issue as to whether the alleged malpractice proximately caused any damages.

[But] Lynn Kelley's legal expert, Amelia A. Bower, opined that Lynn Kelley suffered damage as a result of Buckley's actions.

Further, Lynn Kelley testified that Buckley's failure to produce the K&F partnership agreement and his advice to settle quickly with Ferraro caused her emotional distress.

DECISION AND REMEDY *A state intermediate appellate court reversed the summary judgment in the defendants' favor and remanded the case for additional discovery and a trial. The court found genuine issues of material fact relating to all of Lynn's claims. The court also awarded Lynn the costs of the appeal.*

THE ETHICAL DIMENSION *Suppose that in the new trial Buckley and the Buckley King firm are held legally liable on all of Lynn's claims of malpractice. What acts of ethical misconduct might this indicate?*

THE ECONOMIC DIMENSION *What sanctions might be appropriate for Sivinski's fraud in his suit against Lynn?*

Liability for Fraud

Recall from Chapter 15 that fraud, or misrepresentation, involves the following elements:

1. A misrepresentation of a material fact.
2. An intent to deceive.
3. Justifiable reliance by the innocent party on the misrepresentation.
4. To obtain damages, an actual injury to the innocent party.

A professional may be held liable for *actual* fraud when (1) he or she intentionally misstates a material fact to mislead a client and (2) the client is injured as a result of justifiably relying on the misstated fact. A material fact is one that a reasonable person would consider important in deciding whether to act.

In contrast, a professional may be held liable for *constructive* fraud whether or not he or she acted with fraudulent intent. Constructive fraud may be found when an accountant is grossly negligent in performing his or her duties. ▶ **Example 47.5** Paula, an accountant, is conducting an audit of ComCo, Inc. Paula accepts the explanations of Ron, an ComCo officer, regarding certain financial irregularities, despite evidence that contradicts those explanations and indicates that the irregularities may be illegal. Paula's conduct could be characterized as an inten-

tional failure to perform a duty in reckless disregard of the consequences of such failure. This would constitute gross negligence and could be held to be constructive fraud. ◀

Both actual and constructive fraud are potential sources of legal liability for an accountant or other professional.

SECTION 2
POTENTIAL LIABILITY TO THIRD PARTIES

Traditionally, an accountant or other professional owed a duty only to those with whom she or he had a direct contractual relationship—that is, those with whom she or he was in *privity of contract*. A professional's duty was only to her or his client. Violations of statutes, fraud, and other intentional or reckless acts of wrongdoing were the only exceptions to this general rule.

Today, numerous third parties—including investors, shareholders, creditors, corporate managers and directors, and regulatory agencies—rely on the opinions of auditors (accountants) when making decisions. In view of this extensive reliance, many courts have all but abandoned the privity requirement in regard to accountants' liability to third parties.

In this section, we focus primarily on the potential liability of auditors to third parties. Understanding an auditor's common law liability to third parties is critical. Often, when a business fails, its independent auditor (accountant) may be one of the few potentially *solvent* (able to pay expenses and debts) defendants. The majority of courts now hold that auditors can be held liable to third parties for negligence, but the standard for the imposition of this liability varies.

The *Ultramares* Rule

The traditional rule regarding an accountant's liability to third parties based on privity of contract was enunciated by Chief Judge Benjamin Cardozo in 1931. ▶ **Case in Point 47.6** Fred Stern & Company had hired the public accounting firm of Touche, Niven & Company to review Stern's financial records and prepare a balance sheet for the year ending December 31, 1923.[5] Touche prepared the balance sheet and supplied Stern with thirty-two certified copies. According to the certified balance sheet, Stern had a net worth (assets less liabilities) of $1,070,715.26.

In reality, however, Stern's liabilities exceeded its assets—the company's records had been falsified by insiders at Stern to reflect a positive net worth. In reliance on the certified balance sheets, Ultramares Corporation loaned substantial amounts to Stern. After Stern was declared bankrupt, Ultramares brought an action against Touche for negligence in an attempt to recover damages.

The New York Court of Appeals (that state's highest court) refused to impose liability on Touche. The court concluded that Touche's accountants owed a duty of care only to those persons for whose "primary benefit" the statements were intended. In this case, the statements were intended only for the primary benefit of Stern. The court held that in the absence of privity or a relationship "so close as to approach that of privity," a party could not recover from an accountant.[6] ◀

THE REQUIREMENT OF PRIVITY The requirement of privity has since been referred to as the *Ultramares* rule, or the New York rule. It continues to be used in some states. ▶ **Case in Point 47.7** Toro Company

supplied equipment and credit to Summit Power Equipment Distributors and required Summit to submit audited reports indicating its financial condition. Accountants at Krouse, Kern & Company prepared the reports, which allegedly contained mistakes and omissions regarding Summit's financial condition.

Toro extended large amounts of credit to Summit in reliance on the audited reports. When Summit was unable to repay these amounts, Toro brought a negligence action against Krouse and proved that the accountants knew the reports would be used by Summit to induce Toro to extend credit. Nevertheless, under the *Ultramares* rule, the court refused to hold the accounting firm liable because the firm was not in privity with Toro.[7] ◀

MODIFICATION TO ALLOW "NEAR PRIVITY" The *Ultramares* rule was restated and somewhat modified in a 1985 New York case, *Credit Alliance Corp. v. Arthur Andersen & Co.*[8] In that case, the court held that if a third party has a sufficiently close relationship or *nexus* (link or connection) with an accountant, then the *Ultramares* privity requirement may be satisfied without the establishment of an accountant-client relationship. The rule enunciated in the *Credit Alliance* case is often referred to as the "near privity" rule. Only a minority of states have adopted this rule of accountants' liability to third parties.

The *Restatement* Rule

The *Ultramares* rule has been severely criticized. Its critics assert that because much of the work performed by auditors is intended for use by persons who are not parties to the contract, auditors should owe a duty to these third parties. As support for this position has grown, there has been an erosion of the *Ultramares* rule to expose accountants to liability to third parties in some situations.

The majority of courts have adopted the position taken by the *Restatement (Third) of Torts*. This rule states that accountants are subject to liability for negligence not only to their clients but also to foreseen, or known, users of their reports or financial statements. Under the *Restatement (Third) of Torts*, an accountant's liability extends to:

---

5. Banks, creditors, stockholders, purchasers, and sellers often rely on balance sheets when making decisions related to a company's business.

6. *Ultramares Corp. v. Touche,* 255 N.Y. 170, 174 N.E. 441 (1931).

7. *Toro Co. v. Krouse, Kern & Co.,* 827 F.2d 155 (7th Cir. 1987). See also *Citibank, F.S.B. v. McGladrey & Pullen,* LLP, 2007 WL 7134666 (Ill. 2007).

8. 65 N.Y.2d 536, 483 N.E.2d 110 (1985). A "relationship sufficiently intimate to be equated with privity" is enough for a third party to sue another's accountant for negligence.

1. Persons for whose benefit and guidance the accountant intends to supply the information or knows that the recipient intends to supply it.
2. Persons whom the accountant intends the information to influence or knows that the recipient so intends.

▶ **Example 47.8** Steve, an accountant, prepares a financial statement for Tech Software, Inc., a client, knowing that Tech will submit that statement when it applies for a loan from First National Bank. If Steve makes negligent misstatements or omissions in the statement, the bank may hold Steve liable because he knew that the bank would rely on his work product when deciding whether to make the loan. ◀

The "Reasonably Foreseeable Users" Rule

A small minority of courts hold accountants liable to any users whose reliance on an accountant's statements or reports was *reasonably foreseeable*. This standard has been criticized as extending liability too far and exposing accountants to massive liability.

The majority of courts have concluded that the *Restatement's* approach is more reasonable because it allows accountants to control their exposure to liability. Liability is "fixed by the accountants' particular knowledge at the moment the audit is published," not by the foreseeability of the harm that might occur to a third party after the report is released.

Liability of Attorneys to Third Parties

Like accountants, attorneys may be held liable under the common law to third parties who rely on legal opinions to their detriment. Generally, an attorney is not liable to a nonclient unless the attorney has committed fraud (or malicious conduct). The liability principles stated in the *Restatement (Third) of Torts*, however, may apply to attorneys as well as to accountants.

Should an attorney's duty of care extend to third party beneficiaries whose rights were harmed by the attorney's malpractice? That question was at issue in the following case.

CASE ANALYSIS

Case 47.2 Perez[a] v. Stern
Nebraska Supreme Court, 279 Neb. 187, 777 N.W.2d 545 (2010).

IN THE LANGUAGE OF THE COURT
GERRARD, J. [Justice]
* * * *

[Reyna] Guido is the mother of two minor children. [Domingo] Martinez, the children's father, died after he was run over by a car on July 8, 2001. Martinez was the victim of a hit-and-run accident.

Guido, as personal representative of Martinez's estate, retained [Sandra] Stern to file a wrongful death lawsuit. On July 8, 2003, Stern filed a wrongful death complaint in the district court. But Stern admits that she never perfected service of the complaint, and because the complaint was not served

within six months of filing, the case was dismissed by operation of law.

* * * On February 6, 2007, Guido filed these legal malpractice claims against Stern on behalf of herself, the children, and the estate. Guido alleged that the wrongful death claim expired as a result of Stern's failure to timely perfect service of the complaint. Stern moved for summary judgment on the ground that the malpractice claims were barred by the two-year statute of limitations for professional negligence. Before the court ruled on the motion, Guido voluntarily dismissed her individual claim, but maintained claims as personal representative of the estate and next friend of the children.

The district court found that the malpractice claims accrued on May 7, 2004, when the wrongful death claim

was dismissed. The court found that the estate's claim against Stern was time barred. In response to Guido's argument that the children's minority tolled [suspended] the statute of limitations with respect to them, the court found that because the children could not have brought the underlying wrongful death claim in their own names, the statute of limitations for the legal malpractice claims was not tolled by reason of the children's minority. The court granted summary judgment in favor of Stern and dismissed the complaint.

* * * *

Guido [appealed, claiming] that the district court erred in granting Stern's motion for summary judgment on her affirmative defense of the

CASE 47.2 CONTINUES ▶

---
a. Estaban Perez was one of the minor children of Domingo Martinez, the man killed in the accident.

statute of limitations and, specifically, determining that the children had no independent standing to sue Stern and that Stern owed no independent duty to the minor children to protect their rights and interests.

We note that neither Guido's assignments of error nor the argument in her appellate brief challenges the district court's dismissal of Guido's claims as an individual and as personal representative of Martinez's estate. Therefore, those aspects of the court's judgment will be affirmed.

* * * *

The issue in this case is whether Stern owed an independent duty to the children, as Martinez's next of kin, to timely prosecute the underlying wrongful death claim.

* * * *

In Nebraska, *a lawyer owes a duty to his or her client to use reasonable care and skill in the discharge of his or her duties, but ordinarily this duty does not extend to third parties, absent facts establishing a duty to them.* [Emphasis added.]

But that does not end our analysis. * * * We have never said that privity [of contract] is an absolute requirement of a legal malpractice claim. Instead, we have said that a lawyer's duty to use reasonable care and skill in the discharge of his or her duties *ordinarily* does not extend to third parties, *absent facts establishing a duty to them.* On the facts of this case, we conclude, as have other courts to have addressed this issue in the context of a wrongful death action, that the facts establish an independent legal duty from Stern to Martinez's statutory beneficiaries. [Emphasis in the original]

* * * Courts have repeatedly emphasized that *the starting point for analyzing an attorney's duty to a third party is determining whether the third party was a direct and intended beneficiary of the attorney's services.* [Emphasis added.]

* * * *

In this case, we conclude that Stern owed a duty to the children, as direct and intended beneficiaries of her services, to competently represent their interests. To hold otherwise would deny legal recourse to the children for whose benefit Stern was hired in the first place.

* * * Stern owed a legal duty to Martinez's minor children to exercise reasonable care in representing their interests. Therefore, they have standing to sue Stern for neglecting that duty, and their claims against Stern were tolled by their minority. The district court erred in concluding that their claims were time barred. We affirm the court's dismissal of Guido's individual claim and its determination that the estate's claim against Stern was time barred. But with respect to the children, this cause is reversed and remanded for further proceedings to fully adjudicate Guido's claims on behalf of the children * * * .

Affirmed in part, and in part reversed and remanded for further proceedings.

LEGAL REASONING QUESTIONS

1. If the children had suffered no harm as a result of the attorney's malpractice, would the outcome of this case have been different? Why or why not?

2. Why did the court affirm the dismissal of Guido's individual claim but not the claims that she had brought on behalf of the children?

3. If one of the children had not been a minor at the time of the father's death, the court would have dismissed that child's claims against Stern, even though the child was an intended beneficiary. Is it fair for the law to treat minors differently from other children with regard to a statute of limitations? Why or why not?

4. How might Stern, or anyone in a similar position, have avoided the negative result in this case?

Concept Summary 47.1 on the following page reviews the common law rules under which accountants, attorneys, and other professionals may be held liable.

SECTION 3

THE SARBANES-OXLEY ACT OF 2002

The Sarbanes-Oxley Act (discussed in Chapters 5 and 42) imposes a number of strict requirements on both domestic and foreign public accounting firms. These requirements apply to firms that provide auditing services to companies ("issuers") whose securities are sold to public investors. The act defines the term *issuer* as a company that has securities that are registered under Section 12 of the Securities Exchange Act of 1934, that is required to file reports under Section 15(d) of the 1934 act, or that has filed a registration statement that has not yet become effective under the Securities Act of 1933.

CONCEPT SUMMARY 47.1

Common Law Liability of Accountants and Other Professionals

CONCEPT	NATURE OF LIABILITY
Liability to Clients	1. *Breach of contract*—A professional who fails to perform according to his or her contractual obligations can be held liable for breach of contract and resulting damages. 2. *Negligence*—An accountant, attorney, or other professional, in performing her or his duties, must use the care, knowledge, and judgment generally used by professionals in the same or similar circumstances. Failure to do so is negligence. An accountant's violation of generally accepted accounting principles and generally accepted auditing standards is *prima facie* evidence of negligence. 3. *Fraud*—Intentionally misrepresenting a material fact to a client, when the client relies on the misrepresentation, is actual fraud. Gross negligence in performance of duties is constructive fraud.

Liability to Third Parties	1. *Liability of accountants*—An accountant may be liable for negligence to any third person the accountant knows or should have known will benefit from the accountant's work. The standard for imposing this liability varies, but generally courts follow one of the following rules:
	  a. The *Ultramares rule*—An accountant owes a duty of care to those persons for whose primary benefit the accountant's statements were intended. Liability will be imposed only if the accountant is in privity, or near privity, with the third party.
	  b. The *Restatement rule*—Extends liability to third parties whose reliance is foreseen or known and to third parties in a class of foreseen or known users. This includes persons for whose benefit and guidance the accountant intends to supply the information, and persons whom the accountant intends the information to influence. The majority of courts have adopted this rule.
	  c. The reasonably foreseeable user rule—Liability will be imposed if the third party's use was reasonably foreseeable.
	2. *Liability of attorneys*—An attorney generally is not liable to a nonclient unless the attorney committed fraud or other malicious conduct, although in some situations an attorney may be liable to persons whose reliance is foreseen or known.

The Public Company Accounting Oversight Board

The Sarbanes-Oxley Act increased government oversight of public accounting practices by creating the Public Company Accounting Oversight Board, which reports to the Securities and Exchange Commission. The board oversees the audit of public companies that are subject to securities laws. The goal is to protect public investors and to ensure that public accounting firms comply with the provisions of the act. The act defines *public accounting firms* as firms "engaged in the practice of public accounting or preparing or issuing audit reports."[9]

The key provisions relating to the duties of the oversight board and the requirements relating to public accounting firms are summarized in in Exhibit 47–1 on the next page. (Provisions relating to corporate fraud and the responsibilities of corporate officers and directors were described and listed in Exhibit 42–3.)

Requirements for Maintaining Working Papers

In performing an audit for a client, an accountant accumulates various **working papers**—the documents used and developed during the audit. These include notes, computations, memoranda, copies, and other papers that make up the work product of an accountant's services to a client.

---

9. Recall from Chapter 42 that as of 2010, smaller companies with a public float of less than $75 million no longer need to file an auditor's report on management's assessment of internal controls under Section 404(b).

EXHIBIT 47–1 Key Provisions of the Sarbanes-Oxley Act Relating to Public Accounting Firms

AUDITOR INDEPENDENCE

To help ensure that auditors remain independent of the firms that they audit, Title II of the Sarbanes-Oxley Act does the following:

1. Makes it unlawful for Registered Public Accounting Firms (RPAFs) to perform both audit and nonaudit services for the same company at the same time. Nonaudit services include the following:
   • Bookkeeping or other services related to the accounting records or financial statements of the audit client.
   • Financial information systems design and implementation.
   • Appraisal or valuation services.
   • Fairness opinions.
   • Management functions.
   • Broker or dealer, investment adviser, or investment banking services.
2. Requires preapproval for most auditing services from the issuer's (the corporation's) audit committee.
3. Requires audit partner rotation by prohibiting RPAFs from providing audit services to an issuer if either the lead audit partner or the audit partner responsible for reviewing the audit has provided such services to that corporation in each of the prior five years.
4. Requires RPAFs to make timely reports to the audit committees of the corporations. The report must indicate all critical accounting policies and practices to be used; all alternative treatments of financial information within generally accepted accounting principles that have been discussed with the corporation's management officials, the ramifications of the use of such alternative treatments, and the treatment preferred by the auditor; and other material written communications between the auditor and the corporation's management.
5. Makes it unlawful for an RPAF to provide auditing services to an issuer if the corporation's chief executive officer, chief financial officer, chief accounting officer, or controller was previously employed by the auditor and participated in any capacity in the audit of the corporation during the one-year period preceding the date when the audit began.

DOCUMENT RETENTION AND DESTRUCTION

The Sarbanes-Oxley Act provides that anyone who destroys, alters, or falsifies records with the intent to obstruct or influence a federal investigation or in relation to bankruptcy proceedings can be criminally prosecuted and sentenced to a fine, imprisonment for up to twenty years, or both.

The act also requires accountants who audit or review publicly traded companies to retain all working papers related to the audit or review for a period of five years (now amended to seven years). Violators can be sentenced to a fine, imprisonment for up to ten years, or both.

Under the common law, which in this instance has been codified in a number of states, working papers remain the accountant's property. It is important for accountants to retain such records in the event that they need to defend against lawsuits for negligence or other actions in which their competence is challenged. The client also has a right to access an accountant's working papers because they reflect the client's financial situation. On a client's request, an accountant must return any of the client's records or journals to the client, and failure to do so may result in liability.

Section 802(a)(1) of the Sarbanes-Oxley Act provides that accountants must maintain working papers relating to an audit or review for five years—subsequently increased to seven years—from the end of the fiscal period in which the audit or review was concluded. A knowing violation of this requirement will subject the accountant to a fine, imprisonment for up to ten years, or both.

SECTION 4

POTENTIAL LIABILITY OF ACCOUNTANTS UNDER SECURITIES LAWS

Both civil and criminal liability may be imposed on accountants under the Securities Act of 1933, the Securities Exchange Act of 1934, and the Private Securities Litigation Reform Act of 1995.[10]

---

10. Civil and criminal liability may also be imposed on accountants and other professionals under other statutes, including the Racketeer Influenced and Corrupt Organizations Act (RICO). RICO was discussed in Chapter 10.

Liability under the Securities Act of 1933

The Securities Act of 1933 requires registration statements to be filed with the Securities and Exchange Commission (SEC) prior to an offering of securities (see Chapter 42).[11] Accountants frequently prepare and certify the issuer's financial statements that are included in the registration statement.

LIABILITY UNDER SECTION 11 Section 11 of the Securities Act of 1933 imposes civil liability on accountants for misstatements and omissions of material facts in registration statements. An accountant may be held liable if he or she prepared any financial statements included in the registration statement that "contained an untrue statement of a material fact or omitted to state a material fact required to be stated therein or necessary to make the statements therein not misleading."[12]

An accountant may be liable to anyone who acquires a security covered by the registration statement. A purchaser of a security need only demonstrate that she or he has suffered a loss on the security. Proof of reliance on the materially false statement or misleading omission ordinarily is not required, nor is there a requirement of privity between the accountant and the security purchaser.

The Due Diligence Standard. Section 11 imposes a duty on accountants to use **due diligence** in preparing financial statements included in the filed registration statements. After the purchaser has proved a loss on the security, the accountant has the burden of showing that he or she exercised due diligence in preparing the financial statements. To prove due diligence, an accountant must demonstrate that she or he followed generally accepted standards and did not commit negligence or fraud.

To avoid liability, the accountant must show that he or she:

1. Conducted a reasonable investigation.
2. Had reasonable grounds to believe and did believe, at the time the registration statement became effective, that the statements therein were true and that there was no omission of a material fact that would be misleading.[13]

In particular, the due diligence standard places a burden on accountants to verify information furnished by a corporation's officers and directors. Merely asking questions is not always sufficient to satisfy the requirement of due diligence. Accountants may be held liable, for instance, for failing to detect danger signals in documents furnished by corporate officers that, under GAAS or IFRS, required further investigation.[14]

Other Defenses to Liability. Besides proving that he or she has acted with due diligence, an accountant may raise the following defenses to Section 11 liability:

1. There were no misstatements or omissions.
2. The misstatements or omissions were not of material facts.
3. The misstatements or omissions had no causal connection to the plaintiff's loss.
4. The plaintiff-purchaser invested in the securities knowing of the misstatements or omissions.

LIABILITY UNDER SECTION 12(2) Section 12(2) of the Securities Act of 1933 imposes civil liability for fraud in relation to offerings or sales of securities.[15] Liability is based on communication to an investor, whether orally or in the written prospectus,[16] of an untrue statement or omission of a material fact.

Those who purchase securities and suffer harm as a result of a false or omitted statement, or some other violation, may bring a suit in a federal court to recover their losses and other damages. The U.S. Department of Justice brings criminal actions against those who commit willful violations.

The penalties include fines up to $10,000, imprisonment up to five years, or both. The SEC is authorized to seek an injunction against a willful violator to prevent further violations. The SEC can also ask a court to grant other relief, such as an order to a violator to refund profits derived from an illegal transaction.

Liability under the Securities Exchange Act of 1934

Under Sections 18 and 10(b) of the Securities Exchange Act of 1934 and SEC Rule 10b-5, an accountant may be found liable for fraud. A plaintiff has a substantially heavier burden of proof under the 1934 act than

---

11. Many securities and transactions are expressly exempted from the 1933 act.
12. 15 U.S.C. Section 77k(a).
13. 15 U.S.C. Section 77k(b)(3).
14. See, for example, *Escott v. BarChris Construction Corp.,* 283 F.Supp. 643 (S.D.N.Y. 1968); *In re Cardinal Health, Inc. Securities Litigation,* 426 F.Supp.2d 688 (S.D. Ohio 2006); and *In re WorldCom, Inc. Securities Litigation,* 352 F.Supp.2d 472 (S.D.N.Y. 2005).
15. 15 U.S.C. Section 77*l*.
16. As discussed in Chapter 42, a *prospectus* contains financial disclosures about the corporation for the benefit of potential investors.

under the 1933 act because an accountant does not have to prove due diligence to escape liability under the 1934 act. The 1934 act relieves an accountant from liability if the accountant acted in "good faith."

LIABILITY UNDER SECTION 18 Section 18 of the 1934 act imposes civil liability on an accountant who makes or causes to be made in any application, report, or document a statement that at the time and in light of the circumstances was false or misleading with respect to any material fact.[17]

Section 18 liability is narrow in that it applies only to applications, reports, documents, and registration statements filed with the SEC. In addition, it applies only to sellers and purchasers. Under Section 18, a seller or purchaser must prove one of the following:

1. The false or misleading statement affected the price of the security.
2. The purchaser or seller relied on the false or misleading statement in making the purchase or sale and was not aware of the inaccuracy of the statement.

Good Faith Defense. An accountant will not be liable for violating Section 18 if he or she acted in good faith in preparing the financial statement. To demonstrate good faith, an accountant must show that he or she had no knowledge that the financial statement was false or misleading and that he or she lacked any intent to deceive, manipulate, defraud, or seek unfair advantage over another party. (Note that "mere" negligence in preparing a financial statement does not lead to liability under the 1934 act. This differs from the 1933 act, under which an accountant is liable for all negligent acts.)

Other Defenses. In addition to the good faith defense, accountants can escape liability by proving that the buyer or seller of the security in question knew the financial statement was false and misleading. Sellers and purchasers must bring a cause of action "within one year after the discovery of the facts constituting the cause of action and within three years after such cause of action accrued."[18] A court also has the discretion to assess reasonable costs, including attorneys' fees, against accountants who violate this section.

LIABILITY UNDER SECTION 10(B) AND SEC RULE 10B-5 Accountants additionally face potential legal liability under the antifraud provisions contained in the Securities Exchange Act of 1934 and SEC Rule 10b-5. The scope of these antifraud provisions is very broad and allows private parties to bring civil actions against violators.

Prohibited Conduct. Section 10(b) makes it unlawful for any person, including an accountant, to use, in connection with the purchase or sale of any security, any manipulative or deceptive device or plan that is counter to SEC rules and regulations.[19] Rule 10b-5 further makes it unlawful for any person, by use of any means or instrumentality of interstate commerce, to do the following:

1. Employ any device, scheme, or strategy to defraud.
2. Make any untrue statement of a material fact or omit to state a material fact necessary to make the statements made, in light of the circumstances, not misleading.
3. Engage in any act, practice, or course of business that operates or would operate as a fraud or deceit on any person, in connection with the purchase or sale of any security.[20]

Extent of Liability. Accountants may be held liable only to sellers or purchasers of securities under Section 10(b) and Rule 10b-5. Privity is not necessary for a recovery. An accountant may be liable not only for fraudulent misstatements of material facts in written material filed with the SEC, but also for any fraudulent oral statements or omissions made in connection with the purchase or sale of any security.

For a plaintiff to succeed in recovering damages under these antifraud provisions, he or she must prove intent (scienter) to commit the fraudulent or deceptive act. Ordinary negligence is not enough.

Under Section 10(b) and Rule 10b-5, do accountants have a duty to correct misstatements that they discover in previous financial statements if they know that potential investors are relying on those statements? That was the question in the following case.

17. 15 U.S.C. Section 78r(a).
18. 15 U.S.C. Section 17r(c).
19. 15 U.S.C. Section 78j(b).
20. 17 C.F.R. Section 240.10b-5.

SP TLIGHT on Accountant's Duty to Correct Mistakes

Case 47.3   Overton v. Todman & Co., CPAs

United States Court of Appeals, Second Circuit, 478 F.3d 479 (2007).

BACKGROUND AND FACTS From 1999 through 2002, Todman & Company, CPAs, P.C., audited the financial statements of Direct Brokerage, Inc. (DBI), a broker-dealer in New York registered with the Securities and Exchange Commission (SEC). Each year, Todman issued an unqualified opinion that DBI's financial statements were accurate. DBI filed its statements and Todman's opinions with the SEC. Despite the certifications of accuracy, Todman made significant errors that concealed DBI's largest liability—its payroll taxes—in the 1999 and 2000 audits. The errors came to light in 2003 when the New York State Division of Taxation subpoenaed DBI's payroll records, and it became clear that the company had not filed or paid its payroll taxes for 1999 and 2000. This put DBI in a precarious financial position, owing the state more than $3 million in unpaid taxes, interest, and penalties.

To meet its needs, DBI sought outside investors, including David Overton, who relied on DBI's statements and Todman's opinion for 2002 to invest in DBI. When DBI collapsed under the weight of its liabilities in 2004, Overton and others filed a suit in a federal district court against Todman, asserting, among other things, fraud under Section 10(b) and Rule 10b-5. The court dismissed the complaint. The plaintiffs appealed to the U.S. Court of Appeals for the Second Circuit.

IN THE LANGUAGE OF THE COURT
STRAUB, Circuit Judge.

* * * *

A fundamental principle of securities law is that before an individual becomes liable for his silence, he must have an underlying duty to speak. [Emphasis added.]

* * * *

* * * The Supreme Court [has] held that [Section] 10(b) does not authorize aiding and abetting liability. In order to be liable under [Section] 10(b), the Court held, an actor must himself "mak[e] . . . a material misstatement (or omission) or . . . commit . . . a manipulative act." The rationale underpinning this holding was that (1) by its terms, [Section] 10(b) requires the making of a statement or omission and (2) without such a statement or omission, the "critical" element of reliance would be absent.

Although the Court did not specifically discuss an auditor's duty to correct, it made clear that * * * secondary actors such as accountants may incur primary liability based on their omissions * * * .

* * * For many years we have recognized the existence of an accountant's duty to correct its certified opinions, but never squarely held that such a duty exists for the purposes of primary liability under [Section] 10(b) of the 1934 Act and Rule 10b-5. Presented with an opportunity to do so, we now so hold. Specifically, we hold that an accountant violates the "duty to correct" and becomes primarily liable under [Section] 10(b) and Rule 10b-5 when it (1) makes a statement in its certified opinion that is false or misleading when made; (2) subsequently learns or was reckless in not learning that the earlier statement was false or misleading; (3) knows or should know that potential investors are relying on the opinion and financial statements; yet (4) fails to take reasonable steps to correct or withdraw its opinion and/or the financial statements; and (5) all the other requirements for liability are satisfied.

* * * *

In light of the above principles, we conclude that the District Court erred in dismissing the complaint. Plaintiffs pled that Todman's certified opinion and DBI's 2002 financial statements were misleading at the time they were issued, especially with respect to DBI's payroll tax liability; Todman * * * subsequently learned that its certified opinion was false; Todman also knew that DBI was soliciting outside investors based in part on its 2002 certified financial

CASE 47.3 CONTINUES ▶

CASE 47.3 CONTINUED statements and Todman's accompanying opinion; and that despite this knowledge, Todman took no action to correct or withdraw its opinion and/or DBI's financial statements. These allegations adequately state a claim of primary accountant liability under [Section] 10(b) and Rule 10b-5.

DECISION AND REMEDY *The U.S. Court of Appeals for the Second Circuit held that an accountant is liable in these circumstances under Section 10(b) and Rule 10b-5. The court vacated the lower court's dismissal and remanded the case.*

WHAT IF THE FACTS WERE DIFFERENT? *If Todman had conducted an audit for DBI but had not issued a certified opinion about DBI's financial statements, would the result in this case have been the same? Explain.*

THE LEGAL ENVIRONMENT DIMENSION *Did Overton have a valid reason to sue DBI's auditors? Why or why not?*

The Private Securities Litigation Reform Act of 1995

The Private Securities Litigation Reform Act of 1995 made some changes to the potential liability of accountants and other professionals in securities fraud cases. Among other things, the act imposed a statutory obligation on accountants. An auditor must use adequate procedures in an audit to detect any illegal acts of the company being audited. If something illegal is detected, the auditor must disclose it to the company's board of directors, the audit committee, or the SEC, depending on the circumstances.[21]

PROPORTIONATE LIABILITY The act provides that, in most situations, a party is liable only for the proportion of damages for which he or she is responsible.[22] In other words, the parties are subject to proportionate liability rather than joint and several liability. An accountant who participates in, but is unaware of, illegal conduct may not be liable for the entire amount of the loss caused by the illegality. ▶ **Example 47.9** Nina Chavez, an accountant, helped the president and owner of Midstate Trucking Company draft financial statements that misrepresented Midstate's financial condition. If Nina was not actually aware of the fraud, she can still be held liable, but the amount of her liability could be proportionately less than the entire loss. ◀

AIDING AND ABETTING The act also made it a crime to aid and abet a violation of the Securities Exchange Act of 1934, such as by knowingly participating in or assisting in some improper activity or keeping quiet about it.

If an accountant knowingly aids and abets a primary violator, the SEC can seek an injunction or monetary damages. ▶ **Example 47.10** Smith & Jones, an accounting firm, performs an audit for Belco Sales Company that is so inadequate as to constitute gross negligence. Belco uses the financial statements provided by Smith & Jones as part of a scheme to defraud investors. When the scheme is uncovered, the SEC can bring an action against Smith & Jones for aiding and abetting. The firm knew or should have known that its audited statements contained material misrepresentations on which investors were likely to rely. ◀

Criminal Liability of Accountants

An accountant may be found criminally liable for violations of securities laws and tax laws. In addition, most states make it a crime to (1) knowingly certify false reports, (2) falsify, alter, or destroy books of account, and (3) obtain property or credit through the use of false financial statements.

CRIMINAL VIOLATIONS OF SECURITIES LAWS Accountants may be subject to criminal penalties for *willful* violations of the Securities Act of 1933 and the Securities Exchange Act of 1934. If convicted, they face imprisonment for up to five years and/or a fine of up to $10,000 under the 1933 act and imprisonment for up to ten years and a fine of $100,000 under the 1934 act.

---

21. 15 U.S.C. Section 78j-1.
22. 15 U.S.C. Section 78u-4(g).

Under the Sarbanes-Oxley Act of 2002, if an accountant's false or misleading certified audit statement is used in a securities filing, the accountant may be held criminally liable. The accountant may be fined up to $5 million, imprisoned for up to twenty years, or both.

CRIMINAL VIOLATIONS OF TAX LAWS The Internal Revenue Code makes it a felony to aid or assist in the preparation of a false tax return. Violations are punishable by a fine of $100,000 ($500,000 for a corporation's return) and imprisonment for up to three years.[23] This provision applies to anyone who prepares tax returns for others for compensation, not just to accountants.[24]

A penalty of $250 per tax return is levied on tax preparers for negligent understatement of the client's tax liability. For willful understatement of tax liability or reckless or intentional disregard of rules or regulations, a penalty of $1,000 is imposed.[25]

A tax preparer may also be subject to penalties for failing to furnish the taxpayer with a copy of the return, failing to sign the return, or failing to furnish the appropriate tax identification numbers.[26] In addition, those who prepare tax returns for others may be fined $1,000 per document for aiding and abetting another's understatement of tax liability (the penalty is increased to $10,000 for corporate returns).[27] The tax preparer's liability is limited to one penalty per taxpayer per tax year.

Concept Summary 47.2 below outlines the potential statutory liability of accountants and other professionals.

---

23. 26 U.S.C. Section 7206(2).
24. 26 U.S.C. Section 7701(a)(36).

25. 26 U.S.C. Section 6694.
26. 26 U.S.C. Section 6695.
27. 26 U.S.C. Section 6701.

CONCEPT SUMMARY 47.2

Statutory Liability of Accountants and Other Professionals

STATUTE	NATURE OF LIABILITY
Sarbanes-Oxley Act of 2002	See Exhibit 47–1 on page 922 for the provisions of the act on auditor independence and document retention.
Securities Act of 1933, Sections 11 and 12(2)	Under Section 11 of the 1933 Securities Act, an accountant who makes a false statement or omits a material fact in audited financial statements required for registration of securities under the law may be liable to anyone who acquires securities covered by the registration statement. The accountant's defense is basically the use of due diligence and the reasonable belief that the work was complete and correct. The burden of proof is on the accountant. Willful violations of this act may be subject to criminal penalties. Section 12(2) of the 1933 act imposes civil liability for fraud on anyone who makes an untrue statement or omits a material fact when offering or selling a security to any purchaser of the security.
Securities Exchange Act of 1934, Sections 10(b) and 18	Under Sections 10(b) and 18 of the 1934 Securities Exchange Act, accountants are held liable for false and misleading applications, reports, and documents required under the act. The burden is on the plaintiff, and the accountant has numerous defenses, including good faith and lack of knowledge that what was submitted was false. Willful violations of this act may be subject to criminal penalties.
Internal Revenue Code	1. Aiding or assisting in the preparation of a false tax return is a felony. Aiding and abetting an individual's understatement of tax liability is a separate crime. 2. Tax preparers who negligently or willfully understate a client's tax liability or who recklessly or intentionally disregard Internal Revenue Code rules or regulations are subject to penalties. 3. Tax preparers who fail to provide a taxpayer with a copy of the return, fail to sign the return, or fail to furnish the appropriate tax identification numbers may also be subject to penalties.

SECTION 5
CONFIDENTIALITY AND PRIVILEGE

Professionals are restrained by the ethical tenets of their professions to keep all communications with their clients confidential.

Attorney-Client Relationships

The confidentiality of attorney-client communications is protected by law, which confers a *privilege* on such communications. This privilege exists because of the need for full disclosure to the attorney of the facts of a client's case.

To encourage frankness, confidential attorney-client communications relating to representation are normally held in strictest confidence and protected by law. The attorney and her or his employees may not discuss the client's case with anyone—even under court order—without the client's permission. The client holds the privilege, and only the client may waive it—by disclosing privileged information to someone outside the privilege, for example.

Note, however, that the SEC has implemented rules requiring attorneys who become aware that a client has violated securities laws to report the violation to the SEC. Reporting a client's misconduct could be a breach of the attorney-client privilege, however, so these rules have created a potential conflict for some attorneys.

Accountant-Client Relationships

In a few states, accountant-client communications are privileged by state statute. In these states, accountant-client communications may not be revealed even in court or in court-sanctioned proceedings without the client's permission.

The majority of states, however, abide by the common law, which provides that, if a court so orders, an accountant must disclose information about his or her client to the court. Physicians and other professionals may similarly be compelled to disclose in court information given to them in confidence by patients or clients.

Communications between professionals and their clients—other than those between an attorney and her or his client—are not privileged under federal law. In cases involving federal law, state-provided rights to confidentiality of accountant-client communications are not recognized. Thus, in those cases, in response to a court order, an accountant must provide the information sought.

Reviewing: Professional Liability and Accountability

Superior Wholesale Corporation planned to purchase Regal Furniture, Inc., and wished to determine Regal's net worth. Superior hired Lynette Shuebke, of the accounting firm Shuebke Delgado, to review an audit that had been prepared by Norman Chase, the accountant for Regal. Shuebke advised Superior that Chase had performed a high-quality audit and that Regal's inventory on the audit dates was stated accurately on the general ledger. As a result of these representations, Superior went forward with its purchase of Regal. After the purchase, Superior discovered that the audit by Chase had been materially inaccurate and misleading, primarily because the inventory had been grossly overstated on the balance sheet. Later, a former Regal employee who had begun working for Superior exposed an e-mail exchange between Chase and former Regal chief executive officer Buddy Gantry. The exchange revealed that Chase had cooperated in overstating the inventory and understating Regal's tax liability. Using the information presented in the chapter, answer the following questions.

1. If Shuebke's review was conducted in good faith and conformed to generally accepted accounting principles, can Superior hold Shuebke Delgado liable for negligently failing to detect material omissions in Chase's audit? Why or why not?
2. According to the rule adopted by the majority of courts to determine accountants' liability to third parties, could Chase be liable to Superior? Explain.

3. Generally, what requirements must be met before Superior can recover damages under Section 10(b) of the Securities Exchange Act of 1934 and SEC Rule 10b-5? Can Superior meet these requirements? Why or why not?

4. Suppose that a court determined that Chase had aided Regal in willfully understating its tax liability. What is the maximum penalty that could be imposed on Chase?

DEBATE THIS . . . *Only the largest publicly held companies should be subject to the Sarbanes-Oxley Act.*

Terms and Concepts

auditor 914

defalcation 914

due diligence 923

generally accepted accounting principles (GAAP) 914

generally accepted auditing standards (GAAS) 914

International Financial Reporting Standards (IFRS) 914

working papers 921

ExamPrep

Issue Spotters

1. Dave, an accountant, prepares a financial statement for Excel Company, a client, knowing that Excel will use the statement to obtain a loan from First National Bank. Dave makes negligent omissions in the statement that result in a loss to the bank. Can the bank successfully sue Dave? Why or why not? **(See page 919.)**

2. Nora, an accountant, prepares a financial statement as part of a registration statement that Omega, Inc., files with the Securities and Exchange Commission before making a public offering of securities. The statement contains a misstatement of material fact that is not attributable to Nora's fraud or negligence. Pat relies on the misstatement, buys some of the securities, and suffers a loss. Can Nora be held liable to Pat? Explain. **(See page 923.)**

• **Check your answers to the Issue Spotters against the answers provided in Appendix E at the end of this text.**

Before the Test

Go to **www.cengagebrain.com**, enter the ISBN 9781285185248, and click on "Find" to locate this textbook's Web site. Then, click on "Access Now" under "Study Tools," and select Chapter 47 at the top. There, you will find a Practice Quiz that you can take to assess your mastery of the concepts in this chapter, as well as Flashcards and a Glossary of important terms.

Business Scenarios

47–1. The *Ultramares* Rule. Larkin, Inc., retains Howard Patterson to manage its books and prepare its financial statements. Patterson, a certified public accountant, lives in Indiana and practices there. After twenty years, Patterson has become a bit bored with generally accepted accounting principles (GAAP) and has adopted more creative accounting methods. Now, though, Patterson has a problem, as he is being sued by Molly Tucker, one of Larkin's creditors. Tucker alleges that Patterson either knew or should have known that Larkin's financial statements would be distributed to various individuals. Furthermore, she asserts that these financial statements were negligently prepared and seriously inaccurate. What are the consequences of Patterson's failure to follow GAAP?

Under the traditional *Ultramares* rule, can Tucker recover damages from Patterson? Explain. **(See page 918.)**

47–2. The *Restatement* Rule. The accounting firm of Goldman, Walters, Johnson & Co. prepared financial statements for Lucy's Fashions, Inc. After reviewing the various financial statements, Happydays State Bank agreed to loan Lucy's Fashions $35,000 for expansion. When Lucy's Fashions declared bankruptcy under Chapter 11 six months later, Happydays State Bank promptly filed an action against Goldman, Walters, Johnson & Co., alleging negligent preparation of financial statements. Assuming that the court has abandoned the *Ultramares* approach, what is the result? What are the policy reasons for holding accountants liable to third parties with whom they are not in privity? **(See page 918.)**

47–3. Accountant's Liability under Rule 10b-5. In early 2014, Bennett, Inc., offered a substantial number of new common shares to the public. Harvey Helms had a long-standing interest in Bennett because his grandfather had once been president of the company. On receiving a pro-spectus prepared and distributed by Bennett, Helms was dismayed by the pessimism it embodied. Helms decided to delay purchasing stock in the company. Later, Helms asserted that the prospectus prepared by the accountants was overly pessimistic and contained materially mislead-ing statements. Discuss fully how successful Helms would be in bringing a cause of action under Rule 10b-5 against the accountants of Bennett, Inc. **(See page 923.)**

Business Case Problems

47–4. Accountant's Liability for Audit. A West Virginia bank ran its asset value from $100 million to $1 billion over seven years by aggressively marketing subprime loans. The Office of the Comptroller of the Currency, a federal regulator, audited the bank and discovered that the books had been falsified for several years and that the bank was insolvent. The Comptroller closed the bank and brought criminal charges against its managers. The Comptroller fined Grant Thornton, the bank's accounting firm, $300,000 for recklessly failing to meet generally accepted auditing standards during the years it audited the bank. The Comptroller claimed Thornton violated federal law by "participating in . . . unsafe and unsound banking practice." Thornton appealed, contending that it was not involved in bank operations to that extent based on its audit function. What would be the key to determining if the accounting firm could be held liable for that viola-tion of federal law? [*Grant Thornton, LLP v. Office of the Comptroller of the Currency*, 514 F.3d 1328 (D.C. Cir. 2008)] **(See page 914.)**

47–5. Professional's Liability. Soon after Teresa DeYoung's husband died, her mother-in-law also died, leaving an inheritance of more than $400,000 for DeYoung's children. DeYoung hired John Ruggerio, an attorney, to ensure that her children would receive it. Ruggerio advised her to invest the funds in his real estate business. She declined. A few months later, $300,000 of the inheri-tance was sent to Ruggerio. Without telling DeYoung, he deposited the $300,000 in his account and began to use the funds in his real estate business. Nine months later, $109,000 of the inheritance was sent to Ruggerio. He paid this to DeYoung. She asked about the remaining amount. Ruggerio lied to hide his theft. Unable to access these funds, DeYoung's children changed their college plans to attend less expensive institutions. Nearly three years later, DeYoung learned the truth. Can she bring a suit against Ruggerio? If so, on what ground? If not, why not? Did Ruggerio violate any standard of professional ethics? Discuss. [*DeYoung v. Ruggerio*, 185 Vt. 267, 971 A.2d 627 (2009)] **(See page 915.)**

47–6. Professional Malpractice. Jeffery Guerrero hired James McDonald, a certified public accountant, to rep-resent him and his business in an appeal to the Internal Revenue Service. The appeal was about audits that showed Guerrero owed more taxes. When the appeal failed, McDonald helped Guerrero prepare materials for an appeal to the Tax Court, which was also unsuc-cessful. Guerrero then sued McDonald for professional negligence in the preparation of his evidence for the court. Guerrero claimed that McDonald had failed to adequately prepare witnesses and to present all the argu-ments that could have been made on his behalf so that he could have won the case. Guerrero contended that McDonald was liable for all of the additional taxes he was required to pay. Is Guerrero's claim likely to result in liability on McDonald's part? What factors would the court consider? [*Guerrero v. McDonald*, 302 Ga.App. 164, 690 S.E.2d 486 (2010)] **(See page 916.)**

47–7. BUSINESS CASE PROBLEM WITH SAMPLE ANSWER: Potential Liability to Third Parties.
 In 2006, twenty-seven people and entities became limited partners in two hedge funds that had invested with Bernard Madoff and his investment firm. The partners' investment adviser gave them various investment information, including a memorandum indicating that an independent certified public accountant, KPMG, LLP, had audited the hedge funds' annual reports. Since 2004, KPMG had also prepared annual reports addressed to the funds' "Partners." Each report stated that KPMG had investi-gated the funds' financial statements, had followed generally accepted auditing principles, and had concluded that the state-ments fairly summarized the funds' financial conditions. Moreover, KPMG used the information from its audits to pre-pare individual tax statements for each fund partner. In 2008, Madoff was charged with securities fraud for running a mas-sive Ponzi scheme. In a 2009 report, the Securities and Exchange Commission identified numerous "red flags" that should have been discovered by investment advisers and audi-tors. Unfortunately, the auditors did not find them, and the hedge funds' partners lost millions of dollars. Is KPMG poten-tially liable to the funds' partners under the Restatement (Third) of Torts? *Why or why not?* [*Askenazy v. Tremont Group Holdings, Inc.*, 2012 WL 440675 (Mass.Super. 2012)] **(See page 917.)**

- **For a sample answer to Problem 47–7, go to Appendix F at the end of this text.**

47–8. A QUESTION OF ETHICS: Liability for Negligence.

 Portland Shellfish Co. processes live shellfish in Maine. As one of the firm's two owners, Frank Wetmore held 300 voting and 150 nonvoting shares of the stock. Donna Holden held the other 300 voting shares. Donna's husband, Jeff, managed the company's daily operations, including production, procurement, and sales. The board of directors consisted of Frank and Jeff. In 2001, disagreements arose over the company's management. The Holdens invoked the "Shareholders' Agreement," which provided that "[i]n the event of a deadlock, the directors shall hire an accountant at [Macdonald, Page, Schatz, Fletcher & Co., LLC] to determine the value of the outstanding shares. . . . [E]ach shareholder shall have the right to buy out the other shareholder(s)' interest."

Macdonald Page estimated the stock's "fair market value" at $1.09 million. Donna offered to buy Frank's shares at a price equal to his proportionate share. Frank countered by offering $1.25 million for Donna's shares. Donna rejected Frank's offer and insisted that he sell his shares to her or she would sue. In the face of this threat, Frank sold his shares to Donna for $750,705. Believing the stock to be worth more than twice Macdonald Page's estimate, Frank filed a suit in a federal district court against the accountant. [Wetmore v. Macdonald, Page, Schatz, Fletcher & Co., LLC, 476 F.3d 1 (1st Cir. 2007)] **(See page 914.)**

(a) Frank claimed that in valuing the stock, the accountant disregarded "commonly accepted and reliable methods of valuation in favor of less reliable methods." He alleged negligence, among other things. Macdonald Page filed a motion to dismiss the complaint. What are the elements that establish negligence? Which is the most critical element in this case?

(b) Macdonald Page evaluated the company's stock by identifying its "fair market value," defined as "the price at which the property would change hands between a willing buyer and a willing seller, neither being under a compulsion to buy or sell and both having reasonable knowledge of relevant facts." The accountant knew that the shareholders would use its estimate to determine the price that one would pay to the other. Under these circumstances, was Frank's injury foreseeable? Discuss.

(c) What factor might have influenced Frank to sell his shares to Donna even though he thought that Macdonald Page's "fair market value" figure was less than half of what it should have been? Does this factor represent an unfair, or unethical, advantage? Explain.

Legal Reasoning Group Activity

47–9. Attorney-Client Privilege. Napster, Inc., offered a service that allowed its users to browse digital music files on other users' computers and download selections for free. Music industry principals sued Napster for copyright infringement, and the court ordered Napster to remove from its service files that were identified as infringing. When Napster failed to comply, it was shut down.

A few months later, Bertelsmann, a German corporation, loaned Napster $85 million to fund its anticipated transition to a licensed digital music distribution system. The terms allowed Napster to spend the loan on "general, administrative and overhead expenses." In an e-mail, Napster's chief executive officer referred to a "side deal" under which Napster could use up to $10 million of the loan to pay litigation expenses. Napster failed to launch the new system before declaring bankruptcy. The plaintiffs filed a suit against Bertelsmann, alleging that by its loan, it prolonged Napster's infringement. The plaintiffs asked the court to order the disclosure of all attorney-client communications related to the loan. **(See page 928.)**

(a) The first group will identify the principle that Bertelsmann could assert to protect these communications and outline the purpose of this protection.

(b) The second group will decide whether this principle should protect a client who consults an attorney for advice that will help the client commit fraud.

(c) A third group will determine whether the court should grant the plaintiffs' request.

UNIT NINE Focus on Ethics

Government Regulation

If this text had been written a hundred years ago, it would have had little to say about federal government regulation. Today, in contrast, just about every area of economic activity is regulated by the government. Ethical issues in government regulation arise because regulation, by its very nature, means that some traditional rights and freedoms must be given up to ensure that other rights and freedoms are protected.

Essentially, government regulation brings two ethical principles into conflict. On the one hand, deeply embedded in American culture is the idea that the government should play a limited role in directing our lives. On the other hand, one of the basic functions of government is to protect the welfare of individuals and the environment in which they live.

Ultimately, nearly every law or rule regulating business represents a decision to give up certain rights in order to protect other perceived rights. In this *Focus on Ethics* feature, we look at some of the ethical aspects of government regulation.

Television Programmers and Antitrust Law

When consumers want cable or satellite television programming, they can choose among various cable and satellite providers, or distributors, but each distributor will offer multichannel packages. In other words, a consumer cannot order just the channels that she or he watches regularly. All of the multichannel packages include some very popular channels and some other channels that have very low viewership. Thus, consumers are forced to pay for some unwanted channels in order to get the ones they do want.

A group of consumers sued NBC Universal, the Walt Disney Company, and other programmers, as well as cable and satellite distributors. The consumers claimed that the defendants, because of their full or partial ownership of broadcast channels and their ownership or control of multiple cable or satellite channels, had a higher degree of market power vis-à-vis all distributors. They also claimed that the programmers had exploited this power by requiring the "bundling" of numerous channels in each multichannel package offered to consumers.

The U.S. Court of Appeals for the Ninth Circuit disagreed. The court pointed out that the Sherman Act applies to actions that diminish competition and, in this instance, there was still competition among programmers and distributors.[1]

LEGAL REASONING

1. *Should TV programmers and distributors be held in violation of the Sherman Act for requiring consumers to buy multichannel packages? Why or why not?*

Credit Reporting Agencies and "Blacklisting"

Today, some consumer credit reporting agencies will also conduct an online investigation of a person's history of credit

disputes and litigation. Physicians and landlords frequently use such services to learn whether prospective patients or tenants have a history of suing their physicians or their landlords.

One service, for example, allows physicians, for a fee, to perform more than two hundred online name searches to find out if a prospective patient was ever a plaintiff in a malpractice suit. Other services available to merchants (such as BadCustomer.com) keep a running tally of customers who have requested a credit-card reversal, called a *chargeback*, after paying a merchant. Even a single chargeback can cause merchants to reject a consumer's card in the future.

Users say that these services are an ideal way to screen out undesirable patients and applicants, and thereby reduce the risk of being sued. Consumer rights advocates, however, claim that the sale of such information is akin to "blacklisting"—discriminating against potential customers, patients, or tenants on the basis of previous disputes and litigation. These practices have led to complaints of unfairness, as well as lawsuits against reporting agencies. By and large, though, consumers have little recourse unless what is being reported about them is inaccurate.

Privacy Concerns and the Fair Debt Collection Practices Act

Debt-collection practices have often raised privacy concerns. There have been many lawsuits against collection agencies over voice messages or voice mails left by debt collectors. The Fair Debt Collection Practices Act (FDCPA) prohibits disclosures about a debt to third parties.

Does leaving a voice message regarding a debt collection on an answering machine constitute such a disclosure? That depends on the jurisdiction and the situation. In one case, a Florida court ruled in favor of the debtor. It stated that if a collection agency leaves a voice message for a consumer on an answering machine—even at home—other people (third parties) could hear the message.[2] In another case, a federal district court in California held that a debt-collection company had violated the FDCPA by leaving a voice message for the debtor. The message announcing that the debtor had failed to pay his auto insurance was overheard by his mother.[3]

In contrast, a federal court in Minnesota held that leaving voice messages on a debtor's cell phone did not violate the FDCPA, even though the debtor's children listened to them. Because the messages did not identify the debtor or the debt, the court reasoned that "they conveyed no more information than would have been obvious in caller ID." The suit against the debt collector was dismissed.[4]

---

1. *Brantley v. NBC Universal, Inc.*, 675 F.3d 1192 (9th Cir. 2012).

2. *Berg v. Merchants Association Collection Division, Inc.*, 586 F.Supp.2d 1336 (S.D.Fla. 2008).
3. *Branco v. Credit Collection Services, Inc.*, 2011 WL 3684503 (E.D.Cal. 2011).
4. *Zortman v. J.C. Christensen & Associates, Inc.*, 2012 WL 1563918 (D.Minn. 2012).

LEGAL REASONING

2. *Do you think that debt collectors should be able to leave voice messages regarding the debt on a debtor's phone? Why or why not? Does the fact that many people today only have cell phones affect your answer? Explain.*

Environmental Law

Questions of fairness inevitably arise in regard to environmental law. Has the government gone too far—or not far enough—in regulating businesses in the interest of protecting the environment? At what point do the costs of environmental regulations become too burdensome for society to bear? Consider the problem of toxic waste. Although everybody is in favor of cleaning up America's toxic waste dumps, nobody knows what this task will ultimately cost. Moreover, there is no agreed-on standard as to how clean a site must be before it no longer poses any threat. Must 100 percent of the contamination be removed, or would removal of some lesser amount achieve a reasonable degree of environmental quality?

Concerns over Pharmaceuticals in Drinking Water

The amount of pharmaceuticals used by the U.S. public and in agriculture (antibiotics and hormones given to livestock) has grown substantially in recent years. Widespread trace amounts of many drugs have been detected in our nation's water supply. The drinking water of at least 41 million Americans in twenty-four regions across the country has been found to contain small amounts of prescription drugs.

Some of these trace amounts came from unmetabolized drugs that had passed through the humans and animals that ingested them, but the rest had been flushed down the toilet. For many years, pharmacists, physicians, and the federal government have recommended that people dispose of unused medications by flushing them away. This prevents children from accidentally ingesting the drugs and keeps controlled substances such as the painkillers oxycodone and morphine from falling into the hands of people who might abuse them. At the time, no one considered the long-term effect on the environment of adding pharmaceuticals to the water supply.

The quantities present in water now are far below medicinal doses, but no one knows how long-term exposure to random combinations of drugs will affect humans or wildlife. As yet, there is little scientific evidence about the long-term effects. The federal government does not require drinking water to be tested for drugs, so Americans do not know whether their drinking water is contaminated. Requiring that water be tested and that all traces of drugs be filtered from it would be enormously expensive.

LEGAL REASONING

3. *Should the government wait until there is scientific proof of the harmful effects on humans and wildlife before attempting to regulate pharmaceuticals in drinking water? Or should the*

government enact legislation to address the problem now—before it becomes worse? Discuss fully.

Global Environmental Issues

Pollution does not respect geographic borders. Indeed, one of the reasons that the federal government became involved in environmental protection was that state regulation alone apparently could not solve the problem of air or water pollution. Pollutants generated in one state move in the air and water to other states. Similarly, pollution crosses national borders.

Environmental issues, perhaps more than any others, bring home to everyone the fact that the world today is truly a global community. What one country does or does not do with respect to environmental preservation may be felt by citizens in countries thousands of miles away.

Climate Change. Another challenging—and controversial—issue is potential global climate change. The fear is that emissions, largely from combustion of fossil fuels, will remain in the atmosphere and create a "greenhouse effect" by preventing heat from radiating outward.

Concerns over this issue have led to many attempts to force all world polluters to "clean up their acts." For example, leaders of 187 nations have already agreed to reduce emissions of greenhouse gases in their respective countries. They did this when they ratified the Kyoto Protocol, which was drawn up at a world summit meeting held in Kyoto, Japan, in 1997.

The Kyoto Protocol, which is often referred to as the global warming treaty, established different rates of reduction in greenhouse emissions for different countries or regions. Most nations, however, including the United States, will not meet the treaty's objectives. Many claim the treaty is not effective because it does not address the problem of curbing greenhouse gases in most of the developing world.

LEGAL REASONING

4. *Can you think of a better way that the law can address the problem of climate change, which is clearly not just a national issue? Explain.*

Is Economic Development the Answer? Economists have shown that economic development is the quickest way to reduce pollution worldwide. After a nation reaches a certain per capita income level, the more economic growth the nation experiences, the lower the pollution output. This occurs because richer nations have the resources to pay for pollution reduction.

For example, industries in the United States pollute much less per unit of output than do industries in developing nations—because we are willing to pay for pollution abatement. Even among developed nations, the United States is a leader in curbing pollution. Indeed, in the last ten years, the United States saw a much smaller increase in greenhouse gases than did the European Union.

BUSINESS LAW
CLARKSON · MILLER · CROSS

CHAPTER 48

PERSONAL PROPERTY AND BAILMENTS

Property consists of the legally protected rights and interests a person has in anything with an ascertainable value that is subject to ownership. Property would have little value, however, if the law did not define the rights of owners to use, sell, dispose of, control, and prevent others from trespassing on their property rights.

In the United States, a substantial body of law protects the rights of property owners, but that protection is not absolute. As you will read in this chapter and the next, property owners may have to prove that their ownership rights in a particular item of property are superior to the claims of others. In addition, through its police powers, the government can impose regulations and taxes on property, and can take or seize private property under certain circumstances.

In this chapter, we first examine the differences between personal and real property. We then look at the methods of acquiring ownership of personal property and issues relating to mislaid, lost, and abandoned personal property. In the second half of this chapter, we discuss bailment relationships. A *bailment* is created when personal property is temporarily delivered into the care of another without a transfer of title, such as when a person takes an item of clothing to the dry cleaners. The fact that there is no passage of title and no intent to transfer title is what distinguishes a bailment from a sale or a gift.

PERSONAL PROPERTY VERSUS REAL PROPERTY

Real property (sometimes called *realty* or *real estate*) means the land and everything permanently attached to it, including structures and anything permanently attached to the structures. Everything else is **personal property** (sometimes referred to in case law as *personalty* or **chattel**). In essence, real property is immovable, whereas personal property is capable of being moved.

Personal property can be tangible or intangible. Tangible personal property, such as a flat-screen TV, heavy construction equipment, or a car, has physical substance. Intangible personal property represents some set of rights and interests, but it has no real physical existence. Stocks and bonds are intangible personal property. So, too, are patents, trademarks, and copyrights (discussed in Chapter 8), as well as digital and virtual property, such as the objects used in virtual worlds like Entropia Universe and Second Life.

Both personal property and real property can be owned by an individual person or by an entity. When two or more persons own real or personal property together, concurrent ownership exists. (The different types of joint or concurrent ownership will be discussed in Chapter 49.)

Why Is the Distinction Important?

How property is taxed and what is required to transfer or acquire the property is determined by whether the property is classified as real or personal property.

TAXATION The two types of property are usually subject to different types of taxes. Generally, each state assesses property taxes on real property. Typically, the tax rate is based on the market value of the real property and the various services provided by the city, state, and county in which the property is located. For instance, higher taxes may be imposed on real property located within the city limits to pay for schools, roads, and libraries.

Businesses usually pay taxes (both federal and state) on the personal property they own, use, or lease, including office or farm equipment and supplies. Individuals may pay sales tax when purchasing personal property, but generally they are not required to pay annual taxes on personal property that is not used for business.

ACQUISITION Another reason for distinguishing between real and personal property has to do with the way the property is acquired or transferred. Personal property can be transferred with a minimum of formality. In contrast, real property transfers generally involve a written sales contract and a *deed* that is recorded with the state (deeds and real property transfers are discussed in Chapter 49).

Similarly, establishing ownership rights is simpler for personal property than for real property. ▶ **Example 48.1**   If Mia gives Shawn an iPad as a gift, Shawn does not need to have any paperwork evidencing title. (The ways to acquire ownership of personal property will be discussed shortly.) ◀

Conversion of Real Property to Personal Property

Sometimes, real property can be turned into personal property by detaching it from the land. For instance, the trees, bushes, and plants growing on land are considered part of the real property (with the exception of crops that must be planted every year, such as wheat). If the property is sold, all the vegetation growing on the land normally is transferred to the new owner of the real property.

Once the items are severed (removed) from the land, however, they become personal property. If the trees are cut from the land, the timber is personal property. If apples, grapes, or raspberries are picked from trees or vines growing on real property, they become personal property. Similarly, if land contains minerals (including oil) or other natural resources such as silica or marble, the resources are part of the real property. But once removed, they become personal property.

Conversely, personal property may be converted into real property by attaching it to the real property, as discussed next.

Fixtures

Certain personal property can become so closely associated with the real property to which it is

attached that the law views it as real property. Such property is known as a **fixture**—an item affixed to realty, meaning that it is attached to the real property in a permanent way. The item may be embedded into the land or permanently attached to the property or to another fixture on the property by means of cement, plaster, bolts, nails, or screws. It can even sit on the land without being attached, such as a statue, as long as the owner *intends* the property to be a fixture.

Fixtures normally are included in the sale of land unless the sales contract specifies otherwise. The issue of whether an item is a fixture (and thus real estate) or not a fixture (and thus personal property) often arises with respect to land sales, real property taxation, insurance coverage, and divorces. How the issue is resolved can have important consequences for the parties involved.

TYPICAL FIXTURES Some items can only be attached to property permanently—such as a tile floor, cabinets, and carpeting. It is assumed that the owner intended such items to be fixtures because they had to be permanently attached to the property. Also, when an item of property is custom-made for installation on real property, as storm windows are, the item usually is classified as a fixture.

In addition, an item that is firmly attached to the land and integral to its use may be deemed a fixture. For instance, a mobile home or a complex irrigation system bolted to a cement slab on a farm can be a fixture. The courts assume that owners, in making such installations, intend the objects to become part of their real property.

THE ROLE OF INTENT Generally, when the courts need to determine whether a certain item is a fixture, they examine the intention of the party who placed the object on the real property. When the intent of the party who placed the item on the realty is in dispute, the courts will usually deem that the item is a fixture if either or both of the following are true:

1. The property attached cannot be removed without causing substantial damage to the remaining realty.
2. The property attached is so adapted to the rest of the realty as to become a part of it.

The following case illustrates the importance of intent in determining whether property is a fixture.

CASE ANALYSIS

Case 48.1 APL Limited v. Washington State Department of Revenue

Court of Appeals of Washington, Division 1, 154 Wash.App. 1020 (2010).

IN THE LANGUAGE OF THE COURT
GROSSE, J. [Judge]
* * * *

On September 26, 1985, the Port of Seattle (Port) entered into a thirty-year lease with APL Limited, American President Lines, LTD, and Eagle Marine Services, LTD (collectively, APL) for premises at Terminal 5 for loading and unloading shipping container ships. Terminal 5 was substantially rebuilt and cranes were constructed and installed. The cranes at issue here are built to run on steel crane rails 100 feet apart, embedded in a concrete apron, and supported by specially designed steel-reinforced concrete and piers engineered specifically to support the cranes. The cranes themselves are steel structures that are 198 feet tall, 85 feet wide, more than 370 feet long and each weighs over 800 tons. They are hard wired to a dedicated high voltage electrical system that includes a power substation built specifically for Terminal 5 to power the cranes. The cranes are attached to the power substation by cables that are more than two inches thick. The cranes have been in use continuously on Terminal 5 since their construction over twenty years ago.

APL brought suit * * * for a refund of sales tax paid on the rent for the cranes. The State moved for summary judgment, arguing that the cranes were personalty [personal property] and, as such, subject to sales tax. The trial court granted the motion * * * .

APL appeals * * * .
* * * *

*Real property, for tax purposes, is defined as "the land itself * * * and all buildings, structures or improvements or other fixtures of whatsoever kind thereon."* [Emphasis added.]
* * * *

Case law dictates that to determine whether the cranes are personal property or real property, [that is,] fixtures, we apply the common law test. Under this test, we must consider the following three prongs:

(1) Actual annexation to the realty, or something appurtenant thereto; (2) application to the use or purpose to which that part of the realty with which it is connected is appropriated; and (3) the intention of the party making the annexation to make a permanent accession to the freehold.

All three prongs must be met for a chattel [movable property] to become a fixture. Both parties agree that the second prong is met in this instance but dispute the first and third prongs. [Emphasis added.]

Applying a confusing factual scenario, the trial court decided that the first prong, annexation, was not met and therefore it need not consider any of the other facts presented. This was error because *the determinative factor for whether a chattel annexed to real property becomes part of the real property or retains its character as personal property is the third prong: the intent with which the chattel was annexed to the land.* Intent can be determined from the nature of the chattel attached and its relation or necessity to the activity conducted on the land and the manner in which it is annexed. When the owner and the person that annexes the chattel are one and the same, a rebuttable presumption arises that the owner's intention was for the chattel to become part of the realty. [Emphasis added.]
* * * *

In its oral ruling, the trial court itself recognized that it had not examined the facts regarding the Port's intent to annex these cranes. Because annexation is so intertwined with the intent to annex, one cannot be examined without the other. * * * The factual inferences that can be drawn from the evidence presented should be permitted to be argued to the trial court. Because the trial court did not consider these inferences, summary judgment was inappropriate. We reverse.

LEGAL REASONING QUESTIONS

1. Why did it matter to the parties in this lawsuit whether the cranes were fixtures or not?

2. Did the fact that the appellate court reversed the judgment of the trial court mean that the cranes were fixtures? Explain.

3. What is the key factor in determining whether property is a fixture, and how did that factor determine the outcome in this case?

4. What might the court conclude if the Port of Seattle had rebuilt the terminal to accommodate the cranes with the intent that they be removed after the end of APL's lease term?

TRADE FIXTURES ARE PERSONAL PROPERTY Trade fixtures are an exception to the rule that fixtures are a part of the real property. A **trade fixture** is personal property that is installed for a commercial purpose by a tenant (one who rents real property from the owner, or landlord, discussed in Chapter 49).

Trade fixtures remain the property of the tenant, unless removal would irreparably damage the building or realty. A walk-in cooler, for example, purchased and installed by a tenant who uses the premises for a restaurant, is a trade fixture. The tenant can remove the cooler from the premises when the lease terminates but ordinarily must repair any damage that the removal causes or compensate the landlord for the damage.

SECTION 2
ACQUIRING OWNERSHIP OF PERSONAL PROPERTY

The most common way of acquiring personal property is by purchasing it. We have already discussed the purchase and sale of personal property (goods) in Chapters 20 through 23. Often, property is acquired by will or inheritance, a topic we cover in Chapter 51. Here, we look at additional ways in which ownership of personal property can be acquired, including acquisition by possession, production, gift, accession, and confusion.

Possession

Sometimes, a person can become the owner of personal property merely by possessing it. One example of acquiring ownership through possession is the capture of wild animals. Wild animals belong to no one in their natural state, and the first person to take possession of a wild animal normally owns it. A hunter who kills a deer, for instance, has assumed ownership of it (unless he or she acted in violation of the law).

Those who find lost or abandoned property can also acquire ownership rights through mere possession of the property, as will be discussed later in this chapter. (Ownership rights in real property can also be acquired through *adverse possession*—to be discussed in Chapter 49.)

Production

Production—the fruits of labor—is another means of acquiring ownership of personal property. For instance, writers, inventors, manufacturers, and others who produce personal property may thereby acquire title to it. (In some situations, though, as when a researcher is hired to invent a new product or technique, the researcher may not own what is produced—see Chapter 32.)

Gift

A **gift** is another fairly common means of acquiring or transferring ownership of property. A gift is essentially a *voluntary* transfer of property ownership for which no consideration is given. As discussed in Chapter 13, the presence of consideration is what distinguishes a contract from a gift.

For a gift to be effective, the following three elements are required:

1. Donative intent on the part of the *donor* (the one giving the gift).
2. Delivery.
3. Acceptance by the *donee* (the one receiving the gift).

Until these three requirements are met, no effective gift has been made. ▶ **Example 48.2** Gary's Aunt Celia tells him that she is going to give him a new Mercedes-Benz for his next birthday. Aunt Celia has simply made a promise to make a gift. There is no gift until the Mercedes-Benz is delivered and accepted. ◀

DONATIVE INTENT When a gift is challenged in court, the court will determine whether donative intent exists by looking at the language of the donor and the surrounding circumstances. A court may look at the relationship between the parties and the size of the gift in relation to the donor's other assets. When a person has given away a large portion of her or his assets, the court will scrutinize the transaction closely. The court will analyze the donor's mental capacity and look for indications of fraud or duress.

▶ **Case in Point 48.3** Over a period of three months, Jean Knowles Goodman, who was eighty-five years old, gave Steven Atwood several checks that totaled $56,100. Atwood was a veterinarian who had cared for Goodman's dogs for nearly twenty years, and he and Goodman had become friends. Shortly after writing the last check, Goodman was hospitalized and diagnosed with dementia (loss of brain function) and alcohol dependency.

The guardian who was appointed to represent Goodman filed a lawsuit to invalidate the gifts, claiming that Atwood had lacked mental capacity and donative intent. At trial, a psychiatrist who had examined Goodman testified on behalf of Atwood that while Goodman lacked the capacity to care for herself, she would have understood that she was giving away her funds. Therefore, the court concluded that Goodman had donative intent to make the gifts to Atwood.[1] ◀

DELIVERY The gift must be delivered to the donee. Delivery may be accomplished by means of a third person who is the agent of either the donor or the donee. Naturally, no delivery is necessary if the gift is already in the hands of the donee (provided there is donative intent and acceptance). Delivery is obvious in most cases, but some objects cannot be relinquished physically. Then the question of delivery depends on the surrounding circumstances.

Constructive Delivery. When the physical object itself cannot be delivered, a symbolic, or constructive, delivery will be sufficient. **Constructive delivery** does not confer actual possession of the object in question, only the right to take actual possession. It is a general term for all of those acts that the law holds to be equivalent to acts of real delivery.

▶ **Example 48.4** Teresa wants to make a gift of various rare coins that she has stored in a safe-deposit box at her bank. Teresa certainly cannot deliver the

box itself to the donee, and she does not want to take the coins out of the bank. In this situation, she can simply deliver the key to the box to the donee and authorize the donee's access to the box and its contents. This constitutes symbolic, or constructive, delivery of the contents of the box. ◀

Constructive delivery is always necessary for gifts of intangible personal property—such as stocks, bonds, insurance policies, and contracts. The documents representing the rights are delivered (such as a copy of the policy) rather than the true property.

Relinquishing Dominion and Control. An effective delivery also requires that the donor give up control and **dominion** (ownership rights) over the subject matter of the gift. The outcome of disputes often turns on whether control has actually been relinquished. The Internal Revenue Service carefully examines transactions between relatives, especially when one has given income-producing property to another who is in a lower marginal tax bracket. Unless complete control over the property has been relinquished, the "donor"—not the family member who received the "gift"—will have to pay taxes on the income from that property.

In the following classic case, the court focused on the requirement that a donor must relinquish complete control and dominion over property before a gift can be effectively delivered.

1. *Goodman v. Atwood,* 78 Mass.App.Ct. 655, 940 N.E.2d 514 (2011).

CLASSIC CASE 48.2

In re Estate of Piper
Missouri Court of Appeals, 676 S.W.2d 897 (1984).

BACKGROUND AND FACTS Gladys Piper died intestate (without a will). At the time of her death, she owned miscellaneous personal property worth $5,150 and had in her purse $206.75 in cash and two diamond rings. Wanda Brown, Piper's niece, took the contents of her purse, allegedly to preserve the items for the estate. Clara Kauffman, a friend of Gladys Piper, filed a claim against the estate for $4,800. For several years before Piper's death, Kauffman had taken Piper to the doctor, beauty salon, and grocery store. She had also written Piper's checks to pay her bills and helped her care for her home. Kauffman maintained that Piper had promised to pay her for these services and that Piper had given her the diamond rings as a gift. The trial court denied Kauffman's request for payment of $4,800 on the basis that the services had been voluntary. Kauffman then filed a petition for delivery of personal property (the rings), which was granted by the trial court. The defendants—Piper's heirs and the administrator of Piper's estate—appealed.

IN THE LANGUAGE OF THE COURT
GREENE, Judge.

* * * *

While no particular form is necessary to effect a delivery, and while the delivery may be actual, constructive, or symbolical, there must be some evidence to support a delivery theory.

CASE 48.2 CONTINUED

What we have here, at best, * * * was an intention on the part of Gladys, at some future time, to make a gift of the rings to Clara. Such an intention, no matter how clearly expressed, which has not been carried into effect, confers no ownership rights in the property in the intended donee. *Language written or spoken, expressing an intention to give, does not constitute a gift, unless the intention is executed by a complete and unconditional delivery of the subject matter, or delivery of a proper written instrument evidencing the gift.* There is no evidence in this case to prove delivery, and, for such reason, the trial court's judgment is erroneous. [Emphasis added.]

DECISION AND REMEDY *The judgment of the trial court was reversed. No effective gift of the rings had been made because Piper had never delivered the rings to Kauffman.*

WHAT IF THE FACTS WERE DIFFERENT? *Suppose that Piper had told Kauffman that she was giving the rings to Kauffman but wished to keep them in her possession for a few more days. Would this have affected the court's decision in this case? Explain.*

IMPACT OF THIS CASE ON TODAY'S LAW *This classic case clearly illustrates the delivery requirement for making a gift. Assuming that Piper did, indeed, intend for Kauffman to have the rings, it was unfortunate that Kauffman had no right to receive them after Piper's death. Yet the alternative could possibly lead to even more unfairness. The policy behind the delivery requirement is to protect alleged donors and their heirs from fraudulent claims based solely on parol evidence. If not for this policy, an alleged donee could easily claim that a gift was made when, in fact, it was not.*

ACCEPTANCE The final requirement of a valid gift is acceptance by the donee. This rarely presents any problems because most donees readily accept their gifts. The courts generally assume acceptance unless the circumstances indicate otherwise.

GIFTS *INTER VIVOS* AND GIFTS *CAUSA MORTIS* A gift made during the donor's lifetime is called a **gift *inter vivos*.** A **gift *causa mortis*** is a gift made in contemplation of imminent death. To be effective, a gift *causa mortis* must meet the three requirements of intent, delivery, and acceptance.

A gift *causa mortis* does not become absolute until the donor dies from the contemplated illness or other peril.[2] ▶ **Example 48.5** Yang, who is about to undergo surgery to remove a cancerous tumor, delivers an envelope to Chao, a close business associate. The envelope contains a letter saying, "I want to give you $1 million in U.S. government bonds in the event of my death from this operation." Chao redeems (cashes in) the bonds. The surgeon performs the operation and removes the tumor. Yang recovers fully from the operation, but the day after he leaves the hospital, he is killed when his home is struck by a tornado.

If the administrator of Yang's estate (see Chapter 51) tries to recover the $1 million, she will normally suc-

ceed. The gift *causa mortis* to Chao is automatically revoked if Yang survives the operation. The *specific event* that was contemplated in making the gift was death from a particular operation. Because Yang's death was not the result of this event, the gift is revoked, and the $1 million passes to Yang's estate. ◀ A gift *causa mortis* may also be revoked if the prospective donee dies before the donor.

Accession

Accession means "something added." Accession occurs when someone adds value to an item of personal property by the use of either labor or materials.

Generally, there is no dispute about who owns the property after accession occurs, especially when the accession is accomplished with the owner's consent. ▶ **Example 48.6** Hoshi buys all the materials necessary to customize his Corvette. He hires Zach, a customizing specialist, to come his house to perform the work. Hoshi pays Zach for the value of the labor, obviously retaining title to the property. ◀

If the improvement was made wrongfully—without the permission of the owner—the owner retains title to the property and normally does not have to pay for the improvement. This is true even if the accession increased the value of the property substantially. ▶ **Example 48.7** Colton steals a car and puts expensive new tires on it. If the rightful owner

---

2. For a classic case on the requirement that the donor must die from the contemplated peril, see *Brind v. International Trust Co.,* 66 Colo. 60, 179 P. 148 (1919).

later recovers the car, the owner obviously will not be required to compensate Colton, a car thief, for the value of the new tires. ◀

If the improvement was made due to an honest mistake of judgment, however, the owner usually must pay for the improvement. The owner normally still retains title to the property, though, except in rare instances, when the improvement greatly increases the value of the property or changes its identity. In those rare situations, ownership passes to the improver, and the improver must compensate the original owner for the value of the property before the accession occurred.

Confusion

Confusion is the commingling (mixing together) of goods to such an extent that one person's personal property cannot be distinguished from another's. Confusion frequently occurs with *fungible*

goods, such as grain or oil, which consist of identical units.[3]

If confusion occurs as a result of agreement, an honest mistake, or the act of some third party, the owners share ownership in the commingled goods in proportion to the amount each contributed. ▶ **Example 48.8** Five farmers in a small Iowa community enter into a cooperative arrangement. Each fall, the farmers harvest the same amount of number 2–grade yellow corn and store it in silos that are held by the cooperative. Each farmer thus owns one-fifth of the total corn in the silos. If a fire burns down one of the silos, each farmer will bear one-fifth of the loss. ◀ If goods are confused due to an intentional wrongful act, then the innocent party ordinarily acquires title to the whole.

Concept Summary 48.1 below provides a review of the various ways in which personal property can be acquired.

---

3. See Section 1–201(17) of the Uniform Commercial Code (UCC).

CONCEPT SUMMARY 48.1
Acquisition of Personal Property

TYPE OF ACQUISITION	HOW ACQUISITION OCCURS
By Purchase or by Will	The most common means of acquiring ownership in personal property is by purchasing it (see Chapters 20 through 23). Another way in which personal property is often acquired is by will or inheritance (see Chapter 51).
Possession	Ownership may be acquired by possession if no other person has ownership title (for example, capturing wild animals or finding abandoned property).
Production	Any product or item produced by an individual (with minor exceptions) becomes the property of that individual.
Gift	An effective gift is made when the following three requirements are met: 1. *Intent*—There is evidence of *intent* to make a gift of the property in question. 2. *Delivery*—The gift is delivered (physically or constructively) to the donee or the donee's agent. 3. *Acceptance*—The gift is accepted by the donee or the donee's agent.
Accession	When someone adds value to a piece of property by use of labor or materials, the added value generally becomes the property of the owner of the original property (when accessions are made in bad faith or wrongfully). Good faith accessions that substantially increase the property's value or change the identity of the property may cause title to pass to the improver, who compensates the original owner.
Confusion	If a person commingles fungible goods with those of another, the owners normally share ownership of the commingled goods in proportion to the amount each contributed.

MISLAID, LOST, AND ABANDONED PROPERTY

As already noted, one of the methods of acquiring ownership of property is to possess it. Simply finding something and holding onto it, however, does not *necessarily* give the finder any legal rights in the property. Different rules apply, depending on whether the property was mislaid, lost, or abandoned.

Mislaid Property

Property that has been voluntarily placed somewhere by the owner and then inadvertently forgotten is **mislaid property.** A person who finds mislaid property does not obtain title to the goods.

Instead, the owner of the place where the property was mislaid becomes the caretaker of the property because it is highly likely that the true owner will return.[4] ▶ **Example 48.9** Maya goes to a movie theater. While paying for popcorn at the concessions stand, she sets her iPhone 5 on the counter and then leaves it there. The phone is mislaid property, and the theater owner is entrusted with the duty of reasonable care for it. ◀

Lost Property

Property that is *involuntarily* left is **lost property.** A finder of lost property can claim title to the property against the whole world—*except the true owner.*[5] If the true owner is identified and demands that the lost property be returned, the finder must return it. In contrast, if a third party attempts to take possession of the lost property, the finder will have a better title than the third party.

▶ **Example 48.10** Kayla works in a large library at night. As she crosses the courtyard on her way home, she finds a gold bracelet set with what seem to be precious stones. She takes the bracelet to a jeweler to have it appraised. While pretending to weigh the bracelet, the jeweler's employee removes several of the stones. If Kayla brings an action to recover the stones from the jeweler, she normally will win because she found lost property and holds title against everyone *except the true owner.* ◀

CONVERSION OF LOST PROPERTY When a finder of lost property knows the true owner and fails to return the property to that person, the finder is guilty of the tort of *conversion* (see Chapter 6). In *Example 48.10,* if Kayla knows that the gold bracelet she found belongs to Geneva and does not return the bracelet, Kayla is guilty of conversion. Many states require the finder to make a reasonably diligent search to locate the true owner of lost property.

ESTRAY STATUTES Many states have **estray statutes,** which encourage and facilitate the return of property to its true owner and reward the finder for honesty if the property remains unclaimed. These laws provide an incentive for finders to report their discoveries by making it possible for them, after passage of a specified period of time, to acquire legal title to the found property.

Generally, the item must be lost property, not merely mislaid property, for estray statutes to apply. Estray statutes usually require the finder or the county clerk to advertise the property in an attempt to help the owner recover what has been lost.

▶ **Case in Point 48.11** Drug smugglers often enter the United States illegally from Canada via a frozen river that flows through Van Buren, Maine. When two railroad employees in Van Buren found a duffel bag that contained $165,580 in cash, they reported their find to U.S. Customs agents, who took custody of it. A drug-sniffing dog gave a positive alert on the bag for the scent of drugs. The federal government claimed the property under forfeiture laws, which provide that cash and property involved in illegal drug transactions are forfeited to the government.

The two employees argued that they were entitled to the $165,580 under Maine's estray statute. The statute required finders to (1) provide written notice to the town clerk within seven days after finding the property, (2) post a public notice, and (3) advertise in the town's newspaper. Because the employees had not fulfilled these requirements, the court ruled that they had not acquired title to the property. Thus, the U.S. government had a right to seize the cash.[6] ◀

---

4. The finder of mislaid property is an *involuntary bailee* (as will be discussed later in this chapter).
5. For a landmark English case establishing finders' rights in property, see *Armory v. Delamirie,* 93 Eng.Rep. 664 (K.B. [King's Bench] 1722).

6. *United States v. One Hundred Sixty-Five Thousand Five Hundred Eighty Dollars ($165,580) in U.S. Currency,* 502 F.Supp.2d 114 (D.Me. 2007).

Abandoned Property

Property that has been *discarded* by the true owner, who has *no intention* of reclaiming title to it, is **abandoned property.** Someone who finds abandoned property acquires title to it, and that title is good against the whole world, *including the original owner.* If a person finds abandoned property while trespassing on another's property, however, the trespasser will not acquire title.

The owner of lost property who eventually gives up any further attempt to find it is frequently held to have abandoned the property. ▶ **Example 48.12** Alexis is driving in her car on the freeway when a valuable scarf blows out the window. She retraces her route and looks for the scarf but cannot find it. She finally gives up her search and proceeds to her destination five hundred miles away. When Frye, a hitchhiker, finds the scarf two weeks later, he acquires title to it that is good even against Alexis. By completely giving up her search, Alexis abandoned the scarf just as effectively as if she had intentionally discarded it. ◀

See *Concept Summary 48.2* below for a comparison of mislaid, lost, and abandoned property.

SECTION 4
BAILMENTS

Many routine personal and business transactions involve bailments. A **bailment** is formed by the delivery of personal property, without transfer of title, by one person (called a **bailor**) to another (called a **bailee**). Bailment agreements usually are made for a particular purpose—for example, to loan, lease, store, repair, or transport the property. On completion of the purpose, the bailee is obligated to return the bailed property in the same or better condition to the bailor or a third person or to dispose of it as directed.

Although bailments typically arise by agreement, not all of the elements of a contract must necessarily be present (such as mutual assent and consideration). If Darnell lends his business law textbook to a friend, a bailment is created, but not by contract, because there is no consideration. Nevertheless, many commercial bailments, such as the delivery of clothing to the cleaners for dry cleaning, do involve contracts.

A bailment differs from a sale or a gift in that possession is transferred without passage of title or intent to transfer title. In a sale or a gift, title is intentionally transferred from the seller or donor to the buyer or donee.

Elements of a Bailment

Not all transactions involving the delivery of property from one person to another create a bailment. For such a transfer to become a bailment, the following three elements must be present:

1. Personal property.
2. Delivery of possession (without title).
3. Agreement that the property will be returned to the bailor or otherwise disposed of according to its owner's directions.

PERSONAL PROPERTY REQUIREMENT Only personal property, not real property or persons, can be the subject of a bailment. ▶ **Example 48.13** When you

---

CONCEPT SUMMARY 48.2
Mislaid, Lost, and Abandoned Property

CONCEPT	DESCRIPTION
Mislaid Property	Property that is placed somewhere voluntarily by the owner and then inadvertently forgotten. A finder of mislaid property will not acquire title to the goods, and the owner of the place where the property was mislaid becomes a caretaker of the mislaid property.
Lost Property	Property that is involuntarily left and forgotten. A finder of lost property can claim title to the property against the whole world *except the true owner.*
Abandoned Property	Property that has been discarded by the true owner, who has no intention of reclaiming title to the property in the future. A finder of abandoned property can claim title to it against the whole world, *including the original owner.*

check your bags at the airport, a bailment of your luggage is created because it is personal property. You, as a person, however, cannot be the subject of a bailment. ◄

Although bailments commonly involve *tangible* items—jewelry, cattle, automobiles, and the like—*intangible* personal property, such as promissory notes and shares of corporate stock, may also be bailed.

DELIVERY OF POSSESSION *Delivery of possession* means transfer of possession of the property to the bailee. For delivery to occur, the bailee must be given *exclusive possession and control* over the property, and the bailee must *knowingly* accept the personal property.[7] In other words, the bailee must *intend* to exercise control over it.

If either delivery of possession or knowing acceptance is lacking, there is no bailment relationship. ▶ **Example 48.14** Delacroix goes to a five-star restaurant and checks her coat. She forgets that there is a $20,000 diamond necklace in the coat pocket. In accepting the coat, the bailee does not *knowingly* also accept the necklace. Thus, a bailment of the coat exists—because the restaurant has exclusive possession and control over the coat and knowingly accepted it—but not a bailment of the necklace. ◄

Physical versus Constructive Delivery. Either *physical* or *constructive* delivery will result in the bailee's exclusive possession of and control over the property. As discussed earlier, in the context of gifts, constructive delivery is a substitute, or symbolic, delivery. What is delivered to the bailee is not the actual property bailed (such as a car) but something so related to the property (such as the car keys) that the requirement of delivery is satisfied.

Involuntary Bailments. In certain situations, a court will find that a bailment exists despite the apparent lack of the requisite elements of control and knowledge. One situation in which this occurs is when the bailee acquires the property accidentally or by mistake—as in finding someone else's lost or mislaid property. A bailment is created even though the bailor did not voluntarily deliver the property to the bailee. Such bailments are referred to as *constructive* or *involuntary* bailments.

▶ **Example 48.15** Several corporate managers attend a meeting at the law firm of Jacobs & Matheson.

One of the corporate officers, Kyle Gustafson, inadvertently leaves his briefcase behind at the conclusion of the meeting. In this situation, a court could find that an involuntary bailment was created even though Gustafson did not voluntarily deliver the briefcase and the law firm did not intentionally accept it. If an involuntary bailment exists, the firm is responsible for taking care of the briefcase and returning it to Gustafson. ◄

The Bailment Agreement

A bailment agreement can be express or implied. Although a written or electronic contract is not required for bailments for less than one year (see Chapter 16), it is a good idea to have one, especially when valuable property is involved.

The bailment agreement expressly or impliedly provides for the return of the bailed property to the bailor, or to a third person, or for disposal of the property by the bailee. It is assumed that the bailee will return the identical goods originally given by the bailor. In certain types of bailments, though, such as bailments of fungible goods,[8] the property returned need only be equivalent property.

▶ **Example 48.16** If Hobson stores his grain (fungible goods) in Kwan's grain elevator, a bailment is created. At the end of the storage period, the grain elevator company is not obligated to return to Hobson exactly the same grain that was stored. As long as the company returns grain of the same type, grade, and quantity, the bailee company has performed its obligation. ◄

SECTION 5
ORDINARY BAILMENTS

Bailments are either *ordinary* or *special (extraordinary)*. There are three types of ordinary bailments. They are distinguished according to *which party receives a benefit from the bailment*. This factor will dictate the rights and liabilities of the parties, and the courts may use it to determine the standard of care required of the bailee in possession of the personal property. The three types of ordinary bailments are listed below and described in the following subsections:

1. Bailment for the sole benefit of the bailor.
2. Bailment for the sole benefit of the bailee.

---

7. We are dealing here with *voluntary bailments*. This rule does not apply to *involuntary bailments*.

8. As mentioned earlier, *fungible goods* are goods that consist of identical particles, such as wheat. Fungible goods are defined in UCC 1–201(17).

3. Bailment for the mutual benefit of the bailee and the bailor.

Bailment for the Sole Benefit of the Bailor

A bailment for the sole benefit of the bailor is a type of *gratuitous bailment*—meaning that it involves no consideration. The bailment is for the convenience and benefit of the bailor. Basically, the bailee is caring for the bailor's property as a favor. Therefore, the bailee owes only a slight duty of care and will be liable only if she or he is grossly negligent in caring for the property. (Negligence was discussed in Chapter 6.)

▶ **Example 48.17** Allen asks Sumi to store his car in her garage while he is away. If Sumi agrees to do so, then a gratuitous bailment is created because the bailment is for the sole benefit of the bailor (Allen). If the car is damaged while in Sumi's garage, Sumi will not be responsible for the damage unless it was caused by her gross negligence. ◀

Bailment for the Sole Benefit of the Bailee

When one person lends an item to another person (the bailee) solely for that person's convenience and benefit, a bailment for the sole benefit of the bailee is created. Because the bailee is borrowing the item for her or his own benefit, the bailee owes a duty to exercise the utmost care and will be liable for even slight negligence.

▶ **Example 48.18** Allen asks to borrow Sumi's boat so that he can take his girlfriend sailing over the weekend. The bailment of the boat is for Allen's (the bailee's) sole benefit. If Allen fails to pay attention and runs the boat aground, damaging its hull, he is liable for the costs of repairing the boat. ◀

Mutual-Benefit Bailments

The most common kind of bailment is for the mutual benefit of the bailee and the bailor, and involves some form of compensation for storing items or holding property. It is a contractual bailment and is often referred to as a *bailment for hire* or a *commercial bailment*.

In a commercial bailment, the bailee must exercise ordinary care, which is the care that a reasonably prudent (careful) person would use under the circumstances. If the bailee fails to exercise reasonable care, he or she will be liable for ordinary negligence.

▶ **Example 48.19** Allen leaves his car at Midas for an oil change. Because Midas will be paid to change

Allen's oil, this is a mutual-benefit bailment. If Midas fails to put the correct amount of oil back into Allen's car and the engine is damaged as a result, Midas will be liable for failure to exercise reasonable care. ◀

Rights of the Bailee

Certain rights are implicit in the bailment agreement. Generally, the bailee has the right to take possession of the property and to utilize it for accomplishing the purpose of the bailment. The bailee also has a right to receive compensation (unless the bailment is intended to be gratuitous) and may be able to limit her or his liability for the bailed goods. These rights of the bailee are present (with some limitations) in varying degrees in all bailment transactions.

RIGHT OF POSSESSION A hallmark of the bailment agreement is that the bailee acquires the *right to control and possess the property temporarily*. The duration of a bailment depends on the terms of the agreement. If the bailment agreement specifies a particular period, then the bailment is continuous for that time period, and earlier termination by the bailor is a breach of contract. If no duration is specified, the bailment ends when either the bailor or the bailee requests its termination and the bailed property is returned to the bailor.

A bailee's right of possession, even though temporary, permits the bailee to recover damages from any third parties for damage or loss to the property. ▶ **Example 48.20** No-Spot Dry Cleaners sends all suede leather garments to Cleanall Company for special processing. If Cleanall loses or damages any leather goods, No-Spot has the right to recover from Cleanall. ◀ If the bailed property is stolen, the bailee has a legal right to regain possession of it.

RIGHT TO USE BAILED PROPERTY In some bailments, a bailee may also have a right to use the bailed property. When no express provision is made, the extent of use depends on how necessary it is for the goods to be at the bailee's disposal for the ordinary purpose of the bailment to be carried out.

▶ **Example 48.21** If Shyanne borrows a car to drive a friend to the airport, she, as the bailee, would obviously be expected to use the car. In a bailment involving the long-term storage of a car, however, the bailee is not expected to use the car because the ordinary purpose of a storage bailment does not include use of the property. The bailee would be expected to use or move the car if necessary in an emergency (such as a hurricane or flood) to protect it from harm. ◀

RIGHT OF COMPENSATION Except in a gratuitous bailment, a bailee has a right to be compensated as provided for in the bailment agreement. The bailee also has the right to be reimbursed for costs incurred and services rendered in keeping the bailed property (even in a gratuitous bailment).

In mutual-benefit bailments, the amount of compensation is often stated in the bailment contract. ▶ **Example 48.22** In the rental (bailment) of a car, the contract provides for charges on the basis of time, mileage, or a combination of the two, plus other possible charges. In nonrental bailments, such as when a car is left at a dealership for repairs, the bailee earns a service charge for the work performed. ◀

To enforce the right of compensation, the bailee has a right to place a *possessory lien* (claim) on the specific bailed property until she or he has been fully compensated. Such a lien is sometimes referred to as a **bailee's lien,** or artisan's lien (discussed in Chapter 29). If the bailor refuses to pay or cannot pay the charges (compensation), in most states the bailee is entitled to foreclose on the lien and sell the property to recover the amount owed.

RIGHT TO LIMIT LIABILITY In ordinary bailments, bailees have the right to limit their liability provided that both of the following are true:

1. *The limitations are called to the attention of the bailor.* It is essential that the bailor be informed of the limitation in some way. ▶ **Example 48.23** A sign in Nikolai's garage states that Nikolai will not be responsible "for loss due to theft, fire, or vandalism." Whether the sign will constitute notice will depend on the size of the sign, its location, and any other circumstances affecting the likelihood that customers will see it. ◀
2. *The limitations are not against public policy.* Even when the bailor knows of the limitation, courts consider certain types of disclaimers of liability to be against public policy and therefore illegal. As was discussed in Chapter 14, the courts carefully scrutinize *exculpatory clauses,* which limit a person's liability for her

or his own wrongful acts. In bailments, especially mutual-benefit bailments, exculpatory clauses are often held to be illegal. ▶ **Example 48.24** A receipt from a parking garage expressly disclaims liability for any damage to parked cars, regardless of the cause. Because the bailee (garage) has attempted to exclude liability for the bailee's own negligence, the clause will likely be deemed unenforceable because it is against public policy. ◀

Duties of the Bailee

The bailee's duties are based on a mixture of tort law and contract law and include the following two basic responsibilities:

1. To take appropriate care of the property.
2. To surrender the property to the bailor or dispose of it in accordance with the bailor's instructions at the end of the bailment.

THE DUTY OF CARE The bailee must exercise reasonable care in preserving the bailed property (the duty of care was discussed in Chapter 6). What constitutes reasonable care in a bailment situation normally depends on the nature and specific circumstances of the bailment.

The courts determine the appropriate standard of care on the basis of the type of bailment involved. In a bailment for the sole benefit of the bailor, the bailee need exercise only a slight degree of care, whereas in a bailment for the sole benefit of the bailee, the bailee must exercise great care.

Exhibit 48–1 below illustrates the degree of care required of bailees in bailment relationships. Determining whether a bailee exercised an appropriate degree of care is usually a question of fact for the jury or judge (in a nonjury trial). A bailee's failure to exercise appropriate care in handling the bailor's property results in tort liability.

In the following case, the court had to decide whether a bailee that lost computer data while replacing a hard drive had been negligent.

EXHIBIT 48-1 Degree of Care Required of a Bailee

CASE 48.3

Bridge Tower Dental, P.A. v. Meridian Computer Center, Inc.
Supreme Court of Idaho, 272 P.3d 541 (2012).

BACKGROUND AND FACTS Bridge Tower Dental contracted with Meridian Computer Center to develop a computer system for its dental practice. Bridge Tower then paid a computer consultant, Al Colson, to install the system and later to provide maintenance and support. Beginning in 2004, Colson noticed that one of the server's two hard drives had stopped working and that the system was backing up data only on the mirrored hard drive. After telling Bridge Tower about the problem, Colson took the server to Meridian Computer to be repaired. The owner of Meridian Computer, Jason Patten, agreed to replace the failing hard drive under the warranty.

In attempting to copy data from the mirrored hard drive, however, Patten accidentally erased all the data. Patten had not backed up the mirrored drive because he was not asked to and it is the industry standard not to back up client data unless specifically requested. As a result, Bridge Tower lost all of its patients' records and contact information. Bridge Tower sued Meridian Computer for negligence, and the jury found for Meridian Computer. Bridge Tower appealed.

 IN THE LANGUAGE OF THE COURT
W. *JONES*, Justice.

* * * *

Both parties agreed that a bailment was created when Colson, acting as an agent for Bridge Tower, entrusted Meridian Computer with the server and two hard drives. The scope of the bailment included not only the machine, but all of its contents, including the data contained on the mirrored hard drive. *Under the law of bailment, a bailee has a duty to exercise reasonable care to return the bailed property in the same condition it was in when delivered.* Here, Colson entrusted Meridian Computer with a server containing a failing hard drive and a fully functional mirrored hard drive with data on it. The expectation of both parties was for Meridian Computer to replace the failing hard drive with a new drive, and return the server with its good drive and data intact. Yet, due to an admitted mistake, Patten erased the mirrored drive's data and Meridian Computer returned the server in a much different condition than when it was originally delivered. Meridian Computer returned Bridge Tower's bailed server without any of the functional mirrored drive's data. [Emphasis added.]

Because Meridian Computer returned Bridge Tower's property in a damaged state, there is a presumption of negligence and Meridian Computer bears the burden of proving that the damage was not a result of its own negligence. At trial, Patten admitted that he mistakenly erased the data contained on the functional mirrored hard drive because he accidentally mixed up the source drive with the destination drive. Patten also admitted that he did not back up the functioning drive prior to servicing the hard drives.

Patten attempts to excuse his carelessness by claiming that Meridian Computer belongs to an industry that has no duty to back up data. While this may be true, such a standard does not extinguish its duty not to destroy clients' data. Patten's mistake affirmatively destroyed and damaged Bridge Tower's property, and whether or not Patten had a duty to back up the hard drives is of no bearing in this matter. *This Court recognizes a distinction between not having a duty to back up and having a duty to protect and safeguard bailed property in order to return it in the same condition as it was delivered.* The evidence adduced at trial unquestionably supports that Meridian Computer made a mistake by inadvertently erasing Bridge Tower's mirrored drive, constituting negligence. [Emphasis added.]

DECISION AND REMEDY *The Idaho Supreme Court held that Meridian Computer had breached its duty of care. The court therefore reversed the judgment for Meridian Computer and held that Bridge Tower was entitled to recover.*

THE SOCIAL DIMENSION *What kind of bailment existed in this case? Explain your answer.*

THE LEGAL ENVIRONMENT DIMENSION *Could Meridian have effectively limited its bailment liability? Explain.*

DUTY TO RETURN BAILED PROPERTY At the end of the bailment, the bailee normally must hand over the original property to either the bailor or someone the bailor designates, or must otherwise dispose of it as directed.[9] Failure to give up possession at the time the bailment ends is a breach of contract and could result in a tort lawsuit for conversion or negligence.

A bailee may be liable for conversion or misdelivery if the goods are given to the wrong person. Hence, a bailee should verify that the person (other than the bailor) to whom the goods are given is authorized to take possession.

LOST OR DAMAGED PROPERTY If the bailed property has been lost or is returned damaged, a court will presume that the bailee was negligent. The bailee's obligation is excused, however, if the property was destroyed, lost, or stolen through no fault of the bailee (or claimed by a third party with a superior claim). In other words, the bailee can rebut the presumption of negligence by showing that he or she exercised due care.

▶ **Case in Point 48.25** Michael LaPlace boarded a horse at Pierre Briere's stable, where Charlene Bridgwood also boarded a horse. LaPlace had previously boarded horses at the farm owned by Bridgwood's husband, and Bridgwood had often exercised LaPlace's horses there. One day, Bridgwood helped exercise the horses at Briere's stable.

During the exercise, LaPlace's horse suddenly collapsed and died. LaPlace sued Briere for negligence. The court found that there was a presumption of negligence because the horse died in Briere's care during its bailment. Nevertheless, Briere had successfully rebutted that presumption by showing that Bridgwood was an experienced handler and exercised the horse in an ordinary manner. Thus, Briere was not liable for the horse's death.[10] ◀

Duties of the Bailor

The duties of a bailor are essentially the same as the rights of a bailee. A bailor has a duty to compensate the bailee either as agreed or as reimbursement for costs incurred by the bailee in keeping the bailed property. A bailor also has an all-encompassing duty to provide the bailee with goods or chattels that are free from known defects that could cause injury to the bailee.

BAILOR'S DUTY TO REVEAL DEFECTS The bailor's duty to reveal defects to the bailee translates into two rules:

1. In a *mutual-benefit bailment,* the bailor must notify the bailee of all known defects and any hidden defects that the bailor knows of or could have discovered with reasonable diligence and proper inspection.

2. In a *bailment for the sole benefit of the bailee,* the bailor must notify the bailee of any known defects.

The bailor's duty to reveal defects is based on a negligence theory of tort law. A bailor who fails to give the appropriate notice is liable to the bailee and to any other person who might reasonably be expected to come into contact with the defective article.

▶ **Example 48.26** Rentco (the bailor) rents a tractor to Hal Iverson. Unknown to Rentco (but *discoverable* by reasonable inspection), the brake mechanism on the tractor is defective at the time the bailment is made. Iverson uses the defective tractor without knowledge of the brake problem and is injured along with two other field workers when the tractor rolls out of control. In this situation, Rentco is liable for the injuries sustained by Iverson and the other workers because it negligently failed to discover the defect and notify Iverson. ◀

WARRANTY LIABILITY FOR DEFECTIVE GOODS A bailor can also incur warranty liability based on contract law (see Chapter 23) for injuries resulting from the bailment of defective articles. Property that is leased from a bailor must be *fit for the intended purpose of the bailment.* The bailor's knowledge of or ability to discover any defects is immaterial.

Warranties of fitness arise by law in sales contracts, and courts have held that these warranties apply to bailments "for hire." Article 2A of the Uniform Commercial Code (UCC) extends the implied warranties of merchantability and fitness for a particular purpose to those bailments that include rights to use the bailed goods.[11]

SECTION 6
SPECIAL TYPES OF BAILMENTS

A business is likely to engage in some special types of bailment transactions. These include bailments in which the bailee's duty of care is *extraordinary* and the bailee's liability for loss or damage to the property is absolute. These situations usually involve common carriers and hotel operators. Warehouse companies

---

9. As mentioned earlier, if the bailment involves fungible goods, such as grain, then the bailee is not required to return exactly the same goods to the bailor. Instead, the bailee must return goods of the same type, grade, and quantity.
10. *LaPlace v. Briere,* 404 N.J.Super. 585, 962 A.2d 1139 (2009).
11. UCC 2A–212, 2A–213.

have the same duty of care as ordinary bailees, but like carriers, they are subject to extensive federal and state laws, including Article 7 of the UCC.

Common Carriers

Common carriers are publicly licensed to provide transportation services to the general public. They are legally bound to carry all passengers or freight as long as there is enough space, the fee is paid, and there are no reasonable grounds to refuse service.

Common carriers differ from private carriers, which operate transportation facilities for only a select clientele. A private carrier is not required to provide service to every person or company making a request.

STRICT LIABILITY APPLIES The delivery of goods to a common carrier creates a bailment relationship between the shipper (bailor) and the common carrier (bailee). Unlike ordinary bailees, the common carrier is held to a standard of care based on *strict liability,* rather than reasonable care, in protecting the bailed personal property. This means that the common carrier is absolutely liable, regardless of due care, for all loss or damage to goods except when damage was caused by a natural disaster or war.

LIMITATIONS ON LIABILITY Common carriers cannot contract away their liability for damaged goods. Subject to government regulations, however, they are permitted to limit their dollar liability to an amount stated on the shipment contract or rate filing.[12]

▶ **Case in Point 48.27** A jewelry store (Treiber & Straub, Inc.) used UPS to ship a diamond ring worth $105,000. The owner of the jewelry store arranged for the shipment on UPS's Web site, which required him to click on two on-screen boxes to agree to "My UPS Terms and Conditions." In these terms, UPS and its insurer limited their liability and the amount of insurance coverage on packages to $50,000, and refused to ship items worth more than $50,000. Both UPS and its insurer disclaimed liability *entirely* for such items. Nevertheless, the store owner purchased $50,000 in insurance for the package.

When the ring was lost, the jewelry store filed suit against UPS to recover $50,000 under the insurance policy. The court held that UPS's disclaimer of liability was enforceable. It also found that the jewelry store had breached the contract by indicating that the ship-

ment was worth less than $50,000 when the ring was worth much more.[13] ◄

Warehouse Companies

Warehousing is the business of providing storage of property for compensation. Like ordinary bailees, warehouse companies are liable for loss or damage to property resulting from *negligence*. But because a warehouse company is a professional bailee, it is expected to exercise a high degree of care to protect and preserve the goods.

LIMITATIONS ON LIABILITY A warehouse company can limit the dollar amount of its liability. Under the UCC, however, it must give the bailor the option of paying a higher storage rate for an increase in the liability limit.[14]

WAREHOUSE RECEIPTS Unlike ordinary bailees, a warehouse company can issue *documents of title*—in particular, *warehouse receipts*—and is subject to extensive government regulation, including Article 7 of the UCC.[15] A warehouse receipt describes the bailed property and the terms of the bailment contract. It can be negotiable or nonnegotiable, depending on how it is written. It is negotiable if its terms provide that the warehouse company will deliver the goods "to the bearer" of the receipt or "to the order of" a person named on the receipt.[16]

The warehouse receipt represents the goods (that is, it indicates title) and hence has value and utility in financing commercial transactions. ▶ **Example 48.28** Ossip delivers 6,500 cases of canned corn to Chaney, the owner of a warehouse. Chaney issues a negotiable warehouse receipt payable "to bearer" and gives it to Ossip. Ossip sells and delivers the warehouse receipt to Better Foods, Inc. Better Foods is now the owner of the corn and can obtain the cases by simply presenting the warehouse receipt to Chaney. ◄

Hotel Operators

At common law, hotel owners were strictly liable for the loss of any cash or property that guests brought

---

12. Federal laws require common carriers to offer shippers the opportunity to obtain higher dollar limits for loss by paying a higher fee for the transport.

13. *Treiber & Straub, Inc. v. United Parcel Service, Inc.,* 474 F.3d 379 (7th Cir. 2007).

14. UCC 7–204(1), (2).

15. A *document of title* is defined in UCC 1–201(15) as any "document which in the regular course of business or financing is treated as adequately evidencing that the person in possession of it is entitled to receive, hold, and dispose of the document and the goods it covers." A *warehouse receipt* is a document of title issued by a person engaged for hire in the business of storing goods.

16. UCC 7–104.

into their rooms. Today, state statutes continue to apply strict liability to hotel operators for any loss or damage to their guests' personal property. In many states, hotel operators can avoid strict liability for loss of guests' cash and valuables by:

1. Providing a safe in which to keep guests' valuables.
2. Notifying guests that a safe is available.

In addition, statutes often limit the liability of innkeepers with regard to articles that are not kept in the safe and may limit the availability of damages in the absence of negligence. Most statutes require that the hotel post these limitations on the doors of the rooms or otherwise notify guests.

▶ **Case in Point 48.29** A guest at the Four Seasons hotel was traveling with jewelry valued

at $1.2 million. She put the jewelry in the safe in her room, but someone came into the room and removed the jewelry from the safe without the use of force. The woman sued the hotel, which asserted that it was not liable under the state statute. A court ruled that the Four Seasons had not complied with the state statute, which required it to post the law in the guest rooms and public rooms. Therefore, the hotel could not assert the statute's limitation on liability.[17] ◀

Concept Summary 48.3 below reviews the rights and duties of bailees and bailors.

---

17. *Paraskevaides v. Four Seasons Washington*, 292 F.3d 886 (D.C.Cir. 2002).

CONCEPT SUMMARY 48.3
Rights and Duties of the Bailee and the Bailor

CONCEPT	DESCRIPTION
Rights of a Bailee (Duties of a Bailor)	1. The right of possession allows actions against third parties who damage or convert the bailed property and allows actions against the bailor for wrongful breach of the bailment. 2. A bailee has the right to be compensated or reimbursed for keeping bailed property. 3. If the compensation or reimbursement is not paid, the bailee has a right to place a possessory lien on the bailed property and to foreclose on the lien. 4. A bailee has the right to limit his or her liability. An ordinary bailee can limit the types of risk, monetary amount, or both, provided proper notice is given and the limitation is not against public policy. In special bailments, limitations on the types of risk are usually not allowed, but limitations on the monetary amount of loss are permitted by regulation.
Duties of a Bailee (Rights of a Bailor)	1. A bailee must exercise reasonable care over property entrusted to her or him. A common carrier (special bailee) is held to a standard of care based on strict liability except when damage was caused by a natural disaster or war. 2. Bailed goods in a bailee's possession must be returned to the bailor or be disposed of according to the bailor's directions. Failure to return the property gives rise to a presumption of negligence. 3. A bailee cannot use or profit from bailed goods except by agreement or in situations in which the use is implied to further the bailment purpose.

Reviewing: Personal Property and Bailments

Vanessa Denai purchased forty acres of land in rural Louisiana with a 1,600-square-foot house on it and a metal barn near the house. Denai later met Lance Finney, who had been seeking a small plot of rural property to rent. After several meetings, Denai invited Finney to live on a corner of her property in exchange for Finney's assistance in cutting wood and tending her property. Denai agreed to store Finney's sailboat in her barn.

Continued

With Denai's consent, Finney constructed a concrete and oak foundation on Denai's property. Finney then purchased a 190-square-foot dome from Dome Baja for $3,395. The dome was shipped by Doty Express, a transportation company licensed to serve the public. When it arrived, Finney installed the dome frame and fabric exterior so that the dome was detachable from the foundation. A year after Finney installed the dome, Denai wrote Finney a note stating, "I've decided to give you four acres of land surrounding your dome as drawn on this map." This gift violated no local land-use restrictions. Using the information presented in the chapter, answer the following questions.

1. Is the dome real property or personal property? Explain.
2. Is Denai's gift of land to Finney a testamentary gift, a gift *causa mortis,* or a gift *inter vivos?*
3. What type of bailment relationship was created when Denai agreed to store Finney's boat? What degree of care was Denai required to exercise in storing the boat?
4. What standard of care applied to the shipment of the dome by Doty Express?

DEBATE THIS . . . *Common carriers should not be able to limit their liability.*

Terms and Concepts

abandoned property 944
accession 941
bailee 944
bailee's lien 947
bailment 944
bailor 944
chattel 936

confusion 942
constructive delivery 940
dominion 940
estray statute 943
fixture 937
gift 939
gift *causa mortis* 941

gift *inter vivos* 941
lost property 943
mislaid property 943
personal property 936
property 936
real property 936
trade fixture 939

ExamPrep

Issue Spotters

1. Quintana Corporation sends important documents to Regal Nursery, Inc., via Speedy Messenger Service. While the documents are in Speedy's care, a third party causes an accident to Speedy's delivery vehicle that results in the loss of the documents. Does Speedy have a right to recover from the third party for the loss of the documents? Why or why not? **(See page 946.)**
2. Rosa de la Mar Corporation ships a load of goods via Southeast Delivery Company. The load of goods is lost in a hurricane in Florida. Who suffers the loss? Explain your answer. **(See page 950.)**

• Check your answers to the Issue Spotters against the answers provided in Appendix E at the end of this text.

Before the Test

Go to **www.cengagebrain.com**, enter the ISBN 9781285185248, and click on "Find" to locate this textbook's Web site. Then, click on "Access Now" under "Study Tools," and select Chapter 48 at the top. There, you will find a Practice Quiz that you can take to assess your mastery of the concepts in this chapter, as well as Flashcards and a Glossary of important terms.

Business Scenarios

48–1. Gifts. Jaspal has a serious heart attack and is taken to the hospital. He is aware that he is not expected to live. Because he is a bachelor with no close relatives nearby, Jaspal gives his car keys to his close friend, Friedrich, telling Friedrich that he is expected to die and that the car is Friedrich's. Jaspal survives the heart attack, but two months later he dies from pneumonia. Jaspal's uncle, Sam, the executor of Jaspal's estate, wants Friedrich to return the car. Friedrich refuses, claiming that Jaspal gave the car to him as a gift. Discuss whether Friedrich will be required to return the car to Jaspal's estate. **(See page 939.)**

48–2. Bailments. Curtis is an executive on a business trip to the West Coast. He has driven his car on this trip and checks into the Hotel Ritz. The hotel has a guarded underground parking lot. Curtis gives his car keys to the parking lot attendant but fails to notify the attendant that his wife's $10,000 fur coat is in a box in the trunk. The next day, on checking out, he discovers that his car has been stolen. Curtis wants to hold the hotel liable for both the car and the coat. Discuss the probable success of his claim. **(See page 949.)**

48–3. Duties of the Bailee. Atka owns a valuable speedboat. She is going on vacation and asks her neighbor, Regina, to store the boat in one stall of Regina's double garage. Regina consents, and the boat is moved into the garage. Regina, in need of some grocery items for dinner, drives to the store. She leaves the garage door open, as is her custom. While she is at the store, the speedboat is stolen. What standard of care is required in this situation? Has Atka breached that duty? **(See page 947.)**

48–4. Duties of the Bailee. Orlando borrows a gasoline-driven lawn edger from his neighbor, Max. Max has not used the lawn edger for two years. Orlando has never owned a lawn edger and is not familiar with its use. Max previously used this edger often, and if he had made a reasonable inspection, he would have discovered that the blade was loose. Orlando is injured when the blade becomes detached while he is edging his yard. **(See page 947.)**

(a) Can Orlando hold Max liable for his injuries? Why or why not?

(b) Would your answer be different if Orlando had rented the edger from Max and paid a fee? Explain.

Business Case Problems

48–5. Found Property. A. D. Lock owned Lock Hospitality, Inc., which in turn owned the Best Western Motel in Conway, Arkansas. Joe Terry and David Stocks were preparing the motel for renovation. As they were removing the ceiling tiles in room 118, with Lock present in the room, they noticed a dusty cardboard box near the heating and air-supply vent, where it had apparently been concealed. Terry climbed a ladder to reach the box, opened it, and handed it to Stocks. The box was filled with more than $38,000 in old currency. Lock took possession of the box and its contents. Terry and Stocks filed a suit in an Arkansas state court against Lock and his corporation to obtain the money. Should the money be characterized as lost, mislaid, or abandoned property? To whom should the court award it? Explain. [*Terry v. Lock,* 343 Ark. 452, 37 S.W.3d 202 (2001)] **(See page 943.)**

48–6. Gifts. John Wasniewski opened a brokerage account with Quick and Reilly, Inc., in his son James's name. Twelve years later, when the balance was $52,085, the account was closed, and the funds were transferred to a joint account in the names of John and James's brother. Only after the transfer, when James received a tax form for the prior account's final year, did James learn of its existence. He filed a suit in a Connecticut state court against Quick and Reilly, alleging breach of contract and seeking to recover the account's principal and interest. What are the elements of a valid gift? Did John's opening of the account with Quick and Reilly constitute a gift to James? What is the likely result in this case, and why? [*Wasniewski v. Quick and Reilly, Inc.,* 292 Conn. 98, 971 A.2d 8 (2009)] **(See page 939.)**

48–7. BUSINESS CASE PROBLEM WITH SAMPLE ANSWER: Bailment Obligation.

Bob Moreland left his plane at Don Gray's aircraft repair shop to be painted. When Moreland picked up the airplane, he was disappointed in the quality of the work and pointed out numerous defects. Moreland refused to pay Gray and flew the plane to another shop to have the work redone. Gray sued to collect, contending that Moreland had no right to take the plane to another shop without giving Gray a chance to fix any defects. Gray further argued that by taking the plane, Moreland had accepted Gray's work. Moreland counterclaimed for his expenses. Which party should be awarded damages and why? [Gray v. Moreland, 2010 Ark. App. 207, 374 S.W.3d 178 (2010)] **(See page 944.)**

• For a sample answer to Problem 48–7, go to Appendix F at the end of this text.

48–8. A QUESTION OF ETHICS: Gifts.

Jason Crippen and Catharyn Campbell of Knoxville, Tennessee, were involved in a romantic relationship for many months. Their relationship culminated in an engagement on December 25, 2005, when Crippen placed an engagement ring on Campbell's finger and simultaneously proposed marriage. Campbell accepted the proposal, and the parties were engaged to be married. The engagement did not last, however. The parties broke up, their romantic relationship ended, and neither had any intent to marry the other. Crippen asked Campbell to return the ring. She refused. Crippen filed a suit in a Tennessee state court against Campbell to recover the ring. Both parties filed motions for summary judgment. The court ruled in Campbell's favor. Crippen appealed to a state intermediate appellate court. [Crippen v. Campbell, __ S.W.3d __ (Tenn.App. 2007)] **(See page 939.)**

(a) Under what reasoning could the court affirm the award of the ring to Campbell? On what basis could the court reverse the judgment and order Campbell to return the ring? (Hint: Is an engagement ring a completed gift immediately on its delivery?) Which principles do you support and why?

(b) Should the court determine who was responsible for breaking off the engagement before awarding ownership of the ring? Why or why not?

(c) If, instead of Crippen, one of his creditors had sought the ring in satisfaction of one of his debts, how should the court have ruled? Why?

Legal Reasoning Group Activity

48–9. Bailments. On learning that Sébastien planned to travel abroad, Roslyn asked him to deliver $25,000 in cash to her family in Mexico. During a customs inspection at the border, Sébastien told the customs inspector that he carried less than $10,000. The officer discovered the actual amount of cash that Sébastien was carrying, seized it, and arrested Sébastien. Roslyn asked the government to return what she claimed were her funds, arguing that the arrangement with Sébastien was a bailment and that she still held title to the cash. **(See page 944.)**

(a) The first group will argue that Roslyn is entitled to the cash.

(b) The second group will take the position of the government and develop an argument that Roslyn's agreement with Sébastien does not qualify as a bailment.

CHAPTER 49

REAL PROPERTY AND LANDLORD-TENANT LAW

From the earliest times, property has provided a means for survival. Primitive peoples lived off the fruits of the land, eating the vegetation and wildlife. Later, as the wildlife was domesticated and the vegetation cultivated, property provided pastures and farmland. Throughout history, property has continued to be an indicator of family wealth and social position. In the Western world, the protection of an individual's right to his or her property has become one of our more important rights.

In this chapter, we look at the nature of real property and the ways in which it can be owned. We examine the legal requirements involved in the transfer of real property. We even consider whether the buyer of a haunted house can rescind the sale in this chapter's *Spotlight Case.*

Realize that real property rights are never absolute. There is a higher right—that of the government to take, for compensation, private land for public use. This chapter discusses this right, as well as other restrictions on the ownership or use of property, including zoning laws. We conclude the chapter with a discussion of landlord-tenant relationships.

SECTION 1
THE NATURE OF REAL PROPERTY

As discussed in Chapter 48, real property (or realty) consists of land and everything permanently attached to it, including structures and other fixtures. Real property includes airspace and subsurface rights, as well as rights to plants and vegetation. In essence, real property is immovable.

Land and Structures

Land includes the soil on the surface of the earth and the natural products or artificial structures that are attached to it. Land further includes all the waters contained on or under its surface and much, but not necessarily all, of the airspace above it. The exterior boundaries of land extend down to the center of the earth and up to the farthest reaches of the atmosphere (subject to certain qualifications).

Airspace and Subsurface Rights

The owner of real property has relatively exclusive rights to both the airspace above the land and the soil and minerals underneath it. Any limitations on either airspace rights or subsurface rights, called *encumbrances,* normally must be indicated on the document that transfers title at the time of purchase. The ways in which ownership rights in real property can be limited will be examined later in this chapter.

AIRSPACE RIGHTS Disputes concerning airspace rights may involve the right of commercial and private planes to fly over property and the right of individuals and governments to seed clouds and produce artificial rain. Flights over private land normally do not violate property rights unless the flights are so low and so frequent that they directly interfere with the owner's enjoyment and use of the land. Leaning walls or projecting eave spouts or roofs may also violate the airspace rights of an adjoining property owner.

SUBSURFACE RIGHTS In many states, ownership of land can be separated from ownership of its subsurface. In other words, the owner of the surface may sell subsurface rights to another person. Subsurface rights can be extremely valuable, as these rights include the ownership of minerals, oil, or natural gas. But a subsurface owner's rights would be of little value if he or she could not use the surface to exercise those rights. Hence, a subsurface owner has a right, called a *profit* (see page 959) to go onto the surface of the land to, for example, find and remove minerals.

When ownership is separated into surface and sub-surface rights, each owner can pass title to what she or he owns without the consent of the other owner. Of course, conflicts can arise between the surface owner's use of the property and the subsurface owner's need to extract minerals, oil, or natural gas. In that situation, one party's interest may become subservient (second-ary) to the other party's interest either by statute or by case law. If the owners of the subsurface rights excavate, they are absolutely liable if their excavation causes the surface to collapse. Many states have statutes that also make the excavators liable for any damage to structures on the land. Typically, these statutes set out precise requirements for excavations of various depths.

Plant Life and Vegetation

Plant life, both natural and cultivated, is also consid-ered to be real property. In many instances, the natu-ral vegetation, such as trees, adds greatly to the value of realty. When a parcel of land is sold and the land has growing crops on it, the sale includes the crops, unless otherwise specified in the sales contract. When crops are sold by themselves, however, they are con-sidered to be personal property or goods, as noted in Chapter 48. Consequently, the sale of crops is a sale of goods and is governed by the Uniform Commercial Code (UCC, discussed in Chapters 20 through 23) rather than by real property law.

SECTION 2
OWNERSHIP AND OTHER INTERESTS IN REAL PROPERTY

Ownership of property is an abstract concept that cannot exist independently of the legal system. No one can actually possess, or *hold,* a piece of land, the air above, the earth below, and all the water con-tained on it. One can only possess *rights* in real prop-erty. Numerous rights are involved in real property ownership, which is why property ownership is often viewed as a bundle of rights. One who possesses the entire bundle of rights is said to hold the property in *fee simple,* which is the most complete form of owner-ship. When only some of the rights in the bundle are transferred to another person, the effect is to limit the ownership rights of both the transferor of the rights and the recipient.

Traditionally, ownership interests in real property were referred to as *estates in land,* which include fee simple estates, life estates, and leasehold estates. We examine these estates in land, forms of concurrent ownership, and certain other interests in real property that is owned by others in the following subsections.

Ownership in Fee Simple

In a **fee simple absolute,** the owner has the greatest aggregation of rights, privileges, and power possible. The owner can give the property away or dispose of the property by *deed* (see page 963) or by *will* (see Chapter 51). When there is no will, the fee simple passes to the owner's legal heirs on her or his death. A fee simple absolute is potentially infinite in duration and is assigned forever to a person and her or his heirs without limitation or condition.[1] The owner has the rights of *exclusive* possession and use of the property.

The rights that accompany a fee simple absolute include the right to use the land for whatever purpose the owner sees fit. Of course, other laws, including applicable zoning, noise, and environmental laws, may limit the owner's ability to use the property in certain ways. A person who uses his or her property in a manner that unreasonably interferes with others' right to use or enjoy their own property can be liable for the tort of *nuisance* (discussed in Chapter 45).

▶ **Case in Point 49.1**   Nancy and James Biglane owned and lived in a building next door to a popular bar called the Under the Hill Saloon that featured live music. During the summer, the Saloon, which had no air-conditioning, opened its windows and doors, and live music echoed up and down the street. The Biglanes installed extra insulation, thicker windows, and air-conditioning units in their building. Nevertheless, the noise from the Saloon kept the Biglanes awake at night. Eventually, they sued the owners of the Saloon for nuisance. The court held that the noise from the bar unreasonably interfered with the Biglanes' right to enjoy their property and enjoined (prevented) the Saloon from opening its windows and doors while playing music.[2] ◀

---

1. In another type of estate, the *fee simple defeasible,* ownership in fee simple automatically terminates if a stated event occurs. For example, property might be conveyed (transferred) to a school only as long as it is used for school purposes. In addition, the fee simple may be subject to a *condition subsequent.* This means that if a stated event occurs, the prior owner of the property can bring an action to regain possession of the property.
2. *Biglane v. Under the Hill Corp.,* 949 So.2d 9 (Miss.Sup. 2007).

Life Estates

A **life estate** is an estate that lasts for the life of some specified individual. A **conveyance,** or transfer of real property, "to A for his life" creates a life estate.[3] In a life estate, the life tenant's ownership rights cease to exist on the life tenant's death. The life tenant has the right to use the land, provided that he or she commits no **waste** (injury to the land). In other words, the life tenant cannot use the land in a manner that would adversely affect its value. The life tenant can use the land to harvest crops or, if mines and oil wells are already on the land, can extract minerals and oil from it, but the life tenant cannot exploit the land by creating new wells or mines.

The life tenant can create liens, *easements* (see page 959), and leases. None can extend beyond the life of the tenant, however. In addition, with few exceptions, the owner of a life estate has an exclusive right to possession during his or her lifetime.

Along with these rights, the life tenant also has some duties—to keep the property in repair and to pay property taxes. In short, the owner of the life estate has the same rights as a fee simple owner except that she or he must maintain the value of the property during her or his tenancy.

Concurrent Ownership

Persons who share ownership rights simultaneously in particular property (including real property and personal property) are said to have **concurrent ownership.** There are two principal types of concurrent ownership: *tenancy in common* and *joint tenancy.* Concurrent ownership rights can also be held in a *tenancy by the entirety* or as *community property,* although these types of concurrent ownership are less common.

TENANCY IN COMMON The term **tenancy in common** refers to a form of co-ownership in which each of two or more persons owns an undivided interest in the property. The interest is undivided because each tenant shares rights in the whole property. On the death of a tenant in common, that tenant's interest in the property passes to her or his heirs.

▶ **Example 49.2** Four friends purchase a condominium unit in Hawaii together as tenants in common. This means that each of them has an ownership interest (one-fourth) in the whole. If one of the four owners dies a year after the purchase, his ownership interest passes to his heirs (his wife and children, for example) rather than to the other tenants in common. ◀

Unless the co-tenants have agreed otherwise, a tenant in common can transfer her or his interest in the property to another without the consent of the remaining co-owners. In most states, it is presumed that a co-tenancy is a tenancy in common unless there is specific language indicating the intent to establish a joint tenancy (discussed next).

JOINT TENANCY In a **joint tenancy,** each of two or more persons owns an undivided interest in the property, but a deceased joint tenant's interest passes to the surviving joint tenant or tenants.

Right of Survivorship. The right of a surviving joint tenant to inherit a deceased joint tenant's ownership interest—referred to as a *right of survivorship*—distinguishes a joint tenancy from a tenancy in common. ▶ **Example 49.3** Jerrold and Eva are married and purchase a house as joint tenants. The title to the house clearly expresses the intent to create a joint tenancy because it says "to Jerrold and Eva as joint tenants with right of survivorship." Jerrold has three children from a prior marriage. If Jerrold dies, his interest in the house automatically passes to Eva rather than to his children from the prior marriage. ◀

Termination of a Joint Tenancy. Although a joint tenant can transfer her or his rights by sale or gift to another without the consent of the other joint tenants, doing so terminates the joint tenancy. The person who purchases the property or receives it as a gift becomes a tenant in common, not a joint tenant. ▶ **Example 49.4** Three brothers, Brody, Saul, and Jacob, own a parcel as joint tenants. Brody is experiencing financial difficulties and sells his interest in the property to Beth. The sale terminates the joint tenancy, and now Beth, Saul, and Jacob hold the property as tenants in common. ◀

A joint tenant's interest can also be levied against (seized by court order, see Chapter 29) to satisfy the tenant's judgment creditors. If this occurs, the joint tenancy terminates, and the remaining owners hold the property as tenants in common. (Judgment creditors can also seize the interests of tenants in a tenancy in common.)

TENANCY BY THE ENTIRETY A less common form of shared ownership of real property by husband and

---

3. A less common type of life estate is created by the conveyance "to A for the life of B." This is known as an estate *pur autre vie*—that is, an estate for the duration of the life of another.

wife is a **tenancy by the entirety.** It differs from a joint tenancy in that neither spouse may separately transfer his or her interest during his or her lifetime unless the other spouse consents. In some states in which statutes give the wife the right to convey her property, this form of concurrent ownership has effectively been abolished. A divorce, either spouse's death, or mutual agreement will terminate a tenancy by the entirety.

COMMUNITY PROPERTY A limited number of states[4] allow property to be owned by a married couple as **community property.** If property is held as community property, each spouse technically owns an undivided one-half interest in the property. This type of ownership applies to most property acquired by the husband or the wife during the course of the marriage. It generally does *not* apply to property acquired prior to the marriage or to property acquired by gift or inheritance as separate property during the marriage. After a divorce, community property is divided equally in some states and according to the discretion of the court in other states.

Leasehold Estates

A **leasehold estate** is created when a real property owner or lessor (landlord) agrees to convey the right to possess and use the property to a lessee (tenant) for a certain period of time. In every leasehold estate, the tenant has a *qualified* right to exclusive, though *temporary,* possession. (The tenant's rights are qualified by the landlord's right to enter onto the premises to ensure that the tenant is not causing damage to the property.) The tenant can use the land—for instance, by harvesting crops—but cannot injure it by such activities as cutting down timber to sell or by extracting oil.

The respective rights and duties of the landlord and tenant that arise under a lease agreement will be discussed later in this chapter. Here, we look at the types of leasehold estates, or tenancies, that can be created when real property is leased.

FIXED-TERM TENANCY A **fixed-term tenancy,** also called a *tenancy for years,* is created by an express contract stating that the property is leased for a specified period of time, such as a month, a year, or a period

of years. Signing a one-year lease to occupy an apartment, for instance, creates a tenancy for years.

Note that the term need not be specified by date and can be conditioned on the occurrence of an event, such as leasing a cabin for the summer or an apartment during Mardi Gras. At the end of the period specified in the lease, the lease ends (without notice), and possession of the property returns to the lessor. If the tenant dies during the period of the lease, the lease interest passes to the tenant's heirs as personal property. Often, leases include renewal or extension provisions.

PERIODIC TENANCY With a **periodic tenancy,** the lease does not specify how long it is to last but does specify that rent is to be paid at certain intervals. This type of tenancy is automatically renewed for another rental period unless properly terminated. ▶ **Example 49.5** Jewel, LLC, enters into a lease with Capital Properties. The lease states, "Rent is due on the tenth day of every month." This provision creates a periodic tenancy from month to month. ◀ This type of tenancy can also extend from week to week or from year to year. A periodic tenancy sometimes arises after the lease term ends when the landlord allows the tenant to retain possession and continue paying monthly or weekly rent.

Under the common law, the landlord or tenant must give at least one period's notice to the other party before terminating a periodic tenancy. If the tenancy is month to month, for instance, one month's notice must be given. Today, however, state statutes often require a different period of notice before the termination of a tenancy.

TENANCY AT WILL With a **tenancy at will,** either party can terminate the tenancy without notice. This type of tenancy can arise if a landlord rents property to a tenant "for as long as both agree" or allows a person to live on the premises without paying rent. Tenancy at will is rare today because, as mentioned, most state statutes require a landlord to provide some period of notice to terminate a tenancy. States may also require a landowner to have sufficient cause (reason) to end a residential tenancy.

TENANCY AT SUFFERANCE The mere possession of land without right is called a **tenancy at sufferance.** A tenancy at sufferance is not a true tenancy because it is created when a tenant *wrongfully* retains possession of property. Whenever a tenancy for years or a periodic tenancy ends and the tenant continues

---

4. These states include Alaska, Arizona, California, Idaho, Louisiana, Nevada, New Mexico, Texas, Washington, and Wisconsin. Puerto Rico allows property to be owned as community property as well.

to retain possession of the premises without the owner's permission, a tenancy at sufferance is created.

Nonpossessory Interests

In contrast to the types of property interests just described, some interests in land do not include any rights to possess the property. These interests, known as **nonpossessory interests,** include *easements, profits,* and *licenses.* Nonpossessory interests are basically interests in real property owned by others.

An **easement** is the right of a person to make limited use of another person's real property without taking anything from the property. The right to walk across another's property, for example, is an easement. In contrast, a **profit** is the right to go onto land owned by another and take away some part of the land itself or some product of the land. ▶ **Example 49.6** Akmed owns real property known as the Dunes. Akmed gives Carmen the right to go there and remove all of the sand and gravel that she needs for her cement business. Carmen has a profit. ◀

Easements and profits can be classified as either *appurtenant* or *in gross.* Because easements and profits are similar and the same rules apply to both, we discuss them together.

EASEMENT OR PROFIT APPURTENANT An easement (or profit) *appurtenant* arises when the owner of one piece of land has a right to go onto (or remove something from) an adjacent piece of land owned by another. The land that is benefited by the easement is called the *dominant estate,* and the land that is burdened is called the *servient estate.*

Because easements appurtenant are intended to *benefit the land,* they run (are conveyed) with the land when it is transferred. ▶ **Example 49.7** Owen has a right to drive his car across Green's land, which is adjacent to Owen's property. This right-of-way over Green's property is an easement appurtenant to Owen's land. If Owen sells his land, the easement runs with the land to benefit the new owner. ◀

EASEMENT OR PROFIT IN GROSS In an easement or profit *in gross,* the right to use or take things from another's land is given to one who does not own an adjacent tract of land. These easements are intended to *benefit a particular person or business,* not a particular piece of land, and cannot be transferred.

▶ **Example 49.8** Avery owns a parcel of land with a marble quarry. Avery conveys to Classic Stone Corporation the right to come onto her land and remove up to five hundred pounds of marble per day. Classic Stone owns a profit in gross and cannot transfer this right to another. Similarly, when a utility company is granted an easement to run its power lines across another's property, it obtains an easement in gross. ◀

CREATION OF AN EASEMENT OR PROFIT Most easements and profits are created by an express grant in a contract, deed, or will. This allows the parties to include terms defining the extent and length of time of use. In some situations, an easement or profit can also be created without an express agreement.

An easement or profit may arise by **implication** when the circumstances surrounding the division of a parcel of property imply its creation. ▶ **Example 49.9** Barrow divides a parcel of land that has only one well for drinking water. If Barrow conveys the half without a well to Dean, a profit by implication arises because Dean needs drinking water. ◀

An easement may also be created by **necessity.** An easement by necessity does not require division of property for its existence. A person who rents an apartment, for instance, has an easement by necessity in the private road leading up to it.

An easement arises by **prescription** when one person exercises an easement, such as a right-of-way, on another person's land without the landowner's consent. The use must be apparent and continue for the length of time required by the applicable statute of limitations. (In much the same way, title to property may be obtained by adverse possession, as will be discussed later in this chapter.)

TERMINATION OF AN EASEMENT OR PROFIT An easement or profit can be terminated or extinguished in several ways. The simplest way is to deed it back to the owner of the land that is burdened by it.

Another way is to abandon it and provide evidence of the intent to relinquish the right to use it. Mere nonuse will not extinguish an easement or profit, however, *unless the nonuse is accompanied by an overt act showing the intent to abandon.* An overt act might be, for instance, installing and using a different access road to one's property and discontinuing using an easement across the neighboring property. A court must be convinced that there was an intent to abandon the easement or profit, though. Also, if the owner of an easement or profit acquires the property burdened by it, then it is merged into the property.

LICENSE In the context of real property, a **license** is the revocable right of a person to come onto another person's land. It is a personal privilege that arises from the consent of the owner of the land and can be revoked by the owner. A ticket to attend a movie at a theater or a concert is an example of a license.

In essence, a license grants a person the authority to enter the land of another and perform a specified act or series of acts without obtaining any permanent interest in the land. When a person with a license exceeds the authority granted and undertakes some action on the property that is not permitted, the property owner can sue that person for trespass (discussed in Chapter 6).

▶ **Case in Point 49.10**   A Catholic church granted Prince Realty Management, LLC, a three-month license to use a three-foot strip of its property adja-cent to Prince's property. The license authorized Prince to "put up plywood panels," creating a temporary fence to protect Prince's property during the construction of a new building. During the license's term, Prince installed steel piles and beams on the licensed property. When Prince ignored the church's demands that these structures be removed, the church sued Prince for trespass. The court concluded that the license allowed only temporary structures and that Prince had exceeded its authority by installing steel piles and beams. Therefore, the church was entitled to damages.[5] ◀

See *Concept Summary 49.1* below for a review of the interests that can exist in real property.

---

5. *Roman Catholic Church of Our Lady of Sorrows v. Prince Realty Management, LLC,* 47 A.D.3d 909, 850 N.Y.S.2d 569 (2008).

CONCEPT SUMMARY 49.1
Interests in Real Property

TYPE OF INTEREST	DESCRIPTION

Ownership Interests	1. *Fee simple absolute*—The most complete form of ownership.
	2. *Life estate*—An estate that lasts for the life of a specified individual.
	3. *Concurrent interests*—When two or more persons hold title to property together, concurrent ownership exists.
	  a. A tenancy in common exists when two or more persons own an undivided interest in property. On a tenant's death, that tenant's property interest passes to his or her heirs.
	  b. A joint tenancy exists when two or more persons own an undivided interest in property, with a right of survivorship. On the death of a joint tenant, that tenant's property interest transfers to the remaining tenant(s), not to the heirs of the deceased.
	  c. A tenancy by the entirety is a form of co-ownership between a husband and wife that is similar to a joint tenancy, except that a spouse cannot separately transfer her or his interest during her or his lifetime.
	  d. Community property is a form of co-ownership between a husband and wife in which each spouse technically owns an undivided one-half interest in property acquired during the marriage. This type of ownership occurs in only a few states.

Leasehold Estates	A leasehold estate is an interest in real property that is held for only a limited period of time, as specified in the lease agreement. Types of tenancies relating to leased property include the following: 1. *Fixed-term tenancy (tenancy for years)*—Tenancy for a period of time stated by express contract. 2. *Periodic tenancy*—Tenancy for a period determined by the frequency of rent payments. It is automatically renewed unless proper notice is given. 3. *Tenancy at will*—Tenancy for as long as both parties agree. No notice of termination is required. 4. *Tenancy at sufferance*—Possession of land without legal right.
Nonpossessory Interests	Interests that involve the right to use real property but not to possess it. Easements, profits, and licenses are nonpossessory interests.

TRANSFER OF OWNERSHIP

Ownership interests in real property are frequently transferred by sale, and the terms of the transfer are specified in a real estate sales contract. Often, real estate brokers or agents (see Chapter 32) who are licensed by the state assist the buyers and sellers during the sales transaction.

Real property ownership can also be transferred by gift, by will or inheritance, by possession, or by eminent domain. In the subsections that follow, we focus primarily on voluntary sales of real property. We then consider adverse possession, which is an involuntary method of transferring title to real property. Eminent domain will be discussed later in this chapter, and transfers by will or inheritance will be discussed in Chapter 51.

Real Estate Sales Contracts

In some ways, a sale of real estate is similar to a sale of goods because it involves a transfer of ownership, often with specific warranties. A sale of real estate, however, is a more complicated transaction that involves certain formalities that are not required in a sale of goods. Usually, after substantial negotiation (offers, counteroffers, responses), the parties enter into a detailed contract setting forth their agreement. A contract for a sale of land includes such terms as the purchase price, the type of deed the buyer will receive, the condition of the premises, and any items that will be included.

Unless the buyer pays cash for the property, the buyer must obtain financing through a mortgage loan (see Chapter 30). Real estate sales contracts are often made contingent on the buyer's ability to obtain financing at or below a specified rate of interest. The contract may also be contingent on the buyer selling other real property, the seller obtaining a survey and title insurance, and the property passing one or more inspections. Normally, the buyer is responsible for having the premises inspected for physical or mechanical defects and for insect infestation.

CLOSING DATE AND ESCROW The contract usually fixes a date for performance, or **closing,** that frequently is four to twelve weeks after the contract is signed. On this day, the seller conveys the property to the buyer by delivering the deed to the buyer in exchange for payment of the purchase price.

Deposits toward the purchase price normally are held in a special account, called an **escrow account,** until all of the conditions of sale have been met. Once the closing takes place, the funds in the escrow account are transferred to the seller. The *escrow agent* may be a title company, bank, or special escrow company that acts as a neutral party in the sales transaction to facilitate the sale and exchange of documents.

MARKETABLE TITLE The question of title to a particular parcel of property is especially important to the buyer. A grantor (seller) is obligated to transfer **marketable title,** or good title, to the grantee (buyer). Marketable title means that the grantor's ownership is free from encumbrances (except those disclosed by the grantor) and free of defects.

If the buyer signs a purchase contract and then discovers that the seller does not have a marketable title, the buyer can withdraw from the contract. ▶ **Example 49.11** Chan enters into an agreement to buy Fortuna Ranch from Hal. Chan then discovers that Hal has previously given Pearl an unexpired option to purchase the ranch. In this situation, the title is not marketable because Pearl could exercise the option and Hal would be compelled to sell the ranch to her. Therefore, Chan can withdraw from the contract to buy the property. ◀

The most common way of ensuring title is through **title insurance,** which insures the buyer against loss from defects in title to real property. When financing the purchase of real property, almost all lenders require title insurance to protect their interests in the collateral for the loan.

IMPLIED WARRANTIES IN THE SALE OF NEW HOMES The common law rule of *caveat emptor* ("let the buyer beware") held that the seller of a home made no warranty as to its soundness or fitness (unless the contract or deed stated otherwise). Today, however, most states imply a warranty—the **implied warranty of habitability**—in the sale of new homes. The seller of a new house warrants that it will be fit for human habitation even if the deed or contract of sale does not include such a warranty.

Essentially, the seller is warranting that the house is in reasonable working order and is of reasonably sound construction. Under this theory, the seller of a new home can be liable if the home is defective. In some states, the warranty protects not only the first purchaser but any subsequent purchaser as well.

SELLER'S DUTY TO DISCLOSE HIDDEN DEFECTS In most jurisdictions, courts impose on sellers a duty to disclose any known defect that materially affects the value of the property and that the buyer could not reasonably discover. Failure to disclose such a material defect gives the buyer a right to rescind the contract and to sue for damages based on fraud or misrepresentation.

A dispute may arise over whether the seller knew of the defect before the sale, and there is normally a limit to the time within which the buyer can bring a suit against the seller based on the defect. For instance, in Louisiana, the prescribed limit for a suit against a seller who knew, or can be presumed to have known, of the defect is one year from the day that the buyer discovered it. If the seller did not know of the defect, the limit is one year from the date of the sale. ► **Case in Point 49.12**   Matthew Humphrey partially renovated a house in Louisiana and sold it to Terry and Tabitha Whitehead for $67,000. A few months after the Whiteheads moved in, they discovered rotten wood behind the tile in the bathroom and experienced problems with the fireplace and the plumbing.

Two years later, the Whiteheads filed a suit against Humphrey seeking to rescind the sale. They argued that the plumbing problems were a latent defect that the seller had failed to disclose. Evidence revealed that prior to the sale, the parties were made aware of issues regarding the sewer system and that corrective actions were taken. At the time of the sale, the toilets flushed, and neither side realized that the latent defects had not been resolved. The court ruled that rescission was not warranted for the sewer problems because the Whiteheads had waited too long after their discovery to file a claim against Humphrey. The court did order Humphrey to pay damages for the repairs to the fireplace and for replacing some of the rotten wood, however, because Humphrey knew about these defects at the time of the sale.[6] ◄

In the following *Spotlight Case,* the court had to decide whether the buyer of a house had the right to rescind the sales contract because he was not told that the house was allegedly haunted.

---

6. *Whitehead v. Humphrey,* 954 So.2d 859 (La.App. 2007).

SP TLIGHT on Sales of Haunted Houses

Case 49.1   Stambovsky v. Ackley
Supreme Court, Appellate Division, New York, 572 N.Y.S.2d 672, 169 A.D.2d 254 (1991).

BACKGROUND AND FACTS   Jeffrey Stambovsky signed a contract to buy Helen Ackley's home in Nyack, New York. After the contract was signed, Stambovsky discovered that the house was widely reputed to be haunted. The Ackley family claimed to have seen poltergeists on numerous occasions over the prior nine years. The Ackleys had been interviewed and quoted in both a national publication *(Reader's Digest)* and the local newspaper. The house was described as "a riverfront Victorian (with ghost)" when it was part of a walking tour of Nyack, New York. When Stambovsky discovered the house's reputation, he sued to rescind the contract and recover his down payment. He alleged that Ackley and her real estate agent made material misrepresentations when they failed to disclose Ackley's belief that the home was haunted. Ackley argued that, under the doctrine of *caveat emptor,* she was under no duty to disclose to the buyer the home's haunted reputation. The trial court dismissed Stambovsky's case. Stambovsky appealed.

IN THE LANGUAGE OF THE COURT
Justice *RUBIN* delivered the opinion of the court.

* * * *

While I agree with [the trial court] that the real estate broker, as agent for the seller, is under no duty to disclose to a potential buyer the phantasmal [haunted] reputation of the premises and that, in his pursuit of a legal remedy for fraudulent misrepresentation against the seller, plaintiff hasn't a ghost of a chance, I am nevertheless moved by the spirit of equity to allow the buyer to seek rescission of the contract of sale and recovery of his down payment. New York law fails to recognize any remedy for damages incurred as a result of the seller's mere silence, applying instead the strict rule of *caveat emptor.* Therefore, the theoretical basis

CASE 49.1 CONTINUED for granting relief, even under the extraordinary facts of this case, is elusive if not ephemeral [short-lived].

* * * *

The doctrine of caveat emptor *requires that a buyer act prudently to assess the fitness and value of his purchase and operates to bar the purchaser who fails to exercise due care from seeking the equitable remedy of rescission.* * * * Applying the strict rule of *caveat emptor* to a contract involving a house possessed by poltergeists conjures up visions of a psychic or medium routinely accompanying the structural engineer and Terminix man on an inspection of every home subject to a contract of sale. It portends [warns] that the prudent attorney will establish an escrow account lest the subject of the transaction come back to haunt him and his client—or pray that his malpractice insurance coverage extends to supernatural disasters. In the interest of avoiding such untenable [unsound] consequences, the notion that a haunting is a condition which can and should be ascertained upon reasonable inspection of the premises is a hobgoblin which should be exorcised from the body of legal precedent and laid quietly to rest. [Emphasis added.]

* * * *

In the case at bar [under consideration], defendant seller deliberately fostered the public belief that her home was possessed. Having undertaken to inform the public at large, to whom she has no legal relationship, about the supernatural occurrences on her property, she may be said to owe no less a duty to her contract vendee. It has been remarked that the occasional modern cases, which permit a seller to take unfair advantage of a buyer's ignorance so long as he is not actively misled are "singularly unappetizing" [unfounded]. Where, as here, the seller not only takes unfair advantage of the buyer's ignorance but has created and perpetuated a condition about which he is unlikely to even inquire, enforcement of the contract (in whole or in part) is offensive to the court's sense of equity. Application of the remedy of rescission, within the bounds of the narrow exception to the doctrine of *caveat emptor* set forth herein, is entirely appropriate to relieve the unwitting purchaser from the consequences of a most unnatural bargain.

DECISION AND REMEDY *The New York appellate court found that the doctrine of* caveat emptor *did not apply in this case. The court allowed Stambovsky to rescind the purchase contract and recover the down payment.*

THE ETHICAL DIMENSION *In not disclosing the house's reputation to Stambovsky, was Ackley's behavior unethical? If so, was it unethical because she knew something he did not, or was it unethical because of the nature of the information she omitted? What if Ackley had failed to mention that the roof leaked or that the well was dry—conditions that a buyer would normally investigate? Explain your answer.*

THE LEGAL ENVIRONMENT DIMENSION *Why did the court decide that applying the strict rule of* caveat emptor *was inappropriate in this case? How would applying this doctrine increase costs for the purchaser?*

Deeds

Possession and title to land are passed from person to person by means of a **deed**—the instrument used to transfer real property. Deeds must meet certain requirements, but unlike a contract, a deed does not have to be supported by legally sufficient consideration. Gifts of real property are common, and they require deeds even though there is no consideration for the gift.

To be valid, a deed must include the following:

1. *The names of the* grantor *(the giver or seller) and the* grantee *(the donee or buyer).*

2. *Words evidencing the intent to convey* (for instance, "I hereby bargain, sell, grant, or give"). No specific words are necessary, and if the deed does *not* specify the type of estate being transferred, it presumptively transfers the property in fee simple absolute.

3. *A legally sufficient description of the land.* The description must include enough detail to distinguish the

property being conveyed from every other parcel of land. The property can be identified by reference to an official survey or recorded plat map, or each boundary can be described by *metes and bounds*. **Metes and bounds** is a system of measuring boundary lines by the distance between two points, often using physical features of the local geography—for example, "beginning at the southwesterly intersection of Court and Main Streets, then West 40 feet to the fence, then South 100 feet, then Northeast approximately 120 feet back to the beginning."

4. *The grantor's (and usually his or her spouse's) signature.*

5. *Delivery of the deed.*

WARRANTY DEEDS Different types of deeds provide different degrees of protection against defects of title. A **warranty deed** makes the greatest number of warranties and thus provides the most extensive protection against defects of title. In most states, special language is required to create a warranty deed.

Warranty deeds include a number of *covenants,* or promises, that the grantor makes to the grantee. These covenants include a covenant that the grantor has the title to, and the power to convey, the property; a covenant of quiet enjoyment (a warranty that the buyer will not be disturbed in her or his possession of the land); and a covenant that transfer of the property is made without knowledge of adverse claims of third parties.

Generally, the warranty deed makes the grantor liable for all defects of title by the grantor and previous titleholders. ▶ **Example 49.13** Julio sells a two-acre lot and office building by warranty deed. Subsequently, a third person appears, shows that she has better title than Julio had, and forces the buyer off the property. Here, the covenant of quiet enjoyment has been breached. Thus, the buyer can sue Julio to recover the purchase price of the land, plus any other damages incurred as a result. ◀

SPECIAL WARRANTY DEED In contrast to a warranty deed, a **special warranty deed,** which is also referred to as a *limited warranty deed,* warrants only that the grantor or seller held good title during his or her ownership of the property. In other words, the grantor does not warrant that there were no defects of title when the property was held by previous owners.

If the special warranty deed discloses all liens or other encumbrances, the seller will not be liable to the buyer if a third person subsequently interferes with the buyer's ownership. If the third person's claim arises out of, or is related to, some act of the seller, however, the seller will be liable to the buyer for damages.

QUITCLAIM DEED A **quitclaim deed** offers the least protection against defects in the title. Basically, a quitclaim deed conveys to the grantee whatever interest the grantor had. So, if the grantor had no interest, then the grantee receives no interest. Naturally, if the grantor had a defective title or no title at all, a conveyance by warranty deed or special warranty deed would not cure the defects. Such deeds, however, will give the buyer a cause of action to sue the seller.

A quitclaim deed can and often does serve as a release of the grantor's interest in a particular parcel of property. ▶ **Example 49.14** Sanchez owns a strip of waterfront property on which he wants to build condominiums. Lanz has an easement on a portion of the property, which might interfere with Sanchez's plans for the development. Sanchez can negotiate with Lanz to deed the easement back to Sanchez. A quitclaim deed from Lanz would constitute such a transfer. ◀

GRANT DEED With a **grant deed,** the grantor simply states, "I grant the property to you" or "I convey, or bargain and sell, the property to you." By state statute, grant deeds carry with them an implied warranty that the grantor owns the property and has not previously transferred it to someone else or encumbered it, except as set out in the deed.

Recording Statutes

Once the seller delivers the deed to the buyer (at closing), legal title to the property is conveyed. Nevertheless, the buyer should promptly record the deed with the state records office to establish superior ownership rights against any third parties who might make a claim to the property. Every state has a **recording statute,** which allows deeds to be recorded in the public record. Deeds generally are recorded in the county in which the property is located. The buyer typically pays the required fee because he or she is the one who will be protected by recording the deed.

Recording a deed gives notice to the public that a certain person is now the owner of a particular parcel of real estate. By putting everyone on notice as to the true owner, recording a deed prevents the previous owners from fraudulently conveying the land to other purchasers. Many state statutes require that the grantor sign the deed in the presence of two witnesses before it can be recorded.

Adverse Possession

A person who wrongfully possesses (by occupying or using) the real property of another may eventually acquire title to it through adverse possession. **Adverse possession** is a means of obtaining title to land without delivery of a deed and without the consent of—or payment to—the true owner. Thus, adverse possession is a method of *involuntarily* transferring title to the property from the true owner to the adverse possessor.

Essentially, when one person possesses the real property of another for a certain statutory period of time (three to thirty years, depending on the state, with ten years being most common), that person acquires title to the land.

ELEMENTS OF ADVERSE POSSESSION   For property to be held adversely, four elements must be satisfied:

1. *Possession must be actual and exclusive.* This means that the possessor must physically occupy the property. This requirement is clearly met if the possessor lives on the property, but it may also be met if the possessor builds fences, erects structures, plants crops, or even grazes animals on the land.
2. *The possession must be open, visible, and notorious, not secret or clandestine.* The possessor must occupy the land for all the world to see. This requirement of obviousness ensures that the true owner is on notice that someone is possessing the owner's property wrongfully.
3. *Possession must be continuous and peaceable for the required period of time.* This requirement means that the possessor must not be interrupted in the occupancy by the true owner or by the courts. *Continuous* does not mean constant—it simply means that the possessor has continuously occupied the property in some fashion for the statutory time. *Peaceable* means that no force was used to possess the land.
4. *Possession must be hostile and adverse.* In other words, the possessor cannot be living on the property with the owner's permission and must claim the property as against the whole world.

PURPOSE OF THE DOCTRINE   There are a number of public-policy reasons for the adverse possession doctrine. These include society's interest in resolving boundary disputes, in determining title when title to property is in question, and in assuring that real property remains in the stream of commerce. More fundamentally, the doctrine punishes owners who do not take action when they see adverse possession and rewards possessors for putting land to productive use.

In the following case, the question before the court was whether a landowner had obtained title to a portion of adjacent land by adverse possession.

CASE 49.2

Scarborough v. Rollins
Court of Appeals of Mississippi, 44 So.3d 381 (2010).

BACKGROUND AND FACTS   Charles T. Scarborough and Mildred T. Rollins were adjoining landowners, sharing one common boundary. Based on her survey of the property, Rollins believed that she owned a portion of a gravel road located to the south of the apartment buildings she owned. On the contrary, Scarborough believed that the gravel road was located totally on his property and that he owned some property north of the gravel road toward Rollins's apartment buildings. In July 2006, Scarborough filed a complaint seeking to quiet and confirm his title to the property. Rollins filed a counterclaim seeking to quiet and confirm her title. The court entered judgment for Rollins. Scarborough appealed.

 IN THE LANGUAGE OF THE COURT
ISHEE, J. [Judge]

* * * *

Scarborough asserts that the trial court erred in finding that Rollins proved that she owned the property in dispute by adverse possession. Scarborough claims that Rollins failed to prove

CASE 49.2 CONTINUES ▶

by clear and convincing evidence that her possession of the disputed grassy area down to the northern edge of the gravel road has been hostile, open, notorious, visible, continuing, exclusive, and peaceful. Scarborough also claims that Rollins's paying taxes and mowing the grass north of the gravel road by her and her predecessors in title, as well as [a prior owner's] installation of a gas line are not such adverse actions that gave him sufficient notice that he would know that Rollins was claiming the disputed area and that she was attempting to deny him ownership thereof and exclude him therefrom. Scarborough asserts that both he and Rollins used the disputed land, thus exercising joint use of the land; therefore, a claim of adverse possession is not supported. Scarborough also asserts that Rollins paid taxes only on the land situated north of her monumented south boundary line while he paid taxes on all of the land called for in his deed, including the gravel road and the land north of the gravel road up to Rollins's south boundary.

To succeed on a claim of adverse possession, the claimant has the burden to prove each element by clear and convincing evidence. * * * *Adverse possession requires the claimant to prove that her possession or occupancy was: (1) under claim of ownership; (2) actual or hostile; (3) open, notorious, and visible; (4) continuous and uninterrupted for a period of ten years; (5) exclusive; and (6) peaceful.* [Emphasis added.]

1. Under Claim of Ownership

The deed to Rollins's property presented to the chancery court indicated that she owned the property at or near the disputed property. Evidence was provided to show that Rollins and her predecessors-in-title paid the taxes on all of the property north of the gravel road. However, Scarborough only paid taxes on the property that was south of the gravel road.

2. Actual or Hostile

Evidence was provided to the chancery court that for more than thirty-five years, no one other than Rollins and her predecessors-in-title, the Blacks, used this property.

3. Open, Notorious, and Visible

[One witness] testified at trial that his family's ownership of that land was open and obvious. He stated that everyone in Starkville, who was around the apartments, knew that the apartment complex owned the yard up to the edge of the gravel road.

4. Continuous and Uninterrupted for a Period of Ten Years

Testimony at trial from [three witnesses] all provided that Rollins and her predecessors-in-title used the property for more than thirty-five years.

5. Exclusive

Testimony at trial * * * indicated that no one, until Scarborough, claimed to have used any part of the property in dispute.

6. Peaceful

Rollins testified that until September 2007, she and her predecessors-in-title enjoyed peaceful possession of the property.

We find that Rollins satisfied the elements required for adverse possession.

* * * *

The chancery court properly held that the gravel road which is to the north of Scarborough's property and to the south of Rollins's property was the boundary between the parties and that Rollins was entitled to an award of actual and punitive damages and attorney's fees due to the conversion of her property by Scarborough.

DECISION AND REMEDY   *The Court of Appeals of Mississippi affirmed the lower court's judgment and assessed all costs of the appeal to Scarborough. Rollins had proved title to the land by adverse possession.*

WHAT IF THE FACTS WERE DIFFERENT?   *Suppose that Rollins had not paid any taxes on the disputed land and that Scarborough had done so. Would the result have been different? Explain.*

THE E-COMMERCE DIMENSION   *How might the Internet have facilitated either party's claim to the disputed property?*

SECTION 4
LIMITATIONS ON THE RIGHTS OF PROPERTY OWNERS

No ownership rights in real property can ever really be absolute—that is, an owner of real property cannot always do whatever she or he wishes on or with the property. Nuisance and environmental laws, for example, restrict certain types of activities. Holding the property is also conditional on the payment of property taxes. Zoning laws and building permits frequently restrict one's use of realty. In addition, if a property owner fails to pay debts, the property may be seized to satisfy judgment creditors. In short, the rights of every property owner are subject to certain conditions and limitations. We look here at some of the important ways in which owners' rights in real property can be limited.

Eminent Domain

Even ownership in fee simple absolute is limited by a superior ownership. Just as the king was the ultimate landowner in medieval England, today the government has an ultimate ownership right in all land in the United States. This right, known as **eminent domain,** is sometimes referred to as the *condemnation power* of government to take land for public use. It gives the government the right to acquire possession of real property in the manner directed by the U.S. Constitution and the laws of the state whenever the public interest requires it.

PUBLIC USE REQUIREMENT Property may be taken only for public use, not for private benefit.

▶ **Example 49.15**   When a new public highway is to be built, the government decides where to build it and how much land to condemn. After the government determines that a particular parcel of land is necessary for the highway, it will first offer to buy the property. If the owner refuses the offer, the government brings a judicial (**condemnation**) proceeding to obtain title to the land. Then, in another proceeding, the court determines the *fair value* of the land, which usually is approximately equal to its market value. ◀

When the government uses its power of eminent domain to acquire land owned by a private party, a **taking** occurs. Under the *takings clause* of the Fifth Amendment to the U.S. Constitution, the government must pay "just compensation" to the owner. State constitutions contain similar provisions.

ECONOMIC DEVELOPMENT   In 2005, the United States Supreme Court ruled that the power of eminent domain may be used to further economic development.[7] Since that decision, a majority of state legislatures have passed laws limiting the power of state governments to use eminent domain, particularly for urban redevelopment projects that benefit private developers.

The following case involved a town's condemnation action to acquire rights-of-way for a natural gas pipeline to be constructed through the town. The issue was whether the pipeline was for public use, even though it was not built to furnish natural gas to the residents of that town.

---

7. *Kelo v. City of New London, Connecticut,* 545 U.S. 469, 125 S.Ct. 2655, 162 L.Ed.2d 439 (2005).

CASE ANALYSIS

Case 49.3   Town of Midland v. Morris
Court of Appeals of North Carolina, 704 S.E.2d 329 (2011).

IN THE LANGUAGE OF THE COURT
STEPHENS, Judge.

The Transcontinental Pipeline transports and distributes natural gas from the Gulf of Mexico to the northeastern United States. In April 2002, the City of Monroe, North Carolina, decided to supply the citizens of Monroe and the surrounding area with natural gas by a direct connection between its natural gas distribution system and the Transcontinental Pipeline. To directly connect to the Transcontinental Pipeline, Monroe needed to acquire the rights to property through which to run a pipeline along the forty-two miles between

CASE 49.3 CONTINUES ▶

Monroe and the direct connection on the Transcontinental Pipeline located in Iredell County.

To facilitate the acquisition of land for the construction of the new pipeline ("Pipeline"), Monroe, located in Union County, entered into interlocal agreements with the Town of Mooresville, located in Iredell County, and the Town of Midland, located in Cabarrus County.

The relevant terms of the interlocal agreement between Midland and Monroe * * * provide as follows:

4. Midland shall be responsible for obtaining either by acquisition or by the power of eminent domain and holding in its name for the benefit of the parties and this Interlocal Agreement all easements (both permanent and temporary construction), rights of way, and real property required for the project in Cabarrus County.

* * * *

20. * * * Midland shall retain a perpetual right to locate and install one (1) tap in the pipeline within the corporate limits of Midland from which to operate and supply its own natural gas distribution utility for the benefit of Midland's utility customers in Cabarrus County only. The one tap for Midland's use shall be subject to a right of first refusal granted to a private natural gas provider to serve customers that would otherwise be served by Midland. . . .

* * * *

In 2008 Midland began the process of acquiring the property necessary for the construction of the Pipeline. When negotiations for voluntary acquisitions for the rights of way failed, Midland exercised its eminent domain authority to condemn the needed property.

The present controversy stems from fifteen condemnation actions filed by the Town of Midland in Cabarrus County Superior Court. In those fifteen actions, the opposing parties (hereinafter "Property Owners") filed defenses and counter-

claims, challenging Midland's power to condemn the properties in question * * * .

* * * *

Property Owners first argue that because Midland neither currently provides natural gas services to its citizens, nor currently has any plans to provide natural gas to its citizens in the future, the condemnations were undertaken in violation of the statutes governing eminent domain. We disagree.

* * * *

* * * *We find it manifest [obvious] that Midland may acquire property by condemnation to establish a gas transmission and distribution system, even in the absence of a concrete, immediate plan to furnish gas services to its citizens.* [Emphasis added.]

While we acknowledge the existence of the requirement that the public enterprise be established and conducted for the city and its citizens, we conclude that this requirement is satisfied by Midland's placement of a tap on the Pipeline and by Midland's acquisition of the right to low-cost natural gas. Further, * * * *there is nothing in the record to indicate that Midland will never offer natural gas services to its citizens. In fact, Midland's contracted-for right to install a tap on the Pipeline "from which to operate and supply its own natural gas distribution utility for the benefit of Midland's utility customers" indicates just the opposite:* that Midland will, eventually, furnish natural gas services to its citizens. [Emphasis added.]

* * * *

Property Owners further argue that Midland's condemnations violate [the state's statute] because the condemnations are not "for the public use or benefit."

* * * *

It is clear from the statutory language that establishing a gas transmission and distribution system is an appropriate purpose for the condemnation of property under [the relevant provisions].

Despite the disjunctive language of this statutory requirement, our courts have determined the propriety of a condemnation under [the statute] based on the condemnation's satisfaction of both a "public use test" and a "public benefit test."

The first approach—the public use test—asks whether the public has a right to a definite use of the condemned property. The second approach—the public benefit test— asks whether some benefit accrues to the public as a result of the desired condemnation.

Under the public use test, "the principal and dispositive determination is whether the general public has a right to a definite use of the property sought to be condemned." * * * Applying this test to the present case in the appropriate context, there is nothing to indicate that gas services—were they to be provided by Midland—would be available to anything less than the entire population. Accordingly, there can be no doubt that the Midland condemnations would pass the public use test * * * .

* * * *

Under the public benefit test, *"a given condemnor's desired use of the condemned property in question is for 'the public use or benefit' if that use would contribute to the general welfare and prosperity of the public at large."* In this case, we must take care in defining Midland's "desired use" of the property. Midland is condemning the property to run the Pipeline and to control a tap on the Pipeline, not to immediately provide gas to the citizens of Midland. Accordingly, it is the *availability* of natural gas that must contribute to the general welfare and prosperity of the public at large. [Emphasis added.]

As noted by our Courts, the construction and extension of public utilities, and especially the concomitant commercial and residential growth, provide a clear public benefit to local citizens. * * * Midland's tap

CASE 49.3 CONTINUED

on the Pipeline, and its potential to provide natural gas service, likely will spur growth, as well as provide Midland with an advantage in industrial recruitment. These opportunities must be seen as public benefits accruing to the citizens of Midland, such that Midland's condemnations are for the public benefit.

* * * *

Accordingly, we conclude that the Midland condemnations were not undertaken to provide a solely private benefit.

* * * *

We hold that Midland lawfully exercised its eminent domain power.

LEGAL REASONING QUESTIONS

1. Was Midland's condemnation of property in this case for a public benefit? Explain.

2. Is it fair that a city can exercise its eminent domain power to take property even though the property will not be used immediately to benefit the city's residents? Why or why not?

3. The town of Midland—and its taxpaying citizens—had to pay fair value to fifteen property owners for property it acquired through eminent domain. Is it right to make the citizens of one town pay for a pipeline constructed primarily to benefit another town? Explain.

4. Suppose that Midland had used its eminent domain authority to acquire property for the town to lease to a private resort that would provide a large number of jobs and bring tourist dollars into the community. What are the arguments for and against this use of the power of eminent domain?

Inverse Condemnation

Typically, a government agency exercises the power of eminent domain through litigation or negotiation and pays compensation to the landowner whose property is seized. **Inverse condemnation,** in contrast, occurs when a government simply takes private property from a landowner without paying any compensation, thereby forcing the landowner to sue the government for compensation.

The taking can be physical, as when a government agency uses or occupies the land, or it may be constructive, as when an agency regulation results in loss of property value. The United States Supreme Court has held that even temporary flooding of land by the government may result in liability under the takings clause.[8]

▶ **Case in Point 49.16** In Walton County, Florida, water flows through a ditch from Oyster Lake to the Gulf of Mexico. When Hurricane Opal caused the water to rise in Oyster Lake, Walton County reconfigured the drainage to divert the overflow onto the nearby property of William and Patricia Hemby. The flow was eventually restored to pre-Opal conditions, but during a later emergency, water was diverted onto the Hembys' property again. This diversion was not restored.

The Hembys filed a suit against the county. After their deaths, their daughter Cozette Drake pursued the claim. The court found that by allowing the water diversion, created during emergency conditions, to remain on Drake's property long after the emergency had passed, the county had engaged in a permanent or continuous physical invasion. This invasion rendered Drake's property useless and deprived her of its beneficial enjoyment. Drake was therefore entitled to receive compensation from the county.[9] ◀

Restrictive Covenants

A private restriction on the use of land is known as a **restrictive covenant.** If the restriction is binding on the party who purchases the property originally and on subsequent purchasers as well, it is said to "run with the land." A covenant running with the land must be in writing (usually it is in the deed), and subsequent purchasers must have reason to know about it.

▶ **Example 49.17** In the course of developing a fifty-lot suburban subdivision, Levitt records a declaration of restrictions that effectively limits construction on each lot to one single-family house. Each lot's deed includes a reference to the declaration with a provision that the purchaser and her or his successors are bound to those restrictions. Thus, each purchaser assumes ownership with notice of the restrictions. If

---

8. *Arkansas Game and Fish Commission v. United States*, ___ U.S. ___, 133 S.Ct. 511, 184 L.Ed.2d 417 (2012).

9. *Drake v. Walton County*, 6 So.3d 717 (Fla.App. 2009).

an owner attempts to build a duplex (or any structure that does not comply with the restrictions) on a lot, the other owners may obtain a court order enjoining the construction.

Alternatively, Levitt might simply have included the restrictions on the subdivision's map, filed the map in the appropriate public office, and included a reference to the map in each deed. In this way, each owner would also have been held to have constructive notice of the restrictions. ◀

SECTION 5
ZONING AND GOVERNMENT REGULATIONS

The rules and regulations that collectively manage the development and use of land are known as **zoning laws.** Zoning laws were first used in the United States to segregate slaughterhouses, distilleries, kilns, and other businesses that might pose a nuisance to nearby residences. The growth of modern urban areas has led to an increased need to organize uses of land. Today, zoning laws enable the government of a municipality —a town, city, or county—to control the speed and type of development within its borders by creating different zones and regulating the use of property allowed in each zone.

The United States Supreme Court has held that zoning is a constitutional exercise of a government's police powers.[10] Therefore, as long as its zoning ordinances are rationally related to the health, safety, or welfare of the community, a municipal government has broad discretion to carry out zoning as it sees fit.

Purpose and Scope of Zoning Laws

The purpose of zoning laws is to manage the land within a community in a way that encourages sustainable and organized development while controlling growth in a manner that serves the interests of the community. One of the basic elements of zoning is the classification of land by permissible use as part of a comprehensive municipal plan, but zoning extends to other aspects of land use as well.

PERMISSIBLE USES OF LAND Municipalities generally divide their available land into districts according to the land's present and potential future uses. Typically, land is classified into the following types of permissible uses:

1. *Residential.* In areas dedicated for **residential use,** landowners can construct buildings for human habitation.
2. *Commercial.* Land assigned for business activities is designated as being for **commercial use,** sometimes called business use. An area with a number of retail stores, offices, supermarkets, and hotels might be designated as a commercial or business district. Land used for entertainment purposes, such as movie theaters and sports stadiums, also falls into this category, as does land used for government activities.
3. *Industrial.* Areas designated for **industrial use** typically encompass light and heavy manufacturing, shipping, and heavy transportation. For instance, undeveloped land with easy access to highways and railroads might be classified as suitable for future use by industry. Although industrial uses can be profitable for a city seeking to raise tax revenue, such uses can also result in noise, smoke, or vibrations that interfere with others' enjoyment of their property. Consequently, areas zoned for industrial use generally are kept as far as possible from residential districts and some commercial districts.
4. *Conservation districts.* Some municipalities also establish certain areas that are dedicated to carrying out local soil and water conservation efforts—for instance, wetlands (see Chapter 45) might be designated as a conservation district.

A city's residential, commercial, and industrial districts may be divided, in turn, into subdistricts. For instance, zoning ordinances regulate the type, density, size, and approved uses of structures within a given district. Thus, a residential district may be divided into low-density (single-family homes with large lots), high-density (single- and multiple-family homes with small lots), and planned-unit (condominiums or apartments) subdistricts.

OTHER ZONING RESTRICTIONS Zoning rules extend to much more than the permissible use of land. In residential districts, for instance, an ordinance may require a house or garage to be set back a specific number of feet from a neighbor's property line.

In commercial districts, zoning rules may attempt to maintain a certain visual aesthetic. Therefore, businesses may be required to construct buildings of a cer-

---

10. *Village of Euclid v. Ambler Realty Co.,* 272 U.S. 365, 47 S.Ct. 114, 71 L.Ed. 303 (1926).

tain height and width so that they conform to the style of other commercial buildings in the area.

Businesses may also be required to provide parking for patrons or take other measures to manage traffic. Sometimes, municipalities limit construction of new businesses to prevent traffic congestion. Zoning laws may even attempt to regulate the public morals of the community. For instance, cities commonly impose severe restrictions on the location and operation of adult businesses.

Exceptions to Zoning Laws

Zoning restrictions are not absolute. It is impossible for zoning laws to account for every contingency. The purpose of zoning is to enable the municipality to control development but not to prevent it altogether or limit the government's ability to adapt to changing circumstances or unforeseen needs. Hence, legal processes have been developed to allow for exceptions to zoning laws. Here, we look at these exceptions, known as *variances* and *special-use permits,* as well as at the *special incentives* that governments may offer to encourage certain kinds of development.

VARIANCES When a property owner wants to use his or her land in a manner not permitted by zoning rules, she or he can request a **variance,** which allows an exception to the rules. The property owner requesting the variance must demonstrate that the requested variance:

1. Is necessary for reasonable development.
2. Is the least intrusive solution to the problem.
3. Will not alter the essential character of the neighborhood.

Hardship Situations. Property owners normally request variances in *hardship situations* (when complying with the zoning rules would be too difficult or costly due to existing property conditions). ▶ **Example 49.18** Lin Wang, a homeowner, wants to replace her single-car garage with a two-car garage, but if she does so, the garage will be closer to her neighbor's property than is permitted by the zoning rules. In this situation, she may ask for a variance. She can claim that the configuration of her property (where the current garage is located) makes it difficult and costly to comply with the zoning code, so compliance would create a hardship for her. ◀ Similarly, a church might request a variance from height restrictions in order to erect a new steeple. Or a furniture store might ask for a vari-

ance from *footprint* limitations so that it can expand its showroom (a building's footprint is the area of ground that it covers).

Note that the hardship may not be self-created. In other words, a person usually cannot buy property with zoning regulations in effect and then argue that a variance is needed for the property to be used for the owner's intended purpose.

Public Hearing. In almost all instances, before a variance is granted, there must be a public hearing with adequate notice to neighbors who may object to the exception. After the public hearing, a hearing examiner appointed by the municipality (or the local zoning board or commission) determines whether to grant the exception. When a variance is granted, it applies only to the specific parcel of land for which it was requested and does not create a regulation-free zone.

SPECIAL-USE PERMITS Sometimes, zoning laws permit a use, but only if the property owner complies with specific requirements to ensure that the proposed use does not harm the immediate neighborhood. In such instances, the zoning board will issue **special-use permits,** also called conditional-use permits.

▶ **Example 49.19** An area is designated as a residential district, but small businesses are permitted to operate there so long as they do not affect the characteristics of the neighborhood. A bank asks the zoning board for a special-use permit to open a branch in the area. At the public hearing, the bank's managers demonstrate that the branch will be housed in a building that conforms to the style of other structures in the area. The bank also shows that adequate parking will be available and that landscaping will shield the parking lot from public view. Unless there are strong objections from the branch's prospective neighbors, the board will likely grant the permit. ◀

SPECIAL INCENTIVES In addition to granting exceptions to zoning regulations, municipalities may also wish to encourage certain kinds of development. To do so, they offer incentives, often in the form of lower tax rates or tax credits. For instance, to attract new businesses that will provide jobs for local citizens and increase the tax base, a city may offer incentives in the form of lower property tax rates for a period of years. Similarly, homeowners may receive tax credits for historical preservation if they renovate and maintain older homes.

Tax credits provided by cities and towns may encourage construction firms to utilize "green" construction techniques that are more sustainable.

▶ **Example 49.20** Ryan Orley, of Orley Construction, LLC, knows that a building's thermal load (the amount of heat that must be removed over a given time period) depends, in part, on its orientation to the sun. A change in the building's orientation may entail a higher cost initially but save on air-conditioning expenses later. Ryan convinces his client that it is worth the extra cost to have the building redesigned to minimize the long-term cost of air-conditioning. Ryan also conducts research and discovers that the tax credit available from the city will help cover the additional construction costs. ◀

SECTION 6

LANDLORD-TENANT RELATIONSHIPS

The property interest involved in a landlord-tenant relationship is known as a leasehold estate, as discussed earlier in this chapter. A landlord-tenant relationship is established by a lease contract. A **lease** contract arises when a property owner (landlord) agrees to give another party (the tenant) the exclusive right to possess the property—usually for a price and for a specified term. In most states, statutes require leases for terms exceeding one year to be in writing. The lease should describe the property and indicate the length of the term, the amount of the rent, and how and when it is to be paid.

State or local law often dictates permissible lease terms. For instance, a statute or ordinance might prohibit the leasing of a structure that is in a certain physical condition or is not in compliance with local building codes. As in other areas of law, the National Conference of Commissioners on Uniform State Laws has issued a model act to create more uniformity in the law governing landlord-tenant relations. Twenty-one states have adopted variations of the Uniform Residential Landlord and Tenant Act (URLTA).

Parties' Rights and Duties

The rights and duties of landlords and tenants generally pertain to four broad areas of concern—the possession, use, maintenance, and, of course, rent of leased property.

POSSESSION A landlord is obligated to give a tenant possession of the property that the tenant has agreed to lease. After obtaining possession, the tenant retains the property exclusively until the lease expires, unless the lease states otherwise.

The covenant of quiet enjoyment mentioned previously also applies to leased premises. Under this covenant, the landlord promises that during the lease term, neither the landlord nor anyone having a superior title to the property will disturb the tenant's use and enjoyment of the property. This covenant forms the essence of the landlord-tenant relationship, and if it is breached, the tenant can terminate the lease and sue for damages.

If the landlord deprives the tenant of possession of the leased property or interferes with the tenant's use or enjoyment of it, an **eviction** occurs. An eviction occurs, for instance, when the landlord changes the lock and refuses to give the tenant a new key. A **constructive eviction** occurs when the landlord wrongfully performs or fails to perform any of the duties the lease requires, thereby making the tenant's further use and enjoyment of the property exceedingly difficult or impossible. Examples of constructive eviction include a landlord's failure to provide heat in the winter, light, or other essential utilities.

USE AND MAINTENANCE OF THE PREMISES The tenant normally may make any use of the leased property, provided the use is legal and does not injure the landlord's interest. The parties are free to limit by agreement the uses to which the property may be put. A tenant is not entitled to create a nuisance by substantially interfering with others' quiet enjoyment of their property rights (see *Case in Point 49.1* for an example).

The tenant is responsible for any damage to the premises that he or she causes, intentionally or negligently. The landlord can hold the tenant liable for the cost of returning the property to the physical condition it was in at the lease's inception. The tenant usually is not responsible for ordinary wear and tear, and the property's consequent depreciation in value.

In some jurisdictions, landlords of residential property are required by statute to maintain the premises in good repair. Landlords must also comply with applicable state statutes and city ordinances regarding maintenance and repair of commercial buildings.

IMPLIED WARRANTY OF HABITABILITY A landlord who leases residential property is required to ensure that the premises are habitable—that is, in a safe and suitable condition for people to live there. Additionally, the landlord must make repairs to maintain the premises in that condition for the lease's duration.

Some state legislatures have enacted this warranty into law. In other jurisdictions, courts have based the warranty on the existence of a landlord's statutory duty to keep leased premises in good repair, or they have simply applied it as a matter of public policy. Generally, this warranty applies to major, or *substantial,* physical defects that the landlord knows or should know about and has had a reasonable time to repair—such as a large hole in the roof.

RENT *Rent* is the tenant's payment to the landlord for the tenant's occupancy or use of the landlord's real property. Usually, the tenant must pay the rent even if she or he refuses to occupy the property or moves out for unjustified reasons while the lease is in force. Under the common law, if the leased premises were destroyed by fire or flood, the tenant still had to pay rent. Today, however, if an apartment building burns down, most states' laws do not require tenants to continue to pay rent.

In some situations, such as when a landlord breaches the implied warranty of habitability, a tenant may be allowed to withhold rent as a remedy. When rent withholding is authorized under a statute, the tenant must usually put the amount withheld into an *escrow account.* This account is held in the name of the depositor (the tenant) and an *escrow agent* (usually, the court or a government agency), and the funds are returned to the depositor if the third party (the landlord) fails to make the premises habitable.

Transferring Rights to Leased Property

Either the landlord or the tenant may wish to transfer her or his rights to the leased property during the term of the lease. If the landlord sells the leased property, the tenant becomes the tenant of the new owner. The new owner may collect subsequent rent but must abide by the terms of the existing lease.

ASSIGNMENT The tenant's transfer of his or her entire interest in the leased property to a third person is an *assignment of the lease.* Many leases require that an assignment have the landlord's written consent. The landlord can nullify (avoid) an assignment made

without the required consent. State statutes may specify that the landlord may not unreasonably withhold consent, though. Furthermore, a landlord who knowingly accepts rent from the assignee may be held to have waived the consent requirement.

When an assignment is valid, the assignee acquires all of the tenant's rights under the lease. An assignment, however, does not release the original tenant (assignor) from the obligation to pay rent if the assignee defaults. Also, if the assignee exercises an option under the original lease to extend the term, the original tenant remains liable for the rent during the extension, unless the landlord agrees otherwise.

SUBLEASE The tenant's transfer of all or part of the premises for a period shorter than the lease term is a **sublease.** The same restrictions that apply to an assignment of the tenant's interest in leased property apply to a sublease. If the landlord's consent is required, a sublease without such permission is ineffective. Also, like an assignment, a sublease does not release the tenant from her or his obligations under the lease.

▶ **Example 49.21** Derek, a student, leases an apartment for a two-year period. Although Derek had planned on attending summer school, he decides to accept a job offer in Europe for the summer months instead. Derek therefore obtains his landlord's consent to sublease the apartment to Ava. Ava is bound by the same terms of the lease as Derek, and the landlord can hold Derek liable if Ava violates the lease terms. ◀

Termination of the Lease

Usually, a lease terminates when its term ends. The tenant surrenders the property to the landlord, who retakes possession. If the lease states the time it will end, the landlord is not required to give the tenant notice. The lease terminates automatically

A lease may also be terminated in several other ways. If the tenant purchases the leased property from the landlord during the term of the lease, for instance, the lease will be terminated. The parties may also agree to end a tenancy before it would otherwise terminate. The tenant may also *abandon* the premises—move out completely with no intention of returning before the lease term expires.

At common law, a tenant who abandoned leased property was still obligated to pay the rent for the full term of the lease. The landlord could let the property stand vacant and charge the tenant for the remainder of the term. This is still the rule in some states. In most states today, however, the landlord has a duty to *mitigate* his or her damages—that is, to make a reasonable attempt to lease the property to another party. Consequently, the tenant's liability for unpaid rent is restricted to the period of time that the landlord would reasonably need to lease the property to another tenant. Damages may also be allowed for the landlord's costs in leasing the property again.

Reviewing: Real Property and Landlord-Tenant Law

Vern Shoepke purchased a two-story home from Walter and Eliza Bruster in the town of Roche, Maine. The warranty deed did not specify what covenants would be included in the conveyance. The property was adjacent to a public park that included a popular Frisbee golf course. (Frisbee golf is a sport similar to golf but using Frisbees.) Wayakichi Creek ran along the north end of the park and along Shoepke's property. The deed allowed Roche citizens the right to walk across a five-foot-wide section of the lot beside Wayakichi Creek as part of a two-mile public trail system. Teenagers regularly threw Frisbee golf discs from the walking path behind Shoepke's property over his yard to the adjacent park. Shoepke habitually shouted and cursed at the teenagers, demanding that they not throw objects over his yard. Two months after moving into his Roche home, Shoepke leased the second floor to Lauren Slater for nine months. (The lease agreement did not specify that Shoepke's consent would be required to sublease the second floor.) After three months of tenancy, Slater sublet the second floor to a local artist, Javier Indalecio. Over the remaining six months, Indalecio's use of oil paints damaged the carpeting in Shoepke's home. Using the information presented in the chapter, answer the following questions.

1. What is the term for the right of Roche citizens to walk across Shoepke's land on the trail?
2. What covenants would most courts infer were included in the warranty deed that was used in the property transfer from the Brusters to Shoepke?
3. Suppose that Shoepke wants to file a trespass lawsuit against some teenagers who continually throw Frisbees over his land. Shoepke discovers, however, that when the city put in the Frisbee golf course, the neighborhood homeowners signed an agreement that limited their right to complain about errant Frisbees. What is this type of promise or agreement called in real property law?
4. Can Shoepke hold Slater financially responsible for the damage to the carpeting caused by Indalecio? Why or why not?

DEBATE THIS . . . *Under no circumstances should a local government be able to condemn property in order to sell it later to real estate developers for private use.*

Terms and Concepts

adverse possession 965
closing 961
commercial use 970
community property 958
concurrent ownership 957
condemnation 967
constructive eviction 972
conveyance 957

deed 963
easement 959
eminent domain 967
escrow account 961
eviction 972
fee simple absolute 956
fixed-term tenancy 958
grant deed 964

implication 959
implied warranty of habitability 961
industrial use 970
inverse condemnation 969
joint tenancy 957
lease 972
leasehold estate 958
license 960

ExamPrep

Issue Spotters

1. Bernie sells his house to Consuela under a warranty deed. Later, Delmira appears, holding a better title to the house than Consuela has. Delmira wants to have Consuela evicted from the property. What can Consuela do? **(See page 964.)**

2. Grey owns a commercial building in fee simple. Grey transfers temporary possession of the building to Haven Corporation. Can Haven transfer possession for even less time to Idyll Company? Explain. **(See page 956.)**

- Check your answers to the Issue Spotters against the answers provided in Appendix E at the end of this text.

Before the Test

Go to **www.cengagebrain.com**, enter the ISBN 9781285185248, and click on "Find" to locate this textbook's Web site. Then, click on "Access Now" under "Study Tools," and select Chapter 49 at the top. There, you will find a Practice Quiz that you can take to assess your mastery of the concepts in this chapter, as well as Flashcards and a Glossary of important terms.

Business Scenarios

49–1. Property Ownership. Madison owned a tract of land, but he was not sure that he had full title to the property. When Rafael expressed an interest in buying the land, Madison sold it to Rafael and executed a quitclaim deed. Rafael properly recorded the deed immediately. Several months later, Madison learned that he had had full title to the tract of land. He then sold the land to Linda by warranty deed. Linda knew of the earlier purchase by Rafael but took the deed anyway and later sued to have Rafael evicted from the land. Linda claimed that because she had a warranty deed, her title to the land was better than that conferred by Rafael's quitclaim deed. Will Linda succeed in claiming title to the land? Explain. **(See page 964.)**

49–2. Eviction. James owns a three-story building. He leases the ground floor to Juan's Mexican restaurant. The lease is to run for a five-year period and contains an express covenant of quiet enjoyment. One year later, James leases the top two stories to the Upbeat Club, a dance club for teens. The club's hours run from 5:00 P.M. to 11:00 P.M. The noise from the Upbeat Club is so loud that it is driving customers away from Juan's restaurant. Juan has notified

James of the interference and has called the police on a number of occasions. James refuses to talk to the owners of the Upbeat Club or to do anything to remedy the situation. Juan abandons the premises. James files a suit for breach of the lease agreement and for the rental payments still due under the lease. Juan claims that he was constructively evicted and files a countersuit for damages. Discuss who will be held liable. **(See page 972.)**

49–3. Implied Warranty of Habitability. Sarah has rented a house from Frank. The house is only two years old, but the roof leaks every time it rains. The water that has accumulated in the attic has caused plaster to fall off ceilings in the upstairs bedrooms, and one ceiling has started to sag. Sarah has complained to Frank and asked him to have the roof repaired. Frank says that he has caulked the roof, but the roof still leaks. Frank claims that because Sarah has sole control of the leased premises, she has the duty to repair the roof. Sarah insists that repairing the roof is Frank's responsibility. Discuss fully who is responsible for repairing the roof and, if the responsibility belongs to Frank, what remedies are available to Sarah. **(See page 972.)**

Business Case Problems

49–4. Ownership in Fee Simple. Thomas and Teresa Cline built a house on a 76-acre parcel of real estate next to Roy Berg's home and property in Augusta County, Virginia. The homes were about 1,800 feet apart but in view of each other. After several disagreements between the parties, Berg equipped an 11-foot tripod with motion sensors and floodlights that intermittently illuminated the Clines' home. Berg also installed surveillance cameras that tracked some of the movement on the Clines' property. The cameras transmitted on an open frequency that could be received by any television within range. The Clines asked Berg to turn off, or at least redirect, the lights. When he refused, they erected a fence for 200 feet along the parties' common property line. The 32-foot-high fence consisted of 20 utility poles spaced 10 feet apart with plastic wrap stretched between the poles. This effectively blocked the lights and cameras. Berg filed a suit against the Clines in a Virginia state court, complaining that the fence interfered unreasonably with his use and enjoyment of his property. He asked the court to order the Clines to take the fence down. What are the limits on an owner's use of property? How should the court rule in this case? Why? [*Cline v. Berg*, 273 Va. 142, 639 S.E.2d 231 (2007)] **(See page 956.)**

49–5. Commercial Lease Terms. Gi Hwa Park entered into a lease with Landmark HHH, LLC, for retail space in the Plaza at Landmark, a shopping center in Virginia. The lease required the landlord to keep the roof "in good repair" and the tenant to obtain insurance on her inventory and absolve the landlord from any losses to the extent of the insurance proceeds. Park opened a store—The Four Seasons—in the space, specializing in imported men's suits and accessories. Within a month and continuing for nearly eight years, water intermittently leaked through the roof, causing damage. Landmark eventually had a new roof installed, but water continued to leak into The Four Seasons. On a night of record rainfall, the store suffered substantial water damage, and Park was forced to close. On what basis might Park seek to recover from Landmark? What might Landmark assert in response? Which party's argument is more likely to succeed, and why? [*Landmark HHH, LLC v. Gi Hwa Park*, 277 Va. 50, 671 S.E.2d 143 (2009)] **(See page 972.)**

49–6. Adverse Possession. In 1974, the Mansells built a garage with a dirt floor at the back of their property. The structure went beyond the Mansells' property line and encroached approximately fourteen feet on the neighboring property. The neighbor knew of the encroachment and informally approved it, but did not transfer ownership of the property. In 2001, Betty Hunter bought the neighbor's property. The survey done at that time revealed the encroachment. In 2003, Hunter's attorney notified the Mansells about the encroachment, and the parties held some informal conversations but did not reach an agreement. In 2006, the Mansells installed a concrete foun-

dation and ran electricity to the structure. Hunter then sought a declaratory judgment that she was the fee simple owner of the property partially covered by the garage that encroached on her property. She demanded the removal of the encroaching structure. The Mansells filed a counterclaim, arguing that their possession of the property from 1974 to 2001 gave them ownership by adverse possession. The trial court held that the property still belonged to Hunter, but did not order removal of the garage. Hunter and Mrs. Mansell (whose husband had died in the meantime) both appealed. Did the open occupation of the property for twenty-eight years give Mansell title by adverse possession? Why or why not? [*Hunter v. Mansell*, 240 P.3d 469 (Colo.App. 2010)] **(See page 965.)**

49–7. BUSINESS CASE PROBLEM WITH SAMPLE ANSWER: Adverse Possession.

 The McKeag family operated a marina on their lakefront property in Bolton, New York. For more than forty years, the McKeags used a section of property belonging to their neighbors, the Finleys, as a beach for the marina's customers. The McKeags also stored a large float on the beach during the winter months, built their own retaining wall, and planted bushes and flowers there. The McKeags prevented others from using the property, including the Finleys. Nevertheless, the families always had a friendly relationship, and one of the Finleys gave the McKeags permission to continue using the beach in 1992. He also reminded them of his ownership several times, to which they said nothing. The McKeags also asked for permission to mow grass on the property and once apologized for leaving a jet ski there. Can the McKeags establish adverse possession over the statutory period of ten years? Why or why not? [McKeag v. Finley, 939 N.Y.S.2d 644 (N.Y.App.Div. 2012)] **(See page 965.)**

- **For a sample answer to Problem 49–7, go to Appendix F at the end of this text.**

49–8. SPECIAL CASE ANALYSIS: Eminent Domain.

 Go to Case Analysis Case 49.3, *Town of Midland v. Morris*, on pages 967–969. Read the excerpt and answer the following questions.

(a) **Issue:** On what issue did the parties ask the court to focus?

(b) **Rule of Law:** What rule or test did the court apply?

(c) **Applying the Rule of Law:** How did the court apply the rule to the facts in this case?

(d) **Conclusion:** What did the court conclude? Why?

49–9. A QUESTION OF ETHICS: Seller's Duty to Disclose.

 In 1999, Stephen and Linda Kailin bought the Monona Center, a mall in Madison, Wisconsin, from Perry Armstrong for $760,000. The contract provided, "Seller represents to Buyer that as of the date of acceptance Seller had no notice or knowledge of condi-

tions affecting the Property or transaction" other than certain items disclosed at the time of the offer. Armstrong told the Kailins of the Center's eight tenants, their lease expiration dates, and the monthly and annual rent due under each lease. One of the lessees, Ring's All-American Karate, occupied about a third of the Center's space under a five-year lease. Because of Ring's financial difficulties, Armstrong had agreed to reduce its rent for nine months in 1997. By the time of the sale to the Kailins, Ring owed $13,910 in unpaid rent, but Armstrong did not tell the Kailins, who did not ask. Ring continued to fail to pay rent and finally vacated the Center. The Kailins filed a suit in a Wisconsin state court against Armstrong and others, alleging, among other things, misrepresentation. [Kailin v. Armstrong, *2002 WI App 70, 252 Wis.2d 676, 643 N.W.2d 132 (2002)*] **(See page 962.)**

(a) Did Armstrong have a duty to disclose Ring's delinquency and default to the Kailins? Explain.

(b) What obligation, if any, did Ring have to the Kailins or Armstrong after failing to pay the rent and eventually defaulting on the lease? Discuss.

Legal Reasoning Group Activity

49–10. Adverse Possession. The Wallen family owned a cabin on Lummi Island in the state of Washington. A driveway ran from the cabin across their property to South Nugent Road. Floyd Massey bought the adjacent lot and built a cabin on it in 1980. To gain access to his property, Massey used a bulldozer to extend the driveway, without the Wallens' permission but also without their objection. In 2005, the Wallens sold their property to Wright Fish Company. Massey continued to use and maintain the driveway without permission or objection. In 2011, Massey sold his property to Robert Drake. Drake and his employees continued to use and maintain the driveway without permission or objection, although Drake knew it was located largely on Wright's property. In 2013, Wright sold its lot to Robert Smersh. The next year, Smersh told Drake to stop using the driveway. Drake filed a suit against Smersh, claiming an easement by prescription (which is created by meeting the same requirements as adverse possession). **(See page 965.)**

(a) The first group will decide whether Drake's use of the driveway meets all of the requirements for adverse possession (easement by prescription).

(b) The second group will determine how the court should rule in this case and why. Does it matter that Drake knew the driveway was located largely on Wright's (and then Smersh's) property? Should it matter? Why or why not?

(c) A third group will evaluate the underlying policy and fairness of adverse possession laws. Should the law reward persons who take possession of someone else's land for their own use? Does it make sense to punish owners who allow someone else to use their land without complaint? Explain.

CHAPTER 50

INSURANCE

Protecting against loss is a fore-most concern of all property owners. No one can predict whether an accident or a fire will occur, so individuals and businesses typically protect their personal and financial interests by obtaining insurance.

Insurance is a contract in which the insurance company (the insurer) promises to pay or otherwise compensate another (either the insured or the benefi-ciary) for a particular loss. Insurance may provide for compensation in the event of (1) the injury or death of the insured or another, (2) damage to the insured's property, or (3) other types of losses, such as those resulting from lawsuits. Basically, insurance is an arrangement for *transferring and allocating risk*. In general, **risk** can be described as a prediction concerning potential loss based on known and unknown factors.

Risk management normally involves the transfer of certain risks from the individual to the insurance company by a contractual agreement. We examine the insurance contract and its provisions in this chapter. First, how-ever, we look at some basic insurance terminology and concepts.

SECTION 1
INSURANCE TERMINOLOGY AND CONCEPTS

Like other legal areas, insurance has its own special concepts and terminology. An insurance contract is called a **policy.** The consideration paid to the insurer is called a **premium,** and the insurance company is sometimes called an **underwriter.** The parties to an insurance policy are the *insurer* (the insurance company) and the *insured* (the person covered by its provisions).

Insurance contracts usually are obtained through an *agent,* who normally works for the insurance company, or through a *broker,* who is ordinarily an *independent contractor.* When a broker deals with an applicant for insurance, the broker is, in effect, the applicant's agent (and not an agent of the insurance company).

In contrast, an insurance agent is an agent of the insurance company, not an agent of the applicant. Thus, the agent owes fiduciary duties to the insurer (the insurance company), but not to the person who is applying for insurance. As a general rule, the insur-ance company is bound by the acts of its agents when they act within the scope of the agency relationship (see Chapters 32 and 33). In most situations, state law determines the status of all parties writing or obtain-ing insurance.

Classifications of Insurance

Insurance is classified according to the nature of the risk involved. Fire insurance, casualty insurance, life insur-ance, and title insurance apply to different types of risk and protect different persons and interests. This is rea-sonable because the types of losses that are expected and the types that are foreseeable or unforeseeable vary with the nature of the activity. Exhibit 50–1 on the following page provides a list of common insurance classifications.

Insurable Interest

A person must have an **insurable interest** in some-thing in order to insure it. Without an insurable interest, there is no enforceable contract, and a trans-action to purchase insurance coverage would have to be treated as a wager. The existence of an insurable interest is a primary concern in determining liability under an insurance policy.

LIFE INSURANCE In regard to life insurance, a person must have a reasonable expectation of benefit from the

EXHIBIT 50–1 Selected Insurance Classifications

Type of Insurance	Coverage
Accident	Covers expenses, losses, and suffering incurred by the insured because of accidents causing physical injury and any consequent disability; sometimes includes a specified payment to heirs of the insured if death results from an accident.
All-Risk	Covers all losses that the insured may incur except those that are specifically excluded. Typical exclusions are losses due to war, pollution, earthquakes, and floods.
Automobile	May cover damage to automobiles resulting from specified hazards or occurrences (such as fire, vandalism, theft, or collision); normally provides protection against liability for personal injuries and property damage resulting from the operation of the vehicle.
Casualty	Protects against losses incurred by the insured as a result of being held liable for personal injuries or property damage sustained by others.
Decreasing-Term Life	Provides life insurance; requires uniform payments over the life (term) of the policy, but with a decreasing face value (amount of coverage).
Disability	Replaces a portion of the insured's monthly income from employment in the event that illness or injury causes a short- or long-term disability. Some states require employers to provide short-term disability insurance. Benefits typically last a set period of time, such as six months for short-term coverage or five years for long-term coverage.
Employer's Liability	Insures an employer against liability for injuries or losses sustained by employees during the course of their employment. Covers claims not covered under workers' compensation insurance.
Fire	Covers losses to the insured caused by fire.
Floater	Covers movable property, as long as the property is within the territorial boundaries specified in the contract.
Health	Covers expenses incurred by the insured resulting from physical injury or illness and other expenses relating to health and life maintenance.
Homeowners'	Protects homeowners against some or all risks of loss to their residences and the residences' contents or liability arising from the use of the property.
Key-Person	Protects a business in the event of the death or disability of a key employee.
Liability	Protects against liability imposed on the insured as a result of injuries to the person or property of another.
Life	Covers the death of the policyholder. On the death of the insured, the insurer pays the amount specified in the policy to the insured's beneficiary.
Major Medical	Protects the insured against major hospital, medical, or surgical expenses.
Malpractice	A form of liability insurance that protects professionals (physicians, lawyers, and others) against malpractice claims brought against them by their patients or clients.
Mortgage	Covers a mortgage loan. The insurer pays the balance of the mortgage to the creditor on the death or disability of the debtor.
Term Life	Provides life insurance for a specified period of time (term) with no cash surrender value. It usually is renewable.

continued life of another to have an insurable interest in that person's life. The insurable interest must exist *at the time the policy is obtained*. The benefit may be pecuniary (monetary), or it may be founded on the relationship between the parties (by blood or affinity).

Close family relationships give a person an insurable interest in the life of another. For instance, a husband can take out an insurance policy on his wife and vice versa, or parents can take out life insurance policies on their children. A policy that a person takes out on his or her spouse remains valid even if they divorce, unless a specific provision in the policy calls for its termination on divorce.

KEY-PERSON LIFE INSURANCE *Key-person insurance* is insurance obtained by an organization on the life of a person who is important to that organization. Because the organization expects to experience some financial gain from the continuation of the key person's life or some financial loss from the key person's death, the organization has an insurable interest. Typically, a small company will insure the lives of its important employees because the firm will sustain some degree of loss if they die. Similarly, a corporation has an insurable interest in the life of a key executive (such as a talented CEO) whose death would result in financial loss to the company. If a firm insures a key person's life and that person leaves the firm and subsequently dies, the firm can collect on the insurance policy, provided that it has continued to pay the premiums.

PROPERTY INSURANCE For property insurance, the insurable interest must exist at the time the loss occurs but need not exist when the policy is purchased. The existence of an insurable interest is a primary concern in determining liability under an insurance policy.

▶ **Case in Point 50.1** ABM Industries, Inc., operated the heating, ventilation, and air-conditioning systems at the World Trade Center (WTC) in New York City in 2001. ABM also maintained all of the WTC's common areas. At the time, ABM employed more than eight hundred workers at the WTC. Zurich American Insurance Company insured ABM against losses resulting from "business interruption" caused by direct physical loss or damage "to property owned, controlled, used, leased or intended for use" by ABM.

After the terrorist attacks on September 11, ABM filed a claim to recover for the loss of all income derived from its WTC operations. Zurich argued that the recovery should be limited to the income lost as a result of the destruction of ABM's office and storage space and supplies. A federal appellate court, however, ruled that ABM was entitled to compensation for the loss of all of its WTC operations. The court reasoned that the "policy's scope expressly includes real or personal property that the insured 'used,' 'controlled,' or 'intended for use.' " Because ABM's income depended on "the common areas and leased premises in the WTC complex," it had an insurable interest in that property at the time of the loss.[1] ◀

1. *Zurich American Insurance Co. v. ABM Industries, Inc.,* 397 F.3d 158 (2d Cir. 2005).

THE INSURANCE CONTRACT

An insurance contract is governed by the general principles of contract law, although the insurance industry is heavily regulated by each state.[2] Customarily, a party offers to purchase insurance by submitting an application to the insurance company.

The company can either accept or reject the offer. Sometimes, the insurance company's acceptance is conditional—on the results of a life insurance applicant's medical examination, for instance. For the insurance contract to be binding, consideration (in the form of a premium) must be given, and the parties forming the contract must have the required contractual capacity to do so.

Application for Insurance

The filled-in application form for insurance is usually attached to the policy and made a part of the insurance contract. Thus, an insurance applicant is bound by any false statements that appear in the application (subject to certain exceptions). Because the insurance company evaluates the risk based on the information included in the insurance application, misstatements or misrepresentations can void a policy, especially if the insurance company can show that it would not have extended insurance if it had known the facts.

Effective Date

The effective date of an insurance contract—that is, the date on which the insurance coverage begins—is important. In some situations, the insurance applicant is not protected until a formal written policy is issued. For instance, if the parties agree that the policy will be issued and delivered at a later time, the contract is not effective until the policy is issued and delivered. Thus, any loss sustained between the time of application and the delivery of the policy is not covered.

Also, remember that a broker is an agent of the applicant, not an agent of the insurance company. Therefore, if a person hires a broker to obtain insurance, and the broker fails to procure a policy, the applicant normally is not insured.

2. The states were given authority to regulate the insurance industry by the McCarran-Ferguson Act of 1945, 15 U.S.C. Sections 1011–1015.

BINDER In other situations, the applicant is protected between the time the application is received and the time the insurance company either accepts or rejects it. A person who is obtaining insurance from an insurance company's agent is usually protected from the moment the application is made, provided that some form of premium has been paid. Usually, the agent will write a memorandum, or **binder,** indicating that a policy is pending and stating its essential terms. The binder provides temporary coverage until a formal policy is accepted or denied.

LIFE INSURANCE Parties may agree that a life insurance policy will be binding at the time the insured pays the first premium, or the policy may be expressly contingent on the applicant's passing a physical examination. If the applicant pays the premium and passes the examination, then the policy coverage is continuously in effect. If the applicant pays the premium but dies before having the physical examination, the policy may still be effective. Then, in order to collect, the applicant's estate normally must show that the applicant would have passed the examination had he or she not died.

Provisions and Clauses

Some of the important provisions and clauses contained in insurance contracts are discussed in the following subsections and listed in Exhibit 50–2 below.

PROVISIONS MANDATED BY STATUTE If a statute mandates that a certain provision be included in insurance contracts, a court will interpret the insurance policy as containing that provision. If a statute requires that any limitations regarding coverage be stated in the contract, a court will not allow an insurer to avoid liability for a claim through reliance on an unexpressed restriction.

INCONTESTABILITY CLAUSES Statutes commonly require that a policy for life or health insurance include an **incontestability clause.** Such a clause provides that after the policy has been in force for a specified length of time—often two or three years—the insurer cannot contest statements made in the application.

Once a policy becomes incontestable, the insurer cannot later avoid a claim on the basis of, for instance, fraud on the part of the insured, unless the clause provides an exception for that circumstance. The clause does not prevent an insurer from asserting other defenses to a claim, such as the nonpayment of premiums, failure to file proof of death, or lack of an insurable interest.

COINSURANCE CLAUSES Often, when taking out fire insurance policies, property owners insure their property

EXHIBIT 50–2 Insurance Contract Provisions and Clauses

Type of Clause	Definition
Antilapse Clause	An antilapse clause provides that a life insurance policy will not automatically lapse if no payment is made on the date due. Ordinarily, under such a provision, the insured has a *grace period* of thirty or thirty-one days within which to pay an overdue premium before the policy is canceled.
Appraisal Clause	Insurance policies frequently provide that if the parties cannot agree on the amount of a loss covered under the policy or the value of the property lost, an appraisal, or estimate, by an impartial and qualified third party can be demanded.
Arbitration Clause	Many insurance policies include clauses that call for arbitration of any disputes that arise between the insurer and the insured concerning the settlement of claims.
Coinsurance Clause	Many property insurance policies include a coinsurance clause that applies in the event of a partial loss and determines what percentage of the value of the property must be insured for an owner to be fully reimbursed for a loss. If the owner insures the property up to a specified percentage (typically 80 percent) of its value, she or he will recover any loss up to the face amount of the policy.
Incontestability Clause	An incontestability clause provides that after a policy has been in force for a specified length of time—usually two or three years—the insurer cannot contest statements made in the application.
Multiple Insurance Clause	Many insurance policies include a clause providing that if the insured has multiple insurance policies that cover the same property and the amount of coverage exceeds the loss, the loss will be shared proportionately by the insurance companies.

for less than full value because most fires do not result in a total loss. To encourage owners to insure their property for an amount as close to full value as possible, fire insurance policies generally include a coinsurance clause.

Typically, a **coinsurance clause** provides that if the owner insures the property up to a specified percentage—usually 80 percent—of its value, she or he will recover any loss up to the face amount of the policy. If the insurance is for less than the fixed percentage, the owner is responsible for a proportionate share of the loss. In effect, the owner becomes a coinsurer.

Coinsurance applies only in instances of partial loss. The amount of the recovery is calculated by using the following formula:

$$\text{Loss} \times \left(\frac{\text{Amount of Insurance Coverage}}{\text{Coinsurance Percentage} \times \text{Property Value}} \right) = \frac{\text{Amount of}}{\text{Recovery}}$$

▶ **Example 50.2** Madison, who owns property valued at $200,000, takes out a policy in the amount of $100,000. If Madison then suffers a loss of $80,000, her recovery will be $50,000. Madison will be responsible for (coinsure) the balance of the loss, or $30,000, which is the amount of loss ($80,000) minus the amount of recovery ($50,000).

$$\$80,000 \times \left(\frac{\$100,000}{0.8 \times \$200,000} \right) = \$50,000$$

If Madison had taken out a policy in the amount of 80 percent of the value of the property, or $160,000, then according to the same formula, she would have recovered the full amount of the loss (the face amount of the policy). ◀

APPRAISAL AND ARBITRATION CLAUSES Most fire insurance policies provide that if the parties cannot agree on the amount of a loss covered under the policy or on the value of the property lost, an *appraisal* can be demanded. An appraisal is an estimate of the property's value determined by a suitably qualified individual who has no interest in the property. Typically, two appraisers are used, with one appointed by each party. A third party, or umpire, may be called on to resolve differences. Other types of insurance policies also contain provisions for appraisal and arbitration when the insured and insurer disagree on the value of a loss.

MULTIPLE INSURANCE COVERAGE Sometimes, an insured has *multiple insurance coverage*—that is, policies with several companies covering the same insurable interest. If the amount of coverage exceeds the loss, the insured can collect from each insurer only the company's proportionate share of the liability, relative to the total amount of insurance.

Many fire insurance policies include a pro rata clause, which requires that all carriers proportionately share in any loss. ▶ **Example 50.3** Green insured $50,000 worth of property with two companies. Each policy had a liability limit of $40,000. If the property is totally destroyed, Green can collect only $25,000 from each insurer. ◀

ANTILAPSE CLAUSES A life insurance policy may provide, or a statute may require a policy to provide, that it will not automatically lapse if no payment is made on the date due. Ordinarily, under an **antilapse provision,** the insured has a *grace period* of thirty or thirty-one days within which to pay an overdue premium.

If the insured fails to pay a premium altogether, there are alternatives to cancellation:

1. The insurer may be required to extend the insurance for a period of time.
2. The insurer may issue a policy with less coverage to reflect the amount of the payments made.
3. The insurer may pay to the insured the policy's **cash surrender value**—the amount the insurer has agreed to pay on the policy's cancellation before the insured's death. (This value depends on the period that the policy has already run, the amount of the premium, the insured's age and life expectancy, and amounts to be repaid on any outstanding loans taken out against the policy.)

When the insurance contract states that the insurer cannot cancel the policy, these alternatives are important.

Interpreting Provisions of an Insurance Contract

The courts recognize that most people do not have the special training necessary to understand the intricate terminology used in insurance policies. Therefore, when disputes arise, the courts will interpret the words used in an insurance contract according to their ordinary meanings in light of the nature of the coverage involved.

When there is an ambiguity in the policy, the provision generally is interpreted *against the insurance company*. Also, when it is unclear whether an insurance contract actually exists because the written policy has not been delivered, the uncertainty normally is resolved against the insurance company. The court presumes that the policy is in effect unless the company can show otherwise. Similarly, an insurer must make sure that the insured is adequately notified of any change in coverage under an existing policy.

Disputes over insurance often focus on the application of exclusions in the policy, as the following case illustrates.

CASE 50.1

Valero v. Florida Insurance Guaranty Association, Inc.
District Court of Appeal of Florida, Fourth District, 59 So.3d 1166 (2011).

COMPANY PROFILE Florida Insurance Guaranty Association, Inc. (FIGA), is a nonprofit corporation created by the Florida legislature. FIGA evaluates the outstanding claims of Florida policyholders of property and casualty insurance companies that have become insolvent and have been ordered to liquidate. FIGA attempts to resolve those claims that must be paid to avoid hardship for the claimants. Similar guaranty associations exist in every state, the District of Columbia, Puerto Rico, and the Virgin Islands. Since the start of the property and casualty guaranty association system, there have been about six hundred insolvencies. The system has paid out about $24.2 billion.

BACKGROUND AND FACTS Alberto and Karelli Mila were insured under a liability policy. The policy, in "exclusion k," stated that coverage did not apply to "bodily injury arising out of sexual molestation, corporal punishment or physical or metal abuse." Verushka Valero, on behalf of her child, filed a suit in a Florida state court against the Milas, charging them with negligent supervision of a perpetrator who sexually molested Valero's child. The Milas filed a claim with their insurer to provide a defense against the charges. The insurer had become insolvent. The claim was submitted to FIGA. The association refused to pay the Milas' claim and asked the court to rule that it had no obligation under the policy to provide such a defense. The court issued a summary judgment in FIGA's favor. Valero and the Milas appealed, arguing that exclusion k was ambiguous.

 IN THE LANGUAGE OF THE COURT
GERBER, J. [Judge]

* * * *

The policy at issue contains a list of twelve enumerated exclusions stating that coverage did not apply to bodily injury [arising out of certain circumstances].

* * * *

The insureds argued in the [lower] court that exclusion k. is ambiguous because exclusion *l.* expressly states that it applies to bodily injury "arising out of the use or sale * * * by any person of a Controlled Substance," whereas exclusion k. does not expressly refer to sexual molestation "by any person." However, reading all twelve exclusions together, we believe that the insurer's use of the phrase "by any person" in exclusion *l.* is merely superfluous [unessential] and does not create an ambiguity [vagueness] in exclusion k. or in exclusions d. through i., which also do not use the phrase "by any person." For example, exclusion i. states that coverage does not apply to bodily injury "caused * * * by war." It would make no sense for that exclusion to apply only if war was caused "by an insured."

In practical terms, assuming that "any person" who commits sexual molestation can be an uninsured person, a situation logically must exist in which the insurer then can apply the sexual molestation exclusion to deny coverage to an insured person. That situation presumably would occur where the sexual molestation victim seeks to impose liability against the insured person on

CASE 50.1 CONTINUES ➡

CASE 50.1 CONTINUED some theory of indirect liability such as negligent supervision. In that situation, the insurer would be able to apply the sexual molestation exclusion to deny coverage to an insured person, regardless of the theory pled. That is the situation which exists here. Thus, the [lower] court reached the right result by recognizing the insurer's ability to deny coverage in this case. [Emphasis added.]

* * * *

Both sides have encouraged us to interpret the exclusion at issue in isolation by comparing other jurisdictions' interpretations of identical or similar exclusions. For example, the insurer has cited cases from other jurisdictions holding that identical or similar exclusions preclude coverage for an insured. Conversely, the alleged victim and the insureds have cited cases from other jurisdictions holding that similar exclusions do not preclude coverage for an insured.

We respect other jurisdictions' decisions. However, those decisions are not helpful here because the other jurisdictions examined the exclusions at issue only in isolation. We have had the benefit of considering the exclusion at issue in context with the entire exclusions section. Thus, we leave for another day the interpretation of an identical or similar exclusion for which we lack the context available to us here.

DECISION AND REMEDY *A state intermediate appellate court affirmed the lower court's judgment. The court agreed that the language in the Milas' policy excluding coverage for "bodily injury arising out of sexual molestation" was clear and unambiguous. The exclusion applied to preclude coverage in this case.*

WHAT IF THE FACTS WERE DIFFERENT? *Suppose that exclusion k, instead of exclusion l, has used the phrase "by any person." Would the result have been different? Explain.*

THE ECONOMIC DIMENSION *Why did Valero and the Milas appeal the lower court's judgment in the insurer's favor?*

Cancellation

The insured can cancel a policy at any time, and the insurer can cancel under certain circumstances. When an insurance company can cancel its insurance contract, the policy or a state statute usually requires that the insurer give advance written notice of the cancellation. The same requirement applies when only part of a policy is canceled. Any premium paid in advance and not yet earned may be refundable on the policy's cancellation. The insured may also be entitled to a life insurance policy's cash surrender value.

The insurer may cancel an insurance policy for various reasons, depending on the type of insurance. For example:

1. Automobile insurance can be canceled for nonpayment of premiums or suspension of the insured's driver's license.
2. Property insurance can be canceled for nonpayment of premiums or for other reasons, including the insured's fraud or misrepresentation, gross negligence, or conviction for a crime that increases the risk assumed by the insurer.
3. Life and health policies can be canceled because of false statements made by the insured in the appli-

cation, but the cancellation must take place before the effective date of an incontestability clause.

An insurer cannot cancel—or refuse to renew—a policy for discriminatory reasons or other reasons that violate public policy. Also, an insurer cannot cancel a policy because the insured has appeared as a witness in a case brought against the company.

Duties and Obligations of the Parties

Both parties to an insurance contract are responsible for the obligations they assume under the contract (contract law was discussed in Chapters 11 through 19). In addition, both the insured and the insurer have an implied duty to act in good faith.

DUTIES OF THE INSURED Good faith requires the party who is applying for insurance to reveal everything necessary for the insurer to evaluate the risk. In other words, the applicant must disclose all material facts, including all facts that an insurer would consider in determining whether to charge a higher premium or to refuse to issue a policy altogether. Many insurance companies today require that an applicant give the company permission to access other information, such as private medical records and credit ratings, for the purpose of evaluating the risk.

Once the insurance policy is issued, the insured has three basic duties under the contract:

1. To pay the premiums as stated in the contract.
2. To notify the insurer within a reasonable time if an event occurs that gives rise to a claim.
3. To cooperate with the insurer during any investigation or litigation.

DUTIES OF THE INSURER Once the insurer has accepted the risk, and some event occurs that gives rise to a claim, the insurer has a *duty to investigate* to determine the facts. When a policy provides insur-ance against third party claims, the insurer is obligated to make reasonable efforts to settle such a claim.

If a settlement cannot be reached, then regardless of the claim's merit, the insurer has a *duty to defend* any suit against the insured. Usually, a policy provides that in this situation the insured must *cooperate* in the defense and attend hearings and trials if necessary. The insurer also owes a *duty to pay* any legitimate claims up to the face amount of the policy.

An insurer has a duty to provide or pay an attorney to defend its insured when a complaint alleges facts that could, if proved, impose liability on the insured within the policy's coverage. In the following case, the question was whether a policy covered a dentist's potential liability arising from a practical joke that he played on an employee while performing a dental procedure.

CASE 50.2

Woo v. Fireman's Fund Insurance Co.
Supreme Court of Washington, 161 Wash.2d 43, 164 P.3d 454 (2007).

BACKGROUND AND FACTS   Tina Alberts worked for Robert Woo as a dental surgical assistant. Her family raised potbellied pigs, and she often talked about them at work. Sometimes, Woo mentioned the pigs, intending to encourage a "friendly working environment." Alberts interpreted the comments as offensive. Alberts asked Woo to replace two of her teeth with implants. The procedure required the installation of temporary partial bridges called "flippers." While Alberts was anesthetized, Woo installed a set of flippers shaped like boar tusks, as a joke, and took photos. Before Alberts regained consciousness, he inserted the normal flippers. A month later, Woo's staff gave Alberts the photos at a gathering to celebrate her birthday. Stunned, Alberts refused to return to work. Woo tried to apologize. Alberts filed a suit in a Washington state court against him, alleging battery and other torts. He asked Fireman's Fund Insurance Company to defend him, claiming coverage under his policy. The insurer refused. Woo settled the suit with Alberts for $250,000 and filed a suit against Fireman's, claiming that it had breached its duty to defend him. The court awarded him $750,000 in damages plus the amount of the settlement and attorneys' fees and costs. A state intermediate appellate court reversed the award. Woo appealed to the Washington Supreme Court.

🔨 **IN THE LANGUAGE OF THE COURT**
FAIRHURST, J. [Justice]

* * * *

The professional liability provision states that Fireman's will defend any claim brought against the insured "even if the allegations of the claim are groundless, false or fraudulent." It defines "dental services" as "all services which are performed in the practice of the dentistry profession as defined in the business and professional codes of the state where you are licensed." [Revised Code of Washington (RCW) Section] 18.32.020 * * * states:

> A person practices dentistry * * * who * * * undertakes by any means or methods to diagnose, treat, remove stains or concretions from teeth, operate or prescribe for any disease, pain, injury, deficiency, deformity, or physical condition of the same, or take impressions of the teeth or jaw, or * * * owns, maintains or operates an office for the practice of dentistry * * * .

CASE 50.2 CONTINUES ➡

CASE 50.2 CONTINUED

* * * [Woo] claims the joke was "intertwined with employee and patient relationships, areas of Woo's ownership and operation of the dental office." Fireman's responds that the allegations in Alberts' complaint unambiguously establish that Woo's practical joke was not connected to treating Alberts' condition. It asserts the boar tusk flippers were not intended to replace Alberts' teeth—they were intended only as a practical joke. Fireman's also asserts that insertion of the boar tusk flippers was not covered under the professional liability provision because Woo "interrupted his rendering of dental services."

* * * *

* * * In addition to covering the rendering of dental services, *the professional liability provision covers ownership, maintenance, or operation of an office for the practice of dentistry* and Alberts' complaint alleged Woo's practical joke took place while Woo was conducting his dental practice. The insertion of the boar tusk flippers was also intertwined with Woo's dental practice because it involved an interaction with an employee. [Emphasis added.]

Moreover, Woo's practical joke did not interrupt the dental surgery procedure, as Fireman's argues. * * * The acts that comprised the practical joke were integrated into and inseparable from the overall procedure.

In sum, Alberts' complaint alleges that Woo inserted a flipper, albeit oddly shaped, during a dental surgery procedure while he was operating an office for the practice of dentistry. * * * Because [Revised Code of Washington Section] 18.32.020 defines the practice of dentistry so broadly, the fact that his acts occurred during the operation of a dental practice conceivably brought his actions within the professional liability provision of his insurance policy.

DECISION AND REMEDY *The Washington Supreme Court held that Fireman's had a duty to defend Woo under the professional liability provision of his policy because "the insertion of boar tusk flippers in Alberts' mouth conceivably fell within the policy's broad definition of the practice of dentistry." The state supreme court reversed the decision of the lower court.*

THE ETHICAL DIMENSION *Are the acts of the principal parties—Woo, Alberts, and Fireman's—ethically justifiable in the circumstances of this case? Discuss.*

THE LEGAL ENVIRONMENT DIMENSION *In determining if an insurer has a duty to defend an insured, should a court ask whether the insured had a "reasonable expectation" of coverage? Explain.*

BAD FAITH ACTIONS Although insurance law generally follows contract law, most states now recognize a "bad faith" tort action against insurers. Thus, if an insurer in bad faith denies coverage of a claim, the insured may sue. If successful, the insured can recover an amount exceeding the policy's coverage limits and may also recover punitive damages. Some courts have held insurers liable for a bad faith refusal to settle claims for reasonable amounts within the policy limits.[3]

Defenses against Payment

An insurance company can raise any of the defenses that would be valid in an ordinary action on a contract, as well as the following defenses:

1. *Fraud or misrepresentation.* If the insurance company can show that the policy was procured through fraud or misrepresentation, it may have a valid defense for not paying on a claim. (The insurance company may also have the right to disaffirm or rescind the insurance contract.)

2. *Lack of insurable interest.* An absolute defense exists if the insurer can show that the insured lacked an insurable interest—thus rendering the policy void from the beginning.

3. *Illegal actions of the insured.* Improper actions, such as those that are against public policy or that are otherwise illegal, can also give the insurance company a defense against the payment of a claim or allow it to rescind the contract.

In some situations, the insurance company may be prevented, or estopped, from asserting defenses that normally are available. For instance, an insur-

---

3. See *Columbia National Insurance Co. v. Freeman,* 347 Ark. 423, 64 S.W.3d 720 (2002); and *Selman v. Metropolitan Life Insurance Co.,* 372 Ark. 420, 277 S.W.3d 196 (2008).

ance company ordinarily cannot escape payment on the death of an insured on the ground that the person's age was stated incorrectly on the application. Also, incontestability clauses prevent the insurer from asserting certain defenses.

SECTION 3
TYPES OF INSURANCE

There are four general types of insurance coverage: life insurance, fire and homeowners' insurance, automobile insurance, and business liability insurance. We now examine briefly the coverage available under each of these types of insurance.

Life Insurance

There are five basic types of life insurance:

1. **Whole life** provides protection with an accumulated cash surrender value that can be used as collateral for a loan. The insured pays premiums during his or her entire lifetime, and the beneficiary receives a fixed payment on the death of the insured. (It is also sometimes referred to as straight life, ordinary life, or cash-value insurance.)
2. **Limited-payment life** is a type of policy under which premiums are paid for a stated number of years. After that time, the policy is paid up and fully effective during the insured's life. For instance, a policy might call for twenty payments. Naturally, premiums are higher than for whole life. This insurance also has a cash surrender value.
3. **Term insurance** is a type of policy for which premiums are paid for a specified term. Payment on the policy is due only if death occurs within the term period. Premiums are lower than for whole life or limited-payment life, and there usually is no cash surrender value. Frequently, this type of insurance can be converted to another type of life insurance.
4. **Endowment insurance** involves fixed premium payments that are made for a definite term. At the end of the term, a fixed amount is paid to the insured or, on the death of the insured during the specified period, to a beneficiary. Thus, this type of insurance represents both term insurance and a form of **annuity** (the right to receive fixed, periodic payments for life or—as in this instance—for a term of years). Endowment insurance has a rapidly increasing cash surrender value,

but premiums are high because a payment must be made at the end of the term even if the insured is still living.
5. **Universal life** combines aspects of both term insurance and whole life insurance. From every payment, usually called a "contribution," the issuing life insurance company makes two deductions. The first is a charge for term insurance protection. The second is for company expenses and profit. The funds that remain after these deductions earn interest for the policyholder at a rate determined by the company. The interest-earning amount is called the policy's *cash value,* but that term does not mean the same thing as it does for a traditional whole life insurance policy. With a universal life policy, the cash value grows at a variable interest rate rather than at a predetermined rate.

The rights and liabilities of the parties to life insurance contracts are basically dependent on the specific contract. A few features deserve special attention.

LIABILITY The life insurance contract determines not only the extent of the insurer's liability but also, generally, whether the insurer is liable on the death of the insured. Most life insurance contracts exclude liability for death caused by suicide, military action during war, execution by a state or federal government, and even an event that occurs while the insured is a passenger in a commercial vehicle. In the absence of contractual exclusion, most courts today construe any cause of death to be one of the insurer's risks.

ADJUSTMENT DUE TO MISSTATEMENT OF AGE The insurance policy constitutes the agreement between the parties. The application for insurance is part of the policy and is usually attached to the policy. When the insured misstates his or her age on the application, an error is introduced, particularly as to the amount of premiums paid. As mentioned, misstatement of age is not a material error sufficient to allow the insurer to void the policy. Instead, on discovery of the error, the insurer will adjust the premium payments and/or benefits accordingly.

ASSIGNMENT Most life insurance policies allow the insured to change beneficiaries. When this is permitted, in the absence of any prohibition or notice requirement, the insured can assign the rights to the policy (for instance, as security for a loan) without the consent of the insurer or the beneficiary.

If the beneficiary's right is *vested*—that is, has become absolute, entitling the beneficiary to payment of the proceeds—the policy cannot be assigned without the beneficiary's consent. For the most part, life insurance contracts permit assignment and require notice only to the insurer to be effective.

CREDITORS' RIGHTS Unless insurance proceeds are exempt under state law, the insured's interest in life insurance is an asset that is subject to the rights of judgment creditors. These creditors generally can reach all of the following:

1. Insurance proceeds payable to the insured's estate.
2. Insurance proceeds payable to anyone if the payment of premiums constituted a fraud on creditors.
3. Insurance proceeds payable to a named beneficiary unless the beneficiary's rights have vested.

Creditors, however, cannot compel the insured to make available the cash surrender value of the policy or to change the named beneficiary to that of the creditor. Almost all states exempt at least a part of the proceeds of life insurance from creditors' claims.

TERMINATION Although the insured can cancel and terminate the policy, the insurer generally cannot do so. Therefore, termination usually takes place only if one of the following occurs:

1. Default in premium payments, which causes the policy to lapse.
2. Death and payment of benefits.
3. Expiration of the term of the policy.
4. Cancellation by the insured.

Fire and Homeowners' Insurance

There are basically two types of insurance policies for a home: standard fire insurance policies and homeowners' policies.

STANDARD FIRE INSURANCE POLICIES The standard fire insurance policy protects the homeowner against fire and lightning, as well as damage from smoke and water caused by the fire or the fire department. Most fire insurance policies are classified according to the type of property covered and the extent (amount) of the issuer's liability. Exhibit 50–3 below lists typical fire insurance policies, discussed in the following subsections.

Liability. The insurer's liability is determined from the terms of the policy. Most policies limit recovery to losses resulting from *hostile* fires—basically, those that break out or begin in places where no fire was intended to burn. A *friendly* fire—one burning in a place where it was intended to burn—is not covered. Therefore, smoke from a fireplace is not covered, but smoke from a fire caused by a defective electrical outlet is covered. Sometimes, owners add "extended coverage" to the fire policy to cover losses from "friendly" fires.

If the policy is a *valued* policy (see Exhibit 50–3 below) and the subject matter is completely destroyed, the insurer is liable for the amount specified in the policy. If it is an *open* policy, then the extent of the actual loss must be determined, and the insurer is liable only for the amount of the loss or for the maximum amount specified in the policy, whichever is less. For

EXHIBIT 50–3 Typical Fire Insurance Policies

Type of Policy	Coverage
Blanket	Covers a class of property rather than specific property, because the property is expected to shift or vary in nature. A policy covering the inventory of a business is an example.
Floater	Usually supplements a specific policy. It is intended to cover property that may change in either location or quantity. To illustrate, if the painting mentioned below under "specific policy" is to be exhibited during the year at numerous locations throughout the state, a floater policy would be desirable.
Open	A policy that does not state an agreed-on value for the property. The policy usually provides for a maximum liability of the insurer, but payment for loss is restricted to the fair market value of the property at the time of loss or to the insurer's limit, whichever is less.
Specific	Covers a specific item of property at a specific location. An example is a particular painting located in a residence or a piece of machinery located in a factory or business.
Valued	A policy that, by agreement, places a specific value on the subject to be insured to cover the eventuality of its total loss.

partial losses, actual loss must always be determined, and the insurer's liability is limited to that amount. Most insurance policies permit the insurer to either restore or replace the property destroyed or to pay for the loss.

Proof of Loss. As a condition for recovery, fire insurance policies require the insured to file a proof of loss with the insurer within a specified period or immediately (within a reasonable time). Failure to comply *could* allow the insurance carrier to avoid liability. Courts vary somewhat on the enforcement of such clauses.

Occupancy Clause. Most standard policies require that the premises be occupied at the time of the loss. The relevant clause states that if the premises are vacant or unoccupied for a given period and the insurer's consent to the vacancy is not obtained, the coverage is suspended until the premises are reoccupied. Persons going on extended vacations should check their policies regarding this point.

In the following case, the court had to consider how long a house must be left vacant before it can be considered "unoccupied" and whether the risk of hazard is always greater when a home is unoccupied.

CASE ANALYSIS

Case 50.3   Estate of Luster v. Allstate Insurance Co.

United States Court of Appeals, Seventh Circuit, 598 F.3d 903 (2010).

IN THE LANGUAGE OF THE COURT
POSNER, Circuit Judge.
* * * *

This diversity suit for breach of an insurance contract was dismissed on summary judgment * * * , and the plaintiff's [Estate of Luster's] appeal presents issues of both contract interpretation and Indiana insurance law.

[Wavie] Luster was a widow living alone in her house in Merrillville, Indiana. She had a homeowner's insurance policy from Allstate [Insurance Company]. In October 2001, when she was eighty-three, she was injured in a fall, and after being released from the hospital moved into an extended-care facility. She executed a power of attorney to her lawyer, Rick Gikas, who is the representative of her estate in this litigation. She never returned home and died in April 2006, some four and a half years after her fall. Gikas had notified Allstate of his power of attorney and had directed the company to bill the insurance premiums to his law office. No one lived in the house after she left it.

Three months after her death—her house still unoccupied—a fire caused

extensive damage. Gikas submitted a claim on behalf of the estate. An investigation indicated that the fire may well have been started by burglars, but the plaintiff denies this and the district judge made no finding.

In the course of the investigation Allstate discovered that the house had been unoccupied for four and a half years before Mrs. Luster's death and denied the claim, precipitating [hastening] this suit. Allstate continued billing Gikas for premiums, however, and he continued paying them until October 2008, more than two years after the fire, when Allstate—which claims not to have known that the policy was still in force until its lawyers read the estate's summary-judgment brief that month—purported to cancel the policy retroactively to November 2001, and returned the premiums for the subsequent period to the estate.

The appeal requires us to consider [certain] provisions of the insurance policy: [The policy required the insured to notify Allstate of any change in occupancy of the premises and excluded coverage for property loss caused by "any substantial change or increase in hazard" or by

"vandalism or malicious mischief" if the insured's dwelling was unoccupied for more than thirty consecutive days immediately prior to the vandalism or malicious mischief.]
* * * *

Gikas argues that * * * the house was *not* unoccupied, because right up until her death Luster expressed the intention of returning to live there when her health permitted.

*Regardless of the owner's intentions, * * * four and a half years of continuous absence of human occupation constitutes a change in occupancy.* [Emphasis added.]

The duty-to-notify provision entitled Allstate to cancel the policy in the event the house became unoccupied.

Although the policy expressly authorizes the insurer to cancel it for a violation of any of its terms, it also requires the insurer to give thirty days' notice of intention to cancel, and Allstate failed to do that after discovering in the wake of the fire that the house had been unoccupied for years. *The requirement of notice of intent to cancel is important; it gives the*

CASE 50.3 CONTINUES ▶

CASE 50.3 CONTINUED

insured an opportunity to prevent a lapse of coverage, by taking steps to reinstate the policy or obtain a substitute policy from another insurer. Retroactive termination is inconsistent with the requirement of advance notice. [Emphasis added.]

＊ ＊ ＊ ＊

The district judge ruled that leaving the house unoccupied constituted a "substantial change or increase in hazard" within the meaning [of the policy]. The judge seems to have thought that to leave a house unoccupied for however short a time causes an "increase in hazard" as a matter of law. Allstate takes the more moderate position that any gap in occupation of more than thirty days increases hazard as a matter of law.

Neither position is correct. Houses are rarely occupied continuously. A homeowner might take a thirty-one-day trip; Allstate implies that if a fire occurred during that period the

insured would be uncovered. That is not the law.

Allstate's argument thus implies that if you have a second home the homeowner's policy on your primary residence is illusory; you're away a lot and so coverage lapses. That's nonsense. And even if the house is unoccupied in the relevant sense—the sense that triggers the duty to notify the insurance company of a change in occupancy—it doesn't follow that you have created a "substantial ＊ ＊ ＊ increase in hazard." Maybe you fitted the house with an array of locks and alarms and hired a security company to check on the house daily and so made the house more secure than when you were living there—an especially plausible inference if you happen to be an elderly person who might if in residence damage it inadvertently by leaving appliances on or failing to remove combustibles [flammable items] like cans containing paint or oil-soaked rags or to attend

to defects in the electrical wiring of the house. *There is no rule that moving out of a house per se [in itself] increases the hazards against which the insurance company has insured you.* [Emphasis added.]

＊ ＊ ＊ ＊

There may well have been vandalism, by burglars, and if so it occurred more than thirty days after the house became unoccupied, whenever precisely occupancy ceased—sometime during the four and a half years between Luster's fall and her death. But we do not know whether the vandalism caused the loss—there is no judicial finding that the fire that was the immediate cause of the loss was the result of vandalism. To decide whether it was will require an evidentiary [relating to evidence] hearing, as will Allstate's alternative ground that nonoccupancy substantially increased the risk of loss.

＊ ＊ ＊ ＊

REVERSED AND REMANDED.

LEGAL REASONING QUESTIONS

1. Why did the court conclude that an unoccupied house did not necessarily create a substantial increase in hazard?
2. Why did the court hold that Allstate's cancellation of the policy, retroactive to November 2001 (when Luster moved to an extended-care facility), was ineffective?
3. Was Luster's intent to return to her home when her health permitted sufficient to constitute occupancy? Why or why not?
4. What fact, if it had been different, might have persuaded the court to rule in Allstate's favor in this case? Discuss.

Assignment. Before a loss has occurred, a fire insurance policy is not assignable without the consent of the insurer. The theory is that the fire insurance policy is a personal contract between the insured and the insurer. The nonassignability of a policy is extremely important when a house is purchased. The purchaser must procure his or her own insurance. If the purchaser wishes to assume the seller's remaining period of insurance coverage, the insurer's consent is essential.

▶ **Example 50.4** Kiana is selling her home and lot to Jayden. Kiana has a one-year fire policy with Ajax Insurance Company, with six months of coverage remaining at the date on which the sale is to close. Kiana agrees to assign the balance of her policy,

but Ajax has not given its consent. One day after passage of the deed, a fire totally destroys the house. Can Jayden recover from Ajax?

The answer is no, as the policy is actually voided on the closing of the transaction and the deeding of the property. The reason the policy is voided is that Kiana no longer has an insurable interest at the time of loss, and Jayden has no rights in a nonassignable policy. ◀

HOMEOWNERS' POLICIES A homeowners' policy provides protection against a number of risks under a single policy, allowing the policyholder to avoid the cost of buying each protection separately. There are two basic types of homeowners' coverage: property coverage and liability coverage.

Property Coverage. *Property coverage* includes the garage, house, and other private buildings on the policyholder's lot. It also includes the personal possessions and property of the policyholder at home, while traveling, or at work. It pays additional expenses for living away from home because of a fire or some other covered peril.

Perils insured under property coverage often include fire, lightning, wind, hail, vandalism, and theft (of personal property). Standard homeowners' insurance typically does not cover flood damage. In the absence of a specific provision, such items of personal property as motor vehicles, farm equipment, airplanes, and boats normally are not included under property coverage. Coverage for other property, such as jewelry and securities, usually is limited to a specified dollar amount.

Liability Coverage. *Liability coverage* is for personal liability in the event that someone is injured on the insured's property. It also applies when the insured damages someone else's property or injures someone else (unless the injury involves an automobile, which would be covered by automobile insurance).

Liability coverage under a homeowners' policy applies when others are injured or property is damaged because of the unsafe condition of the policyholder's premises. It also applies when the policyholder is negligent.

Liability coverage normally does not apply, however, if the liability arises from business or professional activities or from the operation of a motor vehicle, which are subjects for separate policies. Also excluded is liability arising from intentional misconduct. Similar to liability coverage is coverage for the medical payments of others who are injured on the policyholder's property and for the property of others that is damaged by a member of the policyholder's family.

Renters' Policies. Renters also take out insurance policies to protect against losses to personal property. Renters' insurance covers personal possessions against various perils and includes coverage for additional living expenses and liability.

Automobile Insurance

There are two basic kinds of automobile insurance: liability insurance and collision and comprehensive insurance.

LIABILITY INSURANCE Automobile liability insurance covers liability for bodily injury and property damage. Liability limits are usually described by a series of three numbers, such as 100/300/50. This means that, for one accident, the policy will pay a maximum of $100,000 for bodily injury to one person, a maximum of $300,000 for bodily injury to more than one person, and a maximum of $50,000 for property damage. Many insurance companies offer liability coverage in amounts up to $500,000 and sometimes higher.

Individuals who are dissatisfied with the maximum liability limits offered by regular automobile insurance coverage can purchase separate coverage under an *umbrella policy*. Umbrella limits sometimes go as high as $10 million. Umbrella policies also cover personal liability in excess of the liability limits of a homeowners' policy.

COLLISION AND COMPREHENSIVE INSURANCE Collision insurance covers damage to the insured's car in any type of collision. Usually, it is not advisable to purchase full collision coverage (otherwise known as *zero deductible*). The price per year is relatively high because it is likely that some small repair jobs will be required each year. Most people prefer to take out policies with a deductible of $250, $500, or $1,000, which cost substantially less than zero-deductible coverage.

Comprehensive insurance covers loss, damage, and destruction due to fire, hurricane, hail, vandalism, and theft. It can be obtained separately from collision insurance.

OTHER AUTOMOBILE INSURANCE Other types of automobile insurance coverage include the following:

1. *Uninsured motorist coverage.* Uninsured motorist coverage insures the driver and passengers against injury caused by any driver without insurance or by a hit-and-run driver. Some states require that it be included in all auto insurance policies sold.
2. *Accidental death benefits.* Sometimes referred to as *double indemnity,* accidental death benefits provide for a payment of twice the policy's face amount if the policyholder dies in an accident. This coverage generally costs very little, but it may not be necessary if the insured has a sufficient amount of life insurance.
3. *Medical payment coverage.* Medical payment coverage provided by an auto insurance policy pays hospital and other medical bills and sometimes funeral expenses. This type of insurance protects

all the passengers in the insured's car when the insured is driving.

4. *Other-driver coverage.* An **omnibus clause,** or *other-driver clause,* protects the vehicle owner who has taken out the insurance and anyone who drives the vehicle with the owner's permission. This coverage may be held to extend to a third party who drives the vehicle with the permission of the person to whom the owner gave permission.

Business Liability Insurance

A business may be vulnerable to all sorts of risks. A key employee may die or become disabled, a customer may be injured when using a manufacturer's product, or a professional may overlook some important detail and be liable for malpractice. If a key employee (for instance, the company president) dies, the firm may have some protection under a key-person insurance policy, discussed earlier. In the other circumstances, other types of insurance may apply.

GENERAL LIABILITY Comprehensive general liability insurance can encompass as many risks as the insurer agrees to cover. It can protect a business from liability for injuries arising from on-premises events held after work hours, such as company social functions. It can protect bars and liquor stores, which in many jurisdictions are liable when a buyer of liquor becomes intoxicated as a result of the sale and injures a third party. General liability insurance can protect a business not only from liability for physical injuries, but also from liability for the loss of financial support suffered by a family because of the injuries.

PRODUCT LIABILITY Manufacturers and retailers may be subject to liability for injuries resulting from the products they sell, and product liability insurance can be written to match specific products' risks. Coverage can be procured under a comprehensive general liability policy or under a separate policy. The coverage may include payment for expenses incurred to recall and replace a product that has proved to be defective. (For a comprehensive discussion of product liability, see Chapter 7.)

PROFESSIONAL MALPRACTICE Attorneys, physicians, architects, engineers, and other professionals often become the targets of negligence suits. Professionals purchase malpractice insurance to protect themselves against such claims. The large judgments in some malpractice suits have received considerable publicity and are sometimes cited in discussions of what has been called "the insurance crisis," because they have contributed to a significant increase in malpractice insurance premiums.

WORKERS' COMPENSATION Workers' compensation insurance covers payments to employees who are injured in accidents arising out of and in the course of employment (that is, on the job). State statutes govern workers' compensation, as discussed in Chapter 34.

Reviewing: Insurance

Provident Insurance, Inc., issued an insurance policy to a company providing an employee, Steve Matlin, with disability insurance. Soon thereafter, Matlin was diagnosed with "panic disorder and phobia of returning to work." He lost his job and sought disability coverage. Provident denied coverage, doubting the diagnosis of disability. Matlin and his employer sued Provident. During pretrial discovery, the insurer learned that Matlin had stated on the policy application that he had never been treated for any "emotional, mental, nervous, urinary, or digestive disorder" or any kind of heart disease. In fact, before Matlin filled out the application, he had visited a physician for chest pains and general anxiety, and the physician had prescribed an antidepressant and recommended that Matlin stop smoking. Using the information presented in the chapter, answer the following questions.

1. Did Matlin commit a misrepresentation on his policy application? Explain.
2. If there was any ambiguity on the application, should it be resolved in favor of the insured or the insurer? Why?

3. Assuming that the policy is valid, does Matlin's situation fall within the terms of the disability policy? Why or why not?

4. If Matlin is covered by the policy but is also disqualified by his misrepresentation on the application for coverage, might the insurer still be liable for bad faith denial of coverage? Explain.

DEBATE THIS . . . *Whenever an insurance company can prove that the applicant committed fraud during the application process, it should not have to pay on the policy.*

Terms and Concepts

annuity 987
antilapse provision 982
binder 981
cash surrender value 982
coinsurance clause 982
endowment insurance 987
incontestability clause 981

insurable interest 978
insurance 978
limited-payment life 987
omnibus clause 992
policy 978
premium 978

risk 978
risk management 978
term insurance 987
underwriter 978
universal life 987
whole life 987

ExamPrep

Issue Spotters

1. Neal applies to Farm Insurance Company for a life insurance policy. On the application, Neal understates his age. Neal obtains the policy, but for a lower premium than he would have had to pay had he disclosed his actual age. The policy includes an incontestability clause. Six years later, Neal dies. Can the insurer refuse payment? Why or why not? **(See page 981.)**

2. Al is divorced and owns a house. Al has no reasonable expectation of benefit from the life of Bea, his former spouse, but applies for insurance on her life anyway. Al obtains a fire insurance policy on the house and then sells the house. Al continues to pay the premiums on both the life insurance policy and the fire

insurance policy. Ten years later, Bea dies and the house is destroyed by fire. Can Al obtain payment for these events? Explain your answers. **(See page 978.)**

• Check your answers to the Issue Spotters against the answers provided in Appendix E at the end of this text.

Before the Test

Go to **www.cengagebrain.com**, enter the ISBN 9781285185248, and click on "Find" to locate this textbook's Web site. Then, click on "Access Now" under "Study Tools," and select Chapter 50 at the top. There, you will find a Practice Quiz that you can take to assess your mastery of the concepts in this chapter, as well as Flashcards and a Glossary of important terms.

Business Scenarios

50–1. Insurable Interest. Adia owns a house and has an elderly third cousin living with her. Adia decides she needs fire insurance on the house and a life insurance policy on her third cousin to cover funeral and other expenses that will result from her cousin's death. Adia takes out a fire insurance policy from Ajax Insurance Co. and a $10,000 life insurance policy from Beta Insurance Co. on her third cousin. Six months later, Adia sells the house to John and transfers title to him. Adia and her cousin move into an apartment. With two months remaining on the Ajax policy, a fire totally destroys the house. At the same time,

Adia's third cousin dies. Both insurance companies say that they have no liability under the insurance contracts because Adia did not have an insurable interest, and they tender back (return) the premiums. Discuss the companies' claims. **(See page 978.)**

50–2. Insurer's Defenses. Patrick contracts with an Ajax Insurance Co. agent for a $50,000 ordinary life insurance policy. The application form is filled in to show Patrick's age as thirty-two. In addition, the application form asks whether Patrick has ever had any heart ailments or problems. Patrick answers no, forgetting that as a young child he was diagnosed as having a slight heart murmur. A policy is issued. Three years later, Patrick becomes seriously ill and dies. A review of the policy discloses that Patrick was actually thirty-three at the time of the application and the issuance of the policy and that he erred in answering the question about a history of heart ailments. Discuss whether Ajax can void the policy and escape liability on Patrick's death. **(See page 986.)**

50–3. Assignment. Sapata has an ordinary life insurance policy on her life and a fire insurance policy on her house. Both policies have been in force for a number of years. Sapata's life insurance names her son, Rory, as beneficiary. Sapata has specifically removed her right to change beneficiaries, and the life insurance policy is silent on the right of assignment. Sapata is going on a one-year European vacation and borrows money from Leonard to finance the trip. Leonard takes an assignment of the life insurance policy as security for the loan, as the policy has accumulated a substantial cash surrender value. Sapata also rents out her house to Leonard and assigns her fire insurance policy to him. Discuss fully whether Sapata's assignment of these policies is valid. **(See page 987.)**

50–4. Fire Insurance. Fritz has an open fire insurance policy on his home for a maximum liability of $60,000. The policy has a number of standard clauses, including the right of the insurer to restore or rebuild the property in lieu of a monetary payment, and it has a standard coinsurance clause. A fire in Fritz's house destroys a utility room and part of the kitchen. The fire was caused by the overheating of an electric water heater. The total damage to the property is $10,000. The property at the time of loss is valued at $100,000. Fritz files a proof-of-loss claim for $10,000. Discuss the insurer's liability in this situation. **(See page 988.)**

Business Case Problems

50–5. Interpreting Provisions. Richard Vanderbrook's home in New Orleans, Louisiana, was insured through Unitrin Preferred Insurance Co. His policy excluded coverage for "flood, surface water, waves, tidal water, overflow of a body of water, or spray from any of these, whether or not driven by wind." The policy did not define the term *flood.* In 2005, Hurricane Katrina struck along the coast of the Gulf of Mexico, devastating portions of Louisiana. In New Orleans, some of the most significant damage occurred when the levees along three canals ruptured, and water submerged about 80 percent of the city, including Vanderbrook's home. He filed a claim for the loss, but Unitrin refused to pay.

Vanderbrook and others whose policies contained similar exclusions asked a federal district court to order their insurers to pay. They contended that their losses were due to the negligent design, construction, and maintenance of the levees and that the policies did not clearly exclude coverage for an inundation of water induced by negligence. On what does a decision in this case hinge? What reasoning supports a ruling in the plaintiffs' favor? In the defendants' favor? [*In re Katrina Canal Breaches Litigation,* 495 F.3d 191 (5th Cir. 2007)] **(See page 982.)**

50–6. Duty to Cooperate. James Bubenik, a dentist, had two patients die while under sedation within six months. Bubenik had medical malpractice insurance with Medical Protective Co. (MPC). The families of both patients sued Bubenik for malpractice. MPC pointed out to Bubenik that a clause in his policy stated that the "Insured shall at all times fully cooperate with the Company in any claim hereunder and shall attend and assist in the preparation and trial of any such claim." During the litigation, however, Bubenik refused to submit to depositions, answer interrogatories, or testify at trial, invoking the privilege against self-incrimination. He also refused to communicate with MPC and instead agreed to assist the patients in obtaining payment. MPC filed suit. Under these circumstances, did MPC have a legal or ethical duty to defend against the claim? Could MPC refuse to pay it? Explain. [*Medical Protective Co. v. Bubenik,* 594 F.3d 1047 (8th Cir. 2010)] **(See page 984.)**

50–7. Bad Faith Actions. Leo and Mary Deters owned Deters Tower Service, Inc., in Iowa. Deters Tower serviced television and radio towers and antennas in a multistate area. The firm obtained a commercial general liability policy issued by USF Insurance Co. to provide coverage for its officers, including Leo. One afternoon, Leo and two Deters Tower employees were working on a TV tower in Council Bluffs when they fell from the tower to their deaths. The workers' families filed a negligence suit against Leo's estate. USF refused to defend the Deters estate against the suit and pay any resulting claim but did not provide a reason for its refusal. Is USF liable to the Deters estate for this refusal? If so, on what basis might the Deters estate recover, and how much? [*Deters v. USF Insurance Co.,* 797 N.W.2d 621 (Iowa App. 2011)] **(See page 986.)**

50–8. BUSINESS CASE PROBLEM
WITH SAMPLE ANSWER: Insurance Provisions and Clauses.

Darling's Rent-a-Car carried property insurance on its cars under a policy issued by Philadelphia Indemnity Insurance Co. The policy listed Darling's as the "insured." Darling's rented a car to Joshuah Farrington. In the rental contract, Farrington agreed to be responsible for any damage to the car and declined the optional insurance. Later, Farrington collided with a moose. Philadelphia paid Darling's for the damage to the car and sought to collect this amount from Farrington. Farrington argued that he was an "insured" under Darling's policy. How should "insured" be

interpreted in this case? Why? [Philadelphia Indemnity Insurance Co. v. Farrington, *37 A.3d 305 (Me. 2012)]* **(See page 981.)**

- **For a sample answer to Problem 50–8, go to Appendix F at the end of this text.**

50–9. A QUESTION OF ETHICS: Insurance Coverage.

 Paul and Julie Leonard's two-story home in Pascagoula, Mississippi, is only twelve feet above sea level and fewer than two hundred yards from the Gulf of Mexico. In 1989, the Leonards bought a homeowners' insurance policy from Jay Fletcher, an agent for Nationwide Mutual Insurance Co. The policy covered any damage caused by wind. It excluded all damage caused by water, including flooding. With each annual renewal, Nationwide reminded the Leonards that their policy did not cover flood damage, but that such coverage was available. The policy also contained an anti-concurrent-causation (ACC) clause that excluded coverage for damage caused by the synergistic action of a covered peril such as wind and an excluded peril such as water. In August 2005, Hurricane Katrina battered Pascagoula

with torrential rain and sustained winds in excess of one hundred miles per hour. Wind damage to the Leonards' home was modest, but the storm drove ashore a seventeen-foot storm surge that flooded the ground floor. When Nationwide refused to pay for the damage to the ground floor, the Leonards filed a suit in a federal district court against the insurer. [Leonard v. Nationwide Mutual Insurance Co., 499 F.3d 419 (5th Cir. 2007)] **(See page 984.)**

(a) Nationwide argued that the storm surge was a concurrently caused peril—a wall of water pushed ashore by hurricane winds—and thus its damage was excluded under the ACC clause. How would you rule on this point? Should a court "enlarge" an insurer's policy obligations? Why or why not?

(b) When the Leonards bought their policy in 1989, Fletcher told them that all hurricane damage was covered. Ten years later, Fletcher told Paul Leonard that they did not need additional flood coverage. Did these statements materially misrepresent or alter the policy? Were they unethical? Discuss.

Legal Reasoning Group Activity

50–10. Insurance Coverage. PAJ, Inc., a jewelry company, had a commercial general liability (CGL) policy from Hanover Insurance Co. The policy required PAJ to notify Hanover of any claim or suit against PAJ "as soon as practicable." Yurman Designs sued PAJ for copyright infringement because of the design of a particular jewelry line. Because PAJ did not realize that the CGL policy had a clause that covered infringement claims, it did not notify Hanover of the suit until four to six months after litigation began. Hanover contended that the policy did not apply to this incident because the late notification had

violated its terms. PAJ sued Hanover, seeking a declaration that it was obligated to defend and indemnify PAJ. **(See page 984.)**

(a) The first group will decide whether Hanover had an obligation to provide PAJ with legal assistance.

(b) The second group will determine the effect that PAJ's late notice to the insurance company had on its ability to provide assistance and mount a defense. Should the court require the insurance company to indemnify PAJ in this situation? Why or why not?

CHAPTER 51

WILLS AND TRUSTS

As the adage says, "You can't take it with you." After you die, all of the real and personal property that you own will be transferred to others. A person can direct the passage of his or her property after death by *will,* subject to certain limitations imposed by the state.

A person who dies without having created a valid will is said to have died **intestate.** In this situation, state **intestacy laws** prescribe the distribution of the property among heirs or next of kin. If no heirs or kin can be found,

the property will **escheat**[1] (title will be transferred to the state).

In addition, a person can transfer property through a *trust.* When a trust is created, the owner (who may be called the *grantor* or the *settlor*) of the property transfers legal title to a trustee. The trustee has a duty imposed by law to hold the property for the use or benefit of another (the beneficiary).

Wills and trusts are two basic devices used in the process of **estate**

---

1. Pronounced is-*cheet.*

planning—determining in advance how one's property and obligations should be transferred on death. Estate planning may also involve powers of attorney and living wills, which we discuss at the conclusion of this chapter. It might even involve decisions concerning social media and one's online identity, as discussed in a feature later in this chapter. Other estate-planning devices include life insurance (discussed in Chapter 50) and joint-tenancy arrangements (described in Chapter 49).

SECTION 1
WILLS

A **will** is the final declaration of how a person desires to have her or his property disposed of after death. It is a formal instrument that must follow exactly the requirements of state law to be effective.

A will can serve other purposes besides the distribution of property. It can appoint a guardian for minor children or incapacitated adults. It can also appoint a personal representative to settle the affairs of the deceased.

Exhibit 51–1 on the following page presents excerpts from the will of Michael Jackson, the "King of Pop," who died from cardiac arrest in 2009 at the age of fifty. Jackson held a substantial amount of tangible and intangible property, including the publishing rights to most of the Beatles' music catalogue. The will is a "pour-over" will, meaning that it transfers all of his property (that is not already held in the name of the trust) into the Michael Jackson Family

Trust (trusts will be discussed later in this chapter). Jackson's will also appoints his mother, Katherine Jackson, as the guardian of his three minor children.

Terminology of Wills

A person who makes a will is known as a **testator** (from the Latin *testari,* "to make a will"). A will is referred to as a *testamentary disposition* of property, and one who dies after having made a valid will is said to have died **testate.** The court responsible for administering any legal problems surrounding a will is called a *probate court,* as mentioned in Chapter 2. When a person dies, a personal representative administers the estate and settles all of the decedent's (deceased person's) affairs.

An **executor** is a personal representative named in a will. An **administrator** is a personal representative appointed by the court for a decedent who dies without a will. The court will also appoint a representative if the will does not name an executor or if the named person lacks the capacity to serve as an executor.

EXHIBIT 51-1 Excerpts from Michael Jackson's Will

Last Will of Michael Joseph Jackson

I, MICHAEL JOSEPH JACKSON, a resident of the State of California, declare this to be my last Will, and do hereby revoke all former wills and codicils made by me.

I.   I declare that I am not married. My marriage to DEBORAH JEAN ROWE JACKSON has been dissolved. I have three children now living, PRINCE MICHAEL JACKSON, JR., PARIS MICHAEL KATHERINE JACKSON and PRINCE MICHAEL JOSEPH JACKSON, II. I have no other children, living or deceased.

II.   It is my intention by this Will to dispose of all property which I am entitled to dispose of by will. I specifically refrain from exercising all powers of appointment that I may possess at the time of my death.

III.   I give my entire estate to the Trustee or Trustees then acting under that certain Amended and Restated Declaration of Trust executed on March 22, 2002 by me as Trustee and Trustor which is called the MICHAEL JACKSON FAMILY TRUST, giving effect to any amendments thereto made prior to my death. All such assets shall be held, managed and distributed as a part of said Trust according to its terms and not as a separate testamentary trust.

If for any reason this gift is not operative or is invalid, or if the aforesaid Trust fails or has been revoked, I give my residuary estate to the Trustee or Trustees named to act in the MICHAEL JACKSON FAMILY TRUST, as Amended and Restated on March 22, 2002, and I direct said Trustee or Trustees to divide, administer, hold and distribute the trust estate pursuant to the provisions of said Trust * * * .

* * * *

IV.   I direct that all federal estate taxes and state inheritance or succession taxes payable upon or resulting from or by reason of my death (herein "Death Taxes") attributable to property which is part of the trust estate of the MICHAEL JACKSON FAMILY TRUST, including property which passes to said trust from my probate estate shall be paid by the Trustee of said trust in accordance with its terms. Death Taxes attributable to property passing outside this Will, other than property constituting the trust estate of the trust mentioned in the preceding sentence, shall be charged against the taker of said property.

V.   I appoint JOHN BRANCA, JOHN McCLAIN and BARRY SIEGEL as co-Executors of this Will. In the event of any of their deaths, resignations, inability, failure or refusal to serve or continue to serve as a co-Executor, the other shall serve and no replacement need be named. The co-Executors serving at any time after my death may name one or more replacements to serve in the event that none of the three named individuals is willing or able to serve at any time.

The term "my executors" as used in this Will shall include any duly acting personal representative or representatives of my estate. No individual acting as such need past a bond.

I hereby give to my Executors, full power and authority at any time or times to sell, lease, mortgage, pledge, exchange or otherwise dispose of the property, whether real or personal comprising my estate, upon such terms as my Executors shall deem best, to continue any business enterprises, to purchase assets from my estate, to continue in force and pay any insurance policy * * * .

VI.   Except as otherwise provided in this Will or in the Trust referred to in Article III hereof, I have intentionally omitted to provide for my heirs. I have intentionally omitted to provide for my former wife, DEBORAH JEAN ROWE JACKSON.

* * * *

VIII.   If any of my children are minors at the time of my death, I nominate my mother, KATHERINE JACKSON as guardian of the persons and estates of such minor children. If KATHERINE JACKSON fails to survive me, or is unable or unwilling to act as guardian, I nominate DIANA ROSS as guardian of the persons and estates of such minor children.

* * * *

Laws Governing Wills

Probate is the court process by which a will is proved valid or invalid. Probate laws vary from state to state. The National Conference of Commissioners on Uniform State Laws issued the Uniform Probate Code (UPC) to promote more uniformity among the states. The UPC codifies general principles and procedures for the resolution of conflicts in settling estates.

The UPC also relaxes some of the requirements for a valid will contained in earlier state laws.

Almost half of the states have enacted some part of the UPC and incorporated it into their own probate codes. Nonetheless, succession and inheritance laws still vary widely among the states, and one should always check the particular laws of the state involved.[2]

---

2. For example, California law differs substantially from the UPC.

Gifts by Will

A gift of real estate by will is generally called a **devise,** and a gift of personal property under a will is called a **bequest,** or **legacy.** The recipient of a gift by will is a *devisee* or a *legatee,* depending on whether the gift was a devise or a legacy.

TYPES OF GIFTS Whether they are devises or bequests, gifts in a will can be specific, general, or residuary.

Specific. A *specific* devise or bequest (legacy) describes particular property (such as "Eastwood Estate" or "my Cartier watch") that can be distinguished from the rest of the testator's property.

General. A *general* devise or bequest (legacy) uses less restrictive terminology. For instance, "I devise all my lands" is a general devise. A general bequest often specifies a sum of cash instead of a particular item of property, such as a watch or an automobile. For instance, "I give to my nephew, Carleton, $30,000" is a general bequest.

If a testamentary gift is conditioned on the commission of an illegal act or an act that is legally impossible to fulfill, the condition will be invalid. ▶ **Case in Point 51.1** A testator made a charitable bequest of $29 million to a nursing home on the condition that the funds be used only to help white patients. Because this condition was impossible to fulfill without violating laws prohibiting discrimination, the court ruled that the illegal portion of the gift was invalid. Essentially, the court invalidated the condition (that the funds be used for only white patients) and allowed the nursing home to receive the funds without any conditions on their use.[3] ◀

Residuary. If any assets remain after specific gifts have been made and debts have been paid, they are called the *residuary* (or *residuum*) of the estate. A will may provide that these assets are to be given to the testator's spouse, distributed to the testator's descendants, or disposed of in some other way. If the testator has not indicated what party or parties should receive the residuary of the estate, the residuary passes according to state laws of intestacy.

ABATEMENT If the assets of an estate are insufficient to pay in full all general bequests provided for in the will, an *abatement* takes place. An abatement means that the legatees receive reduced benefits. ▶ **Example 51.2** Julie's will leaves $15,000 to each of her children, Tamara and Lynn. On Julie's death, only $10,000 is available to honor these bequests. By abatement, each child will receive $5,000. ◀ If bequests are more complicated, abatement may be more complex. The testator's intent, as expressed in the will, controls.

LAPSED LEGACIES If a legatee dies before the death of the testator or before the legacy is payable, a *lapsed legacy* results. At common law, the legacy failed. Today, the legacy may not lapse if the legatee is in a certain blood relationship to the testator (such as a child, grandchild, brother, or sister) and has left a child or other surviving descendant.

Note that if the testator has included a provision in the will addressing lapsed legacies, courts generally will enforce the provision in the way the testator intended. ▶ **Case in Point 51.3** Katherine Hagan executed a will in 1994 that left the residuary of her estate, including all lapsed legacies, to various organizations, such as the Humane Society. In 2001, Hagan inherited $830,000 from a relative. At this time, Hagan did not have the mental capacity to revise or modify her will. When she died in 2005, her residuary estate was worth $1.48 million.

Hagan's relatives, including Janice Benjamin, tried to invalidate the will's provisions regarding the residuary estate so that the funds would pass to them by intestacy laws. The court, however, found that Hagan's intent controlled. She had not intended to give any portion of her estate to her relatives. Because the will specifically stated that lapsed legacies should go into the residuary estate and be distributed to the charities, the court enforced these provisions (and Hagan's relatives received nothing).[4] ◀

Requirements for a Valid Will

A will must comply with statutory formalities designed to ensure that the testator understood his or her actions at the time the will was made. These formalities are intended to help prevent fraud. Unless they are followed, the will is declared void, and the decedent's property is distributed according to the laws of intestacy of that state.

---

3. *Home for Incurables of Baltimore City v. University of Maryland Medical System Corp.,* 369 Md. 67, 797 A.2d 746 (2002). Note that the same rule applies to *testamentary trusts* (see page 1009) that include conditions that are illegal or against public policy. See, for example, *In re Estate of Robertson,* 859 N.E.2d 772 (Ind.App. 2007).

4. *Benjamin v. JPMorgan Chase Bank, N.A.,* 305 S.W.3d 446 (Ky.App. 2010).

Although the required formalities vary among jurisdictions, most states uphold certain basic requirements for executing a will. We now look at the basic requirements for a valid will, including references to the UPC when appropriate.

TESTAMENTARY CAPACITY AND INTENT For a will to be valid, the testator must have testamentary capacity—that is, the testator must be of legal age and sound mind *at the time the will is made*. The legal age for executing a will varies, but in most states and under the UPC, the minimum age is eighteen years [UPC 2–501]. Thus, the will of a twenty-one-year-old decedent written when the person was sixteen is invalid if, under state law, the legal age for executing a will is eighteen.

The concept of "being of sound mind" refers to the testator's ability to formulate and to comprehend a personal plan for the disposition of property. Persons who have been declared incompetent in a legal proceeding do not meet the sound mind requirement.

A valid will is one that represents the maker's intention to transfer and distribute her or his property. Generally, a testator must:

1. Know the nature of the act (intend to make a will).
2. Comprehend and remember the people to whom the testator would naturally leave his or her estate (such as family members and friends).
3. Know the nature and extent of her or his property.
4. Understand the distribution of assets called for by the will.

Undue Influence. When it can be shown that the decedent's plan of distribution was the result of fraud or undue influence, the will is declared invalid. A court may sometimes infer undue influence when the named beneficiary was in a position to influence the making of the will. A presumption of undue influence might arise if the testator ignored blood relatives and named as a beneficiary a nonrelative who was in constant close contact with the testator.

▶ **Example 51.4** Frieda is a nurse who was responsible for caring for Julie, the testator, during the last years of her life. After Julie's death, her family discovers that her will names Frieda as sole beneficiary and excludes all family members. If Julie's family challenges the validity of the will, which was executed a year before her death, the court might infer that Frieda unduly influenced Julie and declare the will invalid. ◀

In the following case, a testator's children and grandchildren claimed that his third wife had unduly influenced him to create a new will that did not provide for them. After a jury trial, the court declared the will invalid. An appellate court had to determine if there was sufficient evidence of undue influence to support the jury's verdict.

CASE 51.1

In re Estate of Johnson
Court of Appeals of Texas, San Antonio, 340 S.W.3d 769 (2011).

BACKGROUND AND FACTS Belton Kleberg Johnson was a descendant of the founders of the King Ranch, a famous ranch in Texas that dates back to the 1850s. He was married three times and had three children from his first marriage, as well as eight grandchildren. Johnson executed a will in 1991, when he was married to his second wife. That will provided for her during her lifetime and left the remainder of his estate in a trust for his grandchildren and children. When his second wife died in 1994, he changed the will to give each grandchild $1 million and to give the remainder to five charities. His children were provided for in a separate trust.

Johnson met his third wife, Laura, shortly after the death of his second wife, and they were married in 1996. In 1997, Johnson executed a will that left $1 million to each grandchild and the remainder to Laura. In 1999, Johnson executed a new will that left his entire estate in trust to Laura for her life and then to a foundation that she controlled. After Johnson died in 2001, his attorney submitted the will from 1999 to probate. Johnson's children and grandchildren (the plaintiffs) challenged the will in court. A jury concluded that the will was invalid as a result of undue influence by Laura. She appealed, claiming that there was insufficient evidence to support the jury's finding.

CASE 51.1 CONTINUES ▶

CASE 51.1 CONTINUED

IN THE LANGUAGE OF THE COURT
Opinion by Catherine *STONE*, Chief Justice.

* * * *

Not every influence exerted by a person on the will of another is undue. *Influence is not undue unless the free agency of the testator was destroyed and a testament produced that expresses the will of the one exerting the influence.* [Emphasis added.]

The exertion of undue influence is usually a subtle thing, and by its very nature usually involves an extended course of dealings and circumstances. Undue influence may be shown by direct or circumstantial evidence, but will usually be established by the latter. [Emphasis added.]

* * * The evidence established that B [throughout the opinion, the court refers to the testator as B, which stands for Belton, his first name] was an alcoholic, and psychological and medical tests showed that the alcohol had an adverse effect on his mental state. Although B received both in-patient and out-patient alcohol rehabilitation services several times before his marriage to Laura, the record contains no evidence that Laura made any effort to stop B's drinking, which he admitted was on-going when he was hospitalized in 2000 and diagnosed with pancreatic cancer.

* * * Ceci [B's daughter] testified that B would disappear for weeks when he was on a binge and could wind up in a different county, state, or country. Testimony was introduced that any flight B chartered was stocked with vodka, and in a nine-month period in 1999, B spent almost $7,000 on liquor and wine. Evidence was also introduced about B's mental abilities while intoxicated. For example, several witnesses testified that B would call late at night or early in the morning after he had been drinking and want to have long, rambling conversations. * * * One time B ordered an employee to purchase tickets to Santiago, Chile, but when the employee called B about going to the airport, B had no recollection of requesting the trip. *In contrast to this evidence of B's significant drinking and its effect on his conduct, Laura denied that B had a drinking problem or was ever intoxicated in her presence.* [Emphasis added.]

* * * *

Appellees contend the evidence also established a habitual subjection of B to Laura's control. Although B had a prenuptial agreement with his second wife, Lynne, Laura refused to consider a prenuptial agreement * * * .

* * * *

Prior to B and Laura's marriage, one note by Copley [Johnson's attorney] stated that Laura wanted to know what the children were getting under the estate plan. One letter summarizing certain estate planning documents had writing in the brown felt tip pen B traditionally used, but also had writing in a red pen. The jury could infer from the evidence and testimony that Laura had reviewed the document and made comments.

On a few occasions, B requested that Copley investigate whether the King Ranch royalties and a house in Cabo San Lucas could be left to his children, but subsequently called and stated that he changed his mind. The jury could infer that B changed his mind after discussions with Laura. * * * With regard to the King Ranch royalties, *evidence was presented that B stated in a conversation with his children in 1999 that the King Ranch royalties were to be kept in the family, and that Laura, who overheard the discussion, stated she would never take a family heirloom. By 1999, however, the King Ranch royalties had been transferred to BKJ Interests, and under the estate plan, the King Ranch royalties would not remain in the family but would eventually be controlled by the foundation.* Evidence was presented that in 2000 B again broached Copley with the idea of leaving the King Ranch royalties to the children. [Emphasis added.]

* * * *

Considering whether the disposition was unnatural, we must consider evidence of B's stated desires and actions. *The evidence established that B made several comments about the interest in the Hyatt being passed to the children/grandchildren. Similarly, evidence established that B was very proud of his heritage and wanted his descendants to inherit the King Ranch royalties. The majority interest in both of those assets, however, was not inherited by the grandchildren.* Instead, Laura initially would benefit from the income from those assets during her life, and the interest would then pass to the foundation. [Emphasis added.]

CASE 51.1 CONTINUED

Perhaps more importantly, *the 1997 Management Trust expressly lists five charities as the remainder beneficiary after Laura's life estate consistent with the charities B had listed in his prior documents * * * .* The evidence established that B had strong ties with these five charities. *The documents found to be the product of undue influence eliminate a mandatory distribution to these favored charities.* Instead, the remainder beneficiary after Laura's life estate became a perpetual foundation. [Emphasis added.]

DECISION AND REMEDY *The state appellate court affirmed the lower court's judgment in favor of the plaintiffs. The court concluded that the evidence was legally and factually sufficient to support the jury's finding of undue influence.*

WHAT IF THE FACTS WERE DIFFERENT? *Suppose that Johnson, in his 1999 will, had specifically stated that it was his intention that his children and grandchildren would not receive any portion of his estate. Would that have changed the outcome? Why or why not?*

THE ETHICAL DIMENSION *No evidence was presented to indicate that Johnson was intoxicated at the time he executed the will. So why did the court's analysis focus on the evidence of Johnson's alcoholism?*

Disinheritance. Although a testator must be able to remember the persons who would naturally be heirs to the estate, there is no requirement that testators give their estate to the natural heirs. A testator may decide to disinherit, or leave nothing to, an individual for various reasons. Most states have laws that attempt to prevent accidental disinheritance, however. There are also laws that protect minor children from the loss of the family residence. Therefore, the testator's intent to disinherit needs to be clear.

The following case involved a will in the form of a testamentary letter that left the decedent's entire estate to a friend and explicitly disinherited his family. The friend died before the decedent, so the court had to decide whether to follow the state's intestacy laws or enforce the disinheritance clause.

CASE 51.2

In re Estate of Melton
Supreme Court of Nevada, 272 P.3d 668 (2012).

BACKGROUND AND FACTS In 1975, William Melton executed a will that, among other things, stated that his daughter, Vicki Palm, was to receive nothing. In 1979, he added a handwritten note to the will, saying that his friend, Alberta Kelleher, was to receive a small portion of his estate. In 1995, Melton sent a signed, handwritten letter to Kelleher. The letter said that Melton was returning from his mother's funeral and, because she had died suddenly in an auto accident, he wanted to put "something in writing" leaving Kelleher his "entire estate." Melton also said, "I *do not* want my brother Larry J. Melton or Vicki Palm or any of my other relatives to have one penny of my estate." When Melton died in 2008, Kelleher had already passed away, and Melton's daughter, Vicki Palm, was his only natural heir. The state of Nevada argued that it should receive everything because Palm had been disinherited. Nevertheless, the trial court applied the state's intestacy laws (discussed later in this chapter) and distributed the entire estate to Palm. The state appealed.

 IN THE LANGUAGE OF THE COURT
PER CURIAM: [By the Whole Court]
* * * *

Under the common law, two general rules, known as the "English rule" and the "American rule," have been developed by courts considering whether to enforce disinheritance provisions

CASE 51.2 CONTINUES ➡

CASE 51.2 CONTINUED as to property passing by intestate succession. Under the English rule, a disinheritance provision, or a so-called "negative will[,]" was enforceable only if "the testator clearly expressed an intent to limit an heir * * * , and at least one other heir remained eligible to receive the intestate property." Under the American rule, a testator could "prevent an heir from receiving his share of any property that passes by intestacy only by affirmatively disposing of the entire estate through a will."

* * * *

Courts following the American rule have espoused three rationales for doing so: (1) enforcing disinheritance provisions as to intestate property "would create an undesirable 'mixing' of the probate and intestacy systems by requiring courts to alter the distribution scheme provided in the intestacy statute"; (2) because disinheritance clauses do not expressly name devisees, "their enforcement would in effect require courts to draft new wills for testators"; and (3) disinheritance clauses are simply "inconsistent with the law of succession."

* * * *

Not surprisingly, because the common law disinheritance rules distort testamentary intent and conflict with testamentary freedom, the modern trend is to reject the traditional rules.

* * * *

* * * [The Nevada statute] defines a "will" broadly. In stark contrast to the common law disinheritance rules, [the statute] imposes no requirement that an instrument affirmatively devise property in order to be enforceable. Rather, a will includes an instrument that "merely" limits an individual or class from inheriting. *The plain language of [the statute] thus demonstrates that the Legislature envisioned a probate system in which disinheritance provisions can be enforced as to intestate property.* Though Palm considers [the statute] unwise, under well-established canons of statutory interpretation, we must not render it nugatory [not valid] or a mere surplusage [excess words]. [Emphasis added.]

DECISION AND REMEDY *The Nevada Supreme Court reversed the judgment of the lower court. It held that the disinheritance clause was enforceable and that Melton's estate should go to the state of Nevada.*

THE LEGAL ENVIRONMENT DIMENSION *Based on the facts presented here, did Melton have testamentary intent when he wrote his letter? Why or why not?*

THE ETHICAL DIMENSION *Why do most states have strict requirements for the execution of a valid will? How did Nevada's requirements affect the outcome in this case?*

WRITING Generally, a will must be in writing. The writing itself can be informal as long as it substantially complies with the statutory requirements. In some states, a will can be handwritten in crayon or ink. It can be written on a sheet or scrap of paper, on a paper bag, or on a piece of cloth. A will that is completely in the handwriting of the testator is called a **holographic will** (sometimes referred to as an *olographic will*).

A **nuncupative will** is an oral will made before witnesses. Oral wills are not permitted in most states. Where authorized by statute, such wills are generally valid only if made during the last illness of the testator and are therefore sometimes referred to as *deathbed wills*. Normally, only personal property can be transferred by a nuncupative will. Statutes may also permit members of the military to make nuncupative wills when on active duty.

SIGNATURE A fundamental requirement is that the testator's signature must appear on the will, generally at the end. Each jurisdiction dictates by statute and court decision what constitutes a signature. Initials, an X or other mark, and words such as "Mom" have all been upheld as valid when it was shown that the testators *intended* them to be signatures.

WITNESSES A will normally must be *attested* (sworn to) by two, and sometimes three, witnesses. The number of witnesses, their qualifications, and the manner in which the witnessing must be done are generally set out in a statute. A witness may be required to be disinterested—that is, not a beneficiary under the will. The UPC, however, allows even interested witnesses to attest to a will [UPC 2–505]. There are no age requirements for witnesses, but they must be mentally competent.

The purpose of the witnesses is to verify that the testator actually executed (signed) the will and had the requisite intent and capacity at the time. A witness need not read the contents of the will. Usually, the testator and all witnesses sign in the sight or the presence of one another. The UPC does not require all parties to sign in the presence of one another, however, and deems it sufficient if the testator acknowledges her or his signature to the witnesses [UPC 2–502].

Revocation of Wills

The testator can revoke a will at any time during her or his life, either by a physical act, such as tearing up the will, or by a subsequent writing. Wills can also be revoked by operation of law. Revocation can be partial or complete, and it must follow certain strict formalities.

REVOCATION BY A PHYSICAL ACT OF THE MAKER A testator can revoke a will by *intentionally* burning, tearing, canceling, obliterating, or otherwise destroy-

ing it or by having someone else do so in the testator's presence and at the testator's direction.[5]

In some states, partial revocation by a physical act of the testator is recognized. Thus, those portions of a will that are lined out or torn away are dropped, and the remaining parts of the will are valid. At no time, however, can a provision be crossed out and an additional or substitute provision added. Such altered portions require that the will be reexecuted (signed again) and reattested (rewitnessed).

To revoke a will by a physical act, it is necessary to follow the mandates of a state statute exactly. When a state statute prescribes the specific methods for revoking a will by a physical act, those are the only methods that will revoke the will.

In the following case, the court had to decide whether the testator had intended to revoke part or all of her will by making certain changes to it after it was executed.

---

5. The destruction cannot be inadvertent. The testator must have intent to revoke the will.

CASE ANALYSIS

Case 51.3   Peterson v. Harrell
Supreme Court of Georgia, 690 S.E.2d 151 (2010).

IN THE LANGUAGE OF THE COURT
THOMPSON, Justice.

Testator Marion E. Peterson died in 2008. She was survived by her two siblings [brother and sister], Arvin Peterson and Carolyn Peterson Basner (caveators[a]). After testator's death, Vasta Lucas, testator's longtime companion and executor of testator's estate, filed a petition to probate testator's will in solemn form. Lucas died during the pendency [pending period] of this appeal, and appellee Richard Harrell was appointed as successor executor and trustee for the estate. Caveators filed a caveat to the petition to probate, alleging the will was

not properly executed or had been revoked due to obliterations. The trial court admitted the will to probate and caveators appealed.

OCGA [the Official Code of Georgia Annotated] Section 53-4-20(b) of the Revised Probate Code of 1998 provides that "a will shall be attested and subscribed in the presence of the testator by two or more competent witnesses." The record evidence in this case establishes that testator executed a will on June 9, 1976. The will was witnessed by two subscribing witnesses, only one of whom was living at the time of trial. Having been provided a copy of testator's will, the surviving witness testified to its due execution by deposition testimony presented at trial and via written interrogatories filed with the court. Caveators presented no evi-

dence challenging either the validity of the signatures on the will or testator's capacity at the time the will was executed. Accordingly, the evidence supports the trial court's finding that the will was duly executed.

The will contained a bequest to Lucas in the form of a trust and provided that upon Lucas's death the trustee shall distribute any remaining assets to four beneficiaries, including caveators. Some time after the will was executed, testator struck through with an ink pen the names of all successor beneficiaries of the trust estate, as well as language in the will nominating Richard Harrell as successor executor and trustee. None of the strike-throughs were witnessed or attested to. Near the end of the will, testator

---

a. In the context of wills, a *caveator* is one who files a *caveat* attacking the validity of an alleged will.

CASE 51.3 CONTINUES ➡

wrote, "My executrix is Julie Peterson." Caveators contend these alterations constitute material cancellations that effect a revocation of the will.

To effect a revocation of a will by obliteration [elimination], caveators must show that testator made material obliterations to her will or directed another to do so and that testator intended for this act to revoke the will. *Joint operation of act and intention is necessary to revoke a will. The intent to revoke the will in its entirety shall be presumed from the obliteration or cancellation of a material portion of the will, but such presumption may be overcome by a preponderance of the evidence.* [Emphasis added.]

Even assuming, arguendo [for the sake of argument], that the alterations to testator's will constituted

a material cancellation within the meaning of OCGA Section 53-4-44, we find no error in the trial court's conclusion that testator did not intend to revoke her entire will. The record supports the trial court's findings that caveators had no knowledge of the circumstances surrounding what they allege to be the revocation of the will, that testator never discussed revoking her will with caveators, and that caveators were not present when testator made the alterations to the will. Caveators presented no evidence of testator's intent other than the alterations themselves, and they satisfied their initial burden only by proving that testator made alterations to the will.

The record also shows, however, that the will was found in good condi-

tion on testator's desk among her personal papers. It bore the signatures of both testator and her subscribing witnesses and set out a primary bequest to Lucas which remained intact. Handwritten alterations crossing out the names of the successor beneficiaries with a single line were initialed by testator and she added language to the will indicating her desire to substitute Julie Peterson as her executrix. As found by the trial court, this evidence clearly indicates testator's intent to cancel only certain provisions of the will, not an intent to revoke the will in its entirety as required for revocation under OCGA Section 53-4-44.

* * * *

Judgment affirmed.

LEGAL REASONING QUESTIONS

1. Why would the caveators argue that the entire will should be revoked? How would the will's revocation benefit them?

2. What could the testator have done differently to clarify her intentions in her will?

3. Suppose that shortly before her death, Peterson had asked Lucas to tear up her will, and Lucas had done so. Would the result in this case have been different? Discuss.

4. How might the availability of a secure online repository for a person's will affect a challenge to the will?

REVOCATION BY A SUBSEQUENT WRITING A will may also be wholly or partially revoked by a **codicil,** a written instrument separate from the will that amends or revokes provisions in the will. A codicil eliminates the necessity of redrafting an entire will merely to add to it or amend it.

A codicil can also be used to revoke an entire will. The codicil must be executed with the same formalities required for a will, and it must refer expressly to the will. In effect, it updates a will because the will is "incorporated by reference" into the codicil.

A new will (second will) can be executed that may or may not revoke the first or a prior will, depending on the language used. To revoke a prior will, the second will must use language specifically revoking other wills, such as, "This will hereby revokes all prior wills." If the second will is otherwise valid and properly executed, it will revoke all prior wills. If the express *declaration of revocation* is missing, then both

wills are read together. If there are any discrepancies between the wills, the second will controls.

REVOCATION BY OPERATION OF LAW Revocation by operation of law occurs when a marriage, a divorce, an annulment, or the birth of a child takes place after a will has been executed.

Marriage and Divorce. When a testator marries after executing a will and the will does not provide for the new spouse, the new spouse may still receive part of the estate. In most states, a subsequent marriage revokes a portion of the will to allow the new spouse to share in the estate. On the testator's death, the spouse can still receive the amount he or she would have taken had the testator died intestate (intestacy laws will be discussed shortly). The rest of the estate is passed under the will [UPC 2–301, 2–508].

If, however, the new spouse is otherwise provided for in the will (or by transfer of property outside the will), he or she will not be given an intestate amount. Also, if the parties had a valid *prenuptial agreement* (see Chapter 16), its provisions dictate what the surviving spouse receives.

At common law and under the law of most states, divorce does not necessarily revoke the entire will. A divorce or an annulment occurring after a will has been executed revokes those dispositions of property made under the will to the former spouse [UPC 2–508].

Children. When a child is born after a will has been executed, she or he may be entitled to a portion of the estate. Most state laws allow a child (born before or after execution of the will) to receive some portion of a parent's estate even if no provision is made in the parent's will. An exception is made when it is clear from the will's terms that the testator intended to disinherit the child (see *Case 51.2,* presented earlier). Under the UPC, the rule is the same.

Rights under a Will

The law imposes certain limitations on the way a person can dispose of property in a will. For instance, a married person who makes a will generally cannot avoid leaving a certain portion of the estate to the surviving spouse unless there is a valid prenuptial agreement. In most states, this is called an *elective share* or a *forced share,* and it is often one-third of the estate or an amount equal to a spouse's share under intestacy laws.

Beneficiaries under a will have rights as well. A beneficiary can renounce (disclaim) his or her share of the property given under a will. Further, a surviving spouse can renounce the amount given under a will and elect to take the forced share when the forced share is larger than the amount of the gift. State statutes provide the methods by which a surviving spouse accomplishes renunciation. The purpose of these statutes is to allow the spouse to obtain whichever distribution would be more advantageous. The UPC gives the surviving spouse an elective right to take a percentage of the total estate determined by the length of time that the spouse and the decedent were married to each other [UPC 2–201].

Probate Procedures

Typically, the procedures used to probate a will depend on the size of the decedent's estate.

INFORMAL PROBATE For smaller estates, most state statutes provide for the distribution of assets without formal probate proceedings. Faster and less expensive methods are then used. Property can be transferred by *affidavit* (a written statement taken in the presence of a person who has authority to affirm it). Problems or questions can be handled during an administrative hearing. Some states allow title to cars, savings and checking accounts, and certain other property to be transferred simply by filling out forms.

A majority of states also provide for *family settlement agreements,* which are private agreements among the beneficiaries. Once a will is admitted to probate, the family members can agree to settle among themselves the distribution of the decedent's assets. Although a family settlement agreement speeds the settlement process, a court order is still needed to protect the estate from future creditors and to clear title to the assets involved. The use of these and other types of summary procedures in estate administration can save time and expenses.

FORMAL PROBATE For larger estates, formal probate proceedings normally are undertaken, and the probate court supervises every aspect of the settlement of the decedent's estate. Additionally, in some situations—such as when a guardian for minor children must be appointed—more formal probate procedures cannot be avoided.

Formal probate proceedings may take several months or several years to complete, depending on the size and complexity of the estate and whether the will is contested. Factors that affect probate include the types of assets owned, the form of ownership, tax issues, the difficulty in locating the beneficiaries who inherit under the will, and marital property issues. When the will is contested, or someone objects to the actions of the personal representative, the duration of probate is extended. As a result, a sizable portion of the decedent's assets (as much as 10 percent) may go to pay the fees charged by attorneys and personal representatives, as well as court costs.

Property Transfers outside the Probate Process

In the ordinary situation, a person can employ various **will substitutes** to avoid the cost of probate—including *living trusts* (discussed later in this chapter), life insurance policies, or individual retirement accounts

(IRAs) with named beneficiaries. One way to transfer property outside the probate process is to make gifts to children or others while one is still living.

Another method of accomplishing a property transfer without a will is through the joint ownership of property. For instance, a person can hold title to certain real or personal property as a joint tenant with a spouse or other person. Recall from Chapter 49 that in a joint tenancy, when one joint tenant dies, the other joint tenant or tenants automatically inherit the deceased tenant's share of the property. This is true even if the deceased tenant has provided otherwise in her or his will.

In all of these situations, the person who sets up a living trust, arranges for a joint tenancy, or names a beneficiary for an IRA should be careful to ensure that the arrangement will benefit the intended person. A court will not apply the same principles when it reviews a transfer outside probate as it would apply to a testamentary transfer.

See *Concept Summary 51.1* below for a review of basic information about wills.

CONCEPT SUMMARY 51.1
Wills

CONCEPT	DESCRIPTION
Terminology	1. *Intestate*—Describes one who dies without a valid will. 2. *Testator*—A person who makes a will. 3. *Personal representative*—A person appointed in a will or by a court to settle the affairs of a decedent. A personal representative named in the will is an *executor*. A personal representative appointed by the court for an intestate decedent is an *administrator*. 4. *Devise*—A gift of real estate by will, whether general or specific. The recipient of a devise is a *devisee*. 5. *Bequest, or legacy*—A gift of personal property by will, which can be general or specific. The recipient of a bequest (legacy) is a *legatee*.
Requirements for a Valid Will	1. The testator must have testamentary capacity (be of legal age and sound mind at the time the will is made). 2. A will must be in writing (except for nuncupative wills). 3. A will must be signed by the testator, and usually several people must witness the signing, depending on the state statute.

Revocation of Wills	1. *By a physical act of the maker*—Intentionally tearing up, canceling, obliterating, or deliberately destroying part or all of a will revokes it.
	2. *By subsequent writing*—
	  a. Codicil—A formal, separate document that amends or revokes an existing will.
	  b. Second will, or new will—A new, properly executed will expressly revoking the existing will.
	3. *By operation of law*—
	  a. Marriage—Generally revokes a will written before the marriage to the extent of providing for the spouse.
	  b. Divorce or annulment—Revokes dispositions of property made to the former spouse under a will made before the divorce or annulment.
	  c. Subsequently born child—It is inferred that the child is entitled to receive the portion of the estate granted under intestacy distribution laws.

Probate Procedures	To *probate* a will means to establish its validity and to carry out the administration of the estate through a court process. Probate laws vary from state to state. Probate procedures may be informal or formal, depending on the size of the estate and other factors, such as whether a guardian for minor children must be appointed.

INTESTACY LAWS

Each state regulates by statute how property will be distributed when a person dies intestate (without a valid will). These statutes are sometimes called statutes of descent and distribution or, more simply, intestacy laws, as mentioned in this chapter's introduction. Intestacy laws attempt to carry out the likely intent and wishes of the decedent.

These laws assume that deceased persons would have intended that their natural heirs (spouses, children, grandchildren, or other family members) inherit their property. Therefore, intestacy statutes set out rules and priorities under which these heirs inherit the property. If no heirs exist, the state will assume ownership of the property. The rules of descent vary widely from state to state. It is thus important to refer to the exact language of the applicable state statutes when addressing any problem of intestacy distribution.

Surviving Spouse and Children

Usually, state statutes provide that first the debts of the decedent must be satisfied out of the estate. Then the remaining assets pass to the surviving spouse and to the children. A surviving spouse usually receives only a share of the estate—typically, one-half if there is also a surviving child and one-third if there are two or more children.[6] Only if no children or grandchildren survive the decedent will a surviving spouse receive the entire estate.

▶ **Example 51.5** Allen dies intestate and is survived by his wife, Betty, and his children, Duane and Tara. Allen's property passes according to intestacy laws. After his outstanding debts are paid, Betty will receive the family home (either in fee simple or as a life estate) and ordinarily a one-third to one-half interest in all other property. The remaining real and personal property will pass to Duane and Tara in equal portions. ◀

Under most state intestacy laws and under the UPC, in-laws do not share in an estate. If a child dies before his or her parents, the child's spouse will not receive an inheritance on the parents' death. Thus, in *Example*

51.5, if Duane died before his father (Allen), Duane's widow would not inherit his share of Allen's estate.

When There Is No Surviving Spouse or Child

When there is no surviving spouse or child, the order of inheritance is grandchildren, then parents of the decedent. These relatives usually are called *lineal descendants.*

If there are no lineal descendants, then *collateral heirs*—brothers and sisters, nieces and nephews, and aunts and uncles of the decedent—are the next groups that share. If there are no survivors in any of these groups, most statutes provide for the property to be distributed among the next of kin of the collateral heirs.

Stepchildren, Adopted Children, and Illegitimate Children

Under intestacy laws, stepchildren are not considered kin. Legally adopted children, however, are recognized as lawful heirs of their adoptive parents (as are children who are in the process of being adopted at the time of a prospective parent's death).

Statutes vary from state to state in regard to the inheritance rights of illegitimate children, or children born out of wedlock. Generally, an illegitimate child is treated as the child of the mother and can inherit from her and her relatives. Traditionally, the child usually was not regarded as the legal child of the father for inheritance purposes—unless paternity had been established through some legal proceeding.

Because of the dramatic increase in the number of children born out of wedlock today, many states have relaxed their laws of inheritance. A majority of states now consider a child born of any union that has the characteristics of a formal marriage relationship (such as unmarried parents who cohabit) to be legitimate.

Under the revised UPC, a child is the child of the natural (biological) parents, regardless of their marital status, as long as the natural parent has openly treated the child as her or his offspring [UPC 2–114]. Although illegitimate children have inheritance rights in most states, their rights are not necessarily identical to those of legitimate children.[7]

---

6. UPC 2–102 has a formula for computing a surviving spouse's share that is contingent on the number of surviving children and parents. For example, if the decedent has no surviving children and one surviving parent, the surviving spouse takes the first $200,000, plus three-fourths of any balance of the intestate estate. UPC 2–102(2).

7. In the landmark case *Trimble v. Gordon,* 430 U.S. 762, 97 S.Ct. 1459, 52 L.Ed.2d 31 (1977), the United States Supreme Court ruled that state limitations on the inheritance rights of illegitimate children must be rationally related to a legitimate state interest.

Grandchildren

Usually, a will provides for how the decedent's estate will be distributed to descendants of deceased children (grandchildren). If a will does not include such a provision—or if a person dies intestate—the question arises as to what share the grandchildren of the decedent will receive. Each state designates one of two methods of distributing the assets of intestate decedents.

PER STIRPES DISTRIBUTION One method of dividing an intestate's estate is ***per stirpes***.[8] Under this method, within a class or group of distributees (such as grandchildren), the children of any one descendant take the share that their deceased parent *would have been* entitled to inherit.

▶ **Example 51.6** Michael, a widower, has two children, Scott and Jillian. Scott has two children (Becky and Holly), and Jillian has one child (Paul). Scott and Jillian die before their father. When Michael dies, if his estate is distributed *per stirpes,* Becky and Holly each receive one-fourth of the estate (dividing Scott's one-half share). Paul receives one-half of the estate (taking Jillian's one-half share). Exhibit 51–2 below illustrates the *per stirpes* method of distribution. ◀

PER CAPITA DISTRIBUTION An estate may also be distributed on a ***per capita***[9] basis—that is, each person in a class or group takes an equal share of the estate.

---

8. *Per stirpes* is a Latin term meaning "by the roots" or "by stock." When used in estate law, it means proportionally divided between beneficiaries according to each beneficiary's deceased ancestor's share.
9. *Per capita* is a Latin term meaning "per person" or "for each head." When used in estate law, it means divided equally among beneficiaries within a class.

▶ **Example 51.7** If Michael's estate is distributed *per capita*, Becky, Holly, and Paul will each receive a one-third share. Exhibit 51–3 on the following page illustrates the *per capita* method of distribution. ◀

SECTION 3
TRUSTS

A **trust** is any arrangement by which property is transferred from one person to a trustee to be administered for the transferor's or another party's benefit. It can also be defined as a right of property (real or personal) held by one party for the benefit of another. A trust can be created to become effective during a person's lifetime or after a person's death. Trusts may be established for any purpose that is not illegal or against public policy, and they may be express or implied.

The essential elements of a trust are as follows:

1. A designated beneficiary (except in charitable trusts, discussed shortly).
2. A designated trustee.
3. A fund sufficiently identified to enable title to pass to the trustee.
4. Actual delivery by the *settlor* or *grantor* (the person creating the trust) to the trustee with the intention of passing title.

Express Trusts

An express trust is created or declared in explicit terms, usually in writing. There are numerous types of express trusts, each with its own special characteristics.

EXHIBIT 51–2 *Per Stirpes* **Distribution**

Under this method of distribution, an heir takes the share that his or her deceased parent would have been entitled to inherit, had the parent lived. This may mean that a class of distributees—the grandchildren in this example—will not inherit in equal portions. Note that Becky and Holly receive only one-fourth of Michael's estate while Paul inherits one-half.

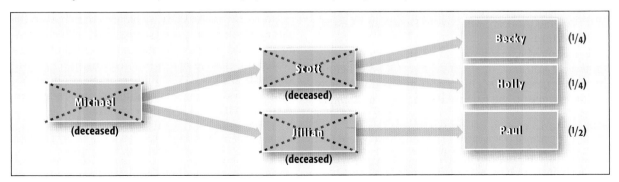

EXHIBIT 51–3 *Per Capita* Distribution

Under this method of distribution, all heirs in a certain class—in this example, the grandchildren—inherit equally. Note that Becky and Holly in this situation each inherit one-third, as does Paul.

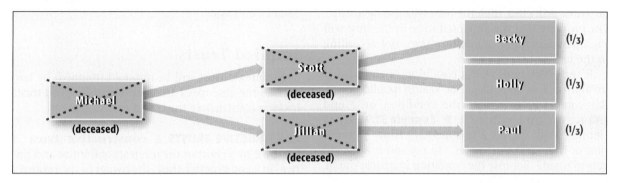

LIVING TRUSTS A **living trust**—or *inter vivos* trust (*inter vivos* is Latin for "between or among the living")—is a trust created by a grantor during her or his lifetime. Living trusts have become a popular estate-planning option because at the grantor's death, assets held in a living trust can pass to the heirs without going through probate.

Note, however, that living trusts do not necessarily shelter assets from estate taxes. The grantor may also have to pay income taxes on trust earnings, depending on whether the trust is revocable or irrevocable.

Revocable Living Trusts. Living trusts can be revocable or irrevocable. In a *revocable* living trust, which is the most common type, the grantor retains control over the trust property during her or his lifetime. The grantor deeds the property to the trustee but retains the power to amend, alter, or revoke the trust during her or his lifetime.

The grantor may also serve as a trustee or co-trustee and can arrange to receive income earned by the trust assets during her or his lifetime. Because the grantor is in control of the funds, she or he is required to pay income taxes on the trust earnings. Unless the trust is revoked, the principal of the trust is transferred to the trust beneficiary on the grantor's death.

▶ **Example 51.8** James Cortez owns and operates a large farm. After his wife dies, James decides to create a living trust for the benefit of his three children, Alicia, Emma, and Jacob. He contacts his attorney, who prepares the documents creating the trust, executes a deed conveying the farm to the trust, and transfers the farm's bank accounts into the name of the trust.

The trust designates James as the trustee and names his son Jacob as the *successor trustee,* who will take over the management of the trust when James dies or becomes incapacitated. Each of the children (as *income beneficiaries*) will receive an income from the trust while James is alive. When James dies, the farm will pass to them without having to go through probate. By holding the property in a revocable living trust, James still has control over the farm during his life (and can make changes to the trust at any time). ◀

Irrevocable Living Trusts. In an *irrevocable* living trust, the grantor permanently gives up control over the property to the trustee. The grantor executes a trust deed, and legal title to the trust property passes to the named trustee. The trustee has a duty to administer the property as directed by the grantor for the benefit and in the interest of the beneficiaries.

The trustee must preserve the trust property and make it productive. If required by the terms of the trust agreement, the trustee must pay income to the beneficiaries in accordance with the terms of the trust. Because the grantor has, in effect, given over the property for the benefit of the beneficiaries, he or she is no longer responsible for paying income taxes on the trust earnings.

TESTAMENTARY TRUSTS A **testamentary trust** is created by will and comes into existence on the grantor's death. Although a testamentary trust has a trustee who maintains legal title to the trust property, the trustee's actions are subject to judicial approval. The trustee can be named in the will or appointed by the court if the trust does not name a trustee. The legal responsibilities of the trustee are the same as in a living trust.

If a court finds that the will setting up a testamentary trust is invalid, then the trust will also be invalid. The property that was supposed to be in the trust will then pass according to intestacy laws, not according to the terms of the trust.

If the court finds that a condition of the trust is invalid because it is illegal or against public policy, the court will invalidate the condition only and enforce the trust without it. ▶ **Example 51.9** Linzy Herman's will creates a testamentary trust. A condition of Herman's trust states, "to my son if he never gets married." Because the condition is against public policy, the court will read the terms of the trust as not including the invalid restraint on marriage. ◀

CHARITABLE TRUSTS A **charitable trust** is an express trust designed for the benefit of a segment of the public or the public in general. It differs from other types of trusts in that the identities of the beneficiaries are uncertain and it can be established to last indefinitely. Usually, to be deemed a charitable trust, a trust must be created for charitable, educational, religious, or scientific purposes.

SPENDTHRIFT TRUSTS A **spendthrift trust** is created to provide for the maintenance of a beneficiary by preventing him or her from being careless with the bestowed funds. Unlike the beneficiaries of other trusts, the beneficiary in a spendthrift trust is not permitted to transfer or assign (see Chapter 17) his or her rights to the trust's principal or future payments from the trust.

Essentially, the beneficiary can draw only a certain portion of the total amount to which he or she is entitled at any one time. The majority of states allow spendthrift trust provisions that prohibit creditors from attaching such trusts, with a few exceptions, such as for payment of a beneficiary's domestic-support obligations.

TOTTEN TRUSTS A **Totten trust**[10] is created when a grantor deposits funds into an account in her or his own name with instructions that in the event of the grantor's death, whatever is in that account should go to a specific beneficiary. This type of trust is revocable at will until the depositor dies or completes the gift in her or his lifetime (by delivering the funds to the intended beneficiary, for instance). The beneficiary has no access to the funds until the depositor's death, when the beneficiary obtains property rights to the balance on hand.

Implied Trusts

Sometimes, a trust will be imposed (implied) by law, even in the absence of an express trust. Implied trusts include constructive trusts and resulting trusts.

CONSTRUCTIVE TRUSTS A **constructive trust** is imposed by a court in the interests of fairness and justice. In a constructive trust, the owner of the property is declared to be a trustee for the parties who are, in equity, actually entitled to the benefits that flow from the trust. Courts often impose constructive trusts when someone who is in a confidential or fiduciary relationship with another person, such as a guardian to a ward, has breached a duty to that person.

If someone wrongfully holds legal title to property—because the property was obtained through fraud or in breach of a legal duty, for instance—a court may impose a constructive trust. ▶ **Case in Point 51.10** Stella Jankowski added her niece Genevieve Viarengo as a joint owner on bank accounts and other financial assets valued at $500,000. Jankowski also executed a will that divided her estate equally among her ten nieces, nephews, and cousins, and named Viarengo and Richard Golebiewski as coexecutors. She did not tell the attorney who drafted the will about the jointly held accounts.

When Jankowski died, Viarengo emptied Jankowski's safe and removed her financial records. Viarengo also claimed that the funds in the accounts were hers. Jankowski's other relatives filed a suit and asked the court to impose a constructive trust. The court found that Viarengo had committed fraud in obtaining the assets that she had held jointly with Jankowski and would be unjustly enriched if she were allowed to retain them. Therefore, the court imposed a constructive trust.[11] ◀

RESULTING TRUSTS A **resulting trust** arises from the conduct of the parties. Here, the trust results, or is created, when circumstances raise an inference that the party holding legal title to the property does so for the benefit of another. The trust will result unless the inference is refuted.

---

10. This type of trust derives its unusual name from *In the Matter of Totten,* 179 N.Y. 112, 71 N.E. 748 (1904).

11. *Garrigus v. Viarengo,* 112 Conn.App. 655, 963 A.2d 1065 (2009).

▶ **Example 51.11**   Gabriela Fuentes wants to put one acre of land she owns on the market for sale. Because she is going out of the country for two years and will not be available to deed the property to a buyer during that period, she conveys the property to her good friend Raul Cruz. Cruz can then attempt to sell the property while Fuentes is gone.

The transaction in which Fuentes conveyed the property to Cruz was intended to be neither a sale nor a gift. Consequently, Cruz will hold the property in a resulting trust for the benefit of Fuentes. When Fuentes returns, Cruz will be required either to deed the property back to her or, if the property has been sold, to turn over the proceeds (held in trust) to her. ◀

Concept Summary 51.2 below provides a synopsis of basic information about trusts.

The Trustee

The trustee is the person holding the trust property. Anyone legally capable of holding title to, and dealing in, property can be a trustee. If a trust fails to name a trustee, or if a named trustee cannot or will not serve, the trust does not fail. An appropriate court can appoint a trustee.

TRUSTEE'S DUTIES   A trustee must act with honesty, good faith, and prudence in administering the trust and must exercise a high degree of loyalty toward the trust beneficiary. The general standard of care is the degree of care a prudent person would exercise in his or her personal affairs.[12] The duty of loyalty requires that the trustee act in the exclusive interest of the beneficiary.

A trustee's specific duties include the following:

1. Maintain clear and accurate accounts of the trust's administration.
2. Furnish complete and correct information to the beneficiary.
3. Keep trust assets separate from her or his own assets.
4. Pay to an income beneficiary the net income of the trust assets at reasonable intervals.

---

12. Revised Uniform Principal and Income Act, Section 2(a)(3); and *Restatement (Third) of Trusts (Prudent Investor Rule)*, Section 227. This rule is in force in a majority of the states by statute and a small number of states under common law.

CONCEPT SUMMARY 51.2
Trusts

CONCEPT	DESCRIPTION
Definition and Essential Elements	A trust is any arrangement by which property is transferred from one person to a trustee to be administered for another's benefit. The essential elements of a trust are (1) a designated beneficiary, (2) a designated trustee, (3) a fund sufficiently identified to enable title to pass to the trustee, and (4) actual delivery to the trustee with the intention of passing title.
Types of Trusts	1. *Living (inter vivos) trust*—A trust executed by a grantor during his or her lifetime. A living trust may be revocable or irrevocable. 2. *Testamentary trust*—A trust created by will and coming into existence on the death of the grantor. 3. *Charitable trust*—A trust designed for the benefit of a segment of the public or the public in general. 4. *Spendthrift trust*—A trust created to provide for the maintenance of a beneficiary by allowing her or him to receive only a certain portion of the total amount at any one time. 5. *Totten trust*—A trust created when one person deposits funds in his or her own name with instructions that the funds should go to a beneficiary on the depositor's death.
Implied Trusts	Implied trusts, which are imposed by law in the interests of fairness and justice, include the following: 1. *Constructive trust*—Arises by operation of law when a transaction occurs in which the person who takes title to property is, in equity, not entitled to enjoy the benefits from it. 2. *Resulting trust*—Arises from the conduct of the parties when an *apparent intention* to create a trust is present.

5. Limit the risk of loss from investments by reasonable diversification and dispose of assets that do not represent prudent investments. (Prudent investment choices might include federal, state, or municipal bonds and some corporate bonds and stocks.)

TRUSTEE'S POWERS When a grantor creates a trust, he or she may set forth the trustee's powers and performance. State law governs in the absence of specific terms in the trust, and the states often restrict the trustee's investment of trust funds.

Typically, statutes confine trustees to investments in conservative debt securities such as government, utility, and railroad bonds and certain real estate loans. Frequently, though, a grantor gives a trustee discretionary investment power. In that circumstance, any statute may be considered only advisory, with the trustee's decisions subject in most states to the prudent person rule.

Of course, a trustee is responsible for carrying out the purposes of the trust. If the trustee fails to comply with the terms of the trust or the controlling statute, he or she is personally liable for any loss.

ALLOCATIONS BETWEEN PRINCIPAL AND INCOME Often, a grantor will provide one beneficiary with a life estate and another beneficiary with the remainder interest in the trust. A farmer, for instance, may create a testamentary trust providing that the farm's income be paid to the surviving spouse and that, on the surviving spouse's death, the farm be given to their children. In this situation, the surviving spouse has a *life estate* in the farm's income, and the children have a *remainder interest* in the farm (the principal).

When a trust is set up in this manner, questions may arise as to how the receipts and expenses for the farm's management and the trust's administration should be allocated between income and principal. When a trust instrument does not provide instructions, a trustee must refer to applicable state law.

The general rule is that ordinary receipts and expenses are chargeable to the income beneficiary, whereas extraordinary receipts and expenses are allocated to the principal beneficiaries.[13] The receipt of rent from trust realty would be ordinary, as would the expense of paying the property's taxes. The cost of long-term improvements and proceeds from the property's sale, however, would be extraordinary.

---

13. Revised Uniform Principal and Income Act, Sections 3, 6, 8, and 13; and *Restatement (Third) of Trusts, (Prudent Investor Rule)*, Section 233.

Trust Termination

The terms of a trust should expressly state the event on which the grantor wishes it to terminate—for instance, the beneficiary's or the trustee's death. If the trust instrument does not provide for termination on the beneficiary's death, the beneficiary's death will not end the trust. Similarly, without an express provision, a trust will not terminate on the trustee's death.

Typically, a trust instrument specifies a termination date. For instance, a trust created to educate the grantor's child may provide that the trust ends when the beneficiary reaches the age of twenty-five. If the trust's purpose is fulfilled before that date, a court may order the trust's termination. If no date is specified, a trust will terminate when its purpose has been fulfilled. Of course, if a trust's purpose becomes impossible or illegal, the trust will terminate.

SECTION 4
OTHER ESTATE-PLANNING ISSUES

Estate planning involves making difficult decisions about the future, such as who will inherit the family home and other assets and who will take care of minor children. Individuals today should also consider formulating a social media estate plan, as discussed in this chapter's *Insight into Social Media* feature on the following page.

Estate planning also involves preparing in advance for other contingencies, such as illness and incapacity. For instance, what happens if you become incapacitated and cannot make your own decisions? Who will take care of your finances and other affairs? Do you want to be kept alive by artificial means, and who do you trust to make decisions about your health care in the event that you cannot? In this section, we discuss powers of attorney and living wills, both of which are frequently executed in conjunction with a will or trust.

Power of Attorney

As discussed in Chapter 33, a power of attorney is often used in business situations to give a person (an agent) authority to act on another's behalf. The powers usually are limited to a specific context, such as negotiating a deal with a buyer or entering into various contracts necessary to achieve a particular objec-

---

INSIGHT INTO SOCIAL MEDIA
Social Media Estate Planning

People are generally quite careful about choosing the personal representatives who will deal with their real estate, bank accounts, and investments after they have died. Today, the same care should be taken in choosing an online executor to deal with a deceased's online identity, particularly in social media.

What an Online Executor Should Do

An online executor is responsible for dealing with a decedent's e-mail addresses, social media profiles, and blogs. E-mail accounts should be closed, but some people do not want their social media profiles to be erased after they die. They want the profiles to be maintained, at least for some specified time after death, so that family and friends can visit them. Some people ask that the online executor place a memorial profile in their social media accounts.

Why Social Media Estate Planning Is Important

Online estate planning is essential because the deceased can still be a victim of identity theft. Unscrupulous fraud-

sters often use dead people's online identities to defraud private companies, individuals, and federal and state governments. If all of a person's e-mail addresses and social media accounts are closed, it is harder for online fraudsters to use them for identity theft.

In addition, closing an e-mail account protects family members from being harassed with continuing spam after the person's death and prevents spammers from hijacking the account. Spammers can use a dead person's e-mail account as the sender of billions of unwanted bulk e-mails.

LEGAL CRITICAL THINKING

INSIGHT INTO THE LEGAL ENVIRONMENT

Why might an online executor need a copy of the deceased's death certificate?

---

tive. Powers of attorney are commonly used in estate planning.

DURABLE POWER OF ATTORNEY One method of providing for future disability is to use a durable power of attorney. A **durable power of attorney** authorizes an individual to act on behalf of another when he or she becomes incapacitated. It can be drafted to take effect immediately or only after a physician certifies that the person is incapacitated. The person to whom the power is given can then write checks, collect insurance proceeds, and otherwise manage the incapacitated person's affairs, including health care.

Adult children may seek a durable power of attorney from their aging parents, particularly if the parents are becoming mentally incompetent or afflicted by Alzheimer's disease. A husband and wife may give each other a power of attorney to make decisions in the event that one of them is hospitalized and unable to express her or his wishes. A person who is undergoing an operation may sign a durable power of attorney to a loved one who can take over his or her affairs in the event of incapacity.

If you become incapacitated without having executed a durable power of attorney, a court may need to appoint a conservator to handle your financial affairs. Although a spouse may have some ability to write checks on joint accounts, her or his power is often significantly limited. In most situations, it is better to have named a person you wish to handle your affairs in the event that you cannot.

HEALTH-CARE POWER OF ATTORNEY A **health-care power of attorney** designates a person who will have the power to choose what type of and how much medical treatment a person who is unable to make such decisions will receive. The importance of appointing a person to make health-care decisions has grown as medical technology enables physicians and hospitals to keep people technically alive for ever-increasing periods of time.

▶ **Example 51.12** Terri Schiavo, a Florida woman, was kept alive in a vegetative state from 1990 to 2005. It took more than twenty court hearings for her husband to convince the court that he had a right to ask physicians to remove her feeding tube and let her die.

If Schiavo had given her husband a health-care power of attorney, he would have had the right to make the decision to remove the feeding tube without going to court. ◄

Living Will

A living will is not a will in the usual sense—that is, it does not appoint an estate representative, dispose of property, or establish a trust. Rather, a **living will** is an advance health directive that allows a person to control what medical treatment may be used after a serious accident or illness. Through a living will, a person can indicate whether he or she wants certain lifesaving procedures to be undertaken in situations in which the treatment will not result in a reasonable quality of life.

Most states have enacted statutes permitting living wills, and it is important that the requirements of state law be followed exactly in creating such wills. Typically, state statutes require physicians to abide by the terms of living wills, and living wills are often included with a patient's medical records.

Reviewing: Wills and Trusts

In June 2013, Bernard Ramish set up a $48,000 trust fund through West Plains Credit Union to provide tuition for his nephew, Nathan Covacek, to attend Tri-State Polytechnic Institute. The trust was established under Ramish's control and went into effect that August. In December, Ramish suffered a brain aneurysm that caused frequent, severe headaches with no other symptoms. Shortly thereafter, Ramish met with an attorney to formalize in writing that he wanted no artificial life-support systems to be used should he suffer a serious illness. He also designated his cousin, Lizzie Johansen, to make decisions on his behalf should he become incapacitated. In August 2015, Ramish developed heatstroke on the golf course at La Prima Country Club.

After recuperating at the clubhouse, Ramish quickly wrote his will on the back of a wine list. It stated, "My last will and testament: Upon my death, I give all of my personal property to my friend Steve Eshom and my home to Lizzie Johansen." He signed the will at the bottom in the presence of five men in the La Prima clubhouse, and all five men signed as witnesses.

A week later, Ramish suffered a second aneurysm and died in his sleep. He was survived by his mother (Dorris Ramish), his son-in-law (Bruce Lupin), and his granddaughter (Tori Lupin). Using the information presented in the chapter, answer the following questions.

1. What type of trust did Ramish create for the benefit of Covacek? Was it revocable or irrevocable?
2. Would Ramish's testament on the back of the wine list meet the requirements for a valid will? Why or why not?
3. What would the order of inheritance have been if Ramish had died intestate?
4. Was Johansen granted a durable power of attorney or a health-care power of attorney for Ramish? Had Ramish created a living will? Explain.

DEBATE THIS ... *Any changes to existing, fully witnessed wills should also have to be witnessed.*

Terms and Concepts

administrator 996
bequest 998
charitable trust 1010
codicil 1004
constructive trust 1010

devise 998
durable power of attorney 1013
escheat 996
estate planning 996
executor 996

health-care power of attorney 1013
holographic will 1002
intestacy laws 996
intestate 996
legacy 998

living trust 1009	probate 997	testator 996
living will 1014	resulting trust 1010	Totten trust 1010
nuncupative will 1002	spendthrift trust 1010	trust 1008
per capita 1008	testamentary trust 1009	will 996
per stirpes 1008	testate 996	will substitutes 1005

ExamPrep

Issue Spotters

1. Sheila makes out a will, leaving her property in equal thirds to Toby and Umeko, her children, and Velda, her niece. Two years later, Sheila is adjudged mentally incompetent, and that same year, she dies. Can Toby and Umeko have Sheila's will revoked on the ground that she did not have the capacity to make a will? Why or why not? **(See page 999.)**

2. Rafael dies without having made a will. He is survived by many relatives—a spouse, children, adopted children, sisters, brothers, uncles, aunts, cousins, nephews, and nieces. What determines who gets what? **(See page 1007.)**

- Check your answers to the Issue Spotters against the answers provided in Appendix E at the end of this text.

Before the Test

Go to **www.cengagebrain.com**, enter the ISBN 9781285185248, and click on "Find" to locate this textbook's Web site. Then, click on "Access Now" under "Study Tools," and select Chapter 51 at the top. There, you will find a Practice Quiz that you can take to assess your mastery of the concepts in this chapter, as well as Flashcards and a Glossary of important terms.

Business Scenarios

51–1. Wills and Intestacy Laws. Benjamin is a widower who has two married children, Edward and Patricia. Patricia has two children, Perry and Paul. Edward has no children. Benjamin dies, and his typewritten will leaves all of his property equally to his children, Edward and Patricia, and provides that should a child predecease him, the grandchildren are to take *per stirpes*. The will was witnessed by Patricia and by Benjamin's lawyer, and it was signed by Benjamin in their presence. Patricia has predeceased Benjamin. Edward claims the will is invalid. **(See page 1007.)**

(a) Discuss whether the will is valid.

(b) Discuss the distribution of Benjamin's estate if the will is invalid.

(c) Discuss the distribution of Benjamin's estate if the will is valid.

51–2. Specific Bequests. Gary Mendel drew up a will in which he left his favorite car, a 1966 red Ferrari, to his daughter, Roberta. A year prior to his death, Mendel sold the 1966 Ferrari and purchased a 1969 Ferrari. Discuss whether Roberta will inherit the 1969 Ferrari under the terms of her father's will. **(See page 998.)**

51–3. Revocation of Wills. While single, James made out a will naming his mother, Carol, as sole beneficiary. Later, James married Lisa. **(See page 1003.)**

(a) If James died while married to Lisa without changing his will, would the estate go to his mother, Carol? Explain.

(b) Assume that James made out a new will on his marriage to Lisa, leaving his entire estate to Lisa. Later, he divorced Lisa and married Mandis, but he did not change his will. Discuss the rights of Lisa and Mandis to James's estate after his death.

(c) Assume that James divorced Lisa, married Mandis, and changed his will, leaving his estate to Mandis. Later, a daughter, Claire, was born. James died without having included Claire in his will. Discuss fully whether Claire has any rights in the estate.

51–4. Intent Requirement. Merlin Winters had three sons. Merlin and his youngest son, Abraham, had a falling out in 1994 and stopped speaking to each other. Merlin made a formal will in 1996, leaving all of his property to the two older sons and explicitly excluding Abraham. Merlin's health began to deteriorate, and by 1997, he was under the full-time care of a nurse, Julia. In 1998, he made a new will expressly revoking the 1996 will and leaving all of his property to Julia. On Merlin's death, the two older sons contest the 1998 will, claiming that Julia exercised undue influence over their father. Abraham claims that both wills are invalid because the first will was revoked by the second will, and the second will is invalid on the ground of undue influence. Is Abraham's contention correct? Explain. **(See page 999.)**

Business Case Problems

51–5. Intestacy Laws. A Florida statute provides that the right of election of a surviving spouse can be waived by written agreement: "A waiver of 'all rights,' or equivalent language, in the property or estate of a present or prospective spouse . . . is a waiver of all rights to elective share." The day before Mary Ann Taylor married Louis Taylor in Florida, they entered into a prenuptial agreement. The agreement stated that all property belonging to each spouse would "forever remain his or her personal estate," "said property shall remain forever free of claim by the other," and the parties would retain "full rights and authority" over their property as they would have "if not married." After Louis died without a will, his only child, Joshua Taylor, filed a petition in a Florida state court for a determination of the beneficiaries of Louis's estate. How much of the estate can Mary Ann elect to receive? Explain. [*Taylor v. Taylor*, 1 So.3d 348 (Fla.App. 1 Dist. 2009)] **(See page 1007.)**

51–6. Wills. Elnora Maxey became the guardian of Sean Hall after his parents died. In 1996, Maxey died, and her will left the two houses in her estate to Hall. Julia Jordan became Hall's new guardian, and when she died, her husband, John Jordan, became Hall's guardian. In 1998, when Hall was eighteen years old, he died intestate, and Jordan was appointed as the administrator of Hall's estate. The two houses had remained in Maxey's estate, but Jordan paid the mortgage and tax payments on the houses for Hall's estate because Hall had inherited the houses. Anthony Cooper, a relative of Maxey, petitioned the probate court to be appointed executor of Maxey's estate, stating that there was now no heir. The court granted the request. Jordan was not aware of the proceedings. Cooper then sold both houses for the incredibly low price of $20,000 each to Quan Smith, without informing Jordan. The houses were then resold to JSD Properties, LLC, for a total of $190,000. Learning of the sale, Jordan sued, contending that Cooper had breached his fiduciary duty and had lied to the court, as Maxey's will had clearly left the houses to Hall. Does Jordan have the right to demand that JSD return the property? What factors would be considered in making this decision? [*Witcher v. JSD Properties, LLC*, 286 Ga. 717, 690 S.E.2d 855 (2010)] **(See page 996.)**

51–7. BUSINESS CASE PROBLEM WITH SAMPLE ANSWER: Undue Influence.

 Susie Walker executed a will that left her entire estate to her grandson. When her grandson died, Susie executed a new will that named her great-grandson as her sole beneficiary and specifically disinherited her son, Tommy. At the time, Tommy's ex-wife was living with Susie. After Susie died, Tommy filed a suit, claiming that her will was the product of undue influence on the part of his ex-wife. Several witnesses testified that Susie had been mentally competent when she executed her will. Does undue influence appear likely based on these facts? Why or why not? [In re Estate of Walker, 80 A.D.3d 865, 914 N.Y.S.2d 379 (3 Dept. 2011)] **(See page 999.)**

- **For a sample answer to Problem 51–7, go to Appendix F at the end of this text.**

51–8. A QUESTION OF ETHICS: Wills.

 Vickie Lynn Smith, an actress and model also known as Anna Nicole Smith, met J. Howard Marshall II in 1991. During their courtship, J. Howard lavished gifts and large sums of money on Anna Nicole, and they married on June 27, 1994. J. Howard died on August 4, 1995. According to Anna Nicole, J. Howard intended to provide for her financial security through a trust, but under the terms of his will, all of his assets were transferred to a trust for the benefit of E. Pierce Marshall, one of J. Howard's sons. While J. Howard's estate was subject to probate proceedings in a Texas state court, Anna Nicole filed for bankruptcy in a federal bankruptcy court. Pierce filed a claim in the bankruptcy proceeding, alleging that Anna Nicole had defamed him when her lawyers told the media that Pierce had engaged in forgery and fraud to gain control of his father's assets. Anna Nicole filed a counterclaim, alleging that Pierce prevented the transfer of his father's assets to a trust for her by, among other things, imprisoning J. Howard against his wishes, surrounding him with security guards to prevent contact with her, and transferring property against his wishes. [Marshall v. Marshall, 547 U.S. 293, 126 S.Ct. 1735, 164 L.Ed.2d 480 (2006)] **(See page 996.)**

- (a) What is the purpose underlying the requirements for a valid will? Which of these requirements might be at issue in this case? How should it apply here? Why?

- (b) State courts generally have jurisdiction over the probate of a will and the administration of an estate. Does the Texas state court thus have the sole authority to adjudicate all of the claims in this case? Why or why not?

- (c) How should Pierce's claim against Anna Nicole and her counterclaim be resolved?

- (d) Anna Nicole executed her will in 2001. The beneficiary—Daniel, her son, who was not J. Howard's child—died in 2006, shortly after Anna Nicole gave birth to a daughter, Dannielynn. In 2007, before executing a new will, Anna Nicole died. What happens if a will's beneficiary dies before the testator? What happens if a child is born after a will is executed?

Legal Reasoning Group Activity

51–9. Intestacy Laws. Three and a half years after Lauren and Warren Woodward were married, they were informed that Warren had leukemia. At the time, the couple had no children, and physicians told the Woodwards that the leukemia treatment might leave Warren sterile. The couple arranged for Warren's sperm to be collected and placed in a sperm bank for later use.

Two years after Warren died, Lauren gave birth to twin girls who had been conceived through artificial insemination using his sperm. The following year, Lauren applied for Social Security survivor benefits for the two children. Her application was rejected on the ground that she had not established that the twins were the husband's children within the meaning of the Social Security Act. Woodward then filed a paternity action in Massachusetts, and the probate court determined that Warren Woodward was the twins' father. She then filed an action in court to determine the inheritance rights of the twins. **(See page 1007.)**

(a) The first group will outline how a court should decide the inheritance rights of children conceived from the sperm of a deceased individual and his surviving spouse.

(b) The second group will decide if children conceived after a parent's death (by means of artificial insemination or *in vitro* fertilization) still inherit under intestate succession laws. Explain the reasoning.

(c) The third group will consider the inheritance rights of a child who was conceived by means of artificial insemination, *in vitro* fertilization, or a surrogate. Should they be different from the rights of a child conceived in the traditional manner? Assuming the biological parent is not part of the child's life, should the child still be able to inherit from the biological parent? Why or why not?

UNIT TEN Focus on Ethics

Property and Its Protection

Property rights have long been given extensive legal protection under both English and U.S. law. In the United States, the right to own property is closely associated with liberty, the pursuit of happiness, and other concepts that have played an integral role in American life. At the same time, conflicts often arise over who owns what and over how property should be used. In this *Focus on Ethics* feature, we explore some of the ethical dimensions of the laws pertaining to property, insurance, and inheritance.

Inheritance Rights and Virtual Property

Many people participate in virtual worlds in cyberspace through avatars (alter egos). Often, these avatars amass virtual property that has an actual value in the real world. For example, in Second Life, a popular virtual world created by Linden Lab, Linden dollars are traded for real dollars.

The virtual goods market in the United States is estimated to be worth at least $1 billion, and worldwide the value may be much as $5 billion. But who really owns the value of this virtual property? If you own a gold coin in the real world, it has a market value and can be passed on to your heirs. But if you own a "gold coin" in Second Life or Bitcoin, will your heirs be able to inherit it after you die?

The fate of a decedent's virtual estate depends, in part, on the virtual world in which it was created. The administrators of some virtual worlds and some Internet service providers allow a new account holder to designate a person who can access the account in the event of his or her death. If the account holder chooses not to do so, the account is simply erased.

To create a virtual world in Second Life, however, the user has to agree to Linden Lab's terms of service, which give the company the right to erase all of the user's virtual property after his or her death. One way to avoid such a fate is to name a *digital executor* through Digital Beyond, a clearinghouse for the distribution of virtual assets after the owner's death. After the owner dies, Digital Beyond transfers her or his most recent passwords to the person named as digital executor, thereby providing access to all of the decedent's accounts.

LEGAL REASONING

1. *A Facebook game, FarmVille, allows members to manage virtual crops together. Would there be any benefit in being able to pass on to one's heirs "the fruits of one's virtual labor"? Why or why not?*

Finders' Rights

The children's adage "finders keepers, losers weepers" is actually written into law—assuming, of course, that the loser (the rightful owner) cannot be found. A finder may acquire good title to found personal property against everyone *except the true owner.*

An early English case, *Armory v. Delamirie,*[1] is a landmark in Anglo-American jurisprudence concerning actions in *trover*—an early form of recovery of damages for the conversion of property. The plaintiff in this case was Armory, a chimney sweep who found a jewel in its setting during the course of his work. He took the jewel to a goldsmith to have it appraised. The goldsmith refused to return the jewel to Armory, claiming that Armory was not the rightful owner of the property.

The court held that the finder, as prior possessor of the item, had rights to the jewel superior to those of all others except the rightful owner. The court said, "The finder of a jewel, though he does not by such finding acquire an absolute property or ownership, yet . . . has such a property as will enable him to keep it against all but the rightful owner, and consequently maintain trover."

The *Armory* case illustrates the doctrine of the *relativity of title.* Under this doctrine, if two contestants, neither of whom can claim absolute title to the property, come before the court, the one who can claim prior possession will likely have established sufficient rights to the property to win the case.

LEGAL REASONING

2. *Does the law strike a fair balance between the rights of parties with respect to found property? Why or why not?*

Bailee's Duty of Care

The standard of care expected of a bailee clearly illustrates how property law reflects ethical principles. For example, a friend asks to borrow your business law text for the weekend. You agree to loan your friend the book. In this situation, which is a bailment for the sole benefit of the bailee (your friend), most people would agree that your friend has an ethical obligation to take great care of your book. After all, if your friend lost your book, you would incur damages. You would have to purchase another one, and if you could not, you might find it difficult to do well on your homework assignments and examinations.

The situation would be different if you had loaned your book to your friend totally for your own benefit. Suppose that you are leaving town during the summer, and your friend offers to store several boxes of books for you until you return in the fall. In this situation, a bailment for the sole benefit of the bailor (you) exists. If your books are destroyed through the bailee's (your friend's) negligence and you sue the bailee for damages, a court will likely take into consideration the fact that the bailee was essentially doing you a favor by storing the books.

Although bailees generally have a duty to exercise reasonable care over bailed property, what constitutes reasonable care in a specific situation normally depends on the surround-

---

1. 93 Eng.Rep. 664 (K.B. [King's Bench] 1722).

ing circumstances. In particular, the duty of care depends on the reason for the bailment and who stood to benefit from the arrangement.

LEGAL REASONING

3. *Do the different standards of care that apply to bailed goods reflect underlying ethical values? If so, how?*

Land-Use Regulations and the "Takings Clause"

When property owners claim that a "regulatory taking" has occurred, the courts decide the issue on a case-by-case basis. In other words, there is no general rule that indicates whether a specific situation will be deemed a taking. In a case decided in 2010, a group of Florida beachfront property owners challenged the constitutionality of the state's decision to add seventy-five feet of sand to the shoreline.

Under Florida law, the boundary between private beachfront property and state-owned land is ordinarily the average high-water line. The state owns any land submerged beneath the ocean or other navigable waters. It is common for storms to cause some fluctuation in the shoreline, however, as sand is deposited or washed away by waves. A change that occurs gradually and imperceptibly over time is called an *accretion,* whereas a sudden change is called an *avulsion*. If an accretion deposits more sand on the shore, the owners of private beachfront property automatically acquire ownership rights to more land—to the new high-water line. If an avulsion occurs, however, the property owners' boundaries remain the same, so the state owns the land abutting the water's edge.

As a result of several hurricanes, 6.9 miles of beach were eroded (an avulsion) in the city of Destin and Walton County. The state therefore requested and received a permit from the Florida Department of Environmental Protection to add seventy-five feet of dry sand on its side (the seaward side) of the high-water line. Owners of the private beachfront property in the area formed a nonprofit corporation to fight the proposed addition of sand, but they lost at an administrative hearing. They then filed a lawsuit claiming that the state's action constituted an unlawful taking of their beachfront property.

The Courts Disagree A Florida appellate court agreed with the property owners that the state had taken their rights to

receive accretions and to have their property remain in contact with the water. The Florida Supreme Court reversed, and the United States Supreme Court granted *certiorari*.

The United States Supreme Court held that Florida had not engaged in an unconstitutional taking. According to the Court, there was no taking because the property owners did not show that their rights to future accretions and to contact with the water were superior to Florida's right to fill in its submerged land.

The state did not relocate the property line to take private property, but simply added sand to property that it already owned (on the side toward the water). Therefore, the state had a right to restore the beach even though the addition of sand interfered with the property owners' rights to have their property touch the water.[2] Although a majority of the Supreme Court justices concurred in the result, there were substantial differences in their reasoning.

A Question of Fairness The question of whether private landowners should be compensated when their land is essentially "taken" for public use by environmental and land-use regulations clearly involves issues of fairness. On the one hand, states, cities, and other local governments want to preserve their natural resources and need some authority to regulate land use to achieve this goal.

On the other hand, private property owners complain that they alone should not have to bear the costs of creating a benefit—such as more sandy beaches for recreation or environmental preservation. These are benefits that all members of the public enjoy. In addition, as a different group of Florida beachfront property owners complained in 2013, if the state adds sand to beaches in front of their property, it may lower the property's value.

LEGAL REASONING

4. *Is it fair for courts to decide whether a regulatory taking has occurred on a case-by-case basis, rather than articulating a general rule on which landowners can rely? Why or why not?*

---

2. *Stop the Beach Renourishment, Inc. v. Florida Department of Environmental Protection,* ___ U.S. ___, 130 S.Ct. 2592, 177 L.Ed.2d 184 (2010).

How to Brief Cases and Analyze Case Problems

How to Brief Cases

To fully understand the law with respect to business, you need to be able to read and understand court decisions. To make this task easier, you can use a method of case analysis that is called *briefing*. There is a fairly standard procedure that you can follow when you "brief" any court case. You must first read the case opinion carefully. When you feel you understand the case, you can prepare a brief of it.

Although the format of the brief may vary, typically it will present the essentials of the case under headings such as those listed below.

1. **Citation.** Give the full citation for the case, including the name of the case, the date it was decided, and the court that decided it.
2. **Facts.** Briefly indicate (a) the reasons for the lawsuit; (b) the identity and arguments of the plaintiff(s) and defendant(s), respectively; and (c) the lower court's decision—if appropriate.
3. **Issue.** Concisely phrase, in the form of a question, the essential issue before the court. (If more than one issue is involved, you may have two—or even more—questions here.)
4. **Decision.** Indicate here—with a "yes" or "no," if possible—the court's answer to the question (or questions) in the *Issue* section above.
5. **Reason.** Summarize as briefly as possible the reasons given by the court for its decision (or decisions) and the case or statutory law relied on by the court in arriving at its decision.

An Example of a Briefed Sample Court Case

As an example of the format used in briefing cases, we present here a briefed version of the sample court case that was presented in Chapter 1 in Exhibit 1–6.

APPLE INC. v. AMAZON.COM INC.
United States District Court, Northern District of California, __ F.Supp.2d __, 2013 WL 11896 (2013).

FACTS In July 2008, Apple Inc. began to sell applications for its mobile devices through its APP STORE service. In March 2011, Amazon.com Inc. launched the Amazon Appstore for Android. Apple filed a suit in a federal district court against Amazon in the same month, asserting false advertising. Apple alleged that that by using the word "Appstore" in the name of Amazon's store, Amazon implied that its store was affili-

ated with or sponsored by Apple. Apple argued that Amazon's service did not have the characteristics and qualities that the public had come to expect from the name APP STORE. For this reason, Apple contended, Amazon's use of "Appstore" misled the public. Amazon filed a motion for summary judgment.

ISSUE Can a vendor use the term "Appstore" to designate a site for buying apps without representing that the nature, characteristics, or quality of the site is the same as that of another vendor's "APP STORE"?

DECISION Yes. The court granted Amazon's motion for summary judgment.

REASON The court pointed out that a false advertising claim requires either a false statement of fact in an ad or evidence showing "exactly what message was conveyed that was sufficient to constitute false advertising." Here, Apple failed to show that Amazon made any false statement and presented no evidence that consumers were misled. Apple did not show that consumers understood "app store" to include specific qualities, characteristics, or attributes of the Apple APP STORE or were otherwise misled by Amazon's use of the term. Nothing indicated that a consumer would expect the two sites to be identical—especially considering that Apple sold apps solely for Apple devices and Amazon sold apps solely for Android and Kindle devices. Apple did not make clear how Amazon's use of Appstore constituted a "statement" that implied something false about Apple's APP STORE. Apple "made no showing that such (implied) statement deceived or had a tendency to deceive users of Amazon's Appstore."

Review of Sample Court Case

Here we provide a review of the briefed version to indicate the kind of information that is contained in each section.

CITATION The name of the case is *Apple Inc. v. Amazon.com Inc.* Apple is the plaintiff. Amazon is the defendant. The U.S. District Court for the Northern District of California (a trial court) decided this case in 2013. The citation states that this case can be found in volume __ of the *Federal Supplement, Second Series,* on page __, and on Westlaw® at 2013 WL 11896.

FACTS The *Facts* section identifies the plaintiff and the defendant, describes the events leading up to this suit and the allegations made by the plaintiff in the suit. If this case were a decision of one of the U.S. courts of appeals, the lower court's ruling, the party appealing, and the appellant's contention on appeal would also be included here.

ISSUE The *Issue* section presents the central issue (or issues) decided by the court. This case involves a false advertising claim. The court considers whether a vendor can use the term "Appstore" to designate a site for buying apps without representing that the nature, characteristics, or quality of the site is the same as that of another vendor's "APP STORE."

DECISION The *Decision* section includes the court's decision on the issues before it. The decision reflects the opinion of the judge or justice hearing the case. Here, the court determined that consumers were not deceived by the two vendors' use of the same term. There was no evidence that consumers understood "app store" to include specific qualities, characteristics, or attributes or were otherwise misled by the use of the term. Decisions by appellate courts are frequently phrased in reference to the lower court's decision. That is, the appellate court may "affirm" the lower court's ruling or "reverse" it.

REASON The *Reason* section includes references to the relevant laws and legal principles that were applied in coming to the conclusion arrived at in the case before the court. The relevant law here included the principle that a false advertising claim requires either a false statement of fact in an ad or evidence showing "exactly what message was conveyed that was sufficient to constitute false advertising." This section also explains the court's application of the law to the facts in this case.

Analyzing Case Problems

In addition to learning how to brief cases, students of business law and the legal environment also find it helpful to know how to analyze case problems. Part of the study of business law and the legal environment usually involves analyzing case problems, such as those included in this text at the end of each chapter.

For each case problem in this book, we provide the relevant background and facts of the lawsuit and the issue before the court. When you are assigned one of these problems, your job will be to determine how the court should decide the issue, and why. In other words, you will need to engage in legal analysis and reasoning. Here, we offer some suggestions on how to make this task less daunting. We begin by presenting a sample problem:

> While Janet Lawson, a famous pianist, was shopping in Quality Market, she slipped and fell on a wet floor in one of the aisles. The floor had recently been mopped by one of the store's employees, but there were no signs warning customers that the floor in that area was wet. As a result of the fall, Lawson injured her right arm and was unable to perform piano concerts for the next six months. Had she been able to perform the scheduled concerts, she would have earned approximately $60,000 over that period of time. Lawson sued Quality Market for this amount, plus another $10,000 in medical expenses. She claimed that the store's failure to warn customers of the wet floor constituted

negligence and therefore the market was liable for her injuries. Will the court agree with Lawson? Discuss.

Understand the Facts

This may sound obvious, but before you can analyze or apply the relevant law to a specific set of facts, you must clearly understand those facts. In other words, you should read through the case problem carefully—more than once, if necessary—to make sure you understand the identity of the plaintiff(s) and defendant(s) in the case and the progression of events that led to the lawsuit.

In the sample case problem just given, the identity of the parties is fairly obvious. Janet Lawson is the one bringing the suit; therefore, she is the plaintiff. Quality Market, against whom she is bringing the suit, is the defendant. Some of the case problems you may work on have multiple plaintiffs or defendants. Often, it is helpful to use abbreviations for the parties. To indicate a reference to a plaintiff, for example, the *pi* symbol—π—is often used, and a defendant is denoted by a *delta*—Δ—a triangle.

The events leading to the lawsuit are also fairly straightforward. Lawson slipped and fell on a wet floor, and she contends that Quality Market should be liable for her injuries because it was negligent in not posting a sign warning customers of the wet floor.

When you are working on case problems, realize that the facts should be accepted as they are given. For example, in our sample problem, it should be accepted that the floor was wet and that there was no sign. In other words, avoid making conjectures, such as "Maybe the floor wasn't too wet," or "Maybe an employee was getting a sign to put up," or "Maybe someone stole the sign." Questioning the facts as they are presented only adds confusion to your analysis.

Legal Analysis and Reasoning

Once you understand the facts given in the case problem, you can begin to analyze the case. Recall from Chapter 1 that the IRAC method is a helpful tool to use in the legal analysis and reasoning process. IRAC is an acronym for Issue, Rule, Application, Conclusion. Applying this method to our sample problem would involve the following steps:

1. First, you need to decide what legal **issue** is involved in the case. In our sample case, the basic issue is whether Quality Market's failure to warn customers of the wet floor constituted negligence. As discussed in Chapter 6, negligence is a *tort*—a civil wrong. In a tort lawsuit, the plaintiff seeks to be compensated for another's wrongful act. A defendant will be deemed negligent if he or she breached a duty of care owed to the plaintiff and the breach of that duty caused the plaintiff to suffer harm.

2. Once you have identified the issue, the next step is to determine what **rule of law** applies to the issue. To make this determination, you will want to review carefully the text of the chapter in which the relevant rule of law for the problem appears. Our sample case problem involves the tort of

negligence, which is covered in Chapter 6. The applicable rule of law is the tort law principle that business owners owe a duty to exercise reasonable care to protect their customers ("business invitees"). Reasonable care, in this context, includes either removing—or warning customers of—*foreseeable* risks about which the owner *knew* or *should have known*. Business owners need not warn customers of "open and obvious" risks, however. If a business owner breaches this duty of care (fails to exercise the appropriate degree of care toward customers), and the breach of duty causes a customer to be injured, the business owner will be liable to the customer for the customer's injuries.

3. The next—and usually the most difficult—step in analyzing case problems is the **application** of the relevant rule of law to the specific facts of the case you are studying. In our sample problem, applying the tort law principle just discussed presents few difficulties. An employee of the store had mopped the floor in the aisle where Lawson slipped and fell, but no sign was present indicating that the floor was wet. That a customer might fall on a wet floor is clearly a foreseeable risk. Therefore, the failure to warn customers about the wet floor was a breach of the duty of care owed by the business owner to the store's customers.

4. Once you have completed Step 3 in the IRAC method, you should be ready to draw your **conclusion.** In our sample problem, Quality Market is liable to Lawson for her injuries, because the market's breach of its duty of care caused Lawson's injuries.

The fact patterns in the case problems presented in this text are not always as simple as those presented in our sample problem. Often, for example, a case has more than one plaintiff or defendant. A case may also involve more than one issue and have more than one applicable rule of law. Furthermore, in some case problems the facts may indicate that the general rule of law should not apply. For example, suppose that a store employee advised Lawson not to walk on the floor in the aisle because it was wet, but Lawson decided to walk on it anyway. This fact could alter the outcome of the case because the store could then raise the defense of assumption of risk (see Chapter 7). Nonetheless, a careful review of the chapter should always provide you with the knowledge you need to analyze the problem thoroughly and arrive at accurate conclusions.

Preamble

We the People of the United States, in Order to form a more perfect Union, establish Justice, insure domestic Tranquility, provide for the common defence, promote the general Welfare, and secure the Blessings of Liberty to ourselves and our Posterity, do ordain and establish this Constitution for the United States of America.

Article I

Section 1. All legislative Powers herein granted shall be vested in a Congress of the United States, which shall consist of a Senate and House of Representatives.

Section 2. The House of Representatives shall be composed of Members chosen every second Year by the People of the several States, and the Electors in each State shall have the Qualifications requisite for Electors of the most numerous Branch of the State Legislature.

No Person shall be a Representative who shall not have attained to the Age of twenty five Years, and been seven Years a Citizen of the United States, and who shall not, when elected, be an Inhabitant of that State in which he shall be chosen.

Representatives and direct Taxes shall be apportioned among the several States which may be included within this Union, according to their respective Numbers, which shall be determined by adding to the whole Number of free Persons, including those bound to Service for a Term of Years, and excluding Indians not taxed, three fifths of all other Persons. The actual Enumeration shall be made within three Years after the first Meeting of the Congress of the United States, and within every subsequent Term of ten Years, in such Manner as they shall by Law direct. The Number of Representatives shall not exceed one for every thirty Thousand, but each State shall have at Least one Representative; and until such enumeration shall be made, the State of New Hampshire shall be entitled to chuse three, Massachusetts eight, Rhode Island and Providence Plantations one, Connecticut five, New York six, New Jersey four, Pennsylvania eight, Delaware one, Maryland six, Virginia ten, North Carolina five, South Carolina five, and Georgia three.

When vacancies happen in the Representation from any State, the Executive Authority thereof shall issue Writs of Election to fill such Vacancies.

The House of Representatives shall chuse their Speaker and other Officers; and shall have the sole Power of Impeachment.

Section 3. The Senate of the United States shall be composed of two Senators from each State, chosen by the Legislature thereof, for six Years; and each Senator shall have one Vote.

Immediately after they shall be assembled in Consequence of the first Election, they shall be divided as equally as may be into three Classes. The Seats of the Senators of the first Class shall be vacated at the Expiration of the second Year, of the second Class at the Expiration of the fourth Year, and of the third Class at the Expiration of the sixth Year, so that one third

may be chosen every second Year; and if Vacancies happen by Resignation, or otherwise, during the Recess of the Legislature of any State, the Executive thereof may make temporary Appointments until the next Meeting of the Legislature, which shall then fill such Vacancies.

No Person shall be a Senator who shall not have attained to the Age of thirty Years, and been nine Years a Citizen of the United States, and who shall not, when elected, be an Inhabitant of that State for which he shall be chosen.

The Vice President of the United States shall be President of the Senate, but shall have no Vote, unless they be equally divided.

The Senate shall chuse their other Officers, and also a President pro tempore, in the Absence of the Vice President, or when he shall exercise the Office of President of the United States.

The Senate shall have the sole Power to try all Impeachments. When sitting for that Purpose, they shall be on Oath or Affirmation. When the President of the United States is tried, the Chief Justice shall preside: And no Person shall be convicted without the Concurrence of two thirds of the Members present.

Judgment in Cases of Impeachment shall not extend further than to removal from Office, and disqualification to hold and enjoy any Office of honor, Trust, or Profit under the United States: but the Party convicted shall nevertheless be liable and subject to Indictment, Trial, Judgment, and Punishment, according to Law.

Section 4. The Times, Places and Manner of holding Elections for Senators and Representatives, shall be prescribed in each State by the Legislature thereof; but the Congress may at any time by Law make or alter such Regulations, except as to the Places of chusing Senators.

The Congress shall assemble at least once in every Year, and such Meeting shall be on the first Monday in December, unless they shall by Law appoint a different Day.

Section 5. Each House shall be the Judge of the Elections, Returns, and Qualifications of its own Members, and a Majority of each shall constitute a Quorum to do Business; but a smaller Number may adjourn from day to day, and may be authorized to compel the Attendance of absent Members, in such Manner, and under such Penalties as each House may provide.

Each House may determine the Rules of its Proceedings, punish its Members for disorderly Behavior, and, with the Concurrence of two thirds, expel a Member.

Each House shall keep a Journal of its Proceedings, and from time to time publish the same, excepting such Parts as may in their Judgment require Secrecy; and the Yeas and Nays of the Members of either House on any question shall, at the Desire of one fifth of those Present, be entered on the Journal.

Neither House, during the Session of Congress, shall, without the Consent of the other, adjourn for more than three days, nor to any other Place than that in which the two Houses shall be sitting.

Section 6. The Senators and Representatives shall receive a Compensation for their Services, to be ascertained by Law, and paid out of the Treasury of the United States. They shall in all Cases, except Treason, Felony and Breach of the Peace, be privileged from Arrest during their Attendance at the Session of their respective Houses, and in going to and returning from the same; and for any Speech or Debate in either House, they shall not be questioned in any other Place.

No Senator or Representative shall, during the Time for which he was elected, be appointed to any civil Office under the Authority of the United States, which shall have been created, or the Emoluments whereof shall have been increased during such time; and no Person holding any Office under the United States, shall be a Member of either House during his Continuance in Office.

Section 7. All Bills for raising Revenue shall originate in the House of Representatives; but the Senate may propose or concur with Amendments as on other Bills.

Every Bill which shall have passed the House of Representatives and the Senate, shall, before it become a Law, be presented to the President of the United States; If he approve he shall sign it, but if not he shall return it, with his Objections to the House in which it shall have originated, who shall enter the Objections at large on their Journal, and proceed to reconsider it. If after such Reconsideration two thirds of that House shall agree to pass the Bill, it shall be sent together with the Objections, to the other House, by which it shall likewise be reconsidered, and if approved by two thirds of that House, it shall become a Law. But in all such Cases the Votes of both Houses shall be determined by Yeas and Nays, and the Names of the Persons voting for and against the Bill shall be entered on the Journal of each House respectively. If any Bill shall not be returned by the President within ten Days (Sundays excepted) after it shall have been presented to him, the Same shall be a Law, in like Manner as if he had signed it, unless the Congress by their Adjournment prevent its Return in which Case it shall not be a Law.

Every Order, Resolution, or Vote, to which the Concurrence of the Senate and House of Representatives may be necessary (except on a question of Adjournment) shall be presented to the President of the United States; and before the Same shall take Effect, shall be approved by him, or being disapproved by him, shall be repassed by two thirds of the Senate and House of Representatives, according to the Rules and Limitations prescribed in the Case of a Bill.

Section 8. The Congress shall have Power To lay and collect Taxes, Duties, Imposts and Excises, to pay the Debts and provide for the common Defence and general Welfare of the United States; but all Duties, Imposts and Excises shall be uniform throughout the United States;

To borrow Money on the credit of the United States;

To regulate Commerce with foreign Nations, and among the several States, and with the Indian Tribes;

To establish an uniform Rule of Naturalization, and uniform Laws on the subject of Bankruptcies throughout the United States;

To coin Money, regulate the Value thereof, and of foreign Coin, and fix the Standard of Weights and Measures;

To provide for the Punishment of counterfeiting the Securities and current Coin of the United States;

To establish Post Offices and post Roads;

To promote the Progress of Science and useful Arts, by securing for limited Times to Authors and Inventors the exclusive Right to their respective Writings and Discoveries;

To constitute Tribunals inferior to the supreme Court;

To define and punish Piracies and Felonies committed on the high Seas, and Offenses against the Law of Nations;

To declare War, grant Letters of Marque and Reprisal, and make Rules concerning Captures on Land and Water;

To raise and support Armies, but no Appropriation of Money to that Use shall be for a longer Term than two Years;

To provide and maintain a Navy;

To make Rules for the Government and Regulation of the land and naval Forces;

To provide for calling forth the Militia to execute the Laws of the Union, suppress Insurrections and repel Invasions;

To provide for organizing, arming, and disciplining, the Militia, and for governing such Part of them as may be employed in the Service of the United States, reserving to the States respectively, the Appointment of the Officers, and the Authority of training the Militia according to the discipline prescribed by Congress;

To exercise exclusive Legislation in all Cases whatsoever, over such District (not exceeding ten Miles square) as may, by Cession of particular States, and the Acceptance of Congress, become the Seat of the Government of the United States, and to exercise like Authority over all Places purchased by the Consent of the Legislature of the State in which the Same shall be, for the Erection of Forts, Magazines, Arsenals, dock-Yards, and other needful Buildings;—And

To make all Laws which shall be necessary and proper for carrying into Execution the foregoing Powers, and all other Powers vested by this Constitution in the Government of the United States, or in any Department or Officer thereof.

Section 9. The Migration or Importation of such Persons as any of the States now existing shall think proper to admit, shall not be prohibited by the Congress prior to the Year one thousand eight hundred and eight, but a Tax or duty may be imposed on such Importation, not exceeding ten dollars for each Person.

The privilege of the Writ of Habeas Corpus shall not be suspended, unless when in Cases of Rebellion or Invasion the public Safety may require it.

No Bill of Attainder or ex post facto Law shall be passed.

No Capitation, or other direct, Tax shall be laid, unless in Proportion to the Census or Enumeration herein before directed to be taken.

No Tax or Duty shall be laid on Articles exported from any State.

No Preference shall be given by any Regulation of Commerce or Revenue to the Ports of one State over those of another: nor shall Vessels bound to, or from, one State be obliged to enter, clear, or pay Duties in another.

No Money shall be drawn from the Treasury, but in Consequence of Appropriations made by Law; and a regular Statement and Account of the Receipts and Expenditures of all public Money shall be published from time to time.

No Title of Nobility shall be granted by the United States: And no Person holding any Office of Profit or Trust under them, shall, without the Consent of the Congress, accept of any present, Emolument, Office, or Title, of any kind whatever, from any King, Prince, or foreign State.

Section 10. No State shall enter into any Treaty, Alliance, or Confederation; grant Letters of Marque and Reprisal; coin Money; emit Bills of Credit; make any Thing but gold and silver Coin a Tender in Payment of Debts; pass any Bill of Attainder, ex post facto Law, or Law impairing the Obligation of Contracts, or grant any Title of Nobility.

No State shall, without the Consent of the Congress, lay any Imposts or Duties on Imports or Exports, except what may be absolutely necessary for executing its inspection Laws: and the net Produce of all Duties and Imposts, laid by any State on Imports or Exports, shall be for the Use of the Treasury of the United States; and all such Laws shall be subject to the Revision and Controul of the Congress.

No State shall, without the Consent of Congress, lay any Duty of Tonnage, keep Troops, or Ships of War in time of Peace, enter into any Agreement or Compact with another State, or with a foreign Power, or engage in War, unless actually invaded, or in such imminent Danger as will not admit of delay.

Article II

Section 1. The executive Power shall be vested in a President of the United States of America. He shall hold his Office during the Term of four Years, and, together with the Vice President, chosen for the same Term, be elected, as follows:

Each State shall appoint, in such Manner as the Legislature thereof may direct, a Number of Electors, equal to the whole Number of Senators and Representatives to which the State may be entitled in the Congress; but no Senator or Representative, or Person holding an Office of Trust or Profit under the United States, shall be appointed an Elector.

The Electors shall meet in their respective States, and vote by Ballot for two Persons, of whom one at least shall not be an Inhabitant of the same State with themselves. And they shall make a List of all the Persons voted for, and of the Number of Votes for each; which List they shall sign and certify, and transmit sealed to the Seat of the Government of the United States, directed to the President of the Senate. The President of the Senate shall, in the Presence of the Senate and House of Representatives, open all the Certificates, and the Votes shall then be counted. The Person having the greatest Number of Votes shall be the President, if such Number be a Majority of the whole Number of Electors appointed; and if there be more than one who have such Majority, and have an equal Number of Votes, then the House of Representatives shall immediately chuse by Ballot one of them for President; and if no Person have a Majority, then from the five highest on the List the said House shall in like Manner chuse the President. But in chusing the President, the Votes shall be taken by States, the Representation from each State having one Vote; A quorum for this Purpose shall consist of a Member or Members from two thirds of the States, and a Majority of all the States shall be necessary to a Choice. In every Case, after the Choice of the President, the Person having the greater Number of Votes of the Electors shall be the Vice President. But if there should remain two or more who have equal Votes, the Senate shall chuse from them by Ballot the Vice President.

The Congress may determine the Time of chusing the Electors, and the Day on which they shall give their Votes; which Day shall be the same throughout the United States.

No person except a natural born Citizen, or a Citizen of the United States, at the time of the Adoption of this Constitution, shall be eligible to the Office of President; neither shall any Person be eligible to that Office who shall not have attained to the Age of thirty five Years, and been fourteen Years a Resident within the United States.

In Case of the Removal of the President from Office, or of his Death, Resignation or Inability to discharge the Powers and Duties of the said Office, the same shall devolve on the Vice President, and the Congress may by Law provide for the Case of Removal, Death, Resignation or Inability, both of the President and Vice President, declaring what Officer shall then act as President, and such Officer shall act accordingly, until the Disability be removed, or a President shall be elected.

The President shall, at stated Times, receive for his Services, a Compensation, which shall neither be increased nor diminished during the Period for which he shall have been elected, and he shall not receive within that Period any other Emolument from the United States, or any of them.

Before he enter on the Execution of his Office, he shall take the following Oath or Affirmation: "I do solemnly swear (or affirm) that I will faithfully execute the Office of President of the United States, and will to the best of my Ability, preserve, protect and defend the Constitution of the United States."

Section 2. The President shall be Commander in Chief of the Army and Navy of the United States, and of the Militia of the several States, when called into the actual Service of the United States; he may require the Opinion, in writing, of the principal Officer in each of the executive Departments, upon any Subject relating to the Duties of their respective Offices, and he shall have Power to grant Reprieves and Pardons for Offenses against the United States, except in Cases of Impeachment.

He shall have Power, by and with the Advice and Consent of the Senate to make Treaties, provided two thirds of the Senators present concur; and he shall nominate, and by and with the Advice and Consent of the Senate, shall appoint Ambassadors, other public Ministers and Consuls, Judges of the supreme Court, and all other Officers of the United States, whose Appointments are not herein otherwise provided for, and which shall be established by Law; but the Congress may by Law vest the Appointment of such inferior Officers, as they think proper, in the President alone, in the Courts of Law, or in the Heads of Departments.

The President shall have Power to fill up all Vacancies that may happen during the Recess of the Senate, by granting Commissions which shall expire at the End of their next Session.

Section 3. He shall from time to time give to the Congress Information of the State of the Union, and recommend to their Consideration such Measures as he shall judge necessary and expedient; he may, on extraordinary Occasions, convene both Houses, or either of them, and in Case of Disagreement between them, with Respect to the Time of Adjournment, he may adjourn them to such Time as he shall think proper; he shall receive Ambassadors and other public Ministers; he shall take Care that the Laws be faithfully executed, and shall Commission all the Officers of the United States.

Section 4. The President, Vice President and all civil Officers of the United States, shall be removed from Office on Impeachment for, and Conviction of, Treason, Bribery, or other high Crimes and Misdemeanors.

Article III

Section 1. The judicial Power of the United States, shall be vested in one supreme Court, and in such inferior Courts as the Congress may from time to time ordain and establish. The Judges, both of the supreme and inferior Courts, shall hold their Offices during good Behaviour, and shall, at stated Times, receive for their Services a Compensation, which shall not be diminished during their Continuance in Office.

Section 2. The judicial Power shall extend to all Cases, in Law and Equity, arising under this Constitution, the Laws of the United States, and Treaties made, or which shall be made, under their Authority;—to all Cases affecting Ambassadors, other public Ministers and Consuls;—to all Cases of admiralty and maritime Jurisdiction;—to Controversies to which the United States shall be a Party;—to Controversies between two or more States;—between a State and Citizens of another State;—between Citizens of different States;—between Citizens of the same State claiming Lands under Grants of different States, and between a State, or the Citizens thereof, and foreign States, Citizens or Subjects.

In all Cases affecting Ambassadors, other public Ministers and Consuls, and those in which a State shall be a Party, the supreme Court shall have original Jurisdiction. In all the other Cases before mentioned, the supreme Court shall have appellate Jurisdiction, both as to Law and Fact, with such Exceptions, and under such Regulations as the Congress shall make.

The Trial of all Crimes, except in Cases of Impeachment, shall be by Jury; and such Trial shall be held in the State where the said Crimes shall have been committed; but when not committed within any State, the Trial shall be at such Place or Places as the Congress may by Law have directed.

Section 3. Treason against the United States, shall consist only in levying War against them, or, in adhering to their Enemies, giving them Aid and Comfort. No Person shall be convicted of Treason unless on the Testimony of two Witnesses to the same overt Act, or on Confession in open Court.

The Congress shall have Power to declare the Punishment of Treason, but no Attainder of Treason shall work Corruption of Blood, or Forfeiture except during the Life of the Person attainted.

Article IV

Section 1. Full Faith and Credit shall be given in each State to the public Acts, Records, and judicial Proceedings of every other State. And the Congress may by general Laws prescribe the Manner in which such Acts, Records and Proceedings shall be proved, and the Effect thereof.

Section 2. The Citizens of each State shall be entitled to all Privileges and Immunities of Citizens in the several States.

A Person charged in any State with Treason, Felony, or other Crime, who shall flee from Justice, and be found in another State, shall on Demand of the executive Authority of the State from which he fled, be delivered up, to be removed to the State having Jurisdiction of the Crime.

No Person held to Service or Labour in one State, under the Laws thereof, escaping into another, shall, in Consequence of any Law or Regulation therein, be discharged from such Service or Labour, but shall be delivered up on Claim of the Party to whom such Service or Labour may be due.

Section 3. New States may be admitted by the Congress into this Union; but no new State shall be formed or erected within the Jurisdiction of any other State; nor any State be formed by the Junction of two or more States, or Parts of States, without the Consent of the Legislatures of the States concerned as well as of the Congress.

The Congress shall have Power to dispose of and make all needful Rules and Regulations respecting the Territory or other Property belonging to the United States; and nothing in this Constitution shall be so construed as to Prejudice any Claims of the United States, or of any particular State.

Section 4. The United States shall guarantee to every State in this Union a Republican Form of Government, and shall protect each of them against Invasion; and on Application of the Legislature, or of the Executive (when the Legislature cannot be convened) against domestic Violence.

Article V

The Congress, whenever two thirds of both Houses shall deem it necessary, shall propose Amendments to this Constitution, or, on the Application of the Legislatures of two thirds of the several States, shall call a Convention for proposing Amendments, which, in either Case, shall be valid to all Intents and Purposes, as part of this Constitution, when ratified by the Legislatures of three fourths of the several States, or by Conventions in three fourths thereof, as the one or the other Mode of Ratification may be proposed by the Congress; Provided that no Amendment which may be made prior to the Year One thousand eight hundred and eight shall in any Manner affect the first and fourth Clauses in the Ninth Section of the first Article; and that no State, without its Consent, shall be deprived of its equal Suffrage in the Senate.

Article VI

All Debts contracted and Engagements entered into, before the Adoption of this Constitution shall be as valid against the United States under this Constitution, as under the Confederation.

This Constitution, and the Laws of the United States which shall be made in Pursuance thereof; and all Treaties made, or which shall be made, under the Authority of the United States, shall be the supreme Law of the Land; and the Judges in every State shall be bound thereby, any Thing in the Constitution or Laws of any State to the Contrary notwithstanding.

The Senators and Representatives before mentioned, and the Members of the several State Legislatures, and all executive and judicial Officers, both of the United States and of the several States, shall be bound by Oath or Affirmation, to support this Constitution; but no religious Test shall ever be required as a Qualification to any Office or public Trust under the United States.

Article VII

The Ratification of the Conventions of nine States shall be sufficient for the Establishment of this Constitution between the States so ratifying the Same.

Amendment I [1791]

Congress shall make no law respecting an establishment of religion, or prohibiting the free exercise thereof; or abridging the freedom of speech, or of the press; or the right of the people peaceably to assembly, and to petition the Government for a redress of grievances.

Amendment II [1791]

A well regulated Militia, being necessary to the security of a free State, the right of the people to keep and bear Arms, shall not be infringed.

Amendment III [1791]

No Soldier shall, in time of peace be quartered in any house, without the consent of the Owner, nor in time of war, but in a manner to be prescribed by law.

Amendment IV [1791]

The right of the people to be secure in their persons, houses, papers, and effects, against unreasonable searches and seizures, shall not be violated, and no Warrants shall issue, but upon probable cause, supported by Oath or affirmation, and particularly describing the place to be searched, and the persons or things to be seized.

Amendment V [1791]

No person shall be held to answer for a capital, or otherwise infamous crime, unless on a presentment or indictment of a Grand Jury, except in cases arising in the land or naval forces, or in the Militia, when in actual service in time of War or public danger; nor shall any person be subject for the same offence to be twice put in jeopardy of life or limb; nor shall be compelled in any criminal case to be a witness against himself, nor be deprived of life, liberty, or property, without due process of law; nor shall private property be taken for public use, without just compensation.

Amendment VI [1791]

In all criminal prosecutions, the accused shall enjoy the right to a speedy and public trial, by an impartial jury of the State and district wherein the crime shall have been committed, which district shall have been previously ascertained by law, and to be informed of the nature and cause of the accusation; to be confronted with the witnesses against him; to have compulsory process for obtaining witnesses in his favor, and to have the Assistance of Counsel for his defence.

Amendment VII [1791]

In Suits at common law, where the value in controversy shall exceed twenty dollars, the right of trial by jury shall be preserved, and no fact tried by jury, shall be otherwise re-examined in any Court of the United States, than according to the rules of the common law.

Amendment VIII [1791]

Excessive bail shall not be required, nor excessive fines imposed, nor cruel and unusual punishments inflicted.

Amendment IX [1791]

The enumeration in the Constitution, of certain rights, shall not be construed to deny or disparage others retained by the people.

Amendment X [1791]

The powers not delegated to the United States by the Constitution, nor prohibited by it to the States, are reserved to the States respectively, or to the people.

Amendment XI [1798]

The Judicial power of the United States shall not be construed to extend to any suit in law or equity, commenced or prosecuted against one of the United States by Citizens of another State, or by Citizens or Subjects of any Foreign State.

Amendment XII [1804]

The Electors shall meet in their respective states, and vote by ballot for President and Vice-President, one of whom, at least, shall not be an inhabitant of the same state with themselves; they shall name in their ballots the person voted for as President, and in distinct ballots the person voted for as Vice-President, and they shall make distinct lists of all persons voted for as President, and of all persons voted for as Vice-President, and of the number of votes for each, which lists they shall sign and certify, and transmit sealed to the seat of the government of the United States, directed to the President of the Senate;—The President of the Senate shall, in the presence of the Senate and House of Representatives, open all the certificates and the votes shall then be counted;—The person having the greatest number of votes for President, shall be the President, if such number be a majority of the whole number of Electors appointed; and if no person have such majority, then from the persons having the highest numbers not exceeding three on the list of those voted for as President, the House of Representatives shall choose immediately, by ballot, the President. But in choosing the President, the votes shall be taken by states, the representation from each state having one vote; a quorum for this purpose shall consist of a member or members from two-thirds of the states, and a majority of all states shall be necessary to a choice. And if the House of Representatives shall not choose a President whenever the right of choice shall devolve upon them, before the fourth day of March next following, then the Vice-President shall act as President, as in the case of the death or other constitutional disability of the President.—The person having the greatest number of votes as Vice-President, shall be the Vice-President, if such number be a majority of the whole number of Electors appointed, and if no person have a majority, then from the two highest numbers on the list, the Senate shall choose the Vice-President; a quorum for the purpose shall consist of two-thirds of the whole number of Senators, and a majority of the whole number shall be necessary to a choice. But no person constitutionally ineligible to the office of President shall be eligible to that of Vice-President of the United States.

Amendment XIII [1865]

Section 1. Neither slavery nor involuntary servitude, except as a punishment for crime whereof the party shall have been duly convicted, shall exist within the United States, or any place subject to their jurisdiction.

Section 2. Congress shall have power to enforce this article by appropriate legislation.

Amendment XIV [1868]

Section 1. All persons born or naturalized in the United States, and subject to the jurisdiction thereof, are citizens of the United States and of the State wherein they reside. No State shall make or enforce any law which shall abridge the privileges or immunities of citizens of the United States; nor shall any State deprive any person of life, liberty, or property, without due process of law; nor deny to any person within its jurisdiction the equal protection of the laws.

Section 2. Representatives shall be apportioned among the several States according to their respective numbers, counting the whole number of persons in each State, excluding Indians not taxed. But when the right to vote at any election for the choice of electors for President and Vice President of the United States, Representatives in Congress, the Executive and Judicial officers of a State, or the members of the Legislature thereof, is denied to any of the male inhabitants of such State, being twenty-one years of age, and citizens of the United States, or in any way abridged, except for participation in rebellion, or other crime, the basis of representation therein shall be reduced in the proportion which the number of such male citizens shall bear to the whole number of male citizens twenty-one years of age in such State.

Section 3. No person shall be a Senator or Representative in Congress, or elector of President and Vice President, or hold any office, civil or military, under the United States, or under any State, who having previously taken an oath, as a member of Congress, or as an officer of the United States, or as a member of any State legislature, or as an executive or judicial officer of any State, to support the Constitution of the United States, shall have engaged in insurrection or rebellion against the same, or given aid or comfort to the enemies thereof. But Congress may by a vote of two-thirds of each House, remove such disability.

Section 4. The validity of the public debt of the United States, authorized by law, including debts incurred for payment of pensions and bounties for services in suppressing insurrection or rebellion, shall not be questioned. But neither the United States nor any State shall assume or pay any debt or obligation incurred in aid of insurrection or rebellion against the United States, or any claim for the loss or emancipation of any slave; but all such debts, obligations and claims shall be held illegal and void.

Section 5. The Congress shall have power to enforce, by appropriate legislation, the provisions of this article.

Amendment XV [1870]

Section 1. The right of citizens of the United States to vote shall not be denied or abridged by the United States or by any State on account of race, color, or previous condition of servitude.

Section 2. The Congress shall have power to enforce this article by appropriate legislation.

Amendment XVI [1913]

The Congress shall have power to lay and collect taxes on incomes, from whatever source derived, without apportionment among the several States, and without regard to any census or enumeration.

Amendment XVII [1913]

Section 1. The Senate of the United States shall be composed of two Senators from each State, elected by the people thereof, for six years; and each Senator shall have one vote. The electors in each State shall have the qualifications requisite for electors of the most numerous branch of the State legislatures.

Section 2. When vacancies happen in the representation of any State in the Senate, the executive authority of such State shall issue writs of election to fill such vacancies: *Provided,* That the legislature of any State may empower the executive thereof to make temporary appointments until the people fill the vacancies by election as the legislature may direct.

Section 3. This amendment shall not be so construed as to affect the election or term of any Senator chosen before it becomes valid as part of the Constitution.

Amendment XVIII [1919]

Section 1. After one year from the ratification of this article the manufacture, sale, or transportation of intoxicating liquors within, the importation thereof into, or the exportation thereof from the United States and all territory subject to the jurisdiction thereof for beverage purposes is hereby prohibited.

Section 2. The Congress and the several States shall have concurrent power to enforce this article by appropriate legislation.

Section 3. This article shall be inoperative unless it shall have been ratified as an amendment to the Constitution by the legislatures of the several States, as provided in the Constitution, within seven years from the date of the submission hereof to the States by the Congress.

Amendment XIX [1920]

Section 1. The right of citizens of the United States to vote shall not be denied or abridged by the United States or by any State on account of sex.

Section 2. Congress shall have power to enforce this article by appropriate legislation.

Amendment XX [1933]

Section 1. The terms of the President and Vice President shall end at noon on the 20th day of January, and the terms of Senators and Representatives at noon on the 3d day of January, of the years in which such terms would have ended if this article had not been ratified; and the terms of their successors shall then begin.

Section 2. The Congress shall assemble at least once in every year, and such meeting shall begin at noon on the 3d day of January, unless they shall by law appoint a different day.

Section 3. If, at the time fixed for the beginning of the term of the President, the President elect shall have died, the Vice President elect shall become President. If the President shall not have been chosen before the time fixed for the beginning of his term, or if the President elect shall have failed to qualify, then the Vice President elect shall act as President until a President shall have qualified; and the Congress may by law provide for the case wherein neither a President elect nor a Vice President elect shall have qualified, declaring who shall then act as President, or the manner in which one who is to act shall be selected, and such person shall act accordingly until a President or Vice President shall have qualified.

Section 4. The Congress may by law provide for the case of the death of any of the persons from whom the House of Representatives may choose a President whenever the right of choice shall have devolved upon them, and for the case of the death of any of the persons from whom the Senate may choose a Vice President whenever the right of choice shall have devolved upon them.

Section 5. Sections 1 and 2 shall take effect on the 15th day of October following the ratification of this article.

Section 6. This article shall be inoperative unless it shall have been ratified as an amendment to the Constitution by the legislatures of three-fourths of the several States within seven years from the date of its submission.

Amendment XXI [1933]

Section 1. The eighteenth article of amendment to the Constitution of the United States is hereby repealed.

Section 2. The transportation or importation into any State, Territory, or possession of the United States for delivery or use therein of intoxicating liquors, in violation of the laws thereof, is hereby prohibited.

Section 3. This article shall be inoperative unless it shall have been ratified as an amendment to the Constitution by conventions in the several States, as provided in the Constitution, within seven years from the date of the submission hereof to the States by the Congress.

Amendment XXII [1951]

Section 1. No person shall be elected to the office of the President more than twice, and no person who has held the office of President, or acted as President, for more than two years of a term to which some other person was elected President shall be elected to the office of President more than once. But this Article shall not apply to any person holding the office of President when this Article was proposed by the Congress, and shall not prevent any person who may be holding the office of President, or acting as President, during the term within which this Article becomes operative from holding the office of President or acting as President during the remainder of such term.

Section 2. This article shall be inoperative unless it shall have been ratified as an amendment to the Constitution by the legislatures of three-fourths of the several States within seven years from the date of its submission to the States by the Congress.

Amendment XXIII [1961]

Section 1. The District constituting the seat of Government of the United States shall appoint in such manner as the Congress may direct:

A number of electors of President and Vice President equal to the whole number of Senators and Representatives in Congress to which the District would be entitled if it were a State, but in no event more than the least populous state; they shall be in addition to those appointed by the states, but they shall be considered, for the purposes of the election of President and Vice President, to be electors appointed by a state; and they shall meet in the District and perform such duties as provided by the twelfth article of amendment.

Section 2. The Congress shall have power to enforce this article by appropriate legislation.

Amendment XXIV [1964]

Section 1. The right of citizens of the United States to vote in any primary or other election for President or Vice President, for electors for President or Vice President, or for Senator or Representative in Congress, shall not be denied or abridged by the United States, or any State by reason of failure to pay any poll tax or other tax.

Section 2. The Congress shall have power to enforce this article by appropriate legislation.

Amendment XXV [1967]

Section 1. In case of the removal of the President from office or of his death or resignation, the Vice President shall become President.

Section 2. Whenever there is a vacancy in the office of the Vice President, the President shall nominate a Vice President who shall take office upon confirmation by a majority vote of both Houses of Congress.

Section 3. Whenever the President transmits to the President pro tempore of the Senate and the Speaker of the House of Representatives his written declaration that he is unable to discharge the powers and duties of his office, and until he transmits to them a written declaration to the contrary, such powers and duties shall be discharged by the Vice President as Acting President.

Section 4. Whenever the Vice President and a majority of either the principal officers of the executive departments or of such other body as Congress may by law provide, transmit to the President pro tempore of the Senate and the Speaker of the House of Representatives their written declaration that the President is unable to discharge the powers and duties of his office, the Vice President shall immediately assume the powers and duties of the office as Acting President.

Thereafter, when the President transmits to the President pro tempore of the Senate and the Speaker of the House of Representatives his written declaration that no inability exists, he shall resume the powers and duties of his office unless the Vice President and a majority of either the principal officers of the executive department or of such other body as Congress may by law provide, transmit within four days to the President pro tempore of the Senate and the Speaker of the House of Representatives their written declaration that the President is unable to discharge the powers and duties of his office. Thereupon Congress shall decide the issue, assembling within forty-eight hours for that purpose if not in session. If the Congress, within twenty-one days after receipt of the latter written declaration, or, if Congress is not in session, within twenty-one days after Congress is required to assemble, deter-mines by two-thirds vote of both Houses that the President is unable to discharge the powers and duties of his office, the Vice President shall continue to discharge the same as Acting President; otherwise, the President shall resume the powers and duties of his office.

Amendment XXVI [1971]

Section 1. The right of citizens of the United States, who are eighteen years of age or older, to vote shall not be denied or abridged by the United States or by any State on account of age.

Section 2. The Congress shall have power to enforce this article by appropriate legislation.

Amendment XXVII [1992]

No law, varying the compensation for the services of the Senators and Representatives, shall take effect, until an election of Representatives shall have intervened.

(Adopted in fifty-two jurisdictions—all fifty States, although Louisiana has adopted only Articles 1, 3, 4, 7, 8, and 9; the District of Columbia; and the Virgin Islands.)

The Code consists of the following articles:

Article
1. General Provisions
2. Sales
2A. Leases
3. Negotiable Instruments
4. Bank Deposits and Collections
4A. Funds Transfers
5. Letters of Credit
6. Repealer of Article 6—Bulk Transfers and [Revised] Article 6—Bulk Sales
7. Warehouse Receipts, Bills of Lading and Other Documents of Title
8. Investment Securities
9. Secured Transactions
10. Effective Date and Repealer
11. Effective Date and Transition Provisions

ARTICLE 1: GENERAL PROVISIONS

Part 1—General Provisions

§ 1–101. Short Titles.
(a) This [Act] may be cited as Uniform Commercial Code.
(b) This article may be cited as Uniform Commercial Code-Uniform Provisions.

§ 1–102. Scope of Article.
This article applies to a transaction to the extent that it is governed by another article of [the Uniform Commercial Code].

§ 1–103. Construction of [Uniform Commercial Code] to Promote Its Purpose and Policies; Applicability of Supplemental Principles of Law.
(a) [The Uniform Commercial Code] must be liberally construed and applied to promote its underlying purposes and policies, which are:
  (1) to simplify, clarify, and modernize the law govern-ing commercial transactions;
  (2) to permit the continued expansion of commercial practices through custom, usage, and agreement of the parties; and
  (3) to make uniform the law among the various jurisdictions.
(b) Unless displaced by the particular provisions of [the Uniform Commercial Code], the principles of law and equity, including the law merchant and the law relative to capacity to

contract, principal and agent, estoppel, fraud, misrepresentation, duress, coercion, mistake, bankruptcy, and other validating or invalidating cause, supplement its provisions.

§ 1–104. Construction Against Implicit Repeal.
This Act being a general act intended as a unified coverage of its subject matter, no part of it shall be deemed to be impliedly repealed by subsequent legislation if such construction can reasonably be avoided.

§ 1–105. Severability.
If any provision or clause of [the Uniform Commercial Code] or its application to any person or circumstance is held invalid, the invalidity does not affect other provisions or applications of [the Uniform Commercial Code] which can be given effect without the invalid provision or application, and to this end the provisions of [the Uniform Commercial Code] are severable.

§ 1–106. Use of Singular and Plural; Gender.
In [the Uniform Commercial Code], unless the statutory context otherwise requires:
(1) words in the singular number include the plural, and those in the plural include the singular; and
(2) words of any gender also refer to any other gender.

§ 1–107. Section Captions.
Section captions are part of [the Uniform Commercial Code].

§ 1–108. Relation to Electronic Signatures in Global and National Commerce Act.
This article modifies, limits, and supersedes the Federal Electronic Signatures in Global and National Commerce Act, 15 U.S.C. Sections 7001 *et seq.*, except that nothing in this article modifies, limits, or supersedes Section 7001(c) of that act or authorizes electronic delivery of any of the notices described in Section 7003(b) of that Act.

Part 2—General Definitions and Principles of Interpretation

§ 1–201. General Definitions.
Subject to additional definitions contained in the subsequent Articles of this Act which are applicable to specific Articles or Parts thereof, and unless the context otherwise requires, in this Act:
(1) "Action", in the sense of a judicial proceeding, includes recoupment, counterclaim, set-off, suit in equity, and any other proceedings in which rights are determined.
(2) "Aggrieved party" means a party entitled to resort to a remedy.
(3) "Agreement", as distinguished from "contract", means the bargain of the parties in fact, as found in their language or by implication from other circumstances, including course of performance, course of dealing, or usage of trade as provided in Section 1–303.
(4) "Bank" means a person engaged in the business of banking and includes a savings bank, savings and loan association, credit union, and trust company.

(5) "Bearer" means a person in control of a negotiable electronic document of title or a person in possession of a negotiable instrument, negotiable tangible document of title, or certificated security that is payable to bearer or indorsed in blank.

(6) "Bill of lading" means a document of title evidencing the receipt of goods for shipment issued by a person engaged in the business of directly or indirectly transporting or forwarding goods. The term does not include a warehouse receipt.

(7) "Branch" includes a separately incorporated foreign branch of a bank.

(8) "Burden of establishing" a fact means the burden of persuading the trier of fact that the existence of the fact is more probable than its nonexistence.

(9) "Buyer in ordinary course of business" means a person that buys goods in good faith, without knowledge that the sale violates the rights of another person in the goods, and in the ordinary course from a person, other than a pawnbroker, in the business of selling goods of that kind. A person buys goods in the ordinary course if the sale to the person comports with the usual or customary practices in the kind of business in which the seller is engaged or with the seller's own usual or customary practices. A person that sells oil, gas, or other minerals at the wellhead or minehead is a person in the business of selling goods of that kind. A buyer in ordinary course of business may buy for cash, by exchange of other property, or on secured or unsecured credit, and may acquire goods or documents of title under a pre-existing contract for sale. Only a buyer that takes possession of the goods or has a right to recover the goods from the seller under Article 2 may be a buyer in ordinary course of business. A person that acquires goods in a transfer in bulk or as security for or in total or partial satisfaction of a money debt is not a buyer in ordinary course of business.

(10) "Conspicuous", with reference to a term, means so written, displayed, or presented that a reasonable person against which it is to operate ought to have noticed it. Whether a term is "conspicuous" or not is a decision for the court. Conspicuous terms include the following:

(A) a heading in capitals equal to or greater in size than the surrounding text, or in contrasting type, font, or color to the surrounding text of the same or lesser size; and

(B) language in the body of a record or display in larger type than the surrounding text, or in contrasting type, font, or color to the surrounding text of the same size, or set off from surrounding text of the same size by symbols or other marks that call attention to the language.

(11) "Consumer" means an individual who enters into a transaction primarily for personal, family, or household purposes.

(12) "Contract", as distinguished from "agreement", means the total legal obligation that results from the parties' agreement as determined by [the Uniform Commercial Code] as supplemented by any other laws.

(13) "Creditor" includes a general creditor, a secured creditor, a lien creditor and any representative of creditors, including an assignee for the benefit of creditors, a trustee in bankruptcy, a receiver in equity and an executor or administrator of an insolvent debtor's or assignor's estate.

(14) "Defendant" includes a person in the position of defendant in a counterclaim, cross-action, or third-party claim.

(15) "Delivery" with respect to an electronic document of title means voluntary transfer of control and with respect to an instrument, a tangible document of title, or chattel paper means voluntary transfer of possession.

(16) "Document of title" means a record (i) that in regular course of business or financing is treated as adequately evidencing that the person in possession or control of the record is entitled to receive, control, hold, and dispose of the record and the goods the record covers and (ii) that purports to be issued by or addressed to a bailee and to cover goods in the bailee's possession which are either identified or are fungible portions of an identified mass. The term includes a bill of lading, transport document, dock warrant, dock receipt, warehouse receipt, and order for delivery of goods. An electronic document of title means a document of title evidenced by a record consisting of information stored in an electronic medium. A tangible document of title means a document of title evidenced by a record consisting of information that is inscribed on a tangible medium.

(17) "Fault" means a default, breach, or wrongful act or omission.

(18) "Fungible goods" means:

(A) goods of which any unit, by nature or usage of trade, is the equivalent of any other like unit; or

(B) goods that by agreement are treated as equivalent.

(19) "Genuine" means free of forgery or counterfeiting.

(20) "Good faith," except as otherwise provided in Article 5, means honesty in fact and the observance of reasonable commercial standards of fair dealing.

(21) "Holder" means:

(A) the person in possession of a negotiable instrument that is payable either to bearer or to an identified person that is the person in possession;

(B) the person in possession of a negotiable tangible document of title if the goods are deliverable either to bearer or to the order of the person in possession; or

(C) the person in control of a negotiable electronic document of title.

(22) "Insolvency proceeding" includes an assignment for the benefit of creditors or other proceeding intended to liquidate or rehabilitate the estate of the person involved.

(23) "Insolvent" means:

(A) having generally ceased to pay debts in the ordinary course of business other than as a result of bona fide dispute;

(B) being unable to pay debts as they become due; or

(C) being insolvent within the meaning of federal bankruptcy law.

(24) "Money" means a medium of exchange currently authorized or adopted by a domestic or foreign government. The term includes a monetary unit of account established by an intergovernmental organization or by agreement between two or more countries.

(25) "Organization" means a person other than an individual.

(26) "Party", as distinguished from "third party", means a person that has engaged in a transaction or made an agreement subject to [the Uniform Commercial Code].

(27) "Person" means an individual, corporation, business trust, estate, trust, partnership, limited liability company, association, joint venture, government, governmental subdivision, agency, or instrumentality, public corporation, or any other legal or commercial entity.

(28) "Present value" means the amount as of a date certain of one or more sums payable in the future, discounted to the date certain by use of either an interest rate specified by the parties if that rate is not manifestly unreasonable at the time the transaction is entered into or, if an interest rate is not so specified, a commercially reasonable rate that takes into account the facts and circumstances at the time the transaction is entered into.

(29) "Purchase" means taking by sale, lease, discount, negotiation, mortgage, pledge, lien, security interest, issue or reissue, gift, or any other voluntary transaction creating an interest in property.

(30) "Purchaser" means a person that takes by purchase.

(31) "Record" means information that is inscribed on a tangible medium or that is stored in an electronic or other medium and is retrievable in perceivable form.

(32) "Remedy" means any remedial right to which an aggrieved party is entitled with or without resort to a tribunal.

(33) "Representative" means a person empowered to act for another, including an agent, an officer of a corporation or association, and a trustee, executor, or administrator of an estate.

(34) "Right" includes remedy.

(35) "Security interest" means an interest in personal property or fixtures which secures payment or performance of an obligation. "Security interest" includes any interest of a consignor and a buyer of accounts, chattel paper, a payment intangible, or a promissory note in a transaction that is subject to Article 9. "Security interest" does not include the special property interest of a buyer of goods on identification of those goods to a contract for sale under Section 2–401, but a buyer may also acquire a "security interest" by complying with Article 9. Except as otherwise provided in Section 2–505, the right of a seller or lessor of goods under Article 2 or 2A to retain or acquire possession of the goods is not a "security interest", but a seller or lessor may also acquire a "security interest" by complying with Article 9. The retention or reservation of title by a seller of goods notwithstanding shipment or delivery to the buyer under Section 2–401 is limited in effect to a reservation of a "security interest." Whether a transaction in the form of a lease creates a "security interest" is determined pursuant to Section 1–203.

(36) "Send" in connection with a writing, record, or notice means:

> **(A)** to deposit in the mail or deliver for transmission by any other usual means of communication with postage or cost of transmission provided for and properly addressed and, in the case of an instrument, to an address specified thereon or otherwise agreed, or if there be none to any address reasonable under the circumstances; or

> **(B)** in any other way to cause to be received any record or notice within the time it would have arrived if properly sent.

(37) "Signed" includes using any symbol executed or adopted with present intention to adopt or accept a writing.

(38) "State" means a State of the United States, the District of Columbia, Puerto Rico, the United States Virgin Islands, or any territory or insular possession subject to the jurisdiction of the United States.

(39) "Surety" includes a guarantor or other secondary obligor.

(40) "Term" means a portion of an agreement that relates to a particular matter.

(41) "Unauthorized signature" means a signature made without actual, implied, or apparent authority. The term includes a forgery.

(42) "Warehouse receipt" means a document of title issued by a person engaged in the business of storing goods for hire.

(43) "Writing" includes printing, typewriting, or any other intentional reduction to tangible form. "Written" has a corresponding meaning.
As amended in 2003.

§ 1–202. Notice; Knowledge.

(a) Subject to subsection (f), a person has "notice" of a fact if the person:

> **(1)** has actual knowledge of it;

> **(2)** has received a notice or notification of it; or

> **(3)** from all the facts and circumstances known to the person at the time in question, has reason to know that it exists.

(b) "Knowledge" means actual knowledge. "Knows" has a corresponding meaning.

(c) "Discover", "learn", or words of similar import refer to knowledge rather than to reason to know.

(d) A person "notifies" or "gives" a notice or notification to another person by taking such steps as may be reasonably required to inform the other person in ordinary course, whether or not the other person actually comes to know of it.

(e) Subject to subsection (f), a person "receives" a notice or notification when:

> **(1)** it comes to that person's attention; or

> **(2)** it is duly delivered in a form reasonable under the circumstances at the place of business through which the contract was made or at another location held out by that person as the place for receipt of such communications.

(f) Notice, knowledge, or a notice or notification received by an organization is effective for a particular transaction from the time it is brought to the attention of the individual conducting that transaction and, in any event, from the time it would have been brought to the individual's attention if the organization had exercised due diligence. An organization exercises due diligence if it maintains reasonable routines for communicating significant information to the person conducting the transaction and there is reasonable compliance with the routines. Due diligence does not require an individual acting for the organization to communicate information unless the communication is part of the individual's regular duties or the individual has reason to know of the transaction and that the transaction would be materially affected by the information.

§ 1–203. Lease Distinguished from Security Interest.

(a) Whether a transaction in the form of a lease creates a lease or security interest is determined by the facts of each case.

(b) A transaction in the form of a lease creates a security interest if the consideration that the lessee is to pay the lessor for the right to possession and use of the goods is an obligation for the term of the lease and is not subject to termination by the lessee, and:

(1) the original term of the lease is equal to or greater than the remaining economic life of the goods;

(2) the lessee is bound to renew the lease for the remaining economic life of the goods or is bound to become the owner of the goods;

(3) the lessee has an option to renew the lease for the remaining economic life of the goods for no additional consideration or for nominal additional consideration upon compliance with the lease agreement; or

(4) the lessee has an option to become the owner of the goods for no additional consideration or for nominal additional consideration upon compliance with the lease agreement.

(c) A transaction in the form of a lease does not create a security interest merely because:

(1) the present value of the consideration the lessee is obligated to pay the lessor for the right to possession and use of the goods is substantially equal to or is greater than the fair market value of the goods at the time the lease is entered into;

(2) the lessee assumes risk of loss of the goods;

(3) the lessee agrees to pay, with respect to the goods, taxes, insurance, filing, recording, or registration fees, or service or maintenance costs;

(4) the lessee has an option to renew the lease or to become the owner of the goods;

(5) the lessee has an option to renew the lease for a fixed rent that is equal to or greater than the reasonably predictable fair market rent for the use of the goods for the term of the renewal at the time the option is to be performed; or

(6) the lessee has an option to become the owner of the goods for a fixed price that is equal to or greater than the reasonably predictable fair market value of the goods at the time the option is to be performed.

(d) Additional consideration is nominal if it is less than the lessee's reasonably predictable cost of performing under the lease agreement if the option is not exercised. Additional consideration is not nominal if:

(1) when the option to renew the lease is granted to the lessee, the rent is stated to be the fair market rent for the use of the goods for the term of the renewal determined at the time the option is to be performed; or

(2) when the option to become the owner of the goods is granted to the lessee, the price is stated to be the fair market value of the goods determined at the time the option is to be performed.

(e) The "remaining economic life of the goods" and "reasonably predictable" fair market rent, fair market value, or cost of performing under the lease agreement must be determined with reference to the facts and circumstances at the time the transaction is entered into.

§ 1–204. Value.

Except as otherwise provided in Articles 3, 4, [and] 5, [and 6], a person gives value for rights if the person acquires them:

(1) in return for a binding commitment to extend credit or for the extension of immediately available credit, whether or not drawn upon and whether or not a charge-back is provided for in the event of difficulties in collection;

(2) as security for, or in total or partial satisfaction of, a preexisting claim;

(3) by accepting delivery under a preexisting contract for purchase; or

(4) in return for any consideration sufficient to support a simple contract.

§ 1–205. Reasonable Time; Seasonableness.

(a) Whether a time for taking an action required by [the Uniform Commercial Code] is reasonable depends on the nature, purpose, and circumstances of the action.

(b) An action is taken seasonably if it is taken at or within the time agreed or, if no time is agreed, at or within a reasonable time.

§ 1–206. Presumptions.

Whenever [the Uniform Commercial Code] creates a "presumption" with respect to a fact, or provides that a fact is "presumed," the trier of fact must find the existence of the fact unless and until evidence is introduced that supports a finding of its nonexistence.

Part 3—Territorial Applicability and General Rules

§ 1–301. Territorial Applicability; Parties' Power to Choose Applicable Law.

(a) In this section:

(1) "Domestic transaction" means a transaction other than an international transaction.

(2) "International transaction" means a transaction that bears a reasonable relation to a country other than the United States.

(b) This section applies to a transaction to the extent that it is governed by another article of the [Uniform Commercial Code].

(c) Except as otherwise provided in this section:

(1) an agreement by parties to a domestic transaction that any or all of their rights and obligations are to be determined by the law of this State or of another State is effective, whether or not the transaction bears a relation to the State designated; and

(2) an agreement by parties to an international transaction that any or all of their rights and obligations are to be determined by the law of this State or of another State or country is effective, whether or not the transaction bears a relation to the State or country designated.

(d) In the absence of an agreement effective under subsection (c), and except as provided in subsections (e) and (g), the rights and obligations of the parties are determined by the law that would be selected by application of this State's conflict of laws principles.

(e) If one of the parties to a transaction is a consumer, the following rules apply:

(1) An agreement referred to in subsection (c) is not effective unless the transaction bears a reasonable relation to the State or country designated.

(2) Application of the law of the State or country determined pursuant to subsection (c) or (d) may not deprive the consumer of the protection of any rule of law governing a matter within the scope of this section, which both is protective of consumers and may not be varied by agreement: (A) of the State or country in which the consumer principally resides, unless subparagraph (B) applies; or (B) if the transaction is a sale of goods, of the State or country in which the consumer both makes the contract and take delivery of those goods, if such State or country is not the State or country in which the consumer principally resides.

(f) An agreement otherwise effective under subsection (c) is not effective to the extent that application of the law of the State or country designated would be contrary to a fundamental policy of the State or country whose law would govern in the absence of agreement under subsection (d).

(g) To the extent that [the Uniform Commercial Code] governs a transaction, if one of the following provisions of [the Uniform Commercial Code] specifies the applicable law, that provision governs and a contrary agreement is effective only to the extent permitted by the law so specified: (1) Section 2–402; (2) Sections 2A–105 and 2A–106; (3) Section 4–102; (4) Section 4A–507; (5) Section 5–116; [(6) Section 6–103;] (7) Section 8–110; (8) Sections 9–301 through 9–307.

§ 1–302. Variation by Agreement.

(a) Except as otherwise provided in subsection (b) or elsewhere in [the Uniform Commercial Code], the effect of provisions of [the Uniform Commercial Code] may be varied by agreement.

(b) The obligations of good faith, diligence, reasonableness, and care prescribed by [the Uniform Commercial Code] may not be disclaimed by agreement. The parties, by agreement, may determine the standards by which the performance of those obligations is to be measured if those standards are not manifestly unreasonable. Whenever [the Uniform Commercial Code] requires an action to be taken within a reasonable time, a time that is not manifestly unreasonable may be fixed by agreement.

(c) The presence in certain provisions of [the Uniform Commercial Code] of the phrase "unless otherwise agreed", or words of similar import, does not imply that the effect of other provisions may not be varied by agreement under this section.

§ 1–303. Course of Performance, Course of Dealing, and Usage of Trade.

(a) A "course of performance" is a sequence of conduct between the parties to a particular transaction that exists if:

>   **(1)** the agreement of the parties with respect to the transaction involves repeated occasions for performance by a party; and
>   **(2)** the other party, with knowledge of the nature of the performance and opportunity for objection to it, accepts the performance or acquiesces in it without objection.

(b) A "course of dealing" is a sequence of conduct concerning previous transactions between the parties to a particular transaction that is fairly to be regarded as establishing a common basis of understanding for interpreting their expressions and other conduct.

(c) A "usage of trade" is any practice or method of dealing having such regularity of observance in a place, vocation, or trade as to justify an expectation that it will be observed with respect to the transaction in question. The existence and scope of such a usage must be proved as facts. If it is established that such a usage is embodied in a trade code or similar record, the interpretation of the record is a question of law.

(d) A course of performance or course of dealing between the parties or usage of trade in the vocation or trade in which they are engaged or of which they are or should be aware is relevant in ascertaining the meaning of the parties' agreement, may give particular meaning to specific terms of the agreement, and may supplement or qualify the terms of the agreement. A usage of trade applicable in the place in which part of the performance under the agreement is to occur may be so utilized as to that part of the performance.

(e) Except as otherwise provided in subsection (f), the express terms of an agreement and any applicable course of performance, course of dealing, or usage of trade must be construed whenever reasonable as consistent with each other. If such a construction is unreasonable:

>   **(1)** express terms prevail over course of performance, course of dealing, and usage of trade;
>   **(2)** course of performance prevails over course of dealing and usage of trade; and
>   **(3)** course of dealing prevails over usage of trade.

(f) Subject to Section 2–209 and Section 2A–208, a course of performance is relevant to show a waiver or modification of any term inconsistent with the course of performance.

(g) Evidence of a relevant usage of trade offered by one party is not admissible unless that party has given the other party notice that the court finds sufficient to prevent unfair surprise to the other party.

§ 1–304. Obligation of Good Faith.

Every contract or duty within [the Uniform Commercial Code] imposes an obligation of good faith in its performance and enforcement.

§ 1–305. Remedies to be Liberally Administered.

(a) The remedies provided by [the Uniform Commercial Code] must be liberally administered to the end that the aggrieved party may be put in as good a position as if the other party had fully performed but neither consequential or special damages nor penal damages may be had except as specifically provided in [the Uniform Commercial Code] or by other rule of law.

(b) Any right or obligation declared by [the Uniform Commercial Code] is enforceable by action unless the provision declaring it specifies a different and limited effect.

§ 1–306. Waiver or Renunciation of Claim or Right After Breach.

A claim or right arising out of an alleged breach may be discharged in whole or in part without consideration by agreement of the aggrieved party in an authenticated record.

§ 1–307. *Prima Facie* Evidence by Third-Party Documents.

A document in due form purporting to be a bill of lading, policy or certificate of insurance, official weigher's or inspector's certificate, consular invoice, or any other document authorized or required by the contract to be issued by a third party is *prima facie* evidence of its own authenticity and genuineness and of the facts stated in the document by the third party.

§ 1–308. Performance or Acceptance Under Reservation of Rights.

(a) A party that with explicit reservation of rights performs or promises performance or assents to performance in a manner demanded or offered by the other party does not thereby prejudice the rights reserved. Such words as "without prejudice," "under protest," or the like are sufficient.

(b) Subsection (a) does not apply to an accord and satisfaction.

§ 1–309. Option to Accelerate at Will.

A term providing that one party or that party's successor in interest may accelerate payment or performance or require collateral or additional collateral "at will" or when the party "deems itself insecure," or words of similar import, means that the party has power to do so only if that party in good faith believes that the prospect of payment or performance is impaired. The burden of establishing lack of good faith is on the party against which the power has been exercised.

§ 1–310. Subordinated Obligations.

An obligation may be issued as subordinated to performance of another obligation of the person obligated, or a creditor may subordinate its right to performance of an obligation by agreement with either the person obligated or another creditor of the person obligated. Subordination does not create a security interest as against either the common debtor or a subordinated creditor.

ARTICLE 2: SALES

Part 1—Short Title, General Construction and Subject Matter

§ 2–101. Short Title.

This Article shall be known and may be cited as Uniform Commercial Code—Sales.

§ 2–102. Scope; Certain Security and Other Transactions Excluded From This Article.

Unless the context otherwise requires, this Article applies to transactions in goods; it does not apply to any transaction which although in the form of an unconditional contract to sell or present sale is intended to operate only as a security transaction nor does this Article impair or repeal any statute regulating sales to consumers, farmers or other specified classes of buyers.

§ 2–103. Definitions and Index of Definitions.

(1) In this Article unless the context otherwise requires

    (a) "Buyer" means a person who buys or contracts to buy goods.

    (b) "Good faith" in the case of a merchant means honesty in fact and the observance of reasonable commercial standards of fair dealing in the trade.

    (c) "Receipt" of goods means taking physical possession of them.

    (d) "Seller" means a person who sells or contracts to sell goods.

(2) Other definitions applying to this Article or to specified Parts thereof, and the sections in which they appear are:

"Acceptance". Section 2–606.
"Banker's credit". Section 2–325.
"Between merchants". Section 2–104.
"Cancellation". Section 2–106(4).
"Commercial unit". Section 2–105.
"Confirmed credit". Section 2–325.
"Conforming to contract". Section 2–106.
"Contract for sale". Section 2–106.
"Cover". Section 2–712.
"Entrusting". Section 2–403.
"Financing agency". Section 2–104.
"Future goods". Section 2–105.
"Goods". Section 2–105.
"Identification". Section 2–501.
"Installment contract". Section 2–612.
"Letter of Credit". Section 2–325.
"Lot". Section 2–105.
"Merchant". Section 2–104.
"Overseas". Section 2–323.
"Person in position of seller". Section 2–707.
"Present sale". Section 2–106.
"Sale". Section 2–106.
"Sale on approval". Section 2–326.
"Sale or return". Section 2–326.
"Termination". Section 2–106.

(3) The following definitions in other Articles apply to this Article:
"Check". Section 3–104.
"Consignee". Section 7–102.
"Consignor". Section 7–102.
"Consumer goods". Section 9–109.
"Dishonor". Section 3–507.
"Draft". Section 3–104.

(4) In addition Article 1 contains general definitions and principles of construction and interpretation applicable throughout this Article.

As amended in 1994 and 1999.

§ 2–104. Definitions: "Merchant"; "Between Merchants"; "Financing Agency".

(1) "Merchant" means a person who deals in goods of the kind or otherwise by his occupation holds himself out as having knowledge or skill peculiar to the practices or goods involved in the transaction or to whom such knowledge or skill may be attributed by his employment of an agent or broker or other intermediary who by his occupation holds himself out as having such knowledge or skill.

(2) "Financing agency" means a bank, finance company or other person who in the ordinary course of business makes advances against goods or documents of title or who by arrangement with either the seller or the buyer intervenes in ordinary course to make or collect payment due or claimed under the contract for sale, as by purchasing or paying the seller's draft or making advances against it or by merely taking it for collection whether or not documents of title accompany the draft. "Financing agency" includes also a bank or other person who similarly intervenes between persons who are in the position of seller and buyer in respect to the goods (Section 2–707).

(3) "Between merchants" means in any transaction with respect to which both parties are chargeable with the knowledge or skill of merchants.

§ 2–105. Definitions: Transferability; "Goods"; "Future" Goods; "Lot"; "Commercial Unit".

(1) "Goods" means all things (including specially manufactured goods) which are movable at the time of identification to the contract for sale other than the money in which the price is to be paid, investment securities (Article 8) and things in action. "Goods" also includes the unborn young of animals and growing crops and other identified things attached to realty as described in the section on goods to be severed from realty (Section 2–107).

(2) Goods must be both existing and identified before any interest in them can pass. Goods which are not both existing and identified are "future" goods. A purported present sale of future goods or of any interest therein operates as a contract to sell.

(3) There may be a sale of a part interest in existing identified goods.

(4) An undivided share in an identified bulk of fungible goods is sufficiently identified to be sold although the quantity of the bulk is not determined. Any agreed proportion of such a bulk or any quantity thereof agreed upon by number, weight or other measure may to the extent of the seller's interest in the bulk be sold to the buyer who then becomes an owner in common.

(5) "Lot" means a parcel or a single article which is the subject matter of a separate sale or delivery, whether or not it is sufficient to perform the contract.

(6) "Commercial unit" means such a unit of goods as by commercial usage is a single whole for purposes of sale and division of which materially impairs its character or value on the market or in use. A commercial unit may be a single article (as a machine) or a set of articles (as a suite of furniture or an assortment of sizes) or a quantity (as a bale, gross, or carload) or any other unit treated in use or in the relevant market as a single whole.

§ 2–106. Definitions: "Contract"; "Agreement"; "Contract for Sale"; "Sale"; "Present Sale"; "Conforming" to Contract; "Termination"; "Cancellation".

(1) In this Article unless the context otherwise requires "contract" and "agreement" are limited to those relating to the present or future sale of goods. "Contract for sale" includes both a present sale of goods and a contract to sell goods at a future time. A "sale" consists in the passing of title from the seller to the buyer for a price (Section 2–401). A "present sale" means a sale which is accomplished by the making of the contract.

(2) Goods or conduct including any part of a performance are "conforming" or conform to the contract when they are in accordance with the obligations under the contract.

(3) "Termination" occurs when either party pursuant to a power created by agreement or law puts an end to the contract otherwise than for its breach. On "termination" all obligations which are still executory on both sides are discharged but any right based on prior breach or performance survives.

(4) "Cancellation" occurs when either party puts an end to the contract for breach by the other and its effect is the same as that of "termination" except that the cancelling party also retains any remedy for breach of the whole contract or any unperformed balance.

§ 2–107. Goods to Be Severed From Realty: Recording.

(1) A contract for the sale of minerals or the like (including oil and gas) or a structure or its materials to be removed from realty is a contract for the sale of goods within this Article if they are to be severed by the seller but until severance a purported present sale thereof which is not effective as a transfer of an interest in land is effective only as a contract to sell.

(2) A contract for the sale apart from the land of growing crops or other things attached to realty and capable of severance without material harm thereto but not described in subsection (1) or of timber to be cut is a contract for the sale of goods within this Article whether the subject matter is to be severed by the buyer or by the seller even though it forms part of the realty at the time of contracting, and the parties can by identification effect a present sale before severance.

(3) The provisions of this section are subject to any third party rights provided by the law relating to realty records, and the contract for sale may be executed and recorded as a document transferring an interest in land and shall then constitute notice to third parties of the buyer's rights under the contract for sale. As amended in 1972.

Part 2—Form, Formation and Readjustment of Contract

§ 2–201. Formal Requirements; Statute of Frauds.

(1) Except as otherwise provided in this section a contract for the sale of goods for the price of $500 or more is not enforceable by way of action or defense unless there is some writing sufficient to indicate that a contract for sale has been made between the parties and signed by the party against whom enforcement is sought or by his authorized agent or broker. A writing is not insufficient because it omits or incorrectly states a term agreed upon but the contract is not enforceable under this paragraph beyond the quantity of goods shown in such writing.

(2) Between merchants if within a reasonable time a writing in confirmation of the contract and sufficient against the sender is received and the party receiving it has reason to know its contents, its satisfies the requirements of subsection (1) against such party unless written notice of objection to its contents is given within ten days after it is received.

(3) A contract which does not satisfy the requirements of subsection (1) but which is valid in other respects is enforceable

    (a) if the goods are to be specially manufactured for the buyer and are not suitable for sale to others in the ordinary course of the seller's business and the seller, before notice of repudiation is received and under circumstances which reasonably indicate that the goods are for the buyer, has made either a substantial beginning of their manufacture or commitments for their procurement; or

    (b) if the party against whom enforcement is sought admits in his pleading, testimony or otherwise in court that a contract for sale was made, but the contract is not enforceable under this provision beyond the quantity of goods admitted; or

    (c) with respect to goods for which payment has been made and accepted or which have been received and accepted (Sec. 2–606).

§ 2–202. Final Written Expression: Parol or Extrinsic Evidence.

Terms with respect to which the confirmatory memoranda of the parties agree or which are otherwise set forth in a writing intended by the parties as a final expression of their agreement with respect to such terms as are included therein may not be contradicted by evidence of any prior agreement or of a contemporaneous oral agreement but may be explained or supplemented

    (a) by course of dealing or usage of trade (Section 1–205) or by course of performance (Section 2–208); and

    (b) by evidence of consistent additional terms unless the court finds the writing to have been intended also as a complete and exclusive statement of the terms of the agreement.

§ 2–203. Seals Inoperative.
The affixing of a seal to a writing evidencing a contract for sale or an offer to buy or sell goods does not constitute the writing a sealed instrument and the law with respect to sealed instruments does not apply to such a contract or offer.

§ 2–204. Formation in General.
(1) A contract for sale of goods may be made in any manner sufficient to show agreement, including conduct by both parties which recognizes the existence of such a contract.

(2) An agreement sufficient to constitute a contract for sale may be found even though the moment of its making is undetermined.

(3) Even though one or more terms are left open a contract for sale does not fail for indefiniteness if the parties have intended to make a contract and there is a reasonably certain basis for giving an appropriate remedy.

§ 2–205. Firm Offers.
An offer by a merchant to buy or sell goods in a signed writing which by its terms gives assurance that it will be held open is not revocable, for lack of consideration, during the time stated or if no time is stated for a reasonable time, but in no event may such period of irrevocability exceed three months; but any such term of assurance on a form supplied by the offeree must be separately signed by the offeror.

§ 2–206. Offer and Acceptance in Formation of Contract.
(1) Unless other unambiguously indicated by the language or circumstances

    (a) an offer to make a contract shall be construed as inviting acceptance in any manner and by any medium reasonable in the circumstances;

    (b) an order or other offer to buy goods for prompt or current shipment shall be construed as inviting acceptance either by a prompt promise to ship or by the prompt or current shipment of conforming or nonconforming goods, but such a shipment of non-conforming goods does not constitute an acceptance if the seller seasonably notifies the buyer that the shipment is offered only as an accommodation to the buyer.

(2) Where the beginning of a requested performance is a reasonable mode of acceptance an offeror who is not notified of acceptance within a reasonable time may treat the offer as having lapsed before acceptance.

§ 2–207. Additional Terms in Acceptance or Confirmation.
(1) A definite and seasonable expression of acceptance or a written confirmation which is sent within a reasonable time operates as an acceptance even though it states terms additional to or different from those offered or agreed upon, unless acceptance is expressly made conditional on assent to the additional or different terms.

(2) The additional terms are to be construed as proposals for addition to the contract. Between merchants such terms become part of the contract unless:

    (a) the offer expressly limits acceptance to the terms of the offer;

    (b) they materially alter it; or

    (c) notification of objection to them has already been given or is given within a reasonable time after notice of them is received.

(3) Conduct by both parties which recognizes the existence of a contract is sufficient to establish a contract for sale although the writings of the parties do not otherwise establish a contract. In such case the terms of the particular contract consist of those terms on which the writings of the parties agree, together with any supplementary terms incorporated under any other provisions of this Act.

§ 2–208. Course of Performance or Practical Construction.
(1) Where the contract for sale involves repeated occasions for performance by either party with knowledge of the nature of the performance and opportunity for objection to it by the other, any course of performance accepted or acquiesced in without objection shall be relevant to determine the meaning of the agreement.

(2) The express terms of the agreement and any such course of performance, as well as any course of dealing and usage of trade, shall be construed whenever reasonable as consistent with each other; but when such construction is unreasonable, express terms shall control course of performance and course of performance shall control both course of dealing and usage of trade (Section 1–205).

(3) Subject to the provisions of the next section on modification and waiver, such course of performance shall be relevant to show a waiver or modification of any term inconsistent with such course of performance.

§ 2–209. Modification, Rescission and Waiver.
(1) An agreement modifying a contract within this Article needs no consideration to be binding.

(2) A signed agreement which excludes modification or rescission except by a signed writing cannot be otherwise modified or rescinded, but except as between merchants such a requirement on a form supplied by the merchant must be separately signed by the other party.

(3) The requirements of the statute of frauds section of this Article (Section 2–201) must be satisfied if the contract as modified is within its provisions.

(4) Although an attempt at modification or rescission does not satisfy the requirements of subsection (2) or (3) it can operate as a waiver.

(5) A party who has made a waiver affecting an executory portion of the contract may retract the waiver by reasonable notification received by the other party that strict performance will be required of any term waived, unless the retraction would be unjust in view of a material change of position in reliance on the waiver.

§ 2–210. Delegation of Performance; Assignment of Rights.

(1) A party may perform his duty through a delegate unless otherwise agreed or unless the other party has a substantial interest in having his original promisor perform or control the acts required by the contract. No delegation of performance relieves the party delegating of any duty to perform or any liability for breach.

(2) Except as otherwise provided in Section 9–406, unless otherwise agreed, all rights of either seller or buyer can be assigned except where the assignment would materially change the duty of the other party, or increase materially the burden or risk imposed on him by his contract, or impair materially his chance of obtaining return performance. A right to damages for breach of the whole contract or a right arising out of the assignor's due performance of his entire obligation can be assigned despite agreement otherwise.

(3) The creation, attachment, perfection, or enforcement of a security interest in the seller's interest under a contract is not a transfer that materially changes the duty of or increases materially the burden or risk imposed on the buyer or impairs materially the buyer's chance of obtaining return performance within the purview of subsection (2) unless, and then only to the extent that, enforcement actually results in a delegation of material performance of the seller. Even in that event, the creation, attachment, perfection, and enforcement of the security interest remain effective, but (i) the seller is liable to the buyer for damages caused by the delegation to the extent that the damages could not reasonably by prevented by the buyer, and (ii) a court having jurisdiction may grant other appropriate relief, including cancellation of the contract for sale or an injunction against enforcement of the security interest or consummation of the enforcement.

(4) Unless the circumstances indicate the contrary a prohibition of assignment of "the contract" is to be construed as barring only the delegation to the assignee of the assignor's performance.

(5) An assignment of "the contract" or of "all my rights under the contract" or an assignment in similar general terms is an assignment of rights and unless the language or the circumstances (as in an assignment for security) indicate the contrary, it is a delegation of performance of the duties of the assignor and its acceptance by the assignee constitutes a promise by him to perform those duties. This promise is enforceable by either the assignor or the other party to the original contract.

(6) The other party may treat any assignment which delegates performance as creating reasonable grounds for insecurity and may without prejudice to his rights against the assignor demand assurances from the assignee (Section 2–609).
As amended in 1999.

Part 3—General Obligation and Construction of Contract

§ 2–301. General Obligations of Parties.

The obligation of the seller is to transfer and deliver and that of the buyer is to accept and pay in accordance with the contract.

§ 2–302. Unconscionable Contract or Clause.

(1) If the court as a matter of law finds the contract or any clause of the contract to have been unconscionable at the time it was made the court may refuse to enforce the contract, or it may enforce the remainder of the contract without the unconscionable clause, or it may so limit the application of any unconscionable clause as to avoid any unconscionable result.

(2) When it is claimed or appears to the court that the contract or any clause thereof may be unconscionable the parties shall be afforded a reasonable opportunity to present evidence as to its commercial setting, purpose and effect to aid the court in making the determination.

§ 2–303. Allocations or Division of Risks.

Where this Article allocates a risk or a burden as between the parties "unless otherwise agreed", the agreement may not only shift the allocation but may also divide the risk or burden.

§ 2–304. Price Payable in Money, Goods, Realty, or Otherwise.

(1) The price can be made payable in money or otherwise. If it is payable in whole or in part in goods each party is a seller of the goods which he is to transfer.

(2) Even though all or part of the price is payable in an interest in realty the transfer of the goods and the seller's obligations with reference to them are subject to this Article, but not the transfer of the interest in realty or the transferor's obligations in connection therewith.

§ 2–305. Open Price Term.

(1) The parties if they so intend can conclude a contract for sale even though the price is not settled. In such a case the price is a reasonable price at the time for delivery if
  (a) nothing is said as to price; or
  (b) the price is left to be agreed by the parties and they fail to agree; or
  (c) the price is to be fixed in terms of some agreed market or other standard as set or recorded by a third person or agency and it is not so set or recorded.

(2) A price to be fixed by the seller or by the buyer means a price for him to fix in good faith.

(3) When a price left to be fixed otherwise than by agreement of the parties fails to be fixed through fault of one party the other may at his option treat the contract as cancelled or himself fix a reasonable price.

(4) Where, however, the parties intend not to be bound unless the price be fixed or agreed and it is not fixed or agreed there is no contract. In such a case the buyer must return any goods already received or if unable so to do must pay their reasonable value at the time of delivery and the seller must return any portion of the price paid on account.

§ 2–306. Output, Requirements and Exclusive Dealings.

(1) A term which measures the quantity by the output of the seller or the requirements of the buyer means such actual output or requirements as may occur in good faith, except that no quantity unreasonably disproportionate to any stated estimate or in the absence of a stated estimate to any normal or otherwise comparable prior output or requirements may be tendered or demanded.

(2) A lawful agreement by either the seller or the buyer for exclusive dealing in the kind of goods concerned imposes unless otherwise agreed an obligation by the seller to use best efforts to supply the goods and by the buyer to use best efforts to promote their sale.

§ 2–307. Delivery in Single Lot or Several Lots.
Unless otherwise agreed all goods called for by a contract for sale must be tendered in a single delivery and payment is due only on such tender but where the circumstances give either party the right to make or demand delivery in lots the price if it can be apportioned may be demanded for each lot.

§ 2–308. Absence of Specified Place for Delivery.
Unless otherwise agreed
(a) the place for delivery of goods is the seller's place of business or if he has none his residence; but
(b) in a contract for sale of identified goods which to the knowledge of the parties at the time of contracting are in some other place, that place is the place for their delivery; and
(c) documents of title may be delivered through customary banking channels.

§ 2–309. Absence of Specific Time Provisions; Notice of Termination.
(1) The time for shipment or delivery or any other action under a contract if not provided in this Article or agreed upon shall be a reasonable time.
(2) Where the contract provides for successive performances but is indefinite in duration it is valid for a reasonable time but unless otherwise agreed may be terminated at any time by either party.
(3) Termination of a contract by one party except on the happening of an agreed event requires that reasonable notification be received by the other party and an agreement dispensing with notification is invalid if its operation would be unconscionable.

§ 2–310. Open Time for Payment or Running of Credit; Authority to Ship Under Reservation.
Unless otherwise agreed
(a) payment is due at the time and place at which the buyer is to receive the goods even though the place of shipment is the place of delivery; and
(b) if the seller is authorized to send the goods he may ship them under reservation, and may tender the documents of title, but the buyer may inspect the goods after their arrival before payment is due unless such inspection is inconsistent with the terms of the contract (Section 2–513); and
(c) if delivery is authorized and made by way of documents of title otherwise than by subsection (b) then payment is due at the time and place at which the buyer is to receive the documents regardless of where the goods are to be received; and
(d) where the seller is required or authorized to ship the goods on credit the credit period runs from the time of shipment but post-dating the invoice or delaying its dis-

patch will correspondingly delay the starting of the credit period.

§ 2–311. Options and Cooperation Respecting Performance.
(1) An agreement for sale which is otherwise sufficiently definite (subsection (3) of Section 2–204) to be a contract is not made invalid by the fact that it leaves particulars of performance to be specified by one of the parties. Any such specification must be made in good faith and within limits set by commercial reasonableness.
(2) Unless otherwise agreed specifications relating to assortment of the goods are at the buyer's option and except as otherwise provided in subsections (1)(c) and (3) of Section 2–319 specifications or arrangements relating to shipment are at the seller's option.
(3) Where such specification would materially affect the other party's performance but is not seasonably made or where one party's cooperation is necessary to the agreed performance of the other but is not seasonably forthcoming, the other party in addition to all other remedies
(a) is excused for any resulting delay in his own performance; and
(b) may also either proceed to perform in any reasonable manner or after the time for a material part of his own performance treat the failure to specify or to cooperate as a breach by failure to deliver or accept the goods.

§ 2–312. Warranty of Title and Against Infringement; Buyer's Obligation Against Infringement.
(1) Subject to subsection (2) there is in a contract for sale a warranty by the seller that
(a) the title conveyed shall be good, and its transfer rightful; and
(b) the goods shall be delivered free from any security interest or other lien or encumbrance of which the buyer at the time of contracting has no knowledge.
(2) A warranty under subsection (1) will be excluded or modified only by specific language or by circumstances which give the buyer reason to know that the person selling does not claim title in himself or that he is purporting to sell only such right or title as he or a third person may have.
(3) Unless otherwise agreed a seller who is a merchant regularly dealing in goods of the kind warrants that the goods shall be delivered free of the rightful claim of any third person by way of infringement or the like but a buyer who furnishes specifications to the seller must hold the seller harmless against any such claim which arises out of compliance with the specifications.

§ 2–313. Express Warranties by Affirmation, Promise, Description, Sample.
(1) Express warranties by the seller are created as follows:
(a) Any affirmation of fact or promise made by the seller to the buyer which relates to the goods and becomes part of the basis of the bargain creates an express warranty that the goods shall conform to the affirmation or promise.
(b) Any description of the goods which is made part of the basis of the bargain creates an express warranty that the goods shall conform to the description.

(c) Any sample or model which is made part of the basis of the bargain creates an express warranty that the whole of the goods shall conform to the sample or model.

(2) It is not necessary to the creation of an express warranty that the seller use formal words such as "warrant" or "guarantee" or that he have a specific intention to make a warranty, but an affirmation merely of the value of the goods or a statement purporting to be merely the seller's opinion or commendation of the goods does not create a warranty.

§ 2–314. Implied Warranty: Merchantability; Usage of Trade.

(1) Unless excluded or modified (Section 2–316), a warranty that the goods shall be merchantable is implied in a contract for their sale if the seller is a merchant with respect to goods of that kind. Under this section the serving for value of food or drink to be consumed either on the premises or elsewhere is a sale.

(2) Goods to be merchantable must be at least such as

(a) pass without objection in the trade under the contract description; and

(b) in the case of fungible goods, are of fair average quality within the description; and

(c) are fit for the ordinary purposes for which such goods are used; and

(d) run, within the variations permitted by the agreement, of even kind, quality and quantity within each unit and among all units involved; and

(e) are adequately contained, packaged, and labeled as the agreement may require; and

(f) conform to the promises or affirmations of fact made on the container or label if any.

(3) Unless excluded or modified (Section 2–316) other implied warranties may arise from course of dealing or usage of trade.

§ 2–315. Implied Warranty: Fitness for Particular Purpose.

Where the seller at the time of contracting has reason to know any particular purpose for which the goods are required and that the buyer is relying on the seller's skill or judgment to select or furnish suitable goods, there is unless excluded or modified under the next section an implied warranty that the goods shall be fit for such purpose.

§ 2–316. Exclusion or Modification of Warranties.

(1) Words or conduct relevant to the creation of an express warranty and words or conduct tending to negate or limit warranty shall be construed wherever reasonable as consistent with each other; but subject to the provisions of this Article on parol or extrinsic evidence (Section 2–202) negation or limitation is inoperative to the extent that such construction is unreasonable.

(2) Subject to subsection (3), to exclude or modify the implied warranty of merchantability or any part of it the language must mention merchantability and in case of a writing must be conspicuous, and to exclude or modify any implied warranty of fitness the exclusion must be by a writing and conspicuous. Language to exclude all implied warranties of fitness is sufficient if it states, for example, that "There are no warranties which extend beyond the description on the face hereof."

(3) Notwithstanding subsection (2)

(a) unless the circumstances indicate otherwise, all implied warranties are excluded by expressions like "as is", "with all faults" or other language which in common understanding calls the buyer's attention to the exclusion of warranties and makes plain that there is no implied warranty; and

(b) when the buyer before entering into the contract has examined the goods or the sample or model as fully as he desired or has refused to examine the goods there is no implied warranty with regard to defects which an examination ought in the circumstances to have revealed to him; and

(c) an implied warranty can also be excluded or modified by course of dealing or course of performance or usage of trade.

(4) Remedies for breach of warranty can be limited in accordance with the provisions of this Article on liquidation or limitation of damages and on contractual modification of remedy (Sections 2–718 and 2–719).

§ 2–317. Cumulation and Conflict of Warranties Express or Implied.

Warranties whether express or implied shall be construed as consistent with each other and as cumulative, but if such construction is unreasonable the intention of the parties shall determine which warranty is dominant. In ascertaining that intention the following rules apply:

(a) Exact or technical specifications displace an inconsistent sample or model or general language of description.

(b) A sample from an existing bulk displaces inconsistent general language of description.

(c) Express warranties displace inconsistent implied warranties other than an implied warranty of fitness for a particular purpose.

§ 2–318. Third Party Beneficiaries of Warranties Express or Implied.

Note: If this Act is introduced in the Congress of the United States this section should be omitted. (States to select one alternative.)

Alternative A

A seller's warranty whether express or implied extends to any natural person who is in the family or household of his buyer or who is a guest in his home if it is reasonable to expect that such person may use, consume or be affected by the goods and who is injured in person by breach of the warranty. A seller may not exclude or limit the operation of this section.

Alternative B

A seller's warranty whether express or implied extends to any natural person who may reasonably be expected to use, consume or be affected by the goods and who is injured in person by breach of the warranty. A seller may not exclude or limit the operation of this section.

Alternative C

A seller's warranty whether express or implied extends to any person who may reasonably be expected to use, consume or be affected by the goods and who is injured by breach of the warranty. A seller may not exclude or limit the operation of this

section with respect to injury to the person of an individual to whom the warranty extends.
As amended 1966.

§ 2–319. F.O.B. and F.A.S. Terms.
(1) Unless otherwise agreed the term F.O.B. (which means "free on board") at a named place, even though used only in connection with the stated price, is a delivery term under which
(a) when the term is F.O.B. the place of shipment, the seller must at that place ship the goods in the manner provided in this Article (Section 2–504) and bear the expense and risk of putting them into the possession of the carrier; or
(b) when the term is F.O.B. the place of destination, the seller must at his own expense and risk transport the goods to that place and there tender delivery of them in the manner provided in this Article (Section 2–503);
(c) when under either (a) or (b) the term is also F.O.B. vessel, car or other vehicle, the seller must in addition at his own expense and risk load the goods on board. If the term is F.O.B. vessel the buyer must name the vessel and in an appropriate case the seller must comply with the provisions of this Article on the form of bill of lading (Section 2–323).
(2) Unless otherwise agreed the term F.A.S. vessel (which means "free alongside") at a named port, even though used only in connection with the stated price, is a delivery term under which the seller must
(a) at his own expense and risk deliver the goods alongside the vessel in the manner usual in that port or on a dock designated and provided by the buyer; and
(b) obtain and tender a receipt for the goods in exchange for which the carrier is under a duty to issue a bill of lading.
(3) Unless otherwise agreed in any case falling within subsection (1)(a) or (c) or subsection (2) the buyer must seasonally give any needed instructions for making delivery, including when the term is F.A.S. or F.O.B. the loading berth of the vessel and in an appropriate case its name and sailing date. The seller may treat the failure of needed instructions as a failure of cooperation under this Article (Section 2–311). He may also at his option move the goods in any reasonable manner preparatory to delivery or shipment.
(4) Under the term F.O.B. vessel or F.A.S. unless otherwise agreed the buyer must make payment against tender of the required documents and the seller may not tender nor the buyer demand delivery of the goods in substitution for the documents.

§ 2–320. C.I.F. and C. & F. Terms.
(1) The term C.I.F. means that the price includes in a lump sum the cost of the goods and the insurance and freight to the named destination. The term C. & F. or C.F. means that the price so includes cost and freight to the named destination.
(2) Unless otherwise agreed and even though used only in connection with the stated price and destination, the term C.I.F. destination or its equivalent requires the seller at his own expense and risk to
(a) put the goods into the possession of a carrier at the port for shipment and obtain a negotiable bill or bills of lading covering the entire transportation to the named destination; and

(b) load the goods and obtain a receipt from the carrier (which may be contained in the bill of lading) showing that the freight has been paid or provided for; and
(c) obtain a policy or certificate of insurance, including any war risk insurance, of a kind and on terms then current at the port of shipment in the usual amount, in the currency of the contract, shown to cover the same goods covered by the bill of lading and providing for payment of loss to the order of the buyer or for the account of whom it may concern; but the seller may add to the price the amount of the premium for any such war risk insurance; and
(d) prepare an invoice of the goods and procure any other documents required to effect shipment or to comply with the contract; and
(e) forward and tender with commercial promptness all the documents in due form and with any indorsement necessary to perfect the buyer's rights.
(3) Unless otherwise agreed the term C. & F. or its equivalent has the same effect and imposes upon the seller the same obligations and risks as a C.I.F. term except the obligation as to insurance.
(4) Under the term C.I.F. or C. & F. unless otherwise agreed the buyer must make payment against tender of the required documents and the seller may not tender nor the buyer demand delivery of the goods in substitution for the documents.

§ 2–321. C.I.F. or C. & F.: "Net Landed Weights"; "Payment on Arrival"; Warranty of Condition on Arrival.
Under a contract containing a term C.I.F. or C. & F.
(1) Where the price is based on or is to be adjusted according to "net landed weights", "delivered weights", "out turn" quantity or quality or the like, unless otherwise agreed the seller must reasonably estimate the price. The payment due on tender of the documents called for by the contract is the amount so estimated, but after final adjustment of the price a settlement must be made with commercial promptness.
(2) An agreement described in subsection (1) or any warranty of quality or condition of the goods on arrival places upon the seller the risk of ordinary deterioration, shrinkage and the like in transportation but has no effect on the place or time of identification to the contract for sale or delivery or on the passing of the risk of loss.
(3) Unless otherwise agreed where the contract provides for payment on or after arrival of the goods the seller must before payment allow such preliminary inspection as is feasible; but if the goods are lost delivery of the documents and payment are due when the goods should have arrived.

§ 2–322. Delivery "Ex-Ship".
(1) Unless otherwise agreed a term for delivery of goods "ex-ship" (which means from the carrying vessel) or in equivalent language is not restricted to a particular ship and requires delivery from a ship which has reached a place at the named port of destination where goods of the kind are usually discharged.
(2) Under such a term unless otherwise agreed
(a) the seller must discharge all liens arising out of the carriage and furnish the buyer with a direction which puts the carrier under a duty to deliver the goods; and

(b) the risk of loss does not pass to the buyer until the goods leave the ship's tackle or are otherwise properly unloaded.

§ 2–323. Form of Bill of Lading Required in Overseas Shipment; "Overseas".
(1) Where the contract contemplates overseas shipment and contains a term C.I.F. or C. & F. or F.O.B. vessel, the seller unless otherwise agreed must obtain a negotiable bill of lading stating that the goods have been loaded on board or, in the case of a term C.I.F. or C. & F., received for shipment.
(2) Where in a case within subsection (1) a bill of lading has been issued in a set of parts, unless otherwise agreed if the documents are not to be sent from abroad the buyer may demand tender of the full set; otherwise only one part of the bill of lading need be tendered. Even if the agreement expressly requires a full set

   (a) due tender of a single part is acceptable within the provisions of this Article on cure of improper delivery (subsection (1) of Section 2–508); and

   (b) even though the full set is demanded, if the documents are sent from abroad the person tendering an incomplete set may nevertheless require payment upon furnishing an indemnity which the buyer in good faith deems adequate.

(3) A shipment by water or by air or a contract contemplating such shipment is "overseas" insofar as by usage of trade or agreement it is subject to the commercial, financing or shipping practices characteristic of international deep water commerce.

§ 2–324. "No Arrival, No Sale" Term.
Under a term "no arrival, no sale" or terms of like meaning, unless otherwise agreed,

   (a) the seller must properly ship conforming goods and if they arrive by any means he must tender them on arrival but he assumes no obligation that the goods will arrive unless he has caused the non-arrival; and

   (b) where without fault of the seller the goods are in part lost or have so deteriorated as no longer to conform to the contract or arrive after the contract time, the buyer may proceed as if there had been casualty to identified goods (Section 2–613).

§ 2–325. "Letter of Credit" Term; "Confirmed Credit".
(1) Failure of the buyer seasonably to furnish an agreed letter of credit is a breach of the contract for sale.
(2) The delivery to seller of a proper letter of credit suspends the buyer's obligation to pay. If the letter of credit is dishonored, the seller may on seasonable notification to the buyer require payment directly from him.
(3) Unless otherwise agreed the term "letter of credit" or "banker's credit" in a contract for sale means an irrevocable credit issued by a financing agency of good repute and, where the shipment is overseas, of good international repute. The term "confirmed credit" means that the credit must also carry the direct obligation of such an agency which does business in the seller's financial market.

§ 2–326. Sale on Approval and Sale or Return; Rights of Creditors.
(1) Unless otherwise agreed, if delivered goods may be returned by the buyer even though they conform to the contract, the transaction is

   (a) a "sale on approval" if the goods are delivered primarily for use, and

   (b) a "sale or return" if the goods are delivered primarily for resale.

(2) Goods held on approval are not subject to the claims of the buyer's creditors until acceptance; goods held on sale or return are subject to such claims while in the buyer's possession.
(3) Any "or return" term of a contract for sale is to be treated as a separate contract for sale within the statute of frauds section of this Article (Section 2–201) and as contradicting the sale aspect of the contract within the provisions of this Article on parol or extrinsic evidence (Section 2–202).
As amended in 1999.

§ 2–327. Special Incidents of Sale on Approval and Sale or Return.
(1) Under a sale on approval unless otherwise agreed

   (a) although the goods are identified to the contract the risk of loss and the title do not pass to the buyer until acceptance; and

   (b) use of the goods consistent with the purpose of trial is not acceptance but failure seasonably to notify the seller of election to return the goods is acceptance, and if the goods conform to the contract acceptance of any part is acceptance of the whole; and

   (c) after due notification of election to return, the return is at the seller's risk and expense but a merchant buyer must follow any reasonable instructions.

(2) Under a sale or return unless otherwise agreed

   (a) the option to return extends to the whole or any commercial unit of the goods while in substantially their original condition, but must be exercised seasonably; and

   (b) the return is at the buyer's risk and expense.

§ 2–328. Sale by Auction.
(1) In a sale by auction if goods are put up in lots each lot is the subject of a separate sale.
(2) A sale by auction is complete when the auctioneer so announces by the fall of the hammer or in other customary manner. Where a bid is made while the hammer is falling in acceptance of a prior bid the auctioneer may in his discretion reopen the bidding or declare the goods sold under the bid on which the hammer was falling.
(3) Such a sale is with reserve unless the goods are in explicit terms put up without reserve. In an auction with reserve the auctioneer may withdraw the goods at any time until he announces completion of the sale. In an auction without reserve, after the auctioneer calls for bids on an article or lot, that article or lot cannot be withdrawn unless no bid is made within a reasonable time. In either case a bidder may retract his bid until the auctioneer's announcement of completion of the sale, but a bidder's retraction does not revive any previous bid.
(4) If the auctioneer knowingly receives a bid on the seller's behalf or the seller makes or procures such as bid, and notice has not been given that liberty for such bidding is reserved, the buyer may at his option avoid the sale or take the goods at the price of the last good faith bid prior to the completion of the sale. This subsection shall not apply to any bid at a forced sale.

Part 4—Title, Creditors and Good Faith Purchasers

§ 2–401. Passing of Title; Reservation for Security; Limited Application of This Section.

Each provision of this Article with regard to the rights, obligations and remedies of the seller, the buyer, purchasers or other third parties applies irrespective of title to the goods except where the provision refers to such title. Insofar as situations are not covered by the other provisions of this Article and matters concerning title became material the following rules apply:

(1) Title to goods cannot pass under a contract for sale prior to their identification to the contract (Section 2–501), and unless otherwise explicitly agreed the buyer acquires by their identification a special property as limited by this Act. Any retention or reservation by the seller of the title (property) in goods shipped or delivered to the buyer is limited in effect to a reservation of a security interest. Subject to these provisions and to the provisions of the Article on Secured Transactions (Article 9), title to goods passes from the seller to the buyer in any manner and on any conditions explicitly agreed on by the parties.

(2) Unless otherwise explicitly agreed title passes to the buyer at the time and place at which the seller completes his performance with reference to the physical delivery of the goods, despite any reservation of a security interest and even though a document of title is to be delivered at a different time or place; and in particular and despite any reservation of a security interest by the bill of lading

    (a) if the contract requires or authorizes the seller to send the goods to the buyer but does not require him to deliver them at destination, title passes to the buyer at the time and place of shipment; but

    (b) if the contract requires delivery at destination, title passes on tender there.

(3) Unless otherwise explicitly agreed where delivery is to be made without moving the goods,

    (a) if the seller is to deliver a document of title, title passes at the time when and the place where he delivers such documents; or

    (b) if the goods are at the time of contracting already identified and no documents are to be delivered, title passes at the time and place of contracting.

(4) A rejection or other refusal by the buyer to receive or retain the goods, whether or not justified, or a justified revocation of acceptance revests title to the goods in the seller. Such revesting occurs by operation of law and is not a "sale".

§ 2–402. Rights of Seller's Creditors Against Sold Goods.

(1) Except as provided in subsections (2) and (3), rights of unsecured creditors of the seller with respect to goods which have been identified to a contract for sale are subject to the buyer's rights to recover the goods under this Article (Sections 2–502 and 2–716).

(2) A creditor of the seller may treat a sale or an identification of goods to a contract for sale as void if as against him a retention of possession by the seller is fraudulent under any rule of law of the state where the goods are situated, except that retention of possession in good faith and current course of trade by a merchant-seller for a commercially reasonable time after a sale or identification is not fraudulent.

(3) Nothing in this Article shall be deemed to impair the rights of creditors of the seller

    (a) under the provisions of the Article on Secured Transactions (Article 9); or

    (b) where identification to the contract or delivery is made not in current course of trade but in satisfaction of or as security for a pre-existing claim for money, security or the like and is made under circumstances which under any rule of law of the state where the goods are situated would apart from this Article constitute the transaction a fraudulent transfer or voidable preference.

§ 2–403. Power to Transfer; Good Faith Purchase of Goods; "Entrusting".

(1) A purchaser of goods acquires all title which his transferor had or had power to transfer except that a purchaser of a limited interest acquires rights only to the extent of the interest purchased. A person with voidable title has power to transfer a good title to a good faith purchaser for value. When goods have been delivered under a transaction of purchase the purchaser has such power even though

    (a) the transferor was deceived as to the identity of the purchaser, or

    (b) the delivery was in exchange for a check which is later dishonored, or

    (c) it was agreed that the transaction was to be a "cash sale", or

    (d) the delivery was procured through fraud punishable as larcenous under the criminal law.

(2) Any entrusting of possession of goods to a merchant who deals in goods of that kind gives him power to transfer all rights of the entruster to a buyer in ordinary course of business.

(3) "Entrusting" includes any delivery and any acquiescence in retention of possession regardless of any condition expressed between the parties to the delivery or acquiescence and regardless of whether the procurement of the entrusting or the possessor's disposition of the goods have been such as to be larcenous under the criminal law.

(4) The rights of other purchasers of goods and of lien creditors are governed by the Articles on Secured Transactions (Article 9), Bulk Transfers (Article 6) and Documents of Title (Article 7). As amended in 1988.

Part 5—Performance

§ 2–501. Insurable Interest in Goods; Manner of Identification of Goods.

(1) The buyer obtains a special property and an insurable interest in goods by identification of existing goods as goods to which the contract refers even though the goods so identified are non-conforming and he has an option to return or reject them. Such identification can be made at any time and in any manner explicitly agreed to by the parties. In the absence of explicit agreement identification occurs

    (a) when the contract is made if it is for the sale of goods already existing and identified;

    (b) if the contract is for the sale of future goods other than those described in paragraph (c), when goods are shipped, marked or otherwise designated by the seller as goods to which the contract refers;

(c) when the crops are planted or otherwise become growing crops or the young are conceived if the contract is for the sale of unborn young to be born within twelve months after contracting or for the sale of crops to be harvested within twelve months or the next normal harvest season after contracting whichever is longer.

(2) The seller retains an insurable interest in goods so long as title to or any security interest in the goods remains in him and where the identification is by the seller alone he may until default or insolvency or notification to the buyer that the identification is final substitute other goods for those identified.

(3) Nothing in this section impairs any insurable interest recognized under any other statute or rule of law.

§ 2–502. Buyer's Right to Goods on Seller's Insolvency.

(1) Subject to subsections (2) and (3) and even though the goods have not been shipped a buyer who has paid a part or all of the price of goods in which he has a special property under the provisions of the immediately preceding section may on making and keeping good a tender of any unpaid portion of their price recover them from the seller if:

(a) in the case of goods bought for personal, family, or household purposes, the seller repudiates or fails to deliver as required by the contract; or

(b) in all cases, the seller becomes insolvent within ten days after receipt of the first installment on their price.

(2) The buyer's right to recover the goods under subsection (1)(a) vests upon acquisition of a special property, even if the seller had not then repudiated or failed to deliver.

(3) If the identification creating his special property has been made by the buyer he acquires the right to recover the goods only if they conform to the contract for sale.

As amended in 1999.

§ 2–503. Manner of Seller's Tender of Delivery.

(1) Tender of delivery requires that the seller put and hold conforming goods at the buyer's disposition and give the buyer any notification reasonably necessary to enable him to take delivery. The manner, time and place for tender are determined by the agreement and this Article, and in particular

(a) tender must be at a reasonable hour, and if it is of goods they must be kept available for the period reasonably necessary to enable the buyer to take possession; but

(b) unless otherwise agreed the buyer must furnish facilities reasonably suited to the receipt of the goods.

(2) Where the case is within the next section respecting shipment tender requires that the seller comply with its provisions.

(3) Where the seller is required to deliver at a particular destination tender requires that he comply with subsection (1) and also in any appropriate case tender documents as described in subsections (4) and (5) of this section.

(4) Where goods are in the possession of a bailee and are to be delivered without being moved

(a) tender requires that the seller either tender a negotiable document of title covering such goods or procure acknowledgment by the bailee of the buyer's right to possession of the goods; but

(b) tender to the buyer of a non-negotiable document of title or of a written direction to the bailee to deliver is sufficient tender unless the buyer seasonably objects, and receipt by the bailee of notification of the buyer's rights fixes those rights as against the bailee and all third persons; but risk of loss of the goods and of any failure by the bailee to honor the non-negotiable document of title or to obey the direction remains on the seller until the buyer has had a reasonable time to present the document or direction, and a refusal by the bailee to honor the document or to obey the direction defeats the tender.

(5) Where the contract requires the seller to deliver documents

(a) he must tender all such documents in correct form, except as provided in this Article with respect to bills of lading in a set (subsection (2) of Section 2–323); and

(b) tender through customary banking channels is sufficient and dishonor of a draft accompanying the documents constitutes non-acceptance or rejection.

§ 2–504. Shipment by Seller.

Where the seller is required or authorized to send the goods to the buyer and the contract does not require him to deliver them at a particular destination, then unless otherwise agreed he must

(a) put the goods in the possession of such a carrier and make such a contract for their transportation as may be reasonable having regard to the nature of the goods and other circumstances of the case; and

(b) obtain and promptly deliver or tender in due form any document necessary to enable the buyer to obtain possession of the goods or otherwise required by the agreement or by usage of trade; and

(c) promptly notify the buyer of the shipment.

Failure to notify the buyer under paragraph (c) or to make a proper contract under paragraph (a) is a ground for rejection only if material delay or loss ensues.

§ 2–505. Seller's Shipment under Reservation.

(1) Where the seller has identified goods to the contract by or before shipment:

(a) his procurement of a negotiable bill of lading to his own order or otherwise reserves in him a security interest in the goods. His procurement of the bill to the order of a financing agency or of the buyer indicates in addition only the seller's expectation of transferring that interest to the person named.

(b) a non-negotiable bill of lading to himself or his nominee reserves possession of the goods as security but except in a case of conditional delivery (subsection (2) of Section 2–507) a non-negotiable bill of lading naming the buyer as consignee reserves no security interest even though the seller retains possession of the bill of lading.

(2) When shipment by the seller with reservation of a security interest is in violation of the contract for sale it constitutes an improper contract for transportation within the preceding section but impairs neither the rights given to the buyer by shipment and identification of the goods to the contract nor the seller's powers as a holder of a negotiable document.

§ 2–506. Rights of Financing Agency.
(1) A financing agency by paying or purchasing for value a draft which relates to a shipment of goods acquires to the extent of the payment or purchase and in addition to its own rights under the draft and any document of title securing it any rights of the shipper in the goods including the right to stop delivery and the shipper's right to have the draft honored by the buyer. **(2)** The right to reimbursement of a financing agency which has in good faith honored or purchased the draft under commitment to or authority from the buyer is not impaired by subsequent discovery of defects with reference to any relevant document which was apparently regular on its face.

§ 2–507. Effect of Seller's Tender; Delivery on Condition.
(1) Tender of delivery is a condition to the buyer's duty to accept the goods and, unless otherwise agreed, to his duty to pay for them. Tender entitles the seller to acceptance of the goods and to payment according to the contract. **(2)** Where payment is due and demanded on the delivery to the buyer of goods or documents of title, his right as against the seller to retain or dispose of them is conditional upon his making the payment due.

§ 2–508. Cure by Seller of Improper Tender or Delivery; Replacement.
(1) Where any tender or delivery by the seller is rejected because non-conforming and the time for performance has not yet expired, the seller may seasonably notify the buyer of his intention to cure and may then within the contract time make a conforming delivery. **(2)** Where the buyer rejects a non-conforming tender which the seller had reasonable grounds to believe would be acceptable with or without money allowance the seller may if he seasonably notifies the buyer have a further reasonable time to substitute a conforming tender.

§ 2–509. Risk of Loss in the Absence of Breach.
(1) Where the contract requires or authorizes the seller to ship the goods by carrier
   (a) if it does not require him to deliver them at a particular destination, the risk of loss passes to the buyer when the goods are duly delivered to the carrier even though the shipment is under reservation (Section 2–505); but
   (b) if it does require him to deliver them at a particular destination and the goods are there duly tendered while in the possession of the carrier, the risk of loss passes to the buyer when the goods are there duly so tendered as to enable the buyer to take delivery.
(2) Where the goods are held by a bailee to be delivered without being moved, the risk of loss passes to the buyer
   (a) on his receipt of a negotiable document of title covering the goods; or
   (b) on acknowledgment by the bailee of the buyer's right to possession of the goods; or
   (c) after his receipt of a non-negotiable document of title or other written direction to deliver, as provided in subsection (4)(b) of Section 2–503.

(3) In any case not within subsection (1) or (2), the risk of loss passes to the buyer on his receipt of the goods if the seller is a merchant; otherwise the risk passes to the buyer on tender of delivery. **(4)** The provisions of this section are subject to contrary agreement of the parties and to the provisions of this Article on sale on approval (Section 2–327) and on effect of breach on risk of loss (Section 2–510).

§ 2–510. Effect of Breach on Risk of Loss.
(1) Where a tender or delivery of goods so fails to conform to the contract as to give a right of rejection the risk of their loss remains on the seller until cure or acceptance. **(2)** Where the buyer rightfully revokes acceptance he may to the extent of any deficiency in his effective insurance coverage treat the risk of loss as having rested on the seller from the beginning. **(3)** Where the buyer as to conforming goods already identified to the contract for sale repudiates or is otherwise in breach before risk of their loss has passed to him, the seller may to the extent of any deficiency in his effective insurance coverage treat the risk of loss as resting on the buyer for a commercially reasonable time.

§ 2–511. Tender of Payment by Buyer; Payment by Check.
(1) Unless otherwise agreed tender of payment is a condition to the seller's duty to tender and complete any delivery. **(2)** Tender of payment is sufficient when made by any means or in any manner current in the ordinary course of business unless the seller demands payment in legal tender and gives any extension of time reasonably necessary to procure it. **(3)** Subject to the provisions of this Act on the effect of an instrument on an obligation (Section 3–310), payment by check is conditional and is defeated as between the parties by dishonor of the check on due presentment.
As amended in 1994.

§ 2–512. Payment by Buyer Before Inspection.
(1) Where the contract requires payment before inspection non-conformity of the goods does not excuse the buyer from so making payment unless
   (a) the non-conformity appears without inspection; or
   (b) despite tender of the required documents the circumstances would justify injunction against honor under this Act (Section 5–109(b)).
(2) Payment pursuant to subsection (1) does not constitute an acceptance of goods or impair the buyer's right to inspect or any of his remedies.
As amended in 1995.

§ 2–513. Buyer's Right to Inspection of Goods.
(1) Unless otherwise agreed and subject to subsection (3), where goods are tendered or delivered or identified to the contract for sale, the buyer has a right before payment or acceptance to inspect them at any reasonable place and time and in any reasonable manner. When the seller is required or authorized to send the goods to the buyer, the inspection may be after their arrival. **(2)** Expenses of inspection must be borne by the buyer but may be recovered from the seller if the goods do not conform and are rejected.

(3) Unless otherwise agreed and subject to the provisions of this Article on C.I.F. contracts (subsection (3) of Section 2–321), the buyer is not entitled to inspect the goods before payment of the price when the contract provides

(a) for delivery "C.O.D." or on other like terms; or

(b) for payment against documents of title, except where such payment is due only after the goods are to become available for inspection.

(4) A place or method of inspection fixed by the parties is presumed to be exclusive but unless otherwise expressly agreed it does not postpone identification or shift the place for delivery or for passing the risk of loss. If compliance becomes impossible, inspection shall be as provided in this section unless the place or method fixed was clearly intended as an indispensable condition failure of which avoids the contract.

§ 2–514. When Documents Deliverable on Acceptance; When on Payment.

Unless otherwise agreed documents against which a draft is drawn are to be delivered to the drawee on acceptance of the draft if it is payable more than three days after presentment; otherwise, only on payment.

§ 2–515. Preserving Evidence of Goods in Dispute.

In furtherance of the adjustment of any claim or dispute

(a) either party on reasonable notification to the other and for the purpose of ascertaining the facts and preserving evidence has the right to inspect, test and sample the goods including such of them as may be in the possession or control of the other; and

(b) the parties may agree to a third party inspection or survey to determine the conformity or condition of the goods and may agree that the findings shall be binding upon them in any subsequent litigation or adjustment.

Part 6—Breach, Repudiation and Excuse

§ 2–601. Buyer's Rights on Improper Delivery.

Subject to the provisions of this Article on breach in installment contracts (Section 2–612) and unless otherwise agreed under the sections on contractual limitations of remedy (Sections 2–718 and 2–719), if the goods or the tender of delivery fail in any respect to conform to the contract, the buyer may

(a) reject the whole; or

(b) accept the whole; or

(c) accept any commercial unit or units and reject the rest.

§ 2–602. Manner and Effect of Rightful Rejection.

(1) Rejection of goods must be within a reasonable time after their delivery or tender. It is ineffective unless the buyer seasonably notifies the seller.

(2) Subject to the provisions of the two following sections on rejected goods (Sections 2–603 and 2–604),

(a) after rejection any exercise of ownership by the buyer with respect to any commercial unit is wrongful as against the seller; and

(b) if the buyer has before rejection taken physical possession of goods in which he does not have a security interest under the provisions of this Article (subsection (3) of Section 2–711), he is under a duty after rejection to hold them with reasonable care at the seller's disposition for a time sufficient to permit the seller to remove them; but

(c) the buyer has no further obligations with regard to goods rightfully rejected.

(3) The seller's rights with respect to goods wrongfully rejected are governed by the provisions of this Article on Seller's remedies in general (Section 2–703).

§ 2–603. Merchant Buyer's Duties as to Rightfully Rejected Goods.

(1) Subject to any security interest in the buyer (subsection (3) of Section 2–711), when the seller has no agent or place of business at the market of rejection a merchant buyer is under a duty after rejection of goods in his possession or control to follow any reasonable instructions received from the seller with respect to the goods and in the absence of such instructions to make reasonable efforts to sell them for the seller's account if they are perishable or threaten to decline in value speedily. Instructions are not reasonable if on demand indemnity for expenses is not forthcoming.

(2) When the buyer sells goods under subsection (1), he is entitled to reimbursement from the seller or out of the proceeds for reasonable expenses of caring for and selling them, and if the expenses include no selling commission then to such commission as is usual in the trade or if there is none to a reasonable sum not exceeding ten per cent on the gross proceeds.

(3) In complying with this section the buyer is held only to good faith and good faith conduct hereunder is neither acceptance nor conversion nor the basis of an action for damages.

§ 2–604. Buyer's Options as to Salvage of Rightfully Rejected Goods.

Subject to the provisions of the immediately preceding section on perishables if the seller gives no instructions within a reasonable time after notification of rejection the buyer may store the rejected goods for the seller's account or reship them to him or resell them for the seller's account with reimbursement as provided in the preceding section. Such action is not acceptance or conversion.

§ 2–605. Waiver of Buyer's Objections by Failure to Particularize.

(1) The buyer's failure to state in connection with rejection a particular defect which is ascertainable by reasonable inspection precludes him from relying on the unstated defect to justify rejection or to establish breach

(a) where the seller could have cured it if stated seasonably; or

(b) between merchants when the seller has after rejection made a request in writing for a full and final written statement of all defects on which the buyer proposes to rely.

(2) Payment against documents made without reservation of rights precludes recovery of the payment for defects apparent on the face of the documents.

§ 2–606. What Constitutes Acceptance of Goods.

(1) Acceptance of goods occurs when the buyer

(a) after a reasonable opportunity to inspect the goods signifies to the seller that the goods are conforming or that he will take or retain them in spite of their nonconformity; or

(b) fails to make an effective rejection (subsection (1) of Section 2–602), but such acceptance does not occur until the buyer has had a reasonable opportunity to inspect them; or

(c) does any act inconsistent with the seller's ownership; but if such act is wrongful as against the seller it is an acceptance only if ratified by him.

(2) Acceptance of a part of any commercial unit is acceptance of that entire unit.

§ 2–607. Effect of Acceptance; Notice of Breach; Burden of Establishing Breach After Acceptance; Notice of Claim or Litigation to Person Answerable Over.

(1) The buyer must pay at the contract rate for any goods accepted.

(2) Acceptance of goods by the buyer precludes rejection of the goods accepted and if made with knowledge of a non-conformity cannot be revoked because of it unless the acceptance was on the reasonable assumption that the non-conformity would be seasonably cured but acceptance does not of itself impair any other remedy provided by this Article for non-conformity.

(3) Where a tender has been accepted

(a) the buyer must within a reasonable time after he discovers or should have discovered any breach notify the seller of breach or be barred from any remedy; and

(b) if the claim is one for infringement or the like (subsection (3) of Section 2–312) and the buyer is sued as a result of such a breach he must so notify the seller within a reasonable time after he receives notice of the litigation or be barred from any remedy over for liability established by the litigation.

(4) The burden is on the buyer to establish any breach with respect to the goods accepted.

(5) Where the buyer is sued for breach of a warranty or other obligation for which his seller is answerable over

(a) he may give his seller written notice of the litigation. If the notice states that the seller may come in and defend and that if the seller does not do so he will be bound in any action against him by his buyer by any determination of fact common to the two litigations, then unless the seller after seasonable receipt of the notice does come in and defend he is so bound.

(b) if the claim is one for infringement or the like (subsection (3) of Section 2–312) the original seller may demand in writing that his buyer turn over to him control of the litigation including settlement or else be barred from any remedy over and if he also agrees to bear all expense and to satisfy any adverse judgment, then unless the buyer after seasonable receipt of the demand does turn over control the buyer is so barred.

(6) The provisions of subsections (3), (4) and (5) apply to any obligation of a buyer to hold the seller harmless against infringement or the like (subsection (3) of Section 2–312).

§ 2–608. Revocation of Acceptance in Whole or in Part.

(1) The buyer may revoke his acceptance of a lot or commercial unit whose non-conformity substantially impairs its value to him if he has accepted it

(a) on the reasonable assumption that its nonconformity would be cured and it has not been seasonably cured; or

(b) without discovery of such non-conformity if his acceptance was reasonably induced either by the difficulty of discovery before acceptance or by the seller's assurances.

(2) Revocation of acceptance must occur within a reasonable time after the buyer discovers or should have discovered the ground for it and before any substantial change in condition of the goods which is not caused by their own defects. It is not effective until the buyer notifies the seller of it.

(3) A buyer who so revokes has the same rights and duties with regard to the goods involved as if he had rejected them.

§ 2–609. Right to Adequate Assurance of Performance.

(1) A contract for sale imposes an obligation on each party that the other's expectation of receiving due performance will not be impaired. When reasonable grounds for insecurity arise with respect to the performance of either party the other may in writing demand adequate assurance of due performance and until he receives such assurance may if commercially reasonable suspend any performance for which he has not already received the agreed return.

(2) Between merchants the reasonableness of grounds for insecurity and the adequacy of any assurance offered shall be determined according to commercial standards.

(3) Acceptance of any improper delivery or payment does not prejudice the party's right to demand adequate assurance of future performance.

(4) After receipt of a justified demand failure to provide within a reasonable time not exceeding thirty days such assurance of due performance as is adequate under the circumstances of the particular case is a repudiation of the contract.

§ 2–610. Anticipatory Repudiation.

When either party repudiates the contract with respect to a performance not yet due the loss of which will substantially impair the value of the contract to the other, the aggrieved party may

(a) for a commercially reasonable time await performance by the repudiating party; or

(b) resort to any remedy for breach (Section 2–703 or Section 2–711), even though he has notified the repudiating party that he would await the latter's performance and has urged retraction; and

(c) in either case suspend his own performance or proceed in accordance with the provisions of this Article on the seller's right to identify goods to the contract notwithstanding breach or to salvage unfinished goods (Section 2–704).

§ 2–611. Retraction of Anticipatory Repudiation.

(1) Until the repudiating party's next performance is due he can retract his repudiation unless the aggrieved party has since the repudiation cancelled or materially changed his position or otherwise indicated that he considers the repudiation final.

(2) Retraction may be by any method which clearly indicates to the aggrieved party that the repudiating party intends to perform, but must include any assurance justifiably demanded under the provisions of this Article (Section 2–609).

(3) Retraction reinstates the repudiating party's rights under the contract with due excuse and allowance to the aggrieved party for any delay occasioned by the repudiation.

§ 2–612. "Installment Contract"; Breach.

(1) An "installment contract" is one which requires or authorizes the delivery of goods in separate lots to be separately accepted, even though the contract contains a clause "each delivery is a separate contract" or its equivalent.

(2) The buyer may reject any installment which is non-conforming if the non-conformity substantially impairs the value of that installment and cannot be cured or if the non-conformity is a defect in the required documents; but if the non-conformity does not fall within subsection (3) and the seller gives adequate assurance of its cure the buyer must accept that installment.

(3) Whenever non-conformity or default with respect to one or more installments substantially impairs the value of the whole contract there is a breach of the whole. But the aggrieved party reinstates the contract if he accepts a non-conforming installment without seasonably notifying of cancellation or if he brings an action with respect only to past installments or demands performance as to future installments.

§ 2–613. Casualty to Identified Goods.

Where the contract requires for its performance goods identified when the contract is made, and the goods suffer casualty without fault of either party before the risk of loss passes to the buyer, or in a proper case under a "no arrival, no sale" term (Section 2–324) then

    (a) if the loss is total the contract is avoided; and

    (b) if the loss is partial or the goods have so deteriorated as no longer to conform to the contract the buyer may nevertheless demand inspection and at his option either treat the contract as voided or accept the goods with due allowance from the contract price for the deterioration or the deficiency in quantity but without further right against the seller.

§ 2–614. Substituted Performance.

(1) Where without fault of either party the agreed berthing, loading, or unloading facilities fail or an agreed type of carrier becomes unavailable or the agreed manner of delivery otherwise becomes commercially impracticable but a commercially reasonable substitute is available, such substitute performance must be tendered and accepted.

(2) If the agreed means or manner of payment fails because of domestic or foreign governmental regulation, the seller may withhold or stop delivery unless the buyer provides a means or manner of payment which is commercially a substantial equivalent. If delivery has already been taken, payment by the means or in the manner provided by the regulation discharges the buyer's obligation unless the regulation is discriminatory, oppressive or predatory.

§ 2–615. Excuse by Failure of Presupposed Conditions.

Except so far as a seller may have assumed a greater obligation and subject to the preceding section on substituted performance:

    (a) Delay in delivery or non-delivery in whole or in part by a seller who complies with paragraphs (b) and (c) is not a breach of his duty under a contract for sale if performance as agreed has been made impracticable by the occurrence of a contingency the nonoccurrence of which was a basic assumption on which the contract was made or by compliance in good faith with any applicable foreign or domestic governmental regulation or order whether or not it later proves to be invalid.

    (b) Where the causes mentioned in paragraph (a) affect only a part of the seller's capacity to perform, he must allocate production and deliveries among his customers but may at his option include regular customers not then under contract as well as his own requirements for further manufacture. He may so allocate in any manner which is fair and reasonable.

    (c) The seller must notify the buyer seasonably that there will be delay or non-delivery and, when allocation is required under paragraph (b), of the estimated quota thus made available for the buyer.

§ 2–616. Procedure on Notice Claiming Excuse.

(1) Where the buyer receives notification of a material or indefinite delay or an allocation justified under the preceding section he may by written notification to the seller as to any delivery concerned, and where the prospective deficiency substantially impairs the value of the whole contract under the provisions of this Article relating to breach of installment contracts (Section 2–612), then also as to the whole,

    (a) terminate and thereby discharge any unexecuted portion of the contract; or

    (b) modify the contract by agreeing to take his available quota in substitution.

(2) If after receipt of such notification from the seller the buyer fails so to modify the contract within a reasonable time not exceeding thirty days the contract lapses with respect to any deliveries affected.

(3) The provisions of this section may not be negated by agreement except in so far as the seller has assumed a greater obligation under the preceding section.

Part 7—Remedies

§ 2–701. Remedies for Breach of Collateral Contracts Not Impaired.

Remedies for breach of any obligation or promise collateral or ancillary to a contract for sale are not impaired by the provisions of this Article.

§ 2–702. Seller's Remedies on Discovery of Buyer's Insolvency.

(1) Where the seller discovers the buyer to be insolvent he may refuse delivery except for cash including payment for all goods theretofore delivered under the contract, and stop delivery under this Article (Section 2–705).

(2) Where the seller discovers that the buyer has received goods on credit while insolvent he may reclaim the goods upon demand made within ten days after the receipt, but if misrepresentation of solvency has been made to the particular seller in writing within three months before delivery the ten day limitation does not apply. Except as provided in this subsection the seller may not base a right to reclaim goods on the buyer's fraudulent or innocent misrepresentation of solvency or of intent to pay.

(3) The seller's right to reclaim under subsection (2) is subject to the rights of a buyer in ordinary course or other good faith purchaser under this Article (Section 2–403). Successful reclamation of goods excludes all other remedies with respect to them.

§ 2–703. Seller's Remedies in General.

Where the buyer wrongfully rejects or revokes acceptance of goods or fails to make a payment due on or before delivery or repudiates with respect to a part or the whole, then with respect to any goods directly affected and, if the breach is of the whole contract (Section 2–612), then also with respect to the whole undelivered balance, the aggrieved seller may

(a) withhold delivery of such goods;

(b) stop delivery by any bailee as hereafter provided (Section 2–705);

(c) proceed under the next section respecting goods still unidentified to the contract;

(d) resell and recover damages as hereafter provided (Section 2–706);

(e) recover damages for non-acceptance (Section 2–708) or in a proper case the price (Section 2–709);

(f) cancel.

§ 2–704. Seller's Right to Identify Goods to the Contract Notwithstanding Breach or to Salvage Unfinished Goods.

(1) An aggrieved seller under the preceding section may

    (a) identify to the contract conforming goods not already identified if at the time he learned of the breach they are in his possession or control;

    (b) treat as the subject of resale goods which have demonstrably been intended for the particular contract even though those goods are unfinished.

(2) Where the goods are unfinished an aggrieved seller may in the exercise of reasonable commercial judgment for the purposes of avoiding loss and of effective realization either complete the manufacture and wholly identify the goods to the contract or cease manufacture and resell for scrap or salvage value or proceed in any other reasonable manner.

§ 2–705. Seller's Stoppage of Delivery in Transit or Otherwise.

(1) The seller may stop delivery of goods in the possession of a carrier or other bailee when he discovers the buyer to be insolvent (Section 2–702) and may stop delivery of carload, truckload, planeload or larger shipments of express or freight when the buyer repudiates or fails to make a payment due before delivery or if for any other reason the seller has a right to withhold or reclaim the goods.

(2) As against such buyer the seller may stop delivery until

    (a) receipt of the goods by the buyer; or

    (b) acknowledgment to the buyer by any bailee of the goods except a carrier that the bailee holds the goods for the buyer; or

    (c) such acknowledgment to the buyer by a carrier by reshipment or as warehouseman; or

    (d) negotiation to the buyer of any negotiable document of title covering the goods.

(3) (a) To stop delivery the seller must so notify as to enable the bailee by reasonable diligence to prevent delivery of the goods.

(b) After such notification the bailee must hold and deliver the goods according to the directions of the seller but the seller is liable to the bailee for any ensuing charges or damages.

(c) If a negotiable document of title has been issued for goods the bailee is not obliged to obey a notification to stop until surrender of the document.

(d) A carrier who has issued a non-negotiable bill of lading is not obliged to obey a notification to stop received from a person other than the consignor.

§ 2–706. Seller's Resale Including Contract for Resale.

(1) Under the conditions stated in Section 2–703 on seller's remedies, the seller may resell the goods concerned or the undelivered balance thereof. Where the resale is made in good faith and in a commercially reasonable manner the seller may recover the difference between the resale price and the contract price together with any incidental damages allowed under the provisions of this Article (Section 2–710), but less expenses saved in consequence of the buyer's breach.

(2) Except as otherwise provided in subsection (3) or unless otherwise agreed resale may be at public or private sale including sale by way of one or more contracts to sell or of identification to an existing contract of the seller. Sale may be as a unit or in parcels and at any time and place and on any terms but every aspect of the sale including the method, manner, time, place and terms must be commercially reasonable. The resale must be reasonably identified as referring to the broken contract, but it is not necessary that the goods be in existence or that any or all of them have been identified to the contract before the breach.

(3) Where the resale is at private sale the seller must give the buyer reasonable notification of his intention to resell.

(4) Where the resale is at public sale

    (a) only identified goods can be sold except where there is a recognized market for a public sale of futures in goods of the kind; and

    (b) it must be made at a usual place or market for public sale if one is reasonably available and except in the case of goods which are perishable or threaten to decline in value speedily the seller must give the buyer reasonable notice of the time and place of the resale; and

    (c) if the goods are not to be within the view of those attending the sale the notification of sale must state the place where the goods are located and provide for their reasonable inspection by prospective bidders; and

    (d) the seller may buy.

(5) A purchaser who buys in good faith at a resale takes the goods free of any rights of the original buyer even though the seller fails to comply with one or more of the requirements of this section.

(6) The seller is not accountable to the buyer for any profit made on any resale. A person in the position of a seller (Section 2–707) or a buyer who has rightfully rejected or justifiably revoked acceptance must account for any excess over the amount of his security interest, as hereinafter defined (subsection (3) of Section 2–711).

§ 2–707. "Person in the Position of a Seller".

(1) A "person in the position of a seller" includes as against a principal an agent who has paid or become responsible for the price of goods on behalf of his principal or anyone who otherwise holds a security interest or other right in goods similar to that of a seller.

(2) A person in the position of a seller may as provided in this Article withhold or stop delivery (Section 2–705) and resell (Section 2–706) and recover incidental damages (Section 2–710).

§ 2–708. Seller's Damages for Non-Acceptance or Repudiation.

(1) Subject to subsection (2) and to the provisions of this Article with respect to proof of market price (Section 2–723), the measure of damages for non-acceptance or repudiation by the buyer is the difference between the market price at the time and place for tender and the unpaid contract price together with any incidental damages provided in this Article (Section 2–710), but less expenses saved in consequence of the buyer's breach.

(2) If the measure of damages provided in subsection (1) is inadequate to put the seller in as good a position as performance would have done then the measure of damages is the profit (including reasonable overhead) which the seller would have made from full performance by the buyer, together with any incidental damages provided in this Article (Section 2–710), due allowance for costs reasonably incurred and due credit for payments or proceeds of resale.

§ 2–709. Action for the Price.

(1) When the buyer fails to pay the price as it becomes due the seller may recover, together with any incidental damages under the next section, the price

(a) of goods accepted or of conforming goods lost or damaged within a commercially reasonable time after risk of their loss has passed to the buyer; and

(b) of goods identified to the contract if the seller is unable after reasonable effort to resell them at a reasonable price or the circumstances reasonably indicate that such effort will be unavailing.

(2) Where the seller sues for the price he must hold for the buyer any goods which have been identified to the contract and are still in his control except that if resale becomes possible he may resell them at any time prior to the collection of the judgment. The net proceeds of any such resale must be credited to the buyer and payment of the judgment entitles him to any goods not resold.

(3) After the buyer has wrongfully rejected or revoked acceptance of the goods or has failed to make a payment due or has repudiated (Section 2–610), a seller who is held not entitled to the price under this section shall nevertheless be awarded damages for non-acceptance under the preceding section.

§ 2–710. Seller's Incidental Damages.

Incidental damages to an aggrieved seller include any commercially reasonable charges, expenses or commissions incurred in stopping delivery, in the transportation, care and custody of goods after the buyer's breach, in connection with return or resale of the goods or otherwise resulting from the breach.

§ 2–711. Buyer's Remedies in General; Buyer's Security Interest in Rejected Goods.

(1) Where the seller fails to make delivery or repudiates or the buyer rightfully rejects or justifiably revokes acceptance then with respect to any goods involved, and with respect to the whole if the breach goes to the whole contract (Section 2–612), the buyer may cancel and whether or not he has done so may in addition to recovering so much of the price as has been paid

(a) "cover" and have damages under the next section as to all the goods affected whether or not they have been identified to the contract; or

(b) recover damages for non-delivery as pro-vided in this Article (Section 2–713).

(2) Where the seller fails to deliver or repudiates the buyer may also

(a) if the goods have been identified recover them as pro-vided in this Article (Section 2–502); or

(b) in a proper case obtain specific performance or replevy the goods as provided in this Article (Section 2–716).

(3) On rightful rejection or justifiable revocation of acceptance a buyer has a security interest in goods in his possession or control for any payments made on their price and any expenses reasonably incurred in their inspection, receipt, transportation, care and custody and may hold such goods and resell them in like manner as an aggrieved seller (Section 2–706).

§ 2–712. "Cover"; Buyer's Procurement of Substitute Goods.

(1) After a breach within the preceding section the buyer may "cover" by making in good faith and without unreasonable delay any reasonable purchase of or contract to purchase goods in substitution for those due from the seller.

(2) The buyer may recover from the seller as damages the difference between the cost of cover and the contract price together with any incidental or consequential damages as hereinafter defined (Section 2–715), but less expenses saved in consequence of the seller's breach.

(3) Failure of the buyer to effect cover within this section does not bar him from any other remedy.

§ 2–713. Buyer's Damages for Non-Delivery or Repudiation.

(1) Subject to the provisions of this Article with respect to proof of market price (Section 2–723), the measure of damages for non-delivery or repudiation by the seller is the difference between the market price at the time when the buyer learned of the breach and the contract price together with any incidental and consequential damages provided in this Article (Section 2–715), but less expenses saved in consequence of the seller's breach.

(2) Market price is to be determined as of the place for tender or, in cases of rejection after arrival or revocation of acceptance, as of the place of arrival.

§ 2–714. Buyer's Damages for Breach in Regard to Accepted Goods.

(1) Where the buyer has accepted goods and given notification (subsection (3) of Section 2–607) he may recover as damages for any non-conformity of tender the loss resulting in the ordinary course of events from the seller's breach as determined in any manner which is reasonable.

(2) The measure of damages for breach of warranty is the difference at the time and place of acceptance between the value of the goods accepted and the value they would have had if they had been as warranted, unless special circumstances show proximate damages of a different amount.

(3) In a proper case any incidental and consequential damages under the next section may also be recovered.

§ 2–715. Buyer's Incidental and Consequential Damages.

(1) Incidental damages resulting from the seller's breach include expenses reasonably incurred in inspection, receipt, transportation and care and custody of goods rightfully rejected, any commercially reasonable charges, expenses or commissions in connection with effecting cover and any other reasonable expense incident to the delay or other breach.

(2) Consequential damages resulting from the seller's breach include

> **(a)** any loss resulting from general or particular requirements and needs of which the seller at the time of contracting had reason to know and which could not reasonably be prevented by cover or otherwise; and

> **(b)** injury to person or property proximately resulting from any breach of warranty.

§ 2–716. Buyer's Right to Specific Performance or Replevin.

(1) Specific performance may be decreed where the goods are unique or in other proper circumstances.

(2) The decree for specific performance may include such terms and conditions as to payment of the price, damages, or other relief as the court may deem just.

(3) The buyer has a right of replevin for goods identified to the contract if after reasonable effort he is unable to effect cover for such goods or the circumstances reasonably indicate that such effort will be unavailing or if the goods have been shipped under reservation and satisfaction of the security interest in them has been made or tendered. In the case of goods bought for personal, family, or household purposes, the buyer's right of replevin vests upon acquisition of a special property, even if the seller had not then repudiated or failed to deliver. As amended in 1999.

§ 2–717. Deduction of Damages From the Price.

The buyer on notifying the seller of his intention to do so may deduct all or any part of the damages resulting from any breach of the contract from any part of the price still due under the same contract.

§ 2–718. Liquidation or Limitation of Damages; Deposits.

(1) Damages for breach by either party may be liquidated in the agreement but only at an amount which is reasonable in the light of the anticipated or actual harm caused by the breach, the difficulties of proof of loss, and the inconvenience or nonfeasibility of otherwise obtaining an adequate remedy. A term fixing unreasonably large liquidated damages is void as a penalty.

(2) Where the seller justifiably withholds delivery of goods because of the buyer's breach, the buyer is entitled to restitution of any amount by which the sum of his payments exceeds

> **(a)** the amount to which the seller is entitled by virtue of terms liquidating the seller's damages in accordance with subsection (1), or

> **(b)** in the absence of such terms, twenty per cent of the value of the total performance for which the buyer is obligated under the contract or $500, whichever is smaller.

(3) The buyer's right to restitution under subsection (2) is subject to offset to the extent that the seller establishes

> **(a)** a right to recover damages under the provisions of this Article other than subsection (1), and

> **(b)** the amount or value of any benefits received by the buyer directly or indirectly by reason of the contract.

(4) Where a seller has received payment in goods their reasonable value or the proceeds of their resale shall be treated as payments for the purposes of subsection (2); but if the seller has notice of the buyer's breach before reselling goods received in part performance, his resale is subject to the conditions laid down in this Article on resale by an aggrieved seller (Section 2–706).

§ 2–719. Contractual Modification or Limitation of Remedy.

(1) Subject to the provisions of subsections (2) and (3) of this section and of the preceding section on liquidation and limitation of damages,

> **(a)** the agreement may provide for remedies in addition to or in substitution for those provided in this Article and may limit or alter the measure of damages recoverable under this Article, as by limiting the buyer's remedies to return of the goods and repayment of the price or to repair and replacement of nonconforming goods or parts; and

> **(b)** resort to a remedy as provided is optional unless the remedy is expressly agreed to be exclusive, in which case it is the sole remedy.

(2) Where circumstances cause an exclusive or limited remedy to fail of its essential purpose, remedy may be had as provided in this Act.

(3) Consequential damages may be limited or excluded unless the limitation or exclusion is unconscionable. Limitation of consequential damages for injury to the person in the case of consumer goods is *prima facie* unconscionable but limitation of damages where the loss is commercial is not.

§ 2–720. Effect of "Cancellation" or "Rescission" on Claims for Antecedent Breach.

Unless the contrary intention clearly appears, expressions of "cancellation" or "rescission" of the contract or the like shall not be construed as a renunciation or discharge of any claim in damages for an antecedent breach.

§ 2–721. Remedies for Fraud.

Remedies for material misrepresentation or fraud include all remedies available under this Article for non-fraudulent breach. Neither rescission or a claim for rescission of the contract for sale nor rejection or return of the goods shall bar or be deemed inconsistent with a claim for damages or other remedy.

§ 2–722. Who Can Sue Third Parties for Injury to Goods.

Where a third party so deals with goods which have been identified to a contract for sale as to cause actionable injury to a party to that contract

(a) a right of action against the third party is in either party to the contract for sale who has title to or a security interest or a special property or an insurable interest in the goods; and if the goods have been destroyed or converted a right of action is also in the party who either bore the risk of loss under the contract for sale or has since the injury assumed that risk as against the other;

(b) if at the time of the injury the party plaintiff did not bear the risk of loss as against the other party to the contract for sale and there is no arrangement between them for disposition of the recovery, his suit or settlement is, subject to his own interest, as a fiduciary for the other party to the contract;

(c) either party may with the consent of the other sue for the benefit of whom it may concern.

§ 2–723. Proof of Market Price: Time and Place.

(1) If an action based on anticipatory repudiation comes to trial before the time for performance with respect to some or all of the goods, any damages based on market price (Section 2–708 or Section 2–713) shall be determined according to the price of such goods prevailing at the time when the aggrieved party learned of the repudiation.

(2) If evidence of a price prevailing at the times or places described in this Article is not readily available the price prevailing within any reasonable time before or after the time described or at any other place which in commercial judgment or under usage of trade would serve as a reasonable substitute for the one described may be used, making any proper allowance for the cost of transporting the goods to or from such other place.

(3) Evidence of a relevant price prevailing at a time or place other than the one described in this Article offered by one party is not admissible unless and until he has given the other party such notice as the court finds sufficient to prevent unfair surprise.

§ 2–724. Admissibility of Market Quotations.

Whenever the prevailing price or value of any goods regularly bought and sold in any established commodity market is in issue, reports in official publications or trade journals or in newspapers or periodicals of general circulation published as the reports of such market shall be admissible in evidence. The circumstances of the preparation of such a report may be shown to affect its weight but not its admissibility.

§ 2–725. Statute of Limitations in Contracts for Sale.

(1) An action for breach of any contract for sale must be commenced within four years after the cause of action has accrued. By the original agreement the parties may reduce the period of limitation to not less than one year but may not extend it.

(2) A cause of action accrues when the breach occurs, regardless of the aggrieved party's lack of knowledge of the breach. A breach of warranty occurs when tender of delivery is made, except that where a warranty explicitly extends to future performance of the goods and discovery of the breach must await the time of such performance the cause of action accrues when the breach is or should have been discovered.

(3) Where an action commenced within the time limited by subsection (1) is so terminated as to leave available a remedy by another action for the same breach such other action may be commenced after the expiration of the time limited and within six months after the termination of the first action unless the termination resulted from voluntary discontinuance or from dismissal for failure or neglect to prosecute.

(4) This section does not alter the law on tolling of the statute of limitations nor does it apply to causes of action which have accrued before this Act becomes effective.

ARTICLE 2A: LEASES

Part 1—General Provisions

§ 2A–101. Short Title.

This Article shall be known and may be cited as the Uniform Commercial Code—Leases.

§ 2A–102. Scope.

This Article applies to any transaction, regardless of form, that creates a lease.

§ 2A–103. Definitions and Index of Definitions.

(1) In this Article unless the context otherwise requires:

(a) "Buyer in ordinary course of business" means a person who in good faith and without knowledge that the sale to him [or her] is in violation of the ownership rights or security interest or leasehold interest of a third party in the goods buys in ordinary course from a person in the business of selling goods of that kind but does not include a pawnbroker. "Buying" may be for cash or by exchange of other property or on secured or unsecured credit and includes receiving goods or documents of title under a preexisting contract for sale but does not include a transfer in bulk or as security for or in total or partial satisfaction of a money debt.

(b) "Cancellation" occurs when either party puts an end to the lease contract for default by the other party.

(c) "Commercial unit" means such a unit of goods as by commercial usage is a single whole for purposes of lease and division of which materially impairs its character or value on the market or in use. A commercial unit may be a single article, as a machine, or a set of articles, as a suite of furniture or a line of machinery, or a quantity, as a gross or carload, or any other unit treated in use or in the relevant market as a single whole.

(d) "Conforming" goods or performance under a lease contract means goods or performance that are in accordance with the obligations under the lease contract.

(e) "Consumer lease" means a lease that a lessor regularly engaged in the business of leasing or selling makes to a lessee who is an individual and who takes under the lease primarily for a personal, family, or household purpose [, if the total payments to be made under the lease contract, excluding payments for options to renew or buy, do not exceed $_____].

(f) "Fault" means wrongful act, omission, breach, or default.

(g) "Finance lease" means a lease with respect to which:

(i) the lessor does not select, manufacture or supply the goods;

(ii) the lessor acquires the goods or the right to possession and use of the goods in connection with the lease; and

(iii) one of the following occurs:

(A) the lessee receives a copy of the contract by which the lessor acquired the goods or the right to possession and use of the goods before signing the lease contract;

(B) the lessee's approval of the contract by which the lessor acquired the goods or the right to possession and use of the goods is a condition to effectiveness of the lease contract;

(C) the lessee, before signing the lease contract, receives an accurate and complete statement designating the promises and warranties, and any disclaimers of warranties, limitations or modifications of remedies, or liquidated damages, including those of a third party, such as the manufacturer of the goods, provided to the lessor by the person supplying the goods in connection with or as part of the contract by which the lessor acquired the goods or the right to possession and use of the goods; or

(D) if the lease is not a consumer lease, the lessor, before the lessee signs the lease contract, informs the lessee in writing (a) of the identity of the person supplying the goods to the lessor, unless the lessee has selected that person and directed the lessor to acquire the goods or the right to possession and use of the goods from that person, (b) that the lessee is entitled under this Article to any promises and warranties, including those of any third party, provided to the lessor by the person supplying the goods in connection with or as part of the contract by which the lessor acquired the goods or the right to possession and use of the goods, and (c) that the lessee may communicate with the person supplying the goods to the lessor and receive an accurate and complete statement of those promises and warranties, including any disclaimers and limitations of them or of remedies.

(h) "Goods" means all things that are movable at the time of identification to the lease contract, or are fixtures (Section 2A–309), but the term does not include money, documents, instruments, accounts, chattel paper, general intangibles, or minerals or the like, including oil and gas, before extraction. The term also includes the unborn young of animals.

(i) "Installment lease contract" means a lease contract that authorizes or requires the delivery of goods in separate lots to be separately accepted, even though the lease contract contains a clause "each delivery is a separate lease" or its equivalent.

(j) "Lease" means a transfer of the right to possession and use of goods for a term in return for consideration, but a sale, including a sale on approval or a sale or return, or retention or creation of a security interest is not a lease. Unless the context clearly indicates otherwise, the term includes a sublease.

(k) "Lease agreement" means the bargain, with respect to the lease, of the lessor and the lessee in fact as found in their language or by implication from other circumstances including course of dealing or usage of trade or course of performance as provided in this Article. Unless the context clearly indicates otherwise, the term includes a sublease agreement.

(l) "Lease contract" means the total legal obligation that results from the lease agreement as affected by this Article and any other applicable rules of law. Unless the context clearly indicates otherwise, the term includes a sublease contract.

(m) "Leasehold interest" means the interest of the lessor or the lessee under a lease contract.

(n) "Lessee" means a person who acquires the right to possession and use of goods under a lease. Unless the context clearly indicates otherwise, the term includes a sublessee.

(o) "Lessee in ordinary course of business" means a person who in good faith and without knowledge that the lease to him [or her] is in violation of the ownership rights or security interest or leasehold interest of a third party in the goods, leases in ordinary course from a person in the business of selling or leasing goods of that kind but does not include a pawnbroker. "Leasing" may be for cash or by exchange of other property or on secured or unsecured credit and includes receiving goods or documents of title under a pre-existing lease contract but does not include a transfer in bulk or as security for or in total or partial satisfaction of a money debt.

(p) "Lessor" means a person who transfers the right to possession and use of goods under a lease. Unless the context clearly indicates otherwise, the term includes a sublessor.

(q) "Lessor's residual interest" means the lessor's interest in the goods after expiration, termination, or cancellation of the lease contract.

(r) "Lien" means a charge against or interest in goods to secure payment of a debt or performance of an obligation, but the term does not include a security interest.

(s) "Lot" means a parcel or a single article that is the subject matter of a separate lease or delivery, whether or not it is sufficient to perform the lease contract.

(t) "Merchant lessee" means a lessee that is a merchant with respect to goods of the kind subject to the lease.

(u) "Present value" means the amount as of a date certain of one or more sums payable in the future, discounted to the date certain. The discount is determined by the interest rate specified by the parties if the rate was not manifestly unreasonable at the time the transaction was entered into; otherwise, the discount is determined by a commercially reasonable rate that takes into account the facts and circumstances of each case at the time the transaction was entered into.

(v) "Purchase" includes taking by sale, lease, mortgage, security interest, pledge, gift, or any other voluntary transaction creating an interest in goods.

(w) "Sublease" means a lease of goods the right to possession and use of which was acquired by the lessor as a lessee under an existing lease.

(x) "Supplier" means a person from whom a lessor buys or leases goods to be leased under a finance lease.

(y) "Supply contract" means a contract under which a lessor buys or leases goods to be leased.

(z) "Termination" occurs when either party pursuant to a power created by agreement or law puts an end to the lease contract otherwise than for default.

(2) Other definitions applying to this Article and the sections in which they appear are:

"Accessions". Section 2A–310(1).
"Construction mortgage". Section 2A–309(1)(d).
"Encumbrance". Section 2A–309(1)(e).
"Fixtures". Section 2A–309(1)(a).
"Fixture filing". Section 2A–309(1)(b).
"Purchase money lease". Section 2A–309(1)(c).

(3) The following definitions in other Articles apply to this Article:

"Accounts". Section 9–106.
"Between merchants". Section 2–104(3).
"Buyer". Section 2–103(1)(a).
"Chattel paper". Section 9–105(1)(b).
"Consumer goods". Section 9–109(1).
"Document". Section 9–105(1)(f).
"Entrusting". Section 2–403(3).
"General intangibles". Section 9–106.
"Good faith". Section 2–103(1)(b).
"Instrument". Section 9–105(1)(i).
"Merchant". Section 2–104(1).
"Mortgage". Section 9–105(1)(j).
"Pursuant to commitment". Section 9–105(1)(k).
"Receipt". Section 2–103(1)(c).
"Sale". Section 2–106(1).
"Sale on approval". Section 2–326.
"Sale or return". Section 2–326.
"Seller". Section 2–103(1)(d).

(4) In addition Article 1 contains general definitions and principles of construction and interpretation applicable throughout this Article.
As amended in 1990 and 1999.

§ 2A–104. Leases Subject to Other Law.
(1) A lease, although subject to this Article, is also subject to any applicable:
    (a) certificate of title statute of this State: (list any certificate of title statutes covering automobiles, trailers, mobile homes, boats, farm tractors, and the like);
    (b) certificate of title statute of another jurisdiction (Section 2A–105); or
    (c) consumer protection statute of this State, or final consumer protection decision of a court of this State existing on the effective date of this Article.
(2) In case of conflict between this Article, other than Sections 2A–105, 2A–304(3), and 2A–305(3), and a statute or decision referred to in subsection (1), the statute or decision controls.

(3) Failure to comply with an applicable law has only the effect specified therein.
As amended in 1990.

§ 2A–105. Territorial Application of Article to Goods Covered by Certificate of Title.
Subject to the provisions of Sections 2A–304(3) and 2A–305(3), with respect to goods covered by a certificate of title issued under a statute of this State or of another jurisdiction, compliance and the effect of compliance or noncompliance with a certificate of title statute are governed by the law (including the conflict of laws rules) of the jurisdiction issuing the certificate until the earlier of (a) surrender of the certificate, or (b) four months after the goods are removed from that jurisdiction and thereafter until a new certificate of title is issued by another jurisdiction.

§ 2A–106. Limitation on Power of Parties to Consumer Lease to Choose Applicable Law and Judicial Forum.
(1) If the law chosen by the parties to a consumer lease is that of a jurisdiction other than a jurisdiction in which the lessee resides at the time the lease agreement becomes enforceable or within 30 days thereafter or in which the goods are to be used, the choice is not enforceable.
(2) If the judicial forum chosen by the parties to a consumer lease is a forum that would not otherwise have jurisdiction over the lessee, the choice is not enforceable.

§ 2A–107. Waiver or Renunciation of Claim or Right After Default.
Any claim or right arising out of an alleged default or breach of warranty may be discharged in whole or in part without consideration by a written waiver or renunciation signed and delivered by the aggrieved party.

§ 2A–108. Unconscionability.
(1) If the court as a matter of law finds a lease contract or any clause of a lease contract to have been unconscionable at the time it was made the court may refuse to enforce the lease contract, or it may enforce the remainder of the lease contract without the unconscionable clause, or it may so limit the application of any unconscionable clause as to avoid any unconscionable result.
(2) With respect to a consumer lease, if the court as a matter of law finds that a lease contract or any clause of a lease contract has been induced by unconscionable conduct or that unconscionable conduct has occurred in the collection of a claim arising from a lease contract, the court may grant appropriate relief.
(3) Before making a finding of unconscionability under subsection (1) or (2), the court, on its own motion or that of a party, shall afford the parties a reasonable opportunity to present evidence as to the setting, purpose, and effect of the lease contract or clause thereof, or of the conduct.
(4) In an action in which the lessee claims unconscionability with respect to a consumer lease:
    (a) If the court finds unconscionability under subsection (1) or (2), the court shall award reasonable attorney's fees to the lessee.
    (b) If the court does not find unconscionability and the lessee claiming unconscionability has brought or maintained

an action he [or she] knew to be groundless, the court shall award reasonable attorney's fees to the party against whom the claim is made.

(c) In determining attorney's fees, the amount of the recovery on behalf of the claimant under subsections (1) and (2) is not controlling.

§ 2A–109. Option to Accelerate at Will.

(1) A term providing that one party or his [or her] successor in interest may accelerate payment or performance or require collateral or additional collateral "at will" or "when he [or she] deems himself [or herself] insecure" or in words of similar import must be construed to mean that he [or she] has power to do so only if he [or she] in good faith believes that the prospect of payment or performance is impaired.

(2) With respect to a consumer lease, the burden of establishing good faith under subsection (1) is on the party who exercised the power; otherwise the burden of establishing lack of good faith is on the party against whom the power has been exercised.

Part 2—Formation and Construction of Lease Contract

§ 2A–201. Statute of Frauds.

(1) A lease contract is not enforceable by way of action or defense unless:

(a) the total payments to be made under the lease contract, excluding payments for options to renew or buy, are less than $1,000; or

(b) there is a writing, signed by the party against whom enforcement is sought or by that party's authorized agent, sufficient to indicate that a lease contract has been made between the parties and to describe the goods leased and the lease term.

(2) Any description of leased goods or of the lease term is sufficient and satisfies subsection (1)(b), whether or not it is specific, if it reasonably identifies what is described.

(3) A writing is not insufficient because it omits or incorrectly states a term agreed upon, but the lease contract is not enforceable under subsection (1)(b) beyond the lease term and the quantity of goods shown in the writing.

(4) A lease contract that does not satisfy the requirements of subsection (1), but which is valid in other respects, is enforceable:

(a) if the goods are to be specially manufactured or obtained for the lessee and are not suitable for lease or sale to others in the ordinary course of the lessor's business, and the lessor, before notice of repudiation is received and under circumstances that reasonably indicate that the goods are for the lessee, has made either a substantial beginning of their manufacture or commitments for their procurement;

(b) if the party against whom enforcement is sought admits in that party's pleading, testimony or otherwise in court that a lease contract was made, but the lease contract is not enforceable under this provision beyond the quantity of goods admitted; or

(c) with respect to goods that have been received and accepted by the lessee.

(5) The lease term under a lease contract referred to in subsection (4) is:

(a) if there is a writing signed by the party against whom enforcement is sought or by that party's authorized agent specifying the lease term, the term so specified;

(b) if the party against whom enforcement is sought admits in that party's pleading, testimony, or otherwise in court a lease term, the term so admitted; or

(c) a reasonable lease term.

§ 2A–202. Final Written Expression: Parol or Extrinsic Evidence.

Terms with respect to which the confirmatory memoranda of the parties agree or which are otherwise set forth in a writing intended by the parties as a final expression of their agreement with respect to such terms as are included therein may not be contradicted by evidence of any prior agreement or of a contemporaneous oral agreement but may be explained or supplemented:

(a) by course of dealing or usage of trade or by course of performance; and

(b) by evidence of consistent additional terms unless the court finds the writing to have been intended also as a complete and exclusive statement of the terms of the agreement.

§ 2A–203. Seals Inoperative.

The affixing of a seal to a writing evidencing a lease contract or an offer to enter into a lease contract does not render the writing a sealed instrument and the law with respect to sealed instruments does not apply to the lease contract or offer.

§ 2A–204. Formation in General.

(1) A lease contract may be made in any manner sufficient to show agreement, including conduct by both parties which recognizes the existence of a lease contract.

(2) An agreement sufficient to constitute a lease contract may be found although the moment of its making is undetermined.

(3) Although one or more terms are left open, a lease contract does not fail for indefiniteness if the parties have intended to make a lease contract and there is a reasonably certain basis for giving an appropriate remedy.

§ 2A–205. Firm Offers.

An offer by a merchant to lease goods to or from another person in a signed writing that by its terms gives assurance it will be held open is not revocable, for lack of consideration, during the time stated or, if no time is stated, for a reasonable time, but in no event may the period of irrevocability exceed 3 months. Any such term of assurance on a form supplied by the offeree must be separately signed by the offeror.

§ 2A–206. Offer and Acceptance in Formation of Lease Contract.

(1) Unless otherwise unambiguously indicated by the language or circumstances, an offer to make a lease contract must be construed as inviting acceptance in any manner and by any medium reasonable in the circumstances.

(2) If the beginning of a requested performance is a reasonable mode of acceptance, an offeror who is not notified of acceptance within a reasonable time may treat the offer as having lapsed before acceptance.

§ 2A–207. Course of Performance or Practical Construction.

(1) If a lease contract involves repeated occasions for performance by either party with knowledge of the nature of the performance and opportunity for objection to it by the other, any course of performance accepted or acquiesced in without objection is relevant to determine the meaning of the lease agreement.

(2) The express terms of a lease agreement and any course of performance, as well as any course of dealing and usage of trade, must be construed whenever reasonable as consistent with each other; but if that construction is unreasonable, express terms control course of performance, course of performance controls both course of dealing and usage of trade, and course of dealing controls usage of trade.

(3) Subject to the provisions of Section 2A–208 on modification and waiver, course of performance is relevant to show a waiver or modification of any term inconsistent with the course of performance.

§ 2A–208. Modification, Rescission and Waiver.

(1) An agreement modifying a lease contract needs no consideration to be binding.

(2) A signed lease agreement that excludes modification or rescission except by a signed writing may not be otherwise modified or rescinded, but, except as between merchants, such a requirement on a form supplied by a merchant must be separately signed by the other party.

(3) Although an attempt at modification or rescission does not satisfy the requirements of subsection (2), it may operate as a waiver.

(4) A party who has made a waiver affecting an executory portion of a lease contract may retract the waiver by reasonable notification received by the other party that strict performance will be required of any term waived, unless the retraction would be unjust in view of a material change of position in reliance on the waiver.

§ 2A–209. Lessee under Finance Lease as Beneficiary of Supply Contract.

(1) The benefit of the supplier's promises to the lessor under the supply contract and of all warranties, whether express or implied, including those of any third party provided in connection with or as part of the supply contract, extends to the lessee to the extent of the lessee's leasehold interest under a finance lease related to the supply contract, but is subject to the terms warranty and of the supply contract and all defenses or claims arising therefrom.

(2) The extension of the benefit of supplier's promises and of warranties to the lessee (Section 2A–209(1)) does not: (i) modify the rights and obligations of the parties to the supply contract, whether arising therefrom or otherwise, or (ii) impose any duty or liability under the supply contract on the lessee.

(3) Any modification or rescission of the supply contract by the supplier and the lessor is effective between the supplier and the lessee unless, before the modification or rescission, the supplier has received notice that the lessee has entered into a finance lease related to the supply contract. If the modification or rescission is effective between the supplier and the lessee, the lessor is deemed to have assumed, in addition to the obligations of the lessor to the lessee under the lease contract, promises of the supplier to the lessor and warranties that were so modified or rescinded as they existed and were available to the lessee before modification or rescission.

(4) In addition to the extension of the benefit of the supplier's promises and of warranties to the lessee under subsection (1), the lessee retains all rights that the lessee may have against the supplier which arise from an agreement between the lessee and the supplier or under other law.
As amended in 1990.

§ 2A–210. Express Warranties.

(1) Express warranties by the lessor are created as follows:

(a) Any affirmation of fact or promise made by the lessor to the lessee which relates to the goods and becomes part of the basis of the bargain creates an express warranty that the goods will conform to the affirmation or promise.

(b) Any description of the goods which is made part of the basis of the bargain creates an express warranty that the goods will conform to the description.

(c) Any sample or model that is made part of the basis of the bargain creates an express warranty that the whole of the goods will conform to the sample or model.

(2) It is not necessary to the creation of an express warranty that the lessor use formal words, such as "warrant" or "guarantee," or that the lessor have a specific intention to make a warranty, but an affirmation merely of the value of the goods or a statement purporting to be merely the lessor's opinion or commendation of the goods does not create a warranty.

§ 2A–211. Warranties Against Interference and Against Infringement; Lessee's Obligation Against Infringement.

(1) There is in a lease contract a warranty that for the lease term no person holds a claim to or interest in the goods that arose from an act or omission of the lessor, other than a claim by way of infringement or the like, which will interfere with the lessee's enjoyment of its leasehold interest.

(2) Except in a finance lease there is in a lease contract by a lessor who is a merchant regularly dealing in goods of the kind a warranty that the goods are delivered free of the rightful claim of any person by way of infringement or the like.

(3) A lessee who furnishes specifications to a lessor or a supplier shall hold the lessor and the supplier harmless against any claim by way of infringement or the like that arises out of compliance with the specifications.

§ 2A–212. Implied Warranty of Merchantability.

(1) Except in a finance lease, a warranty that the goods will be merchantable is implied in a lease contract if the lessor is a merchant with respect to goods of that kind.

(2) Goods to be merchantable must be at least such as

(a) pass without objection in the trade under the description in the lease agreement;

(b) in the case of fungible goods, are of fair average quality within the description;

(c) are fit for the ordinary purposes for which goods of that type are used;

(d) run, within the variation permitted by the lease agreement, of even kind, quality, and quantity within each unit and among all units involved;

(e) are adequately contained, packaged, and labeled as the lease agreement may require; and

(f) conform to any promises or affirmations of fact made on the container or label.

(3) Other implied warranties may arise from course of dealing or usage of trade.

§ 2A–213. Implied Warranty of Fitness for Particular Purpose.

Except in a finance of lease, if the lessor at the time the lease contract is made has reason to know of any particular purpose for which the goods are required and that the lessee is relying on the lessor's skill or judgment to select or furnish suitable goods, there is in the lease contract an implied warranty that the goods will be fit for that purpose.

§ 2A–214. Exclusion or Modification of Warranties.

(1) Words or conduct relevant to the creation of an express warranty and words or conduct tending to negate or limit a warranty must be construed wherever reasonable as consistent with each other; but, subject to the provisions of Section 2A–202 on parol or extrinsic evidence, negation or limitation is inoperative to the extent that the construction is unreasonable.

(2) Subject to subsection (3), to exclude or modify the implied warranty of merchantability or any part of it the language must mention "merchantability", be by a writing, and be conspicuous. Subject to subsection (3), to exclude or modify any implied warranty of fitness the exclusion must be by a writing and be conspicuous. Language to exclude all implied warranties of fitness is sufficient if it is in writing, is conspicuous and states, for example, "There is no warranty that the goods will be fit for a particular purpose".

(3) Notwithstanding subsection (2), but subject to subsection (4),

(a) unless the circumstances indicate otherwise, all implied warranties are excluded by expressions like "as is" or "with all faults" or by other language that in common understanding calls the lessee's attention to the exclusion of warranties and makes plain that there is no implied warranty, if in writing and conspicuous;

(b) if the lessee before entering into the lease contract has examined the goods or the sample or model as fully as desired or has refused to examine the goods, there is no implied warranty with regard to defects that an examination ought in the circumstances to have revealed; and

(c) an implied warranty may also be excluded or modified by course of dealing, course of performance, or usage of trade.

(4) To exclude or modify a warranty against interference or against infringement (Section 2A–211) or any part of it, the language must be specific, be by a writing, and be conspicuous, unless the circumstances, including course of performance, course of dealing, or usage of trade, give the lessee reason to know that the goods are being leased subject to a claim or interest of any person.

§ 2A–215. Cumulation and Conflict of Warranties Express or Implied.

Warranties, whether express or implied, must be construed as consistent with each other and as cumulative, but if that construction is unreasonable, the intention of the parties determines which warranty is dominant. In ascertaining that intention the following rules apply:

(a) Exact or technical specifications displace an inconsistent sample or model or general language of description.

(b) A sample from an existing bulk displaces inconsistent general language of description.

(c) Express warranties displace inconsistent implied warranties other than an implied warranty of fitness for a particular purpose.

§ 2A–216. Third-Party Beneficiaries of Express and Implied Warranties.

Alternative A

A warranty to or for the benefit of a lessee under this Article, whether express or implied, extends to any natural person who is in the family or household of the lessee or who is a guest in the lessee's home if it is reasonable to expect that such person may use, consume, or be affected by the goods and who is injured in person by breach of the warranty. This section does not displace principles of law and equity that extend a warranty to or for the benefit of a lessee to other persons. The operation of this section may not be excluded, modified, or limited, but an exclusion, modification, or limitation of the warranty, including any with respect to rights and remedies, effective against the lessee is also effective against any beneficiary designated under this section.

Alternative B

A warranty to or for the benefit of a lessee under this Article, whether express or implied, extends to any natural person who may reasonably be expected to use, consume, or be affected by the goods and who is injured in person by breach of the warranty. This section does not displace principles of law and equity that extend a warranty to or for the benefit of a lessee to other persons. The operation of this section may not be excluded, modified, or limited, but an exclusion, modification, or limitation of the warranty, including any with respect to rights and remedies, effective against the lessee is also effective against the beneficiary designated under this section.

Alternative C

A warranty to or for the benefit of a lessee under this Article, whether express or implied, extends to any person who may reasonably be expected to use, consume, or be affected by the goods and who is injured by breach of the warranty. The operation of this section may not be excluded, modified, or limited with respect to injury to the person of an individual to whom the warranty extends, but an exclusion, modification, or limitation of the warranty, including any with respect to rights and remedies, effective against the lessee is also effective against the beneficiary designated under this section.

§ 2A–217. Identification.

Identification of goods as goods to which a lease contract refers may be made at any time and in any manner explicitly agreed to by the parties. In the absence of explicit agreement, identification occurs:

(a) when the lease contract is made if the lease contract is for a lease of goods that are existing and identified;

(b) when the goods are shipped, marked, or otherwise designated by the lessor as goods to which the lease contract refers, if the lease contract is for a lease of goods that are not existing and identified; or

(c) when the young are conceived, if the lease contract is for a lease of unborn young of animals.

§ 2A–218. Insurance and Proceeds.

(1) A lessee obtains an insurable interest when existing goods are identified to the lease contract even though the goods identified are nonconforming and the lessee has an option to reject them.

(2) If a lessee has an insurable interest only by reason of the lessor's identification of the goods, the lessor, until default or insolvency or notification to the lessee that identification is final, may substitute other goods for those identified.

(3) Notwithstanding a lessee's insurable interest under subsections (1) and (2), the lessor retains an insurable interest until an option to buy has been exercised by the lessee and risk of loss has passed to the lessee.

(4) Nothing in this section impairs any insurable interest recognized under any other statute or rule of law.

(5) The parties by agreement may determine that one or more parties have an obligation to obtain and pay for insurance covering the goods and by agreement may determine the beneficiary of the proceeds of the insurance.

§ 2A–219. Risk of Loss.

(1) Except in the case of a finance lease, risk of loss is retained by the lessor and does not pass to the lessee. In the case of a finance lease, risk of loss passes to the lessee.

(2) Subject to the provisions of this Article on the effect of default on risk of loss (Section 2A–220), if risk of loss is to pass to the lessee and the time of passage is not stated, the following rules apply:

(a) If the lease contract requires or authorizes the goods to be shipped by carrier

(i) and it does not require delivery at a particular destination, the risk of loss passes to the lessee when the goods are duly delivered to the carrier; but

(ii) if it does require delivery at a particular destination and the goods are there duly tendered while in the possession of the carrier, the risk of loss passes to the lessee when the goods are there duly so tendered as to enable the lessee to take delivery.

(b) If the goods are held by a bailee to be delivered without being moved, the risk of loss passes to the lessee on acknowledgment by the bailee of the lessee's right to possession of the goods.

(c) In any case not within subsection (a) or (b), the risk of loss passes to the lessee on the lessee's receipt of the goods if the lessor, or, in the case of a finance lease, the supplier, is a merchant; otherwise the risk passes to the lessee on tender of delivery.

§ 2A–220. Effect of Default on Risk of Loss.

(1) Where risk of loss is to pass to the lessee and the time of passage is not stated:

(a) If a tender or delivery of goods so fails to conform to the lease contract as to give a right of rejection, the risk of their loss remains with the lessor, or, in the case of a finance lease, the supplier, until cure or acceptance.

(b) If the lessee rightfully revokes acceptance, he [or she], to the extent of any deficiency in his [or her] effective insurance coverage, may treat the risk of loss as having remained with the lessor from the beginning.

(2) Whether or not risk of loss is to pass to the lessee, if the lessee as to conforming goods already identified to a lease contract repudiates or is otherwise in default under the lease contract, the lessor, or, in the case of a finance lease, the supplier, to the extent of any deficiency in his [or her] effective insurance coverage may treat the risk of loss as resting on the lessee for a commercially reasonable time.

§ 2A–221. Casualty to Identified Goods.

If a lease contract requires goods identified when the lease contract is made, and the goods suffer casualty without fault of the lessee, the lessor or the supplier before delivery, or the goods suffer casualty before risk of loss passes to the lessee pursuant to the lease agreement or Section 2A–219, then:

(a) if the loss is total, the lease contract is avoided; and

(b) if the loss is partial or the goods have so deteriorated as to no longer conform to the lease contract, the lessee may nevertheless demand inspection and at his [or her] option either treat the lease contract as avoided or, except in a finance lease that is not a consumer lease, accept the goods with due allowance from the rent payable for the balance of the lease term for the deterioration or the deficiency in quantity but without further right against the lessor.

Part 3—Effect of Lease Contract

§ 2A–301. Enforceability of Lease Contract.

Except as otherwise provided in this Article, a lease contract is effective and enforceable according to its terms between the parties, against purchasers of the goods and against creditors of the parties.

§ 2A–302. Title to and Possession of Goods.

Except as otherwise provided in this Article, each provision of this Article applies whether the lessor or a third party has title to the goods, and whether the lessor, the lessee, or a third party has possession of the goods, notwithstanding any statute or rule of law that possession or the absence of possession is fraudulent.

§ 2A–303. Alienability of Party's Interest Under Lease Contract or of Lessor's Residual Interest in Goods; Delegation of Performance; Transfer of Rights.

(1) As used in this section, "creation of a security interest" includes the sale of a lease contract that is subject to Article 9, Secured Transactions, by reason of Section 9–109(a)(3).

(2) Except as provided in subsections (3) and Section 9–407, a provision in a lease agreement which (i) prohibits the voluntary or involuntary transfer, including a transfer by sale, sublease, creation or enforcement of a security interest, or attachment, levy, or other judicial process, of an interest of a party under the lease contract or of the lessor's residual interest in the goods, or (ii) makes such a transfer an event of default, gives rise to the rights and remedies provided in subsection (4), but a transfer that is prohibited or is an event of default under the lease agreement is otherwise effective.

(3) A provision in a lease agreement which (i) prohibits a transfer of a right to damages for default with respect to the whole lease contract or of a right to payment arising out of the transferor's due performance of the transferor's entire obligation, or (ii) makes such a transfer an event of default, is not enforceable, and such a transfer is not a transfer that materially impairs the propsect of obtaining return performance by, materially changes the duty of, or materially increases the burden or risk imposed on, the other party to the lease contract within the purview of subsection (4).

(4) Subject to subsection (3) and Section 9–407:

(a) if a transfer is made which is made an event of default under a lease agreement, the party to the lease contract not making the transfer, unless that party waives the default or otherwise agrees, has the rights and remedies described in Section 2A–501(2);

(b) if paragraph (a) is not applicable and if a transfer is made that (i) is prohibited under a lease agreement or (ii) materially impairs the prospect of obtaining return performance by, materially changes the duty of, or materially increases the burden or risk imposed on, the other party to the lease contract, unless the party not making the transfer agrees at any time to the transfer in the lease contract or otherwise, then, except as limited by contract, (i) the transferor is liable to the party not making the transfer for damages caused by the transfer to the extent that the damages could not reasonably be prevented by the party not making the transfer and (ii) a court having jurisdiction may grant other appropriate relief, including cancellation of the lease contract or an injunction against the transfer.

(5) A transfer of "the lease" or of "all my rights under the lease", or a transfer in similar general terms, is a transfer of rights and, unless the language or the circumstances, as in a transfer for security, indicate the contrary, the transfer is a delegation of duties by the transferor to the transferee. Acceptance by the transferee constitutes a promise by the transferee to perform those duties. The promise is enforceable by either the transferor or the other party to the lease contract.

(6) Unless otherwise agreed by the lessor and the lessee, a delegation of performance does not relieve the transferor as against the other party of any duty to perform or of any liability for default.

(7) In a consumer lease, to prohibit the transfer of an interest of a party under the lease contract or to make a transfer an event of default, the language must be specific, by a writing, and conspicuous.

As amended in 1990 and 1999.

§ 2A–304. Subsequent Lease of Goods by Lessor.

(1) Subject to Section 2A–303, a subsequent lessee from a lessor of goods under an existing lease contract obtains, to the extent of the leasehold interest transferred, the leasehold interest in the goods that the lessor had or had power to transfer, and except as provided in subsection (2) and Section 2A–527(4), takes subject to the existing lease contract. A lessor with voidable title has power to transfer a good leasehold interest to a

good faith subsequent lessee for value, but only to the extent set forth in the preceding sentence. If goods have been delivered under a transaction of purchase the lessor has that power even though:

(a) the lessor's transferor was deceived as to the identity of the lessor;

(b) the delivery was in exchange for a check which is later dishonored;

(c) it was agreed that the transaction was to be a "cash sale"; or

(d) the delivery was procured through fraud punishable as larcenous under the criminal law.

(2) A subsequent lessee in the ordinary course of business from a lessor who is a merchant dealing in goods of that kind to whom the goods were entrusted by the existing lessee of that lessor before the interest of the subsequent lessee became enforceable against that lessor obtains, to the extent of the leasehold interest transferred, all of that lessor's and the existing lessee's rights to the goods, and takes free of the existing lease contract.

(3) A subsequent lessee from the lessor of goods that are subject to an existing lease contract and are covered by a certificate of title issued under a statute of this State or of another jurisdiction takes no greater rights than those provided both by this section and by the certificate of title statute.

As amended in 1990.

§ 2A–305. Sale or Sublease of Goods by Lessee.

(1) Subject to the provisions of Section 2A–303, a buyer or sublessee from the lessee of goods under an existing lease contract obtains, to the extent of the interest transferred, the leasehold interest in the goods that the lessee had or had power to transfer, and except as provided in subsection (2) and Section 2A–511(4), takes subject to the existing lease contract. A lessee with a voidable leasehold interest has power to transfer a good leasehold interest to a good faith buyer for value or a good faith sublessee for value, but only to the extent set forth in the preceding sentence. When goods have been delivered under a transaction of lease the lessee has that power even though:

(a) the lessor was deceived as to the identity of the lessee;

(b) the delivery was in exchange for a check which is later dishonored; or

(c) the delivery was procured through fraud punishable as larcenous under the criminal law.

(2) A buyer in the ordinary course of business or a sublessee in the ordinary course of business from a lessee who is a merchant dealing in goods of that kind to whom the goods were entrusted by the lessor obtains, to the extent of the interest transferred, all of the lessor's and lessee's rights to the goods, and takes free of the existing lease contract.

(3) A buyer or sublessee from the lessee of goods that are subject to an existing lease contract and are covered by a certificate of title issued under a statute of this State or of another jurisdiction takes no greater rights than those provided both by this section and by the certificate of title statute.

§ 2A–306. Priority of Certain Liens Arising by Operation of Law.

If a person in the ordinary course of his [or her] business furnishes services or materials with respect to goods subject to a lease contract, a lien upon those goods in the possession of that person given by statute or rule of law for those materials or services takes priority over any interest of the lessor or lessee under the lease contract or this Article unless the lien is created by statute and the statute provides otherwise or unless the lien is created by rule of law and the rule of law provides otherwise.

§ 2A–307. Priority of Liens Arising by Attachment or Levy on, Security Interests in, and Other Claims to Goods.

(1) Except as otherwise provided in Section 2A–306, a creditor of a lessee takes subject to the lease contract.

(2) Except as otherwise provided in subsection (3) and in Sections 2A–306 and 2A–308, a creditor of a lessor takes subject to the lease contract unless the creditor holds a lien that attached to the goods before the lease contract became enforceable.

(3) Except as otherwise provided in Sections 9–317, 9–321, and 9–323, a lessee takes a leasehold interest subject to a security interest held by a creditor of the lessor.
As amended in 1990 and 1999.

§ 2A–308. Special Rights of Creditors.

(1) A creditor of a lessor in possession of goods subject to a lease contract may treat the lease contract as void if as against the creditor retention of possession by the lessor is fraudulent under any statute or rule of law, but retention of possession in good faith and current course of trade by the lessor for a commercially reasonable time after the lease contract becomes enforceable is not fraudulent.

(2) Nothing in this Article impairs the rights of creditors of a lessor if the lease contract (a) becomes enforceable, not in current course of trade but in satisfaction of or as security for a pre-existing claim for money, security, or the like, and (b) is made under circumstances which under any statute or rule of law apart from this Article would constitute the transaction a fraudulent transfer or voidable preference.

(3) A creditor of a seller may treat a sale or an identification of goods to a contract for sale as void if as against the creditor retention of possession by the seller is fraudulent under any statute or rule of law, but retention of possession of the goods pursuant to a lease contract entered into by the seller as lessee and the buyer as lessor in connection with the sale or identification of the goods is not fraudulent if the buyer bought for value and in good faith.

§ 2A–309. Lessor's and Lessee's Rights When Goods Become Fixtures.

(1) In this section:

(a) goods are "fixtures" when they become so related to particular real estate that an interest in them arises under real estate law;

(b) a "fixture filing" is the filing, in the office where a mortgage on the real estate would be filed or recorded, of a financing statement covering goods that are or are to become fixtures and conforming to the requirements of Section 9–502(a) and (b);

(c) a lease is a "purchase money lease" unless the lessee has possession or use of the goods or the right to possession or use of the goods before the lease agreement is enforceable;

(d) a mortgage is a "construction mortgage" to the extent it secures an obligation incurred for the construction of an improvement on land including the acquisition cost of the land, if the recorded writing so indicates; and

(e) "encumbrance" includes real estate mortgages and other liens on real estate and all other rights in real estate that are not ownership interests.

(2) Under this Article a lease may be of goods that are fixtures or may continue in goods that become fixtures, but no lease exists under this Article of ordinary building materials incorporated into an improvement on land.

(3) This Article does not prevent creation of a lease of fixtures pursuant to real estate law.

(4) The perfected interest of a lessor of fixtures has priority over a conflicting interest of an encumbrancer or owner of the real estate if:

(a) the lease is a purchase money lease, the conflicting interest of the encumbrancer or owner arises before the goods become fixtures, the interest of the lessor is perfected by a fixture filing before the goods become fixtures or within ten days thereafter, and the lessee has an interest of record in the real estate or is in possession of the real estate; or

(b) the interest of the lessor is perfected by a fixture filing before the interest of the encumbrancer or owner is of record, the lessor's interest has priority over any conflicting interest of a predecessor in title of the encumbrancer or owner, and the lessee has an interest of record in the real estate or is in possession of the real estate.

(5) The interest of a lessor of fixtures, whether or not perfected, has priority over the conflicting interest of an encumbrancer or owner of the real estate if:

(a) the fixtures are readily removable factory or office machines, readily removable equipment that is not primarily used or leased for use in the operation of the real estate, or readily removable replacements of domestic appliances that are goods subject to a consumer lease, and before the goods become fixtures the lease contract is enforceable; or

(b) the conflicting interest is a lien on the real estate obtained by legal or equitable proceedings after the lease contract is enforceable; or

(c) the encumbrancer or owner has consented in writing to the lease or has disclaimed an interest in the goods as fixtures; or

(d) the lessee has a right to remove the goods as against the encumbrancer or owner. If the lessee's right to remove terminates, the priority of the interest of the lessor continues for a reasonable time.

(6) Notwithstanding paragraph (4)(a) but otherwise subject to subsections (4) and (5), the interest of a lessor of fixtures, including the lessor's residual interest, is subordinate to the conflicting interest of an encumbrancer of the real estate under a construction mortgage recorded before the goods become fixtures if the goods become fixtures before the completion of the construction. To the extent given to refinance a construction mortgage, the conflicting interest of an encumbrancer of the real estate under a mortgage has this priority to the same extent as the encumbrancer of the real estate under the construction mortgage.

(7) In cases not within the preceding subsections, priority between the interest of a lessor of fixtures, including the lessor's residual interest, and the conflicting interest of an encumbrancer or owner of the real estate who is not the lessee is determined by the priority rules governing conflicting interests in real estate.

(8) If the interest of a lessor of fixtures, including the lessor's residual interest, has priority over all conflicting interests of all owners and encumbrancers of the real estate, the lessor or the lessee may (i) on default, expiration, termination, or cancellation of the lease agreement but subject to the agreement and this Article, or (ii) if necessary to enforce other rights and remedies of the lessor or lessee under this Article, remove the goods from the real estate, free and clear of all conflicting interests of all owners and encumbrancers of the real estate, but the lessor or lessee must reimburse any encumbrancer or owner of the real estate who is not the lessee and who has not otherwise agreed for the cost of repair of any physical injury, but not for any diminution in value of the real estate caused by the absence of the goods removed or by any necessity of replacing them. A person entitled to reimbursement may refuse permission to remove until the party seeking removal gives adequate security for the performance of this obligation.

(9) Even though the lease agreement does not create a security interest, the interest of a lessor of fixtures, including the lessor's residual interest, is perfected by filing a financing statement as a fixture filing for leased goods that are or are to become fixtures in accordance with the relevant provisions of the Article on Secured Transactions (Article 9).

As amended in 1990 and 1999.

§ 2A–310. Lessor's and Lessee's Rights When Goods Become Accessions.

(1) Goods are "accessions" when they are installed in or affixed to other goods.

(2) The interest of a lessor or a lessee under a lease contract entered into before the goods became accessions is superior to all interests in the whole except as stated in subsection (4).

(3) The interest of a lessor or a lessee under a lease contract entered into at the time or after the goods became accessions is superior to all subsequently acquired interests in the whole except as stated in subsection (4) but is subordinate to interests in the whole existing at the time the lease contract was made unless the holders of such interests in the whole have in writing consented to the lease or disclaimed an interest in the goods as part of the whole.

(4) The interest of a lessor or a lessee under a lease contract described in subsection (2) or (3) is subordinate to the interest of

    (a) a buyer in the ordinary course of business or a lessee in the ordinary course of business of any interest in the whole acquired after the goods became accessions; or

    (b) a creditor with a security interest in the whole perfected before the lease contract was made to the extent that the creditor makes subsequent advances without knowledge of the lease contract.

(5) When under subsections (2) or (3) and (4) a lessor or a lessee of accessions holds an interest that is superior to all interests in the whole, the lessor or the lessee may (a) on default, expiration, termination, or cancellation of the lease contract by the other party but subject to the provisions of the lease contract and this Article, or (b) if necessary to enforce his [or her] other rights and remedies under this Article, remove the goods from the whole, free and clear of all interests in the whole, but he [or she] must reimburse any holder of an interest in the whole who is not the lessee and who has not otherwise agreed for the cost of repair of any physical injury but not for any diminution in value of the whole caused by the absence of the goods removed or by any necessity for replacing them. A person entitled to reimbursement may refuse permission to remove until the party seeking removal gives adequate security for the performance of this obligation.

§ 2A–311. Priority Subject to Subordination.

Nothing in this Article prevents subordination by agreement by any person entitled to priority.

As added in 1990.

Part 4—Performance of Lease Contract: Repudiated, Substituted and Excused

§ 2A–401. Insecurity: Adequate Assurance of Performance.

(1) A lease contract imposes an obligation on each party that the other's expectation of receiving due performance will not be impaired.

(2) If reasonable grounds for insecurity arise with respect to the performance of either party, the insecure party may demand in writing adequate assurance of due performance. Until the insecure party receives that assurance, if commercially reasonable the insecure party may suspend any performance for which he [or she] has not already received the agreed return.

(3) A repudiation of the lease contract occurs if assurance of due performance adequate under the circumstances of the particular case is not provided to the insecure party within a reasonable time, not to exceed 30 days after receipt of a demand by the other party.

(4) Between merchants, the reasonableness of grounds for insecurity and the adequacy of any assurance offered must be determined according to commercial standards.

(5) Acceptance of any nonconforming delivery or payment does not prejudice the aggrieved party's right to demand adequate assurance of future performance.

§ 2A–402. Anticipatory Repudiation.

If either party repudiates a lease contract with respect to a performance not yet due under the lease contract, the loss of which performance will substantially impair the value of the lease contract to the other, the aggrieved party may:

(a) for a commercially reasonable time, await retraction of repudiation and performance by the repudiating party;

(b) make demand pursuant to Section 2A–401 and await assurance of future performance adequate under the circumstances of the particular case; or

(c) resort to any right or remedy upon default under the lease contract or this Article, even though the aggrieved party has notified the repudiating party that the aggrieved party would await the repudiating party's performance and assurance and has urged retraction. In addition, whether or not the aggrieved party is pursuing one of the foregoing remedies, the aggrieved party may suspend performance or, if the aggrieved party is the lessor, proceed in accordance with the provisions of this Article on the lessor's right to identify goods to the lease contract notwithstanding default or to salvage unfinished goods (Section 2A–524).

§ 2A–403. Retraction of Anticipatory Repudiation.

(1) Until the repudiating party's next performance is due, the repudiating party can retract the repudiation unless, since the repudiation, the aggrieved party has cancelled the lease contract or materially changed the aggrieved party's position or otherwise indicated that the aggrieved party considers the repudiation final.

(2) Retraction may be by any method that clearly indicates to the aggrieved party that the repudiating party intends to perform under the lease contract and includes any assurance demanded under Section 2A–401.

(3) Retraction reinstates a repudiating party's rights under a lease contract with due excuse and allowance to the aggrieved party for any delay occasioned by the repudiation.

§ 2A–404. Substituted Performance.

(1) If without fault of the lessee, the lessor and the supplier, the agreed berthing, loading, or unloading facilities fail or the agreed type of carrier becomes unavailable or the agreed manner of delivery otherwise becomes commercially impracticable, but a commercially reasonable substitute is available, the substitute performance must be tendered and accepted.

(2) If the agreed means or manner of payment fails because of domestic or foreign governmental regulation:

(a) the lessor may withhold or stop delivery or cause the supplier to withhold or stop delivery unless the lessee provides a means or manner of payment that is commercially a substantial equivalent; and

(b) if delivery has already been taken, payment by the means or in the manner provided by the regulation discharges the lessee's obligation unless the regulation is discriminatory, oppressive, or predatory.

§ 2A–405. Excused Performance.

Subject to Section 2A–404 on substituted performance, the following rules apply:

(a) Delay in delivery or nondelivery in whole or in part by a lessor or a supplier who complies with paragraphs (b) and (c) is not a default under the lease contract if performance as agreed has been made impracticable by the occurrence of a contingency the nonoccurrence of which was a basic assumption on which the lease contract was made or by compliance in good faith with any applicable foreign or domestic governmental regulation or order, whether or not the regulation or order later proves to be invalid.

(b) If the causes mentioned in paragraph (a) affect only part of the lessor's or the supplier's capacity to perform, he [or she] shall allocate production and deliveries among his [or her] customers but at his [or her] option may include regular customers not then under contract for sale or lease as well as his [or her] own requirements for further manufacture. He [or she] may so allocate in any manner that is fair and reasonable.

(c) The lessor seasonably shall notify the lessee and in the case of a finance lease the supplier seasonably shall notify the lessor and the lessee, if known, that there will be delay or nondelivery and, if allocation is required under paragraph (b), of the estimated quota thus made available for the lessee.

§ 2A–406. Procedure on Excused Performance.

(1) If the lessee receives notification of a material or indefinite delay or an allocation justified under Section 2A–405, the lessee may by written notification to the lessor as to any goods involved, and with respect to all of the goods if under an installment lease contract the value of the whole lease contract is substantially impaired (Section 2A–510):

(a) terminate the lease contract (Section 2A–505(2)); or

(b) except in a finance lease that is not a consumer lease, modify the lease contract by accepting the available quota in substitution, with due allowance from the rent payable for the balance of the lease term for the deficiency but without further right against the lessor.

(2) If, after receipt of a notification from the lessor under Section 2A–405, the lessee fails so to modify the lease agreement within a reasonable time not exceeding 30 days, the lease contract lapses with respect to any deliveries affected.

§ 2A–407. Irrevocable Promises: Finance Leases.

(1) In the case of a finance lease that is not a consumer lease the lessee's promises under the lease contract become irrevocable and independent upon the lessee's acceptance of the goods.

(2) A promise that has become irrevocable and independent under subsection (1):

(a) is effective and enforceable between the parties, and by or against third parties including assignees of the parties, and

(b) is not subject to cancellation, termination, modification, repudiation, excuse, or substitution without the consent of the party to whom the promise runs.

(3) This section does not affect the validity under any other law of a covenant in any lease contract making the lessee's promises irrevocable and independent upon the lessee's acceptance of the goods.

As amended in 1990.

Part 5—Default

A. In General

§ 2A–501. Default: Procedure.

(1) Whether the lessor or the lessee is in default under a lease contract is determined by the lease agreement and this Article.

(2) If the lessor or the lessee is in default under the lease contract, the party seeking enforcement has rights and remedies as provided in this Article and, except as limited by this Article, as provided in the lease agreement.

(3) If the lessor or the lessee is in default under the lease contract, the party seeking enforcement may reduce the party's claim to judgment, or otherwise enforce the lease contract by self-help or any available judicial procedure or nonjudicial procedure, including administrative proceeding, arbitration, or the like, in accordance with this Article.

(4) Except as otherwise provided in Section 1–106(1) or this Article or the lease agreement, the rights and remedies referred to in subsections (2) and (3) are cumulative.

(5) If the lease agreement covers both real property and goods, the party seeking enforcement may proceed under this Part as to the goods, or under other applicable law as to both the real property and the goods in accordance with that party's rights and remedies in respect of the real property, in which case this Part does not apply.

As amended in 1990.

§ 2A–502. Notice After Default.

Except as otherwise provided in this Article or the lease agreement, the lessor or lessee in default under the lease contract is not entitled to notice of default or notice of enforcement from the other party to the lease agreement.

§ 2A–503. Modification or Impairment of Rights and Remedies.

(1) Except as otherwise provided in this Article, the lease agreement may include rights and remedies for default in addition to or in substitution for those provided in this Article and may limit or alter the measure of damages recoverable under this Article.

(2) Resort to a remedy provided under this Article or in the lease agreement is optional unless the remedy is expressly agreed to be exclusive. If circumstances cause an exclusive or limited remedy to fail of its essential purpose, or provision for an exclusive remedy is unconscionable, remedy may be had as provided in this Article.

(3) Consequential damages may be liquidated under Section 2A–504, or may otherwise be limited, altered, or excluded unless the limitation, alteration, or exclusion is unconscionable. Limitation, alteration, or exclusion of consequential damages for injury to the person in the case of consumer goods is *prima facie* unconscionable but limitation, alteration, or exclusion of damages where the loss is commercial is not *prima facie* unconscionable.

(4) Rights and remedies on default by the lessor or the lessee with respect to any obligation or promise collateral or ancillary to the lease contract are not impaired by this Article.

As amended in 1990.

§ 2A–504. Liquidation of Damages.

(1) Damages payable by either party for default, or any other act or omission, including indemnity for loss or diminution of anticipated tax benefits or loss or damage to lessor's residual interest, may be liquidated in the lease agreement but only at an amount or by a formula that is reasonable in light of the then anticipated harm caused by the default or other act or omission.

(2) If the lease agreement provides for liquidation of damages, and such provision does not comply with subsection (1), or such provision is an exclusive or limited remedy that circumstances cause to fail of its essential purpose, remedy may be had as provided in this Article.

(3) If the lessor justifiably withholds or stops delivery of goods because of the lessee's default or insolvency (Section 2A–525 or 2A–526), the lessee is entitled to restitution of any amount by which the sum of his [or her] payments exceeds:

(a) the amount to which the lessor is entitled by virtue of terms liquidating the lessor's damages in accordance with subsection (1); or

(b) in the absence of those terms, 20 percent of the then present value of the total rent the lessee was obligated to pay for the balance of the lease term, or, in the case of a consumer lease, the lesser of such amount or $500.

(4) A lessee's right to restitution under subsection (3) is subject to offset to the extent the lessor establishes:

(a) a right to recover damages under the provisions of this Article other than subsection (1); and

(b) the amount or value of any benefits received by the lessee directly or indirectly by reason of the lease contract.

§ 2A–505. Cancellation and Termination and Effect of Cancellation, Termination, Rescission, or Fraud on Rights and Remedies.

(1) On cancellation of the lease contract, all obligations that are still executory on both sides are discharged, but any right based on prior default or performance survives, and the cancelling party also retains any remedy for default of the whole lease contract or any unperformed balance.

(2) On termination of the lease contract, all obligations that are still executory on both sides are discharged but any right based on prior default or performance survives.

(3) Unless the contrary intention clearly appears, expressions of "cancellation," "rescission," or the like of the lease contract may not be construed as a renunciation or discharge of any claim in damages for an antecedent default.

(4) Rights and remedies for material misrepresentation or fraud include all rights and remedies available under this Article for default.

(5) Neither rescission nor a claim for rescission of the lease contract nor rejection or return of the goods may bar or be deemed inconsistent with a claim for damages or other right or remedy.

§ 2A–506. Statute of Limitations.

(1) An action for default under a lease contract, including breach of warranty or indemnity, must be commenced within 4 years after the cause of action accrued. By the original lease contract the parties may reduce the period of limitation to not less than one year.

(2) A cause of action for default accrues when the act or omission on which the default or breach of warranty is based is or should have been discovered by the aggrieved party, or when the default occurs, whichever is later. A cause of action for indemnity accrues when the act or omission on which the claim for indemnity is based is or should have been discovered by the indemnified party, whichever is later.

(3) If an action commenced within the time limited by subsection (1) is so terminated as to leave available a remedy by another action for the same default or breach of warranty or indemnity, the other action may be commenced after the expiration of the time limited and within 6 months after the termination of the first action unless the termination resulted from voluntary discontinuance or from dismissal for failure or neglect to prosecute.

(4) This section does not alter the law on tolling of the statute of limitations nor does it apply to causes of action that have accrued before this Article becomes effective.

§ 2A–507. Proof of Market Rent: Time and Place.

(1) Damages based on market rent (Section 2A–519 or 2A–528) are determined according to the rent for the use of the goods concerned for a lease term identical to the remaining lease term of the original lease agreement and prevailing at the times specified in Sections 2A–519 and 2A–528.

(2) If evidence of rent for the use of the goods concerned for a lease term identical to the remaining lease term of the original lease agreement and prevailing at the times or places described in this Article is not readily available, the rent prevailing within any reasonable time before or after the time described or at any other place or for a different lease term which in commercial judgment or under usage of trade would serve as a reasonable substitute for the one described may be used, making any proper allowance for the difference, including the cost of transporting the goods to or from the other place.

(3) Evidence of a relevant rent prevailing at a time or place or for a lease term other than the one described in this Article offered by one party is not admissible unless and until he [or she] has given the other party notice the court finds sufficient to prevent unfair surprise.

(4) If the prevailing rent or value of any goods regularly leased in any established market is in issue, reports in official publications or trade journals or in newspapers or periodicals of general circulation published as the reports of that market are admissible in evidence. The circumstances of the preparation of the report may be shown to affect its weight but not its admissibility.

As amended in 1990.

B. Default by Lessor

§ 2A–508. Lessee's Remedies.

(1) If a lessor fails to deliver the goods in conformity to the lease contract (Section 2A–509) or repudiates the lease contract (Section 2A–402), or a lessee rightfully rejects the goods (Section 2A–509) or justifiably revokes acceptance of the goods (Section 2A–517), then with respect to any goods involved, and with respect to all of the goods if under an installment lease contract the value of the whole lease contract is substantially impaired (Section 2A–510), the lessor is in default under the lease contract and the lessee may:

    (a) cancel the lease contract (Section 2A–505(1));

    (b) recover so much of the rent and security as has been paid and is just under the circumstances;

    (c) cover and recover damages as to all goods affected whether or not they have been identified to the lease contract (Sections 2A–518 and 2A–520), or recover damages for nondelivery (Sections 2A–519 and 2A–520);

    (d) exercise any other rights or pursue any other remedies provided in the lease contract.

(2) If a lessor fails to deliver the goods in conformity to the lease contract or repudiates the lease contract, the lessee may also:

    (a) if the goods have been identified, recover them (Section 2A–522); or

    (b) in a proper case, obtain specific performance or replevy the goods (Section 2A–521).

(3) If a lessor is otherwise in default under a lease contract, the lessee may exercise the rights and pursue the remedies provided in the lease contract, which may include a right to cancel the lease, and in Section 2A–519(3).

(4) If a lessor has breached a warranty, whether express or implied, the lessee may recover damages (Section 2A–519(4)).

(5) On rightful rejection or justifiable revocation of acceptance, a lessee has a security interest in goods in the lessee's possession or control for any rent and security that has been paid and any expenses reasonably incurred in their inspection, receipt, transportation, and care and custody and may hold those goods and dispose of them in good faith and in a commercially reasonable manner, subject to Section 2A–527(5).

(6) Subject to the provisions of Section 2A–407, a lessee, on notifying the lessor of the lessee's intention to do so, may deduct all or any part of the damages resulting from any default under the lease contract from any part of the rent still due under the same lease contract.

As amended in 1990.

§ 2A–509. Lessee's Rights on Improper Delivery; Rightful Rejection.

(1) Subject to the provisions of Section 2A–510 on default in installment lease contracts, if the goods or the tender or delivery fail in any respect to conform to the lease contract, the lessee may reject or accept the goods or accept any commercial unit or units and reject the rest of the goods.

(2) Rejection of goods is ineffective unless it is within a reasonable time after tender or delivery of the goods and the lessee seasonably notifies the lessor.

§ 2A–510. Installment Lease Contracts: Rejection and Default.

(1) Under an installment lease contract a lessee may reject any delivery that is nonconforming if the nonconformity substantially impairs the value of that delivery and cannot be cured or the nonconformity is a defect in the required documents; but if the nonconformity does not fall within subsection (2) and the lessor or the supplier gives adequate assurance of its cure, the lessee must accept that delivery.

(2) Whenever nonconformity or default with respect to one or more deliveries substantially impairs the value of the installment lease contract as a whole there is a default with respect to the whole. But, the aggrieved party reinstates the installment lease contract as a whole if the aggrieved party accepts a nonconforming delivery without seasonably notifying of cancellation or brings an action with respect only to past deliveries or demands performance as to future deliveries.

§ 2A–511. Merchant Lessee's Duties as to Rightfully Rejected Goods.

(1) Subject to any security interest of a lessee (Section 2A–508(5)), if a lessor or a supplier has no agent or place of business at the market of rejection, a merchant lessee, after rejection of goods in his [or her] possession or control, shall follow any reasonable instructions received from the lessor or the supplier with respect to the goods. In the absence of those instructions, a merchant lessee shall make reasonable efforts to sell, lease, or otherwise dispose of the goods for the lessor's account if they threaten to decline in value speedily. Instructions are not reasonable if on demand indemnity for expenses is not forthcoming.

(2) If a merchant lessee (subsection (1)) or any other lessee (Section 2A–512) disposes of goods, he [or she] is entitled to reimbursement either from the lessor or the supplier or out of the proceeds for reasonable expenses of caring for and disposing of the goods and, if the expenses include no disposition commission, to such commission as is usual in the trade, or if there is none, to a reasonable sum not exceeding 10 percent of the gross proceeds.

(3) In complying with this section or Section 2A–512, the lessee is held only to good faith. Good faith conduct hereunder is neither acceptance or conversion nor the basis of an action for damages.

(4) A purchaser who purchases in good faith from a lessee pursuant to this section or Section 2A–512 takes the goods free of any rights of the lessor and the supplier even though the lessee fails to comply with one or more of the requirements of this Article.

§ 2A–512. Lessee's Duties as to Rightfully Rejected Goods.

(1) Except as otherwise provided with respect to goods that threaten to decline in value speedily (Section 2A–511) and subject to any security interest of a lessee (Section 2A–508(5)):

    (a) the lessee, after rejection of goods in the lessee's possession, shall hold them with reasonable care at the lessor's or the supplier's disposition for a reasonable time after the lessee's seasonable notification of rejection;

    (b) if the lessor or the supplier gives no instructions within a reasonable time after notification of rejection, the lessee may store the rejected goods for the lessor's or the supplier's account or ship them to the lessor or the supplier or dispose of them for the lessor's or the supplier's account with reimbursement in the manner provided in Section 2A–511; but

    (c) the lessee has no further obligations with regard to goods rightfully rejected.

(2) Action by the lessee pursuant to subsection (1) is not acceptance or conversion.

§ 2A–513. Cure by Lessor of Improper Tender or Delivery; Replacement.

(1) If any tender or delivery by the lessor or the supplier is rejected because nonconforming and the time for performance has not yet expired, the lessor or the supplier may seasonably notify the lessee of the lessor's or the supplier's intention to cure and may then make a conforming delivery within the time provided in the lease contract.

(2) If the lessee rejects a nonconforming tender that the lessor or the supplier had reasonable grounds to believe would be acceptable with or without money allowance, the lessor or the supplier may have a further reasonable time to substitute a conforming tender if he [or she] seasonably notifies the lessee.

§ 2A–514. Waiver of Lessee's Objections.

(1) In rejecting goods, a lessee's failure to state a particular defect that is ascertainable by reasonable inspection precludes the lessee from relying on the defect to justify rejection or to establish default:

    (a) if, stated seasonably, the lessor or the supplier could have cured it (Section 2A–513); or

    (b) between merchants if the lessor or the supplier after rejection has made a request in writing for a full and final written statement of all defects on which the lessee proposes to rely.

(2) A lessee's failure to reserve rights when paying rent or other consideration against documents precludes recovery of the payment for defects apparent on the face of the documents.

§ 2A–515. Acceptance of Goods.

(1) Acceptance of goods occurs after the lessee has had a reasonable opportunity to inspect the goods and

    (a) the lessee signifies or acts with respect to the goods in a manner that signifies to the lessor or the supplier that the goods are conforming or that the lessee will take or retain them in spite of their nonconformity; or

    (b) the lessee fails to make an effective rejection of the goods (Section 2A–509(2)).

(2) Acceptance of a part of any commercial unit is acceptance of that entire unit.

§ 2A–516. Effect of Acceptance of Goods; Notice of Default; Burden of Establishing Default after Acceptance; Notice of Claim or Litigation to Person Answerable Over.

(1) A lessee must pay rent for any goods accepted in accordance with the lease contract, with due allowance for goods rightfully rejected or not delivered.

(2) A lessee's acceptance of goods precludes rejection of the goods accepted. In the case of a finance lease, if made with knowledge of a nonconformity, acceptance cannot be revoked because of it. In any other case, if made with knowledge of a nonconformity, acceptance cannot be revoked because of it unless the acceptance was on the reasonable assumption that the nonconformity would be seasonably cured. Acceptance does not of itself impair any other remedy provided by this Article or the lease agreement for nonconformity.

(3) If a tender has been accepted:

    (a) within a reasonable time after the lessee discovers or should have discovered any default, the lessee shall notify the lessor and the supplier, if any, or be barred from any remedy against the party notified;

    (b) except in the case of a consumer lease, within a reasonable time after the lessee receives notice of litigation for infringement or the like (Section 2A–211) the lessee shall notify the lessor or be barred from any remedy over for liability established by the litigation; and

    (c) the burden is on the lessee to establish any default.

(4) If a lessee is sued for breach of a warranty or other obligation for which a lessor or a supplier is answerable over the following apply:

    (a) The lessee may give the lessor or the supplier, or both, written notice of the litigation. If the notice states that the person notified may come in and defend and that if the person notified does not do so that person will be bound in any action against that person by the lessee by any determination of fact common to the two litigations, then unless the person notified after seasonable receipt of the notice does come in and defend that person is so bound.

(b) The lessor or the supplier may demand in writing that the lessee turn over control of the litigation including settlement if the claim is one for infringement or the like (Section 2A–211) or else be barred from any remedy over. If the demand states that the lessor or the supplier agrees to bear all expense and to satisfy any adverse judgment, then unless the lessee after seasonable receipt of the demand does turn over control the lessee is so barred.

(5) Subsections (3) and (4) apply to any obligation of a lessee to hold the lessor or the supplier harmless against infringement or the like (Section 2A–211).

As amended in 1990.

§ 2A–517. Revocation of Acceptance of Goods.

(1) A lessee may revoke acceptance of a lot or commercial unit whose nonconformity substantially impairs its value to the lessee if the lessee has accepted it:

    (a) except in the case of a finance lease, on the reasonable assumption that its nonconformity would be cured and it has not been seasonably cured; or

    (b) without discovery of the nonconformity if the lessee's acceptance was reasonably induced either by the lessor's assurances or, except in the case of a finance lease, by the difficulty of discovery before acceptance.

(2) Except in the case of a finance lease that is not a consumer lease, a lessee may revoke acceptance of a lot or commercial unit if the lessor defaults under the lease contract and the default substantially impairs the value of that lot or commercial unit to the lessee.

(3) If the lease agreement so provides, the lessee may revoke acceptance of a lot or commercial unit because of other defaults by the lessor.

(4) Revocation of acceptance must occur within a reasonable time after the lessee discovers or should have discovered the ground for it and before any substantial change in condition of the goods which is not caused by the nonconformity. Revocation is not effective until the lessee notifies the lessor.

(5) A lessee who so revokes has the same rights and duties with regard to the goods involved as if the lessee had rejected them.

As amended in 1990.

§ 2A–518. Cover; Substitute Goods.

(1) After a default by a lessor under the lease contract of the type described in Section 2A–508(1), or, if agreed, after other default by the lessor, the lessee may cover by making any purchase or lease of or contract to purchase or lease goods in substitution for those due from the lessor.

(2) Except as otherwise provided with respect to damages liquidated in the lease agreement (Section 2A–504) or otherwise determined pursuant to agreement of the parties (Sections 1–102(3) and 2A–503), if a lessee's cover is by lease agreement substantially similar to the original lease agreement and the new lease agreement is made in good faith and in a commercially reasonable manner, the lessee may recover from the lessor as damages (i) the present value, as of the date of the commencement of the term of the new lease agreement, of the rent under the new lease agreement applicable to that period of the new lease term which is comparable to the then remaining term of the original lease agreement minus the present value as of the same date of the total rent for the then remaining lease term of the original lease agreement, and (ii) any incidental or consequential damages, less expenses saved in consequence of the lessor's default.

(3) If a lessee's cover is by lease agreement that for any reason does not qualify for treatment under subsection (2), or is by purchase or otherwise, the lessee may recover from the lessor as if the lessee had elected not to cover and Section 2A–519 governs.

As amended in 1990.

§ 2A–519. Lessee's Damages for Non-Delivery, Repudiation, Default, and Breach of Warranty in Regard to Accepted Goods.

(1) Except as otherwise provided with respect to damages liquidated in the lease agreement (Section 2A–504) or otherwise determined pursuant to agreement of the parties (Sections 1–102(3) and 2A–503), if a lessee elects not to cover or a lessee elects to cover and the cover is by lease agreement that for any reason does not qualify for treatment under Section 2A–518(2), or is by purchase or otherwise, the measure of damages for non-delivery or repudiation by the lessor or for rejection or revocation of acceptance by the lessee is the present value, as of the date of the default, of the then market rent minus the present value as of the same date of the original rent, computed for the remaining lease term of the original lease agreement, together with incidental and consequential damages, less expenses saved in consequence of the lessor's default.

(2) Market rent is to be determined as of the place for tender or, in cases of rejection after arrival or revocation of acceptance, as of the place of arrival.

(3) Except as otherwise agreed, if the lessee has accepted goods and given notification (Section 2A–516(3)), the measure of damages for non-conforming tender or delivery or other default by a lessor is the loss resulting in the ordinary course of events from the lessor's default as determined in any manner that is reasonable together with incidental and consequential damages, less expenses saved in consequence of the lessor's default.

(4) Except as otherwise agreed, the measure of damages for breach of warranty is the present value at the time and place of acceptance of the difference between the value of the use of the goods accepted and the value if they had been as warranted for the lease term, unless special circumstances show proximate damages of a different amount, together with incidental and consequential damages, less expenses saved in consequence of the lessor's default or breach of warranty.

As amended in 1990.

§ 2A–520. Lessee's Incidental and Consequential Damages.

(1) Incidental damages resulting from a lessor's default include expenses reasonably incurred in inspection, receipt, transportation, and care and custody of goods rightfully rejected or goods the acceptance of which is justifiably revoked, any commercially reasonable charges, expenses or commissions in connection with effecting cover, and any other reasonable expense incident to the default.

(2) Consequential damages resulting from a lessor's default include:

(a) any loss resulting from general or particular requirements and needs of which the lessor at the time of contracting had reason to know and which could not reasonably be prevented by cover or otherwise; and

(b) injury to person or property proximately resulting from any breach of warranty.

§ 2A–521. Lessee's Right to Specific Performance or Replevin.

(1) Specific performance may be decreed if the goods are unique or in other proper circumstances.

(2) A decree for specific performance may include any terms and conditions as to payment of the rent, damages, or other relief that the court deems just.

(3) A lessee has a right of replevin, detinue, sequestration, claim and delivery, or the like for goods identified to the lease contract if after reasonable effort the lessee is unable to effect cover for those goods or the circumstances reasonably indicate that the effort will be unavailing.

§ 2A–522. Lessee's Right to Goods on Lessor's Insolvency.

(1) Subject to subsection (2) and even though the goods have not been shipped, a lessee who has paid a part or all of the rent and security for goods identified to a lease contract (Section 2A–217) on making and keeping good a tender of any unpaid portion of the rent and security due under the lease contract may recover the goods identified from the lessor if the lessor becomes insolvent within 10 days after receipt of the first installment of rent and security.

(2) A lessee acquires the right to recover goods identified to a lease contract only if they conform to the lease contract.

C. Default by Lessee

§ 2A–523. Lessor's Remedies.

(1) If a lessee wrongfully rejects or revokes acceptance of goods or fails to make a payment when due or repudiates with respect to a part or the whole, then, with respect to any goods involved, and with respect to all of the goods if under an installment lease contract the value of the whole lease contract is substantially impaired (Section 2A–510), the lessee is in default under the lease contract and the lessor may:

    (a) cancel the lease contract (Section 2A–505(1));

    (b) proceed respecting goods not identified to the lease contract (Section 2A–524);

    (c) withhold delivery of the goods and take possession of goods previously delivered (Section 2A–525);

    (d) stop delivery of the goods by any bailee (Section 2A–526);

    (e) dispose of the goods and recover damages (Section 2A–527), or retain the goods and recover damages (Section 2A–528), or in a proper case recover rent (Section 2A–529)

    (f) exercise any other rights or pursue any other remedies provided in the lease contract.

(2) If a lessor does not fully exercise a right or obtain a remedy to which the lessor is entitled under subsection (1), the lessor may recover the loss resulting in the ordinary course of events from the lessee's default as determined in any reasonable manner, together with incidental damages, less expenses saved in consequence of the lessee's default.

(3) If a lessee is otherwise in default under a lease contract, the lessor may exercise the rights and pursue the remedies provided in the lease contract, which may include a right to cancel the lease. In addition, unless otherwise provided in the lease contract:

    (a) if the default substantially impairs the value of the lease contract to the lessor, the lessor may exercise the rights and pursue the remedies provided in subsections (1) or (2); or

    (b) if the default does not substantially impair the value of the lease contract to the lessor, the lessor may recover as provided in subsection (2).

As amended in 1990.

§ 2A–524. Lessor's Right to Identify Goods to Lease Contract.

(1) After default by the lessee under the lease contract of the type described in Section 2A–523(1) or 2A–523(3)(a) or, if agreed, after other default by the lessee, the lessor may:

    (a) identify to the lease contract conforming goods not already identified if at the time the lessor learned of the default they were in the lessor's or the supplier's possession or control; and

    (b) dispose of goods (Section 2A–527(1)) that demonstrably have been intended for the particular lease contract even though those goods are unfinished.

(2) If the goods are unfinished, in the exercise of reasonable commercial judgment for the purposes of avoiding loss and of effective realization, an aggrieved lessor or the supplier may either complete manufacture and wholly identify the goods to the lease contract or cease manufacture and lease, sell, or otherwise dispose of the goods for scrap or salvage value or proceed in any other reasonable manner.

As amended in 1990.

§ 2A–525. Lessor's Right to Possession of Goods.

(1) If a lessor discovers the lessee to be insolvent, the lessor may refuse to deliver the goods.

(2) After a default by the lessee under the lease contract of the type described in Section 2A–523(1) or 2A–523(3)(a) or, if agreed, after other default by the lessee, the lessor has the right to take possession of the goods. If the lease contract so provides, the lessor may require the lessee to assemble the goods and make them available to the lessor at a place to be designated by the lessor which is reasonably convenient to both parties. Without removal, the lessor may render unusable any goods employed in trade or business, and may dispose of goods on the lessee's premises (Section 2A–527).

(3) The lessor may proceed under subsection (2) without judicial process if that can be done without breach of the peace or the lessor may proceed by action.

As amended in 1990.

§ 2A–526. Lessor's Stoppage of Delivery in Transit or Otherwise.

(1) A lessor may stop delivery of goods in the possession of a carrier or other bailee if the lessor discovers the lessee to be insolvent and may stop delivery of carload, truckload, planeload, or larger shipments of express or freight if the lessee repudiates or fails to make a payment due before delivery, whether for rent, security or otherwise under the lease contract, or for any other reason the lessor has a right to withhold or take possession of the goods.

(2) In pursuing its remedies under subsection (1), the lessor may stop delivery until

> **(a)** receipt of the goods by the lessee;

> **(b)** acknowledgment to the lessee by any bailee of the goods, except a carrier, that the bailee holds the goods for the lessee; or

> **(c)** such an acknowledgment to the lessee by a carrier via reshipment or as warehouseman.

(3) (a) To stop delivery, a lessor shall so notify as to enable the bailee by reasonable diligence to prevent delivery of the goods.

> **(b)** After notification, the bailee shall hold and deliver the goods according to the directions of the lessor, but the lessor is liable to the bailee for any ensuing charges or damages.

> **(c)** A carrier who has issued a nonnegotiable bill of lading is not obliged to obey a notification to stop received from a person other than the consignor.

§ 2A–527. Lessor's Rights to Dispose of Goods.

(1) After a default by a lessee under the lease contract of the type described in Section 2A–523(1) or 2A–523(3)(a) or after the lessor refuses to deliver or takes possession of goods (Section 2A–525 or 2A–526), or, if agreed, after other default by a lessee, the lessor may dispose of the goods concerned or the undelivered balance thereof by lease, sale, or otherwise.

(2) Except as otherwise provided with respect to damages liquidated in the lease agreement (Section 2A–504) or otherwise determined pursuant to agreement of the parties (Sections 1–102(3) and 2A–503), if the disposition is by lease agreement substantially similar to the original lease agreement and the new lease agreement is made in good faith and in a commercially reasonable manner, the lessor may recover from the lessee as damages (i) accrued and unpaid rent as of the date of the commencement of the term of the new lease agreement, (ii) the present value, as of the same date, of the total rent for the then remaining lease term of the original lease agreement minus the present value, as of the same date, of the rent under the new lease agreement applicable to that period of the new lease term which is comparable to the then remaining term of the original lease agreement, and (iii) any incidental damages allowed under Section 2A–530, less expenses saved in consequence of the lessee's default.

(3) If the lessor's disposition is by lease agreement that for any reason does not qualify for treatment under subsection (2), or is by sale or otherwise, the lessor may recover from the lessee as if the lessor had elected not to dispose of the goods and Section 2A–528 governs.

(4) A subsequent buyer or lessee who buys or leases from the lessor in good faith for value as a result of a disposition under this section takes the goods free of the original lease contract and any rights of the original lessee even though the lessor fails to comply with one or more of the requirements of this Article.

(5) The lessor is not accountable to the lessee for any profit made on any disposition. A lessee who has rightfully rejected or justifiably revoked acceptance shall account to the lessor for any excess over the amount of the lessee's security interest (Section 2A–508(5)).

As amended in 1990.

§ 2A–528. Lessor's Damages for Non-acceptance, Failure to Pay, Repudiation, or Other Default.

(1) Except as otherwise provided with respect to damages liquidated in the lease agreement (Section 2A–504) or otherwise determined pursuant to agreement of the parties (Section 1–102(3) and 2A–503), if a lessor elects to retain the goods or a lessor elects to dispose of the goods and the disposition is by lease agreement that for any reason does not qualify for treatment under Section 2A–527(2), or is by sale or otherwise, the lessor may recover from the lessee as damages for a default of the type described in Section 2A–523(1) or 2A–523(3)(a), or if agreed, for other default of the lessee, (i) accrued and unpaid rent as of the date of the default if the lessee has never taken possession of the goods, or, if the lessee has taken possession of the goods, as of the date the lessor repossesses the goods or an earlier date on which the lessee makes a tender of the goods to the lessor, (ii) the present value as of the date determined under clause (i) of the total rent for the then remaining lease term of the original lease agreement minus the present value as of the same date of the market rent as the place where the goods are located computed for the same lease term, and (iii) any incidental damages allowed under Section 2A–530, less expenses saved in consequence of the lessee's default.

(2) If the measure of damages provided in subsection (1) is inadequate to put a lessor in as good a position as performance would have, the measure of damages is the present value of the profit, including reasonable overhead, the lessor would have made from full performance by the lessee, together with any incidental damages allowed under Section 2A–530, due allowance for costs reasonably incurred and due credit for payments or proceeds of disposition.

As amended in 1990.

§ 2A–529. Lessor's Action for the Rent.

(1) After default by the lessee under the lease contract of the type described in Section 2A–523(1) or 2A–523(3)(a) or, if agreed, after other default by the lessee, if the lessor complies with subsection (2), the lessor may recover from the lessee as damages:

> **(a)** for goods accepted by the lessee and not repossessed by or tendered to the lessor, and for conforming goods lost or damaged within a commercially reasonable time after risk of loss passes to the lessee (Section 2A–219), (i) accrued and unpaid rent as of the date of entry of judgment in favor of the lessor (ii) the present value as of the same date of the rent for the then remaining lease term of the lease agreement, and (iii) any incidental damages allowed under Section 2A–530, less expenses saved in consequence of the lessee's default; and

> **(b)** for goods identified to the lease contract if the lessor is unable after reasonable effort to dispose of them at a reasonable price or the circumstances reasonably indicate that effort will be unavailing, (i) accrued and unpaid rent as of the date of entry of judgment in favor of the lessor, (ii) the present value as of the same date of the rent for the then remaining lease term of the lease agreement, and (iii) any incidental damages allowed under Section 2A–530, less expenses saved in consequence of the lessee's default.

(2) Except as provided in subsection (3), the lessor shall hold for the lessee for the remaining lease term of the lease agreement any goods that have been identified to the lease contract and are in the lessor's control.

(3) The lessor may dispose of the goods at any time before collection of the judgment for damages obtained pursuant to subsection (1). If the disposition is before the end of the remaining lease term of the lease agreement, the lessor's recovery against the lessee for damages is governed by Section 2A–527 or Section 2A–528, and the lessor will cause an appropriate credit to be provided against a judgment for damages to the extent that the amount of the judgment exceeds the recovery available pursuant to Section 2A–527 or 2A–528.

(4) Payment of the judgment for damages obtained pursuant to subsection (1) entitles the lessee to the use and possession of the goods not then disposed of for the remaining lease term of and in accordance with the lease agreement.

(5) After default by the lessee under the lease contract of the type described in Section 2A–523(1) or Section 2A–523(3)(a) or, if agreed, after other default by the lessee, a lessor who is held not entitled to rent under this section must nevertheless be awarded damages for non-acceptance under Sections 2A–527 and 2A–528.

As amended in 1990.

§ 2A–530. Lessor's Incidental Damages.

Incidental damages to an aggrieved lessor include any commercially reasonable charges, expenses, or commissions incurred in stopping delivery, in the transportation, care and custody of goods after the lessee's default, in connection with return or disposition of the goods, or otherwise resulting from the default.

§ 2A–531. Standing to Sue Third Parties for Injury to Goods.

(1) If a third party so deals with goods that have been identified to a lease contract as to cause actionable injury to a party to the lease contract (a) the lessor has a right of action against the third party, and (b) the lessee also has a right of action against the third party if the lessee:

(i) has a security interest in the goods;

(ii) has an insurable interest in the goods; or

(iii) bears the risk of loss under the lease contract or has since the injury assumed that risk as against the lessor and the goods have been converted or destroyed.

(2) If at the time of the injury the party plaintiff did not bear the risk of loss as against the other party to the lease contract and there is no arrangement between them for disposition of the recovery, his [or her] suit or settlement, subject to his [or her] own interest, is as a fiduciary for the other party to the lease contract.

(3) Either party with the consent of the other may sue for the benefit of whom it may concern.

§ 2A–532. Lessor's Rights to Residual Interest.

In addition to any other recovery permitted by this Article or other law, the lessor may recover from the lessee an amount that will fully compensate the lessor for any loss of or damage to the lessor's residual interest in the goods caused by the default of the lessee.

As added in 1990.

REVISED ARTICLE 3: NEGOTIABLE INSTRUMENTS

Part 1—General Provisions and Definitions

§ 3–101. Short Title.

This Article may be cited as Uniform Commercial Code–Negotiable Instruments.

§ 3–102. Subject Matter.

(a) This Article applies to negotiable instruments. It does not apply to money, to payment orders governed by Article 4A, or to securities governed by Article 8.

(b) If there is conflict between this Article and Article 4 or 9, Articles 4 and 9 govern.

(c) Regulations of the Board of Governors of the Federal Reserve System and operating circulars of the Federal Reserve Banks supersede any inconsistent provision of this Article to the extent of the inconsistency.

§ 3–103. Definitions.

(a) In this Article:

(1) "Acceptor" means a drawee who has accepted a draft.

(2) "Drawee" means a person ordered in a draft to make payment.

(3) "Drawer" means a person who signs or is identified in a draft as a person ordering payment.

(4) "Good faith" means honesty in fact and the observance of reasonable commercial standards of fair dealing.

(5) "Maker" means a person who signs or is identified in a note as a person undertaking to pay.

(6) "Order" means a written instruction to pay money signed by the person giving the instruction. The instruction may be addressed to any person, including the person giving the instruction, or to one or more persons jointly or in the alternative but not in succession. An authorization to pay is not an order unless the person authorized to pay is also instructed to pay.

(7) "Ordinary care" in the case of a person engaged in business means observance of reasonable commercial standards, prevailing in the area in which the person is located, with respect to the business in which the person is engaged. In the case of a bank that takes an instrument for processing for collection or payment by automated means, reasonable commercial standards do not require the bank to examine the instrument if the failure to examine does not violate the bank's prescribed procedures and the bank's procedures do not vary unreasonably from general banking usage not disapproved by this Article or Article 4.

(8) "Party" means a party to an instrument.

(9) "Promise" means a written undertaking to pay money signed by the person undertaking to pay. An acknowledgment of an obligation by the obligor is not a promise unless the obligor also undertakes to pay the obligation.

(10) "Prove" with respect to a fact means to meet the burden of establishing the fact (Section 1–201(8)).

(11) "Remitter" means a person who purchases an instrument from its issuer if the instrument is payable to an identified person other than the purchaser.

(b) [Other definitions' section references deleted.]

(c) [Other definitions' section references deleted.]

(d) In addition, Article 1 contains general definitions and principles of construction and interpretation applicable throughout this Article.

§ 3–104. Negotiable Instrument.

(a) Except as provided in subsections (c) and (d), "negotiable instrument" means an unconditional promise or order to pay a fixed amount of money, with or without interest or other charges described in the promise or order, if it:

> **(1)** is payable to bearer or to order at the time it is issued or first comes into possession of a holder;
>
> **(2)** is payable on demand or at a definite time; and
>
> **(3)** does not state any other undertaking or instruction by the person promising or ordering payment to do any act in addition to the payment of money, but the promise or order may contain (i) an undertaking or power to give, maintain, or protect collateral to secure payment, (ii) an authorization or power to the holder to confess judgment or realize on or dispose of collateral, or (iii) a waiver of the benefit of any law intended for the advantage or protection of an obligor.

(b) "Instrument" means a negotiable instrument.

(c) An order that meets all of the requirements of subsection (a), except paragraph (1), and otherwise falls within the definition of "check" in subsection (f) is a negotiable instrument and a check.

(d) A promise or order other than a check is not an instrument if, at the time it is issued or first comes into possession of a holder, it contains a conspicuous statement, however expressed, to the effect that the promise or order is not negotiable or is not an instrument governed by this Article.

(e) An instrument is a "note" if it is a promise and is a "draft" if it is an order. If an instrument falls within the definition of both "note" and "draft," a person entitled to enforce the instrument may treat it as either.

(f) "Check" means (i) a draft, other than a documentary draft, payable on demand and drawn on a bank or (ii) a cashier's check or teller's check. An instrument may be a check even though it is described on its face by another term, such as "money order."

(g) "Cashier's check" means a draft with respect to which the drawer and drawee are the same bank or branches of the same bank.

(h) "Teller's check" means a draft drawn by a bank (i) on another bank, or (ii) payable at or through a bank.

(i) "Traveler's check" means an instrument that (i) is payable on demand, (ii) is drawn on or payable at or through a bank, (iii) is designated by the term "traveler's check" or by a substantially similar term, and (iv) requires, as a condition to payment, a countersignature by a person whose specimen signature appears on the instrument.

(j) "Certificate of deposit" means an instrument containing an acknowledgment by a bank that a sum of money has been received by the bank and a promise by the bank to repay the sum of money. A certificate of deposit is a note of the bank.

§ 3–105. Issue of Instrument.

(a) "Issue" means the first delivery of an instrument by the maker or drawer, whether to a holder or nonholder, for the purpose of giving rights on the instrument to any person.

(b) An unissued instrument, or an unissued incomplete instrument that is completed, is binding on the maker or drawer, but nonissuance is a defense. An instrument that is conditionally issued or is issued for a special purpose is binding on the maker or drawer, but failure of the condition or special purpose to be fulfilled is a defense.

(c) "Issuer" applies to issued and unissued instruments and means a maker or drawer of an instrument.

§ 3–106. Unconditional Promise or Order.

(a) Except as provided in this section, for the purposes of Section 3–104(a), a promise or order is unconditional unless it states (i) an express condition to payment, (ii) that the promise or order is subject to or governed by another writing, or (iii) that rights or obligations with respect to the promise or order are stated in another writing. A reference to another writing does not of itself make the promise or order conditional.

(b) A promise or order is not made conditional (i) by a reference to another writing for a statement of rights with respect to collateral, prepayment, or acceleration, or (ii) because payment is limited to resort to a particular fund or source.

(c) If a promise or order requires, as a condition to payment, a countersignature by a person whose specimen signature appears on the promise or order, the condition does not make the promise or order conditional for the purposes of Section 3–104(a). If the person whose specimen signature appears on an instrument fails to countersign the instrument, the failure to countersign is a defense to the obligation of the issuer, but the failure does not prevent a transferee of the instrument from becoming a holder of the instrument.

(d) If a promise or order at the time it is issued or first comes into possession of a holder contains a statement, required by applicable statutory or administrative law, to the effect that the rights of a holder or transferee are subject to claims or defenses that the issuer could assert against the original payee, the promise or order is not thereby made conditional for the purposes of Section 3–104(a); but if the promise or order is an instrument, there cannot be a holder in due course of the instrument.

§ 3–107. Instrument Payable in Foreign Money.

Unless the instrument otherwise provides, an instrument that states the amount payable in foreign money may be paid in the foreign money or in an equivalent amount in dollars calculated by using the current bank-offered spot rate at the place of payment for the purchase of dollars on the day on which the instrument is paid.

§ 3–108. Payable on Demand or at Definite Time.

(a) A promise or order is "payable on demand" if it (i) states that it is payable on demand or at sight, or otherwise indicates that it is payable at the will of the holder, or (ii) does not state any time of payment.

(b) A promise or order is "payable at a definite time" if it is payable on elapse of a definite period of time after sight or acceptance or at a fixed date or dates or at a time or times readily ascertainable at the time the promise or order is issued, subject to rights of (i) prepayment, (ii) acceleration, (iii) extension at the option of the holder, or (iv) extension to a further definite time at the option of the maker or acceptor or automatically upon or after a specified act or event.

(c) If an instrument, payable at a fixed date, is also payable upon demand made before the fixed date, the instrument is payable on demand until the fixed date and, if demand for payment is not made before that date, becomes payable at a definite time on the fixed date.

§ 3–109. Payable to Bearer or to Order.
(a) A promise or order is payable to bearer if it:

(1) states that it is payable to bearer or to the order of bearer or otherwise indicates that the person in possession of the promise or order is entitled to payment;

(2) does not state a payee; or

(3) states that it is payable to or to the order of cash or otherwise indicates that it is not payable to an identified person.

(b) A promise or order that is not payable to bearer is payable to order if it is payable (i) to the order of an identified person or (ii) to an identified person or order. A promise or order that is payable to order is payable to the identified person.

(c) An instrument payable to bearer may become payable to an identified person if it is specially indorsed pursuant to Section 3–205(a). An instrument payable to an identified person may become payable to bearer if it is indorsed in blank pursuant to Section 3–205(b).

§ 3–110. Identification of Person to Whom Instrument Is Payable.
(a) The person to whom an instrument is initially payable is determined by the intent of the person, whether or not authorized, signing as, or in the name or behalf of, the issuer of the instrument. The instrument is payable to the person intended by the signer even if that person is identified in the instrument by a name or other identification that is not that of the intended person. If more than one person signs in the name or behalf of the issuer of an instrument and all the signers do not intend the same person as payee, the instrument is payable to any person intended by one or more of the signers.

(b) If the signature of the issuer of an instrument is made by automated means, such as a check-writing machine, the payee of the instrument is determined by the intent of the person who supplied the name or identification of the payee, whether or not authorized to do so.

(c) A person to whom an instrument is payable may be identified in any way, including by name, identifying number, office, or account number. For the purpose of determining the holder of an instrument, the following rules apply:

(1) If an instrument is payable to an account and the account is identified only by number, the instrument is payable to the person to whom the account is payable. If an instrument is payable to an account identified by number and by the name of a person, the instrument is payable to the named person, whether or not that person is the owner of the account identified by number.

(2) If an instrument is payable to:

(i) a trust, an estate, or a person described as trustee or representative of a trust or estate, the instrument is payable to the trustee, the representative, or a successor of either, whether or not the beneficiary or estate is also named;

(ii) a person described as agent or similar representative of a named or identified person, the instrument is payable to the represented person, the representative, or a successor of the representative;

(iii) a fund or organization that is not a legal entity, the instrument is payable to a representative of the members of the fund or organization; or

(iv) an office or to a person described as holding an office, the instrument is payable to the named person, the incumbent of the office, or a successor to the incumbent.

(d) If an instrument is payable to two or more persons alternatively, it is payable to any of them and may be negotiated, discharged, or enforced by any or all of them in possession of the instrument. If an instrument is payable to two or more persons not alternatively, it is payable to all of them and may be negotiated, discharged, or enforced only by all of them. If an instrument payable to two or more persons is ambiguous as to whether it is payable to the persons alternatively, the instrument is payable to the persons alternatively.

§ 3–111. Place of Payment.
Except as otherwise provided for items in Article 4, an instrument is payable at the place of payment stated in the instrument. If no place of payment is stated, an instrument is payable at the address of the drawee or maker stated in the instrument. If no address is stated, the place of payment is the place of business of the drawee or maker. If a drawee or maker has more than one place of business, the place of payment is any place of business of the drawee or maker chosen by the person entitled to enforce the instrument. If the drawee or maker has no place of business, the place of payment is the residence of the drawee or maker.

§ 3–112. Interest.
(a) Unless otherwise provided in the instrument, (i) an instrument is not payable with interest, and (ii) interest on an interest-bearing instrument is payable from the date of the instrument.

(b) Interest may be stated in an instrument as a fixed or variable amount of money or it may be expressed as a fixed or variable rate or rates. The amount or rate of interest may be stated or described in the instrument in any manner and may require reference to information not contained in the instrument. If an instrument provides for interest, but the amount of interest payable cannot be ascertained from the description, interest is payable at the judgment rate in effect at the place of payment of the instrument and at the time interest first accrues.

§ 3–113. Date of Instrument.
(a) An instrument may be antedated or postdated. The date stated determines the time of payment if the instrument is payable at a fixed period after date. Except as provided in Section 4–401(c), an instrument payable on demand is not payable before the date of the instrument.

(b) If an instrument is undated, its date is the date of its issue or, in the case of an unissued instrument, the date it first comes into possession of a holder.

§ 3–114. Contradictory Terms of Instrument.

If an instrument contains contradictory terms, typewritten terms prevail over printed terms, handwritten terms prevail over both, and words prevail over numbers.

§ 3–115. Incomplete Instrument.

(a) "Incomplete instrument" means a signed writing, whether or not issued by the signer, the contents of which show at the time of signing that it is incomplete but that the signer intended it to be completed by the addition of words or numbers.

(b) Subject to subsection (c), if an incomplete instrument is an instrument under Section 3–104, it may be enforced according to its terms if it is not completed, or according to its terms as augmented by completion. If an incomplete instrument is not an instrument under Section 3–104, but, after completion, the requirements of Section 3–104 are met, the instrument may be enforced according to its terms as augmented by completion.

(c) If words or numbers are added to an incomplete instrument without authority of the signer, there is an alteration of the incomplete instrument under Section 3–407.

(d) The burden of establishing that words or numbers were added to an incomplete instrument without authority of the signer is on the person asserting the lack of authority.

§ 3–116. Joint and Several Liability; Contribution.

(a) Except as otherwise provided in the instrument, two or more persons who have the same liability on an instrument as makers, drawers, acceptors, indorsers who indorse as joint payees, or anomalous indorsers are jointly and severally liable in the capacity in which they sign.

(b) Except as provided in Section 3–419(e) or by agreement of the affected parties, a party having joint and several liability who pays the instrument is entitled to receive from any party having the same joint and several liability contribution in accordance with applicable law.

(c) Discharge of one party having joint and several liability by a person entitled to enforce the instrument does not affect the right under subsection (b) of a party having the same joint and several liability to receive contribution from the party discharged.

§ 3–117. Other Agreements Affecting Instrument.

Subject to applicable law regarding exclusion of proof of contemporaneous or previous agreements, the obligation of a party to an instrument to pay the instrument may be modified, supplemented, or nullified by a separate agreement of the obligor and a person entitled to enforce the instrument, if the instrument is issued or the obligation is incurred in reliance on the agreement or as part of the same transaction giving rise to the agreement. To the extent an obligation is modified, supplemented, or nullified by an agreement under this section, the agreement is a defense to the obligation.

§ 3–118. Statute of Limitations.

(a) Except as provided in subsection (e), an action to enforce the obligation of a party to pay a note payable at a definite time must be commenced within six years after the due date or dates stated in the note or, if a due date is accelerated, within six years after the accelerated due date.

(b) Except as provided in subsection (d) or (e), if demand for payment is made to the maker of a note payable on demand, an action to enforce the obligation of a party to pay the note must be commenced within six years after the demand. If no demand for payment is made to the maker, an action to enforce the note is barred if neither principal nor interest on the note has been paid for a continuous period of 10 years.

(c) Except as provided in subsection (d), an action to enforce the obligation of a party to an unaccepted draft to pay the draft must be commenced within three years after dishonor of the draft or 10 years after the date of the draft, whichever period expires first.

(d) An action to enforce the obligation of the acceptor of a certified check or the issuer of a teller's check, cashier's check, or traveler's check must be commenced within three years after demand for payment is made to the acceptor or issuer, as the case may be.

(e) An action to enforce the obligation of a party to a certificate of deposit to pay the instrument must be commenced within six years after demand for payment is made to the maker, but if the instrument states a due date and the maker is not required to pay before that date, the six-year period begins when a demand for payment is in effect and the due date has passed.

(f) An action to enforce the obligation of a party to pay an accepted draft, other than a certified check, must be commenced (i) within six years after the due date or dates stated in the draft or acceptance if the obligation of the acceptor is payable at a definite time, or (ii) within six years after the date of the acceptance if the obligation of the acceptor is payable on demand.

(g) Unless governed by other law regarding claims for indemnity or contribution, an action (i) for conversion of an instrument, for money had and received, or like action based on conversion, (ii) for breach of warranty, or (iii) to enforce an obligation, duty, or right arising under this Article and not governed by this section must be commenced within three years after the [cause of action] accrues.

§ 3–119. Notice of Right to Defend Action.

In an action for breach of an obligation for which a third person is answerable over pursuant to this Article or Article 4, the defendant may give the third person written notice of the litigation, and the person notified may then give similar notice to any other person who is answerable over. If the notice states (i) that the person notified may come in and defend and (ii) that failure to do so will bind the person notified in an action later brought by the person giving the notice as to any determination of fact common to the two litigations, the person notified is so bound unless after seasonable receipt of the notice the person notified does come in and defend.

Part 2—Negotiation, Transfer, and Indorsement

§ 3–201. Negotiation.

(a) "Negotiation" means a transfer of possession, whether voluntary or involuntary, of an instrument by a person other than the issuer to a person who thereby becomes its holder.

(b) Except for negotiation by a remitter, if an instrument is payable to an identified person, negotiation requires transfer of possession of the instrument and its indorsement by the holder. If an instrument is payable to bearer, it may be negotiated by transfer of possession alone.

§ 3–202. Negotiation Subject to Rescission.
(a) Negotiation is effective even if obtained (i) from an infant, a corporation exceeding its powers, or a person without capacity, (ii) by fraud, duress, or mistake, or (iii) in breach of duty or as part of an illegal transaction.

(b) To the extent permitted by other law, negotiation may be rescinded or may be subject to other remedies, but those remedies may not be asserted against a subsequent holder in due course or a person paying the instrument in good faith and without knowledge of facts that are a basis for rescission or other remedy.

§ 3–203. Transfer of Instrument; Rights Acquired by Transfer.
(a) An instrument is transferred when it is delivered by a person other than its issuer for the purpose of giving to the person receiving delivery the right to enforce the instrument.

(b) Transfer of an instrument, whether or not the transfer is a negotiation, vests in the transferee any right of the transferor to enforce the instrument, including any right as a holder in due course, but the transferee cannot acquire rights of a holder in due course by a transfer, directly or indirectly, from a holder in due course if the transferee engaged in fraud or illegality affecting the instrument.

(c) Unless otherwise agreed, if an instrument is transferred for value and the transferee does not become a holder because of lack of indorsement by the transferor, the transferee has a specifically enforceable right to the unqualified indorsement of the transferor, but negotiation of the instrument does not occur until the indorsement is made.

(d) If a transferor purports to transfer less than the entire instrument, negotiation of the instrument does not occur. The transferee obtains no rights under this Article and has only the rights of a partial assignee.

§ 3–204. Indorsement.
(a) "Indorsement" means a signature, other than that of a signer as maker, drawer, or acceptor, that alone or accompanied by other words is made on an instrument for the purpose of (i) negotiating the instrument, (ii) restricting payment of the instrument, or (iii) incurring indorser's liability on the instrument, but regardless of the intent of the signer, a signature and its accompanying words is an indorsement unless the accompanying words, terms of the instrument, place of the signature, or other circumstances unambiguously indicate that the signature was made for a purpose other than indorsement. For the purpose of determining whether a signature is made on an instrument, a paper affixed to the instrument is a part of the instrument.

(b) "Indorser" means a person who makes an indorsement.

(c) For the purpose of determining whether the transferee of an instrument is a holder, an indorsement that transfers a security interest in the instrument is effective as an unqualified indorsement of the instrument.

(d) If an instrument is payable to a holder under a name that is not the name of the holder, indorsement may be made by the holder in the name stated in the instrument or in the holder's name or both, but signature in both names may be required by a person paying or taking the instrument for value or collection.

§ 3–205. Special Indorsement; Blank Indorsement; Anomalous Indorsement.
(a) If an indorsement is made by the holder of an instrument, whether payable to an identified person or payable to bearer, and the indorsement identifies a person to whom it makes the instrument payable, it is a "special indorsement." When specially indorsed, an instrument becomes payable to the identified person and may be negotiated only by the indorsement of that person. The principles stated in Section 3–110 apply to special indorsements.

(b) If an indorsement is made by the holder of an instrument and it is not a special indorsement, it is a "blank indorsement." When indorsed in blank, an instrument becomes payable to bearer and may be negotiated by transfer of possession alone until specially indorsed.

(c) The holder may convert a blank indorsement that consists only of a signature into a special indorsement by writing, above the signature of the indorser, words identifying the person to whom the instrument is made payable.

(d) "Anomalous indorsement" means an indorsement made by a person who is not the holder of the instrument. An anomalous indorsement does not affect the manner in which the instrument may be negotiated.

§ 3–206. Restrictive Indorsement.
(a) An indorsement limiting payment to a particular person or otherwise prohibiting further transfer or negotiation of the instrument is not effective to prevent further transfer or negotiation of the instrument.

(b) An indorsement stating a condition to the right of the indorsee to receive payment does not affect the right of the indorsee to enforce the instrument. A person paying the instrument or taking it for value or collection may disregard the condition, and the rights and liabilities of that person are not affected by whether the condition has been fulfilled.

(c) If an instrument bears an indorsement (i) described in Section 4–201(b), or (ii) in blank or to a particular bank using the words "for deposit," "for collection," or other words indicating a purpose of having the instrument collected by a bank for the indorser or for a particular account, the following rules apply:

(1) A person, other than a bank, who purchases the instrument when so indorsed converts the instrument unless the amount paid for the instrument is received by the indorser or applied consistently with the indorsement.

(2) A depositary bank that purchases the instrument or takes it for collection when so indorsed converts the instrument unless the amount paid by the bank with respect to the instrument is received by the indorser or applied consistently with the indorsement.

(3) A payor bank that is also the depositary bank or that takes the instrument for immediate payment over the counter from a person other than a collecting bank converts the instrument unless the proceeds of the instrument are received by the indorser or applied consistently with the indorsement.

(4) Except as otherwise provided in paragraph (3), a payor bank or intermediary bank may disregard the indorsement and is not liable if the proceeds of the instrument are not received by the indorser or applied consistently with the indorsement.

(d) Except for an indorsement covered by subsection (c), if an instrument bears an indorsement using words to the effect that payment is to be made to the indorsee as agent, trustee, or other fiduciary for the benefit of the indorser or another person, the following rules apply:

(1) Unless there is notice of breach of fiduciary duty as provided in Section 3–307, a person who purchases the instrument from the indorsee or takes the instrument from the indorsee for collection or payment may pay the proceeds of payment or the value given for the instrument to the indorsee without regard to whether the indorsee violates a fiduciary duty to the indorser.

(2) A subsequent transferee of the instrument or person who pays the instrument is neither given notice nor otherwise affected by the restriction in the indorsement unless the transferee or payor knows that the fiduciary dealt with the instrument or its proceeds in breach of fiduciary duty.

(e) The presence on an instrument of an indorsement to which this section applies does not prevent a purchaser of the instrument from becoming a holder in due course of the instrument unless the purchaser is a converter under subsection (c) or has notice or knowledge of breach of fiduciary duty as stated in subsection (d).

(f) In an action to enforce the obligation of a party to pay the instrument, the obligor has a defense if payment would violate an indorsement to which this section applies and the payment is not permitted by this section.

§ 3–207. Reacquisition.
Reacquisition of an instrument occurs if it is transferred to a former holder, by negotiation or otherwise. A former holder who reacquires the instrument may cancel indorsements made after the reacquirer first became a holder of the instrument. If the cancellation causes the instrument to be payable to the reacquirer or to bearer, the reacquirer may negotiate the instrument. An indorser whose indorsement is canceled is discharged, and the discharge is effective against any subsequent holder.

Part 3—Enforcement of Instruments
§ 3–301. Person Entitled to Enforce Instrument.
"Person entitled to enforce" an instrument means (i) the holder of the instrument, (ii) a nonholder in possession of the instrument who has the rights of a holder, or (iii) a person not in possession of the instrument who is entitled to enforce the instrument pursuant to Section 3–309 or 3–418(d). A person may be a person entitled to enforce the instrument even though the person is not the owner of the instrument or is in wrongful possession of the instrument.

§ 3–302. Holder in Due Course.
(a) Subject to subsection (c) and Section 3–106(d), "holder in due course" means the holder of an instrument if:

(1) the instrument when issued or negotiated to the holder does not bear such apparent evidence of forgery or alteration or is not otherwise so irregular or incomplete as to call into question its authenticity; and

(2) the holder took the instrument (i) for value, (ii) in good faith, (iii) without notice that the instrument is overdue or has been dishonored or that there is an uncured default with respect to payment of another instrument issued as part of the same series, (iv) without notice that the instrument contains an unauthorized signature or has been altered, (v) without notice of any claim to the instrument described in Section 3–306, and (vi) without notice that any party has a defense or claim in recoupment described in Section 3–305(a).

(b) Notice of discharge of a party, other than discharge in an insolvency proceeding, is not notice of a defense under subsection (a), but discharge is effective against a person who became a holder in due course with notice of the discharge. Public filing or recording of a document does not of itself constitute notice of a defense, claim in recoupment, or claim to the instrument.

(c) Except to the extent a transferor or predecessor in interest has rights as a holder in due course, a person does not acquire rights of a holder in due course of an instrument taken (i) by legal process or by purchase in an execution, bankruptcy, or creditor's sale or similar proceeding, (ii) by purchase as part of a bulk transaction not in ordinary course of business of the transferor, or (iii) as the successor in interest to an estate or other organization.

(d) If, under Section 3–303(a)(1), the promise of performance that is the consideration for an instrument has been partially performed, the holder may assert rights as a holder in due course of the instrument only to the fraction of the amount payable under the instrument equal to the value of the partial performance divided by the value of the promised performance.

(e) If (i) the person entitled to enforce an instrument has only a security interest in the instrument and (ii) the person obliged to pay the instrument has a defense, claim in recoupment, or claim to the instrument that may be asserted against the person who granted the security interest, the person entitled to enforce the instrument may assert rights as a holder in due course only to an amount payable under the instrument which, at the time of enforcement of the instrument, does not exceed the amount of the unpaid obligation secured.

(f) To be effective, notice must be received at a time and in a manner that gives a reasonable opportunity to act on it.

(g) This section is subject to any law limiting status as a holder in due course in particular classes of transactions.

§ 3–303. Value and Consideration.
(a) An instrument is issued or transferred for value if:

(1) the instrument is issued or transferred for a promise of performance, to the extent the promise has been performed;

(2) the transferee acquires a security interest or other lien in the instrument other than a lien obtained by judicial proceeding;

(3) the instrument is issued or transferred as payment of, or as security for, an antecedent claim against any person, whether or not the claim is due;

(4) the instrument is issued or transferred in exchange for a negotiable instrument; or

(5) the instrument is issued or transferred in exchange for the incurring of an irrevocable obligation to a third party by the person taking the instrument.

(b) "Consideration" means any consideration sufficient to support a simple contract. The drawer or maker of an instrument has a defense if the instrument is issued without consideration. If an instrument is issued for a promise of performance, the issuer has a defense to the extent performance of the promise is due and the promise has not been performed. If an instrument is issued for value as stated in subsection (a), the instrument is also issued for consideration.

§ 3–304. Overdue Instrument.

(a) An instrument payable on demand becomes overdue at the earliest of the following times:

(1) on the day after the day demand for payment is duly made;

(2) if the instrument is a check, 90 days after its date; or

(3) if the instrument is not a check, when the instrument has been outstanding for a period of time after its date which is unreasonably long under the circumstances of the particular case in light of the nature of the instrument and usage of the trade.

(b) With respect to an instrument payable at a definite time the following rules apply:

(1) If the principal is payable in installments and a due date has not been accelerated, the instrument becomes overdue upon default under the instrument for nonpayment of an installment, and the instrument remains overdue until the default is cured.

(2) If the principal is not payable in installments and the due date has not been accelerated, the instrument becomes overdue on the day after the due date.

(3) If a due date with respect to principal has been accelerated, the instrument becomes overdue on the day after the accelerated due date.

(c) Unless the due date of principal has been accelerated, an instrument does not become overdue if there is default in payment of interest but no default in payment of principal.

§ 3–305. Defenses and Claims in Recoupment.

(a) Except as stated in subsection (b), the right to enforce the obligation of a party to pay an instrument is subject to the following:

(1) a defense of the obligor based on (i) infancy of the obligor to the extent it is a defense to a simple contract, (ii) duress, lack of legal capacity, or illegality of the transaction which, under other law, nullifies the obligation of the obligor, (iii) fraud that induced the obligor to sign the instrument with neither knowledge nor reasonable opportunity to learn of its character or its essential terms, or (iv) discharge of the obligor in insolvency proceedings;

(2) a defense of the obligor stated in another section of this Article or a defense of the obligor that would be available if the person entitled to enforce the instrument were enforcing a right to payment under a simple contract; and

(3) a claim in recoupment of the obligor against the original payee of the instrument if the claim arose from the transaction that gave rise to the instrument; but the claim of the obligor may be asserted against a transferee of the instrument only to reduce the amount owing on the instrument at the time the action is brought.

(b) The right of a holder in due course to enforce the obligation of a party to pay the instrument is subject to defenses of the obligor stated in subsection (a)(1), but is not subject to defenses of the obligor stated in subsection (a)(2) or claims in recoupment stated in subsection (a)(3) against a person other than the holder.

(c) Except as stated in subsection (d), in an action to enforce the obligation of a party to pay the instrument, the obligor may not assert against the person entitled to enforce the instrument a defense, claim in recoupment, or claim to the instrument (Section 3–306) of another person, but the other person's claim to the instrument may be asserted by the obligor if the other person is joined in the action and personally asserts the claim against the person entitled to enforce the instrument. An obligor is not obliged to pay the instrument if the person seeking enforcement of the instrument does not have rights of a holder in due course and the obligor proves that the instrument is a lost or stolen instrument.

(d) In an action to enforce the obligation of an accommodation party to pay an instrument, the accommodation party may assert against the person entitled to enforce the instrument any defense or claim in recoupment under subsection (a) that the accommodated party could assert against the person entitled to enforce the instrument, except the defenses of discharge in insolvency proceedings, infancy, and lack of legal capacity.

§ 3–306. Claims to an Instrument.

A person taking an instrument, other than a person having rights of a holder in due course, is subject to a claim of a property or possessory right in the instrument or its proceeds, including a claim to rescind a negotiation and to recover the instrument or its proceeds. A person having rights of a holder in due course takes free of the claim to the instrument.

§ 3–307. Notice of Breach of Fiduciary Duty.

(a) In this section:

(1) "Fiduciary" means an agent, trustee, partner, corporate officer or director, or other representative owing a fiduciary duty with respect to an instrument.

(2) "Represented person" means the principal, beneficiary, partnership, corporation, or other person to whom the duty stated in paragraph (1) is owed.

(b) If (i) an instrument is taken from a fiduciary for payment or collection or for value, (ii) the taker has knowledge of the fiduciary status of the fiduciary, and (iii) the represented person makes a claim to the instrument or its proceeds on the basis that the transaction of the fiduciary is a breach of fiduciary duty, the following rules apply:

(1) Notice of breach of fiduciary duty by the fiduciary is notice of the claim of the represented person.

(2) In the case of an instrument payable to the represented person or the fiduciary as such, the taker has notice of the breach of fiduciary duty if the instrument is (i) taken in payment of or as security for a debt known by the taker to be the personal debt of the fiduciary, (ii) taken in a transaction known by the taker to be for the personal benefit of the fiduciary, or (iii) deposited to an account other than an account of the fiduciary, as such, or an account of the represented person.

(3) If an instrument is issued by the represented person or the fiduciary as such, and made payable to the fiduciary personally, the taker does not have notice of the breach of fiduciary duty unless the taker knows of the breach of fiduciary duty.

(4) If an instrument is issued by the represented person or the fiduciary as such, to the taker as payee, the taker has notice of the breach of fiduciary duty if the instrument is (i) taken in payment of or as security for a debt known by the taker to be the personal debt of the fiduciary, (ii) taken in a transaction known by the taker to be for the personal benefit of the fiduciary, or (iii) deposited to an account other than an account of the fiduciary, as such, or an account of the represented person.

§ 3–308. Proof of Signatures and Status as Holder in Due Course.

(a) In an action with respect to an instrument, the authenticity of, and authority to make, each signature on the instrument is admitted unless specifically denied in the pleadings. If the validity of a signature is denied in the pleadings, the burden of establishing validity is on the person claiming validity, but the signature is presumed to be authentic and authorized unless the action is to enforce the liability of the purported signer and the signer is dead or incompetent at the time of trial of the issue of validity of the signature. If an action to enforce the instrument is brought against a person as the undisclosed principal of a person who signed the instrument as a party to the instrument, the plaintiff has the burden of establishing that the defendant is liable on the instrument as a represented person under Section 3–402(a).

(b) If the validity of signatures is admitted or proved and there is compliance with subsection (a), a plaintiff producing the instrument is entitled to payment if the plaintiff proves entitlement to enforce the instrument under Section 3–301, unless the defendant proves a defense or claim in recoupment. If a defense or claim in recoupment is proved, the right to payment of the plaintiff is subject to the defense or claim, except to the extent the plaintiff proves that the plaintiff has rights of a holder in due course which are not subject to the defense or claim.

§ 3–309. Enforcement of Lost, Destroyed, or Stolen Instrument.

(a) A person not in possession of an instrument is entitled to enforce the instrument if (i) the person was in possession of the instrument and entitled to enforce it when loss of possession occurred, (ii) the loss of possession was not the result of a transfer by the person or a lawful seizure, and (iii) the person cannot reasonably obtain possession of the instrument because the instrument was destroyed, its whereabouts cannot be determined, or it is in the wrongful possession of an unknown person or a person that cannot be found or is not amenable to service of process.

(b) A person seeking enforcement of an instrument under subsection (a) must prove the terms of the instrument and the person's right to enforce the instrument. If that proof is made, Section 3–308 applies to the case as if the person seeking enforcement had produced the instrument. The court may not enter judgment in favor of the person seeking enforcement unless it finds that the person required to pay the instrument is adequately protected against loss that might occur by reason of a claim by another person to enforce the instrument. Adequate protection may be provided by any reasonable means.

§ 3–310. Effect of Instrument on Obligation for Which Taken.

(a) Unless otherwise agreed, if a certified check, cashier's check, or teller's check is taken for an obligation, the obligation is discharged to the same extent discharge would result if an amount of money equal to the amount of the instrument were taken in payment of the obligation. Discharge of the obligation does not affect any liability that the obligor may have as an indorser of the instrument.

(b) Unless otherwise agreed and except as provided in subsection (a), if a note or an uncertified check is taken for an obligation, the obligation is suspended to the same extent the obligation would be discharged if an amount of money equal to the amount of the instrument were taken, and the following rules apply:

(1) In the case of an uncertified check, suspension of the obligation continues until dishonor of the check or until it is paid or certified. Payment or certification of the check results in discharge of the obligation to the extent of the amount of the check.

(2) In the case of a note, suspension of the obligation continues until dishonor of the note or until it is paid. Payment of the note results in discharge of the obligation to the extent of the payment.

(3) Except as provided in paragraph (4), if the check or note is dishonored and the obligee of the obligation for which the instrument was taken is the person entitled to enforce the instrument, the obligee may enforce either the instrument or the obligation. In the case of an instrument of a third person which is negotiated to the obligee by the obligor, discharge of the obligor on the instrument also discharges the obligation.

(4) If the person entitled to enforce the instrument taken for an obligation is a person other than the obligee, the obligee may not enforce the obligation to the extent the obligation is suspended. If the obligee is the person entitled to enforce the instrument but no longer has possession of it because it was lost, stolen, or destroyed, the obligation may not be enforced to the extent of the amount payable on the instrument, and to that extent the obligee's rights against the obligor are limited to enforcement of the instrument.

(c) If an instrument other than one described in subsection (a) or (b) is taken for an obligation, the effect is (i) that stated in subsection (a) if the instrument is one on which a bank is liable as maker or acceptor, or (ii) that stated in subsection (b) in any other case.

§ 3–311. Accord and Satisfaction by Use of Instrument.

(a) If a person against whom a claim is asserted proves that (i) that person in good faith tendered an instrument to the claimant as full satisfaction of the claim, (ii) the amount of the claim was unliquidated or subject to a bona fide dispute, and (iii) the claimant obtained payment of the instrument, the following subsections apply.

(b) Unless subsection (c) applies, the claim is discharged if the person against whom the claim is asserted proves that the instrument or an accompanying written communication contained a conspicuous statement to the effect that the instrument was tendered as full satisfaction of the claim.

(c) Subject to subsection (d), a claim is not discharged under subsection (b) if either of the following applies:

(1) The claimant, if an organization, proves that (i) within a reasonable time before the tender, the claimant sent a conspicuous statement to the person against whom the claim is asserted that communications concerning disputed debts, including an instrument tendered as full satisfaction of a debt, are to be sent to a designated person, office, or place, and (ii) the instrument or accompanying communication was not received by that designated person, office, or place.

(2) The claimant, whether or not an organization, proves that within 90 days after payment of the instrument, the claimant tendered repayment of the amount of the instrument to the person against whom the claim is asserted. This paragraph does not apply if the claimant is an organization that sent a statement complying with paragraph (1)(i).

(d) A claim is discharged if the person against whom the claim is asserted proves that within a reasonable time before collection of the instrument was initiated, the claimant, or an agent of the claimant having direct responsibility with respect to the disputed obligation, knew that the instrument was tendered in full satisfaction of the claim.

§ 3–312. Lost, Destroyed, or Stolen Cashier's Check, Teller's Check, or Certified Check.*

(a) In this section:

(1) "Check" means a cashier's check, teller's check, or certified check.

(2) "Claimant" means a person who claims the right to receive the amount of a cashier's check, teller's check, or certified check that was lost, destroyed, or stolen.

(3) "Declaration of loss" means a written statement, made under penalty of perjury, to the effect that (i) the declarer lost possession of a check, (ii) the declarer is the drawer or payee of the check, in the case of a certified check, or the remitter or payee of the check, in the case of a cashier's check or teller's check, (iii) the loss of possession was not the result of a transfer by the declarer or a lawful seizure, and (iv) the declarer cannot reasonably obtain possession of the check because the check was destroyed, its whereabouts cannot be determined, or it is in the wrongful possession of an unknown person or a person that cannot be found or is not amenable to service of process.

(4) "Obligated bank" means the issuer of a cashier's check or teller's check or the acceptor of a certified check.

(b) A claimant may assert a claim to the amount of a check by a communication to the obligated bank describing the check with reasonable certainty and requesting payment of the amount of the check, if (i) the claimant is the drawer or payee of a certified check or the remitter or payee of a cashier's check or teller's check, (ii) the communication contains or is accompanied by a declaration of loss of the claimant with respect to the check, (iii) the communication is received at a time and in a manner affording the bank a reasonable time to act on it before the check is paid, and (iv) the claimant provides reasonable identification if requested by the obligated bank. Delivery of a declaration of loss is a warranty of the truth of the statements made in the declaration. If a claim is asserted in compliance with this subsection, the following rules apply:

(1) The claim becomes enforceable at the later of (i) the time the claim is asserted, or (ii) the 90th day following the date of the check, in the case of a cashier's check or teller's check, or the 90th day following the date of the acceptance, in the case of a certified check.

(2) Until the claim becomes enforceable, it has no legal effect and the obligated bank may pay the check or, in the case of a teller's check, may permit the drawee to pay the check. Payment to a person entitled to enforce the check discharges all liability of the obligated bank with respect to the check.

(3) If the claim becomes enforceable before the check is presented for payment, the obligated bank is not obliged to pay the check.

(4) When the claim becomes enforceable, the obligated bank becomes obliged to pay the amount of the check to the claimant if payment of the check has not been made to a person entitled to enforce the check. Subject to Section 4–302(a)(1), payment to the claimant discharges all liability of the obligated bank with respect to the check.

(c) If the obligated bank pays the amount of a check to a claimant under subsection (b)(4) and the check is presented for payment by a person having rights of a holder in due course, the claimant is obliged to (i) refund the payment to the obligated bank if the check is paid, or (ii) pay the amount of the check to the person having rights of a holder in due course if the check is dishonored.

(d) If a claimant has the right to assert a claim under subsection (b) and is also a person entitled to enforce a cashier's check, teller's check, or certified check which is lost, destroyed, or stolen, the claimant may assert rights with respect to the check either under this section or Section 3–309.

Added in 1991.

Part 4—Liability of Parties

§ 3–401. Signature.

(a) A person is not liable on an instrument unless (i) the person signed the instrument, or (ii) the person is represented by an agent or representative who signed the instrument and the signature is binding on the represented person under Section 3–402.

*[Section 3–312 was not adopted as part of the 1990 Official Text of Revised Article 3. It was officially approved and recommended for enactment in all states in August 1991 by the National Conference of Commissioners on Uniform State Laws.]

(b) A signature may be made (i) manually or by means of a device or machine, and (ii) by the use of any name, including a trade or assumed name, or by a word, mark, or symbol executed or adopted by a person with present intention to authenticate a writing.

§ 3–402. Signature by Representative.

(a) If a person acting, or purporting to act, as a representative signs an instrument by signing either the name of the represented person or the name of the signer, the represented person is bound by the signature to the same extent the represented person would be bound if the signature were on a simple contract. If the represented person is bound, the signature of the representative is the "authorized signature of the represented person" and the represented person is liable on the instrument, whether or not identified in the instrument.

(b) If a representative signs the name of the representative to an instrument and the signature is an authorized signature of the represented person, the following rules apply:

(1) If the form of the signature shows unambiguously that the signature is made on behalf of the represented person who is identified in the instrument, the representative is not liable on the instrument.

(2) Subject to subsection (c), if (i) the form of the signature does not show unambiguously that the signature is made in a representative capacity or (ii) the represented person is not identified in the instrument, the representative is liable on the instrument to a holder in due course that took the instrument without notice that the representative was not intended to be liable on the instrument. With respect to any other person, the representative is liable on the instrument unless the representative proves that the original parties did not intend the representative to be liable on the instrument.

(c) If a representative signs the name of the representative as drawer of a check without indication of the representative status and the check is payable from an account of the represented person who is identified on the check, the signer is not liable on the check if the signature is an authorized signature of the represented person.

§ 3–403. Unauthorized Signature.

(a) Unless otherwise provided in this Article or Article 4, an unauthorized signature is ineffective except as the signature of the unauthorized signer in favor of a person who in good faith pays the instrument or takes it for value. An unauthorized signature may be ratified for all purposes of this Article.

(b) If the signature of more than one person is required to constitute the authorized signature of an organization, the signature of the organization is unauthorized if one of the required signatures is lacking.

(c) The civil or criminal liability of a person who makes an unauthorized signature is not affected by any provision of this Article which makes the unauthorized signature effective for the purposes of this Article.

§ 3–404. Impostors; Fictitious Payees.

(a) If an impostor, by use of the mails or otherwise, induces the issuer of an instrument to issue the instrument to the impostor, or to a person acting in concert with the impostor, by impersonating the payee of the instrument or a person authorized to act for the payee, an indorsement of the instrument by any person in the name of the payee is effective as the indorsement of the payee in favor of a person who, in good faith, pays the instrument or takes it for value or for collection.

(b) If (i) a person whose intent determines to whom an instrument is payable (Section 3–110(a) or (b)) does not intend the person identified as payee to have any interest in the instrument, or (ii) the person identified as payee of an instrument is a fictitious person, the following rules apply until the instrument is negotiated by special indorsement:

(1) Any person in possession of the instrument is its holder.

(2) An indorsement by any person in the name of the payee stated in the instrument is effective as the indorsement of the payee in favor of a person who, in good faith, pays the instrument or takes it for value or for collection.

(c) Under subsection (a) or (b), an indorsement is made in the name of a payee if (i) it is made in a name substantially similar to that of the payee or (ii) the instrument, whether or not indorsed, is deposited in a depositary bank to an account in a name substantially similar to that of the payee.

(d) With respect to an instrument to which subsection (a) or (b) applies, if a person paying the instrument or taking it for value or for collection fails to exercise ordinary care in paying or taking the instrument and that failure substantially contributes to loss resulting from payment of the instrument, the person bearing the loss may recover from the person failing to exercise ordinary care to the extent the failure to exercise ordinary care contributed to the loss.

§ 3–405. Employer's Responsibility for Fraudulent Indorsement by Employee.

(a) In this section:

(1) "Employee" includes an independent contractor and employee of an independent contractor retained by the employer.

(2) "Fraudulent indorsement" means (i) in the case of an instrument payable to the employer, a forged indorsement purporting to be that of the employer, or (ii) in the case of an instrument with respect to which the employer is the issuer, a forged indorsement purporting to be that of the person identified as payee.

(3) "Responsibility" with respect to instruments means authority (i) to sign or indorse instruments on behalf of the employer, (ii) to process instruments received by the employer for bookkeeping purposes, for deposit to an account, or for other disposition, (iii) to prepare or process instruments for issue in the name of the employer, (iv) to supply information determining the names or addresses of payees of instruments to be issued in the name of the employer, (v) to control the disposition of instruments to be issued in the name of the employer, or (vi) to act otherwise with respect to instruments in a responsible capacity. "Responsibility" does not include authority that merely allows an employee to have access to instruments or blank or incomplete instrument forms that are being stored or transported or are part of incoming or outgoing mail, or similar access.

(b) For the purpose of determining the rights and liabilities of a person who, in good faith, pays an instrument or takes it for value or for collection, if an employer entrusted an employee with responsibility with respect to the instrument and the employee or a person acting in concert with the employee makes a fraudulent indorsement of the instrument, the indorsement is effective as the indorsement of the person to whom the instrument is payable if it is made in the name of that person. If the person paying the instrument or taking it for value or for collection fails to exercise ordinary care in paying or taking the instrument and that failure substantially contributes to loss resulting from the fraud, the person bearing the loss may recover from the person failing to exercise ordinary care to the extent the failure to exercise ordinary care contributed to the loss.

(c) Under subsection (b), an indorsement is made in the name of the person to whom an instrument is payable if (i) it is made in a name substantially similar to the name of that person or (ii) the instrument, whether or not indorsed, is deposited in a depositary bank to an account in a name substantially similar to the name of that person.

§ 3–406. Negligence Contributing to Forged Signature or Alteration of Instrument.

(a) A person whose failure to exercise ordinary care substantially contributes to an alteration of an instrument or to the making of a forged signature on an instrument is precluded from asserting the alteration or the forgery against a person who, in good faith, pays the instrument or takes it for value or for collection.

(b) Under subsection (a), if the person asserting the preclusion fails to exercise ordinary care in paying or taking the instrument and that failure substantially contributes to loss, the loss is allocated between the person precluded and the person asserting the preclusion according to the extent to which the failure of each to exercise ordinary care contributed to the loss.

(c) Under subsection (a), the burden of proving failure to exercise ordinary care is on the person asserting the preclusion. Under subsection (b), the burden of proving failure to exercise ordinary care is on the person precluded.

§ 3–407. Alteration.

(a) "Alteration" means (i) an unauthorized change in an instrument that purports to modify in any respect the obligation of a party, or (ii) an unauthorized addition of words or numbers or other change to an incomplete instrument relating to the obligation of a party.

(b) Except as provided in subsection (c), an alteration fraudulently made discharges a party whose obligation is affected by the alteration unless that party assents or is precluded from asserting the alteration. No other alteration discharges a party, and the instrument may be enforced according to its original terms.

(c) A payor bank or drawee paying a fraudulently altered instrument or a person taking it for value, in good faith and without notice of the alteration, may enforce rights with respect to the instrument (i) according to its original terms, or (ii) in the case of an incomplete instrument altered by unauthorized completion, according to its terms as completed.

§ 3–408. Drawee Not Liable on Unaccepted Draft.

A check or other draft does not of itself operate as an assignment of funds in the hands of the drawee available for its payment, and the drawee is not liable on the instrument until the drawee accepts it.

§ 3–409. Acceptance of Draft; Certified Check.

(a) "Acceptance" means the drawee's signed agreement to pay a draft as presented. It must be written on the draft and may consist of the drawee's signature alone. Acceptance may be made at any time and becomes effective when notification pursuant to instructions is given or the accepted draft is delivered for the purpose of giving rights on the acceptance to any person.

(b) A draft may be accepted although it has not been signed by the drawer, is otherwise incomplete, is overdue, or has been dishonored.

(c) If a draft is payable at a fixed period after sight and the acceptor fails to date the acceptance, the holder may complete the acceptance by supplying a date in good faith.

(d) "Certified check" means a check accepted by the bank on which it is drawn. Acceptance may be made as stated in subsection (a) or by a writing on the check which indicates that the check is certified. The drawee of a check has no obligation to certify the check, and refusal to certify is not dishonor of the check.

§ 3–410. Acceptance Varying Draft.

(a) If the terms of a drawee's acceptance vary from the terms of the draft as presented, the holder may refuse the acceptance and treat the draft as dishonored. In that case, the drawee may cancel the acceptance.

(b) The terms of a draft are not varied by an acceptance to pay at a particular bank or place in the United States, unless the acceptance states that the draft is to be paid only at that bank or place.

(c) If the holder assents to an acceptance varying the terms of a draft, the obligation of each drawer and indorser that does not expressly assent to the acceptance is discharged.

§ 3–411. Refusal to Pay Cashier's Checks, Teller's Checks, and Certified Checks.

(a) In this section, "obligated bank" means the acceptor of a certified check or the issuer of a cashier's check or teller's check bought from the issuer.

(b) If the obligated bank wrongfully (i) refuses to pay a cashier's check or certified check, (ii) stops payment of a teller's check, or (iii) refuses to pay a dishonored teller's check, the person asserting the right to enforce the check is entitled to compensation for expenses and loss of interest resulting from the nonpayment and may recover consequential damages if the obligated bank refuses to pay after receiving notice of particular circumstances giving rise to the damages.

(c) Expenses or consequential damages under subsection (b) are not recoverable if the refusal of the obligated bank to pay occurs because (i) the bank suspends payments, (ii) the obligated bank asserts a claim or defense of the bank that it has reasonable grounds to believe is available against the person entitled to enforce the instrument, (iii) the obligated bank has a reasonable doubt whether the person demanding payment is the person entitled to enforce the instrument, or (iv) payment is prohibited by law.

§ 3–412. Obligation of Issuer of Note or Cashier's Check.

The issuer of a note or cashier's check or other draft drawn on the drawer is obliged to pay the instrument (i) according to its terms at the time it was issued or, if not issued, at the time it first came into possession of a holder, or (ii) if the issuer signed an incomplete instrument, according to its terms when completed, to the extent stated in Sections 3–115 and 3–407. The obligation is owed to a person entitled to enforce the instrument or to an indorser who paid the instrument under Section 3–415.

§ 3–413. Obligation of Acceptor.

(a) The acceptor of a draft is obliged to pay the draft (i) according to its terms at the time it was accepted, even though the acceptance states that the draft is payable "as originally drawn" or equivalent terms, (ii) if the acceptance varies the terms of the draft, according to the terms of the draft as varied, or (iii) if the acceptance is of a draft that is an incomplete instrument, according to its terms when completed, to the extent stated in Sections 3–115 and 3–407. The obligation is owed to a person entitled to enforce the draft or to the drawer or an indorser who paid the draft under Section 3–414 or 3–415.

(b) If the certification of a check or other acceptance of a draft states the amount certified or accepted, the obligation of the acceptor is that amount. If (i) the certification or acceptance does not state an amount, (ii) the amount of the instrument is subsequently raised, and (iii) the instrument is then negotiated to a holder in due course, the obligation of the acceptor is the amount of the instrument at the time it was taken by the holder in due course.

§ 3–414. Obligation of Drawer.

(a) This section does not apply to cashier's checks or other drafts drawn on the drawer.

(b) If an unaccepted draft is dishonored, the drawer is obliged to pay the draft (i) according to its terms at the time it was issued or, if not issued, at the time it first came into possession of a holder, or (ii) if the drawer signed an incomplete instrument, according to its terms when completed, to the extent stated in Sections 3–115 and 3–407. The obligation is owed to a person entitled to enforce the draft or to an indorser who paid the draft under Section 3–415.

(c) If a draft is accepted by a bank, the drawer is discharged, regardless of when or by whom acceptance was obtained.

(d) If a draft is accepted and the acceptor is not a bank, the obligation of the drawer to pay the draft if the draft is dishonored by the acceptor is the same as the obligation of an indorser under Section 3–415(a) and (c).

(e) If a draft states that it is drawn "without recourse" or otherwise disclaims liability of the drawer to pay the draft, the drawer is not liable under subsection (b) to pay the draft if the draft is not a check. A disclaimer of the liability stated in subsection (b) is not effective if the draft is a check.

(f) If (i) a check is not presented for payment or given to a depositary bank for collection within 30 days after its date, (ii) the drawee suspends payments after expiration of the 30-day period without paying the check, and (iii) because of the suspension of payments, the drawer is deprived of funds maintained with the drawee to cover payment of the check, the drawer to the extent deprived of funds may discharge its obligation to pay the check by assigning to the person entitled to enforce the check the rights of the drawer against the drawee with respect to the funds.

§ 3–415. Obligation of Indorser.

(a) Subject to subsections (b), (c), and (d) and to Section 3–419(d), if an instrument is dishonored, an indorser is obliged to pay the amount due on the instrument (i) according to the terms of the instrument at the time it was indorsed, or (ii) if the indorser indorsed an incomplete instrument, according to its terms when completed, to the extent stated in Sections 3–115 and 3–407. The obligation of the indorser is owed to a person entitled to enforce the instrument or to a subsequent indorser who paid the instrument under this section.

(b) If an indorsement states that it is made "without recourse" or otherwise disclaims liability of the indorser, the indorser is not liable under subsection (a) to pay the instrument.

(c) If notice of dishonor of an instrument is required by Section 3–503 and notice of dishonor complying with that section is not given to an indorser, the liability of the indorser under subsection (a) is discharged.

(d) If a draft is accepted by a bank after an indorsement is made, the liability of the indorser under subsection (a) is discharged.

(e) If an indorser of a check is liable under subsection (a) and the check is not presented for payment, or given to a depositary bank for collection, within 30 days after the day the indorsement was made, the liability of the indorser under subsection (a) is discharged.

As amended in 1993.

§ 3–416. Transfer Warranties.

(a) A person who transfers an instrument for consideration warrants to the transferee and, if the transfer is by indorsement, to any subsequent transferee that:

> **(1)** the warrantor is a person entitled to enforce the instrument;
>
> **(2)** all signatures on the instrument are authentic and authorized;
>
> **(3)** the instrument has not been altered;
>
> **(4)** the instrument is not subject to a defense or claim in recoupment of any party which can be asserted against the warrantor; and
>
> **(5)** the warrantor has no knowledge of any insolvency proceeding commenced with respect to the maker or acceptor or, in the case of an unaccepted draft, the drawer.

(b) A person to whom the warranties under subsection (a) are made and who took the instrument in good faith may recover from the warrantor as damages for breach of warranty an amount equal to the loss suffered as a result of the breach, but not more than the amount of the instrument plus expenses and loss of interest incurred as a result of the breach.

(c) The warranties stated in subsection (a) cannot be disclaimed with respect to checks. Unless notice of a claim for breach of warranty is given to the warrantor within 30 days after the claimant has reason to know of the breach and the identity of the warrantor, the liability of the warrantor under subsection (b) is discharged to the extent of any loss caused by the delay in giving notice of the claim.

(d) A [cause of action] for breach of warranty under this section accrues when the claimant has reason to know of the breach.

§ 3–417. Presentment Warranties.

(a) If an unaccepted draft is presented to the drawee for payment or acceptance and the drawee pays or accepts the draft, (i) the person obtaining payment or acceptance, at the time of presentment, and (ii) a previous transferor of the draft, at the time of transfer, warrant to the drawee making payment or accepting the draft in good faith that:

(1) the warrantor is, or was, at the time the warrantor transferred the draft, a person entitled to enforce the draft or authorized to obtain payment or acceptance of the draft on behalf of a person entitled to enforce the draft;

(2) the draft has not been altered; and

(3) the warrantor has no knowledge that the signature of the drawer of the draft is unauthorized.

(b) A drawee making payment may recover from any warrantor damages for breach of warranty equal to the amount paid by the drawee less the amount the drawee received or is entitled to receive from the drawer because of the payment. In addition, the drawee is entitled to compensation for expenses and loss of interest resulting from the breach. The right of the drawee to recover damages under this subsection is not affected by any failure of the drawee to exercise ordinary care in making payment. If the drawee accepts the draft, breach of warranty is a defense to the obligation of the acceptor. If the acceptor makes payment with respect to the draft, the acceptor is entitled to recover from any warrantor for breach of warranty the amounts stated in this subsection.

(c) If a drawee asserts a claim for breach of warranty under subsection (a) based on an unauthorized indorsement of the draft or an alteration of the draft, the warrantor may defend by proving that the indorsement is effective under Section 3–404 or 3–405 or the drawer is precluded under Section 3–406 or 4–406 from asserting against the drawee the unauthorized indorsement or alteration.

(d) If (i) a dishonored draft is presented for payment to the drawer or an indorser or (ii) any other instrument is presented for payment to a party obliged to pay the instrument, and (iii) payment is received, the following rules apply:

(1) The person obtaining payment and a prior transferor of the instrument warrant to the person making payment in good faith that the warrantor is, or was, at the time the warrantor transferred the instrument, a person entitled to enforce the instrument or authorized to obtain payment on behalf of a person entitled to enforce the instrument.

(2) The person making payment may recover from any warrantor for breach of warranty an amount equal to the amount paid plus expenses and loss of interest resulting from the breach.

(e) The warranties stated in subsections (a) and (d) cannot be disclaimed with respect to checks. Unless notice of a claim for breach of warranty is given to the warrantor within 30 days after the claimant has reason to know of the breach and the identity of the warrantor, the liability of the warrantor under subsection (b) or (d) is discharged to the extent of any loss caused by the delay in giving notice of the claim.

(f) A [cause of action] for breach of warranty under this section accrues when the claimant has reason to know of the breach.

§ 3–418. Payment or Acceptance by Mistake.

(a) Except as provided in subsection (c), if the drawee of a draft pays or accepts the draft and the drawee acted on the mistaken belief that (i) payment of the draft had not been stopped pursuant to Section 4–403 or (ii) the signature of the drawer of the draft was authorized, the drawee may recover the amount of the draft from the person to whom or for whose benefit payment was made or, in the case of acceptance, may revoke the acceptance. Rights of the drawee under this subsection are not affected by failure of the drawee to exercise ordinary care in paying or accepting the draft.

(b) Except as provided in subsection (c), if an instrument has been paid or accepted by mistake and the case is not covered by subsection (a), the person paying or accepting may, to the extent permitted by the law governing mistake and restitution, (i) recover the payment from the person to whom or for whose benefit payment was made or (ii) in the case of acceptance, may revoke the acceptance.

(c) The remedies provided by subsection (a) or (b) may not be asserted against a person who took the instrument in good faith and for value or who in good faith changed position in reliance on the payment or acceptance. This subsection does not limit remedies provided by Section 3–417 or 4–407.

(d) Notwithstanding Section 4–215, if an instrument is paid or accepted by mistake and the payor or acceptor recovers payment or revokes acceptance under subsection (a) or (b), the instrument is deemed not to have been paid or accepted and is treated as dishonored, and the person from whom payment is recovered has rights as a person entitled to enforce the dishonored instrument.

§ 3–419. Instruments Signed for Accommodation.

(a) If an instrument is issued for value given for the benefit of a party to the instrument ("accommodated party") and another party to the instrument ("accommodation party") signs the instrument for the purpose of incurring liability on the instrument without being a direct beneficiary of the value given for the instrument, the instrument is signed by the accommodation party "for accommodation."

(b) An accommodation party may sign the instrument as maker, drawer, acceptor, or indorser and, subject to subsection (d), is obliged to pay the instrument in the capacity in which the accommodation party signs. The obligation of an accommodation party may be enforced notwithstanding any statute of frauds and whether or not the accommodation party receives consideration for the accommodation.

(c) A person signing an instrument is presumed to be an accommodation party and there is notice that the instrument is signed for accommodation if the signature is an anomalous indorsement or is accompanied by words indicating that the signer is acting as surety or guarantor with respect to the obligation of another party to the instrument. Except as provided in Section 3–605, the obligation of an accommodation party to pay the instrument is not affected by the fact that the person enforcing the obligation had notice when the instrument was taken by that person that the accommodation party signed the instrument for accommodation.

(d) If the signature of a party to an instrument is accompanied by words indicating unambiguously that the party is guaranteeing collection rather than payment of the obligation of another party to the instrument, the signer is obliged to pay the amount due on the instrument to a person entitled to enforce the instrument only if (i) execution of judgment against the other party has been returned unsatisfied, (ii) the other party is insolvent or in an insolvency proceeding, (iii) the other party cannot be served with process, or (iv) it is otherwise apparent that payment cannot be obtained from the other party.

(e) An accommodation party who pays the instrument is entitled to reimbursement from the accommodated party and is entitled to enforce the instrument against the accommodated party. An accommodated party who pays the instrument has no right of recourse against, and is not entitled to contribution from, an accommodation party.

§ 3–420. Conversion of Instrument.

(a) The law applicable to conversion of personal property applies to instruments. An instrument is also converted if it is taken by transfer, other than a negotiation, from a person not entitled to enforce the instrument or a bank makes or obtains payment with respect to the instrument for a person not entitled to enforce the instrument or receive payment. An action for conversion of an instrument may not be brought by (i) the issuer or acceptor of the instrument or (ii) a payee or indorsee who did not receive delivery of the instrument either directly or through delivery to an agent or a co-payee.

(b) In an action under subsection (a), the measure of liability is presumed to be the amount payable on the instrument, but recovery may not exceed the amount of the plaintiff's interest in the instrument.

(c) A representative, other than a depositary bank, who has in good faith dealt with an instrument or its proceeds on behalf of one who was not the person entitled to enforce the instrument is not liable in conversion to that person beyond the amount of any proceeds that it has not paid out.

Part 5—Dishonor

§ 3–501. Presentment.

(a) "Presentment" means a demand made by or on behalf of a person entitled to enforce an instrument (i) to pay the instrument made to the drawee or a party obliged to pay the instrument or, in the case of a note or accepted draft payable at a bank, to the bank, or (ii) to accept a draft made to the drawee.

(b) The following rules are subject to Article 4, agreement of the parties, and clearing-house rules and the like:

    (1) Presentment may be made at the place of payment of the instrument and must be made at the place of payment if the instrument is payable at a bank in the United States; may be made by any commercially reasonable means, including an oral, written, or electronic communication; is effective when the demand for payment or acceptance is received by the person to whom presentment is made; and is effective if made to any one of two or more makers, acceptors, drawees, or other payors.

    (2) Upon demand of the person to whom presentment is made, the person making presentment must (i) exhibit the instrument, (ii) give reasonable identification and, if pre-

sentment is made on behalf of another person, reasonable evidence of authority to do so, and (. . .) sign a receipt on the instrument for any payment made or surrender the instrument if full payment is made.

    (3) Without dishonoring the instrument, the party to whom presentment is made may (i) return the instrument for lack of a necessary indorsement, or (ii) refuse payment or acceptance for failure of the presentment to comply with the terms of the instrument, an agreement of the parties, or other applicable law or rule.

    (4) The party to whom presentment is made may treat presentment as occurring on the next business day after the day of presentment if the party to whom presentment is made has established a cut-off hour not earlier than 2 p.m. for the receipt and processing of instruments presented for payment or acceptance and presentment is made after the cut-off hour.

§ 3–502. Dishonor.

(a) Dishonor of a note is governed by the following rules:

    (1) If the note is payable on demand, the note is dishonored if presentment is duly made to the maker and the note is not paid on the day of presentment.

    (2) If the note is not payable on demand and is payable at or through a bank or the terms of the note require presentment, the note is dishonored if presentment is duly made and the note is not paid on the day it becomes payable or the day of presentment, whichever is later.

    (3) If the note is not payable on demand and paragraph (2) does not apply, the note is dishonored if it is not paid on the day it becomes payable.

(b) Dishonor of an unaccepted draft other than a documentary draft is governed by the following rules:

    (1) If a check is duly presented for payment to the payor bank otherwise than for immediate payment over the counter, the check is dishonored if the payor bank makes timely return of the check or sends timely notice of dishonor or nonpayment under Section 4–301 or 4–302, or becomes accountable for the amount of the check under Section 4–302.

    (2) If a draft is payable on demand and paragraph (1) does not apply, the draft is dishonored if presentment for payment is duly made to the drawee and the draft is not paid on the day of presentment.

    (3) If a draft is payable on a date stated in the draft, the draft is dishonored if (i) presentment for payment is duly made to the drawee and payment is not made on the day the draft becomes payable or the day of presentment, whichever is later, or (ii) presentment for acceptance is duly made before the day the draft becomes payable and the draft is not accepted on the day of presentment.

    (4) If a draft is payable on elapse of a period of time after sight or acceptance, the draft is dishonored if presentment for acceptance is duly made and the draft is not accepted on the day of presentment.

(c) Dishonor of an unaccepted documentary draft occurs according to the rules stated in subsection (b)(2), (3), and (4), except that payment or acceptance may be delayed without dishonor until no later than the close of the third business day of the drawee following the day on which payment or acceptance is required by those paragraphs.

(d) Dishonor of an accepted draft is governed by the following rules:

> **(1)** If the draft is payable on demand, the draft is dishonored if presentment for payment is duly made to the acceptor and the draft is not paid on the day of presentment.
>
> **(2)** If the draft is not payable on demand, the draft is dishonored if presentment for payment is duly made to the acceptor and payment is not made on the day it becomes payable or the day of presentment, whichever is later.

(e) In any case in which presentment is otherwise required for dishonor under this section and presentment is excused under Section 3–504, dishonor occurs without presentment if the instrument is not duly accepted or paid.

(f) If a draft is dishonored because timely acceptance of the draft was not made and the person entitled to demand acceptance consents to a late acceptance, from the time of acceptance the draft is treated as never having been dishonored.

§ 3–503. Notice of Dishonor.

(a) The obligation of an indorser stated in Section 3–415(a) and the obligation of a drawer stated in Section 3–414(d) may not be enforced unless (i) the indorser or drawer is given notice of dishonor of the instrument complying with this section or (ii) notice of dishonor is excused under Section 3–504(b).

(b) Notice of dishonor may be given by any person; may be given by any commercially reasonable means, including an oral, written, or electronic communication; and is sufficient if it reasonably identifies the instrument and indicates that the instrument has been dishonored or has not been paid or accepted. Return of an instrument given to a bank for collection is sufficient notice of dishonor.

(c) Subject to Section 3–504(c), with respect to an instrument taken for collection by a collecting bank, notice of dishonor must be given (i) by the bank before midnight of the next banking day following the banking day on which the bank receives notice of dishonor of the instrument, or (ii) by any other person within 30 days following the day on which the person receives notice of dishonor. With respect to any other instrument, notice of dishonor must be given within 30 days following the day on which dishonor occurs.

§ 3–504. Excused Presentment and Notice of Dishonor.

(a) Presentment for payment or acceptance of an instrument is excused if (i) the person entitled to present the instrument cannot with reasonable diligence make presentment, (ii) the maker or acceptor has repudiated an obligation to pay the instrument or is dead or in insolvency proceedings, (iii) by the terms of the instrument presentment is not necessary to enforce the obligation of indorsers or the drawer, (iv) the drawer or indorser whose obligation is being enforced has waived presentment or otherwise has no reason to expect or right to require that the instrument be paid or accepted, or (v) the drawer instructed the drawee not to pay or accept the draft or the drawee was not obligated to the drawer to pay the draft.

(b) Notice of dishonor is excused if (i) by the terms of the instrument notice of dishonor is not necessary to enforce the obligation of a party to pay the instrument, or (ii) the party whose obligation is being enforced waived notice of dishonor. A waiver of presentment is also a waiver of notice of dishonor.

(c) Delay in giving notice of dishonor is excused if the delay was caused by circumstances beyond the control of the person giving the notice and the person giving the notice exercised reasonable diligence after the cause of the delay ceased to operate.

§ 3–505. Evidence of Dishonor.

(a) The following are admissible as evidence and create a presumption of dishonor and of any notice of dishonor stated:

> **(1)** a document regular in form as provided in subsection (b) which purports to be a protest;
>
> **(2)** a purported stamp or writing of the drawee, payor bank, or presenting bank on or accompanying the instrument stating that acceptance or payment has been refused unless reasons for the refusal are stated and the reasons are not consistent with dishonor;
>
> **(3)** a book or record of the drawee, payor bank, or collecting bank, kept in the usual course of business which shows dishonor, even if there is no evidence of who made the entry.

(b) A protest is a certificate of dishonor made by a United States consul or vice consul, or a notary public or other person authorized to administer oaths by the law of the place where dishonor occurs. It may be made upon information satisfactory to that person. The protest must identify the instrument and certify either that presentment has been made or, if not made, the reason why it was not made, and that the instrument has been dishonored by nonacceptance or nonpayment. The protest may also certify that notice of dishonor has been given to some or all parties.

Part 6—Discharge and Payment

§ 3–601. Discharge and Effect of Discharge.

(a) The obligation of a party to pay the instrument is discharged as stated in this Article or by an act or agreement with the party which would discharge an obligation to pay money under a simple contract.

(b) Discharge of the obligation of a party is not effective against a person acquiring rights of a holder in due course of the instrument without notice of the discharge.

§ 3–602. Payment.

(a) Subject to subsection (b), an instrument is paid to the extent payment is made (i) by or on behalf of a party obliged to pay the instrument, and (ii) to a person entitled to enforce the instrument. To the extent of the payment, the obligation of the party obliged to pay the instrument is discharged even though payment is made with knowledge of a claim to the instrument under Section 3–306 by another person.

(b) The obligation of a party to pay the instrument is not discharged under subsection (a) if:

> **(1)** a claim to the instrument under Section 3–306 is enforceable against the party receiving payment and (i) payment is made with knowledge by the payor that payment is prohibited by injunction or similar process of a court of competent jurisdiction, or (ii) in the case of an

instrument other than a cashier's check, teller's check, or certified check, the party making payment accepted, from the person having a claim to the instrument, indemnity against loss resulting from refusal to pay the person entitled to enforce the instrument; or

(2) the person making payment knows that the instrument is a stolen instrument and pays a person it knows is in wrongful possession of the instrument.

§ 3–603. Tender of Payment.

(a) If tender of payment of an obligation to pay an instrument is made to a person entitled to enforce the instrument, the effect of tender is governed by principles of law applicable to tender of payment under a simple contract.

(b) If tender of payment of an obligation to pay an instrument is made to a person entitled to enforce the instrument and the tender is refused, there is discharge, to the extent of the amount of the tender, of the obligation of an indorser or accommodation party having a right of recourse with respect to the obligation to which the tender relates.

(c) If tender of payment of an amount due on an instrument is made to a person entitled to enforce the instrument, the obligation of the obligor to pay interest after the due date on the amount tendered is discharged. If presentment is required with respect to an instrument and the obligor is able and ready to pay on the due date at every place of payment stated in the instrument, the obligor is deemed to have made tender of payment on the due date to the person entitled to enforce the instrument.

§ 3–604. Discharge by Cancellation or Renunciation.

(a) A person entitled to enforce an instrument, with or without consideration, may discharge the obligation of a party to pay the instrument (i) by an intentional voluntary act, such as surrender of the instrument to the party, destruction, mutilation, or cancellation of the instrument, cancellation or striking out of the party's signature, or the addition of words to the instrument indicating discharge, or (ii) by agreeing not to sue or otherwise renouncing rights against the party by a signed writing.

(b) Cancellation or striking out of an indorsement pursuant to subsection (a) does not affect the status and rights of a party derived from the indorsement.

§ 3–605. Discharge of Indorsers and Accommodation Parties.

(a) In this section, the term "indorser" includes a drawer having the obligation described in Section 3–414(d).

(b) Discharge, under Section 3–604, of the obligation of a party to pay an instrument does not discharge the obligation of an indorser or accommodation party having a right of recourse against the discharged party.

(c) If a person entitled to enforce an instrument agrees, with or without consideration, to an extension of the due date of the obligation of a party to pay the instrument, the extension discharges an indorser or accommodation party having a right of recourse against the party whose obligation is extended to the extent the indorser or accommodation party proves that the extension caused loss to the indorser or accommodation party with respect to the right of recourse.

(d) If a person entitled to enforce an instrument agrees, with or without consideration, to a material modification of the obligation of a party other than an extension of the due date, the modification discharges the obligation of an indorser or accommodation party having a right of recourse against the person whose obligation is modified to the extent the modification causes loss to the indorser or accommodation party with respect to the right of recourse. The loss suffered by the indorser or accommodation party as a result of the modification is equal to the amount of the right of recourse unless the person enforcing the instrument proves that no loss was caused by the modification or that the loss caused by the modification was an amount less than the amount of the right of recourse.

(e) If the obligation of a party to pay an instrument is secured by an interest in collateral and a person entitled to enforce the instrument impairs the value of the interest in collateral, the obligation of an indorser or accommodation party having a right of recourse against the obligor is discharged to the extent of the impairment. The value of an interest in collateral is impaired to the extent (i) the value of the interest is reduced to an amount less than the amount of the right of recourse of the party asserting discharge, or (ii) the reduction in value of the interest causes an increase in the amount by which the amount of the right of recourse exceeds the value of the interest. The burden of proving impairment is on the party asserting discharge.

(f) If the obligation of a party is secured by an interest in collateral not provided by an accommodation party and a person entitled to enforce the instrument impairs the value of the interest in collateral, the obligation of any party who is jointly and severally liable with respect to the secured obligation is discharged to the extent the impairment causes the party asserting discharge to pay more than that party would have been obliged to pay, taking into account rights of contribution, if impairment had not occurred. If the party asserting discharge is an accommodation party not entitled to discharge under subsection (e), the party is deemed to have a right to contribution based on joint and several liability rather than a right to reimbursement. The burden of proving impairment is on the party asserting discharge.

(g) Under subsection (e) or (f), impairing value of an interest in collateral includes (i) failure to obtain or maintain perfection or recordation of the interest in collateral, (ii) release of collateral without substitution of collateral of equal value, (iii) failure to perform a duty to preserve the value of collateral owed, under Article 9 or other law, to a debtor or surety or other person secondarily liable, or (iv) failure to comply with applicable law in disposing of collateral.

(h) An accommodation party is not discharged under subsection (c), (d), or (e) unless the person entitled to enforce the instrument knows of the accommodation or has notice under Section 3–419(c) that the instrument was signed for accommodation.

(i) A party is not discharged under this section if (i) the party asserting discharge consents to the event or conduct that is the basis of the discharge, or (ii) the instrument or a separate agreement of the party provides for waiver of discharge under this section either specifically or by general language indicating that parties waive defenses based on suretyship or impairment of collateral.

ADDENDUM TO REVISED ARTICLE 3
Notes to Legislative Counsel

1. If revised Article 3 is adopted in your state, the reference in Section 2–511 to Section 3–802 should be changed to Section 3–310.

2. If revised Article 3 is adopted in your state and the Uniform Fiduciaries Act is also in effect in your state, you may want to consider amending Uniform Fiduciaries Act § 9 to conform to Section 3–307(b)(2)(iii) and (4)(iii). See Official Comment 3 to Section 3–307.

REVISED ARTICLE 4: BANK DEPOSITS AND COLLECTIONS

Part 1—General Provisions and Definitions

§ 4–101. Short Title.

This Article may be cited as Uniform Commercial Code—Bank Deposits and Collections.
As amended in 1990.

§ 4–102. Applicability.

(a) To the extent that items within this Article are also within Articles 3 and 8, they are subject to those Articles. If there is conflict, this Article governs Article 3, but Article 8 governs this Article.

(b) The liability of a bank for action or non-action with respect to an item handled by it for purposes of presentment, payment, or collection is governed by the law of the place where the bank is located. In the case of action or non-action by or at a branch or separate office of a bank, its liability is governed by the law of the place where the branch or separate office is located.

§ 4–103. Variation by Agreement; Measure of Damages; Action Constituting Ordinary Care.

(a) The effect of the provisions of this Article may be varied by agreement, but the parties to the agreement cannot disclaim a bank's responsibility for its lack of good faith or failure to exercise ordinary care or limit the measure of damages for the lack or failure. However, the parties may determine by agreement the standards by which the bank's responsibility is to be measured if those standards are not manifestly unreasonable.

(b) Federal Reserve regulations and operating circulars, clearing-house rules, and the like have the effect of agreements under subsection (a), whether or not specifically assented to by all parties interested in items handled.

(c) Action or non-action approved by this Article or pursuant to Federal Reserve regulations or operating circulars is the exercise of ordinary care and, in the absence of special instructions, action or non-action consistent with clearing-house rules and the like or with a general banking usage not disapproved by this Article, is *prima facie* the exercise of ordinary care.

(d) The specification or approval of certain procedures by this Article is not disapproval of other procedures that may be reasonable under the circumstances.

(e) The measure of damages for failure to exercise ordinary care in handling an item is the amount of the item reduced by an amount that could not have been realized by the exercise of ordinary care. If there is also bad faith it includes any other damages the party suffered as a proximate consequence.

As amended in 1990.

§ 4–104. Definitions and Index of Definitions.

(a) In this Article, unless the context otherwise requires:

(1) "Account" means any deposit or credit account with a bank, including a demand, time, savings, passbook, share draft, or like account, other than an account evidenced by a certificate of deposit;

(2) "Afternoon" means the period of a day between noon and midnight;

(3) "Banking day" means the part of a day on which a bank is open to the public for carrying on substantially all of its banking functions;

(4) "Clearing house" means an association of banks or other payors regularly clearing items;

(5) "Customer" means a person having an account with a bank or for whom a bank has agreed to collect items, including a bank that maintains an account at another bank;

(6) "Documentary draft" means a draft to be presented for acceptance or payment if specified documents, certificated securities (Section 8–102) or instructions for uncertificated securities (Section 8–102), or other certificates, statements, or the like are to be received by the drawee or other payor before acceptance or payment of the draft;

(7) "Draft" means a draft as defined in Section 3–104 or an item, other than an instrument, that is an order;

(8) "Drawee" means a person ordered in a draft to make payment;

(9) "Item" means an instrument or a promise or order to pay money handled by a bank for collection or payment. The term does not include a payment order governed by Article 4A or a credit or debit card slip;

(10) "Midnight deadline" with respect to a bank is midnight on its next banking day following the banking day on which it receives the relevant item or notice or from which the time for taking action commences to run, whichever is later;

(11) "Settle" means to pay in cash, by clearing-house settlement, in a charge or credit or by remittance, or otherwise as agreed. A settlement may be either provisional or final;

(12) "Suspends payments" with respect to a bank means that it has been closed by order of the supervisory authorities, that a public officer has been appointed to take it over, or that it ceases or refuses to make payments in the ordinary course of business.

(b) [Other definitions' section references deleted.]

(c) [Other definitions' section references deleted.]

(d) In addition, Article 1 contains general definitions and principles of construction and interpretation applicable throughout this Article.

§ 4–105. "Bank"; "Depositary Bank"; "Payor Bank"; "Intermediary Bank"; "Collecting Bank"; "Presenting Bank".

In this Article:

(1) "Bank" means a person engaged in the business of banking, including a savings bank, savings and loan association, credit union, or trust company;

(2) "Depositary bank" means the first bank to take an item even though it is also the payor bank, unless the item is presented for immediate payment over the counter;

(3) "Payor bank" means a bank that is the drawee of a draft;

(4) "Intermediary bank" means a bank to which an item is transferred in course of collection except the depositary or payor bank;

(5) "Collecting bank" means a bank handling an item for collection except the payor bank;

(6) "Presenting bank" means a bank presenting an item except a payor bank.

§ 4–106. Payable Through or Payable at Bank: Collecting Bank.

(a) If an item states that it is "payable through" a bank identified in the item, (i) the item designates the bank as a collecting bank and does not by itself authorize the bank to pay the item, and (ii) the item may be presented for payment only by or through the bank.

Alternative A

(b) If an item states that it is "payable at" a bank identified in the item, the item is equivalent to a draft drawn on the bank.

Alternative B

(b) If an item states that it is "payable at" a bank identified in the item, (i) the item designates the bank as a collecting bank and does not by itself authorize the bank to pay the item, and (ii) the item may be presented for payment only by or through the bank.

(c) If a draft names a nonbank drawee and it is unclear whether a bank named in the draft is a co-drawee or a collecting bank, the bank is a collecting bank.

As added in 1990.

§ 4–107. Separate Office of Bank.

A branch or separate office of a bank is a separate bank for the purpose of computing the time within which and determining the place at or to which action may be taken or notices or orders shall be given under this Article and under Article 3.

As amended in 1962 and 1990.

§ 4–108. Time of Receipt of Items.

(a) For the purpose of allowing time to process items, prove balances, and make the necessary entries on its books to determine its position for the day, a bank may fix an afternoon hour of 2 P.M. or later as a cutoff hour for the handling of money and items and the making of entries on its books.

(b) An item or deposit of money received on any day after a cutoff hour so fixed or after the close of the banking day may be treated as being received at the opening of the next banking day.

As amended in 1990.

§ 4–109. Delays.

(a) Unless otherwise instructed, a collecting bank in a good faith effort to secure payment of a specific item drawn on a payor other than a bank, and with or without the approval of any person involved, may waive, modify, or extend time limits imposed or permitted by this [act] for a period not exceeding two additional banking days without discharge of drawers or indorsers or liability to its transferor or a prior party.

(b) Delay by a collecting bank or payor bank beyond time limits prescribed or permitted by this [act] or by instructions is excused if (i) the delay is caused by interruption of communication or computer facilities, suspension of payments by another bank, war, emergency conditions, failure of equipment, or other circumstances beyond the control of the bank, and (ii) the bank exercises such diligence as the circumstances require.

§ 4–110. Electronic Presentment.

(a) "Agreement for electronic presentment" means an agreement, clearing-house rule, or Federal Reserve regulation or operating circular, providing that presentment of an item may be made by transmission of an image of an item or information describing the item ("presentment notice") rather than delivery of the item itself. The agreement may provide for procedures governing retention, presentment, payment, dishonor, and other matters concerning items subject to the agreement.

(b) Presentment of an item pursuant to an agreement for presentment is made when the presentment notice is received.

(c) If presentment is made by presentment notice, a reference to "item" or "check" in this Article means the presentment notice unless the context otherwise indicates.

As added in 1990.

§ 4–111. Statute of Limitations.

An action to enforce an obligation, duty, or right arising under this Article must be commenced within three years after the [cause of action] accrues.

As added in 1990.

Part 2—Collection of Items: Depositary and Collecting Banks

§ 4–201. Status of Collecting Bank as Agent `and Provisional Status of Credits; Applicability of Article; Item Indorsed "Pay Any Bank".

(a) Unless a contrary intent clearly appears and before the time that a settlement given by a collecting bank for an item is or becomes final, the bank, with respect to an item, is an agent or sub-agent of the owner of the item and any settlement given for the item is provisional. This provision applies regardless of the form of indorsement or lack of indorsement and even though credit given for the item is subject to immediate withdrawal as of right or is in fact withdrawn; but the continuance of ownership of an item by its owner and any rights of the owner to proceeds of the item are subject to rights of a collecting bank, such as those resulting from outstanding advances on the item and rights of recoupment or setoff. If an item is handled by banks for purposes of presentment, payment, collection, or return, the relevant provisions of this Article apply even though action of the parties clearly establishes that a particular bank has purchased the item and is the owner of it.

(b) After an item has been indorsed with the words "pay any bank" or the like, only a bank may acquire the rights of a holder until the item has been:

    (1) returned to the customer initiating collection; or

    (2) specially indorsed by a bank to a person who is not a bank.

As amended in 1990.

§ 4–202. Responsibility for Collection or Return; When Action Timely.

(a) A collecting bank must exercise ordinary care in:

(1) presenting an item or sending it for presentment;

(2) sending notice of dishonor or nonpayment or returning an item other than a documentary draft to the bank's transferor after learning that the item has not been paid or accepted, as the case may be;

(3) settling for an item when the bank receives final settlement; and

(4) notifying its transferor of any loss or delay in transit within a reasonable time after discovery thereof.

(b) A collecting bank exercises ordinary care under subsection (a) by taking proper action before its midnight deadline following receipt of an item, notice, or settlement. Taking proper action within a reasonably longer time may constitute the exercise of ordinary care, but the bank has the burden of establishing timeliness.

(c) Subject to subsection (a)(1), a bank is not liable for the insolvency, neglect, misconduct, mistake, or default of another bank or person or for loss or destruction of an item in the possession of others or in transit.

As amended in 1990.

§ 4–203. Effect of Instructions.

Subject to Article 3 concerning conversion of instruments (Section 3–420) and restrictive indorsements (Section 3–206), only a collecting bank's transferor can give instructions that affect the bank or constitute notice to it, and a collecting bank is not liable to prior parties for any action taken pursuant to the instructions or in accordance with any agreement with its transferor.

§ 4–204. Methods of Sending and Presenting; Sending Directly to Payor Bank.

(a) A collecting bank shall send items by a reasonably prompt method, taking into consideration relevant instructions, the nature of the item, the number of those items on hand, the cost of collection involved, and the method generally used by it or others to present those items.

(b) A collecting bank may send:

(1) an item directly to the payor bank;

(2) an item to a nonbank payor if authorized by its transferor; and

(3) an item other than documentary drafts to a nonbank payor, if authorized by Federal Reserve regulation or operating circular, clearing-house rule, or the like.

(c) Presentment may be made by a presenting bank at a place where the payor bank or other payor has requested that presentment be made.

As amended in 1990.

§ 4–205. Depositary Bank Holder of Unindorsed Item.

If a customer delivers an item to a depositary bank for collection:

(1) the depositary bank becomes a holder of the item at the time it receives the item for collection if the customer at the time of delivery was a holder of the item, whether or not the customer indorses the item, and, if the bank satisfies the other requirements of Section 3–302, it is a holder in due course; and

(2) the depositary bank warrants to collecting banks, the payor bank or other payor, and the drawer that the amount of the item was paid to the customer or deposited to the customer's account.

As amended in 1990.

§ 4–206. Transfer Between Banks.

Any agreed method that identifies the transferor bank is sufficient for the item's further transfer to another bank.

As amended in 1990.

§ 4–207. Transfer Warranties.

(a) A customer or collecting bank that transfers an item and receives a settlement or other consideration warrants to the transferee and to any subsequent collecting bank that:

(1) the warrantor is a person entitled to enforce the item;

(2) all signatures on the item are authentic and authorized;

(3) the item has not been altered;

(4) the item is not subject to a defense or claim in recoupment (Section 3–305(a)) of any party that can be asserted against the warrantor; and

(5) the warrantor has no knowledge of any insolvency proceeding commenced with respect to the maker or acceptor or, in the case of an unaccepted draft, the drawer.

(b) If an item is dishonored, a customer or collecting bank transferring the item and receiving settlement or other consideration is obliged to pay the amount due on the item (i) according to the terms of the item at the time it was transferred, or (ii) if the transfer was of an incomplete item, according to its terms when completed as stated in Sections 3–115 and 3–407. The obligation of a transferor is owed to the transferee and to any subsequent collecting bank that takes the item in good faith. A transferor cannot disclaim its obligation under this subsection by an indorsement stating that it is made "without recourse" or otherwise disclaiming liability.

(c) A person to whom the warranties under subsection (a) are made and who took the item in good faith may recover from the warrantor as damages for breach of warranty an amount equal to the loss suffered as a result of the breach, but not more than the amount of the item plus expenses and loss of interest incurred as a result of the breach.

(d) The warranties stated in subsection (a) cannot be disclaimed with respect to checks. Unless notice of a claim for breach of warranty is given to the warrantor within 30 days after the claimant has reason to know of the breach and the identity of the warrantor, the warrantor is discharged to the extent of any loss caused by the delay in giving notice of the claim.

(e) A cause of action for breach of warranty under this section accrues when the claimant has reason to know of the breach.

As amended in 1990.

§ 4–208. Presentment Warranties.

(a) If an unaccepted draft is presented to the drawee for payment or acceptance and the drawee pays or accepts the draft, (i) the person obtaining payment or acceptance, at the time of presentment, and (ii) a previous transferor of the draft, at the time of transfer, warrant to the drawee that pays or accepts the draft in good faith that:

(1) the warrantor is, or was, at the time the warrantor transferred the draft, a person entitled to enforce the draft or authorized to obtain payment or acceptance of the draft on behalf of a person entitled to enforce the draft;

(2) the draft has not been altered; and

(3) the warrantor has no knowledge that the signature of the purported drawer of the draft is unauthorized.

(b) A drawee making payment may recover from a warrantor damages for breach of warranty equal to the amount paid by the drawee less the amount the drawee received or is entitled to receive from the drawer because of the payment. In addition, the drawee is entitled to compensation for expenses and loss of interest resulting from the breach. The right of the drawee to recover damages under this subsection is not affected by any failure of the drawee to exercise ordinary care in making payment. If the drawee accepts the draft (i) breach of warranty is a defense to the obligation of the acceptor, and (ii) if the acceptor makes payment with respect to the draft, the acceptor is entitled to recover from a warrantor for breach of warranty the amounts stated in this subsection.

(c) If a drawee asserts a claim for breach of warranty under subsection (a) based on an unauthorized indorsement of the draft or an alteration of the draft, the warrantor may defend by proving that the indorsement is effective under Section 3–404 or 3–405 or the drawer is precluded under Section 3–406 or 4–406 from asserting against the drawee the unauthorized indorsement or alteration.

(d) If (i) a dishonored draft is presented for payment to the drawer or an indorser or (ii) any other item is presented for payment to a party obliged to pay the item, and the item is paid, the person obtaining payment and a prior transferor of the item warrant to the person making payment in good faith that the warrantor is, or was, at the time the warrantor transferred the item, a person entitled to enforce the item or authorized to obtain payment on behalf of a person entitled to enforce the item. The person making payment may recover from any warrantor for breach of warranty an amount equal to the amount paid plus expenses and loss of interest resulting from the breach.

(e) The warranties stated in subsections (a) and (d) cannot be disclaimed with respect to checks. Unless notice of a claim for breach of warranty is given to the warrantor within 30 days after the claimant has reason to know of the breach and the identity of the warrantor, the warrantor is discharged to the extent of any loss caused by the delay in giving notice of the claim.

(f) A cause of action for breach of warranty under this section accrues when the claimant has reason to know of the breach.
As amended in 1990.

§ 4–209. Encoding and Retention Warranties.

(a) A person who encodes information on or with respect to an item after issue warrants to any subsequent collecting bank and to the payor bank or other payor that the information is correctly encoded. If the customer of a depositary bank encodes, that bank also makes the warranty.

(b) A person who undertakes to retain an item pursuant to an agreement for electronic presentment warrants to any subsequent collecting bank and to the payor bank or other payor that retention and presentment of the item comply with the agreement. If a customer of a depositary bank undertakes to retain an item, that bank also makes this warranty.

(c) A person to whom warranties are made under this section and who took the item in good faith may recover from the warrantor as damages for breach of warranty an amount equal to the loss suffered as a result of the breach, plus expenses and loss of interest incurred as a result of the breach.
As added in 1990.

§ 4–210. Security Interest of Collecting Bank in Items, Accompanying Documents and Proceeds.

(a) A collecting bank has a security interest in an item and any accompanying documents or the proceeds of either:

(1) in case of an item deposited in an account, to the extent to which credit given for the item has been withdrawn or applied;

(2) in case of an item for which it has given credit available for withdrawal as of right, to the extent of the credit given, whether or not the credit is drawn upon or there is a right of charge-back; or

(3) if it makes an advance on or against the item.

(b) If credit given for several items received at one time or pursuant to a single agreement is withdrawn or applied in part, the security interest remains upon all the items, any accompanying documents or the proceeds of either. For the purpose of this section, credits first given are first withdrawn.

(c) Receipt by a collecting bank of a final settlement for an item is a realization on its security interest in the item, accompanying documents, and proceeds. So long as the bank does not receive final settlement for the item or give up possession of the item or accompanying documents for purposes other than collection, the security interest continues to that extent and is subject to Article 9, but:

(1) no security agreement is necessary to make the security interest enforceable (Section 9–203(1)(a));

(2) no filing is required to perfect the security interest; and

(3) the security interest has priority over conflicting perfected security interests in the item, accompanying documents, or proceeds.
As amended in 1990 and 1999.

§ 4–211. When Bank Gives Value for Purposes of Holder in Due Course.

For purposes of determining its status as a holder in due course, a bank has given value to the extent it has a security interest in an item, if the bank otherwise complies with the requirements of Section 3–302 on what constitutes a holder in due course.
As amended in 1990.

§ 4–212. Presentment by Notice of Item Not Payable by, Through, or at Bank; Liability of Drawer or Indorser.

(a) Unless otherwise instructed, a collecting bank may present an item not payable by, through, or at a bank by sending to the party to accept or pay a written notice that the bank holds the item for acceptance or payment. The notice must be sent in time to be received on or before the day when presentment is due and the bank must meet any requirement of the party to accept or pay under Section 3–501 by the close of the bank's next banking day after it knows of the requirement.

(b) If presentment is made by notice and payment, acceptance, or request for compliance with a requirement under Section 3–501 is not received by the close of business on the day after maturity or, in the case of demand items, by the close of business on the third banking day after notice was sent, the presenting bank may treat the item as dishonored and charge any drawer or indorser by sending it notice of the facts.

As amended in 1990.

§ 4–213. Medium and Time of Settlement by Bank.

(a) With respect to settlement by a bank, the medium and time of settlement may be prescribed by Federal Reserve regulations or circulars, clearing-house rules, and the like, or agreement. In the absence of such prescription:

    (1) the medium of settlement is cash or credit to an account in a Federal Reserve bank of or specified by the person to receive settlement; and

    (2) the time of settlement is:

        (i) with respect to tender of settlement by cash, a cashier's check, or teller's check, when the cash or check is sent or delivered;

        (ii) with respect to tender of settlement by credit in an account in a Federal Reserve Bank, when the credit is made;

        (iii) with respect to tender of settlement by a credit or debit to an account in a bank, when the credit or debit is made or, in the case of tender of settlement by authority to charge an account, when the authority is sent or delivered; or

        (iv) with respect to tender of settlement by a funds transfer, when payment is made pursuant to Section 4A–406(a) to the person receiving settlement.

(b) If the tender of settlement is not by a medium authorized by subsection (a) or the time of settlement is not fixed by subsection (a), no settlement occurs until the tender of settlement is accepted by the person receiving settlement.

(c) If settlement for an item is made by cashier's check or teller's check and the person receiving settlement, before its midnight deadline:

    (1) presents or forwards the check for collection, settlement is final when the check is finally paid; or

    (2) fails to present or forward the check for collection, settlement is final at the midnight deadline of the person receiving settlement.

(d) If settlement for an item is made by giving authority to charge the account of the bank giving settlement in the bank receiving settlement, settlement is final when the charge is made by the bank receiving settlement if there are funds available in the account for the amount of the item.

As amended in 1990.

§ 4–214. Right of Charge-Back or Refund; Liability of Collecting Bank: Return of Item.

(a) If a collecting bank has made provisional settlement with its customer for an item and fails by reason of dishonor, suspension of payments by a bank, or otherwise to receive settlement for the item which is or becomes final, the bank may revoke the settlement given by it, charge back the amount of any credit given for the item to its customer's account, or obtain refund from its customer, whether or not it is able to return the item, if by its midnight deadline or within a longer reasonable time after it learns the facts it returns the item or sends notification of the facts. If the return or notice is delayed beyond the bank's midnight deadline or a longer reasonable time after it learns the facts, the bank may revoke the settlement, charge back the credit, or obtain refund from its customer, but it is liable for any loss resulting from the delay. These rights to revoke, charge back, and obtain refund terminate if and when a settlement for the item received by the bank is or becomes final.

(b) A collecting bank returns an item when it is sent or delivered to the bank's customer or transferor or pursuant to its instructions.

(c) A depositary bank that is also the payor may charge back the amount of an item to its customer's account or obtain refund in accordance with the section governing return of an item received by a payor bank for credit on its books (Section 4–301).

(d) The right to charge back is not affected by:

    (1) previous use of a credit given for the item; or

    (2) failure by any bank to exercise ordinary care with respect to the item, but a bank so failing remains liable.

(e) A failure to charge back or claim refund does not affect other rights of the bank against the customer or any other party.

(f) If credit is given in dollars as the equivalent of the value of an item payable in foreign money, the dollar amount of any charge-back or refund must be calculated on the basis of the bank-offered spot rate for the foreign money prevailing on the day when the person entitled to the charge-back or refund learns that it will not receive payment in ordinary course.

As amended in 1990.

§ 4–215. Final Payment of Item by Payor Bank; When Provisional Debits and Credits Become Final; When Certain Credits Become Available for Withdrawal.

(a) An item is finally paid by a payor bank when the bank has first done any of the following:

    (1) paid the item in cash;

    (2) settled for the item without having a right to revoke the settlement under statute, clearing-house rule, or agreement; or

    (3) made a provisional settlement for the item and failed to revoke the settlement in the time and manner permitted by statute, clearing-house rule, or agreement.

(b) If provisional settlement for an item does not become final, the item is not finally paid.

(c) If provisional settlement for an item between the presenting and payor banks is made through a clearing house or by debits or credits in an account between them, then to the extent that provisional debits or credits for the item are entered in accounts between the presenting and payor banks or between the presenting and successive prior collecting banks seriatim, they become final upon final payment of the item by the payor bank.

(d) If a collecting bank receives a settlement for an item which is or becomes final, the bank is accountable to its customer for the amount of the item and any provisional credit given for the item in an account with its customer becomes final.

(e) Subject to (i) applicable law stating a time for availability of funds and (ii) any right of the bank to apply the credit to an obligation of the customer, credit given by a bank for an item in a customer's account becomes available for withdrawal as of right:

(1) if the bank has received a provisional settlement for the item, when the settlement becomes final and the bank has had a reasonable time to receive return of the item and the item has not been received within that time;

(2) if the bank is both the depositary bank and the payor bank, and the item is finally paid, at the opening of the bank's second banking day following receipt of the item.

(f) Subject to applicable law stating a time for availability of funds and any right of a bank to apply a deposit to an obligation of the depositor, a deposit of money becomes available for withdrawal as of right at the opening of the bank's next banking day after receipt of the deposit.

As amended in 1990.

§ 4– 216. Insolvency and Preference.

(a) If an item is in or comes into the possession of a payor or collecting bank that suspends payment and the item has not been finally paid, the item must be returned by the receiver, trustee, or agent in charge of the closed bank to the presenting bank or the closed bank's customer.

(b) If a payor bank finally pays an item and suspends payments without making a settlement for the item with its customer or the presenting bank which settlement is or becomes final, the owner of the item has a preferred claim against the payor bank.

(c) If a payor bank gives or a collecting bank gives or receives a provisional settlement for an item and thereafter suspends payments, the suspension does not prevent or interfere with the settlement's becoming final if the finality occurs automatically upon the lapse of certain time or the happening of certain events.

(d) If a collecting bank receives from subsequent parties settlement for an item, which settlement is or becomes final and the bank suspends payments without making a settlement for the item with its customer which settlement is or becomes final, the owner of the item has a preferred claim against the collecting bank.

As amended in 1990.

Part 3—Collection of Items: Payor Banks

§ 4–301. Deferred Posting; Recovery of Payment by Return of Items; Time of Dishonor; Return of Items by Payor Bank.

(a) If a payor bank settles for a demand item other than a documentary draft presented otherwise than for immediate payment over the counter before midnight of the banking day of receipt, the payor bank may revoke the settlement and recover the settlement if, before it has made final payment and before its midnight deadline, it

(1) returns the item; or

(2) sends written notice of dishonor or non-payment if the item is unavailable for return.

(b) If a demand item is received by a payor bank for credit on its books, it may return the item or send notice of dishonor and may revoke any credit given or recover the amount thereof

withdrawn by its customer, if it acts within the time limit and in the manner specified in subsection (a).

(c) Unless previous notice of dishonor has been sent, an item is dishonored at the time when for purposes of dishonor it is returned or notice sent in accordance with this section.

(d) An item is returned:

(1) as to an item presented through a clearing house, when it is delivered to the presenting or last collecting bank or to the clearing house or is sent or delivered in accordance with clearing-house rules; or (2) in all other cases, when it is sent or delivered to the bank's customer or transferor or pursuant to instructions.

As amended in 1990.

§ 4–302. Payor Bank's Responsibility for Late Return of Item.

(a) If an item is presented to and received by a payor bank, the bank is accountable for the amount of:

(1) a demand item, other than a documentary draft, whether properly payable or not, if the bank, in any case in which it is not also the depositary bank, retains the item beyond midnight of the banking day of receipt without settling for it or, whether or not it is also the depositary bank, does not pay or return the item or send notice of dishonor until after its midnight deadline; or

(2) any other properly payable item unless, within the time allowed for acceptance or payment of that item, the bank either accepts or pays the item or returns it and accompanying documents.

(b) The liability of a payor bank to pay an item pursuant to subsection (a) is subject to defenses based on breach of a presentment warranty (Section 4–208) or proof that the person seeking enforcement of the liability presented or transferred the item for the purpose of defrauding the payor bank.

As amended in 1990.

§ 4–303. When Items Subject to Notice, Stop-Payment Order, Legal Process, or Setoff; Order in Which Items May Be Charged or Certified.

(a) Any knowledge, notice, or stop-payment order received by, legal process served upon, or setoff exercised by a payor bank comes too late to terminate, suspend, or modify the bank's right or duty to pay an item or to charge its customer's account for the item if the knowledge, notice, stop-payment order, or legal process is received or served and a reasonable time for the bank to act thereon expires or the setoff is exercised after the earliest of the following:

(1) the bank accepts or certifies the item;

(2) the bank pays the item in cash;

(3) the bank settles for the item without having a right to revoke the settlement under statute, clearing-house rule, or agreement;

(4) the bank becomes accountable for the amount of the item under Section 4–302 dealing with the payor bank's responsibility for late return of items; or

(5) with respect to checks, a cutoff hour no earlier than one hour after the opening of the next banking day after the banking day on which the bank received the check and no later than the close of that next banking day or, if no cutoff

hour is fixed, the close of the next banking day after the banking day on which the bank received the check.

(b) Subject to subsection (a), items may be accepted, paid, certified, or charged to the indicated account of its customer in any order.

As amended in 1990.

Part 4—Relationship Between Payor Bank and Its Customer

§ 4–401. When Bank May Charge Customer's Account.

(a) A bank may charge against the account of a customer an item that is properly payable from the account even though the charge creates an overdraft. An item is properly payable if it is authorized by the customer and is in accordance with any agreement between the customer and bank.

(b) A customer is not liable for the amount of an overdraft if the customer neither signed the item nor benefited from the proceeds of the item.

(c) A bank may charge against the account of a customer a check that is otherwise properly payable from the account, even though payment was made before the date of the check, unless the customer has given notice to the bank of the postdating describing the check with reasonable certainty. The notice is effective for the period stated in Section 4–403(b) for stop-payment orders, and must be received at such time and in such manner as to afford the bank a reasonable opportunity to act on it before the bank takes any action with respect to the check described in Section 4–303. If a bank charges against the account of a customer a check before the date stated in the notice of postdating, the bank is liable for damages for the loss resulting from its act. The loss may include damages for dishonor of subsequent items under Section 4–402.

(d) A bank that in good faith makes payment to a holder may charge the indicated account of its customer according to:

    (1) the original terms of the altered item; or

    (2) the terms of the completed item, even though the bank knows the item has been completed unless the bank has notice that the completion was improper.

As amended in 1990.

§ 4–402. Bank's Liability to Customer for Wrongful Dishonor; Time of Determining Insufficiency of Account.

(a) Except as otherwise provided in this Article, a payor bank wrongfully dishonors an item if it dishonors an item that is properly payable, but a bank may dishonor an item that would create an overdraft unless it has agreed to pay the overdraft.

(b) A payor bank is liable to its customer for damages proximately caused by the wrongful dishonor of an item. Liability is limited to actual damages proved and may include damages for an arrest or prosecution of the customer or other consequential damages. Whether any consequential damages are proximately caused by the wrongful dishonor is a question of fact to be determined in each case.

(c) A payor bank's determination of the customer's account balance on which a decision to dishonor for insufficiency of available funds is based may be made at any time between the time the item is received by the payor bank and the time that the payor bank returns the item or gives notice in lieu of return, and no more than one determination need be made. If, at the election of the payor bank, a subsequent balance determination is made for the purpose of reevaluating the bank's decision to dishonor the item, the account balance at that time is determinative of whether a dishonor for insufficiency of available funds is wrongful.

As amended in 1990.

§ 4–403. Customer's Right to Stop Payment; Burden of Proof of Loss.

(a) A customer or any person authorized to draw on the account if there is more than one person may stop payment of any item drawn on the customer's account or close the account by an order to the bank describing the item or account with reasonable certainty received at a time and in a manner that affords the bank a reasonable opportunity to act on it before any action by the bank with respect to the item described in Section 4–303. If the signature of more than one person is required to draw on an account, any of these persons may stop payment or close the account.

(b) A stop-payment order is effective for six months, but it lapses after 14 calendar days if the original order was oral and was not confirmed in writing within that period. A stop-payment order may be renewed for additional six-month periods by a writing given to the bank within a period during which the stop-payment order is effective.

(c) The burden of establishing the fact and amount of loss resulting from the payment of an item contrary to a stop-payment order or order to close an account is on the customer. The loss from payment of an item contrary to a stop-payment order may include damages for dishonor of subsequent items under Section 4–402.

As amended in 1990.

§ 4–404. Bank Not Obliged to Pay Check More Than Six Months Old.

A bank is under no obligation to a customer having a checking account to pay a check, other than a certified check, which is presented more than six months after its date, but it may charge its customer's account for a payment made thereafter in good faith.

§ 4–405. Death or Incompetence of Customer.

(a) A payor or collecting bank's authority to accept, pay, or collect an item or to account for proceeds of its collection, if otherwise effective, is not rendered ineffective by incompetence of a customer of either bank existing at the time the item is issued or its collection is undertaken if the bank does not know of an adjudication of incompetence. Neither death nor incompetence of a customer revokes the authority to accept, pay, collect, or account until the bank knows of the fact of death or of an adjudication of incompetence and has reasonable opportunity to act on it.

(b) Even with knowledge, a bank may for 10 days after the date of death pay or certify checks drawn on or before the date unless ordered to stop payment by a person claiming an interest in the account.

As amended in 1990.

§ 4–406. Customer's Duty to Discover and Report Unauthorized Signature or Alteration.

(a) A bank that sends or makes available to a customer a statement of account showing payment of items for the account shall either return or make available to the customer the items paid or provide information in the statement of account sufficient to allow the customer reasonably to identify the items paid. The statement of account provides sufficient information if the item is described by item number, amount, and date of payment.

(b) If the items are not returned to the customer, the person retaining the items shall either retain the items or, if the items are destroyed, maintain the capacity to furnish legible copies of the items until the expiration of seven years after receipt of the items. A customer may request an item from the bank that paid the item, and that bank must provide in a reasonable time either the item or, if the item has been destroyed or is not otherwise obtainable, a legible copy of the item.

(c) If a bank sends or makes available a statement of account or items pursuant to subsection (a), the customer must exercise reasonable promptness in examining the statement or the items to determine whether any payment was not authorized because of an alteration of an item or because a purported signature by or on behalf of the customer was not authorized. If, based on the statement or items provided, the customer should reasonably have discovered the unauthorized payment, the customer must promptly notify the bank of the relevant facts.

(d) If the bank proves that the customer failed, with respect to an item, to comply with the duties imposed on the customer by subsection (c), the customer is precluded from asserting against the bank:

(1) the customer's unauthorized signature or any alteration on the item, if the bank also proves that it suffered a loss by reason of the failure; and

(2) the customer's unauthorized signature or alteration by the same wrongdoer on any other item paid in good faith by the bank if the payment was made before the bank received notice from the customer of the unauthorized signature or alteration and after the customer had been afforded a reasonable period of time, not exceeding 30 days, in which to examine the item or statement of account and notify the bank.

(e) If subsection (d) applies and the customer proves that the bank failed to exercise ordinary care in paying the item and that the failure substantially contributed to loss, the loss is allocated between the customer precluded and the bank asserting the preclusion according to the extent to which the failure of the customer to comply with subsection (c) and the failure of the bank to exercise ordinary care contributed to the loss. If the customer proves that the bank did not pay the item in good faith, the preclusion under subsection (d) does not apply.

(f) Without regard to care or lack of care of either the customer or the bank, a customer who does not within one year after the statement or items are made available to the customer (subsection (a)) discover and report the customer's unauthorized signature on or any alteration on the item is precluded from asserting against the bank the unauthorized signature or alteration. If there is a preclusion under this subsection, the payor bank may not recover for breach or warranty under Section 4–208 with respect to the unauthorized signature or alteration to which the preclusion applies. As amended in 1990.

§ 4–407. Payor Bank's Right to Subrogation on Improper Payment.

If a payor has paid an item over the order of the drawer or maker to stop payment, or after an account has been closed, or otherwise under circumstances giving a basis for objection by the drawer or maker, to prevent unjust enrichment and only to the extent necessary to prevent loss to the bank by reason of its payment of the item, the payor bank is subrogated to the rights

(1) of any holder in due course on the item against the drawer or maker;

(2) of the payee or any other holder of the item against the drawer or maker either on the item or under the transaction out of which the item arose; and

(3) of the drawer or maker against the payee or any other holder of the item with respect to the transaction out of which the item arose.

As amended in 1990.

Part 5—Collection of Documentary Drafts

§ 4–501. Handling of Documentary Drafts; Duty to Send for Presentment and to Notify Customer of Dishonor.

A bank that takes a documentary draft for collection shall present or send the draft and accompanying documents for presentment and, upon learning that the draft has not been paid or accepted in due course, shall seasonably notify its customer of the fact even though it may have discounted or bought the draft or extended credit available for withdrawal as of right. As amended in 1990.

§ 4–502. Presentment of "On Arrival" Drafts.

If a draft or the relevant instructions require presentment "on arrival", "when goods arrive" or the like, the collecting bank need not present until in its judgment a reasonable time for arrival of the goods has expired. Refusal to pay or accept because the goods have not arrived is not dishonor; the bank must notify its transferor of the refusal but need not present the draft again until it is instructed to do so or learns of the arrival of the goods.

§ 4–503. Responsibility of Presenting Bank for Documents and Goods; Report of Reasons for Dishonor; Referee in Case of Need.

Unless otherwise instructed and except as provided in Article 5, a bank presenting a documentary draft:

(1) must deliver the documents to the drawee on acceptance of the draft if it is payable more than three days after presentment, otherwise, only on payment; and

(2) upon dishonor, either in the case of presentment for acceptance or presentment for payment, may seek and follow instructions from any referee in case of need designated in the draft or, if the presenting bank does not choose to utilize the referee's services, it must use diligence and good faith to ascertain the reason for dishonor, must notify its transferor of the dishonor and of the results of its effort to ascertain the reasons therefor, and must request instructions.

However, the presenting bank is under no obligation with respect to goods represented by the documents except to follow any reasonable instructions seasonably received; it has a right to reimbursement for any expense incurred in following instructions and to prepayment of or indemnity for those expenses.
As amended in 1990.

§ 4–504. Privilege of Presenting Bank to Deal With Goods; Security Interest for Expenses.

(a) A presenting bank that, following the dishonor of a documentary draft, has seasonably requested instructions but does not receive them within a reasonable time may store, sell, or otherwise deal with the goods in any reasonable manner.

(b) For its reasonable expenses incurred by action under subsection (a) the presenting bank has a lien upon the goods or their proceeds, which may be foreclosed in the same manner as an unpaid seller's lien.
As amended in 1990.

ARTICLE 4A: FUNDS TRANSFERS

Part 1—Subject Matter and Definitions

§ 4A–101. Short Title.

This Article may be cited as Uniform Commercial Code—Funds Transfers.

§ 4A–102. Subject Matter.

Except as otherwise provided in Section 4A–108, this Article applies to funds transfers defined in Section 4A–104.

§ 4A–103. Payment Order–Definitions.

(a) In this Article:

(1) "Payment order" means an instruction of a sender to a receiving bank, transmitted orally, electronically, or in writing, to pay, or to cause another bank to pay, a fixed or determinable amount of money to a beneficiary if:

   (i) the instruction does not state a condition to payment to the beneficiary other than time of payment,

   (ii) the receiving bank is to be reimbursed by debiting an account of, or otherwise receiving payment from, the sender, and

   (iii) the instruction is transmitted by the sender directly to the receiving bank or to an agent, funds-transfer system, or communication system for transmittal to the receiving bank.

(2) "Beneficiary" means the person to be paid by the beneficiary's bank.

(3) "Beneficiary's bank" means the bank identified in a payment order in which an account of the beneficiary is to be credited pursuant to the order or which otherwise is to make payment to the beneficiary if the order does not provide for payment to an account.

(4) "Receiving bank" means the bank to which the sender's instruction is addressed.

(5) "Sender" means the person giving the instruction to the receiving bank.

(b) If an instruction complying with subsection (a)(1) is to make more than one payment to a beneficiary, the instruction is a separate payment order with respect to each payment.

(c) A payment order is issued when it is sent to the receiving bank.

§ 4A–104. Funds Transfer–Definitions.

In this Article:

(a) "Funds transfer" means the series of transactions, beginning with the originator's payment order, made for the purpose of making payment to the beneficiary of the order. The term includes any payment order issued by the originator's bank or an intermediary bank intended to carry out the originator's payment order. A funds transfer is completed by acceptance by the beneficiary's bank of a payment order for the benefit of the beneficiary of the originator's payment order.

(b) "Intermediary bank" means a receiving bank other than the originator's bank or the beneficiary's bank.

(c) "Originator" means the sender of the first payment order in a funds transfer.

(d) "Originator's bank" means (i) the receiving bank to which the payment order of the originator is issued if the originator is not a bank, or (ii) the originator if the originator is a bank.

§ 4A–105. Other Definitions.

(a) In this Article:

(1) "Authorized account" means a deposit account of a customer in a bank designated by the customer as a source of payment of payment orders issued by the customer to the bank. If a customer does not so designate an account, any account of the customer is an authorized account if payment of a payment order from that account is not inconsistent with a restriction on the use of that account.

(2) "Bank" means a person engaged in the business of banking and includes a savings bank, savings and loan association, credit union, and trust company. A branch or separate office of a bank is a separate bank for purposes of this Article.

(3) "Customer" means a person, including a bank, having an account with a bank or from whom a bank has agreed to receive payment orders.

(4) "Funds-transfer business day" of a receiving bank means the part of a day during which the receiving bank is open for the receipt, processing, and transmittal of payment orders and cancellations and amendments of payment orders.

(5) "Funds-transfer system" means a wire transfer network, automated clearing house, or other communication system of a clearing house or other association of banks through which a payment order by a bank may be transmitted to the bank to which the order is addressed.

(6) "Good faith" means honesty in fact and the observance of reasonable commercial standards of fair dealing.

(7) "Prove" with respect to a fact means to meet the burden of establishing the fact (Section 1–201(8)).

(b) Other definitions applying to this Article and the sections in which they appear are:

"Acceptance"	Section 4A–209
"Beneficiary"	Section 4A–103
"Beneficiary's bank"	Section 4A–103
"Executed"	Section 4A–301

"Execution date"	Section 4A–301
"Funds transfer"	Section 4A–104
"Funds-transfer system rule"	Section 4A–501
"Intermediary bank"	Section 4A–104
"Originator"	Section 4A–104
"Originator's bank"	Section 4A–104
"Payment by beneficiary's bank to beneficiary"	Section 4A–405
"Payment by originator to beneficiary"	Section 4A–406
"Payment by sender to receiving bank"	Section 4A–403
"Payment date"	Section 4A–401
"Payment order"	Section 4A–103
"Receiving bank"	Section 4A–103
"Security procedure"	Section 4A–201
"Sender"	Section 4A–103

(c) The following definitions in Article 4 apply to this Article:

"Clearing house"	Section 4–104
"Item"	Section 4–104
"Suspends payments"	Section 4–104

(d) In addition, Article 1 contains general definitions and principles of construction and interpretation applicable throughout this Article.

§ 4A–106. Time Payment Order Is Received.
(a) The time of receipt of a payment order or communication cancelling or amending a payment order is determined by the rules applicable to receipt of a notice stated in Section 1–201(27). A receiving bank may fix a cut-off time or times on a funds-transfer business day for the receipt and processing of payment orders and communications cancelling or amending payment orders. Different cut-off times may apply to payment orders, cancellations, or amendments, or to different categories of payment orders, cancellations, or amendments. A cut-off time may apply to senders generally or different cut-off times may apply to different senders or categories of payment orders. If a payment order or communication cancelling or amending a payment order is received after the close of a funds-transfer business day or after the appropriate cut-off time on a funds-transfer business day, the receiving bank may treat the payment order or communication as received at the opening of the next funds-transfer business day.
(b) If this Article refers to an execution date or payment date or states a day on which a receiving bank is required to take action, and the date or day does not fall on a funds-transfer business day, the next day that is a funds-transfer business day is treated as the date or day stated, unless the contrary is stated in this Article.

§ 4A–107. Federal Reserve Regulations and Operating Circulars.
Regulations of the Board of Governors of the Federal Reserve System and operating circulars of the Federal Reserve Banks supersede any inconsistent provision of this Article to the extent of the inconsistency.

§ 4A–108. Exclusion of Consumer Transactions Governed by Federal Law.
This Article does not apply to a funds transfer any part of which is governed by the Electronic Fund Transfer Act of 1978 (Title XX, Public Law 95–630, 92 Stat. 3728, 15 U.S.C. § 1693 *et seq.)* as amended from time to time.

Part 2—Issue and Acceptance of Payment Order
§ 4A–201. Security Procedure.
"Security procedure" means a procedure established by agreement of a customer and a receiving bank for the purpose of (i) verifying that a payment order or communication amending or cancelling a payment order is that of the customer, or (ii) detecting error in the transmission or the content of the payment order or communication. A security procedure may require the use of algorithms or other codes, identifying words or numbers, encryption, callback procedures, or similar security devices. Comparison of a signature on a payment order or communication with an authorized specimen signature of the customer is not by itself a security procedure.

§ 4A–202. Authorized and Verified Payment Orders.
(a) A payment order received by the receiving bank is the authorized order of the person identified as sender if that person authorized the order or is otherwise bound by it under the law of agency.
(b) If a bank and its customer have agreed that the authenticity of payment orders issued to the bank in the name of the customer as sender will be verified pursuant to a security procedure, a payment order received by the receiving bank is effective as the order of the customer, whether or not authorized, if (i) the security procedure is a commercially reasonable method of providing security against unauthorized payment orders, and (ii) the bank proves that it accepted the payment order in good faith and in compliance with the security procedure and any written agreement or instruction of the customer restricting acceptance of payment orders issued in the name of the customer. The bank is not required to follow an instruction that violates a written agreement with the customer or notice of which is not received at a time and in a manner affording the bank a reasonable opportunity to act on it before the payment order is accepted.
(c) Commercial reasonableness of a security procedure is a question of law to be determined by considering the wishes of the customer expressed to the bank, the circumstances of the customer known to the bank, including the size, type, and frequency of payment orders normally issued by the customer to the bank, alternative security procedures offered to the customer, and security procedures in general use by customers and receiving banks similarly situated. A security procedure is deemed to be commercially reasonable if (i) the security procedure was chosen by the customer after the bank offered, and the customer refused, a security procedure that was commercially reasonable for that customer, and (ii) the customer expressly agreed in writing to be bound by any payment order, whether or not authorized, issued in its name and accepted by the bank in compliance with the security procedure chosen by the customer.
(d) The term "sender" in this Article includes the customer in whose name a payment order is issued if the order is the authorized order of the customer under subsection (a), or it is effective as the order of the customer under subsection (b).
(e) This section applies to amendments and cancellations of payment orders to the same extent it applies to payment orders.

(f) Except as provided in this section and in Section 4A–203(a)(1), rights and obligations arising under this section or Section 4A–203 may not be varied by agreement.

§ 4A–203. Unenforceability of Certain Verified Payment Orders.

(a) If an accepted payment order is not, under Section 4A–202(a), an authorized order of a customer identified as sender, but is effective as an order of the customer pursuant to Section 4A–202(b), the following rules apply:

    (1) By express written agreement, the receiving bank may limit the extent to which it is entitled to enforce or retain payment of the payment order.

    (2) The receiving bank is not entitled to enforce or retain payment of the payment order if the customer proves that the order was not caused, directly or indirectly, by a person (i) entrusted at any time with duties to act for the customer with respect to payment orders or the security procedure, or (ii) who obtained access to transmitting facilities of the customer or who obtained, from a source controlled by the customer and without authority of the receiving bank, information facilitating breach of the security procedure, regardless of how the information was obtained or whether the customer was at fault. Information includes any access device, computer software, or the like.

(b) This section applies to amendments of payment orders to the same extent it applies to payment orders.

§ 4A–204. Refund of Payment and Duty of Customer to Report with Respect to Unauthorized Payment Order.

(a) If a receiving bank accepts a payment order issued in the name of its customer as sender which is (i) not authorized and not effective as the order of the customer under Section 4A–202, or (ii) not enforceable, in whole or in part, against the customer under Section 4A–203, the bank shall refund any payment of the payment order received from the customer to the extent the bank is not entitled to enforce payment and shall pay interest on the refundable amount calculated from the date the bank received payment to the date of the refund. However, the customer is not entitled to interest from the bank on the amount to be refunded if the customer fails to exercise ordinary care to determine that the order was not authorized by the customer and to notify the bank of the relevant facts within a reasonable time not exceeding 90 days after the date the customer received notification from the bank that the order was accepted or that the customer's account was debited with respect to the order. The bank is not entitled to any recovery from the customer on account of a failure by the customer to give notification as stated in this section.

(b) Reasonable time under subsection (a) may be fixed by agreement as stated in Section 1–204(1), but the obligation of a receiving bank to refund payment as stated in subsection (a) may not otherwise be varied by agreement.

§ 4A–205. Erroneous Payment Orders.

(a) If an accepted payment order was transmitted pursuant to a security procedure for the detection of error and the payment order (i) erroneously instructed payment to a beneficiary not intended by the sender, (ii) erroneously instructed payment in an amount greater than the amount intended by the sender, or (iii) was an erroneously transmitted duplicate of a payment order previously sent by the sender, the following rules apply:

    (1) If the sender proves that the sender or a person acting on behalf of the sender pursuant to Section 4A–206 complied with the security procedure and that the error would have been detected if the receiving bank had also complied, the sender is not obliged to pay the order to the extent stated in paragraphs (2) and (3).

    (2) If the funds transfer is completed on the basis of an erroneous payment order described in clause (i) or (iii) of subsection (a), the sender is not obliged to pay the order and the receiving bank is entitled to recover from the beneficiary any amount paid to the beneficiary to the extent allowed by the law governing mistake and restitution.

    (3) If the funds transfer is completed on the basis of a payment order described in clause (ii) of subsection (a), the sender is not obliged to pay the order to the extent the amount received by the beneficiary is greater than the amount intended by the sender. In that case, the receiving bank is entitled to recover from the beneficiary the excess amount received to the extent allowed by the law governing mistake and restitution.

(b) If (i) the sender of an erroneous payment order described in subsection (a) is not obliged to pay all or part of the order, and (ii) the sender receives notification from the receiving bank that the order was accepted by the bank or that the sender's account was debited with respect to the order, the sender has a duty to exercise ordinary care, on the basis of information available to the sender, to discover the error with respect to the order and to advise the bank of the relevant facts within a reasonable time, not exceeding 90 days, after the bank's notification was received by the sender. If the bank proves that the sender failed to perform that duty, the sender is liable to the bank for the loss the bank proves it incurred as a result of the failure, but the liability of the sender may not exceed the amount of the sender's order.

(c) This section applies to amendments to payment orders to the same extent it applies to payment orders.

§ 4A–206. Transmission of Payment Order through Funds-Transfer or Other Communication System.

(a) If a payment order addressed to a receiving bank is transmitted to a funds-transfer system or other third party communication system for transmittal to the bank, the system is deemed to be an agent of the sender for the purpose of transmitting the payment order to the bank. If there is a discrepancy between the terms of the payment order transmitted to the system and the terms of the payment order transmitted by the system to the bank, the terms of the payment order of the sender are those transmitted by the system. This section does not apply to a funds-transfer system of the Federal Reserve Banks.

(b) This section applies to cancellations and amendments to payment orders to the same extent it applies to payment orders.

§ 4A–207. Misdescription of Beneficiary.

(a) Subject to subsection (b), if, in a payment order received by the beneficiary's bank, the name, bank account number, or other identification of the beneficiary refers to a nonexistent or unidentifiable person or account, no person has rights as a beneficiary of the order and acceptance of the order cannot occur.

(b) If a payment order received by the beneficiary's bank identifies the beneficiary both by name and by an identifying or bank account number and the name and number identify different persons, the following rules apply:

(1) Except as otherwise provided in subsection (c), if the beneficiary's bank does not know that the name and number refer to different persons, it may rely on the number as the proper identification of the beneficiary of the order. The beneficiary's bank need not determine whether the name and number refer to the same person.

(2) If the beneficiary's bank pays the person identified by name or knows that the name and number identify different persons, no person has rights as beneficiary except the person paid by the beneficiary's bank if that person was entitled to receive payment from the originator of the funds transfer. If no person has rights as beneficiary, acceptance of the order cannot occur.

(c) If (i) a payment order described in subsection (b) is accepted, (ii) the originator's payment order described the beneficiary inconsistently by name and number, and (iii) the beneficiary's bank pays the person identified by number as permitted by subsection (b)(1), the following rules apply:

(1) If the originator is a bank, the originator is obliged to pay its order.

(2) If the originator is not a bank and proves that the person identified by number was not entitled to receive payment from the originator, the originator is not obliged to pay its order unless the originator's bank proves that the originator, before acceptance of the originator's order, had notice that payment of a payment order issued by the originator might be made by the beneficiary's bank on the basis of an identifying or bank account number even if it identifies a person different from the named beneficiary. Proof of notice may be made by any admissible evidence. The originator's bank satisfies the burden of proof if it proves that the originator, before the payment order was accepted, signed a writing stating the information to which the notice relates.

(d) In a case governed by subsection (b)(1), if the beneficiary's bank rightfully pays the person identified by number and that person was not entitled to receive payment from the originator, the amount paid may be recovered from that person to the extent allowed by the law governing mistake and restitution as follows:

(1) If the originator is obliged to pay its payment order as stated in subsection (c), the originator has the right to recover.

(2) If the originator is not a bank and is not obliged to pay its payment order, the originator's bank has the right to recover.

§ 4A–208. Misdescription of Intermediary Bank or Beneficiary's Bank.

(a) This subsection applies to a payment order identifying an intermediary bank or the beneficiary's bank only by an identifying number.

(1) The receiving bank may rely on the number as the proper identification of the intermediary or beneficiary's bank and need not determine whether the number identifies a bank.

(2) The sender is obliged to compensate the receiving bank for any loss and expenses incurred by the receiving bank as a result of its reliance on the number in executing or attempting to execute the order.

(b) This subsection applies to a payment order identifying an intermediary bank or the beneficiary's bank both by name and an identifying number if the name and number identify different persons.

(1) If the sender is a bank, the receiving bank may rely on the number as the proper identification of the intermediary or beneficiary's bank if the receiving bank, when it executes the sender's order, does not know that the name and number identify different persons. The receiving bank need not determine whether the name and number refer to the same person or whether the number refers to a bank. The sender is obliged to compensate the receiving bank for any loss and expenses incurred by the receiving bank as a result of its reliance on the number in executing or attempting to execute the order.

(2) If the sender is not a bank and the receiving bank proves that the sender, before the payment order was accepted, had notice that the receiving bank might rely on the number as the proper identification of the intermediary or beneficiary's bank even if it identifies a person different from the bank identified by name, the rights and obligations of the sender and the receiving bank are governed by subsection (b)(1), as though the sender were a bank. Proof of notice may be made by any admissible evidence. The receiving bank satisfies the burden of proof if it proves that the sender, before the payment order was accepted, signed a writing stating the information to which the notice relates.

(3) Regardless of whether the sender is a bank, the receiving bank may rely on the name as the proper identification of the intermediary or beneficiary's bank if the receiving bank, at the time it executes the sender's order, does not know that the name and number identify different persons. The receiving bank need not determine whether the name and number refer to the same person.

(4) If the receiving bank knows that the name and number identify different persons, reliance on either the name or the number in executing the sender's payment order is a breach of the obligation stated in Section 4A–302(a)(1).

§ 4A–209. Acceptance of Payment Order.

(a) Subject to subsection (d), a receiving bank other than the beneficiary's bank accepts a payment order when it executes the order.

(b) Subject to subsections (c) and (d), a beneficiary's bank accepts a payment order at the earliest of the following times:

(1) When the bank (i) pays the beneficiary as stated in Section 4A–405(a) or 4A–405(b), or (ii) notifies the beneficiary of receipt of the order or that the account of the beneficiary has been credited with respect to the order unless the notice indicates that the bank is rejecting the order or that funds with respect to the order may not be withdrawn or used until receipt of payment from the sender of the order;

(2) When the bank receives payment of the entire amount of the sender's order pursuant to Section 4A–403(a)(1) or 4A–403(a)(2); or

(3) The opening of the next funds-transfer business day of the bank following the payment date of the order if, at that time, the amount of the sender's order is fully covered by a withdrawable credit balance in an authorized account of the sender or the bank has otherwise received full payment from the sender, unless the order was rejected before that time or is rejected within (i) one hour after that time, or (ii) one hour after the opening of the next business day of the sender following the payment date if that time is later. If notice of rejection is received by the sender after the payment date and the authorized account of the sender does not bear interest, the bank is obliged to pay interest to the sender on the amount of the order for the number of days elapsing after the payment date to the day the sender receives notice or learns that the order was not accepted, counting that day as an elapsed day. If the withdrawable credit balance during that period falls below the amount of the order, the amount of interest payable is reduced accordingly.

(c) Acceptance of a payment order cannot occur before the order is received by the receiving bank. Acceptance does not occur under subsection (b)(2) or (b)(3) if the beneficiary of the payment order does not have an account with the receiving bank, the account has been closed, or the receiving bank is not permitted by law to receive credits for the beneficiary's account.

(d) A payment order issued to the originator's bank cannot be accepted until the payment date if the bank is the beneficiary's bank, or the execution date if the bank is not the beneficiary's bank. If the originator's bank executes the originator's payment order before the execution date or pays the beneficiary of the originator's payment order before the payment date and the payment order is subsequently cancelled pursuant to Section 4A–211(b), the bank may recover from the beneficiary any payment received to the extent allowed by the law governing mistake and restitution.

§ 4A–210. Rejection of Payment Order.

(a) A payment order is rejected by the receiving bank by a notice of rejection transmitted to the sender orally, electronically, or in writing. A notice of rejection need not use any particular words and is sufficient if it indicates that the receiving bank is rejecting the order or will not execute or pay the order. Rejection is effective when the notice is given if transmission is by a means that is reasonable in the circumstances. If notice of rejection is given by a means that is not reasonable, rejection is effective when the notice is received. If an agreement of the sender and receiving bank establishes the means to be used to reject a payment order, (i) any means complying with the agreement is reasonable and (ii) any means not complying is not reasonable unless no significant delay in receipt of the notice resulted from the use of the noncomplying means.

(b) This subsection applies if a receiving bank other than the beneficiary's bank fails to execute a payment order despite the existence on the execution date of a withdrawable credit balance in an authorized account of the sender sufficient to cover the order. If the sender does not receive notice of rejection of the order on the execution date and the authorized account of the sender does not bear interest, the bank is obliged to pay interest to the sender on the amount of the order for the number of days elapsing after the execution date to the earlier of the day the order is cancelled pursuant to Section 4A–211(d) or the day the sender receives notice or learns that the order was not executed, counting the final day of the period as an elapsed day. If the withdrawable credit balance during that period falls below the amount of the order, the amount of interest is reduced accordingly.

(c) If a receiving bank suspends payments, all unaccepted payment orders issued to it are are deemed rejected at the time the bank suspends payments.

(d) Acceptance of a payment order precludes a later rejection of the order. Rejection of a payment order precludes a later acceptance of the order.

§ 4A–211. Cancellation and Amendment of Payment Order.

(a) A communication of the sender of a payment order cancelling or amending the order may be transmitted to the receiving bank orally, electronically, or in writing. If a security procedure is in effect between the sender and the receiving bank, the communication is not effective to cancel or amend the order unless the communication is verified pursuant to the security procedure or the bank agrees to the cancellation or amendment.

(b) Subject to subsection (a), a communication by the sender cancelling or amending a payment order is effective to cancel or amend the order if notice of the communication is received at a time and in a manner affording the receiving bank a reasonable opportunity to act on the communication before the bank accepts the payment order.

(c) After a payment order has been accepted, cancellation or amendment of the order is not effective unless the receiving bank agrees or a funds-transfer system rule allows cancellation or amendment without agreement of the bank.

(1) With respect to a payment order accepted by a receiving bank other than the beneficiary's bank, cancellation or amendment is not effective unless a conforming cancellation or amendment of the payment order issued by the receiving bank is also made.

(2) With respect to a payment order accepted by the beneficiary's bank, cancellation or amendment is not effective unless the order was issued in execution of an unauthorized payment order, or because of a mistake by a sender in the funds transfer which resulted in the issuance of a payment order (i) that is a duplicate of a payment order previously issued by the sender, (ii) that orders payment to a beneficiary not entitled to receive payment from the originator, or (iii) that orders payment in an amount greater than the amount the beneficiary was entitled to receive from the originator. If the payment order is cancelled or amended, the beneficiary's bank is entitled to recover from the beneficiary any amount paid to the beneficiary to the extent allowed by the law governing mistake and restitution.

(d) An unaccepted payment order is cancelled by operation of law at the close of the fifth funds-transfer business day of the receiving bank after the execution date or payment date of the order.

(e) A cancelled payment order cannot be accepted. If an accepted payment order is cancelled, the acceptance is nullified and no person has any right or obligation based on the acceptance. Amendment of a payment order is deemed to be cancellation of the original order at the time of amendment and issue of a new payment order in the amended form at the same time.

(f) Unless otherwise provided in an agreement of the parties or in a funds-transfer system rule, if the receiving bank, after accepting a payment order, agrees to cancellation or amendment of the order by the sender or is bound by a funds-transfer system rule allowing cancellation or amendment without the bank's agreement, the sender, whether or not cancellation or amendment is effective, is liable to the bank for any loss and expenses, including reasonable attorney's fees, incurred by the bank as a result of the cancellation or amendment or attempted cancellation or amendment.

(g) A payment order is not revoked by the death or legal incapacity of the sender unless the receiving bank knows of the death or of an adjudication of incapacity by a court of competent jurisdiction and has reasonable opportunity to act before acceptance of the order.

(h) A funds-transfer system rule is not effective to the extent it conflicts with subsection (c)(2).

§ 4A–212. Liability and Duty of Receiving Bank Regarding Unaccepted Payment Order.

If a receiving bank fails to accept a payment order that it is obliged by express agreement to accept, the bank is liable for breach of the agreement to the extent provided in the agreement or in this Article, but does not otherwise have any duty to accept a payment order or, before acceptance, to take any action, or refrain from taking action, with respect to the order except as provided in this Article or by express agreement. Liability based on acceptance arises only when acceptance occurs as stated in Section 4A–209, and liability is limited to that provided in this Article. A receiving bank is not the agent of the sender or beneficiary of the payment order it accepts, or of any other party to the funds transfer, and the bank owes no duty to any party to the funds transfer except as provided in this Article or by express agreement.

Part 3—Execution of Sender's Payment Order by Receiving Bank

§ 4A–301. Execution and Execution Date.

(a) A payment order is "executed" by the receiving bank when it issues a payment order intended to carry out the payment order received by the bank. A payment order received by the beneficiary's bank can be accepted but cannot be executed.

(b) "Execution date" of a payment order means the day on which the receiving bank may properly issue a payment order in execution of the sender's order. The execution date may be determined by instruction of the sender but cannot be ear-

lier than the day the order is received and, unless otherwise determined, is the day the order is received. If the sender's instruction states a payment date, the execution date is the payment date or an earlier date on which execution is reasonably necessary to allow payment to the beneficiary on the payment date.

§ 4A–302. Obligations of Receiving Bank in Execution of Payment Order.

(a) Except as provided in subsections (b) through (d), if the receiving bank accepts a payment order pursuant to Section 4A–209(a), the bank has the following obligations in executing the order:

(1) The receiving bank is obliged to issue, on the execution date, a payment order complying with the sender's order and to follow the sender's instructions concerning (i) any intermediary bank or funds-transfer system to be used in carrying out the funds transfer, or (ii) the means by which payment orders are to be transmitted in the funds transfer. If the originator's bank issues a payment order to an intermediary bank, the originator's bank is obliged to instruct the intermediary bank according to the instruction of the originator. An intermediary bank in the funds transfer is similarly bound by an instruction given to it by the sender of the payment order it accepts.

(2) If the sender's instruction states that the funds transfer is to be carried out telephonically or by wire transfer or otherwise indicates that the funds transfer is to be carried out by the most expeditious means, the receiving bank is obliged to transmit its payment order by the most expeditious available means, and to instruct any intermediary bank accordingly. If a sender's instruction states a payment date, the receiving bank is obliged to transmit its payment order at a time and by means reasonably necessary to allow payment to the beneficiary on the payment date or as soon thereafter as is feasible.

(b) Unless otherwise instructed, a receiving bank executing a payment order may (i) use any funds-transfer system if use of that system is reasonable in the circumstances, and (ii) issue a payment order to the beneficiary's bank or to an intermediary bank through which a payment order conforming to the sender's order can expeditiously be issued to the beneficiary's bank if the receiving bank exercises ordinary care in the selection of the intermediary bank. A receiving bank is not required to follow an instruction of the sender designating a funds-transfer system to be used in carrying out the funds transfer if the receiving bank, in good faith, determines that it is not feasible to follow the instruction or that following the instruction would unduly delay completion of the funds transfer.

(c) Unless subsection (a)(2) applies or the receiving bank is otherwise instructed, the bank may execute a payment order by transmitting its payment order by first class mail or by any means reasonable in the circumstances. If the receiving bank is instructed to execute the sender's order by transmitting its payment order by a particular means, the receiving bank may issue its payment order by the means stated or by any means as expeditious as the means stated.

(d) Unless instructed by the sender, (i) the receiving bank may not obtain payment of its charges for services and expenses in connection with the execution of the sender's order by issuing a payment order in an amount equal to the amount of the sender's order less the amount of the charges, and (ii) may not instruct a subsequent receiving bank to obtain payment of its charges in the same manner.

§ 4A–303. Erroneous Execution of Payment Order.

(a) A receiving bank that (i) executes the payment order of the sender by issuing a payment order in an amount greater than the amount of the sender's order, or (ii) issues a payment order in execution of the sender's order and then issues a duplicate order, is entitled to payment of the amount of the sender's order under Section 4A–402(c) if that subsection is otherwise satisfied. The bank is entitled to recover from the beneficiary of the erroneous order the excess payment received to the extent allowed by the law governing mistake and restitution.

(b) A receiving bank that executes the payment order of the sender by issuing a payment order in an amount less than the amount of the sender's order is entitled to payment of the amount of the sender's order under Section 4A–402(c) if (i) that subsection is otherwise satisfied and (ii) the bank corrects its mistake by issuing an additional payment order for the benefit of the beneficiary of the sender's order. If the error is not corrected, the issuer of the erroneous order is entitled to receive or retain payment from the sender of the order it accepted only to the extent of the amount of the erroneous order. This subsection does not apply if the receiving bank executes the sender's payment order by issuing a payment order in an amount less than the amount of the sender's order for the purpose of obtaining payment of its charges for services and expenses pursuant to instruction of the sender.

(c) If a receiving bank executes the payment order of the sender by issuing a payment order to a beneficiary different from the beneficiary of the sender's order and the funds transfer is completed on the basis of that error, the sender of the payment order that was erroneously executed and all previous senders in the funds transfer are not obliged to pay the payment orders they issued. The issuer of the erroneous order is entitled to recover from the beneficiary of the order the payment received to the extent allowed by the law governing mistake and restitution.

§ 4A–304. Duty of Sender to Report Erroneously Executed Payment Order.

If the sender of a payment order that is erroneously executed as stated in Section 4A–303 receives notification from the receiving bank that the order was executed or that the sender's account was debited with respect to the order, the sender has a duty to exercise ordinary care to determine, on the basis of information available to the sender, that the order was erroneously executed and to notify the bank of the relevant facts within a reasonable time not exceeding 90 days after the notification from the bank was received by the sender. If the sender fails to perform that duty, the bank is not obliged to pay interest on any amount refundable to the sender under Section 4A–402(d) for the period before the bank learns of the execution error. The bank is not entitled to any recovery from the sender on account of a failure by the sender to perform the duty stated in this section.

§ 4A–305. Liability for Late or Improper Execution or Failure to Execute Payment Order.

(a) If a funds transfer is completed but execution of a payment order by the receiving bank in breach of Section 4A–302 results in delay in payment to the beneficiary, the bank is obliged to pay interest to either the originator or the beneficiary of the funds transfer for the period of delay caused by the improper execution. Except as provided in subsection (c), additional damages are not recoverable.

(b) If execution of a payment order by a receiving bank in breach of Section 4A–302 results in (i) noncompletion of the funds transfer, (ii) failure to use an intermediary bank designated by the originator, or (iii) issuance of a payment order that does not comply with the terms of the payment order of the originator, the bank is liable to the originator for its expenses in the funds transfer and for incidental expenses and interest losses, to the extent not covered by subsection (a), resulting from the improper execution. Except as provided in subsection (c), additional damages are not recoverable.

(c) In addition to the amounts payable under subsections (a) and (b), damages, including consequential damages, are recoverable to the extent provided in an express written agreement of the receiving bank.

(d) If a receiving bank fails to execute a payment order it was obliged by express agreement to execute, the receiving bank is liable to the sender for its expenses in the transaction and for incidental expenses and interest losses resulting from the failure to execute. Additional damages, including consequential damages, are recoverable to the extent provided in an express written agreement of the receiving bank, but are not otherwise recoverable.

(e) Reasonable attorney's fees are recoverable if demand for compensation under subsection (a) or (b) is made and refused before an action is brought on the claim. If a claim is made for breach of an agreement under subsection (d) and the agreement does not provide for damages, reasonable attorney's fees are recoverable if demand for compensation under subsection (d) is made and refused before an action is brought on the claim.

(f) Except as stated in this section, the liability of a receiving bank under subsections (a) and (b) may not be varied by agreement.

Part 4—Payment

§ 4A–401. Payment Date.

"Payment date" of a payment order means the day on which the amount of the order is payable to the beneficiary by the beneficiary's bank. The payment date may be determined by instruction of the sender but cannot be earlier than the day the order is received by the beneficiary's bank and, unless otherwise determined, is the day the order is received by the beneficiary's bank.

§ 4A–402. Obligation of Sender to Pay Receiving Bank.

(a) This section is subject to Sections 4A–205 and 4A–207.

(b) With respect to a payment order issued to the beneficiary's bank, acceptance of the order by the bank obliges the sender to pay the bank the amount of the order, but payment is not due until the payment date of the order.

(c) This subsection is subject to subsection (e) and to Section 4A–303. With respect to a payment order issued to a receiving bank other than the beneficiary's bank, acceptance of the order by the receiving bank obliges the sender to pay the bank the amount of the sender's order. Payment by the sender is not due until the execution date of the sender's order. The obligation of that sender to pay its payment order is excused if the funds transfer is not completed by acceptance by the beneficiary's bank of a payment order instructing payment to the beneficiary of that sender's payment order.

(d) If the sender of a payment order pays the order and was not obliged to pay all or part of the amount paid, the bank receiving payment is obliged to refund payment to the extent the sender was not obliged to pay. Except as provided in Sections 4A–204 and 4A–304, interest is payable on the refundable amount from the date of payment.

(e) If a funds transfer is not completed as stated in subsection (c) and an intermediary bank is obliged to refund payment as stated in subsection (d) but is unable to do so because not permitted by applicable law or because the bank suspends payments, a sender in the funds transfer that executed a payment order in compliance with an instruction, as stated in Section 4A–302(a)(1), to route the funds transfer through that intermediary bank is entitled to receive or retain payment from the sender of the payment order that it accepted. The first sender in the funds transfer that issued an instruction requiring routing through that intermediary bank is subrogated to the right of the bank that paid the intermediary bank to refund as stated in subsection (d).

(f) The right of the sender of a payment order to be excused from the obligation to pay the order as stated in subsection (c) or to receive refund under subsection (d) may not be varied by agreement.

§ 4A–403. Payment by Sender to Receiving Bank.

(a) Payment of the sender's obligation under Section 4A–402 to pay the receiving bank occurs as follows:

(1) If the sender is a bank, payment occurs when the receiving bank receives final settlement of the obligation through a Federal Reserve Bank or through a funds-transfer system.

(2) If the sender is a bank and the sender (i) credited an account of the receiving bank with the sender, or (ii) caused an account of the receiving bank in another bank to be credited, payment occurs when the credit is withdrawn or, if not withdrawn, at midnight of the day on which the credit is withdrawable and the receiving bank learns of that fact.

(3) If the receiving bank debits an account of the sender with the receiving bank, payment occurs when the debit is made to the extent the debit is covered by a withdrawable credit balance in the account.

(b) If the sender and receiving bank are members of a funds-transfer system that nets obligations multilaterally among participants, the receiving bank receives final settlement when settlement is complete in accordance with the rules of the system. The obligation of the sender to pay the amount of a payment order transmitted through the funds-transfer system may be satisfied, to the extent permitted by the rules of the system, by setting off and applying against the sender's obligation the right of the sender to receive payment from the receiving bank of the amount of any other payment order transmitted to the sender by the receiving bank through the funds-transfer system. The aggregate balance of obligations owed by each sender to each receiving bank in the funds-transfer system may be satisfied, to the extent permitted by the rules of the system, by setting off and applying against that balance the aggregate balance of obligations owed to the sender by other members of the system. The aggregate balance is determined after the right of setoff stated in the second sentence of this subsection has been exercised.

(c) If two banks transmit payment orders to each other under an agreement that settlement of the obligations of each bank to the other under Section 4A–402 will be made at the end of the day or other period, the total amount owed with respect to all orders transmitted by one bank shall be set off against the total amount owed with respect to all orders transmitted by the other bank. To the extent of the setoff, each bank has made payment to the other.

(d) In a case not covered by subsection (a), the time when payment of the sender's obligation under Section 4A–402(b) or 4A–402(c) occurs is governed by applicable principles of law that determine when an obligation is satisfied.

§ 4A–404. Obligation of Beneficiary's Bank to Pay and Give Notice to Beneficiary.

(a) Subject to Sections 4A–211(e), 4A–405(d), and 4A–405(e), if a beneficiary's bank accepts a payment order, the bank is obliged to pay the amount of the order to the beneficiary of the order. Payment is due on the payment date of the order, but if acceptance occurs on the payment date after the close of the funds-transfer business day of the bank, payment is due on the next funds-transfer business day. If the bank refuses to pay after demand by the beneficiary and receipt of notice of particular circumstances that will give rise to consequential damages as a result of nonpayment, the beneficiary may recover damages resulting from the refusal to pay to the extent the bank had notice of the damages, unless the bank proves that it did not pay because of a reasonable doubt concerning the right of the beneficiary to payment.

(b) If a payment order accepted by the beneficiary's bank instructs payment to an account of the beneficiary, the bank is obliged to notify the beneficiary of receipt of the order before midnight of the next funds-transfer business day following the payment date. If the payment order does not instruct payment to an account of the beneficiary, the bank is required to notify the beneficiary only if notice is required by the order. Notice may be given by first class mail or any other means reasonable in the circumstances. If the bank fails to give the required notice, the bank is obliged to pay interest to the beneficiary on the amount of the payment order from the day notice should have been given until the day the beneficiary learned of receipt of the payment order by the bank. No other damages are recoverable. Reasonable attorney's fees are also recoverable if demand for interest is made and refused before an action is brought on the claim.

(c) The right of a beneficiary to receive payment and damages as stated in subsection (a) may not be varied by agreement or a funds-transfer system rule. The right of a beneficiary to be notified as stated in subsection (b) may be varied by agreement of the beneficiary or by a funds-transfer system rule if the beneficiary is notified of the rule before initiation of the funds transfer.

§ 4A–405. Payment by Beneficiary's Bank to Beneficiary.

(a) If the beneficiary's bank credits an account of the beneficiary of a payment order, payment of the bank's obligation under Section 4A–404(a) occurs when and to the extent (i) the beneficiary is notified of the right to withdraw the credit, (ii) the bank lawfully applies the credit to a debt of the beneficiary, or (iii) funds with respect to the order are otherwise made available to the beneficiary by the bank.

(b) If the beneficiary's bank does not credit an account of the beneficiary of a payment order, the time when payment of the bank's obligation under Section 4A–404(a) occurs is governed by principles of law that determine when an obligation is satisfied.

(c) Except as stated in subsections (d) and (e), if the beneficiary's bank pays the beneficiary of a payment order under a condition to payment or agreement of the beneficiary giving the bank the right to recover payment from the beneficiary if the bank does not receive payment of the order, the condition to payment or agreement is not enforceable.

(d) A funds-transfer system rule may provide that payments made to beneficiaries of funds transfers made through the system are provisional until receipt of payment by the beneficiary's bank of the payment order it accepted. A beneficiary's bank that makes a payment that is provisional under the rule is entitled to refund from the beneficiary if (i) the rule requires that both the beneficiary and the originator be given notice of the provisional nature of the payment before the funds transfer is initiated, (ii) the beneficiary, the beneficiary's bank, and the originator's bank agreed to be bound by the rule, and (iii) the beneficiary's bank did not receive payment of the payment order that it accepted. If the beneficiary is obliged to refund payment to the beneficiary's bank, acceptance of the payment order by the beneficiary's bank is nullified and no payment by the originator of the funds transfer to the beneficiary occurs under Section 4A–406.

(e) This subsection applies to a funds transfer that includes a payment order transmitted over a funds-transfer system that (i) nets obligations multilaterally among participants, and (ii) has in effect a loss-sharing agreement among participants for the purpose of providing funds necessary to complete settlement of the obligations of one or more participants that do not meet their settlement obligations. If the beneficiary's bank in the funds transfer accepts a payment order and the system fails to complete settlement pursuant to its rules with respect to any payment order in the funds transfer, (i) the acceptance by the beneficiary's bank is nullified and no person has any right or obligation based on the acceptance, (ii) the beneficiary's bank is entitled to recover payment from the beneficiary, (iii) no payment by the originator to the beneficiary occurs under Section 4A–406, and (iv) subject to Section 4A–402(e), each sender in

the funds transfer is excused from its obligation to pay its payment order under Section 4A–402(c) because the funds transfer has not been completed.

§ 4A–406. Payment by Originator to Beneficiary; Discharge of Underlying Obligation.

(a) Subject to Sections 4A–211(e), 4A–405(d), and 4A–405(e), the originator of a funds transfer pays the beneficiary of the originator's payment order (i) at the time a payment order for the benefit of the beneficiary is accepted by the beneficiary's bank in the funds transfer and (ii) in an amount equal to the amount of the order accepted by the beneficiary's bank, but not more than the amount of the originator's order.

(b) If payment under subsection (a) is made to satisfy an obligation, the obligation is discharged to the same extent discharge would result from payment to the beneficiary of the same amount in money, unless (i) the payment under subsection (a) was made by a means prohibited by the contract of the beneficiary with respect to the obligation, (ii) the beneficiary, within a reasonable time after receiving notice of receipt of the order by the beneficiary's bank, notified the originator of the beneficiary's refusal of the payment, (iii) funds with respect to the order were not withdrawn by the beneficiary or applied to a debt of the beneficiary, and (iv) the beneficiary would suffer a loss that could reasonably have been avoided if payment had been made by a means complying with the contract. If payment by the originator does not result in discharge under this section, the originator is subrogated to the rights of the beneficiary to receive payment from the beneficiary's bank under Section 4A–404(a).

(c) For the purpose of determining whether discharge of an obligation occurs under subsection (b), if the beneficiary's bank accepts a payment order in an amount equal to the amount of the originator's payment order less charges of one or more receiving banks in the funds transfer, payment to the beneficiary is deemed to be in the amount of the originator's order unless upon demand by the beneficiary the originator does not pay the beneficiary the amount of the deducted charges.

(d) Rights of the originator or of the beneficiary of a funds transfer under this section may be varied only by agreement of the originator and the beneficiary.

Part 5—Miscellaneous Provisions

§ 4A–501. Variation by Agreement and Effect of Funds-Transfer System Rule.

(a) Except as otherwise provided in this Article, the rights and obligations of a party to a funds transfer may be varied by agreement of the affected party.

(b) "Funds-transfer system rule" means a rule of an association of banks (i) governing transmission of payment orders by means of a funds-transfer system of the association or rights and obligations with respect to those orders, or (ii) to the extent the rule governs rights and obligations between banks that are parties to a funds transfer in which a Federal Reserve Bank, acting as an intermediary bank, sends a payment order to the beneficiary's bank. Except as otherwise provided in this Article, a funds-transfer system rule governing rights and obligations between participating banks using the system may be effective even if the rule conflicts with this Article and indirectly affects another party to the funds transfer who does not consent to the rule. A funds-transfer system rule may also govern rights and obligations of parties other than participating banks using the system to the extent stated in Sections 4A–404(c), 4A–405(d), and 4A–507(c).

§ 4A–502. Creditor Process Served on Receiving Bank; Setoff by Beneficiary's Bank.

(a) As used in this section, "creditor process" means levy, attachment, garnishment, notice of lien, sequestration, or similar process issued by or on behalf of a creditor or other claimant with respect to an account.

(b) This subsection applies to creditor process with respect to an authorized account of the sender of a payment order if the creditor process is served on the receiving bank. For the purpose of determining rights with respect to the creditor process, if the receiving bank accepts the payment order the balance in the authorized account is deemed to be reduced by the amount of the payment order to the extent the bank did not otherwise receive payment of the order, unless the creditor process is served at a time and in a manner affording the bank a reasonable opportunity to act on it before the bank accepts the payment order.

(c) If a beneficiary's bank has received a payment order for payment to the beneficiary's account in the bank, the following rules apply:

(1) The bank may credit the beneficiary's account. The amount credited may be set off against an obligation owed by the beneficiary to the bank or may be applied to satisfy creditor process served on the bank with respect to the account.

(2) The bank may credit the beneficiary's account and allow withdrawal of the amount credited unless creditor process with respect to the account is served at a time and in a manner affording the bank a reasonable opportunity to act to prevent withdrawal.

(3) If creditor process with respect to the beneficiary's account has been served and the bank has had a reasonable opportunity to act on it, the bank may not reject the payment order except for a reason unrelated to the service of process.

(d) Creditor process with respect to a payment by the originator to the beneficiary pursuant to a funds transfer may be served only on the beneficiary's bank with respect to the debt owed by that bank to the beneficiary. Any other bank served with the creditor process is not obliged to act with respect to the process.

§ 4A–503. Injunction or Restraining Order with Respect to Funds Transfer.

For proper cause and in compliance with applicable law, a court may restrain (i) a person from issuing a payment order to initiate a funds transfer, (ii) an originator's bank from executing the payment order of the originator, or (iii) the beneficiary's bank from releasing funds to the beneficiary or the beneficiary from withdrawing the funds. A court may not otherwise restrain a person from issuing a payment order, paying or receiving payment of a payment order, or otherwise acting with respect to a funds transfer.

§ 4A–504. Order in Which Items and Payment Orders May Be Charged to Account; Order of Withdrawals from Account.

(a) If a receiving bank has received more than one payment order of the sender or one or more payment orders and other items that are payable from the sender's account, the bank may charge the sender's account with respect to the various orders and items in any sequence.

(b) In determining whether a credit to an account has been withdrawn by the holder of the account or applied to a debt of the holder of the account, credits first made to the account are first withdrawn or applied.

§ 4A–505. Preclusion of Objection to Debit of Customer's Account.

If a receiving bank has received payment from its customer with respect to a payment order issued in the name of the customer as sender and accepted by the bank, and the customer received notification reasonably identifying the order, the customer is precluded from asserting that the bank is not entitled to retain the payment unless the customer notifies the bank of the customer's objection to the payment within one year after the notification was received by the customer.

§ 4A–506. Rate of Interest.

(a) If, under this Article, a receiving bank is obliged to pay interest with respect to a payment order issued to the bank, the amount payable may be determined (i) by agreement of the sender and receiving bank, or (ii) by a funds-transfer system rule if the payment order is transmitted through a funds-transfer system.

(b) If the amount of interest is not determined by an agreement or rule as stated in subsection (a), the amount is calculated by multiplying the applicable Federal Funds rate by the amount on which interest is payable, and then multiplying the product by the number of days for which interest is payable. The applicable Federal Funds rate is the average of the Federal Funds rates published by the Federal Reserve Bank of New York for each of the days for which interest is payable divided by 360. The Federal Funds rate for any day on which a published rate is not available is the same as the published rate for the next preceding day for which there is a published rate. If a receiving bank that accepted a payment order is required to refund payment to the sender of the order because the funds transfer was not completed, but the failure to complete was not due to any fault by the bank, the interest payable is reduced by a percentage equal to the reserve requirement on deposits of the receiving bank.

§ 4A–507. Choice of Law.

(a) The following rules apply unless the affected parties otherwise agree or subsection (c) applies:

(1) The rights and obligations between the sender of a payment order and the receiving bank are governed by the law of the jurisdiction in which the receiving bank is located.

(2) The rights and obligations between the beneficiary's bank and the beneficiary are governed by the law of the jurisdiction in which the beneficiary's bank is located.

(3) The issue of when payment is made pursuant to a funds transfer by the originator to the beneficiary is governed by the law of the jurisdiction in which the beneficiary's bank is located.

(b) If the parties described in each paragraph of subsection (a) have made an agreement selecting the law of a particular jurisdiction to govern rights and obligations between each other, the law of that jurisdiction governs those rights and obligations, whether or not the payment order or the funds transfer bears a reasonable relation to that jurisdiction.

(c) A funds-transfer system rule may select the law of a particular jurisdiction to govern (i) rights and obligations between participating banks with respect to payment orders transmitted or processed through the system, or (ii) the rights and obligations of some or all parties to a funds transfer any part of which is carried out by means of the system. A choice of law made pursuant to clause (i) is binding on participating banks. A choice of law made pursuant to clause (ii) is binding on the originator, other sender, or a receiving bank having notice that the funds-transfer system might be used in the funds transfer and of the choice of law by the system when the originator, other sender, or receiving bank issued or accepted a payment order. The beneficiary of a funds transfer is bound by the choice of law if, when the funds transfer is initiated, the beneficiary has notice that the funds-transfer system might be used in the funds transfer and of the choice of law by the system. The law of a jurisdiction selected pursuant to this subsection may govern, whether or not that law bears a reasonable relation to the matter in issue.

(d) In the event of inconsistency between an agreement under subsection (b) and a choice-of-law rule under subsection (c), the agreement under subsection (b) prevails.

(e) If a funds transfer is made by use of more than one funds-transfer system and there is inconsistency between choice-of-law rules of the systems, the matter in issue is governed by the law of the selected jurisdiction that has the most significant relationship to the matter in issue.

REVISED ARTICLE 5: LETTERS OF CREDIT

§ 5–101 Short Title.
This article may be cited as Uniform Commercial Code—Letters of Credit.

§ 5–102. Definitions.
(a) In this article:

(1) "Adviser" means a person who, at the request of the issuer, a confirmer, or another adviser, notifies or requests another adviser to notify the beneficiary that a letter of credit has been issued, confirmed, or amended.

(2) "Applicant" means a person at whose request or for whose account a letter of credit is issued. The term includes a person who requests an issuer to issue a letter of credit on behalf of another if the person making the request undertakes an obligation to reimburse the issuer.

(3) "Beneficiary" means a person who under the terms of a letter of credit is entitled to have its complying presentation honored. The term includes a person to whom drawing rights have been transferred under a transferable letter of credit.

(4) "Confirmer" means a nominated person who undertakes, at the request or with the consent of the issuer, to honor a presentation under a letter of credit issued by another.

(5) "Dishonor" of a letter of credit means failure timely to honor or to take an interim action, such as acceptance of a draft, that may be required by the letter of credit.

(6) "Document" means a draft or other demand, document of title, investment security, certificate, invoice, or other record, statement, or representation of fact, law, right, or opinion (i) which is presented in a written or other medium permitted by the letter of credit or, unless prohibited by the letter of credit, by the standard practice referred to in Section 5–108(e) and (ii) which is capable of being examined for compliance with the terms and conditions of the letter of credit. A document may not be oral.

(7) "Good faith" means honesty in fact in the conduct or transaction concerned.

(8) "Honor" of a letter of credit means performance of the issuer's undertaking in the letter of credit to pay or deliver an item of value. Unless the letter of credit otherwise provides, "honor" occurs

(i) upon payment,

(ii) if the letter of credit provides for acceptance, upon acceptance of a draft and, at maturity, its payment, or

(iii) if the letter of credit provides for incurring a deferred obligation, upon incurring the obligation and, at maturity, its performance.

(9) "Issuer" means a bank or other person that issues a letter of credit, but does not include an individual who makes an engagement for personal, family, or household purposes.

(10) "Letter of credit" means a definite undertaking that satisfies the requirements of Section 5–104 by an issuer to a beneficiary at the request or for the account of an applicant or, in the case of a financial institution, to itself or for its own account, to honor a documentary presentation by payment or delivery of an item of value.

(11) "Nominated person" means a person whom the issuer (i) designates or authorizes to pay, accept, negotiate, or otherwise give value under a letter of credit and (ii) undertakes by agreement or custom and practice to reimburse.

(12) "Presentation" means delivery of a document to an issuer or nominated person for honor or giving of value under a letter of credit.

(13) "Presenter" means a person making a presentation as or on behalf of a beneficiary or nominated person.

(14) "Record" means information that is inscribed on a tangible medium, or that is stored in an electronic or other medium and is retrievable in perceivable form.

(15) "Successor of a beneficiary" means a person who succeeds to substantially all of the rights of a beneficiary by operation of law, including a corporation with or into which the beneficiary has been merged or consolidated, an administrator, executor, personal representative, trustee in bankruptcy, debtor in possession, liquidator, and receiver.

(b) Definitions in other Articles applying to this article and the sections in which they appear are:

"Accept" or "Acceptance" Section 3–409

"Value" Sections 3–303, 4–211

(c) Article 1 contains certain additional general definitions and principles of construction and interpretation applicable throughout this article.

§ 5–103. Scope.
(a) This article applies to letters of credit and to certain rights and obligations arising out of transactions involving letters of credit.
(b) The statement of a rule in this article does not by itself require, imply, or negate application of the same or a different rule to a situation not provided for, or to a person not specified, in this article.
(c) With the exception of this subsection, subsections (a) and (d), Sections 5–102(a)(9) and (10), 5–106(d), and 5–114(d), and except to the extent prohibited in Sections 1–102(3) and 5–117(d), the effect of this article may be varied by agreement or by a provision stated or incorporated by reference in an undertaking. A term in an agreement or undertaking generally excusing liability or generally limiting remedies for failure to perform obligations is not sufficient to vary obligations prescribed by this article.
(d) Rights and obligations of an issuer to a beneficiary or a nominated person under a letter of credit are independent of the existence, performance, or nonperformance of a contract or arrangement out of which the letter of credit arises or which underlies it, including contracts or arrangements between the issuer and the applicant and between the applicant and the beneficiary.

§ 5–104. Formal Requirements.
A letter of credit, confirmation, advice, transfer, amendment, or cancellation may be issued in any form that is a record and is authenticated (i) by a signature or (ii) in accordance with the agreement of the parties or the standard practice referred to in Section 5–108(e).

§ 5–105. Consideration.
Consideration is not required to issue, amend, transfer, or cancel a letter of credit, advice, or confirmation.

§ 5–106. Issuance, Amendment, Cancellation, and Duration.
(a) A letter of credit is issued and becomes enforceable according to its terms against the issuer when the issuer sends or otherwise transmits it to the person requested to advise or to the beneficiary. A letter of credit is revocable only if it so provides.
(b) After a letter of credit is issued, rights and obligations of a beneficiary, applicant, confirmer, and issuer are not affected by an amendment or cancellation to which that person has not consented except to the extent the letter of credit provides that it is revocable or that the issuer may amend or cancel the letter of credit without that consent.
(c) If there is no stated expiration date or other provision that determines its duration, a letter of credit expires one year after its stated date of issuance or, if none is stated, after the date on which it is issued.
(d) A letter of credit that states that it is perpetual expires five years after its stated date of issuance, or if none is stated, after the date on which it is issued.

§ 5–107. Confirmer, Nominated Person, and Adviser.
(a) A confirmer is directly obligated on a letter of credit and has the rights and obligations of an issuer to the extent of its confirmation. The confirmer also has rights against and obligations to the issuer as if the issuer were an applicant and the confirmer had issued the letter of credit at the request and for the account of the issuer.
(b) A nominated person who is not a confirmer is not obligated to honor or otherwise give value for a presentation.
(c) A person requested to advise may decline to act as an adviser. An adviser that is not a confirmer is not obligated to honor or give value for a presentation. An adviser undertakes to the issuer and to the beneficiary accurately to advise the terms of the letter of credit, confirmation, amendment, or advice received by that person and undertakes to the beneficiary to check the apparent authenticity of the request to advise. Even if the advice is inaccurate, the letter of credit, confirmation, or amendment is enforceable as issued.
(d) A person who notifies a transferee beneficiary of the terms of a letter of credit, confirmation, amendment, or advice has the rights and obligations of an adviser under subsection (c). The terms in the notice to the transferee beneficiary may differ from the terms in any notice to the transferor beneficiary to the extent permitted by the letter of credit, confirmation, amendment, or advice received by the person who so notifies.

§ 5–108. Issuer's Rights and Obligations.
(a) Except as otherwise provided in Section 5–109, an issuer shall honor a presentation that, as determined by the standard practice referred to in subsection (e), appears on its face strictly to comply with the terms and conditions of the letter of credit. Except as otherwise provided in Section 5–113 and unless otherwise agreed with the applicant, an issuer shall dishonor a presentation that does not appear so to comply.
(b) An issuer has a reasonable time after presentation, but not beyond the end of the seventh business day of the issuer after the day of its receipt of documents:
  (1) to honor,
  (2) if the letter of credit provides for honor to be completed more than seven business days after presentation, to accept a draft or incur a deferred obligation, or
  (3) to give notice to the presenter of discrepancies in the presentation.
(c) Except as otherwise provided in subsection (d), an issuer is precluded from asserting as a basis for dishonor any discrepancy if timely notice is not given, or any discrepancy not stated in the notice if timely notice is given.
(d) Failure to give the notice specified in subsection (b) or to mention fraud, forgery, or expiration in the notice does not preclude the issuer from asserting as a basis for dishonor fraud or forgery as described in Section 5–109(a) or expiration of the letter of credit before presentation.
(e) An issuer shall observe standard practice of financial institutions that regularly issue letters of credit. Determination of the issuer's observance of the standard practice is a matter of interpretation for the court. The court shall offer the parties a reasonable opportunity to present evidence of the standard practice.

(f) An issuer is not responsible for:

(1) the performance or nonperformance of the underlying contract, arrangement, or transaction,

(2) an act or omission of others, or

(3) observance or knowledge of the usage of a particular trade other than the standard practice referred to in subsection (e).

(g) If an undertaking constituting a letter of credit under Section 5–102(a)(10) contains nondocumentary conditions, an issuer shall disregard the nondocumentary conditions and treat them as if they were not stated.

(h) An issuer that has dishonored a presentation shall return the documents or hold them at the disposal of, and send advice to that effect to, the presenter.

(i) An issuer that has honored a presentation as permitted or required by this article:

(1) is entitled to be reimbursed by the applicant in immediately available funds not later than the date of its payment of funds;

(2) takes the documents free of claims of the beneficiary or presenter;

(3) is precluded from asserting a right of recourse on a draft under Sections 3–414 and 3–415;

(4) except as otherwise provided in Sections 5–110 and 5–117, is precluded from restitution of money paid or other value given by mistake to the extent the mistake concerns discrepancies in the documents or tender which are apparent on the face of the presentation; and

(5) is discharged to the extent of its performance under the letter of credit unless the issuer honored a presentation in which a required signature of a beneficiary was forged.

§ 5–109. Fraud and Forgery.

(a) If a presentation is made that appears on its face strictly to comply with the terms and conditions of the letter of credit, but a required document is forged or materially fraudulent, or honor of the presentation would facilitate a material fraud by the beneficiary on the issuer or applicant:

(1) the issuer shall honor the presentation, if honor is demanded by (i) a nominated person who has given value in good faith and without notice of forgery or material fraud, (ii) a confirmer who has honored its confirmation in good faith, (iii) a holder in due course of a draft drawn under the letter of credit which was taken after acceptance by the issuer or nominated person, or (iv) an assignee of the issuer's or nominated person's deferred obligation that was taken for value and without notice of forgery or material fraud after the obligation was incurred by the issuer or nominated person; and

(2) the issuer, acting in good faith, may honor or dishonor the presentation in any other case.

(b) If an applicant claims that a required document is forged or materially fraudulent or that honor of the presentation would facilitate a material fraud by the beneficiary on the issuer or applicant, a court of competent jurisdiction may temporarily or permanently enjoin the issuer from honoring a presentation or grant similar relief against the issuer or other persons only if the court finds that:

(1) the relief is not prohibited under the law applicable to an accepted draft or deferred obligation incurred by the issuer;

(2) a beneficiary, issuer, or nominated person who may be adversely affected is adequately protected against loss that it may suffer because the relief is granted;

(3) all of the conditions to entitle a person to the relief under the law of this State have been met; and

(4) on the basis of the information submitted to the court, the applicant is more likely than not to succeed under its claim of forgery or material fraud and the person demanding honor does not qualify for protection under subsection (a)(1).

§ 5–110. Warranties.

(a) If its presentation is honored, the beneficiary warrants:

(1) to the issuer, any other person to whom presentation is made, and the applicant that there is no fraud or forgery of the kind described in Section 5–109(a); and

(2) to the applicant that the drawing does not violate any agreement between the applicant and beneficiary or any other agreement intended by them to be augmented by the letter of credit.

(b) The warranties in subsection (a) are in addition to warranties arising under Article 3, 4, 7, and 8 because of the presentation or transfer of documents covered by any of those articles.

§ 5–111. Remedies.

(a) If an issuer wrongfully dishonors or repudiates its obligation to pay money under a letter of credit before presentation, the beneficiary, successor, or nominated person presenting on its own behalf may recover from the issuer the amount that is the subject of the dishonor or repudiation. If the issuer's obligation under the letter of credit is not for the payment of money, the claimant may obtain specific performance or, at the claimant's election, recover an amount equal to the value of performance from the issuer. In either case, the claimant may also recover incidental but not consequential damages. The claimant is not obligated to take action to avoid damages that might be due from the issuer under this subsection. If, although not obligated to do so, the claimant avoids damages, the claimant's recovery from the issuer must be reduced by the amount of damages avoided. The issuer has the burden of proving the amount of damages avoided. In the case of repudiation the claimant need not present any document.

(b) If an issuer wrongfully dishonors a draft or demand presented under a letter of credit or honors a draft or demand in breach of its obligation to the applicant, the applicant may recover damages resulting from the breach, including incidental but not consequential damages, less any amount saved as a result of the breach.

(c) If an adviser or nominated person other than a confirmer breaches an obligation under this article or an issuer breaches an obligation not covered in subsection (a) or (b), a person to whom the obligation is owed may recover damages resulting from the breach, including incidental but not consequential damages, less any amount saved as a result of the breach. To the extent of the confirmation, a confirmer has the liability of an issuer specified in this subsection and subsections (a) and (b).

(d) An issuer, nominated person, or adviser who is found liable under subsection (a), (b), or (c) shall pay interest on the amount owed thereunder from the date of wrongful dishonor or other appropriate date.

(e) Reasonable attorney's fees and other expenses of litigation must be awarded to the prevailing party in an action in which a remedy is sought under this article.

(f) Damages that would otherwise be payable by a party for breach of an obligation under this article may be liquidated by agreement or undertaking, but only in an amount or by a formula that is reasonable in light of the harm anticipated.

§ 5–112. Transfer of Letter of Credit.

(a) Except as otherwise provided in Section 5–113, unless a letter of credit provides that it is transferable, the right of a beneficiary to draw or otherwise demand performance under a letter of credit may not be transferred.

(b) Even if a letter of credit provides that it is transferable, the issuer may refuse to recognize or carry out a transfer if:

(1) the transfer would violate applicable law; or

(2) the transferor or transferee has failed to comply with any requirement stated in the letter of credit or any other requirement relating to transfer imposed by the issuer which is within the standard practice referred to in Section 5–108(e) or is otherwise reasonable under the circumstances.

§ 5–113. Transfer by Operation of Law.

(a) A successor of a beneficiary may consent to amendments, sign and present documents, and receive payment or other items of value in the name of the beneficiary without disclosing its status as a successor.

(b) A successor of a beneficiary may consent to amendments, sign and present documents, and receive payment or other items of value in its own name as the disclosed successor of the beneficiary. Except as otherwise provided in subsection (e), an issuer shall recognize a disclosed successor of a beneficiary as beneficiary in full substitution for its predecessor upon compliance with the requirements for recognition by the issuer of a transfer of drawing rights by operation of law under the standard practice referred to in Section 5–108(e) or, in the absence of such a practice, compliance with other reasonable procedures sufficient to protect the issuer.

(c) An issuer is not obliged to determine whether a purported successor is a successor of a beneficiary or whether the signature of a purported successor is genuine or authorized.

(d) Honor of a purported successor's apparently complying presentation under subsection (a) or (b) has the consequences specified in Section 5–108(i) even if the purported successor is not the successor of a beneficiary. Documents signed in the name of the beneficiary or of a disclosed successor by a person who is neither the beneficiary nor the successor of the beneficiary are forged documents for the purposes of Section 5–109.

(e) An issuer whose rights of reimbursement are not covered by subsection (d) or substantially similar law and any confirmer or nominated person may decline to recognize a presentation under subsection (b).

(f) A beneficiary whose name is changed after the issuance of a letter of credit has the same rights and obligations as a successor of a beneficiary under this section.

§ 5–114. Assignment of Proceeds.

(a) In this section, "proceeds of a letter of credit" means the cash, check, accepted draft, or other item of value paid or delivered upon honor or giving of value by the issuer or any nominated person under the letter of credit. The term does not include a beneficiary's drawing rights or documents presented by the beneficiary.

(b) A beneficiary may assign its right to part or all of the proceeds of a letter of credit. The beneficiary may do so before presentation as a present assignment of its right to receive proceeds contingent upon its compliance with the terms and conditions of the letter of credit.

(c) An issuer or nominated person need not recognize an assignment of proceeds of a letter of credit until it consents to the assignment.

(d) An issuer or nominated person has no obligation to give or withhold its consent to an assignment of proceeds of a letter of credit, but consent may not be unreasonably withheld if the assignee possesses and exhibits the letter of credit and presentation of the letter of credit is a condition to honor.

(e) Rights of a transferee beneficiary or nominated person are independent of the beneficiary's assignment of the proceeds of a letter of credit and are superior to the assignee's right to the proceeds.

(f) Neither the rights recognized by this section between an assignee and an issuer, transferee beneficiary, or nominated person nor the issuer's or nominated person's payment of proceeds to an assignee or a third person affect the rights between the assignee and any person other than the issuer, transferee beneficiary, or nominated person. The mode of creating and perfecting a security interest in or granting an assignment of a beneficiary's rights to proceeds is governed by Article 9 or other law. Against persons other than the issuer, transferee beneficiary, or nominated person, the rights and obligations arising upon the creation of a security interest or other assignment of a beneficiary's right to proceeds and its perfection are governed by Article 9 or other law.

§ 5–115. Statute of Limitations.

An action to enforce a right or obligation arising under this article must be commenced within one year after the expiration date of the relevant letter of credit or one year after the [claim for relief] [cause of action] accrues, whichever occurs later. A [claim for relief] [cause of action] accrues when the breach occurs, regardless of the aggrieved party's lack of knowledge of the breach.

§ 5–116. Choice of Law and Forum.

(a) The liability of an issuer, nominated person, or adviser for action or omission is governed by the law of the jurisdiction chosen by an agreement in the form of a record signed or otherwise authenticated by the affected parties in the manner provided in Section 5–104 or by a provision in the person's letter of credit, confirmation, or other undertaking. The jurisdiction whose law is chosen need not bear any relation to the transaction.

(b) Unless subsection (a) applies, the liability of an issuer, nominated person, or adviser for action or omission is governed by the law of the jurisdiction in which the person is located. The person is considered to be located at the address indicated in the person's undertaking. If more than one address is indicated, the person is considered to be located at the address from which the person's undertaking was issued. For the purpose of jurisdiction, choice of law, and recognition of interbranch letters of credit, but not enforcement of a judgment, all branches of a bank are considered separate juridical entities and a bank is considered to be located at the place where its relevant branch is considered to be located under this subsection.

(c) Except as otherwise provided in this subsection, the liability of an issuer, nominated person, or adviser is governed by any rules of custom or practice, such as the Uniform Customs and Practice for Documentary Credits, to which the letter of credit, confirmation, or other undertaking is expressly made subject. If (i) this article would govern the liability of an issuer, nominated person, or adviser under subsection (a) or (b), (ii) the relevant undertaking incorporates rules of custom or practice, and (iii) there is conflict between this article and those rules as applied to that undertaking, those rules govern except to the extent of any conflict with the nonvariable provisions specified in Section 5–103(c).

(d) If there is conflict between this article and Article 3, 4, 4A, or 9, this article governs.

(e) The forum for settling disputes arising out of an undertaking within this article may be chosen in the manner and with the binding effect that governing law may be chosen in accordance with subsection (a).

§ 5–117. Subrogation of Issuer, Applicant, and Nominated Person.

(a) An issuer that honors a beneficiary's presentation is subrogated to the rights of the beneficiary to the same extent as if the issuer were a secondary obligor of the underlying obligation owed to the beneficiary and of the applicant to the same extent as if the issuer were the secondary obligor of the underlying obligation owed to the applicant.

(b) An applicant that reimburses an issuer is subrogated to the rights of the issuer against any beneficiary, presenter, or nominated person to the same extent as if the applicant were the secondary obligor of the obligations owed to the issuer and has the rights of subrogation of the issuer to the rights of the beneficiary stated in subsection (a).

(c) A nominated person who pays or gives value against a draft or demand presented under a letter of credit is subrogated to the rights of:

> **(1)** the issuer against the applicant to the same extent as if the nominated person were a secondary obligor of the obligation owed to the issuer by the applicant;
>
> **(2)** the beneficiary to the same extent as if the nominated person were a secondary obligor of the underlying obligation owed to the beneficiary; and
>
> **(3)** the applicant to same extent as if the nominated person were a secondary obligor of the underlying obligation owed to the applicant.

(d) Notwithstanding any agreement or term to the contrary, the rights of subrogation stated in subsections (a) and (b) do not arise until the issuer honors the letter of credit or otherwise pays and the rights in subsection (c) do not arise until the nominated person pays or otherwise gives value. Until then, the issuer, nominated person, and the applicant do not derive under this section present or prospective rights forming the basis of a claim, defense, or excuse.

§ 5–118. Security Interest of Issuer or Nominated Person.

(a) An issuer or nominated person has a security interest in a document presented under a letter of credit to the extent that the issuer or nominated person honors or gives value for the presentation.

(b) So long as and to the extent that an issuer or nominated person has not been reimbursed or has not otherwise recovered the value given with respect to a security interest in a document under subsection (a), the security interest continues and is subject to Article 9, but:

> **(1)** a security agreement is not necessary to make the security interest enforceable under Section 9–203(b)(3);
>
> **(2)** if the document is presented in a medium other than a written or other tangible medium, the security interest is perfected; and
>
> **(3)** if the document is presented in a written or other tangible medium and is not a certificated security, chattel paper, a document of title, an instrument, or a letter of credit, the security interest is perfected and has priority over a conflicting security interest in the document so long as the debtor does not have possession of the document.

As added in 1999.

Transition Provisions

§ [ ]. Effective Date.

This [Act] shall become effective on _____, 20__.

§ [ ]. Repeal.

This [Act] [repeals] [amends] [insert citation to existing Article 5].

§ [ ]. Applicability.

This [Act] applies to a letter of credit that is issued on or after the effective date of this [Act]. This [Act] does not apply to a transaction, event, obligation, or duty arising out of or associated with a letter of credit that was issued before the effective date of this [Act].

§ [ ]. Savings Clause.

A transaction arising out of or associated with a letter of credit that was issued before the effective date of this [Act] and the rights, obligations, and interests flowing from that transaction are governed by any statute or other law amended or repealed by this [Act] as if repeal or amendment had not occurred and may be terminated, completed, consummated, or enforced under that statute or other law.

REPEALER OF ARTICLE 6

BULK TRANSFERS and [Revised] ARTICLE 6 BULK SALES (States to Select One Alternative)

Alternative A

§ 1. Repeal

Article 6 and Section 9–111 of the Uniform Commercial Code are hereby repealed, effective _____.

§ 2. Amendment

Section 1–105(2) of the Uniform Commercial Code is hereby amended to read as follows:

(2) Where one of the following provisions of this Act specifies the applicable law, that provision governs and a contrary agreement is effective only to the extent permitted by the law (including the conflict of laws rules) so specified:

Rights of creditors against sold goods. Section 2–402.

Applicability of the Article on Leases. Section 2A–105 and 2A–106.

Applicability of the Article on Bank Deposits and Collections. Section 4–102.

Applicability of the Article on Investment Securities. Section 8–106.

Perfection provisions of the Article on Secured Transactions. Section 9–103.

§ 3. Amendment.

Section 2–403(4) of the Uniform Commercial Code is hereby amended to read as follows:

(4) The rights of other purchasers of goods and of lien creditors are governed by the Articles on Secured Transactions (Article 9) and Documents of Title (Article 7).

§ 4. Savings Clause.

Rights and obligations that arose under Article 6 and Section 9–111 of the Uniform Commercial Code before their repeal remain valid and may be enforced as though those statutes had not been repealed.]

§ 6–101. Short Title.

This Article shall be known and may be cited as Uniform Commercial Code—Bulk Sales.

§ 6–102. Definitions and Index of Definitions.

(1) In this Article, unless the context otherwise requires:

(a) "Assets" means the inventory that is the subject of a bulk sale and any tangible and intangible personal property used or held for use primarily in, or arising from, the seller's business and sold in connection with that inventory, but the term does not include:

(i) fixtures (Section 9–102(a)(41)) other than readily removable factory and office machines;

(ii) the lessee's interest in a lease of real property; or

(iii) property to the extent it is generally exempt from creditor process under nonbankruptcy law.

(b) "Auctioneer" means a person whom the seller engages to direct, conduct, control, or be responsible for a sale by auction.

(c) "Bulk sale" means:

(i) in the case of a sale by auction or a sale or series of sales conducted by a liquidator on the seller's behalf, a sale or series of sales not in the ordinary course of the seller's business of more than half of the seller's inventory, as measured by value on the date of the bulk-sale agreement, if on that date the auctioneer or liquidator has notice, or after reasonable inquiry would have had notice, that the seller will not continue to operate the same or a similar kind of business after the sale or series of sales; and

(ii) in all other cases, a sale not in the ordinary course of the seller's business of more than half the seller's inventory, as measured by value on the date of the bulk-sale agreement, if on that date the buyer has notice, or after reasonable inquiry would have had notice, that the seller will not continue to operate the same or a similar kind of business after the sale.

(d) "Claim" means a right to payment from the seller, whether or not the right is reduced to judgment, liquidated, fixed, matured, disputed, secured, legal, or equitable. The term includes costs of collection and attorney's fees only to the extent that the laws of this state permit the holder of the claim to recover them in an action against the obligor.

(e) "Claimant" means a person holding a claim incurred in the seller's business other than:

(i) an unsecured and unmatured claim for employment compensation and benefits, including commissions and vacation, severance, and sick-leave pay;

(ii) a claim for injury to an individual or to property, or for breach of warranty, unless:

(A) a right of action for the claim has accrued;

(B) the claim has been asserted against the seller; and

(C) the seller knows the identity of the person asserting the claim and the basis upon which the person has asserted it; and

(States to Select One Alternative)

Alternative A

[**(iii)** a claim for taxes owing to a governmental unit.]

Alternative B

[**(iii)** a claim for taxes owing to a governmental unit, if:

(A) a statute governing the enforcement of the claim permits or requires notice of the bulk sale to be given to the governmental unit in a manner other than by compliance with the requirements of this Article; and

(B) notice is given in accordance with the statute.]

(f) "Creditor" means a claimant or other person holding a claim.

(g)(i) "Date of the bulk sale" means:

(A) if the sale is by auction or is conducted by a liquidator on the seller's behalf, the date on which more than ten percent of the net proceeds is paid to or for the benefit of the seller; and

(B) in all other cases, the later of the date on which:

(I) more than ten percent of the net contract price is paid to or for the benefit of the seller; or

(II) more than ten percent of the assets, as measured by value, are transferred to the buyer.

(ii) For purposes of this subsection:

(A) delivery of a negotiable instrument (Section 3–104(1)) to or for the benefit of the seller in exchange for assets constitutes payment of the contract price pro tanto;

(B) to the extent that the contract price is deposited in an escrow, the contract price is paid to or for the benefit of the seller when the seller acquires the unconditional right to receive the deposit or when the deposit is delivered to the seller or for the benefit of the seller, whichever is earlier; and

(C) an asset is transferred when a person holding an unsecured claim can no longer obtain through judicial proceedings rights to the asset that are superior to those of the buyer arising as a result of the bulk sale. A person holding an unsecured claim can obtain those superior rights to a tangible asset at least until the buyer has an unconditional right, under the bulk-sale agreement, to possess the asset, and a person holding an unsecured claim can obtain those superior rights to an intangible asset at least until the buyer has an unconditional right, under the bulk-sale agreement, to use the asset.

(h) "Date of the bulk-sale agreement" means:

(i) in the case of a sale by auction or conducted by a liquidator (subsection (c)(i)), the date on which the seller engages the auctioneer or liquidator; and

(ii) in all other cases, the date on which a bulk-sale agreement becomes enforceable between the buyer and the seller.

(i) "Debt" means liability on a claim.

(j) "Liquidator" means a person who is regularly engaged in the business of disposing of assets for businesses contemplating liquidation or dissolution.

(k) "Net contract price" means the new consideration the buyer is obligated to pay for the assets less:

(i) the amount of any proceeds of the sale of an asset, to the extent the proceeds are applied in partial or total satisfaction of a debt secured by the asset; and

(ii) the amount of any debt to the extent it is secured by a security interest or lien that is enforceable against the asset before and after it has been sold to a buyer. If a debt is secured by an asset and other property of the seller, the amount of the debt secured by a security interest or lien that is enforceable against the asset is determined by multiplying the debt by a fraction, the numerator of which is the value of the new consideration for the asset on the date of the bulk sale and the denominator of which is the value of all property securing the debt on the date of the bulk sale.

(l) "Net proceeds" means the new consideration received for assets sold at a sale by auction or a sale conducted by a liquidator on the seller's behalf less:

(i) commissions and reasonable expenses of the sale;

(ii) the amount of any proceeds of the sale of an asset, to the extent the proceeds are applied in partial or total satisfaction of a debt secured by the asset; and

(iii) the amount of any debt to the extent it is secured by a security interest or lien that is enforceable against the asset before and after it has been sold to a buyer. If a debt is secured by an asset and other property of the seller, the amount of the debt secured by a security interest or lien that is enforceable against the asset is determined by multiplying the debt by a fraction, the numerator of which is the value of the new consideration for the asset on the date of the bulk sale and the denominator of which is the value of all property securing the debt on the date of the bulk sale.

(m) A sale is "in the ordinary course of the seller's business" if the sale comports with usual or customary practices in the kind of business in which the seller is engaged or with the seller's own usual or customary practices.

(n) "United States" includes its territories and possessions and the Commonwealth of Puerto Rico.

(o) "Value" means fair market value.

(p) "Verified" means signed and sworn to or affirmed.

(2) The following definitions in other Articles apply to this Article:

(a) "Buyer."	Section 2–103(1)(a).
(b) "Equipment."	Section 9–102(a)(33).
(c) "Inventory."	Section 9–102(a)(48).
(d) "Sale."	Section 2–106(1).
(e) "Seller."	Section 2–103(1)(d).

(3) In addition, Article 1 contains general definitions and principles of construction and interpretation applicable throughout this Article.

As amended in 1999.

§ 6–103. Applicability of Article.

(1) Except as otherwise provided in subsection (3), this Article applies to a bulk sale if:

(a) the seller's principal business is the sale of inventory from stock; and

(b) on the date of the bulk-sale agreement the seller is located in this state or, if the seller is located in a jurisdiction that is not a part of the United States, the seller's major executive office in the United States is in this state.

(2) A seller is deemed to be located at his [or her] place of business. If a seller has more than one place of business, the seller is deemed located at his [or her] chief executive office.

(3) This Article does not apply to:

(a) a transfer made to secure payment or performance of an obligation;

(b) a transfer of collateral to a secured party pursuant to Section 9–503;

(c) a disposition of collateral pursuant to Section 9–610;

(d) retention of collateral pursuant to Section 9–620;

(e) a sale of an asset encumbered by a security interest or lien if (i) all the proceeds of the sale are applied in partial or total satisfaction of the debt secured by the security interest or lien or (ii) the security interest or lien is enforceable against the asset after it has been sold to the buyer and the net contract price is zero;

(f) a general assignment for the benefit of creditors or to a subsequent transfer by the assignee;

(g) a sale by an executor, administrator, receiver, trustee in bankruptcy, or any public officer under judicial process;

(h) a sale made in the course of judicial or administrative proceedings for the dissolution or reorganization of an organization;

(i) a sale to a buyer whose principal place of business is in the United States and who:

(i) not earlier than 21 days before the date of the bulk sale, (A) obtains from the seller a verified and dated list of claimants of whom the seller has notice three days before the seller sends or delivers the list to the buyer or (B) conducts a reasonable inquiry to discover the claimants;

(ii) assumes in full the debts owed to claimants of whom the buyer has knowledge on the date the buyer receives the list of claimants from the seller or on the date the buyer completes the reasonable inquiry, as the case may be;

(iii) is not insolvent after the assumption; and

(iv) gives written notice of the assumption not later than 30 days after the date of the bulk sale by sending or delivering a notice to the claimants identified in subparagraph (ii) or by filing a notice in the office of the [Secretary of State];

(j) a sale to a buyer whose principal place of business is in the United States and who:

(i) assumes in full the debts that were incurred in the seller's business before the date of the bulk sale;

(ii) is not insolvent after the assumption; and

(iii) gives written notice of the assumption not later than 30 days after the date of the bulk sale by sending or delivering a notice to each creditor whose debt is assumed or by filing a notice in the office of the [Secretary of State];

(k) a sale to a new organization that is organized to take over and continue the business of the seller and that has its principal place of business in the United States if:

(i) the buyer assumes in full the debts that were incurred in the seller's business before the date of the bulk sale;

(ii) the seller receives nothing from the sale except an interest in the new organization that is subordinate to the claims against the organization arising from the assumption; and

(iii) the buyer gives written notice of the assumption not later than 30 days after the date of the bulk sale by sending or delivering a notice to each creditor whose debt is assumed or by filing a notice in the office of the [Secretary of State];

(l) a sale of assets having:

(i) a value, net of liens and security interests, of less than $10,000. If a debt is secured by assets and other property of the seller, the net value of the assets is determined by subtracting from their value an amount equal to the product of the debt multiplied by a fraction, the numerator of which is the value of the assets on the date of the bulk sale and the denominator of which is the value of all property securing the debt on the date of the bulk sale; or

(ii) a value of more than $25,000,000 on the date of the bulk-sale agreement; or

(m) a sale required by, and made pursuant to, statute.

(4) The notice under subsection (3)(i)(iv) must state: (i) that a sale that may constitute a bulk sale has been or will be made; (ii) the date or prospective date of the bulk sale; (iii) the individual, partnership, or corporate names and the addresses of the seller and buyer; (iv) the address to which inquiries about the sale may be made, if different from the seller's address; and (v) that the buyer has assumed or will assume in full the debts owed to claimants of whom the buyer has knowledge on the date the buyer receives the list of claimants from the seller or completes a reasonable inquiry to discover the claimants.

(5) The notice under subsections (3)(j)(iii) and (3)(k)(iii) must state: (i) that a sale that may constitute a bulk sale has been or will be made; (ii) the date or prospective date of the bulk sale; (iii) the individual, partnership, or corporate names and the addresses of the seller and buyer; (iv) the address to which inquiries about the sale may be made, if different from the seller's address; and (v) that the buyer has assumed or will assume the debts that were incurred in the seller's business before the date of the bulk sale.

(6) For purposes of subsection (3)(l), the value of assets is presumed to be equal to the price the buyer agrees to pay for the assets. However, in a sale by auction or a sale conducted by a liquidator on the seller's behalf, the value of assets is presumed to be the amount the auctioneer or liquidator reasonably estimates the assets will bring at auction or upon liquidation.
As amended in 1999.

§ 6–104. Obligations of Buyer.

(1) In a bulk sale as defined in Section 6–102(1)(c)(ii) the buyer shall:

(a) obtain from the seller a list of all business names and addresses used by the seller within three years before the date the list is sent or delivered to the buyer;

(b) unless excused under subsection (2), obtain from the seller a verified and dated list of claimants of whom the seller has notice three days before the seller sends or delivers the list to the buyer and including, to the extent known by the seller, the address of and the amount claimed by each claimant;

(c) obtain from the seller or prepare a schedule of distribution (Section 6–106(1));

(d) give notice of the bulk sale in accordance with Section 6–105;

(e) unless excused under Section 6–106(4), distribute the net contract price in accordance with the undertakings of the buyer in the schedule of distribution; and

(f) unless excused under subsection (2), make available the list of claimants (subsection (1)(b)) by:

(i) promptly sending or delivering a copy of the list without charge to any claimant whose written request is received b]y the buyer no later than six months after the date of the bulk sale;

(ii) permitting any claimant to inspect and copy the list at any reasonable hour upon request received by the buyer no later than six months after the date of the bulk sale; or

(iii) filing a copy of the list in the office of the [Secretary of State] no later than the time for giving a notice of the bulk sale (Section 6–105(5)). A list filed in accordance with this subparagraph must state the individual, partnership, or corporate name and a mailing address of the seller.

(2) A buyer who gives notice in accordance with Section 6–105(2) is excused from complying with the requirements of subsections (1)(b) and (1)(f).

§ 6–105. Notice to Claimants.

(1) Except as otherwise provided in subsection (2), to comply with Section 6–104(1)(d) the buyer shall send or deliver a written notice of the bulk sale to each claimant on the list of claimants (Section 6–104(1)(b)) and to any other claimant of which the buyer has knowledge at the time the notice of the bulk sale is sent or delivered.

(2) A buyer may comply with Section 6–104(1)(d) by filing a written notice of the bulk sale in the office of the [Secretary of State] if:

(a) on the date of the bulk-sale agreement the seller has 200 or more claimants, exclusive of claimants holding secured or matured claims for employment compensation and benefits, including commissions and vacation, severance, and sick-leave pay; or

(b) the buyer has received a verified statement from the seller stating that, as of the date of the bulk-sale agreement, the number of claimants, exclusive of claimants holding secured or matured claims for employment compensation and benefits, including commissions and vacation, severance, and sick-leave pay, is 200 or more.

(3) The written notice of the bulk sale must be accompanied by a copy of the schedule of distribution (Section 6–106(1)) and state at least:

(a) that the seller and buyer have entered into an agreement for a sale that may constitute a bulk sale under the laws of the State of _____ ;

(b) the date of the agreement;

(c) the date on or after which more than ten percent of the assets were or will be transferred;

(d) the date on or after which more than ten percent of the net contract price was or will be paid, if the date is not stated in the schedule of distribution;

(e) the name and a mailing address of the seller;

(f) any other business name and address listed by the seller pursuant to Section 6–104(1)(a);

(g) the name of the buyer and an address of the buyer from which information concerning the sale can be obtained;

(h) a statement indicating the type of assets or describing the assets item by item;

(i) the manner in which the buyer will make available the list of claimants (Section 6–104(1)(f)), if applicable; and

(j) if the sale is in total or partial satisfaction of an antecedent debt owed by the seller, the amount of the debt to be satisfied and the name of the person to whom it is owed.

(4) For purposes of subsections (3)(e) and (3)(g), the name of a person is the person's individual, partnership, or corporate name.

(5) The buyer shall give notice of the bulk sale not less than 45 days before the date of the bulk sale and, if the buyer gives notice in accordance with subsection (1), not more than 30 days after obtaining the list of claimants.

(6) A written notice substantially complying with the requirements of subsection (3) is effective even though it contains minor errors that are not seriously misleading.

(7) A form substantially as follows is sufficient to comply with subsection (3):

Notice of Sale

(1) _____, whose address is _____, is described in this notice as the "seller."

(2) _____, whose address is _____, is described in this notice as the "buyer."

(3) The seller has disclosed to the buyer that within the past three years the seller has used other business names, operated at other addresses, or both, as follows: _____

_____ .

(4) The seller and the buyer have entered into an agreement dated _____, for a sale that may constitute a bulk sale under the laws of the state of _____.

(5) The date on or after which more than ten percent of the assets that are the subject of the sale were or will be transferred is _____, and [if not stated in the schedule of distribution] the date on or after which more than ten percent of the net contract price was or will be paid is _____ .

(6) The following assets are the subject of the sale: _____ .

(7) [If applicable] The buyer will make available to claimants of the seller a list of the seller's claimants in the following manner: _____ .

(8) [If applicable] The sale is to satisfy $ _____ of an antecedent debt owed by the seller to _____ .

(9) A copy of the schedule of distribution of the net contract price accompanies this notice.

[End of Notice]

§ 6–106. Schedule of Distribution.

(1) The seller and buyer shall agree on how the net contract price is to be distributed and set forth their agreement in a written schedule of distribution.

(2) The schedule of distribution may provide for distribution to any person at any time, including distribution of the entire net contract price to the seller.

(3) The buyer's undertakings in the schedule of distribution run only to the seller. However, a buyer who fails to distribute the net contract price in accordance with the buyer's undertakings in the schedule of distribution is liable to a creditor only as provided in Section 6–107(1).

(4) If the buyer undertakes in the schedule of distribution to distribute any part of the net contract price to a person other than the seller, and, after the buyer has given notice in accordance with Section 6–105, some or all of the anticipated net contract price is or becomes unavailable for distribution as a consequence of the buyer's or seller's having complied with an order of court, legal process, statute, or rule of law, the buyer is excused from any obligation arising under this Article or under any contract with the seller to distribute the net contract price in accordance with the buyer's undertakings in the schedule if the buyer:

(a) distributes the net contract price remaining available in accordance with any priorities for payment stated in the schedule of distribution and, to the extent that the price is insufficient to pay all the debts having a given priority, distributes the price pro rata among those debts shown in the schedule as having the same priority;

(b) distributes the net contract price remaining available in accordance with an order of court;

(c) commences a proceeding for interpleader in a court of competent jurisdiction and is discharged from the proceeding; or

(d) reaches a new agreement with the seller for the distribution of the net contract price remaining available, sets forth the new agreement in an amended schedule of distribution, gives notice of the amended schedule, and distributes the net contract price remaining available in accordance with the buyer's undertakings in the amended schedule.

(5) The notice under subsection (4)(d) must identify the buyer and the seller, state the filing number, if any, of the original notice, set forth the amended schedule, and be given in accordance with subsection (1) or (2) of Section 6–105, whichever is applicable, at least 14 days before the buyer distributes any part of the net contract price remaining available.

(6) If the seller undertakes in the schedule of distribution to distribute any part of the net contract price, and, after the buyer has given notice in accordance with Section 6–105, some or all of the anticipated net contract price is or becomes unavailable for distribution as a consequence of the buyer's or seller's having complied with an order of court, legal process, statute, or rule of law, the seller and any person in control of the seller are excused from any obligation arising under this Article or under any agreement with the buyer to distribute the net contract price in accordance with the seller's undertakings in the schedule if the seller:

(a) distributes the net contract price remaining available in accordance with any priorities for payment stated in the schedule of distribution and, to the extent that the price is insufficient to pay all the debts having a given priority, distributes the price pro rata among those debts shown in the schedule as having the same priority;

(b) distributes the net contract price remaining available in accordance with an order of court;

(c) commences a proceeding for interpleader in a court of competent jurisdiction and is discharged from the proceeding; or

(d) prepares a written amended schedule of distribution of the net contract price remaining available for distribution, gives notice of the amended schedule, and distributes the net contract price remaining available in accordance with the amended schedule.

(7) The notice under subsection (6)(d) must identify the buyer and the seller, state the filing number, if any, of the original notice, set forth the amended schedule, and be given in accordance with subsection (1) or (2) of Section 6–105, whichever is applicable, at least 14 days before the seller distributes any part of the net contract price remaining available.

§ 6–107. Liability for Noncompliance.

(1) Except as provided in subsection (3), and subject to the limitation in subsection (4):

(a) a buyer who fails to comply with the requirements of Section 6–104(1)(e) with respect to a creditor is liable to the creditor for damages in the amount of the claim,

reduced by any amount that the creditor would not have realized if the buyer had complied; and

(b) a buyer who fails to comply with the requirements of any other subsection of Section 6–104 with respect to a claimant is liable to the claimant for damages in the amount of the claim, reduced by any amount that the claimant would not have realized if the buyer had complied.

(2) In an action under subsection (1), the creditor has the burden of establishing the validity and amount of the claim, and the buyer has the burden of establishing the amount that the creditor would not have realized if the buyer had complied.

(3) A buyer who:

(a) made a good faith and commercially reasonable effort to comply with the requirements of Section 6–104(1) or to exclude the sale from the application of this Article under Section 6–103(3); or

(b) on or after the date of the bulk-sale agreement, but before the date of the bulk sale, held a good faith and commercially reasonable belief that this Article does not apply to the particular sale is not liable to creditors for failure to comply with the requirements of Section 6–104. The buyer has the burden of establishing the good faith and commercial reasonableness of the effort or belief.

(4) In a single bulk sale the cumulative liability of the buyer for failure to comply with the requirements of Section 6–104(1) may not exceed an amount equal to:

(a) if the assets consist only of inventory and equipment, twice the net contract price, less the amount of any part of the net contract price paid to or applied for the benefit of the seller or a creditor; or

(b) if the assets include property other than inventory and equipment, twice the net value of the inventory and equipment less the amount of the portion of any part of the net contract price paid to or applied for the benefit of the seller or a creditor which is allocable to the inventory and equipment.

(5) For the purposes of subsection (4)(b), the "net value" of an asset is the value of the asset less (i) the amount of any proceeds of the sale of an asset, to the extent the proceeds are applied in partial or total satisfaction of a debt secured by the asset and (ii) the amount of any debt to the extent it is secured by a security interest or lien that is enforceable against the asset before and after it has been sold to a buyer. If a debt is secured by an asset and other property of the seller, the amount of the debt secured by a security interest or lien that is enforceable against the asset is determined by multiplying the debt by a fraction, the numerator of which is the value of the asset on the date of the bulk sale and the denominator of which is the value of all property securing the debt on the date of the bulk sale. The portion of a part of the net contract price paid to or applied for the benefit of the seller or a creditor that is "allocable to the inventory and equipment" is the portion that bears the same ratio to that part of the net contract price as the net value of the inventory and equipment bears to the net value of all of the assets.

(6) A payment made by the buyer to a person to whom the buyer is, or believes he [or she] is, liable under subsection (1) reduces pro tanto the buyer's cumulative liability under subsection (4).

(7) No action may be brought under subsection (1)(b) by or on behalf of a claimant whose claim is unliquidated or contingent.

(8) A buyer's failure to comply with the requirements of Section 6–104(1) does not (i) impair the buyer's rights in or title to the assets, (ii) render the sale ineffective, void, or voidable, (iii) entitle a creditor to more than a single satisfaction of his [or her] claim, or (iv) create liability other than as provided in this Article.

(9) Payment of the buyer's liability under subsection (1) discharges pro tanto the seller's debt to the creditor.

(10) Unless otherwise agreed, a buyer has an immediate right of reimbursement from the seller for any amount paid to a creditor in partial or total satisfaction of the buyer's liability under subsection (1).

(11) If the seller is an organization, a person who is in direct or indirect control of the seller, and who knowingly, intentionally, and without legal justification fails, or causes the seller to fail, to distribute the net contract price in accordance with the schedule of distribution is liable to any creditor to whom the seller undertook to make payment under the schedule for damages caused by the failure.

§ 6–108. Bulk Sales by Auction; Bulk Sales Conducted by Liquidator.

(1) Sections 6–104, 6–105, 6–106, and 6–107 apply to a bulk sale by auction and a bulk sale conducted by a liquidator on the seller's behalf with the following modifications:

    (a) "buyer" refers to auctioneer or liquidator, as the case may be;

    (b) "net contract price" refers to net proceeds of the auction or net proceeds of the sale, as the case may be;

    (c) the written notice required under Section 6–105(3) must be accompanied by a copy of the schedule of distribution (Section 6–106(1)) and state at least:

        (i) that the seller and the auctioneer or liquidator have entered into an agreement for auction or liquidation services that may constitute an agreement to make a bulk sale under the laws of the State of _____ ;

        (ii) the date of the agreement;

        (iii) the date on or after which the auction began or will begin or the date on or after which the liquidator began or will begin to sell assets on the seller's behalf;

        (iv) the date on or after which more than ten percent of the net proceeds of the sale were or will be paid, if the date is not stated in the schedule of distribution;

        (v) the name and a mailing address of the seller;

        (vi) any other business name and address listed by the seller pursuant to Section 6–104(1)(a);

        (vii) the name of the auctioneer or liquidator and an address of the auctioneer or liquidator from which information concerning the sale can be obtained;

        (viii) a statement indicating the type of assets or describing the assets item by item;

        (ix) the manner in which the auctioneer or liquidator will make available the list of claimants (Section 6–104(1)(f), if applicable; and

        (x) if the sale is in total or partial satisfaction of an antecedent debt owed by the seller, the amount of the debt to be satisfied and the name of the person to whom it is owed; and

    (d) in a single bulk sale the cumulative liability of the auctioneer or liquidator for failure to comply with the requirements of this section may not exceed the amount of the net proceeds of the sale allocable to inventory and equipment sold less the amount of the portion of any part of the net proceeds paid to or applied for the benefit of a creditor which is allocable to the inventory and equipment.

(2) A payment made by the auctioneer or liquidator to a person to whom the auctioneer or liquidator is, or believes he [or she] is, liable under this section reduces pro tanto the auctioneer's or liquidator's cumulative liability under subsection (1)(d).

(3) A form substantially as follows is sufficient to comply with subsection (1)(c):

Notice of Sale

(1) _____, whose address is _____, is described in this notice as the "seller."

(2) _____, whose address is _____ , is described in this notice as the "auctioneer" or "liquidator."

(3) The seller has disclosed to the auctioneer or liquidator that within the past three years the seller has used other business names, operated at other addresses, or both, as follows: _____ .

(4) The seller and the auctioneer or liquidator have entered into an agreement dated _____ for auction or liquidation services that may constitute an agreement to make a bulk sale under the laws of the State of _____ .

(5) The date on or after which the auction began or will begin or the date on or after which the liquidator began or will begin to sell assets on the seller's behalf is _____, and [if not stated in the schedule of distribution] the date on or after which more than ten percent of the net proceeds of the sale were or will be paid is _____ .

(6) The following assets are the subject of the sale: _____ .

(7) [If applicable] The auctioneer or liquidator will make available to claimants of the seller a list of the seller's claimants in the following manner: _____ .

(8) [If applicable] The sale is to satisfy $ _____ of an antecedent debt owed by the seller to _____ .

(9) A copy of the schedule of distribution of the net proceeds accompanies this notice.

[End of Notice]

(4) A person who buys at a bulk sale by auction or conducted by a liquidator need not comply with the requirements of Section 6–104(1) and is not liable for the failure of an auctioneer or liquidator to comply with the requirements of this section.

§ 6–109. What Constitutes Filing; Duties of Filing Officer; Information from Filing Officer.

(1) Presentation of a notice or list of claimants for filing and tender of the filing fee or acceptance of the notice or list by the filing officer constitutes filing under this Article.

(2) The filing officer shall:

    (a) mark each notice or list with a file number and with the date and hour of filing;

    (b) hold the notice or list or a copy for public inspection;

    (c) index the notice or list according to each name given for the seller and for the buyer; and

(d) note in the index the file number and the addresses of the seller and buyer given in the notice or list.

(3) If the person filing a notice or list furnishes the filing officer with a copy, the filing officer upon request shall note upon the copy the file number and date and hour of the filing of the original and send or deliver the copy to the person.

(4) The fee for filing and indexing and for stamping a copy furnished by the person filing to show the date and place of filing is $ _____ for the first page and $ _____ for each additional page. The fee for indexing each name beyond the first two is $ _____ .

(5) Upon request of any person, the filing officer shall issue a certificate showing whether any notice or list with respect to a particular seller or buyer is on file on the date and hour stated in the certificate. If a notice or list is on file, the certificate must give the date and hour of filing of each notice or list and the name and address of each seller, buyer, auctioneer, or liquidator. The fee for the certificate is $ _____ if the request for the certificate is in the standard form prescribed by the [Secretary of State] and otherwise is $ _____ . Upon request of any person, the filing officer shall furnish a copy of any filed notice or list for a fee of $ _____ .

(6) The filing officer shall keep each notice or list for two years after it is filed.

§ 6–110. Limitation of Actions.

(1) Except as provided in subsection (2), an action under this Article against a buyer, auctioneer, or liquidator must be commenced within one year after the date of the bulk sale.

(2) If the buyer, auctioneer, or liquidator conceals the fact that the sale has occurred, the limitation is tolled and an action under this Article may be commenced within the earlier of (i) one year after the person bringing the action discovers that the sale has occurred or (ii) one year after the person bringing the action should have discovered that the sale has occurred, but no later than two years after the date of the bulk sale. Complete noncompliance with the requirements of this Article does not of itself constitute concealment.

(3) An action under Section 6–107(11) must be commenced within one year after the alleged violation occurs.

Conforming Amendment to Section 2–403

States adopting Alternative B should amend Section 2–403(4) of the Uniform Commercial Code to read as follows:

(4) The rights of other purchasers of goods and of lien creditors are governed by the Articles on Secured Transactions (Article 9), Bulk Sales (Article 6) and Documents of Title (Article 7).

ARTICLE 7: WAREHOUSE RECEIPTS, BILLS OF LADING AND OTHER DOCUMENTS OF TITLE

Part 1—General

§ 7–101. Short Title.

This Article shall be known and may be cited as Uniform Commercial Code–Documents of Title.

§ 7–102. Definitions and Index of Definitions.

(1) In this Article, unless the context otherwise requires:

(a) "Bailee" means the person who by a warehouse receipt, bill of lading or other document of title acknowledges possession of goods and contracts to deliver them.

(b) "Consignee" means the person named in a bill to whom or to whose order the bill promises delivery.

(c) "Consignor" means the person named in a bill as the person from whom the goods have been received for shipment.

(d) "Delivery order" means a written order to deliver goods directed to a warehouseman, carrier or other person who in the ordinary course of business issues warehouse receipts or bills of lading.

(e) "Document" means document of title as defined in the general definitions in Article 1 (Section 1–201).

(f) "Goods" means all things which are treated as movable for the purposes of a contract of storage or transportation.

(g) "Issuer" means a bailee who issues a document except that in relation to an unaccepted delivery order it means the person who orders the possessor of goods to deliver. Issuer includes any person for whom an agent or employee purports to act in issuing a document if the agent or employee has real or apparent authority to issue documents, notwithstanding that the issuer received no goods or that the goods were misdescribed or that in any other respect the agent or employee violated his instructions.

(h) "Warehouseman" is a person engaged in the business of storing goods for hire.

(2) Other definitions applying to this Article or to specified Parts thereof, and the sections in which they appear are:
"Duly negotiate". Section 7–501.
"Person entitled under the document". Section 7–403(4).

(3) Definitions in other Articles applying to this Article and the sections in which they appear are:
"Contract for sale". Section 2–106.
"Overseas". Section 2–323.
"Receipt" of goods. Section 2–103.

(4) In addition Article 1 contains general definitions and principles of construction and interpretation applicable throughout this Article.

§ 7–103. Relation of Article to Treaty, Statute, Tariff, Classification or Regulation.

To the extent that any treaty or statute of the United States, regulatory statute of this State or tariff, classification or regulation filed or issued pursuant thereto is applicable, the provisions of this Article are subject thereto.

§ 7–104. Negotiable and Non-Negotiable Warehouse Receipt, Bill of Lading or Other Document of Title.

(1) A warehouse receipt, bill of lading or other document of title is negotiable

(a) if by its terms the goods are to be delivered to bearer or to the order of a named person; or

(b) where recognized in overseas trade, if it runs to a named person or assigns.

(2) Any other document is nonnegotiable. A bill of lading in which it is stated that the goods are consigned to a named person is not made negotiable by a provision that the goods are to be delivered only against a written order signed by the same or another named person.

§ 7–105. Construction Against Negative Implication.

The omission from either Part 2 or Part 3 of this Article of a provision corresponding to a provision made in the other Part does not imply that a corresponding rule of law is not applicable.

Part 2—Warehouse Receipts: Special Provisions

§ 7–201. Who May Issue a Warehouse Receipt; Storage Under Government Bond.

(1) A warehouse receipt may be issued by any warehouseman.

(2) Where goods including distilled spirits and agricultural commodities are stored under a statute requiring a bond against withdrawal or a license for the issuance of receipts in the nature of warehouse receipts, a receipt issued for the goods has like effect as a warehouse receipt even though issued by a person who is the owner of the goods and is not a warehouseman.

§ 7–202. Form of Warehouse Receipt; Essential Terms; Optional Terms.

(1) A warehouse receipt need not be in any particular form.

(2) Unless a warehouse receipt embodies within its written or printed terms each of the following, the warehouseman is liable for damages caused by the omission to a person injured thereby:

(a) the location of the warehouse where the goods are stored;

(b) the date of issue of the receipt;

(c) the consecutive number of the receipt;

(d) a statement whether the goods received will be delivered to the bearer, to a specified person, or to a specified person or his order;

(e) the rate of storage and handling charges, except that where goods are stored under a field warehousing arrangement a statement of that fact is sufficient on a non-negotiable receipt;

(f) a description of the goods or of the packages containing them;

(g) the signature of the warehouseman, which may be made by his authorized agent;

(h) if the receipt is issued for goods of which the warehouseman is owner, either solely or jointly or in common with others, the fact of such ownership; and

(i) a statement of the amount of advances made and of liabilities incurred for which the warehouseman claims a lien or security interest (Section 7–209). If the precise amount of such advances made or of such liabilities incurred is, at the time of the issue of the receipt, unknown to the warehouseman or to his agent who issues it, a statement of the fact that advances have been made or liabilities incurred and the purpose thereof is sufficient.

(3) A warehouseman may insert in his receipt any other terms which are not contrary to the provisions of this Act and do not impair his obligation of delivery (Section 7–403) or his duty of care (Section 7–204). Any contrary provisions shall be ineffective.

§ 7–203. Liability for Non-Receipt or Misdescription.

A party to or purchaser for value in good faith of a document of title other than a bill of lading relying in either case upon the description therein of the goods may recover from the issuer damages caused by the nonreceipt or misdescription of the goods, except to the extent that the document conspicuously indicates that the issuer does not know whether any part or all of the goods in fact were received or conform to the description, as where the description is in terms of marks or labels or kind, quantity or condition, or the receipt or description is qualified by "contents, condition and quality unknown", "said to contain" or the like, if such indication be true, or the party or purchaser otherwise has notice.

§ 7–204. Duty of Care; Contractual Limitation of Warehouseman's Liability.

(1) A warehouseman is liable for damages for loss of or injury to the goods caused by his failure to exercise such care in regard to them as a reasonably careful man would exercise under like circumstances but unless otherwise agreed he is not liable for damages which could not have been avoided by the exercise of such care.

(2) Damages may be limited by a term in the warehouse receipt or storage agreement limiting the amount of liability in case of loss or damage, and setting forth a specific liability per article or item, or value per unit of weight, beyond which the warehouseman shall not be liable; provided, however, that such liability may on written request of the bailor at the time of signing such storage agreement or within a reasonable time after receipt of the warehouse receipt be increased on part or all of the goods thereunder, in which event increased rates may be charged based on such increased valuation, but that no such increase shall be permitted contrary to a lawful limitation of liability contained in the warehouseman's tariff, if any. No such limitation is effective with respect to the warehouseman's liability for conversion to his own use.

(3) Reasonable provisions as to the time and manner of presenting claims and instituting actions based on the bailment may be included in the warehouse receipt or tariff.

(4) This section does not impair or repeal . . .

Note: *Insert in subsection (4) a reference to any statute which imposes a higher responsibility upon the warehouseman or invalidates contractual limitations which would be permissible under this Article.*

§ 7–205. Title Under Warehouse Receipt Defeated in Certain Cases.

A buyer in the ordinary course of business of fungible goods sold and delivered by a warehouseman who is also in the business of buying and selling such goods takes free of any claim under a warehouse receipt even though it has been duly negotiated.

§ 7–206. Termination of Storage at Warehouseman's Option.

(1) A warehouseman may on notifying the person on whose account the goods are held and any other person known to claim an interest in the goods require payment of any charges and removal of the goods from the warehouse at the termination of the period of storage fixed by the document, or, if no period is fixed, within a stated period not less than thirty days after the notification. If the goods are not removed before the date specified in the notification, the warehouseman may sell them in accordance with the provisions of the section on enforcement of a warehouseman's lien (Section 7–210).

(2) If a warehouseman in good faith believes that the goods are about to deteriorate or decline in value to less than the amount of his lien within the time prescribed in subsection (1) for notification, advertisement and sale, the warehouseman may specify in the notification any reasonable shorter time for removal of the goods and in case the goods are not removed, may sell them at public sale held not less than one week after a single advertisement or posting.

(3) If as a result of a quality or condition of the goods of which the warehouseman had no notice at the time of deposit the goods are a hazard to other property or to the warehouse or to persons, the warehouseman may sell the goods at public or private sale without advertisement on reasonable notification to all persons known to claim an interest in the goods. If the warehouseman after a reasonable effort is unable to sell the goods he may dispose of them in any lawful manner and shall incur no liability by reason of such disposition.

(4) The warehouseman must deliver the goods to any person entitled to them under this Article upon due demand made at any time prior to sale or other disposition under this section.

(5) The warehouseman may satisfy his lien from the proceeds of any sale or disposition under this section but must hold the balance for delivery on the demand of any person to whom he would have been bound to deliver the goods.

§ 7–207. Goods Must Be Kept Separate; Fungible Goods.

(1) Unless the warehouse receipt otherwise provides, a warehouseman must keep separate the goods covered by each receipt so as to permit at all times identification and delivery of those goods except that different lots of fungible goods may be commingled.

(2) Fungible goods so commingled are owned in common by the persons entitled thereto and the warehouseman is severally liable to each owner for that owner's share. Where because of overissue a mass of fungible goods is insufficient to meet all the receipts which the warehouseman has issued against it, the persons entitled include all holders to whom overissued receipts have been duly negotiated.

§ 7–208. Altered Warehouse Receipts.

Where a blank in a negotiable warehouse receipt has been filled in without authority, a purchaser for value and without notice of the want of authority may treat the insertion as authorized. Any other unauthorized alteration leaves any receipt enforceable against the issuer according to its original tenor.

§ 7–209. Lien of Warehouseman.

(1) A warehouseman has a lien against the bailor on the goods covered by a warehouse receipt or on the proceeds thereof in his possession for charges for storage or transportation (including demurrage and terminal charges), insurance, labor, or charges present or future in relation to the goods, and for expenses necessary for preservation of the goods or reasonably incurred in their sale pursuant to law. If the person on whose account the goods are held is liable for like charges or expenses in relation to other goods whenever deposited and it is stated in the receipt that a lien is claimed for charges and expenses in relation to other goods, the warehouseman also has a lien against him for such charges and expenses whether or not the other goods have been delivered by the warehouseman. But against a person to whom a negotiable warehouse receipt is duly negotiated a warehouseman's lien is limited to charges in an amount or at a rate specified on the receipt or if no charges are so specified then to a reasonable charge for storage of the goods covered by the receipt subsequent to the date of the receipt.

(2) The warehouseman may also reserve a security interest against the bailor for a maximum amount specified on the receipt for charges other than those specified in subsection (1), such as for money advanced and interest. Such a security interest is governed by the Article on Secured Transactions (Article 9).

(3)(a) A warehouseman's lien for charges and expenses under subsection (1) or a security interest under subsection (2) is also effective against any person who so entrusted the bailor with possession of the goods that a pledge of them by him to a good faith purchaser for value would have been valid but is not effective against a person as to whom the document confers no right in the goods covered by it under Section 7–503.

(b) A warehouseman's lien on household goods for charges and expenses in relation to the goods under subsection (1) is also effective against all persons if the depositor was the legal possessor of the goods at the time of deposit. "Household goods" means furniture, furnishings and personal effects used by the depositor in a dwelling.

(4) A warehouseman loses his lien on any goods which he voluntarily delivers or which he unjustifiably refuses to deliver.

§ 7–210. Enforcement of Warehouseman's Lien.

(1) Except as provided in subsection (2), a warehouseman's lien may be enforced by public or private sale of the goods in bloc or in parcels, at any time or place and on any terms which are commercially reasonable, after notifying all persons known to claim an interest in the goods. Such notification must include a statement of the amount due, the nature of the proposed sale and the time and place of any public sale. The fact that a better price could have been obtained by a sale at a different time or in a different method from that selected by the warehouseman is not of itself sufficient to establish that the sale was not made in a commercially reasonable manner. If the warehouseman either sells the goods in the usual manner in any recognized market therefor, or if he sells at the price current in such market at the time of his sale, or if he has otherwise sold in conformity with commercially reasonable practices among dealers in the type of goods sold, he has sold in a commercially reasonable manner. A sale of more goods than apparently necessary to be offered to ensure satisfaction of the obligation is not commercially reasonable except in cases covered by the preceding sentence.

(2) A warehouseman's lien on goods other than goods stored by a merchant in the course of his business may be enforced only as follows:

(a) All persons known to claim an interest in the goods must be notified.

(b) The notification must be delivered in person or sent by registered or certified letter to the last known address of any person to be notified.

(c) The notification must include an itemized statement of the claim, a description of the goods subject to the lien, a demand for payment within a specified time not less than ten days after receipt of the notification, and a conspicuous statement that unless the claim is paid within the time the goods will be advertised for sale and sold by auction at a specified time and place.

(d) The sale must conform to the terms of the notification.

(e) The sale must be held at the nearest suitable place to that where the goods are held or stored.

(f) After the expiration of the time given in the notification, an advertisement of the sale must be published once a week for two weeks consecutively in a newspaper of general circulation where the sale is to be held. The advertisement must include a description of the goods, the name of the person on whose account they are being held, and the time and place of the sale. The sale must take place at least fifteen days after the first publication. If there is no newspaper of general circulation where the sale is to be held, the advertisement must be posted at least ten days before the sale in not less than six conspicuous places in the neighborhood of the proposed sale.

(3) Before any sale pursuant to this section any person claiming a right in the goods may pay the amount necessary to satisfy the lien and the reasonable expenses incurred under this section. In that event the goods must not be sold, but must be retained by the warehouseman subject to the terms of the receipt and this Article.

(4) The warehouseman may buy at any public sale pursuant to this section.

(5) A purchaser in good faith of goods sold to enforce a warehouseman's lien takes the goods free of any rights of persons against whom the lien was valid, despite noncompliance by the warehouseman with the requirements of this section.

(6) The warehouseman may satisfy his lien from the proceeds of any sale pursuant to this section but must hold the balance, if any, for delivery on demand to any person to whom he would have been bound to deliver the goods.

(7) The rights provided by this section shall be in addition to all other rights allowed by law to a creditor against his debtor.

(8) Where a lien is on goods stored by a merchant in the course of his business the lien may be enforced in accordance with either subsection (1) or (2).

(9) The warehouseman is liable for damages caused by failure to comply with the requirements for sale under this section and in case of willful violation is liable for conversion.

As amended in 1962.

Part 3—Bills of Lading: Special Provisions

§ 7–301. Liability for Non-Receipt or Misdescription; "Said to Contain"; "Shipper's Load and Count"; Improper Handling.

(1) A consignee of a non-negotiable bill who has given value in good faith or a holder to whom a negotiable bill has been duly negotiated relying in either case upon the description therein of the goods, or upon the date therein shown, may recover from the issuer damages caused by the misdating of the bill or the nonreceipt or misdescription of the goods, except to the extent that the document indicates that the issuer does not know whether any part of all of the goods in fact were received or conform to the description, as where the description is in terms of marks or labels or kind, quantity, or condition or the receipt or description is qualified by "contents or condition of contents of packages unknown", "said to contain", "shipper's weight, load and count" or the like, if such indication be true.

(2) When goods are loaded by an issuer who is a common carrier, the issuer must count the packages of goods if package freight and ascertain the kind and quantity if bulk freight. In such cases "shipper's weight, load and count" or other words indicating that the description was made by the shipper are ineffective except as to freight concealed by packages.

(3) When bulk freight is loaded by a shipper who makes available to the issuer adequate facilities for weighing such freight, an issuer who is a common carrier must ascertain the kind and quantity within a reasonable time after receiving the written request of the shipper to do so. In such cases "shipper's weight" or other words of like purport are ineffective.

(4) The issuer may by inserting in the bill the words "shipper's weight, load and count" or other words of like purport indicate that the goods were loaded by the shipper; and if such statement be true the issuer shall not be liable for damages caused by the improper loading. But their omission does not imply liability for such damages.

(5) The shipper shall be deemed to have guaranteed to the issuer the accuracy at the time of shipment of the description, marks, labels, number, kind, quantity, condition and weight, as furnished by him; and the shipper shall indemnify the issuer against damage caused by inaccuracies in such particulars. The right of the issuer to such indemnity shall in no way limit his responsibility and liability under the contract of carriage to any person other than the shipper.

§ 7–302. Through Bills of Lading and Similar Documents.

(1) The issuer of a through bill of lading or other document embodying an undertaking to be performed in part by persons acting as its agents or by connecting carriers is liable to anyone entitled to recover on the document for any breach by such other persons or by a connecting carrier of its obligation under the document but to the extent that the bill covers an undertaking to be performed overseas or in territory not contiguous to the continental United States or an undertaking including matters other than transportation this liability may be varied by agreement of the parties.

(2) Where goods covered by a through bill of lading or other document embodying an undertaking to be performed in part by persons other than the issuer are received by any such person, he is subject with respect to his own performance while the goods are in his possession to the obligation of the issuer. His obligation is discharged by delivery of the goods to another such person pursuant to the document, and does not include liability for breach by any other such persons or by the issuer.

(3) The issuer of such through bill of lading or other document shall be entitled to recover from the connecting carrier or such other person in possession of the goods when the breach of the obligation under the document occurred, the amount it may be required to pay to anyone entitled to recover on the document therefor, as may be evidenced by any receipt, judgment, or transcript thereof, and the amount of any expense reasonably incurred by it in defending any action brought by anyone entitled to recover on the document therefor.

§ 7–303. Diversion; Reconsignment; Change of Instructions.

(1) Unless the bill of lading otherwise provides, the carrier may deliver the goods to a person or destination other than that stated in the bill or may otherwise dispose of the goods on instructions from

(a) the holder of a negotiable bill; or

(b) the consignor on a non-negotiable bill not-withstanding contrary instructions from the consignee; or

(c) the consignee on a non-negotiable bill in the absence of contrary instructions from the consignor, if the goods have arrived at the billed destination or if the consignee is in possession of the bill; or

(d) the consignee on a non-negotiable bill if he is entitled as against the consignor to dispose of them.

(2) Unless such instructions are noted on a negotiable bill of lading, a person to whom the bill is duly negotiated can hold the bailee according to the original terms.

§ 7–304. Bills of Lading in a Set.

(1) Except where customary in overseas transportation, a bill of lading must not be issued in a set of parts. The issuer is liable for damages caused by violation of this subsection.

(2) Where a bill of lading is lawfully drawn in a set of parts, each of which is numbered and expressed to be valid only if the goods have not been delivered against any other part, the whole of the parts constitute one bill.

(3) Where a bill of lading is lawfully issued in a set of parts and different parts are negotiated to different persons, the title of the holder to whom the first due negotiation is made prevails as to both the document and the goods even though any later holder may have received the goods from the carrier in good faith and discharged the carrier's obligation by surrender of his part.

(4) Any person who negotiates or transfers a single part of a bill of lading drawn in a set is liable to holders of that part as if it were the whole set.

(5) The bailee is obliged to deliver in accordance with Part 4 of this Article against the first presented part of a bill of lading lawfully drawn in a set. Such delivery discharges the bailee's obligation on the whole bill.

§ 7–305. Destination Bills.

(1) Instead of issuing a bill of lading to the consignor at the place of shipment a carrier may at the request of the consignor procure the bill to be issued at destination or at any other place designated in the request.

(2) Upon request of anyone entitled as against the carrier to control the goods while in transit and on surrender of any outstanding bill of lading or other receipt covering such goods, the issuer may procure a substitute bill to be issued at any place designated in the request.

§ 7–306. Altered Bills of Lading.

An unauthorized alteration or filling in of a blank in a bill of lading leaves the bill enforceable according to its original tenor.

§ 7–307. Lien of Carrier.

(1) A carrier has a lien on the goods covered by a bill of lading for charges subsequent to the date of its receipt of the goods for storage or transportation (including demurrage and terminal charges) and for expenses necessary for preservation of the goods incident to their transportation or reasonably incurred in their sale pursuant to law. But against a purchaser for value of a negotiable bill of lading a carrier's lien is limited to charges stated in the bill or the applicable tariffs, or if no charges are stated then to a reasonable charge.

(2) A lien for charges and expenses under subsection (1) on goods which the carrier was required by law to receive for transportation is effective against the consignor or any person entitled to the goods unless the carrier had notice that the consignor lacked authority to subject the goods to such charges and expenses. Any other lien under subsection (1) is effective against the consignor and any person who permitted the bailor to have control or possession of the goods unless the carrier had notice that the bailor lacked such authority.

(3) A carrier loses his lien on any goods which he voluntarily delivers or which he unjustifiably refuses to deliver.

§ 7–308. Enforcement of Carrier's Lien.

(1) A carrier's lien may be enforced by public or private sale of the goods, in bloc or in parcels, at any time or place and on any terms which are commercially reasonable, after notifying all persons known to claim an interest in the goods. Such notification must include a statement of the amount due, the nature of the proposed sale and the time and place of any public sale. The fact that a better price could have been obtained by a sale at a different time or in a different method from that selected by the carrier is not of itself sufficient to establish that the sale was not made in a commercially reasonable manner. If the carrier either sells the goods in the usual manner in any recognized market therefor or if he sells at the price current in such market at the time of his sale or if he has otherwise sold in conformity with commercially reasonable practices among dealers in the type of goods sold he has sold in a commercially reasonable manner. A sale of more goods than apparently necessary to be offered to ensure satisfaction of the obligation is not commercially reasonable except in cases covered by the preceding sentence.

(2) Before any sale pursuant to this section any person claiming a right in the goods may pay the amount necessary to satisfy the lien and the reasonable expenses incurred under this section. In that event the goods must not be sold, but must be retained by the carrier subject to the terms of the bill and this Article.

(3) The carrier may buy at any public sale pursuant to this section.

(4) A purchaser in good faith of goods sold to enforce a carrier's lien takes the goods free of any rights of persons against whom the lien was valid, despite noncompliance by the carrier with the requirements of this section.

(5) The carrier may satisfy his lien from the proceeds of any sale pursuant to this section but must hold the balance, if any, for delivery on demand to any person to whom he would have been bound to deliver the goods.

(6) The rights provided by this section shall be in addition to all other rights allowed by law to a creditor against his debtor.

(7) A carrier's lien may be enforced in accordance with either subsection (1) or the procedure set forth in subsection (2) of Section 7–210.

(8) The carrier is liable for damages caused by failure to comply with the requirements for sale under this section and in case of willful violation is liable for conversion.

§ 7–309. Duty of Care; Contractual Limitation of Carrier's Liability.

(1) A carrier who issues a bill of lading whether negotiable or nonnegotiable must exercise the degree of care in relation to the goods which a reasonably careful man would exercise under like circumstances. This subsection does not repeal or change any law or rule of law which imposes liability upon a common carrier for damages not caused by its negligence.

(2) Damages may be limited by a provision that the carrier's liability shall not exceed a value stated in the document if the carrier's rates are dependent upon value and the consignor by the carrier's tariff is afforded an opportunity to declare a higher value or a value as lawfully provided in the tariff, or where no tariff is filed he is otherwise advised of such opportunity; but no such limitation is effective with respect to the carrier's liability for conversion to its own use.

(3) Reasonable provisions as to the time and manner of presenting claims and instituting actions based on the shipment may be included in a bill of lading or tariff.

Part 4—Warehouse Receipts and Bills of Lading: General Obligations

§ 7–401. Irregularities in Issue of Receipt or Bill or Conduct of Issuer.

The obligations imposed by this Article on an issuer apply to a document of title regardless of the fact that

(a) the document may not comply with the requirements of this Article or of any other law or regulation regarding its issue, form or content; or

(b) the issuer may have violated laws regulating the conduct of his business; or

(c) the goods covered by the document were owned by the bailee at the time the document was issued; or

(d) the person issuing the document does not come within the definition of warehouseman if it purports to be a warehouse receipt.

§ 7–402. Duplicate Receipt or Bill; Overissue.

Neither a duplicate nor any other document of title purporting to cover goods already represented by an outstanding document of the same issuer confers any right in the goods, except as provided in the case of bills in a set, overissue of documents for fungible goods and substitutes for lost, stolen or destroyed documents. But the issuer is liable for damages caused by his overissue or failure to identify a duplicate document as such by conspicuous notation on its face.

§ 7–403. Obligation of Warehouseman or Carrier to Deliver; Excuse.

(1) The bailee must deliver the goods to a person entitled under the document who complies with subsections (2) and (3), unless and to the extent that the bailee establishes any of the following:

(a) delivery of the goods to a person whose receipt was rightful as against the claimant;

(b) damage to or delay, loss or destruction of the goods for which the bailee is not liable [, but the burden of establishing negligence in such cases is on the person entitled under the document];

Note: *The brackets in (1)(b) indicate that State enactments may differ on this point without serious damage to the principle of uniformity.*

(c) previous sale or other disposition of the goods in lawful enforcement of a lien or on warehouseman's lawful termination of storage;

(d) the exercise by a seller of his right to stop delivery pursuant to the provisions of the Article on Sales (Section 2–705);

(e) a diversion, reconsignment or other disposition pursuant to the provisions of this Article (Section 7–303) or tariff regulating such right;

(f) release, satisfaction or any other fact affording a personal defense against the claimant;

(g) any other lawful excuse.

(2) A person claiming goods covered by a document of title must satisfy the bailee's lien where the bailee so requests or where the bailee is prohibited by law from delivering the goods until the charges are paid.

(3) Unless the person claiming is one against whom the document confers no right under Sec. 7–503(1), he must surrender for cancellation or notation of partial deliveries any outstanding negotiable document covering the goods, and the bailee must cancel the document or conspicuously note the partial delivery thereon or be liable to any person to whom the document is duly negotiated.

(4) "Person entitled under the document" means holder in the case of a negotiable document, or the person to whom delivery is to be made by the terms of or pursuant to written instructions under a non-negotiable document.

§ 7–404. No Liability for Good Faith Delivery Pursuant to Receipt or Bill.

A bailee who in good faith including observance of reasonable commercial standards has received goods and delivered or otherwise disposed of them according to the terms of the document of title or pursuant to this Article is not liable therefor. This rule applies even though the person from whom he received the goods had no authority to procure the document or to dispose of the goods and even though the person to whom he delivered the goods had no authority to receive them.

Part 5—Warehouse Receipts and Bills of Lading: Negotiation and Transfer

§ 7–501. Form of Negotiation and Requirements of "Due Negotiation".

(1) A negotiable document of title running to the order of a named person is negotiated by his indorsement and delivery. After his indorsement in blank or to bearer any person can negotiate it by delivery alone.

(2)(a) A negotiable document of title is also negotiated by delivery alone when by its original terms it runs to bearer.

(b) When a document running to the order of a named person is delivered to him the effect is the same as if the document had been negotiated.

(3) Negotiation of a negotiable document of title after it has been indorsed to a specified person requires indorsement by the special indorsee as well as delivery.

(4) A negotiable document of title is "duly negotiated" when it is negotiated in the manner stated in this section to a holder who purchases it in good faith without notice of any defense against or claim to it on the part of any person and for value, unless it is established that the negotiation is not in the regular course of business or financing or involves receiving the document in settlement or payment of a money obligation.

(5) Indorsement of a nonnegotiable document neither makes it negotiable nor adds to the transferee's rights.

(6) The naming in a negotiable bill of a person to be notified of the arrival of the goods does not limit the negotiability of the bill nor constitute notice to a purchaser thereof of any interest of such person in the goods.

§ 7–502. Rights Acquired by Due Negotiation.

(1) Subject to the following section and to the provisions of Section 7–205 on fungible goods, a holder to whom a negotiable document of title has been duly negotiated acquires thereby:

(a) title to the document;

(b) title to the goods;

(c) all rights accruing under the law of agency or estoppel, including rights to goods delivered to the bailee after the document was issued; and

(d) the direct obligation of the issuer to hold or deliver the goods according to the terms of the document free of any defense or claim by him except those arising under the terms of the document or under this Article. In the case of a delivery order the bailee's obligation accrues only upon acceptance and the obligation acquired by the holder is that the issuer and any indorser will procure the acceptance of the bailee.

(2) Subject to the following section, title and rights so acquired are not defeated by any stoppage of the goods represented by the document or by surrender of such goods by the bailee, and are not impaired even though the negotiation or any prior negotiation constituted a breach of duty or even though any person has been deprived of possession of the document by misrepresentation, fraud, accident, mistake, duress, loss, theft or conversion, or even though a previous sale or other transfer of the goods or document has been made to a third person.

§ 7–503. Document of Title to Goods Defeated in Certain Cases.

(1) A document of title confers no right in goods against a person who before issuance of the document had a legal interest or a perfected security interest in them and who neither

(a) delivered or entrusted them or any document of title covering them to the bailor or his nominee with actual or apparent authority to ship, store or sell or with power to obtain delivery under this Article (Section 7–403) or with power of disposition under this Act (Sections 2–403 and 9–307) or other statute or rule of law; nor

(b) acquiesced in the procurement by the bailor or his nominee of any document of title.

(2) Title to goods based upon an unaccepted delivery order is subject to the rights of anyone to whom a negotiable warehouse receipt or bill of lading covering the goods has been duly negotiated. Such a title may be defeated under the next section to the same extent as the rights of the issuer or a transferee from the issuer.

(3) Title to goods based upon a bill of lading issued to a freight forwarder is subject to the rights of anyone to whom a bill issued by the freight forwarder is duly negotiated; but delivery by the carrier in accordance with Part 4 of this Article pursuant to its own bill of lading discharges the carrier's obligation to deliver. As amended in 1999.

§ 7–504. Rights Acquired in the Absence of Due Negotiation; Effect of Diversion; Seller's Stoppage of Delivery.

(1) A transferee of a document, whether negotiable or nonnegotiable, to whom the document has been delivered but not duly negotiated, acquires the title and rights which his transferor had or had actual authority to convey.

(2) In the case of a nonnegotiable document, until but not after the bailee receives notification of the transfer, the rights of the transferee may be defeated

(a) by those creditors of the transferor who could treat the sale as void under Section 2–402; or

(b) by a buyer from the transferor in ordinary course of business if the bailee has delivered the goods to the buyer or received notification of his rights; or

(c) as against the bailee by good faith dealings of the bailee with the transferor.

(3) A diversion or other change of shipping instructions by the consignor in a nonnegotiable bill of lading which causes the bailee not to deliver to the consignee defeats the consignee's title to the goods if they have been delivered to a buyer in ordinary course of business and in any event defeats the consignee's rights against the bailee.

(4) Delivery pursuant to a nonnegotiable document may be stopped by a seller under Section 2–705, and subject to the requirement of due notification there provided. A bailee honoring the seller's instructions is entitled to be indemnified by the seller against any resulting loss or expense.

§ 7–505. Indorser Not a Guarantor for Other Parties.

The indorsement of a document of title issued by a bailee does not make the indorser liable for any default by the bailee or by previous indorsers.

§ 7–506. Delivery Without Indorsement: Right to Compel Indorsement.

The transferee of a negotiable document of title has a specifically enforceable right to have his transferor supply any necessary indorsement but the transfer becomes a negotiation only as of the time the indorsement is supplied.

§ 7–507. Warranties on Negotiation or Transfer of Receipt or Bill.

Where a person negotiates or transfers a document of title for value otherwise than as a mere intermediary under the next following section, then unless otherwise agreed he warrants to his immediate purchaser only in addition to any warranty made in selling the goods

(a) that the document is genuine; and

(b) that he has no knowledge of any fact which would impair its validity or worth; and

(c) that his negotiation or transfer is rightful and fully effective with respect to the title to the document and the goods it represents.

§ 7–508. Warranties of Collecting Bank as to Documents.

A collecting bank or other intermediary known to be entrusted with documents on behalf of another or with collection of a draft or other claim against delivery of documents warrants by such delivery of the documents only its own good faith and authority. This rule applies even though the intermediary has purchased or made advances against the claim or draft to be collected.

§ 7–509. Receipt or Bill: When Adequate Compliance With Commercial Contract.

The question whether a document is adequate to fulfill the obligations of a contract for sale or the conditions of a credit is governed by the Articles on Sales (Article 2) and on Letters of Credit (Article 5).

Part 6—Warehouse Receipts and Bills of Lading: Miscellaneous Provisions

§ 7–601. Lost and Missing Documents.

(1) If a document has been lost, stolen or destroyed, a court may order delivery of the goods or issuance of a substitute document and the bailee may without liability to any person comply with such order. If the document was negotiable the claimant must post security approved by the court to indemnify any person who may suffer loss as a result of non-surrender of the document. If the document was not negotiable, such security may be required at the discretion of the court. The court may also in its discretion order payment of the bailee's reasonable costs and counsel fees.

(2) A bailee who without court order delivers goods to a person claiming under a missing negotiable document is liable to any person injured thereby, and if the delivery is not in good faith becomes liable for conversion. Delivery in good faith is not conversion if made in accordance with a filed classification or tariff or, where no classification or tariff is filed, if the claimant posts security with the bailee in an amount at least double the value of the goods at the time of posting to indemnify any person injured by the delivery who files a notice of claim within one year after the delivery.

§ 7–602. Attachment of Goods Covered by a Negotiable Document.

Except where the document was originally issued upon delivery of the goods by a person who had no power to dispose of them, no lien attaches by virtue of any judicial process to goods in the possession of a bailee for which a negotiable document of title is outstanding unless the document be first surrendered to the bailee or its negotiation enjoined, and the bailee shall not be compelled to deliver the goods pursuant to process until the document is surrendered to him or impounded by the court. One who purchases the document for value without notice of the process or injunction takes free of the lien imposed by judicial process.

§ 7–603. Conflicting Claims; Interpleader.

If more than one person claims title or possession of the goods, the bailee is excused from delivery until he has had a reasonable time to ascertain the validity of the adverse claims or to bring an action to compel all claimants to interplead and may compel such interpleader, either in defending an action for nondelivery of the goods, or by original action, whichever is appropriate.

REVISED (1994) ARTICLE 8: INVESTMENT SECURITIES

Part 1—Short Title and General Matters

§ 8–101. Short Title.

This Article may be cited as Uniform Commercial Code—Investment Securities.

§ 8–102. Definitions.

(a) In this Article:

(1) "Adverse claim" means a claim that a claimant has a property interest in a financial asset and that it is a violation of the rights of the claimant for another person to hold, transfer, or deal with the financial asset.

(2) "Bearer form," as applied to a certificated security, means a form in which the security is payable to the bearer of the security certificate according to its terms but not by reason of an indorsement.

(3) "Broker" means a person defined as a broker or dealer under the federal securities laws, but without excluding a bank acting in that capacity.

(4) "Certificated security" means a security that is represented by a certificate.

(5) "Clearing corporation" means:
(i) a person that is registered as a "clearing agency" under the federal securities laws;
(ii) a federal reserve bank; or
(iii) any other person that provides clearance or settlement services with respect to financial assets that would require it to register as a clearing agency under the federal securities laws but for an exclusion or exemption from the registration requirement, if its activities as a clearing corporation, including promulgation of rules, are subject to regulation by a federal or state governmental authority.

(6) "Communicate" means to:
(i) send a signed writing; or
(ii) transmit information by any mechanism agreed upon by the persons transmitting and receiving the information.

(7) "Entitlement holder" means a person identified in the records of a securities intermediary as the person having a security entitlement against the securities intermediary. If a person acquires a security entitlement by virtue of Section 8–501(b)(2) or (3), that person is the entitlement holder.

(8) "Entitlement order" means a notification communicated to a securities intermediary directing transfer or redemption of a financial asset to which the entitlement holder has a security entitlement.

(9) "Financial asset," except as otherwise provided in Section 8–103, means:

(i) a security;

(ii) an obligation of a person or a share, participation, or other interest in a person or in property or an enterprise of a person, which is, or is of a type, dealt in or traded on financial markets, or which is recognized in any area in which it is issued or dealt in as a medium for investment; or

(iii) any property that is held by a securities intermediary for another person in a securities account if the securities intermediary has expressly agreed with the other person that the property is to be treated as a financial asset under this Article.

As context requires, the term means either the interest itself or the means by which a person's claim to it is evidenced, including a certificated or uncertificated security, a security certificate, or a security entitlement.

(10) "Good faith," for purposes of the obligation of good faith in the performance or enforcement of contracts or duties within this Article, means honesty in fact and the observance of reasonable commercial standards of fair dealing.

(11) "Indorsement" means a signature that alone or accompanied by other words is made on a security certificate in registered form or on a separate document for the purpose of assigning, transferring, or redeeming the security or granting a power to assign, transfer, or redeem it.

(12) "Instruction" means a notification communi-cated to the issuer of an uncertificated security which directs that the transfer of the security be registered or that the security be redeemed.

(13) "Registered form," as applied to a certificated security, means a form in which:

(i) the security certificate specifies a person entitled to the security; and

(ii) a transfer of the security may be registered upon books maintained for that purpose by or on behalf of the issuer, or the security certificate so states.

(14) "Securities intermediary" means:

(i) a clearing corporation; or

(ii) a person, including a bank or broker, that in the ordinary course of its business maintains securities accounts for others and is acting in that capacity.

(15) "Security," except as otherwise provided in Section 8–103, means an obligation of an issuer or a share, participation, or other interest in an issuer or in property or an enterprise of an issuer:

(i) which is represented by a security certificate in bearer or registered form, or the transfer of which may be registered upon books maintained for that purpose by or on behalf of the issuer;

(ii) which is one of a class or series or by its terms is divisible into a class or series of shares, participations, interests, or obligations; and

(iii) which:

(A) is, or is of a type, dealt in or traded on securities exchanges or securities markets; or

(B) is a medium for investment and by its terms expressly provides that it is a security governed by this Article.

(16) "Security certificate" means a certificate representing a security.

(17) "Security entitlement" means the rights and property interest of an entitlement holder with respect to a financial asset specified in Part 5.

(18) "Uncertificated security" means a security that is not represented by a certificate.

(b) Other definitions applying to this Article and the sections in which they appear are:

Appropriate person	Section 8–107
Control	Section 8–106
Delivery	Section 8–301
Investment company security	Section 8–103
Issuer	Section 8–201
Overissue	Section 8–210
Protected purchaser	Section 8–303
Securities account	Section 8–501

(c) In addition, Article 1 contains general definitions and principles of construction and interpretation applicable throughout this Article.

(d) The characterization of a person, business, or transaction for purposes of this Article does not determine the characterization of the person, business, or transaction for purposes of any other law, regulation, or rule.

§ 8–103. Rules for Determining Whether Certain Obligations and Interests Are Securities or Financial Assets.

(a) A share or similar equity interest issued by a corporation, business trust, joint stock company, or similar entity is a security.

(b) An "investment company security" is a security. "Investment company security" means a share or similar equity interest issued by an entity that is registered as an investment company under the federal investment company laws, an interest in a unit investment trust that is so registered, or a face-amount certificate issued by a face-amount certificate company that is so registered. Investment company security does not include an insurance policy or endowment policy or annuity contract issued by an insurance company.

(c) An interest in a partnership or limited liability company is not a security unless it is dealt in or traded on securities exchanges or in securities markets, its terms expressly provide that it is a security governed by this Article, or it is an investment company security. However, an interest in a partnership or limited liability company is a financial asset if it is held in a securities account.

(d) A writing that is a security certificate is governed by this Article and not by Article 3, even though it also meets the requirements of that Article. However, a negotiable instrument governed by Article 3 is a financial asset if it is held in a securities account.

(e) An option or similar obligation issued by a clearing corporation to its participants is not a security, but is a financial asset.

(f) A commodity contract, as defined in Section 9–102(a)(15), is not a security or a financial asset.
As amended in 1999.

§ 8–104. Acquisition of Security or Financial Asset or Interest Therein.
(a) A person acquires a security or an interest therein, under this Article, if:
>**(1)** the person is a purchaser to whom a security is delivered pursuant to Section 8–301; or
>**(2)** the person acquires a security entitlement to the security pursuant to Section 8–501.

(b) A person acquires a financial asset, other than a security, or an interest therein, under this Article, if the person acquires a security entitlement to the financial asset.

(c) A person who acquires a security entitlement to a security or other financial asset has the rights specified in Part 5, but is a purchaser of any security, security entitlement, or other financial asset held by the securities intermediary only to the extent provided in Section 8–503.

(d) Unless the context shows that a different meaning is intended, a person who is required by other law, regulation, rule, or agreement to transfer, deliver, present, surrender, exchange, or otherwise put in the possession of another person a security or financial asset satisfies that requirement by causing the other person to acquire an interest in the security or financial asset pursuant to subsection (a) or (b).

§ 8–105. Notice of Adverse Claim.
(a) A person has notice of an adverse claim if:
>**(1)** the person knows of the adverse claim;
>**(2)** the person is aware of facts sufficient to indicate that there is a significant probability that the adverse claim exists and deliberately avoids information that would establish the existence of the adverse claim; or
>**(3)** the person has a duty, imposed by statute or regulation, to investigate whether an adverse claim exists, and the investigation so required would establish the existence of the adverse claim.

(b) Having knowledge that a financial asset or interest therein is or has been transferred by a representative imposes no duty of inquiry into the rightfulness of a transaction and is not notice of an adverse claim. However, a person who knows that a representative has transferred a financial asset or interest therein in a transaction that is, or whose proceeds are being used, for the individual benefit of the representative or otherwise in breach of duty has notice of an adverse claim.

(c) An act or event that creates a right to immediate performance of the principal obligation represented by a security certificate or sets a date on or after which the certificate is to be presented or surrendered for redemption or exchange does not itself constitute notice of an adverse claim except in the case of a transfer more than:
>**(1)** one year after a date set for presentment or surrender for redemption or exchange; or
>**(2)** six months after a date set for payment of money against presentation or surrender of the certificate, if money was available for payment on that date.

(d) A purchaser of a certificated security has notice of an adverse claim if the security certificate:
>**(1)** whether in bearer or registered form, has been indorsed "for collection" or "for surrender" or for some other purpose not involving transfer; or
>**(2)** is in bearer form and has on it an unambiguous statement that it is the property of a person other than the transferor, but the mere writing of a name on the certificate is not such a statement.

(e) Filing of a financing statement under Article 9 is not notice of an adverse claim to a financial asset.

§ 8–106. Control.
(a) A purchaser has "control" of a certificated security in bearer form if the certificated security is delivered to the purchaser.

(b) A purchaser has "control" of a certificated security in registered form if the certificated security is delivered to the purchaser, and:
>**(1)** the certificate is indorsed to the purchaser or in blank by an effective indorsement; or
>**(2)** the certificate is registered in the name of the purchaser, upon original issue or registration of transfer by the issuer.

(c) A purchaser has "control" of an uncertificated secu-rity if:
>**(1)** the uncertificated security is delivered to the purchaser; or
>**(2)** the issuer has agreed that it will comply with instructions originated by the purchaser without further consent by the registered owner.

(d) A purchaser has "control" of a security entitlement if:
>**(1)** the purchaser becomes the entitlement holder;
>**(2)** the securities intermediary has agreed that it will comply with entitlement orders originated by the purchaser without further consent by the entitlement holder; or
>**(3)** another person has control of the security entitlement on behalf of the purchaser or, having previously acquired control of the security entitlement, acknowledges that it has control on behalf of the purchaser.

(e) If an interest in a security entitlement is granted by the entitlement holder to the entitlement holder's own securities intermediary, the securities intermediary has control.

(f) A purchaser who has satisfied the requirements of subsection (c) or (d) has control, even if the registered owner in the case of subsection (c) or the entitlement holder in the case of subsection (d) retains the right to make substitutions for the uncertificated security or security entitlement, to originate instructions or entitlement orders to the issuer or securities intermediary, or otherwise to deal with the uncertificated security or security entitlement.

(g) An issuer or a securities intermediary may not enter into an agreement of the kind described in subsection (c)(2) or (d)(2) without the consent of the registered owner or entitlement holder, but an issuer or a securities intermediary is not required to enter into such an agreement even though the registered owner or entitlement holder so directs. An issuer or securities intermediary that has entered into such an agreement is not required to confirm the existence of the agreement to another party unless requested to do so by the registered owner or entitlement holder.
As amended in 1999.

§ 8–107. Whether Indorsement, Instruction, or Entitlement Order Is Effective.

(a) "Appropriate person" means:

(1) with respect to an indorsement, the person specified by a security certificate or by an effective special indorsement to be entitled to the security;

(2) with respect to an instruction, the registered owner of an uncertificated security;

(3) with respect to an entitlement order, the entitlement holder;

(4) if the person designated in paragraph (1), (2), or (3) is deceased, the designated person's successor taking under other law or the designated person's personal representative acting for the estate of the decedent; or

(5) if the person designated in paragraph (1), (2), or (3) lacks capacity, the designated person's guardian, conservator, or other similar representative who has power under other law to transfer the security or financial asset.

(b) An indorsement, instruction, or entitlement order is effective if:

(1) it is made by the appropriate person;

(2) it is made by a person who has power under the law of agency to transfer the security or financial asset on behalf of the appropriate person, including, in the case of an instruction or entitlement order, a person who has control under Section 8–106(c)(2) or (d)(2); or

(3) the appropriate person has ratified it or is otherwise precluded from asserting its ineffectiveness.

(c) An indorsement, instruction, or entitlement order made by a representative is effective even if:

(1) the representative has failed to comply with a controlling instrument or with the law of the State having jurisdiction of the representative relationship, including any law requiring the representative to obtain court approval of the transaction; or

(2) the representative's action in making the indorsement, instruction, or entitlement order or using the proceeds of the transaction is otherwise a breach of duty.

(d) If a security is registered in the name of or specially indorsed to a person described as a representative, or if a securities account is maintained in the name of a person described as a representative, an indorsement, instruction, or entitlement order made by the person is effective even though the person is no longer serving in the described capacity.

(e) Effectiveness of an indorsement, instruction, or entitlement order is determined as of the date the indorsement, instruction, or entitlement order is made, and an indorsement, instruction, or entitlement order does not become ineffective by reason of any later change of circumstances.

§ 8–108. Warranties in Direct Holding.

(a) A person who transfers a certificated security to a purchaser for value warrants to the purchaser, and an indorser, if the transfer is by indorsement, warrants to any subsequent purchaser, that:

(1) the certificate is genuine and has not been materially altered;

(2) the transferor or indorser does not know of any fact that might impair the validity of the security;

(3) there is no adverse claim to the security;

(4) the transfer does not violate any restriction on transfer;

(5) if the transfer is by indorsement, the indorsement is made by an appropriate person, or if the indorsement is by an agent, the agent has actual authority to act on behalf of the appropriate person; and

(6) the transfer is otherwise effective and rightful.

(b) A person who originates an instruction for registration of transfer of an uncertificated security to a purchaser for value warrants to the purchaser that:

(1) the instruction is made by an appropriate person, or if the instruction is by an agent, the agent has actual authority to act on behalf of the appropriate person;

(2) the security is valid;

(3) there is no adverse claim to the security; and

(4) at the time the instruction is presented to the issuer:

(i) the purchaser will be entitled to the registration of transfer;

(ii) the transfer will be registered by the issuer free from all liens, security interests, restrictions, and claims other than those specified in the instruction;

(iii) the transfer will not violate any restriction on transfer; and

(iv) the requested transfer will otherwise be effective and rightful.

(c) A person who transfers an uncertificated security to a purchaser for value and does not originate an instruction in connection with the transfer warrants that:

(1) the uncertificated security is valid;

(2) there is no adverse claim to the security;

(3) the transfer does not violate any restriction on transfer; and

(4) the transfer is otherwise effective and rightful.

(d) A person who indorses a security certificate warrants to the issuer that:

(1) there is no adverse claim to the security; and

(2) the indorsement is effective.

(e) A person who originates an instruction for registration of transfer of an uncertificated security warrants to the issuer that:

(1) the instruction is effective; and

(2) at the time the instruction is presented to the issuer the purchaser will be entitled to the registration of transfer.

(f) A person who presents a certificated security for registration of transfer or for payment or exchange warrants to the issuer that the person is entitled to the registration, payment, or exchange, but a purchaser for value and without notice of adverse claims to whom transfer is registered warrants only that the person has no knowledge of any unauthorized signature in a necessary indorsement.

(g) If a person acts as agent of another in delivering a certificated security to a purchaser, the identity of the principal was known to the person to whom the certificate was delivered, and the certificate delivered by the agent was received by the agent from the principal or received by the agent from another person at the direction of the principal, the person delivering the security certificate warrants only that the delivering person has authority to act for the principal and does not know of any adverse claim to the certificated security.

(h) A secured party who redelivers a security certificate received, or after payment and on order of the debtor delivers the security certificate to another person, makes only the warranties of an agent under subsection (g).

(i) Except as otherwise provided in subsection (g), a broker acting for a customer makes to the issuer and a purchaser the warranties provided in subsections (a) through (f). A broker that delivers a security certificate to its customer, or causes its customer to be registered as the owner of an uncertificated security, makes to the customer the warranties provided in subsection (a) or (b), and has the rights and privileges of a purchaser under this section. The warranties of and in favor of the broker acting as an agent are in addition to applicable warranties given by and in favor of the customer.

§ 8–109. Warranties in Indirect Holding.

(a) A person who originates an entitlement order to a securities intermediary warrants to the securities intermediary that:

(1) the entitlement order is made by an appropriate person, or if the entitlement order is by an agent, the agent has actual authority to act on behalf of the appropriate person; and

(2) there is no adverse claim to the security entitlement.

(b) A person who delivers a security certificate to a securities intermediary for credit to a securities account or originates an instruction with respect to an uncertificated security directing that the uncertificated security be credited to a securities account makes to the securities intermediary the warranties specified in Section 8–108(a) or (b).

(c) If a securities intermediary delivers a security certificate to its entitlement holder or causes its entitlement holder to be registered as the owner of an uncertificated security, the securities intermediary makes to the entitlement holder the warranties specified in Section 8–108(a) or (b).

§ 8–110. Applicability; Choice of Law.

(a) The local law of the issuer's jurisdiction, as specified in subsection (d), governs:

(1) the validity of a security;

(2) the rights and duties of the issuer with respect to registration of transfer;

(3) the effectiveness of registration of transfer by the issuer;

(4) whether the issuer owes any duties to an adverse claimant to a security; and

(5) whether an adverse claim can be asserted against a person to whom transfer of a certificated or uncertificated security is registered or a person who obtains control of an uncertificated security.

(b) The local law of the securities intermediary's jurisdiction, as specified in subsection (e), governs:

(1) acquisition of a security entitlement from the securities intermediary;

(2) the rights and duties of the securities intermediary and entitlement holder arising out of a security entitlement;

(3) whether the securities intermediary owes any duties to an adverse claimant to a security entitlement; and

(4) whether an adverse claim can be asserted against a person who acquires a security entitlement from the securities intermediary or a person who purchases a security entitlement or interest therein from an entitlement holder.

(c) The local law of the jurisdiction in which a security certificate is located at the time of delivery governs whether an adverse claim can be asserted against a person to whom the security certificate is delivered.

(d) "Issuer's jurisdiction" means the jurisdiction under which the issuer of the security is organized or, if permitted by the law of that jurisdiction, the law of another jurisdiction specified by the issuer. An issuer organized under the law of this State may specify the law of another jurisdiction as the law governing the matters specified in subsection (a)(2) through (5).

(e) The following rules determine a "securities intermediary's jurisdiction" for purposes of this section:

(1) If an agreement between the securities intermediary and its entitlement holder specifies that it is governed by the law of a particular jurisdiction, that jurisdiction is the securities intermediary's jurisdiction.

(2) If an agreement between the securities intermediary and its entitlement holder does not specify the governing law as provided in paragraph (1), but expressly specifies that the securities account is maintained at an office in a particular jurisdiction, that jurisdiction is the securities intermediary's jurisdiction.

(3) If neither paragraph (1) nor paragraph (2) applies and an agreement between the securities intermediary and its entitlement holder governing the securities account expressly provides that the securities account is maintained at an office in a particular jurisdiction, that jurisdiction is the securities intermediary's jurisdiction.

(4) If none of the preceding paragraph applies, the securities intermediary's jurisdiction is the jurisdiction in which the office identified in an account statement as the office serving the entitlement holder's account is located.

(5) If none of the preceding paragraphs applies, the securities intermediary's jurisdiction is the jurisdiction in which the chief executive office of the securities intermediary is located.

(f) A securities intermediary's jurisdiction is not determined by the physical location of certificates representing financial assets, or by the jurisdiction in which is organized the issuer of the financial asset with respect to which an entitlement holder has a security entitlement, or by the location of facilities for data processing or other record keeping concerning the account.
As amended in 1999.

§ 8–111. Clearing Corporation Rules.

A rule adopted by a clearing corporation governing rights and obligations among the clearing corporation and its participants in the clearing corporation is effective even if the rule conflicts with this [Act] and affects another party who does not consent to the rule.

§ 8–112. Creditor's Legal Process.

(a) The interest of a debtor in a certificated security may be reached by a creditor only by actual seizure of the security certificate by the officer making the attachment or levy, except as otherwise provided in subsection (d). However, a certificated security for which the certificate has been surrendered to the issuer may be reached by a creditor by legal process upon the issuer.

(b) The interest of a debtor in an uncertificated security may be reached by a creditor only by legal process upon the issuer at its chief executive office in the United States, except as otherwise provided in subsection (d).

(c) The interest of a debtor in a security entitlement may be reached by a creditor only by legal process upon the securities intermediary with whom the debtor's securities account is maintained, except as otherwise provided in subsection (d).

(d) The interest of a debtor in a certificated security for which the certificate is in the possession of a secured party, or in an uncertificated security registered in the name of a secured party, or a security entitlement maintained in the name of a secured party, may be reached by a creditor by legal process upon the secured party.

(e) A creditor whose debtor is the owner of a certificated security, uncertificated security, or security entitlement is entitled to aid from a court of competent jurisdiction, by injunction or otherwise, in reaching the certificated security, uncertificated security, or security entitlement or in satisfying the claim by means allowed at law or in equity in regard to property that cannot readily be reached by other legal process.

§ 8–113. Statute of Frauds Inapplicable.

A contract or modification of a contract for the sale or purchase of a security is enforceable whether or not there is a writing signed or record authenticated by a party against whom enforcement is sought, even if the contract or modification is not capable of performance within one year of its making.

§ 8–114. Evidentiary Rules Concerning Certificated Securities.

The following rules apply in an action on a certificated security against the issuer:

(1) Unless specifically denied in the pleadings, each signature on a security certificate or in a necessary indorsement is admitted.

(2) If the effectiveness of a signature is put in issue, the burden of establishing effectiveness is on the party claiming under the signature, but the signature is presumed to be genuine or authorized.

(3) If signatures on a security certificate are admitted or established, production of the certificate entitles a holder to recover on it unless the defendant establishes a defense or a defect going to the validity of the security.

(4) If it is shown that a defense or defect exists, the plaintiff has the burden of establishing that the plaintiff or some person under whom the plaintiff claims is a person against whom the defense or defect cannot be asserted.

§ 8–115. Securities Intermediary and Others Not Liable to Adverse Claimant.

A securities intermediary that has transferred a financial asset pursuant to an effective entitlement order, or a broker or other agent or bailee that has dealt with a financial asset at the direction of its customer or principal, is not liable to a person having an adverse claim to the financial asset, unless the securities intermediary, or broker or other agent or bailee:

(1) took the action after it had been served with an injunction, restraining order, or other legal process enjoining it from doing so, issued by a court of competent jurisdiction,

and had a reasonable opportunity to act on the injunction, restraining order, or other legal process; or

(2) acted in collusion with the wrongdoer in violating the rights of the adverse claimant; or

(3) in the case of a security certificate that has been stolen, acted with notice of the adverse claim.

§ 8–116. Securities Intermediary as Purchaser for Value.

A securities intermediary that receives a financial asset and establishes a security entitlement to the financial asset in favor of an entitlement holder is a purchaser for value of the financial asset. A securities intermediary that acquires a security entitlement to a financial asset from another securities intermediary acquires the security entitlement for value if the securities intermediary acquiring the security entitlement establishes a security entitlement to the financial asset in favor of an entitlement holder.

Part 2—Issue and Issuer

§ 8–201. Issuer.

(a) With respect to an obligation on or a defense to a security, an "issuer" includes a person that:

(1) places or authorizes the placing of its name on a security certificate, other than as authenticating trustee, registrar, transfer agent, or the like, to evidence a share, participation, or other interest in its property or in an enterprise, or to evidence its duty to perform an obligation represented by the certificate;

(2) creates a share, participation, or other interest in its property or in an enterprise, or undertakes an obligation, that is an uncertificated security;

(3) directly or indirectly creates a fractional interest in its rights or property, if the fractional interest is represented by a security certificate; or

(4) becomes responsible for, or in place of, another person described as an issuer in this section.

(b) With respect to an obligation on or defense to a security, a guarantor is an issuer to the extent of its guaranty, whether or not its obligation is noted on a security certificate.

(c) With respect to a registration of a transfer, issuer means a person on whose behalf transfer books are maintained.

§ 8–202. Issuer's Responsibility and Defenses; Notice of Defect or Defense.

(a) Even against a purchaser for value and without notice, the terms of a certificated security include terms stated on the certificate and terms made part of the security by reference on the certificate to another instrument, indenture, or document or to a constitution, statute, ordinance, rule, regulation, order, or the like, to the extent the terms referred to do not conflict with terms stated on the certificate. A reference under this subsection does not of itself charge a purchaser for value with notice of a defect going to the validity of the security, even if the certificate expressly states that a person accepting it admits notice. The terms of an uncertificated security include those stated in any instrument, indenture, or document or in a constitution, statute, ordinance, rule, regulation, order, or the like, pursuant to which the security is issued.

(b) The following rules apply if an issuer asserts that a security is not valid:

(1) A security other than one issued by a government or governmental subdivision, agency, or instrumentality, even though issued with a defect going to its validity, is valid in the hands of a purchaser for value and without notice of the particular defect unless the defect involves a violation of a constitutional provision. In that case, the security is valid in the hands of a purchaser for value and without notice of the defect, other than one who takes by original issue.

(2) Paragraph (1) applies to an issuer that is a government or governmental subdivision, agency, or instrumentality only if there has been substantial compliance with the legal requirements governing the issue or the issuer has received a substantial consideration for the issue as a whole or for the particular security and a stated purpose of the issue is one for which the issuer has power to borrow money or issue the security.

(c) Except as otherwise provided in Section 8–205, lack of genuineness of a certificated security is a complete defense, even against a purchaser for value and without notice.

(d) All other defenses of the issuer of a security, including nondelivery and conditional delivery of a certificated security, are ineffective against a purchaser for value who has taken the certificated security without notice of the particular defense.

(e) This section does not affect the right of a party to cancel a contract for a security "when, as and if issued" or "when distributed" in the event of a material change in the character of the security that is the subject of the contract or in the plan or arrangement pursuant to which the security is to be issued or distributed.

(f) If a security is held by a securities intermediary against whom an entitlement holder has a security entitlement with respect to the security, the issuer may not assert any defense that the issuer could not assert if the entitlement holder held the security directly.

§ 8–203. Staleness as Notice of Defect or Defense.

After an act or event, other than a call that has been revoked, creating a right to immediate performance of the principal obligation represented by a certificated security or setting a date on or after which the security is to be presented or surrendered for redemption or exchange, a purchaser is charged with notice of any defect in its issue or defense of the issuer, if the act or event:

(1) requires the payment of money, the delivery of a certificated security, the registration of transfer of an uncertificated security, or any of them on presentation or surrender of the security certificate, the money or security is available on the date set for payment or exchange, and the purchaser takes the security more than one year after that date; or

(2) is not covered by paragraph (1) and the purchaser takes the security more than two years after the date set for surrender or presentation or the date on which performance became due.

§ 8–204. Effect of Issuer's Restriction on Transfer.

A restriction on transfer of a security imposed by the issuer, even if otherwise lawful, is ineffective against a person without knowledge of the restriction unless:

(1) the security is certificated and the restriction is noted conspicuously on the security certificate; or

(2) the security is uncertificated and the registered owner has been notified of the restriction.

§ 8–205. Effect of Unauthorized Signature on Security Certificate.

An unauthorized signature placed on a security certificate before or in the course of issue is ineffective, but the signature is effective in favor of a purchaser for value of the certificated security if the purchaser is without notice of the lack of authority and the signing has been done by:

(1) an authenticating trustee, registrar, transfer agent, or other person entrusted by the issuer with the signing of the security certificate or of similar security certificates, or the immediate preparation for signing of any of them; or

(2) an employee of the issuer, or of any of the persons listed in paragraph (1), entrusted with responsible handling of the security certificate.

§ 8–206. Completion of Alteration of Security Certificate.

(a) If a security certificate contains the signatures necessary to its issue or transfer but is incomplete in any other respect:

(1) any person may complete it by filling in the blanks as authorized; and

(2) even if the blanks are incorrectly filled in, the security certificate as completed is enforceable by a purchaser who took it for value and without notice of the incorrectness.

(b) A complete security certificate that has been improperly altered, even if fraudulently, remains enforceable, but only according to its original terms.

§ 8–207. Rights and Duties of Issuer with Respect to Registered Owners.

(a) Before due presentment for registration of transfer of a certificated security in registered form or of an instruction requesting registration of transfer of an uncertificated security, the issuer or indenture trustee may treat the registered owner as the person exclusively entitled to vote, receive notifications, and otherwise exercise all the rights and powers of an owner.

(b) This Article does not affect the liability of the registered owner of a security for a call, assessment, or the like.

§ 8–208. Effect of Signature of Authenticating Trustee, Registrar, or Transfer Agent.

(a) A person signing a security certificate as authenticating trustee, registrar, transfer agent, or the like, warrants to a purchaser for value of the certificated security, if the purchaser is without notice of a particular defect, that:

(1) the certificate is genuine;

(2) the person's own participation in the issue of the security is within the person's capacity and within the scope of the authority received by the person from the issuer; and

(3) the person has reasonable grounds to believe that the certificated security is in the form and within the amount the issuer is authorized to issue.

(b) Unless otherwise agreed, a person signing under subsection (a) does not assume responsibility for the validity of the security in other respects.

§ 8–209. Issuer's Lien.

A lien in favor of an issuer upon a certificated security is valid against a purchaser only if the right of the issuer to the lien is noted conspicuously on the security certificate.

§ 8–210. Overissue.

(a) In this section, "overissue" means the issue of securities in excess of the amount the issuer has corporate power to issue, but an overissue does not occur if appropriate action has cured the overissue.

(b) Except as otherwise provided in subsections (c) and (d), the provisions of this Article which validate a security or compel its issue or reissue do not apply to the extent that validation, issue, or reissue would result in overissue.

(c) If an identical security not constituting an overissue is reasonably available for purchase, a person entitled to issue or validation may compel the issuer to purchase the security and deliver it if certificated or register its transfer if uncertificated, against surrender of any security certificate the person holds.

(d) If a security is not reasonably available for purchase, a person entitled to issue or validation may recover from the issuer the price the person or the last purchaser for value paid for it with interest from the date of the person's demand.

Part 3—Transfer of Certificated and Uncertificated Securities

§ 8–301. Delivery.

(a) Delivery of a certificated security to a purchaser occurs when:

(1) the purchaser acquires possession of the security certificate;

(2) another person, other than a securities intermediary, either acquires possession of the security certificate on behalf of the purchaser or, having previously acquired possession of the certificate, acknowledges that it holds for the purchaser; or

(3) a securities intermediary acting on behalf of the purchaser acquires possession of the security certificate, only if the certificate is in registered form and is (i) registered in the name of the purchaser, (ii) payable to the order of the purchaser, or (iii) specially indorsed to the purchaser by an effective indorsement and has not been indorsed to the securities intermediary or in blank.

(b) Delivery of an uncertificated security to a purchaser occurs when:

(1) the issuer registers the purchaser as the registered owner, upon original issue or registration of transfer; or

(2) another person, other than a securities intermediary, either becomes the registered owner of the uncertificated security on behalf of the purchaser or, having previously become the registered owner, acknowledges that it holds for the purchaser.

As amended in 1999.

§ 8–302. Rights of Purchaser.

(a) Except as otherwise provided in subsections (b) and (c), upon delivery of a certificated or uncertificated security to a purchaser, the purchaser acquires all rights in the security that the transferor had or had power to transfer.

(b) A purchaser of a limited interest acquires rights only to the extent of the interest purchased.

(c) A purchaser of a certificated security who as a previous holder had notice of an adverse claim does not improve its position by taking from a protected purchaser.

As amended in 1999.

§ 8–303. Protected Purchaser.

(a) "Protected purchaser" means a purchaser of a certificated or uncertificated security, or of an interest therein, who:

(1) gives value;

(2) does not have notice of any adverse claim to the security; and

(3) obtains control of the certificated or uncertificated security.

(b) In addition to acquiring the rights of a purchaser, a protected purchaser also acquires its interest in the security free of any adverse claim.

§ 8–304. Indorsement.

(a) An indorsement may be in blank or special. An indorsement in blank includes an indorsement to bearer. A special indorsement specifies to whom a security is to be transferred or who has power to transfer it. A holder may convert a blank indorsement to a special indorsement.

(b) An indorsement purporting to be only of part of a security certificate representing units intended by the issuer to be separately transferable is effective to the extent of the indorsement.

(c) An indorsement, whether special or in blank, does not constitute a transfer until delivery of the certificate on which it appears or, if the indorsement is on a separate document, until delivery of both the document and the certificate.

(d) If a security certificate in registered form has been delivered to a purchaser without a necessary indorsement, the purchaser may become a protected purchaser only when the indorsement is supplied. However, against a transferor, a transfer is complete upon delivery and the purchaser has a specifically enforceable right to have any necessary indorsement supplied.

(e) An indorsement of a security certificate in bearer form may give notice of an adverse claim to the certificate, but it does not otherwise affect a right to registration that the holder possesses.

(f) Unless otherwise agreed, a person making an indorsement assumes only the obligations provided in Section 8–108 and not an obligation that the security will be honored by the issuer.

§ 8–305. Instruction.

(a) If an instruction has been originated by an appropriate person but is incomplete in any other respect, any person may complete it as authorized and the issuer may rely on it as completed, even though it has been completed incorrectly.

(b) Unless otherwise agreed, a person initiating an instruction assumes only the obligations imposed by Section 8–108 and not an obligation that the security will be honored by the issuer.

§ 8–306. Effect of Guaranteeing Signature, Indorsement, or Instruction.

(a) A person who guarantees a signature of an indorser of a security certificate warrants that at the time of signing:

  (1) the signature was genuine;

  (2) the signer was an appropriate person to indorse, or if the signature is by an agent, the agent had actual authority to act on behalf of the appropriate person; and

  (3) the signer had legal capacity to sign.

(b) A person who guarantees a signature of the originator of an instruction warrants that at the time of signing:

  (1) the signature was genuine;

  (2) the signer was an appropriate person to originate the instruction, or if the signature is by an agent, the agent had actual authority to act on behalf of the appropriate person, if the person specified in the instruction as the registered owner was, in fact, the registered owner, as to which fact the signature guarantor does not make a warranty; and

  (3) the signer had legal capacity to sign.

(c) A person who specially guarantees the signature of an originator of an instruction makes the warranties of a signature guarantor under subsection (b) and also warrants that at the time the instruction is presented to the issuer:

  (1) the person specified in the instruction as the registered owner of the uncertificated security will be the registered owner; and

  (2) the transfer of the uncertificated security requested in the instruction will be registered by the issuer free from all liens, security interests, restrictions, and claims other than those specified in the instruction.

(d) A guarantor under subsections (a) and (b) or a special guarantor under subsection (c) does not otherwise warrant the rightfulness of the transfer.

(e) A person who guarantees an indorsement of a security certificate makes the warranties of a signature guarantor under subsection (a) and also warrants the rightfulness of the transfer in all respects.

(f) A person who guarantees an instruction requesting the transfer of an uncertificated security makes the warranties of a special signature guarantor under subsection (c) and also warrants the rightfulness of the transfer in all respects.

(g) An issuer may not require a special guaranty of signature, a guaranty of indorsement, or a guaranty of instruction as a condition to registration of transfer.

(h) The warranties under this section are made to a person taking or dealing with the security in reliance on the guaranty, and the guarantor is liable to the person for loss resulting from their breach. An indorser or originator of an instruction whose signature, indorsement, or instruction has been guaranteed is liable to a guarantor for any loss suffered by the guarantor as a result of breach of the warranties of the guarantor.

§ 8–307. Purchaser's Right to Requisites for Registration of Transfer.

Unless otherwise agreed, the transferor of a security on due demand shall supply the purchaser with proof of authority to transfer or with any other requisite necessary to obtain registration of the transfer of the security, but if the transfer is not for value, a transferor need not comply unless the purchaser pays the necessary expenses. If the transferor fails within a reasonable time to comply with the demand, the purchaser may reject or rescind the transfer.

Part 4—Registration

§ 8–401. Duty of Issuer to Register Transfer.

(a) If a certificated security in registered form is presented to an issuer with a request to register transfer or an instruction is presented to an issuer with a request to register transfer of an uncertificated security, the issuer shall register the transfer as requested if:

  (1) under the terms of the security the person seeking registration of transfer is eligible to have the security registered in its name;

  (2) the indorsement or instruction is made by the appropriate person or by an agent who has actual authority to act on behalf of the appropriate person;

  (3) reasonable assurance is given that the indorsement or instruction is genuine and authorized (Section 8–402);

  (4) any applicable law relating to the collection of taxes has been complied with;

  (5) the transfer does not violate any restriction on transfer imposed by the issuer in accordance with Section 8–204;

  (6) a demand that the issuer not register transfer has not become effective under Section 8–403, or the issuer has complied with Section 8–403(b) but no legal process or indemnity bond is obtained as provided in Section 8–403(d); and

  (7) the transfer is in fact rightful or is to a protected purchaser.

(b) If an issuer is under a duty to register a transfer of a security, the issuer is liable to a person presenting a certificated security or an instruction for registration or to the person's principal for loss resulting from unreasonable delay in registration or failure or refusal to register the transfer.

§ 8–402. Assurance That Indorsement or Instruction Is Effective.

(a) An issuer may require the following assurance that each necessary indorsement or each instruction is genuine and authorized:

  (1) in all cases, a guaranty of the signature of the person making an indorsement or originating an instruction including, in the case of an instruction, reasonable assurance of identity;

  (2) if the indorsement is made or the instruction is originated by an agent, appropriate assurance of actual authority to sign;

  (3) if the indorsement is made or the instruction is originated by a fiduciary pursuant to Section 8–107(a)(4) or (a)(5), appropriate evidence of appointment or incumbency;

  (4) if there is more than one fiduciary, reasonable assurance that all who are required to sign have done so; and

  (5) if the indorsement is made or the instruction is originated by a person not covered by another provision of this subsection, assurance appropriate to the case corresponding as nearly as may be to the provisions of this subsection.

(b) An issuer may elect to require reasonable assurance beyond that specified in this section.

(c) In this section:

(1) "Guaranty of the signature" means a guaranty signed by or on behalf of a person reasonably believed by the issuer to be responsible. An issuer may adopt standards with respect to responsibility if they are not manifestly unreasonable.

(2) "Appropriate evidence of appointment or incumbency" means:

(i) in the case of a fiduciary appointed or qualified by a court, a certificate issued by or under the direction or supervision of the court or an officer thereof and dated within 60 days before the date of presentation for transfer; or

(ii) in any other case, a copy of a document showing the appointment or a certificate issued by or on behalf of a person reasonably believed by an issuer to be responsible or, in the absence of that document or certificate, other evidence the issuer reasonably considers appropriate.

§ 8–403. Demand That Issuer Not Register Transfer.

(a) A person who is an appropriate person to make an indorsement or originate an instruction may demand that the issuer not register transfer of a security by communicating to the issuer a notification that identifies the registered owner and the issue of which the security is a part and provides an address for communications directed to the person making the demand. The demand is effective only if it is received by the issuer at a time and in a manner affording the issuer reasonable opportunity to act on it.

(b) If a certificated security in registered form is presented to an issuer with a request to register transfer or an instruction is presented to an issuer with a request to register transfer of an uncertificated security after a demand that the issuer not register transfer has become effective, the issuer shall promptly communicate to (i) the person who initiated the demand at the address provided in the demand and (ii) the person who presented the security for registration of transfer or initiated the instruction requesting registration of transfer a notification stating that:

(1) the certificated security has been presented for registration of transfer or the instruction for registration of transfer of the uncertificated security has been received;

(2) a demand that the issuer not register transfer had previously been received; and

(3) the issuer will withhold registration of transfer for a period of time stated in the notification in order to provide the person who initiated the demand an opportunity to obtain legal process or an indemnity bond.

(c) The period described in subsection (b)(3) may not exceed 30 days after the date of communication of the notification. A shorter period may be specified by the issuer if it is not manifestly unreasonable.

(d) An issuer is not liable to a person who initiated a demand that the issuer not register transfer for any loss the person suffers as a result of registration of a transfer pursuant to an effective indorsement or instruction if the person who initiated the demand does not, within the time stated in the issuer's communication, either:

(1) obtain an appropriate restraining order, injunction, or other process from a court of competent jurisdiction enjoining the issuer from registering the transfer; or

(2) file with the issuer an indemnity bond, sufficient in the issuer's judgment to protect the issuer and any transfer agent, registrar, or other agent of the issuer involved from any loss it or they may suffer by refusing to register the transfer.

(e) This section does not relieve an issuer from liability for registering transfer pursuant to an indorsement or instruction that was not effective.

§ 8–404. Wrongful Registration.

(a) Except as otherwise provided in Section 8–406, an issuer is liable for wrongful registration of transfer if the issuer has registered a transfer of a security to a person not entitled to it, and the transfer was registered:

(1) pursuant to an ineffective indorsement or instruction;

(2) after a demand that the issuer not register transfer became effective under Section 8–403(a) and the issuer did not comply with Section 8–403(b);

(3) after the issuer had been served with an injunction, restraining order, or other legal process enjoining it from registering the transfer, issued by a court of competent jurisdiction, and the issuer had a reasonable opportunity to act on the injunction, restraining order, or other legal process; or

(4) by an issuer acting in collusion with the wrongdoer.

(b) An issuer that is liable for wrongful registration of transfer under subsection (a) on demand shall provide the person entitled to the security with a like certificated or uncertificated security, and any payments or distributions that the person did not receive as a result of the wrongful registration. If an overissue would result, the issuer's liability to provide the person with a like security is governed by Section 8–210.

(c) Except as otherwise provided in subsection (a) or in a law relating to the collection of taxes, an issuer is not liable to an owner or other person suffering loss as a result of the registration of a transfer of a security if registration was made pursuant to an effective indorsement or instruction.

§ 8–405. Replacement of Lost, Destroyed, or Wrongfully Taken Security Certificate.

(a) If an owner of a certificated security, whether in registered or bearer form, claims that the certificate has been lost, destroyed, or wrongfully taken, the issuer shall issue a new certificate if the owner:

(1) so requests before the issuer has notice that the certificate has been acquired by a protected purchaser;

(2) files with the issuer a sufficient indemnity bond; and

(3) satisfies other reasonable requirements imposed by the issuer.

(b) If, after the issue of a new security certificate, a protected purchaser of the original certificate presents it for registration of transfer, the issuer shall register the transfer unless an overissue would result. In that case, the issuer's liability is governed by Section 8–210. In addition to any rights on the indemnity bond, an issuer may recover the new certificate from a person to whom it was issued or any person taking under that person, except a protected purchaser.

§ 8–406. Obligation to Notify Issuer of Lost, Destroyed, or Wrongfully Taken Security Certificate.

If a security certificate has been lost, apparently destroyed, or wrongfully taken, and the owner fails to notify the issuer of that fact within a reasonable time after the owner has notice of it and the issuer registers a transfer of the security before receiving notification, the owner may not assert against the issuer a claim for registering the transfer under Section 8–404 or a claim to a new security certificate under Section 8–405.

§ 8–407. Authenticating Trustee, Transfer Agent, and Registrar.

A person acting as authenticating trustee, transfer agent, registrar, or other agent for an issuer in the registration of a transfer of its securities, in the issue of new security certificates or uncertificated securities, or in the cancellation of surrendered security certificates has the same obligation to the holder or owner of a certificated or uncertificated security with regard to the particular functions performed as the issuer has in regard to those functions.

Part 5 Security Entitlements

§ 8–501. Securities Account; Acquisition of Security Entitlement from Securities Intermediary.

(a) "Securities account" means an account to which a financial asset is or may be credited in accordance with an agreement under which the person maintaining the account undertakes to treat the person for whom the account is maintained as entitled to exercise the rights that comprise the financial asset.
(b) Except as otherwise provided in subsections (d) and (e), a person acquires a security entitlement if a securities intermediary:
  (1) indicates by book entry that a financial asset has been credited to the person's securities account;
  (2) receives a financial asset from the person or acquires a financial asset for the person and, in either case, accepts it for credit to the person's securities account; or
  (3) becomes obligated under other law, regulation, or rule to credit a financial asset to the person's securities account.
(c) If a condition of subsection (b) has been met, a person has a security entitlement even though the securities intermediary does not itself hold the financial asset.
(d) If a securities intermediary holds a financial asset for another person, and the financial asset is registered in the name of, payable to the order of, or specially indorsed to the other person, and has not been indorsed to the securities intermediary or in blank, the other person is treated as holding the financial asset directly rather than as having a security entitlement with respect to the financial asset.
(e) Issuance of a security is not establishment of a security entitlement.

§ 8–502. Assertion of Adverse Claim against Entitlement Holder.

An action based on an adverse claim to a financial asset, whether framed in conversion, replevin, constructive trust, equitable lien, or other theory, may not be asserted against a person who acquires a security entitlement under Section 8–501 for value and without notice of the adverse claim.

§ 8–503. Property Interest of Entitlement Holder in Financial Asset Held by Securities Intermediary.

(a) To the extent necessary for a securities intermediary to satisfy all security entitlements with respect to a particular financial asset, all interests in that financial asset held by the securities intermediary are held by the securities intermediary for the entitlement holders, are not property of the securities intermediary, and are not subject to claims of creditors of the securities intermediary, except as otherwise provided in Section 8–511.
(b) An entitlement holder's property interest with respect to a particular financial asset under subsection (a) is a pro rata property interest in all interests in that financial asset held by the securities intermediary, without regard to the time the entitlement holder acquired the security entitlement or the time the securities intermediary acquired the interest in that financial asset.
(c) An entitlement holder's property interest with respect to a particular financial asset under subsection (a) may be enforced against the securities intermediary only by exercise of the entitlement holder's rights under Sections 8–505 through 8–508.
(d) An entitlement holder's property interest with respect to a particular financial asset under subsection (a) may be enforced against a purchaser of the financial asset or interest therein only if:
  (1) insolvency proceedings have been initiated by or against the securities intermediary;
  (2) the securities intermediary does not have sufficient interests in the financial asset to satisfy the security entitlements of all of its entitlement holders to that financial asset;
  (3) the securities intermediary violated its obligations under Section 8–504 by transferring the financial asset or interest therein to the purchaser; and
  (4) the purchaser is not protected under sub-section (e).
The trustee or other liquidator, acting on behalf of all entitlement holders having security entitlements with respect to a particular financial asset, may recover the financial asset, or interest therein, from the purchaser. If the trustee or other liquidator elects not to pursue that right, an entitlement holder whose security entitlement remains unsatisfied has the right to recover its interest in the financial asset from the purchaser.
(e) An action based on the entitlement holder's property interest with respect to a particular financial asset under subsection (a), whether framed in conversion, replevin, constructive trust, equitable lien, or other theory, may not be asserted against any purchaser of a financial asset or interest therein who gives value, obtains control, and does not act in collusion with the securities intermediary in violating the securities intermediary's obligations under Section 8–504.

§ 8–504. Duty of Securities Intermediary to Maintain Financial Asset.

(a) A securities intermediary shall promptly obtain and thereafter maintain a financial asset in a quantity corresponding to the aggregate of all security entitlements it has established in favor of its entitlement holders with respect to that financial asset. The securities intermediary may maintain those financial assets directly or through one or more other securities intermediaries.

(b) Except to the extent otherwise agreed by its entitlement holder, a securities intermediary may not grant any security interests in a financial asset it is obligated to maintain pursuant to subsection (a).

(c) A securities intermediary satisfies the duty in subsection (a) if:

(1) the securities intermediary acts with respect to the duty as agreed upon by the entitlement holder and the securities intermediary; or

(2) in the absence of agreement, the securities intermediary exercises due care in accordance with reasonable commercial standards to obtain and maintain the financial asset.

(d) This section does not apply to a clearing corporation that is itself the obligor of an option or similar obligation to which its entitlement holders have security entitlements.

§ 8–505. Duty of Securities Intermediary with Respect to Payments and Distributions.

(a) A securities intermediary shall take action to obtain a payment or distribution made by the issuer of a financial asset. A securities intermediary satisfies the duty if:

(1) the securities intermediary acts with respect to the duty as agreed upon by the entitlement holder and the securities intermediary; or

(2) in the absence of agreement, the securities intermediary exercises due care in accordance with reasonable commercial standards to attempt to obtain the payment or distribution.

(b) A securities intermediary is obligated to its entitlement holder for a payment or distribution made by the issuer of a financial asset if the payment or distribution is received by the securities intermediary.

§ 8–506. Duty of Securities Intermediary to Exercise Rights as Directed by Entitlement Holder.

A securities intermediary shall exercise rights with respect to a financial asset if directed to do so by an entitlement holder. A securities intermediary satisfies the duty if:

(1) the securities intermediary acts with respect to the duty as agreed upon by the entitlement holder and the securities intermediary; or

(2) in the absence of agreement, the securities intermediary either places the entitlement holder in a position to exercise the rights directly or exercises due care in accordance with reasonable commercial standards to follow the direction of the entitlement holder.

§ 8–507. Duty of Securities Intermediary to Comply with Entitlement Order.

(a) A securities intermediary shall comply with an entitlement order if the entitlement order is originated by the appropriate person, the securities intermediary has had reasonable opportunity to assure itself that the entitlement order is genuine and authorized, and the securities intermediary has had reasonable opportunity

to comply with the entitlement order. A securities intermediary satisfies the duty if:

(1) the securities intermediary acts with respect to the duty as agreed upon by the entitlement holder and the securities intermediary; or

(2) in the absence of agreement, the securities intermediary exercises due care in accordance with reasonable commercial standards to comply with the entitlement order.

(b) If a securities intermediary transfers a financial asset pursuant to an ineffective entitlement order, the securities intermediary shall reestablish a security entitlement in favor of the person entitled to it, and pay or credit any payments or distributions that the person did not receive as a result of the wrongful transfer. If the securities intermediary does not reestablish a security entitlement, the securities intermediary is liable to the entitlement holder for damages.

§ 8–508. Duty of Securities Intermediary to Change Entitlement Holder's Position to Other Form of Security Holding.

A securities intermediary shall act at the direction of an entitlement holder to change a security entitlement into another available form of holding for which the entitlement holder is eligible, or to cause the financial asset to be transferred to a securities account of the entitlement holder with another securities intermediary. A securities intermediary satisfies the duty if:

(1) the securities intermediary acts as agreed upon by the entitlement holder and the securities intermediary; or

(2) in the absence of agreement, the securities intermediary exercises due care in accordance with reasonable commercial standards to follow the direction of the entitlement holder.

§ 8–509. Specification of Duties of Securities Intermediary by Other Statute or Regulation; Manner of Performance of Duties of Securities Intermediary and Exercise of Rights of Entitlement Holder.

(a) If the substance of a duty imposed upon a securities intermediary by Sections 8–504 through 8–508 is the subject of other statute, regulation, or rule, compliance with that statute, regulation, or rule satisfies the duty.

(b) To the extent that specific standards for the performance of the duties of a securities intermediary or the exercise of the rights of an entitlement holder are not specified by other statute, regulation, or rule or by agreement between the securities intermediary and entitlement holder, the securities intermediary shall perform its duties and the entitlement holder shall exercise its rights in a commercially reasonable manner.

(c) The obligation of a securities intermediary to perform the duties imposed by Sections 8–504 through 8–508 is subject to:

(1) rights of the securities intermediary arising out of a security interest under a security agreement with the entitlement holder or otherwise; and

(2) rights of the securities intermediary under other law, regulation, rule, or agreement to withhold performance of its duties as a result of unfulfilled obligations of the entitlement holder to the securities intermediary.

(d) Sections 8–504 through 8–508 do not require a securities intermediary to take any action that is prohibited by other statute, regulation, or rule.

§ 8–510. Rights of Purchaser of Security Entitlement from Entitlement Holder.

(a) An action based on an adverse claim to a financial asset or security entitlement, whether framed in conversion, replevin, constructive trust, equitable lien, or other theory, may not be asserted against a person who purchases a security entitlement, or an interest therein, from an entitlement holder if the purchaser gives value, does not have notice of the adverse claim, and obtains control.

(b) If an adverse claim could not have been asserted against an entitlement holder under Section 8–502, the adverse claim cannot be asserted against a person who purchases a security entitlement, or an interest therein, from the entitlement holder.

(c) In a case not covered by the priority rules in Article 9, a purchaser for value of a security entitlement, or an interest therein, who obtains control has priority over a purchaser of a security entitlement, or an interest therein, who does not obtain control. Except as otherwise provided in subsection (d), purchasers who have control rank according to priority in time of:

> **(1)** the purchaser's becoming the person for whom the securities account, in which the security entitlement is carried, is maintained, if the purchaser obtained control under Section 8–106(d)(1);

> **(2)** the securities intermediary's agreement to comply with the purchaser's entitlement orders with respect to security entitlements carried or to be carried in the securities account in which the security entitlement is carried, if the purchaser obtained control under Section 8–106(d)(2); or

> **(3)** if the purchaser obtained control through another person under Section 8–106(d)(3), the time on which priority would be based under this subsection if the other person were the secured party.

(d) A securities intermediary as purchaser has priority over a conflicting purchaser who has control unless otherwise agreed by the securities intermediary.

As amended in 1999.

§ 8–511. Priority among Security Interests and Entitlement Holders.

(a) Except as otherwise provided in subsections (b) and (c), if a securities intermediary does not have sufficient interests in a particular financial asset to satisfy both its obligations to entitlement holders who have security entitlements to that financial asset and its obligation to a creditor of the securities intermediary who has a security interest in that financial asset, the claims of entitlement holders, other than the creditor, have priority over the claim of the creditor.

(b) A claim of a creditor of a securities intermediary who has a security interest in a financial asset held by a securities intermediary has priority over claims of the securities intermediary's entitlement holders who have security entitlements with respect to that financial asset if the creditor has control over the financial asset.

(c) If a clearing corporation does not have sufficient financial assets to satisfy both its obligations to entitlement holders who have security entitlements with respect to a financial asset and its obligation to a creditor of the clearing corporation who has a security interest in that financial asset, the claim of the creditor has priority over the claims of entitlement holders.

Part 6—Transition Provisions for Revised Article 8

§ 8–601. Effective Date.
This [Act] takes effect . . . .

§ 8–602. Repeals.
This [Act] repeals . . . .

§ 8–603. Savings Clause.
(a) This [Act] does not affect an action or proceeding commenced before this [Act] takes effect.

(b) If a security interest in a security is perfected at the date this [Act] takes effect, and the action by which the security interest was perfected would suffice to perfect a security interest under this [Act], no further action is required to continue perfection. If a security interest in a security is perfected at the date this [Act] takes effect but the action by which the security interest was perfected would not suffice to perfect a security interest under this [Act], the security interest remains perfected for a period of four months after the effective date and continues perfected thereafter if appropriate action to perfect under this [Act] is taken within that period. If a security interest is perfected at the date this [Act] takes effect and the security interest can be perfected by filing under this [Act], a financing statement signed by the secured party instead of the debtor may be filed within that period to continue perfection or thereafter to perfect.

REVISED ARTICLE 9: SECURED TRANSACTIONS

Part 1—General Provisions

[Subpart 1. Short Title, Definitions, and General Concepts]

§ 9–101. Short Title.
This article may be cited as Uniform Commercial Code—Secured Transactions.

§ 9–102. Definitions and Index of Definitions.
(a) In this article:

> **(1)** "Accession" means goods that are physically united with other goods in such a manner that the identity of the original goods is not lost.

> **(2)** "Account", except as used in "account for", means a right to payment of a monetary obligation, whether or not earned by performance, (i) for property that has been or is to be sold, leased, licensed, assigned, or otherwise disposed of, (ii) for services rendered or to be rendered, (iii) for a policy of insurance issued or to be issued, (iv) for a secondary obligation incurred or to be incurred, (v) for energy provided or to be pro-vided, (vi) for the use or hire of a vessel under a charter or other contract, (vii) arising out of the use of a credit or charge card or information contained on or for use with the card, or (viii) as winnings in a lottery or other game of chance operated or sponsored by a State, governmental unit of a State, or person licensed or authorized to operate the game by a State or governmental unit

of a State. The term includes health-care insurance receivables. The term does not include (i) rights to payment evidenced by chattel paper or an instrument, (ii) commercial tort claims, (iii) deposit accounts, (iv) investment property, (v) letter-of-credit rights or letters of credit, or (vi) rights to payment for money or funds advanced or sold, other than rights arising out of the use of a credit or charge card or information contained on or for use with the card.

(3) "Account debtor" means a person obligated on an account, chattel paper, or general intangible. The term does not include persons obligated to pay a negotiable instrument, even if the instrument constitutes part of chattel paper.

(4) "Accounting", except as used in "accounting for", means a record:

  (A) authenticated by a secured party;

  (B) indicating the aggregate unpaid secured obligations as of a date not more than 35 days earlier or 35 days later than the date of the record; and

  (C) identifying the components of the obligations in reasonable detail.

(5) "Agricultural lien" means an interest, other than a security interest, in farm products:

  (A) which secures payment or performance of an obligation for:

    (i) goods or services furnished in connection with a debtor's farming operation; or

    (ii) rent on real property leased by a debtor in connection with its farming operation;

  (B) which is created by statute in favor of a person that:

    (i) in the ordinary course of its business furnished goods or services to a debtor in connection with a debtor's farming operation; or

    (ii) leased real property to a debtor in connection with the debtor's farming operation; and

  (C) whose effectiveness does not depend on the person's possession of the personal property.

(6) "As-extracted collateral" means:

  (A) oil, gas, or other minerals that are subject to a security interest that:

    (i) is created by a debtor having an interest in the minerals before extraction; and

    (ii) attaches to the minerals as extracted; or

  (B) accounts arising out of the sale at the wellhead or minehead of oil, gas, or other minerals in which the debtor had an interest before extraction.

(7) "Authenticate" means:

  (A) to sign; or

  (B) to execute or otherwise adopt a symbol, or encrypt or similarly process a record in whole or in part, with the present intent of the authenticating person to identify the person and adopt or accept a record.

(8) "Bank" means an organization that is engaged in the business of banking. The term includes savings banks, savings and loan associations, credit unions, and trust companies.

(9) "Cash proceeds" means proceeds that are money, checks, deposit accounts, or the like.

(10) "Certificate of title" means a certificate of title with respect to which a statute provides for the security interest in question to be indicated on the certificate as a condition or result of the security interest's obtaining priority over the rights of a lien creditor with respect to the collateral.

(11) "Chattel paper" means a record or records that evidence both a monetary obligation and a security interest in specific goods, a security interest in specific goods and software used in the goods, a security interest in specific goods and license of software used in the goods, a lease of specific goods, or a lease of specific goods and license of software used in the goods. In this paragraph, "monetary obligation" means a monetary obligation secured by the goods or owed under a lease of the goods and includes a monetary obligation with respect to software used in the goods. The term does not include (i) charters or other contracts involving the use or hire of a vessel or (ii) records that evidence a right to payment arising out of the use of a credit or charge card or information contained on or for use with the card. If a transaction is evidenced by records that include an instrument or series of instruments, the group of records taken together constitutes chattel paper.

(12) "Collateral" means the property subject to a security interest or agricultural lien. The term includes:

  (A) proceeds to which a security interest attaches;

  (B) accounts, chattel paper, payment intangibles, and promissory notes that have been sold; and

  (C) goods that are the subject of a consignment.

(13) "Commercial tort claim" means a claim arising in tort with respect to which:

  (A) the claimant is an organization; or

  (B) the claimant is an individual and the claim:

    (i) arose in the course of the claimant's business or profession; and

    (ii) does not include damages arising out of personal injury to or the death of an individual.

(14) "Commodity account" means an account maintained by a commodity intermediary in which a commodity contract is carried for a commodity customer.

(15) "Commodity contract" means a commodity futures contract, an option on a commodity futures contract, a commodity option, or another contract if the contract or option is:

  (A) traded on or subject to the rules of a board of trade that has been designated as a contract market for such a contract pursuant to federal commodities laws; or

  (B) traded on a foreign commodity board of trade, exchange, or market, and is carried on the books of a commodity intermediary for a commodity customer.

(16) "Commodity customer" means a person for which a commodity intermediary carries a commodity contract on its books.

(17) "Commodity intermediary" means a person that:

  (A) is registered as a futures commission merchant under federal commodities law; or

  (B) in the ordinary course of its business provides clearance or settlement services for a board of trade that has been designated as a contract market pursuant to federal commodities law.

(18) "Communicate" means:

    (A) to send a written or other tangible record;

    (B) to transmit a record by any means agreed upon by the persons sending and receiving the record; or

    (C) in the case of transmission of a record to or by a filing office, to transmit a record by any means prescribed by filing-office rule.

(19) "Consignee" means a merchant to which goods are delivered in a consignment.

(20) "Consignment" means a transaction, regardless of its form, in which a person delivers goods to a merchant for the purpose of sale and:

    (A) the merchant:

        (i) deals in goods of that kind under a name other than the name of the person making delivery;

        (ii) is not an auctioneer; and

        (iii) is not generally known by its creditors to be substantially engaged in selling the goods of others;

    (B) with respect to each delivery, the aggregate value of the goods is $1,000 or more at the time of delivery;

    (C) the goods are not consumer goods immediately before delivery; and

    (D) the transaction does not create a security interest that secures an obligation.

(21) "Consignor" means a person that delivers goods to a consignee in a consignment.

(22) "Consumer debtor" means a debtor in a consumer transaction.

(23) "Consumer goods" means goods that are used or bought for use primarily for personal, family, or household purposes.

(24) "Consumer-goods transaction" means a consumer transaction in which:

    (A) an individual incurs an obligation primarily for personal, family, or household purposes; and

    (B) a security interest in consumer goods secures the obligation.

(25) "Consumer obligor" means an obligor who is an individual and who incurred the obligation as part of a transaction entered into primarily for personal, family, or household purposes.

(26) "Consumer transaction" means a transaction in which (i) an individual incurs an obligation primarily for personal, family, or household purposes, (ii) a security interest secures the obligation, and (iii) the collateral is held or acquired primarily for personal, family, or household purposes. The term includes consumer-goods transactions.

(27) "Continuation statement" means an amendment of a financing statement which:

    (A) identifies, by its file number, the initial financing statement to which it relates; and

    (B) indicates that it is a continuation statement for, or that it is filed to continue the effectiveness of, the identified financing statement.

(28) "Debtor" means:

    (A) a person having an interest, other than a security interest or other lien, in the collateral, whether or not the person is an obligor;

    (B) a seller of accounts, chattel paper, payment intangibles, or promissory notes; or

    (C) a consignee.

(29) "Deposit account" means a demand, time, savings, passbook, or similar account maintained with a bank. The term does not include investment property or accounts evidenced by an instrument.

(30) "Document" means a document of title or a receipt of the type described in Section 7–201(2).

(31) "Electronic chattel paper" means chattel paper evidenced by a record or records consisting of information stored in an electronic medium.

(32) "Encumbrance" means a right, other than an ownership interest, in real property. The term includes mortgages and other liens on real property.

(33) "Equipment" means goods other than inventory, farm products, or consumer goods.

(34) "Farm products" means goods, other than standing timber, with respect to which the debtor is engaged in a farming operation and which are:

    (A) crops grown, growing, or to be grown, including:

        (i) crops produced on trees, vines, and bushes; and

        (ii) aquatic goods produced in aquacultural operations;

    (B) livestock, born or unborn, including aquatic goods produced in aquacultural operations;

    (C) supplies used or produced in a farming operation; or

    (D) products of crops or livestock in their unmanufactured states.

(35) "Farming operation" means raising, cultivating, propagating, fattening, grazing, or any other farming, livestock, or aquacultural operation.

(36) "File number" means the number assigned to an initial financing statement pursuant to Section 9–519(a).

(37) "Filing office" means an office designated in Section 9–501 as the place to file a financing statement.

(38) "Filing-office rule" means a rule adopted pursuant to Section 9–526.

(39) "Financing statement" means a record or records composed of an initial financing statement and any filed record relating to the initial financing statement.

(40) "Fixture filing" means the filing of a financing statement covering goods that are or are to become fixtures and satisfying Section 9–502(a) and (b). The term includes the filing of a financing statement covering goods of a transmitting utility which are or are to become fixtures.

(41) "Fixtures" means goods that have become so related to particular real property that an interest in them arises under real property law.

(42) "General intangible" means any personal property, including things in action, other than accounts, chattel paper, commercial tort claims, deposit accounts, documents, goods, instruments, investment property, letter-of-credit rights, letters of credit, money, and oil, gas, or other minerals before extraction. The term includes payment intangibles and software.

(43) "Good faith" means honesty in fact and the observance of reasonable commercial standards of fair dealing.

(44) "Goods" means all things that are movable when a security interest attaches. The term includes (i) fixtures, (ii) standing timber that is to be cut and removed under a conveyance or contract for sale, (iii) the unborn young of animals, (iv) crops grown, growing, or to be grown, even if the crops are produced on trees, vines, or bushes, and (v) manufactured homes. The term also includes a computer program embedded in goods and any supporting information provided in connection with a transaction relating to the program if (i) the program is associated with the goods in such a manner that it customarily is considered part of the goods, or (ii) by becoming the owner of the goods, a person acquires a right to use the program in connection with the goods. The term does not include a computer program embedded in goods that consist solely of the medium in which the program is embedded. The term also does not include accounts, chattel paper, commercial tort claims, deposit accounts, documents, general intangibles, instruments, investment property, letter-of-credit rights, letters of credit, money, or oil, gas, or other minerals before extraction.

(45) "Governmental unit" means a subdivision, agency, department, county, parish, municipality, or other unit of the government of the United States, a State, or a foreign country. The term includes an organization having a separate corporate existence if the organization is eligible to issue debt on which interest is exempt from income taxation under the laws of the United States.

(46) "Health-care-insurance receivable" means an interest in or claim under a policy of insurance which is a right to payment of a monetary obligation for health-care goods or services provided.

(47) "Instrument" means a negotiable instrument or any other writing that evidences a right to the payment of a monetary obligation, is not itself a security agreement or lease, and is of a type that in ordinary course of business is transferred by delivery with any necessary indorsement or assignment. The term does not include (i) investment property, (ii) letters of credit, or (iii) writings that evidence a right to payment arising out of the use of a credit or charge card or information contained on or for use with the card.

(48) "Inventory" means goods, other than farm products, which:

  (A) are leased by a person as lessor;

  (B) are held by a person for sale or lease or to be furnished under a contract of service;

  (C) are furnished by a person under a contract of service; or

  (D) consist of raw materials, work in process, or materials used or consumed in a business.

(49) "Investment property" means a security, whether certificated or uncertificated, security entitlement, securities account, commodity contract, or commodity account.

(50) "Jurisdiction of organization", with respect to a registered organization, means the jurisdiction under whose law the organization is organized.

(51) "Letter-of-credit right" means a right to payment or performance under a letter of credit, whether or not the beneficiary has demanded or is at the time entitled to demand payment or performance. The term does not include the right of a beneficiary to demand payment or performance under a letter of credit.

(52) "Lien creditor" means:

  (A) a creditor that has acquired a lien on the property involved by attachment, levy, or the like;

  (B) an assignee for benefit of creditors from the time of assignment;

  (C) a trustee in bankruptcy from the date of the filing of the petition; or

  (D) a receiver in equity from the time of appointment.

(53) "Manufactured home" means a structure, transportable in one or more sections, which, in the traveling mode, is eight body feet or more in width or 40 body feet or more in length, or, when erected on site, is 320 or more square feet, and which is built on a permanent chassis and designed to be used as a dwelling with or without a permanent foundation when connected to the required utilities, and includes the plumbing, heating, air-conditioning, and electrical systems contained therein. The term includes any structure that meets all of the requirements of this paragraph except the size requirements and with respect to which the manufacturer voluntarily files a certification required by the United States Secretary of Housing and Urban Development and complies with the standards established under Title 42 of the United States Code.

(54) "Manufactured-home transaction" means a secured transaction:

  (A) that creates a purchase-money security interest in a manufactured home, other than a manufactured home held as inventory; or

  (B) in which a manufactured home, other than a manufactured home held as inventory, is the primary collateral.

(55) "Mortgage" means a consensual interest in real property, including fixtures, which secures payment or performance of an obligation.

(56) "New debtor" means a person that becomes bound as debtor under Section 9–203(d) by a security agreement previously entered into by another person.

(57) "New value" means (i) money, (ii) money's worth in property, services, or new credit, or (iii) release by a transferee of an interest in property previously transferred to the transferee. The term does not include an obligation substituted for another obligation.

(58) "Noncash proceeds" means proceeds other than cash proceeds.

(59) "Obligor" means a person that, with respect to an obligation secured by a security interest in or an agricultural lien on the collateral, (i) owes payment or other performance of the obligation, (ii) has provided property other than the collateral to secure payment or other performance of the obligation, or (iii) is otherwise accountable in whole or in part for payment or other performance of the obligation. The term does not include issuers or nominated persons under a letter of credit.

(60) "Original debtor", except as used in Section 9–310(c), means a person that, as debtor, entered into a security agreement to which a new debtor has become bound under Section 9–203(d).

(61) "Payment intangible" means a general intangible under which the account debtor's principal obligation is a monetary obligation.

(62) "Person related to", with respect to an individual, means:

(A) the spouse of the individual;

(B) a brother, brother-in-law, sister, or sister-in-law of the individual;

(C) an ancestor or lineal descendant of the individual or the individual's spouse; or

(D) any other relative, by blood or marriage, of the individual or the individual's spouse who shares the same home with the individual.

(63) "Person related to", with respect to an organization, means:

(A) a person directly or indirectly controlling, controlled by, or under common control with the organization;

(B) an officer or director of, or a person performing similar functions with respect to, the organization;

(C) an officer or director of, or a person performing similar functions with respect to, a person described in subparagraph (A);

(D) the spouse of an individual described in subparagraph (A), (B), or (C); or

(E) an individual who is related by blood or marriage to an individual described in subparagraph (A), (B), (C), or (D) and shares the same home with the individual.

(64) "Proceeds", except as used in Section 9–609(b), means the following property:

(A) whatever is acquired upon the sale, lease, license, exchange, or other disposition of collateral;

(B) whatever is collected on, or distributed on account of, collateral;

(C) rights arising out of collateral;

(D) to the extent of the value of collateral, claims arising out of the loss, nonconformity, or interference with the use of, defects or infringement of rights in, or damage to, the collateral; or

(E) to the extent of the value of collateral and to the extent payable to the debtor or the secured party, insurance payable by reason of the loss or nonconformity of, defects or infringement of rights in, or damage to, the collateral.

(65) "Promissory note" means an instrument that evidences a promise to pay a monetary obligation, does not evidence an order to pay, and does not contain an acknowledgment by a bank that the bank has received for deposit a sum of money or funds.

(66) "Proposal" means a record authenticated by a secured party which includes the terms on which the secured party is willing to accept collateral in full or partial satisfaction of the obligation it secures pursuant to Sections 9–620, 9–621, and 9–622.

(67) "Public-finance transaction" means a secured transaction in connection with which:

(A) debt securities are issued;

(B) all or a portion of the securities issued have an initial stated maturity of at least 20 years; and

(C) the debtor, obligor, secured party, account debtor or other person obligated on collateral, assignor or assignee of a secured obligation, or assignor or assignee of a security interest is a State or a governmental unit of a State.

(68) "Pursuant to commitment", with respect to an advance made or other value given by a secured party, means pursuant to the secured party's obligation, whether or not a subsequent event of default or other event not within the secured party's control has relieved or may relieve the secured party from its obligation.

(69) "Record", except as used in "for record", "of record", "record or legal title", and "record owner", means information that is inscribed on a tangible medium or which is stored in an electronic or other medium and is retrievable in perceivable form.

(70) "Registered organization" means an organization organized solely under the law of a single State or the United States and as to which the State or the United States must maintain a public record showing the organization to have been organized.

(71) "Secondary obligor" means an obligor to the extent that:

(A) the obligor's obligation is secondary; or

(B) the obligor has a right of recourse with respect to an obligation secured by collateral against the debtor, another obligor, or property of either.

(72) "Secured party" means:

(A) a person in whose favor a security interest is created or provided for under a security agreement, whether or not any obligation to be secured is outstanding;

(B) a person that holds an agricultural lien;

(C) a consignor;

(D) a person to which accounts, chattel paper, payment intangibles, or promissory notes have been sold;

(E) a trustee, indenture trustee, agent, collateral agent, or other representative in whose favor a security interest or agricultural lien is created or provided for; or

(F) a person that holds a security interest arising under Section 2–401, 2–505, 2–711(3), 2A–508(5), 4–210, or 5–118.

(73) "Security agreement" means an agreement that creates or provides for a security interest.

(74) "Send", in connection with a record or notification, means:

(A) to deposit in the mail, deliver for transmission, or transmit by any other usual means of communication, with postage or cost of transmission provided for, addressed to any address reasonable under the circumstances; or

(B) to cause the record or notification to be received within the time that it would have been received if properly sent under subparagraph (A).

(75) "Software" means a computer program and any supporting information provided in connection with a transaction relating to the program. The term does not include a computer program that is included in the definition of goods.

(76) "State" means a State of the United States, the District of Columbia, Puerto Rico, the United States Virgin Islands, or any territory or insular possession subject to the jurisdiction of the United States.

(77) "Supporting obligation" means a letter-of-credit right or secondary obligation that supports the payment or performance of an account, chattel paper, a document, a general intangible, an instrument, or investment property.

(78) "Tangible chattel paper" means chattel paper evidenced by a record or records consisting of information that is inscribed on a tangible medium.

(79) "Termination statement" means an amendment of a financing statement which:

(A) identifies, by its file number, the initial financing statement to which it relates; and

(B) indicates either that it is a termination statement or that the identified financing statement is no longer effective.

(80) "Transmitting utility" means a person primarily engaged in the business of:

(A) operating a railroad, subway, street railway, or trolley bus;

(B) transmitting communications electrically, electromagnetically, or by light;

(C) transmitting goods by pipeline or sewer; or

(D) transmitting or producing and transmitting electricity, steam, gas, or water.

(b) The following definitions in other articles apply to this article:

"Applicant."	Section 5–102
"Beneficiary."	Section 5–102
"Broker."	Section 8–102
"Certificated security."	Section 8–102
"Check."	Section 3–104
"Clearing corporation."	Section 8–102
"Contract for sale."	Section 2–106
"Customer."	Section 4–104
"Entitlement holder."	Section 8–102
"Financial asset."	Section 8–102
"Holder in due course."	Section 3–302
"Issuer" (with respect to a letter of credit or letter-of-credit right).	Section 5–102
"Issuer" (with respect to a security).	Section 8–201
"Lease."	Section 2A–103
"Lease agreement."	Section 2A–103
"Lease contract."	Section 2A–103
"Leasehold interest."	Section 2A–103
"Lessee."	Section 2A–103
"Lessee in ordinary course of business."	Section 2A–103
"Lessor."	Section 2A–103
"Lessor's residual interest."	Section 2A–103
"Letter of credit."	Section 5–102
"Merchant."	Section 2–104
"Negotiable instrument."	Section 3–104
"Nominated person."	Section 5–102
"Note."	Section 3–104
"Proceeds of a letter of credit."	Section 5–114
"Prove."	Section 3–103
"Sale."	Section 2–106
"Securities account."	Section 8–501
"Securities intermediary."	Section 8–102
"Security."	Section 8–102
"Security certificate."	Section 8–102
"Security entitlement."	Section 8–102
"Uncertificated security."	Section 8–102

(c) Article 1 contains general definitions and principles of construction and interpretation applicable throughout this article. Amended in 1999 and 2000.

§ 9–103. Purchase-Money Security Interest; Application of Payments; Burden of Establishing.

(a) In this section:

(1) "purchase-money collateral" means goods or software that secures a purchase-money obligation incurred with respect to that collateral; and

(2) "purchase-money obligation" means an obligation of an obligor incurred as all or part of the price of the collateral or for value given to enable the debtor to acquire rights in or the use of the collateral if the value is in fact so used.

(b) A security interest in goods is a purchase-money security interest:

(1) to the extent that the goods are purchase-money collateral with respect to that security interest;

(2) if the security interest is in inventory that is or was purchase-money collateral, also to the extent that the security interest secures a purchase-money obligation incurred with respect to other inventory in which the secured party holds or held a purchase-money security interest; and

(3) also to the extent that the security interest secures a purchase-money obligation incurred with respect to software in which the secured party holds or held a purchase-money security interest.

(c) A security interest in software is a purchase-money security interest to the extent that the security interest also secures a purchase-money obligation incurred with respect to goods in which the secured party holds or held a purchase-money security interest if:

(1) the debtor acquired its interest in the software in an integrated transaction in which it acquired an interest in the goods; and

(2) the debtor acquired its interest in the software for the principal purpose of using the software in the goods.

(d) The security interest of a consignor in goods that are the subject of a consignment is a purchase-money security interest in inventory.

(e) In a transaction other than a consumer-goods transaction, if the extent to which a security interest is a purchase-money security interest depends on the application of a payment to a particular obligation, the payment must be applied:

> **(1)** in accordance with any reasonable method of application to which the parties agree;
>
> **(2)** in the absence of the parties' agreement to a reasonable method, in accordance with any intention of the obligor manifested at or before the time of payment; or
>
> **(3)** in the absence of an agreement to a reasonable method and a timely manifestation of the obligor's intention, in the following order:
>
> > **(A)** to obligations that are not secured; and
> >
> > **(B)** if more than one obligation is secured, to obligations secured by purchase-money security interests in the order in which those obligations were incurred.

(f) In a transaction other than a consumer-goods transaction, a purchase-money security interest does not lose its status as such, even if:

> **(1)** the purchase-money collateral also secures an obligation that is not a purchase-money obligation;
>
> **(2)** collateral that is not purchase-money collateral also secures the purchase-money obligation; or
>
> **(3)** the purchase-money obligation has been renewed, refinanced, consolidated, or restructured.

(g) In a transaction other than a consumer-goods transaction, a secured party claiming a purchase-money security interest has the burden of establishing the extent to which the security interest is a purchase-money security interest.

(h) The limitation of the rules in subsections (e), (f), and (g) to transactions other than consumer-goods transactions is intended to leave to the court the determination of the proper rules in consumer-goods transactions. The court may not infer from that limitation the nature of the proper rule in consumer-goods transactions and may continue to apply established approaches.

§ 9–104. Control of Deposit Account.

(a) A secured party has control of a deposit account if:

> **(1)** the secured party is the bank with which the deposit account is maintained;
>
> **(2)** the debtor, secured party, and bank have agreed in an authenticated record that the bank will comply with instructions originated by the secured party directing disposition of the funds in the deposit account without further consent by the debtor; or
>
> **(3)** the secured party becomes the bank's customer with respect to the deposit account.

(b) A secured party that has satisfied subsection (a) has control, even if the debtor retains the right to direct the disposition of funds from the deposit account.

§ 9–105. Control of Electronic Chattel Paper.

A secured party has control of electronic chattel paper if the record or records comprising the chattel paper are created, stored, and assigned in such a manner that:

> **(1)** a single authoritative copy of the record or records exists which is unique, identifiable and, except as otherwise provided in paragraphs (4), (5), and (6), unalterable;

> **(2)** the authoritative copy identifies the secured party as the assignee of the record or records;
>
> **(3)** the authoritative copy is communicated to and maintained by the secured party or its designated custodian;
>
> **(4)** copies or revisions that add or change an identified assignee of the authoritative copy can be made only with the participation of the secured party;
>
> **(5)** each copy of the authoritative copy and any copy of a copy is readily identifiable as a copy that is not the authoritative copy; and
>
> **(6)** any revision of the authoritative copy is readily identifiable as an authorized or unauthorized revision.

§ 9–106. Control of Investment Property.

(a) A person has control of a certificated security, uncertificated security, or security entitlement as provided in Section 8–106.

(b) A secured party has control of a commodity contract if:

> **(1)** the secured party is the commodity intermediary with which the commodity contract is carried; or
>
> **(2)** the commodity customer, secured party, and commodity intermediary have agreed that the commodity intermediary will apply any value distributed on account of the commodity contract as directed by the secured party without further consent by the commodity customer.

(c) A secured party having control of all security entitlements or commodity contracts carried in a securities account or commodity account has control over the securities account or commodity account.

§ 9–107. Control of Letter-of-Credit Right.

A secured party has control of a letter-of-credit right to the extent of any right to payment or performance by the issuer or any nominated person if the issuer or nominated person has consented to an assignment of proceeds of the letter of credit under Section 5–114(c) or otherwise applicable law or practice.

§ 9–108. Sufficiency of Description.

(a) Except as otherwise provided in subsections (c), (d), and (e), a description of personal or real property is sufficient, whether or not it is specific, if it reasonably identifies what is described.

(b) Except as otherwise provided in subsection (d), a description of collateral reasonably identifies the collateral if it identifies the collateral by:

> **(1)** specific listing;
>
> **(2)** category;
>
> **(3)** except as otherwise provided in subsection (e), a type of collateral defined in [the Uniform Commercial Code];
>
> **(4)** quantity;
>
> **(5)** computational or allocational formula or procedure; or
>
> **(6)** except as otherwise provided in subsection (c), any other method, if the identity of the collateral is objectively determinable.

(c) A description of collateral as "all the debtor's assets" or "all the debtor's personal property" or using words of similar import does not reasonably identify the collateral.

(d) Except as otherwise provided in subsection (e), a description of a security entitlement, securities account, or commodity account is sufficient if it describes:

> **(1)** the collateral by those terms or as investment property; or

(2) the underlying financial asset or commodity contract.

(e) A description only by type of collateral defined in [the Uniform Commercial Code] is an insufficient description of:

(1) a commercial tort claim; or

(2) in a consumer transaction, consumer goods, a security entitlement, a securities account, or a commodity account.

[Subpart 2. Applicability of Article]

§ 9–109. Scope.

(a) Except as otherwise provided in subsections (c) and (d), this article applies to:

(1) a transaction, regardless of its form, that creates a security interest in personal property or fixtures by contract;

(2) an agricultural lien;

(3) a sale of accounts, chattel paper, payment intangibles, or promissory notes;

(4) a consignment;

(5) a security interest arising under Section 2–401, 2–505, 2–711(3), or 2A–508(5), as provided in Section 9–110; and

(6) a security interest arising under Section 4–210 or 5–118.

(b) The application of this article to a security interest in a secured obligation is not affected by the fact that the obligation is itself secured by a transaction or interest to which this article does not apply.

(c) This article does not apply to the extent that:

(1) a statute, regulation, or treaty of the United States preempts this article;

(2) another statute of this State expressly governs the creation, perfection, priority, or enforcement of a security interest created by this State or a governmental unit of this State;

(3) a statute of another State, a foreign country, or a governmental unit of another State or a foreign country, other than a statute generally applicable to security interests, expressly governs creation, perfection, priority, or enforcement of a security interest created by the State, country, or governmental unit; or

(4) the rights of a transferee beneficiary or nominated person under a letter of credit are independent and superior under Section 5–114.

(d) This article does not apply to:

(1) a landlord's lien, other than an agricultural lien;

(2) a lien, other than an agricultural lien, given by statute or other rule of law for services or materials, but Section 9–333 applies with respect to priority of the lien;

(3) an assignment of a claim for wages, salary, or other compensation of an employee;

(4) a sale of accounts, chattel paper, payment intangibles, or promissory notes as part of a sale of the business out of which they arose;

(5) an assignment of accounts, chattel paper, payment intangibles, or promissory notes which is for the purpose of collection only;

(6) an assignment of a right to payment under a contract to an assignee that is also obligated to perform under the contract;

(7) an assignment of a single account, payment intangible, or promissory note to an assignee in full or partial satisfaction of a preexisting indebtedness;

(8) a transfer of an interest in or an assignment of a claim under a policy of insurance, other than an assignment by or to a health-care provider of a health-care-insurance receivable and any subsequent assignment of the right to payment, but Sections 9–315 and 9–322 apply with respect to proceeds and priorities in proceeds;

(9) an assignment of a right represented by a judgment, other than a judgment taken on a right to payment that was collateral;

(10) a right of recoupment or set-off, but:

(A) Section 9–340 applies with respect to the effectiveness of rights of recoupment or set-off against deposit accounts; and

(B) Section 9–404 applies with respect to defenses or claims of an account debtor;

(11) the creation or transfer of an interest in or lien on real property, including a lease or rents thereunder, except to the extent that provision is made for:

(A) liens on real property in Sections 9–203 and 9–308;

(B) fixtures in Section 9–334;

(C) fixture filings in Sections 9–501, 9–502, 9–512, 9–516, and 9–519; and

(D) security agreements covering personal and real property in Section 9–604;

(12) an assignment of a claim arising in tort, other than a commercial tort claim, but Sections 9–315 and 9–322 apply with respect to proceeds and priorities in proceeds; or

(13) an assignment of a deposit account in a consumer transaction, but Sections 9–315 and 9–322 apply with respect to proceeds and priorities in proceeds.

§ 9–110. Security Interests Arising under Article 2 or 2A.

A security interest arising under Section 2–401, 2–505, 2–711(3), or 2A–508(5) is subject to this article. However, until the debtor obtains possession of the goods:

(1) the security interest is enforceable, even if Section 9–203(b)(3) has not been satisfied;

(2) filing is not required to perfect the security interest;

(3) the rights of the secured party after default by the debtor are governed by Article 2 or 2A; and

(4) the security interest has priority over a conflicting security interest created by the debtor.

Part 2—Effectiveness of Security Agreement; Attachment of Security Interest; Rights of Parties to Security Agreement

[Subpart 1. Effectiveness and Attachment]

§ 9–201. General Effectiveness of Security Agreement.

(a) Except as otherwise provided in [the Uniform Commercial Code], a security agreement is effective according to its terms between the parties, against purchasers of the collateral, and against creditors.

(b) A transaction subject to this article is subject to any applicable rule of law which establishes a different rule for consumers and [insert reference to (i) any other statute or regulation that regulates the rates, charges, agreements, and practices for loans, credit sales, or other extensions of credit and (ii) any consumer-protection statute or regulation].

(c) In case of conflict between this article and a rule of law, statute, or regulation described in subsection (b), the rule of law, statute, or regulation controls. Failure to comply with a statute or regulation described in subsection (b) has only the effect the statute or regulation specifies.

(d) This article does not:

> **(1)** validate any rate, charge, agreement, or practice that violates a rule of law, statute, or regulation described in subsection (b); or
>
> **(2)** extend the application of the rule of law, statute, or regulation to a transaction not otherwise subject to it.

§ 9–202. Title to Collateral Immaterial.

Except as otherwise provided with respect to consignments or sales of accounts, chattel paper, payment intangibles, or promissory notes, the provisions of this article with regard to rights and obligations apply whether title to collateral is in the secured party or the debtor.

§ 9–203. Attachment and Enforceability of Security Interest; Proceeds; Supporting Obligations; Formal Requisites.

(a) A security interest attaches to collateral when it becomes enforceable against the debtor with respect to the collateral, unless an agreement expressly postpones the time of attachment.

(b) Except as otherwise provided in subsections (c) through (i), a security interest is enforceable against the debtor and third parties with respect to the collateral only if:

> **(1)** value has been given;
>
> **(2)** the debtor has rights in the collateral or the power to transfer rights in the collateral to a secured party; and
>
> **(3)** one of the following conditions is met:
>
>> **(A)** the debtor has authenticated a security agreement that provides a description of the collateral and, if the security interest covers timber to be cut, a description of the land concerned;
>>
>> **(B)** the collateral is not a certificated security and is in the possession of the secured party under Section 9–313 pursuant to the debtor's security agreement;
>>
>> **(C)** the collateral is a certificated security in registered form and the security certificate has been delivered to the secured party under Section 8–301 pursuant to the debtor's security agreement; or
>>
>> **(D)** the collateral is deposit accounts, electronic chattel paper, investment property, or letter-of-credit rights, and the secured party has control under Section 9–104, 9–105, 9–106, or 9–107 pursuant to the debtor's security agreement.

(c) Subsection (b) is subject to Section 4–210 on the security interest of a collecting bank, Section 5–118 on the security interest of a letter-of-credit issuer or nominated person, Section 9–110 on a security interest arising under Article 2 or 2A, and Section 9–206 on security interests in investment property.

(d) A person becomes bound as debtor by a security agreement entered into by another person if, by operation of law other than this article or by contract:

> **(1)** the security agreement becomes effective to create a security interest in the person's property; or
>
> **(2)** the person becomes generally obligated for the obligations of the other person, including the obligation secured under the security agreement, and acquires or succeeds to all or substantially all of the assets of the other person.

(e) If a new debtor becomes bound as debtor by a security agreement entered into by another person:

> **(1)** the agreement satisfies subsection (b)(3) with respect to existing or after-acquired property of the new debtor to the extent the property is described in the agreement; and
>
> **(2)** another agreement is not necessary to make a security interest in the property enforceable.

(f) The attachment of a security interest in collateral gives the secured party the rights to proceeds provided by Section 9–315 and is also attachment of a security interest in a supporting obligation for the collateral.

(g) The attachment of a security interest in a right to payment or performance secured by a security interest or other lien on personal or real property is also attachment of a security interest in the security interest, mortgage, or other lien.

(h) The attachment of a security interest in a securities account is also attachment of a security interest in the security entitlements carried in the securities account.

(i) The attachment of a security interest in a commodity account is also attachment of a security interest in the commodity contracts carried in the commodity account.

§ 9–204. After-Acquired Property; Future Advances.

(a) Except as otherwise provided in subsection (b), a security agreement may create or provide for a security interest in after-acquired collateral.

(b) A security interest does not attach under a term constituting an after-acquired property clause to:

> **(1)** consumer goods, other than an accession when given as additional security, unless the debtor acquires rights in them within 10 days after the secured party gives value; or
>
> **(2)** a commercial tort claim.

(c) A security agreement may provide that collateral secures, or that accounts, chattel paper, payment intangibles, or promissory notes are sold in connection with, future advances or other value, whether or not the advances or value are given pursuant to commitment.

§ 9–205. Use or Disposition of Collateral Permissible.

(a) A security interest is not invalid or fraudulent against creditors solely because:

> **(1)** the debtor has the right or ability to:
>
>> **(A)** use, commingle, or dispose of all or part of the collateral, including returned or repossessed goods;
>>
>> **(B)** collect, compromise, enforce, or otherwise deal with collateral;
>>
>> **(C)** accept the return of collateral or make repossessions; or
>>
>> **(D)** use, commingle, or dispose of proceeds; or

(2) the secured party fails to require the debtor to account for proceeds or replace collateral.

(b) This section does not relax the requirements of possession if attachment, perfection, or enforcement of a security interest depends upon possession of the collateral by the secured party.

§ 9–206. Security Interest Arising in Purchase or Delivery of Financial Asset.

(a) A security interest in favor of a securities intermediary attaches to a person's security entitlement if:

(1) the person buys a financial asset through the securities intermediary in a transaction in which the person is obligated to pay the purchase price to the securities intermediary at the time of the purchase; and

(2) the securities intermediary credits the financial asset to the buyer's securities account before the buyer pays the securities intermediary.

(b) The security interest described in subsection (a) secures the person's obligation to pay for the financial asset.

(c) A security interest in favor of a person that delivers a certificated security or other financial asset represented by a writing attaches to the security or other financial asset if:

(1) the security or other financial asset:

(A) in the ordinary course of business is transferred by delivery with any necessary indorsement or assignment; and

(B) is delivered under an agreement between persons in the business of dealing with such securities or financial assets; and

(2) the agreement calls for delivery against payment.

(d) The security interest described in subsection (c) secures the obligation to make payment for the delivery.

[Subpart 2. Rights and Duties]

§ 9–207. Rights and Duties of Secured Party Having Possession or Control of Collateral.

(a) Except as otherwise provided in subsection (d), a secured party shall use reasonable care in the custody and preservation of collateral in the secured party's possession. In the case of chattel paper or an instrument, reasonable care includes taking necessary steps to preserve rights against prior parties unless otherwise agreed.

(b) Except as otherwise provided in subsection (d), if a secured party has possession of collateral:

(1) reasonable expenses, including the cost of insurance and payment of taxes or other charges, incurred in the custody, preservation, use, or operation of the collateral are chargeable to the debtor and are secured by the collateral;

(2) the risk of accidental loss or damage is on the debtor to the extent of a deficiency in any effective insurance coverage;

(3) the secured party shall keep the collateral identifiable, but fungible collateral may be commingled; and

(4) the secured party may use or operate the collateral:

(A) for the purpose of preserving the collateral or its value;

(B) as permitted by an order of a court having competent jurisdiction; or

(C) except in the case of consumer goods, in the manner and to the extent agreed by the debtor.

(c) Except as otherwise provided in subsection (d), a secured party having possession of collateral or control of collateral under Section 9–104, 9–105, 9–106, or 9–107:

(1) may hold as additional security any proceeds, except money or funds, received from the collateral;

(2) shall apply money or funds received from the collateral to reduce the secured obligation, unless remitted to the debtor; and

(3) may create a security interest in the collateral.

(d) If the secured party is a buyer of accounts, chattel paper, payment intangibles, or promissory notes or a consignor:

(1) subsection (a) does not apply unless the secured party is entitled under an agreement:

(A) to charge back uncollected collateral; or

(B) otherwise to full or limited recourse against the debtor or a secondary obligor based on the nonpayment or other default of an account debtor or other obligor on the collateral; and

(2) subsections (b) and (c) do not apply.

§ 9–208. Additional Duties of Secured Party Having Control of Collateral.

(a) This section applies to cases in which there is no outstanding secured obligation and the secured party is not committed to make advances, incur obligations, or otherwise give value.

(b) Within 10 days after receiving an authenticated demand by the debtor:

(1) a secured party having control of a deposit account under Section 9–104(a)(2) shall send to the bank with which the deposit account is maintained an authenticated statement that releases the bank from any further obligation to comply with instructions originated by the secured party;

(2) a secured party having control of a deposit account under Section 9–104(a)(3) shall:

(A) pay the debtor the balance on deposit in the deposit account; or

(B) transfer the balance on deposit into a deposit account in the debtor's name;

(3) a secured party, other than a buyer, having control of electronic chattel paper under Section 9–105 shall:

(A) communicate the authoritative copy of the electronic chattel paper to the debtor or its designated custodian;

(B) if the debtor designates a custodian that is the designated custodian with which the authoritative copy of the electronic chattel paper is maintained for the secured party, communicate to the custodian an authenticated record releasing the designated custodian from any further obligation to comply with instructions originated by the secured party and instructing the custodian to comply with instructions originated by the debtor; and

(C) take appropriate action to enable the debtor or its designated custodian to make copies of or revisions to the authoritative copy which add or change an identified assignee of the authoritative copy without the consent of the secured party;

(4) a secured party having control of investment property under Section 8–106(d)(2) or 9–106(b) shall send to the securities intermediary or commodity intermediary with which the security entitlement or commodity contract is maintained an authenticated record that releases the securities intermediary or commodity intermediary from any further obligation to comply with entitlement orders or directions originated by the secured party; and

(5) a secured party having control of a letter-of-credit right under Section 9–107 shall send to each person having an unfulfilled obligation to pay or deliver proceeds of the letter of credit to the secured party an authenticated release from any further obligation to pay or deliver proceeds of the letter of credit to the secured party.

§ 9–209. Duties of Secured Party If Account Debtor Has Been Notified of Assignment.

(a) Except as otherwise provided in subsection (c), this section applies if:

(1) there is no outstanding secured obligation; and

(2) the secured party is not committed to make advances, incur obligations, or otherwise give value.

(b) Within 10 days after receiving an authenticated demand by the debtor, a secured party shall send to an account debtor that has received notification of an assignment to the secured party as assignee under Section 9–406(a) an authenticated record that releases the account debtor from any further obligation to the secured party.

(c) This section does not apply to an assignment constituting the sale of an account, chattel paper, or payment intangible.

§ 9–210. Request for Accounting; Request Regarding List of Collateral or Statement of Account.

(a) In this section:

(1) "Request" means a record of a type described in paragraph (2), (3), or (4).

(2) "Request for an accounting" means a record authenticated by a debtor requesting that the recipient provide an accounting of the unpaid obligations secured by collateral and reasonably identifying the transaction or relationship that is the subject of the request.

(3) "Request regarding a list of collateral" means a record authenticated by a debtor requesting that the recipient approve or correct a list of what the debtor believes to be the collateral securing an obligation and reasonably identifying the transaction or relationship that is the subject of the request.

(4) "Request regarding a statement of account" means a record authenticated by a debtor requesting that the recipient approve or correct a statement indicating what the debtor believes to be the aggregate amount of unpaid obligations secured by collateral as of a specified date and reasonably identifying the transaction or relationship that is the subject of the request.

(b) Subject to subsections (c), (d), (e), and (f), a secured party, other than a buyer of accounts, chattel paper, payment intangibles, or promissory notes or a consignor, shall comply with a request within 14 days after receipt:

(1) in the case of a request for an accounting, by authenticating and sending to the debtor an accounting; and

(2) in the case of a request regarding a list of collateral or a request regarding a statement of account, by authenticating and sending to the debtor an approval or correction.

(c) A secured party that claims a security interest in all of a particular type of collateral owned by the debtor may comply with a request regarding a list of collateral by sending to the debtor an authenticated record including a statement to that effect within 14 days after receipt.

(d) A person that receives a request regarding a list of collateral, claims no interest in the collateral when it receives the request, and claimed an interest in the collateral at an earlier time shall comply with the request within 14 days after receipt by sending to the debtor an authenticated record:

(1) disclaiming any interest in the collateral; and

(2) if known to the recipient, providing the name and mailing address of any assignee of or successor to the recipient's interest in the collateral.

(e) A person that receives a request for an accounting or a request regarding a statement of account, claims no interest in the obligations when it receives the request, and claimed an interest in the obligations at an earlier time shall comply with the request within 14 days after receipt by sending to the debtor an authenticated record:

(1) disclaiming any interest in the obligations; and

(2) if known to the recipient, providing the name and mailing address of any assignee of or successor to the recipient's interest in the obligations.

(f) A debtor is entitled without charge to one response to a request under this section during any six-month period. The secured party may require payment of a charge not exceeding $25 for each additional response.

As amended in 1999.

Part 3—Perfection and Priority

[Subpart 1. Law Governing Perfection and Priority]

§ 9–301. Law Governing Perfection and Priority of Security Interests.

Except as otherwise provided in Sections 9–303 through 9–306, the following rules determine the law governing perfection, the effect of perfection or nonperfection, and the priority of a security interest in collateral:

(1) Except as otherwise provided in this section, while a debtor is located in a jurisdiction, the local law of that jurisdiction governs perfection, the effect of perfection or nonperfection, and the priority of a security interest in collateral.

(2) While collateral is located in a jurisdiction, the local law of that jurisdiction governs perfection, the effect of perfection or nonperfection, and the priority of a possessory security interest in that collateral.

(3) Except as otherwise provided in paragraph (4), while negotiable documents, goods, instruments, money, or tangible chattel paper is located in a jurisdiction, the local law of that jurisdiction governs:

(A) perfection of a security interest in the goods by filing a fixture filing;

(B) perfection of a security interest in timber to be cut; and

(C) the effect of perfection or nonperfection and the priority of a nonpossessory security interest in the collateral.

(4) The local law of the jurisdiction in which the wellhead or minehead is located governs perfection, the effect of perfection or nonperfection, and the priority of a security interest in as-extracted collateral.

§ 9–302. Law Governing Perfection and Priority of Agricultural Liens.

While farm products are located in a jurisdiction, the local law of that jurisdiction governs perfection, the effect of perfection or nonperfection, and the priority of an agricultural lien on the farm products.

§ 9–303. Law Governing Perfection and Priority of Security Interests in Goods Covered by a Certificate of Title.

(a) This section applies to goods covered by a certificate of title, even if there is no other relationship between the jurisdiction under whose certificate of title the goods are covered and the goods or the debtor.

(b) Goods become covered by a certificate of title when a valid application for the certificate of title and the applicable fee are delivered to the appropriate authority. Goods cease to be covered by a certificate of title at the earlier of the time the certificate of title ceases to be effective under the law of the issuing jurisdiction or the time the goods become covered subsequently by a certificate of title issued by another jurisdiction.

(c) The local law of the jurisdiction under whose certificate of title the goods are covered governs perfection, the effect of perfection or nonperfection, and the priority of a security interest in goods covered by a certificate of title from the time the goods become covered by the certificate of title until the goods cease to be covered by the certificate of title.

§ 9–304. Law Governing Perfection and Priority of Security Interests in Deposit Accounts.

(a) The local law of a bank's jurisdiction governs perfection, the effect of perfection or nonperfection, and the priority of a security interest in a deposit account maintained with that bank.

(b) The following rules determine a bank's jurisdiction for purposes of this part:

(1) If an agreement between the bank and the debtor governing the deposit account expressly provides that a particular jurisdiction is the bank's jurisdiction for purposes of this part, this article, or [the Uniform Commercial Code], that jurisdiction is the bank's jurisdiction.

(2) If paragraph (1) does not apply and an agreement between the bank and its customer governing the deposit account expressly provides that the agreement is governed by the law of a particular jurisdiction, that jurisdiction is the bank's jurisdiction.

(3) If neither paragraph (1) nor paragraph (2) applies and an agreement between the bank and its customer governing the deposit account expressly provides that the deposit account is maintained at an office in a particular jurisdiction, that jurisdiction is the bank's jurisdiction.

(4) If none of the preceding paragraphs applies, the bank's jurisdiction is the jurisdiction in which the office identified in an account statement as the office serving the customer's account is located.

(5) If none of the preceding paragraphs applies, the bank's jurisdiction is the jurisdiction in which the chief executive office of the bank is located.

§ 9–305. Law Governing Perfection and Priority of Security Interests in Investment Property.

(a) Except as otherwise provided in subsection (c), the following rules apply:

(1) While a security certificate is located in a jurisdiction, the local law of that jurisdiction governs perfection, the effect of perfection or nonperfection, and the priority of a security interest in the certificated security represented thereby.

(2) The local law of the issuer's jurisdiction as specified in Section 8–110(d) governs perfection, the effect of perfection or nonperfection, and the priority of a security interest in an uncertificated security.

(3) The local law of the securities intermediary's jurisdiction as specified in Section 8–110(e) governs perfection, the effect of perfection or nonperfection, and the priority of a security interest in a security entitlement or securities account.

(4) The local law of the commodity intermediary's jurisdiction governs perfection, the effect of perfection or nonperfection, and the priority of a security interest in a commodity contract or commodity account.

(b) The following rules determine a commodity intermediary's jurisdiction for purposes of this part:

(1) If an agreement between the commodity intermediary and commodity customer governing the commodity account expressly provides that a particular jurisdiction is the commodity intermediary's jurisdiction for purposes of this part, this article, or [the Uniform Commercial Code], that jurisdiction is the commodity intermediary's jurisdiction.

(2) If paragraph (1) does not apply and an agreement between the commodity intermediary and commodity customer governing the commodity account expressly provides that the agreement is governed by the law of a particular jurisdiction, that jurisdiction is the commodity intermediary's jurisdiction.

(3) If neither paragraph (1) nor paragraph (2) applies and an agreement between the commodity intermediary and commodity customer governing the commodity account expressly provides that the commodity account is maintained at an office in a particular jurisdiction, that jurisdiction is the commodity intermediary's jurisdiction.

(4) If none of the preceding paragraphs applies, the commodity intermediary's jurisdiction is the jurisdiction in which the office identified in an account statement as the office serving the commodity customer's account is located.

(5) If none of the preceding paragraphs applies, the commodity intermediary's jurisdiction is the jurisdiction in which the chief executive office of the commodity intermediary is located.

(c) The local law of the jurisdiction in which the debtor is located governs:

> **(1)** perfection of a security interest in investment property by filing;
>
> **(2)** automatic perfection of a security interest in investment property created by a broker or securities intermediary; and
>
> **(3)** automatic perfection of a security interest in a commodity contract or commodity account created by a commodity intermediary.

§ 9–306. Law Governing Perfection and Priority of Security Interests in Letter-of-Credit Rights.

(a) Subject to subsection (c), the local law of the issuer's jurisdiction or a nominated person's jurisdiction governs perfection, the effect of perfection or nonperfection, and the priority of a security interest in a letter-of-credit right if the issuer's jurisdiction or nominated person's jurisdiction is a State.

(b) For purposes of this part, an issuer's jurisdiction or nominated person's jurisdiction is the jurisdiction whose law governs the liability of the issuer or nominated person with respect to the letter-of-credit right as provided in Section 5–116.

(c) This section does not apply to a security interest that is perfected only under Section 9–308(d).

§ 9–307. Location of Debtor.

(a) In this section, "place of business" means a place where a debtor conducts its affairs.

(b) Except as otherwise provided in this section, the following rules determine a debtor's location:

> **(1)** A debtor who is an individual is located at the individual's principal residence.
>
> **(2)** A debtor that is an organization and has only one place of business is located at its place of business.
>
> **(3)** A debtor that is an organization and has more than one place of business is located at its chief executive office.

(c) Subsection (b) applies only if a debtor's residence, place of business, or chief executive office, as applicable, is located in a jurisdiction whose law generally requires information concerning the existence of a nonpossessory security interest to be made generally available in a filing, recording, or registration system as a condition or result of the security interest's obtaining priority over the rights of a lien creditor with respect to the collateral. If subsection (b) does not apply, the debtor is located in the District of Columbia.

(d) A person that ceases to exist, have a residence, or have a place of business continues to be located in the jurisdiction specified by subsections (b) and (c).

(e) A registered organization that is organized under the law of a State is located in that State.

(f) Except as otherwise provided in subsection (i), a registered organization that is organized under the law of the United States and a branch or agency of a bank that is not organized under the law of the United States or a State are located:

> **(1)** in the State that the law of the United States designates, if the law designates a State of location;
>
> **(2)** in the State that the registered organization, branch, or agency designates, if the law of the United States authorizes the registered organization, branch, or agency to designate its State of location; or

> **(3)** in the District of Columbia, if neither paragraph (1) nor paragraph (2) applies.

(g) A registered organization continues to be located in the jurisdiction specified by subsection (e) or (f) notwithstanding:

> **(1)** the suspension, revocation, forfeiture, or lapse of the registered organization's status as such in its jurisdiction of organization; or
>
> **(2)** the dissolution, winding up, or cancellation of the existence of the registered organization.

(h) The United States is located in the District of Columbia.

(i) A branch or agency of a bank that is not organized under the law of the United States or a State is located in the State in which the branch or agency is licensed, if all branches and agencies of the bank are licensed in only one State.

(j) A foreign air carrier under the Federal Aviation Act of 1958, as amended, is located at the designated office of the agent upon which service of process may be made on behalf of the carrier.

(k) This section applies only for purposes of this part.

[Subpart 2. Perfection]

§ 9–308. When Security Interest or Agricultural Lien Is Perfected; Continuity of Perfection.

(a) Except as otherwise provided in this section and Section 9–309, a security interest is perfected if it has attached and all of the applicable requirements for perfection in Sections 9–310 through 9–316 have been satisfied. A security interest is perfected when it attaches if the applicable requirements are satisfied before the security interest attaches.

(b) An agricultural lien is perfected if it has become effective and all of the applicable requirements for perfection in Section 9–310 have been satisfied. An agricultural lien is perfected when it becomes effective if the applicable requirements are satisfied before the agricultural lien becomes effective.

(c) A security interest or agricultural lien is perfected continuously if it is originally perfected by one method under this article and is later perfected by another method under this article, without an intermediate period when it was unperfected.

(d) Perfection of a security interest in collateral also perfects a security interest in a supporting obligation for the collateral.

(e) Perfection of a security interest in a right to payment or performance also perfects a security interest in a security interest, mortgage, or other lien on personal or real property securing the right.

(f) Perfection of a security interest in a securities account also perfects a security interest in the security entitlements carried in the securities account.

(g) Perfection of a security interest in a commodity account also perfects a security interest in the commodity contracts carried in the commodity account.

Legislative Note: Any statute conflicting with subsection (e) must be made expressly subject to that subsection.

§ 9–309. Security Interest Perfected upon Attachment.

The following security interests are perfected when they attach:

> **(1)** a purchase-money security interest in consumer goods, except as otherwise provided in Section 9–311(b)

with respect to consumer goods that are subject to a statute or treaty described in Section 9–311(a);

(2) an assignment of accounts or payment intangibles which does not by itself or in conjunction with other assignments to the same assignee transfer a significant part of the assignor's outstanding accounts or payment intangibles;

(3) a sale of a payment intangible;

(4) a sale of a promissory note;

(5) a security interest created by the assignment of a health-care-insurance receivable to the provider of the health-care goods or services;

(6) a security interest arising under Section 2–401, 2–505, 2–711(3), or 2A–508(5), until the debtor obtains possession of the collateral;

(7) a security interest of a collecting bank arising under Section 4–210;

(8) a security interest of an issuer or nominated person arising under Section 5–118;

(9) a security interest arising in the delivery of a financial asset under Section 9–206(c);

(10) a security interest in investment property created by a broker or securities intermediary;

(11) a security interest in a commodity contract or a commodity account created by a commodity intermediary;

(12) an assignment for the benefit of all creditors of the transferor and subsequent transfers by the assignee thereunder; and

(13) a security interest created by an assignment of a beneficial interest in a decedent's estate; and

(14) a sale by an individual of an account that is a right to payment of winnings in a lottery or other game of chance.

§ 9–310. When Filing Required to Perfect Security Interest or Agricultural Lien; Security Interests and Agricultural Liens to Which Filing Provisions Do Not Apply.

(a) Except as otherwise provided in subsection (b) and Section 9–312(b), a financing statement must be filed to perfect all security interests and agricultural liens.

(b) The filing of a financing statement is not necessary to perfect a security interest:

(1) that is perfected under Section 9–308(d), (e), (f), or (g);

(2) that is perfected under Section 9–309 when it attaches;

(3) in property subject to a statute, regulation, or treaty described in Section 9–311(a);

(4) in goods in possession of a bailee which is perfected under Section 9–312(d)(1) or (2);

(5) in certificated securities, documents, goods, or instruments which is perfected without filing or possession under Section 9–312(e), (f), or (g);

(6) in collateral in the secured party's possession under Section 9–313;

(7) in a certificated security which is perfected by delivery of the security certificate to the secured party under Section 9–313;

(8) in deposit accounts, electronic chattel paper, investment property, or letter-of-credit rights which is perfected by control under Section 9–314;

(9) in proceeds which is perfected under Section 9–315; or

(10) that is perfected under Section 9–316.

(c) If a secured party assigns a perfected security interest or agricultural lien, a filing under this article is not required to continue the perfected status of the security interest against creditors of and transferees from the original debtor.

§ 9–311. Perfection of Security Interests in Property Subject to Certain Statutes, Regulations, and Treaties.

(a) Except as otherwise provided in subsection (d), the filing of a financing statement is not necessary or effective to perfect a security interest in property subject to:

(1) a statute, regulation, or treaty of the United States whose requirements for a security interest's obtaining priority over the rights of a lien creditor with respect to the property preempt Section 9–310(a);

(2) [list any certificate-of-title statute covering automobiles, trailers, mobile homes, boats, farm tractors, or the like, which provides for a security interest to be indicated on the certificate as a condition or result of perfection, and any non-Uniform Commercial Code central filing statute]; or

(3) a certificate-of-title statute of another jurisdiction which provides for a security interest to be indicated on the certificate as a condition or result of the security interest's obtaining priority over the rights of a lien creditor with respect to the property.

(b) Compliance with the requirements of a statute, regulation, or treaty described in subsection (a) for obtaining priority over the rights of a lien creditor is equivalent to the filing of a financing statement under this article. Except as otherwise provided in subsection (d) and Sections 9–313 and 9–316(d) and (e) for goods covered by a certificate of title, a security interest in property subject to a statute, regulation, or treaty described in subsection (a) may be perfected only by compliance with those requirements, and a security interest so perfected remains perfected notwithstanding a change in the use or transfer of possession of the collateral.

(c) Except as otherwise provided in subsection (d) and Section 9–316(d) and (e), duration and renewal of perfection of a security interest perfected by compliance with the requirements prescribed by a statute, regulation, or treaty described in subsection (a) are governed by the statute, regulation, or treaty. In other respects, the security interest is subject to this article.

(d) During any period in which collateral subject to a statute specified in subsection (a)(2) is inventory held for sale or lease by a person or leased by that person as lessor and that person is in the business of selling goods of that kind, this section does not apply to a security interest in that collateral created by that person.

Legislative Note: *This Article contemplates that perfection of a security interest in goods covered by a certificate of title occurs upon receipt by appropriate State officials of a properly tendered application for a certificate of title on which the security interest is to be indicated, without a relation back to an earlier time. States whose certificate-of-title statutes provide for perfection at a different time or contain a relation-back provision should amend the statutes accordingly.*

§ 9–312. Perfection of Security Interests in Chattel Paper, Deposit Accounts, Documents, Goods Covered by Documents, Instruments, Investment Property, Letter-of-Credit Rights, and Money; Perfection by Permissive Filing; Temporary Perfection without Filing or Transfer of Possession.

(a) A security interest in chattel paper, negotiable documents, instruments, or investment property may be perfected by filing.

(b) Except as otherwise provided in Section 9–315(c) and (d) for proceeds:

(1) a security interest in a deposit account may be perfected only by control under Section 9–314;

(2) and except as otherwise provided in Section 9–308(d), a security interest in a letter-of-credit right may be perfected only by control under Section 9–314; and

(3) a security interest in money may be perfected only by the secured party's taking possession under Section 9–313.

(c) While goods are in the possession of a bailee that has issued a negotiable document covering the goods:

(1) a security interest in the goods may be perfected by perfecting a security interest in the document; and

(2) a security interest perfected in the document has priority over any security interest that becomes perfected in the goods by another method during that time.

(d) While goods are in the possession of a bailee that has issued a nonnegotiable document covering the goods, a security interest in the goods may be perfected by:

(1) issuance of a document in the name of the secured party;

(2) the bailee's receipt of notification of the secured party's interest; or

(3) filing as to the goods.

(e) A security interest in certificated securities, negotiable documents, or instruments is perfected without filing or the taking of possession for a period of 20 days from the time it attaches to the extent that it arises for new value given under an authenticated security agreement.

(f) A perfected security interest in a negotiable document or goods in possession of a bailee, other than one that has issued a negotiable document for the goods, remains perfected for 20 days without filing if the secured party makes available to the debtor the goods or documents representing the goods for the purpose of:

(1) ultimate sale or exchange; or

(2) loading, unloading, storing, shipping, transshipping, manufacturing, processing, or otherwise dealing with them in a manner preliminary to their sale or exchange.

(g) A perfected security interest in a certificated security or instrument remains perfected for 20 days without filing if the secured party delivers the security certificate or instrument to the debtor for the purpose of:

(1) ultimate sale or exchange; or

(2) presentation, collection, enforcement, renewal, or registration of transfer.

(h) After the 20-day period specified in subsection (e), (f), or (g) expires, perfection depends upon compliance with this article.

§ 9–313. When Possession by or Delivery to Secured Party Perfects Security Interest without Filing.

(a) Except as otherwise provided in subsection (b), a secured party may perfect a security interest in negotiable documents, goods, instruments, money, or tangible chattel paper by taking possession of the collateral. A secured party may perfect a security interest in certificated securities by taking delivery of the certificated securities under Section 8–301.

(b) With respect to goods covered by a certificate of title issued by this State, a secured party may perfect a security interest in the goods by taking possession of the goods only in the circumstances described in Section 9–316(d).

(c) With respect to collateral other than certificated securities and goods covered by a document, a secured party takes possession of collateral in the possession of a person other than the debtor, the secured party, or a lessee of the collateral from the debtor in the ordinary course of the debtor's business, when:

(1) the person in possession authenticates a record acknowledging that it holds possession of the collateral for the secured party's benefit; or

(2) the person takes possession of the collateral after having authenticated a record acknowledging that it will hold possession of collateral for the secured party's benefit.

(d) If perfection of a security interest depends upon possession of the collateral by a secured party, perfection occurs no earlier than the time the secured party takes possession and continues only while the secured party retains possession.

(e) A security interest in a certificated security in registered form is perfected by delivery when delivery of the certificated security occurs under Section 8–301 and remains perfected by delivery until the debtor obtains possession of the security certificate.

(f) A person in possession of collateral is not required to acknowledge that it holds possession for a secured party's benefit.

(g) If a person acknowledges that it holds possession for the secured party's benefit:

(1) the acknowledgment is effective under subsection (c) or Section 8–301(a), even if the acknowledgment violates the rights of a debtor; and

(2) unless the person otherwise agrees or law other than this article otherwise provides, the person does not owe any duty to the secured party and is not required to confirm the acknowledgment to another person.

(h) A secured party having possession of collateral does not relinquish possession by delivering the collateral to a person other than the debtor or a lessee of the collateral from the debtor in the ordinary course of the debtor's business if the person was instructed before the delivery or is instructed contemporaneously with the delivery:

(1) to hold possession of the collateral for the secured party's benefit; or

(2) to redeliver the collateral to the secured party.

(i) A secured party does not relinquish possession, even if a delivery under subsection (h) violates the rights of a debtor. A person to which collateral is delivered under subsection (h) does not owe any duty to the secured party and is not required to confirm the delivery to another person unless the person otherwise agrees or law other than this article otherwise provides.

§ 9–314. Perfection by Control.

(a) A security interest in investment property, deposit accounts, letter-of-credit rights, or electronic chattel paper may be perfected by control of the collateral under Section 9–104, 9–105, 9–106, or 9–107.

(b) A security interest in deposit accounts, electronic chattel paper, or letter-of-credit rights is perfected by control under Section 9–104, 9–105, or 9–107 when the secured party obtains control and remains perfected by control only while the secured party retains control.

(c) A security interest in investment property is perfected by control under Section 9–106 from the time the secured party obtains control and remains perfected by control until:

    (1) the secured party does not have control; and

    (2) one of the following occurs:

        (A) if the collateral is a certificated security, the debtor has or acquires possession of the security certificate;

        (B) if the collateral is an uncertificated security, the issuer has registered or registers the debtor as the registered owner; or

        (C) if the collateral is a security entitlement, the debtor is or becomes the entitlement holder.

§ 9–315. Secured Party's Rights on Disposition of Collateral and in Proceeds.

(a) Except as otherwise provided in this article and in Section 2–403(2):

    (1) a security interest or agricultural lien continues in collateral notwithstanding sale, lease, license, exchange, or other disposition thereof unless the secured party authorized the disposition free of the security interest or agricultural lien; and

    (2) a security interest attaches to any identifiable proceeds of collateral.

(b) Proceeds that are commingled with other property are identifiable proceeds:

    (1) if the proceeds are goods, to the extent provided by Section 9–336; and

    (2) if the proceeds are not goods, to the extent that the secured party identifies the proceeds by a method of tracing, including application of equitable principles, that is permitted under law other than this article with respect to commingled property of the type involved.

(c) A security interest in proceeds is a perfected security interest if the security interest in the original collateral was perfected.

(d) A perfected security interest in proceeds becomes unperfected on the 21st day after the security interest attaches to the proceeds unless:

    (1) the following conditions are satisfied:

        (A) a filed financing statement covers the original collateral;

        (B) the proceeds are collateral in which a security interest may be perfected by filing in the office in which the financing statement has been filed; and

        (C) the proceeds are not acquired with cash proceeds;

    (2) the proceeds are identifiable cash proceeds; or

    (3) the security interest in the proceeds is perfected other than under subsection (c) when the security interest attaches to the proceeds or within 20 days thereafter.

(e) If a filed financing statement covers the original collateral, a security interest in proceeds which remains perfected under subsection (d)(1) becomes unperfected at the later of:

    (1) when the effectiveness of the filed financing statement lapses under Section 9–515 or is terminated under Section 9–513; or

    (2) the 21st day after the security interest attaches to the proceeds.

§ 9–316. Continued Perfection of Security Interest Following Change in Governing Law.

(a) A security interest perfected pursuant to the law of the jurisdiction designated in Section 9–301(1) or 9–305(c) remains perfected until the earliest of:

    (1) the time perfection would have ceased under the law of that jurisdiction;

    (2) the expiration of four months after a change of the debtor's location to another jurisdiction; or

    (3) the expiration of one year after a transfer of collateral to a person that thereby becomes a debtor and is located in another jurisdiction.

(b) If a security interest described in subsection (a) becomes perfected under the law of the other jurisdiction before the earliest time or event described in that subsection, it remains perfected thereafter. If the security interest does not become perfected under the law of the other jurisdiction before the earliest time or event, it becomes unperfected and is deemed never to have been perfected as against a purchaser of the collateral for value.

(c) A possessory security interest in collateral, other than goods covered by a certificate of title and as-extracted collateral consisting of goods, remains continuously perfected if:

    (1) the collateral is located in one jurisdiction and subject to a security interest perfected under the law of that jurisdiction;

    (2) thereafter the collateral is brought into another jurisdiction; and

    (3) upon entry into the other jurisdiction, the security interest is perfected under the law of the other jurisdiction.

(d) Except as otherwise provided in subsection (e), a security interest in goods covered by a certificate of title which is perfected by any method under the law of another jurisdiction when the goods become covered by a certificate of title from this State remains perfected until the security interest would have become unperfected under the law of the other jurisdiction had the goods not become so covered.

(e) A security interest described in subsection (d) becomes unperfected as against a purchaser of the goods for value and is deemed never to have been perfected as against a purchaser of the goods for value if the applicable requirements for perfection under Section 9–311(b) or 9–313 are not satisfied before the earlier of:

    (1) the time the security interest would have become unperfected under the law of the other jurisdiction had the goods not become covered by a certificate of title from this State; or

(2) the expiration of four months after the goods had become so covered.

(f) A security interest in deposit accounts, letter-of-credit rights, or investment property which is perfected under the law of the bank's jurisdiction, the issuer's jurisdiction, a nominated person's jurisdiction, the securities intermediary's jurisdiction, or the commodity intermediary's jurisdiction, as applicable, remains perfected until the earlier of:

(1) the time the security interest would have become unperfected under the law of that jurisdiction; or

(2) the expiration of four months after a change of the applicable jurisdiction to another jurisdiction.

(g) If a security interest described in subsection (f) becomes perfected under the law of the other jurisdiction before the earlier of the time or the end of the period described in that subsection, it remains perfected thereafter. If the security interest does not become perfected under the law of the other jurisdiction before the earlier of that time or the end of that period, it becomes unperfected and is deemed never to have been perfected as against a purchaser of the collateral for value.

[Subpart 3. Priority]

§ 9–317. Interests That Take Priority over or Take Free of Security Interest or Agricultural Lien.

(a) A security interest or agricultural lien is subordinate to the rights of:

(1) a person entitled to priority under Section 9–322; and

(2) except as otherwise provided in subsection (e), a person that becomes a lien creditor before the earlier of the time:

(A) the security interest or agricultural lien is perfected; or

(B) one of the conditions specified in Section 9–203(b)(3) is met and a financing statement covering the collateral is filed.

(b) Except as otherwise provided in subsection (e), a buyer, other than a secured party, of tangible chattel paper, documents, goods, instruments, or a security certificate takes free of a security interest or agricultural lien if the buyer gives value and receives delivery of the collateral without knowledge of the security interest or agricultural lien and before it is perfected.

(c) Except as otherwise provided in subsection (e), a lessee of goods takes free of a security interest or agricultural lien if the lessee gives value and receives delivery of the collateral without knowledge of the security interest or agricultural lien and before it is perfected.

(d) A licensee of a general intangible or a buyer, other than a secured party, of accounts, electronic chattel paper, general intangibles, or investment property other than a certificated security takes free of a security interest if the licensee or buyer gives value without knowledge of the security interest and before it is perfected.

(e) Except as otherwise provided in Sections 9–320 and 9–321, if a person files a financing statement with respect to a purchase-money security interest before or within 20 days after the debtor receives delivery of the collateral, the security interest takes priority over the rights of a buyer, lessee, or lien creditor which arise between the time the security interest attaches and the time of filing.

As amended in 2000.

§ 9–318. No Interest Retained in Right to Payment That Is Sold; Rights and Title of Seller of Account or Chattel Paper with Respect to Creditors and Purchasers.

(a) A debtor that has sold an account, chattel paper, payment intangible, or promissory note does not retain a legal or equitable interest in the collateral sold.

(b) For purposes of determining the rights of creditors of, and purchasers for value of an account or chattel paper from, a debtor that has sold an account or chattel paper, while the buyer's security interest is unperfected, the debtor is deemed to have rights and title to the account or chattel paper identical to those the debtor sold.

§ 9–319. Rights and Title of Consignee with Respect to Creditors and Purchasers.

(a) Except as otherwise provided in subsection (b), for purposes of determining the rights of creditors of, and purchasers for value of goods from, a consignee, while the goods are in the possession of the consignee, the consignee is deemed to have rights and title to the goods identical to those the consignor had or had power to transfer.

(b) For purposes of determining the rights of a creditor of a consignee, law other than this article determines the rights and title of a consignee while goods are in the consignee's possession if, under this part, a perfected security interest held by the consignor would have priority over the rights of the creditor.

§ 9–320. Buyer of Goods.

(a) Except as otherwise provided in subsection (e), a buyer in ordinary course of business, other than a person buying farm products from a person engaged in farming operations, takes free of a security interest created by the buyer's seller, even if the security interest is perfected and the buyer knows of its existence.

(b) Except as otherwise provided in subsection (e), a buyer of goods from a person who used or bought the goods for use primarily for personal, family, or household purposes takes free of a security interest, even if perfected, if the buyer buys:

(1) without knowledge of the security interest;

(2) for value;

(3) primarily for the buyer's personal, family, or household purposes; and

(4) before the filing of a financing statement covering the goods.

(c) To the extent that it affects the priority of a security interest over a buyer of goods under subsection (b), the period of effectiveness of a filing made in the jurisdiction in which the seller is located is governed by Section 9–316(a) and (b).

(d) A buyer in ordinary course of business buying oil, gas, or other minerals at the wellhead or minehead or after extraction takes free of an interest arising out of an encumbrance.

(e) Subsections (a) and (b) do not affect a security interest in goods in the possession of the secured party under Section 9–313.

§ 9–321. Licensee of General Intangible and Lessee of Goods in Ordinary Course of Business.

(a) In this section, "licensee in ordinary course of business" means a person that becomes a licensee of a general intangible in good faith, without knowledge that the license violates the rights of another person in the general intangible, and in the ordinary course from a person in the business of licensing general intangibles of that kind. A person becomes a licensee in the ordinary course if the license to the person comports with the usual or customary practices in the kind of business in which the licensor is engaged or with the licensor's own usual or customary practices.

(b) A licensee in ordinary course of business takes its rights under a nonexclusive license free of a security interest in the general intangible created by the licensor, even if the security interest is perfected and the licensee knows of its existence.

(c) A lessee in ordinary course of business takes its leasehold interest free of a security interest in the goods created by the lessor, even if the security interest is perfected and the lessee knows of its existence.

§ 9–322. Priorities among Conflicting Security Interests in and Agricultural Liens on Same Collateral.

(a) Except as otherwise provided in this section, priority among conflicting security interests and agricultural liens in the same collateral is determined according to the following rules:

(1) Conflicting perfected security interests and agricultural liens rank according to priority in time of filing or perfection. Priority dates from the earlier of the time a filing covering the collateral is first made or the security interest or agricultural lien is first perfected, if there is no period thereafter when there is neither filing nor perfection.

(2) A perfected security interest or agricultural lien has priority over a conflicting unperfected security interest or agricultural lien.

(3) The first security interest or agricultural lien to attach or become effective has priority if conflicting security interests and agricultural liens are unperfected.

(b) For the purposes of subsection (a)(1):

(1) the time of filing or perfection as to a security interest in collateral is also the time of filing or perfection as to a security interest in proceeds; and

(2) the time of filing or perfection as to a security interest in collateral supported by a supporting obligation is also the time of filing or perfection as to a security interest in the supporting obligation.

(c) Except as otherwise provided in subsection (f), a security interest in collateral which qualifies for priority over a conflicting security interest under Section 9–327, 9–328, 9–329, 9–330, or 9–331 also has priority over a conflicting security interest in:

(1) any supporting obligation for the collateral; and

(2) proceeds of the collateral if:

(A) the security interest in proceeds is perfected;

(B) the proceeds are cash proceeds or of the same type as the collateral; and

(C) in the case of proceeds that are proceeds of proceeds, all intervening proceeds are cash proceeds, proceeds of the same type as the collateral, or an account relating to the collateral.

(d) Subject to subsection (e) and except as otherwise provided in subsection (f), if a security interest in chattel paper, deposit accounts, negotiable documents, instruments, investment property, or letter-of-credit rights is perfected by a method other than filing, conflicting perfected security interests in proceeds of the collateral rank according to priority in time of filing.

(e) Subsection (d) applies only if the proceeds of the collateral are not cash proceeds, chattel paper, negotiable documents, instruments, investment property, or letter-of-credit rights.

(f) Subsections (a) through (e) are subject to:

(1) subsection (g) and the other provisions of this part;

(2) Section 4–210 with respect to a security interest of a collecting bank;

(3) Section 5–118 with respect to a security interest of an issuer or nominated person; and

(4) Section 9–110 with respect to a security interest arising under Article 2 or 2A.

(g) A perfected agricultural lien on collateral has priority over a conflicting security interest in or agricultural lien on the same collateral if the statute creating the agricultural lien so provides.

§ 9–323. Future Advances.

(a) Except as otherwise provided in subsection (c), for purposes of determining the priority of a perfected security interest under Section 9–322(a)(1), perfection of the security interest dates from the time an advance is made to the extent that the security interest secures an advance that:

(1) is made while the security interest is perfected only:

(A) under Section 9–309 when it attaches; or

(B) temporarily under Section 9–312(e), (f), or (g); and

(2) is not made pursuant to a commitment entered into before or while the security interest is perfected by a method other than under Section 9–309 or 9–312(e), (f), or (g).

(b) Except as otherwise provided in subsection (c), a security interest is subordinate to the rights of a person that becomes a lien creditor to the extent that the security interest secures an advance made more than 45 days after the person becomes a lien creditor unless the advance is made:

(1) without knowledge of the lien; or

(2) pursuant to a commitment entered into without knowledge of the lien.

(c) Subsections (a) and (b) do not apply to a security interest held by a secured party that is a buyer of accounts, chattel paper, payment intangibles, or promissory notes or a consignor.

(d) Except as otherwise provided in subsection (e), a buyer of goods other than a buyer in ordinary course of business takes free of a security interest to the extent that it secures advances made after the earlier of:

(1) the time the secured party acquires knowledge of the buyer's purchase; or

(2) 45 days after the purchase.

(e) Subsection (d) does not apply if the advance is made pursuant to a commitment entered into without knowledge of the buyer's purchase and before the expiration of the 45-day period.

(f) Except as otherwise provided in subsection (g), a lessee of goods, other than a lessee in ordinary course of business, takes the leasehold interest free of a security interest to the extent that it secures advances made after the earlier of:

(1) the time the secured party acquires knowledge of the lease; or

(2) 45 days after the lease contract becomes enforceable.

(g) Subsection (f) does not apply if the advance is made pursuant to a commitment entered into without knowledge of the lease and before the expiration of the 45-day period.

As amended in 1999.

§ 9–324. Priority of Purchase-Money Security Interests.

(a) Except as otherwise provided in subsection (g), a perfected purchase-money security interest in goods other than inventory or livestock has priority over a conflicting security interest in the same goods, and, except as otherwise provided in Section 9–327, a perfected security interest in its identifiable proceeds also has priority, if the purchase-money security interest is perfected when the debtor receives possession of the collateral or within 20 days thereafter.

(b) Subject to subsection (c) and except as otherwise provided in subsection (g), a perfected purchase-money security interest in inventory has priority over a conflicting security interest in the same inventory, has priority over a conflicting security interest in chattel paper or an instrument constituting proceeds of the inventory and in proceeds of the chattel paper, if so provided in Section 9–330, and, except as otherwise provided in Section 9–327, also has priority in identifiable cash proceeds of the inventory to the extent the identifiable cash proceeds are received on or before the delivery of the inventory to a buyer, if:

(1) the purchase-money security interest is perfected when the debtor receives possession of the inventory;

(2) the purchase-money secured party sends an authenticated notification to the holder of the conflicting security interest;

(3) the holder of the conflicting security interest receives the notification within five years before the debtor receives possession of the inventory; and

(4) the notification states that the person sending the notification has or expects to acquire a purchase-money security interest in inventory of the debtor and describes the inventory.

(c) Subsections (b)(2) through (4) apply only if the holder of the conflicting security interest had filed a financing statement covering the same types of inventory:

(1) if the purchase-money security interest is perfected by filing, before the date of the filing; or

(2) if the purchase-money security interest is temporarily perfected without filing or possession under Section 9–312(f), before the beginning of the 20-day period thereunder.

(d) Subject to subsection (e) and except as otherwise provided in subsection (g), a perfected purchase-money security interest in livestock that are farm products has priority over a conflicting security interest in the same livestock, and, except as otherwise provided in Section 9–327, a perfected security interest in their identifiable proceeds and identifiable products in their unmanufactured states also has priority, if:

(1) the purchase-money security interest is perfected when the debtor receives possession of the livestock;

(2) the purchase-money secured party sends an authenticated notification to the holder of the conflicting security interest;

(3) the holder of the conflicting security interest receives the notification within six months before the debtor receives possession of the livestock; and

(4) the notification states that the person sending the notification has or expects to acquire a purchase-money security interest in livestock of the debtor and describes the livestock.

(e) Subsections (d)(2) through (4) apply only if the holder of the conflicting security interest had filed a financing statement covering the same types of livestock:

(1) if the purchase-money security interest is perfected by filing, before the date of the filing; or

(2) if the purchase-money security interest is temporarily perfected without filing or possession under Section 9–312(f), before the beginning of the 20-day period thereunder.

(f) Except as otherwise provided in subsection (g), a perfected purchase-money security interest in software has priority over a conflicting security interest in the same collateral, and, except as otherwise provided in Section 9–327, a perfected security interest in its identifiable proceeds also has priority, to the extent that the purchase-money security interest in the goods in which the software was acquired for use has priority in the goods and proceeds of the goods under this section.

(g) If more than one security interest qualifies for priority in the same collateral under subsection (a), (b), (d), or (f):

(1) a security interest securing an obligation incurred as all or part of the price of the collateral has priority over a security interest securing an obligation incurred for value given to enable the debtor to acquire rights in or the use of collateral; and

(2) in all other cases, Section 9–322(a) applies to the qualifying security interests.

§ 9–325. Priority of Security Interests in Transferred Collateral.

(a) Except as otherwise provided in subsection (b), a security interest created by a debtor is subordinate to a security interest in the same collateral created by another person if:

(1) the debtor acquired the collateral subject to the security interest created by the other person;

(2) the security interest created by the other person was perfected when the debtor acquired the collateral; and

(3) there is no period thereafter when the security interest is unperfected.

(b) Subsection (a) subordinates a security interest only if the security interest:

(1) otherwise would have priority solely under Section 9–322(a) or 9–324; or

(2) arose solely under Section 2–711(3) or 2A–508(5).

§ 9–326. Priority of Security Interests Created by New Debtor.

(a) Subject to subsection (b), a security interest created by a new debtor which is perfected by a filed financing statement that is effective solely under Section 9–508 in collateral in which a new debtor has or acquires rights is subordinate to a security interest in the same collateral which is perfected other than by a filed financing statement that is effective solely under Section 9–508.

(b) The other provisions of this part determine the priority among conflicting security interests in the same collateral perfected by filed financing statements that are effective solely under Section 9–508. However, if the security agreements to which a new debtor became bound as debtor were not entered into by the same original debtor, the conflicting security interests rank according to priority in time of the new debtor's having become bound.

§ 9–327. Priority of Security Interests in Deposit Account.

The following rules govern priority among conflicting security interests in the same deposit account:

(1) A security interest held by a secured party having control of the deposit account under Section 9–104 has priority over a conflicting security interest held by a secured party that does not have control.

(2) Except as otherwise provided in paragraphs (3) and (4), security interests perfected by control under Section 9–314 rank according to priority in time of obtaining control.

(3) Except as otherwise provided in paragraph (4), a security interest held by the bank with which the deposit account is maintained has priority over a conflicting security interest held by another secured party.

(4) A security interest perfected by control under Section 9–104(a)(3) has priority over a security interest held by the bank with which the deposit account is maintained.

§ 9–328. Priority of Security Interests in Investment Property.

The following rules govern priority among conflicting security interests in the same investment property:

(1) A security interest held by a secured party having control of investment property under Section 9–106 has priority over a security interest held by a secured party that does not have control of the investment property.

(2) Except as otherwise provided in paragraphs (3) and (4), conflicting security interests held by secured parties each of which has control under Section 9–106 rank according to priority in time of:

(A) if the collateral is a security, obtaining control;

(B) if the collateral is a security entitlement carried in a securities account and:

(i) if the secured party obtained control under Section 8–106(d)(1), the secured party's becoming the person for which the securities account is maintained;

(ii) if the secured party obtained control under Section 8–106(d)(2), the securities intermediary's agreement to comply with the secured party's entitlement orders with respect to security entitlements carried or to be carried in the securities account; or

(iii) if the secured party obtained control through another person under Section 8–106(d)(3), the time on which priority would be based under this paragraph if the other person were the secured party; or

(C) if the collateral is a commodity contract carried with a commodity intermediary, the satisfaction of the requirement for control specified in Section 9–106(b)(2) with respect to commodity contracts carried or to be carried with the commodity intermediary.

(3) A security interest held by a securities intermediary in a security entitlement or a securities account maintained with the securities intermediary has priority over a conflicting security interest held by another secured party.

(4) A security interest held by a commodity intermediary in a commodity contract or a commodity account maintained with the commodity intermediary has priority over a conflicting security interest held by another secured party.

(5) A security interest in a certificated security in registered form which is perfected by taking delivery under Section 9–313(a) and not by control under Section 9–314 has priority over a conflicting security interest perfected by a method other than control.

(6) Conflicting security interests created by a broker, securities intermediary, or commodity intermediary which are perfected without control under Section 9–106 rank equally.

(7) In all other cases, priority among conflicting security interests in investment property is governed by Sections 9–322 and 9–323.

§ 9–329. Priority of Security Interests in Letter-of-Credit Right.

The following rules govern priority among conflicting security interests in the same letter-of-credit right:

(1) A security interest held by a secured party having control of the letter-of-credit right under Section 9–107 has priority to the extent of its control over a conflicting security interest held by a secured party that does not have control.

(2) Security interests perfected by control under Section 9–314 rank according to priority in time of obtaining control.

§ 9–330. Priority of Purchaser of Chattel Paper or Instrument.

(a) A purchaser of chattel paper has priority over a security interest in the chattel paper which is claimed merely as proceeds of inventory subject to a security interest if:

(1) in good faith and in the ordinary course of the purchaser's business, the purchaser gives new value and takes possession of the chattel paper or obtains control of the chattel paper under Section 9–105; and

(2) the chattel paper does not indicate that it has been assigned to an identified assignee other than the purchaser.

(b) A purchaser of chattel paper has priority over a security interest in the chattel paper which is claimed other than merely as proceeds of inventory subject to a security interest if the purchaser gives new value and takes possession of the chattel paper or obtains control of the chattel paper under Section 9–105 in good faith, in the ordinary course of the purchaser's business, and without knowledge that the purchase violates the rights of the secured party.

(c) Except as otherwise provided in Section 9–327, a purchaser having priority in chattel paper under subsection (a) or (b) also has priority in proceeds of the chattel paper to the extent that:

(1) Section 9–322 provides for priority in the proceeds; or

(2) the proceeds consist of the specific goods covered by the chattel paper or cash proceeds of the specific goods, even if the purchaser's security interest in the proceeds is unperfected.

(d) Except as otherwise provided in Section 9–331(a), a purchaser of an instrument has priority over a security interest in the instrument perfected by a method other than possession if the purchaser gives value and takes possession of the instrument in good faith and without knowledge that the purchase violates the rights of the secured party.

(e) For purposes of subsections (a) and (b), the holder of a purchase-money security interest in inventory gives new value for chattel paper constituting proceeds of the inventory.

(f) For purposes of subsections (b) and (d), if chattel paper or an instrument indicates that it has been assigned to an identified secured party other than the purchaser, a purchaser of the chattel paper or instrument has knowledge that the purchase violates the rights of the secured party.

§ 9–331. Priority of Rights of Purchasers of Instruments, Documents, and Securities under Other Articles; Priority of Interests in Financial Assets and Security Entitlements under Article 8.

(a) This article does not limit the rights of a holder in due course of a negotiable instrument, a holder to which a negotiable document of title has been duly negotiated, or a protected purchaser of a security. These holders or purchasers take priority over an earlier security interest, even if perfected, to the extent provided in Articles 3, 7, and 8.

(b) This article does not limit the rights of or impose liability on a person to the extent that the person is protected against the assertion of a claim under Article 8.

(c) Filing under this article does not constitute notice of a claim or defense to the holders, or purchasers, or persons described in subsections (a) and (b).

§ 9–332. Transfer of Money; Transfer of Funds from Deposit Account.

(a) A transferee of money takes the money free of a security interest unless the transferee acts in collusion with the debtor in violating the rights of the secured party.

(b) A transferee of funds from a deposit account takes the funds free of a security interest in the deposit account unless the transferee acts in collusion with the debtor in violating the rights of the secured party.

§ 9–333. Priority of Certain Liens Arising by Operation of Law.

(a) In this section, "possessory lien" means an interest, other than a security interest or an agricultural lien:

(1) which secures payment or performance of an obligation for services or materials furnished with respect to goods by a person in the ordinary course of the person's business;

(2) which is created by statute or rule of law in favor of the person; and

(3) whose effectiveness depends on the person's possession of the goods.

(b) A possessory lien on goods has priority over a security interest in the goods unless the lien is created by a statute that expressly provides otherwise.

§ 9–334. Priority of Security Interests in Fixtures and Crops.

(a) A security interest under this article may be created in goods that are fixtures or may continue in goods that become fixtures. A security interest does not exist under this article in ordinary building materials incorporated into an improvement on land.

(b) This article does not prevent creation of an encumbrance upon fixtures under real property law.

(c) In cases not governed by subsections (d) through (h), a security interest in fixtures is subordinate to a conflicting interest of an encumbrancer or owner of the related real property other than the debtor.

(d) Except as otherwise provided in subsection (h), a perfected security interest in fixtures has priority over a conflicting interest of an encumbrancer or owner of the real property if the debtor has an interest of record in or is in possession of the real property and:

(1) the security interest is a purchase-money security interest;

(2) the interest of the encumbrancer or owner arises before the goods become fixtures; and

(3) the security interest is perfected by a fixture filing before the goods become fixtures or within 20 days thereafter.

(e) A perfected security interest in fixtures has priority over a conflicting interest of an encumbrancer or owner of the real property if:

(1) the debtor has an interest of record in the real property or is in possession of the real property and the security interest:

(A) is perfected by a fixture filing before the interest of the encumbrancer or owner is of record; and

(B) has priority over any conflicting interest of a predecessor in title of the encumbrancer or owner;

(2) before the goods become fixtures, the security interest is perfected by any method permitted by this article and the fixtures are readily removable:

(A) factory or office machines;

(B) equipment that is not primarily used or leased for use in the operation of the real property; or

(C) replacements of domestic appliances that are consumer goods;

(3) the conflicting interest is a lien on the real property obtained by legal or equitable proceedings after the security interest was perfected by any method permitted by this article; or

(4) the security interest is:

(A) created in a manufactured home in a manufactured-home transaction; and

(B) perfected pursuant to a statute described in Section 9–311(a)(2).

(f) A security interest in fixtures, whether or not perfected, has priority over a conflicting interest of an encumbrancer or owner of the real property if:

(1) the encumbrancer or owner has, in an authenticated record, consented to the security interest or disclaimed an interest in the goods as fixtures; or

(2) the debtor has a right to remove the goods as against the encumbrancer or owner.

(g) The priority of the security interest under paragraph (f)(2) continues for a reasonable time if the debtor's right to remove the goods as against the encumbrancer or owner terminates.

(h) A mortgage is a construction mortgage to the extent that it secures an obligation incurred for the construction of an improvement on land, including the acquisition cost of the land, if a recorded record of the mortgage so indicates. Except as otherwise provided in subsections (e) and (f), a security interest in fixtures is subordinate to a construction mortgage if a record of the mortgage is recorded before the goods become fixtures and the goods become fixtures before the completion of the construction. A mortgage has this priority to the same extent as a construction mortgage to the extent that it is given to refinance a construction mortgage.

(i) A perfected security interest in crops growing on real property has priority over a conflicting interest of an encumbrancer or owner of the real property if the debtor has an interest of record in or is in possession of the real property.

(j) Subsection (i) prevails over any inconsistent provisions of the following statutes:

[List here any statutes containing provisions inconsistent with subsection (i).]

Legislative Note: *States that amend statutes to remove provisions inconsistent with subsection (i) need not enact subsection (j).*

§ 9–335. Accessions.

(a) A security interest may be created in an accession and continues in collateral that becomes an accession.

(b) If a security interest is perfected when the collateral becomes an accession, the security interest remains perfected in the collateral.

(c) Except as otherwise provided in subsection (d), the other provisions of this part determine the priority of a security interest in an accession.

(d) A security interest in an accession is subordinate to a security interest in the whole which is perfected by compliance with the requirements of a certificate-of-title statute under Section 9–311(b).

(e) After default, subject to Part 6, a secured party may remove an accession from other goods if the security interest in the accession has priority over the claims of every person having an interest in the whole.

(f) A secured party that removes an accession from other goods under subsection (e) shall promptly reimburse any holder of a security interest or other lien on, or owner of, the whole or of the other goods, other than the debtor, for the cost of repair of any physical injury to the whole or the other goods. The secured party need not reimburse the holder or owner for any diminution in value of the whole or the other goods caused by the absence of the accession removed or by any necessity for replacing it. A person entitled to reimbursement may refuse permission to remove until the secured party gives adequate assurance for the performance of the obligation to reimburse.

§ 9–336. Commingled Goods.

(a) In this section, "commingled goods" means goods that are physically united with other goods in such a manner that their identity is lost in a product or mass.

(b) A security interest does not exist in commingled goods as such. However, a security interest may attach to a product or mass that results when goods become commingled goods.

(c) If collateral becomes commingled goods, a security interest attaches to the product or mass.

(d) If a security interest in collateral is perfected before the collateral becomes commingled goods, the security interest that attaches to the product or mass under subsection (c) is perfected.

(e) Except as otherwise provided in subsection (f), the other provisions of this part determine the priority of a security interest that attaches to the product or mass under subsection (c).

(f) If more than one security interest attaches to the product or mass under subsection (c), the following rules determine priority:

(1) A security interest that is perfected under subsection (d) has priority over a security interest that is unperfected at the time the collateral becomes commingled goods.

(2) If more than one security interest is perfected under subsection (d), the security interests rank equally in proportion to the value of the collateral at the time it became commingled goods.

§ 9–337. Priority of Security Interests in Goods Covered by Certificate of Title.

If, while a security interest in goods is perfected by any method under the law of another jurisdiction, this State issues a certificate of title that does not show that the goods are subject to the security interest or contain a statement that they may be subject to security interests not shown on the certificate:

(1) a buyer of the goods, other than a person in the business of selling goods of that kind, takes free of the security interest if the buyer gives value and receives delivery of the goods after issuance of the certificate and without knowledge of the security interest; and

(2) the security interest is subordinate to a conflicting security interest in the goods that attaches, and is perfected under Section 9–311(b), after issuance of the certificate and without the conflicting secured party's knowledge of the security interest.

§ 9–338. Priority of Security Interest or Agricultural Lien Perfected by Filed Financing Statement Providing Certain Incorrect Information.

If a security interest or agricultural lien is perfected by a filed financing statement providing information described in Section 9–516(b)(5) which is incorrect at the time the financing statement is filed:

(1) the security interest or agricultural lien is subordinate to a conflicting perfected security interest in the collateral to the extent that the holder of the conflicting security interest gives value in reasonable reliance upon the incorrect information; and

(2) a purchaser, other than a secured party, of the collateral takes free of the security interest or agricultural lien to the extent that, in reasonable reliance upon the incorrect information, the purchaser gives value and, in the case of chattel paper, documents, goods, instruments, or a security certificate, receives delivery of the collateral.

§ 9–339. Priority Subject to Subordination.

This article does not preclude subordination by agreement by a person entitled to priority.

[Subpart 4. Rights of Bank]

§ 9–340. Effectiveness of Right of Recoupment or Set-Off against Deposit Account.

(a) Except as otherwise provided in subsection (c), a bank with which a deposit account is maintained may exercise any right of recoupment or set-off against a secured party that holds a security interest in the deposit account.

(b) Except as otherwise provided in subsection (c), the application of this article to a security interest in a deposit account does not affect a right of recoupment or set-off of the secured party as to a deposit account maintained with the secured party.

(c) The exercise by a bank of a set-off against a deposit account is ineffective against a secured party that holds a security interest in the deposit account which is perfected by control under Section 9–104(a)(3), if the set-off is based on a claim against the debtor.

§ 9–341. Bank's Rights and Duties with Respect to Deposit Account.

Except as otherwise provided in Section 9–340(c), and unless the bank otherwise agrees in an authenticated record, a bank's rights and duties with respect to a deposit account maintained with the bank are not terminated, suspended, or modified by:

(1) the creation, attachment, or perfection of a security interest in the deposit account;

(2) the bank's knowledge of the security interest; or

(3) the bank's receipt of instructions from the secured party.

§ 9–342. Bank's Right to Refuse to Enter into or Disclose Existence of Control Agreement.

This article does not require a bank to enter into an agreement of the kind described in Section 9–104(a)(2), even if its customer so requests or directs. A bank that has entered into such an agreement is not required to confirm the existence of the agreement to another person unless requested to do so by its customer.

Part 4—Rights of Third Parties

§ 9–401. Alienability of Debtor's Rights.

(a) Except as otherwise provided in subsection (b) and Sections 9–406, 9–407, 9–408, and 9–409, whether a debtor's rights in collateral may be voluntarily or involuntarily transferred is governed by law other than this article.

(b) An agreement between the debtor and secured party which prohibits a transfer of the debtor's rights in collateral or makes

the transfer a default does not prevent the transfer from taking effect.

§ 9–402. Secured Party Not Obligated on Contract of Debtor or in Tort.

The existence of a security interest, agricultural lien, or authority given to a debtor to dispose of or use collateral, without more, does not subject a secured party to liability in contract or tort for the debtor's acts or omissions.

§ 9–403. Agreement Not to Assert Defenses against Assignee.

(a) In this section, "value" has the meaning provided in Section 3–303(a).

(b) Except as otherwise provided in this section, an agreement between an account debtor and an assignor not to assert against an assignee any claim or defense that the account debtor may have against the assignor is enforceable by an assignee that takes an assignment:

(1) for value;

(2) in good faith;

(3) without notice of a claim of a property or possessory right to the property assigned; and

(4) without notice of a defense or claim in recoupment of the type that may be asserted against a person entitled to enforce a negotiable instrument under Section 3–305(a).

(c) Subsection (b) does not apply to defenses of a type that may be asserted against a holder in due course of a negotiable instrument under Section 3–305(b).

(d) In a consumer transaction, if a record evidences the account debtor's obligation, law other than this article requires that the record include a statement to the effect that the rights of an assignee are subject to claims or defenses that the account debtor could assert against the original obligee, and the record does not include such a statement:

(1) the record has the same effect as if the record included such a statement; and

(2) the account debtor may assert against an assignee those claims and defenses that would have been available if the record included such a statement.

(e) This section is subject to law other than this article which establishes a different rule for an account debtor who is an individual and who incurred the obligation primarily for personal, family, or household purposes.

(f) Except as otherwise provided in subsection (d), this section does not displace law other than this article which gives effect to an agreement by an account debtor not to assert a claim or defense against an assignee.

§ 9–404. Rights Acquired by Assignee; Claims and Defenses against Assignee.

(a) Unless an account debtor has made an enforceable agreement not to assert defenses or claims, and subject to subsections (b) through (e), the rights of an assignee are subject to:

(1) all terms of the agreement between the account debtor and assignor and any defense or claim in recoupment arising from the transaction that gave rise to the contract; and

(2) any other defense or claim of the account debtor against the assignor which accrues before the account debtor receives a notification of the assignment authenticated by the assignor or the assignee.

(b) Subject to subsection (c) and except as otherwise provided in subsection (d), the claim of an account debtor against an assignor may be asserted against an assignee under subsection (a) only to reduce the amount the account debtor owes.

(c) This section is subject to law other than this article which establishes a different rule for an account debtor who is an individual and who incurred the obligation primarily for personal, family, or household purposes.

(d) In a consumer transaction, if a record evidences the account debtor's obligation, law other than this article requires that the record include a statement to the effect that the account debtor's recovery against an assignee with respect to claims and defenses against the assignor may not exceed amounts paid by the account debtor under the record, and the record does not include such a statement, the extent to which a claim of an account debtor against the assignor may be asserted against an assignee is determined as if the record included such a statement.

(e) This section does not apply to an assignment of a health-care-insurance receivable.

§ 9–405. Modification of Assigned Contract.

(a) A modification of or substitution for an assigned contract is effective against an assignee if made in good faith. The assignee acquires corresponding rights under the modified or substituted contract. The assignment may provide that the modification or substitution is a breach of contract by the assignor. This subsection is subject to subsections (b) through (d).

(b) Subsection (a) applies to the extent that:

(1) the right to payment or a part thereof under an assigned contract has not been fully earned by performance; or

(2) the right to payment or a part thereof has been fully earned by performance and the account debtor has not received notification of the assignment under Section 9–406(a).

(c) This section is subject to law other than this article which establishes a different rule for an account debtor who is an individual and who incurred the obligation primarily for personal, family, or household purposes.

(d) This section does not apply to an assignment of a health-care-insurance receivable.

§ 9–406. Discharge of Account Debtor; Notification of Assignment; Identification and Proof of Assignment; Restrictions on Assignment of Accounts, Chattel Paper, Payment Intangibles, and Promissory Notes Ineffective.

(a) Subject to subsections (b) through (i), an account debtor on an account, chattel paper, or a payment intangible may discharge its obligation by paying the assignor until, but not after, the account debtor receives a notification, authenticated by the assignor or the assignee, that the amount due or to become due has been assigned and that payment is to be made to the assignee. After receipt of the notification, the account debtor may discharge its obligation by paying the assignee and may not discharge the obligation by paying the assignor.

(b) Subject to subsection (h), notification is ineffective under subsection (a):

(1) if it does not reasonably identify the rights assigned;

(2) to the extent that an agreement between an account debtor and a seller of a payment intangible limits the account debtor's duty to pay a person other than the seller and the limitation is effective under law other than this article; or

(3) at the option of an account debtor, if the notification notifies the account debtor to make less than the full amount of any installment or other periodic payment to the assignee, even if:

(A) only a portion of the account, chattel paper, or payment intangible has been assigned to that assignee;

(B) a portion has been assigned to another assignee; or

(C) the account debtor knows that the assignment to that assignee is limited.

(c) Subject to subsection (h), if requested by the account debtor, an assignee shall seasonably furnish reasonable proof that the assignment has been made. Unless the assignee complies, the account debtor may discharge its obligation by paying the assignor, even if the account debtor has received a notification under subsection (a).

(d) Except as otherwise provided in subsection (e) and Sections 2A–303 and 9–407, and subject to subsection (h), a term in an agreement between an account debtor and an assignor or in a promissory note is ineffective to the extent that it:

(1) prohibits, restricts, or requires the consent of the account debtor or person obligated on the promissory note to the assignment or transfer of, or the creation, attachment, perfection, or enforcement of a security interest in, the account, chattel paper, payment intangible, or promissory note; or

(2) provides that the assignment or transfer or the creation, attachment, perfection, or enforcement of the security interest may give rise to a default, breach, right of recoupment, claim, defense, termination, right of termination, or remedy under the account, chattel paper, payment intangible, or promissory note.

(e) Subsection (d) does not apply to the sale of a payment intangible or promissory note.

(f) Except as otherwise provided in Sections 2A–303 and 9–407 and subject to subsections (h) and (i), a rule of law, statute, or regulation that prohibits, restricts, or requires the consent of a government, governmental body or official, or account debtor to the assignment or transfer of, or creation of a security interest in, an account or chattel paper is ineffective to the extent that the rule of law, statute, or regulation:

(1) prohibits, restricts, or requires the consent of the government, governmental body or official, or account debtor to the assignment or transfer of, or the creation, attachment, perfection, or enforcement of a security interest in the account or chattel paper; or

(2) provides that the assignment or transfer or the creation, attachment, perfection, or enforcement of the security interest may give rise to a default, breach, right of recoupment, claim, defense, termination, right of termination, or remedy under the account or chattel paper.

(g) Subject to subsection (h), an account debtor may not waive or vary its option under subsection (b)(3).

(h) This section is subject to law other than this article which establishes a different rule for an account debtor who is an individual and who incurred the obligation primarily for personal, family, or household purposes.

(i) This section does not apply to an assignment of a health-care-insurance receivable.

(j) This section prevails over any inconsistent provisions of the following statutes, rules, and regulations:

[List here any statutes, rules, and regulations containing provisions inconsistent with this section.]

Legislative Note: *States that amend statutes, rules, and regulations to remove provisions inconsistent with this section need not enact subsection (j).*

As amended in 1999 and 2000.

§ 9–407. Restrictions on Creation or Enforcement of Security Interest in Leasehold Interest or in Lessor's Residual Interest.

(a) Except as otherwise provided in subsection (b), a term in a lease agreement is ineffective to the extent that it:

(1) prohibits, restricts, or requires the consent of a party to the lease to the assignment or transfer of, or the creation, attachment, perfection, or enforcement of a security interest in an interest of a party under the lease contract or in the lessor's residual interest in the goods; or

(2) provides that the assignment or transfer or the creation, attachment, perfection, or enforcement of the security interest may give rise to a default, breach, right of recoupment, claim, defense, termination, right of termination, or remedy under the lease.

(b) Except as otherwise provided in Section 2A–303(7), a term described in subsection (a)(2) is effective to the extent that there is:

(1) a transfer by the lessee of the lessee's right of possession or use of the goods in violation of the term; or

(2) a delegation of a material performance of either party to the lease contract in violation of the term.

(c) The creation, attachment, perfection, or enforcement of a security interest in the lessor's interest under the lease contract or the lessor's residual interest in the goods is not a transfer that materially impairs the lessee's prospect of obtaining return performance or materially changes the duty of or materially increases the burden or risk imposed on the lessee within the purview of Section 2A–303(4) unless, and then only to the extent that, enforcement actually results in a delegation of material performance of the lessor.

As amended in 1999.

§ 9–408. Restrictions on Assignment of Promissory Notes, Health-Care-Insurance Receivables, and Certain General Intangibles Ineffective.

(a) Except as otherwise provided in subsection (b), a term in a promissory note or in an agreement between an account debtor and a debtor which relates to a health-care-insurance receivable or a general intangible, including a contract, permit, license, or franchise, and which term prohibits, restricts, or requires the consent of the person obligated on the promissory note or the account debtor to, the assignment or transfer of, or creation, attachment, or perfection of a security interest in, the promissory note, health-care-insurance receivable, or general intangible, is ineffective to the extent that the term:

(1) would impair the creation, attachment, or perfection of a security interest; or

(2) provides that the assignment or transfer or the creation, attachment, or perfection of the security interest may give rise to a default, breach, right of recoupment, claim, defense, termination, right of termination, or remedy under the promissory note, health-care-insurance receivable, or general intangible.

(b) Subsection (a) applies to a security interest in a payment intangible or promissory note only if the security interest arises out of a sale of the payment intangible or promissory note.

(c) A rule of law, statute, or regulation that prohibits, restricts, or requires the consent of a government, governmental body or official, person obligated on a promissory note, or account debtor to the assignment or transfer of, or creation of a security interest in, a promissory note, health-care-insurance receivable, or general intangible, including a contract, permit, license, or franchise between an account debtor and a debtor, is ineffective to the extent that the rule of law, statute, or regulation:

(1) would impair the creation, attachment, or perfection of a security interest; or

(2) provides that the assignment or transfer or the creation, attachment, or perfection of the security interest may give rise to a default, breach, right of recoupment, claim, defense, termination, right of termination, or remedy under the promissory note, health-care-insurance receivable, or general intangible.

(d) To the extent that a term in a promissory note or in an agreement between an account debtor and a debtor which relates to a health-care-insurance receivable or general intangible or a rule of law, statute, or regulation described in subsection (c) would be effective under law other than this article but is ineffective under subsection (a) or (c), the creation, attachment, or perfection of a security interest in the promissory note, health-care-insurance receivable, or general intangible:

(1) is not enforceable against the person obligated on the promissory note or the account debtor;

(2) does not impose a duty or obligation on the person obligated on the promissory note or the account debtor;

(3) does not require the person obligated on the promissory note or the account debtor to recognize the security interest, pay or render performance to the secured party, or accept payment or performance from the secured party;

(4) does not entitle the secured party to use or assign the debtor's rights under the promissory note, health-care-insurance receivable, or general intangible, including any related information or materials furnished to the debtor in the transaction giving rise to the promissory note, health-care-insurance receivable, or general intangible;

(5) does not entitle the secured party to use, assign, possess, or have access to any trade secrets or confidential information of the person obligated on the promissory note or the account debtor; and

(6) does not entitle the secured party to enforce the security interest in the promissory note, health-care-insurance receivable, or general intangible.

(e) This section prevails over any inconsistent provisions of the following statutes, rules, and regulations:
[List here any statutes, rules, and regulations containing provisions inconsistent with this section.]

Legislative Note: *States that amend statutes, rules, and regulations to remove provisions inconsistent with this section need not enact subsection (e).*

As amended in 1999.

§ 9–409. Restrictions on Assignment of Letter-of-Credit Rights Ineffective.

(a) A term in a letter of credit or a rule of law, statute, regulation, custom, or practice applicable to the letter of credit which prohibits, restricts, or requires the consent of an applicant, issuer, or nominated person to a beneficiary's assignment of or creation of a security interest in a letter-of-credit right is ineffective to the extent that the term or rule of law, statute, regulation, custom, or practice:

> **(1)** would impair the creation, attachment, or perfection of a security interest in the letter-of-credit right; or

> **(2)** provides that the assignment or the creation, attachment, or perfection of the security interest may give rise to a default, breach, right of recoupment, claim, defense, termination, right of termination, or remedy under the letter-of-credit right.

(b) To the extent that a term in a letter of credit is ineffective under subsection (a) but would be effective under law other than this article or a custom or practice applicable to the letter of credit, to the transfer of a right to draw or otherwise demand performance under the letter of credit, or to the assignment of a right to proceeds of the letter of credit, the creation, attachment, or perfection of a security interest in the letter-of-credit right:

> **(1)** is not enforceable against the applicant, issuer, nominated person, or transferee beneficiary;

> **(2)** imposes no duties or obligations on the applicant, issuer, nominated person, or transferee beneficiary; and

> **(3)** does not require the applicant, issuer, nominated person, or transferee beneficiary to recognize the security interest, pay or render performance to the secured party, or accept payment or other performance from the secured party.

As amended in 1999.

Part 5—Filing

[Subpart 1. Filing Office; Contents and Effectiveness of Financing Statement]

§ 9–501. Filing Office.

(a) Except as otherwise provided in subsection (b), if the local law of this State governs perfection of a security interest or agricultural lien, the office in which to file a financing statement to perfect the security interest or agricultural lien is:

> **(1)** the office designated for the filing or recording of a record of a mortgage on the related real property, if:
> > **(A)** the collateral is as-extracted collateral or timber to be cut; or
> > **(B)** the financing statement is filed as a fixture filing and the collateral is goods that are or are to become fixtures; or

> **(2)** the office of [ ] [or any office duly authorized by [ ]], in all other cases, including a case in which the collateral is goods that are or are to become fixtures and the financing statement is not filed as a fixture filing.

(b) The office in which to file a financing statement to perfect a security interest in collateral, including fixtures, of a transmitting utility is the office of [ ]. The financing statement also constitutes a fixture filing as to the collateral indicated in the financing statement which is or is to become fixtures.

Legislative Note: *The State should designate the filing office where the brackets appear. The filing office may be that of a governmental official (e.g., the Secretary of State) or a private party that maintains the State's filing system.*

§ 9–502. Contents of Financing Statement; Record of Mortgage as Financing Statement; Time of Filing Financing Statement.

(a) Subject to subsection (b), a financing statement is sufficient only if it:
(1) provides the name of the debtor;
(2) provides the name of the secured party or a representative of the secured party; and
(3) indicates the collateral covered by the financing statement.

(b) Except as otherwise provided in Section 9–501(b), to be sufficient, a financing statement that covers as-extracted collateral or timber to be cut, or which is filed as a fixture filing and covers goods that are or are to become fixtures, must satisfy subsection (a) and also:

> **(1)** indicate that it covers this type of collateral;
> **(2)** indicate that it is to be filed [for record] in the real property records;
> **(3)** provide a description of the real property to which the collateral is related [sufficient to give constructive notice of a mortgage under the law of this State if the description were contained in a record of the mortgage of the real property]; and
> **(4)** if the debtor does not have an interest of record in the real property, provide the name of a record owner.

(c) A record of a mortgage is effective, from the date of recording, as a financing statement filed as a fixture filing or as a financing statement covering as-extracted collateral or timber to be cut only if:

> **(1)** the record indicates the goods or accounts that it covers;
> **(2)** the goods are or are to become fixtures related to the real property described in the record or the collateral is related to the real property described in the record and is as-extracted collateral or timber to be cut;
> **(3)** the record satisfies the requirements for a financing statement in this section other than an indication that it is to be filed in the real property records; and
> **(4)** the record is [duly] recorded.

(d) A financing statement may be filed before a security agreement is made or a security interest otherwise attaches.

Legislative Note: Language in brackets is optional. Where the State has any sp*ecial recording system for real property other than the usual grantor-grantee index (as, for instance, a tract system or a title registration or Torrens system) local adaptations of subsection (b) and Section 9–519(d) and (e) may be necessary. See, e.g., Mass. Gen. Laws Chapter 106, Section 9–410.*

§ 9–503. Name of Debtor and Secured Party.

(a) A financing statement sufficiently provides the name of the debtor:

> **(1)** if the debtor is a registered organization, only if the financing statement provides the name of the debtor indicated on the public record of the debtor's jurisdiction of organization which shows the debtor to have been organized;
>
> **(2)** if the debtor is a decedent's estate, only if the financing statement provides the name of the decedent and indicates that the debtor is an estate;
>
> **(3)** if the debtor is a trust or a trustee acting with respect to property held in trust, only if the financing statement:
>
> > **(A)** provides the name specified for the trust in its organic documents or, if no name is specified, provides the name of the settlor and additional information sufficient to distinguish the debtor from other trusts having one or more of the same settlors; and
> >
> > **(B)** indicates, in the debtor's name or otherwise, that the debtor is a trust or is a trustee acting with respect to property held in trust; and
>
> **(4)** in other cases:
>
> > **(A)** if the debtor has a name, only if it provides the individual or organizational name of the debtor; and
> >
> > **(B)** if the debtor does not have a name, only if it provides the names of the partners, members, associates, or other persons comprising the debtor.
> >
> > **(b)** A financing statement that provides the name of the debtor in accordance with subsection (a) is not rendered ineffective by the absence of:
>
> **(1)** a trade name or other name of the debtor; or
>
> **(2)** unless required under subsection (a)(4)(B), names of partners, members, associates, or other persons comprising the debtor.

(c) A financing statement that provides only the debtor's trade name does not sufficiently provide the name of the debtor.

(d) Failure to indicate the representative capacity of a secured party or representative of a secured party does not affect the sufficiency of a financing statement.

(e) A financing statement may provide the name of more than one debtor and the name of more than one secured party.

§ 9–504. Indication of Collateral.

A financing statement sufficiently indicates the collateral that it covers if the financing statement provides:

> **(1)** a description of the collateral pursuant to Section 9–108; or
>
> **(2)** an indication that the financing statement covers all assets or all personal property.

As amended in 1999.

§ 9–505. Filing and Compliance with Other Statutes and Treaties for Consignments, Leases, Other Bailments, and Other Transactions.

(a) A consignor, lessor, or other bailor of goods, a licensor, or a buyer of a payment intangible or promissory note may file a financing statement, or may comply with a statute or treaty described in Section 9–311(a), using the terms "consignor", "consignee", "lessor", "lessee", "bailor", "bailee", "licensor", "licensee", "owner", "registered owner", "buyer", "seller", or words of similar import, instead of the terms "secured party" and "debtor".

(b) This part applies to the filing of a financing statement under subsection (a) and, as appropriate, to compliance that is equivalent to filing a financing statement under Section 9–311(b), but the filing or compliance is not of itself a factor in determining whether the collateral secures an obligation. If it is determined for another reason that the collateral secures an obligation, a security interest held by the consignor, lessor, bailor, licensor, owner, or buyer which attaches to the collateral is perfected by the filing or compliance.

§ 9–506. Effect of Errors or Omissions.

(a) A financing statement substantially satisfying the requirements of this part is effective, even if it has minor errors or omissions, unless the errors or omissions make the financing statement seriously misleading.

(b) Except as otherwise provided in subsection (c), a financing statement that fails sufficiently to provide the name of the debtor in accordance with Section 9–503(a) is seriously misleading.

(c) If a search of the records of the filing office under the debtor's correct name, using the filing office's standard search logic, if any, would disclose a financing statement that fails sufficiently to provide the name of the debtor in accordance with Section 9–503(a), the name provided does not make the financing statement seriously misleading.

(d) For purposes of Section 9–508(b), the "debtor's correct name" in subsection (c) means the correct name of the new debtor.

§ 9–507. Effect of Certain Events on Effectiveness of Financing Statement.

(a) A filed financing statement remains effective with respect to collateral that is sold, exchanged, leased, licensed, or otherwise disposed of and in which a security interest or agricultural lien continues, even if the secured party knows of or consents to the disposition.

(b) Except as otherwise provided in subsection (c) and Section 9–508, a financing statement is not rendered ineffective if, after the financing statement is filed, the information provided in the financing statement becomes seriously misleading under Section 9–506.

(c) If a debtor so changes its name that a filed financing statement becomes seriously misleading under Section 9–506:

> **(1)** the financing statement is effective to perfect a security interest in collateral acquired by the debtor before, or within four months after, the change; and
>
> **(2)** the financing statement is not effective to perfect a security interest in collateral acquired by the debtor more than four months after the change, unless an amendment to the financing statement which renders the financing statement not seriously misleading is filed within four months after the change.

§ 9–508. Effectiveness of Financing Statement If New Debtor Becomes Bound by Security Agreement.

(a) Except as otherwise provided in this section, a filed financing statement naming an original debtor is effective to perfect a security interest in collateral in which a new debtor has or acquires rights to the extent that the financing statement would have been effective had the original debtor acquired rights in the collateral.

(b) If the difference between the name of the original debtor and that of the new debtor causes a filed financing statement that is effective under subsection (a) to be seriously misleading under Section 9–506:

> **(1)** the financing statement is effective to perfect a security interest in collateral acquired by the new debtor before, and within four months after, the new debtor becomes bound under Section 9B–203(d); and
>
> **(2)** the financing statement is not effective to perfect a security interest in collateral acquired by the new debtor more than four months after the new debtor becomes bound under Section 9–203(d) unless an initial financing statement providing the name of the new debtor is filed before the expiration of that time.

(c) This section does not apply to collateral as to which a filed financing statement remains effective against the new debtor under Section 9–507(a).

§ 9–509. Persons Entitled to File a Record.

(a) A person may file an initial financing statement, amendment that adds collateral covered by a financing statement, or amendment that adds a debtor to a financing statement only if:

> **(1)** the debtor authorizes the filing in an authenticated record or pursuant to subsection (b) or (c); or
>
> **(2)** the person holds an agricultural lien that has become effective at the time of filing and the financing statement covers only collateral in which the person holds an agricultural lien.

(b) By authenticating or becoming bound as debtor by a security agreement, a debtor or new debtor authorizes the filing of an initial financing statement, and an amendment, covering:

> **(1)** the collateral described in the security agreement; and
>
> **(2)** property that becomes collateral under Section 9–315(a)(2), whether or not the security agreement expressly covers proceeds.

(c) By acquiring collateral in which a security interest or agricultural lien continues under Section 9–315(a)(1), a debtor authorizes the filing of an initial financing statement, and an amendment, covering the collateral and property that becomes collateral under Section 9–315(a)(2).

(d) A person may file an amendment other than an amendment that adds collateral covered by a financing statement or an amendment that adds a debtor to a financing statement only if:

> **(1)** the secured party of record authorizes the filing; or
>
> (2) the amendment is a termination statement for a financing statement as to which the secured party of record has failed to file or send a termination statement as required by Section 9–513(a) or (c), the debtor authorizes the filing, and the termination statement indicates that the debtor authorized it to be filed.

(e) If there is more than one secured party of record for a financing statement, each secured party of record may authorize the filing of an amendment under subsection (d).
As amended in 2000.

§ 9–510. Effectiveness of Filed Record.

(a) A filed record is effective only to the extent that it was filed by a person that may file it under Section 9–509.

(b) A record authorized by one secured party of record does not affect the financing statement with respect to another secured party of record.

(c) A continuation statement that is not filed within the six-month period prescribed by Section 9–515(d) is ineffective.

§ 9–511. Secured Party of Record.

(a) A secured party of record with respect to a financing statement is a person whose name is provided as the name of the secured party or a representative of the secured party in an initial financing statement that has been filed. If an initial financing statement is filed under Section 9–514(a), the assignee named in the initial financing statement is the secured party of record with respect to the financing statement.

(b) If an amendment of a financing statement which provides the name of a person as a secured party or a representative of a secured party is filed, the person named in the amendment is a secured party of record. If an amendment is filed under Section 9–514(b), the assignee named in the amendment is a secured party of record.

(c) A person remains a secured party of record until the filing of an amendment of the financing statement which deletes the person.

§ 9–512. Amendment of Financing Statement.

[Alternative A]

(a) Subject to Section 9–509, a person may add or delete collateral covered by, continue or terminate the effectiveness of, or, subject to subsection (e), otherwise amend the information provided in, a financing statement by filing an amendment that:

> **(1)** identifies, by its file number, the initial financing statement to which the amendment relates; and
>
> **(2)** if the amendment relates to an initial financing statement filed [or recorded] in a filing office described in Section 9–501(a)(1), provides the information specified in Section 9–502(b).

[Alternative B]

(a) Subject to Section 9–509, a person may add or delete collateral covered by, continue or terminate the effectiveness of, or, subject to subsection (e), otherwise amend the information provided in, a financing statement by filing an amendment that:

> **(1)** identifies, by its file number, the initial financing statement to which the amendment relates; and
>
> **(2)** if the amendment relates to an initial financing statement filed [or recorded] in a filing office described in Section 9–501(a)(1), provides the date [and time] that the initial financing statement was filed [or recorded] and the information specified in Section 9–502(b).

[End of Alternatives]

(b) Except as otherwise provided in Section 9–515, the filing of an amendment does not extend the period of effectiveness of the financing statement.

(c) A financing statement that is amended by an amendment that adds collateral is effective as to the added collateral only from the date of the filing of the amendment.

(d) A financing statement that is amended by an amendment that adds a debtor is effective as to the added debtor only from the date of the filing of the amendment.

(e) An amendment is ineffective to the extent it:

(1) purports to delete all debtors and fails to provide the name of a debtor to be covered by the financing statement; or

(2) purports to delete all secured parties of record and fails to provide the name of a new secured party of record.

Legislative Note: *States whose real-estate filing offices require additional information in amendments and cannot search their records by both the name of the debtor and the file number should enact Alternative B to Sections 9–512(a), 9–518(b), 9–519(f), and 9–522(a).*

§ 9–513. Termination Statement.

(a) A secured party shall cause the secured party of record for a financing statement to file a termination statement for the financing statement if the financing statement covers consumer goods and:

(1) there is no obligation secured by the collateral covered by the financing statement and no commitment to make an advance, incur an obligation, or otherwise give value; or

(2) the debtor did not authorize the filing of the initial financing statement.

(b) To comply with subsection (a), a secured party shall cause the secured party of record to file the termination statement:

(1) within one month after there is no obligation secured by the collateral covered by the financing statement and no commitment to make an advance, incur an obligation, or otherwise give value; or

(2) if earlier, within 20 days after the secured party receives an authenticated demand from a debtor.

(c) In cases not governed by subsection (a), within 20 days after a secured party receives an authenticated demand from a debtor, the secured party shall cause the secured party of record for a financing statement to send to the debtor a termination statement for the financing statement or file the termination statement in the filing office if:

(1) except in the case of a financing statement covering accounts or chattel paper that has been sold or goods that are the subject of a consignment, there is no obligation secured by the collateral covered by the financing statement and no commitment to make an advance, incur an obligation, or otherwise give value;

(2) the financing statement covers accounts or chattel paper that has been sold but as to which the account debtor or other person obligated has discharged its obligation;

(3) the financing statement covers goods that were the subject of a consignment to the debtor but are not in the debtor's possession; or

(4) the debtor did not authorize the filing of the initial financing statement.

(d) Except as otherwise provided in Section 9–510, upon the filing of a termination statement with the filing office, the financing statement to which the termination statement relates ceases to be effective. Except as otherwise provided in Section 9–510, for purposes of Sections 9–519(g), 9–522(a), and 9–523(c), the filing with the filing office of a termination statement relating to a financing statement that indicates that the debtor is a transmitting utility also causes the effectiveness of the financing statement to lapse.

As amended in 2000.

§ 9–514. Assignment of Powers of Secured Party of Record.

(a) Except as otherwise provided in subsection (c), an initial financing statement may reflect an assignment of all of the secured party's power to authorize an amendment to the financing statement by providing the name and mailing address of the assignee as the name and address of the secured party.

(b) Except as otherwise provided in subsection (c), a secured party of record may assign of record all or part of its power to authorize an amendment to a financing statement by filing in the filing office an amendment of the financing statement which:

(1) identifies, by its file number, the initial financing statement to which it relates;

(2) provides the name of the assignor; and

(3) provides the name and mailing address of the assignee.

(c) An assignment of record of a security interest in a fixture covered by a record of a mortgage which is effective as a financing statement filed as a fixture filing under Section 9–502(c) may be made only by an assignment of record of the mortgage in the manner provided by law of this State other than [the Uniform Commercial Code].

§ 9–515. Duration and Effectiveness of Financing Statement; Effect of Lapsed Financing Statement.

(a) Except as otherwise provided in subsections (b), (e), (f), and (g), a filed financing statement is effective for a period of five years after the date of filing.

(b) Except as otherwise provided in subsections (e), (f), and (g), an initial financing statement filed in connection with a public-finance transaction or manufactured-home transaction is effective for a period of 30 years after the date of filing if it indicates that it is filed in connection with a public-finance transaction or manufactured-home transaction.

(c) The effectiveness of a filed financing statement lapses on the expiration of the period of its effectiveness unless before the lapse a continuation statement is filed pursuant to subsection (d). Upon lapse, a financing statement ceases to be effective and any security interest or agricultural lien that was perfected by the financing statement becomes unperfected, unless the security interest is perfected otherwise. If the security interest or agricultural lien becomes unperfected upon lapse, it is deemed never to have been perfected as against a purchaser of the collateral for value.

(d) A continuation statement may be filed only within six months before the expiration of the five-year period specified in subsection (a) or the 30-year period specified in subsection (b), whichever is applicable.

(e) Except as otherwise provided in Section 9–510, upon timely filing of a continuation statement, the effectiveness of the initial financing statement continues for a period of five years commencing on the day on which the financing statement would have become ineffective in the absence of the filing. Upon the expiration of the five-year period, the financing statement lapses in the same manner as provided in subsection (c), unless, before the lapse, another continuation statement is filed pursuant to subsection (d). Succeeding continuation statements may be filed in the same manner to continue the effectiveness of the initial financing statement.

(f) If a debtor is a transmitting utility and a filed financing statement so indicates, the financing statement is effective until a termination statement is filed.

(g) A record of a mortgage that is effective as a financing statement filed as a fixture filing under Section 9–502(c) remains effective as a financing statement filed as a fixture filing until the mortgage is released or satisfied of record or its effectiveness otherwise terminates as to the real property.

§ 9–516. What Constitutes Filing; Effectiveness of Filing.

(a) Except as otherwise provided in subsection (b), communication of a record to a filing office and tender of the filing fee or acceptance of the record by the filing office constitutes filing.

(b) Filing does not occur with respect to a record that a filing office refuses to accept because:

   (1) the record is not communicated by a method or medium of communication authorized by the filing office;

   (2) an amount equal to or greater than the applicable filing fee is not tendered;

   (3) the filing office is unable to index the record because:

      (A) in the case of an initial financing statement, the record does not provide a name for the debtor;

      (B) in the case of an amendment or correction statement, the record:

         (i) does not identify the initial financing statement as required by Section 9–512 or 9–518, as applicable; or

         (ii) identifies an initial financing statement whose effectiveness has lapsed under Section 9–515;

      (C) in the case of an initial financing statement that provides the name of a debtor identified as an individual or an amendment that provides a name of a debtor identified as an individual which was not previously provided in the financing statement to which the record relates, the record does not identify the debtor's last name; or

      (D) in the case of a record filed [or recorded] in the filing office described in Section 9–501(a)(1), the record does not provide a sufficient description of the real property to which it relates;

   (4) in the case of an initial financing statement or an amendment that adds a secured party of record, the record does not provide a name and mailing address for the secured party of record;

   (5) in the case of an initial financing statement or an amendment that provides a name of a debtor which was not previously provided in the financing statement to which the amendment relates, the record does not:

      (A) provide a mailing address for the debtor;

      (B) indicate whether the debtor is an individual or an organization; or

      (C) if the financing statement indicates that the debtor is an organization, provide:

         (i) a type of organization for the debtor;

         (ii) a jurisdiction of organization for the debtor; or

         (iii) an organizational identification number for the debtor or indicate that the debtor has none;

   (6) in the case of an assignment reflected in an initial financing statement under Section 9–514(a) or an amendment filed under Section 9–514(b), the record does not provide a name and mailing address for the assignee; or

   (7) in the case of a continuation statement, the record is not filed within the six-month period prescribed by Section 9–515(d).

(c) For purposes of subsection (b):

   (1) a record does not provide information if the filing office is unable to read or decipher the information; and

   (2) a record that does not indicate that it is an amendment or identify an initial financing statement to which it relates, as required by Section 9–512, 9–514, or 9–518, is an initial financing statement.

(d) A record that is communicated to the filing office with tender of the filing fee, but which the filing office refuses to accept for a reason other than one set forth in subsection (b), is effective as a filed record except as against a purchaser of the collateral which gives value in reasonable reliance upon the absence of the record from the files.

§ 9–517. Effect of Indexing Errors.

The failure of the filing office to index a record correctly does not affect the effectiveness of the filed record.

§ 9–518. Claim Concerning Inaccurate or Wrongfully Filed Record.

(a) A person may file in the filing office a correction statement with respect to a record indexed there under the person's name if the person believes that the record is inaccurate or was wrongfully filed.

[Alternative A]

(b) A correction statement must:

   (1) identify the record to which it relates by the file number assigned to the initial financing statement to which the record relates;

   (2) indicate that it is a correction statement; and

   (3) provide the basis for the person's belief that the record is inaccurate and indicate the manner in which the person believes the record should be amended to cure any inaccuracy or provide the basis for the person's belief that the record was wrongfully filed.

[Alternative B]

(b) A correction statement must:

   (1) identify the record to which it relates by:

      (A) the file number assigned to the initial financing statement to which the record relates; and

      (B) if the correction statement relates to a record filed [or recorded] in a filing office described in Section 9–501(a)(1), the date [and time] that the initial financing statement was filed [or recorded] and the information specified in Section 9–502(b);

(2) indicate that it is a correction statement; and

(3) provide the basis for the person's belief that the record is inaccurate and indicate the manner in which the person believes the record should be amended to cure any inaccuracy or provide the basis for the person's belief that the record was wrongfully filed.

[End of Alternatives]

(c) The filing of a correction statement does not affect the effectiveness of an initial financing statement or other filed record.

Legislative Note: States whose real-estate filing offices require additional information in amendments and cannot search their records by both the name of the debtor and the file number should enact Alternative B to Sections 9–512(a), 9–518(b), 9–519(f), and 9–522(a).

[Subpart 2. Duties and Operation of Filing Office]

§ 9–519. Numbering, Maintaining, and Indexing Records; Communicating Information Provided in Records.

(a) For each record filed in a filing office, the filing office shall:

(1) assign a unique number to the filed record;

(2) create a record that bears the number assigned to the filed record and the date and time of filing;

(3) maintain the filed record for public inspection; and

(4) index the filed record in accordance with subsections (c), (d), and (e).

(b) A file number [assigned after January 1, 2002,] must include a digit that:

(1) is mathematically derived from or related to the other digits of the file number; and

(2) aids the filing office in determining whether a number communicated as the file number includes a single-digit or transpositional error.

(c) Except as otherwise provided in subsections (d) and (e), the filing office shall:

(1) index an initial financing statement according to the name of the debtor and index all filed records relating to the initial financing statement in a manner that associates with one another an initial financing statement and all filed records relating to the initial financing statement; and

(2) index a record that provides a name of a debtor which was not previously provided in the financing statement to which the record relates also according to the name that was not previously provided.

(d) If a financing statement is filed as a fixture filing or covers as-extracted collateral or timber to be cut, [it must be filed for record and] the filing office shall index it:

(1) under the names of the debtor and of each owner of record shown on the financing statement as if they were the mortgagors under a mortgage of the real property described; and

(2) to the extent that the law of this State provides for indexing of records of mortgages under the name of the mortgagee, under the name of the secured party as if the secured party were the mortgagee thereunder, or, if index-

ing is by description, as if the financing statement were a record of a mortgage of the real property described.

(e) If a financing statement is filed as a fixture filing or covers as-extracted collateral or timber to be cut, the filing office shall index an assignment filed under Section 9–514(a) or an amendment filed under Section 9–514(b):

(1) under the name of the assignor as grantor; and

(2) to the extent that the law of this State provides for indexing a record of the assignment of a mortgage under the name of the assignee, under the name of the assignee.

[Alternative A]

(f) The filing office shall maintain a capability:

(1) to retrieve a record by the name of the debtor and by the file number assigned to the initial financing statement to which the record relates; and

(2) to associate and retrieve with one another an initial financing statement and each filed record relating to the initial financing statement.

[Alternative B]

(f) The filing office shall maintain a capability:

(1) to retrieve a record by the name of the debtor and:

(A) if the filing office is described in Section 9–501(a)(1), by the file number assigned to the initial financing statement to which the record relates and the date [and time] that the record was filed [or recorded]; or

(B) if the filing office is described in Section 9–501(a)(2), by the file number assigned to the initial financing statement to which the record relates; and

(2) to associate and retrieve with one another an initial financing statement and each filed record relating to the initial financing statement.

[End of Alternatives]

(g) The filing office may not remove a debtor's name from the index until one year after the effectiveness of a financing statement naming the debtor lapses under Section 9–515 with respect to all secured parties of record.

(h) The filing office shall perform the acts required by subsections (a) through (e) at the time and in the manner prescribed by filing-office rule, but not later than two business days after the filing office receives the record in question.

[(i) Subsection[s] [(b)] [and] [(h)] do[es] not apply to a filing office described in Section 9–501(a)(1).]

Legislative Notes:

1. States whose filing offices currently assign file numbers that include a verification number, commonly known as a "check digit," or can implement this requirement before the effective date of this Article should omit the bracketed language in subsection (b).

2. In States in which writings will not appear in the real property records and indices unless actually recorded the bracketed language in subsection (d) should be used.

3. States whose real-estate filing offices require additional information in amendments and cannot search their records by both the name of the debtor and the file number should enact Alternative B to Sections 9–512(a), 9–518(b), 9–519(f), and 9–522(a).

4. A State that elects not to require real-estate filing offices to comply with either or both of subsections (b) and (h) may adopt an applicable variation of subsection (i) and add "Except as otherwise provided in subsection (i)," to the appropriate subsection or subsections.

§ 9–520. Acceptance and Refusal to Accept Record.

(a) A filing office shall refuse to accept a record for filing for a reason set forth in Section 9–516(b) and may refuse to accept a record for filing only for a reason set forth in Section 9–516(b).

(b) If a filing office refuses to accept a record for filing, it shall communicate to the person that presented the record the fact of and reason for the refusal and the date and time the record would have been filed had the filing office accepted it. The communication must be made at the time and in the manner prescribed by filing-office rule but [, in the case of a filing office described in Section 9–501(a)(2),] in no event more than two business days after the filing office receives the record.

(c) A filed financing statement satisfying Section 9–502(a) and (b) is effective, even if the filing office is required to refuse to accept it for filing under subsection (a). However, Section 9–338 applies to a filed financing statement providing information described in Section 9–516(b)(5) which is incorrect at the time the financing statement is filed.

(d) If a record communicated to a filing office provides information that relates to more than one debtor, this part applies as to each debtor separately.

Legislative Note: *A State that elects not to require real-property filing offices to comply with subsection (b) should include the bracketed language.*

§ 9–521. Uniform Form of Written Financing Statement and Amendment.

(a) A filing office that accepts written records may not refuse to accept a written initial financing statement in the following form and format except for a reason set forth in Section 9–516(b):

[NATIONAL UCC FINANCING STATEMENT (FORM UCC1) (REV. 7/29/98)]

[NATIONAL UCC FINANCING STATEMENT ADDENDUM (FORM UCC1Ad)(REV. 07/29/98)]

(b) A filing office that accepts written records may not refuse to accept a written record in the following form and format except for a reason set forth in Section 9–516(b):

[NATIONAL UCC FINANCING STATEMENT AMENDMENT (FORM UCC3)(REV. 07/29/98)]

[NATIONAL UCC FINANCING STATEMENT AMENDMENT ADDENDUM (FORM UCC3Ad)(REV. 07/29/98)]

§ 9–522. Maintenance and Destruction of Records.

[Alternative A]

(a) The filing office shall maintain a record of the information provided in a filed financing statement for at least one year after the effectiveness of the financing statement has lapsed under Section 9–515 with respect to all secured parties of record. The record must be retrievable by using the name of the debtor and by using the file number assigned to the initial financing statement to which the record relates.

[Alternative B]

(a) The filing office shall maintain a record of the information provided in a filed financing statement for at least one year after the effectiveness of the financing statement has lapsed under Section 9–515 with respect to all secured parties of record. The record must be retrievable by using the name of the debtor and:

(1) if the record was filed [or recorded] in the filing office described in Section 9–501(a)(1), by using the file number assigned to the initial financing statement to which the record relates and the date [and time] that the record was filed [or recorded]; or

(2) if the record was filed in the filing office described in Section 9–501(a)(2), by using the file number assigned to the initial financing statement to which the record relates.

[End of Alternatives]

(b) Except to the extent that a statute governing disposition of public records provides otherwise, the filing office immediately may destroy any written record evidencing a financing statement. However, if the filing office destroys a written record, it shall maintain another record of the financing statement which complies with subsection (a).

Legislative Note: *States whose real-estate filing offices require additional information in amendments and cannot search their records by both the name of the debtor and the file number should enact Alternative B to Sections 9–512(a), 9–518(b), 9–519(f), and 9–522(a).*

§ 9–523. Information from Filing Office; Sale or License of Records.

(a) If a person that files a written record requests an acknowledgment of the filing, the filing office shall send to the person an image of the record showing the number assigned to the record pursuant to Section 9–519(a)(1) and the date and time of the filing of the record. However, if the person furnishes a copy of the record to the filing office, the filing office may instead:

(1) note upon the copy the number assigned to the record pursuant to Section 9–519(a)(1) and the date and time of the filing of the record; and

(2) send the copy to the person.

(b) If a person files a record other than a written record, the filing office shall communicate to the person an acknowledgment that provides:

(1) the information in the record;

(2) the number assigned to the record pursuant to Section 9–519(a)(1); and

(3) the date and time of the filing of the record.

(c) The filing office shall communicate or otherwise make available in a record the following information to any person that requests it:

(1) whether there is on file on a date and time specified by the filing office, but not a date earlier than three business days before the filing office receives the request, any financing statement that:

(A) designates a particular debtor [or, if the request so states, designates a particular debtor at the address specified in the request];

(B) has not lapsed under Section 9–515 with respect to all secured parties of record; and

(C) if the request so states, has lapsed under Section 9–515 and a record of which is maintained by the filing office under Section 9–522(a);

(2) the date and time of filing of each financing statement; and

(3) the information provided in each financing statement.

(d) In complying with its duty under subsection (c), the filing office may communicate information in any medium. However, if requested, the filing office shall communicate information by issuing [its written certificate] [a record that can be admitted into evidence in the courts of this State without extrinsic evidence of its authenticity].

(e) The filing office shall perform the acts required by subsections (a) through (d) at the time and in the manner prescribed by filing-office rule, but not later than two business days after the filing office receives the request.

(f) At least weekly, the [insert appropriate official or governmental agency] [filing office] shall offer to sell or license to the public on a nonexclusive basis, in bulk, copies of all records filed in it under this part, in every medium from time to time available to the filing office.

Legislative Notes:

1. States whose filing office does not offer the additional service of responding to search requests limited to a particular address should omit the bracketed language in subsection (c)(1)(A).

2. A State that elects not to require real-estate filing offices to comply with either or both of subsections (e) and (f) should specify in the appropriate subsection(s) only the filing office described in Section 9–501(a)(2).

§ 9–524. Delay by Filing Office.

Delay by the filing office beyond a time limit prescribed by this part is excused if:

(1) the delay is caused by interruption of communication or computer facilities, war, emergency conditions, failure of equipment, or other circumstances beyond control of the filing office; and

(2) the filing office exercises reasonable diligence under the circumstances.

§ 9–525. Fees.

(a) Except as otherwise provided in subsection (e), the fee for filing and indexing a record under this part, other than an initial financing statement of the kind described in subsection (b), is [the amount specified in subsection (c), if applicable, plus]:

(1) $[X] if the record is communicated in writing and consists of one or two pages;

(2) $[2X] if the record is communicated in writing and consists of more than two pages; and

(3) $[1/2X] if the record is communicated by another medium authorized by filing-office rule.

(b) Except as otherwise provided in subsection (e), the fee for filing and indexing an initial financing statement of the following kind is [the amount specified in subsection (c), if applicable, plus]:

(1) $_____ if the financing statement indicates that it is filed in connection with a public-finance transaction;

(2) $_____ if the financing statement indicates that it is filed in connection with a manufactured-home transaction.

[Alternative A]

(c) The number of names required to be indexed does not affect the amount of the fee in subsections (a) and (b).

[Alternative B]

(c) Except as otherwise provided in subsection (e), if a record is communicated in writing, the fee for each name more than two required to be indexed is $_____.

[End of Alternatives]

(d) The fee for responding to a request for information from the filing office, including for [issuing a certificate showing] [communicating] whether there is on file any financing statement naming a particular debtor, is:

(1) $_____ if the request is communicated in writing; and

(2) $_____ if the request is communicated by another medium authorized by filing-office rule.

(e) This section does not require a fee with respect to a record of a mortgage which is effective as a financing statement filed as a fixture filing or as a financing statement covering as-extracted collateral or timber to be cut under Section 9–502(c). However, the recording and satisfaction fees that otherwise would be applicable to the record of the mortgage apply.

Legislative Notes:

1. To preserve uniformity, a State that places the provisions of this section together with statutes setting fees for other services should do so without modification.

2. A State should enact subsection (c), Alternative A, and omit the bracketed language in subsections (a) and (b) unless its indexing system entails a substantial additional cost when indexing additional names.

As amended in 2000.

§ 9–526. Filing-Office Rules.

(a) The [insert appropriate governmental official or agency] shall adopt and publish rules to implement this article. The filing-office rules must be[:

(1)] consistent with this article[; and

(2) adopted and published in accordance with the [insert any applicable state administrative procedure act]].

(b) To keep the filing-office rules and practices of the filing office in harmony with the rules and practices of filing offices in other jurisdictions that enact substantially this part, and to keep the technology used by the filing office compatible with the technology used by filing offices in other jurisdictions that enact substantially this part, the [insert appropriate governmental official or agency], so far as is consistent with the purposes, policies, and provisions of this article, in adopting, amending, and repealing filing-office rules, shall:

(1) consult with filing offices in other jurisdictions that enact substantially this part; and

(2) consult the most recent version of the Model Rules promulgated by the International Association of Corporate Administrators or any successor organization; and

(3) take into consideration the rules and practices of, and the technology used by, filing offices in other jurisdictions that enact substantially this part.

§ 9–527. Duty to Report.

The [insert appropriate governmental official or agency] shall report [annually on or before _____] to the [Governor and Legislature] on the operation of the filing office. The report must contain a statement of the extent to which:

(1) the filing-office rules are not in harmony with the rules of filing offices in other jurisdictions that enact substantially this part and the reasons for these variations; and

(2) the filing-office rules are not in harmony with the most recent version of the Model Rules promulgated by the International Association of Corporate Administrators, or any successor organization, and the reasons for these variations.

Part 6—Default

[Subpart 1. Default and Enforcement of Security Interest]

§ 9–601. Rights after Default; Judicial Enforcement; Consignor or Buyer of Accounts, Chattel Paper, Payment Intangibles, or Promissory Notes.

(a) After default, a secured party has the rights provided in this part and, except as otherwise provided in Section 9–602, those provided by agreement of the parties. A secured party:

　(1) may reduce a claim to judgment, foreclose, or otherwise enforce the claim, security interest, or agricultural lien by any available judicial procedure; and

　(2) if the collateral is documents, may proceed either as to the documents or as to the goods they cover.

(b) A secured party in possession of collateral or control of collateral under Section 9–104, 9–105, 9–106, or 9–107 has the rights and duties provided in Section 9–207.

(c) The rights under subsections (a) and (b) are cumulative and may be exercised simultaneously.

(d) Except as otherwise provided in subsection (g) and Section 9–605, after default, a debtor and an obligor have the rights provided in this part and by agreement of the parties.

(e) If a secured party has reduced its claim to judgment, the lien of any levy that may be made upon the collateral by virtue of an execution based upon the judgment relates back to the earliest of:

　(1) the date of perfection of the security interest or agricultural lien in the collateral;

　(2) the date of filing a financing statement covering the collateral; or

　(3) any date specified in a statute under which the agricultural lien was created.

(f) A sale pursuant to an execution is a foreclosure of the security interest or agricultural lien by judicial procedure within the meaning of this section. A secured party may purchase at the sale and thereafter hold the collateral free of any other requirements of this article.

(g) Except as otherwise provided in Section 9–607(c), this part imposes no duties upon a secured party that is a consignor or is a buyer of accounts, chattel paper, payment intangibles, or promissory notes.

§ 9–602. Waiver and Variance of Rights and Duties.

Except as otherwise provided in Section 9–624, to the extent that they give rights to a debtor or obligor and impose duties on a secured party, the debtor or obligor may not waive or vary the rules stated in the following listed sections:

　(1) Section 9–207(b)(4)(C), which deals with use and operation of the collateral by the secured party;

　(2) Section 9–210, which deals with requests for an accounting and requests concerning a list of collateral and statement of account;

　(3) Section 9–607(c), which deals with collection and enforcement of collateral;

　(4) Sections 9–608(a) and 9–615(c) to the extent that they deal with application or payment of noncash proceeds of collection, enforcement, or disposition;

　(5) Sections 9–608(a) and 9–615(d) to the extent that they require accounting for or payment of surplus proceeds of collateral;

　(6) Section 9–609 to the extent that it imposes upon a secured party that takes possession of collateral without judicial process the duty to do so without breach of the peace;

　(7) Sections 9–610(b), 9–611, 9–613, and 9–614, which deal with disposition of collateral;

　(8) Section 9–615(f), which deals with calculation of a deficiency or surplus when a disposition is made to the secured party, a person related to the secured party, or a secondary obligor;

　(9) Section 9–616, which deals with explanation of the calculation of a surplus or deficiency;

　(10) Sections 9–620, 9–621, and 9–622, which deal with acceptance of collateral in satisfaction of obligation;

　(11) Section 9–623, which deals with redemption of collateral;

　(12) Section 9–624, which deals with permissible waivers; and

　(13) Sections 9–625 and 9–626, which deal with the secured party's liability for failure to comply with this article.

§ 9–603. Agreement on Standards Concerning Rights and Duties.

(a) The parties may determine by agreement the standards measuring the fulfillment of the rights of a debtor or obligor and the duties of a secured party under a rule stated in Section 9–602 if the standards are not manifestly unreasonable.

(b) Subsection (a) does not apply to the duty under Section 9–609 to refrain from breaching the peace.

§ 9–604. Procedure If Security Agreement Covers Real Property or Fixtures.

(a) If a security agreement covers both personal and real property, a secured party may proceed:

　(1) under this part as to the personal property without prejudicing any rights with respect to the real property; or

　(2) as to both the personal property and the real property in accordance with the rights with respect to the real property, in which case the other provisions of this part do not apply.

(b) Subject to subsection (c), if a security agreement covers goods that are or become fixtures, a secured party may proceed:

　(1) under this part; or

　(2) in accordance with the rights with respect to real property, in which case the other provisions of this part do not apply.

(c) Subject to the other provisions of this part, if a secured party holding a security interest in fixtures has priority over all own-

ers and encumbrancers of the real property, the secured party, after default, may remove the collateral from the real property.
(d) A secured party that removes collateral shall promptly reimburse any encumbrancer or owner of the real property, other than the debtor, for the cost of repair of any physical injury caused by the removal. The secured party need not reimburse the encumbrancer or owner for any diminution in value of the real property caused by the absence of the goods removed or by any necessity of replacing them. A person entitled to reimbursement may refuse permission to remove until the secured party gives adequate assurance for the performance of the obligation to reimburse.

§ 9–605. Unknown Debtor or Secondary Obligor.
A secured party does not owe a duty based on its status as secured party:
>   (1) to a person that is a debtor or obligor, unless the secured party knows:
>>   (A) that the person is a debtor or obligor;
>>   (B) the identity of the person; and
>>   (C) how to communicate with the person; or
>   (2) to a secured party or lienholder that has filed a financing statement against a person, unless the secured party knows:
>>   (A) that the person is a debtor; and
>>   (B) the identity of the person.

§ 9–606. Time of Default for Agricultural Lien.
For purposes of this part, a default occurs in connection with an agricultural lien at the time the secured party becomes entitled to enforce the lien in accordance with the statute under which it was created.

§ 9–607. Collection and Enforcement by Secured Party.
(a) If so agreed, and in any event after default, a secured party:
>   (1) may notify an account debtor or other person obligated on collateral to make payment or otherwise render performance to or for the benefit of the secured party;
>   (2) may take any proceeds to which the secured party is entitled under Section 9–315;
>   (3) may enforce the obligations of an account debtor or other person obligated on collateral and exercise the rights of the debtor with respect to the obligation of the account debtor or other person obligated on collateral to make payment or otherwise render performance to the debtor, and with respect to any property that secures the obligations of the account debtor or other person obligated on the collateral;
>   (4) if it holds a security interest in a deposit account perfected by control under Section 9–104(a)(1), may apply the balance of the deposit account to the obligation secured by the deposit account; and
>   (5) if it holds a security interest in a deposit account perfected by control under Section 9–104(a)(2) or (3), may instruct the bank to pay the balance of the deposit account to or for the benefit of the secured party.

(b) If necessary to enable a secured party to exercise under subsection (a)(3) the right of a debtor to enforce a mortgage nonjudicially, the secured party may record in the office in which a record of the mortgage is recorded:
>   (1) a copy of the security agreement that creates or provides for a security interest in the obligation secured by the mortgage; and
>   (2) the secured party's sworn affidavit in recordable form stating that:
>>   (A) a default has occurred; and
>>   (B) the secured party is entitled to enforce the mortgage nonjudicially.

(c) A secured party shall proceed in a commercially reasonable manner if the secured party:
>   (1) undertakes to collect from or enforce an obligation of an account debtor or other person obligated on collateral; and
>   (2) is entitled to charge back uncollected collateral or otherwise to full or limited recourse against the debtor or a secondary obligor.

(d) A secured party may deduct from the collections made pursuant to subsection (c) reasonable expenses of collection and enforcement, including reasonable attorney's fees and legal expenses incurred by the secured party.

(e) This section does not determine whether an account debtor, bank, or other person obligated on collateral owes a duty to a secured party.

As amended in 2000.

§ 9–608. Application of Proceeds of Collection or Enforcement; Liability for Deficiency and Right to Surplus.
(a) If a security interest or agricultural lien secures payment or performance of an obligation, the following rules apply:
>   (1) A secured party shall apply or pay over for application the cash proceeds of collection or enforcement under Section 9–607 in the following order to:
>>   (A) the reasonable expenses of collection and enforcement and, to the extent provided for by agreement and not prohibited by law, reasonable attorney's fees and legal expenses incurred by the secured party;
>>   (B) the satisfaction of obligations secured by the security interest or agricultural lien under which the collection or enforcement is made; and
>>   (C) the satisfaction of obligations secured by any subordinate security interest in or other lien on the collateral subject to the security interest or agricultural lien under which the collection or enforcement is made if the secured party receives an authenticated demand for proceeds before distribution of the proceeds is completed.
>   (2) If requested by a secured party, a holder of a subordinate security interest or other lien shall furnish reasonable proof of the interest or lien within a reasonable time. Unless the holder complies, the secured party need not comply with the holder's demand under paragraph (1)(C).
>   (3) A secured party need not apply or pay over for application noncash proceeds of collection and enforcement under Section 9–607 unless the failure to do so would be commercially unreasonable. A secured party that applies or pays over for application noncash proceeds shall do so in a commercially reasonable manner.

(4) A secured party shall account to and pay a debtor for any surplus, and the obligor is liable for any deficiency.

(b) If the underlying transaction is a sale of accounts, chattel paper, payment intangibles, or promissory notes, the debtor is not entitled to any surplus, and the obligor is not liable for any deficiency.

As amended in 2000.

§ 9–609. Secured Party's Right to Take Possession after Default.

(a) After default, a secured party:
    (1) may take possession of the collateral; and
    (2) without removal, may render equipment unusable and dispose of collateral on a debtor's premises under Section 9–610.

(b) A secured party may proceed under subsection (a):
    (1) pursuant to judicial process; or
    (2) without judicial process, if it proceeds without breach of the peace.

(c) If so agreed, and in any event after default, a secured party may require the debtor to assemble the collateral and make it available to the secured party at a place to be designated by the secured party which is reasonably convenient to both parties.

§ 9–610. Disposition of Collateral after Default.

(a) After default, a secured party may sell, lease, license, or otherwise dispose of any or all of the collateral in its present condition or following any commercially reasonable preparation or processing.

(b) Every aspect of a disposition of collateral, including the method, manner, time, place, and other terms, must be commercially reasonable. If commercially reasonable, a secured party may dispose of collateral by public or private proceedings, by one or more contracts, as a unit or in parcels, and at any time and place and on any terms.

(c) A secured party may purchase collateral:
    (1) at a public disposition; or
    (2) at a private disposition only if the collateral is of a kind that is customarily sold on a recognized market or the subject of widely distributed standard price quotations.

(d) A contract for sale, lease, license, or other disposition includes the warranties relating to title, possession, quiet enjoyment, and the like which by operation of law accompany a voluntary disposition of property of the kind subject to the contract.

(e) A secured party may disclaim or modify warranties under subsection (d):
    (1) in a manner that would be effective to disclaim or modify the warranties in a voluntary disposition of property of the kind subject to the contract of disposition; or
    (2) by communicating to the purchaser a record evidencing the contract for disposition and including an express disclaimer or modification of the warranties.

(f) A record is sufficient to disclaim warranties under subsection (e) if it indicates "There is no warranty relating to title, possession, quiet enjoyment, or the like in this disposition" or uses words of similar import.

§ 9–611. Notification before Disposition of Collateral.

(a) In this section, "notification date" means the earlier of the date on which:

    (1) a secured party sends to the debtor and any secondary obligor an authenticated notification of disposition; or
    (2) the debtor and any secondary obligor waive the right to notification.

(b) Except as otherwise provided in subsection (d), a secured party that disposes of collateral under Section 9–610 shall send to the persons specified in subsection (c) a reasonable authenticated notification of disposition.

(c) To comply with subsection (b), the secured party shall send an authenticated notification of disposition to:
    (1) the debtor;
    (2) any secondary obligor; and
    (3) if the collateral is other than consumer goods:
        (A) any other person from which the secured party has received, before the notification date, an authenticated notification of a claim of an interest in the collateral;
        (B) any other secured party or lienholder that, 10 days before the notification date, held a security interest in or other lien on the collateral perfected by the filing of a financing statement that:
            (i) identified the collateral;
            (ii) was indexed under the debtor's name as of that date; and
            (iii) was filed in the office in which to file a financing statement against the debtor covering the collateral as of that date; and
        (C) any other secured party that, 10 days before the notification date, held a security interest in the collateral perfected by compliance with a statute, regulation, or treaty described in Section 9–311(a).

(d) Subsection (b) does not apply if the collateral is perishable or threatens to decline speedily in value or is of a type customarily sold on a recognized market.

(e) A secured party complies with the requirement for notification prescribed by subsection (c)(3)(B) if:
    (1) not later than 20 days or earlier than 30 days before the notification date, the secured party requests, in a commercially reasonable manner, information concerning financing statements indexed under the debtor's name in the office indicated in subsection (c)(3)(B); and
    (2) before the notification date, the secured party:
        (A) did not receive a response to the request for information; or
        (B) received a response to the request for information and sent an authenticated notification of disposition to each secured party or other lienholder named in that response whose financing statement covered the collateral.

§ 9–612. Timeliness of Notification before Disposition of Collateral.

(a) Except as otherwise provided in subsection (b), whether a notification is sent within a reasonable time is a question of fact.

(b) In a transaction other than a consumer transaction, a notification of disposition sent after default and 10 days or more before the earliest time of disposition set forth in the notification is sent within a reasonable time before the disposition.

§ 9–613. Contents and Form of Notification before Disposition of Collateral: General.

Except in a consumer-goods transaction, the following rules apply:

(1) The contents of a notification of disposition are sufficient if the notification:

(A) describes the debtor and the secured party;

(B) describes the collateral that is the subject of the intended disposition;

(C) states the method of intended disposition;

(D) states that the debtor is entitled to an accounting of the unpaid indebtedness and states the charge, if any, for an accounting; and

(E) states the time and place of a public disposition or the time after which any other disposition is to be made.

(2) Whether the contents of a notification that lacks any of the information specified in paragraph (1) are nevertheless sufficient is a question of fact.

(3) The contents of a notification providing substantially the information specified in paragraph (1) are sufficient, even if the notification includes:

(A) information not specified by that paragraph; or

(B) minor errors that are not seriously misleading.

(4) A particular phrasing of the notification is not required.

(5) The following form of notification and the form appearing in Section 9–614(3), when completed, each provides sufficient information:

NOTIFICATION OF DISPOSITION OF COLLATERAL

To: [Name of debtor, obligor, or other person to which the notification is sent]

From: [Name, address, and telephone number of secured party]

Name of Debtor(s): [Include only if debtor(s) are not an addressee]

[For a public disposition:]

We will sell [or lease or license, as applicable] the [describe collateral] [to the highest qualified bidder] in public as follows:

Day and Date: _____

Time: _____

Place: _____

[For a private disposition:]

We will sell [or lease or license, as applicable] the [describe collateral] privately sometime after [day and date].

You are entitled to an accounting of the unpaid indebtedness secured by the property that we intend to sell [or lease or license, as applicable] [for a charge of $_____]. You may request an accounting by calling us at [telephone number].

[End of Form]

As amended in 2000.

§ 9–614. Contents and Form of Notification before Disposition of Collateral: Consumer-Goods Transaction.

In a consumer-goods transaction, the following rules apply:

(1) A notification of disposition must provide the following information:

(A) the information specified in Section 9–613(1);

(B) a description of any liability for a deficiency of the person to which the notification is sent;

(C) a telephone number from which the amount that must be paid to the secured party to redeem the collateral under Section 9–623 is available; and

(D) a telephone number or mailing address from which additional information concerning the disposition and the obligation secured is available.

(2) A particular phrasing of the notification is not required.

(3) The following form of notification, when completed, provides sufficient information:

[Name and address of secured party]
[Date]

NOTICE OF OUR PLAN TO SELL PROPERTY

[Name and address of any obligor who is also a debtor]

Subject: [Identification of Transaction]

We have your [describe collateral], because you broke promises in our agreement.

[For a public disposition:]

We will sell [describe collateral] at public sale. A sale could include a lease or license. The sale will be held as follows:

Date: _____

Time: _____

Place: _____

If you need more information about the sale call us at [telephone number] [or write us at [secured party's address]].

We are sending this notice to the following other people who have an interest in [describe collateral] or who owe money under your agreement:

[Names of all other debtors and obligors, if any]

[End of Form]

(4) A notification in the form of paragraph (3) is sufficient, even if additional information appears at the end of the form.

(5) A notification in the form of paragraph (3) is sufficient, even if it includes errors in information not required by paragraph (1), unless the error is misleading with respect to rights arising under this article.

(6) If a notification under this section is not in the form of paragraph (3), law other than this article determines the effect of including information not required by paragraph (1).

§ 9–615. Application of Proceeds of Disposition; Liability for Deficiency and Right to Surplus.

(a) A secured party shall apply or pay over for application the cash proceeds of disposition under Section 9–610 in the following order to:

(1) the reasonable expenses of retaking, holding, preparing for disposition, processing, and disposing, and, to the extent provided for by agreement and not prohibited by law, reasonable attorney's fees and legal expenses incurred by the secured party;

(2) the satisfaction of obligations secured by the security interest or agricultural lien under which the disposition is made;

(3) the satisfaction of obligations secured by any subordinate security interest in or other subordinate lien on the collateral if:

(A) the secured party receives from the holder of the subordinate security interest or other lien an authenticated demand for proceeds before distribution of the proceeds is completed; and

(B) in a case in which a consignor has an interest in the collateral, the subordinate security interest or other lien is senior to the interest of the consignor; and

(4) a secured party that is a consignor of the collateral if the secured party receives from the consignor an authenticated demand for proceeds before distribution of the proceeds is completed.

(b) If requested by a secured party, a holder of a subordinate security interest or other lien shall furnish reasonable proof of the interest or lien within a reasonable time. Unless the holder does so, the secured party need not comply with the holder's demand under subsection (a)(3).

(c) A secured party need not apply or pay over for application noncash proceeds of disposition under Section 9–610 unless the failure to do so would be commercially unreasonable. A secured party that applies or pays over for application noncash proceeds shall do so in a commercially reasonable manner.

(d) If the security interest under which a disposition is made secures payment or performance of an obligation, after making the payments and applications required by subsection (a) and permitted by subsection (c):

(1) unless subsection (a)(4) requires the secured party to apply or pay over cash proceeds to a consignor, the secured party shall account to and pay a debtor for any surplus; and

(2) the obligor is liable for any deficiency.

(e) If the underlying transaction is a sale of accounts, chattel paper, payment intangibles, or promissory notes:

(1) the debtor is not entitled to any surplus; and

(2) the obligor is not liable for any deficiency.

(f) The surplus or deficiency following a disposition is calculated based on the amount of proceeds that would have been realized in a disposition complying with this part to a transferee other than the secured party, a person related to the secured party, or a secondary obligor if:

(1) the transferee in the disposition is the secured party, a person related to the secured party, or a secondary obligor; and

(2) the amount of proceeds of the disposition is significantly below the range of proceeds that a complying disposition to a person other than the secured party, a person related to the secured party, or a secondary obligor would have brought.

(g) A secured party that receives cash proceeds of a disposition in good faith and without knowledge that the receipt violates the rights of the holder of a security interest or other lien that is not subordinate to the security interest or agricultural lien under which the disposition is made:

(1) takes the cash proceeds free of the security interest or other lien;

(2) is not obligated to apply the proceeds of the disposition to the satisfaction of obligations secured by the security interest or other lien; and

(3) is not obligated to account to or pay the holder of the security interest or other lien for any surplus.

As amended in 2000.

§ 9–616. Explanation of Calculation of Surplus or Deficiency.

(a) In this section:

(1) "Explanation" means a writing that:

(A) states the amount of the surplus or deficiency;

(B) provides an explanation in accordance with subsection (c) of how the secured party calculated the surplus or deficiency;

(C) states, if applicable, that future debits, credits, charges, including additional credit service charges or interest, rebates, and expenses may affect the amount of the surplus or deficiency; and

(D) provides a telephone number or mailing address from which additional information concerning the transaction is available.

(2) "Request" means a record:

(A) authenticated by a debtor or consumer obligor;

(B) requesting that the recipient provide an explanation; and

(C) sent after disposition of the collateral under Section 9–610.

(b) In a consumer-goods transaction in which the debtor is entitled to a surplus or a consumer obligor is liable for a deficiency under Section 9–615, the secured party shall:

(1) send an explanation to the debtor or consumer obligor, as applicable, after the disposition and:

(A) before or when the secured party accounts to the debtor and pays any surplus or first makes written demand on the consumer obligor after the disposition for payment of the deficiency; and

(B) within 14 days after receipt of a request; or

(2) in the case of a consumer obligor who is liable for a deficiency, within 14 days after receipt of a request, send to the consumer obligor a record waiving the secured party's right to a deficiency.

(c) To comply with subsection (a)(1)(B), a writing must provide the following information in the following order:

(1) the aggregate amount of obligations secured by the security interest under which the disposition was made, and, if the amount reflects a rebate of unearned interest or credit service charge, an indication of that fact, calculated as of a specified date:

(A) if the secured party takes or receives possession of the collateral after default, not more than 35 days before the secured party takes or receives possession; or

(B) if the secured party takes or receives possession of the collateral before default or does not take possession of the collateral, not more than 35 days before the disposition;

(2) the amount of proceeds of the disposition;

(3) the aggregate amount of the obligations after deducting the amount of proceeds;

(4) the amount, in the aggregate or by type, and types of expenses, including expenses of retaking, holding, preparing for disposition, processing, and disposing of the collateral, and attorney's fees secured by the collateral which are known to the secured party and relate to the current disposition;

(5) the amount, in the aggregate or by type, and types of credits, including rebates of interest or credit service charges, to which the obligor is known to be entitled and which are not reflected in the amount in paragraph (1); and

(6) the amount of the surplus or deficiency.

(d) A particular phrasing of the explanation is not required. An explanation complying substantially with the requirements of subsection (a) is sufficient, even if it includes minor errors that are not seriously misleading.

(e) A debtor or consumer obligor is entitled without charge to one response to a request under this section during any six-month period in which the secured party did not send to the debtor or consumer obligor an explanation pursuant to subsection (b)(1). The secured party may require payment of a charge not exceeding $25 for each additional response.

§ 9–617. Rights of Transferee of Collateral.

(a) A secured party's disposition of collateral after default:

(1) transfers to a transferee for value all of the debtor's rights in the collateral;

(2) discharges the security interest under which the disposition is made; and

(3) discharges any subordinate security interest or other subordinate lien [other than liens created under [cite acts or statutes providing for liens, if any, that are not to be discharged]].

(b) A transferee that acts in good faith takes free of the rights and interests described in subsection (a), even if the secured party fails to comply with this article or the requirements of any judicial proceeding.

(c) If a transferee does not take free of the rights and interests described in subsection (a), the transferee takes the collateral subject to:

(1) the debtor's rights in the collateral;

(2) the security interest or agricultural lien under which the disposition is made; and

(3) any other security interest or other lien.

§ 9–618. Rights and Duties of Certain Secondary Obligors.

(a) A secondary obligor acquires the rights and becomes obligated to perform the duties of the secured party after the secondary obligor:

(1) receives an assignment of a secured obligation from the secured party;

(2) receives a transfer of collateral from the secured party and agrees to accept the rights and assume the duties of the secured party; or

(3) is subrogated to the rights of a secured party with respect to collateral.

(b) An assignment, transfer, or subrogation described in subsection (a):

(1) is not a disposition of collateral under Section 9–610; and

(2) relieves the secured party of further duties under this article.

§ 9–619. Transfer of Record or Legal Title.

(a) In this section, "transfer statement" means a record authenticated by a secured party stating:

(1) that the debtor has defaulted in connection with an obligation secured by specified collateral;

(2) that the secured party has exercised its post-default remedies with respect to the collateral;

(3) that, by reason of the exercise, a transferee has acquired the rights of the debtor in the collateral; and

(4) the name and mailing address of the secured party, debtor, and transferee.

(b) A transfer statement entitles the transferee to the transfer of record of all rights of the debtor in the collateral specified in the statement in any official filing, recording, registration, or certificate-of-title system covering the collateral. If a transfer statement is presented with the applicable fee and request form to the official or office responsible for maintaining the system, the official or office shall:

(1) accept the transfer statement;

(2) promptly amend its records to reflect the transfer; and

(3) if applicable, issue a new appropriate certificate of title in the name of the transferee.

(c) A transfer of the record or legal title to collateral to a secured party under subsection (b) or otherwise is not of itself a disposition of collateral under this article and does not of itself relieve the secured party of its duties under this article.

§ 9–620. Acceptance of Collateral in Full or Partial Satisfaction of Obligation; Compulsory Disposition of Collateral.

(a) Except as otherwise provided in subsection (g), a secured party may accept collateral in full or partial satisfaction of the obligation it secures only if:

(1) the debtor consents to the acceptance under subsection (c);

(2) the secured party does not receive, within the time set forth in subsection (d), a notification of objection to the proposal authenticated by:

(A) a person to which the secured party was required to send a proposal under Section 9–621; or

(B) any other person, other than the debtor, holding an interest in the collateral subordinate to the security interest that is the subject of the proposal;

(3) if the collateral is consumer goods, the collateral is not in the possession of the debtor when the debtor consents to the acceptance; and

(4) subsection (e) does not require the secured party to dispose of the collateral or the debtor waives the requirement pursuant to Section 9–624.

(b) A purported or apparent acceptance of collateral under this section is ineffective unless:

(1) the secured party consents to the acceptance in an authenticated record or sends a proposal to the debtor; and

(2) the conditions of subsection (a) are met.

(c) For purposes of this section:

(1) a debtor consents to an acceptance of collateral in partial satisfaction of the obligation it secures only if the debtor agrees to the terms of the acceptance in a record authenticated after default; and

(2) a debtor consents to an acceptance of collateral in full satisfaction of the obligation it secures only if the debtor agrees to the terms of the acceptance in a record authenticated after default or the secured party:

(A) sends to the debtor after default a proposal that is unconditional or subject only to a condition that collateral not in the possession of the secured party be preserved or maintained;

(B) in the proposal, proposes to accept collateral in full satisfaction of the obligation it secures; and

(C) does not receive a notification of objection authenticated by the debtor within 20 days after the proposal is sent.

(d) To be effective under subsection (a)(2), a notification of objection must be received by the secured party:

(1) in the case of a person to which the proposal was sent pursuant to Section 9–621, within 20 days after notification was sent to that person; and

(2) in other cases:

(A) within 20 days after the last notification was sent pursuant to Section 9–621; or

(B) if a notification was not sent, before the debtor consents to the acceptance under subsection (c).

(e) A secured party that has taken possession of collateral shall dispose of the collateral pursuant to Section 9–610 within the time specified in subsection (f) if:

(1) 60 percent of the cash price has been paid in the case of a purchase-money security interest in consumer goods; or

(2) 60 percent of the principal amount of the obligation secured has been paid in the case of a non-purchase-money security interest in consumer goods.

(f) To comply with subsection (e), the secured party shall dispose of the collateral:

(1) within 90 days after taking possession; or

(2) within any longer period to which the debtor and all secondary obligors have agreed in an agreement to that effect entered into and authenticated after default.

(g) In a consumer transaction, a secured party may not accept collateral in partial satisfaction of the obligation it secures.

§ 9–621. Notification of Proposal to Accept Collateral.

(a) A secured party that desires to accept collateral in full or partial satisfaction of the obligation it secures shall send its proposal to:

(1) any person from which the secured party has received, before the debtor consented to the acceptance, an authenticated notification of a claim of an interest in the collateral;

(2) any other secured party or lienholder that, 10 days before the debtor consented to the acceptance, held a security interest in or other lien on the collateral perfected by the filing of a financing statement that:

(A) identified the collateral;

(B) was indexed under the debtor's name as of that date; and

(C) was filed in the office or offices in which to file a financing statement against the debtor covering the collateral as of that date; and

(3) any other secured party that, 10 days before the debtor consented to the acceptance, held a security interest in the collateral perfected by compliance with a statute, regulation, or treaty described in Section 9–311(a).

(b) A secured party that desires to accept collateral in partial satisfaction of the obligation it secures shall send its proposal to any secondary obligor in addition to the persons described in subsection (a).

§ 9–622. Effect of Acceptance of Collateral.

(a) A secured party's acceptance of collateral in full or partial satisfaction of the obligation it secures:

(1) discharges the obligation to the extent consented to by the debtor;

(2) transfers to the secured party all of a debtor's rights in the collateral;

(3) discharges the security interest or agricultural lien that is the subject of the debtor's consent and any subordinate security interest or other subordinate lien; and

(4) terminates any other subordinate interest.

(b) A subordinate interest is discharged or terminated under subsection (a), even if the secured party fails to comply with this article.

§ 9–623. Right to Redeem Collateral.

(a) A debtor, any secondary obligor, or any other secured party or lienholder may redeem collateral.

(b) To redeem collateral, a person shall tender:

(1) fulfillment of all obligations secured by the collateral; and

(2) the reasonable expenses and attorney's fees described in Section 9–615(a)(1).

(c) A redemption may occur at any time before a secured party:

(1) has collected collateral under Section 9–607;

(2) has disposed of collateral or entered into a contract for its disposition under Section 9–610; or

(3) has accepted collateral in full or partial satisfaction of the obligation it secures under Section 9–622.

§ 9–624. Waiver.

(a) A debtor or secondary obligor may waive the right to notification of disposition of collateral under Section 9–611 only by an agreement to that effect entered into and authenticated after default.

(b) A debtor may waive the right to require disposition of collateral under Section 9–620(e) only by an agreement to that effect entered into and authenticated after default.

(c) Except in a consumer-goods transaction, a debtor or secondary obligor may waive the right to redeem collateral under Section 9–623 only by an agreement to that effect entered into and authenticated after default.

[Subpart 2. Noncompliance with Article]

§ 9–625. Remedies for Secured Party's Failure to Comply with Article.

(a) If it is established that a secured party is not proceeding in accordance with this article, a court may order or restrain collection, enforcement, or disposition of collateral on appropriate terms and conditions.

(b) Subject to subsections (c), (d), and (f), a person is liable for damages in the amount of any loss caused by a failure to comply with this article. Loss caused by a failure to comply may include loss resulting from the debtor's inability to obtain, or increased costs of, alternative financing.

(c) Except as otherwise provided in Section 9–628:

(1) a person that, at the time of the failure, was a debtor, was an obligor, or held a security interest in or other lien on the collateral may recover damages under subsection (b) for its loss; and

(2) if the collateral is consumer goods, a person that was a debtor or a secondary obligor at the time a secured party failed to comply with this part may recover for that failure in any event an amount not less than the credit service charge plus 10 percent of the principal amount of the obligation or the time-price differential plus 10 percent of the cash price.

(d) A debtor whose deficiency is eliminated under Section 9–626 may recover damages for the loss of any surplus. However, a debtor or secondary obligor whose deficiency is eliminated or reduced under Section 9–626 may not otherwise recover under subsection (b) for noncompliance with the provisions of this part relating to collection, enforcement, disposition, or acceptance.

(e) In addition to any damages recoverable under subsection (b), the debtor, consumer obligor, or person named as a debtor in a filed record, as applicable, may recover $500 in each case from a person that:

(1) fails to comply with Section 9–208;

(2) fails to comply with Section 9–209;

(3) files a record that the person is not entitled to file under Section 9–509(a);

(4) fails to cause the secured party of record to file or send a termination statement as required by Section 9–513(a) or (c);

(5) fails to comply with Section 9–616(b)(1) and whose failure is part of a pattern, or consistent with a practice, of noncompliance; or

(6) fails to comply with Section 9–616(b)(2).

(f) A debtor or consumer obligor may recover damages under subsection (b) and, in addition, $500 in each case from a person that, without reasonable cause, fails to comply with a request under Section 9–210. A recipient of a request under Section 9–210 which never claimed an interest in the collateral or obligations that are the subject of a request under that section has a reasonable excuse for failure to comply with the request within the meaning of this subsection.

(g) If a secured party fails to comply with a request regarding a list of collateral or a statement of account under Section 9–210, the secured party may claim a security interest only as shown in the list or statement included in the request as against a person that is reasonably misled by the failure.

As amended in 2000.

§ 9–626. Action in Which Deficiency or Surplus Is in Issue.

(a) In an action arising from a transaction, other than a consumer transaction, in which the amount of a deficiency or surplus is in issue, the following rules apply:

(1) A secured party need not prove compliance with the provisions of this part relating to collection, enforcement, disposition, or acceptance unless the debtor or a secondary obligor places the secured party's compliance in issue.

(2) If the secured party's compliance is placed in issue, the secured party has the burden of establishing that the collection, enforcement, disposition, or acceptance was conducted in accordance with this part.

(3) Except as otherwise provided in Section 9–628, if a secured party fails to prove that the collection, enforcement, disposition, or acceptance was conducted in accordance with the provisions of this part relating to collection, enforcement, disposition, or acceptance, the liability of a debtor or a secondary obligor for a deficiency is limited to an amount by which the sum of the secured obligation, expenses, and attorney's fees exceeds the greater of:

(A) the proceeds of the collection, enforcement, disposition, or acceptance; or

(B) the amount of proceeds that would have been realized had the noncomplying secured party proceeded in accordance with the provisions of this part relating to collection, enforcement, disposition, or acceptance.

(4) For purposes of paragraph (3)(B), the amount of proceeds that would have been realized is equal to the sum of the secured obligation, expenses, and attorney's fees unless the secured party proves that the amount is less than that sum.

(5) If a deficiency or surplus is calculated under Section 9–615(f), the debtor or obligor has the burden of establishing that the amount of proceeds of the disposition is significantly below the range of prices that a complying disposition to a person other than the secured party, a person related to the secured party, or a secondary obligor would have brought.

(b) The limitation of the rules in subsection (a) to transactions other than consumer transactions is intended to leave to the court the determination of the proper rules in consumer transactions. The court may not infer from that limitation the nature of the proper rule in consumer transactions and may continue to apply established approaches.

§ 9–627. Determination of Whether Conduct Was Commercially Reasonable.

(a) The fact that a greater amount could have been obtained by a collection, enforcement, disposition, or acceptance at a different time or in a different method from that selected by the secured party is not of itself sufficient to preclude the secured party from establishing that the collection, enforcement, disposition, or acceptance was made in a commercially reasonable manner.

(b) A disposition of collateral is made in a commercially reasonable manner if the disposition is made:

(1) in the usual manner on any recognized market;

(2) at the price current in any recognized market at the time of the disposition; or

(3) otherwise in conformity with reasonable commercial practices among dealers in the type of property that was the subject of the disposition.

(c) A collection, enforcement, disposition, or acceptance is commercially reasonable if it has been approved:

(1) in a judicial proceeding;

(2) by a bona fide creditors' committee;

(3) by a representative of creditors; or

(4) by an assignee for the benefit of creditors.

(d) Approval under subsection (c) need not be obtained, and lack of approval does not mean that the collection, enforcement, disposition, or acceptance is not commercially reasonable.

§ 9–628. Nonliability and Limitation on Liability of Secured Party; Liability of Secondary Obligor.

(a) Unless a secured party knows that a person is a debtor or obligor, knows the identity of the person, and knows how to communicate with the person:

(1) the secured party is not liable to the person, or to a secured party or lienholder that has filed a financing statement against the person, for failure to comply with this article; and

(2) the secured party's failure to comply with this article does not affect the liability of the person for a deficiency.

(b) A secured party is not liable because of its status as secured party:

(1) to a person that is a debtor or obligor, unless the secured party knows:

(A) that the person is a debtor or obligor;

(B) the identity of the person; and

(C) how to communicate with the person; or

(2) to a secured party or lienholder that has filed a financing statement against a person, unless the secured party knows:

(A) that the person is a debtor; and

(B) the identity of the person.

(c) A secured party is not liable to any person, and a person's liability for a deficiency is not affected, because of any act or omission arising out of the secured party's reasonable belief that a transaction is not a consumer-goods transaction or a consumer transaction or that goods are not consumer goods, if the secured party's belief is based on its reasonable reliance on:

(1) a debtor's representation concerning the purpose for which collateral was to be used, acquired, or held; or

(2) an obligor's representation concerning the purpose for which a secured obligation was incurred.

(d) A secured party is not liable to any person under Section 9–625(c)(2) for its failure to comply with Section 9–616.

(e) A secured party is not liable under Section 9–625(c)(2) more than once with respect to any one secured obligation.

Part 7—Transition

§ 9–701. Effective Date.

This [Act] takes effect on July 1, 2001.

§ 9–702. Savings Clause.

(a) Except as otherwise provided in this part, this [Act] applies to a transaction or lien within its scope, even if the transaction or lien was entered into or created before this [Act] takes effect.

(b) Except as otherwise provided in subsection (c) and Sections 9–703 through 9–709:

(1) transactions and liens that were not governed by [former Article 9], were validly entered into or created before this [Act] takes effect, and would be subject to this [Act] if they had been entered into or created after this [Act] takes effect, and the rights, duties, and interests flowing from those transactions and liens remain valid after this [Act] takes effect; and

(2) the transactions and liens may be terminated, completed, consummated, and enforced as required or permitted by this [Act] or by the law that otherwise would apply if this [Act] had not taken effect.

(c) This [Act] does not affect an action, case, or proceeding commenced before this [Act] takes effect.

As amended in 2000.

§ 9–703. Security Interest Perfected before Effective Date.

(a) A security interest that is enforceable immediately before this [Act] takes effect and would have priority over the rights of a person that becomes a lien creditor at that time is a perfected security interest under this [Act] if, when this [Act] takes effect, the applicable requirements for enforceability and perfection under this [Act] are satisfied without further action.

(b) Except as otherwise provided in Section 9–705, if, immediately before this [Act] takes effect, a security interest is enforceable and would have priority over the rights of a person that becomes a lien creditor at that time, but the applicable requirements for enforceability or perfection under this [Act] are not satisfied when this [Act] takes effect, the security interest:

(1) is a perfected security interest for one year after this [Act] takes effect;

(2) remains enforceable thereafter only if the security interest becomes enforceable under Section 9–203 before the year expires; and

(3) remains perfected thereafter only if the applicable requirements for perfection under this [Act] are satisfied before the year expires.

§ 9–704. Security Interest Unperfected before Effective Date.

A security interest that is enforceable immediately before this [Act] takes effect but which would be subordinate to the rights of a person that becomes a lien creditor at that time:

(1) remains an enforceable security interest for one year after this [Act] takes effect;

(2) remains enforceable thereafter if the security interest becomes enforceable under Section 9–203 when this [Act] takes effect or within one year thereafter; and

(3) becomes perfected:

(A) without further action, when this [Act] takes effect if the applicable requirements for perfection under this [Act] are satisfied before or at that time; or

(B) when the applicable requirements for perfection are satisfied if the requirements are satisfied after that time.

§ 9–705. Effectiveness of Action Taken before Effective Date.

(a) If action, other than the filing of a financing statement, is taken before this [Act] takes effect and the action would have resulted in priority of a security interest over the rights of a person that becomes a lien creditor had the security interest become enforceable before this [Act] takes effect, the action is effective to perfect a security interest that attaches under this [Act] within one year after this [Act] takes effect. An attached security interest becomes unperfected one year after this [Act] takes effect unless the security interest becomes a perfected security interest under this [Act] before the expiration of that period.

(b) The filing of a financing statement before this [Act] takes effect is effective to perfect a security interest to the extent the filing would satisfy the applicable requirements for perfection under this [Act].

(c) This [Act] does not render ineffective an effective financing statement that, before this [Act] takes effect, is filed and satisfies the applicable requirements for perfection under the law of the jurisdiction governing perfection as provided in [former Section 9–103]. However, except as otherwise provided in subsections (d) and (e) and Section 9–706, the financing statement ceases to be effective at the earlier of:

> **(1)** the time the financing statement would have ceased to be effective under the law of the jurisdiction in which it is filed; or
>
> **(2)** June 30, 2006.

(d) The filing of a continuation statement after this [Act] takes effect does not continue the effectiveness of the financing statement filed before this [Act] takes effect. However, upon the timely filing of a continuation statement after this [Act] takes effect and in accordance with the law of the jurisdiction governing perfection as provided in Part 3, the effectiveness of a financing statement filed in the same office in that jurisdiction before this [Act] takes effect continues for the period provided by the law of that jurisdiction.

(e) Subsection (c)(2) applies to a financing statement that, before this [Act] takes effect, is filed against a transmitting utility and satisfies the applicable requirements for perfection under the law of the jurisdiction governing perfection as provided in [former Section 9–103] only to the extent that Part 3 provides that the law of a jurisdiction other than the jurisdiction in which the financing statement is filed governs perfection of a security interest in collateral covered by the financing statement.

(f) A financing statement that includes a financing statement filed before this [Act] takes effect and a continuation statement filed after this [Act] takes effect is effective only to the extent that it satisfies the requirements of Part 5 for an initial financing statement.

§ 9–706. When Initial Financing Statement Suffices to Continue Effectiveness of Financing Statement.

(a) The filing of an initial financing statement in the office specified in Section 9–501 continues the effectiveness of a financing statement filed before this [Act] takes effect if:

> **(1)** the filing of an initial financing statement in that office would be effective to perfect a security interest under this [Act];
>
> **(2)** the pre-effective-date financing statement was filed in an office in another State or another office in this State; and
>
> **(3)** the initial financing statement satisfies subsection (c).

(b) The filing of an initial financing statement under subsection (a) continues the effectiveness of the pre-effective-date financing statement:

> **(1)** if the initial financing statement is filed before this [Act] takes effect, for the period provided in [former Section 9–403] with respect to a financing statement; and
>
> **(2)** if the initial financing statement is filed after this [Act] takes effect, for the period provided in Section 9–515 with respect to an initial financing statement.

(c) To be effective for purposes of subsection (a), an initial financing statement must:

> **(1)** satisfy the requirements of Part 5 for an initial financing statement;
>
> **(2)** identify the pre-effective-date financing statement by indicating the office in which the financing statement was filed and providing the dates of filing and file numbers, if any, of the financing statement and of the most recent continuation statement filed with respect to the financing statement; and
>
> **(3)** indicate that the pre-effective-date financing statement remains effective.

§ 9–707. Amendment of Pre-Effective-Date Financing Statement.

(a) In this section, "Pre-effective-date financing statement" means a financing statement filed before this [Act] takes effect.

(b) After this [Act] takes effect, a person may add or delete collateral covered by, continue or terminate the effectiveness of, or otherwise amend the information provided in, a pre-effective-date financing statement only in accordance with the law of the jurisdiction governing perfection as provided in Part 3. However, the effectiveness of a pre-effective-date financing statement also may be terminated in accordance with the law of the jurisdiction in which the financing statement is filed.

(c) Except as otherwise provided in subsection (d), if the law of this State governs perfection of a security interest, the information in a pre-effective-date financing statement may be amended after this [Act] takes effect only if:

> **(1)** the pre-effective-date financing statement and an amendment are filed in the office specified in Section 9–501;
>
> **(2)** an amendment is filed in the office specified in Section 9–501 concurrently with, or after the filing in that office of, an initial financing statement that satisfies Section 9–706(c); or
>
> **(3)** an initial financing statement that provides the information as amended and satisfies Section 9–706(c) is filed in the office specified in Section 9–501.

(d) If the law of this State governs perfection of a security interest, the effectiveness of a pre-effective-date financing statement may be continued only under Section 9–705(d) and (f) or 9–706.

(e) Whether or not the law of this State governs perfection of a security interest, the effectiveness of a pre-effective-date financing statement filed in this State may be terminated after this [Act] takes effect by filing a termination statement in the office in which the pre-effective-date financing statement is filed, unless an initial financing statement that satisfies Section 9–706(c) has been filed in the office specified by the law of the jurisdiction governing perfection as provided in Part 3 as the office in which to file a financing statement.

As amended in 2000.

§ 9–708. Persons Entitled to File Initial Financing Statement or Continuation Statement.

A person may file an initial financing statement or a continuation statement under this part if:

(1) the secured party of record authorizes the filing; and

(2) the filing is necessary under this part:

(A) to continue the effectiveness of a financing statement filed before this [Act] takes effect; or

(B) to perfect or continue the perfection of a security interest.

As amended in 2000.

§ 9–709. Priority.

(a) This [Act] determines the priority of conflicting claims to collateral. However, if the relative priorities of the claims were established before this [Act] takes effect, [former Article 9] determines priority.

(b) For purposes of Section 9–322(a), the priority of a security interest that becomes enforceable under Section 9–203 of this [Act] dates from the time this [Act] takes effect if the security interest is perfected under this [Act] by the filing of a financing statement before this [Act] takes effect which would not have been effective to perfect the security interest under [former Article 9]. This subsection does not apply to conflicting security interests each of which is perfected by the filing of such a financing statement.

As amended in 2000.

Note: The author's explanatory comments appear in italics following the excerpt from each section.

SECTION 302
Corporate responsibility for financial reports[1]

(a) Regulations required

The Commission shall, by rule, require, for each company filing periodic reports under section 13(a) or 15(d) of the Securities Exchange Act of 1934 (15 U.S.C. 78m, 78o(d)), that the principal executive officer or officers and the principal financial officer or officers, or persons performing similar functions, certify in each annual or quarterly report filed or submitted under either such section of such Act that—

(1) the signing officer has reviewed the report;

(2) based on the officer's knowledge, the report does not contain any untrue statement of a material fact or omit to state a material fact necessary in order to make the statements made, in light of the circumstances under which such statements were made, not misleading;

(3) based on such officer's knowledge, the financial statements, and other financial information included in the report, fairly present in all material respects the financial condition and results of operations of the issuer as of, and for, the periods presented in the report;

(4) the signing officers—

(A) are responsible for establishing and maintaining internal controls;

(B) have designed such internal controls to ensure that material information relating to the issuer and its consolidated subsidiaries is made known to such officers by others within those entities, particularly during the period in which the periodic reports are being prepared;

(C) have evaluated the effectiveness of the issuer's internal controls as of a date within 90 days prior to the report; and

(D) have presented in the report their conclusions about the effectiveness of their internal controls based on their evaluation as of that date;

(5) the signing officers have disclosed to the issuer's auditors and the audit committee of the board of directors (or persons fulfilling the equivalent function)—

(A) all significant deficiencies in the design or operation of internal controls which could adversely affect the issuer's ability to record, process, summarize, and report financial data and have identified for the issuer's auditors any material weaknesses in internal controls; and

(B) any fraud, whether or not material, that involves management or other employees who have a significant role in the issuer's internal controls; and

(6) the signing officers have indicated in the report whether or not there were significant changes in internal controls or in other factors that could significantly affect internal controls subsequent to the date of their evaluation, including any corrective actions with regard to significant deficiencies and material weaknesses.

(b) Foreign reincorporations have no effect

Nothing in this section shall be interpreted or applied in any way to allow any issuer to lessen the legal force of the statement required under this section, by an issuer having reincorporated or having engaged in any other transaction that resulted in the transfer of the corporate domicile or offices of the issuer from inside the United States to outside of the United States.

(c) Deadline

The rules required by subsection (a) of this section shall be effective not later than 30 days after July 30, 2002.

* * * *

Explanatory Comments:

Section 302 requires the chief executive officer (CEO) and chief financial officer (CFO) of each public company to certify that they have reviewed the company's quarterly and annual reports to be filed with the Securities and Exchange Commission (SEC). The CEO and CFO must certify that, based on their knowledge, the reports do not contain any untrue statement of a material fact or any half-truth that would make the report misleading, and that the information contained in the reports fairly presents the company's financial condition.

In addition, this section also requires the CEO and CFO to certify that they have created and designed an internal control system for their company and have recently evaluated that system to ensure that it is effectively providing them with relevant and accurate financial information. If the signing officers have found any significant deficiencies or weaknesses in the company's system or have discovered any evidence of fraud, they must have reported the situation, and any corrective actions they have taken, to the auditors and the audit committee.

SECTION 306
Insider trades during pension fund blackout periods[2]

(a) Prohibition of insider trading during pension fund blackout periods

(1) In general

Except to the extent otherwise provided by rule of the Commission pursuant to paragraph (3), it shall be unlawful for any director or executive officer of an issuer of any

---

1. This section of the Sarbanes-Oxley Act is codified at 15 U.S.C. Section 7241.

2. Codified at 15 U.S.C. Section 7244.

equity security (other than an exempted security), directly or indirectly, to purchase, sell, or otherwise acquire or transfer any equity security of the issuer (other than an exempted security) during any blackout period with respect to such equity security if such director or officer acquires such equity security in connection with his or her service or employment as a director or executive officer.

(2) Remedy

(A) In general

Any profit realized by a director or executive officer referred to in paragraph (1) from any purchase, sale, or other acquisition or transfer in violation of this subsection shall inure to and be recoverable by the issuer, irrespective of any intention on the part of such director or executive officer in entering into the transaction.

(B) Actions to recover profits

An action to recover profits in accordance with this subsection may be instituted at law or in equity in any court of competent jurisdiction by the issuer, or by the owner of any security of the issuer in the name and in behalf of the issuer if the issuer fails or refuses to bring such action within 60 days after the date of request, or fails diligently to prosecute the action thereafter, except that no such suit shall be brought more than 2 years after the date on which such profit was realized.

(3) Rulemaking authorized

The Commission shall, in consultation with the Secretary of Labor, issue rules to clarify the application of this subsection and to prevent evasion thereof. Such rules shall provide for the application of the requirements of paragraph (1) with respect to entities treated as a single employer with respect to an issuer under section 414(b), (c), (m), or (o) of Title 26 to the extent necessary to clarify the application of such requirements and to prevent evasion thereof. Such rules may also provide for appropriate exceptions from the requirements of this subsection, including exceptions for purchases pursuant to an automatic dividend reinvestment program or purchases or sales made pursuant to an advance election.

(4) Blackout period

For purposes of this subsection, the term "blackout period", with respect to the equity securities of any issuer—

(A) means any period of more than 3 consecutive business days during which the ability of not fewer than 50 percent of the participants or beneficiaries under all individual account plans maintained by the issuer to purchase, sell, or otherwise acquire or transfer an interest in any equity of such issuer held in such an individual account plan is temporarily suspended by the issuer or by a fiduciary of the plan; and

(B) does not include, under regulations which shall be prescribed by the Commission—

(i) a regularly scheduled period in which the participants and beneficiaries may not purchase, sell, or otherwise acquire or transfer an interest in any equity of such issuer, if such period is—

(I) incorporated into the individual account plan; and

(II) timely disclosed to employees before becoming participants under the individual account plan or as a subsequent amendment to the plan; or

(ii) any suspension described in subparagraph (A) that is imposed solely in connection with persons becoming participants or beneficiaries, or ceasing to be participants or beneficiaries, in an individual account plan by reason of a corporate merger, acquisition, divestiture, or similar transaction involving the plan or plan sponsor.

(5) Individual account plan

For purposes of this subsection, the term "individual account plan" has the meaning provided in section 1002(34) of Title 29, except that such term shall not include a one-participant retirement plan (within the meaning of section 1021(i)(8)(B) of Title 29).

(6) Notice to directors, executive officers, and the Commission

In any case in which a director or executive officer is subject to the requirements of this subsection in connection with a blackout period (as defined in paragraph (4)) with respect to any equity securities, the issuer of such equity securities shall timely notify such director or officer and the Securities and Exchange Commission of such blackout period.

* * * *

Explanatory Comments:

Corporate pension funds typically prohibit employees from trading shares of the corporation during periods when the pension fund is undergoing significant change. Before 2002, however, these blackout periods did not affect the corporation's executives, who frequently received shares of the corporate stock as part of their compensation. Section 306 was Congress's solution to the basic unfairness of this situation. This section of the act required the SEC to issue rules that prohibit any director or executive officer from trading during pension fund blackout periods. (The SEC later issued these rules, entitled Regulation Blackout Trading Restriction, or Reg BTR.)

Section 306 also provided shareholders with a right to file a shareholder's derivative suit against officers and directors who have profited from trading during these blackout periods (provided that the corporation has failed to bring a suit). The officer or director can be forced to return to the corporation any profits received, regardless of whether the director or officer acted with bad intent.

SECTION 402
Periodical and other reports[3]

* * * *

(i) Accuracy of financial reports

Each financial report that contains financial statements, and that is required to be prepared in accordance with (or reconciled to) generally accepted accounting principles under this chapter and filed with the Commission shall reflect all material correcting adjustments that have been identified by a registered

---

3. This section of the Sarbanes-Oxley Act amended some of the provisions of the 1934 Securities Exchange Act and added the paragraphs reproduced here at 15 U.S.C. Section 78m.

public accounting firm in accordance with generally accepted accounting principles and the rules and regulations of the Commission.

(j) Off-balance sheet transactions

Not later than 180 days after July 30, 2002, the Commission shall issue final rules providing that each annual and quarterly financial report required to be filed with the Commission shall disclose all material off-balance sheet transactions, arrangements, obligations (including contingent obligations), and other relationships of the issuer with unconsolidated entities or other persons, that may have a material current or future effect on financial condition, changes in financial condition, results of operations, liquidity, capital expenditures, capital resources, or significant components of revenues or expenses.

(k) Prohibition on personal loans to executives

(1) In general

It shall be unlawful for any issuer (as defined in section 7201 of this title), directly or indirectly, including through any subsidiary, to extend or maintain credit, to arrange for the extension of credit, or to renew an extension of credit, in the form of a personal loan to or for any director or executive officer (or equivalent thereof) of that issuer. An extension of credit maintained by the issuer on July 30, 2002, shall not be subject to the provisions of this subsection, provided that there is no material modification to any term of any such extension of credit or any renewal of any such extension of credit on or after July 30, 2002.

(2) Limitation

Paragraph (1) does not preclude any home improvement and manufactured home loans (as that term is defined in section 1464 of Title 12), consumer credit (as defined in section 1602 of this title), or any extension of credit under an open end credit plan (as defined in section 1602 of this title), or a charge card (as defined in section 1637(c)(4)(e) of this title), or any extension of credit by a broker or dealer registered under section 78o of this title to an employee of that broker or dealer to buy, trade, or carry securities, that is permitted under rules or regulations of the Board of Governors of the Federal Reserve System pursuant to section 78g of this title (other than an extension of credit that would be used to purchase the stock of that issuer), that is—

(A) made or provided in the ordinary course of the consumer credit business of such issuer;

(B) of a type that is generally made available by such issuer to the public; and

(C) made by such issuer on market terms, or terms that are no more favorable than those offered by the issuer to the general public for such extensions of credit.

(3) Rule of construction for certain loans

Paragraph (1) does not apply to any loan made or maintained by an insured depository institution (as defined in section 1813 of Title 12), if the loan is subject to the insider lending restrictions of section 375b of Title 12.

(l) Real time issuer disclosures

Each issuer reporting under subsection (a) of this section or section 78o(d) of this title shall disclose to the public on a rapid and current basis such additional information concerning material changes in the financial condition or operations of the issuer, in plain English, which may include trend and qualitative information and graphic presentations, as the Commission determines, by rule, is necessary or useful for the protection of investors and in the public interest.

Explanatory Comments:

Before this act, many corporate executives typically received extremely large salaries, significant bonuses, and abundant stock options, even when the companies for which they worked were suffering. Executives were also routinely given personal loans from corporate funds, many of which were never paid back. The average large company during that period loaned almost $1 million a year to top executives, and some companies loaned hundreds of millions of dollars to their executives every year. Section 402 amended the 1934 Securities Exchange Act to prohibit public companies from making personal loans to executive officers and directors.

There are a few exceptions to this prohibition, such as home-improvement loans made in the ordinary course of business. Note also that while loans are forbidden, outright gifts are not. A corporation is free to give gifts to its executives, including cash, provided that these gifts are disclosed on its financial reports. The idea is that corporate directors will be deterred from making substantial gifts to their executives by the disclosure requirement—particularly if the corporation's financial condition is questionable—because making such gifts could be perceived as abusing their authority.

SECTION 403
Directors, officers, and principal stockholders[4]

(a) Disclosures required

(1) Directors, officers, and principal stockholders required to file

Every person who is directly or indirectly the beneficial owner of more than 10 percent of any class of any equity security (other than an exempted security) which is registered pursuant to section 78l of this title, or who is a director or an officer of the issuer of such security, shall file the statements required by this subsection with the Commission (and, if such security is registered on a national securities exchange, also with the exchange).

(2) Time of filing

The statements required by this subsection shall be filed—

(A) at the time of the registration of such security on a national securities exchange or by the effective date of a registration statement filed pursuant to section 78l(g) of this title;

(B) within 10 days after he or she becomes such beneficial owner, director, or officer;

(C) if there has been a change in such ownership, or if such person shall have purchased or sold a security-based swap agreement (as defined in section 206(b) of the Gramm-Leach-Bliley Act (15 U.S.C. 78c note)) involving such equity security, before the end of the second business day following the day on which the subject transaction has been executed, or at such other

---

4. This section of the Sarbanes-Oxley Act amended the disclosure provisions of the 1934 Securities Exchange Act, at 15 U.S.C. Section 78p.

time as the Commission shall establish, by rule, in any case in which the Commission determines that such 2-day period is not feasible.

(3) Contents of statements

A statement filed—

(A) under subparagraph (A) or (B) of paragraph (2) shall contain a statement of the amount of all equity securities of such issuer of which the filing person is the beneficial owner; and

(B) under subparagraph (C) of such paragraph shall indicate ownership by the filing person at the date of filing, any such changes in such ownership, and such purchases and sales of the security-based swap agreements as have occurred since the most recent such filing under such subparagraph.

(4) Electronic filing and availability

Beginning not later than 1 year after July 30, 2002—

(A) a statement filed under subparagraph (C) of paragraph (2) shall be filed electronically;

(B) the Commission shall provide each such statement on a publicly accessible Internet site not later than the end of the business day following that filing; and

(C) the issuer (if the issuer maintains a corporate website) shall provide that statement on that corporate website, not later than the end of the business day following that filing.

* * * *

Explanatory Comments:

This section dramatically shortens the time period provided in the Securities Exchange Act of 1934 for disclosing transactions by insiders. The prior law stated that most transactions had to be reported within ten days of the beginning of the following month, although certain transactions did not have to be reported until the following fiscal year (within the first forty-five days).

In several instances, some insider trading was not disclosed (and was therefore not discovered) until long after the transactions. So Congress added this section to reduce the time period for making disclosures. Under Section 403, most transactions by insiders must be electronically filed with the SEC within two business days.

Also, any company that maintains a Web site must post these SEC filings on its site by the end of the next business day. Congress enacted this section in the belief that if insiders are required to file reports of their transactions promptly with the SEC, companies will do more to police themselves and prevent insider trading.

SECTION 404
Management assessment of internal controls[5]

(a) Rules required

The Commission shall prescribe rules requiring each annual report required by section 78m(a) or 78o(d) of this title to contain an internal control report, which shall—

(1) state the responsibility of management for establishing and maintaining an adequate internal control structure and procedures for financial reporting; and

(2) contain an assessment, as of the end of the most recent fiscal year of the issuer, of the effectiveness of the internal

control structure and procedures of the issuer for financial reporting.

(b) Internal control evaluation and reporting

With respect to the internal control assessment required by subsection (a) of this section, each registered public accounting firm that prepares or issues the audit report for the issuer shall attest to, and report on, the assessment made by the management of the issuer. An attestation made under this subsection shall be made in accordance with standards for attestation engagements issued or adopted by the Board. Any such attestation shall not be the subject of a separate engagement.

* * * *

Explanatory Comments:

This section was enacted to prevent corporate executives from claiming they were ignorant of significant errors in their companies' financial reports. For instance, several CEOs testified before Congress that they simply had no idea that the corporations' financial statements were off by billions of dollars. Congress therefore passed Section 404, which requires each annual report to contain a description and assessment of the company's internal control structure and financial reporting procedures. The section also requires that an audit be conducted of the internal control assessment, as well as the financial statements contained in the report. This section goes hand in hand with Section 302 (which, as discussed previously, requires various certifications attesting to the accuracy of the information in financial reports).

Section 404 has been one of the more controversial and expensive provisions in the Sarbanes-Oxley Act because it requires companies to assess their own internal financial controls to make sure that their financial statements are reliable and accurate. A corporation might need to set up a disclosure committee and a coordinator, establish codes of conduct for accounting and financial personnel, create documentation procedures, provide training, and outline the individuals who are responsible for performing each of the procedures. Companies that were already well managed have not experienced substantial difficulty complying with this section. Other companies, however, have spent millions of dollars setting up, documenting, and evaluating their internal financial control systems. Although initially creating the internal financial control system is a one-time-only expense, the costs of maintaining and evaluating it are ongoing. Some corporations that spent considerable sums complying with Section 404 have been able to offset these costs by discovering and correcting inefficiencies or frauds within their systems. Nevertheless, it is unlikely that any corporation will find compliance with this section to be inexpensive.

SECTION 802(A)
Destruction, alteration, or falsification of records in Federal investigations and bankruptcy[6]

Whoever knowingly alters, destroys, mutilates, conceals, covers up, falsifies, or makes a false entry in any record, document, or tangible object with the intent to impede, obstruct, or influence the investigation or proper administration of any matter within the jurisdiction of any department or agency of the United States or any case filed under title 11, or in relation to or

---

5. Codified at 15 U.S.C. Section 7262.

6. Codified at 15 U.S.C. Section 1519.

contemplation of any such matter or case, shall be fined under this title, imprisoned not more than 20 years, or both.

Destruction of corporate audit records[7]

(a) **(1)** Any accountant who conducts an audit of an issuer of securities to which section 10A(a) of the Securities Exchange Act of 1934 (15 U.S.C. 78j-1(a)) applies, shall maintain all audit or review workpapers for a period of 5 years from the end of the fiscal period in which the audit or review was concluded.

(2) The Securities and Exchange Commission shall promulgate, within 180 days, after adequate notice and an opportunity for comment, such rules and regulations, as are reasonably necessary, relating to the retention of relevant records such as workpapers, documents that form the basis of an audit or review, memoranda, correspondence, communications, other documents, and records (including electronic records) which are created, sent, or received in connection with an audit or review and contain conclusions, opinions, analyses, or financial data relating to such an audit or review, which is conducted by any accountant who conducts an audit of an issuer of securities to which section 10A(a) of the Securities Exchange Act of 1934 (15 U.S.C. 78j-1(a)) applies. The Commission may, from time to time, amend or supplement the rules and regulations that it is required to promulgate under this section, after adequate notice and an opportunity for comment, in order to ensure that such rules and regulations adequately comport with the purposes of this section.

(b) Whoever knowingly and willfully violates subsection (a)(1), or any rule or regulation promulgated by the Securities and Exchange Commission under subsection (a)(2), shall be fined under this title, imprisoned not more than 10 years, or both.

(c) Nothing in this section shall be deemed to diminish or relieve any person of any other duty or obligation imposed by Federal or State law or regulation to maintain, or refrain from destroying, any document.

* * * *

Explanatory Comments:

Section 802(a) enacted two new statutes that punish those who alter or destroy documents. The first statute is not specifically limited to securities fraud cases. It provides that anyone who alters, destroys, or falsifies records in federal investigations or bankruptcy may be criminally prosecuted and sentenced to a fine or to up to twenty years in prison, or both. The second statute requires auditors of public companies to keep all audit or review working papers for five years but expressly allows the SEC to amend or supplement these requirements as it sees fit. The SEC has, in fact, amended this section by issuing a rule that requires auditors who audit reporting companies to retain working papers for seven years from the conclusion of the review. Section 802(a) further provides that anyone who knowingly and willfully violates this statute is subject to criminal prosecution and can be sentenced to a fine, imprisoned for up to ten years, or both if convicted.

This portion of the Sarbanes-Oxley Act implicitly recognizes that persons who are under investigation often are tempted to respond by

destroying or falsifying documents that might prove their complicity in wrongdoing. The severity of the punishment should provide a strong incentive for these individuals to resist the temptation.

SECTION 804
Time limitations on the commencement of civil actions arising under Acts of Congress[8]

(a) Except as otherwise provided by law, a civil action arising under an Act of Congress enacted after the date of the enactment of this section may not be commenced later than 4 years after the cause of action accrues.

(b) Notwithstanding subsection (a), a private right of action that involves a claim of fraud, deceit, manipulation, or contrivance in contravention of a regulatory requirement concerning the securities laws, as defined in section 3(a)(47) of the Securities Exchange Act of 1934 (15 U.S.C. 78c(a)(47)), may be brought not later than the earlier of—

(1) 2 years after the discovery of the facts constituting the violation; or

(2) 5 years after such violation.

* * * *

Explanatory Comments:

Before the enactment of this section, Section 10(b) of the Securities Exchange Act of 1934 had no express statute of limitations. The courts generally required plaintiffs to have filed suit within one year from the date that they should (using due diligence) have discovered that a fraud had been committed but no later than three years after the fraud occurred. Section 804 extends this period by specifying that plaintiffs must file a lawsuit within two years after they discover (or should have discovered) a fraud but no later than five years after the fraud's occurrence. This provision has prevented the courts from dismissing numerous securities fraud lawsuits.

SECTION 806
Civil action to protect against retaliation in fraud cases[9]

(a) Whistleblower protection for employees of publicly traded companies.—

No company with a class of securities registered under section 12 of the Securities Exchange Act of 1934 (15 U.S.C. 78l), or that is required to file reports under section 15(d) of the Securities Exchange Act of 1934 (15 U.S.C. 78o(d)), or any officer, employee, contractor, subcontractor, or agent of such company, may discharge, demote, suspend, threaten, harass, or in any other manner discriminate against an employee in the terms and conditions of employment because of any lawful act done by the employee—

(1) to provide information, cause information to be provided, or otherwise assist in an investigation regarding any conduct which the employee reasonably believes constitutes a violation of section 1341, 1343, 1344, or 1348, any rule or regulation of the Securities and Exchange Commission, or any provision of Federal law relating to fraud against shareholders, when the information or assistance is provided to or the investigation is conducted by—

---

7. Codified at 15 U.S.C. Section 1520.

8. Codified at 28 U.S.C. Section 1658.
9. Codified at 18 U.S.C. Section 1514A.

(A) a Federal regulatory or law enforcement agency;

(B) any Member of Congress or any committee of Congress; or

(C) a person with supervisory authority over the employee (or such other person working for the employer who has the authority to investigate, discover, or terminate misconduct); or

(2) to file, cause to be filed, testify, participate in, or otherwise assist in a proceeding filed or about to be filed (with any knowledge of the employer) relating to an alleged violation of section 1341, 1343, 1344, or 1348, any rule or regulation of the Securities and Exchange Commission, or any provision of Federal law relating to fraud against shareholders.

(b) Enforcement action.—

(1) In general.—A person who alleges discharge or other discrimination by any person in violation of subsection (a) may seek relief under subsection (c), by—

(A) filing a complaint with the Secretary of Labor; or

(B) if the Secretary has not issued a final decision within 180 days of the filing of the complaint and there is no showing that such delay is due to the bad faith of the claimant, bringing an action at law or equity for de novo review in the appropriate district court of the United States, which shall have jurisdiction over such an action without regard to the amount in controversy.

(2) Procedure.—

(A) In general.—An action under paragraph (1)(A) shall be governed under the rules and procedures set forth in section 42121(b) of title 49, United States Code.

(B) Exception.—Notification made under section 42121(b)(1) of title 49, United States Code, shall be made to the person named in the complaint and to the employer.

(C) Burdens of proof.—An action brought under paragraph (1)(B) shall be governed by the legal burdens of proof set forth in section 42121(b) of title 49, United States Code.

(D) Statute of limitations.—An action under paragraph (1) shall be commenced not later than 90 days after the date on which the violation occurs.

(c) Remedies.—

(1) In general.—An employee prevailing in any action under subsection (b)(1) shall be entitled to all relief necessary to make the employee whole.

(2) Compensatory damages.—Relief for any action under paragraph (1) shall include—

(A) reinstatement with the same seniority status that the employee would have had, but for the discrimination;

(B) the amount of back pay, with interest; and

(C) compensation for any special damages sustained as a result of the discrimination, including litigation costs, expert witness fees, and reasonable attorney fees.

(d) Rights retained by employee.—Nothing in this section shall be deemed to diminish the rights, privileges, or remedies of any employee under any Federal or State law, or under any collective bargaining agreement.

Explanatory Comments:

Section 806 is one of several provisions that were included in the Sarbanes-Oxley Act to encourage and protect whistleblowers—that is, employees who report their employer's alleged violations of securities law to the authorities. This section applies to employees, agents, and independent contractors who work for publicly traded companies or testify about such a company during an investigation. It sets up an administrative procedure at the U.S. Department of Labor for individuals who claim that their employer retaliated against them (fired or demoted them, for example) for blowing the whistle on the employer's wrongful conduct. It also allows the award of civil damages—including back pay, reinstatement, special damages, attorneys' fees, and court costs—to employees who prove that they suffered retaliation. Since this provision was enacted, whistleblowers have filed numerous complaints with the U.S. Department of Labor under this section.

SECTION 807
Securities fraud[10]

Whoever knowingly executes, or attempts to execute, a scheme or artifice—

(1) to defraud any person in connection with any security of an issuer with a class of securities registered under section 12 of the Securities Exchange Act of 1934 (15 U.S.C. 78l) or that is required to file reports under section 15(d) of the Securities Exchange Act of 1934 (15 U.S.C. 78o(d)); or

(2) to obtain, by means of false or fraudulent pretenses, representations, or promises, any money or property in connection with the purchase or sale of any security of an issuer with a class of securities registered under section 12 of the Securities Exchange Act of 1934 (15 U.S.C. 78l) or that is required to file reports under section 15(d) of the Securities Exchange Act of 1934 (15 U.S.C. 78o(d)); shall be fined under this title, or imprisoned not more than 25 years, or both.

* * * *

Explanatory Comments:

Section 807 adds a new provision to the federal criminal code that addresses securities fraud. Before 2002, federal securities law had already made it a crime—under Section 10(b) of the Securities Exchange Act of 1934 and SEC Rule 10b-5, both of which were discussed in Chapter 42—to intentionally defraud someone in connection with a purchase or sale of securities, but the offense was not listed in the federal criminal code.

Also, paragraph 2 of Section 807 goes beyond what is prohibited under securities law by making it a crime to obtain by means of false or fraudulent pretenses any money or property from the purchase or sale of securities. This new provision allows violators to be punished by up to twenty-five years in prison, a fine, or both.

SECTION 906
Failure of corporate officers to certify financial reports[11]

(a) Certification of periodic financial reports.—Each periodic report containing financial statements filed by an issuer with the Securities Exchange Commission pursuant to section 13(a)

---

10. Codified at 18 U.S.C. Section 1348.

11. Codified at 18 U.S.C. Section 1350.

or 15(d) of the Securities Exchange Act of 1934 (15 U.S.C. 78m(a) or 78o(d)) shall be accompanied by a written statement by the chief executive officer and chief financial officer (or equivalent thereof) of the issuer.

(b) Content.—The statement required under subsection (a) shall certify that the periodic report containing the financial statements fully complies with the requirements of section 13(a) or 15(d) of the Securities Exchange Act of 1934 (15 U.S.C. 78m or 78o(d)) and that information contained in the periodic report fairly presents, in all material respects, the financial condition and results of operations of the issuer.

(c) Criminal penalties.—Whoever—

   (1) certifies any statement as set forth in subsections (a) and (b) of this section knowing that the periodic report accompanying the statement does not comport with all the requirements set forth in this section shall be fined not more than $1,000,000 or imprisoned not more than 10 years, or both; or

   (2) willfully certifies any statement as set forth in subsections (a) and (b) of this section knowing that the periodic report accompanying the statement does not comport with all the requirements set forth in this section shall be fined not more than $5,000,000, or imprisoned not more than 20 years, or both.

Explanatory Comments:

As previously discussed, under Section 302 a corporation's CEO and CFO are required to certify that they believe the quarterly and annual reports their company files with the SEC are accurate and fairly present the company's financial condition. Section 906 adds "teeth" to these requirements by authorizing criminal penalties for those officers who intentionally certify inaccurate SEC filings.

Knowing violations of the requirements are punishable by a fine of up to $1 million, ten years' imprisonment, or both. Willful violators may be fined up to $5 million, sentenced to up to twenty years' imprisonment, or both. Although the difference between a knowing and a willful violation is not entirely clear, the section is obviously intended to remind corporate officers of the serious consequences of certifying inaccurate reports to the SEC.

CHAPTER 1

1. Under what circumstances might a judge rely on case law to determine the intent and purpose of a statute? Case law includes courts' interpretations of statutes, as well as constitutional provisions and administrative rules. Statutes often codify common law rules. For these reasons, a judge might rely on the common law as a guide to the intent and purpose of a statute.

2. Assuming that these convicted war criminals had not disobeyed any law of their country and had merely been following their government's orders, what law had they violated? Explain. At the time of the Nuremberg trials, "crimes against humanity" were new international crimes. The laws criminalized such acts as murder, extermination, enslavement, deportation, and other inhumane acts committed against any civilian population. These international laws derived their legitimacy from "natural law."

Natural law, which is the oldest and one of the most significant schools of jurisprudence, holds that governments and legal systems should reflect the moral and ethical ideals that are inherent in human nature. Because natural law is universal and discoverable by reason, its adherents believe that all other law is derived from natural law. Natural law therefore supersedes laws created by humans (national, or "positive," law), and in a conflict between the two, national or positive law loses its legitimacy.

The Nuremberg defendants asserted that they had been acting in accordance with German law. The judges dismissed these claims, reasoning that the defendants' acts were commonly regarded as crimes and that the accused must have known that the acts would be considered criminal. The judges clearly believed the tenets of natural law and expected that the defendants, too, should have been able to realize that their acts ran afoul of it. The fact that the "positivist law" of Germany at the time required them to commit these acts is irrelevant. Under natural law theory, the international court was justified in finding the defendants guilty of crimes against humanity.

CHAPTER 2

1. Does the court in Sue's state have jurisdiction over Tipton? What factors will the court consider? A corporation normally is subject to personal jurisdiction in the state in which it is incorporated, has its principal office, and/or is doing business. Under the authority of a state long arm statute, a court can exercise personal jurisdiction over certain out-of-state defendants based on activities that took place within the state. Before a court can exercise jurisdiction, though, it must be demonstrated that the defendant had minimum contacts with the state to justify the jurisdiction.

The minimum-contacts requirement is usually met if the corporation advertises or sells its products within the state, or places its goods into the "stream of commerce" with the intent that the goods be sold in the state. Therefore, a court will consider whether Tipton advertised or sold its product within Sue's state. The court may also look at whether the contract between Sue and Tipton was negotiated or signed within the state.

2. If the dispute is not resolved, or if either party disagrees with the decision of the mediator or arbitrator, will a court hear the case? Explain. Yes. Submission of the dispute to mediation or nonbinding arbitration is mandatory, but compliance with a decision of the mediator or arbitrator is voluntary.

CHAPTER 3

1. Tom can call his first witness. What else might he do? Tom could file a motion for a directed verdict. This motion asks the judge to direct a verdict for Tom on the ground that Sue presented no evidence that would justify granting Jan relief. The judge grants the motion if there is insufficient evidence to raise an issue of fact.

2. Who can appeal to a higher court? Either a plaintiff or a defendant, or both, can appeal a judgment to a higher court. An appellate court can affirm, reverse, or remand a case, or take any of these actions in combination. To appeal successfully, it is best to appeal on the basis of an error of law, because appellate courts do not usually reverse on findings of fact.

CHAPTER 4

1. Can a state, in the interest of energy conservation, ban all advertising by power utilities if conservation could be accomplished by less restrictive means? Why or why not? No. Even if commercial speech is not related to illegal activities nor misleading, it may be restricted if a state has a substantial interest that cannot be achieved by less restrictive means. In this case, the interest in energy conservation is substantial, but it could be achieved by less restrictive means. That would be the utilities' defense against the enforcement of this state law.

2. Is this a violation of equal protection if the only reason for the tax is to protect the local firms from out-of-state competition? Explain. Yes. The tax would limit the liberty of some persons (out of state businesses), so it is subject to a review under the equal protection clause. Protecting local businesses from out-of-state competition is not a legitimate government objective. Thus, such a tax would violate the equal protection clause.

CHAPTER 5

1. *Are there ethical concerns about putting trauma- tized children on the news immediately after an event like this? Why or why not?* In determining whether it is ethical to interview these children soon after a tragic event, it is important to analyze the competing interests and reasons behind the interviews. The interviews may generate more view- ers, which may lead to higher ratings and more advertising rev- enue for the company and its shareholders. Alternatively, the value of the interview to the public or to any investigation may be minimal. The children may not have accurate information and may be further traumatized by the interview process.

2. *Is it ethical for Johnny to take a performance- enhancing drug that has not been banned? Why or why not?* Maybe. Individuals and businesses often face ethical dilemmas when the letter of the law seems clear but alternatives exist that may violate what is known as the spirit of the law or the purpose for the law. In this case, the restrictions exist to stop athletes from performing better than they would naturally because of a foreign substance. The list of banned substances may not be able to keep up with the advances in technology and science in developing performance enhancing drugs.

Some might argue that it is ethical for him to take any- thing that is not formally banned and that all competitors have the same ability to access and take those substances and therefore any advantage is eliminated. Because there seems to be no unfair advantage, the purpose of the restriction is not frustrated. There is an implicit assumption, however, that all performers have the connections and the resources to obtain the non-banned substance. Because this assumption is not nec- essarily true, it is more likely an ethical violation to take the non-banned performance enhancing drugs, even if it is not technically against the rules.

CHAPTER 6

1. *Can Lou recover from Jana? Why or why not?* Probably. To recover on the basis of negligence, the injured party as a plaintiff must show that the truck's owner owed the plaintiff a duty of care, that the owner breached that duty, that the plain- tiff was injured, and that the breach caused the injury.

In this situation, the owner's actions breached the duty of reasonable care. The billboard falling on the plaintiff was the direct cause of the injury, not the plaintiff's own negligence. Thus, liability turns on whether the plaintiff can connect the breach of duty to the injury. This involves the test of proximate cause—the question of foreseeability. The consequences to the injured party must have been a foreseeable result of the owner's carelessness.

2. *What might the firm successfully claim in defense?* The company might defend against this electrician's claim by asserting that the electrician should have known of the risk and, therefore, the company had no duty to warn. According to the problem, the danger is common knowledge in the electri- cian's field and should have been apparent to this electrician, given his years of training and experience. In other words, the

company most likely had no need to warn the electrician of the risk.

The firm could also raise comparative negligence. Both parties' negligence, if any, could be weighed and the liability distributed proportionately. The defendant could also assert assumption of risk, claiming that the electrician voluntarily entered into a dangerous situation, knowing the risk involved.

CHAPTER 7

1. *Is Superior Vehicles liable? Explain your answer.* Yes. The manufacturer is liable for the injuries to the user of the product. A manufacturer is liable for its failure to exercise due care to any person who sustains an injury proximately caused by a negligently made (defective) product.

2. *If Real, Sweet, and Tasty were not negligent, can they be liable for the injury? Why or why not?* Yes. Under the doctrine of strict liability, persons may be liable for the results of their acts regardless of their intentions or their exercise of reasonable care (that is, regardless of fault).

CHAPTER 8

1. *Has Roslyn violated any of the intellectual property rights discussed in this chapter? Explain.* Yes, Roslyn has committed theft of trade secrets. Lists of suppliers and custom- ers cannot be patented, copyrighted, or trademarked, but the information they contain is protected against appropriation by others as trade secrets. And most likely, Roslyn signed a con- tract, agreeing not to use this information outside her employ- ment by Organic. But even without this contract, Organic could have made a convincing case against its ex-employee for a theft of trade secrets.

2. *Is this patent infringement? If so, how might Global save the cost of suing World for infringement and at the same time profit from World's sales?* This is patent infringement. A software maker in this situation might best protect its product, save litigation costs, and profit from its patent by the use of a license. In the context of this problem, a license would grant permission to sell a patented item. (A license can be limited to certain purposes and to the licensee only.)

CHAPTER 9

1. *Has Karl done anything wrong? Explain.* Karl may have committed trademark infringement. Search engines compile their results by looking through Web sites' key-word fields. Key words, or meta tags, increase the likelihood that a site will be included in search engine results, even if the words have no connection to the site.

A site that appropriates the key words of other sites with more frequent hits will appear in the same search engine results as the more popular sites. But using another's trademark as a key word without the owner's permission normally constitutes trademark infringement. Of course, some uses of another's trade- mark as a meta tag may be permissible if the use is reasonably necessary and does not suggest that the owner authorized or sponsored the use.

2. Can Eagle Corporation stop this use of eagle? If so, what must the company show? Explain. Yes. This may be an instance of trademark dilution. Dilution occurs when a trademark is used, without permission, in a way that diminishes the distinctive quality of the mark. Dilution does not require proof that consumers are likely to be confused by the use of the unauthorized mark. The products involved do not have to be similar. Dilution does require, however, that a mark be famous when the dilution occurs.

CHAPTER 10

1. With respect to the gas station, has she committed a crime? If so, what is it? Yes. With respect to the gas station, she has obtained goods by false pretenses. She might also be charged with larceny and forgery, and most states have special statutes covering illegal use of credit cards.

2. Has Ben committed a crime? If so, what is it? Yes. The Counterfeit Access Device and Computer Fraud and Abuse Act provides that a person who accesses a computer online, without permission, to obtain classified data—such as consumer credit files in a credit agency's database—is subject to criminal prosecution. The crime has two elements: accessing the computer without permission and taking data. It is a felony if done for private financial gain. Penalties include fines and imprisonment for up to twenty years. The victim of the theft can also bring a civil suit against the criminal to obtain damages and other relief.

CHAPTER 11

1. What standard determines whether these parties have a contract? Under the objective theory of contracts, if a reasonable person would have thought that Joli had accepted Kerin's offer when she signed and returned the letter, then a contract was made, and Joli is obligated to buy the book. This depends, in part, on what was said in the letter and what was said in response. For instance, did the letter contain a valid offer, and did the response constitute a valid acceptance? Under any circumstances, the issue is not whether either party subjectively believed that they did, or did not, have a contract.

2. Can Ed recover? Why or why not? No. This contract, although not fully executed, is for an illegal purpose and therefore is void. A void contract gives rise to no legal obligation on the part of any party. A contract that is void is no contract. There is nothing to enforce.

CHAPTER 12

1. Do Fidelity and Ron have a contract? Why or why not? No. Revocation of an offer may be implied by conduct inconsistent with the offer. When the corporation hired someone else, and the offeree learned of the hiring, the offer was revoked. The acceptance was too late.

2. Under the Uniform Electronic Transactions Act, what determines the effect of the electronic documents evi-

dencing the parties' deal? Is a party's "signature" necessary? Explain. First, it might be noted that the UETA does not apply unless the parties to a contract agree to use e-commerce in their transaction. In this deal, of course, the parties used e-commerce. The UETA removes barriers to e-commerce by giving the same legal effect to e-records and e-signatures as to paper documents and signatures. The UETA it does not include rules for those transactions, however.

CHAPTER 13

1. Is the new contract binding? Explain. Yes. The original contract was executory. The parties rescinded it and agreed to a new contract. If Sharyn had broken the contract to accept a contract with another employer, she might have been held liable for damages for the breach.

2. Is Fred's promise binding? Explain. Yes. Under the doctrine of detrimental reliance, or promissory estoppel, the promisee is entitled to payment of $5,000 from the promisor on graduation. There was a promise, on which the promisee relied, the reliance was substantial and definite (the promisee went to college for the full term, incurring considerable expenses, and will likely graduate), and it would only be fair to enforce the promise.

CHAPTER 14

1. Can Kenwood enforce the lease against Joan? Why or why not? No. Joan is a minor and may disaffirm this contract. Because the apartment was a necessary, however, she remains liable for the reasonable value of her occupancy of the apartment.

2. If the cause of an accident is found to be the airline's negligence, can it use the clause as a defense to liability? Why or why not? No. Generally, an exculpatory clause (a clause attempting to absolve parties of negligence or other wrongs) is not enforced if the party seeking its enforcement is involved in a business that is important to the public as a matter of practical necessity, such as an airline. Because of the essential nature of such services, the parties have an advantage in bargaining strength and could insist that anyone contracting for its services agree not to hold it liable.

CHAPTER 15

1. Can she rescind the deal? Why or why not? Yes. Rescission may be granted on the basis of fraudulent misrepresentation. The elements of fraudulent misrepresentation include intent to deceive, or *scienter*. *Scienter* exists if a party makes a statement recklessly, without regard to whether it is true or false, or if a party says or implies that a statement is made on some basis such as personal knowledge or personal investigation when it is not.

2. Can Elle be held liable to GCC? Why or why not? Yes. The accountant may be liable on the ground of negligent misrepresentation. A misrepresentation is negligent if a person fails to exercise reasonable care in disclosing material facts or does not use the skill and competence required by his or her business or profession.

CHAPTER 16

1. Can Midstate enforce a deal for $350 more? Explain your answer. No. Under the UCC, a contract for a sale of goods priced at $500 or more must be in writing to be enforceable. In this case, the contract is not enforceable beyond the quantity already delivered and paid for.

2. Next Corporation argues that there is no written contract between them. What will the court say? The court might conclude that under the doctrine of promissory estoppel, the employer is estopped from claiming the lack of a written contract as a defense. The oral contract may be enforced because the employer made a promise on which the employee justifiably relied in moving to New York, the reliance was foreseeable, and injustice can be avoided only by enforcing the promise. If the court strictly enforces the Statute of Frauds, however, the employee may be without a remedy.

CHAPTER 17

1. Can Jeff successfully sue Ed for the $100? Yes. When one person makes a promise with the intention of benefiting a third person, the third person can sue to enforce it. This is a third party beneficiary contract. The third party in this problem is an intended beneficiary.

2. Can Good Credit enforce the contract against Frank? Why or why not? Yes. Generally, if a contract clearly states that a right is not assignable, no assignment will be effective, but there are exceptions. Assignment of the right to receive monetary payment cannot be prohibited.

CHAPTER 18

1. Before Ready or Stealth starts performing, can the parties call off the deal? What if Stealth has already shipped the pizzas? Explain your answers. Contracts that are executory on both sides—contracts on which neither party has performed—can be rescinded solely by agreement. Contracts that are executed on one side—contracts on which one party has performed—can be rescinded only if the party who has performed receives consideration for the promise to call off the deal.

2. What type of agreement is this? Are Ace's obligations discharged? Why or why not? This is a novation because it substitutes a new party for an original party, by agreement of all the parties. The requirements are a previous valid obligation, an agreement of all the parties to a new contract, extinguishment of the old obligation, and a new, valid contract. Ace's obligations are discharged.

CHAPTER 19

1. If Haney sues Greg, what would be the measure of recovery? A nonbreaching party is entitled to his or her benefit of the bargain under the contract. Here, the innocent party is entitled to be put in the position she would have been in if the contract had been fully performed. The measure of the benefit is the cost to complete the work ($500). These are compensatory damages.

2. Is Lyle liable for Marley's expenses in providing for the cattle? Why or why not? No. To recover damages that flow from the consequences of a breach but that are caused by circumstances beyond the contract (consequential damages), the breaching party must know, or have reason to know, that special circumstances will cause the nonbreaching party to suffer the additional loss. That was not the circumstance in this problem.

CHAPTER 20

1. Is this an acceptance of the offer or a counteroffer? If it is an acceptance, is it a breach of the contract? What if Fav-O-Rite told E-Design it was sending the printer stands as "an accommodation"? A shipment of nonconforming goods constitutes an acceptance of the offer and a breach, unless the seller seasonably notifies the buyer that the nonconforming shipment does not constitute an acceptance and is offered only as an accommodation. Thus, since there was no notification here, the shipment was both an acceptance and a breach. If, however, Fav-O-Rite had notified E-Design that it was sending the printer stands as an accommodation, the shipment would not constitute an acceptance and Fav-O-Rite would not be in breach.

2. Is there an enforceable contract between them? Why or why not? Yes. In a transaction between merchants, the requirement of a writing is satisfied if one of them sends to the other a signed written confirmation that indicates the terms of the agreement, and the merchant receiving it has reason to know of its contents. If the merchant who receives the confirmation does not object in writing within ten days after receipt, the writing will be enforceable against him or her even though he or she has not signed anything.

CHAPTER 21

1. What are the consequences if Silk bore the risk? If Adams bore the risk? Buyers and sellers can have an insurable interest in identical goods at the same time. If the buyer (Silk & Satin) bore the risk, it must pay and seek reimbursement from its insurance company. If the seller (Adams Textiles) bore the risk, it must seek reimbursement from its insurance company and may still have an obligation to deliver the identified goods (the fabric) to Silk & Satin.

2. If Karlin files a lawsuit, will she prevail? Why or why not? When a person "entrusts" goods to a merchant (a person who deals in goods of that kind), the merchant has the power to transfer a good title to any purchaser who acquires the goods in the *ordinary course of business*. Karlin entrusted her set to merchant Orken. Orken deals in goods of that kind. Therefore, Orken could pass good title to the set sold to a customer (Grady) because Grady purchased the goods in the ordinary course of business. Consequently, Karlin cannot get the set back from Grady. (But the merchant is liable to the true owner, Karlin, for the equivalent value of the set).

CHAPTER 22

1. Does Country have the right to reject the shipment? Explain. Yes. A seller is obligated to deliver goods in conformity with a contract in every detail. This is the perfect tender rule. The exception of the seller's right to cure does not apply here, because the seller delivered too little too late to take advantage of this exception.

2. Can Poster Planet sue Brite without waiting until May 1? Why or why not? Yes. When anticipatory repudiation occurs, a buyer (or lessee) can resort to any remedy for breach even if the buyer tells the seller (the repudiating party in this problem) that the buyer will wait for the seller's performance.

CHAPTER 23

1. When it does not perform to GCC's specifications, GCC sues Industrial, which claims, "We didn't expressly promise anything." What should GCC argue? The buyer should argue that the seller breached an implied warranty of fitness for a particular purpose. An implied warranty of fitness for a particular purpose arises when a seller knows a particular purpose for which a buyer will use goods and that the buyer is relying on the seller's skill and judgment to select suitable goods.

2. Can Stella recover for breach of the implied warranty of merchantability? Why or why not? Yes, Stella can recover from Roasted Bean for breach of the implied warranty of merchantability. An implied warranty of merchantability arises in every sale of goods sold by a merchant who deals in goods of the kind. Goods that are merchantable are fit for the ordinary purposes for which such goods are used. A sale of food or drink is a sale of goods. Merchantable food is food that is fit to eat or drink on the basis of consumer expectations. A consumer should reasonably expect hot coffee to be hot, but not to be so scalding that it causes third-degree burns.

CHAPTER 24

1. Under what circumstances would a U.S. court enforce the judgment of the Ecuadoran court? Under the principle of comity, a U.S court would defer and give effect to foreign laws and judicial decrees that are consistent with U.S. law and public policy.

2. How can this attempt to undersell U.S. businesses be defeated? The practice described in this problem is known as dumping, which is regarded as an unfair international trade practice. Dumping is the sale of imported goods at "less than fair value." Based on the price of those goods in the exporting country, an extra tariff—known as an antidumping duty—can be imposed on the imports.

CHAPTER 25

1. If included on that instrument, which of the following would prevent its negotiability—"I.O.U. $600," "I promise to pay $600," or an instruction to Sash's bank stating, "I wish you would pay $600 to Yale"? A statement that "I.O.U." money (or anything else) or an instruction to a bank stating, "I wish you would pay," would render any instrument nonnegotiable. To be negotiable, an instrument must contain an express promise to pay. An I.O.U. is only an acknowledgment of indebtedness. An order stating, "I wish you would pay," is not sufficiently precise.

2. Is Marit's note a demand note? Explain. Yes. Instruments that are payable on demand may state "Payable on demand." The nature of an instrument may indicate that it is payable on demand. If no time for payment is specified, then the instrument is also payable on demand. Here, the note required installments but did not state a date for their payment. That Donald did not make a demand for payment did not affect this characteristic of the note.

CHAPTER 26

1. What type of indorsement is this? What effect does this indorsement have on whether the check is considered an order instrument or a bearer instrument? Explain. This is a special indorsement, which names the indorsee (Kurt). No special words are needed. A special indorsement makes an instrument order paper. Thus, further negotiation requires Kurt's indorsement.

2. Can Carl become an HDC? Why or why not? No. One of the requirements for HDC status is that the holder must have performed the promise for which the instrument was issued. A holder takes the instrument for value only to the extent that the promise has been performed. Because Ben did not perform his promise to repair Amy's roof, he is not an HDC. Thus, Carl—who took the instrument from Ben—cannot trace his title back to an HDC, so he is not be protected as an HDC under the shelter principle.

CHAPTER 27

1. Does Suchin have any recourse against the bank for the payment? Why or why not? No. When a drawer's employee provides the drawer with the name of a fictitious payee (a payee whom the drawer does not actually intend to have any interest in an instrument), a forgery of the payee's name is effective to pass good title to subsequent transferees.

2. Is the bookstore a holder in due course (HDC) of Skye's check? Yes. One of the requirements for HDC status is a lack of notice that an instrument is defective. A party will not attain this status if he or she knows, or has reason to know, that an incomplete instrument was later completed in an unauthorized manner. Notice of a defective instrument is given when a holder has reason to know that a defect exists, given all of the facts known at the time. Here, the bookstore did not have notice that Skye's check was incomplete when it was issued. The bookstore saw only a properly completed instrument.

CHAPTER 28

1. Is Lyn liable to Nan? Could Lyn be subject to criminal prosecution? Why or why not? Yes, to both questions. In a civil suit, a drawer (Lyn) is liable to a payee (Nan) or to a holder of a check that is not honored. If intent to defraud can be proved, the drawer (Lyn) can also be subject to criminal prosecution for writing a bad check.

2. How much, if anything, can Roni recover? From whom can the bank recover this amount? The drawer is entitled to $6,300—the amount to which the check was altered ($7,000) less the amount that the drawer ordered the bank to pay ($700). The bank may recover this amount from the party who presented the altered check for payment.

CHAPTER 29

1. What can Larry and Midwest do? Each of the parties can place a mechanic's lien on the debtor's property. If the debtor does not pay what is owed, the property can be sold to satisfy the debt. The only requirements are that the lien be filed within a specific time from the time of the work, depending on the state statute, and notice of the foreclosure and sale must be given to the debtor in advance.

2. If the employer complies with the order and Al stays on the job, is one order enough to garnish all of Al's wages for each pay period until the debt is paid? Why? No. In some states, a creditor must go back to court for a separate order of garnishment for each pay period. Also, federal and state laws limit the amount of money that can be garnished from a debtor's pay.

CHAPTER 30

1. How can Olivia let other creditors know of her interest in the computer? A creditor can put other creditors on notice by perfecting its interest: by filing a financing statement in the appropriate public office, or by taking possession of the collateral until the debtor repays the loan.

2. Liberty could repossess and keep the car, but the bank does not want it. What are the alternatives? When collateral is consumer goods with a PMSI, and the debtor has paid less than 60 percent of the debt or the purchase price, the creditor can dispose of the collateral in a commercially reasonable manner, which generally requires notice to the debtor of the place, time, and manner of sale. A debtor can waive the right to notice, but only after default. Before the disposal, a debtor can redeem the collateral by tendering performance of all of the obligations secured by it and by paying the creditor's reasonable expenses in retaking and maintaining it.

CHAPTER 31

1. Are these debts dischargeable in bankruptcy? Explain. No. Besides the claims listed in this problem, the debts that cannot be discharged in bankruptcy include amounts borrowed to pay back taxes, goods obtained by fraud, debts that were not listed in the petition, domestic support obligations, certain cash advances, and others.

2. Can Quentin recover the $10,000 paid to Ogden on June 1? Why or why not? Yes. A debtor's payment to a creditor made for a preexisting debt, within ninety days (one year in the case of an insider or fraud) of a bankruptcy filing, can be recovered if it gives a creditor more than he or she would have received in the bankruptcy proceedings. A trustee can recover this preference using his or her specific avoidance powers.

CHAPTER 32

1. Was Winona an independent contractor? Yes. An independent contractor is a person who contracts with another— the principal—to do something but who is neither controlled by the other nor subject to the other's right to control with respect to the performance. Independent contractors are not employees, because those who hire them have no control over the details of their performance.

2. When Nadine learns the difference between the price that Dimka is willing to pay and the price at which the owner is willing to sell, she wants to buy the land and sell it to Dimka herself. Can she do this? Discuss. No. Nadine, as an agent, is prohibited from taking advantage of the agency relationship to obtain property that the principal (Dimka Corporation) wants to purchase. This is the duty of loyalty that arises with every agency relationship.

CHAPTER 33

1. Can Davis hold Estee liable for whatever damages he has to pay? Why or why not? Yes. A principal has a duty to indemnify an agent for liabilities incurred because of authorized and lawful acts and transactions and for losses suffered because of the principal's failure to perform his or her duties.

2. In what circumstance is Vivian liable on the note? When a person enters into a contract on another's behalf without the authority to do so, the other may be liable on the contract if he or she approves or affirms that contract. In other words, the employer-principal would be liable for the note in this problem on ratifying it. Whether the employer-principal ratifies the note or not, the unauthorized agent is most likely also liable for it.

CHAPTER 34

1. For Erin to obtain workers' compensation, does her injury have to have been caused by Fine Print's negligence? Does it matter whether the action causing the injury was intentional? Explain. Workers' compensation laws establish a procedure for compensating workers who are injured on the job. Instead of suing to collect benefits, an injured worker notifies the employer of an injury and files a claim with the appropriate state agency.

The right to recover is normally determined without regard to negligence or fault, but intentionally inflicted injuries are not covered. Unlike the potential for recovery in a lawsuit based on negligence or fault, recovery under a workers' compensation statute is limited to the specific amount designated in the statute for the employee's injury.

2. Are these conditions legal? Why or why not? No. A closed shop (a company that requires union membership as a condition of employment) is illegal. A union shop (a company that does not require union membership as a condition of employment but requires workers to join the union after a certain time on the job) is illegal in a state with a right-to-work law, which makes it illegal to require union membership for continued employment.

CHAPTER 35

1. *Is this sexual harassment? Why or why not?* Yes. One type of sexual harassment occurs when a request for sexual favors is a condition of employment, and the person making the request is a supervisor or acts with the authority of the employer. A tangible employment action, such as continued employment, may also lead to the employer's liability for the supervisor's conduct. That the injured employee is a male and the supervisor a female, instead of the other way around, would not affect the outcome. Same-gender harassment is also actionable.

2. *Could Koko succeed in a suit against Lively for discrimination? Explain.* Yes, if she can show that she was not hired solely because of her disability. The other elements for a discrimination suit based on a disability are that the plaintiff (1) has a disability and (2) is otherwise qualified for the job. Both of these elements appear to be satisfied in this problem.

CHAPTER 36

1. *Which form of business organization would be most appropriate?* When a business is relatively small and is not diversified, employs relatively few people, has modest profits, and is not likely to expand significantly or require extensive financing in the immediate future, the most appropriate form for doing business may be a sole proprietorship.

2. *Does this constitute "cause" for termination? Why or why not?* Yes. Failing to meet a specified sales quota can constitute a breach of a franchise agreement. If the franchisor is acting in good faith, "cause" may also include the death or disability of the franchisee, the insolvency of the franchisee, and a breach of another term of the franchise agreement.

CHAPTER 37

1. *When Darnell dies, his widow claims that as Darnell's heir, she is entitled to take his place as Eliana's partner or to receive a share of the firm's assets. Is she right? Why or why not?* No. A widow (or widower) has no right to take a dead partner's place. A partner's death causes dissociation after which the partnership must purchase the dissociated partner's partnership interest. Therefore, the surviving partners must pay the decedent's estate (for his widow) the value of the deceased partner's interest in the partnership.

2. *Because the vehicles would otherwise be sitting idle in a parking lot, can Finian keep the income that results from leasing the delivery vehicles? Explain your answer.* No. Under the partners' fiduciary duty, a partner must account to the partnership for any personal profits or benefits derived without the consent of all the partners in connection with the use of any partnership property. Here, the leasing partner may not keep the money.

CHAPTER 38

1. *What are their options with respect to the management of their firm?* The members of a limited liability company (LLC) may designate a group to run their firm, in which situation the firm would be considered a manager-managed LLC. The group may include only members, only nonmembers, or members and nonmembers. If instead, all members participate in management, the firm would be a member-managed LLC. In fact, unless the members agree otherwise, all members are considered to participate in the management of the firm.

2. *What do these forms of business organization have in common?* Although there are differences, all of these forms of business organizations resemble corporations. A joint stock company, for example, features ownership by shares of stock, it is managed by directors and officers, and it has perpetual existence. A business trust, like a corporation, distributes profits to persons who are not personally responsible for the debts of the organization. Management of a business trust is in the hands of trustees, just as the management of a corporation is in the hands of directors and officers. An incorporated cooperative, which is subject to state laws covering nonprofit corporations, distributes profits to its owners.

CHAPTER 39

1. *Is there a way for Northwest Brands to avoid this double taxation? Explain your answer.* Yes. Small businesses that meet certain requirements can qualify as S corporations, created specifically to permit small businesses to avoid double taxation. The six requirements of an S corporation are (1) the firm must be a domestic corporation, (2) the firm must not be a member of an affiliated group of corporations, (3) the firm must have less than a certain number of shareholders, (4) the shareholders must be individuals, estates, or qualified trusts (or corporations in some cases), (5) there can be only one class of stock, and (6) no shareholder can be a nonresident alien.

2. *Can they grant this authority to their firm? If so, how? If not, why not?* Broad authority to conduct business can be granted in a corporation's articles of incorporation. For example, the term "any lawful purpose" is often used. This can be important because acts of a corporation that are beyond the authority given to it in its articles or charter (or state statutes) are considered illegal, *ultra vires* acts.

CHAPTER 40

1. *Yvon, a Wonder shareholder, learns of the purchase and wants to sue the directors on Wonder's behalf. Can she do it? Explain.* Yes. A shareholder can bring a derivative suit on behalf of a corporation, if some wrong is done to the corporation. Normally, any damages recovered go into the corporate treasury.

2. *Discuss whether Nico owes a duty to Omega or the minority shareholders in selling his shares.* Yes. A single shareholder—or a few shareholders acting together—who owns enough stock to exercise *de facto* control over a corporation owes the corporation and minority shareholders a fiduciary duty when transferring those shares.

CHAPTER 41

1. *What is the term for this type of combination? What happens to the assets, property, and liabilities of Micro?* This combination is a consolidation (a new entity takes the place of the consolidating, disappearing firms). In a merger, one of the merging entities continues to exist. In a consolidation, the new corporation, MM, Inc., inherits all of Micro's assets, property, and liabilities.

2. *Can McClellan hold Peppertree's shareholders personally liable for the debt? Why or why not?* Maybe. If a corporation organizes another corporation with practically the same shareholders and directors and transfers all the assets but does not pay all the first corporation's debts, a court can hold the new corporation liable. Here, the new corporation continued to carry on the same business as Peppertree with all of Peppertree's assets, so it would be fair for a court to hold the new corporation liable for Peppertree's obligations.

CHAPTER 42

1. *What sort of information would an investor consider material?* The average investor is not concerned with minor inaccuracies but with facts that if disclosed would tend to deter him or her from buying the securities. This would include facts that have an important bearing on the condition of the issuer and its business—liabilities, loans to officers and directors, customer delinquencies, and pending lawsuits.

2. *Can Lee take advantage of this information to buy and sell Magma stock? Why or why not?* No. The Securities Exchange Act of 1934 extends liability to officers and directors in their personal transactions for taking advantage of inside information when they know it is unavailable to the persons with whom they are dealing.

CHAPTER 43

1. *What safeguards promote the ALJ's fairness?* Under the Administrative Procedure Act (APA), the administrative law judge (ALJ) must be separate from the agency's investigative and prosecutorial staff. *Ex parte* communications between the ALJ and a party to a proceeding are prohibited. Under the APA, an ALJ is exempt from agency discipline except on a showing of good cause.

2. *Does the firm have any opportunity to express its opinion about the pending rule? Explain.* Yes. Administrative rulemaking starts with the publication of a notice of the rulemaking in the *Federal Register*. A public hearing is held at which proponents and opponents can offer evidence and question witnesses. After the hearing, the agency considers what was presented at the hearing and drafts the final rule.

CHAPTER 44

1. *To market the drug, what must United prove to the Food and Drug Administration?* Under an extensive set of procedures established by the U.S. Food and Drug Administration, which administers the federal Food, Drug, and Cosmetic Act, drugs must be shown to be effective as well as safe before they may be marketed to the public. In general, manufacturers are responsible for ensuring that the drugs they offer for sale are free of any substances that could injure consumers.

2. *What can Gert do?* Under the Truth-in-Lending Act, a buyer who wishes to withhold payment for a faulty product purchased with a credit card must follow specific procedures to settle the dispute. The credit card issuer then must intervene and attempt to settle the dispute.

CHAPTER 45

1. *Are there any reasons that the court might refuse to issue an injunction against Resource's operation? Explain.* Yes. On the ground that the hardships that would be imposed on the polluter and on the community are greater than the hardships suffered by the residents, the court might deny an injunction. If the plant is the core of the local economy, for instance, the residents may be awarded only damages.

2. *If the Environmental Protection Agency cleans up the site, from whom can it recover the cost?* The Comprehensive Environmental Response, Compensation, and Liability Act of 1980 regulates the clean-up of hazardous waste disposal sites. Any potentially responsible party can be charged with the entire cost of cleaning up a site. Potentially responsible parties include the person that generated the waste (ChemCorp) the person that transported the waste to the site (Disposal), the person that owned or operated the site at the time of the disposal (Eliminators), and the current owner or operator of the site (Fluid). A party held responsible for the entire cost may be able to recoup some of it in a lawsuit against other potentially responsible parties.

CHAPTER 46

1. *If Pop's is a monopolist, is it in violation of Section 2 of the Sherman Act? Why or why not?* Size alone does not determine whether a firm is a monopoly—size in relation to the market is what matters. A small store in a small, isolated town is a monopolist if it is the only store serving that market. Monopoly involves the power to affect prices and output. If a firm has sufficient market power to control prices and exclude competition, that firm has monopoly power. Monopoly power in itself is not a violation of Section 2 of the Sherman Act. The offense also requires that the defendant intended to acquire or maintain that power through anticompetitive means.

2. *What factors would a court consider to decide whether this arrangement violates the Clayton Act?* This agreement is a tying arrangement. The legality of a tying arrangement depends the purpose of the agreement, the agreement's likely effect on competition in the relevant markets (the market for the tying product and the market for the tied product), and other factors. Tying arrangements for commodities are subject to Section 3 of the Clayton Act. Tying arrangements for services can be agreements in restraint of trade in violation of Section 1 of the Sherman Act.

CHAPTER 47

1. Can the bank successfully sue Dave? Why or why not? Yes. In these circumstances, when the accountant knows that the bank will use the statement, the bank is a foreseeable user. A foreseeable user is a third party within the class of parties to whom an accountant may be liable for negligence.

2. Can Nora be held liable to Pat? Explain. No. In the circumstances described, the accountant will not be held liable to a purchaser of the securities. Although an accountant may be liable under securities laws for including untrue statements or omitting material facts from financial statements, due diligence is a defense to liability.

Due diligence requires an accountant to conduct a reasonable investigation and have reason to believe that the financial statements were true at the time. The facts say that the misstatement of material fact in Omega's financial statement was not attributable to any fraud or negligence on Nora's part. Therefore, Nora can show that she used due diligence and will not be held liable to Pat.

CHAPTER 48

1. Does Speedy have a right to recover from the third party for the loss of the documents? Why or why not? Yes. A bailee's right of possession, even though temporary, permits the bailee to recover damages from any third persons for damage or loss to the property.

2. Who suffers the loss? Explain your answer. Rosa de la Mar Corporation, the shipper, suffers the loss. A common carrier is liable for damage caused by the willful acts of third persons or by an accident. Other losses must be borne by the shipper (or the recipient, depending on the terms of their contract). This shipment was lost due to an act of God.

CHAPTER 49

1. Delmira wants to have Consuela evicted from the property. What can Consuela do? This is a breach of the warranty deed's covenant of quiet enjoyment. The buyer can sue the seller and recover the purchase price of the house, plus any damages.

2. Can Haven transfer possession for even less time to Idyll Company? Explain. Yes. An owner of a fee simple has

the most rights possible—he or she can give the property away, sell it, transfer it by will, use it for almost any purpose, possess it to the exclusion of all the world, or as in this case, transfer possession for any period of time. The party to whom possession is transferred can also transfer his or her interest (usually only with the owner's permission) for any lesser period of time.

CHAPTER 50

1. Can the insurer refuse payment? Why or why not? No. An incorrect statement as to the age of an insured is a misrepresentation. Under an incontestability clause, however, after a policy has been in force for a certain time (usually two or three years), the insurer cannot cancel the policy or avoid a claim on the basis of statements made in the application.

2. Can Al obtain payment for these events? Explain your answers. No. To obtain insurance, one must have a sufficiently substantial interest in whatever is to be insured. One has an insurable interest in property if one would suffer a pecuniary loss from its destruction. This interest must exist *when the loss occurs.*

To obtain insurance on another's life, one must have a reasonable expectation of benefit from the continued life of the other. The benefit may be founded on a relationship, but "ex-spouse" alone is not such a relationship. An interest in someone's life must exist *when the policy is obtained.*

CHAPTER 51

1. Can Toby and Umeko have Sheila's will revoked on the ground that she did not have the capacity to make a will? Why or why not? No. To have testamentary capacity, a testator must be of legal age and sound mind *at the time the will is made.* Generally, the testator must (1) know the nature of the act, (2) comprehend and remember the "natural objects of his or her bounty," (3) know the nature and extent of her or his property, and (4) understand the distribution of assets called for by the will. In this situation, Sheila had testamentary capacity at the time she made the will. The fact that she was ruled mentally incompetent two years after making the will does not provide sufficient grounds to revoke it.

2. What determines who gets what? The estate will pass according to the state's intestacy laws. Intestacy laws set out how property is distributed when a person dies without a will. Their purpose is to carry out the likely intent of the decedent. The laws determine which of the deceased's natural heirs (including first the surviving spouse, second lineal descendants, third parents, and finally collateral heirs) inherit his or her property.

PROBLEM 1–6. *Reading Citations.* The court's opinion in this case—*United States v. Yi*, 704 F.3d 800 (9th Cir. 2013)—can be found in volume 704 of West's *Federal Reporter,* Third Series, on page 800. The United States Court of Appeals for the Ninth Circuit issued this opinion in 2013.

PROBLEM 2–3. *Arbitration Clause.* Based on a recent holding by the Washington state supreme court, the federal appeals court held that the arbitration provision was unconscionable and therefore invalid. Because it was invalid, the restriction on class-action suits was also invalid.

The state court held that placing class action restrictions in arbitrations agreements with consumers improperly stripped consumers of rights they would normally have to attack certain industry practices. Class-action suits are often brought in cases alleging deceptive or unfair industry practices when the losses suffered by the individual consumer are too small to warrant the consumer bringing suit. In other words, the supposed added cell phone fees were so small that no individual consumer would be likely to litigate or arbitrate the matter due to the expenses involved. Therefore, the clause in the arbitration agreement preventing consumers from joining together in a class-action suit violates public policy and is void and unenforceable.

PROBLEM 3–8. *Discovery.* Yes, the items that were deleted from a Facebook page can be recovered. Normally, a party must hire an expert to recover material in an electronic format, and this can be time consuming and expensive.

Electronic evidence, or e-evidence, consists of all computer-generated or electronically recorded information, such as posts on Facebook and other social media sites. The effect that e-evidence can have in a case depends on its relevance and what it reveals. In the facts presented in this problem, Isaiah should be sanctioned—he should be required to cover Allied's cost of hiring the recovery expert and attorneys' fees for confronting the misconduct. In a jury trial, the court might also instruct the jury to presume that any missing items are harmful to Isaiah's case. If all of the material is retrieved and presented at the trial, any prejudice to Allied's case might thereby be mitigated. If not, the court might go so far as to order a new trial.

In the actual case on which this problem is based, Allied hired an expert, who determined that Isaiah had in fact removed some photos and other items from his Facebook page. After the expert testified about the missing material, Isaiah provided Allied with all of it, including the photos that he had deleted. Allied requested a retrial, but the court instead reduced the amount of Isaiah's damages by the amount that it cost Allied to address his "misconduct."

PROBLEM 4–6. *Establishment Clause.* The establishment clause prohibits the government from passing laws or taking actions that promote religion or show a preference for one religion over another. In assessing a government action, the courts look at the predominant purpose of the action and ask whether the action has the effect of endorsing religion.

Although here DeWeese claimed to have a nonreligious purpose for displaying the poster of the Ten Commandments in a courtroom, his own statements showed a religious purpose. These statements reflected his views about "warring" legal philosophies and his belief that "our legal system is based on moral absolutes from divine law handed down by God through the Ten Commandments." This plainly constitutes a religious purpose that violates the establishment clause because it has the effect of endorsing Judaism or Christianity over other religions. In the case on which this problem is based, the court ruled in favor of the American Civil Liberties Union.

PROBLEM 5–5. *Online Privacy.* Facebook created a program that makes decisions for users. Many believe that privacy is an extremely important right that should be fiercely protected. Thus, using duty-based ethics, any program that has a default setting of giving out information is unethical. Facebook should create the program as an opt-in program.

In addition, under the Kantian categorical imperative, if every company used opt-out programs that allowed the disclosure of potentially personal information, privacy might become merely theoretical. If privacy were reduced or eliminated, the world might not be a better place. From a utilitarian or outcome-based approach, an opt-out program might offer the benefits of being easy to created and start, as well as making it easy to recruit partner programs. On the negative side, the program would eliminate users' ability to chose whether to disclose information about themselves. An opt-in program would maintain that user control but might entail higher start-up costs because it would require more marketing to users up front to persuade them to opt in.

PROBLEM 6–8. *Negligence.* Negligence requires proof that (a) the defendant owed a duty of care to the plaintiff, (b) the defendant breached that duty, (c) the defendant's breach caused the plaintiff's injury, and (d) the plaintiff suffered a legally recognizable injury. With respect to the duty of care, a business owner has a duty to use reasonable care to protect business invitees. This duty includes an obligation to discover and correct or warn of unreasonably dangerous conditions that the owner of the premises should reasonably foresee might endanger an invitee. Some risks are so obvious that an owner need not warn of them. But even if a risk is obvious, a business owner may not be excused from the duty to protect its customers from foreseeable harm.

Because Lucario was the Weatherford's business invitee, the hotel owed her a duty of reasonable care to make its premises safe for her use. The balcony ran nearly the entire width of the window in Lucario's room. She could have reasonably believed that the window was a means of access to the balcony. The window/ balcony configuration was dangerous, however, because the window opened wide enough for an adult to climb out, but the twelve-inch gap between one side of the window and the balcony was unprotected. This unprotected gap opened to a drop of more than three stories to a concrete surface below.

Should the hotel have anticipated the potential harm to a guest opening the window in Room 59 and attempting to access the balcony? The hotel encouraged guests to "step out onto the balcony" to smoke. The dangerous window/balcony configuration could have been remedied at a minimal cost. These circumstances could be perceived as creating an "unreasonably dangerous" condition. And it could be concluded that the hotel created or knew of the condition and failed to take reasonable steps to warn of it or correct it. Of course, the Weatherford might argue that the window/ balcony configuration was so obvious that the hotel was not liable for Lucario's fall.

In the actual case on which this problem is based, the court concluded that the Weatherford did not breach its duty of care to Lucario. On McMurtry's appeal, a state intermediate appellate court held that this conclusion was in error, vacated the lower court's judgment in favor of the hotel on this issue, and remanded the case.

PROBLEM 7–8. *Product Liability.* Here, the accident was caused by Jett's inattention, not by the texting device in the cab of his truck. In a product liability case based on a design defect, the plaintiff has to prove that the product was defective at the time it left the hands of the seller or lessor. The plaintiff must also show that this defective condition made the product "unreasonably dangerous" to the user or consumer. If the product was delivered in a safe condition and subsequent mishandling made it harmful to the user, the seller or lessor normally is not liable. To successfully assert a design defect, a plaintiff has to show that a reasonable alternative design was available and that the defendant failed to use it.

The plaintiffs could contend that the defendant manufacturer of the texting device owed them a duty of care because injuries to vehicle drivers and passengers, and others on the roads, were reasonably foreseeable due to the product's design that (a) required the driver to divert his eyes from the road to view an incoming text from the dispatcher and (b) permitted the receipt of texts while the vehicle was moving. But manufacturers are not required to design a product incapable of distracting a driver. The duty owed by a manufacturer to the user or consumer of a product does not require guarding against hazards that are commonly known or obvious or protecting against injuries that result from a user's careless conduct. That is what happened here.

In the actual case on which this problem is based, the court reached the same conclusion, based on the reasoning stated above, and an intermediate appellate court affirmed the judgment.

PROBLEM 8–5. *Trade Secrets.* Some business information that cannot be protected by trademark, patent, or copyright law is protected against appropriation by competitors as trade secrets. Trade secrets consist of anything that makes a company unique and that would have value to a competitor—customer lists, plans, research and development, pricing information, marketing techniques, and production techniques, for example. Theft of trade secrets is a federal crime.

In this problem, the documents in the boxes in the car could constitute trade secrets. But a number of factors suggest that a finding of theft and imposition of liability would not be appropriate. The boxes were not marked in any way that would indicate they contained confidential information. The boxes were stored in an employee's car. The alleged thief was the employee's spouse, not a CPR competitor, and she apparently had no idea what was in the boxes. Leaving trade secrets so accessible does not show an effort to protect the information.

In the case on which this problem is based, the court dismissed Jones's claim, in part on the reasoning stated above.

PROBLEM 9–6. *Privacy.* No, Rolfe did not have a privacy interest in the information obtained by the subpoenas issued to Midcontinent Communications. The courts have held that the right to privacy is guaranteed by the U.S. Constitution's Bill of Rights, and some state constitutions contain an explicit guarantee of the right. A person must have a reasonable expectation of privacy, though, to maintain a suit or to assert a successful defense for an invasion of privacy.

People clearly have a reasonable expectation of privacy when they enter their personal banking or credit-card information online. They also have a reasonable expectation that online companies will follow their own privacy policies. But people do not a reasonable expectation of privacy in statements made on Twitter and other data that they publicly disseminate. In other words, there is no violation of a subscriber's right to privacy when a third party Internet service provider receives a subpoena and discloses the subscriber's information.

Here, Rolfe supplied his e-mail address and other personal information, including his Internet protocol address, to Midcontinent. In other words, Rolfe publicly disseminated this information. Law enforcement officers obtained this information from Midcontinent through the subpoenas issued by the South Dakota state court. Rolfe provided his information to Midcontinent—he has no legitimate expectation of privacy in that information.

In the actual case on which this problem is based, Rolfe was charged with, and convicted of, possessing, manufacturing, and distributing child pornography, as well as other crimes. As part of the proceedings, the court found that Rolfe had no expectation of privacy in the information that he made available to Midcontinent. On appeal, the South Dakota Supreme Court upheld the conviction.

PROBLEM 10–8. *Criminal Liability.* Yes, Green exhibited the required mental state to establish criminal liability. A wrongful mental state *(mens rea)* is one of the elements typically required to establish criminal liability. The required mental state, or intent, is indicated in an applicable statute or law. For example, for murder, the required mental state is the intent to take another's life. A court can also find that the required mental state is present when a defendant's acts are reckless or criminally negligent. A defendant is criminally reckless if he or she consciously disregards a substantial and unjustifiable risk.

In this problem, Green was clearly aware of the danger to which he was exposing people on the street below, but he did not indicate that he specifically intended to harm anyone. The risk of death created by his conduct, however, was obvious. He must have known what was likely to happen if a bottle or plate thrown from the height of twenty-six stories hit a pedestrian or the windshield of an occupied motor vehicle on the street below. Despite his claim that he was intoxicated, he was sufficiently aware to stop throwing things from the balcony when he saw police in the area, and he later recalled what he had done and what had happened.

In the actual case on which this problem is based, after a jury trial, Green was convicted of reckless endangerment. On appeal, a state intermediate appellate court affirmed the conviction, based in part on the reasoning stated above.

PROBLEM 11–7. *Quasi Contract.* Gutkowski does not have a valid claim for payment, nor should he recover on the basis of a quasi contract. Courts impose quasi contracts on parties in the interest of fairness and justice.

Usually, a quasi contract is imposed to avoid the unjust enrichment of one party at the expense of another. Here, Gutkowski was compensated as a consultant. To establish a claim that he is due more compensation based on unjust enrichment, he must have proof. As it is, he has only his claim that there were discussions about him being a part owner of YES. Discussions and negotiations are not a basis for recovery on a quasi contract.

In the actual case on which this problem is based, the court dismissed Gutkowski's claim for payment.

PROBLEM 12–5. *Offer and Acceptance.* No, a contract was not formed in this case. As the Iowa Supreme Court pointed out, the parties must voluntarily agree to enter into a contract. Courts determine whether an offer has been made objectively—not subjectively.

Under the *Restatement of Contracts (Second)*, "the test for an offer is whether it induces a reasonable belief in the recipient that [the recipient] can, by accepting, bind the sender." The offeror may decide to whom to extend the offer. According to the *Restatement,* an offer may create a power of acceptance in a specified person or in one or more of a specified group or class of persons, acting separately or together.

The court hearing this case explained: "In this situation, Prairie Meadows is the offeror. It makes an offer to its patrons that, if accepted by wagering an amount and the patron wins, it will pay off the wager. Simply stated, the issue is whether Prairie Meadows made an offer to Blackford. Because Prairie Meadows has the ability to determine the class of individuals to whom the offer is made, it may also exclude certain individuals. Blackford had been banned for life from the casino. . . . Under an objective test, unless the ban had been lifted, Blackford could not have reasonably believed he was among the class of individuals invited to accept Prairie Meadows's offer."

In the actual case on which this problem is based, the jury found that the ban against Blackford had not been lifted and, therefore, Prairie Meadows had not extended him an offer to wager. Because there was no offer to him, no contract could result. The state supreme court therefore reversed the decision of the state appellate court and affirmed the trial court's judgment.

PROBLEM 13–6. *Rescission.* As the reviewing court noted, "rescission is intended to restore the parties as nearly as possible to their former positions and 'to bring about substantial justice by adjusting the equities between the parties.'" Rescission does not occur if a contract is affirmed—it means the contract is repudiated.

Here, rescission is appropriate because the contracting parties were mutually mistaken as to the condition of the property. The environmental contamination substantially reduced the property's value. When an agreement to purchase property is subject to rescission, "the seller must refund all payments received in connection with the sale." Hence, the award of damages to the Berensteins was reversed, and the Sharabianlous' deposit was refunded.

PROBLEM 14–5. *Unconscionable Contracts or Clauses.* In this case, the agreement restricted the buyer's options for resolution of a dispute to arbitration and limited the amount of damages. This agreement was both procedurally and substantively unconscionable. Procedural unconscionability concerns the manner in which the parties enter into a contract. Substantive unconscionability can occur when a contract leaves one party to the agreement without a remedy for the nonperformance of the other.

Here, GeoEx told customers that the arbitration terms in its release form were nonnegotiable and that climbers would encounter the same requirements with any other travel company. This amounted to procedural unconscionability, underscoring the customers' lack of bargaining power. The imbalance resulted in oppressive terms, with no real negotiation and an absence of meaningful choice. Furthermore, the restriction on forum (San Francisco) and the limitation on damages (the cost of the trip)—with no limitation on GeoEx's damages—amounted to substantive unconscionability. In the actual case on which this problem is based, the court ruled that the agreement was unconscionable.

PROBLEM 15–5. *Fraudulent Misrepresentation.* Esprit's argument is not credible because the fact that the house was later sold for a good price had nothing to do with the extra costs incurred by the Wilcoxes. The Wilcoxes had borrowed about a million dollars to finance the project, and Esprit knew that. The court determined that "a promise made without a present intent to perform is a misrepresentation of a material fact and is sufficient to support a cause of action for fraud."

Esprit had promised to deliver precut and predrilled logs that could be assembled quickly. It knew the delivery of unfinished logs would cause problems. "After the logs arrived at the home, Esprit further misrepresented that there would be only a two- or three-day delay while the logs where cut and drilled on site. The jury could conclude that Esprit's actions amounted to fraud or such indifference to negative consequences for the buyers as to support an award for punitive damages." The judgment of the lower court was affirmed.

PROBLEM 16–5. *The Parol Evidence Rule.* Vaks and Mangano may not recover for breach of an oral contract. Under the parol evidence rule, if there is a written contract representing the complete and final statement of the parties' agreement, a party may not introduce any evidence of past agreements. Here, the written agreement was an integrated contract because the parties intended it to be a complete and final statement of the terms of their agreement. Vaks and Mangano therefore may not introduce evidence of any inconsistent oral representations made before the contract was executed.

PROBLEM 17–5. *Duties That Cannot Be Delegated.* No. As a general rule, any duty can be delegated. Delegation is prohibited, however, when the contract expressly prohibits delegation. An attempted delegation will render the contract void. But the other party to the contract can consent to the delegation by accepting the delegatee's performance, and the contract will remain valid. If so, that party cannot later object that the delegation breached the contract.

An antidelegation clause, as in the contract in this problem, must be enforced when the delegation is attempted, not after the delegatee's performance is accepted. Because Albea consented to the delegation of APAC's duties under the subcontract to Matthews, Albea is liable to APAC for the labor and materials expended before that delegation.

In the actual case on which this problem is based, the court granted a judgment to APAC.

PROBLEM 18–6. *Conditions of Performance.* Maciel was not correct. In this problem, the performance of a legal obligation under the parties' contract was contingent on a condition—the occurrence of a certain event. If the condition was not satisfied, the obligations of the parties were discharged. Here, Regent University promised to provide an apartment in its housing facility to Maciel as long as he maintained his status as a Regent student. Maintaining student status was the condition for the university's provision of an apartment. On the termination of that status, Regent was entitled to require Maciel to vacate the apartment.

Maciel chose to withdraw from the university at the end of the spring semester, which rendered him ineligible to remain in the apartment. In other words, this decision resulted in noncompliance with the condition for the university's provision of an apartment, and the university was thus no longer bound to perform. Contrary to Maciel's argument in court, he did not have the "legal authority" to continue to occupy the apartment.

In the actual case on which this problem is based, the court convicted Maciel of trespassing. In response to Maciel's argument, a state intermediate appellate court applied the reasoning set out above to affirm the conviction.

PROBLEM 19–6. *Consequential Damages.* Simard is liable only for the losses and expenses related to the first resale. Simard could reasonably anticipate that his breach would require another sale and that the sales price might be less than what he agreed to pay. Therefore, he should be liable for the difference between his sales price and the first resale price ($29,000), plus any expenses arising from the first resale. Simard is not liable, however, for any expenses and losses related to the second resale. After all, Simard did not cause the second purchaser's default, and he could not reasonably foresee that default as a probable result of his breach.

PROBLEM 20–4. *Additional Terms.* No. The Uniform Commercial Code (UCC) dispenses with the common law mirror image rule, which requires that the terms of an acceptance exactly mirror the terms of the offer. Under the UCC, a contract is formed if the offeree makes a definite expression of acceptance even though the terms of the acceptance modify or add to the terms of the offer.

When both parties to the contract are merchants, the additional terms become part of their contract *unless* (a) the original offer expressly required acceptance of its terms, (b) the new or changed terms materially alter the contract, or (c) the offeror rejects the new or changed terms within a reasonable time.

In this problem, the UCC applies because the transactions involve sales of goods. The original offer stated, "By signing below, you agree to the terms." This statement could be construed to expressly require acceptance of the terms to make the offer a binding contract (exception a above).

The contract stated that JMAM was to receive credit for any rejected merchandise. Nothing indicated that the merchandise would be returned to BSI. Baracsi, BSI's owner (the offeree), signed JMAM's (the offeror's) letter in the appropriate location, thereby indicating BSI's agreement to the terms. Thus, BSI made a definite expression of acceptance. The practice of the parties—for six years rejected items were not returned—further supports the conclusion that their contract did not contemplate the return of those items. The "PS" could be interpreted as materially altering the contract (exception b above).

In the actual case on which this problem is based, the court dismissed BSI's complaint.

PROBLEM 21–6. *Passage of Title.* Altieri held title to the car that she was driving at the time of the accident in which Godfrey was injured. Once goods exist and are identified, title can be determined. Under the Uniform Commercial Code (UCC), any explicit understanding between the buyer and the seller determines when title passes. If there is no such agreement, title passes to the buyer at the time and place that the seller physically delivers the goods. In lease contracts, title to the goods is retained by the lessor-owner of the goods. The UCC's provisions relating to passage to title do not apply to leased goods.

Here, Altieri originally leased the car from G.E. Capital Auto Lease, Inc., but by the time of the accident, she had bought it. Even though she had not fully paid for the car or completed the transfer-of-title paperwork, she owned it. Title to the car passed to Altieri when she bought it and took delivery of it. Thus, Altieri, not G.E., was the owner of the car at the time of the accident. In the actual case on which this problem is based, the court concluded that G.E. was not the owner of the vehicle when Godfrey was injured.

PROBLEM 22–8. *Nonconforming Goods.* Padma Paper Mills notified Universal Exports about its breach, so Padma has two ways to recover even though it accepted the goods.

Padma's first option is to argue that it revoked its acceptance, giving it the right to reject the goods. To revoke acceptance, Padma would have to show that (a) the nonconformity substantially impaired the value of the shipment, (b) it predicated its acceptance on a reasonable assumption that Universal Exports would cure the nonconformity, and (c) Universal Exports did not cure the nonconformity within a reasonable time.

Padma's second option is to keep the goods and recover for the damages caused by Universal Exports' breach. Under this option, Padma could recover at least the difference between the value of the goods as promised and their value as accepted.

PROBLEM 23-3. *Express Warranties.* The statements that the tapes would last a lifetime were statements of opinion (puffery) and did not constitute an express warranty. Puffery is not actionable. Therefore, the court should rule in favor of the defendants.

As the court hearing this case explained, calling something the "Gold Collection" or "Masterpiece Collection" is not an affirmation of fact or a promise that the tapes will last for generations or otherwise have an extraordinary life span. A "collection" is "a number of objects or persons or a quantity of a substance that has been collected or has collected often according to some unifying principle or orderly arrangement." Thus, use of the word *collection* did not convey a promise of a lengthy life span.

Also, the use of statements such as "Give Your Children the Memories of a Lifetime—Collect Each Timeless Masterpiece!" or "Available for a Limited Time Only!" did not constitute an express warranty. The court reasoned that even if ads had stated that the tapes would last a lifetime, this would have been an expression of opinion or puffery. The court dismissed the plaintiffs' complaint, and on the plaintiffs' appeal, a state intermediate appellate court affirmed the dismissal.

PROBLEM 24-6. *Sovereign Immunity.* The doctrine of sovereign immunity exempts foreign nations from the jurisdiction of U.S. courts, subject to certain conditions. The Foreign Sovereign Immunities Act (FSIA) of 1976 codifies this doctrine and exclusively governs the circumstances in which an action may be brought in a U.S. court against a foreign nation.

A foreign state is not immune from the jurisdiction of U.S. courts when the state (a) waives immunity, (b) engages in commercial activity, or (c) commits a tort in the United States or violates certain international laws. Under the FSIA, a foreign state includes its political subdivisions and "instrumentalities"—departments and agencies. A commercial activity is a regular course of commercial conduct, transaction, or act that is carried out by the foreign state within the United States or has a direct effect in the United States.

The details of what constitutes a commercial activity are left to the courts. But it seems clear that a foreign government can be considered to engage in commercial activity when, instead of regulating a market, the government participates in it. In other words, when a foreign state, or its political subdivisions or instrumentalities, performs the type of actions in which a private party engages in commerce, the state's actions are likewise commercial.

In the facts of this problem, Iran engaged in commercial activity outside the United States by making and marketing its counterfeit versions of Bell's Model 206 Series helicopters. This activity caused a direct effect in the United States by the consumer confusion that will likely result from Iran's unauthorized use of Bell's trade dress. Thus, the court can exercise jurisdiction in these circumstances, and Iran may be as liable as a private party would be for the same acts.

In the actual case on which this problem is based, Iran did not respond to Bell's complaint. The court held that it had jurisdiction under the FSIA's commercial activity exception, as explained above. The court entered a default judgment against Iran and awarded damages and an injunction to Bell.

PROBLEM 25-7. *Payable on Demand or at a Definite Time.* No. Novel is not correct. The instrument is a note, and Novel is bound to pay it. For an instrument to be negotiable under Section 3–104 of the Uniform Commercial Code, it must meet the following requirements: (a) be in writing, (b) be signed by the maker or the drawer, (c) be an unconditional promise or order to pay, (d) state a fixed amount of money, (e) be payable on demand or at a definite time, and (g) be payable to order or to bearer unless it is a check. When no time for payment is stated on an instrument, the instrument is payable on demand.

Applying these principles to the facts in this problem, all of the requirements to establish the instrument as negotiable are met: (a) the instrument is in writing, (b) it is signed by Novel, (c) there are no conditions or promises other than the unconditional promise to pay, (d) the instrument states a fixed amount ($10,000), (e) the instrument does not include a definite repayment date, and thus is payable on demand, and (f) the instrument is payable to Gallwitz. In the actual case on which this problem is based, the court ruled in favor of Gallwitz for payment of the note.

PROBLEM 26-7. *Negotiation.* A negotiable instrument can be transferred by assignment or by negotiation. An assignment is a transfer of rights by contract. A transfer by assignment to an assignee gives the assignee only those rights that the assignor possessed. Any defenses that can be raised against the assignor can be raised against the assignee. When an instrument is transferred by negotiation, the transferee becomes a holder. A holder receives at least the rights of the previous possessor.

Unlike an assignment, a transfer by negotiation can make it possible for the holder to receive more rights in the instrument than the prior possessor had. A holder who receives greater rights is a holder in due course (HDC) and takes the instrument free of any claims to it and defenses against its payment.

Negotiating order instruments requires delivery and indorsement. If a party to whom a negotiable note is made payable signs it and delivers it to a bank, the transfer is a negotiation, and the bank becomes a holder. If the party does not sign it, however, the transfer would be treated as an assignment, and the bank would become an assignee instead of a holder.

In this problem, Argent was the payee of the note and its holder. Argent transferred the note to Wells Fargo without an indorsement. Thus, the transfer was not a negotiation but an assignment. Wells Fargo became an assignee and not a holder of the note. As an assignee, the bank acquired only those rights that the lender possessed before the assignment. And any defenses—including fraud in connection with the note—that Ford could assert against the lender could also be asserted by the borrower against the bank.

If Argent indorsed the note to Wells Fargo now, after the defendant's response to the complaint, the bank could become a holder of the note, but it could not become an HDC. One of the requirements for HDC status is that a holder must take an instrument without notice of defenses against payment. The bank could not do this, because it is now aware of the borrower's defenses.

In the actual case on which this problem is based, the court issued a judgment in Wells Fargo's favor, and Ford appealed. A state intermediate appellate court reversed the judgment and remanded the case for trial, finding that the bank had failed to prove that it was a holder, an assignee, or even a transferee of the note.

PROBLEM 27–4. *Defenses.* When an instrument is transferred by negotiation, the transferee becomes a holder. A holder can become a holder in due course (HDC) if the holder takes the instrument for value, in good faith, and without notice of any defects. An HDC takes an instrument free of most defenses against payment that could be asserted against the transferor. Defenses against payment fall into two categories. Universal defenses are good against all holders, including HDCs. Personal defenses are used to avoid payment to an ordinary holder, but not an HDC. Personal defenses include breach of contract, ordinary fraud, and any other defenses that can be asserted to avoid payment on a contract. Between the maker and the payee, a promissory note is a contract to pay money. Defenses that may be asserted by the maker against payment on a note include the personal defenses.

In this problem, Klutz does not qualify as an HDC. Thorbecke signed a note as the maker for most of the price for the purchase of the restaurant. Klutz may have taken Thorbecke's note for value—at least to the extent that he performed the part of the contract for the sale of the restaurant—but he did not take it in good faith or without notice. He misrepresented his authority to sell the franchise. In other words, under the facts as presented, Klutz appears to have committed fraud in the inducement and to have breached the contract of sale. Thorbeck appears to have reasonably relied on the misrepresentation and to be entitled to damages as a result. Thorbecke may also be justified in asserting these defenses against payment on the note.

In the actual case on which this problem is based, the court issued a decision in Thorbecke's favor to allow the suit to go to trial to determine whether Klutz misrepresented his authority to transfer the franchise, whether Thorbeck reasonably relied on the misrepresentation, the extent of any damages, and the amount due on the note.

PROBLEM 28–6. *Honoring Checks.* Wells Fargo is liable to W Financial for the amount of the check. A bank that pays a customer's check bearing a forged indorsement must recredit the customer's account or be liable to the customer-drawer for breach of contract. The bank must recredit the account because it failed to carry out the drawer's order to pay to the order of the named party. Eventually, the loss falls on the first party to take the instrument bearing the forged indorsement because

a forged indorsement does not transfer title. Thus, whoever takes an instrument with a forged indorsement cannot become a holder.

Under these rules, Wells Fargo is liable to W Financial for the amount of the check. The bank had an obligation to ensure that the check was properly indorsed. The bank did not pay the check to the order of Lateef, the named payee, but accepted the check for deposit into the account of CA Houston without Lateef's indorsement. The bank did not obtain title to the instrument and could not become a holder, nor was it entitled to enforce the instrument on behalf of any other party who was entitled to enforce it. In the actual case on which this problem is based, the court held that the bank was liable to pay the amount of the check to W Financial.

PROBLEM 29–4. *Guaranty.* When a third person promises to pay a debt owed by another in the event the debtor does not pay, a suretyship or guaranty relationship is created. With a guaranty arrangement, the guarantor is secondarily liable. The guarantor can be required to pay the obligation after the debtor defaults. A guaranty contract between the guarantor and the creditor must be in writing to be enforceable unless the main purpose rule applies. This occurs if the main purpose of the guaranty agreement is to benefit the guarantor. The guarantor's defenses against payment include fraud. Failure to inform the guarantor of material facts known by the creditor that would substantially increase the guarantor's risk is fraud and makes the guaranty obligation voidable.

In this problem, the Kims signed personal guaranties for Majestic's loan. The main purpose exception does not appear to apply, but in any event the guaranties were in writing. The terms appear to have been clear. Those terms provided that the signatories guaranteed full payment of the loan. The signer of an agreement is conclusively bound to its terms whether or not she has read it. The Kims, including Hee, were thus liable to pay the obligation after Majestic defaulted unless there was a defense against payment. There do not appear to have been any defenses here.

In the actual case on which this problem, the court issued a judgment in OPIC's favor.

PROBLEM 30–7. *Perfecting a Security Interest.* Yes, these financing statements were sufficient to perfect the bank's security interests in Tille's equipment. In most situations, perfection is accomplished by filing a financing statement with the appropriate official. To effectively perfect a security interest, a financing statement must contain (a) the debtor's signature, (b) the debtor's and creditor's addresses, and (c) a description of the collateral by type or item.

In this case, all of Union's financing statements were sufficient to perfect security interests. They each provided the name and address of the debtor (Tille), the name and address of the secured party (Union Bank), and a description of the collateral covered by the financing statement. The collateral for one loan consisted of all of Tille's equipment, including after-acquired property. For the second loan, the collateral was the truck crane, and for the third, a Bobcat mini excavator. These descriptions were clearly sufficient to put a prospective creditor on notice that the collateral was the subject of a security interest.

In the actual case on which this problem is based, the court concluded that all of the statements created perfected security interests.

PROBLEM 31–6. *Automatic Stay.* Gholston can recover damages because EZ Auto willfully violated the automatic stay. EZ Auto repossessed the car even though it received notice of the automatic stay from the bankruptcy court. Moreover, EZ Auto retained the car even after it was reminded of the stay by Gholston's attorney. Thus, EZ Auto knew about the automatic stay and violated it intentionally. Because Gholston suffered direct damages as a result, she can recover from EZ Auto.

PROBLEM 32–7. *Employment Relationships.* The facts support a conclusion that Jonathan was an independent contractor and not an employee. In deciding whether a worker is categorized as an employee or an independent contractor, the courts generally consider the amount of control that the employer exercises over the details of the work. Is the work done under the employer's direction or by a specialist without supervision? Control indicates employee status.

In this problem, Jonathan could argue that he was under William's direction and control. It was his first day on the new job. There was no way for him to know what to do without William's direction. He might assert that William told him to load certain tires on a trailer and that thus he was an employee. But this instruction is minimal. The relationship between the parties before the accident was independent contractor and employer. For a decade, Jonathan operated his own business. His accumulated skill, experience, and judgment in the business established that he controlled his work without oversight.

In the actual case on which this problem is based, the court held that Jonathan was an independent contractor.

PROBLEM 33–7. *Liability for Contracts.* Hall may be held personally liable. Hall could not be an agent for House Medic because it was a fictitious name and not a real entity. Moreover, when the contract was formed, Hall did not disclose his true principal, which was Hall Hauling, Ltd. Thus, Hall may be held personally liable as a party to the contract.

PROBLEM 34–6. *Workers' Compensation.* Fairbanks's claim qualifies for workers' compensation benefits. To recover benefits under state workers' compensation laws, the requirements are that the injury (a) was accidental and (b) occurred on the job or in the course of employment. Fault is not an issue. The employee must file a claim with the appropriate state agency or board that administers local workers' compensation claims.

In this problem, Fairbanks's claim for workers' compensation benefits appears to have been timely filed with the appropriate state agency. The focus of the dispute is on the second requirement listed above—an accidental injury that occurred on the job or in the course of employment. Dynea required its employees to wear certain boots as a safety measure. One of the boots caused a sore on Fairbanks's leg. The sore developed into a pustule and broke into a lesion. Within a week, Fairbanks was hospitalized with an MRSA infection.

Dynea argued that the bacteria were on Fairbanks's skin before he came to work. Even if this were true, however, it was the rubbing of the boot that caused the sore through which the bacteria entered his body. This fact fulfills the second requirement for the recovery of workers' compensation benefits.

In the actual case on which this problem is based, the court issued a decision in favor of Fairbanks's claim for benefits.

PROBLEM 35–5. *Retaliation by Employers.* Yes. Dawson could establish a claim for retaliation. Title VII prohibits retaliation. In a retaliation claim, an individual asserts that she or he suffered harm as a result of making a charge, testifying, or participating in a Title VII investigation or proceeding. To prove retaliation, a plaintiff must show that the challenged action was one that would likely have dissuaded a reasonable worker from making or supporting a charge of discrimination.

In this problem, under applicable state law, it was unlawful for an employer to discriminate against an individual based on sexual orientation. Dawson was subjected to derision on the part of co-workers, including his supervisor, based on his sexual orientation. He filed a complaint with his employer's human resources department. Two days later, he was fired. The proximity in time and the other circumstances, especially the supervisor's conduct, would support a retaliation claim. Also, the discharge would likely have dissuaded Dawson, or any reasonable worker, from making a claim of discrimination. In the actual case on which this problem is based, the court held that Dawson offered enough evidence that "a reasonable trier of fact could find in favor of Dawson on his retaliation claim."

PROBLEM 36–6. *Franchise Termination.* Oshana and GTO have stated a claim for wrongful termination of their franchise. A franchisor must act in good faith when terminating a franchise agreement. If the termination is arbitrary or unfair, a franchisee may have a claim for wrongful termination. In this case, Oshana and GTO have alleged that Buchanan acted in bad faith. Their failure to pay rent would ordinarily be a valid basis for termination, but not if the failure was entirely precipitated by Buchanan. Thus, Oshana and GTO may recover if they can prove that their allegations are true.

PROBLEM 37–7. *Partnership Formation.* Garcia and Lucero probably satisfied all three requirements for forming a partnership. They owned the two properties equally, agreed to share both profits and losses, and enjoyed equal management rights. Moreover, it is immaterial that they lacked a written partnership agreement. The writing requirement (Statute of Frauds) does not apply to these facts, and a partnership agreement can be oral or implied by the parties' conduct.

PROBLEM 38–6. *LLC Operation.* No. One Bluewater member could not unilaterally "fire" another member without providing a reason. Part of the attractiveness of the limited liability company (LLC) as a form of business enterprise is its flexibility. The members can decide how to operate the business through an operating agreement. For example, the agreement can set forth procedures for choosing or removing members or managers.

Here, the Bluewater operating agreement provided for a "super majority" vote to remove a member under circumstances that would jeopardize the firm's contractor status. Thus, one Bluewater member could not unilaterally "fire" another member without providing a reason. In fact, a majority of the members could not terminate the other's interest in the firm without providing a reason. Moreover, the only acceptable reason would be a circumstance that undercut the firm's status as a contractor.

The flexibility of the LLC business form relates to its framework, not to its members' capacity to violate its operating agreement. In the actual case on which this problem is based, Smith attempted to "fire" Williford without providing a reason. In Williford's suit, the court issued a judgment in his favor.

PROBLEM 39–7. Close Corporations. Yes, Pourgol's acts may likely have constituted misconduct. In this problem, Burnett charged Pourgol with the submission of incorrect plans to obtain the building permit, misrepresentation of the extent of the renovations, and failure to fix the house. The submission of incorrect plans might arguably have been a mistake, and the misrepresentation might have been a misstatement in good faith. But these acts may instead have been intentional and fraudulent. Assuming the charges are true and all of the acts were wrongful, including the misrepresentation and failure to fix the house, they certainly form the basis for a finding of misconduct.

A close corporation is a private corporation with a small number of shareholders. Close corporations are often managed by their shareholders. To prevent such situations as the one that arose in this problem, shareholders must take an active role in the governance of a corporation. The corporate articles or bylaws might be amended to, for example, require more than a single shareholder or a simple majority to approve an action. A minority shareholder, or a dominated shareholder, or a formerly disinterested shareholder may also pursue a remedy through a direct or derivative (on behalf of the corporation) suit.

Here, the facts do not state which shareholder, if either, held a majority of the shares. But Burnett might have taken any of the steps mentioned above to prevent misconduct. In the problem, Burnett has taken the step of filing a suit against Pourgol. In the actual case on which this problem is based, the court denied Pourgol's motion to dismiss Burnett's complaint.

PROBLEM 40–6. Rights of Shareholders. Yes. Woods has a right to inspect Biolustre's books and records. Every shareholder is entitled to examine corporate records. A shareholder can inspect the books in person or through an agent such as an attorney, accountant, or other authorized assistant.

The right of inspection is limited to the inspection and copying of corporate books and records for a proper purpose. This is because the power of inspection is fraught with potential for abuse—for example, it can involve the disclosure of trade secrets and other confidential information. Thus, a corporation is allowed to protect itself.

Here, Woods, through Hair Ventures, has the right to inspect Biolustre's books and records. She has a proper purpose for the inspection—to obtain information about Biolustre's financial situation. She, and other shareholders, had not received notice of shareholders' meetings or corporate financial reports for years, or notice of Biolustre's plan to issue additional stock. Hair Ventures had a substantial investment in the company. In the actual case on which this problem is based,

the court ordered Biolustre to produce its books and records for Hair Ventures' inspection.

PROBLEM 41–7. Purchase of Assets. Yes. Most likely, Interline is liable for the unpaid amount on the GATT contract with Call Center. An acquiring corporation will be held to have assumed the liabilities of the selling corporation in the following situations:

(a) The purchasing corporation expressly or impliedly assumes the seller's liabilities.

(b) The sale transaction is in effect a merger or consolidation of the two companies.

(c) The purchaser continues the seller's business and retains the same personnel (shareholders, directors, and officers).

(d) The sale is entered into fraudulently for the purpose of escaping liability.

In this problem, Interline acquired GATT's assets at a public sale. There is no indication that Interline agreed to assume GATT's liabilities, there was no merger or other combination of the two companies, and it does not appear that the sale was fraudulently entered into to escape liability.

Thus, the focus is on the third item listed above—whether Interline was liable for GATT's debts because it continued GATT's business with the same personnel. Boyd was not a GATT employee, but he was a former GATT director. Other members of Interline's staff were former GATT employees. GATT and Interline operated out of the same office building. Both companies were in the business of providing travel services to many of the same customers. These factors indicate that Interline is responsible for GATT's liabilities, including its debt to Call Center. In the actual case on which this problem is based, the court focused on the same principles discussed here to issue a judgment in Call Center's favor.

PROBLEM 42–6. Violations of the 1934 Act. An omission or misrepresentation of a material fact in connection with the purchase or sale of a security may violate Section 10(b) of the Securities Exchange Act of 1934 and SEC Rule 10b-5. The key question is whether the omitted or misrepresented information is material. A fact, by itself, is not automatically material.

A fact will be regarded as material only if it is significant enough that it would likely affect an investor's decision as to whether to buy or sell the company's securities. For example, a company's potential liability in a product liability suit and the financial consequences to the firm are material facts that must be disclosed because they affect an investor's decision to buy stock in the company.

In this case, the plaintiffs' claim should not be dismissed. To prevail on their claim that the defendants made material omissions in violation of Section 10(b) and SEC Rule 10-5, the plaintiffs must prove that the omission was material. Their complaint alleged the omission of information linking Zicam and anosmia (loss of the sense of smell) and plausibly suggested that reasonable investors would have viewed this information as material. Zicam products account for 70 percent of Matrixx's sales. Matrixx received reports of consumers who suffered anosmia after using Zicam Cold Remedy.

In public statements discussing revenues and product safety, Matrixx did not disclose this information. But the information was significant enough to likely affect a consumer's decision to use the product, and this would affect the company's revenue and ultimately the commercial viability of the product. The information was therefore significant enough to likely affect an investor's decision whether to buy or sell Matrixx's stock, and this would affect the stock price. Thus, the plaintiffs' allegations were sufficient. Contrary to the defendants' assertion, statistical sampling is not required to show materiality—reasonable investors could view reports of adverse events as material even if the reports did not provide statistically significant evidence.

PROBLEM 43–5. *Agency Powers.* The United States Supreme Court held that greenhouse gases fit within the Clean Air Act's (CAA's) definition of "air pollutant." Thus, the Environmental Protection Agency (EPA) has the authority under that statute to regulate the emission of such gases from new motor vehicles. According to the Court, the definition, which includes "any" air pollutant, embraces all airborne compounds "of whatever stripe."

The EPA's focus on Congress's 1990 amendments (or their lack) does not indicate the original intent behind the statute (and its amendments before 1990). Nothing in the statute suggests that Congress meant to curtail the agency's power to treat greenhouse gases as air pollutants. In other words, the agency has a preexisting mandate to regulate "any air pollutant" that may endanger the public welfare.

The EPA also argued that, even if it had the authority to regulate greenhouse gases, the agency would not exercise that authority because any regulation would conflict with other administration priorities. The Court acknowledged that the CAA conditions EPA action on the agency's formation of a "judgment," but explained that judgment must relate to whether a pollutant "cause[s], or contribute[s] to, air pollution which may reasonably be anticipated to endanger public health or welfare."

Thus, the EPA can avoid issuing regulations only if the agency determines that greenhouse gases do not contribute to climate change (or if the agency reasonably explains why it cannot or will not determine whether they do). The EPA's refusal to regulate was thus "arbitrary, capricious, or otherwise not in accordance with law." The Court remanded the case for the EPA to "ground its reasons for action or inaction in the statute."

PROBLEM 44–7. *Fair Debt-Collection Practices.* Engler may recover under the Fair Debt Collection Practices Act (FDCPA). Atlantic is subject to the FDCPA because it is a debt-collection agency, and it was attempting to collect a debt on behalf of Bank of America. Atlantic also used offensive tactics to collect from Engler. After all, Atlantic gave Engler's employer the false impression that Engler was a criminal, had a pending case, and was about to be arrested. Finally, Engler suffered harm because he experienced discomfort, embarrassment, and distress as a result of Atlantic's abusive conduct. Engler may recover actual damages, statutory damages, and attorneys' fees from Atlantic.

PROBLEM 45–5. *Environmental Impact Statement.* When an agency acts in an arbitrary and capricious manner, then the court has grounds for intervention. Otherwise, the court defers to the expertise of the agency, as revealed in the record.

Here, the environmental impact statement (EIS) was comprehensive, and the National Park Service (NPS) had credible reason to believe that the use of rafts on the river did not damage the wilderness status of portions of the park. Since the NPS acted within its statutory guidelines and followed proper procedure in its decision making, the court would not intervene in the agency's decision. The appellate court found that the plaintiffs had failed to establish that the NPS acted in an arbitrary and capricious manner when it adopted the plan.

PROBLEM 46–6. *Price Discrimination.* Spa Steel satisfies most of the requirements for a price discrimination claim under Section 2 of the Clayton Act. Dayton Superior is engaged in interstate commerce, and it sells goods of like grade and quality to at least three purchasers. Moreover, Spa Steel can show that, because it sells Dayton Superior's products at a higher price, it lost business and thus suffered an injury.

To recover, however, Spa Steel will also need to prove that Dayton Superior charged Spa Steel's competitors a lower price for the same product. Spa Steel cannot recover if its prices were higher for reasons related to its own business, such as having a higher overhead or seeking a larger profit.

PROBLEM 47–7. *Potential Liability to Third Parties.* KPMG is potentially liable to the hedge funds' partners under the *Restatement (Second) of Torts.* Under Section 552 of the Restatement, an auditor owes a duty to "persons for whose benefit and guidance the accountant intends to supply . . . information."

In this case, KPMG prepared annual reports on the hedge funds and addressed them to the funds' "Partners." Additionally, KPMG knew who the partners were because it prepared individual tax forms for them each year. Thus, KPMG's annual reports were for the partners' benefit and guidance. The partners relied on the reports, including their representations that they complied with generally accepted accounting principles. As a result, the partners lost millions of dollars, which exposes KPMG to possible liability under Section 552.

PROBLEM 48–7. *Bailment Obligation.* Moreland should be awarded damages, and Gray should take nothing. The bailee must exercise reasonable care in preserving the bailed property. What constitutes reasonable care in a bailment situation normally depends on the nature and specific circumstances of the bailment. If the bailed property has been lost or is returned damaged, a court will presume that the bailee was negligent.

In this problem, when the bailor (Moreland, the owner of the aircraft) entrusted the plane to the bailee's (Gray's) repair shop for painting, the work was not properly performed. This violated the bailee's duty to exercise reasonable care and breached the bailment contract. The plane was returned damaged, which may also constitute negligence. In the event of a breach, the bailor may sue for damages. The measure of damages is the difference between the value of the bailed property in its present condition and what it would have been worth if the work had been properly performed.

Thus, Gray is liable to Moreland for failing to properly paint the plane. In the actual case on which this problem is based, the court upheld a jury award to Moreland of damages and attorneys' fees.

PROBLEM 49–7. *Adverse Possession.* The McKeags satisfied the first three requirements for adverse possession:

(a) Their possession was actual and exclusive because they used the beach and prevented others from doing so, including the Finleys,

(b) Their possession was open, visible, and notorious because they made improvements to the beach and regularly kept their belongings there.

(c) Their possession was continuous and peaceable for the required ten years. They possessed the property for more than four decades, and they even kept a large float there during the winter months.

Nevertheless, the McKeags' possession was *not* hostile and adverse, which is the fourth requirement. The Finleys had substantial evidence that they gave the McKeags permission to use the beach. Rather than reject the Finleys' permission as unnecessary, the McKeags sometimes said nothing and other times seemingly affirmed that the property belonged to the Finleys. Thus, because the McKeags did not satisfy all four requirements, they cannot establish adverse possession.

PROBLEM 50–8. *Insurance Provisions and Clauses.* Farrington should not be included as an insured within the meaning of the property insurance policy between Darling's and Philadelphia. The existence of an insurable interest is a primary concern when determining liability under an insurance policy. For personal property, an insurable interest exists when the insured derives a pecuniary benefit from the preservation and continued existence of the property. A person has an insurable interest in property when he or she would sustain a financial loss from its destruction. As for an insurance policy's language, courts interpret the words according to their ordinary meanings and in light of the nature of the coverage involved.

Darling's is entitled to recover the value of the loss to the covered vehicle by virtue of its ownership of that vehicle and the fact that it is the owner that suffers the loss when its vehicle is damaged. In other words, under the Philadelphia policy, Darling's had an insurable interest in the car when Farrington smashed into the moose. Farrington might have had an insurable interest as well when he agreed to be responsible for any damage to the car, but he declined the insurance coverage offered in the rental contract.

In the actual case on which this problem is based, in Philadelphia's suit against Farrington, the court entered a judgment in the insurer's favor.

PROBLEM 51–7. *Undue Influence.* No, undue influence does not appear to have occurred in this problem. To invalidate a will on the basis of undue influence, a plaintiff must show that the decedent's plan of distribution was the result of improper pressure brought by another person. Undue influence may be inferred if the testator ignores blood relatives and names as a beneficiary a nonrelative who is in constant close contact and in a position to influence the making of the will.

In this problem, although Tommy's ex-wife lived with Susie and was thus in a position to influence Susie's will, the ex-wife was not a beneficiary under it, so there is no inference of undue influence. Moreover, neither of the wills that Suzie executed left any property to her son, so there was no indication that she had been influenced to change her mind regarding the distribution of her estate. Additionally, she expressly disinherited her son, and several witnesses testified that she was mentally competent at the time she made the will.

In the actual case on which this problem is based, the court presumed that the will was valid.

GLOSSARY

A

Abandoned property Property with which the owner has voluntarily parted, with no intention of recovering it.

Abandonment In landlord-tenant law, a tenant's complete departure from leased premises, with no intention of returning before the end of the lease term.

Abatement A process by which legatees receive reduced benefits if the assets of an estate are insufficient to pay in full all general bequests provided for in the will.

Acceleration clause (1) A clause in an installment contract that provides for all future payments to become due immediately on the failure to tender timely payments or on the occurrence of a specified event. (2) A clause in a mortgage loan contract that makes the entire loan balance become due if the borrower misses or is late making monthly mortgage payments.

Acceptance (1) In contract law, the offeree's notification to the offeror that the offeree agrees to be bound by the terms of the offeror's proposal. Although historically the terms of acceptance had to be the mirror image of the terms of the offer, the Uniform Commercial Code provides that even modified terms of the offer in a definite expression of acceptance constitute a contract. (2) In negotiable instruments law, the drawee's signed agreement to pay a draft when presented.

Acceptor The person (the drawee) who accepts a draft and who agrees to be primarily responsible for its payment.

Accession Occurs when an individual adds value to personal property by either labor or materials. In some situations, a person may acquire ownership rights in another's property through accession.

Accommodation party A person who signs an instrument for the purpose of lending his or her name as credit to another party on the instrument.

Accord and satisfaction An agreement for payment (or other performance) between two parties, one of whom has a right of action against the other. After the payment has been accepted or other performance has been made, the "accord and satisfaction" is complete and the obligation is discharged.

Accredited investors In the context of securities offerings, "sophisticated" investors, such as banks, insurance companies, investment companies, the issuer's executive officers and directors, and persons whose income or net worth exceeds certain limits.

Acquittal A certification or declaration following a trial that the individual accused of a crime is innocent, or free from guilt, and is thus absolved of the charges.

Act of state doctrine A doctrine that provides that the judicial branch of one country will not examine the validity of public acts committed by a recognized foreign government within its own territory.

Actionable Capable of serving as the basis of a lawsuit.

Actual authority Authority of an agent that is express or implied.

Actual malice A condition that exists when a person makes a statement with either knowledge of its falsity or a reckless disregard for the truth. In a defamation suit, a statement made about a public figure normally must be made with actual malice for liability to be incurred.

Actus reus (pronounced *ak*-tus *ray*-uhs) A guilty (prohibited) act. The commission of a prohibited act is one of the two essential elements required for criminal liability, the other element being the intent to commit a crime.

Adequate protection doctrine In bankruptcy law, a doctrine that protects secured creditors from losing their security as a result of an automatic stay on legal proceedings by creditors against the debtor once the debtor petitions for bankruptcy relief. In certain circumstances, the bankruptcy court may provide adequate protection by requiring the debtor or trustee to pay the creditor or provide additional guaranties to protect the creditor against the losses suffered by the creditor as a result of the stay.

Adhesion contract A "standard-form" contract, such as that between a large retailer and a consumer, in which the stronger party dictates the terms.

Adjudication The process of resolving a dispute by presenting evidence and arguments before a neutral third party decision maker in a court or an administrative law proceeding.

Adjustable-rate mortgage (ARM) A mortgage in which the rate of interest paid by the borrower changes periodically, often with reference to a predetermined government interest rate (the index). Usually, the interest rate for ARMs is initially low and increases over time, but there is a cap on the amount that the rate can increase during any adjustment period.

Administrative agency A federal, state, or local government agency established to perform a specific function. Administrative agencies are authorized by legislative acts to make and enforce rules to administer and enforce the acts.

Administrative law The body of law created by administrative agencies (in the form of rules, regulations, orders, and decisions) in order to carry out their duties and responsibilities.

Administrative law judge (ALJ) One who presides over an administrative agency hearing and who has the power to administer oaths, take testimony, rule on questions of evidence, and make determinations of fact.

Administrative process The procedure used by administrative agencies in the administration of law.

Administrator One who is appointed by a court to handle the probate (disposition) of a person's estate if that person dies intestate (without a valid will) or if the executor named in the will cannot serve.

Adverse possession The acquisition of title to real property by occupying it openly, without the consent of the owner, for a period of time specified by a state statute. The occupation must be actual, open, notorious, exclusive, and in opposition to all others, including the owner.

Affidavit A written or printed voluntary statement of facts, confirmed by the oath or affirmation of the party making it and made before a person having the authority to administer the oath or affirmation.

Affirm To validate; to give legal force to. *See also* Ratification

Affirmative action Job-hiring policies that give special consideration to members of protected classes in an effort to overcome present effects of past discrimination.

Affirmative defense A response to a plaintiff's claim that does not deny the plaintiff's facts but attacks the plaintiff's legal right to bring an action. An example is the running of the statute of limitations.

After-acquired evidence A type of evidence submitted in support of an affirmative defense in employment discrimination cases. Evidence that, prior to the employer's discriminatory act, the employee engaged in misconduct sufficient to warrant dismissal had the employer known of it earlier.

After-acquired property Property of the debtor that is acquired after the execution of a security agreement.

Age of majority The age at which an individual is considered legally capable of conducting himself or herself responsibly. A person of this age is entitled to the full rights of citizenship, including the right to vote. In contract law, the age at which one is no longer an infant and can no longer disaffirm a contract.

Agency A relationship between two parties in which one party (the agent) agrees to represent or act for the other (the principal).

Agency by estoppel An agency that arises when a principal negligently allows an agent to exercise powers not granted to the agent, thus justifying others in believing that the agent possesses the requisite agency authority.

Agency coupled with an interest An agency relationship in which the agent has some legal right to (an interest in) the property that is the subject of the agency, and thus the agency is created for the agent's benefit instead of the principal's. Because the agent has an additional interest in the property beyond the normal commission for selling it, the agent's position cannot be terminated until the agent's interest ends.

Agent A person who agrees to represent or act for another, called the principal.

Agreement A meeting of two or more minds in regard to the terms of a contract; usually broken down into two events—an offer by one party to form a contract, and an acceptance of the offer by the person to whom the offer is made.

Alien corporation A designation in the United States for a corporation formed in another country but doing business in the United States.

Alienation In real property law, the voluntary transfer of property from one person to another (as opposed to a transfer by operation of law).

Allegation A statement, claim, or assertion.

Allege To state, recite, assert, or charge.

Alternative dispute resolution (ADR) The resolution of disputes in ways other than those involved in the traditional judicial process. Negotiation, mediation, and arbitration are forms of ADR.

Amend To change through a formal procedure.

American Arbitration Association (AAA) The major organization offering arbitration services in the United States.

Analogy In logical reasoning, an assumption that if two things are similar in some respects, they will be similar in other respects also. Often used in legal reasoning to infer the appropriate application of legal principles in a case being decided by referring to previous cases involving different facts but considered to come within the policy underlying the rule.

Annual percentage rate (APR) The cost of credit on a yearly basis, typically expressed as an annual percentage.

Annuity An insurance policy that pays the insured fixed, periodic payments for life or for a term of years, as stipulated in the policy, after the insured reaches a specified age.

Annul To cancel or to make void.

Answer Procedurally, a defendant's response to the plaintiff's complaint.

Antecedent claim A preexisting claim. In negotiable instruments law, taking an instrument in satisfaction of an antecedent claim is taking the instrument for value—that is, for valid consideration.

Anticipatory repudiation An assertion or action by a party indicating that he or she will not perform an obligation that the party is contractually obligated to perform at a future time.

Antilapse provision A clause in an insurance contract that gives the insured a grace period (usually thirty days) within which to pay an overdue premium.

Antitrust law The body of federal and state laws and statutes protecting trade and commerce from unlawful restraints, price discrimination, price fixing, and monopolies. The principal federal antitrust statues are the Sherman Act of 1890, the Clayton Act of 1914, and the Federal Trade Commission Act of 1914.

Apparent authority Authority that is only apparent, not real. In agency law, a person may be deemed to have had the power to act as an agent for another party if the other party's manifestations to a third party led the third party to believe that an agency existed when, in fact, it did not.

Appeal Resort to a superior court, such as an appellate court, to review the decision of an inferior court, such as a trial court or an administrative agency.

Appellant The party who takes an appeal from one court to another.

Appellate court A court having appellate jurisdiction.

Appellate jurisdiction Courts having appellate jurisdiction act as reviewing courts, or appellate courts. Generally, cases can be brought before appellate courts only on appeal from an order or a judgment of a trial court or other lower court.

Appellee The party against whom an appeal is taken—that is, the party who opposes setting aside or reversing the judgment.

Appraisal right The right of a dissenting shareholder, if he or she objects to an extraordinary transaction of the corporation (such as a merger or consolidation), to have his or her shares appraised and to be paid the fair value of his or her shares by the corporation.

Appraiser An individual who specializes in determining the value of certain real or personal property.

Appropriation In tort law, the use by one person of another person's name, likeness, or other identifying characteristic without permission and for the benefit of the user.

Arbitrary and capricious test A court reviewing an informal administrative agency action applies this test to determine whether or not that action was in clear error. The court gives wide discretion to the expertise of the agency and decides if the agency had sufficient factual information on which to base its action. If no clear error was made, then the agency's action stands.

Arbitration The settling of a dispute by submitting it to a disinterested third party (other than a court), who renders a decision. The decision may or may not be legally binding.

Arbitration clause A clause in a contract that provides that, in the event of a dispute, the parties will submit the dispute to arbitration rather than litigate the dispute in court.

Arraignment A procedure in which an accused person is brought before the court to answer criminal charges. The charge is read to the person, and he or she is asked to enter a plea—such as "guilty" or "not guilty."

Arson The malicious burning of another's dwelling. Some statutes have expanded this to include any real property regardless of ownership and the destruction of property by other means—for example, by explosion.

Articles of incorporation The document filed with the appropriate governmental agency, usually the secretary of state, when a business is incorporated; state statutes usually prescribe what kind of information must be contained in the articles of incorporation.

Articles of merger A document, filed with the secretary of state, that sets forth the terms and conditions of the merger.

Articles of organization The document filed with a designated state official by which a limited liability company is formed.

Articles of partnership A written agreement that sets forth each partner's rights and obligations with respect to the partnership.

Artisan's lien A possessory lien given to a person who has made improvements and added value to another person's personal property as security for payment for services performed.

Assault Any word or action intended to make another person fearful of immediate physical harm; a reasonably believable threat.

Assignee The person to whom contract rights are assigned.

Assignment The act of transferring to another all or part of one's rights arising under a contract.

Assignor The person who assigns contract rights.

Assumption of risk A defense against negligence that can be used when the plaintiff was aware of a danger and voluntarily assumed the risk of injury from that danger.

Attachment (1) In the context of secured transactions, the process by which a security interest in the property of another becomes enforceable. (2) In the context of judicial liens, a court-ordered seizure and taking into custody of property prior to the securing of a judgment for a past-due debt.

Attempted monopolization Any actions by a firm to eliminate competition and gain monopoly power.

Auditor An accountant qualified to perform audits (systematic inspections) of a business's financial records.

Authenticate To sign a record, or with the intent to sign a record, to execute or to adopt an electronic sound, symbol, or the like to link with the record. A *record* is retrievable information inscribed on a tangible medium or stored in an electronic or other medium.

Authority In agency law, the agent's permission to act on behalf of the principal. An agent's authority may be actual (express or implied) or apparent. *See also* Actual authority; Apparent authority

Authorization card A card signed by an employee that gives a union permission to act on his or her behalf in negotiations with management. Unions typically use authorization cards as evidence of employee support during union organization.

Authorized means In contract law, the means of acceptance authorized by the offeror.

Automatic stay In bankruptcy proceedings, the suspension of virtually all litigation and other action by creditors against the debtor or the debtor's property; the stay is effective the moment the debtor files a petition in bankruptcy.

Award In the context of litigation, the amount of money awarded to a plaintiff in a civil lawsuit as damages. In the context of arbitration, the arbitrator's decision.

B

Bailee One to whom goods are entrusted by a bailor. Under the Uniform Commercial Code, a party who, by a bill of lading, warehouse receipt, or other document of title, acknowledges possession of goods and contracts.

Bailee's lien A possessory lien, or claim, that a bailee entitled to compensation can place on the bailed property to ensure that he or she will be paid for the services provided. The lien is effective as long as the bailee retains possession of the bailed goods and has not agreed to extend credit to the bailor. Sometimes referred to as an artisan's lien.

Bailment A situation in which the personal property of one person (a bailor) is entrusted to another (a bailee), who is obligated to return the bailed property to the bailor or dispose of it as directed.

Bailor One who entrusts goods to a bailee.

Bait-and-switch advertising Advertising a product at a very attractive price (the bait) and then informing the consumer, once he or she is in the store, that the advertised product is either not available or is of poor quality; the customer is then urged to purchase (switched to) a more expensive item.

Balloon mortgage A loan that allows the debtor to make small monthly payments for an initial period, such as eight years, but then requires a large balloon payment for the entire remaining balance of the mortgage loan at the end of that period.

Banker's acceptance A negotiable instrument that is commonly used in international trade. A banker's acceptance is drawn by a creditor against the debtor, who pays the draft at maturity. The drawer creates a draft without designating a payee. The draft can pass through many parties' hands before a bank (drawee) accepts it, transforming the draft into a banker's acceptance. Acceptances can be purchased and sold in a way similar to securities.

Bankruptcy court A federal court of limited jurisdiction that handles only bankruptcy proceedings. Bankruptcy proceedings are governed by federal bankruptcy law.

Bankruptcy trustee A person who is either appointed by the U.S. Department of Justice or by creditors in bankruptcy cases. In all bankruptcies under Chapters 7, 12, or 13, a trustee is appointed by the U.S. Trustee, who is an officer of the Department of Justice. Chapter 11 bankruptcies allow the debtor to continue to manage the property as a "debtor in possession," but this person can be replaced for cause with a bankruptcy trustee.

Bargain A mutual undertaking, contract, or agreement between two parties; to negotiate over the terms of a purchase or contract.

Basis of the bargain In contract law, the affirmation of fact or promise on which the sale of goods is predicated, creating an express warranty.

Battery The unprivileged, intentional touching of another.

Bearer A person in the possession of an instrument payable to bearer or indorsed in blank.

Bearer instrument Any instrument that is not payable to a specific person, including instruments payable to the bearer or to "cash."

Beneficiary One to whom life insurance proceeds are payable or for whose benefit a trust has been established or property under a will has been transferred.

Benefit corporation A for-profit corporation that seeks to have a material positive impact on society and the environment. This new business form is available by statute in a growing number of states.

Bequest A gift by will of personal property (from the verb to bequeath).

Beyond a reasonable doubt The standard used to determine the guilt or innocence of a person criminally charged. To be guilty of a crime, one must be proved guilty "beyond and to the exclusion of every reasonable doubt." A reasonable doubt is one that would cause a prudent person to hesitate before acting in matters important to him or her.

Bilateral contract A type of contract that arises when a promise is given in exchange for a return promise.

Bill of lading A document that serves both as evidence of the receipt of goods for shipment and as documentary evidence of title to the goods.

Bill of Rights The first ten amendments to the U.S. Constitution.

Binder A written, temporary insurance policy.

Binding authority Any source of law that a court must follow when deciding a case. Binding authorities include constitutions, statutes, and regulations that govern the issue being decided, as well as court decisions that are controlling precedents within the jurisdiction.

Blank indorsement An indorsement that specifies no particular indorsee and can consist of a mere signature. An order instrument that is indorsed in blank becomes a bearer instrument.

Blue sky laws State laws that regulate the offer and sale of securities.

Bona fide Good faith. A bona fide obligation is one made in good faith—that is, sincerely and honestly.

Bona fide occupational qualification (BFOQ) Identifiable characteristics reasonably necessary to the normal operation of a particular business. These characteristics can include gender, national origin, and religion, but not race.

Bond A certificate that evidences a corporate (or government) debt. It is a security that involves no ownership interest in the issuing entity.

Bond indenture A written agreement between a bond issuer and the bondholders, normally consisting of a specified interest rate, maturity date, and other terms; sometimes simply called an indenture.

Botnet Short for *robot network*—a group of computers that run an application that is controlled and manipulated only by the software source. Although sometimes a legitimate network, usually this term is reserved for a group of computers that have been infected by malicious robot software. In a botnet, each connected computer becomes a zombie, or drone.

Boycott A concerted refusal to do business with a particular person or entity in order to obtain concessions or to express displeasure with certain acts or practices of that person or business. *See also* Secondary boycott

Breach To violate a law, by an act or an omission, or to break a legal obligation that one owes to another person or to society.

Breach of contract The failure, without legal excuse, of a promisor to perform the obligations of a contract.

Bribery The offering, giving, receiving, or soliciting of anything of value with the aim of influencing an official action or an official's discharge of a legal or public duty or (with respect to commercial bribery) a business decision.

Bridge loan A short-term loan that allows a buyer to make a down payment on a new home before selling her or his current home (the current home is used as collateral).

Brief A formal legal document submitted by the attorney for the appellant—or the appellee (in answer to the appellant's brief)—to an appellate court when a case is appealed. The appellant's brief outlines the facts and issues of the case, the judge's rulings or jury's findings that should be reversed or modified, the applicable law, and the arguments on the client's behalf.

Browse-wrap terms Terms and conditions of use that are presented to an Internet user at the time certain products, such as software, are being downloaded but that need not be agreed to (by clicking "I agree," for example) before being able to install or use the product.

Bureaucracy A large organization that is structured hierarchically to carry out specific functions.

Burglary The unlawful entry into a building with the intent to commit a felony. (Some state statutes expand this to include the intent to commit any crime.)

Business ethics Ethics in a business context; a consensus of what constitutes right or wrong behavior in the world of business and the application of moral principles to situations that arise in a business setting.

Business invitees Those people, such as customers or clients, who are invited onto business premises by the owner of those premises for business purposes.

Business judgment rule A rule that immunizes corporate management from liability for actions that result in corporate losses or damages if the actions are undertaken in good faith and are within both the power of the corporation and the authority of management to make.

Business necessity A defense to allegations of employment discrimination in which the employer demonstrates that an employment practice that discriminates against members of a protected class is related to job performance.

Business plan A document describing a company, its products, and its anticipated future performance. Creating a business plan is normally the first step in obtaining loans or venture-capital funds for a new business enterprise.

Business tort Wrongful interference with the business rights of another.

Business trust A voluntary form of business organization in which investors (trust beneficiaries) transfer cash or property to trustees in exchange for trust certificates that represent their investment shares. Management of the business and trust property is handled by the trustees for the use and benefit of the investors. The certificate holders have limited liability (are not responsible for the debts and obligations incurred by the trust) and share in the trust's profits.

Buyer in the ordinary course of business A buyer who, in good faith and without knowledge that the sale violates the ownership rights or security interest of a third party in the goods, purchases goods in the ordinary course of business from a person in the business of selling goods of that kind.

Buyout price The amount payable to a partner on his or her dissociation from a partnership, based on the amount distributable to that partner if the firm were wound up on that date, and offset by any damages for wrongful dissociation.

Buy-sell agreement In the context of partnerships, an express agreement made at the time of partnership formation for one or more of the partners to buy out the other or others should the situation warrant—and thus provide for the smooth dissolution of the partnership.

Bylaws A set of governing rules adopted by a corporation or other association.

Bystander A spectator, witness, or person who was standing nearby when an event occurred and who did not engage in the business or act leading to the event.

C

C.I.F. or C.&F. Cost, insurance, and freight—or just cost and freight. A pricing term in a contract for the sale of goods requiring, among other things, that the seller place the goods in the possession of a carrier before risk passes to the buyer.

C.O.D. Cash on delivery. In sales transactions, a term meaning that the buyer will pay for the goods on delivery and before inspecting the goods.

Callable bond A bond that may be called in and the principal repaid at specified times or under conditions specified in the bond when it is issued.

Cancellation The act of nullifying, or making void. *See also* Rescission

Capital Accumulated goods, possessions, and assets used for the production of profits and wealth; the equity of owners in a business.

Carrier An individual or organization engaged in transporting passengers or goods for hire. *See also* Common carrier

Case law The rules of law announced in court decisions. Case law includes the aggregate of reported cases that interpret judicial precedents, statutes, regulations, and constitutional provisions.

Case on point A previous case involving factual circumstances and issues that are similar to those in the case before the court.

Cash surrender value The amount that the insurer has agreed to pay to the insured if a life insurance policy is canceled before the insured's death.

Cashier's check A check drawn by a bank on itself.

Categorical imperative A concept developed by the philosopher Immanuel Kant as an ethical guideline for behavior. In deciding whether an action is right or wrong, or desirable or undesirable, a person should evaluate the action in terms of what would happen if everybody else in the same situation, or category, acted the same way.

Causation in fact An act or omission without ("but for") which an event would not have occurred.

Cause of action A situation or set of facts sufficient to justify a right to sue.

Cease-and-desist order An administrative or judicial order prohibiting a person or business firm from conducting activities that an agency or court has deemed illegal.

Certificate of deposit (CD) A note of a bank in which a bank acknowledges a receipt of money from a party and promises to repay the money, with interest, to the party on a certain date.

Certificate of limited partnership The basic document filed with a designated state official by which a limited partnership is formed.

Certification mark A mark used by one or more persons, other than the owner, to certify the region, materials, mode of manufacture, quality, or accuracy of the owner's goods or services. When used by members of a cooperative, association, or other organization, such a mark is referred to as a collective mark. Examples of certification marks include the "Good Housekeeping Seal of Approval" and "UL Tested."

Certified check A check that has been accepted by the bank on which it is drawn. Essentially, the bank, by certifying (accepting) the check, promises to pay the check at the time the check is presented.

Certiorari See Writ of certiorari

Chain-style business franchise A franchise that operates under a franchisor's trade name and that is identified as a member of a select group of dealers that engage in the franchisor's business. The franchisee is generally required to follow standardized or prescribed methods of operation. Examples of this type of franchise are McDonald's and most other fast-food chains.

Chancellor An adviser to the king at the time of the early king's courts of England. Individuals petitioned the king for relief when they could not obtain an adequate remedy in a court of law, and these petitions were decided by the chancellor.

Charging order In partnership law, an order granted by a court to a judgment creditor that entitles the creditor to attach profits or assets of a partner on dissolution of the partnership.

Charitable trust A trust in which the property held by a trustee must be used for a charitable purpose, such as the advancement of health, education, or religion.

Chattel All forms of personal property.

Chattel paper Any writing or writings that show both a debt and the fact that the debt is secured by personal property. In many instances, chattel paper consists of a negotiable instrument coupled with a security agreement.

Check A draft drawn by a drawer ordering the drawee bank or financial institution to pay a certain amount of money to the holder on demand.

Checks and balances The system by which each of the three branches of the national government (executive, legislative, and judicial) exercises checks on the powers of the other branches.

Choice-of-language clause A clause in a contract designating the official language by which the contract will be interpreted in the event of a future disagreement over the contract's terms.

Choice-of-law clause A clause in a contract designating the law (such as the law of a particular state or nation) that will govern the contract.

Citation A reference to a publication in which a legal authority—such as a statute or a court decision—or other source can be found.

Civil law The branch of law dealing with the definition and enforcement of all private or public rights, as opposed to criminal matters.

Civil law system A system of law derived from that of the Roman Empire and based on a code rather than case law; the predominant system of law in the nations of continental Europe and the nations that were once their colonies. In the United States, Louisiana is the only state that has a civil law system.

Claim As a verb, to assert or demand. As a noun, a right to payment.

Clearinghouse A system or place where banks exchange checks and drafts drawn on each other and settle daily balances.

Click-on agreement An agreement that arises when a buyer, engaging in a transaction on a computer, indicates his or her assent to be bound by the terms of an offer by clicking on a button that says, for example,

"I agree"; sometimes referred to as a click-on license or a click-wrap agreement.

Close corporation A corporation whose shareholders are limited to a small group of persons, often only family members. The rights of shareholders of a close corporation usually are restricted regarding the transfer of shares to others.

Closed shop A firm that requires union membership by its workers as a condition of employment. The closed shop was made illegal by the Labor-Management Relations Act of 1947.

Closely held corporation A corporation whose shareholders are limited to a small group of persons, often only family members.

Closing The final step in the sale of real estate—also called settlement or closing escrow. The escrow agent coordinates the closing with the recording of deeds, the obtaining of title insurance, and other concurrent closing activities. A number of costs must be paid, in cash, at the time of closing, and they can range from several hundred to several thousand dollars, depending on the amount of the mortgage loan and other conditions of the sale.

Closing argument An argument made after the plaintiff and defendant have rested their cases. Closing arguments are made prior to the jury charges.

Cloud computing The delivery to users of on-demand services from third-party servers over a network. Cloud computing is a delivery model. The most widely used cloud computing services are Software as a Service (SaaS), which offers companies a cheaper way to buy and use packaged applications that are no longer run on servers in house.

Codicil A written supplement or modification to a will. A codicil must be executed with the same formalities as a will.

Coinsurance clause A clause in an insurance contract that encourages property owners to insure their property for an amount as close to full value as possible. If the owner insures the property up to a specified percentage—usually 80 percent—of its value, she or he will recover any loss up to the face amount of the policy.

Collateral Under Article 9 of the Uniform Commercial Code, the property subject to a security interest.

Collateral promise A secondary promise that is ancillary (subsidiary) to a principal transaction or primary contractual relationship, such as a promise made by one person to pay the debts of another if the latter fails to perform. A collateral promise normally must be in writing to be enforceable.

Collecting bank Any bank handling an item for collection, except the payor bank.

Collective bargaining The process by which labor and management negotiate the terms and conditions of employment, including working hours and workplace conditions.

Collective mark A mark used by members of a cooperative, association, or other organization to certify the region, materials, mode of manufacture, quality, or accuracy of the specific goods or services. Examples of collective marks include the labor union marks found on tags of certain products and the credits of movies, which indicate the various associations and organizations that participated in the making of the movies.

Comity A deference by which one nation gives effect to the laws and judicial decrees of another nation. This recognition is based primarily on respect.

Comment period A period of time following an administrative agency's publication or a notice of a proposed rule during which private parties may comment in writing on the agency proposal in an effort to influence agency policy. The agency takes any comments received into consideration when drafting the final version of the regulation.

Commerce clause The provision in Article I, Section 8, of the U.S. Constitution that gives Congress the power to regulate interstate commerce.

Commercial impracticability A doctrine under which a seller may be excused from performing a contract when (1) a contingency occurs, (2) the contingency's occurrence makes performance impracticable, and (3) the nonoccurrence of the contingency was a basic assumption on which the contract was made. Despite the fact that UCC 2–615 expressly frees only sellers under this doctrine, courts have not distinguished between buyers and sellers in applying it.

Commercial paper *See* Negotiable instrument

Commercial use Use of land for business activities only; sometimes called business use.

Commingle To put funds or goods together into one mass so that the funds or goods are so mixed that they no longer have separate identities. In corporate law, if personal and corporate interests are commingled to the extent that the corporation has no separate identity, a court may "pierce the corporate veil" and expose the shareholders to personal liability.

Common area In landlord-tenant law, a portion of the premises over which the landlord retains control and maintenance responsibilities. Common areas may include stairs, lobbies, garages, hallways, and other areas in common use.

Common carrier A carrier that transfers people or goods for hire to the general public.

Common law That body of law developed from custom or judicial decisions in English and U.S. courts, not attributable to a legislature.

Common stock Shares of ownership in a corporation that give the owner of the stock a proportionate interest in the corporation with regard to control, earnings, and net assets; shares of common stock are lowest in priority with respect to payment of dividends and distribution of the corporation's assets on dissolution.

Community property A form of concurrent ownership of property in which each spouse technically owns an undivided one-half interest in property acquired during the marriage. This form of joint ownership occurs in only a minority of states and Puerto Rico.

Comparative negligence A theory in tort law under which the liability for injuries resulting from negligent acts is shared by all parties who were negligent (including the injured party), on the basis of each person's proportionate negligence.

Compelling government interest A test of constitutionality that requires the government to have compelling reasons for passing any law that restricts fundamental rights, such as free speech, or distinguishes between people based on a suspect trait.

Compensatory damages A money award equivalent to the actual value of injuries or damages sustained by the aggrieved party.

Complaint The pleading made by a plaintiff alleging wrongdoing on the part of the defendant; the document that, when filed with a court, initiates a lawsuit.

Complete performance Performance of a contract strictly in accordance with the contract's terms.

Composition agreement *See* Creditors' composition agreement

Computer crime Any violation of criminal law that involves knowledge of computer technology for its perpetration, investigation, or prosecution.

Concentrated industry An industry in which a large percentage of market sales is controlled by either a single firm or a small number of firms.

Concurrent conditions Conditions in a contract that must occur or be performed at the same time; they are mutually dependent. No obligations arise until these conditions are simultaneously performed.

Concurrent jurisdiction Jurisdiction that exists when two different courts have the power to hear a case. For example, some cases can be heard in either a federal or a state court.

Concurrent ownership Joint ownership.

Concurring opinion A written opinion outlining the views of a judge or justice to make or emphasize a point that was not made or emphasized in the majority opinion.

Condemnation The process of taking private property for public use through the government's power of eminent domain.

Condition A possible future event, the occurrence or nonoccurrence of which will trigger the performance of a legal obligation or terminate an existing obligation under a contract.

Condition precedent A condition in a contract that must be met before a party's promise becomes absolute.

Condition subsequent A condition in a contract that operates to terminate a party's absolute promise to perform.

Confiscation A government's taking of privately owned business or personal property without a proper public purpose or an award of just compensation.

Conforming goods Goods that conform to contract specifications.

Confusion The mixing together of goods belonging to two or more owners so that the separately owned goods cannot be identified.

Conglomerate merger A merger between firms that do not compete with each other because they are in different markets (as opposed to horizontal and vertical mergers).

Consent Voluntary agreement to a proposition or an act of another. A concurrence of wills.

Consequential damages Special damages that compensate for a loss that is not direct or immediate (for example, lost profits). The special damages must have been reasonably foreseeable at the time the breach or injury occurred in order for the plaintiff to collect them.

Consideration Generally, the value given in return for a promise or a performance. The consideration, which must be present to make the contract legally binding, must be something of legally sufficient value and bargained for.

Consignment A transaction in which an owner of goods (the consignor) delivers the goods to another (the consignee) for the consignee to sell. The consignee pays the consignor for the goods when they are sold by the consignee.

Consolidation A contractual and statutory process in which two or more corporations join to become a completely new corporation. The original corporations cease to exist, and the new corporation acquires all their assets and liabilities.

Constitutional law Law that is based on the U.S. Constitution and the constitutions of the various states.

Construction loan A loan obtained by the borrower to finance the building of a new home. Construction loans are often set up to release funds at particular stages of the project.

Constructive condition A condition in a contract that is neither expressed nor implied by the contract but rather is imposed by law for reasons of justice.

Constructive delivery An act equivalent to the actual, physical delivery of property that cannot be physically delivered because of difficulty or impossibility; for example, the transfer of a key to a safe constructively delivers the contents of the safe.

Constructive discharge A termination of employment brought about by making an employee's working conditions so intolerable that the employee reasonably feels compelled to leave.

Constructive eviction A form of eviction that occurs when a landlord fails to perform adequately any of the undertakings (such as providing heat in the winter) required by the lease, thereby making the tenant's further use and enjoyment of the property exceedingly difficult or impossible.

Constructive trust An equitable trust that is imposed in the interests of fairness and justice when someone wrongfully holds legal title to property. A court may require the owner to hold the property in trust for the person or persons who rightfully should own the property.

Consumer credit Credit extended primarily for personal or household use.

Consumer-debtor An individual whose debts are primarily consumer debts (debts for purchases made primarily for personal or household use).

Consumer goods Goods that are primarily for personal or household use.

Consumer law The body of statutes, agency rules, and judicial decisions protecting consumers of goods and services from dangerous manufacturing techniques, mislabeling, unfair credit practices, deceptive advertising, and so on. Consumer laws provide remedies and protections that are not ordinarily available to merchants or to businesses.

Contingency fee An attorney's fee that is based on a percentage of the final award received by his or her client as a result of litigation.

Continuation statement A statement that, if filed within six months prior to the expiration date of the original financing statement, continues the perfection of the original security interest for another five years. The perfection of a security interest can be continued in the same manner indefinitely.

Contract An agreement that can be enforced in court; formed by two or more parties, each of whom agrees to perform or to refrain from performing some act now or in the future.

Contract implied in law *See* Quasi contract

Contract under seal A formal agreement in which the seal is a substitute for consideration.

Contractual capacity The legal ability to enter into contracts. The threshold mental capacity required by law for a party who enters into a contract to be bound by that contract.

Contribution *See* Right of contribution

Contributory negligence A theory in tort law under which a complaining party's own negligence contributed to or caused his or her injuries. Contributory negligence is an absolute bar to recovery in a minority of jurisdictions.

Conversion The wrongful taking, using, or retaining possession of personal property that belongs to another.

Convertible bond A bond that can be exchanged for a specified number of shares of common stock under certain conditions.

Conveyance The transfer of a title to land from one person to another by deed; a document (such as a deed) by which an interest in land is transferred from one person to another.

Conviction The outcome of a criminal trial in which the defendant has been found guilty of the crime.

"Cooling-off" laws A set of federal and state laws designed to protect purchasers and lessees of goods or property. For example, the Federal Trade Commission's cooling-off period is three business days for purchases of goods or services from door-to-door salespersons. Cooling off periods vary for loans, mortgages, leases, etc.

Cooperative An association that is organized to provide an economic service to its members (or shareholders). An incorporated cooperative is a nonprofit corporation. It will make distributions of dividends, or profits, to its owners on the basis of their transactions with the cooperative rather than on the basis of the amount of capital they contributed. Examples of cooperatives are consumer purchasing cooperatives, credit cooperatives, and farmers' cooperatives.

Co-ownership Joint ownership.

Copyright The exclusive right of authors to publish, print, or sell an intellectual production for a statutory period of time. A copyright has the same monopolistic nature as a patent or trademark, but it differs in that it applies exclusively to works of art, literature, and other works of authorship, including computer programs.

Corporate governance The relationship between a corporation and its shareholders—specifically, a system that details the distribution of rights and responsibilities of those within the corporation and spells out the rules and procedures for making corporate decisions.

Corporate social responsibility The concept that corporations can and should act ethically and be accountable to society for their actions.

Corporation A legal entity formed in compliance with statutory requirements. The entity is distinct from its shareholders-owners.

Cosign The act of signing a document (such as a note promising to pay another in return for a loan or other benefit) jointly with another person and thereby assuming liability for performing what was promised in the document.

Cost-benefit analysis A decision-making technique that involves weighing the costs of a given action against the benefits of the action.

Co-surety A joint surety. One who assumes liability jointly with another surety for the payment of an obligation.

Counteradvertising New advertising that is undertaken pursuant to a Federal Trade Commission order for the purpose of correcting earlier false claims that were made about a product.

Counterclaim A claim made by a defendant in a civil lawsuit that in effect sues the plaintiff.

Counteroffer An offeree's response to an offer in which the offeree rejects the original offer and at the same time makes a new offer.

Course of dealing Prior conduct between parties to a contract that establishes a common basis for their understanding.

Course of performance The conduct that occurs under the terms of a particular agreement; such conduct indicates what the parties to an agreement intended it to mean.

Court of equity A court that decides controversies and administers justice according to the rules, principles, and precedents of equity.

Court of law A court in which the only remedies that could be granted were things of value, such as money damages. In the early English king's courts, courts of law were distinct from courts of equity.

Covenant against encumbrances A grantor's assurance that there are no encumbrances on land conveyed—that is, that no third parties have rights to or interests in the land that would diminish its value to the grantee.

Covenant not to compete A contractual promise to refrain from competing with another party for a certain period of time and within a certain geographic area. Although covenants not to compete restrain trade, they are commonly found in partnership agreements, business sale agreements, and employment contracts. If they are ancillary to such agreements, covenants not to compete will normally be enforced by the courts unless the time period or geographic area is deemed unreasonable.

Covenant not to sue An agreement to substitute a contractual obligation for some other type of legal action based on a valid claim.

Covenant of quiet enjoyment A promise by a grantor (or landlord) that the grantee (or tenant) will not be evicted or disturbed by the grantor or a person having a lien or superior title.

Covenant of the right to convey A grantor's assurance that he or she has sufficient capacity and title to convey the estate that he or she undertakes to convey by deed.

Covenant running with the land An executory promise made between a grantor and a grantee to which they and subsequent owners of the land are bound.

Cover A buyer or lessee's purchase on the open market of goods to substitute for those promised but never delivered by the seller. Under the Uniform Commercial Code, if the cost of cover exceeds the cost of the contract goods, the buyer or lessee can recover the difference, plus incidental and consequential damages.

Cram-down provision A provision of the Bankruptcy Code that allows a court to confirm a debtor's Chapter 11 reorganization plan even though only one class of creditors has accepted it. To exercise the court's right under this provision, the court must demonstrate that the plan does not discriminate unfairly against any creditors and is fair and equitable.

Creditor A person to whom a debt is owed by another person (the debtor).

Creditor beneficiary A third party beneficiary who has rights in a contract made by the debtor and a third person. The terms of the contract obligate the third person to pay the debt owed to the creditor. The creditor beneficiary can enforce the debt against either party.

Creditors' composition agreement An agreement formed between a debtor and his or her creditors in which the creditors agree to accept a lesser sum than that owed by the debtor in full satisfaction of the debt.

Crime A wrong against society proclaimed in a statute and punishable by society through fines and/or imprisonment—or, in some cases, death.

Criminal act *See Actus reus*

Criminal intent *See Mens rea*

Criminal law Law that defines and governs actions that constitute crimes. Generally, criminal law has to do with wrongful actions committed against society for which society demands redress.

Cross-border pollution Pollution across national boundaries; air and water degradation in one nation resulting from pollution-causing activities in a neighboring country.

Cross-collateralization The use of an asset that is not the subject of a loan to collateralize that loan.

Cross-examination The questioning of an opposing witness during a trial.

Crowdfunding A cooperative activity in which people network and pool funds and other resources via the Internet to assist a cause (such as disaster relief) or invest in a venture (business).

Cumulative voting A method of shareholder voting designed to allow minority shareholders to be represented on the board of directors. With cumulative voting, the number of members of the board to be elected is multiplied by the total number of voting shares held. The result equals the number of votes a shareholder has, and this total can be cast for one or more nominees for director.

Cure Under the Uniform Commercial Code, the right of a party who tenders nonconforming performance to correct his or her performance within the contract period.

Cyber crime A crime that occurs online, in the virtual community of the Internet, as opposed to the physical world.

Cyber fraud Fraud that involves the online theft of credit card information, banking details, and other information for criminal use.

Cyber mark A trademark in cyberspace.

Cyber tort A tort committed via the Internet.

Cyberlaw An informal term used to refer to all laws governing electronic communications and transactions, particularly those conducted via the Internet.

Cybersquatting The act of registering a domain name that is the same as, or confusingly similar to, the trademark of another and then offering to sell that domain name back to the trademark owner.

Cyberterrorist A hacker whose purpose is to exploit a target computer for a serious impact, such as the corruption of a program to sabotage a business.

D

Damages Money sought as a remedy for a breach of contract or for a tortious act.

Debenture bond A bond backed only by the general credit rating of the corporation, plus any assets that can be seized if the corporation allows the debentures to go into default.

Debtor Under Article 9 of the Uniform Commercial Code, any party who owes payment or performance of a secured obligation, whether or not the party actually owns or has rights in the collateral.

Debtor in possession (DIP) In Chapter 11 bankruptcy proceedings, a debtor who is allowed to continue in possession of the estate in property (the business) and to continue business operations.

Deceptive advertising Advertising that misleads consumers, either by making unjustified claims concerning a product's performance or by omitting a material fact concerning the product's composition or performance.

Declaratory judgment A court's judgment on a justiciable controversy when the plaintiff is in doubt as to his or her legal rights; a binding adjudication of the rights and status of litigants even though no consequential relief is awarded.

Decree The judgment of a court of equity.

Deed A document by which title to property (usually real property) is passed.

Deed in lieu of foreclosure An alternative to foreclosure in which the mortgagor, rather than fighting to retain possession, voluntarily conveys the property to the lender in satisfaction of the mortgage.

Defalcation The misuse of funds.

Defamation Any published or publicly spoken false statement that causes injury to another's good name, reputation, or character.

Default judgment A judgment entered by a court against a defendant who has failed to appear in court to answer or defend against the plaintiff's claim.

Defendant One against whom a lawsuit is brought; the accused person in a criminal proceeding.

Defense Reasons that a defendant offers in an action or suit as to why the plaintiff should not obtain what he or she is seeking.

Deficiency judgment A judgment against a debtor for the amount of a debt remaining unpaid after collateral has been repossessed and sold.

Delegatee One to whom contract duties are delegated by another, called the delegator.

Delegation The transfer of a contractual duty to a third party. The party delegating the duty (the delegator) to the third party (the delegatee) is still obliged to perform on the contract should the delegatee fail to perform.

Delegation doctrine A doctrine based on Article I, Section 8, of the U.S. Constitution, which has been construed to allow Congress to delegate some of its power to make and implement laws to administrative agencies. The delegation is considered to be proper as long as Congress sets standards outlining the scope of the agency's authority.

Delegator One who delegates his or her duties under a contract to another, called the delegatee.

Delivery In contract law, one party's act of placing the subject matter of the contract within the other party's possession or control.

Delivery order A written order to deliver goods directed to a warehouser, carrier, or other person who, in the ordinary course of business, issues warehouse receipts or bills of lading [UCC 7–102(1)(d)].

Demand deposit Funds (accepted by a bank) subject to immediate withdrawal, in contrast to a time deposit, which requires that a depositor wait a specific time before withdrawing or pay a penalty for early withdrawal.

De novo Anew; afresh; a second time. In a hearing *de novo,* an appellate court hears the case as a court of original jurisdiction—that is, as if the case had not previously been tried and a decision rendered.

Depositary bank The first bank to receive a check for payment.

Deposition The testimony of a party to a lawsuit or a witness taken under oath before a trial.

Destination contract A contract in which the seller is required to ship the goods by carrier and deliver them at a particular destination. The seller assumes liability for any losses or damage to the goods until they are tendered at the destination specified in the contract.

Devise To make a gift of real property by will.

Digital cash Funds contained on computer software, in the form of secure programs stored on microchips and other computer devices.

Dilution With respect to trademarks, a doctrine under which distinctive or famous trademarks are protected from certain unauthorized uses of the marks regardless of a showing of competition or a likelihood of confusion. Congress created a federal cause of action for dilution in 1995 with the passage of the Federal Trademark Dilution Act.

Direct examination The examination of a witness by the attorney who calls the witness to the stand to testify on behalf of the attorney's client.

Directed verdict *See* Motion for a directed verdict

Disaffirmance The legal avoidance, or setting aside, of a contractual obligation.

Discharge The termination of an obligation. (1) In contract law, discharge occurs when the parties have fully performed their contractual obligations or when events, conduct of the parties, or operation of the law releases the parties from performance. (2) In bankruptcy proceedings, the extinction of the debtor's dischargeable debts.

Discharge in bankruptcy The release of a debtor from all debts that are provable, except those specifically excepted from discharge by statute.

Disclosed principal A principal whose identity is known to a third party at the time the agent makes a contract with the third party.

Discovery A phase in the litigation process during which the opposing parties may obtain information from each other and from third parties prior to trial.

Dishonor To refuse to accept or pay a draft or a promissory note when it is properly presented. An instrument is dishonored when presentment is properly made and acceptance or payment is refused or cannot be obtained within the prescribed time.

Disparagement of property An economically injurious false statement made about another's product or property. A general term for torts that are more specifically referred to as slander of quality or slander of title.

Disparate-impact discrimination A form of employment discrimination that results from certain employer practices or procedures that, although not discriminatory on their face, have a discriminatory effect.

Disparate-treatment discrimination A form of employment discrimination that results when an employer intentionally discriminates against employees who are members of protected classes.

Dissenting opinion A written opinion by a judge or justice who disagrees with the majority opinion.

Dissociation The severance of the relationship between a partner and a partnership when the partner ceases to be associated with the carrying on of the partnership business.

Dissolution The formal disbanding of a partnership or a corporation. It can take place by (1) acts of the partners or, in a corporation, of the shareholders and board of directors; (2) the death of a partner; (3) the expiration of a time period stated in a partnership agreement or a certificate of incorporation; or (4) judicial decree.

Distributed network A network that can be used by persons located (distributed) around the country or the globe to share computer files.

Distribution agreement A contract between a seller and a distributor of the seller's products setting out the terms and conditions of the distributorship.

Distributorship A business arrangement that is established when a manufacturer licenses a dealer to sell its product. An example of a distributorship is an automobile dealership.

Diversity of citizenship Under Article III, Section 2, of the Constitution, a basis for federal court jurisdiction over a lawsuit between (1) citizens of different states, (2) a foreign country and citizens of a state or of different states, or (3) citizens of a state and citizens or subjects of a foreign country. The amount in controversy must be more than $75,000 before a federal court can take jurisdiction in such cases.

Divestiture The act of selling one or more of a company's parts, such as a subsidiary or plant; often mandated by the courts in merger or monopolization cases.

Dividend A distribution to corporate shareholders of corporate profits or income, disbursed in proportion to the number of shares held.

Docket The list of cases entered on a court's calendar and thus scheduled to be heard by the court.

Document of title Paper exchanged in the regular course of business that evidences the right to possession of goods (for example, a bill of lading or a warehouse receipt).

Domain name The series of letters and symbols used to identify site operators on the Internet; Internet "addresses."

Domestic corporation In a given state, a corporation that does business in, and is organized under the laws of, that state.

Domestic relations court A court that deals with domestic (household) relationships, such as adoption, divorce, support payments, child custody, and the like.

Dominion Perfect control in the right of ownership of property; typically implies both title and possession. It requires the complete retention of control over the disposition of property.

Donee beneficiary A third party beneficiary who has rights under a contract as a direct result of the intention of the contract parties to make a gift to the third party.

Double jeopardy A situation occurring when a person is tried twice for the same criminal offense; prohibited by the Fifth Amendment to the Constitution.

Double taxation A feature (and disadvantage) of the corporate form of business. Because a corporation is a separate legal entity, corporate profits are taxed by state and federal governments. Dividends are again taxable as ordinary income to the shareholders receiving them.

Down payment The part of the purchase price of real property that is paid in cash up front, reducing the amount of the loan or mortgage.

Draft Any instrument (such as a check) drawn on a drawee (such as a bank) that orders the drawee to pay a certain sum of money, usually to a third party (the payee), on demand or at a definite future time.

Dram shop act A state statute that imposes liability on the owners of bars and taverns, as well as those who serve alcoholic drinks to the public, for injuries resulting from accidents caused by intoxicated persons when the sellers or servers of alcoholic drinks contributed to the intoxication.

Drawee The party that is ordered to pay a draft or check. With a check, a financial institution is always the drawee.

Drawer The party that initiates a draft (writes a check, for example), thereby ordering the drawee to pay.

Due diligence A required standard of care that certain professionals, such as accountants, must meet to avoid liability for securities violations. Under securities law, an accountant will be deemed to have exercised due diligence if he or she followed generally accepted accounting principles and generally accepted auditing standards and had, "after reasonable investigation, reasonable grounds to believe and did believe, at the time such part of the registration statement became effective, that the statements therein were true and that there was no omission of a material fact required to be stated therein or necessary to make the statements therein not misleading."

Due process clause The provisions of the Fifth and Fourteenth Amendments to the Constitution that guarantee that no person shall be deprived of life, liberty, or property without due process of law. Similar clauses are found in most state constitutions.

Dumping The selling of goods in a foreign country at a price below the price charged for the same goods in the domestic market.

Durable power of attorney A document that authorizes a person to act on behalf of an incompetent person—write checks, collect insurance proceeds, and otherwise manage the disabled person's affairs, including health care—when he or she becomes incapacitated. Spouses often give each other durable power of attorney and, if they are advanced in age, may give a second such power of attorney to an older child.

Duress Unlawful pressure brought to bear on a person, causing the person to perform an act that he or she would not otherwise perform.

Duty-based ethics An ethical philosophy rooted in the idea that every person has certain duties to others, including both humans and the planet. Those duties may be derived from religious principles or from other philosophical reasoning.

Duty of care The duty of all persons, as established by tort law, to exercise a reasonable amount of care in their dealings with others. Failure to exercise due care, which is normally determined by the "reasonable person standard," constitutes the tort of negligence.

E

E-agent A semiautonomous computer program that is capable of executing specific tasks.

E-commerce Business transacted in cyberspace.

E-contract A contract that is entered into in cyberspace and is evidenced only by electronic impulses (such as those that make up a computer's memory), rather than, for example, a typewritten form.

E-evidence A type of evidence that consists of computer-generated or electronically recorded information, including e-mail, voice mail, spreadsheets, word-processing documents, and other data.

E-money Prepaid funds recorded on a computer or a card (such as a *smart card*).

E-signature As defined by the Uniform Electronic Transactions Act, "an electronic sound, symbol, or process attached to or logically associated with a record and executed or adopted by a person with the intent to sign the record."

Early neutral case evaluation A form of alternative dispute resolution in which a neutral third party evaluates the strengths and weakness of the disputing parties' positions; the evaluator's opinion forms the basis for negotiating a settlement.

Easement A nonpossessory right to use another's property in a manner established by either express or implied agreement.

Electronic fund transfer (EFT) A transfer of funds with the use of an electronic terminal, a telephone, a computer, or magnetic tape.

Emancipation In regard to minors, the act of being freed from parental control; occurs when a child's parent or legal guardian relinquishes the legal right to exercise control over the child. Normally, a minor who leaves home to support himself or herself is considered emancipated.

Embezzlement The fraudulent appropriation of money or other property by a person to whom the money or property has been entrusted.

Eminent domain The power of a government to take land for public use from private citizens for just compensation.

Employee A person who works for an employer for a salary or for wages.

Employer An individual or business entity that hires employees, pays them salaries or wages, and exercises control over their work.

Employment at will A common law doctrine under which either party may terminate an employment relationship at any time for any reason, unless a contract specifies otherwise.

Employment discrimination Treating employees or job applicants unequally on the basis of race, color, national origin, religion, gender, age, or disability; prohibited by federal statutes.

Enabling legislation A statute enacted by Congress that authorizes the creation of an administrative agency and specifies the name, composition, purpose, and powers of the agency being created.

Encryption The process by which a message (plaintext) is transformed into something (ciphertext) that the sender and receiver intend third parties not to understand.

Endowment insurance A type of insurance that combines life insurance with an investment so that if the insured outlives the policy, the face value is paid to him or her; if the insured does not outlive the policy, the face value is paid to his or her beneficiary.

Entrapment In criminal law, a defense in which the defendant claims that he or she was induced by a public official—usually an undercover agent or police officer—to commit a crime that he or she would otherwise not have committed.

Entrepreneur One who initiates and assumes the financial risks of a new enterprise and who undertakes to provide or control its management.

Entrustment The transfer of goods to a merchant who deals in goods of that kind and who may transfer those goods and all rights to them to a buyer in the ordinary course of business [UCC 2–403(2)].

Environmental impact statement (EIS) A statement required by the National Environmental Policy Act for any major federal action that will significantly affect the quality of the environment. The statement must analyze the action's impact on the environment and explore alternative actions that might be taken.

Environmental law The body of statutory, regulatory, and common law relating to the protection of the environment.

Equal dignity rule In most states, a rule stating that express authority given to an agent must be in writing if the contract to be made on behalf of the principal is required to be in writing.

Equal protection clause The provision in the Fourteenth Amendment to the Constitution that guarantees that no state will "deny to any person within its jurisdiction the equal protection of the laws." This clause mandates that state governments treat similarly situated individuals in a similar manner.

Equitable maxims General propositions or principles of law that have to do with fairness (equity).

Equitable right of redemption The right of a mortgagor who has breached the mortgage agreement to redeem or purchase the property prior to foreclosure proceedings.

Equity of redemption The right of a mortgagor who has breached the mortgage agreement to redeem or purchase the property prior to foreclosure proceedings.

Equity participation loan A loan that allows the lender to participate in some percentage of the increase in the equity value of a business or property; any loan that gives the lender the right to obtain an ownership interest in the project being financed.

Escheat The transfer of property to the state when the owner of the property dies without heirs.

Escrow account An account that is generally held in the name of the depositor and escrow agent; the funds in the account are paid to a third person only on fulfillment of the escrow condition.

Establishment clause The provision in the First Amendment to the U.S. Constitution that prohibits Congress from creating any law "respecting an establishment of religion."

Estate The interest that a person has in real and personal property.

Estate planning Planning in advance how one's property and obligations should be transferred on one's death. Wills and trusts are two basic devices used in the process of estate planning.

Estop To bar, impede, or preclude.

Estopped Barred, impeded, or precluded.

Estoppel The principle that a party's own acts prevent him or her from claiming a right to the detriment of another who was entitled to and did rely on those acts. *See also* Agency by estoppel; Promissory estoppel

Estray statute A statute defining finders' rights in property when the true owners are unknown.

Ethical reasoning A reasoning process in which an individual links his or her moral convictions or ethical standards to the particular situation at hand.

Ethics Moral principles and values applied to social behavior.

Eviction A landlord's act of depriving a tenant of possession of the leased premises.

Evidence Proof offered at trial—in the form of testimony, documents, records, exhibits, objects, and so on—for the purpose of convincing the court or jury of the truth of a contention.

Exclusionary rule In criminal procedure, a rule under which any evidence that is obtained in violation of the accused's constitutional rights guaranteed by the Fourth, Fifth, and Sixth Amendments, as well as any evidence derived from illegally obtained evidence, will not be admissible in court.

Exclusive agency An agency in which a principal grants an agent an exclusive territory and does not allow another agent to compete in that territory.

Exclusive distributorship A distributorship in which the seller and the distributor of the seller's products agree that the distributor has the exclusive right to distribute the seller's products in a certain geographic area.

Exclusive jurisdiction Jurisdiction that exists when a case can be heard only in a particular court or type of court, such as a federal court or a state court.

Exclusive-dealing contract An agreement under which a seller forbids a buyer to purchase products from the seller's competitors.

Exculpatory clause A clause that releases a contractual party from liability in the event of monetary or physical injury, no matter who is at fault.

Executed contract A contract that has been completely performed by both parties.

Execution An action to carry into effect the directions in a court decree or judgment.

Executive agency An administrative agency within the executive branch of government. At the federal level, executive agencies are those within the cabinet departments.

Executor A person appointed by a testator to see that his or her will is administered appropriately.

Executory contract A contract that has not as yet been fully performed.

Export To sell products to buyers located in other countries.

Express authority Authority expressly given by one party to another. In agency law, an agent has express authority to act for a principal if both parties agree, orally or in writing, that an agency relationship exists in which the agent had the power (authority) to act in the place of, and on behalf of, the principal.

Express contract A contract in which the terms of the agreement are fully and explicitly stated in words, oral or written.

Express warranty A seller's or lessor's oral or written promise, ancillary to an underlying sales or lease agreement, as to the quality, description, or performance of the goods being sold or leased.

Expropriation The seizure by a government of privately owned business or personal property for a proper public purpose and with just compensation.

Extension clause A clause in a time instrument that allows the instrument's date of maturity to be extended into the future.

Extrinsic evidence Evidence that relates to a contract but is not contained within the document itself, such as the testimony of parties and witnesses, or additional agreements or communications. A court may consider extrinsic evidence only when a contract term is ambiguous and the evidence does not contradict the express terms of the contract.

F

F.A.S. Free alongside. A contract term that requires the seller, at his or her own expense and risk, to deliver the goods alongside the ship before risk passes to the buyer.

F.O.B. Free on board. A contract term that indicates that the selling price of the goods includes transportation costs (and that the seller carries the risk of loss) to the specific F.O.B. place named in the contract. The place can be either the place of initial shipment (for example, the seller's city or place of business) or the place of destination (for example, the buyer's city or place of business).

Family limited liability partnership (FLLP) A limited liability partnership (LLP) in which the majority of the partners are persons related to each other, essentially as spouses, parents, grandparents, siblings, cousins, nephews, or nieces. A person acting in a fiduciary capacity for persons so related could also be a partner. All of the partners must be natural persons or persons acting in a fiduciary capacity for the benefit of natural persons.

Federal form of government A system of government in which the states form a union and the sovereign power is divided between a central government and the member states.

Federal question A question that pertains to the U.S. Constitution, acts of Congress, or treaties. A federal question provides a basis for federal jurisdiction.

Federal Reserve System A network of twelve central banks, located around the country and headed by the Federal Reserve Board of Governors. Most banks in the United States have Federal Reserve accounts.

Federal Rules of Civil Procedure (FRCP) The rules controlling procedural matters in civil trials brought before the federal district courts.

Fee simple absolute An ownership interest in land in which the owner has the greatest possible aggregation of rights, privileges, and power. The owner can use, possess, or dispose of the property as he or she chooses during his or her lifetime. On death, the interest in the property passes to the owner's heirs.

Felony A crime—such as arson, murder, rape, or robbery—that carries the most severe sanctions, usually ranging from one year in a state or federal prison to the forfeiture of one's life.

Fictitious payee A payee on a negotiable instrument whom the maker or drawer does not intend to have an interest in the instrument. Indorsements by fictitious payees are not treated as unauthorized under Article 3 of the Uniform Commercial Code.

Fiduciary As a noun, a person having a duty created by his or her undertaking to act primarily for another's benefit in matters connected with the undertaking. As an adjective, a relationship founded on trust and confidence.

Fiduciary duty The duty, imposed on a fiduciary by virtue of his or her position, to act primarily for another's benefit.

Filtering software A computer program that includes a pattern through which data are passed. When designed to block access to certain Web sites, the pattern blocks the retrieval of a site whose URL or key words are on a list within the program.

Final order The final decision of an administrative agency on an issue. If no appeal is taken, or if the case is not reviewed or considered anew by the agency commission, the administrative law judge's initial order becomes the final order of the agency.

Financial institution An organization authorized to do business under state or federal laws relating to financial institutions. Financial institutions may include banks, savings and loan associations, credit unions, and other business entities that directly or indirectly hold accounts belonging to consumers.

Financing statement A document prepared by a secured creditor and filed with the appropriate government official to give notice to the public that the creditor claims an interest in collateral belonging to the debtor named in the statement. The financing statement must contain the names and addresses of both the debtor and the creditor, and describe the collateral by type or item.

Firm offer An offer (by a merchant) that is irrevocable without consideration for a period of time (not longer than three months). A firm offer by a merchant must be in writing and must be signed by the offeror.

Fitness for a particular purpose *See* Implied warranty of fitness for a particular purpose

Fixed-rate mortgage A standard mortgage with a fixed, or unchanging, rate of interest. The loan payments on these mortgages remain the same for the duration of the loan, which ranges between fifteen and forty years.

Fixed-term tenancy A type of tenancy under which property is leased for a specified period of time, such as a month, a year, or a period of years; also called a *tenancy for years*.

Fixture A thing that was once personal property but that has become attached to real property in such a way that it takes on the characteristics of real property and becomes part of that real property.

Floating lien A security interest in proceeds, after-acquired property, or property purchased under a line of credit (or all three); a security interest in collateral that is retained even when the collateral changes in character, classification, or location.

Forbearance The act of refraining from exercising a legal right. An agreement between the lender and the borrower in which the lender agrees to temporarily cease requiring mortgage payments, to delay foreclosure, or to accept smaller payments than previously scheduled.

Force majeure (pronounced mah-*zhure*) **clause** A provision in a contract stipulating that certain unforeseen events—such as war, political upheavals, acts of

God, or other events—will excuse a party from liability for nonperformance of contractual obligations.

Foreclosure A proceeding in which a mortgagee either takes title to or forces the sale of the mortgagor's property in satisfaction of a debt.

Foreign corporation In a given state, a corporation that does business in the state without being incorporated therein.

Foreseeable risk In negligence law, the risk of harm or injury to another that a person of ordinary intelligence and prudence should have reasonably anticipated or foreseen when undertaking an action or refraining from undertaking an action.

Forfeiture The termination of a lease, according to its terms or the terms of a statute, when one of the parties fails to fulfill a condition under the lease and thereby breaches it.

Forgery The fraudulent making or altering of any writing in a way that changes the legal rights and liabilities of another.

Formal contract A contract that by law requires a specific form, such as being executed under seal, to be valid.

Forum A jurisdiction, court, or place in which disputes are litigated and legal remedies are sought.

Forum-selection clause A provision in a contract designating the court, jurisdiction, or tribunal that will decide any disputes arising under the contract.

Franchise Any arrangement in which the owner of a trademark, trade name, or copyright licenses another to use that trademark, trade name, or copyright, under specified conditions or limitations, in the selling of goods and services.

Franchise tax A state or local government tax on the right and privilege of carrying on a business in the form of a corporation.

Franchisee One receiving a license to use another's (the franchisor's) trademark, trade name, or copyright in the sale of goods and services.

Franchisor One licensing another (the franchisee) to use his or her trademark, trade name, or copyright in the sale of goods or services.

Fraud Any misrepresentation, either by misstatement or omission of a material fact, knowingly made with the intention of deceiving another and on which a reasonable person would and does rely to his or her detriment.

Fraud in the execution In the law of negotiable instruments, a type of fraud that occurs when a person is deceived into signing a negotiable instrument, believing that he or she is signing something else (such as a receipt); also called fraud in the inception. Fraud in the execution is a universal defense to payment on a negotiable instrument.

Fraud in the inducement Ordinary fraud. In the law of negotiable instruments, fraud in the inducement occurs when a person issues a negotiable instrument based on false statements by the other party. The issuing party will be able to avoid payment on that instrument unless the holder is a holder in due course; in other words, fraud in the inducement is a personal defense to payment on a negotiable instrument.

Fraudulent misrepresentation (fraud) Any misrepresentation, either by misstatement or omission of a material fact, knowingly made with the intention of deceiving another and on which a reasonable person would and does rely to his or her detriment.

Free exercise clause The provision in the First Amendment to the U.S. Constitution that prohibits Congress from making any law "prohibiting the free exercise" of religion.

Free writing prospectus Any type of written, electronic, or graphic offer of securities that describes the issuing corporation or its securities and includes a legend indicating that the investor may obtain the prospectus at the SEC's Web site.

Frustration of purpose A court-created doctrine under which a party to a contract will be relieved of his or her duty to perform when the objective purpose for performance no longer exists (due to reasons beyond that party's control).

Full faith and credit clause A clause in Article IV, Section 1, of the Constitution that provides that "Full Faith and Credit shall be given in each State to the public Acts, Records, and Judicial Proceedings of every other State." The clause ensures that rights established under deeds, wills, contracts, and the like in one state will be honored by the other states and that any judicial decision with respect to such property rights will be honored and enforced in all states.

Full warranty A warranty as to full performance covering generally both labor and materials.

Fungible goods Goods that are alike by physical nature, by agreement, or by trade usage. Examples of fungible goods are wheat, oil, and wine that are identical in type and quality.

G

Garnishment A legal process used by a creditor to collect a debt by seizing property of the debtor (such as wages) that is being held by a third party (such as the debtor's employer).

General jurisdiction Exists when a court's subject-matter jurisdiction is not restricted. A court of general jurisdiction normally can hear any type of case.

General partner In a limited partnership, a partner who assumes responsibility for the management of the partnership and liability for all partnership debts.

General partnership *See* Partnership

Generally accepted accounting principles (GAAP) The conventions, rules, and procedures that define accepted accounting practices at a particular time. The source of the principles is the Financial Accounting Standards Board.

Generally accepted auditing standards (GAAS) Standards concerning an auditor's professional qualities and the judgment exercised by him or her in the performance of an examination and report. The source of the standards is the American Institute of Certified Public Accountants.

Genuineness of assent Knowing and voluntary assent to the terms of a contract. If a contract is formed as a result of a mistake, misrepresentation, undue influence, or duress, genuineness of assent is lacking, and the contract will be voidable.

Gift Any voluntary transfer of property made without consideration, past or present.

Gift *causa mortis* A gift made in contemplation of death. If the donor does not die of that ailment, the gift is revoked.

Gift *inter vivos* A gift made during one's lifetime and not in contemplation of imminent death, in contrast to a gift *causa mortis*.

Good faith Under the Uniform Commercial Code, good faith means honesty in fact; with regard to merchants, good faith means honesty in fact *and* the observance of reasonable commercial standards of fair dealing in the trade.

Good faith purchaser A purchaser who buys without notice of any circumstance that would put a person of ordinary prudence on inquiry as to whether the seller has valid title to the goods being sold.

Good Samaritan statute A state statute that provides that persons who rescue or provide emergency services to others in peril—unless they do so recklessly, thus causing further harm—cannot be sued for negligence.

Goodwill In the business context, the valuable reputation of a business viewed as an intangible asset.

Grand jury A group of citizens called to decide, after hearing the state's evidence, whether a reasonable basis (probable cause) exists for believing that a crime has been committed and whether a trial ought to be held.

Grant deed A deed that simply recites words of consideration and conveyance. Under statute, a grant deed may impliedly warrant that at least the grantor has not conveyed the property's title to someone else.

Grantee One to whom a grant (of land or property, for example) is made.

Grantor A person who makes a grant, such as a transferor of property or the creator of a trust.

Group boycott The refusal to deal with a particular person or firm by a group of competitors; prohibited by the Sherman Act.

Guarantor A person who agrees to satisfy the debt of another (the debtor) only after the principal debtor defaults; a guarantor's liability is thus secondary.

H

Habitability *See* Implied warranty of habitability

Hacker A person who uses one computer to break into another. Professional computer programmers refer to such persons as "crackers."

Health-care power of attorney A document that designates a person who will have the power to choose what type of and how much medical treatment a person who is unable to make such a choice will receive.

Hearsay An oral or written statement made out of court that is later offered in court by a witness (not the person who made the statement) to prove the truth of the matter asserted in the statement. Hearsay is generally inadmissible as evidence.

Herfindahl-Hirschman Index (HHI) An index measuring market concentration for purposes of antitrust enforcement; calculated by summing the squares of the percentage market shares held by the respective firms.

Historical school A school of legal thought that emphasizes the evolutionary process of law and that looks to the past to discover what the principles of contemporary law should be.

Holder Any person in the possession of an instrument drawn, issued, or indorsed to him or her, to his or her order, to bearer, or in blank.

Holder in due course (HDC) A holder who acquires a negotiable instrument for value; in good faith; and without notice that the instrument is overdue, that it

has been dishonored, that any person has a defense against it or a claim to it, or that the instrument contains unauthorized signatures, alterations, or is so irregular or incomplete as to call into question its authenticity.

Holding company A company whose business activity is holding shares in another company.

Holographic will A will written entirely in the signer's handwriting and usually not witnessed.

Home equity loan A loan in which the lender accepts a person's home equity (the portion of the home's value that is paid off) as collateral, which can be seized if the loan is not repaid on time. Borrowers often take out home equity loans to finance the renovation of the property or to pay off debt that carries a higher interest rate, such as credit-card debt.

Homeowners' insurance Insurance that protects a homeowner's property against damage from storms, fire, and other hazards. Lenders may require that a borrower carry homeowners' insurance on mortgaged property.

Homestead exemption A law permitting a debtor to retain the family home, either in its entirety or up to a specified dollar amount, free from the claims of unsecured creditors or trustees in bankruptcy.

Horizontal merger A merger between two firms that are competing in the same market.

Horizontal restraint Any agreement that in some way restrains competition between rival firms competing in the same market.

Hot-cargo agreement An agreement in which employers voluntarily agree with unions not to handle, use, or deal in nonunion-produced goods of other employers; a type of secondary boycott explicitly prohibited by the Labor-Management Reporting and Disclosure Act of 1959.

Hybrid (two-step) mortgage A mortgage that starts as a fixed-rate mortgage and then converts to an adjustable-rate mortgage.

I

I-551 Alien Registration Receipt Proof that a noncitizen has obtained permanent residency in the United States; the so-called green card.

I-9 verification A form from the Department of Homeland Security, U.S. Citizenship and Immigration Services, used for employment eligibility verification; a form that documents that each new employee is authorized to work in the United States

Identification In a sale of goods, the express designation of the specific goods provided for in the contract.

Identity theft The act of stealing another's identifying information—such as a name, date of birth, or Social Security number—and using that information to access the victim's financial resources.

Illusory promise A promise made without consideration, which renders the promise unenforceable.

Immunity A status of being exempt, or free, from certain duties or requirements. In criminal law, the state may grant an accused person immunity from prosecution—or agree to prosecute for a lesser offense—if the accused person agrees to give the state information that would assist the state in prosecuting other individuals for crimes. In tort law, freedom from liability for defamatory speech. *See also* Privilege

Impeach To challenge the credibility of a person's testimony or attempt to discredit a party or witness.

Implication A way of creating an easement or profit in real property when it is reasonable to imply its existence from the circumstances surrounding the division of the property.

Implied authority Authority that is created not by an explicit oral or written agreement but by implication. In agency law, implied authority (of the agent) can be conferred by custom, inferred from the position the agent occupies, or implied by virtue of being reasonably necessary to carry out express authority.

Implied warranty A warranty that the law derives by implication or inference from the nature of the transaction or the relative situation or circumstances of the parties.

Implied warranty of fitness for a particular purpose A warranty that goods sold or leased are fit for a particular purpose. The warranty arises when any seller or lessor knows the particular purpose for which a buyer or lessee will use the goods and knows that the buyer or lessee is relying on the skill and judgment of the seller or lessor to select suitable goods.

Implied warranty of habitability An implied promise by a landlord that rented residential premises are fit for human habitation—that is, in a condition that is safe and suitable for people to live in.

Implied warranty of merchantability A warranty that goods being sold or leased are reasonably fit for the ordinary purpose for which they are sold or leased, are properly packaged and labeled, and are of fair quality. The warranty automatically arises in every sale or lease of goods made by a merchant who deals in goods of the kind sold or leased.

Implied contract A contract formed in whole or in part from the conduct of the parties (as opposed to an express contract). Also known as implied-in-fact contract.

Impossibility of performance A doctrine under which a party to a contract is relieved of his or her duty to perform when performance becomes impossible or totally impracticable (through no fault of either party).

Imposter One who, by use of the mail, telephone, or personal appearance, induces a maker or drawer to issue an instrument in the name of an impersonated payee. Indorsements by imposters are not treated as unauthorized under Article 3 of the Uniform Commercial Code.

***In personam* jurisdiction** Court jurisdiction over the "person" involved in a legal action; personal jurisdiction.

***In rem* jurisdiction** Court jurisdiction over a defendant's property.

Incidental beneficiary A third party who incidentally benefits from a contract but whose benefit was not the reason the contract was formed; an incidental beneficiary has no rights in a contract and cannot sue to have the contract enforced.

Incontestability clause A clause within a life or health insurance policy that states that after the policy has been in force for a specified length of time—most often two or three years—the insurer cannot contest statements made in the policyholder's application.

Indemnify To compensate or reimburse another for losses or expenses incurred.

Independent contractor One who works for, and receives payment from, an employer but whose working conditions and methods are not controlled by the employer. An independent contractor is not an employee but may be an agent.

Independent regulatory agency An administrative agency that is not considered part of the government's executive branch and is not subject to the authority of the president. Independent agency officials cannot be removed without cause.

Indictment (pronounced in-*dyte*-ment) A charge by a grand jury that a reasonable basis (probable cause) exists for believing that a crime has been committed and that a trial should be held.

Indorsee A person to whom a negotiable instrument is transferred by indorsement.

Indorsement A signature placed on an instrument for the purpose of transferring one's ownership rights in the instrument.

Indorser A person who transfers an instrument by signing (indorsing) it and delivering it to another person.

Industrial use Land use for light or heavy manufacturing, shipping, or heavy transportation.

Informal contract A contract that does not require a specified form or formality in order to be valid.

Information A formal accusation or complaint (without an indictment) issued in certain types of actions (usually criminal actions involving lesser crimes) by a law officer, such as a magistrate.

Information return A tax return submitted by a partnership that reports the income earned by the business. The partnership as an entity does not pay taxes on the income received by the partnership. A partner's profit from the partnership (whether distributed or not) is taxed as individual income to the individual partner.

Infringement A violation of another's legally recognized right. The term is commonly used with reference to the invasion by one party of another party's rights in a patent, trademark, or copyright.

Initial order In the context of administrative law, an agency's disposition in a matter other than a rulemaking. An administrative law judge's initial order becomes final unless it is appealed.

Injunction A court decree ordering a person to do or refrain from doing a certain act or activity.

Innkeeper An owner of an inn, hotel, motel, or other lodging.

Innkeeper's lien A possessory or statutory lien allowing an innkeeper to take the personal property of a guest, brought into the hotel, as security for nonpayment of the guest's bill (debt).

Innocent misrepresentation A false statement of fact or an act made in good faith that deceives and causes harm or injury to another.

Inside director A person on the board of directors who is also an officer of the corporation.

Insider A corporate director or officer, or other employee or agent, with access to confidential information and a duty not to disclose that information in violation of insider-trading laws.

Insider trading The purchase or sale of securities on the basis of "inside information" (information that has not been made available to the public) in violation of a duty owed to the company whose stock is being traded.

Insolvent Under the Uniform Commercial Code, a term describing a person who ceases to pay "his debts in the ordinary course of business or cannot pay his debts as they become due or is insolvent within the meaning of federal bankruptcy law" [UCC 1–201(23)].

Installment contract Under the Uniform Commercial Code, a contract that requires or authorizes delivery in two or more separate lots to be accepted and paid for separately.

Instrument *See* Negotiable instrument

Insurable interest An interest either in a person's life or well-being or in property that is sufficiently substantial that insuring against injury to (or the death of) the person or against damage to the property does not amount to a mere wagering (betting) contract.

Insurance A contract in which, for a stipulated consideration, one party agrees to compensate the other for loss on a specific subject by a specified peril.

Intangible property Property that is incapable of being apprehended by the senses (such as by sight or touch); intellectual property is an example of intangible property.

Integrated contract A written contract that constitutes the final expression of the parties' agreement. If a contract is integrated, evidence extraneous to the contract that contradicts or alters the meaning of the contract in any way is inadmissible.

Intellectual property Property resulting from intellectual, creative processes. Patents, trademarks, and copyrights are examples of intellectual property.

Intended beneficiary A third party for whose benefit a contract is formed; an intended beneficiary can sue the promisor if such a contract is breached.

Intentional tort A wrongful act knowingly committed.

***Inter vivos* gift** *See* Gift *inter vivos*

***Inter vivos* trust** A trust created by the grantor (settlor) and effective during the grantor's lifetime (that is, a trust not established by a will).

Interest-only (IO) mortgage A mortgage that gives the borrower the option of paying only the interest portion of the monthly payment and forgoing the payment of principal for a specified period of time, such as five years. After the interest-only payment option is exhausted, the borrower's payment will increase to include payments on the principal.

Intermediary bank Any bank to which an item is transferred in the course of collection, except the depositary or payor bank.

International Financial Reporting Standards (IFRS) A set of global accounting standards created by the International Accounting Standards Board (IASB) that are being phased in by companies in the United States. The Securities and Exchange Commission is working towards a convergence between the IASB and U.S. accounting standards.

International law The law that governs relations among nations. International customs and treaties are generally considered to be two of the most important sources of international law.

International organization In international law, a term that generally refers to an organization composed mainly of nations and usually established by treaty. The United States is a member of more than one hundred multilateral and bilateral organizations, including at least twenty through the United Nations.

Internet service provider (ISP) A business or organization that offers users access to the Internet and related services.

Interpretive rule An administrative agency rule that simply declares a policy or explains the agency's position and does not establish any legal rights or obligations.

Interrogatories A series of written questions for which written answers are prepared and then signed under oath by a party to a lawsuit, usually with the assistance of the party's attorney.

Intestacy laws State statutes that specify how property will be distributed when a person dies intestate (without a valid will); statutes of descent and distribution.

Intestate As a noun, one who has died without having created a valid will; as an adjective, the state of having died without a will.

Inverse condemnation The taking of private property by the government without payment of just compensation as required by the U.S. Constitution. The owner must sue the government to recover just compensation.

Investment company A company that acts on behalf of many smaller shareholder-owners by buying a large portfolio of securities and professionally managing that portfolio.

Investment contract In securities law, a transaction in which a person invests in a common enterprise reasonably expecting profits that are derived primarily from the efforts of others.

Invitee A person who, either expressly or impliedly, is privileged to enter onto another's land. The inviter owes the invitee (for example, a customer in a store) the duty to exercise reasonable care to protect the invitee from harm.

Irrevocable offer An offer that cannot be revoked or recalled by the offeror without liability. A merchant's firm offer is an example of an irrevocable offer.

Issue The first transfer, or delivery, of an instrument to a holder.

J

Joint and several liability In partnership law, a doctrine under which a plaintiff may sue, and collect a judgment from, one or more of the partners separately (severally, or individually) or all of the partners together (jointly). This is true even if one of the partners sued did not participate in, ratify, or know about whatever gave rise to the cause of action.

Joint liability Shared liability. In partnership law, partners incur joint liability for partnership obligations and debts. For example, if a third party sues a partner on a partnership debt, the partner has the right to insist that the other partners be sued with him or her.

Joint stock company A hybrid form of business organization that combines characteristics of a corporation (shareholder-owners, management by directors and officers of the company, and perpetual existence) and a partnership (it is formed by agreement, not statute; property is usually held in the names of the members; and the shareholders have personal liability for business debts). Usually, the joint stock company is regarded as a partnership for tax and other legally related purposes.

Joint tenancy The joint ownership of property by two or more co-owners in which each co-owner owns an undivided portion of the property. On the death of one of the joint tenants, his or her interest automatically passes to the surviving joint tenants.

Joint venture A joint undertaking of a specific commercial enterprise by an association of persons. A joint venture is normally not a legal entity and is treated like a partnership for federal income tax purposes.

Judgment The final order or decision resulting from a legal action.

Judgment *n.o.v.* *See* Motion for judgment *n.o.v.*

Judgment rate of interest A rate of interest fixed by statute that is applied to a monetary judgment from the moment the judgment is awarded by a court until the judgment is paid or terminated.

Judicial foreclosure A court-supervised foreclosure proceeding in which the court determines the validity of the debt and, if the borrower is in default, issues a judgment for the lender.

Judicial lien A lien on property created by a court order.

Judicial process The procedures relating to, or connected with, the administration of justice through the judicial system.

Judicial review The process by which courts decide on the constitutionality of legislative enactments and actions of the executive branch.

Junior lienholder A person or business that holds a lien that is subordinate to one or more other liens on the same property.

Jurisdiction The authority of a court to hear and decide a specific action.

Jurisprudence The science or philosophy of law.

Justiciable controversy A controversy that is not hypothetical or academic but real and substantial. A requirement that must be satisfied before a court will hear a case.

K

King's court A medieval English court. The king's courts, or *curiae regis,* were established by the Norman conquerors of England. The body of law that developed in these courts was common to the entire English realm and thus became known as the common law.

L

Laches The equitable doctrine that bars a party's right to legal action if the party has neglected for an unreasonable length of time to act on his or her rights.

Landlord An owner of land or rental property who leases it to another person, called the tenant.

Larceny The wrongful taking and carrying away of another person's personal property with the intent to permanently deprive the owner of the property. Some states classify larceny as either grand or petit, depending on the property's value.

Last clear chance A doctrine under which a plaintiff may recover from a defendant for injuries or damages suffered, notwithstanding the plaintiff's own negligence, when the defendant had an opportunity—a last clear chance—to avoid harming the plaintiff through the exercise of reasonable care but failed to do so.

Latent defects A defect that is not obvious or cannot readily be ascertained.

Law A body of enforceable rules governing relationships among individuals and between individuals and their society.

Lawsuit The litigation process. *See* Litigation

Lease In real property law, a contract by which the owner of real property (the landlord, or lessor) grants to a person (the tenant, or lessee) an exclusive right to use and possess the property, usually for a specified period of time, in return for rent or some other form of payment.

Lease agreement In regard to the lease of goods, an agreement in which one person (the lessor) agrees to transfer the right to the possession and use of property to another person (the lessee) in exchange for rental payments.

Leasehold estate An estate in realty held by a tenant under a lease. In every leasehold estate, the tenant has a qualified right to possess and/or use the land.

Legacy A gift of personal property under a will.

Legal positivism A school of legal thought centered on the assumption that there is no law higher than the laws created by a national government. Laws must be obeyed, even if they are unjust, to prevent anarchy.

Legal positivists Adherents to the positivist school of legal thought who believe that there can be no higher law than a nation's positive law—law created by a particular society at a particular point in time. In contrast to the natural law school, the positivist school maintains that there are no "natural" rights. Rights come into existence only when there is a sovereign power (government) to confer and enforce those rights.

Legal rate of interest A rate of interest fixed by statute as either the maximum rate of interest allowed by law or a rate of interest applied when the parties to a contract intend, but do not fix, an interest rate in the contract. In the latter case, the rate is frequently the same as the statutory maximum rate permitted.

Legal realism A school of legal thought that was popular in the 1920s and 1930s and that challenged many existing jurisprudential assumptions, particularly the assumption that subjective elements play no part in judicial reasoning. Legal realists generally advocated a less abstract and more pragmatic approach to the law, an approach that would take into account customary practices and the circumstances in which transactions take place. The school left a lasting imprint on American jurisprudence.

Legal reasoning The process of reasoning by which a judge harmonizes his or her decision with the judicial decisions of previous cases.

Legatee One designated in a will to receive a gift of personal property.

Legislative rule An administrative agency rule that affects substantive legal rights and carries the same weight as a congressionally enacted statute.

Letter of credit A written instrument, usually issued by a bank on behalf of a customer or other person, in which the issuer promises to honor drafts or other demands for payment by third persons in accordance with the terms of the instrument.

Leveraged buyout (LBO) A corporate takeover financed by loans secured by the acquired corporation's assets or by the issuance of corporate bonds, resulting in a high debt load for the corporation.

Levy The obtaining of money by legal process through the seizure and sale of property, usually done after a writ of execution has been issued.

Liability Any actual or potential legal obligation, duty, debt, or responsibility.

Libel Defamation in writing or other form (such as in a digital recording) having the quality of permanence.

License A revocable right or privilege of a person to come on another person's land.

Licensee One who receives a license to use, or enter onto, another's property.

Lien (pronounced *leen*) A claim against specific property to satisfy a debt.

Lien creditor One whose claim is secured by a lien on particular property, as distinguished from a general creditor, who has no such security.

Life estate An interest in land that exists only for the duration of the life of some person, usually the holder of the estate.

Limited jurisdiction Exists when a court's subject-matter jurisdiction is limited. Bankruptcy courts and probate courts are examples of courts with limited jurisdiction.

Limited liability Exists when the liability of the owners of a business is limited to the amount of their investments in the firm.

Limited liability company (LLC) A hybrid form of business enterprise that offers the limited liability of the corporation but the tax advantages of a partnership.

Limited liability limited partnership (LLLP) A type of limited partnership. The difference between a limited partnership and an LLLP is that the liability of the general partner in an LLLP is the same as the liability of the limited partner. That is, the liability of all partners is limited to the amount of their investments in the firm.

Limited liability partnership (LLP) A form of partnership that allows professionals to enjoy the tax benefits of a partnership while limiting their personal liability for the malpractice of other partners.

Limited partner In a limited partnership, a partner who contributes capital to the partnership but has no right to participate in the management and operation of the business. The limited partner assumes no liability for partnership debts beyond the capital contributed.

Limited partnership (LP) A partnership consisting of one or more general partners (who manage the business and are liable to the full extent of their personal assets for debts of the partnership) and one or more limited partners (who contribute only assets and are liable only to the extent of their contributions).

Limited-payment life A type of life insurance for which premiums are payable for a definite period, after which the policy is fully paid.

Limited warranty A written warranty that fails to meet one or more of the minimum standards for a full warranty.

Liquidated damages An amount, stipulated in the contract, that the parties to a contract believe to be a reasonable estimation of the damages that will occur in the event of a breach.

Liquidated debt A debt that is due and certain in amount.

Liquidation (1) In regard to bankruptcy, the sale of all of the nonexempt assets of a debtor and the distribution of the proceeds to the debtor's creditors. Chapter 7 of the Bankruptcy Code provides for liquidation bankruptcy proceedings. (2) In regard to corporations, the process by which corporate assets are converted into cash and distributed among creditors and shareholders according to specific rules of preference.

Litigant A party to a lawsuit.

Litigation The process of resolving a dispute through the court system.

Living trust A trust created by the grantor (settlor) and effective during his or her lifetime. Also called an *inter vivos* trust.

Living will A document that allows a person to control the methods of medical treatment that may be used after a serious accident or illness.

Lockout Occurs when an employer shuts down to prevent employees from working typically because it cannot reach a collective bargaining agreement with the union.

Long arm statute A state statute that permits a state to obtain personal jurisdiction over nonresident defendants. A defendant must have "minimum contacts" with that state for the statute to apply.

Lost property Property with which the owner has involuntarily parted and then cannot find or recover.

M

Magistrate's court A court of limited jurisdiction that is presided over by a public official (magistrate) with certain judicial authority, such as the power to set bail.

Mailbox rule A rule providing that an acceptance of an offer becomes effective on dispatch. Acceptance takes effect, thus completing formation of the contract, at the time the offeree sends or delivers the communication via the mode expressly or impliedly authorized by the offeror.

Main purpose rule A rule of contract law under which an exception to the Statute of Frauds is made if the main purpose in accepting secondary liability under a contract is to secure a personal benefit. If this situation exists, the contract need not be in writing to be enforceable.

Majority *See* Age of majority

Majority opinion A court's written opinion, outlining the views of the majority of the judges or justices deciding the case.

Maker One who promises to pay a certain sum to the holder of a promissory note or certificate of deposit (CD).

Malpractice Professional misconduct or the failure to exercise the requisite degree of skill as a professional. Negligence—the failure to exercise due care—on the part of a professional, such as a physician or an attorney, is commonly referred to as malpractice.

Malware Malicious software programs designed to disrupt or harm a computer, network, smartphone, or other device.

Manufacturing or processing-plant franchise A franchise that is created when the franchisor transmits to the franchisee the essential ingredients or formula to make a particular product. The franchisee then markets the product either at wholesale or at retail in accordance with the franchisor's standards. Examples of this type of franchise are Coca-Cola and other soft-drink bottling companies.

Mark *See* Trademark

Market concentration A situation that exists when a small number of firms share the market for a particular good or service. For example, if the four largest grocery stores in Chicago accounted for 80 percent of all retail food sales, the market clearly would be concentrated in those four firms.

Market power The power of a firm to control the market price of its product. A monopoly has the greatest degree of market power.

Marketable title Title to real estate that is reasonably free from encumbrances, defects in the chain of title, and other matters that affect title, such as adverse possession.

Market-share test The primary measure of monopoly power. A firm's market share is the percentage of a market that the firm controls.

Marshalling assets The arrangement or ranking of assets in a certain order toward the payment of debts. In equity, when two creditors have recourse to the same property of the debtor, but one has recourse to other property of the debtor, that creditor must resort first to those assets of the debtor that are not available to the other creditor.

Material alteration An alteration to a negotiable instrument that changes the contract terms between two parties in any way.

Material fact A fact to which a reasonable person would attach importance in determining his or her course of action. In regard to tender offers, for example, a fact is material if there is a substantial likelihood that a reasonable shareholder would consider it important in deciding how to vote.

Mechanic's lien A statutory lien on the real property of another, created to ensure payment for work performed and materials furnished in the repair or improvement of real property, such as a building.

Mediation A method of settling disputes outside of court by using the services of a neutral third party, called a mediator. The mediator acts as a communicating agent between the parties and suggests ways in which the parties can resolve their dispute.

Member The term used to designate a person who has an ownership interest in a limited liability company.

Mens rea (pronounced *mehns ray*-uh) Criminal intent. A wrongful mental state, which is as necessary as a wrongful act, to establish criminal liability. What constitutes a guilty mental state varies according to the wrongful action. Thus, for murder, the *mens rea* is the intent to take a life. For theft, the *mens rea* must involve both the knowledge that the property belongs to another and the intent to deprive the owner of it.

Merchant A person who is engaged in the purchase and sale of goods. Under the Uniform Commercial Code, a person who deals in goods of the kind involved in the sales contract; for further definitions, see UCC 2–104.

Merger A contractual and statutory process in which one corporation (the surviving corporation) acquires all of the assets and liabilities of another corporation (the merged corporation). The shareholders of the merged corporation receive either payment for their shares or shares in the surviving corporation.

Meta tags Words inserted into a Web site's key-words field to increase the site's appearance in search engine results.

Metadata Data that are automatically recorded by electronic devices and provide information about who created a file and when, and who accessed, modified, or transmitted it on their hard drives. Can be described as data about data.

Minimum-contacts requirement The requirement that before a state court can exercise jurisdiction over a foreign corporation, the foreign corporation must have sufficient contacts with the state. A foreign corporation that has its home office in the state or that has manufacturing plants in the state meets this requirement.

Minimum wage The lowest wage, either by government regulation or union contract, that an employer may pay an hourly worker.

Mini-trial A private proceeding in which each party to a dispute argues its position before the other side and vice versa. A neutral third party may be present and act as an adviser if the parties fail to reach an agreement.

Mirror image rule A common law rule that requires, for a valid contractual agreement, that the terms of the offeree's acceptance adhere exactly to the terms of the offeror's offer.

Misdemeanor A lesser crime than a felony, punishable by a fine or imprisonment for up to one year in other than a state or federal penitentiary.

Mislaid property Property with which the owner has voluntarily parted and then cannot find or recover.

Misrepresentation A false statement of fact or an action that deceives and causes harm or injury to another. *See also* Fraudulent misrepresentation (fraud); Innocent misrepresentation

Mitigation of damages A rule requiring a plaintiff to have done whatever was reasonable to minimize the damages caused by the defendant.

Money laundering Falsely reporting income that has been obtained through criminal activity as income obtained through a legitimate business enterprise—in effect, "laundering" the "dirty money."

Monopolization The possession of monopoly power in the relevant market and the willful acquisition or maintenance of that power, as distinguished from growth or development as a consequence of a superior product, business acumen, or historic accident.

Monopoly A term generally used to describe a market in which there is a single seller or a limited number of sellers.

Monopoly power The ability of a monopoly to dictate what takes place in a given market.

Moral minimum The minimum degree of ethical behavior expected of a business firm, which is usually defined as compliance with the law.

Mortgage A written instrument that gives a creditor (the mortgagee) an interest in, or lien on, the debtor's (mortgagor's) real property as security for a debt. If the debt is not paid, the property can be sold by the creditor and the proceeds used to pay the debt.

Mortgage assignee An entity that purchases a mortgage from the current mortgage holder and assumes all rights and liabilities of that mortgage, including the right to collect and foreclose.

Mortgage bond A bond that pledges specific property. If the corporation defaults on the bond, the bondholder can take the property.

Motion A procedural request or application presented by an attorney to the court on behalf of a client.

Motion for a directed verdict In a state court, a party's request that the judge enter a judgment in her or his favor before the case is submitted to a jury because the other party has not presented sufficient evidence to support the claim. The federal courts refer to this request as a *motion for judgment as a matter of law*.

Motion for a new trial A motion asserting that the trial was so fundamentally flawed (because of error, newly discovered evidence, prejudice, or other reason) that a new trial is necessary to prevent a miscarriage of justice.

Motion for judgment as a matter of law In a federal court, a party's request that the judge enter a judgment in her or his favor before the case is submitted to a jury because the other party has not presented sufficient evidence to support the claim. The state courts refer to this request as a *motion for a directed verdict*.

Motion for judgment *n.o.v.* A motion requesting the court to grant judgment in favor of the party making the motion on the ground that the jury verdict against him or her was unreasonable and erroneous.

Motion for judgment on the pleadings A motion by either party to a lawsuit at the close of the pleadings requesting the court to decide the issue solely on the pleadings without proceeding to trial. The motion will be granted only if no facts are in dispute.

Motion for summary judgment A motion requesting the court to enter a judgment without proceeding to trial. The motion can be based on evidence outside the pleadings and will be granted only if no facts are in dispute.

Motion to dismiss A pleading in which a defendant asserts that the plaintiff's claim fails to state a cause of action (that is, has no basis in law) or that there are other grounds on which a suit should be dismissed.

Multiple product order An order issued by the Federal Trade Commission to a firm that has engaged in deceptive advertising by which the firm is required to cease and desist from false advertising not only in regard to the product that was the subject of the action but also in regard to all the firm's other products.

Municipal court A city or community court with criminal jurisdiction over traffic violations and, less frequently, with civil jurisdiction over other minor matters.

Mutual assent The element of agreement in the formation of a contract. The manifestation of contract parties' mutual assent to the same bargain is required to establish a contract.

Mutual fund A specific type of investment company that continually buys or sells to investors shares of ownership in a portfolio.

Mutual rescission An agreement between the parties to cancel their contract, releasing the parties from further obligations under the contract. The object of the agreement is to restore the parties to the positions they would have occupied had no contract ever been formed. *See also* Rescission

N

National law Law that pertains to a particular nation (as opposed to international law).

Natural law The belief that government and the legal system should reflect universal moral and ethical principles that are inherent in human nature. The natural law school is the oldest and one of the most significant schools of legal thought.

Necessaries Necessities required for life, such as food, shelter, clothing, and medical attention; may include whatever is believed to be necessary to maintain a person's standard of living or financial and social status.

Necessity In criminal law, a defense against liability; under Section 3.02 of the Model Penal Code, this defense is justifiable if "the harm or evil sought to be avoided" by a given action "is greater than that sought to be prevented by the law defining the offense charged."

Negative amortization Occurs when the payment made by the borrower is less than the interest due on the loan and the difference is added to the principal. The result of negative amortization is that the balance owed on the loan increases rather than decreases over time.

Negligence The failure to exercise the standard of care that a reasonable person would exercise in similar circumstances.

Negligence *per se* An act (or failure to act) in violation of a statutory requirement.

Negligent misrepresentation Any manifestation through words or conduct that amounts to an untrue statement of fact made in circumstances in which a reasonable and prudent person would not have done (or failed to do) that which led to the misrepresentation. A representation made with an honest belief in its truth may still be negligent due to (1) a lack of reasonable care in ascertaining the facts, (2) the manner of expression, or (3) the absence of the skill or competence required by a particular business or profession.

Negotiable instrument A signed writing that contains an unconditional promise or order to pay an exact sum of money, on demand or at an exact future time, to a specific person or order, or to bearer.

Negotiation (1) In regard to dispute settlement, a process in which parties attempt to settle their dispute without going to court, with or without attorneys to represent them. (2) In regard to instruments, the transfer of an instrument in such a way that the transferee (the person to whom the instrument is transferred) becomes a holder.

Nominal damages A small monetary award (often one dollar) granted to a plaintiff when no actual damage was suffered or when the plaintiff is unable to show such loss with sufficient certainty.

Nonconforming goods Goods that do not conform to contract specifications.

No-par shares Corporate shares that have no face value—that is, no specific dollar amount is printed on their face.

Normal trade relations (NTR) status A status granted through an international treaty by which each member nation must treat other members at least as well as it treats the country that receives its most favorable treatment. This status was formerly known as most-favored-nation status.

Notary public A public official authorized to attest to the authenticity of signatures.

Note A written instrument signed by a maker unconditionally promising to pay a fixed amount of money to a payee or a holder on demand or on a specific date.

Notice-and-comment rulemaking An administrative rulemaking procedure that involves the publication of a notice of a proposed rulemaking in the *Federal Register*, a comment period for interested parties to express their views on the proposed rule, and the publication of the agency's final rule in the *Federal Register.*

Notice of default A formal notice to a borrower who is behind in making mortgage payments that the borrower is in default and may face foreclosure if the payments are not brought up to date. The notice is filed by the lender in the county where the property is located.

Notice of Proposed Rulemaking A notice published (in the *Federal Register*) by an administrative agency describing a proposed rule. The notice must include information on when and where agency proceedings on the proposed rule will be held, a description of the nature of the proceedings, the legal authority for the proceedings (which usually is the agency's enabling legislation), and the terms or the subject matter of the proposed rule.

Notice of sale A formal notice to a borrower who is in default on a mortgage that the mortgaged property will be sold in a foreclosure proceeding. The notice is sent to the borrower by the lender and is also typically recorded with the county, posted on the property, and published in a newspaper.

Novation The substitution, by agreement, of a new contract for an old one, with the rights under the old one being terminated. Typically, there is a substitution of a new person who is responsible for the contract and the removal of an original party's rights and duties under the contract.

Nuisance A common law doctrine under which persons may be held liable for using their property in a manner that unreasonably interferes with others' rights to use or enjoy their own property.

Nuncupative will An oral will (often called a death-bed will) made before witnesses; usually limited to transfers of personal property.

O

Objective theory of contracts A theory under which the intent to form a contract will be judged by outward, objective facts (what the party said when entering into the contract, how the party acted or appeared, and the circumstances surrounding the transaction) as interpreted by a reasonable person, rather than by the party's own secret, subjective intentions.

Obligee One to whom an obligation is owed.

Obligor One who owes an obligation to another.

Offer A promise or commitment to perform or refrain from performing some specified act in the future.

Offeree A person to whom an offer is made.

Offeror A person who makes an offer.

Omnibus clause A provision in an automobile insurance policy that protects the vehicle owner who has taken out the insurance policy and anyone who drives the vehicle with the owner's permission.

Online dispute resolution (ODR) The resolution of disputes with the assistance of organizations that offer dispute-resolution services via the Internet.

Opening statement A statement made to the jury at the beginning of a trial by a party's attorney, prior to the presentation of evidence. The attorney briefly outlines the evidence that will be offered and the legal theory that will be pursued.

Operating agreement In a limited liability company, an agreement in which the members set forth the details of how the business will be managed and operated.

Opinion A statement by the court expressing the reasons for its decision in a case.

Option contract A contract under which the offeror cannot revoke his or her offer for a stipulated time period and the offeree can accept or reject the offer during this period without fear that the offer will be made to another person. The offeree must give consideration for the option (the irrevocable offer) to be enforceable.

Order for relief A court's grant of assistance to a complainant. In bankruptcy proceedings, the order relieves the debtor of the immediate obligation to pay the debts listed in the bankruptcy petition.

Order instrument A negotiable instrument that is payable "to the order of an identified person" or "to an identified person or order."

Ordinance A law passed by a local governing unit, such as a municipality or a county.

Original jurisdiction Courts having original jurisdiction are courts of the first instance, or trial courts—that is, courts in which lawsuits begin, trials take place, and evidence is presented.

Outcome-based ethics An ethical philosophy that focuses on the impacts of a decision on society or on key stakeholders.

Output contract An agreement in which a seller agrees to sell and a buyer agrees to buy all or up to a stated amount of what the seller produces.

Outside director A person on the board of directors who does not hold a management position at the corporation.

Overdraft A check written on a checking account in which there are insufficient funds to cover the amount of the check.

P

Parent corporation A corporation that owns *all* of the shares of another corporation (known as its subsidiary).

Parent-subsidiary merger A merger of companies in which one company (the parent corporation) owns most of the stock of the other (the subsidiary corporation). A parent-subsidiary merger (short-form merger) can use a simplified procedure when the parent corporation owns at least 90 percent of the outstanding shares of each class of stock of the subsidiary corporation.

Parol evidence A term that originally meant "oral evidence," but that has come to refer to any negotiations or agreements made prior to a contract or any contemporaneous oral agreements made by the parties.

Parol evidence rule A substantive rule of contracts under which a court will not receive into evidence the parties' prior negotiations, prior agreements, or contemporaneous oral agreements if that evidence contradicts or varies the terms of the parties' written contract.

Partially disclosed principal A principal whose identity is unknown by a third person, but the third person knows that the agent is or may be acting for a principal at the time the agent and the third person form a contract.

Participation loan A loan that gives the lender some equity rights in the property, such as the right to receive a percentage of revenue, rental income, or resale income. Also called an equity participation loan.

Partner A co-owner of a partnership.

Partnering agreement An agreement between a seller and a buyer who frequently do business with each other on the terms and conditions that will apply to all subsequently formed electronic contracts.

Partnership An agreement by two or more persons to carry on, as co-owners, a business for profit.

Partnership by estoppel A judicially created partnership that may, at the court's discretion, be imposed for purposes of fairness. The court can prevent those who present themselves as partners (but who are not) from escaping liability if a third person relies on an alleged partnership in good faith and is harmed as a result.

Par-value shares Corporate shares that have a specific face value, or formal cash-in value, written on them, such as one dollar.

Pass-through entity Any entity that does not have its income taxed at the level of that entity; examples are partnerships, S corporations, and limited liability companies.

Past consideration Something given or some act done in the past, which cannot ordinarily be consideration for a later bargain.

Patent A government grant that gives an inventor the exclusive right or privilege to make, use, or sell his or her invention for a limited time period. The word *patent* usually refers to some invention and designates either the instrument by which patent rights are evidenced or the patent itself.

Payee A person to whom an instrument is made payable.

Payor bank The bank on which a check is drawn (the drawee bank).

Peer-to-peer (P2P) networking The sharing of resources (such as files, hard drives, and processing styles) among multiple computers without necessarily requiring a central network server.

Penalty A sum inserted into a contract, not as a measure of compensation for its breach but rather as punishment for a default. The agreement as to the amount will not be enforced, and recovery will be limited to actual damages.

Per capita A Latin term meaning "per person." In the law governing estate distribution, a method of distributing the property of an intestate's estate in which each heir in a certain class (such as grandchildren) receives an equal share.

Per curiam By the whole court; a court opinion written by the court as a whole instead of being authored by a judge or justice.

Per se A Latin term meaning "in itself" or "by itself."

Per se violation A type of anticompetitive agreement—such as a horizontal price-fixing agreement—that is considered to be so injurious to the public that there is no need to determine whether it actually injures market competition; rather, it is in itself (*per se*) a violation of the Sherman Act.

Per stirpes A Latin term meaning "by the roots." In the law governing estate distribution, a method of distributing an intestate's estate in which each heir in a certain class (such as grandchildren) takes the share to which his or her deceased ancestor (such as a mother or father) would have been entitled.

Perfect tender rule A common law rule under which a seller was required to deliver to the buyer goods that conformed perfectly to the requirements stipulated in the sales contract. A tender of nonconforming goods would automatically constitute a breach of contract. Under the Uniform Commercial Code, the rule has been greatly modified.

Perfection The legal process by which secured parties protect themselves against the claims of third parties who may wish to have their debts satisfied out of the same collateral; usually accomplished by the filing of a financing statement with the appropriate government official.

Performance In contract law, the fulfillment of one's duties arising under a contract with another; the normal way of discharging one's contractual obligations.

Periodic tenancy A lease interest in land for an indefinite period involving payment of rent at fixed intervals, such as week to week, month to month, or year to year.

Personal defense A defense that can be used to avoid payment to an ordinary holder of a negotiable instrument but not a holder in due course (HDC) or a holder with the rights of an HDC.

Personal identification number (PIN) A number given to the holder of an access card (debit card, credit card, ATM card, or the like) that is used to conduct financial transactions electronically. Typically, the card will not provide access to a system without the number, which is meant to be kept secret to inhibit unauthorized use of the card.

Personal jurisdiction *See In personam* jurisdiction

Personal property Property that is movable; any property that is not real property.

Personalty Personal property.

Persuasive authority Any legal authority or source of law that a court may look to for guidance but need not follow when making its decision.

Petition in bankruptcy The document that is filed with a bankruptcy court to initiate bankruptcy proceedings. The official forms required for a petition in bankruptcy must be completed accurately, sworn to under oath, and signed by the debtor.

Petitioner In equity practice, a party that initiates a lawsuit.

Petty offense In criminal law, the least serious kind of criminal offense, such as a traffic or building-code violation.

Phishing Online fraud in which criminals pretend to be legitimate companies by using e-mails or malicious Web sites that trick individuals and companies into providing useful information, such as bank account numbers, Social Security numbers, and credit card numbers.

Pierce the corporate veil To disregard the corporate entity, which limits the liability of shareholders, and hold the shareholders personally liable for a corporate obligation.

Plaintiff One who initiates a lawsuit.

Plea In criminal law, a defendant's allegation, in response to the charges brought against him or her, of guilt or innocence.

Plea bargaining The process by which a criminal defendant and the prosecutor in a criminal case work out a mutually satisfactory disposition of the case, subject to court approval; usually involves the defendant's pleading guilty to a lesser offense in return for a lighter sentence.

Pleadings Statements made by the plaintiff and the defendant in a lawsuit that detail the facts, charges, and defenses involved in the litigation; the complaint and answer are part of the pleadings.

Pledge A common law security device (retained in Article 9 of the Uniform Commercial Code) in which personal property is turned over to a creditor as security for the payment of a debt and retained by the creditor until the debt is paid.

Plurality opinion A court opinion that is joined by the largest number of the judges or justices hearing the case, but less than half of the total number.

Police powers Powers possessed by states as part of their inherent sovereignty. These powers may be exercised to protect or promote the public order, health, safety, morals, and general welfare.

Policy In insurance law, a contract between the insurer and the insured in which, for a stipulated consideration, the insurer agrees to compensate the insured for loss on a specific subject by a specified peril.

Positive law The body of conventional, or written, law of a particular society at a particular point in time.

Positivist school A school of legal thought whose adherents believe that there can be no higher law than a nation's positive law—the body of conventional, or written, law of a particular society at a particular time.

Possessory lien A lien that allows one person to retain possession of another's property as security for a debt or obligation owed by the owner of the property to the lienholder. An example of a possessory lien is an artisan's lien.

Potentially responsible party (PRP) A potentially liable party under the Comprehensive Environmental Response, Compensation and Liability Act (CERCLA). Any person who generated the hazardous waste, transported the waste, owned or operated the site at the time of disposal, or currently owns or operates the site may be responsible for some or all of the cleanup costs involved.

Power of attorney A written document, which is usually notarized, authorizing another to act as one's agent; can be special (permitting the agent to do specified acts only) or general (permitting the agent to transact all business for the principal).

Power of sale foreclosure A foreclosure procedure that is not court supervised; available only in some states.

Preauthorized transfer A transfer of funds authorized in advance to recur at substantially regular intervals. The terms and procedures for preauthorized electronic fund transfers through certain financial institutions are subject to the Electronic Fund Transfer Act.

Precedent A court decision that furnishes an example or authority for deciding subsequent cases involving identical or similar facts.

Predatory pricing The pricing of a product below cost with the intent to drive competitors out of the market.

Predominant-factor test A test courts use to determine whether a contract is primarily for the sale of goods or for the sale of services.

Preemption A doctrine under which certain federal laws preempt, or take precedence over, conflicting state or local laws.

Preemptive rights Rights held by shareholders that entitle them to purchase newly issued shares of a corporation's stock, equal in percentage to shares presently held, before the stock is offered to any outside buyers. Preemptive rights enable shareholders to maintain their proportionate ownership and voice in the corporation.

Preference In bankruptcy proceedings, property transfers or payments made by the debtor that favor (give preference to) one creditor over others. The bankruptcy trustee is allowed to recover payments made both voluntarily and involuntarily to one creditor in preference over another.

Preferred creditor One who has received a preferential transfer from a debtor.

Preferred stock Classes of stock that have priority over common stock as to payment of dividends and distribution of assets on the corporation's dissolution.

Prejudgment interest Interest that accrues on the amount of a court judgment from the time of the filing of a lawsuit to the court's issuance of a judgment.

Preliminary hearing An initial hearing used in many felony cases to establish whether it is proper to detain the defendant. A magistrate reviews the evidence and decides if there is probable cause to believe that the defendant committed the crime with which he or she has been charged.

Premium In insurance law, the price paid by the insured for insurance protection for a specified period of time.

Prenuptial agreement An agreement made before marriage that defines each partner's ownership rights in the other partner's property. Prenuptial agreements must be in writing to be enforceable.

Prepayment penalty A provision in a mortgage loan contract that requires the borrower to pay a penalty if the mortgage is repaid in full within a certain period.

Preponderance of the evidence A standard in civil law cases under which the plaintiff must convince the court that, based on the evidence presented by both parties, it is more likely than not that the plaintiff's allegation is true.

Prescription A way of creating an easement or profit in real property by openly using the property, without the true owner's consent, for the required period of time (similar to adverse possession).

Presentment The act of presenting an instrument to the party liable on the instrument to collect payment; presentment also occurs when a person presents an instrument to a drawee for acceptance.

Presentment warranties Implied warranties made by any person who presents an instrument for payment or acceptance that (1) he or she is entitled to enforce the instrument or authorized to obtain payment or acceptance on behalf of a person who is entitled, (2) the instrument has not been altered, and (3) he or she has no knowledge that the signature of the drawer is unauthorized.

Pretrial conference A conference, scheduled before the trial begins, between the judge and the attorneys litigating the suit. The parties may settle the dispute, clarify the issues, schedule discovery, and so on during the conference.

Pretrial motion A written or oral application to a court for a ruling or order, made before trial.

Price discrimination Setting prices in such a way that two competing buyers pay two different prices for an identical product or service.

Price-fixing agreement An agreement between competitors in which the competitors agree to fix the prices of products or services at a certain level; prohibited by the Sherman Act.

***Prima facie* case** A case in which the plaintiff has produced sufficient evidence of his or her conclusion that the case can go to a jury; a case in which the evidence compels the plaintiff's conclusion if the defendant produces no evidence to disprove it.

Primary liability In negotiable instruments law, absolute responsibility for paying a negotiable instrument. Makers and acceptors are primarily liable.

Prime offer rate An interest rate that banks historically charged their most reliable customers. Today, it serves as a basis for pricing other commercial and residential loans.

Principal In agency law, a person who agrees to have another, called the agent, act on his or her behalf.

Principle of rights The principle that human beings have certain fundamental rights (to life, freedom, and the pursuit of happiness, for example). Those who adhere to this "rights theory" believe that a key factor in determining whether a business decision is ethical is how that decision affects the rights of others. These others include the firm's owners, its employees, the consumers of its products or services, its suppliers, the community in which it does business, and society as a whole.

Private equity capital Equity capital that is not quoted on a public exchange. Funds invested in a private company in exchange for an ownership interest in that company. Capital for private equity is raised from retail and institutional investors, and can be used to fund new technologies, expand working capital within an owned company, make acquisitions, or to strengthen a balance sheet.

Privilege In tort law, the ability to act contrary to another person's right without that person's having legal redress for such acts. Privilege may be raised as a defense to defamation.

Privileges and immunities clause Article IV, Section 2, of the Constitution requires states not to discriminate against one another's citizens. A resident of one state cannot be treated as an alien when in another state; he or she may not be denied such privileges and immunities as legal protection, access to courts, travel rights, and property rights.

Privity of contract The relationship that exists between the promisor and the promisee of a contract.

Pro rata Proportionately; in proportion.

Probable cause Reasonable grounds to believe the existence of facts warranting certain actions, such as the search or arrest of a person.

Probate The process of proving and validating a will and the settling of all matters pertaining to administration, guardianship, and the like.

Probate court A state court of limited jurisdiction that conducts proceedings relating to the settlement of a deceased person's estate.

Procedural due process The requirement that any government decision to take life, liberty, or property must be made fairly. For example, fair procedures must be used in determining whether a person will be subjected to punishment or have some burden imposed on him or her.

Procedural law Rules that define the manner in which the rights and duties of individuals may be enforced.

Procedural unconscionability Occurs when one contractual party lacks knowledge or understanding of the contract terms, often due to inconspicuous print or the lack of an opportunity to read the contract or to ask questions about its meaning. Procedural unconscionability often involves an *adhesion contract,* which is a contract drafted by the dominant party and then presented to the other—the adhering party—on a take-it-or-leave-it basis.

Proceeds Under Article 9 of the Uniform Commercial Code, whatever is received when the collateral is sold or otherwise disposed of, such as by exchange.

Product liability The legal liability of manufacturers, sellers, and lessors of goods to consumers, users, and bystanders for injuries or damages that are caused by the goods.

Product misuse A defense against product liability that may be raised when the plaintiff used a product in a manner not intended by the manufacturer. If the misuse is reasonably foreseeable, the seller will not escape liability unless measures were taken to guard against the harm that could result from the misuse.

Professional corporation A corporation formed by professional persons, such as physicians, lawyers, dentists, or accountants, to gain tax benefits. Subject to certain exceptions (when a court may treat a professional corporation as a partnership for liability purposes), the shareholders of a professional corporation have the limited liability characteristic of the corporate form of business.

Profit In real property law, the right to enter onto and remove things from the property of another (for example, the right to enter onto a person's land and remove sand and gravel therefrom).

Promise A person's assurance that he or she will or will not do something.

Promisee A person to whom a promise is made.

Promisor A person who makes a promise.

Promissory estoppel A doctrine that applies when a promisor makes a clear and definite promise on which the promisee justifiably relies; such a promise is binding if justice will be better served by the enforcement of the promise. *See also* Estoppel

Promissory note A written promise made by one person (the maker) to pay a fixed sum of money to another person (the payee or a subsequent holder) on demand or on a specified date.

Promoter A person who takes the preliminary steps in organizing a corporation, including (usually) issuing a prospectus, procuring stock subscriptions, making contract purchases, securing a corporate charter, and the like.

Property Legally protected rights and interests in anything with an ascertainable value that is subject to ownership.

Prospectus A document required by federal or state securities laws that describes the financial operations of a corporation, thus allowing investors to make informed decisions.

Protected class A class of persons with identifiable characteristics who historically have been victimized by discriminatory treatment for certain purposes. Depending on the context, these characteristics include age, color, gender, national origin, race, and religion.

Proximate cause Legal cause; exists when the connection between an act and an injury is strong enough to justify imposing liability.

Proxy In corporation law, a written agreement between a stockholder and another under which the stockholder authorizes the other to vote the stockholder's shares in a certain manner.

Proxy fight A conflict between an individual, group, or firm attempting to take control of a corporation and the corporation's management for the votes of the shareholders.

Public corporation A corporation owned by a federal, state, or municipal government—not to be confused with a publicly held corporation.

Public figures Individuals who are thrust into the public limelight. Public figures include government officials and politicians, movie stars, well-known businesspersons, and generally anybody who becomes known to the public because of his or her position or activities.

Public policy A government policy based on widely held societal values and (usually) expressed or implied in laws or regulations.

Public prosecutor An individual, acting as a trial lawyer, who initiates and conducts criminal cases in the government's name and on behalf of the people.

Publicly held corporation A corporation for which shares of stock have been sold to the public.

Puffery A salesperson's exaggerated claims concerning the quality of goods offered for sale. Such claims involve opinions rather than facts and are not considered to be legally binding promises or warranties.

Punitive damages Money damages that may be awarded to a plaintiff to punish the defendant and deter future similar conduct.

Purchase-money security interest (PMSI) A security interest that arises when a seller or lender extends credit for part or all of the purchase price of goods purchased by a buyer.

Q

Qualified indorsement An indorsement on a negotiable instrument in which the indorser disclaims any contract liability on the instrument; the notation "without recourse" is commonly used to create a qualified indorsement.

Quantum meruit (pronounced *kwahn*-tuhm *mehr*-oo-wuht) Literally, "as much as he deserves"—an expression describing the extent of liability on a contract implied in law (quasi contract). An equitable doctrine based on the concept that one who benefits from another's labor and materials should not be unjustly enriched thereby but should be required to pay a reasonable amount for the benefits received, even absent a contract.

Quasi contract A fictional contract imposed on parties by a court in the interests of fairness and justice; usually, quasi contracts are imposed to avoid the unjust enrichment of one party at the expense of another.

Question of fact In a lawsuit, an issue involving a factual dispute that can only be decided by a judge (or, in a jury trial, a jury).

Question of law In a lawsuit, an issue involving the application or interpretation of a law; therefore, the judge, and not the jury, decides the issue.

Quiet enjoyment *See* Covenant of quiet enjoyment

Quitclaim deed A deed intended to pass any title, interest, or claim that the grantor may have in the property but not warranting that such title is valid. A quitclaim deed offers the least amount of protection against defects in the title.

Quorum The number of members of a decision-making body that must be present before business may be transacted.

Quota An assigned import limit on goods.

R

Ratification The act of accepting and giving legal force to an obligation that previously was not enforceable.

Reaffirmation agreement An agreement between a debtor and a creditor in which the debtor reaffirms, or promises to pay, a debt dischargeable in bankruptcy. To be enforceable, the agreement must be made prior to the discharge of the debt by the bankruptcy court.

Real property Land and everything attached to it, such as foliage and buildings.

Reamortize Restart the amortization schedule (a table of the periodic payments the borrower makes to pay off a debt), changing the way the payments are configured.

Reasonable care The degree of care that a person of ordinary prudence would exercise in the same or similar circumstances.

Reasonable doubt *See* Beyond a reasonable doubt

Reasonable person standard The standard of behavior expected of a hypothetical "reasonable person." The standard against which negligence is measured and that must be observed to avoid liability for negligence.

Rebuttal The refutation of evidence introduced by an adverse party's attorney.

Receiver In a corporate dissolution, a court-appointed person who winds up corporate affairs and liquidates corporate assets.

Record According to the Uniform Electronic Transactions Act, information that is either inscribed on a tangible medium or stored in an electronic or other medium and that is retrievable. The Uniform Computer Information Transactions Act uses the term *record* instead of *writing*.

Recording statutes Statutes that allow deeds, mortgages, and other real property transactions to be recorded so as to provide notice to future purchasers or creditors of an existing claim on the property.

Red herring prospectus A preliminary prospectus that can be distributed to potential investors after the registration statement (for a securities offering) has been filed with the Securities and Exchange Commission. The name derives from the red legend printed across the prospectus stating that the registration has been filed but has not become effective.

Redemption A repurchase, or buying back. In secured transactions law, a debtor's repurchase of collateral securing a debt after a creditor has taken title to the collateral due to the debtor's default but before the secured party disposes of the collateral.

Reformation A court-ordered correction of a written contract so that it reflects the true intentions of the parties.

Regulation E A set of rules issued by the Federal Reserve System's Board of Governors under the authority of the Electronic Fund Transfer Act to protect users of electronic fund transfer systems.

Regulation Z A set of rules promulgated by the Federal Reserve Board to implement the provisions of the Truth-in-Lending Act.

Rejection In contract law, an offeree's express or implied manifestation not to accept an offer. In the law governing contracts for the sale of goods, a buyer's manifest refusal to accept goods on the ground that they do not conform to contract specifications.

Rejoinder The defendant's answer to the plaintiff's rebuttal.

Release A contract in which one party forfeits the right to pursue a legal claim against the other party.

Relevant evidence Evidence tending to make a fact at issue in the case more or less probable than it would be without the evidence. Only relevant evidence is admissible in court.

Remainder A future interest in property held by a person other than the original owner.

Remanded Sent back. If an appellate court disagrees with a lower court's judgment, the case may be remanded to the lower court for further proceedings in which the lower court's decision should be consistent with the appellate court's opinion on the matter.

Remedy The relief given to an innocent party to enforce a right or compensate for the violation of a right.

Remedy at law A remedy available in a court of law. Money damages are awarded as a remedy at law.

Remedy in equity A remedy allowed by courts in situations where remedies at law are not appropriate. Remedies in equity are based on settled rules of fairness, justice, and honesty, and include injunction, specific performance, rescission and restitution, and reformation.

Remitter A person who sends money, or remits payment.

Rent The consideration paid for the use or enjoyment of another's property. In landlord-tenant relationships, the payment made by the tenant to the landlord for the right to possess the premises.

Rent escalation clause A clause providing for an increase in rent during a lease term.

Repair-and-deduct statutes Statutes providing that a tenant may pay for repairs and deduct the cost of the repairs from the rent, as a remedy for a landlord's failure to maintain leased premises.

Replevin (pronounced rih-*pleh*-vin) An action to recover specific goods in the hands of a party who is wrongfully withholding them from the other party.

Reply Procedurally, a plaintiff's response to a defendant's answer.

Reporter A publication in which court cases are published, or reported.

Repudiation The renunciation of a right or duty; the act of a buyer or seller in rejecting a contract either partially or totally. *See also* Anticipatory repudiation

Requirements contract An agreement in which a buyer agrees to purchase and the seller agrees to sell all or up to a stated amount of what the buyer needs or requires.

Res ipsa loquitur (pronounced *rehs ehp*-suh *low*-quuh-tuhr) A doctrine under which negligence may be inferred simply because an event occurred, if it is the type of event that would not occur in the absence of negligence. Literally, the term means "the facts speak for themselves."

Resale price maintenance agreement An agreement between a manufacturer and a retailer in which the manufacturer specifies the minimum retail price of its products. Resale price maintenance agreements are illegal *per se* under the Sherman Act.

Rescind (pronounced rih-*sihnd*) To cancel. *See also* Rescission

Rescission (pronounced rih-*sih*-zhen) A remedy whereby a contract is canceled and the parties are returned to the positions they occupied before the contract was made; may be effected through the mutual consent of the parties, by their conduct, or by court decree.

Residential use Use of land for construction of buildings for human habitation only.

Residuary The surplus of a testator's estate remaining after all of the debts and particular legacies have been discharged.

Respondeat superior (pronounced ree-*spahn*-dee-uht soo-*peer*-ee-your) In Latin, "Let the master respond." A doctrine under which a principal or an employer is held liable for the wrongful acts committed by agents or employees while acting within the course and scope of their agency or employment.

Respondent In equity practice, the party who answers a bill or other proceeding.

Restitution An equitable remedy under which a person is restored to his or her original position prior to loss or injury, or placed in the position he or she would have been in had the breach not occurred.

Restraint of trade Any contract or combination that tends to eliminate or reduce competition, effect a monopoly, artificially maintain prices, or otherwise hamper the course of trade and commerce as it would be carried on if left to the control of natural economic forces.

Restrictive covenant A private restriction on the use of land. If its benefit or obligation passes with the land's ownership, it is said to "run with the land."

Restrictive indorsement Any indorsement on a negotiable instrument that requires the indorsee to comply with certain instructions regarding the funds involved. A restrictive indorsement does not prohibit the further negotiation of the instrument.

Resulting trust An implied trust arising from the conduct of the parties. A trust in which a party holds the actual legal title to another's property but only for that person's benefit.

Retained earnings The portion of a corporation's profits that has not been paid out as dividends to shareholders.

Retainer An advance payment made by a client to a law firm to cover part of the legal fees and/or costs that will be incurred on that client's behalf.

Retaliatory eviction The eviction of a tenant because of the tenant's complaints, participation in a tenant's union, or similar activity with which the landlord does not agree.

Reverse To reject or overrule a court's judgment. An appellate court, for example, might reverse a lower court's judgment on an issue if it feels that the lower court committed an error during the trial or that the jury was improperly instructed.

Reverse discrimination Discrimination against majority groups, such as white males, that results from affirmative action programs, in which preferences are given to minority members and women.

Reverse mortgage A loan product typically provided to older homeowners that allows them to extract cash (in either a lump sum or multiple payments) for the equity in their home. The mortgage does not need to be repaid until the home is sold or the owner leaves or dies.

Reversible error An error by a lower court that is sufficiently substantial to justify an appellate court's reversal of the lower court's decision.

Revocation In contract law, the withdrawal of an offer by an offeror. Unless an offer is irrevocable, it can be revoked at any time prior to acceptance without liability.

Right of contribution The right of a co-surety who pays more than his or her proportionate share on a debtor's default to recover the excess paid from other co-sureties.

Right of entry The right to peaceably take or resume possession of real property.

Right of first refusal The right to purchase personal or real property—such as corporate shares or real estate—before the property is offered for sale to others.

Right of redemption The right of a defaulting borrower to redeem property before a foreclosure sale by paying the full amount of the debt, plus any interest and costs that have accrued.

Right of reimbursement The legal right of a person to be restored, repaid, or indemnified for costs, expenses, or losses incurred or expended on behalf of another.

Right of subrogation The right of a person to stand in the place of (be substituted for) another, giving the substituted party the same legal rights that the original party had.

Right-to-work law A state law providing that employees are not to be required to join a union as a condition of obtaining or retaining employment.

Risk A prediction concerning potential loss based on known and unknown factors.

Risk management Planning that is undertaken to protect one's interest should some event threaten to undermine its security. In the context of insurance, risk management involves transferring certain risks from the insured to the insurance company.

Robbery The act of forcefully and unlawfully taking personal property of any value from another; force or intimidation is usually necessary for an act of theft to be considered a robbery.

Rule of four A rule of the United States Supreme Court under which the Court will not issue a writ of *certiorari* unless at least four justices approve of the decision to issue the writ.

Rule of reason A test by which a court balances the positive effects (such as economic efficiency) of an agreement against its potentially anticompetitive effects. In antitrust litigation, many practices are analyzed under the rule of reason.

Rule 10b-5 *See* SEC Rule 10b-5

Rulemaking The process undertaken by an administrative agency when formally adopting a new regulation or amending an old one. Rulemaking involves notifying the public of a proposed rule or change and receiving and considering the public's comments.

Rules of evidence Rules governing the admissibility of evidence in trial courts.

S

S corporation A close business corporation that has met certain requirements as set out by the Internal Revenue Code and thus qualifies for special income tax treatment. Essentially, an S corporation is taxed the same as a partnership, but its owners enjoy the privilege of limited liability.

Sale The passing of title (evidence of ownership rights) from the seller to the buyer for a price.

Sale on approval A type of conditional sale in which the buyer may take the goods on a trial basis. The sale becomes absolute only when the buyer approves of (or is satisfied with) the goods being sold.

Sale or return A type of conditional sale in which title and possession pass from the seller to the buyer; however, the buyer retains the option to return the goods during a specified period even though the goods conform to the contract.

Sales contract A contract for the sale of goods under which the ownership of goods is transferred from a seller to a buyer for a price.

Satisfaction *See* Accord and satisfaction

Scienter (pronounced *sy-en-*ter) Knowledge by the misrepresenting party that material facts have been falsely represented or omitted with an intent to deceive.

Search warrant An order granted by a public authority, such as a judge, that authorizes law enforcement personnel to search particular premises or property.

Seasonably Within a specified time period. If no period is specified, within a reasonable time.

SEC Rule 10b-5 A rule of the Securities and Exchange Commission that makes it unlawful, in connection with the purchase or sale of any security, to make any untrue statement of a material fact or to omit a material fact if such omission causes the statement to be misleading.

Secondary boycott A union's refusal to work for, purchase from, or handle the products of a secondary employer, with whom the union has no dispute, for the purpose of forcing that employer to stop doing business with the primary employer, with whom the union has a labor dispute.

Secondary liability In negotiable instruments law, the contingent liability of drawers and indorsers. A secondarily liable party becomes liable on an instrument only if the party that is primarily liable on the instrument dishonors it or, in regard to drafts and checks, the drawee fails to pay or to accept the instrument, whichever is required.

Secured party A lender, seller, or any other person in whose favor there is a security interest, including a person to whom accounts or chattel paper has been sold.

Secured transaction Any transaction in which the payment of a debt is guaranteed, or secured, by personal property owned by the debtor or in which the debtor has a legal interest.

Securities Generally, corporate stocks and bonds. A security may also be a note, debenture, stock warrant, or any document given as evidence of an ownership interest in a corporation or as a promise of repayment by a corporation.

Security agreement An agreement that creates or provides for a security interest between the debtor and a secured party.

Security interest Any interest "in personal property or fixtures which secures payment or performance of an obligation" [UCC 1–201(37)].

Self-defense The legally recognized privilege to protect one's self or property against injury by another. The privilege of self-defense protects only acts that are reasonably necessary to protect one's self or property.

Seniority system In regard to employment relationships, a system in which those who have worked longest for the company are first in line for promotions, salary increases, and other benefits; they are also the last to be laid off if the workforce must be reduced.

Service mark A mark used in the sale or the advertising of services, such as to distinguish the services of one person from the services of others. Titles, character names, and other distinctive features of radio and television programs may be registered as service marks.

Service of process The delivery of the complaint and summons to a defendant.

Settlor One creating a trust; also called a *grantor.*

Severance pay A payment by an employer to an employee that exceeds the employee's wages due on termination.

Sexual harassment In the employment context, the granting of job promotions or other benefits in return for sexual favors or conduct that is so sexually offensive that it creates a hostile working environment.

Share A unit of stock. *See also* Stock

Share exchange In a share exchange, some or all of the shares of one corporation are exchanged for some or all of the shares of another corporation, but both corporations continue to exist. Share exchanges are often used to create *holding companies* (companies that own part or all of other companies' stock).

Shareholder One who purchases shares of a corporation's stock, thus acquiring an equity interest in the corporation.

Shareholder's derivative suit A suit brought by a shareholder to enforce a corporate cause of action against a third person.

Sharia Civil law principles of some Middle Eastern countries that are based on the Islamic directives that follow the teachings of the prophet Muhammad.

Shelter principle The principle that the holder of a negotiable instrument who cannot qualify as a holder in due course (HDC), but who derives his or her title through an HDC, acquires the rights of an HDC.

Sheriff's deed The deed given to the purchaser of property at a sheriff's sale as part of the foreclosure process against the owner of the property.

Shipment contract A contract in which the seller is required to ship the goods by carrier. The buyer assumes liability for any losses or damage to the goods after they are delivered to the carrier. Generally, all contracts are assumed to be shipment contracts if nothing to the contrary is stated in the contract.

Short-form merger A merger between a subsidiary corporation and a parent corporation that owns at least 90 percent of the outstanding shares of each class of stock issued by the subsidiary corporation. Short-form mergers can be accomplished without the approval of the shareholders of either corporation.

Short sale A sale of real property for an amount that is less than the balance owed on the mortgage loan, usually due to financial hardship. Both the lender and the borrower must consent to a short sale. Following a short sale, the borrower still owes the balance of the mortgage debt (after the sale proceeds are applied) to the lender unless the lender agrees to forgive the remaining debt.

Short-swing profits Profits made by officers, directors, and certain large stockholders resulting from the use of nonpublic (inside) information about their companies; prohibited by Section 12 of the 1934 Securities Exchange Act.

Shrink-wrap agreement An agreement whose terms are expressed in a document located inside a box in which goods (usually software) are packaged; sometimes called a *shrink-wrap license.*

Sight draft In negotiable instruments law, a draft payable on sight—that is, when it is presented for payment.

Signature Under the Uniform Commercial Code, "any symbol executed or adopted by a party with a present intention to authenticate a writing."

Slander Defamation in oral form.

Slander of quality The publication of false information about another's product, alleging that it is not what its seller claims.

Slander of title The publication of a statement that denies or casts doubt on another's legal ownership of any property, causing financial loss to that property's owner. Also called trade libel.

Small claims courts Special courts in which parties may litigate small claims (usually, claims involving $2,500 or less). Attorneys are not required in small claims courts, and in many states attorneys are not allowed to represent the parties.

Smart card Prepaid funds recorded on a microprocessor chip embedded on a card. One type of *e-money.*

Social media The means by which people can create, share, and exchange ideas and comments via the Internet.

Sociological school A school of legal thought that views the law as a tool for promoting justice in society.

Sole proprietorship The simplest form of business, in which the owner is the business; the owner reports business income on his or her personal income tax return and is legally responsible for all debts and obligations incurred by the business.

Sovereign immunity A doctrine that immunizes foreign nations from the jurisdiction of U.S. courts when certain conditions are satisfied.

Sovereignty The quality of having independent authority over a geographic area. For instance, state governments have the authority to regulate affairs within their border.

Spam Bulk, unsolicited (junk) e-mail.

Special indorsement An indorsement on an instrument that indicates the specific person to whom the indorser intends to make the instrument payable; that is, it names the indorsee.

Special-use permit A permit that allows for a specific exemption to zoning regulations for a particular piece of land in a location that has a particular zoning characteristic. Local zoning authorities grant special-use permits.

Special warranty deed A deed that warrants that the grantor or seller held good title during his or her ownership of the property. This deed (sometimes called a limited warranty deed) does not warrant against defects of title when the property was held by previous owners.

Specific performance An equitable remedy requiring the breaching party to perform as promised under the contract; usually granted only when money damages would be an inadequate remedy and the subject matter of the contract is unique (for example, real property).

Spendthrift trust A trust created to prevent the beneficiary from spending all the money to which he or she is entitled. Only a certain portion of the total amount is given to the beneficiary at any one time, and most states prohibit creditors from attaching assets of the trust.

Spot zoning A zoning classification granted to a parcel of land that is different from the classification given to other land in the immediate area.

Stakeholders Groups, other than the company's shareholders, that are affected by corporate decisions. Stakeholders include employees, customers, creditors, suppliers, and the community in which the corporation operates.

Stale check A check, other than a certified check, that is presented for payment more than six months after its date.

Standing to sue The requirement that an individual must have a sufficient stake in a controversy before he or she can bring a lawsuit. The plaintiff must demonstrate that he or she either has been injured or threatened with injury.

Stare decisis (pronounced *ster*-ay dih-*si*-ses) A common law doctrine under which judges are obligated to follow the precedents established in prior decisions.

Statute of Frauds A state statute under which certain types of contracts must be in writing to be enforceable.

Statute of limitations A federal or state statute setting the maximum time period during which a certain action can be brought or certain rights enforced.

Statute of repose Basically, a statute of limitations that is not dependent on the happening of a cause of action. Statutes of repose generally begin to run at an earlier date and run for a longer period of time than statutes of limitations.

Statutory law The body of law enacted by legislative bodies (as opposed to constitutional law, administrative law, or case law).

Statutory lien A lien created by statute.

Statutory period of redemption A time period (usually set by state statute) during which the property subject to a defaulted mortgage, land contract, or other contract can be redeemed by the debtor after foreclosure or judicial sale.

Statutory right of redemption A right provided by statute in some states under which mortgagors can redeem or purchase their property back after a judicial foreclosure for a limited period of time, such as one year.

Stock An equity (ownership) interest in a corporation, measured in units of shares.

Stock buyback Sometimes, publicly held companies use funds from their own treasuries to repurchase their own stock. The result is that the price of the stock usually goes up.

Stock certificate A certificate issued by a corporation evidencing the ownership of a specified number of shares in the corporation.

Stock option *See* Stock warrant

Stock warrant A certificate that grants the owner the option to buy a given number of shares of stock, usually within a set time period.

Stockholder *See* Shareholder

Stop-payment order An order by a bank customer to his or her bank not to pay or certify a certain check.

Strict liability Liability regardless of fault. In tort law, strict liability may be imposed on defendants in cases involving abnormally dangerous activities, dangerous animals, or defective products.

Strike An extreme action undertaken by unionized workers when collective bargaining fails; the workers leave their jobs, refuse to work, and (typically) picket the employer's workplace.

Subject-matter jurisdiction Jurisdiction over the subject matter of a lawsuit.

Sublease A lease executed by the lessee of real estate to a third person, conveying the same interest that the lessee enjoys but for a shorter term than that held by the lessee.

Subpoena A document commanding a person to appear at a certain time and place or give testimony concerning a certain matter.

Subprime mortgage A high-risk loan made to a borrower who does not qualify for a standard mortgage because of his or her poor credit rating or high debt-to-income ratio. Lenders typically charge a higher interest rate on subprime mortgages.

Subrogation *See* Right of subrogation

Subscriber An investor who agrees, in a subscription agreement, to purchase capital stock in a corporation.

Subsidiary corporation A corporation that wholly owned by another corporate entity (the parent corporation).

Substantial performance Performance that does not vary greatly from the performance promised in a contract; the performance must create substantially the same benefits as those promised in the contract.

Substantive due process A requirement that focuses on the content, or substance, of legislation. If a law or other governmental action limits a fundamental right, such as the right to travel or to vote, it will be held to violate substantive due process unless it promotes a compelling or overriding state interest.

Substantive law Law that defines the rights and duties of individuals with respect to each other, as opposed to procedural law, which defines the manner in which these rights and duties may be enforced.

Substantive unconscionability Occurs when contracts, or portions of contracts, are oppressive or overly harsh. Courts generally focus on provisions that deprive one party of the benefits of the agreement or leave that party without remedy for nonperformance by the other. An example of substantive unconscionability is the agreement by a welfare recipient with a fourth-grade education to purchase a refrigerator for $2,000 under an installment contract.

Substitute check A negotiable instrument that is a paper reproduction of the front and back of an original check and contains all of the same information required on checks for automated processing.

Suit *See* Lawsuit; Litigation

Summary judgment *See* Motion for summary judgment

Summary jury trial (SJT) A method of settling disputes in which a trial is held, but the jury's verdict is not binding. The verdict acts only as a guide to both sides in reaching an agreement during the mandatory negotiations that immediately follow the summary jury trial.

Summons A document informing a defendant that a legal action has been commenced against him or her and that the defendant must appear in court on a certain date to answer the plaintiff's complaint. The document is delivered by a sheriff or any other person so authorized.

Superseding cause An intervening force or event that breaks the connection between a wrongful act and an injury to another; in negligence law, a defense to liability.

Supremacy clause The provision in Article VI of the Constitution that provides that the Constitution, laws, and treaties of the United States are "the supreme Law of the Land." Under this clause, state and local laws that directly conflict with federal law will be rendered invalid.

Surety A person, such as a cosigner on a note, who agrees to be primarily responsible for the debt of another.

Suretyship An express contract in which a third party to a debtor-creditor relationship (the surety) promises to be primarily responsible for the debtor's obligation.

Surviving corporation The remaining, or continuing, corporation following a merger. The surviving corporation is vested with the merged corporation's legal rights and obligations.

Syllogism A form of deductive reasoning consisting of a major premise, a minor premise, and a conclusion.

Symbolic speech Nonverbal conduct that expresses opinions or thoughts about a subject. Symbolic speech is protected under the First Amendment's guarantee of freedom of speech.

Syndicate An investment group of persons or firms brought together for the purpose of financing a project that they would not or could not undertake independently.

T

Tag In the context of the World Wide Web, a code in an HTML document. *See* Meta tags.

Takeover The acquisition of control over a corporation through the purchase of a substantial number of the voting shares of the corporation.

Taking The taking of private property by the government for public use. Under the Fifth Amendment to the Constitution, the government may not take private property for public use without "just compensation."

Tangible employment action A significant change in employment status, such as firing or failing to promote an employee, reassigning the employee to a position with significantly different responsibilities, or effecting a significant change in employment benefits.

Tangible property Property that has physical existence and can be distinguished by the senses of touch, sight, and so on. A car is tangible property; a patent right is intangible property.

Target corporation The corporation to be acquired in a corporate takeover; a corporation to whose shareholders a tender offer is submitted.

Tariff A tax on imported goods.

Technology licensing Allowing another to use and profit from intellectual property (patents, copyrights, trademarks, innovative products or processes, and so on) for consideration. In the context of international business transactions, technology licensing is sometimes an attractive alternative to the establishment of foreign production facilities.

Tenancy at sufferance A type of tenancy under which one who, after rightfully being in possession of leased premises, continues (wrongfully) to occupy the property after the lease has been terminated. The tenant has no rights to possess the property and occupies it only because the person entitled to evict the tenant has not done so.

Tenancy at will A type of tenancy under which either party can terminate the tenancy without notice; usually arises when a tenant who has been under a tenancy for years retains possession, with the landlord's consent, after the tenancy for years has terminated.

Tenancy by the entirety The joint ownership of property by a husband and wife. Neither party can transfer his or her interest in the property without the consent of the other.

Tenancy in common Co-ownership of property in which each party owns an undivided interest that passes to his or her heirs at death.

Tenant One who has the temporary use and occupation of real property owned by another person, called the landlord; the duration and terms of the tenancy are usually established by a lease.

Tender An unconditional offer to perform an obligation by a person who is ready, willing, and able to do so.

Tender of delivery Under the Uniform Commercial Code, a seller's or lessor's act of placing conforming goods at the disposal of the buyer or lessee and giving the buyer or lessee whatever notification is reasonably necessary to enable the buyer or lessee to take delivery.

Tender offer An offer to purchase made by one company directly to the shareholders of another (target) company; often referred to as a "takeover bid."

Term insurance A type of life insurance policy for which premiums are paid for a specified term. Payment on the policy is due only if death occurs within the term period. Premiums are less expensive than for whole life or limited-payment life, and there is usually no cash surrender value.

Testamentary trust A trust that is created by will and therefore does not take effect until the death of the testator.

Testate The condition of having died with a valid will.

Testator One who makes and executes a will.

Third party beneficiary One for whose benefit a promise is made in a contract but who is not a party to the contract.

Time draft A draft that is payable at a definite future time.

Tippee A person who receives inside information.

Title insurance Insurance commonly purchased by a purchaser of real property to protect against loss in the event that the title to the property is not free from liens or superior ownership claims.

Tolling Temporary suspension of the running of a prescribed period (such as a statute of limitations). For instance, a statute of limitations may be tolled until the party suffering an injury has discovered it or should have discovered it.

Tombstone ad An advertisement, historically in a format resembling a tombstone, of a securities offering. The ad informs potential investors of where and how they may obtain a prospectus.

Tort A civil wrong not arising from a breach of contract. A breach of a legal duty that proximately causes harm or injury to another.

Tortfeasor One who commits a tort.

Totten trust A trust created by the deposit of a person's own money in his or her own name as a trustee for another. It is a tentative trust, revocable at will until the depositor dies or completes the gift in his or her lifetime by some unequivocal act or declaration.

Toxic tort A personal injury caused by exposure to a toxic substance, such as asbestos or hazardous waste. Victims can sue for medical expenses, lost wages, and pain and suffering.

Trade acceptance A draft that is drawn by a seller of goods ordering the buyer to pay a specified sum of money to the seller, usually at a stated time in the future. The buyer accepts the draft by signing the face of the draft, thus creating an enforceable obligation to pay the draft when it comes due. On a trade acceptance, the seller is both the drawer and the payee.

Trade dress The image and overall appearance of a product—for example, the distinctive decor, menu, layout, and style of service of a particular restaurant. Basically, trade dress is subject to the same protection as trademarks.

Trade fixture The personal property of a commercial tenant that has been installed or affixed to real property for a business purpose. When the lease ends, the tenant can remove the fixture but must repair any damage to the real property caused by the fixture's removal.

Trade libel The publication of false information about another's product, alleging it is not what its seller claims; also referred to as slander of quality.

Trade name A term that is used to indicate part or all of a business's name and that is directly related to the business's reputation and goodwill. Trade names are protected under the common law (and under trademark law, if the name is the same as the firm's trademark).

Trade secret Information or a process that gives a business an advantage over competitors who do not know the information or process.

Trademark A distinctive mark, motto, device, or implement that a manufacturer stamps, prints, or otherwise affixes to the goods it produces so that they may be identified on the market and their origins made known. Once a trademark is established (under the common law or through registration), the owner is entitled to its exclusive use.

Transfer warranties Implied warranties, made by any person who transfers an instrument for consideration to subsequent transferees and holders who take the instrument in good faith, that (1) the transferor is entitled to enforce the instrument, (2) all signatures are authentic and authorized, (3) the instrument has not been altered, (4) the instrument is not subject to a defense or claim of any party that can be asserted against the transferor, and (5) the transferor has no knowledge of any insolvency proceedings against the maker, the acceptor, or the drawer of the instrument.

Transferee In negotiable instruments law, one to whom a negotiable instrument is transferred (delivered).

Transferor In negotiable instruments law, one who transfers (delivers) a negotiable instrument to another.

Traveler's check A check that is payable on demand, drawn on or payable through a bank, and designated as a traveler's check.

Treasure trove Cash or coin, gold, silver, or bullion found hidden in the earth or other private place, the owner of which is unknown; literally, treasure found.

Treasury securities Government debt issued by the U.S. Department of the Treasury. The interest rate on Treasury securities is often used as a baseline for measuring the rate on loan products with higher interest rates.

Treasury shares Corporate shares that are authorized by the corporation but that have not been issued.

Treaty An agreement formed between two or more independent nations.

Treble damages Damages consisting of three times the amount of damages determined by a jury in certain cases as required by statute.

Trespass to land The entry onto, above, or below the surface of land owned by another without the owner's permission or legal authorization.

Trespass to personal property The unlawful taking or harming of another's personal property; interference with another's right to the exclusive possession of his or her personal property.

Trespasser One who commits the tort of trespass in one of its forms.

Trial court A court in which trials are held and testimony taken.

Triple bottom line The idea that investors and others should consider not only corporate profits, but also the corporation's impact on people and on the planet in assessing the firm. (The bottom line is people, planet, and profits.)

Trust An arrangement in which title to property is held by one person (a trustee) for the benefit of another (a beneficiary).

Trust indorsement An indorsement for the benefit of the indorser or a third person; also known as an agency indorsement. The indorsement results in legal title vesting in the original indorsee.

Tying arrangement An agreement between a buyer and a seller in which the buyer of a specific product or service becomes obligated to purchase additional products or services from the seller.

Typosquatting A form of cybersquatting that relies on mistakes, such as typographical errors, made by Internet users when inputting information into a Web browser.

U

U.S. trustee A government official who performs certain administrative tasks that a bankruptcy judge would otherwise have to perform.

Ultra vires (pronounced *uhl*-trah *vye*-reez) A Latin term meaning "beyond the powers"; in corporate law, acts of a corporation that are beyond its express and implied powers to undertake.

Unanimous opinion A court opinion in which all of the judges or justices of the court agree to the court's decision.

Unconscionable (pronounced un-*kon*-shun-uh-bul) **contract or clause** A contract or clause that is void on the basis of public policy because one party, as a result of his or her disproportionate bargaining power, is forced to accept terms that are unfairly burdensome and that unfairly benefit the dominating party. *See also* Procedural unconscionability; Substantive unconscionability

Underwriter In insurance law, the insurer, or the one assuming a risk in return for the payment of a premium.

Undisclosed principal A principal whose identity is unknown by a third person, and the third person has no knowledge that the agent is acting for a principal at the time the agent and the third person form a contract.

Unenforceable contract A valid contract rendered unenforceable by some statute or law.

Uniform law A model law created by the National Conference of Commissioners on Uniform State Laws and/or the American Law Institute for the states to consider adopting. If the state adopts the law, it becomes statutory law in that state. Each state has the option of adopting or rejecting all or part of a uniform law.

Unilateral contract A contract that results when an offer can only be accepted by the offeree's performance.

Union shop A place of employment in which all workers, once employed, must become union members within a specified period of time as a condition of their continued employment.

Universal defense A defense that is valid against all holders of a negotiable instrument, including holders in due course (HDCs) and holders with the rights of HDCs. Universal defenses are also called real defenses.

Universal life A type of insurance that combines some aspects of term insurance with some aspects of whole life insurance.

Unlawful detainer The unjustifiable retention of the possession of real property by one whose right to possession has terminated—as when a tenant holds over after the end of the lease term in spite of the landlord's demand for possession.

Unliquidated debt A debt that is uncertain in amount.

Unreasonably dangerous product In product liability, a product that is defective to the point of threatening a consumer's health and safety. A product will be considered unreasonably dangerous if it is dangerous beyond the expectation of the ordinary consumer or if a less dangerous alternative was economically feasible for the manufacturer, but the manufacturer failed to produce it.

Usage of trade Any practice or method of dealing having such regularity of observance in a place, vocation, or trade as to justify an expectation that it will be observed with respect to the transaction in question.

Usurpation In corporation law, the taking advantage of a corporate opportunity by a corporate officer or director for his or her personal gain and in violation of his or her fiduciary duties.

Usury Charging an illegal rate of interest.

Utilitarianism An approach to ethical reasoning in which ethically correct behavior is related to an evaluation of the consequences of a given action on those who will be affected by it. In utilitarian reasoning, a "good" decision is one that results in the greatest good for the greatest number of people affected by the decision.

V

Valid contract A contract that results when elements necessary for contract formation (agreement, consideration, legal purpose, and contractual capacity) are present.

Validation notice An initial notice to a debtor from a collection agency informing the debtor that he or she has thirty days to challenge the debt and request verification.

Variance A form of relief or exception from zoning and other laws that is granted to a property owner.

Vendee One who purchases property from another, called the vendor.

Vendor One who sells property to another, called the vendee.

Venture capital Capital (funds and other assets) provided by professional, outside investors (*venture capitalists,* usually groups of wealthy investors and investment banks) to start new business ventures.

Venture capitalist A person or entity that seeks out promising entrepreneurial ventures and funds them in exchange for equity stakes.

Venue (pronounced *ven*-yoo) The geographical district in which an action is tried and from which the jury is selected.

Verdict A formal decision made by a jury.

Vertical merger The acquisition by a company at one stage of production of a company at a higher or lower stage of production (such as its supplier or retailer).

Vertical restraint Any restraint on trade created by agreements between firms at different levels in the manufacturing and distribution process.

Vertically integrated firm A firm that carries out two or more functional phases—such as manufacture, distribution, retailing—of a product.

Vesting Under the Employee Retirement Income Security Act of 1974, a pension plan becomes vested when an employee has a legal right to the benefits purchased with the employer's contributions, even if the employee is no longer working for this employer.

Vicarious liability Legal responsibility placed on one person for the acts of another.

Virtual courtroom A courtroom that is conceptual and not physical. In the context of cyberspace, a virtual courtroom could be a location on the Internet at which judicial proceedings take place.

Virtual property Property that exists in cyberspace and thus is conceptual, as opposed to physical. Intellectual property that exists on the Internet is virtual property.

Virus A type of malware that is transmitted between computers and attempts to do deliberate damage to systems and data.

Vishing The voice counterpart of phishing; vishers use an e-mail or a notice on a Web site that encourage persons to make a phone call which then triggers a voice response system that asks for valuable personal information such as credit card numbers.

Void contract A contract having no legal force or binding effect.

Voidable contract A contract that may be legally avoided (canceled, or annulled) at the option of one of the parties.

Voidable preference In bankruptcy law, a preference that may be avoided, or set aside, by the trustee.

Voir dire (pronounced *vwahr deehr*) A French phrase meaning, literally, "to see, to speak." In jury trials, the phrase refers to the process in which the attorneys question prospective jurors to determine whether they are biased or have any connection with a party to the action or with a prospective witness.

Voting trust An agreement (trust contract) under which legal title to shares of corporate stock is transferred to a trustee who is authorized by the shareholders to vote the shares on their behalf.

W

Waiver An intentional, knowing relinquishment of a legal right.

Warehouse receipt A document of title issued by a bailee-warehouser to cover the goods stored in the warehouse.

Warehouser One in the business of operating a warehouse.

Warranty A promise that certain facts are truly as they are represented to be.

Warranty deed A deed in which the grantor guarantees to the grantee that the grantor has title to the property conveyed in the deed, that there are no encumbrances on the property other than what the grantor has represented, and that the grantee will enjoy quiet possession of the property; a deed that provides the greatest amount of protection for the grantee.

Warranty disclaimer A seller's or lessor's negation or qualification of a warranty.

Warranty of fitness *See* Implied warranty of fitness for a particular purpose.

Warranty of merchantability *See* Implied warranty of merchantability.

Warranty of title An implied warranty made by a seller that the seller has good and valid title to the goods sold and that the transfer of the title is rightful.

Waste The abuse or destructive use of real property by one who is in rightful possession of the property but who does not have title to it. Waste does not include ordinary depreciation due to age and normal use.

Watered stock Shares of stock issued by a corporation for which the corporation receives, as payment, less than the fair market value of the shares.

Wetlands Areas of land designated by government agencies (such as the Army Corps of Engineers or the Environmental Protection Agency) as protected areas that support wildlife and that therefore cannot be filled in or dredged by private contractors or parties.

Whistleblowing An employee's disclosure to government, the press, or upper-management authorities that the employer is engaged in unsafe or illegal activities.

White-collar crime Nonviolent crime committed by individuals or corporations to obtain a personal or business advantage.

Whole life A life insurance policy in which the insured pays a level premium for his or her entire life and in which there is a constantly accumulating cash value that can be withdrawn or borrowed against by the borrower. Sometimes referred to as straight life insurance.

Will An instrument directing what is to be done with the testator's property on his or her death, made by the testator and revocable during his or her lifetime. No interests in the testator's property pass until the testator dies.

Willful Intentional.

Winding up The second of two stages involved in the termination of a partnership or corporation. Once the firm is dissolved, it continues to exist legally until the process of winding up all business affairs (collecting and distributing the firm's assets) is complete.

Workers' compensation laws State statutes establishing an administrative procedure for compensating workers' injuries that arise out of—or in the course of—their employment, regardless of fault.

Working papers The various documents used and developed by an accountant during an audit. Working papers include notes, computations, memoranda, copies, and other papers that make up the work product of an accountant's services to a client.

Workout agreement A formal contract between a debtor and his or her creditors in which the parties agree to negotiate a payment plan for the amount due on the loan instead of proceeding to foreclosure.

Worm A type of malware that is designed to copy itself from one computer to another without human interaction. A worm can copy itself automatically and can replicate in great volume and with great speed. Worms, for example, can send out copies of themselves to every contact in your e-mail address book.

Writ of attachment A court's order, prior to a trial to collect a debt, directing the sheriff or other officer to seize nonexempt property of the debtor; if the creditor prevails at trial, the seized property can be sold to satisfy the judgment.

Writ of *certiorari* (pronounced sur-shee-uh-*rah*-ree) A writ from a higher court asking the lower court for the record of a case.

Writ of execution A court's order, after a judgment has been entered against the debtor, directing the sheriff to seize (levy) and sell any of the debtor's nonexempt real or personal property. The proceeds of the sale are used to pay off the judgment, accrued interest, and costs of the sale; any surplus is paid to the debtor.

Wrongful discharge An employer's termination of an employee's employment in violation of an employment contract or laws that protect employees.

Z

Zoning The division of a city by legislative regulation into districts and the application in each district of regulations having to do with structural and architectural designs of buildings and prescribing the use to which buildings within designated districts may be put.

Zoning laws The rules and regulations that collectively manage the development and use of land.

TABLE OF CASES

Following is a list of all the cases mentioned in this text, including those within the footnotes, features, and case problems. Any case that was an excerpted case for a chapter is given special emphasis by having its title **boldfaced**.

exclusionary rule and, 209
Slander, 122
    damages for, 122
    per se, 122–123
    of quality, 130
    of title, 130
Slavery, 356n
Sliding-scale standard, for Internet-based
    jurisdiction, 33–34, 35–36
Small business. *See also* Business(es);
    Partnership
    business organization selection for,
        740–756
    business trust as, 749–750
    cooperative as, 750
    crowdfunding of, 755
    cyber thieves and, 751
    financial capital for, 754–756
    forms of, 750
    general considerations for, 750–754
    joint stock company as, 749
    joint venture as, 748–749
    liability considerations and, 752
    loan for, 754
    special forms of, 748–750
    syndicate as, 749
    venture capital for, 754–755
Small Business Administration (SBA), 740
    loans from, 754
    Office of the National Enforcement
        Ombudsman at, 857
Small Business Liability Relief and
    Brownfields Revitalization Act
    (2002), 880
Small Business Regulatory Enforcement
    Fairness Act (SBREFA, 1996), 857
Small claims courts, state, 39
Smart cards, 549
Smartphone
    international cyber attacks on, 215
    malware infection of, 215
    payment systems on, 480
Social hosts, 134
Social media, 184–188
    breach of contract and, 350
    business ethics and, 100–101
    company-wide networks, 188
    Electronic Communications Privacy
        Act and, 187
    employee rights and, 673
    employer policies for, 187, 673
    estate planning and, 1013
    legal issues in, 185–187
    password protection and, 187–188
    privacy rights and, 189–190
    tweeting in courtroom, 64
Social networks, free speech and, 82
Social responsibility, corporate, 103–104,
    114–115
Social Security, 664
Social Security Act (OASDI, 1935), 664
Société anonyme (S.A.), 460
Society
    contract law and, 224

corporation's duty to, 114–115
    crimes as offenses against, 194
Sociological school of thought, 12
Software
    copyright protection for, 167–169
    filtering, 86
    licensing of, 181
    limitations on exported, 163
    patents for, 163
    warning labels for video games, 150
Sole proprietorships, 88, 706–708, 750
    advantages of, 706–707
    compared with other forms of
        business, 811
    disadvantages of, 707–708
Sovereign immunity, 458
Sovereignty, of state governments, 74
Spam (junk e-mail), 177–178
    as advertising, 863
Special (extraordinary) bailments, 945,
    949–951
Special damages, 118, 122
Special indorsement, 496
Special power of attorney, 640
Special qualified indorsement, 496–497
Special-use permits, for zoning, 971
Special warranty deed, 964
Specific devise, 998
Specific fire insurance policy, 988
Specific performance, 7
    agent's rights and, 635
    of contracts, 351
    as remedy for breach of contract, 348,
        355–356
    right to obtain, 428–429
Speech, freedom of, 80–86
Spending powers, of Congress, 79
Spendthrift trust, 1010
Spouse
    community property and, 958
    intestacy laws and surviving, 1007
    life estate of, 957, 1012
Stakeholder approach, 101, 104
Stale check, 536
Standard(s), for water pollution, 882
Standard-form contracts, 300
Standard measure, of compensatory
    damages, 350–351
Standard of care
    by agent, 630–631
    of bailee, 945
Standing to sue, 36–37
Stare decisis
    doctrine of, 8–9
    legal reasoning and, 9–10
    legal stability and, 8–9
Start-ups
    crowdfunding for, 755
    financial capital for, 754–756
State(s). *See also* Alternative dispute
    resolution; Workers' compensation
    administrative agencies in, 842
    Bill of Rights limits on, 79–80
    codes of, 14

community property in, 958
    corporate certificate of authority in,
        762
    courts of (*See* State court systems)
    crimes in, 197
    discrimination based on disability, 693
    employees not covered by ADEA, 693
    environmental regulation by, 879–880
    filing articles of incorporation with,
        769
    franchise regulation in, 710
    immigration legislation in, 671–672
    incorporation procedures in, 767–769
    LLC jurisdiction and, 743, 746
    LLP liability by, 734
    M'Naghten test and, 206
    powers concurrent with federal
        government, 78
    powers reserved to, 74
    protection from disclosing social
        media passwords, 188
    regulatory powers of, 74–75
    relations among, 75
    securities laws of, 830
    spam regulation by, 177
    statutes of frauds in, 305
    tort reform in, 119–120
    trade secret laws of, 169
    wills and, 996
    workers' compensation laws of, 664
State agencies, 5
State court systems, 30, 37–39
    appellate courts of, 37–38, 39
    budget cuts for, 38
    decisions of, 14–15
    federal system compared with, 37
    reading case citations for, 17
    supreme (highest) courts of, 39
    trial courts of, 37, 39
State Department (U.S.), 844
State law, 12
    for criminal act punishment, 198–199
    statutory liens created under, 558–559
Statement(s). *See also* Financial
    statements
    creating express warranties, 440–441
    of fact, 122
        fraudulent misrepresentation and,
            126
    of future intent, 242
    of opinion, 122, 293, 441
        fraudulent misrepresentation and,
            126, 293
    of value, 441
State of mind, 197
Stationary sources, of air pollutants, 881
Statute(s). *See also* Law(s); specific statutes
    areas of consumer law regulated by, 862
    assignment prohibited by, 321
    contracts contrary to, 277–279
    court interpretation of, 11
    environmental, 879, 880
    estray, 943
    federal, 4, 79